THE NEW COGNITIVE NEUROSCIENCES

THE NEW COGNITIVE NEUROSCIENCES

Second Edition

Michael S. Gazzaniga, *Editor-in-Chief*

Section Editors: Emilio Bizzi

Ira B. Black

Colin Blakemore

Leda Cosmides

Gregory J. DiGirolamo

Stephen M. Kosslyn

Joseph E. LeDoux

Willem J. M. Levelt

J. Anthony Movshon

Michael I. Posner

Pasko Rakic

Daniel L. Schacter

Edward E. Smith

John Tooby

Endel Tulving

A BRADFORD BOOK

THE MIT PRESS

CAMBRIDGE, MASSACHUSETTS

LONDON, ENGLAND

© 2000 Massachusetts Institute of Technology

All rights reserved. No part of this book may be reproduced in any form by any electronic or mechanical means (including photocopying, recording, or information storage and retrieval) without permission in writing from the publisher.

This book was set in Baskerville by Publication Services, Champaign, Illinois, and was printed and bound in the United States of America.

Library of Congress Cataloging-in-Publication Data

The new cognitive neurosciences / Michael S. Gazzaniga, editor-in-chief.
    p.   cm.
  "A Bradford book."
  Rev. ed. of: The cognitive neurosciences. c1995.
  Includes bibliographical references and index.
  ISBN 0-262-07195-9 (hc : alk. paper)
  1. Cognitive neuroscience. I. Gazzaniga, Michael S.
II. Cognitive neurosciences.
  QP360.5.N4986 1999
  153–dc21   98-52869
                                     CIP

CONTENTS

IV MOTOR SYSTEMS

V   ATTENTION

VI   MEMORY

VII LANGUAGE

VIII HIGHER COGNITIVE FUNCTIONS

IX EMOTION

X EVOLUTION

XI CONSCIOUSNESS

PREFACE

Here we are on the brink of the twenty-first century. While the history of neurological and psychological research goes back at least two hundred years, the heavy work commenced in the twentieth century. In a hundred short years the basic outlines of the nervous system have been articulated. The biochemical, physiological, pharmacological, and structural features of the vertebrate brain have been described and in many instances defined. So too have the basic perceptual, emotional, mnemonic, attentional, and cognitive functions. In the past 20 years these fundamentals have accelerated at an exponential rate, leaving the field of brain and cognitive science swamped with riches of information.

As we stand poised for the Century of the Brain, never mind the Decade of the Brain, our aspirations have expanded, our know-how has been refined, and our will to tackle the central mysteries of mind/brain relationships has been energized. Five years after the first edition of *The Cognitive Neurosciences* was published, another Summer Institute convened in Squaw Valley to produce its successor: this book. Once again the distinguished section editors led their handpicked colleagues through the maze of new data on the brain and mind. For 18 days, with six lectures a day, the story unfolded. It was a breathtaking experience, and the objective of this book is to bring the benefits of that experience to the world.

For the speakers, it was a chance to meet with friends and colleagues both in their immediate area of expertise and in areas related to the institute's agenda, to trade tales of new developments, and to swat balls around in the California sun. For the fellows and myself, who stayed for the entire three weeks, it was a magnificent smorgasbord, a systematic sampling of a sprawling field.

The forced leisure of being cloistered away from labs, beepers, and coworkers encouraged the fellows' promiscuous attendance at the talks and their exposure to topics and perspectives that otherwise might not have made the cut for their busy schedules. In the words of one, "I never would have sat through all this under any other circumstances." But he was glad he did and, like a lot of others, came away with new perspectives on his own work and new insights into the brain.

This interdisciplinary cross-pollination seems inevitable in a field whose subject is itself both a coherent whole and a motley conglomerate of components. Understanding each nucleus or program of the brain can only be helped by examining the pieces with which it interlocks in this scrupulously well-tuned machine. In fact, this collection demonstrates how many central mysteries of the subject remain outstanding. Despite 40 years of truly impressive elaboration of the molecular biology and cellular effects of the neurotrophins, it is still not known just how these critical chemicals are exchanged between neurons, and why. Four decades after H.M.'s debut, it is not clear whether the hippocampus proper is even necessary for "episodic" memory, whether this form of memory is a truly distinct one, and even, as questioned by an audacious few, whether long-term potentiation is important for memory at all.

The basic functional connectivity that gives rise to the contextual and attentional modulation observed throughout the cortex is almost completely unknown. But the brain is fixed, and our understanding is expanding exponentially. Powerful technological advances and increasingly sophisticated experimental designs have resulted in an extravagant proliferation of extraordinary discoveries: reach neurons, mirror neurons, rampant attentional effects in V1, linguistic imprinting by absurdly young infants. The behaviorists' oversimplifications and the Freudians' titillated fascinations have been largely tempered with concepts that are necessarily more grounded in experimental fact but which will undoubtedly themselves be eventually transcended. Biology almost defies conceptualization; the limitless complexity of a living system will always outstrip the chunking and abstracting that is our species' peculiar and powerful talent.

The secret of success of this unlikely ape is its ability to stare into a tangle of detail and to see just the things that are most useful, and to use them with its sticky little hands. Any system that can be is simplified, and the ones that can't–if deemed of sufficient importance–are thought about some more until the concepts are close enough to reality for the hands to reach in and pick up a new tool.

An effort this massive is made possible by the hard work of literally hundreds of people. First the section editors and their colleagues devoted dozens of hours if not days and weeks to this project. The beauty of their work is self-evident and tangible as it is represented in this book. Thanks also to the group of outstanding fellows who grilled each speaker with wit and wisdom and also a certain awe. What is not represented is the hard work of dozens of other people behind the scene. These include the indefatigable Darleen Mimaugh and Deborah Holmes of the Dartmouth Continuing Education Program who planned the logistics of the meeting down to the last detail. Thanks also go to Marin Gazzaniga. She has served as the managing editor of this volume and had the horrendous job of not only organizing the 94 chapters in this book but also beating people into making their deadlines. Her constant good cheer, mixed with the occasional look of an assassin, combined with her editorial and managerial talents, made it all possible.

One must also say a word about MIT Press. This organization has continually been there to promote cognitive science and neuroscience, and now cognitive neuroscience. They produce a beautiful product, distribute it around the world, and keep the price as low as possible. Our new editor, Michael Rutter, has been extremely supportive and helpful and has guided this book to fruition.

Needless to say, the field is indebted for the continuing support of the James S. McDonnell Foundation. Starting in 1986, John T. Bruer and his colleague Michael Witunski saw the importance of cognitive neuroscience, and they have been generously supportive ever since. More recently, Susan Fitszpatrick has taken over the management of the cognitive neuroscience effort and in many ways has deepened the Foundation's commitment to this new field. The Foundation has now been joined in its support of the Summer Institutes by the National Institutes of Health and the National Institute of Drug Abuse. Both of these agencies deal with massive problems that will be enlightened by the advancements reported in this book and in the field at large. We thank them all.

Finally, I would like to comment on the thrill and fulfillment I feel in orchestrating this book. I am frequently asked if the task of serving as steward for this enterprise is not overtaxing. The short answer is that it is a huge pleasure, mixed with moments of sheer frustration at having to deal with the details. But all of life is full of boring details. The trick is to have them in the service of something of importance. My hope is that this book will serve as a guidepost for young and old scientists alike for the first years of the twenty-first century.

Michael S. Gazzaniga
Dartmouth College
Hanover, New Hampshire

THE NEW COGNITIVE
NEUROSCIENCES

I DEVELOPMENT

Introduction

PASKO RAKIC

Developmental neurobiology provides cognitive neuro-science with the rules that govern brain development and set the limits of its capacity for cognition. It also offers clues as to how the brain may have evolved as a biological substrate of cognition. Therefore, this section was designed with the goal of promoting communication between developmental biologists working at the cellular and molecular level in experimental animals and cognitive neuroscientists working on development of behavior in humans.

Five years ago, in the introduction to the Development section of the first edition of *Cognitive Neuroscience*, I expressed my conviction that a badly needed correlation between developmental biology and cognitive sciences would come to pass. Have we narrowed the gap between these two fields of research in the past few years? On the one hand, it could be argued that the gap is actually becoming wider. Developmental neurobiology is becoming more molecular as the use of recombinant technology allows us to study directly the role of individual genes in specific developmental events. We can neutralize selected genes or add new genes, and study the biological consequences. However, the work on the cascades of molecular events and action of various transcription or growth factors is, by necessity, compelling neurobiologists to use simpler organisms, reduced preparations, and in vitro model systems. Moreover, developmental biologists are also concentrating more heavily on early and basic cellular events, such as the determinants of neuronal number through regulation of cell cycle kinetics, programmed cell death, cell lineage pedigree, and the molecular mechanisms of neuronal migration or axonal navigation. They are working less on the challenging, time-consuming task of deciphering the formation of region-specific synaptic circuitry underlying higher brain function in mammalian brain—particularly in primate cerebral cortex, which resembles the human cortex in the size, complexity, and organization (e.g., see Crick and Jones, 1993; Montcastle, 1995).

The objectives of cognitive neuroscientists are also changing rapidly. Unlike the past generation of developmental psychologists, many of whom were not really interested in the workings of the "black box," the present generation is eager to have more information from developmental neuroanatomy and neurophysiology. Such information is critical for the interpretation of sophisticated data obtained from powerful imaging techniques—techniques that were unavailable a scant five years ago. However, the cognitive neuroscientists lack sufficiently detailed and relevant information that is essential or useful for understanding behavior in mammals, and especially primates. Furthermore, the anatomical data are usually not quantitative enough to be useful (e.g., see Crick and Jones, 1993). In the absence of adequate information from neuroanatomy, psychologists are seeking help from modelers, computational neuroscientists, and theorists; or they are moving toward the philosophy (e.g., see Crick and Koch, 1998).

At one level, then, it appears that the gap between developmental biology and cognitive neuroscience has not diminished over the past five years, and may, in fact, be widening. I do not, however, take a pessimistic view. In spite of these trends, I am convinced that we are learning from each other, and that we will come upon empirical generalizations from a common perspective. Furthermore, I believe that the prospect for progress is bright, provided we keep discussing issues of common interest, as has been done at this meeting. A vigorous and continuous exchange of ideas will permit us to elude at least two major sources of impediments: First, that researchers in one field may embrace the data generated from the other without critical evaluation of their significance and real value; second, that simple-minded reductionism may distract researchers from the essential interplay between minute details and the organism as whole—a temptation that arises when the deciphering of narrow issues supersedes functionally meaningful experiments.

Perhaps there are too few "bridge people"—people who can and will synthesize diverse factual information obtained from different levels of analysis (see, for example, Shulman, 1988). Nevertheless, several conceptual issues have been examined and discussed with surprising consensus. The importance of genes and environment cannot and should not be minimized, as both are essential. Without precise genetic programs, we could not develop the extraordinary uniformity evident in the complex system of the human cerebrum. Yet without exposure to sensory stimulation, this system cannot be fully formed. This concept need not be defended today as it was two decades ago (see Goldman and Rakic, 1978). However, it is becoming clear that the environment can only utilize the capacity provided by genes. Similarly, we agree that critical periods in behavior must correspond to specific developmental stages in neuronal differentiation such as the formation of synaptic connections and signaling molecules. Although neuronal activity and functional validation of neuronal circuitry are essential for development of mental skills, synaptic remodeling during development is compatible with selective stabilization among species-specific synaptic patterns that are initially formed by intrinsic genetic information. Finally, there is consensus that our understanding of the causes, pathogenesis, and treatments of mental diseases can be best achieved with full cooperation of the two fields.

REFERENCES

CRICK, F., and E. G. JONES, 1993. Backwardness of human neuroanatomy, *Nature* 361:106–110.

CRICK, F., and C. KOCH, 1998. Consciousness and neuroscience. *Cerebral Cortex* 8:97–107.

GOLDMAN, P. S., and P. RAKIC, 1979. Impact of the outside world upon the developing primate brain. Perspective from neurobiology. *Bull. Menninger Found.* 43:20–28.

MOUNTCASTLE, V., 1995. The evolution of ideas concerning the function of the neocortex. *Cerebral Cortex* 5:289–295.

SHULMAN, R. G., 1998. Hard days in the trenches. *FASEB J.* 12:255–258.

1 Setting the Stage for Cognition: Genesis of the Primate Cerebral Cortex

PASKO RAKIC

ABSTRACT Understanding the development of the cerebral cortex is central to our understanding of human intelligence and creativity. Modern developmental neurobiology provides insight into how this complex structure may have evolved, how it develops, and how this finely tuned process may go astray. The initial developmental events, which are the subject of this review, are the production, migration, and appropriate allocation of neurons to their final laminar and areal positions within the developing cortical plate. The genes and morpho-regulatory molecules that control these early cellular events are being identified and their functions tested, both in vitro and in vivo, in transgenic animals. The data suggest that the early stages of corticogenesis set the stage for the formation of the final pattern of synaptic connections.

The cerebral cortex in humans makes up about two-thirds of the neuronal mass of the brain and contains almost three-quarters of all our synapses. It is also the structure that most distinctively sets us apart from other species. Therefore, the principles governing the development of the cerebral cortex may hold the key to explaining our cognitive capacity and the evolution of human intelligence and creativity. One of the most prominent features of the cerebral cortex in all species—and particularly in primates—is its parcellation into distinct laminar, radial, and areal domains (Eccles, 1984; Mountcastle, 1995; Goldman-Rakic, 1987, 1988; Rakic and Singer, 1988; Szenthagothai, 1987). But although the surface of the neocortex has expanded enormously during phylogeny (e.g., the surface of the human neocortex is 10 times larger than that of a macaque monkey and 1,000 times than that of a rat), its thickness and basic pattern of cytoarchitectonic organization has changed relatively little (Rakic, 1995b).

Understanding the development of the cerebral cortex and its expansion in size and complexity depends critically on answering some fundamental questions: When and where are cortical neurons generated? How is their number regulated in each species and in each individual? What accounts for the expansion of the cortical surface without concomitant increase in thickness?

PASKO RAKIC Section of Neurobiology, Yale University School of Medicine, New Haven, Conn.

How do postmitotic cells attain their proper laminar and areal position within the cortex? When and how are different cell phenotypes generated and the regional differences in the cerebral cortex established? Elucidation of these issues is an essential prerequisite for understanding the subsequent formation of neuronal connections and synaptic architecture that underlie our cognitive capacity as well as the pathogenesis of congenital mental disorders.

This account is largely based on studies of neocortical development in the mouse, macaque, and human brain—studies carried out in my laboratory over the past three decades. Although the principles of cortical development are similar in all three of these species, the differences that do exist, however small, offer some very real clues as to how this structure has evolved. The functions of neurotransmitters, receptors, and ion channels do not change substantially over the phylogenetic scale. Thus we can reasonably attribute the secret of *Homo sapiens'* success to an increased number of neurons, more elaborate connections, and functional specialization of cortical areas. In this review, we focus on the early developmental events that lead to the formation of cellular constituents of the cortical plate. Other communications in this volume deal with subsequent formation of neuronal connections and synaptic junctions.

Basic principles

Neurobiologists generally agree that the basic cellular events and main principles of cortical development are similar to those underlying the formation of other parts of the central nervous system (Sidman and Rakic, 1982). Some of these principles and basic developmental events are diagrammatically illustrated in figure 1.1. Initial cellular events (such as the proliferation, migration, aggregation, and death of cells that form the brain), the subsequent outgrowth of axons, and the establishment of neuronal connections proceed in an orderly fashion in each individual according to a species-specific timetable and are regulated by differential gene expression (figure 1.1A, B). In contrast, the later phases

7

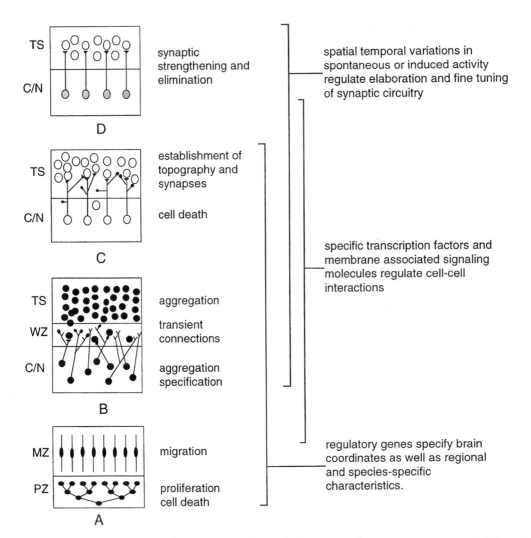

FIGURE 1.1 The complex organization of the adult central nervous system is the end product of sequential, interdependent cellular events that occur during embryonic development. Starting from the bottom (A) and proceeding to the top of the diagram (D), individual neurons are generated in specific proliferative zones (PZ) and, after last cell division, migrate across the migratory zone (MZ) to attain their final locations. There they form cortical sheets or aggregate into nuclei (C/N). Some cells form transient connections in the waiting zones (WZ) before they enter their appropriate target structures (TS). The final set of neuronal connections, which are initially more numerous and diffuse, is established by elimination of cells and excess synapses, as shown at the top of the diagram. These basic cellular events can be observed in most regions of the developing brain. As indicated on the right side of the diagram, a major goal of modern developmental neurobiology is to uncover specific genes and molecules that regulate these cellular events in specific structures as well as to understand the mechanisms that enable the environment to influence the formation of neural connections.

of development, including the selective elimination of neurons, axons, and synapses, as well as the shaping of the final circuits within topographical maps, are influenced by activity-dependent mechanisms which–after birth–involve individual experience (figure 1.1C, D). As indicated on the right side of the diagram, analysis of these events can be carried out at the genetic, molecular, and cellular levels. This article focuses exclusively on those aspects of the early events that are represented at the bottom of figure 1.1A and B.

Time and place of neuronal origin

Early studies of neurogenesis found neither dividing nor migrating neurons in the newborn child, suggesting that cortical neurons in human cerebrum must be generated before birth. However, precise data on the onset and termination of corticogenesis could not be established with the available techniques (see Conel, 1939, for example). Use of sensitive and reliable methods to label dividing cells revealed that the neocortical neurons in the macaque monkey are produced during midgestation (Rakic, 1974, 1988a). In contrast, neurogenesis has been shown to continue after birth both in the cerebellum and the hippocampus (Rakic, 1973; Rakic and Nowakowski, 1981). In the monkey neocortex, however, no additional neurons are added during the animal's 30-year life span (Rakic, 1985). In our own species, comparative cytologic analysis, as well as supravital labeling of dividing neurons in human embryos, indicates that neurons destined for the neocortex are also generated during midgestation (Rakic and Sidman, 1968; Sidman and Rakic, 1973, 1982).

The presence of large numbers of mitotic figures near the lumen of the cerebral cavity of the embryonic human cerebrum and their absence in the cortical plate itself, led to the suggestion that cortical neurons are produced in the germinal matrix situated at the ventricular surface (His, 1904). This hypothesis was substantiated by the application of modern methods for labeling dividing cells in mice (Angevine and Sidman, 1961), monkeys (Rakic, 1974), and humans (Rakic and Sidman, 1968). Proliferative cells in the ventricular zone are organized as a pseudostratified epithelium in which precursor cells divide asynchronously; their nuclei move away from the ventricular surface to replicate their DNA, then move back to the surface to undergo another mitotic cycle (reviewed in Sidman and Rakic, 1973; Rakic, 1988a). Electron microscopic and immunocytochemical analyses revealed the coexistence of neuronal and glial cell lines from the onset of corticogenesis (Levitt, Cooper, and Rakic, 1981; Rakic, 1972). This early divergence of basic cell types has been confirmed using the retroviral gene transfer method, which enables the study of cell lineages in the developing mammalian telencephalon (Luskin, Pearlman, and Sanes, 1988; Cameron and Rakic, 1991).

Transient embryonic zones

During embryonic and fetal development, the telencephalic wall consists of several cellular layers, or zones, that do not exist in the mature brain. Moving outward from the ventricle to the pial surface, these are, in order: the ventricular, subventricular, intermediate and subplate zones; the cortical plate; and the marginal zone (figure 1.2). Although most of these zones were described and characterized in the classical literature at the turn of the century (cf. His, 1904), the subplate zone has been recognized as a separate entity relatively recently (Kostovic and Molliver, 1974; reviewed in Kostovic and Rakic, 1990). This zone consists of early-generated subplate neurons scattered among numerous axons, dendrites, glial fibers, and migrating neurons. Most of these subplate neurons eventually degenerate, but some persist in the adult cerebrum as a set of interstitial cells (Kostovic and Rakic, 1980; Luskin and Shatz, 1985). Although it has been suggested that the subplate zone provides an opportunity for interactions between incoming afferent fibers and early-generated neurons, the significance of these transient contacts is not fully understood.

One possibility is that the subplate zone serves as a cellular substrate for competition among the initial contingent of cortical afferents and that this competition serves to regulate their distribution to appropriate regions of the overlying cortical plate (Rakic, 1976a, 1977; Kostovic and Rakic, 1984; Shatz, Chun, and Luskin, 1988; McConnell, Ghosh, and Shatz, 1994). Subsequent autoradiographic, electron microscopic, and histochemical studies revealed that the axons observed in the subplate zone originate sequentially from the brainstem, basal forebrain, thalamus, and the ipsi- and contralateral cerebral hemispheres (Kostovic and Rakic, 1990). After a variable and partially overlapping period, these diverse fiber systems enter the cortical plate, and the subplate zone disappears, leaving only a vestige of cells– known as interstitial neurons–scattered throughout the subcortical white matter (Kostovic and Rakic, 1980; Chun and Shatz, 1989). A comparison among various species indicates that the size of this transient zone, as well as its role, increases during mammalian evolution. And this increase culminates in the developing association areas of the human fetal cortex concomitant with the enlargement of the corticocortical fiber systems (Kostovic and Rakic, 1990; Kostovic and Goldman-Rakic, 1983). The regional differences in the size, pattern, and resolution of the subplate zone also correlate with the pattern and elaboration of cerebral convolutions (Goldman-Rakic and Rakic, 1984).

Control of cortical size

The size of the cerebral cortex varies greatly among mammals, reaching a peak surface area in primates. Understanding the principles and mechanisms controlling the production of cells destined for the cerebral cortex may be the key to understanding the evolution of human intelligence. Based on the data on the time of cell origin and cell proliferation kinetics, we proposed that the number of cortical cells depends on the mode of mitotic division (symmetric vs. asymmetric), the duration of the cell cycle, and the degree of programmed cell death in the proliferative zones (Rakic, 1988a, 1995b). In the past few years, technologic advances have allowed us to study the regulation of these cellular events in transgenic mice as well as in nonhuman primates using the retroviral gene transfer method (e.g., Kornack and Rakic, 1995; Kuida et

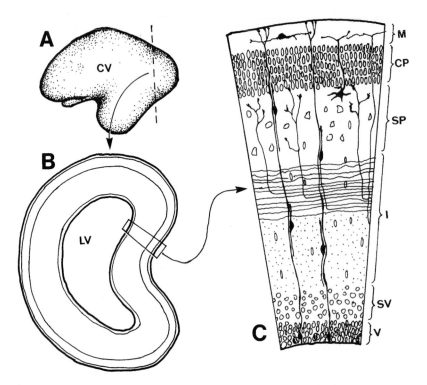

FIGURE 1.2 Cytological organization of the primate cerebral wall during the first half of gestation. (A) The cerebral vesicle of 60–65-day-old monkey fetuses is still smooth and lacks the characteristic convolutions that will emerge in the second half of gestation. (B) Coronal section across the occipital lobe at the level indicated by a vertical dashed line in A. The lateral cerebral ventricle at this age is still relatively large, and only the incipient calcarine fissure marks the position of the prospective visual cortex. (C) A block of the tissue dissected from the upper bank of the calcarine fissure. At this early stage one can recognize six transient embryonic zones from the ventricular surface (bottom) to the pial surface (top): ventricular zone (V), subventricular zone (SV), intermediate zone (I), subplate zone (SP), cortical plate (CP), and marginal zone (M). Note the presence of spindle-shaped migrating neurons moving along the elongated radial glial fibers, which span the full thickness of the cerebral wall. The early afferents originating from the brain stem, thalamus, and other cortical areas invade the cerebral wall and accumulate initially in the subplate zone where they make transient synapses before entering the overlying cortical plate. (Reprinted from Rakic, 1995b, by permission.)

al., 1996, 1998; Zhong et al., 1996). Since most genes and their products involved in cell production and fate determination seem to be preserved during evolution, one might expect that the control of neuronal number and differentiation would be basically similar in all species (Williams and Herrup, 1988). For example, one mechanism that regulates the number of cells produced in the ventricular zone is programmed cell death (PCD) or apoptosis. Although PCD has been considered a major factor contributing to the formation of the vertebrate brain (Glucksmann, 1951), contemporary research has focused mainly on the histogenetic cell death involved in the elimination of inappropriate axonal connections in the later stages of development (e.g., Rakic and Riley, 1983a, 1983b; Oppenheim, 1991). However, the discovery of several classes of genes involved in PCD, which were initially identified in invertebrates, afforded the opportunity to study this phenomenon in the mammalian cerebrum. For example, a family of enzymes called caspases has been shown to play an important role in PCD in a variety of organs and tissues (Ellis and Horwitz, 1991). We have recently demonstrated that in mouse embryos deficient in caspase 9 and 3, fewer cells are eliminated than in their littermates (Kuida et al., 1996, 1998). Reduction of apoptosis in the knockout mice results in the formation of supernumerary founder cells in the cerebral ventricular zone. As a consequence, these mice form ectopic cells in the intermediate zone as well as a larger cortical plate with more radial units. Remarkably, the cerebral cortex in these transgenic mice has a larger surface area and begins to form convolutions. These new approaches provide an example of how the mutation of a few genes that control the reduction of cell death in the proliferative zone could result in the expansion of the cortex during evolution (Rakic, 1995b).

Neuronal cell migration

Since all cortical neurons originate near the ventricular surface of the cerebral vesicle, they must all move to their final positions in the cortex, which develops in the outer regions of the cerebral wall, just below the pia. Initially, while the cerebral wall is still thin, cells move just a short distance. But the length of their pathway increases with the enlargement of the cerebral hemispheres, particularly in the large primate cerebrum in which a massive migration of neurons occurs concomitantly with the rapid growth of the cerebral wall during midgestation (reviewed in Sidman and Rakic, 1982; Rakic, 1988a). This magnitude of cell movement is perhaps the reason that neuronal cell migration was first observed in human embryos (His, 1874). In the early 1970s, advances in methods yielded the discovery that postmitotic neurons find their way to the cortex by following the elongated shafts of radial glial cells (figure 1.3; Rakic, 1972; Rakic, Stensaas, and Sayre, 1974). These elongated cells, which span the fetal cerebral wall from the beginning of corticogenesis, stop transiently to divide during midgestation at the peak of neuronal migration (Schmechel and Rakic, 1979).

While moving along the glial surface, migrating neurons remain preferentially attached to glial fibers, which suggests a "gliophilic" mode of migration (Rakic, 1985, 1990) that is mediated by heterotypic adhesion molecules (Rakic, Cameron, and Komura, 1994). However, some postmitotic cells do not obey glial constraints and move along tangentially oriented axonal fascicles. (See, for example, the black horizontally oriented cell aligned with TR in figure 1.3.) We suggested the term "neurophilic" to characterize the mode of migration of this cell class (Rakic, 1985, 1990). The lateral dispersion of postmitotic neurons was initially observed in Golgi-stained preparations (see figure 1 of the report of the Boulder Committee, 1970), but it attracted renewed attention after the discovery that a specific, presumably neurophilic, cell class moves from the telencephalon to the olfactory bulb (Menezes and Luskin, 1994; Lois and Alvarez-Buylla, 1994). Moreover, studies in rodents have suggested more widespread dispersion of clonally related cortical cells (reviewed in Rakic, 1995a; Tan et al., 1998; Reid, Liang, and Walsh, 1995). However, we must underscore the fact that application of the same methods in the convoluted primate cortex revealed that the majority of migrating cells obey the radial constraints imposed by the radial glial scaffolding (Kornack and Rakic, 1995; see also the section below: Radial Glial Hypothesis).

Considerable progress has been made in understanding the molecular mechanisms behind neuronal migration and the physical displacement of cell perikarya during translocation of the cell nucleus and soma across the densely packed tissue. Initially, based on an observation in situ, it was proposed that a single pair of binding, complementary molecules with gliophilic properties can account for the recognition of glial guides (Rakic, 1981). In the last decade, however, several candidates for recognition and adhesion molecules have been discovered and are being tested (e.g., Cameron and Rakic, 1994; Anton, Camaron, and Rakic, 1996; Hatten and Mason, 1990; Schachner, Faissner, and Fischer, 1985). It has also been shown that voltage- and ligand-gated ion channels on the leading process and cell soma of migrating neurons regulate the influx of calcium ions into migrating neurons (Komuro and Rakic, 1992, 1993, 1996; Rakic and Komuro, 1995). Calcium fluctuations, in turn, may trigger polymerization of the cytoskeletal and contractile proteins essential for cell motility and translocation of the nucleus and surrounding cytoplasm (Rakic, Knyihar-Csillik, and Csillik, 1996). These studies indicate that neuronal migration is a multifaceted developmental event, involving cell–cell recognition, differential adhesion, transmembrane signaling, and intracytoplasmic structural changes (Rakic, Cameron, and Komura, 1994). A simple model of molecular components involved in cell migration is provided on the diagram in figure 1.4. The discovery of the glial-guided radial migration led to the proposal of the radial unit hypothesis (Rakic, 1988a), which has served as a useful working model for research on the cellular and molecular mechanisms involved in normal and abnormal cortical development.

Radial unit hypothesis

The cellular mechanisms underlying expansion of cerebral cortex during individual development and evolution can be explained in the context of the radial unit hypothesis (Rakic, 1988a, 1995b). The neocortex in all species consists of an array of iterative neuronal groups called, interchangeably, radial columns or modules. These groups share a common intrinsic and extrinsic connectivity and subserve the same function (Mountcastle, 1997; Szenthagothai, 1987; Goldman-Rakic, 1987). The larger the cortex in a given species, the larger the number of participating columnar units (Rakic, 1978, 1995b). The radial unit hypothesis of cortical development postulates that the embryonic cortical plate forms from vertically oriented cohorts of neurons generated at the same site in the proliferative ventricular zone of the cerebral vesicle (Rakic, 1978). Each radial unit consists of several clones (polyclones) that migrate to the cortex following glial fascicles spanning the cerebral wall (Rakic, 1988a). In the cortical plate, later-generated cells bypass early-generated ones and settle in an inside-out gradient of neurogenesis (Rakic, 1974). Thus, the two-dimensional positional information of the proliferative units in the ventricular zone is transformed into a three-

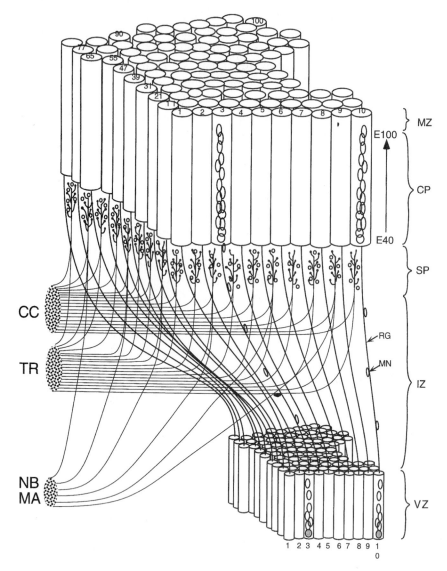

FIGURE 1.3   A three-dimensional illustration of the basic developmental events and types of cell–cell interactions occurring during the early stages of corticogenesis before formation of the final pattern of cortical connections. This cartoon emphasizes radial migration, a predominant mode of neuronal movement which, in primates, underlies the elaborate columnar organization of the neocortex. After their last division, cohorts of migrating neurons (MN) first traverse the intermediate zone (IZ) and then the subplate zone (SP). There they have an opportunity to interact with "waiting" afferents arriving sequentially from the nucleus basalis and monoamine subcortical centers (NB, MA), from the thalamic radiation (TR), and from several ipsilateral and contralateral corticocortical bundles (CC). After the newly generated neurons bypass the earlier generated ones which are situated in the deep cortical layers, they settle at the interface between the developing cortical plate (CP) and the marginal zone (MZ), eventually forming a radial stack of cells that share a common site of origin but generated at different times. For example, neurons produced between E40 and E100 in radial unit 3 follow the same radial glial fascicle and form ontogenetic column 3. Although some cells, presumably neurophilic in their surface affinities, may detach from the cohort and move laterally, guided by an axonal bundle (cf. the horizontally oriented, black cell leaving radial unit 3 and horizontally oriented fibers), most postmitotic cells are gliophilic; i.e., they have an affinity for the glial surface and strictly obey constraints imposed by transient radial glial scaffolding (RG). This cellular arrangement preserves the relationships between the proliferative mosaic of the ventricular zone (VZ) and the corresponding protomap within the SP and CP, even though the cortical surface in primates shifts considerably during the massive cerebral growth encountered in midgestation (for details, see Rakic, 1988a).

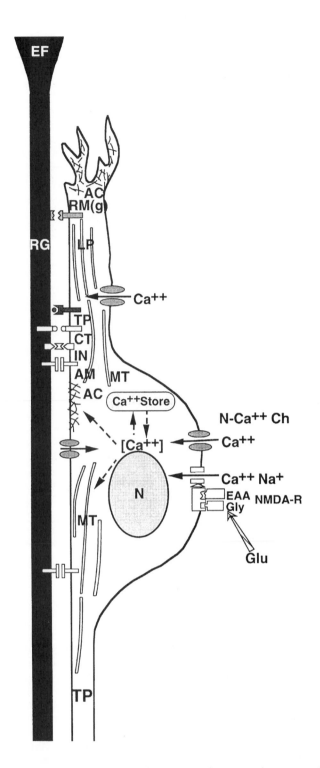

FIGURE 1.4 Model of a proposed cascade of cellular and molecular events that take place during the migration of postmitotic cells in the developing cerebral wall. After their last mitotic division in the ventricular zone, migrating cells extend a leading process (LP) that follows the contours of the radial glial fiber (RG) as it spans the expanding cerebral wall. The cytoskeleton within the LP and trailing process (TP) contain microtubules (MT) and actin-like contractile proteins (AC) which are involved in translocation of the cell nucleus (N) and the surrounding cytoplasm within the leading process until the cell enters the cortical plate. This system, maintained in vitro in slice preparations or imprint culture, provides an opportunity to examine the role of the various molecules that are engaged in recognition, adhesion, transmembrane signaling, and motility that underlies directed neuronal migration. The voltage-gated (N-type) and ligand-gated (NMDA-type) receptors/channels are thought to control calcium influx, which serves as messengers for execution of this movement. Abbreviations: AM, homotypic adhesion molecule; CT, catenin; EAA, excitatory amino acid; EF, end foot of the radial glial fiber; Gly, glycine; IN, integrin; LP, leading process; MT, microtubule; N, cell nucleus; TP, trailing process; RG, radial glial fiber; RM(g) gliophilic recognition molecule; TP, tyrosine phosphorylation. (Modified from Rakic, 1997.)

dimensional cortical architecture: the x- and y-axes of the cells are provided by their site of origin whereas the z-axis is provided by their time of origin (see figure 1.3).

The radial unit hypothesis accounts for the large expansion of cortical surface that occurred without a concomitant increase in thickness during phylogenetic and ontogenetic development (Rakic, 1988a). It also shows how the genes controlling the number of founder cells at the ventricular surface limit the size of the cortical sur-

face both during individual development and during the evolution of mammalian species (Rakic, 1995b). Thus, a relatively small change in the timing of developmental cellular events could have large functional consequences. For example, a minor increase in the length of the cell cycle or the magnitude of cell death in the ventricular zone could result in a large increase in the number of founder cells that form proliferative units (Rakic, 1988a). Since proliferation in the ventricular zone initially proceeds exponentially owing to the prevalence of symmetric divisions, an additional round of mitotic cycles during this phase doubles the number of founder cells and hence the number of radial columns (figure 1.5; Rakic, 1995b). According to this model, fewer than four extra rounds of symmetric cell division in the ventricular zone before the onset of corticogenesis can account for a tenfold difference in the size of the cortical surface. The mode of cell division changes to predominantly asymmetric after the onset of corticogenesis. That allows us to predict that the extended cell production in humans, which is about two weeks longer than in macaques, should result in an enlargement of the cortical thickness by just 10 to 15%—a prediction that has been observed (Rakic, 1995b). Thus, as illustrated in figure 9.5, even a small delay in the onset of the second phase of corticogenesis results in an order-of-magnitude larger cortical surface owing to the increasing number of founder cells at the ventricular zone.

The proposal that neurons comprising a given radial column may be clonally related could be tested

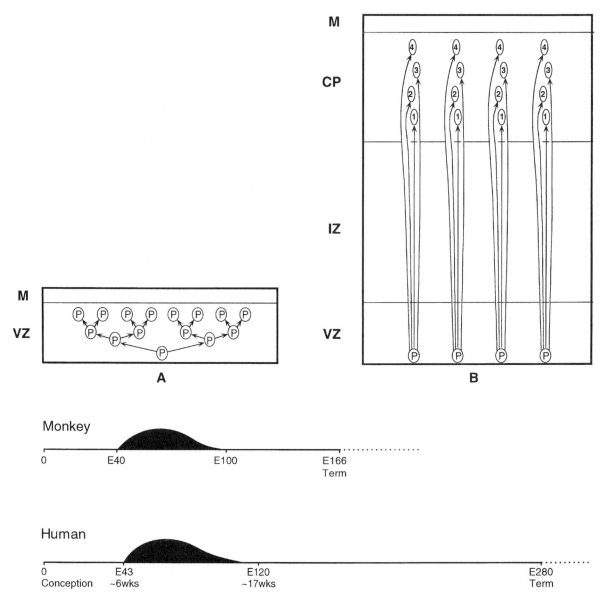

FIGURE 1.5 (A) Schematic model of symmetric cell divisions, which predominate before the E40. At this early embryonic age, the cerebral wall comprises the ventricular zone (VZ), where all the cells are proliferating, and the marginal zone (M), into which some cells extend radial processes. Symmetric division produces two progenitors (P) during each cycle and causes rapid horizontal lateral spread. (B) Model of asymmetric or stem division, which becomes predominant in the monkey embryo after E40. During each asymmetric division a progenitor (P) produces one postmitotic neuron which leaves the ventricular zone and another progenitor which remains within the proliferative zone and continues to divide. Postmitotic neurons migrate rapidly across the intermediate zone (IZ) and become arranged vertically in the cortical plate (CP) in reverse order of their arrival (1, 2, 3, 4). (C) Diagrammatic representation of the time of neuron origin in the macaque monkey. The data were obtained from ^{3}H-thymidine autoradiographic analyses (Rakic, 1974). (D) Estimate of the time of neuron origin in the human neocortex based on the number of mitotic figures within the ventricular zone, supravital DNA synthesis in slice preparations of fetal tissue, and the presence of migrating neurons in the intermediate zone of the human fetal cerebrum. (Reprinted from Rakic, 1995b, by permission.)

experimentally after the introduction of the retroviral gene transfer method for in vivo analysis of cell lineages in the mammalian brain (Sanes, 1989). Use of this approach suggested that most progenitors originating in the same site of the ventricular zone remain radically deployed in the cortex (Luskin, Pearlman, and Sanes, 1988; Kornack and Rakic, 1995; Tan et al., 1998; but see Reid, Liang, and Walsh, 1995). Furthermore, a number of studies in chimeric and transgenic mice have provided evidence that a majority of postmitotic, clonally related neurons move and remain radially distributed in the cortex (e.g., Nakatsuji,

Kadokawa, Suemori, 1991; Soriano et al., 1995; reviewed in Rakic, 1995a). The use of the retroviral gene transfer method in the embryonic primate brain showed that even in the large and highly convoluted cerebrum, radial deployment of many clones is remarkably well preserved (Kornack and Rakic, 1995).

Protomap hypothesis

A major challenge to students of the cerebral cortex is how individual and species-specific cytoarchitectonic areas have emerged from the initial, seemingly uniform ventricular zone and cortical plate. Both intrinsic and extrinsic factors have been suggested. One attractive hypothesis is that all cortical neurons are equipotential and that laminar and areal differences are induced by extrinsic influences exerted via thalamic afferents (Creutzfeldt, 1977). However, there is also considerable evidence that the cells generated within the embryonic cerebral wall contain some intrinsic information about their prospective species-specific cortical organization. To reconcile existing experimental and descriptive data, we formulated a protomap hypothesis (Rakic, 1988a). This hypothesis suggests that the basic pattern of cytoarchitectonic areas emerges through synergistic, interdependent interactions between developmental programs intrinsic to cortical neurons and extrinsic signals supplied by specific inputs from subcortical structures. According to this hypothesis, neurons in the embryonic cortical plate—indeed even in the proliferative ventricular zone where they originate—set up a primordial map that preferentially attracts appropriate afferents, and has a capacity to respond to this input in a specific manner. The prefix proto was introduced to emphasize the primordial, provisionary, and essentially malleable character of the protomap, which is subject to considerable modification by the extrinsic influences exerted at later stages (Rakic, 1988a).

The initial indication that developmental events in the proliferative ventricular zone foreshadow prospective regional differences in the overlying cerebral mantle comes from the observation that the neurogenesis of the primary visual cortex, which contains more neurons per radial unit than the adjacent areas, lasts longer (Rakic, 1976b). Furthermore, it has also been demonstrated that the mitotic index in the ventricular region subjacent to this area is higher than in the adjacent regions (Dehay et al., 1993). Therefore, region-specific differences in production of the ventricular zone can be detected even before neurons arrive at the cortex (Kennedy and Dehay, 1993; Algan and Rakic, 1997). Several lines of evidence indicate that, during the final cell division, one or both daughter cells start to express a variety of neuron class-specific signaling molecules (LoTurco et al., 1995; Lidow and Rakic, 1994). Postmitotic cells not only become committed to a neuronal fate, but also become restricted in their repertoire of possible fates (McConnell, 1988). There have been numerous studies in which the cytology of postmitotic cells has been examined (e.g., Schwartz, Rakic, and Goldman-Rakic, 1991; LoTurco et al., 1995) and/or manipulated by a variety of methods, including spontaneous mutations (e.g., Caviness and Rakic, 1978; Rakic, 1995b), ionizing radiation (Algan and Rakic, 1997), retroviral gene transfer labeling (Parnavelas et al., 1991), transgenic mice (Kuida et al., 1996), and heterochronic transplantations (McConnell, 1988; McConnell and Kasanowski, 1991). All of these studies indicate that certain cell class-specific attributes are expressed before migrating neurons arrive at the cortical plate and become synaptically connected. In addition, retroviral tracing experiments and some clonal analyses suggest that the ventricular zone comprises a heterogeneous population of cells, and that cell lineage contributes substantially to the cell fate determination of neurons (Aklin and van der Kooy, 1993; Parnavelas et al., 1991; Kornack and Rakic, 1995; Williams and Price, 1995; Kuan et al., 1997).

These findings raise the question of whether laminar and areal identities of cortical plate cells provide cues or chemotactic attractants for incoming afferent axons. Data from axonal tracing indicate that afferent connections from subcortical structures and other cortical regions find their way to the specific regions of the cortical plate either directly and/or via the subplate zone (Kostovic and Rakic, 1984, 1990; DeCarlos and O'Leary, 1992; McConnell, Ghosh, and Shatz, 1994; Agmon et al., 1995; Catalano, Robertson, Killackey, 1996; Richards et al., 1997), suggesting the existence of region-specific attractants for pathfinding and target recognition. In support of this idea, the development of correct topologic connections in anophthalmic mice and in early enucleated animals indicates that basic connections and chemoarchitectonic characteristics can form in the absence of information from the periphery (e.g., Kaiserman-Abramof, Graybiel, and Nauta, 1980; Olivaria and Van Sluyters, 1984; Rakic, 1988a; Kennedy and DeHay, 1993; Kuljis and Rakic, 1990; Rakic and Lidow, 1995; Lidow and Rakic, 1992). Region-specific and morpho-regulatory molecules (e.g., Arimatsu et al., 1992; Levitt, Barbe, and Eagleson, 1997; Ferri and Levitt, 1992; Proteus et al., 1991; Buffone et al., 1993; Cohen-Tannoudji, Babinet, and Wassef, 1994; Emerling and Lander, 1994; see also Levitt, chapter 2 of this volume), or layer-specific expression of POU-homeodomain genes (e.g., Frantz et al., 1994; Meissirel et al., 1997) may also contribute to the formation of specified axonal pathways.

Thus, tangentially and radially distinct landmarks in the postmitotic cells facilitate axonal pathfinding and target recognition that eventually lead to parcellation of the cerebral cortex.

It should be underscored that although the embryonic cerebral wall exhibits gradients of several morphoregulatory molecules, as well as other area-specific molecular differences, the protomap within the embryonic cerebrum provides only a set of species-specific genetic instructions and biological constraints. The precise position of interareal borders, the overall size of each cytoarchitectonic area, and the details of their cellular and synaptic characteristics in the adult cerebral cortex are achieved through a cascade of reciprocal interactions between cortical neurons and the cues they receive from afferents arriving from a variety of extracortical sources (Rakic, 1988a). Such afferents may serve to coordinate and adjust the ratio of various cell classes with the subcortical structures, as has been shown in the primary visual system (Meissirel et al., 1997; Rakic et al., 1991; Kennedy and Dehay, 1993; Rakic and Lidow, 1995). In summary, the concept of the cortical protomap includes the role of both intrinsic and extrinsic determinants in shaping the final pattern and relative sizes of the cytoarchitectonic areas.

Timing of cortical genesis in humans

To elucidate the development of the neocortex in humans, it is useful to compare selected cellular features of the human cortex from different prenatal stages with those of the macaque monkey. In so doing, we trace the corresponding times and sequences of developmental events in these species—an essential procedure if we are to apply the findings obtained from experimental animas to the understanding of human cortical development (e.g., Chalupa and Wefers, chapter 3 of this volume). To this end, we make use of Poliakov's comprehensive histologic studies of cortical development in human fetuses, published originally in the Russian literature (e.g., Poliakov, 1959, 1965). These studies have been reviewed in detail elsewhere (Sidman and Rakic, 1982); here, however, these data are summarized in figure 1.6 and compared with the timing of corresponding events in the macaque monkey.

Stage I. Initial formation of the cortical plate (from approximately the 6th to the 10th fetal weeks). During the 7th fetal week, postmitotic cells begin to migrate from the ventricular zone outward to form a new accumulation of cells at the junction of the intermediate and marginal zones. By the middle of this period, synapses of unknown origin are present above and below the cortical plate (Molliver, Kostovic, and Van der Loos, 1973; Zecevic, 1998). This stage corresponds approximately to

the level of cortical development found in the monkey fetus between E40 and E54, depending on the region.

Stage II. Primary condensation of the cortical plate (through approximately the 10th and 11th fetal weeks). At this stage the cortical plate increases in thickness, becomes more compact, and is clearly demarcated from the fiber-rich part of the intermediate zone. This zone seems to have fewer cells per unit volume, indicating that the first major wave of migration is almost spent (figure 1.6). The end of this stage roughly corresponds to the E55-E59 period in the monkey when the majority of efferent neurons of layers 5 and 6 are generated in most regions of the cortex (Sidman and Rakic, 1982; Marin-Padilla, 1988).

Stage III. Bilaminate cortical plate (most pronounced during the 11th to the 13th fetal weeks). The uniform and compact cortical plate of the second stage becomes subdivided into an inner and outer zone: The inner zone is occupied mainly by cells with relatively large, somewhat widely spaced oval nuclei, and the outer zone by cells with densely packed, smaller, bipolar nuclei (figure 1.6). This heterogeneity results from the more advanced maturation of the deep-lying neurons that arrived at the cortical plate during earlier developmental stages, plus the addition of a new wave of somas of immature neurons that take up more superficial positions. This period is also characterized by the appearance of the cell-sparse, fiber-rich subplate zone situated below the cortical plate. This transient embryonic zone in the human fetus is particularly wide in the regions subjacent to the association areas (Kostovic and Rakic, 1990). The third stage corresponds roughly to the level of development achieved in the monkey between E59 and E64.

Stage IV. Secondary condensation (from the 13th to the 15th fetal week). During this period of gestation, the ventricular zone becomes progressively thinner, while the subventricular zone remains relatively wide (figure 1.6). The cortical plate again becomes homogeneous in appearance and resembles, in a sense, a thickened version of stage II. The reason for this change may be that, in stage IV, most of the young neurons in the cortex become considerably larger as they differentiate, while relatively few new immature neurons enter the cortical plate. The result is a more uniform appearance. At the end of this stage, an accumulation of large cells appears below the cortical plate and the subplate zone enlarges further (Kostovic and Rakic, 1990). Depending on the cortical region, this stage appears in the monkey between E64 and E75.

Stage V. Prolonged stage of cortical maturation (from the 16th fetal week continuing well into the postnatal period). Morphological data are inadequate to determine for how long, or how many, neurons continue to migrate

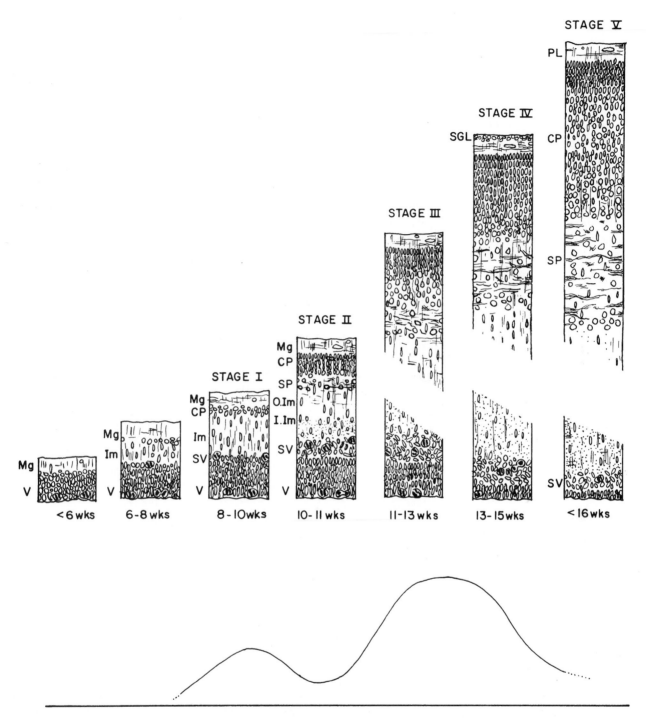

FIGURE 1.6 Semidiagrammatic drawings of the human cerebral wall at various gestational ages listed in fetal weeks below
each column. The stages refer specifically to an arbitrarily chosen cortical area situated midway along the lateral surface of
the hemisphere (detailed in Sidman and Rakic, 1982). In addition, the subplate zone, situated below the cortical plate, appears in the last three stages (Kostovic and Rakic, 1990).
Because there is a gradient of maturation, as many as three of
five stages of cortical development may be observed in different regions of the neocortex in the same fetal brain. In the
three columns on the right, the intermediate zone is not drawn

in full because the thickness of the cerebral wall has increased
markedly compared with earlier stages and cannot fit into the
drawing. The curve below the drawing schematically indicates
waves of cell migration to the neocortex assessed by the density of migrating neurons in the intermediate zone. Abbreviations: CP, cortical plate; Im, intermediate zone; I.Im and
O.Im, inner and outer intermediate zones, respectively; MG,
marginal zone; PL, plexiform layer; SGL, subpial granular
layer; SP, subplate zone; SV, subventricular zone; V, ventricular zone; wks, age in fetal weeks. (Reprinted from Rakic,
1988b.)

to the human neocortex after 16 weeks–hence the dotted line at the right side of the curve in figure 1.6. By the 5th month, relatively few neuronal precursors seem to be proliferating in the reduced ventricular zone of the human cerebral hemispheres, although many neurons generated prior to the 16th week have yet to reach the cortical plate. A comparison of the autoradiographic results in the monkey (Rakic, 1974, 1977) with corresponding stages in human (Rakic and Sidman, 1968; Marin-Padilla, 1988; Kostovic and Rakic, 1990) indicates that most neurons of the human neocortex are generated by the middle of gestation. Toward term, the ventricular zone disappears, the subplate zone dissolves; and, as the intermediate zone transforms into the white matter, only a vestige of the subplate cells remains as interstitial neurons (Kostovic and Rakic, 1980). After all cortical neurons have been generated and attained their final positions, their differentiation, including the formation of synapses, proceeds for a long time, not peaking until the second postnatal year. The subject of synaptogenesis in the cerebral cortex of both monkey and human is described by Bourgeois, Goldman-Rakic, and Rakic in chapter 4 of this volume.

ACKNOWLEDGMENTS   This work was supported U.S. Public Health Service Grants.

REFERENCES

AGMON, A. A., L. T. YANG, E. G. JONES, and D. K. DOWD, 1995. Topologic precision in the thalamic projection to the neonatal mouse. *J. Neurosci.* 13:5365–5382.

AKLIN, S. E., and D. VAN DER KOOY, 1993. Clonal heterogeneity in the germinal zone of the developing telencephalon. *Development* 118:175–192.

ALGAN, O., and P. RAKIC, 1997. Radiation-induced area- and lamina-specific deletion of neurons in the primate visual cortex. *J. Comp. Neurol.* 381:335–352.

ANGEVINE, L. B., and R. L. SIDMAN, 1961. Autoradiographic study of cell migration during histogenesis of cerebral cortex in the mouse. *Nature* 192:766–768.

ANTON, S. A., R. S. CAMERON, and P. RAKIC, 1996. Role of neuron-glial junctional proteins in the maintenance and termination of neuronal migration across the embryonic cerebral wall. *J. Neurosci.* 16:2283–2293.

ARIMATSU, Y., M. MIYAMOTO, I. NIHONMATSU, K. HIRATA, Y. URATAINI, Y. HATANKA, and K. TAKIGUCHI-HOYASHI, 1992. Early regional specification for a molecular neuronal phenotype in the rat neocortex. *Proc. Natl. Acad. Sci. U.S.A.* 89:8879–8883.

BOULDER COMMITTEE, 1970. Embryonic vertebrate central nervous system. Revised terminology. *Anat. Rec.* 166:257–261.

BUFFONE, A., H. J. KIM, L. PUELLES, M. H. PROTEUS, M. A. FROHMAN, G. R. MARTIN, and J. L. R. RUBINSTEIN, 1993. The mouse DLX-2 (Tes-1) Gbx-2 and Wnt-3 in the embryonic day 12.5 mouse forebrain defines potential transverse and longitudinal segmental boundaries. *Mech. Dev.* 40:129–140.

BUGBEE, N. M., and P. S. GOLDMAN-RAKIC, 1983. Columnar organization of cortico-cortical projections in squirrel and rhesus monkeys: Similarity of column width in species differing in cortical volume. *J. Comp. Neurol.* 220:355–364.

CAMERON, R. S., and P. RAKIC, 1991. Glial cell lineage in the cerebral cortex: Review and synthesis. *Glia* 4:124–137.

CAMERON, R. S., and P. RAKIC, 1994. Polypeptides that comprise the plasmalemmal microdomain between migrating neuronal and glial cells. *J. Neurosci.* 14:3139–3155.

CATALANO, S. M., R. T. ROBERTSON, and H. P. KILLACKEY, 1996. Individual axon morphology and thalamocortical topography in developing rat somatosensory cortex. *J. Comp. Neurol.* 366:36–53.

CAVINESS, V. S., JR., and P. RAKIC, 1978. Mechanisms of cortical development: A view from mutations in mice. *Annu. Rev. Neurosci.* 1:297–326.

CHUN, J. M., and C. J. SHATZ, 1989. Interstitial cells of the adult neocortical white matter are the remnant of the early-generated subplate neuron population. *J. Comp. Neurol.* 282:555–569.

COHEN-TANNOUDJI, M., C. BABINET, and M. WASSEF, 1994. Early intrinsic regional specification of the mouse somatosensory cortex. *Nature* 368:460–463.

CONEL, J. L., 1939. *The Postnatal Development of the Human Cerebral Cortex. I. The Cortex of the Newborn.* Cambridge, Mass.: Harvard University Press.

CREUTZFELDT, O. D., 1977. Generality of the functional structure of the neocortex. *Naturwissenschaften* 64:507–517.

DE CARLOS, J. A., and D. D. M. O'LEARY, 1992. Growth and targeting of subplate axons and establishment of major cortical pathways. *J. Neurosci.* 12:1194–1211.

DEHAY, C., P. GIROUD, M. BERLAND, I. SMART, and H. KENNEDY, 1993. Modulation of the cell cycle contributes to the parcellation of the primate visual cortex. *Nature* 366:464–466.

ECCLES, J. C., 1984. The cerebral neocortex: A theory of its operation. In *Cerebral Cortex* (Vol. 2), E. G. JONES and A. PETERS, eds. New York: Plenum Press, pp. 1–36.

ELLIS, R. E., and H. R. HORVITZ, 1991. Two *C. elegans* genes control the programmed deaths of specific cells in the pharynx. *Development* 112:591–603.

EMERLING, D. E., and A. D. LANDER, 1994. Laminar specific attachment and neurite outgrowth of thalamic neurons on cultured slices of developing cerebral cortex. *Development* 120:2811–2822.

FERRI, R. T., and P. LEVITT, 1993. Cerebral cortical progenitors are fated to produce region-specific neuronal populations. *Cerebral Cortex* 3(3):187–198.

FRANTZ, G. D., A. P. BOHNER, R. M. AKERS, and S. K. MCCONNELL, 1994. Regulation of the POU domain gene SCIP during cerebral cortical development. *J. Neurosci.* 14:472–485.

GLUCKSMANN, A., 1951. Cell deaths in normal vertebrate ontogeny. *Biol. Rev.* 26:59–86.

GOLDMAN-RAKIC, P. S., 1987. Circuitry of primate prefrontal cortex and regulation of behavior by representational memory. In *Handbook of Physiology*, F. Plum and V. Mountcastle, eds. Bethesda, Md.: American Physiology Society, pp. 373–417.

GOLDMAN-RAKIC, P. S., 1988. Topography of cognition: Parallel distributed networks in primate association cortex. *Annu. Rev. Neurosci.* 11:137–156.

GOLDMAN-RAKIC, P. S., and P. RAKIC, 1984. Experimental modification of gyral patterns. In *Cerebral Dominance: The*

Biological Foundation, N. Geschwind and A. M. Galaburda, eds. Cambridge, Mass.: Harvard University Press, pp. 179–192.

HATTEN, M. E., and C. A. MASON, 1990. Mechanism of glial-guided neuronal migration *in vitro* and i*n vivo. Experientia* 46:907–916.

HIS, W., 1874. *Unserer Koperform und das Physiologishe Problem inrer Enstehung.* Leipzig: Engelman.

HIS, W., 1904. *Die Entwicklung des Monschlichen Gehirns Wahrend der Ersten Monate.* Leipzig: Hirzel.

KAISERMAN-ABRAMOFF, I. R., A. M. GRAYBIEL, and W. J. H. NAUTA, 1980. The thalamic projection to cortical area 17 in a congenitally anophthalmic mouse strain. *Neuroscience* 5:41–52.

KENNEDY, H., and C. DEHAY, 1993. Cortical specification of mice and men. *Cerebral Cortex* 3:171–186.

KOMURO, H., and P. RAKIC, 1992. Specific role of N-type calcium channels in neuronal migration. *Science* 257:806–809.

KOMURO, H., and P. RAKIC, 1993. Modulation of neuronal migration by NMDA receptors. *Science* 260:95–97.

KOMURO, H., and P. RAKIC, 1996. Calcium oscillations provide signals for the saltatory movement of CNS neurons. *Neuron* 17:257–285.

KORNACK, D. R., and P. RAKIC, 1995. Radial and horizontal deployment of clonally related cells in the primate neocortex: Relationship to distinct mitotic lineages. *Neuron* 15:311–321.

KOSTOVIC, I., and P. S. GOLDMAN-RAKIC, 1983. Transient cholinesterase staining in the mediodorsal nucleus of the thalamus and its connections in the developing human and monkey brain. *J. Comp. Neurol.* 219:431–447.

KOSTOVIC, I., and M. E. MOLLIVER, 1974. A new interpretation of the laminar development of cerebral cortex: Synaptogenesis in different layers of neopalium in the human fetus. *Anat. Rec.* 178:395.

KOSTOVIC, I., and P. RAKIC, 1980. Cytology and time of origin of interstitial neurons in the white matter in infant and adult human and monkey telencephalon. *J. Neurocytol.* 9:219–242.

KOSTOVIC, I., and P. RAKIC, 1984. Development of prestriate visual projections in the monkey and human fetal cerebrum revealed by transient acetylcholinesterase staining. *J. Neurosci.* 4:25–42.

KOSTOVIC, I., and P. RAKIC, 1990. Developmental history of transient subplate zone in the visual and somatosensory cortex of the macaque monkey and human brain. *J. Comp. Neurol.* 297:441–470.

KUAN, C., E. ELLIOT, R. FLAVELL, and P. RAKIC, 1997. Restrictive clonal allocation in the chimeric mouse brain. *Proc. Natl. Acad. Sci. U.S.A.* 94:3374–3379.

KUIDA, K., T. F. HAYDAR, C. KUAN, G. YONG, C. TAYA, H. KARASUYAMA, M. S.-S. SU, P. RAKIC, and R. A. FLAVELL, 1998. Reduced apoptosis and cytochrome c-mediated caspase activation in mice lacking caspase-9. *Cell* 94:325–337.

KUIDA, K., T. S. ZHENG, S. NA, C. KUANG, D. YAN, H. KARASUYAMA, P. RAKIC, and R. A. FLAVELL, 1996. Decreased apoptosis in the brain and premature lethality in CPP32-deficient mice. *Nature* 384:368–372.

KULJIS, R. O., and P. RAKIC, 1990. Hypercolumns in the monkey visual cortex can develop in the absence of cues from photoreceptors. *Proc. Natl. Acad. Sci. U.S.A.* 87:5303–5306.

LEVITT, P., M. L. COOPER, and P. RAKIC, 1981. Coexistence of neuronal and glial precursor cells in the cerebral ventricular zone of the fetal monkey: An ultrastructural immunoperoxidase analysis. *J Neurosci.* 1:27–39.

LEVITT, P., M. F. BARBE, and K. L. EAGLESON, 1997. Patterning and specification of the cerebral cortex. *Annu. Rev. Neurobiol.* 20:1–24.

LIDOW, M. S., and P. RAKIC, 1992. Postnatal development of monoaminergic neurotransmitter receptors with primate neocortex. *Cerebral Cortex* 2:401–415.

LIDOW, M. S., and P. RAKIC, 1994. Unique profiles of α1-, α2-, and β-adrenergic receptors in the developing cortical plate and transient embryonic zones of the rhesus monkey. *J. Neurosci.* 14:4064–4078.

LOIS, C., and A. ALVAREZ-BUYLLA, 1994. Long-distance neuronal migration in the adult mammalian brain. *Science* 264:1145–1148.

LOTURCO, J. J., D. F. OWENS, M. J. S. HEATH, M. B. E. DAVIS, and A. R. KRIEGSTEIN, 1995. GABA and glutamate depolarize cortical progenitor cells and inhibit DNA synthesis. *Neuron* 15:1287–1298.

LUSKIN, M. B., A. L. PEARLMAN, and J. R. SANES, 1988. Cell lineage in the cerebral cortex of the mouse studied in vivo and in vitro with a recombinant retrovirus. *Neuron* 1:635–647.

LUSKIN, M. B., and C. J. SHATZ, 1985. Studies of the earliest generated cells of the cat's visual cortex: Cogeneration of subplate and marginal zones. *J. Neurosci.* 5:1062–1075.

MARIN-PADILLA, M., 1988. Early ontogenesis of the human cerebral cortex. In *Cerebral Cortex. Development and Maturation of Cerebral Cortex*, A. Peters and E.G. Jones, eds. New York: Plenum Press, pp. 1–34.

MCCONNELL, S. K., 1988. Development and decision-making in the mammalian cerebral cortex. *Brain Res. Rev.* 13:1–23.

MCCONNELL, S. K., A. GHOSH, and C. J. SHATZ, 1994. Subplate pioneers and the formation of descending connections from cerebral cortex. *J. Neurosci.* 14:1892–1907.

MCCONNELL, S. K., and C. E. KASANOWSKI, 1991. Cell cycle dependence of laminar determination in developing cerebral cortex. *Science* 254:282–285.

MEISSIREL, C., K. C. WIKLER, L. M. CHALUPA, and P. RAKIC, 1997. Early divergence of M and P visual subsystems in the embryonic primate brain. *Proc. Natl. Acad. Sci. U.S.A.* 94:5900–5905.

MENEZES, J. R. L., and M. B. LUSKIN, 1994. Expression of neuron-specific tubulin defines a novel population in the proliferative layers of the developing telencephalon. *J. Neurosci.* 14:5399–5416.

MOLLIVER, M. E., I. KOSTOVIC, and H. VAN DER LOOS, 1973. The development of synapses in cerebral cortex of the human fetus. *Brain Res.* 50:403–407.

MOUNTCASTLE, V., 1995. The evolution of ideas concerning the function of the neocortex. *Cerebral Cortex* 5:289–295.

MOUNTCASTLE, V. B., 1997. The columnar organization of the neocortex. *Brain* 120:701–722.

NAKATSUJI, M., Y. KADOKAWA, and H. SUEMORI, 1991. Radial columnar patches in the chimeric cerebral cortex visualized by use of mouse embryonic stem cells expressing β-galactosidase. *Dev. Growth Differentiation* 33:571–578.

OLIVARIA, J., and R. C. VAN SLUYTERS, 1984. Callosal connections of the posterior neocortex in normal-eyed, congenitally anophthalmic and neonatally enucleated mice. *J. Comp. Neurol.* 230:249–268.

OPPENHEIM, R. W., 1991. Cell death during development of the nervous system. *Annu. Rev. Neurosci.* 14:453–501.

PARNAVELAS, J. G., J. A. BARFIELD, E. FRANKE, and M. B. LUSKIN, 1991. Separate progenitor cells give rise to pyramidal and nonpyramidal neurons in the rat telencephalon. *Cerebral Cortex* 1:463–491.

POLIAKOV, G. I., 1959. Progressive neuron differentiation of the human cerebral cortex in ontogenesis. In *Development of the Central Nervous System*, S. A. Sarkisov and S. N. Preobrazenskaya, eds. Moscow: Medgiz, pp. 11–26 (in Russian).

POLIAKOV, G. I., 1965. Development of the cerebral neocortex during the first half of intrauterine life. In *Development of the Child's Brain*, S. A. Sarkisov, ed. Leningrad: Medicinam, pp. 22–52 (in Russian).

PROTEUS, M. H., E. J. BRICE, A. BUFFONE, T. B. USDIN, R. D. CIARANELLO, and J. R. RUBINSTEIN, 1991. Isolation and characterization of a library of cDNA clones that are preferentially expressed in the embryonic telencephalon. *Neuron* 7:221.

RAKIC, P., 1972. Mode of cell migration to the superficial layers of fetal monkey neocortex. *J. Comp. Neurol.* 145:61–84.

RAKIC, P., 1973. Kinetics of proliferation and latency between final cell division and onset of differentiation of cerebellar stellate and basket neurons. *J. Comp. Neurol.* 147:523–546.

RAKIC, P., 1974. Neurons in the monkey visual cortex: Systematic relation between time of origin and eventual disposition. *Science* 183:425–427.

RAKIC, P., 1976a. Prenatal genesis of connections subserving ocular dominance in the rhesus monkey. *Nature* 261:467–471.

RAKIC, P., 1976b. Differences in the time of origin and in eventual distribution of neurons in areas 17 and 18 of the visual cortex in the rhesus monkey. *Exp. Brain Res. Suppl.* 1:244–248.

RAKIC, P., 1977. Prenatal development of the visual system in the rhesus monkey. *Philos. Trans. R. Soc. Lond. [Biol.]* 278:245–260.

RAKIC, P., 1978. Neuronal migration and contact interaction in primate telencephalon. *J. Postgrad. Med.* 54:25–40.

RAKIC, P., 1981. Neuron-glial interaction during brain development. *Trends Neurosci.* 4:184–187.

RAKIC, P., 1985. Limits of neurogenesis in primates. *Science* 227:154–156.

RAKIC, P., 1988a. Specification of cerebral cortical areas. *Science* 241:170–176.

RAKIC, P., 1988b. Defects of neuronal migration and pathogenesis of cortical malformations. *Prog. Brain Res.* 73:15–37.

RAKIC, P., 1990. Principles of neuronal cell migration. *Experientia* 46:882–891.

RAKIC, P., 1995a. Radial versus tangential migration of neuronal clones in the developing cerebral cortex *Proc. Natl. Acad. Sci. U.S.A.* 92:11323–11327.

RAKIC, P., 1995b. A small step for the cell–a giant leap for mankind: A hypothesis of neocortical expansion during evolution. *Trends Neurosci.* 18:383–388.

RAKIC, P., 1997. Intra- and extracellular control of neuronal migration: Relevance to cortical malformations. In *Normal and Abnormal Development of the Cortex,* M. Galaburda and Y. Christen, eds. *Research and Perspectives in Neurosciences.* New York: Springer-Verlag, pp. 81–89.

RAKIC, P., R. S. CAMERON, and H. KOMURO, 1994. Recognition, adhesion, transmembrane signaling, and cell motility in guided neuronal migration. *Curr. Opin. Neurobiol.* 4:63–69.

RAKIC, P., E. KNYIHAR-CSILLIK, and B. CSILLIK, 1996. Polarity of microtubule assembly during neuronal migration. *Proc. Natl. Acad. Sci. U.S.A.* 93:9218–9222.

RAKIC, P., and H. KOMURO, 1995.The role of receptor-channel activity during neuronal cell migration. *J. Neurobiol.* 26:299–315.

RAKIC, P., and M. LIDOW, 1995. Distribution and density of neurotransmitter receptors in the absence of retinal input from early embryonic stages. *J. Neurosci.* 15:2561–2574.

RAKIC, P., and R. S. NOWAKOWSKI, 1981. Time of origin of neurons in the hippocampal region of the rhesus monkey. *J. Comp. Neurol.* 196:99–124.

RAKIC, P., and K. P. RILEY, 1983a. Overproduction and elimination of retinal axons in the fetal rhesus monkey. *Science* 209:1441–1444.

RAKIC, P., and K. P. RILEY, 1983b. Regulation of axon numbers in the primate optic nerve by prenatal binocular competition. *Nature* 305:135–137.

RAKIC, P., and R. L. SIDMAN, 1968. Supravital DNA synthesis in the developing human and mouse brain. *J. Neuropath. Exp. Neurol.* 27:246–276.

RAKIC, P., and W. SINGER, 1988. *Neurobiology of the Neocortex.* New York: Wiley.

RAKIC, P., L. J. STENSAAS, and E. P. SAYRE, 1974. Computer-aided three-dimensional reconstruction and quantitative analysis of cells from serial electron microscopic montages of fetal monkey brain. *Nature* 250:31–34.

RAKIC, P., I. SUNER, and R. W. WILLIAMS, 1991. Novel cytoarchitectonic areas induced experimentally within primate striate cortex. *Proc. Natl. Acad. Sci. U.S.A.* 88:2083–2987.

REID, C., I. LIANG, and C. WALSH, 1995. Systematic widespread clonal organization in cerebral cortex. *Neuron* 15:299–310.

RICHARDS, L. J., D. E. KOESTER, R. TUTTLE, and D. D. M. O'LEARY, 1997. Directed growth of early cortical axons is influenced by a chemoattractant released from an intermediate target. *J. Neurosci.* 17:2445–2458.

SANES, J. R., 1989. Analyzing cell lineages with a recombinant retrovirus. *Trends Neurosci.* 12:21–28.

SCHACHNER, M., A. FAISSNER, and G. FISCHER, 1985. Functional and structural aspects of the cell surface in mammalian nervous system development. In *The Cell in Contact: Adhesions and Junctions as Morphogenetic Determinants*, G. M. Edelman, W. E. Gall, and J. P. Thiery, eds. New York: Wiley.

SCHMECHEL, D. E., and P. RAKIC, 1979. Arrested proliferation of radial glial cells during midgestation in rhesus monkey. *Nature* 227:303–305.

SCHWARTZ, M. L., P. RAKIC, and P. S. GOLDMAN-RAKIC, 1991. Early phenotype of cortical neurons: Evidence that a subclass of migrating neurons have callosal axons. *Proc. Natl. Acad. Sci. U.S.A.* 88:1354–1358.

SHATZ, C. J., J. J. M. CHUN, and M. B. LUSKIN, 1988. The role of the subplate in the development of mammalian telencephalon. In *Cerebral Cortex*, A. Peters and E.G. Jones, eds. New York: Plenum Press, pp. 35–38.

SIDMAN, R. L., and P. RAKIC, 1973. Neuronal migration with special reference to developing human brain: A review. *Brain Res.* 62:1–35.

SIDMAN, R. L., and P. RAKIC, 1982. Development of the human central nervous system. In *Histology and Histopathology of the Nervous System*, W. Haymaker and R. D. Adams, eds. Springfield, Ill.: Charles C. Thomas, pp. 3–145.

SORIANO, E., N. DUMESNIL, C. AULADELL, M. COHEN-TANNOUDJI, and C. SOTELO, 1995. Molecular heterogeneity of progenitors and radial migration in the developing cerebral cortex revealed by transgenic expression. *Proc. Natl. Acad. Sci. U.S.A.* 92:11676–11680.

SZENTHAGOTHAI, J., 1987. The neuronal network of the cerebral cortex: A functional interpretation. *Prog. Brain Res.* 201:219–248.

TAN, S.-S., M. KALLONIATIS, K. STURM, P. P. L. TAM, B. E. REESE, and B. FAULKNER-JONES, 1998. Separate progenitors for radial and tangential cell dispersion during development of the cerebral neocortex. *Neuron* 21:295–304.

WILLIAMS, B. P., and J. PRICE, 1995. Evidence for multiple precursor cell types in the embryonic rat cerebral cortex. *Neuron* 14:1181–1188.

WILLIAMS, R. W., and K. HERRUP, 1988. Control of neuron number. *Annu. Rev. Neurosci.* 278:344–352.

ZECEVIC, N., 1998. Synaptogenesis in Layer I of the human cerebral cortex in the first half of gestation. *Cerebral Cortex* 8:245–252.

ZHONG, W., J. N. FEDER, M.-M. JIANG, L.Y. JAN, and Y. N. JAN, 1996. Asymmetric localization of a mammalian Numb homolog during mouse cortical neurogenesis. *Neuron* 17:43–53.

2 Molecular Determinants of Regionalization of the Forebrain and Cerebral Cortex

PAT LEVITT

ABSTRACT   Recent advances in molecular and developmental biology have facilitated the discovery of genes and diffusible factors that control regionalization of the central nervous system. The forebrain arises early through a series of inductive interactions between neuroectoderm and underlying mesendoderm—interactions that produce unique gene expression patterns and cytoarchitecture. Environmental challenges to cell fate by transplantation of early embryonic tissues and molecular studies of gene expression patterns also reveal early specification of regions of the cerebral cortex. Early patterning may be responsible for subsequent, restricted expression of axon guidance cues that are necessary for the formation of functional circuits.

Milestone events of cell proliferation, migration, differentiation, and circuit formation underlie the establishment of functional systems in the central nervous system (CNS). A recent explosion of studies has demonstrated that each ontogenetic event is both temporally and spatially regulated by molecular interactions that control the formation of neuronal populations with unique functional properties. In just the four-year period since a related chapter on the topic of cortical regionalization appeared in *Cognitive Neuroscience* (Levitt, 1994), some of the signaling systems that control pattern formation in the CNS have been defined. During early development, a series of morphologic and molecular changes within the forerunner of the CNS, the neural plate, establishes major regions of the neuraxis as the plate rolls up to form a tube. This begins a hierarchical process in which the early neuraxis undergoes regionalization due to anatomically restricted expression of transcription factors and their inducers (Lumsden and Krumlauf, 1996; Rubenstein et al., 1994; Rubenstein et al., 1998; Tanabe and Jessell, 1996). Thus, the differentiation of region-appropriate neuronal phenotypes occurs subsequent to and is dependent upon parcellation of domains in the CNS. The ability of the projection neurons to interconnect within and between brain regions relies on the further expression of molecules involved in axon guidance (Goodman, 1996; Jessell, 1988; Tessier-Lavinge and Goodman, 1996).

The interactions of diffusible signaling molecules, which arise from nonneural ectoderm and mesendoderm, with neuroectodermal cells begins the complex process of regional specialization that is essential for the subsequent milestone events to take place (Rubenstein and Beachy, 1998). During this process, the basic subdivisions of the neuraxis arise [from rostral to caudal: telencephalon and diencephalon (forebrain), mesencephalon, metencephalon, myelencephalon], with the emergence of dorsoventral and anteroposterior axes. This review focuses on the processes that establish the rostral end of the neural tube, the telencephalon and, in particular, the mechanisms that underlie the regional identity of the cerebral cortex. It is in the context of establishing major brain regions that a framework is built for development of functional specialization in the cortex. Recent research has shown that unique regional properties are expressed early in prenatal development, governed by expression of genes that control neuronal phenotype and the guidance of axon populations to their proper destinations (Levitt, Barbe, and Eagleson, 1997).

Inductive interactions produce the forebrain

Nonneural tissue contributes heavily to the formation of structures that are uniquely found in the forebrain. The notochord, a midline embryonic structure formed during gastrulation, is composed of mesendodermal tissue. Neural-inducing activity has been associated with the notochord; and, in the past decade, studies have shown that a diffusible protein, sonic hedgehog (Shh), is responsible for the initial differentiation of ectoderm into neuroectodermal tissue (Echelard et al., 1993; Tanabe and Jessell, 1996). At the anterior end of the tube, prechordal mesendodermal cells accumulate rostral to the

PAT LEVITT   Department of Neurobiology, University of Pittsburgh School of Medicine, Pittsburgh, Pa.

notochord. These cells serve as a source of Shh; and, through activation of the Shh receptor, an initial regionalization of the rostral neural tube occurs. What is accomplished during the early inductive events? Initial differentiation of the neuroectoderm is thought to involve the patterned expression of transcription factors–proteins that bind to specific DNA sequences and thereby control, in a very powerful fashion, the expression of specific genes (figure 2.1). The expression of Shh results in the induction of Nkx2.1, a transcription factor found only in the ventral part of the anterior neural tube (Qiu et al., 1998). This region will form the hypothalamus, basal ganglia, and other regions of the basal forebrain. Nonneural ectodermal tissue appears to be required for induction of dorsal structures in the prosencephalon, including the telencephalic vesicles that contain the cerebral wall, the dorsal thalamus, and the epithalamus. It appears that FGF8, a secreted member of the fibroblast growth factor family, is responsible for dorsalization of the anterior neural tube (Rubenstein and Beachy, 1998). The involvement of FGF8 is particularly interesting, because this growth factor is expressed by ectoderm throughout the anteroposterior extent of the neural tube, yet only induces forebrain structures rostrally. In the region of the midbrain, for example, FGF8 induces expression of engrailed 2, a gene that marks the anterior

boundary of the midbrain at the level of the isthmus (Crossley, Martinez, and Martin, 1996). The distinct effects caused by the activation of the same receptor (FGF8r) on different populations of cells underscores the critical role of cell location in developmental processes. Thus, cellular context, the spatial and temporal state of any particular cell, has a significant impact on the response of that cell to any particular set of cues that influence differentiation (see Lillien, 1998, for review). When one considers the distinct, local changes induced by FGF8, it is clear that the neuroepithelial cells in the anterior neural tube are distinct from those in the isthmus. Explants of neural plate stage embryos directly demonstrated the different inductive potential of axial mesendoderm (Dale et al., 1997) and differing competence of neural plate cells along the neuraxis (Shimamura and Rubenstein, 1997).

The major dorsal structure of the forebrain, the cerebral cortex, is distinguished from surrounding regions by its laminar appearance, with organized populations of neurons in layers based on their time of origin during fetal development (see Rakic, chapter 1 of this volume). This is in contrast to ventral forebrain structures, which are organized as nuclei or large aggregates of neurons that comprise the basal ganglia, amygdala, and septal region. Studies using explants of early neural tissue have

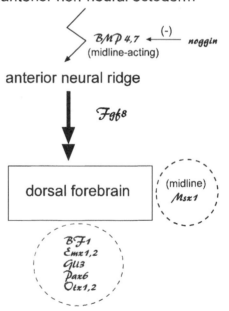

FIGURE 2.1 Schematic diagram illustrating the role of diffusible signals from nonneural tissues in inducing forebrain structures and transcription factors. Prechordal mesoderm is the site of origin of sonic hedgehog, which acts on anterior neural plate tissue to induce ventral forebrain genes such as Nkx2.1 and Pax2. Pax6 expression is suppressed by sonic hedgehog. Anterior nonneural ectoderm produces bone morphogenetic proteins (BMP) 4 and 7, which act on midline anterior neural ridge to induce dorsal forebrain marker Msx1. Note that noggin, which is produced in the forebrain, can act as a negative regulator of BMPs. The anterior neural ridge is the site of Fgf8 production, which acts on the prosencephalic neural plate to induce dorsal forebrain structures and the subsequent expression of transcription factors BF1. Emx1 and 2, Gli3, Pax6, and Otx1 and 2.

shown that soon after Nkx2.1 appears in the ventral neuroectodermal cells, Dlx genes are turned on within the same cell populations (Shimamura and Rubenstein, 1997). Dorsally, Bf1, a transcription factor of the winged helix family, is expressed by neuroectodermal cells that give rise to the cerebral hemispheres and dorsal thalamus. These early molecular changes are critical for subsequent specialization of structures because mutations in early ventral or dorsal genes result in severe malformations or even the absence of specific structures (see, for example, Schmahl et al., 1993; Stoykova et al., 1996; Xuan et al., 1995).

Other transcription factors—including members of the otx and emx family—are expressed in a very rapid fashion just subsequent to Bf1 gene induction. These genes are the vertebrate homologs of drosophila genes that are involved in head formation. It has been shown experimentally that isolated anterior neuroectoderm will not develop dorsal structures in the absence of FGF8, suggesting that this molecule may be involved in early telencephalic patterning. Members of the bone morphogenetic protein (BMP) family are expressed in midline neuroectoderm and the anterior neural ridge, the forerunner of the dorsal telencephalon. It has been suggested that both BMP4 and 7 may be involved in dorsal patterning. Mutation of Bmp4 results in abnormal dorsal midline development (Furuta, Piston, and Hogan, 1997).

Several complicating issues arise in assigning a particular morphologic defect directly to the absence of one specific factor. Many of the genes noted above are expressed in different regions of the early neural tube and participate in multiple inductive events. The hierarchical nature of the molecular interactions is likely to result in complex changes when one gene is mutated. For example, mutations of Otx genes result in the anterior movement of FGF8 expression and the posteriorization of the neural tube (Acampora et al., 1997; Suda et al., 1996). In addition, growth factors have pleotrophic effects (reviewed in Lillien, 1998). Thus, a molecule may be mitogenic for one particular cell population, but cause phenotypic differentiation of that same cell population at a later time [see the example of epidermal growth factor (EGF) below]. Such multiple activities complicate the interpretation of defects that arise from the deletion of any one particular gene.

Regionalization of the cerebral cortex

Progress in understanding the molecular and subsequent anatomic specification of the neuraxis has been both rapid and dramatic in the past few years. But that progress has been, and remains, difficult. What, then, has been the difficulty in determining the extent to which different functional domains of the cerebral cortex are determined prior to experiencing subcortical influences? In fact, studies examining the basic patterning of the neural tube employ an experimental design that relies on the ability to assay specific features, or phenotypes, of the tissue in order to evaluate the extent to which cells in that region express unique features. At a rather global level, one focuses particularly on those characteristics that distinguish regions of the CNS, which themselves may contain heterogeneous nuclei and laminated structures. In the cortex, it is somewhat enigmatic that the establishment of unique cortical cytoarchitectonics, by similar populations of neuronal subclasses [glutaminergic projection and GABAergic interneurons, at a consistent ratio of approximately 6:1 (Beaulieu, 1993; Hendry et al., 1987)], occurs rather late in development, well after connections from the thalamus are established. We have hypothesized that the early decisions made by cortical progenitors to differentiate into specific types of projection neurons provide the framework upon which unique functional areas and their associated connections form. This hypothesis is based on data demonstrating that projections from thalamus to cortex (and those reciprocal connections) form without errors in a very specific fashion (Agmon et al., 1995; DeCarlos and O'Leary, 1992; Erzurumlu and Jhaveri, 1992; Miller, Chou, and Finlay, 1993). The specific targeting suggests that there are molecular differences (both positive and repulsive cues) in the cerebral wall that guide axons to their appropriate functional area. While the molecular mechanisms that control the decisions pertaining to cell fate in different cortical regions are beginning to be understood, recent studies using experimental manipulations of the environment in which cells develop indicate that cortical regionalization may be a complex process.

The cellular environment influences phenotypic potential

Experimental embryologists have utilized a time-honored method to approach the question of how the potential of a cell or tissue to differentiate and express particular phenotypic characteristics is established. One can test the differentiative potential of a piece of tissue or individual cells by placing them into an environment that they normally do not experience (heterotopic). This type of experimental approach is particularly useful when the novel environment is sufficiently different from the normal (homotopic) location of the tissue or cells that are harvested for transplantation. The timing of the manipulation is critical: Grafting the tissue or cells prior to expression of the particular phenotype tests the ability of the tissue or cells to express the feature in a foreign environment, while moving the tissue after expression tests the ability of the tissue to maintain the phenotypic feature in a different environment. This experimental strategy has been used at the cellular and tissue levels with cortical material, and some common mechanisms of development have emerged (Levitt, 1994; Levitt, Barbe, and Eagleson, 1997). Progenitor cells by definition are mitotically active and have not yet differentiated into postmitotic neurons. Progenitors appear to have the greatest potential to develop into a variety of neural cell types. For example, forebrain progenitors will integrate into heterotopic sites of the telencephalon, brainstem, and cerebellum and differentiate into neurons appropriate for each site (Brustle, Maskos, and McKay, 1995; Campbell, Olsson, and Bjorklund, 1995; Fishell, 1995). The neurons even form correct connections. Within the forebrain, progenitors have the capacity to respond to novel environmental cues that alter their predicted cell fate. Laminar position in the cerebral cortex is a predictor of particular neuronal phenotypes because cells in different layers project to different targets. Progenitors obtained at a time when deep-layer neurons are produced can be transplanted to older host brains and will migrate to superficial layers, like their host counterparts, even making connections specific for superficial neurons (McConnell and Kaznowski, 1991). The complementary experiment, in which progenitor cells from older fetal brains are harvested and transplanted into younger hosts, failed to generate the same result (Frantz and McConnell, 1996). The older progenitor cells produced neurons that migrated to more middle and superficial layers. These data suggest that even progenitors can change with time, becoming more restricted in terms of what they can become. This restriction may be due in part to altered expression of growth factor receptors that make a cell more or less responsive to a particular environmental cue (Burrows et al., 1997; Lillien, 1995; Lillien, 1998).

Experiments focusing on regional properties of cortical tissue have been done in parallel with those examining individual cellular characteristics. In the late 1980s, transplantation of small pieces of fetal tissue was performed between occipital (visual) and dorsal fronto-parietal (sensorimotor) cortex. When descending projection patterns of the transplanted neurons were analyzed, it was found that even transplants of late fetal tissue could alter their "normal" normal projections and, instead, develop efferents to brain regions most appropriate for their new location (O'Leary and Stanfield, 1986). The number of neurons that exhibited this capacity was not known at the time; however, recent quantitative studies using a similar transplant strategy have shown that the majority of neurons project subcortically in a manner reflecting their origin rather than their new environment (Castro et al., 1991; Ebrahimi-Gaillard and Roger, 1996; Garnier, Arnault, and Roger, 1997; Garnier et al., 1997). It is therefore likely that, for some projection patterns, many postmitotic neurons can maintain features characteristic of their donor location, the area in which they initially differentiated. This implies that younger transplants, containing more progenitor cells, would exhibit more plasticity. Does this make sense functionally? It is reasonable to predict deficits in functional recovery with transplanted tissue that exhibits mostly aberrant projections based on a new location. Indeed, recent studies have shown that late fetal tissue harvested from occipital cortex cannot subserve functional recovery of somatosensory tissue that it replaced in host animals (Barth and Stanfield, 1994).

Studies in which molecular markers have been used to monitor differentiation of cortical tissue have led to similar conclusions. The expression of the limbic system–associated membrane protein (LAMP), a cell adhesion molecule involved in the development of limbic circuitry (Keller et al., 1989; Levitt, 1984; Pimenta et al., 1995; Zacco et al., 1990), is restricted in the cortex to limbic regions such as medial prefrontal, anterior cingulate, and perirhinal areas (Ferri and Levitt, 1993; Horton and Levitt, 1988; Pimenta, Reinoso, and Levitt, 1996; Reinoso, Pimenta, and Levitt, 1996). Progenitor cells from neocortical regions can express LAMP when placed into a neonatal host environment in which neurons normally express the protein. The change in cell fate of neocortical progenitors is more pronounced when harvested from very young (E12-14) fetal tissue, a time when neuron production is just beginning (Barbe and Levitt, 1991). Perhaps the most striking outcome of these transplant studies was the finding that changes in molecular expression of LAMP by the tissue was paralleled by predictable patterns of thalamocortical and corticocortical projections (Barbe and Levitt, 1992; Barbe and Levitt, 1995). Thus, grafts that contained substantial numbers of LAMP[+] neurons also exhibited limbic thalamic and corticocortical connections. LAMP[−] grafts of somatosensory tissue formed primary sensory neocortical and thalamic connections in the host (Barbe and Levitt, 1992, 1995). Other, subsequent, studies used different molecular markers to document a link between specification of cell populations destined for certain domains of the cerebral cortex and proliferative potential of the cells (Arimatsu et al., 1992, 1994; Cohen-Tannoudji, Babinet, and Wassef, 1994; Soriano et al., 1995).

Cellular dispersion and cortical specification

The radial deployment of cells from the ventricular zone, where neuronal birth occurs, to a final location in the cortical plate is central to the protomap concept, in which the general position of the cell in the neuroepithelium defines the areal destiny of the neuron (Rakic, 1988). This has important implications for the mechanisms that ultimately control the formation of functional circuits involving the cerebral cortex. The concept has been challenged recently, primarily because of studies that document cell dispersion across the cerebral cortex. Retroviral lineage tracing with complex virus libraries has shown that clonally related cells, arising from individual progenitors, can be dispersed to distant locations in the mature cerebral cortex (Walsh and Cepko, 1992). Coupled with this finding, videomicroscopy has shown that one-quarter to one-third of the cells labeled in the ventricular zone of the cerebral wall will move nonradially to the cortical plate, dispersing to locations distant from the radial domain (O'Rourke et al., 1992, 1995). This is not the case for very early progenitors, prior to cortical plate formation; similar labeling studies in explants show that progenitor cells disperse, either by active migration or nuclear translocation, to overlying radial locations (O'Leary, personal communication). Recently, a third piece of evidence suggested that tangential dispersion of subpopulations of neurons is likely to occur in cortical development (Anderson et al., 1998). The fate of progenitor cells in the subventricular zone of the lateral ganglionic eminence (LGE), the region traditionally thought to give rise solely to basal ganglia structures, was monitored in explants of the forebrain from normal and Dlx-1/Dlx-2 mutant mice. In normal mice, GABAergic neurons from the LGE migrate across the pallido-cortical boundary into the cerebral wall to seed widespread cortical areas with interneurons. This fails to occur in the Dlx double knockout mice. Using chimeric animals in which an X-inactivated transgene marks cortical columns (Tan and Breen, 1993; Tan et al., 1995), Tan et al. (1998) showed that glutaminergic (projection) neurons settle in strictly radial patterns, whereas GABAergic interneurons disperse relatively randomly, both within and outside marked columns in the neocortex. These data suggest that cellular dispersion in the cerebral cortex may be more precisely controlled than originally thought, with neurons responsible for establishing area-specific subcortical and corticocortical projections migrating radially from defined regions of the ventricular zone, consistent with the protomap hypothesis (Rakic, 1988).

The dispersion of neurons in the cerebral wall appears to take place in different zones. The lineage studies showed that many retrovirally labeled progenitors moved tangentially within the ventricular zone (Walsh and Cepko, 1993). We suggested that this movement would result in respecification of progenitors that reside in a new microenvironment, prior to exiting the cell cycle (Ferri and Levitt, 1995). This hypothesis is consistent with transplant studies showing that the phenotypic fate of mitotically active cells can be altered in different environments (Barbe and Levitt, 1991; Brustle, Maskos, and McKay, 1995; McConnell and Kaznowski, 1991; reviewed in Levitt, Barbe, and Eagleson, 1997). The specific phenotypes of the cells that migrate tangentially within the fiber-rich intermediate zone may be complex and could include interneurons and nonneuronal cells. The findings do suggest that not all postmitotic neurons exhibit immutable area fates and hence that cells can be influenced to express particular area-specific features later in development. We do not know, as yet, the signals that guide these choices made by neurons in late gestation. In fact, only recently has the use of model culture systems helped dissect mechanisms that control early events of cellular differentiation.

Molecular basis of cortical regionalization

Different molecular, structural, and organizational features of a neuron help define its particular phenotype. The analysis of signals that control cell fate choices is beginning to reveal that different phenotypic characteristics may be regulated by fundamentally different mechanisms. Why is this an important issue for understanding cortical development? As noted above, we have suggested that the early decisions made by cortical progenitors to differentiate into specific types of neurons provide the framework upon which unique functional areas and associated connections form. Transplant studies support this idea (Barbe and Levitt, 1992, 1995; Barth and Stanfield, 1994; Ebrahimi-Gaillard and Roger, 1996; Garnier, Arnault, and Roger, 1997; Garnier et al., 1997). As in drosophila and vertebrate forebrain and brain stem, it is likely that a hierarchy of molecular specification is established early, which controls patterns of gene expression within regional structures. Diffusible signals are likely to establish early patterns of expression of transcription factors (see above), which act further to promote patterns of inductive signals that control cellular diversity. Prochiantz and colleagues (Volovitch et al., 1993) suggested such a hierarchy in which the generation of diversity is tantamount to the formation of specific connections.

Genes involved in regulating dorsoventral and anteroposterior patterning in the forebrain have been discovered (see above and Bulfone et al., 1993; Rubenstein and Beachy, 1998). The development of transverse domains in the forebrain is much less clear, and is particularly relevant to regionalization of the cerebral cortex. Boncinelli and co-workers (Boncinelli, Gulisano, and Broccoli, 1993; Simeone et al., 1992) have suggested that Otx and Emx family members, whose patterns of expression are overlapping, may participate. There is little evidence, however, for transcription factors that are expressed discretely in functional domains of the cerebral cortex. In fact, the broad patterns of expression reflect the general disruption of forebrain development that occurs upon mutation of Otx1 and 2, Emx-2 and Bf-1 in mice (Suda, Matsuo, and Aizawa, 1997; Xuan et al., 1995). Mutation of Emx-1, which is expressed in all neo-, meso-, allo-, and palleocortical regions (Fernandez et al., 1998; Simeone et al., 1992), results in a very mild phenotype (Qiu et al., 1996; Yoshida et al., 1997). One possible mechanism driving cortical specification would involve regulation of gene expression by transcription factors that are expressed in complex, overlapping anatomic patterns. Specification of motor neuron pools occurs in this fashion (Pfaff and Kintner, 1998; Tanabe and Jessell, 1996). Thus, no single gene expression pattern can account for the unique characteristics of a specific set of motor neurons.

Neighboring cell–cell and subcortical–cortical interactions may promote cortical specification. Each of these could control the recently discovered regionalized patterns of expression of axon guidance molecules, which may mediate the formation of cortical circuits. At least four different families of guidance molecules exhibit regionalized patterns in the cerebral cortex during development (figure 2.2):

1. LAMP in meso- and allocortex (Horton and Levitt, 1988; Pimenta et al., 1995; Pimenta, Reinoso, and Levitt, 1996; Reinoso, Pimenta, and Levitt, 1996; Zacco et al., 1990) and neurotrimin (Ntm), a related Ig superfamily molecule, in a pattern complementary to LAMP in primary sensory regions (Struyk et al., 1995; Gil et al., 1997);

2. Eph receptor A5 in limbic cortical regions (Zhang et al., 1997) and its ligand, EphrinA5, with the most dense expression complementary in primary somatosensory cortex (Gao et al., 1998);

3. Cadherin family members cad-6 and cad-8, which are expressed in restricted parts of parietal and limbic cortex, respectively (Redies and Takeichi, 1996);

4. Semaphorin family members, which exhibit complex patterns of expression in different regions of the cortex (Skaliora et al., 1998).

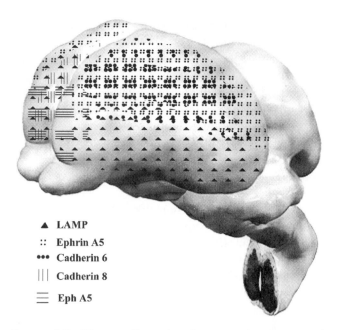

▲ LAMP
:: Ephrin A5
••• Cadherin 6
||| Cadherin 8
≡ Eph A5

FIGURE 2.2 Diagram illustrating the expression patterns of several different guidance molecules in the cerebral cortex during embryonic development. Note that LAMP is expressed both in lateral regions of the cortex along the rhinal sulcus and medially in the prefrontal and anterior cingulate regions. LAMP does not extend into posterior midline regions. EphrinA5 is expressed heavily in dorsolateral parietal areas, complementary to the mostly rostral frontal expression of EphA5. Cadherin 6 has overlapping expression domains with EphrinA5, and cadherin 8 medially in a region of the cerebral wall that overlaps with both LAMP and EphA5. Patterns are drawn on a figure of the rat brain at embryonic day 17. (Reprinted with permission from Altman and Bayer, 1995.)

LAMP, Ntm and EphrinA5 have been shown specifically to mediate the growth of different populations of cortical and subcortical neurons (Gao et al., 1998; Gil et al., 1997; Mann et al., 1998).

What regulates the expression patterns of axon guidance molecules? We have focused on the potential inductive cues that control LAMP expression because the transplant studies showed that changes in the environment of cortical progenitor cells can alter their limbic areal fate. Thus, under the appropriate conditions in vivo, progenitors that normally give rise to sensorimotor neurons can generate LAMP+ neurons with limbic connections. The transplant paradigm is not designed to identify the specific molecular components that mediate these changes in progenitor cell fate. We developed a cell culture system in which we harvested progenitors from the early cerebral wall (embryonic day 12), prior to neuron production in the rat cerebral cortex (Ferri and Levitt, 1993). The studies initially documented a rather remarkable interaction between a diffusible growth factor, transforming growth factor alpha (TGFα) and collagen type IV, which collaborate to induce LAMP expression by neocortical progenitors when they differentiate into neurons (Ferri and Levitt, 1993). TGFα is the CNS ligand that activates the EGF (ErbB1) receptor. The growth factor–matrix interaction was not as surprising as the type of matrix that was required. This is because collagen type IV is usually associated with basement membranes, as in blood vessels. Laminin, fibronectin, and polylysine or polyornithine were unable to substitute for collagen type IV. A mapping study confirmed that collagen type IV is expressed heavily, but transiently, in the ventricular zone of the rat cerebral wall by E11 (Eagleson, Ferri, and Levitt, 1996). The inductive nature of EGFr activation is exhibited only on progenitor cells; neurons fail to respond. The induction of LAMP by EGFr activation is cell cycle–dependent; this is because progenitors must be exposed for a complete cell cycle in order to respond to the inductive signal (Eagleson et al., 1997; Ferri and Levitt, 1995). In fact, cells undergoing their final cycle failed to express LAMP, even though they had been exposed to the inductive signal (Eagleson, Ferri, and Levitt, 1997). Furthermore, we found that induction resulted in LAMP expression in all daughter cells. Clonal analysis using retroviruses that express a reporter gene allows sibling cells to be followed over time through subsequent generations in vitro. The studies showed that of all the progenitor cells that responded to TGFα, more than 90% of the clones generated by these cells were homogeneous in reference to LAMP expression. The data suggest that the inductive response is represented by faithful inheritance of the LAMP phenotype. This feature is even exhibited in the absence of inductive signals in vitro by limbic progenitors. Those progenitors isolated from presumptive limbic regions of the cerebral wall produced LAMP$^+$ neurons. Moreover, all the cells comprising multicell neuronal clones, arising from limbic progenitors, were LAMP$^+$. Multicell clones are formed by progenitors that divide more than once in vitro, demonstrating that even through several cell divisions, all limbic progeny upon differentiation expressed LAMP. These results suggested that limbic progenitor cells received an inductive signal in vivo, prior to harvesting, and were able to remember this signal through several cell divisions (Eagleson et al., 1997).

LAMP is clearly a phenotypic marker that is expressed early. But are all features that are unique to areas of cortex specified? This has not been examined in detail for Ntm or the cadherins; however, recent studies in our laboratory indicate that EphrinA5 expression, which begins at about embryonic day 16 in the rat dorsal parietal region, is regulated differently than LAMP. Progenitor cells isolated from the presumptive sensorimotor domain of the cerebral wall at embryonic day 12 do not express EphrinA5 when neuronal differentiation occurs

(K. Eagleson, R. Zhou, and P. Levitt, unpublished observations). Harvesting of the same region of the cerebral wall 4–5 days later results in robust EphrinA5 expression. It is possible that the inductive signals that regulate EphrinA5 expression were not active at the time of progenitor cell harvesting. Clearly, however, each axon guidance cue may be under different regulation.

Consequences of anomalies in cortical development

Defects in development of the CNS are now believed to underlie, in part, the etiology of neuropsychiatric disorders, such as schizophrenia (Bloom, 1993; Kotrla, Sater, and Weinberger, 1997; Raedler, Knable, and Weinberger, 1998; Weinberger, 1995). The cerebral cortex is an obvious candidate site of developmental alterations because the establishment of lamination and functional areas is required for normal circuit formation. In particular, it has been suggested that regions of the cerebral cortex that mediate cognition, emotional state, and learning and memory (so-called limbic system structures) may be involved in developmental defects leading to pronounced psychopathology. In particular, the absence of pronounced cortical neuropathology in neuropsychiatric disorders suggests that there probably are not major defects in the milestone events of cell proliferation, migration, and cellular differentiation. We are only beginning to learn the consequences of how modest changes in cell cycle regulation or early inductive events in the forebrain might affect pattern formation. For example, gene knockout studies of individual transcription factors may result in little or no altered phenotype (Rubenstein and Beachy, 1998). There are examples of a range of defects, from the mild to the profound. Mutations in Emx-2 or Bf-1 result in severe forebrain malformations. Double knockout of Dlx1 and Dlx2 is required in order to see changes in forebrain organization (Anderson et al., 1998); single mutations of either gene result in minimal changes in brain organization. In the double knockout, Anderson et al. (1998) found that interneuron populations that arise from the ganglion eminence fail to form, and thus the cerebral cortex in the double mutant have reduced numbers of interneurons. Such alterations in early events of neurogenesis could generate functional defects. There are only a few examples of gene mutations that may be involved in the formation of specific cortical circuits, and they have yet to yield identifiable phenotypes (for example, Semaphorin III; see Catalano et al., 1998). As with the Dlx genes, abnormal phenotypes may arise through the mutation of several genes that encode different guidance cues, which normally work in concert to mediate circuit formation in the cerebral cortex. The discovery of transcription factors that are expressed in discrete, but overlapping patterns may be an important element in future investigations. It is possible that mutations in any one or combination of these factors may result in altered cortical phenotypes, which, when examined at the cellular level, may yield clues that link psychopathology with developmental alterations during formation of the cerebral cortex.

REFERENCES

ACAMPORA, D., V. AVANTAGGIATO, F. TUORTO, and A. SIMEONE, 1997. Genetic control of brain morphogenesis through Otx gene dosage requirement. *Development* 124:3639–3650.

AGMON, A., L. T. YANG, E. G. JONES, and D. K. O'DOWD, 1995. Topological precision in the thalamic projection to neonatal mouse barrel cortex. *J. Neurosci.* 15:549–561.

ALTMAN, J., and S. A. BAYER, 1995. *Atlas of Prenatal Rat Brain Development.* Boca Raton, Fla.: CRC Press.

ANDERSON, S. A., D. D. EISENSTAT, L. SHI, and J. L. R. RUBENSTEIN, 1998. Interneuron migration from basal forebrain to neocortex: Dependence on Dlx genes. *Science* 278:474–476.

ARIMATSU, Y., M. MIYAMOTO, I. NIHONMATSU, K. HIRATA, Y. URATANI, and Y. HATANAKA, 1992. Early regional specification for a molecular specification for a molecular neuronal phenotype in the rat neocortex. *Proc. Natl. Acad. Sci. U.S.A.* 89:8879–8883.

ARIMATSU, Y., I. NIHONMATSU, K. HIRATA, and K. TAKIGUCHI-HAYASHI, 1994. Cogeneration of neurons with a unique molecular phenotype in layers V and VI of widespread lateral neocortical areas in the rat. *J. Neurosci.* 14:2020–2031.

BARBE, M. F., and P. LEVITT, 1991. The early commitment of fetal neurons to limbic cortex. *J. Neurosci.* 11: 519–533.

BARBE, M. F., and P. LEVITT, 1992. Attraction of specific thalamic input by cerebral grafts depends on the molecular identity of the implant. *Proc. Natl. Acad. Sci. U.S.A.* 89:3706–3710.

BARBE, M. F., and P. LEVITT, 1995. Age-dependent specification of the cortico-cortical connections of cerebral grafts. *J. Neurosci.* 15:1819–1834.

BARTH, T. M., and B. B. STANFIELD, 1994. Homotopic, but not heterotopic, fetal cortical transplants can result in functional sparing following neonatal damage to the frontal cortex. *Cerebral Cortex* 4:271–278.

BEAULIEU, C., 1993. Numerical data on neocortical neurons in adult rat, with special reference to the GABA population. *Brain Res.* 609:284–292.

BLOOM, F. E., 1993. Advancing a neurodevelopmental origin for schizophrenia. *Arch. Gen. Psychiatry* 50:224–227.

BONCINELLI, E., M. GULISANO, and V. BROCCOLI, 1993. Emx and Otx homeobox genes in the developing mouse brain. *J. Neurobiol.* 24:1356–1366.

BRUSTLE, O., U. MASKOS, and R. D. MCKAY, 1995. Host-guided migration allows targeted introduction of neurons into the embryonic brain. *Neuron* 15:1275–1285.

BULFONE, A., L. PUELLES, M. H. PORTEUS, M. A. FROHMAN, G. R. MARTIN, and J. L. R. RUBENSTEIN, 1993. Spatially restricted expression of Dlx-1, Dlx-2 (Tes-1), Gbx-2, and Wnt-3 in the embryonic day 12.5 mouse forebrain defines potential transverse and longitudinal segmental boundaries. *J. Neurosci.* 13:3155–3172.

BURROWS, R. C., D. WANCIO, P. LEVITT, and L. LILLIEN, 1997. Response diversity and the timing of progenitor cell maturation are regulated by developmental changes in EGF-R expression in the cortex. *Neuron* 19:251–267.

CAMPBELL, K., M. OLSSON, and A. BJORKLUND, 1995. Regional incorporation and site-specific differentiation of striatal precursors transplanted into the embryonic forebrain ventricle. *Neuron* 15:1259–1273.

CASTRO, A. J., T. P. HOGAN, J. C. SØRENSEN, B. S. KLAUSEN, E. H. DANIELSEN, and J. ZIMMER, 1991. Heterotopic neocortical transplants: An anatomical and electrophysiological analysis of host projections to occipital cortical grafts placed into sensorimotor cortical lesions made in newborn rat. *Dev. Brain Res.* 58:231–236.

CATALANO, S., E. K. MESSERSMITH, C. S. GOODMAN, C. J. SHATZ, and A. CHEDOTAL, 1998. Many major CNS axon projections develop normally in the absence of semaphorin III. *Molec. Cell. Neurosci.* 11:173–182.

COHEN-TANNOUDJI, M., C. BABINET, and M. WASSEF, 1994. Early determination of a mouse somatosensory cortex marker. *Nature* 368:460–463.

CROSSLEY, P.H., S. MARTINEZ, and G.R. MARTIN, 1996. Midbrain development induced by FGF8 in the chick embryo. *Nature* 380:66–68.

DALE, J. K., C. VESQUE, T. J. LINTS, T. K. SAMPATH, A. FURLEY, J. DODD, and M. PLACZEK, 1997. Cooperation of BMP7 and SHH in the induction of forebrain ventral midline cells by prechordal mesoderm. *Cell* 90:257–269.

DECARLOS, J. A., and D. D. M. O'LEARY, 1992. Growth and targeting of subplate axons and establishment of major cortical pathways. *J. Neurosci.* 12:1194–1211.

DRESCHER, U., 1997. The Eph family in the patterning of neural development. *Curr. Biol.* 7:R799–R807.

EAGLESON, K. L., R. T. FERRI, and P. LEVITT, 1996. Complementary distribution of collagen type IV and the epidermal growth factor receptor in the rat embryonic telencephalon. *Cerebral Cortex* 6:540–549.

EAGLESON, K. L., and P. LEVITT, 1998. The role of ErbB receptor signaling in cell fate decisions by cortical progenitors: Evidence for a biased, lineage-based responsiveness to different ligands. *Molec. Cell Neurosci.* 12: 349–362.

EAGLESON, K. L., L. LILLIEN, A.V. CHAN, and P. LEVITT, 1997. Mechanisms specifying area fate in cortex include cell-cycle-dependent decisions and the capacity of progenitors to express phenotype memory. *Development* 124:1623–1630.

EBRAHIMI-GAILLARD, A., and M. ROGER, 1996. Development of spinal cord projections from neocortical transplants heterotopically placed in the neocortex of newborn hosts is highly dependent on the embryonic locus of origin of the graft. *J. Comp. Neurol.* 365:129–140.

ECHELARD, Y., D. J. EPSTEIN, B. ST-JACQUES, L. SHEN, J. MOHLER, J. A. MCMAHON, and A. P. MCMAHON, 1993. Sonic hedgehog, a member of a family of putative signaling molecules, is implicated in the regulation of CNS polarity. *Cell* 75:1417–1430.

ERZURUMLU, R. S., and S. JHAVERI, 1992. Emergence of connectivity in the embryonic rat parietal cortex. *Cerebral Cortex* 2:336–352.

FERNANDEZ, A. S., C. PIEAU, J. REPERANT, E. BONCINELLI, and M. WASSEF, 1998. Expression of the Emx-1 and Dlx-1 homeobox genes defines three molecularly distinct domains in the telencephalon of mouse, chick, turtle and frog embryos: Implications for the evolution of telencephalic subdivisions in amniotes. *Development* 125:2099–2111.

FERRI, R. T., and P. LEVITT, 1993. Cerebral cortical progenitors are fated to produce region-specific neuronal populations. *Cerebral Cortex* 3:187–198.

FERRI, R. T., and P. LEVITT, 1995. Regulation of regional differences in the differentiation of cerebral cortical neurons by EGF family-matrix interactions. *Development* 121:1151–1160.

FISHELL, G., 1995. Striatal precursors adopt cortical identities in response to local cues. *Development* 121:803–812.

FRANTZ, G. D., and S. K. MCCONNELL, 1996. Restriction of late cerebral cortical progenitor cells to an upper-layer fate. *Neuron* 17:55–61.

FURUTA, Y., D. W. PISTON, and B. L. HOGAN, 1997. Bone morphogenetic proteins (BMPs) as regulators of dorsal forebrain development. *Development* 124:2203–2212.

GAO, P.-P., Y. YUE, J.-H. ZHANG, D. P. CERRETTI, P. LEVITT, and R. ZHOU, 1998. Regulation of thalamic neurite outgrowth by the Eph ligand ephrin-A-5: Implications in the development of thalamocortical projections. *Proc. Natl. Acad. Sci. U.S.A.* 95: 5329–5334.

GAO, P.-P., J.-H. ZHANG, M. YOKOYAMA, B. RACEY, C.F. DREYFUS, I. B. BLACK, and R. ZHOU, 1996. Regulation of topographic projection in the brain: Elf-1 in the hippocamposeptal system. *Proc. Natl. Acad. Sci. U.S.A.* 93:11161–11166.

GARNIER, C., P. ARNAULT, J. LETANG, and M. ROGER, 1997. Development of projections from transplants of embryonic medial or lateral frontal cortex placed in the lateral frontal cortex of newborn hosts. *Neuroscience Lett.* 213:33–36.

GARNIER, C., P. ARNAULT, and M. ROGER, 1997. Development of the striatal projection from embryonic neurons from the lateral or medial frontal cortex grafted homo- or heterotopically into the medial frontal cortex of newborn rats. *Neuroscience Lett.* 235:41–44.

GIL, O. D., G. ZANAZZI, A. STRUYK, V. ZHUKAREVA, A. PIMENTA, P. LEVITT, and J. SALZER, 1997. Heterophilic interactions between members of a family of cell adhesion molecules: LAMP, OBCAM and neurotrimin that are differentially expressed in the nervous system. *Neurosci. Abstr.* 20:1297.

GOODMAN, C. S., 1996. Mechanisms and molecules that control growth cone guidance. *Annu. Rev. Neurosci.* 19:341–377.

GUISANO, M., V. BROCCOLI, C. PARDINI, and E. BONCINELLI, 1996. Emx1 and Emx2 show different patterns of expression during proliferation and differentiation of the developing cerebral cortex in the mouse. *Eur. J. Neurosci.* 8:1037–1050.

HENDRY, S. H. C., H. D. SCHWARK, E. G. JONES, and J. YAN, 1987. Numbers and proportions of GABA-immunoreactive neurons in different areas of monkey cerebral cortex. *J. Neurosci.* 7:1503–1519.

HORTON, H. L., and P. LEVITT, 1988. A unique membrane protein is expressed on early developing limbic system axons and cortical targets. *J. Neurosci.* 8:4653–4661.

JESSELL, T. M., 1988. Adhesion molecules and the hierarchy of neural development. *Neuron* 1:3–13.

KELLER, F., K. RIMVALL, M. F. BARBE, and P. LEVITT, 1989. A membrane protein associated with the limbic system mediates the formation of the septohippocampal pathway in vitro. *Neuron* 3:551–661.

KOTRLA, K. J., A. K. SATER, and D. R. WEINBERGER, 1997. Neuropathology, neurodevelopment and schizophrenia. In *Neurodevelopment and Adult Psychopathology*, M.S. Keshavan and R.M. Murray, eds. Cambridge, U.K.: Cambridge University Press, pp. 187–198.

LEVITT, P., 1984. A monoclonal antibody to limbic system neurons. *Science* 223:299–301.

LEVITT, P., 1994. Experimental approaches that reveal principles of cerebral cortical development. In *The Cognitive Neurosciences*, M.S. Gazzaniga, ed. Cambridge, Mass.: MIT Press, pp. 147–163.

LEVITT, P., M. F. BARBE, and K. E. EAGLESON, 1997. Patterning and specification of the cerebral cortex. *Annu. Rev. Neurosci.* 20:1–24.

LILLIEN, L., 1995. Changes in retinal cell fate induced by overexpression of EGF receptor. *Nature* 337:158–162.

LILLIEN, L., 1998. Neural progenitors and stem cells: Mechanisms of progenitor heterogeneity. *Curr. Opin. Neurobiol.* 8:37–44.

LUMSDEN, A., and R. KRUMLAUF, 1996. Patterning the vertebrate neuraxis. *Science* 274:1109–1115.

MANN, F., V. ZHUKAREVA, A. PIMENTA, P. LEVITT, and J. BOLZ, 1998. Membrane-associated molecules guide limbic and non-limbic thalamocortical projections. *J. Neurosci.* 18:9409–9419.

MCCONNELL, S. K., and C. E. KAZNOWSKI, 1991. Cell cycle dependence of laminar determination in developing neocortex. *Science* 254: 282–285.

MILLER, B., L. CHOU, and B. L. FINLAY, 1993. The early development of thalamocortical and corticothalamic projections. *J. Comp. Neurol.* 335:16–41.

O'LEARY, D. D. M., B. L. SCHLAGGAR, and R. TUTTLE, 1994. Specification of neocortical areas and thalamocortical connections. *Annu. Rev. Neurosci.* 17:419–439.

O'LEARY, D. D. M., and B. B. STANFIELD, 1986. A transient pyramidal tract projection from the visual cortex in the hamster and its removal by selective collateral elimination. *Dev. Brain Res.* 27:87–99.

O'ROURKE, N. A., M. E. DAILEY, S. J. SMITH, and S. K. MCCONNELL, 1992. Diverse migratory pathways in the developing cerebral cortex. *Science* 258:299–302.

O'ROURKE, N. A., D. P. SULLIVAN, C. E. KAZNOWSKI, A. A. JACOBS, and S. K. MCCONNELL, 1995. Tangential migration of neurons in the developing cerebral cortex. *Development* 121:2165–2176.

PFAFF, S., and C. KINTNER, 1998. Neuronal diversification: Development of motor neuron subtypes. *Curr. Opin. Neurobiol.* 8:27–36.

PIMENTA, A. F., B. S. REINOSO, and P. LEVITT, 1996. Expression of the mRNAs encoding the limbic system-associated membrane protein (LAMP). II. Fetal rat brain. *J. Comp. Neurol.* 375:289–302.

PIMENTA, A., V. ZHUKAREVA, M. F. BARBE, B. REINOSO, C. GRIMLEY, W. HENZEL, I. FISCHER, and P. LEVITT, 1995. The limbic system-associated membrane protein is an Ig superfamily member that mediates selective neuronal growth and axon targeting. *Neuron* 15:287–297.

QIU, M., S. ANDERSON, S. CHEN, J. J. MENESES, R. HEVNER, E. KUWAMA, R. A. PEDERSEN, and J. L. RUBENSTEIN, 1996. Mutation of the Emx-1 homeo box gene disrupts the corpus callosum. *Dev. Biol.* 178:174–178.

QIU, M., K. SHIMAMURA, L. SUSSEL, S. CHEN, and J. L. R. RUBENSTEIN, 1998. Control of anteroposterior and dorsoventral domains of Nkx6.1 gene expression relative to Nkx genes during vertebrate CNS. *Mech. Dev.* 72:77–88.

RAEDLER, T. J., M. B. KNABLE, and D. R. WEINBERGER, 1998. Schizophrenia as a developmental disorder of the cerebral cortex. *Curr. Opin. Neurobiol.* 8:157–161.

RAKIC, P., 1988. Specification of cerebral cortical areas. *Science* 241:170–176.

REDIES, C., and M. TAKEICHI, 1996. Cadherins in the developing central nervous system: An adhesive code for segmental and functional subdivisions. *Dev. Biol.* 180:413–423.

REINOSO, B. S., A. F. PIMENTA, and P. LEVITT, 1996. Expression of the mRNAs encoding the limbic system-associated membrane protein (LAMP). I. Adult rat brain. *J. Comp. Neurol.* 375:274–288.

RUBENSTEIN, J. L. R., and P. A. BEACHY, 1998. Patterning of the embryonic forebrain. *Curr. Opin. Neurobiol.* 8:18–26.

RUBENSTEIN, J. L. R., S. MARTINEZ, K. SHIMAMURA, and L. PUELLES, 1994. The embryonic vertebrate forebrain: The prosomeric model. *Science* 266:578–580.

RUBENSTEIN, J. L. R., K. SHIMAMURA, S. MARTINEZ, and L. PUELLES, 1998. Regionalization of the prosencephalic neural plate. *Annu. Rev. Neurosci.* 2:445–477.

SCHMAHL, W., M. KNOEDLSEDER, J. FAVOR, and D. DAVIDSON, 1993. Defects of neuronal migration and pathogenesis of cortical malformations are associated with Small eye (Sey) in the mouse, a point mutation at the Pax-6 locus. *Acta Neuropathol.* 86:126–135.

SHIMAMURA, K., and J. L. R. RUBENSTEIN, 1997. Inductive interactions direct early regionalization of the mouse forebrain. *Development* 124:2709–2718.

SIMEONE, A., M. GULISANO, D. ACAMPORA, A. STORNAIUOLO, M. RAMBALDI, and E. BONCINELLI, 1992. Two vertebrate homeobox genes related to the *Drosophila empty spiracles* gene are expressed in the embryonic cerebral cortex. *EMBO J.* 11:2541–2550.

SKALIORA, I., W. SINGER, H. BETZ, and A. W. PUSCHE, 1998. Differential patterns of semaphorin expression in the developing rat brain. *Eur. J. Neurosci.* 10:1215–1229.

SORIANO, E., N. DUMESNIL, C. AULADELL, M. COHEN-TANNOUDJI, and C. SOTELO, 1995. Molecular heterogeneity of progenitors and radial migration in the developing cerebral cortex revealed by transgene expression. *Proc. Natl. Acad. Sci. U.S.A.* 92:11676–11680.

STOYKOVA, A., C. WALTHER, R. FRITSCH, and P. GRUSS, 1996. Forebrain patterning defects in Pax6/Small eye mutant mice. *Development* 122:3453–3465.

STRUYK, A. F., P. D. CANNOL, M. J. WOLFGANG, C. L. ROSEN, P. D'EUSTACHIO, and J. L. SALZER, 1995. Cloning of neurotrimin defines a new subfamily of differentially expressed neural cell adhesion molecules. *J. Neurosci.* 15:2141–2156.

SUDA, Y., I. MATSUO, and S. AIZAWA, 1997. Cooperation between Otx1 and Otx2 genes in developmental patterning of rostral brain. *Mech. Dev.* 69:125–141.

SUDA, Y., I. MATSUO, S. KURATANI, and S. AIZAWA, 1996. Otx1 function overlaps with Otx2 in development of mouse forebrain and midbrain. *Genes Cells* 1:1031–1044.

TAN, S. S., and S. BREEN, 1993. Radial mosaicism and tangential cell dispersion both contribute to mouse neocortical development. *Nature* 362:638–640.

TAN, S. S., B. FAULKNER-JONES, S. J. BREEN, M. WALSH, J. F. BERTRAM, and B.E. REESE, 1995. Cell dispersion patterns in different cortical regions studied with an X-inactivated transgenic marker. *Development* 121:1029–1039.

TAN, S., M. KALLONIATIS, K. STURM, P. P. L. TAM, B. E. REESE, and B. FAULKNER-JONES, 1998. Separate progenitors for radial and tangential cell dispersion during development of the cerebral neocortex. *Neuron* 21:295–304.

TANABE, Y., and T. M. JESSELL, 1996. Diversity and pattern in the developing spinal cord. *Science* 274:1115–1123.

TAO, W., and E. LAI, 1992. Telencephalon-restricted expression of BF-1, a new member of the HNF-3/fork head gene family, in the developing rat brain. *Neuron* 8:957–966.

TESSIER-LAVIGNE, M., and C. S. GOODMAN, 1996. The molecular biology of axon guidance. *Science* 274:1123–1133.

VOLOVITCH, M., I. LE ROUX, A. H. JOLIOT, E. BLOCH-GALLEGO, and A. PROCHIANTZ, 1993. Control of neuronal morphogenesis by homeoproteins: Consequences for the making of neuronal networks. *Perspect. Dev. Neurobiol.* 1:133–138.

WALSH, C., and C. L. CEPKO, 1992. Widespread dispersion of neuronal clones across functional regions of the cerebral cortex. *Science* 255:434–440.

WALSH, C., and C. L. CEPKO, 1993. Clonal dispersion in proliferative layers of developing cerebral cortex. *Nature* 362:632–635.

WEINBERGER, D. R., 1995. From neuropathology to neurodevelopment. *The Lancet* 346:552–557.

XUAN, S., C. A. BAPTISTA, G. BALAS, W. TAO, V. C. SOARES, and E. LAI, 1995. Winged helix transcription factor BF-1 is essential for the development of the cerebral hemispheres. *Neuron* 14:1141–1152.

YOSHIDA, M., Y. SUDA, I. MATSUO, N. MIYAMOTO, N. TAKEDA, S. KURATANI, and S. AIZAWA, 1997. Emx1 and Emx2 functions in development of dorsal telencephalon. *Development* 124:101–111.

ZACCO, A., V. COOPER, S. HYLAND-FISHER, P. D. CHANTLER, H. L. HORTON, and P. LEVITT, 1990. Isolation, biochemical characterization and ultrastructural localization of the limbic system associated membrane protein (LAMP), a protein expressed on neurons comprising functional neural circuits. *J. Neurosci.* 10:73–90.

ZHANG, J.-H., A. F. PIMENTA, P. LEVITT, and R. ZHOU, 1997. Dynamic expression suggests multiple roles of the eph family receptor brain-specific kinase (Bsk) during mouse neurogenesis. *Molec. Brain Res.* 47:202–214.

3 A Comparative Perspective on the Formation of Retinal Connections in the Mammalian Brain

LEO M. CHALUPA AND CARA J. WEFERS

ABSTRACT   Recent studies dealing with the formation of retinal projections reveal that mammalian species employ diverse ontogenetic strategies to attain the connectional specificity evident at maturity. Here we review work from our lab on the topographic organization of the retinocollicular pathway in carnivores showing a remarkable degree of precision throughout development, and contrast this with the diffuse mistargeting found in this pathway in the developing rat. We also consider the formation of retinogeniculate projections in the embryonic monkey. In this species, the early divergence of magnocellular and parvocellular pathways reflects the expression of cell-specific markers. The segregation of initially intermingled binocular projections occurs at a later stage, and during this period retinogeniculate fibers are in a state of continuous growth and elaboration. Unlike in the fetal cat, axonal side-branches are few and relatively constant in number throughout prenatal development. Thus, the formation of eye-specific inputs in the primate can best be accounted for by the loss of retinal ganglion cells whose fibers have innervated inappropriate territories rather than resorption of axonal processes. These phylogenetic differences may provide new insights into the multiple factors underlying the formation of connections in the mammalian visual system.

The quest to further our understanding of how the brain gets wired has involved the study of many different systems. In this daunting endeavor the connections of the eyes to retinorecipient structures in the midbrain and thalamus have long been considered favorite models. Consequently, we know a great deal about what occurs from the time that ganglion cells first innervate their target structures until the highly precise projection patterns found at maturity are established. A tacit assumption in this field has been the notion that the developmental events responsible for the formation of retinal connections are basically the same in different mammalian species. What occurs during the formation of the visual system in the rat is thought to apply, albeit at a different time scale, to the cat, monkey, and by extension to the

LEO M. CHALUPA and CARA J. WEFERS   Section of Neurobiology, Physiology and Behavior, University of California, Davis, Calif.

human. At the same time, no one doubts that at maturity the salient features of the visual system are strikingly different among species. This is certainly manifest when one compares the organization of retinal projections in the animals most commonly studied by developmental neurobiologists—the rat, cat, ferret, and monkey.

Here, we consider the results of recent experiments dealing with the development of the retinocollicular pathway in carnivores and retinogeniculate projections in the monkey. The results of these studies, when considered with respect to related work on these pathways in other species, suggest that different developmental strategies have evolved in animals occupying diverse phylogenetic and ecological niches for establishing their unique patterns of connections.

Topographic organization of developing retinocollicular pathways

Shortly after the introduction of axoplasmic-based tracing techniques, it was established that retinal projections initially innervate widespread regions of their target structures before becoming gradually restricted to eye-specific territories (reviewed in Chalupa and Dreher, 1991). For instance, in the retinocollicular pathway it was shown that, in the developing rat (Land and Lund, 1979) and cat (Williams and Chalupa, 1982), the projections of the left and right eyes initially innervate virtually the entire rostrocaudal extent of the superior colliculus. Particularly pronounced is the restructuring exhibited during ontogeny by the ipsilateral pathway which, at maturity, is limited to a patchy distribution within the rostral portion of the colliculus. The overall sequence of events depicted in these studies gave the impression that the early retinocollicular projection pattern was quite diffuse.

This impression was subsequently confirmed by retrograde and anterograde tracing studies of the rat's retinocollicular projection. After making a focal deposit of a fluorescent dye into the caudal pole of the superior colliculus of the newborn rat, O'Leary and colleagues (1986) found a large number of labeled ganglion cells scattered throughout the contralateral retina. Some degree of order was evident, however, since the topographically appropriate peripheral nasal retina contained the highest density of labeled cells. On the basis of such results, it was estimated that for every 100 retinal ganglion cells projecting to the topographically appropriate portion of the superior colliculus, about 14 neurons make gross topographic errors. Consistent with such a high error rate, the initial ingrowth pattern of retinocollicular fibers in the developing rat was also found to be diffuse in anterograde tracing experiments. After crystals of DiI were placed into a region of the temporal retina, crossed retinocollicular fibers were found to initially mistarget widely across both the rostrocaudal and the mediolateral axes of the colliculus (Simon and O'Leary, 1990, 1992).

When identical techniques were employed to study the developing retinocollicular pathway of carnivores (Chalupa, Snider, and Kirby, 1996; Chalupa and Snider, 1998), a very different impression of developmental specificity was obtained. Focal deposits of retrograde tracers into the superficial layers of the superior colliculus of fetal cats revealed that at all stages of development labeled cells were confined, with few exceptions, to a delimited region of the contralateral and ipsilateral retinas. Moreover, the location of retinal regions with a high density of labeled ganglion cells varied with the locus of the tracer deposit in the colliculus in a manner consistent with the topographic organization of the mature cat's retinocollicular pathway. Although some labeled ganglion cells were found to be scattered throughout the contralateral and ipsilateral retinas, such ectopic cells were very sparse in the fetal cat. Throughout development for every 100 cells projecting to the appropriate region of the colliculus, less than one ganglion cell was estimated to make a projection error. Surprisingly, the incidence of ectopic cells did not differ between the contralateral and ipsilateral retina, even though the overall density of crossed labeled cells was consistently greater than that of uncrossed cells.

A high degree of topographic specificity was also found when retinocollicular projections of developing ferrets were visualized by means of anterograde tracings following focal tracer deposits into the developing retina (Chalupa and Snider, 1998). Beginning with the period when the first axons enter the midbrain at embryonic day (E) 30, there is remarkable degree of order, both in the pattern of innervation and in the formation of terminal arbors within topographically appropriate regions

(figures 3.1 and 3.2). Although some misprojecting fibers were evident at all stages of development, these were relatively few and remained fairly constant throughout development.

Taken together, the results of the studies summarized above reveal striking differences in the degree of precision exhibited by the developing retinocollicular pathway of the rat as compared to that of the cat and ferret. There is evidence of massive gross mistargeting in the rat, while in carnivores such projection errors are the exception rather than the rule. These observations have clear implications for the factors that may be responsible for establishing orderly retinal projection patterns. Because the initial ingrowth pattern of retinal axons in the rat is very diffuse, topographic specificity must be instilled by some factor(s) other than directed axonal ingrowth. More specifically, the establishment of topographic specificity in the rat undoubtedly involves "pruning" of extensive collateral branches and axonal arborizations. By contrast, the precise projection pattern seen during development in carnivores would seem to suggest that axon ingrowth plays a major role in establishing retinotopic maps, although some refinement is required to establish the high degree of order found at maturity.

What accounts for the initially widespread ipsilateral retinocollicular projection revealed by intraocular tracing studies? Our investigations of the topographic organization of this pathway in developing cats and ferrets point to multiple factors. First, early in ontogeny uncrossed retinocollicular axons are characterized by widespread terminal arbors which gradually become restricted to attain their mature size. Second, some ganglion cells in the nasal retina project to the caudal portion of the ipsilateral colliculus. Such ganglion cells, which are normally lost during the course of development, appear to innervate the appropriate topographic location of the superior colliculus, but on the wrong side of the brain. Other factors, such as the elimination of axonal side-branches and the loss of ectopic ganglion cells, also contribute to this process; however, such refinements appear to be much less prominent in the carnivore retinocollicular pathway than has been shown to be the case in the developing rat (Simon and O'Leary, 1990, 1992).

Development of retinogeniculate projections in the fetal monkey

Retinogeniculate projections in the mature primate are characterized by several distinguishing features. In the primate, ganglion cells are separated into nasal and temporal hemi-retinas on the basis of their decussation patterns, so that all cells in the temporal retina project

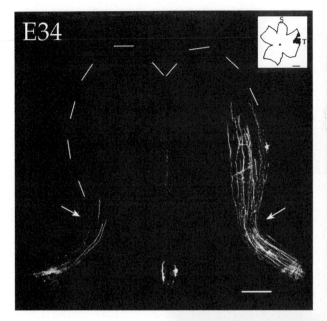

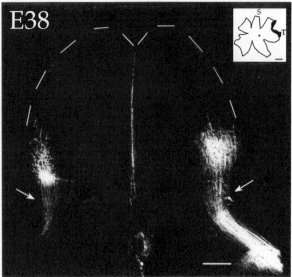

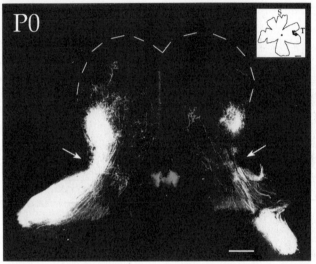

FIGURE 3.1 Confocal montages of wholemounted superior colliculi at three developmental ages. In all panels the collicular border is outlined by a dashed line with the rostral edges denoted by arrows. The left side of each montage is contralateral to the implanted eye. The upper right corner of each panel shows flatmount of retina with black area denoting the DiI implant site. Filled circle represents the optic disk. T, temporal; S, superior. At E34, a contingent of retinal fibers has grown into ipsilateral colliculus, while only a few crossed fibers have reached the colliculus. Note the parallel trajectory of the fibers within the superficial layers. By E38, fibers have begun to ter-minate in the topographically appropriate loci within the contralateral and ipsilateral superior colliculus. Although smaller in area, the contralateral terminal zone is much denser than the ipsilateral terminal zone. At the latest age, P0, a well-defined terminal zone is evident in both the contralateral and ipsilateral superior colliculus in topographically appropriate regions. Compared to E38 the ipsilateral terminal zone has restricted while the contralateral terminal zone has expanded. A few mistargeting fibers can be seen traveling past their respective terminal zones at each age. Scale bars: 1 mm for retina; 500 μm for wholemount.

ipsilaterally while those in the nasal retina project to the contralateral side of the brain. In all other species some ganglion cells, distributed across the entire retina, project to the contralateral hemisphere, so that cells with crossed and uncrossed projections are intermingled within the temporal retina. Upon reaching the thalamus, primate ganglion cells project to the dorsal lateral genic-ulate nucleus in an eye-specific manner, so that the contralateral eye innervates layers 1, 4, and 6 while the ipsilateral eye projects to layers 2, 3, and 5. Eye-specific projection patterns are found in other species with highly developed binocular vision, such as the cat and ferret. What distinguishes the primate from other species is that the major classes of ganglion cells also project in a

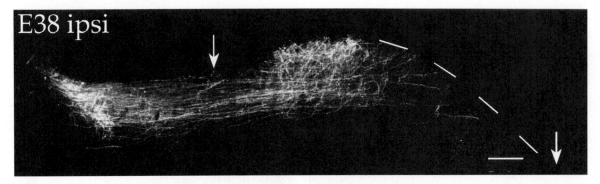

E38 ipsi

FIGURE 3.2 Sagittal section through the densest region of the ipsilateral terminal zone of the E38 animal shown in figure 11.1. The collicular border is outlined by a broken line, with the rostral (left) and the caudal (right) edges denoted by ar-rows. Note the perpendicular turn of the ipsilateral fibers to-ward the dorsal surface of the superior colliculus where they terminate in upper layers. Scale bar = 250 μm.

laminar-specific pattern, with the large Pα cells innervat-ing magnocellular layers, 1 and 2, and the smaller Pβ neurons projecting to parvocellular layers, 3 through 6. Thus, the primate retinogeniculate pathway is character-ized by laminar specificity defined in terms of ocular do-mains as well as cell-specific patterns (figure 3.3). In some species, the inputs of ON and OFF subclasses of ganglion cells are further segregated within sublaminae of the dorsal lateral geniculate nucleus (Stryker and Zahs, 1983), but this is not the case in the primate where the projections of both subclasses are intermingled within a single geniculate layer.

Studies on fetal monkeys have provided informa-tion about the formation of retinal decussation pat-terns, eye-specific laminar projections, as well as magno and parvo pathways. Below, we discuss the de-velopment of these fundamental features of the pri-mate visual system and compare our findings to what has been learned from related studies on nonprimate species.

Retinal decussation

The organization of the fetal monkey's retinal decussa-tion pattern was examined by plotting the distributions of labeled cells in both retinas in animals of known ges-tational ages that received large injections of HRP into the retinorecipient structures of one hemisphere (Cha-lupa and Lia, 1991). This revealed that throughout devel-opment virtually all retinal ganglion cells in the macaque monkey make a correct chiasmatic decision. Thus, even as early as E69, about 100 days before birth, less than 0.5% of all retinal ganglion cells innervate the inappro-priate hemisphere. The fact that the nasotemporal decus-sation pattern of the fetal rhesus monkey is nearly identical to that observed at maturity indicates that reti-nal positional markers must play a key role in specifying the laterality of ganglion cell projections. Thus, it is likely that ganglion cells generated in the temporal retina are characterized by molecular markers different from those of cells in the nasal retina. Such position-derived cues could guide the distinct behaviors of ganglion cell axons when they arrive at the optic chiasm.

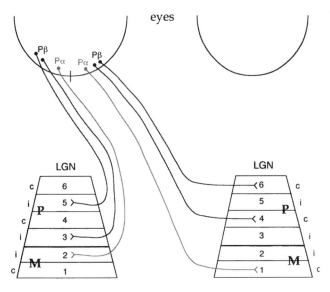

FIGURE 3.3 Schematic illustration of neuronal connections between the eyes and the LGN in the macaque monkey. The connections serving the left and right eyes might be parvocel-lular (P, about 80%), magnocellular (M, about 10%), or others (K, I, or S, about 10%; not shown). The different types of gan-glion cells in the retina are intermixed although the percentage of P cells is higher in the central retina than at the periphery. In the LGN, layers 1 and 2 are magnocellular and layers 3 to 6 are parvocellular. In a given eye, the set of M ganglion cells that project to the contralateral LGN terminates in layer 1, whereas the cells that project ipsilaterally terminate in layer 2. The P ganglion cells project to layers 3 and 5 to the LGN on the same side, and 4 and 6 on the opposite side. For clarity, projections from just one eye are shown.

To gain further insight into this problem, we examined the organization of pioneer retinal axons in the embryonic rhesus monkey (Meissirel and Chalupa, 1994). The initial contingents of crossed and uncrossed optic axons were labeled by two different carbocyanine dyes which permitted their differentiation with confocal microscopy. This revealed that in the embryonic monkey, the uncrossed retinal fibers enter the optic tract well in advance of the crossed fibers, an observation noted previously in the embryonic mouse (Godement, Salaün, and Métin, 1987). When the crossed axons begin to enter the tract, they remain largely segregated from the uncrossed contingent of fibers. This shows that crossed and uncrossed retinal projections, which initially form the primate optic tract, follow distinct temporal and spatial ingrowth patterns. Such an orderly sequential ingrowth of pioneer retinal axons would be expected if chiasmatic cues were expressed very early in development. In the embryonic mouse it has been suggested that a combination of outgrowth promoting and inhibiting molecules (termed L1/CD44 array) is expressed by neurons in the developing optic chiasm and that this acts as a template for guiding the initial decussation pattern (Sretavan et al., 1994). It would seem reasonable to think that similar molecular cues are expressed by chiasmatic neurons in primate embryos, but this remains to be established. Moreover, the temporal and spatial segregation of crossed and uncrossed fibers indicates that the ingrowth of axons into the optic tract is not dependent upon interactions between fibers from the ipsilateral and contralateral eyes. Such an interaction has been inferred from studies on the developing mouse in which one eye was removed before the optic axons arrived at the chiasm (Godement, Salaün, and Métin, 1987), but this idea has not been supported by time-lapse video analysis of navigational patterns of crossed and uncrossed optic fibers (Sretavan and Reichardt, 1993).

Formation of retinogeniculate M and P pathways

The results summarized in this section have been described in greater detail by Meissirel (Meissirel et al., 1997), from which this account is derived.

Tritiated thymidine studies have revealed a curious mismatch between the birth order of Pα and Pβ retinal ganglion cells and that of their target neurons in the M and P layers of the dorsal lateral geniculate nucleus. Within a given region of the retina, Pβ cells are born earlier than Pα cells (Rapaport et al., 1992), but in the geniculate anlage neurons destined for the M layers are generated prior to those that will form the P laminae (Rakic, 1977). In the macaque embryo, the first retinal fibers (stemming from the contralateral eye) reach the geniculate anlage by E48. By this age all geniculate neurons have been generated and have completed their migration, but despite this availability of target cells, the initial contingent of axons bypasses the dorsal thalamus to innervate the midbrain (figure 3.4A). The innervation of the geniculate begins several days later, when retinal fibers sprout short branches which terminate selectively within the medial segment of the nucleus (figure 3.4B). Crossed fibers innervate the medial segment first, and the uncrossed fibers follow this specific ingrowth pattern several days later (figure 3.4C). During this time period the geniculate undergoes a progressive rotation (figure 3.4E), and it is only when this process is largely completed (at E74) that the ventral region of the nucleus (formerly the lateral segment) begins to receive retinal inputs. At this stage, lamination of the geniculate has not occurred, so it is not possible to differentiate between parvo and magno layers. However, based on the outside-to-inside pattern of geniculate cell generation (Rakic, 1977), it can be inferred that the early innervated segment corresponds to what will become the parvo layers, while the later innervated lateral portion of the nucleus will differentiate into the magno laminae (figure 3.4E). Thus, the temporal sequence for "hooking-up" the retinogeniculate pathway in the primate embryo follows the order of ganglion cell generation (i.e., Pβ before Pα) rather than the temporal sequence of target cell generation, in which magno cells are generated before parvo neurons.

At maturity, retinogeniculate arbors stemming from the Pα and Pβ ganglion cells can be differentiated on the basis of their distinctive morphologic features (Conley and Fitzpatrick, 1989). Remarkably, such morphologic differences become evident in the primate embryo as soon as terminal arbors become elaborated (by E95).

The highly specific ingrowth pattern characterizing the formation of parvocellular and magnocellular retinogeniculate pathways was unexpected because left and right eye inputs to the different laminae of this structure were shown to be initially completely intermingled (Rakic, 1976). Indeed, the retinogeniculate pathway of the fetal primate has long been considered the classic example of exuberant projections and subsequent refinement in the developing brain. Our findings reveal, however, that when functional components of this pathway are considered, namely parvocellular and magnocellular inputs, a different picture emerges. Refinements of early projections may not be required in this case because the parvo and magno subsystems seem to follow laminar-specific cues which appear to guide the axons of Pα and Pβ cells to the appropriate segments of the primate geniculate.

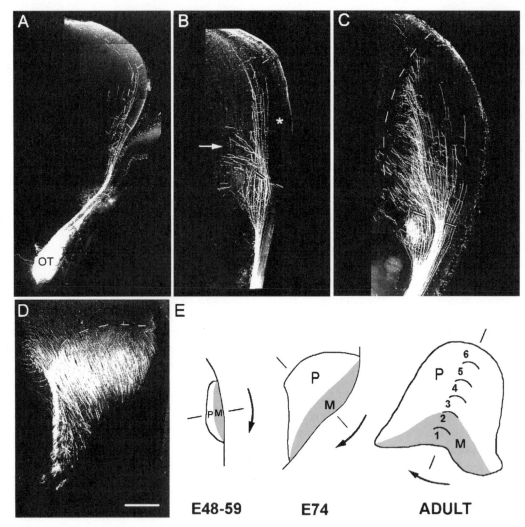

FIGURE 3.4 Photomontages of confocal images through representative coronal sections of the diencephalon showing the distribution of DiI-labeled retinal axons in the embryonic thalamus. (A–D) Dashed lines indicate the border of the dorsal lateral geniculate (dLGN) with a dorsal orientation to the top and a lateral orientation to the right. (A–C) The contralateral side to the DiI optic nerve implants. (A) At E48, retinal axons navigate the contralateral optic tract before being deflected away from the pial surface as they approach the geniculate. A few axons course dorsally past the dLGN toward the midbrain. (B) At E53, there is greater ingrowth of retinal fibers, some of them elaborating medially directed branches. Note that the lateral aspect of the dLGN remains totally devoid of retinal axons (*). Branches derived from the axon trunks are concentrated at the bottom third of the dLGN, and in some cases these extend past its medial border in the external medullary lamina (arrow). (C) At E64, an increasing number of axonal branches invade the medial region of the nucleus. Note that, at this age, the lateral segment of the dLGN is still virtually free of retinal afferents. The section shown is from the rostral part of the dLGN, but essentially the same pattern is observed throughout the rostrocaudal extent of the nucleus. (D) At E74, DiI crystals were implanted into the optic tract to reduce the distance of diffusion. Virtually the entire extent of the nucleus now receives a retinal innervation. The coronal section is from the caudal aspect of the dLGN. (E) Schematic representation of the dLGN rotation (arrows) from E48 to adulthood. The presumptive M layers (shaded area) rotate from a lateral to a ventral position whereas the presumptive P layers rotate from a medial to a dorsal position. Scale bar: A–C, and E, 500 μm; D, 400 μm.

Such observations imply that these two main classes of primate retinal ganglion cells must express different molecular markers that permit their axons to react differentially to putative laminar-specific cues. In the adult macaque retina, antibodies generated against two different gene products (termed Brn-3a and Brn-3b) have been shown to differentially label Pα and Pβ ganglion cell populations (Xiang et al., 1995). Application of these antibodies to the embryonic retina revealed that Brn-3a and Brn-3b positive cells could be visualized at very early stages of development. This was observed shortly after ganglion cells had undergone their final division, and even before they had migrated from the ventricular layer to the ganglion cell layer. These findings provide evidence for the early divergence of Pα and Pβ ganglion cells. Furthermore, they reveal an essential link between distinct cell classes and the high specificity exhibited by these neurons when their fibers innervate the parvo and magno segments of the geniculate.

This suggests that M and P streams in the primate retinogeniculate pathway could be established on the basis of the expression of molecular cues, without the involvement of activity-mediated refinements. This inference is certainly consistent with the evidence summarized above. This interpretation is also in line with what is known about the functional development of mammalian retinal ganglion cells. Patch-clamp recordings from ganglion cells isolated from the fetal cat retina indicate that very early in development these neurons are incapable of generating action potentials (Skaliora, Scobey, and Chalupa, 1993). To a large degree this reflects the low density of sodium channels at early stages of development (Skaliora, Scobey, and Chalupa, 1993), but ontogenetic fluctuations in other conductances and channel properties associated with spike generation have also been documented by means of voltage-clamp recordings (Skaliora et al., 1995; Wang et al., 1997; Robinson and Wang, in press). By extrapolation from these studies on the fetal cat, it seems unlikely that ganglion cells in the embryonic primate are capable of firing action potentials at the time that the parvo and magno pathways are being established. By contrast, several weeks before the segregation of overlapping binocular projections has begun all retinal ganglion cells can discharge action potentials to depolarizing current injections (Skaliora, Scobey, and Chalupa, 1993).

Formation of eye-specific projections

More than twenty years ago, Rakic (1976) discovered, by means of intraocular injections of tritiated amino acids, that the projections of the two eyes innervate the entire dorsal lateral geniculate before segregating into eye-specific laminae. The separation of initially intermingled binocular projections occurs later in development (from about E85 until E120) than the formation of parvo and magno pathways, as discussed above. Analogous experiments on numerous species have shown that such binocular overlap of retinal projections is a common feature of mammalian development, although the degree of binocular overlap exhibited by different species can vary substantially (cf. Chalupa and Dreher, 1991). There is also evidence that the segregation process reflects binocular interactions. Removal of one eye at the time that projections overlap results in the maintenance of the

widespread pattern from the remaining eye (Rakic, 1976; Chalupa and Williams, 1984). Such binocular interactions are thought to reflect activity-mediated events since blockade of spontaneously generated retinal activity induces marked changes in the geniculate territory innervated by the two eyes (Penn et al., 1998).

At a cellular level the early intermingling of left and right eye inputs could be accounted for by two non–mutually exclusive mechanisms. As shown diagrammatically in figure 3.5, one possibility is that individual retinal fibers could be more extensive during development than at maturity, with axons from the two eyes innervating overlapping territories. Such exuberance at the single fiber level could reflect larger terminal arbors as well as the presence of transient axonal side-branches. An alternative hypothesis is that terminal arbors of individual fibers are not exuberant, but some innervate inappropriate territories destined to be the exclusive domain of the other eye. Thus, fibers from the ipsilateral eye might innervate layer 1, and subsequently such inappropriate projections would be eliminated during the period of developmental cell death.

A morphologic analysis of single retinal fibers in the fetal cat revealed that during the prenatal binocular

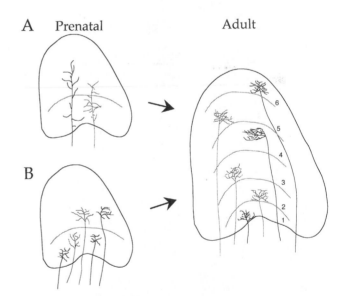

FIGURE 3.5 Schematic of two possible scenarios for the formation of retinogeniculate axons into eye-specific layers in the dlgn. The black outline represents a coronal section of the lgn. The black lines represent contralateral projections; ipsilateral projections are shown in gray. In the adult, the layers of the lgn (numbered) are denoted by stippled lines. In the prenatal sections, a layer is represented for clarity. One possibility is a loss of side branches, and a restructuring of the terminal arborizations (A). The alternative is that optic fiber loss underlies the formation of mature projection patterns (B). Our data suggest the latter alternative.

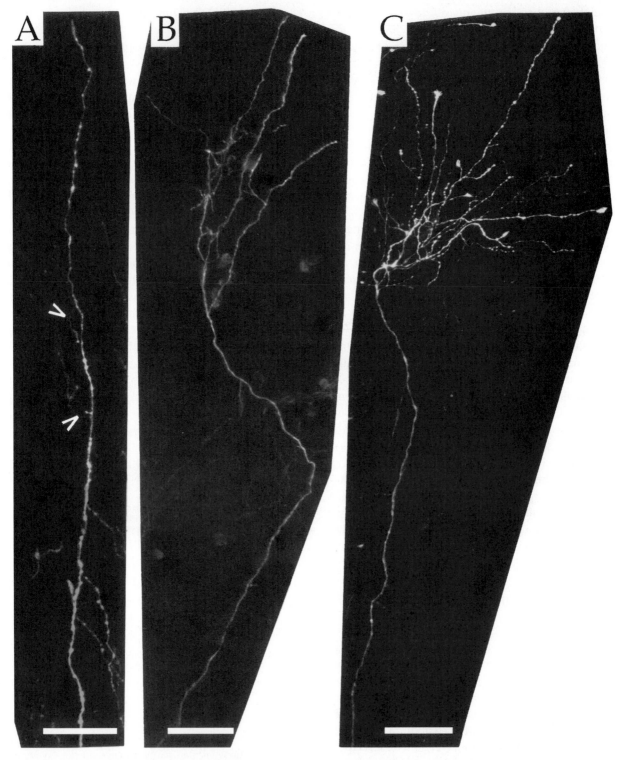

FIGURE 3.6 Confocal photomontages of retinogeniculate axons at different embryonic days (E): E77 (A), E95 (B), and E112 (C). Note that throughout prenatal development these axons are nearly devoid of side branches and show continuous growth and elaboration of the terminal arborization. Cal bars = 50 μm. White arrowheads point to side branches in A.

overlap period there are numerous axonal side-branches (Sretavan and Shatz, 1984). These often span across territories destined to become eye-specific during the course of normal development. Furthermore, the loss of such axonal processes corresponds to the time when binocular segregation occurs. Interestingly, the terminal arbors did not show any transient increase in size during the binocular overlap period. These findings provide a clear-cut account of the cellular basis of binocular overlap and segregation: The overlap reflects the presence of axonal side-branches, while the segregation is due to the loss of such processes.

In the more than two decades since Pasko Rakic showed binocular overlap of retinogeniculate projections in the fetal monkey, it seems remarkable that no one has studied retinogeniculate fibers in the prenatal primate. To some degree, this lacuna reflects the common assumption that what was found in the cat also applies to the monkey.

Recently, we undertook a study of the morphologic characteristics of single retinogeniculate axons in fetal monkeys (Snider et al., 1999). Such an investigation seemed a logical extension of the work described above. We were also motivated by increasing evidence of species differences in the developmental specificity exhibited by other components of the mammalian visual systems (Chalupa and Dreher, 1991). In particular, we were interested in determining whether the axonal side-branches, found to be prevalent in the cat during the binocular overlap period, would also be present in the fetal monkey. Retinal fibers were labeled by implanting single crystals of the fluorescent tracer DiI into the fixed optic tract, yielding complete labeling of single axons as visualized by confocal microscopy.

To date, we have analyzed more than 90 retinogeniculate fibers obtained from fetal animals spanning in age from E78 through E120. The youngest age is near the peak of the binocular overlap period and the oldest is when segregation is already well underway (Rakic, 1976). Examples of retinogeniculate fibers at E77, E95, and E112 are shown in the photomontages in figure 3.6. Several key features are clearly evident. First, axon terminals are yet to form in the youngest animal, while at older ages they become increasingly more complex and elaborate. Importantly, there is no indication that terminal arbors are greater in size at the time when binocular overlap is near its peak. Detailed measurements of a number of salient parameters, including the size and complexity of terminal arbors at four different ages, provided quantitative support for the impression obtained from the raw data (not shown). This was not unexpected since, as indicated above, retinogeniculate fibers of the fetal cat also showed no sign of retrenchment during the course of development. What was distinctive in the monkey embryos was the paucity of axonal side-branches. Throughout the binocular overlap period, retinal fibers in the magno and parvo segments of the geniculate were characterized by very few such processes. Moreover, the low incidence of axonal side-branches remained relatively constant throughout the development period of binocular segregation.

To convince ourselves that this lack of transient axonal branches reflected a genuine species difference rather than some spurious methodological factor, we made similar deposits of DiI into the fixed optic tract of the fetal cat at E50, near the peak of the binocular overlap period. This revealed numerous axonal side-branches, in agreement with the report of Sretavan and Shatz who used HRP deposits in an in vitro preparation to label fetal cat optic fibers. This indicates that there are genuine differences between the cat and monkey in the cellular factors responsible for the binocular overlap and subsequent segregation of retinogeniculate projections: Resorption of axonal side-branches plays a role in this process in the fetal cat, but not in the monkey embryo.

During the segregation of binocular projections, there is a massive loss of optic axons in both the fetal monkey (Rakic and Riley, 1983a) and the fetal cat (Williams et al., 1986). Such loss of axons, which reflects the normal death of ganglion cells, could account entirely for the formation of eye-specific projection patterns. This idea was originally put forth by Rakic (1986), and our findings are entirely in accord with his suggestion. Moreover, this would also explain the observation that prenatal removal of one eye results in an increase of optic fibers in the remaining eye (Rakic and Riley, 1983b), which is concomitant with an expansion of the retinogeniculate projections stemming from the remaining eye. Monocular enucleation in the fetal cat during the binocular overlap period also results in an increase in the ganglion cell population (Chalupa, Williams, and Henderson, 1984) and a corresponding increase in the number of fibers (Williams, Bastiani, and Chalupa, 1983) in the remaining eye and optic nerve as well as an expanded retinogeniculate projection (Chalupa and Williams, 1984). Thus, it seems reasonable to think that loss of retinogeniculate axons is involved in forming eye-specific projection patterns in both the monkey and cat. The key feature distinguishing the monkey from the cat is the presence of transient axonal side-branches in carnivores.

Concluding remarks

The available evidence clearly indicates that there are marked species differences in the developmental events leading to the formation of certain key attributes of retinal projection patterns. In one respect, this complicates our efforts to understand how neuronal connections are formed in the developing brain. On the other hand, the ontogenetic variations exhibited by different species provide an opportunity for developmental neurobiologists to assess the problem from a fresh perspective. By considering why one class of cells (for instance, the retinocollicular projection of the rat as compared to that of the cat) behaves differently from another could expand the scope of the enquiry to a new level of analysis. To understand how retinal ganglion cells make their precise patterns of connections, it could prove illuminating to consider why ganglion cells in different animals (and even different classes of cells in the same animal) hook up with their target neurons by means of different strategies. What's different and what's common during the development of mammalian retinofugal pathways? Until this issue is resolved, the task of developmental neurobiologists will not be completed.

REFERENCES

CHALUPA, L. M., and B. DREHER, 1991. High precision systems require high precision "blueprints": A new view regarding the formation of connections in the mammalian visual system. *J. Cogn. Neurol.* 3:209–219.

CHALUPA, L. M., and B. L. LIA, 1991. The nasotemporal division of retinal ganglion cells with crossed and uncrossed projections in the fetal rhesus monkey. *J. Neurosci.* 11(1):191–202.

CHALUPA, L. M., and C. J. SNIDER, 1998. Topographic specificity in the retinocollicular projection of the developing ferret: An anterograde tracing study. *J. Comp. Neurol.* 392:35–47.

CHALUPA, L. M., C. J. SNIDER, and M. A. KIRBY, 1996. Topographic organization in the retinocollicular pathway of the fetal cat demonstrated by retrograde labeling of ganglion cells. *J. Comp. Neurol.* 368:295–303.

CHALUPA, L. M., and R. W. WILLIAMS, 1984. Organization of the cat's lateral geniculate nucleus following interruption of prenatal binocular competition. *Human Neurobiol.* 3:103–107.

CHALUPA, L. M., R. W. WILLIAMS, and Z. HENDERSON, 1984. Binocular interaction in the fetal cat regulated the size of the ganglion cell population. *Neurosci.* 12:1139–1146.

CONLEY, M., and D. FITZPATRICK, 1989. Morphology of retinogeniculate axons in the macaque. *Visual Neurosci.* 2:287–296.

GODEMENT, P., J. SALAÜN, and C. MASON, 1990. Retinal axon pathfinding in the optic chiasm: Divergence of crossed and uncrossed fibers. *Neuron* 5:173–186.

GODEMENT, P., J. SALAÜN, and C. MÉTIN, 1987. Fate of uncrossed retinal projections following early or late prenatal monocular enucleation in the mouse. *J. Comp. Neurol.* 225:97–109.

LAND, P. W., and R. D. LUND, 1979. Development of the rat's uncrossed retinotectal pathway and its relation to plasticity studies. *Science* 205:698–700.

MEISSIREL, C., and L. M. CHALUPA, 1994. Organization of pioneer retinal axons within the optic tract of the rhesus monkey. *Proc. Natl. Acad. Sci. U.S.A.* 91:3906–3910.

MEISSIREL, C., K. C. WIKLER, L. M. CHALUPA, and P. RAKIC, 1997. Early divergence of magnocellular and parvocellular functional subsystems in the embryonic primate visual system. *Proc. Natl. Acad. Sci. U.S.A.* 94:5900–5905.

O'LEARY, D. D. M., J. W. FAWCETT, and W. M. COWAN, 1986. Topographic targeting errors in the retinocollicular projection and their elimination by selective ganglion cell death. *J. Neurosci.* 6:3692–3705.

PENN, A. A., A. R. PATRICIO, M. B. FELLER, and C. J. SHATZ, 1998. Competition in retinogeniculate patterning driven by spontaneous activity. *Science* 279:2108–2112.

RAKIC, P., 1976. Prenatal genesis of connections subserving ocular dominance in the rhesus monkey. *Nature* 261:467–471.

RAKIC, P., 1977. Prenatal development of the visual system in rhesus monkey. *Phil. Trans. R. Soc. Lond. (Biol.)* 278:245–260.

RAKIC, P., 1986. Mechanism of ocular dominance segregation in the lateral geniculate nucleus: Competitive elimination hypothesis. *Trends Neurosci.* 9:11–15.

RAKIC, P., and K. P. RILEY, 1983a. Overproduction and elimination of retinal axons in the fetal rhesus monkey. *Science* 209:1441–1444.

RAKIC, P., and K. P. RILEY, 1983b. Regulation of axon numbers in the primate optic nerve by prenatal binocular competition. *Nature* 305:135–137.

RAPAPORT, D. H., J. T. FLETCHER, M. M. LaVAIL, and P. RAKIC, 1992. Genesis of neurons in the retinal ganglion cell layer of the monkey. *J. Comp. Neurol.* 322(4):577–588.

ROBINSON, D. W., and G.-Y. WANG, in press. Development of intrinsic membrane properties in mammalian retinal ganglion cells. *Semin. Cell Dev. Biol.*

SIMON, D. K., and D. D. M. O'LEARY, 1990. Limited topographic specificity in the targeting and branching of mammalian retinal axons. *Dev. Biol.* 137:125–134.

SIMON, D. K., and D. D. M. O'LEARY, 1992. Development of topographic order in the mammalian retinocollicular projection. *J. Neurosci.* 12:1212–1232.

SKALIORA, I., D. W. ROBINSON, R. P. SCOBEY, and L. M. CHALUPA, 1995. Properties of K^+ conductances in cat retinal ganglion cells during the period of activity-mediated refinements in retinofugal pathways. *Eur. J. Neurosci.* 7:1558–1568.

SKALIORA, I., R. P. SCOBEY, and L. M. CHALUPA, 1993. Prenatal development of excitability in cat retinal ganglion cells: Action potentials and sodium currents. *J. Neurosci.* 13:313–323.

SNIDER, C. J., C. DEHAY, M. BERLAND, H. KENNEDY, and L. M. CHALUPA, 1999. Prenatal development of retinogeniculate axons in the macaque monkey during segregation of binocular inputs. *J. Neurosci.* 19(1):220–228.

SRETAVAN, D. W., L. FENG, E. PURE, and L. F. REICHARDT, 1994. Embryonic neurons of the developing optic chiasm express L1 and CD44, cell surface molecules with opposing effects on retinal axon growth. *Neuron* 12:957–975.

SRETAVAN, D. W., and L. F. REICHARDT, 1993. Time-lapse video analysis of retinal ganglion cell axon pathfinding at the mammalian optic chiasm: Growth cone guidance using intrinsic chiasm cues. *Neuron* 10:761–777.

SRETAVAN, D. W., and C. J. SHATZ, 1984. Prenatal development of individual retinogeniculate axons during the period of segregation. *Nature* 306:845–848.

STRYKER, M. P., and K. R. ZAHS, 1983. ON and OFF sublaminae in the lateral geniculate nucleus of the ferret. *J. Neurosci.* 3:1943–1951.

WANG, G.-Y., G.-M. RATTO, S. BISTI, and L. M. CHALUPA, 1997. Functional development of intrinsic properties in ganglion cells of the mammalian retina. *J. Neurophysiol.* 78:2895–2903.

WILLIAMS, R. W., M. J. BASTIANI, and L. M. CHALUPA, 1983. Loss of axons in the cat optic nerve following fetal unilateral enucleation: An electron microscope analysis. *J. Neurosci.* 3:133–144.

WILLIAMS, R. W., M. J. BASTIANI, B. LIA, and L. M. CHALUPA, 1986. Growth cones, dying axons, and developmental fluctuations in the fiber population of the cat's optic nerve. *J. Comp. Neurol.* 246:32–69.

WILLIAMS, R. W., and L. M. CHALUPA, 1982. Prenatal development of retinocollicular projections in the cat: An anterograde tracer transport study. *J. Neurosci.* 2:604–622.

XIANG, M., L. ZHOU, J. MACKE, T. YOSHIOKA, S. H. C. HENDRY, R. EDDY, T. B. SHOWS, and J. NATHANS, 1995. Genesis of neurons in the retinal ganglion cell layer of the monkey. *J. Neurosci.* 15:4762–4785.

4 Formation, Elimination, and Stabilization of Synapses in the Primate Cerebral Cortex

JEAN-PIERRE BOURGEOIS, PATRICIA S. GOLDMAN-RAKIC, AND PASKO RAKIC

ABSTRACT The formation of synaptic connections in the primate brain is a protracted and complex process that lasts for decades. We have performed a systematic examination of synaptogenesis in the cerebral cortex of the macaque monkey from the fortieth day of the six-month embryonic period through 30 years of age, identifying five distinct phases of synaptogenesis. In the five major cytoarchitectonic areas so far examined (visual, somatosensory, motor, limbic, and prefrontal), the first three phases of synaptogenesis proceed concurrently in different areas at a rate resistant to experimental manipulation. In contrast, the fourth phase, in which there is high synaptic density, is more malleable, i.e., subject to activity-dependent stabilization and presumed molecular changes in synaptic strength. This phase begins shortly after birth and continues until puberty. The fifth phase, which begins after sexual maturity and extends into old age, is characterized by a very slow decline in synaptic density. The absence of ultrastructural signs of synaptogenesis in the fifth phase indicates either a lack of new synapse formation or an extremely low turnover of synapses in the normal adult primate neocortex. The stability of synaptic contacts throughout adult life would be a biological advantage for the storage and preservation of acquired knowledge.

The cerebral cortex contains by far the largest proportion of synapses in the human brain (Szenthagothai, 1978). Although the timing and status of synaptic connections form the basis of all theories of human psychological development, quantitative information on synaptogenesis has been lacking. To provide insight into mechanisms of development and maintenance of cortical synapses in primates, we have examined the course of synaptogenesis in the macaque monkey under normal and experimental conditions. The cellular organization and functional parcellation of cerebral cortex in this Old World monkey is remarkably similar to that of the hu-

man neocortex (e.g., Polyak, 1957; Shkol'nik-Yarros, 1971; Mountcastle, 1997). The primary visual cortex of the macaque monkey has proved an extremely useful model for analyzing developing connections, synaptoarchitectonics, chemoarchitectonics, plasticity, and the physiology of the primate neocortex (e.g., Hubel, Wiesel, and LeVay, 1977; Zielinski and Hendrickson, 1992; Rakic, Gallager, and Goldman-Rakic, 1988; Meissirel et al., 1997). It is also considered an unexcelled model for understanding human perceptual development (e.g., Teller, 1997, and chapter 6 of this volume).

The biological development of the primate neocortex entails a prolonged and highly orchestrated cascade of cellular events including, successively, the production, migration, and differentiation of neurons (for review, see Rakic, 1988, and chapter 1 of this volume). These early developmental events are followed by a more region-specific elaboration of dendritic and axonal processes (Rakic, 1976; Goldman-Rakic, 1987; Schwartz and Goldman-Rakic, 1991; Barone et al., 1995), culminating in an intricate pattern of synaptic contacts formed between ensembles of local and distant neurons. Using quantitative electron microscopy, we have delineated the kinetics of synaptogenesis in five major functionally distinct cortical areas of the macaque monkeys from conception to old age (Rakic et al., 1986; Bourgeois and Rakic, 1993; Bourgeois, Goldman-Rakic, and Rakic, 1994; Zecevic and Rakic, 1991; Zecevic, Bourgeois, and Rakic, 1989; Granger et al., 1995). The density of synapses per unit volume of neuropil has been estimated using stereological corrections for changes in synaptic size during development. This approach has also provided information on the overall density and number of synapses as well as synaptic localization (on dendritic spines or shafts, and cell somas) and nature (symmetric/asymmetric). These parameters pertain to the entire spectrum of synapses within the areas of interest–those arising locally as well as those from distant sources through long-tract afferents. Thus, our approach does not specify how individual pathways

JEAN-PIERRE BOURGEOIS Laboratoire de Neurobiologie Moleculaire, Departement des Biotechnologies, Institut Pasteur, Paris, France
PATRICIA S. GOLDMAN-RAKIC and PASKO RAKIC Section of Neurobiology, Yale University School of Medicine, New Haven, Conn.

or circuits contribute to the overall changes observed. However, quantification of the course of synaptogenesis across various functional domains sets the stage for more specific analyses and is essential for understanding the interactions between genetic and experiential influences on the scheduling, number, and pattern of synaptic connections. To that end, we have manipulated visual sensory input in two ways—advancing it through premature delivery on the one hand, and eliminating it by early enucleation in utero on the other—then examined the effect of these manipulations on the course of synaptogenesis in the cerebral cortex. We have also tracked synaptogenesis into old age—from puberty to 30-plus years. This chapter describes these various findings and discusses them in the context of human cognitive development.

Kinetics of synaptogenesis

Examination of the quantitative data obtained in a series of studies conducted in the past decade indicates that the course of synaptogenesis can be subdivided into several distinct phases, schematically illustrated in figure 4.1. The methodological details and data are available in the original publications (Bourgeois and Rakic, 1993; Bourgeois, Goldman-Rakic, and Rakic, 1994; Zecevic and Rakic, 1991; Zecevic, Bourgeois, and Rakic, 1989; Granger et al., 1995).

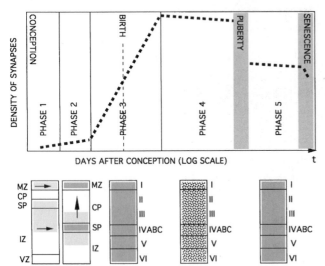

FIGURE 4.1 Changes in the relative density of synapses (dotted line in the upper frame) as a function of days after conception expressed on a log scale on the abscissa (t), in the primary visual cortex of the macaque monkey, during normal development. Five different phases of synaptogenesis are identified between conception and death. Each phase is superimposed above the density distribution of synapses in the cortical layers of the neocortex represented at the bottom of the figure. Abbreviations: CP, cortical plate; IZ intermediate zone; MZ, marginal zone; SP, subplate.

Phase 1: The *precortical phase* of synaptogenesis in macaque embryos begins around embryonic (E) day 40 and lasts for two to three weeks, coinciding with the onset of neurogenesis and the formation of the cortical plate (Rakic, 1981, and chapter 1 of this volume). This phase is termed the precortical phase because synapses are first observed (in low density) in the marginal zone (prospective layer I) and in the subplate zone situated below cortical plate before emerging in the cortical plate itself. These early synapses are formed in part by axons originating from subcortical structures (horizontal arrows in figure 4.1). A similar distribution of early synapses has been observed in the initial phases of synaptogenesis in the human fetal cerebrum (Molliver, Kostovic, and Van der Loos, 1973; Zecevic, 1998).

Phase 2: The *early cortical phase* from E70 through E100 is characterized by the emergence of synapses in the cortical plate. These synapses are formed during the peak of neurogenesis and active migration of neuroblasts through the developing cortical plate (Rakic, 1972, 1988). An inside-out sequence of synaptic appearance appears to follow the radial penetration of axonal projections from the thalamus and from other cortical areas, either preceding (as in the primary visual cortex; cf. Bourgeois and Rakic, 1993), or following (as in the prefrontal cortex; cf. Bourgeois, Goldman-Rakic, and Rakic, 1994), their segregation into cortical columns (vertical arrow in figure 4.1; see also Rakic, 1981). Virtually all synapses during this phase are formed on the dendritic shafts of neurons.

Phase 3: This, the *rapid phase* of synaptogenesis, begins two months before birth (between E90 and E100) after most neurons have been generated; however, our data indicate that it is not directly linked to the end of neurogenesis (Granger et al., 1995). These new synaptic junctions are formed mainly on the dendritic spines coincident with the proliferative growth of dendritic and axonal arbors of intracortical and extracortical neurons (figures 4.2 and 4.3). Once initiated, this phase proceeds uninterruptedly until the maximal density of synapses per unit volume of neuropil is reached, during the second and third months of postnatal life.

Phase 4: This phase of *high synaptic density* in the macaque monkey lasts for about two years, from infancy to adolescence, and ends with a decline during puberty in the third year of life. We refer to it as the "plateau" phase because the mean density of synapses (about 600–900 million synapses per cubic millimeter of neuropil) is substantially above the adult level during most of this phase (Bourgeois and Rakic, 1993). The end of phase 4 is dominated by a significant decline in synaptic density, mainly due to the loss of asymmetric synapses located on dendritic spines (figures 4.2 and 4.3). Interestingly,

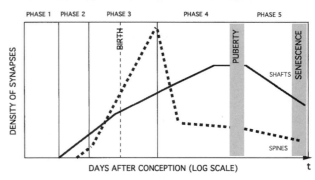

SYNAPTOGENESIS IN LAYER III OF PRIMARY VISUAL CORTEX

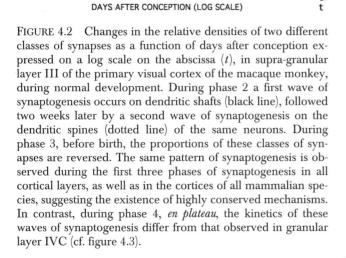

FIGURE 4.2 Changes in the relative densities of two different classes of synapses as a function of days after conception expressed on a log scale on the abscissa (*t*), in supra-granular layer III of the primary visual cortex of the macaque monkey, during normal development. During phase 2 a first wave of synaptogenesis occurs on dendritic shafts (black line), followed two weeks later by a second wave of synaptogenesis on the dendritic spines (dotted line) of the same neurons. During phase 3, before birth, the proportions of these classes of synapses are reversed. The same pattern of synaptogenesis is observed during the first three phases of synaptogenesis in all cortical layers, as well as in the cortices of all mammalian species, suggesting the existence of highly conserved mechanisms. In contrast, during phase 4, *en plateau*, the kinetics of these waves of synaptogenesis differ from that observed in granular layer IVC (cf. figure 4.3).

the number of symmetric synapses on shafts remains relatively steady throughout this period (Bourgeois, Goldman-Rakic, and Rakic, 1994; Bourgeois and Rakic, 1993; Zecevic, Bourgeois, and Rakic, 1989; Zecevic and Rakic, 1991).

It should be mentioned that the decline in synaptic density appears to begin earlier in the visual and somatosensory cortex than in the prefrontal association cortex. Nevertheless, at the time of sexual maturity synaptic density descends to adult levels in all areas of the macaque cortex examined to date, both in our laboratory (see above) and in other laboratories (e.g., see Zielinski and Hendrickson, 1992; Anderson et al., 1995). A similar magnitude of synapse loss during puberty has also been observed in electron microscopic studies in human (see figure 4.5 and Huttenlocher and Dabholkar, 1997) and mouse cortex (De Felipe et al., 1997)–a finding that has received indirect support from brain imaging studies in the macaque (Jacobs et al., 1995) and human cortices (Chugani, Phelps, and Mazziotta, 1987).

Although arbitrarily included in phase 4, we recognize that the period of rapid loss of synapses occurring during puberty could be considered a separate phase with its own cellular mechanisms. Our findings indicate that labile synapses that will not stabilize during

FIGURE 4.3 Changes in the relative densities of two different classes of synapses as a function of days after conception expressed on a log scale on the abscissa (*t*), in granular layer IVC of the primary visual cortex of the macaque monkey, during normal development. The same pattern of synaptogenesis is observed during the first three phases of synaptogenesis as in cortical layer III (see figure 4.2). However, during phase 4, *en plateau*, these two classes of synapses display distinct waves: a short wave of synapses on dendritic spines, and a protracted wave of synapses on dendritic shafts. This is different from the protracted plateau phase 4 of synaptogenesis on dendritic spines observed in supragranular layer III (see figure 4.2).

the long phase 4 are being eliminated during this phase. As frequently mentioned in textbooks, the period around puberty corresponds to a "freezing" of personality and a decline in neural plasticity for acquisition of certain capacities or skills. For example, 12 years of age in humans corresponds to the age at which second languages are no longer acquired with relative ease and without an accent (Johnson and Newport, 1989). Such observations may be explained by the stabilization of the final number of synapses at this period of life.

Phase 5: This last phase of *synaptic stability* begins in the third year of macaque life and lasts for the next three decades of adulthood until the density of synapses slowly but steadily declines with apparent acceleration during senescence (figure 4.1). The stages of synaptogenesis, as they have been discriminated in the studies of the human neocortex, are not entirely concordant with the five phases we have described in monkeys (Huttenlocher and Dabholkar, 1997). Although there is as yet no universal convention for comparative purposes, it is nevertheless clear that the phases of neocortical synaptogenesis in humans are analogous to those in monkeys and also significantly protracted in time as in the macaque (figure 4.5; see also Bourgeois, 1997). Importantly, major aspects of synaptoarchitecture in cortical networks during this period remain unchanged. As adulthood is the most prolonged period of primate life and adult synaptogenesis is of great interest, we have

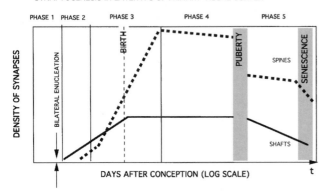

SYNAPTOGENESIS IN LAYER IVC OF PRIMARY VISUAL CORTEX

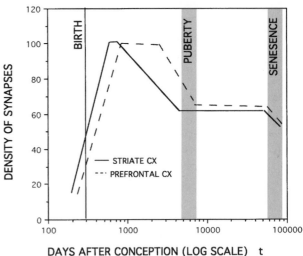

SYNAPTOGENESIS IN HUMAN CEREBRAL CORTEX

FIGURE 4.4 Changes in the relative densities of two different classes of synapses as a function of days after conception expressed on a log scale on the abscissa (t), in granular layer IVC of the primary visual cortex of the macaque monkey after an early bilateral enucleation was performed during phase 1 of synaptogenesis (arrow). The same pattern of synaptogenesis unfolds normally during the first three phases (see figures 12.2 and 12.3). However, during phase 4, *en plateau*, the second reversal of densities of synapses on dendritic spines (dotted line) and shafts (black line) does not take place.

FIGURE 4.5 Changes in the relative density of synapses in the human cerebral cortex as a function of days after conception expressed on a log scale on the abscissa (t). Data are from Huttenlocher and Dabholkar (1997). Only phases 3, 4, and 5 are represented here. The same phases of synaptogenesis are observed in both the primary visual cortex (black line) and prefrontal cortex (dashed line). Note that phase 4 is longer in the prefrontal cortex than in the striate cortex.

examined several thousand photomicrographs in search of ultrastructural evidence of new synaptic connections or their turnover during this period. While we observed growth cones and immature types of contacts or degenerating forms of connections during the formative stages (phases 1–4), we failed to observe any of these markers of new synaptic connections during this three-decade period of adult life. We cannot exclude the possibility that a small number of such events may escape detection. However, the addition of synapses is certainly not cumulative in the primate cerebral cortex since both the density of synapses and their numbers remain stationary during the long life span and, if anything, their numbers slowly decline. A similar lack of evidence for any increase in the density or absolute number of synapses has been observed in other primates (Zielinski and Hendrickson, 1992; Anderson et al., 1995), human (Huttenlocher and Dabholkar, 1997), and in mouse cerebral cortex (De Felipe et al., 1997).

NUMERICAL STABILITY OF SYNAPSES DURING ADULTHOOD The finding that the density and number of synapses becomes stabilized after puberty stands in contrast to earlier reports that learning induces the formation of additional synapses in vertebrate and invertebrates (e.g., Greenough and Bailey, 1988; Bailey and Kandel, 1993). More specifically, observations in rats suggest that experience, both in developing and adult rodents, can induce de novo formation of synapses, resulting in a net in-

crease in their absolute number after each episode of associative learning (Greenough and Alcantara, 1993). These changes should be particularly evident in primates whose life span lasts for decades. However, this mechanism of experience-induced synaptogenesis is not supported by any study in primates including human, whose adult brain is characterized more by homeostasis or a slow but steady decrease of synapses in all layers and areas of the cerebral cortex during adult life (see phase 5 and figures 4.1 to 4.5; see also Bourgeois and Rakic, 1993; Bourgeois, Goldman-Rakic, and Rakic, 1994; Zecevic and Rakic, 1991; Zecevic, Bourgeois, and Rakic, 1989; Zielinski and Hendrickson, 1992; Anderson et al., 1995; Huttenlocher and Dabholkar, 1997). Significantly, a recent study in mice also failed to reveal evidence of an increase in density or absolute number of synapses in the rodent cerebral cortex after sexual maturity (De Felipe et al., 1997). Thus, when estimates of synaptic number or density are based on stereological methodology, the results fail to show net increases in cortical synapses after puberty in any of the species studied to date, despite the extensive opportunities, particularly in humans, for acquisition and accumulation of long-term memories.

This model of synaptic plasticity, without formation of additional synapses, is also supported by the recent experimental and ultrastructural analysis of this issue in the hippocampal neuronal fields of rats in which long-term potentiation had been induced (Geinisman, DeToledo-Morrell, et al., 1996) as well as of rabbits that had been subjected to eyeblink conditioning (Geinisman et al., in press). The latter study is of particular interest because it examined the consequences of conditioning experienced in vivo. Again, using a stereological quantitative approach (Geinisman, Gundersen, et al., 1996), the two independent studies provided evidence of modification of synaptic shape, but the total number of synapses in the target regions affected by the experimental procedure remained unaltered. The conclusion drawn by the authors was that associative learning is unlikely to involve the formation of new synapses and a net increase in synaptic number, but rather a remodeling of existing synapses. Based on the available literature and on our own extensive database in non-human primates, we are also compelled to conclude that learning and memory in the adult primate cortex are, under normal conditions, likely to be achieved mainly through the strengthening and modification of existing connections rather than by the formation of new ones. This conclusion is in harmony with the general conceptualization of learning and memory as due to the induction of molecular changes, which strengthen the efficacy of existing synapses, as initially postulated by Donald Hebb (1949).

Concurrent synaptogenesis in the cortical mantle

Quantitative description of synaptogenesis in several cortical areas sampled from the same cerebral hemisphere of a series of developing macaque monkeys revealed a remarkably similar course of synaptogenesis during phase 3 in two sensory (visual and somatic), one motor, and one limbic cortical area (Rakic et al., 1986; Granger et al., 1995). Similarly rapid and synchronous accretion of both excitatory and inhibitory synapses have also been found during phase 3 in layer III of the prefrontal cortex of the macaque (Anderson et al., 1995). It has generally been implied, and we also had assumed, based in part on the classical studies of myelin staining in the developing human cerebrum, that the neocortex develops in a distinct hierarchical order, from the sensory to motor to association areas (Flechsig, 1920). Therefore, our initial finding of the concurrent acquisition of synapses in functionally diverse and anatomically separated areas of the cerebrum was unexpected (Rakic et al., 1986). In the past decade, however, additional evidence for concurrent development has been gained from brain imaging studies of the maturation of metabolic activity in the macaque cortical mantle (Jacobs et al., 1995) and the human cerebrum (Chugani, Phelps, and Mazziotta,

1987). Furthermore, quantitative studies of the presence of neurotransmitter receptors in the cortex (Lidow, Goldman-Rakic, and Rakic, 1991; Lidow and Rakic, 1992) also reveal identical profiles of receptor density within the range of human biological variation. Recently, Shankle et al. (1998) reanalyzed the classical cytoarchitectonic studies of Conel and concluded that the differentiation of a variety of morphological and laminar features are remarkably similar across cortical areas, and that developmental patterns in many cortical areas are not distinguishable from one another. Finally, the first two phases of synaptogenesis were also recently found to be synchronous across cortical areas in the human embryo, as they are in the macaque (Zecevic, 1998).

Although the rate of decline to adult levels in phase 4 varies in different areas, this phase of high synaptic density also exhibits an overlap in timing across the cortical regions (Rakic, Bourgeois, and Goldman-Rakic, 1994). We have suggested that this overlap may be essential for competitive interactions and the validation of synaptic connections during experience-dependent development. It should be pointed out that not all evidence is supportive of concurrent synaptogenesis, however. In particular, Huttenlocher and Dabholkar (1997) have reported that during the ascending phase of synaptogenesis in the human brain (phase 3 in macaque), the prefrontal association cortex appears to acquire synaptic junctions more slowly than in the primary visual and auditory cortices. This finding has appeal in its concordance with the general notion that executive functions based on language appear to mature latest in development. We have discussed the technical issues related to this conclusion in considerable detail in several previous publications (Rakic, Bourgeois, and Goldman-Rakic, 1994; Goldman-Rakic, Bourgeois, and Rakic, 1997). At present, neither the sample size (due to scarcity of human tissue) nor the magnitude of the effect is sufficient to challenge the idea of concurrent synaptogenesis.

FUNCTIONAL IMPLICATIONS OF CONCURRENT SYNAPTOGENESIS Studies in human infants show that virtually all cortical functions, including language, have anlage in early infancy and do not arise de novo at a late stage of maturation. In humans, evoked activity in response to the maternal voice is present even before birth (Lecanuet and Granier-Deferre, 1993), and the development of visual acuity and depth perception begins in newborn infants (Teller, 1997, and chapter 6 of this volume). Human infants also evidence expectations based on auditory and visual stimuli that depend on the association cortex. Human infants also show competence to represent numerical entities, including action sequences (for review, see Wynn, 1998). In the macaque, likewise, early signs of competencies that will later be fully developed are already in evidence. Thus, adult-like properties of neurons in the inferotemporal cortex, such as selective responses to face recognition, are present at only a few weeks after birth (Rodman, Gross, and Scalaidhe, 1993; Rodman, 1994). The critical periods for obtaining social skills and learning simple discriminations also take place as early as two months after birth in macaque infants (Harlow and Harlow, 1962). The cognitive process of working memory, which is subserved by the dorsolateral prefrontal association cortex, likewise emerges in monkeys soon after birth and before the end of phase 3 (Diamond and Goldman-Rakic, 1989), when basic synaptoarchitectonic features are still being laid down (Bourgeois, Goldman-Rakic, and Rakic, 1994; Goldman-Rakic, Bourgeois, and Rakic, 1997; Goldman-Rakic, 1987). Although monkeys obviously do not possess language, they do have specializations for working memory processes that are common to all informational domains, and are considered essential for language competence (e.g., Baddeley, 1986; Just and Carpenter, 1992; King and Just, 1991; Miyake, 1994).

Based on our own data and consideration of the literature, we have proposed that the integration of sensory, motor, limbic, and associative areas occurs *pari passu* with the structural development of the cortex as a unified structure, i.e., as "whole cloth" (Goldman-Rakic, Bourgeois, and Rakic, 1997). Further, we would argue that the level and complexity of processing advances with each progressive stage of development. Our working hypothesis is that concurrent synaptogenesis in the whole cortical mantle during the rapid phase 3 allows the early coordinated emergence of all cortical functions (Rakic, Bourgeois, and Goldman-Rakic, 1994; Rakic et al., 1986). In agreement with others, we would argue that concurrency is essential for the competitive and selective interactions among the very heterogeneous cortical inputs arriving at each point of the cortex (e.g., Changeux and Danchin, 1976; Katz and Shatz, 1996; Antonini and Stryker, 1998). However, full maturation of cortical functions is a protracted process that may require many years to be achieved in the macaque (Goldman-Rakic, Bourgeois, and Rakic, 1997) and more than a decade in the human (Rakic, Bourgeois, and Goldman-Rakic, 1994; Huttenlocher and Dabholkar, 1997).

Genetic versus environmental control of synaptogenesis

The onset, the rate, and the concurrent course of synaptogenesis in various areas and layers during its initial phases occur before birth and are likely to be determined by mechanisms intrinsic and common to the whole cortical mantle (Rakic et al., 1986; Rakic, Bourgeois, and Goldman-Rakic, 1994; Goldman-Rakic, Bourgeois, and Rakic, 1997). We have experimentally tested the independence of these early developmental events from peripheral inputs using several different approaches. In the first approach, we delivered monkeys prematurely three weeks before birth and compared the synaptic density in their visual cortex to that in full-term infants during phase 3 of rapid synaptogenesis. This study showed that premature exposure to a visual environment in preterm infant monkeys neither accelerates nor delays the overall rate of synaptic accretion during the rapid phase 4 in the primary visual cortex (Bourgeois, Jastreboff, and Rakic, 1989). Rather, the rate of synaptogenesis in phase 3 proceeds in relation to the time of conception and not the time of birth or the onset of visual stimulation.

In a second experiment, we enucleated monkeys bilaterally in utero and returned the fetuses to the womb to be delivered by Cesarean section at term (Bourgeois and Rakic, 1996). This study showed that early bilateral enucleation performed before the onset of phase 3 does not alter the mean density of synapses in the visual cortex at the end of this phase or during the plateau phase 4 (Bourgeois and Rakic, 1996). In the enucleated animals the distribution of the major neurotransmitter receptors and cytochrome oxidase patches related to color vision develop normally in spite of the absence of stimulation from the retina during the early prenatal stages (Kuljis and Rakic, 1990; Rakic and Lidow, 1995). In addition, our electron microscopic analysis of the type of synapses in the visual cortex revealed that the proportion of synaptic contacts situated on dendritic spines (75%) and shafts (25%), at the end of phase 3, is not significantly different in enucleated animals compared with normal sighted infants (figures 4.2 and 4.3; see also Bourgeois and Rakic, 1996). However, these proportions, which are normally reversed during infancy (figure 4.3) in the sublayers IVAB and IVC, are not reversed in the enucleates (figure 4.4). Our findings indicate that the onset, time course, and magnitude of cortical synaptogenesis in the primate visual cortex can proceed normally without any visual stimulation or retinal input. On the other hand, we have also provided the only ultrastructural evidence in the primate that the final adjustments in synaptoarchitecture, including the proportions of synapses on spines and shafts in thalamorecipient layer IV seem to depend on normal functional input (Bourgeois and Rakic, 1996).

Finally, using a genetic approach, one of us (JPB) has examined a mouse strain bearing a null mutation for the

Otx1 gene, in which the total surface of the cortical mantle is significantly reduced. That is, although all cortical domains are still present in this mutant (Acampora et al., 1996), preliminary data suggest that in the primary visual cortex of this abnormal cortical mantle, the onset and timing of phase 3 of synaptogenesis nevertheless proceed normally in relation to the time of conception (Bourgeois, in preparation).

These quantitative ultrastructural studies indicate that the onset, duration, rate of synapse production, and pattern of synaptogenesis (i.e., the percentages of diverse classes of synapses as a function of postconception age) remain essentially unchanged despite significant developmental perturbations during the first three phases of synaptogenesis, supporting the hypothesis that these phases are determined and coordinated by mechanisms intrinsic and common to the whole cortical mantle. Phases 1 and 2, as well as the first half of phase 3, seem to be dominated by "experience-independent" mechanisms, using the terminology of Greenough and Alcantara (1993). Eventually, the initial intrinsic mechanisms become epigenetically modulated by "experience," i.e., patterned inputs reaching the neocortex from the external world (Bourgeois, 1997). During the second part of phase 3 and plateau phase 4, the mechanisms of synaptogenesis become "experience-expectant" (Greenough and Alcantara, 1993). This means that the presence and repetition of visual, auditory, and other sensory parameters of stimulation and other experience, such as motor activity, become necessary for the proper final adjustment of the cortical circuitry. The transition from intrinsic to extrinsic regulation of synaptogenesis in the cerebral cortex most likely involves the cellular mechanisms underlying learning and memory, which are dealt with in later sections of this volume. Understanding whether learning involves synaptogenesis in adult primates will entail quantitative ultrastructural analysis comparable to that used by Geinisman (in press) in the adult rat.

ACKNOWLEDGMENTS We thank Professor Jean-Pierre Changeux for helpful discussions about the role of genes and epigenesis in formation of synapses. This work was supported initially by the Fogarty International Fellowship, and continuously by the Centre National de la Recherche Scientifique, France (JPB) and U.S. Public Health Service (PGR and PR).

REFERENCES

ACAMPORA, D., S. MAZAN, V. AVANTAGGIATO, P. BARONE, F. TUORTO, Y. LALLEMAND, P. BRULET, and A. SIMEONE, 1996. Epilepsy and brain abnormalities in mice lacking the Otx1 gene. *Nature Genetics* 14:218–222.

ANDERSON, S. A., J. D. CLASSEY, E. F. CONDÉ, J. S. LUND, and D. A. LEWIS, 1995. Synchronous development of pyramidal neuron dendritic spines and parvalbumin-immunoreactive chandelier neuron axon terminals in layer III of monkey prefrontal cortex. *Neuroscience* 67(1):7–22.

ANTONINI, A., and M. P. STRYKER, 1998. Effect of sensory disuse on geniculate afferents to cat visual cortex. *Vis. Neurosci.* 15:401–403.

BADDELEY, A., 1986. *Working Memory.* New York: Oxford University Press.

BAILEY, C. H., and E. R. KANDEL, 1993. Structural changes accompanying memory storage. *Annu. Rev. Physiol.* 55:397–426.

BARONE, P., C. DEHAY, M. BERLAND, J. BULLIER, and H. KENNEDY, 1995. Developmental remodeling of primate visual cortical pathways. *Cerebral Cortex* 5:22–38.

BOURGEOIS, J. P., 1997. Synaptogenesis, heterochrony and epigenesis in the mammalian neocortex. *Acta Pediatrica* 422 (suppl.):27–33.

BOURGEOIS, J. P., P. S. GOLDMAN-RAKIC, and P. RAKIC, 1994. Synaptogenesis in the prefrontal cortex of rhesus monkey. *Cerebral Cortex* 4:78–96.

BOURGEOIS, J. P., P. J. JASTREBOFF, and P. RAKIC, 1989. Synaptogenesis in visual cortex of normal and preterm monkeys: Evidence for intrinsic regulation of synaptic overproduction. *Proc. Natl. Acad. Sci. U.S.A.* 86: 4297–4301.

BOURGEOIS, J. P., and P. RAKIC, 1993. Changes of synaptic density in the primary visual cortex of the macaque monkey from fetal to adult stage. *J. Neurosci.* 13:2801–2820.

BOURGEOIS, J. P., and P. RAKIC, 1996. Synaptogenesis in the occipital cortex of macaque monkey devoid of retinal input from early embryonic stages. *Eur. J. Neurosci.* 8:942–950.

CHANGEUX, J. P., and A. DANCHIN, 1976. Selective stabilization of developing synapses as a mechanism for the specification of neural network. *Nature* 264:705–712.

CHUGANI, H. T., M. E. PHELPS, and J. C. MAZZIOTTA, 1987. Positron emission tomography study of human brain functional development. *Ann. Neurol.* 22:487–497.

DE FELIPE, J., P. MARCO, A. FAIRÉN, and E. G. JONES, 1997. Inhibitory synaptogenesis in mouse somatosensory cortex. *Cerebral Cortex* 7:619–634.

DIAMOND, A., and P. S. GOLDMAN-RAKIC, 1989. Comparison of human infants and rhesus monkeys on Piaget's AB task: Evidence for dependence on dorsolateral prefrontal cortex. *Exp. Brain Res.* 74:24–40.

FLECHSIG, P., 1920. *Anatomie des Menchlichen Gehirn und Ruckenmarks auf Myelonetischer.* Leipzig: GrundlageThieme.

GEINISMAN, Y., L. DETOLEDO-MORRELL, F. MORRELL, I. S. PERSINA, and M. A. BEATTY, 1966. Synapses restructuring associated with the maintenance phase of hippocampal long-term potentiation. *J. Comp. Neurol.* 368:413–423.

GEINISMAN, Y., J. F. DISTERHOF, H. J. G. GUNDERSEN, M. MCECHORN, I. S. PERSINA, and J. M. POWER, in press. Structural substrate of hippocampus-dependent associative learning: Remodelling of synapses. *J. Comp. Neurol.*

GEINISMAN, Y., H. J. G. GUNDERSEN, E. VAN DER ZEE, and M. J. WEST, 1996. Unbiased stereological estimation of the total number of synapses in a brain region. *J. Neurocytol.* 25:805–819.

GOLDMAN-RAKIC, P. S., 1987. Development of cortical circuitry and cognitive function. *Child Development* 58:642–691.

GOLDMAN-RAKIC, P. S., J.-P. BOURGEOIS, and P. RAKIC, 1997. Synaptic substrate of cognitive development: Lifespan analysis of synaptogenesis in the prefrontal cortex of the nonhuman primate. In *Development of Prefrontal Cortex. Evolution,*

Neurobiology and Behavior, N. A. Krasnegor, G. Reid Lyon, and P. S. Goldman-Rakic, eds. Baltimore, Md.: Paul H. Brukes, pp. 27–47.

GRANGER, B., A. M. LESOURD, P. RAKIC, and J.-P. BOURGEOIS, 1995. Tempo of neurogenesis and synaptogenesis in the primate cingulate mesocortex: Comparison with the neocortex. *J. Comp. Neurol.* 360: 363–376.

GREENOUGH, W. T., and A. A. ALCANTARA, 1993. The roles of experience in different developmental information stage processes. In *Developmental Neurocognition,* B. de Boysson-Bardies, S. de Schonen, P. Jusczyk, P. McNeilage, and J. Morton, eds. Dordrecht: Kluwer, pp. 3–16.

GREENOUGH, W. T., and C. H. BAILEY, 1988. The anatomy of a memory: Convergence of results across a diversity of tests. *Trends Neurosci.* 11:142–147.

HARLOW, H. F., and HARLOW, M. K., 1962. Social deprivation in monkeys. *Sci. Am.* 207:136–146.

HEBB, D. O., 1949. *The Organization of Behavior.* New York: Wiley.

HUBEL, D. H., T. N. WIESEL, and S. LEVAY, 1977. Plasticity of ocular dominance columns in monkey striate cortex. *Phil. Trans. R. Soc. Lond.* 278:377–409.

HUTTENLOCHER, P. R., and A. S. DABHOLKAR, 1997. Regional differences in synaptogenesis in human cerebral cortex. *J. Comp. Neurol.* 387:167–178.

JACOBS, B., H. T. CHUGANI, V. ALLADA, S. CHEN, M. E. PHELPS, D. B. POLLACK, and M. J. RALEIGH, 1995. Developmental changes in brain metabolism in sedated rhesus macaques and vervet monkeys revealed by positron emission tomography. *Cerebral Cortex* 3:222–233.

JOHNSON, J. S., and E. L. NEWPORT, 1989. Critical period effects in second language learning: The influence of maturational state on the acquisition of English as a second language. *Cogn. Psychology* 21:60–99.

JUST, M. A., and P. CARPENTER, 1992. A capacity theory of comprehension: Individual differences in working memory. *Psych. Rev.* 99:122–149.

KATZ, L. C., and C. J. SHATZ, 1996. Synaptic activity and the construction of cortical circuits. *Science* 274:1133–1138.

KING, J., and M. A. JUST, 1991. Individual differences in syntactic processing: The role of working memory. *J. Mem. Lang.* 30:580–602.

KULJIS, R. O., and P. RAKIC, 1990. Hypercolumns in primate visual cortex develop in the absence of cues from photoreceptors. *Proc. Natl. Acad. Sci. U.S.A.* 87:5303–5306.

LECANUET, J. P., and C. GRANIER-DEFERRE, 1993. Speech stimuli in the fetal environment. In *Developmental Neurocognition,* B. de Boysson-Bardies, S. de Schonen, P. Jusczyk, P. McNeilage, and J. Morton, eds. Dordrecht: Kluwer, pp. 237–248.

LIDOW, M. S., P. S. GOLDMAN-RAKIC, and P. RAKIC, 1991. Synchronized overproduction of neurotransmitter receptors in diverse regions of the primate cerebral cortex. *Proc. Natl. Acad. Sci. U.S.A.* 88:10218–10221.

LIDOW, M. S., and P. RAKIC, 1992. Postnatal development of monoaminergic neurotransmitter receptors with primate neocortex. *Cerebral Cortex* 2:401–415.

MEISSIREL, C., K. C. WIKLER, L. M. CHALUPA, and P. RAKIC, 1997. Early divergence of M and P visual subsystems in the embryonic primate brain. *Proc. Natl. Acad. Sci. U.S.A.* 94: 5900–5905. ·

MIYAKE, A., 1994. Toward a unified theory of capacity constraints: The role of working memory in complex cognition. *Bull. Jpn. Cogn. Sci. Soc.* 1:43–62.

MOLLIVER, M. E., I. KOSTOVIC, and H. VAN DER LOOS, 1973. The development of synapses in cerebral cortex of the human fetus. *Brain Res.* 50:403–407.

MOUNTCASTLE, V. B., 1997. The columnar organization of the neocortex. *Brain* 120:701–722.

POLYAK, S., 1957. *The Vertebrate Visual System.* Chicago: University of Chicago Press.

RAKIC, P., 1972. Mode of cell migration to the superficial layers of fetal monkey neocortex. *J. Comp. Neurol.* 145:61–84.

RAKIC, P., 1976. Prenatal genesis of connections subserving ocular dominance in the rhesus monkey. *Nature* 261:467–471.

RAKIC, P., 1981. Developmental events leading to laminar and areal organization of the neocortex. In *The Organization of Cerebral Cortex,* F. O. Schmitt, F. G. Worden, G. Adelman, and S. G. Dennis, eds. Cambridge, Mass.: MIT Press, pp. 7–28.

RAKIC, P., 1988. Specification of cerebral cortical areas. *Science* 241:170–176.

RAKIC, P., J.-P. BOURGEOIS, M. E. ECKENHOFF, N. ZECEVIC, and P. S. GOLDMAN-RAKIC, 1986. Concurrent overproduction of synapses in diverse regions of the primate cerebral cortex. *Science* 232:232–235.

RAKIC, P., J.-P. BOURGEOIS, and P. S. GOLDMAN-RAKIC, 1994. Synaptic development of the cerebral cortex: Implications for learning, memory, and mental illness. *Prog. Brain Res.* 102:227–243.

RAKIC, P., D. GALLAGER, and P. S. GOLDMAN-RAKIC, 1988. Areal and laminar distribution of major neurotransmitter receptors in the monkey visual cortex. *J. Neurosci.* 8:3670–3690.

RAKIC, P., and M. S. LIDOW, 1995. Distribution and density of neurotransmitter receptors in the visual cortex devoid of retinal input from early embryonic stages. *J. Neurosci.* 15:2561–2574.

RODMAN, H. R., 1994. Development of inferior temporal cortex in the monkey. *Cerebral Cortex* 5:484–498.

RODMAN, H. R., C. G. GROSS, and S. P. SCALAIDHE, 1993. Development of brain substrates for pattern recognition in primates: Physiological and connectional studies of inferior temporal cortex in infant monkeys. In *Developmental Neurocognition,* B. de Boysson-Bardies, S. de Schonen, P. Jusczyk, P. McNeilage, and J. Morton, eds. Dordrecht: Kluwer, pp. 63–75.

SCHWARTZ, M. L., and P. S. GOLDMAN-RAKIC, 1991. Prenatal specification of callosal connections in rhesus monkey. *J. Comp. Neurol.* 307:144–162.

SHANKLE, W. R., A. K. ROMNEY, B. H. LANDING, and J. HARA, 1998. Developmental patterns in the cytoarchitecture of the human cerebral cortex from birth to 6 years examined by correspondence analysis. *Proc. Natl. Acad. Sci. U.S.A.* 95:4023–4028.

SHKOL'NIK-YARROS, E. G., 1971. *Neurons and Interneuronal Connections of the Central Visual System.* New York: Plenum Press.

SZENTHAGOTHAI, J., 1978. The neuronal network of the cerebral cortex: A functional interpretation. *Proc. R. Soc. Lond.* 201:219–248.

TELLER, D. Y., 1997. First glances: The vision of infants. *Invest. Ophthalmol. Vis. Sci.* 38:2183–2203.

WYNN, K., 1998. Psychological foundations of number: Numerical competence in human infants. *Trends Cogn. Sci.* 2:296–303.

ZECEVIC, N., 1998. Synaptogenesis in Layer I of the human cerebral cortex in the first half of gestation. *Cerebral Cortex* 8:245–252.

ZECEVIC, N., J.-P. BOURGEOIS, and P. RAKIC, P., 1989. Synaptic density in motor cortex of rhesus monkey during fetal and postnatal life. *Dev. Brain Res.* 50:11–32.

ZECEVIC, N., and P. RAKIC, 1991. Synaptogenesis in monkey somatosensory cortex. *Cerebral Cortex* 1:510–523.

ZIELINSKI, B. S., and A. HENDRICKSON, 1992. Development of synapses in macaque monkey striate cortex. *Vis. Neurosci.* 8:491–504.

5 Merging Sensory Signals in the Brain: The Development of Multisensory Integration in the Superior Colliculus

BARRY E. STEIN, MARK T. WALLACE, AND TERRENCE R. STANFORD

ABSTRACT During early brain development, systems emerge that are capable of integrating information from different senses. These "multisensory" systems parallel the well-known primary projection systems in which information is segregated on a sense-by-sense basis. The midbrain superior colliculus (SC) is an excellent example of a multisensory system, and recent experiments have shown that its multisensory integration capabilities are not present at birth, but appear gradually during postnatal development. Initially, SC neurons are strictly unimodal and it is not until 12 postnatal days that some of them begin responding to more than a single sensory input. However, it takes several additional weeks before these multisensory neurons are able to integrate their different sensory inputs to enhance or degrade their responses as do their adult counterparts. Among the most significant events that precede the development of this cross-modality integrative ability is the formation of functional inputs from particular regions of the neocortex. It is believed that the timing of this corticotectal development determines the kinds of multisensory information that can be integrated in the SC, and hence the SC-mediated multisensory behaviors that can be expressed at different stages of postnatal development.

All animals are faced with the same daunting task: detecting changes in the external world and interpreting these changes so that they can react appropriately. Their survival depends on it. It is no surprise, then, that the task of accurately representing external "reality" has been a powerful driving force in evolutionary biology and has resulted in animals that possess an impressive array of highly specialized senses. Each of these senses has unique peripheral receptors capable of transducing a specific form of energy into a neural code and a dedicated neural machinery in the central nervous system to represent and interpret these inputs.

By maintaining multiple sensory systems an animal substantially enhances its likelihood of detecting relevant events. These systems not only substitute for one another when necessary (e.g., hearing can substitute for vision in the dark), but also provide multiple modality-specific "views" that reduce the ambiguity of some signals. For example, two objects or events that cannot be distinguished in one physical dimension (they look alike) may be readily differentiated in another (they feel different). Yet sensory modalities have evolved to work in concert; and although the combination of two dissimilar physical cues, say light and sound, may have little direct effect on each other in the external world, they can profoundly alter each other's influence on the brain. Thus, the neural consequences of a stimulus in a given modality may depend on which stimuli from other modalities are present at that same moment. That such intersensory interactions have substantial effects on perception and behavior is obvious from the numerous examples in the literature in which an observer's perception and speed of reaction to one modality-specific stimulus are significantly altered in the presence of another.

At first, such interactions seem surprising. Although some of the sensory modalities may have had similar evolutionary origins (e.g., see Gregory, 1967; Northcutt, 1986), each has become associated with unique subjective attributes, or qualia. These qualia (e.g., hue, pitch, tickle, itch) are inextricably linked to their own sensory systems and have no equivalents in other modalities. Their apparent independence gives the very strong impression that the different sensory systems are also functionally independent—an impression that is quite wrong.

Hosts of perceptual studies demonstrate that stimuli in one modality can significantly alter experiences in another. One broad class of these perceptual effects is called the "ventriloquism effect" (Howard and Templeton, 1966), a phenomenon of intersensory bias in which a stimulus from one sensory modality influences judgments about the location of a stimulus in another modality. The most familiar example, of course, is the situation in which the visual cues associated with the movement of a dummy's mouth evoke the compelling illusion that

BARRY E. STEIN, MARK T. WALLACE, and TERRENCE R. STANFORD Department of Neurobiology and Anatomy, Wake Forest University School of Medicine, Winston-Salem, N.C.

the sound also originates from the dummy. However, we experience this effect far more commonly while watching a movie or television program. The sounds all originate from the same speakers, and these are comparatively far from the visual images on the screen. Yet each voice seems to originate from the appropriate actor.

There are many other examples of the perceptual effects of cross-modality synthesis (see Stein and Meredith, 1993, and Welch and Warren, 1986, for a more detailed discussion). It should, however, be noted that synthesizing inputs from the same event increases the likelihood that the event will be detected and produce a reaction (Stein et al., 1989). In humans and nonhuman primates, where eye movements are frequently used as a measure of attentive and orientation reactions, response latencies to a visual or auditory cue can be reduced significantly by presenting both cues simultaneously (Frens, Van Opstal, and Van der Willigen, 1995; Goldring et al., 1996; Hughes et al., 1994; Lee et al., 1991).

Because the sensory environment is constantly in flux, multisensory integration is an ongoing process. Yet, it is a process of which we are completely unaware. Cross-modality phenomena have fascinated observers of human behavior and perception since the time of ancient Greece. While this fascination has led to a wealth of relevant perceptual and behavioral observations, there have been comparatively few corresponding neural studies. The lack of neural data was due, in part, to inherent difficulties involved in assessing the interactions among modalities and linking them to specific perceptual and/or behavioral events, and to placing these observations in a meaningful developmental context.

In recent years, however, the cat superior colliculus (SC) has been used as a model system with which to explore these processes. The choice of this system was based, in large part, on the high incidence of multisensory neurons, and the well-documented involvement of the SC in overt attentive and orientation behaviors (see Stein and Meredith, 1993, for a review). The use of this model affords some intriguing insights into the principles by which individual neurons in the brain synthesize their multiple sensory inputs and how this product may be used to guide behavior. Similar principles operating in other multisensory structures are likely to underlie higher-order cross-modality perceptions. Before discussing how SC neurons develop their multisensory integrative abilities, it is helpful first to examine what is known about this structure and about the principles guiding multisensory integration in mature SC neurons. Because it is the deep layers of the SC that house its multisensory neurons (superficial layer neurons are purely visual) and

the circuitry through which it effects overt responses, it is this division of the structure that will be discussed.

Observations from adult animals

MAP ALIGNMENT   The SC—perhaps more so than any other brain structure—functions at the interface of sensory and motor processing. It receives inputs from multiple sensory modalities (i.e., visual, auditory, and somatosensory) and issues motor commands to produce coordinated orienting movements of the eyes, ears, head, and body toward stimuli in each of these modalities. Information about stimulus location is represented topographically within the structure by virtue of an orderly arrangement of neurons according to the location of their respective receptive fields (RFs). The result is a map-like arrangement of the sensory representations wherein the rostral portion of the SC is devoted to representing forward (central) visual and auditory space and the front of the body, whereas peripheral visual and auditory space and the rear body parts are represented in the caudal aspect. Similarly, the inferior-superior axis of sensory space is laid out along the medial-lateral axis of the structure. The spatial register among the different sensory maps is formed, in large part, by multisensory neurons whose different RFs are in register with one another (Stein and Meredith, 1993).

Analogously, the SC contains a "motor map" (Harris, 1980; McHaffie and Stein, 1982; Sparks, 1986; Stein and Clamann, 1981; see also McIlwain, 1991; Roucoux and Crommelinck, 1976) composed of output neurons having "movement fields." Rather than encoding the position of a sensory stimulus in space, the locus of activity in the motor map encodes a displacement vector, a movement command that reorients the eyes, ears, head, or body a given distance in a particular direction. Given that the goal is to translate a sensory signal into an appropriate motor command, the alignment of the individual sensory maps to each other and to the motor map must surely be a critical factor.

The notion that different sensory modalities access a common motor map dictates the need for mechanisms that establish and maintain spatial registration among modality-specific RFs. Evidence for spatial correspondence among visual, auditory, and somatosensory maps came first from studies of anesthetized animals and has been reported for many species (e.g., see Stein and Meredith, 1993). In these studies, the modality-specific RFs of SC neurons are recorded from animals in which the eyes, ears, head, and body are in alignment. In these circumstances, the coordinate frames of visual (referred to the retina), auditory (referred to the head), and tactile (referred to the body) "space" co-align. Without exception, these studies suggest close spatial correspondence between RFs representing different modalities. This is particularly evident in individual multisensory neurons. Similar observations have now been made in alert animals whose peripheral sensory organs are aligned (e.g., see Wallace, McHaffie, and Stein, 1997). Considered from a sensorimotor perspective, these findings indicate that when different modality-specific stimuli appear in spatially aligned regions of visual, auditory, or tactile space, they lead to similar spatial distributions of SC activity and, appropriately, specify the same movement vector.

Maintaining map alignment

But what happens when one set of sensory organs is moved relative to the others? As alluded to above, the coordinate systems of visual, auditory, and tactile space use distinctly different referents: Visual space is coded in retinal coordinates, auditory space is coded with respect to the head (and pinnae), and somatosensory space is referred to the body surface. Given that these reference frames can move independently of one another (e.g., when the eyes move but the head remains fixed), there is no unique relationship between a coordinate in one reference frame and that in another. As a result, modality-specific sensory maps in the SC cannot be encoded in their original reference frames (e.g., head-centered, body-centered), if RF registration is to be maintained. For example, eye movements deviate the eyes in the orbit, and each eye movement changes the relationship between the various frames of reference. So, if the eyes are deviated in the orbit 15 degrees to the left, a sensory stimulus 5 degrees to the right of the head would now be 20 degrees right in retinocentric coordinates, but still only 5 degrees right in craniocentric coordinates. If the SC encoded visual information in retinocentric coordinates and auditory information in craniocentric coordinates, a visual and auditory stimulus in the same location in external space would be represented at different loci. Clearly, this would make RF register impossible and make the problem of interfacing with the SC motor map much more complicated.

One possible solution, as discussed by Sparks and colleagues (e.g., Sparks and Nelson, 1987), is that SC sensory maps may be the end-product of coordinate transformations designed to represent modality-specific information in a common frame of reference more closely aligned with the motor representation. In such a scheme, the site of sensory-contingent activity is more closely related to the movement vector required to orient to the stimulus than it is to the spatial location of the stimulus itself. Thus, in the example given above, both visual- and auditory-evoked activity would produce activation at a site appropriate for producing a 20-degree rightward shift in gaze. Evidence that many SC auditory and somatosensory RFs are, indeed, dynamically remapped (as a function of eye position) to maintain RF alignment has been obtained in both monkeys and cats (Groh and Sparks, 1996; Hartline et al., 1995; Jay and Sparks, 1984; Peck, Baro, and Warder, 1995).

Common coordinates and multisensory integration

Cross-modality topographic register is also critical for the proper synthesis of cross-modality information when multiple sensory cues are available. The multisensory SC neurons that perform this synthesis form a substantial portion of the output pathways of the SC that connect to the brain stem's motor circuitry, and presumably are engaged in premotor signaling (Meredith, Wallace, and Stein, 1992; Wallace, Meredith, and Stein, 1993). As will be shown below, misaligning the different RFs of multisensory neurons substantially alters their integrative products and the behaviors that depend on them.

Operationally, "multisensory integration" is defined as a statistically significant difference between the neuron's response to a stimulus combination compared to its response to the individual component stimuli (Meredith and Stein, 1983). The integration can result in a dramatic increase in the number of impulses evoked above that elicited by the individual stimuli (a "response enhancement" that can exceed the sum of the two modality-specific responses), or a significant decrement below that elicited by either of the individual stimuli (a "response depression" that sometimes eliminates responses altogether). Both effects can be exhibited by the same neuron and depend on a variety of factors, the most obvious of which is the spatial relationship among the stimuli (Meredith and Stein, 1996; Wallace, Wilkinson, and Stein, 1996). When two different sensory stimuli originate from the same spatial location, as when they arise from the same event, they fall within the respective (overlapping) RFs of a given multisensory neuron, and usually yield a substantially enhanced response. If, however, the stimuli are spatially disparate (e.g., causally unrelated), so that one stimulus originates from a location outside its modality-specific excitatory RF, no enhancement of the response to the other stimulus occurs. And, if that stimulus falls within the inhibitory region of its RF, it will depress (and may eliminate) responses to the other (Kadunce et al., 1997). Note that response enhancement could serve to facilitate orienting responses to a particular spatial location, whereas response depression suggests the existence of competitive interactions

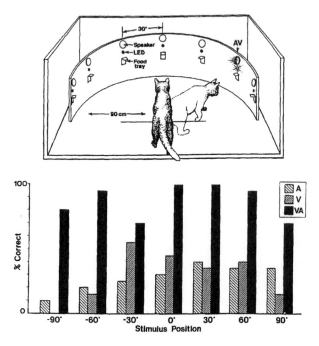

FIGURE 5.1 Enhancement of multisensory attentive/orientation behaviors to spatially coincident visual and auditory stimuli. Top: Animals are trained and tested in a perimetry device in which visual (LED) and auditory (speaker) stimuli are spaced at regular intervals. Animals were rewarded with a food pellet for correctly approaching the active stimulus site. Trials began with the cat fixated on the central LED. In this paradigm, visual, auditory, and spatially coincident visual-auditory (VA) stimuli were delivered in an interleaved manner and the percentage of correct responses was scored. Bottom: Data show that at all locations, behavioral responses to the spatially coincident visual-auditory combination were strongly enhanced when compared with the responses to either of the stimuli presented alone. (From Stein et al., 1989.)

designed to prevent the simultaneous representation of more than one movement goal within the SC (figure 5.1).

Other factors governing multisensory integration

The magnitude of a response enhancement can also vary depending on the timing of the stimuli. Studies in which the onset asynchronies of two stimuli are manipulated have shown that there is a surprisingly long period after one stimulus is presented during which an interaction with another stimulus is possible. Although some visual-auditory neurons exhibit their greatest enhancements when both stimuli occur simultaneously, others prefer an onset asynchrony of 50 ms or more (with the visual stimulus leading the auditory). Generally, there is a progressive decrease in the magnitude of the interaction as the onset asynchrony increases or decreases from the optimum (Meredith, Nemitz, and Stein, 1987; Wallace, Wilkinson, and Stein, 1996; Wallace and Stein, 1997a).

The magnitude of a multisensory enhancement also varies significantly depending on the level of effectiveness of the unimodal stimuli being combined. This relationship is an inverse one. Hence, the combination of weakly effective unimodal stimuli results in the greatest proportionate response enhancement, whereas combinations of very effective unimodal stimuli produce response enhancements that are proportionately quite small. These observations emphasize that the usefulness of multisensory enhancement in the SC is greatest when the intensity of the initiating event is weakest. This makes intuitive sense, as highly effective stimuli already produce strong signals in the central nervous system. Consequently, their detection and likelihood of evoking overt behaviors are already high.

It might seem reasonable to suppose that as long as a neuron receives inputs from multiple sensory modalities, it will integrate those inputs and show the characteristic multisensory enhancement (or depression) described above. However, this is not the case. SC neurons appear to require specific inputs in order to produce these cross-modality integrative products. The most important of these come from an area of cortex, the anterior ectosylvian sulcus (AES).

The AES is a corticotectal (Stein, Spencer, and Edwards, 1983) "association" area composed of visual (AEV; see Mucke et al., 1982; Olson and Graybiel, 1987), auditory (field AES, or "FAES"; see Clarey and Irvine, 1990), and somatosensory (SIV; see Clemo and Stein, 1982) regions. Multisensory neurons in the SC receive convergent inputs from unimodal cells in these different subregions (figure 5.2; see Wallace, Meredith, and Stein, 1993), as well as from unimodal ascending pathways (for a review, see Edwards et al., 1979). Thus, a visual-auditory SC neuron may receive ascending inputs from the retina and inferior colliculus and descending inputs from the AEV and FAES subdivisions of the AES. Yet, the inputs from AES are quite special, and their elimination produces remarkably specific effects on the great majority of multisensory SC neurons that have been examined: Their unimodal responses may be only modestly affected, but their capacity to engage in multisensory integration can be markedly suppressed (Wallace and Stein, 1994). The suppression of multisensory integration is such that even the seemingly straightforward addition of the responses normally evoked by the two unimodal stimuli is lost (figure 5.3). Apparently, then, additive (and even subadditive) multisensory enhancement is not as straightforward as it might first appear; and regardless of magnitude, the multisensory enhancement produced by coupling two unimodal stimuli is generally dependent on integrative mechanisms facilitated by corticotectal influences.

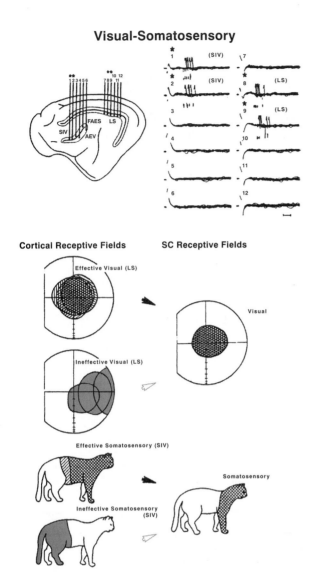

Visual-Somatosensory

Cortical Receptive Fields   SC Receptive Fields

Effective Visual (LS)

Visual

Ineffective Visual (LS)

Effective Somatosensory (SIV)

Somatosensory

Ineffective Somatosensory (SIV)

FIGURE 5.2 Visual and somatosensory cortical inputs converge on an individual SC neuron. Top: Electrode implantation sites in cortex are shown on the left and the evoked activity of a multisensory SC neuron is shown on the right. Note that stimulation of sites in somatosensory (SIV) and visual (LS) cortices orthodromically activated this visual-somatosensory SC neuron, whereas stimulation in auditory (FAES) cortex was ineffective. Bottom: The effective cortical stimulation sites also had multiunit receptive fields that were well matched with the receptive fields of the activated SC neuron. (From Wallace, Meredith, and Stein, 1993.)

The specificity of the corticotectal influences from AES on multisensory integration was quite unexpected. It turns out that what has been considered, in classical terminology, an area of "association cortex" does, indeed, associate among the senses, but does so through a connection to a subcortical structure very far away. In this manner AES not only controls multisensory integration in the SC, but also exerts substantial influence on the attentive and orientation functions the SC mediates.

This became particularly evident from a parallel study using behavioral techniques.

Cats were first trained in a perimetry device to orient to a visual stimulus. In some instances they were taught to orient to an auditory stimulus, in others they were taught to ignore it, and in still others the auditory stimulus was neutral (some animals were trained and tested in all paradigms sequentially). Regardless of the training paradigm, or the area of sensory space examined, the results obtained were substantially the same. When visual and auditory cues were presented together in time and space, there was a significant enhancement in correct responding that exceeded statistical predictions based on combining response probabilities to the unimodal stimuli (figure 5.4). When the cues were spatially disparate, correct responding was markedly decreased (Stein et al., 1989). However, when a broad region of the AES was temporarily deactivated (both AEV and FAES were affected), both the salutary effects of spatially coincident combinations of cross-modality stimuli and the inhibitory effects of spatially disparate cross-modality stimuli were profoundly degraded without affecting unimodal behaviors (Wilkinson, Meredith, and Stein, 1996). Often there were no significant differences between the response probabilities to a visual cue alone and the visual-auditory stimulus combinations.

Developing multisensory processes

An issue that has been of considerable interest to neuroscientists for some time now is whether the newborn brain is capable of engaging in this sort of cross-modality integration or if this capability appears only after extensive postnatal experience with these (or similar) cues. Of some relevance to the development of current thought regarding this issue are discussions in the perceptual literature, particularly those related to a syndrome called "synesthesia." Individuals with synesthesia have sensory experiences that may seem strange to most of us. A modality-specific stimulus can trigger an entire complex of impressions that cross sensory boundaries. For example, a particular sound may trigger a specific visual impression, a well-characterized tactile experience, or even a distinct taste. The term itself means "joining the senses," and investigators have compiled and described a fascinating array of synesthetic experiences (see Cytowic, 1989; Marks, 1975). Although the neural mechanisms underlying this syndrome remain unknown, new imaging studies in synesthetes show great promise in identifying the brain regions that become active during synesthetic experiences (e.g., Paulesu et al., 1995).

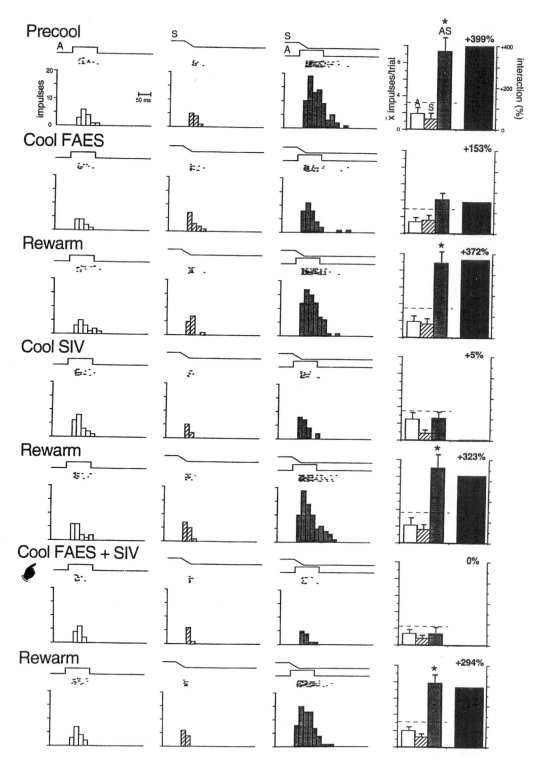

FIGURE 5.3   AES deactivation abolishes SC multisensory integration. Rasters, peristimulus time histograms, and summary bar graphs depict the responses of this auditory-somatosensory SC neuron under various conditions. The top panel (precool) shows the control responses of this neuron to: the auditory stimulus alone (left; the square wave represents the stimulus and is labeled A), the somatosensory stimulus alone (ramp labeled S), and the auditory-somatosensory (AS) stimulus combination. The summary bar graph shows that the response to the stimulus combination was enhanced far above that to either stimulus alone, and well above the sum of the two unimodal stimuli (dashed line). Note that when the auditory (FAES) and somatosensory (SIV) divisions of AES cortex were deactivated by cooling, response enhancement was degraded. During rewarming trials the normal levels of enhancement were reinstated. When both FAES and SIV were deactivated, multisensory enhancement was abolished, even though unimodal auditory and somatosensory responses remained. (From Wallace and Stein, 1994.)

Spatially Coincident Stimuli

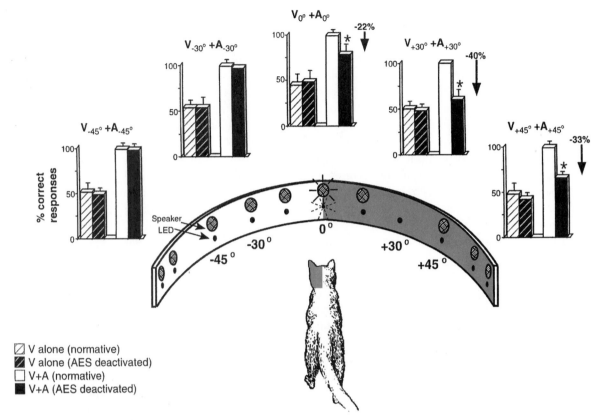

FIGURE 5.4 Deactivating AES impairs multisensory attentive/orientation behaviors. The behavioral paradigm is the same as that described in figure 13.1. The bar graphs above the perimeter display the percentage of correct responses to the visual stimulus alone and the spatially coincident visual-auditory stimulus combination, under both normative and AES deactivation conditions (deactivation was accomplished via lidocaine delivered through indwelling cannulae implanted in AES). Responses were examined to stimuli at five spatial locations. During testing, the intensity of the visual stimulus (LED) was ad-

justed so that the animal approached the correct location on approximately 50% of the unimodal trials. However, pairing this visual stimulus with a spatially coincident auditory stimuli resulted in near-perfect scores at all locations. When AES was deactivated, orientation to contralateral multisensory stimuli was disrupted, even though responses to the contralateral unimodal visual stimulus were unaffected. The percentage of correct responses to all ipsilateral stimuli was also unchanged. The shading depicts the deactivated hemisphere and the region of space affected. *$p < .05$. (From Wilkinson, Meredith, and Stein, 1996.)

Yet regardless of the critical sites involved in the syndrome, some researchers believe that synesthetic experiences are the norm in neonates, becoming degraded with maturation and sensory experience. These researchers believe that sensory impressions form a "primitive unity" at birth (see Bower, 1977; Gibson, 1966; Ryan, 1940; von Hornbostel, 1938), so that a modality-specific stimulus can produce ". . . sensations [that] spill from one sensory system into another" (Maurer and Maurer, 1988). This presupposes that many intersensory phenomena are inborn. Not all investigators accept this idea; many contend, as did Piaget and von Helmoltz, that the sensory modalities are already well-differentiated from one another at birth and that associations

among them must be learned (e.g., see Piaget, 1952; von Helmholtz, 1884/1968). This would lead one to expect that intersensory processes develop only gradually with learning and/or experience. This latter "epigenetic" view may seem the more conservative of the two; however, many observations do not fit easily within established learning paradigms, or are inconsistent with a gradual acquisition of intersensory capabilities (see also Lewkowicz and Lickliter, 1994). One of the most provocative of these was described by Meltzoff and his colleagues (e.g., Meltzoff and Moore, 1983a,b), who showed that within minutes of birth, human babies could imitate the facial expressions of the investigator. When the investigator opened his mouth, the baby opened its mouth; when the investigator stuck out his tongue at the baby, the baby returned the favor. Obviously, the infants had little chance to learn these apparent cross-modality associations, yet they appeared to be matching what they saw to what they felt, a process that Meltzoff called "active intermodal mapping."

For some, this issue remains a contentious one. But regardless of whether or not the newborn brain is capable of sophisticated forms of intersensory experience, multisensory integration, and/or cross-modal transfer, little doubt remains that modality-specific experiences during early life can have an impact on the later use of other modalities. This is evident from experiments in which patterned vision has been induced earlier than normal, either by surgically opening the eyelids in very young mammals or by making small openings in eggs so that bird embryos can receive patterned visual stimuli (Gottlieb, Tomlinson, and Radell, 1989). These earlier-than-normal visual experiences disrupt the normal postnatal auditory dominance and even interfere with the tendency to exhibit normal preferences for species-specific sounds. Similarly, early postnatal experience with nonlocalized auditory cues can interfere with later use of spatially restricted auditory cues (see Lickliter and Banker, 1994), and the lack of coincident auditory-visual experience disrupts normal intersensory development (Lickliter, Lewkowicz, and Columbus, 1996).

Early sensory experiences may even help determine which sensory convergence patterns survive in the brain (Rauschecker, 1996). Exuberant connections that cross modality-specific boundaries have been demonstrated in the cortex in newborn rodents and carnivores. Many of these inputs are "inappropriate" (e.g., visual inputs to auditory or somatosensory structures) as they are not maintained into adulthood. Their transience is believed to be a consequence of their competitive disadvantage with other inputs, but they can be retained if these other inputs are disrupted (Frost, 1984; Innocenti and Clarke, 1984; Sur, Garraghty, and Roe, 1988).

In altricial mammals like the cat, the brain requires a great deal of postnatal maturation before it can underlie adult-like behaviors. The minimal sensory and sensorimotor capabilities of the neonatal kitten reflect an immaturity of many CNS structures, including the SC, affording little hint of the impressive skills it will develop later. It seems hopelessly inept. However, from the perspective of the investigator, the gradual postnatal development of the cat SC provides an opportunity to examine how its neurons develop their sensory responses and especially their striking ability to synthesize cross-modality cues. Thus, the discussion below makes primary use of the cat model, and, unless otherwise stated, the data described below refer to this species.

The immaturity of the newborn cat SC is evident in its paucity of electrical activity. Few of its neurons exhibit spontaneous activity, and fewer still are responsive to sensory stimuli. However, as if to prepare the animal for its most immediate postnatal task of nuzzling its mother in search of milk, at least some tactile-responsive neurons in the SC (and other somatosensory structures) become active in late fetal stages (Stein, Labos, and Kruger, 1973a). The ability to distinguish perioral tactile cues is critical for the kitten to find the nipple and get it into its mouth (Larson and Stein, 1984). These early sensory-responsive SC neurons have weak responses that fatigue quite readily during the first few postnatal days. From a functional perspective, the structure is purely unimodal (i.e., somatosensory) at this time. It is not until about 5 dpn that neurons responsive to auditory cues appear (though none of these neurons are multisensory), and the first deep-layer visual neurons are not active until about 3 weeks postnatal (visual neurons in the purely visual superficial layers are active at 6–7 dpn; see Kao et al., 1994; Stein, Labos, and Kruger, 1973a,b; Wallace and Stein, 1997a).

These neonatal neurons do not yet receive descending (i.e., cortical) inputs; therefore their response properties reflect only ascending and intrinsic influences (Wallace and Stein, 1997a; Stein and Gallagher, 1981). The RFs of early SC neurons are extremely large, whether they are unimodal or multisensory. Visual RFs cover much of the contralateral visual field and somatosensory RFs cover most of the contralateral body. Auditory RFs are completely unformed (i.e., omnidirectional), so that responses are evoked to stimuli anywhere in space. As postnatal maturation proceeds, there is a progressive shrinking of RFs until the characteristic adult-like tuning

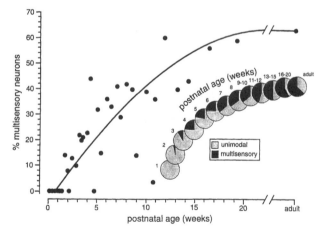

FIGURE 5.5 The incidence of multisensory SC neurons increases during the first 3–4 postnatal months. Plotted is the proportion of multisensory neurons (as a percentage of all sensory-responsive SC neurons) as a function of postnatal age. (From Wallace and Stein, 1997.)

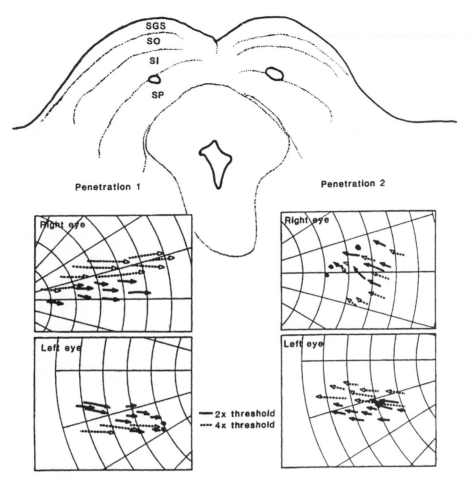

FIGURE 5.6 Eye movements can be evoked via electrical stimulation of the SC prior to the appearance of visual responses. The data shown are taken from a 2-day-old cat in which electrodes were placed in the left (penetration 1) and right (penetration 2) SC. Stimulation at these sites evoked conjugate contralateral eye movements. The direction of movement and excursion length are depicted by the arrows. (From Stein, Clamann, and Goldberg, 1980.)

and topographic alignment among the RFs of multisensory neurons (and among the maps) become evident (Wallace, Meredith, and Stein, 1993; Wallace and Stein, 1996; Wallace and Stein, 1997a,b). A similar developmental contraction of RFs has been noted in monkey (Wallace, McHaffie, and Stein, 1997), ferret (King et al., 1996), owl (Brainard and Knudsen, 1995), and mouse (Benedetti, 1991). If similar mechanisms are operative during human development, it might help explain observations that the spatial concordance of visual and auditory stimuli becomes increasingly important to infants as they age (Morrongiello, 1994).

The functional ontogeny of multisensory neurons in cat SC parallels that of their unimodal counterparts, with the first being auditory-somatosensory neurons that appear at 12 dpn, while visual multisensory (including trimodal) neurons do not appear until about 3 postnatal weeks. However, achieving the adult-like number of multisensory neurons is a very gradual developmental process that is not completed until about 12 postnatal weeks (figure 5.5; see Wallace and Stein, 1997a).

Very little is known about the maturation of the motor or sensorimotor aspects of the SC. Some eye movements can be effected via direct electrical stimulation of the SC as early as 2 days postnatal (figure 5.6), before its neurons are visually responsive; but the thresholds for evoking these movements are quite high, and only few sites are effective. As noted above, visually responsive neurons do not appear until 6–7 dpn in the superficial layers, and not until much later in the deeper layers of the SC, in keeping with the late maturation of visually guided behaviors (Fox, 1970; Norton, 1974). Interestingly, the electrically evoked movements from the neonatal SC show at least the rudiments of adult-like topography, suggesting that premotor connections are being established even before sensory inputs are present. Specifically, in neonatal kittens, stimulating in the left SC moves the two eyes rightward, and stimulation of the homotopic site in the opposite SC produces a

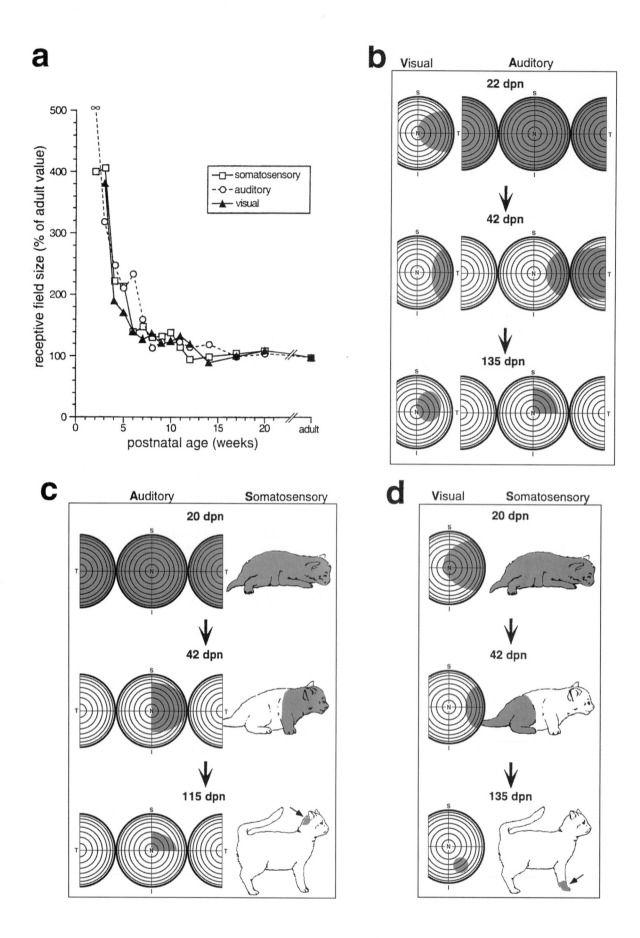

mirror-image leftward eye movement, just as in the adult (Stein, Clamann, and Goldberg, 1980; Stein, Goldberg, and Clamann, 1976).

Maturation of cross-modality receptive field alignment

By the end of the second postnatal month, neurons in the cat SC appear to have properties very much like those found in the adult. Natural sensory stimuli evoke vigorous responses, the animal engages in rapid orienting movements to novel stimuli, and appropriately directed movements can be evoked easily by electrical stimulation of the structure (see Norton, 1974; Stein, 1984; Stein, Clamann, and Goldberg, 1980; Stein, Labos, and Kruger, 1973a,b; Wallace and Stein, 1996; Wallace and Stein, 1997a). Furthermore, the sensory (and motor) maps have established their close topographic register as individual RFs decline in size with development (figure 5.7). The development of the alignment among the various sensory maps, which are constructed from spatially matched ascending and descending projections in each modality, has already been shown to be essential for SC neurons to engage in meaningful multisensory integration (see Wallace, Meredith, and Stein, 1993; Wallace and Stein, 1994, 1997a), and active processes ensure that the different sensory maps align with one another (Benedetti, 1995; King and Carlile, 1993; Knudsen and Brainard, 1991). Presumably, this is because the alignment of sensory maps, and especially the alignment of RFs in multisensory neurons, has substantial adaptive value. As discussed earlier, the spatial alignment among a given neuron's modality-specific RFs is critical to the production of response enhancement to spatially coincident stimuli and response depression to spatially discordant stimuli. These physiological effects, in turn, enhance the salience of related or meaningful events and degrade the salience of unrelated events—with the obvious parallels in the likelihood of generating an overt response (Stein et al., 1989; Wilkinson, Meredith, and Stein, 1996).

FIGURE 5.7 Receptive field size declines with development. (a) Plot of receptive field size as a function of postnatal age for each modality of SC multisensory neurons. (b) Receptive fields (shading) of visual-auditory neurons at three representative developmental stages. Note the decline in size and the increasingly apparent spatial register of receptive fields with age. Each concentric circle represents 10°. In the convention for auditory space, caudal space is depicted by the semicircular "wings," which have been split and folded forward. (c) Receptive fields of auditory-somatosensory neurons at three ages. (d) Receptive fields of visual-somatosensory neurons at three ages. (From Wallace and Stein, 1997.)

Current thinking is that the development of the refined auditory map that characterizes the normal adult requires early visual-auditory experience. This conclusion is based on the data from experiments in which visual or auditory inputs are manipulated during development. For example, some experiments have been conducted in which animals are raised with a sound-attenuating plug in one ear. This renders the inputs from that ear substantially less effective in driving central auditory neurons than those from the open ear and disrupts the normal balance of binaural cues used to construct a computational map of auditory space in the SC (i.e., interaural level difference). Yet the auditory map that is formed looks surprisingly like the one found in normal animals, and is in excellent register with the visual map (figure 5.8; see King et al., 1988; Knudsen, 1983). The alignment of visual and auditory RFs in individual multisensory neurons is also excellent. Apparently, the brain is able to compensate for the imbalance between the two ears by changing their relative influence on SC neurons. In order to do so, it is believed to use the visual map as a template, or comparator, with which to calculate how much it must alter the timing and/or weight of the inputs from each ear to produce a matching map of auditory space. Powerful evidence for this idea also comes from studies in which the visual axis is shifted relative to the auditory axis either by placing prisms on the eyes or surgically shortening the extraocular muscles so that the eyes themselves are deviated. Under such conditions, a seemingly normal visual-auditory register develops because the auditory axis shifts to accommodate the change in the visual axis (King et al., 1988; Knudsen and Knudsen, 1989). Presumably, coincident visual and auditory experiences derived from discrete cues that are closely linked to one another are essential for the precision of intermap calibration both in normal animals and in animals with altered visual experience. Thus, eliminating the opportunity for such experience during development (e.g., dark rearing, omnidirectional sound rearing) prevents the formation of a precise auditory map and precise intermap register (Withington-Wray, Binns, and Keating, 1990a; Withington-Wray et al., 1990b).

But where is this visual template that is used to align the auditory map? The most obvious visual referent is the deep-layer visual map. After all, a significant component of this map is derived from visual-auditory neurons, and the substantial visual-auditory interactions in deep-layer neurons have been the subject of much of this chapter. A complication, however, is that the auditory responses of SC neurons develop much earlier than their visual responses. Furthermore, the omnidirectional early auditory "receptive fields" already have contracted significantly before functional visual inputs are

NORMAL   **NEONATAL EAR PLUG**

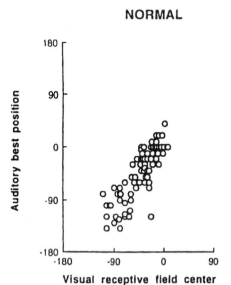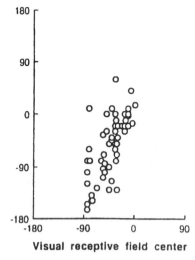

FIGURE 5.8   The auditory map in the ferret SC develops even in animals raised without normal binaural inputs. Data are plotted both for normal animals and for those in which one ear was plugged prior to the onset of hearing. In both populations, there were similar systematic and covarying shifts in the visual and auditory receptive fields at different locations in the SC. (From King et al., 1988.)

demonstrable in deep-layer neurons (Wallace and Stein, 1997a); and even after visual inputs can drive these neurons, it is quite some time before there is any evidence of visual-auditory interactions (Wallace and Stein, 1997a)—an issue that will be discussed in detail in the next section. Such observations offer no support for the hypothesis that the visual template is in the multisensory layers of the SC. Yet, neither are they confutative. A crude auditory map can develop in the absence of visual input, making a visual referent unnecessary for the initial contraction of auditory RFs. Thus, it may be that only the later refinement in auditory RFs is dependent on coincident visual inputs (e.g., see King and Carlile, 1993; Knudsen, Esterly, and du Lac, 1991).

While there is a good deal of face validity to the postulate that the deep-layer visual map is the template for the formation of an auditory map, there is also reason to suspect that the visual template resides in the superficial layers of the SC. This overlying and purely visual region develops visually responsive neurons at 6–7 days postnatal (Stein, Labos, and Kruger, 1973a), and their RFs are already organized into a well-defined map of visual space at 8–10 days postnatal (Kao et al., 1994; also see Wallace, McHaffie, and Stein, 1997), which is long before the auditory map is organized. Furthermore, vertically oriented superficial-deep layer visual connections have been demonstrated in a variety of species, including the cat (Behan and Appell, 1992; Mooney et al., 1988), and partial lesions of the superficial layers in neonatal ferrets produce a disorganized auditory map just below the lesion site (King et al., 1996). Further evidence

for a role for the superficial visual map in the development of deep-layer auditory topography comes from studies in which chronic application of the NMDA receptor antagonist MK801 to the superficial SC layers disrupts the development of the auditory space map (Schnupp et al., 1995).

Clearly, many issues have yet to be fully resolved regarding the development of multimodal RF properties. Indeed, some of the issues may be even more complex than apparent from the discussion thus far. For example, while the majority of studies provide evidence that a visual referent is used to calibrate computationally derived auditory maps, there is evidence in mouse to suggest that visual and auditory maps are adjusted to compensate for altered tactile experience. In one experiment, Benedetti (1995) bent the left vibrissae into the right hemifield, thereby disrupting the normal correspondences among visual, auditory, and tactile cues. Remarkably, in animals subjected to the altered experience from birth, the visual RFs that normally would have represented vibrissae-related regions in the left hemifield were found to be shifted to represent regions in right visual space. Taken together with the observations made in other species, the data suggest that the relative ecological importance of a sensory modality may be a critical factor in determining which sensory map serves as the referent to the others. It might be argued that, unlike the cat or owl, the mouse places more "value" on tactile than on either visual or auditory information, hence the use of a somatosensory rather than a visual or auditory referent for SC map construction. Even in species in which somatosensation is not the "dominant" modality, tactile input has been shown to influence the spatial organization of visual information in cortex (see Fogassi et al., 1996; Graziano, Hu, and Gross, 1997).

Regardless of which modality serves as the mapping template, the establishment of sensory map registration ensures a consistent, modality-independent relationship among the sensory maps and between the sensory and motor maps in the SC. Although much is known about the generation and maintenance of sensory map register, we know very little about the developmental sequences that lead to topographic register between the sensory and motor maps. Most likely, the recalibration of motor output following altered sensory input (e.g., via prisms or vibrissal deformation) requires a flexible linkage between sensory and motor topographies, a linkage that is adaptable only as a consequence of sensorimotor behavioral experience. Dynamic processes also must play a role in calibrating the mechanisms that maintain map alignment during normal behavior. Such calibrations must make use of proprioceptive or efference copy information to effect the coordinate transformations necessary to maintain map alignment despite changes in the relative position of the eyes, ears, head, and body.

Maturation of multisensory integration

One might reasonably postulate that at the point at which an individual SC neuron develops the ability to respond to inputs from different modalities (i.e., becomes multisensory), it would also exhibit the ability to integrate them. However, this postulate proved to be incorrect. In both cat (Wallace and Stein, 1997a) and monkey (Wallace, McHaffie, and Stein, 1997), the youngest multisensory neurons are unable to integrate their different sensory inputs to produce the response enhancement or depression that characterizes adult multisensory integration (figure 5.9). Their responses to the combination of two different sensory cues generally do not differ substantially when one or the other cue is presented individually. Presumably, these neonatal multisensory responses reflect the absence of functional corticotectal inputs. At this stage, then, the neonate might represent the developmental counterpart of an adult animal whose AES has been deactivated. Several weeks later the situation has changed dramatically, with multisensory neurons exhibiting adult-like interactions, presumably reflecting the maturation of the essential corticotectal circuits (figure 5.10).

The observation that the multisensory properties of the SC develop only gradually in postnatal life contrasts with expectations based on the idea of a "primitive

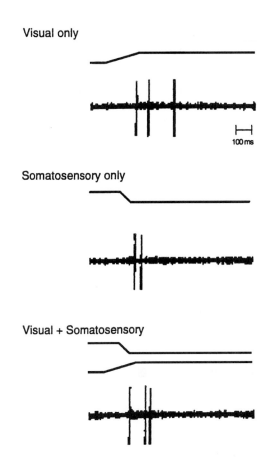

FIGURE 5.9 SC neurons in young cats do not exhibit multisensory enhancement. In this example of a visual-somatosensory neuron in a 20-day-old cat, the combination of visual and somatosensory cues resulted in a response that was neither better nor worse than the response to either of the unimodal stimuli. (From Wallace and Stein, 1997.)

unity" among the senses. However, the sequential appearance of somatosensory, auditory, then visual responses in this structure (see Stein, Labos, and Kruger, 1973a,b; Wallace and Stein, 1997a) is consistent with the idea of a temporal window during which the fundamental organization and information-processing capabilities of one sensory modality are developed before repeating this process for another, and before dealing with the most complicated task of integrating their different signals (see Turkewitz and Kenny, 1985 for a discussion of the possible adaptive significance of sequential sensory development). However, it remains to be seen whether the developmental profile so apparent in the cat SC is also present in other CNS structures and other species.

Concluding remarks

William James (1890) described our initial impression of the world as a "blooming, buzzing confusion" of sensory stimuli—a description implying that it is only after we are

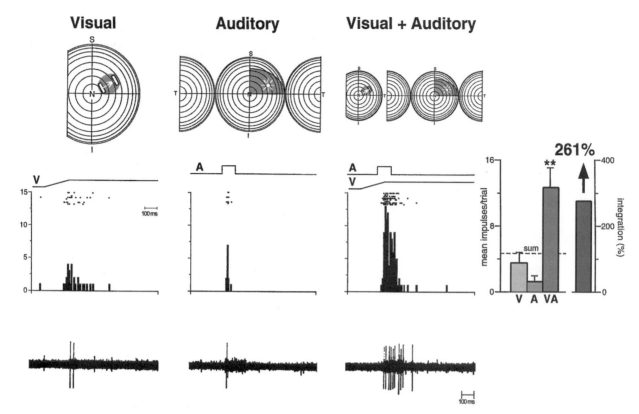

FIGURE 5.10 As soon as they develop the capacity for multisensory integration, neonatal SC neurons look like their adult counterparts. Receptive fields for this visual-auditory neuron in a 30-day-old animal are shown at top. Rasters, histograms, oscillographs, and summary bar graphs show the strongly enhanced responses of this neuron to the visual-auditory combination. Conventions are the same as in figure 13.3. (From Wallace and Stein, 1997.)

able to sort among stimuli, relating them to one another and to specific consequences, that we begin to learn about our world. It is interesting to note, however, that the experience of using the senses to do just that is an important determinant of their ultimate organization and functional capability. In the current context the experience of coordinating information from different senses has been shown to play an essential role in aligning and calibrating multisensory SC RFs and in the representation of auditory space.

Although it seems reasonable to suppose that the impact of specific cues, and perhaps even the magnitude and sign of an interaction in multisensory neurons, also depends on the frequency and consequences of early stimulus pairings, we really know very little about these issues. Nevertheless, at this point it seems most likely that the effects of early experience operate within the framework of the spatial and temporal principles that have already been shown to govern SC multisensory integration in normal adult animals. Based on data from experiments in polysensory cortex (see Jiang et al., 1994; Ramachandran et al., 1993; Wallace, Wilkinson, and Stein, 1996), at least some of these principles appear to be general features of multisensory structures (though they must surely have very different impacts on behav-

ior and perception). Employing similar principles of multisensory integration at different levels of the neuraxis is a parsimonious way to increase or decrease the salience of the same stimulus complex. It is also an effective way to link SC-mediated immediate behaviors with the "higher" perceptual and cognitive processes that coincide with these behaviors and provide conscious dimension to the experience.

ACKNOWLEDGMENTS We thank Nancy London for editorial assistance. The research described here was supported by NIH grants EY 06562 and NS 22543.

REFERENCES

BEHAN, M., and P. P. APPELL, 1992. Intrinsic circuitry in the cat superior colliculus: Projections from the superficial layers. *J. Comp. Neurol.* 315:230–243.

BENEDETTI, F., 1991. The postnatal emergence of a functional somatosensory representation in the superior colliculus of the mouse. *Dev. Brain Res.* 60:51–57.

BENEDETTI, F., 1995. Orienting behaviour and superior colliculus sensory representations in mice with the vibrissae bent into the contralateral hemispace. *Eur. J. Neurosci.* 7:1512–1519.

BOWER, T. G. R., 1977. *A Primer of Infant Development*, San Francisco: W. H. Freeman.

BRAINARD, M. A., and E. I. KNUDSEN, 1995. Dynamics of visually guided auditory plasticity in the optic tectum of the barn owl. *J. Neurophysiol.* 73:595–614.

CLAREY, J. C., and D. R. F. IRVINE, 1990. The anterior ectosylvian sulcal auditory field in the cat: I. An electrophysiological study of its relationship to surrounding auditory cortical fields. *J. Comp. Neurol.* 301:289–303.

CLEMO, H. R., and B. E. STEIN, 1982. Somatosensory cortex: A 'new' somatotopic representation. *Brain Res.* 235:162–168.

CYTOWIC, R. E., 1989. *Synesthesia: A Union of the Senses.* New York: Springer-Verlag.

EDWARDS, S. B., C. L. GINSBURGH, C. K. HENKEL, and B. E. STEIN, 1979. Sources of subcortical projections to the superior colliculus in the cat. *J. Comp. Neurol.* 184:309–330.

FOGASSI, L., V. GALLESE, L. FADIGA, G. LUPPINO, M. MATELLI, and G. RIZZOLATTI, 1996. Coding of peripersonal space in inferior premotor cortex (area F4). *J. Neurophysiol.* 76:141–157.

FOX, M. W., 1970. Reflex development and behavioral organization. In *Developmental Neurobiology*, W. A. Himwich, ed. Springfield, Ill.: Thomas, pp. 553–580.

FRENS, M. A., A. J. VAN OPSTAL, and R. F. VAN DER WILLIGEN, 1995. Spatial and temporal factors determine audio-visual interactions in saccadic eye movements. *Percept. Psychophysics* 57:802–816.

FROST, D. O., 1984. Axonal growth and target selection during development: Retinal projections to the ventrobasal complex and other "nonvisual" structures in neonatal Syrian hamsters. *J. Comp. Neurol.* 230:576–592.

GIBSON, J. J., 1966. *The Senses Considered as Perceptual Systems,* Boston: Houghton Mifflin.

GOLDRING, J. E., M. C. DORRIS, B. D. CORNEIL, P. A. BALLANTYNE, and D. P. MUNOZ, 1996. Combined eye-head gaze shifts to visual and auditory targets in humans. *Exp. Brain Res.* 111:68–78.

GOTTLIEB, G., W. R. TOMLINSON, and P. L. RADELL, 1989. Developmental intersensory interference: Premature visual experience suppresses auditory learning in ducklings. *Infant Behav. Dev.* 12:1–12.

GRAZIANO, M. S., X. T. HU, and C. G. GROSS, 1997. Visuospatial properties of ventral premotor cortex. *J. Neurophysiol.* 77:2268–2292.

GREGORY, R. L., 1967. Origin of eyes and brains. *Nature* 213:369–372.

GROH, J. M., and D. L. SPARKS, 1996. Saccades to somatosensory targets. III. Eye-position-dependent somatosensory activity in primate superior colliculus. *J. Neurophysiol.* 75:439–453.

HARRIS, L. R., 1980. The superior colliculus and movements of the head and eyes in cats. *J. Physiol.* 300:367–391.

HARTLINE, P. H., R. L. VIMAL, A. J. KING, D. D. KURYLO, and D. P. NORTHMORE, 1995. Effects of eye position on auditory localization and neural representation of space in superior colliculus of cats. *Exp. Brain Res.* 104:402–408.

HOWARD, I. P., and W. B. TEMPLETON, 1966. *Human Spatial Orientation.* London: Wiley.

HUGHES, H. C., P. A. REUTER-LORENZ, G. NOZAWA, and R. FENDRICH, 1994. Visual-auditory interactions in sensorimotor processing: Saccades versus manual responses. *J. Exp. Psychol. Human Percept. Perf.* 20:131–153.

INNOCENTI, G. M., and S. CLARKE, 1984. Bilateral transitory projection to visual areas from auditory cortex in kittens. *Dev. Brain Res.* 14:143–148.

JAMES, W., 1890. *Principles of Psychology* (Vol. 1), New York: Holtz (reprinted 1983), Cambridge, Mass.: Harvard University Press.

JAY, M. F., and D. L. SPARKS, 1984. Auditory receptive fields in primate superior colliculus shift with changes in eye position. *Nature* 309:345–347.

JIANG, H., F. LEPORE, M. PTITO, and J.-P. GUILLEMOT, 1994. Sensory interactions in the anterior ectosylvian cortex of cats. *Exp. Brain Res.* 101:385–396.

KADUNCE, D. C., J. W. VAUGHAN, M. T. WALLACE, G. BENEDEK, and B. E. STEIN, 1997. Mechanisms of within- and cross-modality suppression in the superior colliculus. *J. Neurophysiol.* 78:2834–2847.

KAO, C.-Q., J. G. MCHAFFIE, M. A. MEREDITH, and B. E. STEIN, 1994. Functional development of a central visual map in cat. *J. Neurophysiol.* 72:266–272.

KING, A. J., and S. CARLILE, 1993. Changes induced in the representation of auditory space in the superior colliculus by rearing ferrets with binocular lid suture. *Exp. Brain Res.* 94:444–455.

KING, A. J., M. E. HUTCHINGS, D. R. MOORE, and C. BLAKEMORE, 1988. Developmental plasticity in the visual and auditory representations in the mammalian superior colliculus. *Nature* 332:73–76.

KING, A. J., J. W. SCHNUPP, S. CARLILE, A. L. SMITH, and I. D. THOMPSON, 1996. The development of topographically-aligned maps of visual and auditory space in the superior colliculus. *Prog. Brain Res.* 112:335–350.

KNUDSEN, E. I., 1983. Early auditory experience aligns the auditory map of space in the optic tectum of the barn owl. *Science* 222:939–942.

KNUDSEN, E. I., and M. S. BRAINARD, 1991. Visual instruction of the neural map of auditory space in the developing optic tectum. *Science* 253:85–87.

KNUDSEN, E. I., S. D. ESTERLY, and S. DU LAC, 1991. Stretched and upside-down maps of auditory space in the optic tectum of blind-reared owls; acoustic basis and behavioral correlates. *J. Neurosci.* 11:1727–1747.

KNUDSEN, E. I., and P. F. KNUDSEN, 1989. Vision calibrates sound localization in developing barn owls. *J. Neurosci.* 9:3306–3313.

LARSON, M. A., and B. E. STEIN, 1984. The use of tactile and olfactory cues in neonatal orientation and localization of the nipple. *Dev. Psychobiol.* 17:423–436.

LEE, C., S. CHUNG, J. KIM, and J. PARK, 1991. Auditory facilitation of visually guided saccades. *Soc. Neurosci. Abst.* 17:862.

LEWKOWICZ, D. J., and R. LICKLITER, 1994. Insights into mechanisms of intersensory development: The value of a comparative, convergent-operations approach. In *The Development of Intersensory Perception: Comparative Perspectives*, D. J. Lewkowicz and R. Lickliter, eds. Hillsdale, N.J.: Erlbaum, pp. 403–413.

LICKLITER, R,. and H. BANKER, 1994. Prenatal components of intersensory development in precocial birds. In *The Development of Intersensory Perception: Comparative Perspectives*, D. J. Lewkowicz and R. Lickliter, eds. Hillsdale, N.J.: Erlbaum, pp. 59–80.

LICKLITER, R., D. J. LEWKOWICZ, and R. F. COLUMBUS, 1996. Intersensory experience and early perceptual development: The role of spatial contiguity in bobwhite quail chick's responsiveness to multimodal maternal cues. *Dev. Psychobiol.* 29:403–416.

MARKS, L. E., 1975. On colored-hearing synesthesia: Cross-modal translations of sensory dimensions. *Psychol. Bull.* 82:303–331.

MAURER, D., and C. MAURER, 1988. *The World of the Newborn.* New York: Basic Books.

MCHAFFIE, J. G,. and B. E. STEIN, 1982. Eye movements evoked by electrical stimulation in the superior colliculus of rats and hamsters. *Brain Res.* 247:243–253.

MCILWAIN, J. T., 1991. Distributed spatial coding in the superior colliculus: A review. *Visual Neurosci.* 6:3–13.

MELTZOFF, A. N., and M. K. MOORE, 1983a. The origins of imitation in infancy: Paradigm, phenomena, and theories. In *Advances in Infancy Research* (Vol. 2), L.P. Lipsitt, ed. Norwood, N.J.: Ablex, pp. 265–301.

MELTZOFF, A. N., and M. K. MOORE, 1983b. Newborn infants imitate adult facial gestures. *Child Dev.* 54:702–709.

MEREDITH, M. A., J. W. NEMITZ, and B. E. STEIN, 1987. Determinants of multisensory integration in superior colliculus neurons. I. Temporal factors. *J. Neurosci.* 7:3215–3229.

MEREDITH, M. A., and B. E. STEIN, 1983. Interactions among converging sensory inputs in the superior colliculus. *Science* 221:389–391.

MEREDITH, M. A., and B. E. STEIN, 1996. Spatial determinants of multisensory integration in cat superior colliculus neurons. *J. Neurophysiol.* 75:1843–1857.

MEREDITH, M. A., M. T. WALLACE, and B. E. STEIN, 1992. Visual, auditory and somatosensory convergence on output neurons of the cat superior colliculus: Multisensory properties of the tecto-reticulo-spinal projection. *Exp. Brain Res.* 88:181–186.

MOONEY, R. D., M. M. NIKOLETSEAS, P. R. HESS, Z. ALLEN, A. C. LEWIN, and R. W. RHOADES, 1988. The projection from the superficial to the deep layers of the superior colliculus: An intracellular horseradish peroxidase injection study in the hamster. *J. Neurosci.* 8:1384–1399.

MORRONGIELLO, B. A., 1994. The effects of co-location of auditory-visual interactions and cross-modal perception in infants. In *The Development of Intersensory Perception: Comparative Perspectives*, D.J. Lewkowitz and R. Lickliter, eds. Hillsdale, N.J.: Erlbaum, pp. 235–263.

MUCKE, L., M. NORITA, G. BENEDEK, and O. CREUTZ-FELDT, 1982. Physiologic and anatomic investigation of a visual cortical area situated in the ventral bank of the anterior ectosylvian sulcus of the cat. *Exp. Brain Res.* 46:1–11.

NORTHCUTT, R. G., 1986. Evolution of the octavolateralis system: Evaluation and heuristic value of phylogenetic hypotheses. In *The Biology of Change in Otolaryngology*, R. Vanderwater and E. Rubel, eds. New York: Excerpta Medica, pp. 3–14.

NORTON, T. T., 1974. Receptive-field properties of superior colliculus cells and development of visual behavior in kittens. *J. Neurophysiol.* 37:674–690.

OLSON, C. R., and A. M. GRAYBIEL, 1987. Ectosylvian visual area of the cat: Location, retinotopic organization, and connections. *J. Comp. Neurol.* 261:277–294.

PAULESU, E., J. HARRISON, S. BARON-COHEN, J. D. WATSON, L. GOLDSTEIN, J. HEATHER, R. S. FRACKOWIAK, and C. D. FRITH, 1995. The physiology of coloured hearing. A PET activation study of colour-word synaesthesia. *Brain* 118:661–676.

PECK, C. K., J. A. BARO, and S. M. WARDER, 1995. Effects of eye position on saccadic eye movements and on the neuronal responses to auditory and visual stimuli in cat superior colliculus. *Exp. Brain Res.* 103:227–242.

PIAGET, J., 1952. *The Origins of Intelligence in Children.* New York: International Universities Press.

RAMACHANDRAN, R., M. T. WALLACE, H. R. CLEMO, and B. E. STEIN, 1993. Multisensory convergence and integration in rat cortex. *Soc. Neurosci. Abst.* 19:1447.

RAUSCHECKER, J. P., 1996. Substitution of visual by auditory inputs in the cat's anterior ectosylvian cortex. *Prog. Brain Res.* 112:313–323.

ROUCOUX, A., and M. CROMMELINCK, 1976. Eye movements evoked by superior colliculus stimulation in the alert cat. *Brain Res.* 106:349–363.

RYAN, T. A., 1940. Interrelations of the sensory systems in perception. *Psychol. Bull.* 37:659–698.

SCHNUPP, J. W. H., A. J. KING, A. L. SMITH, and I. D. THOMPSON, 1995. NMDA-receptor antagonists disrupt the formation of the auditory space map in the mammalian superior colliculus. *J. Neurosci.* 15:1516–1531.

SPARKS, D. L., 1986. Translation of sensory signals into commands for control of saccadic eye movements: Role of primate superior colliculus. *Physiol. Rev.* 66:116–177.

SPARKS, D. L., and J. S. NELSON, 1987. Sensory and motor maps in the mammalian superior colliculus. *Trends Neurosci.* 10:312–317.

STEIN, B. E., 1984. Development of the superior colliculus. *Annu. Rev. Neurosci.* 7:95–125.

STEIN, B. E., and H.P. CLAMANN, 1981. Control of pinna movements and sensorimotor register in cat superior colliculus. *Brain Behav. Evol.* 19:180–192.

STEIN, B. E., H. P. CLAMANN, and S. J. GOLDBERG, 1980. Superior colliculus: Control of eye movements in neonatal kittens. *Science* 210:78–80.

STEIN, B. E., and H. L. GALLAGHER, 1981. Maturation of cortical control over superior colliculus cells in cat. *Brain Res.* 223:429–435.

STEIN, B. E., S. J. GOLDBERG, and H. P. CLAMANN, 1976. The control of eye movements by the superior colliculus in the alert cat. *Brain Res.* 118:469–474.

STEIN, B. E., E. LABOS, and L. KRUGER, 1973a. Sequence of changes in properties of neurons of superior colliculus of the kitten during maturation. *J. Neurophysiol.* 36:667–679.

STEIN, B. E., E. LABOS, and L. KRUGER, 1973b. Determinants of response latency in neurons of superior colliculus in kittens. *J. Neurophysiol.* 36:680–689.

STEIN, B. E., and M. A. MEREDITH, 1993. *The Merging of the Senses.* Cambridge, Mass.: MIT Press.

STEIN, B. E., M. A. MEREDITH, W. S. HUNEYCUTT, and L. MCDADE, 1989. Behavioral indices of multisensory integration: Orientation to visual cues is affected by auditory stimuli. *J. Cogn. Neurosci.* 1:12–24.

STEIN, B. E., R. F. SPENCER, and S. B. EDWARDS, 1983. Corticotectal and corticothalamic efferent projections of SIV somatosensory cortex in cat. *J. Neurophysiol.* 50:896–909.

SUR, M., P. E. GARRAGHTY, and A. W. ROE, 1988. Experimentally induced visual projections into auditory thalamus and cortex. *Science* 242:1437–1441.

TURKEWITZ, G., and P. A. KENNY, 1982. Limitations on input as a basis for neural organization and perceptual development: A preliminary theoretical statement. *Develop. Psychobiol.* 15:357–368.

VON HELMHOLTZ, H., 1968. The origin of the correct interpretation of our sensory impressions. In *Helmholtz on Perception:*

Its Physiology and Development, R.M. Warren and R.P. Warren, eds. New York: Wiley, pp. 247–266.

VON HORNBOSTEL, E. M., 1938. The unity of the senses. In *A Sourcebook of Gestalt Psychology*, W. D. Ellis, ed. New York: Harcourt Brace, pp. 211–216.

WALLACE, M. T., J. G. MCHAFFIE, and B. E. STEIN, 1997. Visual response properties and visuotopic representation in the newborn monkey superior colliculus. *J. Neurophysiol.* 78:2732–2741.

WALLACE, M. T., M. A. MEREDITH, and B. E. STEIN, 1993. Converging influences from visual, auditory and somatosensory cortices onto output neurons of the superior colliculus. *J. Neurophysiol.* 69:1797–1809.

WALLACE, M. T., and B. E. STEIN, 1994. Cross-modal synthesis in the midbrain depends on input from association cortex. *J. Neurophysiol.* 71:429–432.

WALLACE, M. T., and B. E. STEIN, 1996. Development of auditory responsiveness, topography, and functional convergence with visual inputs in cat superior colliculus (SC). *Soc. Neurosci. Abst.* 22:636.

WALLACE, M. T., and B. E. STEIN, 1997a. Development of multisensory integration in cat superior colliculus. *J. Neurosci.* 17:2429–2444.

WALLACE, M. T., and B. E. STEIN, 1997b. Development of somatosensory responses, topography and interactions with other sensory modalities in cat superior colliculus (SC). *Soc. Neurosci. Abst.* 23:1541.

WALLACE, M. T., L. K. WILKINSON, and B. E. STEIN, 1996. Representation and integration of multiple sensory inputs in primate superior colliculus. *J. Neurophysiol.* 76:1246–1266.

WELCH, R. B., and D. H. WARREN, 1986. Intersensory interactions. In *Handbook of Perception and Human Performance, Vol. I: Sensory Processes and Perception*, K.R. Off, L. Kaufmanns, and J.P. Thomas, eds. New York: Wiley, pp. 1–36.

WILKINSON, L. K., M. A. MEREDITH, and B. E. STEIN, 1996. The role of anterior ectosylvian cortex in cross-modality orientation and approach behavior. *Exp. Brain Res.* 112:1–10.

WITHINGTON-WRAY, D. J., K. E. BINNS, and M. J. KEATING, 1990a. The maturation of the superior collicular map of auditory space in the guinea pig is disrupted by developmental visual deprivation. *Eur. J. Neurosci.* 2:682–692.

WITHINGTON-WRAY, D. J., K. E. BINNS, S. S. DHANJAL, S. G. BRICKLEY, and M. J. KEATING, 1990b. The maturation of the collicular map of auditory space in the guinea pig is disrupted by developmental auditory deprivation. *Eur. J. Neurosci.* 2:693–703.

6 Visual Development: Psychophysics, Neural Substrates, and Causal Stories

DAVIDA Y. TELLER

ABSTRACT This chapter addresses the development of vision in human and monkey infants, as well as the complexities of explaining the development of visual function on the basis of anatomical and physiological development of the visual system. The literature on the development of several visual functions–grating acuity, critical flicker frequency, stereoacuity, vernier acuity, and spatial and temporal contrast sensitivity functions–is selectively reviewed. A distinction is introduced between a *critical locus*–a neural stage at which information is importantly transformed in adults–and a *critical immaturity*–a neural stage at which the visual capacity of the infant is importantly reduced below that of the adult; and it is argued that critical immaturities need not be confined to critical loci. Examples of current theoretical accounts of visual development are discussed from this perspective.

The goals of visual neuroscience are threefold: to describe what and how well we see; to describe the characteristics of the neural substrate that make seeing possible; and to explain the characteristics of vision on the basis of the characteristics of its neural substrate. The goals of developmental visual neuroscience are similarly threefold: to establish the time course of emergence of the various visual functions; to explore the developmental time course of elements of the neural substrate; and to explain the development of vision on the basis of the development of its neural substrate. Visual neuroscience and visual development are arguably among the most advanced of the disciplines that make up the cognitive and developmental behavioral neurosciences, and it is hoped that some of the successes in the visual realm can provide useful precedents for work in related fields.

The current chapter offers a brief progress report on the strategies and accomplishments of developmental visual neuroscience. The first section introduces techniques for testing vision in human and monkey infants, and shows the parallel emergence of grating acuity in both species. In the next two sections, the development of several additional visual functions is described. Finally, these data are compared with selected anatomical and physiological data on development of the visual system in infant primates, and some current models of visual development are briefly analyzed. More extensive reviews can be found elsewhere (Movshon and Kiorpes, 1993; Simons, 1993; Teller, 1997, 1998; Vital-Durand, Atkinson, and Braddick, 1996).

Behavioral techniques and a monkey model

The most common technique used for testing the development of visual function is forced-choice preferential looking, or FPL (Teller, 1979). The FPL technique is based on the infant's propensity to stare at boldly patterned objects. Briefly, the infant is held in front of a visual display. To test grating acuity, squarewave gratings–sets of black and white stripes of various spatial frequencies–are presented randomly on either the right or the left side of the display in a series of trials. An observer who cannot see the stimuli observes the infant via a peephole or a video monitor. On each trial the observer must use the infant's staring behavior to judge the left–right location of the grating. The finest grating for which the observer can do better than chance at judging the location of the grating is taken as the estimate of the infant's acuity. For older ages, operant reinforcers are added. The combination of FPL and operant techniques yields reliable data at all ages throughout infancy, up to the ages at which adult psychophysical measures can be used.

Our approach to establishing the validity of infant monkeys as an animal model for human visual development has been to collect developmental data with similar stimuli and techniques from both species. If the two species have similar visual capacities and go through similar sequences of developmental change, albeit on different time scales, it should be possible to establish an age conversion factor between the two species. Such an age conversion allows one to generalize the results of invasive work on the monkey infant to the human infant, and use the invasive data taken on the monkey to model human visual development.

Early studies showed that human and pigtail macaque monkey infants could be tested with similar behavioral

DAVIDA Y. TELLER   Departments of Psychology and Physiology/Biophysics, University of Washington, Seattle, Wash.

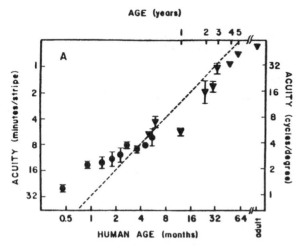
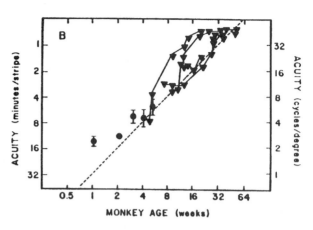

FIGURE 6.1 The development of forced-choice preferential looking (FPL) acuity (closed circles) and operant acuity (closed triangles) in human infants (left) and pigtail macaque infants (right). Human age is plotted in months, and monkey age in weeks. Both species show similar acuity values near birth. Acuity increases steadily with age in both species, but about a fac-

tor of 4 faster in the infant monkeys. The dotted line represents a mnemonic: Acuity in cycles per degree is roughly equal to age, in months for human infants and in weeks for monkey infants. (Reprinted from Teller, 1981, with permission of Elsevier Science.)

techniques (Teller et al., 1978; Teller, 1981). Figure 6.1 shows the growth of behaviorally measured grating acuity in both species, with age plotted in months for human infants and in weeks for monkey infants.

Two interesting trends are illustrated by these data. First, grating acuity is initially very poor—more than an order of magnitude poorer than adult acuity—and emerges gradually over a very long, slow time course, reaching adult levels only at three to five years for human infants and at about a year for monkey infants. Second, the growth curves for human and monkey infants are similar when plotted in months and weeks, respectively. The growth of grating acuity thus conforms well to the 4:1 rule often seen in measures of sensory and cognitive development: Human and macaque infants are similar at birth and have similar growth curves, but a week in the life of an infant monkey is like a month in the life of a human infant. To the precision at which they have been tested, other visual functions also conform reasonably well to this rule (e.g., Kiorpes, 1992). Accordingly, data from both species will be used interchangeably to illustrate the general developmental trends described below.

The development of spatial and temporal resolution

In this section, the development of grating acuity is compared with the development of three additional measures of spatial and temporal resolution: critical flicker frequency, stereoacuity, and vernier acuity.

CRITICAL FLICKER FREQUENCY The term critical flicker frequency (CFF) refers to the fastest *temporal* al-

ternation, or flicker, that an infant of a given age can discriminate from a steady (nonflickering) light. Regal (1981) showed that, surprisingly, even very young infants stare at rapidly flickering stimuli. A 1-month-old's CFF is about 40 Hz (cycles per second), while 2-month-olds, 3-month-olds, and adults have CFFs of about 50, 52, and 55 Hz, respectively. These data are important because they are so different from the long, slow time course of development of grating acuity. To our knowledge, CFFs have not yet been studied in infant monkeys.

STEREOACUITY Stereovision—the capacity to perceive depth on the basis of binocular disparity—was also an early target of developmental studies. The results of three early studies, using three very different experimental paradigms are summarized in figure 6.2. All three studies agree that responses to binocular disparity are absent in almost all infants under the age of 3 months, having their onset between 3 and 6 months postnatal. A similar time course of onset, in weeks rather than months, has also been demonstrated recently in infant monkeys (O'Dell and Boothe, 1997).

In the case of stereoacuity, the data from individual infants are also of interest. Figure 6.3 shows longitudinal data on the development both of grating acuity and stereoacuity in individual human infants (Held, Birch, and Gwiazda, 1980; Held, 1993). The onset of responsiveness to binocular disparity occurs at slightly different postnatal ages in different individual infants; but once the response appears, stereoacuity develops rapidly, reaching 1' disparity within a few weeks of the first response to large disparities. Such a rapid increase in vi-

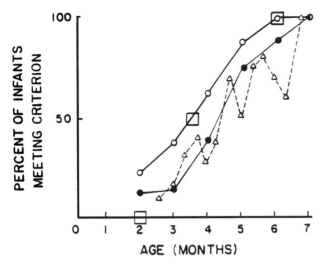

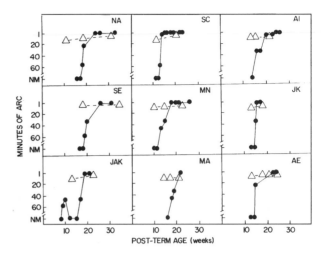

FIGURE 6.2 Summary of early data on the development of responsiveness to binocular disparity. The circles show forced-choice preferential looking data from Birch, Gwiazda, and Held (1982) for crossed disparities of 58' (open circles) and 1' (closed circles). The large open squares show visual evoked potential data from Petrig et al. (1981). The triangles show behavioral data, including the data of Fox et al. (1979), plus additional unpublished data originally supplied by R. Aslin. (Reprinted with permission from Teller, 1982.)

FIGURE 6.3 Longitudinal development of stereoacuity (closed circles) and grating acuity (open triangles) in the same individual infants. The ordinate shows stereoacuity in minutes of arc, and also grating acuity in minutes per 1/2 cycle (stripe) of the grating. The rapid growth in stereoacuity occurs at different ages in different infants, occurring as early as the 13th week in some infants (subject SC), and as late as the 19th week in others (subject SE). Within each infant, the growth of stereoacuity from 58' to 1' occurs remarkably rapidly, and more rapidly than suggested by the group averages in figure 6.2. During the same period, grating acuity changes little if at all in each case. (Reprinted with permission from Held, 1993.)

sual function is unique to the case of binocularity. It is particularly striking, as shown in the figure, that large changes in stereoacuity occur over a time span that produces only minimal changes in grating acuity within the same infant.

VERNIER ACUITY Vernier acuity is a measure of sensitivity to small spatial offsets. For example, two vertical lines or gratings can be presented, one just above the other, with the top pattern offset slightly from exact alignment with the bottom. The subject's vernier acuity is the smallest visible offset between the two stimuli. Figure 6.4 summarizes data for both grating and vernier acuity in infant monkeys (Kiorpes, 1992). These data show a typical developmental time course for grating acuity and a larger developmental change with a consistently more rapid time course for vernier acuity. Both functions probably approach adult levels at about the same age, approximately 40–60 weeks. Longitudinal data from within each animal show a developmental course similar to that of the group average rather than the more abrupt developmental course seen in the case of stereopsis.

Comparisons to earlier human infant data (Manny and Klein, 1985; Shimojo et al, 1984) are also shown in figure 6.4, with ages converted by the 4:1 rule. While grating acuities agree well across species, vernier acuity is apparently higher at each age in infant monkeys than in human infants. However, both earlier studies used

moving vernier offsets, while Kiorpes used stationary offsets; in all probability, a closer identity of stimulus parameters would yield a closer identity of developmental time courses (cf. Skoczensky and Aslin, 1992).

COMPARISONS OF RESOLUTION MEASURES ACROSS VISUAL FUNCTIONS Figure 6.5 shows a comparison of developmental time courses for grating acuity, vernier acuity, stereoacuity, and critical flicker frequency for human infants. In each case, the measured or estimated *adult* value is shown at the top of the graph, at zero on the ordinate. The acuity values at each age are then plotted as decrements with respect to the adult value on a logarithmically spaced ordinate. In such a plot, all values are plotted in log relative terms, so that physical units are eliminated. Such a plot (J. Palmer, personal communication) allows a basis for comparing the relative maturational time courses of different visual functions.

For CFF, the initial decrement is less than an octave—a factor of 2—and CFF rapidly approaches adult levels in early infancy. For grating acuity, in sharp contrast, the initial decrement is about seven octaves; and the developmental curve assumes the long, slow time course described earlier, reaching adult levels only at three to five years after birth. Stereoacuity shows a third pattern—it is

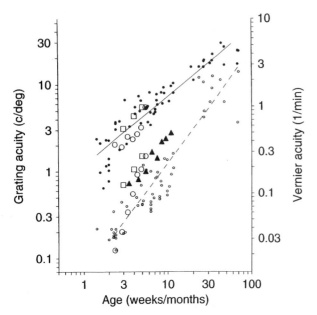

FIGURE 6.4 Longitudinal development of vernier acuity (right ordinate; lower points and dashed line) and grating acuity (left ordinate; upper points and solid line) in the same infant monkeys, plotted as a function of age in weeks. The two functions develop during a similar period, but vernier acuity starts out with a larger deficit and develops more rapidly. The larger symbols show data from earlier studies on human infants, plotted in months. The higher vernier acuity values seen in human infants in some studies are probably an artifact of stimulus differences among the studies. (Reprinted from Kiorpes, 1992, with permission of Cambridge University Press.)

unmeasurable until about three months postnatal. When first measurable, it is about eight octaves below estimated adult levels; but it rises rapidly to within two octaves of adult levels by six months in the group data, and even faster for each individual infant. Finally, vernier acuity shows an initial decrement of perhaps seven octaves, improving at first rapidly and then more slowly with age, with a time course reminiscent of that for grating acuity, but delayed in time (cf. Carkeet, Levi, and Manny, 1997).

Contrast sensitivity functions

Next we examine more extensive data on the development of spatial and temporal vision–spatial and temporal contrast sensitivity functions. The spatial contrast sensitivity function (CSF) describes a subject's sensitivity to sinusoidal gratings of various spatial frequencies. Similarly, the temporal contrast sensitivity function (tCSF) describes a subject's sensitivity to sinusoidal modulations of various temporal frequencies. Logically, there are several ways in which a CSF or a tCSF could change during development: it could shift vertically in sensitivity, or horizontally in spatial or temporal scale; or it could remain constant in sensitivity and scale, but mani-

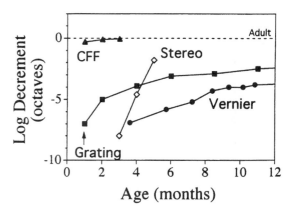

FIGURE 6.5 Summary of maturational rates for four different kinds of visual resolution: critical flicker frequency (from Regal, 1981), grating acuity, stereoacuity, and vernier acuity (from Gwiazda, Bower, and Held, 1989). The dotted line shows the measured or estimated adult acuity value. The log acuity decrement shown by infants in relation to the adult value is plotted as a function of age (from J. Palmer and D. Peterzell, personal communication). (Reprinted from Teller, 1997, with permission of the Association for Research in Vision and Ophthalmology.)

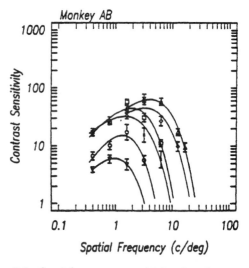

FIGURE 6.6 Spatial contrast sensitivity functions measured longitudinally in a single infant monkey, at six ages between 10 weeks (lowest curve) and 38 weeks (highest curve). The contrast sensitivity function exhibits shifts upward, in sensitivity, and rightward, in spatial scale. (Reprinted from Boothe et al., 1988, with permission of Elsevier Science.)

fest changes in fundamental curve shape. These different kinds of change have different implications within well-established theories of adult visual function (see Teller, 1998, for further discussion). In fact, CSFs and tCSFs show different patterns of change.

SPATIAL CONTRAST SENSITIVITY FUNCTIONS (CSFs) A set of CSFs collected longitudinally from a single infant monkey is shown in figure 6.6 (Boothe et al., 1988). Interestingly, the CSF shifts both vertically and horizon-

Luminance Gratings

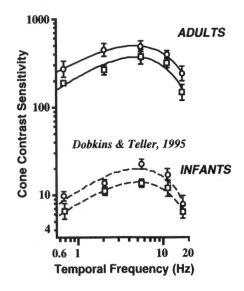

Chromatic Gratings

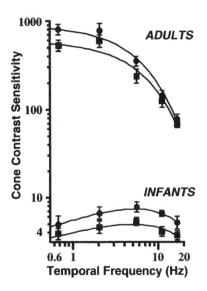

○ MOVING
□ COUNTERPHASE

● MOVING
■ COUNTERPHASE

FIGURE 6.7 Temporal contrast sensitivity functions for 3-month-old infants and adults, for both luminance-modulated (left) and red/green chromatic gratings (right). For luminance-modulated gratings, infants show a simple shift in sensitivity.

For chromatic gratings, there is a major change in curve shape, with adults showing a low-pass function and infants showing a band-pass function. (Reprinted from Dobkins, Lia, and Teller, 1997, with permission of Elsevier Science.)

tally during development. It has been argued that when test conditions are held constant, CSFs at all ages can be fitted with the same shape-invariant curve, shifted only vertically in sensitivity and horizontally in spatial scale (Movshon and Kiorpes, 1988). The same rule seems to hold for CSFs for red/green chromatic stimuli (e.g., Kelly, Borchert, and Teller, 1997).

TEMPORAL CONTRAST SENSITIVITY FUNCTIONS (tCSFs) tCSFs from 3-month-old infants and adults (Dobkins, Lia, and Teller, 1997) are shown in the left panel of figure 6.7. With respect to those of adults, infant tCSFs show a large loss of sensitivity. In both infants and adults, tCSFs peak near 6 Hz and are nearly identical in shape. Thus, while infant spatial CSFs manifest shifts in spatial scale as discussed above, no analogous shift in temporal scale seems to occur.

In addition to sensitivity to variations in intensity, or luminance, human infants show sensitivity to variations in chromaticity, or color (reviewed in Teller and Bornstein, 1987; Brown, 1990; Teller, 1998). Dobkins, Lia, and Teller (1997) tested tCSFs for red/green isoluminant gratings–that is, red/green gratings in which the red and green bars were matched in luminance, and varied only in chromaticity. The red/green gratings flickered in

counterphase; that is, the red and green bars reversed in location, at a rate of 12 reversals per second (6 Hz). In adults, tCSFs for isoluminant red/green gratings are low-pass, as shown in the right panel of figure 6.7. However, tCSFs for red/green gratings are band-pass in 3-month-olds. Thus, infants' responses to flickering red/green gratings provide the first example of a change in curve shape between infancy and adulthood.

In summary, the development of vision is complex rather than simple. Different visual functions emerge over different postnatal epochs, with different time courses and different kinds of changes of functional relationships.

Mechanisms of visual development

These behavioral data on vision and visual development immediately raise questions about neural mechanisms. What and where are the immaturities in the young infant's visual system that allow temporal resolution to be almost adult-like, grating acuity to be reduced by an order of magnitude, and the response to binocular disparity not to happen at all?

As discussed by Rakic (chapter 1 of this volume) and Bourgeois, Goldman-Rakic, and Rakic (chapter 4 of this volume), many postnatal anatomical changes are well documented in the visual system of infant primates; consider, for example, the period of intense synaptogenesis and the segregation of ocular dominance columns during the first two to three postnatal months in infant monkeys, the long slow development of the fovea (Yuodelis and Hendrickson, 1986), and the late maturation of local cortical circuits (Burkhalter, Bernardo, and Charles, 1993) documented in human infant tissue. Physiological development is much less well documented, with only a dozen or so studies in print at present.

Moreover, causal relationships between behavior and substrate are notoriously difficult to establish. Visual functions mature because the neural substrate matures, and the causes of functional maturation undoubtedly lie in neural maturation. But the length of the big toe matures too, yet we do not see it as causal in relation to the development of grating acuity. The puzzle is, which of the many immaturities of the neural substrate provide the *critical immaturities* (Brown, 1990) that limit a particular visual capacity at a particular age? Temporal coincidences become convincing causal stories only as a result of quantitative theoretical argument. The following paragraphs provide brief vignettes of some of the models and speculations that currently attempt to provide bridges between anatomy, physiology, and behavior.

OPTICS AND ACCOMMODATION   The optical quality of the primate eye is excellent at birth, and places no major limitations on visual acuity or other visual functions (see Banks and Bennett, 1988, for a review). Moreover, the development of accommodation (the capacity of the lens of the eye to change its focal length in order to focus on objects at varying distances) provides an example of an immaturity that is probably not a critical immaturity. Newborn infants typically do not accommodate differentially for objects at different distances (Haynes, White, and Held, 1965), and it might be thought that the resulting blur in the retinal image would contribute to their reduced grating acuity. However, the opposite direction of causality is more likely. That is, if the infant's visual system cannot process high spatial frequencies (see below), the infant has no need to accommodate, and no basis for generating signals that would lead to changes in accommodation.

FOVEAL IMMATURITIES AND SPATIAL VISION   The profound and long-lasting anatomical immaturities of the primate fovea (Yuodelis and Hendrickson, 1986) provide a more likely critical immaturity for limiting infant acuity and contrast sensitivity. At birth, infants' foveal cones are coarsely packed, having very short outer segments and probably inferior waveguide properties.

These characteristics drastically reduce the foveal quantal catch in infants compared to adults, and should therefore (due to quantal fluctuations) reduce the overall sensitivity of infants' vision by tenfold or more (Banks and Bennett, 1988). In addition, the change in cone packing density (in combination with changes in eye size) affords a predicted change in spatial scale of about 1:4 between birth and adulthood, in remarkably good correspondence with the spatial scale shift seen in infant CSFs (see figure 6.6; Kelly, Borchert, and Teller, 1997). Several exemplary quantitative models of the effects of foveal immaturity on infant acuity and contrast sensitivity have been developed (Banks and Bennett, 1988; Banks and Crowell, 1993; Brown, Dobson, and Maier, 1987; Jacobs and Blakemore, 1988; Movshon and Kiorpes, 1993; Wilson, 1988, 1993).

Single unit recordings from monkey lateral geniculate nucleus (LGN) show that the LGN neurons with the best spatial resolution have acuities of only about a factor of 2 higher than the behaviorally measured acuities of infant monkeys (Blakemore and Vital-Durand, 1986; Hawken, Blakemore, and Morley, 1997). Thus most, but not all, of the limit on infant grating acuity and the reductions in sensitivity and spatial scale seen in infants' CSFs are probably caused at the earliest stages of visual processing.

Moreover, these losses of sensitivity and spatial scale will doubtless play through importantly to influence the development of many other visual functions. For example, Banks and Bennett (1988) have argued quantitatively that the known foveal immaturities are sufficient to predict the development of vernier acuity in infants. This conclusion is initially surprising, because the visual processing required to analyze vernier offsets in adults is often attributed to visual cortex. However, a function limited by a particular critical locus in the adult can nonetheless be limited by a critical immaturity *at a different locus* in the infant. An adequate model for the development of each visual function will have to incorporate the effects of foveal immaturities before an argument for more central critical immaturities can be maintained.

TEMPORAL PROCESSING   The anatomical and physiological elements that control infants' temporal processing capabilities (CFFs and tCSFs) remain obscure, and data are scarce. The only available temporal response functions of single neurons in early infancy, obtained in neonatal vervet monkey LGN, peak at low temporal frequencies (Hawken, Blakemore, and Morley, 1997), and these authors conclude that the temporal resolution of single LGN cells increases considerably postnatally. These data would lead one to expect changes in temporal scale–rightward shifts of the tCSF–with development, but no such shift is seen in the behavioral data (figure 6.7). The discrepancy between the physiologically based prediction and the behavioral facts remains to be reconciled.

M VS. P PATHWAYS IN EARLY VISUAL PROCESSING Modern anatomical and physiological studies suggest the presence of (at least) two distinct pathways from the retina to cortical area V1 (for a review see Merigan and Maunsell, 1993). These are the M or *magnocellular* pathway, and the P or *parvocellular* pathway. Global models of visual development have occasionally been proposed in which the P pathway precedes the M pathway in development or vice versa. It seems more likely that each pathway has its own course of development, with different functional capabilities of each pathway developing at different rates.

In adults, M-initiated signals are thought to dominate the tCSF for luminance-modulated stimuli, while P-initiated signals are thought to dominate the tCSF for chromatic stimuli. On the basis of their observation of band-pass tCSFs for red/green chromatic modulation in infants, Dobkins, Lia, and Teller (1997) speculated that in the immature visual system, temporally modulated red/green gratings might be detected via M- rather than P-initiated signals. Such an outcome suggests either that temporal resolution in the M pathway matures earlier than temporal resolution in the P pathway, or that the tCSF of P cells changes from band-pass to low-pass during development. In any case, the change in shape of the chromatic tCSF between infancy and adulthood is unique in the infant vision literature, and clearly invites study and modeling at the physiological level.

STEREOPSIS The development of stereopsis provides a final example. Anatomically, ocular dominance columns in primates are not fully segregated at birth, and continue to segregate over the early postnatal weeks or months (Hubel, Wiesel, and LeVay, 1977; Horton and Hocking, 1996). Thus, there is a general temporal coincidence between the end of anatomical segregation of ocular dominance columns and the onset of responses to large binocular disparities.

On this basis, Held (1985) proposed a model of the development of stereovision. In the adult, neurons in layer 4 of cortical area V1 are monocular, with some neurons driven by the left eye and others by the right. Held hypothesized that in very young infants, left-eye and right-eye inputs might converge too early, on the neurons in layer 4, making them binocular rather than monocular. This convergence was hypothesized to cause a loss of eye-of-origin information, and a conse-

quent disabling of disparity selectivity of neurons in the upper cortical layers. In this view, the onset of stereopsis could be caused by the sorting out of left-eye and right-eye inputs in layer 4, enabling disparity detectors to work.

Surprisingly, it took 12 years before physiological data bearing on this hypothesis became available. Using a binocular phase paradigm, Chino et al. (1997) showed recently that in infant monkeys, in contradiction to the hypothesis, both the ocular dominance properties and the disparity selectivity of neurons in V1 are adult-like at birth. The Chino study also confirmed earlier findings (Blakemore and Vital-Durand, 1981) that the sensitivity and spatial tuning properties of V1 neurons are immature (as they are at the LGN and presumably at the retina). Chino and colleagues argue that changes in sensitivity and spatial scale alone are sufficient in principle to produce changes in the infant's behavioral response to binocular disparity. For example, sensitivity to a fixed interocular phase difference, in combination with a shift of the CSFs of neurons toward higher spatial frequencies, will yield sensitivity to smaller absolute disparities.

A quantitative theoretical account of how the early changes in sensitivity and spatial scale should play through to influence stereoacuity remains to be developed. Such a theory might suggest that foveal immaturities should yield quantitatively different developmental time courses for grating acuity and disparity sensitivity (as Banks and Bennett, 1988, argue for grating acuity and vernier acuity). But even so, it is difficult to see how the same changes in sensitivity and scale could allow both the negligible changes of grating acuity and the very rapid improvement of stereoacuity seen in postnatal months 3–6 (figures 14.2, 14.3, and 14.5).

It seems likely that a second critical immaturity will be needed to account for the rapid development of stereopsis. This mechanism did not reveal itself in Chino's binocular-phase–based study of V1 neurons. The rapid development of stereoacuity (like the change in the shape of the chromatic tCSF) cries out for further theoretical and experimental analysis, particularly with stimuli that more closely resemble the stimuli used in the behavioral studies.

In sum, in a curious modern repetition of the history of visual science at the adult level, we know much more about the development of visual functions than we do about the development of visual physiology. It seems certain that the tentative causal stories presented here will be rewritten as more extensive physiological data become available, and as more and more sophisticated experimental paradigms are used (e.g., Chino et al., 1996; Movshon et al., 1997; Hatta et al., 1998).

Summary and conclusions

Infant vision research provides an interesting model for the neurobiology of development. It highlights a set of well-understood techniques for measuring the visual capacities of infants, basic descriptions of the development of many visual functions, and a behaviorally established animal model for asking causal questions. Quantitative anatomical and physiological data are becoming available; and quantitative visual theory is being imported into the discipline and used to evaluate hypotheses about the dependence of visual behavior on visual physiology and visual substrate in the developmental context.

And yet, there is work to be done at the metatheoretical level. Coincidences of time scale and similarities of curve shape between psychophysical, anatomical, and physiological data are the beginning, not the end, of theoretical explanations; and the concept of critical immaturity (Brown, 1990), like that of critical locus (Teller, 1980), will require continuing scrutiny, both at the abstract level and when imbedded implicitly or explicitly in causal stories intended to relate visual function to visual substrate. Similar analyses might be useful in other domains of cognitive neuroscience.

One final question can be raised: Why do vision and the visual system bootstrap themselves in the particular sequence that they do? Why is a visual world with poor visual acuity and contrast sensitivity, poor sensitivity to color differences, and no stereopsis sufficient for young infants, while excellent representation of the temporal properties of stimuli is apparently required? Which of these developmental time courses are direct products of natural selection acting on infant behavior, and which are accidental consequences of other evolutionary pressures? It is easy to speculate that natural selection favors infants who perceive depth and distance before they can crawl; but beyond this, we know little about the reasons for the pattern of emergence of different visual functions over the course of infancy.

ACKNOWLEDGMENTS   Portions of this paper are excerpted with permission from Teller, D. Y., 1997. First glances: The vision of infants. The Friedenwald Lecture. *Investigative Ophthalmology and Visual Science* 38: 2183–2203.

Preparation of this review was partially supported by NIH grant EY 04470. I thank David Corina, J. Anthony Movshon, and Yuzo Chino for comments on an earlier version of the manuscript, and Barry Lia for continuing discussions of the developmental neurobiology of primate vision.

REFERENCES

BANKS, M., and P. BENNETT, 1988. Optical and photoreceptor immaturities limit the spatial and chromatic vision of human neonates. *J. Opt. Soc. Amer. A* 5:2059–2079.

BANKS, M., and J. CROWELL, 1993. Front-end limitations to infant spatial vision: Examination of two analyses. In *Early Visual Development, Normal and Abnormal*, K. Simons, ed. New York: Oxford University Press, pp. 91–116.

BIRCH, E., J. GWIAZDA, and R. HELD, 1982. Stereoacuity development for crossed and uncrossed disparities in human infants. *Vis. Res.* 22:507–513.

BLAKEMORE, C., and F. VITAL-DURAND, 1981. Postnatal development of the monkey's visual system. In *Ciba Foundation Symposium: The Fetus and Independent Life*, 1986, London: Pitman, pp. 152–171.

BLAKEMORE, C., and F. VITAL-DURAND, 1986. Effects of visual deprivation on the development of the monkey's lateral geniculate nucleus. *J. Physiol.* 380:493–511.

BOOTHE, R., L. KIORPES, R. WILLIAMS, and D. TELLER, 1988. Operant measurements of contrast sensitivity in infant macaque monkeys during normal development. *Vis. Res.* 28:387–396.

BROWN, A., 1990. Development of visual sensitivity to light and color vision in human infants: A critical review. *Vis. Res.* 30:1159–1188.

BROWN, A., V. DOBSON, and J. MAIER, 1987. Visual acuity of human infants at scotopic, mesopic and photopic luminances. *Vis. Res.* 27:1845–1858.

BURKHALTER, A., K. BERNARDO, and V. CHARLES, 1993. Development of local circuits in human visual cortex. *J. Neurosci.* 13:1916–1931.

CARKEET, A., D. LEVI, and R. MANNY, 1997. Development of vernier acuity in childhood. *Optom. Vis. Sci.* 74:741–750.

CHINO, Y. M., E. L. SMITH, S. HATTA, and H. CHENG, 1996. Suppressive binocular interactions in the primary visual cortex of infant rhesus monkeys. *Abstr. Soc. Neurosci.* 22: 645.

CHINO, Y. M., E. L. SMITH, S. HATTA, and H. CHENG, 1997. Postnatal development of binocular disparity sensitivity in neurons of the primate visual cortex. *J. Neurosci.* 17:296–307.

DOBKINS, K. R., B. LIA, and D. Y. TELLER, 1997. Infant color vision: Temporal contrast sensitivity functions for chromatic (red/green) stimuli in 3-month-olds. *Vis. Res.* 37:2699–2716.

FOX, R., R. N. ASLIN, S. L. SHEA, and S. T. DUMAIS, 1979. Stereopsis in human infants. *Science* 207:323–324.

GWIAZDA, J., J. BAUER, and R. HELD, 1989. From visual acuity to hyperactivity: A 10-year update. *Can. J. Psych.* 43:109–120.

HATTA, S., T. KUMAGAMI, J. QIAN, M. THORNTON, E. L. SMITH, and Y. M. CHINO, 1998. Naso-temporal directional bias of V1 neurons in young infant monkeys. *Invest. Ophthalmol. Vis. Sci.* 39:2259–2267.

HAWKEN, M. J., C. BLAKEMORE, and J. W. MORLEY, 1997. Development of contrast sensitivity and temporal-frequency selectivity in primate lateral geniculate nucleus. *Exp. Brain Res.* 114:86–98.

HAYNES, H., B. L. WHITE, and R. HELD, 1965. Visual accommodation in human infants. *Science* 148: 528–530.

HELD, R., 1985. Binocular vision–Behavioral and neural development. In *Neonate Cognition: Beyond the Blooming, Buzzing Confusion*, J. Mehler and R. Fox, eds. Hillsdale, N.J.: Erlbaum, pp. 37–44.

HELD, R., 1993. What can rates of development tell us about underlying mechanisms? In *Visual Perception and Cognition in Infancy*, C. Granrud, ed. Hillsdale, N.J.: Erlbaum, pp. 75–89.

HELD, R., E. E. BIRCH, and J. GWIAZDA, 1980. Stereoacuity of human infants. *Proc. Natl. Acad. Sci. U.S.A.* 77:5572–5574.

HORTON, J. C., and D. R. HOCKING, 1996. An adult-like pattern of ocular dominance columns in striate cortex of newborn monkeys prior to visual experience. *J. Neurosci.* 16:1791–1807.

HUBEL, D. H., T. N. WIESEL, and S. LEVAY, 1977. Plasticity of ocular dominance columns in monkey striate cortex. *Phil. Trans. R. Soc. Lond. B* 278:377–409.

JACOBS, D. S., and C. BLAKEMORE, 1988. Factors limiting the postnatal development of visual acuity in the monkey. *Vis. Res.* 28:947–958.

KELLY, J., K. BORCHERT, and D. Y. TELLER, 1997. The development of chromatic and achromatic contrast sensitivity in infancy as tested with sweep VEP. *Vis. Res.* 37:2057–2072.

KIORPES, L., 1992. Effect of strabismus on the development of vernier acuity and grating acuity in monkeys. *Vis. Neurosci.* 9:253–259.

MANNY, R. E., and S. A. KLEIN, 1985. A three alternative tracking paradigm to measure vernier acuity of older infants. *Vis. Res.* 25:1245–1252.

MERIGAN, W. H., and J. H. R. MAUNSELL, 1993. How parallel are the primate visual pathways? *Ann. Rev. Neurosci.* 16:369–402.

MOVSHON, J. A., and L. KIORPES, 1988. Analysis of the development of spatial contrast sensitivity in monkey and human infants. *J. Opt. Soc. Am. A* 5: 2166–2172.

MOVSHON, J. A., and L. KIORPES, 1993. Biological limits on visual development in primates. In *Early Visual Development, Normal and Abnormal*, K. Simons, ed. New York: Oxford University Press, pp. 296–305.

MOVSHON, J. A., L. KIORPES, J. J. HAWKEN, A. M. SKOCZENSKI, J. R. CAVANAUGH, and N. V. GRAHAM, 1997. Sensitivity of LGN neurons in infant macaque monkeys. *Invest. Ophthalmol. Vis. Sci. Suppl.* 38:S498.

O'DELL, C., and R. G. BOOTHE, 1997. The development of stereoacuity in infant rhesus monkeys. *Vis. Res.* 37:2675–2684.

PETRIG, B., B. JULESZ, W. KROPFL, G. BAUMGARTNER, and M. ANLIKER, 1982. Development of stereopsis and cortical binocularity in human infants: Electrophysiological evidence. *Science* 213:1402–1405.

REGAL, D. M., 1981. Development of critical flicker frequency in human infants. *Vis. Res.* 21:549–555.

SHIMOJO, S., E. E. BIRCH, J. GWIAZDA, and R. HELD, 1984. Development of vernier acuity in infants. *Vis. Res.* 24:721–728.

SIMONS, K., 1993. *Early Visual Development, Normal and Abnormal.* New York: Oxford University Press.

SKOCZENSKI, A. M., and R. N. ASLIN, 1992. Spatiotemporal factors in infant position sensitivity: Single bar stimuli. *Vis. Res.* 32:1761–1769.

TELLER, D. Y., 1979. The forced-choice preferential looking procedure: A psychophysical technique for use with human infants. *Infant Behav. Dev.* 2:135–153.

TELLER, D. Y., 1980. Locus questions in visual science. In *Visual Coding and Adaptability*, C. S. Harris, ed. Hillsdale, N.J.: Erlbaum, pp. 151–176.

TELLER, D. Y., 1981. The development of visual acuity in human and monkey infants. *Trends Neurosci.* 4:21–24.

TELLER, D. Y., 1982. Scotopic vision, color vision, and stereopsis in infants. *Current Eye Res.* 2:199–210.

TELLER, D. Y., 1984. Linking propositions. *Vis. Res.* 24:1233–1246.

TELLER, D. Y., 1997. First glances: The vision of infants. The Friedenwald Lecture. *Invest. Ophthamol. Vis. Sci.* 38:2183–2203.

TELLER, D. Y., 1998. Spatial and temporal aspects of infant color vision. *Vis. Res.* 38:3275–3282.

TELLER, D. Y., and M. BORNSTEIN, 1987. Infant color vision and color perception. In *Handbook of Infant Perception, I: From Sensation to Perception*, P. Salapatek and L. Cohen, eds. New York: Academic Press, pp. 185–235.

TELLER, D. Y., D. M. REGAL, T. O. VIDEEN, and E. PULOS, 1978. Development of visual acuity in infant monkeys (Macaca nemestrina) during the early postnatal weeks. *Vis. Res.* 18:561–566.

VITAL-DURAND, F., J. ATKINSON, and O. J. BRADDICK, 1996. *Infant Vision.* New York: Oxford University Press.

WILSON, H. R., 1988. Development of spatiotemporal mechanisms in infant vision. *Vis. Res.* 28:611–628.

WILSON, H. R., 1993. Theories of infant visual development. In *Early Visual Development, Normal and Abnormal*, K. Simons, ed. New York: Oxford University Press, pp. 560–572.

YUODELIS, C., and A. HENDRICKSON, 1986. A qualitative and quantitative analysis of the human fovea during development. *Vis. Res.* 26:847–855.

7 Specificity and Plasticity in Neurocognitive Development in Humans

HELEN J. NEVILLE AND DAPHNE BAVELIER

ABSTRACT Brain imaging studies of adults who have had altered sensory and language experience and studies of normally developing children during sensory and language processing tasks are summarized. The results suggest that different subsystems within vision and within language display different degrees of experience-dependent modification of cortical organization. Within vision, the organization of systems important in processing peripheral space and motion information is most altered following auditory deprivation. Within language, delayed exposure to a language has pronounced effects on the development of systems important in grammatical processing, and has many fewer effects on lexical development. Hypotheses concerning the origins of these differential effects of early experience are discussed.

Cognitive neuroscience has rapidly expanded during the decade of the brain. Progress in cognitive science and in the development of techniques that permit noninvasive monitoring of the human brain have permitted extensive, ongoing mapping and differentiation of sensory and cognitive systems in the mature human mind/brain. The burgeoning literature on the normal adult brain serves as the point of departure for a major opportunity and challenge for the coming decade and century—the characterization of the processes that lead to the development and differentiation of the mature brain (developmental cognitive neuroscience).

Discussions of neurocognitive development have long been dominated (and stifled) by the "nature–nurture" debate. Most current investigators acknowledge both the role of biological constraints imposed by the genotype and the role of environmental inputs in gene expression and other chemical and physiological developmental events. It is clear that neurocognitive development relies on a dynamic and complex interplay between predetermined genetic events and environmental events. In this chapter we argue that the degree of interplay is highly variable across different neurocognitive systems, leading to different degrees and timing of sensitivities to environmental inputs for different brain functions. These differences in developmental specificity and plasticity prevent simple generalization and call for a careful characterization of the developmental events within each system and subsystem.

This chapter offers (1) evidence on the development of the anatomy of the developing cerebral cortex in humans; (2) a review of developmental plasticity of higher visual functions, considering separately functions of the ventral and dorsal visual pathways; (3) a brief discussion of reports on plasticity within the development of other sensory systems; and (4) a consideration of developmental plasticity and specificity of language functions with an emphasis on the comparison of lexical and grammatical functions.

Anatomy and physiology of the developing human brain

Although a thorough review of the structural, chemical, and physiological development of the human brain is beyond the scope of this chapter, this section aims at summarizing the state of knowledge on postnatal human development from infancy to adulthood.

In most species, including humans, the developing brain displays progressive and regressive events during which axons, dendrites, synapses, and neurons show exuberant growth and major loss leading to a remodeling of the neural circuitry. This period of remodeling is hypothesized to be a time during which environmental factors can have a major impact on cortical organization. Several studies of primary sensory areas have shown that sensory inputs are of central importance in selecting the axons, dendrites, synapses, and neurons that form functional neural circuits (Rakic, 1976; Hubel and Wiesel, 1977; Sur, Pallas, and Roe,

HELEN J. NEVILLE   University of Oregon, Eugene, Ore.
DAPHNE BAVELIER   University of Rochester, Rochester, N.Y.

1990). For example, during a specific time period (the sensitive period), visual deprivation induced by monocular eyelid suture results in shrinkage of ocular dominance columns serving the closed eye. Outside the critical period, visual deprivation has little effect on the pattern of ocular dominance (Blakemore, Garey, and Vital-Durand, 1978; Hubel and Wiesel, 1977; Horton and Hocking, 1997). Little is known about the factors that control the duration and timing of sensitive periods; however, the onset of the sensitive period is affected by input. For example, in cats, binocular deprivation results in delayed onset of the sensitive period for ocular dominance formation (Cynader and Mitchell, 1980; Mitchell, 1981). Similar observations have been made in the auditory system of songbirds (Marler, 1970) and humans. The maturation of an early auditory evoked response displays an extended time course of development after cochlear implantation in congenitally deaf children (Ponton et al., 1996). The number of years of auditory experience, rather than chronological age per se, was predictive of the maturational time course.

Different neural systems and associated behavioral capabilities are affected by environmental input at highly variable time periods, supporting the idea that they develop along distinct time courses (Mitchell, 1981; Harwerth, et al., 1986; Curtiss, 1989; Neville, Mills, and Lawson, 1992; Maurer and Lewis, 1998). For example, visual processes thought to arise within the retina (cf. the sensitivity of the scotopic visual system) display relatively short sensitive periods. By contrast, binocular functions that rely on later developing cortical neurons display considerably longer sensitive periods (Harwerth et al., 1986). This variability in the timing of experience-dependent modification may depend upon the rate of maturation of the neural systems that mediate different functions, with later developing cortical areas having more opportunity to be affected by incoming input.

The proposal that different brain systems in the human display distinct developmental time courses is supported by anatomical and physiological measurements. Recently developed neuroanatomical techniques can be used to provide estimates of the density of neurons, axons, dendrites, or synapses in tissue. Huttenlocher and collaborators (Huttenlocher, 1994; Huttenlocher and Dabholkar, 1997) have used electron microscopy to map out the synaptic remodeling that occurs during human development. These authors have compared synaptogenesis and synapse elimination within several different brain areas (Huttenlocher, 1994). In primary visual cortex a burst in synaptogenesis occurs at about 3 to 4 months of age, with the maximum density reached at 4

months. In contrast, synaptogenesis in the middle prefrontal cortex takes longer, reaching a maximum synaptic density at about 3.5 years of age. Furthermore, the time course for synapse elimination occurs significantly later in the middle frontal gyrus (until age 20) than in the primary visual cortex (converged on adult levels by age 4; see figure 7.1; Huttenlocher and Dabholkar, 1997). Recently, Huttenlocher and colleagues have described developmental changes in synaptic density for different cortical areas important in language processing–primary auditory cortex, the angular gyrus (Broadman's area 40), and Broca's area (Huttenlocher, 1994; Huttenlocher and Dabholkar, 1997). At birth synaptic development (as measured by the time course of synaptic density) in the auditory cortex is more advanced than in the two language areas; but by 4 years of age, synaptic density is similar in these areas and is significantly greater than in the adult (by about a factor of 2). These findings suggest different time courses of synaptogenesis for different brain systems. A recent report suggests there may also be considerable postnatal variability in neuron loss and neurogenesis in the human brain (Shankle et al., 1998b). However, other neuroanatomic features of the human brain appear to show concurrent developmental patterns from region to region (Shankle et al., 1998a). In macaque monkeys, Rakic and colleagues (1986) have reported concurrent time courses of synaptogenesis across several different brain areas. However, there is variability between areas in the duration of the maximum densities of synapses, in the elimination phases, and in the timing of synaptogenesis on dendritic shafts and spines (see chapter 4 of this volume).

Anatomical measures of synapse proliferation in the human brain (Huttenlocher and Dabholkar, 1997) describe developmental time courses similar to those observed in physiological studies using PET with FDG, a technique that traces glucose metabolism. Chugani and collaborators (1996) have described the patterns of brain glucose utilization during human development. These studies show a rapid rise in cerebral metabolism during infancy, perhaps reflecting the burst of synaptogenesis described in the structural studies. This is followed by a decrease in brain glucose metabolism later in childhood, in much the same time frame as is observed for the loss of synapses. In the metabolic studies, primary sensory and motor cortex, the hippocampal region, and the cingulate cortex have an earlier increase in glucose metabolism than other cortical regions; and the prefrontal cortex is one of the latest structures to show increased glucose metabolism. These structural and physiological findings support the view of different maturational timetables for distinct brain structures with primary cortices developing before higher association cortices.

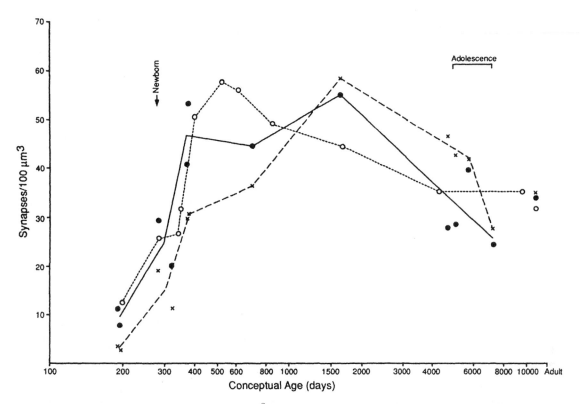

FIGURE 7.1 Mean synaptic density in synapses/100 μm³ in auditory (filled circles), calcarine (open circles), and prefrontal (×s) cortex at various ages. (Reprinted from Huttenlocher and Dabholkar, 1997, by permission of Wiley-Liss, Inc., a subsidiary of John Wiley & Sons, Inc.)

Much more research is necessary to characterize the structural and physiological development of the human brain and to link variability in the development of these parameters to variability in the time course of sensory, motor, and cognitive development in the child.

Developmental specificity of visual functions in humans

We now have powerful brain imaging methods to study aspects of the physiology of sensory and language processing in humans. Event-related brain potentials (ERPs) and functional magnetic resonance imaging (fMRI) are two such techniques. ERPs are voltage fluctuations in the EEG in response to a controlled stimulus. The latencies of different positive and negative components in an ERP reveal the time course of activation (within microseconds) of the neuronal populations that are recruited during the processing of that stimulus. The fMRI technique measures changes in blood flow and oxygenation, permitting mapping of brain regions metabolically active following the presentation of a controlled stimulus. In contrast to the ERP, this technique has a good spatial resolution (about 1 mm) but a restricted temporal resolution.

DORSAL AND VENTRAL VISUAL SUBSYSTEMS   In several experiments employing ERPs, we have observed that sensory and attentional processing of visual information presented to the central and peripheral visual fields elicit activity in different neural pathways in normal hearing subjects. Congenital auditory deprivation is associated with specific enhancements of behavioral performance and ERPs in response to visual information presented in the peripheral (but not the foveal) visual fields (Neville, Schmidt, and Kutas, 1983; Neville and Lawson, 1987a, b, c). These data suggest that the systems mediating the representation of peripheral visual space may be more modifiable than those representing central visual space. There is anatomical evidence that the visual periphery is represented most strongly along the dorsal visual pathway that projects from V1 toward the posterior parietal cortex and includes areas important for the processing of spatial location and motion information. By contrast, central space is largely represented along the ventral pathway that projects from V1 to anterior regions of the inferior temporal lobe and includes areas important for processing form and color information (Ungerleider and Mishkin, 1982; Baizer, Ungerleider, and Desimone, 1991). These results prompted the hypothesis that there may be a greater sensitivity to altered experience for other dorsal visual pathway functions.

In order to investigate this hypothesis, we employed stimuli designed to selectively activate either the magnocellular system (M stimuli) which projects strongly to the dorsal pathway, or the parvocellular system which projects strongly (but not solely: see Stoner and Albright, 1993; Sawatari and Callaway, 1996) to the ventral pathway (P stimuli). The parvo system is highly responsive to color information and to stimuli of high spatial frequency, while the magno system is highly responsive to motion and to stimuli of low spatial frequency and low contrast (Livingstone and Hubel, 1988; Merigan and Maunsell, 1993).

Stimuli were presented at five different locations including the fovea and 8 degrees from the foveal stimulus in the upper and lower left and right visual fields. The parvo (P) stimuli were isoluminant blue and green high spatial frequency gratings (adjusted for the cortical magnification factor) continuously visible at all locations. ERPs were evoked by a brief change in color; randomly at one location the blue bars changed to red for 100 ms. The magno (M) stimuli consisted of low spatial frequency gratings of light and dark gray bars with a low luminance contrast. The evoking stimulus consisted of the bars at one location (random) moving transversely to the right. Subjects fixated centrally and monitored all locations for the rare occurrence of a black square at one of the locations. We first asked whether ERPs to these different stimuli would provide evidence for the activation of distinct neural systems in normal hearing subjects and then asked whether congenital auditory deprivation would have selective effects on these different aspects of processing (Armstrong et al., 1995; Neville and Bavelier, 1998).

In normal hearing subjects the distribution of the ERPs elicited by the parvo and magno stimuli displayed many similarities, and this may be attributable to the spatial proximity (within 1 cm) of the ventral and dorsal stream areas in humans, as indicated in recent fMRI studies (Sereno et al., 1995; Tootell et al., 1995). On the other hand, there were reliable differences in the activity patterns elicited by the stimuli. Magno stimuli elicited responses that were larger dorsally than were responses to parvo stimuli, consistent with our initial hypotheses. Additionally, both the current source density maps and the grand averaged waveforms demonstrate that, whereas the peripheral M stimuli elicited ERPs largest over cortex contralateral to the field of presentation, the P stimuli evoked a bilateral response. This pattern of results may be attributable in part to the deep ventromedial location of V4 which could generate a bilateral

pattern of activation. Area MT, on the other hand, is located more laterally and would therefore generate a stronger contralateral response. Thus, these differences are consistent with anatomical differences of ventral and dorsal stream areas.

In addition, magno stimuli elicited ERP responses with considerably earlier latencies than those elicited by parvo stimuli, consistent with evidence from animal studies that show faster conduction within the magnocellular pathway. In addition, for several early components (beginning at 110 ms), P stimuli presented in the upper and lower visual fields (VF) evoked different response amplitudes while magno stimuli did not. These results may be accounted for by the retinotopic organization of V4 and MT/MST. fMRI data from humans (Sereno et al., 1995) have shown that upper and lower VF representations in several ventral stream areas including V4 are centimeters apart; however, in areas MT and MST, the representations are adjacent. Thus, a difference in response to parvo stimuli in the upper and lower VF is consistent with ventral stream activation, and the similarity of responses to magno stimuli in the upper and lower VF is consistent with dorsal stream activation. In summary, these stimuli were successful in evoking distinct ERP responses that may index the activation of separate streams or modes of visual processing in normal hearing subjects.

EFFECTS OF AUDITORY DEPRIVATION Our prior research, coupled with evidence that different systems within vision display different developmental time courses and modification by visual experience (Sherman, 1985), led us to hypothesize that processing of the magno stimuli would be selectively enhanced in congenitally deaf subjects.

Subjects were 11 congenitally, profoundly and bilaterally deaf subjects born to deaf parents. Whereas hearing subjects' reaction times were faster to targets occurring in the central than in the peripheral visual field, deaf subjects responded equally quickly to targets in the central and peripheral fields. Several specific group differences occurred in the amplitude and distribution of early sensory responses recorded over anterior and temporal regions. Deaf subjects displayed significantly greater amplitudes than hearing subjects–but this effect occurred only for magno stimuli, not for parvo stimuli (see figure 7.2). Further, whereas in hearing subjects, P stimuli elicited larger responses than did M stimuli, in deaf subjects responses to M stimuli were as large as those to P stimuli. In addition, at 150 ms ERPs to the M stimuli displayed a source–sink generator in temporal cortex that was clearly present in the deaf subjects but not in the hearing subjects. Currently, we are acquiring

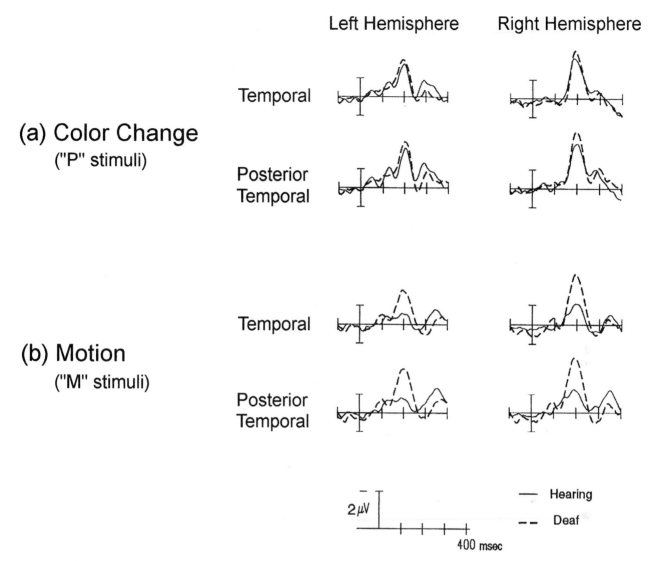

Left Hemisphere   Right Hemisphere

(a) Color Change
("P" stimuli)

Temporal

Posterior
Temporal

(b) Motion
("M" stimuli)

Temporal

Posterior
Temporal

2 µV

—— Hearing
- - Deaf

400 msec

FIGURE 7.2 ERPs elicited by (a) color change and (b) motion in normally hearing and congenitally deaf adults. Recordings from temporal and posterior temporal regions of the left and right hemispheres. (Reprinted with permission from Neville and Bavelier, 1998.)

results from a group of hearing subjects born to deaf parents who acquired ASL as a first language. This research should allow us to determine whether certain group effects observed in this experiment are attributable to auditory deprivation and others to acquisition of a visuospatial language (ASL) since, in previous research, we have observed separate effects of these two factors (Neville and Lawson, 1987c).

These data suggest that there is considerable specificity in the aspects of visual processing that are altered following auditory deprivation; specifically, the dorsal visual processing stream may be more modifiable in response to alterations in afferent input than is the ventral processing pathway. This hypothesis is in broad agreement with the proposal put forward by Chalupa and Dreher (1991) that components of the visual pathway

that are specialized for high acuity vision exhibit fewer developmental redundancies ("errors"), decreased modifiability, and more specificity than do those displaying less acuity and precision. It may also be that the dorsal visual pathway has a more prolonged maturational time course than the ventral pathway, permitting extrinsic influences to exert an effect over a longer time. While little evidence bears directly on this hypothesis, anatomical data suggest that, in humans, neurons in the parvocellular layers of the LGN mature earlier than those in the magnocellular laminae (Hickey, 1977) and, in nonhuman primates, the peripheral retina is slower to mature (Lachica and Casagrande, 1988; Packer, Hendrickson, and Curcio, 1990; Van Driel, Provis, and Billson, 1990). Additionally, data suggest that the development of the Y-cell pathway (which is strongest in the periphery of

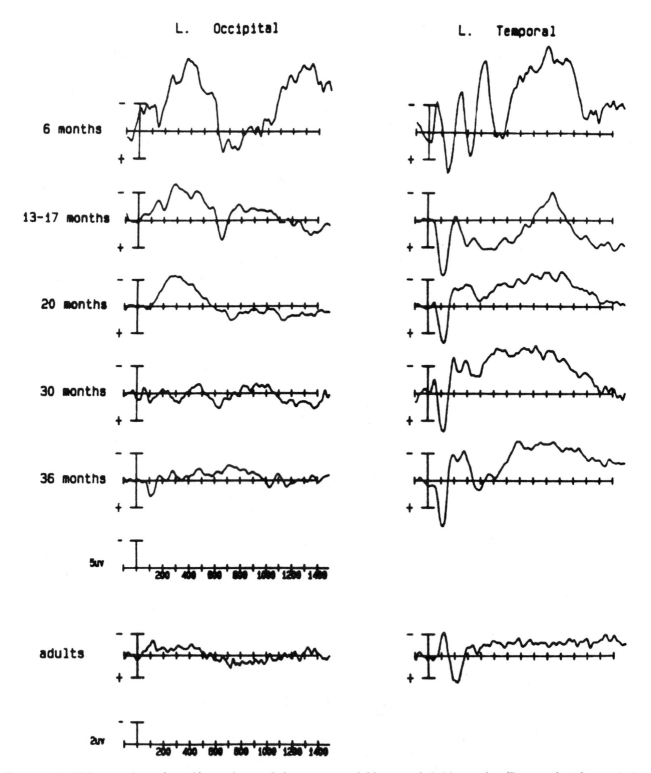

FIGURE 7.3 ERPs to auditory (speech) stimuli recorded over temporal and occipital regions in normal adults (bottom) and in children aged 6–36 months. (Reprinted with permission from Neville, 1995.)

the retina) is more affected by visual deprivation than is development of the W- and X-cell pathways (Sherman and Spear, 1982). Investigators have also reported that the effects of congenital visual deprivation (due to cataracts) are more pronounced on peripheral than foveal vision (and by implication on the dorsal pathway) (Mioche and Perenin, 1986; Bowering et al., 1997). Moreover, in developmental disabilities including dyslexia, specific language impairment, and Williams syndrome, visual deficits are more pronounced for dorsal than ventral visual pathway functions (Lovegrove, Garzia, and Nicholson, 1990; Eden et al., 1996; Atkinson et al., 1997). An additional hypothesis that may account for the greater effects on peripheral vision is that in development the effects of deprivation and enhancement are equivalent within all cortical regions. Those areas with less extent to begin with (e.g., MT, peripheral visual representations) would display the largest proportional effects of both enhancement and vulnerability. A similar hypothesis has been proposed to account for the larger effects of visual deprivation on ocular dominance formation within the periphery in monkeys (Horton and Hocking, 1997).

SENSITIVE PERIOD EFFECTS AND MECHANISMS We have observed that individuals who became deaf after the age of 4 years (due to delayed expression of the gene that leads to cochlear degeneration) typically do not display the increased visual ERPs that we attributed to auditory deprivation (Neville, Schmidt, and Kutas, 1983; Neville and Lawson, 1987c). We considered several mechanisms that might mediate the effects themselves and the developmental time limits on them. One possibility is that they are mediated by an early, normally transient, redundancy of connections between the auditory and visual systems (as has been observed in cats and hamsters: see Dehay, Bullier, and Kennedy, 1984; Frost, 1984; Innocenti and Clarke, 1984). In the absence of competition from auditory input, visual afferents may be maintained on what would normally be auditory neurons. Our results from studies of later deafened individuals suggest that in humans this redundancy may diminish by the fourth year of life. One way we tested this hypothesis was to study the differentiation of visual and auditory sensory responses in normal development (see figure 7.3). In normal adults, auditory stimuli elicit ERP responses that are large over temporal brain regions but small or absent over occipital regions. By contrast, in 6-month-old children we observed that auditory ERPs are equally large over temporal and visual brain regions, consistent with the idea that there is less specificity and more redundancy of connections between auditory and visual cortex at this time. Between 6 and 36 months, however, we ob-

served a gradual decrease in the amplitude of the auditory ERP over visual areas, while the amplitude over the temporal areas was unchanged. These results suggest that early in human development there exists a redundancy of connections between auditory and visual areas and that this overlap gradually decreases between birth and 3 years of age. This loss of redundancy may be the boundary condition that determines when auditory deprivation can result in alterations in the organization of the visual system. Ongoing studies of hearing and deaf infants and children employing the parvo and magno stimuli described above will test for the specificity of these effects.

fMRI STUDY OF MOTION PERCEPTION We have further pursued the hypothesis that deafness alters the functional organization of the dorsal visual stream, by employing fMRI (Tomann et al., 1998). Specifically, we assessed whether early auditory deprivation alters cerebral activation during motion processing. In addition, we hypothesized that these changes would be most marked when visual attention was required in view of the central role of dorsal parietal regions in spatial attention. Motion processing was compared between congenitally deaf (native signers/born to deaf parents) and hearing individuals as visual attention was manipulated. Subjects fixated centrally and viewed an alternation of radial flow fields (converging and diverging) and static dots. While the first run required only passive viewing, visual attention was manipulated in all other runs by asking subjects to detect velocity and/or luminance changes.

Under conditions of active attention, deaf individuals showed a greater number of voxels activated and a larger percent signal change than did hearing subjects in temporal cortex including areas MT-MST (figure 7.4; see color plate 1). Thus, congenital deafness alters the cortical organization of motion processing, especially when attention is required. Interestingly, the recruitment of the intraparietal sulcus was also significantly larger in deaf than in hearing subjects. This result, like our earlier ERP study of spatial attention (Neville and Lawson, 1987b; Neville, 1995), suggests that early auditory deprivation may also alter the cortical organization of visual attention. Ongoing studies will determine the precise location and the specificity of these effects.

Developmental specificity in other neurocognitive domains

Developmental plasticity has also been documented in humans within other sensory modalities. There are several reports that early peripheral blindness leads to changes in the visually deprived cortex. Measures of glucose utilization have shown an increased metabolism

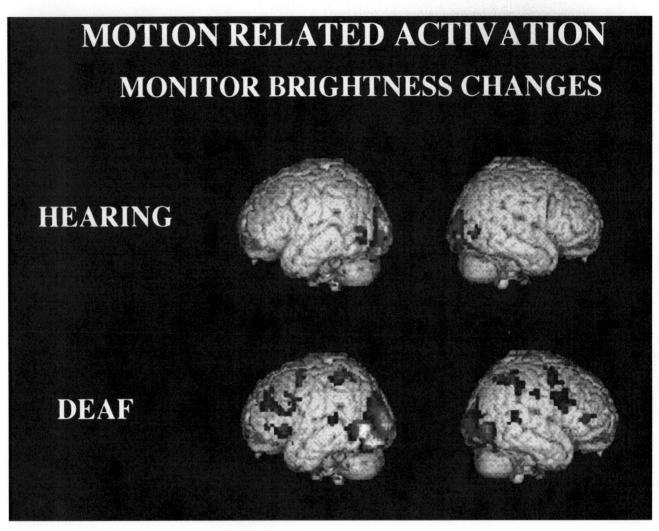

FIGURE 7.4 Activation (fMRI, 1.5T) in normally hearing and congenitally deaf adults in response to visual motion.

in the visual cortex of early blind humans as compared to subjects who became blind after the completion of visual development. These studies report that metabolic activity within the occipital cortex of early blind individuals is higher than that found in blindfolded sighted subjects and equivalent to that of sighted subjects with their eyes open (Wanet-Defalque et al., 1988; Veraart et al., 1990; Uhl et al., 1994). Additionally, ERP studies indicate a larger slow negative DC potential shift over the occipital lobe in early blind than in sighted persons during tactile and auditory tasks (Uhl et al., 1991, 1994; Röder et al., 1996, 1997). Recently, a number of studies have confirmed the functional participation of visual areas during somatosensory tasks in early blind individuals. Using PET, Sadato and colleagues (Sadato et al., 1996) compared tactile discrimination in early blind braille readers and control subjects. Blind subjects revealed activation of visual cortical areas whereas these regions were deactivated in controls. The functional relevance of visual areas in tactile discrimination was further established in a transcranial magnetic stimulation experiment (Cohen et al., 1997). Transient stimulation of the occipital cortex induced errors on a tactile task in early blind subjects but had no effect on the sighted controls. It is worth noting that not all aspects of somatosensory processing recruit visual areas in blind subjects. For example, simple tactile stimuli that did not require discrimination produced little activation in visual areas of blind subjects (Sadato et al., 1996). This finding is in agreement with the hypothesis that different neurocognitive systems and subsystems exhibit different sensitivities to altered experience.

This point is further supported by the research of Röder and colleagues (1997) who have studied auditory localization abilities in blind humans. ERPs were recorded as congenitally blind adults and sighted controls attended either to central or peripheral sound sources in order to detect a rare noise burst either at the 0- or the 90-degree loudspeaker (on different blocks). Behavioral data revealed a higher spatial resolution in the blind, particularly when they were attending to the periphery. Gradients of ERP amplitudes suggested a sharper auditory spatial attention focus in the blind compared to the sighted for peripheral sounds. The results suggest that across auditory and visual modalities the representation of peripheral space is more altered by early sensory experience than is the representation of central space. It is interesting that, on close examination of the behavioral data presented in Rice (1965) on blind humans and Rauschecker and Kneipert (1993) on blind cats, a similar effect is observed–i.e., an advantage in sound localization for the blind that is largest at peripheral locations.

Developmental specificity of language functions in human

It is reasonable to assume that the rules and principles that govern the development of the sensory systems also guide the development of language-relevant brain systems. Thus, differences in the rate of differentiation and degree of specification may be apparent within language and help to identify different functional subsystems. In a series of experiments we have studied the development of the neural systems important in lexical semantic and grammatical processing. In normal, right-handed, monolingual adults nouns and verbs ("open-class" words) that provide lexical/semantic information elicit a different pattern of brain activity (as measured by ERPs) than do function words including prepositions and conjunctions ("closed-class" words) that provide grammatical information in English (Neville, Mills, and Lawson, 1992; Nobre and McCarthy, 1994). In addition, sentences that are semantically nonsensical (but grammatically intact) elicit a different pattern of ERPs than do sentences that contain a violation of syntactic structure (but leave the meaning intact) (Neville et al., 1991; Osterhout, McLaughlin, and Bersick, 1997). These results are consistent with several other types of evidence suggesting that different neural systems mediate the processing of lexical/semantic and grammatical information in adults. Specifically, they imply a greater role for more posterior temporal-parietal systems in lexical/semantic processing and for frontal-temporal systems within the left hemisphere in grammatical processing. This overall pattern appears ubiquitous in adults, and many investigators have suggested that the central role of the left hemisphere in language processing is strongly genetically determined. Certainly, the fact that most individuals, regardless of the language they learn, display left-hemisphere dominance for that language indicates that this aspect of neural development is strongly biased. Nonetheless, it is likely that language-relevant aspects of cerebral organization are dependent on and modified by language experience. Many investigators have studied this question by comparing cerebral organization in individuals who learned a second language at different times in development (Perani et al., 1996; Dehaene et al., 1997; Kim et al., 1997). In general, age of exposure to language appears to affect cerebral organization for that language. Moreover, there appears to be specificity in these effects: In Chinese-English bilinguals delays of as long as 16 years in exposure to English had very little effect on the organization of the brain systems active in lexical/semantic processing. In contrast, delays of just 4 years had significant effects on those aspects of brain organization linked to grammatical processing (figure 7.5; see color plate 2) (Weber-Fox and Neville, 1996). These results and parallel behavioral results from the same study suggest that aspects of semantic and grammatical processing differ markedly in the degree to which they depend upon language input. Specifically, grammatical processing appears more vulnerable to delays in language experience.

STUDIES OF DEAF ADULTS Further evidence on this point was provided by ERP studies of English sentence processing by congenitally deaf individuals who learned English late and as a second language (American Sign Language or ASL was the first language of these subjects; Neville, Mills, and Lawson, 1992). Deaf subjects displayed ERP responses to nouns and to semantically anomalous sentences in written English that were indistinguishable from those of normal hearing subjects who learned English as a first language. These data are consistent with the hypothesis that some aspects of lexical/semantic processing are largely unaffected by the many aspects of language experience that differ between normally hearing and congenitally deaf individuals. By contrast, deaf subjects displayed aberrant ERP responses to grammatical information like that presented in function words in English. Specifically, they did not display the specialization of the anterior regions of the left hemisphere characteristic of native hearing/speaking learners. These data suggest that the systems mediating the processing of grammatical information are more modifiable and vulnerable in response to altered language experience than are those associated with lexical/semantic processing.

STUDIES OF ASL Recently, we have employed the ERP and fMRI techniques to pursue this hypothesis further and also to obtain evidence on the question of whether the strongly biased role of the left hemisphere

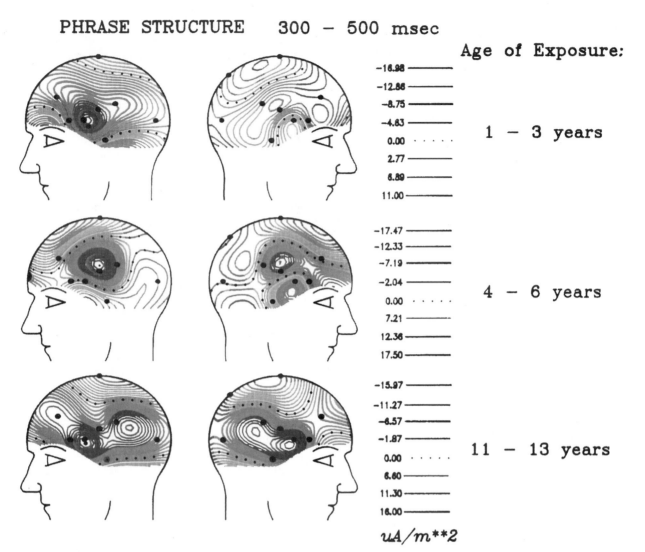

PHRASE STRUCTURE   300 – 500 msec

Age of Exposure:

-16.98
-12.86
-8.75
-4.63
0.00 · · · · ·
2.77
6.89
11.00

1 – 3 years

-17.47
-12.33
-7.19
-2.04
0.00 · · · · ·
7.21
12.36
17.50

4 – 6 years

-15.97
-11.27
-6.57
-1.87
0.00 · · · · ·
6.60
11.30
16.00

11 – 13 years

uA/m**2

FIGURE 7.5 Current source density (CSD) analyses of responses to grammatical anomalies (violations of phrase structure) in English. Early learners of English (1–3 years) display a left lateralized activation, but delays in age of exposure (4–13 years) are associated with bilateral activation.

in language occurs independently of the structure and modality of the language first acquired (Neville et al., 1997, 1998). ERPs recorded to response to open- and closed-class signs in ASL sentences displayed similar timing and anterior/posterior distributions to those observed in previous studies of English. But, whereas in native speakers of English responses to closed-class English words were largest over anterior regions of the left hemisphere, in native signers closed-class ASL signs elicited bilateral activity that extended posteriorly to include parietal regions of both the left and right hemispheres. These results imply that the acquisition of a language that relies on spatial contrasts and the perception of motion may result in the inclusion of right-hemisphere regions into the language system. As seen in figure 7.6, both hearing and deaf native signers displayed this effect. However, hearing people who ac-

quired ASL in the late teens did not show this effect, suggesting there may be a limited time (sensitive) period when this type of organization for grammatical processing can develop. By contrast, the response to semantic information was not affected by age of acquisition of ASL, in keeping with the results from studies of English suggesting that these different subsystems within language display different degrees of developmental plasticity.

In fMRI studies comparing sentence processing in English and ASL we also observed evidence for biological constraints and effects of experience on the mature organization of the language systems of the brain. As seen at the top of figure 7.7 (color plate 3), when hearing adults read English (their first language), there is robust activation within the left (but not the right) hemisphere and in particular within the inferior frontal (Broca's) regions.

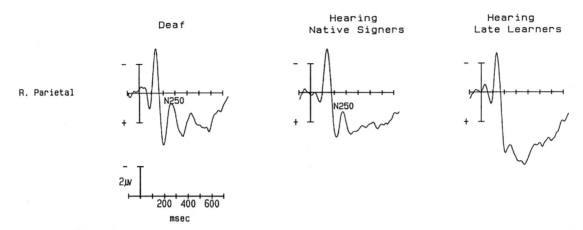

FIGURE 7.6 ERPs to closed-class signs in ASL sentences from 10 deaf, 10 hearing native signers, and 10 late learners of ASL. Recordings from parietal areas of the right hemisphere.

When deaf people read English (their second language, learned late and imperfectly), we did not observe activation of these regions within the left hemisphere (figure 7.7, middle). Is the absence of left-hemisphere activation in the deaf linked to lack of auditory experience with language or to incomplete acquisition of the grammar of the language? ASL is not sound-based, but displays each of the characteristics of all formal languages including a complex grammar (that makes extensive use of spatial location and hand motion) (Klima and Bellugi, 1979). Studies of the same deaf subjects when viewing sentences in their native ASL clearly show activation within the same inferior frontal regions of the left hemisphere that are active when native speakers of English process English (figure 7.7, bottom). These data suggest a strong biological bias for these neural systems to mediate grammatical language regardless of the structure and modality of the language acquired. However, if the language is not acquired within the appropriate time window, this strong bias is not expressed. Biological constraints and language experience interact epigenetially, as has been described for many other systems described in developmental biology.

The fMRI data also indicate a robust role for the right hemisphere in processing ASL. These results suggest that the nature of the language input, in this case the co-occurrence of location and motion information with language, shapes the organization of the language systems of the brain. Further research is necessary to specify the different times in human development when particular types of input are required for optimal development of the many systems and subsystems important in language processing.

EFFECTS OF PRIMARY LANGUAGE ACQUISITION ON CEREBRAL ORGANIZATION The research summarized above implies that language experience determines the development and organization of language-relevant systems of the brain. A strong test of this hypothesis would be to chart the changes in brain organization as children acquire primary language, and to separate these from more general maturational changes (Mills, Coffey-Corina, and Neville, 1993, 1997; Neville and Mills, 1997). We compared patterns of neural activity relevant to language processing in 13- and 20-month-old infants to determine whether or not changes in cerebral organization occur as a function of specific changes in language development when chronological age is held constant. ERPs were recorded as children listened to a series of words whose meaning was understood by the child, words whose meaning the child did not understand, and backward words. Specific and different ERP components discriminated comprehended words from unknown and from backward words. Distinct lateral and anterior-posterior specializations were apparent in ERP responses to the different types of words. At 13 months of age the effects of word comprehension were apparent over anterior and posterior regions of both the left and right hemispheres. However, at 20 months of age the effects occurred only over temporal and parietal regions of the left hemisphere. This increasing specialization of language-relevant systems is not, however, solely dependent on chronological age. In comparisons of children of the same age who differ in size of vocabulary it is clear that language experience/knowledge is strongly predictive of the maturity of cerebral organization: 13-month-

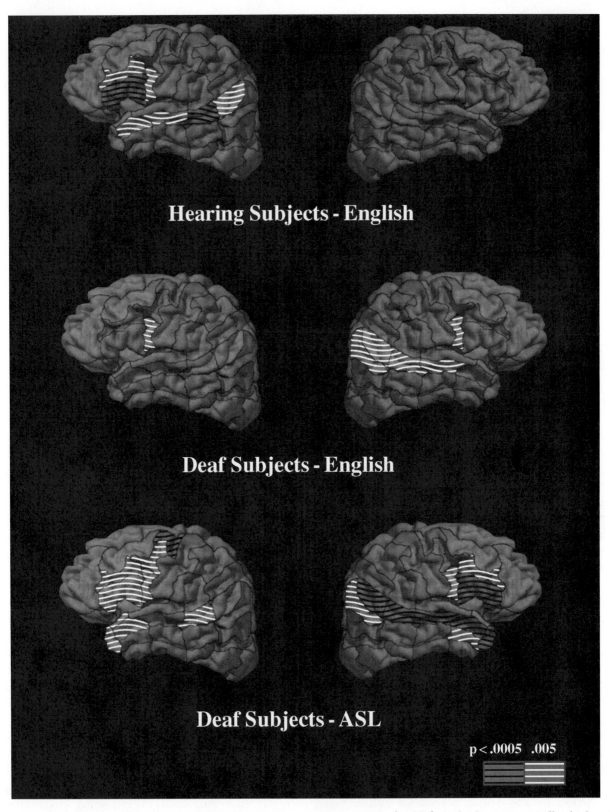

Hearing Subjects - English

Deaf Subjects - English

Deaf Subjects - ASL

p < .0005   .005

FIGURE 7.7 Cortical areas showing increases in blood oxygenation on fMRI when normal hearing adults read English sentences (top), when congenitally deaf native signers read English sentences (middle), and when congenitally deaf native signers view sentences in their native sign language (American Sign Language).

old infants with large vocabularies also display more focal left temporal/parietal effects of word meaning than do those with small vocabularies.

A similar effect is found in the development of the differential processing of open- and closed-class words. We compared ERPs to open- and closed-class words in infants and young children from 20 to 42 months of age. All children understood and produced both the open- and closed-class words presented. At 20 months, ERPs in response to open- and closed-class words did not differ. However, both types of words elicited ERPs that differed from those elicited by unknown and backward words. These data suggest that in the earliest stages of language development, when children are typically speaking in single-word utterances or beginning to put two words together, open- and closed-class words elicit similar patterns of brain activity. At 28–30 months of age, when children typically begin to speak in short phrases, ERPs to open- and closed-class words elicited different patterns of brain activity. However, the more mature left-hemisphere asymmetry to closed-class words was not observed. By 3 years of age most children speak in sentences and use closed-class words appropriately to specify grammatical relations and, like adults, ERPs from 3-year-olds displayed a left-hemisphere asymmetry to closed-class words. Figure 7.8 (color plate 4) illustrates the development of the left-hemisphere asymmetry to closed-class words in current source density maps across the three age groups. The results across the three groups are consistent with the hypothesis that, initially, open- and closed-class words are processed by similar brain systems, and that these systems become progressively specialized with increasing language experience. Further evidence on this hypothesis comes from an examination of ERPs from children who were the same age but differed in language abilities. The 20-month-old children who scored below the 50th percentile for vocabulary size did not show ERP differences to open- and closed-

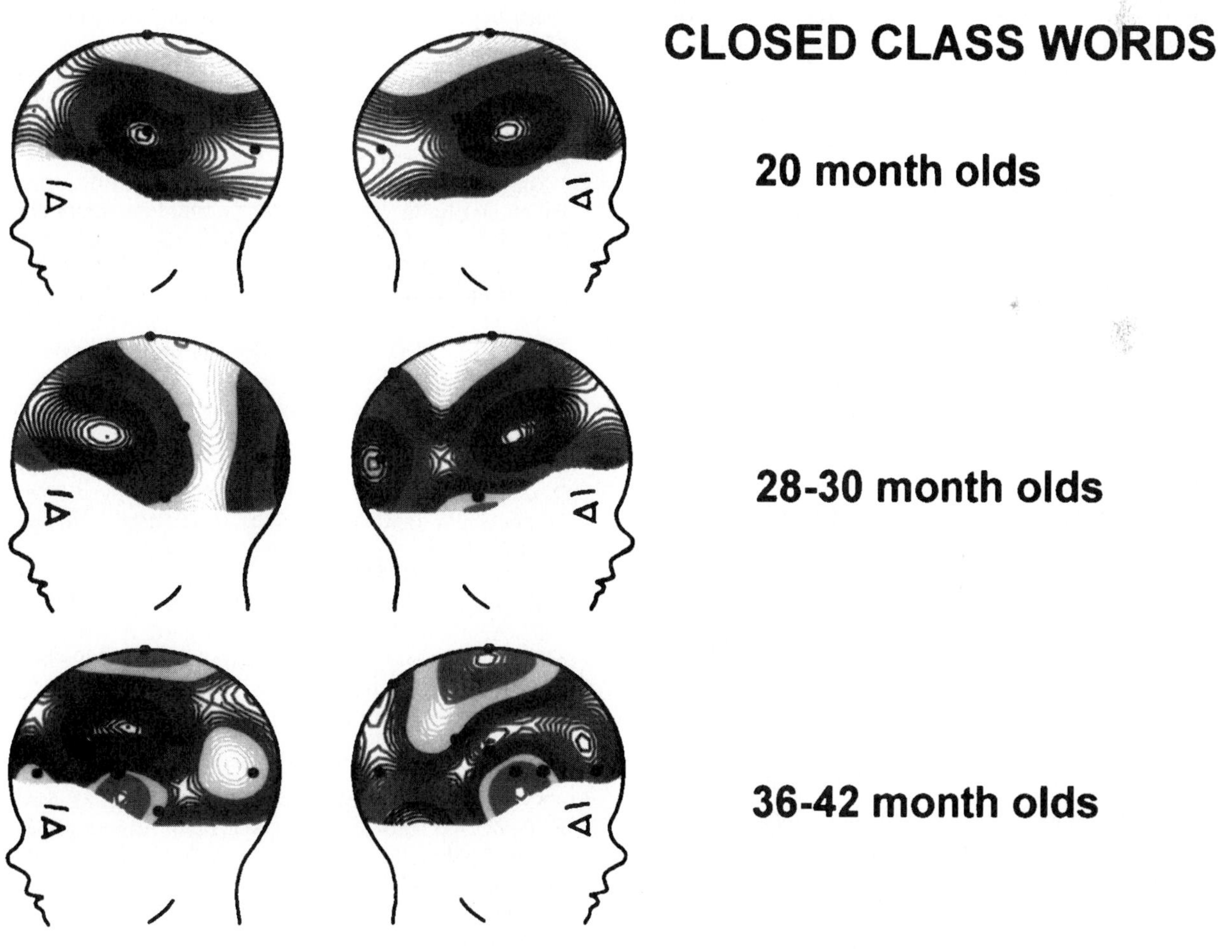

CLOSED CLASS WORDS

20 month olds

28-30 month olds

36-42 month olds

FIGURE 7.8   Current source density (CSD) analyses of neural activity to closed-class words at 200 ms. The CSDs illustrate sinks [i.e., activity flowing into the head (purple)] and sources [i.e., activity flowing out of the head (orange)] at three age groups. Top: At 20 months the CSD shows sinks over both the left and the right hemispheres. Middle: At 28–30 months the CSD shows sinks that are bilateral but slightly more prominent over the right than the left hemisphere. Bottom: At 36–42 months the CSD shows a sink over left anterior regions.

class words. In contrast, those above the 50th percentile displayed ERP differences to open- and closed-class words that were similar to the patterns shown in 28–30-month-olds. These data strongly suggest that the organization of brain activity is linked to language abilities rather than to chronological age per se.

Summary and conclusions

The results from the language studies, taken as a whole, point to different developmental time courses and developmental vulnerabilities of aspects of grammatical and semantic/lexical processing. They thus provide support for conceptions of language that distinguish these subprocesses within language. Similarly, following auditory deprivation, processes associated with the dorsal visual pathway were more altered than were functions associated with the ventral pathway, providing support for conceptions of visual system organization that distinguish functions along these lines. A general hypothesis that may account for the different patterns of plasticity within both vision and language is that systems employing fundamentally different learning mechanisms display different patterns of developmental plasticity. It may be that systems displaying experience-dependent change throughout life–including the topography of sensory maps (Merzenich et al., 1988; Gilbert, 1995; Kaas, 1995), lexical acquisition (i.e., object–word associations), and the establishment of form, face, and object representations (i.e. ventral pathway functions)–rely upon very general, associative learning mechanisms that permit learning and adaptation throughout life. By contrast, systems important for computing dynamically shifting relations between locations, objects, and events (including the dorsal visual pathway and the systems of the brain that mediate grammar) appear dependent on and modifiable by experience primarily during more limited periods in development. This could account both for the greater developmental deficits and enhancements of dorsal pathway function following various developmental anomalies and for the greater effects of altered language experience on grammatical functions. Further research is necessary to characterize systems that become constrained in this way and those that can be modified throughout life. This type of developmental evidence can contribute to fundamental descriptions of the architecture of different cognitive systems. Additionally, in the long run, they may contribute to the design of educational and habilitative programs for both normally and abnormally developing children.

ACKNOWLEDGMENTS This research has been supported by grants from National Institutes of Health, DC00128, and DC00481. We are grateful to our many collaborators on the several studies summarized here, and to Linda Heidenreich for manuscript preparation. We thank Jeff Goodhill for his careful reading of this manuscript.

REFERENCES

ARMSTRONG, B., T. MITCHELL, S. A. HILLYARD, and H. J. NEVILLE, 1995. Effects of auditory deprivation on color and motion processing: An ERP study. Ph.D. diss., University of California.

ATKINSON, J., J. KING, O. BRADDICK, L. NOKES, S. ANKER, and F. BRADDICK, 1997. A specific deficit of dorsal stream function in Williams' syndrome. *NeuroReport* 8:1919–1922.

BAIZER, J. S., L. G. UNGERLEIDER, and R. DESIMONE, 1991. Organization of visual inputs to the inferior temporal and posterior parietal cortex in macaques. *J. Neurosci.* 11:168–190.

BLAKEMORE, C., L. J. GAREY, and F. VITAL-DURAND, 1978. The physiological effects of monocular deprivation and their reversal in the monkey's visual cortex. *Physiol.* (London) 283:223–262.

BOWERING, E. R., D. MAURER, T. L. LEWIS, and H. P. BRENT, 1997. Constriction of the visual field of children after early visual deprivation. *J. Pediatr. Ophthalmol. Strabismus* 34:347–356.

CHALUPA, L., and B. DREHER, 1991. High precision systems require high precision "blueprints": A new view regarding the formation of connections in the mammalian visual system. *J. Cogn. Science* 3:209–219.

CHUGANI, H. T., R.-A. MÜLLER, and D. C. CHUGANI, 1996. Functional brain reorganization in children. *Brain Dev.* 18:347–356.

COHEN, L. G., P. CELNIK, A. PASCUAL-LEONE, B. CORWELL, L. FAIZ, J. DAMBROSIA, M. HONDA, N. SADATO, C. GERLOFF, M. D. CATALA´, and M. HALLETT, 1997. Functional relevance of cross-modal plasticity in blind humans. *Nature* 389:180–183.

CURTISS, S., 1989. The independence and task-specificity of language. In *Interaction in Human Development*, M. Bornstein and J. Bruner, eds. Hillsdale, N.J.: Erlbaum, pp. 105–137.

CYNADER, M., and D. MITCHELL, 1980. Prolonged sensitivity to monocular deprivation in dark reared cats. *J. Neurophysiol.* 43:1026–1040.

DEHAENE, S., E. DUPOUX, J. MEHLER, L. COHEN, D. PERANI, P.-F. VAN DE MOORTELE, S. LEHÉRICI, and D. LE BIHAN, 1997. Anatomical variability in the cortical representation of first and second languages. *NeuroReport* 17:3809–3815.

DEHAY, C., J. BULLIER, and H. KENNEDY, 1984. Transient projections from the fronto-parietal and temporal cortex to areas 17, 18, and 19 in the kitten. *Exp. Brain Res.* 57:208–212.

EDEN, G. F., J. W. VANMETER, J. M. RUMSEY, J. M. MAISOG, R. P. WOODS, and T. A. ZEFFIRO, 1996. Abnormal processing of visual motion in dyslexia revealed by functional brain imaging. *Nature* 382:66–69.

FROST, D. O., 1984. Axonal growth and target selection during development: Retinal projections to the ventrobasal complex and other "nonvisual" structures in neonatal Syrian hamsters. *J. Comp. Neurol.* 230:576–592.

GILBERT, C. D., 1995. Dynamic properties of adult visual cortex. In *The Cognitive Neurosciences,* M. S. Gazzaniga, ed. Cambridge, Mass.: MIT Press, pp. 73–89.

HARWERTH, R., E. SMITH, G. DUNCAN, M. CRAWFORD, and G. VON NOORDEN, 1986. Multiple sensitive periods in the development of the primate visual system. *Science* 232:235–238.

HICKEY, T. L., 1977. Postnatal development of the human lateral geniculate nucleus: Relationship to a critical period for the visual system. *Science* 198:836–838.

HORTON, J. C., and D. R. HOCKING, 1997. Timing of the critical period for plasticity of ocular dominance columns in macaque straite cortex. *J. Neurosci.* 17:3684–3709.

HUBEL, D. H., and T. N. WIESEL, 1977. Functional architecture of macaque monkey visual cortex. *Proc. R. Soc. Lond.* 198:1–59.

HUTTENLOCHER, P. R., 1994. Synaptogenesis, synapse elimination, and neural plasticity in human cerebral cortex. In *Threats to Optimal Development: Integrating Biological, Psychological, and Social Risk Factors*, Vol. 27, C. A. Nelson, ed. Hillsdale, N.J.: Erlbaum, pp. 35–54.

HUTTENLOCHER, P. R., and A. S. DABHOLKAR, 1997. Regional differences in synaptogenesis in human cerebral cortex. *J. Comp. Neurol.* 387:167–178.

INNOCENTI, G., and S. CLARKE, 1984. Bilateral transitory projection to visual areas from auditory cortex in kittens. *Dev. Brain Res.* 14:143–148.

KAAS, J. H., 1995. The reorganization of sensory and motor maps in adult mammals. In *The Cognitive Neurosciences*, M. S. Gazzaniga, ed. Cambridge, Mass.: MIT Press, pp. 51–71.

KIM, K. H. S., N. R. RELKIN, K.-M. LEE, and J. HIRSCH, 1997. Distinct cortical areas associated with native and second languages. *Nature* 388:171–174.

KLIMA, E. S., and U. BELLUGI, 1979. *The Signs of Language.* Cambridge, Mass.: Harvard University Press.

LACHICA, E. A., and V. A. CASAGRANDE, 1988. Development of primate retinogeniculate axon arbors. *Vis. Neurosci.* 1:103–123.

LIVINGSTONE, M., and D. HUBEL, 1988. Segregation of form, color, movement and depth: Anatomy, physiology, and perception. *Science* 240:740–749.

LOVEGROVE, W., R. GARZIA, and S. NICHOLSON, 1990. Experimental evidence for a transient system deficit in specific reading disability. *J. Amer. Optom. Assoc.* 61:137–146.

MARLER, P., 1970. A comparative approach to vocal learning: Song development in white-crowned sparrows. *J. Comp. Physiol. Psych. Monograph* 71:1–25.

MAURER, D., and T. L. LEWIS, 1998. Overt orienting toward peripheral stimuli: Normal development and underlying mechanisms. In *Cognitive Neuroscience of Attention: A Developmental Perspective*, J. E. Richards, ed. Hillsdale, N.J.: Erlbaum, pp. 51–102.

MERIGAN, W., and J. MAUNSELL, 1993. How parallel are the primate visual pathways? *Annu. Rev. Neurosci.* 16:369–402.

MERZENICH, M., G. RECANZONE, W. JENKINS, T. ALLARD, and R. NUDO, 1988. Cortical representational plasticity. In *Neurobiology of Neocortex*, P. Rakic and W. Singer, eds. Chichester, U.K.: John Wiley & Sons, pp. 41–67.

MILLS, D. L., S. A. COFFEY-CORINA, and H. J. NEVILLE, 1993. Language acquisition and cerebral specialization in 20-month-old infants. *J. Cogn. Neurosci.* 5:317–334.

MILLS, D. L., S. A. COFFEY-CORINA, and H. J. NEVILLE, 1997. Language comprehension and cerebral specialization from 13 to 20 months. *Dev. Neuropsychology* 13:397–445.

MIOCHE, L., and M. PERENIN, 1986. Central and peripheral residual vision in humans with bilateral deprivation amblyopia. *Exp. Brain Res.* 62:259–272.

MITCHELL, D., 1981. Sensitive periods in visual development. In *Development of Perception*, R. Aslin, J. Alberts, and M. Petersen, eds. New York: Academic Press, pp. 3–43.

NEVILLE, H. J., 1995. Developmental specificity in neurocognitive development in humans. In *The Cognitive Neurosciences*, M. Gazzaniga, ed. Cambridge, Mass.: MIT Press, pp. 219–231.

NEVILLE, H. J., and D. BAVELIER, 1998. Variability of developmental plasticity within sensory and language systems: Behavioral, ERP and fMRI studies. *Proceedings of the Conference on Advancing Research on Developmental Plasticity: Integrating the Behavioral Science and the Neuroscience of Mental Health.* Washington, D.C.: U.S. Government Printing Office, pp. 174–184.

NEVILLE, H. J., D. BAVELIER, D. CORINA, J. RAUSCHECKER, A. KARNI, A. LALWANI, A. BRAUN, V. CLARK, P. JEZZARD, and R. TURNER, 1998. Cerebral organization for language in deaf and hearing subjects: Biological constraints and effects of experience. *Proc. Natl. Acad. Sci. U.S.A.* 95:922–929.

NEVILLE, H. J., S. A. COFFEY, D. S. LAWSON, A. FISCHER, K. EMMOREY, and U. BELLUGI, 1997. Neural systems mediating American Sign Language: Effects of sensory experience and age of acquisition. *Brain Lang.* 57:285–308.

NEVILLE, H. J., and D. LAWSON, 1987a. Attention to central and peripheral visual space in a movement detection task: An event-related potential and behavioral study. I. Normal hearing adults. *Brain Res.* 405:253–267.

NEVILLE, H. J., and D. LAWSON, 1987b. Attention to central and peripheral visual space in a movement detection task: An event-related and behavioral study. II. Congenitally deaf adults. *Brain Res.* 405:268–283.

NEVILLE, H. J., and D. LAWSON, 1987c. Attention to central and peripheral visual space in a movement detection task. III. Separate effects of auditory deprivation and acquisition of a visual language. *Brain Res.* 405:284–294.

NEVILLE, H. J., and D. MILLS, 1997. Epigenesis of language. *Mental Retardation Dev. Disabilities Res. Rev.* 3:282–292.

NEVILLE, H. J., D. MILLS, and D. LAWSON, 1992. Fractionating language: Different neural subsystems with different sensitive periods. *Cerebral Cortex* 2:244–258.

NEVILLE, H. J., J. NICOL, A. BARSS, K. FORSTER, and M. GARRETT, 1991. Syntactically based sentence processing classes: Evidence from event-related brain potentials. *J. Cogn. Neurosci.* 3:155–170.

NEVILLE, H. J., A. SCHMIDT, and M. KUTAS, 1983. Altered visual evoked potentials in congenitally deaf adults. *Brain Res.* 266:127–132.

NOBRE, A., and G. MCCARTHY, 1994. Language-related ERPs: Scalp distributions and modulation by word type and semantic priming. *J. Cogn. Neurosci.* 6:233–255.

OSTERHOUT, L., J. MCLAUGHLIN, and M. BERSICK, 1997. Event-related brain potentials and human language. *Trends Cogn. Sci.* 1:203–209.

PACKER, O., A. HENDRICKSON, and A. CURCIO, 1990. Developmental redistribution of photoreceptors across the *Macaca nemestrina* (pigtail macaque) retina. *J. Comp. Neurol.* 298:472–493.

PERANI, D., S. DEHAENE, F. GRASSI, L. COHEN, S. F. CAPPA, E. DUPOUX, F. FAZIO, and J. MEHLER, 1996. Brain processing of native and foreign languages. *NeuroReport* 7:2439–2444.

PONTON, C. W., M. DON, J. J. EGGERMONT, M. D. WARING, B. KWONG, and A. MASUDA, 1996. Auditory system plasticity in children after long periods of complete deafness. *NeuroReport* 8:61–65.

RAKIC, P., 1976. Prenatal genesis of connections subserving ocular dominance in the rhesus monkey. *Nature* 261:467–471.

RAKIC, P., J. BOURGEOIS, M. ECKENHOFF, N. ZECEVIC, and P. GOLDMAN-RAKIC, 1986. Concurrent overproduction of synapses in diverse regions of the primate cerebral cortex. *Science* 232:232–235.

RAUSCHECKER, J., and U. KNIEPERT, 1993. Auditory localization behaviour in visually deprived cats. *Eur. J. Neurosci.* 6:149–160.

RICE, C., S. FEINSTEIN, and R. SCHUSTERMAN, 1965. Echo-detection ability of the blind: Size and distance factors. *J. Exp. Psychol.* 70:246–251.

RÖDER, B., F. RÖSLER, and E. HENNIGHAUSEN, 1997. Different cortical activation patterns in blind and sighted humans during encoding and transformation of haptic images. *Psychophysiology* 34:292–307.

RÖDER, B., F. RÖSLER, E. HENNIGHAUSEN, and F. NÄCKER, 1996. Event-related potentials during auditory and somatosensory discrimination in sighted and blind human subjects. *Cogn. Brain Res.* 4:77–93.

RÖDER, B., W. TEDER-SALEJARVI, A. STERR, F. RÖSLER, S. A. HILLYARD, and H. J. NEVILLE, 1997. Auditory-spatial tuning in sighted and blind adults: Behavioral and electrophysiological evidence. *Soc. Neurosci.* 23:1590.

SADATO, N., A. PASCUAL-LEONE, J. GRAFMAN, V. IBANEZ, M.-P. DEIBER, G. DOLD, and M. HALLET, 1996. Activation of the primary visual cortex by braille reading in blind subjects. *Nature* 380:526–528.

SAWATARI, A., and E. M. CALLAWAY, 1996. Convergence of magno- and parvocellular pathways in layer 4B of macaque primary visual cortex. *Nature* 380:442–446.

SERENO, M. I., A. M. DALE, J. B. REPPAS, K. K. KWONG, J. W. BELLIVEAU, T. J. BRADY, B. R. ROSEN, and R. G. TOOTELL, 1995. Borders of multiple visual areas in humans revealed by functional magnetic resonance imaging. *Science* 268:889–893.

SHANKLE, W. R., R. A. KIMBALL, B. H. LANDING, and J. HARA, 1998a. Developmental patterns in the cytoarchitecture of the human cerebral cortex from birth to 6 years examined by correspondence analysis. *Proc. Natl. Acad. Sci. U.S.A.* 95:4023–4028.

SHANKLE, W. R., B. H. LANDING, M. S. RAFII, A. SCHIANO, J. M. CHEN, and J. HARA, 1998b. Evidence for a postnatal doubling of neuron number in the developing human cerebral cortex between 15 months and 6 years. *J. Theor. Biol.* 191:115–140.

SHERMAN, S., 1985. Development of retinal projections to the cat's lateral geniculate nucleus. *TINS* 8:350–355.

SHERMAN, S., and P. SPEAR, 1982. Organization of visual pathways in normal and visually deprived cats. *Psychol. Rev.* 62:738–855.

STONER, G. B., and T. D. ALBRIGHT, 1993. Image segmentation cues in motion processing: Implications for modularity in vision. *J. Cogn. Neurosci.* 5:129–149.

SUR, M., S. PALLAS, and A. ROE, 1990. Cross-modal plasticity in cortical development: Differentiation and specification of sensory neocortex. *TINS* 13:227–233.

TOMANN, A., T. MITCHELL, H. J. NEVILLE, D. CORINA, G. LIU, and D. BAVELIER, 1998. Cortical reorganization for motion processing in congenitally deaf subjects. *Cogn. Neurosci. Soc.* 5:14.

TOOTELL, R. B., J. B. REPPAS, K. K. KWONG, R. MALACH, R. T. BORN, T. J. BRADY, B. R. ROSEN, and J. W. BELLIVEAU, 1995. Functional analysis of human MT and related visual cortical areas using magnetic resonance imaging. *J. Neurosci.* 15:3215–3230.

UHL, F., P. FRANZEN, G. LINDINGER, W. LANG, and L. DEECKE, 1991. On the functionality of the visually deprived occipital cortex in early blind persons. *Neurosci. Lett.* 124:256–259.

UHL, F., T. KRETSCHMER, G. LINDINGER, G. GOLDENBERG, W. LANG, W. ODER, and L. DEECKE, 1994. Tactile mental imagery in sighted persons and in patients suffering from peripheral blindness early in life. *Electroencephalogr. Clin. Neurophysiol.* 91:249–255.

UNGERLEIDER, L. G., and M. MISHKIN, 1982. Two cortical visual systems. In *Analysis of Visual Behavior*, D. J. Ingle, M. A. Goodale, and R. J. Mansfield, eds. Cambridge, Mass.: MIT Press, pp. 549–586.

VAN DRIEL, D., J. M. PROVIS, and F. A. BILLSON, 1990. Early differentiation of ganglion, amacrine, bipolar, and Muller cells in the developing fovea of human retina. *J. Comp. Neurol.* 291:203–219.

VERAART, C., A. DEVOLDER, M. WANET-DEFALQUE, A. BOL, C. MICHEL, and A. GOFFINET, 1990. Glucose utilization in human visual cortex is abnormally elevated in blindness of early onset but decreased in blindness of late onset. *Brain Res.* 510:115–121.

WANET-DEFALQUE, M., C. VERAART, A. DEVOLDER, R. METZ, C. MICHEL, G. DOOMS, and A. GOFFINET, 1988. High metabolic activity in the visual cortex of early blind human subjects. *Brain Res.* 446:369–373.

WEBER-FOX, C., and H. J. NEVILLE, 1996. Maturational constraints on functional specializations for language processing: ERP and behavioral evidence in bilingual speakers. *J. Cogn. Neurosci.* 8:231–256.

8 Language, Mind, and Brain: Experience Alters Perception

PATRICIA K. KUHL

ABSTRACT How does one individual acquire a specific language? Is it appropriate to call it "learning" in the traditional sense? Historically, two dramatically opposed views formed the cornerstones of the debate on language. In one view, a universal grammar and phonology are innately provided and input serves to trigger the appropriate version. In the other view, no innate knowledge is provided and language is acquired through a process of external feedback and reinforcement. Both theories are based on assumptions about the nature of language input to the child and the nature of the developmental change induced by input. New data reviewed here, showing the effects of early language experience on infants, suggest a theoretical revision. By one year of age, prior to the time infants begin to master higher levels of language, infants' perceptual and perceptual-motor systems have been altered by linguistic experience. Phonetic perception has changed dramatically to conform to the native-language pattern, and language-specific speech production has emerged. According to the model described here, this developmental change is caused by a complex "mapping" of linguistic input. This account is different in two respects from traditional views: (1) Language input is not conceived of as triggering innately provided options; (2) the kind of developmental change that occurs does not involve traditional Skinnerian learning, in which change is brought about through reinforcement contingencies. The consequences of this are described in a developmental theory at the phonetic level that may apply to higher levels of language.

Nature, nurture, and a historical debate

Forty-one years ago, a historic confrontation occurred between a strong nativist and a strong learning theorist. Chomsky's (1957) reply to Skinner's (1957) *Verbal Behavior* had just been published, re-igniting the debate on the nature of language. In Chomsky's (1965, 1981) nativist view, universal rules encompassing the grammars and phonologies of all languages were innately specified. Language input served to "trigger" the appropriate subset of rules, and developmental change in language ability was viewed as biological growth akin to that of bodily organs, rather than learning. In the Skinnerian view, language was explicitly learned. Language was brought about in the child through a process of explicit

PATRICIA K. KUHL Department of Speech and Hearing Sciences, University of Washington, Seattle, Wash.

feedback and external control of reinforcement contingencies (Skinner, 1957).

Both views made assumptions about three critical parameters: (1) the biological preparation that infants bring to the task of language learning, (2) the nature of language input, and (3) the nature of developmental change. Chomsky asserted, through the "poverty of the stimulus" argument, that language input to the child is greatly underspecified. Critical elements are missing, hence the necessity for innately specified information. Skinner viewed speech as simply another operant behavior, shaped through parental feedback and reinforcement like all other behaviors.

In the decades that have passed since these positions were developed, the debate has been played out for language at the syntactic, semantic, and phonological levels. In this chapter, I concentrate primarily on the phonetic level of language, using the elementary components of sounds—the consonants and vowels that make up words—to structure an argument about what is given by nature and gained by experience in the acquisition of language. Studying the sound structure of language allows us to test the perception of language in infants just hours old, addressing the question of what language capacities are innate in infants. Then, by tracking the development of infants raised in various cultures listening to different languages, we can determine, again using tests of perception, when infants begin to diverge as a function of experience with a particular language. These methods provide a strong test of the historically opposing views, and the results of these tests deliver dramatic evidence of the interaction between biology and culture, leading to a new view.

Origins of conceptual distinctions and the modern view

The discussion among linguists and psychologists regarding language is only one forum in which the nature–nurture issue has been debated. Begun by philosophers hundreds of years ago, the nativism–empiricism debate or the nativist–constructivist debate concerned the origins of knowledge and whether it stemmed from native abilities or was empirically derived. The debate is of continuing interest across a wide variety of disciplines: ethology (Bateson, 1991; Hauser, 1997), neuroscience (Carew, Menzel, and Shatz, 1998), language science (Kuhl, 1994, 1998a; Pinker, 1994), and developmental psychology (Bates and Elman, 1996; Carey, 1985; Gopnik and Meltzoff, 1997; Karmiloff-Smith, 1995).

These groups use different terms to distinguish complex behaviors that appear relatively immune to, as opposed to wholly dependent on, experience. The terminology reflects differences in emphasis between groups. In ethology for example, the distinction has traditionally been drawn between *innate* or *instinctual* behaviors, considered to be genetically determined, and those *learned* as a function of exposure to the environment (Lorenz, 1965; Thorpe, 1959; Tinbergen, 1951). The emphasis in early ethological writings was on explaining behaviors that existed at birth in the absence of experience (Lorenz's "innate release mechanisms").

In the early psychological literature on the mental development of the child (James, 1890; Koffka, 1924; Vygotsky, 1962), and also in the neuroscience literature (Cajal, 1906), the distinction was drawn using the terms "development" and "learning." *Development* included changes in the organism over time that depend primarily on maturation or internal factors leading to the expression of information specified in the genome. The term development and the term innate are therefore similar, but not identical. *Development* (as opposed to *innate*) emphasized complex behaviors, thought to be un-

der genetic control, that unfold well after birth rather than those existing at birth (innate behavior). *Learning* encompassed processes that depend on explicit experience and produce long-lasting changes. Neuroscientists currently debate how experience alters the brain and whether experience induces *selection*, where options are chosen from a set of innate possibilities, or *instruction*, where experience sculpts a wide open brain (see Doupe and Kuhl's 1999 discussion of birdsong and speech).

Modern writers in all the aforementioned fields agree that behavior unfolds under the control of both a genetic blueprint and the environment, and that the debate now centers on the precise nature of the interplay between the two. Using the development/learning terminology, four alternative models—A through D—can be conceptualized, as illustrated in figure 8.1. The first two are not interactionist accounts, whereas the last two can be described in this way.

Development and learning can be thought of as completely separable processes (figure 8.1, model A). Development follows a maturational course guided by a genetic blueprint, and learning neither follows from nor leads to changes in the pre-established course of development. Alternatively, they can be thought of as two processes so inseparable that they cannot be pulled apart, even conceptually (figure 8.1, model B).

More commonly, development and learning are thought of as separate and distinguishable processes that interact in one way or another (figure 8.1, models C and D). Developmental psychologists, neuroscientists, and neurobiologists largely agree that the interactionist view is the correct one (Bates and Elman, 1996; Bonhoeffer

Conceptual relations between development and learning

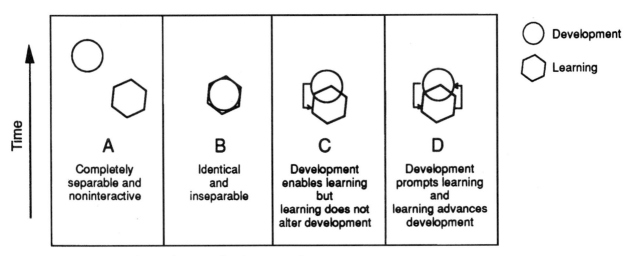

FIGURE 8.1   Conceptual relations between development and learning.

and Shatz, 1998; Carey, 1985; Doupe, 1998; Doupe and Kuhl, 1999; Fanselow and Rudy, 1998; Gopnik and Meltzoff, 1997; Karmiloff-Smith, 1995; Kuhl, 1994, 1998a; Marler, 1990). At issue, however, is exactly how the two systems interact, and particularly whether the interaction between development and learning is bidirectional.

Among the interactionist views, one model is that development enables learning, but that learning does not change the course of development, which unfolds more or less on its own timetable (figure 8.1, model C). Learning is seen as capitalizing on the achievements of development, and cannot occur unless a certain level of development has been achieved. The interaction is unidirectional, however. Development is not affected by learning. In classical developmental psychology, this position is closest to the view of Piaget (1954). In modern neurobiology, the notion that there are "constraints" on learning, that development both prepares the organism and sets limits on learning, is consistent with this model (see Marler, 1974, and Doupe, 1998, for the case of birdsong). Greenough and Black's (1992) "experience-expectant" plasticity, wherein changes in neural development are thought to precede and prepare an organism to react to a reliably present environmental stimulus, provides a detailed example of this model. In each of these cases, development is conceived of as both enabling and limiting learning, but learning does not alter the course of development.

There is an alternative interactionist view. This model describes development and learning as mutually affecting one another (figure 8.1, model D). Development enables and even prompts learning, and learning in turn advances development. This view is closest to that developed by Vygotsky (1979). Vygotsky's theory, the "zone of proximal development" (ZPD), described development at two levels. One was the infant's actual developmental level, the level already achieved. The second was the level that was just within reach. The ZPD was the difference between the two. In Vygotsky's view, environmental stimulation slightly in advance of current development (in the ZPD) resulted in learning and, when this occurred, learning prompted development. Recent theories proposed by developmental psychologists to account for a wide variety of cognitive and linguistic tasks converge on the point that there is mutual interaction between development and learning (Carey, 1985; Gopnik and Meltzoff, 1997; Karmiloff-Smith, 1991).

In linguistic theory, Chomsky's classic view that the growth of language is largely determined by a maturational process fits model C. Experience plays a role, but it is seen as triggering prespecified options or as setting innately determined parameters (Chomsky, 1981). The data reviewed here at the phonetic level of language come closer to the mutual interaction of model D. In the model of speech development I describe, language input plays more than a triggering role in the process. Language input is mapped in a complex process that appears to code its subtle details. Input thus goes beyond setting the parameters of prespecified options. Moreover, early mapping of the perceptual regularities of language input is argued to allow infants to recognize words and phrases, thus advancing development.

In summary, there is a great deal of support for interactionist views (models C and D) over noninteractionist views (models A and B). While the relations between learning and development may differ across species and systems, there is an emerging consensus across diverse disciplines (including neurobiology, psychology, linguistics, and neuroscience) that development and learning are not independent entities. Speech falls clearly on the interactionist side. However, the form of the interaction remains a question, with a cutting-edge issue being whether (and how) learning can alter development. The model proposed here on the basis of recent research on speech development goes some distance toward addressing this issue.

Explanations for developmental change in speech

One of the puzzles in language development is to explain the orderly transitions that all infants go through during development. Infants the world over achieve certain milestones in linguistic development at roughly the same time, regardless of the language they are exposed to. Moreover, developmental change can also include cases in which infants' early skills exceed their later ones. Explaining these transitions is one of the major goals of developmental linguistic theory.

One of these transitions occurs in speech perception. At birth, infants discern differences between all the phonetic units used in the world's languages (Eimas, Miller, and Jusczyk, 1987). All infants show these universal skills, regardless of the language environment in which they are being raised. Data on nonhuman animals' perception of speech suggest that the ability to partition the basic building blocks of speech is deeply rooted in our evolutionary history (Kuhl, 1991a).

When do infants from different cultures begin to diverge? Infants' initial language-universal perceptual abilities are highly constrained just one year later. By the end of the first year, infants fail to discriminate foreign language contrasts they once discriminated (Werker and Tees, 1984), resembling the adult pattern. Adults often find it difficult to perceive differences between sounds not used to distinguish words in their native language. Adult native speakers of Japanese, for example, have great difficulty discriminating American English /r/ and /l/ (Strange, 1995; Best, 1993), and American English listeners have great difficulty hearing the difference between Spanish /b/ and /p/ (Abramson and Lisker, 1970).

Infants' abilities change dramatically over a 6-month period. A recent study completed in Japan shows, for example, that at 6 months Japanese infants respond to the /r-l/ distinction and are as accurate in perceiving it as American 6-month-old infants. By 12 months, Japanese infants no longer demonstrate this ability, even though American infants at that same age have become much better at discriminating the two sounds (Kuhl, Kirtani, et al., 1997).

A similar transition occurs in speech production. Regardless of culture, all infants show a universal progression in the development of speech which encompasses five distinct phases: *Cooing* (1 to 4 months), in which infants produce sounds that resemble vowels; *Canonical Babbling* (5 to 10 months), during which infants produce strings of consonant–vowel syllables, such as "bababababa" or "mamamama"; *First Words* (10 to 15 months), wherein infants use a consistent phonetic form to refer to an object; *Two Word Utterances* (18 to 24 months), in which two words are combined in a meaningful way; and *Meaningful Speech* (15 months and beyond), in which infants produce both babbling and meaningful speech to produce long intonated utterances (Ferguson, Menn, and Stoel-Gammon, 1992). Interestingly, deaf infants exposed to a natural sign language, such as American Sign Language (ASL), are purported to follow the same progression using a visual–manual mode of communication (Petitto, 1993).

While infants across cultures begin life producing a universal set of utterances that cannot be distinguished, their utterances soon begin to diverge, reflecting the influence of the ambient language. By the end of the first year, the utterances of infants reared in different countries begin to be separable; infants show distinct patterns of speech production, both in the prosodic (intonational patterns) and phonetic aspects of language, that are unique to the culture in which they are being raised (de Boysson-Bardies, 1993). In adulthood, the distinctive speech motor patterns initially learned contribute to "accents" in speaking another language (Flege, 1988).

The transition in speech perception and production from a pattern that is initially universal across languages to one that is highly specific to a particular language presents one of the most intriguing problems in language acquisition: What causes the transition? We know it is not simply maturational change. In the absence of natural language input, as in the case of socially isolated children (Fromkin et al., 1974; Curtiss, 1977) or cases in which abandoned children were raised quite literally in the wild (Lane, 1976), full-blown linguistic skills do not develop. Linguistic input and social interaction provided early in life appear to be necessary.

The thesis developed here, using the phonetic level, is that linguistic experience produces a special kind of developmental change. Language input alters the brain's processing of the signal, resulting in the creation of complex mental maps. The mapping "warps" underlying dimensions, altering perception in a way that highlights distinctive categories. This mapping is not like traditional psychological learning. In the psychological literature, for example, this kind of learning depends on the presence of specific contingencies that reward certain responses, feedback about the correctness of the response, and step-by-step shaping of the response (Skinner, 1957). The kind of learning reflected in language is very different. While it depends on external information from the environment (language input), it requires neither explicit teaching nor reinforcement contingencies. Given exposure to language in a normal and socially interactive environment, language learning occurs; and the knowledge gained about a specific language is long-lasting and difficult to undo.

Language experience alters perception

The thesis developed here for the phonetic level of language is that ambient language experience produces a "mapping" that alters perception. A research finding that helps explain how this occurs is called the "perceptual magnet effect." It is observed when tokens perceived as exceptionally good representatives of a phonetic category (prototypes) are used in tests of speech perception (Kuhl, 1991b). The notion that categories have prototypes stems from cognitive psychology. Findings in that field show that the members of common categories (like the category bird or dog) are not equal: An ostrich is not as representative of the category bird as a robin; a terrier is not as representative of the category dog as a collie. These prototypes, or best instances of categories, are easier to remember, show shorter reaction times when identified, and are often preferred in tests that tap our favorite instances of categories (Rosch, 1977). This literature motivated us to test the concept that phonetic categories had prototypes, or best instances, in the early 1980s.

Our results demonstrated that phonetic prototypes did exist (Grieser and Kuhl, 1989; Kuhl, 1991b), that they differed in speakers of different languages (Kuhl,

1992; Näätänen et al., 1997; Willerman and Kuhl, 1996), and that phonetic prototypes function like perceptual magnets for other sounds in the category (Kuhl, 1991b). When listeners hear a phonetic prototype and attempt to discriminate it from sounds that surround it in acoustic space, the prototype displays an attractor effect on the surrounding sounds (figure 8.2). It perceptually pulls other members of the category toward it, making it difficult to hear differences between the prototype and surrounding stimuli. Poor instances from the category (nonprototypes) do not function in this way. A variety of experimental tasks produced this result with both consonants and vowels (Iverson and Kuhl, 1995, 1996; Sussman and Lauckner-Morano, 1995). Other studies confirm listeners' skills in identifying phonetic prototypes and show that they are language specific (Kuhl, 1992; Miller, 1994; Willerman and Kuhl, 1996).

Developmental tests revealed that the perceptual magnet effect was exhibited by 6-month-old infants for the sounds of their native language (Kuhl, 1991b). In later studies, cross-language experiments suggest that the magnet effect is the product of linguistic experience (Kuhl et al., 1992). In the cross-language experiment, infants in the United States and Sweden were tested. The infants from both countries were tested with two vowel prototypes, an American English vowel prototype, /i/ (as in "peep"), and a Swedish vowel prototype, /y/ (as in "fye"). The results demonstrated that the perceptual magnet effect in 6-month-old infants was influenced by exposure to a particular language. American infants demonstrated the magnet effect only for the American English /i/; they treated the Swedish /y/ as a nonprototype. Swedish infants showed the opposite pattern, demonstrating the magnet effect for the Swedish /y/ and treating the American English /i/ as a nonprototype. This is the youngest age at which language experience has been shown to affect phonetic perception.

The perceptual magnet effect thus occurs prior to word learning. What this means is that in the absence of formal language understanding or use–before infants utter or understand their first words–infants' perceptual systems strongly conform to the characteristics of the ambient language. We previously believed that word learning caused infants to recognize that phonetic changes they could hear, such as the change that Japanese infants perceived between /r/ and /l/, did not change the meaning of a word in their language. This discovery was thought to cause the change in phonetic perception. We now know that just the opposite is true. Language input sculpts the brain to create a perceptual system that highlights the contrasts used in the language, while de-emphasizing those that do not, and this happens prior to word learning. The change in phonetic perception thus assists word learning, rather than the reverse.

Further tests on adults suggested that the magnet effect distorted perception to highlight sound contrasts in the native language. Studies on the perception of the phonetic units /r/ and /l/, as in the words "rake" and "lake," illustrate this point. The /r-l/ distinction is one notoriously difficult for Japanese speakers, and our studies sought to determine how adults from different cultures perceive these two sounds. To conduct the study, we used computer-synthesized syllables beginning with /r/ and /l/, spacing them at equal physical intervals in a two-dimensional acoustic grid (Iverson and Kuhl, 1996) (figure 8.3A). American listeners identified each syllable as beginning with either /r/ or /l/, rated its category goodness, and estimated the perceived similarity for all possible pairs of stimuli using a scale from "1" (very dissimilar) to "7" (very similar). Similarity ratings were scaled using multidimensional scaling (MDS) techniques. The results provide a map that indicates perceived distance between stimuli. The results revealed that perception distorts physical space. The physical

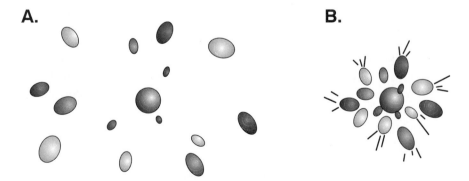

FIGURE 8.2   The perceptual magnet effect. When a variety of sounds in a category surround the category prototype (A), they are perceptually drawn toward the prototype (B). The prototype appears to function like a magnet for other stimuli in the category.

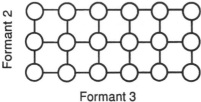

A. **Physical World**

Formant 2

Formant 3

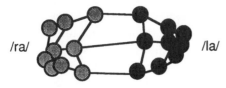

B. Perceptual World: Americans

/ra/ /la/

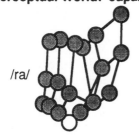

C. Perceptual World: Japanese

/ra/

FIGURE 8.3 Physical (acoustic) versus perceptual distance. Consonant tokens of /r/ and /l/ were generated to be equally distant from one another in acoustic space (A). However, American listeners perceive perceptual space as shrunken near the best instances of /r/ (gray dots) and /l/ (black dots) and stretched at the boundary between the two (B). Japanese listeners' perceptual world differs dramatically; neither magnet effects nor a boundary between the two categories are seen (C).

(acoustic) differences between pairs of stimuli were equal; however, perceived distance was "warped" (figure 8.3B). The perceptual space around the best /r/ and the best /l/ was greatly reduced for American listeners, as predicted by the perceptual magnet effect, while the space near the boundary between the two categories was expanded.

This experiment has now been done using Japanese monolingual listeners (Kuhl et al., submitted) and the results show a strong contrast in the way the /r-l/ stimuli are perceived by American and Japanese adults (figure 8.3C). Japanese adults hear almost all the sounds as /r/; there is no /l/ in Japanese. More striking is the complete absence of these magnet and boundary effects in the Japanese MDS solution. The results suggest that linguistic experience forms perceptual maps specifying the perceived distances between speech stimuli, and that these maps differ greatly in people of different cultures.

The critical point for theory is that neither group perceives physical reality, the actual physical differences between sounds. For each language group, experience has altered perception to create a language-specific map of auditory similarities and differences. The map highlights sound contrasts of the speaker's native language by increasing internal category cohesion and maximizing the difference between categories.

The theoretical position developed here is that speech maps are developed early in infancy, prior to the development of word acquisition. The mapping of phonetic information is seen as enabling infants to recognize word candidates. For example, our work shows that Japanese infants fail to discriminate American English /r/ from /l/ at 12 months of age, though they did so perfectly well at 6 months of age (Kuhl, Andruski, et al., 1997). This would assist Japanese infants in word recognition by collapsing /r/- and /l/-like sounds into a single category, making it possible for Japanese infants to perceive their parents' productions of these sounds as one entity at 12 months, when the process of word acquisition begins. If they did not do so, it would presumably make it more difficult to map sound patterns onto objects and events. Mental maps for speech are the front end of the language mechanism. They point infants in the direction needed to focus on the aspects of the acoustic signal that will separate categories in their own native language. They provide a kind of attentional network that may function as a highly tuned filter for language. Such a network would promote semantic and syntactic analysis.

The view that phonetic mapping supports the recognition of higher order units is supported by data showing that slightly later in development infants use information about phonetic units to recognize word-like forms. Work by Jusczyk and his colleagues shows that just prior to word learning, infants prefer word forms that are typical of the native language, ones in which the stress patterns and phoneme combinations conform to the native-language pattern (Jusczyk et al., 1993). At about this age, infants have also been shown capable of learning the statistical probabilities of sound combinations contained in artificial words (Saffran, Aslin, and Newport, 1996). Infants' mapping at the phonetic level is thus seen as assisting infants in chunking the sound stream into higher order units, suggesting that "learning" promotes "development."

The form of learning we are describing is different from historical versions of learning described by psychologists. It does not involve external reinforcement and contingency learning, as in Skinner. It is automatic and unconscious. During the first year of life, infants come to recognize the recurring properties of their native language and mentally store those properties in some form. Uncovering the underlying neural mechanisms that control this kind of learning may aid our general understanding of the kind of learning that makes us unique as a species.

A theory of speech development

Given these findings, how do we reconceptualize infants' innate predispositions as preparing them for experience? One view can be summarized as a three-step model of speech development, called the Native Language Magnet (NLM) model (Kuhl, 1994, 1998a). NLM describes infants' initial state as well as changes brought about by experience with language (figure 8.4). The model demonstrates how infants' developing native-language speech representations might alter both speech perception and production. The same principles apply to both vowel and consonant perception, and the example developed here is for vowels.

Phase 1 describes infants' initial abilities. At birth, infants discriminate the phonetic distinctions of all lan-

guages of the world. This is illustrated by a hypothetical F1/F2 coordinate vowel space partitioned into categories (figure 8.4A). These divisions separate perceptually the vowels of all languages. According to NLM, infants' abilities to hear all the relevant differences at this stage do not depend on specific language experience. Infants discriminate language sounds they have never heard.

The boundaries shown in phase 1 initially structure perception in a phonetically relevant way. However, these predispositions seen in humans at birth are not likely to be due to a "language module." This notion is buttressed by the fact that nonhuman animals also show this phenomenon, displaying abilities that were once thought to be exclusively human (Kuhl and Miller, 1975, 1978; Kuhl, 1991a; see also Kluender, Diehl, and Killeen, 1987, and Dooling, Best, and Brown, 1995, for demonstrations of speech perception abilities in nonhumans). This has been interpreted as evidence that the evolution of speech capitalized on sound distinctions well separated by the auditory system (Kuhl, 1989, 1991a).

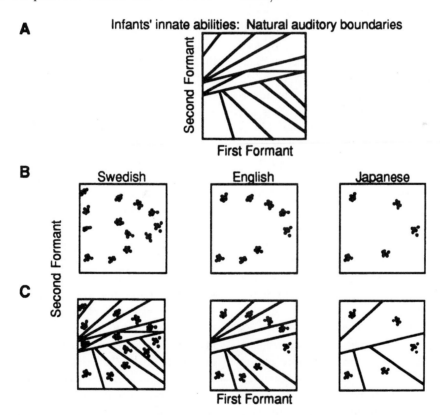

FIGURE 8.4 The native language magnet (NLM) model. (A) At birth, infants perceptually partition the acoustic space underlying phonetic distinctions in a language-universal way. They are capable of discriminating all phonetically relevant differences in the world's languages. (B) By 6 months of age, infants reared in different linguistic environments show an effect of language experience. Infants store incoming vowel informa-

tion in memory in some form. The resulting representations (shown by the dots) are language-specific, and reflect the distributional properties of vowels in the three different languages. (C) After language-specific magnet effects appear, some of the natural boundaries that existed at birth "disappear." Infants now fail to discriminate foreign-language contrasts they once discriminated.

Phase 2 describes the vowel space at 6 months of age for infants reared in three very different language environments, Swedish, English, and Japanese (figure 8.4B). By 6 months of age, infants show more than the ability to perceptually separate all phonetic categories, as shown in phase 1. The distributional properties of vowels heard by infants being raised in Sweden, America, and Japan differ. According to NLM, infants mentally represent this ambient language information (as shown in figure 8.4B), and their mental representations produce language-specific magnet effects. Thus, by 6 months, language-specific perceptual maps have begun to form.

Interesting questions about phase 2 magnet effects are: How much language input does it take to map speech in this way, and is all language heard by the child (including that from a radio or television) effective in producing this kind of learning? In fact, this was the question asked of me by President William J. Clinton at the White House Conference on "Early Learning and the Brain" in April of 1997. My answer was that at present we have no idea how much language input it takes to show these effects. Moreover, we do not know whether language from a disembodied source (TV, radio) would be sufficient to produce it. By 6 months of age, the earliest age for which we have evidence of magnet effects, our estimates suggest that infants have heard thousands of instances of vowels in *en face* communication with their parents (Kuhl, 1994), but that does not tell us what amount is necessary or whether TV is effective. These questions will require a great deal more work, and we have studies underway that will provide some interesting information.

Phase 3 shows how magnet effects recursively alter the initial state of speech perception, and affect the processing of foreign-language stimuli. Magnet effects cause certain perceptual distinctions to be minimized (those near the magnet attractors) while others are maximized (those near the boundaries between two magnets). The consequence is that some of the boundaries that initially divided the space disappear as the perceptual space is reconfigured to incorporate a language's particular magnet placement (figure 8.4C). Magnet effects functionally erase certain boundaries–those relevant to foreign but not native languages. Listeners' auditory systems still process the acoustic differences that separate categories, but their maps indicate that listeners no longer attend to these differences.

In Phase 3, a perceptual space once characterized by basic "auditory cuts"–boundaries that divide all speech categories, and ones demonstrated in nonhuman animals–has been replaced by a dramatically warped space dominated by magnet effects that completely restructure

the space. It is at this phase that infants fail to discriminate foreign-language contrasts that were once discriminable. The mapping of incoming speech has altered which stimulus differences infants respond to, producing a language-specific listener for the first time.

A natural question arising from these data is, what would happen to infants exposed to two different languages. The theory predicts that infants will develop magnet effects for the sound categories of both languages. Interestingly, preliminary data from studies underway suggest that development of two sets of magnet effects is particularly likely when the two languages are spoken by different speakers (mother speaks one language, father speaks another). Presumably, mapping two languages, each spoken by a different speaker, is made easier when infants can separate perceptually the maps for the two languages.

NLM theory offers an explanation for the developmental change observed in speech perception. A developing magnet pulls sounds that were once discriminable toward it, making them less discriminable. Magnet effects should therefore developmentally precede changes in infants' perception of foreign-language contrasts; data indicate that they do (Werker and Polka, 1993). The magnet effect also helps account for the results of studies on the perception of sounds from a foreign language by adults (Best, 1993; Flege, 1993). For example, NLM theory may help explain Japanese listeners' difficulty with American /r/ and /l/. The magnet effect for the Japanese /r/ category prototype (which is neither American /r/ nor /l/) will attract both /r/ and /l/, making the two sounds difficult for native-speaking Japanese people to discriminate (Kuhl et al., submitted). NLM theory argues that early experience establishes a complex perceptual network through which language passes. On this view, one's primary language, and the map that results from early experience, will determine how other languages are perceived.

From a neuroscience perspective, it is of interest to ask whether the developmental change seen in infants' perception of speech is *selective* or *instructive*. Neuroscientists are tempted to relate the finding that synaptic connections are overproduced and then pruned to the developmental time course seen in infants listening to speech, arguing that experience results in selection. But the comparison may not capture the essence of the process. If infants' initial abilities, shared by animals, are simply due to general auditory perceptual mechanisms, while their eventual failures to discriminate are due to the attentional filters produced by magnet effects, what we have to explain physiologically is how the neural system codes these mental maps. The maps would appear to require instruction–some new neural entity sculpted by experience. Could the development of mental maps be accounted for by physiological processes we now understand, such as synaptic pruning, or is something else needed? These questions will undoubtedly keep us busy for some time.

Reinterpreting "critical periods"

The interaction between genetic programming and environmental stimulation is nowhere more evident than in the literature on critical periods in learning (Thorpe, 1961; Marler, 1970). Critical periods are no longer viewed as strictly timed developmental processes with rigid cut-off periods that restrict learning to a specific time frame. Recent studies showing that learning can be stretched by a variety of factors have caused a shift in the terminology used to refer to this period. It is now understood that during "sensitive periods" exposure to specific kinds of information may be more effective than at other times, but that a variety of factors can alter the period of learning. Knudsen's work, for example, on the sound-localization system in the barn owl, shows that the sensitive period for learning the auditory-visual map in the optic tectum can be altered by a variety of factors that either shorten or extend the learning period; the learning period closes much earlier, for instance, if experience occurs in a more natural environment (Knudsen and Knudsen, 1990; Knudsen and Brainerd, 1995).

The idea that sensitive periods define "windows of opportunity" for learning, during which environmental stimulation is highly effective in producing developmental change, remains well supported both in the human and the animal literature. The ability to learn is not equivalent over time. The question is: What causes a decline in the ability to learn over the life span?

The sensitive period denotes a process of learning that is constrained primarily by time, or factors such as hormones, that are outside the learning process itself. There is an alternative possibility suggested by the studies on speech: Later learning may be limited by the fact that learning itself alters the brain, and the brain's resulting structure may produce a kind of interference effect that impacts later learning. For instance, if NLM's argument that learning involves the creation of mental maps for speech is true, this would mean that learning "commits" neural structure in some way. According to the model, speech processing is affected by this neural structure, and future learning is as well. The mechanisms governing an organism's general ability to learn may not have changed. Rather, initial learning may result in a structure that reflects environmental input and, once committed, the learned structure may interfere with the processing of information that does not conform to the learned pattern. On this account, initial learning can alter future learning independent of a strictly timed period.

On this *interference* account, brain "plasticity" (ability to change) would be governed from a statistical standpoint. When additional input does not cause the overall statistical distribution to change substantially, the organism becomes less sensitive to input. Hypothetically, for instance, the infant's representation of the vowel /a/ might not change when the millionth token of the vowel /a/ is heard. Plasticity might thus be independent of time, but dependent on the amount and variability provided by experience. At some time in the life of an organism, one could conceive of a point beyond which new input no longer alters the underlying distribution, and this could, at least in principle, reduce the system's plasticity.

The interference view may account for some aspects of second language learning. When acquiring a second language, certain phonetic distinctions are notoriously difficult to master both in speech perception and production. Take the case of the /r-l/ distinction for native speakers of Japanese. Both hearing the distinction and producing it are very difficult for native speakers of Japanese (Goto, 1971; Miyawaki et al., 1975; Yamada and Tohkura, 1992). According to NLM, this is because exposure to Japanese early in life altered the Japanese infant's perceptual system, resulting in magnet effects for the Japanese phoneme /r/, but not for the American English /r/ or /l/. Once in place, Japanese magnet effects would not make it easy to process American English. American English /r/ and /l/ would be assimilated to Japanese /r/ (Kuhl et al., submitted).

A second language learned later in life (after puberty) may require separation between the two systems to avoid interference. Data gathered using fMRI techniques indicate that adult bilinguals who learned both languages early in life activate overlapping regions of the brain when processing the two languages, while those who learned the second language later activate two distinct regions of the brain for the two languages (Kim et al., 1997). This is consistent with the idea that the brain's processing of a primary language can interfere with the second language. This problem is avoided if both are learned early in development.

The general thesis is that acquiring new phonetic categories as adults is difficult because the brain's mental maps for speech, formed on the basis of the primary language, are incompatible with those required for the new language; hence, interference results. Early in life, interference effects are minimal and new categories can be acquired because input continues to revise the statistical distribution. As mentioned earlier, limited evidence suggests that infants exposed to two languages do much better if each parent speaks one of the two languages than when both parents speak both languages. This may be because it is easier to map two different sets of phonetic categories (one for each of the two languages) if there is some way to keep them perceptually separate. Males and females produce speech in different frequency ranges, and this could make it easier to maintain separation.

These two factors–a maturationally defined temporal window governed by genetic factors, and the neural commitment that results from initial learning–could both be operating to produce constraints on learning a second language later in life. If a maturational process induces neural readiness at a particular time, input that misses this timing could reduce learning. At the same time, an interference factor produced by mapping language input might provide an independent mechanism that contributes to the difficulty in readily learning a second language in adulthood.

Vocal learning

Vocal learning–an organism's dependence on auditory input both from itself and others to acquire a vocal repertoire–is not common among mammals, but is exhibited strikingly in songbirds (Marler 1990; Konishi, 1989). In certain songbirds, and in humans, young members of the species not only learn the perceptual properties of their conspecific communicative signals, but also become proficient producers of those signals. A great deal of research on birds (see Doupe, 1998, for review) and infants (Stoel-Gammon and Otomo, 1986; Oller et al., 1976) has shown that hearing the vocalizations of others, and hearing oneself produce sound, are both essential to the development of vocalizations. Deaf infants, for ex-

ample, do not babble normally (Oller and MacNeilage, 1983), nor do deafened birds (Konishi, 1965; Nottebohm, 1967). And infants tracheotomized at the time at which they would normally be babbling also results in abnormal patterns of development that persist (Locke and Pearson, 1990).

In the case of humans, speech motor patterns learned at the appropriate time become difficult to alter later in life. Speakers who learn a second language after puberty, for example, produce it with an accent typical of their primary language (Flege, 1993). Most speakers of a second language would like to speak like a native speaker, without an accent, but this is difficult to do, even with long-term instruction.

When do we adopt the indelible speech patterns that will mark us as native speakers of a particular language for our entire lives? Developmental studies suggest that by one year of age language-specific patterns of speech production appear in infants' spontaneous utterances (de Boysson-Bardies, 1993; Vihman and de Boysson-Bardies, 1994). However, the fundamental capacity to reproduce the sound patterns one hears is in place much earlier. In a recent study, Kuhl and Meltzoff (1996) recorded infant utterances at 12, 16, and 20 weeks of age while the infants watched and listened to a video recording of a woman producing a vowel, /a/, /i/, or /u/. Infants watched the video for 5 minutes on each of three consecutive days. The results showed a developmental change in infants' vowel productions between 12 and 20 weeks of age. The areas of vowel space occupied by infants' /a/, /i/, and /u/ vowels become progressively more tightly clustered at each age, and by 20 weeks, a "vowel triangle" typical of that produced in every language of the world, had emerged in the infants' own region of the vowel space (figure 8.5). This demonstrated that between 12 and 20 weeks of age, infants' sound pro-

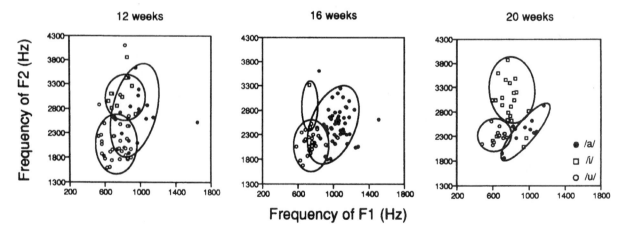

FIGURE 8.5 The location of /a/, /i/, and /u/ vowels produced by 12-, 16-, and 20-week-old infants. Infants' vowel productions show progressively tighter clustering in vowel space over the 8-week period and reflect differences between the three vowel categories seen in adults' productions.

ductions were changing in a way that brought them closer to the adult pattern.

Direct evidence that infants were vocally imitating was also obtained in the study. By 20 weeks, infants were shown to reproduce the vowels they heard. Infants exposed to /a/ were more likely to produce /a/ than when exposed to either /i/ or /u/; similarly, infants exposed to either /i/ or /u/ were more likely to produce the vowel in that condition than when listening to either of the two alternate vowels. The total amount of exposure to a specific vowel in the laboratory was just 15 minutes; yet this was sufficient to influence infants' productions. If 15 minutes of laboratory exposure to a vowel is sufficient to influence infants' vocalizations, then listening to ambient language for weeks would be expected to provide a powerful influence on infants' production of speech. These data suggest that infants' stored representations of speech not only alter infant perception, but alter production as well, serving as auditory patterns that guide motor production. Stored representations are thus viewed as the common cause for both the tighter clustering observed in infant vowel production and the tighter clustering observed in infant vowel perception (figure 8.6).

This pattern of learning and self-organization, in which perceptual patterns stored in memory serve as guides for production, is strikingly similar for birdsong and speech (Doupe and Kuhl, 1999), in visual-motor learning in which such nonspeech oral movements as tongue protrusion and mouth opening are imitated

(Meltzoff and Moore, 1977, 1994), and in language involving both sign (Petitto and Marentette, 1991) and speech (Kuhl and Meltzoff, 1996). In each of these cases, perceptual experience establishes a representation that guides sensorimotor learning. In the case of infants and speech, perception affects production in the earliest stages of language learning, reinforcing the idea that the speech motor patterns of a specific language are formed very early in life. Once learned, motor patterns may also further development by altering the probability that infants will acquire words that contain items they are capable of producing.

The role of vision in speech perception

The link between perception and production can be seen in another experimental situation in speech, and there is some suggestion that this is mirrored in birdsong learning. Speech perception in adults is strongly affected by the sight of a talker's mouth movements during speech, indicating that our representational codes for speech contain both auditory and visual information. One of the most compelling examples of the polymodal nature of speech representations is auditory-visual illusions that result when discrepant information is sent to two separate modalities. One such illusion occurs when auditory information for /b/ is combined with visual information for /g/ (McGurk and MacDonald, 1976; Green et al., 1991; Kuhl et al., 1994; Massaro, 1987). Perceivers report the phenomenal

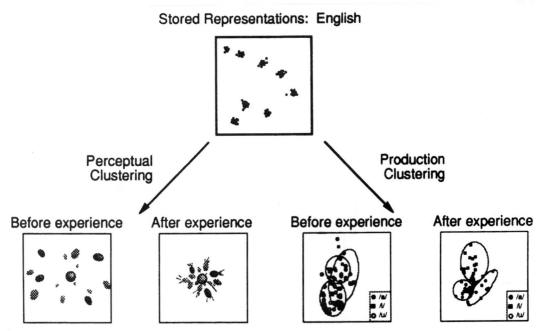

FIGURE 8.6 Stored representations of native-language speech affect both speech perception, producing the perceptual clustering evidenced by the magnet effect, as well as speech pro-

duction, producing the increased clustering seen in infants' vocalizations over time.

impression of an intermediate articulation (/da/ or /tha/) despite the fact that this information was not delivered by or to either sense modality. This is a very robust phenomenon and is readily obtained even when the information from the two modalities comes from different speakers, such as when a male voice is combined with a female face (Green et al., 1991). In this case, there is no doubt that the auditory and visual signals do not belong together. Yet the illusion is still unavoidable—our perceptual systems combine the multimodal information (auditory and visual) to give a unified percept.

Young infants are also affected by visual information. Infants just 18–20 weeks old recognize auditory-visual correspondences for speech, akin to what adults do when lipreading. In these studies, infants looked longer at a matching face—one pronouncing a vowel that matched the vowel sound they heard—than at a mismatched face (Kuhl and Meltzoff, 1982). Young infants demonstrate knowledge about both the auditory and visual information contained in speech, supporting the notion that infants' stored speech representations contain information of both kinds. Additional demonstrations of auditory-visual speech perception in infants suggest that there is a left-hemisphere involvement in the process (MacKain et al., 1983), and more recent data by Rosenblum, Schmuckler, and Johnson (1997) and Walton and Bower (1993) suggest that the ability to match auditory and visual speech is present in newborns.

Visual information thus plays a very strong role in speech perception. When listeners watch the face of the talker, studies show that perception of the message is greatly enhanced, in effect contributing the equivalent of

a 20-dB boost (quite substantial) in the signal. This supports the view that speech in humans is polymodally represented, and that this is the case very early in development.

Nature of language input to the child

Research supports the idea that caretakers around the world use a near-universal speaking style when addressing infants and that infants prefer it over other complex acoustic signals (Fernald, 1985; Fernald and Kuhl, 1987). Estimates indicate that a typical listening day for a 2-year-old includes 20,000–40,000 words (Chapman et al., 1992). Speech addressed to infants (often called "motherese" or "parentese") is unique: It has a characteristic prosodic structure with a higher pitch, a slower tempo, and exaggerated intonation contours, and it is syntactically and semantically simplified.

In new studies, we have uncovered another modification parents make when addressing infants—one that may be important to infant learning. We examined natural language input at the phonetic level to infants in the United States, Russia, and Sweden (Kuhl, Andruski, et al., 1997). The study shows that across three very diverse languages, infant-directed speech exhibited a universal alteration of phonetic units when compared to adult-directed speech. Parents addressing their infants produced acoustically more extreme tokens of vowel sounds, resulting in a "stretching" of the acoustic space encompassing the vowel triangle (figure 8.7). A stretched vowel triangle not only makes speech more discriminable for infants, it also highlights critical spectral parameters that allow speech to be produced by the child. The results suggest that at

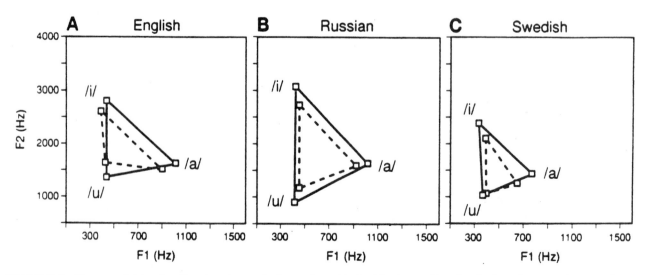

FIGURE 8.7 The vowel triangle of maternal speech directed toward infants (solid line) across three diverse languages shows a "stretching" relative to the adult-directed vowel triangle (dashed line), an effect that both makes vowels more discriminable and highlights the abstract features that infants must use to produce speech themselves.

the phonetic level of language, linguistic input to infants provides exceptionally well-specified information about the units that form the building blocks for words.

Thus, when adults speak to normally developing infants, they enhance phonetic distinctions. In recent studies, language-delayed children showed substantial improvements in measures of speech and language after treatment in a program in which they listened to speech altered by computer to exaggerate phonetic differences (Merzenich et al., 1996; Tallal et al., 1996). This kind of speech may aid infants' discovery of the dimensions of sound that they need to attend to in order to process speech efficiently. In the study, mothers' vowels in speech to children were what acousticians call "hyperarticulated" (Lindblom, 1990), ones that are perceived by adults as better instances of vowel categories (Iverson and Kuhl, 1995; Johnson, Flemming, and Wright, 1993). Parental speech thus contains more prototypical instances, and as shown in the work reviewed previously, these are the very kinds of sounds that produce the perceptual magnet effect. Language input to infants may therefore provide an ideal signal for constructing perceptual maps.

Brain correlates

Since the classic reports of Broca and Wernicke on patients with language deficits typical of aphasia, we have known that the two hemispheres are not equal in the extent to which they subserve language. In the 1960s, behavioral studies on language processing in normal adults contributed additional evidence of the left-hemisphere specialization for language, showing a dissociation for processing speech (left hemisphere) and nonspeech (right hemisphere) signals (Kimura, 1961).

Studies of the brain's organization of language have appeared in increasing numbers with the advent of modern neuroimaging techniques such as PET, positron emission tomography (Peterson et al., 1990; Posner et al., 1988); fMRI, functional magnetic resonance imaging, (Neville et al., 1998); ERP, event-related potentials (Neville, Mills, and Lawson, 1992; Osterhout and Holcomb, 1992); and MEG, magnetoencephalography (Näätänen et al., 1997). While this field is still emergent, there are some conclusions that take us beyond what early studies have shown regarding language and the brain. The new studies suggest, for example, that there is not one unified "language area" in the brain where linguistic signals are processed. Different brain systems subserve different aspects of language processing, and the language processing areas of the brain include many more regions than the classic Broca's and Wernicke's areas.

The imaging studies confirm a dissociation for processing speech and nonspeech signals found in earlier behavioral studies. One study (Zatorre et al., 1992) used PET scans to examine phonetic as opposed to pitch processing. Subjects in the study had to judge the final consonant of the syllable in the phonetic task and the pitch of the syllable (high or low) in the pitch task. The results showed that phonetic processing engaged the LH while pitch processing engaged the RH. This dissociation between the phonetic and nonphonetic processing of auditory dimensions is mirrored in studies using vowels at different pitches and MEG (Poeppel et al., 1997).

Given these results, an important question from the standpoint of development is when the left hemisphere becomes dominant in the processing of linguistic information. Lenneberg (1967) hypothesized that the two hemispheres are equipotential for language until approximately two years of age, at which time LH dominance begins to develop and continues until puberty. However, this theory is contradicted by data suggesting that children with LH versus RH damage at an early age displayed different deficits in language abilities: Early LH damage affects language abilities more than early RH damage (Witelson, 1987).

Behavioral studies have established the right-ear advantage (REA) for speech for verbal stimuli and the left-ear advantage (LEA) for musical and environmental sounds using the dichotic listening task in children as young as 2.5 years (Bever, 1971; Kimura, 1963). But what of infants? Glanville, Best, and Levenson (1977) reported an REA for speech contrasts and an LEA for musical sounds using a cardiac orienting procedure in 3-month-olds. Only two studies provide data on infants' differential responses to speech and music at ages younger than 2 months. In one study, infants' discriminative capacities for speech and music were examined in 2-, 3-, and 4-month-old infants using a cardiac-orienting procedure. The results demonstrated an REA for speech discrimination in 3-month and 4-month-old infants, but not in 2-month-old infants. In addition, an LEA was shown for musical-note discrimination at all three ages. Finally, tests on 2-month-olds conducted by Vargha-Khadem and Corballis (1979) showed infants discriminated speech contrasts equally with both hemispheres. In other words, the results suggest that speech may not be lateralized in 2-month-old infants, but becomes so by 4 months of age.

This issue of the onset of laterality and the extent to which it depends on linguistic experience may be resolved with future research using techniques that can be used throughout the life span. One such technique is the mismatched negativity (MMN), a component of the auditorily evoked event-related potential (ERP). The MMN is automatically elicited by a discriminable change in a repetitive sound pattern and its generation appears to represent the detection of a change in the neural sensory-memory representation established by the repeated stimulus (see Näätänen, 1990, 1992, for review). MMNs to a change in a speech stimulus have been well documented in adult listeners (e.g., Kraus et al., 1992). The MMN has been established in children (Kraus et al., 1993) and most recently in infants (Cheour-Luhtanen et al., 1995; Kuhl, 1998b; Pang et al., 1998). In adult ERP studies, a left-hemisphere asymmetry is evident (Pang et al., 1998), but it has not been observed in newborns (Cheour-Luhtanen et al., 1995).

In summary, there is no strong evidence at present that the bias toward left-hemisphere processing for language is present at birth. The data suggest that it may take experience with linguistically patterned information to produce the left-hemisphere specialization. Thus, there is support for a specialization for language in infancy, but one that develops, rather than one that exists at birth. Moreover, the input that is eventually lateralized to the left hemisphere can be either speech or sign, indicating that it is the linguistic/communicative significance of the signals, rather than their specific form, that accounts for the specialization.

Conclusions

Research has shown that in the first year of life infants learn a great deal about the perceptual characteristics of their native language, and this subsequently alters the perception and production of speech. According to the native language magnet model, perceptual learning early in life results in the formation of stored representations that capture native-language regularities. The theory emphasizes the role of linguistic input. Input does not act like a trigger for innately stored information. Rather, it is mapped in such a way as to "warp" the underlying acoustic space. Stored representations act like perceptual magnets for similar patterns of sound, resulting in maps that specify perceived distances between sounds, and create categories. The map shrinks perceptual distances near a category's most typical instances and stretches perceptual distances between categories. Perceptual maps differ in adults who speak different languages and are polymodally mapped, containing auditory, visual, and motor information. The magnet effects and the mental maps they produce help explain how native-language speech develops, as well as the relative inability of adults to readily acquire a foreign language.

ACKNOWLEDGMENTS Supported by grants to the author from the National Institutes of Health (DC00520, HD18286).

REFERENCES

ABRAMSON, A. S., and L. LISKER, 1970. Discriminability along the voicing continuum: Cross-language tests. In *Proceedings of the Sixth International Congress of Phonetic Sciences Prague 1967*. Prague: Academia, pp. 569–573.

BATES, E., and J. ELMAN, 1996. Learning rediscovered. *Science* 274:1849–1850.

BATESON, P., 1991. Are there principles of behavioral development? In *The Development and Integration of Behaviour*, P. Bateson, ed. Cambridge, U.K.: Cambridge University Press, pp. 19–39.

BEST, C. T., 1993. Language-specific changes in non-native speech perception: A window on early phonological development. In *Developmental Neurocognition: Speech and Face Processing in the First Year of Life*, B. de Boysson-Bardies, S. de Schonen, P. Jusczyk, P. McNeilage, and J. Morton, eds. Dordrecht: Kluwer, pp. 289–304.

BEVER, T. G., 1971. The nature of cerebral dominance in speech behavior of the child and adult. In *Language Acquisition: Models and Methods*, R. Huxley and R. Ingham, eds. London: Academic Press.

BONHOEFFER, T., and C. J. SHATZ, 1998. Neurotrophins and visual system plasticity. In *Mechanistic Relationships between Development and Learning*, T. J. Carew, R. Menzel, and C. J. Shatz, eds. New York: Wiley, pp. 93–112.

CAJAL, R. S., 1906 [1967]. The structure and connections of neurons. In *Nobel Lectures in Physiology or Medicine 1901–1921*. New York: Elsevier, pp. 220–253.

CAREW, T. J., R. MENZEL, and C. J. SHATZ, 1998. *Mechanistic Relationships between Development and Learning*. New York: Wiley.

CAREY, S., 1985. *Conceptual Change in Childhood*. Cambridge, Mass.: MIT Press.

CHAPMAN, R. S., N. W. STREIM, E. R. CRAIS, D. SALMON, E. A. STRAND, and N. A. NEGRI, 1992. Child talk: Assumptions of a developmental process model for early language learning. In *Processes in Language Acquisition and Disorders*, R. S. Chapman, ed. St. Louis: Mosby, pp. 3–19.

CHEOUR-LUHTANEN, M., K. ALHO, T. KUJALA, K. SAINIO, K. REINIKAINEN, M. RENLUND, O. AALTONEN, O. EEROLA, and R. NÄÄTÄNEN, 1995. Mismatch negativity indicates vowel discrimination in newborns. *Hearing Res.* 82:53–58.

CHOMSKY, N., 1957. A review of B. F. Skinner's *Verbal Behavior. Language* 35:26–58.

CHOMSKY, N., 1965. *Aspects of the Theory of Syntax*. Cambridge, Mass.: MIT Press.

CHOMSKY, N., 1981. *Rules and Representations*. New York: Columbia University Press.

CURTISS, S., 1977. *Genie: A Psycholinguistic Study of a Modern Day "Wild Child."* New York: Academic Press.

DE BOYSSON-BARDIES, B., 1993. Ontogeny of language-specific syllabic productions. In *Developmental Neurocognition: Speech and Face Processing in the First Year of Life*, B. de Boysson-Bardies, S. de Schonen, P. Jusczyk, P. McNeilage, and J. Morton, eds. Dordrecht: Kluwer, pp. 353–363.

DOOLING, R. J., C. T. BEST, and S. D. BROWN, 1995. Discrimination of synthetic full-formant and sinewave /ra-la/ continua by budgerigars (*Melopsittacus undulatus*) and zebra finches (*Taeniopygia guttata*). *J. Acoust. Soc. Amer.* 97:1839–1846.

DOUPE, A., 1998. Development and learning in the bird-song system: Are there shared mechanisms? In *Mechanistic Relationships between Development and Learning*, T. J. Carew, R. Menzel, and C. J. Shatz, eds. New York: Wiley, pp. 29–52.

DOUPE, A., and P. K. KUHL, 1999. Birdsong and speech: Common themes and mechanisms. *Annu. Rev. Neurosci.* 22:567–631.

EIMAS, P. D., J. L. MILLER, and P. W. JUSCZYK, 1987. On infant speech perception and the acquisition of language. In *Categorical Perception: The Groundwork of Cognition*, S. Harnad, ed. New York: Cambridge University Press, pp. 161–195.

FANSELOW, M. S., and J. W. RUDY, 1998. Convergence of experimental and developmental approaches to animal learning and memory processes. In *Mechanistic Relationships between Development and Learning*, T. J. Carew, R. Menzel, and C. J. Shatz, eds. New York: Wiley, pp. 15–28.

FERGUSON, C. A., L. MENN, and C. STOEL-GAMMON (eds.), 1992. *Phonological Development: Models, Research, Implications.* Timonium, Md.: York.

FERNALD, A., 1985. Four-month-old infants prefer to listen to motherese. *Infant Behav. Dev.* 8:181–195.

FERNALD, A., and P. KUHL, 1987. Acoustic determinants of infant preference for motherese speech. *Infant Behav. Dev.* 10: 279–293.

FLEGE, J. E., 1988. Factors affecting degree of perceived foreign accent in English sentences. *J. Acoust. Soc. Amer.* 84:70–79.

FLEGE, J. E., 1993. Production and perception of a novel, second-language phonetic contrast. *J. Acoust. Soc. Amer.* 93:1589–1608.

FROMKIN, V., S. KRASHEN, S. CURTIS, D. RIGLER, and M. RIGLER, 1974. The development of language in Genie: A case of language acquisition beyond the "critical period." *Brain Lang.* 1:81–107.

GLANVILLE, B. B., C. T. BEST, and R. LEVENSON, 1977. A cardiac measure of cerebral asymmetries in infant auditory perception. *Dev. Psych.* 13:54–59.

GOPNIK, A., and A. N. MELTZOFF, 1997. *Words, Thoughts, and Theories.* Cambridge, Mass.: MIT Press.

GOTO, H., 1971. Auditory perception by normal Japanese adults of the sounds "l" and "r." *Neuropsychologia* 9:317–323.

GREEN, K. P., P. K. KUHL, A. N. MELTZOFF, and E. B. STEVENS, 1991. Integrating speech information across talkers, gender, and sensory modality: Female faces and male voices in the McGurk effect. *Percept. Psychophysiol.* 50:524–536.

GREENOUGH, W. T., and J. E. BLACK, 1992. Induction of brain structure by experience: Substrates for cognitive development. In *The Minnesota Symposia on Child Psychology, Vol. 24: Developmental Behavioral Neuroscience*, M. Gunnar and C. Nelson, eds. Hillsdale, N.J.: Erlbaum, pp. 155–200.

GRIESER, D., and P. K. KUHL, 1989. Categorization of speech by infants: Support for speech-sound prototypes. *Dev. Psych.* 25:577–588.

HAUSER, M. D., 1997. *The Evolution of Communication.* Cambridge, Mass.: MIT Press.

IVERSON, P., and P. K. KUHL, 1995. Mapping the perceptual magnet effect for speech using signal detection theory and multidimensional scaling. *J. Acoust. Soc. Amer.* 97:553–562.

IVERSON, P., and P. K. KUHL, 1996. Influences of phonetic identification and category goodness on American listeners' perception of /r/ and /l/. *J. Acoust. Soc. Amer.* 99:1130–1140.

JAMES, W., 1890 [1958]. *Principles of Psychology.* New York: Holt.

JOHNSON, K., E. FLEMMING, and R. WRIGHT, 1993. The hyperspace effect: Phonetic targets are hyperarticulated. *Language* 69:505–528.

JUSCZYK, P. W., A. D. FRIEDERICI, J. M. I. WESSELS, V. Y. SVENKERUD, and A. M. JUSCZYK, 1993. Infants' sensitivity to the sound patterns of native language words. *J. Mem. Lang.* 32:402–420.

KARMILOFF-SMITH, A., 1991. Beyond modularity: Innate constraints and developmental change. In *The Epigenesis of Mind: Essays on Biology and Cognition*, S. Carey and R. Gelman, eds. Hillsdale, N.J.: Erlbaum, pp. 171–197.

KARMILOFF-SMITH, A., 1995. Annotation: The extraordinary cognitive journey from foetus through infancy. *J. Child Psych. Psychiat. All. Disc.* 36:1293–1313.

KIM, K. H. S., N. R. RELKIN, K. M. LEE, and J. HIRSCH, 1997. Distinct cortical areas associated with native and second languages. *Nature* 388:172–174.

KIMURA, D., 1961. Cerebral dominance and the perception of verbal stimuli. *Can. J Psychol.* 15:166–171.

KIMURA, D., 1963. Speech lateralization in young children as determined by an auditory test. *J. Comp. Physiol. Psych.* 56:899–902.

KLUENDER, K. R., R. L. DIEHL, and P. R. KILLEEN, 1987. Japanese quail can learn phonetic categories. *Science* 237:1195–1197.

KNUDSEN, E. I., and M. S. BRAINERD, 1995. Creating a unified representation of visual and auditory space in the brain. *Annu. Rev. Neurosci.* 18:19–43.

KNUDSEN, E. I., and P. F. KNUDSEN, 1990. Sensitive and critical periods for visual calibration of sound localization by barn owls. *J. Neurosci.* 10:222–232.

KOFFKA, K., 1924. *The Growth of the Mind.* New York: Harcourt Brace.

KONISHI, M., 1965. Effects of deafening on song development in American robins and black-headed grosbeaks. *Zeitschrift Tierpsychol.* 22:584–599.

KONISHI, M., 1989. Birdsong for neurobiologists. *Neuron* 3:541–549.

KRAUS, N., T. MCGEE, A. MICCO, A. SHARMA, T. CARRELL, and T. NICOL, 1993. Mismatch negativity in school-age children to speech stimuli that are just perceptibly different. *Electroenceph. Clin. Neurophysiol.* 88:123–130.

KRAUS, N., T. MCGEE, A. SHARMA, T. CARRELL, and T. NICOL, 1992. Mismatch negativity event-related potential elicited by speech stimuli. *Ear and Hearing* 13:158–164.

KUHL, P. K., 1989. On babies, birds, modules, and mechanisms: A comparative approach to the acquisition of vocal communication. In *The Comparative Psychology of Audition: Perceiving Complex Sounds*, R. J. Dooling and S. H. Hulse, eds. Hillsdale, N.J.: Erlbaum, pp. 379–419.

KUHL, P. K., 1991a. Human adults and human infants show a "perceptual magnet effect" for the prototypes of speech categories, monkeys do not. *Percept. Psychophysiol.* 50:93–107.

KUHL, P. K., 1991b. Perception, cognition, and the ontogenetic and phylogenetic emergence of human speech. In

Plasticity of Development, S. E. Brauth, W. S. Hall, and R. J. Dooling, eds. Cambridge, Mass.: MIT Press, pp. 73–106.

KUHL, P. K., 1992. Infants' perception and representation of speech: Development of a new theory. In *Proceedings of the International Conference on Spoken Language Processing*, J. J. Ohala, T. M. Nearey, B. L. Derwing, M. M. Hodge, and G. E. Wiebe, eds. Edmonton, Alberta: University of Alberta, pp. 449–456.

KUHL, P. K., 1994. Learning and representation in speech and language. *Curr. Opin. Neurobiol.* 4:812–822.

KUHL, P. K., 1998a. The development of speech and language. In *Mechanistic Relationships between Development and Learning*, T. J. Carew, R. Menzel, C. J. Shatz, eds. New York: Wiley, pp. 53–73.

KUHL, P. K., 1998b. Effects of language experience on speech perception. *J. Acoust. Soc. Amer.* 103:29–31.

KUHL, P. K., J. E. ANDRUSKI, I. A. CHISTOVICH, L. A. CHISTOVICH, E. V. KOZHEVNIKOVA, V. L. RYSKINA, E. I. STOLYAROVA, U. SUNDBERG, and F. LACERDA, 1997. Cross-language analysis of phonetic units in language addressed to infants. *Science* 277:684–686.

KUHL, P. K., S. KIRTANI, T. DEGUCHI, A. HAYASHI, E. B. STEVENS, C. D. DUGGER, and P. IVERSON, 1997. Effects of language experience on speech perception: American and Japanese infants' perception of /ra/ and /la/. *J. Acoust. Soc. Amer.* 102:3135.

KUHL, P. K., and A. N. MELTZOFF, 1982. The bimodal perception of speech in infancy. *Science* 218:1138–1141.

KUHL, P. K., and A. N. MELTZOFF, 1996. Infant vocalizations in response to speech: Vocal imitation and developmental change. *J. Acoust. Soc. Amer.* 100:2425–2438.

KUHL, P. K., and J. D. MILLER, 1975. Speech perception by the chinchilla: Voiced-voiceless distinction in alveolar plosive consonants. *Science* 190:69–72.

KUHL, P. K., and J. D. MILLER, 1978. Speech perception by the chinchilla: Identification functions for synthetic VOT stimuli. *J. Acoust. Soc. Amer.* 63:905–917.

KUHL, P. K., M. TSUZAKI, Y. TOHKURA, and A. N. MELTZOFF, 1994. Human processing of auditory-visual information in speech perception: Potential for multimodal human-machine interfaces. In *Proceedings of the International Conference on Spoken Language Processing*. Tokyo: Acoustical Society of Japan, pp. 539–542.

KUHL, P. K., K. A. WILLIAMS, F. LACERDA, K. N. STEVENS, and B. LINDBLOM, 1992. Linguistic experience alters phonetic perception in infants by 6 months of age. *Science* 255:606–608.

KUHL, P. K., R. A. YAMADA, Y. TOHKURA, P. IVERSON, and E. B. STEVENS, submitted. Linguistic experience and the perception of American English /r/ and /l/: A comparison of Japanese and American listeners.

LANE, H. L., 1976. *The Wild Boy of Aveyron*. Cambridge, Mass.: Harvard University Press.

LENNEBERG, E. H., 1967. *Biological Foundations of Language*. New York: Wiley.

LINDBLOM, B., 1990. Explaining phonetic variation: A sketch of the HandH theory. In *Speech Production and Speech Modeling*, W. J. Hardcastle and A. Marchal, eds. Dordrecht: Kluwer, pp. 403–439.

LOCKE, J. L., and D. M. PEARSON, 1990. Linguistic significance of babbling: Evidence from a tracheostomized infant. *J. Child Lang.* 17:1–16.

LORENZ, K., 1965. *Evolution and Modification of Behavior*. Chicago: Chicago University Press.

MACKAIN, K., M. STUDDERT-KENNEDY, S. SPIEKER, and D. STERN, 1983. Infant intermodal speech perception is a left-hemisphere function. *Science* 219:1347–1349.

MARLER, P., 1970. A comparative approach to vocal learning: Song development in white-crowned sparrows. *J. Comp. Physiol. Psych.* 71:1–25.

MARLER, P., 1974. Constraints on learning: Development of bird song. In *Ethology and Psychiatry*, W. F. Norman, ed. Toronto: University of Toronto, pp. 69–83.

MARLER, P., 1990. Innate learning preferences: Signals for communication. *Dev. Psychobiol.* 23:557–568.

MASSARO, D. W., 1987. *Speech Perception by Ear and Eye: A Paradigm for Psychological Inquiry*. Hillsdale, N.J.: Erlbaum.

MCGURK, H., and J. MACDONALD, 1976. Hearing lips and seeing voices. *Nature* 264:746–748.

MELTZOFF, A. N., and M. K. MOORE, 1977. Imitation of facial and manual gestures by human neonates. *Science* 198:75–78.

MELTZOFF, A. N., and M. K. MOORE, 1994. Imitation, memory, and the representation of persons. *Infant Behav. Dev.* 17:83–99.

MERZENICH, M. M., W. M. JENKINS, P. JOHNSTON, C. SCHREINER, S. L. MILLER, and P. TALLAL, 1996. Temporal processing deficits of language-learning impaired children ameliorated by training. *Science* 271:77–81.

MILLER, J. L., 1994. On the internal structure of phonetic categories: A progress report. *Cognition* 50:271–285.

MIYAWAKI, K., W. STRANGE, R. VERBRUGGE, A. M. LIBERMAN, J. J. JENKINS, and O. FUJIMURA, 1975. An effect of linguistic experience: The discrimination of [r] and [l] by native speakers of Japanese and English. *Percept. Psychophysiol.* 18:331–340.

NÄÄTÄNEN, R., 1990. The role of attention in auditory information processing as revealed by event-related potentials and other brain measures of cognitive function. *Behav. Brain Sci.* 13:201–288.

NÄÄTÄNEN, R., 1992. The mismatch negativity (MMN). In *Attention and Brain Function*. Hillsdale, N.J.: Erlbaum, pp. 137–210.

NÄÄTÄNEN, R., A. LEHTOKOSKI, M. LENNES, M. CHEOUR, M. HUOTILAINEN, A. IIVONEN, M. VAINIO, P. ALKU, R.-J. ILMONIEMI, A. LUUK, J. ALLIK, J. SINKKONEN, and K. ALHO, 1997. Language-specific phoneme representations revealed by electric and magnetic brain responses. *Nature* 385:432–434.

NEVILLE, H. J., D. BAVELIER, D. CORINA, J. RAUSCHECKER, A. KARNI, A. LALWANI, A. BRAUN, V. CLARK, P. JEZZARD, and R. TURNER, 1998. Cerebral organization for language in deaf and hearing subjects: Biological constraints and effects of experience. *Proc. Natl. Acad. Sci. U.S.A.* 95:922–929.

NEVILLE, H. J., D. L. MILLS, and D. S. LAWSON, 1992. Fractionating language: Different neural subsystems with different sensitive periods. *Cerebral Cortex* 2:244–258.

NOTTEBOHM, F., 1967. The role of sensory feedback in the development of avian vocalizations. *Proceedings of the 14th International Ornithological Congress*, pp. 265–280.

OLLER, D. K., and P. F. MACNEILAGE, 1983. Development of speech production: Perspectives from natural and perturbed speech. In *The Production of Speech*, P. F. MacNeilage, ed. New York: Springer-Verlag, pp. 91–108.

OLLER, D. K., L. A. WIEMAN, W. J. DOYLE, and C. ROSS, 1976. Infant babbling and speech. *J. Child Lang.* 3:1–11.

OSTERHOUT, L., and P. L. HOLCOMB, 1992. Event-related brain potentials elicited by syntactic anomaly. *J. Mem. Lang.* 31:785–806.

PANG, E. W., G. E. EDMONDS, R. DESJARDINS, S. C. KHAN, L. J. TRAINOR, and M. J. TAYLOR, 1998. Mismatch negativity to speech stimuli in 8-month-old infants and adults. *Int. J. Psychophysiol.* 29:227–236.

PETERSEN, S. E., P. T. FOX, A. Z. SNYDER, and M. E. RAICHLE, 1990. Activation of extrastriate and frontal cortical areas by visual words and word-like stimuli. *Science* 249:1041–1044.

PETITTO, L. A., 1993. On the ontogenetic requirements for early language acquisition. In *Developmental Neurocognition: Speech and Face Processing in the First Year of Life*, B. de Boysson-Bardies, S. de Schonen, P. Jusczyk, P. McNeilage, and J. Morton, eds. Dordrecht: Kluwer, pp. 365–383.

PETITTO, L. A., and P. F. MARENTETTE, 1991. Babbling in the manual mode: Evidence for the ontogeny of language. *Science* 251:1493–1496.

PIAGET, J., 1954. *The Construction of Reality in the Child*. New York: Basic Books.

PINKER, S., 1994. *The Language Instinct*. New York: Morrow.

POEPPEL, D., C. PHILLIPS, E. YELLIN, H. A. ROWLEY, T. P. ROBERTS, and A. MARANTZ, 1997. Processing of vowels in supratemporal auditory cortex. *Neurosci. Lett.* 221:145–148.

POSNER, M. I., S. E. PETERSEN, P. T. FOX, and M. E. RAICHLE, 1988. Localization of cognitive operations in the human brain. *Science* 240:1627–1631.

ROSCH, E. H., 1977. Human categorization. In *Studies in Cross-Cultural Psychology*, Vol. 1, N. Warren, ed. New York: Academic Press, pp. 1–49.

ROSENBLUM, L. D., M. A. SCHMUCKLER, and J. A. JOHNSON, 1997. The McGurk effect in infants. *Percept. Psychophysiol.* 59:347–357.

SAFFRAN, J. R., R. N. ASLIN, and E. L. NEWPORT, 1996. Statistical learning by 8-month-old infants. *Science* 274:1926–1928.

SKINNER, B. F., 1957. *Verbal Behavior*. New York: Appleton-Century-Crofts.

STOEL-GAMMON, C., and K. OTOMO, 1986. Babbling development of hearing-impaired and normally hearing subjects. *J. Speech Hear. Disord.* 51:33–41.

STRANGE, W. (ed.), 1995. *Speech Perception and Linguistic Experience: Issues in Cross-Language Research*. Timonium, Md.: York.

SUSSMAN, J. E., and V. J. LAUCKNER-MORANO, 1995. Further tests of the "perceptual magnet effect" in the perception of [i]: Identification and change/no-change discrimination. *J. Acoust. Soc. Amer.* 97:539–552.

TALLAL, P., S. L. MILLER, G. BEDI, G. BYMA, X. WANG, S. S. NAGARAJAN, C. SCHREINER, W. M. JENKINS, and M. M. MERZENICH, 1996. Language comprehension in language-learning impaired children improved with acoustically modified speech. *Science* 271:81–84.

THORPE, W. H., 1959. Talking birds and the mode of action of the vocal apparatus of birds. *Proc. Zoolog. Soc. Lond.* 132:441–455.

THORPE, W. H., 1961. *Bird Song: The Biology of Vocal Communication and Expression in Birds*. New York: Cambridge University Press.

TINBERGEN, N., 1951. *The Study of Instinct*. New York: Clarendon.

VARGHA-KHADEM, F., and M. C. CORBALLIS, 1979. Cerebral asymmetry in infants. *Brain Lang.* 8:1–9.

VIHMAN, M. M., and B. DE BOYSSON-BARDIES, 1994. The nature and origins of ambient language influence on infant vocal production and early words. *Phonetica* 51:159–169.

VYGOTSKY, L. S., 1962. *Thought and Language*. Cambridge, Mass.: MIT Press.

VYGOTSKY, L. S., 1979. Interaction between learning and development. In *Mind in Society: The Development of Higher Psychological Processes*, M. Cole, V. John-Steiner, S. Scribner, and E. Souberman, eds. Cambridge, Mass.: Harvard University Press, pp. 79–91.

WALTON, G. E., and T. G. R. BOWER, 1993. Newborns form "prototypes" in less than 1 minute. *Psych. Sci.* 4:203–205.

WERKER, J. F., and L. POLKA, 1993. The ontogeny and developmental significance of language-specific phonetic perception. In *Developmental Neurocognition: Speech and Face Processing in the First Year of Life*, B. de Boysson-Bardies, S. de Schonen, P. Jusczyk, P. McNeilage, and J. Morton, eds. Dordrecht: Kluwer, pp. 275–288.

WERKER, J. F., and R. C. TEES, 1984. Cross-language speech perception: Evidence for perceptual reorganization during the first year of life. *Inf. Behav. Dev.* 7:49–63.

WILLERMAN, R., and P. K. KUHL, 1996. Cross-language speech perception: Swedish, English, and Spanish speakers' perception of front rounded vowels. *Proc. Int. Conf. Spoken Lang.* 1:442–445.

WITELSON, S. F., 1987. Neurobiological aspects of language in children. *Child Dev.* 58:653–688.

YAMADA, R. A., and Y. TOHKURA, 1992. The effects of experimental variables on the perception of American English /r/ and /l/ by Japanese listeners. *Percept. Psychophysiol.* 52:376–392.

ZATORRE, R. J., A. C. EVANS, E. MEYER, and A. GJEDDE, 1992. Lateralization of phonetic and pitch discrimination in speech processing. *Science* 256:846–849.

II PLASTICITY

Introduction

IRA B. BLACK

PLASTICITY, the collective mechanisms that underlie brain mutability and flexibility, enables cognition. Relatively rapid change in brain structure and function generates mind. Characteristic cognitive processes, include-in perception, learning, and memory, are expressions of brain plasticity. What is the substance of adaptability? In brain and mind that function simultaneously on the molecular, cellular, systems, and cognitive levels, where does plasticity emerge?

The chapters in this section present a unified, emphatic answer. Plasticity is built into the fabric of brain and mind at multiple levels, from the molecular to the cognitive. Indeed, our growing awareness of the continuity and integration of plastic mechanisms across functional levels represents one of the most exciting advances since the last edition of this text. We now can tentatively (though incompletely) trace a number of cognitive functions from experience to gene action, molecular mechanism, system function, and cognitive output.

The emerging unity also suggests that characterization of cognition requires description of plastic mechanisms at multiple levels. The characteristics of specific molecular, cellular, and systems plastic interactions shape the particular cognitive function generated. Conversely, systems and cognitive function regulate underlying molecular and cellular processes. In sum, the form and specific traits of a cognitive function are conferred by multilevel plastic mechanisms.

Analysis, characterization, and classification of plastic functions may provide general insights into the large-scale organization of cognitive architecture. The discovery of common plastic mechanisms underlying apparently disparate cognitive functions may reveal unsuspected commonalities. In contrast, apparently similar cognitive domains may prove to be based on

119

qualitatively different plastic mechanisms. This knowledge may lead to a taxonomy of cognitive functions currently unavailable.

To illustrate the coherence of plastic mechanisms across multiple domains, this section follows a bottom-up sequence, proceeding from the molecular to the cognitive. Initially, basic molecular and cellular plastic mechanisms associated with learning, memory, and cortical structure are considered. A universal feature of brain and cognitive architecture, the organization of maps, is examined as a prototypical fundamental neurocognitive strategy. Molecular processes underlying map formation are described, and experience-driven plasticity of maps is analyzed. Finally, the perceptual plasticity resulting from map plasticity emphasizes the continuity of plastic mechanisms from the molecular to the cognitive.

Martin, Brattish, Bailey, and Kindle focus on synaptic plasticity associated with long-term memory. They describe changes in gene action, leading to messenger RNA and protein synthesis that alter long-term synaptic function. A number of plastic molecular mechanisms that contribute to long-lasting forms of synaptic plasticity are defined.

Lynch uses the model of long-term potentiation (LTP) to explore the phenomenon of memory consolidation. During the process of consolidation, newly encoded information gradually becomes resistant to disruption. He presents evidence that consolidation is dependent on the action of synaptic cell adhesion molecules, specifically integrin receptors, that alter synaptic function. Lynch hypothesizes that specific patterns of synaptic transmission activate latent integrin receptors that stabilize LTP and memory function over time, constituting consolidation. The therapeutic implications of these insights are discussed.

Levine and Black describe recently discovered novel mechanisms governing hippocampal synaptic plasticity, trophic regulation of synaptic strength. Specific neurotrophins, which are critical for long-term neuronal development, also regulate synaptic function acutely. A neurotrophin known as brain-derived neurotrophic factor (BDNF) increases responsiveness of postsynaptic hippocampal neurons to glutamatergic stimulation by enhancing the responsiveness of NMDA receptors. The relationships among depolarization, gene expression, trophic actions, and transmitter function in synaptic plasticity are explored in detail.

Whereas the previously mentioned chapters focus on molecular and cellular plastic mechanisms localized to the synapse, McEwen reviews hippocampal plasticity elicited by circulating adrenocortical, gonadal, and thyroid hormones. For example, the formation and destruction of synapses during the estrous cycle and the effects of glucocorticoids on declarative and contextual memory are described. In sum, hippocampal plasticity is placed in the larger context of somatic physiology, allowing experience to access cognitive processes through the endocrine system.

The broad issue of permissive versus instructive stimulus regulation of the development of functional cortical architecture is examined by Katz, Weliky, and Crowley. Using the visual system as a model, the interaction of spontaneous correlated electrical activity and innate information in the genesis of ocular dominance and orientation columns is explored. Employing new approaches, they conclude that elaboration of cortical circuits requires patterned activity in a permissive rather than instructive sense, and that additional intrinsic signals may guide the formation of functional cortical architecture.

The mechanisms generating map formation, a central feature of brain and cognitive architecture, are described by Zhou and Black. Multiple molecular cues guide axons in a topographically precise fashion, resulting in the formation of sequences of maps. The cues are attractive or repulsive and diffusible or membrane bound. Among multiple guidance molecules, two groups play central roles: the tyrosine kindness receptors and legends, and cell adhesion molecules. The former include the attractive neurotoxins and the repulsive EpH family of ligands and receptors. Gradients of membrane-bound EpH receptors and ligands on innervating and target fields confer specificity, and cell adhesion molecules stabilize the connections.

Maps are characterized by striking plasticity. Altered cognitive experience, including changes in sensory input and learning, elicit marked changes in map structure and function, described by Kaas. Map plasticity occurs in cortex and in subcortical structures, including the thalamus and brain stem, and involves the somatosensory, visual, auditory, and motor systems. Some alterations are virtually instantaneous, whereas others evolve over months. Map plasticity may result in misperception or in improvement of sensorimotor skill with practice, for example. Thus experience regulates map plasticity, which, in turn, evokes cognitive plasticity. It is currently not known whether underlying molecular mechanisms include those described by Zhou and Black. Map plasticity represents one set of processes in which cognitive function regulates molecular plastic mechanisms governing brain architectural plasticity.

Recanzone presents evidence that reorganization of cortical representations improves perceptions and the acquisition of a variety of skills throughout life. Cortical plasticity is central to cognition.

To epitomize, this section provides examples of plastic mechanisms—from the molecular, cellular, and systems to the cognitive—that interact to generate mind.

9 Molecular Mechanisms Underlying Learning-Related Long-Lasting Synaptic Plasticity

KELSEY C. MARTIN, DUSAN BARTSCH, CRAIG H. BAILEY, AND ERIC R. KANDEL

ABSTRACT Learning is the process whereby we acquire information about the world, and memory is the process whereby we retain that information. Memory can be divided into at least two temporally distinct components: short-term memory that lasts for minutes to hours and long-term memory that lasts for days, weeks, or even years. Over the past several decades, molecular and cell biological studies of learning and memory have indicated that these behavioral processes are reflected at the cellular level by changes in synaptic plasticity–the ability of neurons to modulate the strength and structure of their synaptic connections with experience (Bliss and Collingridge, 1993; Martin and Kandel, 1996). Thus, in the simplest terms, what these studies have shown is that memories are stored as increases in the strength and, at least in some cases, the number or pattern of synapses in the brain. Like memory, learning-related synaptic plasticity can exist in at least two different forms. First, there is a short-term form that has been found to depend on the covalent modification of already synthesized molecules, leading to an alteration in the strength of preexisting connections. Second, there is a long-term form that has been shown to depend on the synthesis of new messenger RNAs and new proteins, leading to the growth of new synaptic connections. Here we consider the storage of long-term memory by examining the changes in gene expression in the nucleus, the changes in the structure and function of the synapse, and the communication between the synapse and the nucleus that underlie the induction and stabilization of long-lasting forms of synaptic plasticity.

The gill-withdrawal reflex in Aplysia as a model system for studies of learning-related synaptic plasticity

We will focus on studies of learning, memory, and synaptic plasticity in the central nervous system of a higher invertebrate, the marine mollusc *Aplysia*. *Aplysia* has proven advantageous for cellular studies of memory for a variety of reasons. First, the animal can undergo simple forms of learning. Second, it has a tractable nervous system, consisting of approximately 20,000 neurons, many of which are large, invariant, and readily identifiable. As a result, the neural circuitry underlying many of its behaviors has been partially characterized. One such behavior involves the reflex in which the animal withdraws its gill in response to tactile stimulus of the gill. This gill-withdrawal reflex is mediated to a large extent by mechanoreceptor sensory neurons from the siphon that make synaptic contact with motor neurons from the gill. As with defensive behaviors in other species, the gill-withdrawal reflex can undergo several types of behavioral modification, including both nonassociative forms such as habituation and sensitization, and associative forms such as classical conditioning.

Like other forms of learning, habituation and sensitization can exist in both short-term and long-term forms. A single tail shock produces short-term sensitization of the gill-withdrawal reflex that lasts for minutes. Repeated tail shocks given at spaced intervals produce long-term sensitization of the gill-withdrawal reflex that lasts for days or even weeks (Frost et al., 1985).

Of particular value for studies of the cellular and molecular mechanisms underlying sensitization, the critical components of the neuronal circuitry that mediates the gill-withdrawal reflex can be reconstituted in cell culture, where a single presynaptic sensory neuron makes synaptic contact with a single postsynaptic motor neuron. These synaptic connections in culture are stable and exhibit both short- and long-lasting forms of synaptic plasticity. This plasticity can be modified by application of serotonin (5-HT), the modulatory neurotransmitter released by facilitatory interneurons in the intact animal. A single application of 5-HT to the culture dish produces *short-term* facilitation: an increase in the magnitude of the excitatory postsynaptic potential (EPSP) formed between

KELSEY C. MARTIN   Center for Neurobiology and Behavior, College of Physicians and Surgeons of Columbia University, New York, N.Y.
DUSAN BARTSCH   Center for Neurobiology and Behavior, College of Physicians and Surgeons of Columbia University, New York, N.Y.
CRAIG H. BAILEY   Center for Neurobiology and Behavior, College of Physicians and Surgeons of Columbia University, New York, N.Y.
ERIC R. KANDEL   Howard Hughes Medical Institute and Center for Neurobiology and Behavior, College of Physicians and Surgeons of Columbia University, New York, N.Y.

the sensory and motor neuron that lasts for minutes and that does not depend on new protein synthesis.

In contrast, five repeated applications of serotonin given at timed intervals produce long-term facilitation: an increase in the strength of the EPSP that persists for at least 24 hours that requires new RNA and protein synthesis and involves the growth of new synaptic connections between the sensory and motor neurons. To test the role of specific molecules in both short- and long-term facilitation, and in the conversion of the short-term form to one of longer duration, the large *Aplysia* nerve cells can be microinjected with a variety of compounds. As a result, the *Aplysia* sensory–to–motor neuron culture system provides an experimentally accessible model system for analysis of the cellular and molecular mechanisms underlying learning-related synaptic plasticity.

In the past several years, studies of learning and memory in other species have converged to indicate the generality of many cellular and molecular mechanisms used during long-term sensitization in *Aplysia*. Two particularly well-developed systems for the analysis of learning and memory include olfactory learning in *Drosophila* (Davis, 1996) and hippocampal-mediated long-term potentiation (LTP) in rodents (Bliss and Collingridge, 1993). These studies show that similar mechanisms of learning and memory formation are used in species as diverse as *Aplysia*, *Drosophila*, and rodents, and that similar cellular mechanisms underlie a variety of forms of memory, including the implicit or nondeclarative acquisition of motor skills and other tasks, and the explicit, hippocampus-based acquisition of knowledge about people, places, and things (Squire, 1992).

Long-term memory requires changes in gene expression

Neither short-term behavioral sensitization in the animal nor short-term facilitation in dissociated cell culture requires ongoing macromolecular synthesis (Montarolo et al., 1986; Schwartz, Castellucci, and Kandel, 1971). Long-lasting synaptic plasticity differs from short-term in requiring translation and transcription. Inhibitors of RNA and protein synthesis selectively block the induction of the long-term changes in both the semi-intact preparation (Castellucci et al., 1989) and in primary cell culture (Montarolo et al., 1986). Importantly, the induction of long-term facilitation at this single synapse exhibits a critical time window in its requirement for protein and RNA synthesis characteristic of that necessary for learning in both vertebrate and invertebrate animals (Agranoff, 1972; Barondes, 1975; Davis and Squire, 1984; Flexner, Flexner, and Stellar, 1965; Montarolo et

al., 1986). This fact indicates that there is a critical consolidation period during which new genes must be expressed in order to convert transient changes in synaptic strength to more enduring modifications.

PROTEIN KINASE A IS CRITICAL FOR THE TRANSMISSION OF SIGNALS FROM THE SYNAPSE TO THE NUCLEUS Serotonin released by interneurons in vivo or applied directly to sensorimotor cocultures binds to 5-HT receptors on the sensory neuron membrane and activates adenylyl cyclase. The resulting increase in cAMP, in turn, activates the cAMP-dependent protein kinase (PKA). PKA plays a critical role in both short- and long-term facilitation. Indeed, cAMP analogues can evoke both short- and long-term facilitation, and inhibitors of PKA block both forms of facilitation (Ghirardi et al., 1992; Montarolo et al., 1986). How PKA participates in the RNA and protein synthesis–dependent process was illustrated by an experiment carried out by Bacskai and associates (1993). They monitored the subcellular localization of the free PKA catalytic subunit and found that with one pulse of serotonin, which produces short-term facilitation, the catalytic subunit was restricted to the cytoplasm. With repeated pulses of serotonin, which induce long-term facilitation, the catalytic subunit translocated to the nucleus, where it presumably phosphorylates transcription factors and thereby regulates gene expression. Both cAMP and PKA are essential components of the signal-transduction pathway for consolidating memories not only in *Aplysia* but also for certain types of memory in *Drosophila* and mammals. Several olfactory learning mutants in *Drosophila* map to the cAMP pathway (R. L. Davis, 1996; R. L. Davis et al., 1995; Drain, Folkers, and Quinn, 1991) indicating that blocking PKA function blocks memory formation in flies. In parallel, the late but not the early phase of LTP of the CA3 to CA1 synapse in the hippocampus is impaired by pharmacological or genetic interference of PKA (Abel et al., 1997; Frey, Huang, and Kandel, 1993; Huang, Lin, and Kandel, 1994). This interference with PKA blocks long-lasting spatial memory in mice without interfering with short-term memory.

CREB: THE GENETIC SWITCH FOR THE CONSOLIDATION OF LONG-TERM MEMORY Increases of cAMP concentration induce gene expression by activating transcription factors that bind to the cAMP-responsive element (CRE) (Montminy et al., 1986). The CRE-binding protein CREB (Hoeffler et al., 1988) is a major target of PKA phosphorylation of a regulatory P-box, which in turn activates transcription by binding to the CREB-binding protein CBP and basal transcription machinery (Gonzalez and Montminy, 1989). During long-term facilitation in *Aplysia* neurons, PKA appears to activate gene expression via an *Aplysia* CREB (Dash, Hochner, and Kandel, 1990; Bartsch et al., 1998). Dash, Hochner, and Kandel first tested the role of CREB in long-term facilitation by microinjecting CRE oligonucleotides into sensory neurons. The CRE oligonucleotide binds to the CREB protein within the cell and thereby prevents it from binding to CRE sites in the regulatory regions of cAMP-responsive genes. While injection of the CRE oligonucleotide had no effect on short-term facilitation, it selectively blocked long-term facilitation (figure 9.1A, B). Kaang, Kandel, and Grant (1993) further explored the mechanisms of CREB activation in long-term facilitation by microinjecting two constructs into *Aplysia* sensory neurons: an expression plasmid containing a chimeric transacting factor made by fusing the GAL4 DNA–binding domain to the mammalian CREB-activation domain and a reporter plasmid containing the chloramphenicol acetyltransferase (CAT) gene under the control of GAL4 binding sites (figure 9.1C, D). The chimeric transcription factor binds to UASg GAL4–binding sites, but only activates transcription when the CREB P-box is phosphorylated. Since the yeast GAL4-binding site is not regulated by *Aplysia* transcription factors, the transcription of the CAT reporter gene is induced only when the activation domain of the GAL4-CREB hybrid protein is phosphorylated. Following coinjection of these two plasmids into sensory neurons, exposure to 5-HT produced a tenfold stimulation of CAT expression (Kaang, Kandel, and Grant, 1993). Finally, Bartsch and associates (1998) directly demonstrated that CREB is essential for long-term facilitation. They cloned the *Aplysia* CREB gene and showed that blocking expression of one of the CREB1 gene products of the CREB1a protein in sensory neurons by microinjection of antisense oligonucleotides or antibodies blocks long-term but not short-term facilitation. Not only is CREB1a activator necessary for long-term facilitation, but it is also sufficient to induce long-term facilitation. Thus, sensory cell injection of recombinant CREB1a phosphorylated in vitro by PKA led to an increase in EPSP amplitude at 24 hours in the absence of any serotonin stimulation.

In mammals and *Drosophila,* CREB messenger RNAs (mRNAs) undergo extensive splicing: At least six different isoforms of CREB have been cloned in both mammals and *Drosophila* (Ruppert et al., 1992; Yin, Wallach, et al., 1995). To determine the role of specific CREB isoforms in the cells that participate in memory storage, Bartsch and colleagues (1998) characterized the CREB isoforms that are expressed in *Aplysia* sensory neurons and established their particular role in long-term facilitation. In addition to the CREB1α mRNA, which encodes the CREB1a activator, they detected a second CREB1β mRNA encoding the additional CREB1 forms CREB1b

and CREB1c. CREB1b encodes a CRE-binding leucine zipper transcriptional repressor that forms heterodimers with CREB1a and blocks activation from the CRE. Thus microinjection of CREB1b into sensory neurons blocks selectively long-term facilitation induced by 5 pulses of serotonin. CREB1c protein is a cytoplasmic modulator of both short- and long-term facilitation: microinjection of CREB1c into sensory cells increases both short-term and long-term facilitation when paired with only one pulse of serotonin. Since unphosphorylated CREB1c inhibits calcium/calmodulin-dependent kinase (CaMK) activity in *Aplysia* neuronal extracts, one possibility is that CREB1c produces its actions by removing inhibitory constraints mediated by calmodulin or CaMKII. Together, these results indicate that in the sensory neuron, a critical site for memory storage, CREB isoforms act together in a coordinated regulatory unit that can switch a covalent-mediated short-term facilitation to a transcriptionally dependent long-term form.

The transcriptional switch in long-term facilitation is not composed of only the CREB1 regulatory unit. Bartsch and associates (1995) have shown that another member of the CREB gene family, ApCREB2, a CRE-binding transcription factor constitutively expressed in sensory neurons, is a critical component of the genetic switch that converts short- to long-term facilitation. ApCREB2 resembles human CREB2 and mouse ATF4 (Hai et al., 1989; Karpinski et al., 1992), and like CREB1β, ApCREB2 functions as a repressor of long-term facilitation. Thus, injection of anti-ApCREB2 antibodies into *Aplysia* sensory neurons causes a single pulse of serotonin, which normally induces only short-term facilitation lasting minutes. To evoke facilitation that lasts more than 1 day requires both transcription and translation, and is accompanied by a growth of new synaptic connections (figure 9.2).

These studies reveal that long-term synaptic changes are governed by both positive and negative regulators, and that the transition from short-term facilitation to long-term facilitation thus requires the simultaneous removal of transcriptional repressors and activation of transcriptional activators. These transcriptional repressors and activators can interact with each other both physically and functionally. It is likely that the transition is a complex process involving temporally distinct phases of gene activation, repression, and regulation of signal transduction. Differences in the kinetics whereby activators are stimulated and repressors relieved could define the optimal time window separating training trials and account for the well-established difference between massed and spaced training (Carew, Pinsker, and Kandel, 1972; Pinsker et al., 1973; Tully et al., 1994; Yin et al., 1994; Yin, Del Vecchio, et al., 1995).

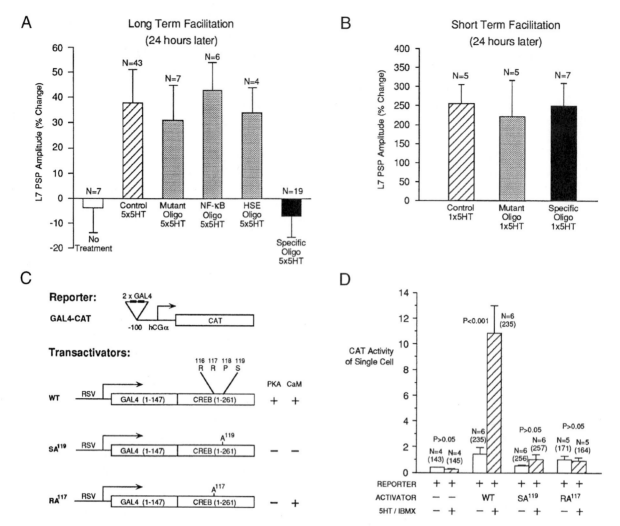

FIGURE 9.1 (A, B) Injection of CRE oligonucleotides blocks 5-HT-induced long-term facilitation. (A) Summary of the blockade of the 5-HT-induced increase in EPSP amplitude by CRE injection. The height of each bar is the percentage change in the EPSP amplitude ± SEM retested 24 hr after treatment. (A two-tailed t-test comparison of means indicated that the decrease in EPSP in cultures injected with CRE oligonucleotide is significantly different [$p < .05$] from the increase in the EPSP in the cells injected with either the mutant or NF–B oligonucleotides.) (B) Summary of the pooled data for short-term facilitation 24 hours after injection. In contrast to long-term facilitation, the 5-HT (5 μM) was applied after the EPSP was first depressed. Five stimuli were given with an interstimulus interval of 30 seconds, resulting in 70–80 percent depression in EPSP amplitude. Application of 5-HT after the fifth stimulus produced an increase in EPSP amplitude by the seventh stimulus. The increase in short-term facilitation was measured by calculating the percentage increase in the seventh EPSP amplitude as compared with the fifth EPSP amplitude. Because the facilitation here was of a depressed EPSP, the percentage facilitation is larger than the long-term, where only the nondepressed EPSP was examined. (From Dash, Hochner, and Kandel, 1990.) (C, D) 5-HT/IBMX leads to activation of CREB through the phosphorylation of PKA. (C) DNA constructs used for transactivation experiments. DNA-binding domain of yeast GAL4 transcription factor (amino acids 1–147)

fused to wild-type or mutated forms of mammalian CREB transactivation domains (amino acids 1–261). Wild-type and mutated phosphorylation consensus sequences are indicated in single-letter amino acid code above constructs. The wild-type sequence (RRPS) is a phosphorylation substrate for both protein kinase A (PKA) and calcium/calmodulin-dependent kinase (CaM) at Ser^{119}. SA^{119} contains a substitution of Ser^{119} with Ala^{119}, preventing phosphorylation by either kinase. RA^{117} contains a substitution of Arg^{117} with Ala^{117}, abolishing the PKA site, but leaving intact the CaMK consensus phosphorylation sequence. GAL4-CREB fusion proteins were constitutively expressed in pNEXδ vector and injected with the reporter construct (GAL4-CAT) containing two copies of the GAL4 site upstream of human chorionic gonadotropin α-subunit gene driving the CAT gene. (D) Quantitative analysis of 5-HT-regulated CREB transactivation. The wild-type (WT) GAL4-CREB transactivator enhances 5-HT/IBMX-mediated expression of CAT, whereas mutant (SA^{119} and RA^{117}) GAL4-CREB show no enhancement. Pairs of sensory clusters were injected and treated in parallel; each lane represents CAT activity of one sensory cluster. CAT activity is expressed as the percentage of substrate acetylated ($\times 10^3$); histograms show pooled area, N = number of animals, and value in parentheses is number of injected neurons. Mean, SEM, and p value from two-tailed paired test are shown. (From Kaang, Kandel, and Grant, 1993.)

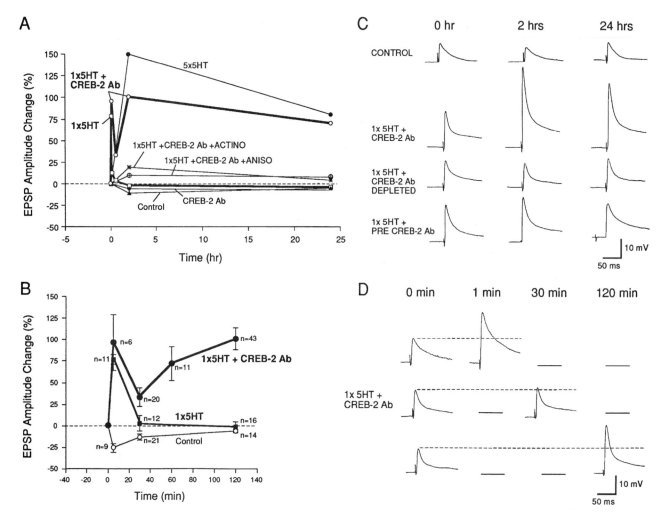

FIGURE 9.2 Time course of the effects of injection of ApCREB2 antiserum on short- and long-term facilitation. (A) Time course of excitatory postsynaptic potential (EPSP) amplitude changes recorded in motor neuron L7 in response to stimulation of the sensory neuron (expressed as percent change in the amplitude of the EPSP) after single and multiple applications of 5-HT to *Aplysia* sensorimotor neuron cocultures. Changes in EPSP amplitude after application of one 5-min pulse of 5-HT (1 × 5-HT, short-term facilitation) and one 5-min pulse of 5-HT paired with injection of anti-ApCREB2 antibodies (1 × 5-HT + CREB-2 Ab, both in boldface lines) are compared with changes in EPSP amplitude induced by five pulses of 5-HT (5 × 5-HT) at 2 and 24 hr. While the EPSP facilitation decays rapidly after one pulse of 5-HT (with a return to base line after 10 min), pairing one pulse with 5-HT with injection of anti-ApCREB2 antibodies induces a long-term facilitation paralleling that of 5 × 5-HT. This long-term facilitation is abolished by the application of the protein synthesis inhibitor anisomycin (1 × 5-HT + CREB-2 Ab + ANISO) or the RNA synthesis inhibitor actinomycin D (1 × 5-HT + CREB-2 Ab + ACTINO) during the training. The difference in EPSP amplitude at 2 hr between 5 × 5-HT and 1 × 5-HT + CREB-2 Ab may reflect the transient protein synthesis–dependent, but RNA synthesis–independent, component of long-term facilitation 2 hr after 5-HT stimulation (29). The controls are either untreated (control) or injected with ApCREB2 antiserum without 5-HT administration (CREB-2 Ab). (B) Comparison of the time course of the EPSP amplitude changes in the first 2 hr after application of a single 5-min pulse of 5-HT with or without injection of CREB-2 antibody. The control cells were not exposed to 5-HT. (C) Example of EPSPs recorded in motoneuron L7 after stimulation of the sensory neuron before (0 hr) and 2 and 24 hr after 5-HT treatment. One pulse of 5-HT paired with the injection of an ApCREB2 antiserum induces a significant increase in EPSP amplitude at 2 and 24 hr, but injection of the preimmune serum (PRE-CREB-2 Ab) or depleted immune serum does not induce long-term facilitation. (D) Examples of EPSPs recorded at indicated times in cocultures injected with ApCREB2 antiserum paired with one 5-min pulse of 5-HT. (Reproduced with permission from Bartsch et al., copyright 1995, *Cell* Press.)

The balance between CREB activator and repressor isoforms is also critically important in long-term behavioral memory, as first shown in *Drosophila*. Expression of an inhibitory form of CREB (dCREB-2b) blocks long-term olfactory memory but does not alter short-term memory (Yin et al., 1994). Overexpression of an activator form of

CREB (dCREB-2a) increases the efficacy of massed training in long-term memory formation (Yin, Del Vecchio, et al., 1995).

The CREB-mediated response to extracellular stimuli can be modulated by a number of kinases (PKA, CaMKII, CaMKIV, RSK2, MAPK, and PKC) and phosphatases (PP1 and calcineurin). The CREB regulatory unit may therefore serve to integrate signals from various signal transduction pathways. This ability to integrate signaling as well as mediate activation or repression may explain why CREB is so central to memory storage (Martin and Kandel, 1996).

MAPK ALSO CARRIES SIGNALS FROM THE SYNAPSE TO THE NUCLEUS   As discussed earlier, the transcriptional switch for the conversion of short- to long-term memory requires not only the activation of CREB1 but also the removal of the repressive action of CREB2, which lacks consensus sites for PKA phosphorylation (Bartsch et al., 1995). It does, however, have two conserved sites for MAPK phosphorylation. A number of features make MAPK an attractive candidate for playing a role in long-term facilitation. First, the MAPK system mediates graded responses to extracellular signals (Marshall, 1995). For example, in PC12 cells, EGF causes transient activation of MAPK that results in cell proliferation, while NGF causes sustained activation of MAPK, which leads to its nuclear translocation and results in neuronal differentiation. This gradation of response may be a molecular parallel to the gradation of synaptic strengthening in response to environmental stimuli, important for learning in both vertebrates and invertebrates. Similar to the PKA translocation, translocation of MAPK to the nucleus provides an attractive potential mechanism for the transition between the covalent short-term forms and transcription-dependent long-term forms of memory. Furthermore, the MAPK pathway interacts with the cAMP pathway in PC12 cells and in neurons, indicating that MAPK might participate with PKA in the consolidation of long-term memory.

To test this possibility, Martin, Michael, and colleagues (1997) and Michael and Martin (1998) examined the subcellular localization of an *Aplysia* ERK2 homologue in sensorimotor neuron cocultures during short- and long-term facilitation. Whereas MAPK immunoreactivity was predominantly localized to the cytoplasm in both sensory and motor neurons during short-term facilitation, MAPK translocated into the nucleus of the presynaptic sensory but not the postsynaptic motor cell during serotonin-induced long-term facilitation (figure 9.3). Presynaptic but not postsynaptic nuclear translocation of MAPK was also triggered by elevations in intracellular cAMP, indicating that the cAMP pathway

activates the MAPK pathway in a neuron-specific manner. Injection of anti-MAPK antibodies or of MAPK kinase inhibitors (PD98059) into the presynaptic sensory cell selectively blocked long-term facilitation without affecting short-term facilitation. Thus, MAPK appears to be necessary for the long-term form of facilitation. The involvement of MAPK in long-term plasticity may be quite general: Martin, Michael, and associates (1997) and Impey and colleagues (1998) found that cAMP also activated MAPK in mouse hippocampal neurons, suggesting that MAPK may play a role in hippocampal long-term potentiation. The requirement for MAPK during hippocampal LTP has been shown by English and Sweatt, (1996, 1997), who demonstrated that ERK1 is activated in CA1 pyramidal cells during LTP and that bath application of MAPK kinase inhibitors blocks LTP.

THE INDUCTION OF IMMEDIATE EARLY GENES   The activation of adenylyl cyclase, the increase in cAMP concentration with the resulting dissociation of the catalytic subunit of PKA and its translocation to the nucleus, and the phosphorylation of CREB are all unaffected by inhibitors of protein synthesis. Where then does the protein synthesis–dependent step that characterizes the consolidation phase appear? Clearly, it must require an additional step–the activation of genes by CREB. To follow further the sequence of steps whereby CREB leads to the stable, self-perpetuating long-term process, Alberini and colleagues (1994) characterized the immediate early genes induced by cAMP and CREB. In a search for possible cAMP-dependent regulatory genes that might be interposed between constitutively expressed transcription factors and stable effector genes, Alberini and colleagues (1994) focused on the CCAAT enhancer-binding protein (C/EBP) transcription factors. They cloned an *Aplysia* C/EBP homologue (ApC/EBP) and found that its expression was induced by exposure to serotonin. Induction of ApC/EBP mRNA is rapid and transient, and occurs in the presence of protein synthesis inhibitors, characteristic of immediate early gene. To determine whether ApC/EBP is necessary for the induction and maintenance of long-term facilitation, Alberini and colleagues (1994) used three different approaches: First, they interfered with the binding of the ApC/EBP to its DNA-binding element (ERE) by injecting oligonucleotides that compete for the binding activity of the endogenous ApC/EBP to its target sequence. Second, they blocked the synthesis of endogenous ApC/EBP by injecting ApC/EBP antisense RNA into the sensory cells. Third, they blocked ApC/EBP by injecting an anti-ApC/EBP antiserum into the sensory neurons. All these blocked long-term facilitation but had no effect on short-term facilitation

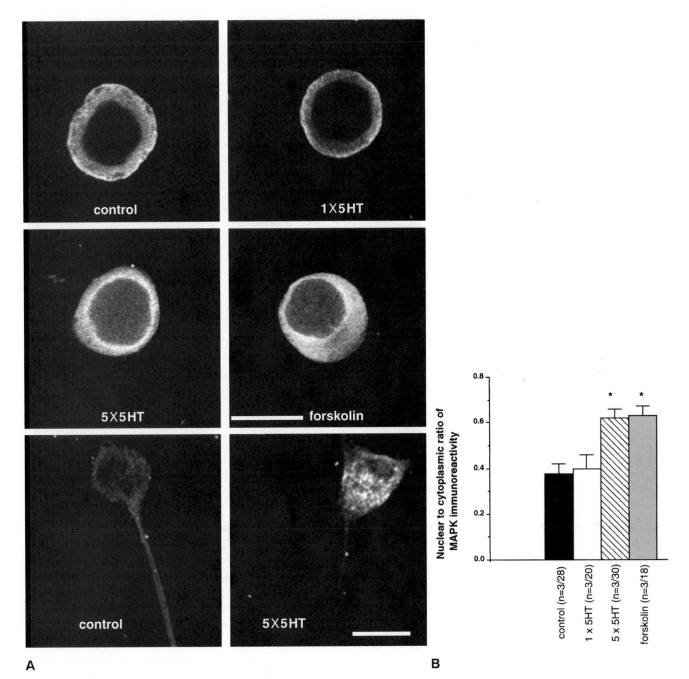

A   B

FIGURE 9.3   MAPK translocates into the nucleus of isolated sensory neurons in culture. Five-day-old cultures of isolated cells were mock treated (control), or treated with one pulse of serotonin (1 × 5-HT), five pulses of serotonin (5 × 5-HT), or 50 μm forskolin in 0.1% DMSO for 30 min. Optical sections were taken through the cell bodies by confocal microscopy, and the mean fluorescence in the nucleus and cytoplasm was determined. (A) In the top four images, examples of optical sections taken through the cell bodies of sensory neurons mock treated (control), treated with one pulse of serotonin (1 × 5-HT), with five pulses of serotonin (5 × 5-HT), or with forskolin. Scale bar = 50 μm. The bottom two images are single optical sections taken through the initial axon segment and cell soma of sensory cells mock treated (control) or treated with five pulses of serotonin (5 × 5-HT), illustrating the apparent translocation of MAPK from the process to the soma. Scale bar = 50 μm. (B) Histogram of the mean nuclear-to-cytoplasmic ratio of MAPK immunoreactivity in sensory neurons in mock-treated cultures (control), cultures treated with one pulse of serotonin (1 × 5-HT), five pulses of serotonin (5 × 5-HT), or forskolin. Error bars represent SE. Asterisk, $p < .01$ compared to control and one pulse of serotonin. The n represents the number of individual culture dishes/total number of individual cells. Averages were obtained from each culture dish, and these were then averaged to obtain the mean presented in the histogram. (From Martin, Michael, et al., 1997.)

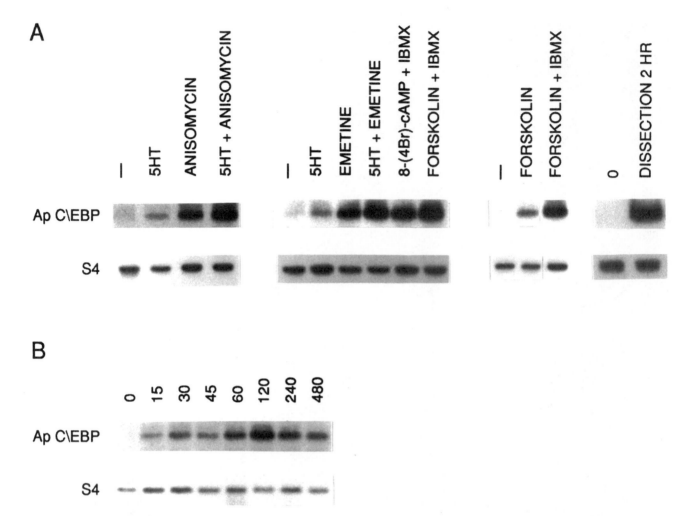

FIGURE 9.4 Induction of ApC/EBP mRNA. (A) ApC/EBP mRNA expression in CNS of untreated *Aplysia*, of *Aplysia* treated in vivo with the indicated drugs for 2 hr at 18°C, or dissected without treatment and kept at 18°C in culture medium. Four independent experiments are shown, in which 10 μg of total RNA extracted from CNSs of untreated (–) or treated *Aplysia*, as indicated, were electrophoresed, blotted, and hybridized with ^{32}P-labeled ApC/EBP (top) or S4 (bottom) probes. The latter encodes the *Aplysia* homologue of S4 riboso- mal protein,[59] which is constitutively expressed and used as a loading control. Zero indicates RNA extracted immediately after dissection of *Aplysia* CNS. Two-hour dissection represents RNA extracted from *Aplysia* CNS dissected and incubated in culture medium for 2 hr at 18°C. (B) Time course of ApC/EBP mRNA induction following 5-HT treatment. Times of treatment are indicated. Five μg of total RNA extracted form total CNS of in vivo treated *Aplysia* were analyzed as described in B. (From Alberini et al., 1994.)

(figure 9.4). Thus the induction of ApC/EBP seems to serve as an intermediate component of a molecular switch activated during the consolidation period.

The existence of C/EBP, a cAMP-regulated immediate early gene that is itself a transcription factor and regulates other genes, leads to a model of sequential gene activation. CREB1a, CREB1b, CREB1c, and CREB2 represent the first level of control, since all are constitutively expressed. Stimuli that lead to long-term facilitation perturb the balance between CREB1-mediated activation and CREB2-mediated repression, through the action of PKA, MAPK, and possibly other kinases. This leads to the up-regulation of a family of immediate early genes. Some of these immediate early genes are tran- scription factors such as C/EBP; others are effectors, such as ubiquitin hydrolase, and contribute to consolidation by extending the inducing signal or by initiating the changes at the synapse that cause long-term facilitation.

Stable long-term facilitation is associated with the synthesis of "late" as well as "early" proteins and with the laying down of new synaptic connections

In addition to ApC/EBP induction, expression of a number of other genes is altered in the sensory neurons of the gill-withdrawal reflex after exposure to repeated pulses of serotonin or long-term behavioral training (Barzilai et al., 1989; Castellucci et al., 1988). One of the early effector genes is ubiquitin C-terminal hydrolase (Hegde et al., 1997). This rapidly induced gene encodes an enzyme that associates with the proteasome and increases its proteolytic activity. This regulated proteolysis is essential for long-term facilitation: Inhibiting the expression or function of the hydrolase blocks induction of long-term but not short-term facilitation. Thus, through induction of the hydrolase and the resulting up-regulation of the ubiquitin pathway, learning recruits a regulated form of proteolysis that removes inhibitory constraints on long-term memory. One of the substrates of ubiquitin-mediated proteolysis is the regulatory subunit of PKA, degradation of which leads to a persistently active PKA (Chain et al., 1999). This persistence in PKA activity continues for up to 24 hours even in the absence of cAMP or serotonin (Greenberg, Bernier, and Schwartz, 1987) and is essential for the consolidation of short- to long-term memory (Chain et al., 1999).

The stable late phase of long-term facilitation involves the growth of new synaptic connections. In *Aplysia*, Bailey and Chen first demonstrated that long-term behavioral sensitization is accompanied by significant structural changes at the level of identified synapses critical to the behavior. By combining selective intracellular labeling with complete serial reconstructions, they showed that storage of the memory for long-term sensitization is accompanied by a family of morphological alterations at identified sensory neuron synapses. These changes reflect structural modifications at two different levels of synaptic organization: alterations in focal regions of membrane specialization of the synapse (the number, size, and vesicle complement of sensory neuron active zones are larger in sensitized than in control animals) and a parallel but more pronounced and widespread modulation of the total number of presynaptic varicosities per sensory neuron (Bailey and Chen, 1983; Bailey and Chen, 1988). Sensory neurons from long-term sensitized animals displayed a twofold increase in the total number of synaptic varicosities as well as an enlargement in the size of each neuron's axonal arbor. The changes in size and vesicle complement of sensory neuron active zones that were present 24 hours after training did not persist as long as the memory. In contrast, the duration of changes in varicosity and active zone number endured in parallel with the behavioral time course of memory, suggesting that only the increases in the number of sensory neuron synapses contribute to the maintenance of long-term sensitization (Bailey and Chen, 1989).

Aspects of the synaptic growth seen during behavioral sensitization in the intact animal can be reconstituted in dissociated cell culture, where serotonin and cAMP lead to a 50% increase in the number of sensory neuron vari-

cosities. In culture, this increase can be correlated with long-term enhancement of the amplitude of the sensory–to–motor synaptic potential and depends on the presence of an appropriate target cell, similar to the synapse formation that occurs during development (Glanzman, Kandel, and Schacher, 1990). Despite the association of structural changes with different forms of memory storage, surprisingly little is known about the intracellular signaling pathways and molecular mechanisms that convert neuronal activity into the formation of new and persistent synaptic connections. This growth also requires protein synthesis (Bailey, Montarolo, et al., 1992) and is paralleled by the increased expression of late effector genes, which included BiP, calreticulin, and clathrin (Bailey and Kandel, 1993; Hu et al., 1993; Kennedy et al., 1992; Kuhl et al., 1992). In addition, there are proteins whose levels decrease following 5-HT treatment, among them different isoforms of an immunoglobulin-related cell adhesion molecule (apCAM), the *Aplysia* homologue of the vertebrate neural cell adhesion molecule, NCAM and Fasciclin II in *Drosophila*. Light and electron microscopic analysis revealed not only that there is a decrease in the transcription of apCAM during long-term facilitation, but also that ApCAM is removed from the surface membrane of the sensory but not from the motor neuron within 1 hour after the addition of serotonin (Bailey, Montarolo, et al., 1992; Mayford et al., 1992). This rapid, presynaptic down-regulation of cell adhesion molecules is achieved by a transient activation of the endocytic pathway, leading to a protein synthesis–dependent internalization of apCAM and its rerouting from a pathway of apparent recycling to a pathway that seems destined for degradation (Bailey, Chen, et al., 1992). Reduction of the membrane concentration of ApCAM by serotonin may represent one of the early molecular steps required for initiating learning-related growth of synaptic connections. Indeed, blocking apCAM mAbs triggers defasciculation, a step that appears to precede normal synapse formation in *Aplysia* (Glanzman, Kandel, and Schacher, 1989; Keller and Schacher, 1990).

To further define the mechanism whereby serotonin leads to apCAM down-regulation, Bailey and colleagues (1997) used epitope tags to examine the fate of the two apCAM isoforms (membrane-bound and GPI-linked) and found that only the transmembrane form is internalized (figure 9.5). This internalization was blocked by overexpression of transmembrane apCAM with a point mutation in the two MAPK phosphorylation consensus sites, as well as by injection of a specific MAPK antagonist into sensory neurons. These data suggest that activation of the MAPK pathway is important for the internalization of apCAMs and may represent one of

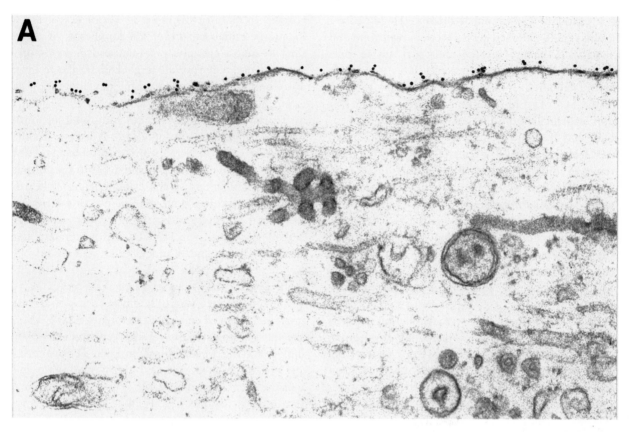

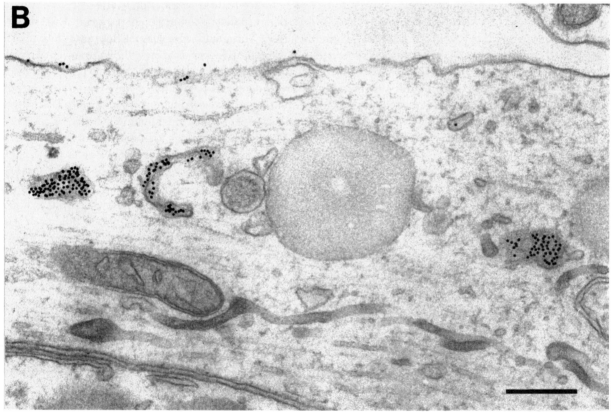

the initial stages of learning-related synaptic growth in *Aplysia*. Furthermore, the combined actions of MAPK both in the cytoplasm and in the nucleus suggest that MAPK plays multiple roles in long-lasting synaptic plasticity and appears to regulate each of the two distinctive processes that characterize the long-term process: activation of transcription and growth of new synaptic connections.

The differential down-regulation of the GPI-linked and transmembrane forms of apCAM raises the interesting possibility that learning-related synaptic growth in the adult may be initiated by an activity-dependent recruitment of specific isoforms of cell adhesion molecules. In conjunction with the recruitment of the family of CREB isoforms described previously, this may provide a regulatory unit capable of acting sequentially at multiple nuclear, cytoplasmic, and plasma membrane sites during the early, inductive phases of the long-term process.

Modulation of cell adhesion molecules appears to be a general mechanism in long-lasting forms of both developmental and learning-related synaptic plasticity (for review see Rutishauser, 1993; Doherty, Fazelli, and Walsh, 1995; Fields and Itoh, 1996; Martin and Kandel, 1996). Thus, in forms of learning and memory in other animals, such as passive avoidance learning, in which chicks learn to suppress pecking behavior toward a bead that is coated with a bitter-tasting liquid, the synthesis of new cell adhesion molecules appears to be critical (Landmesser et al., 1992; Tang, Landmesser, and Rutishauser, 1992). Relatedly, spatial learning and LTP are impaired in NCAM knockout mice (Lüthl et al., 1994). Furthermore, increases in the expression of polysialylated NCAM and in the extracellular concentration of NCAM have been observed after hippocampal LTP, and LTP is inhibited by the application of NCAM antibodies, by NCAM-blocking peptides, or by the removal of polysialic acid by neuraminidase (Rose, 1995). Addition of polysialic acid to NCAM may be functionally equivalent to the internalization of apCAM that occurs

in *Aplysia* neurons in that both processes promote defasciculation, thereby allowing for the growth of new synaptic connections.

Synapse-specific, transcription-dependent plasticity

The finding that long-term memory requires alterations in gene expression poses a cell biological paradox in the study of memory. Does the requirement of transcription and thus the nucleus—a resource shared by all the synapses within a cell—for long-lasting synaptic plasticity mean that long-lasting memory needs to be cellwide, or can the strength of individual synaptic connections be modified independently?

That *synapse-specific* transcription-dependent plasticity does occur has been argued from both theoretical and empirical points of view. Theoretically, since each neuron has a single nucleus but up to thousands of synapses, having the unit of memory storage be the synapse and not the nucleus would greatly maximize the computing power of the brain. Empirically, behavioral studies of classical conditioning in *Aplysia* have shown that there is response specificity in conditioning of the withdrawal reflex (Hawkins et al., 1989). Thus, the gill- and siphon-withdrawal reflex of *Aplysia* undergoes classical conditioning of its amplitude and duration when siphon stimulation (the conditioned stimulus) is paired with tail or mantle shock (the unconditioned stimulus). Whereas the unlearned response to siphon stimulation is straight contraction, the response to tail shock is backward bending, and the response to mantle shock is forward bending. After training for classical conditioning, there is a significant, pairing-specific tendency for the direction of the response to the conditioned stimulus to resemble the response to the unconditioned stimulus (figure 9.6). While this response specificity could be accounted for by branch-specific, activity-dependent facilitation of individual sensory neurons contacting different motor neurons, it is also possible that the response specificity results from facilitation of distinct populations of sensory and motor neurons. Studies in the rodent hippocampus have also shown pathway specificity for the transcription-dependent form of LTP. Thus in "two-pathway" experiments, in which one pathway receives high-frequency stimulation and the other pathway is unstimulated, transcription-dependent LTP is restricted to the tetanized pathway, indicating that it has input specificity (Nguyen, Abel, and Kandel, 1994; Frey and Morris, 1997). However, these studies are at the level not of the single cell, but of populations of cells, and thus the problem of synapse specificity could be solved by recruiting different populations of neurons.

To address these questions at the level of a single cell, Martin, Casadio, and colleagues (1997) modified the

FIGURE 9.5 Differential down-regulation of the GPI-linked versus transmembrane isoforms of apCAM. (A) Neurite of a sensory neuron expressing the GPI-linked isoform of apCAM following a 1-hr exposure to 5-HT. Note that virtually all the gold complexes remain on the surface membrane with none inside, despite a robust 5-HT-induced activation of the endosomal pathway leading to significant accumulations of internal membranous profiles. (B) Neurite of a sensory neuron expressing the transmembrane isoform of apCAM following a 1-hr exposure to 5-HT. In contrast to the lack of down-regulation of the GPI-linked isoform, 5-HT has a dramatic effect on the transmembrane isoform of apCAM removing most of it from the surface membrane, resulting in heavy accumulations of gold complexes within presumptive endocytic compartments. Scale for A and B = 0.25 μm. (From Bailey et al., 1997.)

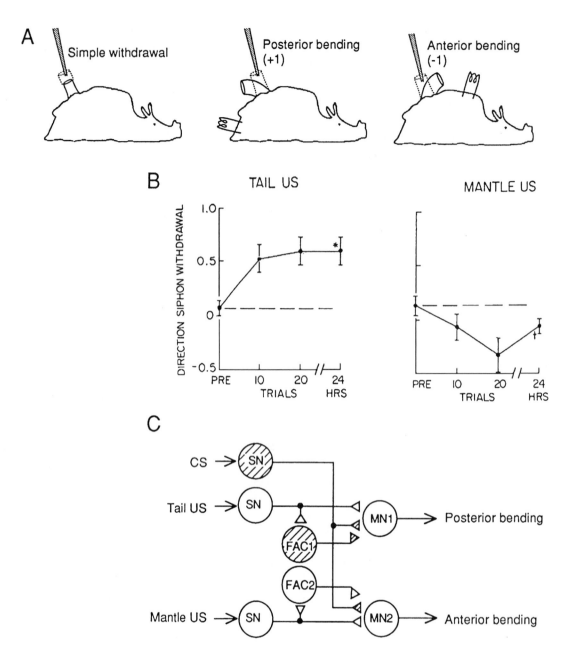

FIGURE 9.6 Response specificity in conditioning of the si-phon-withdrawal reflex. (A) In naive animals, siphon stimulation causes straight contraction of the siphon, tail stimulation causes backward bending, and mantle stimulation causes forward bending. During testing, straight contraction was scored as 0, backward bending was scored as +1, and forward bending was scored as –1. (B) Experiment 1. Different animals received training with siphon stimulation as the CS either paired (P) or unpaired (UP) with tail or mantle shock as the US. The data points indicate the mean direction of siphon withdrawal in response to the CS at each test, and the error bars indicate the SEM. The horizontal dashed line shows the average direction of responding in the pretest (PRE). Significant differences between paired and unpaired training are indicated by an asterisk ($p < .05$) or dagger ($p < .05$, one tailed). (From Hawkins et al., 1989.)

Aplysia culture system by plating a single sensory cell that has a bifurcated axon such that each branch makes synaptic contact with one of two spatially separated motor neurons (figure 9.7). The sensory cell forms stable synapses with each of the motor neurons in culture, and, if serotonin is bath applied to the culture dish, both synaptic connections are strengthened. The advantage of having the synaptic connections spatially separated,

however, is that serotonin can be applied selectively, using perfusion microelectrodes, to the connections made onto a single motor cell, with perfusion of the bath solution adjusted such that neither the sensory cell body nor the connections made onto the second motor neuron are exposed to the serotonin.

As shown in figure 9.7, local application of a single pulse of serotonin onto one set of synaptic connections

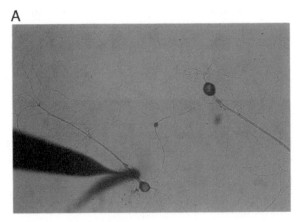

A

B

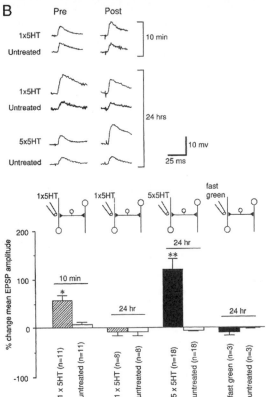

FIGURE 9.7 Synapse-specific short-term and long-term facilitation. (A) Serotonin was applied locally to the synaptic connections formed onto one motor neuron using a perfusion microelectrode. Bulk flow of the perfusate prevented the cell body of the sensory neuron or the synaptic connections made onto the other motor neuron from being exposed to the serotonin. A dye (0.05% fast green) was included to visualize the serotonin perfusion. (B) Application of a single pulse of serotonin increased the amplitude of the EPSP at the serotonin-treated branch 10 min after serotonin application without changing the EPSP at the untreated branch (*$p < .05$, change in EPSP amplitude in serotonin-treated versus untreated branch, Student's t-test). This facilitation was transient: There was no increase in the EPSP at 24 hr at either the serotonin-treated or the untreated branch. In contrast, local perfusion of five spaced pulses of serotonin onto one set of synapses produced long-term facilitation of the EPSP at the serotonin-treated branch without any change at the untreated branch (**$p < .01$, change in EPSP amplitude in serotonin-treated versus untreated branch, Student's t-test). In control experiments, perfusion of the dye alkane (fast green) did not change the EPSP at the perfused or the nonperfused branch. Shown are representative recordings of EPSPs and a histogram of the mean change in EPSP amplitude ±SE. (From Martin, Casadio, et al., 1997.)

specific facilitation has recently been reported in the intact ganglion as well (Gooch and Clark, 1997).

This branch-specific facilitation is dependent on transcription, since it can be blocked by actinomycin D, a transcriptional inhibitor, and by injection of anti-CREB antibodies into the sensory cell body. Thus, a single cell can undergo synaptic plasticity that is both synapse specific and dependent on transcription, specifically on CREB-mediated transcription. Furthermore, this branch-specific facilitation is accompanied by the branch-specific growth of new synaptic connections: Imaging of carboxyfluorescein-filled sensory neurons before and after synapse-specific application of 5 pulses of serotonin reveals the growth of new synaptic varicosities at the serotonin-treated but not at the untreated branch.

How might the products of gene expression be targeted to specific synapses and not others? One possibility is that synapses are "tagged" by synaptic stimulation to capture products of gene expression that are exported throughout the cell but are only functionally incorporated at synapses tagged by previous activity. Experimental support for possible synaptic tagging during learning-related plasticity recently emerged from studies of long-lasting LTP in the hippocampus (Frey and Morris, 1997). The studies were based on populations of neurons and synapses and indicated that, with appropriate timing of activity, the products of the gene expression induced by strong stimulation of one set of synaptic connections can be "captured" by another set of synaptic connections that have been tagged by stimuli that normally produce just

produced a transient facilitation of that synaptic connection without any change in synaptic strength at the synapse that was not exposed to serotonin. Thus, one local application of serotonin produced synapse-specific short-term facilitation, as has previously been demonstrated in the intact ganglion (Clark and Kandel, 1993). To examine long-term facilitation, Martin, Casadio, and colleagues (1997) applied five spaced pulses of serotonin to one of the branches. The treated branch showed long-term facilitation: When measured 24 hours later, repeated serotonin application was found to increase the mean EPSP amplitude of the treated synapse without having any effect on the untreated synapse (figure 9.7). A single presynaptic cell can thus undergo long-lasting facilitation that is branch specific. Long-lasting, branch-

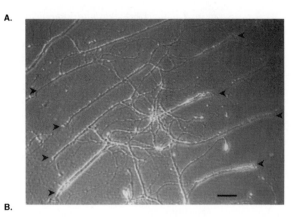

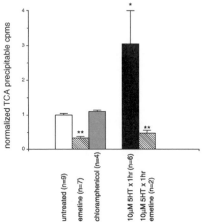

FIGURE 9.8 Translation in isolated presynaptic sensory cell neurites is induced by serotonin. (A, B) Sensory cells (30–40) were cultured for five days. The cell body of each neuron was removed, and the processes were labeled with ^{25}S methionine. Emetine (200 μM) and chloramphenicol (100 μM) were present for 30 min prior to and during the metabolic labeling, and serotonin (10 μM) was present during the metabolic labeling. The cells were then TCA precipitated, and the TCA-insoluble counts were counted on a scintillation counter. Total cpm were divided by the number of cells in each dish. Shown is a histogram of the mean counts plus SE, normalized to the counts in the untreated dishes. The mean cpm/untreated cell was 5.922 ± 1.541, $^*p < .05$, serotonin treated versus untreated processes; $^{**}p < .01$, emetine treated versus untreated and chloramphenicol treated processes, ANOVA followed by Neuman-Keul's multiple range test. (From Martin, Casadio, et al., 1997.)

transient LTP. Martin, Casadio, and associates (1997) performed a similar synaptic capture experiment in our system by giving a single application of serotonin, which produces only transient, short-term facilitation, immediately following five pulses of serotonin to the other synapse, and found that this protocol produced long-lasting facilitation at both branches. Thus a single pulse of serotonin appeared to mark the second set of synapses so that they could capture the products of gene expression induced by five pulses of serotonin at the first set of synapse.

What is the nature of the synaptic tag? One characteristic was that it involved the local synaptic translation of mRNAs. Components of the translational machinery including mRNAs and ribosomes have been detected in the distal processes of invertebrate neurons (Crispino et al., 1997; Scheller et al., 1982; Van Minnen et al., 1997), and an intermediate form of facilitation has been described at the *Aplysia* sensory–to–motor neuron synapse that requires translation but not transcription (Ghirardi, Montarolo, and Kandel, 1995). By locally applying protein synthesis inhibitors, Martin, Casadio, and associates (1997) found that the establishment of synapse-specific long-term facilitation was dependent on local protein synthesis in the sensory but not in the motor neuron. In fact, they found that sensory neuron axons whose cell bodies had been removed were capable of protein synthesis, and that this protein synthesis was stimulated threefold by exposure to serotonin (figure 9.8). This finding adds a new function to the actions of neurotransmitters in the nervous system: the regulation of local protein synthesis to establish synapse-specific changes in synaptic strength.

What these studies begin to indicate is that different temporal and spatial patterns of stimulation can recruit different forms of CREB-mediated transcription-dependent long-term facilitation. Are these differences due to events at the synapse or to differences in gene expression? Future experiments in this system promise to provide answers to many of these questions. The convergence of these cellular and molecular studies with genetic and behavioral studies in *Drosophila* and mice are likely to provide a clearer understanding not only of learning and memory, but of a number of other physiological and pathological phenomena in the brain that are believed to involve changes in synaptic plasticity, including activity-dependent development of the nervous system, age-related memory loss, dependence on and tolerance to drugs of abuse, and epilepsy.

REFERENCES

ABEL, T., P. V. NGUYEN, M. BARAD, T. A. DEUEL, E. R. KANDEL, and R. BOURTCHOULADZE, 1997. Genetic demonstration of a role for PKA in the late phase of LTP and in hippocampus-based long-term memory. *Cell* 88:615–626.

AGRANOFF, B. W., 1972. *The chemistry of mood, motivation, and memory.* New York: Plenum Press.

ALBERINI, C. M., M. GHIRARDI, R. METZ, and E. R. KANDEL, 1994. C/EBP is an immediate-early gene required for the consolidation of long-term facilitation in *Aplysia. Cell* 76:1099–1114.

BACSKAI, B. J., B. HOCHNER, M. MAHAUT-SMITH, S. R. ADAMS, B. K. KAANG, E. R. KANDEL, and R. Y. TSIEN, 1993. Spatially resolved dynamics of cAMP and protein kinase A subunits in *Aplysia* sensory neurons. *Science* 260:222–226.

BAILEY, C. H., and M. CHEN, 1983. Morphological basis of long-term habituation and sensitization in *Aplysia*. *Science* 220:91–93.

BAILEY, C. H., and M. CHEN, 1988. Long-term memory in *Aplysia* modulates the total number of varicosities of single identified sensory neurons. *Proc. Natl. Acad. Sci. U.S.A.* 85:2373–2377.

BAILEY, C. H., and M. CHEN, 1989. Time course of structural changes at identified sensory neuron synapses during long-term sensitization in *Aplysia*. *J. Neurosci.* 9:1774–1780.

BAILEY, C. H., M. CHEN, F. KELLER, and E. R. KANDEL, 1992. Serotonin-mediated endocytosis of apCAM: An early step of learning-related synaptic growth in *Aplysia*. *Science* 256:645–649.

BAILEY, C. H., B. K. KAANG, M. CHEN, K. C. MARTIN, C. S. LIM, A. CASADIO, and E. R. KANDEL, 1997. Mutation in the phosphorylation sites of MAP kinase blocks learning-related internalization of apCAM in *Aplysia* sensory neurons. *Neuron* 18:913–924.

BAILEY, C. H., and E. R. KANDEL, 1993. Structural changes accompanying memory storage. *Annu. Rev. Physiol.* 55:397–426.

BAILEY, C. H., P. MONTAROLO, M. CHEN, E. R. KANDEL, and S. SCHACHER, 1992. Inhibitors of protein and RNA synthesis block structural changes that accompany long-term heterosynaptic plasticity in *Aplysia*. *Neuron* 9:749–758.

BARONDES, S. H., 1975. Protein-synthesis-dependent and protein-synthesis-independent memory storage processes. In *Short-Term Memory*, D. Deutsch and J. A. Deutsch, eds. New York: Academic Press, pp. 379–390.

BARTSCH, D., A. CASADIO, K. A. KARL, P. SERODIO, and E. R. KANDEL, 1998. CREB1 encodes a nuclear activator, a repressor, and a sytoplasmic modulator that form a regulatory unit critical for long-term facilitation. *Cell* 95:211–223.

BARTSCH, D., M. GHIRARDI, P. A. SKEHEL, K. A. KARL, S. P. HERDER, M. CHEN, C. H. BAILEY, and E. R. KANDEL. 1995. *Aplysia* CREB2 represses long-term facilitation: Relief of repression converts transient facilitation into long-term functional and structural change. *Cell* 83:979–992.

BARZILAI, A., T. E. KENNEDY, J. D. SWEATT, and E. R. KANDEL, 1989. 5-HT modulates protein synthesis and the expression of specific proteins during long-term facilitation in *Aplysia* sensory neurons. *Neuron* 2:1577–1586.

BLISS, T. V., and G. L. COLLINGRIDGE, 1993. A synaptic model of memory: Long-term potentiation in the hippocampus. *Nature* 361:31–39.

CAREW, T. J., H. M. PINSKER, and E. R. KANDEL, 1972. Long-term habituation of a defensive withdrawal reflex in *Aplysia*. *Science* 175:451–454.

CASTELLUCCI, V. F., H. BLUMENFELD, P. GOELET, and E. R. KANDEL, 1989. Inhibitor of protein synthesis blocks long-term behavioral sensitization in the isolated gill-withdrawal reflex of *Aplysia*. *J. Neurobiol.* 20:1–9.

CASTELLUCCI, V. F., T. E. KENNEDY, E. R. KANDEL, and P. GOELET, 1988. A quantitative analysis of 2-D gels identifies proteins in which labeling is increased following long-term sensitization in *Aplysia*. *Neuron* 1:321–328.

CHAIN, D. G., A. CASADIO, S. SCHACHER, A. N. HEGDE, M. VALBRUN, N. YAMAMOTO, A. L. GOLDBERG, D. BARTSCH, E. R. KANDEL, and J. H. SCHWARTZ, 1999. Mechanisms for generating the autonomous cAMP-dependent protein kinase required for long-term facilitation in *Aplysia*. *Neuron* 22:147–156.

CLARK, G. A., and E. R. KANDEL, 1993. Induction of long-term facilitation in *Aplysia* sensory neurons by local application of serotonin to remote synapses. *Proc. Natl. Acad. Sci. U.S.A.* 90:11411–11415.

CRISPINO, M., B. B. KAPLAN, R. MARTIN, J. ALVAREZ, J. T. CHUN, J. C. BENECH, and A. GIUDITTA, 1997. Active polysomes are present in the large presynaptic endings of the synaptosomal fraction from squid brain. *J. Neurosci.* 17:7694–7702.

DASH, P. K., B. HOCHNER, and E. R. KANDEL, 1990. Injection of the cAMP-responsive element into the nucleus of *Aplysia* sensory neurons blocks long-term facilitation. *Nature* 345:718–721.

DAVIS, H. P., and L. R. SQUIRE, 1984. Protein synthesis and memory: A review. *Psychol. Bull.* 96:518–559.

DAVIS, R. L., 1996. Physiology and biochemistry of *Drosophila* learning mutants. *Physiol. Rev.* 76:299–317.

DAVIS, R. L., J. CHERRY, B. DAUWALDER, P. L. HAN, and E. SKOULAKIS, 1995. The cyclic AMP system and *Drosophila* learning. *Mol. Cell Biochem.* 149–150, 271–278.

DOHERTY, P., M. S. FAZELLI, and F. S. WALSH, 1995. The neural cell adhesion molecule and synaptic plasticity. *J. Neurobiol.* 26:437–446.

DRAIN, P., E. FOLKERS, and W. G. QUINN, 1991. cAMP-dependent protein kinase and the disruption of learning in transgenic flies. *Neuron* 6:71–82.

ENGLISH, J. D., and J. D. SWEATT, 1996. Activation of p42 mitogen-activated protein kinase in hippocampal long-term potentiation. *J. Biol. Chem.* 271:24329–24332.

ENGLISH, J. D., and J. D. SWEATT, 1997. A requirement for the mitogen-activated protein kinase cascade in hippocampal long-term potentiation. *J. Biol. Chem.* 272:19103–19106.

FIELDS, R. D., and K. ITOH, 1996. Neural cell adhesion molecules in activity-dependent development and synaptic plasticity. *Trends Neurosci.* 19:473–480.

FLEXNER, L. B., J. B. FLEXNER, and E. STELLAR, 1965. Memory and cerebral protein synthesis in mice as affected by graded amounts of puromycin. *Exp. Neurol.* 13:264–272.

FREY, U., Y. Y. HUANG, and E. R. KANDEL, 1993. Effects of cAMP simulate a late stage of LTP in hippocampal CA1 neurons. *Science* 260:1661–1664.

FREY, U., and R. G. MORRIS, 1997. Synaptic tagging and long-term potentiation [see comments]. *Nature* 385:533–536.

FROST, W. N., V. F. CASTELLUCCI, R. D. HAWKINS, and E. R. KANDEL, 1985. Monosynaptic connections from the sensory neurons of the gill- and siphon-withdrawal reflex in *Aplysia* participate in the storage of long-term memory for sensitization. *Proc. Natl. Acad. Sci. U.S.A.* 82:8266–8269.

GHIRARDI, M., O. BRAHA, B. HOCHNER, P. G. MONTAROLO, E. R. KANDEL, and N. DALE, 1992. Roles of PKA and PKC in facilitation of evoked and spontaneous transmitter release at depressed and nondepressed synapses in *Aplysia* sensory neurons. *Neuron* 9:479–489.

GHIRARDI, M., P. G. MONTAROLO, and E. R. KANDEL, 1995. A novel intermediate stage in the transition between short- and long-term facilitation in the sensory to motor neuron synapse of *Aplysia*. *Neuron* 14:413–420.

GLANZMAN, D. L., E. R. KANDEL, and S. SCHACHER, 1990. Target-dependent structural changes accompanying long-term synaptic facilitation in *Aplysia* neurons. *Science* 249:799–802.

GONZALEZ, G. A., and M. R. MONTMINY, 1989. Cyclic AMP stimulates somatostatin gene transcription by phosphorylation of CREB at serine 133. *Cell* 59:675–680.

GOOCH, C. M., and G. A. CLARK, 1997. Synapse-specific long-term facilitation at *Aplysia* sensorimotor connections. *Soc. Neurosci. Abstr.* 23:1415.

GREENBERG, S. M., L. BERNIER, and J. H. SCHWARTZ, 1987. Distribution of cAMP and cAMP-dependent protein kinases in *Aplysia* sensory neurons. *J. Neurosci.* 7:291–301.

HAI, T. W., F. LIU, W. J. COUKOS, and M. R. GREEN, 1989. Transcription factor ATF cDNA clones: An extensive family of leucine zipper proteins able to selectively form DNA-binding heterodimers [published erratum appears in *Genes Dev.* 1990 Apr:4(4):682]. *Genes Dev.* 3:2083–2090.

HAWKINS, R. D., N. LALEVIC, G. A. CLARK, and E. R. KANDEL, 1989. Classical conditioning of the *Aplysia* siphon-withdrawal reflex exhibits response specificity. *Proc. Natl. Acad. Sci. U.S.A.* 86:7620–7624.

HEGDE, A. N., K. INOKUCHI, W. PEI, A. CASADIO, M. GHIRARDI, D. G. CHAIN, K. C. MARTIN, E. R. KANDEL, and J. H. SCHWARTZ, 1997. Ubiquitin C-terminal hydrolase is an immediate-early gene essential for long-term facilitation in *Aplysia*. *Cell* 89:115–126.

HOEFFLER, J. P., T. E. MEYER, Y. YUN, J. L. JAMESON, and J. F. HABENER, 1988. Cyclic AMP-responsive DNA-binding protein: Structure based on a cloned placental cDNA. *Science* 242:1430–1433.

HU, Y., A. BARZILAI, M. CHEN, C. H. BAILEY, and E. R. KANDEL, 1993. 5-HT and cAMP induce the formation of coated pits and vesicles and increase the expression of clathrin light chain in sensory neurons of *Aplysia*. *Neuron* 10:921–929.

HUANG, Y. Y., X. C. LI, and E. R. KANDEL, 1994. cAMP contributes to mossy fiber LTP by initiating both a covalently mediated early phase and macromolecular synthesis-dependent late phase. *Cell* 79:69–79.

IMPEY, S., K. OBRIETAN, S. T. WONG, S. POSER, S. YANO, G. WOYMAN, J. C. DELOUME, G. CHAN, and D. R. STORM, 1998. Cross talk between ERK and PKA is required for CA^{2+} stimulation of CREB-dependent transcription and ERK nuclear translocation. *Neuron* 21:869–883.

KAANG, B. K., E. R. KANDEL, and S. G. GRANT, 1993. Activation of cAMP-responsive genes by stimuli that produce long-term facilitation in *Aplysia* sensory neurons. *Neuron* 10:427–435.

KARPINSKI, B. A., G. D. MORLE, J. HUGGENVIK, M. D. UHLER, and J. M. LEIDEN, 1992. Molecular cloning of human CREB-2: An ATF/CREB transcription factor that can negatively regulate transcription from the cAMP response element. *Proc. Natl. Acad. Sci. U.S.A.* 89:4820–4824.

KELLER, F., and S. SCHACHER, 1990. Neuron-specific membrane glycoproteins promoting neurite fasciculation in *Aplysia californica*. *J. Cell. Biol.* 111:2637–2650.

KENNEDY, T. E., D. KUHL, A. BARZILAI, J. D. SWEATT, and E. R. KANDEL, 1992. Long-term sensitization training in *Aplysia* leads to an increase in calreticulin, a major presynaptic calcium-binding protein. *Neuron* 9:1013–1024.

KUHL, D., T. E. KENNEDY, A. BARZILAI, and E. R. KANDEL, 1992. Long-term sensitization training in *Aplysia* leads to an increase in the expression of BiP, the major protein chaperon of the ER. *J. Cell. Biol.* 119:1069–1076.

LANDMESSER, I., I. DAHM, J. TANG, and U. RUTISHAUSER, 1992. Polysialic acid as a regulator of intramuscular nerve branching during embryonic development. *Neuron* 4:655–667.

LÜTHL, A., J.-P. LAURENT, A. FIGUROV, D. MULLER, and M. SCHACHNER, 1994. Hippocampal long-term potentiation and neural cell adhesion molecules L1 and NCAM. *Nature* 372:777–779.

MARSHALL, C. J., 1995. Specificity of receptor tyrosine kinase signaling: Transient versus sustained extracellular signal-regulated kinase activation. *Cell* 80:179–185.

MARTIN, K. C., A. CASADIO, Y. E, H. ZHU, J. C. ROSE, M. CHEN, C. H. BAILEY, and E. R. KANDEL, 1997. Synapse-specific, long-term facilitation of *Aplysia* sensory to motor synapses: A function for local protein synthesis in memory storage. *Cell* 91:927–938.

MARTIN, K. C., and E. R. KANDEL, 1996. Cell adhesion molecules, CREB, and the formation of new synaptic connections during development and learning [comment]. *Neuron* 17:567–570.

MARTIN, K. C., D. MICHAEL, J. C. ROSE, M. BARAD, A. CASADIO, H. ZHU, and E. R. KANDEL, 1997. MAP kinase translocates into the nucleus of the presynaptic cell and is required for long-term facilitation in *Aplysia*. *Neuron* 18:899–912.

MAYFORD, M., A. BARZILAI, F. KELLER, S. SCHACHER, and E. R. KANDEL, 1992. Modulation of an NCAM-related adhesion molecule with long-term synaptic plasticity in *Aplysia*. *Science* 256:638–644.

MICHAEL, D., and K. C. MARTIN, 1998. Repeated pulses of serotonin required for long-term facilitation activate mitogen-activated protein kinase in sensory neurons of *Aplysia*. *Proc. Natl. Acad. Sci. U.S.A.* 95:1864–1869.

MONTAROLO, P. G., P. GOELET, V. F. CASTELLUCCI, J. MORGAN, E. R. KANDEL, and S. SCHACHER, 1986. A critical period for macromolecular synthesis in long-term heterosynaptic facilitation in *Aplysia*. *Science* 234:1249–1254.

MONTMINY, M. R., K. A. SEVARINO, J. A. WAGNER, G. MANDEL, and R. H. GOODMAN, 1986. Identification of a cyclic-AMP-responsive element within the rat somatostatin gene. *Proc. Natl. Acad. Sci. U.S.A.* 83:6682–6686.

NGUYEN, P. V., T. ABEL, and E. R. KANDEL, 1994. Requirement of a critical period of transcription for induction of a late phase of LTP. *Science* 265:1104–1107.

PINSKER, H. M., W. A. HENING, T. J. CAREW, and E. R. KANDEL, 1973. Long-term sensitization of a defensive withdrawal reflex in *Aplysia*. *Science* 182:1039–1042.

ROSE, S. P., 1995. Cell-adhesion molecules, glucocorticoids, and long-term memory formation. *Trends Neurosci.* 18:502–506.

RUPPERT, S., T. J. COLE, M. BOSHART, E. SCHMID, and G. SCHUTZ, 1992. Multiple mRNA isoforms of the transcription activator protein CREB: Generation by alternative splicing and specific expression in primary spermatocytes. *Embo. J.* 11:1503–1512.

RUTISHAUSER, U., 1993. Adhesion molecules of the nervous system. *Curr. Opin. Neurobiol.* 3:709–715.

SCHELLER, R. H., J. F. JACKSON, L. B. MCALLISTER, J. H. SCHWARTZ, E. R. KANDEL, and R. AXEL, 1982. A family of genes that codes for ELH, a neuropeptide eliciting a stereotyped pattern of behavior in *Aplysia*. *Cell* 28:707–719.

SCHWARTZ, J. H., V. F. CASTELLUCCI, and E. R. KANDEL, 1971. Functioning of identified neurons and synapses in abdominal ganglion of *Aplysia* in absence of protein synthesis. *J. Neurophysiol.* 34:939–953.

SQUIRE, L. R., 1992. Memory and the hippocampus: A synthesis from findings with rats, monkeys, and humans [published erratum appears in *Psychol. Rev.* 1992 Jul:99(3):582]. *Psychol. Rev.* 99:195–231.

TANG, J., L. LANDMESSER, and U. RUTISHAUSER, 1992. Polysialic acid influences specific pathfinding by avian motoneurons. *Neuron* 8:1031–1044.

TULLY, T., T. PREAT, S. C. BOYNTON, and M. DEL VECCHIO, 1994. Genetic dissection of consolidated memory in *Drosophila*. *Cell* 79:35–47.

VAN MINNEN, J., J. J. BERGMAN, E. R. VAN KESTEREN, A. B. SMIT, W. P. M. GERAERTS, K. LUKOWIAK, S. U. HASAN, and N. I. SYED, 1997. De novo protein synthesis in isolated axons of identified neurons. *Neuroscience* 80:1–7.

YIN, J. C., M. DEL VECCHIO, H. ZHOU, and T. TULLY, 1995. CREB as a memory modulator: Induced expression of a dCREB2 activator isoform enhances long-term memory in *Drosophila*. *Cell* 81:107–115.

YIN, J. C., J. S. WALLACH, M. DEL VECCHIO, E. L. WILDER, H. ZHOU, W. G. QUINN, and T. TULLY, 1994. Induction of a dominant negative CREB transgene specifically blocks long-term memory in *Drosophila*. *Cell* 79:49–58.

YIN, J. C., J. S. WALLACH, E. L. WILDER, J. KLINGENSMITH, D. DANG, N. PERRIMON, H. ZHOU, T. TULLY, and W. G. QUINN, 1995. A *Drosophila* CREB/CREM homolog encodes multiple isoforms, including a cyclic AMP-dependent protein kinase-responsive transcriptional activator and antagonist. *Mol. Cell. Biol.* 15:5123–5130.

10 Memory Consolidation and Long-Term Potentiation

GARY LYNCH

ABSTRACT The relationship of long-term potentiation (LTP) to memory is examined with regard to the phenomenon of consolidation, a poorly understood process whereby newly encoded material is gradually made resistant to disruption. Results and ideas from four areas of work are reviewed. First, in vivo and in vitro studies of rat hippocampus have shown that LTP has a consolidation period with many of the same features, including time course, as those classically described for memory. Second, LTP consolidation appears to be mediated by adhesion chemistries and, in particular, by the activation of latent integrin receptors. These discoveries led to the hypothesis that transmission and adhesion–the two functions of synapses–interact, respectively, to express and consolidate potentiation. Third, certain patterns of neuronal activity associated with learning erase potentiation during the consolidation period. This finding raises the possibility that the consolidation period has psychological utility, perhaps with regard to sculpting newly encoded memories. Fourth, recently invented drugs that promote LTP consolidation reduce the number of training trials needed for the formation of lasting memory. These drugs constitute a first application of information about LTP to development of potential therapeutics for memory impairments. In all, the multiple correspondences between physiological and behavioral consolidation point to the conclusion that the two phenomena have the same substrates.

Much, indeed very much, has been written about the relationship between long-term potentiation (LTP) and memory. Clearly some biological mechanism exists with the rapid onset, longevity, and remarkable capacity of memory; that LTP has these and other useful and uncommon encoding properties made inevitable its investigation as a substrate for long-lasting memory, especially in the absence of alternative proposals. Experimental work began with NMDA receptor antagonists (Morris et al., 1986), moved on to correlational analyses using patterned stimulation as a discriminative cue (Roman, Staubli, and Lynch, 1987), and then turned to molecular biological/behavioral approaches (e.g., Mayford, Abel, and Kandel, 1995). Much has been gained from these efforts, including an appreciation of the profound intellectual and practical difficulties attendant to testing the simple proposition "LTP is a substrate of memory." To

GARY LYNCH Department of Psychiatry and Human Behavior, University of California, Irvine, Calif.

note a small example with big consequences, substituting the definite article in this proposition converts it to a form that is manifestly *not* true (it is easily shown that forms of memory exist that do not involve LTP) and yet is widely employed, perhaps unwittingly, in LTP/behavior arguments. These difficulties provide ample reason to be pessimistic about the still popular search for an *experimentum crucis* that "proves" or "disproves" the role of LTP in memory. Testing nontrivial or, better still, counterintuitive predictions arising from the memory/LTP hypothesis is a better strategy: it is less method driven, is likely to generate discoveries about the capabilities of brain networks, and satisfies the normal requirements for accepting (rejecting) a hypothesis.

Testing predictions has, in fact, already uncovered a number of intriguing synaptic phenomena. The LTP-as-memory hypothesis requires synaptic potentiation (like memory) to have multiple decay rates, one of which must be extraordinarily slow. These points have been confirmed: LTP has variants lasting for minutes, hours, and days and, in some circumstances persists without evident change for weeks (Staubli and Lynch, 1987). That naturalistic patterns of stimulation (discussed later) can modify synaptic physiology for periods far longer than the half-life of synaptic proteins is remarkable by any measure. The present review begins with another strong and by no means intuitive prediction of the hypothesis. As has probably been known for as long as people have thought about such things, newly formed memory passes through a period during which it is easily erased and after which it is extremely stable. Consolidation, the name given to the stabilizing process, places severe constraints on LTP as a memory substrate: (a) potentiation has to be erasable without disturbing transmission at neighboring connections; (b) vulnerability has to be time dependent; (c) the pertinent time period should align with that for stabilization of memory. It bears emphasizing that these predictions about LTP arise solely from behavior–there is nothing in neurobiology that necessitates selective vulnerability or specifies the time frame over which potentiation fades. The first section of this chapter, "Consolidation of LTP," deals with results from experiments directed at the three consolidation predictions.

Relationships between macroscopic and microscopic levels of inquiry, as in the case under discussion, are most fruitful when they run in both directions. The "downward" portion of the dialogue is realized in the constraints imposed by the macroscopic level upon the nature of the microscopic, examples of which have been noted for memory/LTP. The "upward" portion has both familiar and not so familiar components. Regarding the former, mechanistic explanations for macroscopic phenomena are acknowledged goals of multilevel studies; in the present context, LTP research began with the assumption that isolation of the substrates of potentiation would yield satisfactory cellular explanations for specific aspects of memory. The second section, "Mechanisms: The adhesion hypothesis of consolidation," will ask if it has fulfilled this expectation with regard to consolidation. The less discussed aspect of the upward side of dialogue (from the micro- to the macro-) concerns understanding or awareness of the phenomena associated with memory. Does LTP predict the existence in memory of phenomena that have gone unnoticed or least under appreciated? This need not be the case. Potentiation isn't isomorphic with memory, and its neurobiological richness might not include details indicative of undiscovered counterparts in psychology. But maybe it will, and a potential case specific to consolidation is described in the third section, "Does the consolidation period have psychological utility?"

The preceding arguments are illustrated in figure 10.1 along with two additional, somewhat more pragmatic, motives for thinking about LTP from a psychological perspective. The first involves "synaptic memory algorithms" for network simulations. These operating rules relating input variables to when, where, and the degree to which contacts will change can be empirically derived through LTP experiments. Work along these lines has yielded novel algorithms and some impressive examples of computation with biological networks. Memory-enhancing drugs are a second potential by-product of LTP research. Potentiation of a preselected set of synapses in an in vitro environment is a much more tractable test system for drug development than behavior. According to the LTP hypothesis, compounds that promote stable potentiation are likely to have positive effects on consolidation of memory. This line of thought led to the discovery of a new class of drugs, and results obtained with these form the fourth subject considered here, in "The pharmacology of consolidation."

Consolidation of LTP

The idea that LTP has a memory-like consolidation period began with the startling (at least to the investigators)

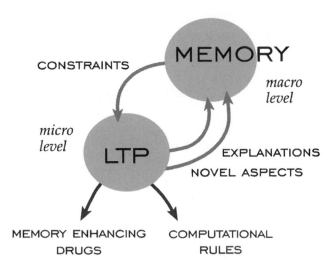

FIGURE 10.1 The dialogue between memory and long-term potentiation (LTP). Memory describes features in potentiation that need to be found before a causal relationship can be assumed (downward arrow). LTP provides explanations for various features of memory–for example, why new memories take minutes, rather than seconds or hours, to stabilize. The upward leg of the dialogue also involves asking if features in LTP can be used to illuminate features of memory that have gone unnoticed. Uncovering nontrivial phenomena often plays an important role in the process whereby microscopic/macroscopic linkages become accepted. Also shown in the figure are two pragmatic advantages in studying LTP and memory together. Potentiation is more easily used than behavior in developing memory-related drugs and provides direct access to the network-level learning rules needed for simulations of brain systems.

discovery in 1980 that potentiation, generated with high-frequency bursts in anesthetized rats, disappears if low-frequency afferent stimulation is applied within a few minutes of induction (Barrionuevo, Schottler, and Lynch, 1980). Too little was known in those early days of LTP to allow for educated guesses as to what types of processes might be involved in the reversal, but three additional observations limited the range of possibilities. First, the effect is synapse specific in that reversing LTP does not disturb neighboring contacts. This result indicates that reversal, like LTP, depends on local biochemical events. Second, reversing stimulation has only transient effects when applied to unpotentiated synapses, indicating that the chemistries triggered by the stimulation interact with those earlier set in motion during the induction of LTP. Third, normal-sized LTP was readily elicited after reversal, as expected if all traces of prior potentiation had been eliminated by the low-frequency stimulation. All three results are explained by the assumption that reversal works by interrupting still active synaptic processes that would (unless disturbed) ultimately produce stable LTP.

A subsequent chronic recording experiment confirmed these points and showed that LTP does not spontaneously recover even after delays of 24 hours (see figure 10.2), again indicating that potentiation was fully erased by low-frequency stimulation (Staubli and Lynch, 1990). The chronic study also showed that the stimulation needed for reversal does not create physiological disturbances in freely moving rats (Staubli and Lynch, 1990). This result reinforced the impression from the earlier, acute experiments that reversal, or at least the activity patterns causing it, could be occurring routinely during behavior. Discussion of this idea will be resumed in a later section.

The first in vitro studies of consolidation deliberately mimicked paradigms used in behavioral studies; that is, a global condition that disrupts physiology was administered at various intervals after LTP had been induced. Hypoxia of a duration just sufficient to transiently block synaptic responses completely eliminated LTP when ap-

plied within the first minute after induction but had only a momentary effect on neighboring, control synapses. Potentiation was resistant to hypoxia applied 30 minutes after induction; indeed, prolonging the episodes to the point at which pathophysiology appeared failed to affect LTP (Arai, Larson, and Lynch, 1990). These results established that LTP has a consolidation period and, moreover, that *the duration of this period is not greatly different than that expected from studies of memory consolidation.* They also prompted efforts to induce LTP reversal in slices using the low-frequency stimulation patterns that had proven effective in animals. Success in this (Larson, Xiao, and Lynch, 1993) made it possible to finally carry out parametric studies of stimulation patterns and to address the all-important question, from the perspective of the memory/LTP hypothesis, of how closely the time course for LTP stabilization matches that for consolidation. The

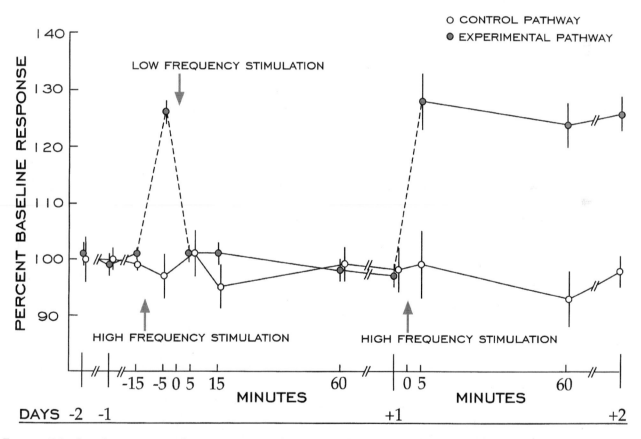

FIGURE 10.2 Low-frequency stimulation erases recently induced long-term potentiation. Chronic recording from freely moving rats was used to test whether LTP reappears once it has been reversed. Two collections of afferents (Schaffer-commissural projections) within the hippocampus were independently stimulated with single pulses at two times per minute. Average response size over two days of testing (days −2 and −1) was used as a baseline. On the experimental day, responses were collected for 15 min, after which "theta bursts" were applied to one of the two outputs. Low-frequency stimulation was applied

within 5 min of LTP induction. The second pathway (open circles) served as a control for any generalized effects of repetitive stimulation. Recording was continued for an hour and the rats returned to their home cages. One day later (day +1), they were returned to the recording apparatus, and tests were made to determine whether LTP had returned. No evidence for spontaneous recovery was found. A second round of theta bursts was then administered. As shown, LTP comparable to that seen 24 hr earlier was obtained. (Modified from Staubli and Lynch, 1990.)

latter issue was taken up by Ursula Staubli and colleagues (Staubli and Chun, 1996); their results along with those from the first memory consolidation experiment (Duncan, 1949) are shown in figure 10.3. The agreement between curves constitutes a striking example in which an otherwise arbitrary property of memory is paralleled in LTP. "Otherwise arbitrary" because there are no known biological or psychological processes that would dictate the illustrated time course for consolidation. Changes in gene expression, for example, are too slow to explain a process that is well under way within a minute and results in an extremely stable state 15–30 minutes later.

An additional point established in the in vitro studies is that reversal can be modulated. Specifically, the probability and magnitude of the effect were increased by high concentrations of norepinephrine (Larson, Xiao, and Lynch, 1993) while the postinduction time frame for robust reversal was substantially lengthened by positive modulators of AMPA-type glutamate receptors (Staubli and Chun, 1996). Independent of their significance for ideas about the substrates of reversal, these results showed that the LTP consolidation period has

some of the same flexibility as its counterpart in memory.

Mechanisms: The adhesion hypothesis of consolidation

What is it, then, that stabilizes LTP and, by inference, memory? Figure 10.4 suggests an answer by recalling that synapses (the locus of potentiation) are junctions with two functions, one highly specialized and the other ubiquitous. The specialized activity–transmission–is the subject of much of neurobiology, while the commonplace function–adhesion–is all but ignored. The simple proposal to be made here is that these functions interact–that transmitter receptors modify adhesion receptors, and adhesion receptors, through their control of junctional organization, regulate the status of transmitter receptors.

INTEGRINS AND CONSOLIDATION Adhesion chemistries were brought into LTP (Staubli, Vanderklish, and Lynch, 1990; Xiao et al., 1991) as a mechanism that

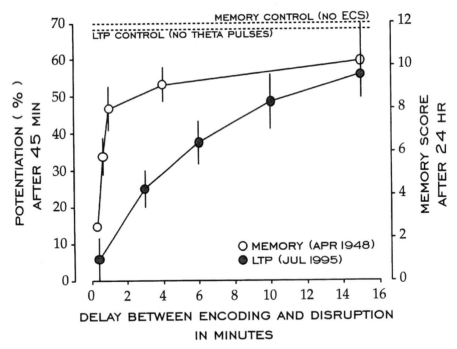

FIGURE 10.3 Memory and LTP consolidate over the same time period. The behavioral data are from Duncan's original description of the time course for consolidation, submitted in April 1948 (Duncan, 1949). Those studies used electroconvulsive shocks (ECS) to disrupt recent learning; that is, rats were trained, given ECS, and tested for retention on the following day. As shown, ECS applied immediately after learning essentially erased memory; the amnestic effect became progressively smaller as the interval between learning and ECS was increased to 5 min, although consolidation did not appear to

be complete even at 15 min. Numerous examples of consolidation over this time frame, though often without the steepness of the curve shown here, have been published. The LTP data are from a paper by Staubli and Chun (1996). In this instance, low-frequency stimulation was delivered at various times after LTP had been induced (see figure 10.2) and the amount of potentiation 45 min later tested. Near complete erasure was obtained when the stimulation was given after a delay of 30 seconds; longer delays resulted in progressively less reversal. Note again that consolidation is not quite complete even at 15 min.

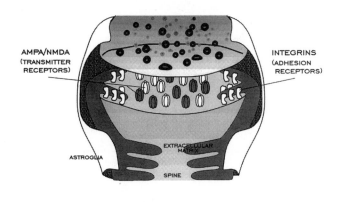

AMPA/NMDA
(TRANSMITTER
RECEPTORS)

INTEGRINS
(ADHESION
RECEPTORS)

EXTRACELLULAR MATRIX

ASTROGLIA

SPINE

ADHESION HYPOTHESIS OF SYNAPTIC PLASTICITY

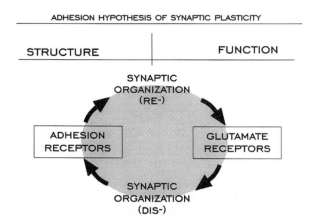

STRUCTURE

FUNCTION

SYNAPTIC ORGANIZATION (RE-)

ADHESION RECEPTORS

GLUTAMATE RECEPTORS

SYNAPTIC ORGANIZATION (DIS-)

FIGURE 10.4   The adhesion hypothesis of consolidation. The figure in the upper panel emphasizes the usually overlooked point that synapses have two very different functions—transmission and adhesion—requiring very different types of receptors. The illustrated ingredients have been described in experimental reports from different laboratories, but the arrangement here is hypothetical. Integrins are shown binding to the extracellular matrix, some part of which is probably generated by the surrounding sheets of astroglial processes. Cadherins and neural cell adhesion molecules, two other types of adhesion receptors found in synapses, are not included in the figure. The bottom panel summarizes the proposal that the two classes of receptors interact, with the result being expression and consolidation of LTP. Glutamate receptors are pictured as driving intracellular chemistries that disassemble the synaptic cytoskeleton and existing adhesive relationships. This process activates latent adhesion receptors that over several minutes reorganize the cytoskeleton and restabilize the synapse. Remodeling the synapse in this way affects the environment in which AMPA-type glutamate receptors are situated; this effect, according to this hypothesis, changes the operating characteristics of the receptors and thus the size and shape of synaptic currents.

could account for three earlier observations: (1) Potentiation is accompanied by changes in synaptic morphology that develop within minutes but then persist indefinitely (Lee et al., 1980, 1981). (2) Consolidation is largely complete within 30 minutes (see preceding section). (3) The minimal stimulation needed to induce potentiation causes partial cleavage of cytoskeletal proteins (see Vanderklish et al., 1995, for direct tests). The first two points required a minutes-range chemistry that can shape morphology into new and stable configurations; the third described how extant structures could be disassembled and indicated that reassembly would have to work on an altered cytoskeleton. Integrins, one of three classes of transmembrane cell adhesion receptors, have properties that match up well with these requirements. They exist in latent states and are brought into play by the sorts of transient events (Du et al., 1991; Newton, Thiel, and Hogg, 1997, for examples) associated with LTP induction; once activated they assemble a remarkable collection of cytoplasmic proteins and thereby reorganize the submembrane cytoskeleton (see Clark and Hynes, 1996, for a review). The time course for this is on the order of several minutes (e.g., van Willigen et al., 1996)–ideal for consolidation–and has as its consequence the formation or modification of a junction that will persist for long stretches of biological time unless actively disturbed.

The first tests for the involvement of integrins in LTP consolidation took advantage of the critical discovery that binding of many of the receptors to their matrix targets is blocked by short peptides containing the amino acid sequence RGD (Pierschbacher and Ruoslahti, 1984). Such peptides block integrin-mediated events (e.g., fibroblast attachment, platelet aggregation, etc.) throughout the body (e.g., Haskel and Abendschein, 1989) and proved to be effective in blocking the consolidation of LTP (Staubli, Vanderklish, and Lynch, 1990; Xiao et al., 1991). Not unexpectedly, given that integrins don't mediate moment-to-moment activities, the antagonists had no measurable effects on baseline physiology, the burst responses used to induce LTP, or the initial degree of potentiation. Nonetheless, LTP induced in their presence failed to stabilize but instead decayed steadily toward baseline over a period of 60 minutes. Later work tested whether integrin activation satisfies one of the most stringent demands that consolidation places on potential substrates, namely, reversal of already established potentiation. Experiments directed at this issue showed that RGD-containing peptides selectively reverse LTP when infused 2 minutes after induction but not when applied after delays of 25 min or longer (figure 10.5). Intermediate results were obtained with applications at 10 min (Staubli, Chun, and Lynch, 1998). The agreement in time courses over which low-frequency stimulation and highly selective peptide antagonists (whose effect is eliminated by single amino acid substitutions) reverse LTP strongly suggests that the two manipulations have a common target. *Integrin activation/engagement thus emerges as that process whose temporal requirements dictate the*

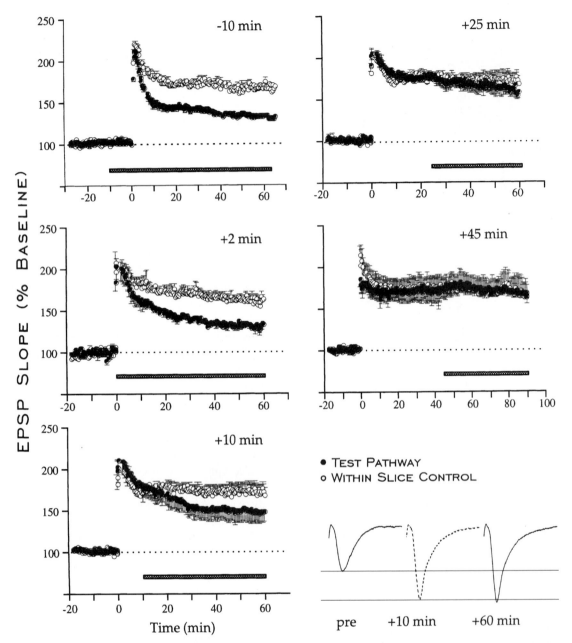

FIGURE 10.5 Integrin receptor antagonists block consolidation. This experiment parallels that summarized in figure 10.3. The antagonists were locally applied to sites within hippocampal slices at various times before or after LTP induction. Controls (open circles) in this case consisted of sites within the slice at which LTP was induced but antagonist was not applied. Blocking integrins even 10 min after induction prevented consolidation. The same treatment had no evident effect when administered 25 min after LTP had been established. (Modified from Staubli et al., 1998.)

particular time courses recently discovered for LTP and repeatedly described for memory.

Two further points should be noted before leaving the topic of integrin antagonists and physiology. First, a mechanism has been identified that explains how low-frequency synaptic responses could block integrin activation; this is considered in a later discussion on the pharmacology of consolidation. Second, RGD peptides block the development of kindling in hippocampal slices (Grooms and Jones, 1997). This recent and important discovery adds a second case in which integrins appear to translate transient high-frequency activity into very stable physiological changes; it will not be surprising if other examples follow.

The results on adhesion and LTP set in motion a search for synaptic integrins in the adult brain. There was virtually no information on this topic at the time of the initial physiological studies, but biochemical experiments soon established that RGD-binding integrins are highly concentrated in forebrain connections (Bahr,

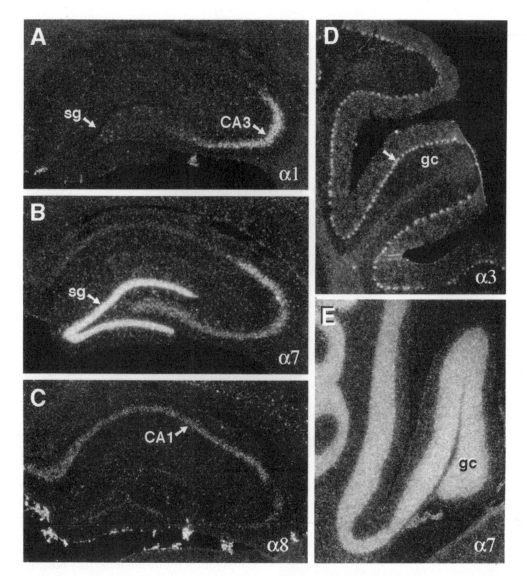

FIGURE 10.6   Brain regions differ in the types of integrins they express. Shown are the distributions of a subgroup of the mRNAs encoding different α subunits used in forming dimeric integrin receptors. Panels A, B, and C show that integrins are differentially expressed across hippocampal subdivisions; CA3 has α1, while dentate gyrus has α7 and CA1 has enriched α8. Regional differences are also found in the cerebellum where α3 is located in the Purkinje neurons while α7 is present in the granule cells. (See Pinkstaff et al., 1999, for further description.)

Sheppard, and Lynch, 1991; Bahr and Lynch, 1992; Bahr et al., 1997). Immunohistochemical work took this investigation much further by localizing known integrin subunits to spines and postsynaptic densities in the hippocampus (Einheber et al., 1996; Nishimura et al., 1998; also see Grooms, Terracio, and Jones, 1993). With the discovery that synapses have integrins, the question of whether different regions or types of neurons utilize different versions of the receptors assumed some importance. Integrins are dimers composed of combinations drawn from more than 16 known α subunits and at least 8 β subunits. Variations in subunit composition have a large effect on the properties of the assembled αβ integrins; peripheral tissues take advantage of this fact to generate collections of functionally distinct adhesion receptors. Recent studies mapping the distribution of the mRNAs encoding the different subunits strongly suggest that brain regions do the same. An example for one subunit is shown in figure 10.6. If these differences are reflected in assembled integrins, then variations in synaptic adhesion receptors would likely be as great as or greater than differences in transmitter receptors. This possibility has important implications for ideas about regional specializations for plasticity and consolidation.

MECHANISMS FOR MODIFYING SYNAPTIC ADHESION. Results connecting integrins to consolidation were followed by reports that cell adhesion molecules (CAMs) and cadherins, the other two classes of adhesion receptors, are also involved in LTP (Rønn et al., 1995; Luthi et al., 1994; Tang, Hung, and Schuman, 1998). These reports provided additional support for, and greatly extended, the general hypothesis that adhesion chemistries are responsible for LTP consolidation. In the case of CAMs, it appears that the relevant changes occur quickly, since blocking agents have little effect when applied immediately after induction (Rønn et al., 1995; Staubli, Chun, and Lynch, 1998). In all likelihood, the three classes of adhesion receptor differ with regard to the following: (1) steps needed to dismantle extant adhesive contacts; (2) steps required to reestablish the contacts; and (3) the influence of the new linkages on emerging changes in synaptic organization and function. In accord with their functions in other systems, and as confirmed by the time course over which their antagonists reduce recent LTP, integrins have a central role in organizing stable changes in the synaptic cytoskeleton and the morphology it supports. The other adhesion receptors minimally provide attachment sites to stabilize remodeled connections and could participate in more active, but so far unknown, ways (point 3).

Regarding disruptive steps (point 1), intracellular proteolysis by calpain (a calcium-sensitive cysteine protease) coupled with extracellular proteolysis by released serine proteases (Hoffman, Larson, et al., 1999; Hoffman, Martinez, and Lynch, 1999) appear to be critical for consolidating LTP. Both types of enzymes are known to recognize an array of proteins that participate in junctional adhesion (Sheppard et al., 1991; Du et al., 1995; Hoffman, Larson, et al., 1999) and therefore have the potential to disengage the adhesive relationships supported by all three classes of receptors. The breakdown products generated by the proteases appear immediately after inducing stimulation but do not increase in concentration thereafter (Vanderklish et al., 1995; Hoffman, Larson, et al., 1999). This finding indicates that the proteolytic events themselves are very brief and restricted to a fraction of the adhesion-related proteins; a limited degree of disengagement can be assumed.

Finally, engaging latent receptors, as discussed for integrins, may not be available to the other two groups of adhesion molecules as a means of reestablishing contacts. Other options include inserting new copies drawn from a local pool, provided by ongoing synthesis, or generated by up-regulating synthesis. Thus there is an interesting possibility that consolidation of synaptic changes is only partially complete after integrins have been activated and synaptic anatomy reorganized. Complete stabilization may come only when cleaved proteins have been replaced and the remodeled synapse left with a normal complement of adhesion molecules. Re-

placement, protein synthesis, and consolidation are considered again in a later section.

CONNECTING CONSOLIDATION AND EXPRESSION.   Stable LTP requires both consolidation and expression events—that is, a change that lasts indefinitely (or is periodically renewed) and a modification to transmission that increases the size of postsynaptic currents. Given that the generators of these currents are continuously broken down and replaced, it is difficult to envision the two functions emerging from a single cellular change. If so, then links between consolidation events and expression events are needed. Links, of course, can only be considered in the context of what has been learned about the basis of expression, aspects of which are noted in the following paragraphs.

An extensive body of evidence points to changes in the AMPA-type glutamate receptors that mediate fast synaptic currents (EPSCs) throughout the brain as the agency of LTP expression:

Argument by exclusion

1. LTP occurs without changing frequency facilitation (Muller and Lynch, 1989) or the effects of other manipulations that influence release probability (Muller et al., 1988). The lack of interaction makes it extremely unlikely that potentiation itself affects probability.

2. Normal LTP can be induced with minimal (Muller, Joly, and Lynch, 1988; Muller and Lynch, 1988) or no (Kauer, Malenka, and Nicoll, 1988) changes in NMDA-receptor-gated currents. NMDA and AMPA receptors are colocalized in synapses; short of a set of unlikely assumptions, it is difficult to picture how changes in transmitter concentration could affect one group of receptors and not the other. These widely replicated results are in accord with the preceding point and rule out changes in transmitter release as the expression mechanism.

3. A change in the thickness of the spine neck is a rare unitary explanation for consolidation and expression; that is, a change that is structural, and therefore could last for as long as the synapse itself, causes a decrease in resistance to synaptic current. Elegant as the idea is, tests of two predictions arising from it proved negative (Jung, Larson, and Lynch, 1991; Larson and Lynch, 1991).

If LTP is not expressed by increases in transmitter or decreases in postsynaptic resistance, then by exclusion it is very probably due to receptor modifications.

Plausibility AMPA-type glutamate receptors, which mediate the synaptic responses that become potentiated, are unusually "plastic." Removing the receptors from their synaptic membranes causes them to shift to a much higher affinity state (Hall, Kessler, and Lynch, 1992), something that does not occur with NMDA receptors. Various experiments indicate that they are influenced by phospholipids (Massicote et al., 1991), intermolecular associations with other proteins (Terramani et al., 1988; Hall et al., 1996), and subsynaptic enzymes (Strack et al., 1997; Barria et al., 1997; Hayashi et al., 1997). In light of these findings, it can be expected that changes in the membrane environment arising from remodeled synaptic anatomy will change the receptors responsible for fast synaptic currents. AMPA receptors are thus plausible candidates for the site of expression.

Correlational evidence

1. Receptor biophysics dictate the shape as well as the size of synaptic current. Changes in waveform are therefore expected for many, but not all, types of receptor modifications. A particular type of waveform shift has in fact been found in studies using field potential (Ambros-Ingerson et al., 1991, 1993; Ambros-Ingerson and Lynch, 1993) or whole-cell recording from slices (Xie et al., 1997), and is evident in data from single-synapse recordings (Stricker, Field, and Redman, 1996; see Kolta, Lynch, and Ambros-Ingerson, 1998).

2. Modifications to receptor biophysics because of LTP should change the effects of other manipulations that independently alter biophysics. This relationship has been confirmed (Xiao et al., 1991; Staubli, Ambros-Ingerson, and Lynch, 1992; Kolta, Lynch, and Ambros-Ingerson, 1998) using the drug aniracetam, which slows certain AMPA receptor rate constants (Ito et al., 1990). The result has been disputed (Asztely et al., 1992) and in any event should be revisited with much more potent AMPA receptor modulators that have recently become available (see the section "Ampakines" below). The point is crucial for two reasons: (1) Interactions between LTP and modulatory drugs would be presumptive evidence that potentiation had modified the operating characteristics of AMPA receptors; (2) coupled with waveform change data, the nature of the interactions could be used to define the nature of the modifications.

Receptor manipulation If AMPA receptors are the agents of expression, then modifying their makeup should in some way modify LTP. This idea was tested using translational suppression of a single receptor subunit to shift receptor composition in favor of the remaining subunits (AMPA receptors are pentamers or tetramers). This experiment was feasible because fully functional AMPA receptors assemble in the absence of the targeted, normally present subunit (Hollman and Heinemann, 1994; see Seeburg, 1993, for reviews). As expected, there were no apparent changes in baseline physiology in slices

with reduced concentrations of the subunit. Expression of LTP, however, was drastically reduced (Vanderklish et al., 1992).

Various proposals based on the evidence summarized here have been made regarding the nature of the receptor change responsible for expression. These include the following:

More receptors The presence of more receptors could be due to the activation of latent receptors or the insertion of copies from a free pool (Lynch and Baudry, 1984, and others). Increases in receptors would almost certainly increase post-synaptic currents.

Clustering Modeling studies by Berger and colleagues suggest that clustering would modify the probabilities of transmitter binding in such a way that a potentiated response would eventuate (Xie et al., 1997).

Modulatory proteins Reorganizing the subsynaptic cytoskeleton could increase the access of proteins that modulate the operational characteristics of AMPA receptors.

Membrane environment As noted, the receptors are very sensitive to their protein and lipid environment, which itself is influenced by the submembrane structural proteins; changing the environment as part of synaptic remodeling would modify receptor biophysics or conductance.

The first two ideas do not involve changes in receptor properties, but the second two do; accordingly, proposals three and four predict interactions between LTP and modulatory drugs, whereas one and two do not. There are already data on this point. The third and fourth ideas can be further tested by defining enzyme and/or lipid influences on the receptors in reduced systems and then searching for comparable effects after LTP induction. Separating the first and second ideas could in principle be done with binding studies (more receptors, more sites). However, past experiments of this type have yielded contradictory results, leaving the question open. Further studies of this kind, together with those on the other listed possibilities, should result in a leading candidate for the mechanism of expression.

Returning to the question of links between consolidation and expression, each of the four expression proposals involves a passive response to a structural change. For example, it is easy to envision a more circular postsynaptic apposition zone increasing the area available for receptors; ongoing processes that insert receptors into the zone would then, without changing their operations, create LTP. Similar morphofunctional arguments can be made for how shifts in the configuration of the subsynaptic cytoskeleton necessarily will influence receptor density, synaptic membrane fluidity, and the movement of modulatory proteins from the spine cytoplasm to the inner face of the synaptic membrane. A very attractive feature of these ideas is that they separate the problem of extreme stability–as manifested by LTP and memory–from the need to adjust the operation of transient receptors. However, it must be stressed that the sequence composed of adhesion chemistry → synaptic morphology → receptor operation, though biologically plausible, remains a hypothesis that posits yet-to-be-demonstrated connections between three independent groups of results. It is for future studies to describe, for example, the connections between adhesion receptors and the postsynaptic density or between the postsynaptic density and clustering of AMPA receptors.

Does the consolidation period have psychological utility?

The memory/LTP hypothesis predicts that naturally occurring patterns of brain activity, as well as patterns related to learning in particular, induce the potentiation effect. The discovery that this is in fact the case (Larson and Lynch, 1986; Larson, Wong, and Lynch, 1986) provided one of the more convincing links between memory and potentiation. The pertinent work has been reviewed elsewhere and will only be noted here as necessary background to a seldom-asked question about consolidation posed by studies on LTP reversal.

A 4–7 Hz rhythm (theta) occurs throughout the cortical telencephalon and is particularly prominent in the hippocampus of small mammals during active behavior. Individual cells commonly emit short bursts of high-frequency activity (3–4 pulses in 30–50 ms) with the bursts being synchronized with the rhythm (Otto et al., 1991). These conditions (bursts separated by 150–250 ms) proved to be ideal for inducing LTP when used as a stimulation pattern. Studies on the reasons for this result showed that theta takes advantage of an IPSP refractory process that reaches its maximum at about 200 ms (Larson, Wong, and Lynch, 1986). Theta thus momentarily releases target neurons from feedforward inhibition (Larson and Lynch, 1986), allowing a second theta burst to generate depolarization sufficient to activate NMDA receptors (Larson and Lynch, 1988) and produce the elevations of internal calcium needed to induce potentiation. Other workers found that the refractory period itself is due to inhibition of GABAergic terminals by GABAb autoreceptors (Mott and Lewis, 1991). In all, the investigations of the LTP-theta relationship provided a first success in coupling brain rhythms to synaptic chemistry. Moreover, the connection of patterns of brain activity with increments in synaptic strength provided

mechanistic explanations for fundamental features of memory including the prominence of temporal contiguity in the forming of associations.

The fact that LTP induction has a deep relationship with a particular rhythm inevitably raised the question of whether this is also true for LTP reversal. Confirmation came in a series of experiments using hippocampal slices (Larson, Xiao, and Lynch, 1993). While the existence of particularly appropriate patterns for reversal was not unexpected, it was indeed surprising that the pertinent rhythm proved to be theta. This discovery strongly implies that erasure requires the prolonged EPSPs that result from IPSP suppression, presumably for altogether different reasons than those involved with induction. Possible mechanisms suggested by theta and other aspects of reversal will be taken up briefly in a later section. But independent of neurobiological issues, the connection of reversal to a prominent rhythm points to the possibility that it is a "real world" event, that is, one that occurs routinely in behaving animals. This impression is strengthened by a more detailed examination of the experiments in which the connection was found. Two inputs (groups of Schaffer-commissural fibers) that converged on a target population of dendrites were used (figure 10.7). Pairs of theta bursts were applied simultaneously to each input; 20 seconds later, *single pulses* at 5 per second (theta) were delivered to one of the two inputs for 30 seconds. This procedure was repeated every 2 minutes for a total of five pairs of theta bursts. Absent theta pulse stimulation, both inputs increment their synaptic strength after each pair of theta bursts until a ceiling is reached after 5–10 pairs; with the pulses, one input grows stronger and the other does not change (see Larson, Xiao, and Lynch, 1993). These results establish that reversal is synapse specific (neighboring inputs were unaffected), occurs with small fiber populations, and involves a commonplace rhythm. Thirty sequential pulses are not likely to occur in vivo, but there is no reason to assume that fewer pulses would not be at least partially effective (30 was the lowest number used in the Larson, Xiao, and Lynch studies). It is also the case that, anecdotally at least, reversal is more robust in vivo than in vitro. In all, conditions needed for reversal may occur routinely during behavior.

The vulnerability of memory to disruption during consolidation is not usually thought of with regard to its psychological utility. But the demonstration that near-normal physiologies can eliminate newly induced synaptic changes is certainly suggestive of a kind of "active forgetting." Something like this could be useful in focusing memory on essential features by erasing over trials the aspects of information that are not reliably detected in successive samplings. Forming a composite memory

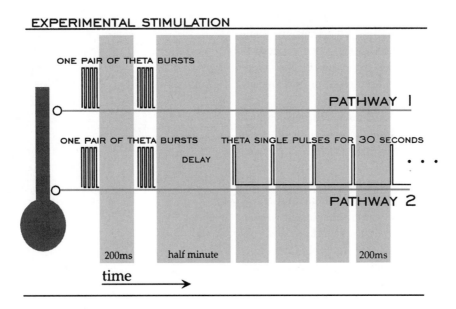

EXPERIMENTAL STIMULATION

ONE PAIR OF THETA BURSTS

PATHWAY 1

ONE PAIR OF THETA BURSTS   THETA SINGLE PULSES FOR 30 SECONDS

DELAY

PATHWAY 2

200ms   half minute   200ms

time

REPEAT STIMULATION FIVE TIMES AT TWO MINUTE INTERVALS

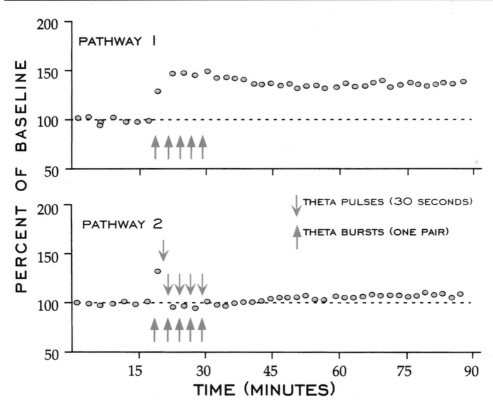

PATHWAY 1

PATHWAY 2

THETA PULSES (30 SECONDS)

THETA BURSTS (ONE PAIR)

PERCENT OF BASELINE

TIME (MINUTES)

FIGURE 10.7   Naturally occurring patterns of afferent activity block consolidation. The illustrated experiments showed that the theta rhythm erases LTP as well as inducing it. Theta burst pairs were delivered simultaneously to two small group of afferents that converged on a population of target neurons (top panel). One population (Pathway 2) received theta pulses beginning 30 seconds later; the other population (Pathway 1) did not. This procedure was repeated five times at 2-min intervals. As shown in the bottom panel, robust and stable LTP developed in Pathway 1, while Pathway 2 was barely changed. (Modified from Larson, Xiao, and Lynch, 1993.)

of a building from different viewpoints could be an example. In any event, the idea that memories are being continuously made and discarded using two versions of the same rhythm (theta bursts, theta pulses) has consequences for network theories, the design of memory-enhancing drugs, and learning theory.

Active forgetting provides a first example in which LTP research suggests something about memory that has not been prominent in psychological studies or theories (the second of the upward links noted in the introductory paragraphs). Moreover, the idea arrives with details that would not have been found with behavioral analyses alone but that nonetheless have behavioral connotations. Theta pulses are an example: these are not detectable as such in behavior but are probably closely associated with a subset of psychological states (Vertis and Kocsis, 1997). Information of this sort not only fleshes out the idea of active forgetting but also provides a correlational approach for testing if it exists; for example, does the presence or absence of the pulses correlate with what is learned (e.g., the steepness of generalization gradients for a complex cue). Pharmacological manipulation provides another approach with which to search for active forgetting, but this is better considered in the general context of LTP and memory enhancement (see the next section). Finally, it bears repeating that the uncovering of interesting phenomena in response to developments at a more microscopic level of analysis has historically proved to be a critical step in the acceptance of theories about mechanisms. In this sense, reversal and forgetting may contribute to the debate on LTP and memory.

The pharmacology of consolidation

Long-term potentiation seen from the perspective of psychology is primarily a tool for explaining and illuminating memory. As noted in the introductory paragraphs and considered here, it can also serve as a test bed with which to develop drugs directed at consolidation.

THREE CLASSES OF SYNAPTIC RECEPTORS The assumption that consolidation involves the sequence "glutamate receptors → adhesion receptors → glutamate receptors" defines two interactions (→) that are obvious targets for memory-enhancing drugs. Figure 10.8 describes another set of possibilities. As illustrated, synapses contain modulatory receptors in addition to the already discussed transmitter and adhesion receptors. There are a variety of these but the two included in the figure—adenosine and platelet-activating factor (PAF) receptors—are of particular interest because they have potent and opposite effects on LTP. Adenosine appears to

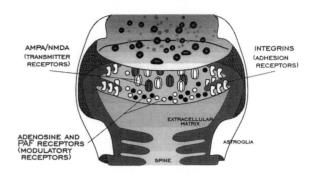

THE SYNAPSE: A JUNCTION WITH THREE TYPES OF RECEPTORS

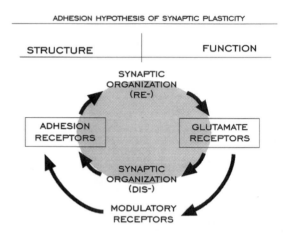

FIGURE 10.8 Incorporating modulatory receptors into the adhesion hypothesis of consolidation. Three types of receptors reported to be present in synapses are shown in the top panel. Possible relationships between them, and how these might influence consolidation, are considered in the bottom schematic. Glutamate receptors are postulated to relax synaptic organization by activating calcium-dependent, intracellular enzymes and to indirectly generate agonists (e.g., adenosine, platelet activating factor) for the modulatory receptors. The modulatory receptors then act on adhesion chemistries engaged by the relatively sudden loss of synaptic organization. The return link (adhesion to transmission) is discussed in the text (also see figure 10.4).

drive the reversal effect: stimulating the receptors immediately after induction reverses LTP (Arai, Kessler, and Lynch, 1990) while blocking them protects consolidation from hypoxia (Arai, Larson, and Lynch, 1990) or theta pulses (Larson, Xiao, and Lynch, 1993; Staubli and Chun, 1996; Abraham and Huggett, 1997). Add the observation that low-frequency stimulation causes a sizable efflux of adenosine (Cunha et al., 1996), and the case for adenosine reversal seems quite good. This opens up the possibility of using centrally active adenosine-receptor antagonists to search for traces of LTP reversal and active forgetting in behavior. Such studies would have to confront a lack of data on the synaptic effects of antagonists in vivo and, as well, develop controls for their notable peripheral influences. With regard to consolidation, any positive effects of adenosine-related drugs would probably come at the expense of what may be a psychologically useful reversal process.

PAF is a potent ether phospholipid that plays a prominent role in inflammatory cascades; it is rapidly generated from brain membranes under a variety of circumstances (see Bazan et al., 1997, for a review). The presence of high-affinity PAF receptors in synaptic membranes (Marcheselli et al., 1990) pointed to the possibility that PAF generated during intense activity somehow contributes to plasticity. This suspicion was confirmed in studies showing that PAF-receptor antagonists block the stabilization of LTP (del Cerro, Arai, and Lynch, 1990; Arai and Lynch, 1992; Bazan et al., 1997). Currently there are no compounds that promote PAF-receptor operations or that would otherwise positively influence the links between synaptic activity, PAF genesis, and PAF-receptor stimulation. Absent these, there are no obvious ways in which PAF's contributions to consolidation can be exploited in developing memory-enhancing drugs.

In passing it should be noted that the opposing effects of PAF and adenosine on LTP, which otherwise have no a priori basis, fit well within the adhesion hypothesis of consolidation. PAF receptors are among the most common triggers for converting latent integrins into an active configuration (Newton, Thiel, and Hogg, 1997)—activation, it will be recalled, was the minutes-long event proposed to reorganize (and restabilize) synaptic morphology. Adenosine receptors, however, are the only receptors so far described that *retard* the engagement of previously latent integrins (Theil et al., 1996). While these results point to the modulatory arrangements diagrammed in figure 10.8, it remains to be established that adenosine and PAF relationships described for peripheral tissues also hold for the brain in general and synapses in particular.

Returning to adhesion and transmitter receptors, there are no compounds available that selectively manipulate the engagement of integrins or facilitate the indirect influence they are postulated to exert on glutamate receptors. The same can be said of the other adhesion molecules (NCAMs, cadherins) and their related chemistries. This situation could change—the study of the links between synaptic adhesion and synaptic plasticity is only just under way, and interest is steadily increasing. But for now, the most obvious route for enhancing LTP is to modulate positively the transmitter receptors that set consolidation chemistries in motion. The obvious problem here is that the receptors mediate the most basic of brain operations with plasticity being a secondary issue.

However, selectivity may not be quite the problem it seems. (1) Prolonged depolarizations are needed for LTP induction, something that afferent bursts produce with strings of closely spaced EPSPs. Temporal summation is critical in that individual EPSPs must persist long enough so that depolarization is maintained, and deepened, by the arrival of the next EPSP. Drugs that extend the duration, but not the amplitude, of the EPSP will have their greatest effects when the responses are not truncated by IPSPs (as they normally are)—that is, during theta pattern activity. It may be possible, then, to develop positive modulators that have larger effects on LTP induction than on baseline transmission. (2) Enhancing excitatory receptors could have a normalizing rather than a disruptive influence when transmission is depressed. This occurrence is likely in humans, a species in which substantial losses of excitatory synapses in cortex are a normal aspect of aging (Masliah et al., 1994). These arguments prompted efforts to design and synthesize centrally active positive modulators of glutamate receptors. As described in the next subsection, the resultant compounds have the predicted memory-enhancing properties.

AMPAKINES   Ampakines have no agonist/antagonist effects in excised patches but instead enhance the response of AMPA receptors to glutamate (figure 10.9). This process involves at least two actions: (1) a slowing of the rate at which the receptor channels stop opening—"desensitize"—in the continuing presence of agonists and (2) reducing the speed with which currents return to baseline—"deactivation"—following a 1-millisecond agonist pulse (Arai et al., 1994, 1996). An effect on opening/closing rates is also possible. The effects of the modulators on deactivation are more predictive of their synaptic actions than are their effects on desensitization (Arai and Lynch, 1998).

The drugs cause a rapid increase in the duration of AMPA-receptor-mediated synaptic responses in hippocampal slices (Staubli et al., 1994) and do so at the same concentrations that enhance AMPA-receptor-gated currents in excised patches. They enter the brain within a minute of interperitoneal injections, prolong the duration of excitatory synaptic responses, and markedly facilitate the induction of LTP in freely moving rats (Staubli, Rogers, and Lynch, 1994). The details of this last result are of interest. Theta bursts with suboptimal numbers of pulses were used to induce a variant of LTP that gradually decayed to baseline over several hours; that is, the initiating conditions were insufficient to produce stable (consolidated) potentiation. Several days later the rats were retested after having been given the ampakine. The same stimulation now

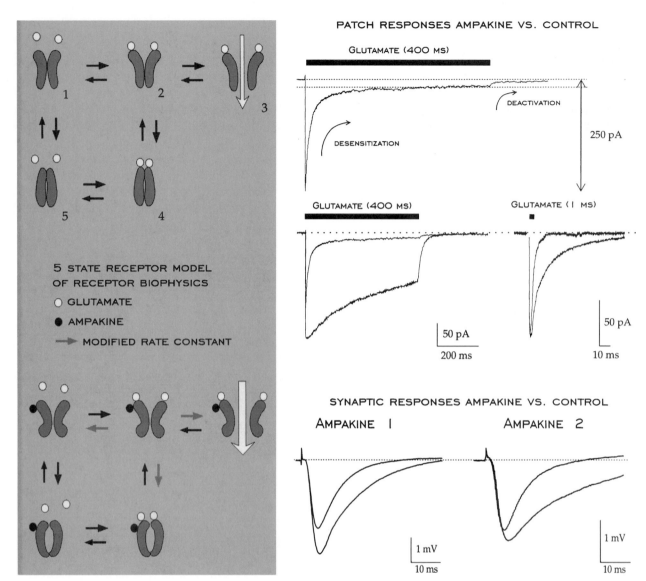

FIGURE 10.9 Centrally active drugs that positively modulate AMPA-type glutamate receptors. The right-hand side shows effects of ampakine drugs on excised patches and hippocampal slices. The top panel is a patch response to a 400-ms application of glutamate. Note that the response drops precipitously despite the continuing presence of agonist. This pattern is "desensitization." The current also takes several milliseconds to return to baseline after glutamate is washed free; this delay is referred to as deactivation. The middle panels describe the effects of an ampakine on patch responses. Desensitization is partly blocked as evidenced by the massive increase in current flow during the sustained application (left side). Responses to 1-ms pulses are shown to the right; under these conditions, which are reasonably close to those obtaining at synapses, it is evident that the ampakine reduces the rate of deactivation. The effects found with brief glutamate pulses are mirrored in synaptic responses, as can be seen in the bottom two tracings.

Results for two ampakines are shown to illustrate that the drugs are not entirely homogeneous in their effects: note that ampakine 1 has a large effect on the amplitude of the response while ampakine 2 increases its duration. Deduced effects of the drugs on the operations of AMPA receptors are illustrated with the models on the left. The five states in the model are (1) receptor baseline; (2) receptor with bound transmitter; (3) receptor opens; (4) desensitized receptor with bound transmitter; (5) desensitized receptor with transmitter dissociated. Ampakines have no effect on the receptor until a binding event (transmitter release) occurs. According to simulation studies, one mode of action that would account for the observed effects on patches and synaptic responses is a reduction in the rate constants (arrows) leading away from state 2. This would allow the receptors to open and close for a longer-than-normal period and thereby increase net current flow. (See Aria et al., 1994, 1996, for further description.)

produced LTP that persisted without evident change for the several hours of the recording session; it thus appears that the positive modulator allowed a marginal degree of theta-driven depolarization to cross the threshold for triggering consolidation chemistries.

Tests for the effects of ampakines on memory consolidation were carried out using a two-odor discrimination task in which well-trained rats typically need ~10 trials to acquire memories that persist for at least three days. A within-subject design was used such that the same rats were given 5 training trials with and without prior administration of an ampakine. The dosage used had no effect on speed of performance or other measures sensitive to arousal and motivation; the selective effects of ampakines at moderate doses on behavior have been described across a variety of testing circumstances. Within the olfactory task, retention scores after several days were well above chance for odor pairs learned in the presence of the ampakines and at chance for those acquired without the drugs (Larson et al., 1995). Evidence that ampakines reduce the requirements for long-term memory was also obtained in eyeblink (Shors et al., 1995) and fear (Rogan, Staubli, and LeDoux, 1997) conditioning studies.

Another series of studies resulted in the intriguing idea that ampakines facilitate the acquisition of "strategies," an extremely stable form of memory. Rats were trained to asymptotic performance on a delayed nonmatch-to-sample paradigm. Beginning in the fifth week of the study an ampakine was administered on every other day of testing. Scores for the rats improved in small increments over two weeks of treatment with the cumulative increase being large. *These improvements lasted for at least a week after drug injections were stopped (longer times weren't tested).* Post hoc analyses showed that the ampakine caused a gradual reduction in the proactive interference caused by a certain type of error; that is, errors on a preceding trial had a lesser effect on the current trial (Hampson et al., 1998a). This result presumably indicates that the rats had acquired a between-trials behavior that minimized the disturbing effects of a wrong choice. Unit recording through an array of chronic electrodes showed that between-trial pattern of firing initiated by the pertinent class of error was reduced by the drug treatments (Hampson et al., 1998b), again as expected if the rats acquired new responses for the delay periods after incorrect choices. In all, it appears that ampakines promote the stable encoding of procedures that otherwise would not become established even with extended training.

Results for ampakines in humans are very limited. Nonetheless, positive effects on memory have been noted in tests using nonsense syllables (Lynch et al.,

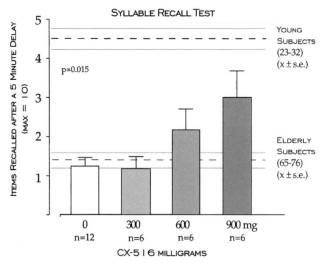

FIGURE 10.10 Effects of an ampakine on the recall of nonsense syllables by 65–75-year-old subjects. Individuals were given drug or placebo at the indicated doses, read a list of 10 nonsense syllables, and asked to recall as many items as possible after a delay of 5 min. Previously collected data indicated that young adults remember between 4 and 5 syllables. As shown in the figure, older subjects do not do as well. The high concentration of ampakine produced a sizable and statistically significant improvement in retention. It is noteworthy that the effective dose, on a mg/kg basis, was at the lower end of the range of concentrations found to be effective in animal studies. (Modified from Lynch et al., 1997.)

1997) as well as more complex measures (Ingvar et al., 1997). The improvements recorded for a small population of elderly subjects were particularly striking (figure 10.10; Lynch et al., 1997). If these results are replicated, then ampakines would constitute a first successful extension of what has been learned about LTP to the development of memory-enhancing drugs.

Summary

The similarities between consolidation of LTP and consolidation of memory described in this chapter are indicative of a very close relationship. The biochemistries recently found to subserve the physiological phenomenon are therefore in all probability the same as those that stabilize newly encoded memory. If so, then the extraordinary 50-year search for the chemistry of consolidation, a scientific episode notable for its singular hypotheses, will in the end have led to the same types of chemistries that mediate such prosaic events as blood clotting. Linking LTP, in all of its specifics, to consolidation also points to new things to look for in memory. One possibility—sculpting recently acquired memory—was discussed and others could have been cited.

Further insights into memory and its consolidation can be expected as more is learned about the adhesion chemistries that appear to stabilize potentiation. Major issues here include the identity of the enzymes that activate latent receptors–a list that presumably includes certain of the lipases and kinases already implicated in LTP–and how modified adhesion affects synaptic architecture and, ultimately, the operation of transmitter receptors. Information on these points is essential for filling out and testing what is now a very sketchy version of an adhesion hypothesis for LTP. It could as well provide a new generation of pharmacologies with which to explore the extent to which consolidation at the behavioral level uses the same cellular processes as physiological consolidation. Of particular relevance to ideas about memory storage is the question of whether the pronounced regional differences in adhesion receptors translate into regional specializations for synaptic plasticity. Analysis of this topic could be a first step in a neurobiological approach to the long-standing questions of whether and by what means brain systems encode qualitatively distinct forms of memory.

A still largely unexplored LTP question with special relevance to the history of consolidation research concerns the cellular events that follow the ~30-minute period during which memory and LTP become firmly entrenched. Beginning with the first years of the field and continuing since, reports have appeared that protein- or RNA-synthesis inhibitors eliminate new learning, in some cases when applied hours or days after training. This often controversial line of work gave rise to the idea that consolidation continues for some time after initial stabilization. If, as current evidence indicates, formation of the lasting variety of LTP requires intracellular and extracellular proteolysis, then the final version of potentiated synapses probably, but not certainly, requires newly synthesized protein. Cytoskeletal and adhesion proteins cleaved during induction presumably must be replaced either from existing pools, by ongoing synthesis, or via up-regulation at transcriptional and/or translational levels. Experiments showing that intense afferent activity increases levels of various mRNAs after about 15 minutes suggest that links with gene expression are available to triggers for LTP. Several studies have tested for contributions by protein synthesis to LTP with positive results (Stanton and Sarvey, 1984; Deadwyler, Dunwiddie, and Lynch, 1987; Nguyen, Abel, and Kandel, 1994; Frey and Morris, 1998); however, various problems, including the potential for unrecognized disturbances to the physiologies that induce potentiation or transmission, underlie the issue.

The argument that synthesis is vital to an hours- or days-long process of completing a remodeled connection raises the issue of whether the new proteins are simply replacement copies for those cleaved during the disassembly phase or instead are in some way novel.

This latter idea of potentiation does not appear to add anything useful to the "disassembly (proteolysis) → reassembly (integrins) → replacement (synthesis)" version of consolidation. This is not to say that neurons and glia lack specialized synthetic machinery used in restabilizing synapses and consolidating potentiation. Dendritic mRNAs encoding cytoskeletal proteins and astroglial genes for matrix proteins are examples of strategically located synthetic systems that could quickly provide substitutes for partially cleaved intra- and extracellular synaptic proteins. But rather than being specialized memory molecules, the proteins in question are better thought of as elements in the brain's version of a general system for modifying and sustaining adhesion junctions. While perhaps lacking the excitement sometimes found in the literature on proteins and memory, this formulation moves the problem closer to areas in which much is known and progress is rapid.

REFERENCES

ABRAHAM, W. C., and A. HUGGETT, 1997. Induction and reversal of long-term potentiation by repeated high-frequency stimulation in rat hippocampal slices. *Hippocampus* 7:137–145.

AMBROS-INGERSON, J., J. LARSON, P. XIAO, and G. LYNCH, 1991. LTP changes the waveform of synaptic responses. *Synapse* 9: 314–316.

AMBROS-INGERSON, J., and G. LYNCH, 1993. Channel gating kinetics and synaptic efficacy: A hypothesis for expression of long-term potentiation. *Proc. Natl. Acad. Sci. U.S.A.* 90: 7903–7907.

AMBROS-INGERSON, J., P. XIAO, J. LARSON, and G. LYNCh, 1993. Waveform analysis suggests that LTP alters the kinetics of synaptic receptor channels. *Brain Res.* 620: 237–244.

ARAI, A., M. KESSLER, J. AMBROS-INGERSON, A. QUAN, E. YIGITER, G. ROGERS, and G. LYNCH, 1996. Effects of a centrally active benzoylpiperidine drug on AMPA receptor kinetics. *Neurosci.* 75:573–585.

ARAI, A., M. KESSLER, and G. LYNCH, 1990. The effects of adenosine on the development of long-term potentiation. *Neurosci. Lett.* 119: 41–44.

ARAI, A., M. KESSLER, P. XIAO, J. AMBROS-INGERSON, G. ROGERS, and G. LYNCH, 1994. A centrally active drug that modulates AMPA receptor gated currents. *Brain Res.* 638:343–346.

ARAI, A., J. LARSON, and G. LYNCH, 1990. Anoxia reveals a vulnerable period in the development of long-term potentiation. *Brain Res.* 511:353–357.

ARAI, A., and G. LYNCH, 1992. Antagonists of the platelet activating factor receptor block long term potentiation in hippocampal slices. *Eur. J. Neurosci.* 4:411–419.

ARAI, A., and G. LYNCH, 1998. The waveform of synaptic transmission at hippocampal synapses is not determined by AMPA receptor desensitization. *Brain Res.* 799:230–234.

ASZTELY, F., E. HANS, H. WIGSTROM, and B. GUSTAFSSON, 1992. Aniracetam-evoked potentiation does not interact with long-term potentiation in the CA1 region of the hippocampus. *Synapse* 11:342–345.

BAHR, B. A., and G. LYNCH, 1992. Purification of an Arg-Gly-Asp selective matrix receptor from brain synaptic plasma membranes. *Biochem. J.* 281 (part 1): 137–142.

BAHR, B. A., A. SHEPPARD, and G. LYNCH, 1991. Fibronectin binding by brain synaptosomal membranes may not involve conventional integrins. *Neuroreport* 2:13–16.

BAHR, B. A., U. STAUBLI, P. XIAO, D. CHUN, Z. X. JI, E. T. ESTEBAN, and G. LYNCH, 1997. Arg-Gly-Asp-Ser-selective adhesion and the stabilization of long-term potentiation: Pharmacological studies and the characterization of a candidate matrix receptor. *J. Neurosci.* 17:1320–1329.

BARRIA, A., D. MULLER, V. DERKACH, L. C. GRIFFITH, and T. R. SODERLING, 1977. Regulatory phosphorylation of AMPA-type glutamate receptors by CaM-KII during long-term potentiation. *Science* 276:2042–2045.

BARRIONUEVO, G., F. SCHOTTLER, and G. LYNCH, 1980. The effects of repetitive low-frequency stimulation on control and "potentiated" synaptic responses in the hippocampus. *Life Sci.* 27:2385–2391.

BAZAN, N. G., M. G. PACKARD, L. TEATHER, and G. ALLAN, 1997. Bioactive lipids in excitatory neurotransmission and neuronal plasticity. *Neurochem. Intern.* 30:225–231.

CLARK, E. A., and R. O. HYNES, 1996. Ras activation is necessary for integrin-mediated activation of extracellular signal-regulated kinase 2 and cytosolic phospholipase A2 but not for cytoskeletal organization. *J. Biol. Chem.* 271:14814–14818.

CUNHA, R. A., E. S. VIZI, J. A. RIBEIRO, and A. M. SEBASTIAO, 1996. Preferential release of ATP and its extra-cellular catabolism as a source of adenosine upon high- but not low-frequency stimulation of rat hippocampal slices. *J. Neurochem.* 67:2180–2187.

DEADWYLER, S. A., T. DUNWIDDIE, and G. LYNCH, 1987. A critical level of protein synthesis is required for long-term potentiation. *Synapse* 1:90–95.

DEL CERRO, S., A. ARAI, and G. LYNCH, 1990. Inhibition of long-term potentiation by an antagonist of platelet-activating factor receptors. *Behav. Neural Biol.* 54:213–217.

DU, X. P., E. F. PLOW, A. L. FRELINGER, T. E. O'TOOLE, J. C. LOFTUS, and M. H. GINSBERG, 1991. Ligands "activate" integrin$_{IIb3}$ (platelet GPIIb-IIIa). *Cell* 65:409–416.

DU, X., T. C. SAIDO, S. TSUBUKI, F. E. INDIG, M. J. WILLIAMS, and M. H. GINSBERG, 1995. Calpain cleavage of the cytoplasmic domain of the integrin beta 3 subunit. *J. Biol. Chem.* 270:26146–26151.

DUNCAN, C. P., 1949. The retroactive effect of electroshock on learning. *J. Comp. Physiol. Psychol.* 42:32–44.

EINHEBER, S., L. M. SCHNAPP, J. L. SALZER, Z. B. CAPPIELLO, and T. A. MILNER, 1996. Regional and ultrastructural distribution of the alpha 8 integrin subunit in developing and adult rat brain suggests a role in synaptic function. *J. Comp. Neurol.* 370:105–134.

FREY, U., and R. G. MORRIS, 1998. Synaptic tagging: Implications for late maintenance of hippocampal long-term potentiation. *Trends Neurosci.* 21:181–188.

GROOMS, S. Y., and L. S. JONES, 1997. RGDS tetrapeptide and hippocampal in vitro kindling in rats: Evidence for integrin-mediated physiological stability. *Neurosci. Let.* 231:139–142.

GROOMS, S. Y., L. TERRACIO, and L. S. JONES, 1993. Anatomical localization of beta 1 integrin-like immunoreactivity in rat brain. *Exp. Neurol.* 122:253–259.

HALL, R. A., M. KESSLER, and G. LYNCH, 1992. Evidence that high- and low-affinity DL-α-amino-3-hydroxy-5-methylisox-azole-4-propionic acid (AMPA) binding sites reflect membrane-dependent states of a single receptor. *J. Neurochem.* 59:1997–2004.

HALL, R. A., A. QUAN, M. KESSLER, and G. LYNCH, 1996. Ultraviolet radiation, thiol reagents, and solubilization enhance AMPA receptor binding affinity via a common mechanism. *Neurochem. Res.* 21:963–968.

HAMPSON, R., G. ROGERS, G. LYNCH, and S. DEADWYLER, 1998a. Facilitative effects of the ampakine CX516 on short-term memory in rats: Enhancement of delayed non-match-to-sample performance. *J. Neurosci.* 18:2740–2747.

HAMPSON, R., G. ROGERS, G. LYNCH, and S. DEADWYLER, 1998b. Facilitative effects of the ampakine CX516 on short-term memory in rats: Correlations with hippocampal unit activity. *J. Neurosci.* 18:2748–2763.

HASKEL, E. J., and D. R. ABENDSCHEIN, 1989. Deaggregation of human platelets in vitro by an RGD analog antagonist of platelet glycoprotein IIb/IIIa receptors. *Thrombosis Res.* 56:687–695.

HAYASHI, Y., A. ISHIDA, H. KATAGIRI, M. MISHINA, H. FUJISAWA, T. MANABE, and T. TAKAHASHI, 1997. Calcium- and calmodulin-dependent phosphorylation of AMPA type glutamate receptor subunits by endogenous protein kinases in the post-synaptic density. *Brain Res., Mol. Brain Res.* 46:338–342.

HOFFMAN, K. B., J. LARSON, B. A. BAHR, and G. LYNCH, 1999. Activation of NMDA receptors stimulates extracellular proteolysis of cell adhesion molecules in hippocampus. *Brain Res.* 811:152–155.

HOFFMAN, K. B., J. MARTINEZ, and G. LYNCH, 1999. Proteolysis of cell adhesion molecules by serine proteases: A role in long-term potentiation. *Brain Res.* 811:29–33.

HOLLMANN, M., and S. HEINEMANN, 1994. Cloned glutamate receptors. *Annu. Rev. Neurosci.* 17: 31–108.

INGVAR, M., J. AMBROS-INGERSON, D. DAVIS, R. GRANGER, M. KESSLER, G. A. ROGERS, R. S. SCHEHR, and G. LYNCH, 1997. Enhancement by an ampakine of memory encoding in humans. *Exp. Neurol.* 146:553–559.

ITO, I., A. TANABE, A. KOHDA, and H. SUGIYAMA, 1990. Allosteric potentiation of quisqualate receptors by a nootropic drug aniracetam. *J. Physiol. (Lond.)* 424:533–543.

JUNG, M. W., J. LARSON, and G. LYNCH, 1991. Evidence that changes in spine neck resistance are not responsible for expression of LTP. *Synapse* 7: 216–220.

KAUER, J. A., R. C. MALENKA, and R. A. NICOLL, 1988. A persistent postsynaptic modification mediates long-term potentiation in the hippocampus. *Neuron* 1: 911–917.

KOLTA, A., G. LYNCH, and J. AMBROS-INGERSON, 1998. Effects of aniracetam after LTP induction are suggestive of interactions on the kinetics of the AMPA receptor channel. *Brain Res.* 788:269–286.

LARSON, J., T. LIEU, V. PETCHPRADUB, B. LEDUC, H. NGO, G. ROGERS, and G. LYNCH, 1995. Facilitation of olfactory learning by a modulator of AMPA receptors. *J. Neurosci.* 15: 8023–8030.

LARSON, J., and G. LYNCH, 1986. Induction of synaptic potentiation in hippocampus by patterned stimulation involves two events. *Science* 232: 985–988.

LARSON, J., and G. LYNCH, 1988. Role of *N*-methyl-D-aspartate receptors in the induction of synaptic potentiation by burst stimulation patterned after the hippocampal theta-rhythm. *Brain Res.* 441:111–118.

LARSON, J., and G. LYNCH, 1991. A test of the spine resistance hypothesis of LTP expression. *Brain Res.* 538: 347–350.

LARSON, J., D. WONG, and G. LYNCH, 1986. Patterned stimulation at the theta frequency is optimal for induction of hippocampal long-term potentiation. *Brain Res.* 368: 347–350.

LARSON, J., P. XIAO, and G. LYNCH, 1993. Reversal of LTP by theta frequency stimulation. *Brain Res.* 600:97–102.

LEE, K., M. OLIVER, F. SCHOTTLER, and G. LYNCH, 1981. Electron microscopic studies of brain slices: The effects of high-frequency stimulation on dendritic ultra structure. In *Electrical Activity in Isolated Mammalian CNS Preparations,* G. Kerkut and H. V. Wheal, eds. New York: Academic Press, pp. 189–212.

LEE, K., F. SCHOTTLER, M. OLIVER, and G. LYNCH, 1980. Brief bursts of high-frequency stimulation produce two types of structural changes in rat hippocampus. *J. Neurophysiol.* 44: 247–258.

LUTHI, A., J.-P. LAURENT, A. FIGUROV, D. MULLER, and M. SCHACHNER, 1994. Hipppocampal long-term potentiation and neural cell adhesion molecules L1 and NCAM. *Nature* 372: 777–779.

LYNCH, G., and M. BAUDRY, 1984. The biochemistry of memory: A new and specific hypothesis. *Science* 224:1057–1063.

LYNCH, G., R. GRANGER, J. AMBROS-INGERSON, C. M. DAVIS, R. SCHEHR, and M. KESSLER, 1997. Evidence that a positive modulator of AMPA-type glutamate receptors affects delayed recall in aged humans. *Exp. Neurol.* 145:89–92.

MARCHESELLI, V. L., M. J. ROSSOWSKA, M.-T. DOMINGO, P. BRAQUET, and N. G. BAZAN, 1990. Distinct platelet-activating factor binding sites in synaptic endings and in intracellular membranes of rat cerebral cortex. *J. Biol. Chem.* 265: 9140–9145.

MASLIAH, E., M. MALLORY, L. HANSEN, R. DETERESA, M. ALFORD, and R. TERRY, 1994. Synaptic and neuritic alterations during the progression of Alzheimer's disease. *Neurosci. Lett.* 174:67–72.

MASSICOTTE, G., P. VANDERKLISH, G. LYNCH, and M. BAUDRY, 1991. Modulation of DL-alpha-Amino-3-Hydroxy-5-Methyl-4-Isoxazolepropionic Acid-Quisqualate receptors by phospholipase-A₂: A necessary step in long-term potentiation. *Proc. Natl. Acad. Sci. U.S.A.* 88:1893–1897.

MAYFORD, M., T. ABEL, and E. R. KANDEL, 1995. Transgenic approaches to cognition. *Curr. Opin. Neurobiol.* 5:141–148.

MORRIS, R. G., E. ANDERSON, G. S. LYNCH, and M. BAUDRY, 1986. Selective impairment of learning and blockade of long-term potentiation by an *N*-methyl-D-aspartate receptor antagonist, AP5. *Nature* 319:774–776.

MOTT, D. D., and D. V. LEWIS, 1991. Facilitation of the induction of long-term potentiation by GABAB receptors. *Science* 252: 1718–1720.

MULLER, D., M. JOLY, and G. LYNCH, 1988. Contributions of quisqualate and NMDA receptors to the induction and expression of LTP. *Science* 242: 1694–1697.

MULLER, D., and G. LYNCH, 1988. Long-term potentiation differentially affects two components of synaptic responses in hippocampus. *Proc. Natl. Acad. Sci. U.S.A.* 85: 9346–9350.

MULLER, D., and G. LYNCH, 1989. Evidence that changes in presynaptic calcium currents are not responsible for long-term potentiation in hippocampus. *Brain Res.* 479: 290–299.

MULLER, D., J. TURNBULL, M. BAUDRY, and G. LYNCH, 1988. Phorbol ester-induced synaptic facilitation is different than long-term potentiation. *Proc. Natl. Acad. Sci. U.S.A.* 85: 6997–7000.

NEWTON, R. A., M. THIEL, and N. HOGG, 1997. Signaling mechanisms and the activation of leukocyte integrins. *J. Leukocyte Biol.* 61:422–426.

NGUYEN, P. V., T. ABEL, and E. R. KANDEL, 1994. Requirement of a critical period of transcription for induction of a late phase of LTP. *Science* 265:1104–1107.

NISHIMURA, S. L., K. P. BOYLEN, S. EINHEBER, T. A. MILNER, D. M. RAMOS, and R. PYTELA, 1998. Synaptic and glial localization of the integrin alpha v beta 8 in mouse and rat brain. *Brain Res.* 791:271–282.

OTTO, T., H. EICHENBAUM, S. I. WIENER, and C. G. WIBLE, 1991. Learning-related patterns of CA1 spike trains parallel stimulation parameters optimal for inducing hippocampal long-term potentiation. *Hippocampus* 1:181–192.

PIERSCHBACHER, M. D., and E. RUOSLAHTI, 1984. Cell attachment activity of fibronectin can be duplicated by small synthetic fragments of the molecule. *Nature* 309:30–33.

PINKSTAFF, J. K., J. DETTERICH, G. LYNCH, and C. M. GALL, 1999. Integrin subunit gene expression is regionally differentiated in adult brain. *J. Neurosci.* 19:1541–1556.

ROGAN, M. T., U. V. STAUBLI, and J. E. LEDOUX, 1997. AMPA receptor facilitation accelerates fear learning without altering the level of conditioned fear acquired. *J. Neurosci.* 17:5928–5935.

ROMAN, F., U. STAUBLI, and G. LYNCH, 1987. Evidence for synaptic potentiation in a cortical network during learning. *Brain Res.* 418:221–226.

RØNN, L. C. B., E. BOCK, D. LINNEMANN, and H. JAHNSEN, 1995. NCAM-antibodies modulate induction of long-term potentiation in rat hippocampal CA1. *Brain Res.* 677:145–151.

SEEBURG, P. H., 1993. The TINS/TIPS Lecture: The molecular biology of mammalian glutamate receptor channels. *Trends Neurosci.* 16:359–365.

SHEPPARD, A., J. WU, U. RUTISHAUSER, and G. LYNCH, 1991. Proteolytic modification of neural cell adhesion molecule (N-CAM) by the intracellular proteinase calpain. *Biochimica Biophysica Acta* 1076:156–160.

SHORS, T. J., R. J. SERVATIUS, R. F. THOMPSON, G. ROGERS, and G. LYNCH, 1995. Enhanced glutamatergic neurotransmission facilitates classical conditioning in the freely moving rat. *Neurosci. Lett.* 186: 153–156.

STANTON, P. K., and J. M. SARVEY, 1984. Blockade of long-term potentiation in rat hippocampal CA1 region by inhibitors of protein synthesis. *J. Neurosci.* 4:3080–3088.

STAUBLI, U., J. AMBROS-INGERSON, and G. LYNCH, 1992. Receptor changes and LTP: An analysis using aniracetam, a drug that reversibly modifies glutamate (AMPA) receptors. *Hippocampus* 2: 49–58.

STAUBLI, U., and D. CHUN, 1996. Factors regulating the reversibility of long-term potentiation. *J. Neurosci.* 16: 853–860.

STAUBLI, U., D. CHUN, and G. LYNCH, 1998. Time-dependent reversal of long-term potentiation by an integrin antagonist. *J. Neurosci.* 18:3460–3469.

STAUBLI, U., and G. LYNCH, 1987. Stable hippocampal long-term potentiation elicited by "theta" pattern stimulation. *Brain Res.* 435:227–234.

STAUBLI, U., and G. LYNCH, 1990. Stable depression of potentiated synaptic responses in the hippocampus with 1–5 Hz stimulation. *Brain Res.* 513:113–118.

STAUBLI, U., Y. PEREZ, F. XU, G. ROGERS, M. INGVAR, S. STONE-ELANDER, and G. LYNCH, 1994. Centrally active modulators of glutamate (AMPA) receptors facilitate the induction of LTP *in vivo. Proc. Natl. Acad. Sci. U.S.A.* 91:11158–11162.

STAUBLI, U., G. ROGERS, and G. LYNCH, 1994. Facilitation of glutamate receptors enhances memory. *Proc. Natl. Acad. Sci. U.S.A.* 91:777–781.

STAUBLI, U., P. VANDERKLISH, and G. LYNCH, 1990. An inhibitor of integrin receptors blocks long-term potentiation. *Behav. Neural Biol.* 53:1–5.

STRACK, S., S. CHOI, D. M. LOVINGER, and R. J. COLBRAN, 1997. Translocation of autophosphorylated calcium/calmodulin-dependent protein kinase II to the postsynaptic density. *J. Biol. Chem.* 272:13467–13470.

STRICKER, C., A. C. FIELD, and S. J. REDMAN, 1996. Changes in the quantal parameters of EPSCs in rat CA1 neurons in vitro after induction of long-term potentiation. *J. Physiol (Lond.)* 490:443–454.

TANG, L., C. P. HUNG, and E. M. SCHUMAN, 1998. A role for the cadherin family of cell adhesion molecules in hippocampal long-term potentiation. *Neuron* 20:1165–1175.

TERRAMANI, T., M. KESSLER, G. LYNCH, and M. BAUDRY, 1988. Effects of thiol-reagents on [$_3$H]-AMPA binding to rat telencephalic membranes. *Mol. Pharmacol.* 34:117–123.

THIEL, M., J. D. CHAMBERS, A. CHOUKER, S. FISCHER, C. ZOURELIDIS, H. J. BARDENHEUER, K. E. ARFORS, and K. PETER, 1996. Effect of adenosine on the expression of beta(2) integrins and L-selectin of human polymorphonuclear leukocytes *in vitro. J. Leukocyte Biol.* 59: 671–682.

VANDERKLISH, P., R. NEVE, B. A. BAHR, A. ARAI, M. HENNEGRIFF, J. LARSON, and G. LYNCH, 1992. Translational suppression of a glutamate receptor subunit impairs long-term potentiation. *Synapse* 12:333–337.

VANDERKLISH, P., T. C. SAIDO, C. GALL, A. ARAI, and G. LYNCH, 1995. Proteolysis of spectrin by calpain accompanies theta-burst stimulation in cultured hippocampal slices. *Mol. Brain Res.* 32: 25–35.

VAN WILLIGEN, G., I. HERS, G. GORTER, and N. AKKERMAN, 1996. Exposure of ligand-binding sites on platelet integrin AIIb/B3 by phosphorylation of the B3 subunit. *Biochem. J.* 314:769–779.

VERTES, R. P., and B. KOCSIS, 1997. Brainstem-diencephalo-septohippocampal systems controlling the theta rhythm in the rat. *Neurosci.* 81:893–926.

XIAO, P., B. A. BAHR, U. STAUBLI, P. W. VANDERKLISH, and G. LYNCH, 1991. Evidence that matrix recognition contributes to stabilization but not induction of LTP. *Neuroreport* 2:461–464.

XIE, X., S.-J. LIAW, M. BAUDRY, and T. BERGER, 1997. Novel expression mechanism for synaptic potentiation: Alignment of presynaptic release site and postsynaptic receptor. *Proc. Natl. Acad. Sci. U.S.A.* 94:6983–6988.

11 Trophic Interactions and Neuronal Plasticity

ERIC S. LEVINE AND IRA B. BLACK

ABSTRACT Increasing evidence suggests that trophic interactions that influence brain ontogeny mediate processes as diverse as learning, memory, and regrowth after injury. This chapter describes recent insights suggesting that impulse activity regulates availability of neurotrophic factors, which in turn modulate neuronal morphology and efficacy of synaptic communication. Through these processes, millisecond-to-millisecond signaling can be converted into long-term changes in neural circuit architecture and function. In addition, different excitatory transmitter receptor subtypes subserve trophic or regressive effects, enabling a neural system to memorialize excitatory or inhibitory experiences precisely. Thus signaling mechanisms that participate in the formation of neuronal circuits during development appear to operate throughout life to modulate interneuronal communication. A variety of open questions are delineated to define provisional future directions.

Emerging evidence suggests that mechanisms underlying developmental plasticity play roles throughout life. For example, processes as diverse as learning, memory, and regrowth after injury may be mediated by cellular and molecular mechanisms that also govern normal development of the nervous system. Commonality of mechanism is exemplified by the increasing awareness of the multiple, critical functions served by brain growth and survival (trophic) factors.

Although growth and survival factors have been the focus of study in developmental biology for decades, their critical roles throughout life have been appreciated only recently. Yet growth factors appear to occupy a central functional niche, potentially integrating experience, impulse activity, synaptic pathway formation (and plasticity), and neural circuit architecture during maturity as well as development. Moreover, traditional distinctions among growth factors, trophic factors, and neurotransmitters are dissolving. To provide perspective for these new views, it may be helpful to summarize salient characteristics of the now-classical agent, nerve growth factor (NGF).

The pioneering studies of Levi-Montalcini, Hamburger, and Cohen established that NGF is required for the survival and normal development of peripheral sensory and sympathetic neurons (Levi-Montalcini and Hamburger, 1953; Cohen and Levi-Montalcini, 1956; Cohen, 1960; Levi-Montalcini and Angeletti, 1968). However, even these initial studies indicated that, in addition to survival, NGF exerted other effects, which could potentially play roles in contexts different from development. For example, the factor elicits neurite outgrowth, and targets treated with NGF become innervated by increased numbers of terminals of responsive neurons (Olson, 1967; Levi-Montalcini and Angeletti, 1968). These experiments clearly suggested that NGF influences neural circuit architecture, at least during development.

The foregoing observations were complemented by the seminal demonstration that target NGF is transported from innervated target to perikarya of innervating neurons in a retrograde fashion (Hendry, Stach, and Herrup, 1974; Hendry et al., 1974; Hendry, 1975). Consequently, NGF may act as a messenger mediating retrograde communication of information from visceral target to innervating neuron in the peripheral nervous system. Since the density of target innervation correlates with the concentration of target NGF messenger RNA (mRNA) (Shelton and Reichardt, 1984), the elaboration of trophic factor by targets may regulate architecture of the pathway and communication between afferent neurons and particular targets.

The recent realization that trophic factors are synthesized in the brain stimulated interest in mechanisms of action and regulation. For example, the observation that NGF regulates the function of basal forebrain cholinergic neurons (Hefti, Dravid, and Hartikka, 1984; Hefti et al., 1985; Martinez et al., 1985; Large et al., 1986; Martinez et al., 1987) and the localization of NGF to hippocampal targets (Whittemore et al., 1986) suggested that trophic functions are critical centrally as well as peripherally. Since the septohippocampal system appears

ERIC S. LEVINE   Department of Pharmacology, University of Connecticut Health Center, Farmington, Conn.
IRA B. BLACK   Department of Neuroscience and Cell Biology, Robert Wood Johnson Medical School, University of Medicine and Dentistry of New Jersey, Piscataway, N.J.

to play an important role in contextual-spatial memory (Eichenbaum, Otto, and Cohen, 1992), trophic and mental functions might somehow be related. Central targets might play roles analogous to those in the periphery, and central interactions might mediate mnemonic function.

The developing trophic field grew more intriguing and complex with the discovery that brain-derived neurotrophic factor (BDNF) and NGF exhibit sequence similarity (Leibrock et al., 1989). The inference that these were members of a neurotrophin gene family was quickly confirmed by the molecular cloning and sequencing of neurotrophin (NT)-3 and NT-4 (Maisonpierre et al., 1990; Hallböök, Ibáñez, and Persson, 1991). Localization of NGF and BDNF, in particular to the hippocampus (Whittemore et al., 1986; Hofer et al., 1990), extended the potential scope of target trophic interactions in the brain.

In turn, critical issues concern the mechanisms that regulate the elaboration of trophic factors by targets, as well as the effects that neurotrophins exert on responsive neurons. Are factors simply produced constitutively by targets, independent of intercellular, environmental stimuli? Alternatively, is expression of trophic factors regulated, potentially allowing the extracellular environment to influence trophic interactions? The latter alternative, of course, may have far-reaching implications, potentially allowing experience to affect trophic interactions, synaptic pathway modulation, and neural communication. Further, if regulation extends beyond development into maturity, environmental influences may access neural pathway architecture throughout life.

A separate issue concerns whether neurotrophins alter pathway efficacy in a dynamic manner. Since such alterations may constitute an important form of plasticity, and even contribute to such critical processes as learning and memory in some systems, trophic modulation of synaptic transmission has attracted increasing attention.

This brief background summary may now permit articulation of some specific questions concerning neurotrophin roles in the brain. Most generally, are trophic gene expression and factor elaboration regulated processes in the brain? Does experience gain access to trophic interactions? More specifically, do pathway use and impulse activity play roles in trophic interactions? Do neurotrophins, in turn, regulate the strength of synaptic communication and neuronal excitability? Which specific transmitter systems and synaptic elements are targeted by neurotrophins? These and related questions have been approached through a combination of in vivo and in vitro techniques.

Trophic gene expression and the balance between excitatory and inhibitory activity

Although trophic interactions in the brain have been intensely studied for nearly a decade, the relationship of trophic gene expression to neural activity has been approached only recently. Experiments performed in vivo initially raised the possibility that innervating neurons might regulate trophic expression in targets. For example, fimbrial transection elevated NGF expression in neonatal hippocampus, suggesting that innervation regulates target elaboration of the trophic factor (Whittemore et al., 1987).

Complementary studies demonstrated that limbic seizures increase hippocampal NGF gene expression (Gall and Isackson, 1989; Gall, Murray, and Isackson, 1991; Isackson et al., 1991). Induction of limbic seizures electrolytically increased NGF mRNA in neurons of the hippocampal dentate gyrus within 1 hour and in neocortical and olfactory forebrain neurons several hours thereafter. Results were quantitated by in situ hybridization and nuclease protection. The NGF message decreased from 1.5 to 15 hours after seizure onset, indicating that the elevation was transient, not long-lasting. These observations raised the possibility that increased impulse activity, in this case pathologic, may increase NGF gene expression, either directly or indirectly. The in vivo nature of the paradigm, and the widespread nature of limbic seizures precluded more detailed analyses. Other approaches have begun to define mediating mechanisms.

Using cultured hippocampus, as neuronal dissociates in fully defined medium or as explants, direct evidence that depolarization regulates NGF gene expression was obtained (Lu et al., 1991a; Elliott et al., 1994). The depolarizing stimuli, elevated K^+ (35 mM) or the Na^+ channel blocker veratridine, evoked a threefold increase in NGF mRNA (figure 11.1). The effect of veratridine was specifically blocked by tetrodotoxin, which antagonizes the channel-blocking actions of the alkaloid, suggesting that depolarization itself increased NGF gene expression. Moreover, using the hippocampal neuronal dissociates, regulation by intrinsic spontaneous impulse activity was analyzed. To increase spontaneous activity in the cultures, inhibitory gamma-aminobutyric acid interneurons were blocked with picrotoxin. Exposure to picrotoxin elicited nearly a threefold increase in NGF message, suggesting that NGF gene expression represents a balance between excitatory and inhibitory impulse activity (figure 11.2). These studies suggested that depolarizing influences and endogenous impulse activity directly regulate trophic gene expression. One natural next set of questions concerned the specific transmitters involved and the mediating receptors.

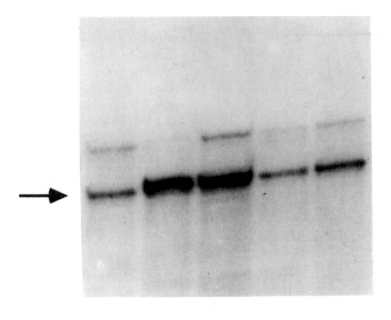

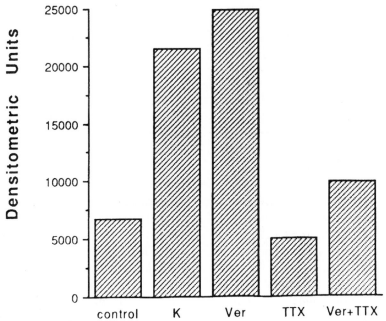

FIGURE 11.1 Regulation of NGF mRNA expression in hippocampal neurons by depolarization. E18 hippocampal neurons were cultured for 6 days in serum-free medium. These cultures were then treated with the following agents for an additional 2 days and harvested for NGF mRNA measurement: K[+], 35 mM; veratridine (Ver), 1 μM; tetrodotoxin (TTX), 1 μM. (Upper) Autoradiogram with 40 μg of total RNA per lane. Arrow indicates the 411-base-pair NGF mRNA fragment protected by RNase T2. (Lower) Densitometric plot of the autoradiogram. The result represents three experiments with independent RNA preparations. (Reprinted from Lu et al., 1991a, by permission.)

Lindholm and colleagues examined a variety of transmitters in cultured hippocampal dissociates (Zafra et al., 1990). Kainic acid, a glutamate receptor agonist, dramatically increased neuronal NGF message. In contrast, N-methyl-D-aspartic acid (NMDA) or inhibitors of NMDA glutamate receptors exerted no effects. Further, the kainate effect was blocked by antagonists of non-NMDA receptors, implying that depolarization of hippocampal neurons by glutamate, through the mediation of non-NMDA receptors, regulates NGF gene expression. The same transmitter-receptor systems also elevated expression of BDNF, suggesting that multiple neurotrophins are regulated by impulse activity in the hippocampus (Zafra et al., 1990).

Recent studies have substantiated this contention and raised the possibility that trophins play roles in

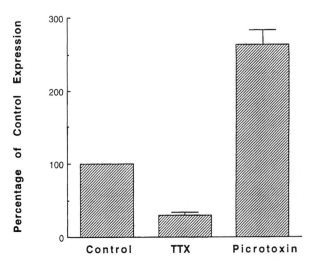

FIGURE 11.2 Regulation of NGF gene expression by spontaneous neuronal activity. E18 hippocampal neurons were cultured in serum-free medium. The control group was cultured for 8 days. The tetrodotoxin (TTX) group was cultured for 2 days and treated with 1 µM TTX for 6 days. The picrotoxin group was cultured for 8 days and treated with the gamma-aminobutyric acid antagonist picrotoxin (1 µM) for 6 hours on the last day. All groups were cultured for the same amount of time before harvest for NGF RNase protection. Autoradiograms were analyzed densitometrically, and numerical values were normalized to percentage of control. (Reprinted from Lu et al., 1991a, by permission.)

physiological processes involved in memory. Long-term potentiation (LTP), an activity-dependent enhancement of synaptic transmission, has attracted attention as one potential mechanism underlying memory function (Bliss and Lomo, 1973). Studies have recently implicated trophic interactions in LTP. Induction of LTP in the hippocampal CA1 pyramidal cell layer increased BDNF and NT-3 messages in CA1 neurons (Patterson et al., 1992). The alterations were apparently cell specific, since nonstimulated regions of the pyramidal cell layer and the dentate exhibited no alterations in mRNA. Moreover, NGF mRNA was unchanged. Since trophins are known to increase transmitter levels and induce axon terminal sprouting, the authors speculate that activity-induced increases in trophin expression may play a role in the relatively stable changes in synaptic transmission that occur in LTP. Evidence for this hypothesis is presented in a subsequent section.

Transmitter-trophic interactions exert both progressive and regressive actions

Whereas the foregoing studies indicate that impulse activity may regulate trophic factor gene expression, other evidence suggests that trophic stimulation and neu-

rotransmitters interact to regulate neuronal form and function. One initial indication of transmitter-trophic interactions derived from an unexpected source, the cerebellum. A number of studies indicated that NGF protein (Large et al., 1986), NGF receptor protein (Eckenstein, 1988; Schatteman et al., 1988; Yan and Johnson, 1988), and NGF receptor mRNA (Buck et al., 1988; Schatteman et al., 1988) are transiently expressed in the cerebellum in several species. These observations raised the possibility that NGF regulates the development of some cerebellar populations. The discovery that Purkinje cells in the developing cerebellum in vivo express high- and low-affinity NGF receptors identified a key population that might be regulated by the trophic factor (Cohen-Cory, Dreyfus, and Black, 1989). This result was of particular interest, since the development of Purkinje cells was known to be regulated by multiple epigenetic factors (Altman, 1972; Altman and Bayer, 1985), including presynaptic innervation (Berry and Bradley, 1976; Sotelo and Arsenio-Nunes, 1976).

To elucidate mechanisms by which trophic and presynaptic stimulation might regulate ontogeny of Purkinje cells, the effects of NGF and excitatory transmitters on survival and morphological maturation were studied in dissociated cell culture (Cohen-Cory, Dreyfus, and Black, 1991). Simultaneous exposure to depolarizing agents and NGF specifically enhanced Purkinje survival. NGF, in combination with either high potassium or veratridine markedly increased Purkinje survival. Moreover, NGF together with the excitatory presynaptic transmitters aspartate or glutamate increased survival twofold (figure 11.3). NGF also increased Purkinje cell size and promoted neurite elaboration. These effects required simultaneous exposure to NGF and either aspartate, glutamate, or pharmacologic depolarizing agents (figure 11.4). Enhanced survival and neurite elaboration were not elicited by exposure to trophic factor or transmitters alone. These results suggest a novel mechanism in which trophic factor and afferent stimulation interact to promote survival and morphogenesis of developing Purkinje cells (see also Morrison and Mason, 1998). The effects on neurite growth were particularly provocative, since this may be a critical determinant of synaptic connections and circuit architecture. In this system, then, the combined action of transmitter and trophic agent may regulate neural system organization. What mechanisms might mediate transmitter-trophic interactions?

We sought to identify the excitatory amino acid (EAA) receptors involved in the regulation of Purkinje survival (Mount, Dreyfus, and Black, 1993). EAAs activate multiple ionotropic receptors as well as a G-protein-linked "metabotropic" receptor. Ionotropic re-

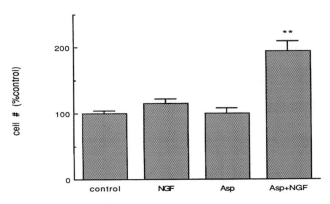

FIGURE 11.3 Effects of aspartate and NGF on Purkinje cell survival. E18 rat cerebellar cells were grown in culture and immunostained for calcium-binding protein to identify Purkinje cells. Duplicates of two independent experiments were analyzed per condition. Doses of 10 μM aspartate (Asp) and 200 units/ml NGF were used for the time in culture. Values depicted (mean ± SEM) are as follows: Control, 100 ± 4.49%; NGF, 115.0 ± 6.72%; Asp, 99.75 ± 8.42%; Asp + NGF, 194.0 ± 15.70%. The actual number of cells in representative control cultures was 1688 ± 99.42.* Differs from control, NGF, and aspartate by $p < .05$. (Reprinted from Cohen-Cory, Dreyfus, and Black, 1991, by permission.)

ceptors are composed of three major subtypes, each named for its preferred agonist (the NMDA, quisqualate/AMPA and kainate receptors). Ionotropic and G-protein-linked receptors have been identified on Purkinje cells (Dupont, Gardette, and Crepel, 1987; Garthwaite, Yamini, and Garthwaite, 1987; Sekiguchi, Okamoto, and Sakai, 1987; Linden et al., 1991; Llano et al., 1991; Masu et al., 1991). To ascertain how receptors modulate survival, Purkinje cells were cultured with NGF, and EAA receptor subtypes were selectively stimulated or antagonized.

Initially, we characterized the potential role of inotropic EAA receptors by exposing cultures to the antagonists MK-801, D-APV (D-2-amino-5-phosphorovaleric acid), and DNQX (6,7-dinitroquinoxaline-2,3-dione). Each increased cell number, suggesting that endogenous ionotropic activity *decreased* survival. To determine whether G-protein-linked EAA receptor stimulation modulates survival, the metabotropic agonist ACPD (1-aminocyclopentane-1,3-dicarboxylic acid) was examined. ACPD alone had no effect on survival. However, simultaneous exposure to ACPD and NGF significantly elevated Purkinje number. Further, increased survival was blocked by the selective metabotropic antagonist L-AP3. In addition, L-AP3 reduced cell number in the absence of exogenous EAA. Thus endogenous metabotropic stimulation is normally necessary for survival.

In sum, excitatory transmitters apparently shape development through a novel mechanism, simulta-

neously exerting trophic actions through G-protein-linked receptors and regressive influences through ionotropic receptors. The ultimate effect of an excitatory transmitter may be determined by the balance between metabotropic-trophic and ionotropic-regressive actions. In the case of Purkinje cells, aspartate, the putative EAA transmitter of innervating climbing fibers, regulates survival through trophic and regressive influences. It is apparent, then, that exquisite precision of regulation may derive from the delicate balance among excitatory, inhibitory, and modulatory actions of transmitters and trophic agents.

Neurotrophins modulate efficacy of synaptic transmission

Recent work indicates that neurotrophins acutely regulate neuronal excitability and synaptic efficacy, greatly expanding potential functional roles. Neurotrophins modulate neuronal activity through multiple mechanisms of action, including induction of ion channel expression, enhancement of presynaptic neurotransmitter release, and modulation of postsynaptic receptor responsiveness. These newly discovered effects have been identified both in the developing and mature nervous systems, indicating that mechanisms responsible for the formation of neural circuits during development also play roles in the dynamic regulation of activity within established circuits.

Neurotrophins can directly regulate neuronal excitability via changes in expression of voltage-gated ion channels. This ability has been most closely examined in PC-12 cells, a pheochromocytoma cell line that differentiates into a sympathetic neuronlike phenotype in response to NGF. In these cells, NGF induces the expression of multiple types of sodium, potassium, and calcium channels (Garber, Hoshi, and Aldrich, 1989; Sharma et al., 1993). The increase in sodium channel expression is mediated at least in part by cyclic AMP-dependent protein kinase (Kalman et al., 1990). Whereas continuous exposure to NGF causes the induction of a family of sodium channels, brief exposure selectively induces expression of the peripheral nerve–type sodium channel gene PN1 (Toledo-Aral et al., 1995). NGF also increases expression of voltage-gated sodium, calcium, and potassium currents in the SK-N-SH neuroblastoma cell line (Lesser and Lo, 1995).

Although these effects have been typically characterized in clonal cell lines, similar mechanisms occur in the brain. One of the best-characterized NGF-responsive cell populations in the brain comprises the cholinergic neurons of the basal forebrain. These neurons provide a dense modulatory input to the hippocampus. Taken

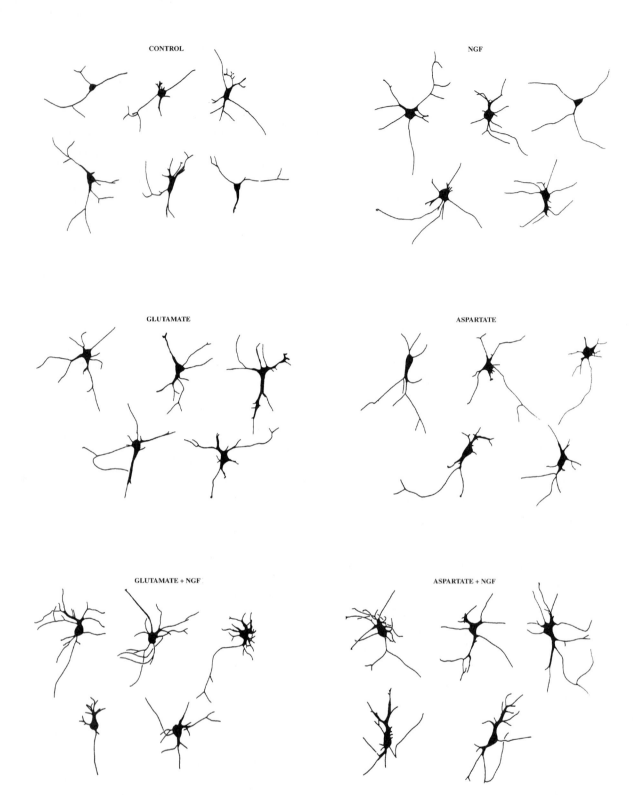

FIGURE 11.4 Morphological maturation of Purkinje cells elicited by excitatory neurotransmitters or NGF or both. Camera lucida tracings of representative CaBP-positive cells were obtained from each experimental condition. Note the marked enhancement in neurite elaboration and in cell size after treatment with glutamate plus NGF or aspartate plus NGF. L-aspartate and L-glutamate were used at a 10-μM final concentration, and NGF was used at 200 units/ml. Scale bar, 40 μm. (Reprinted from Cohen-Cory, Dreyfus, and Black, 1991, by permission.)

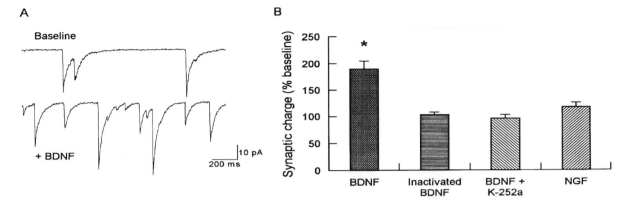

FIGURE 11.5 Potentiation of synaptic transmission by brain-derived neurotrophic factor (BDNF). (A) Whole-cell voltage clamp recordings from a hippocampal neuron before and 3 min after exposure to BDNF ($V_{hold} = -60$ mV). (B) Effects on synaptic charge after bath application of BDNF ($n = 10$ cells), heat-inactivated BDNF ($n = 9$ cells), or nerve growth factor (NGF; $n = 13$ cells; 50 ng/ml). In some experiments, cultures were pretreated for 1 hour with the trk tyrosine kinase inhibitor K-252a in the bath solution (200 nM; $n = 7$ cells). * $p < .001$ compared to baseline levels for that condition. Recordings were obtained from multiple platings. (Reprinted from Levine et al., 1995a, Copyright 1995 National Academy of Sciences, U.S.A.)

together, the basal forebrain–hippocampal system plays a central role in attention, learning, and memory, with a particular emphasis on spatial learning and declarative memory. In basal forebrain cholinergic neurons, NGF increases both L-type and N-type components of voltage-gated calcium currents (Levine et al., 1995b). This effect is specific to NGF, since BDNF does not have a similar effect. Calcium entry via these voltage-dependent channels regulates neurotransmitter release and neuronal firing patterns, and also modulates neuronal gene expression. Thus calcium influx via these channels may mediate some of the well-known trophic actions of NGF. Since these neurons innervate the hippocampus, this effect of NGF may also play a role in modulating hippocampal synaptic transmission.

Direct presynaptic effects of neurotrophins on transmitter release have been best characterized at the neuromuscular junction. The neuromuscular junction is a widely studied model for examining mechanisms of synaptic transmission because it is one of the most accessible and well characterized synapses in the nervous system. At developing *Xenopus* neuromuscular synapses, BDNF and NT-3 potentiate evoked synaptic currents within minutes of exposure by enhancing acetylcholine (ACh) release from presynaptic nerve terminals (Lohof, Ip, and Poo, 1993). In addition to this short-term effect, chronic exposure to BDNF or NT-3 for several days enhances synaptic maturation through effects on presynaptic processes (Wang, Xie, and Lu, 1995). Similar effects are observed in mammalian systems in vitro, where NGF and BDNF directly potentiate the release of ACh and glutamate in the hippocampus and cortex (Knipper, da Penha Berzaghi, et al., 1994). Moreover, this enhanced transmitter release appears to augment synaptic transmission (Knipper, Leung, et al., 1994; Lessmann, Gottmann, and Heumann, 1994).

Neurotrophins also modulate synaptic activity via postsynaptic mechanisms. In the hippocampus, BDNF elicits sustained enhancement of excitatory synaptic activity within minutes of exposure (figure 11.5), leading to increased firing rate (Levine et al., 1995a). The synaptic locus of this effect was determined by making intracellular injections directly in the postsynaptic cell. In these experiments, the effect of BDNF was blocked or enhanced, respectively, by kinase or phosphatase inhibitors (figure 11.6), demonstrating that BDNF modulates postsynaptic responsiveness via phosphorylation-dependent mechanisms. Activation of the high-affinity BDNF receptor, trkB, is critical for this response, since NT-4, another trkB ligand, elicits similar effects. In contrast, the related neurotrophins, NGF and NT-3, as well as the unrelated growth factors epidermal growth factor and basic fibroblast growth factor, do not share this effect (Levine et al., 1996). A postsynaptic locus of action is substantiated by the finding that the biologically active full-length trkB receptor is an intrinsic component of the postsynaptic density (PSD), a specialization of the postsynaptic membrane that anchors neurotransmitter receptors and second-messenger-signaling molecules (Wu et al., 1996).

The postsynaptic effects of BDNF result from modulation of the NMDA subtype of glutamate receptor, which has been directly implicated in learning (Morris, Davis, and Butcher, 1990). BDNF rapidly increases neuronal responses to locally applied glutamate, the major excitatory transmitter in hippocampal circuits, but does not enhance responses to ACh (figure 11.7). Mechanisms responsible for increased

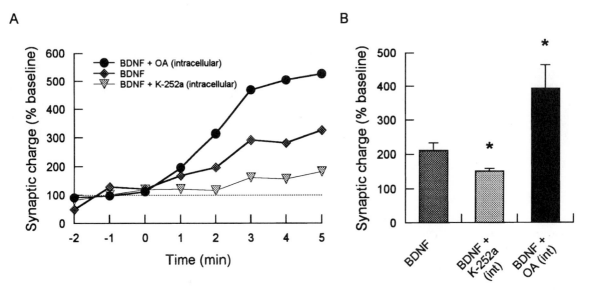

FIGURE 11.6   The effect of BDNF on synaptic charge is modified by postsynaptic manipulations. (A) Time courses of recordings from individual neurons for the effect of either bath-applied BDNF alone (50 ng/ml; diamonds), or in combination with intracellular injection of K-252a (200 nM; triangles) or okadaic acid (OA; 0.5 μM; circles). Recordings were obtained from sister cultures. Each point represents the average synaptic charge for a 1-minute period. (B) Effects of BDNF on synaptic charge. Intracellular injection of K-252a ($n = 8$ cells) decreased the magnitude of the charge effect compared to BDNF alone, while intracellular injection of okadaic acid ($n = 8$ cells) increased the effect. * $p < .05$. Recordings were obtained from multiple platings. (Reprinted from Levine et al., 1995a, Copyright 1995 National Academy of Sciences, U.S.A.)

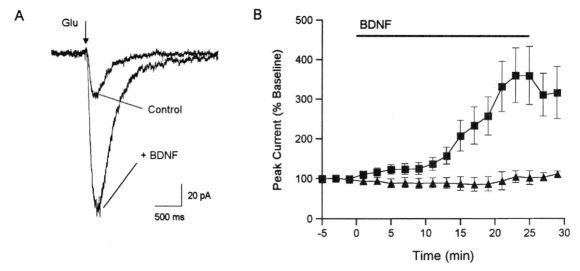

FIGURE 11.7   BDNF enhances responsiveness to iontophoretically applied glutamate but not acetylcholine. (A) Example traces of control response to glutamate iontophoresis (10-ms pulse; indicated by arrow) and response after 20 min of BDNF exposure. Holding potential was –40 mV. The iontophoresis pipette was located in the dendritic region of pyramidal cells. Traces represent the average of five consecutive sweeps. (B) Time course of mean effect of BDNF on glutamate (squares) or acetylcholine (triangles) responsiveness (mean ± SEM). (Reprinted from Levine et al., 1998, Copyright 1998 National Academy of Sciences, U.S.A.)

glutamate responsiveness have been revealed by monitoring the activity of individual NMDA receptor molecules with single-channel recording techniques. These recordings revealed that BDNF enhances the open probability of the NMDA receptor channel (figure 11.8), without changing channel conductance (Levine et al., 1998). BDNF also acutely enhances phosphorylation of NMDA receptor subunits in the PSD (Suen et al., 1997; Lin et al., 1998), an effect which may underlie altered receptor function. Furthermore, modulation of NMDA receptor function plays a direct role in BDNF-induced synaptic plasticity, because this plasticity is blocked by

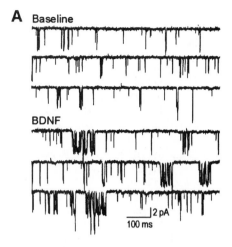

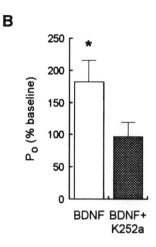

FIGURE 11.8 BDNF increases NMDA-receptor single-channel activity. (A) Example sweeps from a cell-attached single-channel recording before and during application of BDNF (20 ng/ml). This patch contained two channels. The holding potential was –80 mV. (B) Acute exposure to BDNF significantly enhanced NMDA receptor channel open probability (P_o; $p <$ .01; $n = 9$), normalized according to the number of channels in the patch. The trk tyrosine kinase inhibitor K-252a (200 nM) completely blocked the effect of BDNF ($p > .3$; $n = 6$). (Reprinted from Levine et al., 1998, Copyright 1998 National Academy of Sciences, U.S.A.)

pharmacological antagonism of NMDA receptors (Levine et al., 1998).

Thus neurotrophins potentiate synaptic transmission via both pre- and postsynaptic effects, increasing the efficacy of synaptic transmission and the probability of triggering postsynaptic action potentials. The effects of neurotrophins on synaptic activity may have specific consequences for activity-dependent plasticity in the hippocampus, including LTP, a potential cellular substrate of learning and memory. Animals with a targeted deletion of the BDNF gene have deficits in LTP that can be restored by acute reintroduction of BDNF (Korte et al., 1995; Korte et al., 1996; Patterson et al., 1996). Endogenous BDNF also enhances LTP, although specific mechanisms are controversial (Figurov et al., 1996; Akaneya et al., 1997; Kang et al., 1997). Taken together, these data point to an important role for neurotrophins in the regulation of synaptic plasticity and, potentially, the learning and memory processes that are dependent on this plasticity.

Recent studies utilizing a hippocampal lesion model, in fact, suggest that neurotrophin-induced synaptic plasticity may play a part in learning-related changes in hippocampal function. These studies raised the possibility that hippocampal BDNF is associated with spatial memory function. Unilateral hippocampal lesions resulted in deficits in spatial learning tasks in the neonatal rat, while having far lesser effects in the adult, suggesting that the contralateral, unlesioned hippocampus is dysfunctional after neonatal lesions (Van Praag et al., 1998). This model provided the opportunity to examine neurotrophin gene expression in the remaining, apparently dysfunctional hippocampus of rats with deranged memory function. In fact, BDNF mRNA was decreased significantly, while NGF message was unchanged, in the unlesioned hippocampus. Moreover, measures of cholinergic and GABAergic function were normal (Van Praag et al., 1998). These initial studies raise the possibility that BDNF, which regulates synaptic plasticity in vitro, also plays a role in memory mechanisms in vivo. Increasing neurotrophin availability may thus represent a novel approach toward reversing cognitive deficits resulting from injury, disease, or aging.

Some perspectives

The foregoing work provides a view of the emerging complexities of trophic roles in the brain. It is already apparent that impulse activity may influence trophic interactions at multiple loci in different cells and systems. In turn, environmental stimuli that elicit activity in any particular system may, potentially, gain access to trophic regulation and to the long-term changes that result. In principle, then, virtually instantaneous, millisecond-to-millisecond impulses may be converted into quasi-permanent neural circuit changes through distinct, definable molecular mechanisms.

Surprisingly, perhaps, these changes may be either trophic or regressive, depending on the specific EAA receptor subtypes stimulated. Potentially, then, some stimuli may increase pathway efficacy, whereas others may reduce efficacy in some systems. Relationships among experience, impulse activity, and pathway efficacy may be exceedingly complex and fine-tuned. What variables govern the balance between metabotropic-trophic and ionotropic-regressive influences? Is the final biologic effect simply a reflection of relative expression of receptor subtype genes, or do other factors govern access of EAA to already expressed receptors? Is the expression of different receptor subtypes independently regulated at the transcriptional, translational, and posttranslational levels? Approaches to these and related questions may help elucidate the intimate relationships between survival and death, between trophism and regression. More generally, we may inquire whether the coexistent potential for both increased and decreased function is widespread, exhibited by most neuronal systems. Finally, does the trophic-regressive balance contribute to the pathogenesis of disease, and does receptor subtype specificity suggest new therapeutic approaches?

In addition to the trophic-regressive balance, studies with the hippocampal neuronal cultures imply that a balance between excitatory and inhibitory transmitters also regulates trophic factor gene expression. Consequently, experience may potentially increase or decrease pathway efficacy through excitatory or inhibitory transmitter influences. In sum, excitatory-inhibitory, trophic-regressive checks and balances may allow precise modulation of brain neural circuits.

Focusing on trophic effects alone, multiple outstanding questions demand attention. Several may be enunciated as examples to indicate future research directions. While impulse activity and specific EAA transmitters can regulate trophic-factor gene expression, are trophic genes coregulated in most systems, or does regulation occur at different levels in different systems? Since proximate glia express trophic factor in the cerebellar dissociates (Cohen-Cory et al., 1993) as well as in other brain areas in vivo and in vitro (Lu et al., 1991b), should we now envisage a trophic neuron-glia-neuron loop, in addition to the classic neuron-neuron synaptic circuit? With multiple trophic, tropic, and growth factors, in addition to the neurotrophins, how are biologic specificity and selectivity conferred; what is the balance between specificity and redundancy; which factors act sequentially on defined populations; and what are the rules of sequentiality? Are we now in a position to move from environmental stimulus to impulse activity to trophic regulation to mental function and behavior, as implied by the examples of LTP and spatial learning, cited in this chapter?

ACKNOWLEDGMENTS This work was supported by NIH grants P01–HD23315 from the National Institute of Child Health and Human Development and R01–NS10259 from the National Institute of Neurological Disorders and Stroke, by a McKnight Foundation Award in Neuroscience, and by a Juvenile Diabetes Foundation Grant.

REFERENCES

AKANEYA, Y., T. TSUMOTO, S. KINOSHITA, and H. HATANAKA, 1997. Brain-derived neurotrophic factor enhances long-term potentiation in rat visual cortex. *J. Neurosci.* 17:6707–6716.

ALTMAN, J., 1972. Postnatal development of the cerebellar cortex in the rat. II. Phases in the maturation of Purkinje cells and of the molecular layer. *J. Comp. Neurol.* 145:399–463.

ALTMAN, J., and S. A. BAYER, 1985. Embryonic development of the rat cerebellum. III. Regional differences in the time of origin, migration, and settling of Purkinje cells. *J. Comp. Neurol.* 231:42–65.

BERRY, M., and P. BRADLEY, 1976. The growth of the dendritic trees of Purkinje cells in the cerebellum of the rat. *Brain Res.* 112:1–35.

BLISS, T. V., and T. LOMO, 1973. Long-lasting potentiation of synaptic transmission in the dentate area of the anaesthetized rabbit following stimulation of the perforant path. *J. Physiol. (Lond.)* 232:331–356.

BUCK, C. R., H. J. MARTINEZ, M. V. CHAO, and I. B. BLACK, 1988. Differential expression of the nerve growth factor receptor gene in multiple brain areas. *Dev. Brain Res.* 44:259–268.

COHEN, S., 1960. Purification of a nerve-growth promoting protein from the mouse salivary gland and its neuro-cyto-toxic antiserum. *Proc. Natl. Acad. Sci. U.S.A.* 46:302–311.

COHEN, S., and R. LEVI-MONTALCINI, 1956. A nerve growth-stimulating factor isolated from snake venom. *Proc. Natl. Acad. Sci. U.S.A.* 42:571–574.

COHEN-CORY, S., C. F. DREYFUS, and I. B. BLACK, 1989. Expression of high- and low-affinity nerve growth factor receptors by Purkinje cells in the developing rat cerebellum. *Exp. Neurol.* 105:104–109.

COHEN-CORY, S., C. F. DREYFUS, and I. B. BLACK, 1991. NGF and excitatory neurotransmitters regulate survival and morphogenesis of cultured cerebellar Purkinje cells. *J. Neurosci.* 11:462–471.

COHEN-CORY, S., R. C. ELLIOTT, C. F. DREYFUS, and I. B. BLACK, 1993. Depolarizing influences increase low-affinity NGF receptor gene expression in cultured Purkinje neurons. *Exp. Neurol.* 119:165–175.

DUPONT, J. L., R. GARDETTE, and F. CREPEL, 1987. Postnatal development of the chemosensitivity of rat cerebellar Purkinje cells to excitatory amino acids: An in vitro study. *Brain Res.* 431:59–68.

ECKENSTEIN, F., 1988. Transient expression of NGF-receptor-like immunoreactivity in postnatal rat brain and spinal cord. *Brain Res.* 446:149–154.

EICHENBAUM, H., T. OTTO, and N. J. COHEN, 1992. The hippocampus—What does it do? *Behav. Neur. Biol.* 57:2–36.

ELLIOTT, R. C., C. E. INTURRISI, I. B. BLACK, and C. F. DREYFUS, 1994. An improved method detects differential NGF and BDNF gene expression in response to depolarization in cultured hippocampal neurons. *Mol. Brain Res.* 26:81–88.

FIGUROV, A., L. D. POZZO-MILLER, P. OLAFSSON, T. WANG, and B. LU, 1996. Regulation of synaptic responses to high-frequency stimulation and LTP by neurotrophins in the hippocampus. *Nature* 381:706–709.

GALL, C., K. MURRAY, and P. J. ISACKSON, 1991. Kainic acid-induced seizures stimulate increased expression of nerve growth factor mRNA in rat hippocampus. *Mol. Brain Res.* 9:113–123.

GALL, C. M., and P. J. ISACKSON, 1989. Limbic seizures increase neuronal production of messenger RNA for nerve growth factor. *Science* 245:758–761.

GARBER, S. S., T. HOSHI, and R. W. ALDRICH, 1989. Regulation of ionic currents in pheochromocytoma cells by nerve growth factor and dexamethasone. *J. Neurosci.* 9:3976–3987.

GARTHWAITE, G., B. YAMINI, JR., and J. GARTHWAITE, 1987. Selective loss of Purkinje and granule cell responsiveness to N-methyl-D-aspartate in rat cerebellum during development. *Brain Res.* 433:288–292.

HALLBÖÖK, F., C. F. IBÁÑEZ, and H. PERSSON, 1991. Evolutionary studies of the nerve growth factor family reveal a novel member abundantly expressed in *Xenopus* ovary. *Neuron* 6:845–858.

HEFTI, F., A. DRAVID, and J. HARTIKKA, 1994. Chronic intraventricular injections of nerve growth factor elevate hippocampal choline acetyltransferase activity in adult rats with partial septohippocampal lesions. *Brain Res.* 293:305–311.

HEFTI, F., J. HARTIKKA, F. ECKENSTEIN, H. GNAHN, R. HEUMANN, and M. SCHWAB, 1985. Nerve growth factor increases choline acetyltransferase but not survival or fiber outgrowth of cultured fetal septal cholinergic neurons. *Neuroscience* 14:55–68.

HENDRY, I. A., 1975. The retrograde trans-synaptic control of the development of cholinergic terminals in sympathetic ganglia. *Brain Res.* 86:483–487.

HENDRY, I. A., R. STACH, and K. HERRUP, 1974. Characteristics of the retrograde axonal transport system for nerve growth factor in the sympathetic nervous system. *Brain Res.* 82:117–128.

HENDRY, I. A., K. STOCKEL, H. THOENEN, and L. L. IVERSEN, 1974. The retrograde axonal transport of nerve growth factor. *Brain Res.* 68:103–121.

HOFER, M., S. R. PAGLIUSI, A. HOHN, J. LEIBROCK, and Y. A. BARDE, 1990. Regional distribution of brain-derived neurotrophic factor mRNA in the adult mouse brain. *EMBO J.* 9:2459–2464.

ISACKSON, P. J., M. M. HUNTSMAN, K. D. MURRAY, and C. M. GALL, 1991. BDNF mRNA expression is increased in adult rat forebrain after limbic seizures: Temporal patterns of induction distinct from NGF. *Neuron* 6:937–948.

KALMAN, D., B. WONG, A. E. HORVAI, M. J. CLINE, and P. H. O'LAGUE, 1990. Nerve growth factor acts through cAMP-dependent protein kinase to increase the number of sodium channels in PC12 cells. *Neuron* 4:355–366.

KANG, H. J., A. A. WELCHER, D. SHELTON, and E. M. SCHUMAN, 1997. Neurotrophins and time: Different roles for TrkB signaling in hippocampal long-term potentiation. *Neuron* 19:653–664.

KNIPPER, M., M. DA PENHA BERZAGHI, A. BLOCHL, H. BREER, H. THOENEN, and D. LINDHOLM, 1994. Positive feedback between acetylcholine and the neurotrophins nerve growth factor and brain-derived neurotrophic factor in the rat hippocampus. *Eur. J. Neurosci.* 6:668–671.

KNIPPER, M., L. S. LEUNG, D. ZHAO, and R. J. RYLETT, 1994. Short-term modulation of glutamatergic synapses in adult rat hippocampus by NGF. *Neuroreport* 5:2433–2436.

KORTE, M., P. CARROLL, E. WOLF, G. BREM, H. THOENEN, and T. BONHOEFFER, 1995. Hippocampal long-term potentiation is impaired in mice lacking brain-derived neurotrophic factor. *Proc. Natl. Acad. Sci. U.S.A.* 92:8856–8860.

KORTE, M., O. GRIESBECK, C. GRAVEL, P. CARROLL, V. STAIGER, H. THOENEN, and T. BONHOEFFER, 1996. Virus-mediated gene transfer into hippocampal CA1 region restores long-term potentiation in brain-derived neurotrophic factor mutant mice. *Proc. Natl. Acad. Sci. U.S.A.* 93:12547–12552.

LARGE, T. H., S. C. BODARY, D. O. CLEGG, G. WESKAMP, U. OTTEN, and L. F. REICHARDT, 1986. Nerve growth factor gene expression in the developing rat brain. *Science* 234:352–355.

LEIBROCK, J., F. LOTTSPEICH, A. HOHN, M. HOFER, B. HENGERER, P. MASIAKOWSKI, H. THOENEN, and Y. A. BARDE, 1989. Molecular cloning and expression of brain-derived neurotrophic factor. *Nature* 341:149–152.

LESSER, S. S., and D. C. LO, 1995. Regulation of voltage-gated ion channels by NGF and ciliary neurotrophic factor in SK-N-SH neuroblastoma cells. *J. Neurosci.* 15:253–261.

LESSMANN, V., K. GOTTMANN, and R. HEUMANN, 1994. BDNF and NT-4/5 enhance glutamatergic synaptic transmission in cultured hippocampal neurones. *Neuroreport* 6:21–25.

LEVI-MONTALCINI, R., and P. U. ANGELETTI, 1968. Nerve growth factor. *Physiol. Rev* 48:534–569.

LEVI-MONTALCINI, R., and V. HAMBURGER, 1953. A diffusible agent of mouse sarcoma, producing hyperplasia of sympathetic ganglia and hyperneurotization of viscera in the chick embryo. *J. Exp. Zool.* 123:233–288.

LEVINE, E. S., R. A. CROZIER, I. B. BLACK, and M. R. PLUMMER, 1998. Brain-derived neurotrophic factor modulates hippocampal synaptic transmission by increasing N-methyl-D-aspartic acid receptor activity. *Proc. Natl. Acad. Sci. U.S.A.* 95:10235–10239.

LEVINE, E. S., C. F. DREYFUS, I. B. BLACK, and M. R. PLUMMER, 1995a. Brain-derived neurotrophic factor rapidly enhances synaptic transmission in hippocampal neurons via postsynaptic tyrosine kinase receptors. *Proc. Natl. Acad. Sci. U.S.A.* 92:8074–8077.

LEVINE, E. S., C. F. DREYFUS, I. B. BLACK, and M. R. PLUMMER, 1995b. Differential effects of NGF and BDNF on voltage-gated calcium currents in embryonic basal forebrain neurons. *J. Neurosci.* 15:3084–3091.

LEVINE, E. S., C. F. DREYFUS, I. B. BLACK, and M. R. PLUMMER, 1996. Selective role for trkB neurotrophin receptors in rapid modulation of hippocampal synaptic transmission. *Mol. Brain Res.* 38:300–303.

LIN, S. Y., K. WU, E. S. LEVINE, H. T. J. MOUNT, P. C. SUEN, and I. B. BLACK, 1998. BDNF acutely increases tyrosine phosphorylation of the NMDA receptor subunit 2B in cortical and hippocampal postsynaptic densities. *Mol. Brain Res.* 55:20–27.

LINDEN, D. J., M. H. DICKINSON, M. SMEYNE, and J. A. CONNOR, 1991. A long-term depression of AMPA currents in cultured cerebellar Purkinje neurons. *Neuron* 7:81–89.

LLANO, I., J. DREESSEN, M. KANO, and A. KONNERTH, 1991. Intradendritic release of calcium induced by glutamate in cerebellar Purkinje cells. *Neuron* 7:577–583.

LOHOF, A. M., N. Y. IP, and M. M. POO, 1993. Potentiation of developing neuromuscular synapses by the neurotrophins NT-3 and BDNF. *Nature* 363:350–353.

LU, B., M. YOKOYAMA, C. F. DREYFUS, and I. B. BLACK, 1991a. Depolarizing stimuli regulate nerve growth factor gene expression in cultured hippocampal neurons. *Proc. Natl. Acad. Sci. U.S.A.* 88:6289–6292.

LU, B., M. YOKOYAMA, C. F. DREYFUS, and I. B. BLACK, 1991b. NGF gene expression in actively growing brain glia. *J. Neurosci.* 11:318–326.

MAISONPIERRE, P. C., L. BELLUSCIO, S. SQUINTO, N. Y. IP, M. E. FURTH, R. M. LINDSAY, and G. D. YANCOPOULOS, 1990. Neurotrophin-3: A neurotrophic factor related to NGF and BDNF. *Science* 247:1446–1451.

MARTINEZ, H. J., C. F. DREYFUS, G. M. JONAKAIT, and I. B. BLACK, 1985. Nerve growth factor promotes cholinergic development in brain striatal cultures. *Proc. Natl. Acad. Sci. U.S.A.* 82:7777–7781.

MARTINEZ, H. J., C. F. DREYFUS, G. M. JONAKAIT, and I. B. BLACK, 1987. Nerve growth factor selectively increases cholinergic markers but not neuropeptides in rat basal forebrain in culture. *Brain Res.* 412:295–301.

MASU, M., Y. TANABE, K. TSUCHIDA, R. SHIGEMOTO, and S. NAKANISHI, 1991. Sequence and expression of a metabotropic glutamate receptor. *Nature* 349:760–765.

MORRIS, R. G., S. DAVIS, and S. P. BUTCHER, 1990. Hippocampal synaptic plasticity and NMDA receptors: A role in information storage? *Philos. Trans. R. Soc. Lond. B. Biol. Sci.* 329:187–204.

MORRISON, M. E., and C. A. MASON, 1998. Granule neuron regulation of Purkinje cell development: Striking a balance between neurotrophin and glutamate signaling. *J. Neurosci.* 18:3563–3573.

MOUNT, H. T., C. F. DREYFUS, and I. B. BLACK, 1993. Purkinje cell survival is differentially regulated by metabotropic and ionotropic excitatory amino acid receptors. *J. Neurosci.* 13:3173–3179.

OLSON, L., 1967. Outgrowth of sympathetic adrenergic neurons in mice treated with a nerve-growth factor (NGF). *Z. Zellforsch. Mikrosk. Anat.* 81:155–173.

PATTERSON, S. L., T. ABEL, T. A. DEUEL, K. C. MARTIN, J. C. ROSE, and E. R. KANDEL, 1996. Recombinant BDNF rescues deficits in basal synaptic transmission and hippocampal LTP in BDNF knockout mice. *Neuron* 16:1137–1145.

PATTERSON, S. L., L. M. GROVER, P. A. SCHWARTZKROIN, and M. BOTHWELL, 1992. Neurotrophin expression in rat hippocampal slices: A stimulus paradigm inducing LTP in CA1 evokes increases in BDNF and NT-3 mRNAs. *Neuron* 9:1081–1088.

SCHATTEMAN, G. C., L. GIBBS, A. A. LANAHAN, P. CLAUDE, and M. BOTHWELL, 1988. Expression of NGF receptor in the developing and adult central nervous system. *J. Neurosci.* 8:860–873.

SEKIGUCHI, M., K. OKAMOTO, and Y. SAKAI, 1987. NMDA-receptors on Purkinje cell dendrites in guinea pig cerebellar slices. *Brain Res.* 437:402–406.

SHARMA, N., G. D'ARCANGELO, A. KLEINLAUS, S. HALEGOUA, and J. S. TRIMMER, 1993. Nerve growth factor regulates the abundance and distribution of K^+ channels in PC12 cells. *J. Cell Biol.* 123:1835–1843.

SHELTON, D. L., and L. F. REICHARDT, 1984. Expression of the beta-nerve growth factor gene correlates with the density of sympathetic innervation in effector organs. *Proc. Natl. Acad. Sci. U.S.A.* 81:7951–7955.

SOTELO, C., and M. L. ARSENIO-NUNES, 1976. Development of Purkinje cells in absence of climbing fibers. *Brain Res.* 111:289–295.

SUEN, P. C., K. WU, E. S. LEVINE, H. T. J. MOUNT, J. L. XU, S. Y. LIN, and I. B. BLACK, 1997. Brain-derived neurotrophic factor rapidly enhances phosphorylation of the postsynaptic N-methyl-D-aspartate receptor subunit 1. *Proc. Natl. Acad. Sci. U.S.A.* 94:8191–8195.

TOLEDO-ARAL, J. J., P. BREHM, S. HALEGOUA, and G. MANDEL, 1995. A single pulse of nerve growth factor triggers long-term neuronal excitability through sodium channel gene induction. *Neuron* 14:607–611.

VAN PRAAG, H., P. M. QU, R. C. ELLIOTT, H. WU, C. F. DREYFUS, and I. B. BLACK, 1998. Unilateral hippocampal lesions in newborn and adult rats: Effects on spatial memory and BDNF gene expression. *Behav. Brain Res.* 92:21–30.

WANG, T., K. XIE, and B. LU, 1995. Neurotrophins promote maturation of developing neuromuscular synapses. *J. Neurosci.* 15:4796–4805.

WHITTEMORE, S. R., T. EBENDAL, L. LARKFORS, L. OLSON, A. SEIGER, I. STROMBERG, and H. PERSSON, 1986. Development and regional expression of beta nerve growth factor messenger RNA and protein in the rat central nervous system. *Proc. Natl. Acad. Sci. U.S.A.* 83:817–821.

WHITTEMORE, S. R., L. LÄRKFORS, T. EBENDAL, V. R. HOLETS, A. ERICSSON, and H. PERSSON, 1987. Increased ß-nerve growth factor messenger RNA and protein levels in neonatal rat hippocampus following specific cholinergic lesions. *J. Neurosci.* 7:244–251.

WU, K., J. L. XU, P. C. SUEN, E. S. LEVINE, Y. Y. HUANG, H. T. J. MOUNT, S. Y. LIN, and I. B. BLACK, 1996. Functional trkB neurotrophin receptors are intrinsic components of the adult brain postsynaptic density. *Mol. Brain Res.* 43:286–290.

YAN, Q., and E. M. JOHNSON, JR., 1988. An immunohistochemical study of the nerve growth factor receptor in developing rats. *J. Neurosci.* 8:3481–3498.

ZAFRA, F., B. HENGERER, J. LEIBROCK, H. THOENEN, and D. LINDHOLM, 1990. Activity dependent regulation of BDNF and NGF mRNAs in the rat hippocampus is mediated by non-NMDA glutamate receptors. *EMBO J.* 9:3545–3550.

12 Stress, Sex, and the Structural and Functional Plasticity of the Hippocampus

BRUCE S. McEWEN

ABSTRACT The hippocampal formation, which expresses high levels of adrenal steroid receptors, is a plastic brain structure that is important for certain types of learning and memory. It is also vulnerable to insults such as stroke, seizures, and head trauma. The hippocampus is also sensitive and vulnerable to the effects of stress and stress hormones, and it is responsive to the actions of sex hormones as well, both during development and adult life. Stress and sex hormones regulate three types of structural plasticity in the adult hippocampus: synaptogenesis, reorganization of dendrites, and neurogenesis in the dentate gyrus.

Developmentally programmed sex differences are also seen in the hippocampus. Suppression of dentate gyrus neurogenesis and atrophy of dendrites of hippocampal pyramidal neurons are produced by chronic psychosocial stress, involving the actions of adrenal steroids acting in concert with excitatory amino acid neurotransmitters. As far as we can tell, these changes are reversible as long as stress is terminated after a number of weeks. However, there are also reports that much longer durations of psychosocial stress leads to permanent loss of hippocampal pyramidal neurons. In the human hippocampus, MRI studies along with neuropsychological testing have revealed memory impairment and atrophy of the whole human hippocampus in some individuals as they age. This is reminiscent of individual differences in aging in rodents, which appear to reflect life-long patterns of stress hormone reactivity that are developmentally programmed, although a developmental influence on human individual differences is only a matter of speculation. Hippocampal atrophy is also found in Cushing's syndrome, posttraumatic stress disorder, and recurrent depressive illness, indicating that this brain structure is vulnerable and involved in stress- and stress-hormone-related disorders. Knowledge of underlying anatomical changes and the mechanism of hippocampal atrophy may help in developing treatment strategies to either reverse or prevent them.

The brain is sensitive to hormones secreted by the adrenal cortex, gonads, and thyroid in adult life as well as in early development. The earliest evidence for the hormone responsiveness of the nervous system came from the direct implantation of steroid hormones into the brain (Barfield, 1969; Lisk, 1962). Those initial studies in the 1960s used sex hormones because reproductive be-

BRUCE S. McEWEN Harold and Margaret Milliken Hatch Laboratory of Neuroendocrinology, Rockefeller University, New York, N.Y.

haviors were known to be regulated by gonadal steroids. With the introduction of tritiated steroid hormones in the 1960s, it became possible to map the location of steroid hormone receptors in brain tissue by autoradiography and in vitro binding assays (McEwen et al., 1979; Morrell and Pfaff, 1978). This mapping was based upon a model of steroid hormone action introduced in the 1960s centering on intracellular receptors that regulate genes by binding directly to DNA and are located in the cell nucleus (Jensen and Jacobson, 1962). The model of steroid action has been very influential in the current revolution in understanding regulation of gene transcription in eukaryotes (Beato and Sanchez-Pacheco, 1996; Evans, 1988; Yamamoto, 1985). This model not only provided a clear cellular target for localizing steroid receptors in brain cells but also indicated a model by which a chemical messenger could produce long-lasting effects upon neuronal structure and function.

One result of the mapping of steroid receptors was the discovery in 1968 that the hippocampal formation has receptors for adrenal steroids (McEwen, Weiss, and Schwartz, 1968). This finding, first in rats and later in primates (Gerlach et al., 1976) and birds (Rhees, Abel, and Haack, 1972), suggested that the adrenal cortex must have a far-reaching influence on this region of the brain. Indeed it does, but it has been only in the past decade that we have begun to elucidate the multiple hormonal influences in hippocampal structure and function, ranging from adaptive plasticity, which is the subject of this article, to pathophysiological changes. The hippocampal formation plays an important role in spatial and declarative memory as well as in contextual memory (Smriga, Saito, and Nishiyama, 1996). Hippocampal malfunction is implicated in schizophrenia and affective illness (Sheline et al., 1996; Axelson et al., 1993; Bogerts et al., 1993; Arnold et al., 1991; Luchins, 1990). Furthermore, glucocorticoids have a significant impact on the human hippocampus. For example, in Cushing's syndrome and after exogenous glucocorticoid therapy for inflammatory disorders, declarative memory defects have been found (Starkman et al., 1992; Newcomer et al., 1994; Wolkowitz, Reuss, and Weingartner,

1990; Wolkowitz, Rubinow, and Doran, 1990; Martignoni et al., 1992; reviewed in Lupien and McEwen, 1997), and verbal memory scores correlated negatively with elevated cortisol and positively with MRI measures showing decreased hippocampal volume (Starkman et al., 1992). Moreover, the hippocampus is vulnerable to degenerative effects of stress and loss of neurons during aging as well as in response to ischemia, seizures, and head trauma (Hsu and Buzsaki, 1993; Lowenstein et al., 1994; Sloviter, 1994; Landfield and Eldridge, 1994; Sapolsky, 1992).

Besides responding to adrenal steroids, the hippocampus is also a target of sex hormones and thyroid hormone. Male and female rats use different strategies in spatial learning and memory, with males preferring global spatial cues, and females, local contextual information (Williams and Meck, 1991), and the hippocampus displays a number of anatomical sex differences (Gould, Westlind-Danielsson, et al., 1990; Juraska et al., 1985). Moreover, during the estrous cycle of the female rat, new excitatory spine synapses are produced and broken down (Woolley and McEwen, 1992). Developmental thyroid hormone effects have been described on learning, electrophysiology, and anatomical features of the hippocampus (Madeira et al., 1992; Crusio and Schwegler, 1991; Pavlides et al., 1991), and thyroid hormone treatment in adult life produces morphological alterations in pyramidal neurons (Gould, Allan, and McEwen, 1990).

Many of these hormone effects do not occur alone but rather in the context of ongoing neuronal activity. In particular, excitatory amino acids and N-methyl-D-aspartic acid (NMDA) receptors play an important role in the functional and structural changes produced in the hippocampal formation by steroid hormones. At the same time, excitatory amino acids and NMDA receptors are involved in the destructive actions of stress and trauma on the hippocampus, and one of the challenges for future research is to understand what triggers the transition from adaptive plasticity to permanent damage. This chapter reviews the adaptive plasticity in the hippocampus produced by circulating adrenocortical, thyroid, and gonadal hormones acting in many cases in concert with excitatory amino acid neurotransmitters, and it also considers some of the ways in which adaptive plasticity gives way to permanent damage.

Salient features of hippocampal neuroanatomy

The hippocampus is organized as shown in figure 12.1, with two major regions, Ammon's horn and the dentate gyrus. The principal synaptic pathways include input to the granule cells of the dentate gyrus from the entorhinal cortex via the perforant pathway. These in turn project via the mossy fibers to the CA3 pyramidal cells, which then project via the Schaffer collaterals to the CA1 pyramidal cells.

Within the CA3 region are a number of features not shown in the diagram that have considerable significance for its functional activity and vulnerability to damage. These include the collaterals to other CA3 neurons

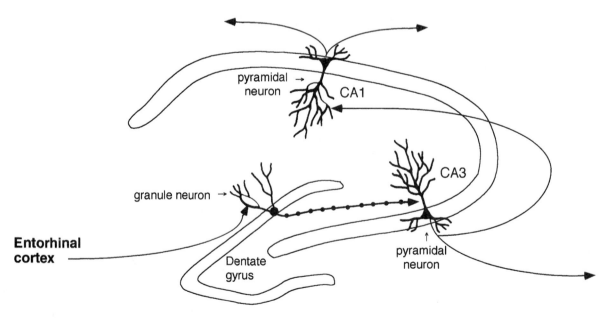

FIGURE 12.1 Basic neuroanatomy of the hippocampal formation, showing the three-cell circuit. This chapter describes studies showing that estrogens stimulate synaptogenesis on spines of dendrites of CA1 pyramidal neurons, whereas repeated stress, acting via glucocorticoids, causes dendritic remodeling of CA3 pyramidal neurons. In addition, adrenal steroids participate in the regulation of neurogenesis in the adult dentate gyrus of the adult.

as well as recurrent projections from CA3 neurons lying closer to the dentate gyrus (Li et al., 1994; Ishizuka, Weber, and Amaral, 1990). Both these collateral systems contribute to the bursting pattern of CA3 neuronal activity (Li et al., 1994) that is a contributing factor to seizure-induced destruction of CA3 pyramidal neurons (Sloviter, 1994).

Besides the principal neurons, the hippocampal formation contains a variety of nonprincipal cells including the excitatory mossy cells of the dentate hilus and the inhibitory interneurons that express a variety of neurochemical features in addition to producing gamma amino butyric acid (GABA). These neurons play an important role in regulating excitability within the hippocampus (Freund and Buzsaki, 1996).

Finally, the dentate gyrus is unique within the brain in having continued neurogenesis of granule neurons during adult life (Cameron, McEwen, and Gould, 1995). The dentate gyrus is formed later than Ammon's horn, and the maturation of the dentate gyrus in the first two weeks of life in the newborn rat (Cameron and Gould, 1996) is related to the development of emotionality, as seen by the effects of neonatal handling (Meaney et al., 1988) as well as by the appearance of "behavioral inhibition" (Takahashi, 1995; Gould and Cameron, 1997). The dentate gyrus is functionally connected to the amygdala, and lesions of the basolateral amygdala impair the formation of long-term potentiation in the dentate gyrus (Ikegaya, Saito, and Abe, 1997).

Sex hormones and the hippocampus

SEX DIFFERENCES   Estrogen and androgen receptors are expressed in the hippocampus of the developing and adult rat. In the developing rat brain, both estrogen receptors and aromatizing enzymes are expressed perinatally at the time of perinatal sexual differentiation and then decline to much lower levels that persist into adulthood (MacLusky et al., 1994; MacLusky et al., 1987; O'Keefe et al., 1995; O'Keefe and Handa, 1990). The cellular pattern of estrogen receptor expression is very similar in developing and adult hippocampus (S. Hayashi and C. Orikasa, personal communication).

Administration of estrogens to newborn female rats mimics the masculine sexual differentiation seen in males as far as the use of global spatial strategies in learning is concerned (Williams and Meck, 1991). Indeed, male and female rats use different strategies in spatial learning and memory, with males preferring global spatial cues, and females, local contextual information (Williams and Meck, 1991).

The hippocampus displays a number of anatomical sex differences. Notably, males have a larger dentate gyrus and more granule neurons, and dentate gyrus volume is increased in developing female rats by neonatal androgen treatment (Roof and Havens, 1992). In addition, sex differences in the pattern of dendritic branching and the density of dendritic spines on CA3 pyramidal neurons have been reported (Gould, Westlind-Danielsson, et al., 1990). Finally, environmental enrichment has different effects on hippocampal morphology in male and female rats (Juraska, Fitch, and Washburne, 1989; Juraska et al., 1985).

OVARIAN HORMONES AND SYNAPTOGENESIS   Adult female rats express low levels of estrogen receptors, and these receptors are expressed in interneurons scattered throughout the hippocampus and cerebral cortex (Weiland et al., 1997). These recent studies confirm and extend earlier findings using steroid autoradiography (Loy, Gerlach, and McEwen, 1988) and immunocytochemistry (DonCarlos, Monroy, and Morrell, 1991). The newly discovered beta estrogen receptor has been reported to be expressed in CA1 and CA2 pyramidal neurons (Li, Schwartz, and Rissman, 1997), but this finding is disputed (Weiland, Alves, and Lopez, personal communication).

During the estrous cycle of the female rat, new excitatory spine synapses are produced and broken down (Woolley and McEwen, 1992; Woolley, Gould, and McEwen, 1990). This finding may help explain the variations in seizure susceptibility of the dorsal hippocampus during the estrous cycle reported in 1968 (Terasawa and Timiras, 1968), with a marked decrease in seizure threshold on the afternoon of proestrus, at the peak of estrogen and progesterone levels. Stimulated by that paper, a morphological study that demonstrated estrogen induction of dendritic spines and new synapses in the ventromedial hypothalamus of the female rat led to the discovery that the density of dendritic spines on CA1 pyramidal neurons was also increased by estradiol (Gould, Woolley, Frankfurt, et al., 1990). These effects were specific for CA1, and dendritic spine density changed cyclically during the estrous cycle of the female rat (Woolley, Gould, and McEwen, 1990). There were also parallel changes in synapse density on dendritic spines, strongly supporting the notion of synapse turnover during the natural reproductive cycle of the rat (Woolley and McEwen, 1992).

There are two particularly important features of synapse formation and breakdown. First, progesterone administration rapidly potentiated estrogen-induced spine formation but then triggered the down-regulation of spines on CA1 neurons; the progesterone antagonist RU38486 blocked the natural down-regulation of spines during the estrous cycle (Woolley and McEwen, 1993).

Second, estrogen induction of new spine synapses on CA1 pyramidal neurons is blocked by concurrent administration of NMDA receptor antagonists (Woolley and McEwen, 1994). A recent study by Woolley showed, by electrophysiological recording, dye filling, and morphometry, that estrogen treatment increases not only spine density on CA1 neurons but also currents mediated by NMDA receptors when AMPA/kainate receptors are blocked (Woolley et al., 1997).

Moreover, a prominent effect of estrogen treatment is to induce NMDA receptor binding sites in the CA1 region of the hippocampus (Gazzaley et al., 1996; Weiland, 1992a). It is therefore possible that activation of NMDA receptors themselves could lead to induction of new synapses, in which case estrogen induction of NMDA receptors would then become a primary event leading to synapse formation.

The problem with all of this plasticity in CA1 pyramidal neurons is that, as noted earlier, the only detectable intracellular estrogen receptors are found in interneurons, not in the CA1 pyramidal neurons themselves. The possible exception is the presence of the beta ER in CA1 and CA2 neurons, discussed previously. There are also no detectable estrogen-inducible intracellular progestin receptors in hippocampus, based upon immunocytochemistry (N. G. Weiland and S. Alves, unpublished); however, there is a binding study showing low levels of such receptors in hippocampal tissue (Parsons et al., 1982). Nevertheless, recent studies with an estrogen antagonist argue strongly for a role of alpha estrogen receptors in interneurons in synapse induction. The estrogen antagonist CI-628 blocks estrogen induction of spines on CA1 neurons and does not produce any agonist effect (McEwen, Tanapat, and Weiland, 1999). This situation is reminiscent of blockade of progestin receptor induction in hypothalamus by CI-628, which is undoubtedly an alpha estrogen receptor–mediated effect (Roy, MacLusky, and McEwen, 1979). This experiment argues against a nongenomic effect of E and is consistent with the presence of alpha, but not beta, estrogen receptors in the inhibitory interneurons (Weiland et al., 1997; McEwen, Tanapat, and Weiland, 1999).

Recent studies on embryonic hippocampal neurons in culture have revealed that estrogens induce spines on dendrites of dissociated hippocampal neurons in culture by a process that is blocked by an NMDA receptor blocker and not by an AMPA/kainate receptor blocker (Murphy and Segal, 1996). In a subsequent study, estrogen treatment was found to increase expression of phosphorylated CREB and CREB-binding protein, and a specific antisense to CREB prevented both the formation of dendritic spines and the elevation in phospho-CREB (Murphy and Segal, 1997a). In agreement with the in vivo data (already discussed), estrogen receptors were located in the cultures on GAD-immunoreactive cells that constitute around 20% of neurons in the culture; estrogen treatment caused GAD content and the number of neurons expressing GAD to decrease, and mimicking this decrease with an inhibitor of GABA synthesis, mercaptopropionic acid, caused an up-regulation of dendritic spine density, mimicking the effects of estradiol (Murphy and Segal, 1997b). However, the situation in the in vivo hippocampus may be somewhat more complicated.

Estrogen induction of the mRNA for glutamic acid decarboxylase (GAD), a GABA synthesizing enzyme, was detected in interneurons residing within the CA1 pyramidal cell layer, a finding consistent with the known localization of estrogen receptors (Weiland, 1992b). Moreover, estrogen treatment induces GABAa receptor binding in the CA1 region of hippocampus, an effect that may be secondary to the action on the interneurons (McCarthy et al., 1992; Schumacher, Coirini, and McEwen, 1989). However, these effects were detected a number of days after estrogen treatment and are not inconsistent with a transient repression of GAD expression, as noted earlier in discussing the cell culture studies.

Concentrating for the moment on the interneurons containing the alpha ER, it is possible that the estrogen effects on formation of synapses on CA1 pyramidal neurons are indirect and mediated through these GABA interneurons. Wong and Moss (1992) reported that two-day estradiol treatment prolongs the EPSP and increases the probability of repetitive firing in some CA1 neurons in response to Schaffer collateral (glutamatergic) stimulation. One explanation is that estrogen actions on inhibitory interneurons might in some manner disinhibit the pyramidal neurons, allowing for removal of the magnesium blockade and activation of NMDA receptors (Orchinik and McEwen, 1995). Two alternative pathways are outlined in figure 12.2. Estrogens may decrease the activity of the GABA inhibitory input to CA1 pyramidal neurons and thus disinhibit the CA1 neurons to allow for up-regulation of NMDA receptors and excitatory synapses; alternatively, estrogens may increase the activity of GABA inhibitory input to other inhibitory interneurons that synapse on CA1 pyramidal neurons, resulting in a disinhibition. As noted previously, the recent evidence from the cell culture model suggests that estrogens transiently suppress expression of glutamic acid decarboxylase in inhibitory interneurons (Murphy and Segal, 1997b), thus supporting the first model shown in figure 12.2. Neuroanatomical data on the type of GABA interneuron that expresses estrogen receptors are consistent with this notion (N. G. Weiland, unpublished).

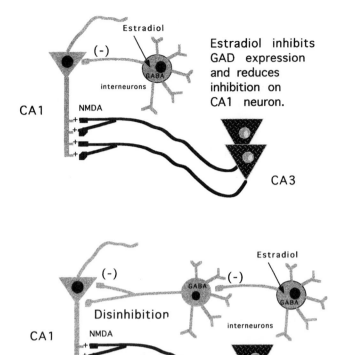

Estradiol inhibits GAD expression and reduces inhibition on CA1 neuron.

Disinhibition

Estradiol enhances GABA activity.

FIGURE 12.2 Alternative schemes for the role of GABA interneurons in synaptogenesis on CA1 pyramidal neurons. Estrogens may act to repress GABA activity in interneurons that synapse on CA1 neurons and produce a state of disinhibition that allows synapse formation to proceed. Alternatively, estrogens may act on GABA interneurons that synapse on other interneurons, in which case the estrogen effect might be to upregulate GABA activity and produce a disinhibition on the CA1 pyramidal neurons.

ANDROGENS AND THE HIPPOCAMPUS   The hippocampus expresses androgen receptors that are prominently localized in CA1 pyramidal neurons (J. E. Kerr et al., 1995). Androgens positively regulate androgen receptor mRNA levels in CA1, although androgen receptor binding is less sensitive to castration and hormone replacement than mRNA levels (J. E. Kerr et al., 1995).

In turn, androgen treatment induces changes in NMDA receptor expression and alters neuronal activity mediated by NMDA receptors in CA1 pyramidal neurons. Electrophysiologically, chronic treatment of castrated rats with the potent androgen dihydrotestosterone (DHT) increased the action potential duration of CA1 pyramidal neurons and decreased the amplitude of the fast hyperpolarization; moreover, DHT treatment promoted recovery of the membrane potential after depolarization with NMDA (Pouliot, Handa, and Beck,

1996). Binding of the antagonist MK801 to NMDA receptors in the CA1 region was elevated by castration, and this increase was prevented by DHT treatment, indicating that the antagonist-binding form of the NMDA receptor is affected by androgen treatment (Kus et al., 1995).

Castration increased levels of the mRNA for GnRH receptor not only on CA1 pyramidal neurons but also in the CA3 region and the dentate gyrus; curiously, however, castration decreased the second-messenger response to GnRH in hippocampal slices (Jennes et al., 1995). Except for electrophysiological studies, there is nothing to suggest a function for GnRH receptors in the hippocampus.

Androgens also have an influence on the adrenocortical response system of the hippocampus. Androgen treatment suppressed expression of Type II (glucocorticoid) receptor mRNA but had no effect on Type I (mineralocorticoid) receptor mRNA levels (J. E. Kerr, Beck, and Handa, 1996a). In this connection, castration has been reported to increase reactivity of the hypothalamo-pituitary-adrenal (HPA) axis (Handa et al., 1993). One possible reason for this effect is that castration increases reactivity of neural circuits involved in regulating HPA function. Consistent with this notion is the finding that castration increased, and androgen replacement suppressed, the immediate early gene responses to novelty in the CA1 region of the hippocampus but not in CA3 or dentate gyrus (J. E. Kerr, Beck, and Handa, 1996b).

Thyroid hormone and the hippocampus

Thyroid hormone receptors (TR) are expressed throughout the forebrain of the developing and adult rat. There are two gene products, TR alpha and TR beta, each of which has several alternately spliced variants. TR alpha 1 binds thyroid hormone, whereas the TR alpha 2 splice variant does not; TR beta 1 and TR beta 2 have identical sequences in their DNA-binding, hinge-region, and ligand-binding domains and differ only at the amino terminal region as a result either of alternative splicing or alternative promotor usage (Lechan et al., 1993). In adult life, TR alpha 1 and TR alpha 2 mRNA are expressed at similar levels in olfactory bulb, hippocampus, and granular layer of the cerebellar cortex, whereas TR beta mRNAs were concentrated in the anterior pituitary and parvocellular paraventricular nucleus (Bradley, Young, and Weinberger, 1989). A related mRNA, REV-ErbA alpha, which fails to bind thyroid hormone, was concentrated in the cerebral cortex (Bradley, Towle, and Young, 1992; Bradley, Young, and Weinberger, 1989). In contrast to the mRNA, immunoreactivity for the TR beta 2 protein was expressed in cerebral cortex, cerebellum, and hypothalamus in areas where the mRNA had not been identified (Lechan et al., 1993). Likewise, TR beta 1 immunoreactivity was found widely expressed in the forebrain, with highest levels in cerebral cortex, particularly parietal cerebral cortex layer 1, olfactory bulb, and hippocampus; thyroidectomy resulted in increased immunoreactivity in a number of brain regions, particularly in habenula and the CA3 region of the hippocampus (Nobrega et al., 1997).

In the developing brain, TR beta 2, which binds to adult anterior pituitary, is expressed in developing hippocampus and striatum, whereas TR alpha 1 and TR alpha 2 mRNAs are expressed in the fetal neocortical plate where there is active neurogenesis (Bradley, Towle, and Young, 1992). Hyperthyroidism early in neonatal life alters hippocampal morphology and the neurochemistry and structure of the basal forebrain cholinergic system of rats (Gould, Woolley, and McEwen, 1991; Westlind-Danielsson, Gould, and McEwen, 1991). In spite of these effects, sex differences in these systems persist in both basal forebrain and hippocampus (Gould, Westlind-Danielsson, et al., 1990; Westlind-Danielsson, Gould, and McEwen, 1991). The same was true for morphological changes in the dendrites of CA3 pyramidal neurons: Hyperthyroid animals had more thorny excrescences in stratum lucidum and longer and more extensively branched apical dendrites (Gould, Westlind-Danielsson, et al., 1990). Astroglial cells in the basal forebrain and septal area were also larger and more extensively branched (Gould, Frankfurt, et al., 1990).

But this hypertrophy is not necessarily to the benefit of the treated animal. On one hand, in the rat experiments cited earlier, both male and female hyperthyroid animals are slower to acquire a hippocampal-dependent spatial learning task and are somewhat impaired in showing long-term potentiation in the hippocampus (Pavlides et al., 1991). On the other hand, a strain of mice that normally shows poor spatial learning and may have a congenital deficiency of thyroid hormone secretion during early development displays a beneficial effect of the same kind of neonatal thyroid hormone treatment (Schwegler et al., 1991). Thus there is an optimal level of thyroid hormone that is associated with optimal cognitive performance, and deviations in the direction of both hyper- and hypothyroidism result in deficiencies in neural development and cognitive function.

A hyperthyroid state in adult life, induced by repeated thyroid hormone treatment, produced morphological alterations in hippocampal pyramidal neurons, involving a reduction in spine density (Gould, Allan, and McEwen, 1990), which is different from and opposite to the effects described for hyperthyroidism in the neonatal

rat brain. Like sexual differentiation, described earlier, this is one more example of how the effects of hormones change as the brain matures.

Changes in response to thyroid hormones have been studied in hippocampus as a function of developmental age. In the CA3 region, the main effect of hypothyroidism involved decreases in volume of the pyramidal cell layer and increases in packing density of pyramidal neurons without reductions in neuronal number (Madeira et al., 1992). These effects were evident whether the hypothyroid condition was during the first 30 days of neonatal life, or between 30 and 180 days, or for the entire 180-day period (Madeira et al., 1992). In the CA1 region, however, there was evidence of neuronal loss (Madeira et al., 1992).

Adrenal steroids and the hippocampus

RECEPTORS AND EFFECTS   The two types of receptors for adrenal steroids in hippocampus are the Type I or mineralocorticoid receptors (MR), and the Type II or glucocorticoid receptors (GR). It is evident from the distribution of mRNA and binding for Type I and Type II adrenal steroid receptor subtypes that neurons in dentate gyrus and Ammon's horn most likely contain both types of receptors (Herman et al., 1989), and indeed this fact has been demonstrated (see DeKloet et al., 1998). Several variants of MR and GR have been demonstrated: for MR, these are located in the untranslated region and may affect regulation of receptor expression (Kwak et al., 1993); for GR, there are receptor variants of the untranslated region, as well as some receptor variants that differ in the translated part of the mRNA (Bamberger et al., 1997; Bamberger, Schulter, and Chrousos, 1996). Another potentially important variable is that MR and GR can form heterodimers, and this activity is likely to affect the nature of the transcriptional regulation that these receptors exert (Trapp and Holsboer, 1996). MR and GR homodimers bind to the same glucocorticoid response elements (GRE) in transfection systems (Arriza et al., 1988), but they have different interactions with proteins coassociated with the receptors (Pearce and Yamamoto, 1993). In the brain and immune system, in cells that express both receptor types, MR and GR show some cross talk with each other as far as regulating their own expression: The primary direction of this effect is for MR occupancy to reduce GR expression at the mRNA (Chao, Ma, et al., 1998) and binding (Miller et al., 1993; Luttge, Rupp, and Davda, 1989) levels.

There are a number of effects mediated by MR and GR in the hippocampus and other brain regions, and most of them reflect unique actions of either MR or GR; see table 12.1. Type II receptors, which are present in the

TABLE 12.1
Neurotransmission

Neurochemical	Brain Region	Receptor Type	Reference
Neuropeptide Y	Hippocampus, hilus	Type I	Watanabe, Akabayashi, and McEwen, 1995
Dynorphin	Hippocampus, DG	Type I	Watanabe, Weiland, and McEwen, 1995
Kainate receptors	Hippocampus, DG	Type I	Watanabe, Weiland, and McEwen, 1995
Vasopressin V1 receptors	Hippocampus	Type I	Saito et al., 1996
Oxytocin receptors	Hippocampus	Type I	Liberzon et al., 1994; Liberzon and Young, 1997
5-HT1A receptors	Hippocampus, DG, CA3	Type I	Kuroda et al., 1994
5-HT2 receptors	Cerebral cortex	Type II	Kuroda et al., 1993
Corticotrophin releasing factor	Hypothalamus, PVN	Type II	Albeck, Hastings, and McEwen, 1994
Neurokinin A (Substance P)	Caudate, bed nucleus	Type I & Type II	Pompei, Riftina, and McEwen, 1995

paraventricular nuclei of the hypothalamus, mediate a profound suppression of CRHmRNA, whereas stimulating the Type I receptor had no effect (Albeck et al., 1997). Both MR and GR mediate increased levels of neurokinin A mRNA in the caudate and bed nucleus of the stria terminalis (Pompei, Riftina, and McEwen, 1995). In contrast to these results, MR activation in the hippocampus is responsible for a number of effects of adrenal steroids on neurochemical features of this brain region, including increased expression of dynorphin mRNA and kainate receptors in the dentate gyrus, increased expression of oxytocin and vasopressin receptors in hippocampus, and repression of neuropeptide Y expression in the dentate hilus as well as repression of 5-HT1A receptor expression in the dentate gyrus and CA3 region (see table 12.1).

Adrenal steroids influence the levels of mRNAs for a number of neurotrophins and do so via the two different receptors. Adrenalectomy increases the expression of BDNF mRNA in CA1 and CA3 regions of the hippocampus and decreases the expression of NT3 and basic FGF mRNA in the CA2 region (Chao, Sakai, et al., 1998). Type I receptor activation reverses the ADX effect and increases expression of basic FGF mRNA and NT3 expression in the CA2 region of the hippocampus, whereas the combination of Type I and Type II receptor activation is most effective in reversing the effect of ADX on BDNF mRNA levels (Chao, Sakai, et al., 1998). The mRNA for a key growth cone and structural marker, GAP43, is increased by ADX, and this effect is reversed by the combination of Type I and Type II receptor activation (Chao, Sakai, et al., 1998), although previous work suggested that this was mainly a Type I receptor effect (Chao and McEwen, 1994).

Type II receptors are not entirely without effects in the hippocampus. Type II receptor activation suppresses neurogenesis in the developing, but not adult, rat dentate gyrus (see the next subsection), and Type II receptors mediate the excitotoxin-induced damage to hip-

pocampal neurons in culture (Packan and Sapolsky, 1990). Type II receptors also mediate inhibitory effects on long-term potentiation in the hippocampus and promote long-term depression (see the next subsection). In general, Type II receptors oppose the actions mediated by Type I receptors on a number of markers of excitability and neurotransmission in the hippocampus (DeKloet et al., 1998).

The findings of distinctly different effects mediated by Type I and Type II receptors have implications for the genomic mechanisms by which these receptors produce their effects on gene transcription. Clearly, the classical GRE, with which both Type I and Type II receptors interact to regulated gene transcription (Arriza et al., 1988), is not a sufficient explanation for the separate actions of these two receptor types on hippocampal processes. Alternative mechanisms involve the differential ability of Type II receptors to interact with fos-jun heterodimers and other proteins (Beato and Sanchez-Pacheco, 1996) as well as the formation of MR-GR heterodimers (Trapp and Holsboer, 1996). See also DeKloet and colleagues (1998) for discussion of this topic.

STRESS, ADRENAL STEROIDS, AND NEURONAL EXCITABILITY   A single burst of high-frequency stimulation to hippocampal afferents can immediately alter the responsiveness of neurons to further stimuli, an effect lasting over a time course of many hours to days. This type of plasticity is called long-term potentiation (LTP) (Bliss and Lomo, 1973). An in vivo study demonstrated in the hippocampal CA1 field that acute stress suppressed LTP (Diamond, Fleshner, and Rose, 1994). An acute injection of glucocorticoids produced an inhibition of LTP in the dentate gyrus (Pavlides, Watanabe, and McEwen, 1993). With regard to glucocorticoid levels, an inverted U-shaped curve was found with regard to induction of plasticity in the CA1 field in relation to circulating corticosterone (CORT) levels; that is, both adrenocortical insufficiency as well as high levels of CORT had a detrimental effect on potentiation, whereas optimal potentiation was obtained within an intermediate range (10–20 µg/dl) of circulating CORT (Diamond et al., 1992).

More recent studies have begun to dissect the underlying mechanism and the role of Type I and Type II receptors. Within the dentate gyrus, LTP can be modulated biphasically by adrenal steroids acting via Type I and Type II receptors; LTP was found to be enhanced within an hour by adrenal steroids acting via Type I receptors, whereas Type II receptor stimulation was found to rapidly suppress LTP (Pavlides, Watanabe, et al., 1995). The enhancement by Type I receptor stimulation lasted for more than 24 hours in awake freely moving animals, whereas LTP disappeared in a few hours in the dentate gyrus of adrenalectomized rats without steroid replacement (Pavlides et al., 1994). The CA1 field responded to corticosteroids in a biphasic manner similar to that of the dentate gyrus (Pavlides et al., 1996); and the same was true of the commissural/associational input to CA3 but not for the mossy fiber input (C. Pavlides and B. McEwen, unpublished). These biphasic effects may help to explain the inverted U-shaped dose response curve with respect to induction of LTP in the CA1 region of Ammon's horn, noted previously (Diamond et al., 1992).

One of the unexpected effects of adrenal steroid receptor stimulation was the finding that, in adrenalectomized rats, Type II receptor activation facilitated the expression of long-term depression (LTD), which is elicited by low-frequency stimulation of afferents to dentate gyrus (Pavlides, Kimura, et al., 1995). Though first demonstrated in dentate gyrus, this effect was recently demonstrated in CA1 and was shown to be mimicked by stress and to involve a transcriptional mechanism (Xu et al., 1998).

It is important to note that the mossy fiber input to the CA3 lacked any facilitation via Type I receptor activation or any inhibition via Type II receptors; instead, Type II receptor stimulation actually facilitated the population spike of LTP after mossy fiber stimulation (Pavlides and McEwen, in press). Because mossy fiber LTP is independent of NMDA receptors (Weisskopf, Zalusky, and Nicoll, 1993; Derrick, Weinberger, and Martinez, 1991) whereas the other forms of LTP involve NMDA receptors, it appears that the biphasic modulation of LTP may involve modulation of NMDA receptors. In this connection, adrenal steroids and stress have been reported to regulate expression of NMDA receptors in the hippocampus (Gottesman, 1997; Bartanusz et al., 1995) and other brain regions (Fitzgerald et al., 1996; Shors et al., 1997).

The precise mechanisms underlying the stress-induced impairments in LTP are not yet established.

While CORT may be modulating LTP directly, via its action on hippocampal cells, the endogenous opiates and neurotransmitters like glutamate and serotonin may also be involved. Tail shock in a restraining tube for 30 minutes caused hippocampal slices from these rats to show significantly less LTP in CA1 pyramidal neurons (Foy et al., 1987). Although LTP was affected, paired-pulse facilitation was not altered, indicating that inhibitory mechanisms were not affected (Shors, Weiss, and Thompson, 1992). Adrenalectomy blocked the stress effect, but this effect was related to the adrenal medulla, since corticosterone did not restore the effect whereas adrenal demedullation mimicked the effect of total adrenalectomy (Shors, Levine, and Thompson, 1990). Moreover, naltrexone, an opiate antagonist, also blocked the effect of stress, suggesting that an endogenous opioid mechanism may be involved (Shors, Seymour, and Thompson, 1990). The inhibitory effects of environmental stressors were found in other paradigms. An inhibitory effect on LTP was found after one week of training to escape low-intensity foot shock in a shuttle box and was more evident in the yoked control, which could not escape the shock (Shors et al., 1989). In another study, exposure of rats to a novel environment resulted in a rapid and reversible impairment of plasticity in vivo in the CA1 region (Diamond, Fleshner, and Rose, 1994).

Recent studies have reported that plasticity in the hippocampus is accompanied by induction of a number of immediate early genes (IEGs; Abraham, Dragunow, and Tate, 1991; Worley et al., 1993). In the hippocampus of unanesthetized, freely behaving animals, it has been shown that IEGs including the fos and jun families, zif/268, and krox, to name but a few, are activated following the induction of LTP. Interestingly, fos and zif/268 have also been shown to increase in a number of brain areas, including the hippocampus, following acute stress (Melia et al., 1994; Watanabe, Stone, and McEwen, 1994; Schreiber et al., 1991). Activation of these IEGs in turn may regulate the expression of various late effector genes, for example, F1/GAP-43, which could then produce structural changes that would be required for the long-term maintenance of plasticity. Because steroid hormone receptors are known to interact with immediate early genes via "composite response elements" on target genes (Miner and Yamamoto, 1991), it is conceivable that the actions of aldosterone to facilitate LTP (Pavlides et al., 1996; Pavlides, Watanabe, et al., 1995; Pavlides et al., 1994) are accompanied by an increased expression of genes that participate in the establishment of new structural connections. Future studies must explore the structural and neurochemical changes that accompany the steroid enhancement of LTP, including possible interactions between glucocorticoids and induction of IEGs, and changes in structural protein and neurotrophin gene expression.

REGULATION OF DENTATE GYRUS NEUROGENESIS AND NEURONAL REPLACEMENT Granule neurons of the adult dentate gyrus depend on adrenal steroids for their survival. This dependence can be seen by the fact that adrenalectomy (ADX) of an adult rat causes increased granule neuron death (Gould, Woolley, and McEwen, 1990; Sloviter et al., 1989). However, neuronal death is only one part of the story because continuous birth of granule neurons occurs in the adult dentate gyrus, and neurogenesis also increases following ADX (Cameron and Gould, 1994).

The first clue as to the magnitude of the ADX effect on neuronal death in dentate gyrus was the finding that, three months after ADX of adult rats, some rats showed almost total loss of dentate gyrus granule neurons (Sloviter et al., 1989). This finding attracted considerable attention because it conflicted with the prevalent view of stress- and glucocorticoid-induced neuronal death in Ammon's horn (see below); it was also very puzzling because only some ADX rats showed the loss of the entire dentate gyrus.

We now have more information that allows us to understand these events better, based on the unique nature of adrenal steroid actions in dentate gyrus. ADX has been shown to induce apoptotic death of dentate granule neurons within 3–7 days in virtually every rat from which all adrenal tissue has been removed (Gould, Woolley, and McEwen, 1990). Loss of the entire dentate gyrus only in some rats may well be explained by absence of accessory adrenal tissue in those rats; when not removed at the time of ADX, this tissue can supply enough adrenal steroids to prevent neuronal loss.

In adult rats, very low levels of adrenal steroids, sufficient to occupy Type I adrenal steroid receptors, completely block dentate gyrus neuronal loss (Woolley et al., 1991). Curiously, however, in newborn rats Type II receptor agonists protect against neuronal apoptosis (Gould, Tanapat, and McEwen, 1997). This finding is consistent with the fact that dentate neuronal loss in the developing rat occurs at much higher circulating steroid levels than in the adult, and it represents another example of the different ways that the two adrenal steroid receptor types are involved in hippocampal function.

It should be noted that granule cell birth is also accelerated by ADX, and that the newly born neurons in the adult dentate gyrus arise in the hilus, very close to the granule cell layer, and then migrate into the granule cell layer, presumably along a vimentin-staining radial glial network that is also enhanced by ADX (Cameron et al.,

1993). Specific antibodies to neuron-specific enolase (NSE) have been used to show that the majority of newly born cells in the adult dentate gyrus are neurons. Using this approach, neurogenesis has been recognized in the adult rat, mouse, tree shrew, and marmoset dentate gyrus (Kempermann, Kuhn, and Gage, 1997; Gould et al., 1998; Gould, McEwen, et al., 1997; Cameron, McEwen, and Gould, 1995), strongly suggesting that this form of plasticity also operates in the adult brain.

In spite of the previously mentioned role for Type I adrenal steroid receptors in suppressing neuronal turnover in adult dentate gyrus, it should be noted that most neuroblasts labeled with [^{3}H] thymidine lack both Type I and Type II adrenal steroid receptors (Cameron et al., 1993) as well as NMDA receptors (Pennartz and Kitai, 1991), indicating that steroidal regulation occurs via messengers from an unidentified steroid-sensitive cell. The possibility that other trophic factors may be involved is currently under investigation. Recent evidence suggests that the EGF receptor may play an important role in the signaling of stem cells to begin division and differentiation into granule neurons (Tanapat and Gould, 1997).

Besides adrenal steroids, excitatory amino acids acting via NMDA receptors regulate neurogenesis in the dentate gyrus (Cameron, McEwen, and Gould, 1995). Blockade of NMDA receptors in an adult rat with a single dose of an antagonist increased neuron number by 20% over a number of weeks; lesions of the entorhinal cortex input to the dentate gyrus also increased neurogenesis (Cameron, McEwen, and Gould, 1995). The increase in neurogenesis is not accompanied by a measurable change in apoptosis. Figure 12.3 summarizes the dual regulation of neuronal turnover by adrenal steroids and excitatory amino acids.

One explanation for why the dentate gyrus makes new cells in adult life, as well as gets rid of them, is that it does so in order to process spatial information and related aspects of memory (Sherry, Jacobs, and Gaulin, 1992). Birds that use space around them to hide and locate food, as well as voles and deer mice that traverse large distances to find mates, have larger hippocampal volumes than closely related species that do not; moreover, there are indications that hippocampal volume may change during the breeding season (Galea et al., 1994; Sherry, Jacobs, and Gaulin, 1992). It remains to be determined whether it is the dentate gyrus that exhibits this plasticity. One clue is that the rate of neurogenesis in the male and female prairie vole varies according to the breeding season (Galea, Tanapat, and Gould, 1996). Moreover, an enriched environment has been found to increase dentate gyrus volume in mice by increasing neuronal survival without altering the rate of

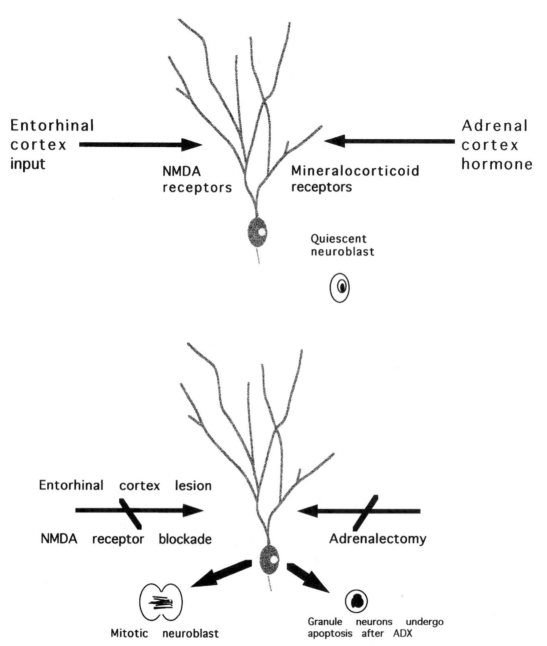

FIGURE 12.3 Regulation of neurogenesis and neuronal turnover in the dentate gyrus by excitatory amino acids acting via NMDA receptors and by adrenal steroids. Adrenalectomy increases both neurogenesis and neuronal apoptosis, whereas the main effect of blocking NMDA receptors or lesioning excitatory input from entorhinal cortex is to increase neurogenesis.

neurogenesis (Kempermann, Kuhn, and Gage, 1997). This finding illustrates in another way the balance between neuronal apoptosis and neurogenesis.

Another aspect of this balance concerns the effects of acute and chronic stress. Acute stress involving the odor of a natural predator, the fox, inhibits neurogenesis in the adult rat (Galea, Tanapat, and Gould, 1996). Acute psychosocial stress in the adult tree shrew, involving largely visual cues, inhibits neurogenesis (Gould et al., 1997). Inhibition of neurogenesis is also seen in the dentate gyrus of the marmoset after acute psychosocial stress (Gould et al., 1998). Chronic psychosocial stress in the tree shrew results in a more substantial inhibition of neurogenesis than after a single acute stressful encounter; moreover, the dentate gyrus is 30% smaller in the chronically stressed tree shrew, although granule neuron number only shows a trend for reduction (Fuchs et al., 1997). This finding suggests that there may be other changes such as atrophy of dendritic branching to account for the decrease in dentate gyrus volume.

Finally, what are the consequences for hippocampal function of altering dentate gyrus volume and the rates of neurogenesis and neuronal apoptosis? In the enriched environment studies (Kempermann, Kuhn, and Gage, 1997), increased dentate gyrus volume was accompanied by better performance on spatial learning tasks. In contrast, chronically stressed tree shrews display impaired spatial learning and memory (Gould et al., 1997), although this impairment might be as much due to atrophy of dendrites of CA3 pyramidal neurons (see the next subsection) as to reduced dentate gyrus neurogenesis (see previous paragraph). Regarding the effects of long-term ADX, several reports have indicated that rats that have substantial granule neuron loss in the dentate gyrus (Sloviter et al., 1989) show modest deficits in spatial memory (Vaher et al., 1994; Conrad and Roy, 1993; Armstrong et al., 1993).

STRESS, ADRENAL STEROIDS, AND NEURONAL ATROPHY   Aus der Muhlen and Ockenfels reported in 1969 that ACTH or cortisone administration to mature guinea pigs caused neurons in hippocampus and other forebrain regions to stain darkly and appear necrotic, as if undergoing atrophy. A similar finding was reported recently for tree shrews undergoing chronic psychosocial stress (Fuchs, Uno, and Flugge, 1995) in which there is also evidence for dendritic atrophy (Magarinos et al., 1996) as well as inhibition of dentate gyrus neurogenesis (see the preceding subsection). While the interpretation of these findings may be questioned in light of more recent findings regarding artifacts that can develop in fixing brains for histological analysis (Cammermeyer, 1978), the findings of aus der Muhlen and Ockenfels were instrumental in stimulating the work of Landfield and colleagues showing that aging in the rat results in some pyramidal neuron loss in hippocampus and that this loss is retarded by adrenalectomy in midlife (for review, see Landfield, 1987).

Robert Sapolsky then demonstrated that 12 weeks of daily CORT injections into young adult rats mimicked the pyramidal neuron loss seen in aging (Sapolsky, Krey, and McEwen, 1985). He went on to demonstrate that excitatory amino acids play an important role in the cell loss by showing, first, that CORT exacerbates kainic acid–induced damage to hippocampus, as well as ischemic damage and, second, that glucocorticoids potentiate excitatory amino acid killing of hippocampal neurons in culture (for review, see Sapolsky, 1992).

In order to examine what actually happens to hippocampal neurons over a shorter time period as a result of glucocorticoid exposure or repeated stress, we used the single-section Golgi technique to demonstrate that, after 21 days of daily corticosterone exposure, the apical dendritic tree of CA3 pyramidal neurons has undergone atrophy (Woolley, Gould, Frankfurt, et al., 1990). A similar atrophy was also produced by 21 days of repeated restraint stress in rats (Watanabe, Gould, and McEwen, 1992) and by 28 days of daily psychosocial stress in tree shrews (Magarinos et al., 1996). In a psychosocial stress model in rats, both dominant and subordinate animals show dendritic atrophy of CA3 pyramidal neurons within 14 days (McKittrick et al., 1996).

Dendritic atrophy caused by corticosterone exposure and by restraint or psychosocial stress was prevented by the daily administration of the antiepileptic drug phenytoin prior to stress or corticosterone treatment (Magarinos et al., 1996; Watanabe, Gould, Cameron, et al., 1992). This finding indicates that neural activity and the release and actions of excitatory amino acids are involved, since phenytoin blocks glutamate release and antagonizes sodium channels and t-type calcium channels that are activated during glutamate induced excitation (see Magarinos et al., 1996; Watanabe, Gould, Cameron, et al., 1992). Subsequent work revealed that NMDA receptor blockade is also effective in preventing stress-induced dendritic atrophy (Magarinos and McEwen, 1995). Thus glucocorticoid treatment can cause atrophy, but, because corticosteroids are released during stress in lower amounts than that which is given exogenously to cause atrophy (Watanabe, Gould, and McEwen, 1992), it was important to determine whether glucocorticoids play a role in stress-induced atrophy.

We used the steroid synthesis inhibitor cyanoketone to reduce the magnitude of corticosterone secretion in response to restraint stress (Magarinos and McEwen, 1995). Cyanoketone attenuates the adrenal steroid stress response but allows basal secretion to occur (Akana et al., 1988). We found that cyanoketone treatment blocked the atrophy of dendrites induced by daily restraint stress (Magarinos and McEwen, 1995).

Several links exist between glucocorticoids and excitatory amino acids. First, excitatory amino acid release is affected by adrenalectomy, which markedly reduces the magnitude of the EAA release evoked by restraint stress (Moghaddam et al., 1994; Lowy, Gault, and Yamamoto, 1993). Second, stress and glucocorticoids increase expression of NMDA receptors or the mRNAs for their subunits (Weiland, Orchinik, and Tanapat, 1997). Finally, adrenal steroids regulate expression of the presynaptic kainate autoreceptor on mossy fiber terminals (Watanabe, Weiland, and McEwen, 1995; Joels et al., 1996), an effect that may enhance the positive feedback of glutamate release upon itself (Chittajallu et al., 1996).

Repeated restraint stress for 21 days causes a suppression of 5-HT1A receptor binding in the dentate gyrus and CA3 region of the hippocampus (Mendelson and

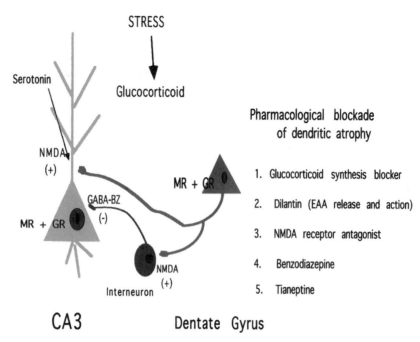

STRESS

Serotonin

Glucocorticoid

NMDA (+)

MR + GR

GABA-BZ (−)

MR + GR

NMDA (+)

Interneuron

CA3   Dentate Gyrus

Pharmacological blockade
of dendritic atrophy

1. Glucocorticoid synthesis blocker

2. Dilantin (EAA release and action)

3. NMDA receptor antagonist

4. Benzodiazepine

5. Tianeptine

FIGURE 12.4 Repeated stress acts via adrenal steroids and NMDA receptors to cause dendrites to atrophy and reorganize on the apical side of CA3 pyramidal neurons. Blocking glucocorticoid synthesis inhibits this process; likewise blocking NMDA receptors or interfering with excitatory neurotransmission with Dilantin prevents stress-induced dendritic atrophy. Finally, treatment of rats undergoing stress with a benzodiaz- epine, adinazolam, or with a serotonin reuptake enhancer, tianeptine, prevents stress-induced dendritic remodeling. The benzodiazepine is presumed to act to enhance inhibitory input to CA3 neurons, whereas the speculative role of tianeptine may be to reduce the effect of extrasynaptic 5-HT to increase NMDA receptor activity.

McEwen, 1992), and psychosocial stress depresses 5-HT transporter expression as well as 5-HT1A receptor binding in these hippocampal subregions (McKittrick et al., 1995, 1996). Because serotonin is released by stressors (Kennet, Dickinson, and Curzon, 1985) and may play a role in the actions of stress on nerve cells, we investigated the actions of agents that facilitate or inhibit serotonin reuptake. Tianeptine is known to enhance serotonin uptake (Whitton et al., 1991; Mennini, Mocaer, and Carattini, 1987), and we compared it with fluoxetine, an inhibitor of 5-HT reuptake (Beasley, Masica, and Potvin, 1992), as well as with desipramine as an inhibitor of noradrenaline uptake. Only tianeptine was effective in preventing atrophy (Watanabe, Gould, Daniels, et al., 1992; Magarinos, Deslandes, and McEwen, in press). Tianeptine also blocked glucocorticoid-induced atrophy of CA3 dendrites (Watanabe, Gould, Daniels, et al., 1992), indicating that this effect is not a result of any interference with glucocorticoid secretion. There is a connection between 5-HT and excitatory amino acids, including evidence of interactions between serotonin and NMDA receptors indicating that serotonin potentiates NMDA receptor binding as well as activity of NMDA receptors and may do so via 5-HT2 receptors (Rahmann and Neumann, 1993; Mennini and Miari, 1991).

Inhibitory interneurons play a major role in regulating excitability of the hippocampus. Indeed, treatment with a benzodiazepine agonist, adinazolam, effectively blocks stress-induced atrophy of CA3 apical dendrites (Magarinos and McEwen, submitted). Figure 12.4 summarizes the present state of knowledge about the multiple control of dendritic atrophy in the CA3 region of the hippocampus.

The interneurons that receive intense innervation from mossy fibers of dentate gyrus granule neurons are especially vulnerable to a variety of insults (Hsu and Buzsaki, 1993). If some of these neurons were to die as a result of repeated restraint stress, then there might be a cumulative effect over time, in which repeated bouts of stress might progressively deplete the dentate gyrus of the buffering action that these inhibitory neurons appear to provide. However, this statement may apply to much longer intervals of repeated stress, because the dendritic atrophy described thus far is reversible.

Stress-induced atrophy of dendrites is reversible within 7–10 days of the termination of stress (C. Conrad, A. Magarinos, J. Ledoux, B. S. McEwen, unpublished); and this stands in contrast to the irreversible damage and neuron loss that have been attributed to head trauma, stroke, seizures, and severe long-term stress (discussed earlier). This reversibility is reminiscent of studies of hippocampal morphology in hibernating animals. Hibernation causes dendritic retraction of CA3 pyramidal neurons in ground squirrels, whereas bringing squirrels out of the hibernating state results in rapid dendrite expansion (Popov and Bocharova, 1992; Popov, Bocharova, and Bragin, 1992). A similar finding was made for hibernating European hamsters (A. Magarinos, B. S. McEwen, and P. Pevet, unpublished). Therefore, with regard to underlying mechanisms, we are drawn toward reversible plasticity and growth processes in the dendritic tree, as will be discussed in the next subsection.

STRESS-INDUCED SYNAPTIC VESICLE REORGANIZATION WITHIN MOSSY FIBER TERMINALS Recent electron microscope studies have provided new insights into the relationship between excitatory amino acids and glucocorticoids and a new morphological end point of repeated stress (Magarinos, Verdugo Garcia, and McEwen, 1997). Because the mossy fibers from dentate granule neurons provide a major excitatory input to the CA3 proximal apical dendrites, which undergo atrophy as a result of repeated stress, we measured ultrastructural parameters associated with the mossy fiber-CA3 synapses in control and 21-day restraint-stressed rats. Whereas mossy fiber terminals (MFT) from control rats were packed with small, clear synaptic vesicles, terminals from stressed animals showed a marked rearrangement of vesicles, with more densely packed clusters localized in the vicinity of active synaptic zones. Moreover, compared with controls, restraint stress increased the area of the mossy fiber terminal occupied by mitochondrial profiles, a configuration which implies a greater, localized energy-generating capacity. A single stress session did not produce these changes either immediately after or the next day following the restraint session.

There are several implications of these findings. First, in MFT from stressed rats, the redistribution of vesicles and their localization near the active synaptic zones, together with more mitochondria, suggests that more vesicles may be available for glutamate release, although this possibility remains to be tested directly by electrophysiology and microdialysis (Magarinos, Verdugo Garcia, and McEwen, 1997). Second, the synaptic vesicle reorganization in MFT provides insights into possible molecular mechanisms of the effects of stress and stress mediators. Neurotransmitter release occurs at discrete active zones containing readily releasable pools of synaptic vesicles; this process requires fusion of vesicles with the presynaptic plasma membrane, and this membrane is retrieved and recycled for subsequent transmitter release (Bajjalieh and Scheller, 1996). Within the presynaptic compartment, synaptic vesicle–associated

phosphoproteins play a key role in regulating the efficiency of the neurotransmitter release from the nerve terminal. Synapsin I, in its dephosphorylated state, keeps the pool of "reserve" synaptic vesicles anchored to the nerve terminal cytoskeleton. Upon cell activation, Ca^{2+}/calmodulin-dependent protein kinase II mediates the phosphorylation of synapsin I, and the "reserve" pool of vesicles is freed from the cytoskeletal matrix, becoming available for neurotransmitter release (Peribone et al., 1997; Llinas et al., 1985; Greengard et al., 1993; Ceccaldi et al., 1995).

High levels of synapsin I protein and mRNA levels are present in the hippocampal MF terminal zone and granule cell neurons, respectively (Melloni et al., 1993; DeCamilli and Greengard, 1986). It is possible that the effect of repeated stress to cause clustering of vesicles close to the active zones could involve an increased expression of phosphorylated synapsin I. This has been observed in the hippocampus and parietal cortex of rats subjected to septal kindling, a model of synaptic plasticity that involves an increase in synaptic efficiency in response to repetitive local stimulations (Yamagata et al., 1995). It is noteworthy that brains of mice lacking the synapsin I gene show smaller mossy fiber terminals and a significant reduction in the number of synaptic vesicles that are not clustered but dispersed throughout the terminal (Takei et al., 1995).

The mossy fiber terminals reside on the proximal regions of the apical dendrites, and their numbers are not reduced in number by chronic stress (Magarinos, Verdugo Garcia, and McEwen, 1997). Therefore, the reduced number of CA3 apical dendritic branch points and total dendritic length observed in Golgi-impregnated material of repeatedly stressed rats and tree shrews might be interpreted as an adaptation to limit the increased excitatory input from recurrent axonal collaterals that are known to project from neighboring CA3 pyramidal neurons (Li et al., 1994; Ishizuka, Weber, and Amaral, 1990). Not only is there a recurrent excitatory input between CA3 pyramidal neurons that can be activated by the mossy fiber system, but also pyramidal neurons in subregion CA3c that lies closest to the hilus send excitatory axons back to the hilar region and affect the dentate gyrus itself (Scharfman, 1994; Kneisler and Dingledine, 1995). Such a feedback loop can presumably reactivate the mossy fiber system and sustain CA3 excitation, as in the so-called SPW or "sharp waves" (Buzsaki, 1986), and such an activation may drive the reorganization of vesicles within the mossy fiber terminals. Moreover, collateral activation of CA3 neurons by other CA3 neurons would help explain the blockade of dendritic atrophy by NMDA receptor blockade (Magarinos and McEwen, 1995), since the stratum lucidum of the

CA3 region does not express NMDA receptors (Monaghan et al., 1983).

CA3 pyramidal neurons display a high vulnerability not only to chronic stress but also to kainic acid administration, an effect that requires the integrity of the mossy fiber pathway (Nadler and Cuthbertson, 1980). As in the case of chronic restraint stress, CA3 region vulnerability is mediated by endogenous glucocorticoids and excitatory amino acid receptors (Armanini et al., 1990); and exogenous glucocorticoids have a potentiating effect (Sapolsky, 1986a, b; Packan and Sapolsky, 1990).

The CA3 hippocampal subregion is also damaged by epileptogenic stimulation of the perforant path, which involves the activation of the DG-MFT-CA3 pathway (Sloviter, 1993). Furthermore, in the epilepsy model, another parallel exists with the chronic stress model in the clustering of synaptic vesicles. It has been reported that synaptic vesicle clustering occurs in MFT of genetically prone epileptic gerbils, and this effect could be totally blocked by the disruption of the perforant pathway (Farias et al., 1992).

Accumulating data has linked epilepsy with excessive excitatory input, resulting in morphological alterations at the synaptic level. Well-characterized animal models of epilepsy, such as kindling and genetically epileptic mice, show that sprouting of mossy fibers generates a recurrent excitatory circuit involving aberrant granule cell–granule cell synapses (Sutula et al., 1996; Parent et al., 1997; Okazaki, Evenson, and Nadler, 1995). This possibility is supported by some electrophysiological evidence (C. Pavlides and B. S. McEwen, unpublished) and demands to be thoroughly tested, because it could account for an amplification of the excitatory input, and therefore, for the extreme sensitivity of mossy fibers to the stress paradigm.

In keeping with the reorganization of dendrites and alteration of synaptic vesicles in mossy fiber terminals, repeated stress produces a variety of effects on the electrophysiological features of the hippocampus (C. Pavlides and B. S. McEwen, unpublished). Forty-eight hours following 21 days of 6 hours-per-day repeated restraint stress, rats were studied under chloropent anaesthesia. Compared to control animals that were briefly handled but not subjected to the restraint stress, there was an inhibition of LTP in the lacunosum/moleculare layer of CA3 of repeatedly stressed rats after stimulation of the commissural/associational pathway. The same inhibition of LTP was seen in the dentate gyrus granule cell layer with stimulation of the medial perforant pathway. The mossy fiber LTP was not affected by repeated stress.

There was another significant finding, namely, that high-frequency stimulation (HFS) produced epileptic afterdischarges in 38% of the repeatedly stressed rats,

while in the nonstressed controls HFS produced epileptic afterdischarges in only 15% of the animals. The rats showing seizures were removed from the analysis described in the previous paragraph. The increased incidence of seizures is consistent with increased mossy fiber sprouting (see preceding discussion).

In a second experiment, animals were subjected to a similar stress paradigm, and a current-source-density analysis was performed. In each of the hippocampal subfields, significant shifts between the control and stressed animals were observed in the sources and sinks.

Hippocampal function

Alterations in hippocampal circuitry and excitability affect a number of brain functions in which the hippocampus plays an important role. These include the regulation of hypothalamo-pituitary-adrenal (HPA) activity, episodic and declarative memory, spatial memory, and processing of emotional information. It is also important to consider the functional implications of sex differences in hippocampal function.

NEUROENDOCRINE REGULATION The hippocampus is involved in the regulation of HPA activity (Jacobson and Sapolsky, 1991), whereas the amygdala has a generally facilitative role (Prewitt and Herman, 1997; Roozendaal, Koolhaas, and Bohus, 1997; Bohus et al., 1996). Hippocampal lesions elevated cortisol secretion under a variety of stressful and nonstressful conditions (Jacobson and Sapolsky, 1991), although the results are not entirely consistent (e.g., see Bradbury, Strack, and Dallman, 1993; Jacobson and Sapolsky, 1991). Glucocorticoid implants into the hippocampus affect HPA activity in ways that are consistent with a feedback role of the hippocampus in HPA regulation (see Jacobson and Sapolsky, 1991). However, lesion and steroid-implant experiments also reveal an equally important role for the medial prefrontal cortex in HPA regulation (Diorio, Viau, and Meaney, 1993). The anatomical links from the hippocampus and medial prefrontal cortex to the hypothalamus are postulated to be via the bed nucleus of the stria terminalis and preoptic area, with an output from these structures to the paraventricular nucleus via inhibitory GABAergic projections (Herman and Cullinan, 1997).

A considerable amount of data has accumulated showing that elevated HPA activity is correlated with reduced levels of Type I or Type II receptors in the hippocampus (Jacobson and Sapolsky, 1991) or prefrontal cortex (Herman and Cullinan, 1997). In general, hippocampal Type I receptors are associated with the maintenance of basal ACTH and glucocorticoid levels

(Bradbury, Akana, and Dallman, 1994; Spencer, Moday, and Miller, 1997; DeKloet et al., 1998); forebrain Type II receptors are also associated with the containment of ACTH secretion (Spencer, Moday, and Miller, 1997; Bradbury, Akana, and Dallman, 1994), although a positive role of hippocampal Type II receptors has recently been reported (DeKloet et al., 1998). It is unclear whether correlations of hippocampal Type I and Type II receptor levels with HPA activity indicate a feedback action of adrenal steroids on the hippocampus, or a priming role for glucocorticoids to make the HPA axis optimally reactive to turning on and turning off a stress response, as suggested by recent studies by Dallman and colleagues (Akana et al., 1988).

Elevated and disregulated HPA activity is seen in depressive illness, but the reasons for this elevation are not entirely clear. Disregulation of the HPA axis associated with major depression is revealed by the dexamethasone suppression test (DST). Although the DST is most likely working at the pituitary level (Miller et al., 1992), the underlying deregulation is undoubtedly of CNS origin and reflects increased drive upon the CRH and AVP systems of the hypothalamus (P. W. Gold et al., 1995) and constitutes a form of endogenously driven stress. A lessening of the adrenal steroid feedback effects on the hippocampus might be a contributing factor to elevated HPA activity in depression, and recent studies of Barden and coworkers with a transgenic mouse strain (Holsboer and Barden, 1996; Barden et al., 1997) have suggested that decreased forebrain Type II receptor expression might be a contributing factor to depression and a potential target of antidepressant therapy (Montkowski et al., 1995; Holsboer and Barden, 1996). It is not clear, however, how much hippocampal Type II receptor expression, as opposed to expression in other brain regions, is a key factor.

There is another linkage of the hippocampus with elevated cortisol levels. Recent studies using MRI imaging have indicated that elevated cortisol levels are associated with some shrinkage of the hippocampal formation and mild cognitive impairment (Lupien et al., 1998; Sheline et al., 1996; Axelson et al., 1993; Starkman et al., 1992). This topic will be discussed in the next subsection.

ADRENAL STEROIDS, STRESS, AND HIPPOCAMPALLY DEPENDENT MEMORY   In animal models, adrenal steroids acutely modulate memory formation through their actions on excitability. Type I receptor activation has been associated with enhanced attention and improved acquisition, whereas Type II receptor activation shows a biphasic effect on memory performance, with low doses of adrenal steroids facilitating and high doses inhibiting the retention of memories dependent on hippocampal

function (Lupien and McEwen, 1997). Single stressful episodes also affect memory (Diamond et al., 1996) and appear to do so via adrenal steroids (Diamond et al., 1996) as well as other pathways (Shors, Seymour, and Thompson, 1990).

Chronically, repeated stresses also cause memory impairment, presumably through their ability to cause dendritic atrophy and suppression of neurogenesis. Functional studies of repeatedly stressed rats revealed impairments in two different tests of hippocampally dependent spatial memory. In an eight-arm radial maze in rats, 21 days of restraint stress prior to maze training led to impaired acquisition and larger numbers of errors, but only when rats were trained and evaluated immediately after the end of the stress sequence; 18 days later, the acquisition was normal (Luine et al., 1994). This impairment was in the same direction, but not as great, as impairment found in aging rats; moreover, stress effects were prevented by prior treatment of rats with phenytoin or with tianeptine under the same conditions in which phenytoin was able to prevent the stress-induced atrophy of CA3 pyramidal neurons (Luine et al., 1994; Watanabe, Gould, Cameron, et al., 1992).

In a subsequent study, a spatial recognition memory task in a Y-maze was used to demonstrate an impairment in rats that received 21 days of restraint stress and were tested immediately at the end of stress (Conrad et al., 1996). Tianeptine treatment prior to daily stress prevented the impairment (Conrad et al., 1996), just as it had prevented the dendritic atrophy. A more recent study examined contextual fear conditioning and found that repeated restraint stress did not impair, but rather enhanced, both tone- and context-dependent fear conditioning (C. Conrad, A. Magarinos, J. Ledoux, and B. S. McEwen, unpublished).

Studies on the tree shrew have shown that 28 days of psychosocial stress impair spatial memory in a modified hole board test (Gould et al., 1997). It should be noted that we have to consider changes in dentate gyrus neurogenesis in explaining memory impairment.

In humans, there is evidence for cognitive impairment associated with adrenal steroid treatment (Newcomer et al., 1994; Wolkowitz, Reuss, and Weingartner, 1990; Wolkowitz, Rubinow, and Doran, 1990; Martignoni et al., 1992). In the most recent of these studies, dexamethasone was given for four consecutive days at 23:00, and cognitive testing was performed at 14:00 on study days 0, 1, 4, and 7 after the last treatment (Newcomer et al., 1994). There was decreased declarative memory recall on study day 4 and day 7 after the last treatment in the DEX-treated subjects compared to placebo-treated subjects (Newcomer et al., 1994). No other cognitive measures were affected by DEX, indicating the specificity to a task that is known to involve hippocampal-temporal lobe function. Because the poorest performance was found on study day 4, along with the lowest levels of endogenous cortisol, it is impossible to say whether the cognitive deficit is associated with the action of DEX on the brain or the reduction in cortisol. Since glucocorticoids have biphasic effects on synaptic plasticity (Pavlides, Watanabe, et al., 1995; Diamond et al., 1992; see "Stress, Adrenal Steroids, and Neuronal Excitability" subsection), which are thought of as neurophysiological models of information storage processes (Bliss and Collingridge, 1993, either explanation is plausible.

Another study employed a bolus injection of cortisol and reported declarative memory deficits acutely after treatment (Kirschbaum et al., 1996). Such bolus administration of cortisol impairs glucose uptake in hippocampus (de Leon et al., 1997), and this action may represent a mechanism for acute memory impairment by glucocorticoids because of the well-known facilitation of memory mechanisms by glucose administration (P. E. Gold, 1987).

Chronically, stressful conditions and elevated HPA activity are associated with selective atrophy in the human brain, based upon MRI imaging. The conditions in which hippocampal atrophy has been reported include Cushing's syndrome, posttraumatic stress disorder, recurrent depressive illness, normal aging preceding dementia, and Alzheimer's disease (McEwen, 1997). Hippocampal shrinkage is usually accompanied by deficits in declarative, episodic, spatial, and contextual memory performance, and the hippocampal changes provide a neural substrate for changes in cognitive function that have been recognized to accompany these various conditions. The hippocampus has long been known as a target of stress hormones, and it is an especially plastic and vulnerable region of the brain. However, the prominence of the hippocampus as a glucocorticoid target has obscured the fact that other factors besides glucocorticoid hormones are involved in the process of hippocampal atrophy. Excitatory amino acids and NMDA receptors are prominent in their involvement in an animal model of hippocampal atrophy as well as in neuronal death. Furthermore, the finding of hippocampal atrophy does not necessarily imply a permanent loss of cells, and this aspect deserves careful investigation, both to analyze the underlying anatomical changes and to investigate the possibility of pharmacological treatment to reverse the process. In cases where atrophy is due to cell loss, the time course of the disease process will provide much useful information about mechanism and offer the possibility of early intervention to arrest or slow the pathological process.

HIPPOCAMPAL FUNCTION IN DEVELOPMENT AND AGING The vulnerability of many systems of the body to stress is influenced by experiences early in life. In animal models, unpredictable prenatal stress causes increased emotionality and increased reactivity of the HPA axis and autonomic nervous system, and these effects last throughout the life span. Postnatal handling in rats, a mild stress involving brief daily separation from the mother, counteracts the effects of prenatal stress and results in reduced emotionality and reduced reactivity of the HPA axis and autonomic nervous system. The vulnerability of the hippocampus to age-related loss of function parallels these effects–prenatal stress increasing and postnatal handling decreasing the rate of brain aging. Concurrently, age-related decline of gonadal function reduces the beneficial and protective actions of these hormones on brain function. At the same time, age-related increases in adrenal steroid activity promote age-related changes in brain cells that can culminate in neuronal damage or cell death. Lifelong patterns of adrenocortical function, determined by early experience, contribute to rates of brain aging, at least in experimental animals.

Unpredictable or uncontrollable stressful experiences of a pregnant rat increase emotionality and stress hormone reactivity in offspring that last for the lifetime of the individual, whereas the gentle and repeated stimulation of newborn rat pups known as postnatal handling produces reductions in emotionality and stress hormone reactivity that also last a lifetime (Vallee et al., 1997; Meaney et al., 1988; Fride et al., 1986; Levine et al., 1967; Denenberg and Haltmeyer, 1967; Ader, 1968). These effects appear to involve mediation by both the mother's behavior and by adrenal and thyroid hormone actions. More is known about the mechanism of neonatal handling. Handling involves separating the pups from the mother for 10 minutes per day for the first two weeks of neonatal life, and the licking of the pup by the mother appears to be an important determinant of the postnatal handling effect (Liu et al., 1997). At the same time, increasing corticosterone levels in the mother's milk mimic some of the effects of neonatal handling (Catalani et al., 1993), and thyroid hormone elevations have been suggested as a possible mediator of the neonatal handling effect, particularly regarding the elevated expression of glucocorticoid receptors in the hippocampus (Meaney, Aitken, and Sapolsky, 1987).

Studies in which both prenatal stress and postnatal handling were compared indicate that these two procedures have opposite effects on food intake, body weight, and anxiety, as well as HPA activity (Vallee et al., 1996, 1997). However the two processes interact, in that prenatal stress effects on HPA activity and emotionality are reversed by early postnatal "adoption" or cross-fostering of pups to new mothers (Barbazanges, Vallee, et al., 1996; Maccari et al., 1995), which is most likely a form of postnatal handling involving intense licking of the pup by the mother (Liu et al., 1997). Prenatal stress during the last week of gestation in rats increases reactivity of the HPA axis and reduces expression of the Type I adrenal steroid receptor in hippocampus, which help to contain basal levels of HPA activity (Vallee et al., 1996; Henry et al., 1994). Prenatal stress also increases anxiety in an open field test and decreases basal food intake and body weight (Vallee et al., 1996, 1997). It is important to note that some of these prenatal stress effects may involve a mediation by adrenal steroids (Barbazanges, Piazza, et al., 1996). Taken together with the fact that postnatal handling effects may also be mimicked by adrenal steroids (Catalani et al., 1993), the specific effects of adrenal steroids on the neural development of emotionality and HPA reactivity may change qualitatively as the nervous system matures.

For prenatal stress and postnatal handling, once the emotionality and the reactivity of the adrenocortical system are established by events early in life, it is the subsequent actions of the hypothalamo-pituitary-adrenal (HPA) axis in adult life that play a major role in determining the rate of brain and body aging. Increased HPA activity is associated with increased brain aging, whereas the opposite is true of animals with reduced HPA reactivity to novel situations. Rats with increased HPA reactivity show early decline of cognitive functions associated with the hippocampus (Dellu et al., 1994) as well as increased propensity to self-administer drugs such as amphetamine and cocaine (Deroche et al., 1993; Piazza et al., 1994). In contrast, rats with a lower HPA reactivity as a result of neonatal handling have a slower rate of cognitive aging and a reduced loss of hippocampal neurons and function (Meaney et al., 1994; Catalani et al., 1993).

With regard to the natural process of aging, long-term stress also accelerates a number of biological markers of aging in rats, including increasing the excitability of CA1 pyramidal neurons via a calcium-dependent mechanism and causing loss of hippocampal pyramidal neurons (Koprowski et al., 1993). An important factor may be the enhancement by glucocorticoids of calcium currents in hippocampus (D. S. Kerr et al., 1992), in view of the key role of calcium ions in destructive as well as plastic processes in hippocampal neurons.

We have seen that adrenal steroids affect the structure and function of the hippocampus in a variety of ways, and we have also seen that, in human subjects, there is evidence for both cognitive impairment and hippocampal atrophy associated with altered levels of adrenal ste-

roids. What are the possible mechanisms for these changes? As discussed previously, the acute inhibition of LTP and PBP by high levels of glucocorticoids represents one mechanism by which this process might occur, while the atrophy of rat hippocampal CA3 neurons after either repeated stress or repeated glucocorticoid treatment, along with the reported atrophy of the hippocampus of Cushing's patients and depressed subjects, constitutes a long-term mechanism for cognitive impairment.

Another aspect of the relationship between adrenal steroid levels, cognitive function and hippocampal volume is illustrated by studies of basal cortisol levels and cognitive deficits in human aging (Lupien et al., 1994, 1998). Aged subjects followed over a four-year period, who showed a significant increase in cortisol levels over the four years and had high basal cortisol levels in year 4, showed deficits on tasks measuring explicit memory as well as selective attention, compared to subjects with either decreasing cortisol levels over four years or subjects with increasing basal cortisol but moderate current cortisol levels (Lupien et al., 1994). They also showed a hippocampus that was 14% smaller than age-matched controls who did not show progressive cortisol increases and were not cognitively impaired (Lupien et al., 1998). Thus, once again, the question of acute versus chronic effects of cortisol is unsettled as a primary cause, and both types of mechanisms may apply. However, this study evokes the model called the glucocorticoid cascade hypothesis (Sapolsky, Zola-Morgan, and Squire, 1991), in which rising cortisol levels compromise the hippocampus by destroying neurons and contribute to cognitive impairment as well as reducing the inhibitory effect of the hippocampus on cortisol secretion. Consistent with this hypothesis is the fact that lesions of the fornix or the hippocampal formation–temporal lobe region of Cynomolgus monkeys produced an elevation of cortisol secretion for at least six months postlesion (Sapolsky, 1992; Sapolsky, Krey, and McEwen, 1986).

A final point to be made about adrenal steroids, stress, and the hippocampus is that adrenal steroids do not act alone. Rather, we have seen that both excitatory amino acids and serotonin release, possibly facilitated by circulating glucocorticoids, play a key role. In fact, the final common path for CA3 dendritic atrophy in rats treated with either corticosterone or by restraint stress involves processes that are blocked by blocking glutamate release or actions using phenytoin or an NMDA antagonist, respectively, or by facilitating serotonin reuptake using tianeptine. The efficacy of these agents raises the attractive possibility of treating individuals–perhaps the depressed elderly–with agents such as phenytoin or tianeptine as a means of improving cognitive function. If such studies are carried out, it will be important to determine the degree to which hippocampal volume may be increased by such treatments and whether long-term treatment protects these same individuals from dementia.

EFFECTS OF ESTROGENS ON LEARNING AND MEMORY   It has been difficult to detect cyclicity of performance in spatial tasks, with no effect reported (Berry, McMahan, and Gallagher, 1996), with differences reported in motivational or attentional parameters (Blasberg et al., 1996), or with an impairment reported in performance on proestrus (Frye, 1995). This lack of agreement and paucity of effects may be a reflection of the relative insensitivity of the measures used to detect behaviors that female rats actually use in their natural environments at the time of mating. However, some success has resulted from studying longer-term effects of ovariectomy and estrogen replacement on hippocampal-dependent learning and memory.

Three types of effects have been reported in animal models. First, E treatment of ovariectomized female rats has been reported to improve acquisition on a radial maze task as well as in a reinforced T-maze alternation task (Daniel et al., 1996; Fader, Hendricson, and Dohanich, 1996). Second, sustained E treatment is reported to improve performance in a working memory task (O'Neal et al., 1996) as well as in the radial arm maze (Luine et al., 1996; Daniel et al., 1996). Third, E treatment is reported to promote a shift in the strategy that female rats use to solve an appetitive two-choice discrimination, with E treatment increasing the probability of using a response as opposed to a spatial strategy (Korol et al., 1996). Fourth, aging female rats that have low E plasma levels in the "estropause" are reported to perform significantly worse in a Morris water maze than female rats with high E levels (Juraska and Warren, 1996).

The effects of estrogen replacement in rats are reminiscent of the effects of E treatment in women whose ovarian function has been eliminated by surgical menopause or by a GnRH antagonist used to shrink the size of fibroids prior to surgery (Sherwin and Tulandi, 1996; Robinson et al., 1994; Sherwin, 1994). In general, these effects are seen within a number of weeks and are reversible. Another aspect of estrogen action in the aging brain is that E treatment of postmenopausal women appears to have a protective effect on the brain with regard to Alzheimer's disease (Tang et al., 1996; Henderson, Watt, and Buckwalter, 1996; Paganini-Hill and Henderson, 1994; Henderson et al., 1994; Birge, 1994). It is likely that these protective actions involve a number of other actions of estrogens besides inducing synapses. These include suppression of the production of the toxic

form of beta amyloid protein (Jaffe et al., 1994) and inhibition of free-radical-induced toxicity (Grindley, Green, and Simpkins, 1997; Behl et al., 1997). It should also be noted that estrogens affect many regions of the brain, including the basal forebrain cholinergic systems, the serotonergic system, the dopaminergic system, and the noradrenergic system (for review, see McEwen et al., 1997; McEwen et al., 1995).

IMPORTANCE OF SEX DIFFERENCES   Sex differences in brain structures and mechanisms occur in other brain regions besides hypothalamus, such as hippocampus, and they appear to be involved in aspects of cognitive function and other processes that go beyond the reproductive process itself, such as the higher incidence of depression in women and of substance abuse in men (Regier et al., 1988). There are also sex differences in the severity of brain damage resulting from transient ischemia (Hall, Pazara, and Linseman, 1991) and sex differences in the response of the brain to lesions (Morse, Dekosky, and Scheff, 1992) and to severe, chronic stress (Mizoguchi et al., 1992; Uno et al., 1989). A recent study has shown that the stress-induced atrophy of apical dendrites of CA3 pyramidal neurons occurs in male rats but not in female rats (Galea et al., 1997). What is not yet clear in this case is whether this atrophy, which is reversible, increases or decreases the vulnerability of the male and female brain to permanent damage.

Conclusions

The hippocampus is a brain site of considerable plasticity, directed by hormones but also involving endogenous excitatory amino acids and NMDA receptors, along with other transmitters. Because the hippocampus performs a similar behavioral role in animals and in humans, what we learn from studies of hormone effects in animals is directly applicable to the human condition. The best examples are the changes in hippocampal volume in humans, detected by MRI, which can be evaluated in terms of the known mechanisms by which stress and stress hormones regulate neurogenesis in the dentate gyrus, dendritic remodeling in the CA3 region, and pyramidal neuron survival. Not all conditions involving hippocampal atrophy need to involve the same detailed neuroanatomical changes—some may involve permanent damage, whereas others may involve potentially reversible changes in the dentate gyrus or Ammon's horn. Yet all these instances of atrophy involve deficits in declarative and spatial memory, which can be found not only in humans but also in animal models in which some form of hippocampal atrophy or damage has been produced.

Another example of the transferability of information between animal models and human subjects pertains to the actions of estrogens on declarative memory in humans that were stimulated by and predicted from the findings in animals that estrogens regulate the formation of excitatory spine synapses in the hippocampus. Indeed, there are studies in humans that show rapid and reversible effects of estrogen deprivation and replacement on verbal memory. Moreover, the study of the neuroprotective actions of estrogens has arisen from animal model studies of the diverse actions of estrogens on nonreproductive systems of the brain, as well as models of neurotoxicity and the amyloid precursor protein.

Sex differences and the process of sexual differentiation constitute another major area of convergence of animal and human studies of hippocampal function. The intriguing sex differences in hippocampal morphology and spatial learning and memory seen in rats are reminiscent of sex differences in human neuropsychological studies with respect to strategies used to solve spatial navigation problems. Equally important for their implications are the sex differences in vulnerability of the hippocampal formation of animals to atrophy and damage from severe stress. At present, there are hints from human clinical studies of differential vulnerability of the male and female human brain to a variety of insults, and much more investigation needs to be done in this regard in terms of the protective efficacy of gonadal hormone replacement therapy in the aging human brain.

Finally, studies of the plasticity of the hippocampus provide a very useful and productive system in which to explore fundamental processes of neurogenesis, synaptogenesis, and dendritic remodeling in the context of highly relevant situations of adaptive plasticity of the adult brain. The studies described in this chapter will provide an excellent foundation for a new generation of investigations of these various forms of plasticity, using transgenic animal models as well as cell culture systems.

ACKNOWLEDGMENTS   Research support for studies in the author's laboratory was provided by NIH grants MH43156 and NS07080 as well as the Health Foundation, New York, and Servier, France. The author wishes to thank his many colleagues and collaborators for their many contributions.

REFERENCES

ABRAHAM, W. C., M. DRAGUNOW, and W. P. TATE, 1991. The role of immediate early genes in the stabilization of long-term potentiation. *Mol. Neurobiol.* 5:297–314.

ADER, R., 1968. Effects of early experiences on emotional and physiological reactivity in the rat. *J. Comp. Physiol. Psychol.* 66:264–268.

AKANA, S. F., L. JACOBSON, C. S. CASCIO, J. SHINSAKO, and M. F. DALLMAN, 1988. Constant corticosterone replacement normalizes basal adrenocorticotropin (ACTH) but permits sustained ACTH hypersecretion after stress in adrenalectomized rats. *Endocrinology* 122:1337.

ALBECK, D. S., N. B. HASTINGS, and B. S. MCEWEN, 1994. Effects of adrenalectomy and Type I and Type II glucocorticoid receptor activation on AVP and CRH mRNA in the rat hypothalamus. *Mol. Brain Res.* 26:129–134.

ALBECK, D. S., C. R. MCKITTRICK, D. C. BLANCHARD, R. J. BLANCHARD, J. NIKULINA, B. S. MCEWEN, and R. R. SAKAI, 1997. Chronic social stress alters levels of corticotropin-releasing factor and arginine vasopressin mRNA in rat brain. *J. Neurosci.* 17:4895–4903.

ARMANINI, M., C. HUTCHINGS, B. STEIN, and R. SAPOLSKY, 1990. Glucocorticoid endangerment of hippocampal neurons is NMDA-receptor dependent. *Brain Res.* 532:7–12.

ARMSTRONG, J. D., D. C. MCINTYRE, S. NEUBORT, and R. S. SLOVITER, 1993. Learning and memory after adrenalectomy-induced hippocampal dentate granule cell degeneration in the rat. *Hippocampus,* 3:359–371.

ARNOLD, S. E., V. M.-Y. LEE, R. E. GUR, and J. Q. TROJANOWSKI, 1991. Abnormal expression of two microtubule-associated proteins (MAP2 and MAP5) in specific subfields of the hippocampal formation in schizophrenia. *Proc. Nat. Acad. Sci. U.S.A.* 88:10850–10854.

ARRIZA, J., R. SIMERLY, L. SWANSON, and R. EVANS, 1988. The neuronal mineralocorticoid receptor as a mediator of glucocorticoid response. *Neuron* 1:887–900.

AUS DER MUHLEN, K., and H. OCKENFELS, 1969. Morphologische veranderungen im diencephalon und telencephalon: Storungen des regelkreises adenohypophysenebennierenrinde. *Z. Zellforsch. Mikrosck. Anat.* 93:126–141.

AXELSON, D., A. DORAISWAMY, W. MCDONALD, O. BOYKO, L. TYPLER, L. PATTERSON, C. B. NEMEROFF, E. H. ELLINWOOD, and K. R. R. KRISHAN, 1993. Hypercortisolemia and hippocampal changes in depression. *Psychiatry Res.* 47:163–173.

BAJJALIEH, S. M., and R. H. SCHELLER, 1996. The Biochemistry of Neurotransmitter Secretion. *J. Biol. Chem.* 270:1971–1974.

BAMBERGER, C. M., H. M. SCHULTE, and G. P. CHROUSOS, 1996. Molecular determinants of glucocorticoid receptor function and tissue sensitivity to glucocorticoids. *Endocr. Rev.* 17:245–261.

BAMBERGER, C. M., A. BAMBERGER, M. WALD, G. P. CHROUSOS, and H. M. SCHULTE, 1997. Inhibition of mineralocorticoid activity by the b-isoform of the human glucocorticoid receptor. *J. Steroid Biochem. Mol. Biol.* 60:43–50.

BARBAZANGES, A., V. P. PIAZZA, M. LE MOAL, and S. MACCARI, 1996. Maternal glucocorticoid secretion mediates long-term effects of prenatal stress. *J. Neurosci.* 15:3943–3949.

BARBAZANGES, A., M. VALLEE, W. MAYO, J. DAY, H. SIMON, M. LE MOAL, and S. MACCARI, 1996. Early and later adoptions have different long-term effects on male rat offspring. *J. Neurosci.* 16:7783–7790.

BARDEN, N., I. S. M. STEC, A. MONTKOWSKI, F. HOLSBOER, and J. M. H. M. REUL, 1997. Endocrine profile and neuroendocrine challenge tests in transgenic mice expressing antisense RNA against the glucocorticoid receptor. *Neuroendocrinology* 66:212–220.

BARFIELD, R., 1969. Activation of copulatory behavior by androgen implanted into the preoptic area of the male fowl. *Horm. Behav.* 1:37–52.

BARTANUSZ, V., J. M. AUBRY, S. PAGLIUSI, D. JEZOVA, J. BAFFI, and J. Z. KISS, 1995. Stress-induced changes in messenger RNA levels of N-methyl-D-aspartate and AMPA receptor subunits in selected regions of the rat hippocampus and hypothalamus. *Neuroscience* 66:247–252.

BEASLEY, C., D. MASICA, and J. POTVIN, 1992. Fluoxetine: A review of receptor and functional effects and their clinical implications. *Psychopharmacology*, 107:1–10.

BEATO, M., and A. SANCHEZ-PACHECO, 1996. Interaction of steroid hormone receptors with the transcription initiation complex. *Endocr. Rev.* 17:587–609.

BEHL, C., T. SKUTELLA, F. LEZOUALC'H, A. POST, M. WIDMANN, C. J. NEWTON, and F. HOLSBOER, 1997. Neuroprotection against oxidative stress by estrogens: Structure-activity relationship. *Mol. Pharm.* 51:535–541.

BERRY, B., R. MCMAHAN, and M. GALLAGHER, 1996. The effects of estrogen on performance of a hippocampal-dependent task. *Abstr. Soc. Neurosci.* 22:547.8–P1386.

BIRGE, S. J., 1994. The role of estrogen deficiency in the aging central nervous system. In *Treatment of the Postmenopausal Woman: Basic and Clinical Aspects,* R. A. Lobo, ed. New York: Raven Press, pp. 153–157.

BLASBERG, M. E., R. W. STACKMAN, C. J. LANGAN, and A. S. CLARK, 1996. Dynamics of working memory across the estrous cycle. *Abstr. Soc. Neurosci.* 22:547.5–P1386.

BLISS, T. V. P., and G. L. COLLINGRIDGE, 1993. A synaptic model of memory: Long-term potentiation in the hippocampus. *Nature* 361:31–39.

BLISS, T. V. P., and T. LOMO, 1973. Long-lasting potentiation of synaptic transmission in the dentate area of the anaesthetized rabbit following stimulation of the perforant path. *J. Physiol.* 232:331–356.

BOGERTS, B., J. A. LIEBERMAN, M. ASHTAIR, R. M. BILDER, G. DE GREEF, G. LERNER, C. JOHNS, and S. MASIAR, 1993. Hippocampus-amygdala volumes and psychopathology in chronic schizophrenia. *Biol. Psychiatry* 33:236–246.

BOHUS, B., J. M. KOOLHAAS, P. G. M. LUITEN, S. M. KORTE, B. ROOZENDAAL, and A. WIERSMA, 1996. The neurobiology of the central nucleus of the amygdala in relation to neuroendocrine and autonomic outflow. *Prog. Brain Res.* 107:447–460.

BRADBURY, M. J., S. F. AKANA, and M. F. DALLMAN, 1994. Roles of Type I and II corticosteroid receptors in regulation of basal activity in the hypothalamo-pituitary-adrenal axis during the diurnal trough and peak: Evidence for a nonadditive effect of combined receptor occupation. *Endocrinology* 134:1286–1296.

BRADBURY, M. J., A. M. STRACK, and M. F. DALLMAN, 1993. Lesions of the hippocampal efferent pathway (fimbria-fornix) do not alter sensitivity of adrenocorticotropin to feedback inhibition by corticosterone in rats. *Neuroendocrinology* 58:396–407.

BRADLEY, D. J., H. C. TOWLE, and W. S. YOUNG III, 1992. Spatial and temporal expression of α- and β-thyroid hormone receptor mRNAs, including the β2-subtype, in the developing mammalian nervous system. *J. Neurosci.* 12:2288–2302.

BRADLEY, D. J., W. S. YOUNG III, and C. WEINBERGER, 1989. Differential expression of α- and β-thyroid hormone receptor genes in rat brain and pituitary. *Proc. Natl. Acad. Sci. U.S.A.* 86:7250–7254.

BUZSAKI, G., 1986. Hippocampal sharp waves: Their origin and significance. *Brain Res.* 398:242–252.

CAMERON, H. A., and E. GOULD, 1994. Adult neurogenesis is regulated by adrenal steroids in the dentate gyrus. *Neuroscience* 61:203–209.

CAMERON, H. A., and E. GOULD, 1996. The control of neuronal birth and survival. In *Receptor Dynamics in Neural Development,* C. A. Shaw, ed. New York: CRC Press, pp. 141–157.

CAMERON, H. A., B. S. MCEWEN, and E. GOULD, 1995. Regulation of adult neurogenesis by excitatory input and NMDA receptor activation in the dentate gyrus. *J. Neurosci.* 15:4687–4692.

CAMERON, H., C. WOOLLEY, B. S. MCEWEN, and E. GOULD, 1993. Differentiation of newly born neurons and glia in the dentate gyrus of the adult rat. *Neuroscience,* 56:337–344.

CAMMERMEYER, J., 1978. Is the solitary dark neuron a manifestation of postmortem trauma to the brain inadequately fixed by perfusion? *Histochemistry* 56:97–115.

CATALANI, A., M. MARINELLI, S. SCACCIANOCE, R. NICOLAI, L. A. A. MUSCOLO, A. PORCU, L. KORANYI, P. V. PIAZZA, and L. ANGELUCCI, 1993. Progeny of mothers drinking corticosterone during lactation has lower stress-induced corticosterone secretion and better cognitive performance. *Brain Res.* 624:209–215.

CECCALDI, P. E., F. GROHOVAZ, F. BENFENATI, E. CHIEREGATTI, P. GREENGARD, and F. VALTORTA, 1995. Dephosphorylated synapsin I anchors synaptic vesicles to actin cytoskeleton: An analysis by videomicroscope. *J. Cell Biol.* 128:905–912.

CHAO, H. M., L. MA, B. S. MCEWEN, and R. R. SAKAI, 1998. Regulation of glucocorticoid receptor and mineralocorticoid receptor messenger ribonucleic acids by selective agonists in the rat hippocampus. *Endocrinology* 139:1810–1814.

CHAO, H., and B. S. MCEWEN, 1994. Glucocorticoids and the expression of mRNAs for neurotrophins, their receptors and GAP-43 in the rat hippocampus. *Mol. Brain Res.* 26:271–276.

CHAO, H. M., R. R. SAKAI, L. MA, and B. S. MCEWEN, 1998. Adrenal steroid regulation of neurotrophic factor expression in the rat hippocampus. *Endocrinology* 139:3112–3118.

CHITTAJALLU, R., M. VIGNES, K. K. DEV, J. M. BARNES, G. L. COLLINGRIDGE, and J. M. HENLEY, 1996. Regulation of glutamate release by presynaptic kainate receptors in the hippocampus. *Nature* 379:78–81.

CONRAD, C. D., L. A. M. GALEA, Y. KURODA, and B. S. MCEWEN, 1996. Chronic stress impairs rat spatial memory on the Y-maze, and this effect is blocked by tianeptine pretreatment. *Behav. Neurosci.* 110:1321–1334.

CONRAD, C. D., and E. J. ROY, 1993. Selective loss of hippocampal granule cells following adrenalectomy: Implications for spatial memory. *J. Neurosci.* 13:2582–2590.

CRUSIO, W. E., and H. SCHWEGLER, 1991. Early postnatal hyperthyroidism improves both working and reference memory in a spatial radial-maze task in adult mice. *Physiol. Behav.* 50:259–261.

DANIEL, J. M., A. J. FADER, A. SPENCER, and B. E. F. WEE, 1996. Effects of estrogen and environment on radial maze acquisition. *Abstr. Soc. Neurosci.* 22:547.7–P1386.

DECAMILLI, P., and P. GREENGARD, 1986. Synapsin I: A synaptic vesicle associated neuronal phosphoprotein. *Biochem. Pharmacol.* 35:4349–4357.

DEKLOET, E. R., E. VREUGDENHIL, M. S. OITZL, and M. JOELS, 1998. Brain corticosteroid receptor balance in health and disease. *Endocr. Rev.* 19:269–301.

DE LEON, M. J., T. MCRAE, H. RUSINEK, A. CONVIT, S. DE SANTI, C. TARSHISH, J. GOLOMB, N. VOLKOW, K. DAISLEY, N. ORENTREICH, and B. S. MCEWEN, 1997. Cortisol reduces hippocampal glucose metabolism in normal elderly, but not in Alzheimer's disease. *J. Clin. Endocr. Metab.* 82:3251–3259.

DELLU, F., W. MAYO, M. VALLEE, M. LEMOAL, and H. SIMON, 1994. Reactivity to novelty during youth as a predictive factor of cognitive impairment in the elderly: A longitudinal study in rats. *Brain Res.* 653:51–56.

DENENBERG, V. H., and G. C. HALTMEYER, 1967. Test of the monotonicity hypothesis concerning infantile stimulation and emotional reactivity. *J. Comp. Physiol. Psychol.* 63:394–396.

DEROCHE, V., P. V. PIAZZA, M. LEMOAL, and H. SIMON, 1993. Individual differences in the psychomotor effects of morphine are predicted by reactivity to novelty and influenced by corticosterone secretion. *Brain Res.* 623:341–344.

DERRICK, B. E., S. B. WEINBERGER, and J. L. MARTINEZ, 1991. Opioid receptors are involved in an NMDA receptor-independent mechanism of LTP induction at hippocampal mossy fiber-CA3 synapses. *Brain Res. Bull.* 27:219–223.

DIAMOND, D. M., M. C. BENNETT, M. FLESHNER, and G. M. ROSE, 1992. Inverted-U relationship between the level of peripheral corticosterone and the magnitude of hippocampal primed burst potentiation. *Hippocampus* 2:421–430.

DIAMOND, D. M., M. FLESHNER, N. INGERSOLL, and G. M. ROSE, 1996. Psychological stress impairs spatial working memory: Relevance to electrophysiological studies of hippocampal function. *Behav. Neurosci.* 110:661–672.

DIAMOND, D. M., M. FLESHNER, and G. M. ROSE, 1994. Psychological stress repeatedly blocks hippocampal primed burst potentiation in behaving rats. *Behav. Brain Res.* 62:1–9.

DIORIO, D., V. VIAU, and M. J. MEANEY, 1993. The role of the medial prefrontal cortex (cingulate gyrus) in the regulation of hypothalamic-pituitary-adrenal responses to stress. *J. Neurosci.* 13:3839–3847.

DONCARLOS, L. L., E. MONROY, and J. I. MORRELL, 1991. Distribution of estrogen receptor-immunoreactive cells in the forebrain of the female guinea pig. *J. Comp. Neurol.* 305:591–612.

EVANS, R., 1988. The steroid and thyroid hormone receptor superfamily. *Science* 240:889–895.

FADER, A. J., A. W. HENDRICSON, and G. P. DOHANICH, 1996. Effects of estrogen treatment on T-maze alternation in female and male rats. *Abstr. Soc. Neurosci.* 22:547.6–P1386.

FARIAS, P. A., S. Q. LOW, G. M. PETERSON, and C. E. RIBAK, 1992. Morphological evidence for altered synaptic organization and structure in the hippocampal formation of seizure-sensitive gerbils. *Hippocampus* 2:229–246.

FITZGERALD, L. W., J. ORTIZ, A. G. HAMEDANI, and E. J. NESTLER, 1996. Drugs of abuse and stress increase the expression of GluR1 and NMDAR1 glutamate receptor subunits in the rat ventral segmental area: Common adaptations among cross-sensitizing agents. *J. Neurosci.* 16: 274–282.

FOY, M., M. STANTON, L. SEYMOUR, and R. THOMPSON, 1987. Behavioral stress impairs long-term potentiation in rodent hippocampus. *Behav. Neur. Biol.* 48:138–149.

FREUND, T. F., and G. BUZSAKI, 1996. Interneurons of the hippocampus. *Hippocampus* 6:345–470.

FRIDE, E., Y. DAN, J. FELDON, G. HALEVY, and M. WEINSTOCK, 1986. Effects of prenatal stress on vulnerability to stress and prepubertal and adult rats. *Physiol. Behav.* 37:681–687.

FRYE, C. A., 1995. Estrus-associated decrements in a water maze task are limited to acquisition. *Physiol. Behav.* 57:5–14.

FUCHS, E., G. FLUGGE, B. S. MCEWEN, P. TANAPAT, and E. GOULD, 1997. Chronic subordination stress inhibits neurogenesis and decreases the volume of the granule cell layer. *Abstr. Soc. Neurosci.* 23:130.10, p. 317.

FUCHS, E., H. UNO, and G. FLUGGE, 1995. Chronic psychosocial stress induces morphological alterations in hippocampal pyramidal neurons of the tree shrew. *Brain Res.* 673:275–282.

GALEA, L. A. M., M. KAVALIERS, K. OSSENKOPP, D. INNES, and E. L. HARGREAVES, 1994. Sexually dimorphic spatial learning varies seasonally in two populations of deer mice. *Brain Res.* 635:18–26.

GALEA, L. A. M., B. S. MCEWEN, P. TANAPAT, T. DEAK, R. L. SPENCER, and F. S. DHABHAR, 1997. Sex differences in dendritic atrophy of CA3 pyramidal neurons in response to chronic restraint stress. *Neuroscience* 81:689–697.

GALEA, L. A. M., P. TANAPAT, and E. GOULD, 1996. Exposure to predator odor suppresses cell proliferation in the dentate gyrus of adult rats via a cholinergic mechanism. *Abstr. Soc. Neurosci.* 22:474.8, p. 1196.

GAZZALEY, A. H., N. G. WEILAND, B. S. MCEWEN, and J. H. MORRISON, 1996. Differential regulation of NMDAR1 mRNA and protein by estradiol in the rat hippocampus. *J. Neurosci.* 16:6830–6838.

GERLACH, J., B. S. MCEWEN, D. W. PFAFF, S. MOSKOVITZ, M. FERIN, P. CARMEL, and E. ZIMMERMAN, 1976. Cells in regions of rhesus monkey brain and pituitary retain radioactive estradiol, corticosterone, and cortisol differently. *Brain Res.* 103:603–612.

GOLD, P. E., 1987. Sweet memories. *Am. Scientist* 75:151–155.

GOLD, P. W., J. LICINIO, M. L. WONG, and G. P. CHROUSOS, 1995. Corticotropin releasing hormone in the pathophysiology of melancholic and atypical depression and in the mechanism of action of antidepressant drugs. *Ann. N.Y. Acad. Sci.* 771:716–729.

GOTTESMAN, I. I., 1997. Twins: En route to QTLs for cognition. *Science* 276:1522–1523.

GOULD, E., M. ALLAN, and B. S. MCEWEN, 1990. Dendritic spine density of adult hippocampal pyramidal cells is sensitive to thyroid hormone. *Brain Res.* 525:327–329.

GOULD, E., and H. A. CAMERON, 1997. Early NMDA receptor blockade impairs defensive behavior and increases cell proliferation in the dentate gyrus of developing rats. *Behav. Neurosci.* 111:49–56.

GOULD, E., M. FRANKFURT, A. WESTLIND-DANIELSSON, and B. S. MCEWEN, 1990. Developing forebrain astrocytes are sensitive to thyroid hormone. *Glia* 3:283–292.

GOULD, E., B. S. MCEWEN, P. TANAPAT, L. A. M. GALEA, and E. FUCHS, 1997. Neurogenesis in the dentate gyrus of the adult tree shrew is regulated by psychosocial stress and NMDA receptor activation. *J. Neurosci.* 17:2492–2498.

GOULD, E., P. TANAPAT, and B. S. MCEWEN, 1997. Activation of the type 2 adrenal steroid receptor can rescue granule cells from death during development. *Devel. Brain Res.* 101: 265–268.

GOULD, E., P. TANAPAT, B. S. MCEWEN, G. FLUGGE, and E. FUCHS, 1998. Proliferation of granule cell precursors in the dentate gyrus of adult monkeys is diminished by stress. *Proc. Natl. Acad. Sci. U.S.A.* 95:3168–3171.

GOULD, E., A. WESTLIND-DANIELSSON, M. FRANKFURT, and B. S. MCEWEN, 1990. Sex differences and thyroid hormone sensitivity of hippocampal pyramidal neurons. *J. Neurosci.* 10:996–1003.

GOULD, E., C. WOOLLEY, M. FRANKFURT, and B. S. MCEWEN, 1990. Gonadal steroids regulate dendritic spine density in hippocampal pyramidal cells in adulthood. *J. Neurosci.* 10:1286–1291.

GOULD, E., C. WOOLLEY, and B. S. MCEWEN, 1990. Short-term glucocorticoid manipulations affect neuronal morphology and survival in the adult dentate gyrus. *Neuroscience* 37:367–375.

GOULD, E., C. WOOLLEY, and B. S. MCEWEN, 1991. The hippocampal formation: Morphological changes induced by thyroid, gonadal, and adrenal hormones. *Psychoneuroendocrinology,* 16:67–84.

GREENGARD, P., F. VALTORTA, A. J. CZERNIK, and F. BENFANATI, 1993. Synaptic vesicle phosphoproteins and regulation of synaptic function. *Science* 259:780–785.

GRINDLEY, K. E., P. S. GREEN, and J. W. SIMPKINS, 1997. Low concentrations of estradiol reduce b-amyloid (25–35) induced toxicity, lipid peroxidation, and glucose utilization in human SK-N-SH neuroblastoma cells. *Brain Res.* 778: 158–165.

HALL, E. D., K. E. PAZARA, and K. L. LINSEMAN, 1991. Sex differences in postischemic neuronal necrosis in gerbils. *J. Cerebral Blood Flow Metab.* 11:292–298.

HANDA, R. J., K. M. NUNLEY, S. A. LORENS, J. P. LOUIE, R. F. MCGIVERN, and M. R. BOLLNOW, 1993. Androgen regulation of adrenocorticotropin and corticosterone secretion in the male rat following novelty and foot shock stressors. *Physiol. Behav.* 55:117–124.

HENDERSON, V. W., A. PAGANINI-HILL, C. K. EMANUEL, M. E. DUNN, and J. G. BUCKWALTER, 1994. Estrogen replacement therapy in older women: Comparisons between Alzheimer's disease cases and nondemented control subjects. *Arch. Neurol.* 51:896–900.

HENDERSON, V. W., L. WATT, and J. G. BUCKWALTER, 1996. Cognitive skills associated with estrogen replacement in women with Alzheimer's disease. *Psychoneuroendocrinology* 12:421–430.

HENRY, C., M. KABBAJ, H. SIMON, M. LEMOAL, and S. MACCARI, 1994. Prenatal stress increases the hypothalamo-pituitary-adrenal axis response in young and adult rats. *J. Neuroendocr.* 6:341–345.

HERMAN, J. P., and W. E. CULLINAN, 1997. Neurocircuitry of stress: Central control of the hypothalamo-pituitary-adrenocortical axis. *Trends Neurosci.* 20:78–84.

HERMAN, J. P., P. D. PATEL, H. AKIL, and S. J. WATSON, 1989. Localization and regulation of glucocorticoid and mineralocorticoid receptor messenger RNAs in the hippocampal formation of the rat. *Mol. Endocr.* 3:1886–1894.

HOLSBOER, F., and N. BARDEN, 1996. Antidepressants and hypothalamic-pituitary-adrenocortical regulation. *Endocr. Rev.* 17:187–205.

HSU, M., and G. BUZSAKI, 1993. Vulnerability of mossy fiber targets in the rat hippocampus to forebrain ischemia. *J. Neurosci.* 13:3964–3979.

IKEGAYA, Y., H. SAITO, and K. ABE, 1997. The basomedial and basolateral amygdaloid nuclei contribute to the induction of long-term potentiation in the dentate gyrus in vivo. *Eur. J. Neurosci.* 8:1833–1839.

ISHIZUKA, N., J. WEBER, and D. G. AMARAL, 1990. Organization of intrahippocampal projections originating from CA3 pyramidal cells in the rat. *J. Comp. Neurol.* 295:580–623.

JACOBSON, L., and R. SAPOLSKY, 1991. The role of the hippocampus in feedback regulation of the hypothalamic-pituitary-adrenocortical axis. *Endocr. Rev.* 12:118–134.

JAFFE, A. B., C. D. TORAN-ALLERAND, P. GREENGARD, and S. E. GANDY, 1994. Estrogen regulates metabolism of Alzheimer amyloid B precursor protein. *J. Biol. Chem.* 269:13065–13068.

JENNES, L., B. BRANE, A. CENTERS, J. A. JANOVICK, and P. M. CONN, 1995. Regulation of hippocampal gonadotropin releasing hormone (GnRH) receptor mRNA and GnRH-stimulated inositol phosphate production by gonadal steroid hormones. *Mol. Brain Res.* 33:104–110.

JENSEN, E., and H. JACOBSON, 1962. Basic guides to the mechanics of estrogen action. *Rec. Prog. Horm. Res.* 18:387–408.

JOELS, M., A. BOSMA, H. HENDRIKSEN, P. DIEGENBACH, and W. KAMPHUIS, 1996. Corticosteroid actions on the expression of kainate receptor subunit mRNAs in rat hippocampus. *Mol. Brain Res.* 37:15–20.

JURASKA, J., J. FITCH, C. HENDERSON, and N. RIVERS, 1985. Sex differences in the dendritic branching of dentate granule cells following differential experience. *Brain Res.* 333:73–80.

JURASKA, J. M., J. M. FITCH, and D. L. WASHBURNE, 1989. The dendritic morphology of pyramidal neurons in the rat hippocampal CA3 area. II. Effects of gender and the environment. *Brain Res.* 479:115–119.

JURASKA, J. M., and S. G. WARREN, 1996. Spatial memory decline in aged, non-cycling female rats varies with the phase of estropause. *Abstr. Soc. Neurosci.* 22:547.12, p. 1387.

KEMPERMANN, G., H. G. KUHN, and F. H. GAGE, 1997. More hippocampal neurons in adult mice living in an enriched environment. *Nature* 586:493–495.

KENNET, G. A., S. L. DICKINSON, and G. CURZON, 1985. Enhancement of some 5-HT dependent behavioral responses following repeated immobilization in rats. *Brain Res.* 330:253–260.

KERR, D. S., L. W. CAMPBELL, O. THIBAULT, and P. W. LANDFIELD, 1992. Hippocampal glucocorticoid receptor activation enhances voltage-dependent Ca^{2+} conductances: Relevance to brain aging. *Proc. Natl. Acad. Sci. U.S.A.* 89:8527–8531.

KERR, J. E., R. J. ALLORE, S. G. BECK, and R. J. HANDA, 1995. Distribution and hormonal regulation of androgen receptor (AR) and AR messenger ribonucleic acid in the rat hippocampus. *Endocrinology* 136:3213–3221.

KERR, J. E., S. G. BECK, and R. J. HANDA, 1996a. Androgens modulate glucocorticoid receptor mRNA, but not mineralocorticoid receptor mRNA levels, in the rat hippocampus. *J. Neuroendocr.* 8:439–447.

KERR, J. E., S. G. BECK, and R. J. HANDA, 1996b. Androgens selectively modulate C-FOS messenger RNA induction in the rat hippocampus following novelty. *Neuroscience* 74:757–766.

KIRSCHBAUM, C., O. T. WOLF, M. MAY, W. WIPPICH, and D. H. HELLHAMMER, 1996. Stress- and treatment-induced elevations of cortisol levels associated with impaired verbal and spatial declarative memory in healthy adults. *Life Sci.* 58:1475–1483.

KNEISLER, T. B., and R. DINGLEDINE, 1995. Synaptic input from Ca3 pyramidal cells to dentate basket cells in rat hippocampus. *J. Physiol.* 487:125–146.

KOPROWSKI, H., Y. M. ZHENG, E. HEBER-KATZ, N. FRASER, L. RORKE, Z. F. FU, C. HANLON, and B. DIETZSCHOLD, 1993. In vivo expression of inducible nitric oxide synthase in experimentally induced neurologic diseases. *Proc. Natl. Acad. Sci. U.S.A.* 90:3024–3027.

KOROL, D. L., J. M. COUPER, C. K. MCINTYRE, and P. E. GOLD, 1996. Strategies for learning across the estrous cycle in female rats. *Abstr. Soc. Neurosci.* 22:547.4–P1386.

KURODA, Y., M. MIKUNI, N. NOMURA, and K. TAKAHASHI, 1993. Differential effect of subchronic dexamethasone treatment on serotonin-2 and beta-adrenergic receptors in the rat cerebral cortex and hippocampus. *Neurosci. Lett.* 155:195–198.

KURODA, Y., Y. WATANABE, D. ALBECK, N. HASTINGS, and B. S. MCEWEN, 1994. Effects of adrenalectomy and type I and type II adrenal steroid receptor activation on 5-HT1A and 5-HT2 receptor binding and 5-HT transporter mRNA expression in rat brain. *Brain Res.* 648:157–161.

KUS, L., R. J. HANDA, J. M. HAUTMAN, and A. J. BEITZ, 1995. Castration increases [125I]MK801 binding in the hippocampus of male rats. *Brain Res.* 683:270–274.

KWAK, S. P., P. D. PATEL, R. C. THOMPSON, H. AKIL, and S. J. WATSON, 1993. 5′-heterogeneity of the mineralocorticoid receptor messenger ribonucleic acid: Differential expression and regulation of splice variants within the rat hippocampus. *Endocrinology* 133:2344–2350.

LANDFIELD, P. W., 1987. Modulation of brain aging correlates by long-term alterations of adrenal steroids and neurally active peptides. *Prog. Brain Res.* 72:279–300.

LANDFIELD, P. W., and J. C. ELDRIDGE, 1994. Evolving aspects of the glucocorticoid hypothesis of brain aging: Hormonal modulation of neuronal calcium homeostasis. *Neurobiol. Aging* 15:579–588.

LECHAN, R. M., Y. QI, T. J. BERRODIN, K. D. DAVIS, H. L. SCHWARTZ, K. A. STRAIT, J. H. OPPENHEIMER, and M. A. LAZAR, 1993. Immunocytochemical delineation of thyroid hormone receptor b-2like immunoreactivity in the rat central nervous system. *Endocrinology* 132:2461–2469.

LEVINE, S., G. C. HALTMEYER, G. G. KARAS, and V. H. DENENBERG, 1967. Physiological and behavioral effects of infantile stimulation. *Physiol. Behav.* 2:55–59.

LI, X., P. E. SCHWARTZ, and E. F. RISSMAN, 1997. Distribution of estrogen receptor beta-like immunoreactivity in rat forebrain. *Neuroendocrinology* 66:63–67.

LI, X. G., P. SOMOGYI, A. YLINEN, and G. BUZSAKI, 1994. The hippocampal CA3 network: An in vivo intracellular labeling study. *J. Comp. Neurol.* 339:181–208.

LIBERZON, I., D. T. CHALMERS, A. MANSOUR, J. F. LOPEZ, S. J. WATSON, and E. A. YOUNG, 1994. Glucocorticoid regulation of hippocampal oxytocin receptor binding. *Brain Res.* 650:317–322.

LIBERZON, I., and E. A. YOUNG, 1997. Effects of stress and glucocorticoids on CNS oxytocin receptor binding. *Psychoneuroendocrinology* 22:411–422.

LISK, R., 1962. Diencephalic placement of estradiol and sexual receptivity in female rat. *Am. J. Physiol.* 203:493–496.

LIU, D., J. DIORIO, B. TANNENBAUM, C. CALDJI, D. FRANCIS, A. FREEDMAN, S. SHARMA, D. PEARSON, P. M. PLOTSKY, and M. J. MEANEY, 1997. Maternal care, hippocampal glucocorticoid receptors, and hypothalamic-pituitary-adrenal responses to stress. *Science* 277:1659–1662.

LLINAS, R., T. L. MCGUINNESS, C. S. LEONARD, M. SUGIMOR, and P. GREENGARD, 1985. Intraterminal injection of synapsin I or calcium/calmodulin-dependent protein kinase II alters neurotransmitter release at the squid giant synapse. *Proc. Natl. Acad. Sci. U.S.A.* 82:3035–3039.

LOWENSTEIN, D., M. J. THOMAS, D. H. SMITH, and T. K. MCINTOSH, 1994. Selective vulnerability of dentate hilar neurons following traumatic brain injury: A potential mechanistic link between head trauma and disorders of the hippocampus. *J. Neurosci.* 12:4846–4853.

LOWY, M. T., L. GAULT, and B. K. YAMAMOTO, 1993. Adrenalectomy attenuates stress-induced elevations in extracellular glutamate concentrations in the hippocampus. *J. Neurochem.* 61:1957–1960.

LOY, R., J. GERLACH, and B. S. MCEWEN, 1988. Autoradiographic localization of estradiol-binding neurons in rat hippocampal formation and entorhinal cortex. *Dev. Brain Res.* 39:245–251.

LUCHINS, D. J., 1990. Comment: A possible role of hippocampal dysfunction in schizophrenic symptomatology. *Biol. Psychiatry* 28:87–91.

LUINE, V. N., J. RENTAS, L. STERBANK, and K. BECK, 1996. Estradiol effects on rat spatial memory. *Abstr. Soc. Neurosci.* 22:547.9–P1387.

LUINE, V., M. VILLEGAS, C. MARTINEZ, and B. S. MCEWEN, 1994. Repeated stress causes reversible impairments of spatial memory performance. *Brain Res.* 639:167–170.

LUPIEN, S. J., M. J. DELEON, S. DE SANTI, A. CONVIT, C. TARSHISH, N. P. V. NAIR, M. THAKUR, B. S. MCEWEN, R. L. HAUGER, and M. J. MEANEY, 1998. Cortisol levels during human aging predict hippocampal atrophy and memory deficits. *Nature Neurosci.* 1:69–73.

LUPIEN, S., A. R. LECOURS, I. LUSSIER, G. SCHWARTZ, N. P. V. NAIR, and M. J. MEANEY, 1994. Basal cortisol levels and cognitive deficits in human aging. *J. Neurosci.* 14:2893–2903.

LUPIEN, S. J., and B. S. MCEWEN, 1997. The acute effects of corticosteroids on cognition: integration of animal and human model studies. *Brain Res. Rev.* 24:1–27.

LUTTGE, W., M. RUPP, and M. DAVDA, 1989. Aldosterone-stimulated down-regulation of both type I and type II adrenocorticosteroid receptors in mouse brain is mediated via type I receptors. *Endocrinology* 125:817–824.

MACCARI, S., P. V. PIAZZA, M. KABBAJ, A. BARBAZANGES, H. SIMON, and M. LEMOAL, 1995. Adoption reverses the long-term impairment in glucocorticoid feedback induced by prenatal stress. *J. Neurosci.* 15:110–116.

MACLUSKY, N., A. S. CLARK, F. NAFTOLIN, and P. S. GOLDMAN-RAKIC, 1987. Oestrogen formation in the mammalian brain: Possible role of aromatase in sexual differentiation of the hippocampus and neocortex. *Steroids* 50:459–474.

MACLUSKY, N. J., M. J. WALTERS, A. S. CLARK, and C. D. TORAN-ALLERAND, 1994. Aromatase in the cerebral cortex, hippocampus, and midbrain: Ontogeny and developmental implications. *Mol. Cell. Neurosci.* 5:691–698.

MADEIRA, M., N. SOUSA, M. LIMA-ANDRADE, F. CALHEIROS, A. CADETE-LEITE, and M. PAULA-BARBOSA, 1992. Selective vulnerability of the hippocampal pyramidal neurons to hypothyroidism in male and female rats. *J. Comp. Neurol.* 322:501–518.

MAGARINOS, A. M., A. DESLANDES, and B. S. MCEWEN, in press. Effects of antidepressants and a benzodiazepine on the dendritic structure of CA3 pyramidal neurons after chronic stress. *Eur. J. Pharmacol.*

MAGARINOS, A. M., and B. S. MCEWEN, 1995. Stress-induced atrophy of apical dendrites of hippocampal CA3c neurons: Involvement of glucocorticoid secretion and excitatory amino acid receptors. *Neuroscience* 69:89–98.

MAGARINOS, A. M., B. S. MCEWEN, G. FLUGGE, and E. FUCHS, 1996. Chronic psychosocial stress causes apical dendritic atrophy of hippocampal CA3 pyramidal neurons in subordinate tree shrews. *J. Neurosci.* 16:3534–3540.

MAGARINOS, A. M., J. M. VERDUGO GARCIA, and B. S. MCEWEN, 1997. Chronic restraint stress alters synaptic terminal structure in hippocampus. *Proc. Natl. Acad. Sci. U.S.A.* 94:14002–14008.

MARTIGNONI, E., A. COSTA, E. SINFORIANI, A. LIUZZI, P. CHIODII, M. MAURI, G. BONO, and G. NAPPI, 1992. The brain as a target for adrenocortical steroids: cognitive implications. *Psychoneuroendocrinology* 17:343–354.

MCCARTHY, M., H. COIRINI, M. SCHUMACHER, A. JOHNSON, D. PFAFF, S. SCHWARTZ-GIBLIN, and B. S. MCEWEN, 1992. Steroid regulation and sex differences in [3H]muscimol binding in hippocampus, hypothalamus, and midbrain in rats. *J. Neuroendocr.* 4:393–399.

MCEWEN, B. S., 1997. Possible mechanisms for atrophy of the human hippocampus. *Mol. Psychiatry* 2:255–262.

MCEWEN, B. S., S. E. ALVES, K. BULLOCH, and N. G. WEILAND, 1997. Ovarian steroids and the brain: Implications for cognition and aging. *Neurology* 48:S8–S15.

MCEWEN, B. S., P. G. DAVIS, B. PARSONS, and D. W. PFAFF, 1979. The brain as a target for steroid hormone action. *Ann. Rev. Neurosci.* 2:65–112.

MCEWEN, B. S., E. GOULD, M. ORCHINIK, N. G. WEILAND, and C. S. WOOLLEY, 1995. Oestrogens and the structural and functional plasticity of neurons: Implications for memory, aging, and neurodegenerative processes. Ciba Foundation Symposium 191. In *The Nonreproductive Actions of Sex Steroids*, J. Goode, ed. London: CIBA Foundation, pp. 52–73.

MCEWEN, B. S., P. TANAPAT, and N. G. WEILAND, 1999. Inhibition of dendritic spine induction on hippocampal CA1 pyramidal neurons by a nonsteroidal estrogen antagonist in female rats. *Endocrinology* 140:1044–1047.

MCEWEN, B. S., J. WEISS, and L. SCHWARTZ, 1968. Selective retention of corticosterone by limbic structures in rat brain. *Nature* 220:911–912.

MCKITTRICK, C. R., D. C. BLANCHARD, R. J. BLANCHARD, B. S. MCEWEN, and R. R. SAKAI, 1995. Serotonin receptor binding in a colony model of chronic social stress. *Biol. Psychiatry* 37:383–393.

MCKITTRICK, C. R., A. M. MAGARINOS, D. C. BLANCHARD, R. J. BLANCHARD, and B. S. MCEWEN, 1996. Chronic social stress decreases binding to 5HT transporter sites and reduces dendritic arbors in CA3 of hippocampus. A*bstr. Soc. Neurosci.* 22:809.18, p. 2060.

MEANEY, M., D. AITKEN, H. BERKEL, S. BHATNAGER, and R. SAPOLSKY, 1988. Effect of neonatal handling of age-related impairments associated with the hippocampus. *Science* 239:766–768.

MEANEY, M., D. AITKEN, and R. SAPOLSKY, 1987. Thyroid hormones influence the development of hippocampal glucocorticoid receptors in the rat: A mechanism for the effects of postnatal handling on the development of the adrenocortical stress response. *Neuroendocrinology* 45:278–285.

MEANEY, M. J., B. TANNENBAUM, D. FRANCIS, S. BHATNAGAR, N. SHANKS, V. VIAU, D. O'DONNELL, and P. M. PLOTSKY, 1994. Early environmental programming hypothalamic-pituitary-adrenal responses to stress. *Seminars Neurosci.* 6:247–259.

MELIA, K. R., A. E. RYABININ, R. SCHROEDER, F. E. BLOOM, and M. C. WILSON, 1994. Induction and habituation of immediate early gene expression in rat brain by acute and repeated restraint stress. *J. Neurosci.* 14:5929–5938.

MELLONI, R. H. J., L. M. HEMMENDINGER, J. E. HAMOS, and L. J. DEGENNARO, 1993. Synapsin I gene expression in the adult brain with Comp. analysis of mRNA and protein in the hippocampus. *J. Comp. Neurol.* 327:507–520.

MENDELSON, S., and B. S. MCEWEN, 1992. Autoradiographic analyses of the effects of adrenalectomy and corticosterone on 5-HT1A and 5-HT1B receptors in the dorsal hippocampus and cortex of the rat. *Neuroendocrinology* 55:444–450.

MENNINI, T., and A. MIARI, 1991. Modulation of 3H glutamate binding by serotonin in rat hippocampus: An autoradiographic study. *Life Sci.* 49:283–292.

MENNINI, T., E. MOCAER, and S. CARATTINI, 1987. Tianeptine, a selective enhancer of serotonin uptake in rat brain. *Naunyn Schmiedebergs Arch. Pharmacol.* 336:478–482.

MILLER, A. H., R. SPENCER, A. HUSAIN, R. RHEE, B. S. MCEWEN, and M. STEIN, 1993. Differential expression of type I adrenal steroid receptors in immune tissues is associated with tissue-specific regulation of type II receptors by aldosterone. *Endocrinology* 133:2133–2140.

MILLER, A. H., R. SPENCER, M. PULERA, S. KANG, B. S. MCEWEN, and M. STEIN, 1992. Adrenal steroid receptor activation in rat brain and pituitary following dexamethasone: Implications for the dexamethasone suppression test. *Biol. Psych.* 32:850–869.

MINER, J. N., and K. R. YAMAMOTO, 1991. Regulatory crosstalk at composite response elements. *Trends Biochem. Sci.* 16:423–426.

MIZOGUCHI, K., T. KUNISHITA, D. H. CHUI, and T. TABIRA, 1992. Stress induces neuronal death in the hippocampus of castrated rats. *Neurosci. Lett.* 138:157–160.

MOGHADDAM, B., M. L. BOLIANO, B. STEIN-BEHRENS, and R. SAPOLSKY, 1994. Glucocorticoids mediate the stress-induced extracellular accumulation of glutamate. *Brain Res.* 655:251–254.

MONAGHAN, D. T., V. R. HOLETS, D. W. TOY, and C. W. COTMAN, 1983. Anatomical distributions of four pharmacologically distinct 3H-L-glutamate binding sites. *Nature* 306:176–179.

MONTKOWSKI, A., N. BARDEN, C. WOTJAK, I. STEC, J. GANSTER, M. MEANEY, M. ENGELMANN, J. M. H. M. REUL, R. LANDGRAF, and F. HOLSBOER, 1995. Long-term antidepressant treatment reduces behavioural deficits in transgenic mice with impaired glucocorticoid receptor function. *J. Neuroendocrinol.* 7:841–845.

MORRELL, J., and D. W. PFAFF, 1978. A neuroendocrine approach to brain function: Localization of sex steroid concentrating cells in vertebrate brains. *Am. Zool.* 18:447–460.

MORSE, J. K., S. T. DEKOSKY, and S. W. SCHEFF, 1992. Neurotrophic effects of steroids on lesion-induced growth in the hippocampus. *Exp. Neurol.* 118:47–52.

MURPHY, D. D., and M. SEGAL, 1996. Regulation of dendritic spine density in cultured rat hippocampal neurons by steroid hormones. *J. Neurosci.* 16:4059–4068.

MURPHY, D. D., and M. SEGAL, 1997a. Morphological plasticity of dendritic spines in central neurons is mediated by activation of cAMP response element binding protein. *Proc. Natl. Acad. Sci. U.S.A.* 94:1482–1487.

MURPHY, D. D., and M. SEGAL, 1997b. Estradiol increases dendritic spine density by reducing GABA in hippocampal interneurons. *Abstr. Soc. Neurosci.* 23:262.15, p. 657.

NADLER, J., and G. CUTHBERTSON, 1980. Kainic acid neurotoxicity toward hippocampal formation: Dependence on specific excitatory pathways. *Brain Res.* 195:47–56.

NEWCOMER, J. W., S. CRAFT, T. HERSHEY, K. ASKINS, and M. E. BARDGETT, 1994. Glucocorticoid-induced impairment in declarative memory performance in adult humans. *J. Neurosci.* 14:2047–2053.

NOBREGA, J. N., R. RAYMOND, J. PUYMIRAT, T. BELEJ, and R. T. JOFFE, 1997. Regional changes in b1 thyroid hormone receptor immunoreactivity in rat brain after thyroidectomy. *Brain Res.* 761:161–164.

OKAZAKI, M. M., D. A. EVENSON, and J. V. NADLER, 1995. Hippocampal mossy fiber sprouting and synapse formation after status epilepticus in rats: Visualization after retrograde transport of biocytin. *J. Comp. Neurol.* 352:515–534.

O'KEEFE, J. A., and R. J. HANDA, 1990. Transient elevation of estrogen receptors in the neonatal rat hippocampus. *Devel. Brain Res.* 57:119–127.

O'KEEFE, J. A., Y. LI, L. H. BURGESS, and R. J. HANDA, 1995. Estrogen receptor mRNA alterations in the developing rat hippocampus. *Mol. Brain Res.* 30:115–124.

O'NEAL, M. F., L. W. MEANS, M. C. POOLE, and R. J. HAMM, 1996. Estrogen affects performance of ovariectomized rats in a two-choice water-escape working memory task. *Psychoneuroendocrinology* 21:51–65.

ORCHINIK, M., and B. S. MCEWEN, 1995. Rapid actions in the brain: A critique of genomic and nongenomic mechanisms. In *Genomic and Nongenomic Effects of Aldosterone,* M. Wehling, ed. Boca Raton, Fla.: CRC Press, pp. 77–108.

PACKAN, D. R., and R. M. SAPOLSKY, 1990. Glucocorticoid endangerment of the hippocampus: Tissue, steroid, and receptor specificity. *Neuroendocrinology* 51:613–618.

PAGANINI-HILL, A., and V. W. HENDERSON, 1994. Estrogen deficiency and risk of Alzheimer's disease in women. *Am. J. Epidemiol.* 3:3–16.

PARENT, J. M., T. W. YU, R. T. LEIBOWITZ, D. H. GESCHWIND, R. S. SLOVITER, and D. H. LOWENSTEIN, 1997. Dentate granule cell neurogenesis is increased by seizures and contributes to aberrant network reorganization in the adult rat hippocampus. *J. Neurosci.* 17:3727–3738.

PARSONS, B., T. C. RAINBOW, N. MACLUSKY, and B. S. MCEWEN, 1982. Progestin receptor levels in rat hypothalamic and limbic nuclei. *J. Neurosci.* 2:1446–1452.

PAVLIDES, C., A. KIMURA, A. M. MAGARINOS, and B. S. MCEWEN, 1994. Type I adrenal steroid receptors prolong hippocampal long-term potentiation. *NeuroReport* 5:2673–2677.

PAVLIDES, C., A. KIMURA, A. M. MAGARINOS, and B. S. MCEWEN, 1995. Hippocampal homosynaptic long-term depression/depotentiation induced by adrenal steroids. *Neuroscience* 68:379–385.

PAVLIDES, C., S. OGAWA, A. KIMURA, and B. MCEWEN, 1996. Role of adrenal steroid mineralocorticoid and glucocorticoid receptors in long-term potentiation in the CA1 field of hippocampal slices. *Brain Res.* 738:229–235.

PAVLIDES, C., Y. WATANABE, A. M. MAGARINOS, and B. S. MCEWEN, 1995. Opposing role of adrenal steroid Type I and Type II receptors in hippocampal long-term potentiation. *Neuroscience* 68:387–394.

PAVLIDES, C., Y. WATANABE, and B. S. MCEWEN, 1993. Effects of glucocorticoids on hippocampal long-term potentiation. *Hippocampus* 3:183–192.

PAVLIDES, C., A. WESTLIND-DANIELSSON, H. NYBORG, and B. S. MCEWEN, 1991. Neonatal hyperthyroidism disrupts hippocampal LTP and spatial learning. *Exp. Brain Res.* 85:559–564.

PEARCE, D., and K. R. YAMAMOTO, 1993. Mineralocorticoid and glucocorticoid receptor activities distinguished by non-receptor factors at a composite response element. *Science* 259:1161–1165.

PENNARTZ, C. M. A., and S. T. KITAI, 1991. Hippocampal inputs to identified neurons in an in vitro slice preparation of the rat nucleus accumbens: Evidence for feed-forward inhibition. *J. Neurosci.* 11:2838–2847.

PERIBONE, V. A., O. SHUPLIAKOV, L. BRODIN, S. HILFIKER-ROTHENFLUH, A. J. CZERNIC, and P. GREENGARD, 1997. Distinct pools of synaptic vesicles in neurotransmitter release. *Nature* 375:493–496.

PIAZZA, P. V., M. MARINELLI, C. JODOGNE, V. DEROCHE, F. ROUGE-PONT, S. MACCARI, M. LEMOAL, and H. SIMON, 1994. Inhibition of corticosterone synthesis by metyrapone decreases cocaine-induced locomotion and relapse of cocaine self-administration. *Brain Res.* 658:259–264.

POMPEI, P., F. RIFTINA, and B. S. MCEWEN, 1995. Effect of adrenal steroids on preproneurokinin-A gene expression in discrete regions of the rat brain. *Mol. Brain Res.* 33:209–216.

POPOV, V. I., and L. S. BOCHAROVA, 1992. Hibernation-induced structural changes in synaptic contacts between mossy fibres and hippocampal pyramidal neurons. *Neuroscience* 48:53–62.

POPOV, V. I., L. S. BOCHAROVA, and A. G. BRAGIN, 1992. Repeated changes of dendritic morphology in the hippocampus of ground squirrels in the course of hibernation. *Neuroscience* 48:45–51.

POULIOT, W. A., R. J. HANDA, and S. G. BECK, 1996. Androgen modulates *N*-methyl-D-aspartate-mediated depolarization in CA1 hippocampal pyramidal cells. *Synapse* 23:10–19.

PREWITT, C. M. F., and J. P. HERMAN, 1997. Hypothalamo-pituitary-adrenocortical regulation following lesions of the central nucleus of the amygdala. *Stress* 1:263–279.

RAHMANN, S., and R. S. NEUMANN, 1993. Activation of 5-HT2 receptors facilitates depolarization of neocortical neurons by *N*-methyl-D-aspartate. *Eur. J. Pharmacol.* 231:347–354.

REGIER, D. A., J. H. BOYD, J. D. BURKE, D. S. RAE, J. K. MYERS, M. KRAMER, L. N. ROBBINS, L. K. GEORGE, M. KARNO, and B. Z. LOCKE, 1988. One-month prevalence of mental disorders in the *U.S. Arch. Gen. Psychiatry* 45:977–986.

RHEES, R. W., J. H. ABEL, and D. W. HAACK, 1972. Uptake of tritiated steroids in the brain of the duck (*Anas platyrhynchos*). *Gen. Comp. Endocr.* 18:292–300.

ROBINSON, D., L. FRIEDMAN, R. MARCUS, J. TINKLENBERG, and J. YESAVAGE, 1994. Estrogen replacement therapy and memory in older women. *J. Am. Geriatr. Soc.* 42:919–922.

ROOF, R. L., and M. D. HAVENS, 1992. Testosterone improves maze performance and induces development of a male hippocampus in females. *Brain Res.* 571:310–313.

ROOZENDAAL, B., J. M. KOOLHAAS, and B. BOHUS, 1997. Central amygdaloid involvement in neuroendocrine correlates of conditioned stress responses. *J. Neuroendocr.* 4:483–489.

ROY, E., N. MACLUSKY, and B. S. MCEWEN, 1979. Antiestrogen inhibits the induction of progestin receptors by estradiol in the hypothalamus, pituitary, and uterus. *Endocrinology* 104:1333–1336.

SAITO, R., N. ISHIHARADA, Y. BAN, K. HONDA, Y. TAKANO, and H. KAMIYA, 1996. Vasopressin V1 receptor in rat hippocampus is regulated by adrenocortical functions. *Brain Res.* 646:170–174.

SAPOLSKY, R., 1986a. Glucocorticoid toxicity in the hippocampus: Reversal by supplementation with brain fuels. *J. Neurosci.* 6:2240–2244.

SAPOLSKY, R., 1986b. Glucocorticoid toxicity in the hippocampus: Temporal aspects of synergy with kainic acid. *Neuroendocrinology* 43:440–444.

SAPOLSKY, R., 1992. *Stress, the Aging Brain, and the Mechanisms of Neuron Death.* Cambridge, Mass.: MIT Press.

SAPOLSKY, R., L. KREY, and B. S. MCEWEN, 1985. Prolonged glucocorticoid exposure reduces hippocampal neuron number: Implications for aging. *J. Neurosci.* 5:1222–1227.

SAPOLSKY, R., L. KREY, and B. S. MCEWEN, 1986. The neuroendocrinology of stress and aging: The glucocorticoid cascade hypothesis. *Endocr. Rev.* 7:284–301.

SAPOLSKY, R. M., S. ZOLA-MORGAN, and L. R. SQUIRE, 1991. Inhibition of glucocorticoid secretion by the hippocampal formation in the primate. *J. Neurosci.* 11:3695–3704.

SCHARFMAN, H. E., 1994. Evidence from simultaneous intracellular recordings in rat hippocampal slices that area Ca3 pyramidal cells innervate dentate hilar mossy cells. *J. Neurophysiol.* 72:2167–2180.

SCHREIBER, S. S., G. TOCCO, T. J. SHORS, and R. F. THOMPSON, 1991. Activation of immediate early genes after acute stress. *NeuroReport* 2:17–20.

SCHUMACHER, M., H. COIRINI, and B. S. MCEWEN, 1989. Regulation of high-affinity GABAa receptors in the dorsal hippocampus by estradiol and progesterone. *Brain Res.* 487:178–183.

SCHWEGLER, H., W. E. CRUSIO, H. P. LIPP, I. BRUST, and G. G. MUELLER, 1991. Early postnatal hyperthyroidism alters hippocampal circuitry and improves radial-maze learning in adult mice. *J. Neurosci.* 11:2102–2106.

SHELINE, Y. I., P. W. WANG, M. H. GADO, J. C. CSERNANSKY, and M. W. VANNIER, 1996. Hippocampal atrophy in recurrent major depression. *Proc. Natl. Acad. Sci. U.S.A.* 93:3908–3913.

SHERRY, D. F., L. F. JACOBS, and S. J. GAULIN, 1992. Spatial memory and adaptive specialization of the hippocampus. *Trends Neurosci.* 15:298–303.

SHERWIN, B. B., 1994. Estrogenic effects on memory in women. *Ann. N.Y. Acad. Sci.* 743:213–231.

SHERWIN, B. B., and T. TULANDI, 1996. "Add-back" estrogen reverses cognitive deficits induced by a gonadotropin-releasing hormone agonist in women with leiomyomata uteri. *J. Clin. Endocr. Metab.* 81:2545–2549.

SHORS, T. J., S. ELKABES, J. C. SELCHER, and I. B. BLACK, 1997. Stress persistently increases NMDA receptor-mediated binding of [3H]PDBu (a marker for protein kinase C) in the amygdala, and reexposure to the stressful context reactivates the increase. *Brain Res.* 750:293–300.

SHORS, T. J., S. LEVINE, and R. F. THOMPSON, 1990. Effect of adrenalectomy and demedullation on the stress-induced impairment of long-term potentiation. *Neuroendocrinology* 51:70–75.

SHORS, T. J., T. B. SEIB, S. LEVINE, and R. F. THOMPSON, 1989. Inescapable versus escapable shock modulates long-

term potentiation in the rat hippocampus. *Science* 244:224–226.

SHORS, T. J., L. SEYMOUR, and R. F. THOMPSON, 1990. Opioid antagonist eliminates the stress-induced impairment of long-term potentiation (LTP). *Brain Res.* 506:316–318.

SHORS, T. J., C. WEISS, and R. F. THOMPSON, 1992. Stress-induced facilitation of classical conditioning. *Science* 257:537–539.

SLOVITER, R. S., 1993. "Epileptic" brain damage in rats induced by sustained electrical stimulation of the perforant path I. Acute electrophysiological and light microscopic studies. *Brain Res. Bull.* 10:675–697.

SLOVITER, R. S., 1994. The functional organization of the hippocampal dentate gyrus and its relevance to the pathogenesis of temporal lobe epilepsy. *Ann. Neurol.* 35:640–654.

SLOVITER, R., G. VALIQUETTE, G. ABRAMS, E. RONK, A. SOLLAS, L. PAUL, and S. NEUBORT, 1989. Selective loss of hippocampal granule cells in the mature rat brain after adrenalectomy. *Science* 243:535–538.

SMRIGA, M., H. SAITO, and N. NISHIYAMA, 1996. Hippocampal long- and short-term potentiation is modulated by adrenalectomy and corticosterone. *Neuroendocr.* 64:35–41.

SPENCER, R. L., H. J. MODAY, and A. H. MILLER, 1997. Maintenance of basal ACTH levels of corticosterone and Ru28362, but not aldosterone: Relationship to available Type I and Type II corticosteroid receptor levels in brain and pituitary. *Stress* 2:51–64.

STARKMAN, M. N., S. S. GEBARSKI, S. BERENT, and D. E. SCHTEINGART, 1992. Hippocampal formation volume, memory dysfunction, and cortisol levels in patients with Cushing's syndrome. *Biol. Psychiatry* 32:756–765.

SUTULA, T., J. KOCH, G. GOLARAI, Y. WATANABE, and J. O. MCNAMARA, 1996. NMDA receptor dependence of kindling and mossy fiber sprouting: Evidence that the NMDA receptor regulates patterning of hippocampal circuits in the adult brain. *J. Neurosci.* 16:7398–7406.

TAKAHASHI, L. K., 1995. Glucocorticoids, the hippocampus, and behavioral inhibition in the preweanling rat. *J. Neurosci.* 15:6023–6034.

TAKEI, Y., A. HARADA, S. TAKEDA, K. KOBAYASHI, S. TERADA, T. NODA, T. TAKAHASHI, and N. HIROKAWA, 1995. Synapsin I deficiency results in the structural change in the presynaptic terminals in the murine nervous system. *J. Cell Biol.* 131:1789–1800.

TANAPAT, P., and E. GOULD, 1997. EGF stimulates proliferation of granule cell precursors in the dentate gyrus of adult rats. *Abstr. Soc. Neurosci.* 23:130.9, p. 317.

TANG, M. X., D. JACOBS, Y. STERN, K. MARDER, P. SCHOFIELD, B. GURLAND, H. ANDREWS, and R. MAYEUX, 1996. Effect of oestrogen during menopause on risk and age at onset of Alzheimer's disease. *Lancet* 348:429–432.

TERASAWA, E., and P. TIMIRAS, 1968. Electrical activity during the estrous cycle of the rat: Cyclic changes in limbic structures. *Endocrinology* 83:207–216.

TRAPP, T., and F. HOLSBOER, 1996. Heterodimerization between mineralocorticoid and glucocorticoid receptors increases the functional diversity of corticosteroid action. *Trends Pharmacol. Sci.* 17:145–149.

UNO, H., T. ROSS, J. ELSE, M. SULEMAN, and R. SAPOLSKY, 1989. Hippocampal damage associated with prolonged and fatal stress in primates. *J. Neurosci.* 9:1709–1711.

VAHER, P. R., V. N. LUINE, E. GOULD, and B. S. MCEWEN, 1994. Effects of adrenalectomy on spatial memory performance and dentate gyrus morphology. *Brain Res.* 656:71–78.

VALLEE, M., W. MAYO, F. DELLU, M. LE MOAL, H. SIMON, and S. MACCARI, 1997. Prenatal stress induces high anxiety, and postnatal handling induces low anxiety in adult offspring: Correlation with stress-induced corticosterone secretion. *J. Neurosci.* 17:2626–2636.

VALLEE, M., W. MAYO, S. MACCARI, M. LE MOAL, and H. SIMON, 1996. Long-term effects of prenatal stress and handling on metabolic parameters: Relationship to corticosterone secretion response. *Brain Res.* 712:287–292.

WATANABE, Y., A. AKABAYASHI, and B. S. MCEWEN, 1995. Adrenal steroid regulation of neuropeptide Y (NPY) mRNA: Differences between dentate hilus and locus coeuleus and arcuate nucleus. *Mol. Brain Res.* 28:135–140.

WATANABE, Y., E. GOULD, H. A. CAMERON, D. C. DANIELS, and B. S. MCEWEN, 1992. Phenytoin prevents stress- and corticosterone-induced atrophy of CA3 pyramidal neurons. *Hippocampus* 2:431–436.

WATANABE, Y., E. GOULD, D. DANIELS, H. CAMERON, and B. S. MCEWEN, 1992. Tianeptine attenuates stress-induced morphological changes in the hippocampus. *Eur. J. Pharmacol.* 222:157–162.

WATANABE, Y., E. GOULD, and B. S. MCEWEN, 1992. Stress induces atrophy of apical dendrites of hippocampus CA3 pyramidal neurons. *Brain Res.* 588:341–344.

WATANABE, Y., E. STONE, and B. S. MCEWEN, 1994. Induction and habituation of c-FOS and ZIF/268 by acute and repeated stressors. *NeuroReport* 5:1321–1324.

WATANABE, Y., N. G. WEILAND, and B. S. MCEWEN, 1995. Effects of adrenal steroid manipulations and repeated restraint stress on dynorphin mRNA levels and excitatory amino acid receptor binding in hippocampus. *Brain Res.* 680:217–225.

WEILAND, N. G., 1992a. Estradiol selectively regulates agonist binding sites on the N-methyl-D-aspartate receptor complex in the CA1 region of the hippocampus. *Endocrinology* 131:662–668.

WEILAND, N. G., 1992b. Glutamic acid decarboxylase messenger ribonucleic acid is regulated by estradiol and progesterone in the hippocampus. *Endocrinology* 131:2697–2702.

WEILAND, N. G., M. ORCHINIK, and P. TANAPAT, 1997. Chronic corticosterone treatment induces parallel changes in N-methyl-D-aspartate receptor subunit messenger RNA levels and antagonist binding sites in the hippocampus. *Neuroscience* 78:653–662.

WEILAND, N. G., C. ORIKASA, S. HAYASHI, and B. S. MCEWEN, 1997. Distribution and hormone regulation of estrogen receptor immunoreactive cells in the hippocampus of male and female rats. *J. Comp. Neurol.* 388:603–612.

WEISSKOPF, M. G., R. A. ZALUTSKY, and R. A. NICOLL, 1993. The opioid peptide dynorphin mediates heterosynaptic depression of hippocampal mossy fibre synapses and modulates long-term potentiation. *Nature* 362:423–428.

WESTLIND-DANIELSSON, A., E. GOULD, and B. S. MCEWEN, 1991. Thyroid hormone causes sexually distinct neurochemical and morphological alterations in rat septal-diagonal band neurons. *J. Neurochem.* 56:119–128.

WHITTON, P., G. SARNA, M. O'CONNELL, and G. CURZON, 1991. The effect of the novel antidepressant tianeptine on the concentration of 5-hydroxytryptamine in rat hippocampal dialysates in vivo. *Psychopharmacology* 104:81–85.

WILLIAMS, C. L., and W. H. MECK, 1991. The organizational effects of gonadal steroids on sexually dimorphic spatial ability. *Psychoneuroendocrinology* 16:155–176.

WOLKOWITZ, O., V. REUSS, and H. WEINGARTNER, 1990. Cognitive effects of corticosteroids. *Am. J. Psychiatry* 147:1297–1303.

WOLKOWITZ, O., D. RUBINOW, and A. DORAN, 1990. Prednisone effects on neurochemistry and behavior: Preliminary findings. *Arch. General Psychiatry* 47:963–968.

WONG, M., and R. L. MOSS, 1992. Long-term and short-term electrophysiological effects of estrogen on the synaptic properties of hippocampal CA1 neurons. *J. Neurosci.* 12:3217–3225.

WOOLLEY, C., E. GOULD, M. FRANKFURT, and B. S. MCEWEN, 1990. Naturally occurring fluctuation in dendritic spine density on adult hippocampal pyramidal neurons. *J. Neurosci.* 10:4035–4039.

WOOLLEY, C. S., E. GOULD, and B. S. MCEWEN, 1990. Exposure to excess glucocorticoids alters dendritic morphology of adult hippocampal pyramidal neurons. *Brain Res.* 531:225–231.

WOOLLEY, C., E. GOULD, R. SAKAI, R. SPENCER, and B. S. MCEWEN, 1991. Effects of aldosterone or RU28362 treatment on adrenalectomy-induced cell death in the dentate gyrus of the adult rat. *Brain Res.* 554:312–315.

WOOLLEY, C., and B. S. MCEWEN, 1992. Estradiol mediates fluctuation in hippocampal synapse density during the estrous cycle in the adult rat. *J. Neurosci.* 12:2549–2554.

WOOLLEY, C., and B. S. MCEWEN, 1993. Roles of estradiol and progesterone in regulation of hippocampal dendritic spine density during the estrous cycle in the rat. *J. Comp. Neurol.* 336:293–306.

WOOLLEY, C., and B. S. MCEWEN, 1994. Estradiol regulates hippocampal dendritic spine density via an N-methyl-D-aspartate receptor dependent mechanism. *J. Neurosci.* 14:7680–7687.

WOOLLEY, C. S., N. G. WEILAND, B. S. MCEWEN, and P. A. SCHWARTZKROIN, 1997. Estradiol increases the sensitivity of hippocampal CA1 pyramidal cells to NMDA receptor-mediated synaptic input: Correlation with dendritic spine density. *J. Neurosci.* 17:1848–1859.

WORLEY, P. F., R. V. BHAT, J. M. BARABAN, C. A. ERICKSON, B. L. MCNAUGHTON, and C. A. BARNES, 1993. Thresholds for synaptic activation of transcription factors in hippocampus-correlation with long-term enhancement. *J. Neurosci.* 13:4776–4786.

XU, L., C. HOLSCHER, R. ANWYL, and M. J. ROWAN, 1998. Glucocorticoid receptor and protein/RNA synthesis-dependent mechanisms underlie the control of synaptic plasticity by stress. *Proc. Natl. Acad. Sci. U.S.A.* 95:3204–3208.

YAMAGATA, Y., K. OBATA, P. GREENGARD, and A. J. CZERNIK, 1995. Increase in synapsin I phosphorylation implicates a presynaptic component in septal kindling. *J. Neurosci.* 64:1–4.

YAMAMOTO, K., 1985. Steroid receptor regulated transcription of specific genes and gene networks. *Ann. Rev. Genet.* 19:209–252.

13 Activity and the Development of the Visual Cortex: New Perspectives

LAWRENCE C. KATZ, MICHAEL WELIKY, AND JUSTIN C. CROWLEY

ABSTRACT Although development of cortical functional architecture has been widely viewed as an activity-dependent process strongly influenced by environmental cues, a growing body of research indicates that the initial establishment of cortical circuits takes place without the influence of visual experience. Increasing attention has focused on the possible roles of spontaneous activity in providing the instructive cues necessary to construct cortical circuits. New recording and stimulation techniques that allow recording and manipulation of spontaneous activity in vivo demonstrate that spontaneous activity in the developing visual pathway exhibits several features inconsistent with simple correlation-based models of cortical development. Moreover, manipulations of endogenous patterns reveal that the initial establishment of ocular dominance and orientation columns is surprisingly resistant to changes in the correlational structure of spontaneous activity. The current emphasis on correlation-based models, which may be appropriate for later plastic changes, could be obscuring the role of intrinsic signals that guide the initial establishment of functional architecture.

Since the pioneering work of Hubel and Wiesel some 30 years ago, development of the functional architecture of the mammalian striate cortex has served as a kind of Rosetta stone for understanding the influences of neuronal activity and environment on the construction and modification of brain circuitry (Wiesel, 1982). Historically, greatest attention has been paid to the mechanisms by which established patterns of neural circuits, such as ocular dominance columns, are modified by visual experience during restricted "critical periods" early in postnatal life (Hubel and Wiesel, 1970; Wiesel and Hubel, 1965a). The well-documented effects of monocular deprivation (Wiesel and Hubel, 1965b) and strabismic rearing (Hubel and Wiesel, 1965) make a compelling argument for the role of visual experience

LAWRENCE C. KATZ Howard Hughes Medical Institute and Department of Neurobiology, Duke University Medical Center, Durham, N.C.
MICHAEL WELIKY Center for Visual Science, University of Rochester, Rochester, N.Y.
JUSTIN C. CROWLEY Howard Hughes Medical Institute and Department of Neurobiology, Duke University Medical Center, Durham, N.C.

and the resulting patterns of neuronal activity in eliciting rearrangements of functional connections. Currently popular theories for how such plastic rearrangements take place focus on the role of correlated neuronal activity and its effects on synaptic strength, perhaps mediated by NMDA-receptor-dependent mechanisms such as long-term potentiation (see Bear and Kirkwood, 1993, for review).

However, it has been less appreciated that the establishment of orientation and ocular dominance columns has at least two distinct phases: the initial establishment of a certain pattern of connectivity, and a subsequent stage during which plastic modifications of existing patterns are possible. The rules and mechanisms guiding these two phases need not be identical. For example, the work of Rakic (1977) and more recently Horton and Hocking (1996) demonstrates that geniculocortical afferents, which form the anatomical underpinning of ocular dominance columns, segregate into eye-specific stripes before birth and before any patterned visual experience is possible. Similarly, early work by Hubel and Wiesel in cats and monkeys (Hubel and Wiesel, 1963; Wiesel and Hubel, 1974) and more recent work in cats (Godecke and Bonhoeffer, 1996) demonstrate that orientation tuning and binocularly aligned maps of orientation columns develop in the absence of visual input.

It seems likely that the key to understanding how cortical architecture is first constructed is to understand how geniculocortical afferents are patterned within layer 4 of the developing cortex. Obviously the segregation of geniculocortical afferents into eye-specific stripes–the basis of ocular dominance columns–takes place in layer 4. In addition, however, there is good evidence that the spatial arrangement of geniculocortical afferents provides a basic outline of orientation selectivity in cortex (Chapman, Zahs, and Stryker, 1991; Ferster, Chung, and Wheat, 1996; Ferster and Koch, 1987; Reid and Alonso, 1995; Sompolinsky and Shapley, 1997). In modeling studies, developmental rules based on patterns of activity and local correlations can produce arrangements of geniculocortical inputs that mimic those actually observed (Linsker, 1986a, 1986b; Miller, 1994a;

Swindale, 1982, 1992). Ideally, therefore, one would like to know the actual patterns of activity in the output neurons of the developing thalamus and in layer 4 of cortex.

Spontaneous activity in the developing visual pathway

The realization that spontaneous activity in developing systems could provide cues necessary for anatomical rearrangements (Stryker and Harris, 1986) provided an important conceptual shift that helped resolve the apparent contradiction between the observation that cortical architecture emerged without visual experience and the observation that it could be modified by such experience. The importance of spontaneous activity has been demonstrated most clearly in the development of eye-specific layers in the cat lateral geniculate nucleus (LGN). Inputs from the two eyes initially overlap in the developing thalamus and gradually segregate into eye-specific layers well before birth. This segregation depends on neuronal activity: Pharmacologically silencing the thalamus or the eyes prevents segregation into separate layers (Sretavan and Shatz, 1986b; Sretavan, Shatz, and Stryker, 1988).

Experiments in the developing retina have provided the bulk of the data available regarding the patterns of spontaneous activity present along the developing visual pathway. In their pioneering experiments Maffei and Galli-Resta (1990) recorded from retinal ganglion cells in prenatal rat pups, using an ex utero preparation. Even before eye opening (and before photoreceptor cells were generated) they observed that retinal ganglion cells were producing regular, spontaneous bursts of action potentials, and that these bursts were highly correlated among nearby neurons. An extensive series of subsequent investigations by Shatz and colleagues used innovative combinations of multielectrode recordings and optical recordings in vitro to demonstrate that retinal activity actually consisted of local waves of activity propagating across limited portions of the retina. At any given time, a relatively small portion of the retina is spontaneously active, but over time the waves essentially "tile" the developing retina (Feller et al., 1997; Meister et al., 1991; Wong, Meister, and Shatz, 1993).

Because the two eyes have no direct connections between them, spontaneous, periodic waves in the two retinas create two independent oscillators. From the standpoint of correlation-based theories of axon segregation, this fact provides an ideal cue for segregating eye-specific layers in the LGN—the activity of groups of retinal ganglion cells from one eye will be well correlated with the activity of nearby cells, while the patterns of activity of groups of retinal ganglion cells from the other

eye will be essentially uncorrelated. In three-eyed frogs the uncorrelated patterns of activity in the normal and ectopic eyes are sufficient to drive segregation of retinotectal terminals into patterns greatly resembling ocular dominance columns (Constantine-Paton and Law, 1978; Law and Constantine-Paton, 1981; Reh and Constantine-Paton, 1985).

Theoretically, such uncorrelated patterns of activity would be ideal not only for segregating layers in the LGN, but also for segregating geniculocortical afferents into eye-specific stripes in layer 4 of the visual cortex. Recordings in rodents (Mooney et al., 1996) suggest that the patterns of waves observed in the retina cause thalamic neurons to fire in similar patterns, thus providing an obvious route for retinal waves to influence geniculocortical termination patterns.

However, despite the suggestive simplicity of such condition-based models, it is not always possible to predict the actual patterns of spontaneous activity driving the cortex in vivo by extrapolating from the patterns present in the retina in vitro. While patterns within the retina itself are immune to modification by connections with the rest of the central nervous system, patterns of spontaneous activity in the thalamus and cortex are shaped by retinal input and by local circuits within each structure, and by feedback connections between different regions. In the LGN, for example, retinal inputs provide only a small proportion—under 15%—of synaptic inputs (Guillery, 1969a, 1969b). Intrinsic GABAergic interneurons, inhibitory inputs from the thalamic reticular nucleus, and feedback connections from layer 6 of primary visual cortex comprise a significant proportion of the synapses. In addition, numerous other brainstem structures provide significant neuromodulatory inputs, especially acetylcholine but also noradrenaline and serotonin (see Sherman and Koch, 1998, for a recent review).

Thus, while it is convenient and appropriate to study spontaneous patterns of retinal activity in an in vitro model of the isolated retina, this approach cannot reveal the transformations that retinal activity may undergo at subsequent stages in the visual pathway. Hence it is important to determine the patterns of spontaneous activity in the developing thalamus in vivo.

Patterns of spontaneous activity in the developing thalamus in vivo

By using multielectrode extracellular recordings, it is possible to record spontaneous activity in the developing thalamus of awake, behaving ferrets (Weliky and Katz, in press). The ferret LGN has a stereotyped organization, with contralateral and ipsilateral inputs segregated into distinct layers (layers A and A1, respectively). Within each layer, retinal axons are segregated by response sub-type, such that ON-center and OFF-center ganglion cells terminate in distinct sublaminae. Thus, with an array of eight closely spaced microwires, spontaneous activity can be simultaneously recorded across eye- and response-type-specific layers. As these inputs are functional well before eye opening, visually evoked responses allow the exact location of each electrode to be determined.

Ferrets typically open their eyes around postnatal day 34. Cortical cells become visually responsive (although the eyes are still closed) by about day 21, and retinal waves are observed in vitro up until about day 30 (Wong, Meister, and Shatz, 1993). Recordings of spontaneous activity in awake, behaving ferrets in vivo between day 21 and 26 reveal robust, patterned spontaneous activity that superficially resembles the patterns of retinal activity observed in vitro. Activity consists of periodic, high-frequency bursts lasting several seconds, followed by 20–30 seconds of quiescence (figure 13.1). Interestingly, these patterns are observed only in unanesthetized animals. Even very low concentrations of inhalation anesthetics (such as isofluorane) completely abolish this spontaneous activity. However, the level and pattern of activity appear insensitive to the animal's overall behavioral state, and do not change dramatically whether the animals are quietly resting or actively exploring their environment.

As might be expected from patterns of retinal activity, analysis of the correlational structure of thalamic spontaneous activity showed that activity within each individual eye-specific layer was highly correlated. The highest correlations occurred between groups of neurons that shared inputs from the same eye and from the same retinal ganglion cell receptive field type (i.e., ON or OFF center). However, in addition to these expected types of correlations, significant binocular correlations were also observed, which were much too high to be generated by independent periodic events in the two retinas. Ablation of the ipsilateral visual cortex specifically abolished the binocular correlations, while leaving the within-eye correlations and patterned activity intact (figure 13.2).

Thalamocortical loops and the generation of patterned spontaneous activity

Most models of the development of cortical functional architecture are based on activity-dependent changes in synaptic connectivity that depend on the levels of correlation between competing groups of afferents. If one accepts this theoretical standpoint, developing thalamocortical axons must satisfy at least two constraints: inputs from the two eyes must be sufficiently uncorrelated such that they segregate into eye-specific domains (ocular dominance columns) yet have sufficient correlation such

that the maps of orientation selectivity are identical in the two eyes (Miller, 1994b; Swindale, 1992, 1996).

The patterns of spontaneous activity in the thalamus appear to meet these basic requirements. In particular, the requisite binocular correlations, which could potentially be generated via any number of local or extrinsic circuits, are specifically mediated by corticothalamic feedback. In the adult, the role of the layer 6 feedback connection to the thalamus has a long, rich, and controversial history. In some studies (Schmielau and Singer, 1977) this connection has been implicated in binocular visual processing and in establishing correlations between nearby cells (Sillito et al., 1994). These results from anesthetized adult animals, especially the role in binocular vision, are certainly consistent with the apparent role of corticothalamic feedback in neonatal animals.

Even in the absence of retinal inputs, the thalamocortical loop sustains robust spontaneous oscillatory activity. If both optic nerves are severed, leaving the thalamocortical connection intact, all spontaneous thalamic activity ceases for several hours. After this time, however, highly correlated, high-frequency bursts of action potentials return (Weliky and Katz, in press) (figure 13.3). Unlike bursts driven by retinal activity, these bursts are very highly correlated across eye-specific layers, although correlations within each eye-specific layer remain the strongest. Nevertheless, even in the absence of retinal input, including drive by retinal waves, highly structured periodic activity is generated. Although the isolated thalamus itself, later in life, sustains oscillatory activity (McCormick, Trent, and Ramoa, 1995), in these younger animals patterned activity results from thalamocortical interactions, as ablation of the cortex completely obliterated bursts. In the thalami of animals with both optic nerves cut and the ipsilateral cortex ablated, the remaining activity consists of isolated, random spikes with no detectable correlations between recording sites.

Thus removing the eyes does not eliminate patterned activity in the developing thalamocortical projection, but does dramatically alter its correlational structure, producing activity patterns in which the two eye-specific layers are much more correlated than normal. This observation is significant for interpreting further experiments on the development of cortical functional architecture, which will be discussed in later sections (see "Activity and the development of ocular dominance columns: A reconsideration").

A contralateral eye bias in patterning thalamic spontaneous activity

From the standpoint of activity in the two retinas, there is no reason to suspect differences in the level or pattern of

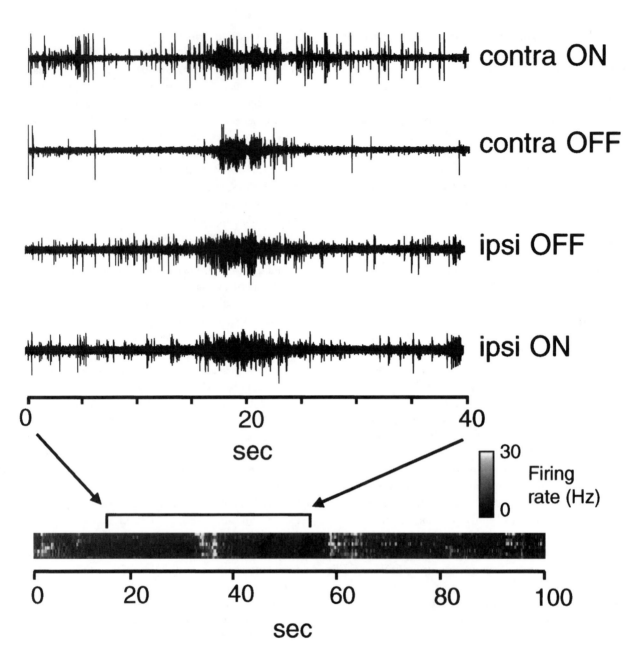

FIGURE 13.1 Spontaneous activity in the lateral geniculate nucleus (LGN) of an awake behaving ferret, approximately 1 week prior to eye opening. The top four traces show neural activity recorded on four different electrodes of an eight-electrode array. Each electrode is located in a different eye-specific LGN layer (ipsi: the eye on the same side as the recording array; contra: the eye contralateral to the array) and response-type-specific layer (i.e., ON center and OFF center), as identified by visual stimulation. Spontaneous activity consists of bursts of action potentials, lasting a few seconds, at roughly 20-second intervals. In the lower portion of the figure, the spike rate at each of the eight electrodes is represented in gray scale; in these time-series graphs bursts are apparent as zones of white. Within the 100-second-long recording illustrated, four bursts occurred. There are clear correlations in the firing patterns across all layers and receptive-field types, although the correlations are highest between electrodes of the same ocularity and receptive field subtype. (Modified from Weliky and Katz, in press.)

activity emerging from the two eyes. Yet there are reasons to suspect that the contributions of the two eyes in driving downstream circuits in the thalamus and cortex are not necessarily equal. For example, the first orientation-selective cells in the developing cortex are driven exclusively by the contralateral eye. Even more dramatically, optically imaged orientation maps are first observed only when the contralateral eye is stimulated, and these responding cells seem to be already grouped into zones—columns—of contralaterally dominated inputs, even when ipsilaterally driven responses are absent (Crair, Gillespie, and Stryker, 1998; Godecke et al., 1997).

In the thalamus, contralateral inputs from the retina reach the thalamus a few days before ipsilateral inputs,

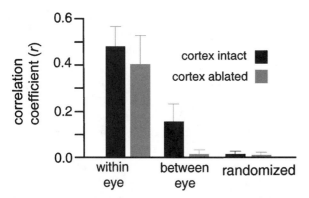

FIGURE 13.2 Histograms of the correlation coefficients in all experiments. With the ipsilateral cortex intact, the strongest correlations are between electrodes that share the same ocularity and receptive field subtype; however, highly significant correlations are present between the two eyes (compare "Between eye" to "Randomized," which shows the absence of correlations when these same spike trains are randomly shifted in time). Aspiration of the visual cortex specifically abolishes binocular correlations while leaving the within-eye correlations unaffected. (Modified from Weliky and Katz, in press.)

although the two sets spatially overlap prior to segregation of eye-specific layers. In recordings from older animals, activity patterns emerging from the contralateral eye dominate, and may in fact determine, the patterns of spontaneous activity in the thalamus (and by implication, in the cortex as well) (Weliky and Katz, in press). If the ipsilateral optic nerve is severed during the period of spontaneous bursting, the overall level and pattern of

spontaneous activity remains virtually unchanged. In contrast, if the contralateral optic nerve is cut, the pattern of activity in the thalamus rapidly assumes the temporal structure of spontaneous activity seen when both optic nerves are cut simultaneously (figure 13.3). Thus, the ipsilateral retinal ganglion cells appear incapable, on their own, of driving spontaneous activity in the thalamus. In the presence of ipsilateral retinal activity alone, the system is strongly dominated by the thalamocortical loop described earlier, and the resulting activity is highly correlated among all electrodes.

Although it is unclear how early this contralateral bias develops, it is in place before eye opening and well before segregation of ocular dominance columns. This bias at the level of the thalamus is probably the basis of the early development of contralateral visual responses in the cortex, and perhaps for the observations that ocular dominance columns representing the contralateral eye appear to be wider even in animals without visual experience (Tychsen and Burkhalter, 1997). As has been pointed out previously (Crair, Gillespie, and Stryker, 1998) this initial bias presents several significant challenges to the standard Hebbian models of ocular dominance column formation. According to current dogma, representations of the two eyes start out equivalent, as indicated by overlapping patterns of geniculocortical input from the two eye-specific layers (LeVay, Stryker, and Shatz, 1978; LeVay, Wiesel, and Hubel, 1980). By a correlation-based process of competition, involving

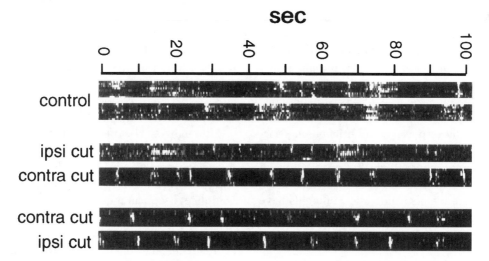

FIGURE 13.3 Time series graphs following manipulations of thalamic input. Under control conditions (top two panels), bursts occur approximately every 20 seconds and last for several seconds; usually only a subset of electrodes are active at any given time. Cutting the ipsilateral optic nerve (middle two panels) has virtually no effect on the pattern of bursting. When both optic nerves are severed, however, the pattern of LGN bursting changes dramatically: Now activity is observed on all electrodes during a burst; the bursts are shorter and occur more frequently

and regularly. Remarkably, these effects are not symmetric, for cutting the contralateral optic nerve first (bottom two panels) immediately causes the pattern of spontaneous activity to resemble that seen after severing both nerves. Cutting the ipsilateral optic nerve does not change the pattern further. Thus it appears that the bursting pattern is driven primarily by inputs from the contralateral optic nerve, and inputs from the ipsilateral optic nerve are by themselves incapable of driving thalamic activity. (Modified from Weliky and Katz, in press.)

strengthening of coactive inputs (presumably from the same eye) and weakening of uncorrelated inputs (from different eyes), ocular dominance stripes are thought to emerge gradually. However, if the inputs from the contralateral and ipsilateral eyes are not equivalent—and, specifically, if those from the contralateral eye are stronger—then it is difficult to account for segregation by a strictly Hebbian mechanism. According to such a mechanism, the stronger contralateral input should wrest territory from the ipsilateral inputs, which are unable to drive cells on their own. Since the contralateral inputs are stronger, earlier, there should be no opportunity for an ipsilateral input to develop. Since it clearly does, it appears that current understanding of the rules of activity-based development, based largely on Hebbian formulations involving long-term potentiation and depression (Kirkwood, Lee, and Bear, 1995; Kirkwood and Bear, 1994; Bear, Cooper, and Ebner, 1987) may not be directly applicable to the initial establishment of columns.

Once the two eyes have established the outlines of their respective territories, however, ipsilateral inputs catch up to contralateral inputs in their ability to drive cells, and the two inputs become roughly equivalent (Crair, Gillespie, and Stryker, 1998). At this point, imbalances in activity, or changes in its correlational structure, do modify cortical representations by a process that is consistent with Hebbian theories. The classic experiments of Hubel and Wiesel on the effects of eyelid closure (Hubel and Wiesel, 1970; Wiesel and Hubel, 1965a, 1965b) were done primarily during this period. Thus it is likely that the rules governing the plasticity of established (or nearly established) ocular dominance columns may be quite different from those that drive the initial formation of the segregated pattern. From this perspective, it is intriguing that Hubel and Wiesel noted that the critical period for modifying ocular dominance columns by visual experience did not begin before 3 weeks postnatal in the cat, although neurons were visually responsive and orientation selective for at least 1 week before this point. This finding suggests that the forces controlling the distribution of geniculocortical afferents are indifferent to changes in activity patterns before the geniculocortical afferents have begun segregating into stripes, a process which is well under way by 3 weeks postnatal.

Activity and the development of orientation selectivity

Neurons in the primary visual cortex are well tuned to respond to lines and bars of particular orientations. Orientation-selective neurons are grouped together into orientation columns, and, across the tangential extent of cortex, orientation selectivity is continuously repre-

sented in an orderly pattern. A substantial body of evidence supports Hubel and Wiesel's original theory (Hubel and Wiesel, 1962) for generating orientation selectivity via the summation of center-surround receptive fields of geniculocortical afferents. Although substantial sharpening of orientation tuning occurs via local cortical circuits (Douglas and Martin, 1991; Ringach, Hawken, and Shapley, 1997; Somers, Nelson, and Sua, 1995; Sompolinsky and Shapley, 1997), there is general agreement that at least a crude bias for particular orientations is formed in layer 4 by the termination patterns of geniculocortical afferents (Chapman, Zahs, and Stryker, 1991; Ferster, Chung, and Wheat, 1996; Reid and Alonso, 1995). Thus, the development of this central aspect of central visual processing architecture, like the development of ocular dominance columns, is at its heart an issue of how geniculocortical afferents acquire a specific termination pattern in layer 4.

Unlike the development of ocular dominance columns, the development of orientation selectivity has never been tightly linked to visual experience. Monkeys have fully developed orientation columns at birth (Wiesel and Hubel, 1974). Oriented neurons are present in cats immediately after eye opening, leading Hubel and Wiesel to posit that orientation tuning was a "genetically" determined property (Hubel and Wiesel, 1963). Manipulations of visual experience (such as stripe rearing) can lead to the selective preservation of certain oriented responses, but do not underlay their initial specification, nor allow respecification of a given neuron's orientation preference (Stryker et al., 1978). Moreover, even if the two eyes have completely unrelated patterns of visual experience (accomplished by alternating lid suture), the patterns of orientation maps driven by each eye are in perfect register—implying that correlated experience is not necessary for alignment (Godecke and Bonhoeffer, 1996).

Although visual experience is almost certainly not involved in creating orientation maps, the role of spontaneous neuronal activity is less clear. Silencing the cortex with pharmacological manipulations leads to an almost complete disappearance of oriented neurons (Chapman and Stryker, 1993). However, such manipulations do not distinguish between instructive and permissive roles of spontaneous neuronal activity. For example, neurons may simply need to be active to some degree in order to grow axon collaterals or to be able to read molecular signals present in the cellular environment. In this case, the amount of activity may be important, but the exact patterns less so. Conversely, if activity is instructive, then the temporal structure of patterned activity, such as the patterns of correlations between different neurons, should carry important information.

In either scenario, silencing the cortex would induce alterations. However, manipulations that alter the pattern of activity can distinguish between permissive and instructive roles: If activity is permissive, then changing the patterns, without changing levels, should have little effect, whereas if activity is instructive, changing the patterns should greatly alter the outcome. For technical reasons, there have been few attempts to alter patterns of endogenous, spontaneous activity during the relevant developmental windows.

Exogenous patterned activity and the development of orientation tuning and maps

As the preceding discussion has demonstrated, the most likely sources of spontaneous, patterned activity in the developing visual pathway are retinal waves (especially in the contralateral retina) and the thalamocortical circuits activated by them. Are such activity patterns instructive or permissive? Based on a limited number of technically challenging experiments, the answer seems to be both: Depending on the cortical layer, central disruption of retinal activity patterns has little effect on orientation tuning in layer 4, while orientation tuning outside this layer is greatly compromised.

This assertion is based on experiments in which cuff electrodes were chronically implanted around the optic nerve of neonatal ferrets (Weliky and Katz, 1997). Stimulation was applied to the entire nerve every 20 seconds for up to two weeks, beginning well before eye opening and during the period that retinal waves are still present. The idea of this paradigm was to massively synchronize the patterned activity in the visual pathway, thereby overriding any local correlations or patterns that the system might be using to set up orientation domains. Conceptually this experiment resembles strobe-rearing experiments (Cynader, Berman, and Hein, 1973; Schmidt and Buzzard, 1993), in which synchronized visually evoked activity was used to manipulate the correlational structure of activity. Using cuff stimulation, however, this could be done at a time prior to the initial establishment of orientation (and ocular dominance) columns.

The effects of massively correlating the geniculocortical input were striking. In the upper and lower layers of cortex, orientation tuning was sharply decreased compared to both normal animals and animals with cuff implants that were not stimulated (figure 13.4). Although almost all neurons showed some orientation bias, the distribution of tuning strengths in the stimulated animals was similar to that of neurons recorded from immature ferrets prior to eye opening. However, in layer 4—the site of geniculocortical afferent termination, and the presumed site where orientation selectivity is first gener-

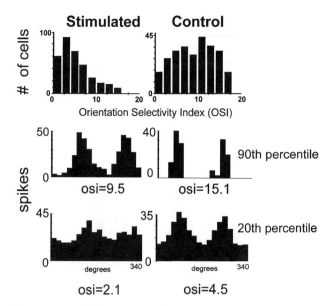

FIGURE 13.4   Effects of chronic optic nerve stimulation on orientation selectivity in ferret visual cortex. For each of several hundred neurons recorded in stimulated or control animals, an orientation selectivity index (OSI) was calculated. Stimulation resulted in a dramatic reduction in orientation selectivity, as manifested by a marked shift in orientation selectivity to lower numbers (<10). The lower four histograms show individual tuning curves to give some indication of the magnitude of this effect. Neurons in the 90th percentile of selectivity were very sharply tuned in control animals, and even cells in the 20th percentile were clearly orientation selective. In contrast, even the best tuned neurons in the stimulated animals were broadly tuned, and those in the 20th percentile were only weakly orientation selective. (Adapted from Weliky and Katz, 1997.)

ated—there was no difference in orientation tuning strength (figure 13.5). In normal ferrets (and cats) cells in layer 4 have weaker orientation tuning than cells in the upper and lower layers, presumably due to contributions of intrinsic circuits outside of layer 4 to tuning. The finding that tuning in layer 4 was largely immune to large changes in the correlational structure of activity suggests that the mechanisms that initially pattern orientation tuning may differ from those that fine-tune this property.

This difference between establishment of tuning and its refinement is highlighted by another finding: In the chronically stimulated animals, the overall map of orientation selectivity is unaltered (Weliky and Katz, 1997). In normal animals, optically imaged maps of orientation selectivity show a complex pattern in which orientation selectivity changes smoothly around singularities called pinwheels (Bonhoeffer and Grinvald, 1991). In stimulated animals, the size, shape, spacing, and organization of orientation-selective domains are normal. The only difference is that the strength of orientation selectivity in any given zone is weaker than normal, reflecting the decreased tuning strength seen on a single-cell level.

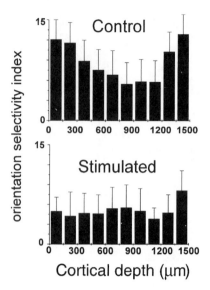

FIGURE 13.5   Effects of laminar position on orientation selectivity in chronically stimulated animals. In normal animals (top histogram) the most sharply tuned neurons are located in the upper and lower layers; layer 4 neurons (roughly 700–1100 μm deep) are much less well tuned. In the stimulated cortex, all neurons exhibited roughly the orientation selectivity seen in layer 4. These results imply that chronic stimulation degraded orientation selectivity outside of layer 4 but not within layer 4, perhaps via effects on local circuits in the layers above and below layer 4. (Adapted from Weliky and Katz, 1997.)

The resistance of layer 4 orientation tuning and overall orientation maps to massive manipulations of activity can be interpreted in a number of ways. Such resistance may simply reflect the fact that manipulations that begin later in the neonatal period may simply be too late. In the case of the experiments described here, activity was altered beginning at postnatal day 25, which, although prior to the time at which orientation maps or selective cells can be seen, is still 10 days after geniculocortical afferents have arrived in layer 4. Thus it is possible that patterns of spontaneous activity at very early ages construct the initial pattern of orientation maps. Numerous theoretical models are consistent with such an assertion. However, at these later stages, activity seems to act permissively, rather than instructively, for maintaining orientation in layer 4 and the basic outline of orientation maps.

Molecular patterning and the establishment of orientation maps

Alternatively, the organization of geniculocortical afferents in layer 4 may be accomplished by entirely different mechanisms. Hubel and Wiesel actually proposed (at a time when much less was known) that orientation selectivity was genetically programmed (Hubel and

Wiesel, 1963). In more modern parlance, this suggestion would be equivalent to proposing that a set of molecular cues present in layer 4, on geniculocortical afferents, or in both could guide the initial formation of orientation maps. Is it really conceivable that a set of such cues (perhaps acting in concert with ongoing activity) could pattern a system as complex as orientation selectivity?

The molecular intricacies of pattern formation during development elsewhere in the animal kingdom make this proposal at least plausible. Extensive experimentation in butterflies has shown that the intricate patterns in this epithelial tissue can be derived by interactions among a very limited number of diffusible morphogens (Nijhout, 1991). The patterning of body segments, cell fates, and epithelial patterns in vertebrates and invertebrates, which are of sometimes startling complexity, have come to be understood as interactions between relatively small numbers of cell-surface and diffusible molecules whose distribution and timing are critical (see Lumsden and Krumlauf, 1996; Tanabe and Jessell, 1996, for recent reviews). In the nervous system, topographic mapping is determined by a small number of ligands and receptors with graded distributions in inputs and targets (Cheng et al., 1995). And perhaps most strikingly, the extraordinarily specific connections between the olfactory epithelium and the olfactory bulb rely on perhaps hundreds of distinct molecular cues that guide spatially scattered receptors to terminate within a single glomerulus (Wang et al., 1998). Neuronal activity appears unimportant in this system (Belluscio et al., 1998). Thus the complexity of the orientation map alone is not a sufficient argument for discarding a molecular mapping strategy. Virtually all experimental approaches to date have manipulated activity, and there has been little effort to design experiments to reveal possible molecular cues that this system could use. If such cues are indeed present, it is likely that they will be transient and present at very early times in development, perhaps when geniculocortical afferents are still arriving.

Activity and the development of ocular dominance columns: A reconsideration

Earlier in this chapter a clear distinction was made between the initial establishment of ocular dominance columns and their subsequent plasticity. Though a long tradition of experimental evidence supports the notion that activity plays an instructive role in ocular dominance plasticity (Chapman et al., 1986; Gu, Bear, and Singer, 1989; Kleinschmidt, Bear, and Singer, 1987; Reiter, Waitzman, and Stryker, 1986; Stryker and Harris, 1986; Wiesel and Hubel, 1965b), much less is known about activity's roles during their initial establishment. The issue of distinguishing instructive ver-

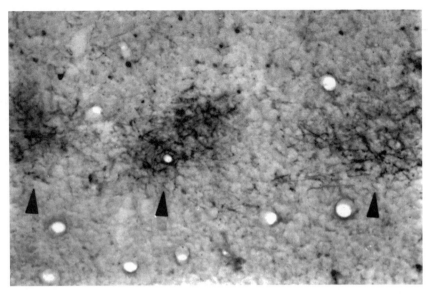

FIGURE 13.6 Segregation of geniculocortical axons into columns in the absence of the eyes. In an animal enucleated at postnatal day 15 (just after thalamic afferents have arrived in layer 4) and allowed to survive until postnatal day 70, injection of an anterograde tracer into one layer of the LGN reveals clearly segregated patches of terminals in layer 4 of visual cortex. These patches have a center-to-center spacing of about 500 μm, indistinguishable from the patches seen in normal animals. Thus thalamic afferents can segregate without any input from the retina, suggesting that cues present in the thalamus, cortex, or both are sufficient to establish segregated columns. (From J. C. Crowley and L. C. Katz, unpublished results.)

sus permissive roles of activity has been discussed, and the same arguments hold for examining ocular dominance columns. Simply silencing either the retina or the cortex implicates neuronal activity in the development of these connections, but such a manipulation cannot determine whether activity patterns are important and, by implication, whether Hebbian or other correlation-based mechanisms are at work.

The results of recordings in neonatal ferret thalamus provided an intriguing hint of an experimental approach for specifically manipulating correlational patterns without significantly disrupting activity levels in the developing visual system. Recall that when both optic nerves were severed in a neonatal ferret, a new pattern of spontaneous activity emerged, driven by the thalamocortical loop (figure 13.3) (Weliky and Katz, 1998). The result of severing the optic nerves was a dramatic increase in correlation of activity in the two eye-specific layers. Thus, in contrast to normal animals, in which the correlations between eye-specific layers were relatively low, in enucleated animals the correlations between the two LGN layers were much higher.

Under such circumstances, can geniculocortical afferents still segregate into eye-specific stripes—the equivalent of ocular dominance columns? Remarkably, they can. Both anterograde and retrograde tracing experiments reveal that in animals binocularly enucleated at P15 (just after geniculocortical afferents have reached layer 4) and examined at P70 (after the close of the criti-

cal period) geniculocortical afferents segregate into eye-specific zones with a periodicity and precision indistinguishable from normal control animals (figure 13.6) (J. C. Crowley and L. C. Katz, unpublished results).

One obvious implication of such a finding is that continuous presence of patterns of activity originating from the retina, whether spontaneous or evoked, are not required for segregation of geniculocortical afferents. What is critical, however, is that removing the eyes is not equivalent to silencing the remaining portions of the visual pathway: In vivo recordings amply demonstrate that enucleation induces a new pattern of spontaneous activity whose correlational structure is very different from normal. In contrast, binocular injections of tetrodotoxin completely silence the thalamus and cortex (Stryker and Harris, 1986). In this case, the silencing of the system prevents or delays emergence of ocular dominance columns. Although it is certainly possible that the patterns of activity in the enucleated animals retain sufficient correlational structure to allow afferents to segregate using Hebbian mechanisms, another interpretation is that neurons must simply be active in a specific pattern in order to express or access molecular cues.

Many features of cortical architecture appear to emerge in enucleated animals. In primates, early enucleation does not prevent normal synaptogenesis (Bourgeois and Rakic, 1996), the differentiation of cortical layers, the laminar-specific organization of monaminergic receptor systems (Rakic and Lidow, 1995), or the appearance of cytochrome oxidase blobs (Kuljis and Rakic, 1990). In the experiments in ferrets described earlier, enucleation also did not prevent appearance of clustered horizontal connections in the upper layers of striate cortex (J. C. Crowley and L. C. Katz, unpublished observations). Similar experiments (Ruthazer and Stryker, 1996) done at somewhat later ages showed similar results. In normal adult animals, such clusters link orientation columns that share orientation preference. The fact that clustered connections can emerge entirely independent of retinal activity, and in the presence of highly correlated thalamic activity, further strengthens the idea that the circuitry involved in orientation tuning may also develop without reference to correlation-based cues.

Investigations in a number of systems, including developing neurons, have shown that periodic patterns of activity produce distinct patterns of intracellular calcium fluxes that in themselves determine patterns of gene expression. This relationship has been clearly shown in developing *Xenopus* spinal cord neurons. Different frequencies of calcium-mediated events–"spikes" versus "waves"–regulate distinct aspects of neuronal differentiation (Gu and Spitzer, 1995). For example, calcium waves appeared to regulate neurite extension, whereas spikes mediated changes in excitability and transmitter expression. In fact, periodic bursts of activity are a ubiquitous feature of neuronal development: Not only are waves present during the development of the retina in all vertebrate species examined thus far (including ferrets, mice, chickens, and turtles), but oscillations with similar properties are also present in the developing spinal cord (Ho and O'Donovan, 1993; O'Donovan, 1989), cortex (Yuste, Peinado, and Katz, 1992), and substantia nigra (Christie, Williams, and North, 1989). In systems like the substantia nigra there is little reason to suspect that the correlational structure of activity is critical, implying that such periodic bursts are critical to the differentiation of the neurons, rather than for providing a substrate for Hebbian segregation (Gu and Spitzer, 1997; Spitzer, Olson, and Gu, 1995).

In the specific context of normal ocular dominance column development, then, one can imagine retinal waves and the patterned downstream activity they induce as having at least two potential roles. The first is the conventional view in this field, namely that the specifics of pre- and postsynaptic correlation patterns critically determine the development of specific patterns of connections. An alternative, albeit extreme, view is that patterns of activity are critical for inducing specific patterns of gene expression and cell differentiation, but that the details of correlations between cells are not carrying instructive information. In this view, bursting in a given

cell is critical for activating important genetic programs, but whether a cell is bursting in concert with neighbors in the same or different layers is irrelevant. Thus, in animals with no eyes, even though correlations between layers are high, all cells are undergoing periodic intracellular calcium fluxes, which enable them to express and decode cues necessary for ocular dominance column formation.

The NMDA receptor may play a critical role in modulating these calcium fluxes. Early in cortical development, this receptor appears to be the dominant glutamate receptor, and the voltage-dependent magnesium block appears to be considerably weaker. Thus, the NMDA receptor may function less as a correlation detector and more as a conduit for periodic calcium fluxes. Blocking this receptor could therefore inhibit initial column formation not by blocking correlated activity per se, but by blocking the calcium oscillations necessary to elicit expression or detection of specific molecular cues. Thus the failure of columns to form in the complete absence of activity can be interpreted not as an elimination of correlations, but as an elimination of this critical permissive cue.

Of course, this view is based on a very limited number of experimental findings. And there are certain observations that flatly contradict the notion that molecular cues are required for segregation of functionally distinct groups of axons. The most compelling of these comes from experiments in three-eyed frogs. In this system, when retinotectal axons from two eyes are forced to innervate a single optic tectum, they segregate in an activity-dependent (and NMDA-receptor-dependent) fashion. The frog optic tectum is normally innervated exclusively by the contralateral retina, so it is absurd to propose that there exists some stripelike endogenous cue for either of the two eyes. However, the fact that correlated activity in frogs *can* induce stripe formation does not mean that the identical mechanism *must* be responsible in the cortex of mammals. Stripes in epithelial structures (and neurons are epithelial in origin) are a general solution to many different biological constraints, and the finding of correlation-based stripes in the frog optic tectum does not prove that stripes in striate cortex have the same mechanistic underpinnings.

The finding of a contralateral bias also indirectly strengthens the notion that molecular cues may be involved. Why do stronger contralateral inputs not take over the inactive areas that later are dominated by ipsilateral inputs? Perhaps some patterned cell surface cue specific to contralaterally derived axons prevents ingrowth. Contralateral inputs are derived from the nasal part of the retina, and the demarcation between nasal and temporal retina is set up very early in development and is almost certainly determined by intrinsic molecular cues. It is not too difficult to imagine that the cues that distinguish nasal and temporal retina can be utilized throughout the visual pathway. Guidance molecules, such as the semaphorins, exist in many different varieties, and have been shown to distinguish between closely related axons in a variety of brain structures (Goodman, 1994). Indeed there are suggestions that even at the level of the LGN, there exist intrinsic molecular cues that can pattern the terminal arbors of retinal axons (Miessirel et al., 1997; Sretavan and Shatz, 1986a).

Molecular signals for cortical functional architecture

For many years, the emphasis of research on the development of cortical architecture has been heavily influenced by the finding that correlation-based, long-term changes in synaptic efficacy, such as LTP and LTD, can be elicited in the developing (and mature) thalamus and visual cortex (Bear, 1995; Bear and Kirkwood, 1993; Bear and Malenka, 1994; Kirkwood and Bear, 1994; Kirkwood, Lee, and Bear, 1995; Mooney, Madison, and Shatz, 1993). Most work has been premised on the belief that such alterations must be largely responsible for structural plasticity in this system. Far less attention has been devoted to the possibility that molecular maps may in some way prefigure the eventual architecture of visual cortex.

Nevertheless, there have been occasional intriguing reports of molecular patterns that are present before architecture is fully formed. For example, in the developing cat visual cortex, specific classes of serotonin receptors form striking, periodic columns with the center-to-center spacing of ocular dominance columns (Dyck and Cynader, 1993b). Such periodicity is difficult to reconcile with the accepted wisdom (required for most correlation-based models of ocular dominance column formation) that all the territory in layer 4 (along with the inputs from the two eye-specific geniculate layers) is functionally equivalent. Zinc (associated with synaptic terminals), cytochrome oxidase (a metabolic marker), and acetylcholinesterase are also distributed in complex, frequently interdigitating patterns (Dyck, Beaulieu, and Cynader, 1993; Dyck and Cynader, 1993a). As early as 2 weeks postnatal, Trepel and colleagues (1998) observed a nonuniform distribution of the NMDA-receptor–immunoreactive neurons, suggesting that certain loci in the early developing cortex are more susceptible to modification by activity.

However, most of these molecules are likely to be downstream of even earlier signals. Neurons in the developing cortex acquire their laminar identity while still in the ventricular zone (McConnell, 1988). In ferrets,

layer 4 neurons reach the cortical plate around postnatal day 10 and geniculocortical afferents arrive soon after (Jackson, Peduzzi, and Hickey, 1989). Cues may also be present in the developing subplate, an early-generated population of neurons that receive a transient connection from the thalamus. Ablation of this population prevents ocular dominance column formation (Ghosh and Shatz, 1994), so it is conceivable that the markers distinguishing ipsilateral and contralateral inputs from the LGN could be present soon after the very first cells of the cortex are postmitotic. There has been little effort—and, until recently, little motivation—to examine whether guidance molecules are inhomogeneously distributed in the cortical plate at such early stages.

Another possible source of cues resides in the retina. There is clear evidence that at least some of the functional segregation that occurs in the developing LGN is based on molecular distinctions and not activity alone. For example, M and P pathways in the primate emerge without significant overlap in the LGN, and this distinction appears to emerge as soon as the respective retinal ganglion cells complete their last division (Miessirel et al., 1997). As discussed previously, retinal ganglion cells in nasal and temporal retina are almost certainly molecularly distinct, and these are the sources of the ipsilateral and contralateral inputs to the LGN. Using modern molecular techniques such as subtraction or differential display, it may be possible to get some hints about the signaling pathways involved in distinguishing these two pathways beginning at the retina.

Conclusions

The currently accepted view of the development of cortical architecture relies heavily on correlation-based mechanisms involving the NMDA receptor and phenomena such as LTP and LTD. While there is little question that activity at some level is crucial for the plasticity of cortical connections, there is a small but growing body of evidence that the initial establishment of cortical architecture may utilize activity in a very different context. Moreover, by analogy with other developing systems, there are reasons to suspect that as-yet-undiscovered molecular cues may frame the detailed connectivity of the developing visual system. Rather than designing more experiments to ratify the existing dogma of correlation-dependent mechanisms, it may be time to design approaches to determine whether such molecular cues indeed exist.

ACKNOWLEDGMENTS Several of the experiments from our laboratory described here were supported in part by National Institutes of Health (National Eye Institute) grant EY07960.

REFERENCES

BEAR, M. F., 1995. Mechanism for a sliding synaptic modification threshold. *Neuron* 15:1–4.

BEAR, M. F., L. N. COOPER, and F. F. EBNER, 1987. A physiological basis for a theory of synapse modification. *Science* 237:42–48.

BEAR, M. F., and A. KIRKWOOD, 1993. Neocortical long-term potentiation. *Curr. Opin. Neurobiol.* 3:197–202.

BEAR, M. F., and R. C. MALENKA, 1994. Synaptic plasticity: LTP and LTD. *Curr. Opin. Neurobiol.* 4:389–399.

BELLUSCIO, L., G. H. GOLD, A. NEMES, and R. AXEL, 1998. Mice deficient in G(olf) are anosmic. *Neuron* 20:69–81.

BONHOEFFER, T., and A. GRINVALD, 1991. Iso-orientation domains in cat visual cortex are arranged in pinwheel-like patterns. *Nature* 353:429–431.

BOURGEOIS, J. P., and P. RAKIC, 1996. Synaptogenesis in the occipital cortex of macaque monkey devoid of retinal input from early embryonic stages. *Eur. J. Neurosci.* 8:942–950.

CHAPMAN, B., M. D. JACOBSON, H. O. REITER, and M. P. STRYKER, 1986. Ocular dominance shift in kitten visual cortex caused by imbalance in retinal electrical activity. *Nature* 324:154–156.

CHAPMAN, B., and M. P. STRYKER, 1993. Development of orientation selectivity in ferret visual cortex and effects of deprivation. *J. Neurosci.* 13:5251–5262.

CHAPMAN, B., K. R. ZAHS, and M. P. STRYKER, 1991. Relation of cortical cell orientation selectivity to alignment of receptive fields of the geniculocortical afferents that arborize within a single orientation column in ferret visual cortex. *J. Neurosci.* 11:1347–1358.

CHENG, H.-J., M. NAKAMOTO, A. D. BERGMANN, and J. G. FLANAGAN, 1995. Complimentary gradients in expression and binding of ELF-1 and Mek4 in development of the topographic retinotectal projection map. *Cell* 82:371–381.

CHRISTIE, M. J., J. T. WILLIAMS, and R. A. NORTH, 1989. Electrical coupling synchronizes subthreshold activity in locus coeruleus neurons in vitro from neonatal rats. *J. Neurosci.* 9:3584–3589.

CONSTANTINE-PATON, M., and M. I. LAW, 1978. Eye-specific termination bands in tecta of three-eyed frogs. *Science* 202:639–641.

CRAIR, M. C., D. C. GILLESPIE, and M. P. STRYKER, 1998. The role of visual experience in the development of columns in cat visual cortex. *Science* 279:566–570.

CROWLEY, J. C., and L. C. KATZ, in press. Segregation of geniculocortical afferents in the absence of retinal input. *Soc. Neurosci. Abstr.*

CYNADER, M., N. BERMAN, and A. HEIN, 1973. Cats reared in stroboscopic illumination: Effects on receptive fields in visual cortex. *Proc. Natl. Acad. Sci. U.S.A.* 70:1353–1354.

DOUGLAS, R. J., and K. A. C. MARTIN, 1991. A functional microcircuit for cat visual cortex. *J. Physiol.* 440:735–769.

DYCK, R., C. BEAULIEU, and M. CYNADER, 1993. Histochemical localization of synaptic zinc in the developing cat visual cortex. *J. Comp. Neurol.* 329:53–67.

DYCK, R., and M. CYNADER, 1993a. An interdigitated columnar mosaic of cytochrome oxidase, zinc, and neurotransmitter-related molecules in cat and monkey visual cortex. *Proc. Natl. Acad. Sci. U.S.A.* 90:9066–9069.

DYCK, R., and M. S. CYNADER, 1993b. Autoradiographic localization of serotonin receptor subtypes in cat visual cortex:

Transient regional, laminar, and columnar distributions during postnatal development. *J. Neurosci.* 13:4316–4338.

FELLER, M. B., D. A. BUTTS, H. L. AARON, D. S. ROKHSAR, and C. J. SHATZ, 1997. Dynamic processes shape spatiotemporal properties of retinal waves. *Neuron* 19:293–306.

FERSTER, D., S. CHUNG, and H. WHEAT, 1996. Orientation selectivity of thalamic input to simple cells of cat visual cortex. *Nature* 380:249–252.

FERSTER, D., and C. KOCH, 1987. Neuronal connections underlying orientation selectivity in cat visual cortex. *Trends Neurosci.* 10:487–492.

GHOSH, A. and C. SHATZ, 1994. Segregation of geniculocortical afferents during the critical period: A role for subplate neurons. *J. Neurosci.* 14:3862–3880.

GODECKE, I., and T. BONHOEFFER, 1996. Development of identical orientation maps for two eyes without common visual experience. *Nature* 379:251–254.

GODECKE, I., D. S. KIM, T. BONHOEFFER, and W. SINGER, 1997. Development of orientation preference maps in area 18 of kitten visual cortex. *Eur. J. Neurosci.* 9:1754–1762.

GOODMAN, C. S., 1994. The likeness of being: Phylogenetically conserved molecular mechanisms of growth cone guidance. *Cell* 78:353–356.

GU, Q. A., M. F. BEAR, and W. SINGER, 1989. Blockade of NMDA-receptors prevents ocularity changes in kitten visual cortex after reversed monocular deprivation. *Dev. Brain Res.* 47:281–288.

GU, X., and N. C. SPITZER, 1995. Distinct aspects of neuronal differentiation encoded by frequency of spontaneous Ca^{2+} transients. *Nature* 375:784–787.

GU, X., and N. C. SPITZER, 1997. Breaking the code: Regulation of neuronal differentiation by spontaneous calcium transients. *Dev. Neurosci.* 19:33–41.

GUILLERY, R. W., 1969a. The organization of synaptic interconnections in the laminae of the dorsal lateral geniculate nucleus of the cat. *Z. Zellforsch. Mikrosk. Anat.* 96:1–38.

GUILLERY, R. W., 1969b. A quantitative study of synaptic interconnections in the dorsal lateral geniculate nucleus of the adult cat. *Z. Zellforsch. Mikrosk. Anat.* 96:39–48.

HO, S., and M. J. O'DONOVAN, 1993. Regionalization and intersegmental coordination of rhythm-generating networks in the spinal cord of the chick embryo. *J. Neurosci.* 13:1354–1371.

HORTON, J. C., and D. R. HOCKING, 1996. An adult-like pattern of ocular dominance columns in striate cortex of newborn monkeys prior to visual experience. *J. Neurosci.* 16:1791–1807.

HUBEL, D. H., and T. N. WIESEL, 1962. Receptive fields, binocular interaction and functional architecture in the cat's visual cortex. *J. Physiol.* 160:106–154.

HUBEL, D. H., and T. N. WIESEL, 1963. Receptive fields of cells in striate cortex of very young, visually inexperienced kittens. *J. Neurophysiol.* 26:994–1002.

HUBEL, D. H., and T. N. WIESEL, 1965. Binocular interaction in striate cortex of kittens reared with artificial squint. *J. Neurophysiol.* 28:1041–1059.

HUBEL, D. H., and T. N. WIESEL, 1970. The period of susceptibility to the physiological effects of unilateral eye closure in kittens. *J. Physiol.* 206:419–436.

JACKSON, C. A., J. D. PEDUZZI, and T. L. HICKEY, 1989. Visual cortex development in the ferret. I. Genesis and migration of visual cortical neurons. *J. Neurosci.* 9:1242–1253.

KIRKWOOD, A., and M. F. BEAR, 1994. Hebbian synapses in visual cortex. *J. Neurosci.* 14:1634–1645.

KIRKWOOD, A., H. K. LEE, and M. F. BEAR, 1995. Coregulation of long-term potentiation and experience-dependent synaptic plasticity in visual cortex by age and experience. *Nature* 375:328–331.

KLEINSCHMIDT, A., M. F. BEAR, and W. SINGER, 1987. Blockade of "NMDA" receptors disrupts experience dependent plasticity of kitten striate cortex. *Science* 238:355–358.

KULJIS, R., and P. RAKIC, 1990. Hypercolumns in primate visual cortex can develop in the absence of cues from photoreceptors. *Proc. Natl. Acad. Sci. U.S.A.* 87:5303–5306.

LAW, M. I., and M. CONSTANTINE-PATON, 1981. Anatomy and physiology of experimentally produced striped tecta. *J. Neurosci.* 1:741–759.

LEVAY, S., M. P. STRYKER, and C. J. SHATZ, 1978. Ocular dominance columns and their development in layer IV of the cat's visual cortex: A quantitative study. *J. Comp. Neurol.* 179:223–244.

LEVAY, S., T. N. WIESEL, and D. H. HUBEL, 1980. The development of ocular dominance columns in normal and visually deprived monkeys. *J. Comp. Neurol.* 191:1–51.

LINSKER, R., 1986a. From basic network principles to neural architecture: Emergence of orientation columns. *Proc. Natl. Acad. Sci. U.S.A.* 83:8779–8783.

LINSKER, R., 1986b. From basic network principles to neural architecture: Emergence of orientation-selective cells. *Proc. Natl. Acad. Sci. U.S.A.* 83:8390–8394.

LUMSDEN, A., and R. KRUMLAUF, 1996. Patterning the vertebrate neuraxis. *Science* 274:1109–1115.

MAFFEI, L., and L. GALLI-RESTA, 1990. Correlation in the discharges of neighboring rat retinal ganglion cells during prenatal life. *Proc. Natl. Acad. Sci. U.S.A.* 87:2861–2864.

MCCONNELL, S. K., 1988. Fates of visual cortical neurons in the ferret after isochronic and heterochronic transplantation. *J. Neurosci.* 8:945–974.

MCCORMICK, D. A., F. TRENT, and A. S. RAMOA, 1995. Postnatal development of synchronized network oscillations in the ferret dorsal lateral geniculate and perigeniculate nuclei. *J. Neurosci.* 15:5739–5752.

MEISTER, M., R. O. L. WONG, D. A. BAYLOR, and C. J. SHATZ, 1991. Synchronous bursts of action potentials in ganglion cells of the developing mammalian retina. *Science* 252:939–943.

MIESSIREL, C., K. C. WIKLER, L. M. CHALUPA, and P. RAKIC, 1997. Early divergence of magnocellular and parvocellular functional subsystems in the embryonic primate visual system. *Proc. Natl. Acad. Sci. U.S.A.* 94:5900–5905.

MILLER, K. D., 1994a. A model for the development of simple cell receptive fields and the ordered arrangement of orientation columns through activity-dependent competition between ON- and OFF-center inputs. *J. Neurosci.* 14:409–441.

MILLER, K. D., 1994b. Models of activity-dependent neural development. *Prog. Brain Res.* 102:303–318.

MOONEY, R., D. V. MADISON, and C. J. SHATZ, 1993. Enhancement of transmission at the developing retinogeniculate synapse. *Neuron* 10:815–825.

MOONEY, R., A. A. PENN, R. GALLEGO, and C. J. SHATZ, 1996. Thalamic relay of spontaneous retinal activity prior to vision. *Neuron* 17:863–874.

NIJHOUT, H. F., 1991. *The Development and Evolution of Butterfly Wing Patterns.* Washington, D.C.: Smithsonian Institution Press.

O'DONOVAN, M. J., 1989. Motor activity in the isolated spinal cord of the chick embryo: Synaptic drive and firing pattern of single motoneurons. *J. Neurosci.* 9:943–958.

RAKIC, P., 1977. Prenatal development of the visual system in rhesus monkey. *Philos. Trans. R. Soc. Lond. B. Biol. Sci.* 278:245–260.

RAKIC, P., and M. S. LIDOW, 1995. Distribution and density of monoamine receptors in the primate visual cortex devoid of retinal input from early embryonic stages. *J. Neurosci.* 15:2561–2574.

REH, T. A., and M. CONSTANTINE-PATON, 1985. Eye-specific segregation requires neural activity in three-eyed *Rana pipiens. J. Neurosci.* 5:1132–1143.

REID, R. C., and J. M. ALONSO, 1995. Specificity of monosynaptic connections from thalamus to visual cortex. *Nature* 378:281–284.

REITER, H. O., D. M. WAITZMAN, and M. P. STRYKER, 1986. Cortical activity blockade prevents ocular dominance plasticity in the kitten visual cortex. *Exp. Brain Res.* 65:182–188.

RINGACH, D. L., M. J. HAWKEN, and R. SHAPLEY, 1997. Dynamics of orientation tuning in macaque primary visual cortex. *Nature* 387:281–284.

RUTHAZER, E. S., and M. P. STRYKER, 1996. The role of activity in the development of long-range horizontal connections in area 17 of the ferret. *J. Neurosci.* 16:7253–7269.

SCHMIDT, J. T., and M. BUZZARD, 1993. Activity-driven sharpening of the retinotectal projection in goldfish: Development under stroboscopic illumination prevents sharpening. *J. Neurobiol.* 24:384–399.

SCHMIELAU, F., and W. SINGER, 1977. The role of visual cortex for binocular interactions in the cat lateral geniculate nucleus. *Brain Res.* 120:354–361.

SHERMAN, S. M., and C. KOCH, 1998. Thalamus. In *The Synaptic Organization of the Brain,* G. M. Shepherd, ed. New York: Oxford University Press, pp. 289–328.

SILLITO, A. M., H. E. JONES, G. L. GERSTEIN, and D. C. WEST, 1994. Feature-linked synchronization of thalamic relay cell firing induced by feedback from the visual cortex. *Nature* 369:479–482.

SOMERS, D. C., S. B. NELSON, and M. SUR, 1995. An emergent model of orientation selectivity in cat visual cortical simple cells. *J. Neurosci.* 15:5448–5465.

SOMPOLINSKY, H., and R. SHAPLEY, 1997. New perspectives on the mechanisms for orientation selectivity. *Curr. Opin. Neurobiol.* 7:514–522.

SPITZER, N. C., E. OLSON, and X. GU, 1995. Spontaneous calcium transients regulate neuronal plasticity in developing neurons. *J. Neurobiol.* 26:316–324.

SRETAVAN, D. W., and C. J. SHATZ, 1986a. Prenatal development of cat retinogeniculate axon arbors in the absence of binocular interactions. *J. Neurosci.* 6:990–1003.

SRETAVAN, D. W., and C. J. SHATZ, 1986b. Prenatal development of retinal ganglion cell axons: Segregation into eye-specific layers within the cat's lateral geniculate nucleus. *J. Neurosci.* 6:234–251.

SRETAVAN, D. W., C. J. SHATZ, and M. P. STRYKER, 1988. Modification of retinal ganglion cell axon morphology by prenatal infusion of tetrodotoxin. *Nature* 336:468–471.

STRYKER, M. P., and W. A. HARRIS, 1986. Binocular impulse blockade prevents the formation of ocular dominance columns in cat visual cortex. *J. Neurosci.* 6:2117–2133.

STRYKER, M. P., H. SHERK, A. G. LEVENTHALAND, and H. V. B. HIRSCH, 1978. Physiological consequences for the cat's visual cortex of effectively restricting early visual experience with oriented contours. *J. Neurophysiol.* 41:896–909.

SWINDALE, N. V., 1982. A model for the formation of orientation columns. *Proc. R. Soc. Lond. B. Biol. Sci.* 215:211–230.

SWINDALE, N. V., 1992. A model for the coordinated development of columnar systems in primate striate cortex. *Biol. Cybern.* 66:217–230.

SWINDALE, N. V., 1996. The development of topography in the visual cortex: A review of models. *Network-Computation in Neural Systems* 7:161–247.

TANABE, Y., and T. M. JESSELL, 1996. Diversity and pattern in the developing spinal cord. *Science* 274:1115–1123.

TREPEL, C., K. R. DUFFY, V. D. PEGADO, and K. M. MURPHY, 1998. Patchy distribution of NMDAR1 subunit immunoreactivity in developing visual cortex. *J. Neurosci.* 18:3404–3415.

TYCHSEN, L., and A. BURKHALTER, 1997. Nasotemporal asymmetries in V1: Ocular dominance columns of infant, adult, and strabismic macaque monkeys. *J. Comp. Neurol.* 388:32–46.

WANG, F., A. NEMES, M. MENDELSOHN, and R. AXEL, 1998. Odorant receptors govern the formation of a precise topographic map. *Cell* 93:47–60.

WELIKY, M., and L. C. KATZ, 1997. Disruption of orientation tuning in visual cortex by artificially correlated neuronal activity. *Nature* 386:680–685.

WELIKY, M., and L. C. KATZ, in press. Correlational structure of spontaneous neuronal activity in the developing lateral geniculate nucleus *in vivo*. *Science*.

WIESEL, T. N., 1982. Postnatal development of the visual cortex and the influence of environment. *Nature* 299:583–591.

WIESEL, T. N., and D. H. HUBEL, 1965a. Extent of recovery from the effects of visual deprivation in kittens. *J. Neurophysiol.* 28:1060–1072.

WIESEL, T. N., and H. D. HUBEL, 1965b. Comparison of the effects of unilateral and bilateral eye closure on cortical unit responses in kittens. *J. Neurophysiol.* 28:1029–1040.

WIESEL, T. N., and D. H. HUBEL, 1974. Ordered arrangement of orientation columns in monkeys lacking visual experience. *J. Comp. Neurol.* 158:307–318.

WONG, R. O., M. MEISTER, and C. J. SHATZ, 1993. Transient period of correlated bursting activity during development of the mammalian retina. *Neuron* 11:923–938.

YUSTE, R., A. PEINADO, and L. C. KATZ, 1992. Neuronal domains in developing neocortex. *Science* 254:665–669.

14 Development of Neural Maps: Molecular Mechanisms

RENPING ZHOU AND IRA B. BLACK

ABSTRACT Neural circuits, the structural basis of cognition, are organized in a highly ordered fashion. The spatial order of neurons is often preserved by their axonal termini in target tissues, forming topographic projection maps. During the development of these maps, axons are guided by multiple mechanisms to travel long distances to specific targets. The guidance cues can be attractive or repulsive, and can be diffusible or membrane bound. Among the many guidance molecules, two families have emerged as key factors regulating topographic map formation: they are tyrosine-kinase-family receptors and ligands, and cell adhesion molecules. In the tyrosine kinase family, neurotrophins are candidates for attractive cues, while the Eph subfamily receptors and ligands are repulsive/inhibitory cues. The specificity of maps comes from the graded distribution of the Eph receptors and ligands in the pre- and postsynaptic fields, and negative effects for axonal growth are generated from the ligand-receptor interactions. Properly distributed axon termini may be stabilized by cell adhesion molecules expressed in both the projecting and target neurons through homophilic interactions. Thus the concerted actions of multiple guidance molecules are necessary for the construction of topographic maps during development.

The concept that sensory information is encoded in the brain as topographic maps, which reflect the external world and morphology of sensory organs, has existed since the time of Descartes (1644, 1647). Such topographic encoding is critical for brain functions, as evidenced by orderly representations of sensory surfaces and body effectors in the sensory and motor systems and by experience-dependent plastic changes of these representations (Kaas, 1991). Recent studies using modern histological and tracing techniques have demonstrated that topographic mapping is a basic principle of brain architecture. Neuronal inputs to the central nervous system (CNS) are topographic in many sensory systems including the visual, the auditory, and the somatosensory projections (reviewed in Udin and Fawcett, 1988). Topographic maps are not restricted to sensory

RENPING ZHOU   Department of Chemical Biology, College of Pharmacy, Rutgers University, and Department of Neuroscience and Cell Biology, Robert Wood Johnson Medical School, Piscataway, N.J.
IRA B. BLACK   Department of Neuroscience and Cell Biology, Robert Wood Johnson Medical School, Piscataway, N.J.

systems. They also exist in the limbic circuits that mediate learning, memory, and emotions. One of the major limbic components, the hippocampus, for example, is connected to its subcortical target, the septum, in a highly organized manner (Swanson, Kohler, and Bjorklund, 1987). Similarity in organizing principles between limbic circuits and sensory systems suggests that learning, memory, and emotions are governed by the same spatial constraints as sensory information processing.

There are at least four stages in the development of topographic neural maps. First, appropriate phenotypic fates must be determined for projecting and target neurons so that specific recognitive surface tags are expressed at proper concentrations by neurons spatially and temporally. Second, axons must navigate appropriate paths to reach their targets. Third, terminals must be guided to proper topographic locations after arriving at the projection targets. Fourth, gross topographic maps must be refined to generate precise functional maps. Very little is known about the initial differentiation of projecting and target fields that express specific guidance tags. In contrast, considerable knowledge has recently been obtained regarding axonal navigation to targets (Tessier-Levigne and Goodman, 1996; Goodman, 1996). This chapter focuses primarily on recent advances elucidating how guidance cues direct axon terminals to proper locations to establish coarse maps. We initially discuss mechanisms for topographic mapping, and then examine the molecular identity of guidance cues. Finally, the concerted actions of various cues in two model systems are presented to demonstrate how neural maps are constructed. Mechanisms for refinement of maps have recently been reviewed by Goodman and Shatz (1993) and will not be discussed here.

Guidance mechanisms

Given the central importance of neural maps in cognition, developmental mechanisms have attracted much attention for over half a century. Several models have been proposed. It was widely believed in the 1930s and 1940s that axons were guided primarily by mechanical

213

patterns in the tissues (Weiss, 1939; Weiss and Taylor, 1944). This hypothesis proposed that axons were oriented by mechanical stresses within the tissue ultrastructure and grew along physical guidelines in the developing tissues. The critical prediction of this hypothesis—that axons growing into the target through different paths would not be able to form proper maps—was refuted by later experimental observations. In salamanders, retinal axons traveled by completely anomalous routes to form correctly ordered retinotectal projections (Harris, 1982). Consequently, the proper positioning of axonal terminals did not rely on the route of growth, but rather was determined by other mechanisms such as addresses in the tectum.

CHEMOAFFINITY THEORY   At the end of the 19th century, Cajal and others proposed that axons might be guided by chemical attraction or trophic mechanisms (Ramon y Cajal, 1893). This proposal was later developed into the chemoaffinity hypothesis by Roger Sperry based on studies of retinotectal projections (Sperry, 1963). Retinal ganglion cells project to the tectum, a visual center in the brain, in a highly ordered manner (Sperry, 1963; Gaze, Jacobson, and Szekely, 1963). The observation that the target positions of retinal ganglion axons were determined strictly by their embryonic spatial origin led Sperry to reject the mechanical theory of axonal guidance. Regenerating axons from different parts of the retina made connections with specific predesignated target zones in the tectum. These axons grew across large sections of nontarget tectal zones without forming synapses. Furthermore, retinal axons traveled through abnormal routes generated by artificial displacement to reach their embryonically defined targets, suggesting that the cells had intrinsic guidance tags and did not rely on physical guidance mechanisms (Sperry, 1944). In one experiment, Sperry rotated the eyes 180° and showed that the regenerating retinal axons still made appropriate connections according to their original locations. These animals also had functional vision, except that their visual world was inverted and reversed. The visual inversion was never corrected by experience, suggesting that learning did not play major roles in the establishment of terminal organization of retinal axons. These observations contradicted the contention that maps were organized by functional selection, a popular concept early in the 20th century (Jacobson, 1991).

These studies lead to the chemoaffinity hypothesis, holding that axons are guided to proper targets by matching cytochemical tags on presynaptic and postsynaptic neurons (Sperry, 1963). Sperry further proposed that the tags might be distributed in the projecting and target fields in gradients, and that only *quantitatively*

matching concentrations of the *complementary tags* allowed synapse formation. Such tag pairs might be oriented along perpendicular axes to define multidimensional maps. The chemoaffinity theory has been supported by numerous developmental, electrophysiological, and molecular studies, and candidate molecular tags have been recently identified.

MULTIPLE MECHANISMS   Sperry's chemoaffinity theory emphasized the critical importance of chemical affinity, implying attractive interactions between axons and targets with matching guidance tags. Recent studies have identified at least four different guidance mechanisms that direct axons to proper targets (reviewed in Goodman, 1996, and Tessier-Levigne and Goodman, 1996). They include diffusible and contact-mediated positive and negative guidance. For the development of topographic neural maps, two additional guidance mechanisms, axonal elimination and activity-dependent refinement, are also involved.

Over a century ago, Ramon y Cajal (1893) first suspected the existence of diffusible chemoattractants released by the targets to guide distant incoming axons. Recent analyses have identified several chemoattractants (Goodman, 1996; Tessier-Levigne and Goodman, 1996). Axons are specifically attracted toward targets by these factors. Growth cone behavior is also influenced by contact-mediated attractive molecules, such as growth-promoting cell adhesion molecules (CAMs). These positive signals may function either by attracting growth cones or by supporting survival of growing axons.

In vitro assays that examine the effect of guidance cues on growth cone extension revealed several diffusible, repulsive signals (Dodd and Schuchardt, 1995; Keynes and Cook, 1995; Goodman, 1996; Tessier-Levigne and Goodman, 1996). Axons grow away from the source of these signals. Similar to the positive guidance cues, negative regulation of axons can also be contact mediated. Bonhoeffer and colleagues elegantly demonstrated that a gradient of contact repulsive signals exists in the visual tectum that specifically repels temporal retinal axons (Walter, Muller, and Bonhoeffer, 1990).

Axons or neurons projecting to improper spatial locations may be eliminated. In rodents, retinal axons initially project to the superior colliculus with little topographic specificity (Simon and O'Leary, 1990, 1992; Nakamura and O'Leary, 1989). Excess axons or branches are removed only later (Simon and O'Leary, 1990, 1992; Nakamura and O'Leary, 1989). In the chicken, refinement of the retinotectal map also occurs by eliminating entire ganglion cells with targeting errors (Rager and Rager, 1978; Hughes and McLoon, 1979). Further refinement of the coarse topographic maps can be achieved by neuronal electrical activity (Goodman and Shatz, 1993).

Molecular identity of topographic mapping cues

Given the importance of neural maps, a major effort in modern neurobiology has been directed to the identification of axonal guidance molecules. The candidates identified so far belong to several distinct families. However, they share a common property: Their signaling components all contain ligands and receptors expressed in the presynaptic and postsynaptic fields. We focus on molecules with clearly demonstrated guidance functions in map formation. They include members of the receptor-tyrosine-kinase family (which phosphorylates proteins on tyrosine) and the cell-adhesion-molecule (CAM) family.

RECEPTOR TYROSINE KINASES AND THEIR LIGANDS Receptor tyrosine kinases, key components in the transduction of extracellular signals across the cell membrane, play critical roles in neuronal growth, survival, and axonal guidance. Numerous receptor kinases have been characterized and typically exhibit an extracellular ligand-binding domain, a transmembrane region, and an intracellular kinase domain (van der Geer, Hunter, and Lindberg, 1994). Upon ligand binding, the kinase is activated and modifies other intracellular signaling proteins. During the development of neural maps, this ability to respond to extracellular signals allows incoming axons to recognize target neurons.

The tyrosine kinase receptors are classified into many different subfamilies according to sequence homology. Members of each subfamily share a higher degree of homology with each other than with members from other families. Although the kinase domains are well conserved, the extracellular domains have diverged among different receptors. The extracellular domains are typically composed of a number of different structural domains such as the IgG-like and the fibronectin type III–like regions (van der Geer, Hunter, and Lindberg, 1994). Members of each receptor subfamily have distinct topological organization of these structure domains (van der Geer, Hunter, and Lindberg, 1994). The unique sequences of the ligand-binding domains allow specific interaction with distinct ligands and consequent diverse responses by neurons to different guidance or survival cues.

The Eph subfamily receptors and ligands The Eph subfamily receptors and ligands have emerged recently as major players in the development of topographic neural maps (Brambilla and Klein, 1995; Tessier-Lavigne, 1995; Friedman and O'Leary, 1996; Pandey, Lindberg, and Dixit, 1995; Orike and Pini, 1996; Muller, Bonhoeffer, and Drescher, 1996; Zhou, 1998). The Eph subfamily is the largest known group of receptors, consisting of at least 14 distinct members. For many years, study of Eph receptor function was hampered by the lack of identified ligands. However, the recent isolation of at least eight distinct ligands (the ephrins) has helped elucidate potential roles of the receptors in many developmental processes, including axon guidance and the formation of topographic projection maps (Zhou, 1998).

The Eph ligands are unique. They are all membrane anchored, either by a glycosylphosphatidylinositol (GPI) linkage or a transmembrane domain. Furthermore, membrane attachment is required for function. Soluble ligands fail to activate the receptors, in contrast to ligands of many other members of the tyrosine-kinase-receptor subfamily. The association with membranes restricts diffusion and confines the Eph ligands to specific spatial locations. Thus the ligands and receptors of this subfamily are uniquely suited for guiding axons to specific targets.

Recent in vitro and in vivo studies indicated that the Eph subfamily receptors and ligands play critical roles at multiple stages of map development. These roles include guiding axons along proper tracks toward the target tissues, axon fasciculation, and topographic mapping of axon termini in the target field (reviewed in Zhou, 1998).

Trophic factors and their receptors Positive guidance cues also appear to be required in developing topographic maps (Boxberg, Deiss, and Schwarz, 1993). Trophic factors are prime candidates for this role. It has been proposed that these factors, supplied in limiting amounts by target tissues, regulate neuronal connectivity by supporting the survival of appropriate axons while eliminating mistargeted or excess axons and/or neurons (Purves, 1988). Trophic factors belong to a variety of different molecular families. Factors in the neurotrophin subfamily, including nerve growth factor (NGF), brain-derived neurotrophic factor (BDNF), and neurotrophin-3 and -4, interact with the trk subfamily tyrosine kinase receptors, as well as a low-affinity receptor, p75 (Chao, 1992; Barbacid, 1995; Bothwell, 1995). The glial cell–derived neurotrophic factor (GDNF) family of trophic factors interact with cell surface coreceptors and the tyrosine kinase receptor Ret. Binding to the coreceptors is necessary before interacting with the signaling receptor Ret (Olson, 1997; Robertson and Mason, 1997). Other neurotrophic factors include fibroblast growth factor (FGF) and the cytokine ciliary neurotrophic factor (CNTF), which are ligands of tyrosine kinase receptors and cytokine receptors, respectively. These neurotrophic factors support the survival of a variety of different neuronal populations and often have partially overlapping activities (Korsching, 1993). Recent studies indicate that neurotrophic factors serve as target-derived positive regulators that attract and stabilize incoming axons (Davies, 1996). A number of neurotrophic factors are found in the peripheral or central target tissues, while their receptors are expressed in the projecting neurons (Davies, 1996), suggesting critical roles in the development of neural maps.

CELL ADHESION MOLECULES   Studies of the cell adhesion molecules indicate that they may participate in the elaboration of maps. There are large numbers of CAMs, and they belong to several gene families, including the immunoglobulin superfamily and cadherins. The roles of CAMs in neurodevelopment have been investigated intensively using several different approaches. Expression analyses revealed that many CAMs have specific patterns of expression in vivo. Some showed expression in discrete sets of nuclei that constitute functional neural circuits (Levitt, 1984; Reinoso, Pimenta, and Levitt, 1996; Redies and Takeichi, 1996; Takeichi, 1995). Culture studies indicated that CAMs generally promote axonal growth and may function in vivo to guide growth cones through contact-mediated attractions (Walsh and Doherty, 1997), although exceptions, such as myelin-associated glycoprotein and connectin, function as contact-mediated repulsive cues (Mukhopadhyay et al., 1994; McKerracher et al., 1994; Nose, Takeichi, and Goodman, 1994). Different CAMs show specific ability to promote neurite growth of specific neurons (Pimenta et al., 1995). Antibody perturbation experiments and genetic analyses showed that inhibition of CAM function leads to targeting errors in a variety of neural circuits. Several CAM molecules have been implicated in neural map formation. They include the limbic system–associated membrane protein (LAMP) (Zhukareva and Levitt, 1995; Pimenta et al., 1995), neural cell adhesion molecule (NCAM) (Walsh and Doherty, 1997), and cadherins (Takeichi, 1995; Ranscht, 1994).

Development of topographic neural maps in the brain

The development of topographic maps in vivo is likely to be guided by combinations of different guidance mechanisms. The Eph subfamily ligand/receptor interaction is well recognized to provide negative guidance. Although other guidance interactions remain to be characterized, several classes of molecules including CAMs and GDNF-related factors appear to serve as positive guidance cues. In this section we discuss two different topographic systems, the hippocamposeptal and the ret-

inotectal maps, to demonstrate how the concerted actions of different guidance mechanisms help to establish topographic neuronal connections.

HIPPOCAMPOSEPTAL MAP   The hippocampus is critical in spatial learning and memory (Zola-Morgan and Squire, 1993), functions that depend on complex topographic connections to a number of related structures (Swanson, Kohler, and Bjorklund, 1987; Lopes da Silva et al., 1990). The hippocampus receives projections from the entorhinal cortex, which receives multimodal input from a wide variety of cortical regions. The entorhinal projection to the hippocampus innervates dentate granule cells, which in turn project to area CA3 through the mossy fibers. The CA3 pyramidal cells project to the CA1 region via Schaffer collaterals, forming a trisynaptic circuit within the hippocampus. The hippocampal efferents are sent to two major forebrain locations. One projection reaches broad parts of the cerebral cortex and influences the long-term storage of memories. The other projection is directed toward the septum (Risold and Swanson, 1996; Swanson and Cowan, 1977), which plays critical roles in modulating hippocampal activity. The connections from the entorhinal cortex to the hippocampus to the lateral septum are arranged topographically, suggesting that ordered projections are crucial for hippocampal cognitive function.

Among the hippocampal circuits, the hippocamposeptal map serves as a useful model system. The ingrowth of hippocampal axons to the septum occurs from embryonic day 21 (E21) to postnatal day 14 (P14) in the rat (Linke, Pabst, and Frotscher, 1995). Although it is not known how the axons are guided through the fornix and fimbria to reach the septal target, LAMP appears to serve as a contact-mediated positive guidance cue for the incoming axons. High levels of LAMP were detected in both the hippocampal neurons and the septal target (Pimenta et al., 1995; Reinoso, Pimenta, and Levitt, 1996). Consistent with this notion, LAMP promotes the growth of hippocampal axons and mediates homophilic binding (Pimenta et al., 1995; Zhukareva and Levitt, 1995).

Hippocampal axons terminate primarily in the lateral portion of the septum. Axons from the medial hippocampus project mostly to the dorsomedial region of the lateral septum, whereas axons from the lateral hippocampus terminate in the ventrolateral target (figure 14.1; see color plate 5). Thus neurons project along the mediolateral axis of the hippocampus to the dorsomedial-to-ventrolateral axis of the septal target. Although LAMP may be important in stabilizing interactions between the connections of hippocampal and septal neu-

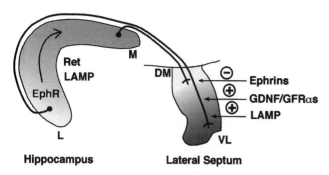

FIGURE 14.1 Regulation of topographic map formation in the hippocamposeptal projection. Medial (M) hippocampal neurons send their axons to the dorsomedial (DM) septal target, while the lateral (L) hippocampal neurons target the ventrolateral (VL) septum. The ligands located in the ventral lateral septum serve to restrict the medial hippocampal neurons (Eph receptor–positive, red) from innervating this region (ligand-positive, blue), which is topographically inappropriate for the medial neurons. However, the ligands allow the innervation of the ventral lateral septum by the lateral hippocampal neurons, because they express few Eph receptors (yellow). In addition to the Eph subfamily receptors and ligands, the GDNF receptor Ret is expressed in the hippocampal neurons, while the ligand-binding coreceptors GFRα1 and 2 are transcribed in the septum. The coreceptors are likely to trap GDNF and/or neurturin and thus serve as target-derived trophic factors for incoming hippocampal axons. Furthermore, both the hippocampal and the target neurons express LAMP, a homophilic cell adhesion molecule, which may serve to stabilize the connection between hippocampal axon terminals and the septal target cells.

rons, the uniform distribution of LAMP indicates that it is unlikely to be responsible for differential topographic mapping of hippocampal axons.

Topographic mapping appears to be regulated by the Eph subfamily ligands and receptors (figure 14.1; see color plate 5). Inhibitory interactions between Eph receptors and ligands that are expressed in gradients in the pre- and postsynaptic neurons are responsible for mapping axon termini with increasing concentrations of receptors over target areas with decreasing amounts of ligands. Analysis of expression of the Eph subfamily receptors showed that several members including EphA3, A5, A6, and A7 are expressed in the hippocampus in lateral (low)–to–medial (high) gradients (Gao et al., 1996; Y. Yue and R. Zhou, unpublished results). Opposing to the gradients of the receptors, at least three ligands, ephrin-A2, A3, and A5, are expressed in the subcortical target of hippocampus, the lateral septum. All three ligands show dorsal (low)–to–ventral (high) expression gradients. However, there are some differences in the spatial distribution of these ligands. Ephrin-A2 and A3 are transcribed in narrow stripes along the lateral edge of the lateral septum, whereas ephrin-A5 appears as diffused signals in the ventral lateral septum

(Zhang et al., 1996). Combination of all three ligands forms a continuous dorsomedial-to-ventrolateral gradient. The septal ligand gradient is complementary (opposing) to the receptor gradient. Hippocampal neurons that express high levels of receptors (medial hippocampus) project to target areas where low levels of ligands are transcribed (dorsal target). Conversely, hippocampal neurons that express low levels of receptors (lateral hippocampus) send axons to the target region with high ligand expression (the ventrolateral target). Thus the gradients of receptor and ligand expression in the projecting and target fields fulfill the requirement of chemoaffinity theory and suggest a function in neuronal mapping.

The countergradients predict that the ligands are repulsive or inhibitory for receptor-positive hippocampal axons. The biological effects of the three ligands on hippocampal neurons were tested using a coculture assay in which medial or lateral hippocampal neurons were cocultured with ligand-expressing cells. All three ligands showed an ability to differentiate the medial versus lateral hippocampal neurons. The growth of neurites from the medial, but not the lateral, hippocampal neurons was specifically inhibited by the ligands (Gao et al., 1996; P.-P. Gao and R. Zhou, unpublished data). Consistent with the inhibition, ephrin-A5 caused growth cone collapse of both the hippocampal and the cortical neurons (Meima et al., 1997). Thus axons with increasingly higher levels of receptor expression are likely to terminate over the septal target with decreasing levels of ligand expression. Once the termini are distributed through selective inhibition via Eph ligand/receptor interaction, homophilic interaction between LAMP expressed in both in the pre- and postsynaptic neurons is likely to stabilize the projection. These observations indicate that the hippocamposeptal map is directed by a combination of positive and negative guidance interactions between the pre- and postsynaptic neurons (figure 14.1; see color plate 5).

RETINOTECTAL MAP Studies of the retinotectal projections, as a model system for neural map development, have been informative in our understanding of the molecular mechanisms (Roskies, Friedman, and O'Leary, 1995). The projection of retinal ganglion cell axons to the tectum is highly organized: Temporal axons terminate in the anterior tectum, and nasal axons map to the posterior tectum (figure 14.2; see color plate 6). To elucidate the nature of guidance cues, Bonhoeffer and colleagues examined the ability of retinal ganglion axons to discriminate between the anterior and posterior tectal target in vitro (Bonhoeffer and Huf, 1985). They observed that temporal retinal axons

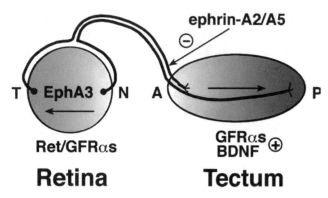

FIGURE 14.2 Specification of retinotectal topographic map. Temporal and nasal retinal ganglion neurons project to the anterior and posterior portions of the chick tectum (superior colliculus in mammals), respectively. The Eph receptor EphA3 is expressed in a nasal (N, low)–to–temporal (T, high) gradient in the retina. The Eph ligands ephrin-A2 and A5 are expressed in the tectum in an anterior (A, low)–to–posterior (P, high) gradient. The ligand gradient serves to repel/eliminate receptor-positive temporal axons. The extent of inhibition may be proportional to the extent of ligand-receptor interaction. In contrast, GDNF entrapped by its binding receptor GFRαs and BDNF may serve as a positive guidance cue to promote the ingrowth of retinal axons in general.

prefer to grow on membrane extracts from the anterior tectum, their topographically correct target, but are repelled by the posterior extracts (Stahl et al., 1990). The selectivity is due to repulsive cues in the posterior target. To identify the negative guidance cue enriched in the posterior tectum, Drescher and colleagues (1995) isolated a 25 kD membrane protein using two-dimensional gel electrophoresis, which they initially named repulsive axon guidance signal, or RAGS. The RAGS protein is distributed in an anterior-to-posterior gradient in the tectum and has stronger repulsion for the temporal axons than the nasal axons in vitro (Monschau et al., 1997). The graded distribution and repulsive activity against the retinal axons indicate that RAGS is a candidate guidance cue and potentially plays a key role in the establishment of retinotectal topographic map.

Sequence analysis revealed that RAGS is the chicken homologue of ephrin-A5, a ligand of the Eph subfamily (Winslow et al., 1995; Drescher et al., 1995). In vivo analysis using gene knockout technique confirmed a critical role of ephrin-A5 in retinotectal topographic map formation (Frisen et al., 1998). Independently, studies by Flanagan and colleagues implicated a different ligand of the Eph subfamily, ephrin-A2, in the guidance of retinal axons (Cheng et al., 1995; Nakamoto et al., 1996). Ephrin-A2 is expressed in an anterior-to-posterior gradient in the tectum and repels the temporal but not the nasal axons in vitro. Counter to the ligand

expression in the tectum, the receptor of ephrin-A2 and A5, EphA3 is distributed in a nasal (low)–to–temporal (high) gradient in the retina. The existence of opposing ligand-receptor gradients in both the retinotectal and hippocamposeptal systems indicates that these molecules use similar mechanisms in specifying different maps in the brain.

To demonstrate a guidance role in vivo, ephrin-A2 was expressed ectopically in the tectum using a retroviral vector (Nakamoto et al., 1996). The temporal axons avoided areas of ectopic ephrin-A2 expression and mapped to abnormally anterior positions, whereas no effect was observed on the nasal axons. These observations provide direct evidence that ephrin-A2 is a guidance molecule that determines target specificity of the temporal axons by inhibiting axon growth through a countergradient of receptors in the presynaptic terminals (figure 14.2; see color plate 6). Together with their function in the hippocamposeptal projection, these findings demonstrate that the Eph receptors and ligands are universal negative regulators in establishing topographic maps.

The cellular mechanisms underlying ephrin function have not been well characterized. Earlier studies indicate that retinal ganglion axons initially explore and project to much broader areas than the final targets (Nakamura and O'Leary, 1989; Simon and O'Leary, 1990, 1992). In rodents, both nasal and temporal axons extend through the entire superior colliculus during early development (Simon and O'Leary, 1990, 1992). However, mistargeted axons are later pruned (Simon and O'Leary, 1990, 1992). We have shown that ephrins have dual effects on hippocampal axons in vitro, initially stimulating axonal extension and branching, but subsequently causing degeneration (unpublished observations). Consequently, ephrins may determine topographic positions by axonal elimination, in contrast to a guidance mechanism. These observations further suggest that ephrins are pruning signals for the elimination of excess axons.

In addition to axonal pruning, selective death of ganglion cells also occurs during the time of target innervation. Cell death is not dependent on the presence of the tectal target, indicating that it may be due to limiting amounts of trophic signals. Consistent with this view, components of the signaling system of the neurotrophic factor GDNF are expressed in the retina and the tectum (Yu et al., 1998). GDNF-family factors support neuronal survival through the interaction with a signal transducing tyrosine kinase receptor Ret and a ligand-binding coreceptor (Lindsay and Yancopoulos, 1996; Robertson and Mason, 1997). One of the coreceptors, GFRα-2, is transcribed at high levels in the tectum, presumably entrapping GDNF-family factors as target-derived neurotrophic activity to support the survival of retinal ganglion cells, which express the signaling receptor Ret (Yu et al., 1998). In addition, a different factor of the neurotrophin family, brain-derived neurotrophic factor, may also play a role in supporting the survival of retina ganglion cells (Herzog and von Bartheld, 1998; Ma et al., 1998). Thus a combination of axonal elimination and selective survival of retinal ganglion cells may be important for the formation of retinotectal map (figure 14.2; see color plate 6).

It remains unclear what signals prevent nasal axons from terminating in the anterior tectum. It has been suggested that other molecules such as trophic factors may be specifically expressed in the posterior tectum and attract only the nasal axons (Boxberg, Deiss, and Schwarz, 1993). Thus the concerted actions of negative signals, such as those from Eph molecules, and potential trophic interactions may be critical for the establishment of topographic maps.

Conclusions and perspectives

The development of topographic neural maps apparently requires the actions of multiple guidance cues and employs multiple guidance mechanisms. Axons are guided to the proper targets by a combination of positive and negative signals working in diffusible or contact-mediated forms, along with elimination of mistargeted axons or neurons. These different mechanisms are used in both pathfinding and precise target selection. The guidance molecules belong to a variety of different families. CAMs are likely to be contact-mediated positive cues that function as permissible axonal growth substrates during pathfinding or serve to stabilize correct projections at the targets. Neurotrophic factors may contribute to the development of neural maps by selectively supporting survival and/or tropic attraction of proper axons. Members of the Eph subfamily ligands and receptors occupy a uniquely important position in determining the topographic specificity of axon terminals. Such specificity may be achieved by repelling or eliminating mistargeted axons from the ligand-expressing inhibitory domains. Research in the past half century has contributed greatly to our understanding of the mechanisms of axonal guidance. However, undoubtedly many guidance cues remain to be discovered, and a true challenge in the future will be to fit all the puzzle pieces together. In addition, little is known about how these signals regulate axonal behavior; the elucidation of the downstream signaling pathways will likely be a major research focus.

REFERENCES

BARBACID, M., 1995. Neurotrophic factors and their receptors. *Curr. Opin. Cell. Biol.* 7:148–155.

BONHOEFFER, F., and J. HUF, 1985. Position-dependent properties of retinal axons and their growth cones. *Nature* 315:409–410.

BOTHWELL, M., 1995. Functional interactions of neurotrophins and neurotrophin receptors. *Annu. Rev. Neurosci.* 18:223–253.

BOXBERG, Y. V., S. DEISS, and U. SCHWARZ, 1993. Guidance and topographic stabilization of nasal chick retinal axons on target-derived components in vitro. *Neuron* 10:345–357.

BRAMBILLA, R., and R. KLEIN, 1995. Telling axons where to grow: A role for Eph receptor tyrosine kinases in guidance. *Mol. Cell. Neurosci.* 6:487–495.

CHAO, M. V., 1992. Neurotrophin receptors: A window into neuronal differentiation. *Neuron* 9:583–593.

CHENG, H.-J., M. NAKAMOTO, A. D. BERGEMANN, and J. G. FLANAGAN, 1995. Complementary gradients in expression and binding of ELF-1 and Mek4 in development of the topographic retinotectal projection map. *Cell* 82:371–381.

DAVIES, A. M., 1996. The neurotrophic hypothesis: Where does it stand? *Philos. Trans. R. Soc. Lond. B Biol. Sci.* 351:389–394.

DESCARTES, R., 1644. Letter to Mesland. In *Oeuvres philosophiques III*, F. Aliquie, ed. Paris: Garnier Frères, 1963.

DESCARTES, R., 1647. Les objections et les responses. In *Oeuvres philosophiques II*, F. Aliquie, ed. Paris: Garnier Frères, 1963.

DODD, J., and A. SCHUCHARDT, 1995. Axon guidance: A compelling case for repelling growth cones. *Cell* 81:471–474.

DRESCHER, U., C. KREMOSER, C. HANDWERKER, J. LOSCHINGER, N. MASAHARU, and F. BONHOEFFER, 1995. In vitro guidance of retinal ganglion cell axons by RAGS, a 25kDa tectal protein related to ligands for Eph receptor tyrosine kinases. *Cell* 82:359–370.

FRIEDMAN, G. C., and D. D. O'LEARY, 1996. Eph receptor tyrosine kinases and their ligands in neural development. *Curr. Opin. Neurobiol.* 6:127–133.

FRISEN, J., P. A. YATES, T. MCLAUGHLIN, G. C. FRIEDMAN, D. D. O'LEARY, and M. BARBACID, 1998. Ephrin-A5 (AL-1/RAGS) is essential for proper retinal axon guidance and topographic mapping in the mammalian visual system. *Neuron* 20:235–243.

GAO, P.-P., J.-H. ZHANG, M. YOKOYAMA, B. RACEY, C. F. DREYFUS, I. B. BLACK, and R. ZHOU, 1996. Regulation of topographic projection in the brain: Elf-1 in the hippocamposeptal system. *Proc. Natl. Acad. Sci. U.S.A.* 93:11161–11166.

GAZE, R. M., M. JACOBSON, and G. SZEKELY, 1963. The retino-tectal projection in *Xenopus* with compound eyes. *J. Physiol.* 165:484–499.

GOODMAN, C. S., 1996. Mechanisms and molecules that control growth cone guidance. *Annu. Rev. Neurosci.* 19:341–377.

GOODMAN, C. S., and C. J. SHATZ, 1993. Developmental mechanisms that generate precise patterns of neuronal connectivity. *Cell* 72/*Neuron* 10 (Suppl.):77–98.

HARRIS, W. A., 1982. The transplantation of eyes to genetically eyeless salamanders: Visual projections and somatosensory interactions. *J. Neurosci.* 2:339–353.

HERZOG, K. H., and C. S. VON BARTHELD, 1998. Contributions of the optic tectum and the retina as sources of brain-derived neurotrophic factor for retinal ganglion cells in the chick embryo. *J. Neurosci.* 18:2891–2906.

HUGHES, W. F., and S. C. MCLOON, 1979. Ganglion cell death during normal retinal development in the chick: Comparisons with cell death induced by early target field destruction. *Exp. Neurol.* 66:587–601.

JACOBSON, M., 1991. *Developmental Neurobiology.* New York and London: Plenum Press.

KAAS, J. H., 1991. Plasticity of sensory and motor maps in adult mammals. *Annu. Rev. Neurosci.* 14:137–167.

KEYNES, R. J., and G. M. W. COOK, 1995. Repulsive and inhibitory signals. *Curr. Opin. Neurobiol.* 5:75–82.

KORSCHING, S., 1993. The neurotrophic factor concept: A re-examination. *J. Neurosci.* 13:2739–2748.

LEVITT, P., 1984. A monoclonal antibody to limbic system neurons. *Science* 223:299–301.

LINDSAY, R. M., and G. D. YANCOPOULOS, 1996. GDNF in a bind with known orphan: Accessory implicated in new twist. *Neuron* 17:571–574.

LINKE, R., T. PABST, and M. FROTSCHER, 1995. Development of the hippocamposeptal projection in the rat. *J. Comp. Neurol.* 351:602–616.

LOPES DA SILVA, F., M. P. WITTER, P. H. BOEIJINGA, and A. H. M. LOHMAN, 1990. Anatomic organization and physiology of the limbic cortex. *Physiol. Rev.* 70:453–511.

MA, Y. T., T. HSIEH, M. E. FORBES, J. E. JOHNSON, and D. O. FROST, 1998. BDNF injected into the superior colliculus reduces developmental retinal ganglion cell death. *J. Neurosci.* 18:2097–2107.

MCKERRACHER, L., S. DAVID, D. L. JACKSON, V. KOTTIS, R. J. DUNN, and P. E. BRAUN, 1994. Identification of myelin-associated glycoprotein as a major myelin-derived inhibitor of neurite growth. *Neuron* 13:805–811.

MEIMA, L., I. J. KLJAVIN, P. MORAN, A. SHIH, J. W. WINSLOW, and I. W. CARAS, 1997. AL-1-induced growth cone collapse of rat cortical neurons is correlated with REK7 expression and rearrangement of the actin cytoskeleton. *Eur. J. Neurosci.* 9:177–188.

MONSCHAU, B., C. KREMOSER, K. OHTA, H. TANAKA, T. KANEKO, T. YAMADA, C. HANDWERKER, M. R. HORNBERGER, J. LOSCHINGER, E. B. PASQUALE, D. A. SIEVER, M. F. VERDERAME, B. K. MULLER, F. BONHOEFFER, and U. DRESCHER, 1997. Shared and distinct functions of RAGS and ELF-1 in guiding retinal axons. *EMBO J.* 16:1258–1267.

MUKHOPADHYAY, G., P. DOHERTY, F. S. WALSH, P. R. CROCKER, and M. T. FILBIN, 1994. A novel role for myelin-associated glycoprotein as an inhibitor of axonal regeneration. *Neuron* 13:757–767.

MULLER, B. K., F. BONHOEFFER, and U. DRESCHER, 1996. Novel gene families involved in neural pathfinding. *Curr. Opin. Genet. Dev.* 6:469–474.

NAKAMOTO, M., H.-J. CHENG, G. C. FRIEDMAN, T. MCLAUGHLIN, M. J. HANSEN, C. H. YOON, D. D. M. O'LEARY, and J. G. FLANAGAN, 1996. Topographically specific effects of ELF-1 on retinal axon guidance in vitro and retinal axon mapping in vivo. *Cell* 86:755–766.

NAKAMURA, H., and D. D. M. O'LEARY, 1989. Inaccuracies in initial growth and arborization of chick retinotectal axons followed by course corrections and axon remodeling to develop topographic order. *J. Neurosci.* 9:3776–3795.

NOSE, A., M. TAKEICHI, and C. S. GOODMAN, 1994. Ectopic expression of connectin reveals a repulsive function during growth cone guidance and synapse formation. *Neuron* 13:525–539.

OLSON, L., 1997. The coming of age of the GDNF family and its receptors: Gene delivery in a rat Parkinson model may have clinical implications. *Trends Neurosci.* 20:277–279.

ORIKE, N., and A. PINI, 1996. Axon guidance: Following the Eph plan. *Curr. Biol.* 6:108–110.

PANDEY, A., R. A. LINDBERG, and V. M. DIXIT, 1995. Cell signaling: Receptor orphans find a family. *Curr. Biol.* 5:986–989.

PIMENTA, A. F., V. ZHUKAREVA, M. F. BARBE, B. S. REINOSO, C. GRIMLEY, W. HENZEL, I. FISCHER, and P. LEVITT, 1995. The limbic system–associated membrane protein is an Ig superfamily member that mediates selective neuronal growth and axon targeting. *Neuron* 15:287–297.

PURVES, D., 1988. *Body and Brain: A Trophic Theory of Neural Connections.* Cambridge, Mass.: Harvard University Press.

RAGER, G., and U. RAGER, 1978. Systems matching by degeneration. I. A quantitative electron microscopic study of the generation and degeneration of ganglion cells in the chicken. *Exp. Brain Res.* 33:65–78.

RAMON Y CAJAL, S., 1893. La rétine des vertébrés. *La Cellule* 9:17–258.

RANSCHT, B., 1994. Cadherins and catenins: Interactions and functions in embryonic development. *Curr. Opin. Cell Biol.* 6:740–746.

REDIES, C., and M. TAKEICHI, 1996. Cadherins in the developing central nervous system: An adhesive code for segmental and functional subdivisions. *Dev. Biol.* 180:413–423.

REINOSO, B. S., A. F. PIMENTA, and P. LEVITT, 1996. Expression of the mRNAs encoding the limbic system-associated membrane protein (LAMP). I. Adult rat brain. *J. Comp. Neurol.* 375:274–288.

RISOLD, P. Y., and L. W. SWANSON, 1996. Structural evidence for functional domains in the rat hippocampus. *Science* 272:1484–1486.

ROBERTSON, K., and I. MASON, 1997. The GDNF-RET signaling partnership. *Trends Genet.* 13:1–3.

ROSKIES, A., G. C. FRIEDMAN, and D. D. O'LEARY, 1995. Mechanisms and molecules controlling the development of retinal maps. *Perspect. Dev. Neurobiol.* 3:63–75.

SIMON, D. K., and D. D. M. O'LEARY, 1990. Limited topographic specificity in the targeting and branching of mammalian retinal axons. *Dev. Biol.* 137:125–134.

SIMON, D. K., and D. D. M. O'LEARY, 1992. Development of topographic order in the mammalian retinocollicular projection. *J. Neurosci.* 12:1212–1232.

SPERRY, R., 1944. Optic nerve regeneration with return of vision in anurans. *J. Neurophysiol.* 7:57–69.

SPERRY, R., 1963. Chemoaffinity in the orderly growth of nerve fiber patterns and connections. *Proc. Natl. Acad. Sci. U.S.A.* 50:703–710.

STAHL, B., B. MULLER, Y. VON BOXBERG, E. C. COX, and F. BONHOEFFER, 1990. Biochemical characterization of a putative axonal guidance molecule of the chick visual system. *Neuron* 5:735–743.

SWANSON, L. W., and W. M. COWAN, 1977. An autoradiographic study of the organization of the efferent connections of the hippocampal formation in the rat. *J. Comp. Neur.* 172:49–84.

SWANSON, L. W., C. KOHLER, and A. BJÖRKLUND, 1987. The limbic region. I. The septohippocampal system. In *Hand-*

book of *Chemical Neuroanatomy*, vol. 5: *Integrated Systems of the CNS*, A. Björklund, T. Hökfelt, and L. W. Swanson, eds. Amsterdam: Elsevier Science Publishers B. V., part 1, pp. 124–278.

TAKEICHI, M., 1995. Morphogenetic roles of classic cadherins. *Curr. Opin. Cell Biol.* 7:619–627.

TESSIER-LAVIGNE, M., 1995. Eph receptor tyrosine kinases, axon repulsion, and the development of topographic maps. *Cell* 82:345–348.

TESSIER-LAVIGNE, M., and C. S. GOODMAN, 1996. The molecular biology of axon guidance. *Science* 274:1123–1133.

UDIN, S., and J. W. FAWCETT, 1988. Formation of topographic maps. *Ann. Rev. Neurosci.* 11:289–327.

VAN DER GEER, P., T. HUNTER, and R. A. LINDBERG, 1994. Receptor protein–tyrosine kinases and their signal transduction pathways. *Annu. Rev. Cell Biol.* 10:251–337.

WALSH, F. S., and P. DOHERTY, 1997. Neural cell adhesion molecules of the immunoglobulin superfamily: Role in axon growth and guidance. *Annu. Rev. Cell Dev. Biol.* 13: 425–456.

WALTER, J., B. K. MULLER, and F. BONHOEFFER, 1990. Axonal guidance by an avoidance mechanism. *J. Physiol. (Paris)* 84: 104–110.

WEISS, P. A., 1939. *Principles of Development*. New York: Holt, part 4.

WEISS, P. A., and A. C. TAYLOR, 1944. Further experimental evidence against "neurotropism" in nerve regeneration. *J. Exp. Zool.* 95:233–257.

WINSLOW, J. W., P. MORAN, J. VALVERDE, A. SHIH, J. Q. YUAN, S. C. WONG, S. P. TSAI, A. GODDARD, W. J. HENZEL, F. HEFTI, et al., 1995. Cloning of AL-1, a ligand for an Eph-related tyrosine kinase receptor involved in axon bundle formation. *Neuron* 14:973–981.

YU, T., S. SCULLY, Y. YU, G. M. FOX, S. JING, and R. ZHOU, 1998. Expression of GDNF family receptor components during development: Implications in the mechanisms of interaction. *J. Neurosci.* 18:4684–4696.

ZHANG, J.-H., D. P. CERRETTI, T. YU, J. G. FLANAGAN, and R. ZHOU, 1996. Detection of ligands in regions anatomically connected to neurons expressing the Eph receptor Bsk: Potential roles in neuron-target interaction. *J. Neurosci.* 16: 7182–7192.

ZHOU, R., 1998. The Eph family receptors and ligands. *Pharmacol. Ther.* 77:151–181.

ZHUKAREVA, V., and P. LEVITT, 1995. The limbic system–associated membrane protein (LAMP) selectively mediates interactions with specific central neuron populations. *Development* 121:1161–1172.

ZOLA-MORGAN, S., and L. R. SQUIRE, 1993. Neuroanatomy of memory. *Annu. Rev. Neurosci.* 16:547–563.

15 The Reorganization of Sensory and Motor Maps after Injury in Adult Mammals

JON H. KAAS

ABSTRACT Sensory and motor maps in the brains of adult mammals are highly plastic. The mutability of the topographic structures of these maps has been most convincingly demonstrated in the larger, two-dimensional maps of sensory surfaces in primary sensory cortex after long-standing deactivations of part of the receptor sheet. More limited modifications of cortical maps have been demonstrated after changes in experience and learning. In addition, convincing changes in subcortical maps have been demonstrated in the thalamus and brain stem, suggesting that all levels of sensory systems are modifiable, even in the mature brain. Changes in maps have been demonstrated in a range of mammalian species and in the somatosensory, visual, auditory, and motor systems. Some alterations are instantaneous, reflecting adjustments in dynamic systems. Others emerge over minutes to weeks as a result of synaptic modifications, the play of neuromodulating systems, and the regulation of the neurotransmitters. In instances of massive deafferentations, such as after the loss of a limb, major reactivations of cortical maps occur, but over longer times of months. These reactivations appear to depend, in part, on the growth of new connections. These massive reactivations lead to misperceptions referred to the missing sensory surface. Rearrangements of sensory and motor maps in the mature brain may be responsible for improvements in sensorimotor skills with practice, useful adjustment to sensory loss and change, and recoveries from central nervous system damage, as well as misperceptions and malfunctions. A fuller understanding of the mechanisms of adult plasticity might lead to improved clinical treatments and the potentiation of favorable outcomes.

One of the major surprises to emerge from research on sensory systems over the last 20 years is that the internal structures of maps of sensory surfaces in the brain are extremely mutable, even in adult mammals. The developing brain was already known to be highly plastic, since the course of development could be greatly altered by injury to part of the pathway or by sensory deprivation. In contrast, some of the same manipulations seemed to have little effect on the mature brain or even brains at later stages of development. In addition, reli-

JON H. KAAS Department of Psychology, Vanderbilt University, Nashville, Tenn.

able sensory perception would appear to depend on a system that is rather stable in organization. Therefore, the organization of much of the mature brain has been considered to be fixed by the end of development. Yet, some capacity for reorganization in sensory-perceptual systems would seem necessary to account for the learning of sensorimotor skills, adjustments to changes in sensory inputs, and the considerable recoveries that often occur after focal brain damage. We now know that the details of cortical representations are dynamically maintained, that changes in sensory inputs and the significance of sensory inputs can alter response properties of neurons and the structure of sensory maps over short to long time courses, and that after injuries major changes in sensory maps are possible. Some alterations are of such extent that they can only be explained by the growth of new connections. The evidence for such flexibility in brain organization leads to some obvious questions. For instance, how do such changes occur? Are they useful or harmful, and, either way, how can we control them? And, are all parts of the cortex, or brain, equally flexible, or do early and higher-order fields differ? While we have only partial answers to these and related questions, the usefulness of answering them is clear. But it is important to recognize that even after 20 or more years of intensive research, we are at the early stages of understanding the extent and nature of plasticity in the adult brain.

One of the current limits on our understanding is that only a few regions of the brain have been extensively studied. Many of the studies have been of the mutability of the hand map in primary somatosensory cortex of monkeys. A concentration of efforts on this cortex might seem strange, until one considers the technical advantages that this cortex offers. First, one needs a convincing way of demonstrating brain changes. The primary somatosensory representation is extremely precise and orderly, and the portion representing the hand in primates is rather large. The representation is two-dimensional, in

223

contrast to the more complex, three-dimensional, smaller subcortical representations, and the hand region of primary somatosensory cortex, at least in some primates, is exposed on the surface of the brain. These advantages allow alterations in cortex to be determined, even with relatively imprecise measuring methods, such as microelectrode mapping procedures.

As a result of concentrated efforts on a few favorable preparations, such as hand cortex in primates, we know a lot about the mutability of these structures. We also have enough evidence to say that many regions of cortex across many species of mammals are changeable, but we are uncertain if primary sensory cortex is more or less changeable than higher-order areas. However, there is evidence that cortical representations can be more mutable than subcortical representations.

The focus of this chapter is the effects of deactivating injuries to sensory systems, especially to the somatosensory system of primates. One reason for this focus is that the alterations in sensory inputs produced by damage have produced the largest changes in cortical organization, and thus the clearest evidence for plasticity in the mature brain has come from such deprivation experiments. Nevertheless, sensory experience and learning produce alterations in cortical circuits, and the accumulated evidence is now rather compelling (see chapter 16). However, we feel that the larger and more obvious changes produced by some types of injuries are especially interesting because they are not easily explained by simple adjustments in synaptic strengths. Thus the larger map reorganizations raise the issue of new neuronal growth in the mature brain. In addition, they raise the possibility of unwanted as well as desirable perceptual consequences.

Normally, sensory representations are relatively stable across time and across individuals

The hallmark of primary sensory cortex is the presence of an orderly and detailed representation of a sensory surface. It is the consistency of this representation across time and individuals that allows compelling evidence for mutability to be obtained. Thus the permanence of map organization allows changes that are due to a manipulation to be demonstrated by means of before-and-after measurements in the same animal, and it is the consistency of map organization across members of the same species that allows a group of normals to serve as controls for a group of manipulated individuals. While the variability of even primary sensory maps has been stressed on occasion (e.g., Merzenich et al., 1987), published maps of sensory cortex reflect measurement errors as well as biological variability. Cortical maps tend

to be highly consistent in instances where measurement error is greatly reduced. Extreme consistency, for example, is apparent in the morphological reflection of the somatotopy of S1 in rats and mice, where the arrangement of the so-called barrel field is remarkably stable across individuals, at least those born with a normal number of facial whiskers (Welker and Van der Loos, 1986). A similar consistency across individuals has been reported for the anatomical isomorph in S1 of the nose of the starnosed mole (Catania and Kaas, 1997). While some might argue that S1 in primates is more variable, we recently discovered that the representations of the fingers and palm are visible in appropriately processed brain sections through area 3b of monkeys, and this easily and accurately measured histological map is extremely consistent across individuals (Jain, Catania, and Kaas, 1998). Furthermore, the morphological map is not altered by manipulations that greatly change the physiological map, and thus the morphological map can serve as a reference for changes induced by manipulations. Even with the possibility of considerable measurement error, studies across laboratories, experimental groups, and recording conditions have revealed little variability in the response properties of neurons, the receptive field sizes of neurons, and the basic somatotopy revealed by neuronal populations in area 3b of macaque monkeys (Pons et al., 1987).

The dynamic nature of sensory maps

Any alteration in the pattern of input from a sensory surface would, of course, be immediately reflected in changes in the central maps activated by those inputs. But the changes are more complex than simple removals or additions because of convergences and divergences in the connection patterns and subtle differences in these patterns for excitatory and inhibitory connections. Thus removing the inputs from a finger with local anesthetic, for example, might not silence cortex or subcortical structures normally devoted to that finger because weak inputs to that cortex related to adjoining fingers might be less inhibited (Rasmussan and Turnbull, 1983; Kelahan and Doetsch, 1984; Calford and Tweedale, 1991; Pettit and Schwark, 1993; Rasmussan, Louw, and Northgrave, 1993; Doetsch et al., 1996). These immediate consequences of rebalancing inhibitory and excitatory circuits (see Xing and Gerstein, 1996; Nicolelis, 1997, for review) have been described as the "unmasking" of silent synapses (P. D. Wall, 1977) or more recently as "disinhibition" (Calford and Tweedale, 1988). The evidence for such immediate changes tells us a great deal about the nature of the circuits in the system and how they normally operate. Similar immediate changes in neuron receptive field properties, including receptive field sizes, can be induced by modifications in the activating stimuli. For example, the responses of visual neurons in visual cortex to line segments within the receptive field may be enhanced by similarly oriented line segments outside the receptive field, but inhibited by such segments of other orientations, suggesting a neural mechanism for the perceptual linking of line segments and the salience of segments of similar orientations. Many features of perception may depend on such dynamic features of cortical circuits (see Gilbert, 1998).

Other features of neurons and sensory maps may change rapidly with stimulus conditions. Many rapid changes may result from the modulation of local circuits by inputs from other structures (Castro-Alamancos and Connors, 1996). Brainstem neuromodulatory centers, such as the raphe nuclei and locus coeruleus, project widely to affect many neurons simultaneously as a result of changes in alertness, motivation, and emotional state (e.g., Juliano et al., 1990). In a similar but more focused manner, the activation of pain afferents by capsaicin injections in the skin appears to produce tonic activity in fibers that influence inhibitory interneurons and thus modulate receptive field sizes of neurons throughout the dorsal column–medial lemniscal system (Calford and Tweedale, 1991; Rasmusson, Louw, and Northgrave, 1993). Finally, synaptic strengths and thus neuronal properties and cortical maps can be rapidly modified by learning and experience (chapter 16; Weinberger, 1995; Ebner et al., 1997). Such stimulus-induced changes in synaptic strengths seem to depend on the entry of calcium into neurons through NMDA receptors following extended Hebbian rules (Bear, Cooper, and Ebner, 1987; Rauschecker, 1991; Benuskova, Diamond, and Ebner, 1994). During experience-related changes in mature brains, the synaptic modifications may be permitted or potentiated by the neuromodulatory actions of acetylcholine release via projections from nucleus basalis (Dykes, 1990, 1997; Juliano, Ma, and Eslin, 1991; Wienberger, 1995; Kilgard and Merzenich, 1998).

Slowly emerging reorganizations of cortical maps

Many alterations in sensory maps occur over longer time periods of hours, weeks, and even months. These more slowly emerging changes are especially interesting because they potentially involve mechanisms in addition to adjustments in the dynamic balance of the neuronal network and rapid synaptic modifications, especially activity-dependent effects on the expression of genes that can lead to neurotransmitter regulation (E. G. Jones, 1993) and the release of trophic factors (Levine and Black,

1997) that alter the growth of dendrites and axons. The products of early gene expression, as a result of increases or decreases in neural activity, can be measured in minutes to hours (e.g., Melzer and Steiner, 1997).

One of the now classic demonstrations of cortical plasticity involved the reorganization of the hand representation in S1 (3b) of monkeys after section of the median nerve to the skin of the thumb half of the glabrous hand (Merzenich et al., 1983a). This procedure deprives about half of the hand representation of its normal source of activation. Although some neurons in this deprived territory acquire new receptive fields on innervated parts of the hand immediately or very rapidly (Silva et al., 1996), probably due to disinhibition, the extent of the reactivation gradually increases over a period of weeks until all deprived neurons are highly responsive to tactile inputs on the hand (figure 15.1; Merzenich et al., 1983b). The recovery is largely from inputs from the hairy back of the hand, and the cortical reactivation is highly somatotopic, with regions formerly devoted to the glabrous surfaces of digits 1–3 activated instead from inputs from the dorsal skin of digits 1–3 in the same sequence.

The original interpretation of this recovery was that it was based on the potentiation of weak and ineffective synapses in the fringes of highly overlapping thalamo-cortical axon arbors, but subsequent studies have revealed that this interpretation is too simple. First, an investigation of the nature of the map of the hand in the first relay of tactile information in the cuneate nucleus of the dorsal column–trigeminal complex suggested an involvement at this initial level. Anatomical studies showed that afferents from each digit terminate in a separate cluster of neurons in the cuneate nucleus, but inputs from the dorsal and glabrous surfaces of the same digit terminate in the same cluster of cells (Florence, Wall, and Kaas, 1991). Thus it would require only a limited rewiring or potentiation of local connections in the cuneate nucleus for neurons responsive to glabrous skin to become responsive to dorsal skin. Second, reactivation of hand cortex can be incomplete if the radial nerve to the dorsal hand is sectioned in addition to the ulnar or median nerve to the glabrous hand (Garraghty et al., 1994), but reactivation is complete if both the ulnar and median nerves are sectioned (Garraghty and Kaas, 1991a). Thus the inputs from the dorsal hand are especially potent in reactivating cortex. Third, recordings obtained in the thalamic target of the cuneate nucleus, the hand subnucleus of the ventroposterior nucleus, revealed that considerable reactivation of deprived neurons occurs at this level of the system after median nerve section (Garraghty and Kaas, 1991b). More directly, reactivation of some of the deprived

A. Location of Map

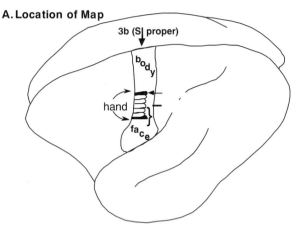

B. Representation Order

C. Normal Map

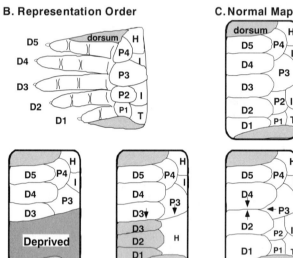

D. Portion deprived by nerve section

E. Reorganization after nerve section

F. Reorganization after D3 removed

FIGURE 15.1   Primary somatosensory cortex (area 3b) reorganizes after median nerve section or finger loss in monkeys. (A) The locations of area 3b and the portion devoted to the hand on a lateral view of the brain of an owl monkey. This New World monkey has only a shallow dimple in cortex medial to the hand representation, rather than a central fissure, as in humans. Thus area 3b is largely in the exposed surface of the brain. (B) The glabrous hand is represented in area 3b as if the palm were split from the ventral wrist toward digit 3, and spread out on cortex with digits 1–5 in a lateromedial sequence and the palm caudal to the digits. The dorsal surface is poorly represented (stippled) in a variable manner. Often, the dorsal skin of the digits and hand are represented in narrow bands of tissue medial and lateral to that of the glabrous hand (see Jain, Florence, and Kaas, 1998, for review). (C) The hand representation is distorted into a roughly rectangular shape in area 3b, with a compression of the length compared to the width of the hand. (D) The median nerve subserves about half of the glabrous hand from the thumb (D1) to part of the middle finger (D3). Thus section of the median nerve deprives most of the lateral half of the hand representation of its normal source of activation (hatched region). (E) The deprived region of the hand representation, the former territory of the median nerve, becomes reactivated over about one month of recovery by inputs largely from the hairy, dorsal surface of the hand via the intact radial nerve. Some expansion of the representations of glabrous D3 and P3 occurs (arrows). The reactivation is somatotopic, with the former territories of glabrous D1–D3 and adjoining pads acquiring responsiveness to stimulation of dorsal skin of D1–D3 and adjoining pads (see Merzenich et al., 1983a, 1983b). (E) In another type of deprivation, the loss or removal of a finger, the deprived territory of the missing finger becomes responsive to inputs from the adjoining fingers and palm (see Merzenich et al., 1984; Jain, Catania, and Kaas, 1998). Digits and pads of the hand are traditionally numbered, and insular (I), hypothenar (H), and thenar (T) pads are indicated.

neurons occurs in the cuneate nucleus (Xu and Wall, 1997), as postulated. Yet, the outcome in cortex is not as simple as switching neurons in the cuneate nucleus from a glabrous to a hairy skin source of activation, together with the relay of this switch in activation to the thalamus and cortex. Instead, it seems likely that an incomplete and relatively weak reactivation of neurons in the cuneate nucleus is relayed and potentiated in the thalamus and potentiated again when relayed to the cortex. Much of this potentiation may depend on NMDA receptors, since chronically blocking these receptors prevented the reactivation and reorganization of somatosensory cortex (Garraghty and Muja, 1996). The reactivation of cortex may also be facilitated by the down-regulation of GABA expression in the deprived cortex as a consequence of a period of reduced neuronal activity (Garraghty, Lachica, and Kaas, 1991).

Whatever the mechanisms, the consequences of nerve damage can be completely reversible. If the median nerve is crushed, rather than sectioned, so that it can regenerate accurately to original skin targets, the regenerated nerve reclaims its lost cortical territory, and neurons in this territory recover receptive fields that are almost identical in skin locations to those they had originally (J. T. Wall, Felleman, and Kaas, 1983).

The series of experiments on the effects of median nerve damage in monkeys leads to several conclusions. First, subcortical structures are clearly subject to reorganization and reactivation. There is a history of earlier evidence for spinal cord and brainstem plasticity in adult mammals, but difficulties of measuring limited changes in the small subcortical maps led to uncertainties about at least some of the claims (see Snow and Wilson, 1991). The reactivation of the large hand subnucleus of the ventroposterior nucleus by preserved inputs from the back of the hand after median and ulnar nerve section provides strong evidence for subcortical plasticity

(Garraghty and Kaas, 1991b), especially in conjunction with comparable results from a number of more recent studies (e.g., Pettit and Schwark, 1993; Rasmusson, 1996; Xu and Wall, 1997; Parker, Wood, and Dostrovsky, 1998). Second, normal map structure may differ from level to level in a processing system, so that relatively minor somatotopic adjustments at one level, such as the substitution of dorsal skin for glabrous skin inputs in the cuneate nucleus, can appear larger at subsequent levels (see Kaas and Florence, 1997). Third, modifications at early stages of processing in a hierarchical system can be amplified by modifications at subsequent stages. Even at early stages of cortical processing, the observed results involve a combination of cortical and subcortical mechanisms. Furthermore, due to feedback connections, cortical changes impact on subcortical representations (Ergenzinger et al., 1998). Nevertheless, we do not suggest that subcortical changes always play a major or even a notable role. We know, for example, that the second somatosensory area of monkeys, S2, depends on inputs from areas of anterior parietal cortex (Pons et al., 1987; Garraghty, Pons, and Kaas, 1990) and that lesions of the hand representations in these areas deactivate the hand portion of S2, which subsequently becomes responsive to other remaining inputs from anterior parietal cortex (Pons, Garraghty, and Mishkin, 1988; figure 15.2). It seems unlikely that the reorganization of S2 depends on subcortical rather than cortical mechanisms. We also know that restricted lesions of the retina in cats or monkeys deactivate the retinotopic portion of the thalamic relay, the lateral geniculate nucleus, and primary visual cortex, but the amount of reactivation by parts of the retina surrounding the lesion is very limited in the lateral geniculate nucleus (e.g., Darian-Smith and Gilbert, 1995; Baekelandt et al., 1994) compared to the extensive reactivation of cortex (figure 15.3; see Chino, 1997).

The subcortical and cortical changes in map organization demonstrated after peripheral nerve section in monkeys constitute only a fragment of an impressive collection of evidence that deactivations of populations of central nervous system neurons by receptor damage are followed by reactivations by remaining inputs. Positive results have been obtained from a range of manipulations across a number of mammalian species. In monkeys with amputated or missing digits, the primary somatosensory cortex normally responsive to those digits typically became responsive to inputs from adjoining digits (figure 15.1F), although some unresponsive cortex may remain (Merzenich et al., 1984; Calford and Tweedale, 1991; Code, Eslin, and Juliano, 1992; Manger, Woods, and Jones, 1996; Jain, Catania, and Kaas, 1998). Similarly, the cortical territories of

A. Location of Anterior Parietal Fields 3a, 3b, 1 and 2 and S2 in Macaque Monkey

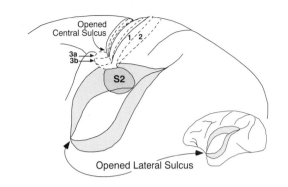

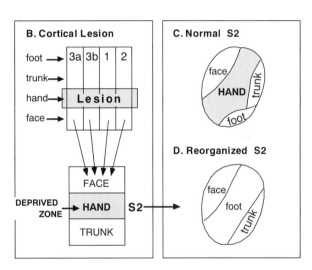

FIGURE 15.2 Reorganization of the second somatosensory area, S2, after lesions of the hand representations in anterior parietal cortex. Each of the four fields of anterior parietal cortex represents the body from foot to face in a mediolateral sequence (see Kaas, 1983). The activation of S2 depends on direct projections from these four fields, especially area 3b (Pons et al., 1987; Garraghty, Pons, and Kaas, 1990). Thus a lesion of the hand regions of these four fields deactivates the hand portion of S2. This cortex recovers responsiveness, largely to the foot (Pons, Garraghty, and Mishkin, 1988). (A) The locations of somatosensory areas on a lateral view of the brain of a macaque monkey. S2 can be seen on the upper bank of the opened lateral sulcus. Areas 3a and 3b are in the opened central sulcus, while areas 1 and 2 are largely on the brain surface. (B) A schematic of the four areas and S2, with the depriving effects of a lesion of hand cortex. (C) The normal somatotopy of S2 including a large representation of the hand. (D) The reorganized S2 with hand cortex reactivated by inputs from the foot.

missing digits of the large hand representations in S1 of raccoons became responsive to inputs from remaining digits (figure 15.4). Comparable results have been reported after digit loss in bats (Calford and Tweedale, 1988) and cats (Kalaska and Pomeranz, 1979) and after

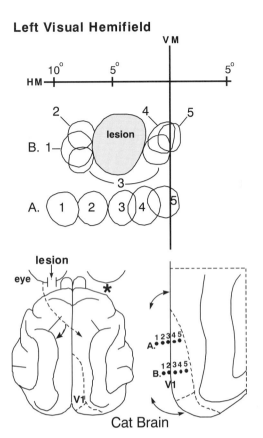

Left Visual Hemifield

Cat Brain

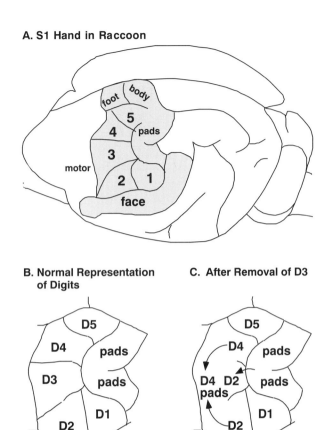

A. S1 Hand in Raccoon

B. Normal Representation of Digits

C. After Removal of D3

FIGURE 15.3 The reorganization of primary visual cortex following lesions of the retina. The deactivated cortex becomes responsive to parts of the retina adjoining the lesion. Because visual cortex is activated by both eyes, either lesions are retinotopically matched in both eyes, or all inputs are removed from the eye without a lesion (*) in order to completely deactivate a region of cortex.

(Lower left) A dorsal view of a cat brain showing a left eye with a 5° retinal lesion and the course of retinal projections (arrows) to the thalamus of both hemispheres. Recordings were made in primary visual cortex (V1–dashed line) of the right hemisphere.

(Lower right) A dorsal view of caudal visual cortex of the left hemisphere with some of V1 of the medial wall folded out, so that two rows of recording sites (numbered dots) are visible.

(Above) A portion of the left visual hemifield, marked in degrees along the zero horizontal meridian (HM), and showing the zero vertical meridian (VM). The projected location of the lesion of the retina of the left eye is outlined, together with receptive fields for neurons in the two rows of recording sites. Receptive fields for row A (see lower right) form a normal and orderly progression from temporal vision to the VM for a mediolateral sequence of recording sites toward the lateral border of V1. Receptive fields for row B, which passes through deprived cortex, are abnormally arranged so that receptive fields pile up on each side of the scotoma caused by the retinal lesion. Neurons at sites 2–4 acquired new receptive fields from retina outside of the lesion. Neurons at site 3 had two receptive fields, one on each side of the lesion. (Based on Kaas et al., 1990.)

FIGURE 15.4 Reorganization of somatosensory cortex after digit removal has also been convincingly demonstrated in raccoons, which have a large, highly orderly representation of the glabrous hand in primary somatosensory cortex, S1. (A) The location of S1 and the hand representation of pads and digits 1–5 on a dorsolateral view of the brain. (B) Normal representation of the digits in S1. (C) After removal of D3, the deprived cortex becomes activated by inputs from D2 and D4, and the palm adjoining D3. (Based on Kelahan and Doetsch, 1984; Rasmusson, 1982).

nerve damage in rats (J. T. Wall and Cusick, 1984). Cortical reorganization has been demonstrated even in humans, but the limited resolution of the noninvasive brain-imaging techniques (fMRI) has meant that only the larger reorganizations following limb amputations are obvious (see next section). While studies of cortex have concentrated on the detailed somatotopic map in S1 (3b), reorganizations have also been demonstrated in areas 3a and 1 of anterior parietal cortex (Merzenich et al., 1983a; Jain, Catania, and Kaas, 1997a) and in S2 (figure 15.2; Pons, Garraghty, and Mishkin, 1988) of monkeys.

As already noted, there have been many demonstrations of the filling in of cortical zones of deactivation after focal lesions of the retina in cats and monkeys (figure 15.3; Chino, 1997), and there is some evidence for the reorganization of the middle tempo-

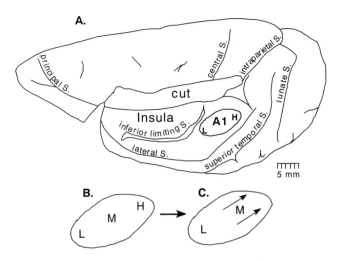

B.

C.

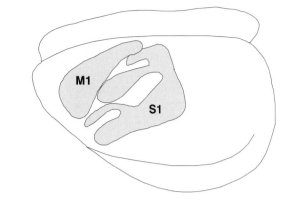

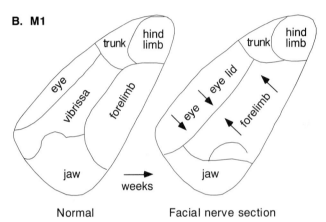

B. M1

FIGURE 15.5 The reorganization of deactivated auditory cortex. (A) A dorsal view of the left hemisphere of a macaque monkey brain with cortex over the lower bank of the lateral sulcus (S) cut away to reveal the location of primary auditory cortex (A1). (B) Primary auditory cortex (oval) normally is tonotopically organized in roughly rostrocaudal fashion with low tones (L) activating rostral locations, middle frequency tones (M) activating middle locations, and high tones (H) activating caudal locations. (C) Months after a high-frequency cochlear hearing loss produced by ototoxic drugs, neurons in caudal A1 no longer responded to high tones. Instead, these neurons responded to middle-frequency tones, and the representation of middle tones expanded (arrows). (Based on Schwaber, Garraghty, and Kaas, 1993).

FIGURE 15.6 The reorganization of primary motor cortex, M1, after section of the motor nerve to the movable vibrissa of the face. (A) A dorsolateral view of a rat brain showing the locations of primary motor cortex, M1, and somatosensory cortex, S1. (B) The normal somatotopy of the motor map in M1 (left) is modified over weeks of recovery after nerve section so that electrical stimulation of vibrissa cortex comes to evoke movements of the forelimb, eyelid, and eye. (Based on Sanes, Suner, and Donoghue, 1990).

ral visual area, MT, of monkeys after partial lesions of MT (Newsome and Pare, 1988; Yamasaki and Wurtz, 1991) or lesions of its activating input from V1 (Kaas and Krubitzer, 1992). An advantage of the visual system for studies of reactivation is that the reactivated neurons can be easily studied quantitatively for changes in response properties. Consistent with the qualitative observations from somatosensory cortex, visual neurons that acquire new receptive fields as a result of retinal lesions are little changed in response properties (Chino et al., 1995; Chino, 1997). Primary auditory cortex has also been shown to reorganize (see Kaas, 1996) after partial hearing loss in adult rodents (Robertson and Irvine, 1989), cats (Rajan et al., 1993), and monkeys (figure 15.5; Schwaber, Garraghty, and Kaas, 1993).

Evidence for plasticity in primary motor cortex comes from microstimulation experiments where a systematic map of movements can be demonstrated by evoking movements from many locations in cortex with low levels of electrical stimulation delivered with microelectrodes. After the loss of the muscle targets of part of motor cortex (Donoghue, Suner, and Sanes, 1990; Sanes, Suner, and Donoghue, 1990) by section of the motor nerve to the movable whiskers of the face in rats,

low levels of electrical stimulation of the vibrissa cortex come to evoke movements of the forelimb and eye (figure 15.6). Similar reorganizations of human motor cortex have been demonstrated with transcranial magnetic stimulation (see Chen et al., 1998), and in monkeys with microstimulation (Schieber and Deuel, 1997). Additionally, lesions of parts of MI for specific movements are followed by recoveries where stimulation of remaining parts of M1 can evoke the movements of the missing cortex (Nudo and Milliken, 1996; Nudo et al., 1996; Nudo, Plantz, and Milliken, 1997). Thus we conclude from these rather dramatic experiments that the mature brain, perhaps especially cortex, is not fixed in functional organization, and cortical areas of several levels in all major systems and across mammalian species can change.

Massive cortical reorganization

Most of the changes in sensory and motor representations described are of a size that is limited enough to be compatible with explanations based largely or solely on alterations in the synaptic strengths of existing connections. Recently, however, there have been a number of demonstrations of cortical reorganizations of a very large scale following the loss of most or all of the afferent inputs from a limb or even larger portions of the body. The first evidence that such massive changes occur come from studies of somatosensory cortex in monkeys 12 years or more after complete deafferentation of the arm by section of the relevant dorsal roots as they enter the spinal cord. Originally, these monkeys were studied behaviorally. Fortunately some were available for a microelectrode mapping study of somatosensory cortex. The surprising and remarkable finding from these recordings was that the large mediolateral extents (10 mm or more) of areas 3b and 1 that formerly represented the hand, wrist, and arm in these monkeys, were completely responsive to inputs from the chin and jaw (Pons et al., 1991). Thus neurons over a large expanse of cortex responded vigorously to the displacement of hairs and light touch on a limited portion of the face. The reactivated cortex was just medial to cortex that normally responds to the face, and this cortex continued to respond to the face. These results raised two important questions. First, what are the perceptual consequences of such an extensive reorganization of the somatosensory system? Second, how is such an extensive reorganization mediated?

The evidence for massive cortical reorganization immediately attracted the attention of investigators interested in the sensation of the existence of a missing limb, the phantom limb, that is typically reported by adult humans with amputations. The existence of such sensations has long been recognized, and they have been attributed to spontaneous or other neural activity in the portions of the somatosensory system formerly related to the missing limb (e.g., Melzack, 1990). Soon after the report on cortical reorganization in monkeys, Ramachandran, Rogers-Ramachandran, and Stewart (1992) drew attention to highly significant behavioral observations on phantom limbs. In brief, they noted that a light touch on the face of a patient with a missing arm led to the sensation of touch, not only on the face, but also on the phantom of the missing arm. Furthermore, touches on different parts of the face resulted in sensations on different parts of the phantom. To explain these observations, Ramachandran, Rogers-Ramachandran, and Stewart (1992) assumed that amputations are followed by massive cortical reorganization, as in deafferented

monkeys. They further postulated that touching the face activates the reorganized cortex, and activation of the reorganized cortex signals touch on the missing limb, rather than the real source of activation, the face. Further study revealed that sensations on the missing limb can also be triggered by touches on the skin of the stump of the missing limb (Ramachandran, 1993; Halligan et al., 1993; Yang et al., 1994; Aglioti, Bonazzi, and Cortese, 1994). However, the hypothesis that the triggered phantom sensations are caused by the activation of reorganized parts of primary somatosensory cortex does not easily account for all observations on phantom limbs. Most notably, trigger zones on the arm can emerge for sensations referred to a missing hand within a day of the loss of the hand (Doetsch, 1997). As yet, there is no evidence for such rapid reactivation of primary somatosensory cortex (see below).

At the time when Ramachandran, Rogers-Ramachandran, and Stewart (1992) proposed that the face activated hand cortex in humans with forelimb amputation, such extensive reorganization of cortex was only known for monkeys with a complete deafferentation of the forelimb (Pons et al., 1991), and it was not certain what would happen after a more limited sensory loss. However, monkeys, like humans, sometimes receive injuries that require a therapeutic amputation of a limb, and it soon became possible to study cortical organization in three such monkeys. Microelectrode recordings from these monkeys with forelimb or hand amputations revealed that hand cortex was completely reactivated by inputs from the stump of the limb, and to some extent the face (Florence and Kaas, 1995). The results indicated that massive reorganization of somatosensory cortex can follow the loss of inputs from the hand or forelimb in primates (also see Florence, Taub, and Lyon, 1997), and thus cortical reorganization could account for the face and stump trigger zones for sensations on the phantom in humans. Unfortunately, the results did not provide any information on the length of time it takes for reorganization, since the monkeys were studied 1–13 years after their amputations. However, the results did provide an important clue about the possible sources of the reactivation. In each monkey, an anatomical tracer was injected into the skin of the stump of the amputated limb. The transportation of this tracer through sensory nerves of the stump to the spinal cord and cuneate subnucleus of the brain stem revealed axon terminations in normal locations for the representation of the arm, but also a sparse distribution of axons in the part of the nucleus where the hand is normally represented. These anatomical results generated the hypothesis that axons from the arm had sprouted to grow into the deafferented part of the cuneate nucleus formerly devoted to the hand. While this sparse reinnervation presumably would activate only some of the deprived neurons on the cuneate nucleus, the divergence and convergence of projections from the cuneate nucleus to the ventroposterior nucleus of the thalamus would result in a larger population of reactivated neurons, and the divergence of thalamocortical projections, together with the framework of lateral, intrinsic connections in somatosensory cortex, would lead to more effective reactivations at these higher levels.

The use of noninvasive imaging methods has allowed the issue of brain reorganization after amputations to be directly examined in humans. Such imaging studies provided further evidence that face and stump inputs come to activate hand cortex in humans with forelimb amputations (Yang et al., 1994; Elbert et al., 1994; Flor et al., 1995; Knecht et al., 1996). Remarkable additional evidence came from a study of the results of recording from neurons in the ventroposterior nucleus of humans with amputations, and electrically stimulating the same neurons (Davis et al., 1998). In normal, undeprived portions of the somatosensory thalamus, these investigators found that the sensations produced by microstimulation were referred to the same locations as the receptive fields of the neurons at the sites of electrical stimulation. But in some amputees, stimulating neurons with receptive fields on the stump of the missing limb produced sensations referred to the missing limb. The results indicate that reorganization of deprived parts of the somatosensory system, as observed in cortex, had already occurred at the level of the thalamus, and that the reactivated neurons continued to retain their original meaning of stimuli on the missing limb. This finding, of course, does not suggest that sensations on the missing limb are mediated in the thalamus, since these neurons are part of a complex system that includes many levels of somatosensory cortex that would also be activated by the electrical stimulation of thalamic neurons. Nevertheless, the evidence is now rather compelling that amputations can produce extensive reorganizations of the somatosensory system. Such reorganizations may be expressed subcortically at the level of the thalamus, and reactivated neurons retain the original significance and signal misperceptions of touch on the phantom limb.

Are such massive reactivations mediated, at least to some critical extent, by the growth of new connections? Further evidence for new growth came from studies of the time it takes for massive cortical reorganization, since new growth would take some time to occur. The time course of reactivation was possible to study in monkeys with unilateral section of forelimb afferents in the dorsal columns of the spinal cord (Jain, Catania, and Kaas, 1997b, 1998a). There is a history of many years of behavioral and electrophysiological studies of the effects of dorsal column section in monkeys, and a surprising finding is that the behavioral consequences are rather mild (e.g., Makous, Friedman, and Vierch, 1996). Thus, soon after unilateral sections, monkeys climb about and retrieve food with the affected limb, although not as skillfully as with the normal limb. Despite these rather limited behavioral changes, the hand region of area 3b of somatosensory cortex of monkeys was completely deactivated by dorsal column section above the level where afferents enter from the hand, while the more lateral cortex devoted to the face responded normally to touch on the face (figure 15.7B). However, if the lesion was incomplete so that a fraction of the afferents from the hand remained, these afferents continued to activate cortical neurons, and the complete hand territory of cortex gradually became reactivated by these preserved inputs from the hand (figure 15.7D, E). If the dorsal column section was complete, no reactivation of this cortex by hand afferents occurred even after months. Instead, the hand cortex became reactivated by preserved inputs from the face and a few preserved afferents from the anterior arm that enter the spinal cord above the level where afferents enter from the hand (figure 15.7C). Indeed, many neurons in hand cortex became responsive to tactile stimuli on either the face or anterior arm. Most importantly, the reactivation of somatosensory cortex by face inputs occurred slowly, emerging only after six to eight months of recovery. This slow development suggests that a critical feature in the reactivation is the sprouting and growth of new connections, possibly the sprouting and growth of axon collaterals of afferents from the face (and stump for amputations) into the portions of the cuneate nucleus of the brain stem normally activated by the hand as proposed by Florence and Kaas (1995).

The proposal that reactivation is based on the formation of new connections is somewhat unconventional, since new growth in the mature central nervous system is expected to be very limited (see Florence and Kaas, in press, for review). Yet, there is evidence that the terminations of crushed nerves sprout in the spinal cord of monkeys (Florence et al., 1993; see Kapfhaminer, 1997, for review of axon sprouting in the spinal cord) and that afferents grow into new brainstem territories after limb amputations (Florence and Kaas, 1995) or dorsal column section (N. Jain, unpublished observations). Since the new growth in the brain stem is sparse, the effects of these reinnervations are most likely enhanced at higher levels in the system so that many neurons are

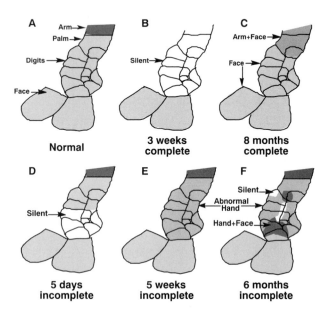

FIGURE 15.7 The reorganization of somatosensory cortex after dorsal column lesions. The dorsal column constitutes the major spinal cord pathway for ascending afferents from cutaneous and muscle receptors. Section of the dorsal column at high cervical levels removes this input from the hand and most of the arm, as well as lower parts of the body, while leaving inputs from the face intact. (A) The normal organization of the lateral portion of area 3b in owl monkeys (see figure 15.1 for locations on brain). The upper and lower face are represented in two ovals of cortex laterally, the digits in a lateromedial sequence from 1–5 more medially and rostrally, the pads of the palm, caudally, and the wrist and arm medially. (B) After a complete dorsal column lesion of one side, the opposite hand region and more medial cortex becomes completely unresponsive to touch and hair movement. Some medial cortex may remain responsive to preserved inputs from the anterior arm, and lateral cortex remains normally responsive to touch and hair movement on the face. This complete deactivation persists for months. (C) After 6–8 months of recovery from contralateral dorsal column section, hand cortex becomes responsive to touch and hair movement on the face. Some of the more medial cortex may respond to both the face and the anterior arm. (D) Incomplete dorsal column lesions leave some of the hand representation responsive to tactile stimulation of the hand. Within the first few days of recovery, this activation is somatotopically appropriate, and much of the hand representation is unresponsive (Silent). (E) Within weeks of an incomplete dorsal column lesion leaving some inputs from the hand intact, these preserved inputs come to activate much or all of hand cortex. (F) After months of recovery after an incomplete dorsal column lesion, many locations in hand cortex respond to both hand and face inputs. This result seems to reflect both the more rapid potentiation of preserved inputs from the hand and the slower potentiation of preserved inputs from the face. (Modified from Jain, Florence, and Kaas, 1998.)

reactivated in the thalamus (Davis et al., 1998), and the cortical reactivation is even more effective. Reactivations in cortex may even depend in part on the growth of new connections in cortex. Darian-Smith and Gilbert (1994) provided anatomical evidence that the horizon-

tal connections in visual cortex sprout to become more dense in regions where neurons have become reactivated after being deprived by long-standing retinal lesions. Similarly, injections of anatomical tracers in somatosensory cortex of monkeys with limb amputations provided evidence for the growth of new and more extensive horizontal connections within the deprived but recovered cortex (Florence, Taub, and Lyon, 1997). New growth may occur at other levels of the somatosensory and visual systems as well (e.g., Baekelandt et al., 1994), and new growth may include the extension of dendrites of cortical and subcortical neurons (e.g., T. A. Jones and Schallert, 1994).

The anatomical results after massive deafferentations demonstrate the possibility of considerable new growth in the mature central nervous system (also, see Aguayo, 1985). Glial cells of the central nervous system appear to generate molecules that normally inhibit axon growth, and thus new growth can be promoted by interfering with these molecules (e.g., Z'Graggen et al., 1998; see Schwab, 1996, for review). It is not certain why new growth of an extensive nature takes so long to emerge, but it may take time for inducing factors (e.g., Cohen-Cory and Fraser, 1995) to be expressed, as well as time for new growth (see Florence and Kaas, in press). While new growth may be important in many reactivations, new growth may provide only a framework for recovery, and many other factors important in less massive reactivations undoubtedly also contribute.

Conclusions

As a result of a large number of studies of cortical and subcortical plasticity of sensory and motor systems in adult mammals, especially during the last few years, a number of conclusions are now supportable.

1. The detailed structure of normal representations is dynamically maintained. Alterations in inputs, activations of modulating systems with emotional state and attention, and even changes in stimulus conditions can produce immediate changes in the dynamic balance within systems so that receptive field properties, receptive field sizes and locations, and map topography change. Such rapid changes are typically quite reversible, but they may lead to changes in synaptic strengths and thus to more persistent alterations.

2. Alterations produced by prolonged, localized sensory or electrical stimulation or by sensory deprivations may lead to activity-induced modifications in neurotransmitter and neuromodulator expression, the local growth of axons and dendrites, and alterations in synaptic strengths. Synaptic weights also may be altered by

experience and learning according to modified Hebbian rules.

3. Reorganizations of sensory and motor maps occur in all major systems and at subcortical as well as cortical levels. Modifications accumulate and amplify across serial levels of processing. Cortical areas, due to a system of horizontal connections, may be more modifiable than subcortical stations.

4. Some types of recovery are best understood in terms of the internal structures of subcortical maps. The substitution of dorsal skin inputs for glabrous skin inputs, for example, appears to involve rather local and limited synaptic changes in the cuneate nucleus of the brain stem that results in an impressively large reorganization of the cortical map.

5. Some types of reorganization, such as those that occur after major sensory deafferentations, take months to emerge. These major reactivations appear to depend on the extensive sprouting and growth of axons to form new connections. The massive reorganizations lead to misperceptions, and often unwanted sensations. Nevertheless, the potential for new growth holds promise for many clinical applications, and new growth may be important in other recoveries, such as those that occur after stroke.

REFERENCES

AGLIOTI, S., A. BONAZZI, and F. CORTESE, 1994. Phantom lower limb as a perceptual marker of neural plasticity in the mature human brain. *Proc. R. Soc. Lond. B.* 255:273–278.

AGUAYO, A. J., 1985. Axonal regeneration from injured neurons in the adult mammalian central nervous system. In *Synaptic Plasticity*, C. W. Cotman, ed. New York: Guilford Press, pp. 457–484.

BAEKELANDT, V., L. ARCKEN, W. ANNAERT, U. T. EYSEL, G. A. ORBAN, and F. VANDESANDE, 1994. Alterations in GAP-43 and synapsin immunoreactivity provide evidence for synaptic reorganization in adult cat dorsal lateral geniculate nucleus following retinal lesions. *Eur. J. Neurosci.* 6:754–765.

BEAR, M. F., L. N. COOPER, and F. F. EBNER, 1987. A physiological basis for a theory of synapse modification. *Science* 237:42–48.

BENUSKOVA, L., M. E. DIAMOND, and F. F. EBNER, 1994. Dynamic synaptic modification threshold: Computational model of experience-dependent plasticity in adult rat barrel cortex. *Proc. Natl. Acad. Sci. U.S.A.* 91:4791–4795.

CALFORD, M. B., and R. TWEEDALE, 1988. Immediate and chronic changes in responses of somatosensory cortex in adult flying-fox after digit amputation. *Nature* 332:446–448.

CALFORD, M. B., and R. TWEEDALE, 1991. Immediate expansion of receptive fields of neurons in area 3b of macaque monkeys after digit denervation. *Somatosens. Mot. Res.* 8:249–260.

CASTRO-ALAMANCOS, M. A., and B. W. CONNORS, 1996. Short-term plasticity of a thalamocortical pathway dynamically modulated by behavioral state. *Science* 272:274–277.

CATANIA, K. C., and J. H. KAAS, 1997. Somatosensory fovea in the star-nosed mole: Behavioral use of the star in relation to innervation patterns and cortical representation. *J. Comp. Neurol.* 387:215–233.

CHEN, R., B. CORNWELL, Z. VASEEN, M. HALLETT, and L. G. COHEN, 1998. Mechanisms of cortical reorganization in lower-limb amputees. *J. Neurosci.* 18:3443–3450.

CHINO, Y. M., 1997. Receptive-field plasticity in the adult visual cortex: Dynamic signal recording or experience-dependent plasticity. *Sem. Neurosci.* 9: 34–46.

CHINO, Y. M., E. I. SMITH III, J. H. KAAS, Y. SASAKI, and H. CHENG, 1995. Receptive-field properties of deafferented visual cortical neurons after topographic map reorganization. *J. Neurosci.* 15:2417–2433.

CODE, R. A., D. E. ESLIN, and S. L. JULIANO, 1992. Expansion of stimulus-evoked metabolic activity in monkey somatosensory cortex after peripheral denervation. *Exp. Brain Res.* 88:341–344.

COHEN-CORY, S., and S. E. FRASER, 1995. Effects of brain-derived neurotrophic factor on optic axon branching and remodelling *in vivo*. *Nature* 378:192–196.

DARIAN-SMITH, C., and C. D. GILBERT, 1994. Axonal sprouting accompanies functional reorganization in adult cat striate cortex. *Nature* 368:737–740.

DARIAN-SMITH, C., and C. D. GILBERT, 1995. Topographic reorganization in the striate cortex of the adult cat and monkey is cortically mediated. *J. Neurosci.* 15:1631–1647.

DAVIS, K. D., Z. H. T. KISS, L. LUO, R. R. TASKAR, A. M. LOZANO, and J. O. DOSTROVSKY, 1998. Phantom sensations generated by thalamic microstimulation. *Nature* 391:385–387.

DOETSCH, G. S., 1997. Progressive changes in cutaneous trigger zones for sensation referred to a phantom hand: A case report and review with implications for cortical reorganization. *Somatosens. Mot. Res.* 14:6–16.

DOETSCH, G. S., T. A. HARRISON, A. C. MacDONALD, and M. S. LITAKER, 1996. Short-term plasticity in primary somatosensory cortex of the rat: Rapid changes in magnitudes and latencies of neuronal response following digit denervation. *Exp. Brain Res.* 112:505–512.

DONOGHUE, J. P., S. SUNER, and J. N. SANES, 1990. Dynamic organization of primary motor cortex output to target muscles in adult rats. II. Rapid reorganization following motor nerve lesions. *Exp. Brain Res.* 79:492–503.

DYKES, R. W., 1990. Acetylcholine and neuronal plasticity in somatosensory cortex. In *Brain Cholinergic Systems*, M. Steriade and D. Biesold, eds. New York: Oxford University Press, pp. 294–313.

DYKES, R. W., 1997. Mechanisms controlling neuronal plasticity in somatosensory cortex. *Can. J. Physiol. Pharmacol.* 75: 535–545.

EBNER, F. F., V. REMA, R. SACHDEV, and F. J. SYMONS, 1997. Activity-dependent plasticity in adult somatic sensory cortex. *Sem. Neurosci.* 9:47–58.

ELBERT, T., H. FLOR, N. BIRBAUMER, et al., 1994. Extensive reorganization of the somatosensory cortex in adult humans after nervous system injury. *NeuroReport* 5:2593–2597.

ERGENZINGER, E. R., M. M. GLASIER, J. O. HAHM, and T. P. PONS, 1998. Cortically induced thalamic plasticity in the primate somatosensory system. *Nature Neurosci.* 1:226–229.

FLOR, H., T. ELBERT, and S. KNECHT, et al., 1995. Phantom-limb pain as a perceptual correlate of cortical reorganization following arm amputation. *Nature* 375:482–484.

FLORENCE, S. L., P. E. GARRAGHTY, M. CARLSON, and J. H. KAAS, 1993. Sprouting of peripheral nerve axons in the spinal cord of monkeys. *Brain Res.* 601:343–348.

FLORENCE, S. L., and J. H. KAAS, 1995. Large-scale reorganization at multiple levels of the somatosensory pathway follows therapeutic amputation of the hand in monkeys. *J. Neurosci.* 15:8083–8095.

FLORENCE, S. L., and J. H. KAAS, in press. Cortical plasticity: Growth of new connections can contribute to reorganization. In *Somatosensory Processing: From Single Neurons to Brain Imaging*, M. J. Rowe, ed. North Ryde, New South Wales: Gordon and Breach Science.

FLORENCE, S. L., H. B. TAUB, and D. C. LYON, 1997. Functional and structural reorganization in somatosensory cortex of adult macaque monkeys after forelimb injury. *Soc. Neurosci. Abstr.* 23:1007.

FLORENCE, S. L., J. T. WALL, and J. H. KAAS, 1991. Central projections from the skin of the hand in squirrel monkeys. *J. Comp. Neurol.* 311:563–578.

FOOTE, S. L., and J. H. MORRISON, 1987. Extrathalamic modulation of cortical function. *Annu. Rev. Neurosci.* 10:67–95.

GARRAGHTY, P. E., D. P. HANES, S. L. FLORENCE, and J. H. KAAS, 1994. Pattern of peripheral deafferentation predicts reorganizational limits in adult primate somatosensory cortex. *Somatosens. Mot. Res.* 11:109–117.

GARRAGHTY, P. E., and J. H. KAAS, 1991a. Large-scale functional reorganization in adult monkey cortex after peripheral nerve injury. *Proc. Natl. Acad. Sci. U.S.A.* 88:6976–6980.

GARRAGHTY, P. E., and J. H. KAAS, 1991b. Functional reorganization in adult monkey thalamus after peripheral nerve injury. *NeuroReport* 2:747–750.

GARRAGHTY, P. E., E. A. LACHICA, and J. H. KAAS, 1991. Injury-induced reorganization of somatosensory cortex is accompanied by reductions in GABA staining. *Somatosens. Mot. Res.* 8:347–354.

GARRAGHTY, P. E., and N. MUJA, 1996. NMDA receptors and plasticity in adult primate somatosensory cortex. *J. Comp. Neurol.* 367:319–326.

GARRAGHTY, P. E., T. P. PONS, and J. H. KAAS, 1990. Ablations of areas 3b (SI proper) and 3a of somatosensory cortex in marmosets deactivate the second and parietal ventral somatosensory areas. *Somatosens. Mot. Res.* 7:125–135.

GILBERT, C. D., 1998. Adult cortical dynamics. *Physiol. Rev.* 78:467–485.

HALLIGAN, P. W., J. C. MARSHALL, D. T. WADE, J. DAVY, and D. MORRISON, 1993. Thumb in cheek? Sensory reorganizations and perceptual plasticity after limb amputation. *NeuroReport* 4:233–236.

JAIN, N., K. C. CATANIA, and J. H. KAAS, 1997a. Reorganization of somatosensory area 3a in owl monkeys following long-term deafferentation by dorsal column section. *Soc. Neurosci. Abstr.* 23:1799.

JAIN, N., K. C. CATANIA, and J. H. KAAS, 1997b. Deactivation and reactivation of somatosensory cortex after dorsal spinal cord injury. *Nature* 386:495–498.

JAIN, N., K. C. CATANIA, and J. H. KAAS, 1998. A histologically visible representation of the fingers and palm in primate area 3b and its immutability following long-term deafferentations. *Cerebral Cortex* 8:227–236.

JAIN, N., S. L. FLORENCE, and J. H. KAAS, 1998. Reorganization of somatosensory cortex after nerve and spinal cord injury. *News Physiol. Sci.* 13:143–149.

JONES, E. G., 1993. GABAergic neurons and their role in cortical plasticity in primates. *Cerebral Cortex* 3:361–372.

JONES, T. A., and T. SCHALLERT, 1994. Use-dependent growth of pyramidal neurons after neocortical damage. *J. Neurosci.* 14:2140–2152.

JULIANO, S. L., W. MA, M. F. BEAR, and D. ESLIN, 1990. Cholinergic manipulation alters stimulus-evoked metabolic activity in cat somatosensory cortex. *J. Comp. Neurol.* 297:106–120.

JULIANO, S. L., W. MA, and D. ESLIN, 1991. Cholinergic depletion prevents expansion of topographic maps in somatosensory cortex. *Proc. Natl. Acad. Sci. U.S.A.* 88:780–784.

KAAS, J. H., 1983. What, if anything, is S-I? The organization of the "first somatosensory area" of cortex. *Physiol. Rev.* 63:206–231.

KAAS, J. H., 1996. Plasticity of sensory representations in the auditory and other systems of adult mammals. In *Auditory System Plasticity and Regeneration*, R. J. Salvi, D. Henderson, F. Fiorino, and J. Colletti, eds. New York: Thieme Medical, pp. 213–223.

KAAS, J. H., and S. L. FLORENCE, 1997. Mechanisms of reorganization in sensory systems of primates after peripheral nerve injury. In *Brain Plasticity,* H. J. Freund, B. A. Sabel, and O. W. Witte, eds. *Advances in Neurology*, vol. 78. Philadelphia: Lippincott–Raven Press, pp. 147–158.

KAAS, J. H., and L. A. KRUBITZER, 1992. Area 17 lesions deactivate area MT in owl monkeys. *Vis. Neurosci.* 9:399–407.

KAAS, J. H., L. A. KRUBITZER, Y. M. CHINO, A. L. LANGSTON, E. H. POLLEY, and N. BLAIR, 1990. Reorganization of retinotopic cortical maps in adult mammals after lesions of the retina. *Science* 248:229–231.

KALASKA, J., and B. POMERANZ, 1979. Chronic paw denervation causes an age-dependent appearance of novel responses from forearm in "paw cortex" of kittens and adult cats. *J. Neurophysiol.* 42:618–633.

KAPFHAMMER, J. P., 1997. Axon sprouting in the spinal cord: Growth promoting and growth inhibitory mechanisms. *Anat. Embryol.* 196:417–426.

KELAHAN, A. M., and G. S. DOETSCH, 1984. Time-dependent changes in the functional organization of somatosensory cerebral cortex following digit amputation in adult raccoons. *Somatosens. Res.* 2:49–81.

KILGARD, M. P., and M. M. MERZENICH, 1998. Cortical map reorganization enabled by nucleus basalis activity. *Science* 279:1714–1718.

KNECHT, S. H., T. HENNINGSEN, H. ELBERT, H. FLOR, C. HOHLING, C. PANTEV, and E. TAUB, 1996. Reorganizational and perceptional changes after amputation. *Brain* 119:1213–1219.

LEVINE, E. S., and I. B. BLACK, 1997. Trophic factor, synaptic plasticity, and memory. *Ann. N.Y. Acad. Sci.* 835:12–19.

MAKOUS, J. C., R. M. FRIEDMAN, and C. J. VIERCH, 1996. Effects of a dorsal column lesion on temporal processing within the somatosensory system of primates. *Exp. Brain Res.* 112: 253–267.

MANGER, P. P., T. M. WOODS, and E. C. JONES, 1996. Plasticity of the somatosensory cortical map in macaque monkeys after chronic partial amputation of a digit. *Proc. R. Soc. Lond. B.* 263:933–939.

MELZACK, R., 1990. Phantom limbs and the concept of a neuromatrix. *Trends Neurosci.* 13:88–92.

MELZER, P., and H. STEINER, 1997. Stimulus-dependent expression of immediate-early genes in rat somatosensory cortex. *J. Comp. Neurol.* 380:145–153.

MERZENICH, M. M., J. H. KAAS, J. WALL, J. J. NELSON, M. SUR, and D. FELLEMAN, 1983a. Topographic reorganization of somatosensory cortical areas 3b and 1 in adult monkeys following restricted deafferentation. *Neurosci.* 8:33–55.

MERZENICH, M. M., J. H. KAAS, J. T. WALL, M. SUR, R. J. NELSON, and D. J. FELLEMAN, 1983b. Progression of change following median nerve section in the cortical representation of the hand in areas 3b and 1 in adult owl and squirrel monkeys. *Neurosci.* 10:639–665.

MERZENICH, M. M., R. J. NELSON, J. H. KAAS, M. P. STRYKER, W. M. JENKINS, J. M. ZOOK, M. S. CYNADER, and A. SCHOPPMANN, 1987. Variability in hand surface representation in areas 3b and 1 in adult owl and squirrel monkeys. *J. Comp. Neurol.* 25:281–296.

MERZENICH, M. M., R. J. NELSON, M. P. STRYKER, M. S. CYNADER, A. SCHOPPMAN, and J. M. ZOOK, 1984. Somatosensory cortical map changes following digit amputation in adult monkeys. *J. Comp. Neurol.* 224:591–605.

NEWSOME, W. T., and E. B. PARE, 1988. A selective impairment of motion perception following lesions of the middle temporal visual area (MT). *J. Neurosci.* 8:2201–2211.

NICOLELIS, M. A. L., 1997. Dynamic and distributed somatosensory representations as the substrate for cortical and subcortical plasticity. *Sem. Neurosci.* 9:24–33.

NUDO, R. J., and G. W. MILLIKEN, 1996. Reorganization of movement representations in primary motor cortex following focal ischemic infarcts in adult squirrel monkeys. *J. Neurophysiol.* 75:2144–2149.

NUDO, R. J., E. J. PLANTZ, and G. W. MILLIKEN, 1997. Adaptive plasticity in primate motor cortex as a consequence of behavioral experience and neuronal injury. *Sem. Neurosci.* 9:13–23.

NUDO, R. J., B. M. WISE, F. SIFUENTES, and G. W. MILLIKEN, 1996. Neural substrates for the effects of rehabilitative training on motor recovery after ischemic infarct. *Science* 272:1791–1794.

PARKER, J. L., M. L. WOOD, and J. O. DOSTROVSKY, 1998. A focal zone of thalamic plasticity. *J. Neurosci.* 18:548–558.

PETTIT, M. J., and H. D. SCHWARK, 1993. Receptive field reorganization in dorsal column nuclei during temporary denervation. *Science* 262:2054–2056.

PONS, T. P., P. E. GARRAGHTY, D. P. FRIEDMAN, and M. MISHKIN, 1987. Physiological evidence for serial processing in somatosensory cortex. *Science* 237:417–420.

PONS, T. P., P. E. GARRAGHTY, and M. MISHKIN, 1988. Lesion-induced plasticity in the second somatosensory cortex of adult macaques. *Proc. Natl. Acad. Sci. U.S.A.* 85:5279–5281.

PONS, T. P., P. E. GARRAGHTY, A. K. OMMAYA, J. H. KAAS, E. TAUB, and M. MISHKIN, 1991. Massive cortical reorganization after sensory deafferentation in adult macaques. *Science* 252:1857–1860.

PONS, T. P., J. T. WALL, P. E. GARRAGHTY, C. G. CUSICK, and J. H. KAAS, 1987. Consistent features of the representation of the hand in area 3b of macaque monkeys. *Somatosens. Mot. Res.* 4:309–331.

RAJAN, R., D. R. F. IRVINE, L. Z. WISE, and P. HEIL, 1993. Effect of unilateral partial cochlear lesions in adult cats on the representation of lesioned and unlesioned cochleas in primary auditory cortex. *J. Comp. Neurol.* 338:17–49.

RAMACHANDRAN, V. S., 1993. Behavioral and magnetoencephalographic correlates of plasticity in the adult brain. *Proc. Natl. Acad. Sci. U.S.A.* 90:10413–10420.

RAMACHANDRAN, V. S., D. ROGERS-RAMACHANDRAN, and M. STEWART, 1992. Perceptual correlates of massive cortical reorganization. *Science* 258:1159–1160.

RASMUSSON, D. D., 1982. Reorganization of raccoon somatosensory cortex following removal of the fifth digit. *J. Comp. Neurol.* 205:313–326.

RASMUSSON, D., 1996. Changes in the organization of the ventroposterior lateral thalamic nucleus after digit removal in adult raccoon. *J. Comp. Neurol.* 364:92–103.

RASMUSSON, D. D., D. F. LOUW, and S. A. NORTHGRAVE, 1993. The immediate effects of peripheral denervation on inhibitory mechanisms in the somatosensory thalamus. *Somatosens. Mot. Res.* 10:69–80.

RASMUSSON, D., and B. G. TURNBULL, 1983. Immediate effects of digit amputation on S1 cortex in raccoon: Unmasking of inhibitory fields. *Brain Res.* 288:368–370.

RAUSCHECKER, J. P., 1991. Mechanisms of visual plasticity: Hebb synapses, SMDA receptors, and beyond. *Physiol. Rev.* 71:587–615.

ROBERTSON, D., and D. R. F. IRVINE, 1989. Plasticity of frequency organization in auditory cortex of guinea pigs with partial unilateral deafness. *J. Comp. Neurol.* 282:456–471.

SANES, J. N., S. SUNER, and J. P. DONOGHUE, 1990. Dynamic organization of primary motor cortex output to target muscles in adult rats. I. Long-term patterns of reorganization following motor or mixed nerve lesions. *Exp. Brain Res.* 79:479–491.

SCHIEBER, M. H., and R. K. DEUEL, 1997. Primary motor cortex reorganization in a long-term monkey amputee. *Somatosens. Mot. Res.* 14:157–167.

SCHWAB, M. E., 1996. Bridging the gap in spinal cord regeneration. *Nature Medicine* 2:976.

SCHWABER, M. K., P. E. GARRAGHTY, and J. H. KAAS, 1993. Neuroplasticity of the adult primate auditory cortex following cochlear hearing loss. *Am. J. Otol.* 14:252–258.

SILVA, A. C., S. K. RASEY, X. WU, and J. T. WALL, 1996. Initial cortical reactions to injury of the median and radial nerves to the hands of adult primates. *J. Comp. Neurol.* 366:700–716.

SNOW, P. J., and P. WILSON, 1991. Plasticity in the somatosensory system of developing and mature mammals. *Progress in Sensory Physiology*, vol. 2. New York: Springer-Verlag.

WALL, J. T., and C. G. CUSICK, 1984. Cutaneous responsiveness in primary somatosensory S-I hindpaw cortex before and after partial hindpaw deafferentation in adult rats. *J. Neurosci.* 4:1499–1515.

WALL, J. T., D. J. FELLEMAN, and J. H. KAAS, 1983. Recovery of normal topography in the somatosensory cortex of monkeys after nerve crush and regeneration. *Science* 221:771–773.

WALL, P. D., 1977. The presence of ineffective synapses and the circumstances which unmask them. *Philos. Trans. R. Soc. Lond. Biol.* 278:361–372.

WEINBERGER, N. W., 1995. Dynamic regulation of receptive fields and maps in the adult sensory cortex. *Annu. Rev. Neurosci.* 18:129–158.

WELKER, E., and H. VAN DER LOOS, 1986. Quantitative correlation between barrel-field size and the sensory denervation of the whiskerpad: A comparative study in six strains of mice bred for different patterns of mystacial vibrissae. *J. Neurosci.* 6:2117–2133.

XING, J., and G. L. GERSTEIN, 1996. Networks with lateral connectivity. I. Dynamic properties mediated by the balance of intrinsic excitation and inhibition. *J. Neurophysiol.* 75:184–199.

XU, J., and J. T. WALL, 1997. Rapid changes in brainstem maps of adult primates after peripheral injury. *Brain Res.* 774:221–215.

YAMASAKI, D. S., and R. W. WURTZ, 1991. Recovery of function after lesions in the superior temporal sulcus in the monkey. *J. Neurophysiol.* 66:651–673.

YANG, T. T., C. C. GALLEN, V. S. RAMACHANDRAN, S. COBB, B. J. SCHWARTZ, and F. E. BLOOM, 1994. Noninvasive detection of cerebral plasticity in adult human somatosensory cortex. *NeuroReport* 5:701–704.

Z'GRAGGEN, W. J., G. A. S. METZ, G. L. KARTJE, M. THALLMAN, and M. E. SCHWAB, 1998. Functional recovery and enhanced corticofugal plasticity after unilateral pyramidal tract lesion and blockage of myelin-associated neurite growth inhibitors in adult rats. *J. Neurosci.* 18:4744–4757.

16 Cerebral Cortical Plasticity: Perception and Skill Acquisition

GREGG H. RECANZONE

ABSTRACT Cerebral cortical plasticity has been demonstrated in a variety of different mammals, following a number of different peripheral and central nervous system manipulations. The reorganization of cortical representations has been implicated in the ability to acquire perceptual and motor skills throughout normal life. This chapter presents evidence from a variety of studies which indicates that cortical plasticity occurs in normal, intact animals and humans, and that these changes in representations are correlated with changes in both motor skills and sensory perceptions.

One of the central goals in neuroscience, particularly in cognitive neuroscience, is to determine the neuronal mechanisms that generate perceptions. Very little is known about how action potentials transmitted throughout the nervous system allow individuals to perceive the complex world around them, to compare this representation of the world to past experience, and to initiate behaviors to achieve goals (e.g., eating, drinking, rest, lively conversation). Although both animal and human studies indicate that the cerebral cortex is integral in processing complex stimuli, very little is known of this structure beyond the presumed relevance of particular areas for specific functions. Although much knowledge has been gained over the past decades on how the individual neurons in a limited number of cortical areas respond to different stimuli, it is still unclear how these responses participate in perception.

While it may be agreed by many that the cerebral cortex is necessary for some perceptions, there is less consensus on how the cerebral cortex is actually functioning to create these perceptions. Further, one of the basic tenets of psychological studies since the late 1800s has been that individuals will improve at virtually any task with continued practice. It was presumed by James (1890) that this improvement in performance was made possible by a change, or "plasticity," of the "organic materials" of the central nervous system.

GREGG H. RECANZONE Center for Neuroscience and Section of Neurobiology, Physiology, and Behavior, University of California at Davis, Calif.

The first real insights into how such changes could be manifest in the cerebral cortex came from studies examining the effects of peripheral nerve injuries on cortical "maps," or representations of the sensory surface, in adult mammals (see Kaas, 1991, and chapter 15). The term *plasticity* is used to describe this capacity to change cortical representations in adults. In such studies denervation, or extensive behavioral use of a restricted sensory surface, results in a change in the central representation of that sensory surface. These results are consistent with the earliest reports of cerebral cortical function performed at the turn of the 20th century by Sir Charles Sherrington and colleagues. Their studies of the motor cortex of monkeys and great apes indicated that movement representations in the motor cortex could be altered over the course of several minutes, and that this effect was reversible (Graham Brown and Sherrington, 1912).

Several other studies have shown that cortical representations most likely reflect the stimulus history of the sensory surface being represented. For example, the cortical representation of the ventral body surface is larger in nursing rat mothers than in non-nursing female rats (Xerri, Stern, and Merzenich, 1994). The selective stimulation of two whiskers either experimentally (DeLacour, Houcine, and Talbi, 1987) or by trimming all but two adjacent whiskers (Armstrong-James, Diamond, and Ebner, 1994) results in many more neurons within the somatosensory cortex responding to both of the two whiskers. In primates, surgical fusion of two digits results in a zone of cortex in area 3b in which neurons have receptive fields that cross the suture line and respond to parts of both fused digits, in contrast to the normal situation where 3b neurons rarely, if ever, respond to stimulation of two digits (Allard et al., 1991; see also Merzenich et al., 1987). Finally, Jenkins and colleagues (1990) showed that training monkeys to attend to stimulation on the tip of one or two fingers results in an increased representation of the stimulated fingertips compared to the unstimulated fingers. Similar kinds of short- and long-term plasticity have been observed in the visual cortex as well as in human subjects performing visual psychophysical tasks (see Gilbert et al., 1996; Gilbert, 1998).

These experiments provide evidence that cortical plasticity is not necessarily a response to the peripheral injury, but can also occur by changing the stimulation pattern across the skin. This finding further suggests that practice at a particular behavioral task, which generally results in an improvement in performance, would similarly be reflected by a change in the cortical representations of the relevant sensory or motor components of the task. For example, it could be reasoned that the increased representation of the ventral surface of the rats (Xerri, Stern, and Merzenich, 1994) or the fingertips of the monkeys (Jenkins et al., 1990) results in better perceptual acuity over that skin surface for that animal. The rest of this chapter will draw on selected examples from a variety of different experimental methodologies to address the central question: Are changes in cortical representations a reflection of normal cortical processes that underlie the ability to acquire new skills and behaviors?

Cortical plasticity and changes in perception invoked by classical conditioning paradigms

Early studies on the effects of classical conditioning on the response properties of neurons in the central auditory system have shown that there is a clear change in the functional tuning properties of neurons throughout the central auditory system. Some of the earliest examples are derived from studies in which awake adult rats were implanted with a series of electrodes that recorded the activity of spatially restricted neurons throughout the brain stem, thalamus, and cortex (Olds et al., 1972; Disterhoft and Stuart, 1976). In these experiments, neuronal activity was recorded during a period in which one of two different tones was presented or a food pellet was dispensed over the course of the first day. There was no temporal relationship between the tone and the food delivery, and thus no association between the two would be expected to be formed (pseudoconditioning). On the second day, however, one of the two tones always preceded the pellet delivery, while the other tone never preceded a food reward (conditioning). In these studies, after the conditioning period, the amount of activity of cortical neurons increased in response to the tone paired with the food delivery. This increase could be extinguished by returning to the pseudoconditioning procedure, now called extinction, where the tones and food delivery were no longer correlated (Disterhoft and Stuart, 1976). Similar kinds of effects were also observed in the noncortical regions as well, particularly the posterior thalamus and pretectal regions. Much smaller differences were noted in the main ascending auditory subcortical regions, the infe-

rior colliculus and the medial geniculate body of the thalamus (Disterhoft and Stuart, 1976).

A similar series of studies using a mild electrical shock to the forepaw as the unconditioned stimulus and the pupillary dilation reflex as the unconditioned response have extended these findings in the cat. The change in the response properties of neurons is more rapid in the auditory cortex than in the cochlear nucleus (Oleson, Ashe, and Weinberger, 1975). These changes are not, however ubiquitous throughout the central nervous system. Comparison of the conditioning effects of multiple-unit activity within the medial, ventral, and dorsal subdivisions of the auditory thalamus, the medial geniculate body (MGB), showed that neuronal responses changed only in the medial subdivision, and not in the ventral or dorsal regions of the MGB (Ryugo and Weinberger, 1978). This result is interesting in that the ventral division of the MGB has the anatomical connections and response properties consistent with those of a thalamic relay or lemniscal nucleus, whereas the medial division is more consistent with a lemniscal adjunct or nonspecific function.

More recent studies have expanded these observations by defining the response properties of single neurons to both conditioned and a series of nonconditioned stimuli (Diamond and Weinberger, 1986; Bakin and Weinberger, 1990; see Weinberger, 1995, 1998). In these paradigms, the responses of single neurons to a series of tone pips at different frequencies are recorded, and then one frequency is chosen to be the conditioned stimulus. A short time after the tone elicits the conditioned response (20–45 paired trials), the response of the neuron to the series of tone pips is again recorded. An example of a typical result is shown in figure 16.1 for neurons recorded in the secondary and ventral ectosylvian auditory cortical fields (Diamond and Weinberger, 1986). This figure is derived from the neurons that were the most sharply tuned for frequency. In most of these cells studied, there was an increase in the response to the tone paired with the foot shock (labeled 0 on the x-axis), with very little increase for other frequencies. This increase was reversed by a period of extinction, when the tone was presented in the absence of the foot shock for 20 trials (figure 16.1).

A similar result was shown in the guinea pig primary auditory cortex (Bakin and Weinberger, 1990), in which many neurons changed their frequency-tuning profile to respond best to the paired frequency (figure 16.2). In this paradigm, by choosing a paired frequency that was slightly different from the best frequency of the neuron, there was an increase in the response to the paired frequency and a parallel decrease in the response to the preconditioning best frequency, resulting in a shifted

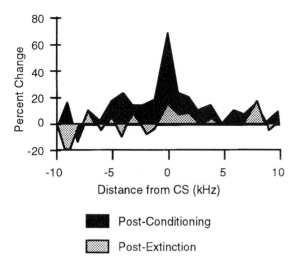

Post-Conditioning

Post-Extinction

FIGURE 16.1 Changes in the activity of auditory cortical neurons following a classical conditioning paradigm. The dark area denotes the percent change in the responses of the neurons as a function of the difference in frequency from the conditioned stimulus (CS) between the preconditioning and postconditioning conditions. The shaded area denotes the change in response between the preconditioning and postextinction conditions. Note that the greatest change occurred at the CS frequency. (Adapted from Diamond and Weinberger, 1986.)

tuning profile for the neuron. This type of change in the tuning profile of the single neuron has also been shown to last for up to eight weeks after training (Weinberger, Javid, and Lapin, 1993). These results indicate that there is an expansion of the representation of the paired frequency that parallels the acquisition of the conditioned response (see Weinberger, 1998). This is expected, given that the perception of the stimulus would surely change from one that has no behavioral relevance to one that signals that a foot shock is imminent.

Similar studies in the MGB have shown that the ventral division (MGBv), which contains the most sharply frequency-tuned neurons and is considered to be the major relay nucleus, does not show the same type of plasticity (Ryugo and Weinberger, 1978). However, the medial division (MGBm), which has more broadly tuned neurons and projects to the primary auditory cortex and other cortical areas, does show a type of plasticity very similar to that of the auditory cortex (Ryugo and Weinberger, 1978; Edeline and Weinberger, 1992). These results suggest that there are two parallel pathways within the auditory system, one which is largely immune to such conditioning effects, and the other which likely mediates the cortical plasticity observed following classical conditioning (for a more complete description of this topic see Weinberger, 1998).

Pharmacological studies suggest that acetylcholine (ACh) plays a key role in modulating the change in corti-

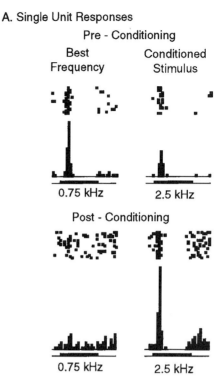

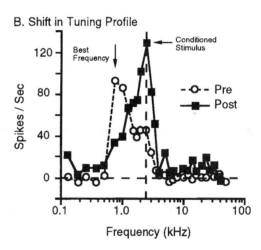

FIGURE 16.2 Change in the response profile of a single auditory cortical neuron following conditioning. (A) Rasters and peristimulus time histograms (PSTHs) of the response to the best frequency of the neuron (0.75 kHz, left) and the frequency of the conditioned stimulus (2.5 kHz, right) before (top) and after (bottom) the conditioning protocol. (B) The complete tuning profile tested before (open circles) and after (closed squares) the conditioning protocol. Note that the postconditioning best frequency of this neuron is now at 2.5 kHz. This shift resulted from an increase in the response to the CS frequency and a decrease in the response to the previous best frequency. (Adapted from Weinberger, 1998.)

cal neuronal responsiveness. Application of ACh at the recording electrode can alter the response of the neuron to specific frequencies (McKenna, Ashe, and Weinberger, 1989). Iontophoresis of acetylcholine paired with the presentation of a tone can result in an increase in the response of the neurons, similar to the effects seen with tone and shock pairings (Metherate and Weinberger, 1990). Similarly, direct stimulation of the nucleus basalis, which contains the neurons that release ACh in the cerebral cortex, shortly after the onset of a tone results in a similar enhancement of the neuronal response to the paired tone in both anesthetized animals (Bakin and Weinberger, 1996) and awake animals (Bjordahl, Dimyan, and Weinberger, 1998), and also results in a greater area of primary auditory cortex that responds to the paired tone (Kilgard and Merzenich, 1998). These data together indicate that (1) cortical responses can be altered over a very short time course and can be long-lasting, (2) these modifications presumably reflect a change in the perception of the stimulus, and (3) neuro-modulatory elements facilitate, and may well be required, to effect such changes.

Cortical plasticity following operant conditioning

A direct test of the hypothesis that cortical representational plasticity reflects changes in perception and skill acquisition was conducted in the somatosensory cortex of adult owl monkeys. In the normal owl monkey, there is a topographically well-organized map of the contralateral hand in the primary somatosensory cortical area 3b. These experiments entailed training monkeys to perform a tactile discrimination task using only a small skin area of a single finger, measuring the improvement in performance at this task over the course of several weeks of training, and then relating this performance to the cortical representation of the small skin area used in the task.

Adult monkeys were trained to remove their hand from a tactile stimulator when they detected that the frequency of the stimulus increased from the standard of 20 Hz (Recanzone, Jenkins, et al., 1992). Initially, monkeys were only able to discriminate stimuli that were at least 5 Hz greater (i.e., 25 Hz). In the early phases of training, the thresholds decreased rapidly, followed by a longer and slower period of improvement during the subsequent weeks until these monkeys were ultimately able to discriminate differences in frequency of only 1–2 Hz. It is likely that the initial, rapid period of improvement is reflecting the ability of the monkeys to generalize to all stimulus frequencies and to develop the most effective "strategy" in performing the task (Recanzone, Jenkins, et al., 1992). When tested on an adjacent finger on two or three occasions throughout the period of extensive practice on a different finger, the thresholds reflected the rapid improvement component, but did not improve significantly during subsequent sessions (see figure 16.3).

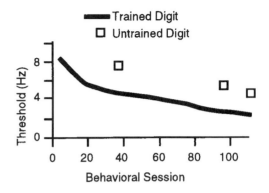

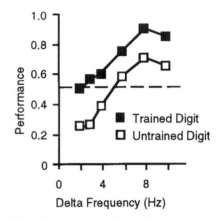

FIGURE 16.3   Improvement in performance measured during the performance of a tactile frequency discrimination task. (A) Schematic of the behavioral data where the threshold rapidly decreased during the first few training sessions, and was then followed by a much slower and progressive decrease in threshold with training. Open symbols denote the thresholds measured for the adjacent finger taken at three different time points over the course of the study. (B) Psychometric functions for both the trained (closed squares) and untrained (open squares) fingers taken the day before the electrophysiological experiment began. (Adapted from Recanzone, Jenkins, et al., 1992.)

The representation of the trained skin, as well as the same skin regions on nontrained fingers of the same and opposite hands, was then defined in cortical area 3b (Recanzone, Merzenich, et al., 1992). One striking difference was the increased area of representation of the trained skin when compared to similar, untrained skin surfaces (figure 16.4A). A second major difference was that the receptive fields on the trained skin surfaces were much larger than those on the untrained skin (figure 16.4B). A third major difference was in the responses of the cortical neurons to the same vibratory tactile stimulation that was used in the behavioral task (Recanzone, Merzenich, and Schreiner, 1992). As would be expected by the larger representation in gen-

A. Area 3b Map Changes

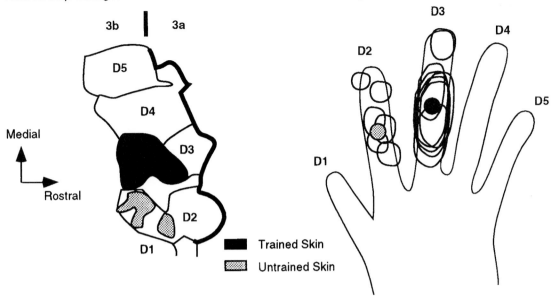

B. Receptive Field Sizes

C. Population Cycle Histograms to 20 Hz Stimuli

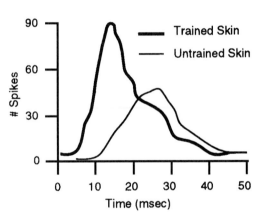

D. Temporal Responses Predict Behavioral Thresholds

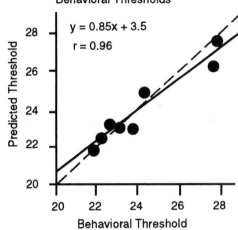

$$y = 0.85x + 3.5$$
$$r = 0.96$$

FIGURE 16.4   Changes in cortical representations of trained and untrained skin regions in monkeys trained at a tactile discrimination task. (A) The cortical area of representation of the trained (black) and adjacent, untrained (shaded) skin regions. (B) Representative receptive fields recorded for each of these fingers. The circles show the region of skin stimulated during the task for the trained (filled) and untrained (shaded) fingers. (A and B adapted from Recanzone, Merzenich, et al., 1992.) (C) Population cycle histograms taken from all locations that responded to stimulation of the trained and untrained skin surfaces in a single monkey. These cycle histograms were obtained by combining the action potentials for all stimulus cycles excluding the first across all cortical locations. Bin size is 1 millisecond. The heavy line shows the responses to stimulation of the trained skin site; the thin line shows the responses to stimulation of the adjacent skin site. (D) Regression analysis between the measured behavioral threshold for both trained and untrained digits as a function of the predicted threshold based on differences in the population cycle histograms between the standard and test frequencies. The solid line shows the best-fit regression line; the dashed line shows perfect correlation. (C and D adapted from Recanzone, Merzenich, and Schreiner, 1992.)

eral, there was a greater number of neurons that responded to stimulation on the trained finger when compared to untrained monkeys or to other fingers on the same hand. Although the responses of the neurons at each cortical location were very similar to stimulation of the trained and untrained fingers, when the responses were pooled across the population of area 3b neurons, there was an increase in the temporal fidelity of the responses to these behaviorally relevant stimuli (figure 16.4C). This increased fidelity was strongly correlated with the behavioral performance of both trained and untrained digits (figure 16.4D). The large representations of the trained skin and the correlated activity across neurons to the same stimulus frequencies indicate that the population of cortical neurons became highly selective in their responses and responded synchronously to the same behaviorally relevant tactile input. As the monkey continued to practice the task over weeks of daily sessions, there was presumably an increase in this population encoding of the stimulus frequency, which resulted in better information on the stimulus frequency and therefore improved performance at the task.

The same result was subsequently found in the primary auditory cortex in monkeys trained to perform an acoustic frequency discrimination task (Recanzone, Schreiner, and Merzenich, 1993). Monkeys performing a similar type of behavioral task showed a progressive improvement in their ability to discriminate small differences in the frequency of sequentially presented acoustic stimuli (figure 16.5A). When the frequency representation was defined in these monkeys, there was a clear increase in the cortical area of representation of the behaviorally relevant stimuli (figure 16.5B, C) compared to controls that were either engaged in the task using a different standard frequency or were untrained in any task. This increased representation was similarly closely correlated with the improved performance and increased frequency discrimination acuity.

In both the somatosensory and auditory experiments, it was found that attention to either the tactile or auditory stimulus was required for the cortical changes to occur. In monkeys that received the same tactile stimulus but were performing the auditory discrimination task, changes were observed in the auditory cortex but not in the somatosensory cortex. Similarly, monkeys that received the same auditory stimuli while performing the tactile task showed changes only in the somatosensory cortex but not in the auditory cortex. These results strongly suggest that attending to the stimuli (and thereby activating neuromodulatory circuits such as ACh) is necessary to change the cortical representations, and presumably to effect a change in the percep-

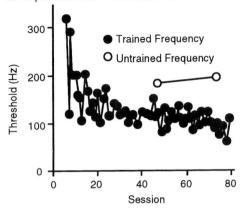

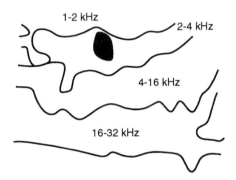

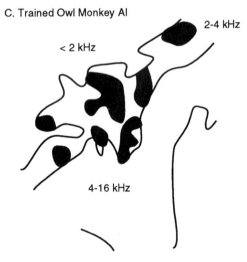

FIGURE 16.5 Auditory frequency discrimination training. (A) Behavioral threshold as a function of session for one monkey. Solid symbols show the threshold measured for the trained frequency. Open symbols show the threshold measured for a different frequency that was only tested on two, widely interspersed, sessions. (B) The region of primary auditory cortex in an untrained monkey that contained cells with a characteristic frequency in the range used in the behavioral task (black regions). (C) Similar map of primary auditory cortex in a monkey trained to discriminate the same frequency shown in B. (Adapted from Recanzone, Merzenich, and Schreiner, 1993).

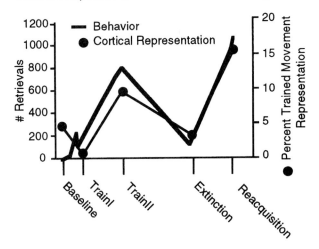

Area of Responses in Motor Cortex with Training

FIGURE 16.6 Changes in motor cortical areas of representation with training. The number of successful pellet retrievals (heavy lines, left *y*-axis) is an indicator of the ability of the monkey to obtain the pellet. The area of representation of the relevant movements in the task (finger flexion and wrist extension) as a percent of the hand representation in the motor cortex is shown as the thin line and solid circles. This monkey went through five different phases of training, extinction, and reacquisition. The cortical area of representation of the relevant movements parallels the monkey's ability to perform the task. (Adapted from Nudo et al., 1996.)

tion, although this assumption was not tested in these animals.

Other studies in the motor cortex show a similar pattern of results. Motor cortical maps can be derived by electrically stimulating the deep cortical layers with small currents (10–30 µA) and observing the elicited movements. Several studies on the motor cortex of squirrel monkeys indicate that the cortical representation of motor movements is related to the ability of the monkey to perform simple motor tasks. For example, there are differences in the organization of the hand representations in the primary motor cortex in individual monkeys, with the representation of the dominant hand being larger and more spatially complex than the representation of the nondominant hand (Nudo et al., 1992), presumably reflecting the greater use and dexterity of the dominant hand. Monkeys trained to make a set of specific movements, whether rotation about the wrist or movement of the wrist and fingers, had a greater representation of the practiced movements (Nudo et al., 1996). The changes in the cortical representations of these movements closely followed the behavioral ability of the monkey to retrieve the pellet, which is based primarily on the dexterity of the movement (figure 16.6). These data showed that the motor cortical representations are

plastic and can change over time in the adult animal and that these changes reflect the acquisition and degradation of the monkey's motor skills during the course of the experiments.

Cortical plasticity demonstrated in human subjects

Functional imaging techniques applied to human subjects have been valuable tools in investigating cortical plasticity in human subjects and indicate that cortical reorganization with training, as seen in the animal experiments, occurs in the human cortex as well. For example, humans who are practiced string players (violin, cello, or guitar) have greater cortical activation (based on MEG dipole strength) from stimulation on the fingertips of their left hands than people who do not play an instrument (Elbert et al., 1995).

Changes in cortical representations that relate to changes in the ability to perform a motor task have also been demonstrated in human subjects (Karni et al., 1995; see also Karni et al., 1998). In this study, the amount of activity in the motor cortex was defined using functional magnetic resonance imaging (fMRI) while the subjects made one of two matched, mirror-reversed sequenced finger movements (e.g., pinkie–middle–ring–index–pinkie). These subjects then practiced only one of these two sequences for 10–20 minutes each day. Over the course of several weeks the speed with which the sequences were performed increased, and the number of errors decreased. When the subjects were scanned again after training, there was more activation of primary motor cortex for the practiced sequence compared to the unpracticed sequence in each subject tested (figure 16.7). This result is predicted by the monkey experiments described earlier (Recanzone, Jenkins, et al., 1992; Recanzone, Merzenich, et al., 1992; Recanzone, Merzenich, and Schreiner, 1992; Recanzone, Schreiner, and Merzenich, 1993; Nudo et al., 1996), where the increased cortical areas of representation were correlated with an improvement in performance at a perceptual or motor task.

A second area of interest has focused on cortical plasticity in blind individuals who read braille. The previously discussed animal work predicts that these individuals would have increased representations of their braille-reading finger pads compared to either sighted or non-braille-reading controls. Evidence to support this hypothesis has been obtained using both scalp-evoked potentials and transcranial magnetic stimulation of the sensorimotor cortex of blind and control human subjects (Pascual-Leone and Torres, 1993; Pascual-Leone et al., 1993). These experiments have shown that there is an increase in the representation of the finger

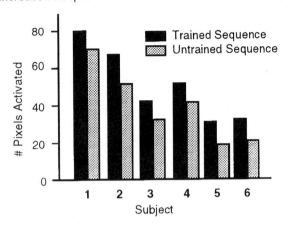

Increased Response Area in Motor Cortex with Training

FIGURE 16.7 Motor cortex activation during a practiced and nonpracticed finger-tapping task. These data show the extent of motor cortex that was activated during the performance of the practiced sequenced finger-movement task (solid bars) compared to a similar but unpracticed sequence (stippled bars). Each subject showed an increase in the number of pixels activated within motor cortex for the practiced task. (Adapted from Karni et al., 1995.)

muscles most used during braille reading in motor cortex, and a greater activation of the sensorimotor cortex during stimulation of the fingertips used during braille reading. Interestingly, subjects who have been blind since infancy or early childhood also commonly have an activation of visual cortex during braille reading (Sadato et al., 1996) that does not occur in sighted individuals. This intriguing result suggests that the neurons in the cerebral cortex are not only capable of altering their responses within a given modality but can also change the modality of their responses if altered experiences occur early enough during development (see also chapter 7).

Experiments on human amputees further suggest that cortical plasticity can account for altered perceptions following the amputation. In many human amputee patients, there is a phenomenon known as the phantom limb (Henderson and Smyth, 1948; Cronholm, 1951; Haber, 1958) in which subjects clearly perceive their missing limb as still being attached, although they are cognitively fully aware that it no longer is. It had been suggested that the phantom limb was the result of the residual representation in the cortex of what used to respond to the arm input, following a "filling in" of the former hand representation by the face and arm representation, which is seen following amputations and deafferentation in monkeys (Merzenich et al., 1984; Pons et al., 1991). The human somatosensory cortex is functionally organized with a topography similar to that of the monkey; namely, the hand representation is bordered medially by the arm representation and laterally by the chin and jaw representation. Since there is no

longer any afferent drive from the missing limb, these cortical neurons would either come to respond to adjacent, intact body regions, or would remain silent as the deafferentation was too large to overcome (see Merzenich et al., 1984).

Functional imaging studies similarly indicate that the region formerly responding to the hand now responds to stimulation of the face (Yang et al., 1994; Elbert et al., 1994; see Ramachandran, 1993). The extent of this reorganization has been shown to be correlated with the amount of pain experienced in the phantom limb (Flor et al., 1995). In a second study (Birbaumer et al., 1997), injection of local anesthetic into the region near the amputation resulted in relief of phantom limb pain in half of the subjects tested. In those subjects that had pain relief, there was a reduction in the amount of apparent cortical reorganization following the injection of the local anesthetic. Interestingly, in the subjects that did not experience any pain relief or had not experienced phantom pain previously, there was no change in the cortical representations before and after the injection of the anesthetic. This result suggests that the amount of cortex that was reorganized from formerly representing the amputated arm and hand to representing the shoulder and face in some way contributes to the phantom pain or, conversely, that phantom pain in some way results in the altered cortical representation. It will be interesting to see how these two factors are related in future experiments.

Implications of cortical plasticity and changes in perception

This chapter has reviewed evidence that changes in perceptual acuity or motor skill are the result of changes in the cortical representations of the relevant sensory or motor aspects of the task. In each of the cases of cortical plasticity there is an increased representation of the relevant stimuli. Given that the size of the cerebral cortex is fixed in the adult, this result implies that the cortical representations of some sensory surfaces or movements have necessarily decreased in order to accommodate the greater representation of other sensory surfaces or movements. This relationship has been noted primarily in animal studies where there is a clear decrease in the cortical representation of adjacent skin surfaces in the somatosensory cortex (see Jenkins et al., 1990; Recanzone, Merzenich, et al., 1992), or the adjacent frequencies in the auditory cortex (Recanzone, Schreiner, and Merzenich, 1993) or different movement representations in the motor cortex (Nudo et al., 1996). Does this result then imply that there is a decrease in performance at some other task? The lim-

Perceptual Acuity Decreases Without Practice

A. Tactile Frequency Discrimination Task

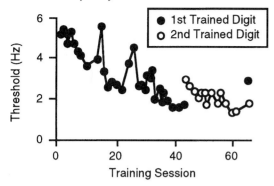

B. Auditory Frequency Discrimination Task

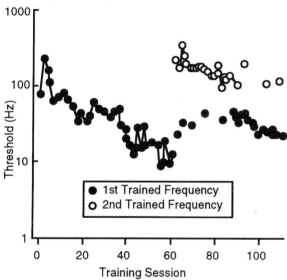

FIGURE 16.8 Changes in perceptual performance as a function of practice. Data taken from one monkey that was trained at a tactile frequency discrimination task (A) taken from Recanzone, Jenkins, et al. (1992) and one trained at an auditory frequency discrimination task (B) taken from Recanzone, Schreiner, and Merzenich, (1993). In both cases, 1–2 weeks of testing on either a different skin surface or a different frequency (open circles) resulted in an increase in threshold for the previously practiced (solid circles) skin surface or auditory frequency.

ited data available suggest that this is indeed the case; performance at one task will change the cortical representations in favor of that task at the expense of some unpracticed task. For example, there was a progressive improvement in performance with training at both a tactile frequency discrimination task or an auditory discrimination task as described previously (figure 16.8; Recanzone, Jenkins, et al., 1992; Recanzone, Schreiner, and Merzenich, 1993). If the task is changed to test a different sensory surface, after the improvement in performance at the first, there is an improvement over time in

the performance for the new skin surface or frequency (open symbols, figure 16.8) and a corresponding decrease in performance at the previously trained skin surface or frequency (closed symbols, figure 16.8). A similar improvement and degradation in performance can be seen in motor tasks with a corresponding change in the cortical representation of the specific movements used in the task (figure 16.6; Nudo et al., 1996).

This is not a simple "zero sum" rule in which learning one thing will necessarily result in forgetting something else; rather, it is a simple reflection of the fact that performance at unpracticed tasks is degraded over time. There are clear anatomical and functional limits to the extent of cortical reorganization and the extent at which performance at a particular task can improve. I do not suggest that continued practice at a frequency discrimination task would ultimately cause only that narrow band of frequencies to be represented across the entire extent of primary auditory cortex at the expense of all other frequencies. The ability to process acoustic information is an important and behaviorally relevant task in most mammals, and there exists a driving force to maintain that ability in spite of a competing need to perform well at a specific task. Therefore, the cerebral cortex must be continuously modifying its central representations in a delicate balance to ensure that all of the behaviorally relevant and important information processing can take place. These dynamic processes are presumably continuing throughout life (e.g., see Merzenich et al., 1991, 1993) and likely account for the normal variability seen in cortical representations of different individuals of a species (Merzenich et al., 1987) and indeed the normal variations in abilities seen across individuals such as ourselves.

ACKNOWLEDGMENTS I would like to thank L. A. Krubitzer, N. M. Weinberger, M. L. Sutter, M. L. Phan, A. R. Tice, and J. A. Langston for helpful suggestions on previous versions of the manuscript. Funding provided in part by NIH grant DC-02371, the Klingenstein Fund, and the Sloan Foundation.

REFERENCES

ALLARD, T., S. A. CLARK, W. M., JENKINS, and M. M. MERZENICH, 1991. Reorganization of somatosensory area 3b representations in adult owl monkeys after digital syndactyly. *J. Neurophysiol.* 66:1048–1058.

ARMSTRONG-JAMES, M., M. E. DIAMOND, and F. F. EBNER, 1994. An innocuous bias in whisker use in adult rats modifies receptive fields of barrel cortex neurons. *J. Neurosci.* 14:6978–6991.

BAKIN, J. S., and N. M. WEINBERGER, 1990. Classical conditioning induces CS-specific receptive field plasticity in the auditory cortex of the guinea pig. *Brain Res.* 536(1–2):271–86.

BAKIN, J. S., and N. M. WEINBERGER, 1996. Induction of a physiological memory in the cerebral cortex by stimulation of the nucleus basalis. *Proc. Natl. Acad. Sci. U.S.A.* 93(20): 11219–11224.

BIRBAUMER, N., W. LUTZENBERGER, P. MONTOYA, W. LARBIG, K. UNERTL, S. TÖPFNER, W. GRODD, E. TAUB, and H. FLOR, 1997. Effects of regional anesthesia on phantom limb pain are mirrored in changes in cortical reorganization. *J. Neurosci.* 17:5503–5508.

BJORDAHL, T. S., M. A. DIMYAN, and N. M. WEINBERGER, 1998. Induction of long-term receptive field plasticity in the auditory cortex of the waking guinea pig by stimulation of the nucleus basalis. *Behav. Neurosci.* 112:467–479.

CRONHOLM, B., 1951. Phantom limbs in amputees: A study of changes in the integration of centripetal impulses with special reference to referred sensations. *Acta Psychiat. Neurological. Scand. Suppl.* 72:1–310.

DELACOUR, J., O. HOUCINE, and B. TALBI, 1987. "Learned" changes in the responses of the rat barrel field neurons. *Neuroscience* 23:63–71.

DIAMOND, D. M., and N. M. WEINBERGER, 1986. Classical conditioning rapidly induces specific changes in frequency receptive fields of single neurons in secondary and ventral ectosylvian auditory cortical fields. *Brain Res.* 372:357–360.

DISTERHOFT, J. F., and D. K. STUART, 1976. Trial sequence of changed unit activity in auditory system of alert rat during conditioned response acquisition and extinction. *J. Neurophysiol.* 39:266–281.

EDELINE, J.-M., and N. M. WEINBERGER, 1992. Associative retuning in the thalamic source of input to the amygdala and auditory cortex: Receptive field plasticity in the medial division of the medial geniculate body. *Behav. Neurosci.* 106:81–105.

ELBERT, T., H. FLOR, N. BIRBAUMER, S. KNECHT, S. HAMPSON, W. LARBIG, and E. TAUB, 1994. Extensive reorganization of the somatosensory cortex on adult humans after nervous system injury. *NeuroReport* 5:2593–2597.

ELBERT, T., C. PANTEV, C. WIENBRUCH, B. ROCKSTROH, and E. TAUB, 1995. Increased cortical representation of the fingers of the left hand in string players. *Science* 270:305–307.

FLOR, H., T. ELBERT, S. KNECHT, C. WIENBRUCH, C. PANTEV, N. BIRBAUMER, W. LARBIG, and E. TAUB, 1995. Phantom-limb pain as a perceptual correlate of cortical reorganization following arm amputation. *Nature* 375:482–484.

GILBERT, C. D., 1998. Adult cortical dynamics. *Physiol. Rev.* 78:467–485.

GILBERT, C. D., A. DAS, M. ITO, M. KAPADIA, and G. WESTHEIMER, 1996. Spatial integration and cortical dynamics. *Proc. Natl. Acad. Sci. U.S.A.* 93:615–622.

GRAHAM BROWN, T., and C. S. SHERRINGTON, 1912. On the instability of a cortical point. *Proc. Roy. Soc. Lond. B* 85:250–277.

HABER, W. B., 1958. Reactions to loss of limb: Physiological and psychological aspects. *Ann. N.Y. Acad. Sci.* 74:14–24.

HENDERSON, W. R., and G. E. SMYTH, 1948. Phantom limbs. *J. Neurol. Neurosurg. Psychiat.* 11:88–112.

JAMES, W., 1890. *The Principles of Psychology.* vol 1. New York: Dover.

JENKINS, W. M., M. M. MERZENICH, M. T. OCHS, T. ALLARD, and E. GUIC-ROBLES, 1990. Functional reorganization of primary somatosensory cortex in adult owl monkeys after behaviorally controlled tactile stimulation. *J. Neurophysiol.* 63:82–104.

KAAS, J. H., 1991. Plasticity of sensory and motor maps in adult mammals. *Annu. Rev. Neurosci.* 14:137–167.

KARNI, A., G. MEYER, P. JEZZARD, M. M. ADAMS, R. TURNER, and L. G. UNGERLEIDER, 1995. Functional MRI evidence for adult motor cortex plasticity during motor skill learning. *Nature* 377:155–158.

KARNI, A., G. MEYER, C. REY-HIPOLITO, P. JEZZARD, M. M. ADAMS, R. TURNER, and L. G. UNGERLEIDER, 1998. The acquisition of skilled motor performance: Fast and slow experience-driven changes in primary motor cortex. *Proc. Natl. Acad. Sci. U.S.A.* 95:861–868.

KILGARD, M. P., and M. M. MERZENICH, 1998. Cortical map reorganization enabled by nucleus basalis activity. *Science* 279:1714–1718.

MCKENNA, T. M., J. H. ASHE, and N. M. WEINBERGER, 1989. Cholinergic modulation of frequency receptive fields in auditory cortex. I. Frequency-specific effects of muscarinic agonists. *Synapse* 4:30–43.

MERZENICH, M. M., K. A. GRAJSKI, W. M. JENKINS, G. H. RECANZONE, and B. PETERSON, 1991. Functional cortical plasticity: Cortical network origins of representations changes. *Cold Spring Harbor Symp. Quant. Biol.* 55:873–887.

MERZENICH, M. M., R. J. NELSON, J. H. KAAS, M. P. STRYKER, W. M. JENKINS, J. M. ZOOK, M. S. CYNADER, and A. SCHOPPMANN, 1987. Variability in hand surface representations in areas 3b and 1 in adult owl and squirrel monkeys. *J. Comp. Neurol.* 258:281–296.

MERZENICH, M. M., R. J. NELSON, M. P. STRYKER, M. S. CYNADER, A. SCHOPPMANN, and J. M. ZOOK, 1984. Somatosensory cortical map changes following digital amputation in adult monkey. *J. Comp. Neurol.* 224:591–605.

MERZENICH, M. M., C. SCHREINER, W. M. JENKINS, and X. WANG, 1993. Neural mechanisms underlying temporal integration, segmentation, and input sequence representation: Some implications for the origin of learning disabilities. *Ann. N.Y. Acad. Sci.* 682:1–22.

METHERATE, R., and N. M. WEINBERGER, 1990. Cholinergic modulation of responses to single tones produces tone-specific receptive field alterations in cat auditory cortex. *Synapse* 6:133–145.

NUDO, R. J., W. M. JENKINS, M. M. MERZENICH, T. PREJEAN, and R. GRENDA, 1992. Neurophysiological correlates of hand preference in primary motor cortex of adult squirrel monkeys. *J. Neurosci.* 12:2918–2947.

NUDO, R. J., G. W. MILLIKEN, W. M. JENKINS, and M. M. MERZENICH, 1996. Use-dependent alterations of movement representations in primary motor cortex of adult squirrel monkeys. *J. Neurosci.* 16:785–807.

OLDS, J., J. F. DISTERHOFT, M. SEGAL, C. L. KORNBLITH, and R. HIRSH, 1972. Learning centers of rat brain mapped by measuring latencies of conditioned unit responses. *J. Neurophysiol.* 35:202–219.

OLESON, T. D., J. H. ASHE, and N. M. WEINBERGER, 1975. Modification of auditory and somatosensory system activity during pupillary conditioning in the paralyzed cat. *J. Neurophysiol.* 38:1114–1139.

PASCUAL-LEONE, A., A. CAMMAROTA, E. M. WASSERMANN, J. P. BRASIL-NETO, L. G. COHEN, and M. HALLETT, 1993. Modulation of motor cortical outputs to the reading hand of braille readers. *Ann. Neurol.* 34:33–37.

PASCUAL-LEONE, A., and F. TORRES, 1993. Plasticity of the sensorimotor cortex representation of the reading finger of braille readers. *Brain* 116:39–52.

PONS, T. P., P. E. GARRAGHTY, A. K. OMMAYA, J. H. KAAS, E. TAUB, and M. MISHKIN, 1991. Massive cortical reorganization after sensory deafferentation in adult macaques. *Science* 252:1857–1860.

RAMACHANDRAN, V. S., 1993. Behavioral and magneto encephalographic correlates of plasticity in the adult human brain. *Proc. Natl. Acad. Sci. U.S.A.* 90:10413–10420.

RECANZONE, G. H., W. M. JENKINS, G. T. HRADEK, and M. M. MERZENICH, 1992. Progressive improvement in discriminative abilities in adult owl monkeys performing a tactile frequency discrimination task. *J. Neurophysiol.* 67:1015–1030.

RECANZONE, G. H., M. M. MERZENICH, W. M. JENKINS, K. A. GRAJSKI, and H. A. DINSE, 1992. Topographic reorganization of the hand representation in cortical area 3b of owl monkeys trained in a frequency discrimination task. *J. Neurophysiol.* 67:1031–1056.

RECANZONE, G. H., M. M. MERZENICH, and C. E. SCHREINER, 1992. Changes in the distributed temporal response properties of SI cortical neurons reflect improvements in performance on a temporally based tactile discrimination task. *J. Neurophysiol.* 67:1071–1091.

RECANZONE, G. H., C. E. SCHREINER, and M. M. MERZENICH, 1993. Plasticity in the frequency representation of primary auditory cortex following discrimination training in adult owl monkeys. *J. Neurosci.* 13:87–103.

RYUGO, D. K., and N. M. WEINBERGER, 1978. Differential plasticity of morphologically distinct neuron populations in the medial geniculate body of the cat during classical conditioning. *Behav. Biol.* 22:275–301.

SADATO, N., A. PASCUAL-LEONE, J. GRAFMAN, V. IBANEZ, M. P. DEIBER, G. DOLD, and M. HALLETT, 1996. Activation of the primary visual cortex by Braille reading in blind subjects. *Nature* 380:526–528.

WEINBERGER, N. M., 1995. Dynamic regulation of receptive fields maps in the adult sensory cortex. *Annu. Rev. Neurosci.* 18:129–158.

WEINBERGER, N. M., 1998. Physiological memory in primary auditory cortex: Characteristics and mechanisms. *Neurobiology of Learning and Memory* 70:226–251.

WEINBERGER, N. M., R. JAVID, and B. LEPAN, 1993. Long-term retention of learning-induced receptive-field plasticity in the auditory cortex. *Proc. Natl. Acad. Sci. U.S.A.* 90:2394–2398.

XERRI, C., J. M. STERN, and M. M. MERZENICH, 1994. Alterations of the cortical representation of the rat ventrum induced by nursing behavior. *J. Neurosci.* 14:1710–1721.

YANG, T. T., C. C. GALLEN, V. S. RAMACHANDRAN, S. COBB, B. J. SCHWARTZ, and F. E. BLOOM, 1994. Noninvasive detection of cerebral plasticity in adult human somatosensory cortex. *NeuroReport* 5:701–704.

III SENSORY SYSTEMS

Introduction

J. ANTHONY MOVSHON
AND COLIN BLAKEMORE

In the context of modern cognitive science, it is easy to overlook the formidable tasks faced, and effortlessly mastered, by sensory mechanisms. The task of sensory systems is to provide a faithful representation of biologically relevant events in the external environment. In most cases, the raw signals transduced by receptors seem woefully inadequate to this task. These raw data are far removed from the complex structures in the world that give rise to them, in the same sense that the numerical values given to the pixels in a computer display are far removed from the true information that the display conveys. Yet our sensory systems all contrive, by subtle and complex calculation, to create efficient and informative representations of their perceptual worlds. These representations are at the same time enormously richer and enormously simpler than the basic measurements of light intensity, force, and chemical composition that support them. They are richer because they contain representations of objects, states, and events that are abstracted from the primitive sensory signals; they are simpler because they represent the distillation of the vast quantities of raw measurement information offered to the central nervous system by each sensory surface. To understand the full richness of sensory processing, we must appreciate both the volume of computation and the sophisticated deductions that give rise to our sensory experience. This section presents a variety of perspectives on the neural foundations of perception, derived from several different methods and several different sensory systems.

The most basic questions considered in this section concern the nature and meaning of the signals carried by single sensory neurons and the maps and areas in which they live. The issues raised and addressed in chapters by Middlebrooks, Newsome, Parker, Shamma, Shapley, and Wandell have roots that extend back seven decades to the earliest recordings of sensory unit activity. How are sensory signals encoded by single neurons? How reliable and efficient is this encoding? How are single-neuron signals transformed and elaborated by successive levels of processing? How are different processing levels and areas represented in large-scale patterns of neural activity? Answers to these questions, and questions about the answers, continue to command the attention of those who study sensory systems. In favorable cases, remarkably sophisticated signals can be discerned in single neurons, and the efficient use of these signals by "higher" processes can in principle be used to reveal much of the information the organism uses to control behavior.

Beyond the basic encoding of the features of a stimulus, crucial questions arise concerning the perceptual context within which a particular element is perceived. These elemental representations must be blended and combined with information from other places and times in the sensory continuum to achieve a representation of the world's objects and events that separates them from the contexts in which they occur. The construction of this kind of elaborated representation is the concern of chapters by Adelson, Kersten, Lamme, and Singer. The task of understanding these representations uncovers a host of questions. How is perceptual context defined; what is "figure" and what is "ground"? How do widely separated elements of a sensory event get combined and articulated in sensory representations? How does the structure of the natural world influence the way in which it is perceived? What methods and mechanisms of statistical inference drive the transition from encoded elements to perceived events and objects?

Sensory processing cannot end with the encoding of a stimulus and its representation of objects and events in a context. The succession of events in a sensory analysis blend gradually from early stages that are purely stimulus-driven to later stages in which signals are modulated by messages from other sensory systems, from memory systems, and from attentional systems. The task of uncovering the nature and role of these signals in higher areas is addressed in chapters by King, Maunsell, McCarthy, and Miyashita. How are different and separately computed kinds of information about the same sensory quality fused to yield fully formed representations of the world? How are those representations modulated by the behavioral state and needs of the animal, and by memories of other states, needs, and events? These issues occupy a no-man's-land between classically "sensory" processes and "cognitive" ones, and it is clear that this no-man's-land is in fact richly inhabited. It is, of course, inevitable that sensory signals will drive cognitive processing, but it is also clear that recurrent cognitive signals play an important role in sensory systems.

Perception is meaningless in the absence of action, and the final stage of understanding any perceptual process is to understand how it is used to initiate and orchestrate purposive behavior. This question is the concern of chapters by Doupe, Goodale, and Sejnowski. Sensorimotor integration is rapidly emerging as a crucial concern that spans the border between perceptual and motor systems. How do sensory representations become transformed into motor commands? How are sensory signals arising from actions of the observer distinguished from signals arising elsewhere in the world? How are motor sequences learned from sensory inputs? Is the information used for the control of action the same as, or different from, the information subserving "pure" perceptual processing?

The grand challenge of understanding perception requires that we be able to answer and address all the different phases of processing represented by the chapters in this section. The key issues in these chapters have wide relevance to cognitive processes, and spill over the traditional borders among sensation, perception, cognition, and action. Our ability to begin to address these questions with rigor and precision is producing a new and integrated view of the relations between perceptual processes and the other elements that form the neural basis of cognition.

17 Dynamics of Responses in Visual Cortex

ROBERT SHAPLEY AND DARIO RINGACH

ABSTRACT In this chapter we discuss our recent research on the dynamics of responses by single neurons in the primary visual cortex of macaque monkeys. Our experiments were designed to test ideas about the nature of cortical information processing. General principles of cortical information processing gleaned from this kind of research should, we hope, have wide applicability in the analysis of cortical function.

To understand vision properly, we need to understand how the cerebral cortex uses the signals that come to it from the lateral geniculate nucleus (LGN)—signals that ultimately derive from retinal signals evoked by patterns of light. This level of understanding would require a complete comprehension of the function of the cortex. A lot is known about neural connections in the visual cortex, the specificity of the input connections (Hubel and Wiesel, 1972; Blasdel and Lund, 1983; Lachica, Beck, and Casagrande, 1992; Yoshioka, Levitt, and Lund, 1994), and the wealth of feedback and lateral connections within V1 and between V1 and other areas (Rockland and Lund, 1983; Gilbert and Wiesel, 1983; Lund, 1988; Lund, Yoshioka, and Levitt, 1993). But why is the cerebral cortex organized in this way—what is the purpose of building a machine with this specific architecture? That question we cannot answer yet. Even while we focus on difficult immediate problems, we should bear this major question in mind.

Orientation tuning and cortical function

One of the crucial facts about what happens at the cortex is the transformation from spatially isotropic to orientation tuned elements (studied first in cat visual cortex by Hubel and Wiesel, 1962; then in monkey cortex by, among others, Hubel and Wiesel, 1968; Schiller, Finlay, and Volman, 1976; De Valois, Yund, and Hepler, 1982). Prior to the cortex, in single neurons in the retina and LGN, there is weak or no orientation selectivity. Some authors have emphasized the ellipticity of the LGN receptive fields as a possible source of orientation bias in the cortex (Shou and Leventhal, 1989; Smith et al., 1990; Vidyasagar, 1992). However, direct comparison of the amount of orientation tuning expected from single

LGN inputs to the amount of orientation tuning seen in cortical cells reveals that the contribution of orientation tuning in individual LGN neurons is a relatively small part of the story (e.g., see Reid and Alonso, 1995). It has been thought from the time of its discovery that orientation tuning of single visual neurons, as an emergent property in visual cortex, must be an important clue to how the cortex works and why it is built the way it is. But a comprehensive and satisfactory explanation of this phenomenon has resisted visual neuroscience even now. Indicative of a resurgence of interest in this problem, several opinions about recent data have been expressed in recent review articles (Das, 1996; Reid and Alonso, 1996; Sompolinsky and Shapley, 1997). The reviews of Das and Reid and Alonso emphasized the significance of the experimental evidence by Ferster and colleagues—data indicating that the LGN input to cortical cells is highly tuned for orientation (Ferster, Chung, and Wheat, 1996). Sompolinsky and Shapley's paper, on the contrary, reviewed the experimental evidence and theoretical arguments for the importance of corticocortical connections in orientation selectivity. The motivation of our work on cortical dynamics is to offer a fresh experimental approach to this problem (Ringach, Hawken, and Shapley, 1997).

From the time of its publication, Hubel and Wiesel's (1962) feedforward model has been a dominant idea in this field. This model is simple and has the great virtue of being explicit and implementable. It involves the addition of signals from LGN cells that are aligned in a row along the long axis of the receptive field of the orientationally selective neuron. For the often-encountered edge-sensitive orientation tuned cells, Hubel and Wiesel postulated that a row of ON cells from the LGN would provide excitatory input and an adjacent parallel row of OFF cells would provide excitation in response to the opposite sign of contrast. There is some indirect support for this kind of neural architecture in the ferret visual cortex (Chapman, Zahs, and Stryker, 1991), and more direct support from recent dual recordings in LGN and cortex in the cat (Reid and Alonso, 1995). The meaning of the Chapman results in ferret cortex is problematic because their later work on the orientation tuning of cortical cells in the input layer of ferret visual cortex indicates that these cells are very broadly tuned

ROBERT SHAPLEY and DARIO RINGACH Center for Neural Science, New York University, N.Y.

for orientation (Chapman and Stryker, 1993); more properly, one would call layer 4 neurons in ferret visual cortex orientation-biased, not really orientation-tuned. Thus not all of the ferret LGN cells, whose synaptic terminations form long rows of aligned visual inputs located near a cortical layer 4 cell, make contact with that individual cortical cell–otherwise the cortical neuron would be much more tuned for orientation than it is. This means that the earlier paper by Chapman and colleagues (1991), the paper usually cited as strong support for the Hubel–Wiesel model, is not persuasive. However, the experimental result on orientation tuning in cat cortex after cortical cooling (Ferster, Chung, and Wheat, 1996) is an important result that indicates that the collective thalamic input to a cortical neuron is tuned for orientation.

Moreover, there is a serious problem with the 1962 Hubel–Wiesel model: It predicts too little orientation selectivity, and it also has as its consequence that none of the cortical cells would be "simple" cells according to Hubel and Wiesel's original definition in that same classic paper. The reason for these problems has been known for a long time. The LGN cells clip at 0 spikes/s even at fairly low stimulus contrast, and therefore would act like nonlinear subunits as inputs to their cortical targets (Palmer and Davis, 1981; Tolhurst and Dean, 1990; Shapley, 1994). The response of the Hubel–Wiesel model would then be the sum of all these rectifying LGN receptive fields. Under these circumstances, there would be no reason for the model to have zero response at 90 degrees from the optimal orientation; in fact, for most reasonable choices of receptive field shape, one would predict a response at the perpendicular orientation at least half as strong as that at peak.

The Hubel–Wiesel model also predicts a qualitative response feature that is *not* observed–a change in the pattern of response to a drifting grating as a function of orientation. The response should be synchronized, at the drift frequency, at the optimum orientation parallel to the long axis of the LGN row. But it should be mainly elevated spike rate with little or no modulation when the stimulus is at the orthogonal orientation. The pattern of response at the optimal orientation, synchronous with the bars of a grating pattern, would be characteristic of what are called "simple" cells, while the elevated discharge rate at the orthogonal-to-optimal orientation–dominated as it is by the nonlinear, thresholded, LGN input–would be termed a response characteristic of "complex" cells.

The dependence of orientation tuning bandwidth on stimulus contrast is another, third, consequence of the Hubel–Wiesel model that is not observed in cortical cells. When contrast is low, the Hubel–Wiesel model predicts sharper orientation tuning than when contrast is high because the LGN nonlinearity would cause much less broadening of the input at low contrast, and the cortical cell's threshold would sharpen the tuning considerably in the cortex when the summed input is relatively weak, as it is at low contrast. None of the three predictions of the Hubel–Wiesel model discussed here is observed in real cortical cells: Orientationally tuned cortical simple cells respond little or not at all at 90° from peak orientation, the response of a simple cell is synchronized to the input drift rate at all orientations where there is a response, and there is approximate contrast invariance of orientation tuning. Real (and fairly typical) data from a representative simple cell in cat cortex are displayed in figure 17.1, from the work of Sclar and Freeman (1982). This figure shows orientation tuning curves measured at four different contrasts, from low to fairly high contrast. The narrow tuning and relative independence of tuning with contrast are notable features of this figure.

To correct the problems of the Hubel–Wiesel model, one can add opponent inhibition as in the "push-pull"

Cat V1 simple cell spike responses Orientation tuning and contrast

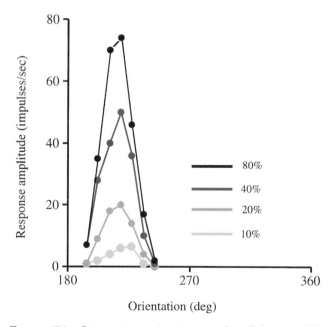

FIGURE 17.1 Orientation tuning in a simple cell from cat V1 at four different contrasts. These are steady-state data collected when a cat simple cell was driven by a single drifting sine grating at the optimal spatial frequency and temporal frequency. Four different contrasts generated the four different curves. The height of the curves is dependent on contrast, but the shape of the curve is relatively invariant with contrast. This cat cortical neuron is about average in the sharpness of its orientation tuning.

model (Palmer and Davis, 1981; Tolhurst and Dean, 1990; Ferster, 1988, 1992). But one must suppose that this inhibition is through cortical interneurons rather than direct from the thalamic afferents. The reason for this qualification is the dogma that there is no direct thalamocortical inhibition, only excitation (see Lund, 1988). Inhibition would have to be mediated through cortical inhibitory interneurons. However, there is a problem with the push-pull model, too. It predicts that there ought to be excitatory *and* inhibitory input when the stimulus is orthogonal to the long axis of the receptive field, with inhibition erasing the excitation. However, intracellular recording in cat cortex revealed that excitatory *and* inhibitory input was minimal at the orthogonal orientation (Ferster, 1986, 1992). So there seem to be problems accounting for major qualitative properties of orientation tuning only in terms of thalamic excitatory and inhibitory inputs, though there is good evidence that these inputs are organized to contribute to orientation tuning to some extent. This is only a problem if orientation tuning is supposed to occur at the first stage in the cortex, as in the Hubel–Wiesel model. Of course, there is the possibility that sharp orientation tuning emerges only in layers of the cortex above and below layer 4, layers of cortical cells in which corticocortical interactions are the major source of orientation tuning. This is in fact what we observed in the monkey striate cortex and will show below.

Experimental work about the importance of corticocortical interactions in causing orientation tuning has proceeded in a different direction. Initially, Sillito's (1975) experiments with bicuculline suggested that intracortical inhibition might be necessary for orientation tuning. But those experiments are confounded by ceiling effects, and the direct experiments of Nelson and colleagues (1994) blocking inhibition intracellularly prove that inhibition onto a single neuron is not necessary for that neuron to be orientation tuned. However, the role of intracortical inhibition as a factor in cortical orientation tuning has been supported by the work of A. B. Bonds and collaborators in their studies of interactions between stimuli at different orientations (Bonds, 1989), of the effects of blocking activity in infragranular layers (Allison, Pfleger, and Bonds, 1995), and of the effects of GABA on orientation selectivity (Allison, Casagrande, and Bonds, 1995). A completely different result supports the idea that corticocortical effects are important–namely, the contrast-invariance of orientation tuning in the results of Sclar and Freeman (1982) and Skottun and collaborators (1987). As described previously in connection with figure 17.1, without corticocortical interaction, one would expect orientation tuning to broaden at high contrasts. That corticocortical recurrent

connections may yield contrast invariant orientation tuning is one of the main conclusions of the theoretical work of Ben-Yishai, Bar-Or, and Sompolinsky (1995), as discussed below.

The idea that corticocortical feedback plays a crucial role in orientation tuning has been put forward most forcefully by theorists of brain function. There are three new papers that make the case for corticocortical feedback. Each emphasizes in its own way the importance of recurrent excitation as well as inhibition. One is the paper by Somers, Nelson, and Sur (1995) which puts forward a complex computational model for orientation tuning. Another is the paper by Douglas and collaborators (1995) which argues for the importance of recurrent excitation in cortical circuits, and its role in orientation tuning as an example. A third paper in this genre is the work of Ben-Yishai, Bar-Or, and Sompolinsky (1995). Ben-Yishai and colleagues offer an analytical model from which they make several qualitative and quantitative predictions. The most important prediction is that with feedforward models you cannot predict contrast invariance of orientation tuning without postulating some intracortical mechanism like a contrast gain control. However, their feedback model with recurrent excitation and inhibition will exhibit contrast invariance. In recent simulations with a model that shares some of the features of the Ben-Yishai model and the Somers model, M. Pugh and colleagues observed that feedback models generate secondary peaks in the orientation tuning curves at 90 degrees away from the optimal orientation, at times after the main peak emerges, and that orientation tuning exhibits some evolution or sharpening of tuning with time (Pugh et al., in press). These features are reminiscent of what can be expected from recurrent lateral inhibitory networks (Ratliff, 1965) because secondary peaks and troughs in activity emerge naturally due to recurrent interaction, and different dynamics of excitation and inhibition in recurrent networks can cause time evolution of tuning. As we report below, we have observed features such as secondary peaks and troughs in the orientation domain for some monkey striate cortical neurons, so we believe that at this point we should take the feedback models seriously. This is the starting point for the research described in detail below on the dynamics of orientation tuning in visual cortex. To make clear the structural differences between a feedforward model, such as the Hubel–Wiesel model, and such feedback models as those of Somers and Ben-Yishai, we offer figure 17.2, a cartoon sketch (from Somers, Nelson, and Sur, 1995) of different cortical models that have been used to explain orientation tuning.

Before embarking on new methods and new results, let us reflect on why it matters whether feedforward

Feedforward   Inhibitory   Recurrent

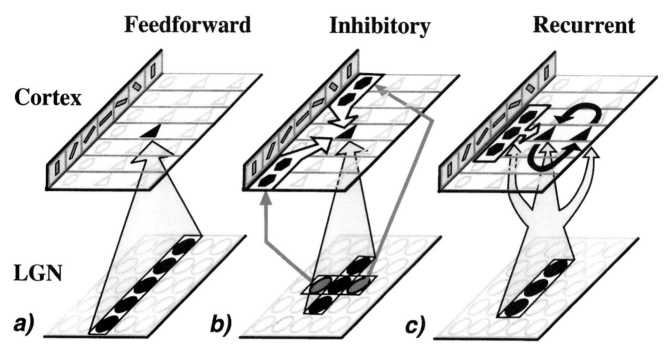

FIGURE 17.2 Sketch of different models for cortical orientation selectivity. At the cortical level, hexagonal shapes stand
for inhibitory neurons and triangular shapes stand for excitatory neurons. The LGN cell are depicted as the circular shapes
at the LGN level in the models. (a) Feedforward. All first-order
cortical cells receive input from a row of LGN cells aligned in
space. (b) In inhibitory models, there is inhibitory input from
orientation-tuned cortical neurons, indicated by the outlined

white arrows. (c) Recurrent excitatory and inhibitory feedback
models have both corticocortical inhibition (white arrows) and
corticocortical excitation (black arrows) impinging on all cortical cells. These corticocortical interactions are supposed to
greatly sharpen a broadly tuned input from LGN (indicated by
the shorter row of aligned LGN cells). (From Somers, Nelson,
and Sur, 1995.)

convergence or lateral cortical interactions generates
orientation selectivity. The difference between these two
explanations matters a lot for our conception of cerebral
cortical function. If orientation selectivity is due mainly to
the specific pattern of convergence of LGN afferents, this
would mean that a fundamental function of the visual
cortex arises from the feedforward filtering of the sensory
input, supporting the view of cortical processing as implementing a hierarchy of feedforward transformations.
However, if intracortical circuitry plays an important role
in orientation tuning, it implies that intracortical interactions shape the nature of the internal representations of
the external world that form in the cortex.

Orientation tuning dynamics

Knowing whether the sharpness of orientation tuning
changes during the time course of the cell's response is
central for the understanding of the mechanism for orientation selectivity. Unfortunately, this issue has been
controversial. The sharpening of the intracellular potential of cortical neurons with time, observed by Pei and
colleagues (1994), suggests that the extracellular responses should show a similar effect. However, Cele-

brini and collaborators (1993) found the opposite result,
that orientation selectivity is fully developed at the very
start of the extracellularly recorded spike train response
in virtually all the recorded cells in V1 of awake monkeys. We sought to investigate this crucial question with
a new methodology.

Reverse correlation in the orientation domain was
used to measure the time evolution of orientation tuning. The stimulus generation and the procedure used in
the data analysis are described first. We then discuss the
method's practical advantages.

For each cell, a set S of sinusoidal gratings of a fixed
spatial frequency (optimal for the cell) and contrast (in
the range 80–99%) but different orientations and spatial
phases was generated and stored in the computer's
memory. The orientation domain was sampled in equal
steps ranging between 3° and 12°. For most of the cells
reported here the angular resolution was fixed at 10°.
For each orientation, sinusoidal gratings at four or eight
spatial phases were included in the set. The spatial
phases were equally spaced and covered the entire 360°
range. In a typical experiment, the total number of images required was 144 (18 orientations times 8 spatial
phases).

The stimulus was generated by randomly selecting, at each video refresh time, a new image from S (with replacement). Unless otherwise noted this was done at a rate of 60 frames/s. The stimulus can be described as a very rapid sequence of gratings with random orientations and spatial phases. Stimulus segments were presented in 30-s trials with interstimulus intervals of approximately 1–2 s. Usually, 30 trials were presented to each cell, making the total experiment time about 15 m. The specific image sequence used in each trial was saved by the computer. During the stimulation period, action potentials were recorded extracellularly and time-stamped by the data acquisition system. In the experiments reported here, the size of the stimulation patch was large compared to the "classical receptive field" size of the cell defined by the peak of an area tuning curve obtained using circular stimulus patches of varying radii. The radius of the circular stimulus patch used in the experiments was between 2 and 6 times the optimal radius. This resulted on an average stimulus size of approximately 4° in diameter. The receptive field of the cell was centered at the middle of the stimulus. Therefore, both the classical receptive field of the cell and its surround were stimulated. This was done so as to include all the functional processes that would contribute visual inputs to cortical neurons and affect their orientation selectivity. Thus, it should be clear that inputs from the surround may contribute to the dynamic responses reported below.

The time course of orientation selectivity was determined according to the following algorithm. First, an array of counters corresponding to each of the orientations present in the stimulus was zeroed. A fixed value of a time-delay parameter τ was selected. For each nerve impulse recorded we went back τ ms in time and obtained the orientation of the grating that was present at that moment in the image sequence. The counter corresponding to that orientation was incremented by 1. Responses at a given orientation but different spatial phases were pooled. Let us denote by $N(\theta)$ the number of counts in the bin indexed by the orientation angle θ, and by M the total number of spikes collected. Notice that the sum of all spikes in the different orientation bins should equal the total number of spikes collected. We define

$$p(\theta,\tau) = N(\theta)/M$$

where $p(\theta,\tau)$ gives the empirical probability (or relative frequency) that an orientation θ was present in the stimulus image sequence τ ms before a nerve impulse was generated by the cell. For a fixed value of τ, $p(\theta,\tau)$ is a probability distribution on the orientation angles present in the stimulus set.

It is worth considering how many data go into the calculations of $p(\theta,\tau)$. We usually run the orientation dy-

namics data collection for 15 minutes—i.e., 900 seconds—or 54,000 stimulus images presented to the monkey. For a typical run where we are using 5° angular resolution, there are 375 presentations of each image to average over because there are 36 angles times 4 spatial phases, or 144 distinct images, in the image set. Another way of looking at it is if a typical cortical neuron fires on the average 5 spikes/s to the image sequence, then the reverse correlation will average over 4500 spikes. Therefore, we can obtain quite smooth, accurate orientation tuning curves.

We can study the dynamics of orientation tuning by studying $p(\theta,\tau)$. For $\tau = 0$, for example, we don't expect to see any influence of the input on the output spike train because visual integration and delay in the retina and subcortical visual pathway are too slow for us to observe anything happening in the cortex. Therefore, $p(\theta,0)$ would be a flat function with respect to orientation. Similarly, for very long τ, we also expect to see a flat distribution of $p(\theta,\tau)$; this is because cells have finite memory. For intermediate values of τ, we expect to see a smooth peaked distribution which represents the preference of the cell for particular orientations. Using these techniques, we have done experiments on dynamics of orientation tuning in different layers of macaque monkey visual cortex (V1). The results indicate two main patterns of dynamics: unimodal and multimodal. Unimodal dynamics means that the response, after a delay, simply increases and relaxes monotonically. We have observed multimodal dynamics of several types: (1) rebound responses, where the response at and around the peak orientation reverses its relative probability compared to the baseline and actually becomes a trough of probability 20–50 ms after the time it was a peak; (2) time evolution (sharpening with time) of orientation tuning; or (3) transient peaks of activity at off-optimal orientation, most often at 90° from the peak. In none of these cases is the orientation tuning function separable (factorable) in the two dimensions of orientation and time.

The method we used allows us to measure orientation tuning when the test stimuli are embedded within a rich stimulus set of temporally adjacent stimuli. We studied neurons in all layers of macaque V1, keeping track of their locations through standard methods of track reconstruction. In these early experiments, we used only high-contrast stimuli in order to get strong responses (contrast >90%). In these experiments the area of the stimulus was chosen to be 4–36 times bigger than that of the conventional receptive field of the neuron under study. Thus our stimuli covered the conventional receptive field as well as the "silent surround." This is what most researchers who have studied orientation tuning with conventional stimuli have done previously (see, for

$r_t(\theta)$ 1/deg

Orientation (deg)

258

example, De Valois, Yund, and Hepler, 1982; Celebrini et al., 1993; among others). It would be very interesting to study the dependence of orientation tuning sharpness and dynamics on stimulus area, and we have begun such a study.

Results

The major findings of our studies are as follows: (1) There is a very strong laminar dependence of orientation tuning sharpness. (2) There is an equally impressive dependence of orientation tuning dynamics on laminar location. (3) The pattern of the dynamics of sharply tuned cells in the output layers of V1 is consistent with a two-mechanism model in which an early, orientation-tuned excitatory signal is summed with a later, somewhat more broadly tuned, orientation-tuned inhibitory signal.

Most cells in the input layers $4C\alpha$ and β have simple, unimodal dynamics and are relatively broadly tuned for orientation. By unimodal dynamics we mean that, after a time delay, the response has a single peak in time and, after the peak, simply relaxes back to baseline. However, cells in layers 2, 3, 4B, 5, and 6 showed multimodal dynamics: rebound responses, sharpening of the orientation tuning with time, and/or transient peaks of activity at off-optimal orientation. Figure 17.3 (from the results of Ringach, Hawken, and Shapley, 1997) illustrates unimodal dynamics in 4C neurons' responses and multimodal dynamics in the response of neurons of the output layers 2, 3, 4B, 5, and 6. We found that these neurons with multimodal dynamics are usually much more sharply tuned in orientation.

Some of the data that suggest the two-mechanism model are given in figure 17.3. It shows orientation tun-

ing functions, derived from reverse correlation measurements, for two neurons (labeled c and d) in macaque V1 layer 4B. Note that in layer 4B, which is located just above layer $4C\alpha$, there is already evidence for complex interactions in the orientation domain: Rebound inhibition in both 4B cells can be observed around the 65-ms delay; and in cell c, there is clear evidence for flanking inhibition around the peak at 55 ms. In cell d's response, there is an especially clear indication of an elevated response orthogonal to the main peak, at a later time, at 65 ms in this case. In both these representative examples, there is a clear suppression, peaking at the formerly preferred orientation, at about 20 ms after the peak excitatory signal.

Implications

These results indicate that lateral interaction in the orientation domain is prevalent in striate cortex. The nature of this interaction is not yet understood. But the sombrero shapes of the orientation tuning distributions—so evident in cell c in figure 17.3 at 55 ms, for instance—suggest that we must consider recurrent or feedback inhibitory mechanisms in a model for the cortex. These sombrero-like distributions in orientation resemble the difference-of-Gaussian sensitivity distributions of center-surround receptive fields in the spatial dimension, and are predicted by feedback models of cortex (see, for instance, Somers, Nelson, and Sur, 1995; Ben-Yishai, Bar-Or, and Sompolinsky, 1995; Carandini and Ringach, 1997).

This work has implications about the validity of the receptive-field idea as a way of understanding cortical function. The implication is that lateral interactions in the cortex shape many aspects of cellular functions. Support for this view comes from quite a lot of work using a very different paradigm—the study of cortical visual interactions across space, also known as "contextual effects." This includes the work on center-surround interactions (reviewed by Allman, 1985), on orientation contrast (Knierim and van Essen, 1992; Sillito et al., 1995; Levitt and Lund, 1997), and on figure–ground effects (e.g., Lamme, 1995; Zipser, Lamme, and Schiller, 1996). There is also the recent work by Bullier and colleagues (reviewed in Salin and Bullier, 1995) that indicates the importance of feedback connections from extrastriate areas into V1. This body of work suggests that the cells in the primary visual cortex are influenced by lateral and feedback interactions in a very significant way, much more so than was imagined when the receptive field concept was first applied to cortex. In perception of natural scenes, even more than in laboratory experiments on simplified stimuli, the effects of context

FIGURE 17.3 Reverse correlation measurements of the time evolution of orientation tuning in macaque V1 neurons from all layers of striate cortex. The vertical scale is probability, the horizontal axis is orientation angle, and each graph in the perspective plot is for a different time offset τ. The orientation distributions before the first perspective plot and after the last perspective plot are all flat across orientation. Cell (a) is from $4C\alpha$, and cell (b) is from $4C\beta$; cells (c) and (d) are two different cells from layer 4B, and they illustrate the types of multimodal dynamics seen outside the input layers. Cell (e) is from layer 2/3; cell (f) is a cell from layer 5 that illustrates the change in preferred orientation tuning with time; cell (g) is an especially sharply tuned cell from 2/3 that has very strong flank suppression with a clear sombrero-like orientation distribution for times between 82 and 114 ms. Cell (h) is a layer-6 cell that has a clear multipeaked orientation tuning curve at time delays of 82–91 ms. M is the number of images shown, so $1/M$ is the uniform probability expected when there is no orientation response. (These data are redrawn from Ringach, Hawken, and Shapley, 1997.)

may play an important role in visual cortical cell responses. This must be quantified in future experiments.

With respect to the visual function of V1 cortex, this work makes it clear that the conventional view—that the cortex is a filter bank of static filters tuned to spatial frequencies and orientations in small regions in the visual environment—is a distortion of the true function of the cortex. Rather, when we use dynamic stimuli to probe the function of the cortical network, we see that cortical cells are alive with possibility. They exhibit near-neighbor inhibition that is slow, and near-neighbor excitation that is very fast. And they reveal dynamic changes in their orientation selectivity, with many neurons sharpening their tuning with time, but very rapidly. What is most striking is that, because of the delayed inhibition clearly evident in the neurons from layer 4B in figure 17.3, there is a marked change in the orientation preference of the neurons during the time evolution of their responses. Early in the response, there is a peak at the same orientation, approximately, as the peak of the steady-state tuning curve measured with conventional drifting stimuli like gratings or bars. However, later in the response, usually about 20 ms later, there is a rapid shift to an orientation preference orthogonal to the initial peak (because the late inhibition is greatest at the early peak orientation). We need to consider the importance of this time variation in preferred orientation for the visual function of the neurons in the cortex. What it means, we think, is that the optimal stimulus for such neurons may not be a line or a grating; rather, it is a time-varying, oriented boundary which is oriented at the initial peak orientation first and then rapidly switches to the orthogonal. What sorts of stimuli are these? Two possibilities occur to us: curved boundaries, and 2D features like corners or junctions. As the eye moves along a curved boundary, the orientation of a boundary that falls on a particular region of the eye, and hence the cortex, changes substantially and systematically. This means that it is the kind of dynamic change of orientation that might be particularly effective in stimulating cortical neurons. The effect of a corner or other 2D junctions could be even more effective because the boundaries at a corner often abruptly jump through 90° of orientation. This would be a most effective stimulus for many cells in layer 4B and in layers 2/3, which project to V2 and thence to many visual areas of the brain. Such speculations will need to be checked with experiments in the coming years. But it is clear that these and other new experiments have completely changed our view of the rich possibilities of information processing in primary visual cortex. And this also offers hope that the cortical mechanisms uncovered in V1 may be useful in comprehending the function of the cerebral cortex as a whole.

ACKNOWLEDGMENTS Our experiments were done in collaboration with Michael Hawken, Ferenc Mechler, Michael Sceniak, and Elizabeth Johnson, and we are very grateful to them for their help and their useful comments. The experimental work was supported by grants from the U.S. National Eye Institute, the U.S. National Science Foundation, and the Sloan Foundation.

REFERENCES

ALLISON, J. D., V. A. CASAGRANDE, and A. B. BONDS, 1995. Dynamic differentiation of GABAA-sensitive influences on orientation selectivity of complex cells in the cat striate cortex. *Exp. Brain Res.* 104:81–88.

ALLISON, J. D., B. PFLEGER, and A. B. BONDS, 1995. The influence of input from the lower cortical layers on the orientation tuning of upper layer V1 cells in a primate. *Vis. Neurosci.* 12:309–320.

ALLMAN, J., 1985. Stimulus specific responses from beyond the classical receptive field: Neurophysiological mechanisms for local-global comparisons in visual neurons. *Annu. Rev. Neurosci.* 8:407–430.

BEN-YISHAI, R., R. L. BAR-OR, and H. SOMPOLINSKY, 1995. Theory of orientation tuning in visual cortex. *Proc. Natl. Acad. Sci. U.S.A.* 92:3844–3848.

BLASDEL, G. G., and J. S. LUND, 1983. Termination of afferent axons in macaque striate cortex. *J. Neurosci.* 3:1389–1413.

BONDS, A. B., 1989. Role of inhibition in the specification of orientation selectivity of cells in the cat striate cortex. *Vis. Neurosci.* 2:41–55.

BRACEWELL, R. N., 1986. *The Fourier Transform and Its Applications* (2d Ed.). New York: McGraw-Hill, p. 385ff.

CARANDINI, M., and D. L. RINGACH, 1997. Predictions of a recurrent model of orientation selectivity. *Vis. Res.* 37:3061–3071.

CELEBRINI S., S. THORPE, Y. TROTTER, and M. IMBERT, 1993. Dynamics of orientation coding in area V1 of the awake primate. *Vis. Neurosci.* 10:811–825.

CHAPMAN, B., and M. P. STRYKER, 1993. Development of orientation selectivity in ferret visual cortex and effects of deprivation. *J. Neurosci.* 13:1347–1358.

CHAPMAN, B., K. ZAHS, and M. P. STRYKER, 1991. Relation of cortical cell orientation selectivity to alignment of receptive fields of the geniculocortical afferents that arborize within a single orientation column in ferret visual cortex. *J. Neurosci.* 11:1347–1358.

DAS, A., 1996. Orientation in visual cortex: A simple mechanism emerges. *Neuron* 16:477–480.

DE VALOIS, R. L., E. W. YUND, and N. HEPLER, 1982. The orientation and direction selectivity of cells in macaque visual cortex. *Vis. Res.* 22:531–544.

DOUGLAS, R. J., C. KOCH, M. MAHOWALD, K. A. MARTIN, and H. H. SUAREZ, 1995. Recurrent excitation in neocortical circuits. *Science* 269:981–985.

FERSTER, D., 1986. Orientation selectivity of synaptic potentials in neurons of cat primary visual cortex. *J. Neurosci.* 6:1284–1301.

FERSTER, D., 1988. Spatially opponent excitation and inhibition in simple cells of the cat visual cortex. *J. Neurosci.* 8:1172–1180.

FERSTER, D., 1992. The synaptic inputs to simple cells of the cat visual cortex. *Prog. Brain Res.* 90:423–441.

FERSTER, D., S. CHUNG, and H. WHEAT, 1996. Orientation selectivity of thalamic input to simple cells of cat visual cortex. *Nature* 380:249–252.

GILBERT, C. D., and T. N. WIESEL, 1983. Clustered intrinsic connections in cat visual cortex. *J. Neurosci.* 3:1116–1133.

HUBEL, D. H., and T. N. WIESEL, 1962. Receptive fields, binocular interaction and functional architecture in the cat's visual cortex. *J. Physiol.* 160:106–154.

HUBEL, D. H., and T. N. WIESEL, 1968. Receptive fields and functional architecture of monkey striate cortex. *J. Physiol. (Lond.)* 195:215–243.

HUBEL, D. H., and T. N. WIESEL, 1972. Laminar and columnar distribution of geniculo-cortical fibers in the macaque monkey. *J. Comp. Neurol.* 146:421–450.

KNIERIM, J. J., and D. C. VAN ESSEN, 1992. Neuronal responses to static texture patterns in area V1 of the alert macaque monkey. *J. Neurophysiol.* 67:961–980.

LACHICA, E. A., P. D. BECK, and V. A. CASAGRANDE, 1992. Parallel pathways in macaque monkey striate cortex: Anatomically defined columns in layer III. *Proc. Natl. Acad. Sci. U.S.A.* 89:3566–3570.

LAMME, V. A., 1995. The neurophysiology of figure–ground segregation in primary visual cortex. *J. Neurosci.* 15:1605–1615.

LEVITT, J. B., and J. S. LUND, 1997. Contrast dependence of contextual effects in primate visual cortex. *Nature* 387:73–76.

LUND, J. S., 1988. Anatomical organization of macaque monkey striate visual cortex. *Annu. Rev. Neurosci.* 11:253–288.

LUND, J. S., T. YOSHIOKA, and J. B. LEVITT, 1993. Comparison of intrinsic connectivity in different areas of macaque monkey cerebral cortex. *Cerebral Cortex* 3:148–162.

NELSON, S., L. TOTH, B. SHETH, and M. SUR, 1994. Orientation selectivity of cortical neurons during intracellular blockade of inhibition. *Science* 265:774–777.

PEI, X., T. R. VIDYASAGAR, M. VOLGUSHEV, and O. CREUTZFELDT, 1994. Receptive field analysis and orientation selectivity of postsynaptic potentials of simple cells in cat visual cortex. *J. Neurosci.* 14:7130–7140.

PUGH, M., M. J. SHELLEY, D. L. RINGACH, and R. SHAPLEY, in press. Computational modeling of orientation tuning dynamics in V1 neurons. *J. Comp. Neurosci.*

RATLIFF, F., 1965. *Mach Bands.* San Francisco: Holden Day.

REID, R. C., and J. M. ALONSO, 1995. Specificity of monosynaptic connections from thalamus to visual cortex. *Nature* 378:281–284.

REID, R. C., and J. M. ALONSO, 1996. The processing and encoding of information in the visual cortex. *Curr. Opin. Neurobiol.* 6:475–480.

RINGACH, D., M. HAWKEN, and R. SHAPLEY, 1997. The dynamics of orientation tuning in the macaque monkey striate cortex. *Nature* 387:281–284.

ROCKLAND, K. S., and J. S. LUND, 1983. Intrinsic laminar lattice connections in primate visual cortex. *J. Comp. Neurol.* 216:303–318.

SALIN, P. A., and J. BULLIER, 1995. Corticocortical connections in the visual system: Structure and function. *Physiol. Rev.* 75:107–154.

SCHILLER, P. H., B. L. FINLAY, and S. F. VOLMAN, 1976. Quantitative studies of single-cell properties in monkey striate cortex. II. Orientation specificity and ocular dominance. *J. Neurophysiol.* 39:1320–1333.

SCLAR, G., and R. D. FREEMAN, 1982. Orientation selectivity in cat's striate cortex is invariant with stimulus contrast. *Exp. Brain Res.* 46:457–461.

SHAPLEY, R. M., 1994. Linearity and non-linearity in cortical receptive fields. In *Higher Order Processing in the Visual System,* Gregory R. Bock and Jamie A. Goode, eds. Ciba Symposium 184. Chichester, England: Wiley, pp. 71–81.

SHOU, T. D., and A. G. LEVENTHAL, 1989. Organized arrangement of orientation-sensitive relay cells in the cat's dorsal lateral geniculate nucleus. *J. Neurosci.* 9:4287–4302.

SILLITO, A. M., 1975. The contribution of inhibitory mechanisms to the receptive field properties of neurons in the striate cortex of the cat. *J. Physiol.* 250:305–329.

SILLITO, A. M., K. L. GRIEVE, H. E. JONES, J. CUDEIRO, and J. DAVIS, 1995. Visual cortical mechanisms detecting focal orientation discontinuities. *Nature* 378:492–496.

SKOTTUN, B. C., A. BRADLEY, G. SCLAR, I. OHZAWA, and R. D. FREEMAN, 1987. The effects of contrast on visual orientation and spatial frequency discrimination: A comparison of single cells and behavior. *J. Neurophysiol.* 57:773–786.

SMITH III, E. L., Y. M. CHINO, W. H. RIDDER, and K. KITAGAWA, 1990. Orientation bias of neurons in the lateral geniculate nucleus of macaque monkeys. *Vis. Neurosci.* 5(6): 525–545.

SOMERS, D. C., S. B. NELSON, and M. SUR, 1995. An emergent model of orientation selectivity in cat visual cortical simple cells. *J. Neurosci.* 15:5448–5465.

SOMPOLINSKY, H., and R. SHAPLEY, 1997. New perspectives on the mechanisms for orientation selectivity. *Curr. Opin. Neurobiol.* 7:514–522.

TOLHURST, D. J., and A. F. DEAN, 1990. The effects of contrast on the linearity of spatial summation of simple cells in the cat's striate cortex. *Exp. Brain Res.* 79:582–588.

VIDYASAGAR, T. R., 1992. Subcortical mechanisms in orientation sensitivity of cat visual cortical cells. *Neuroreport* 3:185–188.

YOSHIOKA, T., J. B. LEVITT, and J. S. LUND, 1994. Independence and merger of thalamocortical channels within macaque monkey primary visual cortex: Anatomy of interlaminar projections. *Vis. Neurosci.* 11:467–489.

ZIPSER, K., V. A. LAMME, and P. H. SCHILLER, 1996. Contextual modulation in primary visual cortex. *J. Neurosci.* 15: 7376–7389.

18 Binocular Neurons and the Perception of Depth

ANDREW J. PARKER, BRUCE G. CUMMING, AND JON V. DODD

ABSTRACT Understanding the links between perception and the activity of single neurons would be a major achievement for cognitive neuroscience. The perception of stereoscopic depth through binocular vision provides a number of opportunities for studying these links. We present the results of recent experiments in the striate visual cortex (V1) and extrastriate visual areas (V2 and V5) that illustrate progress in investigating these issues.

The prevailing paradigm in cognitive neuroscience holds that activity within certain neurons will lead to the perception of a particular quality, such as color, motion, or pitch. It is widely assumed that the critical population of neurons resides within the cerebral cortex. Activity is rather broadly conceived here, so that the pattern of activity across a population of neurons (Recanzone, Merzenich, and Schreiner, 1992) or the presence of characteristic temporal sequences of action potentials (Singer and Gray, 1995) is within the scope of this term. The more specific issues that arise from supposing that the activity within *single neurons* is critical have been discussed elsewhere (Barlow, 1972; Parker and Newsome, 1998). Briefly, the properties of candidate neurons should account for the characteristic features of perceptual performance; loss of the relevant neurons should lead to some behaviorally measurable defect in perception; artificial stimulation of the neurons electrically or chemically should alter behavioral measures of perception; and the trial-to-trial fluctuations in neuronal performance should have measurable consequences for behavioral performance.

The work presented here falls within this prevailing paradigm. Nonetheless, it is worth a pause to consider alternatives. Essentially, the relevant level of analysis would be either more "fine-grained" or more "coarse-grained" than the level of single neurons. More "fine-grained" would mean examining subcellular processes, perhaps from the level of dendrites down to single ion channels or other molecular processes within the neuron and its immediate extracellular environment. More "coarse-grained" would mean examining the pooled signal from spatially neighboring neurons by means such as optical imaging, PET, or fMRI or by measuring the signal at several points within a circuit of neurons (Abeles, 1991). Neither of these alternatives is self-evidently incoherent as a theory of how the nervous system could work. Nonetheless, each alternative would eventually need to arrange for some output in the axons that travel from one cortical region to another (and eventually to the axons of motor neurons). At least in this respect, the signals provided by single neurons are crucial.

Binocular vision

Binocular vision is an excellent model system for investigating the links between neuronal activity and perception. Unlike perceptual phenomena that depend primarily on peripheral mechanisms (for example, the spectral sensitivity curve of scotopic vision), binocular vision requires the central combination of information from the two retinas. This requirement emphasizes the significance of signals at a cortical level. Binocular vision can also be probed with stimuli such as random-dot stereograms that ensure that the observer must use the stereoscopic system to extract the required information (Julesz, 1971). Stereoscopic vision has been studied intensively at the psychophysical and computational level (Poggio and Poggio, 1984): hence, stereo vision is known to exhibit a diverse and characteristic set of phenomena that are well suited for study at the neurophysiological level.

In our view, binocular vision has just about the right degree of complexity for studying the links between neurophysiology and perception. On one hand, simpler systems, such as the photoreceptors and ganglion cells in the retina, have already been examined, and, in any case, they tell us little about the essential cortical processes involved in the act of vision. On the other hand, given our present level of understanding, the study of more complex perceptual phenomena, such as object recognition, leads inevitably to an insufficiently precise specification of the perceptual task facing the observer.

ANDREW J. PARKER, BRUCE G. CUMMING, and JON V. DODD   University Laboratory of Physiology, Oxford, United Kingdom

263

Overview of this chapter

The experimental work presented in this chapter divides into two parts. The first part examines the responses of binocular neurons in the striate visual cortex (V1). The aim is to determine whether some of the characteristic features of the psychophysics of stereoscopic vision can be explained by reference to the properties of V1 neurons. The answer is negative, a result that forces us to look outside V1 in search of an explanation for these characteristics. There is a widespread distribution of disparity-selective neurons in several extrastriate cortical areas. In the second part, we examine findings in two of these extrastriate cortical areas, V2 and V5(MT). Area V2 has been repeatedly implicated as having a special role in binocular stereopsis. By contrast, V5(MT) has been most associated with a role in processing visual motion. Recent evidence implies that these neurons are also responsible for signaling some aspects of binocular depth. Finally, we discuss the currently popular idea that feedback connections from extrastriate cortical areas to V1 might signal perceptually relevant information (see Lamme and Spekreijse, chapter 19 of this volume).

Binocular neurons in V1

The studies in V1 arise out of comparisons between characteristic psychophysical properties of the stereoscopic system and the properties of disparity-selective cortical neurons. Each study reveals a discrepancy between the way in which stereo depth is perceived and how neurons in V1 respond, even those that are highly tuned for binocular disparity. By itself an individual discrepancy of this kind would not mean much. But as it turns out, all four discrepancies consistently support a simpler explanation of the behavior of V1 neurons: namely, that they are acting as a preliminary binocular matching system, with characteristics close to that of a pair of spatial filters that process the output of the left and right retinas and provide for a simple binocular combination of this information.

We will deal with the specific predictions of the binocular filtering model in relation to each experiment. For now, it is sufficient to indicate that in almost all essential characteristics our data from V1 in awake, behaving monkeys can be accommodated by the kind of model advanced by Ohzawa, DeAngelis, and Freeman (1990) for explaining data recorded from the anesthetized cat visual cortex. The fact that this kind of model is suitable has strong implications for the way in which V1 neurons respond in the awake animal. First, perhaps surprisingly, there is relatively little evidence of "top-down" influences on the stereoscopic responses of V1 neurons. Sec-

ond, the way in which V1 neurons fail to match the psychophysical characteristics of stereopsis not only indicates the need for further processing beyond V1 but also illustrates the limited scope of the Ohzawa, DeAngelis, and Freeman model as a physiologically based explanation of the perceptual properties of binocular stereopsis.

ANTICORRELATED STEREOGRAMS The first case that we present makes use of anticorrelated random-dot stereograms (aRDS). These patterns do not lead to a coherent percept of stereoscopic depth, but they evoke responses in V1 neurons that are strongly related to the disparity of the stimulus pattern. In a conventional (correlated) random-dot stereogram (cRDS), each bright dot in one eye's image is paired with a bright dot in the other eye's image. Binocular depth is introduced by altering the horizontal position of dots in the images (Julesz, 1971). If the stereogram is constructed on a midgray background, dark dots may be also be used, and again the pairing of dots between the eyes is matched for brightness (compare the left-hand and central parts of figure 18.1A). In an aRDS, each bright dot in one eye's image is placed in a horizontal position that would pair it with a dark dot in the other eye's image. The effect of this manipulation on the psychophysical appearance is dramatic and can be observed by attempting to fuse the central and right-hand portions of figure 18.1B. At a sufficiently high dot density, stereopsis is impossible: Although observers continue to be able to discriminate anticorrelated patterns from binocularly uncorrelated dots, it is impossible to discriminate different disparities in anticorrelated patterns (Cogan, Lomakin, and Rossi, 1993; Cumming, Shapiro, and Parker, 1998).

The spatial filtering model for binocular neurons has a characteristic behavior when stimulated with aRDS (see Cumming and Parker, 1997). The model predicts an inversion of the disparity tuning function measured with cRDS. This arises from the way in which bright and dark dots differentially stimulate the ON and OFF zones making up the receptive field of the neuron. With cRDS, the neuron is maximally excited when a bright feature falls within an ON region of the receptive field in *both* right and left eyes (or similarly a dark feature falls within an OFF region). At the equivalent disparity with aRDS, all zones of the receptive field are receiving a bright feature through one eye and a dark feature of the same geometry through the other eye. These effects cancel, leading to a weak response, possibly below the background firing rate.

The most effective responses with aRDS are created when a bright dot stimulates an ON region in one eye's receptive field and a dark dot stimulates an OFF region

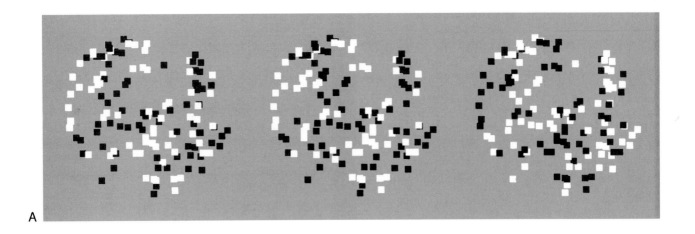

A

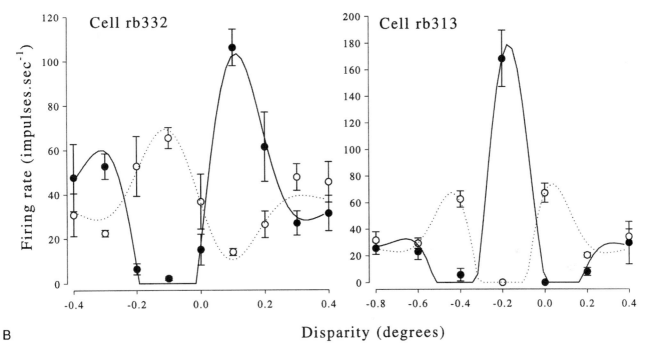

B

Disparity (degrees)

FIGURE 18.1 (A) Sample random-dot stereogram with both correlated and anticorrelated forms (cRDS and aRDS). The left random-dot field and the center field are correlated (so that each dot in one field has a partner of the corresponding contrast in the other field). Binocular fusion of left and center field reveals a foreground region segregated in depth from a surrounding region. The right random-dot field is equivalent to the left field except that the contrast polarity of all dots is inverted. When the right and center field are fused binocularly, there is no segregation of the foreground and surround regions, and no depth is seen. (B) Example tuning curves of two V1 neurons measured with cRDS and aRDS. The ordinate shows firing rate in impulses per second, and the abscissa shows binocular disparity. Firing rates for cRDS are shown with filled symbols and fitted with a solid line; firing rates for aRDS are shown with open symbols and fitted with a dotted line. The tuning curves with cRDS and aRDS are inverted with respect to each other.

in the other eye's receptive field. As the position of a bright dot in one eye's stimulus is linked geometrically to a dark dot in the other eye, the optimal binocular stimulation requires an offset between the positions of the bright and dark dots. The most favorable size of the offset is equal to the separation of the zones of the receptive field. Hence, the binocular filtering model predicts that when a disparity tuning curve is measured with aRDS, the peak of the curve should shift to a new disparity, whose value is predictable based on the spatial separation of ON and OFF zones making up the receptive field. Although this argument has been developed as if the cortical neuron had a simple receptive field, the argument also holds for complex cell behavior, because their responses are compatible with a nonlinear combination of several subunits with properties like those of simple cells (Ohzawa, DeAngelis, and Freeman, 1990).

Broadly, V1 receptive fields conform to the expectations of this model: Their disparity tuning functions are inverted by anticorrelation (Cumming and Parker, 1997; figure 18.1). By contrast, we confirmed that, like human observers, the monkeys from whom the V1 neurons were recorded cannot make depth discrimination judgments with anticorrelated stimuli. The combination of these results demonstrates that it is possible to arrange stimuli that generate a large signal within the disparity-selective cells of V1 but nonetheless fail to provide any perception of depth. Even though the amplitudes of the responses to aRDS and cRDS may differ, it is clear that the mere activation of disparity-selective V1 neurons is insufficient for stereoscopic depth perception: The pattern of neuronal responses must be organized in an appropriate way, so as to stimulate neurons that are presumably at a different cortical site, where binocular correspondence is sorted out. It follows that the processing at this other presumed cortical site must be more sophisticated than a simple weighted pooling of the responses from V1, because the population profile of V1 responses by itself can neither predict the difference in appearance of aRDS and cRDS nor account for binocular correspondence.

WINDOWED GRATING PATCHES   The previous subsection demonstrated that binocular stimuli that do not lead to stereopsis evoke systematic responses from V1 neurons as the disparity is changed. Here we discuss binocular stimuli that are in principle capable of supporting stereopsis but are actually excluded from the current stereoscopic percept, owing to the geometric arrangement of the stimulus. We used a stimulus that provides for multiple local matches between features on the left and right retinas. The stimulus is a sinusoidal grating pattern delimited by a sharp circular window (see figure 18.2A).

As a preliminary, recall that a grating pattern *without* a window is inherently ambiguous as a binocular stimulus because of the periodic nature of the grating. In our stimulus, the binocular disparity is altered by shifting *both* grating and window horizontally in one eye's image with respect to the other. Consider a receptive field of limited spatial extent that is sensitive only to the local features falling directly within the receptive field. It follows that such a receptive field is not affected by the window so that, as far as the receptive field is concerned, the windowed sinusoid is effectively the same as a grating without a window. There is in reality no basis for determining an unambiguous value for the disparity of the bars of the grating, unless the binocular matching process can be influenced by the disparity of the window.

Figure 18.2A shows that, as the disparity approaches a multiple of the spatial period of the sine wave, then there is also a valid local match for several of the bars at zero disparity. The global disparity is unambiguously signaled by the window and the bars of the grating. But the illustrated manipulation reveals that, if only the bars of the grating are considered, there is a multiplicity of local matches that could stimulate the binocular receptive fields of cortical neurons.

This possibility has been appreciated for some time from a psychophysical and computational perspective (Julesz, 1971; Marr and Poggio, 1976; Mitchison, 1988), where it has been termed the correspondence problem. Psychophysically, the outcome is clear: Human observers respond only to the globally specified disparity in this configuration. (Note that there is no question of a discrepancy between the disparity of the window and the grating. The same globally correct disparity is always signaled by both the window and the bars, but the bars also signal a variety of other locally valid matches.) One way of investigating the signal provided by V1 neurons is to assess whether these neurons respond exclusively to globally correct matches or alternatively to any valid local match within their receptive field.

An example of this test applied to a V1 receptive field is shown in figure 18.3. The response of the neuron with patches of sinusoidal grating shows a peak at the optimal disparity measured with dynamic RDS patterns (as expected), but there is also an additional peak at the repeat period of the grating. Such additional peaks represent strong responses to the local disparities within the pattern. We have tested more than 60 V1 neurons, which all respond similarly to the example illustrated. By contrast, both monkeys have been tested psychophysically and respond in the same way as human observers: The perceptual responses are controlled only by the global disparity of the pattern.

SUMS OF SINUSOIDS   There is a potential objection to the previous experiment: It requires some inward propagation of constraints from outside the classical receptive field so that information about the global disparity can influence the processing of local disparities within the receptive field. This process may be impossible within V1, but a more local process could still be at work. Therefore, we have investigated the same question in experiments where the signal that could disambiguate local matches is within the receptive field itself.

In this case, a sum of two spatial sinusoids was used to stimulate the cortical receptive field. The sum of sinusoids results in a spatial pattern of light that has bright and dark features that match up binocularly across the spatial extent of the pattern (see figure 18.2B). This pattern has a

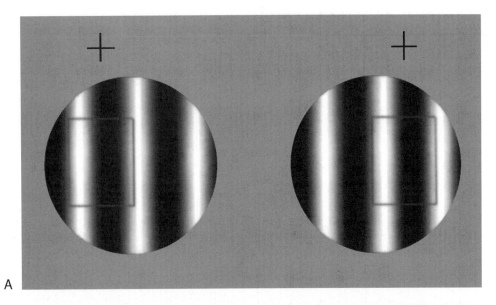

A

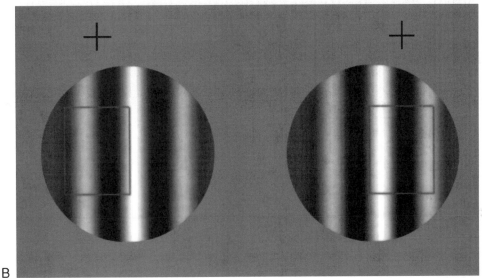

B

FIGURE 18.2 (A) Stereoscopic figure of a binocular sinusoidal grating pattern with a sharp circular window, as used for testing V1 receptive fields. The stimuli are presented on a midgray screen with a dark fixation cross (which the monkey is trained to fixate), and the location of the receptive field is shown schematically by the gray outline box. The shift in position of the window between the left and right eyes defines a binocular disparity, and upon binocular fusion the stimulus appears as a sinusoidal grating occupying a depth plane distinct from the fixation plane. However the local luminance distribution within the receptive field is also consistent with a zero disparity because the disparity of the window is equal to one spatial period of sine wave. (B) Stereoscopic figures of the binocular sum of sinusoids stimulus. The format is similar to A, but sinusoids at two different spatial frequencies are summed together. The overall pattern has a repeat period governed by the difference between the two spatial frequencies, so if the component frequencies are 3 and 4 cycles per degree the pattern will have repeat period of 1 cycle per degree. Psychophysical testing with these stimuli indicates that the stereo depth judgments of observers are influenced by the repeat period. Neurophysiological results from V1 with these two stimulus types are shown in figures 18.3 and 18.4.

repeat period fixed by the *difference* in the spatial frequency of the two component sine waves. If the neurons in V1 were able to combine information from the two different spatial frequencies within the stimulus, their disparity responses should be dominated by the disparity of the repeat period. The psychophysical responses of both humans and monkeys are sensitive to an interaction between the sinusoids because the pattern of depth judgments is firmly linked to the globally correct pattern of binocular matches. Thus, psychophysically, the repeat period is effective in constraining stereoscopic depth perception (Thomas, Cumming, and Parker, 1998).

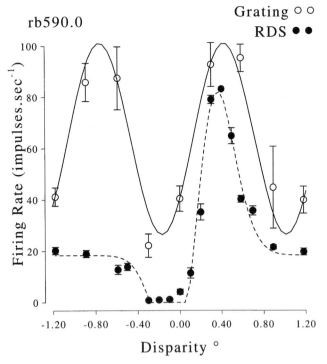

Grating ○ ○
RDS ● ●

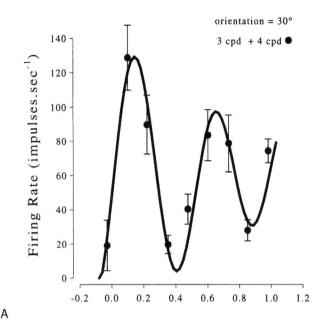

A

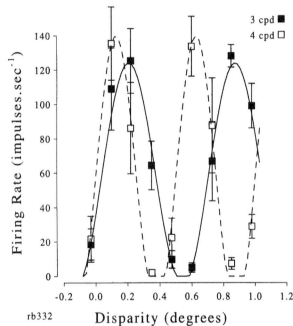

B   rb332

FIGURE 18.3   Data from single cortical neuron recorded in V1 first with dynamic RDS patterns (filled symbols, dashed curve) and then with windowed sinusoidal gratings (open symbols, solid curve). The neuron is clearly tuned for dynamic RDS patterns, but by itself this test does not establish that the neuron responds only to globally correct binocular matches. The data with the windowed sinusoid show two peaks: one at the same position as the peak with dynamic RDS and one at the disparity corresponding to the repeat period of the sinusoid (see figure 18.2A). The stimulus that creates this second peak is perceived by human observers as *nearer* than the fixation plane, whereas the optimal RDS stimulus is *more distant* than the fixation plane.

On the other hand, if the neurons are responsive to purely local information, the simplest prediction is that the neuron's disparity tuning for the sum of sinusoids should be a weighted sum of its responses to each component presented separately (Ohzawa and Freeman, 1986). Qualitatively, the neuron will show peaks in the tuning curve for disparities between noncorresponding features on the stimulus profile.

This pattern of behavior can be seen in the example presented in figure 18.4. The two curves in figure 18.4B show the responses to each sinusoidal component presented separately. Figure 18.4A shows the responses of the same neuron to the two sinusoids presented together, and the curve fitted to this data is a weighted sum of the two sinusoidal curves (from figure 18.4B) that were found to be a satisfactory description of the response to each component presented alone. This result indicates that the neuron responds to each component independently and, as far as disparity tuning is con-

FIGURE 18.4   (A) Data for a single cortical neuron recorded in V1 with the sum of sinusoids stimulus (see figure 18.2B). The peak tuning at about 0.2 degrees of disparity is accompanied by a smaller peak at 0.6–0.7 degrees disparity. The entire tuning curve can be satisfactorily described with a fitted curve defined by a sum of sine waves whose periodicities are fixed by the spatial frequencies of the component sine wave grating patterns. (B) Data from the same cortical neuron as A, showing its response to each component of sinusoid. The responses shown here were collected on trials randomly interleaved with those in A.

cerned, there is no interaction between the sinusoids. This example, like the previous ones, highlights the way in which the disparity-specific responses of V1 neurons are inadequate for explaining the perceptual properties of stereoscopic vision.

RELATIVE VERSUS ABSOLUTE DISPARITY A striking point that emerges from comparing the psychological and the neurophysiological literature on binocular disparity is that each field typically maintains different conceptions of disparity. The point is illustrated in figure 18.5. Neurophysiologists have considered disparity to be the fact that objects at depths other than the fixation plane will project to anatomically noncorresponding points on the left and right retinas (Joshua and Bishop, 1970). Here we will refer to this as *absolute disparity*. Psychologists on the other hand have often considered disparity to be the difference in the projections of two visible features. We will refer to this definition as *relative disparity*.

There are two important respects in which these definitions lead to different properties. First, straightforwardly, at least two visible features are required to define a relative disparity. Second, when the eyes change in convergence in a static 3-D scene, the absolute disparity of features on the retina changes, whereas the relative disparity between features is essentially invariant. Looked at from this point of view, there would be considerable advantage to the binocular visual system in creating a representation of binocular depth based on relative disparity. Such a representation would be stable under changes of fixation in a way that a representation based purely on absolute disparity could never achieve.

It is thus perhaps no surprise that there is considerable psychophysical evidence that the representation effectively used by human observers for binocular depth

judgments is related much more closely to relative disparity than to absolute disparity. The perceived depth of stereoscopic features is typically governed much more by their disparity relative to that of neighboring visual features than by their absolute disparity relative to the binocular point of regard (Westheimer, 1979; Mitchison and Westheimer, 1984; Kumar and Glaser, 1992; Erkelens and Collewijn, 1985; Howard and Rogers, 1995; Glennerster and McKee, in preparation). The problem in assessing the neurophysiological literature on this question is that almost all studies have introduced binocular disparity into the visual stimulus in such a way that absolute and relative disparities have been changed together consistently.

One way to separate the effects of relative and absolute disparity would be to add a surround to a binocular depth target and then manipulate the depth of the surround. This approach allows the relative disparity between the target and its surround to be altered independently. It is straightforward to arrange, but a negative result would be hard to interpret. (We present an example of using this approach in V2 later.) The reason is that, in order to carry out the experiment with an awake behaving primate, the experimenter needs to provide a binocular fixation target. Since we cannot predict in advance how relative disparity is computed, it could be the case that neurons compute relative disparity between the binocular fixation target and the stimulus presented within the receptive field.

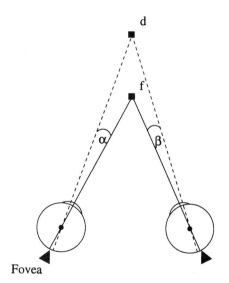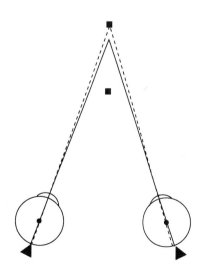

FIGURE 18.5 Diagram to illustrate definitions of absolute and relative disparity. The essence of absolute disparity is that it is calculated in a true retinal coordinate frame between *one* visible feature and the binocular location that the eyes are currently fixating. By contrast, the essence of relative disparity is that it is calculated between *two* visible features. Thus, in the left-hand figure, the eyes are looking at the binocular fixation point *f*, and a binocular feature *d* is present at a different depth. The disparity (both absolute and relative) of *d* with respect to *f* is given by $\alpha + \beta$. In the right-hand figure, the eyes are rotated to a new fixation position. The absolute disparity of *d* has decreased (smaller angles between the binocular lines of sight), but the relative disparity between *d* and the old fixation point *f* remains the same.

Recently we have investigated this question with the use of a feedback strategy to add a controlled amount of extra absolute disparity to a visual target that also contains relative disparity information. This procedure allows us to manipulate absolute disparity independently of relative disparity. The strategy involves adding an extra absolute disparity to all the visible features within the animal's binocular field including the fixation marker. This situation was achieved by altering the angle between the mirrors that formed the stereoscope through which the animal viewed the targets. This alteration is equivalent to stepping the entire binocular field forward or back by an extra absolute disparity equal to the change in angle between the mirrors. The natural reaction of the animal under this manipulation is to alter vergence to reacquire binocular fixation. It is at this point that feedback is exploited. The animal's binocular eye position is monitored with implanted scleral search coils. As the animal alters its eye position, the measured change in vergence is used to alter the positions of the mirrors so as to maintain the required additional absolute disparity.

This use of feedback is a classic device for investigating the function of the disparity-driven vergence system (Rashbass and Westheimer, 1961). It is important to stress that for our purposes the induced vergence movement is essentially an irrelevant side effect. The important aspect is that we have introduced a known amount of extra absolute disparity. This manipulation has a clear prediction in regard to the properties of cortical neurons that are selective for binocular disparity. If the neuron is computing disparity in a coordinate frame defined by absolute disparity, then a consequence of the addition of an extra absolute disparity is that the preferred disparity of the neuronal tuning function should shift by an amount equivalent to the added absolute disparity. If the neuron is computing disparity in a coordinate frame defined by relative disparity, then the extra absolute disparity should have no effect.

Representative results for a V1 neuron are shown in figure 18.6. This neuron shows changes in its preferred disparity when additional absolute disparities are included in the display. Hence the neuron computes disparity as absolute disparity rather than relative disparity. All 54 neurons that we have explored in V1 show this pattern of behavior.

SUMMARY OF V1 RESULTS   We have explored several features of the disparity-related responses of V1 neurons. In all cases, the responses of these neurons are incompatible with predictions based on the hypothesis that these neurons are directly involved in controlling the perceptual process. It appears that V1 represents a preliminary stage in the generation of the stereoscopic process. By analogy with earlier studies of motion processing (Movshon et al., 1985), disparity processing appears to proceed with V1 performing a binocular spatiotemporal filtering of the retinal outputs, which is then followed by the elaboration of higher-order properties in extrastriate cortical areas.

Binocular responses in extrastriate cortex

Some of the earliest studies on the extrastriate cortex indicated the presence of disparity-selective neurons in these visual areas (Hubel and Wiesel, 1970; Maunsell and Van Essen, 1983). By itself this observation is unremarkable. There is a sense in which any binocular neuron may be expected to show some measurable disparity tuning if it has spatially restricted receptive fields in the left and right eyes. When the centers of the receptive fields are determined in the left and right eyes and projection lines are drawn out from those centers, the lines will cross at some point in binocular space (assuming there is no vertical misalignment of the receptive fields). This geometric organization is sufficient to enable the neurophysiologist to measure some disparity tuning from a neuron with this receptive field structure. This fact illustrates quite nicely the general point that no firm conclusions about the role of neurons in perception can be deduced simply from the fact that they are tuned to some particular sensory parameter.

Thus we concentrate on recently acquired evidence that neurons in the extrastriate cortex are indeed more closely involved in controlling the animal's stereoscopic percept than neurons in V1. Cortical area V2 has long been implicated in the processing of binocular information, and we point to some features of disparity processing in V2 that appear qualitatively different from observations in V1. Other evidence from extrastriate cortex comes from cortical area V5(MT), which until now has been chiefly associated with the perceptual processing of motion information.

RESPONSES TO RELATIVE DISPARITY IN V2   We employed the technique of directly probing responses to relative disparity by manipulating the disparity of a surround region while the disparity of a central region covering the receptive field was held constant. This changes dramatically the perceptual appearance of the depth configuration in the dynamic random-dot figure. A neuron that is sensitive to depth relationships should have its disparity-tuning function shifted to different preferred disparity (or otherwise modulated) by this change in configuration.

Figure 18.7 shows the disparity tuning curve of a V2 neuron measured under two conditions. In the first case, the surround region is maintained at a disparity of −0.4° relative to the binocular fixation point (i.e., always more distant); in the second case, the surround is maintained at disparity of +0.4° (in front of the fixation point). In both cases, the disparity tuning is measured by changing the disparity of the center to the values shown on the abscissa. The main (upper) figure shows the responses of the neuron as a function of disparity; the inset (lower) figure shows the animal's vergence state at each disparity.

The main upper figure shows that the neuron's tuning curve is shifted along the abscissa by the change of background configuration in the direction expected for a neuron that is sensitive to relative disparity. However, the size of the shift is too small for this neuron to be considered as purely sensitive to relative disparity: There is some residual sensitivity to absolute disparity.

Another cautionary feature of the results is shown in the lower figure, where there is clear evidence of a change in vergence that is linked to the change in background configuration (see the section "Feedback effects in V1?"). It appears that this change in vergence is too small to account for all of the change in the neuron's tuning curve but undoubtedly contributes to it. The change of vergence is somewhat unexpected, given that the animal has a clear binocular fixation point and that the surround region is limited in size and does not traverse the binocular fixation point. Evidently, measurements of binocular eye position are essential in evaluating claims about sensitivity to relative disparity, since if the animal were always to converge at the same distance as the *surround region* in this experiment, one could falsely conclude that the neuron is sensitive to relative disparity.

In our limited sample so far, only a few neurons in V2 behave like that in figure 18.7 by showing evidence for

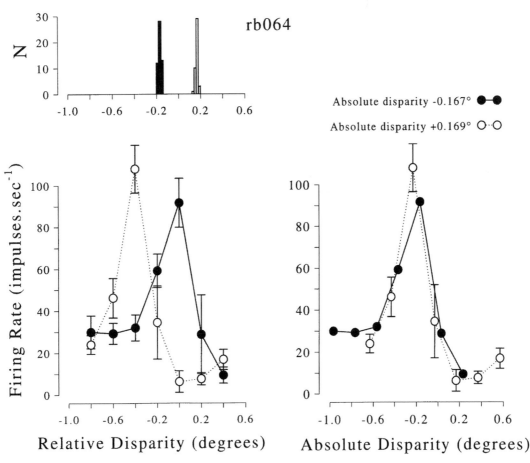

FIGURE 18.6 Responses of a V1 cortical neuron to manipulation of absolute and relative disparity with dynamic random-dot stereogram stimuli. The lower left graph shows the firing rate of the neuron (impulses per second) as a function of relative disparity (degrees) under two different conditions of added absolute disparity. The values of the added absolute disparity were controlled by feedback from the measured vergence position (see text) and are plotted in the upper left graph. The lower right graph shows the same neuronal tuning data replotted with an abscissa with a scale of absolute disparity. The tuning curves from the two conditions now coincide, thus demonstrating that this V1 neuron responds to the absolute not the relative disparity of stereoscopic stimuli.

sensitivity to relative disparity as well as absolute disparity. The majority of neurons in V2 show no sensitivity to the background configuration in this procedure, and we conjecture that they are primarily responsive to absolute disparity. Given existing evidence for the clustering of different types of neuron in V2 (Peterhans and von der Heydt, 1993; Roe and T'so, 1995), it will be interesting to see whether evidence for clustering of neurons with sensitivity to relative disparity emerges as more data are collected.

RESPONSES OF NEURONS IN V5(MT) TO PERCEPTUALLY AMBIGUOUS STIMULI   For this study we employed perceptually ambiguous stimuli: figures that permit two or more distinct perceptual interpretations by the observer. A classic example from perceptual psychology is the Necker cube (figure 18.8). In these experiments, we used a motion stimulus that reverses in depth similarly to the Necker cube. The motion figure consists of a set of dots depicted on a transparent cylindrical surface that is rotating about its axis. Human observers may perceive this cylinder as rotating either clockwise or counterclockwise. The perceived direction of rotation of the cylinder is linked to the relative depth assigned to the moving dots forming the figure. A vertically oriented cylinder will rotate clockwise (as viewed from above) if the leftward moving dots in the pattern are assigned to the nearer surface and the rightward moving dots to the further surface. If the cylinder reverses direction of rotation, the depth relationships necessarily change.

If an observer views a figure of this type with one eye and the display is produced by orthographic projection, there is no information that the observer can use to determine the "true" direction of rotation. If, however, binocular viewing is used, then stereo disparities can be used to indicate to the perceptual system which of the two surfaces is in front of the other. In this case, the direction of rotation becomes unambiguous. We exploited binocular vision to train monkeys to indicate the direction of rotation of cylindrical motion stimuli. The fact that this stimulus is unambiguous allows us to create the appropriate reward contingencies for training the monkey. The training can be taken further by decreasing the size of the stereo disparities down to the neighborhood of stereo threshold.

It is then possible to include occasions on which the animal is presented with a cylinder in which the front and rear surfaces have the same disparity. Such trials are essentially impossible to distinguish from near-threshold examples, which actually include some disparity and thus have a demonstrably correct answer. The responses on the ambiguous trials indicate an unbiased measure of the

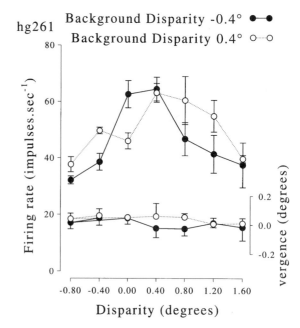

FIGURE 18.7   Responses of a cortical neuron recorded in V2 to dynamic random-dot stereograms, where the foreground (central) region was at the absolute disparities indicated on the abscissa and the background (surround) region was placed at either +0.4° or –0.4° relative to the fixation target. The lower inset graph shows the average state of the monkey's convergence on the fixation target (0.0°) upon the same trials during which the neuron was recorded. The change of background disparity induces a shift in the tuning of the cortical neuron, which is in the correct direction for a response that is exclusive to *relative* disparity but is smaller than the 0.8° shift expected on this basis. Nonetheless the shift in the neuronal tuning is too small to be accounted for by the small shifts in convergence state.

subject's perception of the cylinder with motion cues alone.

The neuronal responses to these rotating cylinder targets (Bradley, Qian, and Andersen, 1995; Dodd et al., 1997; Bradley, Chang, and Andersen, 1998) confirm that many neurons in V5(MT) carry disparity-related signals, as well as their well-known direction selectivity. The response varies systematically as the disparity between the front and back surfaces of the cylinder is altered. Preliminary testing of the receptive field with single planes of dots was used to assess the receptive field location and size, direction selectivity, and disparity preference of the neurons. The cylinder was then placed so that its size and location matched the receptive field and at least one of its surfaces fell within the direction and disparity preference of the neuron. In general, the neuron changed its response monotonically as the disparity of the surfaces within the cylinder changed, so that the output of the neuron could potentially contribute to the animal's judgment about the perceived configuration of the cylindrical target.

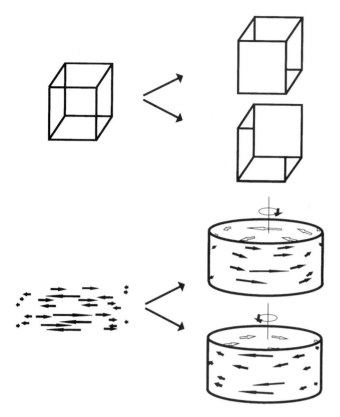

FIGURE 18.8 The upper figure shows a well-known example of a perceptually reversible figure, the Necker cube, for which the alternative 3-D interpretations are indicated diagrammatically at the right of the figure. The lower figure shows the principle behind the perceptually reversible rotating cylinder used in our experiments. The cylinder is depicted with dots placed at random locations on its surface. The moving dots are represented here by arrows that point in the direction of their motion and whose length shows their speed. The motion flow field on the left is inherently ambiguous and can support either of the two interpretations shown on the right. The addition of binocular stereo cues separates the front and rear surfaces of the transparent cylinder and thereby fixes the direction of rotation.

The interesting case is the response of the neuron on trials where all the dots forming the cylinder have zero disparity. The external stimulus is constant, but the animal's report about the configuration differs from trial to trial. Using exactly this approach, Bradley, Chang, and Andersen (1998) have already shown that some MT neurons have enhanced responses when the animal makes a behavioral choice consistent with the properties of the recorded neuron.

We wanted to find out whether the single-trial responses of the neurons were *predictive* of the animal's response, and if so with what statistical reliability. We examined two probability distributions of the neuron's responses: one for trials on which the animal reported that the stimulus was rotating counterclockwise and one for trials on which the report was clockwise (see figure 18.9). This experiment revealed that the neuronal firing

pattern was in general predictive of the animal's responses. More precisely, the response of some neurons yielded a highly reliable index of the animal's choice. In some cases, there was almost no overlap between the two probability distributions. We employed the analyses of choice probability described by Britten and colleagues (1996) and discovered that choice probabilities could be as high as 0.93 with an average value of 0.68. These values are much higher than those found by Britten and colleagues (1996) for neurons in the same cortical area during the performance of a direction discrimination task with moving patterns of dots.

Clearly, this result reflects a strong correlation between the neuronal responses and the animal's perception, but its cause remains to be determined. Recently, DeAngelis, Cumming, and Newsome (1998) have taken matters one step further by employing electrical stimulation while the animal is performing a stereo depth judgment task. They succeeded in shifting the monkey's perceptual decisions such that stimulation in a region of V5(MT) preferring "near" disparities resulted in a greater proportion of "near" responses from the animal (see DeAngelis et al., chapter 21 of this volume). These various results suggest that V5(MT) may have an important role in some aspects of stereoscopic vision.

Feedback effects in V1?

Cortical area V1 receives a large number of afferent connections from extrastriate cortex as well as connections from the visual thalamus. Recently it has been argued that these connections provide a feedback system that creates a modulation of the responses of V1 neurons, in a way that depends upon the perceptual context of the stimulus (Lamme, 1995), including its binocular disparity (Zipser, Lamme, and Schiller, 1996). The experiments presented here are relevant to this discussion. Feedback signals from higher cortical areas are one way in which V1 neurons could disambiguate stereoscopic matches (in the case of the windowed sinusoids) or develop a sensitivity for relative rather than absolute disparity. The fact that no such effects can be observed in V1 argues that contextual modulation of V1 responses does little that is useful for stereoscopic processing. So the first point is that, for the case of stereo vision, contextual modulation fails to achieve what would be a useful perceptual function. In this respect, its functional role remains mysterious.

Nonetheless, contextual modulation adds a complexity to the simple picture of V1 that we advanced earlier. We may identify three possible routes by which the responses of V1 neurons could be modulated. The first is by intracortical connections from within V1, which are

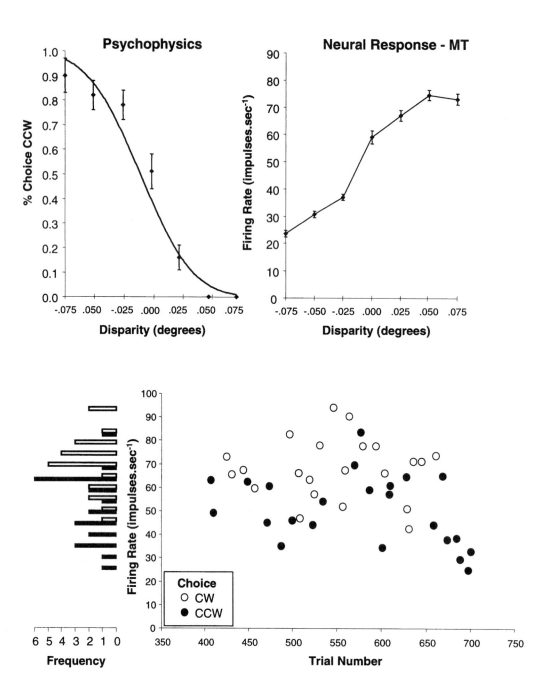

FIGURE 18.9 Simultaneously acquired neurophysiological responses from a single cortical neuron recorded in V5(MT) and psychophysical responses from the same animal to the rotating cylinder stimulus described in figure 18.8 as a function of the binocular disparity between the two surfaces of the cylinder. The upper pair of graphs shows that both the psychophysical and the neural responses change systematically with binocular disparity. The lower graph extracts the responses on trials where the binocular disparity was 0.0° and the cylinder was in-

herently ambiguous. The firing rates are plotted against trial number with the animal's choices of clockwise (CW, $N = 22$) and counterclockwise (CCW, $N = 23$) shown separately. These data are summarized at the left as two frequency distributions of firing rate, one for each type of choice made by the animal. The separation of these two distributions can be summarized by the choice probability (here 0.823), which indicates the tightness of the correlation between the firing of this individual neuron and the perceptual choices made by the animal.

often assumed to be the route by which influences outside the classical receptive field can alter the stimulus specificity and responsivity of the neuron, even when the animal is anesthetized and the eye position is held fixed by paralyzing agents (e.g., Levitt and Lund, 1997).

The second route is by feedback from connections from other locations in the brain, generally assumed to be largely from other extrastriate cortical areas (Lamme, 1995; Zipser, Lamme, and Schiller, 1996; Lamme and Spekreijse, chapter 19 of this volume). The third route is more indirect, via a stimulus-induced change in eye position, which is clearly a potential problem in the awake, behaving animal.

We emphasize two points here. First, when a static random-dot field is presented to the V1 receptive field of an awake, behaving monkey (as in Zipser, Lamme, and Schiller, 1996), there is typically a burst of firing closely following stimulus presentation, and then the firing rate settles down to a much lower rate, which is readily elevated again by the visual consequences of a small eye movement. A great deal of the firing in the later phases of the stimulus duration therefore depends not particularly on the stimulus parameters but on the pattern of eye movements made by the animal. Second, we demonstrated earlier that binocular neurons in V1 are selective for absolute rather than relative disparity, so any shift in vergence position will affect the signals in V1 neurons. Clearly, it is essential to monitor the positions of both eyes. Even when a visual neuron is insensitive to binocular disparity or monocularly driven, a change of vergence can alter the position of the visual stimulus with respect to the receptive field.

Zipser, Lamme, and Schiller (1996) argue that the disparity relationships between a foreground area covering the receptive field and a background area outside the classical receptive field create contextual modulation of V1 responses. This proposal is potentially at variance with our view that V1 neurons do not respond to relative disparity. We have therefore sought to reproduce as closely as possible the conditions under which the responses of V1 cortical cells appear to be modulated by the manipulation of disparities outside the classical receptive field. Although we can observe phenomena similar to those described, in a substantial number of cases we can establish that small shifts in vergence are responsible for the effect. Zipser, Lamme, and Schiller measured the position of only one eye during their experiments, and it is relevant to note that the design of their experiment requires the animal to maintain convergence while an extended field of random dots is introduced at a nonzero disparity.

Such conditions are ideal for evoking a transient change in vergence (as seen in figure 18.10 and studied extensively by Busettini, Miles, and Krauzlis, 1996). In the absence of records of binocular eye position, it is impossible to evaluate the extent to which the data from the Zipser, Lamme, and Schiller study are contaminated with vergence eye-movement artifacts. The data shown in figure 18.10 demonstrate a transient change in vergence induced by the background. The animal's vergence is initially at zero degrees of disparity, moves away from zero degrees when the background is introduced at a nonzero disparity, and then moves back to

zero degrees as the animal reacquires convergence on the fixation target itself. As shown in figure 18.10, the experiment examines the case where the occurrence of the vergence transient is separated in time from the presentation of a perceptually segregated stimulus over the receptive field. If a background of nonzero disparity is presented 700 ms *prior* to the stimulus on the receptive

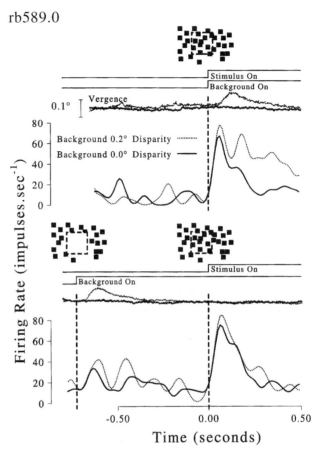

FIGURE 18.10 Responses of V1 neuron to static random-dot stereograms in the manner of Zipser, Lamme, and Schiller (1996). The stereogram consists of a central stimulus that is always at 0° disparity and covers an area about twice the "classical receptive field," and an extensive background region that may be either at 0.2° or at 0.0° disparity and covers a wide area including the animal's binocular fixation point. The figures plot smoothed measures of the instantaneous firing rate in a single neuron and measures of convergent eye position averaged over 8–10 trials. Simultaneous presentation of the receptive field stimulus with background at nonzero disparity causes an enhanced firing from the neuron with a more extended time course (upper graph). This enhancement may be attributable to the small induced vergence movement rather than the perceptual segregation of the stimulus from the background. The lower graph presents the same experiment except that the background is presented 700 ms before the receptive field stimulus. The small induced vergence movement occurs in response to the background presentation, and the stimulus-driven responses of the neuron are now identical regardless of the background disparity.

field, the transient wobble in vergence is complete before the stimulus arrives on the receptive field. This manipulation eliminates the apparent effect of background disparity on the responses to the stimulus in the receptive field.

None of this discussion affects the general question of the existence of modulatory influences from outside the classical receptive field in V1. Such effects have of course been demonstrated in the anesthetized, paralyzed preparation (e.g., Levitt and Lund, 1997), where systematic eye movements are not a problem, and we have confirmed their existence in our own recordings. However, these modulatory influences do not support what would be an important functional role in providing V1 neurons with sensitivity to relative disparity. From the present evidence, we are uncertain whether binocular disparity actually contributes to any contextual modulation effects in V1. What is certain is that a substantial fraction of the disparity-induced modulations previously reported in V1 are most likely attributable to the effect of eye movements.

Conclusions

This study has developed and applied a sequence of challenging tests of binocular processing to the striate cortical (V1) representation of the visual scene. The outcome of all these tests points to the need for additional processing beyond V1 to account for many psychophysical characteristics of binocular stereopsis. Both V2 and V5(MT) are extrastriate cortical areas that may be involved in the elaboration of stereoscopically related signals. V2 appears heterogeneous but may well yield interesting information with more extensive sampling. Recent results from V5(MT) are very striking: Tight correlations between neural activity in V5 and the psychophysically effective signals for binocular depth have been demonstrated here, and clear effects of electrical microstimulation on binocular depth judgments have been found (DeAngelis, Cumming, and Newsome, 1998; see DeAngelis et al., chapter 21 of this volume).

On the other hand, there is relatively little neurophysiological data concerning the processing of fine-grain stereo information in V5(MT), and one lesion study in V5(MT) has reported no loss of performance in a stereoscopic depth task (Schiller, 1993). In view of the fact that at least some single neurons in V1 have sensitivities for stereoscopic depth approaching that of the psychophysical observer (Pointon, Cumming, and Parker, 1998), an educated guess would be that signals serving fine-grain stereopsis are sent to extrastriate sites other than V5(MT). In this regard, the much larger number of neurons in V2 and V4 compared with V5(MT) suggests that some compartments of V2 or V4 may contain highly relevant signals.

ACKNOWLEDGMENTS   This work was supported by the Wellcome Trust, the Royal Society, the Medical Research Council, and the Oxford McDonnell-Pew Center in Cognitive Neuroscience.

REFERENCES

ABELES, M., 1991. *Corticonics: Neural circuits of the cerebral cortex.* Cambridge, U.K.: Cambridge University Press.

BARLOW, H. B., 1972. Single units and sensation: A neuron doctrine for perceptual psychology? *Perception* 1:371–394.

BRADLEY, D. C., G. C. CHANG, and R. A. ANDERSEN, 1998. Encoding of three-dimensional structure-from-motion by primate area MT neurons. *Nature* 392:714–717.

BRADLEY, D. C., N. QIAN, and R. A. ANDERSEN, 1995. Integration of motion and stereopsis in middle temporal cortical area of macaques. *Nature* 373:609–611.

BRITTEN, K. H., W. T. NEWSOME, M. N. SHADLEN, S. CELEBRINI, and J. A. MOVSHON, 1996. A relationship between behavioral choice and the visual responses of neurons in macaque MT. *Vis. Neurosci.* 13:87–100.

BUSETTINI, C., F. A. MILES, and R. J. KRAUZLIS, 1996. Short-latency vergence responses and their dependence on a prior saccadic eye movement. *J. Neurophysiol.* 75:1392–1410.

COGAN, A. I., A. J. LOMAKIN, and A. ROSSI, 1993. Depth in anticorrelated stereograms: Effects of spatial density and interocular delay. *Vision Res.* 33:1959–1975.

CUMMING, B. G., and A. J. PARKER, 1997. Responses of primary visual cortical neurons to binocular disparity without the perception of depth. *Nature* 389:280–283.

CUMMING, B. G., S. E. SHAPIRO, and A. J. PARKER, 1998. Disparity detection in anticorrelated stereograms. *Perception* 27:1367–1377.

DEANGELIS, G., B. G. CUMMING, and W. T. NEWSOME, 1998. Cortical area MT and the perception of stereoscopic depth. *Nature* 394:677–680.

DODD, J. V., B. G. CUMMING, W. T. NEWSOME, and A. J. PARKER, 1997. Firing of V5(MT) neurons reliably covaries with reported 3-D configuration in a perceptually ambiguous structure-from-motion task. *Soc. Neurosci. Abstr.* 23:1125 (no. 447.6).

ERKELENS, C. J., and H. COLLEWIJN, 1985. Motion perception during dichoptic viewing of moving random-dot stereograms. *Vision Res.* 25:583–588.

GLENNERSTER, A., and S. P. MCKEE, in preparation. Bias and sensitivity of stereo judgments in the presence of a slanted reference plane.

HOWARD, I. P., and B. J. ROGERS, 1995. *Binocular Vision and Stereopsis.* New York: Oxford University Press.

HUBEL, D. H., and T. N. WIESEL, 1970. Stereoscopic vision in macaque monkey: Cells sensitive to binocular depth in area 18 of the macaque monkey cortex. *Nature* 225(227): 41–42.

JOSHUA, D. E., and P. O. BISHOP, 1970. Binocular single vision and depth discrimination: Receptive field disparities for central and peripheral vision and binocular interactions on peripheral single units in cat striate cortex. *Exp. Brain Res.* 10:389–416.

JULESZ, B., 1971. *Foundations of Cyclopean Perception.* Chicago: University of Chicago Press.

KUMAR, T., and D. A. GLASER, 1992. Depth discrimination of a line is improved by adding other nearby lines. *Vision Res.* 32:1667–1676.

LAMME, V. A. F., 1995. The neurophysiology of figure-ground segregation in primary visual cortex. *J. Neurophysiol.* 15: 1605–1615.

LEVITT, J. B., and J. S. LUND, 1997. Contrast dependence of contextual effects in primate visual cortex. *Nature* 387:73–76.

MARR, D., and T. POGGIO, 1976. Cooperative computation of stereo disparity. *Science* 194:283–287.

MAUNSELL, J. H. R., and D. C. VAN ESSEN, 1983. Functional properties of neurons in middle temporal visual area (MT) of macaque monkey. II. Binocular interactions and the sensitivity to binocular disparity. *J. Neurophysiol.* 49:1148–1167.

MITCHISON, G. J., 1988. Planarity and segmentation in stereoscopic matching. *Perception* 17:753–782.

MITCHISON, G. J., and G. WESTHEIMER, 1984. The perception of depth in simple figures. *Vision Res.* 24:1063–1073.

MOVSHON, J. A., E. H. ADELSON, M. S. GIZZI, and W. T. NEWSOME, 1985. The analysis of moving visual patterns. *Pontificiae Academiae Scientiarum Scripta Varia* 54:118–151.

OHZAWA, I., G. C. DEANGELIS, and R. D. FREEMAN, 1990. Stereoscopic depth discrimination in the visual cortex: Neurons ideally suited as disparity detectors. *Science* 249:1037–1041.

OHZAWA, I., and R. D. FREEMAN, 1986. The binocular organization of simple cells in the cat's visual cortex. *J. Neurophysiol.* 56: 221–242.

PARKER, A. J., and B. G. CUMMING, 1996. Local vs global stereoscopic matching in neurons of cortical area V1. Supplement to *Invest. Ophthalmol. Vis. Sci.*, 37:S424. (no. 1959).

PARKER, A. J., and W. T. NEWSOME, 1998. Sense and the single neuron: Probing the physiology of perception. *Annu. Rev. Neurosci.* 21:227–277.

PETERHANS, E., and R. VON DER HEYDT, 1993. Functional organization of area V2 in the alert macaque. *Euro. J. Neurosci.* 5:509–524.

POGGIO, G. F., and T. POGGIO, 1984. The analysis of stereopsis. *Annu. Rev. Neurosci.* 7:379–412.

POINTON, A. D., B. G. CUMMING, and A. J. PARKER, 1998. Simultaneous measurement of neuronal and psychophysical performance in binocular stereopsis. Supplement to *Invest. Ophthalmol. Vis. Sci.* 38: S323 (no. 1491).

RASHBASS, C., and G. WESTHEIMER, 1961. Disjunctive eye movements. *J. Physiol.* 159:339–360.

RECANZONE, G. H., M. M. MERZENICH, and C. E. SCHREINER, 1992. Changes in the distributed temporal response properties of SI cortical neurons reflect improvements in performance on a temporally based tactile discrimination task. *J. Neurophysiol.* 67:1071–1091.

ROE, A. W., and D. Y. T'SO, 1995. Visual topography in primate V2: Multiple representation across functional stripes. *J. Neurosci.* 15:3689–3715.

SCHILLER, P. H., 1993. The effects of V4 and middle temporal (MT) area lesions on visual performance in the rhesus monkey. *Vis. Neurosci.* 10:717–746.

SINGER, W., and C. M. GRAY, 1995. Visual feature integration and the temporal correlation hypothesis. *Annu. Rev. Neurosci.* 18:555–586.

THOMAS, O. M., B. G. CUMMING, and A. J. PARKER, 1998. Neural and psychophysical responses to binocular compound gratings. *Perception* 27(Supplement):107.

WESTHEIMER, G., 1979. Cooperative neural processes involved in stereoscopic acuity. *Exp. Brain Res.* 36:585–597.

ZIPSER, K., V. A. F. LAMME, and P. H. SCHILLER, 1996. Contextual modulation in primary visual cortex. *J. Neurosci.* 16:7376–7389.

19 Contextual Modulation in Primary Visual Cortex and Scene Perception

VICTOR A. F. LAMME AND HENK SPEKREIJSE

ABSTRACT   Through the receptive field properties of neurons in the cortical visual areas we mainly observe the feedforward cascade of information processing, transforming visual input into specific outputs. Horizontal and feedback connections are expressed by contextual modulation of neuronal activity. In area V1, where receptive field properties reflect only low-level processing, contextual modulation can be observed that represents fully evaluated perceptual saliency of the features within the receptive field. It is proposed that contextual modulation reflects a process distinct from receptive field–based processing. This process integrates information from distant areas in visual cortex, neurophysiologically "highlighting" those neurons that represent image elements or features of objects that stand out perceptually. It may thus serve as a binding tag, and be a neurophysiological correlate of object-based attention or visual awareness.

Receptive fields and the functions of visual areas

The receptive field of a neuron in visual cortex is classically defined as the part of the visual field from which action potential responses can be elicited by presenting a stimulus. This stimulus has to meet a number of requirements for a cell to respond, and the receptive field is "tuned" to particular features. A well known example is that cells in primary visual cortex (V1) respond better to some orientations of luminance contrast than to others (Hubel and Wiesel, 1968, 1977). Traditionally, the function of a visual area is derived from the set of features to which the receptive fields in the area are tuned. We call area MT a "motion" area because many of its neurons are tuned to direction, speed, or other aspects of motion (Maunsell and Van Essen, 1983; Allman, Miezin, and McGuiness, 1985a; Newsome, Mikami, and Wurtz, 1986; Movshon et al., 1986; Maunsell and Newsome, 1987); we call V4 a "color" or a "form" area because cells are tuned to certain wavelengths (Zeki, 1973, 1980) or elementary shapes (Desimone and Schein, 1987; Gallant et al., 1996); and so on. This view is further substan-

VICTOR A. F. LAMME   The Netherlands Ophthalmic Research Institute, Amsterdam, The Netherlands

HENK SPEKREIJSE   Graduate School of Neurosciences, AMC, University of Amsterdam, Amsterdam, The Netherlands

tiated by the fact that lesions of these areas often cause deficits that are more or less specific to the processing function we attribute to that area by means of its receptive field tuning properties (Dean, 1979; Newsome et al., 1985; Heywood and Cowey, 1987; Maunsell and Newsome, 1987; Wild et al., 1985; Schiller and Lee, 1991; Schiller, 1993). Thus we arrive at a modular organization of visual processing (DeYoe and Van Essen, 1988; Livingstone and Hubel, 1988) that is still disputed in its strictness, but nevertheless has profoundly pervaded our thinking on the roles of cortical areas in vision.

Spatially limited receptive field analysis performed within separate modules requires extensive and dynamic interactions to combine the distributed information. Anatomical connections provide a framework for those interactions (Felleman and Van Essen, 1991). Within each module, horizontal interactions integrate information from separate parts of the visual field (Gilbert and Wiesel, 1989; Gilbert, 1992). Between modules, information is transferred in a feedforward fashion from low-level modules to higher-level ones. But in addition, feedback connections transfer information in the reverse direction (Salin and Bullier, 1995). When going upstream through the hierarchy of visual areas, receptive fields obtain tuning properties of increasing complexity and incorporate information from increasing parts of the visual field (Maunsell and Newsome, 1987). Receptive field properties therefore seem to reflect mostly the convergent-divergent feedforward cascade of information processing. Feedback connections are highly diverging, but their influence on cells in lower areas is not reflected by the small receptive field sizes in an area such as V1 (Salin and Bullier, 1995). The longest of the horizontal connections within V1 spread over distances much larger than the size of receptive fields would suggest (Gilbert, 1992, 1993). We must conclude that a view based solely on receptive field properties and modular processing does not take into account the interactions mediated by a set of connections that numerically outweigh the set of feedforward connections.

Not long after the discovery of cortical receptive fields and their tuning properties, it was recognized that once

279

the receptive field contains some stimulus, the response to this stimulus may be modulated by surrounding stimuli (Jones, 1970). A surprising and key feature of this phenomenon is that the modulating stimuli do not evoke a response when presented alone, and hence are outside the classical receptive field. The early experiments, in area 17 of anesthetized cats, typically used bars or gratings as receptive field and surround stimuli. It was found that modulatory effects can be evoked from large distances, but are strongest at short distances. Both facilitation and inhibition have been reported; these could be either nonspecific or any combination of orientation and direction of motion-specific (Blakemore and Tobin, 1972; Maffei and Fiorentini, 1976; Nelson and Frost, 1978; Allman, Miezin, and McGuiness, 1985b). Also in areas beyond V1, modulation from outside the receptive field has been reported (Desimone et al., 1993; Allman, Miezin, and McGuiness, 1985a, b). The phenomenon thus seems to be a general property of visual processing by cortical cells.

Where does that leave the concept of receptive field–based modular processing? The coding capability of a neuron will merely be weakened when its firing rate can equally well be modulated by a change in receptive field stimulus and by a change in its context. What would be the function of these modulations? Recent findings on the properties of contextual modulation suggest a role entirely distinct from the encoding of receptive field–based information. Its characteristics bear no specific relation to the receptive field tuning properties (Lamme, 1995). Contextual modulation reflects, better than the receptive field properties, the process of combining the information from the many neurons that respond to particular features or parts of an image. This could imply a role for contextual modulation in feature binding, attention or even visual awareness. Within that context, the properties of contextual modulation in primary visual cortex will here be compared with properties of perceptual organization.

V1 is an interesting area in this respect. Its receptive field tuning properties are well characterized. Receptive fields are very small, so global analysis, reflecting perceptual interpretation of the scene as a whole, is least expected here on the basis of receptive field–like processes. On the other hand, V1 is at the top of the hierarchy in terms of feedback connections. Activity representing the convergence of information from all visual areas would be expected to clearly reflect a fully evolved perceptual interpretation. In V1, therefore, we should expect receptive field processing of a sort most detached from scene perception but contextual modulation closely related to it. There is ample evidence for the former; we will now take a look at evidence for the latter.

Phenomenology of contextual modulation in V1

CONTEXTS MODULATING PERCEPTION OF SINGLE IMAGE ELEMENTS A single line segment on a blank background is a visual scene only rarely encountered. In natural scenes, line segments or contrast edges are embedded in many others, forming edges, textures, and object boundaries, the one occluded by the other. The perceptual interpretation of a single line segment strongly depends on its context. Line segments form ideal stimuli for V1 cells. V1 receptive fields are often tuned for their orientation, direction of motion, disparity, size, contrast, or color (Hubel and Wiesel, 1977; Schiller, Finlay, and Volman, 1976; DeValois, Albrecht, and Thorell, 1982; Livingstone and Hubel, 1988; Poggio, 1995). V1 neurons are therefore classically viewed as encoding information about line segments or contrast edges within their receptive fields. But what happens to the neuron's response when the perceptual context of a line segment within the receptive field is manipulated?

Compared to a single line segment (figure 19.1a), multiple line segments (figure 19.1b) have to share perceptual saliency among one another. The single line segment strongly draws attention to itself. The set of line segments, rather, draws attention as a group, such that each individual line segment is of much less importance. In V1, we find a correlate of this in contextual modulation. If we imagine the line segment of figure 19.1a to fall on a V1 receptive field, and the surrounding line segments added in figure 19.1b to fall outside, we see that responses of neurons are generally stronger in the first situation than in the second (Knierim and Van Essen, 1992).

The reduced saliency of the center line segment can be alleviated by having its orientation differ from those of the surrounding elements, creating a perceptual "pop-out" of the center element (Nothdurft, 1991, 1994). This (partial) restoration of perceptual saliency finds a parallel in that the responses of many cells in V1 are larger in figure 19.1c than in figure 19.1b, although not as large as the response would be for a lone element (figure 19.1a) (Knierim and Van Essen, 1992). That this is not a local, mechanistic phenomenon is illustrated by figure 19.1d. Here, too, the center line segment is surrounded by line segments of different orientations. There is no perceptual pop-out, though, because the orientation difference between center and surround does not differ from orientation differences among elements in general (see also Nothdurft, 1985, 1994; Landy and Bergen, 1991). Likewise, responses are not different from the responses to the figure 19.1b stimulus (Knierim and Van Essen, 1992; Kapadia et al., 1995).

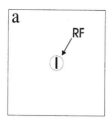

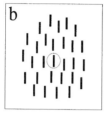

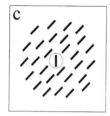

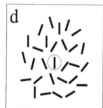

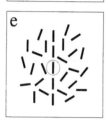

FIGURE 19.1   The context of a line segment changes its perceptual saliency. (a) A lone line segment is perceptually most salient. (b) The same line segment, now embedded in similar ones, draws much less attention as an individual. (c) The line segment may pop out when its orientation differs from that of the surrounding line segments, restoring its perceptual saliency to some extent. (d) Global stimulus aspects are taken into consideration, since a similar local orientation difference does not produce pop-out when surrounding elements all have different orientations. (e) Perceptual grouping by coaxial alignment may cause line segments to segregate, increasing their perceptual saliency. When a V1 neuron is stimulated by presenting these displays, so that its receptive field (dotted circle) covers only the same center line segment in all cases, contextual modulation of its responses signals the perceptual saliency of the center line segment.

When line segments group into elongated chains, they again segregate from a background of randomly oriented line segments (figure 19.1e). Whether such grouping occurs depends on the relative alignment of the line seg-

ments. Coaxial line segments group better than parallel ones. In general, grouping depends on relative distance, angle, and axial offset (Field, Hayes, and Hess, 1993; Kapadia et al., 1995; Kovacs, 1996). It was found that these same factors influence contextual modulation in V1 neurons. Line segments that are flanked by collinear ones (Nelson and Frost, 1985) or, more generally, by line segments that lower detection thresholds, elicit larger responses (Kapadia et al., 1995). It was not fully clear from this study how these enhancements compare to the more general finding of inhibition by surround stimuli (e.g., figure 19.1b). A recent study (Polat et al., 1998) showed that at low contrasts, collinear stimuli result in enhancement, while at high contrast they result in inhibition.

IMAGE ELEMENTS BELONGING TO SURFACES   It is just a small step from the stimuli of figure 19.1e to the stimulus of figure 19.2a. The more or less one-dimensional chain of lines has now been extended to two dimensions. As in figure 19.1c, the grouped line segments, which now group on the basis of similar orientation, segregate from a background of line segments of another orientation. An important feature is added though–the notion of boundary and surface. Where line segments join line segments of the orthogonal orientation, we observe the boundary between the square figure and the background. Line segments within the boundary comprise the surface of the figure.

We have analyzed how contextual modulation modifies responses depending on whether the receptive field contains line segments belonging either to the boundary or surface of the figure or to the background. This can be done by using complementary stimulus pairs, leaving receptive field stimulation identical in all cases (Lamme, 1995; see also figure 19.5a)–a prerequisite for studying contextual modulation separately from receptive field processing as such. Figure 19.2b shows population responses from neurons in V1 of the awake monkey for the three different receptive field contexts: background, boundary, or surface. The response to line segments within the receptive field that belong to the background consists of a transient followed by a slow decay. When the same neurons respond to identical line segments that now comprise the boundary between figure and ground, the same initial transient is observed; but from a latency of about 80 ms on, the response is higher than the response to background elements. We observe the same phenomenon when the receptive field is at the center of the figure, although the latency at which figure and background responses start to diverge is now about 100 ms. In figure 19.2c, these data, combined with data from several other positions of the receptive field relative to figure and ground, are represented in a 3D format. On the front

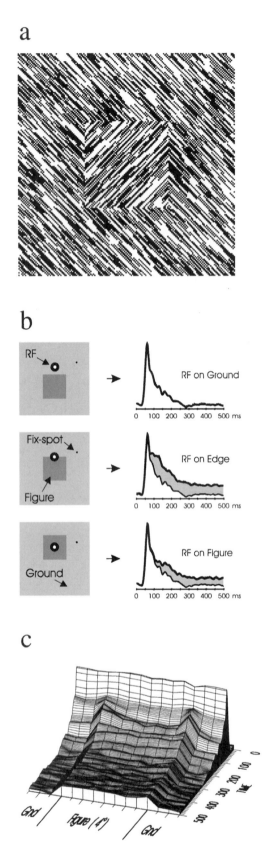

a

b

RF

Fix-spot

Figure

Ground

RF on Ground

0   100 200 300 400 500 ms

RF on Edge

0   100 200 300 400 500 ms

RF on Figure

0   100 200 300 400 500 ms

c

Gnd   Figure (4°)   Gnd

TIME
0
100
200
300
400
500

FIGURE 19.2   The neural correlate of figure–ground segregation in V1. (a) Line segments of similar orientation perceptually group together and segregate from line segments of
another orientation. The center square is considered a textured figure on a textured background, which perceptually
seems to continue behind it. The boundary between figure
and ground belongs to the figure surface. (b) Responses in V1
to the figure–ground display are larger when the receptive
field (open circle; RF) of a neuron is on the boundary or on
the surface of the figure than when it is on the background.
(While receptive field stimulation is left identical in these
three cases, see Lamme, 1995.) Note that contextual modulation (gray shading) only develops after 80–100 ms after stimulus onset; the initial transient is identical in all three cases,
showing that only what happens within the receptive field determines the responses up to 80 ms. (c) Responses in V1 with
the receptive field at 15 different positions relative to figure
and ground, such that the contextual modulation is "scanned"
across a line passing over and through the figure. The 15 positions are on the x-axis (in front), time is on the y-axis (side),
and response strength is on the vertical axis. Responses are
identical up to about 80 ms after stimulus onset (note the horizontal wave at the back of the plot, which is at 50 ms). Then,
responses are "highlighted" at the boundary between figure
and ground first. This is followed by an equal response enhancement for all positions of the receptive field within the
figure, compared to responses for positions of the receptive
field on the background.

served for all positions of the receptive field within the
boundaries between figure and ground. Initially, at 80 ms,
contextual modulation only highlights the boundaries between figure and ground. But from about 100 ms on, all
elements within the figure show contextual modulation
relative to the background, as if a neural image of the figure is stamped out of the neural image of the background,
closely reflecting our figure–ground percept.

These data illustrate an important point, one that is
not self-evident from the results discussed in the previous section: Contextual modulation takes into account
local grouping and segregation criteria, but it can also ignore them, taking into account the figure–ground polarity of the segregating elements as well. At the center of
the figure, the elements are surrounded by similar ones;
nevertheless, contextual modulation is the same as at the
edge, where elements are flanked by orthogonal ones.
Immediately outside the boundary between figure and
ground, elements are similarly flanked by orthogonal
ones, but contextual modulation is absent (that is, responses are identical to background positions farther
away). Instead of reflecting local discontinuities, or differences between receptive field center and surround
stimuli, contextual modulation in these experiments reflects the figure–ground relationships of the surfaces in
the scene. Again, the neurons representing the perceptually most salient elements of the scene, in this case the

horizontal axis, the different positions of receptive field
relative to figure and ground are represented. The contextual modulation observed in figure 19.2b can now be ob-

whole figure, are highlighted relative to neurons representing less important elements.

This kind of figure–ground contextual modulation bears no relation to the receptive field properties of the neurons recorded from Lamme (1995). For example, the effects described above can be recorded in cells without any sharp orientation tuning. Also, it is found that the effects can be elicited by figure–ground displays defined by a variety of cues. On the population response level, contextual modulation is of the same magnitude for figures defined by differences in orientation, direction of motion, disparity, color, or luminance (Lamme, 1995; Zipser, Lamme, and Schiller, 1996). When all these cues are combined, modulation is not additive, but identical to the one-cue situation. This shows again that the modulation signals figure–ground relationships instead of feature-specific differences: A figure is a figure, no matter how it is defined.

Interesting observations were also made using more complex displays than the one of figure 19.2a. For example, when rivalrous patterns are presented to the two eyes, so that segregating squares are visible in either eye alone, contextual modulation is present only when the cyclopean percept (i.e., the combination of the images of the two eyes; see Kolb and Braun, 1995) is that of a figure segregating from ground. This implies that contextual modulation reflects perceptual interpretation of–instead of information present in–the retinal images. Also, when a textured frame is shown on a textured background, the square region within the frame is perceived as continuous with the background surrounding the frame. It has been shown that, in that case, modulation for the center square is absent, as if signaling the perceptual interpretation that this "square" is a continuation of the background (Zipser, Lamme, and Schiller, 1996). Under specific conditions, a stronger modulation right at the geometric center of the figures in figure–ground scenes can sometimes be observed (Lee et al., 1998). It has been proposed that this plays a role in representing the medial axes of objects (Kovacs, 1996; Lee et al., 1998).

Similar modulations of neuronal activity in V1 can be observed in relation to perceived brightness of surfaces. The perceived brightness of a surface can be modulated by the brightness of surrounding surfaces (figure 19.3a). It was found that V1 neurons modulate their activity according to changes in perceived brightness when these changes are induced by luminance modulations of surrounding surfaces that do not impinge on their receptive fields (Rossi, Rittenhouse, and Paradiso, 1996). Perceived brightness can also be changed by presenting a surface, followed by the presentation of a surrounding surface of equal luminance. This is called metacontrast masking (figure 19.3b). Depending on the time interval between the presentation of the first surface and the second sur-

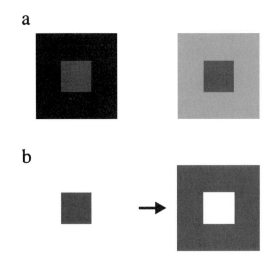

FIGURE 19.3 Changing apparent brightness of a surface. (a) The apparent brightness of a gray square depends on the luminance of the surrounding square. Both the center gray squares are printed at the exact same gray level, but appear brightest when surrounded by a black frame. This is called simultaneous contrast. (b) When a luminance square is followed by the presentation of a frame of equal luminance, the apparent brightness of the preceding square is reduced, depending on the onset asynchrony between first and second stimulus. This is called metacontrast masking. In both cases, it has been observed that V1 neurons modulate their responses according to the reduced saliency of the center square when this is positioned over their RF.

rounding surface, the perceived brightness of the first surface is diminished (Schiller and Smith, 1968). Under ideal conditions perception of the appearance of the first surface may totally vanish. It was reported that the responses of V1 cells, whose receptive fields were centered on the center disk of a metacontrast stimulus, were modulated according to the reduced apparent brightness of that center disk. This modulation was not present in an early part of the response, only in a later one (Bridgeman, 1980).

LATENCY OF CONTEXTUAL MODULATION EFFECTS AND THE ROLE OF FEEDBACK Responses in area V1 have a minimal response onset latency of about 30 ms (Maunsell and Gibson, 1992; Nowak et al., 1995). This can be viewed as the time at which processing in V1 sets off. With respect to the question as to what type of connections, (feedforward, horizontal, or feedback) may mediate contextual modulation, it is important to know how long it takes for these modulations to occur once activity has started in V1. The suppressive effect that arises from presenting a stimulus in the immediate surround of a receptive field stimulus (figure 19.1b) takes a very short time to develop. Results of no latency difference (Müller, Krauskopf, and Lennie, 1997) and a latency difference of just 7 ms (Knierim and Van Essen, 1992) have been reported. Orientation-specific effects [i.e., comparing the effect of an identical background with that of an orthogonal background producing perceptual pop-out (figure 19.1b vs. figure 19.1c)] take about 20 ms (Knierim and Van Essen, 1992). Modulation related to figure–ground segregation of surfaces (figure 19.2a) may start from 30 ms up to about 70 ms after response onset, depending on the cue that segregates figure from ground (Lamme, 1995; Zipser, Lamme, and Schiller, 1996) and on the distance of the receptive field from the edge of the surface (figure 19.2c). For metacontrast masking (figure 19.3b), no effects were found prior to 110 ms (Bridgeman, 1980); and assuming a minimal V1 response latency of 30 ms for these data, one may conclude that contextual modulation related to apparent brightness takes about 80 ms to develop.

Once processing has started in V1, contextual modulation thus takes a wide range of times to express itself. The latency of the effects seems to depend on the complexity of the computations underlying the modulation and the spatial extent of the part of the scene that is taken into consideration. Short latency contextual modulation effects are more likely to be generated by feedforward and horizontal connections than by feedback connections since the latter would presumably take some time to exert their effect. However, for some extrastriate visual areas, minimal response latencies as short as those for V1 have been reported (Nowak et al., 1995; Nowak and Bullier, 1997), so even short latency effects may be caused by feedback. Indeed, it has been shown that more short-range contextual effects, like those described in relation to figure 19.1, depend on feedback from V2 (Bullier et al., 1996; see also Lamme, Supèr, and Spekreijse, 1998, for a review).

More complex or spatially long-range effects that take considerable time to develop are very likely to depend at least in part on feedback. To study this dependency directly, one has to inactivate extrastriate areas while recording from V1. In figure 19.4a, we show the results of recording figure–ground related modulation in an animal that had sustained a large lesion to the extrastriate areas, ipsilateral to the recording site. Contextual modulation is still evoked at the boundary between figure and ground, but is no longer present for the surface elements of the figure. Figure–ground related modulation thus depends on the integrity of the extrastriate areas (Lamme, Zipser, and Spekreijse, 1997).

The role of contextual modulation in visual processing

CONTEXTUAL MODULATION REFLECTS A GENERALIZED NOTION OF PERCEPTUAL SALIENCY   In the above results, contextual modulation is shown to reflect three

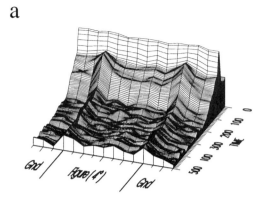

a

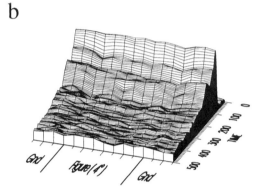

b

FIGURE 19.4   The effects of extrastriate lesions and of anesthesia on figure–ground related contextual modulation. Similar "scans" of contextual modulation across a line passing over and through the figure of figure 19.2a are shown as in figure 19.2c. In (a), the results are shown from recordings from an animal that had sustained a lesion to the peristriate belt of visual cortex. This lesion more or less isolates V1 from feedback from extrastriate areas, with the exception of area V2. Note that contextual modulation is only present for positions of the receptive field overlying the figure–ground boundary, and that responses are the same for background positions and positions inside the square. In (b), the results are shown from recordings in intact animals, but anesthetized with isoflurane. Here, normal receptive field responses are recorded but contextual modulation is absent altogether.

different aspects of image elements: segregation or pop-out, detectability, and apparent brightness. An element is said to pop out when its detection is independent of the number of surrounding elements. For example, in figure 19.1c, the time it takes to recognize that one element differs from the rest would be equal for this amount of distractors and for a far larger amount. In other words, it does not take serial or attentive scrutiny of the individual elements of the scene to recognize that one is different from the rest. Surfaces may also pop out, as in figure 19.2a; this phenomenon is called texture segregation.

Detectability of image elements refers to a different psychophysical measure. By presenting an element at various low contrasts, its detection threshold (for instance, 50% detection chance) can be determined. In this way, it was found that detection threshold lowers, i.e., detectability increases, when line segments are flanked by collinear ones (figure 19.1e) (Polat and Sagi, 1994; Kapadia et al., 1995; Kovacs, 1996). It was also found that detectability is higher within an enclosed area of the scene than outside (Kovacs and Julesz, 1994), which is reminiscent of the contextual modulation effects for surfaces (Lamme, 1995; Lee et al., 1998). Apparent brightness is typically determined by comparing the brightness of one test surface with that of another. In a two-alternative forced-choice procedure, subjects are asked to tell which of two surfaces appears brighter (figure 19.3; Bridgeman, 1980).

These three measures have some essential differences. For example, one analyzes performance at detection thresholds, whereas the other two may be used at more normal levels of contrast. Also, whether popout elements always have lower detection thresholds or increased apparent brightness is an open question. They do share common ground, however, which may be best described as a generalized notion of perceptual saliency. In this context the term is defined as a measure of how well an image element is capable of drawing attention to itself. Elements that pop out, or have lower detection thresholds, or are brighter than others all share a common property—they attract attention. This intuitive relation between the three measures is underscored by the findings of contextual modulation. When context produces pop-out, increases detectability, or increases apparent brightness, contextual modulation always results in an *increase* in the neuronal responses. When single-unit responses are analyzed, cells might, in some cases, exhibit opposite effects (Allman, Miezin, and McGuiness, 1985a; Lamme, 1995; Zipser, Lamme, and Schiller, 1996; Kapadia et al., 1995; Polat et al., 1998). At the multiunit or population level, however, the outcome is always very clear; response amplitude reflects the proposed generalized notion of perceptual saliency. This can be seen as an argument in favor of the thesis that perception takes into account population effects rather than responses of individual neurons.

It is probably also crucial to record these effects in awake animals. The contextual modulation effects described here have been recorded in awake and perceiving animals. But even in anesthetized subjects receptive field surround effects are present (see Allman, Miezin, and McGuiness, 1985b; Sillito et al., 1996; Kastner, Nothdurft, and Pigarev, 1997). The extent to which these are similar to contextual modulation in the awake animal is not fully clear. Thus far, only one investigation has directly compared the awake and anesthetized con-

dition in the same animals and with the same stimuli. Here, it was found that, at the population response level, figure–ground related contextual modulation is present only in the awake and perceiving animal (figure 19.4b; Lamme, Zipser, and Spekreijse, 1998). In the anesthetized monkey, contextual modulation recorded from single units is often both positively and negatively correlated with perceptual saliency; and it might be that on the population level these effects cancel. This could imply that subprocesses underlying normal contextual modulation are still operational under anesthesia, but fail to produce a coherent effect at the population response level.

CONTEXTUAL MODULATION AS A BINDING TAG   Modular processing introduces a problem. The computations performed within the separate modules have to be combined to produce a coherent output. The role of vision is to segregate objects from background and from each other, and to select particular ones for behavioral responses. Image elements and features, processed by cells at different locations, have to be combined so that we are able to manipulate the objects we encounter (the "binding" problem; Singer and Gray, 1995; Treisman, 1996). To some extent this might be explained by the feedforward cascade of increasingly complex receptive field tuning properties observed when going upstream through the hierarchy of visual areas (Barlow, 1995; Maunsell and Newsome, 1987). But strict feedforward processing introduces many problems, particularly in terms of the number of neurons needed to account for every possible combination of inputs and outputs (the "combinatorial explosion"). In this context, many have advocated population coding as opposed to "grandmother" cell hypotheses (Abeles, 1982; Georgopoulos, 1991; Singer and Gray, 1995). In population coding, cells might at some time be engaged in a processing task with one set of neurons (an assembly), but at another time with a different set. Here, the problem is how cells are recognized or "labeled" as belonging to the same assembly. For example, in processing an image such as figure 19.2a, a label should separate the neurons that code for the elements of the figure from the neurons that code for the background.

It has been proposed that synchrony of firing between cells might act as such a label (Singer and Gray, 1995). It has been found that neurons in V1 fire their action potentials in relative synchrony when their receptive fields (RFs) are stimulated with a coherently moving bar. This synchrony is reduced when the neurons are co-stimulated with separate bars (Gray et al., 1989; Freiwald, Kreiter, and Singer, 1995). On the basis of these results, neurons whose RFs fall within the figure region of an image should fire in synchrony with neurons whose RFs fall within the figure, and not fire in synchrony with neurons whose RFs fall on the background. We studied synchrony for neuron pairs when both RFs lie within the figure (in-in) and when the RFs lie on either side of the boundary between figure and ground (in-out), as shown in figure 19.5a. Synchrony depended on low-level parameters such as relative distances between RFs, and relative orientation of line segments stimulating the two RFs. In figure 19.5b, we compare synchrony for the same pairs of V1 neurons under in-in conditions (ordinate) and in-out conditions (abscissa). The stimulus was a moving random dot figure–ground display (Lamme, 1995). For these neuron pairs, there is no difference in synchrony between the two conditions. In combination with our other results on this topic (Lamme and Spekreijse, 1998), this indicates that synchrony in V1 does not label cells as belonging to either figure or ground.

Alternatively, enhanced firing rate could serve as a binding tag. Cells engaged in the processing of features or elements of the same object would have an enhanced firing rate compared to other cells. In figure 19.5c, we compare response amplitudes of the same sites that formed the pairs in figure 19.5b. Almost all neurons had higher responses to elements of the figure than of the background. Also, remember that a particular neuron will typically show an equal amount of response enhancement for all elements of a figure, whether close to the edge or within its center (figure 19.2c; Lamme, 1995). This shows that, indeed, response enhancement may serve as a tag that binds the elements of the figure together. A drawback of firing rate versus synchrony as a binding tag is that with the former it is more difficult to separate several assemblies from each other (Singer and Gray, 1995). It is, however, questionable whether the visual system is capable of representing many objects simultaneously. Experiments on change blindness indicate that not more than two to three objects are represented by the visual system at a time (Irwin, 1997; Rensink, 1997).

CONTEXTUAL MODULATION AND VISUAL ATTENTION AND AWARENESS Perceptually salient elements are strong bottom-up attention grabbers. In that sense, contextual modulation can also be viewed as representing the amount of attention that is *drawn* by elements in the image. Attention is more commonly viewed as being *given*; where many objects may draw attention, only a few can receive it. Attention is often considered a top-down influence on early processing (Rizolatti, Riggio, and Sheliga, 1994). Lesions to extrastriate areas suppress contextual modulation for figure–ground displays (figure 19.4a; Lamme, Zipser, and Spekreijse, 1997), but other types of modulation arise so fast that top-down in-

fluences seem unlikely. Whether contextual modulation reflects attention that is drawn by or given to an object thus awaits further experimentation. The distinction might, however, be nonexistent. Pop-out and segregation were initially considered to be performed preattentively, but now it is becoming clear that these depend on the same attentional resources as serial search tasks. Pop-out and segregation break down when attention is focused on something else (Treisman, 1993; Joseph, Chun, and Nakayama, 1997). In other words, attention that is drawn depends on what is already given. Attention is probably best considered a push-pull between bottom-up and top-down mechanisms.

A further distinction is between spatial and object-based attention (Duncan, 1984; Treisman, 1993, 1996; Vecera and Farah, 1994). In feature integration theory, (Treisman 1993), attentional mechanisms are required to turn features into objects. Features of the same object may be represented in separate maps (e.g., color and orientation), and by focusing attention to the location in space where the two coincide these features can be tagged as belonging to the same object. Parallel search, as in pop-out, or serial search differ only in the size of the spatial attention window (Treisman, 1993; Wolfe and Bennett, 1997). Objects can also overlap in space. Features therefore also need to be tagged as belonging to a particular object. This requires object-based attention (Duncan, 1984; Treisman, 1993; Vecera and Farah, 1994).

Numerous studies have reported modulatory effects of focal spatial attention on neuronal activity in many cortical areas, including V1 (Motter, 1993; for a review, see Desimone and Duncan, 1995). Neural correlates of object-based attention are less well documented, but it has been shown in a PET study that object-based attention has effects on activity in striate cortex (Fink et al., 1997). It is unlikely that contextual modulation is a reflection of focal spatial attention. Two separate and distant textured figures (as in figure 19.2a) on a background evoke the same amount of modulation as one (Lamme, Zipser, and Spekreijse, 1998). On the other hand, figure–ground contextual modulation precisely highlights the elements of an object that segregate from background (figure 19.2), and thus could serve as a correlate of object-based attention. Also, we have recently shown that the responses in V1 to one of two overlapping lines are enhanced when attention is focused on that line by means of a curve tracing task (Roelfsema, Lamme, and Spekreijse, 1998). This object-based attentive enhancement bears strong similarities to the contextual modulations described here, in that they are typically of long latency (~200 ms) and of the same order of magnitude. It might be, therefore, that contextual modulation is a correlate of attention-based feature grouping of elements

a

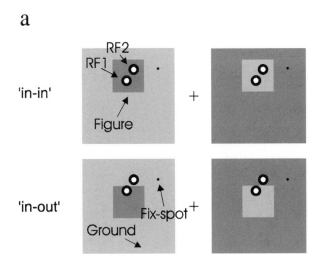

'in-in'

RF2

RF1

Figure

'in-out'

Fix-spot

Ground

FIGURE 19.5 Comparing synchrony and amplitude modulation as a binding tag in figure–ground segregation. (a) Responses of, and cross-correlations between, the multiunit activity (MUA) of pairs of electrodes were obtained with figure–ground stimuli at various positions relative to the receptive fields (RFs). The figure could cover both RFs (in-in), or one of the RFs, but not the other (in-out). In this case, the different shades of gray are meant to represent opposite directions of motion of random dots. (b) The left panel shows normalized cross-correlograms between two electrodes implanted in monkey V1, for the two conditions, in-in, and in-out. The right panel shows normalized cross-correlation coefficients for condition in-out (abscissa) against normalized cross-correlation coefficients for condition in-in (ordinate), both at time lag 0, for all pairs of recording sites in two animals. No significant differences are found between these two conditions. (c) In the left panel responses of one electrode to the stimulus where the RF was within the square figure (in = thick line) are superimposed on those where the RF was outside the figure, i.e., on the background (out = thin line). The right panel shows the amplitudes (average of 0–600 ms) of the responses of all electrodes of the two animals. Amplitude of response to the out condition is on the abscissa, to the in condition on the ordinate. The difference between the two conditions is significant at $p < .000001$.

b

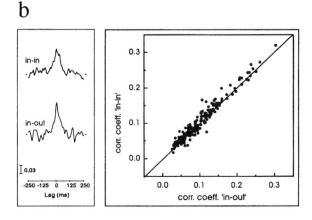

c

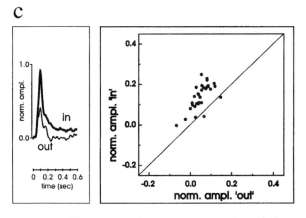

cluded from the neural substrate of visual awareness because activity can be recorded in V1 of which one is not aware (Crick and Koch, 1995; He, Cavanaugh, and Intriligator, 1996). However, some have shown effects of focal attention in V1 (Motter, 1993), and the relation between attention and visual awareness is obvious (Treisman, 1993; Newsome, 1996). In this chapter, we have shown modulations that bear a strong relation to the perceptual interpretation of the scene as a whole. Furthermore, contextual modulation in V1 is selectively suppressed by anesthesia, while RF tuning properties remain unaffected (Lamme, Zipser, and Spekreijse, 1998). Thus, V1 RF tuning properties do not reflect perception, but response amplitudes do. Apparently, some types of V1 activity are more intimately related to perception than others and both types of activity coexist in a single area. In other words, while V1 may host much in the way of perceptually impenetrable signals, this in no way implies that other aspects of its activity should not become accessible to, or even constitute, conscious visual perception. In the end, it will be more fruitful to look for the *processes* that constitute perception than for the *areas* that do so.

Conclusions

Contextual modulation in V1 takes into account information from very distant parts of the visual scene to signal a generalized notion of perceptual saliency of the image elements that fall on the receptive field of the neuron that is recorded. It thus highlights those neurons

into objects. When adopting an attention-based theory of feature binding (Treisman, 1993), this is in fact the same role as suggested in the previous section.

It is a small step from visual object-based attention to visual awareness. Currently, there is a lively debate about the neural correlate of visual awareness (Block, 1996; Stoerig, 1996). In this discussion, a pivotal role seems to be taken by V1. It has been argued that V1 should be ex-in the brain representing features that are, in some way, more important to our behavioral decisions than others. In that sense, it is strongly related to neurophysiological correlates of attention, and possibly of visual awareness. Contextual modulation can be viewed as part of a general class of neurophysiological phenomena that sit on top of the feedforward, receptive field–based, modular processing stream. This class reflects the horizontal and feedback interactions in the brain. Understanding these interactions will be crucial in understanding perceptual organization, attention, and visual awareness.

REFERENCES

ABELES, M., 1982. *Local Cortical Circuits*. Berlin: Springer-Verlag.

ALLMAN, J. M., F. MIEZIN, and E. MCGUINESS, 1985a. Direction and velocity-specific responses from beyond the classical receptive field in the middle temporal visual area (MT). *Perception* 14:105–126.

ALLMAN, J. M., F. MIEZIN, and E. MCGUINESS, 1985b. Stimulus specific responses from beyond the classical receptive field: Neurophysiological mechanisms for local-global comparisons in visual neurons. *Annu. Rev. Neurosci.* 8:407–430.

BARLOW, H. B., 1995. The neuron doctrine in perception. In *The Cognitive Neurosciences*, M. S. Gazzaniga, ed. Cambridge, Mass.: MIT Press, pp. 415–435.

BLAKEMORE, C., and E. A. TOBIN, 1972. Lateral inhibition between orientation detectors in the cat's visual cortex. *Exp. Brain Res.* 15:439–440.

BLOCK, N., 1996. How can we find the neural correlate of consciousness? *Trends Neurosci.* 19:456–459.

BRIDGEMAN, B., 1980. Temporal response characteristics of cells in monkey striate cortex measured with metacontrast masking and brightness discrimination. *Brain Res.* 196:347–364.

BULLIER, J., J. M. HUPÉ, A. C. JAMES, and P. GIRARD, 1996. Functional interactions between areas V1 and V2 in the monkey. *J. Physiol. (Paris)* 90:217–220.

CRICK, F., and C. KOCH, 1995. Are we aware of neural activity in primary visual cortex? *Nature* 375:121–123.

DEAN, P., 1979. Visual cortex ablation and thresholds for successively presented stimuli in rhesus monkeys. II. Hue. *Exp. Brain Res.* 35:69–83.

DESIMONE, R., and J. DUNCAN, 1995. Neural correlates of selective visual attention. *Annu. Rev. Neurosci.* 18:193–222.

DESIMONE, R., J. MORAN, S. J. SCHEIN, and M. MISHKIN, 1993. A role for the corpus callosum in visual area V4 of the macaque. *Vis. Neurosci.* 10:159–171.

DESIMONE, R., and S. J. SCHEIN, 1987. Visual properties of neurons in area V4 of the macaque: Sensitivity to stimulus form. *J. Neurophysiol.* 57:835–868.

DEVALOIS, R. L., D. G. ALBRECHT, and L. G. THORELL, 1982. Spatial frequency selectivity of cells in macaque visual cortex. *Vis. Res.* 22:545–559.

DEYOE, E. A., and D. C. VAN ESSEN, 1988. Concurrent processing streams in monkey visual cortex. *Trends Neurosci.* 11:219–226.

DUNCAN, J., 1984. Selective attention and the organization of visual information. *J. Exp. Psychol. Gen.* 113:501–517.

FELLEMAN, D. J., and D. C. VAN ESSEN, 1991. Distributed hierarchical processing in the primate cerebral cortex. *Cerebral Cortex* 1:1–47.

FIELD, D. J., A. HAYES, and F. HESS, 1993. Contour integration by the human visual system: Evidence for a local 'association field.' *Vision Res.* 33:173–193.

FINK, G. R., R. J. DOLAN, P. W. HALLIGAN, J. C. MARSHALL, and C. D. FRITH, 1997. Space based and object based visual attention: Shared and specific neural domains. *Brain* 120:2013–2028.

FREIWALD, W. A., A. K. KREITER, and W. SINGER, 1995. Stimulus dependent intercolumnar synchronization of single unit responses in cat area 17. *Neuroreport* 6:2348–2352.

GALLANT, J. L., C. E. CONNOR, S. RAKSHIT, J. W. LEWIS, and D. C. VAN ESSEN, 1996. Neural responses to polar, hyperbolic, and Cartesian gratings in area V4 of the macaque monkey. *J. Neurophysiol.* 76:2718–2739.

GEORGOPOULOS, A. P., 1991. Higher order motor control. *Annu. Rev. Neurosci.* 14:361–377.

GILBERT, C. D., 1992. Horizontal integration and cortical dynamics. *Neuron* 9:1–13.

GILBERT, C. D., 1993. Circuitry, architecture and functional dynamics of visual cortex. *Cerebral Cortex* 3:373–386.

GILBERT, C. D., and T. N. WIESEL, 1989. Columnar specificity of intrinsic horizontal and cortico-cortical connections in cat visual cortex. *J. Neurosci.* 9:2432–2442.

GRAY, C. M., A. K. ENGEL, P. KÖNIG, and W. SINGER, 1989. Oscillatory responses in cat visual cortex exhibit intercolumnar synchronization which reflects global stimulus properties. *Nature* 338:334–337.

HE, S., P. CAVANAGH, and J. INTRILIGATOR, 1996. Attentional resolution and the locus of visual awareness. *Nature* 383:334–336.

HEYWOOD, C. A., and A. COWEY, 1987. On the role of cortical area V4 in the discrimination of hue and pattern in macaque monkeys. *J. Neurosci.* 7:2601–2617.

HUBEL, D. H., and T. N. WIESEL, 1968. Receptive fields and functional architecture of monkey striate cortex. *J. Physiol. (Lond.)* 195:215–243.

HUBEL, D. H., and T. N. WIESEL, 1977. Ferrier lecture. Functional architecture of macaque monkey visual cortex. *Proc. R. Soc. Lond. B.* 198:1–59.

IRWIN, D. E., 1997. Eye movements and scene perception: Memory for things observed. *Invest. Ophthalmol. Vis. Sci.* 38:S707 (ARVO abstract #3274).

JONES, B. H., 1970. Responses of single neurons in cat visual cortex to a simple and a more complex stimulus. *Amer. J. Physiol.* 218:1102–1107.

JOSEPH, J. S., M. M. CHUN, and K. NAKAYAMA, 1997. Attentional requirements in a 'preattentive' feature search task. *Nature* 387:805–808.

KAPADIA, M. K., M. ITO, C. D. GILBERT, and G. WESTHEIMER, 1995. Improvement in visual sensitivity by changes in local context: Parallel studies in human observers and in V1 of alert monkeys. *Neuron* 15:843–856.

KASTNER, S., H. C. NOTHDURFT, and I. N. PIGAREV, 1997. Neuronal correlates of pop-out in cat striate cortex. *Vision Res.* 37:371–376.

KNIERIM, J. J., and D. C. VAN ESSEN, 1992. Neuronal responses to static texture patterns in area V1 of the alert macaque monkey. *J. Neurophysiol.* 67:961–980.

KOLB, F. C., and J. BRAUN, 1995. Blindsight in normal observers. *Nature* 377:336–338.

KOVACS, I., 1996. Gestalten of today: Early processing of visual contours and surfaces. *Behav. Brain. Res.* 82:1–11.

KOVACS, I., and B. JULESZ, 1994. Perceptual sensitivity maps within globally defined visual shapes. *Nature* 370:644–646.

LAMME, V. A. F., 1995. The neurophysiology of figure-ground segregation in primary visual cortex. *J. Neurosci.* 15:1605–1615.

LAMME, V. A. F., and H. SPEKREIJSE, 1998. Neuronal synchrony does not represent texture segregation. *Nature* 396:362–366.

LAMME, V. A. F., H. SUPÈR, and H. SPEKREIJSE, 1998. Feedforward, horizontal and feedback processing in the visual cortex. *Curr. Opin. Neurobiol.* 8:529–535.

LAMME, V. A. F., K. ZIPSER, and H. SPEKREIJSE, 1997. Figure-ground signals in V1 depend on extra-striate feedback. *Invest. Ophthalmol. Vis. Sci.* 38:S969 (ARVO abstract #4490).

LAMME, V. A. F., K. ZIPSER, and H. SPEKREIJSE, 1998. Figure-ground activity in primary visual cortex is suppressed by anaesthesia. *Proc. Natl. Acad. Sci. U.S.A.* 95:3263–3268.

LANDY, M. S., and J. R. BERGEN, 1991. Texture segregation and orientation gradient. *Vision Res.* 31:679–691.

LEE, T. S., R. MUMFORD, R. ROMERO, and V. A. F. LAMME, 1998. The role of the primary visual cortex in higher level vision. *Vision Res.* 38:2429–2454.

LIVINGSTONE, M. S., and D. H. HUBEL, 1988. Segregation of form, colour, movement, and depth: Anatomy, physiology, and perception. *Science* 240:740–749.

MAFFEI, L., and A. FIORENTINI, 1976. The unresponsive regions of visual cortical receptive fields. *Vision Res.* 16:1131–1139.

MAUNSELL, J. H. R., and J. R. GIBSON, 1992. Visual response latencies in striate cortex of the macaque monkey. *J. Neurophysiol.* 68:1332–1344.

MAUNSELL, J. H. R., and W. T. NEWSOME, 1987. Visual processing in monkey extrastriate cortex. *Annu. Rev. Neurosci.* 10:363–401.

MAUNSELL, J. H. R., and D. C. VAN ESSEN, 1983. Functional properties of neurons in the middle temporal visual area of the macaque monkey. I. Selectivity for stimulus direction, speed and orientation. *J. Neurophysiol.* 49:1127–1147.

MOVSHON, J. A., E. H. ADELSON, M. S. GIZZI, and W. T. NEWSOME, 1986. The analysis of moving visual patterns. In *Pattern Recognition Mechanisms*, C. Chagas, R. Gatass, and C. Gross, eds. New York: Springer-Verlag, pp. 117–151.

MOTTER, B. C., 1993. Focal attention produces spatially selective processing in visual cortical areas V1, V2, and V4 in the presence of competing stimuli. *J. Neurophysiol.* 70:909–919.

MÜLLER, J. R., J. KRAUSKOPF, and P. LENNIE, 1997. Mechanisms surrounding the classical receptive field in macaque V1. *Invest. Ophthalmol. Vis. Sci.* 38:S969 (ARVO abstract 4489).

NELSON, J. I., and B. FROST, 1978. Orientation selective inhibition from beyond the classic visual receptive field. *Brain Res.* 139:359–365.

NELSON, J. I., and B. FROST, 1985. Intracortical facilitation among co-oriented, co-axially aligned simple cells in cat striate cortex. *Exp. Brain Res.* 6:54–61.

NEWSOME, W. T., 1996. Visual attention: Spotlights, highlights and visual awareness. *Curr. Biol.* 6:357–360.

NEWSOME, W. T., A. MIKAMI, and R. H. WURTZ, 1986. Motion selectivity in macaque visual cortex. III. Psychophysics and physiology of apparent motion. *J. Neurophysiol.* 55:1340–1351.

NEWSOME, W. T., R. H. WURTZ, M. R. DÜRSTELER, and A. MIKAMI, 1985. Deficits in visual motion perception following ibotenic acid lesions of the middle temporal visual area of the macaque monkey. *J. Neurosci.* 5:825–840.

NOTHDURFT, H. C., 1985. Sensitivity for structure gradient in texture discrimination tasks. *Vision Res.* 25:1957–1968.

NOTHDURFT, H. C., 1991. Texture segmentation and pop-out from orientation contrast. *Vision Res.* 31:1073–1078.

NOTHDURFT, H. C., 1992. Feature analysis and the role of similarity in preattentive vision. *Percept. Psychophysics* 52:355–375.

NOTHDURFT, H. C., 1994. Common properties of visual segmentation. In *Higher-Order Processing in the Visual System*, R. Bock and J. A. Goode, eds. Ciba Foundation Symposium 184, Chichester: Wiley, pp. 245–268.

NOWAK, L. G., and J. BULLIER, 1997. The timing of information transfer in the visual system. In *Extrastriate Cortex (Cerebral Cortex*, Vol. 12), J. Kaas, K. Rockland, and A. Peters, eds. New York: Plenum Press, pp. 205–241.

NOWAK, L. G., M. H. J. MUNK, P. GIRARD, and J. BULLIER, 1995. Visual latencies in areas V1 and V2 of the macaque monkey. *Vis. Neurosci.* 12:371–384.

POGGIO, G. F., 1995. Mechanisms of stereopsis in monkey visual cortex. *Cerebral Cortex* 3:193–204.

POLAT, U., K. MIZOBE, M. W. PETTET, T. KASAMATSU, and A. NORCIA, 1998. Collinear stimuli regulate visual responses depending on cell's contrast threshold. *Nature* 391:580–584.

POLAT, U., and D. SAGI, 1994. The architecture of perceptual spatial interactions. *Vision Res.* 34:73–78.

RENSINK, R. A., 1997. How much of a scene is seen? The role of attention in scene perception. *Invest. Ophthalmol. Vis. Sci.* 38:S707 (ARVO abstract #3277).

RIZOLATTI, G., L. RIGGIO, and B. M. SHELIGA, 1994. Space and selective attention. In *Attention and Performance. XV. Conscious and Non-conscious Information Processing*, C. Umiltà and M. Moscovitch, eds. Cambridge, Mass.: MIT Press, pp. 231–265.

ROELFSEMA, P. R., V. A. F. LAMME, and H. SPEKREIJSE, 1998. Object based attention in the primary visual cortex of the macaque monkey. *Nature* 395:376–381.

ROSSI, A. F., C. D. RITTENHOUSE, and M. PARADISO, 1996. The representation of brightness in primary visual cortex. *Science* 273:1104–1107.

SALIN, P., and J. BULLIER, 1995. Corticocortical connections in the visual system: Structure and function. *Physiol. Rev.* 75:107–154.

SCHILLER, P. H., 1993. The effects of V4 and middle temporal (MT) area lesions on visual performance in the rhesus monkey. *Vis. Neurosci.* 10:717–746.

SCHILLER, P. H., B. L. FINLAY, and S. F. VOLMAN, 1976. Quantitative studies of single cell properties in monkey striate cortex. I-V. *J. Neurophysiol.* 39:1288–1374.

SCHILLER, P. H., and K. LEE, 1991. The role of the primate extrastriate area V4 in vision. *Science* 251:1251–1253.

SCHILLER, P. H., and M. SMITH, 1968. Monoptic and dichoptic metacontrast. *Percept. Psychophys.* 3:237–239.

SILLITO, A. M., K. L. GRIEVE, H. E. JONES, J. CUDEIRO, and J. DAVIS, 1996. Visual cortical mechanisms detecting focal orientation discontinuities. *Nature* 378:492–496.

SINGER, W., and C. M. GRAY, 1995. Visual feature integration and the temporal correlation hypothesis. *Annu. Rev. Neurosci.* 18:555–586.

STOERIG, P., 1996. Varieties of vision: From blind responses to conscious recognition. *Trends Neurosci.* 19:401–406.

TREISMAN, A., 1993. The perception of features and objects. In *Attention: Selection, Awareness and Control: A Tribute to Donald Broadbent*, A. Baddeley and L. Weiskrantz, eds. Oxford: Clarendon Press, pp. 5–35.

TREISMAN, A., 1996. The binding problem. *Curr. Opin. Neurobiol.* 6:171–178.

VECERA, S. P., and M. J. FARAH, 1994. Does visual attention select objects or locations? *J. Exp. Psychol. Gen.* 123:146–160.

WILD, H. M., S. R. BUTLER, D. CARDEN, and J. J. KULIKOWSKI, 1985. Primate cortical area V4 important for co-lour constancy but not wavelength discrimination. *Nature* 313:133–135.

WOLFE, J. M., and S. C. BENNETT, 1997. Preattentive object files: Shapeless bundles of basic features. *Vision Res.* 37:25–43.

ZEKI, S. M., 1973. Colour coding in rhesus monkey prestriate cortex. *Brain Res.* 53:422–427.

ZEKI, S. M., 1980. The representation of colours in the cerebral cortex. *Nature* 284:412–418.

ZIPSER, K., V. A. F. LAMME, and P. H. SCHILLER, 1996. Contextual modulation in primary visual cortex. *J. Neurosci.* 16:7376–7389.

20 Computational Neuroimaging: Color Representations and Processing

BRIAN A. WANDELL

ABSTRACT Establishing the relationship between neural activity and private experience requires reasoning that links psychological and neural measurements. Because the experimental variables in these two disciplines differ, rigorously linking the data requires a quantitative analysis of the information represented in corresponding psychological and neural measurements. Color appearance is a good psychological domain for working out the link because several quantifiable rules, such as trichromacy, light adaptation, opponent-colors responses, and low spatiotemporal resolution for color, are well characterized. First, these fundamental color appearance properties are described. Then, current hypotheses linking color appearance and neural activity are discussed. Finally, recent experiments using functional magnetic resonance imaging to analyze the relationship are reviewed.

The brain interprets the retinal image as a collection of objects having various perceptual features, including color, motion, and texture. One important goal of vision science is to discover the computational principles and specific neural mechanisms used by the brain to infer the presence of objects and their properties from the retinal image. This chapter reviews the main ideas concerning how color appearance is derived from the signal encoded within the retina.

Illusions remind us that our visual experience is not a measurement of the physical stimulus, but rather a neural computation. Some visual illusions offer significant insight into these neural computations. The illusion in figure 20.1 demonstrates that even a sensation as simple as brightness is an interpretation of the image and not just a measurement of the number of photon absorptions. The square patches on the left side of the figure appear light; the square patches on the right side appear dark. In fact, the squares on the left reflect the same amount of light and cause the same number of photon absorptions as those on the right. The appearances differs because of neural computations.

The illusion suggests that brightness is a perceptual explanation of surface reflectance. The number of photons reflected from an object confounds the reflectance of the object and the ambient illumination level. The

brightness of the squares is better explained as a comparison between the patch and the background. If we assume that the background reflectance is constant across the page, this comparison estimates the reflectance: Were the background constant, the patch on the left would be more reflective than the one on the right. It is a reasonable guess that the neural computations incorrectly treat the large background as uniform and that the difference in photon absorption rates are caused by an illumination gradient. Hence, we experience the two patches as having different brightness even though they send equal numbers of photons to our eyes.

For two reasons, color appearance is a useful model system for exploring the neural basis of visual experience. First, a great deal is known about the biological basis of color encoding in both human and animal vision (Wandell, 1995). Because we understand many of the fundamental rules concerning the encoding of color, we can begin with a firm understanding of how color information enters the visual pathways. Second, when compared to many other visual sensations, color appearance is simple. Color sensations can be well described using only a few primitive terms–such as hue, saturation, and brightness. By studying the neural basis of color appearance, we may be able to deduce some principles about the neural basis of visual awareness.

In this chapter, I will explore some of the current hypotheses of how color appearance is computed within the visual pathways. The first part of this review summarizes the basic principles of color appearance. The second part introduces recent working hypotheses about the neural computations underlying these color appearance principles.

A central conclusion of the chapter is this: Information about the wavelength composition of light must be represented throughout much of visual cortex. Information about the wavelength composition of the retinal image is used by neural circuits engaged in image segmentation, object recognition, motion, and other important visual tasks. In this way, color information is part of the vast array of unconscious visual processing.

BRIAN A. WANDELL Neuroscience Program and Department of Psychology, Stanford University, Stanford, Calif.

FIGURE 20.1 Color appearance is a neural computation. When uniformly illuminated, the pair of squares on the left and right send the same number of photons to the eye. The pair on the left appears lighter because neural computations of brightness includes information from the surrounding regions, and not just the photon absorptions from the object itself.

To identify the neural circuitry specifically associated with color appearance, we must identify the specific color signals that share the properties of behavioral color appearance judgments. I will suggest some ways functional magnetic resonance imaging can be used to measure cortical signals in human observers and discriminate neural signals that correlate with appearance from those that provide wavelength information for other visual circuits.

Principles of color appearance

Human color appearance judgments are based on three fundamental principles: trichromacy, opponent-color representations, and color constancy. This section contains a brief review of these principles and some discussion of their neural basis.

TRICHROMACY The neural representation of the visual world begins with the responses of four interleaved photoreceptor mosaics: three types of cone photoreceptors and one type of rod photoreceptor. These mosaics simultaneously encode information about pattern, motion, and many other aspects of the visual world. The rods function primarily under very low light levels, where human observers are monochromats, so that any pair of lights can be matched to one another simply by adjusting their relative intensities. Signals initiated within the cones permit us to discriminate between lights of different spectral composition. Hence, in the remainder we will focus on signals initiated by the cone mosaics.

When other factors such as the spatiotemporal properties of the stimuli and ambient viewing conditions are held equal, two lights that cause the same number of absorptions in the three cone classes appear identical. Because there are only three cone types, people have only a modest ability to discriminate among lights with different *spectral power distributions*. The spectral power distribution (SPD) of a light source measures how much power there is at each wavelength. The SPD is commonly used to specify the wavelength composition of a light. When studying color vision, spectra are ordinarily specified over a range from about 370 to 730 nanometers (nm). Figure 20.2 shows the spectral power distributions of three lights that, despite the obvious differences in their SPDs, cause the same number of cone absorptions. These lights are metameric to one another.

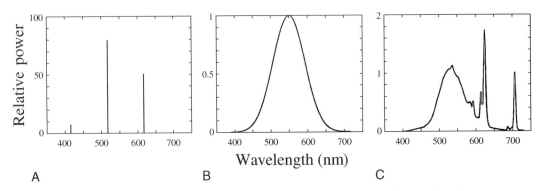

FIGURE 20.2 Three different spectral power distributions that have the same color appearance are shown. (A) The sum of three monochromatic lights, (B) a Gaussian spectrum, and (C) light emitted from a typical television monitor.

Two lights that cause the same number of absorptions in each cone class, but have different spectral power distributions, are called *metamers*. With only a few caveats, it is possible to arrange a match between any test light and a second light that is the sum of three, fixed, primary lights. The ability to arrange a color match using three primary lights is called *trichromacy* and flows from the presence of three cone types. Because photopigment absorptions follow nearly linear rules over a large range of intensities, it has been possible to develop a complete characterization of the set of metameric lights. The ability to control and create metamers is a key aspect of most color reproduction technologies (Brainard, 1995; Wandell, 1995).

The trichromatic character of color matching is a fundamental principle of color appearance. But there is no immediate connection between color matching and common color-appearance terms, such as hue terms like red and green, or general terms like light and dark. Many factors, including the spatiotemporal structure of the stimulus and the ambient background, strongly influence the perceived color appearance. Thus the retinal encoding by three cone types defines a fundamental limit on the range of color experiences, but there is much more to be understood about color appearance than simple matching.

To see this point, consider that during the color-matching measurements the observer never describes the stimulus appearance, but only establishes a match between a pair of stimuli. The difference between setting a match and judging appearance is implicit in figure 20.1. Suppose that we set a color match between a pair of square targets, such as the upper and lower squares on the left. These two squares cause the same pattern of cone absorptions, so they still match in appearance when they are shifted to the right. While the match between the two squares is preserved, the color appearance of both squares changes. Hence, from the point of view of color matching nothing changes as the position shifts from the left to right. From the point of view of color appearance, there is a significant change.

Thus a theory of color appearance requires more information than a theory of color matching. Matches between two common spatial temporal patterns, seen within a common framework, can be explained by knowing only the light absorptions within the cone outer segments. But, measuring and explaining color appearance requires much more.

OPPONENT COLORS A second key concept in color appearance is our inability to experience certain hue combinations. While logically possible, these hue combinations are beyond the scope of our neural apparatus and are never offered as a visual explanation of the retinal image. These forbidden color combinations are called *opponent colors*.

To understand this phenomenon, first consider a pair of color sensations that can co-occur, red and yellow. We have no difficulty perceiving these two components within a single color; orange is the common name for such a color. Nor do we have any trouble identifying hues that appear both reddish and bluish at the same time; purple is the common name for such a color. But, observers never identify a hue as being reddish and greenish at the same time. Similarly, people never report seeing a color that is yellow and blue at the same time. A spot may appear yellow *or* blue or neither. But a spot never appears yellow *and* blue. There is no logical or physical reason that there should be such opponent colors. The cause must be how the brain encodes color appearance.

Since Hering's (1905) initial description of opponent colors, there have been many behavioral and theoretical studies of opponent colors. One way to demonstrate the significance of an opponent-colors representation is to ask subjects to name the colors of spectral test lights. The words red and green are essentially never used together, nor are the words blue and yellow. Other combinations, such as red and yellow, occur frequently (Boynton and Gordon, 1965).

A second way to see the effects of the opponent-colors representation is to measure the detection threshold of various colored test lights. The points in figure 20.3 show the L and M cone contrast levels at detection threshold, and the solid curve is an ellipsoid drawn through these points. These data were measured using a spatially blurry spot whose contrast increased and then decreased slowly over time, as shown by the insets.

To understand why these data suggest a powerful opponent-colors signal, consider how much contrast is needed to see an L cone stimulus, an M cone stimulus, and an L plus M cone stimulus. A test light that excites only the L or M cones can be seen at less than 1 percent contrast. But a test light that excites the L and M cones together requires 6 percent contrast in both cones, considerably more. Hence, stimulating the M cones reduces the visibility of an L cone signal. This opposition of the signals suggests an L-M opponent-colors neural representation. Other sensitivity measurements also suggest a blue-yellow opponency (e.g., Pugh, 1976; Pugh and Mollon, 1979; Mollon, 1982).

Behavioral experiments suggest that color information is represented in an opponent-colors format comprising three neural pathways. One pathway encodes the red-green dimension of color. An increase, say, of activity in this pathway corresponds to a red percept, while a

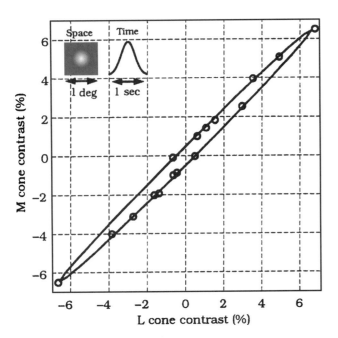

FIGURE 20.3 Detection threshold contour for colored stimuli. The horizontal and vertical axes measure L and M cone contrast levels. Threshold measurements are shown by the open points. When the stimulus modulates only the L cones (horizontal axis) or only the M cones (vertical axis), threshold is much lower than when the stimulus modulates both the L and the M cones (upper right direction). The lowest cone contrast levels occur when the L and M cones are modulated with opposing sign (upper left direction). The solid curve shows an interpolated ellipsoidal curve. The insets in the upper left show spatial and temporal representations of the test stimulus. (Source: Wandell, 1985.)

decrease of neural activity corresponds to a green percept. A second opponent-colors pathway represents blue-yellow, and a third neural pathway represents light-dark. This neural format explains opponent-colors appearance: If different sensations are coded by increments (red) and decrements (green) within a single set of neurons, then red and green cannot be experienced at the same location and time. Similarly, blue and yellow are a forbidden combination.

To study one of the three neural pathways, it is necessary to silence the other two. To do so, it is essential to identify the set of stimuli that *fail* to excite each pathway. Then, by finding a signal that fails to excite, say, the red-green and the light-dark pathways, we can isolate the blue-yellow pathway. A stimulus that appears neither red nor green is said to be in red-green equilibrium. Such a stimulus might appear blue, yellow, or achromatic.

The collection of red-green equilibrium stimuli can be characterized using simple geometric figures. To see how, first consider figure 20.4A (see color plate 7). This drawing shows a method of representing colored stimuli as three-dimensional points. In the representation used

in this figure, the stimuli are described in terms of the red, green, and blue phosphors' intensities, relative to the background. Second, consider a surface that passes through the points representing red-green equilibrium stimuli; figure 20.4B (see color plate 7) shows four different views of such a surface. This red-green equilibrium surface divides those stimuli that appear reddish (concave side) from those that appear greenish. The surface is shaded to suggest the bluish and yellowish appearance of the equilibrium stimuli. Because the equilibrium stimuli appear neither red nor green, they should be invisible to neurons coding red-green color appearance. Hence, the shape of this surface can be used to identify the properties of neurons that might carry the opponent-colors appearance signal for red-green. (Burns et al., 1984; Chichilnisky and Wandell, 1995; Ejima and Takahashi, 1985; Mausfeld and Niederee, 1993).

Spatial resolution Based on the opponent-colors measurements already discussed and others, it is possible to present observers with simple patterns that stimulate one of the three color pathways and fail to stimulate the other two. By isolating such mechanisms, it is possible to study their spatial and temporal properties. Studies of the spatial sensitivity of the red-green and blue-yellow pathways demonstrate that opponent-colors pathways have very poor spatial resolution compared to the light-dark pathway. Consequently, fine spatial patterns higher than roughly 30 cycles per degree (cpd) invariably *appear* to be a light-dark variation around the mean no matter what their true physical composition. Red-green spatial variation does not exceed roughly 20 cpd (correcting for the optics) or 10 cpd (through natural optics). Blue-yellow spatial variations extend only to 5 or 6 cpd. Figure 20.5 summarizes measurements of spatial sensitivity of the red-green opponent-colors pathways from three different laboratories.

At high spatial frequencies, observers have reduced contrast sensitivity to the red-green patterns compared to light-dark patterns. At low spatial frequencies, observers are relatively more sensitive to red-green targets. The same spatial frequency dependence holds for the blue-yellow opponent-color dimension. The poor spatial responsivity of the eye to color is a very large effect. Consequently, it is used widely to create efficient image representations in color-imaging applications (Zhang and Wandell, 1996; Zhang et al., 1997). Hence, the spatial resolution of a neural population should serve as a useful marker for identifying the population of neurons carrying the opponent-colors signals. Neurons carrying the blue-yellow opponent colors image should have relatively large spatial receptive fields, and their receptive field centers should sample the retinal image

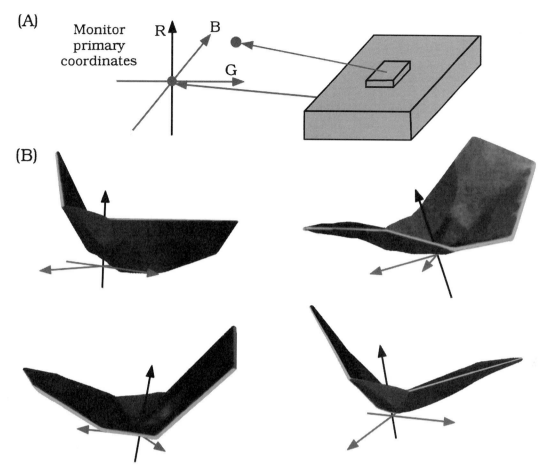

FIGURE 20.4   A geometric description of colored stimuli that appear neither red nor green. (A) The test stimulus is a square patch shown on a uniform background. The background is plotted at the origin of the three-dimensional coordinate system. The test stimulus is represented in a three-dimensional color space in terms of the intensities of the three display primaries relative to the background. The arrows on the three axes indicate the direction of increasing intensity. (B) A surface passing through red-green equilibrium stimuli is shown from four separate views. Stimuli represented on the surface appear blue, yellow, or achromatic. The surface is shaded with these colors to provide a rough guide about their color appearance. (Source: Chichilnisky and Wandell, in press.)

sparsely. Neurons carrying the light-dark image should have small receptive fields and sample the image finely. Neurons carrying red-green information should have a representation intermediate between the other two populations.

CONTRAST, ADAPTATION, AND CONSTANCY   A third fundamental aspect of color is that appearance depends strongly on the spatial and temporal context (see, e.g., figure 20.1). The significance of the spatial and temporal context for color appearance judgments represents an important part of the computational structure of the visual pathways.

Various contextual conditions influence color appearance, and several of these conditions have been given special names. Changes in appearance caused by the immediately surrounding spatial region are usually called *contrast* effects. Appearance effects caused by the eye's adaptation to large, steady backgrounds are called *color adaptation* effects. Appearance shifts caused by changes in the ambient illumination used to view a collection of surfaces are called *color constancy* effects. These stimulus conditions are commonly separated in the literature; but, there is no powerful evidence to show whether these effects are produced by different or similar neural mechanisms.

As stimulus conditions, color adaptation and color constancy have much in common. Both are appearance changes caused by a contextual shift that is spread over large regions of the image and that is stable across time. One important difference between the two conditions is that adaptation is usually associated with conditions in which the target is presented on a uniform background, whereas color constancy involves a patterned background.

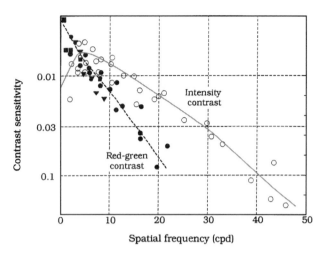

FIGURE 20.5 Comparison of red-green and intensity spatial-contrast sensitivity functions. The filled symbols show contrast sensitivity measurements made using stimuli visible mainly to the red-green opponent-colors mechanisms. The data from Anderson, Mullen, and Hess (1991; inverted triangles) and Sekiguchi, Williams, and Brainard (1993; circles) show absolute contrast. The data from Poison and Wandell (1993; squares) were obtained using a method that does not permit estimation of the absolute sensitivity. These data have been shifted vertically and should be compared only with respect to the falloff in sensitivity. Measurements by Sekiguchi, Williams, and Brainard, and Anderson, Mullen, and Hess compensated for the chromatic aberration of the eye. The Poirson and Wandell measurements did not, but at the relatively low spatial frequencies (below 7 cpd) where the three data sets overlap, red-green chromatic aberration is not a large factor (Marimont and Wandell, 1993). The open circles show contrast sensitivity measurements from three observers to light-dark patterns (Sekiguchi, Williams, and Brainard, 1993). The shaded curves were drawn by hand to emphasize the higher spatial resolution of the light-dark variation measurements.

Given the significance of edges for visual perception, this difference may be important. There is no widely agreed upon method for incorporating both pattern and illumination variation in a single theory. But, some general rules have been observed in cases in which there are relatively few edges in the image and the main effects we must explain are the change in the characteristics of the illumination.

The visual pathways adapt to illumination level changes that span many orders of magnitude and very large changes in the illuminant spectral power distribution. Thus both the overall level of absorptions and the relative cone absorption rates from a surface change under different illuminants. In recent years, a number of studies have shown that the appearance changes caused by changes in the intensity or spectral composition of a uniform background can be approximated by simple rules that modestly extend a proposal from J. von Kries, made in the early 20th century, and

sketched in figure 20.6 (see color plate 8) (von Kries, [1902], 1970).

Consider the simple visual stimulus shown in figure 20.6. The stimulus comprises a uniform background field and a superimposed target. In this case the target is shown as an increment, though in other cases it might be a decrement of the mean field. Modern explanations of von Kries adaptation explain how the background and target interact by assuming that based on spatial and temporal properties the target causes one signal in the photoreceptor array, shown by the main signaling path in the figure. Photons from the background establish the gain, say G_L, G_M, and G_S of the three cone pathways in the main signaling path. For example, increasing the background absorptions in the L cones reduces the gain in the L cone signal.

It is worth spending a moment to consider the implications of this hypothesis rigorously. Stating the rule using symbols is important because the rule contains some surprising subtleties. Suppose that a target t is presented on a background B. Suppose that the background causes a mean level of cone absorptions (L, M, S) which must be

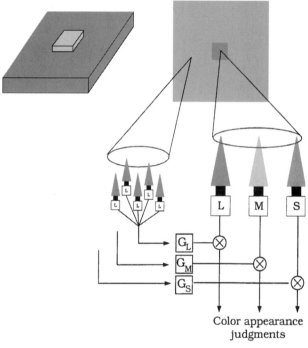

FIGURE 20.6 Schematic of the von Kries model of adaptation. The stimuli are shown as a uniform background field and a small incremental test. Light from the background establishes the gain of the cone signals. Light from the test perturbs the cones. In this version of von Kries adaptation, only background photons absorbed in the L cones influence the gain of the L test signal, and incremental and decremental signals are treated the same. Neither of these assumptions is precisely correct (e.g., Chichilnisky and Wandell, 1996; Mausfeld and Niederee, 1993).

all positive. The target causes a change in the mean level of (l, m, s), and these values may be negative, positive, or zero. Von Kries suggested that *any* target t seen on background B will match a second target $t'=(l', m', s')$ seen on a second background, $B'=(L', M', S')$ when the target cone absorptions are related by

$$l'/l = G_L/G_{L'}, \qquad m'/m = G_M/G_{M'},$$
$$s'/s = G_S/G_{S'}$$

One important part of this hypothesis is as follows: The cone absorptions ratios, say l'/l, are the same for any pair of matching lights seen on backgrounds B and B'. Hence, many different matches can be predicted once we know the scalar values associated with each cone class. The von Kries hypothesis has been tested on several occasions and serves as a good approximation (Bäuml, 1995; Brainard and Wandell, 1992; Chichilnisky and Wandell, 1995).

There is a second important part of the hypothesis that has been rarely studied: How do the gain values, G_L, depend on the background photon absorptions? As the hypothesis is drawn, the value of G_L depends only on the L cone signals. Hence, with this form of the hypothesis, test matches can be predicted by scaling within cone types. It may be the case, however, that the gain values depend on the backgrounds in more complex ways.

The two parts of von Kries's hypothesis are open to empirical examination. When measured on simple, uniform backgrounds, the first part of von Kries's hypothesis holds well for decremental targets and coarsely for all targets. Significant improvements in the predictions of color matches can be obtained by applying different rules to incremental and decremental test targets (Chichilnisky and Wandell, 1996; Mausfeld and Niederee, 1993). The further problem of understanding how the gain factors depend on the spatial pattern of the background or the scene interpretation is not understood.

While open problems remain, enough is known about adaptation on uniform backgrounds so that one can make preliminary comparisons between neural and behavioral measurements. The predictions of von Kries's adaptation are powerful, and we may find that not all neural substrates follow its form. Hence, von Kries can be very helpful when we seek those neural substrates that mediate color appearance.

The neural basis of color appearance

Two main hypotheses have been proposed concerning the link between neural activity and color. One hypothesis emphasizes the flow of information from the retina into cortex. The second emphasizes regions in cortex that may play a special role in color perception.

RETINAL ORIGINS Information is sent from the retina to cortex along several distinct populations of neurons, or pathways. These pathways can be distinguished based on the morphology of the cells, their connections within the retina, and their central projections (see figure 20.7). At present, three fundamentally different pathways have been clearly established.

The *P pathway* leaves the retina via the midget ganglion cells. These cells comprise both on- and off-center neurons, and both on- and off-center cells are driven by the single foveal L and M cones. Based on anatomical studies, it appears that the S cones contribute only to an off-center midget ganglion cell (Klug et al., 1993). It appears, though is not yet certain, that the opposing surround signal is controlled by signals from a mixture of the other cone types (Sterling, 1998; but see Reid and Shapley, 1992). The midget ganglion cells project to the parvocellular layers of the lateral geniculate nucleus, and then to layer 4Cb of primary visual cortex.

The *M pathway* leaves the retina via the parasol cells. These neurons project to the magnocellular layer of the LGN. The L and M cone signals contribute with a common sign to both the center and surround responses of neurons in the M pathway. The output of the parasol cells is sent to layers 4Ca and 4B of primary cortex.

The *K pathway* leaves the retina via the *small bistratified retinal ganglion cells*. These neurons receive an excitatory S cone center and an inhibitory L and M cone surround. They project to *koniocellular* layers of the lateral geniculate nucleus, layers that fall in between the parvocellular and magnocellular layers. The neurons in the koniocellular layers project to the superficial layers of visual cortex.

The receptive field and anatomical connections of neurons within these pathways suggest that each has different specializations for transmitting color information. The clearest association is between the K pathway and blue-yellow color appearance. In addition to their opponent-colors signal between the S and (L,M) cones, these neurons also have low spatial resolution (Dacey and Lee, 1994; Sterling, 1998).

It is often said that color is coded by the P pathway, and luminance is coded in the M pathway (e.g., Spillmann and Werner, 1990). The principal experimental evidence for this hypothesis is that foveal midget ganglion cells' centers are driven by signals from a single cone while the surround is driven by an opposing signal that includes the other cone type. Thus, an L cone center midget cell receives an opposing M cone signal from the surround. The opponency between the L and M cone signals can be measured using large stimuli that cover both the center and surround of the receptive field (Derrington, Krauskopf, and Lennie, 1984). Neurons in

Pathway properties

Pathway	Cone inputs	Ganglion cell type	LGN layer	V1 input layers

P	central:
	    single L, M, S center
	    mixed surround
	peripheral:
	    mixed center
	    mixed surround
		midget	parvocellular	4Cb

M	LM center and surround	parasol	magnocellular	4Ca
K	S on LM off	small bistratified	koniocellular	2,3

FIGURE 20.7   Some properties of the parvocellular, magnocellular, and koniocellular pathways.

the M pathway are not a candidate for representing an opponent-colors signal because they receive a mixture of L and M cone signals in both the center and the surround. Moreover, their properties seem very well suited to carrying high-temporal-frequency information called the *luminance* signal (Lee et al., 1990; but see V. Smith et al., 1992).

There are some problems with this segregation of tasks between the P and M pathways. First, the number and spacing of the mosaic of neurons making up the P pathway is significantly higher than any other retinal mosaic. In the fovea, for example, each cone sends its output to two neurons in the P pathway (one on- and one off-signal). In fact, the midget ganglion cell mosaic that carries the P pathway signal contains 70% of the 1.25 million human retinal ganglion cells (Rodieck, 1998). Consequently, this mosaic is the only one that can represent the high-resolution signal used for achromatic vision. Second, it seems likely that neurons in the K pathway carry blue-yellow signals. This pathway contains a full representation of the visual field, and the spatial receptive field of the pathway matches the blue-yellow signal well. Third, it is odd to argue that the P pathway represents all of blue-yellow color vision given that it contains only an off-center S-cone-driven cell type and the primary on S-cone signal exits via the K pathway.

At present, there appear to be several possibilities concerning the distribution of color signals. First, the blue-yellow signals may be carried on both the P and K path-

ways. Second, a new retinal pathway carrying the red-green signals may be found. Third, the signals within the P pathway may code both achromatic and red-green signals, and the perceptual red-green representation may be formed through a recombination of these signals in cortex. For example, if P-pathway neurons with L and M cone inputs can be distinguished at the level of cortex, then P-pathway signals could be recombined to create both a light-dark and a red-green representation (Ingling and Martinez, 1983; Lennie, Krauskopf, and Sclar, 1990). What the basis for this discrimination between these types of neurons might be, and how the cortical creation of achromatic and red-green signals can be integrated with other novel cortical receptive field properties such as direction selectivity, orientation, and disparity tuning, remain to be worked out.

CORTICAL CENTERS   The second widely discussed hypothesis about the neural basis of color is that there is a cortical "color center." A cortical center for a perceptual feature, such as color or motion, means that visual experience of that feature is represented by the activity of the neurons within that center (Zeki, 1990, 1993).

In monkey, two cortical locations have been suggested for a putative cortical color center. Zeki has argued that area V4 is the color center because single-unit recordings in area V4 covaried with color appearance, and not the wavelength composition of the test light (Zeki, 1993). These measurements have not been re-

298   SENSORY SYSTEMS

peated, and there has been some disagreement concerning V4's role in color (Schein and Desimone, 1990). For example, Cowey and Heywood (1995) have convincing evidence that area V4 is not essential for color constancy, an important appearance task. They suggest that processing in a nearby area, TEO, is essential.

The modern focus on a human color center is rooted in a seminal paper by Meadows (1974), who reviewed descriptions of individuals with cerebral disturbances of color appearance. Several different types of disturbances exist, and he sketched a pathway and lesion sites where damage might impair performance on several different types of color tasks, including discrimination and appearance language. Human neuropsychological and neuroimaging measurements suggest that damage to a cortical region on the ventral surface of the occipital lobe, in the fusiform gyrus, interferes with normal color processing (Meadows, 1974; Zeki et al., 1991). Neuroimaging studies about this hypothesis are reviewed in the next section.

fMRI measurement methods

By juxtaposing the retinal and cortical hypotheses, one can see that to understand the neural basis of color appearance requires tracing the flow of information from retina through cortex. Selecting stimuli that preferentially stimulate one retinal pathway or another, and then measuring the color responses across cortex, can provide important data for a general theory of the neural basis of color appearance. But, how can we trace the neural activity of the color pathways in the human brain?

Functional magnetic resonance imaging (fMRI) is a neuroimaging method that can be used to make inferences about the neural activity in the alert, performing human brain. The physical basis of the method, as well as some recent advances, are reviewed elsewhere (Moseley and Glover, 1995; Tootell et al., 1996; Wandell, 1999). Briefly, the fMRI signal is an indirect measure of neural activity. The fMRI signal varies as a function of the local blood oxygen content which, in turn, covaries with modulations in the neural activity. In some portions of the brain, particularly near primary visual cortex, changes in blood oxygen mirror the spatial pattern of neural activity at a spatial resolution of less than 2 mm (Engel, Glover, and Wandell, 1997). The signal-to-noise ratio (SNR) of the fMRI signal is somewhat higher than earlier neuroimaging methods, and it can be used to measure stimulus-response functions of active cortical regions in the brains of individual subjects.

To integrate fMRI measurements with the extensive literature on the activity of single units in monkey brain,

it is useful to colocate the neuroimaging measurements with visual areas. The spatial resolution of fMRI and certain advances in visualization methods have made it possible to identify retinotopically organized visual areas in individual observers' brains (DeYoe et al., 1996; Engel, Glover, and Wandell, 1997; Sereno et al., 1995; A. T. Smith et al., 1998). Hence, the neuroimaging results can be compared to single-unit measurements from corresponding areas in animal models.

Two developments have made identification of retinotopically organized areas possible. First, a simple class of stimuli have been developed to permit efficient measurement of the retinotopic organization in several visual areas (Engel et al., 1994). Second, novel methods for visualizing the spatial distribution of activity on the cortical surface have been developed (Dale and Sereno, 1993; DeYoe et al., 1996; Drury et al., 1996; Engel, Glover, and Wandell, 1997; Goebel, 1996; Teo, Sapiro, and Wandell, 1997). The visualization methods permit one to segment gray and white matter and reconstruct three-dimensional images of the gray/white boundary (figure 20.8A; see color plate 9). Using the segmentation, it has proven useful to create flattened representations of the gray matter in order to appreciate the retinotopic organization (figure 20.8B). In those cases described in the next subsection when a visual area is mentioned, its location was determined using retinotopic mapping and flattened representations.

COLOR FMRI MEASUREMENTS   Zeki and colleagues (1991; McKeefry and Zeki, 1997; Sakai et al., 1995) have used both PET and fMRI to measure color-related activity in the human brain. In a widely cited set of papers, they measured the difference in activity caused by an achromatic and colored stimulus (Lueck et al., 1989; McKeefry and Zeki, 1997; Zeki et al., 1991). The achromatic version of the spatial stimulus is shown in figure 20.9A, and the colored version has the same lightness but adds various hues. The initial reports were that "the only area showing a significant change of activity was in the region of the lingual and fusiform gyri. This area lies outside the striate cortex and is the same area implicated in achromatopsia (cerebral color blindness)" (Zeki et al., 1991).

This report was puzzling for the following reasons. The achromatic and colored stimuli have equal achromatic signals but different opponent-colors signals. Hence, if we accept the logic of the subtraction methodology, comparisons of the activity caused by the two stimuli should produce activity in all brain regions that respond to opponent-colors signals. The absence of an opponent-colors signal in early cortical areas is puzzling because the parvocellular and koniocellular pathways

(A)　　　　　　　　　　　　　(B)

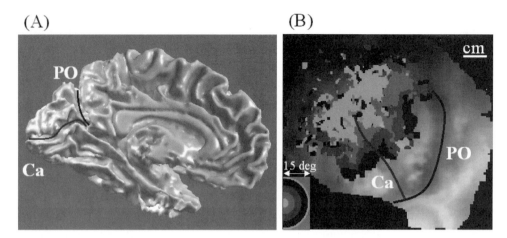

FIGURE 20.8   Methods of visualizing the human brain. (A) A three-dimensional rendering of the gray/white boundary of a human brain is shown. The rendering was created by segmenting gray and white matter and creating a connected representation of the gray matter (Teo, Sapiro, and Wandell, 1997). This medial view shows the location of the calcarine (Ca) and parieto-occipital (PO) sulci. This image was created using software developed by R. Taylor in our laboratory. (B) Distances within the connected gray matter can be measured using Dijkstra's algorithm. From these distances, it is possible to create a flat-tened representation of the gray matter that minimizes the difference between distances measured along the curved gray matter surface and distances on the flattened representation. The underlying gray image represents the gray matter, shaded so that light and dark measure the position along the medial to lateral axis. The colored overlay shows the retinotopic organization with respect to distance from fixation (see the legend at the lower left). A description of the methods as well as software for segmenting and flattening can be obtained from the web site http://white.stanford.edu/wandell.html.

should respond to such a signal, and these pathways represent a large fraction of the neurons in primary visual cortex. Why was their response not measured? The absence of a signal in primary visual cortex poses the further question of how these opponent-colors signals reach the fusiform gyrus on ventral occipital surface.

This puzzle has been solved by new results from several laboratories showing that opponent-colors signals can be measured in early visual areas (e.g., Kleinschmidt et al., 1996; Engel, Zhang, and Wandell, 1997; McKeefry and Zeki, 1997; Hadjikhani et al., 1998). For example, Engel, Zhang, and Wandell (1997) showed that for certain stimuli, the most powerful responses in area V1, per unit cone contrast, are caused by lights that excite opponent-colors mechanisms.

Figure 20.10A shows the color tuning measured in area V1 using a contrast reversal rate of 1 Hz and with the spatial pattern shown in figure 20.9B. The color tuning is plotted using a format that can be compared with behavioral detection thresholds (see figure 20.3). The solid line in the fMRI color tuning curve shows the L and M cone contrast levels that produced the same fMRI signal. The dashed curves are 80% confidence intervals. The isoresponse curve qualitatively matches the

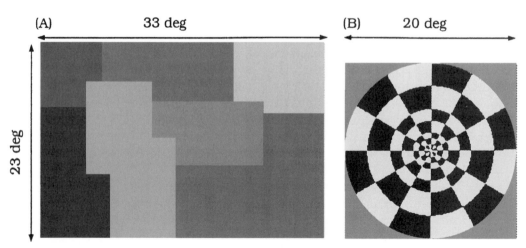

FIGURE 20.9   The spatial structure of (A) the Mondrian stimulus used by McKeefry and Zeki (1997) and (B) the contrast-reversing checkerboard used by Engel, Zhang, and Wandell (1997).

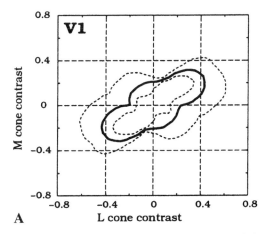
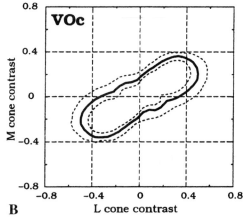

FIGURE 20.10   Comparison of the color tuning in area V1 (A) and an active region located in the ventral occipital region, VOc (B). The solid curves show stimuli that evoked an equal fMRI response. Stimuli with opposing L and M cone contrasts (opponent-colors signals) are more effective at evoking a response than stimuli with convarying L and M cone contrasts. The two regions share a common color tuning; separate measurements suggest that the signal in VOc is slightly stronger.

detection threshold contour measured with the same stimulus.

The original observation of a strong response to chromatic signals within the fusiform gyrus is also confirmed by all groups, and studies of this region may tell us more about the flow of cortical color signals. The retinotopic organization of this region has been probed by McKeefry and Zeki (1997) and by Hadjikhani and colleagues (1998). Both groups find that this location on the ventral occipital surface represents an entire hemisphere. The main difference in their analysis is that McKeefry and Zeki refer to the area as V4, in homology with monkey V4. Hadjikhani and colleagues (1998) suggest the color responsive area falls beyond the fourth retinotopically organized human area and that it should be called V8, and not V4. For the present, the neutral and temporary name *VOc* will be used to refer to the location in ventral-occipital cortex.

Does the color tuning of area V1 differ from that of VOc? Were the opponent-colors signals substantially more powerful in VOc than V1, one might still argue for an enhanced color representation in VOc. Wandell and colleagues (in press) measured the isoresponse curve in VOc to the same stimulus shown in figure 20.9B. For these conditions, they found that the color tuning in VOc and V1 are quite similar. Of course, it remains possible that selecting other spatial patterns or choosing different tasks and viewing conditions will cause differences to emerge.

Measurements with contrast-reversing lights and simple rectangular patterns reveal powerful opponent-colors signals along the pathway from V1, V2, and VOc. But, these are not the only cortical locations that receive opponent-colors signals. Moving stimuli, seen only by opponent-color mechanisms, evoke powerful activations in motion-selective areas located at the lateral portion of the parieto-occipital sulcus (Ffytche, Skidmore, and Zeki, 1995; Poirson, Baseler, and Wandell, 1997). Hence, cortical responses to opponent-colors stimuli, presumably carried by the parvocellular and koniocellular inputs to cortex, appear widely distributed in cortex. The powerful opponent-colors signal in V1, V2, VOc, and motion-selective cortex represent only a portion of the distribution of color signals in cortex.

The ability to make complete color tuning measurements using fMRI offers us one way to measure cortical signals in human observers. By making these measurements with a broader array of stimuli, we should be able to identify the neural signals that correlate with appearance and understand the computations that take place at different cortical locations.

Conclusions

Several quantitative principles describe human color appearance judgments. Color appearance represents three perceptual dimensions (trichromacy); color appearance computations adjust to changes in the ambient illumination, so that appearance depends more on the relative cone absorptions than the absolute number of absorptions; color appearance is organized into one achromatic and two opponent-colors representations; the spatial resolution of the opponent-colors mechanisms is substantially lower than that of the achromatic mechanism.

Using fMRI, it is possible to make measurements of the color sensitivity in various parts of human visual cortex. Although visual cortex contains many different signals coding the spectral composition of the retinal image, these signals do not all match the quantitative principles of human color appearance. The signals measured so far may be significant for color appearance, but no region has been clearly identified as a unique color appearance center. Rather, it seems likely that by expanding the range of measurements and comparing the quantitative responses in visual cortex with the fundamental properties of human color judgments, it may be possible to find a series of neural computations that, taken together, result in our experience of color.

ACKNOWLEDGMENTS The author thanks H. Baseler and S. Engel for comments. This work was supported by National Eye Institute grant RO1EY30614 and a McKnight senior fellowship.

REFERENCES

ANDERSON, S., K. MULLEN, and R. HESS, 1991. Human peripheral spatial resolution for achromatic and chromatic stimuli: Limits imposed by optical and retinal factors. *J. Physiol.* 442:47–64.

BÄUML, K. H., 1995. Illuminant changes under different surface collections: Examining some principles of color appearance. *J. Opt. Soc. Am. A* 12(2):261–271.

BOYNTON, R. M., and J. GORDON, 1965. Bezold-brucke hue shift measured by color-naming technique. *J. Opt. Soc. Am.* 55:78–86.

BRAINARD, D. H., 1995. Colorimetry. In *Handbook of the Optical Society*, M. Bass, ed. New York: McGraw-Hill.

BRAINARD, D. H., and B. A. WANDELL, 1992. Asymmetric color matching: How color appearance depends on the illuminant. *J. Opt. Soc. Am. A* 9(9):1433–1448.

BURNS, S., A. E. ELSNER, J. POKORNY, and V. C. SMITH, 1984. The abney effect: Chromaticity coordinates of unique and other constant hues. *Vision Res.* 24:479–489.

CHICHILNISKY, E. J., and B. A. WANDELL, 1995. Photoreceptor sensitivity changes explain color appearance shifts induced by large uniform backgrounds in dichoptic matching. *Vision Res.* 35(2):239–254.

CHICHILNISKY, E. J., and B. A. WANDELL, 1996. Seeing gray through the on and off pathways. *Vis. Neurosci.* 13:591–596.

CHICHILNISKY, E. J., and B. A. WANDELL, in press. Trichromatic opponent color classification. *Vision Res.*

COWEY, A., and C. A. HEYWOOD, 1995. There's more to colour than meets the eye. *Behav. Brain Res.* 71:89–100.

DACEY, D. M., and B. B. LEE, 1994. The "blue-on" opponent pathway in primate retina originates from a distinct bistratified ganglion cell type. *Nature* 367(6465):731–735.

DALE, A. M., and M. I. SERENO, 1993. Improved localization of cortical activity by combining EEG and MEG with MRI cortical surface reconstruction: A linear approach. *J. Cog. Neurosci.* 5:162–176.

DERRINGTON, A. M., J. KRAUSKOPF, and P. LENNIE, 1984. Chromatic mechanisms in lateral geniculate nucleus of macaque. *J. Physiol.* 357:241–265.

DEYOE, E. A., G. J. CARMAN, P. BANDETTINI, S. GLICKMAN, J. WIESER, R. COX, D. MILLER, and J. NEITZ, 1996. Mapping striate and extrastriate areas in human cerebral cortex. *Proc. Natl. Acad. Sci. U.S.A.* 93:2382–2386.

DRURY, H. A., D. C. VAN ESSEN, C. H. ANDERSON, C. W. LEE, T. A. COOGAN, and J. W. LEWIS, 1996. Computerized mappings of the cerebral cortex: A multiresolution flattening method and a surface-based coordinate system. *J. Cog. Neurosci.* 8:1–28.

EJIMA, Y., and S. TAKAHASHI, 1985. Interaction between short- and longer-wavelength cones in hue cancellation codes: Nonlinearities of hue and cancellation as a function of stimulus intensity. *Vision Res.* 25:1911–1922.

ENGEL, S. A., G. H. GLOVER, and B. A. WANDELL, 1997. Retinotopic organization in human visual cortex and the spatial precision of functional MRI. *Cerebral Cortex* 7(2):181–192.

ENGEL, S. A., D. E. RUMELHART, B. A. WANDELL, A. T. LEE, M. N. SHADLEN, and G. H. GLOVER, 1994. fMRI of human visual cortex. *Nature* 369:525.

ENGEL, S. A., X. ZHANG, and B. A. WANDELL, 1997. Color tuning in human visual cortex measured using functional magnetic resonance imaging. *Nature* 388(6637):68–71.

FFYTCHE, D., B. SKIDMORE, and S. ZEKI, 1995. Motion-from-hue activates area V5 of human visual cortex. *Proc. R. Soc. Lond.* 260(1359):353–358.

GOEBEL, R., 1996. Analyse und visualisierung von magnetresonanztomographiedaten. In *Forschung und wissenschaftliches Rechne*, Th. Plesser and P. Wittenburg, eds. Beiträge zum Heinz-Billing-Preis. Göttingen: GWDG.

HADJIKHANI, N., A. K. LIU, R. TOOTELL, P. CAVANAGH, and A. DALE, 1998. Retinotopy and color sensitivity in human visual cortical area V8. *Nature Neurosci.* 1(3):235–241.

HERING, E., 1905. *Handbuch der gesammter Augenheilkunde*, vol. 3, chapter Gründzuge der Lhre vom Lichtsinn. Berlin.

INGLING, C. R., and E. MARTINEZ, 1983. The spatiochromatic signal of the R-G channel. In *Color Vision*, J. D. Mollon and L. T. Sharpe, eds. London: Academic Press, pp. 433–444.

KLEINSCHMIDT, A., B. B. LEE, M. REQUART, and J. FRAHM, 1996. Functional mapping of color processing by magnetic resonance imaging of responses to selective P- and M-pathway stimulation. *Exp. Brain Res.* 110(2):279–288.

KLUG, K., Y. TUSKAMOTO, P. STERLING, and S. J. SCHEIN, 1993. Blue cone off-midget ganglion cells in macaque. *Invest. Opthalmol. Vis. Sci.* 34(4):1398A.

LEE, B., J. POKORNY, V. SMITH, P. MARTIN, and A. VALBERG, 1990. Luminance and chromatic modulation sensitivity of macaque ganglion cells and human observers. *J. Opt. Soc. Am. A* 7(12):2223–2236.

LENNIE, P., J. KRAUSKOPF, and G. SCLAR, 1990. Chromatic mechanisms in striate cortex of macaque. *J. Neurosci.* 10(2):649–669.

LUECK, C. J., S. ZEKI, K. J. FRISTON, M. P. DIEBER, P. COPE, V. J. CUNNINGHAM, A. A. LAMMERTSMA, C. KENNARD, and R. S. J. FRAKOWIAC, 1989. The color center in the cerebral cortex of man. *Nature* 340(6232):386–389.

MARIMONT, D., and B. A. WANDELL, 1993. Matching color images: The effects of axial chromatic aberration. *J. Opt. Soc. Am. A* 12:3113–3122.

MAUSFELD, R., and R. NIEDEREE, 1993. An inquiry into relational concepts of color, based on incremental principles of color coding for minimal relational stimuli. *Perception* 22(4):427–462.

MCKEEFRY, D. J., and S. M. ZEKI, 1997. The position and topography of the human color center as revealed by functional magnetic resonance imaging. *Brain* 120:2229–2242.

MEADOWS, J., 1974. Disturbed perception of colors associated with localized cerebral lesions. *Brain* 97:615–632.

MOLLON, J. D., 1982. Colour vision. *Ann. Rev. Psychol.* 33:41–85.

MOSELEY, M., and G. H. GLOVER, 1995. Functional MR imaging: Capabilities and limitations. In *Neuroimaging Clinics of North America–Functional Neuroimaging*, Vol. 5. J. Kucharczyk, M. Moseley, T. Roberts, and W. Orrison, eds. Philadelphia: Saunders, pp. 161–191.

POIRSON, A., H. BASELER, and B. A. WANDELL, 1997. Color tuning to moving stimuli in the human visual cortex. *Soc. Neurosci. Abstr.* 23:1396.

POIRSON, A. B., and B. A. WANDELL, 1993. The appearance of colored patterns: Pattern-color separability. *J. Opt. Soc. Am. A* 10(12):2458–2471.

PUGH, E. N., 1976. The nature of the π_1 mechanism of W. S. Stiles. *J. Physiol.* 257:713–747.

PUGH, E. N., and J. D. MOLLON, 1979. A theory of the π_1 and π_3 colour mechanisms of Stiles. *Vision Res.* 19:293–312.

REID, R. C., and R. M. SHAPLEY, 1992. Spatial structure of cone inputs to receptive fields in primate lateral geniculate nucleus. *Nature* 356(6371):716–718.

RODIECK, R. W., 1998. *The First Steps in Seeing.* Sunderland, Mass.: Sinauer Press.

SAKAI, K., E. WATANABE, Y. ONODERA, I. UCHIDA, H. KATO, E. YAMAMOTO, H. KOIZUMI, and Y. MIYASHITA, 1995. Functional mapping of the human color center with echoplanar magnetic resonance imaging. *Proc. R. Soc. Lond. B Biol. Sci.* 261(1360):89–98.

SCHEIN, S. J., and R. DESIMONE, 1990. Spectral properties of V4 neurons in the macaque. *J. Neurosci.* 10(10):3369–3389.

SEKIGUCHI, N., D. R. WILLIAMS, and D. H. BRAINARD, 1993. Efficiency in detection of isoluminant and isochromatic interference fringes. *J. Opt. Soc. Am. A* 10(10):2118–2133.

SERENO, M. I., A. M. DALE, J. B. REPPAS, K. K. KWONG, J. W. BELLIVEAU, T. J. BRADY, B. R. ROSEN, and R. B. TOOTELL, 1995. Borders of multiple human visual areas in humans revealed by functional MRI. *Science* 268:889–893.

SMITH, A. T., M. GREENLEE, K. D. SINGH, F. M. KRAEMER, and J. HENNIG, 1998. The processing of first- and second-order motion in human visual cortex assessed by functional magnetic resonance imaging (fMRI). *J. Neurosci.* 18(10):3816–3830.

SMITH, V., B. LEE, J. POKORNY, P. MARTIN, and A. VALBERG, 1992. Responses of macaque ganglion cells to the relative phase of heterochromatically modulated light. *J. Physiol.* 458:191–221.

SPILLMAN, L., and J. WERNER, eds., 1990. *Visual Perception: The Neurophysiological Foundations.* San Diego: Academic Press.

STERLING, P., 1998. Retina. In *Synaptic Organization of the Brain.*, G. M. Shepherd, ed. New York: Oxford University Press.

TEO, P., G. SAPIRO, and B. A. WANDELL, 1997. Creating connected representations of cortical gray matter for functional MRI visualization. *IEEE Med. Trans.* 16(6):852–863.

TOOTELL, R. B., A. M. DALE, M. I. SERENO, and R. MALACH, 1996. New images from human visual cortex. *Trends Neurosci.* 19(11):481–489.

VON KRIES, J., [1902] 1970. Chromatic adaptation. In *Sources of Color Science*, D. L. MacAdam, ed. Cambridge, Mass.: MIT Press.

WANDELL, B. A., 1985. Color measurement and discrimination. *J. Opt. Soc. Am. A* 2:62–71.

WANDELL, B. A., 1995. *Foundations of Vision.* Sunderland, Mass.: Sinauer Press.

WANDELL, B. A., 1999. *Computational Neuroimaging of Human Visual Cortex.* Palo Alto: Annual Reviews.

WANDELL, B. A., H. BASELER, A. B. POIRSON, and G. M. BOYNTON, in press. Computational neuroimaging: Color tuning in two human cortical areas measured using fMRI. In *Color Vision: From Molecular Genetics to Perception,* K. Gegenfurtner and T. Sharpe, eds. Cambridge, U.K.: Cambridge University Press.

ZEKI, S., 1990. A century of cerebral achromatopsia. *Brain* 113:1721–1777.

ZEKI, S., 1993. *A Vision of the Brain.* Oxford: Blackwell Scientific Publications.

ZEKI, S., J. D. G. WATSON, C. J. LUECK, K. J. FRISTON, C. KENNARD, and R. S. J. FRACKOWIAK, 1991. A direct demonstration of functional specialization in human visual cortex. *J. Neurosci.* 11(3):641–649.

ZHANG, X., D. A. SILVERSTEIN, J. E. FARRELL, and B. A. WANDELL, 1997. Color image quality metric S-CIELAB and its application on halftone texture visibility. *COMPCON97 Digest of Papers,* pp. 44–48.

ZHANG, X., and B. A. WANDELL, 1996. A spatial extension to CIELAB for digital color image reproduction. *Society for Information Display Symposium Technical Digest* 27:731–734.

21   A New Role for Cortical Area MT: The Perception of Stereoscopic Depth

GREGORY C. DEANGELIS, BRUCE G. CUMMING, AND WILLIAM T. NEWSOME

ABSTRACT   Neurons that respond selectively to binocular disparity are widely assumed to play an important role in stereoscopic depth perception, but there is little direct evidence for this presumed link between neurophysiology and perception. Furthermore, it is not clear whether any of the thirty or more known cortical visual areas is specialized for stereopsis, which remains one of the most significant visual functions lacking a clear cortical substrate. We present evidence for a columnar organization of disparity-selective neurons in extrastriate visual area MT of rhesus monkeys. Nearby neurons have similar disparity tuning properties, and the preferred disparity changes smoothly across the cortical surface, suggesting that MT contains a map of binocular disparity. To test whether neurons in this map are involved in depth perception, we electrically stimulated clusters of disparity-selective MT neurons while monkeys discriminated depth in random dot stereograms. Microstimulation systematically biased perceptual judgments of depth toward the preferred disparity of neurons at the stimulation site. These results show that behaviorally relevant signals concerning stereoscopic depth are present in MT. This is the first clear demonstration of specialization for stereoscopic vision in any cortical area.

A central goal of cognitive neuroscience is to reveal how neural activity gives rise to sensory perception. Perhaps the clearest link between a specific perceptual capacity and its cortical substrate has arisen from studies of motion perception and its relation to neural activity in the middle temporal visual area (MT, or V5) of primates. Approximately 90% of MT neurons respond selectively to the direction of motion of a visual stimulus (Dubner and Zeki, 1971; Zeki, 1974), and MT neurons with similar functional properties are clustered together in "columns" such that neurons in each column respond optimally to a particular direction of motion (Albright, Desimone, and Gross, 1984). Numerous experiments have now confirmed that this "functional architecture" for motion direction reflects a prominent role for MT in mediating motion perception. For example, lesions of MT can disrupt motion perception (Newsome and Pare,

1988; Pasternak and Merigan, 1994; Orban, Saunders, and Vandenbussche, 1995), and single neurons in MT are exquisitely sensitive to weak motion signals near psychophysical threshold for motion detection (Britten et al., 1992). Moreover, electrical microstimulation of a column of MT neurons can cause monkeys to report seeing the direction of motion encoded by the stimulated neurons, even though the visual display actually contains motion in a different direction altogether (Salzman et al., 1992; Salzman and Newsome, 1994).

In this chapter, we present evidence that MT also plays an important role in stereoscopic vision. Stereopsis is the perception of depth based on small positional differences (binocular disparity) between images formed on the two retinae. Neurons that respond selectively to binocular disparity were first described three decades ago (Barlow, Blakemore, and Pettigrew, 1967; Pettigrew, Nikara, and Bishop, 1968), and have subsequently been observed in similar numbers in many primate visual areas including V1, V2, V3, MT, and MST (Hubel and Wiesel, 1970; Poggio and Fischer, 1977; Poggio, Gonzalez, and Krause, 1988; Felleman and Van Essen, 1987; Maunsell and Van Essen 1983b; Roy, Komatsu, and Wurtz, 1992). However, evidence for a columnar organization of disparity-selective neurons is limited. Disparity tuned neurons appear to cluster weakly in cat V1 (Blakemore, 1970; LeVay and Voigt, 1988), and preferred disparity may vary systematically within disparity-tuned subregions of V2 in monkeys and sheep (Hubel and Livingstone, 1987; Ts'o, Gilbert, and Wiesel, 1990; Clarke, Donaldson, and Whitteridge, 1976).

We now show that MT contains a columnar organization for binocular disparity in addition to its well known organization for motion direction. Disparity-selective MT neurons tend to occur in discrete patches, and preferred disparity varies systematically from column to column within these patches. Furthermore, we demonstrate that activation of disparity-tuned columns with electrical microstimulation can influence perceptual judgments of depth in a manner consistent with the disparity tuning of the stimulated neurons. Thus, disparity-selective MT neurons appear to play an important role in stereopsis.

GREGORY C. DEANGELIS and WILLIAM T. NEWSOME   Howard Hughes Medical Institute and Department of Neurobiology, Stanford University School of Medicine, Stanford, Calif.
BRUCE G. CUMMING   Laboratory of Physiology, Oxford University, Oxford, United Kingdom

Clustering of disparity-selective neurons in MT

If MT contains an organized map of binocular disparity, then nearby neurons should have similar disparity tuning. To test this possibility, we measured the disparity selectivity of multiunit clusters (MU) and single units (SU) during electrode penetrations through MT. In these experiments, two monkeys (S and P) were simply required to maintain fixation on a small spot of light while a moving random-dot pattern appeared over the multiunit receptive field (RF). Location, size, direction, and movement speed of the pattern were tailored to the preferences of the neurons at each recording site. The horizontal disparity of the moving dots was varied by rendering them in depth as a red/green anaglyph on a standard CRT display (frame rate = 60 Hz). Outside the RF, the remainder of the visual display was filled with zero-disparity dots, which were replotted randomly at 20 Hz to produce a twinkling background. This zero-disparity background helped maintain the monkey's eye vergence at the depth of the fixation point. Vergence angle was monitored in monkey S with the use of binocular scleral search coils (Robinson, 1963; Judge, Richmond, and Chu, 1980), and there was no systematic dependence of vergence on the disparity of the dots.

Figure 21.1 shows MU (filled circles) and SU (open circles) responses measured simultaneously from a single microelectrode. Action potentials from the SU were excluded from the MU response, ensuring that the MU activity arises from several other nearby SUs.[1] The MU response is clearly tuned for disparity, suggesting that its constituent SUs have a similar disparity preference. This conclusion is further supported by the close agreement in shape between the MU and SU tuning curves. Although the SU response is more strongly modulated by disparity, both curves exhibit peaks and troughs at similar disparities. This correspondence between MU and SU tuning curves is typical of most of our recordings in MT.

To quantify this relationship, we fitted the disparity tuning curves with a cubic spline interpolation and we extracted three parameters from each tuning curve. A disparity tuning index (DTI) was defined as $1 - (R_{min} - S)/(R_{max} - S)$, where R_{max} is the maximum fitted response, R_{min} is the minimum fitted response, and S denotes spontaneous activity (in the absence of a visual stimulus). For sites with significant disparity tuning (one-way ANOVA, $P < .05$), the disparity at which the fitted curve reached a maximum defined the preferred disparity (PD), and the disparity difference between the largest peak and the deepest trough was considered to be the disparity tuning width (DTW).

Across our sample of 110 simultaneous recordings, DTI values for SUs and MUs were significantly corre-

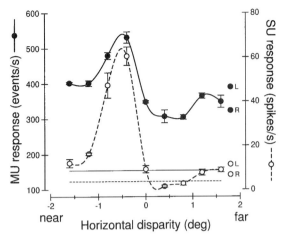

FIGURE 21.1   MT neurons are clustered according to disparity selectivity. Filled circles show MU responses to a drifting random dot pattern (direction = 225°, speed = 2.2°/s) with variable disparity. The solid curve is a cubic spline interpolation, and error bars correspond to 1 standard error. Filled circles labeled L and R denote MU responses to the same visual stimulus presented monocularly to either the left or right eye, respectively. The solid horizontal line gives the MU response in the absence of a visual stimulus (i.e., spontaneous activity). Open circles show responses of an isolated SU that was recorded simultaneously with the MU activity (action potentials from the SU were not included in the MU activity). The dashed horizontal line gives the spontaneous activity level of the SU. Note that the tuning of the SU response compares well with that of the MU response, which reflects the combined activity of several nearby neurons. Eccentricity = 6.3°; RF diameter = 5°. MU response: PD = –0.49°; DTI = 0.62. SU response: PD = –0.50°; DTI = 1.05.

lated ($R = 0.67$, slope = 0.79, $P < .0001$). This result permits the important inference that SUs generally exhibit weak disparity tuning at the same recording sites where MU activity is poorly tuned; we can therefore rule out the possibility that flat MU disparity tuning curves arise from a combination of SUs that are well tuned to widely different disparities. At 77/110 sites with significant disparity tuning (one-way ANOVA, $P < .05$ for both SU and MU), there was a strong correlation between SU and MU data with respect to both the preferred disparity ($R = 0.91$, slope = 1.05, $P < .0001$) and the disparity tuning width ($R = 0.76$, slope = 0.87, $P < .0001$). These results indicate that MT neurons are spatially clustered according to their disparity tuning properties, consistent with the notion of a columnar organization for disparity.

Functional architecture for binocular disparity in MT

Having established that disparity-selective neurons are clustered, we investigated the functional architecture of

MT by measuring MU disparity tuning curves at regularly spaced intervals along electrode penetrations through MT. Data were collected at 411 recording sites (241 in monkey P, 170 in monkey S) along penetrations from two different angles. In *oblique* penetrations, we approached MT from the occipital lobe, passing first through the lunate sulcus. Electrodes traveled in a sagittal plane, tilted ~20° below horizontal. Thus, our electrode passed through MT at an oblique angle, ranging from ~45° to 90° away from the surface normal. Given that MT is organized retinotopically (Maunsell and Van Essen, 1987; Albright and Desimone, 1987) and contains a columnar architecture for direction of motion (Albright, Desimone, and Gross, 1984), we expected both receptive field (RF) position and preferred direction of motion to vary systematically in these penetrations. These known variations could then be used as a reference to evaluate changes in disparity selectivity. In *normal* penetrations, we approached MT from the frontal lobes (near-sagittal plane, tilted ~45° below the horizontal), passing first through the central and intraparietal sulci. The electrodes thus entered MT at an angle roughly normal to the cortical surface. In these penetrations we expected RF positions and preferred directions to remain fairly constant, again providing a useful reference for comparison with disparity tuning.

Figure 21.2a shows a sequence of disparity tuning curves measured at 100-μm intervals along an oblique penetration through MT; figure 21.2b summarizes these data quantitatively. First, note that the disparity tuning was poor both at the beginning and the end of the penetration, but was quite strong in the middle. A similar patchy distribution of disparity-selective responses was observed in many penetrations, suggesting that disparity-selective and -nonselective neurons are spatially segregated within MT. Patches of poor disparity selectivity were short in this penetration, but such patches extended up to 1.5 mm in other oblique penetrations (and were not always at the beginning and end of the penetration). Second, note that the PD changed systematically within the disparity-selective segment of this oblique penetration. Similar gradients of PD from "near" to "far" disparities, or vice versa, occurred along many oblique penetrations, suggesting that MT contains a systematic map of binocular disparities. Finally, as expected for an oblique penetration, the preferred direction of motion changed gradually from one recording site to the next along most of the penetration (figure 21.2b, small arrows), and RF position moved gradually from the lower left quadrant of the visual field up to the horizontal meridian (data not shown).

Figure 21.2c,d shows analogous data from a normal penetration through MT. In contrast to the oblique pen-

etration, the disparity tuning curves were very similar from one recording site to the next (figure 21.2c). The DTI remained roughly constant throughout this penetration, except at the last recording site which was near the boundary with white matter (figure 21.2d). In addition, the PD remained quite constant within a range of near disparities between –0.5° and –0.9°. Both the preferred direction of motion (arrows) and the RF location in space (data not shown) changed little throughout this penetration. We obtained similar results in many of our normal penetrations, including some in which disparity selectivity was poor throughout the penetration.

To summarize these data, we analyzed changes in disparity tuning as a function of distance between recording sites. For 22 oblique penetrations, figure 21.3 (filled circles) shows the mean absolute difference in DTI (|ΔDTI|) plotted against distance. Data were pooled across the 22 oblique penetrations as follows. For each penetration, we computed |ΔDTI| for all unique pairs of recording sites. We then pooled these values across penetrations (for each distance) and plotted the mean |ΔDTI| against distance between sites. The data were then analyzed by a two-way ANOVA, with distance and penetration type as the two factors. The mean |ΔDTI| increases significantly with distance [$F(9,3060) = 22.5$, $P \ll .001$], indicating that nearby recording sites have more similar DTIs than distant recording sites. At large separations, |ΔDTI| for oblique penetrations approaches the value obtained from random pairings of sites (solid line). Similarly, the mean |ΔPD| for oblique penetrations (open circles) also increases with distance [$F(9,2708) = 12.61$, $P \ll .001$]. This confirms that there is a systematic map of preferred disparity in MT, with smooth changes from one site to the next.

Among the 14 normal penetrations, both |ΔDTI| and |ΔPD| tend to increase with distance (filled and open triangles, respectively), as is expected if our "normal" penetrations are not perfectly orthogonal to the cortical surface. At all distances, however, the data from normal penetrations lie well below those from oblique penetrations [$F(1,3060) = 208.9$ for DTI, $F(1,2708) = 122.9$ for PD; $P \ll .001$ for both]. Thus, disparity tuning stays much more constant within normal penetrations, consistent with the idea that disparity-selective neurons are organized in columns that run perpendicular to the cortical surface. A similar finding was previously reported for direction selectivity in MT (Albright, Desimone, and Gross, 1984).

To summarize, the functional architecture for disparity in MT has three main features. First, disparity-tuned neurons are clustered into columns according to preferred disparity. Second, disparity-tuned columns are themselves clustered within MT such that disparity-sensitive

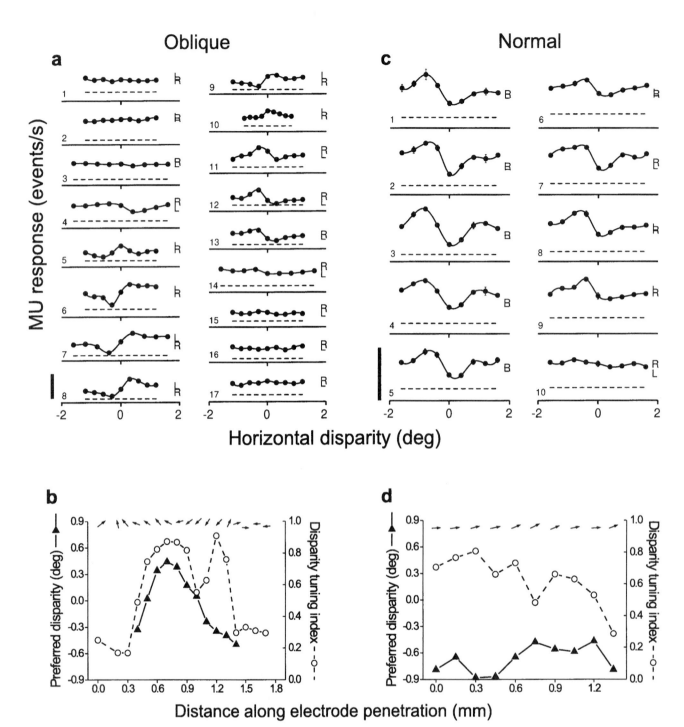

FIGURE 21.2   MT exhibits a columnar architecture for binocular disparity. (a) Sequence of disparity tuning curves recorded at 100-μm intervals along an oblique penetration through MT in monkey S. Each graph shows the MU response as a function of horizontal disparity. Standard error bars are plotted around each mean, but are generally smaller than the data points themselves. Smooth curves are cubic spline interpolations. Dashed lines represent the spontaneous activity level, and the letters L and R give responses obtained during monocular controls. Height of scale bar = 400 events/s. (b) Quantitative summary of disparity tuning for the oblique penetration illustrated in part a. Open circles (right axis) plot disparity tuning index (DTI) as a function of distance along the electrode penetration, whereas filled triangles (left axis) plot the preferred disparity (PD) at each recording site (PD is not plotted in cases where there is no significant disparity tuning; ANOVA, $P > .05$). Arrows denote the preferred direction of motion at each recording site. (c) Sequence of disparity tuning curves recorded at 150-μm intervals along a normal penetration through MT in monkey P. Height of scale bar = 400 events/s. (d) Summary of disparity tuning parameters for the normal penetration in part c. Conventions as in part b.

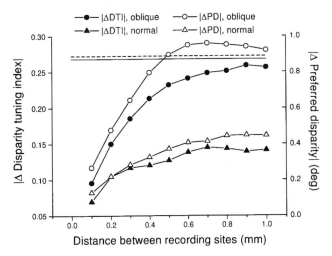

FIGURE 21.3 Quantitative summary of data from oblique and normal penetrations. Filled symbols show the mean absolute difference in disparity tuning index (|ΔDTI|; left axis) between pairs of recording sites as a function of distance between the sites (filled circles, data pooled across 22 oblique penetrations; filled triangles, data pooled across 14 normal penetrations). Open symbols show the mean absolute difference in preferred disparity (|ΔPD|; right axis) plotted as a function of distance (open circles, data from 22 oblique penetrations; open triangles, data from 14 normal penetrations). Because the number of observations that comprise each data point decreases with distance, data are not plotted beyond a distance of 1 mm. The solid and dashed horizontal lines show the values of |ΔDTI| and |ΔPD|, respectively, computed from random pairings of recording sites. These are the values that would be expected if there were no functional organization for disparity. Note that the left and right y-axes were scaled (to the nearest round numbers) so that the solid and dashed horizontal lines were roughly superimposed.

patches of cortex are interspersed among cortex that is poorly tuned for disparity (e.g., figure 21.2a,b). Finally, in patches with good disparity tuning, preferred disparity typically varies smoothly from column to column across the surface of MT. Some aspects of the functional architecture for disparity are poorly understood at present. We do not know the actual shapes of the disparity-selective patches, nor how consistently PD is organized within these patches. In addition, we know very little concerning the alignment of maps for direction and for disparity. Optical imaging or 2-deoxyglucose functional mapping studies may help resolve these issues.

Microstimulation of MT biases depth judgments

We next sought to determine whether MT plays a functional role in depth perception. We tested this possibility by applying electrical microstimulation within disparity columns in MT while monkeys performed the stereoscopic depth discrimination task illustrated in figure 21.4. Two monkeys (R and T) viewed a random-dot vi-

sual display in which a fraction of the dots carried a consistent depth signal ("signal" dots), while the remaining dots were randomly scattered in depth ("noise" dots). Signal dots were presented on each trial at a disparity either "near" or "far" with respect to the fixation point. One of the two disparities was the disparity preferred by the MT neurons near the electrode tip, while the other disparity was a nonoptimal disparity. The location and size of the visual stimulus aperture, as well as the direction and speed of the moving dots, were chosen to maximize the MU response. The monkeys' task was to report seeing near or far depth by making a saccadic eye movement to one of two small saccade targets. By varying the fraction of signal dots in the display (% binocular correlation), task difficulty could be easily adjusted. Importantly, the monkeys were rewarded for reporting the actual depth of the signal dots irrespective of the presence of microstimulation. In these experiments, random-dot stimuli were rendered in depth by presenting stimuli alternately to each eye using LCD shutters synchronized to the frame rate of the CRT display (100 Hz). Again, binocular search coils were implanted in one monkey (R) to detect possible effects of microstimulation on vergence eye movements.

We made oblique penetrations through MT to search for microstimulation sites. An adequate site was considered to be a region where the disparity tuning of MU activity was roughly constant over at least 200–300 μm. Upon identifying a suitable site, we positioned our electrode in the middle of the region of constant preferred disparity for the duration of the experiment. Microstimulation parameters were similar to those used in previous studies from this laboratory (Salzman et al., 1992; Murasugi, Salzman, and Newsome, 1993). The stimulation train consisted of 20-μA biphasic pulses, each consisting of a 200-μs cathodal pulse followed by a 200-μs anodal pulse, with a 100-μs interval between the two. If microstimulation augments the signal carried by the stimulated neurons, and if these neurons provide signals used by the monkey to perform the task, we would expect microstimulation to increase the frequency of perceptual choices toward the depth encoded by neurons at the stimulation site.

Figure 21.5 depicts exactly this result from two microstimulation experiments in MT. Figure 21.5a illustrates the disparity tuning curve for a site that responded optimally to far disparities; the arrowheads indicate the two disparities employed in the depth discrimination task. Figure 21.5b shows how microstimulation at this site affected perceptual judgments. For almost every stimulus condition, the monkey decided in favor of the preferred disparity more often on stimulated trials (filled circles) than on nonstimulated trials

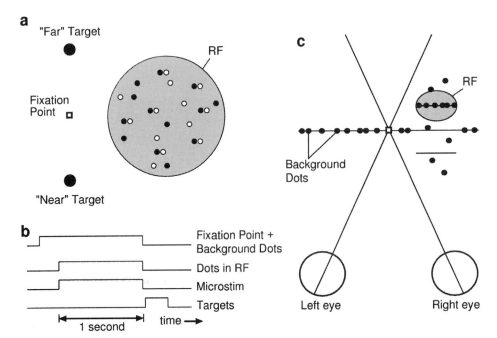

FIGURE 21.4 Depth discrimination task used to measure the effect of microstimulation on depth judgments. (a) Spatial arrangement of the fixation point, visual stimulus, and response targets. The shaded circle (not present in actual display) represents the MU RF. A random dot pattern was presented within a circular aperture approximately the same size as the RF. Filled dots denote the image shown to the left eye, and unfilled dots denote the right eye's image. Here, half of the dots are paired with a fixed disparity (signal dots), and the remaining dots have random horizontal disparities (noise dots). (b) Sequence of events during each trial. The fixation point appeared first, and the monkey was required to maintain fixation within a 1.5° window throughout the trial. After the animal fixated for ~500 ms, the visual stimulus appeared for 1 s within the MU RF of the recorded neurons. On half the trials, selected randomly, microstimulation was applied concurrently with the dots. Subsequently, fixation point, visual stimulus, and microstimulation were turned off, and two small target disks ap-

peared. The monkey made a saccadic eye movement to the upper target to indicate a far stimulus, or to the lower target to indicate near. (c) Top-down view of the visual stimulus. On each trial, signal dots appeared at either of two fixed disparities, one near and one far (short horizontal line segments). One disparity (far, in this example) was chosen to be optimal for the recorded neurons (RF shown shaded); the other disparity was chosen to be nonoptimal. Here, the visual stimulus consists of 50% signal dots and 50% noise dots. Task difficulty was modulated by varying the proportion of signal dots in the display (i.e., percent binocular correlation). Signal and noise dots moved with a velocity (direction and speed) that was optimal for the neurons at the electrode tip. Dots situated along the plane of fixation, but outside the stimulus aperture, were stationary and provided a zero-disparity background. These background dots were plotted at random positions on each trial, and appeared simultaneously with the fixation point. (Adapted from DeAngelis, Cumming, and Newsome, 1998.)

(open circles). This bias toward the preferred disparity is evident as a leftward shift of the psychometric function. We considered the magnitude of this shift to be the horizontal offset between sigmoidal curves fitted to the data points (using logistic regression). This shift was measured as the distance between the two curves at the level of 50% preferred decisions. The effect illustrated in figure 21.5b was equivalent to 22.5% correlated dots, a nearly modal effect for monkey R.

Figures 21.5c and d show similar data from an experiment performed on monkey T. Neurons at this stimulation site responded best to near disparities, as illustrated in figure 21.5c. Consistent with the MU disparity tuning, microstimulation at this site induced a strong choice bias toward the near disparity. The resulting shift of the psychometric function was equivalent to 57.6% correlated

dots, the largest effect that we have observed in any of our experiments.

Figure 21.6 summarizes results from 65 microstimulation experiments. The scattergram plots the amplitude of the microstimulation effect against the disparity-tuning index measured at each stimulation site. Positive values on the ordinate correspond to leftward shifts of the psychometric function, that is, shifts *toward* the optimal disparity of the stimulation site. Filled symbols indicate statistically significant effects (logistic regression, $P <$ .05), which occurred in 43/65 experiments. Among the significant effects, 42/43 were toward the depth preferred by neurons at the stimulation site, the one exception being a site with poor disparity tuning. The histogram at the right depicts the same data collapsed across DTI.

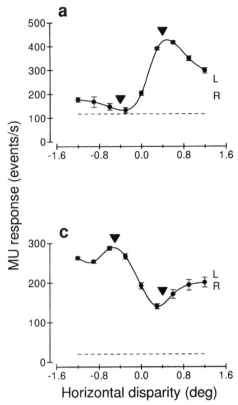

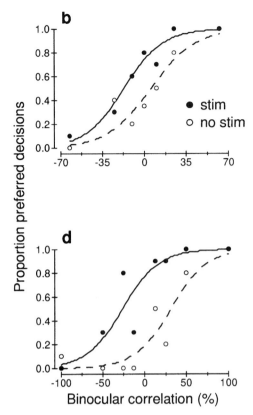

FIGURE 21.5 Microstimulation of MT biases depth judgments. (a) Disparity tuning of MU activity at a site in monkey R preferring far disparities. Arrowheads denote the two disparities used in the depth discrimination task; other conventions as in figure 21.1. (b) Effect of microstimulation on depth judgments for the site depicted in part a. The abscissa represents the strength of the depth signal in percentage of binocularly correlated dots (i.e., percent signal dots). Positive values indicate that signal dots were presented at the preferred disparity (far) of the recorded neurons; negative values correspond to signal dots presented at the nonoptimal disparity. The ordinate is the proportion of decisions that the monkey made in favor of the preferred disparity (each point represents 10 trials). Filled and open circles show psychometric functions obtained during

trials with and without microstimulation, respectively. Each curve was fitted with a sigmoidal function using logistic regression. The net effect of microstimulation was a leftward shift of the psychometric function equivalent to 22.5% correlated dots, and the effect was highly significant ($P < .005$), as determined from logistic regression based on maximum likelihood estimation (Cox and Snell, 1989). (c) Disparity tuning of MU activity at a near-tuned site in monkey T. (d) Effect of microstimulation at the site for which tuning is shown in part c. The leftward shift induced by microstimulation at this site was equivalent to 57.6% correlated dots (logistic regression, $P < .0001$). (Reprinted with permission from DeAngelis, Cumming, and Newsome, 1998.)

The amplitude of the microstimulation effect was significantly correlated with the DTI measured at the stimulation site ($R = .48$, $P < .005$ for monkey R; $R = .45$, $P < .01$ for monkey T). Statistically significant microstimulation effects were generally limited to sites with moderate to strong disparity selectivity. This correlation further demonstrates that microstimulation effects are quite specific; stimulation at sites with weak disparity tuning produces weak effects on depth perception.

Although microstimulation often produced a significant leftward shift of the psychometric function, the slope of the psychometric function changed significantly in only 4/65 experiments (logistic regression, $P < .05$). The average slope ratio (stimulation/no stimulation) of 0.97 did not differ significantly from 1.0 (t-test, $t = -0.68$,

$P > .5$). Thus, microstimulation produces a choice bias toward the preferred disparity without compromising perceptual sensitivity to small variations in binocular correlation.

Microstimulation effects with stationary stimuli

In the experiments described thus far, the motion of the random dots was in the preferred direction of neurons at the stimulation site. Because MT is widely thought to be more important for the analysis of moving than stationary stimuli (Allman, Miezin, and McGuinness, 1985; Albright, 1993), we tested whether the effects of microstimulation on stereo judgments were limited to moving stimuli. After a modest training period, monkey R was

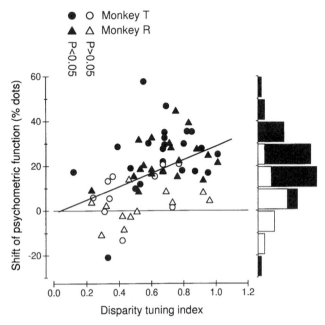

● ○ Monkey T
▲ △ Monkey R

P<0.05 P>0.05

FIGURE 21.6   Summary of microstimulation effects for 65 experiments from two monkeys. The scatterplot shows the shift of the psychometric function (leftward shifts are positive) plotted against the disparity tuning index of MU activity measured at each stimulation site. Filled symbols denote statistically significant effects (logistic regression, $P < .05$). Triangles and circles denote data from monkeys R and T, respectively. The solid line is the best linear fit to the data (linear regression). On the right the data are collapsed across DTI and plotted as a histogram. (Reprinted with permission from DeAngelis, Cumming, and Newsome, 1998.)

able to perform the depth discrimination task (figure 21.4) with all dots stationary. Thus, image motion on the retina could only arise from small eye movements occurring during fixation.

We performed the stationary-dots experiment at 12 sites in MT where microstimulation generated significant effects on depth judgments when the dots were moving. At 9 of these 12 sites, microstimulation also exerted a significant effect on depth judgments involving stationary dots; judgments in the stationary-dots condition were unaffected at the remaining 3 sites. The mean leftward shift of the psychometric function across all 12 sites was 25.8% for moving dots and 27.9% for stationary dots ($P > .5$; paired t-test). We also measured disparity tuning curves using stationary dots at these 12 sites. All exhibited strong disparity selectivity for stationary dots (mean DTI was 0.93 for stationary and 0.70 for moving dots; $P < .001$, paired t-test), although the overall response level was generally larger for moving dots (371 events/s) than for stationary dots (223 events/s) ($P < .001$, paired t-test). Some of the response to stationary dots was almost certainly driven by small eye movements during fixation.

Role of MT in stereopsis

The experiments described here provide two new lines of evidence that primate area MT is an important processing stage for neural signals related to stereoscopic depth perception. First, MT contains a functional architecture for binocular disparity in addition to its well known architecture for direction of motion: MT neurons are clustered according to their disparity selectivity, and preferred disparities vary smoothly across the surface of MT within the disparity-tuned patches. To our knowledge, this is the first clear, quantitative evidence for a systematic map of preferred disparity in primate visual cortex (but see Hubel and Livingstone, 1987; Ts'o, Gilbert, and Wiesel, 1990). Second, microstimulation of disparity columns in MT can bias stereoscopic judgments of depth, and the direction of the bias (near or far) is predictable from the disparity tuning of neurons at the stimulation site. Thus the disparity signals carried by MT neurons are an important part of the neural substrate for depth judgments in our task. This finding establishes the first direct link between the physiological property of disparity selectivity and the stereoscopic perception of depth. Note that the existence of disparity selective neurons alone is not sufficient to establish this link, because disparity signals can be used for other purposes such as guidance of vergence eye movements, a possibility strongly suggested by recent experiments on disparity selective neurons in V1 (Cumming and Parker, 1997; Masson, Busettini, and Miles, 1997). It is possible that disparity signals in MT are also used in the control of vergence eye movements, although careful inspection of data from monkey R revealed no effect of microstimulation on vergence.

Previous work has shown that MT is specialized for processing motion information (Albright, Desimone, and Gross, 1993). In fact, MT is often cited as one of the best examples of functional specialization in cortex. Our results show that the role of MT in vision is not limited to motion analysis. This conclusion is emphasized by the fact that many MT neurons exhibit robust disparity tuning in response to stationary random-dot patterns, and that microstimulation biases depth judgments involving stationary dots. Although the vast majority of MT neurons are selective for direction and speed of visual motion (e.g., Maunsell and Van Essen, 1983a), their activity apparently can be used to judge the depth of stationary objects as well (the *retinal image* is not completely stationary, of course, due to small eye movements around the point of fixation). Our findings concerning the role of MT in stereopsis are complemented by recent evidence that MT may also play a role in the perception of depth from motion cues (Bradley, Chang, and Andersen, 1998; Dodd et al., 1997).

Under the conditions of our experiment, which involves large disparities degraded by noise, MT appears to play an important role in depth perception. This does not mean, however, that *all* aspects of stereopsis depend on MT, nor that any *single* aspect of stereopsis depends *entirely* on MT. Consider, for example, that monkeys are capable of discriminating differences in disparity of less than 20 seconds of arc in the fovea (Sarmiento, 1975; Cowey and Wilkinson, 1991) and 1–3 minutes of arc at 5 degrees eccentricity (Pointon, Cumming, and Parker, 1998). By comparison, the disparity tuning of MT neurons is quite coarse (figure 21.2); thus, discrimination of fine disparities in our visual stimuli may require other cortical areas where neurons are more sharply tuned for disparity. The involvement of other cortical areas may in part explain why lesions of MT have not revealed a stereo deficit (Schiller, 1993). Broadly based investigations, including single-unit recording, microstimulation, and lesion techniques in a number of visual areas, will be necessary to achieve a comprehensive understanding of the neural basis of stereoscopic vision.

ACKNOWLEDGMENTS   We are grateful to Judy Stein and Cynthia Doane for capable technical assistance, and to Andrew Parker, Jon Dodd, Brian Wandell, Jamie Nichols, Eyal Siedemann, Greg Horwitz, and Crista Barberini for critical review of the manuscript. G. C. DeAngelis was supported by a Medical Research Fellowship from the Bank of America/Giannini Foundation, an NRSA from the National Eye Institute, and by a Career Award in the Biomedical Sciences from the Burroughs-Wellcome Fund. B. G. Cumming is a Royal Society Research Fellow, and W. T. Newsome is an Investigator of the Howard Hughes Medical Institute. This work was also supported by the National Eye Institute (EY05603).

NOTE

1. SU action potentials were identified using a template-matching algorithm implemented by a spike-sorting board; MU activity was recorded by means of a time-amplitude window discriminator. SU action potentials were excluded from the MU activity by setting the upper boundary of the window discriminator well below the peak of the SU action potential. For several experiments, the effectiveness of this approach was confirmed off-line by deliberately editing out any event in the multiunit record that occurred within a 3-ms window centered on each spike from the SU response, thereby eliminating any possible "leakage" of SU activity into the MU response. Analysis of the edited MU records yielded results essentially identical to analysis of the unedited MU records.

REFERENCES

ALBRIGHT, T. D., 1993. Cortical processing of visual motion. *Rev. Oculomotor Res.* 5:177–201.

ALBRIGHT, T. D., and R. DESIMONE, 1987. Local precision of visuotopic organization in the middle temporal area (MT) of the macaque. *Exp. Brain Res.* 65:582–592.

ALBRIGHT, T. D., R. DESIMONE, and C. G. GROSS, 1984. Columnar organization of directionally selective cells in visual area MT of the macaque. *J. Neurophysiol.* 51:16–31.

ALLMAN, J., F. MIEZIN, and E. MCGUINNESS, 1985. Stimulus specific responses from beyond the classical receptive field: Neurophysiological mechanisms for local-global comparisons in visual neurons. *Annu. Rev. Neurosci.* 8:407–430.

BARLOW, H. B., C. BLAKEMORE, and J. D. PETTIGREW, 1967. The neural mechanism of binocular depth discrimination. *J. Physiol. (Lond.)* 193:327–342.

BLAKEMORE, C., 1970. The representation of three-dimensional visual space in the cat's striate cortex. *J. Physiol. (Lond)* 209:155–178.

BRADLEY, D. C., G. C. CHANG, and R. A. ANDERSEN, 1998. Encoding of three-dimensional structure-from-motion by primate area MT neurons. *Nature* 392:714–717.

BRITTEN, K. H., M. N. SHADLEN, W. T. NEWSOME, and J. A. MOVSHON, 1992. The analysis of visual motion: A comparison of neuronal and psychophysical performance. *J. Neurosci.* 12:4745–4765.

CLARKE, P. G., I. M. DONALDSON, and D. WHITTERIDGE, 1976. Binocular visual mechanisms in cortical areas I and II of the sheep. *J. Physiol. (Lond.)* 256:509–526.

COWEY, A., and F. WILKINSON, 1991. The role of the corpus callosum and extrastriate visual areas in stereoacuity in macaque monkeys. *Neuropsychologia* 29:465–479.

COX, D. R., and E. J. SNELL, 1989. *Analysis of Binary Data.* London: Chapman and Hall.

CUMMING, B. G., and A. J. PARKER, 1997. Responses of primary visual cortical neurons to binocular disparity without depth perception. *Nature* 389:280–283.

DEANGELIS, G. C., B. G. CUMMING, and W. T. NEWSOME, 1998. Cortical area MT and the perception of stereoscopic depth. *Nature* 394:677–680.

DODD, J. V., B. G. CUMMING, W. T. NEWSOME, and A. J. PARKER, 1997. Firing of V5 (MT) neurons reliably covaries with reported 3-D configuration in a perceptually-ambiguous structure-from-motion task. *Soc. Neurosci. Abstr.* 23:1125.

DUBNER, R., and S. M. ZEKI, 1971. Response properties and receptive fields of cells in an anatomically defined region of the superior temporal sulcus in the monkey. *Brain Res.* 35:528–532.

FELLEMAN, D. J., and D. C. VAN ESSEN, 1987. Receptive field properties of neurons in area V3 of macaque monkey extrastriate cortex. *J. Neurophysiol.* 57:889–920.

HUBEL, D. H., and M. S. LIVINGSTONE, 1987. Segregation of form, color, and stereopsis in primate area 18. *J. Neurosci.* 7:3378–3415.

HUBEL, D. H., and T. N. WIESEL, 1970. Stereoscopic vision in macaque monkey. Cells sensitive to binocular depth in area 18 of the macaque monkey cortex. *Nature* 225:41–42.

JUDGE, S. J., B. J. RICHMOND, and F. C. CHU, 1980. Implantation of magnetic search coils for measurement of eye position: An improved method. *Vision Res.* 20:535–538.

LEVAY, S., and T. VOIGT, 1988. Ocular dominance and disparity coding in cat visual cortex. *Vis. Neurosci.* 1:395–414.

MASSON, G. S., C. BUSETTINI, and F. A. MILES, 1997. Vergence eye movements in response to binocular disparity without depth perception. *Nature* 389:283–286.

MAUNSELL, J. H., and D. C. VAN ESSEN, 1983a. Functional properties of neurons in middle temporal visual area of the macaque monkey. I. Selectivity for stimulus direction, speed, and orientation. *J. Neurophysiol.* 49:1127–1147.

MAUNSELL, J. H., and D. C. VAN ESSEN, 1983b. Functional properties of neurons in middle temporal visual area of the macaque monkey. II. Binocular interactions and sensitivity to binocular disparity. *J. Neurophysiol.* 49:1148–1167.

MAUNSELL, J. H., and D. C. VAN ESSEN, 1987. Topographic organization of the middle temporal visual area in the macaque monkey: Representational biases and the relationship to callosal connections and myeloarchitectonic boundaries. *J. Comp. Neurol.* 266:535–555.

MURASUGI, C. M., C. D. SALZMAN, and W. T. NEWSOME, 1993. Microstimulation in visual area MT: Effects of varying pulse amplitude and frequency. *J. Neurosci.* 13:1719–1729.

NEWSOME, W. T., and E. B. PARE, 1988. A selective impairment of motion perception following lesions of the middle temporal visual area (MT). *J. Neurosci.* 8:2201–2211.

ORBAN, G. A., R. C. SAUNDERS, and E. VANDENBUSSCHE, 1995. Lesions of the superior temporal cortical motion areas impair speed discrimination in the macaque monkey. *Eur. J. Neurosci.* 7:2261–2276.

PASTERNAK, T., and W. H. MERIGAN, 1994. Motion perception following lesions of the superior temporal sulcus in the monkey. *Cerebral Cortex* 4:247–259.

PETTIGREW, J. D., T. NIKARA, and P. O. BISHOP, 1968. Binocular interaction on single units in cat striate cortex: Simultaneous stimulation by single moving slit with receptive fields in correspondence. *Exp. Brain Res.* 6:391–410.

POGGIO, G. F., and B. FISCHER, 1977. Binocular interaction and depth sensitivity in striate and prestriate cortex of behaving rhesus monkey. *J. Neurophysiol.* 40:1392–1405.

POGGIO, G. F., F. GONZALEZ, and F. KRAUSE, 1988. Stereoscopic mechanisms in monkey visual cortex: Binocular correlation and disparity selectivity. *J. Neurosci.* 8:4531–4550.

POINTON, A., B. G. CUMMING, and A. J. PARKER, 1998. Simultaneous measurement of neuronal and psychophysical performance in binocular stereopsis. *Invest. Ophthalmol. Vis. Sci. Abstr.* 39:S323.

ROBINSON, D. A., 1963. A method of measuring eye movement using a scleral search coil in a magnetic field. *IEEE Trans. Biomed. Eng.* 10:137–145.

ROY, J. P., H. KOMATSU, and R. H. WURTZ, 1992. Disparity sensitivity of neurons in monkey extrastriate area MST. *J. Neurosci.* 12:2478–2492.

SALZMAN, C. D., C. M. MURASUGI, K. H. BRITTEN, and W. T. NEWSOME, 1992. Microstimulation in visual area MT: Effects on direction discrimination performance. *J. Neurosci.* 12:2331–2355.

SALZMAN, C. D., and W. T. NEWSOME, 1994. Neural mechanisms for forming a perceptual decision. *Science* 264:231–237.

SARMIENTO, R. F., 1975. The stereoacuity of macaque monkey. *Vision Res.* 15:493–498.

SCHILLER, P. H., 1993. The effects of V4 and middle temporal (MT) area lesions on visual performance in the rhesus monkey. *Vis. Neurosci.* 10:717–746.

TS'O, D. Y., C. D. GILBERT, and T. N. WIESEL, 1990. Functional architecture of color and disparity in visual area 2 of macaque monkey. *Soc. Neurosci. Abstr.* 16:293.

ZEKI, S. M., 1974. Functional organization of a visual area in the posterior bank of the superior temporal sulcus of the rhesus monkey. *J. Physiol.* 236:549–573.

22 Effects of Attention on Neuronal Response Properties in Visual Cerebral Cortex

JOHN H. R. MAUNSELL AND CARRIE J. MCADAMS

ABSTRACT While many studies have shown that attention can affect the strength of neuronal responses in cerebral cortex, little is known about whether attention alters the stimulus selectivities of individual neurons. We have examined this question by recording the responses of isolated neurons in area V4 of monkeys while they performed a task that required them to either attend to or ignore the stimulus in a neuron's receptive field. Comparisons of orientation tuning curves measured in the two modes suggest that attention increases responses to all stimuli proportionately, without sharpening the tuning curve. A proportionate scaling of tuning curves without sharpening has also been reported when stimulus attributes such as contrast or color are varied. Thus, it is possible that ascending sensory signals related to stimulus qualities and descending signals related to behavioral state are treated equivalently in visual cortex.

Attention is a critical determinant of what we perceive. At any moment we can give full attention to just a tiny fraction of the available sensory information. Attention often makes the difference between looking and seeing. Major changes in the visual scene can go unnoticed if attention is not allocated to the site of change (see Rensink, O'Regan, and Clark, 1997; Simons and Levin, 1997). Even when changes are detected, responses to a stimulus are slower or less sensitive when attention is directed to some other spatial location or object attribute (see Duncan, 1984; Hikosaka, Miyauchi, and Shimojo, 1993; Egeth and Yantis, 1997).

In neurophysiological studies, attention has been shown to affect how sensory information is processed in the cerebral cortex. The influence of a subject's level of vigilance on the responses of cortical sensory neurons was obvious in some of the earliest single-cell recordings made from awake animals (Hubel et al., 1959). While some of these effects may be widespread, nonspecific modulations related to the level of arousal, neurons in every part of the visual cortex have been shown to be influenced in highly selective ways that depend on the behavioral significance of the stimulus in their receptive field (see Colby, 1991; Colby, Duhamel, and Goldberg, 1993; Desimone and Duncan, 1995).

Figure 22.1 shows data from our laboratory that illustrate the effects of attention on the activity of a cortical neuron. Responses were collected from a directionally selective cell in the medial superior temporal area (MST) in a monkey that watched two dots move back and forth on a screen (Treue and Maunsell, 1996). Only one of the dots fell in the receptive field of the neuron. On a given trial, the animal was instructed to attend to one of the two stimuli. The animal's eye position was monitored, and the animal was required to attend to the selected dot without looking at it directly, holding its gaze fixed on a small fixation point. In this way we could ensure that the retinal stimulation was the same whether the animal directed its attention to one dot or the other. Like many neurons in the later stages of visual cortex, this cell responded much more strongly to the receptive field stimulus when the animal paid attention to that stimulus than when the animal focused its attention on the other stimulus. Because the retinal stimulation was the same in both conditions, we attribute the difference in the neuron's response to whether the animal was attending to the stimulus inside its receptive field. Thus, this neuron did not signal the motion of any stimulus on its receptive field; rather, it selectively signaled the motion of stimuli to which the animal was attending.

Many studies have shown that attention can change the strength of neuronal responses, in most cases causing cells to respond more strongly when the animal pays attention to the stimulus they represent (see Maunsell, 1995). Little is known, however, about the interactions between attention and the sensory response properties of neurons. Most studies of attention have examined responses to a single stimulus, leaving open the

JOHN H. R. MAUNSELL   Howard Hughes Medical Institute and Division of Neuroscience, Baylor College of Medicine, Houston, Tex.

CARRIE J. MCADAMS   Division of Neuroscience, Baylor College of Medicine, Houston, Tex.

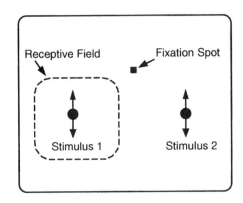

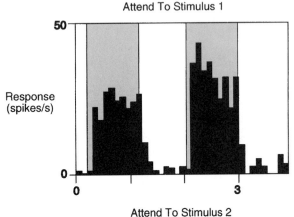

Attend To Stimulus 1

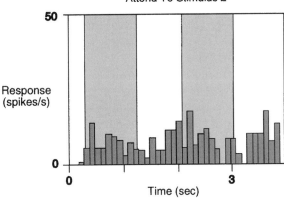

Attend To Stimulus 2

FIGURE 22.1 Attentional modulation of the responses of a neuron in the medial superior temporal area (MST). The upper panel is a schematic representation of the stimulus configuration. Stimulus 1 was positioned to move back and forth across the center of the receptive field of the neuron being recorded. Stimulus 2 moved back and forth outside the receptive field in the other half of the visual field. Gaze was held on the fixation spot throughout all trials. The subject animal could be instructed to attend to either one of these stimuli by a cue presented at the start of each trial. It was trained to release a lever when the cued stimulus changed its speed. The other stimulus might also change speed, but trials ended without reward if the animal responded to the uncued stimulus. The lower panels show the neuron's responses to the receptive field stimulus sorted according to whether the animal was attending to that stimulus. Each histogram shows the rate of firing as a function of time as the stimuli moved back and forth. The shaded portions are intervals when the stimulus inside the receptive field moved in the direction preferred by the neuron. Each plot is the average of many stimulus presentations. The average rate at which this neuron fired spikes was much greater when the animal was attending to the stimulus in its receptive field, although the retinal stimulation was the same in both cases.

question of whether attention alters stimulus selectivity. For example, the data in figure 22.1 show that attention increased responses to motion in the preferred direction for a neuron, but they do not address the question of whether attention changed the directional selectivity of the cell. Sharpening neuronal tuning for behaviorally relevant stimulus dimensions might be a powerful mechanism for improving behavioral detection or discrimination of those stimulus attributes.

We have begun to examine this question by recording the responses of isolated neurons in area V4 of trained monkeys. We selected V4 because it represented a good compromise between earlier stages, in which behavioral modulations are weaker, and later stages, in which tuning curves for simple stimulus dimensions are more diffi-

cult to obtain. Because most neurons in V4 are sensitive to the orientation of stimuli in their receptive field, our experiments have focused on the effects of attention on orientation tuning.

Effects of attention on orientation tuning in area V4

TASK DESIGN AND DATA COLLECTION   Monkeys were trained to do a task that shifted their attention between two stimulus locations. We used a match-to-sample task in which pairs of stimuli were presented as samples and tests (figure 22.2). The displays were generated on a calibrated video monitor under computer control. The stimuli in one location were grating patterns, while those in the other location were patches of color. On each trial, the animal attended to just one location and used a lever to report whether the sample and test stimuli in that location were same or different. The location for attention was signaled to the animal using instruction trials in which stimuli appeared in only one location. The animals learned to continue reporting on this location during a subsequent block of trials when stimuli were presented in both locations.

Matches in the two locations were uncorrelated so that the animal got no advantage from attending to or responding to stimuli in the incorrect location. Because the animals got 80–90% of the trials correct, we can be sure that they kept track of the relevant location. There is no way to know whether the animal allocated some attention to the incorrect location, but any attention allocated to the incorrect location should only reduce the modulations in neuronal response that we observed. For that

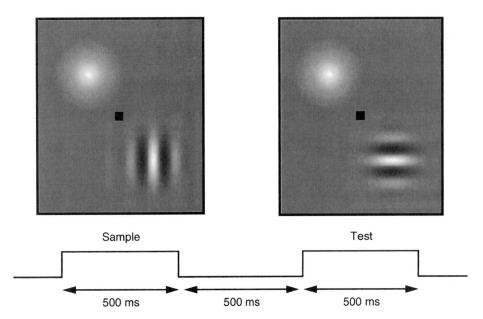

Sample   Test

500 ms   500 ms   500 ms

FIGURE 22.2 The delayed match-to-sample task used to examine the effects of attention in area V4. The stimuli appearing in one location were black and white Gabors that were temporally counterphased at 4 Hz. The stimuli in the other location were two-dimensional colored Gaussians. All stimuli were isoluminant with a midlevel gray background. Pairs of sample and test stimuli were presented for 500 ms and were separated by 500 ms during which only the fixation spot was present. On each trial the animal was instructed to attend to just one location and to report whether the sample and test stimuli in that location were the same. The correct response to a match was to release a lever within 500 ms from the start of the test stimulus. The correct response for nonmatching stimuli was to keep the lever depressed until the test stimulus was removed (700–1000 ms after its appearance).

reason, the effects we describe here should be considered a lower limit on the full range of attentional modulations of responses.

We monitored eye position and required the animals to perform the task while keeping their fixation within 0.5° of a small spot at the center of the screen. Using controlled fixation, the stimuli could be presented to specific locations on the retinas, and were the same whether the animal attended to one stimulus or the other.

While the animal performed the task, extracellular recordings were made from isolated neurons in area V4. For each cell the stimuli were adjusted so that the grating patterns were centered in the receptive field. The size and spatial frequency of the gratings were optimized for each neuron. Over the course of many trials, we collected neuronal responses to a complete range of grating orientations in two conditions: one when the animal was attending to the grating in the receptive field and reporting on its orientation, and one when it was ignoring the grating and reporting on the color of the other stimulus outside the receptive field. The stimuli were exactly the same in both cases, and the animal's attention was cycled back and forth between the two locations many times during data collection from each neuron.

STRONGER RESPONSES WITHOUT NARROWER TUNING Results from a typical V4 neuron are shown in figure 22.3. Like many neurons in V4, this cell responded more strongly to the grating patterns in its receptive field when the animal paid attention to them. The upper panels show the responses of the cell to selected stimulus orientations. These data, and all others presented here, are responses to the presentation of the sample stimulus. The upper row contains responses collected while the animal was attending to the stimulus, and the bottom row contains responses collected while the animal was ignoring those stimuli and attending to the color patches in the other visual hemifield. Although the neuron responded to the receptive field stimulus in both cases, responses were stronger when the animal was attending to that stimulus (with the possible exception of the least favored orientations, which were inhibitory).

The lower panel in figure 22.3 shows the average rate of firing to each of the 12 stimulus orientations tested. In this and other figures we present responses as the average rate of firing during the stimulus presentation without subtracting the spontaneous rate of firing. The curve through each set of points is the best-fitting Gaussian function. The amplitude of the curve when the animal attended to the stimuli was 26 spikes/s, while that for the ignored stimuli was 18 spikes/s. Because the same stimuli

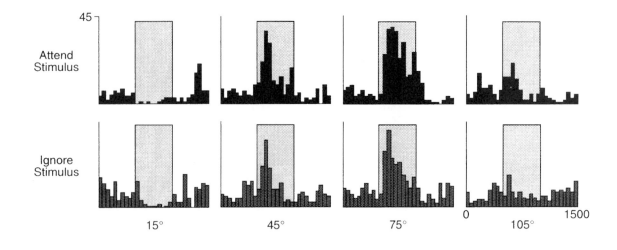

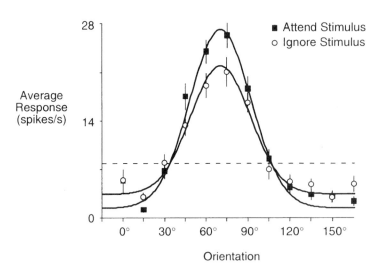

FIGURE 22.3 Effects of attention on the responses of a V4 neuron to oriented stimuli. The histograms in the upper panels plot the response of the neuron to the appearance of the sample stimulus in the receptive field. The pairs of histograms in each column represent responses to 4 different orientations of the Gabor stimulus in the receptive field. The upper row shows responses collected when the animal was attending to the sample stimulus, and the lower row shows responses to the same stimulus was ignored. The shading marks the period when the sample stimulus was present. The axes are scaled in spikes per second (vertical) and milliseconds (horizontal). Each histogram includes 20 repetitions of the stimulus. The lower panel is a plot average rate of firing as a function of sample stimulus orientation. Filled squares mark responses to attended stimuli and open circles mark responses when the stimuli were ignored. The error bars are ±1 standard error of the mean. The dashed line represents spontaneous activity. The curves through the data points are best-fitting Gaussians. The neuron was orientation-selective in both cases, but the amplitude of the fitted function, measured from its peak to its baseline, was greater when the animal was paying attention to the stimuli. There was little change in the width (σ) of the fitted functions.

were presented in both conditions, this difference in response can be attributed to differences in the way the animal allocated its attention between the two conditions. A stronger response to attended stimuli has been reported in many earlier studies of V4 (Moran and Desimone, 1985; Haenny, Maunsell, and Schiller, 1988; Haenny and Schiller, 1988; Spitzer, Desimone, and Moran, 1988; Maunsell et al., 1991; Motter, 1993; Motter, 1994a, b; Connor et al., 1996, 1997; Luck et al., 1997).

By measuring responses to different orientations, we can ask whether attention affects the sharpness of orien-

tation tuning for V4 neurons. Although the amplitude of the orientation tuning curves changed for this neuron, there was little difference in the width of the tuning functions. The widths of the fitted functions in figure 22.3, taken as one standard deviation (σ) of the Gaussian, are 30° for the attended stimuli and 31° for ignored stimuli.

An increase in orientation tuning curve amplitude without a change in width was typical for the V4 neurons we encountered. Data from 262 V4 neurons in two monkeys are summarized in figure 22.4. The statistical significance of each Gaussian fit was determined by per-

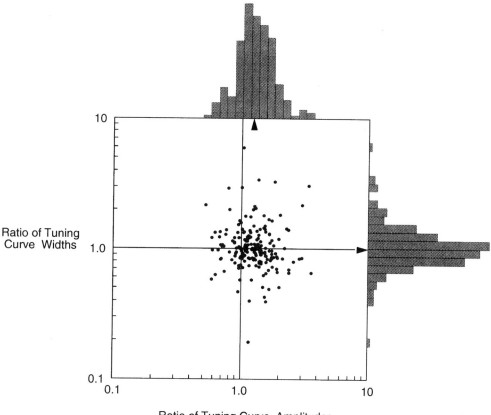

FIGURE 22.4   Effects of attention on the amplitude and width of orientation tuning curves in V4. For the 197 V4 neurons whose responses to different orientations were well-fit by Gaussian in both task modes, ratios of curve amplitudes and widths were computed for each cell. The median ratio for tuning curve amplitude was 1.24, indicating a systematic increase in response modulation in V4 with attention. The median ratio for tuning curve width was 1.00. There is no sign of a systematic relationship between the two ratios. The histograms above and to the right of the scatterplot show the distributions for amplitude and width ratios. The medians of each distribution are marked with small arrows.

forming an F-test that compared the goodness of fit to that for a line. Of the neurons recorded, the orientation tuning data for 197 (75%) reached criterion for the Gaussian fit in both the attended and unattended conditions ($p < .05$; median $r^2 = 0.40$). For these neurons, we computed a ratio for the amplitude of the tuning curves for the attended and ignored stimuli. A corresponding ratio was computed for the width of the curves. For the neuron whose responses are illustrated in figure 22.3, the ratio for amplitude was 1.44, and that for tuning width was 1.03. Across the entire V4 population, attention enhanced responses to oriented stimuli (median amplitude ratio 1.24), but there was no systematic effect on tuning width (median width ratio 1.00). The scatterplot reveals no correlation between the effects of attention on the amplitude and width of the orientation tuning curves.

An alternative way to assess the effects of attention on orientation in V4 is to construct population tuning curves. The response functions in figure 22.5 represent the average effect of attention on the responses of individual neurons in that area. These functions include all the responses collected from the 262 neurons tested in V4. The data points from each cell were shifted left or right to align peak responses at 0°. The data points (and the level of spontaneous activity) were then scaled vertically to bring the peak to 1.0, while the level of 0.0 spikes/s was not moved. Firing rates for each orientation and behavioral state were then averaged across all neurons. The solid curves in figure 22.5 are Gaussian functions that were fitted to the averaged data. The dashed line is the average spontaneous activity. These population tuning curves differ in amplitude by a factor of 1.31, but their widths are the same ($\sigma = 38°$ in both conditions).

MULTIPLICATIVE SCALING OF ORIENTATION TUNING CURVES   These results suggest that attention increases the amplitude of orientation tuning curves without systematically changing their width. A question that remains is whether the effect of attention is a multiplicative scaling, such that responses to all orientations are increased proportionately. The amplitude change described above

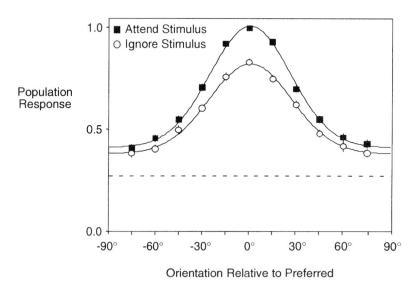

FIGURE 22.5 Population orientation tuning curves for V4. Responses from all 262 V4 neurons are summarized in these curves. They were constructed by shifting each neuron's tuning curves left or right to bring the preferred orientation to 0°, and vertically to bring the peak of the attended orientation tun- ing curve to 1.0. Values at each point were then averaged. The curves represent the average effects of attention on orientation tuning within V4. Attention increased the amplitude of the average orientation tuning curve by about 35%, but did not affect the width of orientation tuning (0%).

does not address this issue because the amplitude could increase even if there were no change in the response to the least preferred orientations.

We can assess whether attention causes a proportional increase in responses to all orientations by plotting responses from the condition where the animal was attending to the stimulus against responses when the animal was ignoring the stimulus. If attention increases all responses proportionately, the points should lie on a straight line whose slope gives the proportional change. Figure 22.6 is such a plot. It replots the data from figure 22.5. Each point represents responses to a particular orientation (relative to preferred orientation), with the normalized response to the attended stimulus on the vertical axis and the normalized response to the ignored stimulus on the horizontal axis. The dashed lines are at ±1 standard error of the mean of spontaneous activity in the two conditions.

The correlation coefficient for these data is 1.00 (0.99 confidence interval: 0.99–1.00). This excellent correlation supports the idea that the effect of attention is a multiplicative scaling of responses. A least-squares regression of the response in the attended condition on the response in the ignored condition gives a line with a slope of 1.31, corresponding to a 31% increase in neural responses when the animal attended to the stimuli in the receptive field. If attention acts by multiplicative scaling of responses, then no-response in one condition should correspond to no-response in the other. The regression line shows that this is the case: It passes through the region representing spontaneous activity in both conditions.

THE MAGNITUDE OF ATTENTION EFFECTS   Although some individual neurons were greatly affected by attention, for most the changes in tuning curve amplitude were modest (figure 22.4). Nevertheless, the modulations reported here should not be taken as an absolute indication of the strength of attentional modulations in V4. Measures of human performance show that the processing of irrelevant stimuli can proceed automatically, suffering only when attentional demands are great (Rees, Frith, and Lavie, 1997). Neurophysiological experiments that have varied the difficulty of tasks suggest that the effects of attention covary with difficulty (Spitzer, Desimone, and Moran, 1988; Spitzer and Richmond, 1991). The performance of our animals suggests that they were not greatly challenged by the task they performed (80–90% correct responses). They may therefore have directed some attention to both stimulus locations at all times, only varying the proportion allocated to each site when different locations were cued. This possibility could be addressed in experiments that manipulate attentional load and include more challenging conditions.

The relationship between sensory and attentional signals in visual cortex

CHANGES IN ATTENTION RESEMBLE CHANGES IN STIMULUS PROPERTIES   Our results suggest that attention acts to selectively strengthen the responses of cortical neurons that convey behaviorally relevant sensory signals without changing their stimulus selectivity. A multiplicative scaling of tuning curves by attention is in-

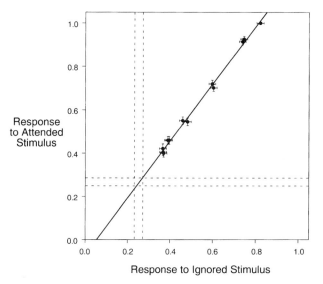

FIGURE 22.6 Multiplicative scaling of responses by attention. This scatterplot replots the data in figure 22.5. Each point represents the population average response to a particular orientation (relative to preferred orientation, ±1 standard error of the mean), with the response to attended stimuli on the vertical axis and the response to ignored stimuli on the horizontal axis. The dashed lines are ±1 standard error of the mean for spontaneous activity in each condition. As predicted by multiplicative scaling, responses are highly correlated (correlation coefficient 1.00). The line through the data is a least-squares regression of the attended response on the ignored response. This line has a slope of 1.31. As expected for multiplicative scaling of responses, this line passes through the region representing spontaneous activity in both conditions.

teresting because it resembles the effects of manipulating stimulus qualities. For example, orientation-selective cells generally respond more strongly to brighter stimuli, and orientation tuning curves derived using stimuli of different brightnesses are multiplicatively scaled versions of each other. It is commonly observed that when a neuron is sensitive to two stimulus attributes, manipulating one attribute will multiplicatively scale the tuning curve for the other without changing the steepness of the tuning function. This has been found for many pairwise manipulations: contrast and orientation or direction, contrast and spatial frequency, contrast and temporal frequency, contrast and spatial position, orientation and direction, speed and direction, and spatial frequency and temporal frequency (Ikeda and Wright, 1972; Tolhurst and Movshon, 1975; Dean, 1980, 1981; Holub and Morton-Gibson, 1981; Albrecht and Hamilton, 1982; Sclar and Freeman, 1982; Bisti et al., 1985; Foster et al., 1985; Rodman and Albright, 1987; Skottun et al., 1987; Galli et al., 1988; Hamilton, Albrecht, and Geisler, 1989; Friend and Baker, 1993; Carandini and Heeger, 1994; McLean and Palmer, 1994a, b; Geisler and Albrecht, 1997).

Our results suggest that the interactions between sensory signals and those related to attention may also be multiplicative. Other types of extraretinal inputs to visual cortex also lead to multiplicative scaling of sensory responses: Signals related to the angle of gaze appear to scale receptive field profiles of neurons in posterior parietal cortex (Andersen, Essick, and Siegel, 1985). Thus, it is possible that multiplicative scaling is the normal mode of interaction between all inputs to visual cortex, whether retinal or extraretinal. Mechanisms that would produce multiplicative scalings of response functions have been described (Albrecht and Geisler, 1991; Carandini and Heeger, 1994), and advantages of this property have been discussed (e.g., Pouget and Sejnowski, 1997; Salinas and Abbott, 1997). It is nevertheless fair to say that we lack a good understanding of the significance of this arrangement for processing of information in cerebral cortex.

The phenomenological similarity between the effects of attention and those of sensory signals raises the possibility that attentional inputs to cortex involve neural mechanisms (e.g., circuits, cell types, neurotransmitters) that are similar, perhaps identical, to those used in processing ascending signals from the retinas. For example, neurons in V4 might receive ascending inputs from earlier stages of visual cortex, which convey information about retinal stimulation (contrast, color, orientation, etc.), and descending signals from higher centers, perhaps prefrontal cortex, which convey information about behavioral state (e.g., whether the region within the neuron's receptive field is behaviorally relevant). The origins of these signals would be unknown and irrelevant to the recipient V4 neurons, which would treat all the inputs equivalently in generating their response.

EXCEPTIONS TO MULTIPLICATIVE SCALING   Some neurons respond best to different temporal frequencies when tested at different spatial frequencies (Ikeda and Wright, 1972; Foster et al., 1985; Friend and Baker, 1993). Such changes in the preferred stimulus are not consistent with multiplicative scaling of responses. Similarly, shifting the locus of spatial attention within or around a receptive field changes the receptive field profile (i.e., tuning in spatial coordinates; see Moran and Desimone, 1985; Connor et al., 1996, 1997). Shifts in the receptive field profile are also inconsistent with multiplicative scaling.

It is possible that multiplicative scaling is the norm for cortex and that exceptions such as these represent unavoidable consequences of the generation of new response properties. For example, an interdependence between spatial frequency and temporal frequency preferences would be expected for neurons that preferred a particular speed of motion. If a neuron's best response always occurred at a particular speed, then tests with drifting sinusoidal gratings would yield an optimum temporal frequency that was higher for high spatial frequencies and lower for low spatial frequencies. Such neurons may nevertheless show multiplicative scaling when speed tuning is examined. For example, speed-selective neurons in the middle temporal visual area (MT) do show multiplicative scaling for tuning curves for speed when direction of motion is varied (Rodman and Albright, 1987).

Changes in receptive field profiles associated with local shifts in spatial attention might similarly arise as an unavoidable consequence of the trend toward larger receptive fields in later stages of visual cortex (see Maunsell and Newsome, 1987). The large receptive fields in V4 are constructed by summing signals from neurons in earlier cortical stages, which have smaller receptive fields (figure 22.7A). If attention to a restricted locus within a V4 receptive field causes a multiplicative scaling of the responses of selected neurons in earlier cortical stages, the limited distribution of attentional effects among the neurons contributing to the V4 cell would shift its receptive field center (figure 22.7B). Because receptive fields grow larger at successive levels of cortical processing, spatially selective attention would be expected to shift receptive field profiles in cortical stages beyond a site where it has its direct effect. A phenomenon of this sort could account for the effects observed by Moran and Desimone in V4 and inferotemporal cortex (1985), which they described as the receptive field contracting around the stimulus the animal was attending to. If attention acted at earlier levels to increase the gain of neurons representing one portion of a V4 receptive field while decreasing the gain of neurons representing another portion, the V4 receptive field could shift or contract.

Receptive field profiles may be special in this regard. Most other response properties have not been found to sharpen or broaden greatly in ascending the cortical hierarchy. If a V4 neuron receives inputs from two neurons with slightly offset receptive fields but the same orientation tuning (figure 22.7C), then selective enhancement of the responses of one of the input neurons would cause the orientation tuning curve of the V4 neuron to increase in amplitude but not in width (figure 22.7D).

Concluding comments

More data are needed before we understand the significance and scope of multiplicative scaling of sensory and behavioral signals in visual cerebral cortex. The current

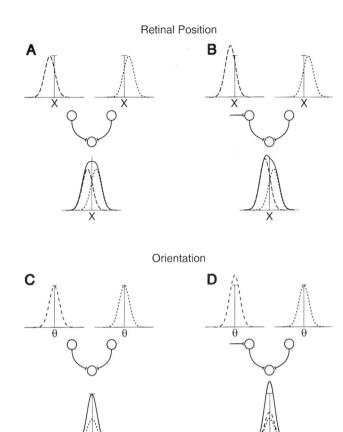

FIGURE 22.7 Different consequences of multiplicative scaling of tuning curves by attention. If attention acts only by multiplicative scaling of responses, it can nevertheless lead to changes in response properties that are not multiplicative scalings. This figure illustrates a hypothetical situation in which inputs from two neurons converge on a third. (A) Two neurons with slightly offset receptive fields converge on a third, which consequently has a receptive field (solid line) that is the sum of the receptive fields of the two input neurons (dashed and dotted lines). (B) If spatially selective attention acts to multiplicatively scale the responses of only one of the input neurons (dashed lines), the response profile of the third neuron (solid line) changes shape, such that the site of greatest sensitivity is offset. (C and D) No change in the response profile of the recipient neuron occurs if the input neurons share a common tuning curve, as might occur for orientation and other stimulus dimensions. If attention acts selectively on either of the input neurons, the third neuron will respond more strongly, but without a shift in its response profile.

experiments have examined just one stimulus attribute in one visual area using one behavioral task. It will be important to learn whether multiplicative scaling of responses by attention occurs for other stimulus attributes, cortical areas, and tasks. If attention does act primarily through scaling of response functions, it would suggest a simple accounting for the behavioral advantages conferred by attention. Attention may alter the cortical representation of the visual scene in a way that is equivalent to increasing the contrast of those stimuli that currently have behavioral relevance. Whether the goal is detection or discrimination, behavioral performance should profit from this manipulation.

ACKNOWLEDGMENTS We thank Erik Cook, Ruth Anne Eatock, and Geoff Ghose for comments on preliminary versions of this chapter. The data for figure 22.1 were provided by Stefan Treue. This work was supported by grants R01 EY05911, T32 EY07001, T32 GM07330, and T32 GM08507 from the National Institutes of Health. JHRM is an investigator with the Howard Hughes Medical Institute.

REFERENCES

ALBRECHT, D. G., and W. S. GEISLER, 1991. Motion selectivity and the contrast-response function of simple cells in the visual cortex. *Vis. Neurosci.* 7:531–546.

ALBRECHT, D. G., and D. B. HAMILTON, 1982. Striate cortex of monkey and cat: Contrast response function. *J. Neurophysiol.* 48:217–237.

ANDERSEN, R. A., G. K. ESSICK, and R. SIEGEL, 1985. The encoding of spatial location by posterior parietal neurons. *Science* 230:456–458.

BISTI, S., G. CARMIGNOTO, L. GALLI, and L. MAFFEI, 1985. Spatial-frequency characteristics of neurones of area 18 in the cat: Dependence on the velocity of the visual stimulus. *J. Physiol. (Lond.)* 359:259–268.

CARANDINI, M., and D. J. HEEGER, 1994. Summation and division by neurons in primate visual cortex. *Science* 264:1333–1336.

COLBY, C. L., 1991. The neuroanatomy and neurophysiology of attention. *J. Child Neurol.* 6:S90–S118.

COLBY, C., J. R. DUHAMEL, and M. E. GOLDBERG, 1993. The analysis of visual space by the lateral intraparietal area of the monkey: The role of extraretinal signals. *Prog. Brain Res.* 95:307–316.

CONNOR, C. E., J. L. GALLANT, D. C. PREDDIE, and D. C. VAN ESSEN, 1996. Responses in area V4 depend on the spatial relationship between stimulus and attention. *J. Neurophysiol.* 75:1306–1308.

CONNOR, C. E., D. C. PREDDIE, J. L. GALLANT, and D. C. VAN ESSEN, 1997. Spatial attention effects in macaque area V4. *J. Neurosci.* 17:3201–3214.

DEAN, A. F., 1980. The contrast-dependence of direction-selectivity. *J. Physiol. (Lond.)* 303:38P–39P.

DEAN, A. F., 1981. The variability of discharge of simple cells in the cat striate cortex. *Exp. Brain Res.* 44:437–440.

DESIMONE, R., and J. DUNCAN, 1995. Neural mechanisms of selective visual attention. *Annu. Rev. Neurosci.* 18:193–222.

DUNCAN, J., 1984. Selective attention and the organization of visual information. *J. Exp. Psychol. Gen.* 113:501–517.

EGETH, H. E., and S. YANTIS, 1997. Visual Attention: Control, representation, and time course. *Annu. Rev. Psych.* 48:269–297.

FOSTER, K. H., J. P. GASKA, M. NAGLER, and D. A. POLLEN, 1985. Spatial and temporal frequency selectivity of neurones in visual cortical areas V1 and V2 of the macaque monkey. *J. Physiol. (Lond.)* 365:331–363.

FRIEND, S. M., and C. L. BAKER, JR., 1993. Spatio-temporal frequency separability in area 18 neurons of the cat. *Vision Res.* 33:1765–1771.

GALLI, L., L. CHALUPA, L. MAFFEI, and S. BISTI, 1988. The organization of receptive fields in area 18 neurones of the cat varies with the spatio-temporal characteristics of the visual stimulus. *Exp. Brain Res.* 71:1–7.

GEISLER, W. S., and D. G. ALBRECHT, 1997. Visual cortex neurons in monkeys and cats: Detection, discrimination and identification. *Vis. Neurosci.* 14:897–919.

HAENNY, P. E., J. H. R. MAUNSELL, and P. H. SCHILLER, 1988. State dependent activity in monkey visual cortex. II. Extraretinal factors in V4. *Exp. Brain Res.* 69:245–259.

HAENNY, P. E., and P. H. SCHILLER, 1988. State dependent activity in monkey visual cortex. I. Single cell activity in V1 and V4 on visual tasks. *Exp. Brain Res.* 69:225–244.

HAMILTON, D. B., D. G. ALBRECHT, and W. S. GEISLER, 1989. Visual cortical receptive fields in monkey and cat: Spatial and temporal phase transfer function. *Vision Res.* 20:1285–1308.

HIKOSAKA, O., S. MIYAUCHI, and S. SHIMOJO, 1993. Visual attention revealed by an illusion of motion. *Neurosci. Res.* 18:11–18.

HOLUB, R. A., and M. MORTON-GIBSON, 1981. Response of visual cortical neurons of the cat to moving sinusoidal gratings: Response-contrast functions and spatiotemporal interactions. *J. Neurophysiol.* 46:1244–1259.

HUBEL, D. H., C. O. HENSON, A. RUBERT, and R. GALAMBOS, 1959. "Attention" units in the auditory cortex. *Science* 129:1279–1280.

IKEDA, H., and M. J. WRIGHT, 1972. Receptive field organisation of 'sustained' and 'transient' retinal ganglion cells which subserve different functional roles. *J. Physiol. (Lond.)* 227:769–800.

LUCK, S. J., L. CHELAZZI, S. A. HILLYARD, and R. DESIMONE, 1997. Neural mechanisms of spatial selective attention in areas V1, V2, and V4 of macaque visual cortex. *J. Neurophysiol.* 77:24–42.

MAUNSELL, J. H. R., 1995. The brain's visual world: Representations of visual targets in cerebral cortex. *Science* 270:764–769.

MAUNSELL, J. H. R., and W. T. NEWSOME, 1987. Visual processing in monkey extrastriate cortex. *Annu. Rev. Neurosci.* 10:363–401.

MAUNSELL, J. H. R., G. SCLAR, T. A. NEALEY, and D. D. DEPRIEST, 1991. Extraretinal representations in area V4 in the macaque monkey. *J. Neurosci.* 7:561–573.

MCLEAN, J., and L. A. PALMER, 1994a. Contribution of linear mechanisms to the specification of local motion by simple cells in areas 17 and 19 of the cat. *Vis. Neurosci.* 11:271–294.

MCLEAN, J., and L. A. PALMER, 1994b. Organization of simple cell responses in the three-dimensional (3-D) frequency domain. *Vis. Neurosci.* 11:295–306.

MORAN, J., and R. DESIMONE, 1985. Selective attention gates visual processing in the extrastriate cortex. *Science* 229:782–784.

MOTTER, B. C., 1993. Focal attention produces spatially selective processing in visual cortical areas V1, V2, and V4 in the presence of competing stimuli. *J. Neurophysiol.* 70:909–919.

MOTTER, B. C., 1994a. Neural correlates of attentive selection for color or luminance in extrastriate area V4. *J. Neurosci.* 14:2178–2189.

MOTTER, B. C., 1994b. Neural correlates of feature selective memory and pop-out in extrastriate area V4. *J. Neurosci.* 14:2190–2199.

POUGET, A., and T. SEJNOWSKI, 1997. Spatial transformations in the parietal cortex using basis function. *J. Cogn. Neurosci.* 9:222–237.

REES, G., C. D. FRITH, and N. LAVIE, 1997. Modulating irrelevant motion perception by varying attentional load in an unrelated task. *Science* 278:1616–1619.

RENSINK, R. A., J. K. O'REGAN, and J. J. CLARK, 1997. To see or not to see: The need for attention to perceive changes in scenes. *Psychol. Sci.* 8:368–373.

RODMAN, H. R., and T. D. ALBRIGHT, 1987. Coding of visual stimulus velocity in area MT of the macaque. *Vision Res.* 27:2035–2048.

SALINAS, E., and L. F. ABBOTT, 1997. Invariant visual responses from attentional gain fields. *J. Neurophysiol.* 77:3267–3272.

SCLAR, G., and R. D. FREEMAN, 1982. Orientation selectivity in the cat's striate cortex is invariant with stimulus contrast. *Exp. Brain Res.* 46:457–461.

SIMONS, D. J., and D. T. LEVIN, 1997. Change blindness. *Trends Cogn. Sci.* 1:261–268.

SKOTTUN, B. C., A. BRADLEY, G. SCLAR, I. OHZAWA, and R. D. FREEMAN, 1987. The effects of contrast on visual orientation and spatial frequency discrimination: A comparison of single cells and behavior. *J. Neurophysiol.* 57: 773–786.

SPITZER, H., R. DESIMONE, and J. MORAN, 1988. Increased attention enhances both behavioral and neuronal performance. *Science* 240:338–340.

SPITZER, H., and B. J. RICHMOND, 1991. Task difficulty: Ignoring, attending to, and discriminating a visual stimulus yield progressively more activity in inferior temporal neurons. *Exp. Brain Res.* 83:340–348.

TOLHURST, D. J., and J. A. MOVSHON, 1975. Spatial and temporal contrast sensitivity of striate cortical neurons. *Nature* 257:674–675.

TREUE, S., and J. H. R. MAUNSELL, 1996. Attentional modulation of visual motion processing in cortical areas MT and MST. *Nature* 382:539–541.

23 Response Synchronization: A Universal Coding Strategy for the Definition of Relations

WOLF SINGER

ABSTRACT   It is proposed that the mammalian brain uses two complementary strategies for the representation of contents. First, items that are frequent, of low complexity, or of great behavioral relevance are represented by cells with specific response properties that acquire their selectivity through recombination of inputs in hierarchically organized feedforward architectures. Second, items that are infrequent, novel, of high complexity, or too diverse to be represented by individual neurons are encoded by dynamically associated assemblies of feature-tuned cells. Based on theoretical arguments and experimental findings, it is suggested that these assemblies are formed by rapid and transient synchronization of the responses of the associated neurons, coincident firing serving as the required signature of relatedness. It is concluded that this coding strategy is fully compatible both with the precision with which cortical networks handle temporally patterned activity and with the significance that nervous systems attribute to synchronized activity in the context of perception and learning. Thus, labeled line codes and assembly codes are complementary strategies, and so are rate codes and temporal codes.

Due to evolutionary selection, highly developed brains tend to employ optimized strategies for encoding and representing relevant environmental variables. However, because constraints often conflict, the implemented solutions are bound to be compromises. Optimal strategies differ for temporal and nontemporal features, processing speed is the rival of coding precision and flexibility, and all solutions are constrained both by the biophysical properties of neurons and the need to economize on neuron numbers. In this chapter we posit a coding strategy that exploits temporal synchrony of responses that defines relations among the responses of distributed neurons. As this coding strategy is essentially constrained by the precision with which neuronal networks can handle temporal patterns, we begin with the question of how well cortical networks can handle temporal patterns, then ask whether these can be used to

convey information in addition to that encoded in the amplitude of responses.

Temporal constraints

PRECISION   Evidence indicates that neuronal networks can encode, transmit, and evaluate the temporal structure of stimuli with astounding precision. The highest degree of temporal resolution is probably reached in the specialized circuits of the auditory system, which exploit latency differences in the submillisecond range for sound localization (for review see Carr, 1993, and Middlebrooks, chapter 30 of this volume). Although signal transduction in the retina is slower than in the ear, the visual system, too, is capable of resolving temporal patterns with a precision in the millisecond range. Thus, timing differences in the millisecond range suffice for the identification of depth cues in rapidly moving patterns (Morgan and Castet, 1995), and stimulus onset asynchronies of <10 ms are readily exploited for perceptual grouping (Leonards, Singer, and Fahle, 1996). The visual system binds simultaneously appearing pattern elements and segregates them from elements presented with temporal offset (Leonards, Singer, and Fahle, 1996; Leonards and Singer, 1998; Alais, Blake, and Lee, 1998; Usher and Donnelly, 1998; but see Kiper, Gegenfurtner, and Movshon, 1996). Interestingly, the small latency differences that support sound localization or figure–ground segregation are not perceivable as temporal cues. There is thus a dissociation between the perceptibility of temporal stimulus features and their effect on early sensory processes.

Electrophysiological evidence confirms the ability of neuronal networks to transmit temporally modulated responses with a precision in the millisecond range over several processing stages. In the auditory cortex of owl monkeys species-specific calls evoke responses whose temporal modulation is so precise that intertrial variability of responses to the same call remains in the range of

WOLF SINGER   Department of Neurophysiology, Max Planck Institute for Brain Research, Frankfurt, Germany

325

a few milliseconds (DeCharms and Merzenich, 1996). The visual system appears to operate with comparable precision. Cross-correlations between simultaneously recorded responses of retinal ganglion cells, relay neurons in the lateral geniculate, and cortical cells show that the oscillatory patterning of retinal responses is reliably transmitted to the cortex (Castelo-Branco, Neuenschwander, and Singer, 1998). Given the high frequency of the retinal oscillations (up to 100 Hz), this implies that the timing of discharges can be transmitted over several synaptic stages with a resolution in the millisecond range, at least when the discharges in parallel channels are precisely synchronized. The well synchronized cortical responses to flicker stimuli point in the same direction (Rager and Singer, 1998). This temporal fidelity of synaptic transmission is not confined to primary sensory pathways but holds, as well, for intracortical interactions. Cortical neurons can engage in oscillatory firing patterns in the γ-frequency range and synchronize their responses with millisecond precision over surprisingly large distances. Thus, cortical networks can handle temporally structured activity with low temporal dispersion (Engel et al., 1992, 1997; Singer and Gray, 1995; König, Engel, and Singer, 1996; see also Buracas et al., 1998, for the monkey).

These studies suggest several important conclusions. First, information about the temporal variables of stimuli can be encoded and transmitted over several processing stages with a precision in the millisecond range and, in specialized systems, in the submillisecond range. Second, there is a mechanism capable of evaluating the temporal covariation of responses—i.e., the degree of their synchronicity—with a resolution that exceeds the temporal resolution of conscious perception. Third, the mechanism that exploits temporal covariation of responses for perceptual grouping interprets simultaneous—i.e., synchronized—responses as related and segregates them from responses that follow a different time course.

Simulation studies indicate that such precision is readily obtained with neurons that operate within conventional time constants if transmission occurs in reciprocally coupled parallel channels—i.e., if a population coding strategy is used (Diesmann, Gewaltig, and Aertsen, 1996). In this case, neurons at the same processing level synchronize their discharges, whereupon these highly coherent pulse packets are conveyed with minimal dispersion across several synaptic stages, as postulated for synfire chains (Abeles, 1991). Population coding also compensates for low discharge rates and fluctuations in firing probability. As indicated in figure 23.1, precise timing information can be encoded in population responses without requiring drastic rate variations in individual

neurons if discharges in parallel channels are synchronized with sufficient precision and if the responses of the whole population are evaluated conjointly. Thus, when temporal patterns need to be transmitted with high precision, population coding is required and information about temporal variables is contained in the relative timing of spikes in parallel channels.

PROCESSING SPEED   Another constraint assigning importance to the timing of discharges in distributed population responses is processing speed. Estimates based on reaction times, evoked potentials, and latencies of single-cell responses suggest that patterns of average complexity can be recognized within less than 100 ms. This leaves only a few tens of milliseconds per processing stage to perform the computations necessary for the selection and grouping of responses (Rolls and Tovee, 1994; Thorpe, Fize, and Marlot, 1996). If discharge rates vary between 0 and 100 Hz and interspike intervals follow a Poisson distribution, a neuron can emit maximally 3–4 spikes on average within the interval of interest, plus a few more spikes if it is bursting. Hence, the dynamic range exploitable for the transmission of rate-coded information about nontemporal stimulus features is very narrow. As proposed by Shadlen and Newsome (1998), this problem can also be overcome by population coding. However, if processing times are indeed in the range of tens of milliseconds, the population vectors need to be defined and read out at comparable time scales; thus it matters when, exactly, a cell participating in the population emits the few spikes that it can contribute within the available time window.

RATE CODING VERSUS TEMPORAL CODING   Considerable disagreement attends the question of rate coding versus temporal coding. That is, do neurons in the central nervous system encode information solely by varying their discharge rate (Shadlen and Newsome, 1994, 1998) or do the temporal relations between the discharges in a population of neurons contain additional information (Softky and Koch, 1993; König, Engel, and Singer, 1996; Softky, 1995; Mainen and Sejnowski, 1995; Stevens and Zador, 1998; Buracas et al., 1998)? The arguments above suggest that this may be an ill-posed question because rate and temporal codes are complementary and convey information at different time scales. If a population of neurons is to signal the temporal features of a stimulus with a precision in the millisecond range, or if information about nontemporal features has to be encoded within short processing intervals, the amplitude of the population response must be modulated with time constants in the range of milliseconds. It must matter, then, when exactly and in which temporal relation the units comprising a

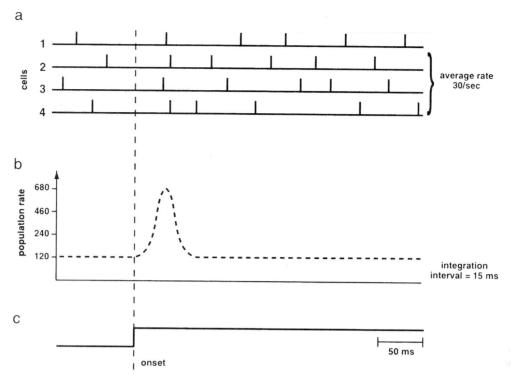

FIGURE 23.1   Signaling of precise timing by population coding and spike synchronization. The precise onset of a stimulus is signaled by a transient increase of spike density in the summed response of the population of four neurons (dotted line) without a noticeable rate change of the individual responses (traces 1–4). This is achieved by synchronization of the first spikes following stimulus onset. In this case, synchronization is assumed to result from stimulus locking, i.e., from a transient increase in firing probability that occurs simultaneously in all four channels. The four neurons discharge with an average rate of 30 per second and the interval over which the population response is summed is assumed to be on the order of 15 ms.

population emit their action potentials because temporal dispersion of input or output spikes would change both the time course and the amplitude of the population response. However, once precise timing of discharges in a population response starts to matter, a fundamental criterion for rate codes is violated. Most, if not all, rate-coding concepts assume that the precise timing of spikes in a discharge sequence is irrelevant and that the frequency of spikes is the only significant parameter. The distinction between the two coding regimes becomes particularly problematic in the case of population coding. Here, the number of spikes in a time slice across the population response can be changed in two complementary ways—either by modulating discharge frequency of individual cells or by shifting the timing of spikes without altering average discharge rate. (A mechanism permitting the shifting of spikes is discussed below.) Thus, if a population of neurons is to transmit precise temporal information and/or to accomplish computations within a few tens of milliseconds, it is bound to operate in a regime where the relative timing of discharges *is* crucial. Why? Because computational results will be affected at least as much by temporal regrouping of discharges as by changing average rates. It

follows that, in population coding, information can, in principle, be encoded both by varying discharge rates and by changing the timing of individual spikes.

At all levels of sensory processing, there is a recurring need to define relations among the responses of simultaneously active neurons with high temporal resolution. We therefore propose that these binding functions are realized by temporal coordination of the discharges of distributed neuronal populations. According to Hebb (1949), such relations can be defined by a coordinated increase of the discharge rate of the selected neurons. This raises the saliency of the responses jointly and ensures that they are processed together at the next stage. Joint enhancement of the saliency of responses is thus equivalent to defining relations and binding selected responses for further joint processing. However, if such binding has to be accomplished rapidly and with high temporal resolution, the coherent rate fluctuations need to be so short that they cannot be adequately described in terms of rate changes. The reason for this is twofold. First, the patterns of coherent rate fluctuations—i.e., the binding patterns—can be changed without altering the average discharge rate of the involved neurons by regrouping of discharges.

Second, a definition of rates becomes meaningless if the intervals over which coherence is defined are shorter than the mean interspike intervals. We therefore advocate the hypothesis that the nervous system exploits the option to synchronize discharges in order to define relations among the responses of distributed neurons and to accomplish binding. Synchronizing the occurrence of spikes emitted by a population of neurons also raises the saliency of responses because coincident inputs drive the population of target cells at the next processing stage more effectively than temporally dispersed inputs (Alonso, Usrey, and Reid, 1996; Stevens and Zador, 1998). Thus, synchronization defines relations among distributed responses and assures binding in the same way that joint rate increases do, but does so with much higher temporal resolution.

Two Complementary Strategies for the Representation of Relations: Smart Neurons and Assemblies   A major challenge for cognitive systems is the combinatorial complexity of the relations that need to be analyzed and represented. In the context of cognitive functions, combinatorial problems arise from the fact that perceptual objects consist of unique, often highly complex constellations of features that, in turn, represent specific relations among elementary sensory signals. Although the variety of basic feature dimensions that nervous systems exploit to classify perceptual objects is limited, the diversity of possible constellations is, for all practical purposes, unlimited. Thus, cognitive systems have to explore a huge combinatorial space when searching for the consistent relations among features that define a perceptual object. Combinatorial problems of similar nature have to be solved for the programming and execution of movements. Although the elementary components of motor acts—the movements of individual muscle fibers—are limited in number, the diversity of movements that can be composed by combining the elementary components in ever-changing constellations is, again, virtually infinite.

Encoding features and their constellations is the equivalent of encoding relations. One way to accomplish this is the recombination of signals via selective convergence of input connections in hierarchically structured feedforward architectures. In the primary visual cortex of mammals, for example, relations among the responses of collinearly aligned retinal ganglion cells are represented by having the output of these ganglion cells converge onto individual cortical neurons (Hubel and Wiesel, 1962; Chapman, Zahs, and Stryker, 1991; Jagadeesh, Wheat, and Ferster, 1993; Reid and Alonso, 1995). In this way, the feature "orientation" is extracted and represented. Iteration of this strategy in prestriate

cortical areas leads to increasingly smart neurons that encode more and more complex relations (Tanaka et al., 1991), including those characteristic for such real-world objects as faces (Gross, 1992). This strategy of representing features and their constellations by the tuned responses of individual cells (labeled line coding) is rapid and reliable because it can be realized by simple feedforward processing. However, if used as the only representational strategy, it requires astronomical numbers of neurons in order to cope with the virtually infinite diversity of possible feature conjunctions (Sejnowski, 1986; Engel et al., 1992). Moreover, it is not easy to see how such a strategy deals with the representation of novel objects at first encounter. These constraints apply not only for the representation of complex perceptual objects but also for the encoding of such elementary features as the precise position, shape, and orientation of a contour segment. Given the high spatial resolution with which these features can be distinguished, a very large number of neurons would be required if all possible conjunctions of these properties were encoded in a one-to-one relation by sharply tuned neurons.

A complementary strategy is needed—one that permits sharing of neurons for the representation of different contents. One such strategy is population coding, also known as "coarse coding." Neurons are broadly tuned and signal with graded responses variations of features along several dimensions, e.g., orientation, location, and contrast of a contour border. Hence, a particular contour drives a large number of cells with overlapping preferences and the precise configuration of the stimulus can be assessed by interpolation from the population response. This coding strategy is common in sensory cortices, requires simple feedforward architectures, and engenders no decoding problem as long as the populations activated by simultaneously presented stimuli do not overlap too much. However, this strategy permits only representation of those features or feature conjunctions that are explicitly represented by the response properties of the cells comprising the population. A different coding strategy is required for the representation of feature constellations for which no specialized neurons exist. Such a strategy has been advocated by Hebb (1949), who proposed that a specific constellation of features should be represented by a dynamically associated assembly of cells which represents the respective feature conjunctions as a whole. The individual features associated in such assemblies can, in turn, be represented either by sharply tuned cells or, more economically, by population codes. This representational strategy also economizes on neuron numbers: The same cells can be bound successively into different assemblies. However, assembly codes differ from simple population codes in that they are based on active association of neurons into functionally coherent representations. Such active binding is necessary because conjunctions are no longer explicitly coded by the specific response properties of individual cells, but rather are defined by the association of cells into assemblies. Because this requires cooperative interactions among the members of an assembly, assembly codes cannot be implemented in architectures that possess only feedforward connections. Assembly formation requires, in addition, association connections that permit flexible binding of neuronal responses within and across processing levels. The fundamental difference between labeled line or population codes on the one hand and assembly codes on the other becomes particularly clear if one considers the processes required for the acquisition of new representations by learning. In the first case, the weight of feedforward connections must be changed to generate neurons that come to prefer new feature conjunctions. In the second case, the association connections need to be changed to permit preferential association of neurons that represent the new conjunction as an ensemble.

In sum, then, assembly coding requires that: (1) feature-selective neurons bind in variable constellations into different assemblies; (2) the rules of binding correspond to common Gestalt principles; (3) particular perceptual objects always activate the same assembly once learning has taken place and the association connections favoring stabilization of this assembly have been strengthened; and (4) the joint responses of cells comprising an assembly be distinguishable by subsequent processing stages as components of one coherent representation, thereby avoiding confusion with simultaneous responses of cells belonging to other assemblies and preventing the signaling of otherwise unrelated contents.

Numerous theoretical studies have addressed the question of how assemblies can self-organize on the basis of cooperative interactions within associative neuronal networks (for review, see Hebb, 1949; Braitenberg, 1978; Edelman, 1987; Palm, 1990; Gerstein and Gochin, 1992). Such studies have provided solutions compatible with the functional architecture of the cerebral cortex (for review, see Singer, 1995), but a critical question remains: How are the responses of cell assemblies tagged as related? An unambiguous signature of relatedness is crucial for assembly codes because the meaning of responses changes with context. Hence, false conjunctions are deleterious. Unfortunately, the risk of false conjunctions is constitutive in assembly coding: Assembly codes economize on neuron numbers only if the same cells can be bound into different assemblies at different times. Since complex scenes usually consist of spatially overlapping and contiguous objects, situations often arise when the same group of neurons must be recruited simultaneously into different assemblies. As a matter of principle, then, assemblies that share common neurons but describe different objects cannot overlap in time. They have to be generated successively to avoid their merging. Processing speed is thus critically limited by the rate at which different assemblies can be formed and dissolved. At peripheral levels of processing where conjunctions are defined for many different, often spatially contiguous features, the alternation rate between assemblies coding for different conjunctions of features must be considerably faster than the rate at which different objects can be perceived and represented. The reason is that the results of the various grouping operations need to be interpreted jointly by higher processing stages for the evaluation of relations of higher order. Hence, the multiplexed results of low-level grouping must alternate fast enough to permit their association at higher processing stages even though they are transmitted as a sequence.

Similar superposition problems could also arise in population coding. If two contours are close or overlapping, there will always be a set of cells that respond to both contours even if these differ in certain features and ought to be processed. Segregating the respective populations spatially is no solution–it would require more neurons than implementing sharply tuned cells right away. The possibility should be considered, therefore, that under certain conditions population codes, too, might require disambiguation by temporal multiplexing.

THE SIGNATURE OF ASSEMBLIES   The simplest way to define relations among the responses of neurons and to bind them together for joint processing is to raise the saliency of the selected responses, either by joint rate increases or by synchronization or both. And, given the constraints of processing speed, the time constants for the reconfiguration of assemblies should be in the order of tens of milliseconds or less. This implies that the saliency of the selected responses must be defined within intervals of just a few tens of milliseconds, and hence a temporal resolution in which coordination of spike timing is more important than modulation of average discharge rate. Thus, for short-lived assemblies, the appropriate signature of relatedness is the synchronization of discharges with a precision in the millisecond range. As with the signaling of rapid stimulus transients by synchronous population responses, synchronization has an additional effect–transmission of signals is accelerated and the temporal signature of the synchronized responses can be preserved across successive processing stages. This increases processing speed further while preserving the signature of assemblies during subsequent processing. Finally, as indicated in figure 23.2, cells can be bound successively

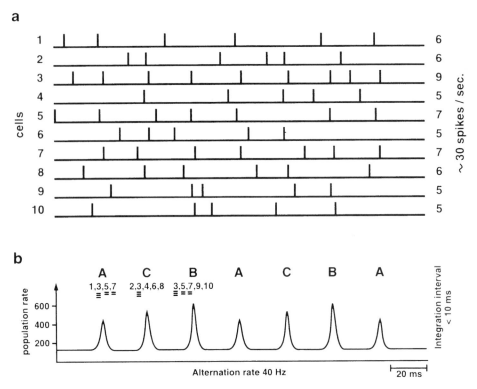

FIGURE 23.2 Disambiguation of temporally overlapping assemblies by synchronization of discharges in selected response segments. Despite the sustained and constant discharge rate (~30 Hz) of the ten depicted cells, the saliency of responses is transiently and repeatedly increased for three different, spatially overlapping assemblies (A, B, C) by synchronization of the discharges of the subpopulations of cells comprising the three assemblies. Note that the individual spike trains appear nonoscillatory while the spike density of the population response fluctuates periodically (lower continuous line). Note also that cells 5 and 7 are shared by two and cell 3 is shared by all three assemblies. Because cell 3 contributes spikes to more assemblies than the others, its discharge frequency is slightly higher. In this case, the different assemblies are interleaved with a rate of 40 Hz and the integration interval for the evaluation of the population response is assumed to be around 10 ms. Faster multiplexing could be achieved by having all assemblies oscillate at 40 Hz and separating them by phase shifts. However, in this case integration time constants would have to be shorter.

into several different assemblies without overt modification of their average discharge rate if their discharges are appropriately grouped in time. This leaves the option to use sustained modifications of average rates in parallel for other functions. Thus, defining relations among distributed responses by synchronization has a number of advantages. It defines relations with high temporal precision, accelerates processing, facilitates transmission of signatures of relatedness across processing stages, and provides the option to use average discharge rate for the encoding of additional information.

Mechanisms for temporal grouping of responses

STIMULUS LOCKING VERSUS INTERNAL PATTERNING In sensory systems, precise synchronization of discharges typically results from the locking of responses to temporally structured stimuli. As discussed, this externally induced synchronicity of discharges is interpreted as a signature of relatedness and supports perceptual grouping. Thus, synchronization of responses, if induced by external stimuli, has exactly the binding function postulated above for the tagging of assemblies. How, then, does the nervous system achieve grouping and segregation of responses when stimuli lack a distinct temporal structure or when the temporal structure of stimuli conflicts with other, nontemporal grouping cues? Does the brain then use an entirely different strategy for the binding of responses, implementing different learning rules, or is there a way to use the synchronization of responses as a signature of relatedness for nontemporal stimulus properties as well?

Consider: (1) The responses of cortical neurons to moving stimuli often exhibit an oscillatory patterning that is not stimulus-locked (Gray and Singer, 1987); (2) these temporally structured discharges can become synchronized for neurons distributed both within (Gray and Singer, 1987, 1989) and across cortical areas (Gray et al., 1989; Engel, König, Kreiter, et al., 1991; Engel, König, and Singer, 1991; Engel, Kreiter, et al., 1991); (3) synchronization probability reflects common Gestalt criteria of perceptual grouping (Gray et al., 1989; Engel,

König, and Singer, 1991; Engel, Kreiter, et al., 1991; Kreiter and Singer, 1992, 1996; Freiwald, Kreiter, and Singer, 1995). In the light of these discoveries, we proposed that the cerebral cortex imposes a temporal microstructure on otherwise sustained responses, using this temporal patterning to express, through synchronization, the degree of relatedness of the responses.

In principle, temporal patterning and synchronization can be achieved in two ways; and, in fact, evidence suggests that both are exploited. First, cells could generate additional, precisely timed spikes as a result of a transient, well synchronized reduction of inhibition or an increase of excitatory drive. Second, spikes that would have occurred anyway could be shifted so that they coincide within the critical window. In the first case, the temporal patterning and synchronization may be associated with a measurable change in discharge rate; in the second case, it is not. In both cases, however, one would measure a transient increase in spike density within the interval where discharges are synchronized if one could record simultaneously from a sufficiently large number of cells and sum across the population. The time of occurrence of synchronized discharges is not locked to any external event when synchronization is caused by internal interactions. Thus, synchronized response segments cannot be detected by compiling histograms from the responses of individual neurons, even if synchronization is achieved by inserting additional spikes and hence is associated with a transient increase in discharge rate. The only way to detect internally generated synchrony is to record simultaneously from more than one unit, then perform correlation analysis.

Studies employing such multicell recordings offer growing evidence that the temporal patterning of responses and their synchronization by internal neuronal interactions are frequent phenomena observable in many cerebral structures (for recent reviews, see Singer and Gray, 1995; Singer et al., 1997). Moreover, these temporal patterns are often seen to have an oscillatory component which is best revealed by recording jointly the activity of several adjacent cells. The better detectability of oscillations in population responses has a twofold explanation. First, individual cells tend to skip oscillation cycles in an irregular manner; second, oscillatory epochs are usually short and oscillation frequencies variable. This suggests that the periodicity of oscillatory population responses is often not apparent in the firing patterns of individual cells, even if their discharges are precisely phase-locked to the oscillatory activity of the population (figure 23.2).

If, like stimulus-locked synchronization, internally generated synchronization is to serve as a signature of relatedness, it must meet several criteria. First, its precision should be in the millisecond range to permit multiplexing of different assemblies at a rate fast enough to be compatible with known processing speed. Second, for the same reason, it must be possible to synchronize responses within a few tens of milliseconds. Third, one should find evidence that synchronized activity is more effective than nonsynchronized activity in driving cells in target structures, because precise synchronization can serve as a tag of relatedness only if it effectively enhances the saliency of the synchronized responses. Fourth, there should be a close correlation between the occurrence of these precise and rapidly changing synchronization patterns on the one hand and perceptual or motor processes on the other.

TEMPORAL CONSTRAINTS   The postulate that internally generated synchronization should be as precise as externally induced synchronization is well supported by cross-correlation data. The widths of the correlation peaks at half-height are typically in the range of <10 ms (for review, see Singer et al., 1997). In particular, when the global EEG is in a desynchronized state, internally generated synchronization is often associated with an oscillatory patterning of the respective responses in the high β- or the γ-frequency range (from 20 to 60 Hz) (Munk et al., 1996; Herculano et al., in press). This reduces the probability of spurious correlations and enhances further the precision with which synchronized responses are distinguished from nonsynchronized responses.

The second postulate that internally generated synchronization must be established very rapidly (within a few tens of milliseconds) has received theoretical and experimental support recently. Simulations with spiking neurons reveal that networks of appropriately coupled units can indeed undergo very rapid transitions from uncorrelated to synchronized states (Hopfield and Hertz, 1995; Deppisch et al., 1993; Bauer and Pawelzik, 1993; Gerstner and Van Hemmen, 1993; Gerstner, 1996; Van Vreeswijk, Abbot, and Ermentrout, 1994). Rapid transitions from independent to synchronized firing are also observed in natural networks (Gray et al., 1992). In visual centers, it is not uncommon that neurons engage in synchronous activity, often with additional oscillatory patterning, at the very same time they increase their discharge rate in response to the light stimulus (Neuenschwander and Singer, 1996; Castelo-Branco, Neuenschwander, and Singer, 1998; Gray et al., 1992).

Recently, combined in vitro and in vivo experiments have suggested a new synchronization mechanism that operates extremely fast and could permit a rapid read-out of the grouping criteria that reside in the functional architecture of cortical connections. This mechanism exploits two properties—first, the ability of oscillating cells to delay their output relative to incoming EPSPs and, second, the oscillatory patterning of ongoing cortical activity.

When the membrane potential of a cell undergoes an oscillatory modulation, EPSPs with an NMDA-receptor–mediated component do not necessarily evoke spikes at the time of occurrence but only when the cell reaches the peak of the next depolarizing cycle. The reason is that NMDA receptors still occupied by glutamate are reactivated by the removal of the voltage-dependent magnesium block (Volgushev, Chistiakova, and Singer, 1998). Thus, responses can be delayed considerably, whereby the maximum delay interval depends on oscillation frequency and can amount to almost the duration of one cycle. With such a mechanism, responses to temporally dispersed EPSPs can be synchronized within less than an oscillation cycle. This option appears to be exploited for the rapid synchronization of responses. Response latencies of cortical neurons fluctuate in the range of about 20 ms for identical, repeatedly presented stimuli; however, recent correlation studies indicate that these fluctuations can be correlated for responses of neurons located in different columns (Fries, Roelfsema, Engel, et al., 1997; Fries, Roelfsema, Singer, et al., 1997). The data suggest that this rapid adjustment of response latencies is due to coherent oscillations of the membrane potential of the respective neurons and hence is, in all likelihood, based on the delay mechanism identified in the slice experiments.

The ongoing fluctuations of cortical activity are not random. Rather–as shown with a different approach by Arieli and colleagues (1996)–they exhibit specific spatiotemporal patterns that are likely to reflect the functional architecture of intracortical connections. These, in turn, are known to preferentially link columns coding for related features that tend to be grouped perceptually (Gilbert and Wiesel, 1989; Ts'o and Gilbert, 1988; Malach et al., 1993; Schmidt et al., 1997). Physiological data suggest that these corticocortical connections contribute to the synchronization of spatially segregated groups of neurons (Engel, König, Kreiter, et al., 1991; Löwel and Singer, 1992; König et al., 1993; Nowak et al., 1995). It is conceivable, then, that the grouping criteria residing in the functional architecture of the intracortical association connections are continuously translated into specific spatiotemporal patterns of membrane potential fluctuations, and these in turn serve the rapid temporal coordination of responses to incoming sensory signals. If the pattern of these fluctuations is also modified by top-down influences from higher cortical areas and by immediately preceding changes of sensory input, these dynamic patterns would be equivalent with the system's updated expectancy against which incoming activity is matched. One of the effects of matching these predic-

tions with incoming signals is a rapid temporal regrouping of output activity (figure 23.3).

Obviously, the grouping of responses by internal adjustment of temporal patterns should not override grouping by stimulus-locking to preserve temporal grouping cues inherent in dynamic scenes. As discussed elsewhere, a solution to this problem is parallel processing of signals about temporal and nontemporal stimulus features (Leonards and Singer, 1997, 1998). In this case, responses signaling the precise temporal structure of stimuli could be exempted from latency adjustments while responses signaling nontemporal features could be subject to internal temporal patterning. This scenario is supported by psychophysical evidence. Experiments on texture segregation suggest, first, that the grouping mechanism exploiting the temporal signature of stimuli relies mainly on the transient responses of the magnocellular system (Leonards and Singer, 1998) and, second, that these temporally precise signals are used to make inferences on the temporal structure of stimuli activating preferentially the parvocellular pathways (Leonards and Singer, 1997). Third, these experiments suggest that the grouping mechanisms relying on external timing and internal patterning, respectively, cooperate synergistically if both temporal and nontemporal cues define the same figure while they compete with one another, provided patterns are presented in which temporal and nontemporal features define different, spatially overlapping figures. Most importantly, however, conflicting temporal cues do not interfere with the binding of nontemporal features if these temporal cues do not define a figure (Leonards, Singer, and Fahle, 1996). Thus, temporal and nontemporal grouping cues appear to be processed in parallel but not independently–a finding consistent with the anatomical organization of the magno- and parvocellular processing streams (for review, see Maunsell, 1995).

RELATIONS BETWEEN RESPONSE SYNCHRONIZATION, COGNITION, AND MOTOR PERFORMANCE   One line of support for a functional role of the oscillatory patterning of responses in the β- and γ-frequency range and for precise synchronization comes from the finding that these phenomena are particularly well expressed when the brain is in an activated state, i.e., when the EEG is desynchronized and exhibits high power in the β- and γ-frequency range (figure 23.4; Munk et al., 1996). Such EEG patterns are characteristic for the aroused and attentive as well as the dreaming brain (see Hobson, 1988) and hence for states in which sensory representations can be activated. Conversely, both the oscillatory patterning of responses in the γ-frequency range (Madler et al., 1991) and the precise synchronization disappear

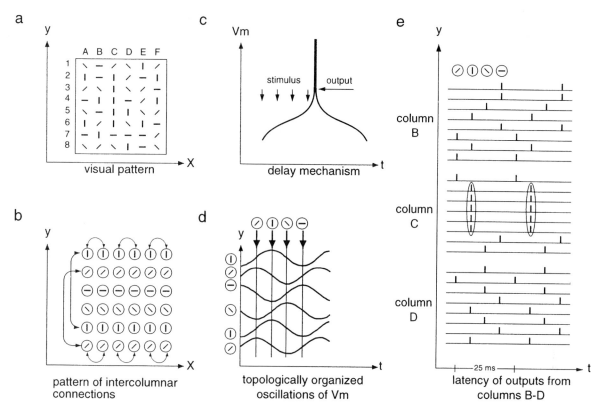

a   visual pattern

c   delay mechanism

b   pattern of intercolumnar
    connections

d   topologically organized
    oscillations of Vm

e   latency of outputs from
    columns B-D

FIGURE 23.3   A putative mechanism for the rapid conversion of perceptual grouping rules into a temporal code. (a) Due to the grouping criterion of collinearity, the vertical bars in column C and the horizontal bars in row 7 are bound together and are perceived as the letter L. (b) In agreement with anatomy it is assumed that cortical columns preferring similar orientations are coupled preferentially. (c) Schematic representation of the mechanism that delays the output of a cell with oscillating membrane potential until the depolarizing peak of the respective next oscillation cycle is reached (horizontal arrow) irrespective of when the EPSPs are generated (vertical arrows). (d) Due to preferential coupling, cells preferring the same orientation are assumed to exhibit coherent oscillations of their membrane potential, but oscillations of cells with different preferences are assumed to be phase-shifted. Thus, cells sharing the same preferences will emit synchronized responses and cells with differing preferences temporally offset responses. (e) Latency distribution of discharges of cells responding to pattern elements in columns B, C, and D of panel a. Latencies correspond to the phase-shifted oscillations of cells preferring different orientations as depicted in d. Note that the cells responding to the collinear bars in column C (panel a) discharge synchronously, which allows for rapid binding of the respective responses.

when anesthesia is deepened and/or if the animal is in slow wave sleep and the EEG exhibits prominent δ activity. In this case, synchronization collapses long before the amplitudes of neuronal responses get attenuated (unpublished observations). Numerous observations, both in animal and human subjects, point in the same direction. For example, synchronous oscillations in the γ-frequency range and their synchronization become more prominent during states of focused attention (Roelfsema et al., 1996; Murthy and Fetz, 1996a,b; De Oliveira, Thiele, and Hoffmann, 1997) or when subjects are engaged in visual discrimination tasks that put strong demands on feature binding or short-term memory functions (Tallon-Baudry et al., 1995, 1996, 1997).

Direct relations between response synchronization and perception have been found in cats who suffered from strabismic amblyopia. Surprisingly, the responses of individual neurons in the cat primary visual cortex fail to reflect the deficits associated with amblyopic vision (see Roelfsema et al., 1994, for references). The only significant correlate of amblyopia was the drastically reduced ability of neurons driven by the amblyopic eye to synchronize their responses. This accounts well for the perceptual disturbances: Impaired synchronization reduces the saliency of responses and therefore can explain the suppression of signals from the amblyopic eye. Moreover, deficiencies in the synchronizing mechanism are bound to impair the disambiguation of population codes, which accounts for the most characteristic disturbances in amblyopia—reduced visual acuity and the crowding phenomenon.

Another close correlation between response synchronization and perception has been found in experiments on binocular rivalry in strabismic animals (Fries,

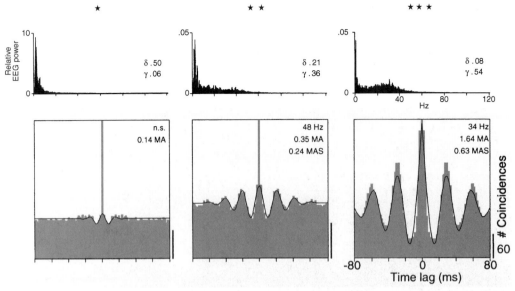

FIGURE 23.4   State dependence of response synchronization. Upper row: Power distribution in the EEG recorded during three episodes from an anesthetized cat. Lower row: Averaged cross-correlograms of multiunit responses evoked by a drifting grating and recorded from two different sites in A17 during corresponding episodes. Note that the synchronization of the responses and the oscillatory modulation in the γ-frequency range increase with increasing γ-activity in the EEG. Inserts in the power spectra give the relative power in the δ- and γ-frequency range. Insets in the cross-correlograms give the oscillation frequency (in hertz), the relative modulation amplitude of the center peak (MA), and of the first side peak (MAS). (From Herculano et al., in press.)

Roelfsema, Engel, et al., 1997). Due to experience-dependent modifications of processing circuitry (Wiesel and Hubel, 1965; Löwel and Singer, 1992), perception in nonamblyopic strabismic subjects always alternates between the two eyes. We have exploited this phenomenon of rivalry to investigate how neuronal responses that are selected and perceived differ from those that are suppressed and excluded from supporting perception (figure 23.5). The outcome of these experiments was surprising. The responses of neurons in areas 17 and 18 were not attenuated during epochs in which they were excluded from controlling eye movements and supporting perception. A close and highly significant correlation existed, however, between changes in the strength of response synchronization and the outcome of rivalry. Cells mediating responses of the eye that won in interocular competition increased the synchronicity of their responses upon presentation of the rivalrous stimulus to the losing eye, while the reverse was true for cells driven by the eye that became suppressed. Thus, selection of responses for further processing appeared to be achieved by modulating the degree of synchronization rather than the amplitude of responses.

These results are direct support for the hypothesis that precise temporal relations between the discharges of spatially distributed neurons matter in cortical processing and that synchronization may be exploited to jointly raise the saliency of the responses selected for further processing. The important point here is that this selec-

tion is apparently achieved without enhancing the average discharge rate of the selected responses or inhibiting the nonselected responses.

The fact that both in amblyopia and binocular rivalry only well synchronized activity supports perception agrees with the notion that well synchronized responses are more salient and have a stronger impact on cells at subsequent processing stages than poorly synchronized responses. Further support comes from a recent multi-electrode study on corticotectal interactions in the cat (Brecht, Singer, and Engel, 1998). Tectal cells get synchronized to responses of cells in visual cortical areas if the respective cell groups are activated by the same contour, suggesting synchronization of tectal responses by corticotectal projections. This synchronizing effect is strongly enhanced when the responses of cortical cells are themselves well synchronized among each other, irrespective of whether the relevant cortical cells are located within a single cortical area or are distributed across different areas, in this case between areas 17, 18, and area PMLS (figure 23.6). This indicates that cortical cells are more effective in driving common tectal target cells when their responses are synchronized than when they fire independently. Again, these changes in functional coupling cannot be explained by rate changes. When neurons synchronize their responses, the discharge rate usually does not increase; rather, average discharge rates either remain unchanged or decrease (Herculano et al., in press).

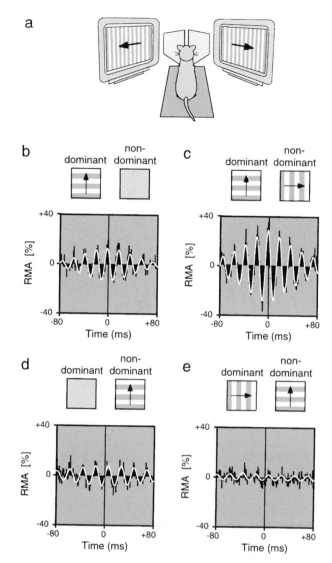

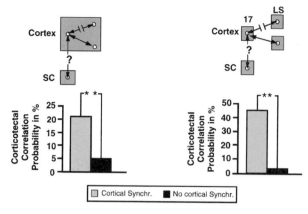

FIGURE 23.6 Dependence of corticotectal synchronization on intracortical synchronization within (left plots) and across (right plots) cortical areas. Left: Percentage of significant corticotectal correlations when cortical cells recorded from two sites in the same cortical area synchronize (shaded column) or do not synchronize (black column) their responses. Right: Percentage of corticotectal interactions between A17 and the tectum when area 17 cells synchronize (shaded column) or do not synchronize (black column) their responses with those of cells in the lateral suprasylvian sulcus. (From Brecht, Singer, and Engel, 1998.)

FIGURE 23.5 Neuronal synchronization under conditions of binocular rivalry. (a) Using two mirrors, different patterns were presented to the two eyes of strabismic cats. (b–e) Normalized cross-correlograms for two pairs of recording sites activated by the eye that won (b and c) and lost (d and e) in interocular competition. Insets above the correlograms indicate stimulation conditions. Under monocular stimulation (b), cells driven by the winning eye show a significant correlation which is enhanced after introduction of the rivalrous stimulus to the other eye (c). The reverse is the case for cells driven by the losing eye (compare conditions d and e). The white continuous line superimposed on the correlograms represents a damped cosine function fitted to the data. The relative modulation amplitude (RMA) of the center peak in the correlogram, is computed as the ratio of peak amplitude over offset of correlogram modulation. This measure reflects the strength of synchrony. (Modified from Fries, Roelfsema, Engel, et al., 1997.)

Further indications for a functional role of precise timing relations between the discharges of distributed neurons have recently been obtained with multielectrode recordings from the motor and prefrontal cortex of monkeys performing a visually cued reaching task. In a study by Riehle and colleagues (1997), the monkeys' anticipation of cued motor responses was deducible from the occurrence of supernumerary coincidences among discharges of neurons in primary motor cortex, while no such inferences could be drawn from rate fluctuations of individual neurons. Other studies (Vaadia et al., 1995; Prut et al., 1998) report a similar relation between a precise temporal coordination of the discharges of simultaneously recorded neurons and cued motor responses in the prefrontal cortex. Finally, Hatsopoulos, Ojakangas, and Donoghue found transient and highly precise synchronization among cells in motor cortex that were related to the direction of motion and the extent to which a particular stimulus–response association had been practiced and learned (Hatsopoulos, Ojakangas, and Donoghue, 1997; Ojakangas, Hatsopoulos, and Donoghue, 1997; Donoghue et al., 1998). Complementary support for a functional role of precise spike timing comes from studies of the insect olfactory system. As in the mammalian olfactory bulb (Freeman and Skarda, 1985), odors evoke oscillatory population responses in the antennal lobes and hence synchronized volleys of spikes in parallel channels. Interestingly, information about the composition of a particular odor is encoded both in the pattern of rate fluctuations in parallel channels and in the distribution of coincident spikes (Macleod and Laurent, 1996; Wehr and Laurent, 1996; Stopfer et al., 1997). When the oscillatory patterning and the resulting synchronization are disrupted by pharmacological manipulations without modification of the spatiotemporal pattern of rate fluctuations, simple, noncomposite odors could still be discriminated while complex, composite odors were confounded (Macleod and Laurent, 1996; Wehr and Laurent, 1996; Stopfer et al., 1997).

Conclusions

Taken together, the data and arguments expounded in this chapter support the notion that neuronal networks are capable of evaluating with a precision in the millisecond range the temporal relations among the discharges of neuronal populations and that they exploit this ability for two purposes: First, for the precise signaling of temporal features across processing stages; and second, for the definition of relations among distributed responses with high temporal resolution. Such a relation defining or binding mechanism is indispensable in ensemble coding because this representational strategy requires flexible and rapid binding of distributed responses in ever-changing constellations. Assembly coding, in turn, appears necessary in order to cope with the representation of the astronomical number of possible relations among features describing real-world objects. It appears, then, as if the cerebral cortex applies two complementary coding strategies: First, an explicit representation of features and their conjunctions in the tuned responses of individual, specialized neurons or populations of such neurons; and second, an implicit representation of conjunctions of such explicitly coded contents in dynamically associated assemblies. The first strategy seems to be applied for the representation of a limited set of features and some of their conjunctions. In all likelihood, this strategy is reserved for items that occur very frequently and/or are of particular behavioral importance, such as faces and expressions. The second strategy seems to be reserved for the representation of all those items for which an explicit representation cannot be realized, either because the explicit representation would require too many neurons or because the contents to be represented are too infrequent to warrant the implementation of specialized neurons. Also, the second strategy seems to be the only way to represent novel contents as there cannot be specialized neurons for them at first encounter. However, if novel items acquire high behavioral significance, as is the case for stimuli used in experiments with trained monkeys, it appears that these do become represented explicitly by specialized neurons (Miyashita, 1993; Logothetis, Pauls, and Poggio, 1995). In conclusion, then, there is no incompatibility between the strategy to encode contents by rate-modulated smart neurons on the one hand and by temporally defined assemblies on the other. Rather, the two regimes are coexistent and ideally complement one another.

REFERENCES

ABELES, M. (ed.), 1991. *Corticonics.* Cambridge: Cambridge University Press.

ALAIS, D., R. BLAKE, and S.-H. LEE, 1998. Visual features that vary together over time group together over space. *Nature Neurosci.* 1(2):160–164.

ALONSO, J.-M., W. M. USREY, and R. C. REID, 1996. Precisely correlated firing in cells of the lateral geniculate nucleus. *Nature* 383:815–819.

ARIELI, A., A. STERKIN, A. GRINVALD, and A. AERTSEN, 1996. Dynamics of ongoing activity: Explanation of the large variability in evoked cortical responses. *Science* 273:1868–1871.

BAUER, H.-U., and K. PAWELZIK, 1993. Alternating oscillatory and stochastic dynamics in a model for a neuronal assembly. *Physica D* 69:380–393.

BRAITENBERG, V., 1978. Cell assemblies in the cerebral cortex. In *Architectonics of the Cerebral Cortex. Lecture Notes in Biomathematics 21, Theoretical Approaches in Complex Systems*, R. Heim and G. Palm, eds. Berlin: Springer-Verlag, pp. 171–188.

BRECHT, M., W. SINGER, and A. K. ENGEL, 1998. Correlation analysis of corticotectal interactions in the cat visual system. *J. Neurophysiol.* 79:2394–2407.

BURACAS, G., A. ZADOR, M. DEWEESE, and T. ALBRIGHT, 1998. Efficient discrimination of temporal patterns by motion-sensitive neurons in primate visual cortex. *Neuron* 20:959–969.

CARR, C. E., 1993. Processing of temporal information in the brain. *Annu. Rev. Neurosci.* 16:223–243.

CASTELO-BRANCO, M., S. NEUENSCHWANDER, and W. SINGER, 1998. Synchronization of visual responses between the cortex, lateral geniculate nucleus, and retina in the anesthetized cat. *J. Neurosci.* 18(16):6395–6410.

CHAPMAN, B., K. R. ZAHS, and M. P. STRYKER, 1991. Relation of cortical cell orientation selectivity to alignment of receptive fields of the geniculocortical afferents that arborize within a single orientation column in ferret visual cortex. *J. Neurosci.* 11:1347–1358.

DECHARMS, R. C., and M. M. MERZENICH, 1996. Primary cortical representation of sounds by the coordination of action-potential timing. *Nature* 381:610–613.

DE OLIVEIRA, S. C., A. THIELE, and K. P. HOFFMANN, 1997. Synchronization of neuronal activity during stimulus expectation in a direction discrimination task. *J. Neurosci.* 17:9248–9260.

DEPPISCH, J., H.-U. BAUER, T. B. SCHILLEN, P. KÖNIG, K. PAWELZIK, and T. GEISEL, 1993. Alternating oscillatory and stochastic states in a network of spiking neurons. *Network* 4:243–257.

DIESMANN, M., M.-O. GEWALTIG, and A. AERTSEN, 1996. Characterization of synfire activity by propagating 'pulse packets.' In *Computational Neuroscience: Trends in Research*, J. Bower, ed. San Diego: Academic Press, pp. 59–64.

DONOGHUE, J. P., J. N. SANES, N. G. HATSOPOULOS, and G. GAÁL, 1998. Neural discharge and local field potential oscillations in primate motor cortex during voluntary movements. *J. Neurophysiol.* 79:159–173.

EDELMAN, G. M., 1987. *Neural Darwinism: The Theory of Neuronal Group Selection.* New York: Basic Books.

ENGEL, A. K., P. KÖNIG, A. K. KREITER, T. B. SCHILLEN, and W. SINGER, 1992. Temporal coding in the visual cortex: New vistas on integration in the nervous system. *Trends Neurosci.* 15:218–226.

ENGEL, A. K., P. KÖNIG, A. K. KREITER, and W. SINGER, 1991. Interhemispheric synchronization of oscillatory neuronal responses in cat visual cortex. *Science* 252:1177–1179.

ENGEL, A. K., P. KÖNIG, and W. SINGER, 1991. Direct physiological evidence for scene segmentation by temporal coding. *Proc. Natl. Acad. Sci. U.S.A.* 88:9136–9140.

ENGEL, A. K., A. K. KREITER, P. KÖNIG, and W. SINGER, 1991. Synchronization of oscillatory neuronal responses between striate and extrastriate visual cortical areas of the cat. *Proc. Natl. Acad. Sci. U.S.A.* 88:6048–6052.

ENGEL, A. K., P. R. ROELFSEMA, P. FRIES, M. BRECHT, and W. SINGER, 1997. Role of the temporal domain for response selection and perceptual binding. *Cerebral Cortex* 7:571–582.

FREEMAN, W. J., and C. A. SKARDA, 1985. Spatial EEG-patterns, non-linear dynamics and perception: The neo-Sherrington view. *Brain Res. Rev.* 10:147–175.

FREIWALD, W. A., A. K. KREITER, and W. SINGER, 1995. Stimulus dependent intercolumnar synchronization of single-unit responses in cat area 17. *NeuroReport* 6:2348–2352.

FRIES, P., P. R. ROELFSEMA, A. K. ENGEL, P. KÖNIG, and W. SINGER, 1997. Synchronization of oscillatory responses in visual cortex correlates with perception in interocular rivalry. *Proc. Natl. Acad. Sci. U.S.A.* 94:12699–12704.

FRIES, P., P. R. ROELFSEMA, W. SINGER, and A. K. ENGEL, 1997. Correlated variations of response latencies due to synchronous subthreshold membrane potential fluctuations in cat striate cortex. *Soc. Neurosci. Abstr.* 23:499.

GERSTEIN, G. L., and P. M. GOCHIN, 1992. Neuronal population coding and the elephant. In *Information Processing in the Cortex: Experiments and Theory*, A. Aertsen and V. Braitenberg, eds. Berlin: Springer-Verlag, pp. 139–173.

GERSTNER, W., and J. L. VAN HEMMEN, 1993. Coherence and incoherence in a globally coupled ensemble of pulse-emitting units. *Phys. Rev. Lett.* 7:312–315.

GERSTNER, W., 1996. Rapid phase locking in systems of pulse-coupled oscillators with delays. *Phys. Rev. Lett.* 76:1755–1758.

GILBERT, C. D., and T. N. WIESEL, 1989. Columnar specificity of intrinsic horizontal and cortico-cortical connections in cat visual cortex. *J. Neurosci.* 9:2432–2442.

GRAY, C. M., A. K. ENGEL, P. KÖNIG, and W. SINGER, 1992. Synchronization of oscillatory neuronal responses in cat striate cortex–Temporal properties. *Vis. Neurosci.* 8:337–347.

GRAY, C. M., P. KÖNIG, A. K. ENGEL, and W. SINGER, 1989. Oscillatory responses in cat visual cortex exhibit intercolumnar synchronization which reflects global stimulus properties. *Nature* 338:334–337.

GRAY, C. M., and W. SINGER, 1987. Stimulus-specific neuronal oscillations in the cat visual cortex: A cortical functional unit. *Soc. Neurosci. Abstr.* 13:404.3.

GRAY, C. M., and W. SINGER, 1989. Stimulus-specific neuronal oscillations in orientation columns of cat visual cortex. *Proc. Natl. Acad. Sci. U.S.A.* 86:1698–1702.

GROSS, C. G., 1992. Representation of visual stimuli in inferior temporal cortex. *Phil. Trans. R. Soc. Lond. (Biol.)* 335:3–10.

HATSOPOULOS, N. G., C. L. OJAKANGAS, and J. P. DONOGHUE, 1997. Planning of sequential arm movements from simultaneously recorded motor cortical neurons. *Soc. Neurosci. Abstr.* 23:1400.

HEBB, D. O., 1949. *The Organization of Behavior: A Neuropsychological Theory.* New York: Wiley.

HERCULANO, S., M. H. J. MUNK, S. NEUENSCHWANDER, and W. SINGER, in press. Precisely synchronized oscillatory firing patterns require cortical activation. *J. Neurosci.*

HOBSON, J. A., 1988. *The Dreaming Brain.* New York: Basic Books.

HOPFIELD, J. J., and A. V. M. HERTZ, 1995. Rapid local synchronization of action potentials: Toward computation with coupled integrate-and-fire neurons. *Proc. Natl. Acad. Sci. U.S.A.* 92:6655–6662.

HUBEL, D. H., and T. N. WIESEL, 1962. Receptive fields, binocular interaction and functional architecture in the cat's visual cortex. *J. Physiol. (Lond.)* 160:106–154.

JAGADEESH, B., H. S. WHEAT, and D. FERSTER, 1993. Linearity of summation of synaptic potentials underlying direction selectivity in simple cells of the cat visual cortex. *Science* 262:1901–1904.

KIPER, D. C., K. R. GEGENFURTNER, and J. A. MOVSHON, 1996. Cortical oscillatory responses do not affect visual segmentation. *Vision Res.* 36:539–544.

KÖNIG, P., A. K. ENGEL, S. LÖWEL, and W. SINGER, 1993. Squint affects synchronization of oscillatory responses in cat visual cortex. *Eur. J. Neurosci.* 5:501–508.

KÖNIG, P., A. K. ENGEL, and W. SINGER, 1996. Integrator or coincidence detector? The role of the cortical neuron revisited. *Trends Neurosci.* 19:130–137.

KREITER, A. K., and W. SINGER, 1992. Oscillatory neuronal responses in the visual cortex of the awake macaque monkey. *Eur. J. Neurosci.* 4:369–375.

KREITER, A. K., and W. SINGER, 1996. Stimulus-dependent synchronization of neuronal responses in the visual cortex of the awake macaque monkey. *J. Neurosci.* 16:2381–2396.

LEONARDS, U., and W. SINGER, 1997. Selective temporal interactions between processing streams with differential sensitivity for colour and luminance contrast. *Vision Res.* 37:1129–1140.

LEONARDS, U., and W. SINGER, 1998. Two segmentation mechanisms with differential sensitivity for colour and luminance contrast. *Vision Res.* 38(1):101–109.

LEONARDS, U., W. SINGER, and M. FAHLE, 1996. The influence of temporal phase differences on texture segmentation. *Vision Res.* 36:2689–2697.

LOGOTHETIS, N. K., J. PAULS, and T. POGGIO, 1995. Shape representation in the inferior temporal cortex of monkeys. *Curr. Biol.* 5:552–563.

LÖWEL, S., and W. SINGER, 1992. Selection of intrinsic horizontal connections in the visual cortex by correlated neuronal activity. *Science* 255:209–212.

MACLEOD, K., and G. LAURENT, 1996. Distinct mechanisms for synchronization and temporal patterning of odor-encoding neural assemblies. *Science* 274:976–979.

MADLER, C., I. KELLER, D. SCHWENDER, and E. PÖPPEL, 1991. Sensory information-processing during general anesthesia–Effect of isoflurane on auditory evoked neuronal oscillations. *Brit. J. Anaesth.* 66:81–87.

MAINEN, Z. F., and T. J. SEJNOWSKI, 1995. Reliability of spike timing in neocortical neurons. *Science* 268:1503–1505.

MALACH, R., Y. AMIR, M. HAREL, and A. GRINVALD, 1993. Relationship between intrinsic connections and functional architecture revealed by optical imaging and in vivo targeted biocytin injections in primate striate cortex. *Proc. Natl. Acad. Sci. U.S.A.* 90:10469–10473.

MAUNSELL, J. H. R., 1995. The brain's visual world: Representation of visual targets in cerebral cortex. *Science* 270:764–769.

MIYASHITA, Y., 1993. Inferior temporal cortex: Where visual perception meets memory. *Annu. Rev. Neurosci.* 16:245–263.

MORGAN, M. J., and E. CASTET, 1995. Stereoscopic depth perception at high velocities. *Nature* 378:380–383.

MUNK, M. H. J., P. R. ROELFSEMA, P. KÖNIG, A. K. ENGEL, and W. SINGER, 1996. Role of reticular activation in the modulation of intracortical synchronization. *Science* 272:271–274.

MURTHY, V. N., and E. E. FETZ, 1996a. Oscillatory activity in sensorimotor cortex of awake monkeys: Synchronization of local field potentials and relation to behavior. *J. Neurophysiol.* 76:3949–3967.

MURTHY, V. N., and E. E. FETZ, 1996b. Synchronization of neurons during local field potential oscillations in sensorimotor cortex of awake monkeys. *J. Neurophysiol.* 76:3968–3982.

NEUENSCHWANDER, S., and W. SINGER, 1996. Long-range synchronization of oscillatory light responses in the cat retina and lateral geniculate nucleus. *Nature* 379:728–733.

NOWAK, L. G., M. H. J. MUNK, J. I. NELSON, A. C. JAMES, and J. BULLIER, 1995. Structural basis of cortical synchronization. I. Three types of interhemispheric coupling. *J. Neurophysiol.* 74:2379–2400.

OJAKANGAS, C. L., N. G. HATSOPOULOS, and J. P. DONOGHUE, 1997. Reorganization of neuronal synchrony in M1 during visuomotor adaptation. *Soc. Neurosci. Abstr.* 23:1399.

PALM, G., 1990. Cell assemblies as a guideline for brain research. *Concepts Neurosci.* 1:133–147.

PRUT, Y., E. VAADIA, H. BERGMAN, I. HAALMAN, H. SLOVIN, and M. ABELES, 1998. Spatiotemporal structure of cortical activity: Properties and behavioral relevance. *J. Neurophysiol.* 79:2857–2874.

RAGER, G., and W. SINGER, 1998. The response of cat visual cortex to flicker stimuli of variable frequency. *Eur. J. Neurosci.* 10:1856–1877.

REID, R. C., and J. M. ALONSO, 1995. Specificity of monosynaptic connections from thalamus to visual cortex. *Nature* 378:281–284.

RIEHLE, A., S. GRÜN, M. DIESMANN, and A. AERTSEN, 1997. Spike synchronization and rate modulation differentially involved in motor cortical function. *Science* 278:1950–1953.

ROELFSEMA, P. R., A. K. ENGEL, P. KÖNIG, and W. SINGER, 1996. The role of neuronal synchronization in response selection: A biologically plausible theory of structured representations in the visual cortex. *J. Cogn. Neurosci.* 8(6):603–625.

ROELFSEMA, P. R., P. KÖNIG, A. K. ENGEL, R. SIRETEANU, and W. SINGER, 1994. Reduced synchronization in the visual cortex of cats with strabismic amblyopia. *Eur. J. Neurosci.* 6:1645–1655.

ROLLS, D. T., and M. J. TOVEE, 1994. Processing speed in the cerebral cortex and the neurophysiology of visual masking. *Proc. R. Soc. Lond. B* 257:9–15.

SCHMIDT, K. E., R. GOEBEL, S. LÖWEL, and W. SINGER, 1997. The perceptual grouping criterion of colinearity is reflected by anisotropies of connections in the primary visual cortex. *Eur. J. Neurosci.* 9:1083–1089.

SEJNOWSKI, T. R., 1986. Open questions about computation in cerebral cortex. In *Parallel Distributed Processing,* Vol. 2., J. L. McClelland and D. E. Rumelhart, eds. Cambridge, Mass.: MIT Press, pp. 372–389.

SHADLEN, M. N., and W. T. NEWSOME, 1994. Noise, neural codes and cortical organization. *Curr. Opin. Neurobiol.* 4:569–579.

SHADLEN, M. N., and W. T. NEWSOME, 1998. The variable discharge of cortical neurons: Implications for connectivity, computation, and information coding. *J. Neurosci.* 18:3870–3896.

SINGER, W., 1995. Development and plasticity of cortical processing architectures. *Science* 270:758–764.

SINGER, W., A. K. ENGEL, A. K. KREITER, M. H. J. MUNK, S. NEUENSCHWANDER, and P. R. ROELFSEMA, 1997. Neuronal assemblies: Necessity, signature and detectability. *Trends Cogn. Sci.* 1:252–261.

SINGER, W., and C. M. GRAY, 1995. Visual feature integration and the temporal correlation hypothesis. *Annu. Rev. Neurosci.* 18:555–586.

SOFTKY, W. R., 1995. Simple codes versus efficient codes. *Curr. Opin. Neurobiol.* 5:239–247.

SOFTKY, W. R., and C. KOCH, 1993. The highly irregular firing of cortical cells is inconsistent with temporal integration of random EPSPs. *J. Neurosci.* 13:334–350.

STEVENS, C. F., and A. M. ZADOR, 1998. Input synchrony and the irregular firing of cortical neurons. *Nature Neurosci.* 1:210–217.

STOPFER, M., S. BHAGAVAN, B. H. SMITH, and G. LAURENT, 1997. Impaired odour discrimination on desynchronization of odour-encoding neural assemblies. *Nature* 390:70–74.

TALLON-BAUDRY, C., O. BERTRAND, P. BOUCHET, and J. PERNIER, 1995. Gamma-range activity evoked by coherent visual stimuli in humans. *Eur. J. Neurosci.* 7:1285–1291.

TALLON-BAUDRY, C., O. BERTRAND, C. DELPUECH, and J. PERNIER, 1996. Stimulus specificity of phase-locked and non-phase-locked 40Hz visual responses in human. *J. Neurosci.* 16:4240–4249.

TALLON-BAUDRY, C., O. BERTRAND, C. DELPUECH, and J. PERNIER, 1997. Oscillatory γ-band (30-70Hz) activity induced by a visual search task in humans. *J. Neurosci.* 17:722–734.

TANAKA, K., H. SAITO, Y. FUKADA, and M. MORIYA, 1991. Coding visual images of objects in the inferotemporal cortex of the macaque monkey. *J. Neurophysiol.* 66:170–189.

THORPE, S., D. FIZE, and C. MARLOT, 1996. Speed of processing in the human visual system. *Nature* 38:520–522.

TS'O, D. Y., and C. D. GILBERT, 1988. The organization of chromatic and spatial interactions in the primate striate cortex. *J. Neurosci.* 8:1712–1727.

USHER, M., and N. DONNELLY, 1998. Visual synchrony affects binding and segmentation in perception. *Nature* 394:179–182.

VAADIA, E., I. HAALMAN, M. ABELES, H. BERGMAN, Y. PRUT, H. SLOVIN, and A. AERTSEN, 1995. Dynamics of neuronal interactions in monkey cortex in relation to behavioural events. *Nature* 373:515–518.

VAN VREESWIJK, D., L. F. ABBOTT, and G. B. ERMENTROUT, 1994. When inhibition not excitation synchronizes neural firing. *J. Comput. Neurosci.* 1:313–321.

VOLGUSHEV, M., M. CHISTIAKOVA, and W. SINGER, 1998. Modification of discharge patterns of neocortical neurons by induced oscillations of the membrane potential. *Neurosci.* 83(1):15–25.

WEHR, M., and G. LAURENT, 1996. Odour encoding by temporal sequences of firing in oscillating neural assemblies. *Nature* 384:162–166.

WIESEL, T. N., and D. H. HUBEL, 1965. Comparison of the effects of unilateral and bilateral eye closure on cortical unit responses in kittens. *J. Neurophysiol.* 28:1029–1040.

24 Lightness Perception and Lightness Illusions

EDWARD H. ADELSON

ABSTRACT A gray surface in sunlight may have much higher luminance than it has in the shade, but it still looks gray. To achieve the task of "lightness constancy," the visual system must discount the illumination and other viewing conditions and estimate the reflectance. Many different physical situations, such as shadows, filters, or haze, can be combined to form a single, simple mapping from luminance to reflectance. The net effect of the viewing conditions, including additive and multiplicative effects, may be termed an "atmosphere." An "atmospheric transfer function" maps reflectance into luminance. To correctly estimate lightness, a visual system must determine a "lightness transfer function" that performs the inverse. Human lightness computation is imperfect, but performs well in most natural situations. Lightness illusions can reveal the inner workings of the estimation process, which may involve low-level, mid-level, and high-level mechanisms. Mid-level mechanisms, involving contours, junctions, and grouping, appear to be critical in explaining many lightness phenomena.

Every light is a shade, compared to the higher lights, 'til you come to the sun; and every shade is a light, compared to the deeper shades, 'til you come to the night.

–John Ruskin (1879)

The amount of light coming to the eye from an object depends on the amount of light striking the surface and on the proportion of light that is reflected. If a visual system made just a single measurement of luminance, acting as a photometer, there would be no way to distinguish a white surface in dim light from a black surface in bright light. Yet humans can usually do just that. This skill is known as *lightness constancy*.

The constancies are central to perception. An organism needs to know about meaningful world-properties–color, size, shape, etc. These properties are not explicitly available in the retinal image, but are extracted by visual processing. The gray shade of a surface is one such property. To extract it, luminance information must be combined across space. In figure 24.1, for example, we see the well known *simultaneous contrast* effect, which demonstrates a spatial interaction in lightness percep-

tion. The two smaller squares are the same shade of gray, but the square in the dark surround appears lighter than the square in the light surround. This is, of course, an illusion, which may be viewed as a quirky failure of perception. But such illusions are also revealing, allowing us to examine the inner workings of a system that functions remarkably well. Here we consider how lightness illusions can inform us about lightness perception.

Levels of processing

The visual system processes information at many levels of sophistication. At the retina, there is *low-level vision*, including light adaptation and the center–surround receptive fields of ganglion cells. At the other extreme is *high-level vision*, which includes cognitive processes that incorporate knowledge about objects, materials, and scenes. In between there is *mid-level vision*. Mid-level vision is simply an ill-defined region between low and high. The representations and the processing in the middle stages are commonly thought to involve surfaces, contours, grouping, and so on. Lightness perception seems to involve all three levels of processing.

The low-level approach to lightness is associated with Ewald Hering. He considered adaptation and local interactions, at a physiological level, as the crucial mechanisms. This approach has long enjoyed popularity because it offers an attractive connection between physiology and psychophysics. Figure 24.2a shows the receptive field of an idealized center–surround cell. The cell exhibits lateral inhibition: light in the center is excitatory while light in the surround is inhibitory. A cross-section of the receptive field is shown in figure 24.2b. This cell performs a local comparison between a given luminance and the neighboring luminances, and thus offers machinery that can help explain the simultaneous contrast (SC) illusion. This idea was formalized by Ernst Mach, who proposed a Laplacian derivative operator as the mechanism.

One of Mach's inspirations was an illusion now known as the Mach band. When a spatial ramp in luminance abruptly changes slope, an illusory light or dark

EDWARD H. ADELSON Department of Brain and Cognitive Sciences, Massachusetts Institute of Technology, Cambridge, Mass.

FIGURE 24.1   The simultaneous contrast effect.

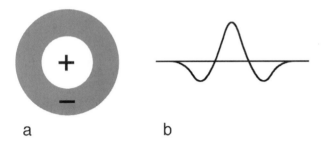

a   b

FIGURE 24.2   Center-surround inhibition.

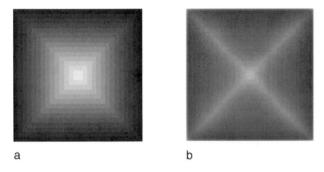

a   b

FIGURE 24.3   An illusion by Vasarely (a) and a bandpass filtered version (b).

band appears. A variant of the Mach band has been used by the op artist Vasarely, as shown in figure 24.3a. The image consists of a set of nested squares. Each square is a constant luminance. The pattern gives the illusion of a glowing X along the diagonals, even though the corners of the squares are no brighter than the straight parts. When a center–surround filter is run over this pattern (i.e., is convolved with it), it produces the image shown in figure 24.3b. The filter output makes the bright diagonals explicit.

A center–surround filter cannot explain a percept by itself: Perception involves the whole brain. However, center–surround responses can go a long way toward explaining certain illusions.

Derivative operators respond especially well to sharp intensity transitions such as edges. The importance of

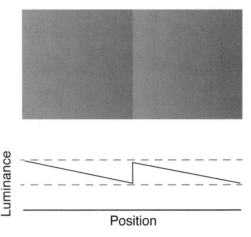

FIGURE 24.4   One version of the Craik-O'Brien-Cornsweet effect.

edges, and the lesser importance of slow gradients, is indicated by the *Craik–O'Brien–Cornsweet effect* (COCE) named after its several discoverers. Figure 24.4 shows one of several COCE variants. The figure appears to contain a dark square next to a light square. Actually, the two squares are ramps, and they are identical, as shown by the luminance profile underneath (the dashed lines show constant luminances). The response of a center–surround cell to this pattern will be almost the same as its response to a true step edge–a big response at the edge and a small response elsewhere. While this doesn't explain why the image looks as it does, it may help explain why one image looks similar to the other (Cornsweet, 1970).

Center–surround processing is presumably in place for a good reason. Land and McCann (1971) developed a model they called Retinex, which placed the processing in a meaningful computational context.

Land and McCann began by considering the nature of scenes and images. They argued that reflectance tends to be constant across space except for abrupt changes at the transitions between objects or pigments. Thus a reflectance change shows itself as a step edge in an image, while illuminance changes gradually over space. By this argument one can separate reflectance change from illuminance change by taking spatial derivatives: High derivatives are due to reflectance and low ones to illuminance.

The Retinex model applies a derivative operator to the image, and thresholds the output to remove illuminance variation. The algorithm then reintegrates edge information over space to reconstruct the reflectance image.

The Retinex model works well for stimuli that satisfy its assumptions, including the Craik–O'Brien–Cornsweet display and the "mondrians" (which roughly resemble paintings by the artist Piet Mondriaan) that Land and McCann used. A mondrian is an array of randomly colored, randomly placed rectangles covering a plane surface, and illuminated nonuniformly.

The real world is more complex than the mondrian world, of course, and the Retinex model has its limits. In its original form, it cannot handle the configural effects to be described later in this chapter. However, the Land–McCann research program articulated some important principles. Vision is possible only because there are constraints in the world; i.e., images are not formed by arbitrary random processes. To function in this world, the visual system must exploit the ecology of images–it must "know" the likelihood of various things in the world, as well as the likelihood that a given image-property could be caused by one or another world-property. This world-knowledge may be hardwired or learned, and may manifest itself at various levels of processing.

Limits on low-level processes

The high-level approach is historically associated with Hermann von Helmholtz, who argued that perception is the product of *unconscious inference*. His dictum was this: What we perceive is our visual system's best guess as to what is in the world. The guess is based on the raw image data plus our prior experience. In the Helmholtz view, lightness constancy is achieved by inferring, and discounting, the illuminant. From this standpoint the details of low-level processing are not the issue. A lightness judgment involves the workings of the whole visual system, and that system is designed to interpret natural scenes. Simultaneous contrast and other illusions are the by-products of such processing.

Hochberg and Beck (1954) and Gilchrist (1977) showed that 3D cues could greatly change the lightness perception in a scene, even when the retinal image remains essentially unchanged, in accord with Helmholtz's approach.

The importance of scene interpretation is also shown by a recent variant on the Craik–O'Brien–Cornsweet effect devised by Knill and Kersten (1991). In figure 24.5a, one sees two identical cylinders. In figure 24.5b one sees a brick painted with two shades of paint. Embedded within each image is a COCE pattern in the vertical direction. The two ramps are interpreted as shading in figure 24.5a, but as paint in figure 24.5b.

The Gestalt approach

The Gestalt psychologists approached lightness perception, and perception generally, in a different manner

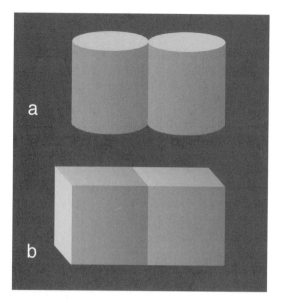

FIGURE 24.5   Knill and Kersten's illusion. Both figures contain the same COCE ramps, but the interpretations are quite different.

from the Hering or Helmholtz schools. They emphasized the importance of perceptual organization, much of it based on mechanisms that might be characterized as midlevel. The key concepts include grouping, belongingness, good continuation, proximity, and so on.

Koffka offered an example of how simultaneous contrast can be manipulated by changing spatial configuration. The ring in figure 24.6a appears almost uniform in color. When the stimulus is split in two, as shown in figure 24.6b, the two half-rings appear to be different shades of gray. The two halves now have separate identities, and each is perceived within its own context.

A novel variant that involves transparency is shown in figure 24.6c. The left and right half-blocks are slid vertically, and the new configuration leads to a very different perceptual organization and a strong lightness illusion. We will return to this stimulus in our later discussion.

Some terminology

Having outlined some basic phenomena, we now return to the basic problems. First, we clarify some terminology (more complete definitions can be found in books on photometry and colorimetry):

Luminance is the amount of visible light that comes to the eye from a surface.

Illuminance is the amount of light incident on a surface.

Reflectance is the proportion of incident light that is reflected from a surface.

Reflectance, also called *albedo*, varies from 0 to 1 or, equivalently, from 0% to 100% where 0% is ideal black

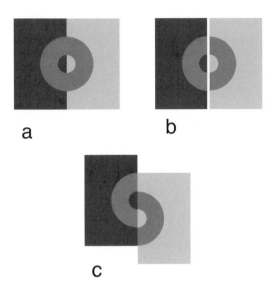

a

b

c

FIGURE 24.6   Variants on the Koffka ring. (a) The ring appears almost uniform. (b) When split, the two half-rings appear distinctly different. (c) When shifted, the two half-rings appear quite different.

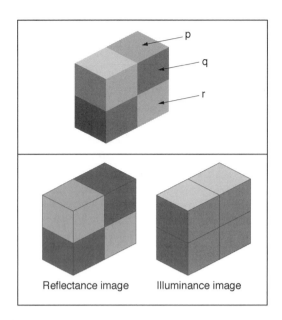

Reflectance image   Illuminance image

FIGURE 24.7   The "checker-block" and its analysis into two intrinsic images.

and 100% is ideal white. In practice, typical black paint is about 5% and typical white paint about 85%. (To keep things simple, we consider only ideal matte surfaces, for which a single reflectance value offers a complete description.)

Luminance, illuminance, and reflectance are physical quantities that can be measured by physical devices. There are also two subjective variables that must be discussed:

Lightness is the perceived reflectance of a surface. It represents the visual system's attempt to extract reflectance based on the luminances in the scene.

Brightness is the perceived intensity of light coming from the image itself, rather than any property of the portrayed scene. Brightness is sometimes defined as perceived luminance.

These terms may be understood by reference to figure 24.7. The block is made of a 2×2 set of cubes, each colored either light or dark gray. We call this the "checkerblock." Illumination comes from an oblique angle, lighting different faces differently. The luminance image can be considered to be the product of two other images–the reflectance image and the illuminance image. These underlying images are termed *intrinsic images* in machine vision (Barrow and Tenenbaum, 1978). Intrinsic image decompositions have been proposed for understanding lightness perception (Arend, 1994; Adelson and Pentland, 1996).

Patches p and q have the same reflectance, but different luminances. Patches q and r have different reflec-

tances and different luminances; they share the same illuminance. Patches p and r happen to have the same luminance, because the lower reflectance of p is counterbalanced by its higher illuminance.

Faces p and q appear to be painted with the same gray, and thus they have the same lightness. However, it is clear that p has more luminance than q in the image, and so the patches differ in brightness. Patches p and r differ in both lightness and brightness, despite having the same luminances.

The problem of lightness constancy

From a physical point of view, the problem of lightness constancy is as follows. An illuminance image, $E(x,y)$, and a reflectance image, $R(x,y)$, are multiplied to produce a luminance image, $L(x,y)$:

$$L(x,y) = E(x,y)\,R(x,y)$$

An observer is given L at each pixel and attempts to determine the two numbers, E and R, that were multiplied to make it. Unfortunately, unmultiplying two numbers is impossible. If $E(x,y)$ and $R(x,y)$ are arbitrary functions, then for any $E(x,y)$ there exists an $R(x,y)$ that produces the observed image. The problem appears impossible, but humans do it pretty well. This must mean that illuminance and reflectance images are not arbitrary functions. They are constrained by statistical properties of the world, as proposed by Land and McCann.

Note that Land and McCann's constraints fail when applied to the checkerblock image. Figure 24.8a shows two light–dark edges. They are exactly the same in the image, and any local edge detector or filter will respond to them in the same way. Retinex will classify both as reflectance steps. Yet they have very different meanings. One is caused by illuminance (due to a change in surface normal); the other is caused by reflectance.

To interpret the edges, the visual system must consider them in a larger context. One good source of information is the junctions, where two or more contours come together. As shown in figure 24.8b, X, Y, L, T, and ψ are some of the simple junction types. The configuration of a junction, as well as the gray levels forming the junction, can offer cues about the shading and reflectance of a surface.

Particularly strong constraints are imposed by a ψ-junction like the one in figure 24.8b. The vertical spine appears to be a dihedral with different illuminance on the two sides. The angled arms appear to represent a reflectance edge that crosses the dihedral. The ratios of the gray levels, and the angles of the arms, are consistent with this interpretation.

The influence of a ψ-junction can propagate along the contours that meet at the ψ. A single light–dark edge, ambiguous by itself, can be pushed toward a particular interpretation by adjoining ψ's (Sinha and Adelson, 1993).

In figure 24.9, the dashed rectangle encloses a set of horizontal light and dark stripes. If we consider only the region within the dashed rectangle, we cannot determine the physical sources of the stripes. However, if we cover the right side of the figure and view the left side, it appears that the stripes are due to paint. If we cover the left side and view the right, it appears that the stripes are due to different lighting on the stair steps. If we view both sides, the percept flip-flops according to where we look.

The ψ-junctions seem to be in control here. If we follow a stripe to the left, it connects to a ψ with a vertical spine and becomes an arm of that ψ. The junction configuration, together with the junction gray levels, suggests that the stripe is due to reflectance. When the same strip is followed to the right, it joins a ψ with a horizontal spine. Again, the configuration and gray levels suggest that illuminance is the cause.

Configurations involving ψ's can modulate brightness illusions. Figure 24.10 shows a stimulus we call the *corrugated plaid* (Adelson, 1993). In figure 24.10a the two marked patches are the same shade of gray. The upper patch appears slightly darker. Figure 24.10b shows another array of gray patches in which the same gray levels are at the same positions as in figure 24.10a; i.e., the raster sequence of grays is the same. Only the geometry has been changed, parallelograms having been substituted for squares and vice versa. The illusion is much enhanced, the upper patch appearing much darker than the lower one. In the laboratory the apparent luminance difference is increased threefold.

A low-level filtering mechanism, or a mechanism based on local edge interactions, cannot explain the change in the illusion. We proposed (Adelson, 1993) a Helmholtzian explanation based on intrinsic images: The change in ψ-junctions causes a change in the perception of 3D surface orientation and shading. In figure 24.10a the two test patches appear to be in the

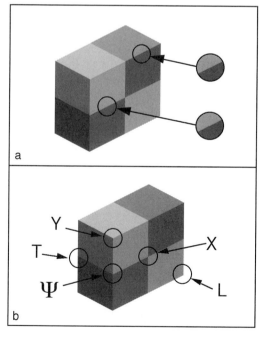

FIGURE 24.8 (a) The local ambiguity of edges. (b) A variety of junctions.

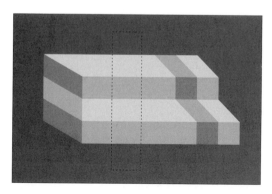

FIGURE 24.9 The impossible steps. On the left, the horizontal stripes appear to be due to paint; on the right, they appear to be due to shading.

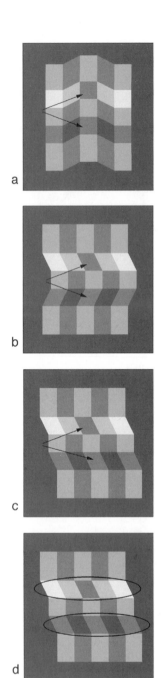

FIGURE 24.10 Variations on the corrugated plaid. (a) The two patches appear nearly the same. (b) The patches appear quite different. (c) The patches appear quite different, but there is no plausible shaded model. (d) Possible grouping induced by junctions.

same illumination, but in figure 24.10b they are differently illuminated. A brightly lit patch of dark gray looks quite different from a dimly lit patch of light gray. This lightness computation could have a strong influence on brightness judgments.

Thus a 3D shaded model can help explain the phenomenon. But is it necessary? Todorovic (1997) has de-

vised a variant, shown in figure 24.10c, that suggests not. The figure was made by mirror-reversing the bottom two rows. For many observers the illusion remains nearly as strong as in figure 24.10b. However, there is no reasonable interpretation in terms of a 3D shaded model. The two strips containing the test patches appear to lie in parallel planes, and so they should be receiving similar illumination.

Perhaps the intrinsic image story can be saved by appealing to the notion of local consistency without global consistency, such as occurs in figure 24.9. However, it may be that the main effects are the result of simpler 2D computations. The ψ-junctions, taken as 2D configurations, could be used as grouping cues that define the context in which lightness is assessed, as indicated in figure 24.10d. If this is correct, the Helmholtzian approach is overkill.

A number of investigators have lately argued for models based on Gestalt-like grouping mechanisms (e.g., Ross and Pessoa, in press). Gilchrist, who in earlier years took a Helmholtzian stance (Gilchrist and Jacobsen, 1983), has recently proposed a model of lightness that emphasizes 2D configuration and grouping mechanisms (Gilchrist et al., in press).

Anchoring and frameworks

Gilchrist's new model took shape in the course of his investigations into *anchoring*. The anchoring problem is this: Suppose an observer determines that patch *x* has four times the reflectance of patch *y*. This solves part of the lightness problem, but not all of it; the absolute reflectances remain unknown. An 80% near-white is four times a 20% gray, but a 20% gray is also four times a 5% black. For absolute judgments one must tie down the gray scale with an anchor, i.e., a luminance that is mapped to a standard reflectance such as midgray or white.

Land and McCann, having encountered this problem with Retinex, proposed that the highest luminance should be anchored to white. All other grays could then be scaled relative to that white. This is known as the *highest-luminance rule.*

Li and Gilchrist (in press) tested the highest-luminance rule using bipartite ganzfelds. They painted the inside of a large hemispherical dome with two shades of gray paint. When subjects put their heads inside, their entire visual fields were filled with just two luminances. A bipartite field painted black and gray appeared to be a bipartite field painted gray and white, as predicted by the highest-luminance rule.

By manipulating the relative areas of the light and dark fields, Gilchrist and Cataliotti (1994) found evi-

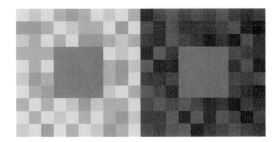

FIGURE 24.11 Simultaneous contrast is enhanced with articulated surrounds, as shown below.

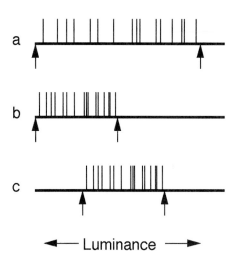

FIGURE 24.12 A collection of random gray surfaces will lead to different luminance distributions in different viewing conditions.

dence for a second, competing anchoring rule: The largest area tends to appear white. They argue that the actual anchor is a compromise between these rules.

Gilchrist also emphasizes the importance of *articulation* and *insulation* in anchoring. Articulation is a term used earlier by Katz (1935); it refers to the number of distinct surfaces or patches within a region. Katz observed that greater articulation leads to better lightness constancy, and Gilchrist proposes that it leads to better local anchoring. We can demonstrate the effect of articulation with a simultaneous contrast display, as in figure 24.11. At the top is a standard display, with an articulated version shown below. The surround mean luminances have not changed, but the surrounds are broken into many squares. The articulated version gives a stronger illusion. In our laboratory we find that the strength of the illusory contrast can be doubled. (As with all the demonstrations in this chapter, the effect may be weaker on the printed page owing to the small image size and limitations in the printing process.)

In Gilchrist's model, anchoring occurs within a *framework*, which is a region containing patches that are grouped. Frameworks can be local or global. In figure 24.11, a local framework would be the patches surrounding the test square, and the global framework would be the entire page, and even the room in which the page is viewed.

If a local framework is well *insulated*, it has strong control over the anchoring. Insulation occurs when the local framework is strongly grouped as a separate entity from the global framework.

Statistical estimation

The various lightness principles might be thought of as heuristics that the visual system has arbitrarily adopted. These principles begin to make sense, however, if we consider the lightness problem from the standpoint of statistical estimation.

Suppose the world consisted of a set of gray patches randomly drawn from some distribution. Then, under a given illuminance, one would observe a distribution of luminance samples such as that shown in figure 24.12a. If the illumination were dimmed by half, then the luminances would follow suit, as shown in figure 24.12b. The arrows bracketing the distributions represent the extremes of 0% and 100% reflectance, i.e., the luminances mapping to ideal black and ideal white.

The observed luminances can also be changed by an additive haze or glare, which slides the distribution upward, as illustrated in figure 24.12c. Again, one can estimate which luminance corresponds to which reflectance; i.e., one can estimate the mapping between the observed luminance and the underlying reflectance. We use the term *atmosphere* to refer to the combined effects of a multiplicative process (e.g., illuminance) and an additive process (e.g., haze).

If one has prior knowledge about distributions of reflectances and atmospheres, one can construct optimal estimates of the locations of various reflectances along the luminance axis. That is, one can estimate the mapping between luminance and reflectance, as is required for lightness constancy.

Estimating this mapping is a central task of lightness perception. The image luminance is given and the perceived reflectance (lightness) must be derived. Anchoring

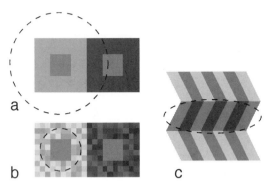

FIGURE 24.13 Lightness computations may employ adaptive windows.

is a way of describing part of this process. We will return to this problem when we discuss lightness transfer functions.

Adaptive windows

A larger number of samples will lead to better estimates of the lightness mapping. To increase N, the visual system can gather samples from a larger window. However, the atmosphere can vary from place to place, so there is a counterargument favoring small windows.

Suppose that the visual system uses an adaptive window to deal with this tradeoff. The window grows when there are too few samples and shrinks when there are more than enough. Consider the examples shown in figure 24.13. In the classical SC display, figure 24.13a, there are only a few large patches, so the window will tend to grow. In the articulated SC display, figure 24.13b, the window can remain fairly small.

Lightness estimates are computed based on the statistics within the adaptive window. In the classic SC display, the window becomes so large that the statistics surrounding either of the test patches are rather similar. (In Gilchrist's terminology, the global framework dominates). In the articulated display, the windows can be small, so that they will not mix statistics from different atmospheres. This predicts the enhancement in the illusion.

It is reasonable to assume that the statistical window has soft edges. For example, it could be a 2D Gaussian hump centered at the location of interest. Since nearby patches are likely to share the same atmosphere, proximity should lead to high weights, with more distant patches getting lower weights (cf. Reid and Shapley, 1988; Spehar, DeBonet, and Zaidi, 1996). The dashed lines in figure 24.13 would indicate a level line of the Gaussian hump.

A further advantage occurs if the adaptive window can change shape. For example, in figure 24.13c, it would be prudent to keep the statistical pooling within the horizontal region shown by the ellipse. This will avoid mixing luminances from the adjacent regions, which are in different lighting.

This reasoning might explain why ψ-junctions are effective at insulating one region from another. A set of ψ's along a contour (and with the appropriate gray levels) gives a strong cue that the contour is an atmospheric boundary. The statistical window should avoid crossing such a boundary in order to avoid mixing distributions. Thus the window should configure itself into a shape like that in figure 24.13c.

Atmospheres

As noted, illuminance is only one of the factors determining the luminance corresponding to a given reflectance. Other factors could include interposed filters (e.g., sunglasses), scattering, glare from a specular surface such as a windshield, and so on. It turns out that most physical effects will lead to linear transforms. Therefore the combined effects can be captured by a single linear transform (characterized by two parameters). This is what we call an atmosphere. The equation we use is

$$L = mR + e$$

where L and R are luminance and reflectance, m is a multiplier on the reflectance, and e is an additive source of light. The value of m is determined by the amount of light falling on the surface, as well as the proportion of light absorbed by the intervening media between the surface and the eye.

The equation here is closely related to the linear equation underlying Metelli's episcotister model (Metelli, 1974) for transparency, except that there is no necessary coupling between the additive and multiplicative terms. The parameters m and e are free to take on any positive values.

An atmosphere may be thought of as a single transparent layer, except that it allows a larger range of parameters. It can be amplifying rather than attenuating, and it can have an arbitrarily large additive component.

In our usage, "atmosphere" simply refers to the mapping, i.e., the mathematical properties established by the viewing conditions without regard to the underlying physical processes. Putting on sunglasses or dimming the lights has the same effect on the luminances, and so leads to the same effect on atmosphere. To be more explicit about this meaning, we define the *atmospheric transfer function*, or *ATF*, as the mapping between reflectance and luminance.

Figure 24.14 shows a set of random vertical lines viewed in three different atmospheres. The large outer

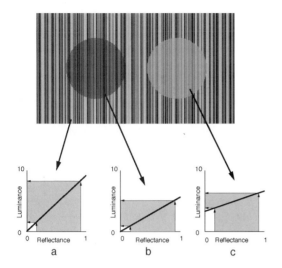

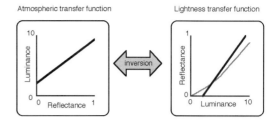

FIGURE 24.15   The inverse relation between the atmospheric transfer function and the ideal lightness transfer function.

FIGURE 24.14   Lines of random gray, viewed under three different atmospheres. The ATF's, shown below, determine the mapping from reflectance to luminance.

lightness transfer function, or *LTF*. The LTF is subjective; it need not be linear and need not be the correct inverse of the ATF. For a given observer it must be determined empirically.

region is in some default atmosphere. The left disk is in an attenuating atmosphere (compared to the default). The right disk is in a hazy atmosphere.

The ATF for the main atmosphere is shown in figure 24.14a. It passes through the origin, meaning that *e* is zero. The slope is specified by *m*. (*Note:* Since reflectance and luminance are in different units, there is also a scale constant that depends on the chosen units.) The small arrows in the panels show how the various reflectances are mapped to their corresponding luminances. The shaded area within the arrows shows how a typical range of reflectances will be mapped into the corresponding range of luminances.

Figure 24.14b shows the ATF for the dimmer atmosphere. The slope is reduced, and the intercept remains zero. On the right, in figure 24.14c, is the ATF of the hazy atmosphere. The output luminance range is compressed by *m* and shifted up by *e*.

Note that there is no such thing as a "non-atmosphere." An observer cannot see the reflectances "directly," but rather requires an atmospheric transfer function to convert reflectances to luminances. The parameters of the ATF always have values.

Finally, note that the (*m,e*) parametrization has no privileged status. Any two numbers will do. For example, a useful alternative would be the white-point and the black-point.

Since the atmosphere maps a reflectance to a luminance, the observer must implicitly reverse the mapping, turning a luminance into a perceived reflectance, as illustrated in figure 24.15. The inverting function, for a given observer in a given condition, may be called the

Atmospheres and X-junctions

The connection between X-junctions and atmospheres is shown in figure 24.16. Different types of atmospheres lead to different ordinal categories of X-junctions (cf. Beck, Prazdny, and Ivry, 1984; Adelson and Anandan, 1990; Anderson, 1997).

Figure 24.16a shows a region with two shades of gray paint. The large light square has 75% reflectance and the small dark square in the corner has 25% reflectance. The two reflectances are marked with arrows on the abscissa of the corresponding ATF diagram, below. Figure 24.16b shows what happens when a new atmosphere is introduced in the central patch. The new ATF is shown in a dashed line in the ATF diagram; it might be produced by a dark filter or a shadow. The resulting luminances form an X-junction of the "sign-preserving" or "nonreversing" type (Adelson and Anandan, 1990), which is consistent with transparency.

Figure 24.16c shows a different category of X-junction: the single-reversing X. It gives the impression of a murky or hazy medium. For a single-reversing X, the new ATF must cross the original ATF at a point between the two reflectances. A crossover ATF can only arise from an additive process combined with an attenuative process, such as would occur with smoke or a dirty window. Another difference between single-reversing and sign-preserving Xs is that either edge of a sign-preserving X is potentially an atmospheric boundary, while only one edge of a single-reversing edge can be an atmospheric boundary. For this reason, the depth ordering of a single-reversing X is unambiguous.

Finally, figure 24.16d shows a double-reversing X, which does not look transparent. The ATF needed to produce this X would require a negative slope. This cannot occur in normal physical circumstances. Double-reversing X-junctions do not signal atmospheric

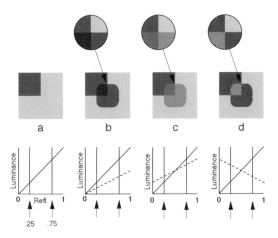

FIGURE 24.16 Transparency involves the imposition of a new atmosphere. The resulting X-junction category depends on the atmospheric transfer function.

boundaries to the visual system, and they typically look like paint rather than transparency. The junctions in a checkerboard are double-reversing Xs.

The ATF diagrams offer a simple graphical analysis of different X-junction types, and show how the X-junctions can be diagnostic of atmospheric boundaries.

Figure 24.17 shows an illusion using X-junctions to make atmospheres perceptible as such. The centers of the two diamond-shaped regions are physically the same shade of light gray. However, the upper one seems to lie in haze, while the lower one seems to lie in clear air.

The single-reversing Xs surrounding the lower diamond indicate that it is a clearer region within a hazier region. The statistics of the upper region are elevated and compressed, indicating the presence of both attenuative and additive processes. Thus the statistical cues and the configural cues point in the same direction: The lower atmosphere is clear while the upper one is hazy.

The shifted Koffka rings

It is useful at this point to recall the modified Koffka display of figure 24.6c. When the two halves are slid vertically, a set of sign-preserving X-junctions is created along the vertical contour. The junctions are consistent with transparency, and the contour becomes a strong atmospheric boundary between the left and right regions. The two semicircles are seen within different frameworks. The statistics on the two sides are different. In addition, grouping cues such as good continuation indicate that the left semicircle is connected to the light region on the right, and the right semicircle is connected to the dark region on the left. Thus there are several cues that conspire to make the two semicircles look quite different.

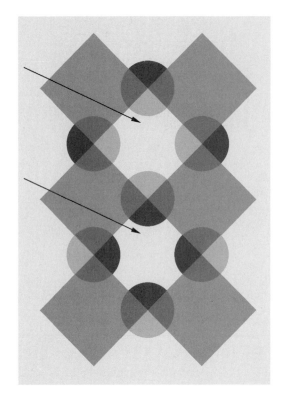

FIGURE 24.17 The haze illusion. The two marked regions are identical shades of gray. One appears clear and the other appears hazy.

T-junctions and White's illusion

White's illusion is shown in figure 24.18. The gray rectangles are the same. This is surprising: By local contrast, the left ones should look darker than the right ones. The left rectangles have a long border with white and a short border with black. The illusion is reversed from the usual direction. This effect has been interpreted in terms of the T-junctions (Todorovic, 1997; Gilchrist et al., in press). Patches straddling the stem of a T are grouped together for the lightness computation, and the crossbar of the T serves as an atmospheric boundary (cf. Anderson, 1997, for an alternative approach).

Zaidi, Spehar, and Shy (1997) have shown that the action of T-junctions can be so strong that it overpowers traditional grouping cues such as coplanarity. Therefore the grouping rules for the lightness computation evidently differ from those underlying subjective belongingness.

Constructing a new illusion

One can intentionally combine statistical and configural cues to produce large contrast illusions. In the "criss-cross" illusion of figure 24.19, the small tilted rectangles in the middle are all the same shade of gray. Many peo-

FIGURE 24.18   White's illusion. The gray rectangles are all the same shade of gray.

ple find this hard to believe. The figure was constructed by the following principles: The multiple ψ-junctions along the vertical edges establish strong atmospheric boundaries. Within each vertical strip there are three luminances and multiple edges to establish articulation. The test patch is the maximum of the distribution within the dark vertical strips, and the minimum of the distribution within the light vertical strips. The combination of tricks leads to a strong illusion.

Each ψ-junction, by itself, would offer evidence of a 3D fold with shading. However, along a given vertical contour the ψ's point in opposite directions, which discourages the folded interpretation. Some observers see the image in terms of transparent strips; others see it merely as a flat painting. However, all subjects see a strong illusion instantly. Thus, a 3D folded percept is not necessary: The illusion works even when "a ψ is just a ψ" (Hupfeld, 1931).

The snake illusion

Similar principles can be used to construct a figure with X-junctions. Figure 24.20a shows an illusion we call the

snake illusion (Somers and Adelson, 1997). The figure is a modification of the simultaneous contrast display shown at the right. The diamonds are the same shade of gray and they are seen against light or dark backgrounds. A set of half-ellipses has been added along the horizontal contours. The X-junctions aligned with the contour are consistent with transparency, and they establish atmospheric boundaries between strips. The statistics within a strip are chosen so that the diamonds are at extrema within the strip distributions. Note that the ellipses do not touch the diamonds, so the edge contrast between each diamond and its surround is unchanged.

Figure 24.20b shows a different modification in which the half-ellipses create a sinuous pattern with no junctions and no sense of transparency. The contrast illusion is weak; for most subjects it is almost gone. Thus, while figures 24.20a and 24.20b have the same diamonds against the same surrounds, the manipulations of the contour greatly change the lightness percept. In effect, we can turn the contrast effect up or down by remote control.

Why should the illusion of figure 24.20b be weaker than in the standard SC? We have various observations suggesting that the best atmospheric boundaries are straight, and that curved contours tend to be interpreted

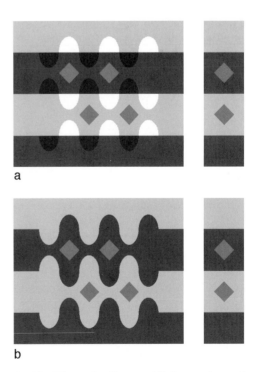

FIGURE 24.20   The snake illusion. All diamonds are the same shade of gray. (a) The regular snake: the diamonds appear quite different. (b) The "anti-snake": the diamonds appear nearly the same. The local contrast relations between diamonds and surrounds are the same in both (a) and (b).

FIGURE 24.19   The crisscross illusion. The small tilted rectangles are all the same shade of gray.

as reflectance. The sinuous contours of figure 24.20b are not seen as atmospheric boundaries, and therefore the adaptive window is free to grow and to mix statistics from both light and dark strips.

Summary

Illusions of lightness and brightness can help reveal the nature of lightness computations in the human visual system. It appears that low-level, mid-level, and high-level factors can all be involved. In this chapter we have emphasized the phenomena related to mid-level processing.

Our evidence, along with the evidence of other researchers, supports the notion that statistical and configural information are combined to estimate the lightness mapping at a given image location. In outline, picture looks like this:

• At every point in an image, there exists an apparent atmospheric transfer function (ATF) mapping reflectance into luminance. To estimate reflectance given luminance, the visual system must invert the mapping, implicitly or explicitly. The inverting function at each point may be called the lightness transfer function (LTF).

• The lightness of a given patch is computed by comparing its luminance to a weighted distribution of neighboring luminances. The exact computation remains unknown.

• Classical mechanisms of perceptual grouping can influence the weights assigned to patches during the lightness computation. The mechanisms may include proximity, good continuation, similarity, and so on. However, the grouping used by the lightness system apparently differs from ordinary perceptual grouping.

• The luminance statistics are gathered within an adaptive window. When the samples are plentiful, the window remains small; but when the samples are sparse, the window expands. The window is soft-edged.

• The adaptive window can change shape and size in order to avoid mixing information from different atmospheres.

• Certain junction types offer evidence that a given contour is the result of a change in atmosphere. The contour then acts as an atmospheric boundary, preventing the information on one side from mixing with that on the other. A series of junctions aligned consistently along a contour produces a strong atmospheric boundary. Some evidence suggests that straight contours make better atmospheric boundaries than curved ones.

REFERENCES

ADELSON, E. H., 1993. Perceptual organization and the judgment of brightness. *Science* 262:2042–2044.

ADELSON, E. H., and P. ANANDAN, 1990. Ordinal characteristics of transparency. *Proceedings of the AAAI-90 Workshop on Qualitative Vision*, pp. 77–81.

ADELSON, E. H., and A. P. PENTLAND, 1996. The perception of shading and reflectance. In *Perception as Bayesian Inference*, D. Knill and W. Richards, eds. New York: Cambridge University Press, pp. 409–423.

ANDERSON, B. L., 1997. A theory of illusory lightness and transparency in monocular and binocular images: The role of contour junctions. *Perception* 26:419–453.

AREND, L., 1994. Surface colors, illumination, and surface geometry: Intrinsic-image models of human color perception. In *Lightness, Brightness, and Transparency*, A. Gilchrist, ed. Hillsdale, N.J.: Erlbaum, pp. 159–213.

BARROW, H. G., and J. TENENBAUM, 1978. Recovering intrinsic scene characteristics from images. In *Computer Vision Systems*, A. R. Hanson and E. M. Riseman, eds. New York: Academic Press, pp. 3–26.

BECK, J., K. PRAZDNY, and R. IVRY, 1984. The perception of transparency with achromatic colors. *Percept. Psychophysics* 35(5):407–422.

CORNSWEET, T., 1970. *Visual Perception*. New York: Academic Press.

GILCHRIST, A. L., 1977. Perceived lightness depends on perceived spatial arrangement. *Science* 195(4274):185–187.

GILCHRIST, A. L., and J. CATALIOTTI, 1994. Anchoring of surface lightness with multiple illumination levels. *Invest. Ophthalmol. Vis. Sci.* (suppl.) 35(4):2165.

GILCHRIST, A. L., and A. JACOBSEN, 1983. Lightness constancy through a veiling luminance. *J. Exp. Psych.* 9(6):936–944.

GILCHRIST, A. L., C. KOSSYFIDIS, F. BONATO, T. AGOSTINI, J. X. L. CATALIOTTI, B. SPEHAR, and J. SZURA, in press. A new theory of lightness perception. *Psych. Rev.*

HOCHBERG, J. E., and J. BECK, 1954. Apparent spatial arrangement and perceived brightness. *J. Exp. Psych.* 47:263–266.

HUPFELD, H., 1931. Lyrics to "As Time Goes By," Harms, Inc., ASCAP. See also *Casablanca*, Warner Brothers, 1942.

KATZ, D., 1935. *The World of Colour*. London: Kegan Paul.

KNILL, D., and D. KERSTEN, 1991. Apparent surface curvature affects lightness perception. *Nature* 351:228–230.

LAND, E. H., and J. J. MCCANN, 1971. Lightness and Retinex theory. *J. Opt. Soc. Amer.* 61:1–11.

LI, X., and A. GILCHRIST, in press. Relative area and relative luminance combine to anchor surface lightness values. *Perception and Psychophysics*.

METELLI, F., 1974. Achromatic color conditions in the perception of transparency. In *Perception, Essays in Honor of J. J. Gibson*, R. B. McLeod and H. L. Pick, eds. Ithaca, N.Y.: Cornell University Press, pp. 93–116.

REID, R. C., and R. SHAPLEY, 1988. Brightness induction by local contrast and the spatial dependence of assimilation. *Vision Res.* 28:115–132.

ROSS, W., and L. PESSOA, in press. A contrast/filling-in model of 3-D lightness perception. *Perception and Psychophysics*.

SINHA, P., and E. H. ADELSON, 1993. Recovering reflectance in a world of painted polyhedra. *Proceedings of Fourth International Conference on Computer Vision*, Berlin; May 11–14, 1993; Los Alamitos, Calif.: IEEE Computer Society Press, pp. 156–163.

SOMERS, D. C., and E. H. ADELSON, 1997. Junctions, transparency, and brightness. *Invest. Ophthalmol. Vis. Sci. (Suppl.)* 38: S453.

SPEHAR, B., I. DeBONET, and Q. ZAIDI, 1996. Brightness induction from uniform and complex surrounds: A general model. *Vision Res.* 36:1893–1906.

TODOROVIC, D., 1997. Lightness and junctions. *Perception* 26(4):379–394.

ZAIDI, Q., B. SPEHAR, and M. SHY, 1997. Induced effects of backgrounds and foregrounds in three-dimensional configurations: The role of T-junctions. *Perception* 26:395–408.

25 High-Level Vision as Statistical Inference

DANIEL KERSTEN

ABSTRACT Human vision is remarkably versatile and reliable, despite the fact that retinal image information is noisy, ambiguous, and confounds the properties of objects that are useful. By treating vision as a problem of statistical inference, three classes of constraints can be identified: the visual task, prior knowledge of scene structure independent of the image, and the relationship between image structure and task requirements. By considering the visual system as an organ for statistical inference, we can test whether and how it uses these constraints. This strategy is illustrated for two high-level visual functions: depth-from-cast-shadows and viewpoint compensation in 3D object recognition.

An object's relative depth can be determined from its cast shadow, even when local image information doesn't uniquely specify shadow edges and global information doesn't determine where the light source is. What information enables a unique estimate of depth from shadows? This chapter shows how the visual task, prior assumptions on light source movement and material properties, and local image cues constrain the perception of depth from shadows.

A 3D object can be recognized from views never seen before, despite the fact that depth information about shape is lost due to projection onto the retina. How does human recognition compensate for variations in viewpoint? By designing a simple recognition task for which optimal statistical decisions are computable, human performance can be normalized with respect to the information in the task, leaving remaining differences diagnostic of brain mechanisms.

High-level vision is often divided into two primary functions: object recognition and localization. Although these visual functions have quite different processing demands, they are linked by a common framework of statistical inference. The need for such a framework spans the levels of visual processing (see figure 25.1), and is due to the inherently statistical relationship between the image measurements at the eye and properties of objects in the world. The statistical problem of vision is both geometric and photometric: The depth dimension is lost owing to projection onto the retina, and information about the geometry of objects gets entangled with photometric information about object ma-

DANIEL KERSTEN Department of Psychology, University of Minnesota, Minneapolis, Minn.

terial and illumination. Image intensity at a point is a complex function of object shapes, materials, illumination, and viewpoint (see figure 25.2). As a result, information about the world is encrypted in the pattern of image intensities and any single source of local image information is only probabilistically related to its causes. This chapter takes seriously the idea that vision consists of brain processes that decrypt image patterns through statistical inference (Kersten, 1990; Yuille and Bülthoff, 1996). Perception as inference has a long history; however, it is with the advent of computer vision that we have begun to understand the inherent complexity of visual inference from natural images and to develop and apply the theoretical principles of perceptual inference (Clark and Yuille, 1990; Knill and Richards, 1996).

Much of our knowledge of the visual system has come through an analysis of early stages of processing in which we try to understand how local contours (defined by intensity, color, texture, disparity, or motion) are grouped to define objects. Consider figure 25.1 for example. Here we see how local constraints of edge collinearity and transparency determine the way contours are grouped in a simple figure, with the result that one sees either overlapping ape faces or nonoverlapping human faces. Research in computer vision has shown, however, that edge detection and object segmentation from natural images is a harder problem. Even apart from ubiquitous image and neural noise, the response of an optimally tuned oriented spatial filter (e.g., simple cell in visual cortex) does not uniquely determine whether the corresponding edge in the scene is due to a shadow, specularity, or a change in depth, orientation, or material (see figure 25.3). Yet such distinctions are crucial for visual function. Adaptive visual behavior depends on reliable decisions regarding object shape, material, and spatial relationships (figure 25.2). Because of the inherent ambiguity in the eye's input regarding these scene properties, vision is sometimes said to be an ill-posed problem. In contrast, the brain has clearly solved the problem–but how? The answers lie both in

353

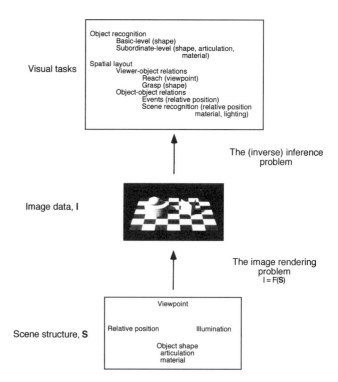

FIGURE 25.1 Different levels of perceptual processing. Vision is often divided into low-, middle-, and high-level levels of processing. Consider the upper left panel, which is usually (but not always) seen as the overlapping profiles of two simians. Low-level vision detects local image features, such as short oriented line segments or corners. Middle-level vision groups image features likely to belong to the same object. High-level vision refers to the type of visual function (e.g., depth perception or object recognition). Here, for example, the grouping is seen either as the overlapping face profiles of two simians or as two human faces. The interpretation of the figure depends on interactions across levels involving visibility of local features, constraints on grouping, and prior expectations on simian and human profiles. For example, middle-level constraints determine how the four lines meeting at the two X-junctions are grouped. A constraint of collinearity interprets the X-junction as two crossing straight lines (rather than touching corners), which is consistent with the simian percept. But a strong prior preference for human profiles can override this middle-level constraint. If the two halves are separated down the middle (lower left panel), one can easily see the other interpretation of two humans. Local constraints on transparency also affect how the contours are grouped (two right panels).

FIGURE 25.2 Constraints on visual inference. Information about object shape, articulation, material, illumination, and viewpoint is encrypted in the image through rendering and projection. Diverse visual tasks depend on estimates of these scene variables. Some scene variable estimates are more important for some tasks than others. The important variables for a task are the *explicit* variables. Variables to be discounted are referred to as *generic*. For example, it is commonly assumed that shape–but not viewpoint, illumination, or material–should be estimated explicitly for basic-level recognition (e.g., deciding whether an image is that of a dog, rather than a particular dog, "Snuggles"). Viewpoint and illumination are generic variables for object recognition at all levels. Hypothesized explicit variables are indicated in parentheses for various visual tasks (top box). The visual task, the nature of the projection of the scene onto the image, and the scene structure probabilities characterize the knowledge required for decoding image data.

1. Natural constraints and visual decisions

One can identify three types of constraints that make reliable visual inference possible: the visual task, prior knowledge of scene structure independent of the image, and the relationship between image structure and task requirements. Bayesian decision theory provides a precise language to model these constraints (Yuille and Bülthoff, 1996). Here we postpone discussion of the visual task and suppose that the image measurements, **I**, and the required scene parameters, **S**, useful for the task have been specified. The knowledge for visual inference is characterized by the posterior probability density, $P(\mathbf{S}|\mathbf{I})$, which models the probability of a scene description **S**, given the image data, **I**. By Bayes' rule,

the nature of visual mechanisms and in the theme of this chapter–the information that enables and constrains reliable visual inference.

the posterior is

$$P(\mathbf{S}|\mathbf{I}) = \frac{P(\mathbf{S})P(\mathbf{I}|\mathbf{S})}{P(\mathbf{I})}$$

$$\propto P(\mathbf{S})P(\mathbf{I}|\mathbf{S}) = P(\mathbf{S})P(\mathbf{I} - F(\mathbf{S}))$$

where $P(\mathbf{I})$ is fixed for a given image measurement.

$P(\mathbf{S})$ is the prior density modeling the scene. In theory, a prior scene model could be realized as an algorithm to produce samples of scenes–including objects, materials, and illuminations–independent of the images that might result. In practice, density models are limited to subdomains such as surface smoothness, shape, contour, or material (Kersten, 1991; Poggio, Torre, and Koch, 1985; Sha'ashua and Ullman, 1988; Zucker and

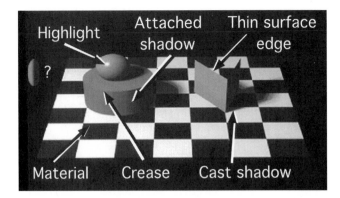

FIGURE 25.3   A measurement of a local change of image intensity, illustrated by the elliptical patch in the upper left, is highly ambiguous as to what in the scene caused it. A change in material, depth, surface orientation, specularity, or shadow can create the same local oriented intensity change, up to a spatial scale factor. (Adapted from Kersten, 1997.)

David, 1988), or specific object domains (e.g., human facial surfaces via principal components analysis; cf. Vetter and Troje, 1997). From the standpoint of inference, knowledge of prior constraints eliminates alternative image interpretations that are consistent with the image data. Once formulated, one can test whether human perception employs the prior constraints (Mamassian and Landy, 1998; Weiss and Adelson, 1998). Later, in section 2, we'll see how the assumption that light sources are usually above objects affects the perception of depth from cast shadows.

$P(\mathbf{I}|\mathbf{S})$ is the likelihood of the image measurements given a scene description. The likelihood is determined by how images are formed–the image rendering problem of computer graphics, $\mathbf{I} = F(\mathbf{S})$.[1] A common example of the likelihood constraint is that straight lines in the scene project to straight lines in the image. The likelihood also provides the tools for reducing ambiguity through cue integration (Landy et al., 1995). *A priori* knowledge of the scene would seem to be required to develop an explicit model of the image. However, Bayes provides tools for learning representations of the image, bottom-up (e.g., Olshausen and Field, 1996; Zhu, Wu, and Mumford, 1997). Mumford (1995) has proposed that minimum description length encoding (formally equivalent to Bayes' maximum *a posteriori* estimation[2]) may provide a general means to discover world structure from images. Specific task requirements can also be used to discover useful image features (e.g., Belhumeur, Hespanha, and Kriegman, 1996). These image-based approaches are important because the problems are posed in a form closer to those of natural adaptation and development. But ultimately, the statistical structure of images derives from how images are formed from the scene.

Let's return to the question of how knowledge of the visual task reduces ambiguity in visual inference.

SPECIFYING THE TASK: EXPLICIT AND GENERIC VARIABLES   Visual problems are often said to be ill-posed when there are more scene parameters to estimate than data. In this case, priors are essential to find unique solutions. However, for specific functional goals, such as visual tracking or face recognition, the number of parameters can be drastically reduced (Blake and Yuille, 1992). With a good representation, the prior is constant, and the decision can be made on the likelihood alone. One still faces the problem that image intensities confound all of the scene variables, both the irrelevant and those required for the task. The relevant and irrelevant scene variables are called explicit and generic, respectively.[3] The general idea is that different visual tasks require a more explicit or precise representation of some scene parameters than others (Brainard and Freeman, 1994; Freeman, 1994; Yuille and Bülthoff, 1996; Hurlbert, Bloj, and Kersten, submitted; figure 25.2, upper box). For example, object recognition relies on an estimation of shape, with viewpoint discounted (section 3). But discounting is not ignoring, and one would like estimates of the scene that are insensitive to the generic variables. In fact, with certain assumptions, finding the most likely estimate of the posterior density of the explicit variable has an appealing intuitive interpretation (Freeman, 1994): Perception's model of the image should be robust over variations in generic variables.[4] This is a generalization of the generic view principle (Lowe, 1985; Nakayama and Shimojo, 1992) and follows from statistical decision theory. Note that, as stated, a literal implementation would be top-down, because it would require measuring variations in the image domain. Section 2 shows how specifying depth and illumination direction as explicit and generic variables, respectively, reduces ambiguity in depth-from-shadows.

The posterior probability defines the visual information available, but one must still extract estimates and decisions according to some criterion. In section 2, we estimate depth from shadows by picking the depth that is most probable. A visual task can also be a simple decision, which makes for good psychophysics. In section 3, we ask humans and a statistically ideal observer to maximize the percent correct in answering the question: Is this the right object?

THE UTILITY OF TREATING VISION AS BAYESIAN INFERENCE   The Bayesian framework has much to offer: It requires one to describe all the assumptions that constrain the visual inference; it specifies quantitative models at a level appropriate for psychophysics, avoiding premature commitment to neural mechanisms; and it provides a common language for psychophysics (Knill and Kersten, 1991) and neural network modeling (Bishop, 1995; Ripley, 1996). A weakness of a Bayesian analysis is that, while prescribing the constraints, it doesn't say how they are embedded in visual mechanisms. However, comparison of human and ideal observers provides hints for neural model implementations, as shown in the object recognition example discussed below.

The rationale for using the Bayesian inversion of the posterior probability is that, although the image rendering constraint is unambiguous, it is usually easier to determine than the inverse. But does Bayes suggest more than a theoretical convenience? It has been argued that the inherent confounding of diverse scene causes in natural patterns, including images, necessitates analysis-by-synthesis through a generative model that tests top-down predictions of the input. One commonly discussed explanation for the pattern of backprojections between cortical areas is that these connections enable the expression of unresolved high-level hypotheses in the language of an earlier level (Mumford, 1994; Dayan et al., 1995). This expression can then be tested with respect to the incoming data at the earlier level. Thus, domain-specific models in memory can be manipulated to check for fits to the incoming data in ways that are difficult bottom-up. We return to this issue below in the discussion of human object recognition mechanisms.

APPLYING THE STATISTICAL INFERENCE APPROACH TO HIGH-LEVEL VISION   We have seen that characterizing the statistical requirements for reliable visual inferences is a complex problem. It requires modeling the signals the world is sending about object shape, material, and location; the way in which the signals get "muddled" in the form of an image; and the optimal means to decode this image. Solving these problems using Bayes' methods for general-purpose vision is not yet feasible. Practical applications to high-level human vision require either (1) a judicious approximation of a natural visual task and qualitative analysis of natural constraints or (2) designing a computable psychophysical task. The latter approach has a successful history in studies of early visual mechanisms (e.g., Barlow, 1962; Geisler, 1989; Knill, 1998; Pelli, 1990; Schrater, Knill, and Simoncelli, 1998) and recent applications to the high-level visual tasks of reading (Legge, Klitz, and Tjan, 1997) and object recognition (Tjan et al., 1995).

Section 2 describes a qualitative analysis of depth-from-cast-shadows, a problem in spatial layout where resolving ambiguity in edge identity is crucial (Knill, Kersten, and Mamassian, 1995). Realistic computer graphics allow the approximation of natural complexity

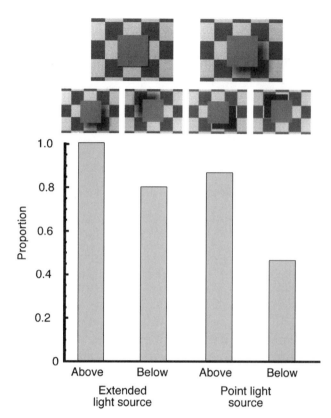

FIGURE 25.4 Depth-from-cast-shadows. Observers viewed computer animations in which a central square was held fixed in the image, while its shadow moved diagonally back and forth from the center outwards. The simulations were produced by moving the central square back and forth directly along the line of sight. By using orthographic projection, the image size is independent of depth and thus remained constant. The upper panel shows first and last frames for the main condition, in which the illumination was from an extended light source above and to the left of the square. The middle panel shows final frames for this condition, as well as three others. From left to right, the conditions are: extended light source from above, extended light source from below, point light source from above, and point light source from below. The extended light source (e.g., a fluorescent panel) produces a penumbra that gets fuzzier as the square gets farther away from the background. Despite the lack of objective image motion of the central square, it almost always appeared to move in depth for the extended-light-from-above condition. The bar graph (lower panel) shows the proportion of times (out of 15) observers reported the central square patch to be moving in depth for extended and point light sources from above or below. There is a significant advantage of an extended light versus a point source ($z = 2.28$, $p < .02$), and of light from above versus below ($z = 3.028$, $p < .002$). A QuickTime™ movie demonstrating illusory motion from shadows can be viewed and downloaded from: http://vision.psych.umn.edu/www/kersten-lab/shadows.html. (Adapted from Kersten et al., 1996.)

while retaining sufficient simplicity to analyze the image ambiguities and identify natural constraints. Section 3 describes an investigation of the problem of viewpoint variation in object recognition, where the second

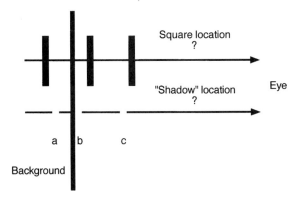

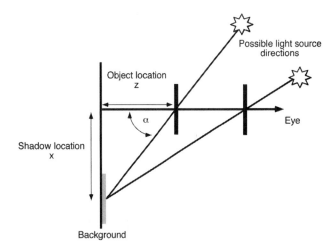

FIGURE 25.5 Ambiguities of material and spatial layout for the depth-from-shadows movies. Assume the central square, the "shadow," and background of figure 25.4 have been segmented, but not labeled according to whether they are opaque material, transparent material, or shadow. Image formation constraints guarantee that the central square and the dark shadow regions lie somewhere along the line of sight—but where? The background could be transparent and in front of the shadow (a), rather than the reverse (b or c). If outside the eye's depth-of-field, the ersatz shadow image would mimic the fuzziness of a penumbra change. If the shadow patch was instead a transparent surface, it could be at location b or c; but if a shadow, it would have to be at b. Occlusion cues place the square in front of the background. For a reliable inference of depth-from-shadows, the shadow has to be labeled as such, localized to the background, and linked to the casting object. And then one is left with two more questions: Where is the light source, and is the motion in the image due to movement of the light source or the central square (see figure 25.6).

FIGURE 25.6 The visual task constrains the estimate of relative depth-from-shadows. This figure shows a very simplified view of the geometric constraints where we've assumed that the remaining unknowns are the light source direction, α, and relative depth, z. By treating light source direction as a generic variable, one can show that the best bet for the target depth is $z = x$.

approach, often called *ideal-observer* analysis, is adopted (Liu and Kersten, 1998; Liu, Knill, and Kersten, 1995). A key issue is how recognition overcomes the geometric problem of projection. Ideal-observer analysis provides a rigorous means to normalize human performance with respect to the informational limits imposed by the task itself, and thereby draw firm conclusions about the underlying mechanisms.

2. Depth-from-cast-shadows: Qualitative analysis of constraints

One can list more than a dozen cues to depth, including stereo disparity, motion parallax, and the pictorial cues. One of the pictorial cues, depth-from-cast-shadows, is particularly interesting because it is surprisingly strong for human perception (under some conditions dominating motion or stereo; Kersten et al., 1996) and seems to involve a complex set of inferences, which we explore below (Kersten, Mamassian, and Knill, 1997; Mamassian, Knill, and Kersten, 1998). From a theoretical standpoint, we do not yet have a quantitative theory of how to compute depth from shadows, even in principle. This is in contrast to depth from stereo disparity or mo-

tion parallax where the computational problems are well-understood.

To investigate depth-from-shadows experimentally, Kersten and colleagues (1996) made a movie of a square in front of a stationary checkerboard illuminated with an extended light source (figure 25.4, top panel). The central square was fixed in the image, and the only movement was that of a shadow translating diagonally away and then back to the square. Despite the square's lack of motion, observers reported an initial strong perception of the square moving in depth. The computer animation looks realistic and the perceptual interpretation unique, yet the image data have significant ambiguities of material and depth (figure 25.5), and of light source motion and direction (figure 25.6). This simple percept involves a range of decisions across several levels of abstraction. Let's consider, in turn, inferences of (1) context, (2) motion event, (3) image region categorization, and (4) depth parameter estimation.

1. A key question of context is: Which of the objects or viewer provides the frame of reference with which to interpret the locations of the other object(s)? Viewpoint should be generic for deciding whether the square is headed away from the checkerboard, but explicit if the task is to reach to the square. The central square, not the background, appears to move. Relative size, enclosure, and occlusion information in the image may all provide support for the decision that the checkerboard provides a stationary frame of reference. The decision that the background is opaque (see figure 25.5) must involve a prior default on material, because the same image could

have resulted from a transparent background and opaque "shadow"–a percept which can be seen given training (Kersten et al., 1992).

2. At some level, an object–shadow "event" must be identified. This could involve combining independent identifications of surface and shadow image regions, or using global image information. Other experiments suggest that characteristic correlated motion, an image formation constraint, may be a global diagnostic for a moving object–shadow pair because of its robustness with respect to viewpoint variation (Kersten, Mamassian, and Knill, 1997). For moving objects, the linkage between the object and its shadow is strongly constrained by a prior assumption that light sources usually don't move. The assumption that light sources are usually from above accounts for the finding that shadows above the object are less effective than those below (figure 25.4)–an assumption well known for shape-from-shading (Gibson, 1950).

3. Computing relative depth depends on either an explicit or implicit categorization of image regions as opaque surface, transparent surface, or shadowed surface. A particularly diagnostic cue for motion in depth is the changing fuzziness of the penumbra caused by an extended light source. This was the most effective condition in figure 25.4. Such a local image measurement has less ambiguity with other scene causes (e.g., it is less likely to be confused with a material change, although it could result from surface edge motion out of the depth-of-field range, or a spreading stain). This cue is also robust over viewpoint, and a large range of types of illumination. In contrast, the sharp shadow is often seen as a transparent surface–a decision also supported by local transparency constraints at X-junctions (Metelli, 1975). Physically unnatural light "shadows" violate local transparency constraints consistent with shadows and lead to less effective apparent motion (Kersten, Mamassian, and Knill, 1997). Occlusion of the shadow by the object is a potentially important constraint for determining which patch of the object–shadow pair is the shadow; however, occlusion isn't necessary for depth-from-cast-shadows.

Local cues supporting a shadow hypothesis have to be weighed against the conflicting cues regarding motion in depth. Size change and velocity in the image are both zero, indicating no motion in depth. This is a consequence of viewpoint's being a generic variable. The alternative interpretation is of a square moving directly along the line of sight, but this is normally ruled out because small changes in viewpoint would produce large changes in the image. The fact that depth change with shadow motion is seen is evidence of a strong prior stationary light source constraint.

4. A visual estimation can be made as to the square's location or velocity from the measured shadow location or velocity. Suppose the object–shadow pair is detected, the shadow identified and localized to the background surface. The stationary light source assumption would resolve ambiguity regarding motion in depth. But what about a stationary case? Where is the light source?

THE VISUAL TASK CONSTRAINS AN ESTIMATE OF RELATIVE DEPTH: ROBUSTNESS WITH RESPECT TO GENERIC VARIABLES   Consider the simple geometric ambiguity illustrated in figure 25.6. The measured displacement, x, between the image of an object and its shadow can be caused by an infinite number of combinations of object distance, z, and light source direction, α: $x = z \tan(\alpha)$. An additional constraint is required to estimate z from x. One could try to measure (or make up) a prior on the light direction that would produce a unique estimate of z. But the task itself provides a sufficient constraint to uniquely estimate z. Assume that the explicit variable is relative depth z, and the generic variable is light source direction α. By differentiating the above geometric constraint on object, shadow, and light source parameters (see note 4), we have $\Delta x = \Delta\alpha(x^2 + z^2)/z$. For a given variation $\Delta\alpha$, the minimum change in Δx would occur for $z = x$. Perception's estimate of shadow displacement is most robust to variations in light direction for relative depths equal to the displacement, i.e., equivalent to assuming the light is at 45 degrees. At this point, we do not know the generality or precision with which the robustness principle predicts human estimates of depth-from-shadows, our point being to illustrate how task requirements reduce ambiguity. However, in the domain of color constancy, treating illumination direction as a generic variable has been shown to quantitatively predict color matches contingent on the mutual illumination between surfaces (Hurlbert, Bloj, and Kersten, submitted).

3. Viewpoint compensation in 3D object recognition: Ideal-observer analysis

A basic component of 3D object recognition is a process that verifies matches between the input stimulus and stored object representations in memory. The problem is that the images of a single object are enormously variable, depending on viewpoint, among other factors. The visual system must somehow compensate for such variations in order to identify an object as the same when seen from another viewpoint. There has been recent debate regarding the nature of these stored representations and the mechanisms that test for a match. On the one hand, certain object properties such as edge straightness are preserved in the image over viewpoint changes, suggesting that the early extraction of such features could be used fairly directly (Biederman, 1987; Hummel and Biederman, 1992). On the other hand, computer vision has shown the difficulties in extracting features such as edges from natural images. Further, the experimental observation that familiar views of an object are processed more effectively than unfamiliar views suggests that the memory of an object may be closely tied to images previously seen of that object (Bülthoff and Edelman, 1992; Tarr and Bülthoff, 1995).

How does the visual system compensate for image variations in size, position, and rotation in depth produced by an object? One can devise schemes to allow for variations in scale and position through feedforward mechanisms (Ullman, 1996). Neurons insensitive to object scale and position have been found in inferotemporal cortex of monkeys (Logothetis et al., 1994). Allowing for rotations in depth, however, seems more problematic because depth information is lost in the 2D projection, so one doesn't know how to transform the image to allow for these rotations. Let's consider two cases that differ in the degree to which 3D information is involved in a test for a match.

Suppose that an object is represented as a collection of independent 2D images or views in memory. These views have, through experience, come to be associated with each other, and have a common label. In order to recognize a novel view, similarity is measured independently between this novel view and each of the familiar views. The combination of the measurements determines if the novel view should be recognized or rejected. Although the measure of similarity has some flexibility, the crucial point is that recognition can be achieved with 2D manipulations of the images without reconstructing the 3D structure of the object either explicitly or implicitly (Bülthoff and Edelman, 1992; Poggio and Edelman, 1990). Below we describe a "smarter" version of such a model for human vision (the 2D/2D observer), which in addition allows for possible rotations in 2D for each template view.

Contrast this with a second case in which there is a candidate 3D object model in memory. Then the appropriate transformation could be applied to the model in memory, and thus compensate for rotations in depth in order to test for a match. Imagine two subcases. The most straightforward identification scheme verifies a match by translating, scaling, and rotating an explicit 3D model of the object in memory, projecting the result in a 2D image space, then using a measure of similarity to test for a satisfactory match with the 2D input (Basri and Weinshall, 1996). The statistically optimal version of this model is called a 3D/2D ideal observer (Liu, Knill, and

Kersten, 1995). Despite its intuitive simplicity, a straightforward implementation is computationally unrealistic even for simple objects–the space of transformations is just too big. However, a clever shortcut was discovered by Ullman and Basri (1991): With as few as two views one could carry out the verification process by checking the linear dependence of the input image on the two stored views.

Liu, Knill, and Kersten (1995) devised a 3D object discrimination task for which they could calculate ideal performance for the 2D/2D and 3D/2D classes of observers. By comparing human with ideal performance, they were able to factor out limitations imposed by the task itself, and thereby investigate how the human visual system compensates for viewpoint change.

Their object world was simple: Five randomly placed vertices (3D points) were connected by four straight cylinders of uniform diameter, making 3D wire prototype objects that looked like bent paper clips. A pair of objects was generated from a prototype by adding independent 3D positional Gaussian noise at the vertex points. One object is called the target, whose Gaussian noise has a fixed variance. The other is called the distractor, whose variance is always larger. In the test phase, the novel views of an object could have any orientation in space–i.e., the prior probability on rotations in 3D was uniform. The 3D/2D observer has complete knowledge of the target object and task. Prior knowledge of the target object is given in the form of 11 views to the 2D/2D observer, and to the human observers through training.

In contrast to the analysis of depth-from-cast-shadows, the task requirements for the ideal and human observers are precisely specified. Optimal recognition performance is based on the shape of the object defined by the image vertex positions (explicit variables), with viewpoint variables being generic. The task is summarized in figure 25.7. Both the human and ideal observers must choose from the two images an object that is more similar (in Euclidean distance) of the feature points to the prototype object.

3D/2D IDEAL OBSERVER   Let's formalize the inference constraints for the 3D/2D ideal observer. Occlusion can be neglected because the vertex feature points for wire objects are visible from almost all viewing angles. Further, because the vertices are connected, one knows how to order the vertices when comparing stimulus to memory. The visual decision is based on a representation of the objects and images in terms of 15 and 10 dimensional vector vertex locations, respectively.

The 3D/2D ideal observer matches the stimulus image against all possible views of a known prototype object.

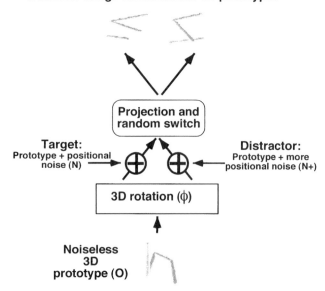

Which 2D image best matches 3D prototype?

Projection and random switch

Target: Prototype + positional noise (N)

Distractor: Prototype + more positional noise (N+)

3D rotation (φ)

Noiseless 3D prototype (O)

FIGURE 25.7 The 3D object classification task presented to human and ideal observers. The observers are required to discriminate between two classes of wire object—one generated by adding a small fixed amount of noise to the vertices of a prototype object (the target), and the other generated by adding a larger amount of noise to the prototype object (distractor). The means for both target and distractor sets are the same prototype object. Two stimuli were generated by a 3D rotation of the noiseless prototype. The standard deviation of the positional noise added to the distractor (prototype + more noise) was greater than that added to the signal (prototype + noise). Knowledge of the wire objects was provided in a prior training session in which the object prototype was first learned from a discrete number (11 rotations) of its images. The 11 training views of a prototype object were created by rotating the object first around the x-axis (horizontal in the screen plane) six times in 60-degree steps, and then around the y-axis (vertical in the screen plane) six times, again with 60-degree rotational steps, resulting in 11 views of the object. The angle with the z-axis was chosen from a uniform density between 0 and 180 degrees and the angle with x-axis was chosen from a uniform density between 0 and 360 degrees.

By definition, the ideal's image rendering model is

$$\mathbf{I} = F_{\Phi}(\mathbf{O}) + \mathbf{N}_p$$

where **I** and **O** are vector representations of the 2D vertex positions of the 2D image and 3D vertex positions of the object, respectively. $F_{\Phi}(\bullet)$ represents the combined effects of an unknown viewpoint transformation in 3D (represented by a three-component vector Φ), followed by orthographic projection. $\mathbf{N}_p$ is the positional noise of the projected vertex positions. An ideal observer can detect only the 2D vertex positions in a stimulus image but has a full 3D model of the prototype. Such an observer would estimate the probability of obtaining image $\mathbf{I}_k$ from the target (smaller noise variance)

by integrating out the generic viewpoint variables to obtain the probability of $\mathbf{I}_k$, $p_t(\mathbf{I}_k)$.[5] To achieve the maximum average percent correct, the ideal observer chooses the image ($k = 1$ or 2) with the larger value of $p_t(\mathbf{I}_k)$.

The essence of the 3D/2D ideal observer is that it provides an exact model of the 3D object, **O**, in memory, as well as precise knowledge of how such an object in the world could be transformed into an image, **I**. This transformation includes the unknown generic variables of rotation. A key component in the ideal calculation is a measurement of similarity; because the noise is Gaussian, this is given by $\|\mathbf{I} - F_{\Phi}(\mathbf{T}_i)\|^2$. In theory, a straightforward implementation of the probability calculation would involve manipulations in a 3D object space followed by backprojection of the model into image space to measure the similarity. (Again, because of the large transformation space, this calculation isn't feasible; see Liu, Knill, and Kersten, 1995, for an approximation). The 2D/2D observer is an alternative way of measuring similarity—one that relies on manipulations that can, in principle, be done entirely in a 2D image space. In efficiency, it is lower than the 3D/2D observer's, but can it account for human performance?

THE 2D/2D OBSERVER In the experimental task, an observer sees 11 distinct views of the object—familiar views from which a 3D/2D observer could, in theory, construct a 3D object model, **O** (11 is more than enough to do this). Suppose, however, that there was no mechanism to construct such a model, and the recognition system had to rely on making matches of the 11 familiar views in memory to the stimulus image. Further suppose the observer had available rigid rotations in the 2D plane to compensate for the normal image variations that arise through 3D rotations. This 2D/2D observer has the wrong image-rendering model. Yet it does its best by optimally combining information from stored multiple views under the constraint of 2D rigid transformations specified by a rotation matrix, R_{ϕ}.

Let **I** represent the coordinates of the vertices in a stimulus image, and $\mathbf{T} = \{\mathbf{T}_1, \mathbf{T}_2, \ldots, \mathbf{T}_{11}\}$ represent the 11 prototype templates. The ideal decision is based on $p_t(\mathbf{I})$ where the viewpoint compensation is restricted to the 2D image domain.[6] Because a rotation of the model ($R_{\phi}(\mathbf{T}_i)$) is equivalent to an inverse rotation of the image ($R_{\phi}^{-1}(\mathbf{I})$) for the 2D/2D observer, variation over viewpoint can be compensated for either by feedforward or backprojection.

HUMAN PERFORMANCE Figure 25.8 shows human performance relative to the 3D/2D and 2D/2D observers for decisions based on both familiar and novel views.

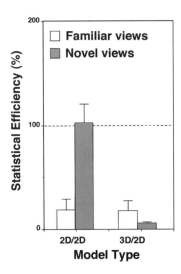

FIGURE 25.8 Statistical efficiencies for human performance relative to the 3D/2D and 2D/2D observers. The error bars show ±1 standard deviation.

Performance is measured in terms of statistical efficiency.[7] The 3D/2D efficiency factors out the limits to performance imposed by the task itself, independent of any algorithm used to compute decisions. The 2D/2D efficiencies are expressed in the same units.

First note that 3D/2D efficiencies are much less than 100%. There are two main sources of inefficiency for humans: intrinsic noise and an inappropriate transformation process. If the only problem were some internal uncertainty added to the artificially introduced positional noise, the efficiencies for familiar and novel views would be the same. The fact that novel views are dealt with less efficiently is consistent with theories of recognition that assume the visual memory for an object is closely tied to its stored familiar views. The 2D/2D observer is a precise definition of one such view-dependent model. But now note that the statistical efficiencies for novel views are too high. In fact, efficiencies exceeding 100% means that we can exclude from the human-performance model any implementation that verifies matches using remembered templates and rigid image manipulations.

These results show that human recognition uses a much "dumber" view-compensation mechanism than the 3D/2D ideal observer, but a "smarter" one than an independent comparison with stored views. One candidate smarter model would be to allow for 2D affine transformations that include translation, rotation, scale, and skew adjustments in the image domain. Recent work shows that this kind of view compensation gets us closer to human performance, but still fails to account for human ability to recognize novel views (Liu and Kersten, 1998).

4. Conclusions

We have seen how two quite different high-level visual functions, perception of depth and object recognition, can be investigated within the common framework of statistical inference. The perception of depth-from-cast-shadows involves a remarkable synthesis of default prior assumptions on material and lighting, local image cues, and global constraints. We've considered just one of more than a dozen sources of information for depth. A quantitative computational model for the perception of spatial layout is an important challenge for future vision research.

A key problem in 3D object recognition is understanding how the brain compensates for variations in viewpoint. By designing a relatively simple visual task for which the optimal inference is computable, one can pit human and ideal observers against each other in the same task. While the computational formulations can be demanding, ideal-observer analysis has the potential to rigorously test well-defined models of human high-level visual functions. Statistical efficiency normalizes performance with respect to the information in the task, with remaining differences diagnostic of processing mechanisms of the visual brain. This research has shown that independent comparisons of images to templates in memory cannot account for human viewpoint compensation, even with some flexibility (via 2D rigid transformations) allowed in the matching process.

For natural images, the information for high-level vision is complex and difficult to model. Our solution to this complexity for depth-from-shadows was a qualitative Bayesian analysis of realistic images. The ideal-observer study of object recognition took a different approach, using a computable but artificial model of uncertainty. A major goal for future research is to develop quantitative ideal observer models for high-level visual functions based on objectively modeled natural image and scene statistics (Zhu, Wu, and Mumford, 1997; Simoncelli, 1997).

ACKNOWLEDGMENTS The author's research is supported by the National Science Foundation (SBR-9631682) and the National Institutes of Health (RO1 EY11507-001). I also thank Zili Liu, Cindee Madison, Paul Schrater, Brian Stankiewicz, and Colin Blakemore for their help.

NOTES

1. If there is no imaging noise, the density $P(\mathbf{I} - F(\mathbf{S}))$ is a delta function, $\delta(\mathbf{I} - F(\mathbf{S}))$. The delta density is a zero-tolerance filter for wrong scenes—it is zero for scenes that don't predict the image data and infinitely high for those that do.
2. The intuition behind the equivalence is due to Shannon—that one can achieve efficient communication (in our case, the brain's decoding of scene properties encrypted in the

image) by seeking shorter image codes, x (in bits), for the more probable scene properties, and longer ones for the less probable ones (i.e., by setting length(x) = $-\log_2 P(x)$). The total message length is the sum of the length of the code itself plus the length of any discrepancies between the code's description of $\mathbf{I}$, and the actual $\mathbf{I}$: length(code, $\mathbf{I}$) = length(code) + length($\mathbf{I} - F$(code)). Applying $\log_2()$ to Bayes' formula shows the equivalence: The shortest code, for image $\mathbf{I}$, will also maximize the posterior probability $p(\mathbf{S}|\mathbf{I})$, which, if the code = $\mathbf{S}$, would be the most likely scene description.

3. More generally, Bayesian decision theory softens the sharp distinction between explicit and generic variables by defining a loss function $L(S, \Sigma)$ which is the penalty for Σ (the estimate of S) when the true scene parameter is S. Then the optimal decision minimizes the risk:

$$R(\Sigma_G, \Sigma_E) = \int L(S_G, \Sigma_G; S_E, \Sigma_E) P(S_E, S_G | I) \, dS_G \, dS_E$$

where the subscripts E and G indicate explicit and generic variables. With a loss function, $-\delta(\Sigma_E - S_E)$, where the cost to errors in the generic variable is constant, minimizing risk is equivalent to marginalizing the posterior with respect to the generic variable (i.e., integrating out the generic variable),

$$P(S_E | I) = \int P(S_G, S_E | I) \, dS_G$$

and choosing the maximum of this posterior density.

4. Suppose we have an image measurement, x, which depends on a generic variable, α, and explicit variable z: $x = F(z, \alpha)$. The problem is that we have two unknowns and only one measurement. Assume that the prior, $p(z, \alpha)$, is constant over some domain; then using Bayes' rule, we have $p(z|x) \propto \int p(x|z, \alpha) \, d\alpha$. Assuming Gaussian measurement noise, we have $p(z|x) \propto \int e^{-(x - F(z, \alpha))^2/2\sigma^2} \, d\alpha$. Let $S(\alpha) = (x - F(z, \alpha))^2$. If α_M is a solution of $S(\alpha_M) = 0$, then the Taylor series expansion of $S(\alpha)$ about α_M is

$$S(\alpha) \approx (\alpha - \alpha_M)^2 \frac{\partial^2 S}{\partial \alpha^2}\bigg|_{\alpha = \alpha_M} = 2(\alpha - \alpha_M)^2 \left(\frac{\partial F}{\partial \alpha}\right)^2\bigg|_{\alpha = \alpha_M},$$

and

$$p(z|x) \propto \int e^{-(\alpha - \alpha_M)^2/2\sigma'^2} \, d\alpha,$$

where

$$\sigma' = \sigma/2\left(\frac{\partial F}{\partial \alpha}\right)^2\bigg|_{\alpha = \alpha_M}.$$

This is a standard Gaussian integral, which evaluates to

$$p(z|x) \propto 1/\left|\frac{\partial F}{\partial \alpha}\right|_{\alpha = \alpha_M}.$$

Thus, more probable values of z result when changes in the generic variable, α, produce small changes in x (= $F(z, \alpha)$).

5. Formally, the 3D/2D ideal observer's probability is

$$p_t(\mathbf{I}_k) = \int p(\mathbf{N}_p = \mathbf{I} - F_\Phi(\mathbf{O})) p(\Phi) \, d\Phi$$

$$\propto \int e^{-\|\mathbf{I} - F_\Phi(\mathbf{T}_i)\|^2/\sigma^2} p(\Phi) \, d\Phi.$$

6. The probability, $p_t(\mathbf{I})$, for the 2D/2D observer is given by

$$p_t(\mathbf{I}) = \sum_{i=1}^{11} \int_0^{2\pi} [p(\mathbf{I} - R_\phi(\mathbf{T}_i)) p(R_\phi(\mathbf{T}_i))] \, d\phi$$

where $p(\mathbf{I}|R_\phi(\mathbf{T}_i))$ is the probability that $\mathbf{I}$ was generated by adding noise to template $\mathbf{T}_i$ at 2D rotation angle ϕ. The prior probability, $p(R_\phi(\mathbf{T}_i))$, is constant (= $1/2\pi$). The actual calculation used was slightly more complicated to allow for uncertainty as to which vertex was first.

7. Statistical efficiency is defined as the ratio of the number of data samples the ideal requires to the number the human observer requires for an identical level of performance, e.g., same percent correct (see Liu, Knill, and Kersten, 1995).

REFERENCES

BARLOW, H. B., 1962. A method of determining the overall quantum efficiency of visual discriminations. *J. Physiol. (Lond.)* 160:155–168.

BASRI, R., and D. WEINSHALL, 1996. Distance metric between 3D models and 2D images for recognition and classification. *IEEE Transactions on Pattern Analysis and Machine Intelligence* 18:465–470.

BELHUMEUR, P. N., J. P. HESPANHA, and D. J. KRIEGMAN, 1996. Eigenfaces vs. fisherfaces: Recognition using class specific linear projection. *IEEE Transactions on Pattern Analysis and Machine Intelligence* 19:711–720.

BIEDERMAN, I., 1987. Recognition-by-components: A theory of human image understanding. *Psychol. Rev.* 94:115–147.

BISHOP, C. M., 1995. *Neural Networks for Pattern Recognition.* Oxford: Oxford University Press.

BLAKE, A., and A. YUILLE, 1992. *Active Vision.* Cambridge, Mass.: MIT Press.

BRAINARD, D. H., and W. T. FREEMAN, 1994. Bayesian method for recovering surface and illuminant properties from photosensor responses. In *Human Vision, Visual Processing, and Digital Display V*, Vol. 2179. Bellingham, Wash.: Society of Photo-Optical Instrumentation Engineers, pp. 364–376.

BÜLTHOFF, H. H., and S. EDELMAN, 1992. Psychophysical support for a two-dimensional view interpolation theory of object recognition. *Proc. Natl. Acad. Sci. U.S.A.* 89:60–64.

CLARK, J. J., and A. L. YUILLE, 1990. *Data Fusion for Sensory Information Processing.* Boston: Kluwer.

DAYAN, P., G. E. HINTON, R. M. NEAL, and R. S. ZEMEL, 1995. The Helmholtz machine. *Neural Computation* 7(5):889–904.

FREEMAN, W. T., 1994. The generic viewpoint assumption in a framework for visual perception. *Nature* 368:542–545.

GEISLER, W., 1989. Sequential ideal-observer analysis of visual discriminations. *Psychol. Rev.* 96(2):267–314.

GIBSON, J. J., 1950. *The Perception of the Visual World.* Boston, Mass.: Houghton Mifflin.

HUMMEL, J. E., and I. BIEDERMAN, 1992. Dynamic binding in a neural network for shape recognition. *Psychol. Rev.* 99(3):480–517.

HURLBERT, A. C., BLOJ, M., and KERSTEN, D., submitted. Visual perception discounts the color of mutual illumination.

KERSTEN, D., 1990. Statistical limits to image understanding. In *Vision: Coding and Efficiency*, C. Blakemore, ed. Cambridge: Cambridge University Press, pp. 32–44.

KERSTEN, D. J., 1991. Transparency and the cooperative computation of scene attributes. In *Computational Models of Visual Processing*, M. Landy and A. Movshon, eds. Cambridge, Mass.: MIT Press, pp. 209–228.

KERSTEN, D., 1997. Inverse 3D graphics: A metaphor for visual perception. *Behavior Research Methods, Instruments, and Computers* 29(1):37–46.

KERSTEN, D., H. H. BÜLTHOFF, B. SCHWARTZ, and K. KURTZ, 1992. Interaction between transparency and structure from motion. *Neural Computation* 4(4):573–589.

KERSTEN, D., D. C. KNILL, P. MAMASSIAN, and I. BÜLTHOFF, 1996. Illusory motion from shadows. *Nature* 379:31.

KERSTEN, D., P. MAMASSIAN, and D. C. KNILL, 1997. Moving cast shadows induce apparent motion in depth. *Perception* 26(2):171–192.

KNILL, D. C., 1998. Surface orientation from texture: Ideal observers, generic observers and the information content of texture cues. *Vision Res.* 38:1655–1682.

KNILL, D. C., and D. KERSTEN, 1991. Ideal perceptual observers for computation, psychophysics, and neural networks. In *Pattern Recognition by Man and Machine*, R. J. Watt, ed. New York: Macmillan, pp. 83–97.

KNILL, D. C., D. KERSTEN, and P. MAMASSIAN, 1996. The Bayesian framework for visual information processing: Implications for psychophysics. In *Perception as Bayesian Inference*, D. C. Knill and W. Richards, eds. Cambridge: Cambridge University Press, pp. 239–286.

KNILL, D. C., and W. RICHARDS, eds., 1996. *Perception as Bayesian Inference*. Cambridge: Cambridge University Press.

LANDY, M. S., L. T. MALONEY, E. B. JOHNSTON, and M. J. YOUNG, 1995. Measurement and modeling of depth cue combination: In defense of weak fusion. *Vision Res.* 35:389–412.

LEGGE, G. E., T. S. KLITZ, and B. S. TJAN, 1997. Mr. Chips: An ideal-observer model of reading. *Psychol. Rev.* 104(3):524–553.

LIU, Z., and D. KERSTEN, 1998. 2D observers for 3D object recognition? *Vision Res.* 38:2507–2519.

LIU, Z., D. C. KNILL, and D. KERSTEN, 1995. Object classification for human and ideal observers. *Vision Res.* 35(4):549–568.

LOGOTHETIS, N. K., J. PAULS, H. H. BÜLTHOFF, and T. POGGIO, 1994. View-dependent object recognition in monkeys. *Curr. Biol.* 4(5):401–414.

LOWE, D. G., 1985. *Perceptual Organization and Visual Recognition*. Kluwer International Series in Engineering and Computer Science. *Robotics: Vision, Manipulation*. Boston: Kluwer Academic.

MAMASSIAN, P., D. C. KNILL, and D. KERSTEN, 1998. The perception of cast shadows. *Trends Cogn. Sci.* 2:288–295.

MAMASSIAN, P., and M. S. LANDY, 1998. Observer biases in the 3D interpretation of line drawings. *Vision Res.* 38:2817–2832.

METELLI, F., 1975. Shadows without penumbra. In *Gestaltentheorie in der modernen Psychologie*, S. Ertel, L. Kemmler, and L.

Stadler, eds. Darmstadt, Germany: Dietrich Steinkopff, pp. 200–209.

MUMFORD, D., 1994. Neuronal architectures for pattern-theoretic problems. In *Large-Scale Neuronal Theories of the Brain*, C. Koch and J. L. Davis, eds. Cambridge, Mass.: MIT Press, pp. 125–152.

MUMFORD, D., 1995. Pattern theory: A unifying perspective. In *Perception as Bayesian Inference*, D. C. Knill and W. Richards, eds. Cambridge: Cambridge University Press, Chapter 2.

NAKAYAMA, K., and S. SHIMOJO, 1992. Experiencing and perceiving visual surfaces. *Science* 257:1357–1363.

OLSHAUSEN, B. A., and D. J. FIELD, 1996. Emergence of simple-cell receptive field properties by learning a sparse code for natural images. *Nature* 381:607–609.

PELLI, D. G., 1990. The quantum efficiency of vision. In *Vision: Coding and Efficiency*, C. Blakemore, ed. Cambridge: Cambridge University Press, pp. 3–24.

POGGIO, T., and S. EDELMAN, 1990. A network that learns to recognize three-dimensional objects. *Nature* 343:263–266.

POGGIO, T., V. TORRE, and C. KOCH, 1985. Computational vision and regularization theory. *Nature* 317:314–319.

RIPLEY, B. D., 1996. *Pattern Recognition and Neural Networks*. Cambridge: Cambridge University Press.

SCHRATER, P. R., D. C. KNILL, and E. P. SIMONCELLI, 1998. Mechanisms of visual motion detection. Unpublished.

SHA'ASHUA, A., and S. ULLMAN, 1988. Structural saliency: The detection of globally salient structures using a locally connected network. In *2nd International Conference on Computer Vision* 88:321–327. Washington, D.C.: IEEE Computer Society Press.

SIMONCELLI, E. P., 1997. Statistical models for images: Compression, restoration, and synthesis. In *31st Asilomar Conference on Signals, Systems, and Computers*. Pacific Grove, Calif.: IEEE Signal Processing Society.

TARR, M. J., and H. H. BÜLTHOFF, 1995. Is human object recognition better described by geon-structural-descriptions or by multiple-views? *J. Exp. Psychol.* 21(6):1494–1505.

TJAN, B., W. BRAJE, G. E. LEGGE, and D. KERSTEN, 1995. Human efficiency for recognizing 3-D objects in luminance noise. *Vision Res.* 35(21):3053–3069.

ULLMAN, S., 1996. *High-Level Vision: Object Recognition and Visual Cognition*. Cambridge, Mass.: MIT Press.

ULLMAN, S., and R. BASRI, 1991. Recognition by linear combinations of models. *IEEE Transactions on Pattern Analysis and Machine Intelligence* 13(10):992–1006.

VETTER, T., and N. F. TROJE, 1997. Separation of texture and shape in images of faces for image coding and synthesis. *J. Opt. Soc. Amer. A* 14(9):2152–2161.

WEISS, Y., and E. H. ADELSON, 1998. Slow and smooth: A Bayesian theory for the combination of local motion signals in human vision (MIT A.I. Memo No. 1624).

YUILLE, A. L., and H. H. BÜLTHOFF, 1996. Bayesian decision theory and psychophysics. In *Perception as Bayesian Inference*, D. C. Knill and W. Richards, eds. Cambridge: Cambridge University Press, pp. 123–166.

ZHU, S. C., Y. WU, and D. MUMFORD, 1997. Minimax entropy principle and its applications to texture modeling. *Neural Computation* 9(8):1627–1660.

ZUCKER, S. W., and C. DAVID, 1988. The organization of curve detection: Coarse tangent fields and fine spline coverings. In *Proceedings 2nd International Conference on Computer Vision*. Tarpon Springs, Fla.: IEEE Computer Society Press.

26 Perception and Action in the Human Visual System

MELVYN A. GOODALE

ABSTRACT Evidence from studies with neurological patients and normal observers has shown that the control of skilled actions depends on visual processes that are quite independent from those that lead to perception-based knowledge of the world. Moreover, this distinction between vision for perception and vision for action is reflected in the organization of the visual pathways in primate cerebral cortex. Two broad "streams" of projections from primary visual cortex have been identified: a ventral stream projecting to the inferotemporal cortex and a dorsal stream projecting to the posterior parietal cortex. Both streams process information about the structure of objects and about their spatial locations—and both are subject to the modulatory influences of attention. Each stream, however, uses this visual information in different ways. The ventral stream transforms the visual information into perceptual representations that embody the enduring characteristics of objects and their relations. Such representations enable us to identify objects, to attach meaning and significance to them, and to establish their causal relations—operations that are essential for accumulating knowledge about the world. In contrast, the transformations carried out by the dorsal stream deal with moment-to-moment information about the location and disposition of objects with respect to the effector being used and thereby mediate the visual control of skilled actions directed at those objects. Both streams work together in the production of adaptive behavior. The selection of appropriate goal objects and the action to be performed depends on the perceptual machinery of the ventral stream, but the execution of a goal-directed action is carried out by dedicated on-line control systems in the dorsal stream.

When we gaze out of our window, we see a world replete with objects and surfaces, textures and movement, light and shade—a world that has an existence separate from ourselves. Without vision, this rich perception of the world would not exist. For the last 200 years, visual scientists have been trying to find out how our eyes and brain create this percept.

But vision does more than deliver our experience of the world. It also guides our movements through that world. The visual control of movement, however, has until recently been relatively neglected. Indeed, traditional accounts of vision, while acknowledging the role of

MELVYN A. GOODALE Department of Psychology and Graduate Program in Neuroscience, University of Western Ontario, London, Ontario

vision in the control of movement, have simply regarded it as part of a larger function—that of constructing an internal model of the external world. Even though such accounts might postulate separate "modules" for the processing of different visual features such as motion, color, texture, and form, there is an implicit assumption that in the end vision delivers some sort of unified representation of the external world—a kind of simulacrum of the real thing that serves as the perceptual foundation for all visually driven thought and action.

Over the last ten years, this idea of a monolithic visual system has begun to be challenged. Vision is no longer regarded as a single system delivering a "general-purpose" representation of the external world. Instead, vision is seen as consisting of a number of separate systems in which the input processing of each system has been shaped by the output mechanisms it serves. In particular, it has been suggested that the visual control of actions—from saccadic eye movements to skilled grasping movements of the hand and limb—depend on visual mechanisms that are functionally and neurally separate from those mediating our perception of the world. In this chapter, I will argue that this distinction between vision for action and vision for perception can help us to understand the complex organization of the visual pathways in the human brain. Before examining the intricacies of human vision, however, it might be useful to examine the origins of vision and the role that vision plays in the life of simple organisms.

The evolution of visuomotor control

Vision did not evolve to enable organisms to perceive. It evolved to provide distal control of their movements. Take the case of Euglena, a single-cell organism that uses light as a source of energy. Euglena has been shown to alter its pattern of swimming as a function of the ambient light levels in different parts of the pond or puddle in which it lives. Such phototactic behavior ensures that the Euglena stays longer in regions of its environment where sunlight is available for the manufacture of food (Gould, 1982). To explain this behavior, it is not necessary to argue that the Euglena "perceives" the light or even that it has some sort of internal model of the outside world. One simply has to talk about a simple input-output device linking the amount of ambient light to the pattern of locomotion. Of course, a mechanism of this sort, although driven by light, is far less complicated than the visual systems of multicellular organisms. But even in more complex organisms, such as vertebrates, much of vision can be understood entirely in terms of the distal control of movement without reference to experiential perception or any general-purpose representation of the outside world.

As vision evolved in simple vertebrates, visual control systems for different kinds of behavior developed relatively independent neural substrates. Thus, in present-day amphibians, like the frog, there is evidence that visually guided prey-catching and visually guided obstacle avoidance are separately mediated by different pathways from the retina right through to the effector systems producing the movements (Ingle, 1973, 1982, 1991). The visual control of prey-catching depends on circuitry involving retinal projections to the optic tectum while the visual control of locomotion around barriers depends on circuitry involving retinal projections to particular regions of the pretectal nuclei. Each of these retinal targets projects in turn to different premotor nuclei in the brain stem and spinal cord. In fact, accumulating evidence from studies in both frog and toad suggest that there are at least five separate visuomotor *modules*, each responsible for a different kind of visually guided behavior and each having distinct processing routes from input to output (Ingle, 1991; Ewert, 1987). The outputs of these different modules certainly have to be coordinated, but in no sense are they guided by a single general-purpose visual representation in the frog's brain. [For a discussion of this issue, see Goodale (1996) and Milner and Goodale (1995).]

Although there is evidence that the same kind of visuomotor modularity found in the frog also exists in the mammalian brain (for review, see Goodale, 1996), the very complexity of the day-to-day living in many mammals, particularly in higher primates, demands much more flexible organization of the circuitry. In monkeys (and thus presumably in humans as well), many of the visuomotor circuits that are shared with simpler vertebrates appear to be modulated by more recently evolved control systems in the cerebral cortex (for review, see Milner and Goodale, 1995). This Jacksonian circuitry (Jackson, 1875), in which a layer of cortical control is superimposed on more ancient subcortical networks, makes possible much more adaptive visuomotor behavior. Of course, the basic subcortical circuitry has also changed to some extent and new visuomotor control systems involving both cortical and subcortical

structures have emerged. But even though these complex visuomotor control systems in the primate brain are capable of generating an almost limitless range of visually guided behavior, there is evidence that these visuomotor modules are functionally and neurally separate from those mediating our perception of the world.

The emergence of visual perception

As interactions with the world became more complicated and subtle, direct sensory control of action was not enough. With the emergence of cognitive systems and complex social behavior, a good deal of motor output has become quite arbitrary with respect to sensory input. Many animals, particularly humans and other primates, behave as though their actions are driven by some sort of internal model of the world in which they live. The representational systems that use vision to generate such models or percepts of the world must carry out very different transformations on visual input from the transformations carried out by the visuomotor modules described earlier. For one thing, they are not linked directly to specific motor outputs, but access these outputs via cognitive systems involving memory, semantics, spatial reasoning, planning, and communication. Such higher-order representational systems allow us to perceive a world beyond our bodies, to share that experience with other members of our species, and to plan a vast range of different actions. But even though perception allows us to choose a particular goal, the actual *execution* of an action carried out to fulfil that goal may nevertheless be mediated by dedicated visuomotor modules that are not dissimilar in principle from those found in frogs and toads. In other words, vision in humans and other primates (and perhaps other animals as well) has two distinct but interacting functions: (1) the perception of objects and their relations, which provides a foundation for the organism's cognitive life; and (2) the control of actions directed at (or with respect to) those objects, in which separate motor outputs are programmed and controlled on-line.

Dorsal and ventral streams

Beyond V1, visual information is conveyed to a bewildering number of extrastriate areas (for review, see Zeki, 1993). Despite the complexity of the interconnections between these different areas, two broad "streams" of projections from V1 have been identified in the macaque monkey brain: a *ventral stream* projecting eventually to the inferotemporal cortex and a *dorsal stream* projecting to the posterior parietal cortex (Ungerleider and Mishkin, 1982). These regions also receive inputs from a number of other subcortical visual structures, such as the superior colliculus, which sends prominent projections to the dorsal stream (via the thalamus). A schematic diagram of these pathways can be found in figure 26.1. Although some caution must be exercised in generalizing from monkey to human (Crick and Jones, 1993), it seems likely that the visual projections from primary visual cortex to the temporal and parietal lobes in the human brain involve a separation into ventral and dorsal streams similar to that seen in the monkey.

In 1982, Ungerleider and Mishkin argued that the two streams of visual processing play different but complementary roles in the processing of incoming visual information. According to their original account, the ventral stream plays a critical role in the identification and recognition of objects, while the dorsal stream mediates the localization of those same objects. Some have referred to this distinction in visual processing as one between object vision and spatial vision–"what" versus "where." Support for this idea came from work with monkeys. Lesions of inferotemporal cortex in monkeys produced deficits in their ability to discriminate between objects on the basis of their visual features but did not affect their performance on a spatially demanding "landmark" task (Pohl, 1973; Ungerleider and Brody, 1977). Conversely, lesions of the posterior parietal cortex produced deficits in performance on the landmark task but did not affect object discrimination learning (for a critique of these studies, see Goodale, 1995; Milner and Goodale, 1995). Although the evidence for the original Ungerleider–Mishkin proposal initially seemed quite compel-ling, recent findings from a broad range of studies in both humans and monkeys has forced a reinterpretation of the division of labor between the two streams. As will be detailed in subsequent sections, David Milner and I have offered an account of the two streams that emphasizes the differences in the requirements of the output systems that each stream serves.

Vision for perception and vision for action

David Milner and I have suggested, in contrast to Ungerleider and Mishkin (1982), that both streams process information about object features and about their spatial relations. Each stream, however, uses this visual information in different ways (Goodale and Milner, 1992). In the ventral stream, the transformations focus on the enduring characteristics of objects and their relations, permitting the formation of long-term perceptual representations. Such representations play an essential role in the identification of objects and enable us to classify objects and events, attach meaning and significance to them, and establish their causal relations. As we saw earlier, such operations are essential for accumulating a knowledge base about the world. In contrast, the transformations carried out by the dorsal stream deal with the moment-to-moment information about the location and disposition of objects with respect to the effector being used and thereby mediate the visual control of skilled actions, such as manual prehension, directed at those objects. As such, the dorsal stream can be regarded as a cortical extension of the dedicated visuomotor modules that

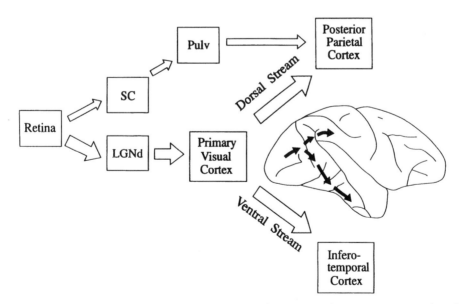

FIGURE 26.1   Major routes whereby retinal input reaches the dorsal and ventral streams. The diagram of the macaque brain (right hemisphere) on the right of the figure shows the approximate routes of the corticocortical projections from primary vi-sual cortex to the posterior parietal and the inferotemporal cortex, respectively. LGNd: lateral geniculate nucleus, pars dorsalis; Pulv: pulvinar; SC: superior colliculus. (Adapted with permission from Goodale et al., 1994.)

mediate visually guided movements in all vertebrates. The perceptual representations constructed by the ventral stream interact with various high-level cognitive mechanisms and enable an organism to select a particular course of action with respect to objects in the world while the visuomotor networks in the dorsal stream (and associated cortical and subcortical pathways) are responsible for the programming and on-line control of the particular movements that action entails.

This division of labor between the two cortical visual pathways requires that different transformations be carried out on incoming visual information. Consider first the task of the perceptual system in the ventral stream. To generate long-term representations of objects and their relations, perceptual mechanisms must be "object-based"; i.e., constancies of size, shape, color, lightness, and relative location need to be maintained across different viewing conditions. Some of these mechanisms might use a network of viewer-centered representations of the same object (e.g., Bülthoff and Edelman, 1992); others might use an array of canonical representations (e.g., Palmer, Rosch, and Chase, 1981); still others might be truly "object-centered" (Marr, 1982). But whatever the particular coding might be, it is the identity of the object, not its disposition with respect to the observer, that is of primary concern to the perceptual system. This is not the case for the visuomotor mechanisms in the dorsal stream and other related structures that support actions directed at that object. In this case, the underlying visuomotor transformations have to be viewer-centered; in other words, both the location of the object and its disposition and motion must be encoded relative to the observer in egocentric coordinates, that is in retinocentric, head-centered, torso-centered, or shoulder-centered coordinates. (One constancy that must operate, however, is object size; in order to scale the grasp during prehension, the underlying visuomotor mechanisms must be able to compute the real size of the object independent of its distance from the observer.) Finally, because the position and disposition of a goal object in the action space of an observer is rarely constant, such computations must take place de novo every time an action occurs (for a discussion of this issue, see Goodale, Jakobson, and Keillor, 1994). In other words, the action systems of the dorsal stream do most of their work on-line; only the perception systems of the ventral stream can afford to work off-line. To summarize then, while similar (but not identical) visual information about object shape, size, local orientation, and location is available to both systems, the transformational algorithms that are applied to these inputs are uniquely tailored to the function of each system. According to our proposal, it is the nature of the functional requirements of perception and ac-

tion that lies at the root of the division of labor in the ventral and dorsal visual projection systems of the primate cerebral cortex.

Neuropsychological evidence for perception and action streams

In the intact brain, the two streams of processing work together in a seamless and integrated fashion. Nevertheless, by studying individuals who have sustained brain damage that spares one of these systems but not the other, it is possible to get a glimpse into how each stream transforms incoming visual information.

PERCEPTION WITHOUT ACTION   It has been known for a long time that patients with lesions in the superior regions of the posterior parietal cortex can have problems using vision to direct a grasp or aiming movement toward the correct location of a visual target placed in different positions in the visual field, particularly the peripheral visual field. This particular deficit is often described as *optic ataxia* (Bálint, 1909). But the failure to locate an object with the hand should not be construed as a problem in spatial vision; many of these patients can, for example, describe the relative position of the object in space quite accurately, even though they cannot direct their hand toward it (Jeannerod, 1988; Perenin and Vighetto, 1988). Moreover, sometimes the deficit will be seen in one hand but not the other. Problems in the visual control of locomotion and the production of voluntary saccades have also been observed following damage to the posterior parietal region (for review, see Milner and Goodale, 1995). It should be pointed out, of course, that these patients typically have no difficulty using input from other sensory systems, such as proprioception or audition, to guide their movements. Their deficit is neither "purely" visual nor "purely" motor but is instead a visuomotor deficit.

Some of these patients are unable to use visual information to rotate their hands or scale the opening of their fingers when reaching out to pick up an object, even though they have no difficulty describing the size or orientation of objects in that part of the visual field (Jakobson et al., 1991; Jeannerod, 1988; Jeannerod, Decety, and Michel, 1994; Goodale et al., 1993; Perenin and Vighetto, 1988). Similarly, as figure 26.2 illustrates, patients with damage to this region can also show deficits in the selection of stable grasp points on the surface of objects of varying shape (Goodale et al., 1994). These results show that the visuomotor disturbances accompanying damage to the posterior parietal cortex need not be limited to deficits in the spatial control of movements but can extend to object features such as size, shape, and

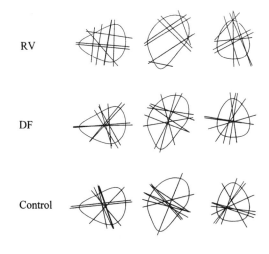

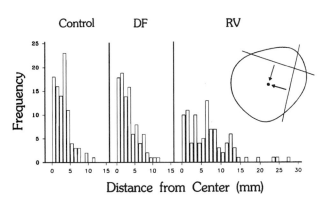

FIGURE 26.2   The diagram at the top of this figure shows the "grasp lines" (joining points where the thumb and index finger first made contact with the shape) selected by the optic ataxia patient (RV), the visual agnosic patient (DF), and the control subject (SH) when picking up three of the twelve shapes used in the study. The four different orientations in which each shape was presented have been rotated so that they are aligned. Notice the similarity between DF's grasp lines and those of the control subject, and how their grasp lines differ from those of RV who often chooses very unstable grasp points. The frequency distributions below illustrate the distance between the grasp lines and the center of mass of the shape for DF, RV, and the control subject (SH) for all twelve shapes. The inset shows how these distances were computed. Notice again that whereas DF and SH's grasp lines tended to pass through or close to the center of mass of the shape, this was not the case for RV. (Adapted with permission from Goodale et al., 1994.)

orientation. Nevertheless, it is worth emphasizing that the deficits are visuomotor in nature not perceptual; the patients have no trouble discriminating between objects of different size or shape or between objects placed in different orientations.

The various visuomotor deficits that have been described in patients with damage to the posterior parietal region are quite dissociable from one another. Some patients are unable to use visual information to control their hand postures but have no difficulty controlling the direction of their grasp; others show the reverse pattern. Some patients are unable to foveate a target object, but have no difficulty directing a well-formed grasp in its direction; others may show no evidence of an oculomotor deficit but be unable to guide their hand toward an object under visual control. Indeed, depending upon the size and locus of the lesion, a patient can demonstrate any combination of these visuomotor deficits (for review, see Milner and Goodale, 1995). Different subregions of the posterior parietal cortex, it appears, are critical for the visual control of different motor outputs. A particular motor act, such as reaching out and grasping an object, presumably would engage visuomotor mechanisms in a number of these different areas, including those involved in the control of saccades, visual pursuit, reaching with the limb, and grasping movements of the hands and fingers (for a discussion of the different components of manual prehension, see Jeannerod, 1988). Just how such mechanisms are coordinated is not well understood–although some models have been proposed (e.g., Hoff and Arbib, 1992). In any case, it is clear that the visual control of each of the constituent actions will require different sensorimotor coordinate transformations and there have been some attempts to specify how the posterior parietal cortex might mediate such transformations (e.g., Flanders, Tillery, and Soechting, 1992; Stein, 1992). But again, even though patients with damage to the posterior parietal region may show a variety of different visuomotor deficits, they can often describe (and hence presumably perceive) the intrinsic visual features and the location of the very object they are unable to grasp, foveate, and/or walk toward.

ACTION WITHOUT PERCEPTION   The fact that patients with damage to posterior parietal cortex can perceive objects but cannot grasp them provides one piece of evidence that there are separate neural substrates for perception and action in the human brain. It also suggests that the superior regions of the posterior parietal cortex, the human homolog of the monkey dorsal stream, is critical for the visual control of action. But even more compelling evidence for separate visual systems for perception and action comes from patients who show the opposite pattern of deficits and spared visual abilities. Take the case of DF, for example.

DF is a woman, now in her early 40s, who had the misfortune at age 34 to suffer irreversible brain damage as a result of near-asphyxiation by carbon monoxide. When she regained consciousness, it was apparent that DF's visual system had been badly damaged by the anoxia. She was unable to recognize the faces of her relatives and friends or identify the visual form of common objects. In fact, she could not even tell the difference between simple geometric shapes such as a square and a triangle. At the same time, she had no difficulty recognizing people from their voices or identifying objects placed in her hands; her perceptual problems appeared to be exclusively visual. Even today, more than ten years after the accident, she remains quite unable to identify objects or drawings on the basis of their visual form.

The damage in DF's brain is quite diffuse, a common pattern in cases of anoxia. Nevertheless, certain areas of her brain, especially those in the posterior region of her cerebral cortex, appear to be more severely damaged than others. Magnetic resonance imaging carried out just over a year after her accident showed that the ventrolateral regions of her occipital lobe are particularly compromised. Primary visual cortex, however, appears to be largely spared in DF (for details, see Milner et al., 1991).

DF's perceptual problems are not simply a case of being unable to associate a visual stimulus with meaningful semantic information. For example, while it is true that she cannot find the right name or semantic association for the objects depicted in the simple line drawings illustrated in the left-hand column of figure 26.3, she is also completely unable to draw what she sees when she looks at the line drawing. Moreover, her inability to copy drawings is not due to a problem in controlling the movements of the pen or pencil. When she is asked to

Model   Copy   Memory

FIGURE 26.3   Patient DF's attempts to draw from models and from memory. DF was unable to identify the line drawings of an apple and an open book shown on the left. In addition, her copies were very poor. Note that she did incorporate some elements of the line drawing (e.g., the dots indicating the text in the book) into her copy. When she was asked on another occasion to draw an apple or an open book from memory, she produced a respectable representation of both items (right-hand column). When she was later shown her own drawings, she had no idea what they were. (Adapted with permission of Elsevier Science from Servos, Goodale, and Humphrey, 1993.)

draw a particular object from memory, she is able to do so reasonably well, as the drawings on the right-hand side of figure 26.3 illustrate.

Nor is DF's inability to perceive the shape and form of objects in the world due to deficits in basic sensory processing (Milner et al., 1991). She remains quite capable of identifying colors, for example. In addition, perimetric testing carried out quite early after her accident showed that she could detect luminance-defined targets at least as far out as 30° into the visual periphery. Her spatial contrast sensitivity was also normal above 5 Hz and was only moderately impaired at lower spatial frequencies. Of course, even though she could detect the presence of the spatial frequency gratings in these tests, she could not report their orientation. In fact, DF has great problems describing or discriminating the orientation and form of any visual contour, no matter how that contour is defined. Thus, she cannot identify shapes whose contours are defined by differences in luminance or color, or by differences in the direction of motion or the plane of depth. Nor can she recognize shapes that are defined by the similarity or proximity of individual elements of the visual array. Nevertheless, information about the spatial distribution of the visual array appeared to reach her primary visual cortex. Thus, when she was shown a high-contrast reversing checkerboard pattern in an electrophysiological assessment carried out just after the accident, the initial components of the evoked response, such as the P100, appeared to be quite normal, suggesting that her primary visual cortex was working normally. In short, DF's deficit seems to be "perceptual" rather than "sensory" in nature. She simply cannot perceive shapes and forms—even though the early stages of her visual system would appear to have access to the requisite low-level sensory information.

What is most remarkable about DF, however, is that despite her profound deficits in form vision, she is able to use visual information about the size, shape, and orientation of objects to control a broad range of visually guided movements. DF will reach out and grasp your hand if you offer it when you first meet her. She is equally adept at reaching out for a door handle—even in an unfamiliar environment. She can walk unassisted across a room or patio, stepping easily over low obstacles and walking around higher ones. Even more amazing is the fact that she can reach out and grasp an object placed in front of her with considerable accuracy and confidence—despite the fact that moments before she was quite unable to identify or describe that same object.

These dissociations between DF's perceptual abilities and her ability to use visual information to control skilled movements are also evident in formal testing (Goodale et al., 1991). For example, when she is presented with a series of rectangular blocks that vary in their dimensions but not in their overall surface area, she is unable to say whether or not any two of these blocks are the same or different. Even when a single block is placed in front of her, she is unable to indicate how wide the block is by opening her index finger and thumb a matching amount. Nevertheless, when she reaches out to pick up the block using a precision grip, the opening between her index finger and thumb is scaled in flight to the width of the object, just as it is in subjects with normal vision.

A similar dissociation can be seen in DF's processing of the orientation of objects (Goodale et al., 1991). Thus, even though she cannot discriminate between objects placed in different orientations on a table in front of her, she can rotate her hand in the correct orientation when she reaches out to grasp one of the objects. When presented with a large slot in a vertical surface, she is unable to rotate a hand-held card to match the orientation of that slot (see figure 26.4). But again, when she attempts to insert the hand-held card into the slot, she rotates the card in the appropriate way as she moves it toward the slot (figure 26.4). She can also use information about the shape of an object to locate stable grasp points on its surface when she picks it up (Goodale et al., 1994). Thus, when grasping an object like those illustrated in figure 26.2, DF will place her finger and thumb so that a line joining the opposing points of contact passes through the object's center of mass. And, unlike the patient with posterior parietal damage whose performance is also illustrated in figure 26.2, DF chooses points on the object's boundary where her fingers are the least likely to slip—such as points of high convexity or concavity—just as the control subject with normal vision does. Needless to say, DF is quite unable to tell these objects apart in a same-different discrimination. In short, DF can use visual information about the size, orientation, and shape of objects to program and control her goal-directed movements even though she has no meaningful perception of those object features.

As I mentioned earlier, these spared visuomotor skills are not limited to reaching and grasping movements; DF can also walk around quite well under visual control. When she was tested more formally, we found that she is able to negotiate obstacles during locomotion as well as control subjects (Patla and Goodale, 1997). Thus, when obstacles of different heights were randomly placed in her path on different trials, she stepped over these obstacles quite efficiently and the elevation of her toe increased linearly as a function of obstacle height, just as it does in neurologically intact individuals. Yet when she was asked to give verbal estimates of the height of the obstacles, the slope of the line relating esti-

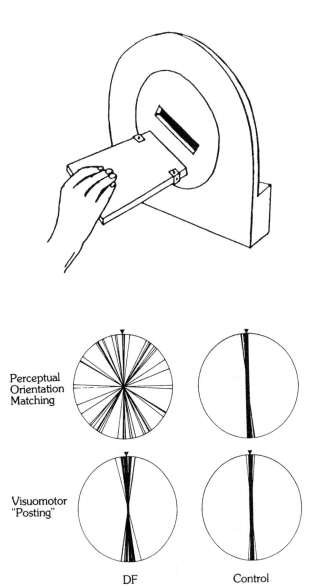

FIGURE 26.4 Top: Apparatus that was used to test sensitivity to orientation in patient DF. The slot could be placed in any one of a number of orientations around the clock. Subjects were required either to rotate a hand-held card to match the orientation of the slot or to "post" the card into the slot as shown in this figure. Bottom: Polar plots of the orientation of the hand-held card on the perceptual matching task and the visuomotor posting task for DF and an age-matched control subject. The correct orientation on each trial has been rotated to vertical. Note that although DF was unable to match the orientation of the card to that of the slot in the perceptual matching card, she did rotate the card to the correct orientation as she attempted to insert it into the slot on the posting task. (Adapted with permission from Goodale, 1995.)

mated and actual obstacle height was much shallower in her case than it was in normal subjects. Similar dissociations between perceptual judgments about the pitch of the visual field and its effect on eye position have also been observed in DF (Servos, Matin, and Goodale, 1995).

There is also evidence for a dissociation between the perception of spatial relations and the use of egocentric spatial information for motor control in DF. When asked, for example, to copy a simple array of colored tokens laid out on a surface by using a similar set of tokens, she generates a rather poor copy. Yet at the same time, when asked to point in turn to each of the colored tokens in the original array, her performance is quite normal (Murphy, Carey, and Goodale, 1998). In other words, despite the fact that she has excellent egocentric coding of the spatial position of objects, her perceptual representation of the relative position of those objects (sometimes called allocentric coding) is clearly abnormal.

To summarize: Even though DF's brain damage has left her unable to perceive the size, shape, and orientation of objects, her visuomotor outputs remain quite sensitive to these same object features. There appears to have been an interruption in the normal flow of shape and contour information into her perceptual system without affecting the processing of shape and contour information by her visuomotor control systems. But where is the damage in DF's brain? If, as was suggested earlier, the perception of objects and events is mediated by the ventral stream of visual projections to inferotemporal cortex, DF should show evidence for damage relatively early in this pathway. Certainly, the pattern of damage revealed by the MRI is consistent with this interpretation; the major focus of cortical damage is in the ventro-lateral region of the occipital cortex, an area thought to be part of the human homolog of the ventral stream. At the same time, her primary visual cortex, which provides input for both the dorsal and ventral streams, appears to be largely intact. Thus, although input from primary visual cortex to the ventral stream has been compromised in DF, input from this structure to the dorsal stream appears to be essentially intact. In addition, the dorsal stream, unlike the ventral stream, also receives important visual input from the superior colliculus via the pulvinar, a nucleus in the thalamus (see figure 26.1). Indeed, recent work by Perenin and Rossetti (1996) suggests that this collicular-pulvinar route to the dorsal stream may be able to support object-directed grasping movements even without input from V1. They tested a patient who was completely blind (by conventional testing) in one-half of his visual field following a medial occipital lesion that included all of V1. The patient could not see any objects in his blind field. Nevertheless, when he was persuaded to reach out and grasp objects placed in his blind field, he showed some evidence of sensitivity to the size and orientation of objects. Thus, there are at least two routes whereby information could reach the dorsal stream in DF: from the superior colliculus (via the pulvinar) and from the lateral geniculate nucleus (via primary visual cortex). Either or both of these pathways could be continuing to mediate well-formed visuomotor responses in DF.

One must be cautious, however, about drawing strong conclusions about anatomy and pathways from patients like DF. Her deficits arose not from a discrete lesion, but from anoxia. As a consequence, the brain damage in DF, while localized to some extent, is much more diffuse than it would be in a patient with a stroke or tumor. Thus, while the striking dissociation between perceptual and visuomotor abilities in DF can be mapped onto the distinction between the ventral and dorsal streams of visual processing that David Milner and I proposed (Goodale and Milner, 1992), that mapping can be only tentative. The proposal is strengthened, however, by observations in patients like those described in the previous section whose pattern of deficits is complementary to DF's and whose brain damage can be confidently localized to the dorsal stream.

In summary, the neuropsychological findings can be accommodated quite well by the proposal that the division of labor between the ventral and dorsal streams of visual processing is based on the distinction between visuomotor control and the more visuocognitive functions of vision. Moreover, as we shall see in the next section, this new way of looking at the organization of the visual system is also consistent with the story that is emerging from anatomical, neurophysiological, and behavioral work in the monkey.

Evidence from monkey studies

A broad range of different studies on the dorsal and ventral streams in the monkey lend considerable support to the distinction outlined above (for a detailed account of this work, see Milner and Goodale, 1995). For example, monkeys with lesions of inferotemporal cortex, who show profound deficits in object recognition, are nevertheless as capable as a normal animal at picking up small objects (Klüver and Bucy, 1939), at catching flying insects (Pribram, 1967), and at orienting their fingers to extract morsels of food embedded in small slots (Buchbinder et al., 1980). Like DF, these monkeys are unable to discriminate between objects on the basis of the same visual features that they apparently use to direct their grasping movements. In addition to the lesion studies, there is a long history of electrophysiological work showing that cells in inferotemporal cortex and neighboring regions of the superior temporal sulcus are tuned to specific objects and object features—and some of them maintain their selectivity irrespective of viewpoint, retinal image size, and even color (for review, see Milner and Goodale, 1995). Moreover, the responses of these cells are not affected by the animal's motor behavior but are instead sensitive to the reinforcement history and significance of the visual stimuli that drive them. It has been suggested that cells in this region might play a role in comparing current visual inputs with internal representations of recalled images (e.g., Eskandar, Richmond, and Optican, 1992), which are themselves presumably stored in other regions, such as neighboring regions of the medial temporal lobe and related limbic areas (Fahy, Riches, and Brown, 1993; Nishijo et al., 1993). In fact, sensitivity to particular objects can be created in ensembles of cells in inferotemporal cortex simply by training the animals to discriminate between different objects (Logothetis, Pauls, and Poggio, 1995). These and other studies too numerous to cite here lend considerable support to the suggestion that the object-based descriptions provided by the ventral stream form the basic raw material for recognition memory and other long-term representations of the visual world.

In sharp contrast to the activity of cells in the ventral stream, the responses of cells in the dorsal stream are greatly dependent on the concurrent motor behavior of the animal. Thus, separate subsets of visual cells in the posterior parietal cortex, the major terminal zone for the dorsal stream, have been shown to be implicated in visual fixation, pursuit and saccadic eye movements, visually guided reaching, and the manipulation of objects (Hyvärinen and Poranen, 1974; Mountcastle et al., 1975). In reviewing these studies, Andersen (1987) has pointed out that most neurons in these areas "exhibit both sensory-related and movement-related activity." Moreover, the motor modulation is quite specific. Recent work in Andersen's laboratory, for example, has shown that visual cells in the posterior parietal cortex that code the location of a target for a saccadic eye movement are quite separate from cells in this region that code the location for a manual aiming movement to the same target (Snyder, Batista, and Andersen, 1997). In other experiments (Taira et al., 1990), cells in the posterior parietal region that fire when the monkey manipulates an object have also been shown to be sensitive to the intrinsic object features, such as size and orientation, that determine the posture of the hand and fingers during a grasping movement. Lesions in this region of the posterior parietal cortex produce deficits in the visual control of reaching and grasping similar in many respects to those seen in humans following damage to the homologous region (e.g., Ettlinger, 1977). The posterior parietal cortex is also intimately linked with premotor cortex, the superior colliculus, and pontine nuclei–brain areas that have also been implicated in various aspects of the visual control of eye, limb, and body movements (for review, see Goodale,

1996). In short, the networks in the dorsal stream have the functional properties and interconnections that one might expect to see in a system concerned with the moment-to-moment control of visually guided actions. [Of necessity, this review of the monkey literature is far from complete. Interested readers are directed to Milner and Goodale (1995) and Jeannerod (1997).]

Perception and action in the normal observer

Although the evidence from neurological patients discussed earlier points to a clear dissociation between the visual pathways supporting perception and action, one might also expect to see evidence for such a dissociation in neurologically intact individuals. In other words, the visual information that is used to calibrate and control a skilled motor act directed at an object might not always match the perceptual judgments that are made about that object. After all, the control of skilled actions imposes requirements on visual processing that are different from those demanded of the mechanisms supporting visual recognition. Efficient grasping, for example, demands rapid and accurate computation of the size, shape, orientation, and location of the object; and the required computations for action must be organized within egocentric frames of reference. For example, while we might *perceive* that one object is larger or closer than another, such relative judgments of size and distance are not enough to calibrate the grasping movement directed at that object; to grasp the object accurately, it is necessary to know its *exact* size and distance.

Although there are numerous examples of such dissociations in the literature, particularly with respect to the spatial location of visual stimuli (for review, see Goodale and Haffenden, 1998), some of the most compelling demonstrations have involved the use of pictorial illusions. Take the Ebbinghaus illusion for example. In this familiar illusion, which is illustrated in figure 26.5, two target circles of equal size, each surrounded by a circular array of either smaller or larger circles, are presented side by side. Subjects typically report that the target circle surrounded by the array of smaller circles appears larger than the one surrounded by the array of larger circles, presumably because of the difference in the contrast in size between the target circles and the surrounding circles. In another version of the illusion, also illustrated in figure 26.5, the target circles can be made to appear identical in size by increasing the actual size of the target circle surrounded by the larger circles.

Although our perceptual judgments are clearly affected by these manipulations of the stimulus array, there is good reason to believe that the calibration of

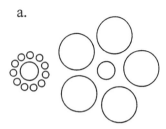

a.

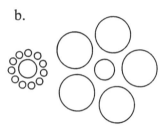

b.

FIGURE 26.5 The Ebbinghaus illusion. Panel a shows the standard version of the illusion in which physically identical target circles appear perceptually different. Most people judge the target circle surrounded by the annulus of smaller circles to be larger than the other target circle. Panel b shows a version of the illusion in which the target circle surrounded by the annulus of larger circles has been made physically larger than the other target, compensating for the effect of the illusion. Most people now see the two target circles as equivalent in size. (Adapted with permission from Aglioti, DeSouza, and Goodale, 1995.)

size-dependent motor outputs, such as grip aperture during grasping, would not be. When we reach out to pick up an object, we must compute its real size if we are to pick it up efficiently. As was mentioned earlier, it is not enough to know that it is larger or smaller than surrounding objects. One might expect, therefore, that grip scaling would be insensitive to size-contrast illusions such as the Ebbinghaus illusion. Such a result was recently found in two experiments that used a three-dimensional version of the illusion in which two thin "poker-chip" disks were arranged as pairs on a standard Ebbinghaus annular circle display (Aglioti, De-Souza, and Goodale, 1995; Haffenden and Goodale, 1998). Trials in which the two disks appeared perceptually identical but were physically different in size were randomly alternated with trials in which the disks appeared perceptually different but were physically identical. Even though subjects showed robust perceptual illusions—even in a matching task in which they opened their index finger and thumb to match the perceived diameter of one of the disks—their grip aperture was correlated with the real size of the disk when they reached out to pick it up (see figure 26.6).

But why should perception be so susceptible to this illusion while the calibration of grasp is not? The mecha-

nisms underlying the size-contrast illusion are not well understood. It is possible that it arises from a straightforward relative size judgment, whereby an object that is smaller than its immediate neighbors is assumed to be smaller than a similar object that is larger than its immediate neighbors. It is also possible that some sort of image-distance equation is contributing to the illusion in which the array of smaller circles is assumed to be more distant than the array of larger circles. As a consequence, the target circle within the array of smaller circles will also be perceived as more distant (and therefore larger) than the target circle of equivalent retinal image size within the array of larger circles. In other words, the illusion may be simply a consequence of the perceptual system's attempt to make size constancy judgments on the basis of an analysis of the entire visual array (Coren, 1971; Gregory, 1963).

Mechanisms such as these, in which the relations between objects in the visual array play a crucial role in scene interpretation, are clearly central to perception. As we look out across a landscape, we cannot help but see some objects as larger or closer than others. In contrast, the execution of a goal-directed act such as grasping depends on computations that are centered on the target itself and must take into account the actual size and distance of that target—and transform that information into the coordinates of the effectors that carry out the actions. The relative size and distance between the target object and others in the scene are of no consequence to the computations mediating action.

The integration of perception and action

Although I have been emphasizing the fact that the dorsal action stream and the ventral perception stream are anatomically and functionally distinct, the two streams must work together in everyday life. Indeed, an argument can be made that the two streams play complementary roles in the production of adaptive behavior.

A useful metaphor for understanding the different contributions of the dorsal and ventral stream to visually guided behavior can be found in robotic engineering. That metaphor is *teleassistance* (Pook and Ballard, 1996). In teleassistance, a human operator identifies the goal and then uses a symbolic language to communicate with a semi-autonomous robot that actually performs the required motor act on the identified goal object. Teleassistance is much more flexible than completely autonomous robotic control, which is limited to the working environment for which it has been programmed and cannot cope easily with novel events. Teleassistance is also more efficient than teleoperation, in which a human operator simply controls the move-

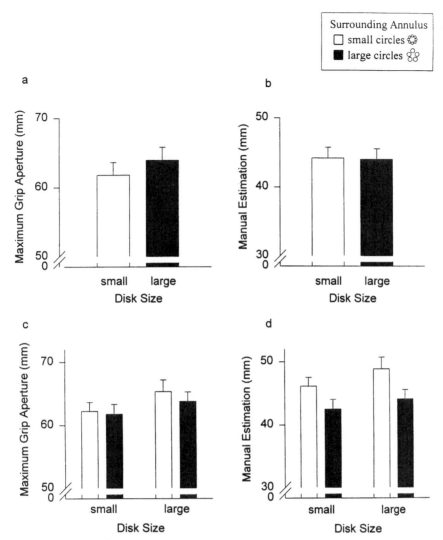

a

b

c

d

FIGURE 26.6 Calibration of the grasp (on left) and manual estimations (on right) for disks surrounded by the illusory annuli: (a and b) Perceptually identical conditions; (c and d) perceptually different conditions. The difference between the maximum grip aperture achieved during a grasping movement was significantly greater for large disks than the maximum grip aperture for small disks independent of whether or not the subject perceived the disks to be the same or different sizes ($p <$ .05). Manual estimations were influenced by the illusory display. The difference between manual estimations of the large and small disks in the perceptually identical condition was not significant ($p >$ .05). Perceptually different, but physically identical disk pairs produced significantly different manual estimations. The small disk surrounded by the small circle annulus was estimated to be larger than the small disk surrounded by the large circle annulus ($p <$ .01). Manual estimations of the pair of large disks produced a similar result. The large disk surrounded by the small circle annulus was estimated to be larger than the large disk surrounded by the large circle annulus ($p <$ .05). Error bars indicate the standard error of the mean averaged within each condition for all subjects. (Adapted with permission from Haffenden and Goodale, 1998.)

ment of a manipulandum at a distance. As Pook and Ballard (1996) have demonstrated, teleoperation (i.e., the human operator) cannot cope with sudden changes in scale or the delay between action and feedback from that action. In short, teleassistance combines the flexibility of teleoperation with the precision of autonomous routines.

The interaction between the ventral and dorsal streams is an excellent example of the principle of teleassistance, but in this case instantiated in biology. The perceptual-cognitive systems in the ventral stream, like the human operator in teleassistance, identify different objects in the scene—using a representational system that is rich and detailed but not metrically precise. When a particular goal object has been flagged, dedicated visuomotor networks in the dorsal stream (in conjunction with related circuits in premotor cortex, basal ganglia, and brain stem) are activated to perform the desired motor act. Thus, the networks in the dorsal stream, with their precise egocentric coding of the location, size, orientation, and shape of the goal object, are like the robotic component of teleassistance. Thus, both systems are required for purposive behavior—one system to select the goal object from the visual array, the other to carry out the required metrical computations for the goal-directed action. One of the most important questions yet to be addressed is how the two streams communicate with one another.

REFERENCES

AGLIOTI, S., J. F. X. DESOUZA, and M. A. GOODALE, 1995. Size-contrast illusions deceive the eye but not the hand. *Curr. Biol.* 5:679–685.

ANDERSEN, R. A., 1987. Inferior parietal lobule function in spatial perception and visuomotor integration. In *Handbook of Physiology.* Section 1: *The Nervous System,* Vol. V: *Higher Functions of the Brain,* Part 2, V. B. Mountcastle, F. Plum, and S. R. Geiger, eds. Bethesda, Md.: American Physiological Association, pp. 483–518.

BÁLINT, R., 1909. Seelenlämung des 'Schauens,' optische Ataxie, räumliche Störung der Aufmerksamkeit. *Monatsch. Psychiatr. Neurol.* 25:51–81.

BUCHBINDER, S., B. DIXON, Y.-W. HYANG, J. G. MAY, and M. GLICKSTEIN, 1980. The effects of cortical lesions on visual guidance of the hand. *Soc. Neurosci. Abstr.* 6:675.

BÜLTHOFF, H. H., and S. EDELMAN, 1992. Psychophysical support for a two-dimensional view interpolation theory of object recognition. *Proc. Natl. Acad. Sci. U.S.A.* 89:60–64.

COREN, S., 1971. A size contrast illusion without physical size differences. *Amer. J. Psychol.* 84:565–566.

CRICK, F., and E. JONES, 1993. Backwardness of human neuroanatomy. *Nature* 361:109–110.

ESKANDAR, E. M., B. J. RICHMOND, and L. M. OPTICAN, 1992. Role of inferior temporal neurons in visual memory. I. Temporal encoding of information about visual images, recalled images, and behavioral context. *J. Neurophysiol.* 68:1277–1295.

ETTLINGER, G., 1977. Parietal cortex in visual orientation. In *Physiological Aspects of Clinical Neurology,* F. C. Rose, ed. Oxford: Blackwell, pp. 93–100.

EWERT, J.-P., 1987. Neuroethology of releasing mechanisms: Prey-catching in toads. *Behav. Brain Sci.* 10:337–405.

FAHY, F. L., I. P. RICHES, and M. W. BROWN, 1993. Neuronal signals of importance to the performance of visual recognition memory tasks: Evidence from recordings of single neurons in the medial thalamus of primates. In *The Visually Responsive Neuron: From Basic Neurophysiology to Behavior. Progress in Brain Research,* Vol. 95, T. P. Hicks, S. Molotchnikoff, and T. Ono, eds. Amsterdam: Elsevier, pp. 401–416.

FLANDERS, M., S. I. H. TILLERY, and J. F. SOECHTING, 1992. Early stages in a sensorimotor transformation. *Behav. Brain Sci.* 15:309–362.

GOODALE, M. A., 1995. The cortical organization of visual perception and visuomotor control. In *An Invitation to Cognitive Science.* Vol. 2: *Visual Cognition and Action* (2nd Ed.), S. Kosslyn, ed. Cambridge, Mass.: MIT Press, pp. 167–213.

GOODALE, M. A., 1996. Visuomotor modules in the vertebrate brain. *Can. J. Physiol. Pharm.* 74:390–400.

GOODALE, M. A., and A. HAFFENDEN, 1998. Frames of reference for perception and action in the human visual system. *Neurosci. Biobehav. Rev.* 22:161–172.

GOODALE, M. A., L. S. JAKOBSON, and J. M. KEILLOR, 1994. Differences in the visual control of pantomimed and natural grasping movements. *Neuropsychologia* 32:1159–1178.

GOODALE, M. A., J. P. MEENAN, H. H. BÜLTHOFF, D. A. NICOLLE, K. S. MURPHY, and C. I. RACICOT, 1994. Separate neural pathways for the visual analysis of object shape in perception and prehension. *Curr. Biol.* 4:604–610.

GOODALE, M. A., and A. D. MILNER, 1992. Separate visual pathways for perception and action. *Trends Neurosci.* 15:20–25.

GOODALE, M. A., A. D. MILNER, L. S. JAKOBSON, and D. P. CAREY, 1991. A neurological dissociation between perceiving objects and grasping them. *Nature* 349:154–156.

GOODALE, M. A., K. MURPHY, J. P. MEENAN, C. I. RACICOT, and D. A. NICOLLE, 1993. Spared object perception but poor object-calibrated grasping in a patient with optic ataxia. *Soc. Neurosci. Abstr.* 19:775.

GREGORY, R. L., 1963. Distortion of visual space as inappropriate constancy scaling. *Nature* 199:678–680.

GOULD, J. L., 1982. *Ethology: The Mechanisms and Evolution of Behavior.* New York: Norton.

HAFFENDEN, A., and M. A. GOODALE, 1998. The effect of pictorial illusion on prehension and perception. *J. Cogn. Neurosci.* 10:122–136.

HOFF, B., and M. A. ARBIB, 1992. A model of the effects of speed, accuracy and perturbation on visually guided reaching. In *Control of Arm Movement in Space: Neurophysiological and Computational Approaches,* R. Caminiti, P. B. Johnson, and Y. Burnod, eds. New York: Springer-Verlag, pp. 285–306.

HYVÄRINEN, J., and A. PORANEN, 1974. Function of the parietal associative area 7 as revealed from cellular discharges in alert monkeys. *Brain* 97:673–692.

INGLE, D. J., 1973. Two visual systems in the frog. *Science* 181:1053–1055.

INGLE, D. J., 1982. Organization of visuomotor behaviors in vertebrates. In *Analysis of Visual Behavior,* D. J. Ingle, M. A. Goodale, and R. J. W. Mansfield, eds. Cambridge, Mass.: MIT Press, pp. 67–109.

INGLE, D. J., 1991. Functions of subcortical visual systems in vertebrates and the evolution of higher visual mechanisms. In *Vision and Visual Dysfunction.* Vol. 2: *Evolution of the Eye and Visual System,* R. L. Gregory and J. Cronly-Dillon, eds. London: Macmillan, pp. 152–164.

JACKSON, J. H., 1875. *Clinical and Physiological Researches on the Nervous System.* London: Churchill.

JAKOBSON, L. S., Y. M. ARCHIBALD, D. P. CAREY, and M. A. GOODALE, 1991. A kinematic analysis of reaching and grasping movements in a patient recovering from optic ataxia. *Neuropsychologia* 29:803–809.

JEANNEROD, M., 1988. *The Neural and Behavioural Organization of Goal-Directed Movements.* Oxford: Oxford University Press.

JEANNEROD, M., 1997. *The Cognitive Neuroscience of Action.* Oxford: Blackwell.

JEANNEROD, M., J. DECETY, and F. MICHEL, 1994. Impairment of grasping movements following bilateral posterior parietal lesion. *Neuropsychologia* 32:369–380.

KLÜVER, H., and P. C. BUCY, 1939. Preliminary analysis of functions of the temporal lobes of monkeys. *Arch. Neurol. Psychiatr.* 42:979–1000.

LOGOTHETIS, N. K., J. PAULS, and T. POGGIO, 1995. Shape representation in the inferior temporal cortex of monkeys. *Curr. Biol.* 5:552–563.

MARR, D., 1982. *Vision.* San Francisco: Freeman.

MILNER, A. D., and M. A. GOODALE, 1995. *The Visual Brain in Action.* Oxford: Oxford University Press.

MILNER, A. D., D. I. PERRETT, R. S. JOHNSTON, P. J. BENSON, T. R. JORDAN, D. W. HEELEY, D. BETTUCCI, F. MORTARA, R. MUTANI, E. TERAZZI, and D. L. W. DAVIDSON, 1991. Perception and action in visual form agnosia. *Brain* 114:405–428.

MOUNTCASTLE, V. B., J. C. LYNCH, A. GEORGOPOULOS, H. SAKATA, and C. ACUNA, 1975. Posterior parietal association cortex of the monkey: Command functions for operations within extrapersonal space. *J. Neurophysiol.* 38:871–908.

MURPHY, K. J., D. P CAREY, and M. A. GOODALE, 1998. The perception of spatial relations in a patient with visual form agnosia. *Cogn. Neuropsychol.* 15:705–722.

NISHIJO, H., T. ONO, R. TAMURA, and K. NAKAMURA, 1993. Amygdalar and hippocampal neuron responses related to recognition and memory in monkey. In *The Visually Responsive Neuron: From Basic Neurophysiology to Behavior. Progress in Brain Research,* Vol. 95, T. P. Hicks, S. Molotchnikoff, and T. Ono, eds. Amsterdam: Elsevier, pp. 339–358.

PALMER, S., E. ROSCH, and P. CHASE, 1981. Canonical perspective and the perception of objects. In *Attention and Performance,* Vol. IX, J. Long and A. Baddeley, eds. Hillsdale, N.J.: Erlbaum, pp. 135–151.

PATLA, A., and M. A. GOODALE, 1997. Visuomotor transformation required for obstacle avoidance during locomotion is unaffected in a patient with visual form agnosia. *NeuroRep.* 8:165–168.

PERENIN, M.-T., and Y. ROSSETTI, 1996. Grasping without form discrimination in a hemianopic field. *NeuroRep.* 7:793–797.

PERENIN, M.-T., and A. VIGHETTO, 1988. Optic ataxia: A specific disruption in visuomotor mechanisms. I. Different aspects of the deficit in reaching for objects. *Brain* 111:643–674.

POHL, W., 1973. Dissociation of spatial discrimination deficits following frontal and parietal lesions in monkeys. *J. Comp. Physiol. Psychol.* 82:227–239.

POOK, P. K., and D. H. BALLARD, 1996. Deictic human/robot interaction. *Robot. Auton. Syst.* 18:259–269.

PRIBRAM, K. H., 1967. Memory and the organization of attention. In *Brain Function and Learning.* Vol. IV. UCLA Forum in Medical Sciences 6, D. B. Lindsley and A. A. Lumsdaine, eds. Berkeley: University of California Press, pp.79–122.

SERVOS, P., M. A. GOODALE, and G. K. HUMPHREY, 1993. The drawing of objects by a visual form agnosic: Contribution of surface properties and memorial representations. *Neuropsychologia* 31:251–259.

SERVOS, P., L. MATIN, and M. A. GOODALE, 1995. Dissociations between two forms of spatial processing by a visual form agnosic. *NeuroRep.* 6:1893–1896.

SNYDER, L. H., A. P. BATISTA, and R. A. ANDERSEN, 1997. Coding of intention in the posterior parietal cortex. *Nature* 386:167–170.

STEIN, J. F., 1992. The representation of egocentric space in the posterior parietal cortex. *Behav. Brain Sci.* 15:691–700.

TAIRA, M., S. MINE, A. P. GEORGOPOULOS, A. MURATA, and H. SAKATA, 1990. Parietal cortex neurons of the monkey related to the visual guidance of hand movement. *Exp. Brain Res.* 83:29–36.

UNGERLEIDER, L. G., and B. A. BRODY, 1977. Extrapersonal spatial orientation: The role of posterior parietal, anterior frontal, and inferotemporal cortex. *Exp. Neurol.* 56:265–280.

UNGERLEIDER, L. G., and M. MISHKIN, 1982. Two cortical visual systems. In *Analysis of Visual Behavior,* D. J. Ingle, M. A. Goodale, and R. J. W. Mansfield, eds. Cambridge, Mass.: MIT Press, pp. 549–586.

ZEKI, S., 1993. *A Vision of the Brain.* Oxford: Blackwell Scientific Publications.

27 Visual Associative Long-Term Memory: Encoding and Retrieval in Inferotemporal Cortex of the Primate

YASUSHI MIYASHITA

ABSTRACT The neural mechanisms that enable manipulation of visual images in mind are examined. To provide a solid neurophysiological basis for the studies devoted to visual imagery, an animal model was devised. Macaque monkeys were trained to memorize visual objects in associative memory and to retrieve the active internal representation ("image") of the objects from long-term storage according to an associative cue. A color switch was used to control the need for image generation and its initiation time, independently of the cue itself. In the inferotemporal cortex, we found a group of neurons whose activity represented the active image of a specific object in mind. The neural representation could be recalled or suppressed according to the need of image generation. How, then, is the association between the cue and the image represented and created? By using an object–object association task, we demonstrate that inferotemporal neurons can encode arbitrarily defined associative relations between objects. We then found that the interaction between the medial temporal lobe and inferotemporal cortex plays an essential role in the encoding process. This interaction was analyzed by electrophysiological single unit recording, combined with neurotoxic lesions and molecular biological methods. These studies opened a new approach for understanding the neural mechanisms of memory encoding and retrieval.

Create an image of the Pantheon in your mind. Can you count the columns that support its pediment?

–E. A. C. Alain (1926)

Our ability to "see with the mind's eye" has been of interest to philosophers and scientists for a long time. When the nature of the reflective consciousness was investigated by reflection, it was often asked whether [strong] "image" and [weak] "perception" are distinguishable in both psychological and epistemological dimensions (Sartre, 1938). Consider the Pantheon and its columns, as shown in figure 27.1 (see color plate 10). Recalling those columns is a well known litmus test for

such a distinction. Mental images are not actual pictures in the brain; obviously, we cannot assume a homunculus in the brain who looks at the images. Nevertheless, the research on imagery is challenging since imagery is one of the first higher cognitive abilities that is firmly rooted in the brain. And it is clearly an important topic, since understanding this ability would provide some constraints on the neural basis of consciousness.

Today many approaches (mostly neuroimaging, as well as electrophysiological, psychophysical, and neuropsychological approaches) are being used to ask where and how pictorial representations of objects, scenes, and living beings are generated, stored, and maintained in the brain (Roland, 1993; Kosslyn, 1994; Miyashita, 1995). Even the question of to what degree the processes involved in visual perception and imagery share a common neural substrate has partially been answered. Here we attempt to provide a solid neurophysiological basis for those studies by using an animal model. In our visual memory tasks, monkeys were asked to encode visual objects in associative long-term memory and to retrieve internal representations of the objects from long-term storage according to an appropriate cue. The monkeys can recall the internal representation even without direct sensory stimulation (Hasegawa et al., 1998). Here we note that the nature of the internal representation that lies in the deepest structure for imagery or image generation has been long debated (Pylyshyn, 1981; Kosslyn, 1994); however, recent neuroscience investigations strongly suggest contributions of depictive representation in both humans and monkeys (Kosslyn, 1994; Miyashita, 1995). In humans, especially when verbal instruction triggers the image generation, propositional representation may also contribute to that generation (Pylyshyn, 1981). Therefore, the word "image," as used in this chapter, indicates a depictive internal representation that lies under the goal-directed behavior in the memory tasks of monkeys.

YASUSHI MIYASHITA Department of Physiology, The University of Tokyo School of Medicine, Hongo, Tokyo; Laboratory of Cognitive Neuroscience, National Institute for Physiological Sciences, Okazaki; Mind Articulation Project, ICORP, Japan Science and Technology Corporation, Yushima, Tokyo

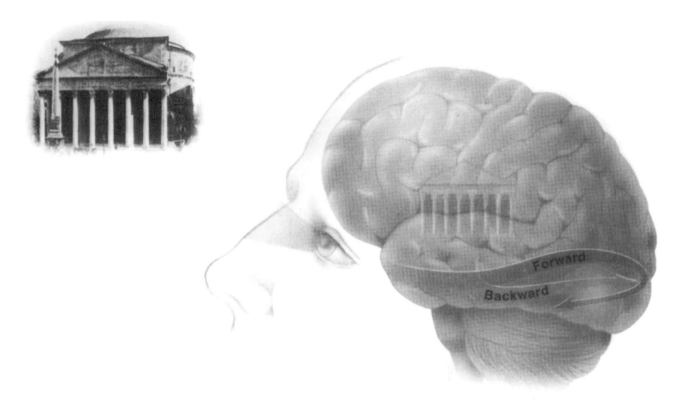

FIGURE 27.1 Visual perception mainly relies on the forward, bottom-up flow of information. Image retrieval or imagery experience, in contrast, highlights the backward projections as an anatomical substrate of top-down mental operations. If an imagery task requires reconstruction of the detailed local geometry of the image (as in counting the columns in a memory of the Pantheon), backward signals from higher-order representations might reach topographically organized visual areas. This cartoon does not indicate that mental images are actual pictures in the brain; obviously, we cannot assume any homunculus in the brain who looks at the images. (Adapted from Miyashita, 1995; artwork by K. Sutliff.)

We start from a neuronal correlate of image generation in monkey inferotemporal cortex. We demonstrate that single neurons become active when the monkey generates from its long-term memory store the image that is instructed by a previous cue stimulus (Miyashita et al., 1998; Naya, Sakai, and Miyashita, 1996). Neurons in inferotemporal cortex can respond to such a prospective object, as well as a retrospective object in memory or a visible object (Miyashita, 1988, 1993). Then we explore the question of where such a prospective activation of an object's image can originate. By using the object–object association task for monkeys, we demonstrate that inferotemporal neurons can encode associative relations between objects and can provide a kind of semantic network among objects (Miyashita, 1993). We found that, in the process of encoding of visual objects, the interaction between the medial temporal lobe and inferotemporal cortex plays an essential role. We analyze this interaction by combination of electrophysiological single unit recording, neurotoxic lesions, and molecular biological methods (Miyashita et al., 1998; Okuno and Miyashita, 1996). These studies clarified how the associative long-term memory of objects is en-

coded and how the prospective activation of an object's image emerges. Comparison with the human imagery system is also discussed.

Neuronal representation of visual long-term memory

Along the occipitotemporal visual pathway from the primary visual cortex (figure 27.1), the physical properties of a visual object are analyzed in the multiple subdivisions of the prestriate and posterior temporal cortices, and the inferotemporal cortex synthesizes the analyzed attributes into a unique configuration (Mishkin, 1982; Van Essen et al., 1992; Miyashita, 1993). The inferotemporal cortex has been proposed to be the memory storehouse for object vision on the basis of behavioral experiments (Mishkin, 1982; Squire, 1987). But how are the memories of objects represented among neuronal networks in the inferotemporal cortex?

Most of our long-term memories of episodes and semantic knowledge are organized so that we can retrieve them by association. We propose that visual memory is organized by the same principle, encoding the forms of objects as structured bundles of associations between elementary views of objects (Miyashita, Date, and Okuno, 1993). We obtained evidence for the associative mechanism by training monkeys to memorize artificial associative relations among visual patterns, then examining whether picture-selective activities of inferotemporal neurons encode the stimulus–stimulus association imposed in the learning (Miyashita, 1988, 1993). One example of such studies used the pair-association (PA) learning task (Sakai and Miyashita, 1991; Higuchi and Miyashita, 1996) by modifying a human declarative memory task (Wechsler, 1987). The results provided strong evidence that inferotemporal neurons acquire stimulus selectivity through associative learning and that the selectivity reflects a stimulus–stimulus association among geometrically different forms. But in this chapter we start from discoveries of retrieval-related neurons in inferotemporal cortex, since the pair-association task requires both encoding and retrieval of the object image.

Neuronal correlate of mental imagery in inferotemporal cortex

In our pair-association task for monkeys, meaningless computer-generated colored pictures were sorted randomly into pairs (G1/B1 to G12/B12), each pair containing a green picture and a blue picture (figure 27.2; see color plate 11). The combination of the paired associates cannot be predicted without memorizing them beforehand, and macaque monkeys (*Macaca fuscata*) were trained to memorize these pairs. In each trial of the task, a cue stimulus was presented, and then the monkey was rewarded when he chose the paired associate of the cue. It should be noted that this task is essentially a memory *recall* task, which demands activation of internal representation of a picture from long-term memory.

In an earlier experiment with monochromatic visual stimuli (Sakai and Miyashita, 1991), we found an interesting category of neurons–*pair-recall neurons*–that exhibited a prospective-type delay activity before the

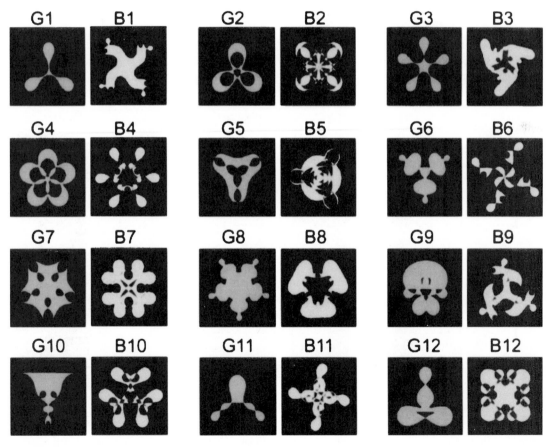

FIGURE 27.2   Image retrieval task for monkeys. The pair-association with color switch (PACS) task uses twelve pairs of colored pictures. When one member of each pair is shown, trained monkeys can retrieve and choose the other member of the paired associates. The first pair consists of the picture G1 (green) and picture B1 (blue), the second pair consists of G2 and B2, and so on.

choice appeared. The delay activity was coupled with the paired associate that is not actually seen but is to be retrieved. This finding led us to a hypothesis that the pair-recall neurons were key elements of the image generation process in the task. Then we tested this hypothesis by developing a novel task, the pair-association with color switch (PACS) task. In this task the necessity for image generation and its initiation time were controlled by a color switch in the middle of the delay period (Naya, Sakai, and Miyashita, 1996). The PACS task consisted of PACS trials and control trials. The control trial, in which there is no color switch, corresponds to a trial of the conventional delayed matching-to-sample (DMS) task where the monkey chooses the same picture as a cue.

The sequence of events in a PACS trial or a DMS trial was as follows (see figure 27.3 and color plate 12). When the monkey pressed a lever in front of the video monitor, a gray square for fixation was presented at the center of the screen for 1 s (warning). Following the cue presentation of one of 24 pictures for 0.5 s, a square was presented during the delay period. The square's color was the same as the cue's color during the first part of the delay period (delay 1) for 2 s in PACS trials or for 5 s in DMS trials. In PACS trials, the square's color changed into the color of the paired associate after delay 1, signaling the initiation of retrieval, and then the second part of the delay period (delay 2) started. Delay 2 was not included in DMS trials. To balance the visual stimulus conditions in the two trials, a gray square was presented for 1 s during the third part of the delay period (delay 3). After delay 3, a choice of two stimuli was shown randomly in two of four possible positions (arranged in two rows of two columns). The choice stimuli were the paired associate of the cue (correct) and a distracter (error) in PACS trials, while the choice stimuli were the same picture as the cue (correct) and a distracter (error) in DMS trials. The animal obtained a reward for touching the correct picture within 1.2 s. PACS trials and DMS trials were randomized. Extracellular discharges of single neurons were recorded with a glass-insulated tungsten microelectrode (Miyashita et al., 1989).

Figure 27.4 demonstrates the activity of a single inferotemporal neuron. The neuron exhibited typical differential responses between the PACS trial and DMS trial in delays 2 and 3, but not in delay 1, indicating that the neuronal firing was switched at the onset of delay 2 in the PACS trial. In this neuron one picture, green 7 (G7), elicited the strongest response during the cue period in both the PACS trial and the DMS trial. (We call this picture the "best picture" throughout the description of this neuron, irrespective of its delay response, although the "best picture" does not necessarily elicit the strongest delay response.) The excitatory response was maintained in delay 1 in both PACS and DMS trials. The paired associate of the best picture, blue 7 (B7), elicited no re-

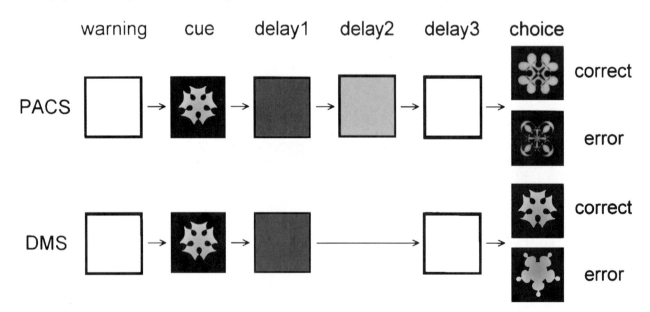

FIGURE 27.3 Sequence of events in the image retrieval task. Both PACS trials and DMS trials use the same color stimuli shown in figure 27.2. In each trial of the task, a cue stimulus is presented, and the monkey is rewarded when he chooses the correct choice stimulus. The correct choice stimulus is the paired associate of the cue in PACS trials and the cue itself in DMS trials. PACS trials and DMS trials were given randomly.

Event sequence is the following: Warning, gray square for fixation (1 s in both trials); cue, one of 24 colored pictures (0.5 s); delay 1, fixation square the same color as the cue picture (2 s in PACS trials, 5 s in the DMS trials); delay 2, fixation square the same color as the paired associate of the cue picture (3 s in PACS trials); delay 3, fixation gray square (1 s in both trials); choice, a choice of two stimuli (1.2 s in both trials).

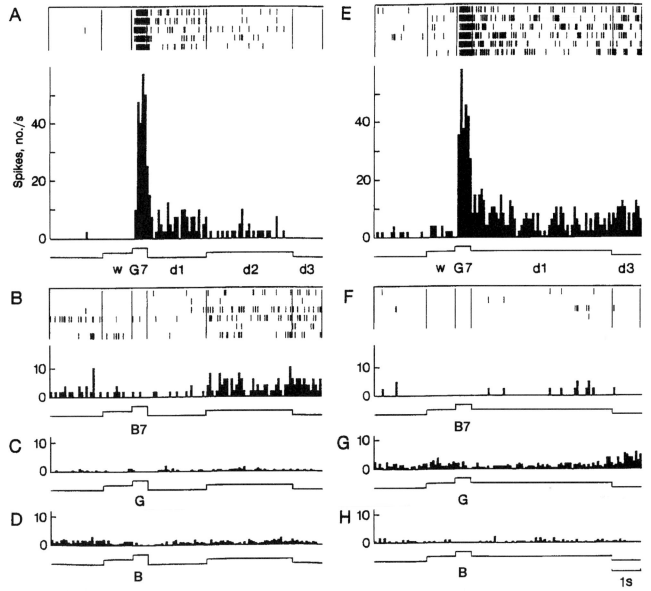

FIGURE 27.4   Neuronal correlate of image retrieval in the temporal cortex. Differential delay responses of a pair-recall neuron in PACS trials and DMS trials. Rastergrams of neural discharges in each trial and spike density histograms were obtained from a single inferotemporal neuron. Bin width, 80 ms. (A–D) Responses in PACS trials. (E–H) Responses in DMS trials. (A, E) Responses in trials for picture G7 as a cue. (B, F) Responses in trials for picture B7 as a cue. (C, G) Responses in trials for picture G1–G12 except G7 as cue pictures (G). (D, H) Responses in trial for picture B1–B12 except B7 as cue pictures (C). Picture G7 elicited the strongest cue response in both tasks

(A, E). Note the suppressed response during delay 2 and delay 3 in PACS trials (A), but not in DMS trials (E). We called this phenomenon the pair-suppression effect. In trials for picture B7 as a cue, no response was observed during the cue period in both tasks (B, F). Note the enhanced response during delay 2 and delay 3 in PACS trials (B), but not in DMS trials (F). We called this phenomenon the pair-recall effect. In trials for picture G and B as cues, no responses were observed in both trials (C, D, G, H), indicating that there was no significant color effect (Naya, Sakai, and Miyashita, 1996).

sponses during the cue period and whole delay period in the DMS trial. In contrast, when B7 was presented as a cue in PACS trial, this neuron started to respond just after the onset of delay 2 when the square's color changed from the cue's color (blue) to that of the paired associate (green).

Figure 27.5 quantifies these stimulus-specific activities of this neuron in PACS trials (see color plate 13). Only the stimulus G7 activated the cell during the cue period (top). In delay 1, this neuron continued to be active only for G7 (middle). However, in delays 2 and 3, when the retrieval of the paired associate was required,

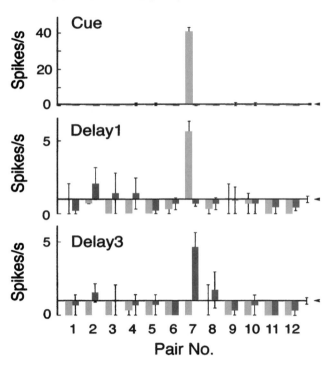

STIMULUS SELECTIVITY OF AIT NEURON IN PACS

FIGURE 27.5 Stimulus selectivity of the inferotemporal neuron (same as that in figure 27.4) is shown in different task periods (top, cue period; middle, delay 1; bottom, delay 3). The ordinate shows the mean discharge rate in each task period after the presentation of a cue stimulus; cue stimuli are labeled as "pair No." on the abscissa (G1 = green histogram bar in No.1; B1 = blue histogram bar in No.1; etc.). This neuron selectively responded to the cue stimulus G7 during the cue period. Note that the cue stimulus B7 does not elicit any response during the cue period and delay 1 in this neuron, but during delays 2 and 3 the same neuron became suddenly active.

the responses were switched from G7 to B7 (bottom). In other words, in the trial when B7 was presented as a cue, the cell was not active until delay 1, but the cell became suddenly active during delays 2 and 3, where the retrieval of G7 was required. Summing up, the cell became active when the image of its best picture (G7) should be recalled from memory. The picture-selective activation after the color switch in PACS trials is called the pair-recall effect.

It is important that the pair-recall effect cannot be due to the effect of the square's color, since other stimuli, either green or blue, did not induce a similar effect (figure 27.5, bottom). This was confirmed by the facts that the pair-recall effect continued from delay 2 into delay 3, in which the square's color was the same gray in both PACS and DMS trials, and that the pair-recall effect was found in PACS trials but not in DMS trials (figure 27.4).

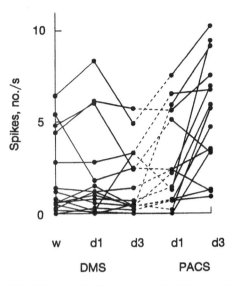

FIGURE 27.6 Pair-recall effect in the PACS task. Discharge rates in trials where the best picture's paired associates were used as a cue in PACS and DMS trials. Each circle denotes the average firing rate for one of single inferotemporal neurons recorded ($n = 15$). In the PACS trials, activities during delay 3 (d3) were higher than those during delay 1 (d1) for most of the 15 cells. In the DMS trials, activities during d3 were not significantly different from those during d1 (Naya, Sakai, and Miyashita, 1996).

Figure 27.6 compares the responses of 15 cells that showed delay responses and were held long enough to complete PACS and DMS trials with all the stimuli. The number of spikes was counted by collecting the trials whose cue picture was the best picture's associate. The effect of the trial classes (PACS vs. DMS) on the delay response was significant [$F(1,14) = 19.8, p < .001$], and there was an interaction between the trial classes and period [$F(1,28) = 12.2, p < .005$]. We further analyzed responses among periods in each trial class (PACS or DMS), and responses between the trial classes in each period. In both PACS and DMS, responses in delay 1 remained equal to warning responses. These delay 1 responses were thus independent of the trial classes. In delay 3 of PACS, the responses were significantly stronger than those in delay 1 ($t = 3.5, p < .005$), while the delay 3 responses in DMS trials remained equal to the delay 1 responses. The delay 3 responses in PACS trials were significantly stronger than those in DMS trials ($t = 5.2, p < .001$). These results confirmed that the pair-recall effect is triggered by the color switch.

All of the above results strongly support the hypothesis that these neural discharges represent the active internal representation of a specific object in mind (the "image" of G7 in the case of figures 27.4 and 27.5). But how does this neural firing arise? What kind of machinery could drive the pair-recall neuron in delay 2/3 in spite of null activity in delay 1? It might depend on a top-down input from the prefrontal cortex. Indeed, we recently found that, under an experimental design with a pair-association paradigm, prefrontal cortex could instruct the inferotemporal cortex to retrieve a correct memory of an object, even without bottom-up sensory input to the inferotemporal cortex (Hasegawa et al., 1998). However, it was also confirmed that only the posterior association cortex could hold the specific information on the paired associates in long-term memory (Hasegawa et al., 1998). Thus the neural mechanism for the image generation should involve specific communication between the pair-recall neurons and the neurons that encode the paired associates in long-term memory.

Let us now consider the neuronal mechanisms that encode the long-term memory of objects.

Inferotemporal neurons that encode the long-term memory of the paired associates

In previous studies (but with monochromatic paired associates), we found neurons that selectively encoded the associative relation between the paired associates (Sakai and Miyashita, 1991). To find out the neuronal correlates of the long-term memory of the paired associates, we trained monkeys to memorize the paired pictures (a monochromatic version of figure 27.2). We recorded single neuron activity and tested whether cells tended to respond preferentially to both of the paired associates, in spite of the fact that both stimuli had no geometric similarity. In the anterior ventral part of area TE (TEav), we found some patchy areas in which many neurons preferentially responded to both of the paired associates (the "pair-coding neuron"). We analyzed sampled cells by calculating response correlation using pair index or correlation coefficients (Sakai and Miyashita, 1991; Higuchi and Miyashita, 1996). The frequency distribution of these indices revealed that the paired associates elicited significantly correlated responses in these areas. This result provides strong evidence that inferotemporal neurons acquire stimulus selectivity through associative learning and that the selectivity reflects a stimulus–stimulus association among geometrically different complex forms.

Role of the interaction between the medial temporal lobe and inferotemporal cortex

Now we can examine the encoding mechanisms—specifically, the role of the interaction between the medial temporal lobe and inferotemporal cortex in the formation of declarative long-term memory (Squire and Zola-Morgan, 1991; Squire, 1987). Using behaving monkey preparation with the pair-association task, we investigated the hypothesis that limbic neurons undergo rapid modification of synaptic connectivity and provide backward signals that guide reorganization of forward neural circuits to (and/or in) the inferotemporal cortex. This hypothesis has anatomical support in that inferotemporal cortex receives massive backward projections from the medial temporal lobe, especially from the perirhinal cortex (Van Hoesen, 1982; Webster et al., 1991; Suzuki and Amaral, 1994a,b). Thus the hypothesis for the role of the backward signal in the consolidation process specifically predicts that a lesion that includes the perirhinal cortex would impair the formation of the associative code for pictures in the inferotemporal neurons (figure 27.7). We now test this prediction.

We combined single-unit recording in the chronic monkey preparation with surgical manipulation so that individual inferotemporal neurons become devoid of the backward signals but can receive forward signals when visual stimuli are presented. We prepared a specific experimental design to run this project (figure 27.7). Backward neuronal connections from the limbic system to the inferotemporal cortex were interrupted by a lesion of the perirhinal cortices. But because a bilateral lesion would impair the monkeys' behavior in the pair-association task (Murray, Gaffan, and Mishkin, 1993), the perirhinal/entorhinal cortices were lesioned unilaterally. With the unilateral lesion, the inferotemporal cortex of the lesioned side could receive information from the contralateral inferotemporal cortex. Receptive fields of inferotemporal neurons cover both hemifields before the lesion. In order to remove the interhemispheric signal from the healthy contralateral inferotemporal cortex, we surgically cut the anterior commissure (AC) at the beginning of the experiment. This surgery disconnected the anterior temporal cortex of each hemisphere from the other, since most commissural fibers of this area traverse the AC rather than the corpus callosum (Pandya, Karol, and Lele, 1973; Demeter et al., 1990). With this surgically manipulated chronic monkey preparation, we tested the ability of inferotemporal neurons to represent associations between picture pairs.

Two adult monkeys (*Macaca fuscata*) were trained in the pair-association task. The AC was transected before the learning of the task (figure 27.8B). After recovery, the monkey was trained with a set (set A) of the paired associates to the criterion performance level; then extracellular spike discharges of single neurons in the anterior inferotemporal cortex were recorded as a prelesion control, as reported in previous studies (Miyashita, 1988; Miyashita and Chang, 1988; Sakai and Miyashita, 1991). Then we deprived inferotemporal neurons of backward neural information by unilateral ibotenic acid lesions of the entorhinal and perirhinal cortices. The lesion covered both the medial and lateral banks of the rhinal sulcus completely, and most of

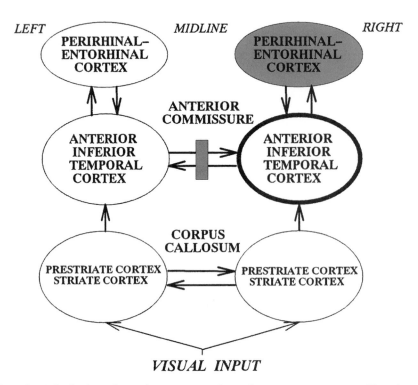

LEFT   MIDLINE   RIGHT

FIGURE 27.7   What is the role of the backward signal in memory formation? The inferotemporal cortex receives a backward signal from the limbic system as well as a forward visual signal from the prestriate cortices. This diagram shows an experimental design to answer the question.

the entorhinal and perirhinal cortex (figure 27.8C–E). The lesioned cortex suffered atrophy, but fibers in the underlying white matter were left unharmed. After the ibotenic acid injection, the monkeys were trained with a new set of paired associates (set B). Then extracellular spike discharges of single neurons were recorded from the same area as that in the prelesion control. Correlation coefficient was used to analyze pair-coding responses of these cells (Higuchi and Miyashita, 1996). The response variability of the cells was evaluated before and after the lesion by a response variability index. The index was defined in each cell as the ratio of the standard deviation of firing rates among the trials for the optimum stimulus over the mean firing rate for the optimum stimulus. Larger values of this index indicate more trial-to-trial fluctuations of the responses.

Figure 27.9 compares the responsiveness of the cells before and after the lesion. The results of two monkeys were not significantly different ($p > .25$) in a two-way ANOVA in any of the indices and have been pooled. Prior to the ibotenic acid lesion, we examined the responses of 92 cells. The distribution of the correlation coefficient showed that the paired associates elicited significantly correlated responses in the control ($p < .01$; Wilcoxon's signed-rank test), confirming the conclusion of our previous report (Sakai and Miyashita, 1991). After the lesion, we examined the responses of 75 cells, and

the cells responded to the pictures (38 ± 2 spikes/s) even more strongly than the control (31 ± 1 spikes/s). However, the correlation coefficients were reduced ($p < .05$) and dropped to chance level after the lesion. The spontaneous discharge rates were not significantly different among the groups ($p > .2$). We also tested with a response variability index whether the cells exhibited any sign of pathological firing after the lesion. The index did not differ significantly between the groups ($p > .6$). We conclude that lesion of the entorhinal and perirhinal cortices disrupted the associative code of the inferotemporal neurons between the paired associates, without impairing the visual response to each stimulus. The results support the view that inferotemporal neurons have the ability to represent the long-term mnemonic code between picture pairs and that this ability is critically dependent on backward connections from the perirhinal cortices to the inferotemporal neurons.

Circuit reorganization in the primate temporal cortex

Then we ask why the limbic–neocortical interactions are so important. By our hypothesis, perirhinal neurons undergo rapid modification of synaptic connectivity and provide backward signals that guide reorganization of forward neural circuits to (and/or in) the inferotemporal

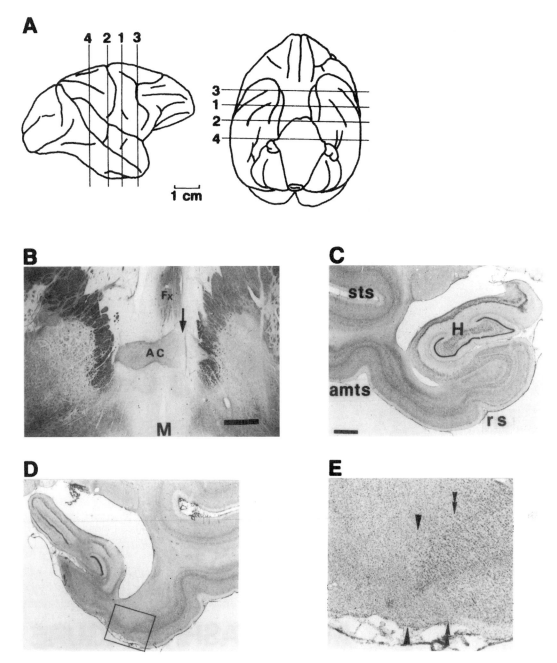

FIGURE 27.8   Unilateral ibotenic acid lesion of the entorhinal and perirhinal cortices. (A) Lateral (left) and ventral (right) view of a monkey brain, indicating the locations of sections used in the following panels (section 1 for panel B, 2 for C–E). Scale bar, 1 cm. (B) Fiber-stained coronal section through the anterior commissure (AC). The AC was surgically cut (arrow) just to the right of the midline (M). The fornix (Fx) was left intact. Scale bar, 2 mm. (C) Cresyl violet–stained coronal section showing the left (intact) entorhinal and perirhinal cortices.

Scale bar, 2 mm. (D) Same section as C, but showing the right entorhinal and perirhinal cortices that were lesioned by ibotenic acid. (E) Higher magnification of the area outlined in D. Double arrowheads indicate the border between intact area (to the right) and incompletely lesioned area. Arrowheads indicate the border between completely (to the left) and incompletely lesioned area. H, hippocampus; amts, anterior middle temporal sulcus; sts, superior temporal sulcus; rs, rhinal sulcus (Higuchi and Miyashita, 1996).

cortex. To explore the first part of this hypothesis, we employed a molecular biological approach. If the hypothesis is true, we should be able to detect the expressions of molecular markers for synaptic plasticity in the monkey temporal cortex (especially perirhinal cortex) during learning of the pair-association task. As the first step, we attempted to test the expression of immediate early genes (IEGs).

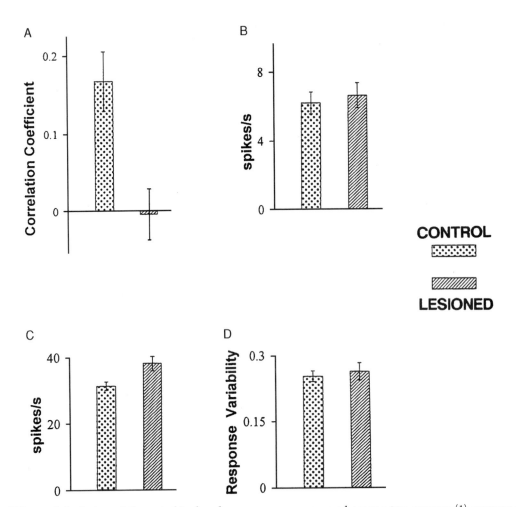

FIGURE 27.9 Effects of the lesion of the entorhinal and per-irhinal cortices upon neuronal responsiveness in the pair-association task: (A) Correlation coefficient; (B) spontaneous discharge rate; (C) maximum discharge rate with spontaneous discharge subtracted; (D) response variability. These indices were compared among two groups: (1) neurons that were recorded prior to the lesion using the set-A stimuli (stippled bar, $n = 92$); (2) those recorded after the lesion using the set-B stimuli (hatched with thin line, $n = 75$). Data are shown as mean ± s.e.m.

IEGs are a class of genes that show rapid and transient, but protein synthesis–independent increases in transcription. Many IEGs encode transcription factors such as Fos, Jun and ZIF268; and these IEGs, especially *zif*268 (the gene that encodes for ZIF268), have been hypothesized to play crucial roles in transduction of neuronal electric signals into more permanent synaptic organization (Morgan and Curran, 1991; Bailey and Kandel, 1993). For example, the induction of *zif*268 in the dentate gyrus is closely correlated with the induction of long-term potentiation (LTP) (Abraham et al., 1993; Worley et al., 1993). We attempted to determine in which temporal cortical areas IEGs were expressed during visual long-term memory formation in the primate. We trained monkeys to learn two different cognitive memory tasks, a visual pair-association task and a visual discrimination task. The visual pair-association task required the monkeys to memorize visual stimulus–stimulus associations (Sakai and Miyashita, 1991; Murray, Gaffan, and Mishkin, 1993). The other task, the visual discrimination task, required them to memorize stimulus–reward associations (Iwai and Mishkin, 1969). The types of learning required in these tasks are different since they are sensitive to lesions in different brain areas and the visual pair-association task was more sensitive to lesions of the medial temporal cortex (Iwai and Mishkin, 1969; Murray, Gaffan, and Mishkin, 1993).

To investigate formation of the stimulus–stimulus association memory but not the skill-based (or habit-like) memory (Mishkin, 1982) incidental to the learning paradigm, we designed a specific learning procedure (figure 27.10). We first trained the monkeys to learn a "rule" or "strategy" of the tasks, which is considered to be related to the skill-based memory, using a set of 24 pictures (the *training set*). After the monkeys' performance reached a plateau level with the training set, a new stimulus set (the *test set*) was introduced. The monkeys' performance was at a chance level in the first day with the test set. The

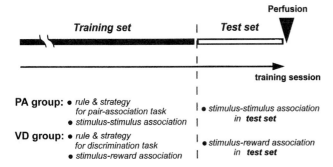

PA group: • rule & strategy
for pair-association task
• stimulus-stimulus association

• stimulus-stimulus association
in **test set**

VD group: • rule & strategy
for discrimination task
• stimulus-reward association

• stimulus-reward association
in **test set**

FIGURE 27.10 Experimental design to detect learning-induced activation of molecular markers in monkeys. To detect the expression of a gene that is specifically related to the paired-associate learning, two different control procedures were introduced. First, the monkeys learned the rule and task strategy during the learning of the *training-set* stimuli, and then the expression of molecular markers was detected during the learning of the *test-set* stimuli. Second, the expression during paired-associate learning was compared with that during visual discrimination learning. The paired-associate learning and visual discrimination learning used the same visual stimuli, the same motor responses, and the same amount of rewards.

performance improved in 5–6 subsequent days, but did not reach a plateau phase. Then the monkeys were perfused immediately after completion of 90 minutes' learning on the perfusion day. The brain blocks were frozen in dry-ice powder and sections (32 μm) were cut using a cryostat and stained immunohistochemically. The specificity and reactivity of the anti-ZIF268 antibody has been described (Okuno, Saffen, and Miyashita, 1995). The anti-ZIF268 antibody specifically recognized an 86-kDa protein in the nuclear extracts from monkey cerebral cortex in immunoprecipitation experiments (Okuno and Miyashita, 1996).

We compared expression of ZIF268 in the anterior temporal cortex of the monkeys during visual paired-associate learning and visual discrimination learning. The presentation of visual stimuli, numbers of emitted motor responses, and amounts of given reward were equalized in the two tasks. In the case of visual paired-associate learning, the intensely ZIF268-immunopositive neurons were accumulated in patches in the ventral surface of the inferior temporal gyrus. The patches were centered in layer IV and spread into both superficial (II/III) and deep (V and VI) layers. The patchy pattern was found in several consecutive sections and was specific to ZIF268, since other IEG products (cFos and JunD) did not show such patterns in adjacent sections (Okuno and Miyashita, 1996).

The distribution of ZIF268 expression in the monkey temporal cortex was quantified by image analysis (Okuno and Miyashita, 1996) and displayed on a two-dimensional unfolded map (figure 27.11; see color plate

14). In each monkey with visual paired-associate learning, ZIF268 was expressed at high levels in a strip parallel to the rhinal sulcus in an anterior–posterior axis, particularly in several patches in this strip (PA1–PA3). ZIF268 was expressed at relatively low levels and was distributed more homogeneously in the monkeys with visual discrimination learning (VD1–VD3). The inferior temporal gyrus is composed of three cytoarchitectonically and connectionally distinct areas (area 35, area 36, and the ventral part of area TE) (Suzuki and Amaral, 1994a). The expression of ZIF268 in the monkeys during visual paired-associate learning was prominent in area 36. By contrast, in area 35, which is medially adjacent to area 36, ZIF268 expression levels were low during both types of visual learning. A two-way ANOVA on the mean expression level (two learning tasks and three brain areas) revealed a significant effect of task [$F(1,4) = 12.05$, $p = .025$] and of area [$F(2,8) = 17.73$, $p = .001$]. The expression in area 36 was significantly higher during visual paired-associate learning than during visual discrimination learning [1.34 ± 0.07 and 0.96 ± 0.04 ($\pm$ s.e.m., arbitrary units), respectively; $p = .01$]. In area 35, the expression levels in the two monkey groups were similar and were not significantly different (pair-association, 0.65 ± 0.09; discrimination, 0.58 ± 0.05; $p > .5$). In ventral TE, the difference did not reach statistical significance ($p = .22$), but there might be a tendency for higher expression of ZIF268 in the monkeys with visual paired-associate learning (pair-association, 1.11 ± 0.15; discrimination, 0.85 ± 0.08). These results support the hypothesis that perirhinal neurons would undergo rapid modification of synaptic connectivity during learning of the visual pair-association task.

Conclusion

In this chapter, we examined neural mechanisms underlying memory retrieval and the consolidation process by single-unit recording and molecular biological methods. For this purpose we devised a visual pair-association memory task for monkeys. The task requires the monkey to encode associative relations between visual objects and to retrieve the high-level internal representation (the "image") of the paired associate according to a cue stimulus. We proposed that the visual memory is organized as structured bundles of associations between objects in the inferotemporal cortex (Miyashita, 1993) and that the retrieved image is activated in the neural network of the inferotemporal cortex. The pair-association with color switch (PACS) task, in which the necessity for image retrieval and its initiation time were controlled by a color switch, provided particularly compelling evidence for the role of inferotemporal neurons

A

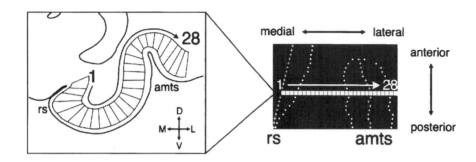

B

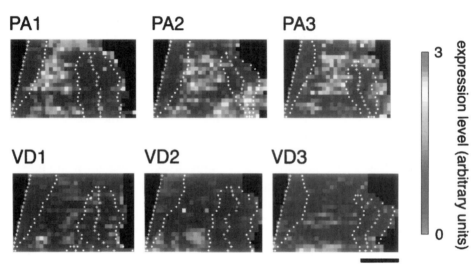

FIGURE 27.11 Two-dimensional unfolded maps of the monkey temporal cortex indicating ZIF268 expression levels. (A) Line drawing of 28 radial, segmented areas in a coronal section through the right medioventral temporal cortex (left). The cortical area in each section was subdivided into a number of radial segments. To display the spatial distribution of ZIF268 expression levels, the segmented areas were reconstructed as a two-dimensional unfolded map (right). The fundus and lip of a sulcus are outlined by white crosses and dots, respectively. Serial sections were aligned along the fundus of the rhinal sulcus. rs = rhinal sulcus; amts = anterior middle temporal sulcus; D, L, V, M = dorsal, lateral, ventral, medial. (B) The expression levels of ZIF268 in the temporal cortex of individual monkeys. The density of reaction products of ZIF268-immunostaining in the segments is indicated on the unfolded maps (similar to the right panel in A) in pseudocolor representation. The maps from monkeys with visual paired-associate learning (PA1–PA3) and visual discrimination learning (VD1–VD3) are shown in upper and lower panels, respectively. The values are normalized so that the mean density of the reaction products of all segments from all six monkeys is 1.0 (Okuno and Miyashita, 1996). The boundaries of cortical areas were indicated by gray dots. Scale bar, 10 mm (Okuno and Miyashita, 1996).

(Naya, Sakai, and Miyashita, 1996). The activated high-level representation in inferotemporal cortex could be the origin of backward signals that appear to reach topographically organized visual areas when an imagery task requires reconstruction of the detailed local geometry of the image (as in counting the columns of the Pantheon), as demonstrated in neuroimaging and psychophysical studies (Ishai and Sagi, 1996; Miyashita, 1995; Kosslyn, 1994; Roland, 1993).

The backward signal from the medial temporal lobe to the inferotemporal cortex plays a distinct role in memory consolidation. We analyzed the interaction between the perirhinal cortex and area TEav during the formation of the visual paired-associate memory in monkeys. We hypothesized that the interaction is critical since perirhinal neurons might undergo rapid modification of synaptic connectivity and could provide a backward signal to guide reorganization of forward neural circuits in (and/or to) area TEav. The results of single-unit recording combined with neurotoxic lesions, as well as detection of the expression of molecular markers for synaptic plasticity, supported the hypothesis. However, the study has completed only the first stage of investigation, and there are many missing links. For example, it is believed that the induced transcription factors regulate expression of late-response genes which probably contribute to the synaptic plasticity, especially to morphological changes (Bailey and Kandel, 1993). So far we have no data in monkey inferotemporal cortex supporting this line of speculation.

In the above studies, we extensively used the visual pair-association memory task for monkeys–an approach that offers many advantages. However, in this task (even in the PACS task), the image was generated in a simple way, in which a subject recalled a previously seen object. We humans use imagery in more flexible ways. First, we can combine or arrange objects in novel configurations in images. Second, we can also mentally draw patterns that we have never actually seen, and we can visualize novel patterns that are not based on rearranging familiar components. To make these image computations possible, an imagery system should contain another subsystem–one that uses associative memory and constructs local representations on the basis of a global image by top-down attentional shift (Farah, 1990; Kosslyn, 1994). Anatomical localization of the subsystem might be hypothesized in the dorsolateral prefrontal cortex, but evidence is still scanty (Fuster, 1989). It is noted that, although we believe depictive representation lies in the deepest structure for image generation (Kosslyn, 1994; Miyashita, 1995), propositional representation may also generate imagery by the use of this subsystem, especially in humans (Pylyshyn, 1981). Characterization and neurophysiological analysis of this subsystem would provide further constraints on the neural basis of imagery and its conscious activation.

REFERENCES

ABRAHAM, W. C., S. E. MASON, J. DEMMER, J. M. WILLIAMS, C. L. RICHARDSON, W. P. TATE, P. A. LAWLOR, and M. DRAGUNOW, 1993. Correlations between immediate early gene induction and the persistence of long-term potentiation. *Neuroscience* 56:717–727.

ALAIN, E. A. C., 1926. *Systeme des Beaux-Art.* Paris: Gallimard.

BAILEY, C. H., and E. R. KANDEL, 1993. Structural changes accompanying memory storage. *Annu. Rev. Physiol.* 55:397–426.

DEMETER, S., D. L. ROSENE, and G. W. VAN HOESEN, 1990. Fields and origin and pathways of the interhemispheric commissures in the temporal lobe of the macaques. *J. Comp. Neurol.* 302:29–53.

FARAH, M. J., 1990. *Visual Agnosia.* Cambridge, Mass.: MIT Press.

FUSTER, J. M., 1989. *The Prefrontal Cortex.* New York: Raven Press.

HASEGAWA, I., T. FUKUSHIMA, T. IHARA, and Y. MIYASHITA, 1998. Callosal window between prefrontal cortices: Cognitive interaction to retrieve long-term memory. *Science* 281: 814–818.

HIGUCHI, S., and Y. MIYASHITA, 1996. Formation of mnemonic neuronal responses to visual paired associates in inferotemporal cortex is impaired by perirhinal and entorhinal lesions. *Proc. Natl. Acad. Sci. U.S.A.* 93:739–743.

ISHAI, A., and D. SAGI, 1995. Common mechanisms of visual imagery and perception. *Science* 268:1772–1774.

IWAI, E., and M. MISHKIN, 1969. Further evidence on the locus of the visual area in the temporal lobe of the monkey. *Exp. Neurol.* 25:585–594.

KOSSLYN, S. M., 1994. *Image and Brain.* Cambridge, Mass.: MIT Press.

MILNER, B., 1968. Visual recognition and recall after right temporal-lobe excision in man. *Neuropsychologia* 6:191–209.

MISHKIN, M., 1982. A memory system in the monkey. *Phil. Trans. R. Soc. Lond. B* 298:85–95.

MIYASHITA, Y., 1988. Neuronal correlate of visual associative long-term memory in the primate temporal cortex. *Nature* 335:817–820.

MIYASHITA, Y., 1993. Inferior temporal cortex: Where visual perception meets memory. *Annu. Rev. Neurosci.* 16:245–263.

MIYASHITA, Y., 1995. How the brain creates imagery. *Science* 268:1719–1720.

MIYASHITA, Y., and H. S. CHANG, 1988. Neuronal correlate of pictorial short-term memory in the primate temporal cortex. *Nature* 331:68–70.

MIYASHITA, Y., A. DATE, and H. OKUNO, 1993. Configuration encoding of complex visual forms by single neurons of monkey temporal cortex. *Neuropsychologia* 31:1119–1131.

MIYASHITA, Y., S. HIGUCHI, K. SAKAI, and N. MASUI, 1991. Generation of fractal patterns for probing the visual memory. *Neurosci. Res.* 12:307–311.

MIYASHITA, Y., M. KAMEYAMA, I. HASEGAWA, and T. FUKUSHIMA, 1998. Consolidation of visual associative long-term memory in the temporal cortex of primates. *Neurobiol. Learn. Memory* 70:197–211.

MIYASHITA, Y., T. ROLLS, P. M. B. CAHUSAC, H. NIKI, and J. D. FEIGENBAUM, 1989. Activity of hippocampal formation neurons in the monkey related to a stimulus-response association task. *J. Neurophysiol.* 61:669–678.

MORGAN, J. I., and T. CURRAN, 1991. Stimulus-transcription coupling in the nervous system: Involvement of the inducible proto-oncogenes fos and jun. *Annu. Rev. Neurosci.* 14: 421–451.

MURRAY, E. A., D. GAFFAN, and M. MISHKIN, 1993. Neural substrates of visual stimulus-stimulus association in rhesus monkeys. *J. Neurosci.* 13:4549–4541.

NAYA, Y., K. SAKAI, and Y. MIYASHITA, 1996. Activity of primate inferotemporal neurons related to a sought target in a pair-association task. *Proc. Natl. Acad. Sci. U.S.A.* 93:2664–2669.

OKUNO, H., and Y. MIYASHITA, 1996. Expression of the transcription factor ZIF268 in the temporal cortex of monkeys during visual paired associate learning. *Eur. J. Neurosci.* 8: 2118–2128.

OKUNO, H., D. W. SAFFEN, and Y. MIYASHITA, 1995. Subdivision-specific expression of Zif268 in the hippocampal formation of the Macaque monkey. *Neuroscience* 66:829–845.

PANDYA, D. N., E. A. KAROL, and P. P. LELE, 1973. The distribution of the anterior commissure in the squirrel monkey. *Brain Res.* 49:177–180.

PYLYSHYN, Z. W., 1981. The imagery debate: Analogue media versus tacit knowledge. *Psychol. Rev.* 87:16–45.

ROLAND, P. E., 1993. *Brain Activation.* New York: Wiley-Liss.

SAKAI, K., and Y. MIYASHITA, 1991. Neural organization for the long-term memory of paired associates. *Nature* 354:152–155.

SARTRE, J. P., 1938. *L'imaginare.* Paris: Gallimard.

SQUIRE, L. R., 1987. *Memory and Brain.* New York: Oxford University Press.

SQUIRE, L. R., and S. ZOLA-MORGAN, 1991. The medial temporal lobe memory system. *Science* 253:1380–1386.

SUZUKI, W. A., and D. G. AMARAL, 1994a. Topographic organization of the reciprocal connections between the monkey entorhinal cortex and the perirhinal and parahippocampal cortices. *J. Neurosci.* 14:1856–1877.

SUZUKI, W. A., and D. G. AMARAL, 1994b. Perirhinal and parahippocampal cortices of the Macaque monkey: Cortical afferents. *J. Comp. Neurol.* 350:497–533.

VAN ESSEN, D. C., C. H. ANDERSON, and D. J. FELLEMAN, 1992. Information processing in the primate visual system: An integrated systems perspective. *Science* 255:419–423.

VAN HOESEN, G. W., 1982. The parahippocampal gyrus: New observations regarding its cortical connections in the monkey. *Trends Neurosci.* 5:345–353.

WEBSTER, M. J., L. G. UNGERLEIDER, and J. BACHEVALIER, 1991. Connections of inferior temporal areas TE and TEO with medial temporal-lobe structures in infant and adult monkeys. *J. Neurosci.* 11:1095–1116.

WECHSLER, D., 1987. *Wechsler Memory Scale–Revised.* San Antonio: The Psychological Corporation.

WORLEY, P. F., R. V. BHAT, J. M. BARABAN, C. A. ERICKSON, B. L. MCNAUGHTON, and C. A. BARNES, 1993. Thresholds for synaptic activation of transcription factors in hippocampus: Correlation with long-term enhancement. *J. Neurosci.* 13:4776–4786.

28 Physiological Studies of Face Processing in Humans

GREGORY MCCARTHY

ABSTRACT Face processing comprises perceptual and cognitive processes required for the recognition of a complex stimulus as a face, the identification of the particular face in view, and the analysis of facial expression. These and other components of face processing can be dissociated by brain lesions, suggesting that face processing relies on a distributed neural system. Recent physiological studies in humans have begun to supplement the lesion data in identifying critical nodes in this distributed system. Neuroimaging studies using positron emission tomography and functional magnetic resonance imaging have demonstrated that discrete regions of the fusiform gyrus are consistently activated when subjects view faces. Electrophysiological recordings from electrodes placed directly on the fusiform gyrus have further demonstrated that face-specific evoked activity occurs within 200 ms of face presentation. Electrical stimulation of these same sites has frequently led to transient prosopagnosia, strongly implicating these discrete brain regions in face processing. However, the specificity of these regions for face processing is still a contentious issue, as is the degree to which these fusiform face regions are modulated by top-down processing.

In addition to ventral occipitotemporal cortex, other brain regions are engaged by face processing. In general, tasks emphasizing face memory activate more anterior regions of the medial temporal lobe, including the parahippocampal gyrus and hippocampus. Faces also evoke activity in and near the superior temporal sulcus. This latter activation may reflect the processing of dynamic information related to the analysis of eye and mouth movements. Finally, the amygdala has been strongly implicated in the analysis of facial expressions, particularly fearful expressions, while the insula has been activated by expressions of disgust. These results suggest that the analysis of specific emotional expressions may be linked to neural systems involved in behaviors relevant to those emotions.

Face processing encompasses a large number of perceptual and cognitive processes including the extraction of the face from among other structures in the visual scene, the identification of the particular face in view, the access of the bearer's name and associated semantic information, and the analysis of facial expression to determine the bearer's intentions and emotional state. The fast and accurate processing of faces confers a survival advantage–kin are easily identified and danger and threat are rapidly conveyed. The apparently effortless ability to identify faces has given rise to the notion that face processing is effected by special neural mechanisms, an idea lent credence by studies of patients showing that brain lesions can sometimes lead to profound deficits in face processing. However, face agnosia, or prosopagnosia, is often associated with other difficulties in object recognition, leading some investigators to conclude that the deficit is not face-specific (Bauer and Trobe, 1984; Damasio, Damasio, and Van Hoesen, 1982) but reflects a more general problem of within-category visual discrimination. This point has been contested in studies reporting patients with visual processing deficits that appear quite specific for faces (De Renzi et al., 1991; Farah et al., 1995). Other studies have demonstrated that aspects of face processing such as gender discrimination, face identity and analysis of facial expression can be dissociated by brain lesions (e.g., Adolphs et al., 1994; Sergent and Villemure, 1989) suggesting that face processing relies upon a distributed neural system.

Functional neuroimaging and neurophysiological studies have begun to supplement studies based upon the analysis of brain lesions in describing the functional neuroanatomy of face processing. Here we review neuroimaging and neurophysiological studies that have investigated the functional properties and specificity of different cortical regions for face processing. We limit our scope to studies of healthy adult humans, although pertinent references to the voluminous literature on prosopagnosia are provided where relevant. We do not attempt to review the many relevant studies concerned with the development of face processing in humans, deficits in face processing associated with psychiatric disorders, or physiological studies in nonhuman primates. The reader is directed to several excellent treatments of this topic (Bruce and Young, 1986; Farah, 1990; Milders and Perrett, 1993).

GREGORY MCCARTHY Brain Imaging and Analysis Center, Duke University Medical Center, and Veterans Affairs Medical Center, Durham, N.C.

Neuroanatomical localization of face and object perception

We first consider studies that have addressed the neuroanatomical basis for visual object recognition and the distinction between faces and nonface objects. Several neuroimaging studies have tested the distinction drawn between visual processing of objects in the ventral portion of the brain, the "what is it" pathway, and of spatial locations in more dorsal brain regions, the "where is it" pathway (Ungerleider and Mishkin, 1982). Haxby and colleagues (Haxby et al., 1991) performed the first neuroimaging studies in humans that explicitly addressed this dichotomy using oxygen-labeled water $(H_2^{15}O)$ and positron emission tomography (PET) to measure task-related changes in regional cerebral blood flow (rCBF). A face-matching task was used to stimulate the ventral object pathway, and dot-location matching was used to stimulate the dorsal spatial location pathway. A third task controlled for visual stimulation and motor responses. As predicted, the face-matching task activated the ventral occipitotemporal cortex while the dot-location task activated the superior parietal lobe. The dorsal–ventral distinction between location and face matching was confirmed in subsequent publications, even when all stimuli contained faces and only task instructions differentiated the object and spatial tasks (Haxby et al., 1993, 1994). As before, the face-matching task activated the ventral occipitotemporal region bilaterally, but the greater magnitude and spatial extent of activation occurred in the right hemisphere, particularly in the fusiform gyrus. This right hemisphere dominance for faces contrasts with a similar study (Köhler et al., 1995) that used objects other than faces. As in Haxby's studies (Haxby et al., 1991, 1993), bilateral occipitotemporal activation was found for objects, but activation was greater and extended more anteriorly in the left fusiform.

Haxby (Haxby et al., 1991, 1993, 1994) and Köhler (Köhler et al., 1995) established that faces and nonface objects activate extensive regions of ventral occipitotemporal cortex bilaterally, with a right hemisphere bias for faces and a left bias for nonface objects. Malach and colleagues (1995) performed a study using functional magnetic resonance imaging (fMRI) to investigate early stages of visual processing that discriminate objects from nonobjects. Objects, including faces, activated a region (termed LO) that was localized to the lateral aspect of the posterior fusiform gyrus bilaterally. While activated by all objects, LO showed little activation for textures or "phase-scrambled" objects (created by scrambling the phase of the 2D Fourier transform of the objects and then performing an inverse transform,

thereby preserving the spatial frequency of the original objects). Malach reported that LO was equally activated by familiar objects and unfamiliar abstract shapes and suggested, therefore, that LO may represent a preliminary stage in object recognition prior to semantic analysis.

Sergent, Ohta, and MacDonald (1992) performed the first neuroimaging studies that attempted systematically to isolate components of face processing from the visual processing of nonface objects and lower visual stimuli such as sinusoidal gratings. A comparison of two discrimination tasks–face gender and sinusoidal grating orientation–yielded extensive posterior right occipital hemisphere activation (including the inferior, middle, and lateral occipital gyri and the right lingual gyrus) and less extensive left hemisphere activation (including the left middle occipital gyrus). A comparison of object discrimination and sinusoidal grating discrimination yielded extensive activation in the left occipitotemporal region, principally the fusiform gyrus, inferior and middle temporal gyri, the middle occipital gyrus, and superior parietal lobe. The areas activated by face gender discrimination that were not also activated during object discrimination included the ventral and inferior lateral occipitotemporal cortex of the right hemisphere, including the fusiform and parahippocampal gyrus, and the anterior medial temporal lobe bilaterally.

Our group (Puce et al., 1995) used fMRI to investigate responses to unfamiliar faces compared to equiluminant control stimuli consisting of the equiluminant piecewise scrambled faces. Faces activated the ventral occipitotemporal cortex bilaterally, primarily within the fusiform gyrus, with lesser activation of the adjacent occipitotemporal sulcus and inferior temporal gyrus. The volume of face-related activation in the right fusiform gyrus and adjacent occipitotemporal sulcus was approximately 160% of that obtained in similar regions of the left hemisphere. Similar activations were reported by Clark (Clark et al., 1996) who performed a fMRI study, using the same face-matching task as that in Haxby's study (Haxby et al., 1993) and found the most reliable activation in the right fusiform gyrus. Also, Kanwisher (Kanwisher et al., 1996) compared faces to everyday objects and found that faces activated the right fusiform while objects activated the fusiform and parahippocampal gyri bilaterally.

The neuroimaging studies just reviewed consistently show that objects primarily activated ventral occipitotemporal cortex. Although the activation was usually bilateral, faces produced stronger activation of the right hemisphere while nonface objects produced stronger activation of the left hemisphere. Prosopagnosia is most frequently associated with bilateral lesions to the occipitotemporal cortex (Damasio, Damasio, and Van Hoesen, 1982), although right hemisphere damage has been shown to be sufficient to produce the deficit (De Renzi et al., 1994). The activation obtained in the PET studies was more spatially extensive than that obtained in the fMRI studies–a fact Clark (Clark et al., 1996) attributed to the spatial smoothing typically employed in PET studies. Across studies, the right fusiform gyrus was most consistently activated. Like Sergent (Sergent, Ohta, and MacDonald, 1992), Puce and colleagues (1995) also noted discrete activation in lateral cortex including the right middle occipital gyrus and lateral occipital sulcus and more anteriorly in the superior temporal sulcus. Lesser activation was noted in the left middle occipital gyrus.

Figure 28.1–an overlay of activation by faces obtained in a fMRI study by Puce and colleagues (1996)–illustrates several of the points raised above (see color plate 15). Bilateral activation of the fusiform gyri by faces (yellow-red overlay) is clearly evident, with some-

what more extensive activation obtained in the right fusiform. Activation by faces of right lateral cortex is also prominent.

While the neuroimaging studies are consistent in showing that faces activate ventral occipitotemporal cortex, they do not establish when such processing occurs. Our group has made electrophysiological recordings from implanted electrodes in extrastriate regions in patients being evaluated for seizure disorders. Allison and colleagues (1994a,c) reported a study of 24 patients who viewed faces, equiluminant piecewise scrambled faces, cars, scrambled cars, and butterflies. Faces, but not the other stimulus categories, evoked a surface-negative potential with a peak latency of approximately 200 ms (N200). Figure 28.2 presents an example of face-specific N200 recorded from a subdural electrode on the right lateral fusiform gyrus. Despite recording from widespread sites within the brain, N200 was evoked only from focal regions of the left and right fusiform, inferior temporal gyri, and from a lateral region centered

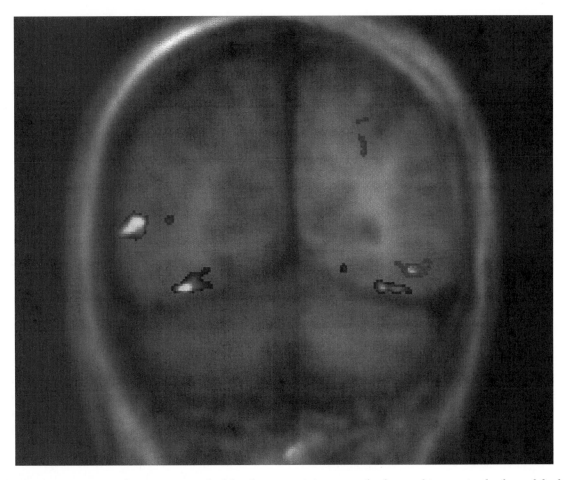

FIGURE 28.1   A comparison of activations evoked by faces (yellow-red overlay) and letterstrings (green overlay). Faces activated the fusiform gyrus bilaterally, and a region of lateral cortex in the right hemisphere. Letterstrings activated the oc-

cipitotemporal sulcus and intraparietal sulcus of the left hemisphere. The overlays shown represent the spatially normalized average of 12 subjects. (From Puce and associates, 1996.)

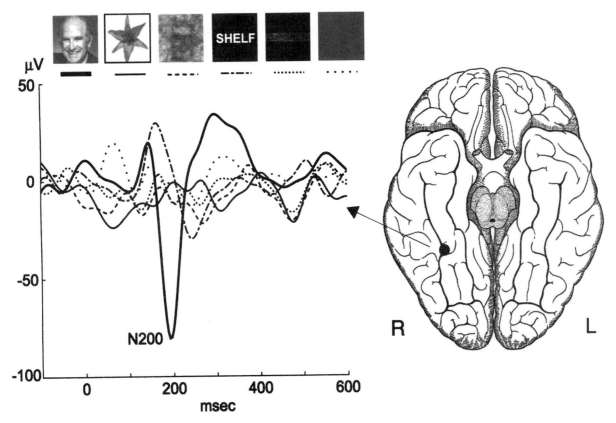

FIGURE 28.2   ERPs recorded from an electrode on the right lateral mid-fusiform gyrus in response to six different stimulus categories shown at the top: faces, flowers, phase-scrambled faces, nouns, phase-scrambled nouns, and gray rectangles. The subject was instructed to respond with a button press when- ever a gray rectangle appeared. A large negative potential at approximately 200 ms (N200) was evoked only by faces. Elec- trodes immediately adjacent to this site (not shown) showed no face-specific ERPs.

upon the middle temporal gyrus (see below). Electrical stimulation of the face-specific N200 sites frequently produced a transient inability to name familiar faces but did not interfere with naming nonface objects (although extensive testing was not possible owing to clinical constraints). Adjacent to the more face-specific sites, color-sensitive ERPs were often recorded from the lateral lingual and medial fusiform gyrus. When these sites were electrically stimulated, color disturbances often resulted. No overlap was found between color and face-specific sites, although their close proximity may explain the frequent association of prosopagnosia and achromatopsia (e.g., Bruyer et al., 1983) in the human lesion literature. Allison's results (Allison et al., 1994a,c) suggest that discrete regions of inferior extrastriate vi- sual cortex, varying in location between individuals, are specialized for the recognition of faces.

Figure 28.3 summarizes the locations of principal acti- vations within the occipitotemporal region reported in ten representative studies using PET (open symbols), fMRI (closed symbols), and intracranial electrophysiol- ogy (asterisk).

Are faces special?

An enduring question in face perception is whether faces are unique objects processed by special neural ma- chinery (Ellis, 1985). This question encompasses two re- lated issues. The first asks whether deficits in face recognition following lesions are related to a general dif- ficulty in discriminating items within a subordinate cate- gory (see Bauer and Trobe, 1984; Damasio, Damasio, and Van Hoesen, 1982). Faces may be special only in that they are usually processed to the subordinate level (the president's face) while other objects are processed to the base category level (a clock). Many prosopagnosic patients have difficulties with within-group discrimina- tions such as cars or flowers (De Haan, Young, and New- combe, 1991). However, some prosopagnosics appear to have a specific deficit for face recognition despite exten- sive testing with other object categories (Farah, Levinson, and Klein, 1995) and other patients have ex- tensive object agnosias with intact face recognition (Moscovitch, Winocur, and Behrmann, 1997). Thus while many prosopagnosics have extensive difficulties in

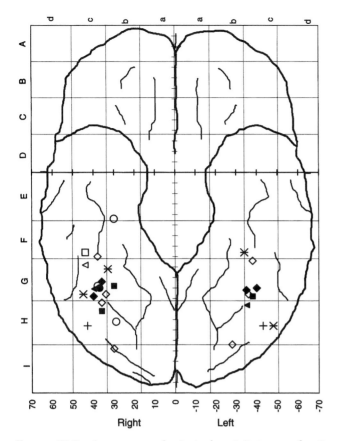

FIGURE 28.3 A summary of principal occipitotemporal activations reported in ten representative studies concerned with face and object perception using different methodologies. Each symbol corresponds to the locations provided in each study in the coordinates of Talairach and Tournoux (1988). Four studies used PET methodology: (○) Face identity minus visual gratings (Sergent et al., 1994); (◇) face identity greater than spatial location (Haxby et al., 1994); (△) faces greater than control (Dolan et al., 1996); (□) degraded faces following exposure to undegraded faces (Dolan et al., 1997). Five studies used fMRI methodology: (+) Area LO (Malach et al., 1995); (●) face matching (Clarke et al., 1996); (■) faces greater than letterstrings (Puce et al., 1996); (▲) faces greater than objects (Kanwisher, McDermott, and Chun, 1997); (✳) faces among objects and nonobjects (McCarthy et al., 1997). One study used intracranial electrophysiological recording: (◆) Face-specific N200s (Allison et al., 1994a).

discriminating among other within-category items, this is not a necessary observation.

The electrophysiological data reviewed above generally support the thesis that specific neural regions are involved in at least the initial stages of face processing. Furthermore, other studies by our group found letterstring-specific sites within ventral occipitotemporal cortex that were clearly distinct from face-specific sites and from which face-specific and letterstring-specific N200 ERPs were evoked. (Allison et al., 1994a,c; Nobre, Allison, and McCarthy, 1994). Fol-

lowing upon these electrophysiological dissociations, Puce and colleagues (1996) contrasted faces, letterstrings, and textures in a fMRI experiment. Consistent with our prior study (Puce et al., 1995), bilateral (right hemisphere dominant) activation of the fusiform gyrus and the adjacent occipitotemporal and inferior occipital sulci was evoked by faces (figure 28.1, yellow-red overlay). In contrast, letterstrings evoked activation that was primarily restricted to the left lateral fusiform gyrus and occipitotemporal sulcus (figure 28.1, green overlay).

Puce and colleagues (1995) confirmed the strong dissociation between faces and letterstrings first observed electrophysiologically. However, it can be argued that letterstrings are themselves a special stimulus category and that the face-selective regions could have been activated by exemplars of other object categories. Kanwisher and colleagues (Kanwisher, McDermott, and Chun, 1997) addressed this and other issues in a series of neuroimaging studies. They first identified candidate face-specific areas by comparing faces to everyday objects. Regions for which faces evoked a stronger response than objects were identified in the fusiform gyrus in twelve of fifteen subjects. Ten of ten right-handed subjects had a right fusiform activation focus, and five of these ten also had a left fusiform focus. The average size of the right fusiform area was more than two times greater than the left fusiform area. Once identified, these fusiform regions were then used as regions of interest in subsequent studies using a subset of the same subjects.

Kanwisher first compared two-tone and scrambled versions of the same faces and found strong face activation despite equal luminance, thus confirming the results of Puce (Puce et al., 1995, 1996), who compared faces to equiluminant piecewise scrambled faces and textures. In a second experiment, Kanwisher compared unfamiliar faces to a set of unfamiliar houses. The faces evoked more than six times greater activation in the face areas than did houses, demonstrating the selectivity of the face areas for faces and further demonstrating that subordinate exemplars of any object category are not sufficient to activate the face region. The face areas responded more strongly to faces than to human hands, demonstrating that face area activation does not generalize to all body parts. Finally, subjects were tested with faces and hands in a task where the subject was required to respond to stimulus repetitions. Again, the face area was not activated by hands, even though the task required fine, within-category discrimination. Kanwisher (Kanwisher, McDermott, and Chun, 1997) concluded that the face area activation does not simply reflect subordinate-level categorization, but rather constitutes a neural module for face perception.

As reviewed above, Sergent, Ohta, and MacDonald (1992) reported that while faces and objects commonly activated the left fusiform gyrus, only faces activated the right fusiform, suggesting that faces may activate both face-specific regions in the right fusiform and more general object recognition regions in the left fusiform. Using similar reasoning, we hypothesized that faces presented in isolation may activate both general and specific recognition systems, and that activations evoked by faces in prior studies reflect both specific and general activation (McCarthy et al., 1997). To test this hypothesis, we presented subjects with a dynamic display in which control stimuli appeared briefly and asynchronously at different spatial locations for the duration of each run. In contrast, faces appeared among the control stimuli according to a periodic schedule. Approximately 1100 stimuli were presented in each 3-minute run—an average of 5 stimuli appeared on screen within each second. In one experimental condition, the control stimuli were examples of common objects. In the other condition, the control stimuli were phase-scrambled versions of the same objects with identical spatial frequency and luminance but otherwise unrecognizable. We predicted that faces among the scrambled nonobjects would evoke activation of the face-specific *and* general object recognition systems. However, faces presented among objects would only activate the face-specific system, as concurrent object processing would saturate the general object recognition system. Consistent with this hypothesis, we found bilateral activation within the fusiform gyrus evoked by faces presented among nonobjects, and more spatially restricted activation of a small region of the right fusiform gyrus for faces presented among objects.

To address the issue of within-category discrimination, additional studies were conducted in which the periodic presentation of faces was replaced by the periodic presentation of different flowers. We predicted that flowers presented among nonobjects would activate the general object recognition system. However, flowers presented among objects should evoke no fusiform activation, as the areas activated by flowers would now be activated continuously by concurrent object processing. The results were as predicted. Flowers evoked extensive fusiform gyrus activity bilaterally (but greater in the left hemisphere) when presented among nonobjects, but showed no activation when presented among objects. Results from a single subject are presented in figure 28.4 (see color plate 16).

Taken together, the results of Allison (Allison et al., 1994a,c), Puce (Puce et al., 1996), Kanwisher (Kanwisher, McDermott, and Chun, 1997), and McCarthy (McCarthy et al., 1997) present a strong case that relatively focal regions within the (primarily right) fusiform gyrus respond specifically to faces and not to exemplars of other categories. However, it is also clear that faces evoke activity that is both specific and nonspecific within the fusiform gyrus; hence it is incumbent upon investigators to establish what portion of their obtained activations are face-specific before generalizing about the properties of this brain region.

While the studies reviewed above demonstrate that individual exemplars of different categories do not activate the face-specific fusiform region, this in itself does not invalidate the notion that within-category, or subordinate-level, processing poses an additional burden upon perceptual processes within the fusiform gyri. Gauthier and colleagues (1997) provide evidence that subordinate-level judgments about stimuli yield greater activation within the fusiform gyrus than base-level judgments about the same stimuli. Whether this result reflects a deeper depth of processing that further engages the fusiform object recognition system, or whether subordinate classification increases attentional demands or task difficulty, is not certain. The influence of attentional and mnemonic factors on processing in the fusiform face areas will be addressed in the next two sections.

A second issue regarding the special nature of face processing is whether the face areas defined in the prior studies represent cortex unique to face processing, or whether these regions have been tuned by long experience with homogeneous stimuli (Gauthier et al., 1997). To date, no neuroimaging study has directly addressed this issue, although behavioral evidence suggests that people can become experts in making fine discriminations among other categories of homogeneous stimuli (Gauthier and Tarr, 1997). Whether this expertise is instantiated in specific cortical regions has not yet been established.

Attention and faces

Neuroimaging studies have previously demonstrated attentional modulation in extrastriate regions specialized for color (Corbetta et al., 1990) and motion processing (O'Craven et al., 1997). Several authors have investigated the influence of attention upon neuroimaging activations evoked by face processing. At issue is the hypothesis that face perception is a fully automatic and obligatory process and, as such, does not require attention for its operation.

Sergent, Ohta, and MacDonald (1992) found that passively viewed faces produced no extrastriate activation relative to visual control stimuli whereas tasks requiring explicit processing of faces produced robust activation. However, subsequent fMRI studies have found discrete activation within the fusiform gyrus in passive viewing

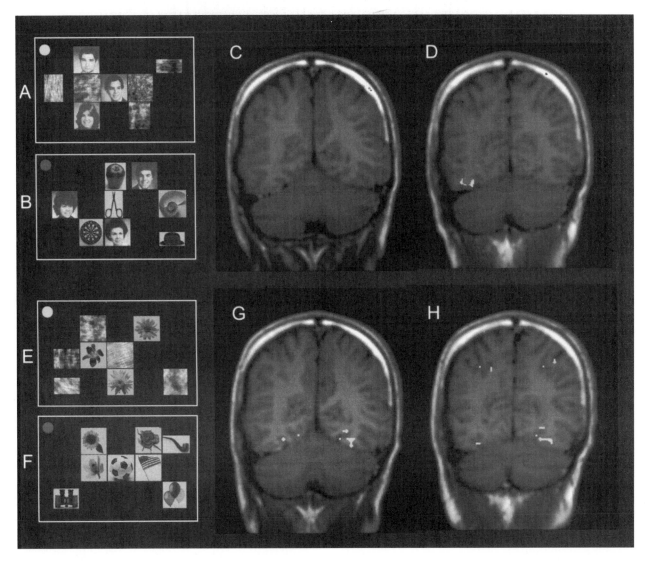

FIGURE 28.4 Results from two adjacent slices in a single-subject study (McCarthy et al., 1997). Faces presented periodically within a dynamic montage of phase-scrambled objects (A) evoked activation within the right fusiform gyrus (D; yellow overlay). Faces presented within a montage of everyday objects (B) activated this same region (D, orange overlay). Bilateral activation (left hemisphere dominant) was observed in the fusiform gyri in both slices (G, H; yellow overlay) for flowers presented within a montage of phase-scrambled objects (E). However, no activation to flowers was obtained in any slice when presented within a montage of everyday objects (F). The activations in all figures were obtained using a split-t procedure; i.e., all colored voxels were significant in each of two replications of each task in which faces and flowers were presented at two different periods.

conditions (Kanwisher et al., 1996; Kanwisher, McDermott, and Chun, 1997; McCarthy et al., 1997; Puce et al., 1995, 1996). Haxby and colleagues (1994) explicitly examined the role of attention by comparing a face-matching task and a spatial judgment task that used identical stimuli. The faces were spatially offset within larger enclosing boxes, and the relative arrangement of the boxes was the basis of the spatial task. Face matching evoked bilateral activation of the fusiform gyrus with the largest magnitude and greatest spatial extent in the right hemisphere. Additionally, face matching activated right prefrontal and orbital frontal cortex. Since both tasks contained the same faces, this activation by the face-matching task above that obtained for the spatial task was presumed to reflect attention or other task-related processing.

One question raised by the preceding study is whether the rather extensive region activated by the face-matching task represented face-specific attentional modulation, or whether it represented a more general attentional modulation for other object features. Using fMRI, Clark and colleagues (1997) performed a study conceptually similar to Haxby's (Haxby et al., 1994) in which subjects were presented with color-washed faces, with attention directed either to the faces or to the color. While many regions were commonly activated by both attention conditions relative to a sensorimotor control task, no areas were activated by attention to faces that were not also activated by attention to color. In contrast, a small region in the right lingual gyrus and collateral sulcus did appear to be selective for attention to color. Clark suggested that the lack of attentional modulation to faces may reflect automatic processing of faces in both attention conditions that did not benefit from additional attention.

In neither of the preceding studies was there independent localization of face-specific cortex prior to the attentional manipulations. Wojciulik (Wojciulik, Kanwisher, and Driver, 1998) first identified face-specific regions of the fusiform gyrus by engaging subjects in a passive viewing task contrasting faces with everyday objects (see Kanwisher, McDermott, and Chun, 1997). ROIs were then drawn for these regions and tested in each of two attention conditions. Each stimulus was composed of a central fixation cross with two faces and two houses arranged in vertical or horizontal pairs. On different trials, the subject was required to determine whether the faces or the houses were identical. The stimuli were briefly exposed to avoid saccades, and the spatial arrangement of stimuli provided no advantage for eccentric fixation. Attention to faces produced a relative increase in the signal intensity of the predefined face-specific ROI. Wojciulik and colleagues (Wojciulik, Kanwisher, and Driver, 1998) argued that while specialized visual machinery may exist for faces, their perceptual processing depends upon attention.

Despite some inconsistencies noted above, the weight of the neuroimaging data suggests that attention can influence the magnitude of activation within fusiform gyrus and challenges the notion that perception of faces is fully automatic. This conclusion is consistent with recent behavioral studies in which upright faces do not show the visual "pop-out" phenomena in displays containing inverted or distorted faces (Brown, Huey, and Findlay, 1997). These results are inconsistent, however, with electrophysiological data in humans that show little change in the N200 face-specific potential to repeated presentations of the same face (Puce, McCarthy, and Allison, 1997); data suggesting that an obligatory response to a face occurs within 200 ms of its appearance. Two issues are relevant. The first is that the neuroimaging studies demonstrating changes in activation by attention have not reported whether the attentional manipulations affected the subjects' abilities to process faces. For example, while Wojciulik (Wojciulik, Kanwisher, and Driver, 1998) provides the best controlled study to date, it is not

certain that attending to houses prevented subjects from recognizing a familiar face, or from discriminating the gender of the faces.

The second issue concerns the timing of the attentional effect. It is possible that an initial phase of activation occurring within a face-specific area in the fusiform is automatic, and that task requirements engender further analysis that extends the duration of activation within the region under descending, or top-down, control. Recent intracranial electrical recordings from the fusiform gyrus in humans have shown that short-latency (~200 ms) ERPs specific to letterstrings are not influenced by attention, but that strong attentional effects occur at 600–800 ms at the same electrodes (Nobre, Allison, and McCarthy, 1998).

Memory for faces

FACE ENCODING AND RECOGNITION   Several studies have distinguished neural systems involved in face encoding and recognition and systems involved with working memory for faces (Andreasen et al., 1996; Courtney et al., 1996; Courtney et al., 1997; Gur et al., 1997; Haxby et al., 1996; Haxby et al., 1995; Kapur et al., 1995). In the Sergent study reviewed above (Sergent, Ohta, and MacDonald, 1992), face gender discrimination primarily activated posterior occipitotemporal cortex. A further comparison of a famous face discrimination task with face gender discrimination yielded bilateral activation of more anterior regions, principally the fusiform gyri, the temporal poles, gyrus rectus, and the left middle temporal gyrus. The greatest activation occurred in the right, but not left, parahippocampal gyrus. Sergent concluded that the perceptual aspects of face processing primarily engaged right occipital regions while face identification engaged more anterior right ventral occipitotemporal regions, principally the mid-fusiform and parahippocampal gyri.

Sergent (1993) compared the results of her PET studies with the pattern of lesions in four prosopagnosic patients, all profoundly deficient in recognizing the identities of faces while reporting normal recognition of objects. Two of the patients sustained damage to the posterior aspect of the right fusiform gyrus, and were deficient in discriminating male and female faces. In contrast, one patient's lesion invaded the white matter near the fusiform gyrus but not the gyrus itself. This patient was able to discriminate male and female faces and match different views of the same face. Thus, Sergent concluded that the extraction of physiognomic invariants (i.e., gender, emotion, and age) occurs posteriorly while the activation of pertinent memories associated with faces must occur anterior to the fusiform gyrus.

Consistent with this hypothesis were the findings from her fourth patient. This patient, who was unable to recognize the identity of faces but performed normally with regard to extraction of physiognomic information, had a postencephalitic lesion that destroyed the anterior right temporal lobe and left temporal pole.

Haxby reported a study contrasting the encoding of unfamiliar faces and the recognition of recently learned faces (Haxby et al., 1996). The face-encoding task primarily activated the right medial temporal region including the hippocampus and adjacent cortex. Additional areas of the left prefrontal cortex, left inferior temporal gyrus, and anterior cingulate cortex were also activated. In contrast, the face recognition task primarily activated the right prefrontal cortex, anterior cingulate cortex, bilateral inferior parietal cortex, bilateral ventral occipital cortex, and cerebellum. Thus, the right medial temporal regions appeared to participate in the encoding of new faces, but not in their subsequent recall. The hemispheric differences noted in the prefrontal region—left hemisphere for face encoding, right hemisphere for face retrieval—is consistent with the hemisphere encoding–retrieval asymmetry (HERA) model proposed by Tulving (Tulving et al., 1994).

Haxby used face matching as the control task; thus faces were included in all comparisons. It is notable, therefore, that no activation of the fusiform gyrus was observed in the face encoding and face recognition tasks above that evoked in the control task (although more posterior activation was noted). Haxby suggested that these areas perform the same perceptual processes independently of additional mnemonic activity (however, see Andreasen et al., 1996). Sergent (Sergent, Ohta, and MacDonald, 1992) and Haxby (Haxby et al., 1996) are consistent in their conclusions that memory for faces occurs at sites anterior to the fusiform regions identified as critical for initial perceptual face processing. They are also consistent in implicating right anterior medial temporal lobe structures in mnemonic processing of faces. However, Sergent implicates these structures in recognition of familiar faces whereas Haxby argues for their involvement in face encoding but not recognition.

The role of the hippocampus in face memory is unclear. Haxby (Haxby et al., 1996) implicates the right hippocampus in face encoding but not recognition. Andreasen (Andreasen et al., 1996) also found no hippocampal activation during face recognition. However, Kapur (Kapur et al., 1995) reported increased left hippocampal activation in both a famous-faces discrimination task and a recent-faces recognition task, when both were compared to a face-gender discrimination task.

This left-retrieval, right-encoding pattern of results reported for hippocampus is the opposite of that argued for prefrontal cortex (Tulving et al., 1994).

WORKING MEMORY FOR FACES Three recent neuroimaging studies from overlapping groups of investigators have been concerned with working memory for faces. Haxby and colleagues (1995) performed a PET study to distinguish areas involved with face perception from areas involved in transient storage of faces. They noted that activation of right inferior frontal cortex had been observed in their prior studies of face processing (Haxby et al., 1994), and hypothesized that this region might maintain the face representation when the face was not in view. Haxby and colleagues performed a delayed match-to-sample task in which the retention interval separating the sample and test faces was increased (1, 6, 11, 16, and 21 s) across runs. Thus the proportion of the interval devoted to viewing a face was diminished while the time required to keep the face in working memory increased. Consistent with their hypothesis, activation within an extensive region of the ventral occipitotemporal cortex showed a negative correlation with delay interval; i.e., the longer the interval, the less activation was obtained. This decreased activation was bilateral, but extended more anteriorly in the right hemisphere. The greatest effect was noted in the right posterior fusiform where activation by faces with retention interval delays beyond 11 s did not differ from sensorimotor control tasks. Haxby's group concluded that their results provided no evidence that striate and ventral extrastriate areas maintained an active, working memory representation of a face.

Haxby and colleagues noted that there was more activation in right anterior medial temporal regions including the hippocampus and parahippocampal gyrus for the face delay task with delays of 1 s than there was for simultaneous matching of faces. These areas were less activated at 6 s, and not at all at longer delay intervals. The interpretation of this finding is the same as that in the study reviewed above (Haxby et al., 1996)—that the right hippocampus is involved in encoding of faces, but not in their retrieval.

Courtney and colleagues used PET to contrast working memory for faces and for spatial locations (Courtney et al., 1996). Subjects were shown three consecutive faces at different spatial locations. A probe face was shown after a 1-s delay at one of the locations. In the location working memory condition, the subject indicated whether the location of the probe matched a location of one of the test stimuli. In the face working memory condition, the subject indicated whether the probe matched one of the test faces. Thus, the stimuli were identical and only the instructions changed. Compared to the location working memory task, face working memory demonstrated significant activation of fusiform, parahippocampal, inferior frontal, and anterior cingulate cortices, as well as right thalamus and midline cerebellum. Since faces were the only objects used in this task, no conclusions can be drawn about the specificity of the working memory results for faces per se. However, since the stimuli were identical for both varieties of the working memory task, it is notable that working memory for faces evoked greater activation bilaterally in the occipitotemporal region. This suggests that some task component—working memory or attention—increased activation of the fusiform over that automatically evoked by faces. Both location and face working memory tasks activated a small region in the right posterior fusiform relative to a sensorimotor control task that did not use faces. Since face stimuli were present in both the location and face working memory tasks, this region may reflect automatic processing of face stimuli; i.e., the face module of Kanwisher, McDermott, and Chun (1997).

In a subsequent study, Courtney and colleagues (1997) performed a fMRI task using a delayed match-to-sample design. A multiple regression analysis was performed to identify the relative weighting at each voxel for three factors: nonselective transient visual responses, "face-selective" transient responses, and sustained activation over the 8-s retention interval. (As Courtney indicates, faces were the only object shown, so the regions designated as "face-selective" may in fact respond to other visual objects.) In general, the most posterior ventral occipital regions showed the highest weightings for nonspecific visual responses and the lowest (and nonsignificant) weightings for sustained activation. The opposite pattern was obtained in prefrontal regions where the anterior middle frontal gyrus showed the highest weighting for sustained activation and nonsignificant activation for nonspecific visual responses. This prefrontal region showed moderate selectivity for faces; however, previous studies have shown this region of the middle frontal gyrus to be active in both spatial and nonspatial working memory tasks (McCarthy et al., 1994, 1996). Face-selective responses were highest in the mid-to-anterior fusiform gyrus and inferior occipital sulcus, particularly in the right hemisphere. The fusiform maintained a small but significant level of activation during the delay, and other regions in the occipitotemporal cortex also showed a significant activation during the delay. Unlike Haxby's group (Haxby et al., 1995), Courtney's group concluded that the fusiform and adjacent regions did participate in the maintenance of working memory. They further speculated that this maintenance would

persist only as long as the region was not recruited in the perception of new stimuli.

The results indicating that working memory for faces influences extrastriate regions involved in face processing present interpretive difficulties insofar as none of the studies independently identified the fusiform face areas. Thus it is not clear whether the enhanced activation of the fusiform observed in some working memory tasks occurred in, or was restricted to, face-specific areas. As faces were the only objects seen in each study, it is possible that the activation observed was nonspecific.

Eye and mouth movements

Single-unit studies in monkeys (Perrett, Rolls, and Caan, 1982) and humans (Ojemann, Ojemann, and Lettich, 1992) have identified temporal lobe neurons that respond selectively to faces. Furthermore, Perrett and colleagues have shown that neurons in the superior temporal sulcus are sensitive to the direction of gaze within the face displayed to the monkey (Perrett et al., 1985). Monkeys can accurately discriminate small shifts in gaze direction in photographs, but they suffer significant deficits in this task following surgical removal of the cortex within the superior temporal sulcus (Campbell et al., 1990). Two prosopagnosic patients tested with this task also showed deficits relative to normal control subjects (Campbell et al., 1990).

Our group's interest in face and eye movements was stimulated by a dissociation between intracranial ERP recordings made from the fusiform gyrus and ERP recordings made from the scalp overlying the posterior temporal area. Intracranial recordings of face-specific N200s showed that full faces evoked larger N200s than those to isolated eyes (Allison et al., 1994b). Scalp recordings, however, revealed that isolated eyes invariably evoked a larger N200 than full faces (Bentin et al., 1996; Taylor, Edmonds, and McCarthy, 1997). This dissociation can be seen in figure 28.5. In fMRI studies, Puce and colleagues (Puce et al., 1995, 1996) had shown a small focus of activation to faces in lateral occipitotemporal cortex in addition to strong fusiform activation (see figure 28.1). Since the scalp electrodes that recorded the larger evoked potential to isolated eyes were placed approximately above the middle temporal gyrus, it was suggested that this part of the temporal lobe might contain a functionally different region for processing dynamic information about eyes. We therefore conducted a fMRI experiment in which subjects viewed moving eyes or moving mouths within an otherwise stationary face, or movements of check patterns that occurred in the same spatial location as the eyes or mouth (Puce et al., 1998). Throughout all stimulus conditions, a moving

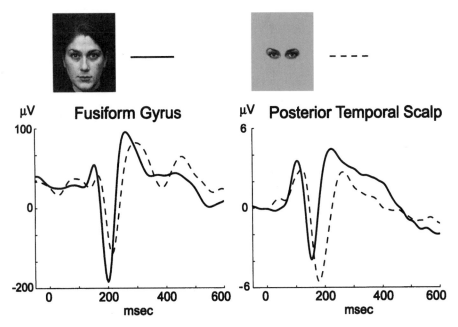

FIGURE 28.5 A comparison of ERPs evoked by full faces (solid line) and isolated eyes (dashed lines) illustrating the different pattern of results reported for recordings from the ventral occipitotemporal brain (Allison et al., 1994b) and from scalp electrodes overlying the posterior temporal scalp (Bentin et al., 1996; Taylor et al., 1997). The ERPs on the left were obtained in a single patient from a site on the fusiform gyrus identified as face-specific in a series of screening tasks using faces and nonface objects (see figure 28.2). Here full faces evoke a larger N200 than do isolated eyes or other face components. The recordings on the right were obtained by Taylor and collaborators (1997) and represent the average response from the right posterior scalp (T6) of 20 subjects viewing the identical stimuli. Here eyes consistently evoke a larger N200 than do full faces. The ERPs to full faces are also earlier in latency than those recorded from the occipitotemporal region.

radial pattern was presented in the background in an attempt to control for the effect of movement per se. Eye and mouth movements, but not the moving check pattern, activated a bilateral region centered in the posterior superior temporal sulcus. The region was anterior to that activated by the moving radial background, which primarily activated the posterior-temporal-occipital fossa and the lateral occipital sulcus–a region corresponding to area MT/V5.

It is notable that the moving eyes and mouth did not activate the fusiform face area. On the basis of neurological lesions, Campbell, Landis, and Regard (1986) demonstrated a double dissociation between face recognition and the ability to lipread. The results of Puce's group suggest, therefore, that the region within the superior temporal sulcus may be both preferentially involved in the perception of gaze direction and mouth movements and related to nearby regions involved in the perception of biological motion.

Emotional expression

Appropriate social communication is dependent upon the correct perception and interpretation of nonverbal cues such as the tone of voice, the emotional expression of a face, and the direction of gaze that both signifies at-

tention and directs the emotional expression to its target. Cross-cultural studies have demonstrated that discrimination among different facial expressions of emotion is universal (for review, see Ekman, 1993; Ekman and Friesen, 1971). Deficiencies in the analysis and/or discrimination of facial expressions have been reported in several psychiatric and neurological disorders such as schizophrenia (Archer, Hay, and Young, 1994; Cutting, 1981), autism (Hobson, Ouston, and Lee, 1988), and Parkinson's disease (Jacobs et al., 1995). Within the physiological literature concerning the perception and analysis of face expression, two issues have been emphasized: whether separate neural regions subserve processing for face identity and facial expression, and whether the analysis of different facial expressions involves different brain structures or shows different patterns of hemispheric activation.

Some prosopagnosic patients can accurately identify the emotional expression of a face but cannot identify the face (e.g., Sergent, 1993). Differences in the pattern of neuropsychological findings have suggested that processing for facial identity and that for facial expression involve different neural pathways (Adolphs et al., 1996; Bowers et al., 1985; Bowers and Heilman, 1984). For example, Bowers and Heilman (1984) reported a patient with a right posterior lesion who could neither name emotions depicted in pictures of faces nor point to examples of emotional expressions. Humphreys and colleagues (Humphreys, Donnelly, and Riddoch, 1993) reported a patient with relatively good performance in facial identification but poor performance in judging emotional expression. Rapcsak and colleagues (Rapcsak, Comer, and Rubens, 1993; Rapcsak, Kaszniak, and Rubens, 1989) report two patients with damage to the right inferior and middle temporal gyrus who demonstrated selective deficits in matching emotional expressions with their names, and with pointing to pictures of faces depicting particular emotions. Single-unit recordings from the superior and middle temporal gyrus in the right temporal lobe of patients undergoing awake craniotomy showed a significant proportion of cells to be responsive when patients were engaged in face matching and the labeling of facial expression (Ojemann, Ojemann, and Lettich, 1992). Bauer (1986) suggested that two distinct neural pathways are involved in the processing of faces—a ventromedial route responsible for processing underlying overt recognition of faces, and a dorsal route initially involving lateral temporal cortex and projecting to parietal lobe and cingulate gyrus related to emotional processing.

Studies of focal brain damage in humans have reported an overall right hemisphere role in processing facial expression (Adolphs et al., 1996; Bowers et al., 1985). For example, Adolphs and colleagues (1996) investigated the neural systems involved in recognizing facial emotional expression in 37 subjects with focal brain lesions to the left or right hemispheres. Subjects with left hemisphere lesions showed no impairment in processing facial expression. Subjects with right hemisphere lesions were impaired in recognizing certain negative emotions, such as the recognition of fear, but not in the recognition of happy expressions. Within the right hemisphere, the regions corresponding to greatest impairment were the inferior parietal cortex and the mesial anterior infracalcarine cortex. Young and colleagues (1993), however, reported four patients deficient in recognizing facial emotion with unilateral left hemisphere lesions.

Behavioral studies using tachistoscopic displays of lateralized faces have shown a similar inconsistent pattern of results regarding laterality. Many show a left visual field/right hemisphere advantage for processing facial expression (e.g., Ley and Bryden, 1979; Wedding and Cyrus, 1986); but this result has been reported to occur for negative expressions only (Moretti, Charlton, and Taylor, 1996), positive expressions only (Duda and Brown, 1984), or not at all (Stalans and Wedding, 1985). One influential model posits that negative emotions are predominantly processed within the right hemisphere

while positive emotions are processed by the left hemisphere (see Davidson, 1992).

Several neuroimaging studies have investigated the neural systems involved in processing facial emotions. Sergent and colleagues (1994) conducted PET studies to investigate whether differences in processing face identity and emotional expression involved different brain regions. Sergent had two active conditions—a famous-face discrimination task, and a face emotion discrimination task with unfamiliar faces. The right fusiform gyrus was activated by face identity but not by face emotion, suggesting that this area did not participate in the analysis of face emotion. The right middle occipital gyrus was, however, activated by the face emotion task, consistent with the right posterior dominance seen for both positive and negative emotions in the study by Gur, Skolnick, and Gur (1994).

Dolan and colleagues (1996) conducted a face-delayed match-to-sample task with a 45-s retention interval and compared conditions involving happy or neutral expressions. Compared to neutral, the positive expressions activated the left inferior frontal gyrus, the left anterior cingulate gyrus, the right fusiform gyrus, and the thalamus. George and colleagues (1993) conducted a task in which subjects were asked to match pictures of faces based on emotional expression or identity. When comparing emotion to identity matching, significant activation was observed bilaterally in the inferior frontal gyri and in the right anterior cingulate.

These results demonstrate a difference in activation related to facial expression processing, but offer little consistency among the structures activated. Two studies obtained activation of the anterior cingulate (although predominantly in different hemispheres) and in the inferior frontal gyri (Dolan et al., 1996; George et al., 1993). One study found that emotional face expression activated the right fusiform gyrus (Dolan et al., 1996), one explicitly found no fusiform activation (Sergent et al., 1994), while the third found no activation of the fusiform even when comparing faces to a spatial control task (George et al., 1993).

Single-unit studies in the amygdala of monkeys (Leonard et al., 1985) and humans (Heit, Smith, and Halgren, 1988) have shown that the amygdala is responsive to faces. Several recent neuropsychological studies have strongly implicated the amygdala in the processing of emotional expression. Adolphs and colleagues (1994, 1995) reported a subject with a genetic disorder resulting in selective bilateral amygdala damage. This patient had greatly impaired judgment in the recognition of fearful expressions—a deficit not found in their patients with unilateral amygdala lesions. The patient with bilateral amygdala damage had no difficulty in recognizing faces and could skillfully draw all facial expressions except fearful expressions. In a subsequent study, Adolphs and colleagues demonstrated that three subjects with bilateral amygdala damage were markedly deficient in their ability to judge the trustworthiness and approachability of faces, particularly with faces ranked as negative by subjects with unilateral amygdala damage and by normal controls (Adolphs, Tranel, and Damasio, 1998). In contrast, the bilateral amygdala subjects had no difficulty in discriminating faces or in making social judgments on the basis of verbal descriptions. On the basis of these results, it was suggested that the amygdala is an important component of a neural system that uses facial expression to retrieve socially relevant knowledge. In addition, Scott and colleagues (1997) reported that bilateral amygdala lesions also impair judgments concerning the emotional intonation of auditorily presented sentences, particularly with regard to fear and anger.

Several recent neuroimaging studies have implicated the amygdala in the processing of emotions and emotional stimuli (Drevets et al., 1992; Irwin et al., 1996; Ketter et al., 1996; Schneider et al., 1997) and in the analysis of facial expression. Breiter and colleagues (1996) reported a fMRI study in which fearful faces activated the amygdala bilaterally when compared to blocks of neutral faces. In a second experiment using a region of interest analysis, Breiter's group again found left amygdala activation for fearful expressions and for happy faces. They observed a somewhat differential pattern of activation for these different emotions within the amygdala, and found that neutral faces also showed some amygdala activation compared to nonface controls. The left amygdala showed rapid habituation for emotional expressions, and the right amygdala was not significantly activated by any face stimuli.

In two PET studies, Morris and collaborators (1996, 1998) showed greater left amygdala activation to fearful faces than to happy faces. The left amygdala and insular cortex showed increasing activation to increasing intensity of fearfulness. As before, the right amygdala showed no activation to faces. Morris also noted that the left amygdala increased its activity as the intensity of happy faces was decreased, suggesting that the left amygdala responds to happy faces by decreasing its activation below baseline. Both Breiter (Breiter et al. 1996) and Morris (Morris et al. 1996, 1998) showed that facial emotion also affected processing in extrastriate regions, suggestive of a backprojection or neuromodulary influence from the amygdala.

Whalen and colleagues (1998) used fMRI to study unconscious emotional processing in the amygdala. Subjects were presented with happy or fearful faces for 33 ms, whereupon they were immediately shown a face de-picting a neutral expression. As a result of this backward-masking procedure, eight of the ten subjects reported seeing only the neutral expressions. Despite the lack of conscious awareness, activation of the amygdala was higher for the masked fearful faces, and lower for the masked happy faces, than for a fixation control. Activation was restricted to the amygdala, but was bilateral and habituated after two runs.

Morris and colleagues further explored the role of conscious and unconscious processing of facial expression by the amygdala and its influence upon the laterality of the activation (Morris, Ohman, and Dolan, 1998). Angry faces previously paired with aversive white noise bursts evoked activity in the right amygdala when a backward mask (a face with neutral expression) was applied and the patient was unaware of the angry face. However, when the angry face was unmasked and consciously perceived, only the left amygdala was activated.

The studies to this point have implicated the amygdala in the analysis of negative, primarily fearful, facial expression. Phillips and collaborators (1997) compared fMRI activations to two negative emotions–fear and disgust–using mildly happy faces as controls. Two intensities of each emotion were tested while subjects performed a gender discrimination task in which facial expression was irrelevant. Consistent with the studies reviewed above, medium-intensity fearful faces evoked activity in the left amygdala and left insula. Disgust did not activate the amygdala; rather, the most prominent activation was found in the right anterior insula, where the level of activation increased with the intensity of the disgusted expression. It was suggested that the facial expression of disgust is closely linked to the region activated by noxious gustatory stimuli. Perception of disgust in another individual was hypothesized to have a selective evolutionary advantage.

The neuroimaging and neuropsychological studies reviewed above clearly dissociate the processing of facial expression from facial identity and strongly implicate the amygdala in the processing of emotional expressions. Across studies, the most consistent amygdala activation was obtained for fearful expressions, with less consistent results noted for positive or happy expressions which may, in fact, reduce amygdala activation (Morris et al., 1996). Overall, the left amygdala was more activated by emotional expressions than the right amygdala, although this may be related to the subject's conscious awareness of the emotional expression (Morris, Ohman, and Dolan, 1998). The role of the amygdala in processing fearful expressions is particularly interesting given its demonstrated role in fear conditioning. In that regard, the selective response of the insula for expressions of disgust (Phillips et al., 1997) is noteworthy given the putative role of that brain region in taste. These results suggest that the perception of different emotions may be closely related to specific neural systems involved in behaviors relevant to that particular emotion.

Summary and conclusions

The studies reviewed strongly implicate the ventral occipitotemporal cortex, and particularly the fusiform gyrus, in the initial processing of faces. Bilateral activation was obtained in almost all studies, but the right hemisphere activation was consistently stronger and spatially more extensive. Faces activated a larger region of ventral occipitotemporal cortex when there were no other objects in the visual field than when the field contained other objects. This suggests that faces may be processed by both face-specific and general object recognition systems. Face-specific cortex therefore represents a more focal region of activation than indicated in most PET and fMRI studies. The face-specific regions were not activated by exemplars of other stimulus categories, including nonface body parts, even when within-category discriminations were required by the task. The electrophysiological data establish that faces are differentiated from other stimulus categories by 200 ms, and that this processing is relatively insensitive to habituation. Taken together, these results suggest the presence of a neural module in fusiform gyrus that responds in a fast and obligatory manner to faces. Whether this putative module is hardwired from birth or develops from long experience with faces is undecided by these data.

The modularity of face processing in the fusiform gyrus is challenged, however, by several studies reporting enhanced activation within the ventral occipitotemporal region as a consequence of top-down processing involving attention (Haxby et al., 1994; Wojciulik, Kanwisher, and Driver, 1998), working memory (Courtney et al., 1996, 1997), and analysis of emotional expression (Breiter et al., 1996; Morris et al., 1998). However, with one exception (Wojciulik, Kanwisher, and Driver, 1998), these studies did not independently identify face-specific cortex within the ventral extrastriate regions. Moreover, these studies provide no information about when the top-down modulation may have occurred. It may be that initial face processing, as reflected by N200, is relatively insensitive to top-down influence, but that later processing at N200 or more anterior sites further engages the face-specific fusiform areas and modulates their activity.

Tasks emphasizing memory for faces differentiated posterior fusiform and more anterior activation of the medial temporal lobe, including the parahippocampal gyrus and hippocampus. The dependence of activation within the medial temporal lobe for face encoding and face retrieval was uncertain and might be differentiated by hemisphere. Taken together, the neuropsychological and neuroimaging data suggest a ventral pathway for face processing where faces are extracted from the visual scene and differentiated from other objects in the posterior and mid-fusiform gyrus, and where the recognition of particular faces is performed in the anterior and medial temporal lobe.

A second pathway for face analysis may occur in more dorsal regions and involve the middle occipital and temporal gyri, and the superior temporal sulcus where activity may be related to the extraction of dynamic features from faces, such as eye movements and mouth movements. The lack of activation in the ventral face areas by moving eyes and mouths suggests that these dorsal regions were activated in parallel to the ventral face regions. The targets of this putative dorsal pathway are unknown. Given the role that dynamic changes in eye and mouth position play in facial expression, we speculate that the amygdala may receive input from this region to integrate the face with its social context.

ACKNOWLEDGMENTS This work was supported by the Department of Veterans Affairs and by NIMH grant MH-05286. I gratefully acknowledge my collaborators Drs. Truett Allison, Aina Puce, and Shlomo Bentin, and thank them for their comments on this paper.

REFERENCES

ADOLPHS, R., H. DAMASIO, D. TRANEL, and A. R. DAMASIO, 1996. Cortical systems for the recognition of emotion in facial expressions. *J. Neurosci.* 16:7678–7687.

ADOLPHS, R., D. TRANEL, and A. R. DAMASIO, 1998. The human amygdala in social judgment. *Nature* 393:470.

ADOLPHS, R., D. TRANEL, H. DAMASIO, and A. DAMASIO, 1994. Impaired recognition of emotion in facial expressions following bilateral damage to the human amygdala. *Nature* 372:669–672.

ADOLPHS, R., D. TRANEL, H. DAMASIO, and A. R. DAMASIO, 1995. Fear and the human amygdala. *J. Neurosci.* 15:5879–5891.

ALLISON, T., H. GINTER, G. MCCARTHY, A. C. NOBRE, A. PUCE, M. LUBY, and D. D. SPENCER, 1994a. Face recognition in human extrastriate cortex. *J. Neurophysiol.* 71:821–825.

ALLISON, T., G. MCCARTHY, A. BELGER, A. PUCE, M. LUBY, D. D. SPENCER, and S. BENTIN, 1994b. What is a face? Electrophysiological responsiveness of human extrastriate visual cortex to human faces, face components, and animal faces. *Soc. Neurosci. Abstr.* 20:316.

ALLISON, T., G. MCCARTHY, A. NOBRE, A. PUCE, and A. BELGER, 1994c. Human extrastriate visual cortex and the perception of faces, words, numbers, and colors. *Cerebral Cortex* 4:544–554.

ANDREASEN, N. C., D. S. O'LEARY, S. ARNDT, T. CIZADLO, R. HURTIG, K. REZAI, G. L. WATKINS, L. B. PONTO, and R. D. HICHWA, 1996. Neural substrates of facial recognition. *J. Neuropsychol. Clin. Neurosci.* 8:139–146.

ARCHER, J., D. C. HAY, and A. W. YOUNG, 1994. Movement, face processing and schizophrenia: Evidence of a differential deficit in expression analysis. *Brit. J. Clin. Psychol.* 33:517–528.

BAUER, R. M., 1986. The cognitive psychophysiology of prosopagnosia. In *Aspects of Face Processing*, H. D. Ellis, M. A. Jeeves, F. Newcombe, and A. Young, eds. Boston: Martinus Nijhoff, pp. 253–267.

BAUER, R. M., and J. D. TROBE, 1984. Visual memory and perceptual impairments in prosopagnosia. *J. Clin. Neuro-Ophthalmol.* 4:39–46.

BENTIN, S., T. ALLISON, A. PUCE, E. PEREZ, and G. MCCARTHY, 1996. Electrophysiological studies of face perception in humans. *J. Cogn. Neurosci.* 8:551–565.

BOWERS, D., R. M. BAUER, H. B. COSLETT, and K. M. HEILMAN, 1985. Processing of faces by patients with unilateral hemisphere lesions. I. Dissociation between judgments of facial affect and facial identity. *Brain & Cognition* 4:258–272.

BOWERS, D., and K. M. HEILMAN, 1984. Dissociation between the processing of affective and nonaffective faces: A case study. *J. Clin. Neuropsychol.* 6:367–379.

BREITER, H. C., N. L. ETCOFF, P. J. WHALEN, W. A. KENNEDY, S. L. RAUCH, R. L. BUCKNER, M. M. STRAUSS, S. E. HYMAN, and B. R. ROSEN, 1996. Response and habituation of the human amygdala during visual processing of facial expression. *Neuron* 17:875–887.

BROWN, V., D. HUEY, and J. M. FINDLAY, 1997. Face detection in peripheral vision–Do faces pop out? *Perception* 26:1555–1570.

BRUCE, V., and A. YOUNG, 1986. Understanding face recognition. *Brit. J. Psychol.* 77:305–327.

BRUYER, R., C. LATERRE, X. SERON, P. FEYEREISEN, E. STRYPSTEIN, E. PIERRARD, and D. RECTEM, 1983. A case of prosopagnosia with some preserved covert remembrance of familiar faces. *Brain & Cognition* 2:257–284.

CAMPBELL, R., C. A. HEYWOOD, A. COWEY, M. REGARD, and T. LANDIS, 1990. Sensitivity to eye gaze in prosopagnosic patients and monkeys with superior temporal sulcus ablation. *Neuropsychologia* 28:1123–1142.

CAMPBELL, R., T. LANDIS, and M. REGARD, 1986. Face recognition and lipreading. A neurological dissociation. *Brain* 109:509–521.

CLARK, V. P., K. KEIL, J. M. MAISOG, S. COURTNEY, L. G. UNGERLEIDER, and J. V. HAXBY, 1996. Functional magnetic resonance imaging of human visual cortex during face matching: A comparison with positron emission tomography. *Neuroimage* 4:1–15.

CLARK, V. P., R. PARASURAMAN, K. KEIL, R. KULANSKY, S. FANNON, J. M. MAISOG, L. G. UNGERLEIDER, and J. V. HAXBY, 1997. Selective attention to face identity and color studied with fMRI. *Human Brain Mapping* 5:293–297.

CORBETTA, M., F. M. MIEZIN, S. DOBMEYER, G. L. SHULMAN, and S. E. PETERSEN, 1990. Attentional modulation of neural processing of shape, color, and velocity in humans. *Science* 248:1556–1559.

COURTNEY, S. M., L. G. UNGERLEIDER, K. KEIL, and J. V. HAXBY, 1996. Object and spatial visual working memory activate separate neural systems in human cortex. *Cerebral Cortex* 6:39–49.

COURTNEY, S. M., L. G. UNGERLEIDER, K. KEIL, and J. V. HAXBY, 1997. Transient and sustained activity in a distributed neural system for human working memory. *Nature* 386:608–611.

CUTTING, J., 1981. Judgement of emotional expression in schizophrenics. *Brit. J. Psychiatry* 139:1–6.

DAMASIO, A. R., H. DAMASIO, and G. W. VAN HOESEN, 1982. Prosopagnosia: Anatomic basis and behavioral mechanisms. *Neurology* 32:331–341.

DAVIDSON, R. J., 1992. Anterior cerebral asymmetry and the nature of emotion. *Brain & Cognition* 20:125–151.

DE HAAN, E. H., A. W. YOUNG, and F. NEWCOMBE, 1991. Covert and overt recognition in prosopagnosia. *Brain* 114:2575–2591.

DE RENZI, E., P. FAGLIONI, D. GROSSI, and P. NICHELLI, 1991. Apperceptive and associative forms of prosopagnosia. *Cortex* 27:213–221.

DE RENZI, E., D. PERANI, G. A. CARLESIMO, M. C. SILVERI, and F. FAZIO, 1994. Prosopagnosia can be associated with damage confined to the right hemisphere–An MRI and PET study and a review of the literature. *Neuropsychologia* 32:893–902.

DOLAN, R. J., G. R. FINK, E. ROLLS, M. BOOTH, A. HOLMES, R. S. J. FRACKOWIAK, and K. J. FRISTON, 1997. How the brain learns to see objects and faces in an impoverished context. *Nature* 389:596–599.

DOLAN, R. J., P. FLETCHER, J. MORRIS, N. KAPUR, J. F. W. DEAKIN, and C. D. FRITH, 1996. Neural activation during covert processing of positive emotional facial expressions. *Neuroimage* 4:194–200.

DREVETS, W. C., T. O. VIDEEN, J. L. PRICE, S. H. PRESKORN, S. T. CARMICHAEL, and M. E. RAICHLE, 1992. A functional anatomical study of unipolar depression. *J. Neurosci.* 12:3628–3641.

DUDA, P. D., and J. BROWN, 1984. Lateral asymmetry of positive and negative emotions. *Cortex* 20:253–261.

EKMAN, P., 1993. Facial expression and emotion. *Amer. Psychologist* 48:384–392.

EKMAN, P., and W. V. FRIESEN, 1971. Constants across cultures in the face and emotion. *J. Personality Soc. Psychol.* 17:124–129.

ELLIS, H. D., 1985. Introduction to aspects of face processing: Ten questions in need of answers. In *Aspects of Face Processing*, H. D. Ellis, M. A. Jeeves, F. Newcombe, and A. Young, eds. Boston: Martinus Nijhoff, pp. 3–13.

FARAH, M. J., 1990. *Visual Agnosia: Disorders of Object Recognition and What They Tell Us about Normal Vision.* Cambridge, Mass.: MIT Press.

FARAH, M. J., K. L. LEVINSON, and K. L. KLEIN, 1995. Face perception and within-category discrimination in prosopagnosia. *Neuropsychologia* 33:661–674.

FARAH, M. J., K. D. WILSON, H. M. DRAIN, and J. R. TANAKA, 1995. The inverted face inversion effect in prosopagnosia: Evidence for mandatory, face-specific perceptual mechanisms. *Vision Res.* 35:2089–2093.

GAUTHIER, I., A.W. ANDERSON, M. J. TARR, P. SKUDLARSKI, and J. C. GORE, 1997. Levels of categorization in visual recognition studied using functional magnetic resonance imaging. *Curr. Biol.* 7:645–651.

GAUTHIER, I., and M. J. TARR, 1997. Becoming a greeble expert–Exploring mechanisms for face recognition. *Vision Res.* 37:1673–1682.

GEORGE, M. S., T. A. KETTER, D. S. GILL, J. V. HAXBY, L. G. UNGERLEIDER, P. HERSCOVITCH, and R. M. POST, 1993. Brain regions involved in recognizing facial emotion or identity: An oxygen-15 PET study. *J. Neuropsychiat. Clin. Neurosci.* 5:384–394.

GUR, R. C., J. D. RAGLAND, L. H. MOZLEY, P. D. MOZLEY, R. SMITH, A. ALAVI, W. BILKER, and R. E. GUR, 1997. Lateralized changes in regional cerebral blood flow during performance of verbal and facial recognition tasks: Correlations with performance and "effort." *Brain & Cognition* 33:388–414.

GUR, R. C., B. E. SKOLNICK, and R. E. GUR, 1994. Effects of emotional discrimination tasks on cerebral blood flow: Regional activation and its relation to performance. *Brain & Cognition* 25:271–286.

HAXBY, J. V., C. L. GRADY, B. HORWITZ, J. SALERNO, L. G. UNGERLEIDER, M. MISHKIN, M. B. SHAPIRO, and S. I. RAPAPORT, 1993. Dissociation of object and spatial visual processing pathways in human extrastriate cortex. In *Functional Organization of the Human Visual Cortex*, B. Gulyas, D. Ottoson, and P. E. Roland, eds. New York: Pergamon, pp. 329–340.

HAXBY, J. V., C. L. GRADY, B. HORWITZ, L. G. UNGERLEIDER, M. MISHKIN, R. E. CARSON, P. HERSCOVITCH, M. B. SCHAPIRO, and S. I. RAPOPORT, 1991. Dissociation of object and spatial visual processing pathways in human extrastriate cortex. *Proc. Natl. Acad. Sci. U.S.A.* 88:1621–1625.

HAXBY, J. V., B. HORWITZ, L. G. UNGERLEIDER, J. M. MAISOG, P. PIETRINI, and C. L. GRADY, 1994. The functional organization of human extrastriate cortex: A PET-rCBF study of selective attention to faces and locations. *J. Neurosci.* 14:6336–6353.

HAXBY, J. V., L. G. UNGERLEIDER, B. HORWITZ, J. M. MAISOG, S. I. RAPOPORT, and C. L. GRADY, 1996. Face encoding and recognition in the human brain. *Proc. Natl. Acad. Sci. U.S.A.* 93:922–927.

HAXBY, J. V., L. G. UNGERLEIDER, B. HORWITZ, S. I. RAPOPORT, and C. L. GRADY, 1995. Hemispheric differences in neural systems for face working memory: A PET-rCBF study. *Human Brain Mapping* 3:68–82.

HEIT, G., M. E. SMITH, and E. HALGREN, 1988. Neural encoding of individual words and faces by the human hippocampus and amygdala. *Nature* 333:773–775.

HOBSON, R. P., J. OUSTON, and A. LEE, 1988. What's in a face? The case of autism. *Brit. J. Psychol.* 79:441–453.

HUMPHREYS, G. W., N. DONNELLY, and M. J. RIDDOCH, 1993. Expression is computed separately from facial identity, and it is computed separately for moving and static faces: Neuropsychological evidence. *Neuropsychologia* 31:173–181.

IRWIN, W., R. J. DAVIDSON, M. J. LOWE, B. J. MOCK, J. A. SORENSON, and P. A. TURSKI, 1996. Human amygdala activation detected with echo-planar functional magnetic resonance imaging. *Neuroreport* 7:1765–1769.

JACOBS, D. H., J. SHUREN, D. BOWERS, and K. M. HEILMAN, 1995. Emotional facial imagery, perception, and expression in Parkinson's disease. *Neurology* 45:1696–1702.

KANWISHER, N., M. M. CHUN, J. McDERMOTT, and P. J. LEDDEN, 1996. Functional imaging of human visual recognition. *Cogn. Brain Res.* 5:55–67.

KANWISHER, N., J. McDERMOTT, and M. M. CHUN, 1997. The fusiform face area: A module in human extrastriate cortex specialized for face perception. *J. Neurosci.* 17:4302–4311.

KAPUR, N., K. J. FRISTON, A. YOUNG, C. D. FRITH, and R. S. FRACKOWIAK, 1995. Activation of human hippocampal formation during memory for faces: A PET study. *Cortex* 31:99–108.

KETTER, T. A., P. J. ANDREASON, M. S. GEORGE, C. LEE, D. S. GILL, P. I. PAREKH, M. W. WILLIS, P. HERSCOVITCH, and R. M. POST, 1996. Anterior paralimbic mediation of procaine-induced emotional and psychosensory experiences. *Arch. Gen. Psychiatry* 53:59–69.

KÖHLER, S., S. KAPUR, M. MOSCOVITCH, G. WINOCUR, and S. HOULE, 1995. Dissociation of pathways for object and spatial vision: A PET study in humans. *Neuroreport* 6:1865–1868.

LEONARD, C. M., E. T. ROLLS, F. A. WILSON, and G. C. BAYLIS, 1985. Neurons in the amygdala of the monkey with responses selective for faces. *Behav. Brain Res.* 15:159–176.

LEY, R. G., and M. P. BRYDEN, 1979. Hemispheric differences in processing emotions and faces. *Brain Lang.* 7:127–138.

MALACH, R., J. B. REPPAS, R. R. BENSON, K. K. KWONG, H. JIANG, W. A. KENNEDY, P. J. LEDDEN, T. J. BRADY, B. R. ROSEN, and R. B. TOOTELL, 1995. Object-related activity revealed by functional magnetic resonance imaging in human occipital cortex. *Proc. Natl. Acad. Sci. U.S.A.* 92:8135–8139.

McCARTHY, G., A. M. BLAMIRE, A. PUCE, A. C. NOBRE, G. BLOCH, F. HYDER, P. GOLDMAN-RAKIC, and R. G. SHULMAN, 1994. Functional magnetic resonance imaging of human prefrontal cortex activation during a spatial working memory task. *Proc. Natl. Acad. Sci. U.S.A.* 91:8690–8694.

McCARTHY, G., A. PUCE, R. T. CONSTABLE, J. H. KRYSTAL, J. C. GORE, and P. GOLDMAN-RAKIC, 1996. Activation of human prefrontal cortex during spatial and nonspatial working memory tasks measured by functional MRI. *Cereb. Cortex* 6:600–611.

McCARTHY, G., A. PUCE, J. C. GORE, and T. ALLISON, 1997. Face-specific processing in the human fusiform gyrus. *J. Cogn. Neurosci.* 9:605–610.

MILDERS, M. V., and D. I. PERRETT, 1993. Recent developments in the neuropsychology and physiology of face processing. *Baillieres Clin. Neurol.* 2:361–388.

MORETTI, M. M., S. CHARLTON, and S. TAYLOR, 1996. The effects of hemispheric asymmetries and depression on the perception of emotion. *Brain & Cognition* 32:67–82.

MORRIS, J. S., K. J. FRISTON, C. BUCHEL, C. D. FRITH, A. W. YOUNG, A. J. CALDER, and R. J. DOLAN, 1998. A neuromodulatory role for the human amygdala in processing emotional facial expressions. *Brain* 121:47–57.

MORRIS, J. S., C. D. FRITH, D. I. PERRETT, D. ROWLAND, A. W. YOUNG, A. J. CALDER, and R. J. DOLAN, 1996. A differential neural response in the human amygdala to fearful and happy facial expressions. *Nature* 383:812–815.

MORRIS, J. S., A. OHMAN, and R. J. DOLAN, 1998. Conscious and unconscious emotional learning in the human amygdala. *Nature* 393:467–470.

MOSCOVITCH, M., G. WINOCUR, and M. BEHRMANN, 1997. What is special about face recognition: Nineteen experiments on a person with visual object agnosia and dyslexia but normal face recognition. *J. Cogn. Neurosci.* 9:555–604.

NOBRE, A. C., T. ALLISON, and G. McCARTHY, 1994. Word recognition in the human inferior temporal lobe. *Nature* 372:260–263.

NOBRE, A. C., T. ALLISON, and G. MCCARTHY, 1998. Modulation of human extrastriate visual processing by selective attention to colours and words. *Brain* 121:1357–1368.

O'CRAVEN, K. M., B. R. ROSEN, K. K. KWONG, A. TREISMAN, and R. L. SAVOY, 1997. Voluntary attention modulates fMRI activity in human MT-MST. *Neuron* 18:591–598.

OJEMANN, J. G., G. A. OJEMANN, and E. LETTICH, 1992. Neuronal activity related to faces and matching in human right nondominant temporal cortex. *Brain* 115:1–13.

PERRETT, D. I., E. T. ROLLS, and W. CAAN, 1982. Visual neurons responsive to faces in the monkey temporal cortex. *Exp. Brain Res.* 47:329–342.

PERRETT, D. I., P. A. SMITH, D. D. POTTER, A. J. MISTLIN, A. S. HEAD, A. D. MILNER, and M. A. JEEVES, 1985. Visual cells in the temporal cortex sensitive to face view and gaze direction. *Proc. R. Soc. Lond. B* 223:293–317.

PHILLIPS, M. L., A. W. YOUNG, C. SENIOR, M. BRAMMER, C. ANDREW, A. J. CALDER, E. T. BULLMORE, D. I. PERRETT, D. ROWLAND, S. C. WILLIAMS, J. A. GRAY, and A. S. DAVID, 1997. A specific neural substrate for perceiving facial expressions of disgust. *Nature* 389:495–498.

PUCE, A., T. ALLISON, M. ASGARI, J. C. GORE, and G. MC-CARTHY, 1996. Differential sensitivity of human visual cortex to faces, letterstrings, and textures: A functional magnetic resonance imaging study. *J. Neurosci.* 16:5205–5215.

PUCE, A., T. ALLISON, S. BENTIN, J. C. GORE, and G. MCCARTHY, 1998. Temporal cortex activation in humans viewing eye and mouth movements. *J. Neurosci.* 18:2188–2199.

PUCE, A., T. ALLISON, J. C. GORE, and G. MCCARTHY, 1995. Face-sensitive regions in human extrastriate cortex studied by functional MRI. *J. Neurophysiol.* 74:1192–1199.

PUCE, A., G. MCCARTHY, and T. ALLISON, 1997. Changes in face-specific intracranial ERP amplitude as a function of repeated stimulus presentation. *Soc. Neurosci. Abstr.* 23:2065.

RAPCSAK, S. Z., J. F. COMER, and A. B. RUBENS, 1993. Anomia for facial expressions: neuropsychological mechanisms and anatomical correlates. *Brain Lang.* 45:233–252.

RAPCSAK, S. Z., A. W. KASZNIAK, and A. B. RUBENS, 1989. Anomia for facial expressions: evidence for a category specific visual-verbal disconnection syndrome. *Neuropsychologia* 27:1031–1041.

SCHNEIDER, F., W. GRODD, U. WEISS, U. KLOSE, K. R. MAYER, T. NAGELE, and R. C. GUR, 1997. Functional MRI reveals left amygdala activation during emotion. *Psychiat. Res. Neuroimaging* 76:75–82.

SCOTT, S. K., A. W. YOUNG, A. J. CALDER, D. J. HELLAWELL, J. P. AGGLETON, and M. JOHNSON, 1997. Impaired auditory recognition of fear and anger following bilateral amygdala lesions. *Nature* 385:254–257.

SERGENT, J., 1993. The processing of faces in cerebral cortex. In *Functional Organization of the Human Visual Cortex*, B. Gulyas, D. Ottoson, and P. E. Roland, eds. New York: Pergamon, pp. 359–372.

SERGENT, J., S. OHTA, and B. MACDONALD, 1992. Functional neuroanatomy of face and object processing. A positron emission tomography study. *Brain* 115:15–36.

SERGENT, J., S. OHTA, B. MACDONALD, and E. ZUCK, 1994. Segregated processing of facial identity and emotion in the human brain: A PET study. In *Object and Face Recognition: A Special Issue of Visual Cognition*, Vol. 1, No. 2/3., Vicki Bruce and G. Humphreys, eds. Hove: Erlbaum, pp. 349–369.

SERGENT, J., and J. G. VILLEMURE, 1989. Prosopagnosia in a right hemispherectomized patient. *Brain* 112:975–995.

STALANS, L., and D. WEDDING, 1985. Superiority of the left hemisphere in the recognition of emotional faces. *Int. J. Neurosci.* 25:219–223.

TALAIRACH, J., and M. TOURNOUX, 1988. *Co-planar Stereotaxic Atlas of the Human Brain.* New York: Thieme Medical Publishers.

TAYLOR, M. J., G. EDMONDS, T. ALLISON, and G. MCCARTHY, 1997. Neurophysiological indices of the development of face perception. *Soc. Neurosci. Abstr.* 23:2112.

TULVING, E., S. KAPUR, F. I. CRAIK, M. MOSCOVITCH, and S. HOULE, 1994. Hemispheric encoding/retrieval asymmetry in episodic memory: Positron emission tomography findings [see comments]. *Proc. Natl. Acad. Sci. U.S.A.* 91:2016–2020.

UNGERLEIDER, L. G., and M. MISHKIN, 1982. Two cortical visual systems. In *Analysis of Visual Behavior*, D. J. Ingle, M. A. Goodale, and R. J. W. Mansfield, eds. Cambridge, Mass.: MIT Press, pp. 549–586.

WEDDING, D., and P. CYRUS, 1986. Recognition of emotion in hemifaces presented to the left and right visual fields. *Int. J. Neurosci.* 30:161–164.

WHALEN, P. J., S. L. RAUCH, N. L. ETCOFF, S. C. MCINERNEY, M. B. LEE, and M. A. JENIKE, 1998. Masked presentations of emotional facial expressions modulate amygdala activity without explicit knowledge. *J. Neurosci.* 18:411–418.

WOJCIULIK, E., N. KANWISHER, and J. DRIVER, 1998. Covert visual attention modulates face-specific activity in the human fusiform gyrus: fMRI study. *J. Neurophysiol.* 79:1574–1578.

YOUNG, A. W., F. NEWCOMBE, E. H. DE HAAN, M. SMALL, and D. C. HAY, 1993. Face perception after brain injury. Selective impairments affecting identity and expression. *Brain* 116:941–959.

29 Physiological Basis of Timbre Perception

SHIHAB A. SHAMMA

ABSTRACT   Speech, music, and other complex sounds are characterized by their pitch, timbre, loudness, forms of modulation, and onset/offset instants. These descriptions of sound quality have a close relationship to the instantaneous spectral properties of the sound waves. Physiological, psychoacoustical, and computational studies reveal that the central auditory system has developed elegant mechanisms to extract and represent this spectrotemporal information. For instance, the primary auditory cortex (A1) employs a multiscale representation in which the dynamic spectrum is repeatedly represented in A1 at various degrees of spectral and temporal resolution. This is accomplished by cells whose responses are selective to a range of spectrotemporal parameters such as the local bandwidth and asymmetry of spectral peaks, and their onset and offset transition rates. These findings are reviewed here, together with their functional implications and applications in sound analysis systems, and the experimental methods developed to collect and interpret them.

In a complex acoustic environment, several sound sources may simultaneously change their loudness, location, timbre, and pitch. Yet, like many other animals, humans are able to integrate effortlessly the multitude of cues arriving at their ears, deriving coherent percepts and judgments about the attributes of each sound source. This facility to analyze an auditory scene is conceptually based on a multistage process in which sound is first analyzed in terms of a relatively few perceptually significant features (the alphabet of auditory perception). Then higher level integrative processes organize and group the extracted features according to specific context-sensitive rules (the syntax of auditory perception).

Much has been learned in recent years about the initial and final stages of this process. Physiological experiments have revealed the neural representations of sound in the early stages of the auditory pathway, and the elementary features that underlie the perception of such attributes as timbre and location (Young and Sachs, 1979; Sullivan and Konishi, 1986; Knudsen, 1984; Blackburn and Sachs, 1990). Similarly, psychoacoustical investigations have shed considerable light

on the way we form and label sound images based on relationships among their physical parameters (Bregman, 1978). However, the crucial transitional stages between the physiological representations and their perceptual correlates remain mysterious and subject to considerable study and debate.

To illustrate these arguments, consider the role of pitch and timbre percepts in grouping the components of a complex sound such as the vowels /a/ and /i/ in figure 29.1, where /a/ represents the vowel sound as in /bat/ and /i/ represents the vowel sound as in /beet/. Each vowel here consists of many harmonics of a fundamental frequency–approximately 95 Hz (for /i/) and 170 Hz (for /a/)–which corresponds to the *pitch* of the vowel heard in each case. The *timbre* of the vowels is broadly defined by the American Standards Association as that "attribute which is not pitch or loudness," a definition that reflects the difficulty in specifying its physical correlates (Plomp, 1976). The most salient of such correlates is the shape of the spectral envelope (or profile) and its dynamics. Thus, to first-order, a particular vowel (e.g., /a/ in figure 29.1) preserves its perceptual identity if the envelope of its spectrum remains stable, regardless of the nature of the underlying spectral components. For

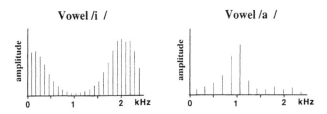

FIGURE 29.1   Schematic of acoustic spectra of speech vowels. The harmonic structure of the spectrum is represented by the equally spaced components on the linear frequency axis. The fundamental frequency is the lowest component, and is equal in this case to the frequency separation between the harmonics. Harmonic series give rise to a pitch percept equal to the fundamental (note that pitch of the vowel /a/ in the figure is about twice as high as that of /i/). The envelope of the spectrum (also called the profile) is the primary cue responsible for its timbre. Different vowels are distinguished by their distinctive profiles, especially the location and shape of the spectral peaks (also called the formants).

SHIHAB A. SHAMMA   Center for Auditory and Acoustic Research, Institute for Systems Research, Department of Electrical Engineering, University of Maryland, College Park, Md.

411

instance, it is perceived as being voiced with a certain pitch if the components are a harmonic series, and perceived as whispered if the underlying spectrum is noisy. Timbre is also determined by the dynamics of the spectral envelope, as in distinguishing between a piano and violin based on the speed of their rise (or onset) and decay times (Plomp, 1976).

Numerous experimental studies have demonstrated that if the two vowels in figure 29.1 are heard simultaneously, they could be segregated based solely on their spectral profiles. However, the segregation is significantly easier when the pitch of the vowels is different, or when their harmonic components have different onset times. These cues (and many others) accumulate to facilitate the sorting and grouping of different sound sources in a complex acoustic environment (Mellinger and Mont-Renaud, 1995; Lyon and Shamma, 1995). To make use of these percepts in acoustic scene analysis, the auditory system must extract and represent the underlying stimulus features in its neural response patterns. To illustrate these neural processes and representations, we focus in this review on the perception of timbre—specifically, on the neural representation of its most important physical correlates in the peripheral and cortical stages of the auditory system. We begin by summarizing the latest findings on how the spectral profile shape and its dynamics are encoded at various levels of the auditory system. We then discuss how the emergence of invariance to certain features may directly reflect our timbre perception, asking how these features might link with higher level analysis and rules whose exact physiological bases remain obscure. In addition, we highlight an important principle of sensory coding—that of multiscale or multiresolution decomposition, which operates in the auditory system both in the early and central stages of analysis and along the spectral and temporal dimensions of the stimuli.

Multiscale analysis of the acoustic spectrum in the early auditory stages

Sound signals undergo a series of complex transformations in the early auditory system, as illustrated in figure 29.2. These stages convert the acoustic spectrum of the stimulus into an internal representation that we call the *auditory spectrum*. The biophysics of these operations is rather elaborate (for a detailed review, see Deng, Geisler, and Greenberg, 1988; Greenberg, 1988; Shamma et al., 1986). Briefly, sound pressure waves impinging upon the eardrum cause vibrations that are transmitted to the fluids of the cochlea via the ossicles of the middle ear. These vibrations induce pressure differences across the basilar membrane, which in turn produce mechanical

displacements whose amplitudes peak at different locations along the cochlea depending on the frequency of the stimulus. For high frequencies the maximum response occurs near the base of the cochlea, while for lower frequencies it occurs near the apex. In this way, the spatial axis of the cochlea may be associated with a *tonotopically* (frequency) ordered axis.

One simple way to visualize the response characteristics of the basilar membrane is to associate each point on it with a frequency-selective (or bandpass) filter, i.e., to model the basilar membrane as an ordered bank of filters. These filters are relatively broadly tuned and significantly asymmetric in shape, with a steep roll-off on their high-frequency sides. The center frequency of each filter is called the characteristic frequency (CF). For much of the audible frequency range (roughly above 500 Hz) the filters' bandwidths are linearly proportional to the CF; i.e., the filters have constant tuning over most of the cochlear length. This property implies that (1) the CFs of the filters are logarithmically mapped along the tonotopic axis, and (2) the cochlear in effect performs a frequency decomposition of the sound signal known as an affine wavelet transform (Yang, Wang, and Shamma, 1992). In this analysis, the increasing bandwidths toward higher CFs imply progressively coarser absolute frequency resolution (but a constant relative resolution). From a perceptual point of view, this multiresolution (also called multiscale) transformation offers a compromise between the temporal and spectral dimensions. Thus, higher (lower) frequencies analyzed by smaller (wider) time-windows facilitate both a good temporal resolution of transient acoustic stimuli in the higher frequency bands and spectral resolution of narrow peaks in the lower frequency bands.

The cochlear filter outputs are then transduced into intracellular receptor potentials by a dense, topographically ordered array of sensory hair cells. For frequencies up to 3–4 kHz, the receptor potentials reflect faithfully the detailed temporal fine structure of the filter outputs. For higher frequencies, only the short-term power in the filter outputs is preserved (Sachs and Young, 1979). The receptor potentials also exhibit a limited dynamic range of about 30–40 dB due to a hair cell nonlinearity. Beyond this level, the hair cell is driven into saturation and the receptor potentials appear heavily compressed. Finally, the receptor potentials are converted into stochastic trains of electrical impulses (firings) that travel down the fibers of the auditory nerve which project to the cochlear nucleus, the first station of the central auditory system. There, recipient neurons in the cochlear nucleus reconstruct estimates of the receptor potentials by effectively computing the ensemble averages of activity in locally adjacent fibers (Shamma, 1989).

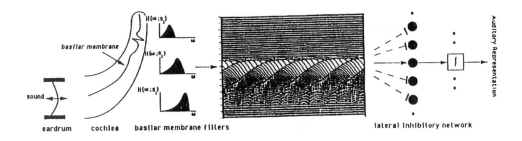

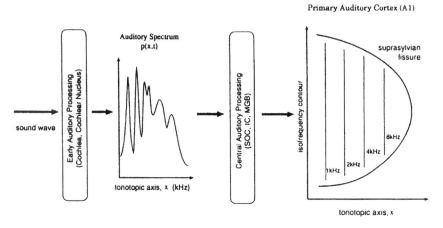

FIGURE 29.2 Overview of some of the auditory transformations of the acoustic signal. Top: Schematic illustrating the major processing stages in the early auditory system. Sound initiates traveling-wave displacements on the basilar membrane. Displacements at each point are modeled as bandpass filters centered on a specific frequency, with high frequencies near the entrance (base) of the cochlea and lower ones towards the apex. The displacements are transduced into neural activity in a topographically ordered array of fibers (the auditory nerve). The response patterns are then conveyed to the cochlear nucleus where it is hypothesized that lateral inhibitory networks extract an enhanced auditory representation of the sound spectrum (Shamma et al., 1986; Shamma, 1985a,b). Bottom: Overview of the auditory nervous pathway, which includes the cochlea, cochlear nucleus, superior olivary complex (SOC), lateral lemniscus, inferior colliculus (IC), the medial geniculate body (MGB), and the tonotopically organized primary auditory cortex and other cortical fields.

Responses of the auditory nerve contain information about all attributes of the sound stimulus, including its timbre, pitch, and other spatial and temporal characteristics. Presumably, various networks and pathways are involved at this point in estimating and encoding the necessary features associated with each of these attributes. Specifically, it has been demonstrated physiologically that the extraction of the spectral profile from the auditory nerve responses occurs at this stage by a population of stellate cells in the anteroventral portion of the cochlear nucleus (AVCN) (Blackburn and Sachs, 1990). The exact network topology that gives rise to this estimate remains uncertain. One possible scheme involves lateral inhibitory interactions which effectively sharpen the responses across the auditory nerve fiber array or, equivalently, decorrelate the activity across the array (Shamma, 1985). Anatomical and physiological support for this lateral inhibition in the cochlear nucleus is discussed in (Shamma, 1989).

The short-time averaged outputs from such a network closely resemble the spectral profile of the stimulus with few important modifications. They include a sharpened representation of the spectral peaks relative to the valleys, and a suppression of background noise that closely resembles the masking phenomenon observed in psychoacoustical experiments (Moore, 1986; Wang and Shamma, 1994). Figure 29.3 illustrates such an auditory spectrum computed for a full sentence, /*come home right away*/, using a computational model of the early auditory stages (available upon request from ftp://zikr.isr. umd.edu/speech/nsltools.tar.gz). Note that for a dynamic spectrum like that of a sentence (as opposed to that of static vowels as shown in figure 29.1), changes or modulations in the spectral profiles in time occur at relatively slow rates (on the order of 10–20 Hz), reflecting the phonetic and/or syllabic structure of the utterance. These modulation rates are typical of music, speech, and many natural sounds, and are well matched to the temporal response sensitivity of higher auditory centers.

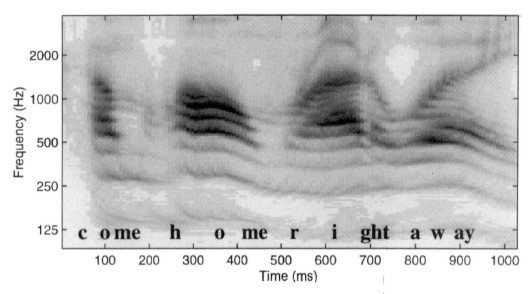

FIGURE 29.3   The auditory spectrogram of the sentence /*come home right away* / generated by a computation model of the early auditory stages. Approximate assignments of the different phonemes are also indicated.

Multiscale representation of the acoustic spectrum in the auditory cortex

The spectral pattern extracted early in the auditory pathway (the cochlea and cochlear nucleus) is relayed to the primary auditory cortex (A1) through several stages of processing, as shown in figure 29.2 (Webster, Popper, and Fay, 1992). Therefore, A1 responses integrate all influences from preceding nuclei, which are likely involved in a host of other perceptual tasks such as binaural localization and pitch estimation. As in other sensory systems, the auditory pathway is topographically (tonotopically) organized all the way up to the A1. Thus, when tested with single tones, neurons along this pathway are found to be selective to a range of frequencies around a "best frequency" (BF). Within this range, responses change from excitatory to inhibitory in a pattern that varies from one cell to another in its width and asymmetry around the BF. This response pattern is usually called the response area, or response field (RF), of the neuron and is illustrated in figure 29.4. The RF is strictly analogous to the notion of a receptive field in retinal and other visual cells, where it usually denotes the incidence angles of the light, or, equivalently, the portion of the sensory epithelium which, when stimulated, induces excitatory and/or inhibitory responses in the cell. In the auditory system, the RF is defined with respect to the tonotopic axis (which effectively labels the sensory epithelium).

It is clear that the detailed shape of a neuron's RF largely dictates its responses. Consequently, the search for a neural representation of a particular sound attribute can be achieved through measurements of a wide variety of RFs, coupled with an interpretation of these RFs in terms of their selectivity to meaningful features of that attribute. As an example, consider the multiscale representation of the spectral profile shown in figures 29.5 and 25.6 and thought to exist in A1 based on extensive neurophysiological data collected over the last decade. Here, the auditory spectrum is repeatedly represented at various degrees of resolution. The basic outlines of this representation are described for stationary spectra first (the vowel /*a*/) (figure 29.5; see color plate 17), and then for full dynamic spectra (figure 29.6; see color plate 18).

In figure 29.5A, the auditory spectral profile of the vowel /*a*/ is shown as would be presumably extracted at the cochlear nucleus. Several versions of this profile

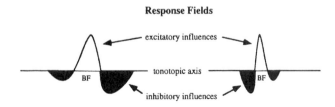

FIGURE 29.4   Schematic of response fields (RFs) of two auditory units defined against the tonotopic axis. In each case, the unit is excited around a particular "best frequency" (BF). The excitatory region of responses is surrounded by other frequencies to which the cell is inhibited (dark regions). The unit to the left has a relatively broad bandwidth (wide RF), and the inhibitory sidebands are asymmetric. The unit to the right is narrowly tuned around the BF, and has the opposite asymmetry of inhibition around its BF.

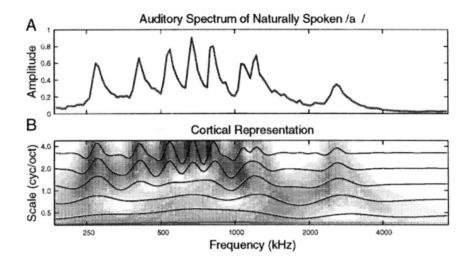

A Auditory Spectrum of Naturally Spoken /a /

B Cortical Representation

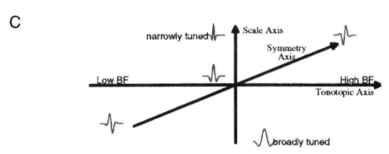

Frequency (kHz)

C

narrowly tuned

Scale Axis

Symmetry Axis

Low BF

High BF

Tonotopic Axis

broadly tuned

FIGURE 29.5   Multiscale representation of spectral profiles in the auditory cortex. (A) The auditory spectral profile of a naturally spoken vowel /*a*/. (B) The cortical representations of the spectral profile of the naturally spoken vowel /*a*/. The tonotopic axis is given in kilohertz. The ordinate is the scale axis (fine to coarse from top to bottom), which reflects the bandwidth of the RF; the axis is labeled by the ripple frequency to which the RF at each scale is most responsive. The strength of the response is indicated by the intensity of the color. For illustrative reasons, the strength of the response at several scales is also shown by the solid profiles superimposed upon this figure. The fine structure of the spectral profiles is seen only at the highest scales, whereas its coarse overall outline appears at the lower scales. Color encodes the local asymmetry of the most

responsive RF: Green indicates that the most responsive RF at this location is symmetric, red (blue) indicates RFs that are odd-symmetric, and purple is an inverted RF. Therefore, color provides a description of the local energy distribution in the spectrum. For example, the tonotopic locations at which the spectrum is locally symmetric (green) closely reflect the positions of the peaks in the auditory spectrum; red (blue) indicates whether the local spectral slope is rising (falling) or if the nearest spectral peak is at a higher (lower) frequency. (C) A schematic of the three RF organizational axes that give rise to the cortical representation: the best frequency (tonotopic axis), the bandwidth (the scale axis), and the asymmetry. Along each axis, the RF changes its shape gradually as indicated.

are displayed in figure 29.5B with various degrees of resolution from the coarsest (smoothest or the most averaged) at the bottom to the finest (most detailed) at the top. Thus, the spectral peaks that dominate this profile—e.g., the resolved harmonics in the low-frequency region (<1 kHz) and the peaks of the overall spectral envelope (called formants, at approximately 700, 1200, and 2700 Hz)—are explicitly analyzed in the cortical representation in terms of their local symmetry and bandwidth. For instance, the formants are relatively broad in bandwidth and thus are represented in the coarse or low scale regions (<1 cycle/octave). In contrast, the fine structure of the harmonics is visible only

at high scales (>1 cycle/octave). One way such patterns of cortical activation can be generated is through repeated layers of tonotopically ordered neurons with RFs of different bandwidths, in effect forming a two-dimensional sheet of A1 neurons (Mendelson and Schreiner, 1990).

The spectral representation in A1, however, is more complex, with a third dimension encoding the local shape (or asymmetry) of the spectrum. This axis is indicated by the color of the most responsive neurons at each CF. Green, red, and blue represent units most responsive to a local spectral profile that is distributed evenly around, skewed mostly above, or skewed mostly

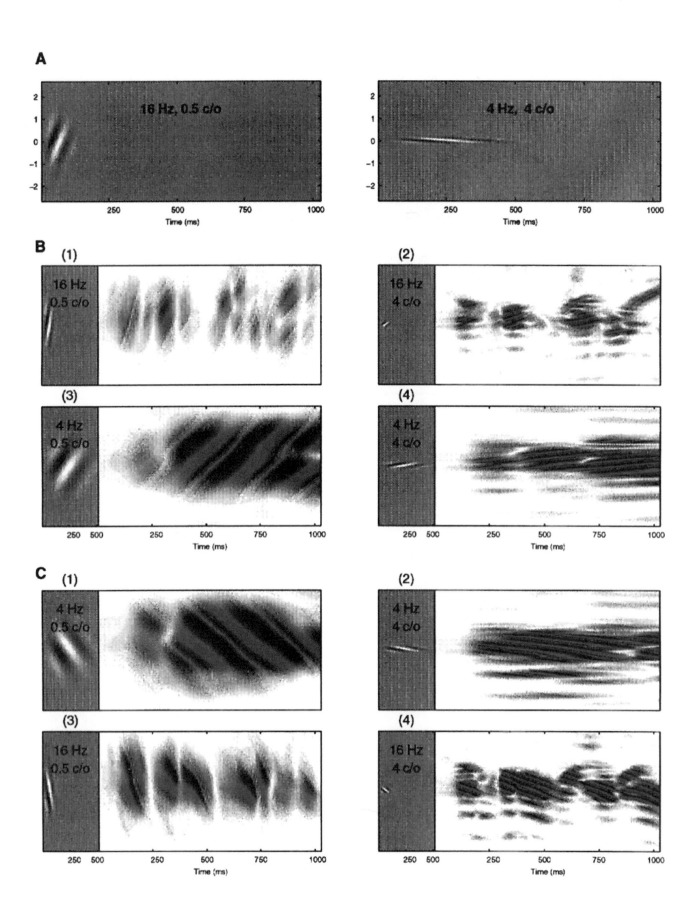

FIGURE 29.6 A1 multiscale analysis of auditory spectra along the spectral and temporal dimensions. (A) Schematic of spectrotemporal response fields (STRF) in A1. The STRF is intuitively an extension of the notion of RF to the temporal dimension. Light (dark) shaded regions indicate excitatory (inhibitory) regions. The left panel illustrates a broadly tuned, dynamically agile, upward sensitive STRF while the right panel illustrates STRF with the opposite properties. The parameters (0.5 cycles/octave and 16 Hz, 4 cycles/octave and 4 Hz) indicate the density and velocity of the most effective ripple spectrum for these units (see also figure 29.7). (B,C) Each panel shows the auditory spectrogram of the sentence / come home right away / (shown earlier in figure 29.3) as represented by the activity of units with directionally selective RFs [downward-sensitive STRFs in (B); upward-sensitive in (C)], with progressively finer spectral resolution (left to right) and increasingly rapid temporal resolution. The insets to each panel depict the STRF used to generate the spectrogram. Colors represent the phase of the response (exactly as in figure 29.5); the intensity of the color is proportional to the strength of the response.

below their CFs, respectively. RFs can easily achieve this response selectivity with inhibitory sidebands of different asymmetries, as illustrated in figure 29.4 (Shamma et al., 1993). In summary, the RFs needed to generate the above-described A1 responses must continuously vary along the three axes shown in figure 29.5C: tonotopic, bandwidth, and asymmetry.

Natural acoustic spectra are rarely stationary, but rather evolve, reflecting the changing characteristics of the source–the succession of different phonemes in a sentence or of different instruments in a symphony for example. Figure 29.3 shows the auditory spectrum of the sentence / come home right away / over approximately one second. Note the rapid onsets and offsets in the energy of the formants, especially near stop consonants such as /c/ and /t/. As with stationary vowel spectra (figure 29.5), the "auditory spectrograms" are represented in A1 in multiple resolutions, as illustrated in figure 29.6. These representations imply cortical RFs that are defined not only with respect to the spectral (tonotopic) axis, as in figure 29.4, but also along a temporal dimension as shown in figure 29.6A. Spectrotemporal RFs (STRFs) may vary in their spectral BFs, bandwidths, and asymmetry, and also in their temporal agility and directional selectivity. For instance, the STRF on the left is relatively broadly tuned (about 2 octaves), dynamically agile, and exhibits an upward directional selectivity. By comparison, the STRF on the right is narrowly tuned spectrally, downward sensitive, and is relatively slow.

A1 units have indeed been found to vary along these multiple dimensions, exhibiting spectral bandwidths from 0.5 to 2 octaves, temporal selectivities that range

from rapid responses (over 16 Hz) to very slow (under 4 Hz), and directional sensitivities to upward, bidirectional, and downward moving spectral energy. Populations of these different kinds of STRFs can support a spectrotemporal multiscale representation of the spectrograms as shown in figure 29.6B,C for the same sentence as in figure 29.3. Each panel here displays the spectrogram viewed at a certain spectral and temporal resolution. Also shown to the left of each panel is the hypothetical STRF of the unit population that generates the activity seen. For instance, units in upper panels (figure 29.6B) are upward-sensitive, and hence exhibit only upward-sweeping spectral energy; the opposite is true for the lower panels (figure 29.6C). Panels B1 and C3 are broadly tuned but temporally rapid, thus highlighting spectrally coarse events in the spectrograms; panels B4 and C2 encode the opposite features (spectrally fine, temporally slow receptive fields). These two pairs of representations are polar opposites of each other perceptually, the latter pair emphasizing the physical correlates of pitch and long vowels (the harmonic peaks and their slow change in time), and the former emphasizing the spectral features and dynamics usually associated with the perception of consonants.

Physiological foundations of the multiscale representations

The auditory system performs a twofold multiscale analysis in which the acoustic signal is first transformed into the auditory spectrum in the cochlea and cochlear nucleus, followed by a transformation of the auditory spectrum into the cortical representation seen in A1. The physiological foundations of the multiscale analysis in the cochlea are well established and will not be elaborated upon here. Perhaps the most persuasive evidence for it is the logarithmic distribution of frequencies along the tonotopic axis, together with the roughly constant Q filtering of the basilar membrane (Webster, Popper, Fay, 1992).

The cortical multiscale representation is based on extensive recordings in A1 employing a wide range of acoustic stimuli, both natural and artificial, spectrally narrow and broad, species-specific and otherwise (Clarey, Barone, and Imig, 1992; Shamma, 1996). Compared to the auditory periphery, the functional organization in A1 has remained uncertain. In large part, this is attributable to the complexity and nonlinearity of the representation their spectra–even the simplest spectra such as those of a single tone at different sound levels (Phillips et al., 1994; Irvine, 1992). Another complicating factor is the multiple overlapping maps of various spectral and temporal features discovered along the isofrequency planes of A1 (Versnel, Kowalski, and Shamma, 1995; Calhoun and Schreiner, 1995; Mendelson and Schreiner, 1990; Suga, 1984). Nevertheless, these results have led to several viable hypotheses regarding the way the spectral profile might be encoded in A1 and other auditory fields (Phillips et al., 1994; Wang and Shamma, 1995; Irvine, 1992).

A basic measurement in the experimental validation of all hypotheses is that of the unit response area, defined roughly as the range of tone frequencies and intensities that elicit excitatory or inhibitory responses. Response areas are usually measured using single or multiple tonal stimuli, and are found to vary considerably from one cell to another in their width and asymmetry around the BF (Shamma et al., 1993). While qualitatively useful as predictors of a unit's responses to arbitrary broadband spectra, response area measurements are significantly affected by a host of measurement difficulties and nonlinear factors (Shamma, Versnel, and Kowalski, 1995; Nelken, Prut, and Vaadia, 1994) that render their parameter estimates (e.g., bandwidth and asymmetry) quantitatively uncertain.

To circumvent some of these problems, new techniques have been employed to measure the spectral and dynamic properties of response areas in A1 and potentially other auditory fields and nuclei (Calhoun and Schreiner, 1995; Shamma, Versnel, and Kowalski, 1995). The stimuli and techniques apply linear system theory to measure the response area of cortical units. In one method, the stimuli used are broadband spectra with sinusoidally modulated profiles against the logarithmic frequency axis–also called ripples as shown in figure 29.7. These stimuli are analogous to the drifting gratings used in receptive field measurements in VI and other visual structures (De Valois and De Valois, 1990). By varying the peak density, amplitude, phase, and the drifting velocity of the ripple, one can measure a ripple transfer function. Using an inverse Fourier transform, we can then obtain a spectrotemporal response field (STRF) function that effectively resembles the response area of the unit, as explained in detail in figures 29.8 and 29.9. In another method (shown in figure 29.10), stimuli with random and dynamic spectral profiles are cross-correlated with the responses to extract the STRF (also known as the reverse-correlation method) (Eggermont, 1993). Using these methods, STRFs of hundreds of units in A1 have been measured, mapped, and compared to those obtained from single and two-tone stimuli (Shamma, Versnel, and Kowalski, 1995; Kowalski, Depireux, and Shamma, 1996a,b).

Figure 29.8 illustrates the responses to moving ripples and the way in which they are analyzed. The raster re-

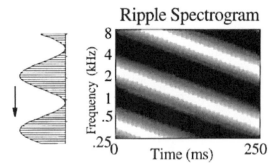

FIGURE 29.7 The ripple spectral profile is shown to the left of the spectrogram. It usually consists of 101 tones equally spaced along the logarithmic frequency axis, spanning 5 octaves (e.g., 0.25–8 kHz). The sinusoidal envelope has a ripple density or frequency Ω, given in cycles per octave. It moves at a constant velocity ω defined as the number of ripple cycles traversing the lower edge of the spectrum per second (hertz). The spectrogram of this moving ripple is shown to the right. Different ripple frequencies, velocities, and direction change the orientation of the sweeps. The ripple in the figure is at $\Omega = 0.4$ cycles/octave, and $w = 4$ Hz.

sponses in figure 29.8A are elicited by a ripple spectrum (0.4 cycle/octave) traveling at a range of velocities ($\omega = 4$–20 Hz). The amplitude and phase of the synchronized response component at each ω are derived and plotted as the magnitude and phase of the transfer function $T_{\Omega}(\omega)$. Figure 29.8B illustrates the complementary test of the response properties to moving ripples; here, ripple velocity is fixed at $\omega = 4$ Hz while the ripple frequency is increased systematically from 0 to 2 cycles/octave. The responses are analyzed as before, and plotted as the magnitude and phase of the ripple transfer function $T_{\omega}(\Omega)$.

The transfer functions thus measured are valid at one ripple frequency or velocity, as indicated by the subscripts ω and Ω, and illustrated in figure 29.9 (bottom) (see color plate 19). In principle, one must measure the two-dimensional transfer function at all Ω and ω, and for both upward and downward directions of moving ripples. However, it has been demonstrated that for a given direction, these functions remain largely unchanged apart from a scale change (Kowalski, Depireux, and Shamma, 1996a,b). Consequently, for each direction, the temporal and ripple transfer functions can be treated separately (i.e., they are quadrant-separable), and the full transfer function can be assumed to equal the products of the two separate measurements (figure 29.9, middle). To obtain the full STRF, the transfer function is then inverse Fourier–transformed as described in more detail by Simon, Depireux, and Shamma (1998).

Very similar overall STRFs are measured using the reverse-correlation method described in figure 29.10 (see color plate 20). Here, the stimuli consist of combinations

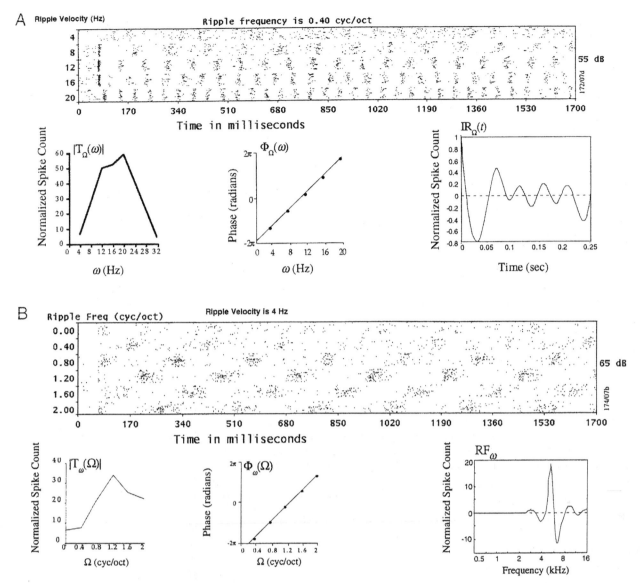

FIGURE 29.8 Analysis of responses to moving ripples. (A) Temporal transfer function. Top: Raster responses to a ripple ($\Omega = 0.8$ cycles/octave) moving at different velocities. The ripple begins moving to the left at 0 ms, and the stimulus is turned on at 50 ms. Bottom: The amplitude $T_\Omega(\omega)$ and phase $\Phi_\Omega(\omega)$ of the temporal transfer functions are measured from period histograms of the data. The inverse Fourier transform of the transfer function gives the impulse response function of the cell at a particular ripple ($IR_\Omega(t)$). (B) Ripple transfer functions. Top: Raster responses to ripples with different densities all moving at $\omega = 4$ Hz. Bottom: The amplitude $T_\omega(\Omega)$ and phase $\Phi_\omega(\Omega)$ of the ripple transfer functions are measured from period histograms of the data. The inverse Fourier transform of the transfer function gives the RF of the cell at a particular velocity (RF_ω).

of moving ripples with random phases, and all combinations of velocities and ripple frequencies. Using the spike-triggered averaging method (Eggermont, 1993), the spectra most effective in producing spikes are computed and displayed as the STRF shown in figure 29.10C. The similarity between the STRFs obtained from the two measurement techniques confirms the important finding of quadrant separability, since the reverse correlation method does not require this assumption. STRFs measured with dynamic ripples exhibit a variety of shapes, reflecting the selectivity of the underlying transfer functions. For example, some are broadly tuned and asymmetric (as illustrated by the unit in figure 29.11B) while others are relatively narrow and symmetric (figure 29.11A); some are relatively rapid in time (figure 29.9, top; figure 29.11A), and others are slow (figure 29.11B) (Simon, Depireux, and Shamma, 1998). These varied types of STRFs are exactly what are needed to generate the multiscale spectrotemporal representations described earlier.

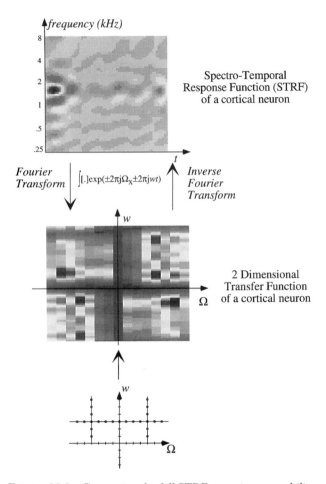

FIGURE 29.9 Computing the full STRF assuming separability. Bottom: The magnitude and phase (not shown) of the two-dimensional transfer function measured as in figure 29.8. Note that measurements are obtained at just one ω and Ω. Middle: Assuming separability, the full transfer function is computed from the product of the two cross sections measured at ω and Ω. Top: The STRF is computed from a two-dimensional inverse Fourier transformation of the transfer function. All colors here indicate the strength of the response. Red (blue) represent the excitatory (inhibitory) fields of the RF.

The ripple analysis techniques assume that the responses to such broadband stimuli are substantially linear in character. The most important correlate of linearity is the *superposition principle*, which implies that responses to combinations of ripples are linearly additive and can be predicted from the responses to single ripples. These assumptions have been verified by successfully predicting responses to arbitrary complex spectra composed of multiple ripples and speech vowels, as illustrated in figure 29.11 (Shamma and Versnel, 1995; Kowalski, Depireux, and Shamma, 1996a,b). It should be emphasized, however, that A1 unit responses still exhibit nonlinear response characteristics such as half-wave rectification, saturation, adaptation, and often non-

monotonic rate-level functions. The effects of these nonlinearities on the STRF measurements are only partially understood and accounted for by these analysis methods (Kowalski, Depireux, and Shamma, 1996a,b).

Perceptual significance of the cortical multiscale representations

What is the perceptual significance of these multiscale representations, and what advantages do they provide to the processing of auditory and other sensory systems? From a scientific and engineering point of view, these representations are valuable since they provide explicit features that are perceptually significant. By understanding the properties of these features, we may be able to account for the stability and noise-robustness of our auditory percepts and facilitate the manipulation of these percepts in various engineering systems. We already discussed the perceptual correlates of noise-suppression in the early auditory stages. Here we elaborate on the perceptual correlates of the segregation of pitch and timbre cues in the cortical representation.

The hypothetical cortical representation of a complex speech segment is described in some detail in figure 29.6. As is evident in these panels, information about the pitch is preserved mostly in the finest spectral scales [panels B,C(2,4)] where the spectral harmonics are resolved. The lower and intermediate scales mostly represent the overall spectral envelope (a correlate of the timbre percept). The segregation of these cues may in turn explain the relative independence of these two percepts, e.g., producing different pitches with a particular instrument or playing the same note (pitch) on different instruments. This is an extremely useful property of the cortical representations in sound processing and recognition systems because it is often the case that one of the percepts is unnecessary. For example, to recognize a word or a phoneme (e.g., a vowel), the voice pitch is largely irrelevant. The opposite is true in recognizing a melody. Similarly, the segregation is useful in applications where a voice (pitch) or a phoneme (timbre) is morphed from one into another. Similar arguments can be advanced for the different temporal scales. For example, fast time scales are associated with sound transients (e.g., plucked instruments and speech consonants), and slow time scales with sustained sounds (e.g., bowed and wind instruments and speech vowels). Once again, the segregation can prove useful in many applications as in morphing.

The multiscale representation offers advantages with respect to robustness against noise. This is because different types of sounds (speech, music, and environmental noise) occupy distinct regions in the cortical multiscale representation, and hence interfering sounds occupying

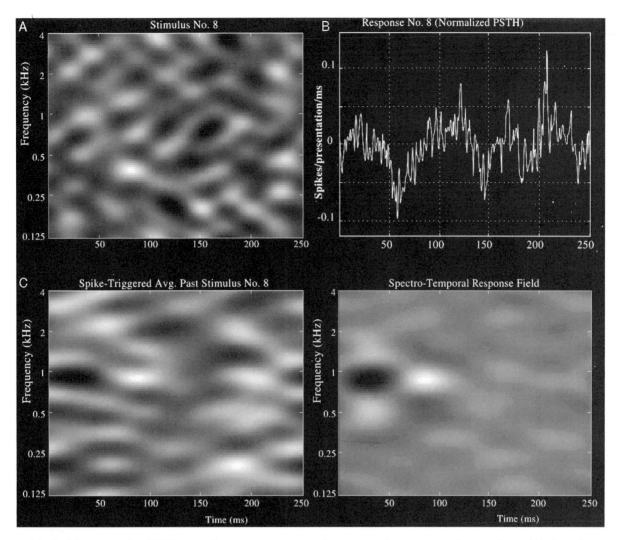

FIGURE 29.10   Measuring the STRF using the reverse correlation method. (A) The spectrogram of one of the "random"
stimuli used in the experiments. The stimulus consists of 200
ripples ranging from 0.2 to 2 cycles/octave, 4 to 40 Hz, and
random starting phases. The results from many such stimuli
are averaged at the end to compute the final STRF. (B) Period

histogram of responses to the stimulus in (A). Stimulus spectra
that precede each spike are averaged to produce the STRF.
(C) At the left is the STRF computed using the reverse-correlation method. The right panel shows the STRF of the same
unit using the ripple analysis method.

different regions can be filtered out. For instance, speech
sounds are largely concentrated in the intermediate
scales (0.25–3 cycles/octave), lower frequency ranges
(0.25–4 kHz) (Hillier, 1991), and with temporal modulations from 5 to 10 Hz (Wu et al., 1997). Consequently, outputs outside of these ranges can be removed to enhance
the signal-to-noise ratio prior to further processing. In the
best performing speech recognition systems to date, modulations in the speech spectrogram are bandpassed
around 10 Hz to eliminate slowly varying background
hums or to minimize the effects of rapid and irregular
transients (Wu et al., 1997).

Finally, it is also possible to perform a variety of experiments with the multiscale representation in which different scales are eliminated in order to estimate their overall

contribution to the intelligibility of the signal. Another interesting manipulation is the translation of the activity
pattern along the three different axes of the multiscale
representation: the tonotopic (log-frequency), scale, and
phase axes. Translations along these axes considerably alter the sound percept, but they do not seem to affect its
intelligibility. For example, shifting the response patterns
up and down the tonotopic axis by more than an octave
produces speech that is easily comprehensible despite the
large changes in the absolute frequencies of the spectral
formants. This may be due to the fact that simple translations do not alter the overall shape of the corresponding
cortical pattern. Similarly, translations along the scale,
phase, and temporal axes produce changes in percept,
but not in intelligibility. An interesting aspect of these

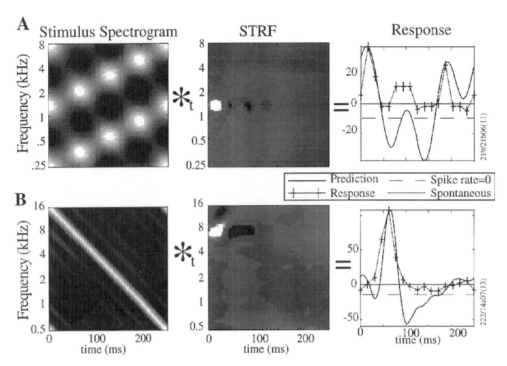

FIGURE 29.11 Predictions of responses to complex dynamic spectra using the STRF. (A) The predicted response is computed by convolving (along the temporal dimension) the STRF and the spectrogram. The stimulus shown is composed of two ripples (0.4 cycles/octave at 12 and −4 Hz). The predicted waveform is shown juxtaposed upon the actual response (crosses) over one period of the stimulus. (B) Same as in (A) except for a stimulus consisting of ripples at (0.2 cycles/octave at 4 Hz + 0.4 cycles/octave at 8 Hz + . . . + 1.2 cycles/octave at 24 Hz, all in cosine phase).

(harmless) translations is that they are naturally produced by variations in the length of the vocal tract, its overall conical shape, or the rate of articulatory motion (speaking rate). Such variations are common across different speakers; consequently, our ability to normalize (and ignore) them may be partly explained by the invariance of our cortical representations to them.

We can identify many other features of the cortical representations whose perceptual correlates remain unexplored. For instance, the direction and rate of motion along the frequency axis are explicitly available. In figure 29.6, for example, B(1) and B(2) display fast, upward-moving energy as opposed to the slow, downward-moving energy of C(1) and C(2). Such information may be extremely useful in tracking and grouping variations common to one sound source, an essential preliminary step to segregating polyphonic signals and organizing a complex auditory scene.

Clearly, to appreciate all of the arguments presented here, we must be able to invert the cortical representation back to the acoustic signal so we can hear it. Procedures to accomplish this inversion are now available using convex-projection methods (Yang, Wang, and Shamma, 1992). The challenging aspects of this inversion are largely due to the several nonlinearities in the early stages of the auditory pathway. From a theoretical point of view, success in inverting the cortical representation back to the acoustic stimulus illustrates the minimal loss of information through the many complex transformations along the auditory pathway (Yang, Wang, and Shamma, 1992). A convenient MATLAB-based package to perform and display the results of the auditory transformations and manipulations, and to invert the representations back to the acoustic stimulus is available upon request on ftp://zikr.isr.umd.edu/speech/nsltools.tar.gz.

ACKNOWLEDGMENTS The material reviewed here is the product of collaborations with many colleagues, among whom are Dr. Didier Depireux, Dr. Jonathan Simon, Dr. Huib Versnel, David Klein, Powen Ru, Nina Kowalski, and Tai-chi. The research is partially funded by the Office of Naval Research and the National Science Foundation.

REFERENCES

BLACKBURN, C., and M. SACHS, 1990. The representation of the steady-state vowel /e/ in the discharge patterns of cat anteroventral cochlear nucleus neurons. *J. Neurophysiol.* 63: 1191–1212.

BREGMAN, A. S., 1978. Auditory streaming: Competition among alternative organization. *Percept. Psychophys.* 23:391–398.

CALHOUN, B., and C. SCHREINER, 1995. Spectral envelope coding in cat primary auditory cortex. *J. Aud. Neurosci.* 1:39–61.

CLAREY, J., P. BARONE, and T. IMIG, 1992. Physiology of thalamus and cortex. In *The Mammalian Auditory Pathway: Neurophysiology*, D. Webster, A. Popper, and R. Fay, eds. New York: Springer-Verlag, pp. 232–334.

DENG, L., C. GEISLER, and S. GREENBERG, 1988. A composite model of the auditory periphery for the processing of speech. *J. Phonetics* 16:93–108.

DE VALOIS, R., and K. DE VALOIS, 1990. *Spatial Vision*. New York: Oxford University Press.

EGGERMONT, J., 1993. Wiener and Volterra analyses applied to the auditory system. *Hear. Res.* 66:177–201.

GREENBERG, S., 1988. The ear as a speech analyzer. *J. Phonetics* 16:139–150.

HILLIER, D., 1991. Auditory processing of sinusoidal spectral envelopes. Ph.D. Dissertation, The Washington University and Severn Institute.

IRVINE, D., 1992. Physiology of the auditory brainstem. In *The Mammalian Auditory Pathway: Neurophysiology*, D. Webster, A. Popper, and R. Fay, eds. New York: Springer-Verlag, pp. 153–231.

KNUDSEN, E., 1984. Synthesis of a neural map of auditory space in the owl. In *Dynamic Aspects of Neocortical Function*, G. Edelman, W. Gall, and W. Cowan, eds. New York: Wiley, pp. 375–396.

KOWALSKI, N., D. DEPIREUX, and S. SHAMMA, 1996a. Analysis of dynamic spectra in ferret primary auditory cortex: Characteristics of single unit responses to moving ripple spectra. *J. Neurophysiol.* 76(5):3503–3523.

KOWALSKI, N., D. DEPIREUX, and S. SHAMMA, 1996b. Analysis of dynamic spectra in ferret primary auditory cortex: Prediction of single unit responses to arbitrary dynamic spectra. *J. Neurophysiol.* 76(5):3524–3534.

LYON, R., and S. SHAMMA, 1995. Auditory representations of timbre and pitch. In *Auditory Computation*, H. Hawkins, T. McMullen, A. Popper, and R. Fay, eds. New York: Springer-Verlag, pp. 221–270.

MELLINGER, M., and B. MONT-RENAUD, 1995. Scene analysis. In *Auditory Computation*, H. Hawkins, T. McMullen, A. Popper, and R. Fay, eds. New York: Springer-Verlag, pp. 271–331.

MENDELSON, J., and C. SCHREINER, 1990. Functional topography of cat primary auditory cortex: Distribution of integrated excitation. *J. Neurophysiol.* 64(5):1442–1459.

MOORE, B., 1986. *Frequency Selectivity in Hearing*. New York: Academic Press.

NELKEN, I., Y. PRUT, and E. VAADIA, 1994. Population responses to multifrequency sounds in the cat auditory cortex: One- and two-parameter families of sounds. *Hear. Res.* 72:206–222.

PHILLIPS, D., M. SEMPLE, M. CALFORD, and L. KITZES, 1994. Level-dependent representation of stimulus frequency in cat primary auditory cortex. *Exp. Br. Res.* 102:210–226.

PLOMP, R., 1976. *Aspects of Tone Sensation*. New York: Academic Press.

SACHS, M., and E. YOUNG, 1979. Encoding of steady state vowels in the auditory nerve: Representation in terms of discharge rate. *J. Acoust. Soc. Amer.* 66:470–479.

SHAMMA, S., 1985a. Speech processing in the auditory system. I. Representation of speech in the responses of the auditory nerve. *J. Acoust. Soc. Amer.* 78:1611–1621.

SHAMMA, S., 1985b. Speech processing in the auditory system. II. Lateral inhibition and the processing of speech evoked activity in the auditory nerve. *J. Acoust. Soc. Amer.* 78:1622–1632.

SHAMMA, S., 1989. Spatial and temporal processing in central auditory networks. In *Methods in Neuronal Modeling*, C. Koch and I. Segev, eds. Cambridge, Mass.: MIT Press, pp. 411–460.

SHAMMA, S., 1996. Auditory cortical representation of complex acoustic spectra as inferred from the ripple analysis method. *Network: Comp. Neural Syst.* 7:439–476.

SHAMMA, S., R. CHADWICK, J. WILBUR, K. MOORISH, and J. RINZEL, 1986. A biophysical model of cochlear processing: Intensity dependence of pure tone responses. *J. Acoust. Soc. Amer.* 80:133–144.

SHAMMA, S. A., J. FLESHMAN, P. WISER, and H. VERSNEL, 1993. Organization of response areas in ferret primary auditory cortex. *J. Neurophysiol.* 69(2):367–383.

SHAMMA, S., and H. VERSNEL, 1995. Ripple analysis in the ferret primary auditory cortex. II. Prediction of unit responses to arbitrary spectral profiles. *J. Aud. Neurosci.* 1:255–270.

SHAMMA, S., H. VERSNEL, and N. KOWALSKI, 1995. Ripple analysis in the ferret primary auditory cortex. I. Response characteristics of single units to sinusoidally rippled spectra. *J. Aud. Neurosci.* 1:233–254.

SIMON, J., D. DEPIREUX, and S. SHAMMA, 1998. Representation of complex spectra in auditory cortex. In *Psychophysical and Physiological Advances in Hearing*, A. Palmer, A. Rees, A. Summerfield, and R. Meddis, eds. London: Whurr Publishers, pp. 513–520.

SUGA, N., 1984. The extent to which biosonar information is represented in the bat auditory cortex. In *Dynamic Aspects of Neocortical Function*, G. M. Edelman, W. E. Gall, and W. M. Cowan, eds. New York: Wiley, pp. 315–373.

SULLIVAN, W., and M. KONISHI, 1986. Neural map of interaural phase difference in the owl's brainstem. *Proc. Natl. Acad. Sci. U.S.A.* 83:8400–8404.

VERSNEL, H., S. SHAMMA, and N. KOWALSKI, 1995. Ripple analysis in the ferret primary auditory cortex. III. Topographic and columnar distribution of ripple response parameters. *J. Aud. Neurosci.* 1:271–285.

WANG, K., and S. SHAMMA, 1994. Self-normalization and noise robustness in early auditory processing. *IEEE Trans. Aud. Speech* 2(3):421–435.

WANG, K., and S. SHAMMA, 1995. Representation of spectral profiles in the primary auditory cortex. *IEEE Trans. Speech Audio Proc.* 3(2):382–395.

WEBSTER, D., 1992. Overview of mammalian auditory pathways with emphasis on humans. In *The Mammalian Auditory Pathway: Neuroanatomy*, D. Webster, A. Popper, and R. Fay, eds. New York: Springer-Verlag, pp. 1–22.

WU, S.-L., M. SHIRE, S. GREENBERG, and N. MORGAN, 1997. Integrating syllable boundary information into speech recognition. *ICASSP-97*, pp. 987–990.

YANG, X., K. WANG, and S. SHAMMA, 1992. Auditory representations of acoustic signals. *IEEE Trans. Inf. Theory* 38(2):824–839.

YOUNG, E., and M. SACHS, 1979. Representation of steady state vowels in the temporal aspects of the discharge patterns of populations of auditory-nerve fibers. *J. Acoust. Soc. Amer.* 66:1381–1403.

30 Cortical Representations of Auditory Space

JOHN C. MIDDLEBROOKS

ABSTRACT   The results of cortical lesions indicate that normal auditory cortical function is necessary for the perception of the location of a sound source. In the midbrain, neuronal maps of auditory space are well known. It is surprising, then, that efforts in several laboratories have failed to demonstrate a conventional topographical representation of sound-source location in the auditory cortex. An alternative view is presented here, in which single neurons are regarded as panoramic localizers. Experimentally, artificial neural networks were used to recognize single-unit spike patterns and, thereby, to identify the locations of sound sources. Spike patterns were shown to carry location-related information not only in their magnitudes but also in the timing of individual spikes. The representation of any particular sound-source location appears to be distributed across large populations of neurons.

Location in space is a conspicuous attribute of a sound source. Animals localize sound sources to track prey or to avoid becoming prey. Listeners exploit location-related information to aid in segregating a sound signal from a noisy background. Confronted with the cacophony of voices in a noisy office or in a cocktail party, humans can focus attention along a specific direction to single out a particular voice. In a typical listening situation, one has a sense of multiple discrete sound sources at well-defined locations.

In the visual and somatosensory systems, stimulus localization is a fairly straightforward matter. The locations of stimuli are mapped directly on the sensory epithelia, either the retina or the skin. Neurons in visual or somatosensory cortex have restricted receptive fields that, in essence, are determined by the area of the sensory epithelium that supplies their input. The locations of visual or somatic receptive fields vary systematically as a function of the locations of neurons in the cortex. Points in visual or somatic space map onto points in the cortex. In the auditory system, localization is much less direct. The auditory sensory epithelium contains a map of stimulus frequency, and consequently, auditory cortical topography is devoted to frequency representation. The locations of sound sources must be computed from acoustical cues provided by the interaction of the incident sound wave with the head and external ears (see review by Middlebrooks and Green, 1991). The principal acoustical cues for the horizontal locations of sound sources are interaural timing differences and interaural level differences. The vertical and front/back locations of sounds are cued by characteristics of sound spectra that are introduced by direction-dependent resonances of the convoluted external ear.

Computation of sound-source locations takes place within structures of the auditory brain stem. Likely brain stem structures for detection of localization cues include the superior olivary complex for interaural difference cues and the dorsal cochlear nucleus for spectral cues. One product of the brain stem location computation is, in the midbrain superior colliculus, a map of auditory space. The auditory map lies in register with maps of visual, somatic, and motor space, and auditory units show restricted spatial receptive fields (see King and Schnupp, chapter 31 of this volume, for review of brain stem mechanisms and superior colliculus maps).

Auditory cortical function is essential for normal sound localization. Human patients that sustain lesions of the temporal lobe show deficits in localization of sounds presented on the side contralateral to the lesion (Greene, 1929; Wortis and Pfeiffer, 1948; Sanchez-Longo and Forster, 1958; Klingon and Bontecou, 1966). In cats, experimental lesions of the auditory cortex have little effect on reflexive head movements toward unexpected sounds (Thompson and Masterton, 1978); such movements probably are mediated by the superior colliculus. Auditory cortical lesions in cats do, however, block purposive behavior that requires sound localization. That is, after experimental unilateral lesions of the auditory cortex, cats are unable to walk to the source of a contralateral noise burst (Jenkins and Masterton, 1982). A unilateral localization deficit is perhaps the most conspicuous sign of a unilateral auditory cortical lesion.

Given that an intact auditory cortex is necessary for normal sound localization and that the brain is capable of constructing an auditory space map (at least in the superior colliculus), a rather obvious hypothesis would be

JOHN C. MIDDLEBROOKS   Kresge Hearing Research Institute, University of Michigan, Ann Arbor, Mich.

425

that the auditory cortex contains a point-to-point map of auditory space. Such a map has been actively sought by several groups of investigators. Surprisingly, the consensus of those groups has been that there is no map, at least not in the form represented by the visual and somatic maps in the cortex or by the auditory space map in the superior colliculus. In this chapter, we begin by reviewing the characteristics of spatial tuning in the auditory cortex, citing some limited evidence for spatial topography. Nevertheless, we argue against the presence of a map of space in the auditory cortex. Then we present an alternative view of auditory spatial coding, in which individual neurons code locations throughout space and information about a particular point in space is distributed among a large population of neurons. Finally, we identify some of the features of neuronal spike patterns that carry auditory location-related information.

Spatial tuning of neuronal spike counts

Spatial coding in the auditory cortex has been studied most systematically in the cat, so this review focuses on that species. Spatial receptive fields have been described in cortical area A1 (Middlebrooks and Pettigrew, 1981; Brugge et al., 1994). Profiles of spike counts versus azimuth have been measured in area A1 (Imig, Irons, and Samson, 1990; Rajan, Aitkin, and Irvine, 1990a); area A2 (Middlebrooks et al., 1994, 1998), the anterior ectosylvian area (area AES: Korte and Rauschecker, 1993; Middlebrooks et al., 1994, 1998); and, to a limited degree, the anterior auditory area (area AAF: Korte and Rauschecker, 1993). The elevation sensitivity of spike counts has been measured in areas A2 and AES (Xu, Furukawa, and Middlebrooks, 1998). One might have predicted that area A1 or AES is specialized for sound localization. In the case of A1, that prediction comes from the observation by Jenkins and Merzenich (1984) that lesions restricted to area A1 impaired cats' localization of sounds presented contralateral to the lesion. In the case of area AES, Meredith and Clemo (1989) found that area AES is the only auditory cortical field that sends strong anatomical projections to the superior colliculus, which contains an auditory space map. Nevertheless, among the cortical areas in which spatial coding has been studied physiologically, no area stands out as obviously containing more spatially selective units or a more consistent spatial topography. Figure 30.1 shows some examples of azimuth and elevation sensitivity for units in area A2. The illustrated examples roughly span the range of sharpness of tuning that we have observed in that area.

The spatial sensitivity of units varies among units and, to a lesser degree, among cortical areas; but one can make some generalizations. First, *spike counts are modulated by the location of a sound source.* Between 39% and 94% of units in areas AES and A2 showed more than 50% modulation of their spike counts by the location in azimuth of a noise burst (Middlebrooks et al., 1998); the exact percentages of units varied with cortical area and with sound level. In area A1, Rajan and colleagues (1990a) reported that 82% of units showed more than 50% modulation of their spike counts, and Imig and colleagues (1990) reported that 66% of units showed more than 75% modulation. Second, *the spatial tuning of units tends to be broad.* One can represent the spatial tuning of a unit by its *maximal receptive field*, which is the region within which a sound source could activate the unit above its resting level. In area A1, 75–85% of units showed maximal receptive fields that either filled a hemifield on one side of the cat or spanned all tested locations (Middlebrooks and Pettigrew, 1981; Brugge et al., 1994). Alternatively, one can represent the spatial tuning of a unit by its *best area* (Knudsen, 1982), which is the region within which stimuli activated the unit to more than 50% of its maximum spike count. Best areas spanned more than 180° for 58–85% of units in area AES and 81–97% of units in area A2 (Middlebrooks et al., 1998); again, the exact percentage of units varied with sound level. In area A1, best areas have been measured only in front of the cat, but so-called omnidirectional and hemifield units accounted for 82% of units (Rajan et al., 1990a). Third, *spatial receptive fields tend to expand in width with increases in stimulus sound level.* At stimulus levels near a unit's threshold, spatial receptive fields tended to be limited to a restricted region near the axis of greatest sensitivity of the external ear, most often the contralateral ear (Middlebrooks and Pettigrew, 1981; Brugge, Reale, and Hind, 1996). As sound levels were increased, receptive fields broadened at least until sound levels at the ipsilateral ear were high enough to activate inhibitory mechanisms. Brugge and colleagues (1996) reported that as sound levels were increased, the receptive fields of some ("unbounded") units in area A1 expanded until they occupied all tested locations, whereas the receptive fields of other ("bounded") units expanded only until they reached a boundary near the vertical midline. In areas AES and A2, the best areas of 88% and 77% of units, respectively, broadened as sound levels were increased from 20 to 40 dB above unit thresholds. The examples in figure 30.1 show spatial tuning that broadened with increasing sound level. Fourth, *the spatial preferences of units can change with changes in sound level.* For units that show sharp enough spatial tuning, one can define a "best-azimuth centroid," which is the spike-count–weighted center of a peak in a unit's azimuth profile, i.e., the azimuth

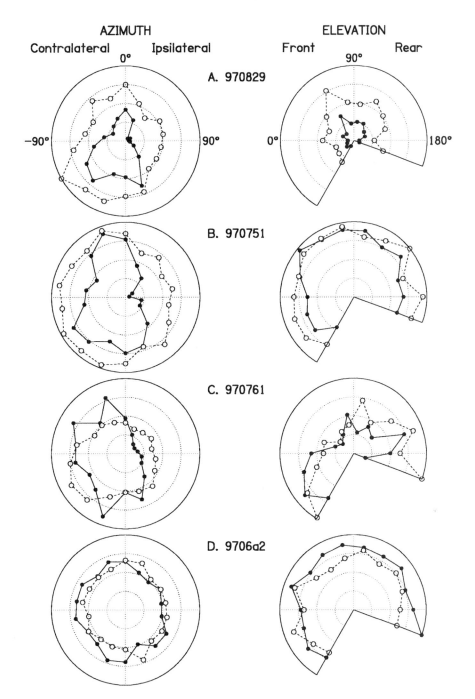

AZIMUTH
Contralateral   Ipsilateral
0°
-90°   90°

ELEVATION
Front   Rear
90°
0°   180°

A. 970829

B. 970751

C. 970761

D. 9706a2

FIGURE 30.1 Spatial tuning of spike counts. Each row represents the azimuth tuning (left) and elevation tuning (right) of one unit recorded in area A2. In these polar plots, the angular dimension shows the sound-source location and the radial dimension shows the spike count averaged across 40 trials and normalized to 100%. The azimuth plots are drawn as if looking down on the cat, and the elevation plots are views from the cat's left side. Filled and open symbols indicate measurements made with sound levels 20 dB and 40 dB, respectively, above units' thresholds.

to which the unit is "tuned" (Middlebrooks et al., 1998). In area AES and A2, more than half of the units that had measurable best-azimuth centroids when stimulus levels were 20 dB above threshold showed substantial changes in their centroids when sound levels were increased by 20 dB. Either the centroid shifted in location by more than 40° or the unit became so broadly tuned that the centroid could no longer be measured. The units represented in figure 30.1B and C are examples that showed such changes in tuning. Similarly, one can see changes in azimuth tuning in illustrated data from area A1. Finally, *spatial profiles of units can show multiple peaks.* The spike-count-versus-azimuth profiles of some units show two or more discrete peaks separated by well-defined valleys. The units represented in figure 30.1A and B are examples. Middlebrooks and colleagues (1998) found that 24% of units in area AES and 15% of units in area A2 had two or more best-azimuth centroids. In many instances, two best-azimuth centroids of a unit would lie in mirror symmetry with respect to the interaural axis, but that was not always the case. One also can see multiple peaks in illustrated data from area A1 (e.g., Imig, Irons, and Samson, 1990, figure 7).

It is a common observation in visual, somatosensory, and motor cortices that receptive fields are substantially larger than behavioral spatial resolution. Several models have addressed this issue under the general topic of "coarse coding" (e.g., Hinton, McClelland, and Rumelhart, 1986). In models of the motor cortex, Georgopolis, Kettner, and Schwartz (1988) have proposed a population code in which each neuron, although broadly tuned, represents a particular movement vector. Specific movements are represented by spike-rate–weighted vector sums of large populations of neurons. We have tried, with little success, to adapt such models to our data from areas AES and A2. The main problems are that the spatial preferences of units tend to change with increases in sound level, that units can show more than one preferred direction, and that many units show such broad spatial tuning that it is impossible to define a preferred direction.

Figure 30.2 shows, as a function of sound-source azimuth, the percentage of units recorded in areas AES and A2 that were activated to more than 25, 50, or 75% of their maximum firing levels. The plots suggest that a sound source at a level 40 dB above threshold located nearly anywhere on the side contralateral to the recording site would activate nearly all units to at least half of their maximal rates. Similarly, sounds at most contralateral locations would activate about 70% of units to more than 75% of their maximum rates. That is, a model that relied on spike counts to code locations in contralateral space would require that nearly all units discriminate locations with counts restricted to the maximum half of their dynamic ranges (i.e., spike counts could range between 50 and 100% of maximum). Indeed, the majority of units would need to operate in the upper quarter of their dynamic ranges (75 to 100% of maximum).

A topographical model of spatial coding in the cortex would require that the spatial preferences of units vary systematically as a function of the locations of units in the cortex. In support of a topographical model, the studies described above found that units that are located close together in the cortex generally tend to show similar spatial sensitivity. For instance, Middlebrooks and

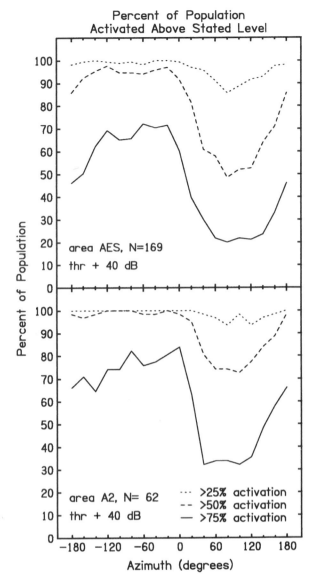

FIGURE 30.2 Percentage of unit population activated by sound sources at various azimuths. These plots are derived from normalized spike-count data from 169 units recorded in area AES (top) or 62 units recorded in area A2 (bottom). The three lines in each panel show the percentages of the units that were activated above 25, 50, or 75% of each unit's maximum spike count by a noise burst that was 40 dB above each unit's threshold. Data are plotted as a function of sound-source azimuth. (Modified from Middlebrooks et al., 1998.)

Pettigrew (1981) found clusters of units that showed the same receptive field class. Units within a particular receptive field class, however, often occupied multiple clusters that were separated by units within a different receptive field class. Subsequent studies have confirmed the tendency of units with similar spatial tuning to aggregate in the cortex (Rajan et al., 1990b; Clarey, Barone, and Imig, 1994). Some studies have demonstrated examples of sequences of units along as much as 1.5 mm of electrode tracks across the cortex that showed systematic changes in spatial preferences (Imig, Irons, and Samson, 1990; Middlebrooks et al., 1998). Such sequences of units, however, were interspersed among sequences of units that showed very different spatial sensitivity. Investigators who have searched for spatial topography in areas A1, A2, or AES have consistently concluded that the organization that they found was not consistent with an integrated cortical map of auditory space.

Spatial information carried by neuronal spike patterns

In a conventional view of spatial coding, one assumes that activity in a single neuron is dedicated to coding a particular location in space. In that view, the broad spatial tuning of most auditory cortical neurons is a liability. Viewed another way, however, broad tuning might be an asset. The raster plot in figure 30.3 shows the spike patterns of a single unit elicited by sound sources at various locations. Throughout 360° of azimuth, the patterns varied in the number of spikes and in the timing within each burst of spikes. To the degree that various spike patterns of a unit are characteristic of specific locations, the activity of a unit might carry information about

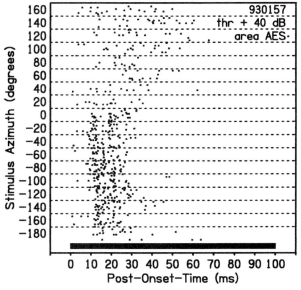

FIGURE 30.3 Responses of unit 930157. This raster plot shows the responses of a unit to 100-ms noise bursts presented at various azimuths. Each dot represents one spike from the unit. Each row of dots represents the spike pattern in response to one stimulus presentation. Stimulus azimuths were varied randomly, but in this plot responses are sorted according to stimulus azimuth as indicated on the vertical axis. Eight trials at each azimuth are represented. The filled bar at the bottom represents the duration of the stimulus. (Modified from Middlebrooks et al., 1998.)

many sound-source locations. That is, single units might code location *panoramically*. We have tested that hypothesis by attempting to identify sound-source locations by recognizing spike patterns of single units (Middlebrooks et al., 1994, 1998).

To test location coding by single units, we recorded multiple responses to sounds at each of a number of locations, then formed a *training set* from the responses in odd-numbered trials and a *test set* from the responses in even-numbered trials. The training set was used to train a computer algorithm to recognize the spike patterns associated with particular sound-source locations, and the test set was used to test the accuracy of such recognition. The isolation of training and test sets provided a form of cross validation of pattern recognition. Spike patterns from single trials proved to be too sparse to provide adequate recognition, often containing only one or two spikes. For that reason we formed multiple bootstrap averages of ensembles of eight trials. Bootstrap averages, formed by drawing multiple samples with replacement from a limited sample of responses, served to estimate the variance within an unlimited population (Efron and Tibshirani, 1991). We tested a variety of computer pattern-recognition algorithms and obtained satisfying results with several. The results presented here were obtained with a two-layer feedforward perceptron, which is a type of artificial neural network (Rumelhart, Hinton, and Williams, 1986). The inputs to the network were spike density functions quantized in fifty 1-ms bins, and the output was a scalar estimate of sound-source azimuth (details of the network architecture are given in Middlebrooks et al., 1998). We used bootstrap-average responses from the training set to train the network, then we presented responses from the test set to the trained network and measured the accuracy with which the network estimated sound-source azimuth.

Figure 30.4 shows the performance of an artificial neural network in estimating sound-source azimuth based on the responses of the unit represented in figure 30.3. Each plus sign represents the network output in response to one bootstrap-average spike pattern. The solid line shows the mean of the estimates at each source location. The dashed line with positive slope represents the loci of perfect estimates and the two dashed lines with negative slope represent loci of perfect front/back confusions (i.e., estimates that were mirror-symmetric to the source location with respect to the interaural axis). The mean-direction line tracks the perfect-performance line throughout most of the 360° of azimuth. The mean-direction line makes an abrupt jump across source locations 0° and ipsilateral 20°. That is the range of azimuths at which this and many other units showed the greatest change in spike counts. The network output discriminated left

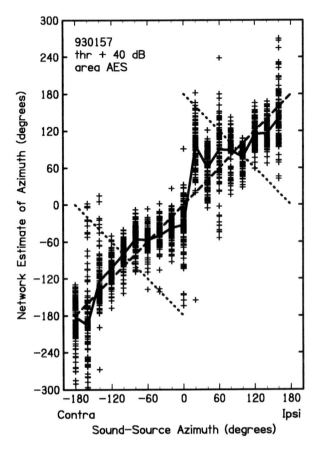

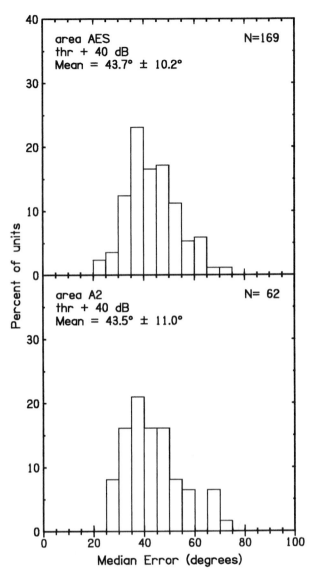

FIGURE 30.4 Network performance for unit 930157. Each plus sign represents the network output in response to input of one bootstrapped pattern. The abscissa represents the actual stimulus azimuth and the ordinate represents the network estimate of azimuth. The solid line connects the mean directions of network estimates for each actual stimulus location. The dashed line with positive slope represents perfect performance, and the two dotted lines with negative slope represent front/back symmetry between stimulus location and network output. (Modified from Middlebrooks et al., 1998.)

FIGURE 30.5 Distributions of median errors. These histograms show the percentages of the units in each sample that produced network performances with particular ranges of median errors. Top and bottom: Areas AES and A2, respectively. Left and right: 20 and 40 dB, respectively, above units' thresholds. (Modified from Middlebrooks et al., 1998.)

from right nearly perfectly except for source locations around the midline, and front/back confusions were fairly infrequent. Contrary to the conventional view that a single neuron is dedicated to coding a single point in space, the responses of this unit distinguished a broad range of locations.

We summarized the localization performance of neural networks by computing the median value of the magnitudes of errors across all trials at all locations. The median error computed in that way is sensitive to both the mean and the dispersion of the network estimates of location. Figure 30.5 shows the distribution of median errors for the units that we studied in areas AES and A2; data are from the condition in which sound levels were fixed at 40 dB above units' thresholds. All of the units in our sample produced median errors smaller than the value of 90° that is predicted given chance performance.

The median errors varied widely, with mean values of 43.7° for area AES and 43.5° for area A2. The distributions were unimodal, so we had no justification for segregating particular classes of units that were more or less location-sensitive. Nevertheless, one might imagine that the units with relatively small median errors have a greater role in location coding than those with larger median errors.

As noted, the spatial tuning of spike counts often changed with changes in stimulus level so, of course, changes in level normally resulted in changes in spike patterns. For that reason, a network that was trained

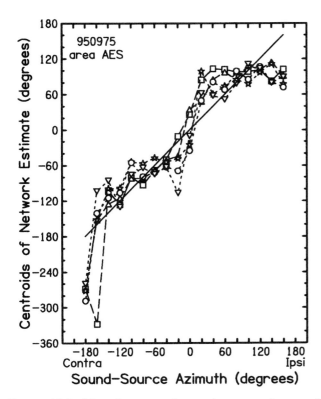

FIGURE 30.6   Mean directions of network output at five sound levels. An artificial neural network was trained with the responses of unit 950975 to noise bursts that roved in level from 20 to 40 dB above threshold in 5-dB steps. A test set contained responses from the same unit to stimuli at those same levels. Each line style indicates the mean direction of network output in recognition of responses in the test set to sounds of a single level. The steep slopes of the lines near –180° and 0° reflect the sharp changes in spike patterns across the rear and front midlines.

with responses to stimuli at one level tended to perform poorly in recognition of responses to stimuli at another level. Nevertheless, when networks were trained with responses to stimuli that roved across multiple levels, they were reasonably successful in recognizing responses to stimuli at any level within the trained range. Figure 30.6 shows the performance of a network that was trained with responses that roved in 5-dB steps between 20 and 40 dB above a unit's threshold. Here, network estimates are represented only by mean-direction lines. Each line represents classification of responses to a single sound level. Even though the same set of network weights was used to test all levels, the network was able to generalize across responses to all five sound levels. Note the sharp discrimination of locations across the front and rear midlines (i.e., near 0 and –180°). Apparently, the training procedure identified level-invariant features of spike patterns that carried azimuth-related information.

We favor the interpretation that the neurons we studied were adapted to code sound-source location. An alternative interpretation, however, is that the neurons

were sensitive only to a particular acoustical cue, such as interaural level difference, that happened to covary with azimuth. We tested the latter hypothesis by measuring the sensitivity of cortical units to the elevation of sound sources in the vertical midline. In the vertical midline, interaural difference cues are negligible and the principal cue for location presumably is the elevation-dependent transformation of spectral shape by one or both external ears. We recorded the responses of units to sound sources at various elevations, then performed a neural-network analysis analogous to our analysis of azimuth coding. Figure 30.7 shows the median errors of units in azimuth and elevation; the dashed lines indicate the means of the samples in each dimension. There was a weak but significant correlation between localization performance in azimuth and elevation. Generally, the units that coded azimuth well also coded elevation well. This suggests that single units can combine information from interaural difference cues and from spectral shape cues. It supports the interpretation that at least some of these neurons are adapted to code sound-source location.

Information-bearing features of neuronal spike patterns

The majority of studies of sensory coding by neurons tend to represent the responses of neurons only by the magnitudes of responses, i.e., either by the spike rate or by a count of spikes within a particular interval. We wished to test whether the magnitudes of responses captured all of the location-related information in spike patterns, or whether the timing of spikes might carry additional information. As an empirical test, we configured artificial neural networks to estimate sound-source azimuth by recognizing spike counts alone. We compared localization performance based on recognition of spike counts with that based on recognition of complete spike patterns, which contained both response magnitude and response timing. Figure 30.8 shows that comparison for units in area AES (top) and area A2 (bottom). On average, median errors were significantly greater when the neural network analyzed only spike counts than when the network analyzed complete spike patterns. A few of the points in the plots lie near the lines that indicates equal performance of spike counts and spike patterns. The bulk of the distributions, however, lay well above the line, in some cases showing median errors for spike-count recognition that were twice as large as the errors for spike-pattern recognition.

We have begun to explore specific features of spike timing that might carry location-related information

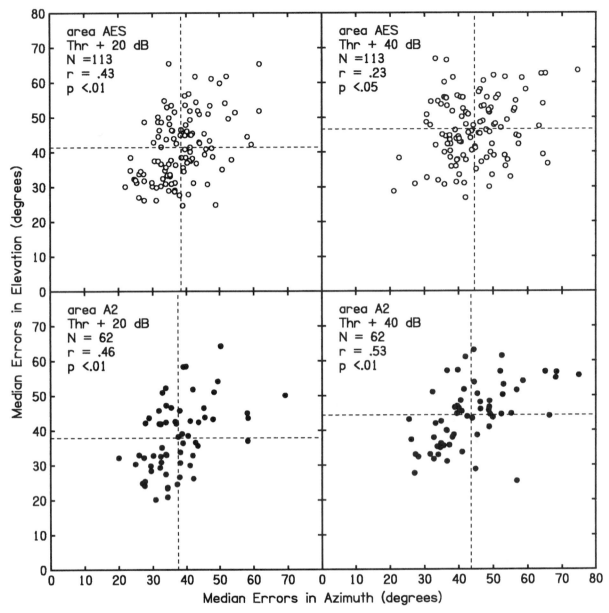

FIGURE 30.7 Correlation between network performance in azimuth and elevation. Each dot in the scatterplots represents, for one unit, the median error of the network performance in elevation versus that in azimuth. The upper and lower rows of panels show data from areas AES and A2, respectively. The left and right columns of panels show data measured with stimuli 20 and 40 dB, respectively, above unit thresholds. The distribution of points in each panel showed a significant positive correlation. (From Xu et al., 1998.)

(Middlebrooks and Xu, 1996). In addition to spike counts, we have had some success with the *mean spike latency*, i.e., the mean of the latencies of all spikes within a spike pattern. Computation of mean latency was possible only because nearly all of the spike patterns that we observed consisted of a discrete burst of spikes, typically 10 to 50 ms in duration, at the onset of the stimulus (see figure 30.3 for an example). The mean latency is influenced by the first-spike latency and by the duration of each spike pattern. Figure 30.9 shows profiles of spike counts and mean latencies of one unit as a function of sound-source azimuth. Across many azimuths, the spike count clearly was modulated by source locations, and mean latencies were rather constant. In other ranges of azimuth, indicated by the solid bars, sound sources produced spike counts that were relatively constant but mean latencies that were modulated by source location. This example shows but one way in which spike timing could provide location-related information that supplements information carried by spike counts.

We have used an analysis-of-variance procedure to compute the percentage of the variance in spike patterns

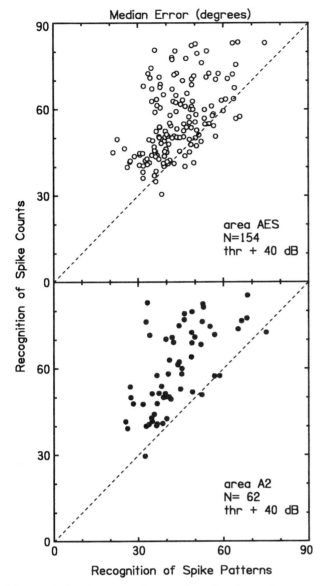

FIGURE 30.8 Accuracy of azimuth coding by spike counts and by complete spike patterns. This plot shows the accuracy of artificial-neural-network estimation of sound-source azimuth based on full spike patterns and spike counts. Full patterns (abscissa) consisted of spike density functions expressed with 1-ms resolution. Spike counts (ordinate) were the total number of spikes in each density function–i.e., the area under the density function. Top and bottom: Areas AES and A2. (From Middlebrooks et al., 1998.)

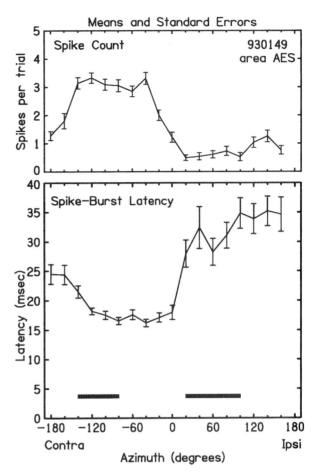

FIGURE 30.9 Azimuth profiles from mean spike count and mean latency. Data are from unit 930149 in area AES. Spike counts were averaged across all trials at each sound-source azimuth. Mean latencies were computed only for trials in which one or more spikes were recorded. Error bars are + or − standard error of the mean.

accounted for by spike counts, by mean latencies, and by some other measures of spike timing. For most of our sample, the spike count was the single term that accounted for the most variance, averaging nearly 40% of the variance. The variance in spike patterns accounted for by mean latencies was substantial, however, averaging around 25% across all units. In a few instances, mean latencies were closely correlated with spike counts, so mean latencies provided no information additional to

that available from spike counts. More often, however, the correlations between spike counts and mean latencies were very low, so the two terms were essentially independent.

We tested the capacity of spike latencies to provide independent location-related information. We configured neural networks either with spike counts as the only input or with two inputs consisting of spike counts and a mean-latency term. Addition of the mean-latency term substantially improved localization performance of the network. Localization based on two inputs was nearly as accurate as localization based on recognition of full spike patterns. We speculate that the difference in localization performance that remained between the two-input and the full-pattern networks was due to information that was carried by details of the timing of spikes within bursts that were not captured by the mean latency.

Throughout the preceding analysis, the timing of spikes was expressed in the form of latencies relative to

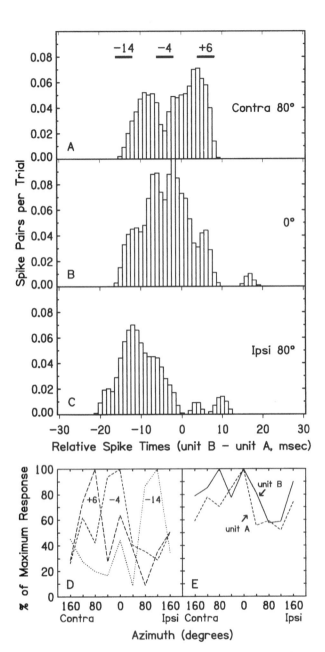

FIGURE 30.10 Relative spike times between two units. (A, B, C) Each bar represents the frequency of occurrence of a particular relative spike time measured between units A and B. Sound-source locations were contralateral 80° (A), 0° (B), and ipsilateral 80° (C) relative to the side of the recording site. The line segments numbered −14, −4, and +6 represent 4-ms relative-time windows centered at the indicated times. (D) Each line style shows, as a function of sound-source azimuth, the probability of recording a pair of spikes with relative times falling within a 4-ms window centered at the specified time. The profiles are normalized to 100%. (E) Different line styles show normalized spike counts versus sound-source azimuth for units A and B individually. (Modified from Middlebrooks, 1998.)

the onset of the stimulus. The onset time was known with microsecond precision to the investigator, but latency information would be of little use to an animal

without an independent signal to mark the sound onset time. We have begun to explore an alternative, that information might be coded by the *relative* timing among spikes in multiple units. We used a silicon-substrate probe (Wise, Angell, and Starr, 1970) to record simultaneously from units at multiple cortical sites. Figure 30.10 shows an analysis of one pair of units. Panels A, B, and C show the distribution of spike times in one unit ("unit B") expressed relative to the times of spikes in another unit ("unit A"). The distributions shifted along the relative-time axis as the sound source location was varied among contralateral 80°, 0° and ipsilateral 80°.

One could imagine that a downstream neuron, or a behaving animal, might respond differently to spike pairs falling at different relative times, and such differential responses have been demonstrated (e.g., Segundo et al., 1963). We modeled an interneuronal comparator by counting the number of spike pairs that fell within restricted relative-time windows as a function of sound-source azimuth. Figure 30.10D plots the result of that computation for three 4-ms time windows centered at relative times of +6, − 4, and −14 ms; those time windows are represented by line segments at the top of figure 30.10A. The probability of spike pairs at particular relative times was in this example substantially more azimuth-sensitive than were the spike counts of units A and B, taken individually (as shown in figure 30.10E). This simple analysis hints of a way to begin thinking about stimulus coding by the coordinated activity among populations of neurons.

Conclusions

Area A1 of the auditory cortex contains a well-known example of a topographic representation, known as "tonotopic organization," in which low-to-high sound frequencies are represented by the caudal-to-rostral position of maximally activated neurons (Merzenich, Knight, and Roth, 1975). In that representation, processing of sounds of a particular frequency appears to be assigned to a restricted region of cortex. In contrast, the representation of sound-source location in any of the auditory cortical areas that have been explored appears not to be topographic. Single units are broadly tuned for source location, their tuning changes with changes in stimulus level, and the progression of preferred locations across the cortical surface is at best fragmented. The results that we have obtained favor a different, *distributed*, organization in which the responses of single neurons code locations across a broad range, and accurate sound localization is derived from information that is distributed among neurons throughout a cortical field.

This distributed organization contrasts with the precise retinotopic organization with which we are familiar in the primary visual cortex. Yet, as one moves higher in the extrastriate visual cortical hierarchy, the precision of retinotopy successively deteriorates. It would be surprising if the object of higher-level cortical processing were to degrade spatial precision. It seems more likely that, at higher levels of the visual hierarchy, visual space is coded in some form that does not require a precise point-to-point cortical topography. In the primary auditory pathway, there is no spatial topography imposed by the organization of the auditory periphery, so it is perhaps not surprising that space coding takes a nontopographical form.

The notion that stimulus-related information might be coded by the timing of neuronal spikes is well established in auditory nerve and auditory brainstem research. Coding by spike timing in the auditory cortex is more novel. In the visual system, information-theoretic analyses have demonstrated that some three to five dimensions of spike patterns, including magnitude and timing dimensions, can carry stimulus-related information (e.g., Richmond and Optican, 1987). The issue of information coding by temporal details of spike patterns is, however, a matter of some controversy in the visual literature (Shadlen and Newsome, 1994; Softky, 1995). In our work in the auditory cortex, raster plots of spike patterns show conspicuous stimulus dependence, and errors in decoding of sound-source locations can double when temporal features of spike patterns are discarded. The stimulus dependence of cortical spike timing presumably is a product of neural transmission delays and membrane time constants, and one might guess that similar mechanisms are available for decoding of information stored in spike times.

If we speculate about mechanisms by which biological neural networks might decode spike patterns, we move perilously close to a model that demands neurons that are sharply tuned for sound-source locations. Such neurons have been sought throughout much of the auditory cortex largely without success. An alternative view, which we favor, is that there is no overt decoding of spike patterns by single neurons and that, instead, the decoded information exists only in the behavior or perception of the whole animal. In ongoing experiments we are exploring the principles by which the magnitude and timing of spike patterns might act to synchronize specific subpopulations of neurons, thereby selecting those subpopulations to contribute to behavioral output.

ACKNOWLEDGMENTS I am pleased to acknowledge the contributions of my colleagues Drs. Ann Clock Eddins, David M. Green, Li Xu, and Shigeto Furukawa in collecting and analyzing data and in helping to develop many of the ideas presented here. Ms. Zekiye Onsan provided expert technical assistance. I am grateful for research funding from the NIDCD.

REFERENCES

BRUGGE, J. F., R. A. REALE, and J. E. HIND, 1996. The structure of spatial receptive fields of neurons in primary auditory cortex of the cat. *J. Neurosci.* 16:4420–4437.

BRUGGE, J. F., R. A. REALE, J. E. HIND, J. C. K. CHAN, A. D. MUSICANT, and P. W. F. POON, 1994. Simulation of free-field sound sources and its application to studies of cortical mechanisms of sound localization in the cat. *Hear. Res.* 73:67–84.

CLAREY, J. C., P. BARONE, and T. J. IMIG, 1994. Functional organization of sound direction and sound pressure level in primary auditory cortex of the cat. *J. Neurophysiol.* 72:2383–2405.

EFRON, B., and R. TIBSHIRANI, 1991. Statistical analysis in the computer age. *Science* 253:390–395.

GEORGOPOULOS, A. T., R. E. KETTNER, and A. B. SCHWARTZ, 1988. Primate motor cortex and free arm movements to visual targets in three-dimensional space. II. Coding of the direction of movement by a neuronal population. *J. Neurosci.* 8:2928–2937.

GREENE, T. C., 1929. The ability to localize sound: A study of binaural hearing in patients with tumor of the brain. *Arch. Surg.* 18:1825–1841.

HINTON, G. E., J. L. McCLELLAND, and D. E. RUMELHART, 1986. Distributed representations. In *Parallel Distributed Processing. Explorations in the Microstructure of Cognition.* Vol. 1: *Foundations*, D. E. Rumelhart, J. L. McClelland, and PDP Research Group, eds. Cambridge, Mass.: MIT Press, pp. 77–109.

IMIG, T. J., W. A. IRONS, and F. R. SAMSON, 1990. Single-unit selectivity to azimuthal direction and sound pressure level of noise bursts in cat high-frequency primary auditory cortex. *J. Neurophysiol.* 63:1448–1466.

JENKINS, W. M., and R. B. MASTERTON, 1982. Sound localization: Effects of unilateral lesions in central auditory system. *J. Neurophysiol.* 47:987–1016.

JENKINS, W. M., and M. M. MERZENICH, 1984. Role of cat primary auditory cortex for sound-localization behavior. *J. Neurophysiol.* 52:819–847.

KLINGON, G. H., and D. C. BONTECOU, 1966. Localization in auditory space. *Neurol.* 16:879–886.

KNUDSEN, E. I., 1982. Auditory and visual maps of space in the optic tectum of the owl. *J. Neurosci.* 2:1177–1194.

KORTE, M., and J. P. RAUSCHECKER, 1993. Auditory spatial tuning of cortical neurons is sharpened in cats with early blindness. *J. Neurophysiol.* 70:1717–1721.

MEREDITH, M. A., and H. R. CLEMO, 1989. Auditory cortical projection from the anterior ectosylvian sulcus (field AES) to the superior colliculus in the cat: An anatomical and electrophysiological study. *J. Comp. Neurol.* 289:687–707.

MERZENICH, M. M., P. L. KNIGHT, and G. L. ROTH, 1975. Representation of cochlea within primary auditory cortex in the cat. *J. Neurophysiol.* 38:231–249.

MIDDLEBROOKS, J. C., 1998. Location coding by auditory cortical neurons. In *Central Auditory Processing and Neural Modeling*, J. F. Brugge and P. Poon, eds. New York: Plenum, pp. 139–148.

MIDDLEBROOKS, J. C., A. E. CLOCK, L. XU, and D. M. GREEN, 1994. A panoramic code for sound location by cortical neurons. *Science* 264:842–844.

MIDDLEBROOKS, J. C., and D. M. GREEN, 1991. Sound localization by human listeners. *Annu. Rev. Psychol.* 42:135–159.

MIDDLEBROOKS, J. C., and J. D. PETTIGREW, 1981. Functional classes of neurons in primary auditory cortex of the cat distinguished by sensitivity to sound location. *J. Neurosci.* 1:107–120.

MIDDLEBROOKS, J. C., and L. XU, 1996. Information-bearing elements of spike trains in the cat's auditory cortex. *Abstr. Neurosci.* 424.16:1068.

MIDDLEBROOKS, J. C., L. XU, A. E. CLOCK, and D. M. GREEN, 1998. Codes for sound-source location in non-tonotopic auditory cortex. *J. Neurophysiol.* 80:863–881.

RAJAN, R., L. M. AITKIN, and D. R. F. IRVINE, 1990a. Azimuthal sensitivity of neurons in primary auditory cortex of cats. II. Organization along frequency-band strips. *J. Neurophysiol.* 64:888–902.

RAJAN, R., L. M. AITKIN, D. R. F. IRVINE, and J. MCKAY, 1990b. Azimuthal sensitivity of neurons in primary auditory cortex of cats. I. Types of sensitivity and the effects of variations in stimulus parameters. *J. Neurophysiol.* 64:872–887.

RICHMOND, B. J., and L. M. OPTICAN, 1987. Temporal encoding of two-dimensional patterns by single units in primate inferior temporal cortex. II. Quantification of response waveform. *J. Neurophysiol.* 57:147–161.

RUMELHART, D. E., G. E. HINTON, and R. J. WILLIAMS, 1986. Learning internal representations by error propagation. In *Parallel Distributed Processing. Explorations in the Microstructure of Cognition.* Vol. 1: *Foundations,* D. E. Rumelhart, J. L. McClelland, and PDP Research Group, eds. Cambridge, Mass.: MIT Press, pp. 318–362.

SANCHEZ-LONGO, L. P., and F. M. FORSTER, 1958. Clinical significance of impairment of sound localization. *Neurol.* 8:119–125.

SEGUNDO, J. P., G. P. MOORE, L. J. STENSAAS, and T. H. BULLOCK, 1963. Sensitivity of neurones in Aplysia to temporal pattern of arriving impulses. *J. Exp. Biol.* 40:643–667.

SHADLEN, M. N., and W. T. NEWSOME, 1995. Is there a signal in the noise? *Curr. Opin. Neurobiol.* 5:248–250.

SOFTKY, W. R., 1995. Simple codes versus efficient codes. *Curr. Opin. Neurobiol.* 5:239–247.

THOMPSON, G. C., and R. B. MASTERTON, 1978. Brain stem auditory pathways involved in reflexive head orientation to sound. *J. Neurophysiol.* 41:1183–1202.

WISE, K. D., J. B. ANGELL, and A. STARR, 1970. An integrated circuit approach to extracellular microelectrodes. *IEEE Trans. Biomed. Eng.* 17:238–247.

WORTIS, S. B., and A. Z. PFEIFFER, 1948. Unilateral auditory-spatial agnosia. *J. Nerv. Ment. Dis.* 108:181–186.

XU, L., S. FURUKAWA, and J. C. MIDDLEBROOKS, 1998. Sensitivity to sound-source elevation in non-tonotopic auditory cortex. *J. Neurophysiol.* 80:882–894.

31 Sensory Convergence in Neural Function and Development

ANDREW J. KING AND JAN W. H. SCHNUPP

ABSTRACT   Perhaps one of the biggest challenges for sensory networks is to permit convergence of information from different processing channels that is both functionally and developmentally appropriate. Neurons in the superior colliculus receive converging inputs from different sensory modalities. This allows excitatory and inhibitory interactions to take place, which process the spatiotemporal relationship between diverse sensory signals. These interactions occur within the framework of topographically aligned sensory maps, which appear to mediate rapid, goal-directed behavior in a multisensory environment. Visual and somatosensory maps arise from spatially ordered projections from their receptor surfaces. In contrast, the synthesis of a computational map of auditory space requires that neurons become tuned to matching values of monaural and binaural localization cues that are initially encoded in separate brainstem pathways. Merging auditory and visual representations in the superior colliculus during development is an activity-dependent process, in which visual signals, possibly arising from the superficial layers of this nucleus, are used to adjust auditory spatial tuning.

Coding of sensory information within and across modalities

A fundamental question in sensory physiology is the manner in which behaviorally significant information is encoded and processed by neurons in the brain (Ferster and Spruston, 1995; Rieke et al., 1997). For single neurons, the parameters of sensory signals can be specified by variations in the frequency at which nerve impulses are generated (rate coding) and by the precise timing of those impulses (temporal coding). Within populations of neurons that differ in their sensitivities, stimulus parameters are represented by spatiotemporal patterns of activity, and, in many areas of the brain, the tuning of neighboring neurons varies systematically to form sensory maps (place coding). Recent work has focused on synchronization of discharges among different groups of neurons as an additional and potentially highly versatile way of signaling sensory events. Identifying whether the brain actually uses these strategies as a means of encoding sensory information is very difficult. Nevertheless,

valuable insights have been obtained from modeling studies and by relating behavioral performance to normal or experimentally induced abnormal patterns of neural activity (Laurent, 1997; Middlebrooks, chapter 30, this volume; Rieke et al., 1997). What does seem certain is that the relative contribution of different coding schemes varies both within and across different sensory systems.

Sensory maps are ubiquitous in the brain and offer several advantages for analyzing information. For example, lateral interactions between neighboring neurons tuned to adjacent positions in stimulus space can compute contrast or generate sensitivity to stimulus motion. Although mapping is certainly not essential for extracting new features in the environment, this arrangement does provide an efficient use of neural connections.

Perhaps the best examples of neural maps that can be related to stimulus coding are so-called computational representations (Knudsen, du Lac, and Esterly, 1987) that are isomorphic with some aspect of the outside world, but which are not directly related to the anatomical arrangement of axons leaving the receptor cells. Among these are maps of auditory space in the midbrain of barn owls (Knudsen, du Lac, and Esterly, 1987; Konishi, 1995) and mammals (King and Carlile, 1995), which are brought into register in the superior colliculus (SC) with projectional maps of visual space and of the body surface (figure 31.1). As a consequence, the different sensory signals from a single object in space converge on common motor output pathways and evoke shifts in gaze toward the location of that target. The alignment of visual, auditory, and somatosensory maps also provides a means by which different sensory modalities can interact to determine the responses of SC neurons. As the distributed representations of the posterior parietal cortex illustrate (Andersen et al., 1997), interfacing sensory and motor processing need not necessarily take place within a topographically organized framework. But in the SC, a nucleus concerned primarily with reflex orienting movements, the presence of congruent sensory and motor maps appears to optimize the neural

ANDREW J. KING and JAN W. H. SCHNUPP   University Laboratory of Physiology, Oxford, United Kingdom

437

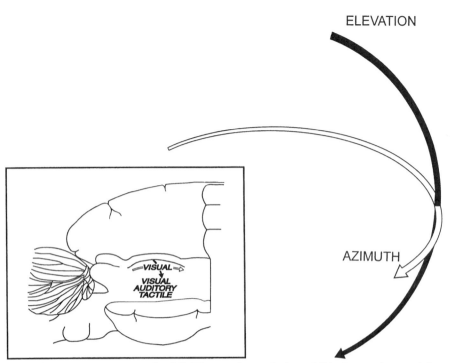

ELEVATION

AZIMUTH

VISUAL
VISUAL
AUDITORY
TACTILE

FIGURE 31.1   Representation of sensory space in the SC. The inset shows a sketch of the SC in the ferret midbrain. The superficial layers are exclusively visual, whereas the deeper layers receive multimodal inputs. Stimulus azimuth is mapped onto the rostrocaudal axis (white arrow), and elevation onto the mediolateral (black arrow) axis of the nucleus. The portion of visual and auditory space represented within the SC is indicated by the arrows to the right, and corresponds approximately to the extent of the visual field of the contralateral eye.

circuitry in ways that are computationally efficient and hence amenable to experimental investigation.

Implications of multisensory convergence at the neuronal level

One of the most interesting properties of multisensory neurons, both in the SC and elsewhere in the brain, is that their responses can be modulated according to the spatiotemporal relationships between converging stimuli from different modalities. Compared to their responses to individual stimuli presented alone, these neurons may exhibit significantly enhanced firing when stimuli of different modality are delivered in close temporal and spatial proximity (reviewed by Stein and Meredith, 1993). This property, which is known as multisensory facilitation, is thought to increase the salience of events that may activate more than one sense organ, potentially making them easier to detect and localize.

The neural basis for multisensory integration is unknown. Enhancement and occlusion between converging signals could arise if signals are added linearly because the spike activity of neurons is typically a nonlinear function of their inputs. Figure 31.2 illustrates a sigmoidal input–output function in which the response evoked by the linear summation of auditory and visual input signals depends on the operating point along this

function, i.e., on the intensity of the stimuli. This simple mathematical model appears to provide a good approximation for the bimodal responses of SC neurons (figure 31.3; Schnupp et al., 1997). For example, the expansive nonlinearity in the rising phase of the sigmoid correctly predicts that the most pronounced enhancements occur for stimuli just above threshold. It has been suggested that the NMDA class of glutamate receptors might be responsible for enhanced bimodal responses (Binns and Salt, 1996; Stein and Meredith, 1993). However, the multisensory properties observed in the SC are perhaps more easily explained in terms of an essentially linear integration of converging inputs. Summation of inputs followed by nonlinear activation functions may also explain interactions between converging inputs in the visual cortex (Freeman and Ohzawa, 1990), posterior parietal cortex (Andersen et al., 1997) and motor cortex (Capaday, 1997).

Because multisensory facilitation in SC neurons is observed only when each stimulus falls within its excitatory receptive field, the alignment of those receptive fields would appear to be a necessary property if response enhancements are to signal multisensory cues associated with a common source (Stein and Meredith, 1993). Different sensory systems represent spatial information in different coordinates, with those of visual space centered on the retina and those of auditory space

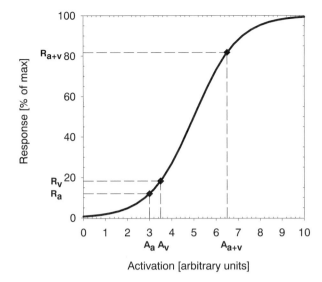

FIGURE 31.2 Schematic illustrating how a neuron with a nonlinear input–output function (sigmoid) might produce greatly facilitated responses ($R_{v+a} > R_v + R_a$) simply by summing input activations linearly ($A_{v+a} = A_v + A_a$). Note that the degree of facilitation depends on the magnitude of the inputs (stimulus intensity), which will determine the operating point along the nonlinear input–output function. For sigmoidal functions, maximum facilitation would be observed for inputs close to unit threshold.

on the ears and head. However, by incorporating signals that relate to the position of the sense organs, the sensory responses of SC neurons appear to be transformed into a single coordinate framework that is commonly referred to as motor-error (Sparks and Groh, 1995). Motor-error coordinates indicate the difference or error between current eye position and the location of the sensory target. This coordinate transformation is a necessary requirement if information from different modalities is to be combined in a meaningful manner and used to guide orientation movements to stimuli irrespective of their modality.

Construction of topographically aligned sensory maps in the superior colliculus

Neural maps of visual and auditory space are constructed in different ways. By acting like a camera, the eye forms a map of visual space on the retina. This map is preserved, albeit in a slightly distorted form, at different levels of the brain as a result of topographically organized projections. Spatially ordered projections also arise from the cochlea, but result in central maps of sound frequency, not source location. The first step in matching the inputs of different modalities in the SC is therefore the synthesis within the brain of a map of auditory space. This is achieved by tuning neurons to acoustic localization cues

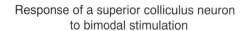
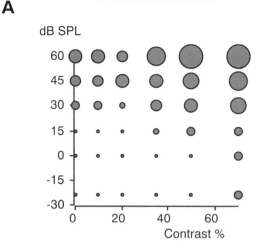
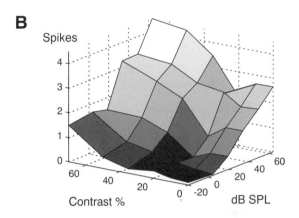
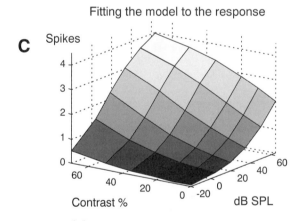

FIGURE 31.3 (A) Visual–auditory joint-sensitivity function of a bimodal unit in the deeper layers of the ferret SC, measured with simultaneously presented visual (sinusoidally modulated luminance) and auditory (broadband noise) stimuli. Each of the gray filled circles has a radius proportional to the spike count (per stimulus presentation) obtained at the contrast/ sound pressure level combination indicated by the axes. (B) Same data as in A, shown as a 3D surface plot. (C) Predicted responses obtained by fitting a sigmoidal model (logistic equation) to the data shown in A and B.

that correspond to different directions in space (King and Carlile, 1995; Konishi, 1995; Middlebrooks and Green, 1991). These cues include interaural time differences (ITDs), which are determined by the distance between the ears, and interaural level differences (ILDs), which result from the directional filtering properties of the external ears plus the shadowing effect of the head. In addition, the direction-dependent changes in the sound spectrum imposed by the external ears can be used, under some circumstances, to localize sounds monaurally (King and Carlile, 1995; Middlebrooks and Green, 1991).

To a large extent, the initial processing of these auditory localization cues takes place within separate pathways of the brain stem. In mammals, auditory nerve fibers carry signals from the cochlea to the ventral (VCN) and dorsal cochlear nuclei (DCN). The processing of binaural localization cues begins in the superior olivary complex, which receives converging inputs from each VCN. As a result of their synaptic and biophysical specializations, some VCN cells transmit temporal information with great fidelity to the medial superior olive (MSO), where sensitivity to ITDs of the order of tens of microseconds emerges (Oertel, 1997). Neurons in the lateral superior olive (LSO) receive a direct excitatory projection from the ipsilateral VCN and an indirect inhibitory projection from the contralateral side. Consequently, they are sensitive to ILDs. MSO and LSO neurons then relay ITD and ILD information, respectively, to the midbrain. The pathways that process monaural spectral cues are still largely unexplored. However, both physiological (Young et al., 1992) and behavioral (May, 1998) studies suggest an involvement of the DCN, which projects directly to the midbrain.

The spatial selectivity of neurons in the mammalian SC appears to be based on ILDs and monaural spectral localization cues (King and Carlile, 1995). The synthesis of a map of auditory space therefore involves the correct merging of spatial information from different brainstem circuits. As part of this process, inputs are also combined across different frequency channels to produce the broad and often complex spectral tuning of SC neurons. Only recently has evidence been obtained to indicate whether in mammals the representation of auditory space first emerges at the level of the SC or is relayed there from other auditory areas.

The mammalian SC is innervated by several auditory areas in the brain stem and cortex (e.g., Edwards et al., 1979; King, Jiang, and Moore, 1998; Meredith and Clemo, 1989). In most species, the largest inputs arise from the ipsilateral inferior colliculus, particularly the nucleus of the brachium (BIN) and the external nucleus (ICX) of that structure. The projection from the ipsilat-

eral BIN to the SC is spatially organized, with rostral and caudal regions of the BIN projecting primarily to corresponding regions of the SC (King, Jiang, and Moore, 1998; figure 31.4). At sound levels high enough to stimulate both ears, a topographic representation of sound azimuth is found along this axis in both nuclei (Schnupp and King, 1997; figure 31.5A,C). In addition to this place code or map of auditory space, some neurons show variations in spike latency and temporal discharge pattern with sound source location. This would suggest

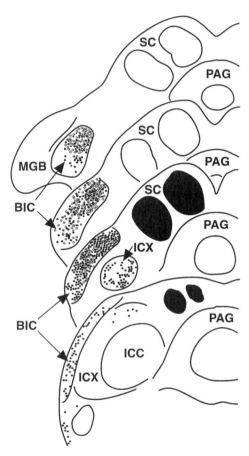

FIGURE 31.4 Distribution of retrograde labeling in subcortical auditory structures after injections of green fluorescent microspheres into rostral SC and red microspheres into caudal SC. The frontal sections are arranged from rostral (top) to caudal (bottom). The open and filled areas in the SC indicate the injection sites of green and red tracers, respectively. The small open and filled circles show the positions of retrogradely green or red labeled cells, respectively. The small asterisks indicate doubly labeled cells. The pattern of labeling indicates that the projection to the SC from the nucleus of the brachium of the inferior colliculus may be spatially ordered along the rostrocaudal axis. More limited labeling is also found in the contralateral auditory midbrain and in other auditory brainstem nuclei. BIC = brachium of the inferior colliculus, MGB = medial geniculate body, ICX = external nucleus of the inferior colliculus, ICC = central nucleus of the inferior colliculus, PAG = periaqueductal gray. (Data from King, Jiang, and Moore, 1998.)

Superior Colliculus

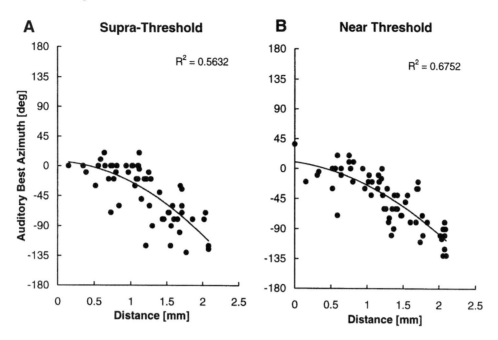

Brachium of the Inferior Colliculus

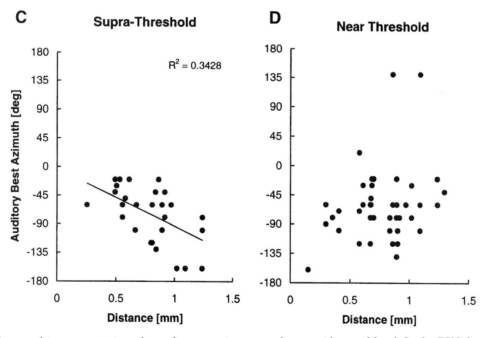

FIGURE 31.5 Topographic representation of sound source azimuth in the SC (A,B) and in the BIN (C,D). The suprathreshold data were obtained at 25–30 dB and the near threshold data at 10–15 dB above unit threshold. The topography in the SC is best described by a second-order polynomial, and does

not change with sound level. In the BIN, however, a systematic relationship between best sound azimuth and recording site is apparent only at suprathreshold sound levels. (From Schnupp and King, 1997, with permission.)

that, as in the auditory cortex (Middlebrooks, chapter 30, this volume), multiple forms of stimulus coding may operate simultaneously in the midbrain (Schnupp and King, 1997).

In comparison to the SC, auditory neurons in the BIN are less sharply tuned for sound direction, exhibit a greater incidence of ambiguous tuning to two or more sound directions and, in terms of the distribution

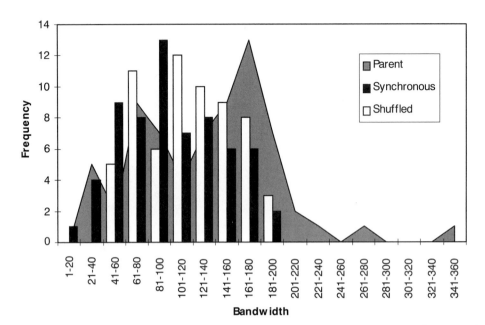

FIGURE 31.6   Convergence of inputs to the SC may sharpen auditory spatial tuning. Distribution of 50% spatial bandwidths (azimuth profile widths in degrees at 50% of maximum response) for single unit (gray area) and "bicellular" (black and white bars) response profiles in the BIN. Bicellular response profiles were obtained by counting only those spikes that occurred within 5 ms of a spike fired by another unit recorded simultaneously with the same electrode. For unit pairs whose firing was significantly correlated (black bars), the bicellular response profiles were significantly more sharply tuned than their parent single-unit response profiles. Possible effects of short-term interactions between single units can be disrupted by "shuffling" the data from repeated presentations of the stimulus. The resulting azimuth profiles (white bars) still show a significant improvement in spatial tuning compared to the single-unit profiles.

of best azimuths, a less precise map of auditory space. Furthermore, although the spatial selectivity of SC neurons remains topographically organized over a range of sound levels (figure 31.5A,B), near-threshold best azimuths do not vary systematically with recording site in the BIN, but are instead clustered around the interaural axis in the contralateral hemifield (figure 31.5D). Sound elevation is also mapped within the SC (King and Carlile, 1993; King, Moore, and Hutchings, 1994), but not apparently in the BIN (Schnupp and King, 1997).

Monaural spectral cues appear to be largely responsible for the azimuth and elevation topography observed in the SC at near threshold sound levels, which is unaffected by occlusion of or cochlear ablation in the ipsilateral ear (King, Moore, and Hutchings, 1994; Palmer and King, 1985). Even at higher sound levels, where SC neurons exhibit a systematic variation in sensitivity to ILDs (Wise and Irvine, 1985), spectral cues are still required to resolve front/back confusions due to the spatially ambiguous nature of binaural cues at individual sound frequencies (Carlile and King, 1994). The lack of both elevation topography and near-threshold azimuth topography, together with the greater incidence of spatially ambiguous response profiles, suggests that a full complement of spectral localization cues may not be en-

coded in the BIN. Presumably, afferents from the ICX, in which a topographic representation of sound azimuth has also been reported (Binns et al., 1992), or other auditory structures contribute additional information that is used in the construction of the two-dimensional map in the SC.

Cues to the importance of converging inputs in the generation of higher-level sensory response properties can be obtained by recording simultaneously from several neurons in the circuit. Recordings from pairs of units in the BIN reveal that azimuth response profiles constructed from spike pairs firing in near synchrony are more sharply tuned than those of the individual neurons of each pair and much more like those of SC neurons (figure 31.6). An improvement in spatial tuning is observed even if short-term correlations in neural activity are removed in the analysis by shuffling the responses to repeated stimulus presentations. This would indicate that active synchronization between neurons is not required, and that simple convergence from different BIN neurons with similar, overlapping response properties could contribute to the more precise representation in the SC. Furthermore, the presence in several auditory brainstem nuclei, including the ICX, of GABAergic neurons that project to the SC (Appell and Behan, 1990), suggests that inhibitory inputs also contribute to shaping the spatial response properties of SC neurons. Given the importance of sensory experience, both auditory and visual, in the development of the auditory space map in the SC (King and Carlile, 1995), it seems likely that activity-dependent mechanisms are involved in selecting the most appropriate combinations of inputs from the BIN and other auditory structures during early life.

Aligning visual and auditory maps during development

The developmental emergence of sensory representations in the brain reflects the maturation of the peripheral sense organs as well as that of the afferent connections and synaptic properties that underlie stimulus processing. Although the projection from the BIN is spatially organized on the day of birth in ferrets (Jiang, King, and Thompson, 1995), the topographic order in the representation of auditory space in the SC matures gradually during the second and third postnatal months (King and Carlile, 1995). Postnatal sharpening of the auditory receptive fields of SC neurons has also been observed both in guinea pigs (Withington-Wray, Binns, and Keating, 1990a) and in cats (Wallace and Stein, 1997). This is likely to be due in part to the maturation of auditory localization cues, which change with the size and shape of the head and ears (King and Carlile, 1995). Nevertheless, the brain stem circuits that process ILDs also undergo maturational changes during normal postnatal development (Sanes, 1993). Moreover, it is now well established that experience-mediated plasticity in the developing auditory representation plays a critical role in establishing the congruence with the map of visual space in the SC (reviewed by King and Carlile, 1995; Knudsen and Brainard, 1995).

A role for vision in refining the development of auditory spatial tuning has emerged from studies in which visual spatial cues have been manipulated during early life. Disrupting the pattern of visual input by binocular eyelid suture in barn owls (Knudsen, Esterly, and du Lac, 1991), guinea pigs (Withington, 1992), and ferrets (King and Carlile, 1993) leads to the development of an auditory representation that tends to possess normal topographic order, but which is nevertheless degraded in various ways. If the visual map is displaced relative to the head by surgical deviation of the eye (King et al., 1988) or by prism rearing (Knudsen and Brainard, 1991), the auditory representation undergoes a corresponding shift so that the two modalities continue to share a common topographic organization.

A similar adaptive change in auditory spatial tuning can be induced by manipulation of the acoustic localization cues available to the developing animal. Occluding one ear will attenuate and change the phase of incoming sounds, thereby altering the ILD and ITD values that correspond to positions in visual space. A period of monaural occlusion in young owls will shift the tuning of neurons in the SC toward these new binaural cue values, particularly if normal visual cues are available (Knudsen and Mogdans, 1992). Removal of the external ear structures, the facial ruff and preaural flap, in this species is also followed by a compensatory change in neuronal tuning to ILDs and especially ITDs (Knudsen, Esterly, and Olsen, 1994). These changes are sufficient to reestablish at least a partial correspondence between the representation of the auditory localization cue values and the map of visual space.

The developing mammalian auditory system appears to possess a similar capacity to adjust to the altered binaural cues produced by occlusion of one ear. If a plug is introduced in infancy, a near normal representation of auditory space develops in the ferret SC (King and Carlile, 1995; King et al., 1988). Unlike in owls, however, disruption of spectral localization cues in infancy does not lead to a compensatory change in mammalian auditory spatial tuning (Schnupp, King, and Carlile, 1998). Even though normal visual cues are present, bilateral removal of the pinna and concha of the external ear in juvenile ferrets degrades the auditory representation in the SC and therefore its alignment with the unchanged visual map (figure 31.7A). Other parts of the auditory pathway are also likely to be affected by abnormal spectral localization cues and, behaviorally, these animals exhibit a similar impairment in their capacity to judge the location of broadband sound sources (Parsons et al., in press; figure 31.7B). Other experimental manipulations that have been carried out in both birds and mammals have revealed a role for sensory experience in aligning the visual and auditory representations in the SC that seems to be quite consistent across different species. The physiological and behavioral consequences of early pinna and concha removal in ferrets appear to indicate a greater dependence on spectral cues provided by the external ears for auditory localization in mammals than in barn owls.

It seems likely that the anatomical projections underlying the auditory map are first established in an experience-independent manner. Correlated visual and auditory activity then appears to be used to refine the auditory spatial tuning of SC neurons, so that map registration is achieved irrespective of individual differences in the size, shape, and relative position of the different

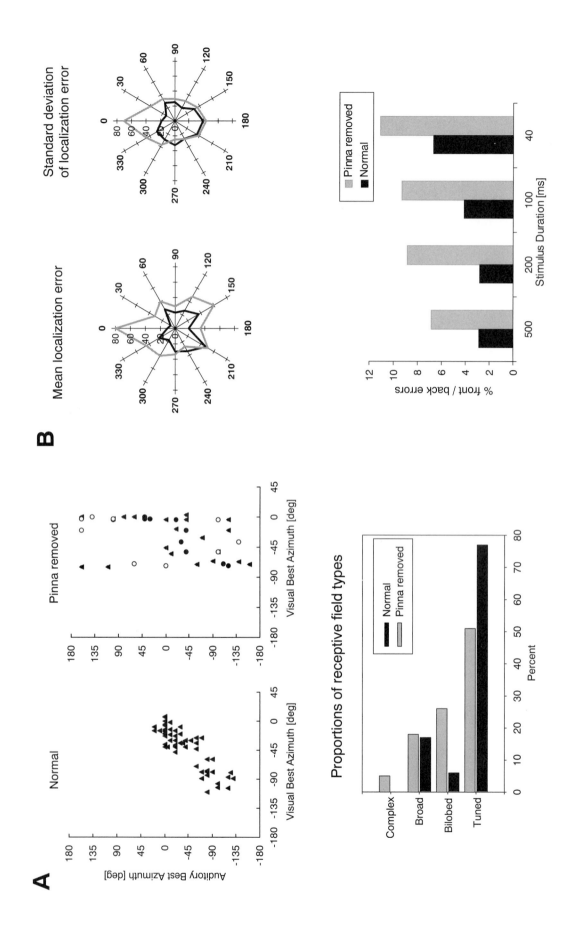

444

sense organs. In each species that has been examined, visual cues play a primary role in calibrating the preferred sound directions of SC auditory neurons. This guiding influence of vision only becomes apparent, however, if sufficient, reliable acoustical information is also available during development.

In recent years, attention has shifted to the neural mechanisms that match auditory and visual signals during development. One possibility is that this may involve a Hebbian mechanism in which auditory inputs are selectively weakened or stabilized according to whether they are active at the same time as visual inputs that converge on the same neuron. In particular, the biophysical properties of NMDA receptors suggest a possible basis for detecting concurrently active synaptic inputs (Fox and Daw, 1993). Much of the evidence implicating NMDA receptors in the development of sensory systems has come from studies showing that blockade of these receptors with appropriate antagonists can prevent the rearrangement of maps that would otherwise occur in response to experimentally manipulated inputs. If synaptic plasticity contributes to normal sensory maturation, and, in particular, to fine-tuning the registration of visual and auditory representations in the SC, it should be possible to disrupt this process through the application of NMDA-receptor antagonists during an appropriate stage of development.

Various techniques are available for the application of drugs to discrete regions of the brain. For example, implants made from Elvax, a slow-release polymer, release agents for a period of up to several months (Schnupp et al., 1995; Smith, Cordery, and Thompson, 1995). Implantation of Elvax containing NMDA-receptor antagonists onto the dorsal surface of the SC in juvenile ferrets specifically interferes with the development of the auditory representation (Schnupp et al., 1995). Chronic application of these antagonists in adult animals does not change the topographic order of either the visual representation in the superficial layers (figure 31.8A) or the auditory representation in the deeper layers (figure 31.8B) of the SC. Consequently, the registration of the maps is unaffected. The visual map is also unaltered in ferrets reared with Elvax implants from before eye opening and the onset of hearing until after the age at which the auditory space map normally emerges (figure 31.8A), most probably because the retinocollicular projection is already mature at implantation (Chalupa and Snider, 1998; King et al., 1996). The auditory representation, in contrast, does not develop normally in these animals (figure 31.8B) and the registration with the unchanged visual map is disrupted. By themselves, these findings do not demonstrate that NMDA receptors subserve a role as coincidence detectors; blocking these receptors may simply reduce synaptic currents to levels below those required to induce plastic changes. Nevertheless, they do confirm the importance of neural activity in establishing the alignment of different sensory maps. As well as providing a possible trigger for the activity-dependent steps that lead to the emergence of a precise and unambiguous representation of auditory space, NMDA-receptor mediated currents appear to be particularly involved in expressing visually guided changes in auditory spatial tuning of midbrain neurons in prism-reared owls (Feldman, Brainard, and Knudsen, 1996).

Besides correlating auditory and visual inputs to the SC, NMDA receptors may play another role in the development of the auditory space map. At sound levels close to unit threshold, the auditory representation in all but the most rostral region of the mammalian SC appears to be derived from monaural pinna cues (King, Moore, and Hutchings, 1994; Palmer and King, 1985), whereas sensitivity to ILDs maintains the topographic order at higher levels (Wise and Irvine, 1985). As discussed above, monaural and binaural localization cues are likely to be processed initially by separate, parallel pathways within the auditory brain stem. The abnormal auditory responses observed following

FIGURE 31.7 Physiological and psychophysical consequences of disrupting spectral localization cues by removal of the pinna and concha of the external ear in juvenile ferrets. (A) In normal adult ferrets more than 75% of SC auditory units are tuned to single azimuthal positions, and most of the others exhibit broad, typically hemifield, response profiles (bottom panel, black bars). The best azimuths of the tuned units are closely aligned with those of visual units in the overlying superficial layers (top left panel). Recordings from adult ferrets in which the pinna and concha had been removed bilaterally in infancy revealed a marked increase in the proportion of auditory units with ambiguous spatial tuning (bottom panel, gray bars, "bilobed" and "complex" categories). This is expected, given that the external ears provide important information for resolving front/back ambiguities in binaural localization cues. These auditory units also exhibited much less topographic order and consequently a poorer alignment with the visual map (top right panel: the best azimuths of tuned units are shown as triangles and two best azimuths for each bilobed unit as filled and open circles). (B) Performance in an absolute localization task. Noise bursts were delivered from one of 12 speakers positioned around the animal. The animals had been trained to approach the active speaker for a water reward. Top panels: Mean (left) and standard deviation (right) of the error in localizing brief (40 ms) sounds for normal ferrets (black lines) and after early pinna and concha removal (gray lines). Bottom panel: Incidence of front/back errors at different stimulus durations. Overall, ferrets perform less well after early removal of the pinna and concha and make more front/back errors. (Single-unit data from Schnupp, King, and Carlile, 1998.)

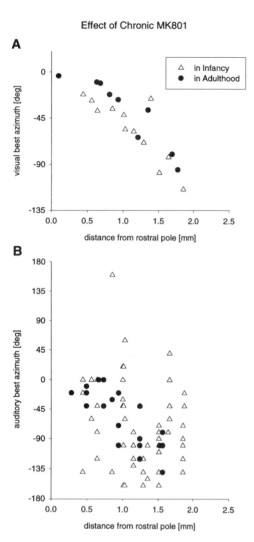

Effect of Chronic MK801

A

B

FIGURE 31.8   Effects of chronic NMDA-receptor blockade on the topographic organization of the representations of visual space in the superficial layers and of auditory space in the deeper layers of the ferret SC. (A) Multiunit visual best azimuths are plotted against the rostrocaudal position of the recording site within the SC. These data are from juvenile (61–70 days old, open triangles) and adult animals (filled circles) that, 5–6 weeks earlier, received Elvax implants containing the non-competitive NMDA antagonist MK801. A clear topographic order is apparent in both cases, which is not significantly different from that found in normal, age-matched ferrets. (B) The auditory best azimuths recorded in the animals that received Elvax implants in adulthood also show a normal topographic order (filled circles). However, those recorded in the animals treated with MK801 during the period over which the auditory space map normally matures (open triangles) show significantly more scatter than their age-matched controls. (Data from Schnupp et al., 1995.)

removal of the pinna and concha in juvenile ferrets suggest that spectral cues play a critical role in establishing the sensitivity of SC neurons to combinations of monaural and binaural cues that unambiguously identify sound source direction (Schnupp, King, and Carlile, 1998). Appropriately combining different localization cues appears to be an activity-dependent process that may also conform to Hebbian rules of synaptic plasticity.

Where does visual calibration of auditory spatial tuning take place?

If visual signals do contribute to the sharpening and ordering of auditory spatial response profiles, it would seem necessary that inputs from the two modalities converge on the same neuron, so that any error between them can be measured. Because most neurons in the deeper layers of the mammalian SC and in the barn owl's optic tectum are responsive to stimuli in more than one modality, one might expect that the interactions would take place in those structures. However, prism-rearing experiments in owls have shown that altered visual cues also affect the ITD tuning of neurons in the ICX (Brainard and Knudsen, 1993), which provides auditory input to the tectum via a topographically organized projection (Knudsen and Knudsen, 1983). These changes, which take several weeks to develop, appear to be brought about by an anatomical reorganization of the projection to the ICX from the central nucleus of the inferior colliculus (Feldman and Knudsen, 1997). How visual signals feed into this circuit is not yet clear, nor is it known whether equivalent changes occur in the mammalian brain.

The representation of auditory space in the ICX of guinea pigs is unaltered by dark rearing (Binns, Withington, and Keating, 1995), a procedure that degrades the development of the map in the SC (Withington-Wray, Binns, and Keating, 1990b). However, the contribution of the ICX to the auditory representation in the SC in mammals is currently uncertain. On the other hand, some of the auditory neurons in the ferret's BIN are also visually responsive (Schnupp and King, 1997). This raises the possibility that, as in owls, the nucleus providing the principal, spatially ordered auditory input to the SC (figure 31.4) may also be influenced by visual experience.

In cats, multisensory neurons in the deeper layers of the SC first respond to visual stimuli more than a week after the first auditory responses appear. With increasing age, both auditory and visual receptive fields become progressively sharpened as the neurons begin to integrate information from different modalities (Wallace and Stein, 1997). Because of these factors, the visual map in the deeper layers would not appear to provide an ideal template for an activity-dependent refinement of auditory spatial selectivity. In contrast, in carnivores, the retinocollicular projection to the superficial layers exhibits a high degree of topographic order throughout development (Chalupa and Snider, 1998; King et al., 1996) and a mature visual map is already present in those layers by the time of natural eye opening (Kao et al., 1994; King and Carlile, 1995; King et al., 1996). Superficial-layer neurons are thought to play a role in visual processing, and their contribution to the sensorimotor function of the SC is uncertain (Casagrande et al., 1972; Edwards et al., 1979). Nevertheless, interlaminar connections between the superficial and deep layers of the SC have now been demonstrated in several species (e.g., Behan and Appell, 1992; Hall and Lee, 1997; Mooney, Huang, and Rhoades, 1992). These

may provide an anatomical substrate by which the relatively small and early developing visual receptive fields of superficial-layer neurons could contribute to the maturation of sensory responses in the deeper layers of the SC.

In ferrets, aspiration of the caudal part of the superficial layers on the day of birth has minimal effects on what is left of the visual map in the remaining rostral region or on the auditory spatial selectivity of neurons found beneath that region (King et al., 1996; King, Schnupp, and Thompson, 1998). Recordings made from the intact rostral part of the SC in adulthood show that both superficial-layer visual and deep-layer auditory neurons are

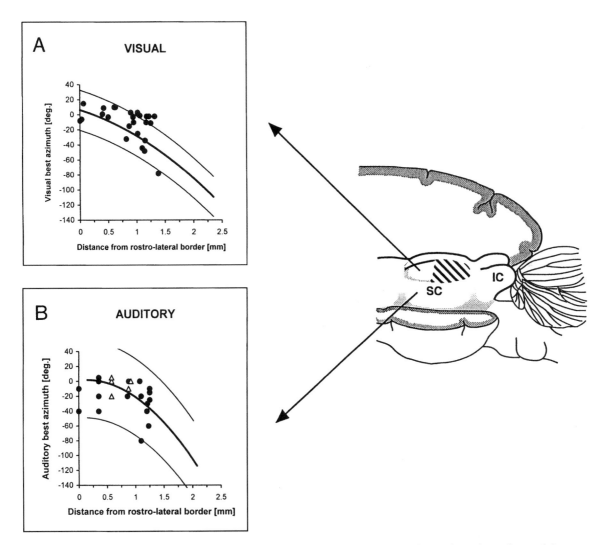

FIGURE 31.9 (A) Visual representation in the remaining superficial layers of the SC in adult ferrets following aspiration of the caudal portion of those layers on the day of birth. The azimuthal best positions are plotted against the distance of their recording sites along the rostrocaudal axis of the SC. (B) Auditory representation beneath the remaining portion of the superficial layers. The open triangles represent the auditory best azimuths of units that were also visually responsive, whereas the filled circles indicate the values obtained from unimodal auditory neurons. The two lines in each panel represent two standard deviations on either side of the polynomial function that provides the best fit to the visual and auditory maps in normal ferrets. The hatched area of the SC in the parasagittal view on the right indicates the aspirated region of the superficial layers. (From King et al., 1996, with permission.)

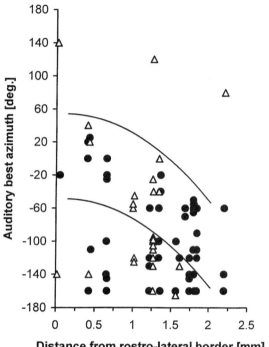

Distance from rostro-lateral border [mm]

FIGURE 31.10 Auditory representation in the deeper layers of the adult ferret SC from which the overlying superficial layers had been removed by aspiration on the day of birth; plotted as in figure 31.9B. The open triangles represent the auditory best azimuths of units that were also visually responsive, whereas the filled circles indicate the values obtained from unimodal auditory neurons. (From King et al., 1996, with permission.)

tuned to azimuthal angles that span a restricted part of anterior space, falling either within or very close to the normal range of values (figure 31.9). Although confined primarily to the contralateral hemifield, the preferred sound directions of units recorded ventral to the superficial-layer lesion exhibit significantly more scatter, with many values falling outside the normal range (figure 31.10). Many deep-layer neurons in this region of the SC still receive visual inputs, presumably originating from extrastriate cortical areas, but these are apparently insufficient to rescue the auditory spatial tuning of bimodal cells. These results identify a potential role for superficial-layer neurons in establishing the alignment of sensory maps in the SC. However, it remains to be seen whether and how visual activity in the superficial layers can fine-tune the developing auditory responses either in the SC or at an earlier stage in the pathway.

Conclusions

The SC has proved to be an extremely useful structure in which to examine the way in which spatial informa-

tion provided by a variety of sensory cues is synthesized and integrated. Where neurons in the SC and in multisensory areas of the cortex receive converging inputs from two or more modalities, they tend to have receptive fields that are roughly aligned in space. In terms of variations in firing rate, SC neurons are tuned to restricted regions of sensory space and it is the alignment of these preferred stimulus directions across different modalities that most clearly characterizes the registration of the maps.

Compared to visual and somatosensory representations, considerable central processing is involved in establishing a neural map of auditory space. Activity-dependent processes appear to play an essential role during development in matching the tuning of individual neurons to different auditory localization cues that correspond to specific positions in visual space. Subsequent transformation of sensory signals into a common coordinate frame, which most likely incorporates efference copy signals, can allow receptive field alignment to be maintained in the face of independent mobility of the sense organs. This enables different sensory cues to be substituted for one another and to be combined in ways that can improve the accuracy with which multimodal events are localized. Many perceptual experiences depend on cooperative interactions between multiple sensory inputs. For example, the improvement in speech perception that results from watching movements of the speaker's lips may involve a synthesis of linguistic visual cues and speech sounds in the auditory cortex (Calvert et al., 1997). It seems highly likely that the principles of sensory convergence and integration exhibited by SC neurons are also relevant to the processing of complex inputs elsewhere in the brain.

ACKNOWLEDGMENTS This work was supported by a Wellcome Senior Research Fellowship to Andrew King and by a Wellcome Prize Studentship and subsequently a Dunhill Research Fellowship (awarded by Defeating Deafness: The Hearing Research Trust) to Jan Schnupp. We are grateful to Roland Baddeley, Simon Carlile, Jim Giles, Ze Dong Jiang, Richard Lanyon, David Moore, Carl Parsons, Adam Smith, and Ian Thompson for their valuable contributions to some of the experiments described in this chapter, and to David Moore, Alan Palmer, and Dan Sanes for their comments on the manuscript.

REFERENCES

ANDERSEN, R. A., L. H. SNYDER, D. C. BRADLEY, and J. XING, 1997. Multimodal representation of space in the posterior parietal cortex and its use in planning movements. *Annu. Rev. Neurosci.* 20:303–330.

APPELL, P. P., and M. BEHAN, 1990. Sources of subcortical GABAergic projections to the superior colliculus in the cat. *J. Comp. Neurol.* 302:143–158.

BEHAN, M., and P. P. APPELL, 1992. Intrinsic circuitry in the cat superior colliculus: Projections from the superficial layers. *J. Comp. Neurol.* 315:230–243.

BINNS, K. E., S. GRANT, D. J. WITHINGTON, and M. J. KEATING, 1992. A topographic representation of auditory space in the external nucleus of the inferior colliculus of the guinea-pig. *Brain Res.* 589:231–242.

BINNS, K. E., and T. E. SALT, 1996. Importance of NMDA receptors for multimodal integration in the deep layers of the cat superior colliculus. *J. Neurophysiol.* 75:920–930.

BINNS, K. E., D. J. WITHINGTON, and M. J. KEATING, 1995. The developmental emergence of the representation of auditory azimuth in the external nucleus of the inferior colliculus of the guinea pig: The effects of visual and auditory deprivation. *Dev. Brain Res.* 85:14–24.

BRAINARD, M. S., and E. I. KNUDSEN, 1993. Experience-dependent plasticity in the inferior colliculus: A site for visual calibration of the neural representation of auditory space in the barn owl. *J. Neurosci.* 13:4589–4608.

CALVERT, G. A., E. T. BULLMORE, M. J. BRAMMER, R. CAMPBELL, S. C. R. WILLIAMS, P. K. MCGUIRE, P. W. R. WOODRUFF, S. D. IVERSEN, and A. S. DAVID, 1997. Activation of auditory cortex during silent lipreading. *Science* 276:593–596.

CAPADAY, C., 1997. Neurophysiological methods for studies of the motor system in freely moving human subjects. *J. Neurosci. Methods* 74:201–218.

CARLILE, S., and A. J. KING, 1994. Monaural and binaural spectrum level cues in the ferret: Acoustics and the neural representation of auditory space. *J. Neurophysiol.* 71:785–801.

CASAGRANDE, V. A., J. K. HARTING, W. C. HALL, I. T. DIAMOND, and G. F. MARTIN, 1972. Superior colliculus of the tree shrew: A structural and functional subdivision into superficial and deep layers. *Science* 177:444–447.

CHALUPA, L. M., and C. J. SNIDER, 1998. Topographic specificity in the retinocollicular projection of the developing ferret: An anterograde tracing study. *J. Comp. Neurol.* 392:35–47.

EDWARDS, S. B., C. L. GINSBURGH, C. K. HENKEL, and B. E. STEIN, 1979. Sources of subcortical projections to the superior colliculus in the cat. *J. Comp. Neurol.* 184:309–330.

FELDMAN, D. E., M. S. BRAINARD, and E. I. KNUDSEN, 1996. Newly learned auditory responses mediated by NMDA receptors in the owl inferior colliculus. *Science* 271:525–528.

FELDMAN, D. E., and E. I. KNUDSEN, 1997. An anatomical basis for visual calibration of the auditory space map in the barn owl's midbrain. *J. Neurosci.* 17:6820–6837.

FERSTER, D., and N. SPRUSTON, 1995. Cracking the neuronal code. *Science* 270:756–757.

FOX, K., and N. W. DAW, 1993. Do NMDA receptors have a critical function in visual cortical plasticity? *Trends Neurosci.* 16:116–122.

FREEMAN, R. D., and I. OHZAWA, 1990. On the neurophysiological organization of binocular vision. *Vision Res.* 30:1661–1676.

HALL, W. C., and P. LEE, 1997. Interlaminar connections of the superior colliculus in the tree shrew. III. The optic layer. *Vis. Neurosci.* 14:647–661.

JIANG, Z. D., A. J. KING, and I. D. THOMPSON, 1995. Organization of auditory brainstem projections to the superior colliculus in neonatal ferrets. *Brit. J. Audiol.* 29:49.

KAO, C.-Q., J. G. MCHAFFIE, M. A. MEREDITH, and B. E. STEIN, 1994. Functional development of a central visual map in cat. *J. Neurophysiol.* 72:266–272.

KING, A. J., and S. CARLILE, 1993. Changes induced in the representation of auditory space in the superior colliculus by rearing ferrets with binocular eyelid suture. *Exp. Brain Res.* 94:444–455.

KING, A. J., and S. CARLILE, 1995. Neural coding for auditory space. In *The Cognitive Neurosciences*, M. S. Gazzaniga, ed. Cambridge, Mass.: MIT Press, pp. 279–293.

KING, A. J., M. E. HUTCHINGS, D. R. MOORE, and C. BLAKEMORE, 1988. Developmental plasticity in the visual and auditory representations in the mammalian superior colliculus. *Nature* 332:73–76.

KING, A. J., Z. D. JIANG, and D. R. MOORE, 1998. Auditory brainstem projections to the ferret superior colliculus: Anatomical contribution to the neural coding of sound azimuth. *J. Comp. Neurol.* 390:342–365.

KING, A. J, D. R. MOORE, and M. E. HUTCHINGS, 1994. Topographic representation of auditory space in the superior colliculus of adult ferrets after monaural deafening in infancy. *J. Neurophysiol.* 71:182–194.

KING, A. J., J. W. H. SCHNUPP, S. CARLILE, A. L. SMITH, and I. D. THOMPSON, 1996. The development of topographically-aligned maps of visual and auditory space in the superior colliculus. *Prog. Brain Res.* 112:335–350.

KING, A. J., J. W. H. SCHNUPP, and I. D. THOMPSON, 1998. Signals from the superficial layers of the superior colliculus enable the development of the auditory space map in the deeper layers. *J. Neurosci.* 18:9394–9408.

KNUDSEN, E. I., and M. S. BRAINARD, 1991. Visual instruction of the neural map of auditory space in the developing optic tectum. *Science* 253:85–87.

KNUDSEN, E. I., and M. S. BRAINARD, 1995. Creating a unified representation of visual and auditory space in the brain. *Annu. Rev. Neurosci.* 18:19–43.

KNUDSEN, E. I., S. DU LAC, and S. D. ESTERLY, 1987. Computational maps in the brain. *Annu. Rev. Neurosci.* 10:41–65.

KNUDSEN, E. I., S. D. ESTERLY, and S. DU LAC, 1991. Stretched and upside-down maps of auditory space in the optic tectum of blind-reared owls; acoustic basis and behavioral correlates. *J. Neurosci.* 11:1727–1747.

KNUDSEN, E. I., S. D. ESTERLY, and J. F. OLSEN, 1994. Adaptive plasticity of the auditory space map in the optic tectum of adult and baby barn owls in response to external ear modification. *J. Neurophysiol.* 71:79–94.

KNUDSEN, E. I., and P. F. KNUDSEN, 1983. Space-mapped auditory projections from the inferior colliculus to the optic tectum in the barn owl (*Tyto alba*). *J. Comp. Neurol.* 218:187–196.

KNUDSEN, E. I., and J. MOGDANS, 1992. Vision-independent adjustment of unit tuning to sound localization cues in response to monaural occlusion in developing owl optic tectum. *J. Neurosci.* 12:3485–3493.

KONISHI, M., 1995. Neural mechanisms of auditory image formation. In *The Cognitive Neurosciences*, M. S. Gazzaniga, ed. Cambridge, Mass.: MIT Press, pp. 269–277.

LAURENT, G., 1997. Olfactory processing: Maps, time and codes. *Curr. Opin. Neurobiol.* 7:547–553.

MAY, B. J., 1998. Lesions of the dorsal cochlear nucleus disrupt sound orientation behavior in cats. *Abstr. Assoc. Res. Otolaryngol.*, p. 170.

MEREDITH, M. A., and H. R. CLEMO, 1989. Auditory cortical projection from the anterior ectosylvian sulcus (Field AES) to the superior colliculus in the cat: An anatomical and electrophysiological study. *J. Comp. Neurol.* 289:687–707.

MIDDLEBROOKS, J. C., and D. M. GREEN, 1991. Sound localization by human listeners. *Annu. Rev. Psychol.* 42:135–159.

MOONEY, R. D., X. HUANG, and R. W. RHOADES, 1992. Functional influence of interlaminar connections in the hamster's superior colliculus. *J. Neurosci.* 12:2417–2432.

OERTEL, D., 1997. Encoding of timing in the brain stem auditory nuclei of vertebrates. *Neuron* 19:959–962.

PALMER, A. R., and A. J. KING, 1985. A monaural space map in the guinea-pig superior colliculus. *Hearing Res.* 17:267–280.

PARSONS, C. H., R. G. LANYON, J. W. H. SCHNUPP, and A. J. KING, in press. The effects of altering spectral cues in infancy on horizontal and vertical sound localization by adult ferrets. *J. Neurophysiol.*

RIEKE, R., D. WARLAND, R. DE RUYTER VAN STEVENINCK, and W. BIALEK, 1997. *Spikes: Exploring the Neural Code.* Cambridge, Mass.: MIT Press.

SANES, D. H., 1993. The development of synaptic function and integration in the central auditory system. *J. Neurosci.* 13:2627–2637.

SCHNUPP, J. W. H., J. D. GILES, R. J. BADDELEY, and A. J. KING, 1997. Multisensory facilitation may be due to non-linearities in the neuron's rate-intensity function. *Soc. Neurosci. Abstr.* 23:1542.

SCHNUPP, J. W. H., and A. J. KING, 1997. Coding for auditory space in the nucleus of the brachium of the inferior colliculus in the ferret. *J. Neurophysiol.* 78:2717–2731.

SCHNUPP, J. W. H., A. J. KING, and S. CARLILE, 1998. Altered spectral localization cues disrupt the development of the auditory space map in the superior colliculus of the ferret. *J. Neurophysiol.* 79:1053–1069.

SCHNUPP, J. W. H., A. J. KING, A. L. SMITH, and I. D. THOMPSON, 1995. NMDA-receptor antagonists disrupt the formation of the auditory space map in the mammalian superior colliculus. *J. Neurosci.* 15:1516–1531.

SMITH, A. L., P. M. CORDERY, and I. D. THOMPSON, 1995. Manufacture and release characteristics of Elvax polymers containing glutamate receptor antagonists. *J. Neurosci. Methods* 60:211–217.

SPARKS, D. L., and J. M. GROH, 1995. The superior colliculus: A window for viewing issues in integrative neuroscience. In *The Cognitive Neurosciences*, M. S. Gazzaniga, ed. Cambridge, Mass.: MIT Press, pp. 565–584.

STEIN, B. E., and M. A. MEREDITH, 1993. *The Merging of the Senses.* Cambridge, Mass.: MIT Press.

WALLACE, M. T., and B. E. STEIN, 1997. Development of multisensory neurons and multisensory integration in cat superior colliculus. *J. Neurosci.* 17:2429–2444.

WISE, L. Z., and D. R. F. IRVINE, 1985. Topographic organization of interaural intensity difference sensitivity in deep layers of cat superior colliculus: Implications for auditory spatial representation. *J. Neurophysiol.* 54:185–211.

WITHINGTON, D. J., 1992. The effect of binocular lid suture on auditory responses in the guinea-pig superior colliculus. *Neurosci. Lett.* 136:153–156.

WITHINGTON-WRAY, D. J., K. E. BINNS, and M. J. KEATING, 1990a. The developmental emergence of a map of auditory space in the superior colliculus of the guinea pig. *Dev. Brain Res.* 51:225–236.

WITHINGTON-WRAY, D. J., K. E. BINNS, and M. J. KEATING, 1990b. The maturation of the superior collicular map of auditory space in the guinea pig is disrupted by developmental visual deprivation. *Eur. J. Neurosci.* 2:682–692.

YOUNG, E. D., G. A. SPIROU, J. J. RICE, and H. F. VOIGT, 1992. Neural organization and responses to complex stimuli in the dorsal cochlear nucleus. *Phil. Trans. Roy. Soc. Lond.* B 336:407–413.

32 The Song System: Neural Circuits Essential throughout Life for Vocal Behavior and Plasticity

ALLISON J. DOUPE, MICHAEL S. BRAINARD, AND NEAL A. HESSLER

ABSTRACT The learned vocal behavior of songbirds provides a useful model system for sensorimotor learning and behavior in general, and for the learning and production of human speech in particular. In young birds in the process of learning, song changes rapidly, and is dramatically sensitive to the removal of auditory feedback. In contrast, the adult song of many species was thought to be quite stable and independent of hearing. In zebra finches, however, it is now clear that stable adult song is actively maintained using auditory feedback, because deafening of these birds as adults causes their song to deteriorate slowly (Nordeen and Nordeen, 1992). Little was known, however, about whether the neural pathways involved in adult song modification and maintenance are similar to those important during learning. By analyzing the song behavior and neurophysiology of adult zebra finches, both in normal and deafened birds, we have found that the anterior forebrain pathway, a circuit crucial for initial song learning, is also essential for the changes in adult song that normally result from deafening, and is highly active during singing in adults. Moreover, singing-related activity in this pathway is strongly modulated by social context, which is known to affect both adult song and song learning. These findings on the regulation of vocal plasticity in the song system of adult birds shed light on the nature of signals for learning at all ages, as well as on developmental changes in the capacity for plasticity.

Birdsong is a complex vocal motor behavior with a number of parallels to human speech, particularly the fact that it is learned early in life with a strong dependence on hearing (Konishi, 1965; Marler, 1970). In adult birds of most species, however, song is highly stable, and was thought to be largely independent of auditory feedback (Konishi, 1965), perhaps being driven solely by a central pattern generator. Recently, however, it has become clear that, at least in zebra finches and related species, adult song requires continued auditory feedback for its stable maintenance: The songs of zebra finches deafened as adults deteriorate slowly over the

ALLISON J. DOUPE, MICHAEL S. BRAINARD, and NEAL A. HESSLER Departments of Physiology and Psychiatry and Keck Center for Integrative Neuroscience, University of California, San Francisco, Calif.

course of weeks to months, although with a great deal of variability between individuals in the speed and amount of deterioration (Nordeen and Nordeen, 1992). This dependence on auditory feedback–though much less dramatic than that seen in young birds, in whom song invariably degrades rapidly after deafening (Nottebohm, 1968; Price, 1979)–nonetheless indicates that sensory feedback functions in adult song. This is true of speech as well: Although humans show much more preservation of speech if they become deaf as adults rather than during childhood, the speech of deaf adults does gradually deteriorate, with a great deal of inter-individual variability (just as in songbirds), but sometimes to the point of unintelligibility (Cowie and Douglas-Cowie, 1992).

The new observations that hearing is essential for maintained vocal production in adult zebra finches raise the questions of how and where the signals from auditory feedback act in the brain. Songbirds, like humans, have a specialized neural circuit devoted to vocal learning and production, known as the song system, which is a likely location for many of the neural mechanisms involved in song. Studies of the adult song system may have advantages for uncovering how neural signals mediate the matching of vocal motor output to sensory feedback. For example, in adult birds, the intended outcome of learning, the adult song, is already known, while in juvenile birds learning for the first time, the ultimate target of learning is of necessity unclear until later. Moreover, in young birds the instructive signals and mechanisms for learning are inevitably entangled with the processes underlying the rapid growth and development of the song system, which occur at the same time as initial song learning. In adults these developmental processes are largely complete and should not confound the mechanisms involved in maintaining learned song. Finally, studying adult birds and comparing them to juveniles can address whether the mechanisms that subserve normal song maintenance parallel those required

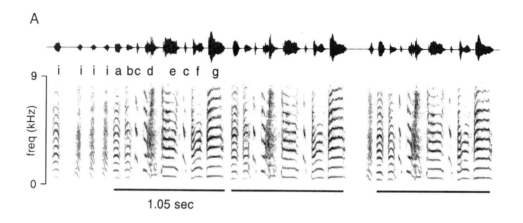

A

i i i i a b c d e c f g

9

freq (kHz)

0

1.05 sec

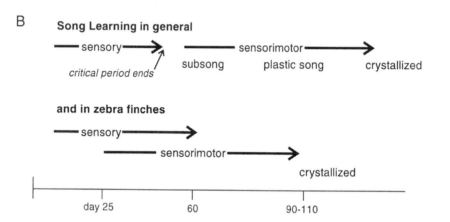

B

Song Learning in general

—sensory—→

critical period ends

subsong

—sensorimotor—→

plastic song

crystallized

and in zebra finches

—sensory—→

—sensorimotor—→

crystallized

day 25   60   90–110

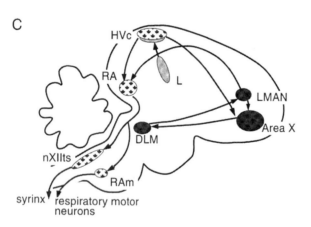

C

HVc

RA   L

LMAN

Area X

DLM

nXIIts

RAm

syrinx respiratory motor neurons

FIGURE 32.1 (A) Birdsong. A spectrogram (frequency vs. time plot, with amplitude indicated by the darkness of the signal) of a typical zebra finch song shows the characteristic features of song. The smallest elements, called "notes," are either sung alone or combined to form "syllables" (marked with lowercase letters); particular stereotyped sequences of syllables, called "motifs" in zebra finches (indicated by dark bars), may be repeated one to many times, preceded by a variable number of short introductory notes (i). (B) Timeline of song learning. The general features of song learning are similar in all songbirds. The initial memorization or sensory learning of the song is followed by sensorimotor learning. During this vocal practice phase, the bird first produces the highly variable and amorphous sounds of subsong, followed by plastic song, in which motor rehearsal of learned song is evident. Finally, the bird develops stable or crystallized song. The details of song learning vary from species to species. Seasonal species generally learn their song over the first year of life, while zebra finches, which mature rapidly (within 3 months), learn to sing during these 3 months and show extensive overlap between the two phases of learning. (C) The song system. Simplified schematic of the song system. Motor pathway nuclei are shown filled with a pattern, and the anterior forebrain (AF) nuclei are dark gray. The field L complex (light gray) provides the major source of auditory input to the song system, via its direct and indirect connections to HVc.

during learning, and whether and how vocal plasticity changes through the life cycle.

Birdsong learning: The behavior

As a prelude to investigating adult song maintenance, it is useful to define birdsong and review what is known about its learning. Birdsong, like speech, consists of ordered strings of sound called syllables, separated by brief silent intervals (figure 32.1A), and is learned by songbirds when they are young. The phenomenology of song learning is strikingly similar to human speech learning. Songbirds do not produce adult-like sounds when they first begin to vocalize, but instead sing rambling immature song akin to the babbling of human infants. Young birds then gradually refine their vocalizations until they sing mature adult song, which strongly resembles the songs of adults that they heard while growing up. Numerous behavioral studies have revealed that this learning occurs in two stages, both of which are critically dependent on hearing (figure 32.1B). In an initial "sensory learning" phase, young birds do not vocalize a great deal, but hear the song of an adult tutor or tutors (usually the male parent and neighboring males), committing much of this song to memory (Marler, 1970). This must occur within a time-limited critical period analogous to sensitive periods for human language learning. Later, during a period of vocal practice or "sensorimotor learning," birds begin to sing, gradually matching their initially immature vocalizations to their memorized song or "template." At the end of this phase, birds produce stereotyped, "crystallized" song, which in many species is stable for the rest of the bird's life (for reviews, see Konishi, 1985; Kroodsma and Miller, 1996).

If deafened prior to sensorimotor learning so they cannot hear their own voices while learning to sing, songbirds never produce normal song (Konishi, 1965). Thus, birds cannot simply internally translate the memorized song into the correct pattern of vocal motor commands; rather, they must actively develop the required motor mapping by evaluating sensory feedback from their own vocalizations (figure 32.2A). Moreover, this dependence on auditory experience is developmentally regulated: Loss of hearing by adult songbirds whose song is stable has much smaller and slower effects on vocal production than the same loss during the active sensorimotor matching of initial song acquisition (Konishi, 1965; Nordeen and Nordeen, 1992; Price, 1979). This, too, is similar to humans, who are strongly dependent on hearing early in life for normal speech acquisition, but show much more preservation of speech if they become deaf as adults (Cowie and Douglas-Cowie, 1992).

Brain structures specialized for song learning and production

Songbirds also resemble humans in having evolved a complex set of neural structures in the forebrain that are essential for song learning and production (figure 32.1C; Nottebohm, Stokes, and Leonard, 1976; Bottjer et al., 1989). The so-called song "motor" pathway controls the midbrain and brainstem areas that regulate the muscles of the vocal tract and of respiration, and is essential throughout life for normal singing. This includes the song motor control nucleus HVc, which projects to the premotor nucleus RA; RA then connects to midbrain vocal control areas, respiratory premotor neurons, and motor neurons for the musculature of the avian vocal organ, the syrinx (see Wild, 1997, for review). Lesions of HVc or RA at any age dramatically disrupt singing, sometimes resulting in complete muteness, akin to that seen in some human aphasias (Nottebohm, Stokes, and Leonard, 1976). This circuit is thus critically involved in song production throughout life.

A second circuit of forebrain nuclei also links HVc to RA, but via an indirect loop through the basal ganglia and thalamus (Bottjer et al., 1989; Okuhata and Saito, 1987). This pathway through the anterior forebrain (AF) includes the striatal-like nucleus area X, the medial portion of a dorsolateral thalamic nucleus (DLM), and a forebrain nucleus perhaps analogous to prefrontal cortex, the lateral magnocellular nucleus of the anterior neostriatum (LMAN). The importance of this AF pathway changes developmentally in a manner similar to that seen for hearing. Lesions or pharmacological inactivation of its component nuclei markedly disrupt initial song learning and production. In contrast, lesions in adult birds singing crystallized song have no obvious effect on song production (Basham, Nordeen, and Nordeen, 1996; Bottjer, Miesner, and Arnold, 1984; Scharff and Nottebohm, 1991; Sohrabji, Nordeen, and Nordeen, 1990). Thus, the AF pathway has some critical function during learning.

Because both the AF circuit and auditory feedback are essential during learning, and less so in adulthood, one role of the AF may be to mediate the auditory feedback critical to normal song development (Doupe, 1993). Consistent with this hypothesis, AF nuclei contain auditory neurons that, in adult zebra finches, are highly song-selective (Doupe, 1997): They respond much more strongly to playback of the bird's own song (BOS) than to songs of conspecifics (other individuals of the same species), and respond better to BOS than to temporally altered versions of this song (that is, played in reverse or with the syllables out of order). Neurons so specialized for song could play a role in the sensory evaluation of

A. Learning

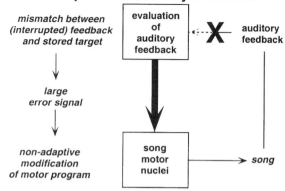

mismatch between developing song and stored target

↓

large error signal

↓

adaptive modification of motor program

B. Normal adult

good match between mature song and stored target

↓

small error signal

↓

stable song

C. Interruption of auditory feedback

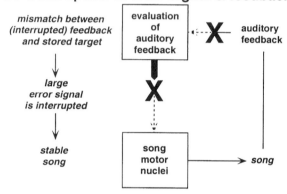

mismatch between (interrupted) feedback and stored target

↓

large error signal

↓

non-adaptive modification of motor program

D. Interruption of error signal & feedback

mismatch between (interrupted) feedback and stored target

↓

large error signal is interrupted

↓

stable song

FIGURE 32.2   Hypothetical flow of auditory feedback through the song system and the potential consequences of disrupting that flow at different stages. (A) During song learning, auditory feedback from the developing song of juvenile birds is compared with a stored song target (or template). Differences between the bird's own song and the target song result in an error signal that drives adaptive modification of song. (B) After song learning in a normal adult bird, the bird's own song closely approximates the target song. Consequently, there is little or no error signal to drive further changes in song, and song remains stable. (C) If auditory feedback is interrupted, then a comparison of feedback with the stored song target will result in a large mismatch and large error signal. This error signal will potentially drive changes in song, which will be nonadaptive. (D) If the error signal itself is interrupted, then the impetus for change in song will be removed, even in the presence of a mismatch between auditory feedback and the stored song target.

BOS that must accompany learning. Moreover, this selectivity emerges during learning. In juvenile zebra finches that have not yet begun to sing, AF neurons respond to all conspecific songs as well as to reversed versions of them. Then, as learning progresses, these neurons rapidly develop strong selectivity for the sounds of the bird's own song, and in some cases for that of its tutor as well (Doupe, 1997; Solis and Doupe, 1997). AF neurons selective for the tutor are well suited to act as a template: They could provide information, encoded in the strength or pattern of their firing rate, about how well certain vocalizations match the memorized song model. Alternatively, AF neurons with selectivity for the bird's emerging song clearly have the potential to provide the developing bird with information about its own vocalizations, which must be a prerequisite for modifying those vocalizations to match the tutor song template. More experiments, including manipulations of this pathway during song development, will be necessary to test the idea that this circuit provides important sensory or sensorimotor feedback during learning and how it does so. Nonetheless, the developmental studies of its auditory properties provide one line of evidence that it carries information useful in song learning.

Active maintenance of song in adulthood and the function of the AF

Adult song is generally very stable: Repeated renditions of an individual bird's song have highly reproducible acoustic structure. Early experiments, using white-crowned sparrows, also showed that adult song was not affected by deafening, in contrast to the marked disruption of song caused by deafening before or during song learning (Konishi, 1965; Nottebohm, 1968). This suggested that stable adult song becomes completely independent of auditory feedback. Recently, however, it has become clear that in some species, auditory feedback is required for adult song maintenance. In adult zebra finches, deafening causes gradual deterioration of song (Nordeen and Nordeen, 1992), while deafening in adult Bengalese finches results in a rapid loss of syllable ordering and a more gradual deterioration of syllable structure (Okanoya and Yamaguchi, 1997; Woolley and Rubel, 1997). This raises the question of whether the mechanisms that subserve normal song maintenance parallel those required during learning. Specifically, is the AF pathway, crucial to learning, also involved in the maintenance of adult song by auditory feedback?

This issue was initially examined by lesioning LMAN bilaterally in normal adult zebra finches, then waiting for weeks to months to see whether interruption of the AF pathway would disrupt song maintenance and result in a gradual deterioration of song similar to that seen in response to deafening. Even 16 weeks after these LMAN lesions, however, song structure remained unchanged (Nordeen and Nordeen, 1993). This indicates that these lesions are not equivalent to removing auditory feedback, and suggests that the AF is not simply a conduit for the auditory feedback utilized in maintaining adult song. These results are consistent, however, with a model in which the AF is involved in evaluating auditory feedback.

The important distinction between these two possibilities is illustrated in figure 32.2, which traces the hypothetical flow of auditory feedback through the song system, and the potential consequences of disrupting that flow at different points. Normally, during song learning, auditory feedback of the bird's own song is encoded by the nervous system and then compared with an internal model of the song target (the song template). To the extent that there is a mismatch between the bird's own song and the song target, the evaluation results in an error or teaching signal that drives adaptive modification of the song motor program (figure 32.2A). After the completion of learning in an adult songbird, auditory feedback matches the song target, and evaluation results in a small error signal that does not cause changes in song (figure 32.2B): At this point the song is stable. Subsequent removal of all auditory feedback, however, causes a large mismatch between expected and actual feedback. This could create a large error signal that drives (nonadaptive) changes in the song (figure 32.2C) such as those seen experimentally in deaf finches (Nordeen and Nordeen, 1992). In contrast, if instead of interrupting auditory feedback prior to its evaluation, the output of the evaluation were interrupted (figure 32.2D), the consequences would be quite different. In this case, no error signal would reach

the motor pathway and song would not change. Indeed, by this hypothesis, interrupting the error signal would occlude the effects of altering auditory feedback (figure 32.2D).

In the context of this model, the failure of LMAN lesions to cause deterioration in song (Nordeen and Nordeen, 1993) indicates that these lesions do not interrupt auditory feedback prior to its evaluation (figure 32.2C). We have begun to test the alternative hypothesis, that the AF participates in evaluating auditory feedback, in a number of ways. In behavioral studies, we compared changes in song that followed deafening with those that followed a combination of deafening and bilateral AF lesions directed at nucleus LMAN (figure 32.2D), to see whether LMAN lesions occlude the effects of deafening. We also recorded neurophysiological activity of the AF in awake birds, to look more directly at the signals present in the AF during singing both in hearing and deaf birds. Preliminary or brief reports of these results have appeared elsewhere (Brainard and Doupe, 1997; Hessler and Doupe, 1997, 1999; Hessler, Kao, and Doupe, 1998).

LMAN lesions occlude the effects of deafening in adult finches

Consistent with prior reports (Nordeen and Nordeen, 1992), we found that songs of normal adult zebra finches were stable over long periods of time, while songs of zebra finches deafened in adulthood gradually deteriorated over a period of weeks to months (figure 32.3A). In marked contrast, songs of birds that received AF lesions at the same time as they were deafened remained relatively unchanged (figure 32.3B).

The effects of experimental manipulations on song were characterized using two separate measures. First, we used human observers to score how well syllables that were initially present in the bird's repertoire were preserved in later songs (similar to the procedures of Morrison and Nottebohm, 1993; Nordeen and Nordeen, 1992). Observers based their judgments on spectrographic representations of syllables that were presented individually. This measure therefore emphasized changes in the phonology of syllables rather than changes in the sequence in which syllables were sung or in the overall temporal pattern of song.

Figure 32.4A summarizes the changes in syllables observed for the different experimental groups. The presongs for each comparison were recorded just prior to experimental manipulation from birds that were at least 3 months of age and had mature songs as judged by the presence of stereotyped sequences of syllables ("motifs") that did not vary from one song rendition to the

A deafened

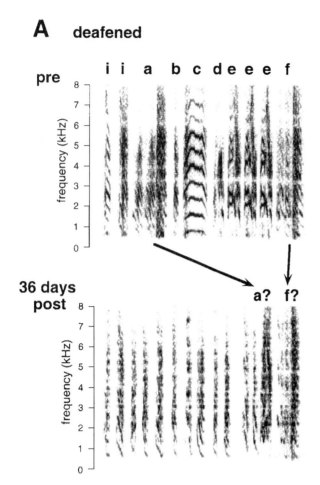

B lesioned & deafened

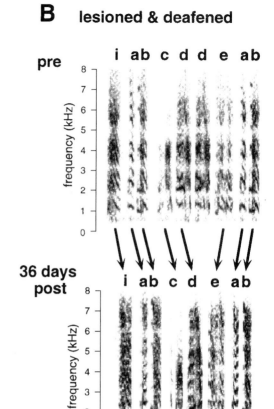

FIGURE 32.3   Effects of deafening on the songs of normal and LMAN lesioned zebra finches. Spectrographic representations of songs recorded at 98 days of age from two normally reared zebra finch brothers. One brother (A) was deafened by bilateral cochlear removal at 107 days of age. This bird's song subsequently deteriorated rapidly, so that by 36 days post-deafening few, if any, of the syllables that had initially been present in the bird's repertoire were retained. The temporal pattern of song is also clearly altered. The second brother (B) was also deafened at 107 days of age. However, four days prior to deafening, this bird received a bilateral electrolytic lesion of nucleus LMAN. In contrast to the bird that had been deafened only, this bird recognizably retained all of the syllables that initially had been present in its song.

next. The postsongs were recorded at least 200 days later in order to allow maximal effects of deafening to develop. The changes in song that followed deafening varied between individuals, and for some birds were no greater than those observed in controls that retained normal hearing. Sources of this variability may include the age at which birds were deafened, the exact conditions under which they were housed, and the complexity of their songs. In some instances we were able to control at least partially for these sources of variability, as well as for any genetic contributions to variation, by studying pairs of brothers. Brothers were housed together throughout the course of the experiment and had similar songs by virtue of exposure to each other and to the same adult tutor. Additionally, all recordings and shared experimental manipulations for brothers were carried out at the same ages. Data that derive from pairs of brothers are connected by lines in figure 32.4. Despite

the variability in the effects of deafening, overall the songs of deafened birds deteriorated significantly relative to those of controls. In contrast, the songs of birds that received LMAN lesions prior to deafening did not change any more than those of control birds. Furthermore, in each instance where there were recordings from pairs of brothers, the syllables of the birds lesioned prior to deafening were more stable than those of their deafened but unlesioned brothers. Thus, the absence of LMAN largely prevented the phonological deterioration normally resulting from deafening in adult zebra finches.

Second, we used a cross-correlation technique to measure changes in the temporal pattern of songs. For this measure, songs were represented by the timing of the start and end of each syllable while the spectral structure of individual syllables was ignored. For each bird, the timing pattern representing the most common motif before any experimental manipulation was first

A

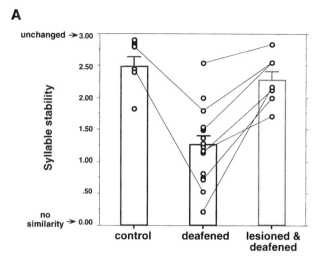

B

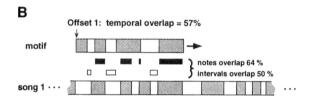

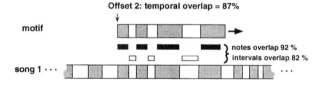

C

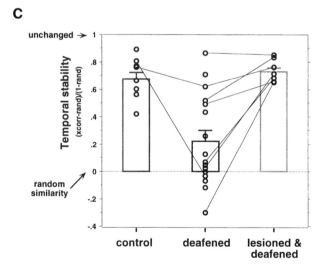

FIGURE 32.4 Summary of song stability following deafening of normal or LMAN-lesioned birds. (A) Syllable stability. Observers that were blind to the experimental manipulation of each bird scored the similarity between syllables from songs recorded before any manipulation and those recorded from later songs. For each "presyllable" initially present in the bird's repertoire, observers identified the most similar syllable present in songs recorded at later dates. Observers additionally judged the degree of similarity between each presyllable and its best match on a scale of 0 (no similarity) to 3 (identical). Each point corresponds to an individual bird and indicates the average similarity between syllables from presongs and those from songs recorded at least 200 days later. Lines connect points corresponding to brothers housed together and treated identically except for the indicated experimental manipulations. Bars show the means for each group. The syllables of deafened-only birds deteriorated significantly relative to those of control birds. In contrast, syllables of birds that were lesioned prior to deafening did not deteriorate relative to controls. (B) Method for quantification of changes in the temporal pattern of song. Songs were represented by the timing of syllables and intervals (shaded and open boxes, respectively) while the spectral structure of individual syllables was ignored. For each bird the timing pattern representing the most common motif before any experimental manipulation was identified. For each possible offset between the motif and songs from later recording sessions, the degree of temporal match was quantified as the average of the percentage overlap of notes and the percentage overlap of intervals. The temporal overlaps for two separate offsets are illustrated. The regions of note overlap are indicated between the representation of the motif–the songs, by solid boxes and the regions of interval overlap, by open boxes. In this case, the maximal overlap between the motif and the song occurred for the second illustrated offset. This maximal overlap was used as a measure of how well the temporal pattern of song was conserved following experimental manipulation. To partially control for the varying complexity of the motifs sung by different birds, the maximum overlaps for each motif were also calculated relative to randomly selected songs from unrelated birds. The temporal stability of song was then expressed as a normalized value ranging from 0 (equal amount of overlap to unrelated songs) to 1 (perfect overlap). (C) Temporal stability following different experimental manipulations. Each point corresponds to an individual bird and indicates the temporal stability between presongs and songs recorded at least 200 days later. Lines connect points corresponding to brothers. Bars show the means for each group. The temporal pattern of songs for deafened-only birds deteriorated significantly relative to those of control birds. In contrast, songs of birds that were lesioned prior to deafening did not deteriorate relative to controls.

identified. Songs from later recording sessions were then searched for the pattern of notes and intervals that most closely matched this motif pattern (figure 32.4B). The best matches for at least 10 songs were then averaged together and normalized (see legend) to yield a

measure of temporal stability. Figure 32.4C illustrates the temporal stability of song observed following the different experimental manipulations. Again, despite a great deal of variability between birds, deafening caused a significant deterioration of the temporal pattern of song relative to controls, and this deterioration was largely prevented by lesions of LMAN. Together with the analysis of syllable structure, these results indicate

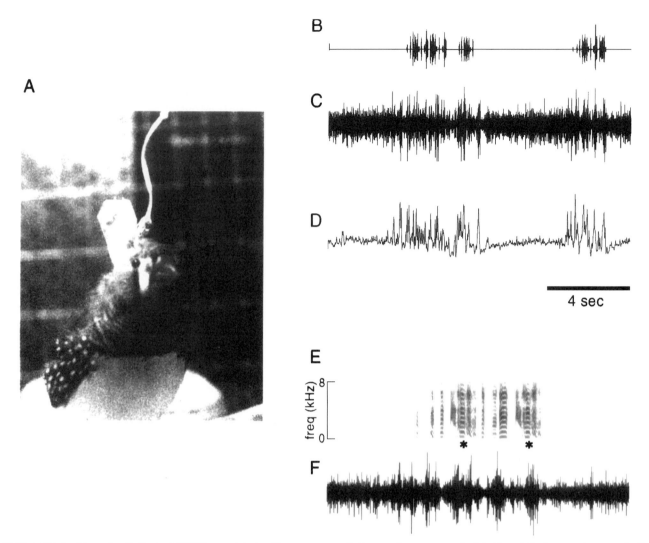

FIGURE 32.5 Neural activity in LMAN associated with song production. The spontaneous vocalizations produced over a period of 10 seconds by a representative bird (A) are displayed as an oscillogram (time-varying amplitude waveform) in B, aligned with simultaneously recorded neural activity in LMAN in C. In D, the waveform of neural activity in panel B has been rectified and integrated, and smoothed with a 10-ms Gaussian kernel, to show the overall pattern of multi-unit activity during singing. The final 4 seconds of singing and associated neural activity are shown expanded in E and F; the spectrogram in E shows the complex temporal and spectral structure of the bird's vocalizations, and the neural activity waveform highlights the characteristic bursty character of singing-related firing. The asterisks indicate a complex syllable repeated twice in this bout of song: Note that although the acoustic production is very similar, the neural activity associated with each rendition of this syllable is different in pattern.

that lesions of LMAN block vocal plasticity in adult birds, both of syllable phonology and of the overall temporal pattern of song.

LMAN is active during singing in adult birds

To characterize signals present in the AF of normal adult birds, and to determine what has been removed in AF-lesioned birds, we recorded single- and multi-unit activity in LMAN and area X during singing in 20 adult zebra finches. Chronic electrodes were stereotaxically implanted in the brain above LMAN and area X, and advanced into the nuclei during recording sessions. In both LMAN and X, neurons fired vigorously during singing (figures 32.5 and 32.6). Strikingly, excitation began prior to song output, indicating that at least some of the activity is independent of reafferent auditory feedback of the bird's own voice. Neural activity in LMAN was also often markedly reduced immediately following song termination.

For a more detailed examination of the relationship of neural firing to song production, we recorded extended periods of singing, during which most birds produced multiple renditions of a stereotyped song. The bird shown in figure 32.7, for example, frequently sang a song type that contained two repeats of an extremely

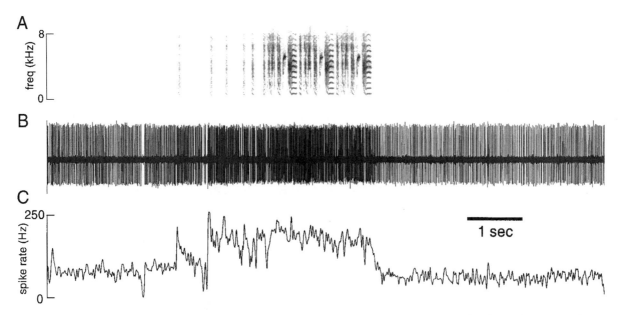

A
freq (kHz)
8

0

B

C
spike rate (Hz)
250

1 sec

0

FIGURE 32.6   Excitation in area X during song production. Spectrogram of a 10-second period including a song produced by bird mx-13 (A), along with simultaneously recorded firing of a single unit in area X (B). This neuron strikingly increased its firing rate, from a steady baseline of ~100 Hz during song production. This can also be seen in panel C, where the instantaneous spike rate of this neuron, calculated by convolving spike arrival times with a 10-ms Gaussian kernel, is displayed.

reproducible five-syllable motif (figure 32.7A–C; note especially the apparent close match between the renditions of the complex syllables d and e in the first and second motifs). The amplitude envelopes of 100 of these song productions are displayed on a grayscale and aligned for maximal overlap of the last four syllables in figure 32.7D. The timing of syllable production over repeated motifs was very stereotyped: For both the first and second motifs, variability in motif duration was approximately 1% [for the first motif, duration = 721 ± 8.2 ms (s.d.); for the second, duration = 736 ± 7.8 ms]. The apparently larger scatter in timing for the first motif is largely due to variability in the interval between the two motifs. Below the 100 motif renditions, the multi-unit neural activity level recorded in LMAN during each song is also plotted on a grayscale (figure 32.7E). This makes evident the consistent increase in neural activity prior to the first song elements as well as the post-singing inhibition.

In addition to the relationship between activity and the initiation and termination of singing, there were on average in all recordings consistent patterns of activity related to individual song elements. Although this was not always obvious on single trials or with single units (e.g., figures 32.5E–F and 32.7G), it can be seen in a plot of average activity level during song motifs (figure 32.7F): Even though syllables in the first motif are not optimally aligned, the patterns of average activity are quite similar during, for example, the repeats of syllables d and e in the first and second motifs. When both motifs were independently well-aligned, mean activity levels during repeated song elements were even more similar. Thus, despite the variability across renditions at the single-neuron level, the simultaneous activity of multiple AF neurons carries a signal with a consistent relationship to song syllables.

Peaks of activity in all recordings also tended to precede syllables (figure 32.7D–E; see also figures 32.10 and 32.11). To compare directly the temporal relationship of activity to song production for LMAN with that in the motor pathway, we calculated the latency from increased neural activity to song onset. For a representative bird, activity preceding 84 song bouts in which the bird had been quiet for at least three seconds prior to singing is displayed in figure 32.8. Firing to song onset latency was measured from the onset of the abrupt activity peak just preceding the first syllable of the song to the onset of this syllable (some birds, like the one in figure 32.8, also showed a slow and variable increase in activity prior to the distinct activity peak, which was not included in this latency measurement). For the site shown, the mean latency was 58 ms; across recordings from all birds, the mean latency was 62 ± 16 ms (s.d.), with means within individual birds ranging from 48 to 95 ms. These values are in the range of those reported in previous studies of singing-related activity in HVc (McCasland, 1987; Yu and Margoliash, 1996). This is therefore consistent with the possibility that much of the singing-related AF activity originates from the song motor circuit, and may represent in part a version of the

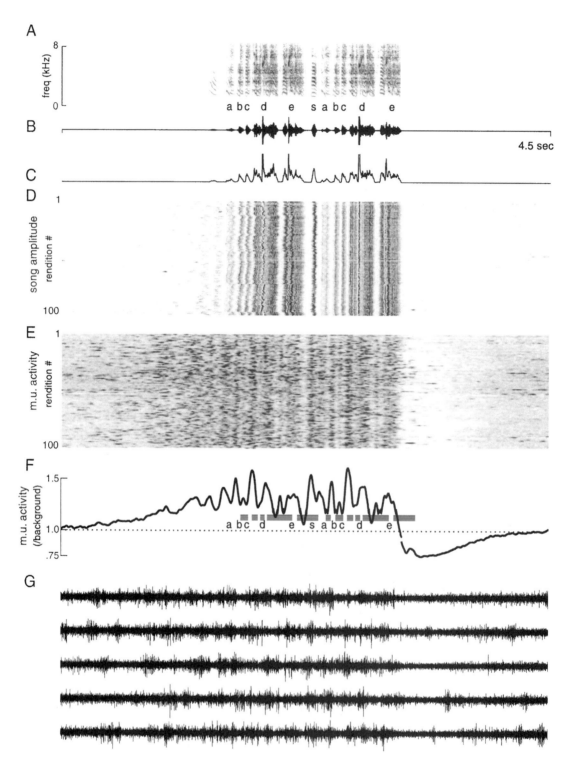

FIGURE 32.7 Neural activity in LMAN associated with repeated song-motif renditions. Spectrogram (A) and oscillogram (B) of a typical song produced by bird dc-18. In order to represent song temporal structure in one dimension, the song oscillogram waveform was rectified and smoothed, as shown in C. These smoothed amplitude envelopes can then be displayed using a grayscale (dark areas represent high intensity), allowing a graphical representation of multiple song renditions, as in D, in which amplitude envelopes of 100 consecutive song renditions recorded in a single session are plotted,

aligned for maximal overlap between the final four syllables. The striking stereotypy of song timing and structure is evident in these plots. Panel E shows the multi-unit neural activity level recorded during each successive song rendition, along with F, the mean neural activity level (normalized by background nonsinging activity level) across 160 song renditions. Mean timing of syllable occurrence is overlaid on panel F for comparison of activity to song production. Neural activity during five representative song renditions is shown in panel G.

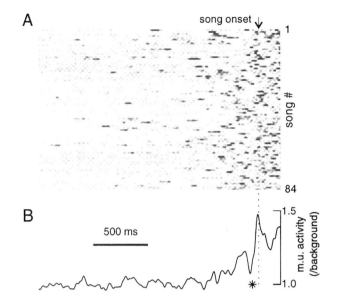

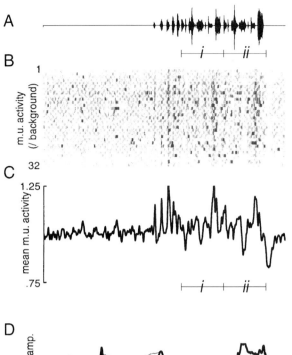

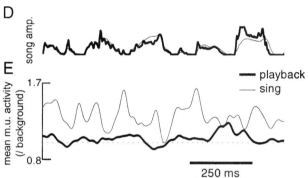

FIGURE 32.8 Temporal relationship of LMAN firing to song initiation. (A) Multi-unit activity level, represented in grayscale, as in figure 32.7, during multiple 2-second presinging epochs, and the initial 200 ms of singing. (B) Below activity levels for individual trials is plotted the mean of all trials, scaled by background activity level. Note the slight and gradual increase in activity several hundred milliseconds prior to song and the abrupt activity peak just prior to singing onset. The onset of this peak, at 58 ms prior to song initiation, is indicated by an asterisk.

premotor signals also sent to the motor output pathway, that is, an "efference copy" of motor commands from the song control nucleus HVc. Such activity patterns are often seen in sensorimotor systems (von Holst and Mittelstaedt, 1950; Bell, 1989; Bridgeman, 1995) and can be useful for providing information about intended motor activity to multiple areas of the brain, and for comparing motor commands with the motor or sensory consequences of these commands.

As an initial investigation of what portion of the activity during singing might reflect sensory input—and because most previous studies of the AF analyzed auditory responses to playback of song (although in anesthetized birds)—we also presented a taped version of the bird's song to awake birds. Playback of the bird's own song did in some cases evoke patterned activity similar to that seen in anesthetized birds. One of the strongest such responses that we recorded is shown in figure 32.9. Passive presentation of a two-motif song version of the bird's own song consistently elicited increases and decreases in multi-unit neural activity (figure 32.9B,C) at this site. This response was clearly smaller, however, than that seen at the same site when the bird produced the same song motif itself (figure 32.9D–E), and a clear relationship between the firing pattern during singing and that during playback was not

FIGURE 32.9 LMAN activity elicited by presentation of a bird's own song and comparison to singing-related activity. Multiple trials of passive presentation of a two-motif version of a bird's own song (A; motifs denoted by i,ii and divided by bar) elicited consistent firing (B) over background levels, as measured by integrated multiple unit activity (grayscale axis: darkness proportional to amplitude). Consistent firing pattern over presentations is indicated by distinct peaks and troughs in the mean activity level (C; scaled by background firing level) over these presentations. Despite the equal overall amplitude of the two songs (D; thin line, average amplitude of motifs sung; thick line, average amplitude of taped song), mean activity levels during playback of the first and second motifs combined (E; thick line) were lower than the activity elicited during singing of the same song motifs at the same site (E; thin line, average multi-unit activity level).

apparent. Such playback responses were not seen in all birds, and were in all cases less consistent than activity during song production. Thus, much of the singing-related firing may be associated with motor production of song, and it may also be critical for maximal and consistent sensory responses that the bird produce the sound itself.

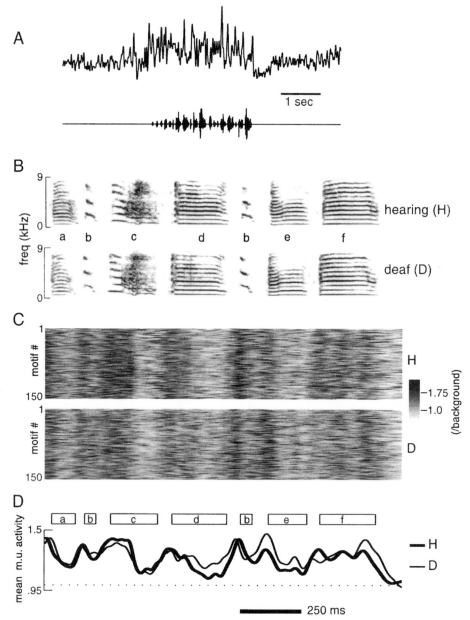

FIGURE 32.10 Singing-related neural activity at sites in LMAN before and after deafening. (A) The waveform and oscillogram show the song and associated increase in LMAN firing in a deaf bird. Between several hours prior to deafening (H) and one day following deafening (P.D.), the production of a stereotyped seven-syllable song motif was not grossly altered. (B) Multi-unit neural activity level (normalized by background nonsinging activity levels; see grayscale to right) in LMAN during repeated motif renditions was likewise very similar in pattern and amplitude between hearing (H) and deafened (P.D.) conditions, despite the fact that this activity was recorded at different sites in the hearing and deaf birds (C). Furthermore, mean activity levels across 150 motif renditions (D) revealed only small differences in the pattern of activity during motif production between the site at which the bird could hear its own voice and the site recorded when it could not. Above the mean activity plot is a representation of the average syllable timing (for the P.D. recording). Note that, as in figure 32.11, the trend for peaks of activity seems to associate with syllable onsets.

AF nuclei are active during singing in deaf birds

To determine whether activity is present in the AF of deaf birds, we recorded multi-unit activity from several sites in LMAN, deafened the birds by cochlear removal, then recorded activity during singing one to three days later. The nucleus was still markedly active during singing (figure 32.10A), and thus AF activity is available to influence the song motor pathway of deaf birds.

We then began to investigate whether AF activity is not only present after deafening but immediately altered in its patterning. As an initial attempt to examine whether patterned AF activity during song production is modulated by the sound of the bird's own voice, we compared the pattern of multi-unit activity during motifs recorded from deaf birds (at a time when song structure had not yet noticeably changed, 1–4 days post-deafening; figure 32.10B) to that recorded at nearby sites before deafening. Strikingly, neither the activity of multi-unit sites (figure 32.10C) nor the activity averaged over many sites (figure 32.10D) was grossly different between pre- and post-deafening recordings. Thus, on average, much of the singing-related AF firing is not dramatically or rapidly altered by deafening. If the sensory feedback from the bird's own voice is of the same order of magnitude as responses to playback (figure 32.9), however, it might be a small fraction of the large singing-related neural activity, and perhaps difficult to detect under normal conditions. More precise measurements of activity of the same sites or even single neurons pre- and post-deafening will be necessary to see if the AF activity of identified neurons or sites shows any immediate, more subtle, alterations in the absence of auditory feedback. In addition, systematic and reversible manipulations of auditory feedback that alter its correlation with singing, rather than simply removing it, may be more useful than deafening for revealing any influence of sounds heard on AF activity. Finally, since song deteriorates very slowly in these birds, it may be that, although auditory feedback changes immediately, the neural implementation of the error signal emerges only gradually in adult finches.

AF activity is modulated by social context

Social factors are critically important to singing, both during song learning and in adult song production. For example, a number of studies have shown that zebra finches will not learn from tutors unless they can interact with them (visually or physically; cf. Slater, Eales, and Clayton, 1988); similarly, they have not been found to learn from tape playback unless they are trained to activate the tapes themselves (Adret, 1993). In adult zebra finches, both singing and overall behavior differ when males sing to a live female or male of the same species, as compared to singing in isolation. The songs in these two situations, which have been called "directed" and "undirected" song, respectively, have been suggested to differ in some way in motivational intensity. We investigated whether the singing-related AF activity of adults might be similarly modulated by social context.

For eight birds, epochs of spontaneous isolated singing were interspersed with presentation of a female or male zebra finch, in a separate cage, to the recorded male. Most birds began singing to the other bird within

seconds. Although in a previous study, directed song motifs were sung more rapidly than undirected ones (Sossinka and Bohner, 1980), we did not consistently observe this in our experiments: Our birds' directed song sped up at most by 1%. Syllable structure also did not differ detectably between the two conditions (figure 32.11, top). Thus, the fine structure of motif production was nearly identical for these songs produced in quite different behavioral contexts.

The pattern of neural activity in anterior forebrain nuclei, however, was strikingly dependent on the behavioral context. One example of such an experiment is seen in figure 32.11. During an eight-hour recording session, almost three hundred renditions of a stereotyped six-syllable song motif (figure 32.11, top) were produced. The multi-unit activity level in LMAN during each rendition, plotted on a grayscale as in figures 32.7–10, is shown beneath the spectrograms in figure 32.11. The responses occurred in two distinct social contexts, either with another bird present (filled bar to right of activity plots), or in isolation (empty bar to right). The pattern of activity during production of identical song elements clearly depended on whether the bird was alone or with another bird. Average activity during singing directed to another bird was consistently of lower overall amplitude, as is seen in the mean activity levels within and across renditions (figure 32.11). Moreover, there was a larger modulation of activity during undirected compared to directed singing, as measured by the coefficient of variation (C.V.) of activity levels within individual song renditions (figure 32.11, within rendition panel). Finally, the activity patterns during the two conditions revealed more variability in the pattern of activity associated with song elements during undirected as compared to directed singing (as measured by the C.V. values across motif renditions for each condition; figure 32.11, across renditions panel). Many of these differences between the two social conditions can be seen not only in the mean activity plots, but also in traces of neural activity such as those recorded during six consecutive motif renditions, spanning a transition from accompanied to solitary social state (figure 32.11, bottom). Spikes during directed singing (the top three waveforms) often appeared discrete and temporally distinct from each other, while firing during singing alone (bottom three waveforms) was often clustered into large bursts of activity, which could be followed by depression below background firing levels. Similar differences in activity were seen between directed and undirected singing for six birds in LMAN, and for five birds in area X. Thus, AF firing is consistently different in distinct social settings.

While AF activity distinguishes between directed and undirected singing in adult birds, preliminary results

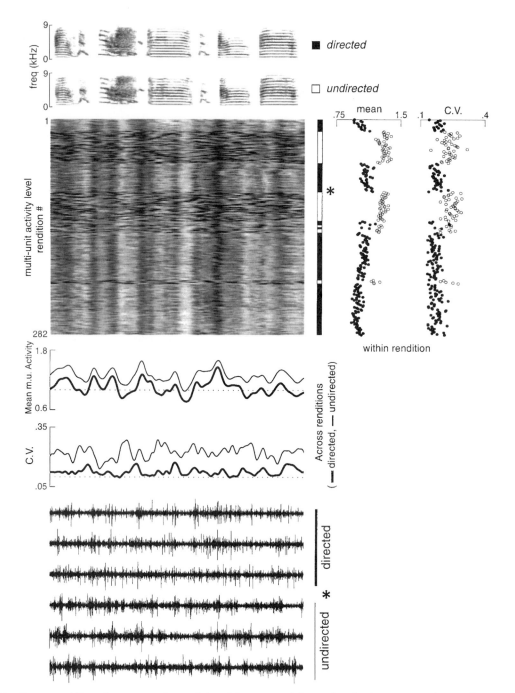

FIGURE 32.11 Firing in AF nuclei is strongly modulated by social factors. Top: Spectrograms of a six-syllable song motif of bird dc-12, sung in the presence of another bird (above, *directed*) and in isolation (below, *undirected*). Plotted below these spectrograms is the multi-unit neural activity recorded during production of consecutive renditions of this motif during an eight-hour session, with amplitude represented by grayscale, as in figures 32.7 through 32.10. Duration of each rendition is 950 ms. The vertical bar to right of the panel indicates social stimuli present during production of each motif rendition, with the filled bar representing the presence of another bird (directed singing), and the empty bar representing isolation (undirected singing). To the right of the social status bar are plotted the mean activity level for each motif rendition and the relative modulation level of activity within each motif (calculated as the C.V. of activity within each rendition, that is, the S.D./mean). Note the strong and reproducible difference in activity during song depending on the behavioral context. Panels below the grayscale activity panel show the mean activity levels and the C.V. of activity over time across all renditions of directed (thick line) and undirected (thin line) motifs. Background levels of mean activity and C.V. are plotted as dotted lines on these panels. Bottom: Neural activity waveforms recorded during production of six consecutive song motifs during a change from directed to undirected singing (these waveforms were drawn from the epoch marked with an asterisk to right of social context bar).

suggest that the direct motor circuit of the adult song system may not (Hessler, Kao, and Doupe, 1998). In recordings of multi-unit neural activity in the nucleus RA of three adult zebra finches, there were no significant differences in firing amplitude or variability between directed and undirected singing. This is consistent with the relative lack of difference in song structure between the two types of singing in our experiments. Thus, the signal influencing the activity of the song system AF circuit as a function of social context may arise elsewhere than HVc, perhaps in the strong projection from mesolimbic dopaminergic neurons to the AF circuit (Lewis et al., 1981; Soha, Shimizu, and Doupe, 1996).

Conclusions

Although initial lesion studies of the AF nuclei suggested that they play a role only during song learning (Bottjer, Miesner, and Arnold, 1984; Nottebohm, Stokes and Leonard, 1976; Scharff and Nottebohm, 1991; Sohrabji, Nordeen, and Nordeen, 1990), this idea must be revised in light of these behavioral studies of adults in whom the normal match between song output and its feedback has been altered. They show that the nucleus LMAN is also essential in adults for vocal motor plasticity, even the marked deterioration associated with deafening. This is consistent with the results of Morrison and Nottebohm (1993), who created an unusual situation in which adult zebra finches could incorporate new syllables into song, and showed that they did not do so after LMAN lesions.

In addition, our neurophysiological studies in awake, behaving birds show that singing is accompanied by patterned activity in the AF, even though this activity is not required for song production. This activity is present in both hearing and deaf adult birds during singing, and thus may provide information necessary for plasticity to the motor pathway. The temporal relationship of AF firing to song suggests that this activity consists in part of an efference copy of the motor commands from the song control nucleus HVc. Finally, singing-related activity in LMAN and area X is also modulated by behavioral context, which is known to be important for song learning in zebra finches: When birds sing to conspecific males or females, AF activity during song is decreased both in magnitude and in variability compared to activity in the same birds singing alone.

In combination, the behavioral and physiological results suggest that the AF provides a neural error signal that actively instructs change in the motor pathway of birds experiencing a sensorimotor mismatch. This "instructive" model for the function of the AF in adult song maintenance, equivalent to the ideas outlined in figure 32.2, is thus the same as that proposed for young birds. Alternatively (or in addition), AF activity may be "permissive" for plasticity by providing critical neural or trophic inputs to the motor pathway. Several lines of evidence offer indirect support for the first (instructive) hypothesis. For one, the AF is clearly active during singing, even in deaf birds, and thus provides input to the RA premotor neurons also receiving direct input from HVc. Moreover, the song-selective auditory properties of neurons in LMAN and area X are well suited to provide feedback to the motor pathways about how well a bird's vocalizations match its intended target (Doupe, 1997; Solis and Doupe, 1997). Surprisingly, however, the overall activity in LMAN during singing did not immediately change dramatically between hearing and deaf birds. Further crucial predictions of this hypothesis therefore remain to be addressed, particularly whether the patterned activity of the AF during singing carries sensory information about the bird's own vocalizations, and whether this changes, perhaps subtly or slowly, in singing birds with sensorimotor mismatch.

Alternatively, the hypothesis that LMAN is permissive for change in song output throughout life proposes that, without LMAN inputs to RA, no change in the connections of the motor pathway (HVc to RA and RA intrinsic connections) can occur. The occlusion of the effects of deafening by LMAN lesions in this model would be the result of withdrawing inputs necessary for plasticity from RA. The putative error signals resulting from sensorimotor mismatch might exist elsewhere in the song circuit, or could also be in the AF; in the latter case, the AF would be instructive as well as permissive. Several existing findings are consistent with the idea that the AF is permissive for vocal plasticity. In young birds, lesions of LMAN have very different effects on song than do lesions of the AF nucleus two steps earlier in the pathway, area X (Scharff and Nottebohm, 1991; Sohrabji, Nordeen, and Nordeen, 1990). Following lesions of area X, the song of young birds remains permanently plastic, perhaps as a result of losing an instructive target signal. In contrast, LMAN lesions in birds of the same age cause a rapid and premature crystallization of an abnormally simplified song. This behavioral difference suggests that area X and LMAN lesions do not cause completely analogous disruptions of patterned information through this pathway, and that LMAN lesions in young birds cause decreased vocal motor plasticity just as in adults. One possibility is that loss of LMAN terminals deprives RA not only of patterned activity, but also of some neural or trophic influence required to change synapses in the motor pathway. Earlier in development (around 20 days posthatch in zebra finches), LMAN clearly has some trophic function, since lesioning LMAN results in cell death in RA (Akutagawa and Konishi, 1994; Johnson and Bottjer, 1994). In addition, in both juvenile and adult birds, the LMAN synapses on RA neurons activate primarily NMDA receptors, rather than the more usual mixture of NMDA and non-NMDA receptors common in most forebrain areas (Mooney, 1992). Such highly NMDAergic synapses are common in developing systems, where their activation and the subsequent influx of calcium is thought to play a trophic role in synaptic growth and stabilization (e.g., Constantine-Paton, Cline, and Debski, 1990), but are much rarer in adults; the presence of significant numbers of such synapses in adult RA makes them a possible candidate for mediating trophic or other permissive effects of LMAN activity.

Finally, song learning in general, and in zebra finches in particular, is strongly dependent on particular behavioral cues, and can be shaped by social factors, both early, during sensory learning (Adret, 1993; Baptista and Petrinovich, 1986; Slater, Eales, and Clayton, 1988), and later, during song crystallization (West and King, 1988; Nelson and Marler, 1994). The consistent change in AF firing in different social settings thus raises the possibility that the AF can regulate song plasticity as a function of behavioral context, and/or contribute to motivational and social aspects of song. The fact that neither song structure nor RA activity in adults appeared to change acutely in response to the socially induced changes in LMAN activity is similar to the slow or absent effects of deafening and LMAN lesions on adult song. This may reflect the weak effect of the LMAN to RA connections in adult birds, which are much diminished compared to those in juvenile birds (Herrmann and Arnold, 1991). Social effects on song and RA neural activity might be much faster and more obvious in young birds, when plasticity is enhanced. Alternatively, social effects on song structure and learning at any age may occur slowly over time and require multiple episodes of a particular behavioral context.

These studies in adults, at a time when the rapid growth and development of the song system is complete and no longer confounds the mechanisms essential to learning, have provided evidence for a role of the AF pathway in vocal plasticity that holds throughout learning as well as in adulthood. Moreover, the problems of social and attentional effects on learning, which are evident in many animals, may be particularly approachable in this system, with its combination of a discrete behavior and a dedicated neural circuit involved in its control.

ACKNOWLEDGMENTS We thank Tony Movshon for comments on the manuscript, Amy Tam and Adria Arteseros for expert technical help, and Ned Molyneaux for excellent editorial assistance. The work described and the preparation of the manuscript were supported by a Life Sciences Research Fellowship (MSB), a National Research Service Award (NAH), the Merck Fund, the EJLB Foundation, and National Institutes of Health grants MH55987 and NS34835.

REFERENCES

ADRET, P., 1993. Operant conditioning, song learning and imprinting to taped song in the zebra finch. *Animal Behav.* 46:149–159.

AKUTAGAWA, E., and M. KONISHI, 1994. Two separate areas of the brain differentially guide the development of a song control nucleus in the zebra finch. *Proc. Natl. Acad. Sci. U.S.A.* 91:12413–12417.

BAPTISTA, L. F., and L. PETRINOVICH, 1986. Song development in the white-crowned sparrow: Social factors and sex differences. *Animal Behav.* 34:1359–1371.

BASHAM, M. E., E. J. NORDEEN, and K. W. NORDEEN, 1996. Blockade of NMDA receptors in the anterior forebrain impairs sensory acquisition in the zebra finch. *Neurobiol. Learning Mem.* 66:295–304.

BELL, C. C., 1989. Sensory coding and corollary discharge effects in mormyrid electric fish. *J. Exp. Biol.* 146:229–253.

BOTTJER, S. W., K. A. HALSEMA, S. A. BROWN, and E. A. MIESNER, 1989. Axonal connections of a forebrain nucleus involved with vocal learning in zebra finches. *J. Comp. Neurol.* 279:312–326.

BOTTJER, S. W., E. A. MIESNER, and A. P. ARNOLD, 1984. Forebrain lesions disrupt development but not maintenance of song in passerine birds. *Science* 224:901–903.

BRAINARD, M. S., and A. J. DOUPE, 1997. Anterior forebrain lesions eliminate deafening-induced song deterioration in adult zebra finches. *Soc. Neurosci. Abstr.* 22:796.

BRIDGEMAN, B., 1995. A review of the role of efference copy in sensory and oculomotor control systems. *Ann. Biomed. Eng.* 23:409–422.

CONSTANTINE-PATON, M., H. T. CLINE, and E. DEBSKI, 1990. Patterned activity, synaptic convergence, and the NMDA receptor in developing visual pathways. *Annu. Rev. Neurosci.* 13:129–154.

COWIE, R., and E. DOUGLAS-COWIE, 1992. *Postlingually Acquired Deafness: Speech Deterioration and the Wider Consequences*, Vol. 62, W. Winter, ed. Berlin: Mouton de Gruyter.

DOUPE, A. J., 1993. A neural circuit specialized for vocal learning. *Curr. Opin. Neurobiol.* 3(1):104–111.

DOUPE, A. J., 1997. Song- and order-selective neurons in the songbird anterior forebrain and their emergence during vocal development. *J. Neurosci.* 17:1147–1167.

DOUPE, A. J., and M. KONISHI, 1991. Song-selective auditory circuits in the vocal control system of the zebra finch. *Proc. Natl. Acad. Sci. U.S.A.* 88:11339–11343.

HERRMANN, K., and A. P. ARNOLD, 1991. The development of afferent projections to the robust archistriatal nucleus in male zebra finches: A quantitative electron microscopic study. *J. Neurosci.* 11:2063–2074.

HESSLER, N. A., and A. J. DOUPE, 1997. Singing-related neural activity in anterior forebrain nuclei of adult zebra finch. *Soc. Neurosci. Abstr.* 22:245.

HESSLER, N. A., and A. J. DOUPE, 1999. Social context modulates singing-related neural activity in the songbird forebrain. *Nature Neurosci.* 2:209–211.

HESSLER, N. A., M. KAO, and A. J. DOUPE, 1998. Singing-related activity of adult anterior forebrain nuclei and its modulation by social context. *Soc. Neurosci. Abstr.* 23:191.

JOHNSON, F., and S. W. BOTTJER, 1994. Afferent influences on cell death and birth during development of a cortical nucleus necessary for learned vocal behavior in zebra finches. *Development* 120:13–24.

KONISHI, M., 1965. The role of auditory feedback in the control of vocalization in the white-crowned sparrow. *Z. f. Tierpsychol.* 22:770–783.

KONISHI, M., 1985. Birdsong: From behavior to neuron. *Annu. Rev. Neurosci.* 8:125–170.

KROODSMA, D., and E. H. MILLER, 1996. *Ecology and Evolution of Acoustic Communication in Birds*. Ithaca, N.Y.: Cornell University Press.

LEWIS, J. W., S. M. RYAN, A. P. ARNOLD, and L. L. BUTCHER, 1981. Evidence for a catecholaminergic projection to area X in the zebra finch. *J. Comp. Neurol.* 196: 347–354.

MARLER, P., 1970. A comparative approach to vocal learning: song development in white-crowned sparrows. *J. Comp. Physiol. Psych.* 71:1–25.

MARLER, P., and S. PETERS, 1989. Species differences in auditory responsiveness in early vocal learning. In *The Comparative Psychology of Audition: Perceiving Complex Sounds*, R. J. Dooling and S. H. Hulse, eds. Hillsdale, N.J.: Erlbaum, pp. 243–273.

MCCASLAND, J. S., 1987. Neuronal control of bird song production. *J. Neurosci.* 7:23–39.

MOONEY, R., 1992. Synaptic basis for developmental plasticity in a birdsong nucleus. *J. Neurosci.* 12:2464–2477.

MORRISON, R. G., and F. NOTTEBOHM, 1993. Role of a telencephalic nucleus in the delayed song learning of socially isolated zebra finches. *J. Neurobiol.* 24:1045–1064.

NELSON, D. A., and P. MARLER, 1994. Selection-based learning in bird song development. *Proc. Natl. Acad. Sci. U.S.A.* 91:10498–10501.

NORDEEN, K. W., and E. J. NORDEEN, 1992. Auditory feedback is necessary for the maintenance of stereotyped song in adult zebra finches. *Behav. Neural Biol.* 57:58–66.

NORDEEN, K. W., and E. J. NORDEEN, 1993. Long-term maintenance of song in adult zebra finches is not affected by lesions of a forebrain region involved in song learning. *Behav. Neural Biol.* 59:79–82.

NOTTEBOHM, F., 1968. Auditory experience and song development in the chaffinch (*Fringilla coelebs*). *Ibis* 11:549–568.

NOTTEBOHM, F., T. M. STOKES, and C. M. LEONARD, 1976. Central control of song in the canary, *Serinus canarius*. *J. Comp. Neurol.* 165:457–486.

OKANOYA, K., and A. YAMAGUCHI, 1997. Adult Bengalese finches (*Lonchura striata* var. *domestica*) require real-time auditory feedback to produce normal song syntax. *J. Neurobiol.* 33:343–356.

OKUHATA, S., and N. SAITO, 1987. Synaptic connections of thalamo-cerebral vocal control nuclei of the canary. *Brain Res. Bull.* 18:35–44.

PRICE, P. H., 1979. Developmental determinants of structure in zebra finch song. *J. Comp. Physiol. Psych.* 93:268–277.

SCHARFF, C., and F. NOTTEBOHM, 1991. Selective impairment of song learning following lesions of a forebrain nucleus in the juvenile zebra finch. *J. Neurosci.* 11:2896–2913.

SLATER, P. J., L. A. EALES, and N. S. CLAYTON, 1988. Song learning in zebra finches (*Taeniopygia guttata*): Progress and prospects. *Adv. Study Behav.* 18:1–33.

SOHA, J. A., T. SHIMIZU, and A. J. DOUPE, 1996. Development of the catecholaminergic innervation of the song system of the male zebra finch. *J. Neurobiol.* 29:473–489.

SOHRABJI, F., E. J. NORDEEN, and K. W. NORDEEN, 1990. Selective impairment of song learning following lesions of a forebrain nucleus in the juvenile zebra finch. *Behav. Neur. Biol.* 53:51–63.

SOLIS, M. M., and A. J. DOUPE, 1997. Anterior forebrain neurons develop selectivity by an intermediate stage of song learning. *J. Neurosci.* 17:6447–6462.

SOSSINKA, R., and J. BOHNER, 1980. Song types in the zebra finch *poephila guttata castanotis*. *Z Tierpsychol.* 53:123–132.

VON HOLST, E., and H. MITTELSTAEDT, 1950. Das Reafferenzprinzip. *Naturwissenschaften* 37:464–476.

WEST, M. J., and A. P. KING, 1988. Female visual displays affect the development of male song in the cowbird. *Nature* 334:244–246.

WILD, J. M., 1997. Neural pathways for the control of birdsong. *J. Neurobiol.* 33:653–670.

WOOLLEY, S. M., and E. W. RUBEL, 1997. Bengalese finches (*Lonchura striata domestica*) depend upon auditory feedback for the maintenance of adult song. *J. Neurosci.* 17:6380–6390.

YU, A. C., and D. MARGOLIASH, 1996. Temporal hierarchical control of singing in birds. *Science* 273:1871–1875.

33 A Computational Model of Avian Song Learning

KENJI DOYA AND TERRENCE J. SEJNOWSKI

ABSTRACT   Oscine song learning has an auditory phase during which a tutor song is learned and a sensorimotor phase of successive improvement that leads to adult song. A theoretical framework for song learning is presented based on the hypothesis that the primary role of the *anterior forebrain pathway* of the song system is to transform an auditory template to a motor program by a form of reinforcement learning. This framework was tested by building a network model of the song-learning system including a model of the syrinx, the avian vocal organ. The model replicated the spectral envelopes of the syllables from zebra finch songs after several hundred trials of learning. The performance of the model was even better when trained on songs generated by another model having the same architecture. Experiments are proposed to further test the biological plausibility of the hypothesis, which may lead to a more detailed model of the song-learning system. Other types of sensorimotor learning based on mimicry could be implemented with a similar type of computational model.

In comparison with our understanding of the preprogrammed central pattern generators found in many invertebrates and lower vertebrates responsible for complex motor behaviors (Cohen, Rossignol, and Grillner, 1988; Harris-Warrick et al., 1992; Kristan, 1992), much less is known about the representation of motor patterns acquired through experience in humans and other vertebrates, such as walking, riding a bicycle, or talking. Singing in oscine birds is a favorable system for studying the acquisition of complex motor patterns. Much is known about the ethology of birdsong learning and the influence of early auditory learning (Marler, 1963; Konishi, 1965; Marler, 1991; Catchpole and Slater, 1995). The major brain nuclei involved in song control and learning have been identified, as schematically shown in figure 33.1 (Nottebohm, Stokes, and Leonard, 1976; Bottjer et al., 1989). New data are accumulating from lesion and recording experiments on these nuclei (for reviews, see Konishi, 1985; Doupe, 1993; Margoliash, 1997; Bottjer and Arnold, 1997).

KENJI DOYA   Kawato Dynamic Brain Project, ERATO, Japan Science and Technology Corporation, Kyoto, Japan, and Howard Hughes Medical Institute, Salk Institute for Biological Studies, La Jolla, Calif.
TERRENCE J. SEJNOWSKI   Department of Biology, University of California, San Diego, and Howard Hughes Medical Institute, Salk Institute for Biological Studies, La Jolla, Calif.

The primary goal of this chapter is to present a theoretical framework and a working model for song learning based on recent experimental findings. Specifically, we focus on the function of the *anterior forebrain pathway*, which is not involved in song production in adult birds, but is necessary for song learning in young birds (Bottjer, Miesner, and Arnold, 1984). Our main hypothesis is that the anterior forebrain pathway works as a reinforcement learning system that is similar to the *adaptive critic* architecture proposed by Barto, Sutton, and Anderson (1983).

The song *template* is a key concept in birdsong learning. A young male bird listens to a *tutor song* during the *critical period* and memorizes a template of the song; later, the bird learns to sing the stored song by comparing its own vocalization to the song template using auditory feedback (Konishi, 1965). However, it is still an open question how the song is encoded and where in the bird's brain the song template is stored. Recent experiments in zebra finch suggest that the song control system has a hierarchical organization: HVc, the high vocal center, is involved in producing a sequence of syllables, whereas its downstream nucleus RA is responsible for the subsyllabic components (Vu, Mazurek, and Kuo, 1994; Yu and Margoliash, 1996).

If we assume that a song is learned in such a hierarchical fashion, the problem of song learning can be decomposed into the following three subproblems:

1. *Sensory encoding:* How to encode the acoustic features of syllables in such a way that they are reliably recognized.
2. *Sequential memory:* How to organize the network so that syllable sequences are stably memorized and reproduced.
3. *Motor decoding:* How to find the motor command patterns needed to replicate the acoustic features of each syllable.

Existing experimental evidence does not provide straightforward solutions to these problems. A computational approach could help in exploring the biological solutions and, in particular, in providing functional

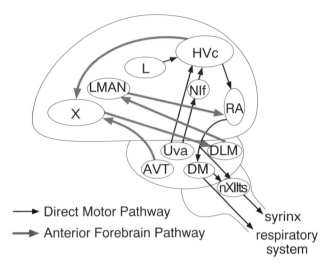

→ Direct Motor Pathway
→ Anterior Forebrain Pathway

FIGURE 33.1 Schematic diagram of the major songbird brain nuclei involved in song control. The thinner arrows show the direct motor control pathway, and the thicker arrows show the anterior forebrain pathway. Abbreviations: Uva, nucleus uvaeformis of thalamus; NIf, nucleus interface of neostriatum; L, field L of forebrain; HVc, high vocal center (formerly called hyperstriatum ventrale, pars caudale); RA, robust nucleus of archistriatum; DM, dorsomedial part of nucleus intercollicularis; nXIIts, tracheosyringeal part of hypoglossal nucleus; AVT, ventral area of Tsai of midbrain; X, area X of lobus parolfactorius; DLM, medial part of dorsolateral nucleus of thalamus; LMAN, lateral magnocellular nucleus of anterior neostriatum.

constraints on the organization of the learning system. For example, theories of unsupervised learning (von der Malsburg, 1973; Amari, 1977; Linsker, 1986; Bell and Sejnowski, 1995) suggest several possible solutions to sensory encoding problems. Studies of associative memory networks (Fukushima, 1973; Sompolinsky and Kanter, 1986; Dehaene, Changeux, and Nadal, 1987; Amari, 1988; Morita, 1996) provide constraints on representation and architectures that enable stable storage of temporal sequences. There have been extensive studies on the "inverse problem" of finding the control input for a nonlinear system to realize a given target output (Miller, Sutton, and Werbos, 1990; Gullapalli, 1995).

In this chapter, we propose a working hypothesis for the functions subserved by song-related brain nuclei in songbirds (figure 33.1), with an emphasis on the role of anterior forebrain pathway in solving the motor decoding problem.

Figure 33.2 illustrates various schemes for solving inverse problems using neural networks. In the first scheme (figure 33.2a), the desired output is converted to a desired motor command by an inverse model of the motor system that enables replication of the desired output in one shot. Although attractive as a model of vocal learning in other species like humans, this is not an appropriate model for vocal learning in songbirds because they require many repetitions of singing trials with auditory feedback. Another possible scheme is error correction learning (figure 33.2b) that uses a linear approximation of the inverse model to convert motor output error into the motor command error for incremental learning of the control network. The problem is that the learning schemes proposed to date either use a biologically implausible algorithm (Jordan and Rumelhart, 1992) or assume the preexistence of an approximate inverse model (Kawato, Furukawa, and Suzuki, 1987; Kawato, 1990). Furthermore, in order to calculate the error in the acoustic output, a replica of the target output, or the tutor song, has to be available.

The third scheme (figure 33.2c) is based on the paradigm of reinforcement learning (Sutton and Barto, 1998). It does not use an inverse model and uses a critic that evaluates the motor output by comparing the present vocal output with the tutor song. Learning is based on the correlation between stochastic changes in the motor command and the increase or decrease in the evaluation (Barto, Sutton, and Anderson, 1983; Gullapalli, 1995). There is no need to maintain a replica of the tutor song. Activation levels of auditory neurons that have selective tuning to the tutor song can be used as the evaluation signal.

Among these alternatives, we argue that the reinforcement learning scheme (figure 33.2c) is the most likely for birdsong learning. We will further propose a hypothesis about how this reinforcement learning scheme can be implemented in the known circuitry of the song control system with the constraints given by anatomy, physiology, and the results of lesion studies. We then describe a neural network model that replicates song learning behavior based on these constraints. Experimental tests of the model and limitations are addressed in the "Discussion."

Earlier versions of this model have appeared elsewhere (Doya and Sejnowski, 1994, 1995).

Model of the song control system

ANATOMY OF THE SONG CONTROL SYSTEM The principal brain nuclei involved in song learning are shown in figure 33.1 (Nottebohm, Stokes, and Leonard, 1976; Bottjer et al., 1989). There are two major pathways: the direct motor pathway and the indirect, anterior forebrain pathway. The direct pathway is composed of Uva, NIf, HVc, RA, DM, and nXIIts. Lesions to these nuclei immediately disrupt singing, although the effects of lesions in Uva and NIf are variable (Nottebohm, Stokes, and Leonard, 1976; Mc-

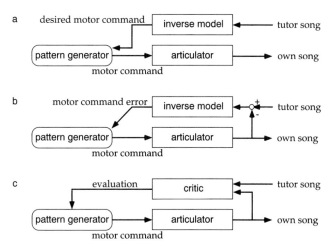

FIGURE 33.2 Different schemes for solving sensorimotor inverse problems. (a) One-shot learning by an inverse model of the motor system. (b) Error correction learning by an approxi-

mate inverse model. (c) Reinforcement learning by a stochastic controller and a critic.

Casland, 1987; Williams and Vicario, 1993; Vu, Kuo, and Chance, 1995). In a recent microstimulation experiment on singing birds, stimulation of HVc produced disruption of the sequence of syllables, whereas stimulation of RA only disrupted the pattern of individual syllables (Vu, Mazurek, and Kuo, 1994). Furthermore, recent study of extracellular recording from singing birds revealed that the activity patterns in HVc are uniquely associated with syllable identity, while precisely timed burst activities in RA are uniquely associated with subsyllabic components (A. C. Yu and Margoliash, 1996). These data suggest that HVc is a candidate site for representing sequences of syllables and that RA is a possible site where the motor patterns for each syllable are stored.

The indirect pathway consists of area X, DLM, and LMAN, forming a bypass from HVc to RA. This pathway is not directly involved in song production because lesions in this pathway in adult birds do not impair their "crystallized" songs (Nottebohm, Stokes, and Leonard, 1976). However, if a lesion is made at any point along the indirect pathway in young birds before the end of vocal learning, their songs become highly abnormal (Bottjer, Miesner, and Arnold, 1984; Sohrabji, Nordeen, and Nordeen, 1990; Scharff and Nottebohm, 1991). There have been a variety of hypotheses for the function of this pathway: comparison of sensory and motor representations of song (Williams, 1989), reinforcement of syllable specific activation patterns within RA (Bottjer et al., 1989), processing of auditory feedback and modulation of plasticity (Scharff and Nottebohm, 1991), a measure of how well a vocalization matches a particular auditory template (Doupe and Konishi, 1991), and selective reinforcement of synaptic connections from HVc to RA (Mooney, 1992).

FUNCTIONS FOR COMPONENTS OF THE SONG CONTROL SYSTEM We propose a functional model of the song control system based on the following experimental evidence:

1. Sequences of syllables are produced at the level of HVc (Vu, Mazurek, and Kuo, 1994; A. C. Yu and Margoliash, 1996).
2. RA is a myotopically organized (Vicario, 1991b).
3. Both the direct and indirect pathways linking HVc and RA are unidirectional (Bottjer et al., 1989).

These facts imply the following constraints on the localization of the computational processes suggested in the preceding list:

1. The representation of syllables suitable for auditory recognition and sequential memory is constructed in the ascending auditory pathway up to the level of HVc.
2. The memory and production of syllable sequences are performed within HVc.
3. The syllable representation in HVc needs to be transformed into muscle-oriented representation in RA.

Figure 33.3 illustrates our current working hypothesis about the functions of song-related nuclei. The ascending auditory pathway from the cochlea through the auditory thalamus and the forebrain auditory nucleus field L to HVc performs hierarchical processing of auditory input, leading to some internal representation of syllables that is useful for recognition and memory. On one hand, it is known that field L has a tonotopical organization (Bonke, Scheich, and Langner, 1979) and that the neurons respond to pure tone or band-limited noises (Margoliash, 1986). On the other hand, no tonotopical organization is found in HVc, whose neurons have more

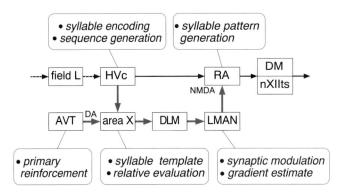

FIGURE 33.3 Schematic diagram indicating the proposed functions for each of the major nuclei of the song system. The direct pathway is shown at the top, starting with auditory input into field L. The anterior forebrain pathway starts at HVc and makes a side loop to RA through area X and LMAN. The bullets in each balloon give the proposed function of the corresponding nucleus. See text for more details.

selective response properties to complex acoustic features, such as frequency modulation, combination of harmonics, sequence of notes, and sequence of syllables (Margoliash, 1983; Margoliash and Fortune, 1992; Lewicki and Konishi, 1995; Lewicki, 1996). Many cells are strongly tuned to the bird's own song (Margoliash, 1986). It has recently been found that the auditory responses of HVc neurons to different syllables have distributed and overlapping spatial patterns (Sutter and Margoliash, 1994), but the functional implication of such a representation remains to be studied.

HVc is regarded as the main center for memory and generation of syllable sequence (Vu, Mazurek, and Kuo, 1994; A. C. Yu and Margoliash, 1996). Sequence production in HVc is probably controlled by timing cues from NIf and Uva (McCasland, 1987; Williams and Vicario, 1993). Neurons in HVc show both auditory and motor responses (McCasland and Konishi, 1981; McCasland, 1987), but neither tonotopical or myotopical organization is seen in HVc. Nor has any simple correlation been reported between the auditory and motor responses for the same syllable (McCasland and Konishi, 1981; McCasland, 1987; C.-H. Yu and Margoliash, 1993). There appears to be a drastic change in the operation of HVc during singing: The spontaneous activity increases (C.-H. Yu and Margoliash, 1993; A. C. Yu and Margoliash, 1996), and the auditory response is suppressed for a few seconds afterward (McCasland and Konishi, 1981).

RA has topographic connection to nXIIts, which topographically projects to the muscles in the syrinx (Vicario, 1988; Vicario, 1991b). The dorsal part of RA projects to DM, which projects to the respiratory control system. Since no myotopical organization is apparent in HVc, the syllable representation in HVc would have to be transformed into a more muscle-oriented representation in the connection from HVc to RA. The anterior

forebrain pathway forms a side path to this motor decoding pathway. Lesions in area X or LMAN in adults do not affect crystallized songs, but disrupt song learning in young birds (Bottjer, Miesner, and Arnold, 1984; Sohrabji, Nordeen, and Nordeen, 1990; Scharff and Nottebohm, 1991). Neurons in area X, DLM, and LMAN have highly selective response to the bird's own song in adult birds (Doupe and Konishi, 1991), but some of them are selective to the tutor song in young birds (Solis and Doupe, 1995). Synaptic connections from LMAN to RA are formed prior to those from HVc (Konishi and Akutagawa, 1985) and are mediated mainly by NMDA-type glutamate receptors (Kubota and Saito, 1991; Mooney and Konishi, 1991), which are involved in development and learning in the mammalian central nervous system (Malenka and Nicoll, 1993; Fox and Zahs, 1994). These facts suggest that the function of the anterior forebrain pathway is to set up appropriate synaptic connections from HVc to RA that lead to a better match between the bird's own vocalization and the song template (Bottjer et al., 1989; Mooney, 1992; Doupe and Konishi, 1991; Doupe, 1993).

Based on these previous suggestions, we hypothesize that the anterior forebrain pathway functions to be a specific reinforcement learning system called an *adaptive critic*, as shown in figure 33.4 (Barto, Sutton, and Anderson, 1983). In a reinforcement learning paradigm, a stochastic perturbation is given to the motor commands, and if it results in better performance, the perturbed motor command is reinforced; that is, the perturbation is made permanent. In order for this learning scheme to work efficiently, it is necessary that the positive and negative reinforcement be balanced. An important role of the critic is to evaluate the present performance relative to the recent average performance, a method known as *reinforcement comparison* (Sutton and Barto, 1998). In the context of syllable vocalization learning, we propose that

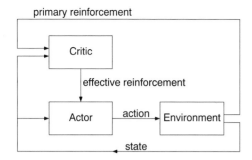

FIGURE 33.4 A block diagram showing the actor-critic architecture for a feedback control task (Barto, Sutton, and Anderson, 1983). The direct control pathway is the closed loop between the actor and the environment. The control policy is learned through interaction with the critic, which evaluates the sensory feedback caused by the action of the actor. A scalar reinforcement signal generated by the critic is used by the actor to modify its future action. The critic receives information used for the evaluation from a primary reinforcer. In the birdsong literature, the term "template" is used for the information used by the critic to perform the evaluation.

LMAN provides stochastic perturbation to the HVc-to-RA connection and that area X evaluates how well the resulting syllable matches the template. The raw similarity index is compared to the recent average similarity index for the syllable, and the relative evaluation signal then determines whether the temporary change in the HVc-to-RA connection is made permanent or not. In this scheme, the evaluation and perturbation modules are on a side path to the main motor control pathway and are not necessary for control when learning is completed.

Several lines of evidence support this hypothesis. Lesions in area X and LMAN in young birds result in contrasting deficits (Scharff and Nottebohm, 1991). Early area X lesion results in unstable singing in the adulthood when songs are normally crystallized. This effect is similar to that of early deafening. Early lesion in LMAN results in stable but poorly structured song with fewer syllables than normal. These observations are nicely explained if we assume that area X serves as the critic, which provides evaluation of vocalization based on auditory feedback, and that LMAN modulates the connection strengths from HVc to RA and provides a random element to the controller.

The hypothesis that area X functions as a critic is supported by the fact that it receives dopaminergic input from a midbrain nucleus AVT, the avian homologue of mammalian ventral tegmental area (Lewis et al., 1981; Casto and Ball, 1994). Activity of the dopamine system is related to reward in many species (Schultz, Apicella, and Ljungberg, 1993). During auditory learning, this dopaminergic input can be used for selection of auditory input that is to be memorized as song template. It has been shown that a young bird does not indiscriminately

memorize all of its auditory experience as its song template. When a young zebra finch is caged with several adult birds, it selects most of its song syllables from the adult that had most frequent interaction with the bird, especially feeding interactions (Williams, 1990). We postulate that this selection of auditory input that is to be memorized as song template happens in area X by association of auditory input from HVc and reward input from AVT. In other words, whereas the auditory tuning of HVc cells should simply reflect auditory experience, responses of area X cells are tuned to the specific songs to be learned. Although the majority of neurons in both HVc and area X in young birds are tuned to the bird's own developing song rather than to the tutor song (Volman, 1993; Doupe, 1993), some of the neurons in area X have preferred tuning to the tutor song (Solis and Doupe, 1995). During the sensorimotor learning phase, the activation level of those neurons could be used to evaluate the match between the vocalization of the bird and that of the tutor. Furthermore, if the function of area X is not simply to detect a match to the stored template but also to provide "relative" evaluation based on recent level of performance, then there should be many cells that are tuned more to the bird's current song than to the tutor song.

As mentioned earlier, synaptic input from LMAN to RA is predominantly mediated by NMDA-type glutamate receptors, whereas input from HVc to RA is mainly mediated by non-NMDA-type receptors (Kubota and Saito, 1991; Mooney and Konishi, 1991). The NMDA-type input from LMAN may enable both short-term and long-term changes in the HVc-to-RA synaptic efficacy during sensorimotor learning. It has been observed in slice preparations that simultaneous stimulation of both HVc and fibers originating in LMAN results in a response larger than the linear summation of individual responses (Mooney, 1992), consistent with some nonlinear interaction between these two inputs. For example, when there is a tonic NMDA-type input, the postsynaptic response to the same non-NMDA-type input is amplified, which effectively modulates the synaptic conductance of the non-NMDA inputs (Thomson and Deuchars, 1994). Although long-term changes of synaptic strengths have not yet been found in RA, activation of NMDA-type receptors triggers plastic synaptic change in many other central nervous systems (Malenka and Nicoll, 1993).

Computer simulations of vocalization learning

We focus on only one of the three computational problems in song learning, namely that of finding the motor commands needed to produce a desired auditory

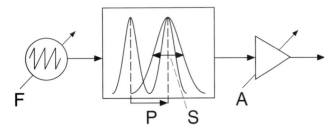

F P S A

FIGURE 33.5 The model of the syrinx used in the song learning model. The sound output was controlled by four input variables: *A*, gain of the amplifier; *F*, fundamental frequency of the sound source; *P*, peak frequency; and *S*, sharpness of the band-pass filter. In addition to these parameters, the output was governed by units with a range of temporal responses (see figure 33.6).

impression. The question we asked is whether the reinforcement learning scheme that we have outlined can be implemented within the known biological constraints and whether such a system can perform sensorimotor learning within a realistic number of trials. We required the model to produce sound that could be compared to real birdsong.

The outline of the simulation system is as follows. We built a simple model of the syrinx, the avian vocal organ, and then constructed a neural network model of RA and HVc that sends a series of motor commands to the syrinx model. We implemented the adaptive critic learning system by assigning the stochastic perturbation to LMAN and the syllable evaluation to area X. Since it was beyond the scope of the present investigation to model the detailed mechanisms of auditory encoding and sequential memory, we used simplified spectrographic template matching for syllable templates and unary encoding of syllables in HVc, which are not necessarily biologically realistic.

SYRINX: SOUND SYNTHESIZER   In order to test the performance of the model of the vocal control system, we designed a computer program that mimics the function of the syrinx, the avian vocal organ located near the junction of the trachea and the bronchi (Brackenbury, 1982; Vicario, 1991a). The sound source for the syrinx is the oscillation of a pair of tympaniform membranes on the medial side of the bronchi. Depending on the tension of the membrane and the airflow around it, which are controlled by the activity of six pairs of syringeal muscles, the syrinx can produce pure tones, harmonic sounds, and nonharmonic sounds with complex frequency modulation (Casey and Gaunt, 1985). Activation of the dorsal syringeal muscles coincides with the air flow in the bronchus, and activation of the ventral syringeal muscles correlates well with the fundamental oscillation frequency of the sound (Goller and Suthers, 1995). The

spectral profile of the sound is also affected by the resonance property of the vocal tract (Nowicki, 1987).

A simple model of the syrinx, shown in figure 33.5, consisted of a variable-frequency sound source, a band-pass filter, and an amplifier. A triangular wave form was used for the sound source because it includes all the integer harmonic components. The output of this sound synthesizer was controlled by the following four variables: the fundamental frequency of the harmonic sound source F, the peak frequency P, the sharpness S of the band-pass filter, and the gain of the amplifier A. The output sound waveform $x(t)$ was calculated from the time course of the variables $(A(t), F(t), P(t), S(t))$, which had values between zero and one:

$$\dot{\phi}(t) = f_0 + (f_1 - f_0)F(t)$$
$$z(t) = [\phi(t) \bmod 1] \times 2 - 1$$
$$\omega(t) = 2\pi[f_2 + (f_3 - f_2)P(t)]$$
$$\mu(t) = \mu_0 + (\mu_1 - \mu_0)S(t)$$
$$\dot{u}(t) = \omega(t)[z(t) - u(t)] - \mu v(t)$$
$$\dot{v}(t) = \mu u(t) - \omega(t)v(t)$$
$$x(t) = A(t)u(t)$$

where $\phi(t)$ and $z(t)$ are the phase and the output of the harmonic oscillator, and $\omega(t)$ and $\mu(t)$ are the angular frequency and damping factor of the band-pass filter, respectively. The values of the parameters were $f_0 = 0.4$ kHz, $f_1 = 1.2$ kHz, $f_2 = 2$ kHz, $f_3 = 8$ kHz, $\mu_0 = 1.0$ ms^{-1}, and $\mu_1 = 0.1$ ms^{-1}. The system was numerically integrated by the Euler method using a time step of $^1/_{32}$ ms. The model could produce "birdlike" chirps and warbles with the time courses of the input variables chosen appropriately (figure 33.9).

RA: SYLLABLE PATTERN GENERATOR   RA is capable of producing a variety of temporal responses in order to produce command outputs for syllables with various spectral features. Several constraints are available from experimental studies. First, RA has a myotopical organization (Vicario, 1991b). Second, in slice preparations, HVc input to RA evokes fast non-NMDA-type, slower NMDA-type, and delayed polysynaptic inhibitory responses (Mooney, 1992). Third, neurotransmitters mediated by second-messenger systems such as norepinephrine and GABA$_B$ agonists also have effects on neurons in RA on slower time scales (Perkel, 1994). Although the details of the local circuits in RA are not yet known, the observed cellular and synaptic time courses could produce the complex temporal responses needed to produce syllables in response to command inputs from HVc.

To mimic myotopical organization, the model of RA had four subnetworks, each of which could exert control

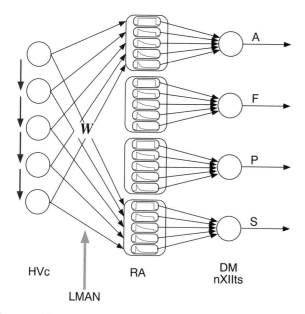

FIGURE 33.6 Model of the direct motor pathway. Syllables were unary coded in HVc, and their sequential activation triggered syllable pattern generation networks in RA. The RA units were divided into four groups corresponding to the four motor command variables (A, F, P, S). Within each group, there were k exponential temporal kernels with different time constants. The sum of their response profiles served as the motor command for the syrinx model.

on one of the four output motor command variables (A, F, P, S). Within each subnetwork, there were $k = 5$ "temporal response kernels," where each unit had a different time course, as shown in figure 33.6. The temporal response of an RA unit $r_j(t)$ to the input from HVc $s_i(t)$ ($i = 1, \ldots, n$) was

$$p_j(t) = \sum_{i=1}^{n} w_{ji} s_i(t)$$

$$\tau_j \dot{q}_j(t) = p_j(t) - q_j(t)$$

$$r_j(t) = p_j(t) - q_j(t)$$

where $p_j(t)$ is the input sum, $q_j(t)$ is delayed inhibition or adaptation, and τ_j is the time constant of the jth unit. The motor command output was synthesized from a combination of these responses:

$$m^C(t) = f\left[\sum_{j=1}^{k} r_j^C(t) + b^C\right]$$

where index C denotes one of the command variables (A, F, P, S), f is a sigmoid function $f(x) = 1/[1 + \exp(-4x)]$, and b is the bias. The time constants of the $k = 5$ kernels were $\tau_1 = \infty$ [i.e., $r_j(t) = p_j(t)$], $\tau_2 = 80$, $\tau_3 =$

40, $\tau_4 = 20$, and $\tau_1 = 10$ (ms). In order to assure clear syllable onset and offset, the bias for the sound amplitude was $b^A = -1$, and the weight for the first kernel was initially set as $w_{1i}^A = 1$. Other biases and initial weights were set to zero. The weights w_{ji} were initialized at the beginning of learning to random values generated with a Gaussian distribution having a standard deviation of 0.1. The reinforcement learning algorithm given in the next subsection incrementally changed the weights corresponding to each syllable.

HVC: SEQUENCE GENERATOR In recordings from HVc in awake birds, some neurons became activated preceding specific syllables (McCasland, 1987; A. C. Yu and Margoliash, 1996). A simple syllable coding was adopted in which all the neurons that become active for the ith syllable were aggregated as the state of a single "unit," s_i. The onset and offset of each syllable in a tutor song was detected by thresholding the sound amplitude and storing the interval in an event table. During the course of a song, each syllable coding unit s_i, was turned on ($s_i = 1$) and off ($s_i = 0$) at the stored onset and offset time. This "unary encoding" scheme is oversimplified, and there is evidence that the motor encoding of syllables has overlaps, so that a single HVc unit would be active during more than one syllable (A. C. Yu and Margoliash, 1996), as in the case of auditory encoding (Sutter and Margoliash, 1994). A distributed encoding could have been used to model HVc, but this was not included in the present model for simplicity.

LMAN: STOCHASTIC GRADIENT ASCENT The vocal output is determined by the connection weight matrix $W = \{w_{ji}^A \ w_{ji}^F \ w_{ji}^P \ w_{ji}^S\}$ based on the preceding models of HVc, RA, and the syrinx. The goal of motor learning then is to find a point in this $4kn$-dimensional weight space that produces a vocalization that maximizes the evaluation of the template-matching measure. In the reinforcement learning algorithm used here, this goal was accomplished by a stochastic method for optimizing the evaluation function.

In the first step of the learning algorithm, the output motor command from RA was stochastically perturbed by temporarily changing the input connection strengths from HVc. Such perturbations in the output of RA units could be produced by the modulation of the HVc-to-RA connection weights by NMDA-type synaptic input from LMAN. The perturbation of the weights was implemented as a static weight change δw_{ji} during each song trial. This produces a perturbation in the RA:

$$\delta p_j(t) = \sum_{i=1}^{n} \delta w_{ji} s_i(t)$$

The second step was to evaluate this perturbed song by comparing it with the song template. By the procedure mentioned in the next section (on area X), a syllable-specific value $\hat{r}$, the "effective" reinforcement, was derived. Finally, the weights were permanently changed based on correlations among the inputs, outputs, and the evaluation (Barto and Jordan, 1987; Barto, 1995):

$$\Delta w_{ji} \propto \hat{r} \times \delta p_j(t) \times s_i(t)$$

With the unary encoding scheme of HVc adopted here, this expression reduces to

$$\Delta w_{ji} \propto \hat{r} \times \delta w_{ji}$$

since only one syllable unit i is active ($s_i = 1$). In other words, the temporary synaptic modulation δw_{ji} persists as a plastic change Δw_{ji} if the effective evaluation is positive, which is a kind of "weight perturbation" optimization algorithm (Alspector et al., 1993; Unnikrishnan and Venugopal, 1994).

A refinement of this basic reinforcement algorithm was used that improved the convergence of the learning. For each trial T, the temporary weight perturbation $\delta w_{ji}(T)$ was the sum of the evaluation gradient estimate $G_{ji}(T)$ defined subsequently and a random perturbation $N_{ji}(T)$ of size η:

$$\delta w_{ji}(T) = G_{ji}(T) + \eta N_{ji}(T)$$

The network with perturbed weights $w_{ji}(T) + \delta W_{ji}(t)$ was used to produce a vocal output, and its evaluation $\hat{r}(T)$ was given by the model of area X described in the next subsection. The weights were then permanently changed only if the trial was successful:

$$w_{ji}(T+1) = w_{ji}(T) + \delta w_{ji}(T) \quad \text{if } \hat{r}(T) > 0$$

The estimate of gradient in the weight space $G_{ji}(T)$ was updated by the sum of the perturbations $\delta W_{ji}(T)$ multiplied by the effective evaluation:

$$G_{ji}(T) = \alpha \hat{r}(T)\delta w_{ji}(T) + (1 - \alpha) G_{ji}(T)$$

where the constant $0 < \alpha < 1$ controls the influence of the new trial on the running average over trials. A geometrical interpretation of this learning algorithm is illustrated in figure 33.7. The weighted running average of the weight change is like the "momentum" that is commonly used in other neural network learning algorithms (Rumelhart, Hinton, and Williams, 1986). We used $\alpha = 0.2$ and $\eta = 0.02$ in all the simulations reported here.

AREA X: EVALUATION BY SPECTROGRAPHIC TEMPLATE MATCHING   The activation levels of the neurons selective for the tutor song that have been observed in area X

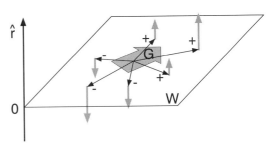

FIGURE 33.7   Estimate of evaluation gradient G from weighted summation of perturbation vectors. The vertical axis is the evaluation $\hat{r}$, and each point in the W plane represents a choice for two of the weights (there were many more in the actual model). The gradient G (central arrow) gives the running average of the evaluation function over the recent history of stochastically chosen weights, represented by the thin vectors from the central thick arrow.

(Solis and Doupe, 1995) could represent the similarity of the recently produced syllable to the corresponding tutor syllable (Doupe and Konishi, 1991). The evaluation of each syllable was assumed to be available separately, and a simple spectrographic template-matching method was used for evaluating its similarity to the tutor syllable, as follows.

First, the sound waveform from the bird was transformed into a spectrogram, which had 80 frequency channels in steps of 100 Hz, sampled every 1 ms. The onset and offset of the syllable were detected by appropriately setting a threshold for the sound amplitude. The spectrographic pattern of each syllable was down-sampled with a Gaussian filter having 40 frequency bins and 20 temporal bins, to accommodate slight variations in both frequency and time domains. The resulting 800-dimensional vector was normalized and then stored as the template vector for each syllable. A sample vector for a synthesized syllable was made in the same way. The correlation $0 \le r \le 1$ between the template and sample vector was used as the raw evaluation score.

We further assumed that area X functions as an "adaptive" critic that provides the evaluation in a form relative to currently expected level of performance. The running average $\bar{r}$ of the evaluation r was updated at each time step:

$$\bar{r}(T+1) = \beta r(T) + (1 - \beta)\bar{r}(T)$$

where $0 < \beta < 1$ is the smoothing constant for the averaging. The "effective evaluation" $\hat{r}$ that was used for learning in LMAN was given by

$$\hat{r}(T) = \tanh\{[r(T) - \bar{r}(T)]/\gamma\}$$

The squashing function tanh was used to regulate the learning process. We used $\beta = 0.1$ and $\gamma = 0.1$ in all simulations.

ZEBRA FINCH SONG SAMPLES Songs of male adult zebra finches were recorded and digitized at 12 bits and with a 32-kHz sampling rate by Michael Lewicki at the California Institute of Technology.

Computer simulation was performed on Sparc Station 10 (Sun Micro Systems) with an audio interface to facilitate evaluation of songs by human ears. The simulation system was programmed in the C language and took approximately 30 minutes to simulate 500 learning trials. The results reported in the next subsection were confirmed in at least five simulation runs using different random seeds for the stochastic learning.

LEARNING A ZEBRA FINCH SONG Figure 33.8 shows an example of how the song learning simulator performed. The spectrogram of a song motif of a zebra finch is displayed in the top row. Ten syllables in the motif were identified (shown in boxes), and their spectrographic patterns were stored as syllable templates. Ten

syllable-coding HVc units were alternately turned on and off at the syllable onset and offset times of the original song motif (upper middle panel). RA units in the model were driven by the HVc output through the synaptic connection strengths w_{ji}. For each of the four motor command variables (A, F, P, S), there were five units with different time constants (middle panel). The sum of the different temporal response profiles determines the time course of the motor command output (lower middle panel), which was sent to the syrinx model. The waveform of the synthesized song was then converted into a spectrogram (bottom panel). The spectrographic patterns of syllables (marked by boxes) were sampled and compared to the templates, yielding an evaluation r for each syllable that was then used for changing the weights w_{ji}.

Initially, the connection weights w_{ji} were set to small random values, so the syllables did not resemble the original song. After about 500 trials, the average correlation

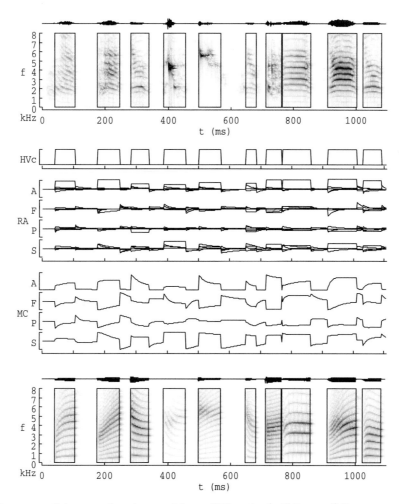

FIGURE 33.8 Input and outputs of the song learning model. (top panel) Spectrogram of the tutor song motif, which consisted of five syllables. (upper middle panel) Activation pattern of HVc units. (middle panel) Responses of the units in RA. (lower middle panel) Four motor command variables. (bottom panel) Spectrogram of the synthesized song produced by the network.

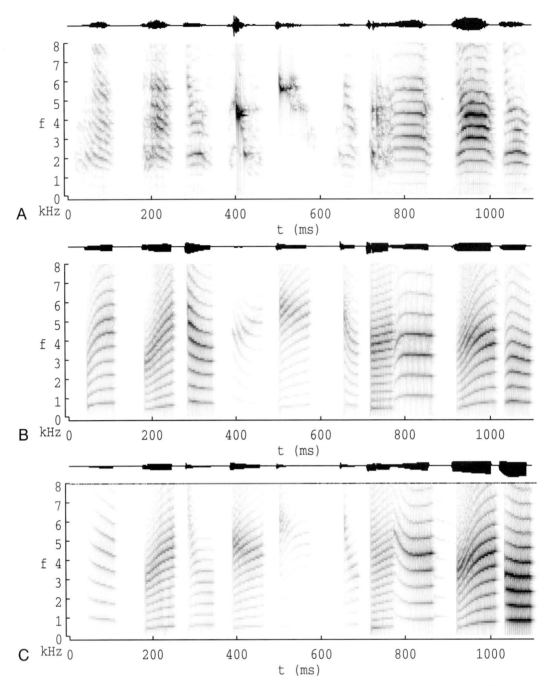

FIGURE 33.9 Sonograms. (A) The original zebra finch song motif. (B) A song produced by the model after 500 trials using the zebra finch song A as the template. (C) A song produced after 500 trials using the model song B as the template.

between the original and synthesized syllables reached about 0.8 (figure 33.10). The final synthesized song motif sounded more similar to the tutor song than the random initial song. As shown in the spectrograms (figure 33.9), the overall frequency profiles of the syllables were similar, although the detailed features in the spectrogram, such as harmonic structures and frequency modulation patterns, were not accurately reproduced.

LEARNING A SYNTHESIZED SONG There are two possible reasons for the imperfect replication of the zebra finch song syllables. One is that our model of the syrinx and the motor control network were much more primitive than those of a real zebra finch, and therefore precise mimicry was impossible. Another is that the reinforcement learning procedure converged to a suboptimal solution. In order to differentiate these possibilities,

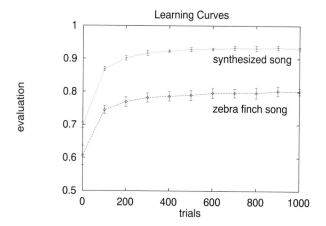

FIGURE 33.10   Learning curves for the song learning model. Two different learning curves are shown, one using a zebra finch song as the tutor (dashed line) and the second using a synthesized song generated by another model as the tutor (dotted line). On each trial, a new set of weight perturbations was chosen, a song produced, and an evaluation carried out as described in the text. The evaluation shown here is the correlation between the syllable and its corresponding template. The curves represent the average evaluation of 50 syllables (10 syllables per song; 5 simulation runs).

we tested the performance of the model when the target song could be exactly reproduced by taking a set of syllable templates from a synthesized song motif and training another model from a random start. The correlation after 500 trials was 0.94 (dotted line in figure 33.10) and the song sounded quite similar to the tutor model as judged by human ears (see figure 33.9B,C). This result implies that the relatively low performance using a real zebra finch song as a template was mainly due to the differences between the vocal system of the real bird and that of the model. However, even with the synthesized song, the reinforcement learning algorithm did not converge to the optimal solution with a correlation of 1.0. Note that imperfect replication of syllables and the resulting individual variability of songs are also seen in real birds.

Discussion

The primary question addressed by our model of song learning is whether a relatively simple reinforcement learning system could converge to a tutor song within the number of trials that are available to a real zebra finch. The model is based on specific hypotheses for how the computational problems could be solved in a way that is consistent with the neural responses that have been observed in song control nuclei. The simulations demonstrate that the proposed learning system can satisfy these constraints and imitate birdsong.

Many simplifying assumptions were made in the present network model: Syllables were unary coded in HVc; the sound synthesizer was much simpler than a real syrinx; simple spectrographic template matching was used for syllable evaluation. However, it is possible to replace these simplified modules with more biologically accurate ones as warranted by further experimental data. Since the number of learning trials needed to reach convergence in the present model was many fewer than the number of vocalizations that occur during real birdsong learning, which have not been counted in the zebra finch but number many thousand, there is adequate margin for elaboration.

Additional experiments are needed to test and improve the model, as outlined in the following subsections.

BLOCKING DA INPUT FROM AVT   We have suggested that dopaminergic input from AVT to area X could be used for selection of a particular auditory input as a song template. Lesion or reversible block of the dopaminergic system in AVT should disrupt memory of tutor syllables if this hypothesis is true. Injection of dopaminergic agonist or antagonist into area X during tutor song presentation should affect selection of songs to be learned. If confirmed, this method would provide strong evidence that the song templates are stored in the anterior forebrain pathway.

TEST OF MODULATION AND PLASTICITY INDUCED BY LMAN   We assumed that NMDA-type synaptic input from LMAN to RA modulated the non-NMDA-type synaptic input from HVc to RA. There has been no direct experimental evidence for plastic changes in RA synapses induced by input from LMAN. Further experiments in slice preparations could reveal when and how such plasticity is induced, or could indicate that such plasticity is not plausible. Another approach is electric stimulation of LMAN in young, singing birds. If altered activity in LMAN results in perturbation of ongoing song or plastic change in the song after perturbation, that would suggest the existence of modulatory or plastic mechanisms in vivo.

SUPPRESSION OF AUDITORY RESPONSE IN HVC DURING SINGING   In HVc neurons that have both auditory and motor responses, the auditory responses are suppressed during and soon after the bird is singing (McCasland and Konishi, 1981; McCasland, 1987). If the suppression is complete and occurs in young birds, we would have to reconsider the use of auditory feedback in the model. One possibility is that the suppression is due to the same mechanisms that induce hyperpolarization in

HVc neurons with the auditory stimulus of the bird's own song (Lewicki, 1996). This may help in narrowing the auditory selectivity of the HVc neurons.

DELAY IN AUDITORY FEEDBACK We assumed that each vocalized syllable was evaluated separately, but this approach may not be possible if there is significant overlap in the motor and auditory responses to adjacent syllables. The auditory response latency is about 30 ms in HVc and 50 ms in LMAN in anesthetized birds (Williams, 1989). If the latency is similar in awake birds, by the time the anterior forebrain pathway processes the auditory feedback, the motor units in HVc and RA should be generating the next syllable. In order to utilize the delayed evaluation signal, the synapses from HVc to RA have to use an "eligibility trace" for plasticity (Barto, Sutton, and Anderson, 1983). Examples of possible biological implementation of eligibility traces can be seen in Houk, Adams, and Barto, (1994), and Schweighofer, Arbib, and Dominey (1996).

Recently, a new hypothesis was proposed for a "forward model" within HVc that predicts the auditory outcome from the HVc motor output. The predicted auditory outcome is then used for immediate reinforcement of ongoing motor activity instead of the actual auditory feedback (Troyer, Doupe, and Miller, 1996). However, it may be difficult for such prediction of auditory outcome to be reliably performed within HVc while the connection from HVc to RA is changed by learning.

FEEDBACK CONNECTION IN THE ANTERIOR FOREBRAIN PATHWAY Recently, novel axonal connections were found from RA to DLM (Wild, 1993) and from LMAN to area X (Vates and Nottebohm, 1995; Nixdorf-Bergweiler, Lips, and Heinemann, 1995). Although we did not take into account these possible feedback connections within the AFP, they are still consistent with our basic assumption that there is no feedback connection back to HVc in the AFP.

The finding of the novel connection from LMAN to area X raises a possibility that correlation between perturbation and evaluation, which is the main factor of stochastic learning, is taken at the level of area X instead of in LMAN as we assumed. It has been shown that the connections from LMAN through area X to DLM (Vates and Nottebohm, 1995) and from DLM through LMAN to RA (Johnson, Sablan, and Bottjer, 1995) are topographically organized. This organization would enable the activity pattern in LMAN to be correlated with the syllable evaluation in area X and then sent back to LMAN through DLM to alter the next activity pattern in LMAN. Together with the finding that the ventral and

middle parts of RA differentially control the dorsal and ventral syringeal muscles and that these muscles control the air flow and the fundamental frequency, respectively (Goller and Suthers, 1995), it is possible that there are distinct channels within the AFP that are involved in evaluation and modulation of different aspects of vocalization. However, data on the activity of AFP neurons during singing would be necessary to test these possibilities.

Conclusions

In this chapter, we have identified computational mechanisms that could account for birdsong learning and shown how these mechanisms could be supported by the known anatomy of the avian brain. We then focused on the issue of sensorimotor learning and tested our specific hypothesis that the anterior forebrain pathway works as a reinforcement learning system. The current theory and simulation results given here could be regarded as an "existence proof" for one solution to the song-learning problem, but it does not exclude other possible solutions. Nevertheless, this is the first computational model of the entire song-learning system that is able to replicate realistic birdsongs. Because the model was based on the recent experimental findings, especially those from the anterior forebrain pathway, experimental tests of the proposed model should provide a better understanding of the mechanisms of song learning and, more generally, the neural principles underlying the acquisition of novel motor patterns based on sensory experience.

ACKNOWLEDGMENTS We thank M. Lewicki for the zebra finch song data and M. Konishi, D. Margoliash, A. Doupe, M. Lewicki, E. Vu, D. Perkel, G. Striedter and S. Volman for their helpful discussions.

REFERENCES

ALSPECTOR, J., R. MIER, B. YUHAS, A. JAYAKUMAR, and D. LIPPE, 1993. A parallel gradient descent method for learning in analog VLSI networks. In *Advances in Neural Information Processing Systems 5*, C. L. Giles, S. J. Hanson, and J. D. Cowan, eds., San Mateo, Calif.: Morgan Kaufmann, pp. 580–587.

AMARI, S., 1977. Neural theory of association and concept formation. *Biol. Cybern.* 26:175–185.

AMARI, S., 1988. Statistical neurodynamics of various versions of correlation associative memory. In *Proceedings of International Conference on Neural Networks* 1988, San Diego, pp. I:633–640.

BARTO, A. G., 1995. Reinforcement learning. In *The Handbook of Brain Theory and Neural Networks,* M. A. Arbib, ed. Cambridge, Mass.: MIT Press, pp. 804–809.

BARTO, A. G., and M. I. JORDAN, 1987. Gradient following without backpropagation. In *Proceedings of the First Interna-*

tional Conference on Neural Networks, San Diego. New York: IEEE, pp. 629–636.

BARTO, A. G., R. S. SUTTON, and C. W. ANDERSON, 1983. Neuronlike adaptive elements that can solve difficult learning control problems. *IEEE Trans. Syst. Man Cybern.* 13:834–846.

BELL, A. J., and T. J. SEJNOWSKI, 1995. An information-maximization approach to blind separation and blind deconvolution. *Neural Computation* 7:1129–1159.

BONKE, D., H. SCHEICH, and G. LANGNER, 1979. Responsiveness of units in the auditory neostriatum of the Guinea fowl *Numida meleagris* to species-specific calls and synthetic stimuli, I. *J. Comp. Physiol.* 132:243–255.

BOTTJER, S. W., and A. P. ARNOLD, 1997. Developmental plasticity in neural circuits for a learned behavior. *Annu. Rev. Neurosci.* 20:459–481.

BOTTJER, S. W., K. A. HALSEMA, S. A. BROWN, and E. A. MIESNER, 1989. Axonal connections of a forebrain nucleus involved with vocal learning in zebra finches. *J. Comp. Neurol.* 279:312–326.

BOTTJER, S. W., E. A. MIESNER, and A. P. ARNOLD, 1984. Forebrain lesions disrupt development but not maintenance of song in passerine birds. *Science* 224:901–903.

BRACKENBURY, J. H., 1982. The structural basis of voice production and its relationship to sound characteristics. In *Evolutionary and Ecological Aspects of Acoustic Communication in Birds*, vol. 1. New York: Academic Press, pp. 53–73.

CASEY, R. M., and A. S. GAUNT, 1985. Theoretical models of the avian syrinx. *J. Theoret. Biol.* 116:45–64.

CASTO, J. M., and G. F. BALL, 1994. Characterization and localization of D1 dopamine receptors in the sexually dimorphic vocal control nucleus, area X, and the basal ganglia of European starlings. *J. Neurobiol.* 225:767–780.

CATCHPOLE, C. K., and P. J. B. SLATER, 1995. *Bird Song: Biological Themes and Variations.* Cambridge, U.K.: Cambridge University Press.

COHEN, A. H., S. R. ROSSIGNOL, and S. GRILLNER, 1988. *Neural Control of Rhythmic Movements in Vertebrates.* New York: John Wiley and Sons.

DEHAENE, S., J.-P. CHANGEUX, and J.-P. NADAL, 1987. Neural networks that learn temporal sequences by selection. *Proc. Natl. Acad. Sci. U.S.A.* 84:2727–2731.

DOUPE, A. J., 1993. A neural circuit specialized for vocal learning. *Curr. Opin. Neurobiol.* 3:104–111.

DOUPE, A. J., and M. KONISHI, 1991. Song-selective auditory circuits in the vocal control system of the zebra finch. *Proc. Natl. Acad. Sci. U.S.A.* 88:11339–11343.

DOYA, K., and T. J. SEJNOWSKI, 1994. A computational model of song learning in the anterior forebrain pathway of the birdsong control system. *Soc. Neurosci. Abstr.* 20:166.

DOYA, K., and T. J. SEJNOWSKI, 1995. A novel reinforcement model of birdsong vocalization learning. In G. Tesauro, D. S. Touretzky, and T. K. Leen, eds., *Advances in Neural Information Processing Systems 7.* Cambridge, MA: MIT Press, pp. 101–108.

FOX, K., and K. ZAHS, 1994. Critical period control in sensory cortex. *Curr. Opin. Neurobiol.* 4:112–119.

FUKUSHIMA, K., 1973. A model of associative memory in the brain. *Kybernetik* 12:58–63.

GOLLER, F., and R. A. SUTHERS, 1995. Implications for lateralization of bird song from unilateral gating of bilateral motor patterns. *Nature* 373:63–66.

GULLAPALLI, V., 1995. Direct associative reinforcement learning methods for dynamic systems control. *Neurocomputing* 9:271–292.

HARRIS-WARRICK, R. M., E. MARDER, A. I. SELVERSTON, and M. MOULINS, 1992. *Dynamic Biological Networks—The Stomatogastric Nervous System.* Cambridge, MA: MIT Press.

HOUK, J. C., J. L. ADAMS, and A. G. BARTO, 1994. A model of how the basal ganglia generate and use neural signals that predict reinforcement. In J. C. Houk, J. L. Davis, and D. G. Beiser, eds., *Models of Information Processing in the Basal Ganglia.* Cambridge, MA: MIT Press, pp. 249–270.

JOHNSON, F., M. M. SABLAN, and S. W. BOTTJER, 1995. Topographic organization of a forebrain pathway involved with vocal learning in zebra finches. *J. Comp. Neurol.* 358:260–278.

JORDAN, M. I., and D. E. RUMELHART, 1992. Forward models: Supervised learning with a distal teacher. *Cognitive Science* 16:307–354.

KAWATO, M., 1990. The feedback-error-learning neural network for supervised motor learning. In R. Eckmiller, ed., *Neural Network for Sensory and Motor Systems.* Amsterdam: Elsevier.

KAWATO, M., K. FURUKAWA, and R. SUZUKI, 1987. A hierarchical neural network model for control and learning of voluntary movement. *Biol. Cybern.* 57:169–185.

KONISHI, M., 1965. The role of auditory feedback in the control of vocalization in the white-crowned sparrow. *Z. Tierpsychol.* 22:770–783.

KONISHI, M., 1985. Birdsong: From behavior to neuron. *Annu. Rev. Neurosci.* 8:125–170.

KONISHI, M., and E. AKUTAGAWA, 1985. Neuronal growth, atrophy and death in a sexually dimorphic song nucleus in the zebra finch brain. *Nature* 315:145–147.

KRISTAN, W. B., JR., 1992. Neuronal basis of behavior. *Curr. Opin. Neurobiol.* 2:781–787.

KUBOTA, M., and N. SAITO, 1991. NMDA receptors participate differentially in two different synaptic inputs in neurons of the zebra finch robust nucleus of the archistriatum in vitro. *Neurosci. Lett.* 125:1107–1109.

LEWICKI, M. S., 1996. Intracellular characterization of song-specific neurons in the zebra finch auditory forebrain. *J. Neurosci.* 16:5854–5863.

LEWICKI, M. S., and M. KONISHI, 1995. Mechanisms underlying the sensitivity of songbird forebrain neurons to temporal order. *Proc. Natl. Acad. Sci. U.S.A.* 92:5582–5586.

LEWIS, J. W., S. M. RYAN, A. P. ARNOLD, and L. L. BUTCHER, 1981. Evidence for a catecholaminergic projection to area X in the zebra finch. *J. Comp. Neurol.* 196:347–354.

LINSKER, R., 1986. From basic network principles to neural architecture. *Proc. Natl. Acad. Sci. U.S.A.* 83:7508–7512, 8390–8394, 8779–8783.

MALENKA, R. C., and R. A. NICOLL, 1993. NMDA-receptor-dependent synaptic plasticity: Multiple forms and mechanisms. *Trends Neurosci.* 16:521–527.

MARGOLIASH, D., 1983. Acoustic parameters underlying the responses of song-specific neurons in the white-crowned sparrow. *J. Neurosci.* 3:1039–1057.

MARGOLIASH, D., 1986. Preference for autogenous song by auditory neurons in a song system nucleus of the white-crowned sparrow. *J. Neurosci.* 6:1643–1661.

MARGOLIASH, D., 1997. Distributed theme-domain representations in the birdsong system. *Neuron* 19:963–966.

MARGOLIASH, D., and E. S. FORTUNE, 1992. Temporal and harmonic combination–sensitive neurons in the zebra finch's HVc. *J. Neurosci.* 12:4309–4326.

MARLER, P., 1963. Inheritance and learning in the development of animal vocalizations. In R.-G. Bunsel, ed., *Acoustic Behavior of Animals.* Amsterdam: Elsevier, pp. 228–243.

MARLER, P., 1991. Song-learning behavior: The interface with neuroethology. *Trends Neurosci.* 14:199–206.

MCCASLAND, J. S., 1987. Neuronal control of birdsong production. *J. Neurosci.* 7:23–39.

MCCASLAND, J. S., and M. KONISHI, 1981. Interaction between auditory and motor activities in an avian song control nucleus. *Proc. Natl. Acad. Sci. U.S.A.* 78:7815–7819.

MILLER, W. T., R. S. SUTTON, and P. J. WERBOS, 1990. *Neural Networks for Control.* Cambridge, MA: MIT Press.

MOONEY, R., 1992. Synaptic basis of developmental plasticity in a birdsong nucleus *J. Neurosci.* 12:2464–2477.

MOONEY, R., and M. KONISHI, 1991. Two distinct inputs to an avian song nucleus activate different glutamate receptor subtypes on individual neurons. *Proc. Natl. Acad. Sci. U.S.A.* 88:4075–4079.

MORITA, M., 1996. Memory and learning of sequential patterns by nonmonotone neural networks. *Neural Networks* 9:1477–1489.

NIXDORF-BERGWEILER, B. E., M. B. LIPS, and U. HEINEMANN, 1995. Electrophysiological and morphological evidence for a new projection of LMAN-neurones toward area X. *NeuroReport* 6:1729.

NOTTEBOHM, F., T. M. STOKES, and C. M. LEONARD, 1976. Central control of song in the canary, *Serinus canarius. J. Comp. Neurol.* 165:457–486.

NOWICKI, S., 1987. Vocal tract resonances in oscine bird sound production: Evidence from bird-songs in a helium atmosphere. *Nature* 325:533–555.

PERKEL, D. J., 1994. Differential modulation of excitatory synaptic transmission by norepinephrine and baclofen in zebra finch nucleus RA. *Soc. Neurosci. Abstr.* 20:165.

RUMELHART, D. E., G. E. HINTON, and R. J. WILLIAMS, 1986. Learning representations by back-propagating errors. *Nature* 323:533–536.

SCHARFF, C., and F. NOTTEBOHM, 1991. A comparative study of the behavioral deficits following lesions of various parts of the zebra finch song systems: Implications for vocal learning. *J. Neurosci.* 11:2896–2913.

SCHULTZ, W., P. APICELLA, and T. LJUNGBERG, 1993. Responses of monkey dopamine neurons to reward and conditioned stimuli during successive steps of learning a delayed response task. *J. Neurosci.* 13:900–913.

SCHWEIGHOFER, N., M. A. ARBIB, and P. F. DOMINEY, 1996. A model of the cerebellum in adaptive control of saccadic gain. I. The model and its biological substrate. *Biol. Cybern.* 75:19–28.

SOHRABJI, F., E. J. NORDEEN, and K. W. NORDEEN, 1990. Selective impairment of song learning following lesions of a forebrain nucleus in the juvenile zebra finch. *Behav. Neural Biol.* 53:51–63.

SOLIS, M. M., and A. J. DOUPE, 1995. The development of song- and order-selectivity in the anterior forebrain of juvenile zebra finches. *Soc. Neurosci. Abstr.* 21:959.

SOMPOLINSKY, H., and I. KANTER, 1986. Temporal association in asymmetric neural networks. *Phys. Rev. Lett.* 57:2861–2864.

SUTTER, M. L., and D. MARGOLIASH, 1994. Global synchronous response to autogenous song in zebra finch HVc. *J. Neurophysiol.* 72(5): 2105–2123.

SUTTON, R. S., and A. G. BARTO, 1998. *Reinforcement Learning.* Cambridge, MA: MIT Press.

THOMSON, A. M., and J. DEUCHARS, 1994. Temporal and spatial properties of local circuits in neocortex. *Trends Neurosci.* 17:119–126.

TROYER, T. W., A. J. DOUPE, and K. D. MILLER, 1996. An associational hypothesis for sensorimotor learning of birdsong. In *Computational Neuroscience.* New York: Academic Press, pp. 409–414.

UNNIKRISHNAN, K. P., and K. P. VENUGOPAL, 1994. Alopex: A correlation-based learning algorithm for feedforward and recurrent neural networks. *Neural Computation* 6:469–490.

VATES, G. E., and F. NOTTEBOHM, 1995. Feedback circuitry within a song-learning pathway. *Proc. Natl. Acad. Sci. U.S.A.* 92:5139–5143.

VICARIO, D. S., 1988. Organization of the zebra finch song control system: I. Representation of syringeal muscles in the hypoglossal nucleus. *J. Comp. Neurol.* 271:346–354.

VICARIO, D. S., 1991a. Neural mechanisms of vocal production in songbirds. *Curr. Opin. Neurobiol.* 1:595–600.

VICARIO, D. S., 1991b. Organization of the zebra finch song control system: II. Functional organization of outputs from nucleus robustus archistriatalis. *J. Comp. Neurol.* 309:486–494.

VOLMAN, S. F., 1993. Development of neural selectivity for birdsong during vocal learning. *J. Neurosci.* 13:4737–4747.

VON DER MALSBURG, C., 1973. Self-organization of orientation sensitive cells in the striate cortex. *Kybernetik* 14:85–100.

VU, E. T., Y.-C. KUO, and F. S. CHANCE, 1995. Effects of lesioning nucleus interfacialis on adult zebra finch song. *Soc. Neurosci. Abstr.* 21:964.

VU, E. T., M. E. MAZUREK, and Y.-C. KUO, 1994. Identification of a forebrain motor programming network for the learned song of zebra finches. *J. Neurosci.* 14:6924–6934.

WILD, J. M., 1993. Descending projections of the songbird nucleus robustus archistriatalis. *J. Comp. Neurol.* 338:225–241.

WILLIAMS, H., 1989. Multiple representations and auditory-motor interactions in the avian song system. *Ann. N.Y. Acad. Sci.* 563:148–164.

WILLIAMS, H., 1990. Models for song learning in the zebra finch: Fathers or others. *Animal Behaviour* 39:745–757.

WILLIAMS, H., and D. S. VICARIO, 1993. Temporal patterning of song production: Participation of nucleus uvaeformis of the thalamus. *J. Neurobiol.* 24:903–912.

YU, A. C., and D. MARGOLIASH, 1996. Temporal hierarchical control of singing birds. *Science* 273:1871–1875.

YU, C.-H., and D. MARGOLIASH, 1993. Differences between motor recruitment and auditory responses in zebra finch HVc. *Soc. Neurosci. Abstr.* 19:1018.

IV MOTOR

SYSTEMS

Introduction

EMILIO BIZZI

This section addresses a series of central issues in motor control, ranging from motor planning and execution to motor learning.

Planning and execution of limb movements

A number of studies in humans and monkeys have demonstrated that the posterior parietal cortex has a role in programming actions and in transforming sensory signals into plans for motor behaviors (Mountcastle et al., 1975; Andersen, Brotchie, and Mazzoni, 1992; Mazzoni et al., 1996; Snyder, Baptista, and Andersen, 1997). Functionally different subdivisions of the posterior parietal cortex have been identified. Among these subdivisions, there is an area specialized for saccades, the lateral intraparietal area (LIP), and a posterior parietal region (PRR) specialized for planning reaching movements. A third area is the anterior intraparietal area (AIP), which is specialized for grasping (Sakata et al., 1997).

Andersen and colleagues (see chapter 36) have shown how the different sensory modalities that originally are represented in different coordinate frames are brought together in the areas of the posterior parietal cortex. LIP and PRR areas encode the spacial location of visual and auditory signals using a common reference frame, that of the eye. The neurons of these areas code a goal for movement in multiple coordinate frames (eye, head, body, and the world). Depending on how these cells are read by other brain areas, different coordinate transformations can be accomplished by the same population of neurons.

Among the brain areas, those of the frontal lobe, especially the premotor cortex, receive signals from the posterior parietal cortex. Metelli and associates (1994) showed that the parietal area AIP and the premotor areas anatomically are connected reciprocally. Sakata and coworkers (1997), who have studied the properties of the AIP neurons, showed that many AIP neurons are selective for object shape and size. In addition, Sakata and associates described neurons that are active during object fixation and grasping movements executed under visual guidance. These neurons do not discharge when the same movement is performed in darkness.

Given the connectivity between the parietal cortex (AIP) and the premotor areas of the frontal lobe, it is not surprising that the neurons of the premotor areas discharge actively during grasping. However, as shown by Rizzolatti, Fogassi, and Gallese in chapter 38, the prefrontal neurons are profoundly different from those in the parietal cortex. The prefrontal neurons are active when grasping is performed, but, remarkably, they also are active when the movement is performed with different effectors, such as the right and the left hand, or the mouth. Other neurons are selective for grasping with a specific grip type.

According to these authors, these neurons store specific knowledge about an action and indicate how to implement it. They represent a "vocabulary" of actions. The existence of anatomic connectivity between the premotor area and the classical motor area 4 facilitates the selection of the most appropriate combination of movements. In addition, the presence of these neurons simplifies the association between a given sensory stimulus, such as a visually presented object, and the appropriate motor response toward it.

In addition to the various types of grasping neurons, there is another class of neurons that becomes active both when the monkey performs an action and when it observes a similar action made by another monkey or by the experimenter. These neurons have been named "mirror neurons." Rizzolatti, Fogassi, and Gallese have related this important and novel observation to a basic system of recognition of actions and the creation of an internal copy of actions.

In chapter 37, Georgopoulos deals with planning and emphasizes that to study the neural mechanisms of cognitive motor processing, a multiplicity of approaches is needed. Behavioral, neurophysiologic, and imaging methods all provide the crucial insights into the neural processes subserving the production of movement. Examples illustrating that each of these methods affords only a partial view of the whole are described.

In chapters 36, 37, and 38, Andersen and associates, Georgopoulos, and Rizzolatti, Fogassi, and Gallese describe the activities of parietal and frontal neurons that clearly are related with some aspect of motor planning. Bizzi and Mussa-Ivaldi (chapter 34) and Jordan and Wolpert (chapter 42) also address the question of planning but focus mainly on the processes that transform a motor plan into the signals that activate the muscles.

To execute movements, the central nervous system must transform information about a small number of variables (direction, amplitude, and velocity) into a large number of signals to many muscles. Any transformation of this type is "ill-posed" in the sense that an exact solution either is not available or is not unique. For instance, if the goal is to move the hand from an initial position (A) to a point (B) in space, then there are a number of possible hand trajectories that could achieve this goal; the solution of this elementary motor problem is not unique. Even after the central nervous system has chosen a particular path for the hand, its implementation can be achieved with multiple combinations of joint motions at the shoulder, elbow, and wrist. Again, the solution is not unique. Finally, because there are many muscles around each joint, the net force generated by their activation can be achieved by a variety of combinations of muscles.

How the central nervous system of vertebrates handles the staggering number of mechanical variables involved even in the simplest movement is one of the central problems in motor control. In their chapter, Jordan and Wolpert describe the computational models that have been proposed by a number of investigators in the last few years.

The complexity inherent in controlling so many degrees of freedom has led researchers to propose that the nervous system must have developed ways to simplify this problem. In their chapter, Bizzi and Mussa-Ivaldi present evidence supporting the idea that the transformations leading to the execution of a motor plan are implemented by a small number of control modules. Recent experiments in the spinalized frog have suggested that these control modules may be organized in the spinal cord as simple synergies of spring-like muscles. Subsequent work has revealed that an extensive variety of movements can be obtained from a simple linear summation of these control modules.

Planning and execution of eye movements

Many regions in the primate brain have been identified where neuronal activity correlates with the generation of saccades. These regions include the frontal and parietal cortices, the basal ganglia, the cerebellum, and the brain stem. A key structure of the saccadic system is the superior colliculus. Areas in the cerebral cortex and basal ganglia project directly to the superior colliculus, which can be seen as a location for the coordination of the varied inputs from the forebrain and as the location for the transformation of these inputs into outputs for the control of eye movements. In chapter 40, Wurtz and associates describe the different types of neurons found within the superior colliculus, the importance of the map of saccadic vectors on the colliculus, and the significance of the change in the population activity within the map for the generation of eye movements. A key point of this chapter is the discussion of the significance of the delay activity in the buildup and fixation neurons. Wurtz and colleagues regard the delay activity observed in collicular neurons as part of the preparation to move.

Another important point is the comparison of the activity of neurons in the superior colliculus with those in the cortex that project to the superior colliculus. One of the most striking observations is that the same type of activity can be identified in both cortex and superior colliculus. This result supports the idea of a distributed processing in which a given transformation does not occur in a particular area but rather progresses across a series of regions.

Motor learning

The chapters by Ghez and associates (chapter 35), Hikosaka and colleagues (chapter 39), and Wilson (chapter 41) deal with the cellular substrates of motor learning. Hikosaka and colleagues describe the brain areas that become active during the acquisition of a visuomotor sequence. He shows that in the early stages of learning of a sequence, there is activation of the supplementary motor area (SMA) and the dorsolateral prefrontal cortex. These areas act together with the anterior part of the basal ganglia. Subsequently, the posterior part of the basal ganglia and the dentate nucleus of the cerebellum become active. Hikosaka also demonstrates that the learning of the sequence was disrupted only partially by the inactivation of one of these areas, suggesting that multiple regions subserve learning concurrently.

Another form of learning is navigation, which involves establishing the initial position of the animal, updating this information by keeping track of self-movement, identifying landmarks, and establishing spacial orientation with respect to them. In 1978, O'Keefe and Nadel outlined several basic systems for rodent's navigation, with the hippocampus as the site of the cognitive map for navigation.

In his chapter, Wilson describes in detail the neural systems that are involved in the acquisition and maintenance of the sense of place and directions. He demonstrates that directional and place information is maintained by distinct hippocampal and thalamic subsystems that are capable of incorporating self-motion signals as well as extrinsic cue information. Interestingly, these sig-

nals are dependent on prior experience demonstrating their dependence from memory.

Ghez and collaborators in chapter 35 examine the neural patterns of activity that are established during different types of motor learning. They describe the internal representations and the learning that underlie the development of accuracy in point-to-point movements of the arm. The observation presented in this chapter demonstrates that reaching for visual targets quickly and accurately depends on three internal representations, each of which is adjusted through sensory feedback. Learning to produce accurate movements involves distinct processes based on visual feedback. In contrast, the transformation of a motor plan coded in extrinsic space coordinates into a system of intrinsic coordinates depends critically on proprioception.

Given that many motor control problems involve interacting with unexpected circumstances in the environment, successful performance is dependent on the motor system's ability to adapt. Through adaptation, the motor control system is able to maintain and update its internal knowledge of external dynamics. In their chapter, Jordan and Wolpert discuss different approaches to the problem of motor learning, such as direct inverse modeling, feedback error learning, distal supervised learning, reinforcement learning, and unsupervised bootstrap learning. All these approaches provide mechanisms for sensory motor transformations, but they differ in the kind of data that they require.

REFERENCES

ANDERSEN, R. A., P. R. BROTCHIE, and P. MAZZONI, 1992. Evidence for the lateral intraparietal area as the parietal eye field. *Curr. Opin. Neurobiol.* 2:840–846.

MAZZONI, P., R. M. BRACEWELL, S. BARASH, and R. A. ANDERSEN, 1996. Motor intention activity in the macaque's lateral intraparietal area. I: Dissociation of motor plan from sensory memory. *J. Neurophysiol.* 76(3):1439–1456.

METELLI, M., G. LUPPINO, A. MURATA, and H. SAKATA, 1994. Independent anatomical circuits for reaching and grasping linking the inferior parietal sulcus and inferior area 6 in macaque monkey. *Soc. Neuroscience Abs.* 20: 404.4.

MOUNTCASTLE, V. B., J. C. LYNCH, A. GEORGOPOULOS, H. SAKATA, and C. ACUNA, 1975. Posterior parietal association cortex of the monkey: Command functions for operations within extrapersonal space. *J. Neurophysiol.* 38:871–908.

O'KEEFE, J., and L. NADEL, 1978. *The Hippocampus as a Cognitive Map.* Oxford: Clarendon.

SAKATA, H., M. TAIRA, M. KUSUNOKI, A. MARATA, and Y. TANAKA, 1997. The TINS Lecture: The parietal association cortex in depth perception and visual control of hand action. *Trends Neurosci.* 20:350–357.

SNYDER, L. H., A. BAPTISTA, and R. A. ANDERSEN, 1997. Coding of intention in the posterior parietal cortex. *Nature* 386:167–170.

34 Toward a Neurobiology of Coordinate Transformations

EMILIO BIZZI AND FERDINANDO A. MUSSA-IVALDI

ABSTRACT The authors discuss a perspective in motor control that is based on the distinction between planning and execution of motor behaviors. This distinction has emerged from experimental observations that suggest that the central nervous system plans movements in terms of spatial or extrinsic coordinates rather than body-centered coordinates. What, then, are the processes that transform a motor plan into the signals that activate the muscles? The authors review a number of theoretical and experimental findings that suggest that the coordinate transformations leading to the execution of a motor plan are implemented by a small number of control modules. In particular, some recent experiments in the spinalized frog have suggested that these control modules may be organized by the spinal cord as simple synergies of spring-like muscles. Subsequent theoretical work has revealed that a wide variety of motor control policies can be obtained from a simple linear combination of these few control modules. The computational framework for representing the generation of movement by a combination of independent modules is presented in this chapter. Finally, the implications of this modular approach for our understanding of motor learning and adaptation are discussed.

In this chapter, we address a conundrum that has long faced investigators in motor control: If movements are specified by the central nervous system (CNS) in terms of goals, as psychophysical evidence seems to imply, what are the processes in the CNS that transform the neural representation of these goals into signals that activate the muscles? In the past few years, psychophysical and electrophysiologic observations made by a number of investigators have indicated that motor goals as simple as reaching and pointing are planned by the CNS in terms of extrinsic coordinates representing the motion of the hand in space. In the first part of this chapter, we review the evidence that motor behavior is represented in the higher centers of the brain in terms of extrinsic coordinates. In the second part, we propose a novel hypothesis describing one possible way in which motor plans could be transformed into motor commands.

EMILIO BIZZI Department of Brain and Cognitive Sciences, The Massachusetts Institute of Technology, Cambridge, Mass.
FERDINANDO A. MUSSA-IVALDI Department of Physiology, Northwestern University, Chicago, Ill.

Evidence for motor planning in spatial (extrinsic) coordinates

In which coordinate frames does the CNS represent movement? Morasso (1981) suggests that the planning of arm movements is carried out in extrinsic coordinates that represent the motion of the hand in space. Morasso instructed human subjects to point with one hand to different visual targets that were activated randomly. His analysis of the movements showed two kinematic invariances: (1) the hand trajectories were approximately straight segments, and (2) the tangential hand velocity for different movements always appeared to have a bell-shaped configuration–the time needed to accelerate the hand was approximately equal to the time needed to bring it back to rest. Because these simple and invariant features were detected in the coordinates of the hand only, these results suggest that CNS planning takes place in terms of hand motion in space. Morasso's observations were extended to more complex curved movements performed by human subjects in an obstacle avoidance task (Abend, Bizzi, and Morasso, 1982). Again, kinematic invariances were present in the hand and not in the joint motion. Later, Flash and Hogan (1985) showed that the kinematic behavior described by Morasso (1981) and Abend, Bizzi, and Morasso (1982) could be derived from a single organizing principle based on optimizing endpoint smoothness. Interestingly, their mathematical model is compatible with a hypothesis based on planning in space but not with that based on joint coordinates.

The idea that movements of the hand are planned by the CNS in terms of extrinsic coordinates is related to the hypothesis that the planning and execution of movements constitute two separate stages of information processing (Bernstein, 1967; Hogan et al., 1987; and Ghez et al., chapter 35, this volume). According to this view, during planning, the brain is concerned with establishing movement kinematics–that is, a sequence of positions that the hand is expected to occupy at different times within the extrapersonal space. During execution, the dynamics of the musculoskeletal system are controlled to enforce the planning of movements within different environmental conditions.

This separation between planning and execution (or between kinematics and dynamics) has been challenged by Uno, Kawato, and Suzuki (1989), who have suggested that the kinematic features observed by Morasso may be accounted for by a model in which the rate of change of joint torque, rather than endpoint smoothness, is minimized. In essence, these authors proposed that the observed kinematics might be a "side effect" of the computational processes underlying the control of dynamics.

In contrast with this view, recent experimental findings by Flash and Gurevich (1992) and by Shadmehr and Mussa-Ivaldi (1994) have demonstrated that the kinematics of movement indeed are planned independently of the dynamic conditions in which movement occurs. Shadmehr and Mussa-Ivaldi (1994) asked human subjects to execute movements of the hand in different directions while holding the handle of a two-joint planar robot. At the beginning of the experiment, the robot acted as a passive device, and the subject produced straight-line hand movements (as described in Morasso's experiment). In a subsequent stage of the experiment, the robot was programmed to generate a field of forces that depended linearly on the measured velocity of the hand.

The effect of the field was rather complex, consisting of a combination of destabilizing forces and a viscous drag in two orthogonal directions. At first, subjects reacted to the unexpected field with a visibly perturbed trajectory of the hand. Subjects then were asked to perform several target acquisition movements within the field of forces, and they were not given any instructions regarding hand trajectory.

Gradually, the kinematics of the hand movements returned to the original straight line with a bell-shaped tangential velocity profile, as observed before the onset of the perturbing field. Flash and Gurevich (1992), who used a spring-like load instead of a velocity-dependent field as a perturbation, observed a similar adaptive behavior.

Thus, in the experiments by Shadmehr and Mussa-Ivaldi and Flash and Gurevich, the basic kinematics—that is, the straight line trajectories and bell-shaped velocity profiles—were restored at the end of the adaptation period despite a totally changed dynamic environment.

Clearly, these findings are not compatible with the idea that the movement kinematics are derived from a single optimization principle applied to the dynamics of the motor system. On the contrary, the results on the adaptation to external force fields strongly suggest that movement kinematics are programmed as a desired trajectory to be enforced in different dynamic conditions.

In addition to the psychophysical evidence, recordings from cells in cortical and subcortical areas of monkeys have shown a correlation between the cells' firing pattern and direction of the hand's motion (Georgopoulos, Kettner, and Schwartz, 1988a,b; Kalaska et al., 1989; Caminiti, Johnson, and Urbano, 1990; Georgopoulos, see chapter 37, this volume). It appears that the activity of certain classes of cortical cells in the motor cortex is represented in spatial coordinates without any specification about how muscles are to be engaged to produce the forces necessary for the movement.

Taken together, the psychophysical and electrophysical evidence points toward a hierarchical organization of the motor system, with the higher centers of the CNS representing motor goals in spatial coordinates. The next step, of course, is the transformation of the motor goals into impulses for the large number of muscles that are activated simultaneously during the execution of even the simplest kind of limb movement.

Execution of planned actions: The production of muscle's forces

To execute movements, the CNS must transform information about a small number of variables (direction, amplitude, and velocity) into a large number of signals to many muscles.

Any transformation of this type is "ill-posed" because an exact solution might not be available or unique. For instance, if the goal is to move the hand from an initial position [A] to a point [B] in space, then clearly there are a number of possible hand trajectories that could achieve this goal: the solution of this elementary motor problem is not unique. Even after the CNS has chosen a particular path for the hand, its implementation can be achieved with multiple combinations of joint motions at the shoulder, elbow and wrist—again, the solution is not unique. Finally, because there are many muscles around each joint, the net force generated by their activation can be achieved by a variety of combinations of muscles.

How the CNS of vertebrates handles the staggering number of mechanical variables involved in even the simplest movement is one of the central problems in motor control. Even a simple task, such as a reaching movement of the arm toward an object, involves the simultaneous activation of many thousands of motor units belonging to a number of muscles. The complexity inherent in controlling so many degrees of freedom has led us and a number of other researchers to propose that the nervous system must have developed ways to simplify this problem.

A variety of proposals have been made to explain these complexities. For instance, Hollerbach and Atkeson (1987), inspired by work in robotics, have suggested that the CNS first derives the motion of the joints from the planned path of the limb's endpoint (inverse kinematics). Next, the CNS computes the necessary joint torques (inverse dynamics) and then distributes the torques to a number of muscles. This hypothesis rests on the assumption that the CNS can estimate accurately limb inertia, center of mass, and the moment arm of muscles about the joints. This line of thinking seems to us improbable because the implied feedforward computations would lead to large motor instabilities every time the small errors in evaluating the various parameters occur. Alternative proposals have been made that do not depend on the solution of the complicated inverse dynamics problem. Specifically, it has been proposed that the CNS may transform the desired hand motion into a series of equilibrium positions (Bizzi et al., 1984). The forces needed to track the equilibrium trajectory result from the intrinsic elastic properties of muscles and from local feedback loops (Feldman, 1974; Bizzi, Polit, and Morasso, 1976, 1992; Hogan, 1984, 1985).

In the past few years, Bizzi, Mussa-Ivaldi, and Giszter (1991), Giszter, Mussa-Ivaldi, and Bizzi (1993), Mussa-Ivaldi, Giszter, and Bizzi (1994), and Saltiel, Tresh, and Bizzi (1998) have asked a specific question. Is the motor behavior of vertebrates based on simple units (motor primitives) that can be combined flexibly to accomplish a variety of motor tasks? This fundamental and long-standing question was addressed by investigating the spinal cord of frogs and rats with an array of approaches, such as microstimulation, N-methyl-D-aspartate (NMDA) iontophoresis, cutaneous stimulation of the hindlimb, and supraspinal stimulation. With these techniques, evidence for a modular organization of the frog and rat's spinal cord has been provided.

Evidence for spinal cord modules

A module is a functional unit in the spinal cord that generates a specific motor output by imposing a specific pattern of muscle activation. One way to elicit a spinal module is through microstimulation of the spinal cord in spinalized frogs. Bizzi, Mussa-Ivaldi, and Giszter (1991) and Giszter, Mussa-Ivaldi, and Bizzi (1993) elicited the activation of the leg's muscles by microstimulating the lateral and intermediate neuropil zone of the lumbar spinal cord.

To measure the mechanical responses of the activated muscles, Bizzi, Mussa-Ivaldi, and Giszter (1991) attached the right ankle of the frog to a six-axis force transducer, as shown in figure 34.1. The transducer held the ankle approximately level with the acetabulum. The transducer was mounted on a two-axis Cartesian manipulator, and the Cartesian location of the frog's ankle was set using this manipulator. The xy-plane corresponded approximately to the horizontal plane. In the experiments described, only the x and y components were considered.

Following the microstimulation of the spinal cord, Bizzi and associates observed a change in the forces at the ankle after a latency of between 30 and 150 msec. (Most response latencies were at approximately 100 msec.) The forces rose to a plateau level and then declined to the baseline level after a variable period (300 msec to 2 sec) after the termination of stimulation. At each ankle location, the net force vector, $\mathbf{F}$, obtained in response to stimulation, was expressed as the sum of two components—the "resting" force vector, $\mathbf{F_r}$, and the "active" force vector, $\mathbf{F_a}$:

$$\mathbf{F} = \mathbf{F_r} + \mathbf{F_a} \qquad (1)$$

The resting force vector corresponded to the force measured before the onset of the stimulus. The active force vector, $\mathbf{F_a} = \mathbf{F} - \mathbf{F_r}$, represented the additional force induced by our stimulus. The active field was generated only by those muscles directly or indirectly activated in response to stimulation.

As the electrode penetrated deeper into the cord, the orientation of the "active," above-baseline force vector recorded at a given leg position generally remained constant. Its magnitude usually varied, reaching a peak at the site of lowest threshold.

To record the spatial variations of forces generated by the leg muscles, Bizzi and colleagues followed a three-part procedure. First, they placed the frog's leg at a location within the leg's workspace. Second, they stimulated a site in the spinal cord and recorded the direction and amplitude of the elicited isometric force at the ankle. Third, they repeated the stimulation procedure with the ankle placed at each of 9 to 16 locations. These locations sampled a large portion of the region of the horizontal plane that could be reached by the frog's ankle (i.e., the leg's workspace). At each location, they stimulated the same site in the spinal cord and recorded the force vector, $\mathbf{F} = (\mathbf{F_x}, \mathbf{F_y})$, at the ankle. Although the site of spinal cord stimulation was constant throughout, they found that the elicited force vector varied as they placed the leg at different locations. These changes in force throughout the workspace resulted from a variety of mechanical factors, such as the

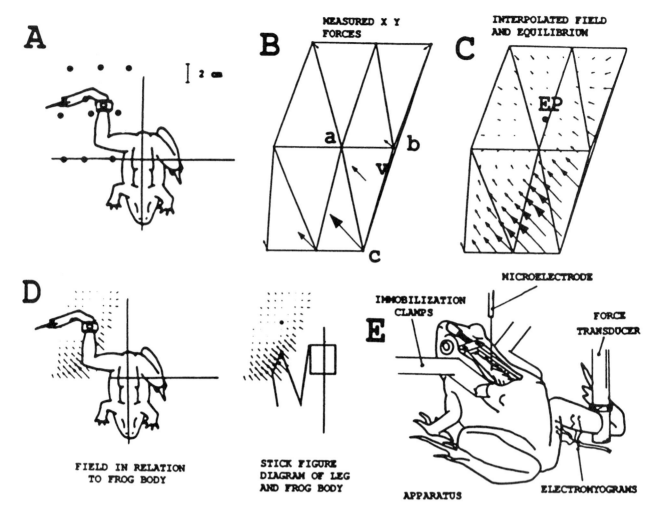

FIGURE 34.1   The apparatus and method of construction of a force field. (A) A collection of forces are recorded at several different spatial locations (black dots). (B) A minimum perimeter (Delaunay) tesselation of the nine points is constructed. Within each triangle, vectors are estimated using an exact linear interpolation based on the three corner vectors. Thus, vector v is calculated using vectors at vertices a, b, and c. (C) The interpolated field is used to find any equilibrium point (EP). (D) On the left, the interpolated force field is shown in relation to the frog in the apparatus. On the right, this representation is reduced to a stylized construction that is used to express the relation of frog axis and leg to the interpolated force field in the remaining figures. (E) The apparatus. The spine is clamped and the pelvis is held clamped by restraints (not shown). With an electrode in the spinal gray matter, the mechanical response to stimulation is recorded at the force sensor, which is attached to the limb at the ankle. The limb configuration is constrained fully by the pelvic restraint and the force sensor. (From Giszter, Mussa-Ivaldi, and Bizzi, 1993.)

length, moment arms, and viscoelastic properties of the muscles. In addition, reflex modulation of the muscles' activations played a role in the development of the forces at the ankle.

The collection of the measured forces corresponded to a force field (figure 34.1). Remarkably, in most instances (80%), the spatial variation of the measured force vectors resulted in a field that was at all times both convergent and characterized by a single equilibrium point (i.e., a point at which the amplitude of the F_x and F_y force components was zero). This equilibrium point represented the locus at which the leg would have been at steady state if it were free to move. The temporal evolution of the total force field caused a smooth movement of the equilibrium point from its position at rest to a new position at peak force magnitude and then back to the resting position. This motion of the equilibrium point constitutes what has been called the "virtual trajectory." The virtual trajectory is defined as the trajectory of positions at which the leg would experience no net force (figure 34.2).

Bizzi and coworkers and Giszter and associates found that the active-field data fell into a few classes or force field types (figure 34.3). After mapping most of the premotor area of the lumbar cord, they reached the conclusion that there are at least four areas from which four

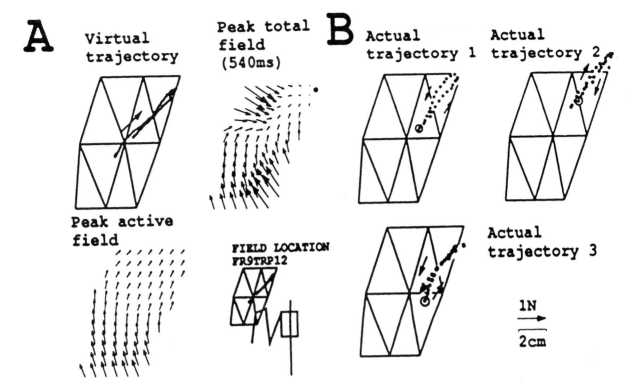

FIGURE 34.2 Comparison of actual and virtual trajectory. (A) Force field measurements. Shown is the virtual trajectory of equilibrium points (upper left), which derives from the time course of the total convergent force field shown at peak amplitude. The active field (lower left) had a pattern of forces that would specify a flow moving caudally and medially. The relation of the trajectory to the frog's body is shown schematically at lower right. (B) Trajectory measurements. Three sample limb trajectories from the suspended limb are shown. These were recorded at 30 Hz using a video system. We related the kinematic data to the grid of points used to collect the forces sampled for the field. The three trajectories begin at different locations in the grid because of different initial resting fields as a result of the leg's suspension (see text). The actual pattern of movement is predicted well by the total field. This was especially evident in the first trajectory, where resting equilibria almost coincide. The direction of the movement was predicted well by the active pattern in those trajectories where initial resting postures differed. (From Giszter, Mussa-Ivaldi, and Bizzi, 1993.)

distinct types of convergence force fields (CFFs) are elicited. Within each region, a qualitatively similar set of x and y forces were produced. This map of postures is shown in figure 34.3.

Force fields elicited by chemical stimulation

With electrical stimulation, it is not clear at which level the cells of the spinal cord are stimulated; somas, dendrites, axons, and nerve terminals all can be depolarized by current. For this reason, Saltiel, Tresh, and Bizzi (1998) induced force output from the spinal cord of the frog by using a compound that is known to activate only somas and dendrites. NMDA microiontophoresis was used with current and duration parameters expected to produce a spread estimated at a 150- to 270-mm radius.

This study confirmed that the spinal cord produces a limited number of discrete motor outputs. NMDA iontophoresis was applied to the lumbar spinal cord gray while monitoring the isometric force output of the ipsilateral hindlimb at the ankle. Tonic and rhythmic forces were generated. The distribution of force orientations was quite comparable to that obtained with electrical stimulation at the same sites. The map of tonic responses revealed a topographic organization; each type of force orientation was elicited from sites that grouped together in zones at distinct rostrocaudal and depth locations. Taken together, these results support the concept of a modular organization of the motor system in the frog's spinal cord and delineate the topography of these modules.

Mapping rhythmic forces showed that each was elicited from two or three regions of the cord. These results suggest that the different types of responses organized within the spinal cord might be combined together to create complex behaviors, such as those produced during rhythmic pattern generation. One mechanism by which these responses might be combined flexibly to create more complex behaviors is described in the next section.

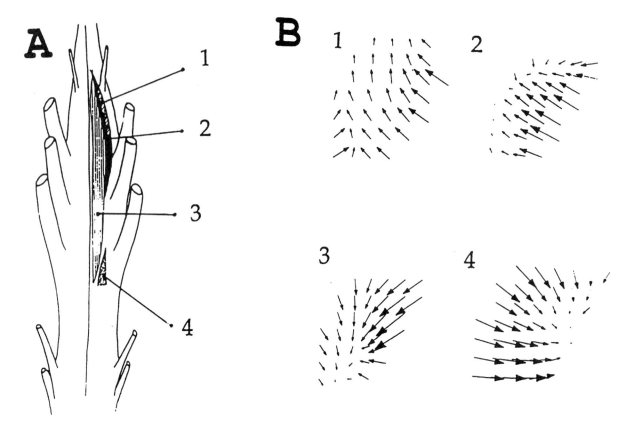

FIGURE 34.3   (A) Regions of the lumbar spinal cord containing the neural circuitries that specify the force fields (1–4). Within each region, similar sets of convergence force fields (CFFs) are produced. The diagram is based on 40 CFFs elicited by microstimulation of premotor regions in three spinalized frogs. (B) Four types of CFFs. To facilitate comparison among CFFs recorded in different animals, we subtracted the passive force field from the force field obtained at steady state. Passive field represents the mechanical behavior generated by the frog's leg (recorded at the ankle) in the absence of any stimulation. The force field is at steady state when the forces induced by the stimulation of the spinal cord have reached their maximal amplitude. (From Bizzi, Mussa-Ivaldi, and Giszter, 1991.)

Vector summation of force fields

One of the most remarkable observations derived from the microstimulation of the frog spinal cord has been that the fields induced by the focal activation of the spinal cord follow a principle of vectorial summation. Specifically, Mussa-Ivaldi, Giszter, and Bizzi (1994) investigated vectorial summation with the following experimental paradigm. First, a focal electrical stimulation was delivered to a site, A, of the spinal cord and the subsequent active field $F_A(x)$ was determined by measuring a set of force vectors at distinct ankle locations. Following the measurement of $F_A(x)$, a second electrical stimulation was applied to a different site, B, and a field $F_B(x)$ was derived. From these two fields, their sum, $F_S(x) = F_A(x) + F_B(x)$, was computed at all the sample points. Finally, another active field, $F_\&(x)$, was measured by stimulating the sites A and B simultaneously. When Mussa-Ivaldi, Giszter, and Bizzi compared the "costimulation fields," $F_\&(x)$, with the corresponding "summation fields," $F_S(x)$, they found that in 80% of cases, the two fields were equivalent (figure 34.4).

The observation that force fields sum vectorially suggests a way to relate natural movements to spinal cord microstimulation. Diverse neural signals conveyed by afferent inputs or descending tracts may gain access to the premotor areas described by Bizzi, Mussa-Ivaldi, and Giszter (1991), Giszter, Mussa-Ivaldi, and Bizzi (1993), and Saltiel, Tresh, and Bizzi (1998) and in this way specify the activation of a set of muscles. Physiologic movements result from patterns of neural activity distributed by afferent fibers or by descending branching fibers throughout fairly wide regions of the spinal cord. The activity conveyed by these branches may stimulate local clusters of cells that in turn generate force fields. Our assumption is that these fields sum like the convergent force fields generated by our electrical or chemical stimulation, leading to the possibility that a wide range of behaviors can be created by the summation of these different force fields.

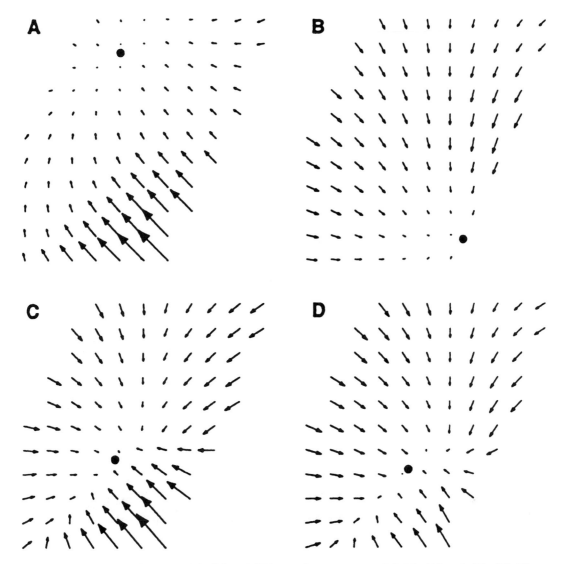

FIGURE 34.4 Combinations of multiple stimuli. (A) and (B) show the individual fields resulting from stimulation at two different sites in the premotor areas of the lumbar spinal cord. The equilibrium of field (A) is in extension, and (B) is in flexion. (C) The computed field [AB] predicted by a simple vecto-rial summation of fields (A) and (B). (D) The actual field evoked by stimulation of (A) and (B) together. The equilibrium point is indicated by a filled circle. (From Bizzi, Mussa-Ivaldi, and Giszter, 1991.)

Force fields as modules of control

The results of microstimulation of the frog's spinal cord have indicated that the spinal premotor circuits are organized in a relatively small number of modules. From an anatomic point of view, each module establishes—presumably via propriospinal connections—a common drive to a set of agonist and antagonist muscles. From a functional point of view, each module generates a field of forces. This field can be regarded as an elementary unit of control because it determines univocally the force generated by the module in response to any externally imposed state of motion of the limb.

A limb's posture is encoded implicitly as a stable equilibrium point within this field. Equilibrium is defined as the point at which force vanishes. Stability is ensured by the module producing a force that pulls the limb back toward the equilibrium point in response to a displacement. This operation leads to a force field that converges toward the equilibrium point. Thus, a module implements a stable posture by generating a force field that converges to that posture. In addition, a module can generate movement by producing a force field that varies in time so that the equilibrium point shifts from an initial to a final position. This concept not only is consistent with the aforementioned equilibrium point hypothesis, but it also provides a more general theoretical framework. Although the equilibrium point hypothesis specifies only the location of the equilibrium point and the local stiffness around this location, the force field specifies the pattern of forces across the entire workspace of a limb. This is an important feature that allows the control system to deal with the nonlinear properties of arm dynamics and to generate a class of behaviors that include the exertion of contact forces against objects in the environment.

Two major findings have emerged from the microstimulation experiments: (1) stimulation of several sites across the lumbar spinal cord produced only a few qualitatively distinct force fields, and (2) the force fields generated by spinal microstimulation added vectorially when two stimuli were applied simultaneously at two different spinal sites. These findings suggest the hypothesis that the motor system may create a variety of movements by the superposition of the force fields produced by a small set of independent spinal modules. The plausibility of this hypothesis has been tested in simulation studies by Mussa-Ivaldi and Giszter (1992) and Mussa-Ivaldi (1997).

The generation of movement by the combination of modules

In robotics (Brady et al., 1982), a desired trajectory is expressed as a temporal sequence of positions to be assumed by the limb. This sequence then is transformed by means of an inverse dynamics computation into a corresponding sequence of joint torques or muscle forces. The underlying assumption is that motor commands operate directly on the muscles and that muscles behave like ideal force generators. This assumption is quite plausible when dealing with conventional robots, whose motion controllers operate on nearly ideal force sources, such as torque motors. The amount of force generated by an ideal source does not depend on the position or the velocity at which it operates.

Our current understanding of muscle mechanics and of the circuits of the spinal cord offer a radically different scenario. Muscles are quite different from ideal force generators because their viscoelastic properties cause the force that they produce to depend on the muscle length and shortening velocity in addition to driving command. Furthermore, the microstimulation experiments and other neurophysiologic evidence indicate that most of the descending commands do not have access to individual muscles but rather to groups of muscles mediated by spinal interneurons. We formalize these notions by stating that the descending neural commands select and add vectorially the force fields generated by independent modules of control. In this new

computational scheme, the desired trajectory of the limb is not translated by the supraspinal circuits into a temporal sequence of force commands but instead into a set of commands that select and tune a corresponding set of modules of control.

Mathematically, this process may be expressed as follows. Let $D(q, \dot{q}, \ddot{q})$ represent the passive nonlinear dynamics of the limb. The variables q, $\dot{q}$ and $\ddot{q}$ are, respectively, the vectors of joint angles, angular velocities, and angular accelerations. The function $D(\cdot)$ is a nonlinear relation that transforms these kinematic variables into a corresponding vector of joint torques. The active force field generated by a spinal module, m, also may be represented as a nonlinear function of the joint angles and angular velocities and of time: $\phi_m(q, \dot{q}, t)$. The dependence of a module's force on position and velocity is a direct consequence of the viscoelastic properties of the muscles. The dependence on time is a consequence of the dynamics of muscle contraction and of the interactions among spinal neurons. The evidence that we have discussed previously suggests that the descending commands do not alter the form of these force fields. Instead, the descending commands operate by recruiting different modules in different amounts. In a first approximation, the recruitment of a module, m, by a central command may be represented as a (nonnegative) scaling factor, c_m, that changes uniformly the amplitude of the forces without altering their direction.[1] Then, a system of K modules leads to a net force field:

$$\sum_{m=1}^{K} c_m \cdot \phi_m(q, \dot{q}, t)$$

The net dynamics of the limb and of the control system may be represented by the differential equation:

$$D(q, \dot{q}, \ddot{q}) = \sum_{m=1}^{K} c_m \cdot \phi_m(q, \dot{q}, t) \qquad (2)$$

Given a particular set of selection coefficients and a specification of the initial position and velocity, this equation admits a unique trajectory $\hat{q}(t)$ as its solution.

In this framework, the central command is represented by a K-dimensional vector of selection parameters, $c = (c_1, c_2, \dots, c_K)$. This is quite different from the pattern of joint torques, which must be computed explicitly in the inverse dynamic methods.

The computational problem with a modular system is that of deriving the selection parameters that lead to the execution of a desired trajectory. This problem may be approached as one of function approximation: given a desired trajectory, find a set of selection coefficients that minimize the error between the desired trajectory and the trajectory that results from the selection coefficients.

In a simulation study, Mussa-Ivaldi (1997) has shown that this approximation problem can be expressed as a problem of linear least-squares in the selection coefficients. Therefore, for any desired trajectory, a unique set of parameters that minimize the error measure can always be found.[2] Obviously this method does not guarantee that an arbitrary movement can be implemented with unlimited accuracy. The force fields produced by the module represent a constraint on the trajectories that may actually be generated by the control system.

Is it possible, given such a constraint, to reproduce the kinematic features of reaching arm movements? The simulation studies of Mussa-Ivaldi (1997) indeed show that by combining a small number of convergent force fields with stereotyped time dependency, it is possible to generate the intersegmental coordination that makes the hand move along a rectilinear path with a bell-shaped velocity profile. In these simulations, the force fields were divided in two classes: "step" fields and "pulse" fields. These two classes differed only by their dependence on time. The forces generated by the step fields started from zero amplitude and reached monotonically a plateau during the movement time. The forces generated by the pulse fields also started from zero amplitude, then they reached a peak value and returned to zero amplitude during the movement time. Models based on similar temporal patterns have been successful in dealing with the control of saccadic eye movements (Robinson, 1981). Figure 34.5 (see also color plate 21) illustrates a simulated arm movement produced by the combination of pulse and step fields. In addition to approximating the desired arm kinematics, this control system generates a temporal sequence of force fields with a moving equilibrium point, that is, a virtual trajectory thus reproducing the stability properties that are typical of observed reaching movements (Bizzi et al., 1984; Hogan, 1985).

Modules as a basis for representing movements: motor learning

Although spinal force fields offer a practical way to generate movement, they also provide the CNS with something equivalent to a movement's representation. This representation is similar geometrically to the representation of space by a set of Cartesian coordinates. In the latter case, we may take three directions–represented by three independent vectors–and then project any point in space along these directions. As a result, an arbitrary point in space is represented by three numbers, the co-

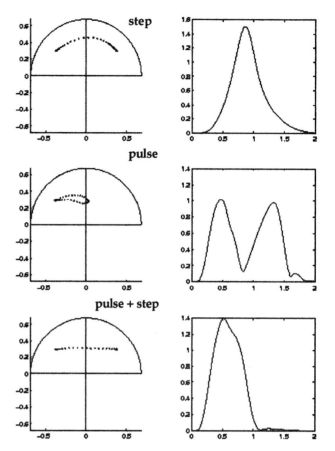

FIGURE 34.5 Simulation of arm movement by the combination of pulse and step fields. The three frames on the left side show the workspace of a two-joint planar arm. The shoulder joint is at the center of the coordinate system. Hand trajectories are shown as dotted curves, with the dots separated by equal sampling intervals. The panels on the right display the velocity profiles of the movements on the left. (Top) Movement resulting from the activation of a step field. The starting position is to the left of the shoulder, the target to the right. This field sets the equilibrium point on the target. (Middle) Movement resulting from the activation of a pulse field. The starting point is the same as for the step. As the field reaches the maximum intensity, the hand moves toward the right side. Then the field amplitude decreases, and the hand returns to the starting position. (Bottom) Movement resulting from the vectorial summation of the step and pulse fields of the top and middle panels. The pulse fields effectively correct the movement curvature produced by the step field (top panel). At the end of the movement, the pulse field ceases to be effective, and the final position is determined by the step field. The resulting movement is nearly rectilinear, and the velocity profile is unimodal. In this simulation, the parameters that modulate the amplitude of the pulse and step fields were chosen to approximate a straight-line movement from left to right with symmetric velocity profiles. Units: space (m), time (sec), velocity (m/sec).

ordinates x, y, and z. The movements of a limb can be considered "points" in an abstract geometrical space. In this abstract geometrical space, the force fields produced by a set of modules play a role equivalent to that of the

Cartesian axes, and the selection parameters that generate a particular movement may be regarded as generalized projections of this movement along the modules' fields.[3] In this view, the representation of a trajectory– that is, the particular set of selection parameters that implement this trajectory– depend both on a limb's passive dynamics and on the set of fields generated by the modules.

If the dynamics change and the modules remain unchanged, then the representation of the movement must change accordingly. This is shown by the following argument. Suppose that a trajectory, $q(t)$, is represented by a selection vector $c = (c_1, c_2, \ldots, c_K)$ for a limb with the dynamics of Equation (1). Now suppose that the limb dynamics are modified by an additional unexpected load, $E(q, \dot{q}, \ddot{q})$. Leaving the representation and the fields unchanged, we now have a new differential equation:

$$D(q, \dot{q}, \ddot{q}) + E(q, \dot{q}, \ddot{q}) = \sum_{m=1}^{K} c_m \cdot \phi_m(q, \dot{q}, t)$$

whose solution is a trajectory, $\tilde{q}(t)$, generally different from the original trajectory $q(t)$. The old selection vector has become a representation for $\tilde{q}(t)$. The old trajectory is recovered by changing the selection coefficients to a new set $c' = c + e$, with

$$E(q(t), \dot{q}(t), \ddot{q}(t)) = \sum_{m=1}^{K} e_m \cdot \phi_m(q(t), \dot{q}(t), t)$$

With these new coefficients, the new dynamics become equivalent to the old dynamics along the original trajectory.[4] The modified coefficients c' are a new representation of the old movement $q(t)$ in the altered dynamics. This procedure for forming a new representation and for recovering the original movement is consistent with the empirical observation of after effects in load adaptation[5] (Shadmehr and Mussa-Ivaldi, 1994).

Is it necessary for the motor system to modify a movement's representation each time the limb dynamics changes, or is there a way for restoring the previously existing representations? From a computational point of view, whenever a dynamic change is permanent–as when we undergo growth or damage–it would seem convenient for the CNS to have the ability to restore the previously learned motor skills (i.e., the previously learned movement representations) without needing to relearn them all. There currently is no strong experimental evidence to resolve this issue. However, the representation of motor primitives as force fields provides a theoretical insight. It may be

possible for the adaptive system to restore, at least partially, the motor representations that preexist a change in dynamics, and to do so, it is necessary to modify the modules and their force fields. A specific modification is obtained when we may express the coefficients $e = e(e_1, e_2, \ldots, e_K)$ as a linear transformation of the original coefficients $c = (c_1, c_2, \ldots, c_K)$:

$$e = Wc$$

This transformation represents a coordinate transformation of the selection vector and may be implemented by a linear associative network. With a minimum of algebra one sees that

$$D(q, \dot{q}, \ddot{q}) + E(q, \dot{q}, q) = \sum_{m=1}^{K} c'_m \cdot \phi_m(q, \dot{q}, t)$$
$$= \sum_{m=1}^{K} (c_m + e_m) \cdot \phi_m(q, \dot{q}, t)$$
$$= \sum_{m=1}^{K} c_m \cdot \overline{\phi}_m(q, \dot{q}, t)$$

where the old fields ϕ_m have been replaced by the new fields

$$\overline{\phi}_m = \sum_{l=1}^{K} (I_{l,m} + W_{l,m}) \cdot \phi_l$$

This again is a coordinate transformation of the original fields, which may be implemented by a neural network intervening between the descending commands and the original fields. By means of this coordinate transformation, one obtains the important result that the movement representation–that is, the selection vector c–can be maintained invariant after a change in limb dynamics.

One may regard this form of invariance as the motor counterpart of the perceptual stability that allows the visual system to identify objects and faces in variable light conditions and from different viewpoints. As in the visual system, the possibility of constructing invariant representations within the motor system rests on the existence of independent primitives–the spinal force fields–that form a basis for constructing a variety of behaviors.

NOTES

1. This simplification is supported by the observation that variable intensities of stimulation in the frog's spinal cord resulted in changes of force field amplitude but not in changes of force directions (Giszter, Mussa-Ivaldi, and Bizzi, 1993).

2. This globally optimum solution is found by minimizing the error

$$\int \left\| D(\hat{q}(t), \dot{\hat{q}}(t), \ddot{\hat{q}}(t)) - \sum_{m=1}^{K} c_m \phi_m(\hat{q}(t), \dot{\hat{q}}(t), t) \right\|^2 \cdot dt$$

over the desired trajectory, $\hat{q}(t)$. This is a quadratic expression in the selection coefficients. The global solution is obtained by solving for c_m the linear system of K equations

$$\int \phi_n(\hat{q}(t), \dot{\hat{q}}(t), t) \bullet D(\hat{q}(t), \dot{\hat{q}}(t), \ddot{\hat{q}}(t)) dt$$

$$= \sum_{m=1}^{K} \left[\int \phi_n(\hat{q}(t), \dot{\hat{q}}(t), t) \bullet \phi_m(\hat{q}(t), \dot{\hat{q}}(t), t) dt \right] c_m$$

where the dot operator indicates the scalar product. This system is guaranteed to have a solution if and only if the determinant of the field autocorrelation matrix

$$\Phi_{m,n} \equiv \int \phi_n(\hat{q}(t), \dot{\hat{q}}(t), t) \bullet \phi_m(\hat{q}(t), \dot{\hat{q}}(t), t) dt$$

does not vanish.

3. This is not just an analogy but a formal equivalence. In analytic geometry, a 3D vector $\vec{r}$ is represented as

$$r = x_1 \cdot \vec{e_1} + x_2 \cdot \vec{e_2} + x_3 \cdot \vec{e_3} \qquad (3)$$

where $\vec{e_1}$, $\vec{e_2}$ and $\vec{e_3}$ are three vectors forming a *basis* for 3D space and x_1, x_2 and x_3 are three numbers, the representation of r with respect to this basis. In the case of movement control, the expression

$$D(q(t), \dot{q}(t), \ddot{q}(t)) = c_1 \cdot \phi_1(q(t), \dot{q}(t), t)$$
$$+ c_2 \cdot \phi_2(q(t), \dot{q}(t), t)$$
$$+ \cdots + c_K \cdot \phi_K(q(t), \dot{q}(t), t)$$

is identically satisfied if and only if the trajectory $q(t)$ is a solution of the differential equation (1). Like x_1, x_2 and x_3, the selection coefficients c_i are real numbers that modulate the functions ϕ_i. Thus, the latter play the same role as the basis vectors in (2). The procedure to calculate the coefficients described in the previous footnote is formally equivalent to a projection operation.

4. Because if

$$D(q(t), \dot{q}(t), \ddot{q}(t)) = \sum_{m=1}^{K} c_m \cdot \phi_m(q(t), \dot{q}(t), t)$$

and

$$E(q(t), \dot{q}(t), \ddot{q}(t)) = \sum_{m=1}^{K} e_m \cdot \phi_m(q(t), \dot{q}(t), t)$$

are both identically satisfied, then also their sum

$$D(q(t), \dot{q}(t), \ddot{q}(t)) + E(q(t), \dot{q}(t), \ddot{q}(t))$$
$$= \sum_{m=1}^{K} (c_m + e_m) \cdot \phi_m(q(t), \dot{q}(t), t)$$

is identically satisfied.

5. If the load is removed after the new representation is formed, the dynamics becomes

$$D(q, \dot{q}, \ddot{q}) = \sum_{m=1}^{K} (c_m + e_m) \cdot \phi_m(q, \dot{q}, t)$$

that can be rewritten as

$$D(q, \dot{q}, \ddot{q}) - \sum_{m=1}^{K} e_m \cdot \phi_m(q, \dot{q}, t)$$
$$= \sum_{m=1}^{K} c_m \cdot \phi_m(q, \dot{q}, t)$$

Therefore, removing the load with the new representation corresponds approximately to applying the opposite load with the old representation.

REFERENCES

ABEND, W., E. BIZZI, and P. MORASSO, 1982. Human arm trajectory formation. *Brain* 105:331–348.

BERNSTEIN, N. A., 1967. *The Coordination and Regulation of Movements.* New York: Pergamon.

BIZZI, E., N. ACCORNERO, W. CHAPPLE, and N. HOGAN, 1984. Posture control and trajectory formation during arm movement. *J. Neurosci.* 4: 2738–2744.

BIZZI, E., N. HOGAN, F. A. MUSSA-IVALDI, and S. GISZTER, 1992. Does the nervous system use equilibrium-point control to guide single and multiple joint movements? *Behav. Brain Sci.* 15:603–613.

BIZZI, E., F. A. MUSSA-IVALDI, and S. F. GISZTER, 1991. Computations underlying the execution of movement: A biological perspective. *Science* 253:287–291.

BIZZI, E., A. POLIT, and P. MORASSO, 1976. Mechanisms underlying achievement of final head position. *J. Neurophysiol.* 39:435–444.

BRADY, M., J. M. HOLLERBACH, T. L. JOHNSON, T. LOZANO-PEREZ, and M. T. MASON, 1982. *Robot Motion: Planning and Control.* Cambridge, Mass.: MIT Press.

CAMINITI, R., P. B. JOHNSON, and A. URBANO, 1990. Making arm movements within different parts of space: Dynamic aspects in the primate motor cortex. *J. Neurosci.* 10:2039–2058.

FELDMAN, A. G., 1974. Change of muscle length due to shift of the equilibrium point of the muscle-load system. *Biofizika* 19:534–538.

FLASH, T., and I. GUREVICH, 1992. Arm movement and stiffness adaptation to external loads. In *Proceedings of the Annual Conference in IEEE Engineering in Medicine and Biology Society.* New York: IEEE Publishing Services, pp. 885–886.

FLASH, T., and N. HOGAN, 1985. The coordination of arm movements: An experimentally confirmed mathematical model. *J. Neurosci.* 5:1688–1703.

GEORGOPOULOUS, A. P., R. E. KETTNER, and A. B. SCHWARTZ, 1988a. Primate motor cortex and free arm movements to visual targets in three-dimensional space: I. Coding of the direction of movement by a neuronal population. *J. Neurosci.* 8:2913–2927.

GEORGOPOULOUS, A. P., R. E. KETTNER, and A. B. SCHWARTZ, 1988b. Primate motor cortex and free arm movements to visual targets in three-dimensional space: II. Coding of the direction of movement by a neuronal population. *J. Neurosci.* 8:2928–2937.

GISZTER, S. F., F. A. MUSSA-IVALDI, and E. BIZZI, 1993. Convergent force fields organized in the frog's spinal cord. *J. Neurosci.* 13:467–491.

HOGAN, N., 1984. An organizing principle for a class of voluntary movement control. *J. Neurosci.* 4:2745–2754.

HOGAN, N., 1985. The mechanics of multi-joint posture and movement control. *Biol. Cybern.* 52:315–331.

HOGAN, N., E. BIZZI, F. A. MUSSA-IVALDI, and T. FLASH, 1987. Controlling multijoint motor behavior. In *Exercise and Sport Science Review 15,* K. B. Pandolf, ed. New York: Macmillan, pp. 153–190.

HOLLERBACH, J. M., and C. G. ATKESON, 1987. Deducing planning variables from experimental arm trajectories: Pitfalls and possibilities. *Biol. Cybern.* 56:279–292.

KALASKA, J. F., D. A. D. COHEN, M. L. HYDE, and M. PRUD'HOMME, 1989. A comparison of movement direction-related versus load direction-related activity in primate motor cortex, using a two-dimensional reaching task. *J. Neurosci.* 9:2080–2102.

MORASSO, P., 1981. Spatial control of arm movements. *Exp. Brain. Res.* 42:223–227.

MUSSA-IVALDI, F. A., 1997. Nonlinear force fields: A distributed system of control primitives for representing and learning movements. In *Proceedings of the 1997 IEEE International Symposium on Computational Intelligence in Robotics and Automation.* New York: IEEE Press, pp. 84–90.

MUSSA-IVALDI, F. A., and S. F. GISZTER, 1992. Vector field approximation: A computational paradigm for motor control and learning. *Biol. Cybern.* 67:491–500.

MUSSA-IVALDI, F. A., S. F. GISZTER, and E. BIZZI, 1994. Linear combinations of primitives in vertebrate motor control. *Proc. Natl. Acad. Sci. U.S.A.* 91:7534–7538.

ROBINSON, D. A., 1981. The use of control system analysis in the neurophysiology of eye movements. *Annu. Rev. Neurosci.* 4:463–503.

SATIEL, P., M. TRESH, and E. BIZZI, 1998. Spinal cord modular organization and rhythm generation: An NMDA iontophoretic study in the frog. *J. Neurophysiol.* 80:2323–2339.

SHADMEHR, R., and F. A. MUSSA-IVALDI, 1994. Adaptive representation of dynamics during learning of a motor task. *J. Neurosci.* 14:3208–3224.

UNO, Y., M. KAWATO, and R. SUZUKI, 1989. Formation and control of optimal trajectory in human multijoint arm movement: Minimum torque-change model. *Biol. Cybern.* 61:89–101.

35 Spatial Representations and Internal Models of Limb Dynamics in Motor Learning

CLAUDE GHEZ, JOHN W. KRAKAUER, ROBERT L. SAINBURG,
AND MARIA-FELICE GHILARDI

ABSTRACT   In this chapter we propose that the planning of reaching movements depends on the learning of three internal representations and that visual and proprioceptive feedback play different roles in this process. Prior studies have shown that movements to visual targets are planned in a vectorial representation of space centered at the hand. Here we show that adaptation to gain changes, which require rescaling a visuomotor transformation, is more rapid than adaptation to rotations, which require rotating the frame of reference. Generalization differs between the two learning conditions. Subjects readily learn new scaling factors after training with a single target and use them to move accurately to targets at different distances and directions from the origin. With rotations, training with a single target allows them to aim movements accurately only if the target is in the same direction. However, they remain accurate in that direction when moving from different initial positions. It is inferred that training results in learning a directional axis that can be translated in the workspace. To learn a complete reference frame requires training to targets in at least 8 directions. Visual feedback is sufficient and proprioception is not necessary to learn new gains and rotations.

The planning of movement as a vector implies a second representation, that of hand position. The finding of systematic position-dependent directional biases indicates that proprioception alone is not sufficient for the origin of movement vectors to be specified with accuracy. Instead we suggest that visual information is necessary to calibrate the proprioceptive representation of hand position in space.

Straight and accurate movements also require learning the dynamic properties of the limb. This third representation is known as an internal model. We studied this process by examining how subjects adapt to a novel inertial load that changes the inertial interactions at the elbow. Training with a single target does not generalize to other directions; however, learning can be applied to new positions in the workspace if the joint angle changes are the same. Thus, unlike learning a new spatial reference frame, new internal models of inertial dynamics are encoded in intrinsic coordinates. Changing the sources of sensory feedback shows that only proprioceptive feedback is necessary for this learning.

The differences in the rules for learning spatial transformations and inertial models suggest that the two processes are independent. This was confirmed by showing that consolidation of newly learned spatial reference frames and new inertial models are independent and interference remains restricted to each form of learning. We therefore suggest that separate working memory buffers are used in the two forms of learning.

CLAUDE GHEZ   Center for Neurobiology and Behavior, N.Y.S. Psychiatric Institute, Columbia University, College of Physicians and Surgeons, New York, N.Y.

JOHN W. KRAKAUER   Department of Neurology, Columbia University, College of Physicians and Surgeons, New York, N.Y.

ROBERT L. SAINBURG   School of Health Related Professions, State University of New York at Buffalo, Buffalo, N.Y.

MARIA-FELICE GHILARDI   Center for Neurobiology and Behavior, Columbia University, New York, N.Y., and INB-CNR, Milan, Italy

It is widely accepted that the nervous system represents and plans reaching movements in extrinsic space: Despite variable joint motions, hand movements aimed to targets throughout peripersonal space remain straight and have stereotyped bell-shaped velocity profiles (Morasso, 1981). Both the velocity and acceleration profiles scale with movement extent (Atkeson and Hollerbach, 1985), even if target distance is unpredictable (Ghez, 1979; Gordon, Ghilardi, and Ghez, 1994). The straightness and linear scaling of early trajectory variables to the distance of the target show that the nervous system controls movement through feedforward mechanisms.

Detailed analyses of trajectory errors indicate further that hand movements are planned vectorially as extents and directions in a hand-centered coordinate system (Ghez et al., 1997; Ghez et al., 1990; Gordon, Ghilardi, and Ghez, 1994; Vindras and Viviani, 1998). These results agree with those from a study of single-cell recordings in primates by Georgopoulos and colleagues, which revealed populations of neurons in primary motor cortex that encode movement direction itself (Georgopoulos, Schwartz, and Kettner, 1986). The vectorial space in which intended movements are coded requires a known origin, that is, the initial hand position, and its relationship to other points in visual space. Visuospatial and hand-centered vectorial maps can differ in terms of scaling or in reference frame depending on the task. Learning new spatial maps is therefore necessary if movements are to remain accurate.

To displace the hand in space along an intended trajectory, extent and direction need to be recoded in intrinsic coordinates to specify the appropriate muscle forces and joint torques (Flanders, Helms Tillery, and Soechting, 1992). Consistent with this, Kalaska and co-workers have identified populations of neurons in primary motor cortex that encode movement direction and joint motion successively (Scott and Kalaska, 1997). The transformation from extrinsic to intrinsic coordinates must take account of the complex mechanical effects of gravity, inertia, and intersegmental interactions (Hollerbach and Flash, 1982; Hoy and Zernicke, 1985; Hoy and Zernicke, 1986; Hoy, Zernicke, and Smith, 1985). Moreover, biomechanical conditions change with fatigue and other time varying factors. It is generally believed that to perform the transformation from extrinsic to intrinsic coordinates the dynamic properties of the limb, which are represented as an internal model by the nervous system, must be learned (Shadmehr and Mussa-Ivaldi, 1994; Ghez, 1979; Ghez et al., 1990; Ghez and Sainburg, 1995; Gordon, Ghilardi, and Ghez, 1995; Sainburg, Ghez, and Kalakanis, 1999). Although concurrent visual and proprioceptive feedback are critical in calibrating internal models of limb dynamics (Ghez, Gordon, and Ghilardi, 1995; Sainburg and Ghez, 1995), the role of proprioception in learning new dynamic models is not known.

In the first section of this chapter, we examine the roles of visual and proprioceptive feedback in adapting to changes in the gain and direction of visual feedback information and to changes in initial position of the hand. In the second section, we examine the learning of new models of inertial dynamics and the roles of proprioceptive and visual feedback in this. Finally, in the third section, we show that learning and consolidation of new spatial transformations and new inertial dynamics are independent.

Learning new spatial transformations

REMAPPING AND ROTATING REFERENCE FRAMES: ROLES OF VISUAL FEEDBACK   Movement planning in a hand-centered vectorial space suggests that errors in extent and direction should be computed and processed separately. To determine whether this is the case, we studied the time course and the effects of changes in visual feedback as subjects adapted to changes in gain and to rotations in hand path displays around the starting position of the hand on a computer monitor. The values for

the gain change and the rotation were chosen to equate the linear error (distance from target to movement end point) of the predicted unadapted movement and presumably its salience. Subjects made out-and-back movements of their hand on a horizontal surface at shoulder level. Targets were displayed on the screen with a cursor indicating the position of their hand while an opaque shield prevented subjects from seeing their arm and hand. After a block of 60 to 90 trials, the motions of the screen cursor were changed unexpectedly. As can be seen in figure 35.1, after an increase in gain to 1.5:1, the first movements were overshot by approximately 150%; when the hand path display was rotated counterclockwise 30°, movements were deviated by 30° in the same direction. Errors in extent and direction decreased rapidly over the first 5 to 10 movements and more slowly thereafter. In both cases, the decay in error was fit by a double exponential function. Subjects use errors detected with each movement to adjust either the extent or direction of the next movement by a given proportion of the error. The double exponential fit could reflect the use of two different strategies over time. In an initial period, when the systematic source of the error is most readily distinguishable from random variability, successive adjustments are large. Later, when systematic errors have become smaller and more difficult to distinguish from variable errors, a different adaptive strategy is chosen.

Time course of learning   Adaptation to changes in gain is more rapid than adaptation to rotations (Pine et al., 1996). This is apparent comparing the initial slopes of the fitted lines in figure 35.1. Additionally, the systematic extent errors produced by the gain change are fully corrected after about 60 movements while with rotation, movements remain significantly deviated even after 90 movements (figure 35.1, top). Since the initial linear error was the same for both perturbations, the more rapid adaptation to the gain change does not result from differences in magnitudes of the errors induced by the perturbation.

Increasing the number of targets influences the time course of adaptation differently for gain and rotation. Adaptation to a new gain is more rapid and errors reach baseline sooner when the number of targets is increased from 1 to 8. In contrast, adaptation to a rotation is slower with 8 targets than with a single target (Krakauer et al., 1997).

The more rapid rate of adaptation to imposed gain changes when moving to multiple targets can be understood by assuming that errors are held temporarily in working memory. Movements to several target distances will then more readily reveal their common origin as scaling errors. The question arises, however, why the

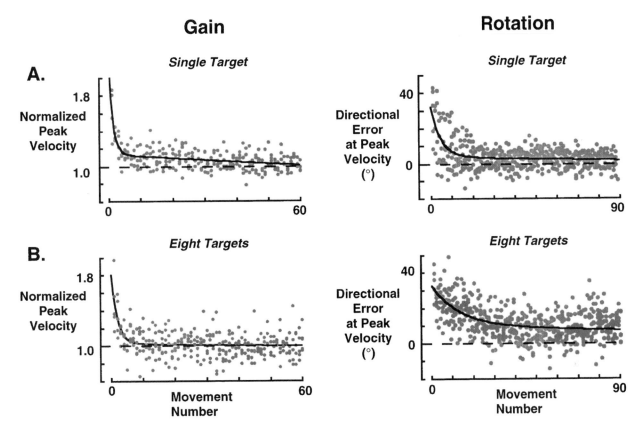

Gain

A.

Single Target

Normalized Peak Velocity

1.8

1.0

0   60

B.

Eight Targets

Normalized Peak Velocity

1.8

1.0

0   60

Movement Number

Rotation

Single Target

Directional Error at Peak Velocity (°)

40

0

0   90

Eight Targets

Directional Error at Peak Velocity (°)

40

0

0   90

Movement Number

FIGURE 35.1 Time course of learning new gains and rotations. (A) Learning of the new gain (1.5) is measured as the scaling of the peak velocity to the target extent. Peak velocity was normalized by dividing it by target extent. Data are fitted by double exponential functions. (B) Learning of the 30° counterclockwise rotation was measured by the progressive reduction in the directional error at peak velocity.

same improvement with multiple targets does not occur with rotation. One explanation might be that errors resulting from gain changes would be improved by rescaling the same pattern of motor neuron activation regardless of the position of the hand in the workspace or the direction of movement. Adjusting for a rotated reference frame may be more difficult. This is because movements in different directions are produced by different muscle patterns and joint rotations. Also the changes in joint rotation appropriate to counter a given directional error are different from those in the original reference frame. Therefore, it may be necessary for all directions to be sampled in order to derive the rule underlying the error. This suggests that adaptation to new gains generalizes across target distances, whereas adaptation to rotations is local.

Generalization of learning To demonstrate differences in generalization of learning gain changes and rotations, we trained subjects to move rapidly to a single target and back and changed the gain or direction of visual feedback. We then examined the errors they made when reaching for targets at different extents or directions without visual feedback.

The data in figure 35.2A show that learning the appropriate extents of movements made to near or to far targets in either of two directions generalizes across target distances and directions. With rotation, however, directional errors increase rapidly as the angle separating the test target from the training target increases (figure 35.2B). The slope of this decline becomes less with two and four training directions. With eight training directions, movements to intermediate targets are as accurate as those in the trained direction (Krakauer, Pine, and Ghez, 1996).

These results demonstrate that although visual feedback enables subjects to rapidly rescale vectorial representations of extrinsic space, learning a rotated reference frame centered on the hand is a more lengthy process and requires targets in several directions. The question of whether learning to move the hand in a single direction reflects a single stimulus-response association or the learning of a more general spatial transformation is considered later in this chapter.

LEARNING HAND POSITION IN VISUAL SPACE: ROLES OF VISUAL AND PROPRIOCEPTIVE INFORMATION   In principle, the position of the hand in space could be computed from proprioception and knowledge of segment

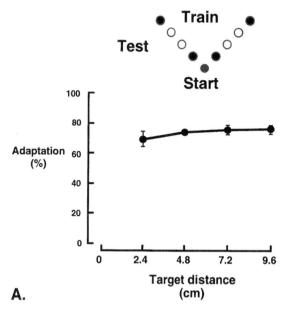

A.

B.

FIGURE 35.2 Generalization of learning after adaptation to gain changes and rotations in hand path displays. (A) Separate groups of subjects were trained, using visual feedback, to move to one or the other of the four black targets shown in the inset. They were then tested without feedback to all eight targets (gray circles). The degree of adaptation is a percentage ratio of the peak velocity in the control and test conditions divided by the gain change (1:1.5). No difference is present in the scaling of peak velocity between the trained and untrained directions indicating complete generalization. (B) As in (A), subjects learned either 1, 2, 4, or 8 targets (*inset*) and were tested to 10 others (1 at 22.5° on either side of the trained direction plus the 8 directions shown in the inset labeled 8). The degree of adaptation is a percentage ratio of the directional error at peak velocity to the imposed rotation (30° counterclockwise). Individual points are averages across subjects for targets on both sides of the trained direction. For target separations greater than 45°, adaptation decays rapidly as target direction deviates from the trained direction.

lengths. However, this seems unlikely. First, the relationship of muscle length or joint angle to the discharge of muscle (Houk and Rymer, 1981; Matthews, 1981b; Matthews and Stein, 1969) is linear only over limited ranges of static positions. Thus, changes in lengths or angles produce different changes in neural activity for different initial conditions. Second, judgments of segment lengths, needed to compute hand position, can be unreliable or biased. Therefore, it is not surprising that estimates of hand position drift over time (Wann and Ibrahim, 1992).

The inadequacy of proprioception alone in motor planning is also demonstrated by the consistent directional biases that occur when subjects reach for visual targets but cannot see their hands before movement (figure 35.3A). These biases increase as the initial position of the hand deviates from its usual location near a forward egocentric axis (Ghilardi, Gordon, and Ghez, 1995; Pine et al., 1998) and are present to the same degree when subjects simply are given verbal instructions to point in a given direction relative to their body.

These position-dependent biases disappear, however, if subjects can see their hand together with the targets directly in the same workspace. These biases could have resulted if, during the each block of trials, the representation of either hand or target location had drifted towards the location in which motor tasks are most frequently performed. Indeed, the precision and accuracy of spatial judgments is influenced by such central tendency biases (Poulton, 1975). Simple dynamic simulations (Pine et al., 1998) support the idea that when the hand is not visible, the brain relies on a remembered location of hand position that systematically underestimates the distance from its usual position by a given percentage.

If the specification of movement direction were based on inaccurately remembered hand positions, extensive training at a single location might be expected to abolish preexisting directional biases. Additionally, if the representation of hand position is biased by recent experience, new errors should be present at different initial hand positions but show the same position dependence as before training. As can be seen in figure 35.3B, the directional bias of movements made without visual feedback from a lateral starting point disappear when subjects are trained to move to the same targets with the hand continuously visible. However, when movements are made in other positions, new directional biases occur but vary with hand position in

504   MOTOR SYSTEMS

A. Mean Directional Error

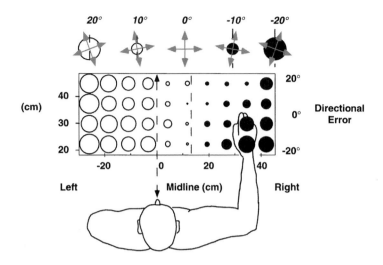

B. Mean directional errors before and after training with visual feedback

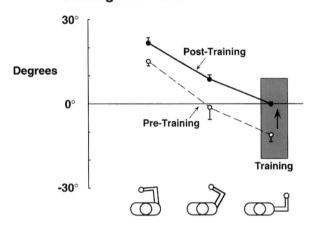

FIGURE 35.3   Position dependent directional biases. Subjects sat in front of a horizontal tablet and made reaching movements to a circular array of 12 targets shown on a vertical computer screen. Vision of the arm was obstructed by a shield. (A) Subjects ($N = 3$) moved to a circular array of 12 targets without visual feedback after their hand was moved passively to the positions indicated by the circles. The diagram shows that mean directional error (across target directions) for each position varies with the position of their hand relative to the body midline. Biases are clockwise in regions to the left and counter-clockwise of the right of an error free region extending forward from the body midline. The degree of bias is shown by the rotated "compass points" and the diameters of the circles. (B) Training with visual feedback in one location eliminates the directional bias present previously in that hand position (gray rectangle) but introduces biases throughout the rest of the workspace. These new biases increase with the mediolateral distance of the hand from the trained location. The three limb configurations are as shown in the schematic drawing.

the same way as before training: The two sets of points parallel each other in figure 35.3B.

These results add further support to the conclusion that the continuous flow of proprioceptive information during successive movements is not adequate to specify the origin of individual movement vectors. Instead, we suggest that vision of the hand and limb is necessary to calibrate these proprioceptive signals.

Learning new musculoskeletal dynamics

To displace the hand in space, the nervous system must also transform the intended direction and extent into feedforward control signals distributed to motor neurons and muscles. For the resulting movement trajectory to conform to the one that was intended, feedforward commands need to anticipate the effects of both environmental forces and of forces arising within the musculoskeletal system itself. Internal forces include ones produced by muscles and by the inertial resistance. In linked mechanical systems such as the arm, dynamic interactions that occur among limb segments produce large time-varying torques at each joint. These depend critically on joint and hand velocities and, more importantly, on angular accelerations occurring during movement. Learning an internal model of these dynamic properties of the musculoskeletal system is essential to transform intended actions into mechanical displacement (Goodbody and Wolpert, 1998; Imamizu, Uno, and Kawato, 1995; Jordan, 1996; Lackner and Dizio, 1994; Sainburg, Ghez, and Kalakanis, 1999; Sainburg et al., 1995; Shadmehr and Mussa-Ivaldi, 1994).

It recently has been demonstrated that normal individuals can develop and store new internal models of both Coriolis forces (Lackner and Dizio, 1994) and of velocity-dependent force fields acting on the hand (Shadmehr and Mussa-Ivaldi, 1994; Shadmehr, Mussa-Ivaldi, and Bizzi, 1993): When the forces are removed unexpectedly, subjects show dramatic hand path curvatures that mirror the directions and magnitudes of the forces imposed during learning ("after-effects").

Studies of deafferented patients, who lack any sensation of joint motion, have shown that proprioceptive feedback is essential to generate or update internal models of limb inertia and intersegmental dynamics (Ghez, Gordon, and Ghilardi, 1995; Ghez et al., 1990; Ghez and Sainburg, 1995; Gordon, Ghilardi, and Ghez, 1990; Gordon, Ghilardi, and Ghez, 1995; Sainburg et al., 1995; Sainburg, Poizner, and Ghez, 1993; Virji-Babul et al., 1997). In fact, muscle spindles and other mechanoreceptors do provide the nervous system with feedback signals that reflect velocities and accelerations of changes in muscle length and joint angles. Patients lacking proprioception because of the degeneration of large diameter afferent axons make large errors in movement amplitude that vary with the inertial configuration of the arm. They also are unable to reverse direction sharply in particular directions. These reversal errors have been found to reflect inadequate control of intersegmental forces which in the patients account entirely for the actual joint motions that take place during movement. Both direction and reversal errors, however, are reduced markedly when patients can see their limb before each movement. This improvement persists for a few minutes after vision is removed again (Ghez, Gordon, and Ghilardi, 1995; Ghez and Sainburg, 1995; Sainburg et al., 1995). Thus, patients can substitute visual for proprioceptive feedback to recalibrate an internal representation of limb dynamic properties. Nevertheless,

even with vision, deafferented patients cannot achieve full control of unconstrained multijoint movements in 3-D space (Sainburg, Poizner, and Ghez, 1993; Rothwell et al., 1982).

CONTROL OF INTERSEGMENTAL DYNAMICS: DIFFERING EFFECTS OF FEEDBACK IN CORRECTING ONGOING MOVEMENTS AND IN LEARNING NEW INTERNAL MODELS The mechanisms used to control intersegmental dynamics of the arm can be studied in both intact and deafferented subjects by altering the relationships between joint motions and torques. The experimental procedure is illustrated in figure 35.4A. The center of mass of the distal limb segment was displaced effectively by attaching a 1-kg load either medially or laterally to the longitudinal axis of the forearm. The subject's task was to make a single overlapping out-and-back motion of the hand to trace a target line rapidly and accurately.

After adaptation to the medial load placement, the load was switched unexpectedly to the lateral position before movement onset, once every four to eight movements ("surprise lateral" condition in figure 35.4). Figure 35.4B illustrates the effect of this change in intersegmental dynamics on the hand trajectory: Just before the switch, the hand path consists of two nearly straight segments lying over the target line. In the surprise trial, however, the initial direction of movement remains straight but deviates clockwise away from the target and does not reverse direction sharply. This early clockwise direction error results from increased elbow extension, whereas the rounding of the trajectory during the movement reversals results from desynchronization of elbow and shoulder joint motions (Sainburg, Ghez, and Kalakanis, 1999).

The changes in elbow and shoulder rotations that produce the hand path deviations can be attributed to feedforward control calibrated to the intersegmental dynamics of the previously adapted condition: This is demonstrated with a simple forward simulation in figure 35.4B (left). The muscle torque profiles calculated from an adapted medial trial were applied to an ideal open-loop controller with inertial properties corresponding to the lateral mass condition. This computation estimated what would have happened if the subject had used the torques needed to control the medial mass accurately throughout the "surprise lateral" trial. The simulation can be seen to predict the initial direction errors accurately; however, the simulated reversals were curved less broadly than the actual ones. This indicates that although the early part of the trajectory resulted exclusively from feedforward processes, with time, feedback signals adjust the trajectory on line. Across subjects, this feedback degraded the sharpness of movement reversals in comparison with ones pro-

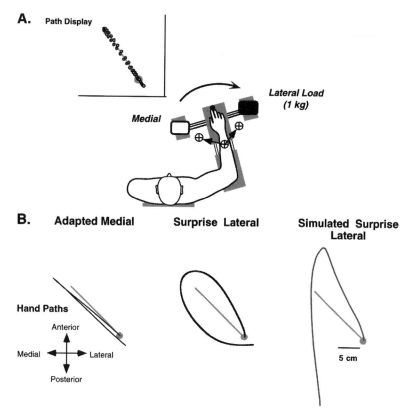

FIGURE 35.4   Errors in hand and joint trajectories when moving lateral loads. (A) Experimental set-up. The subject's arm was supported on air sleds on a horizontal glass surface, and the shoulder was stabilized. Hand position was visible to the subject as a screen cursor between and after movement. Joint angles were computed from potentiometers at the elbow and shoulder. A 1-kg load was placed either 25 cm lateral or medial to the hand, displacing the center of mass of the distal segment as indicated by the arrow. The major mechanical effect of this change of the center of mass of the distal limb segment was to increase the magnitude of the interaction torques produced at the elbow joint by motions at the shoulder. Changes in inertial interactions at the shoulder were balanced by the minor changes in total limb inertia. Middle: Hand paths from the last trial of each adaptation session (left and right columns) and from a typical "surprise" trial in a single subject. Bottom: Elbow and shoulder joint angles corresponding to the trials above. (B) Typical adapted medial (left) and surprise lateral (right) trials are shown in black. The muscle torques computed from trained medial trial were used to simulate a pure aftereffect uncontaminated by on-line correction. This simulation shows the effect of these torques had the mass not been displaced.

duced by the simulated feedforward controller acting alone. Nevertheless, the final position of the hand was achieved much more accurately in the actual than the simulated trajectory.

The ability of the subjects to return to the starting position despite large trajectory errors suggests that movement endpoints are determined by a mechanism that is distinct from the one responsible for the trajectory itself. Feldman and Bizzi (Bizzi, Polit, and Morasso, 1976; Feldman, 1974; Mussa-Ivaldi, Hogan, and Bizzi, 1985; Polit and Bizzi, 1979) described equilibrium control models that exploit the viscoelastic properties of the musculoskeletal system (mediated by muscle properties alone or including reflexes) through simultaneous activation of antagonistic muscle groups to specify a specific equilibrium position in either joint or hand space. In these models the desired final position is attained independently of the trajectory, which may vary depending on task dynamics. Hirayama and coworkers (Hirayama and Jordan, 1993) incorporated a similar positional control mechanism into a two-phase computational model of trajectory control. In that model, initial trajectory features reflected a feedforward mechanism, whereas final position was achieved using a postural controller that used visual feedback to specify levels of stationary motor commands to groups of muscles.

Thus, we conclude that the dynamics of rapid reaching movements are controlled by three distinct mechanisms that operate successively. First, movements are controlled through feedforward mechanisms that are adapted to existing mechanical conditions. Second, as sensory feedback becomes available during movements, corrections are made. Such corrections may be maladaptive if the dynamic properties of the limb are altered. Learning allows such corrections to become appropriate. Third, the final position of the hand is also controlled through postural mechanisms that can be implemented once the limb is no longer moving rapidly at the end of movement.

INTERNAL MODELS OF INTERSEGMENTAL INTERACTIONS ARE ENCODED IN INTRINSIC COORDINATES The results shown in figure 35.4 demonstrate that with practice moving the hand to a single target and back, subjects can adjust both feedforward and feedback mechanisms to control hand trajectory. Does learning to move a given extent in a single direction with a new inertial configuration allow subjects to do so accurately when moving from different starting positions and in different directions? In examining this, we first determined whether accuracy obtained with practice moving a medial or a lateral load to a single target transfers to movements in other directions from the same origin. This was not the case; direction and reversal errors increased as the target direction deviated from the one used for training. Beyond 45° on either side of the trained direction, there no longer was any evidence of this prior practice. Thus, learning shows only limited generalization to new directions from the same position (Gandolfo, Mussa-Ivaldi, and Bizzi, 1996; Sainburg and Ghez, 1995; Sainburg, Ghez, and Kalakanis, 1999). This lack of generalization would be expected if during training subjects learned the dynamic interactions that occur during a specific set of joint motions. Alternatively, subjects might simply have learned to move their hand a particular distance and direction in extrinsic space. To distinguish between these possibilities, subjects were trained to move their hand accurately with the lateral load out and back to a single target from a specific location in the workspace (again without visual feedback). We then examined the accuracy of movements made with the same load but starting from a different position in the workspace presented occasionally as surprise trials (figure 35.5A) and to two new targets. The two targets were selected to require either the same joint excursions or the same extent and direction of hand movement as during training. Figure 35.5B shows that movements made to the target that required the same joint excursions as that of training ("joint space") were substantially more accurate than those made to the other target ("hand space").

These results indicate that learning of inertial dynamics is represented in an intrinsic coordinate system re-

lated to muscle actions or proprioceptive signals, rather than in visual coordinates. This is consistent with our earlier observations, based on similar experimental paradigms, that proprioception plays a critical role in the control interaction forces (Sainburg et al., 1995).

LOCAL LEARNING OF MOVEMENT DIRECTION IN A ROTATED VISUAL FIELD IS ENCODED IN EXTRINSIC SPACE We have seen earlier that when subjects adapt to a rotated display by training to a single target, learning does not generalize to other directions. This is similar to what occurs when moving to a single target with a new inertial configuration of the arm. Thus, adaptation to a rotated hand path display but with a single target in a given direction also may reflect the learning of a more general rule represented either in extrinsic or in intrinsic coordinates.

As previously, we addressed this question by training subjects to move out and back from a single spatial location to a given target with vision of the hand and arm occluded; however, present subjects had continuous visual feedback on the computer screen. After a block of control trials, the displays of hand paths were rotated counterclockwise by 60°. Subjects then were tested without feedback as they moved to the same locations shown on the screen but from a different initial position and arm configuration (figure 35.6A). Figure 35.6B shows that in the displaced position, directional errors clustered around those predicted if subjects had encoded prior learning in extrinsic space rather than the one that would be appropriate if learning was represented in joint coordinates. Figure 35.6C shows the large differences in joint angle changes in trained and test positions in one of the six subjects. Thus, with a rotated display and a single target direction, subjects depend on the directional errors they observe visually on the computer screen to learn to move along a directional axis that can be translated to other locations in the workspace. Unlike in the learning of new inertial dynamics, proprioceptive information representing errors in intrinsic space does not play a significant role (see discussion).

Consolidation and interference in learning rotated reference frames

It is generally accepted that for the brain to learn cognitive and motor tasks, sensory events, and motor commands occurring in the course of task performance are stored in working memory. It has been suggested that the neural space in short or working memory is limited and that individual events or associations compete for this space (Baddeley, 1992; Ballard, Hayhoe, and Pelz, 1995).

A.

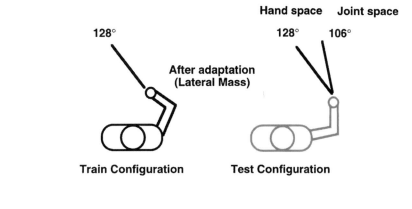

B.

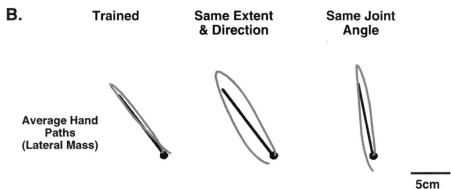

FIGURE 35.5   Inertial dynamics are learned in intrinsic space. (A) Schematic of the experimental paradigm to examine transfer of learning across the workspace. Subjects practiced moving with the lateral mass to the single 128°, 10-cm target on the left of the workspace using visual displays of their hand paths. The shoulder and elbow angles corresponding to the beginning of the target were 55° and 90°, respectively. After 100 trials of practice, occasional trials required subjects to move from a second position to one of the targets on the right of the workspace without visual feedback. One of these targets matched the direction and length of trained target exactly, and the other target required the same angular displacements of the joints as the trained target and therefore was different in direction and length. (B) Ensemble averaged hand paths from a single subject who trained with the lateral mass position to the 128°, 10-cm line in the left of workspace.

Over time, however, items in working memory are transferred to new locations and distributed in multiple brain regions for long-term storage. It is known that if subjects are given a task to relearn hours, days, and weeks after initial practice, learning is more rapid and complete, a process called *consolidation.*

Shadmehr and coworkers discovered that consolidation also occurs in motor learning, in a task requiring subjects to make straight reaching movements to visual targets in a rotating viscous force field (Brashers-Krug, Shadmehr, and Bizzi, 1996). The rate of learning improved when subjects receive two successive sessions of practice separated by one or more days. However, if subjects were given the task of learning a force field rotating in the opposite direction, consolidation failed to occur. This *interference* was greatest at 5 minutes and decreased over the course of 6 to 24 hours, when consolidation was complete (Brashers-Krug, Shadmehr, and Bizzi, 1996;

Shadmehr and Brashers-Krug, 1997; Shadmehr and Holcomb, 1997).

ADAPTING TO DISPLAY ROTATIONS IS UNAFFECTED BY INTERVENING OR CONCURRENT LEARNING OF NOVEL INERTIAL DYNAMICS   The differences in coordinate systems and in sensory feedback channels used to learn new visuomotor transformations and new inertial dynamics described in earlier sections suggests that the two forms of learning might take place independently of each other. If this were true, interference with consolidation would be restricted to each process.

To answer this question, subjects were trained to reach for targets in eight directions with an imposed 30° counterclockwise rotation of hand paths displayed on the screen (as in figure 35.1B, right). Subjects then were retested 24 hours later, and the rates of learning during the two days were compared. Four groups of subjects were

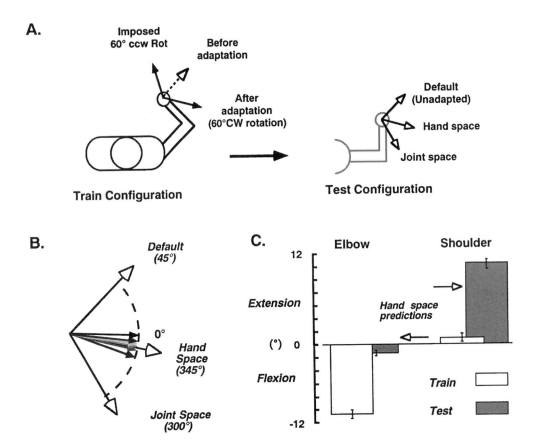

FIGURE 35.6 A rotated direction of hand movement is learned in extrinsic space. (A) Schematic of experimental paradigm to examine transfer of learning across the workspace. *Training:* Subjects faced a vertical display and were instructed to make planar reaching movements to a screen target at the 45° position. Cursor feedback was rotated 60° counterclockwise requiring adaptation for accuracy to be achieved. The actual hand directions before and after adaptation are indicated by the arrows in the training configuration: shoulder at 45°, elbow at 90°. *Testing:* Subjects had their trunk moved while maintaining the same origin of the hand; this resulted in a new arm configuration: shoulder at 90°, elbow at 90°. They were then tested in the novel configuration, without feedback, to the same screen target in the presence of the 60° rotation. The empty arrows in the test configuration indicate the predicted hand directions if adaptation were absent, if learn-

ing were in joint space, or if learning were of a trajectory in hand space. (B) A polar plot of mean hand movement direction for six subjects in the novel configuration after adaptation in the training configuration. Each subject is represented by a single arrow. The larger gray arrows represent predicted performance as described in (A). All six subjects were distributed around the predicted performance if they were to have adapted in hand space. (C) A bar chart of mean elbow and shoulder angle changes for a single subject in the training and testing configurations. The angle changes were computed using the subject's limb segment lengths and handpaths. Note that the joint angle changes differ markedly for the two configurations, suggesting that the subject is not learning in joint space. The arrows represent the expected joint angle changes if the subject were to adapt perfectly in hand space.

studied (figure 35.7). A first group was not given any additional practice between days (figure 35.7A) and represented the control group. A second group learned to move a laterally displaced load 5 minutes after the rotation (figure 35.7B). A third group did so concurrently as they learned the rotation (figure 35.7C, dual task). Finally, a fourth group (figure 35.7D) learned a rotation in the opposite direction (30° clockwise) 5 minutes after the initial 30° counterclockwise rotation. Subjects had visual feedback (screen cursor) at all times.

As can be noted in figure 35.7A there is clear evidence of consolidation in learning the rotated visuomo-

tor transformation: The initial rate of learning was significantly greater on day 2, and the residual error at the end of the training session was significantly less on day 2 than on day 1. These indices of consolidation were unaffected when subjects learned to move a lateral load 5 minutes after the rotation (figure 35.7B) or concurrently with it (figure 35.7D). Conversely, there was no significant difference between the rates of learning a 30° counterclockwise rotation on day 1 and day 2 when subjects learned a rotation in the opposite direction immediately after the first training session (figure 35.7D). Thus, although there is consolidation in the learning of a

Mean Directional Error

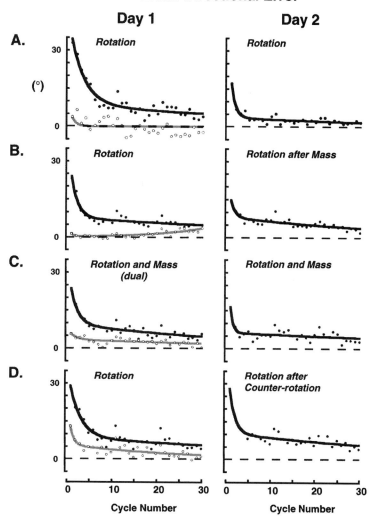

FIGURE 35.7 Consolidation and interference in learning a new reference frame. For each condition the mean directional error per cycle (cycles represent movements to the 8 target directions) is plotted against cycle number during the training block. Points are means across subjects; lines are fitted to the points by double exponential function. The empty circles represent the single familiarization trial before rotations or load changes. The black circles represent training trials. Differences between conditions were evaluated by comparing the means of the first two and the last two cycles using a factorial ANOVA.

spatial rotation and interference when subjects learn an opposite rotation, there is no interference when subjects learn new internal models of inertial dynamics. The opposite is also true: Consolidation in the learning of the same change in limb dynamics is unaffected by learning a 30° counterclockwise rotation, either at the same time or 5 minutes later (Krakauer, Ghilardi, and Ghez, 1998).

Discussion

The observations presented here describe three internal representations that are necessary to plan fast and accurate reaching movements. Each is subject to adaptive learning but uses different feedback signals and obeys different rules. The first representation encodes the spa-

tial features of the task in a vectorial space where target location is represented in terms of extent and direction from the initial hand position. Visual errors detected in successive movements operate to rescale and reorient this spatial map. We have proposed a second representation to locate the hand in peripersonal space. This proprioceptive map requires frequent recalibration by visual or other sensory signals. Finally, the third is a representation of critical biomechanical characteristics of the limb. This representation is needed to transform intended movement vectors into appropriate muscle forces or joint torques. Proprioceptive feedback is critical in establishing such new internal models of inertial dynamics. The terminal portions of hand and joint trajectories are consistent with the idea that movement endpoints may also be determined redundantly by specifying the intended final hand position in space. This planned final position could depend on the same proprioceptive map of task space as the origin of the intended movement vector.

The rules underlying adaptation to altered gains and rotations indicate that errors in extent and direction are used differently in rescaling and in reorienting visuospatial maps of movement vectors. Rescaling is relatively rapid and generalizes throughout the workspace in an approximately linear fashion. Errors in movement direction adjust the orientation of the reference frame; however, this form of learning is local: When directional errors are experienced moving to a single direction, subjects learn a directional axis that can translate in the workspace. For subjects to learn a complete reference frame in a horizontal space centered at the hand, 8 or more equally spaced target directions are necessary. In this case, however, the time course of learning is greatly prolonged. It appears that visual information alone is sufficient to rescale and to reorient spatial reference frames for motor planning. Unpublished data in two patients with large-fiber sensory neuropathy (C. Ghez, J. Gordon, and M. F. Ghilardi, unpublished studies of patients M.A. and I.W.) indicates that learning new scaling factors and spatial reference axes does not require proprioceptive information. Similarly, mirror drawing was found to be unimpaired in a third patient (G.L. in Blouin, Bard, Teasdale et al., 1993).

In contrast to learning gains and rotations, learning new models of limb dynamics depends critically on proprioception. Observations in one deafferented patient indicate that visual feedback alone cannot provide the necessary information. Indeed, the patient was unable to reduce the inertial errors by monitoring either the cursor on the screen or her arm in the workspace (Virji-Babul et al., 1997; N. Virji-Babul et al., in preparation).

The differences in coordinate systems and in sensory signals required suggest that learning new spatial representations depends on different neural channels and different sites for memory storage. While learning a rotated reference frame interferes with the consolidation of a previously learned rotation in the opposite direction, learning a new model of limb dynamics does not. Similarly, the rate at which a new internal model is learned and its consolidation in memory are unaffected by learning a new spatial reference frame. Finally, the rate at which subjects adapt to rotations or to new inertial interactions is unchanged when they learn both concurrently. Thus, learning new representations of extrinsic space and learning new internal models of inertial dynamics involve different neural systems and separate working memory buffers.

Many studies have demonstrated that working memory buffers (Baddeley, 1992; Ballard, Hayhoe, and Pelz, 1995) have a limited capacity. This could be the major determinant of the higher rate of learning and generalization in learning new scaling factors than in learning rotated reference frames or inertial models. Prochazka and his colleagues have pointed out that the amount of proprioceptive information generated during each movement is very large (Prochazka, 1996). Consequently, limited memory capacity should present a particular challenge for acquiring skill in tasks where the motions at many joints must be controlled precisely or in skills, such as golf, in which objects with unusual inertial configurations are to be rapidly displaced.

On the basis of the observations summarized in the section Remapping and Rotating Reference Frames: Roles of Visual Feedback, we proposed that movement accuracy also requires learning a map of extrinsic space represented as joint angles. The special importance of static as opposed to dynamic signals in generating such models is suggested by the more linear coding of static than of dynamic information by muscle spindles (Houk and Rymer, 1981; Matthews, 1981a). Over some range, the same hand position could be specified by scaling the ratio of muscle activations as proposed by equilibrium theories (Feldman, 1974; Bizzi et al., 1984). Nevertheless, such proprioceptive maps of space are apt to be rather coarse, given the time-dependent fluctuations in receptor responses. The specification of an entire trajectory as a large series of equilibrium trajectories seems implausible because of the large nonlinear changes in the contractile forces of muscles during length changes.

Our observations are consistent with computational models that can transform information about intended actions into neural signals that specify torques at joints. Such models propose the existence of inverse and forward internal models that adjust feedforward as well as feedback controllers (Jordan and Rumelhart, 1990; Wolpert, Ghahramani, and Jordan, 1995). With repeated trials, the parameters of these models would be adjusted by comparing expected sensory input, available as corollary discharge signals (Bell, 1982; Matthews, 1982) and sensory feedback acquired in the course of movement. The psychophysical observations presented here suggest that separate sensory motor representations, along with distinct working memory buffers supporting them, do exist in the nervous system.

ACKNOWLEDGMENTS The authors are indebted to Zachary Pine for reading earlier versions of this chapter and for conducting experiments that directly led to the ones presented here. We thank Dr. Dimitrios Kalakanis for scholarly comments and assistance in editing portions of this chapter. We are also grateful to Hao Huang and Walton B. Comer, who developed software for experiment control and data analysis, and to Antony Hacking for expert assistance with illustrations. We are grateful to Professor Jonathan Cole for allowing us to study visuospatial learning in patient I.W. Supported by NS22715 and NS01961.

REFERENCES

ATKESON, C. G., and J. M. HOLLERBACH, 1985. Kinematic features of unrestrained vertical arm movements. *J. Neurosci.* 5:2318–2330.

BADDELEY, A., 1992. Working memory. *Science* 255:556–559.

BALLARD, D. H., M. M. HAYHOE, and J. PELZ, 1995. Memory limits in sensorimotor tasks. In *Models of Information Processing in the Basal Ganglia,* J. C. Houk, J. L. Davis, and D. G. Beiter, eds. Cambridge, Mass.: MIT Press, pp. 295–313.

BELL, C. C., 1982. Properties of a modifiable efference copy in an electric fish. *J. Neurophysiol.* 47:1043–1056.

BIZZI, E., N. ACCORNERO, et al., 1984. Posture control and trajectory formation during arm movement. *J. Neurosci.* 4:2738–2744.

BIZZI, E., A. POLIT, and P. MORASSO, 1976. Mechanisms underlying achievement of final head position. *J. Neurophysiol.* 39:435–444.

BLOUIN, J., C. BARD, and N. TEASDALE, et al., 1993. Reference systems for coding spatial information in normal subjects and a deafferented patient. *Exp. Brain Res.* 93:324–331.

BRASHERS-KRUG, T., R. SHADMEHR, and E. BIZZI, 1996. Consolidation in human motor memory. *Nature* 382:252–255.

FELDMAN, A. G., 1974. Change of muscle length due to shift of the equilibrium point of the muscle-load system. *Biofizika* 19:749–753.

FLANDERS, M., S. I. HELMS TILLERY, and J. F. SOECHTING, 1992. Early stages in a sensorimotor transformation. *Behav. Brain Sci.* 15:309–362.

GANDOLFO, F., F. A. MUSSA-IVALDI, and E. BIZZI, 1996. Motor learning by field approximation. *Proc. Nat. Acad. Sci.* 93: 3843–3846.

GEORGOPOULOS, A. P., A. B. SCHWARTZ, and R. E. KETTNER, 1986. Neuronal population coding of movement direction. *Science* 233:1416–1419.

GHEZ, C., 1979. Contributions of central programs to rapid limb movements in the cat. In *Integration in the Nervous System,* H. Asanuma and V. J. Wilson, eds. Tokyo: Igaku-Shoin, pp. 305–320.

GHEZ, C., M. FAVILLA, M. F. GHILARDI, et al., 1997. Discrete and continuous planning of hand movements and isometric force trajectories. *Exp. Brain Res.* 115:217–233.

GHEZ, C., J. GORDON, and M. F. GHILARDI, 1995. Impairments of reaching movements in patients without proprioception: II. Effects of visual information on accuracy. *J. Neurophysiol.* 73:361–372.

GHEZ, C., J. GORDON, M. F. GHILARDI, et al., 1990. Roles of proprioceptive input in the programming of arm trajectories. *Cold Spring Harb. Symp. Quant. Biol.* 55:837–847.

GHEZ, C., and R. SAINBURG, 1995. Proprioceptive control of interjoint coordination. *Can. J. Physiol. Pharmacol.* 73:273–294.

GHILARDI, M. F., J. GORDON, and C. GHEZ, 1995. Learning a visuomotor transformation in a local area of workspace pro-

duces directional biases in other areas. *J. Neurophysiol.* 73: 2535–2539.

GOODBODY, S. J., and D. M. WOLPERT, 1998. *J. Neurophysiol.* 79:1825–1838.

GORDON, A. M., H. FORSSBERG, R. S. JOHANSSON, et al., 1991. The integration of haptically acquired size information in the programming of precision grip. *Exp. Brain Res.* 83:483–488.

GORDON, J., and C. GHEZ, 1987a. Trajectory control in targeted force impulses: II. Pulse height control. *Exp. Brain Res.* 67:241–252.

GORDON, J., and C. GHEZ, 1987b. Trajectory control in targeted force impulses: III. Compensatory adjustments for initial errors. *Exp. Brain Res.* 67:253–269.

GORDON, J., M. F. GHILARDI, S. E. COOPER, et al., 1994. Accuracy of planar reaching movements: II. Systematic extent errors resulting from inertial anisotropy. *Exp. Brain Res.* 99: 112–130.

GORDON, J., M. F. GHILARDI, and C. GHEZ, 1990. Deafferented subjects fail to compensate for workspace anisotropies in 2-dimensional arm movements. *Soc. Neurosci. Abs.* 16: 1089.

GORDON, J., M. F. GHILARDI, and C. GHEZ, 1994. Accuracy of planar reaching movements: I. Independence of direction and extent variability. *Exp. Brain Res.* 99:97–111.

GORDON, J., M. F. GHILARDI, and C. GHEZ, 1995. Impairments of reaching movements in patients without proprioception: I. Spatial errors. *J. Neurophysiol.* 73:347–360.

HIRAYAMA, M. K. M., and M. I. JORDAN, 1993. The cascade neural network model and speed-accuracy trade-off of arm movement. *J. Motor Behav.* 25:162–174.

HOLLERBACH, J. M., and T. FLASH, 1982. Dynamic interactions between limb segments during planar arm movement. *Biol. Cybern.* 44:67–77.

HOUK, J. C., and W. Z. RYMER, 1981. Neural control of muscle length and tension. In *Handbook of Physiology: Sec. 1. The Nervous System: Vol. 2. Motor Control, Part 1,* V. B. Brooks, ed., Bethesda, Md.: American Physiological Society, pp. 257–323.

HOY, M. G., and R. F. ZERNICKE, 1985. Modulation of limb dynamics in the swing phase of locomotion. *J. Biomech.* 18:49–60.

HOY, M. G., and R. F. ZERNICKE, 1986. The role of intersegmental dynamics during rapid limb oscillations. *J. Biomech.* 19:867–877.

HOY, M. G., R. F. ZERNICKE, and J. L. SMITH, 1985. Contrasting roles of inertial and muscle moments at knee and ankle during paw-shake response. *J. Neurophysiol.* 54:1282–1294.

IMAMIZU, H., Y. UNO, and M. KAWATO, 1995. Internal representations of the motor apparatus: Implications from generalization in visuomotor learning. *J. Exp. Psychol. Hum. Percept. Perform.* 21:1174–1198.

JEANNEROD, M., and C. PRABLANC, 1983. Visual control of reaching movements in man. In *Advances in Neurology, Vol. 39: Motor Control Mechanisms in Health and Disease,* J. E. Desmedt, ed. New York: Raven Press, pp. 13–30.

JORDAN, M. I., 1996. Computational aspects of motor control and motor learning. In *Handbook of Perception and Action, Vol. II: Motor Skills,* H. Heuer and S. W. Keele, eds. San Diego, Calif.: Academic Press, pp. 71–118.

JORDAN, M. I., and D. E. RUMELHART, 1990. *Forward models: Supervised learning with a distal teacher.* Cambridge, Mass.: MIT Center for Cognitive Science.

KRAKAUER, J., M. F. GHILARDI, and C. GHEZ, 1998. Subjects learn novel visuomotor transformations and novel intersegmental dynamics independently. *Soc. Neurosci. Abs.* 24:1157.

KRAKAUER, J. W., Z. M. PINE, and C. GHEZ, 1996. Differences in generalization of adaptation to altered gains and display rotations in reaching movements. *Soc. Neurosci. Abs.* 22:899.

KRAKAUER, J. W., Z. M. PINE, H. HUANG, et al., 1997. Learning a rotated reference frame requires moving in multiple directions and differs with joint system used. *Soc. Neurosci. Abs.* 23:202.

LACKNER, J. R., and P. DIZIO, 1994. Rapid adaptation to coriolis force perturbations of arm trajectory. *J. Neurophysiol.* 72:199–313.

MATTHEWS, P. B. C., 1981a. Evolving views on the internal operation and functional role of the muscle spindle. *J. Physiol. (Lond)* 320:1–30.

MATTHEWS, P. B. C., 1981b. Muscle spindles: Their messages and their fusimotor supply. In *Handbook of Physiology: Sec. 1. The Nervous System: Vol. 2. Motor Control, Part 1,* V. B. Brooks, ed. Bethesda, Md.: American Physiological Society, pp. 189–228.

MATTHEWS, P. B. C., 1982. Where does Sherrington's "muscular sense" originate? Muscles, joints, corollary discharges? *Annu. Rev. Neurosci.* 5:189–218.

MATTHEWS, P. B. C., and R. B. STEIN, 1969. The sensitivity of muscle spindle afferents to small sinusoidal changes of length. *J. Physiol.* 200:723–743.

MORASSO, P., 1981. Spatial control of arm movements. *Exp. Brain Res.* 42:223–227.

MUSSA-IVALDI, F. A., N. HOGAN, and E. BIZZI, 1985. Neural, mechanical, and geometric factors subserving arm posture in humans. *J. Neurosci.* 5:2732–2743.

PINE, Z. M., M. F. GHILARDI, M. L. CHILDRESS, et al., 1998. Directional bias in point-to-point tabletop reaching movements. *Soc. Neurosci. Abs.* 24:419.

PINE, Z. M., J. KRAKAUER, J. GORDON, et al., 1996. Learning of scaling factors and reference axes for reaching movements. *Neuroreport* 7:2357–2361.

POLIT, A., and E. BIZZI, 1979. Characteristics of motor programs underlying arm movements in monkey. *J. Neurophysiol.* 42:183–194.

POULTON, E. C., 1975. Range effects in experiments on people. *Am. J. Psychol.* 88:3–32.

PROCHAZKA, A., 1996. Proprioceptive feedback and movement regulation. In *Handbook of Physiology–Section 12.* New York: Oxford University Press, pp. 89–127.

ROTHWELL, J. L., M. M. TRAUB, B. L. DAY, et al., 1982. Manual motor performance in a deafferented man. *Brain* 105: 515–542.

SAINBURG, R. L., and C. GHEZ, 1995. Limitations in the learning and generalization of multijoint dynamics. *Neurosci. Abs.*

SAINBURG, R. L., C. GHEZ, and K. KALAKANIS, 1999. Intersegmental dynamics are controlled by sequential anticipatory, error correction, and postural mechanisms. *J. Neurophysiol.* 81:1045–1056.

SAINBURG, R. L., M. F. GHILARDI, H. POIZNER, et al., 1995. The control of limb dynamics in normal subjects and patients without proprioception. *J. Neurophysiol.* 73:820–835.

SAINBURG, R. L., H. POIZNER, and C. GHEZ, 1993. Loss of proprioception produces deficits in interjoint coordination. *J. Neurophysiol.* 70:2136–2147.

SCOTT, S. H., and J. F. KALASKA, 1997. Reaching movements with similar hand paths but different arm orientations: I. Activity of individual cells in motor cortex. *J. Neurophysiol.* 77: 826–852.

SHADMEHR, R., and T. BRASHERS-KRUG, 1997. Functional stages in the formation of human long-term motor memory. *J. Neurosci.* 17:409–419.

SHADMEHR, R., and H. H. HOLCOMB, 1997. Neural correlates of motor memory consolidation. *Science.* 277:821–825.

SHADMEHR, R., and F. A. MUSSA-IVALDI, 1994. Adaptive representation of dynamics during learning of a motor task. *J. Neurosci.* 14:3208–3224.

SHADMEHR, R., F. A. MUSSA-IVALDI, and E. BIZZI, 1993. Postural force fields of the human arm and their role in generating multijoint movements. *J. Neurosci.* 13:45–62.

VINDRAS, P., and P. VIVIANI, 1998. Frames of reference and control parameters in visuomanual pointing. *J. Exp. Psychol.* 24:1–23.

VIRJI-BABUL, N., R. L. SAINBURG, H. HUANG, et al., 1997. Visual feedback information enhances learning of novel limb dynamics in deafferented patients. *Soc. Neurosci. Abs.* 23:202.

WANN, J. P., and S. F. IBRAHIM, 1992. Does limb proprioception drift? *Exp. Brain Res.* 91:162–166.

WESTLING, G., and R. S. JOHANSSON, 1987. Responses in glabrous skin mechanoreceptors during precision grip in humans. *Exp. Brain Res.* 66:128–140.

WOLPERT, D. M., Z. GHAHRAMANI, and M. I. JORDAN, 1995. An internal model for sensorimotor integration. *Science.* 269:1880–1882.

36 Programming to Look and Reach in the Posterior Parietal Cortex

R. A. ANDERSEN, A. P. BATISTA, L. H. SNYDER, C. A. BUNEO, AND Y. E. COHEN

ABSTRACT   Classically, the posterior parietal cortex (PPC) has been believed to be an association sensory area responsible for attention and spatial awareness. Over the past few years, however, a new idea has emerged that this area also analyzes sensory information for the purpose of planning actions. Experiments from the authors' laboratory have shown that the PPC has an anatomic map with respect to intentions. The PPC is an "association" cortex in the sense that it must combine different sensory modalities, which are coded in different coordinate frames, within this map for action plans. Interestingly, two different areas of the PPC, one involved with moving the eyes (the lateral intraparietal [LIP] area) and another involved with moving the arms (the parietal reach region [PRR]), both appear to represent the goals for movements using the same set of rules, even though the eventual outcome of their activities are for different behaviors. In both areas, individual neurons code spatial locations using a common reference frame, that is, with respect to the eye, but these responses also are gain-modulated by eye and body position signals. At the population level, this mechanism allows these areas to code concurrently a goal for movement in multiple coordinate frames (eye, head, body, and world). Depending on how this group of cells is sampled by other areas of the brain, different coordinate transformations can be accomplished by this same population of neurons.

The posterior parietal cortex generally is believed to be a high-order sensory region that contributes to spatial awareness. The phenomenon of "neglect," which results after lesions to this area, manifests as a deficit in attending to objects in the affected visual field or in shifting attention and has been used as a prime example of a sensory attention role for PPC (Critchley, 1953; Andersen, 1987, for review). However, another syndrome also common with PPC lesions is apraxia. This deficit is neither sensory, because subjects still have normal visual and other sensory functions, nor motor, because the patients are not paralyzed. However, they seem unable to form the "plan" or "idea" for a movement. Thus, this deficit is interposed between sensation and action and appears to result from a disruption in the early stages of movement planning (Critchley, 1953, for review). In recent years, several studies in humans and monkeys point

to a newly appreciated role of the PPC in programming actions, and more specifically, in transforming sensory signals into plans for motor behaviors (Mountcastle et al., 1975; Gnadt and Andersen, 1988; Goodale and Milner, 1992; Rizzolatti, Riggio, and Sheliga, 1994; Andersen, 1995; Mazzoni et al., 1996b; Sakata et al., 1997; Snyder, Batista, and Andersen, 1997).

A new and emerging view of the PPC is that it contains an anatomic map of intentions (Andersen et al., 1997; Snyder, Batista, and Andersen, 1997) (figure 36.1). Included in this map for movement planning is area LIP, which appears to be specialized for making saccades. A region medial and posterior to area LIP, PRR, is specialized for planning reach movements. This area likely includes the dorsal aspect of the parieto-occipital (PO) area and the medial intraparietal (MIP) area. A third task-specific area is the anterior intraparietal (AIP) area, located just rostral to area LIP, which appears to be specialized for grasping (Sakata et al., 1997). Finally, within the fundus of the intraparietal sulcus is an area with somatosensory receptive fields around the mouth and head and visual receptive fields that in many cases prefer stimuli moving toward the animal's mouth and head (Duhamel, Colby, and Goldberg, 1998). This ventral intraparietal (VIP) area may be specialized for "grasping" with the mouth.

In this review, we cover studies revealing the role of PPC in intention. Also of interest are studies examining the coordinate frame in which space is represented in area LIP and PRR. This work was designed to determine how different modalities that are represented originally in different coordinate frames are brought together in the PPC. We also discuss how communication may be achieved between these different areas, which are highly interconnected anatomically (Andersen et al., 1990; Blatt, Andersen, and Stoner, 1990), and how these areas might incorporate common processing strategies for the orchestration of complex behaviors requiring hand–eye coordination. As we will see, area LIP and PRR appear to use a common mechanism for representing visually and auditorily cued spatial locations. The resulting representation has the computationally powerful

R. A. ANDERSEN, A. P. BATISTA, L. H. SNYDER, C. A. BUNEO, and Y. E. COHEN   Division of Biology, California Institute of Technology, Pasadena, Calif.

515

Anatomical Organization for Actions in the Posterior Parietal Cortex

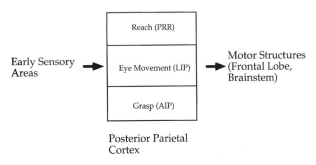

FIGURE 36.1 The posterior parietal cortex contains separate areas specialized for reach movements (area PRR), saccades (area LIP), and grasping (area AIP).

feature that it is distributed and can be read out by other areas of the brain as several different coordinate frames, for example, eye-, head-, body-, or even world-centered. Finally, we review research that finds that the representations of space in both area LIP and PRR are updated across eye movements for the remembered locations of targets for movement.

Intentions to saccade and reach

There is a considerable amount of suggestive evidence that the PPC has an intentional role, but it has been very difficult to design experiments that dissociate intention-related activity from activity related to attention. This difficulty arises from the fact that monkeys (and humans) attend to locations where they plan to make movements. In a recent study, we designed a task specifically to isolate intention-related activity (Snyder, Batista, and Andersen, 1997). We reasoned that activity in the PPC should be indifferent to the type of movement planned by the animal if it is only related to attention. Thus, if the monkey planned a reach or a saccade to the stimulus at the same location, there should be little or no difference in activity if it is primarily dependent on attention. However, if the activity depends strongly on the movement the monkey plans, then this activity would be related to the animal's intention.

Animals were trained to memorize the location of briefly flashed visual stimuli in an otherwise dark room and to plan either an eye or an arm movement to the cued location, the type of movement being instructed by the color of the flashed stimulus. Figure 36.2 demonstrates our typical result—that the activity in the memory period depended largely on the type of movement the animal planned. Approximately two thirds of PPC neurons showed a significant response in the memory pe-

riod for only one of the two movement plans. The remaining one third of the cells responded to both plans. However, approximately one half of the cells responding for both movements appeared to be forming a default plan for a particular type of movement, as shown in an additional control and thus also were intention related. We proposed that these cells were coding "covert" plans for movement. An example of one of these covert planning cells is shown in figure 36.3. This cell had activity during the memory period regardless of whether the animal planned a reach or a saccade into its receptive field. In the control experiment, we had the animal perform a two-movement task, in which he planned and

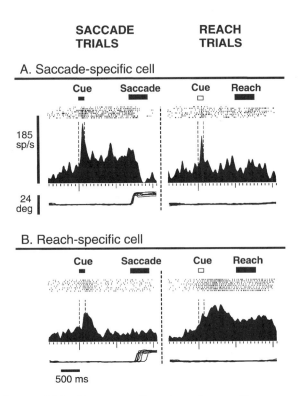

FIGURE 36.2 Responses of two intention-specific neurons in the delayed-saccade (left) and delayed-reach (right) tasks. Each panel shows timing of peripheral flash (Cue: red flashes indicated by filled bars, green flashes by open bars) and response (Saccade or Reach); eight rows of rasters corresponding to every third action potential recorded during each of eight trials; a spike density histogram of neuronal activity, generated by convolution with a triangular kernel aligned on cue presentation, with cue onset and offset indicated by dashed lines; and eight overlaid traces showing vertical eye position. Neuronal responses in the cue interval (50 ms before to 150 ms after cue offset) were nonspecific. However, during the delay interval (150–600 ms), firing depended specifically on motor intent. (A) A cell showing elevated delay period firing before a saccade (left) but not before a reach (right). For illustration purposes, data for this cell were collected using a fixed delay interval. (B) A second cell showing reach rather than saccade specificity during the delay interval. (Reprinted from Snyder, Batista, and Andersen, 1997.)

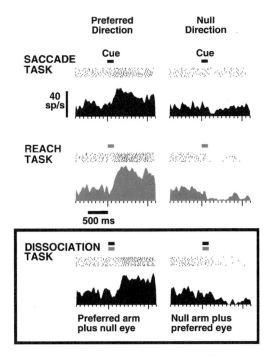

FIGURE 36.3 An intention-specific neuron whose motor specificity was revealed by the dissociation task. Delay activity was greater before movements toward the receptive field (Preferred Direction) compared with away (Null Direction) in both delayed saccade (top row) and reach (middle row) tasks. Thus, in single-movement tasks, the neuron appears to code remembered target location independent of motor intent. However, motor specificity was revealed in the dissociation task (bottom row). Firing was vigorous before a preferred reach combined with a null saccade (bottom left) but nearly absent before a preferred saccade plus null reach (bottom right). Thus, when both a reach and a saccade were planned, delay activity reflected the intended reach and not the intended saccade. Panel formats are similar to figure 36.1. Every other action potential is indicated by one raster mark. (Reprinted from Snyder, Batista, and Andersen, 1997.)

made eye and reach movements simultaneously in opposite directions. The bottom panels of figure 36.3 illustrate that when the animal planned an arm movement into the receptive field but an eye movement outside the receptive field, the cell was active, but when it planned the eye movement into the receptive field and the arm movement outside of the receptive field, the cell was not active. Thus, it would appear that the animal was making a "default" plan to reach that was not executed. Because half of the cells responding to both plans demonstrated a covert preference for either saccades or reaches, overall 84% of the PPC cells tested had activity during the memory period specifying the intent of the animal.

The intended movement activity was anatomically segregated depending on whether it was related to plans for saccades or reach. Perhaps not surprisingly, eye movement planning activity was found predominantly in area LIP. This finding is very consistent with previous research, which has indicated that area LIP can be considered the "posterior eye field" for the processing of saccadic eye movements (Andersen, Brotchie, and Mazzoni, 1992). Area LIP cells have presaccadic bursts of activity (Barash et al., 1991); saccade deficits result after lesions in area LIP (Lynch and McLaren, 1989; Li, Mazzoni, and Andersen, 1999); there are strong anatomic projections from area LIP to other saccade centers, such as the superior colliculus, frontal eye field, and dorsallateral pons (Lynch, Graybiel, and Lobeck, 1985; Asanuma, Andersen, and Cowan, 1985; Blatt, Andersen, and Stoner, 1990; Andersen et al., 1990); and electrical microstimulation of area LIP evokes saccades without other body movements (Thier and Andersen, 1996, 1998). The reach selective responses were found medial and posterior to area LIP, in a band of cortex that likely includes areas MIP to PO. We referred to this functionally defined region of the PPC as the parietal reach region (PRR).

The focus of attention and the planning of eye movements are linked tightly, so it could be argued that the selectivity in area LIP is due to the fact that animals attend to where they plan to saccade but not to where they plan to reach, and the differential activity reflects this difference in attention (Colby and Goldberg, 1999). However, this line of reasoning would require PRR neurons also to be most active when eye movements are planned in their receptive fields; instead, we see the reverse phenomena, with activity being greatest when reaches are planned into their receptive fields. Moreover, in the following experiments, attention was maintained the same and the animals were asked to change their movement plans. As we see, when attention is identical across trials, the activity of PPC neurons changes dramatically depending on the animals' plans.

Changing movement plans without changing the locus of attention

A direct prediction from the aforementioned conclusions is that activity should shift between areas LIP and PRR when monkeys change their movement plans. We have tested this prediction with the paradigm shown in figure 36.4 (Snyder, Batista, and Andersen, 1998). The experiment began in a similar manner to the aforementioned one, with a flash of light instructing a particular type of movement to the location of the flash inside the receptive field of a cell. However, in the later period of some of the trials, this plan either was changed by a second flash of a different color or was reaffirmed by a flash of the same color. The animals did not know what the subsequent flash

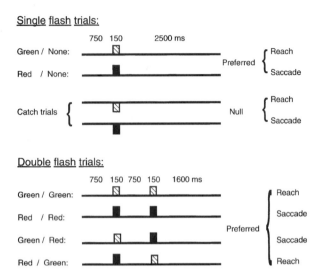

Single flash trials:

Double flash trials:

FIGURE 36.4 Time course of eight single- and double-flash trials. The experiment was designed to force the animal to attend to the spatial location and color of both flashes. A 150-ms flash appeared 750 ms after fixation began. Red and green flashes instructed saccades and reaches, respectively. On half of the trials, a second flash occurred 750 ms later at the same location as the first, sometimes instructing a change in the motor plan but never shifting spatial attention. Fixation light offset, 2.5 s after the first flash, signaled the animal to perform the most recently instructed movement. For one animal, double-flash trials also occurred for the null direction (not shown). (Reprinted from Snyder, Batista, and Andersen, 1998.)

would instruct, and because these second flashes always appeared at the same location as the first flashes, the monkeys' attention was the same whether the plan was changed or reaffirmed.

The response was related strongly to the animals' intentions. Figure 36.5 shows the activity of a reach neuron (figure 36.5A) and a saccade neuron (figure 36.5B) when the monkey changes plans from a reach to a saccade and vice versa. The activity of the neurons is much stronger when the preferred movement is cued. In the reach cell illustrated in figure 36.5A, the activity also is much higher during the first and second delays when the monkey is planning a reach instead of a saccade. These dramatic plan-related changes in neural response during the delay are taking place without the animal emitting any behavior at all. The animal is simply changing his intentions during the delay period.

The plan dependency across the population of PRR cells can be seen in figure 36.6A. The response to the first flash is larger when it is green and therefore is instructing a reach. This reach-planning activity remains high during the first delay period. The middle panel shows the responses to a second, green flash instructing a reach, segregated into two plots, depending on whether this second flash reaffirmed or changed the

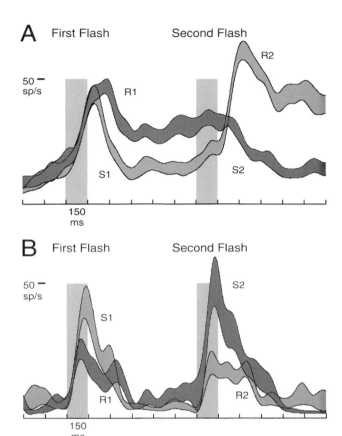

FIGURE 36.5 (A) Intention-selective responses of a parietal reach region (PRR) neuron to changes in motor plan, from a saccade to a reach (light trace) or from a reach to a saccade (dark trace). Sustained activity resulting from an instruction to plan a reach (R1) was abolished when a second flash changed the plan to a saccade (S2). An initial instruction to plan a saccade elicited only a transient response (S1), but when the plan was changed to a reach, activity increased (R2). Instruction to plan a reach elicited a larger response when countermanding a previous plan than when presented alone (R2 transient and sustained responses are larger than R1 responses). The reverse was true for a flash instructing a saccade (S2 transient less than S1 transient). Each flash was presented at the same location inside the response field so that second flashes changed motor intention without shifting spatial attention. All data shown were obtained before movement was cued to begin. (B) Intention-selective responses from a lateral intraparietal (LIP) neuron, complementary to the neuron of (A). Flashes instructing saccades elicited larger responses than those instructing reaches (S1 vs. R1 and S2 vs. R2) with still larger transient responses when the instruction to saccade countermanded a previous instruction (S2 vs. S1). Each ribbon is the mean response of 8 to 12 trials ±1 standard error of the mean (SE). Shading indicates the time of one 150-ms flash. Data were smoothed before plotting (121-point digital low-pass filter, transition band 20–32 Hz). (Reprinted from Snyder, Batista, and Andersen, 1998.)

plan. In this instance, the response to the identical green flash, under identical attention conditions, was much stronger if the animals were required to change their plans. Thus, it can be concluded that a large component of the flash-triggered activity actually reflects a shift in plans. The plots on the right show that this change-in-plan–specific activity is not a result of the novelty. These plots show the responses to the second flash when it is red and instructing an eye movement. These responses were small for the nonpreferred plan, regardless of whether it was a change or reaffirmation of the previous plan. Thus, the enhanced response to the flashes was present only when there was a change of plan to the preferred plan. The same result was found for LIP neurons, but saccades were the preferred plan.

Coding the next planned movement in the lateral intraparietal area and the parietal reach region

Using a memory double saccade paradigm, we found that most of area LIP neurons code the next planned eye movement (Mazzoni et al., 1996b). As shown in figure 36.7D, for a representative neuron, when the second target of the planned sequence of movements fell within the receptive field of the LIP cell but the animal was planning the first eye movement outside of the receptive field, this cell showed only a brief response to the stimulus and was not active in the memory period. However, if the same target fell within the receptive field of the cell and it was the target for the first eye movement, then the cell was active during the memory period (figure 36.7C). This result is typical of most (77%) LIP neurons. There also was a minority of cells with activity for the second target during the memory phase, and these cells appear to hold the memory of the location of the second target.

We recently performed a similar double-movement experiment in the PRR but required the monkey to plan two reaches instead of two saccades (Batista et al., 1998). In this task, we first cued the monkey to a location for a reach within the receptive field of the neuron. However, during the delay period, if we flashed a second target outside the receptive field of the cell, the animal was required to make the reach first to that target. At the end of the delay, the animal reached to this second target and another delay period began in which he then planned a movement to the first flashed target location. At the end of this second delay, the animal made a second limb movement to the remembered location of the first target. We found that, similar to LIP cells, PRR cells ceased firing to the remembered location of the first reach target when the monkey was planning an arm movement to the location of the second target, outside the receptive field of the cell. Moreover, we found when we reversed the sequence of targets so that the second target and first reach were in the receptive field, the activity still was always only present when the next

planned movement was into the receptive field. Thus, PRR shares another similarity with area LIP, with PRR neurons coding the next planned movement in double-movement tasks. This result adds further support for the idea that a large component of both PRR and LIP activity reflects the animals' plans or intentions for movement.

The coordinate frame of the lateral intraparietal area for visual stimuli

Lateral intraparietal neurons have receptive fields much like neurons in other visual areas, which are in the coordinates of the retina or eye–that is, the locations in space that activate these cells move with the eyes. However, we also have found that the activity of these cells is modulated by eye position and head position (Andersen et al., 1990; Brotchie et al., 1995; Snyder, Grieve, et al., 1998). Neural network simulations show that these "gain field" effects can serve as the basis for a distributed coding in other coordinate frames besides an eye-centered frame (Zipser and Andersen, 1988). Thus, for instance, neurons in another part of the brain that receive inputs from area LIP could construct receptive fields in head-centered coordinates by exploiting the eye position gain fields. Likewise, the combination of eye and head position gains can be used to construct body-centered representations (figures 36.8 and 36.9).

Coordinate frame for the lateral intraparietal area for auditory stimuli

Area LIP is considered an extrastriate visual area. It is at approximately the same level as area V4 (Andersen et al., 1990; Blatt, Andersen, and Stoner, 1990) when considered within the hierarchy of visual areas based on feedforward and feedback patterns of corticocortical connections (Maunsell and van Essen, 1983). Thus, it is imbedded deeply in the extrastriate visual cortex and occupies a position relatively early (i.e., close to V1) in the visual pathway. This is reflected in the brisk responses of area LIP to visual stimuli, even when the animal is ignoring the stimulus (Linden, Grunewald, and Andersen, 1997) or is anesthetized (Blatt, Andersen, and Stoner, 1990).

LIP neurons usually do not respond to auditory stimuli. However, because area LIP plays a major role in processing saccades and because monkeys obviously can make saccades to auditory stimuli, we hypothesized that LIP neurons would be active when the monkey used auditory stimuli for the purpose of making eye movements. This is in fact the case (Mazzoni et al.,

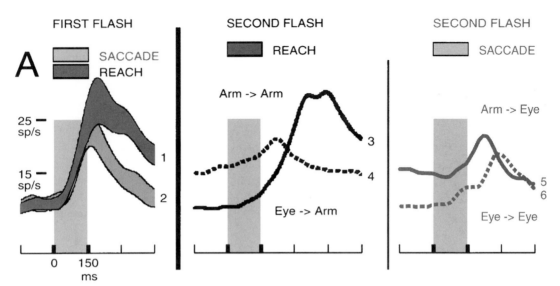

FIGURE 36.6 Population data from the parietal reach region (PRR) ([A] average of 17 cells). Responses to the first (left panel) and second (right and middle panels) flashes, instructing either a saccade (light) or a reach (dark) are shown. Second flashes could instruct a preferred (middle) or nonpreferred (right) movement, and this instruction could countermand (traces 3 and 5) or affirm (traces 4 and 6) the original instruction. Response to a preferred countermanding flash was larger than to a preferred affirming flash (3 vs. 4) and comparable with the response to a preferred first flash (1). For nonpreferred movements, countermanding and affirming flashes elicited similar comparatively small responses (5 vs. 6). Format as in figure 36.5, except that SE was calculated across cells rather than across trials (left). (Reprinted from Snyder, Batista, and Andersen, 1998.)

1996a; Grunewald, Linden, and Andersen, 1997). We also have determined the reference frame of these auditory triggered responses in a memory-guided eye movement task. In very early levels of the brain dedicated to determining the spatial location of auditory stimuli, cells have auditory receptive fields in head-centered coordinates. These head-centered fields are constructed using interaural time, intensity, and spectral cues. Conversely, in area LIP, we found only 33% of the cells had fields in head-centered coordinates whereas a surprising 44% had fields that were in eye-centered coordinates (Stricanne, Andersen, and Mazzoni, 1996). The remaining 23% of the cells had fields that were intermediate between these two coordinate frames. One parsimonious interpretation of these results is that area LIP is responsible for converting head-centered auditory signals into eye-centered coordinates. The neurons with auditory responses in area LIP typically also have eye position gain fields. These gain effects could provide the mechanism for converting auditory signals from a head-centered to an eye-centered representation.

These findings have two important implications. First, the fact that area LIP only responds to auditory stimuli when they are of oculomotor significance to the animal presents a very different view of multimodal integration than is commonly held. It suggests that area LIP usually is a default visual area, involved in transforming visual stimuli into eye movement plans. However, when auditory stimuli are deemed to be targets for saccades, then LIP becomes active. Second, when auditory signals are relayed to area LIP, they are transformed into the eye-centered reference frame of this area. This result suggests that vision provides the basic map for spatial location within area LIP. As we will see, these two ideas also can be extended to PRR. In fact, for many forms of extrapersonal spatial analysis and behavior, space may be represented in eye coordinates and other modalities may be brought into the eye-centered representation when multimodal integration is required. This idea certainly makes good ecological sense for vision and audition because audition can give us the general location of a stimulus but only our high-resolution vision can locate precisely a target of interest. This concept may explain the ventriloquist effect, in which visual stimuli tend to dictate the perceived spatial location of the auditory stimuli. In this illusion, if we see someone's lips moving but the speech source is from a different location in space, we nonetheless perceive the sound as coming from the moving lips.

Reference frame for the parietal reach region

We recently examined the reference frame for reach-planning activity in PRR. One possibility is that the reach activity is in the coordinates of the limb, coding the motor error for a limb movement. Alternatively,

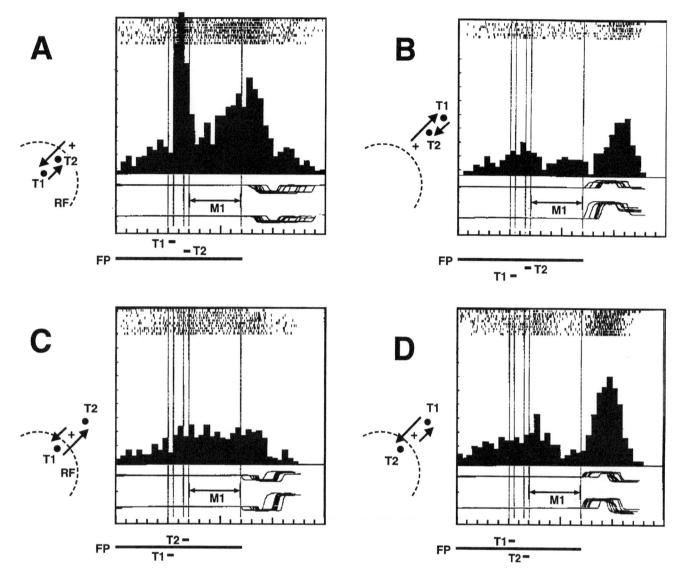

FIGURE 36.7 Activity of a lateral intraparietal (LIP) neuron in four different sequences of a double-saccade paradigm. Each panel has a plot that includes, from top to bottom, the spike rasters for each trial, the time histogram (binwidth, 50 ms) of the firing rate (20 Hz/division in A–C, 25 Hz/division in D), and the horizontal and vertical eye positions (25 degrees/division; abscissa: 100 ms/division). Vertical dotted lines and the thick horizontal lines below each panel again show the onset and offset of the visual stimuli. Diagrams to the left of each panel show the spatial arrangement of the first and second target (T1 and T2, respectively), the first and second saccades (arrows), and the neuron's receptive field (RF). (Reprinted from Mazzoni and associates, 1996b.)

PRR activity could be referenced to the eye, similar to activity in area LIP. We differentiated between these two possibilities by having monkeys make the same reach, but with the eyes gazing in different directions, or alternatively having them reach to the same location with respect to the eyes, but with the limbs starting from different initial positions. If the neurons were coding in eye coordinates, we would expect different activities for the former condition because identical reaches are made to different retinal locations. However, if the cells are coding in limb coordinates, then activity should vary in the latter condition because limb movements in different directions are made to the same location with respect to the retina. We found that most PRR cells code reaches in eye coordinates (Batista et al., 1998). The eye-centered responses often were modulated by eye position (Batista et al., 1998). Thus, PRR appears to have the same distributed representation of space as LIP, with their neurons having eye-centered receptive fields modulated by gain fields for eye and other body part positions (figure 36.8).

Establishing a common coordinate frame for both LIP and PRR led us to a rather nonintuitive prediction–that reaches to the remembered locations of sounds in the

PRR and LIP Share a Common Coordinate Frame

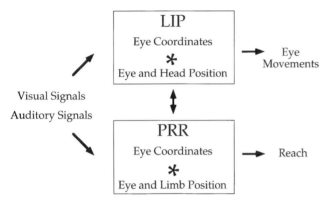

FIGURE 36.8   Both visually and auditorily cued locations are represented in eye coordinates in the lateral intraparietal (LIP) area and the parietal reach region (PRR). Also, both areas have gain modulation of the eye-centered receptive fields by eye and body part positions.

A Distributed Code for the Representation of Space

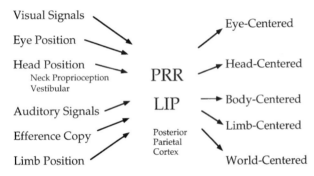

FIGURE 36.9   The eye-centered visual and auditory receptive fields of the parietal reach region (PRR) and the lateral intraparietal (LIP) area are modulated by signals specifying eye, head, and limb position. These modulations produce a common, distributed representation in both areas that can be read out by other parts of the brain in a variety of coordinate frames (including eye, head, body, and even world centered), depending on how the population of neurons in area LIP and PRR are sampled.

dark should be coded in eye-centered coordinates. Of course, in principle, there is no need for this sort of representation. Head-centered auditory signals could be converted directly to limb coordinates for making reaches; there is no need to have an intermediate step of converting these reach signals to eye coordinates. However, if there is a common coordinate frame for both PRR and LIP, then the reach activity should code the target location in eye-centered coordinates and be modulated by eye and limb position signals. Furthermore,

the results from the auditory saccade experiments in area LIP, outlined previously, also predict that the auditory signals would be transformed into eye-centered receptive fields in PRR. This prediction has been substantiated in recent experiments from our laboratory (Cohen and Andersen, 1998). We find that reaches to auditory targets often are coded in eye coordinates in PRR, and these eye-centered receptive fields are strongly gain-modulated by both eye and limb positions. Thus, auditory and visual signals are represented in a similar distributed manner in both LIP and PRR, with eye-centered receptive fields modulated by eye and body position signals (figure 36.8). The advantage of a shared reference frame may be to coordinate communication between the two areas, for instance, during tasks that require the close coordination of the eyes and hands.

Updating lateral intraparietal and parietal reach region spatial representations across saccades

To make an eye movement to a remembered location after intervening saccades requires a mechanism for updating the location of the target. Sparks and Mays (1980) first addressed this intriguing problem in physiologic experiments in the superior colliculus. They found that cells in the intermediate layers updated the location of the next planned eye movement in eye-centered coordinates across saccades. We later showed a similar updating in LIP (Gnadt and Andersen, 1988). Duhamel and

The Remembered Locations Are Maintained in Eye Coordinates Across Saccades in Both PPR and LIP

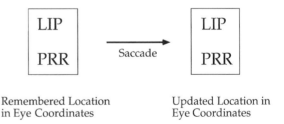

FIGURE 36.10   Remembered locations are updated in eye coordinates in both the lateral intraparietal (LIP) area and the parietal reach region (PRR). This updating is required not only to ensure that eye-centered locations remain invariant across eye movements, but also for other coordinate frames as well. For instance, when the eye position changes, the eye-gain fields change, and if the eye-centered locations of remembered stimuli are not updated, the correct head-centered location cannot be read out from the population of LIP or PRR neurons.

associates (1992) extended these results to show that a second eye movement was not necessary for this updating to take place. Although they interpreted this updated activity to be sensory, the results of Snyder, Batista, and Andersen (1997, 1998) suggest that this activity may in fact represent default plans for eye movements to the flashed second targets.

We recently asked whether this same updating process takes place in PRR. We presented a visual target for a reach that a monkey was required to remember. However, during the memory period, we then had the monkey make a saccade to fixate a new location in space. Routinely, the remembered location of the reach target was updated in eye coordinates to take into account the change in eye position (Batista et al., 1998). For example, if the monkey made a saccade that brought the remembered location of the target into the retinal receptive field of the PRR neuron, then it became active during the delay period before the reach. If the saccade brought the remembered location out of the receptive field of PRR cell, then it fell silent. Again, LIP and PRR were found to share an important similarity, both updating remembered locations in eye coordinates across saccades (figure 36.10). We also have seen the same updating in eye coordinates for locations cued by auditory targets (Cohen and Andersen, 1998).

This finding has important consequences for reading out the distributed representation of space accurately in nonretinal coordinates. If the eyes move, the eye position signals and gain modulations in LIP and PRR change in accordance with the new eye position. If the remembered retinal location of a target remains the same after the eye movement it is coded incorrectly in head- or body-centered coordinates. Thus, the updating of location in eye coordinates is necessary to read out the correct location with respect to the head or body.

Conclusions

The results reviewed previously show that areas LIP and PRR share several common features, even though one area is related to planning eye movements and the other is related to activity in reach movements. These common features include the following:

1. Both code visual and auditory targets in eye centered coordinates (figure 36.8);

2. Both demonstrate gain fields for eye and other body part positions (figure 36.9);

3. Activity in both areas code the next planned movement; and

4. Planned movement activity is updated across eye movements (figure 36.10).

These common features, particularly points 1 and 2, indicate that the two areas use a common coordinate frame. This coordinate frame is distributed and can be read out by other areas in several different reference frames. The specificity of their activity for the type of movement, and the fact that the cells only code the next planned movement (point 3), indicates that both areas code intentions to move. Whether these two areas of the PPC establish the basic rules for processing for other areas in the PPC remains to be seen.

ACKNOWLEDGMENTS   The authors would like to acknowledge Cierina Reyes for editorial assistance and Betty Gillikin for technical assistance. This work was supported by grants from the NIH, Sloan Center for Theoretical Neurobiology at Caltech, and ONR.

REFERENCES

ANDERSEN, R.A., 1987. The role of the inferior parietal lobule in spatial perception and visual-motor integration. In *The Handbook of Physiology. Section 1: The Nervous System, Volume V. Higher Functions of the Brain, Part 2,* F. Plum, V. B. Mountcastle, and S. R. Geiger, eds. Bethesda, Md.: American Physiological Society, pp. 483–518.

ANDERSEN, R. A., 1995. Encoding of intention and spatial location in the posterior parietal cortex. *Cereb. Cortex* 5:457–469.

ANDERSEN, R. A., C. ASANUMA, G. ESSICK, and R. M. SIEGEL, 1990. Cortico-cortical connections of anatomically and physiologically defined subdivisions within the inferior parietal lobule. *J. Comp. Neurol.* 296:65–113.

ANDERSEN, R. A., P. R. BROTCHIE, and P. MAZZONI, 1992. Evidence for the lateral intraparietal area as the parietal eye field. *Curr. Opin. Neurobiol.* 2:840–846.

ANDERSEN, R. A., L. H. SNYDER, D. C. BRADLEY, and J. XING, 1997. Multimodal representation of space in the posterior parietal cortex and its use in planning movements. *Annu. Rev. Neurosci.* 20:303–330.

ASANUMA, C., R. A. ANDERSEN, and W. M. COWAN, 1985. Form of the divergent thalamocortical projections form the medial pulvinar to the caudal inferior parietal lobule and prefrontal cortex: A double-label retrograde fluorescent tracer study in macaque monkey. *J. Comp. Neurol.* 241:357–381.

BARASH, S., R. A. ANDERSEN, R. M. BRACEWELL, L. FOGASSI, and J. GNADT, 1991. Saccade-related activity in the lateral intraparietal area: I. Temporal properties. *J. Neurophysiol.* 66:1095–1108.

BATISTA, A. P., L. H. SNYDER, C. A. BUNEO, and R. A ANDERSEN, 1998. The parietal reach region (PRR) employs a predominantly retinal reference frame which updates across saccades, and encodes only the impending reach. *Soc. Neurosci. Abs.* 24:262.

BROTCHIE, P. R., R. A. ANDERSEN, L. H. SNYDER, and S. J. GOODMAN, 1995. Head position signals used by parietal neurons to encode locations of visual stimuli. *Nature* 375:232–235.

COHEN, Y. E., and R. A. ANDERSEN, 1998. The parietal reach region (PRR) encodes reaches to auditory targets in an eye-centered reference frame. *Soc. Neurosci. Abs.* 24:262.

COLBY, C. L., and M. E. GOLDBERG, 1999. Space and attention in parietal cortex. *Ann. Rev. Neurosci.* 22:319–349.

CRITCHLEY, M., 1953. *The Parietal Lobes.* New York: Hafner Press.

DUHAMEL, J. R., C. L. COLBY, and M. E. GOLDBERG, 1992. The updating of the representation of visual space in parietal cortex by intended eye movements. *Science* 255:90–92.

DUHAMEL, J. R., C. L. COLBY, and M. E. GOLDBERG, 1998. Ventral intraparietal area of macaque–Congruent visual and somatic response properties. *J. Neurophysiol.* 79:126–136.

GNADT, J. W., and R. A. ANDERSEN, 1988. Memory related motor planning activity in posterior parietal cortex of macaque. *Exp. Brain Res.* 70:216–220.

GOODALE, M. A., and A. D. MILNER, 1992. Separate visual pathways for perception and action. *Trends Neurosci.* 15:20–25.

GRUNEWALD, A., J. F. LINDEN, and R. A ANDERSEN, 1997. Auditory responses in LIP II: Behavioral gating. *Soc. Neurosci. Abs.* 23:16.

LI, C.-S. R., P. MAZZONI, and R. A. ANDERSEN, 1999. The effect of reversible inactivation of macaque lateral intraparietal area on visual and memory saccades. *J. Neurophysiol.* 81:1827–1838.

LINDEN, J. F., A. GRUNEWALD, and R. A. ANDERSEN, 1997. Auditory responses in LIP: I. Training effects. *Soc. Neurosci. Abs.* 23:16.

LYNCH, J. C., A. M. GRAYBIEL, and L. J. LOBECK, 1985. The differential projection of two cytoarchitectonic subregions of the inferior parietal lobule of macaque upon the deep layers of the superior colliculus. *J. Comp. Neurol.* 235:241–254.

LYNCH, J. C., and J. W. MCLAREN, 1989. Deficits of visual attention and saccadic eye movements after lesions of parietooccipital cortex in monkeys. *J. Neurophysiol.* 61:74–90.

MAUNSELL, J. H., and D. C. VAN ESSEN, 1983. The connections of the middle temporal visual area (MT) and their relationship to a cortical hierarchy in the macaque monkey. *J. Neurosci.* 3:2563–2586.

MAZZONI, P., R. M. BRACEWELL, S. BARASH, and R. A. ANDERSEN, 1996a. Spatially tuned auditory responses in area LIP of macaques performing delayed memory saccades to acoustic targets. *J. Neurophysiol.* 75:1233–1241.

MAZZONI, P., R. M. BRACEWELL, S. BARASH, and R. A. ANDERSEN, 1996b. Motor intention activity in the macaque's lateral intraparietal area: I. Dissociation of motor plan from sensory memory. *J. Neurophysiol.* 76:1439–1456.

MOUNTCASTLE, V. B., J. C. LYNCH, A. GEORGOPOULOS, H. SAKATA, and C. ACUNA, 1975. Posterior parietal association cortex of the monkey: Command functions for operations within extrapersonal space. *J. Neurophysiol.* 38:871–908.

RIZZOLATTI, G., RIGGIO, L., and SHELIGA, B. M., 1994. Space and selective attention. In *Attention and Performance, XV. Conscious and Nonconscious Information Processing,* C. Umilta and M. Moscovitch, eds. Cambridge, Mass.: MIT Press, pp. 231–265.

SAKATA, H., M. TAIRA, M. KUSUNOKI, A. MARATA, and Y. TANAKA, 1997. The TINS lecture: The parietal association cortex in depth perception and visual control of hand action. *Trends Neurol.* 20:350–357.

SNYDER, L. H., A. P. BATISTA, and R. A. ANDERSEN, 1997. Coding of intention in the posterior parietal cortex. *Nature* 386:167–170.

SNYDER, L. H., A. P. BATISTA, and R. A. ANDERSEN, 1998. Change in motor plan, without a change in the spatial locus of attention, modulates activity in posterior parietal cortex. *J. Neurophysiol.* 79:2814–2819.

SNYDER, L. H., K. L. GRIEVE, P. R. BROTCHIE, and R. A. ANDERSEN, 1998. Separate body- and world-referenced representations of visual space in parietal cortex. *Nature* 394:887–890.

SPARKS, D., and L. E. MAYS, 1980. Movement fields of saccade-related burst neurons in the monkey superior colliculus. *Brain Res.* 190:39–50.

STRICANNE, B., R. A. ANDERSEN, and P. MAZZONI, 1996. Eye-centered, head-centered and intermediate coding of remembered sound locations in area LIP. *J. Neurophysiol.* 76:2071–2076.

THIER, P., and R. A. ANDERSEN, 1996. Electrical microstimulation suggests two different kinds of representation of head-centered space in the intraparietal sulcus of rhesus monkeys. *Proc. Natl. Acad. Sci. U.S.A.* 93:4962–4967.

THIER, P., and R. A. ANDERSEN, 1998. Electrical microstimulation distinguishes distinct saccade-related areas in the posterior parietal cortex. *Am. Psychol. Soc.* 80(5):1713–1735.

ZIPSER, D., and R. A. ANDERSEN, 1988. A back propagation programmed network that simulates response properties of a subset of posterior parietal neurons. *Nature* 331:679–684.

37 Neural Mechanisms of Motor Cognitive Processes: Functional MRI and Neurophysiological Studies

APOSTOLOS P. GEORGOPOULOS

ABSTRACT The neural mechanisms of cognitive processes cannot be elucidated using a single method; instead, useful insight can be gained by employing various approaches. In this chapter, the author attempts a discussion in this direction, namely the investigation of the mechanisms underlying some motor cognitive processes using behavioral, neurophysiological, and functional neuroimaging methods.

At the extremes, pure motor or cognitive processes are separate, for example, in the cases of the stretch reflex or mental calculation. However, they commonly are associated to varying degrees, for example, when you play chess. In fact, chess playing can be regarded as a motor-cognitive task par excellence because it consists essentially of actual and imagined movements of the chess pieces and the hand. During the past several years, we have developed two tasks at the interface of motor and cognitive processing and used them to investigate the neural mechanisms underlying their performance. Specifically, both tasks require the making of hand movements at a different direction from a stimulus direction but based on different rules. In both tasks, human subjects and monkeys moved a two-dimensional (2-D) handle and responded to visual stimuli appearing on a display. In the first task, the movement had to be at a constant angle from the stimulus direction (Georgopoulos and Massey, 1987), whereas in the second task, the movement had to be selected based on the serial order of stimuli in a sequence (Georgopoulos and Lurito, 1991). The mechanisms involved in these two tasks were investigated using classical chronometric, experimental psychological methods (Georgopoulos and Massey, 1987; Georgopoulos and Lurito, 1991), functional magnetic resonance imaging (fMRI) of the brains of human subjects (Tagaris et al., 1998), and recording of the activity of single cells in the brain of behaving monkeys

APOSTOLOS P. GEORGOPOULOS Brain Sciences Center, Veterans Affairs Medical Center and Cognitive Sciences Center, Departments of Neuroscience, Physiology, Neurology, and Psychiatry, University of Minnesota, Minneapolis, Minn.

(Georgopoulos et al., 1989; Lurito, Georgakopoulos, and Georgopoulos, 1991; Pellizzer, Sargent, and Georgopoulos, 1995). Each of these investigations provided unique, crucial insights into the processes involved that were complementary with each other. However, each of these sets of studies gives only a partial view of the whole, and it is only after all the results are looked at together that one can get a more adequate glimpse of the whole problem. Following is a summary of the essential findings from these individual studies, with an attempt at the end to sketch the whole as I see it emerge from these partial views.

Behavior

In the mental rotation task, the subject had to move a handle at an angle (clock- or counterclockwise [CCW]) from a stimulus direction. Thus, the direction of the movement was spatially connected to the direction of the stimulus and was at a constant angular relation to it. Experiments in human subjects (Georgopoulos and Massey, 1987) showed that the response time (RT) increased as a linear function of the instructed angle. This finding suggested that the psychological process in this task involves a mental rotation of the motor intention from the direction of the stimulus to the direction of the movement. This is similar to the mental rotation of visual images proposed by Shepard and colleagues (see Shepard and Cooper, 1982) in a different setting.

In the context-recall memory-scanning task, the subject had to move the handle in a direction specified by a serial order rule with respect to the onset of a particular stimulus in a sequence. Two to seven stimuli were presented successively on a circle (list stimuli), and then one of them (except the last one) was shown again (test stimulus); the subject was required to move in the direction of the stimulus that followed the test stimulus in the list sequence. In this case, the RT was a linear function of the number of list stimuli (Georgopoulos and Lurito,

1991). This finding suggested a memory scanning operation analogous to the one suggested by Sternberg (1969) for a visual recognition task.

Thus, these two tasks required that movements be made away from a stimulus direction but based on different rules, namely a spatial transformation or a temporal order rule. The monotonic increase of the RT with key task variables suggested two different psychological processes as the cardinal features of these tasks, namely mental rotation in the former and memory scanning in the latter task. The next step was to find out which brain areas are involved in these processes and how information is being processed at the neuronal level. For the former objective, we used fMRI; for the latter, we employed single-cell recordings in behaving monkeys.

Functional magnetic resonance imaging of mental rotation and memory scanning

GENERAL CONSIDERATIONS Functional brain imaging provides a means by which the patterns of activation of various brain areas in a task can be determined. The main advantage of these techniques is that they can provide functional activation images of the whole brain, but they lack functional specificity at the cellular level because the "activation" reflects changes in blood flow or metabolic signals that only indirectly relate to neuronal activity. Therefore, the data obtained from such studies are interpretable only in the context of other information (e.g., from neuropsychological or neurophysiological studies) concerning the role of specific areas in particular tasks. These considerations are exemplified in the results of our studies, discussed in a subsequent section.

THE TASKS USED: COGNITIVE OPERATIONS AND THEIR OPERANDA Cognitive processes do not happen in vacuo; essentially, they are operations carried out on operanda. For example, mental arithmetic operates on mental representations of numbers. A major objective of our studies has been to design experimental paradigms in which cognitive operations of interest and their operanda are chosen so as to provide distinct task dimensions. These task dimensions provide, in turn, an abstract space that serves as a guidepost for interpreting the results of functional imaging studies, an explanation of which follows.

We used four cognitive tasks in these experiments (Tagaris et al., 1998). They were combinations of two cognitive processes (mental rotation and memory scanning) operating on two kinds of operanda (visual images and intended arm movement direction). Thus, four operation–operandum combinations were generated, as illustrated in figure 37.1. We wanted to identify the brain activation patterns for each one of the four tasks and, hopefully, relate them in some abstract way to the tasks themselves. The crucial question is: Can we recover the dimensions of the tasks (i.e., operation and operandum) from the brain activation patterns?

Typical trials of the four cognitive tasks used are illustrated in the first column of figure 37.2 (see also color plate 22), and trials of matched "control" tasks are illustrated in the second column. In the visual mental rotation task (figure 37.2A), the letter G was shown rotated from −160° to +160° from the upright at 20° intervals, in a random order in different trials. Normal and mirror images of the letter were presented for each angle above. Subjects responded by pressing the left or the right of two buttons to indicate whether the letter was in normal or mirror image orientation, respectively. In the control task (figure 37.2), the same letter was shown in normal and upright positions, and the subjects responded simply by pressing a button without having to make any judgment. In the movement mental rotation task (figure 37.2B), an instruction angle was shown for 900 ms and was followed by a stimulus in 1 of 12 positions on a circle, every 30°; 12 stimuli were shown for each of five instruction angles (30° to 150° CCW, every 30°) in a randomized block design. Subjects responded by moving a joystick-controlled cursor in a direction away from the stimulus at the instructed angle. In the control task, a zero angle was instructed, and subjects responded by moving the joystick in the direction of the stimulus shown. In the context-recognition visual memory-scanning task (figure 37.2C), a sequence (list) of two to seven visual stimuli was shown in a random order on a circle, and then two consecutive (test) stimuli were shown again in the same or reverse sequence; subjects responded by pressing the left or the right of two buttons to indicate whether the two test stimuli were presented

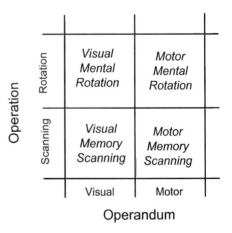

FIGURE 37.1 Experimental task design.

in the original or reverse sequence, respectively. In the control task, two to seven stimuli were shown but only one as a test stimulus, and the subjects responded by pressing a button without having to make any judgment. Finally, in the context-recall movement memory-scanning task (figure 37.2D), a sequence of two to seven stimuli was shown in a random order on a circle, and then one (test) stimulus (except the last) was shown again; subjects responded by moving a joystick-controlled cursor in the direction of the stimulus that was presented next to the test stimulus in the sequence. In the control task, the same display was shown, and the subjects responded by moving the joystick in the direction of the test stimulus. For both memory-scanning tasks, eight circular positions were used, every 45°. Each visual stimulus was shown for 600 ms and then went off while the next stimulus came on; the delay from the end of the presentation of the last stimulus to the onset of the first test stimulus was 900 ms.

Each of these four cognitive tasks was performed during the "task period," which was preceded and followed by a "control period," during which the corresponding control tasks were performed. The sequence of presentation of these four tasks was randomized. Key presses and directed movements were recorded using a nonmagnetic keypad and joystick, respectively. Directed movements were considered correct when they were within +30° from the required direction. The response time was measured with a precision of 1 ms. Eye movements were recorded during performance in the magnet by electro-oculography using Ag/AgCl electrodes and graphite wires. In general, eye movements were infrequent during data acquisition.

THE ISSUE OF CONTROL TASKS As expected, the RT increased as a linear function of the angle of rotation in the two mental rotation tasks or of the number of list stimuli in the two memory-scanning tasks used (data not shown). This suggests that the hypothesized operations were indeed employed in these tasks. The crucial item in interpreting the following results concerns the tasks performed during the control period because the judgment on whether a brain area was involved or not in these tasks rested on a statistical comparison between the fMRI signal during the task period and that during the control period. As explained previously, the control tasks differed for each of the four cases because our objective was to factor out the visuomotor events between the control and task periods, and thus isolate the particular cognitive condition under study, that is, the particular combination of a cognitive operation (i.e., mental rotation or memory scanning) and its operandum (i.e., visual image or intended arm movement direction) (fig-

ure 37.1). This design is crucial because if the control tasks were not matched for the corresponding cognitive ones with respect to simple visuomotor events (e.g., if, during the control period, the subjects simply rested with eyes closed), then the comparison between task and control periods would have reflected differences in simple sensorimotor processing in addition to the aforementioned cognitive aspects. Therefore, for the interpretation of the following results, the brain activation patterns observed refer to the cognitive aspects of the tasks employed.

BRAIN ACTIVATION PATTERNS Functional activation maps were derived from fMRI images acquired at high magnetic field (4 Tesla; see Tagaris et al., 1998, for the technical details of data acquisition and initial statistical processing). Overall, a conservative combination of criteria was used to identify highly consistent activation. The assignment of activated pixels to specific areas was based on anatomic landmarks in 2-D images and in three-dimensional (3-D) reconstructions of brain volumes (VoxelView/Ultra 2.5, Vital Images Inc., Fairfield, IA) as well as on Talairach coordinates (Talairach and Tournoux, 1988). Thirty brain areas were used for these analyses. The percentages of subjects (N = 10 subjects, 5 women and 5 men) in whom a specific area was activated in a given task are shown as shades of gray in figure 37.3; the columns represent brain areas, and the rows represent the four cognitive tasks used. Thus, a whole column shows the varying consistency of involvement of a given area in the four tasks, whereas a whole row shows the varying involvement of the various areas in a given task. This representation can be interpreted as a probability map that depicts the probability that a particular area will be activated during performance of a given task; alternatively, this representation can be interpreted as a consistency map, which shows the consistency by which a particular brain area will be activated in a given task. This is a quantitative way of analyzing binary functional activation maps, that is, brain maps in which an area of interest is considered either activated or not. Usually, such maps are treated descriptively, and little if any use is made of the information pertaining to the consistency of activation of a given area across subjects. In contrast, we used precisely this information in our analyses because it is the primary datum at the level of the population of subjects imaged.

MULTIDIMENSIONAL SCALING: GENERAL CONSIDERATIONS Multidimensional scaling (MDS) is a multivariate analysis technique by which a representation in a high-dimensional space is reduced to a representation in a low-dimensional space while trying to keep the relative

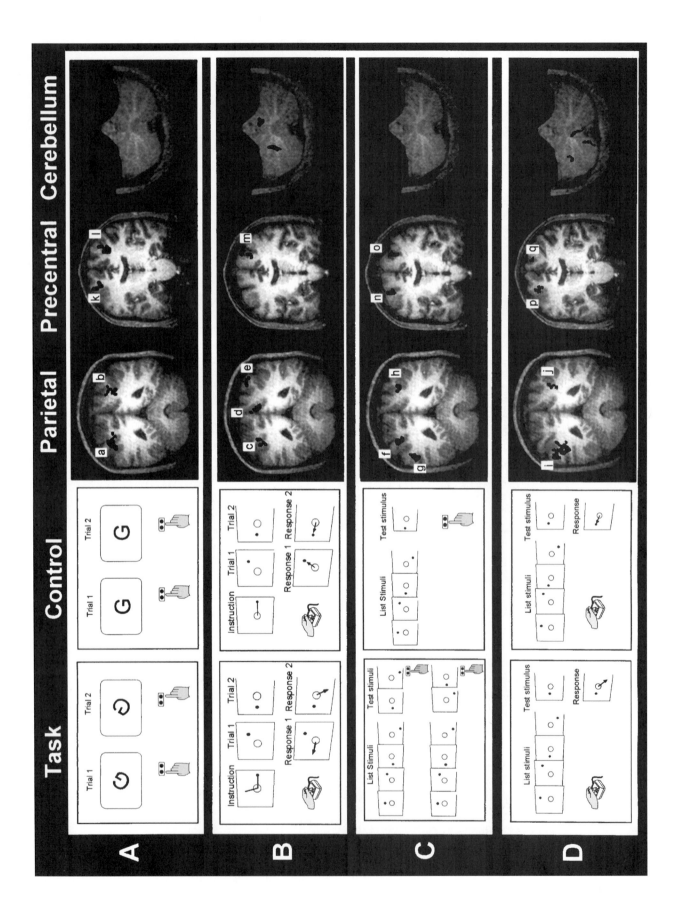

528

FIGURE 37.2 Schematic drawings of the tasks used and functional activation maps from one subject. (A) Visual mental rotation; (B) motor mental rotation; (C) visual memory scanning; (D) motor memory scanning. *Task:* experimental tasks. *Control:* control tasks. The control tasks were designed so that the visual display and the motor responses were very similar with those of the corresponding experimental tasks. Therefore, the functional activation maps reflect the combination of task dimensions and not sensorimotor events. *Activation:* Functional activation maps illustrate typical examples from one subject. Areas a, b, c, f, h, and j correspond to the intraparietal sulcus. Area e corresponds to the right superior parietal lobule. Areas g and h correspond to the left inferior parietal lobule. Areas k through q correspond to the precentral gyrus. Talairach coordinates for the center of activation shown (in mm on mediolateral, anterior-posterior, and inferior-superior axis) are as follows: a:33/-40/ 44; b: 30/-38/ 46; c: 32/-40/ 43; d: 1/-35/-45; e: 32/-39/ 52; f: 32/-40/ 45; g: 46/-43/ 28; h: 31/-39/45; i: 45/-43/ 30; j: 34/-38/ 36; k: 17/-19/ 59; l: 25/-20/-55; m: 23/-16/ 64; n: 22/-15/ 61; o: 24/-16/ 58; p: 18/-20/ 60; q: 12/-21/67.

distances between corresponding points in the two spaces as similar as possible (Shepard, 1980). The data entered in this analysis consist of dissimilarities (e.g., Euclidean distances) between pairs of measurements, commonly arranged in a symmetric "dissimilarity" matrix. The main outcome of MDS is a plot of the variable of interest (e.g., stimuli or tasks) in what is called derived configuration space. The dimensions of this space are usually two, as one strives to reduce the number of original dimensions as much as possible, but the choice of the number of the reduced dimensions is somewhat arbitrary. Therefore, it is especially useful if this choice is guided by considerations other than those of parsimony.

Such considerations existed in the present application, for which the configuration space was that of the four cognitive tasks; because, by design, we had two dimensions in the task domain (one for the cognitive operation and another for the operanda, see figure 37.1), a choice of two dimensions was dictated for the configuration space. This also provided a substantial reduction in dimensionality of the original space, from a 30-dimensional brain area space to the 2-D task configuration MDS space.

The MDS analysis can be performed on a single dissimilarity matrix. However, if several such matrices are available for a given problem, each individual matrix can be weighted separately in the analysis, resulting in what is called weighted MDS (WMDS), or individual scaling (INDSCAL) procedure, which we used. In the present application, we had data concerning the functional activation of each one of 30 brain areas for the four tasks used; therefore, we constructed 30 4 × 4 dissimilarity matrices and used the INDSCAL procedure of the SPSS statistical package (version 7, SPSS, Inc., Chicago, IL, 1996) for a weighted MDS. There are two additional advantages of the WMDS. One is that the position of the points in the derived configuration space is fixed, which makes the dimensions potentially interpretable. And the other is that it yields an additional plot showing what is called derived subject weights. In this plot, the points plotted correspond to the individual "subjects" (in the present case, these are the brain areas), and the axes are exactly the same as those in the task configuration space. Although it looks like a scatter plot, this is a vector plot: all vectors originate from the origin of the axes and end on the plotted points; therefore,

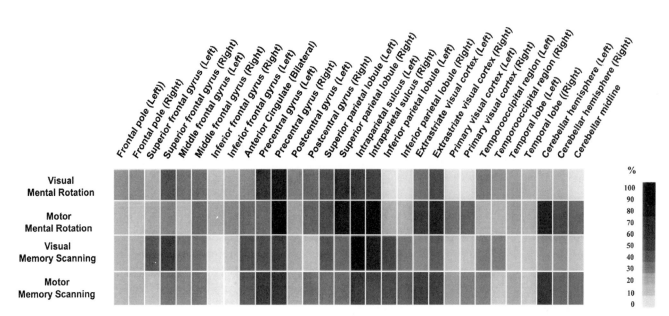

FIGURE 37.3 Schematic diagram showing the percentage of subjects who showed activation of the areas indicated ($N = 10$ subjects). (Reprinted from Tagaris et al., 1998, Copyright 1998, page 110, with permission from Elsevier Science.)

there are as many vectors as points plotted. For the interpretation of this plot, the task configuration space plot is derived by weighting individual dissimilarity matrices, and, therefore, it represents an overall "average" configuration, which may or may not be optimal for a particular "subject." The vectors in the derived subject weight plot concern these aspects, which are reflected in the length of the vector and its angular orientation. Specifically, in our application, the length of a vector (from 0 to 1) indicates how "good" the derived task configuration space is for a particular brain area: the longer the vector, the closer this configuration "suits" this brain area. Conversely, the orientation of the vector indicates the relative importance of the two dimensions for this area, as reflected in the ratio of the projections of the vector on the two axes (i.e., the slope of the line). This means that if the dimensions are interpretable, then a statement can be made about the relative participation of a brain area in the aspect(s) reflected in these dimensions.

MULTIDIMENSIONAL SCALING: RESULTS   The task configuration space derived using INDSCAL and a ratio level of measurement is shown in figure 37.4. Twenty-nine areas contributed to this analysis. (One area was dropped because it yielded a dissimilarity matrix of all zeros. This area was the right middle frontal gyrus, which was activated in exactly the same number of subjects in all four tasks [figure 37.3] and, therefore, could not provide information differentiating these tasks.) It can be seen that the four points corresponding to the

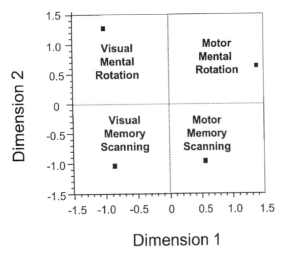

Multidimensional Scaling (INDSCAL): Derived Task Configuration

FIGURE 37.4 Task configuration space derived by multidimensional scaling (MDS), individual scaling (INDSCAL) model (see text for details).

four cognitive tasks used fell in each of the four quadrants such that the two dimensions could be identified as relating to the operation (ordinate) or the operandum (abscissa). In fact, these were the two task dimensions by design, as illustrated in figure 37.1. These results mean that the MDS analysis recaptured the cognitive-psychological dimensions of the tasks from the brain activation patterns. Figure 37.5 recapitulates this correspondence by showing the formal similarity between the planned task dimensions (left panel) and the derived task dimensions (right panel). This is a remarkable finding and a tribute to the power of MDS as a tool by which to analyze complex neuroimaging patterns of activation.

Figure 37.6 plots the derived area weights. It seems that the vectors plotted fall into three groups, as follows. The first group is closer to the abscissa, the second is around the main diagonal, and the third is closer to the ordinate. Our interpretation of this plot is along the lines discussed previously; namely, that the areas in the first group are involved with the dimension of the abscissa (i.e., operandum), those of the third group with the dimension of the ordinate (i.e., operation), whereas those in the middle are involved with both dimensions. The second point concerns the goodness of fit of the derived task configuration space for particular brain areas. As aforementioned, this is indicated by the length of the vector: the longer the vector, the better the goodness of fit. (Other measures also can be used, such as Kruskal's stress formulae or R^2.) Interestingly, in figure 37.6, the vectors closest to the axes were longer than those in the middle, with lengths close to the maximum possible value of one. This suggests that in the context of the tasks used, brain areas are rather specialized in processing information concerning the cognitive operation or its operandum, rather than dealing with both of them. Finally, this plot provides interesting information regarding the possible involvement of particular areas in these functions. Thus, the areas with a good fit (e.g., long vectors) that presumably are concerned with the operandum dimension (group nearest to the abscissa) included occipital (primary visual and extrastriate cortex bilaterally), cerebellar areas (cerebellar hemispheres bilaterally and cerebellar midline), and the left middle frontal gyrus. The areas presumably concerned with the operation dimension (group nearest the ordinate) included parietal areas (inferior parietal lobule bilaterally, right superior parietal lobule), the right temporal cortex, and the anterior cingulate gyrus (this area was not split in left and right). All other areas had shorter vectors or belonged to the group in the middle.

Thus, the MDS analysis provided a novel way by which neurobehavioral relations were explored. It re-

Planned
Task Configuration

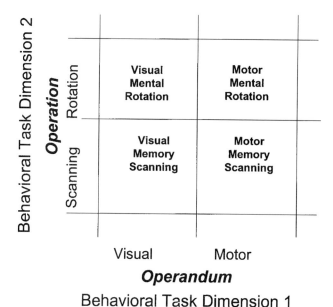

Derived
Task Configuration

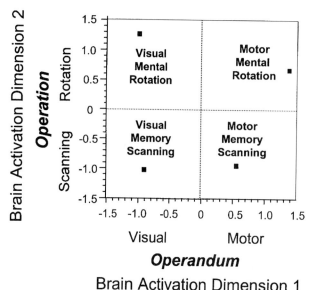

FIGURE 37.5 Interpretation of the results of the multidimensional scaling analysis illustrated in figure 37.4. Left: Experimental task design, as depicted in figure 37.1. Right: Same plot as that of figure 37.4, but here the axes are interpreted to indicate the task dimensions, as on the left panel.

covered the task dimensions from the brain activation patterns and identified areas specifically associated with those dimensions. By necessity, the grain of exploring brain function based on any kind of analysis is constrained by the grain of separating brain areas. In the present analyses, this grain was more coarse for some areas (e.g., extrastriate cortex and cerebellum) than for others (such as the parietal areas). A finer parcellation of anatomic areas can be achieved by several means, such as using finer anatomic landmarks or additional tasks known to activate certain areas. In any case, this is an open-ended problem, and, most probably, it always will be desirable to strive for even finer parcellations. However, as more and more areas are distinguished, correlations in their patterns of activation also are likely to increase, which essentially will limit the usefulness of this approach. Of course, a crucial objective is to determine the level of the coarseness of the grain necessary and sufficient for a given study, and it is likely for this to differ from study to study. Therefore, this remains an active field of investigation. However, the present study captured a bird's eye view of the specific problem, and, given the encouraging results obtained, it seems that the parcellation of brain areas used might have not been very far from the appropriate one for this study.

Single cell neurophysiology of mental rotation and memory scanning

GENERAL CONSIDERATIONS As aforementioned, the signal measured by functional neuroimaging methods is related only indirectly to the electrophysiological activity. Crucial validation studies have shown a correspondence between the expected activation of a brain area (e.g., visual cortex, motor cortex) based on prior neurophysiological evidence and the one actually observed using neuroimaging (e.g., see Ogawa et al., 1992; Kim et al., 1993). However, the situation becomes fairly complicated when more complex tasks are considered because a change in a neuroimaging signal (e.g., blood flow in PET or BOLD activation in fMRI) is not uniquely associated with neurophysiological events, such as excitation or inhibition. The detailed cellular mechanisms can be investigated only by using suitable methods, and one of the finest ones is the recording of single cell activity in behaving animals. The impulse activity is recorded by microelectrodes, and several such electrodes can be employed to record simultaneously the activity of many cells (Eichenbaum and Davis, 1998). The spike trains thus collected then are analyzed with respect to behavioral events, and the relations between these two kinds of data are analyzed. Therefore, the major advantage of this

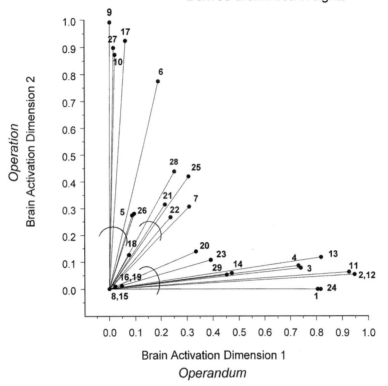

Multidimensional Scaling (INDSCAL):
Derived Brain Area Weights

Operation
Brain Activation Dimension 2

Brain Activation Dimension 1
Operandum

FIGURE 37.6 Brain area weight plot derived by individual scaling (INDSCAL) model. The numbers in the plot correspond to the following areas: *1*, left primary visual cortex; *2*, right primary visual cortex; *3*, left extrastriate visual cortex; *4*, right extrastriate visual cortex; *5*, left superior parietal lobule; *6*, right superior parietal lobule; *7*, left intraparietal sulcus; *8*, right intraparietal sulcus; *9*, left inferior parietal lobule; *10*, right inferior parietal lobule; *11*, left cerebellar hemisphere; *12*, right cerebellar hemisphere; *13*, cerebellar midline; *14*, left temporooccipital region; *15*, right temporooccipital region; *16*, left temporal lobe; *17*, right temporal lobe; *18*, left postcentral gyrus; *19*, right postcentral gyrus; *20*, left precentral gyrus; *21*, right precentral gyrus; *22*, left superior frontal gyrus; *23*, right superior frontal gyrus; *24*, left middle frontal gyrus; *25*, left inferior frontal gyrus; *26*, right inferior frontal gyrus; *27*, bilateral anterior cingulate; *28*, left frontal pole; *29*, right frontal pole.

method is its fine grain and the detail by which it can probe cellular mechanism, but its drawback is that it can only explore a very limited part of the brain (usually of the order of millimeters), especially as compared with neuroimaging methods that can scan the whole brain in a matter of seconds. It is obvious that each of the two methods can provide important, albeit partial, information about the brain mechanisms of behavior. In our studies, we have been using both of these methods to obtain this kind of complementary information. The results of our analyses of fMRI data during mental rotation and memory scanning were described in the preceding section; in what follows, we discuss the results of neurophysiological studies in monkeys trained to perform the aforementioned movement mental rotation and movement memory-scanning tasks. However, we summarize first the neural coding of movement direction by motor cortical cells.

NEURAL CODING OF MOVEMENT DIRECTION   The activity of single cells in the motor cortex is tuned directionally–that is, cell activity is highest for a given direction ("preferred direction") of movement and decreases gradually with directions farther and farther away from the preferred one (Georgopoulos et al., 1982; Amirikian and Georgopoulos, 1998). Typically, the frequency of cell discharge varies as a linear function of the direction cosines of the movement vector (relative to its origin), or, equivalently, of the cosine of the angle formed between the direction of a particular movement and the cell's preferred direction (i.e., the direction of movement for which cell activity would be highest). Preferred directions differ for different cells and are distributed uniformly in 3-D space (Schwartz, Kettner, and Georgopoulos, 1988). Finally, the preferred direction is very similar for movements of different amplitudes (Fu, Suarez, and Ebner, 1993).

Single cells provide only the building elements of the neural construct underlying movement generation and control: this construct invariably involves populations of neurons. The use of neuronal populations in this context differs from common statistical measures of populations, such as averages, variances, and frequency distributions of functional cell properties. Instead, the hypothesis is that a single neuron carries only partial information about a movement parameter that therefore is represented uniquely in the whole neuronal ensemble. This analysis was applied to the coding of the direction of movement, as follows. The broad directional tuning indicates that a given cell participates in movements of many directions; from this result, and from the fact that preferred directions range widely, it follows that a movement in a particular direction engages a whole population of cells. A unique code for the direction of movement was proposed (Georgopoulos et al., 1983; Georgopoulos, Schwartz, and Kettner, 1986; Georgopoulos, Kettner, and Schwartz, 1988) that regarded this population as an ensemble of vectors. Each vector represents the contribution of a directionally tuned cell; it points in the cell's preferred direction and is weighted (i.e., has length) according to the change in cell activity associated with a particular movement direction. The weighted vector sum of these neuronal contributions was called the "neuronal population vector." The population vector points in the direction of reaching (Georgopoulos et al., 1983; Georgopoulos, Schwartz, and Kettner, 1986; Georgopoulos, Kettner, and Schwartz, 1988; Kalaska, Caminiti, and Georgopoulos, 1983; Kalaska et al., 1989; Fortier, Kalaska, and Smith, 1989; Caminiti et al., 1991). Although preferred directions tend to change in the horizontal plane as the origin of the movement changes, the population vector remains an unbiased predictor of the direction of the movement (Caminiti et al., 1991). Three aspects of the population vector analysis are remarkable: its simplicity, its robustness, and its spatial outcome. With respect to simplicity, the ongoing calculation of the population vector is a simple procedure, for it (1) assumes the directional selectivity of single cells, which is apparent, (2) involves weighting of vectorial contributions by single cells on the basis of the change in cell activity, which is reasonable, and (3) relies on the vectorial summation of these contributions, which is practically the simplest procedure to obtain a unique outcome. With respect to robustness, the population vector is a robust measure, for it still can convey a good directional signal even with only 100 cells (Georgopoulos, Kettner, and Schwartz, 1988). Finally, the population vector is a directional measure, isomorphic direction in space. Indeed, the population analysis transforms aggregates of

purely temporal spike trains into a spatiotemporal signal.

These properties of the population vector suggest that it may be robust in the temporal domain as well. Indeed, when it was calculated as a time-varying signal every 20 ms, it provided an accurate prediction during the response time regarding the upcoming movement trajectory (Georgopoulos et al., 1984; Georgopoulos, Kettner, and Schwartz, 1988). This finding demonstrated the feasibility of using the population vector as a measure of the directional tendency of a neuronal ensemble and gave the impetus to new studies in which delays were imposed such that the movement was initiated after a period of time following a cue stimulus and in response to a "go" signal. The first of these studies (Georgopoulos, Crutcher, and Schwartz, 1989) involved an instructed delay period: The cue stimulus came on and stayed on while the monkey waited immobile for the occurrence of the go stimulus, which triggered the movement. Under those conditions, the population vector pointed during the delay in the direction of the cue, which was the same as that of the upcoming movement. Therefore, using this analysis, the directional information in the neuronal ensemble could be identified during the waiting period. The second study (Smyrnis et al., 1992) went a step further and included a memorized delay period: The cue stimulus came on but stayed on for only 300 ms, after which it was turned off. There ensued a memorized delay period during which the monkey waited immobile for the occurrence of the go signal but during which there was no target stimulus on display. The monkey was required to move, at the presentation of the go signal, in the direction of the (now absent) cue. Therefore, this cue direction had to be kept in memory during the delay period. Indeed, the population vector pointed in the direction of the memorized cue direction during the delay period. The results of these delay studies demonstrated the usefulness and power of the population vector analysis by which to monitor in time cognitive operations. In the two subsequent experiments discussed next, the tasks used required transformations of the intended direction of movement, one based on a spatial rule (mental rotation task) and another based on a temporal order rule (context-recall memory scanning task). These two tasks were very similar to the movement mental rotation and memory-scanning tasks used in the fMRI studies, as discussed previously. Therefore, they provide two interesting cases in which to compare the results and their implications for the neural mechanisms involved.

Neurophysiology of motor mental rotation The knowledge gained from single-cell and population analyses with respect to the neural coding of the direction of movement was applied to interpret changes in neuronal activity when a transformation was imposed on the upcoming movement, namely that it points in a direction at and angle from a reference direction indicated by a stimulus on the plane. In these experiments (Georgopoulos et al., 1989; Lurito, Georgakopoulos, and Georgopoulos, 1991), rhesus monkeys were trained to move a handle 90° CCW from a reference direction ("transformation" task); these trials were intermixed with others in which the animals moved in the direction of the target ("direct" task). The cell activity in the arm area of the motor cortex (contralateral to the performing arm) were recorded extracellularly. The neural activity was analyzed at the single-cell and neuronal population levels. We found the following. The changes in the activity of single cells in the direct task were related to the direction of movement, as described previously (Georgopoulos et al., 1982). The cell activity also changed in the transformation task, but there were no cells that changed activity exclusively in this task. Therefore, at the level of the motor cortex, the required transformation did not seem to involve a separate neuronal ensemble. The patterns of single-cell activity in the transformation task frequently differed from those observed in the direct task when the stimulus or the movement was the same. More specifically, cells could not be classified consistently as "movement"- or "stimulus"-related because frequently the activity of a particular cell would seem "movement-related" for a particular stimulus-movement combination, "stimulus-related" for another combination, or unrelated to either movement or stimulus for still another combination. Thus, no obvious insight could be gained from such an analysis of single-cell activity. However, an analysis of the activity of the neuronal population using the time evolution of the neuronal population vector revealed an orderly rotation of the neuronal population vector from the direction of the stimulus toward the direction of the movement through the 90° CCW angle (figure 37.7) (Georgopoulos et al., 1989; Lurito, Georgalopoulos, and Georgopoulos, 1991). There are several points of interest in this analysis that were surprising. First, there was no a priori reason to expect that the population vector would point to any other direction than the direction of the movement, on the simple hypothesis that the motor cortex is involved only in the production of movement. Our interpretation of the population vector as the directional motor intention suggests that in the transformation task, the motor intention is not restricted to the movement direction but occupies intermediate directions during the reaction time. Second, there was no a priori reason to expect that the popula-

tion vector would shift in an orderly fashion in the CCW direction, for no explicit instruction was given to the animals to that effect. The results obtained suggest that the directional motor intention spanned the smallest angle. This could, presumably, minimize the time and computational load involved in the transformation required.

The hypothesis was tested that this apparent rotation of the population vector could be the result of activation of two subsets of cells, one with preferred directions at or near the stimulus direction and another with preferred directions around the direction of movement: if cells of the former type were recruited at the beginning of the reaction time, followed by those of the second type, then the vector sum of the two could provide the rotating population vector. However, such a preferential activation of "stimulus direction"-centered and "movement direction"-centered cells was not observed. Conversely, a true rotation of the population vector could be reflected in the engagement of cells with intermediate preferred directions during the middle of the reaction time. Indeed, such a transient increase in the recruitment of cells with intermediate (i.e., between the stimulus and movement) preferred directions during the middle of the reaction time was observed. This supports the idea of a true rotation of the population signal. Finally, a rotation of the population vector through several angles, including 180°, has been described in a different context (Wise, di Pellegrino, and Boussaoud, 1996).

Neurophysiology of motor memory scanning This task required that a movement be made in a direction away from a stimulus direction based on a temporal, serial order rule (Pellizzer, Sargent, and Georgopoulos, 1995). This is a very different rule from the spatial one applied to the task described in the preceding section. Two monkeys were trained to perform a task that was very similar to the movement memory-scanning task described in the fMRI section. Briefly, two to five list stimuli were presented on a circle every 0.65 s at pseudorandom locations; when one of them (except the last) changed color (test stimulus), the monkeys made a motor response toward the next light in the sequence. Obviously, unlike the mental rotation task, in this task, the direction of the motor response bears no consistent relation to the direction of the test stimulus. Instead, this task seems to involve a memory-scanning process, in which list directions are searched until the test one is identified and the next one in the sequence selected. This kind of process was suggested by the results of early experiments in the visual domain (Sternberg, 1969) and by those of later experiments in the motor

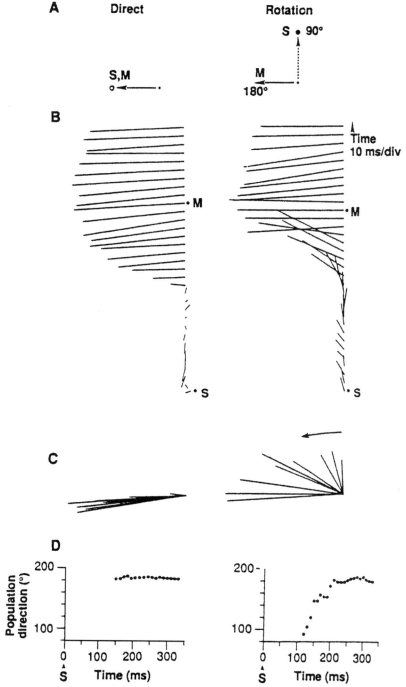

FIGURE 37.7 Results from a "direct" (left) and "rotation" (right) movement. (A) Task. Unfilled and filled circles indicate dim and bright light, respectively. Interrupted and continuous lines with arrows indicate stimulus (*S*) and movement (*M*) direction, respectively. (B) Neuronal population vectors calculated every 10 ms from the onset of the stimulus, *S*, at positions shown in (A) until after the onset of the movement, *M*. When the population vector lengthens, for the direct case (left) it points in the direction of the movement, whereas for the rotation case it points initially in the direction of the stimulus and then rotates counterclockwise (from 12 o'clock to 9 o'clock) and points in the direction of the movement. (C) Ten successive population vectors from (B) are shown in a spatial plot, starting from the first population vector that increased significantly in length. Notice the counterclockwise rotation of the population vector (right). (D) Scatter plots of the direction of the population vector as a function of time, starting from the first population vector that increased significantly in length following stimulus onset (*S*). For the direct case (left), the direction of the population vector is in the direction of the movement (~180°); for the rotation case (right), the direction of the population vector rotates counterclockwise from the direction of the stimulus (~90°) to the direction of the movement (~180°). (From Georgopoulos et al., 1989. Reproduced with permission of the publisher. Copyright AAAS, 1989.)

Control task

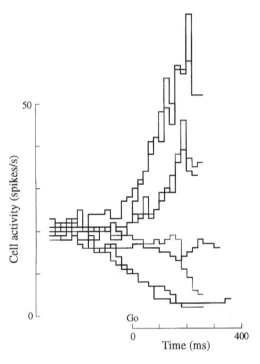

Context recall task

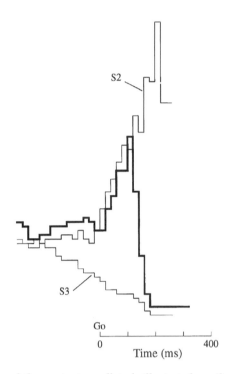

FIGURE 37.8 Peristimulus histograms of activity of a motor cortical cell are shown for eight directions in the control task (left), and one case of the context-recall task (right). In the left panel, histograms of cell activity are color coded for motor responses in different directions in the control task. In the right panel, two of these histograms are reproduced as thinner lines together with the histogram (black) of cell activity in the con-dition of the context-recall task illustrated on the top. After the go signal, cell activity (black) initially increased in the same way as in the control case (thin red line) for the direction toward the test stimulus (*S2*) and then changed abruptly and decreased to the level corresponding to the control activity for the direction of the motor response (toward *S3*). (From Pellizzer, Sargent, and Georgopoulos, 1995.)

field (Georgopoulos and Lurito, 1991); namely, that the response time increases as a linear function of the number of list stimuli. Indeed, this relation also was present in the monkey performance (Carpenter, Pellizzer, and Georgopoulos, 1996). The question, then, is what are the neural mechanisms of this memory scanning process? The results of neurophysiological studies in the motor cortex (Pellizzer, Sargent, and Georgopoulos, 1995) showed that the basic element of these mechanisms involves an abrupt (~40 ms) switching between the directions being searched. This was evident both at the single-cell and population levels. Specifically, single cells showed an abrupt change in activity from the pattern associated with the direction of test stimulus to that associated with the direction of the motor response; an example is shown in figure 37.8 (see also color plate 23). At the ensemble level, the neuronal population vector switch abruptly from test to the motor direction. The difference between the neural mechanisms of this task and that of mental rotation was exemplified further by analyzing the activity of cells with preferred directions intermediate between the stimulus and the movement. As discussed in the preceding section, these cells were recruited selectively during the response time in the mental rotation task. In contrast, they were not engaged in the memory-scanning task. This is shown in figure 37.9. Therefore, the mental rotation and memory-scanning tasks involve fundamentally different kinds of

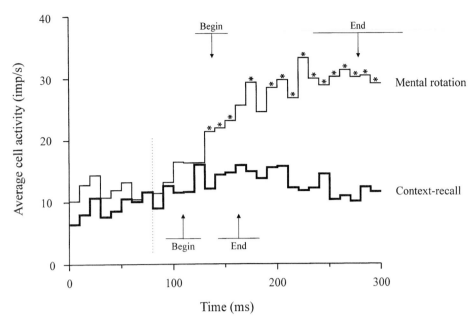

FIGURE 37.9 Peristimulus time histograms (10 ms binwidth) of the activity of cells with preferred direction at the intermediate direction (±10°) between the stimulus and movement directions in the mental rotation task (*2,3*), and between the test stimulus (*S2*) and motor response (*S3*) in the context-recall task (*19*). Histograms start at the onset of the go signal (time zero). In the mental rotation task, the activity of such cells (thin line) increased by more than threefold and was statistically sig-nificant (indicated by *), whereas in the context-recall task, cell activity remained almost constant (thick line) and was not sta-tistically significant compared with cell activity during the first 80 ms (dotted line; *baseline period*) (*20*). The arrows indicate the average time (±SD) at which the population vector began to change direction (*Begin*) and when it attained the direction of the motor response (*End*). (From Pelizzer, Sargent, and Georgopoulos, 1995.)

mechanisms (slow rotation vs. abrupt switching) both of which were identified, remarkably, within the same (proximal arm) area of the motor cortex.

Conclusions

Our studies of the motor mental rotation and memory-scanning tasks using both fMRI and single-cell record-ings provide a useful ground for trying to define the boundaries of the gain in knowledge provided by these methods. The neurophysiological studies showed clearly that the motor cortex is involved in both of these tasks, and this also was documented by the fMRI studies. Therefore, there is an excellent correspondence be-tween the two methods regarding this point. Because of the kind of fMRI signal, this is as far as the fMRI studies can go: they cannot provide information concerning the nature of the cellular information processing mecha-nisms involved. These can be glimpsed at from the re-sults of the neurophysiological studies. These results demonstrate clearly that the neural mechanisms both at the single cell and at the population levels are very dif-ferent in the two cases. Of course, no neuroimaging study could have distinguished between these two differ-ent mechanisms. This consideration brings forward an important point, namely that the "activation" of an area

needs to be considered cautiously, within the context of other information gained from studies using different methods. Conversely, no single-cell recording study could have produced the "bird's eye" view provided by the fMRI study and the insight provided by the MDS analysis, in regard to both the task dimensions and the differential involvement of brain areas with information processing along these dimensions. Neurophysiological studies are appropriate for examining in depth the cellu-lar mechanisms but not the overall activation patterns. Therefore, the two methods are complementary and to-gether can provide a more integrated view of the neural mechanisms of behavior.

ACKNOWLEDGMENTS This study was supported by United States Public Health Service grants NS17413, NS32919, and RR088079, the United States Department of Veterans Affairs, and the American Legion Chair in Brain Sciences.

REFERENCES

AMIRIKIAN, B., and A. P. GEORGOPOULOS, 1998. Directional tuning functions of motor cortical cells. *Soc. Neurosci. Abs.* 24:404.

CAMINITI, R., P. B. JOHNSON, C. GALLI, S. FERRAINA, Y. BURNOD, and A. URBANO, 1991. Making arm movements within different parts of space: The premotor and motorcor-tical representation of a coordinate system for reaching at vi-sual targets. *J. Neurosci.* 11:1182–1197.

CARPENTER, A. F., G. PELLIZZER, and A. P. GEORGOPOULOS, 1996. Context-recall memory scanning in two primate species. *Soc. Neurosci. Abs.* 22:1382.

EICHENBAUM, H., and J. DAVIS, 1998. *Strategies in the Study of Biological Neural Networks.* New York: Wiley.

FORTIER, P. A., J. F. KALASKA, and A. M. SMITH, 1989. Cerebellar neuronal activity related to whole-arm reaching movements in the monkey. *J. Neurophysiol.* 62:198–211.

FU, Q.-G., J. L. SUAREZ, and T. J. EBNER, 1993. Neuronal specification of direction and distance during reaching movements in the superior precentral premotor area and primary motor cortex of monkeys. *J. Neurophysiol.* 70:2097–2116.

GEORGOPOULOS, A. P., R. CAMINITI, J. F. KALASKA, and J. T. MASSEY, 1983. Spatial coding of movement: A hypothesis concerning the coding of movement direction by motor cortical populations. *Exp. Brain Res. Suppl.* 7:327–336.

GEORGOPOULOS, A. P., M. D. CRUTCHER, and A. B. SCHWARTZ, 1989. Cognitive spatial motor processes: 3. Motor cortical prediction of movement direction during an instructed delay period. *Exp. Brain Res.* 75:183–194.

GEORGOPOULOS, A. P., J. F. KALASKA, R. CAMINITI, and J. T. MASSEY, 1982. On the relations between the direction of two-dimensional arm movements and cell discharge in primate motor cortex. *J. Neurosci.* 2:1527–1537.

GEORGOPOULOS, A. P., J. F. KALASKA, M. D. CRUTCHER, R. CAMINITI, and J. T. MASSEY, 1984. The representation of movement direction in the motor cortex: Single cell and population studies. In *Dynamic Aspects of Neocortical Function,* G. M. Edelman, W. M. Cowan, and W. E. Gall, eds. New York: Wiley, pp. 501–524.

GEORGOPOULOS, A. P., R. E. KETTNER, and A. B. SCHWARTZ, 1988. Primate motor cortex and free arm movements to visual targets in three-dimensional space: II. Coding of the direction of movement by a neuronal population. *J. Neurosci.* 8:2928–2937.

GEORGOPOULOS, A. P., and J. T. LURITO, 1991. Cognitive spatial-motor processes: 6. Visuomotor memory scanning. *Exp. Brain Res.* 83:453–458.

GEORGOPOULOS, A. P., J. LURITO, M. PETRIDES, A. B. SCHWARTZ, and J. T. MASSEY, 1989. Mental rotation of the neuronal population vector. *Science* 243:234–236.

GEORGOPOULOS, A. P., and J. T. MASSEY, 1987. Cognitive spatial-motor processes: 1. The making of movements at various angles from a stimulus direction. *Exp. Brain Res.* 65:361–370.

GEORGOPOULOS, A. P., A. B. SCHWARTZ, and R. E. KETTNER, 1986. Neuronal population coding of movement direction. *Science* 233:1416–1419.

KALASKA, J. F., R. CAMINITI, and A. P. GEORGOPOULOS, 1983. Cortical mechanisms related to the direction of two-dimensional arm movements: Relations in parietal area 5 and comparison with motor cortex. *Exp. Brain Res.* 51:247–260.

KALASKA, J. F., D. A. D. COHEN, M. L. HYDE, and M. PRUD'HOMME, 1989. A comparison of movement direction-related versus load direction-related activity in primate motor cortex, using a two-dimensional reaching task. *J. Neurosci.* 9:2080–2102.

KIM, S.-G., J. ASHE, A. P. GEORGOPOULOS, H. MERKLE, J. M. ELLERMANN, R. S. MENON, S. OGAWA, and K. UGURBIL, 1993. Functional imaging of human motor cortex at high magnetic field. *J. Neurophysiol.* 69:297–302.

LURITO, J. T., T. GEORGAKOPOULOS, and A. P. GEORGOPOULOS, 1991. Cognitive spatial-motor processes: 7. The making of movements at an angle from a stimulus direction: studies of motor cortical activity at the single cell and population levels. *Exp. Brain Res.* 87:562–580.

OGAWA, S., D. W. TANK, R. MENON, J. M. ELLERMANN, S.-G. KIM, H. MERKLE, and K. UGURBIL, 1992. Intrinsic signal changes accompanying sensory stimulation: Functional brain mapping using MRI. *Proc. Natl. Acad. Sci. U.S.A.* 89:5951–5955.

PELLIZZER, G., P. SARGENT, and A. P. GEORGOPOULOS, 1995. Motor cortical activity in a context-recall task. *Science* 269: 702–705.

SCHWARTZ, A. B., R. E. KETTNER, and A. P. GEORGOPOULOS, 1988. Primate motor cortex and free arm movements to visual targets in three-dimensional space: I. Relations between single cell discharge and direction of movement. *J. Neurosci.* 8:2913–2927.

SHEPARD, R. N., 1980. Multidimensional scaling, tree-fitting, and clustering. *Science* 210:390–398.

SHEPARD, R. N., and L. COOPER, 1982. *Mental Images and Their Transformations.* Cambridge: MIT Press.

SMYRNIS, N., M. TAIRA, J. ASHE, and A. P. GEORGOPOULOS, 1992. Motor cortical activity in a memorized delay task. *Exp. Brain Res.* 92:139–151.

STERNBERG, S., 1969. Memory-scanning: Mental processes revealed by reaction-time experiments. *Am. Sci.* 54:421–457.

TAGARIS, G. A., W. RICHTER, S.-G. KIM, G. PELLIZZER, P. ANDERSEN, K. UGURBIL, and A. P. GEORGOPOULOS, 1998. Functional magnetic resonance imaging of mental rotation and memory scanning: A multidimensional scaling analysis of brain activation patterns. *Brain Res. Rev.* 26:106–112.

TALAIRACH, J., and P. TOURNOUX, 1988. *Co-planar Stereotaxic Atlas of the Human Brain.* New York: Thieme.

WISE, S. P., G. DI PELLEGRINO, and D. BOUSSAOUD, 1996. The premotor cortex and nonstandard sensorimotor mapping. *Can. J. Physiol. Pharmacol.* 74:469–482.

38 Cortical Mechanisms Subserving Object Grasping and Action Recognition: A New View on the Cortical Motor Functions

GIACOMO RIZZOLATTI, LEONARDO FOGASSI, AND VITTORIO GALLESE

ABSTRACT This chapter provides evidence for a new and broader view of the functions of the cortical motor system. On the basis of the functional properties of a monkey premotor area (area F5), the authors propose that at the core of the cortical motor systems there are vocabularies of motor actions. Neurons forming these vocabularies store knowledge about actions and the description of how this knowledge must be applied. When a specific population of these neurons becomes active, an internal copy of a specific action is generated. This copy may be used for two purposes: (1) planning and executing goal-directed actions or (2) recognizing actions made by another individual. The action recognition is based on a match between an observed action and its internal motor copy. Finally, evidence is reviewed showing that an action observation/execution matching system, similar to that of the monkey, also is present in humans.

"The motor systems of the brain exist to translate thought, sensation and emotion into movement. At present the initial steps of this process lie beyond analysis. We do not know how voluntary movements are engendered, nor where the 'orders' come from" (Henneman, 1984). This sentence, which starts the section on the organization of the motor system in the classic *Medical Physiology*, edited by Mountcastle, expresses well the prevalent ideas about the motor system: The motor system deals with *movements*. The processes that lead to them are remote processes virtually inaccessible to neurophysiologic inquiry.

The view proposed in this chapter is different. First, we challenge the view that *movement* is at the core of the motor system. *Action* is. Unlike movement, action is defined by a goal and by an expectancy. Movements are the final outcome of action and are programmed and controlled as such only when action is set and executed.

Second, motor system is involved not exclusively in action generation but also plays an important role in matching the external reality on the internally produced actions. We submit that in primates, this second role is by no means secondary but has a great importance for recognizing actions made by others.

Although we believe that these concepts are valid in general for the mosaic of motor areas forming the agranular frontal cortex, in this chapter, we use as an example the organization of one monkey premotor area, area F5. In this area, the two aspects of the motor system, action generation and action recognition, clearly emerge.

Motor properties of F5 neurons

Figure 38.1 shows a lateral view of the monkey brain. Area F5 forms the rostral part of inferior area 6. It is located anterior to area F4 and extends into the posterior bank of the inferior arcuate sulcus (Matelli, Luppino, and Rizzolatti, 1985).

Area F5 is not homogeneous. At least two morphologically distinct sectors can be distinguished in it, F5 of the convexity (F5c) and F5 forming the posterior bank of the arcuate sulcus (F5ab) (Matelli et al., 1996). Corticospinal fibers originate from F5ab only (He, Dum, and Strick, 1993).

Intracortical microstimulation studies and neuron recordings showed that area F5 is involved in the control of hand and mouth movements. (Rizzolatti et al., 1981a, 1981b; Kurata and Tanji, 1986; Gentilucci et al., 1988; Rizzolatti et al., 1988; Hepp-Reymond et al., 1994). Although there is a considerable overlap between the two representations, hand movements are located more dorsally, whereas mouth movements are located more ventrally (Gentilucci et al., 1988).

Particularly important for understanding the function of F5 are the results obtained by testing F5 neurons in a

GIACOMO RIZZOLATTI, LEONARDO FOGASSI, and VITTORIO GALLESE Istituto di Fisiologia Umana, Università di Parma, Parma, Italy

539

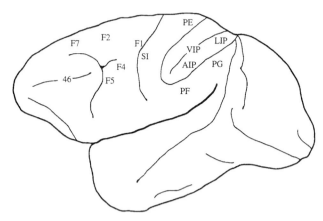

FIGURE 38.1   Lateral view of macaque monkey cerebral cortex showing frontal and parietal areas. The intraparietal sulcus is opened to show areas located in its medial and lateral banks. Frontal agranular cortical areas are classified according to Matelli et al. (1985). The cortical areas of the parietal convexity are classified according to Von Bonin and Bailey (1947). Abbreviations: AIP, anterior intraparietal area; LIP, lateral intraparietal area; MIP, medial intraparietal area; VIP, ventral intraparietal area.

naturalistic context (Rizzolatti et al., 1988). Awake monkeys were seated on a primate chair and presented with various objects (geometric solids, pieces of food of different size and shape). The stimuli were introduced in various spatial locations around the monkey, inside and outside its peripersonal space. After object presentation, the monkey was allowed to reach and grasp the objects.

The results confirmed that most neurons become active in relation to distal movements. However, they also showed that the neuron discharge typically correlates much better with an action or with fragments of an action (motor acts) rather than with the movements forming it. Thus, many neurons discharge when an action (e.g., grasping) is performed with effectors as different as the right hand, the left hand, or the mouth. An example of this behavior is shown in figure 38.2. Furthermore, in most neurons, the same type of movement (e.g., an index finger flexion) effective in triggering a neuron during grasping made with the index finger and the thumb was not effective during grasping made using all fingers. Thus, in these cases, the characterization of neuron activity in terms of individual movements is meaningless.

By using actions as classification criteria, F5 neurons were subdivided into the following main categories: grasping-with-the-hand-and-the-mouth neurons, grasping-with-the-hand neurons, holding neurons, tearing neurons, poking neurons, and manipulating neurons. Grasping neurons were the neuron type most represented (Rizzolatti et al., 1988).

Grasping is a complex action characterized by an initial opening phase, during which fingers are shaped according to the object physical properties (size, shape) and the wrist is adapted to object orientation, and a second, closure phase, in which fingers are flexed around the object until they touch it (Jeannerod, 1988). The type of hand shape depends on the size and shape of the object to be grasped. The three grip types that monkeys most frequently use are: precision grip, which is opposition of the thumb to the index finger (used for grasping small objects); finger prehension, which is opposition of the thumb to the other fingers (used to grasp middle-sized objects or to retrieve them from a narrow container); and whole-hand (or power) prehension, which is opposition of the fingers to the palm (used to grasp large objects). Neurons were recorded while monkeys grasped objects using these three grip types.

The results showed that most (85%) grasping neurons are selective for one of the three main grip types. The most represented type is precision grip, the least represented is whole-hand prehension. There is specificity for different finger configurations even within the same general type of grip. Thus, for example, in the case of whole-hand prehension, the prehension of a sphere, which requires the opposition of all fingers, is encoded by different neurons than the prehension of a cylinder, for which a palm opposition grip, thumb excluded, is required (figure 38.3).

Both neurons selective for a specific grip type and those unspecific showed a variety of temporal relations with the prehension phases. Some F5 neurons discharged during the whole action coded by them, sometimes starting to fire at stimulus presentation. Some were active mostly during the opening of the fingers, some during finger closure (Jeannerod et al., 1995).

A METHODOLOGICAL INTERLUDE   Before discussing the theoretical importance of these findings, a methodological point must be stressed. Typically, in neuron studies of the motor cortex, the behavioral or ethological context in which movements are emitted are considered of little or no importance. The variable that is controlled is movement. Paradigmatic in this sense are the experiments of Evarts, in which the animal had simply to move the wrist or exert a force (Evarts, 1981).

Had this approach been used in the study of F5, the most important characteristics of its neurons would have been lost. For example, it would have been impossible to discover that that same neuron discharges during mouth grasping and hand grasping. Similarly, because many grasping neurons produce a weak response during an inappropriate movement (e.g., a finger flexion), their

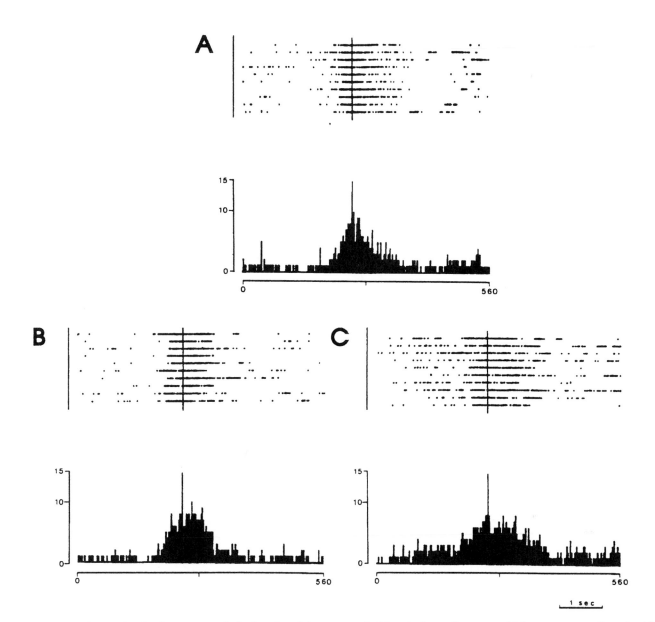

FIGURE 38.2 Example of a "grasping-with-the-hand-and-the-mouth" F5 neuron. (A) Neuron discharge during grasping with the mouth. (B) Neuron discharge during grasping with the hand contralateral to the recorded hemisphere. (C) Neuron discharge during grasping with the hand ipsilateral to the re-corded hemisphere. Rasters and histograms are aligned with the moment in which the monkey touched the food. The histograms are the sum of ten trials. Abscissae: time expressed in bins. Bin width: 10 ms. Ordinates: spikes/bin. (Modified from Rizzolatti et al., 1988.)

main characteristic (e.g., that of firing during specific motor action) also would have passed unnoticed.

The results of F5 study indicate that for cortical motor neurons, the same strategy should be used as that so successfully adopted in the sensory systems. For each neuron, the specific motor triggering feature must be established, and for those responding to passive stimuli, the sensory triggering features also must be assessed. Only, at this point, specific behavioral tasks can be adopted. Without such a strategy, one would never

"know how voluntary movements are engendered, nor where the 'orders' come from."

A "VOCABULARY" OF MOTOR ACTION Some years ago, Arbib (1981) proposed to describe the behavior of individuals in terms of schemas. A schema is both a store of knowledge and the description of a process for applying that knowledge. The schema idea can be applied at the single neuron level. The properties of F5 neurons fit this definition. These neurons store specific

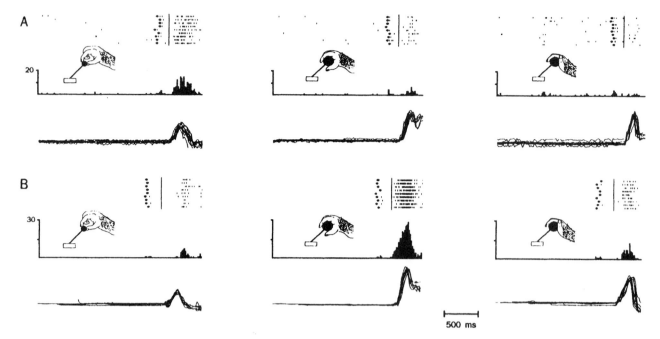

FIGURE 38.3 Examples of two F5 "grasping-with-the-hand" purely motor neurons. Recordings were made during the following behavioral task; the monkey was seated in front of a dark box. Trials began when the monkey pressed a keypad. Pressing the keypad illuminated the box, and a geometric solid located inside of it became visible. After a variable delay, the front door of the box opened, allowing the monkey to reach for and grasp the object. (A) Neuron selective for precision grip. (B) Neuron selective for whole-hand prehension. Rasters and histograms and the distance between the thumb and the index finger (recorded with a computerized movement analyzer) are shown, aligned with the onset of hand movement (vertical bar). Dots indicate the opening of the box front door. The grasped objects were, from left to right: a small sphere, a large sphere, and a horizontally oriented cylinder. Abscissae: time expressed in ms; ordinates: spikes/bin. Bin width: 20 ms. (Modified from Jeannerod et al., 1995.)

knowledge about an action and, when activated, indicate how to implement it.

F5 is a store of motor schemas or, using the terminology of Rizzolatti (Rizzolatti and Gentilucci, 1988; Gentilucci and Rizzolatti, 1990) a "vocabulary" of actions. This motor vocabulary is constituted by "words," each of which is represented by a set of F5 neurons. Some words indicate the general goal of an action (e.g., grasping, holding, tearing); others indicate the way in which a specific action must be executed (e.g., precision grip or finger prehension). Finally, other words are concerned with the temporal segmentation of the action into motor acts, each coding a specific phase of the grip (e.g., hand opening, hand closure).

The view that F5 contains a vocabulary of motor schemas has important functional implications. First, the presence of such a vocabulary strongly facilitates the execution of motor commands. The existence of neurons, which represent specific motor schemas and are anatomically linked (hard-wired) with cortical (F1) and subcortical motor centers, facilitates the selection of the most appropriate combination of movements by reducing the number of variables that the motor system has to control to achieve the action goal. Second, it simplifies the association between a given stimulus (i.e., a visually presented object) and the appropriate motor response toward it. Third, it gives the brain a storage of motor schemas (i.e., a knowledge about actions) that, as we show in the next sections, provides the motor system with functions traditionally attributed to the sensory systems.

Canonical F5 neurons

The motor properties of F5 we described in the previous section are proper to all F5 neurons. Studies of the responsiveness of F5 neurons have shown that many of them respond to visual stimuli. According to the type of effective visual stimulus, the responsive neurons (visuomotor neurons) were subdivided into two main categories. Neurons of the first category discharge when the monkey observes graspable objects. As evident in a forthcoming section, these neurons play a role in object-to-hand movement transformations. Because visuomotor transformation is a function traditionally attributed to the ventral premotor cortex, we refer to them as "canonical" F5 neurons. Neurons of the second category discharge when the monkey observes another individual making an action in front of it. We refer to these neurons as "mirror neurons" (Gallese et al., 1996; Rizzolatti et al., 1996a).

The two categories of F5 neurons are located in two different subregions of area F5: canonical neurons are found mainly in F5ab, whereas mirror neurons are recorded almost exclusively from the cortical convexity (F5c).

VISUAL PROPERTIES OF CANONICAL F5 NEURONS   Experiments in which F5 neurons were tested using natural stimuli showed that many F5 neurons became active in response to object presentation (Rizzolatti et al., 1988). Recently (Murata et al., 1997), the visual responses of F5 neurons to object presentation were re-examined using a formal behavioral paradigm originally devised by Sakata (Murata et al., 1996). The paradigm was basically as follows.

The monkey faced a dark box where geometric objects (e.g., cube, cylinder, sphere) of different size and shape were located. The objects were presented one at a time. The trial started with the presentation of a colored spot of light on the object that remained invisible. At the spot presentation, the monkey had to fixate it and press a bar. The bar pressing illuminated the box and made the object visible. After a variable delay, the spot changed color. This was the signal for the monkey to release the bar and reach and grasp the object ("grasping in light" condition). In a second condition, all the events were as aforementioned, but when the spot changed color, the monkey had only to release the bar. Object grasping was not allowed ("object fixation" condition). The two conditions were run in different blocks, and the spot colors in them were different. In a third condition ("grasping in dark" condition), the same object was presented for many consecutive trials. The monkey saw the object before the beginning of the first experimental trial, and therefore knew its characteristics, but it had to perform the entire task without visual guidance. Eye movements were controlled in all conditions.

The results showed that approximately half of the tested neurons responded to three-dimensional (3-D) object presentation and two thirds of them were selective to one specific object or to a cluster of objects. A strict congruence between visual and motor selectivity was found in most recorded neurons. Figure 38.4 shows the responses of a visually selective neuron. Observation and grasping of the ring produced strong responses (figure 38.4A). Responses to the other five objects were modest (sphere) or virtually absent.

Figures 38.4B and C show the behavior of the same neuron in two other experimental conditions: object fixation and object grasping in dark. In the object fixation condition, the objects were presented as aforementioned,

but at the go signal, instead of grasping the object, the monkey had to release a key. Grasping was not allowed. In this condition, the object is totally irrelevant for task solution, which only requires the detection of the go signal (spot color change). However, the neuron strongly discharged at the presentation of the preferred object (figure 38.4B).

The behavior of the neuron during object grasping in dark is illustrated in figure 38.4C. In the absence of any visual stimulus, the neuron discharged in association with ring grasping. The movement-related discharge was preceded by a sustained activity.

How can these findings be explained? At the onset, the object related visual responses could not be attributed to unspecific factors, such as attention or "intention" (desire to grasp the object). If either of these possibilities were true, the neuron would have not shown object specificity. Attention and "intention" are the same, regardless of which is the object presented. How can the neuron response to the object be interpreted?

Before answering this question, we must consider that a discharge extracellularly recorded from a neuron represents the output of this neuron regardless of how the neuron is excited. Thus, the responses of a given F5 neuron must be either visual, with the responses reflecting the physical aspect of the object, or motor, dealing with the activation of a motor schema—that is, the "idea" of how a motor effector must interact with the object.

The fact that F5 is a premotor area suggests that the object-related F5 neurons responses should represent objects in motor terms. Every time an object is presented, it triggers an immediate retrieval of the specific word of the motor vocabulary related to that object. Therefore, regardless of any intention to move (see "object fixation condition"), the "visual" response to object presentation would be the translation of the object into a potential motor action. The representation of this potential action then is kept active during the period following object presentation (see the sustained response following object presentation) and is transformed in overt movement only when the response is allowed.

Preliminary experiments from our laboratory confirm this interpretation (see also Murata et al., 1997). A large number of visually responsive neurons discharge to the presentation of objects that, although differing in shape (i.e., cube, cone, sphere), nevertheless are grasped in the same way.

The AIP-F5 grasping circuit

VISUAL INPUT TO F5: AREA AIP   Regardless of the interpretation of their discharge, there is no doubt that many F5 neurons respond to visual stimuli. Which is the source of this input? For many years, it has been known that inferior area 6 is connected heavily with the inferior parietal lobe (Petrides and Pandya, 1984; Matelli et al., 1986; Cavada and Goldman-Rakic, 1989). More recently, Sakata and coworkers (Taira et al., 1990) showed that in the rostral half of the lateral bank of the intraparietal sulcus (IPS), there are neurons, located in a particular sector, that become active during hand actions. They called this sector *anterior intraparietal area*, or area AIP (Sakata et al., 1995). Anatomic experiments showed that AIP and F5 are strongly reciprocally connected (Matelli et al., 1994; Matelli and Luppino, 1997).

The properties of AIP neurons have been studied by Sakata and associates (1995) using a paradigm similar to that used for F5 neurons. Neurons active during the task were subdivided into three classes: motor dominant neurons, visual and motor neurons, and visual dominant neurons. Two of them—motor dominant neurons and vi-

sual and motor neurons—have discharge properties similar to those of motor and visuomotor F5 neurons, respectively, whereas the third class—visual dominant neurons—is not present in F5. Visual dominant neurons are active during object fixation and grasping movements executed under visual guidance, but they do not respond when the same movements are executed in darkness (Sakata et al., 1995).

Like F5 neurons, many AIP neurons are selective for object shape and size. Among those classified as visual and motor neurons, many show the same selectivity during both object fixation and object grasping.

Although F5 and AIP share many common features, there also are some differences between them. In particular: (1) visual responses to 3-D objects are observed more frequently in AIP than in F5; (2) virtually all F5 neurons have motor properties, whereas these properties are present only in a set of AIP neu-

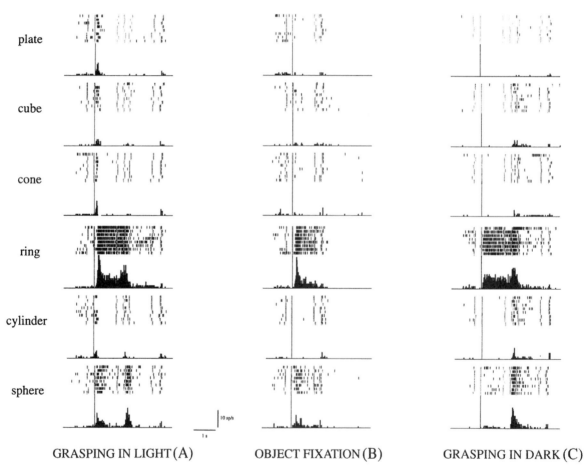

GRASPING IN LIGHT (A)   OBJECT FIXATION (B)   GRASPING IN DARK (C)

FIGURE 38.4 Example of a F5 "grasping-with-the-hand" visuomotor neuron. Panels show neural activity recorded during three different experimental conditions (A–C). Rasters and histograms are aligned (vertical bar) with key press. In (A) and (B), key press determines the illumination of the object. Small gray bars in each raster of (A) and (C) indicate, from left to right: appearance of a spot of light on the object; key press; change of color of the spot; key release; onset of object pulling; further change of color of the spot; onset of object release. Small gray bars in each raster of (B) indicate, from left to right: appearance of a spot of light on the object; key press; change of color of the spot; key release. Abscissae: time expressed in s. Ordinates: spikes/s. (Modified from Murata et al., 1997.)

Control

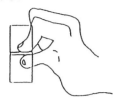  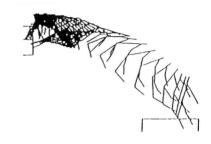

Muscimol (site B)

 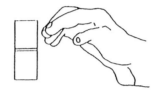 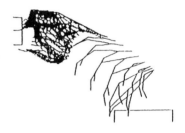

FIGURE 38.5 Preshaping and actual grasping of a small plate in a groove. *Top row:* single frame images redrawn from video and stick diagram of a typical control trial. During preshaping, the monkey extends its index finger and simultaneously flexes the last three fingers. Actual grasping is achieved by opposing the thumb and the index finger (precision grip). *Bottom row:* single frame images redrawn from video and stick diagram of a single trial performed after muscimol microinjection in area AIP. During preshaping, flexion of the last three fingers did not occur, and thumb–index finger opposition could not be executed. (Modified from Gallese et al., 1994.)

rons; (3) visual dominant neurons are present only in AIP; and (4) most AIP neurons discharge during the whole grasping action, whereas this occurs only in some F5 neurons, F5 neurons discharging more frequently only in some of the phases in which grasping is subdivided.

INACTIVATION STUDIES The data discussed thus far strongly suggest that the AIP-F5 circuit is involved in visuomotor transformations for grasping. This role of the AIP-F5 circuit recently was proved directly by inactivation data.

The effect of inactivation of AIP (muscimol injections) on grasping behavior was studied by Gallese and colleagues (1994). They trained a monkey to reach for and grasp geometric solids of different size and shape, each of which required a specific pattern of finger movements to be grasped adequately.

After muscimol injection, the behavior of the hand contralateral to the injection side was markedly impaired. Severe disruption of preshaping of the hand was observed constantly. As a consequence, there was a mismatch between the 3-D features of the objects to be grasped, especially of the small ones, and the posturing of finger movements, leading either to a complete failure of prehension or to an awkward grasping. In the case of

successful grasping, the grip very often was achieved after several correction movements that relied on tactile exploration of the object. A deficit in reaching never was observed.

Figure 38.5 illustrates the grip of a small plate positioned in a groove performed before (upper part) and after (lower part) AIP inactivation. After inactivation, hand preshaping was disrupted completely; the monkey did not flex its last three fingers and very often failed to insert the index finger into the groove. When the monkey occasionally succeeded in inserting it, it nevertheless was unable to oppose the finger to the thumb.

Preliminary experiments in which muscimol was injected into F5ab–that is, in the F5 sector in which canonical neurons are located–produced similar deficits. The impairment was limited to precision grip of the hand contralateral to the lesion when small injections were made. Larger injections produced bilateral deficit concerning all grip types (Gallese et al., 1997).

VISUOMOTOR TRANSFORMATION FOR GRASPING: A POSSIBLE NEURAL MODEL The functional properties of F5 and AIP just reviewed allow one to propose a model that can explain how the AIP-F5 circuit transforms visual information into action. Mainly, the AIP visual

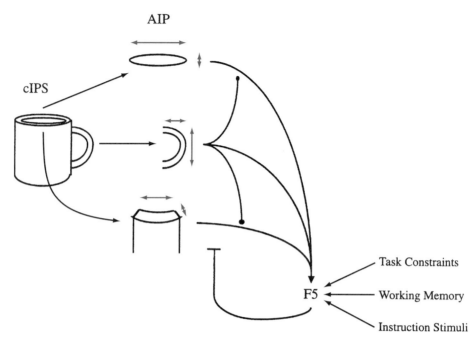

FIGURE 38.6 Cartoon schematically representing a model of AIP-F5 interactions for hand grasping under visual guidance. The figure shows an object that may be grasped in various ways. The object is analyzed by the posterior part of the infe-rior parietal cortex (cIPS area) and by AIP. The selection of prehension type occurs in area F5. (Modified from Fagg and Arbib, 1998.)

dominant neurons receive information on object proper-ties from 3-D object sensitive neurons located in an area posterior to LIP, called caudal IPS (cIPS, see Shikata et al., 1996). The AIP neurons extract from this global ob-ject description some specific aspects. For example, in the case of the mug shown in figure 38.6, AIP neurons respond to the handle of the mug, to its body, or its body upper border. Therefore, they parcellate the global ob-ject into its parts. This multiple description then is sent to F5, "proposing" various grasping possibilities. One of them is chosen. The choice depends on the concomitant information (purpose of the grasping, internal drive, spa-tial relationship with other objects) that F5 receives from the prefrontal lobe by means of other premotor areas or directly. On the basis of joint AIP input and visual and nonvisual contextual information, a grasping schema (e.g., precision grip) is selected. This schema then (1) is sent back to AIP by way of motor dominant neurons, al-lowing matching between the selected movement pat-tern and the visual input during action execution and (2) activates in sequence the various motor act schemas forming the grasping actions (e.g., hand opening, hand closure). These motor act schemas provide the necessary information to F1 and subcortical centers for action exe-cution. A computational model of the AIP-F5 circuit based on principles similar to those just described re-cently was proposed by Fagg and Arbib (1998; Fagg, 1996).

Mirror F5 neurons

In addition to canonical neurons, in F5, there is a second category of visuomotor neurons. These neurons become active both when the monkey performs an action *and* when it observes a similar action made by another mon-key or by the experimenter. The presentation of 3-D ob-jects, even when held by the hand, does not evoke the neuron discharge. These neurons have been named "mirror neurons" (Gallese et al., 1996; Rizzolatti et al., 1996a). An example is shown in figure 38.7.

To discover the trigger features of mirror neurons, Rizzolatti and coworkers (1996a; Gallese et al., 1996) presented the monkey with a series of actions. They were transitive actions (such as grasping, holding, ma-nipulating, or tearing objects), intransitive movements with emotional content (e.g., threatening gestures) or without it (e.g., arms lifting). Furthermore, to control whether a recorded neuron responded specifically to hand–objects interactions, the following actions also were performed: hand movements mimicking object-re-lated actions in the absence of the objects; prehension movements made using tools such as pincers or pliers; simultaneous movements of hands and objects kept spa-tially separated. Finally, to rule out the possibility that mirror neurons activation could be due to unspecific fac-tors such as food expectancy or motor preparation for food retrieval or reward, a group of neurons were stud-

A

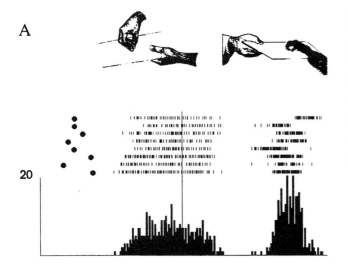

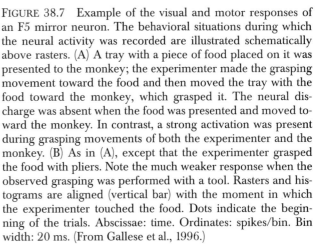

FIGURE 38.7 Example of the visual and motor responses of an F5 mirror neuron. The behavioral situations during which the neural activity was recorded are illustrated schematically above rasters. (A) A tray with a piece of food placed on it was presented to the monkey; the experimenter made the grasping movement toward the food and then moved the tray with the food toward the monkey, which grasped it. The neural discharge was absent when the food was presented and moved toward the monkey. In contrast, a strong activation was present during grasping movements of both the experimenter and the monkey. (B) As in (A), except that the experimenter grasped the food with pliers. Note the much weaker response when the observed grasping was performed with a tool. Rasters and histograms are aligned (vertical bar) with the moment in which the experimenter touched the food. Dots indicate the beginning of the trials. Abscissae: time. Ordinates: spikes/bin. Bin width: 20 ms. (From Gallese et al., 1996.)

B

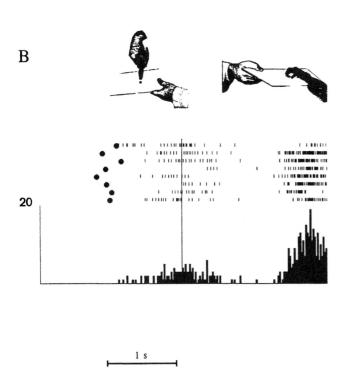

1 s

ied using a second monkey as the agent of the action. Although the second monkey grasped food and ate it, the first monkey (the monkey from which neurons were recorded) observed its action passively.

MIRROR NEURONS PROPERTIES   The visual stimuli most effective in triggering mirror neurons were found to be actions in which an agent (another monkey or an experimenter) interacts with an object using either the hand or, more rarely, the mouth. Object presentation, including interesting stimuli such as food items or the sight of faces or body movements were ineffective. Similarly, ac-

tions made using tools either did not activate the neurons or activated them only very weakly (see figure 38.7).

The observed hand actions most effective in triggering the neurons were grasping, manipulating, and placing. More than half of neurons, among those activated by the observation of hand action, were active during the observation of one action only. The remainders responded to two or, rarely, three of them. Some neurons were selective not only to the general action aim (e.g., grasping) but also to how the action was performed, selectively firing during the observation of one particular type of grip (e.g., precision grip, but not whole-hand prehension).

There was a large amount of generalization in terms of the precise physical aspects of the effective agent. For many neurons, the precise hand orientation was not crucial for activation. Similarly, in most cases, the distance from the monkey at which the action was executed did not influence the response. For most neurons, the effect was the same when the experimenter used the right or the left hand. In one third of tested neurons, however, the discharge consistently was stronger when the action was made by one hand instead of the other.

As far as the objects targets of the observed action are concerned, their significance for the monkey did not influence the neuron discharge. The responses to meaningful objects like food were the same as those to 3-D solids. The sizes of the objects, target of the action, were relevant in one third of the recorded neurons. In these cases, neurons were visually activated only when the object of the effective observed action had a specific size. The selectivity was related to the real size of the object and not to its size on the retina. It is likely, however, that this selectivity was not due to the visual characteristics of the objects, but to the grip that their size evokes. Experiments to dissociate these two variables have not been carried out yet.

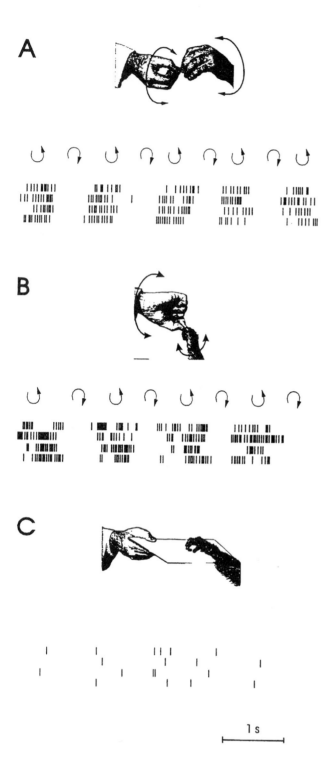

FIGURE 38.8   Example of the visual and motor responses of a highly congruent F5 mirror neuron. The behavioral situations during which the neural activity was recorded are illustrated schematically above neural records. Four continuous recordings are shown in each panel. (A) The monkey observes the experimenter rotating his hands around a small piece of food in opposite directions, alternating clockwise and counterclockwise movements. The response is present only in one rotation direction. (B) The experimenter rotates a piece of food held by the monkey, which opposes the experimenter movement by rotating its wrist in the opposite direction. (C) The monkey grasps a piece of food using a precision grip. Small arrows above the records in (A) and (B) indicate the rotations direction. (From Rizzolatti et al., 1996a.)

precision grip). For other neurons, the congruence was broader. For them, the motor requirements (e.g., precision grip) usually were more strict than the visual ones (any type of hand grasping). An example of a highly congruent mirror neuron is shown in figure 38.8.

OTHER AREAS RESPONDING SELECTIVELY TO BIOLOGICAL STIMULI   Neurons responding to complex biological stimuli had been described previously in the macaque brain. A series of studies showed that neurons that discharge selectively to the presentation of faces or hands are present in the inferotemporal lobe (Gross, Rocha-Miranda, and Bender, 1972; Perrett, Rolls, and Caan, 1982; Desimone et al., 1984; Rodman, O'Scalaidhe, and Gross, 1993) and in the prefrontal lobe below the principal sulcus (Pigarev, Rizzolatti, and Scandolara, 1979; O'Scalaidhe, Wilson, and Goldman-Rakic, 1997). Neurons responding to complex biological visual stimuli such as walking or climbing also were reported in the amygdala (Brothers, Ring, and Kling, 1990). Even more relevant to the present issue is the work of Perrett and co-workers (Perrett, Rolls, and Caan, 1982; Perrett et al., 1989, 1990). These authors showed that in the lower bank of the superior temporal sulcus (STS), there are neurons selectively activated by the observation of hand–object interactions. These properties resemble the visual properties of F5 mirror neurons: both STS and F5 mirror neurons code the same types of actions; they both generalize their responses to the different instances of the same action; and neither are responsive to mimicked hand actions without the target object. However, the distinctive feature of F5 neurons–and, so far, their uniqueness–resides in the fact that they discharge also during active movements of the observer: an observed action and action actively made produce the same neural pattern of activation.

The presence of two brain regions, neurons of which are endowed with similar visual properties, raises the question of their possible relationship. A possibility is

Mirror neurons, like canonical neurons, discharged during active movements. A comparison between the actions they code and the actions that trigger them when seen showed that for almost all the mirror neurons, there was a clear congruence between the observed and executed action. This congruence was for many neurons extremely strict, that is, the effective motor action (e.g., precision grip) coincided with the action that, when seen, triggered the neurons (e.g., again,

that STS and F5 represent distinct stages of the same system. The STS neurons provide an initial "pictorial" description of an action that is then fed (through an intermediate step in the posterior parietal cortex or in the prefrontal lobe) to area F5, where this description is matched with the pattern responsible for the execution of the same action.

THE MIRROR SYSTEM IN HUMANS The first evidence that a mirror system exists in humans was provided by Fadiga and associates (1995), who stimulated the motor cortex of normal human subjects using transcranial magnetic stimulation (TMS). The rationale of the experiment was the following. If the observation of an action activates the premotor cortex in humans, as it does in monkeys, then TMS should induce, during action observation, an enhancement of motor-evoked potentials (MEPs) recorded from the muscles that are active when the observed action is executed. The results confirmed the hypothesis. During the observation of grasping movements, a selective increase of MEPs was observed in the muscles that the subjects used for grasping objects.

Although these data indicate that an action execution/observation matching system exists in humans, they do not give information on the circuits underlying it. Data on this issue were provided by two positron-emission tomography (PET) experiments (Rizzolatti et al., 1996b; Grafton et al. 1996) and, more recently, by a neuromagnetic study (Hari et al., 1998). The two PET experiments differed in many aspects, but both had a condition in which subjects observed the experimenter grasping an object. In this condition, there was an activation of the STS, the inferior parietal lobule, and the inferior frontal gyrus (area 45). All activations were in the left hemisphere. The neuromagnetic study (Hari et al., 1998) was focused on the precentral motor cortex, the basic rhythm of which desynchronizes during active hand movements (Salenius et al., 1997). The results showed that grasping observation produced a similar desynchronization in the absence of any movement. The grasping observation-related desynchronization most likely reflects an activation of motor cortex due to an input to it coming from the inferior frontal gyrus or other premotor areas. The alternative interpretation, that mirror neurons also are present in the precentral motor cortex, is rather unlikely considering their absence in monkey area F1 (area 4) (Gallese et al., 1996).

Thus, the cortical areas active during action observation in humans match well those active in the monkey in the same conditions. In addition to the aforementioned areas containing neurons responding to meaningful biological stimuli, preliminary evidence from our laboratory shows that mirror neurons are present in inferior

parietal cortex (Fogassi et al., 1998). Note also that there is a growing consensus that F5 is the monkey homologue of Broca's area, or of part of it (Von Bonin and Bailey, 1947; Petrides and Pandya, 1994; Preuss, Stepniewska, and Kaas, 1996; and Rizzolatti and Arbib, 1998).

Taken together, these data indicate that a system matching action observation and action execution is present in humans as in monkeys. This system includes frontal, parietal, and temporal lobe areas.

POSSIBLE FUNCTION OF MIRROR NEURONS Primates are social animals living in continuous mutual relationship with conspecifics. Macaque monkeys live in groups characterized by active and intense social interactions, such as parental care, mating, and grooming that usually are disciplined by a well-delineated hierarchical organization. Therefore, it is crucial for each member of a given social group to be able to recognize the presence of another individual performing an action, to discriminate the observed action from others, and to "understand" the meaning of the observed action to react appropriately to it.

The observation of actions made by other individuals has another important function, that of learning their actions. When we learn a new motor skill, we observe and reproduce again and again the same sequence of actions that the teacher is displaying in front of us. The goal is to achieve as much as possible a match between the teacher-skilled motor behavior and our clumsy approximations of it. Evidence from developmental psychology demonstrates that in humans, the capacity to imitate is displayed soon after birth (Meltzoff and Moore, 1977). However, there is controversy about whether monkeys are able to learn by imitation; many authors maintain that a true learning by imitation is present, among primates, only in humans (see references in Galef, 1988; Whiten and Ham, 1992; Tomasello, Kruger, and Ratner, 1993; Byrne, 1995; Galef, 1998).

How do we recognize and imitate actions? One possibility is that action understanding and imitations require a complex cognitive description of the observed act. The existence of the mirror system suggests, however, another and simpler possibility. Everybody agrees that when an individual starts an action, he or she knows (predicts) its consequences. This knowledge is the result of an association between the schema of that action (the aforementioned potential action coded in the premotor cortex) and the consequences of this action. Thanks to mirror neurons, this knowledge can be extended to actions performed by others. When the observation of an action performed by another individual activates neurons that represent that action in the observer's premotor cortex, the observed action is recognized because of the similarity (or even identity) of the evoked representation to that internally generated during its active programming.

Thus, we propose that the mirror system is a basic system for recognition of action. Both monkeys and humans use it for this purpose. In addition humans probably use this system also for action imitation (Jeannerod, 1994). If, as maintained by many, monkeys are unable to imitate actions made by other individuals, this would suggest that, although endowed of a mechanism that generates internal copies of actions made by others, they are unable to use them for replicating those actions. This would suggest that the intentional use of internal copies of actions developed only late in evolution.

Conclusions

What is the use of the motor system? The classical answer to this question is undoubtedly the one cited in the introductory section: "The motor system exists to translate thought, sensation and emotion into movement." The data reviewed in this chapter lead to a different and broader view. In primates, the aim of the motor system is to create internal copies of actions and to use these internal copies for generating actions as well as for understanding motor events.

According to this view, there are "vocabularies" of motor actions at the core of the cortical motor system. Neurons forming these "vocabularies" store both knowledge about an action and the description, at least in general (nonparametric) terms, of how this knowledge should be used. The ensemble of neurons related to a given action forms the global motor schema of that action. When an appropriate stimulus is presented, the relevant schema is activated. This does not imply that the action occurs any time a motor schema is activated. The activation of a motor schema determines only the appearance of an internal copy of that action that may be executed.

In the vocabulary of F5, there are two sets of visuomotor neurons: canonical neurons and mirror neurons. Canonical neurons together with neurons located in the parietal lobe area AIP form a circuit that transforms intrinsic object properties into hand action. They are automatically (regardless of animal intention to act) activated in response to appropriate stimulus presentation. The movements do not necessarily follow this activation. The way in which this internal copy, a potential action, is transformed into a real action currently is not known. Our suggestion is that the lateral parietofrontal circuits are under control of mesial motor areas (Rizzolatti et al., 1990; Rizzolatti, Luppino, and Matelli, 1996). Among

these, particularly suitable for this control role is area F6, which receives a massive input from prefrontal cortex (Luppino et al., 1993; Lu, Preston, and Strick, 1994). When internal and external contingencies are such that it is both desirable and feasible that a potential action becomes a real action, the control exerted by mesial areas is removed and the action may unroll.

From the existence of an internal copy of actions stems the second function of the motor system, that of matching an observed action onto the internal motor copy of the same action. The presence of a common code for a received message (in the case of mirror neurons, actions made by others) and for an action actively emitted by the observing individual gives a cue on how individuals can understand the "pictorial" description of the inferotemporal and parietal areas. The evidence we present concerns event recognition but it is likely that in early periods of life, the same mechanism is used also for giving meaning to other types of percepts (see Rizzolatti and Gallese, 1997). These considerations, although at the moment purely hypothetical, appear to be extremely fascinating because they open the possibility to approach neurophysiologically issues that, like object semantics, were traditionally the domain of philosophical inquiry.

ACKNOWLEDGMENTS This work was supported by EEC Contract Biomed/H4 CT95-0789 and by grants from CNR and Murst to G.R.

REFERENCES

ARBIB, M. A., 1981. Perceptual structures and distributed motor control. In *Handbook of Physiology—The Nervous System, II, Part 1*, V. B. Brooks, ed. Bethesda, Md.: American Physiological Society, pp. 1449–1480.

BROTHERS, L., B. RING, and A. KLING, 1990. Response of neurons in the macaque amygdala to complex social stimuli. *Behav. Brain Res.* 41:199–213.

BYRNE, R., 1995. *The Thinking Ape: Evolutionary Origin of Intelligence.* Oxford: Oxford University Press.

CAVADA, C., P. S. GOLDMAN-RAKIC, 1989. Posterior parietal cortex in rhesus monkey: II. Evidence for segregated corticocortical networks linking sensory and limbic areas with the frontal lobe. *J. Comp. Neurol.* 287:422–445.

DESIMONE, R., T. D. ALBRIGHT, C. G. GROSS, and C. BRUCE, 1984. Stimulus-selective properties of inferior temporal neurons in the macaque. *J. Neurosci.* 8:2051–2062.

EVARTS, E. V., 1981. Role of motor cortex in voluntary movements in primates. In *Handbook of Physiology—The Nervous System, II,* J. M. Brookhart and V. B. Mountcastle, eds. Bethesda, Md.: American Physiological Society, pp. 1083–1120.

FADIGA, L., L. FOGASSI, G. PAVESI, and G. RIZZOLATTI, 1995. Motor facilitation during action observation: a magnetic stimulation study. *J. Neurophysiol.* 73:2608–2611.

FAGG, A. H., 1996. *A Computational Model of the Cortical Mechanisms Involved in Primate Grasping.* University of Southern California. Doctoral (PhD) Thesis. Los Angeles.

FAGG, A. H., and M. A. ARBIB, 1998. Modeling parietal-premotor interactions in primate control of grasping. *Neural Networks* 11:1277–1303.

FOGASSI, L., V. GALLESE, L. FADIGO, and G. RIZZOLATTI, 1998. Neurons responding to the sight of goal directed hand/arm actions in the parietal area PF (7b) of the macaque monkey. *Soc. Neurosci. Abs.* 24:257.5.

GALEF, B. G., JR., 1988. Imitation in animals: History, definitions and interpretation of data from the psychological laboratory. In *Social Learning: Psychological and Biological Perspectives*, T. Zentall and B. G. Galef, Jr., eds. Hillsdale, N.J.: Lawrence Erlbaum, pp. 3–28.

GALEF, B. G., JR., 1988. Recent progress in studies of imitation and social learning in animals. In *Advances in Psychological Science, Vol. 2: Biological and Cognitive Aspects*, M. Sabourin, F. Craick, and M. Robert, eds. Hove, U.K.: Psychology Press, pp. 275–297.

GALLESE, V., L. FADIGA, L. FOGASSI, G. LUPPINO, and A. MURATA, 1997. A parietal-frontal circuit for hand grasping movements in the monkey: evidence from reversible inactivation experiments. In *Parietal Lobe Contributions to Orientation in 3D Space. Exp. Brain Res. Series, vol. 25,* P. Thier and H.-O. Karnath, eds. Berlin, Germany: Springer, pp. 255–270.

GALLESE, V., L. FADIGA, L. FOGASSI, and G. RIZZOLATTI, 1996. Action recognition in the premotor cortex. *Brain* 119:593–609.

GALLESE, V., A. MURATA, M. KASEDA, N. NIKI, and H. SAKATA, 1994. Deficit of hand preshaping after muscimol injection in monkey parietal cortex. *Neuroreport* 5:1525–1529.

GENTILUCCI, M., L. FOGASSI, G. LUPPINO, M. MATELLI, R. CAMARDA, and G. RIZZOLATTI, 1988. Functional organization of inferior area 6 in the macaque monkey: I. Somatotopy and the control of proximal movements. *Exp. Brain Res.* 71:475–490.

GENTILUCCI, M., and G. RIZZOLATTI, 1990. Cortical motor control of arm and hand movements. In *Vision And Action: The Control of Grasping*, M. A. Goodale, ed. Norwood, N.J.: Ablex, pp. 147–162.

GRAFTON, S. T., M. A. ARBIB, L. FADIGA, and G. RIZZOLATTI, 1996. Localization of grasp representations in humans by PET: 2. Observation compared with imagination. *Exp. Brain Res.* 112:103–111.

GROSS, C. G., C. E. ROCHA-MIRANDA, and D. B. BENDER, 1972. Visual properties of neurons in inferotemporal cortex of the monkey. *J. Neurophysiol.* 35:96–111.

HARI, R., N. FORSS, E. KIRVERSKARI, S. AVIKAINEN, S. SALENIUS, and G. RIZZOLATTI, 1998. Activation of human precentral motor cortex during action observation: a neuromagnetic study. *Proc. Natl. Acad. Sci. U.S.A.* 35:15061–15065.

HE, S. Q., R. P. DUM, and P.L. STRICK, 1993. Topographic organization of corticospinal projections from the frontal lobe–Motor areas on the lateral surface of the hemisphere. *J. Neurosci.* 13:952–980.

HENNEMAN, E., 1984. Organization of the motor systems—a preview. In *Medical Physiology, XIV Edition*, B. Mountcastle, ed. St. Louis: C. V. Mosby, pp. 669–673.

HEPP-REYMOND, M-C., E. J. HUSLER, M. A. MAIER, and H.-X. QI, 1994. Force-related neuronal activity in two regions of the primate ventral premotor cortex. *Canad. J. Physiol. Pharmacol.* 72:571–579.

JEANNEROD, M., 1988. *The Neural and Behavioral Organization of Goal-Directed Movements.* Oxford: Clarendon Press.

JEANNEROD, M., 1994. The representing brain: neural correlates of motor intention and imagery. *Behav. Brain Sci.* 17:187–245.

JEANNEROD, M., M. A. ARBIB, G. RIZZOLATTI, and H. SAKATA, 1995. Grasping objects: The cortical mechanisms of visuomotor transformation. *Trends Neurosci.* 18:314–320.

KURATA, K., and J. TANJI, 1986. Premotor cortex neurons in macaques: activity before distal and proximal forelimb movements. *J. Neurosci.* 6:403–411.

LU, M. T., J. B. PRESTON, and P. L. STRICK, 1994. Interconnections between the prefrontal cortex and the premotor areas in the frontal lobe. *J. Comp. Neurol.* 341:375–392.

LUPPINO, G., M. MATELLI, R. CAMARDA, and G. RIZZOLATTI, 1993. Corticocortical connections of area F3 (SMA-Proper) and area F6 (Pre-SMA) in the macaque monkey. *J. Comp. Neurol.* 338:114–140.

MATELLI, M., R. CAMARDA, M. GLICKSTEIN, and G. RIZZOLATTI, 1986. Afferent and efferent projections of the inferior area 6 in the macaque monkey. *J Comp. Neurol.* 251:281–298.

MATELLI, M., and G. LUPPINO, 1997. Functional anatomy of human motor cortical areas. In *Handbook of Neuropsychology, Vol. XI,* F. Boller and J. Grafman, eds. Amsterdam: Elsevier, pp. 9–26.

MATELLI, M., G. LUPPINO, P. GOVONI, and S. GEYER, 1996. Anatomical and functional subdivisions of inferior area 6 in macaque monkey. *Soc. Neurosci. Abs.* 22:796.2.

MATELLI, M., G. LUPPINO, A. MURATA, and H. SAKATA, 1994. Independent anatomical circuits for reaching and grasping linking the inferior parietal sulcus and inferior area 6 in macaque monkey. *Soc. Neurosci. Abs.* 20:404.4.

MATELLI, M., G. LUPPINO, and G. RIZZOLATTI, 1985. Patterns of cytochrome oxidase activity in the frontal agranular cortex of macaque monkey. *Behav. Brain Res.* 18:125–136.

MELTZOFF, A. N., and M. K. MOORE, 1977. Imitation of facial and manual gestures by human neonates. *Science* 198:75–78.

MURATA, A., L. FADIGA, L. FOGASSI, V. GALLESE, V. RAOS, and G. RIZZOLATTI, 1997. Object representation in the ventral premotor cortex (area F5) of the monkey. *J. Neurophysiol.* 78:2226–2230.

MURATA, A., V. GALLESE, M. KASEDA, and H. SAKATA, 1996. Parietal neurons related to memory-guided hand manipulation. *J. Neurophysiol.* 75:2180–2186.

O'SCALAIDHE, S. P. O., F. A. W. WILSON, and P. S. GOLDMAN-RAKIC, 1997. Areal segregation of face-processing neurons in prefrontal cortex. *Science* 278:1135–1138.

PERRETT, D. I., M. H. HARRIES, R. BEVAN, S. THOMAS, P. J. BENSON, A. J. MISTLIN et al., 1989. Frameworks of analysis for the neural representation of animate objects and actions. *J. Exp. Biol.* 146:87–113.

PERRETT, D. I., A. J. MISTLIN, M. H. HARRIES, and A. J. CHITTY, 1990. Understanding the visual appearance and consequence of hand actions. In *Vision and Action: The Control of Grasping*, M. A. Goodale, ed. Norwood, N.J.: Ablex, pp. 163–180.

PERRETT, D.I., E.T. ROLLS, and W. CAAN, 1982. Visual neurones responsive to faces in the monkey temporal cortex. *Exp. Brain Res.* 47:329–342.

PETRIDES, M., and D. N. PANDYA, 1994. Comparative architectonic analysis of the human and the macaque frontal cortex. In *Handbook of Neuropsychology, Volume IX,* F. Boller and J. Grafman, eds. Amsterdam: Elsevier, pp. 17–58.

PETRIDES, M., and D. N. PANDYA, 1984. Projections to the frontal cortex from the posterior parietal region in the rhesus monkey. *J. Comp. Neurol.* 228:105–116.

PIGAREV, I. N., G. RIZZOLATTI, and C. SCANDOLARA, 1979. Neurons responding to visual stimuli in the frontal lobe of macaque monkeys. *Neurosci. Lett.* 12:207–212.

PREUSS, T. M., I. STEPNIEWSKA, and J. H. KAAS, 1996. Movement representation in the dorsal and ventral premotor areas of owl monkeys: A microstimulation study. *J. Comp. Neurol.* 371:649–675.

RIZZOLATTI, G., and M. A. ARBIB, 1998. Language within our grasp. *Trends Neurosci.* 21:188–194.

RIZZOLATTI, G., R. CAMARDA, L. FOGASSI, M. GENTILUCCI, G. LUPPINO, and M. MATELLI, 1988. Functional organization of inferior area 6 in the macaque monkey: II. Area F5 and the control of distal movements. *Exp. Brain Res.* 71:491–507.

RIZZOLATTI, G., L. FADIGA, L. FOGASSI, and V. GALLESE, 1996a. Premotor cortex and the recognition of motor actions. *Cogn. Brain Res.* 3:131–141.

RIZZOLATTI, G., L. FADIGA, M. MATELLI, V. BETTINARDI, E. PAULESU, D. PERANI, and F. FAZIO, 1996b. Localization of grasp representations in humans by PET: 1. Observation versus execution. *Exp. Brain Res.* 111:246–252.

RIZZOLATTI, G., and V. GALLESE, 1997. From action to meaning: A neurophysiological perspective. In *Les Neurosciences et la philosophie de l'action*, J.-L. Petit, ed. Paris: Librairie Philosophique J. Vrin Ed., pp. 217–229.

RIZZOLATTI, G., and M. GENTILUCCI, 1988. Motor and visualmotor functions of the premotor cortex. In *Neurobiology of Neocortex*, P. Rakic and W. Singer, eds. Chichester: Wiley, pp. 269–284.

RIZZOLATTI, G., M. GENTILUCCI, R. CAMARDA, V. GALLESE, G. LUPPINO, M. MATELLI, and L. FOGASSI, 1990. Neurons related to reaching-grasping arm movements in the rostral part of area 6 (area 6ab). *Exp. Brain Res.* 82: 337–350.

RIZZOLATTI, G., G. LUPPINO, and M. MATELLI, 1996. The classic supplementary motor area is formed by two independent areas. In *Supplementary Sensorimotor Area, Vol. 70*, H. O. Luders, ed. Philadelphia: Lippincott-Raven, pp. 45–56.

RIZZOLATTI, G., C. SCANDOLARA, M. GENTILUCCI, and M. MATELLI, 1981a. Afferent properties of periarcuate neurons in macaque monkey. I. Somatosensory responses. *Behav. Brain Res.* 2:125–246.

RIZZOLATTI, G., C. SCANDOLARA, M. MATELLI, and M. GENTILUCCI, 1981b. Afferent properties of periarcuate neurons in macaque monkey. II. Visual responses. *Behav. Brain Res.* 2:147–163.

RODMAN, H. R., S. P. O'SCALAIDHE, and C. G. GROSS, 1993. Response properties of neurons in temporal cortical visual areas of infant monkeys. *J. Neurophysiol.* 70:1115–1136.

SAKATA, H., M. TAIRA, A. MURATA, and S. MINE, 1995. Neural mechanisms of visual guidance of hand action in the parietal cortex of the monkey. *Cereb. Cortex* 5:429–438.

SALENIUS, S., A. SCHNITZLER, R. SALMENIN, V. JOUSMAKI, and R. HARI, 1997. Modulation of human rolandic rhythms during natural sensorimotor tasks. *Neuroimaging* 5:221–228.

SHIKATA, E., Y. TANAKA, H. NAKAMURA, M. TAIRA, and H. SAKATA, 1996. Selectivity of the parietal visual neurons in 3D orientation of surface of stereoscopic stimuli. *Neuroreport* 7:2389–2394.

TAIRA, M., S. MINE, A. P. GEORGOPOULOS, A. MURATA, and H. SAKATA, 1990. Parietal cortex neurons of the monkey related to the visual guidance of hand movement. *Exp. Brain Res.* 83:29–36.

TOMASELLO, M., A. C. KRUGER, and H. H. RATNER, 1993. Cultural learning. *Behav. Brain Sci.* 16:495–552.

VON BONIN, G., and P. BAILEY, 1947. *The Neocortex of Macaca Mulatta*. Urbana, Ill.: University of Illinois Press.

WHITEN, A., and R. HAM, 1992. On the nature and evolution of imitation in the animal kingdom: Reappraisal of a century of research. In *Advances in the Study of Behaviour, Vol. 21*, P. J. B. Slater, J. S. Rosenblatt, C. Beer, and M. Milinski, eds. New York: Academic Press, pp. 239–283.

39 Neural Mechanisms for Learning of Sequential Procedures

O. HIKOSAKA, K. SAKAI, H. NAKAHARA, X. LU, S. MIYACHI, K. NAKAMURA,
AND M. K. RAND

ABSTRACT   Acquisition of procedural skill requires long-term practice with repeated trial-and-error processes during which acquisition of knowledge (what to do) gradually is replaced with acquisition of skill (how to do). Using a visuomotor sequence task with trial-and-error processes for macaque monkeys and humans, the authors have shown that multiple brain areas contribute to different stages and different aspects of procedural learning. The frontal cortex (particularly the pre-supplementary motor area [SMA]) and the anterior part of the basal ganglia contribute to the initial stage of learning, in which knowledge for the procedure is acquired. The authors' data also suggested that procedural skill is acquired simultaneously, in which the SMA plays an important role. In contrast, the posterior part of the basal ganglia and the dentate nucleus of the cerebellum contribute to the long-term learning stage, in which the procedure is executed implicitly with a chain of anticipatory movements.

Based on their results and the results from other laboratories, the authors propose a hypothetical scheme in which a sequential procedure is learned independently by two parallel mechanisms in the cerebral cortex that use the visual and motor coordinates. Both of them are supported by the basal ganglia and the cerebellum: The basal ganglia provided them with reinforcement signals, and the cerebellum provided them with timing information. The proposed neural architecture would operate in an effective and flexible manner to acquire multiple sequential procedures.

Intelligence is based on the ability to learn a complex sequence of movements, as implicated in the usage of tools (Matsuzawa, 1996) and languages (Kuhl, 1994). How we learn such sequential procedures has been a long-standing objective of psychology and currently is a major topic in neuroscience. However, our understanding is far from complete. We hardly are able to pinpoint the brain structures that are critical for the sequential procedural learning. A consensus among neuroscientists is that the brain regions that are critical for declarative memory, including the hippocampus, are not critical for procedural learning or memory (Squire and Zola, 1996). Therefore, the procedural memory has been characterized by exclusion–that is, what is left out of the declarative memory mechanisms. Interestingly, this is the very reason why many neuroscientists currently are interested in disclosing the mystery of procedural learning.

In this review, we first describe the current status of the research on procedural learning, then summarize our study on monkeys and humans, and finally propose a neural network model as an attempt to integrate results from our and other laboratories.[1]

Brain regions that are implicated in procedural learning

As summarized in table 39.1, a number of brain regions have been shown to be involved in different types of learning. Interestingly, learning of sequential procedures currently is a major issue in studies using human subjects, but it rarely has been studied using animal subjects. Sequential procedures have been used in animal studies only after they have been learned to study the control mechanism of sequential movements (Tanji and Shima, 1994).

However, many of the human studies, especially imaging studies using positron-emission tomography (PET) or functional magnetic resonance imaging (fMRI), have focused on learning of sequential movements, such as the serial reaction time (SRT) task (Nissen and Bullemer, 1987). Common to the results of these studies was that several brain areas were active concurrently during learning, including the cerebral cortex, the basal ganglia, and the cerebellum. It has been proposed that there are different stages in learning to which different brain regions contribute (Karni et al., 1998; Petersen et al., 1998; Shadmehr and Brashers-Krug, 1997).

However, it still was unclear whether these brain regions actually contribute to the learning and how they interact with each other during learning. Crucial to answering this question was: (1) to identify the brain regions that were active with learning and (2) to manipulate the activity of each region to see whether learning and retention of memory were disrupted. Our strategy was to combine animal and human experiments

O. HIKOSAKA, K. SAKAI, H. NAKAHARA, X. LU, S. MIYACHI, K. NAKAMURA, and M. K. RAND   Department of Physiology, Juntendo University, School of Medicine, Tokyo, Japan

553

TABLE 39.1

	Species	Area	Experiment	Task
Animal Studies				
Simple Motor Task				
Sasaki and Gemba (1981)	Macaque	M1	Field potential	Visually triggered
Sasaki and Gemba (1982)	Macaque	M1	Field potential	Visually triggered
Sasaki and Gemba (1983)	Macaque	CbII	Field potential	Visually triggered
Aizawa et al. (1991)	Macaque	M1, SMA	Unit recording	Visually triggered
Thaler et al. (1995)	Macaque	SMA	Lesion	Self-paced
Chen et al. (1995)	Macaque	SMA	Lesion	Internal selection
Association Learning				
Petrides (1982)	Macaque	PF	Lesion	S-R association (visual-motor)
Kubota and Komatsu (1985)	Macaque	PF	Unit recording	S-R association (visual–Go/Nogo)
Canavan et al. (1989)	Macaque	Thalamus	Lesion	S-R association (visual-motor)
Watanabe (1990)	Macaque	PF	Unit recording	S-reward association
Mitz et al. (1991)	Macaque	PM	Unit recording	S-R association (visual-motor)
Germain and Lamarre (1993)	Macaque	PM	Unit recording	S-R association (auditory–motor)
Schultz et al. (1993)	Macaque	SN	Unit recording	S-reward association
Aosaki et al. (1994)	Macaque	Str	Unit recording	S-reward association
Chen and Wise (1995)	Macaque	SEF	Unit recording	S-R association (visual–oculomotor)
Rolls et al. (1996)	Macaque	PF (orbitofrontal)	Unit recording	S-S association (olfactory–visual)
Bell et al. (1997)	Fish	Cbl-Ctx	EPSP	S-S association (ES-ES [in vitro])
Adaptation				
Baizer and Glickstein (1974)	Macaque	Cbl-Ctx	Lesion	Prism adaptation
Asanuma and Keller (1991)	Cat	M1	Lesion	Pursuit rotor
Lou and Bloedel (1992)	Ferret	Cbl-Ctx	Unit recording	Perturbed locomotion
Ojakangas and Ebner (1994)	Macaque	Cbl-Ctx	Unit recording	Gain adaptation
Stern and Passingham (1995)	Macaque	Accumbens	Lesion	Reversal adaptation
Motor Sequence				
Nakamura et al. (1998)	Macaque	PreSMA	Unit recording	Visuomotor sequence
Miyashita et al. (1996)	Macaque	PreSMA, SMA	Inactivation	Visuomotor sequence
Miyachi et al. (1997)	Macaque	Str	Inactivation	Visuomotor sequence
Bloedel et al. (1996)	Cat	Cbl-N	Inactivation	Template task
Lu et al. (1998)	Macaque	Cbl-N	Inactivation	Visuomotor sequence
Motor Skill				
Zola-Morgan and Squire (1984)	Macaque	Hip(-)	Lesion	Barrier motor skill and lifesaver motor skill
Sakamoto et al. (1989)	Cat	S1	Lesion	Picking up foods
Fabre-Thorp and Leversque (1991)	Cat	Thalamus	Lesion	Visuomotor reaching
Pavlides et al. (1993)	Macaque	S1	Lesion	Picking up foods
Kleim et al. (1996)	Rat	Cbl-Ctx	Synaptology	Running through obstacles
Kleim et al. (1997)	Rat	M1	Synaptology	Running through obstacles
Others				
Olmstead et al. (1976)	Cat	PF	Lesion	T-maze learning
Malamut et al. (1984)	Macaque	Hip(-)	Lesion	Object-discrimination

using the same task for learning of sequential procedures and examine how different brain regions contribute to the learning process. The results are summarized in the following section.

Strategy for searching the neural correlates of sequence learning

A sequential procedure is complex and therefore difficult to learn. This may be why few studies have been done using animal subjects. Our 2×5 task was designed to overcome this difficulty (figure 39.1) (Hikosaka et al., 1995). A sequence (hyperset) in this task has a hierarchical structure such that the final goal (completion of hyperset) is reached by passing through successive subgoals (completion of set); a successive increase of partial reinforcement led to maximum reinforcement at the final goal. This reinforcement schedule apparently keeps the animals' motivation at a high level and allows them to acquire the procedure for a new sequence in a

TABLE 39.1 *(continued)*

	Experiment	Area	Task
Human Studies			
Association Learning			
Drewe (1975)	Patients	PF	Go/Nogo
Petrides (1985)	Patients	PF, Hip	S-R association (visual-motor)
Halsband and Freund (1990)	Patients	PM	S-R association (visual-motor)
Canavan et al. (1994)	Patients	Cbl	S-R association (visual-motor)
Deiber et al. (1997)	PET	PF, Cing, PM, PA	S-R association (visual-motor)
Adaptation			
Cohen and Squire (1980)	Patients	Hip(-)	Mirror reading
Frith et al. (1986)	Patients	SN	Visuomotor tracking
Lang et al. (1988)	EEG	PF	Visuomotor tracking (reverse adaptation)
Sanes et al. (1990)	Patients	Cbl	Mirror writing
Grafton et al. (1992)	PET	SMA, M1, thalamus	Pursuit rotor
Flament et al. (1996)	fMRI	Str, Cbl-Ctx	Visuomotor tracking
Martin et al. (1996a, b)	Patients	Cbl	Prism adaptation
Timmann et al. (1996)	Patients	Cbl	Visuomotor learning
Imamizu et al. (1997)	fMRI	Cbl-Ctx	Visuomotor tracking (rotation)
Inoue et al. (1997)	PET	PA	Visuomotor reaching (rotation)
Shadmehr et al. (1997)	PET	PF, PA	Force field adaptation
Rand, Wunderlich, et al. (1998)	Patients	Cbl	Response to locomotor perturbation
Motor Sequence			
Knopman and Nissen (1987)	Patients	Hip(-)	SRT
Knopman and Missen (1991)	Patients	Str	SRT
Pascual-Leone et al. (1993)	Patients	SN, Cbl	SRT
Jenkins et al. (1994)	PET	PF, PM, SMA, P, Cbl-Ctx	Motor sequence with trial and error
Pascual-Leone et al. (1994)	TMS	M1	SRT
Seitz et al. (1994)	PET	PM, Cbl-Ctx	Hand writing
Jackson et al. (1995)	Patients	SN	SRT
Karni et al. (1995)	fMRI	M1	Finger sequence
Pascual-Leone et al. (1995)	TMS	M1	SRT
Rauch et al. (1995)	PET	PM, Str, thalamus	SRT
Doyon et al. (1996)	PET	vPF, Cing, PA, Str, Cbl-N	SRT
Hikosaka, Sakai, et al. (1996)	fMRI	PreSMA	Visuomotor sequence with trial and error
Pascual-Leone et al. (1996)	TMS	PF	SRT
Petit et al. (1996)	PET	PF, SMA, PA	Sequential saccades
Dominey et al. (1997)	Patients	SN	SRT
Doyon et al. (1997)	Patients	PF(-), SN, Cbl	SRT
Jueptner, Stephan, et al. (1997)	PET	PF, Cing	Motor sequence with trial and error
Jueptner, Frith, et al. (1997)	PET	BG, Cbl-N	Motor sequence with trial and error
Molinari et al. (1997)	Lesion	Cbl	SRT
Rauch et al. (1997)	fMRI	Str	SRT
Sakai et al. (1998)	fMRI	PF, PreSMA, PA	Visuomotor sequence with trial and error
Verbal			
Fiez et al. (1992)	Patients	Cbl	Verb generation
Raichle et al. (1994)	PET	PF, Cing, Cbl-Ctx	Verb generation
Faglioni et al. (1995)	Patients	SN	Automatic verbal recall
Others			
Saint-Cyr et al. (1988)	Patients	SN	Cognitive skill (Tower of Hanoi)
Knowlton et al. (1996)	Patients	SN	Habbit (Probabilistic)

Studies using animal and human subjects are shown separately. Studies on learning of simple reflexes are not listed. Studies from our laboratory are in italic. Abbreviations: prefrontal cortex (PF), ventral prefrontal cortex (vPF), parietal cortex (PA), cingulate cortex (Cing), S1 (primary somatosensory cortex), cerebellar cortex (Cbll-Ctx), cerebellar nuclei (Cbll-N), cerebellum in general (Cbll), basal ganglia (BG), striatum (Str), substantia nigra (SN). Hip (-) indicates that the hippocampal region was unrelated to learning. See Note 1 for other abbreviations.

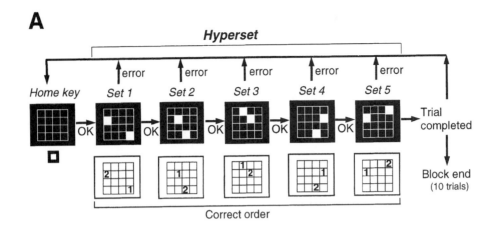

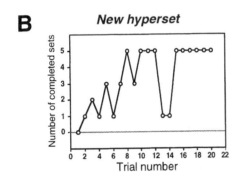

FIGURE 39.1   Procedure of 2×5 task. (A) In front of the monkey is a panel on which 16 LED buttons are arranged in a 4×4 matrix. Beneath the panel is another button called the "home key." If the monkey presses the home key, 2 of the 16 LED buttons are illuminated simultaneously. The monkey has to press them in a correct (predetermined) order, which he has to find out by trial and error. This is called "set." If successful, the LED buttons turn off sequentially and another pair of LEDs, a second set, is illuminated that the monkey has to press again in a correct order. A total of five sets is presented in a fixed order for completion of a trial, which we call "hyperset." If the monkey presses a wrong button, the trial is aborted, and the monkey has to start again from the home key as a new trial. Each hyperset was presented repeatedly in a block until 10 to 20 successful trials were performed. A different hyperset then was used for the next block. (B) An example of a block of practice trials using a new hyperset (left) and a learned hyperset (right). The numbers of completed sets (ordinate) are shown for consecutive trials (abscissa). In the learned hyperset, the monkey completed the block (10 successful trials) with no error. In the new hyperset, the same monkey made errors initially at the first or second set, but the number of completed sets increased gradually.

short period (usually less than 4 min). Furthermore, the 2×5 task allows us to generate new sequences, practically as many as possible.

Our experimental strategy was composed of three lines of experimental procedures: (1) initial training of learning procedures, (2) behavioral experiments, and (3) physiological experiments.

First, we had the monkeys learn a set of sequences repeatedly until they could perform the sequences highly skillfully, presumably based on long-term memories or programs for the sequences. We then would be ready to search for the neural mechanisms that are involved in the memory storage or retrieval processes. Conversely, by having the monkeys learn new sequences repeatedly, we would be ready to search for the neural mechanisms that are involved in learning of new procedures.

The second procedure, behavioral experiments, was performed to correlate the process of learning using the 2×5 task with a large number of human behavioral studies (table 39.1). We showed that the monkeys learned individual sequences in the same way as human subjects do, for example, following the "law of practice" (Newell and Rosenbloom, 1981). In addition, we found interesting observations that would be correlated with underlying neural mechanisms (summarized in table 39.2 and described in detail in the following section).

Finally, we attempted to find the neural correlates of sequence learning using two approaches: activation study (single-unit recording in monkeys and fMRI in humans) and inactivation study (reversible blockade by muscimol injection). The activation and inactivation studies are complementary for the following reasons. The activation study could produce false-positive errors:

TABLE 39.2
Learning stages in 2 × 5 task

Stage	Early	Intermediate	Late
Specific to hand?	No		Yes
Specific to order?	No		Yes
Quick?	No		Yes
Anticipatory movements?	No		Yes
Forget on next day?	Yes		No
Forget after 6 months?	Yes		No
Classification	Declarative		Procedural
	Explicit		Implicit
	Knowledge		Skill
Brain areas			
Cerebral cortex	Pre-SMA	SMA	
	DLPFC	IPS	
		Precuneus	
Basal ganglia	Anterior striatum		Putamen
Cerebellum			Dentate nucleus

Note that the distinction between the early and late learning stages may not be so clear as indicated here (e.g., performance in the late stage is not absolutely specific to the hand). The SMA, IPS, and precuneus are classified as an intermediate group for the following reasons. The SMA, compared with the pre-SMA, contributes to the motor aspect of learning. The IPS and precuneus become active in the later phase of short-term learning.

Abbreviations: Supplementary motor area (SMA), dorsolateral prefrontal cortex (DLPFC), intraparietal sulcus (IPS).

even if a particular set of neurons of brain regions is activated with learning, it may not be actually necessary for learning. Conversely, the inactivation study could produce false-negative errors: even if inactivation of a particular brain region does not disturb learning processes, other intact brain regions could compensate for the function subserved by the inactivated region.

Multiple stages in visuomotor sequence learning

By training monkeys with the 2×5 task, we found that sequence learning is composed of at least three stages (Hikosaka et al., 1995): (1) short-term sequence-selective stage, (2) long-term sequence-selective stage, and (3) long-term sequence-unselective stage.

SHORT-TERM SEQUENCE-SELECTIVE STAGE On encountering a completely new sequence (2×5), our monkeys, after trial-and-error processes, learned to perform the sequence correctly within a few minutes. Although they knew what to do by then, their performance was far from skillful and was slow. On the next day, the monkeys again made some errors for the same sequence (although the number of errors became fewer).

LONG-TERM SEQUENCE-SELECTIVE STAGE After practice of the same sequence for 30 days or more, the monkeys seldom made errors, and the performance became very skillful and fast, like a professional typist. A similar improvement of performance occurred for each new sequence. In this way, the monkeys eventually acquired a set of learned sequences for which they were very skillful. This ability was retained for a long time without practice (e.g., 6 months) (Hikosaka, Miyachi, et al., 1996).

LONG-TERM SEQUENCE-UNSELECTIVE STAGE With a long-term experience of the 2×5 task (e.g., more than 1 year), the monkeys mastered a new sequence with progressively fewer errors. It appeared that they acquired better strategies to learn new sequences.

Emergence of anticipatory movements with long-term practice

There were distinct differences between the short-term learning and the long-term learning (table 39.2) because the performance was much faster in the long-term stage. This was not because the hand movements per se became faster. In fact, the movement time (time between the first and second button presses when the movement was guided fully by visual stimuli) was not different between new and learned sequences or was even shorter for new sequences. A major factor that made the performance faster was the shortening of the button press reaction time (time from stimulus onset to the first button press in each set) (Miyashita et al., 1996). In the short-term stage of learning, the monkeys initiated a saccadic eye movement to one of the two LED buttons after they were illuminated (react-mode). In contrast, in the long-term stage of learning, the monkeys initiated a saccade and hand movement to the correct one of the two LED buttons before they turned on; when the buttons turned on, the gaze already was directed at the correct button, and the hand was positioned close to it (anticipatory mode). Thus, the reaction time was much shortened in the long-term stage compared with the short-term stage, even though the speed of movements was unchanged.

Transition from knowledge to skill with long-term practice

There were additional observations that distinguished the short-term and long-term stages of learning. We had the monkeys use either the right or left hand for a given sequence throughout the learning period. As a result, each monkey had a repertoire of learned sequences, half of which were learned with the right hand and the other half with the left hand. When the monkeys were asked to use the hand that had not been used for long-term practice for a given sequence, their performance became very poor in terms of the number of errors and the performance time, although it was better than the performance for new sequences (Rand, Hikosaka, et al., 1998). However, this was not true for a newly learned sequence. We compared two learning schedules in which a new sequence is learned for two blocks in two consecutive days: (1) using the same hand and (2) using different hands. The performance improved in both cases, although the improvement was somewhat greater in the case of the same hand (Rand et al., unpublished observation). These results suggest that, in the short-term stage of learning, the memory for a visuomotor sequence is accessible to both the trained hand and the untrained hand, implying that the monkeys had explicit knowledge for the sequence, presumably in the visual coordinates. After long-term practice, however, the memory would become largely inaccessible to the untrained hand, implying that the monkeys now relied on implicit skill for performing the sequence.

Human psychological studies have suggested that procedural skill learning involves a declarative-to-procedural transition of learning stages (Fitts, 1964; Anderson, 1982). However, there has been no appropriate experiment using animal subjects to investigate neural mechanisms underlying such a transition of learning stages. Recent human imaging studies have indicated that the pattern of brain activation changes with practice (table 39.1). Some of them may be related to the declarative-to-procedural transition, but there have been few attempts to correlate the brain activation to the transition of learning stages (Sakai et al., 1998). In this sense, our 2×5 task provides an ideal environment to address this issue.

Sequence rather than individual elements is learned

Another interesting observation was on the difference in the nature of memories between the short-term and long-term stages. As already described, each sequence (hyperset) was composed of five sets in which a correct order of button presses was predetermined. After the monkeys acquired a number of learned sequences with long-term practice, we reversed the order of sets while the correct order of button presses remained the same for each sets. Our experiments showed that the performance for the reversed sequences was very poor, as if the monkeys were performing completely new sequences (Rand, Hikosaka, et al., 1998). The result suggests that the monkeys acquired the memories for the whole sequences, rather than the memories for individual elements (sets) separately.

However, this was not necessarily true in the short-term stage of learning. When the monkeys were required to perform the reversed sequence after learning of the original sequence only once, one of the two monkeys tested showed improvement of performance in the same way as when they performed the original sequence again (Rand et al., unpublished observation).

These results suggest that memories are created first for individual elements in a sequence, which then are compiled into a composite memory for the whole sequence after long-term practice. In other words, the monkeys remembered individual elements initially, but not after long-term practice. This is consistent with the aforementioned idea that practice is associated with an explicit-to-implicit transition of procedural memory.

Physiological studies already have disclosed some hints on this issue. That is, neurons that change their activity with particular transitions or combinations of movement sequences, rather than movements per se, have been found in the supplementary motor area (Mushiake, Inase, and Tanji, 1991), caudate nucleus (Kermadi and Joseph, 1995), globus pallidus (Mushiake and Strick, 1996), and dentate nucleus (Mushiake and Strick, 1993).

We wanted to know how such sequential transitions are implemented as neural signals with practice and decided to examine different brain areas using the same 2×5 task, as shown in the following section.

The presupplementary motor area and the supplementary motor area contribute to learning of new sequences, but in different ways

BACKGROUND   The medial part of the frontal cortex includes at least two areas that are related intimately to voluntary movements: the supplementary motor area (SMA) and the pre-SMA (Tanji, 1994). There is evidence that the SMA is related to the *control* of sequential movements (Tanji and Shima, 1994), bimanual coordination (Brinkman, 1984), and internally guided movements (Halsband, Matsuzaka, and Tanji, 1994).

We hypothesized, therefore, that the medial frontal cortex also plays an important role in *learning* of sequential movements. Our study using the 2 × 5 task indicated that the pre-SMA, rather than SMA, contributes to the initial learning of visuomotor sequences (Nakamura, Sakai, and Hikosaka, 1998, 1999). The results were obtained in three lines of experiments (table 39.3): (1) single-unit recording, (2) reversible inactivation (both using monkeys), and (3) fMRI using human subjects.

2 × 5 TASK: SINGLE-UNIT RECORDING   We recorded the activity of single neurons in the medial frontal cortex while the monkeys were performing three to five new sequences and three to five learned sequences (Nakamura, Sakai, and Hikosaka, 1998). We found that many neurons became active preferentially while the monkeys were trying to learn new sequences. Such "new-preferring" neurons were more prevalent in the pre-SMA than in the SMA. A typical pre-SMA neuron would show phasic activity before the first button press for each set if the sequence was new, whereas the same neuron would show almost no activity when the sequence had been learned. The activation for new sequences was unrelated to the side of the hand performing the task; it occurred when either the contralateral or ipsilateral hand was used. There are some neurons that were active preferentially for learned sequences, but their number is smaller and tended to be found in the SMA. These results suggest that the medial frontal cortex, especially the pre-SMA, is related to new learning, rather than long-term memory storage or retrieval.

TABLE 39.3
Summary of 2 × 5 experiments on medial frontal cortex

Brain Region	pre-SMA	SMA
Single-cell activity	New > learned	New = learned
No. of errors		
New	Increase++	Increase ±
Learned	No change	No change
Button-press RT		
New	Increase+	Increase++
Learned	Increase+	Increase+
Anticipatory saccade		
Learned	No change	No change
Hand preference	Bilateral	Contra/bilateral

Hand preference is not absolute; e.g., many neurons in the SMA were preferentially active for the contralateral hand.

Abbreviations: supplementary motor area (SMA), response time (RT).

2 × 5 TASK: REVERSIBLE INACTIVATION   To test this hypothesis, we locally and reversibly inactivated different portions of the pre-SMA and the SMA by injecting a small amount of muscimol unilaterally (Nakamura, Sakai, and Hikosaka, 1999). After a muscimol injection, we had the monkeys perform new and learned sequences. We found that the number of errors (sequence errors) increased for new sequences, but not for learned sequences. This effect was stronger after pre-SMA injections than SMA injections, as expected from the results of single-unit recording. Furthermore, the effect was present when either the contralateral or ipsilateral hand was used, particularly after the pre-SMA injections, again being consistent with the recording data.

Conversely, movement parameters, such as button press reaction time (BP-RT), were affected more clearly by SMA injections. The BP-RT, which is the time from the onset of two target stimuli to the first button press, was much shorter for learned sequences because the hand moved in an anticipatory manner toward the location of the target before it was illuminated (see aforementioned discussion). This parameter thus reflected how anticipatory the performance was, rather than how fast the individual movements were. The BP-RT for new sequences increased after muscimol injections in the SMA more clearly than injections in the pre-SMA. However, anticipatory saccades were not affected by inactivation of either the SMA or the pre-SMA.

2 × 5 TASK: INTERPRETATION   These results, taken together, suggest that both the pre-SMA and the SMA contribute to learning of new sequences, but in different ways. The pre-SMA contributes to the acquisition of correct orders of button presses, whereas the SMA contributes to the acquisition of quicker performance with anticipatory movements. In addition, it was found that more than half of SMA neurons were active preferentially when the contralateral hand was used, whereas most pre-SMA neurons showed no preference for either the contra- or ipsilateral hand.

The difference between the pre-SMA and the SMA led us to propose the following hypothesis: The pre-SMA works to acquire explicit knowledge, whereas the SMA works to acquire implicit skill. Knowledge would be evaluated by the number of errors (in accordance with pre-SMA inactivation), whereas skill would be evaluated by the performance speed (in accordance with SMA inactivation). Knowledge should be unrelated to the performing hand (in accordance with pre-SMA activity), whereas skill may be specific to the hand (in accordance with SMA activity).

2×10 Task: Human Functional Magnetic Resonance Imaging (Medial Frontal Cortex) The aforementioned findings in animal studies are supplemented by the fMRI experiments on human subjects (Hikosaka et al., 1996b). We used basically the same task for human subjects except that the sequence was 2×10 or 3×10 and that the rate of button presses was made constant. For comparison, we used a task in which the subjects were allowed to press buttons in any order. The learning (i.e., learn–any order) was associated with consistent activation of a region in the medial frontal cortex that was slightly anterior to the anterior commissure. We designated this region as a human homologue of the pre-SMA, in accordance with the suggestion proposed by Picard and Strick (1996). The human pre-SMA was not activated with sequential button presses if no learning was involved (any order–rest). Conversely, the SMA, a region posterior to the anterior commissure, was activated with such sensory-motor processes (any order–rest) but not with learning.

Frontal-to-parietal transition of learning-related activation

BACKGROUND   As described in table 39.1, other human imaging studies have shown that multiple brain regions were activated with sequence learning. It therefore is unlikely that only the pre-SMA is related to learning in the 2×10 task. We therefore extended our survey of fMRI by examining the activity of the whole frontal, parietal, and occipital areas.

2×10 Task: Human Functional Magnetic Resonance Imaging   We found that at least four cortical regions were active with learning (Sakai et al., 1998): (1) medial frontal cortex (pre-SMA), (2) lateral frontal cortex (dorsolateral prefrontal cortex), (3) medial parietal cortex (precuneus), and (4) lateral parietal cortex (intraparietal sulcus region) (figure 39.2). Interestingly, there was a global transition of activity from the two frontal regions to the two parietal regions, although the subjects were learning a single visuomotor sequence. Thus, the lateral frontal cortex was active in the early phase, the pre-SMA in the early and intermediate phases, the precuneus in the intermediate phase, and the lateral parietal cortex in the intermediate and advanced stages.

2×10 Task: Interpretation   The frontal activation corresponded to the initial learning phase, during which the performance time increased nearly linearly with the number of targets (if the subjects were asked to perform as quickly as possible), suggesting that the information was processed in a sequential manner–a characteristic feature of attentive processes (Schneider and Shiffrin, 1977). Conversely, the parietal activation corresponded to the intermediate or late phase of learning, during which the performance time decreased, suggesting that the information was processed, at least partly, in a parallel manner–a characteristic feature of automatic processes (Fendrich, Healy, and Bourne, 1991).

2×10 Task: Further Studies   To investigate the nature of pre-SMA activation, we modified the 2×10 task in two ways: (1) a 2×10 color sequence task and (2) a 2×6 position mapping task. In the 2×10 color task, the targets appeared with one of four colors, and the subjects had to press buttons in the correct orders based on their colors, not their positions. The pre-SMA still was active with learning. In the 2×6 mapping task, six pairs of targets (set) with different configurations appeared in a random order so that the subjects had to remember the correct order of button presses depending on the target configuration. The pre-SMA again was active, and this time remained active even after acquisition of button press orders. In short, the pre-SMA becomes active when the response is determined by the current sensory inputs, rather than by the predetermined procedure.

Anterior/posterior functional differentiation of the basal ganglia

BACKGROUND   The basal ganglia have been implicated in reinforcement learning (Robbins and Everitt, 1996; Houk, Adams, and Barto, 1995) and implicit learning (Jackson et al., 1995; Knowlton, Mangels, and Squire, 1996). The role of the basal ganglia in learning also is supported by adaptable changes in neuronal activity in the basal ganglia (Graybiel et al., 1994; Schultz, Apicella, and Ljungberg, 1993; Kawagoe, Takikawa, and Hikosaka, 1998). Neurons in the striatum show activity that anticipates upcoming sensory and motor events (Hikosaka, Sakamoto, and Usui, 1989; Schultz et al., 1992) and show sequence-dependent activation (Kermadi et al., 1993). These results suggest that the basal ganglia are related to learning and memory of sequential procedures.

2×5 Task: Reversible Inactivation   We inactivated different portions of the caudate and putamen by injecting muscimol, usually bilaterally (Miyachi et al., 1997). We classified injection sites into three classes: (1) anterior striatum (head of the caudate and the anterior part of the putamen), (2) mid-posterior putamen, and (3) mid-posterior caudate (figure 39.3; table 39.4). The inactivation of the anterior striatum led to increases in the

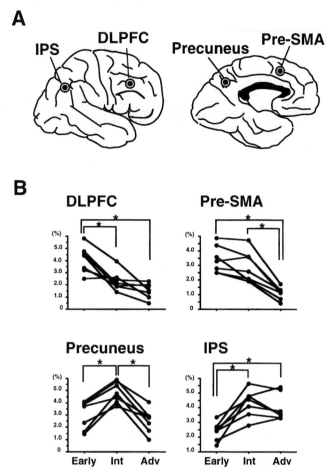

FIGURE 39.2 Transition of learning-related brain activation. Correlation of cortical activation with learning stages. (A) Four cortical areas related to learning of visuomotor sequences: dorsolateral prefrontal cortex (DLPFC), presupplementary motor area (pre-SMA), precuneus, and intraparietal sulcus (IPS). (B) For each cortical area, data obtained from six subjects are shown for the three learning stages: early (left), intermediate (center), and advanced (right) stages. Paired comparisons were made between the learning stages using Wilcoxon's signed rank test; significant differences $(P < .05)$ are indicated by asterisks.

number of sequence errors highly significantly for new sequences and weakly significantly for learned sequences. The inactivation of the mid-posterior putamen led to an increase in the number of errors significantly for learned sequences but not new sequences. The inactivation of the mid-posterior caudate produced effects that were inconsistent and variable.

These results suggest that the anterior striatum is related mainly to acquisition of new sequences, whereas the mid-posterior striatum (putamen) is related to storage or retrieval of long-term memories. The aforementioned suggestion was confirmed by single-unit recordings: neurons in the anterior striatum tended to be more active for new sequences whereas neurons in the mid-posterior putamen tended to be more active for learned sequences.

2×5 TASK: INTERPRETATION The results suggest that the anterior and posterior portions of the basal ganglia

contribute to learning of visuomotor sequences in different ways. What are the relationships between the basal ganglia and the cerebral cortex?

The cerebral cortex and the basal ganglia connect with each other, forming loops of neural circuits, each of which may have a unique function (Alexander and Crutcher, 1990). The anterior-posterior functional differentiation of the basal ganglia suggested by our study may be related to such multiple corticobasal ganglia networks. Thus, the anterior part of the striatum together with the association cortex (especially the dorsolateral prefrontal cortex) form a "cognitive" circuit. However, the mid-posterior portion of the putamen together with the sensory-motor cortex form a "motor" circuit.

Our results are consistent with this view because the anterior striatum (in monkeys) and the dorsolateral prefrontal cortex (in humans) are active in the early stage of

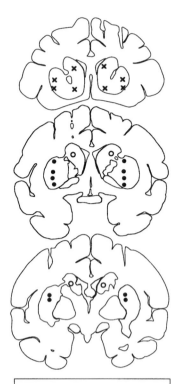

FIGURE 39.3 Sites of muscimol injection in the striatum at three anteroposterior levels (from top to bottom): 6 mm anterior, 2 mm anterior, and 2 mm posterior to the anterior commissure (AC). These injection sites were classified into three groups: anterior striatum (crosses); mid-posterior putamen (filled circles); mid-posterior caudate (open circles). Results are summarized in table 39.4.

learning and that the inactivation of the anterior striatum disrupted new learning. Conversely, it is tempting to presume that the mid-posterior part of the putamen together with some part of the sensory-motor cortex work for storage and retrieval of sequence memories. The SMA is a candidate for this role (Schell and Strick, 1984), but our data suggested that it also contributes to new learning (Nakamura, Sakai, and Hikosaka, 1999). Another possibility is that the presumed role of the mid-posterior putamen in memory storage and retrieval is related to its connection with the primary motor cortex (Künzle, 1975; Hoover and Strick, 1993).

Cerebellar dentate nucleus contributes to long-term memory for procedural skill

BACKGROUND   It is well known that the ability to adjust parameters of reflexes and simple movements is lost without the cerebellum (Thach, Goodkin, and Keathing, 1992). One therefore might assume that the cerebellum

also plays an important role in learning of more complex actions, such as learning of sequential procedures. Although there have been few animal studies focussed on sequence learning, many human imaging studies have shown that the cerebellum is activated during different types of motor and nonmotor learning, including sequence learning (table 39.1). However, in these studies, the precise function and locus for sequence learning were unknown.

2×5 TASK: REVERSIBLE INACTIVATION   We inactivated different portions of the cerebellar nuclei (dentate, interpositus, and fastigial nuclei) by injecting muscimol unilaterally (Lu, Hikosaka, and Miyachi, 1998) (figure 39.4; table 39.5). When the dorsal or central part of the dentate nucleus was inactivated, the number of errors increased significantly for learned sequences but not for new sequences; inactivation of the lateral or ventral portion of the dentate nucleus, interpositus nucleus, or fastigial nucleus produced no effect on learning or memory. Further, the effect was present only when the hand ipsilateral to the injection was used.

Conversely, slowing of movements occurred after any of these inactivations, but again for the ipsilateral hand. This result suggests that the deficits after the inactivation of the dorsal-central portions of the dentate nucleus were not contingent on the movement deficits but reflect the memory deficits.

2×5 TASK: INTERPRETATION   The results suggest that the dorsal and central portions of the dentate nucleus are selectively related to the storage or retrieval of long-term procedural memories for the ipsilateral hand. The unilateral nature of the cerebellar functions is consistent with the former behavioral study showing poor transfer of long-term memory: The monkeys had difficulty in performing learned sequences when they were asked to use the hand that was not used for practice (Rand, Hikosaka, et al., 1998). It also suggests that the cerebellum contributes to implicit skill rather than explicit knowledge. This contrasted with the presumed role of the pre-SMA and dorsolateral prefrontal cortex.

TABLE 39.4
Summary of inactivation experiments on basal ganglia

Brain Region	Anterior Striatum	Posterior Putamen	Posterior Caudate
No. of errors			
New sequences	Increase++	No change	Inconsistent
Learned sequences	Increase+	Increase++	Inconsistent

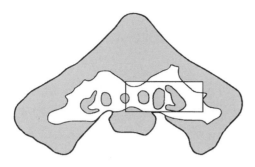

**Increase in Number of Errors
(Learned sequences)**

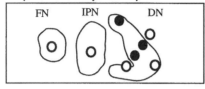

Increase in Movement Time

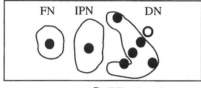

● Effective sites
○ Non-effective sites

FIGURE 39.4 Effects of muscimol injection in the cerebellar nuclei. The cerebellar nuclei on one side (top) are shown enlarged below. The number of errors for learned, but not new, sequences increased after the injections in the dorsomedial, dorsolateral, and central parts of the dentate nucleus (DN). The movement time increased after all injections including the interpositus nucleus (IPN) and fastigial nucleus (FN), except for the injection above the dentate nucleus. See also table 39.5.

The "memory" area of the dentate nucleus, especially the dorsal part, is known to project to the M1 through the thalamus (Middleton and Strick, 1996). It thus is tempting to hypothesize that the cerebello-cerebral network underlies the formation of motor skill. In fact, recent studies have indicated that practice-dependent changes occur in the M1 in animals (Nudo et al., 1996; Asanuma and Pavlides, 1997) and humans (Karni et al., 1995; Classen et al., 1998).

However, human and animal studies have shown that the cerebellum tends to be active in the early stage of learning (table 39.1). We interpret the seeming discrepancy between our results and the results of other studies as follows. The cerebellum may start working from the beginning of learning, but its role is not yet critical because other areas, including the pre-SMA and the anterior striatum, work in parallel to acquire knowledge for correct performance. After long-term practice, however, the performance becomes more dependent on the cerebellar mechanism, which enables quick and skillful movements but is specific to the hand used for the practice. It is unknown, if this is the case, whether the same portion of the dentate nucleus is involved in the early learning process.

Other brain areas also may contribute to sequence learning

Our fMRI study (Sakai et al., 1998) raised the possibility that the medial and lateral parts of the parietal cortex is involved in learning visuomotor sequences. Although the parietal areas were activated after the frontal areas, their activation largely disappeared after an extensive practice (Sakai et al., 1998). This might indicate that the parietal cortex is related to learning in its intermediate stage.

Findings on the medial part of the parietal cortex (precuneus) in human imaging studies might be relevant to our results. Thus, mental navigation of familiar routes was associated with distinct activation of the precuneus (Ghaem et al., 1997; Maguire, Frackowiak, and Firth, 1997). Crucial in navigation is the information on visuomotor sequences, as in our 2×10 task.

Other brain regions to be studied include the premotor cortex, cingulate cortex, hippocampal region, and limbic system. There has been no attempt in animal studies to study these areas in relation to learning of sequential procedures.

Parallel networks for procedural learning– A hypothesis

CONCEPTUAL SCHEME Based on the results of our studies and other related studies, we propose a hypothesis on the neural mechanism for learning of visuomotor sequences. A key feature of our hypothesis, shown in figure 39.5A (see also color plate 24), is that there are separate systems in the brain that contribute to different aspects of visuomotor sequence learning (Nakahara, 1997; Nakahara et al., 1997). Here we postulate "event sequence system" and "action sequence system," which work independently. They use different coordinate systems: the visual and motor coordinates, respectively. There are two ways in which these learning systems communicate with each other: through a "coordinator" and a "translator." The coordinator determines to allow or disallow the opponent system to work, whereas the translator converts information from one coordinate to the other.

We further hypothesize that there are two systems that support the parallel learning systems: (1) the reinforcement learning system and (2) the motor sequence system. The reinforcement system (assigned to the basal

TABLE 39.5
Summary of inactivation experiments on cerebellar nuclei

| | Dentate Nucleus | | | |
Brain Region	Dorsal and Central	Ventral and Lateral	Interpositus Nucleus	Fastigial Nucleus
No. of errors				
New sequences	No change	No change	No change	No change
Learned sequences	Increase++	No change	No change	No change
Movement speed	Decrease++	Decrease++	Decrease++	Decrease++
Anticipatory saccade				
Learned	Decrease+	No change	Decrease+	No change
Hand preference	Ipsilateral	Ipsilateral	Ipsilateral	Ipsilateral

ganglia) determines whether a sequence of events or actions is to be learned; this is based on whether the final outcome of the action sequence is beneficial (or rewarding) for the animal. The motor sequence system (assigned to the cerebellum), by interacting with the event and action sequence systems, works to refine the movements constituting each action.

NETWORK MODEL   Let us elaborate on the hypothesis by relating these functional modules to actual brain areas, as shown in figure 39.5B. We try to reach an agreement based on three sources of information: (1) our experimental findings, (2) experimental findings from other laboratories, and (3) known anatomic connections. There may, of course, be other ways to do so, and the scheme in figure 39.5B is subject to change in the course of future studies.

We assign the event and action sequence systems, respectively, to the dorsolateral prefrontal cortex (DLPF)[2] and the SMA.[3] We have added two pathways that bypass these systems; they would work when no learning is involved: (1) the pathway from the posterior parietal cortex to the frontal eye field for visually guided saccadic eye movements (Schall et al., 1995) and (2) the pathway from the anterior parietal cortex to the motor cortex for hand movements guided by somatosensory means (Strick and Kim, 1978). In figure 39.5A, the coordinator and translator are indicated to be bidirectional, but we consider a unidirectional case in figure 39.5B, from the event sequence system to the action sequence system.

The coordinator (assigned to the pre-SMA) compares the current visual input (Vi) and the predicted visual input (Vp) and, if they do not match (mismatch indicated by ΔV), suppresses the learning function of the action sequence system and at the same time facilitates the translator. The predicted input is provided by the event sequence system.[4] The mismatch between the current and predicted inputs (ΔV) would occur on

two occasions: (1) when the animal starts to learn a new sequence (Nakamura, Sakai, and Hikosaka, 1998) and (2) when the sequence is changed (Shima et al., 1996; Matsuzaka and Tanji, 1996). In this case, the visual input is used directly to guide eye movements through the frontal eye field (FEF) and indirectly to guide hand movements through the translator (assigned to the premotor area [PM][5]), while the event sequence system learns the visual sequence. The translator is needed because the retinotopic information must be translated into the somatotopic information, a process frequently called "inverse kinematics" (Kawato, Furukawa, and Suzuki, 1987).

As the event sequence system learns the visual sequence, its output (predicted visual input) matches the current visual input, so that the coordinator (pre-SMA) becomes inactive[6] and therefore the action sequence system starts to learn the sequence.[7] At this stage, however, the learning of motor sequences still is guided by the visually guided mechanism, which involves the posterior parietal cortex, the FEF, and the PM.[8] By repeating this procedure, the motor sequence system implements the sequence in the motor

FIGURE 39.5   A model for learning of sequential procedures based on our data and the data from other laboratories. (A) Conceptual scheme that postulates two parallel learning systems, one using the visual coordinates (event sequence system) and the other using the motor coordinates (action sequence system). They communicate with each other by means of a coordinator and a translator. We further postulate two subsystems. The reinforcement system acts to decide which sequences are to be learned. The motor sequence system acts to refine individual movements constituting the action sequence. (B) An attempt to correlate the conceptual scheme with actual brain regions. Visual information during the performance of sequence procedures is fed back to the event sequence system (event predictor, assigned to the DLPF) by means of the inferior parietal cortex, whereas motor (or somatosensory) information is fed back to the action sequence system (action predictor, SMA) by means of the superior parietal cortex.

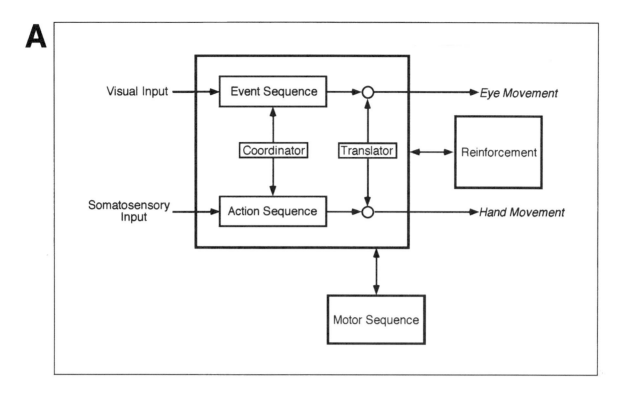

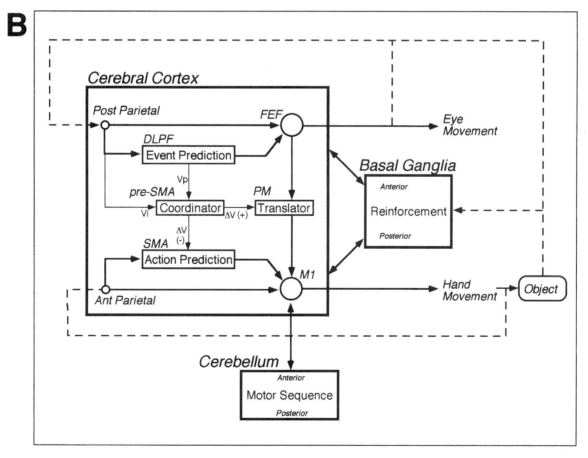

coordinates and finally dominates over the visually guided system.

The key role of the reinforcement system (assigned to the basal ganglia) is to determine whether current or preceding actions are beneficial for the animal. The dopaminergic system in the basal ganglia would carry such reinforcement signals to the striatum to enhance or depress the corticostriatal synapses (Schultz et al., 1992). The evaluated signals would then be fed back to the corresponding cortical regions to modulate the cortical learning processes (Hikosaka, 1994). The ability of the basal ganglia system to predict upcoming reward (Houk, Adams, and Barto, 1995) is very useful in learning of behavioral sequences. Different parts of the basal ganglia would guide different parts of the cerebral cortex. For example, the anterior portion of the striatum is connected with the cortical areas related to the event sequence system, whereas the posterior striatum (putamen) is connected with the cortical areas related to the action sequence system (Parent, 1990), consistent with the results of our inactivation experiments (Miyachi et al., 1997).

The motor sequence system (assigned to the cerebellum) contributes to refinement of individual movements constituting an action, which is the basis of motor skill. Particularly important in such motor skill would be the control and learning of timing.[9] We postulate that the anterior part of the cerebellum learns to implement time sequences, whereas the posterior part detects the difference between the predicted timing and the actual timing[10]—an algorithm similar to that for the DLPF and pre-SMA. After long-term practice, the anterior cerebellum acquires a fixed timing sequence, the predicted timing matches the actual timing, and therefore the posterior cerebellum becomes inactive, and consequently the anterior cerebellum sends the predicted outputs to the M1 (Middleton and Strick, 1994). The performance at this stage is very skillful and stereotyped. It requires little activation of the visual sequence system and therefore is carried out without conscious control. The finely tuned timing information derived from the anterior cerebellum also would be critical in coordinating sequential transitions of different sensory-motor systems (Thach, Goodkin, and Keating, 1992). The anterior cerebellum would control exclusively one side of the hand (i.e., ipsilateral side), as Lu and associates (1998) demonstrated; otherwise, the animal would not be able to acquire skill for each hand.

OPPOSITE HAND EXPERIMENT   Note that the action or motor sequence system is largely specific to the side of the performing hand, whereas the event sequence system is not. After long-term practice using one hand, the

performance is largely dependent on the outputs of the action and motor sequence systems. If the animal then is asked to use the opposite hand, the performance would be very poor because the action or motor sequence system for this hand has little access to the information on the learned sequence. This actually was demonstrated by Rand, Hikosaka, and associates (1998).

RELATION TO INACTIVATION EXPERIMENTS

Pre-SMA   At the beginning of learning, the performance typically should be dependent on the event sequence system, which deals with visual and working memory information. The inactivation of the pre-SMA would have two effects. First, because the action sequence system is not suppressed in the early stage of learning, it acquires sequence information, whether it is correct or not. Such erratic motor signals would distract the correct performance. Second, because the translator (PM) does not receive excitatory inputs from the pre-SMA, visual sequence information would not be converted appropriately to motor information. These two effects, taken together, hinder the initial stage of sequence learning. In contrast, the performance after long-term practice is largely dependent on the action and motor sequence systems so that it hardly would be affected by the inactivation of the pre-SMA. This is exactly what Nakamura, Sakai, and Hikosaka (1999) demonstrated.

Striatum   The anterior and posterior parts of the basal ganglia would provide the event and action sequence systems, respectively, with reinforcement signals. The inactivation of the anterior striatum would disrupt learning of event sequences, which is dominant in the early stage of sequence learning; the inactivation of the posterior striatum would disrupt learning of action sequences, which is dominant in the late stage. The results of Miyachi and associates (1997) correspond to this prediction.

Dentate nucleus of the cerebellum   The dorsal part of the dentate nucleus is connected with the M1 (Middleton and Strick, 1994) to support the skillful and implicit performance. Inactivation of this region thus would affect the performance only after extensive practice and only when the ipsilateral hand is used, as demonstrated by Lu and associates (1998).

The inactivation of the posterior cerebellum and the ventral or lateral portion of the dentate nucleus would affect learning when it still is dependent on the visual sequence. We did not see such effects, perhaps because we did not inactivate the dentate nucleus bilaterally.

Conclusions

Based on behavioral experiments on trained monkeys, we have shown that learning of sequential procedures occurs in at least two stages: (1) a short-term stage (within a session), in which the subject correctly but slowly performs the sequence by reacting to individual visual stimuli (implying an explicit process); and (2) a long-term stage (across days), in which the sequence is performed quickly with a chain of anticipatory movements (implying an implicit process). Subsequent physiological experiments on trained monkeys and human subjects have revealed neural correlates of the transition of the learning stage because multiple brain regions contribute to the learning in different ways and with different time courses. The frontal cortex (pre-SMA and DLPF), together with the anterior part of the basal ganglia, contributes to the initiation of short-term learning, which is guided by visual information. The SMA, another part of the frontal cortex, also contributes to the short-term stage of learning, but more so for improvement of motor performance. The long-term learning stage is supported by the regions including the posterior part of the basal ganglia and the dentate nucleus of the cerebellum. The contribution of the cerebellum is limited to the hand used for practice, suggesting an implicit process (in agreement with the behavioral data).

However, our experiments showed that the learning was disrupted only partially by inactivation of one of these areas, suggesting that multiple regions subserve the learning concurrently. This led us to propose a model for learning of sequential procedures. A key feature of this model is that the information on a sequential procedure is acquired in parallel by two learning systems, one coding the sequence in the visual coordinates (event sequence system, assigned to DLPF) and the other coding the sequence in the motor coordinates (action sequence system, SMA). These systems communicate with each other via a coordinator (pre-SMA) and a translator (PM). In the course of learning, the coordinator acts to shift the weight of contribution from the event sequence system to the action sequence system. After long-term practice, the sequential procedure can be produced largely by the action sequence system, which can produce the sequence directly without visual-to-motor translation.

These two learning systems are supported by two subsystems, one for reinforcement learning (basal ganglia) and the other for motor sequence learning (cerebellum). The reinforcement learning system acts to decide whether the performed sequence is to be learned based on the reward outcome of the procedure. The motor sequence system acts to refine and coordinate individual movements based on timing information.

The model obviously is incomplete but provides a working scheme to consider possible ways in which the brain works in a goal-directed manner because the brain, after all, is composed of parallel, distributed neural networks.

ACKNOWLEDGMENTS The authors thank Makoto Kato for designing the computer programs for animal experiments, Kenji Doya for providing valuable advice in theoretical approaches, and Satoru Miyauchi, Ryousuke Takino, Yuka Sasaki, and Benno Pütz for contributing to the fMRI experiments.

This study was supported by (1) the Uehara Memorial Foundation; (2) Grant-in-Aid for Scientific Research on Priority Areas from The Ministry of Education, Science and Culture of Japan; and (3) The Japan Society for the Promotion of Science (JSPS) Research for the Future program.

NOTES

1. Abbreviations: dorsolateral prefrontal cortex (DLPF), pre-supplementary motor area (pre-SMA), supplementary motor area (SMA), intraparietal sulcus region (IPS), premotor area (PM), frontal eye field (FEF), supplementary eye field (SEF), primary motor cortex (M1).
2. The DLPF is crucial for various processes for working memory (Goldman-Rakic, 1996), including coding of behavioral sequences (Petrides, 1995). However, it seems unlikely that DLPF stores event sequence information as a long-term memory. Such a long-term memory function may be carried out by other brain areas, perhaps including the precuneus or the intraparietal areas (Sakai et al., 1998).
3. Many studies have suggested that motor sequences are coded by neurons in the SMA (Tanji and Shima, 1994) and that the human SMA is activated with learning of motor sequences (Jenkins et al., 1994; Petersen et al., 1998). Our studies also suggest the SMA is related to anticipatory expression of learned motor sequences (Miyashita et al., 1996).
4. The pre-SMA receives inputs from the DLPF (Luppino et al., 1993) which may carry information on event prediction, and from the posterior parietal cortex (Luppino et al., 1993), which may carry current visual inputs.
5. The PM appears to be related to the visuomotor coordinate transformation, as shown by visually guided actions (Passingham, 1985; Rizzolatti et al., 1996), action recognition (Gallese et al., 1996), and object-centered visual responses (Graziano, Hu, and Gross, 1997).
6. Pre-SMA neurons tend to decrease activity as the number of errors decreased with learning (Nakamura, Sakai, and Hikosaka, 1998; Sakai et al., 1998).
7. Note that, after the action sequence system starts learning, the event sequence system would continue to learn the visual sequence to store it as a long-term memory, perhaps outside the DLPF.
8. The SMA may be learning a motor sequence while the performance still is guided by visual inputs (i.e., relative early stage of long-term learning, as our study suggested) (Nakamura, Sakai, and Hikosaka, 1998).

9. Many studies have suggested that the cerebellum is related to the timing process (Ivry and Keele, 1989; Jueptner et al., 1996).
10. Our unpublished observation (Sakai et al., 1999) using fMRI indicates that the posterolateral part of the cerebellum is activated selectively when the timing of response is uncertain, whereas the pre-SMA is active when the kind of response is uncertain. Conversely, it still is unknown whether the anterior cerebellum is involved in storage of timing information.

REFERENCES

AIZAWA, H., M. INASE, H. MUSHIAKE, K. SHIMA, and J. TANJI, 1991. Reorganization of activity in the supplementary motor area associated with motor learning and functional recovery. *Exp. Brain Res.* 84:668–671.

ALEXANDER, G. E., and M. D. CRUTCHER, 1990. Functional architecture of basal ganglia circuits: Neural substrates of parallel processing. *Trends Neurosci.* 13:266–271.

ANDERSON, J. R., 1982. Acquisition of cognitive skill. *Psychol. Rev.* 89:369–406.

AOSAKI, T., H. TSUBOKAWA, A. ISHIDA, K. WATANABE, A. M. GRAYBIEL, and M. KIMURA, 1994. Responses of tonically active neurons in the primate's striatum undergo systematic changes during behavioral sensorimotor conditioning. *J. Neurosci.* 14:3969–3984.

ASANUMA, H., and A. KELLER, 1991. Neuronal mechanisms of motor learning in mammals. *Neuroreport* 2:217–224.

ASANUMA, H., and C. PAVLIDES, 1997. Neurobiological basis of motor learning in mammals. *Neuroreport* 8:i–vi.

BAIZER, J. S., and M. GLICKSTEIN, 1974. Role of cerebellum in prism adaptation. *J. Physiol.* 236:34–35.

BELL, C. C., V. Z. HAN, Y. SUGAWARA, and K. GRANT, 1997. Synaptic plasticity in a cerebellum-like structure depends on temporal order. *Nature* 387:278–281.

BLOEDEL, J. R., V. BRACHA, Y. SHIMANSKY, and M. S. MILAK, 1996. The role of the cerebellum in the acquisition of comoplex volitional forelimb movements. In: *The Acquisition of Motor Behavior in Vertebrates*, J. R. Bloedel, T. J. Ebner, and S. P. Wise, eds. Cambridge: The MIT Press, pp. 319–342.

BRINKMAN, C., 1984. Supplementary motor area of the monkey's cerebral cortex: Short- and long-term deficits after unilateral ablation and the effects of subsequent callosal section. *J. Neurosci.* 4:918–929.

CANAVAN, A. G. M., P. D. NIXON, and R. E. PASSINGHAM, 1989. Motor learning in monkeys (*Macaca fascicularis*) with lesions in motor thalamus. *Exp. Brain Res.* 77:113–126.

CHEN, L. L., and S. P. WISE, 1995. Neuronal activity in the supplementary eye field during acquisition of conditional oculomotor associations. *J. Neurophysiol.* 73:1101–1121.

CHEN, Y.-C., D. THALER, P. D. NIXON, C. E. STERN, and R. E. PASSINGHAM, 1995. The functions of the medial premotor cortex: II. The timing and selection of learned movements. *Exp. Brain Res.* 102:461–473.

CLASSEN, J., J. LIEPERT, S. P. WISE, M. HALLETT, and L. G. COHEN, 1998. Rapid plasticity of human cortical movement representation induced by practice. *J. Neurophysiol.* 79:1117–1123.

COHEN, N. J., and L. R. SQUIRE, 1980. Preserved learning and retention of pattern-analyzing skill in amnesia: Dissociation of knowing how and knowing that. *Science* 210:207–210.

DEIBER, M.-P., S. P. WISE, M. HONDA, M. J. CATALAN, J. GRAFMAN, and M. HALLETT, 1997. Frontal and parietal networks for conditional motor learning: A positron emission tomography study. *J. Neurophysiol.* 78:977–991.

DOMINEY, P. F., J. VENTRE-DOMINEY, E. BROUSSOLLE, and M. JEANNEROD, 1997. Analogical transfer is effective in a serial reaction time task in Parkinson's disease: Evidence for a dissociable form of sequence learning. *Neuropsychologia* 35:1–9.

DOYON, J., D. GAUDREAU, R. LAFORCE, M. CASTONGUAY, P. J. BEDARD, F. BEDARD, and J.-P. BOUCHARD, 1997. Role of the striatum, cerebellum, and frontal lobes in the learning of a visuomotor sequence. *Brain Cogn.* 34:218–245.

DOYON, J., A. M. OWEN, M. PETRIDES, V. SZIKLAS, and A. EVANS, 1996. Functional anatomy of visuomotor skill learning in human subjects examined with positron emission tomography. *Eur. J. Neurosci.* 8:637–648.

DREWE, E. A., 1975. Go/no-go learning after frontal lobe lesions in humans. *Cortex* 11:8–16.

FABRE-THORPE, M., and F. LEVERSQUE, 1991. Visuo-motor relearning after brain damage crucially depends on the integrity of the ventrolateral thalamic nucleus. *Behav. Neurosci.* 105:176–192.

FAGLIONI P., M. SCARPA, C. BOTTI, and V. FERRARI, 1995. Parkinson's disease affects automatic and spares intentional verbal learning a stochastic approach to explicit learning processes. *Cortex* 31:597–617.

FENDRICH, D. W., A. F. HEALY, and L. E. J. BOURNE, 1991. Long-term repetition effects for motoric and perceptual procedures. *J. Exp. Psychol. Learn. Mem. Cogn.* 17:137–151.

FIEZ, J. A., S. E. PETERSEN, M. K. CHENEY, and M. E. RAICHLE, 1992. Impaired non-motor learning and error detection associated with cerebellar damage. *Brain* 115:155–178.

FITTS, P. M., 1964. Perceptual-motor skill learning. In: *Categories of Human Learning*, A. W. Melton, ed. New York: Academic Press, pp. 243–285.

FLAMENT, D., J. M. ELLERMANN, S.-G. KIM, K. UGURBIL, and T. J. EBNER, 1996. Functional magnetic resonance imaging of cerebellar activation during the learning of a visuomotor dissociation task. *Hum. Brain Mapping* 4:210–226.

FRITH, C. D., C. A. BLOXHAM, and K. N. CARPENTER, 1986. Impairments in the learning and performance of a new manual skill in patients with Parkinson's disease. *J. Neurol. Neurosurg. Psychiatry* 49:661–668.

GALLESE, V., L. FADIGA, L. FOGASSI, and G. RIZZOLATTI, 1996. Action recognition in the premotor cortex. *Brain* 119:593–609.

GERMAIN, L., and Y. LAMARRE, 1993. Neuronal activity in the motor and premotor cortices before and after learning the associations between auditory stimuli and motor responses. *Brain Res.* 611:175–179.

GHAEM, O., E. MELLET, F. CRIVELLO, N. TZOURIO, B. MAZOYER, A. BERTHOZ, and M. DENIS, 1997. Mental navigation along memorized routes activates the hippocampus, precuneus and insula. *Neuroreport* 8:739–744.

GOLDMAN-RAKIC, P. S., 1996. Regional and cellular fractionation of working memory. *Proc. Natl. Acad. Sci. U.S.A.* 93:13473–13480.

GRAFTON, S. T., J. C. MAZZIOTTA, S. PRESTY, K. J. FRISTON, R. S. J. FRACKOWIAK, and M. E. PHELPS, 1992. Functional anatomy of human procedural learning determined with regional cerebral blood flow and PET. *J. Neurosci.* 12:2542–2548.

GRAYBIEL, A. M., T. AOSAKI, A. FLAHERTY, and M. KIMURA, 1994. The basal ganglia and adaptive motor control. *Science* 265:1826–1831.

GRAZIANO, M. S. A., X. T. HU, and C. G. GROSS, 1997. Visuospatial properties of ventral premotor cortex. *J. Neurophysiol.* 77:2268–2292.

HALSBAND, U., and H. J. FREUND, 1990. Premotor cortex and conditional motor learning in man. *Brain* 113:207–222.

HALSBAND, U., Y. MATSUZAKA, and J. TANJI, 1994. Neuronal activity in the primate supplementary, pre-supplementary and premotor cortex during externally and internally instructed sequential movements. *Neurosci. Res.* 20:149–155.

HIKOSAKA, O., 1994. Role of basal ganglia in control of innate movements, learned behavior and cognition–A hypothesis. In: *The Basal Ganglia IV: New Ideas and Data on Structure and Function,* G. Percheron, J. S. McKenzie, and J. Feger eds. New York: Plenum Press, pp. 589–596.

HIKOSAKA, O., S. MIYACHI, K. MIYASHITA, and M. K. RAND, 1996. Learning of sequential procedures in monkeys. In: *The Acquisition of Motor Behavior in Vertebrates,* J. R. Bloedel, T. J. Ebner, and S. P. Wise, eds. Cambridge, The MIT Press, pp. 303–317.

HIKOSAKA, O., M. K. RAND, S. MIYACHI, and K. MIYASHITA, 1995. Learning of sequential movements in the monkey–Process of learning and retention of memory. *J. Neurophysiol.* 74:1652–1661.

HIKOSAKA, O., K. SAKAI, S. MIYAUCHI, R. TAKINO, Y. SASAKI, and B. PÜTZ, 1996. Activation of human presupplementary motor area in learning of sequential procedures: A functional MRI study. *J. Neurophysiol.* 76:617–621.

HIKOSAKA, O., M. SAKAMOTO, and S. USUI, 1989. Functional properties of monkey caudate neurons: III. Activities related to expectation of target and reward. *J. Neurophysiol.* 61:814–832.

HOOVER, J. E., and P. L. STRICK, 1993. Multiple output channels in the basal ganglia. *Science* 259:819–821.

HOUK, J. C., J. L. ADAMS, and A. BARTO, 1995. A model of how the basal ganglia generate and use neural signals that predict reinforcement. In: *Models of Information Processing in the Basal Ganglia,* J. C. Houk, J. L. Davis, and D. G. Beiser, eds. Cambridge: MIT Press, pp. 249–270.

IMAMIZU, H., S. MIYAUCHI, Y. SASAKI, R. TAKINO, B. PÜTZ, and M. KAWATO, 1997. Separated modules for visuomotor control and learning in the cerebellum: A functional MRI study. *NeuroImage* 5:S598.

INOUE, K., R. KAWASHIMA, K. SATOH, S. KINOMURA, R. GOTO, M. SUGIURA, M. ITO, and H. FUKUDA, 1997. Activity in the parietal area during visuomotor learning with optical rotation. *Neuroreport* 8:3979–3983.

IVRY, R. I., and S. W. KEELE, 1989. Timing functions of the cerebellum. *J. Cogn. Neurosci.* 1:134–150.

JACKSON, G. M., S. R. JACKSON, J. HARRISON, L. HENDERSON, and C. KENNARD, 1995. Serial reaction time learning and Parkinson's disease: Evidence for a procedural learning deficit. *Neuropsychologia* 33:577–593.

JENKINS, I. H., D. J. BROOKS, P. D. NIXON, R. S. J. FRACKOWIAK, and R. E. PASSINGHAM, 1994. Motor sequence learning: A study with positron emission tomography. *J. Neurosci.* 14:3775–3790.

JUEPTNER, M., L. FLERICH, C. WEILLER, S. P. MUELLER, and H.-C. DIENER, 1996. The human cerebellum and temporal information processing-results from a PET experiment. *Neuroreport* 7:2761–2765.

JUEPTNER, M., C. D. FRITH, D. J. BROOKS, R. S. J. FRACKOWIAK, and R. E. PASSINGHAM, 1997. Anatomy of motor learning. II. Subcortical structures and learning by trial and error. *J Neurophysiol* 77:1325–1337.

JUEPTNER, M., K. M. STEPHAN, C. D. FRITH, D. J. BROOKS, R. S. J. FRACKOWIAK, and R. E. PASSINGHAM, 1997. Anatomy of motor learning: I. Frontal cortex and attention to action. *J. Neurophysiol.* 77:1313–1324.

KARNI, A., G. MEYER, P. JEZZARD, M. M. ADAMS, R. TURNER, and L. G. UNGERLEIDER, 1995. Functional MRI evidence for adult motor cortex plasticity during motor skill learning. *Nature* 377:155–158.

KARNI, A., G. MEYER, C. REY-HIPOLITO, P. JEZZARD, M. M. ADAMS, R. TURNER, and L. G. UNGERLEIDER, 1998. The acquisition of skilled motor performance: Fast and slow experience–driven changes in primary motor cortex. *Proc. Natl. Acad. Sci. U.S.A.* 95:861–868.

KAWAGOE, R., Y. TAKIKAWA, and O. HIKOSAKA, 1998. Expectation of reward modulates cognitive signals in the basal ganglia. *Nat. Neurosci.* 5:411–416.

KAWATO, M., K. FURUKAWA, and R. SUZUKI, 1987. A hierarchical neural-network model for control and learning of voluntary movement. *Biol. Cybern.* 57:169–185.

KERMADI, I., and J. P. JOSEPH, 1995. Activity in the caudate nucleus of monkey during spatial sequencing. *J. Neurophysiol.* 74:911–933.

KERMADI, I., Y. JURQUET, M. ARZI, and J. P. JOSEPH, 1993. Neural activity in the caudate nucleus of monkeys during spatial sequencing. *Exp. Brain Res.* 94:352–356.

KLEIM, J. A., E. LUSSNIG, E. R. SCHWARZ, T. A. COMERY, and W. T. GREENOUGH, 1996. Synaptogenesis and FOS expression in the motor cortex of the adult rat after motor skill learning. *J. Neurosci.* 16:4529–4535.

KLEIM, J. A., K. VIJ, D. H. BALLARD, and W. T. GREENOUGH, 1997. Learning-dependent synaptic modifications in the cerebellar cortex of the adult rat persist for at least four weeks. *J. Neurosci.* 17:717–721.

KNOPMAN, D., and M. J. NISSEN, 1991. Procedural learning is impaired in Huntington's disease: Evidence from the serial reaction time task. *Neuropsychologia* 29:245–254.

KNOPMAN, D. S., and M. J. NISSEN, 1987. Implicit learning in patients with probable Alzheimer's disease. *Neurology* 37:784–788.

KNOWLTON, B. J., J. A. MANGELS, and L. R. SQUIRE, 1996. A neostriatal habit learning system in humans. *Science* 273:1399–1402.

KUBOTA, K., and H. KOMATSU, 1985. Neuron activities of monkey prefrontal cortex during the learning of visual discrimination tasks with GO/NO-GO performances. *Neurosci. Res.* 3:106–129.

KUHL, P. K., 1994. Learning and representation in speech and language. *Curr. Opin. Neurobiol.* 4:812–822.

KÜNZLE, H., 1975. Bilateral projections from the precentral motor cortex to the putamen and other parts of the basal ganglia: An autoradiographic study in *Macaca fascicularis*. *Brain Res.* 88:195–209.

LANG, W., M. LANG, I. PODREKA, M. STEINER, F. UHL, E. SUESS, C. MÜLLER, and L. DEECKE, 1988. DC-potential shifts and regional cerebral flow reveal frontal cortex involvement in human visuomotor learning. *Exp. Brain Res.* 71:353–364.

LOU, J. S., and J. S. BLOEDEL, 1992. Responses of sagittally aligned Purkinje cells during perturbed locomotion: Relation of climbing fiber activation to simple spike modulation. *J. Neurophysiol.* 68:1820–1833.

LU, X., O. HIKOSAKA, and S. MIYACHI, 1998. Role of monkey cerebellar nuclei in skill for sequential movement. *J. Neurophysiol.* 79:2245–2254.

LUPPINO, G., M. MATELLI, R. CAMARDA, and G. RIZZOLATTI, 1993. Corticocortical connections of area F3 (SMA-proper) and area F6 (pre-SMA) in the macaque monkey. *J. Comp. Neurol.* 338:114–140.

MAGUIRE, E. A., R. S. J. FRACKOWIAK, and C. D. FRITH, 1997. Recalling routes around London: Activation of the right hippocampus in taxi drivers. *J. Neurosci.* 15:7103–7110.

MALAMUT, B. L., R. C. SAUNDERS, and M. MISHKIN, 1984. Monkeys with combined amygdalo-hippocampal lesions succeed in object discrimination learning despite 24-hour intertrial intervals. *Behav. Neurosci.* 98:759–769.

MARTIN, T. A., J. G. KEATING, H. P. GOODKIN, A. J. BASTIAN, and W. T. THACH, 1996a. Throwing while looking through prisms: I. Focal olivocerebellar lesions impair adaptation. *Brain* 119:1183–1198.

MARTIN, T. A., J. G. KEATING, H. P. GOODKIN, A. J. BASTIAN, and W. T. THACH, 1996b. Throwing while looking through prisms: II. Specificity and storage of multiple gaze-throw calibrations. *Brain* 119:1199–1211.

MATSUZAKA, Y., and J. TANJI, 1996. Changing directions of forthcoming arm movements: Neuronal activity in the presupplementary and supplementary motor area of monkey cerebral cortex. *J. Neurophysiol.* 76:2327–2342.

MATSUZAWA, T., 1996. Chimpanzee intelligence in nature and in captivity: isomorphism of symbol use and tool use. In: *Great Ape Societies,* W. C. McGrew, L. F. Marchant, and T. Nishida, eds. Cambridge, U.K.: Cambridge University Press, pp. 196–209.

MIDDLETON, F. A., and P. L. STRICK, 1994. Anatomical evidence for cerebellar and basal ganglia involvement in higher cognitive functions. *Science* 266:458–461.

MIDDLETON, F. A., and P. L. STRICK, 1996. New concept regarding the organization of basal ganglia and cerebellar output. In: *Integrative and Molecular Approach to Brain Function,* M. Ito and Y. Miyashita, eds. Amsterdam: Elsevier, pp. 253–269.

MITZ, A. R., M. GODSCHALK, and S. P. WISE, 1991. Learning-dependent neuronal activity in the premotor cortex: Activity during the acquisition of conditional motor associations. *J. Neurosci.* 11:1855–1872.

MIYACHI, S., O. HIKOSAKA, K. MIYASHITA, Z. KARÁDI, and M. K. RAND, 1997. Differential roles of monkey striatum in learning of sequential hand movement. *Exp. Brain Res.* 115:1–5.

MIYASHITA, K., M. K. RAND, S. MIYACHI, and O. HIKOSAKA, 1996. Anticipatory saccades in sequential procedural learning in monkeys. *J. Neurophysiol.* 76:1361–1366.

MOLINARI, M., M. G. LEGGIO, A. SOLIDA, R. CIORRA, S. MISCIAGNA, M. C. SILVERI, and L. PETROSINI, 1997. Cerebellum and procedural learning: Evidence from focal cerebellar lesions. *Brain* 120:1753–1762.

MUSHIAKE, H., M. INASE, and J. TANJI, 1991. Neuronal activity in the primate premotor, supplementary, and precentral motor cortex during visually guided and internally determined sequential movements. *J. Neurophysiol.* 66:705–718.

MUSHIAKE, H., and P. STRICK, 1996. Pallidal neuron activity during sequential arm movements. *J. Neurophysiol.* 74:2754–2758.

MUSHIAKE, H., and P. L. STRICK, 1993. Preferential activity of dentate neurons during limb movements guided by vision. *J. Neurophysiol.* 70:2660–2664.

NAKAHARA, H., 1997. *Sequential Decision Making in Biological Systems: The Role of Nonlinear Dynamical Phenomena in Working Memory and Reinforcement Learning in Long-Term Memory.* Tokyo, University of Tokyo.

NAKAHARA, H., K. DOYA, O. HIKOSAKA, and S. NAGANO, 1997. Multiple representations in the basal ganglia loops for acquisition and execution of sequential motor control. *Soc. Neurosci. Abs.* 23:778.

NAKAMURA, K., K. SAKAI, and O. HIKOSAKA, 1998. Neuronal activity in medial frontal cortex during learning of sequential procedures. *J. Neurophysiol.* 80:2671–2687.

NAKAMURA, K., K. SAKAI, and O. HIKOSAKA, 1999. Effects of local inactivation of monkey medial frontal cortex in learning of sequential procedures. *J. Neurophysiol.* (in press).

NEWELL, A., and P. S. ROSENBLOOM, 1981. Mechanisms of skill acquisition and the law of practice. In: *Cognitive Skills and Their Acquisition,* J. R. Anderson, ed. Hillsdale, N.J.: Erlbaum, pp. 1–55.

NISSEN, M. J., and P. BULLEMER, 1987. Attentional requirements of learning: Evidence from performance measures. *Cogn. Psychol.* 19:1–32.

NUDO, R. J., G. W. MILLIKEN, W. M. JENKINS, and M. M. MERZENICH, 1996. Use-dependent alterations of movement representations in primary motor cortex of adult squirrel monkeys. *J. Neurosci.* 16:785–807.

OJAKANGAS, C. L., and T. J. EBNER, 1994. Purkinje cell complex spike activity during voluntary motor learning: Relationship to kinematics. *J. Neurophysiol.* 72:2617–2630.

OLMSTEAD, C. E., J. R. VILLABLANCA, R. J. MARCUS, and D. L. AVERY, 1976. Effects of caudate nuclei and frontal cortex ablations in cats: IV. Bar pressing, maze learning, and performance. *Exp. Neurol.* 53:670–693.

PARENT, A., 1990. Extrinsic connections of the basal ganglia. *Trends Neurosci.* 13:254–258.

PASCUAL-LEONE, A., N. DANG, L. COHEN, J. P. BRASIL-NETO, A. CAMMAROTA, and M. HALLETT, 1995. Modulation of muscle responses evoked by transcranial magnetic stimulation during the acquisition of new fine motor skills. *J. Neurophysiol.* 74:1037–1045.

PASCUAL-LEONE, A., J. GRAFMAN, K. CLARK, M. STEWART, S. MASSAQUOI, J.-S. LOU, and M. HALLET, 1993. Procedural learning of Parkinson's disease and cerebellar degeneration. *Ann. Neurol.* 34:594–602.

PASCUAL-LEONE, A., J. GRAFMAN, and M. HALLETT, 1994. Modulation of cortical motor output maps during development of implicit and explicit knowledge. *Science* 263:1287–1289.

PASCUAL-LEONE, A., E. M. WASSERMANN, J. GRAFMAN, and M. HALLETT, 1996. The role of the dorsolateral prefrontal cortex in implicit procedural learning. *Exp. Brain Res.* 107:479–485.

PASSINGHAM, R. E., 1985. Premotor cortex: Sensory cues and movement. *Behav. Brain Res.* 18:175–186.

PETERSEN, S. E., H. VAN MIER, J. A. FIEZ, and M. E. RAICHLE, 1998. The effects of practice on the functional anatomy of task performance. *Proc. Natl. Acad. Sci. U.S.A.* 95:853–860.

PETIT, L., C. ORSSAUD, N. TZOURIO, F. CRIVELLO, A. BERTHOZ, and B. MAZOYER, 1996. Functional anatomy of a pre-learned sequence of horizontal saccades in humans. *J. Neurosci.* 16:3714–3726.

PETRIDES, M., 1982. Motor conditional associative-learning after selective prefrontal lesions in the monkey. *Behav. Brain Res.* 5:407–413.

PETRIDES, M., 1985. Deficits on conditional associative-learning tasks after frontal- and temporal-lobe lesions in man. *Neuropsychologia* 23:601–614.

PETRIDES, M., 1995. Impairments on nonspatial self-ordered and externally ordered working memory tasks after lesions of the mid-dorsal part of the lateral frontal cortex in the monkey. *J. Neurosci.* 15:359–375.

PICARD, N., and P. L. STRICK, 1996. Motor areas of the medial wall: A review of their location and functional activation. *Cereb. Cortex* 6:342–353.

RAICHLE, M. E., J. FIEZ, T. O. VIDEEN, A. M. MACLEOD, J. V. PARDO, P. T. FOX, and S. E. PETERSEN, 1994. Practice-related changes in human brain functional anatomy during nonmotor learning. *Cereb. Cortex* 4:8–26.

RAND, M. K., O. HIKOSAKA, S. MIYACHI, X. LU, and K. MIYASHITA, 1998. Characteristics of a long-term procedural skill in the monkey. *Exp. Brain Res.* 118:293–297.

RAND, M. K., D. A. WUNDERLICH, P. E. MARTIN, G. E. STELMACH, and J. R. BLOEDEL, 1998. Adaptive changes in responses to repeated locomotor perturbations in cerebellar patients. *Exp. Brain Res.* 122:31–43.

RAUCH, S. L., C. R. SAVAGE, H. D. BROWN, T. CURRAN, N. M. ALPERT, A. KENDRICK, A. J. FISCHMAN, and S. M. KOSSLYN, 1995. A PET investigation of implicit and explicit sequence learning. *Hum. Brain Mapping* 3:271–286.

RAUCH, S. L., P. J. WHALEN, C. R. SAVAGE, T. CURRAN, A. KENDRICK, H. D. BROWN, G. BUSH, H. C. BREITER, and B. R. ROSEN, 1997. Striatal recruitment during an implicit sequence learning task as measured by functional magnetic resonance imaging. *Hum. Brain Mapping* 5:124–132.

RIZZOLATTI, G., L. FADIGA, V. GALLESE, and L. FOGASSI, 1996. Premotor cortex and the recognition of motor actions. *Cogn. Brain Res.* 3:131–141.

ROBBINS, T. W., and B. J. EVERITT, 1996. Neurobehavioural mechanisms of reward and motivation. *Curr. Opin. Neurobiol.* 6:228–236.

ROLLS, E. T., H. D. CRITCHLEY, R. MASON, and E. A. WAKEMAN, 1996. Orbitofrontal cortex neurons: Role in olfactory and visual association learning. *J. Neurophysiol.* 75:1970–1981.

SAINT-CYR, J. A., A. E. TAYLOR, and A. E. LANG, 1988. Procedural learning and neostriatal dysfunction in man. *Brain* 111:941–959.

SAKAI, K., O. HIKOSAKA, S. MIYAUCHI, R. TAKINO, Y. SASAKI, and B. PÜTZ, 1998. Transition of brain activation from frontal to parietal areas in visuo-motor sequence learning. *J. Neurosci.* 18:1827–1840.

SAKAMOTO, T., K. ARISSIAN, and H. ASANUMA, 1989. Functional role of the sensory cortex in learning motor skills in cats. *Brain Res.* 503:258–264.

SANES, J. N., B. M. DIMITROV, and M. HALLETT, 1990. Motor learning in patients with cerebellar dysfunction. *Brain* 113:103–120.

SASAKI, K., and H. GEMBA, 1981. Changes of premovement field potentials in the cerebral cortex during learning processes of visually initiated hand movements in the monkey. *Neurosci. Lett.* 27:125–130.

SASAKI, K., and H. GEMBA, 1982. Development and change of cortical field potentials during learning processes of visually initiated hand movements in the monkey. *Exp. Brain Res.* 48:429–437.

SASAKI, K., and H. GEMBA, 1983. Learning of fast and stable hand movement and cerebro–cerebellar interactions in the monkey. *Brain Res.* 277:41–46.

SCHALL, J. D., A. MOREL, D. J. KING, and J. BULLIER, 1995. Topography of visual cortex connections with frontal eye field in macaque: Convergence and segregation of processing streams. *J. Neurosci.* 15:4464–4487.

SCHELL, G. R., and P. L. STRICK, 1984. The origin of thalamic inputs to the arcuate premotor and supplementary motor areas. *J. Neurosci.* 4:539–560.

SCHNEIDER, W., and R. M. SHIFFRIN, 1977. Controlled and automatic human information processing: I. Detection, search, and attention. *Psychol. Rev.* 84:1–66.

SCHULTZ, W., P. APICELLA, and T. LJUNGBERG, 1993. Responses of monkey dopamine neurons to reward and conditioned stimuli during successive steps of learning a delayed response task. *J. Neurosci.* 13:900–913.

SCHULTZ, W., P. APICELLA, E. SCARNATI, and T. LJUNGBERG, 1992. Neuronal activity in monkey ventral striatum related to the expectation of reward. *J. Neurosci.* 12:4595–4610.

SEITZ, R. J., A. G. M. CANAVAN, L. YÁGÜEZ, H. HERZOG, L. TELLMANN, U. KNORR, Y. HUANG, and V. HÖMBERG, 1994. Successive roles of the cerebellum and premotor cortices in trajectorial learning. *Neuroreport* 5:2541–2544.

SHADMEHR, R., and T. BRASHERS-KRUG, 1997. Functional stages in the formation of human long-term motor memory. *J. Neurosci.* 17:409–419.

SHADMEHR, R., and H. H. HOLCOMB, 1997. Neural correlates of motor memory consolidation. *Science* 277:821–825.

SHIMA, K., H. MUSHIAKE, N. SAITO, and J. TANJI, 1996. Role for cells in the presupplementary motor area in updating motor plans. *Proc. Natl. Acad. Sci. U.S.A.* 93.

SQUIRE, L. R., and S. M. ZOLA, 1996. Structure and function of declarative and nondeclarative memory systems. *Proc. Natl. Acad. Sci. U.S.A.* 93:13515–13522.

STERN, C. E., and R. E. PASSINGHAM, 1995. The nucleus accumbens in monkeys (*Macaca fascicularis*): III. Reversal learning. *Exp. Brain Res.* 106:239–247.

STRICK, P. L., and C. C. KIM, 1978. Input to primate motor cortex from posterior parietal cortex (area 5): I. Demonstration by retrograde transport. *Brain Res.* 157:325–330.

TANJI, J., 1994. The supplementary motor area in the cerebral cortex. *Neurosci. Res.* 19:251–268.

TANJI, J., and K. SHIMA, 1994. Role for supplementary motor area cells in planning several movements ahead. *Nature* 371:413–416.

THACH, W. T., H. P. GOODKIN, and J. G. KEATING, 1992. The cerebellum and the adaptive coordination of movement. *Annu. Rev. Neurosci.* 15:403–442.

THALER, D., Y.-C. CHEN, P. D. NIXON, C. E. STERN, and R. E. PASSINGHAM, 1995. The functions of the medial premotor cortex. I. Simple learned movements. *Exp. Brain Res.* 102:445–460.

TIMMANN, D., Y. SHIMANSKY, P. S. LARSON, D. A. WUNDERLICH, G. E. STELMACH, and J. R. BLOEDEL, 1996. Visuomotor learning in cerebellar patients. *Behav. Brain Res.* 81:99–113.

WATANABE, M., 1990. Prefrontal unit activity during associative learning in the monkey. *Exp. Brain Res.* 80:296–309.

ZOLA-MORGAN, S., and L. R. SQUIRE, 1984. Preserved learning in monkeys with medial temporal lesions: Sparing of motor and cognitive skills. *J. Neurosci.* 4:1072–1085.

40 The Superior Colliculus and the Cognitive Control of Movement

ROBERT H. WURTZ, MICHELE A. BASSO, MARTIN PARÉ, AND MARC A. SOMMER

ABSTRACT   Normal vision consists of an alternation of saccadic eye movements and periods of visual fixation. This is a relatively simple alternation of movement and nonmovement, but the control of this alternation involves many of the cognitive issues underlying the performance of more complex actions. The superior colliculus (SC) is a nexus in the brain system controlling these saccades and fixations, and recent experiments have shown how this structure and its cortical inputs contribute to their control. Activity on the SC movement map shows that the amplitude and direction of the impending saccade is most likely to be represented by the vector average across a large population of neurons. The control of the alternation of movement and nonmovement, which in the case of the saccadic system is the alternation of saccades and fixation, involves the balance of competition between SC neurons tonically active during visual fixation (fixation neurons) and those active long before saccades (buildup neurons). The preparation to move may be represented by the long lead or delay activity of buildup neurons because, as the probability that a saccade will be made increases, this delay activity increases. Whether the processing preceding movement initiation is discrete for each area or is distributed across areas can be answered by comparing neuronal activity in the SC with that of the neurons in frontal and parietal cortices that project to the SC. The processing is distributed with overlap between neuronal activity in cortex and SC and a shift in the SC toward movement preparation.

Rapid or saccadic eye movements shift our line of sight from one part of the visual field to another and allow us to direct the higher visual acuity provided by the fovea toward successive points in the field. We make these eye movements as frequently as two times per second during such tasks as scanning the visual scene or reading. Just as important as the saccades, however, is the lack of movement between them because it is in these periods of fixation when almost all vision occurs. Thus, saccades and fixations can be regarded as an integrated system that both moves the eye rapidly to the next target and then holds the eye steadily on that target. This alternation of saccades and fixation is particularly evident during reading (figure 40.1).

ROBERT H. WURTZ, MICHELE A. BASSO, MARTIN PARÉ, and MARC A. SOMMER   Laboratory of Sensorimotor Research, National Eye Institute, National Institutes of Health, Bethesda, Md.

Even given that saccades and fixation are necessary for normal vision, why should such a relatively mechanistic system be of any relevance to cognitive neuroscience? There are at least three reasons.

First, saccades are relatively simple movements, and they therefore offer the opportunity to understand a simple system within the brain for generating actions. The saccades involve rotation of each eye by the coordinated activation of only six muscles, have no variation of load—and therefore have no need for load compensation—and have no complexity introduced by the movement of joints (Robinson, 1968). These relatively simple movements do, however, involve most of the cognitive issues underlying the performance of more complex actions. For example, a saccadic eye movement to a visual stimulus requires shifting attention and selecting a target, transforming input from a sensory map to the output on a movement map, and then coordinating the appropriate muscles to execute the movement and hold the eye in the new position.

Second, we have a superb animal model of the human saccadic-fixation system in the old-world monkey, which allows us to study the brain mechanisms controlling the movement. Since the introduction of the now standard techniques for recording neuronal activity from awake behaving monkeys (Evarts, 1966), the accurate recording of eye movements (Fuchs and Robinson, 1966; Judge, Richmond, and Chu, 1980), the training of monkeys to control eye movements (Fuchs, 1967), and the visual stimuli that guide them (Wurtz, 1969), the regions of the monkey brain active before visually guided saccades have been identified. The visual pathway to the striate cortex, to extrastriate areas, and then to the regions of the parietal and frontal cortices have been identified and are included in figure 40.2A. Just as the elaboration of the changes in visual processing at each step in this pathway has contributed to our understanding of the visual input on which further cognitive processing is built, the extensive understanding of the brainstem oculomotor centers for saccade generation (Hepp et al., 1989; Moschovakis and Highstein, 1994) has led to greater understanding of what output is required of cognitive

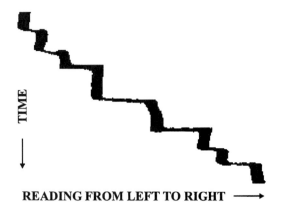

READING FROM LEFT TO RIGHT ——➤

FIGURE 40.1 Interplay between rapid eye movements (saccades) and the pauses between these movements (fixation). In this example of the successive eye positions during the reading of a single line of text, saccades (vertical lines) move the eye across the page but are separated by periods of visual fixation (horizontal lines). Almost all of visual perception occurs during these periods of visual fixation. (Modified from Yarbus, 1967.)

processing for movement generation. Understanding the "spinal cord" for the saccadic system allows us to step backward gradually from the basic mechanics of movement to consider the control of these actions at higher levels.

Third, there is a nexus in the system through which much (although not all) of the information from the cortex flows to the brainstem oculomotor structures, the superior colliculus (SC). The SC receives inputs from the parietal and frontal areas of the cerebral cortex known to be related to saccade generation both directly and through the basal ganglia (Fries, 1984; Hikosaka and Wurtz, 1983) (figure 40.2A) and projects directly to the pontine and midbrain oculomotor areas. The SC can be viewed as a location for the coordination of the varied inputs from the forebrain and as the location for the transformation of these into outputs for the control of movement. It is the last step in the system in which both a visual and a motor map clearly are evident (Robinson, 1972; Schiller and Stryker, 1972; Wurtz and Goldberg, 1972).

In this chapter, we concentrate on several recent developments of our understanding of the saccadic/fixation system and its relation to the control of movement. We first describe how the neuronal elements in the SC are organized, including how only a few neuron types can be organized across a map to provide different output signals. Then we consider how the SC contributes to the alternating pattern of saccades and fixations. Finally we consider the "delay" activity between the neuronal response to the stimulus and the burst before a saccade and consider the transition leading to this activity in the cortical neurons that project to the SC.

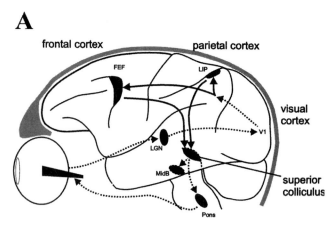

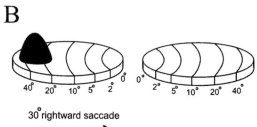

FIGURE 40.2 Brain systems for the generation of saccades and fixation. (A) Outline of the pathway from the visual input through cerebral cortex to oculomotor centers controlling eye muscles. The schematic drawing shows a lateral view of a monkey brain. The afferent visual pathway is indicated by the dotted line arrows passing from the retina to the lateral geniculate nucleus (*LGN*) of the thalamus to the striate cortex (*V1*), and then by a series of steps (not shown) to the parietal cortex (the lateral intraparietal [*LIP*] area) and the frontal cortex (the frontal eye field [*FEF*]). The projections from these areas to the superior colliculus (*SC*) are indicated by the solid line arrows. Omitted from the drawing are several areas (including the supplementary eye field in frontal cortex), reciprocal connections between areas, and the indirect pathway through the basal ganglia (caudate and substantia nigra pars reticulata). The output from the colliculus to the midbrain and pons oculomotor centers and then to the eye muscles also are indicated by dotted lines. (B) The schematic drawing of the organization of the SC on the right and left sides of the brain. Small saccades are represented in the rostral SC (0°) and large saccades are represented in the caudal SC (40°). The activity before a saccade is across a population of neurons, which is represented by a mound in the SC on the side of the brain opposite to the direction of the impending saccade.

Organization of the superior colliculus

The SC lies on the roof of the midbrain and consists of successive gray and white layers. Neurons in the superficial layers respond to visual stimuli and have receptive fields in the field contralateral to their location in the SC. Neurons in the intermediate layers often also respond to visual stimuli, but their most vigorous discharge is before the onset of saccadic eye movements.

We concentrate on these saccade-related neurons because it is in them that we see the transition from sensory to motor-related activity.

SUPERIOR COLLICULUS MAP FOR SACCADES Just as superficial-layer neurons have visual receptive fields, the saccade-related neurons in the intermediate layers have movement fields, that is, they increase their activity before saccades made only to one region of the visual field (Wurtz and Goldberg, 1972). There is a gradient of activity within each movement field, and a neuron's maximum discharge is associated with saccades of specific amplitude and direction–the neuron's optimal saccadic vector. Different neurons have different vectors, and the neurons are organized in a highly regular fashion to produce a neural map of saccadic vectors covering the contralateral visual field (figure 40.2B). On this map, large saccades are represented in the caudal portion, small are in the rostral region, upward are more medial, and downward are more lateral.

NEURON TYPES The activity of all the neurons within the intermediate layers is not identical, however, and to systematically study them, different types have been identified. The classification we use (Munoz and Wurtz, 1995a) is based largely on the activity of these neurons that comes *after* any initial visual response to the saccade target but *before* any burst of activity preceding saccade onset. This intervening activity is best revealed in two behavioral paradigms, the visual and memory-delayed saccade tasks. In these delay tasks, there is a period of active fixation during which we measure the resting discharge rate of the neuron. Then a visual target is presented in the center of the neuron's movement field, but the monkey is required to delay making a saccade to it (the delay period) until the fixation stimulus is extinguished (the cue to move). In the visual task, the target remains until the end of each trial, whereas in the memory task, it is only flashed and the monkey has to make a saccade to the remembered location.

Burst neurons (Munoz and Wurtz, 1995a) are the saccade-related neurons that have been most extensively studied in the SC and those that also have been referred to as saccade-related burst neurons (Sparks, 1978). In the delayed saccade tasks, these neurons frequently display a brief response time-locked to the onset of the visual stimulus, but their salient response is the vigorous burst of activity before a saccade made into their movement field (figure 40.3A). In contrast to other saccade-related neurons, they have next to no discharge during the delay period. The burst neurons are found throughout the rostral to caudal extent of the collicular map, and it is assumed

that their activity is a signal to make a saccade with a vector coded by the position of that neuron on the SC map.

Buildup neurons continue to show sustained activity during the delay period in a delayed saccade task (figure 40.3B). In contrast to the burst neurons, these neurons do not necessarily show a discrete saccade-related burst in activity and certainly must include many, if not all, of the saccade-related neurons other than the burst neurons that have been described in many experiments, beginning with the earliest investigations (Mays and Sparks, 1980; Mohler and Wurtz, 1976; Sparks, 1978; Wurtz and Goldberg, 1972). Because of their delay activity, they originally were referred to as long lead neurons (Sparks, 1978). Munoz and Wurtz (1995a) more recently categorized these neurons as *buildup* neurons because their delay activity often increases gradually as the saccade onset approaches. Note that this neuronal class also may include neurons that were described differently by other groups, for example, quasi-visual neurons (Mays and Sparks, 1980) and prelude bursters (Glimcher and Sparks, 1992). Like the burst neurons, the buildup neurons are found throughout the collicular map. Our working hypothesis is that their buildup or delay activity represents the preparation to make a saccade, and their activation may facilitate saccade production.

Fixation neurons become active tonically when the animal fixates a visual stimulus and pause when a saccade occurs (figure 40.3C). These neurons originally were described in the cat SC (Munoz and Guitton, 1991) and then were identified in the monkey (Munoz and Wurtz, 1993a). In the monkey, the fixation neurons were shown further to sustain their discharge when the fixation stimulus was removed and the monkey continued to fixate, thereby ruling out the possibility that these neurons were simply visual neurons with a foveal receptive field excited by the fixation stimulus. The fixation neurons are found in the rostral region of the SC on both sides of the brain. Their discharge is related to the maintenance of fixation.

CONCLUSION: SUPERIOR COLLICULUS ORGANIZATION It is striking that there may be only a few neuron types within the SC intermediate layers although there may be more variation, particularly among the buildup neurons, than we consider here. The two points to be emphasized on the organization, however, are not new but rather have been recognized for a number of years. First, the map of saccadic vectors, which we have described (see review by Sparks and Hartwich-Young, 1989), conveys the vector for the *change* in eye position produced by the saccade. Second, a change in the activity of a *population* of neurons on the SC map has significant importance, which we

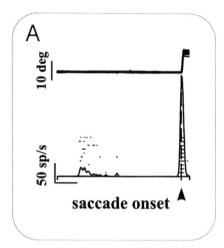

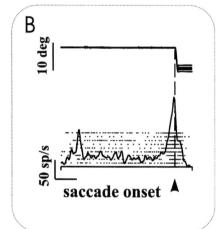

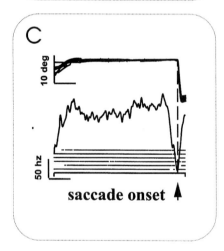

FIGURE 40.3 Classification of neurons in the intermediate layers of the SC into three categories: burst, buildup, and fixation. The top row of each example shows the eye position traces, and below these are rasters, with each tick in the raster representing a single action potential and each row of ticks representing a single trial. The superimposed spike density functions show the sum of the activity across the trials. All traces are aligned on the onset of the saccadic eye movement. (A) An example of a burst neuron with a clear response to the onset of the visual target (start of the line) and a burst of activity before the saccade (arrowhead under the line). (B) An example of a buildup neuron with a slight visual response, continuing activity, and a burst of activity before the saccade. Buildup neurons can be defined as those whose discharge rate during the delay period is significantly higher ($P < .01$) than the resting rate. While the buildup neurons clearly are different from the burst neurons, they may form a continuum with them; the buildup neurons also may be a more heterogeneous as suggested by the broad range of discharge behaviors exhibited in response to the visual stimulus and before the saccade. (C) An example of a fixation neuron with a high rate of discharge while the monkey is fixating on a target.

Interaction of saccades and fixation

One of the striking observations on the SC is the identification of neurons that are related to both the generation of saccades and the maintenance of fixation.

CONTINUITY OF FIXATION AND BUILDUP NEURONS Fixation neurons have been described as a separate class of neurons because of their high discharge rate during fixation, and understanding how they are related to other SC neurons depends on determining what controls their high rate of discharge during active visual fixation. One possibility is that the discharge of these fixation neurons could be influenced by factors similar to those influencing the buildup neurons because although we have described the buildup and fixation neurons as behaving very differently (figure 40.3), they have at least two characteristics in common. First, they both lie somewhat deeper in the SC than the burst neurons (Munoz and Wurtz, 1995a). Second, they both have movement fields; most fixation neurons, like buildup neurons, were shown to have a burst of activity with small contralaterally directed saccades (Munoz and Wurtz, 1995a).

One possibility is that the fixation neurons have delay activity just as buildup neurons do, and that the increased activity during fixation essentially is this delay activity. To investigate this, Krauzlis and associates (1997) recorded from neurons in the rostral SC that had the characteristics of fixation neurons, including continued discharge when the monkey fixated in the absence

have not yet emphasized. Before the onset of a saccade, it is not just a few neurons that become active but roughly 25% of the entire population (Munoz and Wurtz, 1995b), and it is the vector average of these active neurons that appears to determine which saccade is made (Sparks et al., 1990), as represented by the mound of activity on the SC map in figure 40.2B.

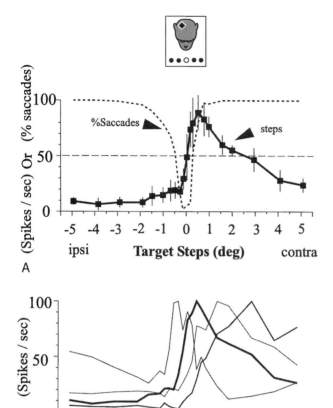

FIGURE 40.4 Fixation neuron activity with small changes in target position. (A) Changes in firing rate of a neuron after small steps of the fixation target into the visual field either ipsilateral or contralateral from the SC in which the neuron was recorded. Symbols show the mean firing rate over an interval beginning 100 ms after the target step and lasting for 100 ms or until 8 ms before the saccade onset. Error bars indicate ±1 SD for the 12 trials. The dotted line indicates the percentage of trials on which each target step elicited a saccade. Dashed line indicates the mean firing rate with no target steps. (B) Change in activity of four fixation neurons from one monkey after the same small steps. The four have been normalized so that the peaks of the curves are 100. The neuron with the darkened trace is the same as in (A). (From Krauzlis and associates, 1997.)

of a fixation target. They stepped the target on which the monkey was fixating to slightly eccentric locations and rewarded the monkey for making a saccade to the target. Fixation neurons showed the largest increases in firing rates with small steps into the contralateral visual field; the neuron in figure 40.4A showed the largest response for steps of approximately 0.5°. Different neurons showed the maximal response for contralateral steps of different sizes (figure 40.4B). Saccades to large target steps were accompanied by a decrease in activity for both ipsilateral and contralateral saccades, as had

been reported previously (Munoz and Wurtz, 1993a). What is particularly relevant is that the increase always was for small steps and that the increase in activity occurred whether the step elicited a saccade or not. Krauzlis and colleagues (1997) concluded that the fixation neurons are tonically active during visual fixation, not because they are carrying a unique fixation signal but because they are indicating target locations very close to the fovea that usually do not elicit a saccade.

What these experiments show is that the activity of the fixation neurons during fixation has two striking similarities to the delay activity in buildup neurons. First, both the fixation and buildup neurons increase their activity for a target at some eccentricity in the contralateral visual field, the fixation neurons for very small target steps and the buildup neurons for larger steps. Second, the delay activity is present even if no saccade is made, as indicated for the fixation neurons by Krauzlis and associates (1997) and for the buildup neurons by Munoz and Wurtz (1995a). Thus, the fixation neurons might be regarded most parsimoniously as a rostral continuation of the buildup neurons. The hypothesis that emerges is that the activity of these fixation and buildup neurons indicates an error between where the eye is and where the target is, and the size of the error represented by the neuron depends on the location of the neuron on the SC movement map. This simplification eliminates the problem of deciding where in the rostral SC the fixation cells end and where buildup neurons begin. The different effects of activating these neurons depends on their interactions within the SC and probably their differential connections outside the SC, as we consider in the next section.

FIXATION AND SACCADE INTERACTION   How does this proposed continuity of fixation and buildup neurons affect the original hypothesis (Munoz and Wurtz, 1993a, 1993b) that the activity of monkey fixation neurons suppresses the generation of saccades? We believe that the interaction between saccades and fixation still is controlled by a system within the brain that includes the SC but that the observations just described show how the neuronal elements are organized to carry out this interaction. The basic observations on the effects of activating or inactivating the rostral SC still hold. Saccades are suppressed by the activation of the SC fixation region by either electrical stimulation or injection of the chemical agent bicuculine, a gamma-aminobutyric acid (GABA) antagonist (Munoz and Wurtz, 1993b). Conversely, saccade production is facilitated by the inactivation of the fixation neurons by injection of the GABA agonist muscimol (Munoz and Wurtz, 1993). Both observations show that alteration of the rostral SC affects when saccades are generated.

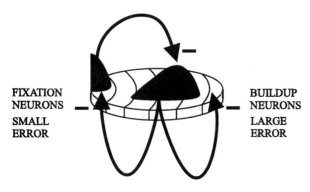

FIXATION
NEURONS
SMALL
ERROR

BUILDUP
NEURONS
LARGE
ERROR

FIGURE 40.5 Mutual inhibition of fixation and buildup neurons. The arrows indicate inhibitory interactions. The fixation neurons in the rostral SC inhibit the saccade-related neurons in the caudal SC whereas the saccade-related neurons inhibit both other saccade neurons and the fixation neurons. Not shown are the inhibitory inputs from the basal ganglia or the presumed excitatory inputs from cerebral cortex.

This leads to a hypothesis of the interaction between fixation and saccades shown schematically in figure 40.5. The basic assumption is that when any population of SC neurons is active anywhere on the SC map, they suppress the activity of all other SC neurons. When buildup neurons in the caudal SC become active, they act to inhibit all other neurons in the SC, including the most rostral fixation-type buildup neurons. They also provide an error signal according to their position on the SC, indicating which saccadic vector would be required to bring the eye to the target to eliminate the error. The output of these neurons may be to adjacent burst neurons as well as directly to neurons in the pons and midbrain outside the SC. When the fixation neurons in the rostral SC become active, they also inhibit all other SC neurons. The fixation activity also indicates that a position error exists, but this error signal is so small that no eye movement is elicited—giving incidentally a physiological basis for the concept of a dead zone for saccade initiation (but considerably larger than that in humans) (Wyman and Steinman, 1973). The outcome of this competition for fixation or saccade (here and probably in other parts of the brain as well) determines the initiation of saccades. There may be differences in the strength of the inhibitory effects in the rostral and caudal regions of the SC, but the neural mechanisms can be regarded as fundamentally the same.

Several lines of evidence are consistent with the interactions between rostral and caudal SC, as outlined in figure 40.5. First, it has become clear that activity in the rostral SC does directly inhibit saccade-related neurons in the caudal SC. Initially, the saccade suppression effect caused by the activation of the SC fixation region logi-cally could be explained by an interaction between fixation and saccade-related elements located downstream of the SC. Indeed, a pause in the activity of brainstem omnipause neurons is necessary to release the burst generator and produce a saccade (Hepp et al., 1989; Moschovakis and Highstein, 1994), and these neurons receive preferential projection from the rostral SC (Büttner-Ennever and Horn, 1994; Paré and Guitton, 1994). The SC fixation neurons therefore could alter the generation of the saccade as an influence onto the activity of omnipause neurons, that is, without acting directly on the SC saccade-related neurons. Munoz and colleagues (1996), however, showed that when electrical stimulation of the rostral SC interrupts saccades in mid-flight, there is a pause in the saccade-related activity of both burst and buildup neurons in caudal SC when the eyes stop momentarily. This indicates that the fixation neuron activity does act on the SC saccade-related activity.

The mutual inhibitory effect of activity in the rostral and caudal SC also has received support from both physiological and anatomic experiments. By electrically stimulating within the monkey SC, Munoz and Istvan (1998) established the inhibitory effect of fixation neurons on burst and buildup neurons and of these saccade-related neurons back onto fixation neurons. In addition, these experiments showed that stimulation of saccade regions also inhibits other remotely located saccade-related neurons. (The only exception to the mutual inhibition between collicular neurons is the connection between the fixation neurons in the two SCs: stimulation of one fixation region excites rather than inhibits the fixation neurons in the other SC.) The presence of GABAergic connections throughout the SC (Mize, 1992) and the recent experiments in the ferret (Meredith and Ramoa, 1998) showing that stimulation at any point in the SC, rostral or caudal, produces an initial inhibition at distant points in the SC, support the hypothesis of inhibitory interactions. Behan and Kime (1996) showed in the cat that biocytin injections label cells within 0.5 mm up to 5.0 mm from the injection site, which provides anatomic evidence for horizontal connections throughout the length of the SC. Thus, the mutual inhibition between different parts of the SC, consistent with the fixation/saccade interactions within the SC, are supported by what is known about the physiological and anatomic connections between these neurons.

EXPRESS SACCADES The interaction between fixation- and saccade-related activity has been explored in a recent series of experiments on an express saccade, a short latency saccade that is critically dependent on an intact SC (Schiller, Sandell, and Maunsell, 1987). These experiments illustrate most clearly the interactions we have considered.

One of the most prominent ideas about the shift in fixation caused by a saccade, which usually is addressed with respect to the accompanying shift of attention, is that there must be an initial disengagement from the current fixation stimulus. This disengagement also was proposed to be critical in the reduction of saccadic reaction time in the gap saccade paradigm and the generation of express saccades (Fischer and Weber, 1993), the latencies of which (~80 ms) approach the conduction time from the retina to the eye muscles (Fischer and Boch, 1983). With the discovery of the SC fixation neurons, a neural correlate for the fixation disengagement was obvious: the disengagement occurs when the fixation neurons reduce their discharge after the disappearance of the fixation stimulus or pause before saccades. The increased incidence of express saccades following rostral SC inactivation (Munoz and Wurtz, 1991) provided experimental support for this hypothesis, as did the finding that a decrease in fixation activity during the gap task correlates with the reduction in saccade reaction time (Dorris, Paré, and Munoz, 1997).

Recording of the activity of SC burst neurons revealed that the saccade-related burst of activity is indistinguishable from the target-related responses of these neurons when an express saccade is produced (Dorris, Paré, and Munoz, 1997; Edelman and Keller, 1996). It was hypothesized that the release of fixation permits the target-related responses of SC neurons to be strong enough to trigger short-latency express saccades (Edelman and Keller, 1996; Sommer, 1994).

Fixation disengagement, however, can only be a part of the mechanism for express saccades in the monkey, as indicated by recent behavioral experiments by Paré and Munoz (1996). Using the gap saccade task, they trained monkeys to make express saccades after presenting the saccade target repeatedly in the same part of the visual field. After this training, express saccades were made only to a restricted region of the visual field centered on the location of the target used for training. The disappearance of the fixation stimulus before target presentation did not lead to express saccade production at the other target locations but simply reduced the mean saccadic reaction time. Overall, these results indicate that it is the neuronal activity associated with the preparation to make saccades to the training target that determines the occurrence of express saccades, not just the release of fixation afforded by the disappearance of the fixation stimulus. In subsequent physiological experiments, Dorris, Paré, and Munoz (1997) showed that fixation neurons decrease their discharge before express saccades, but that these changes are not predictive of express saccade production (figure 40.6A). In contrast, the increased level of discharge of buildup neurons before target presentation was found to be correlated with the occurrence of express saccades when these were made into the movement field of the neurons (figure 40.6B). This increase in the early activity of buildup neurons thus may facilitate the excitability of the corresponding saccade region and thereby allow the target-related responses of the SC neurons to trigger the short-latency express saccades. Additional evidence for this motor preparation hypothesis for express saccade generation comes from another behavioral study. Using a scanning saccade paradigm, Sommer (1997) compared the spatial attributes of saccades produced in response to suddenly appearing stimuli with those made while scanning to unchanging stimuli. He found that the occurrence of express saccades was related to the congruence between the location of the suddenly appearing target and the goal of voluntary saccade planning.

If we generalize the observations made on express saccade generation to all saccades, the decision to make a saccade can be reduced to the competitive interaction between the signals related to planning a saccade and those related to maintaining fixation. Each signal is necessary, but not sufficient, for determining when a saccade will be initiated.

CONCLUSION: SACCADE AND FIXATION INTERACTION The observations described emphasize several points. First, the interactions underlying the alternation of fixation and saccades all may depend on interactions between *one neuronal class* in the SC, what we have referred to as the buildup neuron. This illustrates a case in which one neuronal element can be used to produce quite different effects (fixation or saccades) depending on its relation to other neurons on a neuronal map. Second, the movement generation is a result of *the balance of competition* between the activity of the neurons signaling movement (the buildup neurons and probably the burst neurons as well) and those signaling nonmovement (the fixation neurons). This interaction is based on competing activity on two parts of the SC map (rostral fixation and caudal saccade), and the outcome determines when a saccade will be made.

Superior colliculus delay activity

The SC activity that we have concentrated on in considering fixation is the activity in the delay period that precedes the burst of activity accompanying saccades. Following, we consider factors that alter this delay activity.

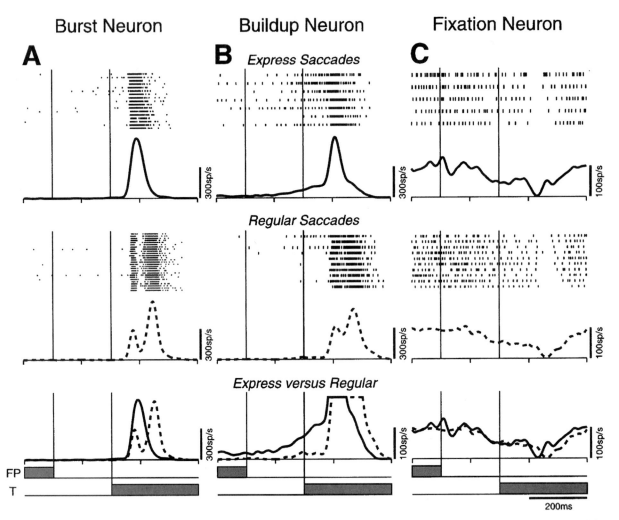

Burst Neuron

A

Buildup Neuron

B *Express Saccades*

Regular Saccades

Express versus Regular

Fixation Neuron

C

FP

T

200ms

FIGURE 40.6   Neuronal activity of burst (A), buildup (B), and fixation (C) neurons during the generation of short-latency express saccades (top) and long-latency regular saccades (middle). The paradigm used was the gap saccade task in which the fixation stimulus (*FP*) is extinguished 200 ms before the target (*T*) presentation (as indicated by the bars along the bottom). Rasters and spike density functions are aligned on target onset. In the bottom panel, the spike density functions of the express (solid line) and the regular (dashed line) trials are superimposed. (A) The activity of burst neurons displayed two bursts before regular saccades: one time-locked to the target onset and a later one time-locked to the saccade onset. In contrast, express saccades were preceded by only one robust burst time-locked to both target and saccade onsets. (B) The discharge rate of buildup neurons during the gap period before the target onset was greater for express saccade trials compared with regular saccades. After the target presentation, the buildup neuron showed activity similar to the burst neuron. (C) The activity of fixation neurons decreased during the gap and paused just before either express or regular saccades. However, the level of activity associated with each type of saccades did not differ. Express saccades were defined as those with latencies between 70 to 120 ms, and regular saccades had latencies between 130 and 180 ms. (After Dorris, Paré, and Munoz, 1997.)

Because this delay period activity is not tied to the occurrence of the saccade, Munoz and Wurtz (1995a) proposed that it represents the preparation to make a saccade. Consistent with this motor preparation hypothesis, Dorris and colleagues (1997) demonstrated that the level of delay activity for a significant proportion of buildup neurons (41%) predicts motor performance. They showed that the level of buildup activity during a gap period (between the time the fixation stimulus was turned off but before presentation of the target) was inversely correlated to the reaction time of the saccade: the greater the discharge, the shorter the reaction time.

If these early neuronal changes are related to preparation to make a saccade, then such changes should be sensitive to the likelihood that a saccade will be made (Riehle and Requin, 1993). Two recent experiments tested whether manipulating the prior knowledge of the monkey as to whether a saccade will be made alters the delay activity of the SC buildup neurons.

TARGET PROBABILITY PARADIGMS Basso and Wurtz (1997, 1998) used two paradigms that required monkeys to make a saccade to a peripheral stimulus while changing the probability that a given stimulus would be the saccade target.

In the first paradigm, varying the number of stimuli presented to the monkey changed the probability that the one located in the movement field of the neuron would become the target. One, two, four, or eight stimuli were presented, and then later the monkey was cued as to which one was the saccade target (figure 40.7). During the preselection period, when the monkey did not know which of the stimuli would be the target, increasing the number of possible targets from one to eight decreased the activity. When the target dimmed, the activity in each condition increased to the level present when only a single target was present. During the preselection period, the mean discharge rate of all buildup neurons studied decreased as target probability decreased.

In a second paradigm, the number of stimuli remained constant so that no changes related to visual interaction could account for the results. Presenting the eight targets in a series of blocked trials, in which the same one of the eight stimuli became the target, increased target probability. After a number of trials, the neurons developed a higher level of activity than in the case when any of the eight stimuli could become the target. Therefore, changes in target probability modulate the buildup activity during a delay period whether those changes result from varying the number of stimuli or varying the monkey's previous experience. In contrast, the burst of activity of burst neurons and the saccade-related burst activity of buildup neurons did not change in either probability experiment.

GO/NOGO PARADIGM In this experiment, the fixation stimulus provided information about whether a saccade would be required to a peripheral stimulus located in the movement field of the neuron. In the two types of trials used, the fixation stimulus first changed color, signaling to the monkey that the upcoming peripheral stimulus should be either ignored (Nogo trials) or should be taken as the target for a saccade (Go trials—see stimulus bars in figure 40.8). Most buildup neurons tested in this paradigm (61%) showed delay activity specific to the Go instruction, as exemplified in figure 40.8 (Sommer, Paré, and Wurtz, 1997). For these neurons, the buildup activity was much higher after target pre-

sentation if the Go instruction was provided, that is, if a saccade was to be executed. For the sample of buildup neurons ($n = 62$), the delay activity in Go trials was 2.4 times greater than that observed in Nogo trials. Other studies have demonstrated similar modulation of early low-frequency discharge in SC neurons in tasks designed to show activity changes with movement selection (Glimcher and Sparks, 1992) or shifts in attention (Kustov and Robinson, 1996).

CONCLUSION: DELAY ACTIVITY Both the target probability and the Go/Nogo experiments show that a greater probability that the monkey will be required to make a saccade on a particular trial leads to a higher level of delay or buildup activity. This increase is consistent with viewing the buildup neuron activity as part of the preparation to make a saccade that precedes the burst of activity at the time of a saccade. This increased activity that precedes the generation of a saccade represents an increase in activity on one part of the SC map, and this activity develops over time during the delay period. We believe that what we refer to loosely as "preparation to move" might best be regarded as the gradual specification over time of one part of the SC map as the center of activity for the next saccade. This localized activity specifies the vector for the next saccade, and the narrowing of activity over time is a narrowing of the selection of this vector.

Cortical input to superior colliculus

Many of the fixation, buildup, and burst neurons are likely to receive input from the cerebral cortex. This opens the possibility of seeing the transition in activity between the cerebral cortex and the superior colliculus. To explore this transition, the cortical neurons that project to the SC must be identified. It is not sufficient to compare the activity of any neuron in the cortical areas that project to the SC with the SC activity because many of the cortical neurons might not project to the SC. We need to study specifically those neurons that project to the SC and have used antidromic stimulation to do so. In this technique, a cortical neuron is identified as projecting to the SC if electrical stimulation of the SC produces spikes in the cortical neuron with short consistent latencies (along with other criteria, Lemon, 1984). We have concentrated on the neurons in the parietal and frontal cortex because neurons in these regions have well-established projections to the SC (Huerta, Krubitzer, and Kaas, 1986; Leichnetz and Goldberg, 1988; Lynch, Graybiel, and Lobeck, 1985).

array on

target dim movement field

pre-selection   selection   Eye

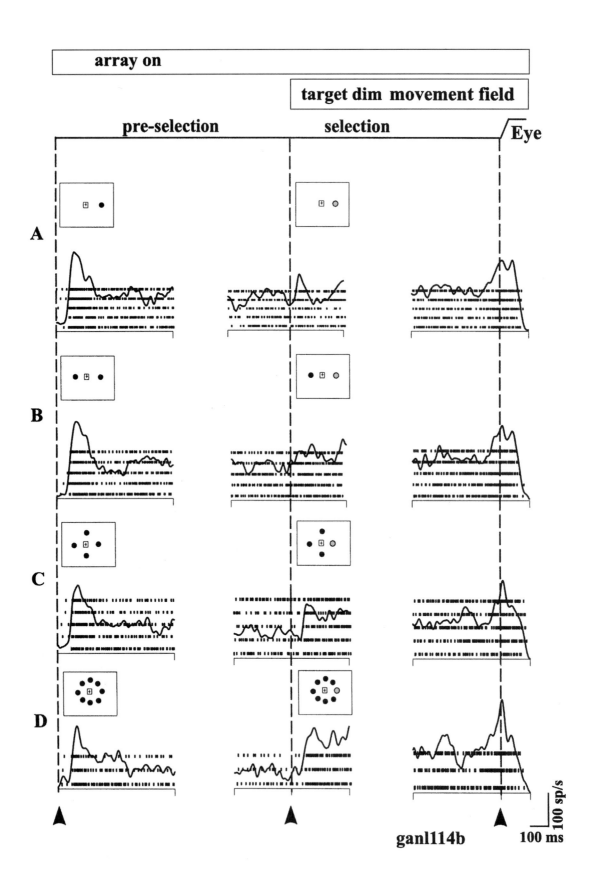

A

B

C

D

ganl114b

100 sp/s

100 ms

FIGURE 40.7 Buildup neuron activity modulated by shifts in target probability. Increases in the number of potential targets for the impending saccade reduced buildup neuron activity. The events of the task are indicated by the labeled periods of time across the top, and the spatial arrangement is indicated by a schematic of the stimulus display in front of the monkey. The first column shows activity on five trials in the rasters and the mean of these in the superimposed spike density trace when one (A), two (B), four (C), or eight (D) targets were presented during the preselection. This example is taken from trials when the target was in the movement field of the neuron. The first column is aligned (vertical dashed lines) on the onset of the possible targets (preselection period), the second on the dimming of one of the targets (selection period), and the third on the onset of the saccade (eye movement period). There is an initial visual response and subsequent sustained or delay period activity. Both of these activities were reduced as the number of stimuli was increased. When the target dimmed, the activity increased. This neuron had a burst of action potentials associated with the onset of the saccade that did not differ substantially between the probability conditions.

PARIETAL CORTEX INPUTS TO SUPERIOR COLLICULUS   The lateral intraparietal (LIP) area is the area in the inferior parietal lobule where saccade-related activity has been described by both the Andersen and Goldberg groups (Andersen and Gnadt, 1989; Andersen, Essick, and Siegel, 1987; Barash et al., 1991; Colby, Du-

hamel, and Goldberg, 1995; Colby, Duhamel, and Goldberg, 1996; Mazzoni et al., 1996). Paré and Wurtz (1997) first identified the LIP neurons that can be activated antidromically from electrical stimulation within the SC. The projection neurons act primarily on the intermediate layers of the SC because antidromic activation thresholds reached minimum values at depths where neurons showed saccade-related activity. The LIP projection to the SC appears to be organized topographically because the most efficient antidromic stimulation typically was obtained at SC sites with movement fields similar to those of the LIP neurons.

Approximately 75% of the identified LIP efferent neurons responded to the onset of the visual target, and approximately 60% of the neurons maintained their activity during the delay period of either the visual or memory-delayed saccade tasks. Several LIP neurons also exhibited a modest saccade-related increase in activity, but none had only a saccade-related burst of activity like the SC burst neurons or some frontal eye field (FEF) efferent neurons. Although the LIP neurons therefore were more similar to the SC buildup neurons than to the SC burst neurons, the LIP neurons differed from the SC neurons in the Go/Nogo task (figure 40.9A). Only about one third of the LIP efferent neurons had delay activity that occurred only after the Go instruction, and the mean

SC buildup neuron

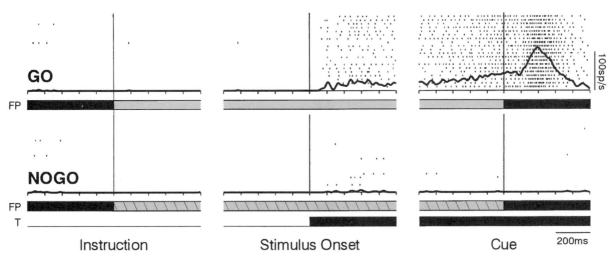

FIGURE 40.8 Neuronal activity of a buildup neuron in a Go/Nogo saccade paradigm. Instructions were given by a change in color of the fixation stimulus (*FP*) before the peripheral stimulus (*T*) appeared. A change from blue to red indicated a Nogo instruction, whereas a change to green indicated a Go instruction. After the peripheral stimulus was presented, there was a delay period. After this, the fixation stimulus returned to its original blue color, cueing the monkey to either maintain fixation for a prolonged duration (Nogo) or execute the saccade (Go). Rasters and spike density functions for Go (top) and

Nogo (bottom) trials are aligned on the instruction (left), target (middle), and cue (right). This neuron started to discharge after the target appearance and exhibited delay activity only if the Go instruction had been given. The discharge peaked at the onset of the saccades made in response to the cue presentation. This neuron was virtually silent during Nogo trials. To quantify the level of delay activity, the discharge rate was measured during a 300-ms epoch ending at the time of the cue presentation. This neuron's delay activity was 33.3 sp/s and 0.2 sp/s in Go and Nogo trials, respectively.

A   LIP efferent neuron

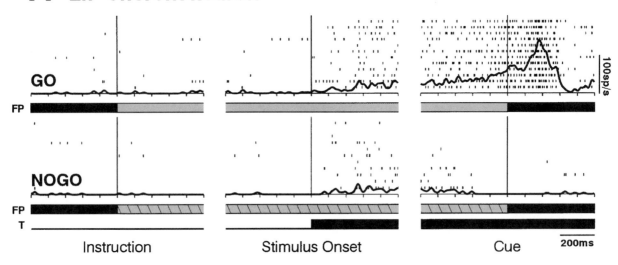

| Instruction | Stimulus Onset | Cue | 200ms |

B   FEF efferent neuron

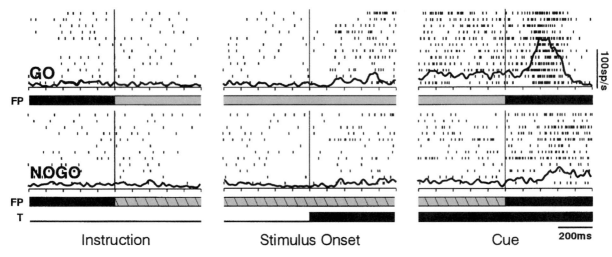

| Instruction | Stimulus Onset | Cue | 200ms |

FIGURE 40.9   Neuronal activity of cortical efferent neurons in a Go/Nogo delayed saccade paradigm. Responses of lateral intraparietal (LIP) (top) and frontal eye field (FEF) (bottom) neurons that were activated antidromically by SC stimulation. In the Go trials, the neurons started discharging after the stimulus onset and maintained their discharge until the saccade was made in response to the cue. In the Nogo trials, less response was observed after the stimulus presentation. Same organization as in figure 40.8.

delay activity in Go trials was only 1.3 times greater than that in the Nogo trials. The delay activity of the LIP neurons started at the time of the visual target and continued for most neurons regardless of whether there was preparation to make the saccade. This is in contrast to the SC neurons, where activity in approximately two thirds of the SC neurons had activity only after the Go instruction, and across the sample there was 2.4 times greater activity on the Go trials. Thus, the SC neurons were substantially more related to the signal to move, and using our inter-

pretation of the Go/Nogo task, were more closely related to the preparation to move whereas the LIP neurons were more dependent on the visual stimulus than the signal to make a saccade.

FRONTAL CORTEX INPUTS TO SUPERIOR COLLICULUS   The FEF is the area in the frontal lobe that, together with the SC, is necessary for saccade generation (Schiller, True, and Conway, 1980). Segraves and Goldberg (1987) previously reported that FEF neurons that are antidromically activated by SC stimulation carry a saccade-related burst signal that sometimes is combined with a response to visual stimulation. We have confirmed this observation and find that approximately 15% of the FEF neurons have only presaccadic bursts. Thus, in contrast to the LIP area, the FEF does have neurons projecting to the SC that have characteristics of the SC burst neurons. As was the case with the LIP region, the FEF projection to SC was topographically organized and directed to the intermediate layers.

In addition to these burst-like neurons, approximately one third of the FEF efferent neurons showed delay activity between the onset of the stimulus and the saccade, which made them similar to the SC buildup neurons. Like the SC buildup neurons, but in contrast to the LIP efferent neurons, nearly two thirds of the FEF efferent neurons with delay activity had activity in Go trails that was higher than in Nogo trials (figure 40.9B). This activity on the Go trials, although frequent, was small, only 1.5 times greater than that observed on Nogo trials (Wurtz and Sommer, 1998). Thus, although the FEF has buildup-like activity as frequently as do the SC neurons, the Go/Nogo effect is smaller, like that in the LIP. The FEF appears to be a more heterogeneous area than is the LIP region and includes both burst- and buildup-type neurons.

While investigating the frontal cortex inputs to the SC, there was an additional finding that raises questions about the unidirectional flow of information from cortex to brainstem outlined in figure 40.2A: electrical stimulation of the SC (Sommer and Wurtz, 1998) showed that many FEF neurons *receive* inputs from the SC, presumably by means of a thalamic synapse (Lynch, Hoover, and Strick, 1994). These FEF neurons always had a phasic visual response, and some also carried signals such as delay activity, a presaccadic burst, or fixation activity. These results suggest that the processes underlying saccade generation involve a bidirectional communication between the SC and cortical areas.

COMPARISON OF SUPERIOR COLLICULUS INPUTS The neurons in the LIP area and the FEF that project directly to the SC carry an amalgam of visual, delay, and saccade signals, although the ratio of these signals differs between the two areas. The efferents from the LIP area have not been found to show activity comparable to the burst neurons in the SC, whereas FEF efferents frequently do. The efferents of both the LIP area and the FEF show delay activity, but in the LIP area the activity is more pronounced. Thus, the delay activity is represented more heavily in LIP efferents than is the burst, and for the FEF, it is approximately

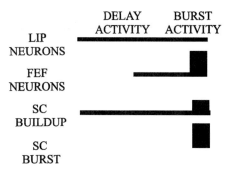

FIGURE 40.10 Summary of the overlap of activity between neurons in the cerebral cortex (LIP and FEF) that project to the SC and the neurons in the SC (burst and buildup). Activity in the delay period is represented by the horizontal line: the greater the activity, the longer the line. The burst is represented by the height of the vertical bar, the higher the bar the larger the burst. The delay activity is consistently present in LIP and SC buildup neurons, but there is little if any burst in the LIP neurons. The delay activity is also present in the FEF neurons, but these neurons also frequently have a burst of activity, as do the SC burst neurons. There are therefore both *differences* between the neurons in the two cortical areas projecting to the SC and *overlap* between the cortical activity and SC activity, the LIP having greater similarity to the SC buildup neurons than to the SC burst neurons and the FEF tending to have the reverse relationship.

the reverse. Figure 40.10 compares schematically this overlap of the activity in the LIP efferents, the FEF efferents, and the SC buildup and burst neurons. Whether this input is directed separately to the burst and buildup neurons in the SC remains to be determined. Because signals also are transmitted from the SC to cortex (and between the FEF and the LIP area as well), the development of saccade-related activity must result from the continuous interaction between multiple brain structures, including the FEF, the LIP area, and the SC.

CONCLUSION: DISTRIBUTED PROCESSING The shifts in processing from one area to the next in the brain logically could be of substantially different types (Miller, 1988). On the one hand, this processing could be discrete: the processing in one area is completed and the result is passed on to the next area, where a new stage of processing begins. Conversely, the processing might be distributed: the same type of processing in one area continues at some higher level in the next area. Comparison of the activity of cortical and SC neurons offers one of the few opportunities in sensorimotor systems to determine which type of transformation occurs. In the visual-oculomotor processing that we have considered, it is distributed processing. One of our most striking observations is that the same type of neuronal activity can be identified in both the cortex and the SC and that there is simply a shift in the characteristics of the processing. For example, the processing conveyed by buildup neurons is carried on in both the parietal cortex and the SC, but analysis of the nature of the continuing activity shows that there is a shift in the dependence of that activity toward the preparation to make a saccade.

REFERENCES

ANDERSEN, R., and J. W. GNADT, 1989. Posterior parietal cortex. In *The Neurobiology of Saccadic Eye Movements, Reviews of Oculomotor Research, Vol. III,* R. H. Wurtz, and M. E. Goldberg, eds. Amsterdam: Elsevier, pp. 315–336.

ANDERSEN, R. A., G. K. ESSICK, and R. M. SIEGEL, 1987. Neurons of area 7 activated by both visual stimuli and oculomotor behavior. *Exp. Brain Res.* 67:316–322.

BARASH, S., R. M. BRACEWELL, L. FOGASSI, J. W. GNADT, and R. A. ANDERSEN, 1991. Saccade-related activity in the lateral intraparietal area: I. Temporal properties. *J. Neurophysiol.* 66:1095–1108.

BASSO, M. A., and R. H. WURTZ, 1997. Modulation of neuronal activity by target uncertainty. *Nature* 389:66–69.

BASSO, M. A., and R. H. WURTZ, 1998. Modulation of neuronal activity in superior colliculus by changes in target probability. *J. Neurosci.* 18:7519–7534.

BEHAN, M., and N. M. KIME, 1996. Intrinsic circuitry in the deep layers of the cat superior colliculus. *Vis. Neurosci.* 13: 1031–1042.

BÜTTNER-ENNEVER, J. A., and A. K. E. HORN, 1994. Neuroanatomy of saccadic omnipause neurons in nucleus raphe interpositus. In *Contemporary Ocular Motor and Vestibular Research: A Tribute to David A. Robinson,* A. F. Fuchs, T. Brandt, U. Büttner, and D. Zee, eds. Stuttgart: Thieme, pp. 488–495.

COLBY, C. L., J.-R. DUHAMEL, and M. E. GOLDBERG, 1995. Oculocentric spatial representation in parietal cortex. *Cereb. Cortex* 5:470–481.

COLBY, C. L., J.-R. DUHAMEL, and M. E. GOLDBERG, 1996. Visual, presaccadic and cognitive activation of single neurons in monkey lateral intraparietal area. *J. Neurophysiol.* 76:2841–2852.

DORRIS, M. C., M. PARÉ, and D. P. MUNOZ, 1997. Neuronal activity in monkey superior colliculus related to the initiation of saccadic eye movements. *J. Neurosci.* 17:8566–8579.

EDELMAN, J. A., and E. L. KELLER, 1996. Activity of visuomotor burst neurons in the superior colliculus accompanying express saccades. *J. Neurophysiol.* 76:908–926.

EVARTS, E. V., 1966. Methods for recording activity of individual neurons in moving animals. In *Methods in Medical Research,* R. F. Rushmer, ed. Chicago: Year Book, pp. 241–250.

FISCHER, B., and R. BOCH, 1983. Saccadic eye movements after extremely short reaction times in the monkey. *Brain Res.* 260:21–26.

FISCHER, B., and H. WEBER, 1993. Express saccades and visual attention. *Behav. Brain Sci.* 16:553–567.

FRIES, W., 1984. Cortical projections to the superior colliculus in the macaque monkey: A retrograde study using horseradish peroxidase. *J. Comp. Neurol.* 230:55–76.

FUCHS, A. F., 1967. Periodic eye tracking in the monkey. *J. Physiol. (Lond.)* 193:161–171.

FUCHS, A. F., and D. A. ROBINSON, 1966. A method for measuring horizontal and vertical eye movement chronically in the monkey. *J. Appl. Physiol.* 21:1068–1070.

GLIMCHER, P. W., and D. L. SPARKS, 1992. Movement selection in advance of action in the superior colliculus. *Nature* 355:542–545.

HEPP, K., V. HENN, T. VILIS, and B. COHEN, 1989. Brainstem regions related to saccade generation. In *The Neurobiology of Saccadic Eye Movements, Reviews of Oculomotor Research, Vol. III,* R. H. Wurtz and M. E. Goldberg, eds. Amsterdam: Elsevier, pp. 105–212.

HIKOSAKA, O., and R. H. WURTZ, 1983. Visual and oculomotor functions of monkey substantia nigra pars reticulata: IV. Relation of substantia nigra to superior colliculus. *J. Neurophysiol.* 49:1285–1301.

HUERTA, M. F., L. A. KRUBITZER, and J. H. KAAS, 1986. Frontal eye field as defined by intracortical microstimulation in squirrel monkeys, owl monkeys, and macaque monkeys: I. Subcortical connections. *J. Comp. Neurol.* 253:415–439.

JUDGE, S. J., B. J. RICHMOND, and F. C. CHU, 1980. Implantation of magnetic search coils for measurement of eye position: An improved method. *Vision Res.* 20:535–538.

KRAUZLIS, R. J., M. A. BASSO, and R. H. WURTZ, 1997. Shared motor error for multiple eye movements. *Science* 276:1693–1695.

KUSTOV, A. A., and D. L. ROBINSON, 1996. Shared neural control of attentional shifts and eye movements. *Nature* 384:74–77.

LEICHNETZ, G. R., and M. E. GOLDBERG, 1988. Higher centers concerned with eye movement and visual attention: Cerebral cortex and thalamus. In *Neuroanatomy of the Oculomotor System,* J. A. Büttner-Ennever, ed. Amsterdam: Elsevier, pp. 365–429.

LEMON, R., 1984. Methods for neuronal recording in conscious animals. In *IBRO Handbook Series: Methods in the Neurosciences, Vol. 4,* New York: J. Wiley & Sons, pp. 95–102.

LYNCH, J. C., A. M. GRAYBIEL, and L. J. LOBECK, 1985. The differential projection of two cytoarchitectonic subregions of the inferior parietal lobule of macaque upon the deep layers of the superior colliculus. *J. Comp. Neurol.* 235:241–254.

LYNCH, J. C., J. E. HOOVER, and P. L. STRICK, 1994. Input to the primate frontal eye field from the substantia nigra, superior colliculus, and dentate nucleus demonstrated by transneuronal transport. *Exp. Brain Res.* 100:181–186.

MAYS, L. E., and D. L. SPARKS, 1980. Dissociation of visual and saccade-related responses in superior colliculus neurons. *J. Neurophysiol.* 43:207–232.

MAZZONI, P., R. M. BRACEWELL, S. BARASH, and R. A. ANDERSEN, 1996. Motor intention activity in the macaque's lateral intraparietal area: I. Dissociation of motor plan from sensory memory. *J. Neurophysiol.* 76:1439–1456.

MEREDITH, M. A., and A. S. RAMOA, 1998. Intrinsic circuitry of the superior colliculus: Pharmacophysiological identification of horizontally oriented inhibitory interneurons. *J. Neurophysiol.* 79:1597–1602.

MILLER, J., 1988. Discrete and continuous models of human information processing: Theoretical distinctions and empirical results. *Acta Psychologica* 67:191–257.

MIZE, R. R., 1992. The organization of GABAergic neurons in the mammalian superior colliculus. *Prog. Brain Res.* 90:219–248.

MOHLER, C. W., and R. H. WURTZ, 1976. Organization of monkey superior colliculus: Intermediate layer cells discharging before eye movements. *J. Neurophysiol.* 39:722–744.

MOSCHOVAKIS, A. K., and S. M. HIGHSTEIN, 1994. The anatomy and physiology of primate neurons that control rapid eye movements. *Annu. Rev. Neurosci.* 17:465–488.

MUNOZ, D. P., and D. GUITTON, 1991. Control of orienting gaze shifts by the tectoreticulospinal system in the head-free cat: II. Sustained discharges during motor preparation and fixation. *J. Neurophysiol.* 66:1624–1641.

MUNOZ, D. P., and P. J. ISTVAN, 1998. Lateral inhibitory interactions in the intermediate layers of the monkey superior colliculus. *J. Neurophysiol.* 79:1193–1209.

MUNOZ, D. P., D. M. WAITZMAN, and R. H. WURTZ, 1996. Activity of neurons in monkey superior colliculus during interrupted saccades. *J. Neurophysiol.* 75:2562–2580.

MUNOZ, D. P., and R. H. WURTZ, 1991. Disruption of visual fixation following injection of GABAergic drugs into the fixation zone of the primate superior colliculus. *Soc. Neurosci. Abs.* 17:544.

MUNOZ, D. P., and R. H. WURTZ, 1993a. Fixation cells in monkey superior colliculus: I. Characteristics of cell discharge. *J. Neurophysiol.* 70:559–575.

MUNOZ, D. P., and R. H. WURTZ, 1993b. Fixation cells in monkey superior colliculus: II. Reversible activation and deactivation. *J. Neurophysiol.* 70:576–589.

MUNOZ, D. P., and R. H. WURTZ, 1995a. Saccade-related activity in monkey superior colliculus: I. Characteristics of burst and buildup cells. *J. Neurophysiol.* 73:2313–2333.

MUNOZ, D. P., and R. H. WURTZ, 1995b. Saccade-related activity in monkey superior colliculus: II. Spread of activity during saccades. *J. Neurophysiol.* 73:2334–2348.

PARÉ, M., and D. GUITTON, 1994. The fixation area of the cat superior colliculus: Effects of electrical stimulation and direct connection with brainstem omnipause neurons. *Exp. Brain Res.* 101:109–122.

PARÉ, M., and D. P. MUNOZ, 1996. Saccadic reaction time in the monkey: Advanced preparation of oculomotor programs is primarily responsible for express saccade occurrence. *J. Neurophysiol.* 76:3666–3681.

PARÉ, M., and R. H. WURTZ, 1997. Monkey posterior parietal cortex neurons antidromically activated from superior colliculus. *J. Neurophysiol.* 78:3493–3497.

RIEHLE, A., and J. REQUIN, 1993. The predictive value for performance speed of preparatory changes in neuronal activity of the monkey motor and premotor cortex. *Behav. Brain Res.* 26:35–49.

ROBINSON, D. A., 1968. Eye movement control in primates. *Science* 161:1219–1224.

ROBINSON, D. A., 1972. Eye movements evoked by collicular stimulation in the alert monkey. *Vision Res.* 12:1795–1808.

SCHILLER, P. H., J. H. SANDELL, and J. H. R. MAUNSELL, 1987. The effect of frontal eye field and superior colliculus lesions on saccadic latencies in the rhesus monkey. *J. Neurophysiol.* 57:1033–1049.

SCHILLER, P. H., and M. STRYKER, 1972. Single-unit recording and stimulation in superior colliculus of the alert rhesus monkey. *J. Neurophysiol.* 35:915–924.

SCHILLER, P. H., S. D. TRUE, and J. L. CONWAY, 1980. Deficits in eye movements following frontal eye field and superior colliculus ablations. *J. Neurophysiol.* 44:1175–1189.

SEGRAVES, M. A., and M. E. GOLDBERG, 1987. Functional properties of corticotectal neurons in the monkey's frontal eye field. *J. Neurophysiol.* 58:1387–1419.

SOMMER, M. A., 1994. Express saccades elicited during visual scan in the monkey. *Vision Res.* 34:2023–2038.

SOMMER, M. A., 1997. The spatial relationship between scanning saccades and express saccades. *Vision Res.* 37:2745–2756.

SOMMER, M. A., M. PARÉ, and R. H. WURTZ, 1997. Instructional dependence of preparatory discharges of superior colliculus neurons. *Soc. Neurosci. Abs.* 23:843.

SOMMER, M. A., and R. H. WURTZ, 1998. Frontal eye field neurons orthodromically activated from the superior colliculus. *J. Neurophysiol.* 80:3331–3335.

SPARKS, D. L., 1978. Functional properties of neurons in the monkey superior colliculus: coupling of neuronal activity and saccade onset. *Brain Res.* 156:1–16.

SPARKS, D. L., and R. HARTWICH-YOUNG, 1989. The deep layers of the superior colliculus. In *The Neurobiology of Saccadic Eye Movements, Reviews of Oculomotor Research, Vol. III,* R. H. Wurtz and M. E. Goldberg, eds. Amsterdam: Elsevier, pp. 213–256.

SPARKS, D. L., C. LEE, W. H. ROHRER, 1990. Population coding of the direction, amplitude, and velocity of saccadic eye movements by neurons in the superior colliculus. *Cold Spring Harbor Symp. Quant. Biol.* 55:805–811.

WURTZ, R. H., 1969. Visual receptive fields of striate cortex neurons in awake monkeys. *J. Neurophysiol.* 32:727–742.

WURTZ, R. H., and M. E. GOLDBERG, 1972. Activity of superior colliculus in behaving monkey: III. Cells discharging before eye movements. *J. Neurophysiol.* 35:575–586.

WURTZ, R. H., and M. A. SOMMER, 1998. Instructional dependence of delay activity in the projection from frontal eye field to superior colliculus in macaque. *Soc. Neurosci. Abs.* 24:1146.

WYMAN, D., and R. M. STEINMAN, 1973. Small step tracking: Implications for the oculomotor "dead zone." *Vision Res.* 13:2165–2172.

YARBUS, A. L., 1967. *Eye Movements and Vision.* New York: Plenum.

41 The Neural Correlates of Place and Direction

M. A. WILSON

ABSTRACT Recent findings have shed new light on the biological mechanisms underlying our sense of direction and place. Distinct brain subsystems in the hippocampus, thalamus, subicular, and parietal regions display direct neural correlates of head orientation and spatial location within specific environments. The behavior of cells in these areas also is affected strongly by prior experience, suggesting a significant mnemonic component to these systems. The trajectory dependence of activity within the hippocampus suggests a role in processing of route or ordered mnemonic information.

Navigation and maps

Navigation can be defined simply as the process of getting from place to place. Although simple to describe, its successful execution can be quite complex. This problem can be solved through a calculation of a trajectory between locations using the determinations of position, course, and distance traveled. Such traversal can involve establishing an initial position and bearing and then updating this information by keeping track of self-movement in a process known as "dead reckoning." Taken in this sense, we see that navigation is fundamentally a process of map traversal and without doubt, many animals are quite adept at carrying out such navigational feats (Gallistel, 1990).

However, the process also can be viewed at another level, one that may strike many as more consonant with their own personal experience. Going from one place to another frequently involves traversing a network of intermediate points—following a route in which familiar landmarks indicate progressive success and dictate new courses of actions. Using such a strategy requires the ability to identify landmarks and to establish spatial orientation with respect to them. This is the navigational strategy not of maps, but of routes. One easily can see how these systems relate to one another. Traversing the

gap between intermediate points of a route can itself become a mapping process.

A distinctive difference between route and map-based navigation is the relaxation of the need for precise metric information, particularly that of distance. This is familiar to those who have viewed a navigational guide to a subway in which distance typically is distorted but nevertheless provides perfectly adequate instruction for achieving the ultimate objective of reaching one place from another. But the two fundamental pieces of information that are shared by both map- and route-based strategy are those of place and heading.

In 1978, O'Keefe and Nadel outlined several basic systems for rodent spatial navigation. Routes and cues were maintained by a *taxon* system, whereas maps were part of the *locale* system. The hippocampus in particular was implicated as the heart of the locale system, the site of the cognitive map. But recently, many other areas involved in the evaluation of distance, location, and directions have been identified. These areas also have been found to contribute to other forms of spatial behavior, such as visual search and reaching, suggesting related features of motor control.

In this chapter, we examine in detail the neural systems that appear to be involved in establishing and maintaining a sense of place and direction.

Our ability to recall childhood memories is limited to those events occurring roughly after the age of 3 years that overlap with the emergence of more mature spatial navigational strategies (Hermer and Spelke, 1996). Thus begins the relationship between our sense of place and our ability to form lasting memories of events, linked through the hippocampus, a brain structure that lies at this intersection of memory and spatial cognition. Figure 41.1 diagrams the pathways that lead to the hippocampus. These include structures in the parietal lobe that have been associated with spatial localization and movement (see chapter 36), areas in the frontal lobe which are responsible for the coordination of actions (see chapter 38), areas in the temporal lobe

M. A. WILSON Departments of Brain and Cognitive Sciences and Biology, Center for Learning and Memory, Massachusetts Institute of Technology, Cambridge, Mass.

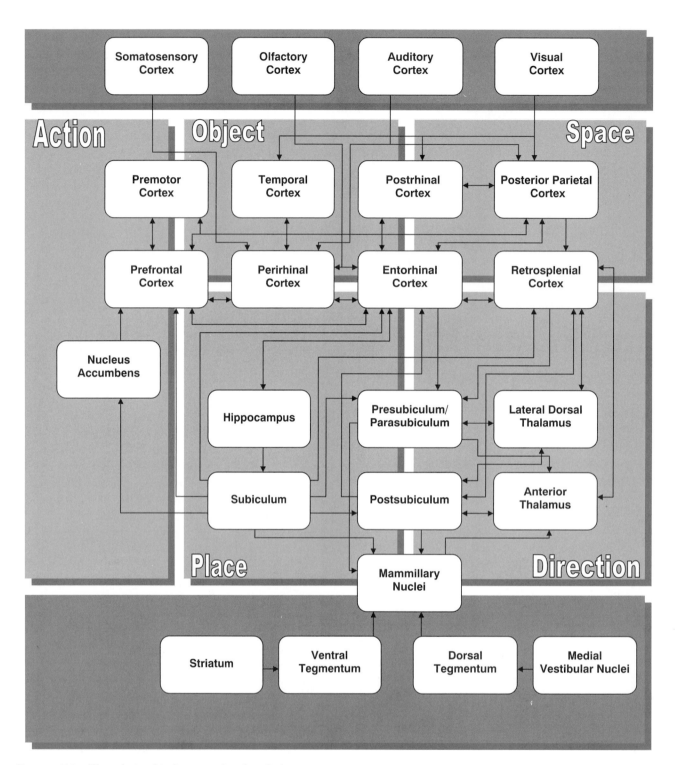

FIGURE 41.1 The relationship between the identified systems
carrying place and directional information.

involved in object identification, and thalamic areas
carrying directional information.

A SENSE OF PLACE *Perirhinal, postrhinal, and entorhinal
cortex* Identification and localization of landmarks are
important for establishing position and bearing during

navigation. In rodents, this landmark information appears to pass through perirhinal and postrhinal cortices
that lie along the rhinal sulcus of the temporal lobe. The
perirhinal cortex receives significant input from sensory
areas that may code for stimulus attributes such as somatosensory, auditory, and olfactory cortices. The postrhi-

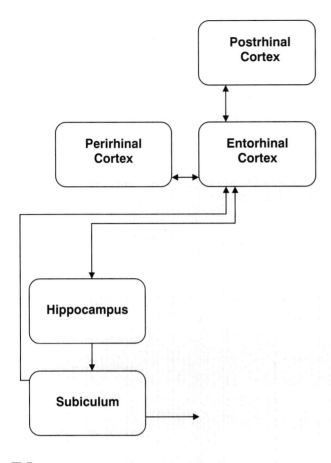

FIGURE 41.2   The systems involved in carrying place information.

nal cortex (corresponding to primate parahippocampal cortex [Burwell, Witter, and Amaral, 1995]) receives input from visual and spatial areas, such as posterior parietal cortex, that may carry information about stimulus location, angle, and distance. The outputs of these structures converge in the entorhinal cortex, where the integration of spatial and attribute information may occur (figure 41.2) (Burwell and Amaral, 1998). Behavioral studies in rodents (Bunsey and Eichenbaum, 1993; Wiig, Cooper, and Bear, 1996; Mumby and Pinel, 1994; Zhu, Brown, and Aggleton, 1995) and in primates (Suzuki et al., 1993; Gaffan and Murray, 1992; Murray and Mishkin, 1986; Zola-Morgan et al., 1989) demonstrate the importance of these structures in spatial and object memory tasks. Human imaging studies have shown that these areas are active during navigation (Aguirre et al., 1996) and viewing of spatial scenes (Epstein and Kanwisher, 1998). Interestingly, combined lesions of perirhinal and postrhinal cortex impair object recognition but still allow rodents to perform some spatial memory tasks, showing that spatial navigation is not entirely de-

pendent on landmark recognition (Aggleton et al., 1997).

The hippocampus   The hippocampus is a brain region that has been implicated in the formation and long-term consolidation of episodic memory (Zola-Morgan and Squire, 1993; Scoville and Milner, 1957). It receives convergent information from unimodal and multimodal association cortices through the entorhinal cortex (figure 41.1). Damage to the hippocampus leads to severe spatial learning deficits in animals (O'Keefe and Nadel 1978), and recent functional imaging studies have related hippocampal activation with spatial navigation and memory in humans (Maguire, Frackowiak, and Frith, 1997; Maguire et al., 1998; Ghaem et al., 1997).

Place cells   Hippocampal pyramidal cells recorded in freely behaving rodents have spatial receptive fields that are restricted to relatively small regions (5%–30%) of specific environments. Different cells are active in different locations, and the region of space in which they are active is referred to as the "place field" of the cell (O'Keefe and Dostrovsky, 1971). Individual cells can show remarkably consistent firing patterns over long periods of time, with repeated placement in the same environment, and cells will have different place fields in different environments (Thompson and Best, 1989; Kubie and Ranck, 1983; O'Keefe and Speakman, 1987). Ensembles of 50 to 100 cells can convey sufficient information over a 1-second interval to precisely locate an animal in space to within a few centimeters, and in any given environment, 30% to 50% of all hippocampal pyramidal cells may have fields (Wilson and McNaughton, 1993) (figure 41.3; see color plate 25). Place cells have been identified in all CA regions of the hippocampus and dentate gyrus (Jung and McNaughton, 1993) and in the subiculum (Sharp and Green, 1994), superficial layers of the entorhinal cortex (Quirk et al., 1992) and parasubiculum (Taube, 1995a). Place cells typically require active locomotion through the field for spatial firing but respond to passive movement of the animal through its place field under certain conditions. Animals moved through their place fields under conditions of severe restraint show an absence of spatially related firing (Foster, Castro, and McNaughton, 1989). This is related to the significant influence of behavioral state on hippocampal activity. Pyramidal cells recorded while an animal is resting quietly or sleeping lose both their characteristic 8- to 10-Hz rhythmic activity and spatial selectivity. Although place fields persist after removal of individual visual cues (O'Keefe and Speakman, 1987), as well as in total darkness (Markus et al., 1994; Quirk, Muller, and Kubie, 1990), rotation of individual cues results in corresponding rotation of place fields,

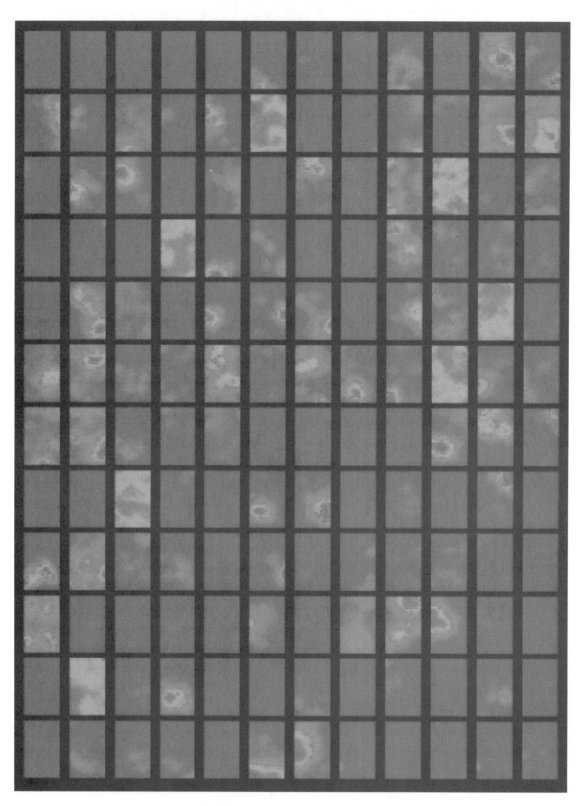

FIGURE 41.3 Spatial firing distributions of 144 hippocampal place cells recorded simultaneously while the rat explored a 60 × 45-cm apparatus. Each panel represents the firing distribution of one cell. Red indicates high firing, dark blue indicates no firing. The 7 high rate cells are inhibitory interneurons, the rest are pyramidal cells. The spatial encoding by hippocampal cells is sufficiently robust that the animal's location in the apparatus can be predicted to within a few centimeters solely on the basis of the mean firing rate distributions and the activity of these cells over a 1-second window.

indicating that visual cues can exert strong influence over spatial firing but can be supplanted by nonvisual, presumably idiothetic information, under certain conditions.

Although place cells can show spatial specificity on the first exposure to a spatial location (Hill, 1978), the robustness of response improves significantly with repeated exposures over the course of 5 to 10 minutes. The coordinated activity of ensembles of neurons also was found to vary as a result of experience (Wilson and McNaughton, 1993). This finding suggests that familiarity may be reflected in the degree of coordinated activation of hippocampal ensembles, which itself may be a function of activity dependent synaptic plasticity.

In a related finding, McHugh and associates (1996) examined the spatial firing characteristics of hippocampal CA1 cells in mice with CA1-specific genetic deletion of N-methyl-D-aspartate (NMDA) receptors. This deletion effectively eliminated NMDA-dependent long-term potentiation (LTP), a primary form of activity dependent on synaptic plasticity in this region. Although these animals still showed place-related firing, the fields themselves were larger and more variable, and ensembles of cells with overlapping place fields showed no significant covariation, in a sense never making the transition from novel to familiar firing patterns due to the absence of synaptic plasticity (figure 41.4; see color plate 26).

Although spatial location is a dominant factor influencing the activity of place cells during random foraging, during repeated traversal of a fixed path—such as running back and forth on a linear track—the firing of these cells becomes highly directional. Cells show high rates of firing when the animal is moving through the location of the field in a particular direction and are silent when it moves through the same location in the opposing direction (McNaughton, Barnes, and O'Keefe, 1983).

This directional dependency does not require linear behavior and emerges whenever an animal repeatedly follows a trajectory. Additionally, this directionality is not constrained by fixed heading and can appear during repeated turns of a given orientation or along circular paths that span 180° (Wilson, unpublished observations). Muller and colleagues (1994) have argued that differences in directional selectivity during linear track and open-field behavior demonstrates that directionality is not a fixed attribute of hippocampal place cells but rather is a function of task and environment.

REFERENCE FRAMES   For navigational purposes, spatial information must be maintained relative to one or more reference frames. Gothard and associates (1996) recorded multiple simultaneous place cells during a task in which the animal made repeated excursions from a start-

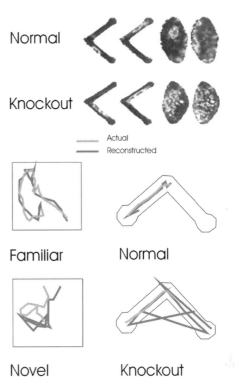

FIGURE 41.4   The effect of blockade of synaptic plasticity on the robustness of the spatial signal in the hippocampus of a mouse. This mouse was engineered genetically to knock out the NMDA receptor selectively in region CA1 (Tsien, Huerta, and Tonegawa, 1996). Trajectory reconstruction is shown for normal and disrupted animals. This also is compared with trajectory reconstruction in normal rats during novel and familiar exposure to an environment. Accurate transmission of spatial information appears to require both experience and synaptic plasticity.

ing box to a goal site, each of which were placed at varied locations in a large environment. They found cells that responded to multiple reference frames as defined by the room, start, and goal boxes. These responses were distributed across largely nonoverlapping populations of cells and were active simultaneously, with some cells responding at fixed locations with respect to the room, and other cells responding as the animal approached or left the start and goal points. These results demonstrate the complex manner in which context must be defined relative to relevant cues.

The reference frames need not be defined purely by spatial or geometric factors. Markus and coworkers (1995) found that different place cells could be activated depending not only on the location and heading of the animals but also based on the task the animal was performing. Rats were trained on an open field either to forage for randomly scattered food pellets or to sequentially visit four locations arranged in a square configuration. Place fields in these two tasks differed, and when the animal was cued to switch between these tasks at random times, the place cells were able to switch rapidly to the appropriate task-dependent representation.

GEOMETRY AND PLACE Burgess and O'Keefe (1996) demonstrated that geometric distortion of a small enclosure through stretching walls in a way that preserved the basic topology of the space but altered relative distance between points resulted in place cells that were stretched similarly. These cells appeared to preserve the topology or connectedness of adjacent locations at the expense of absolute distance. The loss of distance information with preservation of topological and geometric information points, when combined with the emergence of directional firing during repeated path following, points to a strong influence of route or trajectory information over absolute spatial information. Gallistel (1996) has argued that this geometric information is used for both orientating animals in space as well as localizing goals within that space.

A SENSE OF DIRECTION Our ability to perceive and maintain a sense of direction is tied fundamentally to a subsystem of sensory (primarily visual and vestibular) brain areas. Behavioral studies in animals have demonstrated an ability to establish and maintain a sense of direction (Mittelstaedt and Glasauer, 1991; Gallistel, 1990; Etienne, Maurer, and Seguinot, 1996). Berthoz (1997) points out that although it has been shown that humans are capable of acquiring and reproducing spatial trajectories using the integration of linear and angular vestibular information alone, patients with vestibular deficits still could maintain distance information, but directional information was lost. This suggested that vestibular information contributed to the sense of orientation, whereas motor information contributed to estimates of distance.

By integrating both angular and linear self-motion information along a path relative to a starting point, the simple form of navigation known as "dead reckoning" can be carried out. This system of path integration requires that distance and direction be computed. Insects may accomplish this through monitoring visual flow, counting footfalls, or tracking position of the sun (Gallistel, 1990), whereas rodents may use vestibular and motor efferents in conjunction with visual landmark evaluation. The use of this system typically is demonstrated by assessing the ability of an animal to take a meandering outward path from a starting point to a goal and then return along a straight line following the shortest path to the start (Etienne, Maurer, and Seguinot, 1996). Whishaw and Maaswinkel (1998) have argued that the ability to carry out this navigational task in the absence of visual guidance requires intact hippocampal

function. McNaughton and associates (1996) have proposed a model that identifies the hippocampus as a system that is preconfigured to support dead reckoning.

Head direction cells Maintaining orientation, or heading, is a process of establishing a stable angular reference with respect to a particular reference frame in which one wishes to carry out navigational behavior. The relationship between points within these reference frames, such as distance and direction, defines coordinate systems. These reference frames may exist "out there" in the world, independent of the organism. In such "allocentric" reference frames, coordinates are independent of the orientation of the body in space (Tolman, 1948; O'Keefe and Nadel, 1978). Allocentric coordinates are not necessarily of a fixed scale and could encompass a single room, a building, or an entire city. As these examples suggest, they also may be nested and dependent on one another.

Egocentric reference frames are those that are relative to the organism. They may define a space relative to the head, the eye, or the hand, and once again we see that movement through this space relative to the body becomes a matter of traversing multiple, nested frames of reference. Although we largely confine our discussion to issues of allocentric localization and orientation, in chapters 36 and 38, we see similar issues arise in the context of motor control of reaching and gaze.

Although allocentric coordinate systems appear to be defined exclusively by the measured relationships between objects in the world, an organism could use a separate self-constructed coordinate system within that external space. In particular, idiothetic information—those signals generated by the actions of the organism itself—can serve to construct such a self-contained reference system through the process of path integration, allowing an actions to be carried out in the absence of or in the face of unreliable information from the external world. The most familiar of these internal signals are those arising from the vestibular and proprioceptive systems.

Significant progress has been made in identifying both the regions and the factors that influence these directional signals. Head direction cells have been identified in a number of regions of the brain, including the anterior dorsal nucleus of the thalamus (ATN) (Taube, 1995b), the lateral dorsal thalamic nucleus (LDN) (Mizumori and Williams, 1993), the striatum (Wiener, 1993), the retrosplenial or posterior cingulate cortex (Chen et al., 1994), and postsubiculum (PoS) (Taube, Muller, and Ranck, 1990). These regions maintain a precise representation of current heading with narrow tuning characteristics. These head direction cells fire independently of the animal's location within an environment with preferred firing directions distributed over 360°. Although cells in each of these regions respond with similar directional specificity, they do show different sensitivity to visual, vestibular, and motor efferent signals (reviewed in Taube et al., 1996).

Parietal, retrosplenial, striatal head direction cells Only a small fraction of cells in the parietal cortex have been reported to show directional firing (<5%) and therefore are unlikely to represent a significant source of directional information. Head direction cells in the retrosplenial cortex share a number of attributes with the thalamic and PoS cells but show greater variability of response and broader tuning curves and lower frequency of occurrence (<10%) (Chen et al., 1994). These systems probably derive directional information from multiple convergent sources and therefore reflect a higher-order evaluation of direction. Cells with head directional correlates in the striatum are small in number (<10%), with additional behavioral correlates such as spatial preference and task sensitivity. These cells also are unlikely to serve as the basis for a basic directional system and are more likely to relate to task and behavioral elements that have directional attributes. This may be similar to the type of directionality seen in hippocampal cells during repeated path traversal.

In rodents, lesions to the parietal cortex produce long-lasting deficits in tasks that require learning object/spatial relationships but leave object recognition unaffected (Decoteau and Kesner, 1998). Interestingly, such lesions do not seem to impair allocentric distance estimates (Long and Kesner, 1996), suggesting that orientation may be particularly dependent on intact parietal function. Retrosplenial lesions also fail to impair several tasks involving memory for spatial location (Neave et al., 1994) or object identity (Ennaceur, Neave, and Aggleton, 1997). Similarly, in humans, lesions in the retrosplenial and parietal regions produce deficits in memory for directional orientation between objects while leaving the ability to identify those objects intact (Takahashi et al., 1997).

Anterior, lateral dorsal thalamic nuclei, and the postsubiculum The most prominent directional signals arise from thalamic and postsubicular regions. Mizumori and Williams (1993) found that LDN cells required visual input to establish their initial directional specificity but could maintain responsiveness in the absence of visual cues. Additionally, maximal directional firing for individual cells was established after exposure to multiple cues at different headings and locations rather than single cues in the preferred direction, suggesting a contextual as well as perceptual influence on the directional signal.

They also identified a correlation between directional specificity and errors on the radial arm maze.

Dudchenko and Taube (1997) found a similar relationship between head direction cells and errors on a spatial reference memory task. They also reported an absence of goal related modulation of head directional activity.

Taube (1995b) identified a difference between postsubicular (PoS) and anterior thalamic head (ATN) direction cells. PoS cells maintained directional firing during passive rotation of a restrained animal whereas cells in the ATN did not, suggesting that ATN cells require volitional movement signals.

The ability of visual cues to override internal signals was examined by Goodridge and Taube (1995). Animals were presented with conflicting directional information from internal directional sources (e.g., self-motion and vestibular integration) and external sources (visual cues) by reintroducing a familiar landmark at a position that was inconsistent with current directional firing. Cells in both the ATN and PoS shifted their firing to match the direction indicated by prior experience with the landmark.

Interestingly, Taube and Burton (1995) report that these cells can change preferred direction when an animal moves from one environment to the next, suggesting that this directional system is tied to individual frames of reference rather than serving as an absolute measure of heading. They also discovered that repeated conflict between visual and idiothetic cues led to a reduction in the control of visual cues over directional response.

In a related study, Knierim and associates (1995) examined the influence of familiar and salient visual cues on thalamic head direction cells and place cells in the hippocampus (CA1 and CA3) when the relationship between internal and external directional signals was placed repeatedly in conflict through disorientation (repeated rotation in a closed container). Animals were trained to forage for randomly scattered food pellets in a circular gray environment with a single salient visual cue (a white or black cue card covering 90° of the cylinder wall). Under these conditions, the cue card had minimal influence on reorienting the animals' directional and place responses. This disruption of cue-control was evident even in animals that were not subjected immediately to the disorientation procedure but that had been through the experience weeks before testing. These results point to the importance of the animal's perception of cue stability as a factor in predicting the degree of influence the cue has on directional and spatial orientation. After such disorientation, the variation in directional and place firing remains strongly coupled, suggesting that disorientation relates more

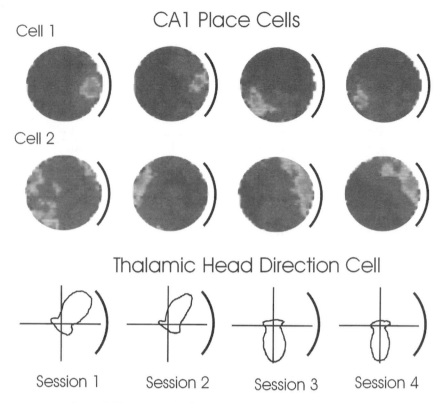

CA1 Place Cells

Cell 1

Cell 2

Thalamic Head Direction Cell

Session 1   Session 2   Session 3   Session 4

FIGURE 41.5 Spontaneous rotation of hippocampal place cells and thalamic directional cells after disorientation.

directly to reference frame orientation than consistency of place or positional information (figure 41.5; see color plate 27). This study also offered some insight into the parameters that may govern the balance between visual versus internal directional cues. Rotation of the cue cards by less than 45° was more likely to produce a correction of head direction cells. This suggests that passively maintained internal heading information may have significant intrinsic error that must be updated frequently to maintain integrity. This is consistent with the observation that place and directional firing in hippocampal and surrounding regions degrades over 5- to 10-minute periods of open-field exploration in the dark, and that the interval can be reduced significantly through further elimination of nonvisual intramaze cues.

Dudchenko, Goodridge, and Taube (1997) found that animals that were impaired in a radial arm maze task after disorientation still followed single distal landmarks. These results suggest that learned association between a landmark and stable experience is not required for a landmark to influence head direction responses. It also suggests that disorientation can influence not only the variability of the directional signal but that the use of the signal in guiding behavioral responses. A similar dissoci-

ation was proposed to exist between spatial firing of hippocampal cells reflecting response specificity and the covariance of place-cell ensembles, reflecting response familiarity or reliability (McHugh et al., 1996).

Although visual cues have been found to exert a variable influence on directional firing, removal of self-motion cues through vestibular system lesions were found to completely abolish directional firing of ATN cells, with only minor impact on locomotive behavior but significant impact on navigational ability (Stackman and Taube, 1997).

Conversely, lesions of the hippocampus had no impact on directional firing of cells in either the postsubiculum or the ATN (Golob and Taube, 1997). In addition, the preferred firing direction of these cells remained stable over several days of repeated exposure to an environment. This suggests that the contextual information required for establishing orientation within an environment may be more limited than the information provided by the hippocampus for establishing spatial location or context. In a complementary manner, Smith (1997) reviewed studies that suggest that hippocampal function may be capable of compensation for the orientation deficits introduced by vestibular dysfunction. These results reinforce the notion that the sense of direction and the sense of place are separate faculties maintained by distinct brain structures.

CONNECTIVITY BETWEEN DIRECTIONAL SUBSYSTEMS
Anatomic studies have identified reciprocal connectivity between many of the regions with head directional cells (figure 41.6). To identify the dependencies between some of these structures, Goodridge and Taube (1997) performed lesions of either the ATN or the PoS and recorded from head direction cells in the remaining structure. They found that ATN cells maintained directional firing after PoS lesions, but that lesions of the ATN abolished directional firing in the PoS. Examination of the directional responses in ATN cells with the PoS removed revealed a reduction in visual cue control and broader directional tuning. These results suggest that the PoS contributes information needed for visual control of orientation, but consistent with earlier results indicating the variable influence of visual cues on directional firing, elimination of this information through PoS lesions did not abolish directional response. Conversely, disruption of ATN lesions, like vestibular system lesions, led to complete disruption of directional response, again pointing to the critical role of vestibular information in orientation.

Lesions of the LDN, which is connected reciprocally with the PoS (Golob, Wolk, and Taube, 1998), did not affect directional firing of PoS head direction cells and did not affect visual cue control.

Two studies have suggested that the firing of ATN cells is correlated more closely with the animal's future head direction (20–30 msec) whereas PoS activity corresponds to current heading (Taube and Muller, 1998; Blair and Sharp, 1996). This effect may result from differential contributions of motor efferent copy signals to the ATN and the PoS or from delay associated with the ATN to PoS-directed drive revealed in earlier lesion studies. Direct motor drive of ATN cells with minimal delay is consistent with earlier discussion of ATN disruption during passive rotation, although continued firing of PoS cells under these conditions indicates a more complex pattern of interaction.

The retrosplenial cortex lies at the convergence of neocortical sensory, thalamic directional, and hippocampal spatial systems. This would provide a convenient site for the integration of distal information, whereas the convergence of self-motion (idiothetic) information, place, and direction in the pre-, post-, and parasubicular areas would provide a convenient site for path integration. The close relationship of retrosplenial and subicular cortices would allow for interaction between distal and ideothetic systems, enabling visual updating of directional sense as well as vestibular correction for egocentric object coordinates.

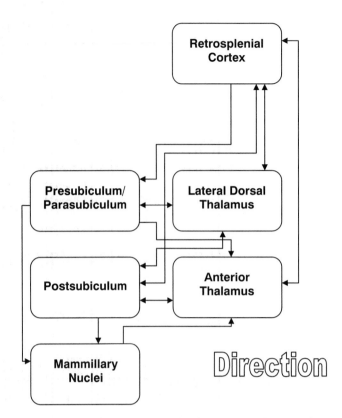

FIGURE 41.6 The systems involved in carrying directional information.

Computational models

Based on many of the findings described, a number of models have been proposed that combine these systems into a comprehensive neural architecture for navigation (see Trullier et al., 1997, for a review).

Brown and Sharp (1995) describe a model of navigation that uses a stimulus-response strategy for route learning. In this model, head direction and place cells activate "motor" cells. The resulting change in position and heading after motor response activates a different set of place and head direction cells, leading to the next response. This approach is similar to the "local view" hypothesis proposed by McNaughton, Chen, and Markus (1991). Although this simple S-R model allows rapid route learning, it does not lend itself well to novel route generation.

Redish and Touretzky (Touretzky and Redish, 1996; Redish and Touretzky, 1997) offer a comprehensive model of navigation based on anatomic segregation and connectivity of structures in the hippocampus, the thalamus, and the neocortex. They divide the problem of navigation into six distinct subproblems–local view, head direction, path integration, place coding, goals, and reference frames.

Foster and associates (1998) describe a computation model of navigation that combines mechanisms of dead reckoning and reward learning with an internal representation of allocentric space to provide a framework for rapid learning of trajectories to goals. Learning in the model is based on the well-established temporal difference rule, and the hippocampus provides crucial map information for optimizing trajectories based on spatial adjacency of paths. The model is particularly interesting because it is able to solve not only a conventional spatial reference memory task in the Morris water maze but also a novel and computationally difficult delay match to place task.

RELATION TO OTHER MOTOR CORTICAL CONTROL SYSTEMS The process of navigation bears similarities to other motor control problems. These include the controlled movement of the eyes during visual exploration of a scene and movement of the limbs during spatial exploration, or reaching for objects in space. Each of these tasks requires the identification of target objects, evaluation of their spatial location within a sensory coordinate system, transformation of that spatial information into a motor output coordinate system, initiation of action based on the target and its location, and maintenance or integration of changes in spatial information resulting from those actions. In chapter 38, Rizzolatti and colleagues describe neurons in the primate premotor area that contain a "vocabulary" of motor actions that can be modulated by activity in parietal cortical areas. In chapter 36, Andersen and associates describe neurons in the posterior parietal cortex that provide the sensory context for execution of planned eye and arm movements. There also is evidence that the hippocampus may be involved in sequences of visually guided memory saccades (Müri et al., 1994).

Summary

Directional and place information is maintained by distinct hippocampal, subicular, and thalamic subsystems that are capable of incorporating intrinsic self-motion signals and extrinsic cue information in a stable representation of orientation and location. These signals also are highly dependent on prior experience, demonstrating their dependence on memory. Cells in the hippocampus that are modulated strongly by spatial location also show strong trajectory dependence, which suggests a role of this system in route- or order-related mnemonic and navigational processing. These systems can be related to more general motor control systems that involve the planning and guidance of actions in space.

REFERENCES

AGGLETON, J. P., S. KEEN, E. C. WARBURTON, and T. J. BUSSEY, 1997. Extensive cytotoxic lesions involving both the rhinal cortices and area TE impair recognition but spare spatial alternation in the rat. *Brain Res. Bull.* 43:279–287.

AGUIRRE, G. K., J. A. DETRE, D. C. ALSOP, and M. D'ESPOSITO, 1996. The parahippocampus subserves topographical learning in man. *Cereb. Cortex* 6:823–829.

BERTHOZ, A., 1997. Parietal and hippocampal contribution to topokinetic and topographical memory. *Philos. Trans. R. Soc. Lond. B Biol. Sci.* 352:1437–1448.

BLAIR, H. T., and P. E. SHARP, 1996. Visual and vestibular influences on head-direction cells in the anterior thalamus of the rat. *Behav. Neurosci.* 110:643–660.

BROWN, M. A., and P. E. SHARP, 1995. Simulation of spatial learning in the Morris water maze by a neural network model of the hippocampal formation and nucleus accumbens. *Hippocampus* 5:171–188.

BUNSEY, M., and H. EICHENBAUM, 1993. Critical role for the parahippocampal region for paired-associate learning in rats. *Behav. Neurosci.* 107:740–747.

BURGESS, N., and J. O'KEEFE, 1996. Neuronal computations underlying the firing of place cells and their role in navigation. *Hippocampus* 6:749–762.

BURWELL, R. D., and D. G. AMARAL, 1998. Perirhinal and postrhinal cortices of the rat: Interconnectivity and connections with the entorhinal cortex. *J. Comp. Neurol.* 391:293–321.

BURWELL, R. D., M. P. WITTER, and D. G. AMARAL, 1995. Perirhinal and postrhinal cortices of the rat: A review of the neuroanatomical literature and comparison with findings from the monkey brain. *Hippocampus* 5:390–408.

CHEN, L. L., L. H. LIN, E. J. GREEN, C. A. BARNES, and B. L. MCNAUGHTON, 1994. Head-direction cells in the rat posterior cortex: I. Anatomical distribution and behavioral modulation. *Exp. Brain Res.* 101:8–23.

DECOTEAU, W. E., and R. P. KESNER, 1998. Effects of hippocampal and parietal cortex lesions on the processing of multiple-object scenes. *Behav. Neurosci.* 112:68–82.

DUDCHENKO, P. A., and J. S. TAUBE, 1997. Correlation between head direction cell activity and spatial behavior on a radial arm maze. *Behav. Neurosci.* 111:3–19.

DUDCHENKO, P. A., J. P. GOODRIDGE, and J. S. TAUBE, 1997. The effects of disorientation on visual landmark control of head direction cell orientation. *Exp. Brain. Res.* 115:375–380.

ENNACEUR, A., N. NEAVE, and J. P. AGGLETON, 1997. Spontaneous object recognition and object location memory in rats: The effects of lesions in the cingulate cortices, the medial prefrontal cortex, the cingulum bundle and the fornix. *Exp. Brain Res.* 113:509–519.

EPSTEIN, R., and N. KANWISHER, 1998. A cortical representation of the local visual environment. *Nature* 392:598–601.

ETIENNE, A. S., R. MAURER, and V. SEGUINOT, 1996. Path integration in mammals and its interaction with visual landmarks. *J. Exp. Biol.* 199:201–209.

FOSTER, D. J., R. G. M. MORRIS, and P. DAYAN, 1998. Hippocampal model of rat spatial abilities using temporal difference learning. In: *Advances in Neural Information Processing 10*, M. I. Jordan, M. J. Kearns, and S. A. Solla, eds. Cambridge, Mass.: MIT Press, pp. 145–151.

FOSTER, T. C., C. A. CASTRO, and B. L. MCNAUGHTON, 1989. Spatial selectivity of rat hippocampal neurons: Dependence on preparedness for movement. *Science* 244:1580–1582.

GAFFAN, D., and E. A. MURRAY, 1992. Monkeys (Macaca fascicularis) with rhinal cortex ablations succeed in object discrimination learning despite 24-hr intertrial intervals and fail at matching to sample despite double sample presentations. *Behav. Neurosci.* 106:30–38.

GALLISTEL, C. R., 1990. *The Organization of Learning.* Cambridge, Mass.: MIT Press.

GALLISTEL, C. R., and A. E. CRAMER, 1996. Computations on metric maps in mammals: Getting oriented and choosing a multi-destination route. *J. Exp. Biol.* 199:211–217.

GHAEM, O., E. MELLET, F. CRIVELLO, N. TZOURIO, B. MAZOYER, A. BERTHOZ, and M. DENIS, 1997. Mental navigation along memorized routes activates the hippocampus, precuneus, and insula. *Neuroreport* 8:739–744.

GOLOB, E. J., D. A. WOLK, and J. S. TAUBE, 1998. Recordings of postsubiculum head direction cells following lesions of the laterodorsal thalamic nucleus. *Brain Res.* 780:9–19.

GOLOB, E. J., and J. S. TAUBE, 1997. Head direction cells and episodic spatial information in rats without a hippocampus. *Proc. Natl. Acad. Sci. U.S.A.* 94:7645–7650.

GOODRIDGE, J. P., and J. S. TAUBE, 1997. Interaction between the postsubiculum and anterior thalamus in the generation of head direction activity. *J. Neurosci.* 17:9315–9330.

GOODRIDGE, J. P., and J. S. TAUBE, 1995. Preferential use of the landmark navigational system by head direction cells in rats. *Behav. Neurosci.* 109:49–61.

GOTHARD, K. M., W. E. SKAGGS, K. M. MOORE, and B. L. MCNAUGHTON, 1996. Binding of hippocampal CA1 neural activity to multiple reference frames in a landmark-based navigation task. *J. Neurosci.* 16:823–835.

HERMER, L., and E. SPELKE, 1996. Modularity and development: The case of spatial reorientation. *Cognition* 61:195–232.

HILL, A. J., 1978. First occurrence of hippocampal spatial firing in a new environment. *Exp. Neurol.* 62:282–297.

JUNG, M. W., and B. L. MCNAUGHTON, 1993. Spatial selectivity of unit activity in the hippocampal granular layer. *Hippocampus* 3:165–182.

KNIERIM, J. J., H. S. KUDRIMOTI, and B. MCNAUGHTON, 1995. Place cells, head direction cells, and the learning of landmark stability. *J. Neurosci.* 15:1648–1659.

KUBIE, J. L., and J. B. J. RANCK, 1983. Sensory-behavioral correlates in individual hippocampus neurons in three situations: Space and context. In: *Neurobiology of the hippocampus,* W. Seifert, ed. New York: Academic Press, pp. 433–447.

LONG, J. M., and R. P. KESNER, 1996. The effects of dorsal versus ventral hippocampal, total hippocampal, and parietal cortex lesions on memory for allocentric distance in rats. *Behav. Neurosci.* 110:922–932.

MAGUIRE, E. A., N. BURGESS, J. G. DONNETT, R. S. FRACKOWIAK, C. D. FRITH, and J. O'KEEFE, 1998. Knowing where and getting there: A human navigational network. *Science* 280:921–924.

MAGUIRE, E. A., R. S. J. FRACKOWIAK, and C. D. FRITH, 1997. Recalling routes around London: Activation of the right hippocampus in taxi drivers. *J. Neurosci.* 17:7103–7110.

MARKUS, E. J., Y. L. QIN, B. LEONARD, W. E. SKAGGS, B. L. MCNAUGHTON, and C. A. BARNES, 1995. Interactions between location and task affect the spatial and directional firig of hippocampal neurons. *J. Neurosci.* 15:7079–7094.

MARKUS, E. J., C. A. BARNES, B. L. MCNAUGHTON, V. L. GLADDEN, and W. E. SKAGGS, 1994. Spatial information content and reliability of hippocampal CA1 neurons: Effects of visual input. *Hippocampus* 4:410–421.

MCHUGH, T. J., K. E. BLUM, J. Z. TSIEN, S. TONEGAWA, and M. A. WILSON, 1996. Impaired hippocampal representation of space in CA1-specific NMDAR 1 knockout mice. *Cell* 87: 1339–1349.

MCNAUGHTON, B., C. BARNES, J. GERRARD, K. GOTHARD, M. JUNG, J. KNIERIM, H. KUDRIMOTI, Y. QIN, W. SKAGGS, M. SUSTER, and K. WEAVER, 1996. Deciphering the hippocampal polyglot: the hippocampus as a path integration system. *J. Exp. Biol.* 199:173–185.

MCNAUGHTON, B. L., C. A. BARNES, and J. O'KEEFE, 1983. The contributions of position, direction, and velocity to single unit activity in the hippocampus of freely-moving rats. *Exp. Brain Res.* 52:41–49.

MCNAUGHTON, B. L., L. L. CHEN, and E. J. MARKUS, 1991. Dead reckoning, landmark learning, and the sense of direction: A neurophysiological and computational hypothesis. *J. Cogn. Neurosci.* 3:190–202.

MITTELSTAEDT, M. L., and S. GLASAUER, 1991. Idiothetic navigation in gerbils and humans. *Zool. J. Physiol.* 95:427–435.

MIZUMORI, S. J., and J. D. WILLIAMS, 1993. Directionally selective mnemonic properties of neurons in the lateral dorsal nucleus of the thalamus of rats. *J. Neurosci.* 13:4015–4028.

MULLER, R. U., E. BOSTOCK, J. S. TAUBE, and J. L. KUBIE, 1994. On the directional firing properties of hippocampal place cells. *J. Neurosci.* 14:7235–7251.

MUMBY, D. G., and J. P. J. PINEL, 1994. Rhinal cortex lesions and object recognition in rats. *Behav. Neurosci.* 108:11–18.

MÜRI, R. M., S. RIVAUD, S. TIMSIT, P. CORNU, and C. PIERROT-DESCILLIGNY, 1994. The role of the right medial temporal lobe in the control of memory-guided saccades. *Exp. Brain Res.* 101:165–168.

MURRAY, E. A., and M. MISHKIN, 1986. Visual recognition in monkeys following rhinal cortical ablations combined with either amygdalectomy or hippocampectomy. *J. Neurosci.* 6: 1991–2003.

NEAVE, N., S. LLOYD, A. SAHGAL, and J. P. AGGLETON, 1994. Lack of effect of lesions in the anterior cingulate cortex and retrosplenial cortex on certain tests of spatial memory in the rat. *Behav. Brain Res.* 65:89–101.

O'KEEFE, J., and J. DOSTROVSKY, 1971. The hippocampus as a spatial map: Preliminary evidence from unit activity in the freely-moving rat. *Brain Res.* 34:171–175.

O'KEEFE, J., and L. NADEL, 1978. *The Hippocampus as a Cognitive Map.* Oxford. Clarendon.

O'KEEFE, J., and A. SPEAKMAN, 1987. Single unit activity in the rat hippocampus during a spatial memory task. *Exp. Brain. Res.* 68:1–27.

QUIRK, G. L., R. U. MULLER, J. L. KUBIE, and J. B. J. RANCK, 1992. The positional firing properties of medial entorhinal neurons: Description and comparison with hippocampal place cells. *J. Neurosci.* 12:1945–1963.

QUIRK, G. J., R. U. MULLER, and J. L. KUBIE, 1990. The firing of hippocampal place cells in the dark depends on the rats recent experience. *J. Neurosci.* 10:2008–2017.

REDISH, A. D., and D. S. TOURETZKY, 1997. Cognitive maps beyond the hippocampus. *Hippocampus* 7:15–35.

SCOVILLE, W. B., and B. MILNER, 1957. Loss of recent memory after bilateral hippocampal lesions. *J. Neurol. Neurosurg. Psychiatry* 20:11–21.

SHARP, P. E., and C. GREEN, 1994. Spatial correlates of firing patterns of single cells in the subiculum of the freely moving rat. *J. Neurosci.* 14:2339–2356.

SMITH, P. F., 1997. Vestibular-hippocampal interactions. *Hippocampus* 7:465–471.

STACKMAN, R. W., and J. S. TAUBE, 1997. Firing properties of head direction cells in the rat anterior thalamic nucleus: Dependence on vestibular input. *J. Neurosci.* 17:4349–4358.

SUZUKI, W. A., S. ZOLA-MORGAN, L. R. SQUIRE, and D. G. AMARAL, 1993. Lesions of the perirhinal and parahippocampal cortices in the monkey produce long-lasting memory imparment in the visual and tactual modalities. *J. Neurosci.* 13:2430–2451.

TAKAHASHI, N., M. KAWAMURA, J. SHIOTA, N. KASAHATA, and K. HIRAYAMA, 1997. Pure topographic disorientation due to right retrosplenial lesion. *Neurology* 49:464–449.

TAUBE, J. S., 1995a. Place cells recorded in the parasubiculum of freely moving rats. *Hippocampus* 5:569–583.

TAUBE, J. S., 1995b. Head direction cells recorded in the anterior thalamic nuclei of freely moving rats. *J. Neurosci.* 15:70–86.

TAUBE, J. S., and H. L. BURTON, 1995. Head direction cell activity monitored in a novel environment and during a cue conflict situation. *J. Neurophysiol.* 74:1953–1971.

TAUBE, J. S., J. P. GOODRIDGE, E. J. GOLOB, P. A. DUDCHENKO, and R. W. STACKMAN, 1996. Processing the head direction cell signal: A review and commentary. *Brain Res Bull.* 40:477–484.

TAUBE, J. S., and R. U. MULLER, 1998. Comparisons of head direction cell activity in the postsubiculum and anterior thalamus of freely moving rats. *Hippocampus* 8:87–108.

TAUBE, J. S., R. U. MULLER, and J. B. J. RANCK, 1990. Head directions cells recorded from the postsubiculum in freely moving rats: I. Description and quantitative analysis. *J. Neurosci.* 10:436–447.

THOMPSON, L. T., and P. J. BEST, 1989. Place cells and silent cells in the hippocampus of freely-behaving rats. *J. Neurosci.* 9:2382–2390.

TOLMAN, E. C., 1948. Cognitive maps in rats and men. *Psychol. Rev.* 55:189–208.

TOURETZKY, D. S., and A. D. REDISH, 1996. Theory of rodent navigation based on interacting representations of space. *Hippocampus* 6:247–270.

TRULLIER, O., S. I. WIENER, A. BERTHOZ, and J. MEYER, 1997. Biologically based artificial navigation systems: Review and prospects. *Progr. Neurobiol.* 51:483–544.

TSIEN, J. Z., P. T. HUERTA, and S. TONEGAWA, 1996. The essential role of hippocampal CA1 NMDA receptor-dependent synaptic plasticity in spatial memory. *Cell* 87: 1327–1338.

WIENER, S. I., 1993. Spatial and behavioral correlates of striatal neurons in rats performing a self-initiated navigation task. *J. Neurosci.* 13:3802–3817.

WIIG, K. A., L. N. COOPER, and M. F. BEAR, 1996. Temporally graded retrograde amnesia following separate and combined lesions of the perirhinal cortex and fornix in the rat. *Learning Memory* 3:313–325.

WILSON, M. A., and B. MCNAUGHTON, 1993. Dynamics of the hippocampal ensemble code for space. *Science* 261:1055–1058.

WHISHAW, I. Q., and H. MAASWINKEL, 1998. Rats with fimbria-fornix lesions are impaired in path integration: A role for the hippocampus in "sense of direction." *J. Neurosci.* 18:3050–3058.

ZHU, X. O., M. O. BROWN, and J. P. AGGLETON, 1995. Neuronal signalling of information important to visual recognition memory in rat rhinal and neighboring cortices. *Eur. J. Neurosci.* 7:753–765.

ZOLA-MORGAN, S., L. R. SQUIRE, D. G. AMARAL, and W. A. SUZUKI, 1989. Lesions of perirhinal and parahippocampal cortex that spare the amygdala and hippocampal formation produce severe memory impairment. *J. Neurosci.* 9:4355–4370.

ZOLA-MORGAN, S., and L. R. SQUIRE, 1993. Neuroanatomy of memory. *Ann. Rev. Neurosci.* 16:547–563.

42 Computational Motor Control

MICHAEL I. JORDAN AND DANIEL M. WOLPERT

ABSTRACT The authors discuss some of the computational approaches that have been developed in the area of motor control. They focus on problems relating to motor planning, internal models, state estimation, motor learning, and modularity. The aim of the chapter is to demonstrate, both at a conceptual level and through consideration of specific models, how computational approaches shed light on problems in the control of movement.

The study of motor control is fundamentally the study of sensorimotor transformations. For the motor control system to move its effectors to apply forces on objects in the world or to position its sensors with respect to objects in the world, it must coordinate a variety of forms of sensory and motor data. These data generally are in different formats and may refer to the same entities but in different coordinate systems. Transformations between these coordinate systems allow motor and sensory data to be related, closing the sensorimotor loop.

Equally fundamental is the fact that the motor control system operates with dynamic systems whose behavior depends on the way that energy is stored and transformed. The study of motor control, therefore, also is the study of dynamics. These two interrelated issues—sensorimotor transformations and dynamics—underlie much of the research in the area of motor control.

From a computational perspective, the motor system can be considered a system whose inputs are the motor commands emanating from the controller within the central nervous system (CNS) (figure 42.1, center). To determine the behavior of the system in response to this input, an additional set of variables, called *state variables*, also must be known. For example, in a robotic model of the arm, the motor command would represent the torques generated around the joints and the state variables would be the joint angles and angular velocities. Taken together, the inputs and the state variables are sufficient to determine the future behavior of the system. It is unrealistic, however, to assume that the controller in the CNS has direct access to the state of the system that

it is controlling; rather, we generally assume that the controller has access to a sensory feedback signal that is a function of the state. This signal is treated as the output of the abstract computational system.

In this chapter, we consider five issues that arise in considering the general computational schema in figure 42.1. The first issue is that of motor planning, which we consider to be the computational process by which the desired outputs of the system are specified, given an extrinsic task goal. Second, we explore the notion of internal models, which are systems that mimic—within the CNS—the behavior of the controlled system. Such models have a variety of roles in motor control that we elucidate. Third, we consider the problem of state estimation, which is the process by which the unknown state of the motor system can be estimated by monitoring both its inputs and its outputs. This process requires the CNS to integrate its internal state estimates, obtained via an internal model, with the sensory feedback. We then consider how internal models are refined through motor learning. Finally, we discuss how multiple internal models can be used in motor control.

Although many of the concepts discussed are applicable to all areas of motor control, including eye movements, speech production, and posture, we focus on arm movements as an illustrative system.

Motor planning

The computational problem of motor planning arises from a fundamental property of the motor system: the reduction in the degrees of freedom from neural commands through muscle activation to movement kinematics (Bernstein, 1967) (figure 42.2). Even for the simplest of tasks, such as moving the hand to a target location, there are an infinite number of possible paths that the hand could move along, and for each of these paths, there are an infinite number of velocity profiles (trajectories) the hand could follow. Having specified the hand path and velocity, each location of the hand along the path can be achieved by multiple combinations of joint angles, and, due to the overlapping actions of muscles and the ability to co-contract, each arm configuration can be achieved by many different muscle activations. Motor planning can be considered as the computational

MICHAEL I. JORDAN Division of Computer Science and Department of Statistics, University of California, Berkeley, Calif.

DANIEL M. WOLPERT Sobell Department of Neurophysiology, Institute of Neurology, University College, London, United Kingdom

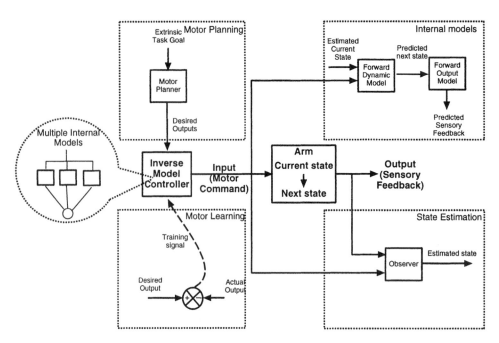

FIGURE 42.1 The motor system is shown schematically, along with the five themes of motor control reviewed in the chapter. The motor system (center) has inputs—the motor commands—

which causes it to change its states and produce an output—the sensory feedback. For clarity, not all lines are shown.

process of selecting a single solution or pattern of behavior at the levels in the motor hierarchy (figure 42.2), from the many alternatives that are consistent with the task.

Given the redundancy in the motor system, it is illuminating that experimental observations of unconstrained point-to-point reaching movements have demonstrated that several aspects of movements tend to remain invariant, despite variations in movement direction, movement speed, and movement location (Morasso, 1981; Flash and Hogan, 1985). First, as shown in figure 42.3a, the motion of the hand tends to follow roughly a straight line in space. This observation is not uniformly true; significant curvature is observed for certain movements, particularly horizontal movements and movements near the boundaries of the workspace (Atkeson and Hollerbach, 1985; Soechting and Lacquaniti, 1981; Uno, Kawato, and Suzuki, 1989). The tendency to make straight-line movements, however, characterizes a reasonably large class of movements and is somewhat surprising given that the muscles act in rotating coordinate systems attached to the joints. Second, the movement of the hand is smooth. Higher derivatives of the hand motion, such as the velocity and acceleration, tend to vary smoothly in time. Consider the plot of tangential speed shown in figure 42.3b. Scrutiny of the curve in the early phase of the motion reveals that the slope of the plot of speed against time is initially zero and increases smoothly. This is striking, given that the positional error is maximal at the beginning of the movement. Third, the

shape of the plot of hand speed is unimodal and roughly symmetric (bell-shaped). There are exceptions to this observation as well, particularly for movements in

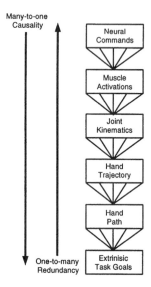

FIGURE 42.2 The levels in the motor hierarchy are shown, with the triangles between the levels indicating the reduction in the degrees of freedom between the higher and lower levels. Specifying a pattern of behavior at any level completely specifies the patterns at the level below (many-to-one: many patterns at the higher level correspond to one pattern at the lower) but is consistent with many patterns at the level above (one-to-many). Planning can be considered as the process by which particular patterns, consistent with the extrinsic task goals, are selected at each level. Reprinted with permission from Wolpert (1997).

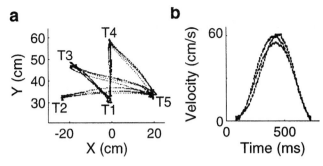

FIGURE 42.3 (a) Observed hand paths for a set of point-to-point movements from Uno and associates (1989) (with permission). The coordinate system is centered on the shoulder with x and y in the transverse and sagittal directions, respectively. (b) Observed velocity profiles for movements from T1 to T3 in (a). Reprinted with permission from Uno and associates (1989).

which the accuracy requirement leads to feedback playing an important role (Beggs and Howarth, 1972; MacKenzie et al., 1987; Milner and Ijaz, 1990), but again this observation characterizes a reasonably large class of movements.

OPTIMAL CONTROL APPROACHES Optimization theory provides a computational framework that is natural for a selection process such as motor planning (Bryson and Ho, 1975). Rather than describing the kinematics of a movement directly, in terms of the time-varying values of positions or angles, the movement is described more abstractly, in terms of a global measure, such as total efficiency, smoothness, accuracy, or duration. This global measure encodes the cost of the movement, and the optimal movement is the movement that minimizes the cost. In this framework, the cost function is a mathematical means for specifying the plan. The variables that determine the cost, and that are therefore planned, determine the patterns of behavior observed. For example, we might postulate that the trajectory followed by the hand is the one that minimizes the total energy expended during the movement. The theoretical goal is to formulate a single such postulate, or a small set of postulates, that accounts for a wide variety of the data on reaching.

Let us begin by considering the mathematical machinery that is needed to describe "optimal" movements. Letting T denote the duration of a movement and letting $x(t)$ denote the value of degree of freedom x at time t, a movement is a *function* $x(t)$, $t \in [0, T]$. There are an infinite number of such functions. An optimization approach proposes to choose between these functions by comparing them on the basis of a measure of cost. The cost function is a *functional*, a function that maps functions into real numbers. For every movement there is a corresponding number, which provides a basis of comparison between movements. The cost function in dynamic optimization generally is taken to be of the following form:

$$J = \int_0^T g(x(t), t)\, dt, \tag{1}$$

where $g(x(t), t)$ is a function that measures the instantaneous cost of the movement. The instantaneous cost g typically quantifies aspects of the movement that are considered undesirable, such as jerkiness, error, or high-energy expenditure. Integrating the instantaneous cost provides the total measure of cost J.

The mathematical techniques that have been developed for optimizing expressions such as Equation 1 fall into two broad classes: those based on calculus of variations and those based on dynamic programming (Bryson and Ho, 1975). Both classes of techniques provide mathematical conditions that characterize optimal trajectories. For certain classes of problems, these conditions provide equations that can be solved once and for all, yielding closed form expressions for optimal trajectories. For other classes of problems, the equations must be solved numerically.

Note that a description of movement in terms of an optimization principle does not necessarily imply that there is a computational process of optimization underlying the actual control of movement. Optimization theory simply stipulates that the system operates at the minimum of the "cost function" (the measure that is optimized) but does not commit itself to any particular computational process that puts the system at the minimum. Although many possible cost functions have been examined (Nelson, 1983), there are two main classes of models proposed for point-to-point movements—kinematic and dynamic-based models.

KINEMATIC COSTS The cost function in kinematic-based models contain only geometrical and time-based properties of motion, and the variables of interest are the positions (e.g., joint angles or hand Cartesian coordinates) and their corresponding velocities, accelerations, and higher derivatives. Based on the observation that point-to-point movements of the hand are smooth when viewed in a Cartesian framework, it was proposed that the squared first derivative of Cartesian hand acceleration or "jerk" is minimized over the movement (Hogan, 1984; Flash and Hogan, 1985). Letting $x(t)$ denote the position at time t, the minimum jerk model is based on the following cost function:

$$J = \int_0^T \left[\frac{d^3 x}{dt^3}\right]^2 dt, \tag{2}$$

where T is the duration of the movement. Using the calculus of variations, Hogan showed that the trajectory that minimizes this cost function is of the following form:

$$x(t) = x_0 + (x_f - x_0)[10(t/T)^3 - 15(t/T)^4 + 6(t/T)^5], \quad (3)$$

where x_0 and x_f are the initial and final positions, respectively.

The minimum jerk model takes the smoothness of motion as the basic primitive and predicts straight-line Cartesian hand paths with bell-shaped velocity profiles that are consistent with empirical data for rapid movements made without accuracy constraints. Flash and Hogan (1985) point out that the natural generalization of Equation 2 to three spatial dimensions involves taking the sum of the squares of the jerk along each dimension, which is equivalent to three independent minimizations. Thus, the resulting trajectories all are of the form of Equation 3, differing only in the values of the initial and final positions. Because these differences simply scale the time-varying part of Equation 3, the result is always a straight-line motion in space. Although penalizing higher derivatives of kinematic variables such as snap, crackle, or pop (the next three derivatives after jerk) produce very similar trajectories, penalizing lower derivatives of kinematic variables, such as acceleration or velocity, lead to nonzero accelerations at the initial time, which is inconsistent with the behavioral data.

One aspect of the minimum jerk model that is unsatisfying is the need to prespecify the duration T. Hoff (1992) has extended the minimum jerk model by allowing the duration to be a free parameter. Because longer movements always can be made smoother than short movements, Hoff created a tradeoff between duration and smoothness by penalizing duration. This is accomplished via the following cost function:

$$J = \int_0^T \left\{ g \left[\frac{d^3 x}{dt^3} \right]^2 + 1 \right\} dt, \quad (4)$$

where T is free. The term of unity in the integrand increases the cost of movements as a function of their duration and trades off against the cost because of smoothness. The parameter γ quantifies the relative magnitudes of these two costs. Hoff has shown that this model can reproduce the results from experiments in which the locations of targets are switched just before the onset of movement (Pelisson et al., 1986; Georgopoulos, Lalaska, and Massey, 1981). The model successfully predicts both movement trajectories and movement duration.

The minimum jerk model recently was used in an attempt to find a unified framework within which to understand two properties of trajectory formation—local isochrony and the two-thirds power law. Whereas "global" isochrony refers to the observation that the average velocity of movements increases with the movement distance, thereby maintaining movement duration nearly constant, "local" isochrony refers to the subunits of movement. For example, if subjects trace out a figure eight in which the two loops are of unequal size, the time to traverse each loop is approximately equal. By approximating the solution of minimum jerk when the path is constrained (only the velocity along the path could be varied), local isochrony becomes an emergent property of the optimization of jerk (Viviani and Flash, 1995). The two-thirds power law, $A \propto C^\beta$ ($\beta \approx \frac{2}{3}$), is based on the observation of the relationship between path curvature (C) and hand angular velocity (A) during drawing or scribbling (Lacquaniti, Terzuolo, and Viviani, 1983) (for a more general formulation of the law, see Viviani and Schneider, 1991). It has been shown that the minimum-jerk solution for movement along a constrained path approximates the solution given by the two-thirds power law (Viviani and Flash, 1995). One area of debate is the extent to which the two-thirds power law is a manifestation of a plan rather than a control constraint. Gribble and Ostry, using a simple dynamic model, have shown that the two-thirds power law could be an emergent property of the viscoelastic properties of the muscles (Gribble and Ostry, 1996). One feature that has not been explained yet by such emergent property models, however, is the fact that the exponent of the power law, β, changes systematically through development, from a value of 0.77 at 6 years of age to an adult value of 0.66 ($\frac{2}{3}$) at approximately 12 years of age (Viviani and Schneider, 1991).

DYNAMIC COSTS   The cost function in dynamic-based models depends on the dynamics of the arm, and the variables of interest include joint torques, forces acting on the hand, and muscle commands. Several models have been proposed in which the cost function depends on dynamic variables, such as torque change, muscle tension, or motor command (Kawato, 1992; Uno, Kawato, and Suzuki, 1989). One critical difference between the kinematic and dynamic-based models is the separability of planning and execution. The specification of the movement in kinematic models, such as minimum jerk, involves the positions and velocities of the arm as a function of time. Therefore, a separate process is required to achieve these specifications, and this model is a hierarchical, serial plan-and-execute model. In contrast, the solution to dynamic models, such as minimum torque change, are the motor commands required to achieve the movement, and, therefore, planning and execution are no longer separate processes.

Uno and associates (1989) have presented data that are problematic for the minimum jerk model. First, they studied trajectories when an external force (a spring) acted on the hand. They found that subjects made curvilinear movements in this case, which is not predicted by the minimum jerk model.[1] Second, they studied movements with via points and observed that symmetrically placed via points did not necessarily lead to symmetric paths of the hand in space. Finally, they studied large range movements and observed significant curvilinearity in the paths of motion. These observations led Uno and coworkers to suggest an alternative optimization principle in which forces play a role. They proposed penalizing the rate of change of torque, a quantity that is locally proportional to jerk (under static conditions). This principle is captured by the following cost function:

$$ J = \int_0^T \sum_{i=1}^n \left[\frac{d\tau_i}{dt}\right]^2 dt, \qquad (5) $$

where $d\tau_i/dt$ is the rate of change of torque at the ith joint. Uno and colleagues showed that this minimum torque-change cost function predicts trajectories that correspond to the trajectories that they observed empirically.

MINIMUM VARIANCE PLANNING Although both minimum jerk and minimum torque-change are able to capture many aspects of observed trajectories, they have several features that make them unsatisfying as models of movement. First, there has been no principled explanation why the CNS should choose to optimize such quantities as jerk or torque-change, other than that these models predict smooth trajectories. These models do not propose any advantage for smoothness of movement but simply assume that smoothness is optimized. Furthermore, it still is unknown whether the CNS could estimate such complex quantities as jerk or torque-change and integrate them over the duration of a trajectory. Lastly, the models provide no principled way of selecting the movement duration, which is a free parameter in both models.

In an attempt to resolve these problems, Harris and Wolpert (1998) recently proposed the minimum-variance theory of motor planning for both eye and arm movements. They suggest that biological noise is the underlying determinant of both eye and arm movement planning. In the model, they assume that the neural control signal is corrupted by noise, thereby causing trajectories to deviate from the desired path. These deviations are accumulated over the duration of a movement, leading to variability in the final position. If the noise were independent of the control signal, then the accumulated error could be minimized by making the movement as

rapidly as possible. However, the key assumption of the hypothesis is that the noise in the neural control signal increases with the mean level of the signal. In the presence of such signal-dependent noise, moving as rapidly as possible actually may increase the variability in the final position. This is because, for low-pass systems such as the eye or arm, moving faster requires larger control signals, which carry more noise. Because the resulting inaccuracy of the movement may require corrective behavior, such as further movements, moving very fast may become counterproductive (Meyer et al., 1988; Harris, 1995). Accuracy could be improved by having small amplitude control signals, but the movement consequently will be slow. Thus, signal-dependent noise inherently imposes a tradeoff between movement duration and terminal accuracy. This is in agreement with the well-known observation that faster arm movements, for a given amplitude, are more inaccurate (Fitts, 1954). The key point is that for given amplitude and duration of movement, the final positional variance depends critically on the actual neural commands and subsequent velocity profile.

Harris and Wolpert (1998) suggest that the feedforward sequence of neural commands are selected to minimize the final positional variance while keeping the duration to the minimum compatible with the accuracy constraints of a particular task. This minimum-variance theory accurately predicts the velocity profiles of both saccades and arm movements (figure 42.4). Moreover, the profiles are relatively insensitive to large changes in the parameters of the arm, so that even when the inertia and viscosity of the arm or the time constants of the muscle are individually halved or doubled, the optimal profile remains essentially unchanged (figure 42.4b). This is consistent with the observation that when the arm is subject to elastic, viscous, or inertial loads, the bell-shaped velocity profile is regained after a period of adaptation (Flash and Gurevich, 1991; Shadmehr and Mussa-Ivaldi, 1994; Lackner and DiZio, 1994; Brashers-Krug, Shadmehr, and Bizzi, 1996; Sainburg and Ghez, 1995; Goodbody and Wolpert, 1998).

The minimum-variance approach has several important ramifications. Primarily, it provides a biologically plausible theoretical underpinning for both eye and arm movements. In contrast, it is difficult to explain the biological relevance of such factors as jerk or torque-change. Moreover, there is no need for the CNS to construct highly derived signals to estimate the cost of the movement, which now is simply variance of the final position or the consequences of this inaccuracy, such as the time spent in making corrective movements (Meyer et al., 1988; Harris, 1995). Such costs are directly available to the nervous system, and the optimal trajectory could

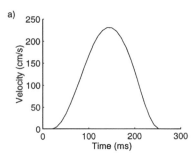

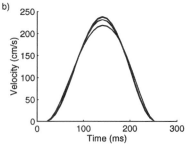

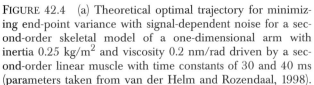

FIGURE 42.4 (a) Theoretical optimal trajectory for minimizing end-point variance with signal-dependent noise for a second-order skeletal model of a one-dimensional arm with inertia 0.25 kg/m^2 and viscosity 0.2 nm/rad driven by a second-order linear muscle with time constants of 30 and 40 ms (parameters taken from van der Helm and Rozendaal, 1998).

(b) Eight velocity profiles for the model in (a) in which the inertia, viscosity, and time constants are individually doubled or halved. The trajectory is essentially invariant to these large changes in the dynamics of the arm. (Reprinted with permission from Harris and Wolpert, 1998.)

be learned from the experience of repeated movements. This model therefore is a combined kinematic and dynamic model. The variance is determined by the dynamics of the system, but the consequences of this variance may be assessed in extrinsic coordinates, such as a visual error. Finally, the model explains why theories based on smoothness have been so successful. To change the velocity of the eye or arm rapidly requires large changes in the driving signal. Because such large signals would generate noise, it pays to avoid abrupt trajectory changes.

Internal models

The basic task of a control system is to manage the relationships between sensory variables and motor variables. There are two basic kinds of transformations that can be considered: sensory-to-motor transformations and motor-to-sensory transformations. The transformation from motor variables to sensory variables is accomplished by the environment and by the musculoskeletal system; these physical systems transform efferent motor actions into reafferent sensory feedback. It is also possible, however, to consider internal transformations, implemented by neural circuitry, that mimic the external motor-to-sensory transformation. Such internal transformations are known as internal forward models. Forward dynamic models predict the next state (e.g., position and velocity), given the current state and the motor command, whereas forward output models predict the sensory feedback. This is in contrast to inverse models, which invert the system by providing the motor command that causes a desired change in state. Because inverse models produce the motor command required to achieve some desired result, they have a natural use as a controller (see the section on Motor Learning).

MOTOR PREDICTION: FORWARD MODELS   In this section, we discuss possible roles for forward models in motor control and motor learning (Miall and Wolpert, 1996). One such role is as an ingredient in a system that uses a copy of the motor command–an "efference copy"–to anticipate and cancel the sensory effects of movement–the "reafference." This role for forward models has been studied extensively in the field of eye movement control (see Jeannerod, 1997, for a review). In the case of limb control, a forward model may subserve the additional function of canceling the effects on sensation induced by self-motion and distinguishing self-produced motion from the sensory feedback caused by contact with objects in the environment.

Another role for forward models is to provide a fast internal loop that helps stabilize feedback control systems. Feedback control in biological systems is subject to potential difficulties with stability because the sensory feedback through the periphery is delayed by a significant amount (Miall et al., 1993). Such delays can result in instability when trying to make rapid movements under feedback control. Two strategies can maintain stability during movement with such delays–intermittence and prediction. Intermittence, in which movement is interspersed with rest, is seen in manual tracking and saccadic eye movement. The intermittence of movement allows time for veridical sensory feedback to be obtained (a strategy often used in adjusting the temperature of a shower, where the time delays are large). Such intermittence can arise either from a psychological refractory period after each movement (Smith, 1967) or from an error deadzone (Wolpert et al., 1992) in which the perceived error must exceed a threshold before a new movement is initiated. Alternatively, in predictive control, a forward model is used to provide internal feedback of the predicted outcome of an action, which can be used before sensory feedback is available, thereby preventing instability (Miall et al., 1993). In effect, the control system controls the forward model rather than the actual system. Because the loop through the forward model is not subject to peripheral delays, the difficulties with stability are lessened. The control signals obtained within this inner loop are sent to the periphery, and the physical system moves along in tandem. Of course, there are inevitable disturbances acting on the physical system that are not modeled by the internal model; thus, the feedback from the actual system cannot be neglected entirely. However, the predictable feedback can be canceled by delaying the output from the forward model. Only the unpredictable components of the feedback, which are likely to be small, are used in correcting errors within the feedback loop through the periphery. This kind of feedback control system, which uses a forward model both for mimicking the plant and for canceling predictable feedback, is known in the engineering literature as a "Smith predictor." Miall and associates (1993) have proposed that the cerebellum acts as a Smith predictor.

Another interesting example of a forward model arises in the literature on speech production. Lindblom, Lubker, and Gay (1979) studied an experimental task in which subjects produced vowel sounds while their jaw was held open by a bite block. Lindblom and associates observed that the vowels produced by the subjects had formant frequencies in the normal range, despite the fact that unusual articulatory postures were required to produce these sounds. Moreover, the formant frequencies were in the normal range during the first pitch period, before any possible influence of acoustic feedback. Lindblom and colleagues proposed a model of the control system for speech production that involved placing a forward model of the vocal tract in an internal feedback pathway.

Finally, forward models also can play a role in both state estimation and motor learning, as discussed in the following section.

INVERSE MODELS   We also can consider internal models that perform a transformation in the opposite direction, from sensory variables to motor variables. Such transformations are known as *internal inverse models*, and they allow the motor control system to transform desired sensory consequences into the motor actions that yield these consequences. Internal inverse models are the basic modules in open-loop control systems.

Internal inverse models also play an important role in motor control. A particularly clear example of an inverse model arises in the vestibulo-ocular reflex (VOR). The VOR couples the movement of the eyes to the motion of the head, thereby allowing an organism to keep its gaze fixed in space. This is achieved by causing the motion of the eyes to be equal and opposite to the motion of the head (Robinson, 1981). In effect, the VOR control system must compute the motor command that is predicted to yield a particular eye velocity. This computation is an internal inverse model of the physical relationship between muscle contraction and eye motion.

There are many other such examples of inverse models. Indeed, inverse models are fundamental modules in open-loop control systems: They allow the control system to compute an appropriate control signal without relying on error-correcting feedback.[2]

An important issue to stress in our discussion of internal models is that internal models are not required to be detailed or accurate models of the external world. Often, an internal model need only provide a rough approximation of some external transformation to play a useful role. For example, an inaccurate inverse model can provide an initial open-loop "push" that is corrected by a feedback controller. Similarly, an inaccurate forward model can be used inside an internal feedback loop because the feedback loop corrects the errors. This issue arises again in the following section, when motor learning is discussed, where we will see that an inaccurate forward model can be used to learn an accurate controller.

State estimation

Although the state of a system is not directly available to the controller, it is possible to estimate the state indirectly. Such a state estimator, known as an "observer" (Goodwin and Sin, 1984), produces its estimate of the current state by monitoring the stream of inputs (motor commands) and outputs (sensory feedback) of the system (figure 42.1). By using both sources of information, the observer can reduce its uncertainty in the state estimate and become robust to sensor failure. In addition, because there are delays in sensory feedback, the observer can use the motor command to produce more timely state estimates than would be possible using sensory feedback alone.

Although many studies have examined integration among purely sensory stimuli (for a psychophysical review, see Welch and Warren, 1986), little is known of how sensory and motor information is integrated during movement. When we move our arm in the absence of visual feedback, there are three basic methods that the CNS can use to obtain an estimate of the current state (e.g., the position and velocity) of the hand. The system can make use of sensory inflow (the information available from proprioception), it can make use of motor outflow (the motor commands sent to the arm), or it can combine these two sources of information. Although sensory signals can directly cue the location of the hand, motor

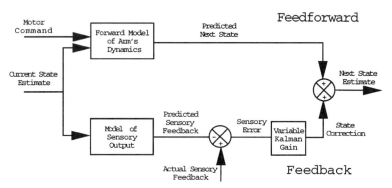

FIGURE 42.5 Sensorimotor integration model. (Reprinted with permission from Wolpert and colleagues, 1995.)

outflow generally does not. For example, given a sequence of torques applied to the arm (the motor outflow), an internal model of the arm's dynamics is needed to estimate the arm's final configuration.

To explore whether an internal model of the arm is used in sensorimotor integration, Wolpert and associates (1995) studied a task in which subjects–after initially viewing their arm in the light–made arm movements in the dark. The subjects' internal estimate of their hand location was assessed by asking them to visually localize the position of their hand (which was hidden from view) at the end of the movement. Wolpert and colleagues developed a model of this sensorimotor integration process (figure 42.5). This Kalman filter model of the sensorimotor integration process is based on a formal engineering model from the optimal state estimation field (Goodwin and Sin, 1984). The Kalman filter is a linear dynamical system that produces an estimate of the location of the hand by using both the motor outflow and sensory feedback in conjunction with a model of the motor system, thereby reducing the overall uncertainty in its estimate (Kalman and Bucy, 1961). This model assumes that the localization errors arise from two sources of uncertainty, the first from the variability in the response of the arm to the motor command and the second in the sensory feedback given the arm's configuration. The Kalman filter model can be considered as the combination of two processes that together contribute to the state estimate. The first, feedforward process (upper part), uses the efferent outflow along with the current state estimate to predict the next state by simulating the movement dynamics with a forward model. The second, feedback process (lower part), compares the sensory inflow with a prediction of the sensory inflow based on the current state. The sensory error, the difference between actual and predicted sensory feedback, is used to correct the state estimate resulting from the forward model. The relative contributions of the internal simulation and sensory correction processes to the final estimate are modulated by the time-varying

Kalman gain to provide optimal state estimates. Unlike simpler models that do not integrate both sensory and motor information, this model could account for the empirical data (Wolpert, Ghahramani, and Jordan, 1995). This suggests that a forward model is used by the CNS to maintain an estimate of the state of the motor system.

Duhamel and colleagues (1992) have presented neurophysiological data that imply a role for an internal forward model in the saccadic system. They have proposed that one of the roles of the lateral intraparietal (LIP) area of the parietal cortex is to maintain a retinal representation of potential saccadic targets. Such a representation simplifies the task of saccade generation because the transformation from a retinal representation to a motor representation is relatively simple. The retinal representation must be updated, however, whenever the eyes move in the head. This updating process requires an internal forward model that embodies knowledge of the retinal effects of eye movements. In particular, for a given eye movement (a motor action), the brain must predict the motion of objects on the retina (the sensory consequences). This predicted motion is added to the current retinal representation to yield an updated retinal representation.

Motor learning

In the previous section, we discussed several ways in which internal models can be used in a control system. Inverse models are the basic building blocks, of open-loop control. Forward models also can be used in open-loop control and have additional roles in state estimation and compensation for delays. An internal model is a form of knowledge about the environment (Ghez et al., 1990; Lacquaniti, Borghese, and Carrozzo, 1992; Shadmehr and Mussa-Ivaldi, 1994). Many motor control problems involve interacting with objects in the external world, and these objects generally have unknown mechanical properties. There also are changes in the musculoskeletal system due to growth or injury. These considerations suggest an important role for adaptive processes. Through adaptation, the motor control system is able to maintain and update its internal knowledge of external dynamics.

Recent work on motor learning has focused on the representation of the inverse dynamic model. When subjects make point-to-point movements in which the dynamics of their arm is altered, for example, by using a robot to generate a force field acting on the hand, they initially show trajectories that deviate from their normal paths and velocity profiles (Shadmehr and Mussa-Ivaldi, 1994; Lackner and DiZio, 1994). However, over time, subjects adapt and move naturally in the presence of the force field. This can be interpreted as adaptation of the inverse model or the incorporation of an auxiliary control system to counteract the novel forces experienced during movement. Several theoretical questions have been addressed using this learning paradigm. The first explored the representation of the controller and in particular whether it was best represented in joint or Cartesian space (Shadmehr and Mussa-Ivaldi, 1994). This was investigated by examining the generalization of motor learning at locations in the workspace remote from where subjects had adapted to the force field. By assessing in which coordinate system the transfer occurred, evidence was provided for joint-based control. Another important advance was made in a study designed to answer whether the order in which states (position and velocities) were visited was important for learning or whether having learned a force field for a set of states subjects would be able to make natural movements when visiting the states in a novel order (Conditt, Gandolfo, and Mussa-Ivaldi, 1997). The findings showed that the order was unimportant and argue strongly against a rote learning of individual trajectories. The learning of novel dynamic has been shown to undergo a period of consolidation after the perturbation has been removed (Brashers-Krug, Shadmehr, and Bizzi, 1996). Subjects' ability to perform in a previously experienced field was disrupted if a different field was presented immediately after this initial experience. Consolidation of this motor learning appears to be a gradual process with a second field after four hours having no effect on subsequent performance in the first field. This suggests that motor learning undergoes a period of consolidation during which time the motor learning or memory is fragile to being disrupted by different motor learning.

In this section, we discuss the computational algorithms by which such motor learning could take place, focusing on five different approaches: direct inverse

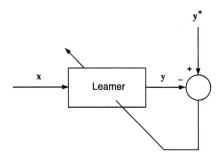

FIGURE 42.6   A generic supervised learning system. The vector $\mathbf{y}$ is the actual output, and the vector $\mathbf{y}^*$ is the target output. The error between the target and the actual output is used to adjust the parameters of the learner.

modeling, feedback error learning, distal supervised learning, reinforcement learning, and unsupervised bootstrap learning. All these approaches provide mechanisms for learning general sensorimotor transformations. They differ principally in the kinds of data and the kinds of auxiliary supporting structure that they require.

The first three schemes that we discuss are instances of a general approach to learning known as supervised learning. A generic supervised learning system is shown in figure 42.6. A supervised learner requires a target output corresponding to each input. The error between the target output and the actual output is computed and is used to drive the changes to the parameters inside the learning system. This process generally is formulated as an optimization problem in which the cost function is one-half the squared error:

$$J = \tfrac{1}{2}\left\| \mathbf{y}^* - \mathbf{y} \right\|^2. \tag{6}$$

The learning algorithm adjusts the parameters of the system to minimize this cost function. For details on particular supervised learning algorithms, refer to the study by Hertz and associates (1991).

In the following, we assume that the controlled system or plant (the musculoskeletal system and any relevant external dynamical systems) is described by a set of state variables $\mathbf{x}[n]$, an input $\mathbf{u}[n]$, and an output $\mathbf{y}[n]$. These variables are related by the following dynamic equation:

$$\mathbf{x}[n+1] = f(\mathbf{x}[n], \mathbf{u}[n]). \tag{7}$$

where n is the time step and f is the *next-state equation*. We also require an *output equation* that specifies how the output $\mathbf{y}[n]$ is obtained from the current state:

$$\mathbf{y}[n] = g(\mathbf{x}[n]), \tag{8}$$

We use the notation $\mathbf{y}*[n]$ to refer to a desired value (a target value) for the output variable and the notation $\hat{\mathbf{x}}[n]$ to refer to an internal estimate of the state of the controlled system.

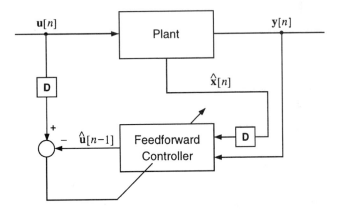

FIGURE 42.7 The direct inverse modeling approach to learning a controller. The state estimate $\hat{\mathbf{x}}[n]$ is assumed to be provided by an observer (not shown).

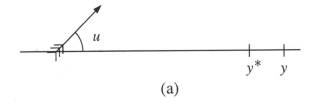

(a)

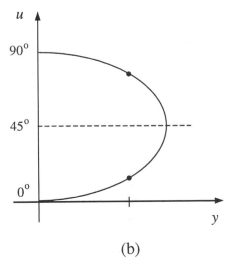

(b)

FIGURE 42.8 (a) An "archery" problem. (b) The parabolic relationship between distance traveled (y) and angle (u) for a projectile. For each value of y, there are two corresponding values of u, symmetrically placed around 45°.

DIRECT INVERSE MODELING How might a system acquire an inverse model of the plant? One approach is to present various test inputs to the plant, observe the outputs, and provide these input–output pairs as training data to a supervised learning algorithm by reversing the role of the inputs and the outputs. That is, the plant output is provided as an input to the learning controller, and the controller is required to produce as output the corresponding plant input. This approach, shown diagrammatically in figure 42.7, is known as direct inverse modeling (Widrow and Stearns, 1985; Atkeson and Reinkensmeyer, 1988; Kuperstein, 1988; Miller, 1987). Note that we treat the plant output as being observed at time n. The input to the learning controller is the current plant output $\mathbf{y}[n]$ and the delayed state estimate $\hat{\mathbf{x}}[n-1]$. The controller is required to produce the plant input that gave rise to the current output, in the context of the delayed estimated state. This is a supervised learning problem, in which the plant input $\mathbf{u}[n]$ serves as the target in the following cost function:

$$J = \tfrac{1}{2}\|\mathbf{u}[n] - \hat{\mathbf{u}}[n]\|^2,\qquad(9)$$

where $\hat{\mathbf{u}}[n]$ denotes the controller output at time n.

An example of a problem for which the direct inverse modeling approach is applicable is the inverse kinematics problem. The problem is to learn a sensorimotor transformation between the desired position of the hand in spatial coordinates and a corresponding set of joint angles for the arm that achieve that position. To learn such a transformation, the system tries a random joint angle configuration (a vector $\mathbf{u}[n]$) and observes the resulting hand position (the vector $\mathbf{y}[n]$). The system gathers a number of such pairs and uses a supervised learning algorithm to learn a mapping from $\mathbf{y}[n]$ to $\mathbf{u}[n]$.

Nonlinear systems and the nonconvexity problem The direct inverse modeling approach is well-behaved for linear systems and indeed can be shown to converge to correct parameter estimates for such systems under certain conditions (Goodwin and Sin, 1984). For nonlinear systems, however, a difficulty arises that is related to the general "degrees-of-freedom problem" in motor control (Bernstein, 1967). The problem is the result of a particular form of redundancy in nonlinear systems (Jordan, 1992). In such systems, the "optimal" parameter estimates (i.e., those that minimize the cost function in Equation 9) in fact may yield an incorrect controller.

Consider the following simple example. Figure 42.8 shows a one degree-of-freedom "archery" problem: A controller chooses an angle u and an arrow is projected at that angle. Figure 42.8b shows the parabolic relationship between distance traveled and angle. Note that for each distance, there are two angles that yield that distance. This implies that a learning system using direct inverse modeling sees two different targets paired with any given input. If a least-squares cost function is used (see Equation 9), then the system produces an output that is the average of the two targets, which, by the symmetry of the problem, is 45°. Thus, the system converges to an incorrect controller that maps each target distance to the same 45° control signal.

FEEDBACK ERROR LEARNING Kawato and colleagues (1987) have developed a direct approach to motor learning known as *feedback error learning*. Feedback error learning makes use of a feedback controller to guide the learning of the feedforward controller.[3] Consider a composite feedback–feedforward control system in which the total control signal is the sum of the feedforward component and the feedback component:

$$\mathbf{u}[n] = \mathbf{u}_{ff}[n] + \mathbf{u}_{fb}[n].$$

In the context of a direct approach to motor learning, the signal $\mathbf{u}[n]$ is the target for learning the feedforward controller (see figure 42.7). The error between the target and the feedforward control signal is $(\mathbf{u}[n] - \mathbf{u}_{ff}[n])$, which in the current case is simply $\mathbf{u}_{fb}[n]$. Thus, an error for learning the feedforward controller can be provided by the feedback control signal (see figure 42.9).

An important difference between feedback error learning and direct inverse modeling regards the signal used as the controller input. In direct inverse modeling, the controller is trained "off-line"; that is, the input to the controller for the purposes of training is the actual plant output, not the desired plant output. For the controller to actually participate in the control process, it must receive the desired plant output as its input. The direct inverse modeling approach therefore requires a switching process—the desired plant output must be switched in for the purposes of control, and the actual plant output must be switched in for the purposes of training. The feedback error learning approach provides a more elegant solution to this problem. In feedback error learning, the desired plant output is used for both control and training. The feedforward controller is trained "on-line"; that is, it is used as a con-

troller while it is being trained. Although the training data that it receives–pairs of actual plant inputs and desired plant outputs–are not samples of the inverse dynamics of the plant, the system nonetheless converges to an inverse model of the plant because of the error-correcting properties of the feedback controller.

By using a feedback controller, the feedback error learning approach also solves another problem associated with direct inverse modeling. Direct inverse modeling is not *goal directed*; that is, it is not sensitive to particular output goals (Jordan and Rosenbaum, 1989). This is seen simply by observing that the goal signal $(\mathbf{y}*[n])$ does not appear in figure 42.7. The learning process samples randomly in the control space, which may or may not yield a plant output near any particular goal. Even if a particular goal is specified before the learning begins, the direct inverse modeling procedure must search throughout the control space until an acceptable solution is found. In the feedback error learning approach, however, the feedback controller serves to guide the system to the correct region of the control space. By using a feedback controller, the system makes essential use of the error between the desired plant output and the actual plant output to guide the learning. This fact links the feedback error learning approach to the indirect approach to motor learning that we discuss in the following section. In the indirect approach, the learning algorithm is based directly on the output error.

DISTAL SUPERVISED LEARNING In this section, an indirect approach to motor learning known as distal supervised learning is discussed. Distal supervised learning avoids the nonconvexity problem and also avoids certain other problems associated with direct approaches to motor learning (Jordan, 1990; Jordan and Rumelhart, 1992). In distal supervised learning, the controller is learned indirectly, through the intermediary of a forward model of the plant. The forward model must itself be learned from observations of the inputs and outputs of the plant. The distal supervised learning approach

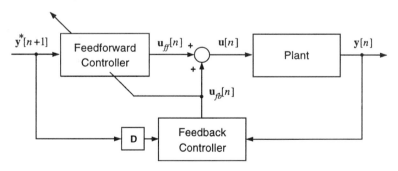

FIGURE 42.9 The feedback error learning approach to learning a feedforward controller. The feedback control signal is the error term for learning the feedforward controller.

therefore is composed of two interacting processes, one process in which the forward model is learned and another process in which the forward model is used in the learning of the controller.

The distal supervised learning approach is illustrated in figure 42.10. There are two interwoven processes depicted in the figure. One process involves the acquisition of an internal forward model of the plant. The forward model is a mapping from states and inputs to predicted plant outputs, and it is trained using the prediction error $(\mathbf{y}[n] - \hat{\mathbf{y}}[n])$, where $\hat{\mathbf{y}}[n]$ is the output of the forward model. The second process involves training the controller. This is accomplished in the following manner. The controller and the forward model are joined together and are treated as a single composite learning system. If the controller is to be an inverse model, then the composite learning system should be an identity transformation (i.e., a transformation whose output is the same as its input). This suggests that the controller can be trained indirectly by training the composite learning system to be an identity transformation. This is a supervised learning problem in which the entire composite learning system (the system inside the dashed box in figure 42.10) corresponds to the box labeled "Learner" in figure 42.6. During this training process, the parameters in the forward model are held fixed. Thus, the composite learning system is trained to be an identity transformation by a constrained learning process in which some of the parameters inside the system are held fixed. By allowing only the controller parameters to be altered, this process trains the controller indirectly.

Training a system to be an identity transformation means that its supervised error signal is the difference between the input and the output. This error signal is just the *performance error* $(\mathbf{y}*[n] - \mathbf{y}[n])$ (see figure 42.10). This is a sensible error term—it is the observed error in motor performance. That is, the learning algorithm trains the controller by correcting the error between the desired plant output and the actual plant output.

Let us return to the "archery" problem. Let us assume that the system already has acquired a perfect forward model of the function relating u to y, as shown in figure 42.11. The system now can use the forward model to recover a solution u for a given target $y*$. This can be achieved in different ways, depending on the particular supervised learning technique that is adopted. One approach involves using the local slope of the forward model to provide a correction to the current best guess for the control signal. (This corresponds to using gradient descent as the algorithm for training the composite learning system.) As seen in figure 42.11, the slope provides information about the direction to adjust the control signal to reduce the performance error $(y* - y)$. The adjustments to the control signal are converted into adjustments to the parameters of the controller using the chain rule.

An advantage of working with a forward model is that the nonconvexity of the problem does not prevent the system from converging to a unique solution. The system simply heads downhill toward one solution or the other (see figure 42.11). Moreover, if particular kinds of solutions are preferred (e.g., the left branch vs. the right branch of the parabola), then additional constraints can be added to the cost function to force the system to search in one branch or the other (Jordan, 1990).

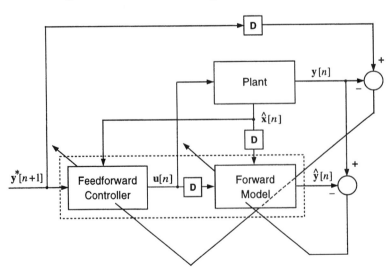

FIGURE 42.10 The distal supervised learning approach. The forward model is trained using the prediction error $(\mathbf{y}[n] - \hat{\mathbf{y}}[n])$. The subsystems in the dashed box constitute the composite learning system. This system is trained by using the performance error $(\mathbf{y}*[n] - \mathbf{y}[n])$ and holding the forward model fixed. The state estimate $\hat{\mathbf{x}}[n]$ is assumed to be provided by an observer (not shown).

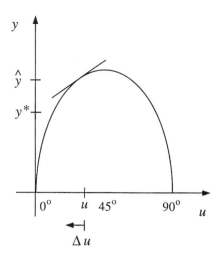

FIGURE 42.11 A forward model for the archery problem. Given a value of u, the forward model allows the output y to be predicted, the error $y^* - y$ to be estimated, and the slope to be estimated at u. The product of the latter two quantities provides information about how to adjust u to make the error smaller.

Suppose finally that the forward model is imperfect. In this case, the error between the desired output and the predicted output is the quantity $(\mathbf{y}*[n] - \hat{\mathbf{y}}[n])$, the *predicted performance error*. Using this error, the best the system can do is to acquire a controller that is an inverse of the forward model. Because the forward model is inaccurate, the controller is inaccurate. However, the predicted performance error is not the only error available for training the composite learning system. Because the actual plant output $(\mathbf{y}[n])$ still can be measured after a learning trial, the true performance error $(\mathbf{y}*[n] - \hat{\mathbf{y}}[n])$ still is available for training the controller. This implies that the output of the forward model can be discarded; the forward model is needed only for the structure that it provides as part of the composite learning system (e.g., the slope that it provides in figure 42.11). Moreover, for this purpose, an exact forward model is not required. Roughly speaking, the forward model need only provide coarse information about how to improve the control signal based on the current performance error, not precise information about how to make the optimal correction. If the performance error is decreased to zero, then an accurate controller has been found, regardless of the path taken to find that controller.

REINFORCEMENT LEARNING   Reinforcement learning algorithms differ from supervised learning algorithms by requiring significantly less information be available to the learner. Rather than requiring a vector performance error or a vector target in the control space, reinforcement learning algorithms require only a scalar evaluation of performance. A scalar evaluation signal simply tells a system whether it is performing well; it does not provide information about how to correct an error. A variety of reinforcement learning algorithms has been developed, and ties have been made to optimal control theory (Sutton and Barto, 1998). A strength of reinforcement learning algorithms is their ability to learn in the face of delayed evaluation.

In the simplest reinforcement learning paradigm, there is a set of possible responses at each point in the state, goal space. Associated with the ith response is a probability of selecting that response as an output on a given trial. Once a response is selected and transmitted to the environment, a scalar evaluation or reinforcement signal is computed as a function of the response and the state of environment. The reinforcement signal then is used in changing the selection probabilities for future trials: If reinforcement is high, the probability of selecting a response is increased; otherwise, the probability is decreased. Typically, the probabilities associated with the remaining (unselected) responses also are adjusted in some manner so that the total probability sums to one.

Reinforcement learning algorithms are able to learn in situations in which very little instructional information is available from the environment. In particular, such algorithms need make no comparison between the input goal (the vector $\mathbf{y}*$) and the result obtained (the vector $\mathbf{y}$) to find a control signal that achieves the goal. When such a comparison can be made, however, reinforcement learning still is applicable but may be slower than other algorithms that make use of such information. Although in many cases in motor control, it appears that a comparison with a goal vector is feasible, the question is empirical and as yet unresolved (Adams, 1984). Does feedback during learning serve to strengthen or weaken the action just emitted or to provide structural information about how to change the action just emitted into a more suitable action?

BOOTSTRAP LEARNING   The techniques discussed until this point all require that either an error signal or an evaluation signal is available for adjusting the controller. It also is possible to consider a form of motor learning that needs no such corrective information. This form of learning improves the controller by building on earlier learning. Such an algorithm is referred to in the adaptive signal processing literature as "bootstrap learning" (Widrow and Stearns, 1985).

How might a system learn without being corrected or evaluated? Let us work within the framework discussed previously for reinforcement learning, in which one of a set of responses is chosen with probability p_i. Suppose that because of prior learning, the system performs a task correctly a certain fraction of the time but still makes errors. The learning algorithm is as follows: The system selects actions according to the probabilities that it already has learned and rewards its actions indiscriminately–that is, it rewards both correct and incorrect actions. We argue that the system still can converge to a control law in which the correct action is chosen with probability one. The reason for this is that the responses of nonselected actions are effectively weakened, because the sum of the p_i must be one. That is, if p_i is strengthened, p_j must be decreased, for all j not equal to i. Because the system starts with the correct action having a larger probability of being selected than the other actions, that action has a larger probability of being strengthened, and thus, an even larger probability of being selected. Thus, if the initial balance in favor of the correct action is strong enough, the system can improve.

We know of no evidence that such a learning process is used by the motor control system, but the possibility appears never to have been investigated directly. The algorithm has intuitive appeal because there are situations in which it seems that mere repetition of a task can lead to improvement. The simplicity of the algorithm certainly is appealing from the point of view of neural implementation.

Modularity

Although the discussion in earlier sections has focused on how a single internal model could be used in motor control, recent models have begun to investigate the computational advantages of using a set of internal models. A general computational strategy for designing modular learning systems is to treat the problem as one of combining multiple models, each of which is defined over a local region of the input space. Such a strategy has been introduced in the "mixture of experts" architecture for supervised learning (Jacobs et al., 1991; Jordan and Jacobs, 1994). The architecture involves a set of function approximators known as "expert networks" (usually neural networks) that are combined by a classifier known as a "gating network" (figure 42.12). These networks are trained simultaneously to split the input space into regions in which particular experts can specialize. The gating network uses a soft split of the input data, thereby allowing data to be processed by multiple experts; the contribution of each is modulated by the gating module's estimate of the probability that each expert is the appropriate one to use. This model has been proposed both as a model of high-level vision (Jacobs, Jordan, and Barto, 1991) and of the role of the basal ganglia during sensorimotor learning (Graybiel et al., 1994).

Ghahramani and Wolpert (1997) have proposed this model to account for experimental data on visuomotor

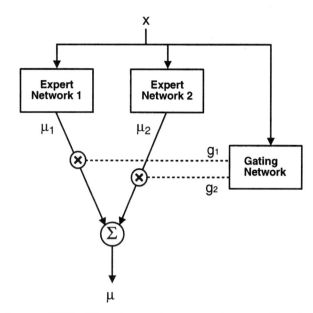

FIGURE 42.12 The mixture of experts architecture. Based on the state vector $\mathbf{x}$, the gating network assigns credit to the expert networks by calculating normalized mixing coefficients g_i. The expert networks implement a mapping from inputs $\mathbf{x}$ to outputs μ_i for the region of the state space in which they are appropriate.

learning. Using a virtual reality system, a single visual target location was remapped to two different hand positions depending on the starting location of the movement. Such a perturbation creates a conflict in the visuomotor map, which captures the (normally 1-to-1) relation between visually perceived and actual hand locations. One way to resolve this conflict is to develop two separate visuomotor maps (i.e., the expert modules), each appropriate for one of the two starting locations. A separate mechanism (i.e., the gating module) then combines, based on the starting location of the movement, the outputs of the two visuomotor maps. The internal structure of the system was probed by investigating the generalization properties in response to novel inputs, which in this case are the starting locations on which it has not been trained. As predicted by the mixture of experts, model subjects were able to learn both conflicting mappings and to interpolate smoothly from one visuomotor map to the other as the starting location was varied.

MULTIPLE PAIRED FORWARD-INVERSE MODEL There are three potential benefits, with regard to motor control, in employing the modularity inherent in the mixture-of-experts models over a nonmodular system when learning inverse models. First, the world essentially is modular–that is, we interact with multiple qualitatively different objects and environments. By using multiple inverse models, each of which might capture the motor commands necessary when acting with a particular object or within a particular environment, we can achieve an efficient coding of the world. In other words, the large set of environmental conditions in which we are required to generate movement requires multiple behaviors or sets of motor commands, each embodied within an inverse model. Second, the use of a modular system allows individual modules to participate in motor learning without affecting the motor behaviors already learned by other modules. Such modularity therefore can reduce interference between what already is learned and what is to be learned, thereby both speeding up motor learning while retaining previously learned behaviors. Third, many situations that we encounter are derived from a combination of previously experienced contexts, such as novel conjoints of manipulated objects and environments. By modulating the contribution to the final motor command of the outputs of the inverse modules, an enormous repertoire of behaviors can be generated. With as few as 32 inverse models, in which the output of each model either contributes or does not contribute to the final motor command, we have 232 or 1010 behaviors—sufficient for a new behavior for every second of one's life. Therefore, multiple internal models can be re-

garded conceptually as motor primitives, which are the building blocks used to construct intricate motor behaviors with an enormous vocabulary.

Given that we wish to use multiple internal models, several questions naturally arise–how are they acquired during motor learning to divide up the repertoire of behaviors for different contexts while preventing new learning from corrupting previously learned behaviors? As at any given time, we usually are faced with a single environment and a single object to be manipulated; the brain must solve the selection problem of issuing a single set of motor commands from its large vocabulary. Thus, how can the outputs of the inverse models be switched on and off appropriately in response to different behavioral contexts to generate a coordinated final motor command?

These issues have been addressed by Wolpert and Kawato (1998) in the multiple paired forward-inverse model. Based on the benefits of a modular approach and the experimental evidence for modularity, Wolpert and Kawato (Wolpert and Kawato, 1998; Kawato and Wolpert, 1998) have proposed that the problem of motor learning and control is best solved using multiple controllers, that is, inverse models. At any given time, one or a subset of these inverse models contributes to the final motor command.

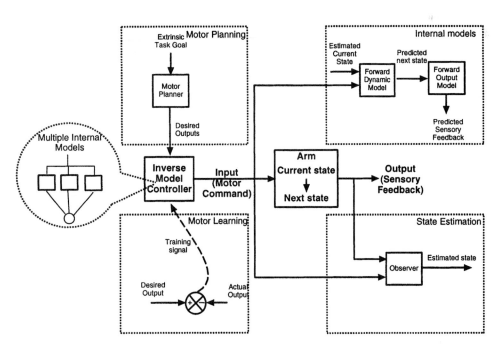

FIGURE 42.13 The multiple paired forward-inverse model. Each inverse model is paired with a corresponding forward model, which is used to convert performance errors into motor errors for training the inverse model. The ensemble of models is controlled by a "responsibility estimator," whose job is to partition the state space into regions corresponding to the different local model pairs. Reprinted with permission from Wolpert and Kawato (1998).

The basic idea of the model is that multiple inverse models exist to control the system, and each is augmented with a forward model. The system therefore contains multiple pairs of corresponding forward and inverse models (see figure 42.13). Within each pair, the inverse and forward internal models are coupled tightly during their acquisition, through motor learning and use, through gating of the inverse models' outputs dependent on the behavioral context. Key to this model are the responsibility signals, which reflect, at any given time, the degree to which each pair of forward and inverse models should be responsible for controlling the current behavior. This responsibility signal is derived from the comparison of the errors in prediction of the forward models—the smaller this prediction error, the higher the module's responsibility. The responsibilities then are used to control the learning within the forward models, with those models with high responsibilities receiving proportionally more of their error signals than modules with low responsibility. Over time, the forward models learn to divide up the system dynamics experienced, and the responsibilities reflect the extent to which each forward model captures the current behavior of the system. By using the same responsibility signal to gate the learning of the inverse models, which are updated by a training system such as feedback-error learning, these models learn the appropriate controls for the context captured by their paired forward model. A final component of the model is a responsibility predictor that tries to predict the responsibility of the module from sensory information alone. The responsibility predictor, whose inputs are sensory signals, estimates the responsibility before movement onset, whereas the forward models generate the responsibility after the consequences of movement are known. These two signals are merged to determine the final responsibility estimate, which determines the contribution of each inverse model's output to the final motor command. This combined model is capable of learning to produce appropriate motor commands under a variety of contexts and is able to switch between controllers as the context changes.

ACKNOWLEDGMENTS Preparation of this paper was supported in part by grants from the Human Frontier Science Program, the McDonnell-Pew Foundation, the Wellcome Trust, the Medical Research Council, the Royal Society, and by grant N00014-90-J-1942 awarded by the Office of Naval Research. Michael Jordan is an NSF Presidential Young Investigator.

NOTES

1. The minimum jerk model is entirely kinematic (forces do not enter into the optimization procedure); thus, it predicts straight-line motion regardless of external forces. This argument assumes that subjects are able in principle to compensate for the external force.

2. Note, however, that inverse models are not the only way to implement open-loop control schemes. As we have seen, an open-loop controller also can be implemented by placing a forward model in an internal feedback loop. See Jordan (1996) for further discussion.

3. A feedforward controller is an internal inverse model of the plant that is used in an open-loop control configuration. See Jordan (1996) for further discussion of feedforward and feedback control.

REFERENCES

ADAMS, J. A., 1984. Learning of movement sequences. *Psychol. Bull.* 96:3–28.

ATKESON, C. G., and J. M. HOLLERBACH, 1985. Kinematic features of unrestrained vertical arm movements. *J. Neurosci.* 5:2318–2330.

ATKESON, C. G., and D. J. REINKENSMEYER, 1988. *Using Associative Content-Addressable Memories to Control Robots.* IEEE Conference on Decision and Control, San Francisco, May, 1988.

BEGGS, W. D. A., and C. I. HOWARTH, 1972. The movement of the hand towards a target. *Q. J. Exp. Psychol.* 24:448–453.

BERNSTEIN, N., 1967. *The Coordination and Regulation of Movements.* London: Pergamon.

BRASHERS-KRUG, T., R. SHADMEHR, and E. BIZZI, 1996. Consolidation in human motor memory. *Nature* 382:252–255.

BRYSON, A. E., and Y.C. HO, 1975. *Applied Optimal Control.* New York: Wiley.

CONDITT, M. A., F. GANDOLFO, and F. A. MUSSA-IVALDI, 1997. The motor system does not learn dynamics of the arm by rote memorization of past experience. *J. Neurophysiol.* 78:1:554–560.

DUHAMEL, J. R., C. L. COLBY, and M. E. GOLDBERG, 1992. The updating of the representation of visual space in parietal cortex by intended eye movements. *Science* 255:90–92.

FITTS, P. M., 1954. The information capacity of the human motor system in controlling the amplitude of movements. *J. Exp. Psychol.* 47:381–391.

FLASH, T., and I. GUREVICH, 1991. Human motor adaptation to external loads. *IEEE Eng. Med. Biol. Soc. Conference* 13:885–886.

FLASH, T., and N. HOGAN, 1985. The co-ordination of arm movements: An experimentally confirmed mathematical model. *J. Neurosci.* 5:1688–1703.

GEORGOPOULOS, A. P., J. F. KALASKA, and J. T. MASSEY, 1981. Spatial trajectories and reaction times of aimed movements: Effects of practice, uncertainty and change in target location. *J. Neurophysiol.* 46:725–743.

GHAHRAMANI, Z., and D. M. WOLPERT, 1997. Modular decomposition in visuomotor learning. *Nature* 386:392–395.

GHEZ, C., J. GORDON, M. F. GHILARDI, C. N. CHRISTAKOS, and S. E. COOPER, 1990. Roles of proprioceptive input in the programming of arm trajectories. *Cold Spring Harb. Symp. Quant. Biol.* 55:837–847.

GOODBODY, S. J., and D. M. WOLPERT, 1998. Temporal and amplitude generalization in motor learning. *J. Neurophysiol.* 79:1825–1838.

GOODWIN, G. C., and K. S. SIN, 1984. *Adaptive Filtering Prediction and Control.* Englewood Cliffs, N.J.: Prentice-Hall.

GRAYBIEL, A. M., T. AOSAKI, A. W. FLAHERTY, and M. KIMURA, 1994. The basal ganglia and adaptive motor control. *Science* 265:1826–1831.

GRIBBLE, P. L., and D. J. OSTRY, 1996. Origins of the power-law relation between movement velocity and curvature–Modeling the effects of muscle mechanics and limb dynamics. *J. Neurophysiol.* 76:2853–2860.

HARRIS, C. M., 1995. Does saccadic under-shoot minimize saccadic flight-time? A Monte-Carlo study. *Vision Res.* 35:691–701.

HARRIS, C. M., and D. M. WOLPERT, 1998. Signal-dependent noise determines motor planning. *Nature* 394:780–784.

HERTZ, J., A. KROGH, and R. G. PALMER, 1991. *Introduction to the Theory of Neural Computation.* Redwood City, Calif.: Addison-Wesley.

HOFF, B. R., 1992. *A Computational Description of the Organization of Human Reaching and Prehension.* University of Southern California, Los Angeles. PhD Thesis.

HOGAN, N., 1984. An organizing principle for a class of voluntary movements. *J. Neurosci.* 4:2745–2754.

JACOBS, R. A., M. I. JORDAN, and A. G. BARTO, 1991. Task decomposition through competition in a modular connectionist architecture: The what and where vision tasks. *Cogn. Sci.* 15:219–250.

JACOBS, R. A., M. I. JORDAN, S. J. NOWLAN, and G. E. HINTON, 1991. Adaptive mixture of local experts. *Neural Comput.* 3:79–87.

JEANNEROD, M., 1997. *The Cognitive Neuroscience of Action.* Oxford: Blackwell.

JORDAN, M. I., 1990. Motor learning and the degrees of freedom problem. In: *Attention and Performance, XIII,* M. Jeannerod, ed. Hillsdale, N.J.: Erlbaum.

JORDAN, M. I., 1992. Constrained supervised learning. *J. Math. Psychol.* 36:396–425.

JORDAN, M. I., 1996. Computational aspects of motor control and motor learning. In: *Handbook of Perception and Action: Motor Skills,* H. Heuer and S. Keele, eds. New York: Academic Press.

JORDAN, M. I., and R. A. Jacobs, 1994. Hierarchical mixtures of experts and the EM algorithm. *Neural Comput.* 6:181–214.

JORDAN, M. I., and D. A. ROSENBAUM, 1989. Action. In: *Foundations of Cognitive Science,* M. I. Posner, ed. Cambridge, Mass.: MIT Press.

JORDAN, M. I., and D. E. RUMELHART, 1992. Forward models: Supervised learning with a distal teacher. *Cogn. Sci.* 16:307–354.

KALMAN, R. E., and R. S. BUCY, 1961. New results in linear filtering and prediction. *J. Basic Engineering (ASME)* 83D:95–108.

KAWATO, M., 1992. Optimization and learning in neural networks for formation and control of coordinated movement. In: *Attention and Performance, XIV: Synergies in Experimental Psychology, Artificial Intelligence, and Cognitive Neuroscience–A Silver Jubilee,* D. Meyer and S. Kornblum, eds. Cambridge, Mass.: MIT Press, pp. 821–849.

KAWATO, M., K. FURAWAKA, and R. SUZUKI, 1987. A hierarchical neural network model for the control and learning of voluntary movements. *Biol. Cybern.* 56:1–17.

KAWATO, M., and D. M. WOLPERT, 1998. Internal models for motor control. In: *Sensory Guidance of Movement,* M. Glickstein and R. Bock, eds. Chichester, U.K.: Novartis, pp. 291–307.

KUPERSTEIN, M., 1988. Neural model of adaptive hand-eye coordination for single postures. *Science* 239:1308–1311.

LACKNER, J. R., and P. DIZIO, 1994. Rapid adaptation to Coriolis force perturbations of arm trajectory. *J. Neurophysiol.* 72:299–313.

LACQUANITI, F., N. A. BORGHESE, and M. CARROZZO, 1992. Internal models of limb geometry in the control of hand compliance. *J. Neurosci.* 12:1750–1762.

LACQUANITI, F., C. A. TERZUOLO, and P. VIVIANI, 1983. The law relating kinematic and figural aspects of drawing movements. *Acta Psychologica* 54:115–130.

LINDBLOM, B., J. LUBKER, and T. GAY, 1979. Formant frequencies of some fixed-mandible vowels and a model of speech motor programming by predictive simulation. *J. Phonetics* 7:147–161.

MACKENZIE, C. L., R. G. MARTENIUK, C. DUGAS, D. LISKE, and B. EICKMEIER, 1987. Three dimensional movement trajectories in Fitts' task: Implications for control. *Q. J. Exp. Psychol.* 39:629–647.

MEYER, D. E., R. A. ABRAMS, S. KORNBLUM, C. E. WRIGHT, and J. E. K. SMITH, 1988. Optimality in human motor performance: Ideal control of rapid aimed movements. *Psychol. Rev.* 98:340–370.

MIALL, R. C., D. J. WEIR, D. M. WOLPERT, and J. F. STEIN, 1993. Is the cerebellum a Smith predictor? *J. Motor Behav.* 25(3):203–216.

MIALL, R. C., and D. M. WOLPERT, 1996. Forward models for physiological motor control. *Neural Networks* 9:8:1265–1279.

MILLER, W. T., 1987. Sensor-based control of robotic manipulators using a general learning algorithm. *IEEE J. Robotics Automation* 3:157–165.

MILNER, T. E., and M. M. IJAZ, 1990. The effect of accuracy constraints on three-dimensional movement kinematics. *Neuroscience* 35:365–374.

MORASSO, P., 1981. Spatial control of arm movements. *Exp. Brain Res.* 42:223–227.

NELSON, W. L., 1983. Physical principles for economies of skilled movements. *Biol. Cybern.* 46:135–147.

PELISSON, D., C. PRABLANC, M. A. GOODALE, and M. JEANNEROD, 1986. Visual control of reaching movements without vision of the limb: II. Evidence of fast unconscious processes correcting the trajectory of the hand to the final position of a double-step stimulus. *Exp. Brain Res.* 62:303–311.

ROBINSON, D. A., 1981. The use of control systems analysis in the neurophysiology of eye movements. *Annu. Rev. Neurosci.* 4:463–503.

SAINBURG, R. L., and C. GHEZ, 1995. Limitations in the learning and generalization of multijoint dynamics. *Soc. Neurosci. Abs.* 21(1):686.

SHADMEHR, R., and F. MUSSA-IVALDI, 1994. Adaptive representation of dynamics during learning of a motor task. *J. Neurosci.* 14:5:3208–3224.

SMITH, M. C., 1967. Theories of the psychological refractory period. *Psychol. Bull.* 67:202–213.

SOECHTING, J. F., and F. LACQUANITI, 1981. Invariant characteristics of a pointing movement in man. *J. Neurosci.* 1:710–720.

SUTTON, R., and A. G. BARTO, 1998. *Reinforcement Learning.* Cambridge, Mass.: MIT Press.

UNO, Y., M. KAWATO, and R. SUZUKI, 1989. Formation and control of optimal trajectories in human multijoint arm movements: Minimum torque-change model. *Biol. Cybern.* 61:89–101.

VAN DER HELM, F. C. T., and L. A. ROZENDAAL, 1998. Musculoskeletal systems with intrinsic and proprioceptive feedback. In: *Biomechanics and Neural Control of Movement*, J. M. Winters and P. E. Crago, eds. New York: Springer-Verlag, pp. 197–234.

VIVIANI, P., and T. FLASH, 1995. Minimum-jerk model, two-thirds power law and isochrony: Converging approaches to the study of movement planning. *J. Exp. Psychol. HPP* 21: 32–53.

VIVIANI, P., and R. SCHNEIDER, 1991. A developmental study of the relationship between geometry and kinematics in drawing movements. *J. Exp. Psychol. HPP* 17:198–218.

WELCH, R. B., and D. H. WARREN, 1986. Intersensory interactions. In: *Handbook of Perception and Human Performance. Volume I: Sensory Processes and Perception*, K. R. Boff, L. Kaufman, and J. P. Thomas, eds. New York: Wiley.

WIDROW, B., and S. D. STEARNS, 1985. *Adaptive Signal Processing*. Englewood Cliffs, N.J.: Prentice-Hall.

WOLPERT, D. M., 1997. Computational approaches to motor control. *Trends Cogn. Sci.* 1:209–216.

WOLPERT, D. M., Z. GHAHRAMANI, and M. I. JORDAN, 1995. An internal model for sensorimotor integration. *Science* 269:1880–1882.

WOLPERT, D. M., and M. KAWATO, 1998. Multiple paired forward and inverse models for motor control. *Neural Networks* 11:1317–1329.

WOLPERT, D. M., R. C. MIALL, J. L. WINTER, and J. F. STEIN, 1992. Evidence for an error deadzone in compensatory tracking. *J. Motor Behav.* 24:4:299–308.

V ATTENTION

Introduction

GREGORY J. DiGIROLAMO AND
MICHAEL I. POSNER

Central to human cognition and performance is the ability to selectively enhance the processing of a salient stimulus, relative to less important aspects, in a complex scene. This section addresses the topic of the cognitive and neural mechanisms involved in such attentional selection. The study of the orienting to and selective enhancement of sensory events has been the most explored of all the areas of attention in cognitive neuroscience and this topic dominates our section.

In several chapters (Posner and DiGirolamo; LaBerge; Luck and Hillyard; Robertson and Rafal) a major theme is the processing of a stimulus when multiple stimuli are presented or responses are competing for selection. Investigations into how the brain accomplishes stimulus selection and enhancement have used most of the major methods available to cognitive neuroscience. In the following chapters, you will read about single-cell studies in monkeys demonstrating relative enhancement for stimuli that are attended (Chelazzi and Corbetta), as well as changes in the time course and amplitude of the electrical signal seen on the human scalp for selected stimuli (Luck and Hillyard).

Attention to a stimulus is also accompanied by changes in regional blood flow to the areas of the brain that perform the computations that are being attended (Chelazzi and Corbetta; Mangun, Jha, Hopfinger, and Handy). In addition, the sources of these attentional effects are discussed in several other chapters. LaBerge, in particular, deals with models of how selection might be orchestrated by the interaction of brain regions.

Further chapters concern attentional dysfunction, which impairs the ability to select stimuli due either to brain injury (Behrmann; Robertson and Rafal). The study of patients with lesions continues to provide an important method for examining the parts of the brain necessary for carrying out attentional functions; it also offers an important basis for applying cognitive neuroscience to the assessment of important human problems and their treatment.

David Marr has pointed out that a complete explanation of any phenomenon must address the mechanisms and the computations involved in carrying out a behavior as well as the behavior itself. Common to all of these chapters, as well as the field of cognitive neuroscience as a whole, is the use of multiple methods of investigation at different levels of analysis to advance our understanding of complex cognitive questions. The problem of integrating data from these multiple levels of analysis remains a frontier for cognitive neuroscience. Mangun and colleagues consider the difficult issue of relating changes in regional cerebral blood flow to the electrical activity recorded from the scalp. These measures also need to be better integrated with the underlying cellular activity and with reaction time studies. Readers need to be careful in following the distinct methods and nomenclatures involved when crossing different levels of analysis. In cognitive psychology, for example, the terms *facilitation* and *inhibition* often refer, respectively, to increases and decreases in reaction time. Improvements in reaction time may be related either to increases in blood flow due to attention (Chelazzi and Corbetta) or decreases in blood flow due to the tuning of the neural population needed to perform the computation, as in priming or practice. Moreover, increases in blood flow may be caused either by excitatory or inhibitory post-synaptic potentials. Thus the terms at one level may be used quite differently at other levels of analysis. These chapters attempt to explore attentional selection at all levels. A fuller understanding of how terms are employed at each level is important for integration to proceed. New findings are apparent in all of these chapters, but full integration between levels remains extremely difficult.

We have endeavored to gather a range of chapters to demonstrate the progress that has been made in specific areas of attention while giving a broad overview of the field. Some aspects of attention are not addressed in these chapters. For example, our knowledge of the neuroanatomical and neurochemical mechanisms of arousal and sustained attention has progressed considerably. This work was summarized in the last edition of *The Cognitive Neurosciences* by Robbins and Everett and has not been repeated here. Nor have we reexamined the work in development of attention since the summary by Johnson in the last volume.

43 Attention in Cognitive Neuroscience: An Overview

MICHAEL I. POSNER AND GREGORY J. DIGIROLAMO

ABSTRACT The chapters of this section are concerned with the problem of attention. During the past several years, the analysis of attention has progressed substantially in terms of cognitive parameters and brain function. Neuroimaging methods have been applied, singly and in combination, most heavily to the question of orienting to visual targets. The results have yielded a wealth of information showing that attentional modulation occurs rapidly within the visual system, identifying which structures are most heavily involved, and indicating what happens to unattended information. As this effort proceeds, it may be possible to understand more about the anatomy of forms of attention that guide our thoughts, regulate our emotions, and integrate our performance.

Early history

The problem of selective attention is one of the oldest in psychology. William James (1890) wrote, at the turn of the century, "Everyone knows what attention is. It is the taking possession by the mind in clear and vivid form of one out of what seem several simultaneous objects or trains of thought." Even at this very early stage in attentional research, James distinguished between sensory attention driven by external stimuli and voluntary attention to the external environment or internal mental representations.

The dominance of behavioral psychology, however, postponed research into the internal mechanisms of selective attention in the first half of this century. Evidence that the integrity of the reticular formation of the brainstem was important to maintain the alert state provided some anatomical reality to the study of arousal mechanisms underlying one aspect of attention (Moruzzi and Magoun, 1949). This anatomical approach has led to many new findings relating the individual subcortical transmitter systems of arousal (e.g., dopamine, norepinephrine) to the computations underlying the selection of information.

MICHAEL I. POSNER Sackler Institute, Weill Medical College of Cornell University, Ithaca, N.Y.
GREGORY J. DIGIROLAMO Beckman Institute, University of Illinois, Urbana, Ill.

The quest for information-processing mechanisms to support the more selective and voluntary aspects of attention began with studies of dichotic listening following World War II. A filter was proposed that limited the information (in the formal sense of information theory) passed between highly parallel sensory systems and a limited-capacity perceptual system (Broadbent, 1958).

Selective listening experiments supported the view of early selection of a relevant message, with nonselected information being lost to conscious processing. Physiological studies (Skinner and Yingling, 1977) suggested that selection of the relevant channels might involve a thalamic gating mechanism using the reticular nucleus of the thalamus controlled by prefrontal sites. Peripheral gating mechanisms still represent a potential source of selection that might be especially important in lower mammals. In human information-processing studies, however, it was clear that unattended information is often processed to a high level, as evidenced by the fact that an important message on the unattended channel can interfere with the selected channel (Posner, 1978). This result suggested that attentional selection involves higher cortical levels. More recent animal studies suggest that thalamic mechanisms might work in conjunction with sensory processing areas to gate information at cortical levels (LaBerge, this volume; Moran and Desimone, 1985). The ability to select input channels and the levels at which selection occurs has remained an active question of current studies of attention.

In the 1970s, psychologists began to distinguish between automatic and controlled processes (Posner, 1978). Visual words can activate other words similar in meaning (semantic associates), even when the person has no awareness of the word's presence. These studies indicated that the parallel organization found for sensory information extends to semantic processing. However, selecting a word meaning for active attention appeared to suppress the availability of other word meanings. Attention was viewed less as an early sensory bottleneck and more as a system for providing priority for motor acts, consciousness, and memory (Allport, 1980). These higher-level mechanisms of attention involve frontal areas and provide important means of coordinating cognitive processes (see Chelazzi and Corbetta, chapter 46).

Another approach to selectivity arose in work on the orienting reflex (Kahneman, 1973; Sokolov, 1963). The use of slow autonomic systems (e.g., skin conductance) as a measure of orienting made it difficult to analyze the cognitive components and neural systems underlying orienting. In the mid-1970s, neurobiologists began to study information processing in alert monkeys (Wurtz, Goldberg, and Robinson, 1980). Because the visual system had been relatively well investigated using microelectrodes, much of this work involved the visual system. The last 15 years have seen a steady advance in our understanding of the neural systems related to visual orienting from studies using single-cell recording in alert monkeys (Chelazzi and Corbetta, chapter 46; Motter, 1998). This work demonstrated a relatively restricted number of neural areas in which the firing rates of neurons were enhanced selectively when monkeys were trained to attend to a location or object. At the level of the superior colliculus, selective enhancement could be obtained only when eye movement was involved. In contrast, neurons in the posterior parietal lobe demonstrated selective enhancement even when the animal maintained fixation. An area of the thalamus, the lateral pulvinar, was similar to the parietal lobe in containing cells that demonstrated selective enhancement when monkeys attended (Colby, 1991). Indeed the thalamic areas relate to the earlier rat models (Skinner and Yingling, 1977) but are believed to perform selection at higher levels of analysis. Vision remains the central system for the integration of cognitive and neuroscience approaches to selectivity.

Until recently, the approaches to human information processing differed from neuroscientific approaches to attention using nonhuman animals. The former tended to describe attention either as a bottleneck that protected limited-capacity central systems from overload, or as a resource (analogous to the use of the term in economics) that could be allocated to various processing systems. On the other hand, neuroscientific views emphasized several separate neural mechanisms that might be involved in orienting and maintaining alertness. Currently, there is an attempt to integrate these two viewpoints within the cognitive neuroscience of attention (Näätänen, 1992; Posner and Peterson, 1990). The chapters in this section all take this approach.

Imaging methods

The effort to link attention to specific brain systems depends on the availability of methods to secure links between cognition and neural processes (Sejnowski and Churchland, 1989). The parameters for classifying methods are based on the spatial resolution and temporal precision of the techniques. Major methods used for spatial resolution include depth electrical recordings, positron emission tomography (PET), and functional magnetic resonance imaging (fMRI). The post-stimulus latency histograms of cells from single- or multi-electrode arrays can provide exquisite temporal and spatial precision, but their invasive nature requires either surgical interventions in humans or the use of animal models. Temporal precision with normal human subjects is a feature of various chronometric methods involving reaction time or speed–accuracy trade-off measures (Bower and Clapper, 1989) and can also be studied by using event-related electrical or magnetic potentials (Näätänen, 1992; Rugg and Coles, 1995).

An important aspect of understanding the current developments in this field is to track converging evidence from multiple methods of study that combine high temporal and spatial resolution (e.g., Heinze et al., 1994). The chapters in this section have been selected to provide a background in various methodologies and perspectives on attention.

Much of the current progress in the cognitive neuroscience of the attention system rests historically on two important methodological developments. First, the use of microelectrodes with alert animals has shown that attention modulates the activity of individual cells (Colby, 1991). Second, anatomical (e.g., computerized tomography or MRI) and physiological (e.g., PET, fMRI) methods of studying parts of the brain have allowed more meaningful investigations of localization of cognitive functions in normal people (Toga and Mazziotta, 1996).

To move beyond the localization of anatomical areas, it is useful to employ methods sensitive to the time dynamics of information processing, and this usually requires analysis in the millisecond range. The temporal precision of various methods is changing rapidly, but the imaging methods based on blood flow or volume require changes in blood vessels, limiting temporal precision to hundreds of milliseconds at best. Currently, combined studies using localization methods (e.g., PET) and time-dynamic methods (e.g., ERPs) provide a convenient way to trace the rapid time-dynamic changes that occur in the course of human information processing (e.g., Heinze et al., 1994).

It would be ideal if imaging methods were developed that provided the desired combination of high temporal and spatial resolution. However, each of the current technologies has its own limitations. Cellular recording is limited to animals and is associated with sampling problems. Magnetoencephalography is expensive and, unless many channels are used, must be repositioned for examination of each area. Scalp electrical recording suffers from difficulty in localizing the generators directly from scalp distributions, and fMRI and PET are limited by the time required for blood vessels to reflect brain activity (hemodynamic lag). Each of the extant methods will, however, afford modifications that may address some or all of these problems; moreover, new methods, such as event-related fMRI, are becoming available (Josephs, Turner, and Friston, 1997).

Issues

With the exception of advances in methods (e.g., event-related fMRI) and the increased effort to integrate data across methods, much of what was summarized in the previous volume remains up-to-date. The progress in the field, then, relates to the ability to reexamine fundamental issues in light of the new data available from the cognitive neuroscience approach. In that light we address three major issues that arose during the cognitive era—issues that are discussed in more detail in the chapters that follow.

EARLY AND LATE SELECTION   One of the oldest issues in the field of attention is how early in processing can attention influence input. Since this issue began during the information-processing period, it often took the following form: Are attentional influences largely changes in criteria (i.e., biases) introduced by the nature of the decisions subjects make based on the sensory evidence, or does attention influence the sensory evidence itself? Many empirical studies were done to determine if attentional changes showed up as alterations in the beta parameter of a signal detection analysis or whether instead they involved changes in the d' parameter (Hawkins et al., 1990). Although many elegant studies were conducted attempting to clarify this issue, no final resolution was reached (although it seems likely that both parameters can be varied by some experimental conditions).

Neuroscience evidence of four types has been brought to bear on these issues: The lesion method (Behrmann, chapter 45; Robertson and Rafal, chapter 44), cellular studies (Chelazzi and Corbetta, chapter 46; Luck and Hillyard, chapter 47), neuroimaging (Chelazzi and Corbetta, chapter 46; Mangun et al., chapter 48) and event-related cortical potentials (Luck and Hillyard, chapter 47; Mangun et al., chapter 48). Lesions of the parietal lobe interfered with the ability to shift attention to the contralesional side and showed a very specific deficit in reaction time experiments (Posner et al., 1987). Stimuli from the affected side appeared to have great difficulty in summoning orienting under conditions when the pa-

tient was already processing something on the ipsilateral side of the lesion (disengage deficit). While normal subjects showed only a small deficit in reaction time when the target appeared in the opposite visual field from the cue (invalid trials), patients were often simply unaware of the target presented in the neglected field. This result seemed decisive evidence of a sensory influence of attention since the subjects with parietal lesions were unable to report the presence of the target.

However, further studies indicated that the neglected stimulus is processed, even if unconsciously, and awareness was still possible. For example, while subjects might miss a contralesional target feature in isolation, they might report the stimulus if integration with material on the ipsilesional side completed an object, even without attention (Driver, Baylis, and Rafal, 1993; Mack and Rock, 1998). Moreover, implicit priming was also reported indicating that many sensory operations were being carried out (McGlinchey-Berroth et al., 1993). In addition to the lesion evidence, both electrical recordings from the scalp and cellular recordings in monkeys in the object recognition pathway indicated that attention could influence portions of the visual systems in V4 and later.

At first, the cellular data were persuasive that V1 could not be influenced by attention. However, attentional modulation in V1 appears to occur when the visual field is cluttered (Posner and Gilbert, 1999). This finding shows how closely the psychological method and the physiological results are integrated. Only in a cluttered field do we usually see extremely strong attentional effects in reaction time experiments in normal subjects. Attentional effects in normals are rarely obtained in an uncluttered field; only neuropsychological patients show a strong effect in an empty field. A cluttered field requires information about the location of the target and also about its surround. This requires selection in a smaller receptive field, and it is then that effects in V1 have been reported (Motter, 1993, 1998).

The early vs. late question can be resolved into three somewhat interdependent issues.

1. How early in the nervous system can attention influence stimulus input? The above results suggest that it can be as early as V1 under some conditions, but it is often later in visual processing (e.g., Moran and Desimone, 1985).

2. How quickly after input can attention influence information processing? Again, the cellular and physiological data indicate that it can be quite early, although in most paradigms the influence is not strong until 80–100 ms after stimulus onset (e.g., Clark and Hillyard, 1996). The timing issue is of particular importance because activation of a particular brain area may be along

the input pathway or could be due to feedback from higher areas.

3. What does early selection mean for the processing of information, both selected and unselected? Here the answer is more complex. It seems to mean that certain aspects of complex scenes may be available for conscious report while other aspects will be available only if they succeed in producing reorienting. Unattended objects, however, may still be processed to fairly high levels, and the processing itself may summon attention. The depth of cognitive processing of unattended objects and the possibility of attentional summoning suggest that early selection does not have the cognitive consequence originally implied. Selecting one stimulus over others does not mean that unselected items will not produce a reorienting of attention (e.g., McCormick, 1997) or still influence behavior (Neill, 1977).

SEPARATE CONTROL SYSTEMS   Basic to understanding attention is the issue of whether the mechanisms that comprise the brain's attentional system are separate (James, 1890; Posner and Dehaene, 1994) or not (Neisser, 1976) from sensory and memory systems. Like the issue of early or late selection, this debate stems from cognitive studies of attention. It was apparent that interference would result between tasks requiring common input or output systems (one cannot look forward and backward at the same time, nor flex and extend a muscle simultaneously). However, some evidence suggested that interference occurred in many cognitive studies even when the modality of input and the motor output were quite separate. Many cognitive studies have been related to these issues. But despite evidence on both sides (Bourke, et al., 1996; Duncan, Humphreys, and Ward, 1997), no clear resolution has been possible.

From an anatomical perspective, we can distinguish two types of brain areas related to attention. By the *source* of attention, we mean those anatomical areas that seem to be specific to attention, not primarily involved in other forms of processing. However, when attention operates during task performance, it will operate at the neural areas (*site* of attention) where the computations involved in the task are usually performed. Thus, when subjects attend to the color, form, or motion of a visual object, they amplify blood flow in various extrastriate areas (Corbetta et al., 1991). These areas are known to be involved in the passive registration of the same information. We expect that most brain areas, especially cortical areas, will show attention effects in this sense, although they are not part of the brain's attentional system.

Most discussions of the site vs. source issue have been in the study of orienting (Cohen et al., 1994; Luck and

Ford, 1998; Posner, 1992). Evidence from neglect patients cited in the last section suggested that orienting in the visual system was achieved by orchestrating changes in the orienting network (involving the posterior parietal lobe, pulvinar, and colliculus) to influence input into the ventral object recognition pathway. Thus, visual search would involve changes in the parietal lobe that reflect disengagement, as well as activation in the superior colliculus involved in moving attention; it also provides a signal into V4, via the pulvinar, that enhances information at attended locations (see also LaBerge, chapter 49, for a different but related view). In favor of this view, PET studies show strong activity in parietal, pulvinar, and frontal areas during attention shifts (Corbetta et al., 1995; LaBerge and Buchsbaum, 1990), and ERP data indicate the role of the dorsal pathway during visual search (Luck, 1994).

A different view suggests that attentional effects are primarily due to competition within the object recognition pathway (largely V4) itself (Duncan, Humphreys, and Ward, 1997). This difference may be largely a matter of emphasis, as Desimone and Duncan (1995) allow for top-down influences to be involved in the decision about which part of the scene should be selected. They do not, however, specify what this top-down influence might be (for suggestions on this, see Chelazzi and Corbetta, chapter 46; LaBerge, chapter 49; and Robertson and Rafal, chapter 44).

Even if one acknowledges top-down influences from parietal and frontal areas on the visual system, one may argue that these activations do not constitute a separate attentional system, but rather reflect real or implicit activity of the eyes or some other movement (Rizzolatti, Riggio, and Sheliga, 1994). This view is represented by Chelazzi and Corbetta, chapter 46. There is considerable evidence for anatomical overlap between the frontal and parietal areas used in the control of saccadic eye movements and the areas active during attentional tasks (Corbetta, 1998). Moreover, many important implications about the nature of selective attention have come from the analogy between saccades and attention shifts (for example, the extra time taken to shift across the midline, or the distinction between shifts to the upper and lower visual fields). However, several important pieces of evidence suggest that there are additional properties of attention that do not relate too closely to saccades. First, attention shifts demonstrate costs and benefits even within the fovea (see LaBerge, chapter 49). Second, a shift of attention from the periphery to the fovea has as large a cost as a shift from the fovea to the periphery (Posner and Cohen, 1984). There is also clear evidence for selection among objects in the same visual location (Weber, Kramer, and Miller, 1997). Whether one thinks of orienting as due to programming of eye movements or as a covert shift within a separate attentional network, the involvement of the parietal area in this process remains to be understood.

The clearest reason for wanting to maintain separation between the brain's attentional system and overt movements, whether of the hands or the eyes, remains situations in which attention is employed to control cognition independent of the effector systems. Searching memory, combining thoughts, selecting information for storage, and monitoring behavior are important attentional operations that require no effector system. These volitional cognitive operations are discussed in the next section.

Executive control

Despite the obvious importance of a means of unifying the processing of anatomically separate cognitive modules, it has been difficult to specify the functions and mechanisms of executive control that lead to coherent behavior. Perhaps for that reason, the cognitive neuroscience literature contains relatively little discussion of these mechanisms. This is also true of this section, although LaBerge (chapter 49 in this volume) discusses some of the frontal input into orienting mechanisms.

Our strongest indication of executive control remains the subjective experience of having control of our thoughts and actions (cf. James, 1890). Lesions of the frontal lobe often produce incoherent behavior and impairment in planning, suggesting an anatomical reality of executive control (Duncan, Burgess, and Emslie, 1995). In this part of our chapter we indicate some effort to extend cognitive models of executive control to neuroimaging studies that explore the anatomy and circuitry of executive control.

It has been hard to define executive control—the term has been used in many ways, and the processes that fall under this umbrella term are not well agreed upon. We try to avoid these difficulties by discussing conflict among stimulus or response elements as one situation in which executive control is needed. Our goal in this section is to review those behavioral and neuroimaging studies of conflict in the Stroop effect, dual task interference, and error detection in the hope of indicating some cognitive and neuroanatomical mechanisms of executive control. At the end, we relate these findings to evidence that the same brain areas may be involved in control of pain, distress, and other emotional responses.

STROOP A classical example of attentional conflict is the well-known Stroop task (Stroop, 1935). In this paradigm, subjects are asked to name the color of ink in which a word is presented. The word can either indicate a different color name from the ink color (incongruent) or the same color name as the ink color (congruent). The resulting reaction times and error rates are compared against a neutral condition in which a noncolor word or a letter string is presented (see Posner and DiGirolamo, 1998, for a discussion of "neutral"). Highly reliable interference is found when the color and word meaning disagree, and a less reliable but often observed facilitation is found when the color and word agree (MacLeod, 1991).

Neuroimaging studies of the Stroop effect have demonstrated activation of a midline attentional system in resolving the word and color conflict (Bench et al., 1993; Carter, Mintun, and Cohen, 1995; Derbyshire, Vogt, and Jones, 1998; George et al., 1994; Pardo et al., 1990; Taylor et al., 1994). Though the correspondence is not exact, all studies find a midline cingulate activation when the word and color disagree (for a review, see Posner and DiGirolamo, 1998). Surprisingly, the congruent condition (relative to a neutral) also activates the cingulate cortex (Bench et al., 1993; Carter, Mintun, and Cohen, 1995). DiGirolamo (DiGirolamo, Heidrich, and Posner, 1998; Posner and DiGirolamo, 1998) has suggested an analysis of the Stroop effect that postulates comparable selective attentional processes to resolve conflict in both the congruent and incongruent conditions. In support of this hypothesis, event-related potential waveforms for the incongruent and congruent condition diverged from the neutral condition, but did not diverge from each other until response (DiGirolamo, Heidrich, and Posner, 1998). Moreover, dipole modeling of the congruent and incongruent conditions produced matching neural solutions consistent with the cingulate gyrus generator seen in the blood flow studies. These results suggest the activity of an executive attentional system during both congruent and incongruent conditions. Color word trials require a selection between information from the word and information from the color, independent of the congruity of the trial type. These data demonstrate that selection of one dimension of a stimulus that has multiple dimensions presents a situation of conflict that requires executive control mechanisms. In the course of this dimensional conflict, the cingulate cortex is active during times requiring conflict resolution between anatomically separate cognitive processing systems.

DUAL-TASK Neuroimaging studies have suggested that the cingulate cortex is also involved in attentional processing during dual-task situations. When subjects are learning a sequencing task or generating a use for a word, the cingulate cortex and dorsolateral frontal areas are highly active. In contrast, once performance is automated and attention is no longer required, the cingulate and dorsolateral frontal areas are no longer active (Frith et al., 1991; Raichle et al., 1994). Dual-task interference also decreases when either of the tasks becomes well learned. During dual-task performance of tasks that share neither input nor response, performance deteriorated compared to either task alone, and there was increased activation in the cingulate cortex. Passingham and colleagues (1996) have suggested that interference occurs centrally, not in either perceptual or response systems; they further suggest that one of the neural areas in which the central bottleneck occurs is the cingulate cortex. In support of this notion, when subjects are asked to attend to a well-learned sequence, increased activation is found only in the cingulate and dorsolateral frontal areas and dual-task interference increases. These areas are the same areas active during the original learning of the movement; these areas come back on-line when subjects attend to the movements following practice (Jueptner et al., 1997).

To investigate the central executive of Baddeley's (1993) working memory model, D'Esposito (1995) and colleagues also compared performance in single vs. dual-task conditions. As in the previous study, activation in the cingulate cortex and dorsolateral frontal regions significantly increased (relative to single-task activity) during the concurrent task condition. D'Esposito and colleagues argued that the cingulate cortex and dorsolateral prefrontal cortex comprise part of the neuroanatomical circuit of the central executive.

ERROR DETECTION   Immediately following an error, subjects are often conscious of making a mistake. When subjects are aware of making an error in speeded tasks, they showed negativity over midfrontal channels on the scalp following the key press (Dehaene, Posner, and Tucker, 1994; Gehring et al., 1993). Using the Brain Electrical Source Analysis (BESA) algorithm (Scherg and Berg, 1995), localization of this error-related negativity suggested activation from the cingulate (see also Badgaiyan and Posner, 1998). Errors can be either slips (incorrect executions of a motor program) or mistakes (selection of an inappropriate intention). Dehaene, Posner, and Tucker (1994) have shown that the negativity generated by the cingulate only follows a slip when the subjects know they've made an error, but not if they've mistakenly selected an incorrect response. Activation of the cingulate related to conflict and error has now been shown in blood flow studies as well (Carter et al., 1998). Monitoring of the selected response and awareness of the response actually made are crucial for coherent and successful behavior. Cingulate activation is directly related to awareness of one's own planned behavior.

The presence of frontal activity, particularly in midline structures in these conflict tasks, suggests a possible common anatomy, at least to some forms of executive control. In this section we have suggested that these structures are related to subjective feelings of voluntary control of thoughts and feelings. More evidence of this issue arises in studies related to aspects of awareness such as stimuli that involved pain.

PAIN   Neuroimaging studies have demonstrated that the processing of pain also activates the anterior cingulate. In a recent study, responses to painful stimuli and to the incongruent trials of the Stroop effect were studied within the same experiment (Derbyshire, Vogt, and Jones, 1998). It was found that areas of the midcingulate were active in both, but that subjects appeared to differ in the specific areas activated to pain and to conflict and the two rarely overlapped in the same subject. Moreover, it appears to be the subjective experience of pain that is encoded in the anterior cingulate. In one study, subjects were hypnotized to experience more or less pain from the same stimulation, dependent on hypnotic suggestion (Rainville et al., 1997). Blood flow changes in the anterior cingulate cortex correlated with subjects' reporting significantly more subjective pain. However, perceived pain did not correlate with activity in primary somatosensory cortex. These findings are intriguing and suggest important interaction between control of cognition and affect (Posner and Rothbart, 1998).

PSYCHIATRIC DISORDERS   Another area of investigation to study awareness is the breakdown of volition and perception in psychiatric disorders. One representative case is the positive symptoms of schizophrenia. Symptoms such as alien control and auditory hallucination suggest a dysfunction of the executive control system in patients with schizophrenia (DiGirolamo and Posner, 1996; Early et al., 1989; Frith, 1992). In the positive symptoms of schizophrenia, many of the deficits suggest a dysfunction in subjective perception. Postmortem histological analysis has revealed abnormalities in cingulate cortex morphology in patients with schizophrenia (Benes, 1993). In Benes' view, the regulatory function of the cingulate is impaired. Neuroimaging studies have suggested that impaired activation in cognitive tasks by patients with schizophrenia are directly related to activation in the cingulate (Dolan et al., 1995). Following neuroleptics, both behavioral performance and blood flow in the cingulate reach the levels seen in subjects with no history of psychiatric disorder. Tracing deficits in the neurocircuitry of psychiatry disorders might better our understanding of the relation of executive attention functions to normal, as well as pathological, cognition and behavior.

The study of these higher forms of attention from a cognitive neuroscience view is still in an early stage of development. Efforts to better understand the operations involved in executive control as well as to explore their anatomy and circuitry are critical goals for the future of attention research.

REFERENCES

ALLPORT, A., 1993. Attention and control: Have we been asking the wrong questions? A critical review of twenty-five years. In *Attention and Performance XIV: Synergies in Experimental Psychology, Artificial Intelligence, and Cognitive Neuroscience,* D. E. Meyer and S. Kornblum, eds., Cambridge, Mass.: MIT Press, pp. 183–218.

ALLPORT, D. A., 1980. Attention and performance. In *Cognitive Psychology,* G. Claxton, ed., London: Routledge and Kegan Paul, pp. 112–153.

BADDELEY, A., 1993. Working memory or working attention. In *Attention: Selection, Awareness, and Control,* A. Baddeley and L. Weiskrantz, eds., Oxford: Clarendon Press, pp. 152–170.

BADGAIYAN, R. D., and M. I. POSNER, 1998. Mapping cingulate cortex in response to selection and monitoring. *Neuroimage* 7: 255–260.

BAYLIS, G. C., J. DRIVER, and R. D. RAFAL, 1993. Visual extinction and stimulus repetition. *J. Cogn. Neurosci.* 5:453–466.

BENCH, C. J., C. D. FRITH, P. M. GRASBY, K. J. FRISTON, E. PAULESU, R. S. J. FRACKOWIAK, and R. J. DOLAN, 1993. Investigations of the functional anatomy of attention using the Stroop test. *Neuropsychologia* 31:907–922.

BENES, F. M., 1993. Relationship of cingulate cortex to schizophrenia and other psychiatric disorders. In *Neurobiology of Cingulate Cortex and Limbic Thalamus: A Comprehensive Handbook,* B. A. Vogt and M. Gabriel eds., Boston: Birkhauser, pp. 581–605.

BOURKE, P. A., J. DUNCAN, and I. NIMMO-SMITH, 1996. A general factor involved in dual-task performance decrement. *Quart. J. Exp. Psychol.* 49A:525–545.

BOWER, G. H., and J. P. CLAPPER, 1989. Experimental methods in cognitive science. In *Foundations of Cognitive Science,* M. I. Posner, ed., Cambridge, Mass.: MIT Press, pp. 245–300.

BROADBENT, D. E., 1958. *Perception and Communication.* London: Pergamon Press.

CARTER, C. S., T. S. BRAVER, D. M. BARCH, M. M. BOTVINICK, D. NOLL, and J. D. COHEN, 1998. Anterior cingulate cortex, error detection, and online monitoring of performance. *Science* 280:747–749.

CARTER, C. S., M. MINTUN, and J. D. COHEN, 1995. Interference and facilitation effects during selective attention: An $H_2{}^{15}O$ PET study of Stroop task performance. *Neuroimage* 2:264–272.

CLARK, V. P., and S. A. HILLYARD, 1996. Spatial selective attention affects early extrastriate but not striate components of the visual evoked potential. *J. Cogn. Neurosci.* 8: 387–402.

COHEN, J. D., R. D. ROMERO, D. SERVAN-SCHREIBER, and M. J. FARAH, 1994. Mechanisms of spatial attention: The relation of macrostructure to microstructure in parietal neglect. *J. Cogn. Neurosci.* 6:377–387.

COLBY, C. L., 1991. The neuroanatomy and neurophysiology of attention. *J. Child Neurol.* 6:90–118.

CORBETTA, M., 1998. Fronto-parietal cortical networks for directing attention and the eye to visual locations: Identical, independent, or overlapping neural systems? *Proc. Nat. Acad. Sci.* 95:831–838.

CORBETTA, M., F. M. MIEZIN, S. DOBMEYER, G. L. SHULMAN, and S. E. PETERSEN, 1991. Selective and divided attention during visual discrimination of shape, color, and speed: Functional anatomy by positron emission tomography. *J. Neurosci.* 11:2383–2402.

CORBETTA, M., G. L. SHULMAN, F. M. MIEZIN, and S. E. PETERSEN, 1995. Superior parietal cortex activation during spatial attention shifts and visual feature conjunction. *Science* 270:802–805.

D'ESPOSITO, M., J. A. DETRE, D. C. ALSOP, R. K. SHIN, S. ATLAS, and M. GROSSMAN, 1995. The neural basis of the central executive system of working memory. *Nature* 378:279–281.

DEHAENE, S., M. I. POSNER, and D. M. TUCKER, 1994. Localization of a neural system for error detection and compensation. *Psychol. Sci.* 5:303–305.

DERBYSHIRE, S. W., A. K. JONES, G. GYULAI, S. CLARK, D. TOWNSEND, and L. L. FIRESTONE, 1997. Pain processing during three levels of noxious stimulation produces differential patterns of central activity. *Pain* 73:431–445.

DERBYSHIRE, S. W., B. A. VOGT, and A. K. JONES, 1998. Pain and Stroop interference tasks activate separate processing modules in anterior cingulate cortex. *Exp. Brain Res.* 118: 52–60.

DESIMONE, R., and J. DUNCAN, 1995. Neural mechanisms of selective attention. *Annu. Rev. Neurosci.* 18:193–222.

DIGIROLAMO, G. J., A. HEIDRICH, and M. I. POSNER, 1998. Similar time course and neural circuitry across congruent and incongruent Stroop conditions. *A poster presented at the 5th Annual Meeting of the Cognitive Neuroscience Society.* San Francisco, Calif.

DIGIROLAMO, G. J., and M. I. Posner, 1996. Attention and schizophrenia: A view from cognitive neuroscience. *Cogn. Neuropsychiatry* 1:95–102.

DOLAN, R. J., P. FLETCHER, C. D. FRITH, K. J. FRISTON, R. S. J. FRACKOWIAK, and P. M. GRASBY, 1995. Dopaminergic modulation of impaired cognitive activation in the anterior cingulate cortex in schizophrenia. *Science* 378:180–182.

DRIVER, J., G. C. BAYLIS, and R. RAFAL, 1993. Perceived figure-ground segmentation and symmetry perception in a patient with neglect. *Nature* 360:73–75.

DUNCAN, J., 1980. The demonstration of capacity limitation. *Cogn. Psychol.* 12:75–96.

DUNCAN, J., P. BURGESS, and H. EMSLIE, 1995. Fluid intelligence after frontal lobe lesion. *Neuropsychologia* 33:261–268.

DUNCAN, J., G. HUMPHREYS, and R. WARD, 1997. Competitive brain activity in visual attention. *Curr. Opin. Neurobiol.* 7: 255–261.

EARLY, T. S., M. I. POSNER, E. M. REIMAN, and M. E. RAICHLE, 1989. Hyperactivity of the left stiato-pallidal projection. *Psych. Devel.* 2:85–121.

FIELDS, H. L., 1987. *Pain.* New York: McGraw-Hill.

FRITH, C. D., 1992. *The Cognitive Neuropsychology of Schizophrenia.* London: Lawrence Erlbaum Associates.

FRITH, C. D., K. FRISTON, P. F. LIDDLE, and R. S. J. FRACKOW-IAK, 1991. Willed action and the prefrontal cortex in man: A study with PET. *Proc. R. Soc. Lond. B* 244:241–246.

GEHRING, W. J., B. GROSS, M. G. H. COLES, D. E. MEYER, and E. DONCHIN, 1993. A neural system for error detection and compensation. *Psychol. Sci.* 4:385–390.

GEORGE, M. S., T. A. KETTER, P. I. PAREKH, N. ROSINSKY, H. RING, B. J. CASEY, M. R. TRIMBLE, B. HORWITZ, P. HERSCOVITCH, and R. M. POST, 1994. Regional brain activity when selecting response despite interference: An $H_2^{15}O$ PET study of the Stroop and an emotional Stroop. *Hum. Brain Map.* 1:194–209.

HAWKINS, H. L., S. A. HILLYARD, S. J. LUCK, M. MOULOUA, C. J. DOWNING, and D. P. WOODWARD, 1990. Visual attention modulates signal detection. *J. Exp. Psychol.: Hum. Percept. Perf.* 16:802–811.

HEINZE, H. J., G. R. MANGUN, W. BURCHERT, H. HINRICHS, M. SCHOLTZ, T. F. MUNTEL, A. GOSEL, M. SCHERG, S. JOHANNES, H. HUNDESHAGEN, M. S. GAZZANIGA, and S. A. HILLYARD, 1994. Combined spatial and temporal imaging of brain activity during visual selective attention in humans. *Nature* 372:543–546.

JAMES, W., 1890. *Principles of Psychology.* New York: Holt.

JOSEPHS, O., R. TURNER, and K. FRISTON, 1997. Event-related fMRI. *Hum. Brain Map.* 5:243–248.

JUEPTNER, M., K. M. STEPHAN, C. D. FRITH, D. J. BROOKS, R. S. J. FRACKOWIAK, and R. E. PASSINGHAM, 1997. Anatomy of motor learning: I. The frontal cortex and attention to action. *J. Neurophysiol.* 77:1313–1324.

KAHNEMAN, D., 1973. *Attention and Effort.* Englewood Cliffs, N.J.: Prentice Hall.

KANWISHER, N., 1987. Repetition blindness: Type recognition without token individuation. *Cognition* 27:117–143.

KANWISHER, N., J. DRIVER, and L. MACHADO, 1995. Spatial repetition blindness is modulated by selective attention to color or shape. *Cogn. Psychol.* 29:303–337.

LABERGE, D., and M. S. BUCHSBAUM, 1990. Positron emission tomography measurements of pulvinar activity during an attention task. *J. Neurosci.* 10:613–619.

LUCK, S. J., 1994. Cognitive and neural mechanisms of visual search. *Curr. Opin. Neurobiol.* 4:183–188.

LUCK, S. J., and M. A. FORD, 1998. On the role of selective attention in visual perception. *Proc. Nat. Acad. Sci.* 95:825–830.

LUMER, E. D., K. J. FRITH, and G. REES, 1998. Neural correlates of perceptual rivalry in the human brain. *Science* 280:1930–1934.

MACK, A., and I. ROCK, 1998. *Inattentional Blindness.* Cambridge, Mass.: MIT Press.

MACLEOD, C. M., 1991. Half a century of research on the Stroop effect: An integrative review. *Psychol. Bull.* 109:163–209.

MCCORMICK, P. A., 1997. Orienting without awareness. *J. Exp. Psychol.: Hum. Percept. Perf.* 23:168–180.

MCGLINCHEY-BERROTH, R., W. P. MILBERG, M. VEFAELLIE, M. ALEXANDER, and P. KILDUFF, 1993. Semantic priming in the neglected visual field: Evidence from a lexical decision task. *Cogn. Neuropsychol.* 10:79–108.

MORAN, J., and R. DESIMONE, 1985. Selective attention gates visual processing in the extrastriate cortex. *Science* 229:782–784.

MORUZZI, G., and H. W. MAGOUN, 1949. Brain stem reticular formation and activation of EEG. *Electroencephalogr. Clin. Neurophysiol.* 1:455–473.

MOTTER, B. C., 1993. Focal attention produces spatially selective processing in visual cortical areas V1, V2, and V4 in the presence of competing stimuli. *J. Neurophysiol.* 70:909–919.

MOTTER, B. C., 1998. Neurophysiology of visual attention. In *The Attentive Brain,* R. Parasuraman, ed., Cambridge, Mass.: MIT Press, pp. 51–70.

NÄÄTÄNEN, R., 1992. *Attention and Brain Function.* Hillsdale, N.J.: Lawrence Erlbaum Associates.

NEILL, W. T., 1977. Inhibitory and facilitatory processes in selective attention. *J. Exp. Psychol.: Hum. Percept. Perf.* 3:444–450.

NEISSER, U., 1976. *Cognition and Reality.* San Francisco: W. H. Freeman.

PARDO, J. V., P. J. PARDO, K. W. JANER, and M. E. RAICHLE, 1990. The anterior cingulate cortex mediates processing selection in the Stroop attentional conflict paradigm. *Proc. Nat. Acad. Sci.* 87:256–259.

PASHLER, H. E., 1998. *The Psychology of Attention.* Cambridge, Mass.: MIT Press.

PASSINGHAM, R. E., 1996. Attention to action. *Proc. R. Soc. Lond. B* 351:1473–1479.

POSNER, M. I., 1978. *Chronometric Explorations of Mind.* Hillsdale, N.J.: Erlbaum.

POSNER, M. I., 1992. Attention as a cognitive and neural system. *Curr. Direct. Psychol. Sci.* 1:11–14.

POSNER, M. I., and Y. COHEN, 1984. Components of visual orienting. In *Attention and Performance X,* H. Bouma and D. Bowhuis, eds., Hillsdale, N.J.: Erlbaum, pp. 531–556.

POSNER, M. I., and S. DEHAENE, 1994. Attentional networks. *Trends Neurosci.* 17:75–79.

POSNER, M. I., and G. J. DIGIROLAMO, 1998. Executive attention: Conflict, target detection and cognitive control. In *The Attentive Brain,* R. Parasuraman, ed., Cambridge, Mass.: MIT Press, pp. 401–423.

POSNER, M. I., and C. D. GILBERT, 1999. Attention and primary visual cortex. *Proc. Natl. Acad. Sci. U.S.A.* 96(6):2585–2587.

POSNER, M. I., and S. E. PETERSON, 1990. The attention system of the human brain. *Annu. Rev. Neurosci.* 13:25–42.

POSNER, M. I., and M. K. ROTHBART, 1998. Attention, self regulation and consciousness. *Trans. Phil. Soc. Lond. B,* in press.

POSNER, M. I., J. A. WALKER, F. A. FRIEDRICH, and R. D. RAFAL, 1987. How do the parietal lobes direct covert attention? *Neuropsychologia* 25(1-A):135–145.

RAICHLE, M. E., J. A. FIEZ, T. O. VIDEEN, A.-M. K. MACLEOD, J. V. PARDO, P. T. FOX, and S. E. PETERSEN, 1994. Practice-related changes in human brain functional anatomy during nonmotor learning. *Cereb. Cortex* 4:8–26.

RAINVILLE, P., G. H. DUNCAN, D. D. PRICE, B. CARRIER, and M. C. BUSHNELL, 1997. Pain affect encoded in human anterior cingulate but not somatosensory cortex. *Science* 277:968–971.

RIZZOLATTI, G., L. RIGGIO, and B. M. SHELIGA, 1994. Space and selective attention. In *Attention and Performance XV: Conscious and Nonconscious Information Processing,* C. Umiltà and M. Moscovitch, eds., Cambridge, Mass.: MIT Press, pp. 232–265.

RUGG, M. D., and M. G. H. COLES, 1995. *Electrophysiology of Mind.* New York: Oxford University Press.

SCHERG, M., and P. BERG, 1995. *Brain Electric Source Analysis Handbook (Version 2.0).* Herndon, Va.: Neuroscan.

SEJNOWSKI, T. J., and P. S. CHURCHLAND, 1989. Brain and cognition. In *Foundations of Cognitive Science,* M. I. Posner, ed., Cambridge, Mass.: MIT Press, pp. 301–356.

SHAPIRO, K. L., K. M. ARNELL, and J. E. RAYMOND, 1997. The attentional blink. *Trends Cogn. Sci.* 8:291–296.

SKINNER, J. E., and C. YINGLING, 1977. Central gating mechanisms that regulate event-related potentials and behavior. In *Attention, Voluntary Contraction, and Event-Related Cerebral Potentials,* J. E. Desmedt, ed., New York: Basal, pp. 30–69.

SOKOLOV, E. N., 1963. Higher nervous functions: The orienting reflex. *Annu. Rev. Physiol.* 25:545–580.

STROOP, J. R., 1935. Studies of interference in serial verbal reactions. *J. Exp. Psychol.* 18:643–662.

TAYLOR, S. F., S. KORNBLUM, S. MINOSHIMA, L. M. OLILVER, and R. A. KOEPPES, 1994. Changes in medial cortical blood flow with a stimulus-response compatibility task. *Neuropsychologia* 32:249–255.

TOGA, A. W., and J. C. MAZZIOTTA, 1996. *Brain Mapping: The Methods.* San Diego: Academic Press.

WEBER, T. A., A. F. KRAMER, and G. A. MILLER, 1997. Selective processing of superimposed objects: An electrophysiological analysis of object-based attentional selection. *Biol. Psychol.* 45:159–182.

WEISKRANTZ, L., 1997. *Consciousness Lost and Found.* Oxford: Oxford University Press.

WURTZ, R. H., M. E. GOLDBERG, and D. L. ROBINSON, 1980. Behavioral modulation of visual responses in the monkey: Stimulus selection for attention and movement. *Prog. Psychobiol. Physiol. Psychol.* 9:43–83.

44 Disorders of Visual Attention

LYNN C. ROBERTSON AND ROBERT RAFAL

ABSTRACT Advances in cognitive science and neuroscience are leading to a clearer understanding of the psychobiology underlying clinical disorders of visual attention. The study of these disorders has made many contributions to theories of normal attentional functioning, as well. In this chapter we discuss how attentional processes may operate in regulating normal visual attentional operations, explore some of the neural substrates of visual attention, and review the cognitive and biological bases of visual attention disabilities in everyday life. Drawing upon syndrome-based observations, lesion data with neurological patients, and transcortical magnetic stimulation data with normal participants, we examine the contributions of each approach to our understanding of the functions of visual attention and the neural substrates subserving these functions.

Meet the gentleman shown in figure 44.1A (see also color plate 28). He had recently suffered a large stroke affecting the right frontal and parietal lobes. Although his visual sensation was intact, he failed to detect signals in the side of space opposite the lesion and was not consciously aware of contralesional objects or parts of objects. He did not, for example, orient to people who approached him from his left side. And when a $10 bill was held a few inches from the left side of his face, it went unnoticed. This striking deficiency in lateralized orienting is known as hemispatial neglect. It most commonly results from lesions of the right cerebral hemisphere (although neglect from left hemisphere lesions has been observed), especially those involving the temporoparietal cortex. This chapter covers some of what is known about the psychobiology underlying hemispatial neglect and other clinical disorders of visual attention. The disabilities of these patients pose a vexing puzzle, sometimes challenging existing theories of attention.

Technical advances such as functional magnetic resonance (fMRI), positron emission tomography (PET), and evoked related potentials (ERP) have made it possible to measure regions of activity during visual attention tasks. Findings from these techniques are converging with those from studies of brain-injured subjects, allowing a more complete picture to emerge. In this effort, neuropsychology makes a special contribution: While ac-

tivation studies can determine what brain structures are activated in a given task, only the lesion method can determine what structures are necessary to perform it.

The interpretation of neuropsychological observations as they relate to normal function must consider the dynamic and interactive operations of the brain. While acute lesions eliminate the functions of the destroyed tissue, they also disrupt the functions of neural structures connected to the damaged area. This remote effect is called diaschesis. For example, acute lesions of the frontal cortex may also produce hypometabolism in the superior colliculus (Deuel and Collins, 1984). Thus, the behavioral effects of acute frontal lesions reflect the dysfunction throughout and help to define a frontocollicular circuit, not just the effect of missing frontal tissue. On the other hand, behavior in the chronic phase of illness, after acute diaschesis effects have abated, may reflect the operations of a reorganized brain. These changes in behavior during the transition from acute to chronic phases of disability can provide precious insights into dynamic brain organization.

The recent application of the technique of transcranial magnetic stimulation (TMS) in cognitive neuroscience provides converging lesion data that can help in interpreting the effects of natural lesions. TMS is used to induce an electric current through the skull on subjacent cortex, and can thus be used with normal subjects. After briefly activating the cortex, there is a silent period, lasting less than a few hundred milliseconds, in which the cortex is transiently inactivated. TMS essentially induces an ultra-acute lesion—one that is very brief and is not susceptible to plastic brain reorganization, so diaschesis of remote structures is not likely.

In this chapter we examine some of the effects of both acute and chronic lesions, and of TMS on selected aspects of visual attention. We first review the role of specific brain structures in orienting attention to locations in the visual field with some potential links to eye movement systems. Then we consider the role objects may play in guiding attention.

The visual grasp reflex

All vertebrates have primitive midbrain circuits for reflexively orienting toward salient events in the visual

LYNN C. ROBERTSON Veterans Affairs Neurology Research and Department of Psychology, University of California, Berkeley, Calif.

ROBERT RAFAL University of Wales, Bangor, U.K.

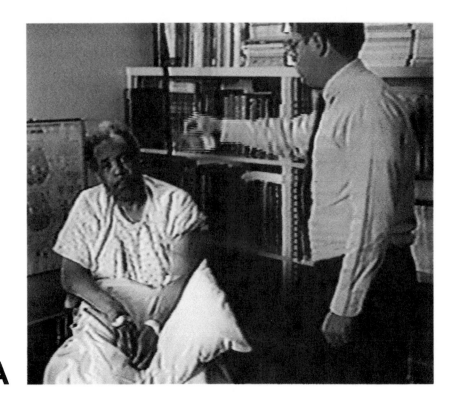

FIGURE 44.1   (A) A patient with left hemispatial neglect from a recent frontoparietal stroke. He is not aware of the examiner approaching from the left side. Note the orienting bias toward his right ipsilesional side. (B) A patient with progressive supra- nuclear palsy (PSP). He is aware of the examiner but has lost the spontaneous visual grasp reflex, even when the examiner looms toward him.

periphery. As mammals, humans have a phylogenetically new visual cortex that receives its dominant input through the thalamus (the lateral geniculate nucleus). The phylogenetically older midbrain pathway in humans is most associated with eye movements that normally accompany visual orienting. Figure 44.1B shows a patient with a neurodegenerative disorder of the brain stem and basal ganglia–a disorder known as progressive supranuclear palsy (PSP). Because the basal ganglia and the substantia nigra are involved, the clinical picture shares many features with Parkinson's disease. In addition, there is degeneration unique to this disease involving the superior colliculus and adjacent peritectal region. This pathology results in the distinctive paralysis of voluntary eye movements. Although there is a loss of the spontaneous visual grasp reflex, the patient is not blind and, unlike the patient with hemispatial neglect in figure 44.1A, he does report seeing the examiner.

In a study of attentional orienting, PSP patients were asked to respond with a key press when they detected a target appearing to the left, right, above, or below fixation (Posner et al., 1985; Rafal et al., 1988). Before each target, a peripheral cue appeared at one of these locations, and the influence of the cue on subsequent detection speed was measured. In normal individuals, the cue produces a biphasic effect on target detection; early facilitation followed by later inhibition, known as inhibition of return or IOR. The PSP patients exhibited a loss of both the initial facilitatory effect and the IOR along the vertical axis where their voluntary eye movement deficits were most severe. Thus both components of reflexive orienting seem to be mediated, at least in part, by midbrain visuomotor pathways.

Another way to investigate midbrain visuomotor reflexes in humans is to determine what visuomotor functions are preserved when damage to primary visual (striate) cortex leaves midbrain pathways intact. Figure 44.2A shows the MRI of an individual whose small stroke in the pericalcerine cortex was largely restricted to this area. Unlike the patients in figure 44.1, this patient is blind in the entire hemifield contralateral to the lesion. The capacity of patients with such visual loss to compensate is striking–a capacity that may be mediated in part by preserved retinotectal pathways. These pathways process information that, while not accessible to awareness, can nevertheless trigger orienting responses toward the hemianopic field. This "blindsight" has been demonstrated by requiring hemianopic subjects to move their eyes or reach toward signals they cannot "see," and by employing forced-choice response methods to show that visual information is processed without awareness (Weiskrantz, 1986).

The physiologic mechanisms responsible for blindsight remain controversial. In some patients there is "residual vision," which could be mediated by spared geniculostriate fibers (Fendrich, Wessinger, and Gazzaniga, 1992). Recently, however, Danziger, Fendrich, and Rafal (1997) showed that IOR was activated in the blind field of a hemianopic patient, even in regions that did not show conventional blindsight on a forced-choice localization task. This finding offers converging evidence that visual orienting is generated through midbrain visuomotor pathways.

CORTICOCOLLICULAR INTERACTIONS There are extensive direct and indirect projections from the cortex to the superior colliculus. This is especially prominent for areas of the dorsolateral prefrontal cortex, most notably the frontal eye field (FEF), but is also true for parietal-occipital areas.

Parietocollicular interactions Parietal influence on collicular activity was demonstrated some time ago in cats (Sprague, 1966). Behavior akin to hemispatial neglect of the contralesional side was induced by removing occipital and parietal cortex on one side. However, subsequent removal of the opposite superior colliculus improved vision in the contralesional field. This phenomenon, known as the Sprague effect, suggests that the parieto-occipital projections into the ipsilateral superior colliculus normally exert tonic facilitation. After parietal lesions, the ipsilesional colliculus loses this tonic activation (Hovda and Villablanca, 1990). At the same time, the opposite (contralesional) colliculus becomes hyperactive due to increased activation from its parietal lobe–the consequence of decreased inhibition through callosal projections from the opposite hemisphere (Seyal, Ro, and Rafal, 1995). The two colliculi are mutually inhibitory under normal conditions; i.e., the more active the colliculus is on one side, the more inhibition it exerts on the other. In this way, the colliculus that is normally activated by ipsilateral parieto-occipital projections receives a double hit with unilateral parietal lesions. Not only does the activation of the ipsilesional colliculus decrease due to the cortical damage, but it also decreases due to increased inhibition from the opposite superior colliculus.

Frontocollicular interactions Hemispatial neglect also occurs with acute frontal lobe damage and is often accompanied by eye deviation toward the ipsilesional side. An acute lesion to the FEF causes a kind of shock to connected regions (i.e., diaschesis), which can be measured experimentally as hypometabolism in remote structures including the superior colliculus (Deuel and Collins,

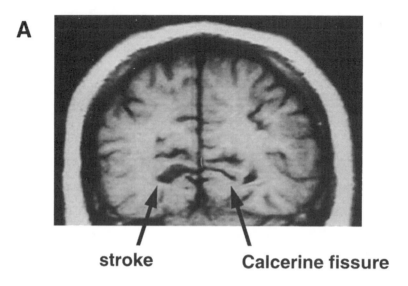

A

stroke   Calcerine fissure

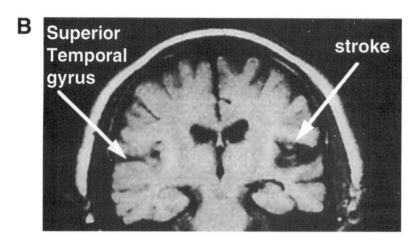

B

Superior Temporal gyrus   stroke

FIGURE 44.2   MRI scans of patients with (A) a small striate cortex lesion causing hemianopia and (B) a small temporal-parietal lesion.

1984). Neglect seen after small acute lesions of the FEF is generally short-term, and may be due in part to transient ipsilesional colliculus dysfunction. In the chronic, compensated state, lesions restricted to the FEF result neither in persistent neglect nor any other evident impairments in daily life. The reorganized state of frontocollicular circuitry after FEF lesions is a complex one. One of the net effects of chronic FEF lesions may be a disinhibited visual grasp reflex toward contralesional signals (i.e., the opposite of what is seen in neglect). This can be seen in the eye movements of recovered patients with frontal lesions in anti-saccade tasks. That is, chronic lesions in the FEF produce a deficit in inhibiting reflexive glances, especially into the contralesional field (Guitton, Buchtel, and Douglas, 1985; Rafal et al., in press).

Henik, Rafal, and Rhodes, 1994 compared the effects of chronic unilateral lesions of the human frontal eye fields on the latencies of reflexive visually guided saccades and of voluntary saccades. The patients in this study were part of a pool of individuals who had suffered brain injuries some time earlier, mostly from strokes, and who have been gracious in helping us investigate the consequences of these injuries. Each was selected for having a single, unilateral lesion restricted to the dorsolateral prefrontal cortex. Nine patients in whom the lesion included the FEF were compared with seven neurological control patients who had frontal lesions that spared what is believed, on the basis of PET studies, to be the human analog to the FEF (Paus, 1996).

The patients were tested in two saccade tasks: visually guided saccades to targets that appeared 10 degrees to the left or right, and voluntary saccades from a symbolic arrow cue at the center of the display that pointed to a marker target 10 degrees to the left or right. For the neurological patients whose frontal lesions spared the FEF, the latencies for voluntary saccades were normal, i.e., longer than for visually guided saccades, and the frontal lesion did not produce an asymmetry in eye movements for one direction over another. In patients with FEF lesions, voluntary saccades were slower to the contralesional field. In contrast, reflexive, visually guided saccades were slower to the ipsilesional field. In addition, in the ipsilesional field the patients' visually guided saccade latencies were no faster than their latencies for voluntary saccades.

These results indicate that FEF lesions have two separate effects on eye movements: (1) They increase the latency of endogenous saccades, and are thus involved in their generation; (2) they reduce the visual grasp reflex in the ipsilesional field relative to the contralesional field after recovery. Thus unilateral lesions of the FEF, in the chronic state, can produce a kind of reverse Sprague effect. One explanation is that FEF lesions disinhibit the ipsilesional substantia nigra pars reticulata, resulting in inhibition of the superior colliculus opposite to the FEF lesion.

A study using transcranial magnetic stimulation (TMS) in normal subjects investigated whether this reverse Sprague effect reflects a reorganization following recovery from brain injury or the immediate effect of FEF inactivation. The effects of TMS are very transient. They presumably do not cause much in the way of remote diaschesis effects and certainly do not allow time for reorganization. When TMS was applied over the FEF, there was an increase in latency for voluntary saccades to the contralateral field—the same pattern that was seen in patients with chronic focal lesions (Ro et al., 1997). However, TMS of the FEF did not have the effect on ipsilesional visually guided saccades that occurs with chronic lesions, suggesting that the reverse Sprague effect after chronic FEF lesions is the result of reorganization or compensation from brain injury.

These findings emphasize the importance of converging approaches to studies in cognitive neuroscience; the study of both acute and chronic lesions can be revealing when the findings of both kinds of investigations are integrated with one another and with other methods for studying brain function in humans. A recent study (Ro et al., 1999) combined TMS and MRI imaging to map the human frontal eye field. The hand area of motor cortex was identified physiologically as the focal region where TMS elicited finger movements. A marker was placed over this scalp site and an MRI scan was taken to co-localize the hand with morphological markers on MRI (see figure 44.3). The region just anterior to the hand area was mapped to identify sites where TMS increased the latency for voluntary saccades. The results confirmed the region as centered about 2 cm anterior to the hand at the junction of the middle frontal gyrus and the precentral gyrus. The excellent spatial resolution of TMS and its ultra-brief effects—which obviate the problems of diaschesis and plastic brain reorganization that can complicate the interpretation of the effects of natural lesions in the acute and chronic stages, respectively—make it a promising technique for providing converging information about brain–behavior relationships.

Disengaging attention and the mechanism of extinction

Extinction is associated with hemispatial neglect. Patients with extinction report no information on the contralesional side but only when there is simultaneous stimulation on the ipsilesional side. One initial explanation of this phenomenon focused on attention and a "disengage deficit"; that is, patients have difficulty disengaging attention from an ipsilesional stimulus to move in the direction of a contralesional stimulus (Posner et al., 1984). Thus, when a cue was presented on the ipsilesional or contralesional side, response time to detect a target at the cued location (valid) was rapid, but response time to detect a target at the uncued location (invalid) was much greater when first cued to the ipsilesional side.

Posner and colleagues (1984) suggested that the deficit was more pronounced in patients with superior parietal lesions. However, a more recent study with patients with chronic focal lesions (Friedrich et al., 1998) has implicated the temporal-parietal junction (TPJ) (figure 44.2B) as the critical region in producing a pattern consistent with a disengage deficit.

Space and objects

What is it that is neglected in patients like the gentleman in figure 44.1A? Marlene Behrmann provides an excellent review in her chapter (chapter 45 in this volume) showing that perceptual processing can proceed in object-centered reference frames (i.e., spatial representations defined by objects, scenes, or groups of items). Here we discuss selected findings that may help determine how reference frames are established and how attention is distributed within these frames.

Object-centered neglect can be observed at bedside when the examiner rotates 90 degrees right or left in

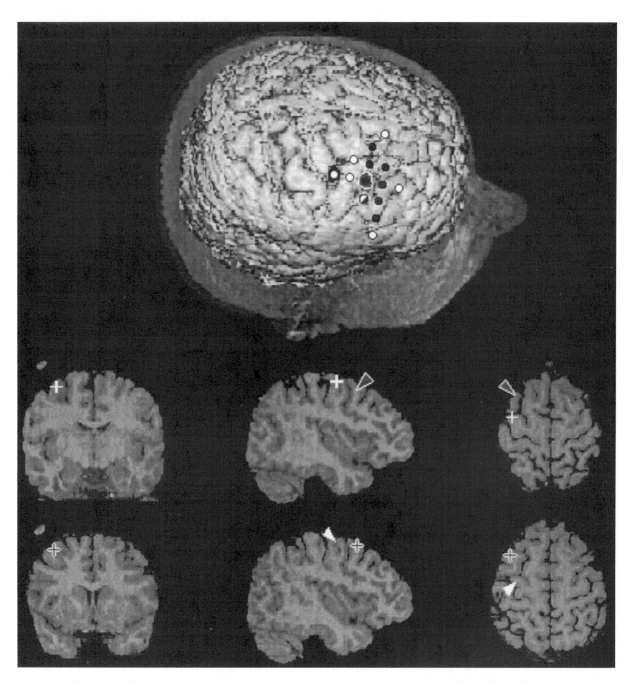

FIGURE 44.3 Structural MRI of normal subject showing the hand area of the motor cortex (white crosshairs), where transcortical magnetic stimulation (TMS) produced finger movements, and oculomotor cortex (outlined crosshairs), where TMS resulted in increased latency for voluntary sac- cades to the contralateral visual field. The white crosshairs are represented in the upper figure as a white dot surrounded by a black square, and the outlined crosshairs are represented by the black form outlined in white to its right. (Adapted from Ro et al., 1999.)

front of a patient, as shown in figure 44.4. In this case, evidence for neglect in nonviewer spatial frames is observed relative to right and left defined by the examiner's orientation. For lack of a better word, such effects are commonly described as "object-based," since neglect for one side of space follows a stimulus—a face, a screen, or even a higher-order collection of parts that form a more global perceptual unit. Object-based neglect highlights a paradox. Neglect is defined as the lack of awareness for space in objects or parts of objects, yet objects are the very things that define the space for object-based neglect. How this occurs is not yet known, but there are several lines of evidence that give some hints about what information may be critical.

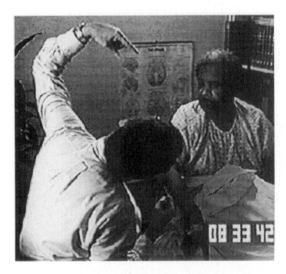 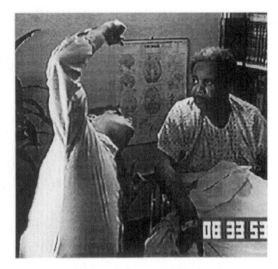

FIGURE 44.4   A patient with unilateral visual neglect who neglects the right hand of the examiner (the hand on the patient's left side when both patient and examiner are upright) in coordinates defined by the orientation of the examiner's body. The

examiner's right hand is neglected even when his body is rotated 90 degrees to the right or the left. This is an example of neglect in object-centered coordinates. (Reprinted from Rafal, 1994.)

Grabowecky, Robertson, and Treisman (1993) demonstrated that the represented center of a display can be manipulated by varying the center of mass. Seven patients with neglect were asked to visually search a diamond-shaped area for a target in the center of a display. The central display was either presented alone or with nontarget flankers on the right or left side or both (figure 44.5). Relative to the no-flanker condition, neglect was magnified when flankers were placed on the ipsilesional side, thereby moving the central diamond display further to the contralesional side in object-centered coordinates. But when flankers were added to both the contralesional and ipsilesional sides, the magnitude of neglect reverted to that observed when no flankers were present. This occurred whether or not the flankers contained features of the target (Grabowecky, 1992). In other words, it was not the absolute amount of information in the ipsilesional or contralesional visual field that was most important in establishing the center of the reference frame—it was the center of mass of the display in object-based coordinates.

Pavlovskaya and colleagues (1997) have shown that one critical determinant of the center of mass is the display's luminance centroid (LC), which they calculate on the basis of the low spatial frequency information in the display. They found that normal participants detected targets located at the LC more readily than they detected targets at the center defined by spatial geometry (when the two defined different locations, and hence were pitted against each other) or at other locations within the display. Targets slightly to the left or right of the LC were detected relatively poorly. And, in two patients with neglect, the patients' attention was shifted to

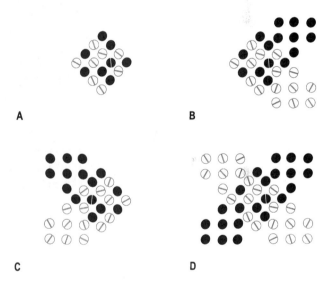

FIGURE 44.5   Example of stimuli used with a group of neglect patients in a conjunction search task where the target was always in a diamond-like 4 × 4 matrix presented in the center of the screen. Flankers where targets never appeared were either not present (A), present on the right or left side only (B, C), or present on both sides (D). The center of mass varies with these different displays and neglect varied with the center of mass.

the right of the LC. These findings suggest there may be a critical role of lower spatial frequencies in determining the center of a reference frame or its origin. Moreover, these effects have implications for the role of the right hemisphere in global processing.

These results are consistent with those of Driver and co-workers (1993), who showed that symmetry of a display influences performance in patients with neglect, even when they cannot report whether or not a stimulus

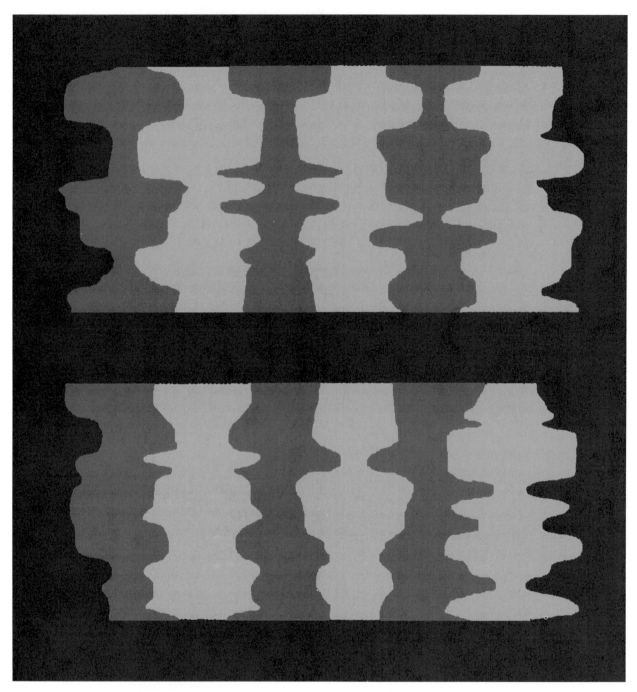

FIGURE 44.6   Example of a figure–ground pattern where the normal propensity is to perceive the symmetric design as figure. A patient with neglect reported by Driver, Baylis, and Ra-

fal (1993) also experienced figure–ground segmentation based on symmetry in this figure, even though he was at chance in explicitly reporting whether or not the shapes were symmetric.

is symmetric. (In a symmetric figure, the center of mass and LC are always in the middle.) They exploited the well known phenomenon in normals that symmetric figures are more likely than asymmetric ones to be seen as figure in a figure–ground display (figure 44.6). A patient with neglect was instructed to report which of two colors appeared in front of the other in a figure–ground pattern. The patient chose the color of the symmetric figure

more often than that of the asymmetric figure, even though he could not correctly report whether the color he chose was that of a symmetric or asymmetric figure.

The foregoing observations add to the evidence that, in the neglected field, preattentive vision can parse a scene to extract figure from ground, group objects, and define their primary axis. The center of mass is then shifted to produce an attentional shift to the right in

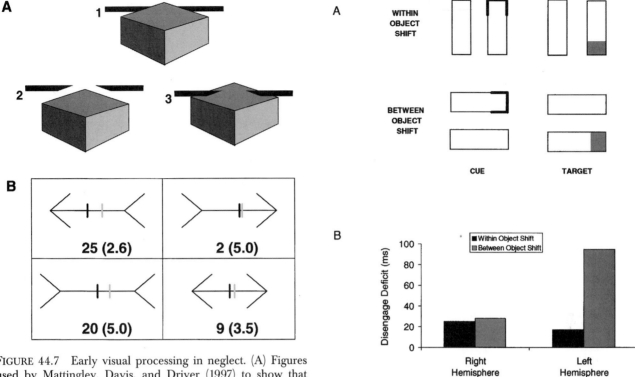

A

B

25 (2.6)	2 (5.0)
20 (5.0)	9 (3.5)

FIGURE 44.7 Early visual processing in neglect. (A) Figures used by Mattingley, Davis, and Driver (1997) to show that amodal completion behind an occluder reduced visual extinction. (B) Figures used by Ro and Rafal (1996) to demonstrate that geometric illusions are generated preattentively. The two figures on the bottom demonstrate the Muller–Lyer illusion, and show that the patient's bisection error (the bisection mark is shown in gray and the true midpoint in black) was proportional to perceived line length as determined by the illusion. The top and bottom figures in each pair differ only on the left (contralesional) side and were reported as looking the "same" by the patient. Nevertheless, her bisection errors differed in top and bottom pairs, demonstrating that the illusions were generated by features on the left for which the patient had no explicit awareness. Bisection errors are indicated in millimeters (standard deviations in parentheses).

FIGURE 44.8 (A) Example of stimuli adapted from Egly, Driver, and Rafal (1994). A location at one end of a rectangle is cued (dark black lines) and a target (gray filled square) appears 300 ms later. The target is more likely to be at the cued location (valid) than uncued location (invalid), which occurs either within the same object or between objects as shown. (B) Data for groups of patients with left parietal lesions ($N = 5$) or right parietal lesions ($N = 8$). The disengage deficit refers to the mean RT costs (invalid minus valid) for ipsilesional minus contralesional shifts of attention. (Adapted from Rafal and Robertson, 1995.)

object-centered reference frames. As observed in unilateral visual neglect, this shift can cause information on the contralesional edge of a stimulus to drop from conscious awareness. Other observations in patients with hemispatial neglect demonstrate that early or preattentive vision generates amodal completion (Mattingley, Davis, and Driver, 1997; figure 44.7A) as well as geometric illusions (Ro and Rafal, 1996; figure 44.7B). What is neglected by some patients appears to be the contralesional side of reference frames within candidate objects.

Finally, other effects have shown hemispheric differences in attentional orienting within rather than between objects of a display. Egly, Driver, and Rafal (1994) used a modification of the covert orienting paradigm to mea-

sure what has come to be called space- and object-based attentional shifts. They tested normal subjects and patients with chronic lesions of the posterior parietal association cortex. The stimuli and procedure are outlined in figure 44.8. In normal subjects, cueing effects (or costs) were greater for shifting attention between than within objects. Several findings in the patient groups are noteworthy. First, both patient groups (those with left- or right-hemisphere lesions) produced larger costs to respond to targets in their contralesional than their ipsilesional fields. This is consistent with the LC and center of mass results just discussed. The important new finding was a difference between the two patient groups in shifting attention between objects. Both patient groups showed problems in disengaging attention from the intact field; however, for between-object shifts of attention from the ipsilesional to the contralesional field, the disengage deficit in patients with left-hemisphere damage was more pronounced than in patients with right-hemisphere damage.

Another study using a similar paradigm confirmed the hemispheric differences in a split-brain patient. When the stimuli were presented in his left visual field, between- and within-object shifts were equivalent (attention was guided by the overall or global stimulus array). But when the stimuli were presented in his right visual field, the normal within- versus between-object differences were observed (Egly, Driver, and Rafal, 1994).

Taken together, these findings suggest that the left parietal lobe is critical for shifting attention between objects (perhaps from one center of mass to another), while the right parietal lobe is more involved in shifting attention within global aspects of a stimulus display. Indeed, shifting attention between global and local objects is also affected by left but not by right parietal lesions (see Robertson, 1996; Rafal and Robertson, 1995), consistent with a problem in shifting attention between LCs defined by global properties of a stimulus and those defined by more local properties.

Objects and parts of objects

In the natural environment, spatial relationships are often complex. Objects are not merely next to each other, with spatial gaps between them; some objects contain other objects or form parts of one another. The focus of attention in any given display may vary. In natural scenes attention can be directed to a house, to its windows and doors, to a wall to the material from which the wall is made, and so on. Neuropsychological evidence has shown that global and local object structure is processed differently by the two hemispheres.

Right-hemisphere damage disrupts (eliminates or slows) the perception of global objects, while left-hemisphere damage disrupts the perception of local objects (or what is typically called parts). Figure 44.9 shows an example of the drawings from patients with unilateral left- or right-hemisphere damage (Delis, Robertson, and Efron, 1986; Robertson and Lamb, 1991). These dramatic differences were observed in patients in acute stages. When groups of well-screened and stable neurological patients were tested well after stroke (from 6 months to 13 years), the hemispheric differences were revealed only in response time measures. In these studies the stimuli were large global letters constructed from smaller local letters shown briefly on a computer screen. The task was to determine, as rapidly as possible, which of two target letters occurred on each trial. The target appeared as either the global or local form and response

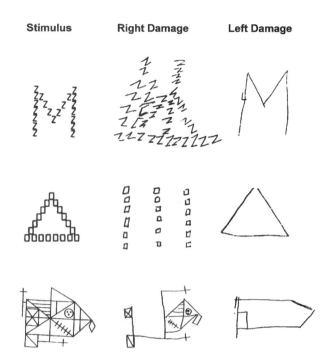

| Stimulus | Right Damage | Left Damage |

FIGURE 44.9 Examples of drawings of a stimulus by patients with left or right hemisphere damage. (Adapted from Robertson and Lamb, 1991.)

time was measured via computer. Six groups of patients ($N = 5$–7) and normal matched controls were tested (Robertson, Lamb, and Knight, 1988, 1991). The hemispheric differences were found only for patients with lesions that were centered in the temporal-parietal junction (TPJ).

The hemispheric differences cannot be attributed to the sensory acuity of the global and local objects. The global/local asymmetry has been observed in TPJ groups whether the stimuli are shown in central vision, where acuity is high, or in peripheral vision, where it is low. Visual resolution falls off rapidly in sensory and primary vision as one moves out from the fovea, and local discrimination suffers more than global discrimination as resolution decreases. Nevertheless, the hemispheric effects remain relatively unaffected. The hemispheric effects also occur in patients whether the stimuli are presented in central vision or in the contralateral or ipsilateral visual field to the lesion (see Ivry and Robertson, 1998, for a complete discussion). Although the baseline speed of response may change (local discrimination is faster in central than peripheral vision), the asymmetry continues to be observed relative to a baseline established by control subjects.

Another study showed that the differences remained strong for centrally presented stimuli even when the stimulus changed in overall size (Lamb, Robertson, and Knight, 1990). Again, the hemispheric asymmetry was relative to the baseline response of normal age-matched controls and was found only for TPJ groups. Together, these results demonstrate that the asymmetry is superimposed on primary visual processes that may favor one stimulus size or spatial scale over another.

Initial studies with normal healthy subjects suggested that the differences were due to the different spatial frequency spectra that define global and local objects. This difference is roughly equivalent to spatial resolution (blurry vs. fine) or spatial scale (large vs. small). The spatial frequency hypothesis was originally proposed by Sergent (1982), who used hierarchical letter patterns presented briefly in either the right or left visual field in normal, college-aged students. Left visual field presentation (projecting stimuli directly to the right hemisphere) produced faster responses for global letters, while right visual field presentation (projecting stimuli directly to the left hemisphere) produced faster responses for local letters.

Kitterle, Christman, and Hellige (1990) tested this hypothesis in healthy normal subjects by presenting sinusoidal gratings with a single spatial frequency per trial in either the right or left visual field. They first used a simple detection task, and found no evidence of visual field differences. However, when subjects had to determine which grating was presented (i.e., attend to the spatial frequencies in the stimulus in order to determine which one it was), response times differed. Response times for lower frequencies were better when presented in the left visual field (LVF) than the right visual field (RVF), while response times for higher frequencies were better when presented in the RVF than the LVF. As global objects include lower frequencies than local objects, these data are consistent with the global/local differences found by Sergent but occur only when the object level is important in performing the task (i.e., attention to particular frequencies is useful).

But if this hypothesis is correct, how do we account for the invariance of the asymmetry in TPJ patients over size and eccentricity? Christman, Kitterle, and Hellige (1991) reported data that shed some light on this question. They presented compound stimuli with two spatial frequency gratings superimposed on one another. In one condition the subjects' task was to determine whether or not a designated frequency (measured in cycles per degree, or cpd) was present. (We call the designated frequency a "medium" frequency since it was paired with a higher frequency in some cases and a lower frequency in others.) When the medium frequency (4 cpd) was present in the context of a higher frequency (9 cpd) grating, performance was better for LVF presentation; but when it was presented in the context of a lower fre-

quency (1 cpd) grating, performance was better in the RVF. Thus, a grating of the same frequency could show a right or left visual field advantage depending on whether it was the relatively high- or the relatively low-frequency component.

In a hierarchical pattern the global object contains lower frequencies relative to local objects independent of visual angle. Absolute frequencies vary with visual angle or stimulus acuity. The data from TPJ patients are consistent with the idea that the global/local hemispheric asymmetry may be a function of the analysis of *relative* spatial frequencies or spatial scale at the two levels of object structure (Ivy and Robertson, 1998).

A major question that arises from this discussion–how an absolute scale is converted to a relative one–is also a problem in object-based neglect. That is, how are absolute spatial attributes (whether locations or spatial scales) converted into relative ones? Conceivably, there is an early–perhaps preattentive–selection of a range of absolute values, a range that serves as input for subsequent analysis biased toward the higher or lower (or left or right) values it receives. Suppose, for instance, early mechanisms selected a frequency range of 1–4 cpd, then relayed this range to channels biased to attend to relatively higher frequencies (as purported for the left hemisphere). In that case, 4 cpd would be responded to more rapidly in the right than in the left visual field because it is the relatively higher frequency within that range. But what if the range selected were 4–9 cpd and that was relayed to secondary channels biased to attend to lower frequencies (as purported for the right hemisphere)? In that case, the 4-cpd grating–now the lower frequency within the range–would be responded to more rapidly in the left than right visual field. These are, in fact, the results observed by Christman, Kitterle, and Hellige (1991), and they are consistent with the global/local effects found in patients.

It is intriguing that recent imaging studies have found more activation of the right hemisphere when responding to global hierarchical patterns and more activation of the left hemisphere when responding to local patterns (Fink et al., 1996; Martinez et al., 1996). Although the exact locus is controversial (some reporting activation in the fusiform gyrus and others reporting activation near the temporal-parietal junction), asymmetry has been observed in posterior areas. ERP data also support a difference in the hemispheres over posterior leads with hierarchically structured letter patterns (Heinze et al., 1994; Proverbio, Minniti, and Zani, 1998), and the expected asymmetry has been observed in split-brain patients as well (Robertson, Lamb, and Zaidel, 1993).

One salient clinical fact is that hemispatial neglect is much more common, severe, and long-lasting after lesions of the right than the left hemisphere. Since lesions of either the left or right TPJ may cause extinction (Vallar, 1993) or an extinction-like RT pattern, some other effect of right hemisphere lesions may account for the disparity in severity. The local bias produced by right TPJ lesions offers one explanation. Any factor that causes attention to become more actively engaged in the ipsilesional field will exacerbate the problem of disengaging attention, and thereby exacerbate visual neglect. In effect, the local bias engendered by right TPJ lesions causes patients to get "stuck" on local details. Since local details generally outnumber global ones, the difficulty in disengaging may be enhanced.

The conjoint effects of the local bias with difficulty in disengaging attention may contribute to some classic signs of neglect on paper-and-pencil tasks. Consider, for example, a patient writing numbers on a clock face. She will be more successful if, as she is writing in each number, she remains oriented to her task with reference to the whole clock. If her attention becomes focused on the number she is writing and she loses sight of the whole clock, she has difficulty in disengaging from that number to fill in the rest of the numbers on the clock face. On the other hand, if the clock face remains uncluttered with other numbers, patients with neglect are better able to remain oriented to the whole clock face. Di Pellegrino (1995) showed that patients with hemispatial neglect can put a single number in the appropriate location on a clock face provided they are given separate sheets for each number.

Halligan and Marshall (1994) asked a patient with left hemispatial neglect to bisect a horizontal line. In one condition they also presented a vertical line at the right end of the horizontal line. Before asking the patient to bisect the horizontal line, they gave the patient a task that required attending to the full extent of the vertical line, thereby obliging the patient to expand attention from the end of the horizontal line. The result was improved performance on the subsequent bisection of the horizontal line. By helping to overcome the tendency of the patient to become hyperengaged in a small focus of attention at the end of the line to be bisected, neglect was improved. Perhaps this expansion of attention to a more global level explains why patients with neglect make fewer errors when bisecting a rectangle than when bisecting a line–and why the higher the vertical extent of the rectangle, the less the bisection error (Vallar, 1994).

Objects and the loss of spatial orienting

Unilateral right parietal lobe lesions can produce hemispatial neglect in object-centered spatial coordinates (for reviews see Rafal, 1998; Robertson, 1998). However, bilateral parietal damage produces different symptoms, collectively known as Balint's syndrome (Balint, 1909; Rafal, 1997). Rather than neglecting both sides of objects, as might be expected if right and left neglect were summed, these patients see nothing but objects (figure 44.10; see also color plate 29). They can see just one object at a time (simultaneous agnosia), and the objects they see seem to appear automatically, only to be replaced randomly with other objects in the visual field. They have no difficulty recognizing faces, colors, single words, or shapes; but they exhibit severe spatial problems. They get lost. They cannot reach correctly; nor can they move their eyes toward a perceived object's location or verbally identify its location as right, left, up, or down relative to themselves or to other objects. They can, however, correctly reach to locations on their own bodies and correctly move their right or left limbs upon command (Robertson et al., 1997).

As a result of these deficits, patients with this syndrome are extremely restricted in their everyday lives: They are spatially disoriented and require care with simple tasks such as eating, dressing, or moving around a room. In pure cases, they show few, if any, signs of aphasia, confusion, memory loss, or lack of judgment. They can be, in fact, cognitively normal except for the severe attentional and spatial deficits that render them functionally blind.

The syndrome is typically seen with bilateral damage in the inferior parietal lobes and adjacent occipital areas. Often, inferior regions of the superior parietal lobes are involved as well. In one patient, RM, whom we have been testing for several years, the lesions are centered in these areas (figure 44.11). The lesions damaged neither the optical fibers nor the primary visual areas, either anatomically or functionally.

Recent evidence suggests that a major underlying problem in these patients is the computation of or access to spatial representations that normally guide attention from one object to another in a cluttered field. It has been reported (Coslett and Saffran, 1991; Robertson et al., 1997) that such patients have difficulty searching for a conjunction target in a cluttered array. Any target that requires an attentional search from one object to another is impaired.

Patients with hemispatial neglect are also extremely slow to search for these types of target patterns, and the search time increases substantially as the number of distracters increases (Eglin et al., 1989). However, a single feature, such as a red dot among blue and yellow distracters, can be detected relatively rapidly in the hemineglected field and the speed of detection is not affected by the number of items in a display (Eglin et

FIGURE 44.10 (A) A patient with Balint's syndrome shown two superimposed objects. This gentleman reported seeing the comb; and when asked about the spoon, he reported he could not see it. These objects were then set aside for a few seconds. When the objects were picked up and presented to the patient again, he reported seeing only the spoon. After the objects were set down and shown a second time, the patient seemed perplexed and had difficulty deciding what he was seeing. When asked if he still saw either the comb or the spoon, he shook his head and said, "I think I see a blackboard with a bunch of writing on it." In fact, there was a blackboard with writing in chalk in the background. (B) A second patient with Balint's syndrome, shown reaching for the handle of a screwdriver. Despite being able to report the object's identity and looking directly at it, he is not able to reach to its accurate location. When this patient was asked to reach for parts of his own body, he was able to do so easily and accurately, showing no evidence of a primary motor deficit or loss of coordination between an egocentric location and reaching.

al., 1989). Patients with Balint's syndrome are also able to detect features rapidly with few errors and are unaffected by the number of distracters in the display (Robertson et al., 1997). Normal subjects' response times to detect features are independent of the number of distracters as well (Treisman and Gelade, 1980).

Treisman and Gelade (1980) proposed that feature search does not require spatial attention while conjunction search does. The evidence from patients with Balint's syndrome and those with hemineglect supports this proposition. With lesions that affect spatial awareness, conjunction search is slow and limited, while

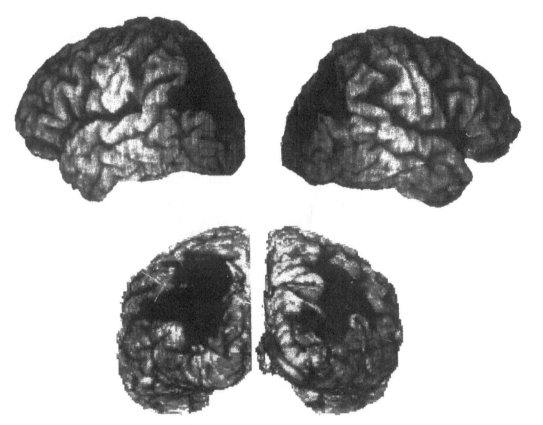

FIGURE 44.11   3D reconstruction of patient RM's MRI. The lesion locations are typical for patients with Balint's syndrome. Note that primary visual cortices and the temporoparietal junction are intact, which is consistent with RM's intact primary visual abilities as documented by formal ophthalmological examination (see Robertson et al., 1997). (Adapted from Friedman-Hill, Robertson, and Treisman, 1995.)

feature search in a similarly cluttered array remains relatively intact.

Electrophysiological, functional, and neuropsychological evidence has shown that primary features such as color, shape, motion, or size are represented more strongly in some areas of cortex (in different regions of posterior temporal lobes) than in others. To account for our perception of correctly conjoined features (e.g., a large green apple as opposed to large, green, and apple) in a cluttered array, we accept that some type of binding occurs. Otherwise, the features would remain separate or be miscombined, producing illusory conjunctions (Treisman and Schmidt, 1982). Treisman proposed that in order to correctly bind features together, spatial attention is required. In support of this theory, consider the patient with Balint's syndrome who perceived illusory conjunctions even when the stimuli were shown for up to 10 seconds in a two-item array (Friedman-Hill, Robertson, and Treisman, 1995; Robertson et al., 1997). Similarly, consider a patient with a unilateral left TPJ lesion who reported more illusory conjunctions in her contralesional field than in her ipsilesional field (Cohen and Rafal, 1991). These findings are consistent with difficulty in serial search—a difficulty which, according to Treisman (1998), reflects a problem in binding the proper features of each item or group of items in a display due to problems in attending to locations.

Other evidence has shown that although these patients cannot explicitly access representations of spatial information in the external environment, their visual systems do contain some spatial maps. Robertson and colleagues (1997) asked patient RM to read, as rapidly as possible, the words UP or DOWN as they appeared on a computer screen. The word showed up in the upper or lower location of a surrounding rectangle and stayed on the screen until a response was made. When the word's meaning and location were consistent, RM responded 142 ms faster than when they were inconsistent. That is, he showed a spatial Stroop effect. But in accord with his spatial deficits, he had great difficulty in reporting whether the word was in the upper or lower portion of the rectangle: He said he was guessing, and his 51% correct performance was consistent with this report. He recovered some ability to explicitly access locations over time (85% correct), but his spatial Stroop effect did not change significantly (162 ms), demonstrating that the effect was not due to the degree of explicit spatial awareness. These data suggest the existence of multiple spatial maps–maps that contain information below the threshold of awareness. These maps may be tied to early visual input that normally feeds into the parietal lobes to create explicit spatial representations. And it is these representations that are used to guide attention in serial search or to other maps, possibly those associated with eye movements or reference frame selection (Robertson, 1998).

It is important to note that RM showed normal facilitation in an exogenous Posner cueing task with uninformative cues (Robert Egly, personal communication). Given the evidence for implicit spatial maps, this suggests that this type of attentional orienting, which is believed to be more automatic, does not require explicit spatial maps or, as seen in patients with extinction, even awareness of the signal evoking the orienting response (Danziger, Fendrich, and Rafal, 1998). RM also shows implicit effects on his response when looking for such things as letters within words, local forms within global forms, and semantic relationships.

It is clear that preattentive processing has a large effect on normal attentional orienting. Patients with neglect or extinction, and those with simultaneous agnosia as in Balint's syndrome, can tell us much about what features of objects and properties of displays of objects are preattentively processed and which require attention.

Visual attention may be summoned to a location reflexively by the midbrain extrageniculate system, by information in the visual scene that is a potential object, or by voluntary processes that guide strategic search from one location or object to another.

Concluding remarks

It is likely that the mammalian nervous system contains several different systems involved in selectively attending to objects and their locations. There is evidence that midbrain and several cortical regions contain spatial maps that can be used to control attentional orienting. Others appear linked to spatial coordinates that reside below awareness and may be more retinally or viewer based. Still others may be associated with spatial scale (i.e., global versus local). There appear to be many different areas of the brain that represent space either implicitly or explicitly, and in some cases other areas that control how attention is allocated within these representations (Rafal and Robertson, 1995). Deficits of attention may reflect direct insult to the control of attentional orienting; or they may reflect indirect insult arising from loss of underlying spatial representations that attentional systems require or from loss of object or feature information. The conse-

quences for the patient can be severe, resulting in limited access to information critical for some of the most basic functions of everyday life.

ACKNOWLEDGMENTS This work was supported by a Career Award from the Veterans Administration, a NIMH grant (RO1 MH55682), and NSF grant (SBR 96-31132) to L. Robertson and NIMH grants (RO1 MH45414, and RO1 MH51400) to R. Rafal. The order of authorship was reversed from the previous edition which was originally determined by coin toss.

REFERENCES

BALINT, R., 1909. Seelenlahmung des "Schauens," optische Ataxie, raumliche Storung der Aufmerksamkeit. *Monatsch. Psychiatr. Neuro.* 25:51–81. Translated in *Cogn. Neuropsychol.* 12:265–281.

CHRISTMAN, S., F. KITTERLE, and J. HELLIGE, 1991. Hemispheric asymmetry in the processing of absolute versus relative spatial frequency. *Brain Cognit.* 16:62–73.

COHEN, A., and R. D. RAFAL, 1991. Attention and feature integration: Illusory conjunctions in a patient with a parietal lobe lesion. *Psychol. Sci.* 2:106–110.

COSLETT, H. B., and E. M. SAFFRAN, 1991. Simultanagnosia: To see but not to see. *Brain* 113:1523–1545.

DANZIGER, S., R. FENDRICH, and R. D. RAFAL, 1997. Inhibitory tagging of locations in the blind field of hemianopic patients. *Consciousness Cognit.* 6:291–307.

DELIS, D. C., L. C. ROBERTSON, and R. EFRON, 1986. Hemispheric specialization of memory for visual hierarchical stimuli. *Neuropsychologia* 24:205–214.

DEUEL, R. K., and R. C. COLLINS, 1984. The functional anatomy of frontal lobe neglect in monkeys: Behavioral and 2-deoxyglucose studies. *Ann. Neurol.* 15:521–529.

DI PELLEGRINO, G., 1995. Clock-drawing in a case of left visuo-spatial neglect: A deficit of disengagement. *Neuropsychologia* 33:353–358.

DRIVER, J., G. BAYLIS, and R. RAFAL, 1993. Preserved figure-ground segmentation and symmetry perception in a patient with neglect. *Nature* 360:73–75.

EGLIN, M., L. C. ROBERTSON, and R. T. KNIGHT, 1989. Visual search performance in the neglect syndrome. *J. Cogn. Neurosci.* 4:372–381.

EGLY, R., J. DRIVER, and R. D. RAFAL, 1994. Shifting visual attention between objects and locations: Evidence from normal and parietal lesion subjects. *J. Exp. Psychol.* 123:127–161.

FENDRICH, R., C. M. WESSINGER, and M. S. GAZZANIGA, 1992. Residual vision in a scotoma: Implications for blindsight. *Science* 258:1489–1491.

FINK, G., P. HALLIGAN, J. MARSHALL, C. FRITH, R. FRACKOWIAK, and R. DOLAN, 1996. Where in the brain does visual attention select the forest and the trees? *Nature* 15:626–628.

FRIEDMAN-HILL, S. R., L. C. ROBERTSON, and A. TREISMAN, 1995. Parietal contributions to visual feature binding: Evidence from a patient with bilateral lesions. *Science* 269:853–855.

FRIEDRICH, F. J., R. EGLY, R. D. RAFAL, and D. BECK, 1998. Spatial attention deficits in humans: A comparison of superior parietal and temporal-parietal junction lesions. *Neuropsychology* 12(2):193–207.

GRABOWECKY, M., 1992. Preattentive processes guide visual attention: Evidence from normals and patients with unilateral visual neglect. Doctoral dissertation, University of California, Berkeley.

GRABOWECKY, M., L. C. ROBERTSON, and A. TREISMAN, 1993. Preattentive processes guide visual search: Evidence from patients with unilateral visual neglect. *J. Cogn. Neurosci.* 5:288–302.

GUITTON, D., H. A. BUCHTEL, and R. M. DOUGLAS, 1985. Frontal lobe lesions in man cause difficulties in suppressing reflexive glances and in generating goal directed saccades. *Exp. Brain Res.* 58:455–472.

HALLIGAN, P. W., and J. C. MARSHALL, 1994. Focal and global attention modulate the expression of visuo-spatial neglect: A case study. *Neuropsychologia* 32:13–21.

HEINZE, H.-J., S. JOHANNES, T. F. MUNTE, and G. R. MANGUN, 1994. The order of global- and local-level information processing: Electrophysiological evidence for parallel perceptual processes. In *Cognitive Electrophysiology,* H.-J. Heinze, T. F. Munte, and G. R. Mangun, eds. Boston, Mass.: Birkhauser, pp. 102–123.

HENIK, A., R. RAFAL, and D. RHODES, 1994. Endogenously generated and visually guided saccades after lesions of the human frontal eye fields. *J. Cogn. Neurosci.* 6:400–411.

HOVDA, D. A., and J. R. VILLABLANCA, 1990. Sparing of visual field perception in neonatal but not adult cerebral hemispherectomized cats. Relationship with oxidative metabolism in the superior colliculus. *Behav. Brain Res.* 37:119–132.

IVRY, R., and L. C. ROBERTSON, 1998. *The Two Sides of Perception.* Cambridge, Mass.: MIT Press.

KITTERLE, F., S. CHRISTMAN, and J. HELLIGE, 1990. Hemispheric differences are found in the identification, but not the detection, of low versus high spatial frequencies. *Percept. Psychophysics* 48:297–306.

LAMB, M. R., L. C. ROBERTSON, and R. T. KNIGHT, 1990. Component mechanisms underlying the processing of hierarchically organized patterns: Inferences from patients with unilateral cortical lesions. *J. Exp. Psychol.: Learn. Mem. Cognit.* 16:471–483.

MARTINEZ, A., P. MOSES, L. FRANK, D. BLAETTLER, J. STILES, E. WONG, and R. BUXTON, 1996. Lateralized differences in spatial processing: Evidence from RT and fMRI. Paper presented at the Second International Conference in Functional Mapping of the Human Brain, Boston.

MATTINGLEY, J. B., G. DAVIS, and J. DRIVER, 1997. Preattentive filling-in of visual surfaces in parietal extinction. *Science* 275:671–673.

PAUS, T., 1996. Location and function of the human frontal eye-field: A selective review. *Neuropsychologia* 34:475–483.

PAVLOVSKAYA, M., I. GLASS, N. SOROKER, B. BLUM, and Z. GROSWASSER, 1997. Coordinate frame for pattern recognition in unilateral spatial neglect. *J. Cogn. Neurosci.* 9:824–834.

POSNER, M. I., R. D. RAFAL, L. CHOATE, and J. VAUGHN, 1985. Inhibition of return: Neural basis and function. *Cogn. Neuropsychol.* 2:211–228.

POSNER, M. I., J. A. WALKER, F. J. FRIEDRICH, and R. D. RAFAL, 1984. Effects of parietal injury on covert orienting of attention. *J. Neurosci.* 4:1863–1874.

PROVERBIO, A. M., A. MINNITI, and A. ZANI, 1998. Electrophysiological evidence of a perceptual precedence of global vs. local visual information. *Cogn. Brain Res.* 6:321–334.

RAFAL, R. D., 1994. Neglect. *Cur. Opin. Neurobiol.* 4:2312–2316.

RAFAL, R. D., 1997. Balint syndrome. In *Behavioral Neurology and Neuropsychology,* T. E. Feinberg and M. J. Farah, eds. New York: McGraw-Hill, pp. 337–356.

RAFAL, R. D., 1998. Neglect. In *The Attentive Brain,* R. Parasuraman, ed. Cambridge, Mass.: MIT Press, pp. 489–525.

RAFAL, R. D., L. J. MACHADO, T. RO, and H. W. INGLE, in press. Looking forward to looking: Saccade preparation and control of the visual grasp reflex. In *Control of Cognitive Operations: Attention and Performance XVIII,* S. Munsell and J. Driver, eds. Cambridge, Mass.: MIT Press.

RAFAL, R. D., M. I. POSNER, J. H. FRIEDMAN, A. W. INHOFF, and E. BERNSTEIN, 1988. Orienting of visual attention in progressive supranuclear palsy. *Brain* 111:267–280.

RAFAL, R., and L. ROBERTSON, 1995. The neurology of visual attention. In *The Cognitive Neurosciences,* M. S. Gazzaniga, ed. Cambridge, Mass.: MIT Press, pp. 625–648.

RO, T., S. CHEIFET, H. INGLE, R. SHOUP, and R. RAFAL, 1999. Localization of the human frontal eye fields and motor hand area with transcranial magnetic stimulation and magnetic resonance imaging. *Neuropsychologia* 37(2):225–231.

RO, T., A. HENIK, L. MACHADO, and R. D. RAFAL, 1997. Transcranial magnetic stimulation of the prefrontal cortex delays contralateral endogenous saccades. *J. Cogn. Neurosci.* 9:433–440.

RO, T., and R. D. RAFAL, 1996. Perception of geometric illusion in visual neglect. *Neuropsychologia* 34:973–978.

ROBERTSON, L. C., 1996. Attentional persistence for features of hierarchical patterns. *J. Exp. Psychol.* 125:227–249.

ROBERTSON, L. C., 1998. Visuospatial attention and parietal function: Their role in object perception. In *The Attentive Brain,* R. Parasuraman, ed. Cambridge, Mass.: MIT Press, pp. 257–278.

ROBERTSON, L. C., and M. R. LAMB, 1991. Neuropsychological contributions to theories of part/whole organization. *Cogn. Psychol.* 23:299–330.

ROBERTSON, L. C., M. R. LAMB, and R. T. KNIGHT, 1988. Effects of lesions of temporal-parietal junction on perceptual and attentional processing in humans. *J. Neurosci.* 8:3757–3769.

ROBERTSON, L. C., M. R. LAMB, and R. T. KNIGHT, 1991. Normal global-local analysis in patients with dorsolateral frontal lobe lesions. *Neuropsychologia* 29:959–967.

ROBERTSON, L. C., M. R. LAMB, and E. ZAIDEL, 1993. Interhemispheric relations in processing hierarchical patterns: Evidence from normal and commissurotomized subjects. *Neuropsychology* 7:325–342.

ROBERTSON, L. C., A. TREISMAN, S. FRIEDMAN-HILL, and M. GRABOWECKY, 1997. The interaction of spatial and object pathways: Evidence from Balint's syndrome. *J. Cogn. Neurosci.* 9:295–317.

SERGENT, J., 1982. The cerebral balance of power: Confrontation or cooperation? *J. Exp. Psychol.: Hum. Percept. Perform.* 8:253–272.

SEYAL, M., T. RO, and R. RAFAL, 1995. Increased sensitivity to ipsilateral cutaneous stimuli following transcranial magnetic stimulation of the parietal lobe. *Ann. Neurol.* 38:264–267.

SPRAGUE, J. M., 1966. Interaction of cortex and superior colliculus in mediation of peripherally summoned behavior in the cat. *Science* 153:1544–1547.

TREISMAN, A., 1988. Features and objects: The fourteenth Bartlett memorial lecture. *Quart. J. Exp. Psychol.* 40A:201–237.

TREISMAN, A., and G. GELADE, 1980. A feature integration theory of attention. *Cogn. Psychol.* 12:97–136.

TREISMAN, A., and H. SCHMIDT, 1982. Illusory conjunctions in the perception of objects. *Cogn. Psychol.* 14:107–141.

VALLAR, G., 1993. The anatomical basis of spatial neglect in humans. In *Unilateral Neglect: Clinical and Experimental Studies,* I. H. Robertson and J. C. Marshall, eds. Hillsdale, N.J.: Lawrence Erlbaum, pp. 27–62.

VALLAR, G., 1994. Left spatial hemineglect: An unmanageable explosion of dissociations? *Neuropsychol. Rehab.* 4:209–212.

WEISKRANTZ, L., 1986. *Blindsight: A Case Study and Implications.* Oxford: Oxford University Press.

45 Spatial Reference Frames and Hemispatial Neglect

MARLENE BEHRMANN

ABSTRACT Acting upon an object requires not only an appreciation of its geometry and meaning, but knowledge of its spatial position as well. However, spatial position cannot be defined absolutely, so an object's location must be represented with respect to a coordinate system or spatial frame of reference. The question is: What coordinate system(s) are used for spatial representation, and what are the psychological and neural mechanisms involved in coding spatial position? To address these issues, evidence is obtained from studying the performance of neuropsychological subjects who, after lesions primarily affecting the right parietal lobe, manifest hemispatial neglect–a deficit in spatial representation. Interestingly, patients neglect contralateral left-sided information where left is defined with respect to multiple reference frames. Furthermore, the relative contribution of different reference frames may be weighted, and task requirements and contingencies may influence the use of various coordinate systems, and hence the manifestation of neglect.

A fundamental function of vision is to provide information such that objects can be acted upon. For example, reaching over to pick up a coffee cup requires not only that the visual scene be segmented into discrete objects, one of which is the cup, and that one appreciate the geometry of the cup and its handle, but also that the spatial location of the cup be adequately computed and represented. One of the most dramatic deficits in spatial perception and action is hemispatial neglect ("neglect" for short) in which a patient fails to orient toward or report information that appears on the contralateral side of space (see Driver and Mattingley, 1998, and Vallar, 1998, for recent reviews of this disorder). Neglect occurs more commonly and with greater severity after right- than left-hemisphere lesions, and the most frequent neural concomitant is the inferior parietal lobule (Bisiach and Vallar, 1988; Stone, Halligan, and Greenwood, 1993; Vallar, 1993). Because of this asymmetry, I will refer to neglect as being "left-sided." Patients with neglect may not notice objects on the left of a scene, may ignore words on the left of a page or food on the left of a plate, and, typically, may fail to copy features on the left of a figure while preserving the corresponding features on the right, as shown in figure 45.1.

MARLENE BEHRMANN   Department of Psychology, Carnegie Mellon University, Pittsburgh, Pa.

Neglect is not restricted to the visual domain: Patients may not orient to contralateral auditory information (Bisiach and Vallar, 1988; De Renzi, Gentilini, and Barbieri, 1989), may not detect a contralateral somatosensory stimulus (Làdavas et al., 1998; Moscovitch and Behrmann, 1994), and may even ignore contralateral odors (Bellas, Novelly, and Eskenazi, 1989; Bellas, et al., 1988). Neglect is also not restricted to sensory input: Patients with neglect may perform movements more poorly to the contralateral than ipsilateral side. This holds both for upper limb movements (Heilman, et al., 1987; Mattingley, Bradshaw, and Phillips, 1992; Mattingley and Driver, 1997; Mattingley, et al., 1998; Meador et al., 1986) and for eye movements (Gainotti, 1993; Girotti et al., 1983). Figure 45.2 shows the eye movements of a control subject and a neglect patient during visual search for the letter A embedded in a random array of letters, presented on a board spanning 45 degrees of visual angle horizontally. Each circle depicts the position of a single fixation in x- and y-coordinates and the size of the circle corresponds to the duration of the fixation. The normal subject searches roughly equally across the entire space; but the patient makes few eye movements into the contralateral space, and those that are made are extremely brief in duration (Behrmann et al., 1997). Interestingly, the patient makes many more fixations to the ipsilateral right side than does the normal control, and these fixations are long in duration. The poor lateralization to the left and increased attention to the right is consistent with many views of a gradient of attention across space from left to right (Behrmann et al., 1990; Kinsbourne, 1977; Mozer and Behrmann, 1990).

The failure to process information on the contralateral side can be attributed neither to a primary motor or sensory impairment nor to a hemianopia (Walker et al., 1991). Even when information is presented to the intact visual field of a neglect patient, information in the contralateral hemispace is still neglected (Làdavas, Petronio, and Umiltà, 1990). Patients may even show neglect in the absence of visual input; for example, patients ignore the left side of a scene constructed in visual mental imagery (Bisiach and Luzzatti, 1978) and fail to search the

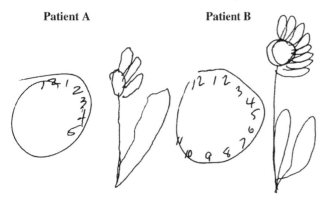

Patient A   **Patient B**

FIGURE 45.1   Copy of a daisy and a clock drawn by two patients with left-sided neglect following a lesion to the middle cerebral artery of the right hemisphere.

left of a dark room (Hornak, 1992; Karnath and Fetter, 1995). Finally, patients can be cued to process information on the contralesional side (Mattingley, Bradshaw, and Bradshaw, 1994; Milner et al., 1993; Riddoch and Humphreys, 1983) through verbal or other visual instructions. Taken together, these findings rule out a primary sensory deficit as being causally linked to neglect.

Although considerable controversy remains concerning the exact underlying mechanisms that give rise to neglect, there is general agreement that these patients do not orient contralaterally of their own volition and thus fail to represent information on that side of space adequately (Bisiach, 1993; Bisiach, 1997; Driver and Mattingley, 1998; Halligan and Marshall, 1994; Làdavas, Carletti, and Gori, 1994; McGlinchey-Berroth, 1997; Milner and Harvey, 1995; Vallar, 1998). In their comprehensive review of disorders of visual attention, Robertson and Rafal (chapter 44 in this volume) discuss neglect and other neuropsychological disorders of ori-

enting, the relationship between attention and eye movements, and the neural substrate that underlies various attentional deficits. The reader is referred to that chapter for more details on these issues. The focus of the present chapter is rather more restricted, centering on the question of the nature of the spatial representations in parietal cortex.

The specific question to be addressed is this: When the patients ignore information on the left, what is it left of? Because "left" and "right" cannot be defined in absolute terms, they must always be qualified with respect to a set of coordinates or spatial reference frame—i.e., relative to an origin and axes. It is these spatial coordinates that are used for organizing spatial information, and for establishing spatial relationships between objects in the scene and between the observer and the objects. By examining what determines the midline such that information to the left of it is neglected, we may understand how spatial position is coded in parietal cortex.

Spatial reference frames coding left and right (horizontal)

A number of potential reference frames can be used to define and code left/right positions in space (Feldman, 1985; Hinton, 1981). These can be divided into two broad classes: Objects and locations can be defined relative to the viewer's vantage point *(egocentrically)*, or they can be defined *allocentrically* from an extrinsic vantage point independent of the viewer's position. If positions were coded egocentrically, patients with left neglect would ignore information to the left of the viewer's midline. If positions were represented in allocentric coordinates, patients with neglect would ignore information to the left

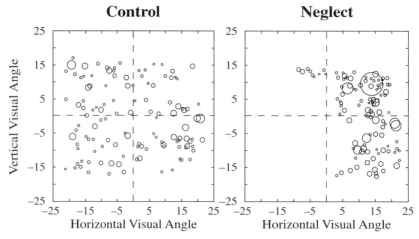

FIGURE 45.2   The location (in *x*- and *y*-coordinates) and duration (reflected as size of the circle) of fixations for a normal control subject and a typical patient with hemispatial neglect during search for the letter A in a random array of letters covering ap-

proximately 45 degrees of horizontal visual angle. Subjects wore a scleral contact annulus in one eye while they viewed the target display. Eye position was sampled every 5 ms (i.e., 200 samples per second). (Adapted from Behrmann et al., 1997.)

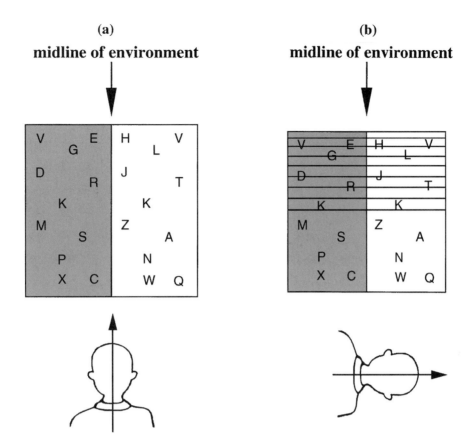

(a)

midline of environment

(b)

midline of environment

FIGURE 45.3 Left-sided neglect in environment- and viewer-based frames. Neglect patients report fewer letters from the shaded region in the panel (a). They report fewer letters from the shaded region in the panel (b), that is, the left of the environment frame, but also fewer letters from the striped region, i.e., the left of the viewer's midline (viewer frame).

of the midline of the environment or scene, or perhaps even to the left of individual objects present in the scene. There are, however, a number of potential reference frames that may be identified within the categories of allocentric and egocentric reference frames. But before examining the evidence for these more specific reference frames, data supporting the initial distinction between the broad classes are presented first.

To determine whether spatial position is defined egocentrically and/or allocentrically, several studies have examined whether the neglected information falls to the left of the midline of the viewer or of the environment. In such studies patients typically perform a task such as simple target detection (e.g., Gazzaniga and Làdavas, 1987; Làdavas, 1987) or reporting of words, letters, colors, or objects (e.g., Behrmann and Moscovitch, 1994; Calvanio, Petrone, and Levine, 1987; Farah et al., 1990). The tasks are generally performed in two different conditions. In the first condition (figure 45.3a), subjects are seated upright, with the midsagittal plane of the trunk, eyes, and head aligned with the midline of the display (scene) or environment. Under this condition, however, the left of the viewer is confounded with the left of the environment (or gravitational upright), and hence it is not possible to de-

termine which spatial reference frame determines what information is neglected. The second condition (figure 45.3b), in which the two frames are dissociated, is critical to deconfound the two reference frames. In this condition, the patient rotates his/her head and/or body in the frontal plane, orthogonal to gravity. Under this arrangement, the left of the viewer maps onto the upper region of the display, but the left of the environment remains as if the viewer were physically upright; thus, one can evaluate the amount of neglect in the viewer and environment reference frames separately.

Findings from most of these studies support the existence of both egocentric and allocentric neglect; even when the midline of the viewer is rotated away from that of the environment, patients report information on the left more poorly than that on the right defined with respect to the upright environment. Importantly, performance is also poorer for information presented to the left than to the right of the viewer's midline. In fact, in the single quadrant that is on the left in both of these frames, performance is poorest (Calvanio, Petrone, and Levine, 1987), as depicted in figure 45.3b (upper left quadrant). These results suggest that neglect may manifest in both egocentric and allocentric reference frames simultaneously. Whether each individual reference frame contributes additively (as a vector sum, for example) or multiplicatively on each trial, or whether one dominates in some trials but not in others, remains to be determined. (For some interesting ideas and simulations using a basis function model, see Pouget and Sejnowski, 1997a,b.) The more specific question concerning the relative contribution of spatial reference frames within each of these two broad classes is considered next.

EGOCENTRIC REFERENCE FRAMES Within an egocentric frame of reference, left is defined with respect to the viewer's own body coordinates. At least four different egocentric frames may be identified, however: "Left" may be defined with respect to the midline of (1) the eyes or vertical meridian of the visual field, (2) the head, (3) the trunk, or (4) the longitudinal axis of the limb involved in executing an action, such as the arm.

Experiments that examine the individual contribution of a single egocentric reference frame adopt the same logic as experiments that differentiate between egocentric and allocentric neglect by rotating one reference frame out of alignment from the other. For example, to examine the individual contribution of a reference frame centered on the eyes, Kooistra and Heilman (1989) compared the visual fields of a single patient in two conditions: (1) when the eyes, head, and trunk all coincided; (2) when the head and trunk were held in the midsagittal plane but the eyes deviated 30 degrees to either the left or right. The critical finding was that the patient failed to detect the stimuli when her gaze was straight ahead or when her gaze deviated to the left; but the patient performed well when her gaze deviated to the right, indicating some amelioration of the neglect with the eyes deviated to the right. We, too, observed a modulation of neglect when we recorded the latency and accuracy of saccades in neglect patients performing a detection task in which targets were presented at 5, 10, or 15 degrees to the left or right of the midline of the eye or retinal axis. When the eyes are pointed straight ahead (0 degrees), the targets fall along a gradient with best detection and latency on the right and poorest on the left. Latency (and also accuracy to some extent) was modulated by position of the eye in the head. When the eyes were deviated 15 degrees to the right, neglect was significantly ameliorated; but there was no real change in detection when the eyes were deviated 15 degrees to the left (Behrmann et al., 1999). Modulation of neglect by the line-of-sight (or orbital position) has also been shown by Bisiach, Capitani, and Porta (1985) in a tactile exploration study and by Duhamel and colleagues (1992), although in this latter study this was so only under certain testing conditions (see also Hillis et al., 1998).

Although these findings suggest that the retinocentric and/or oculocentric axis plays some role in determining what is neglected (see also the section below on related findings from single-unit studies with nonhuman primates), it is unclear whether these are the only egocentric reference frames that are important or whether others might also contribute. Karnath and colleagues, for example, have argued that the midline of the trunk (body-centered reference frame) plays a fundamental (perhaps exclusive) role and serves as the anchor or midline for dividing space into left and right (Karnath, Christ, and Hartje, 1993; Karnath, Fetter, and Dichgans, 1996; Karnath, Schenkel, and Fisher, 1991). In their experiments, subjects performed a target detection task with the eyes, head, and trunk all aligned in the midsagittal plane (baseline) or with either the head or the trunk rotated by 15 degrees. Targets were presented at 7 degrees to the left or right and saccadic latency was measured. Interestingly, there was no difference in RTs between the baseline condition and either condition involving the rotation of the head. There was, however, significant amelioration of neglect when the trunk was rotated to the left compared to the baseline condition. Surprisingly, however, the neglect was not exacerbated by trunk rotations to the right—a result they acknowledge as puzzling. [See also Karnath (1997) for further discussion and consideration of vestibular and optokinetic variables, and Farnè, Ponti, and Làdavas (1998) for a more general evaluation of these findings.] Support for the role of the midline of the trunk is also obtained from a study by Beschin and colleagues (1997), who found a decrease in neglect when the visual display was placed to the right of the trunk but not when it was placed to the right of the head or eyes (although the testing conditions are not perfectly comparable in this experiment). Unfortunately, this study cannot shed light on the possible increase of neglect with the display placed to the left of the trunk as this condition was not tested. It appears, however, that, under certain conditions, neglect can be ameliorated by leftward rotations of the trunk midline and exacerbated by rightward rotations of the trunk midline (Chokron and Imbert, 1993).

But the body midline cannot be the only bisector of space into left and right, as neglect can be observed for information placed solely to the right of the body midline (Làdavas, 1987). Furthermore, some studies have shown that the extent of the deviation error produced by neglect patients in a line bisection task remains the same irrespective of whether the lines to be bisected are placed to the right or left of the trunk's midline (Ishiai, Furukawa, and Tsukagoshi, 1989; Reuter-Lorenz and Posner, 1990). In addition, Morris Moscovitch and I showed that even when the right hand remained on the

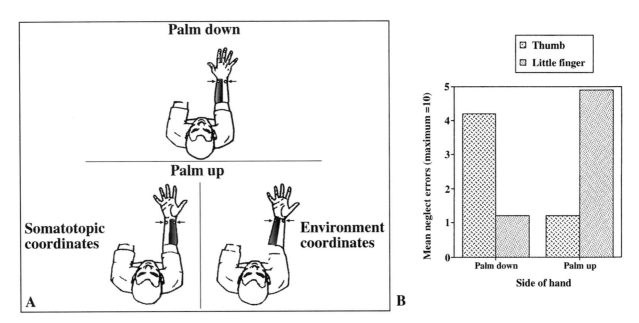

FIGURE 45.4 (A) Depiction of testing conditions of tactile neglect and (B) results showing mean number of errors in tactile detection for targets on the thumb and little finger side in the palm-down and palm-up position when stimuli are delivered to both sides simultaneously. (Adapted from Moscovitch and Behrmann, 1994.)

right of the body midline, tactile neglect was still observed. We designed this last study with two goals in mind: to examine whether tactile neglect could be observed in patients with visual neglect and, if so, to determine the frame of reference of tactile neglect. Using blindfolded patients with visual neglect, we applied a light tactile stimulus to the intact ipsilateral right hand on the thumb and/or little finger side, then directed the patients simply to indicate the location of the tactile stimulation (Moscovitch and Behrmann, 1994). All the patients reported fewer stimuli from the left side of the wrist (toward the thumb) than from the right (toward the little finger) while the hand was palm-down, as shown in figure 45.4 (these data are only from the bilateral simultaneous stimulation condition). When the hand was turned palm-up, the patients neglected the stimulation on the little finger side more than that on the thumb side. These findings indicate that tactile neglect does occur in patients with visual neglect, supporting the view that there is a common or unitary spatial map accessible by more than one sensory modality. More relevant for this discussion, however, is the finding that it is not the somatotopic surface that determines the spatial position of tactile stimuli (i.e., the patients do not always neglect the thumb side); rather, a more abstract, allocentric reference frame—independent of limb orientation—is used for representing the locations of stimuli and for coding what is on the "left." Importantly, it is also not the midline of the body that determines the neglect, as the same result occurs when the hand is right of the body midline.

Rather less research has been done to evaluate the role of the position of the limb on neglect performance. In their tactile exploration study, Bisiach, Capitani, and Porta (1985) manipulated not only eye position but also the placement of the right limb. In two conditions, the workspace of the limb fell along the midline of the trunk; and in the remaining two, the limb extended into the right side of space (as the board to be explored tactually was placed to the right). Performance did not differ in these conditions, suggesting that the limb coordinates are not crucial in affecting neglect (but see Graziano and Gross, 1996, for discussion of how the limb coordinates influence the neuronal activity of putamen and premotor neurons in monkeys). A recent study, however, suggests that there may be some involvement of limb coordinates, although this may primarily involve the spatial position of the limbs in relation to each other. In this study, Aglioti, Smania, and Peru (1999) applied bilateral stimulation to the dorsum of the hands when the hands were either placed straight ahead (anatomical position) or crossed one over the other. When the hands were crossed, the crossing could occur across the midline of the body or just in the right or in the left hemispace. The extinction of the stimulus on the left hand was prevalent in the anatomical position. But in the crossed position, there was both improved detection of the stimulus delivered to the left hand and poorer detection of the right-hand stimulus—and this was the case irrespective of whether the hands were positioned on the left, on the right, or across the midline of the trunk. These findings suggest that spatial position of a tactile stimulus to one hand is coded with some sensitivity to the location of the other limb, and that this is independent of the midsaggital plane of the trunk.

Evidence supporting the contribution of the final egocentric frame, one defined with respect to the midline of the head, is still somewhat controversial. For example, although Karnath, Christ, and Hartje (1993) found no modulation of neglect with changes in head orientation, we have found that the neglect pattern is influenced directly by the position of the head on the trunk, albeit to a lesser extent than some other reference frames (Behrmann et al., 1999; note, however, that the combined influence of target defined retinally and by orbital position codes position with respect to the head). It is also useful to note that in those studies that differentiate egocentric from allocentric coordinates and in which the patient's head (but not body) is tilted to the right or left, neglect may be occurring with respect to the midline of the head (as in figure 45.3). In these paradigms, however, it is not clear whether the neglect is indeed head-centered because the observed neglect may be defined by the position of the eyes or of the head as both are rotated from upright in the frontal plane (see also Hillis et al., 1998).

The studies reviewed thus far clearly point out the modulation of the severity of the neglect as a function of the midline of the trunk, the gaze angle or line-of-sight, and the position of the limb and perhaps, albeit to a lesser extent, the midline of the head. Whether or not these various egocentric frames are truly separable from each other, and hence independent, or whether they are contingent on each other to various degrees remains to be determined.

ALLOCENTRIC REFERENCE FRAMES Just as a number of different reference frames can be defined egocentrically, and can influence performance differentially, so too can different allocentric reference frames be identified and evaluated. The two main allocentric frames include one defined with respect to the midline of a visual scene or environment, and one defined with respect to the midline of individual objects or perceptual units in the scene.

The derivation of an environment-centered frame requires computations involving gravitational forces on the otolith organ of the vestibular system, visual input to define environmental landmarks with respect to gravity, and proprioceptive and tactile information to provide a sense of the body's posture in relation to gravity. As suggested earlier on, several studies have observed that the midline of the environment is important in separating out the left and right of space, as evident from the neglect of the left of the upright environment when the

viewer is tilted (Behrmann and Moscovitch, 1994; Calvanio, Petrone, and Levine, 1987; Farah et al., 1990; Làdavas, 1987). Mennemeier, Chatterjee, and Heilman (1994), however, have argued that the environmental frame is perhaps the most important, and even more salient than a viewer-based frame. Their conclusion is based on a line bisection study with two patients with multidimensional neglect, in which the environmental and body-centered frames were brought into opposition through rotating the subjects' body in left, right, prone, and supine positions. The critical finding was that the patients' bisection errors were predicted better by the environmental than body-centered frames, leading the researchers to conclude that environment coordinates dominate in coding spatial positions.

There is, however, another interpretation of the data invoking the centrality of the environment-based frame, and that concerns the role of gravity. Because visual information was present in all of the studies described above, it is possible that visual, rather than gravitational, information may have played an important role. Thus, when subjects were required to search for a spot of light in the dark with their bodies either upright or tilted to the left or right, forward or backward, subjects exhibited a bias to search the ipsilesional hemispace for this visual stimulus—and this bias held equivalently across the different body rotations. These findings suggest that it is the body midline (and translating the visual information in relation to this midline) rather than a gravity-based environmental display that may potentially underlie the previously reported environment-based neglect (Karnath, Fetter, and Niemeier, 1996).

In the last few years, considerable evidence has accumulated suggesting that spatial position may be coded with respect to another allocentric frame, the midline of an individual object, and that patients neglect the left side of an individual object regardless of its spatial position. Gainotti, Messerli, and Tissot (1972) first observed that, in copying several objects in a scene, some patients failed to copy the left side of an individual object while still copying objects located further to the left of their own incomplete drawings (see also Caramazza and Hillis, 1990; Halligan and Marshall, 1993, for examples). A problem with interpreting this provocative result, however, is that copying is a sequential task. Thus, when a subject copies a single element in a display, that element becomes the entire scene or environment and the subject may neglect information on its left. When the subject moves to copy the next element, this next element then becomes the entire environment and the left of this next object is neglected. Under these conditions, one cannot easily distinguish between object- and environment-based neglect.

Object-based neglect, however, has now been observed in a number of studies using very different paradigms. In one of the first studies to address this issue, Driver and Halligan (1991) asked their patient, PP, to make same–different judgments on two upright, elongated nonsense shapes placed one above the other in the midline of the viewer. Of most relevance is the fact that PP failed to detect the point of difference when it fell on the left under these conditions. Even more dramatic was the finding that the point of difference was still not detected when, for example, the two shapes were rotated 45 degrees to the right and the point of difference fell on the right of the viewer but on the left of the object defined by a longitudinal axis through the midline of the object. This demonstration of object-based neglect is consistent with the report of Caramazza and Hillis (1990) who showed that their patient, NG (who had right-sided neglect after a left hemisphere lesion), failed to read the letters on the right of a word, irrespective of whether the word was written in standard format, was printed vertically, or appeared in mirror-reverse format.

Along the same lines, Young, Hellawell, and Welch (1991) showed that their patient, BQ, neglected the left side of chimeric stimuli (in which the left side of one object is joined to the right side of a second object). Particularly impressive is the fact that BQ reported the identity of the face on the right side of the chimeric stimulus more accurately than the left both when the chimeric stimulus was presented upright in the intact ipsilesional field and when the chimeric stimulus was inverted 180 degrees so the right half of the upright face fell on the left side of space. (But performance was not perfect in this condition, reflecting the fact that this right side of the face was on the left of some other coordinate frame.) The failure to orient toward and process the left half of the chimera is also evident in eye movements; Walker and colleagues (1996) reported that their patient, RR, restricted his fixations to the right side of an individual object. This object-based pattern could not be attributed to the failure to fixate the left of a display, as RR could scan both the left and right of scenes and could also make left saccades when the left half of an object was presented in his left visual field (Walker and Findlay, 1997; Walker et al., 1996). A host of other studies now support these results which, taken together, suggest that the boundaries and properties of an individual object in a scene may play an important role in defining what is "left."

To examine the contribution of a reference frame centered on an individual object, Steve Tipper and I devised an experiment (influenced by some of his previous work with normal subjects on inhibition of re-

turn in object coordinates) in which we could systematically disambiguate the object-based frame from other confounding reference frames. In these studies, we presented neglect patients with computer displays consisting of an object (barbell) in which the two circles were colored differently (see figure 45.5). The barbell appeared in the center of the computer screen (or entirely on the right for patients with a left field defect); then, after a short delay, on two-thirds of the trials, a target or probe in the form of a small white dot appeared in the center of either the left or the right circle. The patients pressed a key as soon as they detected the presence of this target, and we measured their accuracy and speed. As expected, in this "static" condition, patients took much longer or made more errors in detecting the left than the right target. Because the left and right of the barbell are aligned with other reference frames, a decoupling condition was introduced. In this second, "rotating" or moving condition, the midline of the barbell is dissociated from various other reference frames in the following way. First the barbell is presented on the computer screen; then after a short delay, it is rotated 180 degrees around the midpoint of the connecting horizontal rod while the patients watch. When the rotation is complete and the barbell has reached its stationary position, a short delay ensues, whereupon the target appears on the left or right of space. Note that, as shown in the example in figure 45.5, the display in which the target is presented is identical in the static and rotating condition. However, in the rotation condition, the original left circle of the barbell is now on the right side on the computer screen and the original right circle is now on the left side of the screen. This arrangement allows us to determine whether the patients now neglect targets appearing on the "good" right side of space (but on the left of the object) and show good detection of targets appearing on the "poor" left side of space (but on the right of the object).

As is evident from the lighter bars in the graph in figure 45.5, patients are significantly slower to detect left- than right-sided targets in the static condition. The situation is reversed in the rotating condition: Now, patients are faster at detecting the left- than right-sided target, as shown by the darker bars. The explanation that we proposed for this paradoxical reversal of neglect was that patients neglect the information that falls to the left of the object's midline and, conversely, attend well to the information that falls to the object's right. Even when the object moves into a new spatial location or undergoes a complete rotation, information on its left is still at a disadvantage compared to information on its right. This pattern cannot be attributed to an artifact of eye movement; even when eye movement is controlled, the same pattern

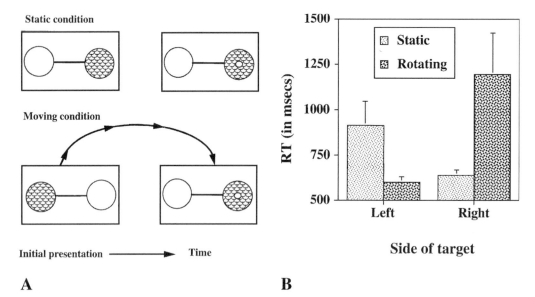

Static condition

Moving condition

Initial presentation ——————▶ Time

A

B

FIGURE 45.5 (A) Depiction of the static and rotating conditions with identical final displays. One circle of the barbell was colored red and one colored blue. (B) Mean reaction time for 4 patients with neglect to detect the target on the left and right in the static and moving conditions. Note that, because the fifth subject made so many errors, his data are not included here in the RT analysis; however, his data reveal the same pattern with accuracy as the dependent measure. (Adapted from Behrmann and Tipper, 1994.)

is observed (Tipper and Behrmann, 1996). Nor is this finding obviously attributable to the covert tracking of the left or right of the object. In fact, relative to the static condition, in the moving condition, the facilitation for targets on the left together with the inhibition of targets on the right critically depends on the two circles' forming a unified object–it is not evident when the two circles are not joined. If the result were simply a function of the patients' covertly tracking, say, the right circle of the barbell (to which their attention is drawn initially), a similar finding should be obtained even when the two circles are not connected. These findings led us to conclude that spatial positions are also defined with respect to an object-based reference frame and hence information to the left of this frame may be neglected.

To examine whether neglect can arise for information defined in multiple coordinates simultaneously (one of which is object-based), we extended this experiment by adding to the barbell display two gray squares (Behrmann and Tipper, 1999). These squares served as stationary markers–they remained fixed to the left and right sides of a second reference frame defined with respect to either the environmental or viewer midline (for short, we refer to this as "location-based") even on trials when the barbell rotated (see figure 45.6A). In this experiment, when the target appeared, it did so with equal probability in the left or right of the barbell or in the left or right square. Trials that probed these four target positions were randomly ordered so that the patients could not predict where the target would appear.

Importantly, as shown in figure 45.6B, the finding of object-based neglect was replicated: Performance was poorer for targets on the left than on the right of the barbell in the static condition, and this was reversed in the moving condition (left panel of graph showing only the data from the barbell). The novel finding, illustrated in the right panel of figure 45.6B, was this: When the target appeared in the left square, detection was always slower than when the target appeared in the right square, irrespective of whether the barbell remained static or rotated.

In a final experiment in this series, we added one further manipulation: Whereas the targets appeared equi-probably on the left or right of the barbell or squares in the previous experiment, we included two additional blocks of trials with the same subjects. In one of these blocks, the proportion of targets that would appear in the object-based frame or the location-based frame was either 20% or 80%, respectively, or the converse in the second block. The results from these additional blocks indicated that, as the probability of a target's appearing in the barbell was increased, so the severity of object-based neglect increased, reflected as a larger reversal of neglect in the static and moving conditions. Taken together, these results suggest two important conclusions. First, patients can neglect the left of the environment and/or viewer frame and, at the very same time, can neglect the left of an object, even when the left of the object is on the right side of space (as demonstrated by the rotating barbell). Second, the distribution of visuospatial attention in

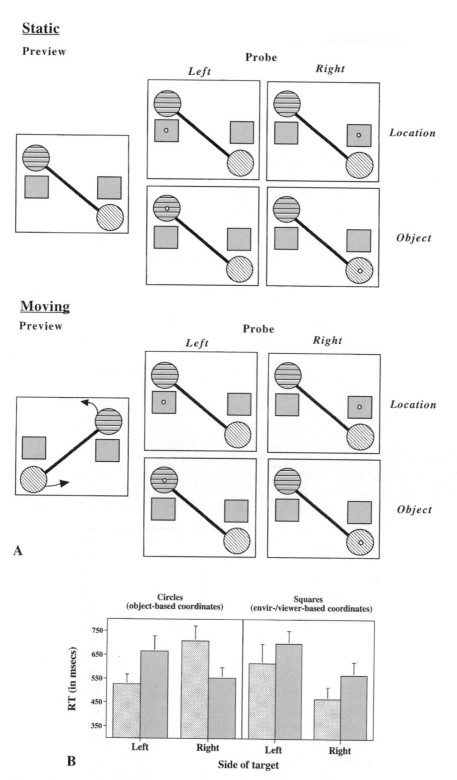

FIGURE 45.6 (A) Depiction of the four types of target-present displays including targets on the left and right of the object and of the environment/viewer (location) frame in the static and moving conditions. (B) Mean reaction time for 5 patients with neglect to detect the target on the left and right in the static and moving conditions in the two different reference frames. (Adapted from Behrmann and Tipper, 1999.)

these two frames of reference is flexible, and may be influenced by task demands or contingencies (see also Hillis, Mordkoff, and Caramazza, in press). These findings suggest that the parietal lobe can code spatial information relative to multiple spatial reference frames simultaneously and flexibly.

Almost all of the studies demonstrating object-based neglect discussed thus far might arguably require some form of mental rotation. Indeed, it has been suggested that there is no such phenomenon as object-based neglect, and hence that all these results could be accounted for by mental rotation. If patients mentally rotated images to the canonical upright before the left and right were coded, and if there were a gradient of attention across space (Kinsbourne, 1987; Mozer and Behrmann, 1990), then the left of an object would always be disadvantaged relative to its right. Indeed, Buxbaum and colleagues (1996) have shown that it is only when the patient is instructed to use mental rotation that the object-based neglect emerges. This explanation, however, is still somewhat controversial for two reasons. First, in none of the studies on object-based neglect reported thus far are the subjects instructed to use mental rotation; yet the neglect for the left of the object was still observed (whereas the effect was observed only when the patient was instructed to use mental rotation in Buxbaum et al., 1996). Second, whether or not these patients can actually make use of mental rotation is also unclear, given that the right parietal cortex (which is damaged in these patients) plays a critical role in mental rotation (Alivasatos and Petrides, 1997) and lesions to it usually impair the ability to perform mental rotation (Farah and Hammond, 1988; Ratcliff, 1979).

There are, moreover, several elegant studies of object-based neglect in which mental rotation is clearly not required. For example, Driver and colleagues showed that a neglect patient failed to detect a small gap that appeared on one side of a triangle (Driver et al., 1994). This was only the case, however, when, the gap fell to the left of the midline of the triangle, and the orientation of the triangle was biased by virtue of surrounding triangles. (See also Reuter-Lorenz, Drain, and Hardy-Morais, 1996, for results with normal subjects showing directionally specific object-based processing.) Several other studies have also shown that perceptual organization or grouping processes can significantly influence the manifestation of neglect and perhaps even reverse it (Driver, Baylis, and Rafal, 1992; Grabowecky, Robertson, and Treisman, 1993; Humphreys and Riddoch, 1995; Riddoch et al., 1995). Recently, for example, Ward, Goodrich, and Driver, (1994) showed that when the contralesional item could be grouped with the ipsilesional information on the basis of Gestalt factors such as

similarity (for example, a bracket on the left and a bracket on the right) or symmetry, report of the left-sided stimulus improved by roughly 50% compared to when the left-sided information could not be grouped with a simultaneous right-sided stimulus. The same pattern was obtained when the two items formed a familiar configuration (for example, an arrow made of a left arrowhead and a right horizontal bar). Similar effects of grouping have been observed with normal subjects in which unattended information is processed better if it forms part of an object defined by uniform connectedness (see, for example, Kramer and Hahn, 1996; Watson and Kramer, 1997).

This amelioration of neglect through grouping has now been replicated in several studies, and better processing of the contralesional information has been shown when the left-sided information can be grouped with corresponding right-sided information by bottom-up factors such as color and proximity (Driver and Halligan, 1991) or brightness, or by the presence of collinear edges (Gilchrist, Humphreys, and Riddoch, 1996; Rorden et al., 1997). Information on the left may also be grouped with the information on the right (and hence preserved) by a global outline (Driver, Baylis, and Rafal, 1992; Farah, Wallace, and Vecera, 1993), by an illusory contour (Kanizsa-type figure) of a partially occluded figure (Mattingley, David, and Driver, 1997), or by any well-configured object or whole (Gilchrist et al., 1996; Humphreys and Riddoch, 1994). One possible mechanism for determining what constitutes an object is a computation of the center of mass of the display. Two recent studies (Grabowecky et al., 1993; Pavlovskaya, et al., 1997) suggest that this might be the case (Robertson and Rafal, chapter 44 in this volume, discuss this in more detail). Both Grabowecky and Pavlovskaya manipulated the center of mass of the stimulus, either by adding features to one or both sides of a central set of features or by altering the luminance of the display. In both cases, patients neglected more information on the contralateral side if the center of mass was shifted rightward, suggesting that a coarse (perhaps preattentive) description of the display provides a basis for further spatial computation.

However, perceptual features are not the only basis on which "objectness" is determined, as semantic cohesiveness can also ameliorate some left-sided neglect. For example, Behrmann and colleagues (1990) showed that patients who failed to read the word COW correctly when presented to the left were able to read it better when the word BOY was presented simultaneously on its right, as in COWBOY—and some advantage was obtained even with a blank space between the two component words, as in COW BOY. The advantage from the right-sided context was observed only when the two words (COW BOY) constituted a real compound word rather than a noncompound item such as COW SUN (see Mozer and Behrmann, 1990, for a computational implementation and explanation of this behavior).

These findings suggest a couple of factors: Both perceptual and more conceptual object properties play a role in determining what is neglected. Information to the left of the midline of an object may be neglected, but this neglect may be offset if the information to the left coheres well with the corresponding right-sided information. Preattentive processes may suffice to bind the left- and right-sided information together in many cases, but top-down factors like semantic or morphological composition may also modulate the distribution of attention (Mozer and Behrmann, 1990).

Spatial reference frames coding up/down and near/far

Thus far, this chapter has focused exclusively on reference frames coding left and right. But similar questions apply with regard to other spatial dimensions, such as up/down (vertical) and near/far (radial). It would be remiss not to include a brief discussion of spatial coding in other dimensions, as patients with parietal lesions show impairments in representing locations in these other planes as well. For example, some patients show "altitudinal neglect," in which they omit more information from the upper than lower portion of the array (Shelton, Bowers, and Heilman, 1990) or vice versa (Butter et al., 1989; Halligan and Marshall, 1989; Mennemeier et al., 1994; Nichelli et al., 1993; Pitzalis, Spinelli, and Zoccolotti, 1997). Performance may also differ along the radial dimension. Some patients show only personal neglect, in which, for example, they fail to brush their hair, shave their faces, or apply makeup on the left (Beschin and Robertson, 1997; Guariglia and Antonucci, 1992; Peru and Pinna, 1997). Other patients show only peripersonal, but not personal, neglect; in this case, they ignore contralateral information presented near but not on the body (Halligan and Marshall, 1991; Mennemeier, Wertman, and Heilman, 1992). Other patients ignore only contralateral information presented in far or extrapersonal space (Bisiach et al., 1986; Cowey, Small, and Ellis, 1994). Interestingly, it may be that neglect along the near–far axis is apparent only when the subject must produce a motor response to the stimulus and not when spatial perception alone is tested (Pizzamiglio et al., 1989). The fact that neglect can be dissociated for various distances suggests that the parietal cortex also incorporates information about the proximal–distal plane (Rizzolatti and Berti, 1990).

CORRESPONDING DATA FROM NONHUMAN PRIMATES   The data obtained from human subjects with hemispatial neglect suggest that there are a number of different reference frames computed by parietal cortex. Whether these different representations are subserved by a single neural region within parietal cortex or whether there are distinct neural substrates is not easily answered in the context of human studies, given that the lesions (usually resulting from a middle cerebral artery infarction) are generally large and multiple parietal regions are implicated. Animal studies, therefore, provide an important source of converging evidence on the issue of spatial representation. There is no direct analog of hemispatial neglect in monkeys, and anatomical and cytoarchitectonic homologies between posterior parietal cortex in monkeys and humans are hardly perfect (Crowne and Mah, 1998); nevertheless, several experimenters have described the occurrence of visual extinction after lesions to the posterior parietal areas (Gaffan and Hornak, 1997; Lynch and McLaren, 1989; Rizzolatti, Gentilucci, and Matelli, 1985). Perhaps more informative for the current purpose are the findings from single-neuron recording studies conducted in the parietal cortex of awake, behaving monkeys. Results of these studies are reviewed here briefly; for further details, the reader is encouraged to consult the many excellent papers by Anderson and colleagues (Andersen et al., 1997, 1993) and by Colby and colleagues (Colby, 1996, 1998; Colby and Goldberg, 1999).

The work with monkeys has provided direct evidence that parietal cortex contains several distinct areas and multiple representations of space. Within the class of egocentric representations, neurons in the lateral intraparietal area have receptive fields that map targets relative to the retina, and the activity of these neurons can be significantly modulated by orbital position (Andersen, Essick, and Siegel, 1985). Interestingly, these neurons can also update their retinal image in conjunction with an eye movement so that their internal representation always matches the current eye position (referred to as an eye-centered representation; Colby, Duhamel, and Goldberg, 1993; Duhamel, Colby, and Goldberg, 1992). Neurons that code stimulus location relative to the head have also been described, this time in the ventral intraparietal sulcus (Brotchie et al., 1995). These neurons can be driven by both visual and somatosensory stimulation, and the tactile and visual receptive fields are in close correspondence.

Directional selectivity of neurons is also evident when monkeys make movements of similar direction but to different parts of the workspace (Caminiti et al., 1991), and neurons in premotor cortex have receptive fields that

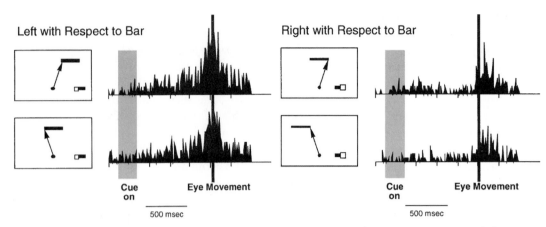

FIGURE 45.7   Histograms of the average firing rate of a single neuron over time showing the directional selectivity for a position on the left of a bar, irrespective of the physical direction of the movement (right or left in the orbit). (Adapted from Olson and Gettner, 1995.)

move with the arm (Graziano, Yap, and Gross, 1994). Neurons in the medial intraparietal area are specialized for responding to stimuli within reaching distance (Colby and Duhamel, 1991) and likely play an important role in deriving arm- and reaching-related spatial representations. Finally, results that converge with the object-based neuropsychological findings have been obtained from recordings of single neurons in monkeys required to move their eyes to the left or right of objects (Olson and Gettner, 1995; Olson, Gettner, and Tremblay, 1998). Interestingly, the results showed that neurons in the supplementary eye field—a premotor area in frontal cortex—are activated selectively when the monkey is planning to make an eye movement to the left of an object, whereas other neurons are activated when the monkey plans an eye movement to the right of an object (see figure 45.7). This object-based directional selectivity occurs regardless of the direction of the eye movement required and the retinal position of the object, regardless of the exact visual features of the object, and regardless of whether the monkey was specifically following an object-centered instruction. These results point directly to a neural mechanism that might be responsible for locating positions in an object-based reference frame. Damage to neurons with object-left spatial selectivity would then give rise to the object-based neglect that is revealed by the patients.

Outstanding questions

Many unanswered questions concerning the frames of reference for coding spatial position remain. Whether or not egocentric and allocentric frames (and the many different frames within each of these categories) are independent of each other in humans remains to be determined. For example, Farah and colleagues (1990) have suggested that in their sample, viewer-centered and environment-centered neglect always co-occurred but there was no evidence of object-based neglect. (But see Hillis and Rapp, 1998, for a re-analysis of the data in which they show that some individual subjects exhibit object-based neglect.) Whether this is coincidence or statistically real–and which exact egocentric and allocentric reference frames are implicated–remains to be determined. A further question concerns the relative contribution of each reference frame when neglect is determined by more than one. In those few studies where the data are analyzed such that this question can be addressed, the contribution of each reference frame sometimes appears to be additive and sometimes multiplicative (Behrmann et al., 1998; Behrmann and Tipper, 1998; Calvanio, Petrone, and Levine, 1987). Further investigation of the coupling and relative contributions of different reference frames to spatial coding is clearly required.

The extent to which different reference frames participate depending on the task requirements is also important to understand. As discussed previously, we have shown that it is possible to differentially weight the contribution of a coordinate system depending on the task to be performed (Behrmann and Tipper, 1998). Consistent with this task dependency is the fact that the activity in neurons in posterior parietal cortex differs depending on the task the animal is intending to perform (eye movements versus reaching; Snyder, Batista, and Andersen, 1997).

A final question concerns the neural substrate supporting the computation of the different reference frames. As is clear in the nonhuman primate literature, several distinct regions in the parietal cortex appear to play somewhat different roles (for possible human analogs, see Milner, 1997). Precise localization in a population of neglect patients is extremely difficult, given that the lesion is typically rather large and involves almost all of parietal cortex (and often, additional lobar structures; Vallar and Perani, 1987). A recent neuroimaging study with normal subjects, however, can shed some light on the issue, suggesting that there might be both common and different regions implicated in location-based and object-based computations. In this study, normal subjects judged the position of a probe on the left or right of an environment frame or of an object frame. Relative to the baseline condition (line length judgment), attending both to an object in left or right space or to the left or right of an individual object revealed an increase in regional cerebral blood flow in left and right superior parietal regions as well as in left inferior parietal regions (as well as some other cortical regions). Additional region activation seen only for the object-based task included left striate and prestriate regions, whereas additional activation associated only with the space-based task included right prefrontal regions and right inferior temporal-occipital cortex (Fink et al., 1997). These findings suggest an overlap in neural mechanisms for different spatial reference representations, but also some divergence between them (see also Egly, Driver, and Rafal, 1994).

The variety of deficits observed following parietal damage suggests that this region of cortex plays a critical role in spatial representation. The parietal cortex, however, does not have a monopoly on spatial processing; regions such as frontal cortex and parahippocampal regions also contribute importantly to spatial representations (see Maguire, 1997; Rainer, Asaad, and Miller, 1998; Robertson and Rafal, chapter 44 in this volume, for more details). How these different areas work together to give rise to our unitary visual experience remains unclear, but neuropsychological studies with patients suffering from hemispatial neglect allow us to observe some of the representations and processes that ultimately contribute to our unified spatial experience.

ACKNOWLEDGMENTS   The author thanks Carol Colby, David Plaut, and Mike Posner for useful comments on this manuscript. This work was supported by a FIRST award from the National Institutes of Mental Health (R01 MH5424-6) and by a NIMH Program project grant (MH47566-06).

REFERENCES

AGLIOTI, S., N. SMANIA, and A. PERU, 1999. Frames of reference for mapping tactile stimuli in brain-damaged patients. *J. Cogn. Neurosci.* 11(1):67–79.

ALIVASATOS, B., and M. PETRIDES, 1997. Functional activation of the human brain during mental rotation. *Neuropsychologia* 35(2):111–118.

ANDERSEN, R. A., G. K. ESSICK, and R. M. SIEGEL, 1985. Encoding of spatial location by posterior parietal neurons. *Science* 230:456–458.

ANDERSEN, R. A., L. H. SNYDER, D. C. BRADLEY, and J. XING, 1997. Multimodal representation of space in the posterior parietal cortex and its use in planning movements. *Annu. Rev. Neurosci.* 20:303–330.

ANDERSEN, R. A., L. H. SNYDER, C.-S. LI, and B. STRICANNE, 1993. Coordinate transformations in the representation of spatial information. *Curr. Opinion Neurobiol.* 3:171–176.

BEHRMANN, M., J. J. S. BARTON, S. WATT, and S. E. BLACK, 1997. Impaired visual search in patients with unilateral neglect: An oculographic analysis. *Neuropsychologia* 35(11): 1445–1458.

BEHRMANN, M., T. GHISELLI-CRIPPA, J. SWEENEY, I. DIMATTEO, and R. KASS, 1999. The relative contribution of different egocentric spatial coordinate frames in hemispatial neglect. Submitted manuscript.

BEHRMANN, M., and M. MOSCOVITCH, 1994. Object-centered neglect in patients with unilateral neglect: Effects of left-right coordinates of objects. *J. Cogn. Neurosci.* 6(1):1–16.

BEHRMANN, M., M. MOSCOVITCH, S. E. BLACK, and M. MOZER, 1990. Perceptual and conceptual factors in neglect dyslexia: Two contrasting case studies. *Brain* 113(4):1163–1883.

BEHRMANN, M., and S. P. TIPPER, 1994. Object-based attentional mechanisms: Evidence from patients with unilateral neglect. In *Attention and Performance XV: Conscious and Nonconscious Information Processing*, C. Umilta and M. Moscovitch, eds. Cambridge, Mass.: MIT Press, pp. 351–375.

BEHRMANN, M., and S. P. TIPPER, 1999. Attention accesses multiple reference frames: Evidence from neglect. *J. Exp. Psychol.: Hum. Percept. Perform.* 25(1):83–101.

BELLAS, D. N., R. A. NOVELLY, and B. ESKENAZI, 1989. Olfactory lateralization and identification in right hemisphere lesion and control patients. *Neuropsychologia* 27(9):1187–1191.

BELLAS, D. N., R. A. NOVELLY, B. ESKENAZI, and J. WASSERSTEIN, 1988. The nature of unilateral olfactory neglect in the olfactory sensory system. *Neuropsychologia* 26:45–52.

BESCHIN, N., R. CUBELLI, S. DELLA SALA, and L. SPINAZZOLA, 1997. Left of what? The role of egocentric coordinates in neglect. *J. Neurol. Neurosurg. Psych.* 63:483–489.

BESCHIN, N., and I. H. ROBERTSON, 1997. Personal versus extrapersonal neglect: A group study of their dissociation using a clinically reliable test. *Cortex* 33:379–384.

BISIACH, E., 1993. Mental representation in unilateral neglect and related disorders: The Twentieth Bartlett Memorial Lecture. *Quart. J. Exp. Psychol.* 46A(3):435–461.

BISIACH, E., 1997. The spatial features of unilateral neglect. In *Parietal Lobe Contributions to Orientation in 3-D Space*, H.-O. Karnath and P. Thier, eds. Heidelberg: Springer-Verlag, pp. 465–495.

BISIACH, E., E. CAPITANI, and E. PORTA, 1985. Two basic properties of space representation in the brain. *J. Neurol. Neurosurg. Psych.* 48:141–144.

BISIACH, E., and C. LUZZATTI, 1978. Unilateral neglect of representational space. *Cortex* 14:129–133.

BISIACH, E., D. PERANI, G. VALLAR, and A. BERTI, 1986. Unilateral neglect: Personal and extra-personal. *Neuropsychologia* 24:759–767.

BISIACH, E., and G. VALLAR, 1988. Hemineglect in humans. In *Handbook of Neuropsychology*, Vol. 1, F. Boller and J. Grafman eds. Amsterdam: Elsevier, pp. 195–222.

BROTCHIE, P. R., R. A. ANDERSEN, L. H. SNYDER, and S. J. GOODMAN, 1995. Head position signals used by parietal neurons to encode locations of visual stimuli. *Nature* 375:232–235.

BUTTER, C. M., J. EVANS, N. KIRSCH, and D. KEWMAN, 1989. Altitudinal neglect following traumatic brain injury: A case report. *Neuropsychologia* 25:135–146.

BUXBAUM, L. J., H. B. COSLETT, M. W. MONTGOMERY, and M. J. FARAH, 1996. Mental rotation may underlie apparent object-based neglect. *Neuropsychologia* 34(2):113–126.

CALVANIO, R., P. N. PETRONE, and D. LEVINE, 1987. Left visual spatial neglect is both environment-centered and body-centered. *Neurology* 37:1179–1183.

CAMINITI, R., P. B. JOHNSON, C. GALLI, S. FERRAINA, and Y. BURNOD, 1991. Making arm movements in different parts of space: The premotor and motor cortical representations of a co-ordinate system for reaching to visual targets. *J. Neurosci.* 11:1182–1197.

CARAMAZZA, A., and A. E. HILLIS, 1990. Spatial representation of words in the brain implied by studies of a unilateral neglect patient. *Nature* 346:267–269.

CHOKRON, S., and M. IMBERT, 1993. Egocentric reference and asymmetric perception of space. *Neuropsychologia* 31(3):267–275.

COLBY, C., 1996. A neurophysiological distinction between attention and intention. In *Attention and Performance VXI*, T. Inui and J. L. McClelland, eds. Cambridge, Mass.: MIT Press, pp. 157–177.

COLBY, C., 1998. Action-oriented spatial reference frames in cortex. *Neuron* 20:15–24.

COLBY, C., and J.-R. DUHAMEL, 1991. Heterogeneity of extrastriate visual areas and multiple parietal areas in the macaque monkey. *Neuropsychologia* 29:517–537.

COLBY, C. L., J.-R. DUHAMEL, and M. E. GOLDBERG, 1993. The analysis of visual space by the lateral intraparietal area of the monkey: The role of extraretinal signals. In *Progress in Brain Research*, vol. 95, T. P. Hicks, S. Molotchnikoff, and T. Ono, eds. Amsterdam: Elsevier-Science, pp. 307–316.

COLBY, C. L., and M. E. GOLDBERG, 1999. Space and attention in parietal cortex. *Annu. Rev. Neurosci.* 22:319–349.

COWEY, A., M. SMALL, and S. ELLIS, 1994. Left visuo-spatial neglect can be worse in far than near space. *Neuropsychologia* 32(9):1059–1066.

CROWNE, D. P., and L. W. MAH, 1998. A comparison of hemispatial neglect from posterior parietal and periarcuate lesions in the monkey. *Psychobiology* 26(2):103–108.

DE RENZI, E., M. GENTILINI, and C. BARBIERI, 1989. Auditory neglect. *J. Neurol. Neurosurg. Psych.* 52:613–617.

DRIVER, J., G. C. BAYLIS, S. GOODRICH, and R. D. RAFAL, 1994. Axis-based neglect of visual shape. *Neuropsychologia* 32(11):1353–1365.

DRIVER, J., G. C. BAYLIS, and R. D. RAFAL, 1992. Preserved figure-ground segregation and symmetry perception in visual neglect. *Nature* 360:73–75.

DRIVER, J., and P. W. HALLIGAN, 1991. Can visual neglect operate in object-centered coordinates: An affirmative study. *Cogn. Neuropsychol.* 8:475–496.

DRIVER, J., and J. B. MATTINGLEY, 1998. Parietal neglect and visual awareness. *Nature Neurosci.* 1:17–22.

DUHAMEL, J. R., C. L. COLBY, and M. E. GOLDBERG, 1992. The updating of representations of visual space in parietal cortex by intended eye movements. *Science* 225:90–92.

DUHAMEL, J. R., M. E. GOLDBERG, E. J. FITZGIBBONS, A. SIRIGU, and J. GRAFMAN, 1992. Saccadic dysmetria in a patient with a right frontoparietal lesion: The importance of corollary discharge for accurate spatial behavior. *Brain* 115:1387–1402.

EGLY, R., J. DRIVER, and R. RAFAL, 1994. Shifting visual attention between objects and locations: Evidence from normal and parietal lesion subjects. *J. Exp. Psychol.* 123:161–177.

FARAH, M. J., J. L. BRUNN, A. B. WONG, M. WALLACE, and P. CARPENTER, 1990. Frames of reference for the allocation of spatial attention: Evidence from the neglect syndrome. *Neuropsychologia* 28:335–347.

FARAH, M. J., and K. M. HAMMOND, 1988. Mental rotation and orientation-invariant object recognition: Dissociable processes. *Cognition* 29:29–46.

FARAH, M. J., M. WALLACE, and S. P. VECERA, 1993. "What" and "where" in visual attention: Evidence from the neglect syndrome. In *Unilateral Neglect: Clinical and Experimental Studies*, I. H. Robertson and J. C. Marshall, eds. Hove, U.K.: Lawrence Erlbaum Associates, pp. 123–138.

FARNÈ, A., F. PONTI, and E. LÀDAVAS, 1998. In search of biased egocentric reference frames in neglect. *Neuropsychologia* 36(7):611–623.

FINK, G. R., R. J. DOLAN, P. W. HALLIGAN, J. C. MARSHALL, and C. D. FRITH, 1997. Space-based and object-based visual attention: Shared and specific neural domains. *Brain* 120:2013–2028.

FELDMAN, J. A., 1985. Four frames suffice: A provisional model of vision and space. *Behavioral and Brain Sciences* 8(2):265–313.

GAFFAN, D., and J. HORNAK, 1997. Visual neglect in the monkey. *Brain* 120:1647–1657.

GAINOTTI, G., 1993. The role of spontaneous eye movements in orienting attention and in unilateral neglect. In *Hemispatial Neglect*, I. Robertson and J. C. Marshall, eds. London: Erlbaum, pp. 107–122.

GAINOTTI, G., P. MESSERLI, and R. TISSOT, 1972. Qualitative analysis of unilateral spatial neglect in relation to laterality of cerebral lesions. *J. Neurol. Neurosurg. Psychiatry* 35:545–550.

GAZZANIGA, M., and E. LÀDAVAS, 1987. Disturbances in spatial attention following lesion or disconnection of the right parietal lobe. In *Neurophysiological and Neuropsychological Aspects of Spatial Neglect*, M. Jeannerod, ed. Amsterdam: North Holland, pp. 203–213.

GILCHRIST, I. D., G. W. HUMPHREYS, and M. J. RIDDOCH, 1996. Grouping and extinction: Evidence for low-level modulation of visual selection. *Cogn. Neuropsychol.* 13(8):1223–1249.

GIROTTI, F., M. CASAZZA, M. MUSICCO, and G. AVANZINI, 1983. Oculomotor disorders in cortical lesions in man: The role of unilateral neglect. *Neuropsychologia* 21(5):543–553.

GRABOWECKY, M., L. C. ROBERTSON, and A. TREISMAN, 1993. Preattentive processes guide visual search: Evidence from patients with unilateral visual neglect. *J. Cogn. Neurosci.* 5(3):288–302.

GRAZIANO, M., and C. G. GROSS, 1996. Multiple pathways for processing visual space. In *Attention and Performance XVI*, T. Inui and J. L. McClelland, eds. Cambridge, Mass.: Bradford Book, MIT Press, pp. 181–207.

GRAZIANO, M. S. A., G. S. YAP, and C. G. GROSS, 1994. Coding of visual space by premotor neurons. *Science* 266:1054–1057.

GUARIGLIA, C., and G. ANTONUCCI, 1992. Personal and extrapersonal space: A case of neglect dissociation. *Neuropsychologia* 30(11):1001–1009.

HALLIGAN, P. W., and J. C. MARSHALL, 1989. Is neglect (only) lateral? A quadrant analysis of line cancellation. *J. Clin. Exp. Neuropsychol.* 11:793–798.

HALLIGAN, P. W., and J. C. MARSHALL, 1991. Left neglect for near but not far space in man. *Nature* 350(6318):498–500.

HALLIGAN, P. W., and J. C. MARSHALL, 1993. When two is one: A case study of spatial parsing in visual neglect. *Perception* 22:309–312.

HALLIGAN, P. W., and J. C. MARSHALL, 1994. Toward a principled explanation of unilateral neglect. *Cogn. Neuropsychol.* 11(2):167–206.

HEILMAN, K. M., D. BOWERS, E. VALENSTEIN, and R. T. WATSON, 1987. Hemispace and hemispatial neglect. In *Neurophysiological and Neuropsychological Aspects of Spatial Neglect*, M. Jeannerod, ed. Amsterdam: Elsevier, pp. 115–150.

HILLIS, A. E., T. MORDKOFF, and A. CARAMAZZA, in press. Mechanisms of spatial attention revealed by hemispatial neglect. *Cortex.*

HILLIS, A. E., and B. RAPP, 1998. Unilateral spatial neglect in dissociable frames of reference: A comment on Farah, Brunn, Wong, Wallace and Carpenter. *Neuropsychologia* 36(11):1257–1262.

HILLIS, A. E., B. RAPP, L. BENZING, and A. CARAMAZZA, 1998. Dissociable coordinate frames of unilateral neglect: "Viewer-centered" neglect. *Brain and Cog.* 37:491–526.

HINTON, G. E., 1981. A parallel computation that assigns canonical object-based frames of reference, *Proceedings of the 7th International Joint Conference on Artificial Intelligence* Vancouver, pp. 683–685.

HORNAK, J., 1992. Ocular exploration in the dark by patients with visual neglect. *Neuropsychologia* 30(2):547–552.

HUMPHREYS, G. W., and M. J. RIDDOCH, 1994. Attention to within-object and between-object spatial representations: Multiple sites for visual selection. *Cogn. Neuropsychol.* 11(2): 207–241.

HUMPHREYS, G. W., and M. J. RIDDOCH, 1995. Separate coding of space within and between perceptual objects: Evidence from unilateral visual neglect. *Cogn. Neuropsychol.* 12(3):283–312.

ISHIAI, S., T. FURUKAWA, and H. TSUKAGOSHI, 1989. Visuospatial processes of line bisection and the mechanisms underlying spatial neglect. *Brain* 112:1485–1502.

KARNATH, H.-O., 1997. Neural encoding of space in egocentric coordinates. In *Parietal Lobe Contributions to Orientation in 3-D Space*, P. Thier and H.-O. Karnath, eds. Heidelberg: Springer-Verlag, pp. 497–520.

KARNATH, H.-O., K. CHRIST, and W. HARTJE, 1993. Decrease of contralateral neglect by neck muscle vibration and spatial orientation of the trunk midline. *Brain* 116:383–396.

KARNATH, H.-O., and M. FETTER, 1995. Ocular space exploration in the dark and its relation to subjective and objective body orientation in neglect patients with parietal lesions. *Neuropsychologia* 33(3):371–377.

KARNATH, H.-O., M. FETTER, and J. DICHGANS, 1996. Ocular exploration of space as a function of neck proprioceptive and vestibular input: Observations in normal subjects and patients with spatial neglect after parietal lesions. *Exp. Brain Res.* 109:333–342.

KARNATH, H.-O., M. FETTER, and M. NIEMEIER, 1996. Disentangling gravitational, environmental and egocentric reference frames in spatial neglect. *J. Cogn. Neurosci.* 10(6):680–690.

KARNATH, H.-O., P. SCHENKEL, and B. FISHER, 1991. Trunk orientation as the determining factor of the contralateral deficit in the neglect syndrome and as the physical anchor of the internal representation of body orientation in space. *Brain* 114:1997–2014.

KINSBOURNE, M., 1977. Hemi-neglect and hemisphere rivalry. In *Hemi-inattention and Hemispheric Specialization: Advances in Neurology*, Vol. 18, E. Weinstein and R. Friedland, eds. New York: Raven Press, pp. 41–49.

KINSBOURNE, M., 1987. Mechanisms of unilateral neglect. In *Neurophysiological and Neuropsychological Aspects of Spatial Neglect*, M. Jeannerod ed. Amsterdam: North Holland, pp. 69–86.

KOOISTRA, C. A, and K. M. HEILMAN, 1989. Hemispatial visual inattention masquerading as hemianopia. *Neurology* 39:1125–1127.

KRAMER, A. F., and S. HAHN, 1996. Splitting the beam: Distribution of attention over noncontiguous regions of the visual field. *Psychol. Sci.* 6(6):381–386.

LÀDAVAS, E., 1987. Is hemispatial deficit produced by right parietal damage associated with retinal or gravitational coordinates. *Brain* 110:167–180.

LÀDAVAS, E., M. CARLETTI, and G. GORI, 1994. Automatic and voluntary orienting of attention in patients with visual neglect: Horizontal and vertical dimensions. *Neuropsychologia* 32(10):1195–1208.

LÀDAVAS, E., G. DI PELLEGRINO, A. FARNE, and G. ZELONI, 1998. Neuropsychological evidence of an integrated visuotactile representation of peripersonal space in humans. *J. Cog. Neurosci.* 10(5):581–589.

LÀDAVAS, E., A. PETRONIO, and C. UMILTÀ, 1990. The deployment of visual attention in the intact field of hemineglect patients. *Cortex* 26:307–317.

LYNCH, J. C., and J. W. MCLAREN, 1989. Deficits of visual attention and saccadic eye movements after lesions of parietooccipital cortex in monkeys. *J. Neurophysiol.* 61(1):74.

MAGUIRE, E. A., 1997. The cerebral representation of space: Insights from functional imaging data. *Trends Cogn. Sci.* 1(2):62–68.

MATTINGLEY, J. B., J. L. BRADSHAW, and J. A. BRADSHAW, 1994. Horizontal visual motion modulates focal attention in left unilateral spatial neglect. *J. Neurol. Neurosurg. Psych.* 57:1228–1235.

MATTINGLEY, J. B., J. L. BRADSHAW, and J. G. PHILLIPS, 1992. Impairments of movement initiation and execution in unilateral neglect. *Brain* 115:1849–1874.

MATTINGLEY, J. B., G. DAVID, and J. DRIVER, 1997. Preattentive filling in of visual surfaces in parietal extinction. *Science* 275:671–674.

MATTINGLEY, J. B., and J. DRIVER, 1997. Distinguishing sensory and motor deficits after parietal damage: An evaluation of response selection biases in unilateral neglect. In *Parietal Contributions to Orientation in 3-D Space*, P. Thier and H.-O. Karnath, eds. Heidelberg: Springer-Verlag, pp. 309–338.

MATTINGLEY, J. B., M. HUSAIN, C. RORDEN, C. KENNARD, and J. DRIVER, 1998. Motor role of human inferior parietal lobe revealed in unilateral neglect patients. *Nature* 392:179–182.

MCGLINCHEY-BERROTH, R., 1997. Visual information processing in hemispatial neglect. *Trends Cogn. Sci.* 1(3):91–97.

MEADOR, K. J., R. T. WATSON, D. BOWERS, and K. M. HEILMAN, 1986. Hypometria with hemispatial and limb motor neglect. *Brain* 109:293–305.

MENNEMEIER, M., A. CHATTERJEE, and K. M. HEILMAN, 1994. A comparison of the influences of body and environment-centered reference frames on neglect. *Brain* 117:1013–1021.

MENNEMEIER, M., E. WERTMAN, and K. M. HEILMAN, 1992. Neglect of near peripersonal space. *Brain* 115:37–50.

MILNER, A. D., and M. HARVEY, 1995. Distortion of size perception in visuospatial neglect. *Curr. Biol.* 5(1):85–89.

MILNER, A. D., M. HARVEY, R. C. ROBERTS, and S. V. FORSTER, 1993. Line bisection errors in visual neglect: Misguided action or size distortion? *Neuropsychologia* 31(1):39–49.

MILNER, A. D., 1997. Neglect, extinction, and the cortical streams of visual processing. In *Parietal Contributions to Orientation in 3-D Space*, P. Thier and H.-O. Karnath, eds. Heidelberg: Springer-Verlag, pp. 3–22.

MOSCOVITCH, M., and M. BEHRMANN, 1994. Coding of spatial information in the somatosensory system: Evidence from patients with right parietal lesions. *J. Cogn. Neurosci.* 6(2):151–155.

MOZER, M. C., and M. BEHRMANN, 1990. On the interaction of selective attention and lexical knowledge: A connectionist account of neglect dyslexia. *J. Cogn. Neurosci.* 2(2):96–123.

NICHELLI, P., A. A. VENNERI, R. PENTORE, and R. CUBELLI, 1993. Horizontal and vertical neglect dyslexia. *Brain Lang.* 44:264–283.

OLSON, C. R., and S. N. GETTNER, 1995. Object-centered directional selectivity in the macaque supplementary eye field. *Nature* 269:985–988.

OLSON, C. R., S. N. GETTNER, and L. TREMBLAY, 1998. Representation of allocentric space in the monkey frontal lobe. In *Spatial Functions of the Hippocampal Formation and Parietal Cortex*, N. Burgess, K. Geffrey, and J. O'Keefe, eds. Oxford University Press, pp. 359–380.

PAVLOVSKAYA, M., I. GLASS, N. SOROKER, B. BLUM, and Z. GROSWASSER, 1997. Coordinate frame for pattern recognition in unilateral spatial neglect. *J. Cogn. Neurosci.* 9(6):824–834.

PERU, A., and G. PINNA, 1997. Right personal neglect following a left hemisphere stroke: A case report. *Cortex* 33:585–590.

PITZALIS, S., D. SPINELLI, and P. ZOCCOLOTTI, 1997. Vertical neglect: Behavioral and electrophysiological data. *Cortex* 33:679–688.

PIZZAMIGLIO, L., S. CAPPA, G. VALLAR, P. ZOCCOLOTTI, G. BOTTINI, P. CLURLL, C. GUARGIA, and G. ANTONUCCI, 1989. Visual neglect for far and near extra-personal space in humans. *Cortex* 25:471–477.

POUGET, A., and T. J. SEJNOWSKI, 1997a. Lesion in a basis function model of parietal cortex: Comparison with hemineglect. In *Parietal Lobe Contributions to Orientation in 3-D Space*, P. Thier and H.-O. Karnath, eds. Heidelberg: Springer-Verlag, pp. 521–538.

POUGET, A., and T. J. SEJNOWSKI, 1997b. Spatial transformations in the parietal cortex using basis functions. *J. Cogn. Neurosci.* 9(2):222–237.

RAINER, G., W. F. ASAAD, and E. K. MILLER, 1998. Memory fields of neurons in the primate prefrontal cortex. *Proc. Natl. Acad. Sci. U.S.A.* 95:15008–15013.

RATCLIFF, G., 1979. Spatial thought, mental rotation and the right cerebral hemisphere. *Neuropsychologia* 17:49–54.

REUTER-LORENZ, P., M. DRAIN, and C. HARDY-MORAIS, 1996. Object-centered attentional biases in the normal brain. *J. Cogn. Neurosci.* 8(6):540–550.

REUTER-LORENZ, P., and M. I. POSNER, 1990. Components of neglect from right-hemisphere damage: An analysis of line bisections. *Neuropsychologia* 28(4):327–333.

RIDDOCH, M. J., and G. W. HUMPHREYS, 1983. The effect of cueing on unilateral neglect. *Neuropsychologia* 21:589–599.

RIDDOCH, M. J., G. W. HUMPHREYS, L. LUCKHURST, E. BURROUGHS, and A. BATEMAN, 1995). "Paradoxical neglect": Spatial representations, hemisphere-specific activation and spatial cueing. *Cogn. Neuropsychol.* 12(6):569–604.

RIZZOLATTI, G., and A. BERTI, 1990. Neglect as a neural representation deficit. *Rev. Neurol. (Paris)* 146(10):626–634.

RIZZOLATTI, G., M. GENTILUCCI, and M. MATELLI, 1985. Selective spatial attention: One center, one circuit, or many circuits. In *Attention and Performance XI,* M. I. Posner and O. S. M. Marin, eds. Hillsdale, N.J.: Erlbaum, pp. 251–265.

RORDEN, C., J. B. MATTINGLEY, H.-O. KARNATH, and J. DRIVER, 1997. Visual extinction and prior entry: Impaired perception of temporal order with intact motion perception after unilateral parietal damage. *Neuropsychologia* 35(4):421–433.

SHELTON, P. A., D. BOWERS, and K. M. HEILMAN, 1990. Peripersonal and vertical neglect. *Brain* 113:191–205.

SNYDER, L. H., A. P. BATISTA, and R. A. ANDERSEN, 1997. Coding of intention in the posterior parietal cortex. *Nature* 386:167–170.

STONE, S. P., P. W. HALLIGAN, and R. J. GREENWOOD, 1993. The incidence of neglect phenomena and related disorders in patients with an acute right or left hemisphere stroke. *Age and Ageing* 22:46–52.

TIPPER, S. P., and M. BEHRMANN, 1996. Object-centered not scene-based visual neglect. *J. Exp. Psychol.* 22(5):1261–1278.

VALLAR, G., 1993. The anatomical basis of spatial hemineglect in humans. In *Unilateral Neglect: Clinical and Experimental Studies.* I. Robertson and J. C. Marshall, eds. Hove: Erlbaum, pp. 27–59.

VALLAR, G., 1998. Spatial hemineglect in humans. *Trends Cogn. Sci.* 2(3):87–96.

VALLAR, G., and D. PERANI, 1987. The anatomy of spatial neglect in humans. In *Neurophysiological and Neuropsychological Aspects of Spatial Neglect*, M. Jeannerod, ed. Amsterdam: Elsevier, pp. 235–258.

WALKER, R., and J. M. FINDLAY, 1997. Eye movement control in spatial- and object-based neglect. In *Parietal Lobe Contributions to Orientation in 3-D Space*, P. Thier and H.-O. Karnath, eds. Heidelberg: Springer-Verlag, pp. 201–218.

WALKER, R., J. M. FINDLAY, A. W. YOUNG, and N. B. LINCOLN, 1996. Saccadic eye movements in object-based neglect. *Cogn. Neuropsychol.* 13(4):569–615.

WALKER, R., J. M. FINDLAY, A. W. YOUNG, and J. WELCH, 1991. Disentangling neglect and hemianopia. *Neuropsychologia* 29(10):1019–1027.

WARD, R., S. GOODRICH, and J. DRIVER, 1994. Grouping reduces visual extinction: Neuropsychological evidence for weight-linkage in visual selection. *Vis. Cog.* 1(1):101–129.

WATSON, S. E., and A. F. KRAMER, 1997. Object-based visual selective attention and perceptual organization. Submitted.

YOUNG, A. W., D. J. HELLAWELL, and J. WELCH, 1991. Neglect and visual recognition. *Brain* 115:51–71.

46 Cortical Mechanisms of Visuospatial Attention in the Primate Brain

LEONARDO CHELAZZI AND MAURIZIO CORBETTA

ABSTRACT Recent functional neuroimaging studies in humans have highlighted a network of cortical regions implicated in the control of visuospatial attention. Critical nodes of this network are regions in the superior frontal and posterior parietal cortices. Single-unit recording experiments in the behaving macaque, together with a number of related functional brain imaging investigations in humans, have further demonstrated that these regions in frontal and parietal cortex house mechanisms for the sensory-controlled guidance of purposeful actions, including motor intention and spatial working memory signals. We propose that these motor intention and spatial working memory signals may correspond to the control signals for the allocation of spatial attention to visual field positions. In addition to modulating sensory processing within the dorsal visual system, control signals for attention have also been shown to bias processing in ventral extrastriate visual areas implicated in the analysis of object features by favoring the processing of objects at attended locations.

Almost without exception, the behavior of humans is governed by an orderly sequence of goals. Some of these correspond to the satisfaction of primary needs, such as providing food and liquids, while others correspond to a virtually endless list of more sophisticated activities and motives born in our modern society, such as picking a book from a bookshelf or locating the correct exit along the highway. Our moment-to-moment cognitive activity is organized around these goals. In this chapter we do not deal with what determines the succession of goals in daily life and its neural correlates. We simply take for granted that goals dominate our mental processes and overt behavior, and that several factors are involved in giving priority to one goal or another at any specific time. Rather, we discuss how implementing a certain goal leads to the selective processing of incoming sensory information—the realm of selective attention. Selective attention is defined as the cognitive function that allows the focusing of processing resources onto the sensory inputs that are relevant in a given context, and the accompanying withdrawal of resources from inputs that are irrelevant or potentially interfering. In the main, we limit our discussion to recent advancements in understanding the neural mechanisms of *visuospatial* selective attention—advancements that have been obtained by the recording of single neurons from the brain of subhuman primates and by the functional imaging of the human brain with positron emission tomography (PET) and functional magnetic resonance imaging (fMRI).

Any visual scene contains multiple objects, where each object is composed of multiple features such as color, shape, motion, and location. Although we can select objects of interest based on any feature or combination of features, the selection of visual objects by location is a powerful way of selecting behaviorally relevant visual information for object recognition. Locations are also selected in the context of a large class of visuomotor behaviors, including orienting to peripheral stimuli by eye (e.g., saccadic), arm (e.g., pointing), or hand (e.g., grasping) movements. Finally, the role of visual locations is emphasized by several theories of higher vision. For instance, Ullman has proposed that the computation of various spatial relations between objects requires the application of visual routines or processes to one or two selected stimulus locations at any given time (Ullman, 1984). The analysis of the whole visual scene therefore requires a mechanism for switching the focus of processing from one location to another. Similarly, Treisman's feature integration theory (Treisman and Gelade, 1980; Treisman, 1991) proposes that the perception of objects in cluttered visual scenes is critically dependent upon an attentional mechanism that selects an object location and binds the features at that location into a unified object percept. Selection of spatial locations, therefore, appears to have broad implications for both perception and action.

One class of paradigms (a class that has enjoyed constant success over the last twenty years) used in exploring visual spatial attention is based on controlled manipulations of stimulus expectancy at specific visual field locations. In these paradigms, observers are induced to focus

LEONARDO CHELAZZI Dipartimento di Scienze Neurologiche e della Visione, University of Verona, Verona, Italy
MAURIZIO CORBETTA Department of Neurology, Radiology, Anatomy and Neurobiology, and the McDonnell Center for Studies of Higher Brain Functions, Washington University, St. Louis, Mo.

their attention on stimuli presented at one location in the visual field and to ignore stimuli presented at other locations while maintaining their gaze on a central fixation target. The direction of the subject's attention can be controlled in two ways: either by means of symbolic cues, usually presented at the center of gaze, in which case we speak of endogenous orienting of attention (e.g., Posner, 1980); or by means of peripheral cues that summon attention automatically to the cued location, i.e., exogenous orienting (e.g., Jonides and Yantis, 1988). Finally, in some studies, instead of using a trial-by-trial cueing procedure, subjects are asked to maintain their attention aligned with a particular spatial location throughout a block of trials, i.e., sustained attention (Van Voorhis and Hillyard, 1977; Tassinari et al., 1987).

Performance is typically enhanced at the attended location, and impaired at the ignored location(s), relative to when attention is uncommitted or evenly distributed across the visual field in advance of stimulus presentation (Posner, 1980). These changes in performance have been shown not only for the simple detection of suprathreshold light stimuli, but also for the detection of near-threshold stimuli and for different types of stimulus identification (e.g., Bashinski and Bacharach, 1984; Downing, 1988). The latter observation is particularly relevant, for it shows that spatial attention has access to functional modules responsible for the specialized processing of visual features and for object perception.

When trying to understand the brain mechanisms underlying spatially selective attention, it is helpful to distinguish the control, or source, signals responsible for directing attention toward a given location from the modulatory effects exerted by these signals on the processing of incoming visual stimuli (attentional modulation of sensory activity). These two sets of signals have different time courses—by definition, control signals must precede the modulation of sensory-driven activity—and, possibly, different distribution within the brain. For example, while the modulation of sensory-driven activity occurs in visual areas implicated in the analysis of the various stimulus features, source signals may additionally involve non–strictly visual areas, which encode and maintain these signals even in the absence of any stimulus in the scene.

In recent years, neuroimaging studies in humans have shown that a network of cortical regions in frontal and parietal cortex is active when attention is directed to visual spatial locations. Similar regions are also recruited during the preparation/execution of eye movements, and possibly other goal-directed motor responses, and when spatial locations are actively remembered for brief periods of time (spatial working memory). Physiological recordings from single neurons in awake behaving primates have demonstrated that neurons in homologous regions show a combination of sensory, attentional, premotor, and memory signals, presumably participating in the sensorimotor transformations necessary for the control of purposeful actions. Thus, source signals implicated in the allocation of attention to a spatial location may be closely related to the intention to move toward that location (motor preparation signals) and/or to the process of actively remembering that location (working memory signals).

The allocation of attention to a spatial location also causes modulatory changes in extrastriate visual areas involved in the analysis of object features. The net effect of these changes is the amplification of neural signals representing stimuli at attended locations relative to neural signals representing stimuli at unattended locations. This relative advantage can result either from enhanced responses to stimuli at the attended location or from suppression of responses to stimuli at unattended locations, or both. We propose that the frontoparietal cortical network, in addition to participating in the sensorimotor transformations necessary for the guidance of overt behaviors, delivers the control signals that modulate activity in the ventral stream of cortical visual processing.

In the next two sections, we mainly use functional imaging data to highlight the location of frontal and parietal areas that are involved in the control of spatial attention, and single-unit data to discuss the nature of attentional signals in these areas. In the subsequent section, the effects of attention on extrastriate visual areas involved in object processing are considered.

Localization of control systems for spatially selective attention

The role of frontal and parietal cortices in the control of spatial attention had long been recognized on the basis of observations with brain-damaged individuals showing attention-related deficits (hemineglect and extinction) and the analysis of the behavioral disturbances following localized brain lesions in nonhuman primates. For instance, Mesulam (1981, 1990) conceptualized spatial orienting as a complex behavior composed of perceptual, exploratory, and motivational components, with each of these components localized to different cortical regions. In particular, posterior parietal cortex was thought to be involved in the spatial (perceptual) encoding of stimuli, frontal cortex in planning exploratory eye and hand movements toward those stimuli, and cingulate cortex in providing the motivational tone necessary for purposeful orienting. Posner and his colleagues (Posner et al., 1984; Posner and Petersen, 1990) suggested that the allocation of attention to locations/objects involves multiple computational stages, and that these stages may be mapped onto different cortical and subcortical regions. Specifically, directing attention from one object to the next involves disengaging attention from the current object of interest, moving attention onto the new object of interest, and engaging it there. Disengage, move, and engage operations of attention were respectively localized to posterior parietal cortex, superior colliculus, and pulvinar nucleus of the thalamus.

These ideas about visuospatial attention have been more recently tested by recording hemodynamic signals from the living human brain with PET during the performance of cognitive tasks in which subjects covertly directed their attention to peripheral visual stimuli in order to perform visual detection or discrimination. Different studies have manipulated spatial attention in various ways. In some studies subjects were cued to direct attention to different peripheral visual locations to detect the onset of a visual stimulus (Corbetta et al., 1993) or to discriminate its identity (Nobre et al., 1997). In others, subjects voluntarily sustained attention at a single peripheral location to discriminate target stimuli presented in a temporal sequence of distractors (Heinze et al., 1994; Woldorff et al., 1997) or to detect certain target features (e.g., a change in stimulus orientation; Vandenberghe et al., 1996, 1997). Finally, some studies varied the degree of attentional commitment to peripheral stimuli (Corbetta et al., 1995; Vandenberghe et al., 1997). In most experiments sensory activity engendered by the visual stimulation and the motor activity related to the preparation/execution of a behavioral response were appropriately controlled to ensure that the obtained activations reflected either control signals to direct attention to a location or their modulatory effect on incoming sensory information.

Figure 46.1 summarizes these studies by projecting foci of activation localized during different peripheral attention tasks, as compared with an appropriate control condition, on a normalized brain atlas (both 3D view and corresponding surface reconstruction), developed at Washington University by Drury and Van Essen (Drury et al., 1996; Van Essen and Drury, 1997) (see also color plate 30). The control condition in each study was either visual fixation or passive presentation of the same stimuli as in the peripheral attention task. Despite differences in the details of each experiment, and anatomical differences between groups of subjects, a common network of frontal and parietal cortical regions seem to be recruited when people direct attention to peripheral stimuli without moving their eyes. Regions of activation include the postcentral and intraparietal sulcus in parietal cortex, and the precentral sul-

cus/gyrus and the posterior tip of the superior frontal sulcus in frontal cortex. Other regions that have been less consistently activated across studies are the cingulate gyrus, the medial frontal gyrus, and the superior temporal gyrus/sulcus. More recently, a more precise anatomical localization of these functional regions in relationship to specific sulcal or gyral landmarks has been obtained by recording task-related hemodynamic changes with fMRI in single subjects and by projecting the functional data on surface representations of their own brain (see, for example, figure 46.4).

It should be noted that these regions represent areas that are commonly active across experiments. Moreover, in each experiment specific visual and motor areas are active as a function of task demands. Interestingly, tasks that require the simple detection of peripheral stimuli seem to involve predominantly areas of the dorsal visual system. In contrast, tasks requiring the discrimination of objects at peripheral locations involve regions within both the dorsal and ventral stream of processing; and the frontoparietal network is active along with multiple occipitotemporal regions specialized in object processing (Heinze et al., 1994; Corbetta et al., 1995; Vandenberghe et al., 1996, 1997; Woldorff et al., 1997). The only exception to this rule is one study (Heinze et al., 1994), in which subjects discriminated peripheral shapes positioned in the upper visual field. In this study only activations in occipitotemporal cortex contralateral to the direction of attention were reported, without accompanying activations in posterior parietal cortex. Woldorff and colleagues (1997) repeated the same experiment by positioning the stimuli in the lower visual field, however, and obtained robust dorsal, frontoparietal activations. The reason for this discrepancy remains unclear. One interpretation of these general findings is that the frontoparietal network is important for the allocation of attention to peripheral objects, and for their localization, independent of the type of object identification task. Furthermore, selective hemodynamic modulations have been recorded in areas of the ventral visual system, contralaterally to the direction of attention, during object discrimination tasks performed at peripheral locations (Heinze et al., 1994; Vandenberghe et al., 1996, 1997; Woldorff et al., 1997). Correspondingly, the allocation of attention facilitates object discrimination at attended locations (Hawkins, Shafto, and Richardson, 1988; Downing, 1988). The dorsal frontal and parietal regions may therefore be the source of selective spatial biasing signals that enhance visual processing in areas of the ventral visual system specialized for object analysis. Later in this chapter we consider the neuronal correlates of these spatially selective modulatory effects in the ventral visual system.

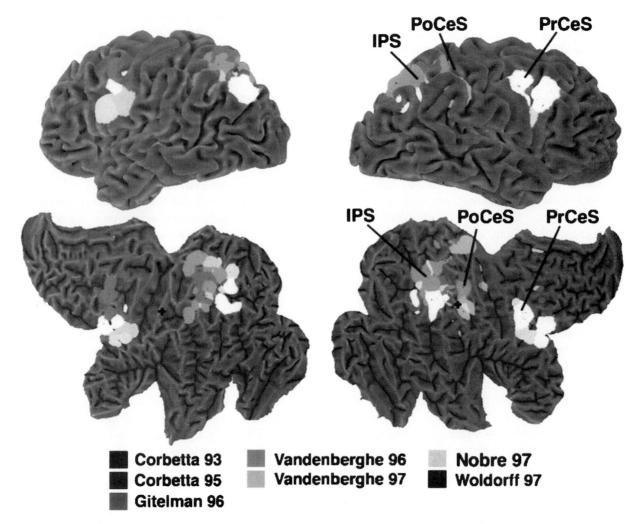

FIGURE 46.1 Frontoparietal cortical network during peripheral visual attention. Common regions of activation across studies include the intraparietal (IPS), postcentral, and precentral sulcus (PrCeS). Foci of activity in each study were mapped onto 3D brain and 2D surface reconstruction of Visible Man brain atlas (Drury et al., 1996). The foci are spatially smoothed with a 10-mm radius filter to account for methodological differences across laboratories in entering the standard atlas space (Talairach and Tournoux, 1988; Van Essen and Drury, 1997).

Overall, these studies support the idea that a common network of parietal and frontal areas is recruited when the focus of attention is directed to peripheral visual objects/ locations, independent of eye movements. Similar regions seem to be recruited when attention is dynamically moved to different locations or maintained for a prolonged time at the same location (shifting vs. sustained attention). Similarly, the same areas are engaged when attention is voluntarily directed toward a visual object and when it is reflexively drawn to its salient visual features (endogenous vs. exogenous attention). While it is possible that some degree of anatomo-functional segregation will eventually emerge within this cortical network by comparing different modes of spatial attention recruitment in the same subject, the strong anatomical overlap across studies suggests that these regions may play a general role in the allocation of attention to spatial locations.

Although the evidence reviewed so far is quite compelling in linking the control systems for spatially selective attention to neuronal activity within a frontoparietal network, these same cortical regions can have other roles in nonspatial forms of attention. This is suggested by some recent functional imaging studies. In one study (Le, Pardo, and Hu, 1998), for instance, subjects were presented with a single stimulus (a colored shape) at the center of gaze, and in separate blocks they were required to perform one of three different tasks: (1) sustained attention to the color of the stimulus, while ignoring its shape; (2) sustained attention to the shape of the stimulus, while ignoring its color; (3) continuous shifts of attention to the color and to the shape of the stimulus in alternating trials. The critical comparison was between the sustained (color or shape) and the shift condition. Regional blood oxygenation in the cerebellum and posterior parietal cortex was measured with fMRI. Attention shifting between visual features produced significant activation bilaterally in superior parietal lobule (extending into the intraparietal sulcus), cuneus, and precuneus, as well as in right lateral cerebellum. Thus, parietal regions may control switches between visual representations even without changes in spatial location. An analogous conclusion has been reached in another study (Lumer, Friston, and Rees, 1998) exploring the neural correlates of perceptual rivalry. In binocular rivalry, dissimilar images are presented to the two eyes and perception alternates spontaneously between each monocular view. Functional brain imaging with fMRI was used to assess the mechanisms underlying the transition between the two alternating perceptual states. Activations specific to shifts in perceptual experience were found in the right inferior and superior parietal lobules and in the right inferior frontal cortex. The right superior parietal activation overlaps with a region active for peripheral attention. Although it is unclear why mechanisms for shifting between visual representations underlying perceptual rivalry should map at least in part onto the same network of areas implicated in visuospatial attention, it is interesting that both cognitive phenomena entail suppression of visual information from conscious perception—information presented at unattended locations in spatial attention tasks, and information relative to either monocular view in binocular rivalry. These frontoparietal cortical networks may therefore play a more general role in regulating the access of competing visual representations to perceptual awareness.

Neuronal signals in frontoparietal cortical networks for spatially selective attention

Data from electrophysiological experiments in the awake monkey can help clarify the neuronal signals in brain networks for spatial attention revealed by functional imaging studies in humans. Single-unit recordings in monkey have shown that spatially directed attention has widespread effects on the responses of neurons in a large number of cortical regions, both in the occipitoparietal and occipitotemporal streams of visual processing, and in functional regions of the frontal lobe. We consider first studies that have investigated how the allocation of attention modifies the neuronal response to visual stimuli during detection or localization tasks (attentional modulation of sensory response); later, we consider neuronal signals that may underlie the allocation and dynamics of attention across the visual field (source or control signals).

ATTENTIONAL MODULATIONS OF SENSORY RESPONSE DURING SPATIALLY SELECTIVE ATTENTION TASKS Cells in different subdivisions of the posterior parietal cortex of the macaque give enhanced responses to a receptive field (RF) stimulus when the animal voluntarily attends to the stimulus to detect its dimming, compared to when the animal's attention is directed to the foveal target (figure 46.2, top) (Robinson, Goldberg, and Stanton, 1978; Bushnell, Goldberg, and Robinson, 1981; Colby, Duhamel, and Goldberg, 1996). These experiments are usually carried out by instructing the animal to maintain attention at one location for prolonged periods of time. The same enhancement is obtained when the RF stimulus is the target for an immediate or delayed saccade (e.g., Colby, Duhamel, and Goldberg, 1996). These effects have been observed within tissue of the lateral bank of the intraparietal sulcus, area LIP, and nearby gyrus of the inferior parietal lobule, area 7a. A similar enhancement of visual responses has also been observed within a subdivision of the pulvinar nucleus of the thalamus, Pdm, which is interconnected with posterior parietal cortex and has been proposed to play a critical role in selective attention (Petersen, Robinson, and Keys, 1985; Robinson and Petersen, 1992). Enhanced visual responses in area LIP and 7a, and in the pulvinar, have been interpreted as correlates of control signals to direct attention to relevant stimulus locations (Wurtz, Goldberg, and Robinson, 1982; Colby, Duhamel, and Goldberg, 1996). However, these effects are unlikely to reflect the voluntary (or endogenous) allocation of attention to a peripheral location, since attention is presumably deployed at the target location prior to stimulus onset. Other neural signals must necessarily mediate the cognitive process of directing the focus of attention to the location of the stimulus before its appearance. More likely, these modulations reflect the neural correlate of a processing facilitation for sensory stimuli that are behaviorally relevant in a given context.

Interestingly, response modulations of this type have been observed in other cortical and subcortical structures, like the superior colliculus (Goldberg and Wurtz, 1972) and the frontal eye field (FEF; Goldberg and Bushnell, 1981; Wurtz and Mohler, 1976), that are connected to parietal cortex and are more closely involved in the preparation and execution of saccadic eye movements. In other words, the neural facilitation for the processing of target stimuli seems to propagate downstream toward areas involved in response selection and initiation. The enhancement in the FEF was initially reported only when selection of the RF stimulus was contingent on the execution of a saccadic eye movement toward its location, suggesting that it was related specifically to selection of the target for a goal-directed motor response

Fixation

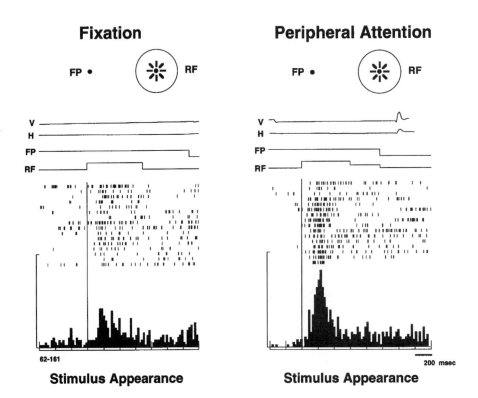

Peripheral Attention

Delayed Saccade

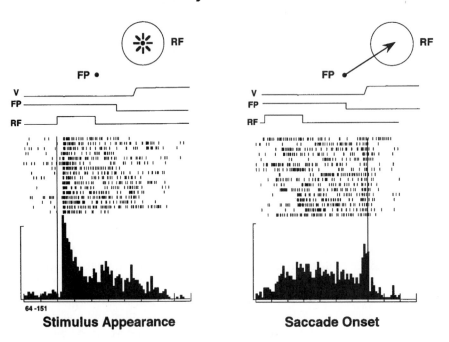

rather than to spatial attention per se (Goldberg and Bushnell, 1981; Wurtz and Mohler, 1976). This notion, however, might have to be modified. In a series of experiments, Schall and his associates have recently investigated the role of FEF neurons in selecting a target

presented in an array of distractors (Schall and Hanes, 1993; Schall et al., 1995a; Thompson et al., 1996). It was shown that visuomovement neurons in FEF of the macaque signal whether the stimulus in their RF is a target or a distractor, and that this effect is present even

FIGURE 46.2   Response properties in monkey area LIP. Top: Enhancement of the visual response in a single cell when the stimulus becomes behaviorally significant. On the left, the monkey simply fixates a central point while an irrelevant peripheral stimulus appears in the receptive field. On the right, the monkey still fixates the central point but must now attend to the peripheral stimulus to detect a slight dimming. The same stimulus is presented in both tasks, but the response is doubled when the stimulus is made task-relevant. Each panel shows a raster and histogram synchronized on stimulus onset. In the raster display, vertical tic marks indicate the time when an action potential occurred, and each horizontal line shows activity during a single trial. Successive correctly performed trials are aligned on the vertical trigger line. The histogram calibration bar at far left signifies a firing rate of 100 spikes/s. Time lines show horizontal and vertical eye position for a single trial and the time of onset, dimming, and offset for the receptive field stimulus. Bottom: Visual, memory, and presaccadic signals in a single LIP neuron. In the delayed saccade task, the monkey fixates a central point and a visual stimulus is presented in the receptive field for 400 ms (left). After a variable delay, the fixation point is extinguished and the monkey makes a saccade to the location where the stimulus had appeared (right). The same set of trials is aligned on stimulus appearance (left) and on saccade onset (right). Separate visual and motor bursts are seen in each trial, as well as tonic activity during the memory period. (Adapted from Goldberg, Colby, and Duhamel, 1990, and Colby and Duhamel, 1996.)

when eye movements to the target are not allowed (Thompson et al., 1997). Similarly, Kodaka, Mikami, and Kubota (1997) recently provided evidence that the visual response of FEF neurons is enhanced when a stimulus presented at an attended location is detected through a manual response. Frontal regions therefore may be involved as well as posterior parietal cortex in the attentive processing of visual targets during detection or localization tasks.

In the same parietal areas that show a visual enhancement effect during sustained peripheral attention, suppressive effects related to target detection have also been documented during visual orienting tasks in which attention is cued to different locations on each trial. Robinson, Bowman, and Kertzman (1995) have shown that responses of neurons in areas LIP and 7a to a RF stimulus are reduced when the stimulus follows a visual cue presented at the same or at a nearby location. Although peripheral cueing did sometimes result in enhanced responses to the forthcoming target, the more common effect was a response reduction. A similar decrease of responses to expected stimuli, compared to unexpected stimuli, has been observed by Steinmetz and his colleagues (Steinmetz et al., 1994; Steinmetz and Constantinidis, 1995) recording from area 7a during a spatial version of a delayed match-to-sample task. Neuronal responses to matching stimuli (at the cued location) were

considerably reduced compared to responses to nonmatching stimuli (at uncued locations), even when several nonmatching stimuli had intervened.

One interpretation of the above results is that the increased responses to unexpected stimuli in the visual field may be part of a mechanism responsible for redirecting attention in space, i.e., disengaging focal attention from its current focus. This type of attentional signal could provide a way to redirect attention to new, salient locations in the visual field, but cannot be the neuronal correlate of an endogenous voluntary signal that allows the organism to direct attention to any arbitrary location in the visual field irrespective of its sensory saliency.

It is important to note that, among other possible variables, one factor that could explain the prevalence of suppression in the latter studies compared to the enhanced effects in other studies (Robinson, Goldberg, and Stanton, 1978; Bushnell, Goldberg, and Robinson, 1981; Colby, Duhamel, and Goldberg, 1996) could be the use of peripheral, local cues. It is well known from psychophysical experiments in humans that peripheral cues, in addition to engendering facilitory effects due to the automatic capture of attention toward the cued location, also produce robust inhibitory effects that tend to favor unstimulated locations in the visual field (a phenomenon known as "inhibition of return"; see, for example, Posner and Cohen, 1984; Maylor and Hockey, 1985; Tassinari et al., 1987; Rafal et al., 1989; Tassinari et al., 1994; Rafal, Egly, and Rhodes, 1994; Tipper et al., 1994; Abrams and Dobkin, 1994; Reuter-Lorenz, Jha, and Rosenquist, 1996).

PUTATIVE CONTROL SIGNALS FOR SPATIALLY SELECTIVE ATTENTION   Two general ideas have been put forward to explain how the brain directs attention to locations and/or objects. In virtually all tasks, the deliberate allocation of attention to a position in the visual field may require some form of active memory of the location to be attended (spatial working memory). Correspondingly, control signals for selective attention in space may functionally overlap with spatial working memory signals (Desimone and Duncan, 1995; Desimone, 1996). In addition, the tight linkage in natural vision between attention and eye movements (and action systems in general) suggests that the covert allocation of attention to a location may be closely related to the intention to move toward the same location (Rizzolatti et al., 1987; Rizzolatti and Craighero, 1998). In other words, neuronal signals for movements of attention may coincide with preparatory motor signals. These two sets of explanations are not mutually exclusive, as either mechanism may be critical under certain behavioral conditions.

Neurons in frontal and parietal cortex have long been shown to display a pattern of activity that is well suited to store a mental representation (working memory) of a location in space in order to bridge a temporal gap in the task sequence. Tasks used in a number of studies to demonstrate this capability of neurons require the monkey to maintain the location of a briefly presented peripheral stimulus in memory during a blank delay interval, and then to produce a motor response (e.g., a saccade) to the remembered location of the stimulus upon presentation of a go signal (e.g., the offset of the fixation point). In parietal cortex location-specific activity in the retention interval of oculomotor and/or skeletomotor tasks has been demonstrated both in area LIP and 7a (Andersen, Essick, and Siegel, 1987; Barash et al., 1991; Colby, Duhamel, and Goldberg, 1996; Constantinidis and Steinmetz, 1996), while in the frontal lobe a similar activity has been shown in premotor cortex (di Pellegrino and Wise, 1991, 1993), in dorsolateral prefrontal cortex (Niki and Watanabe, 1976; Funahashi, Bruce, and Goldman-Rakic, 1989; Quintana and Fuster, 1992; Funahashi, Chafee, and Goldman-Rakic, 1993; Rao, Rainer, and Miller, 1997), and in the FEF (Bruce and Goldberg, 1985). Interestingly, while sustained activity specifying a location seems to be abolished by intervening stimuli in area 7a (Constantinidis and Steinmetz, 1996), the same activity survives the interference exerted by intervening stimuli in dorsolateral prefrontal cortex (di Pellegrino and Wise, 1993). Regions in frontal and posterior parietal cortex implicated in spatial working memory are likely to be part (together with other cortical and subcortical structures; Selemon and Goldman-Rakic, 1988) of a distributed network contributing to this function, consistent with the rich reciprocal connections between prefrontal and posterior parietal tissue (e.g., Petrides and Pandya, 1984; Barbas, 1988; Cavada and Goldman-Rakic, 1989; Schall et al., 1995b).

A functional link between spatial working memory and control signals for the allocation of attention has been recently supported by recordings in parietal area LIP. Colby and her colleagues (Colby, Duhamel, and Goldberg, 1996) have shown that neurons in LIP display elevated background firing rates both when the animal has to remember the location of a target presented in the RF of the recorded neuron within the context of a delayed saccade task, and when the animal can anticipate the onset of a relevant visual stimulus inside the RF in a peripheral attention task. This is strong evidence that forming and storing a mental representation of a relevant location in space is a critical component not only in traditional spatial working memory tasks, but also in tasks requiring the deliberate allocation of attention to a specific region of the visual field.

Additional evidence supporting a functional relationship between spatial working memory signals and spatial attentional control signals comes from functional neuroimaging studies in humans. In particular, a number of PET and fMRI studies in humans have revealed activations in posterior parietal and lateral frontal regions (particularly in the right hemisphere) under task conditions requiring the storage and manipulation of spatial information in working memory (see Ungerleider, 1995; Smith and Jonides, 1997, for reviews). In parietal cortex, these activations were typically centered around the intraparietal sulcus and extended into the superior and inferior parietal lobules. In the frontal lobe, activations were usually localized near the precentral sulcus, superior frontal sulcus, and more anteriorly in lateral prefrontal cortex. Figure 46.3 compares regions of activation during studies of peripheral attention (as in figure 46.1) and selected studies of spatial working memory (Jonides et al., 1993; Courtney et al., 1996, 1997, 1998; Owen et al., 1996; Smith et al., 1995; Smith, Jonides, and Koeppe, 1996) (see also color plate 31). All working memory studies involved conditions in which spatial locations were actively remembered and control conditions for sensorimotor factors. The resulting foci of activation were derived by comparing memory conditions against the control condition. The listed studies have been selected because they report the foci of activation in a standard anatomical space that can be used for comparison across conditions and experiments (Talairach and Tournoux 1988). There appears to be strong overlap in posterior parietal cortex, weaker overlap in the precentral region, and preferential activation of the prefrontal cortex during spatial working memory tasks. Interestingly, prefrontal cortex is active in some peripheral attention tasks that require sustained attention (e.g., Vandenberghe et al., 1997), but not in tasks that involve rapid shifts of attention (Corbetta et al., 1993, 1995; Nobre et al., 1997). It is therefore possible that frontal mechanisms of spatial working memory are preferentially involved when locations are maintained on-line for a substantial amount of time, but less so during rapid shifts of attention that occur during spatial cueing tasks. In addition, the recruitment of anterior prefrontal cortex in typical spatial working memory tasks might be due to a greater demand on central executive functions (manipulation of spatial information) in most of these tasks compared to spatial attention tasks.

An important and related issue is whether areas in frontal and parietal cortex that generate and maintain selective spatial signals for the allocation of attention are better conceptualized as "abstract" spatial maps or as nodes of specific sensorimotor systems necessary to perform stimulus guided actions. One possible schema

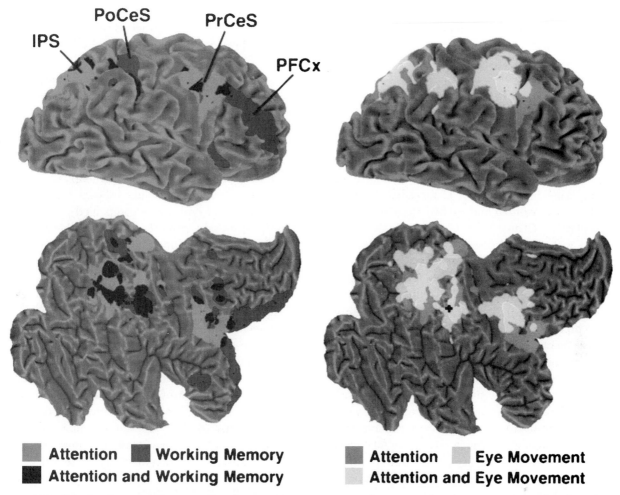

IPS PoCeS PrCeS PFCx

▨ Attention	▨ Working Memory
▨ Attention and Working Memory	

▨ Attention	▨ Eye Movement
▨ Attention and Eye Movement	

FIGURE 46.3 Peripheral attention vs. spatial working memory vs. saccadic eye movement across studies. 3D and surface reconstruction of right hemisphere of the Visible Man brain atlas. Left: Regions active for peripheral attention (red), regions active for spatial working memory (blue), and regions of overlap (magenta). Studies of attention are the same as those in figure 46.1; for studies of spatial working memory, see text. Note the remarkable overlap in parietal cortex, partial overlap in precentral region, and exclusive activation of prefrontal cortex (PFCx) for spatial working memory. Other anatomical abbreviations are as in figure 46.1. Right: Comparison between peripheral attention (red) and saccadic eye movements (green) (see text for list of studies). Note the strong overlap (yellow) in both parietal and precentral region. There is no activation in prefrontal cortex.

of the former idea could be that parietal cortex may contain a map of extrapersonal space in which potential locations of interest are "highlighted" by working memory signals from prefrontal cortex. The spatial output of this representation is abstract in the sense that it is not intimately related to any specific action system. This output can be critical across a variety of perceptual tasks, e.g., to gate sensory responses in the ventral visual system during object recognition (Desimone and Duncan, 1995) and/or to conjoin the elemental features of an object (Treisman, 1996). Likewise, it could be critical to initiate a variety of visuomotor responses, e.g., saccadic or reaching movements to a target location. Alternatively, these spatial representations may be intrinsic to specific visuomotor mechanisms for sen-

sory guided responses (e.g., looking, reaching, grasping, navigation).

A view originally proposed by Rizzolatti and colleagues envisioned that neuronal signals necessary to allocate attention to a visual field location correspond to the intention to move the eyes toward the same location, i.e., to preparatory motor activity in spatial oculomotor maps (Rizzolatti et al., 1987; Sheliga, Riggio, and Rizzolatti, 1994, 1995). More recent developments of this theory have generalized this idea to visuomotor systems involved in other sensory guided responses (Rizzolatti and Craighero, 1998; see below). Under this account, the sustained activity recorded during the delay saccade and peripheral attention tasks in parietal area LIP by Colby and colleagues (Colby, Duhamel, and Goldberg,

1996) would be better described as "sustained intentional activity," reflecting the preparation of an impending eye movement to that location, even when no eye movement is actually performed (Snyder, Batista, and Andersen, 1997).

There is substantial evidence supporting the general view of a tight functional relationship between mechanisms for spatial attention and oculomotor control. First, let us consider the functional properties of neurons in area LIP in posterior parietal cortex and the FEF (area 8) in prefrontal cortex of the macaque, which have long been implicated in the control of saccadic eye movements. Neurons recorded in these two areas display similar properties (Chafee and Goldman-Rakic, 1998), consistent with the dense reciprocal connections (e.g., Petrides and Pandya, 1984), and they have been classified into three distinct classes (Bruce and Goldberg, 1985; Chafee and Goldman-Rakic, 1998)–visual, visuo-movement, and movement neurons. Visual neurons have the predominant role of registering a visual event. Visuomovement neurons likely play an intermediate role in transforming a sensory event into a premotor command. Movement cells are more directly implicated in delivering command signals to subcortical structures responsible for activating the eye muscles. We have discussed how neurons in LIP and FEF are capable of encoding the behavioral relevance or saliency of a visual stimulus (see also Gottlieb, Kusunoki, and Goldberg, 1998). In addition, neurons in LIP and the FEF are able to retain location information in working memory for the guidance of delayed oculomotor responses. Thus, these regions seem to be well equipped to perform all the necessary operations to guide purposeful oculomotor responses: the selective encoding of a potential target; the maintenance of target location in memory, if required; and the delivery of command signals to trigger subcortical structures directly responsible for the control of the eye muscles (see figure 46.2, bottom). One could imagine that for neurons in areas LIP and FEF there is actually little formal difference, if any, between coding the relevance of a location of interest in the visual field and coding the intention to make a saccade toward that location.

Second, recent physiological experiments have demonstrated that control signals for location selection may indeed be oculomotor in nature. Kustov and Robinson (1996) have demonstrated that the vector of saccadic eye movements induced by microelectrical stimulation of the deep layers of the superior colliculus is deviated by the presentation of endogenous cues (e.g., a cue at fixation) directing the monkey's attention toward a visual field location during a manual detection task. Since the monkey was rewarded for maintaining accurate fixation, these findings would suggest that cognitively induced shifts of attention to a visual location manifest themselves as preparatory saccadic activity in the superior colliculus.

Third, psychophysical experiments in humans have established a tight functional relationship between attentional and oculomotor processes. During natural vision objects of interest are immediately foveated; i.e., shifts of attention in space are accompanied or immediately followed by gaze shifts. While some initial attempts provided somewhat ambiguous results (e.g., Klein, 1980), more recent experiments have shown that voluntary shifts of gaze are typically accompanied by shifts of attention toward the same location (Shepherd, Findlay, and Hockey, 1986; Hoffman and Subramaniam, 1995; Kowler et al., 1995; Deubel and Schneider, 1996) or in the same direction (Chelazzi et al., 1995). So, while it has long been known that attention can be moved across the visual field without concomitant eye movements, eye movements toward a selected visual target seem to involve necessarily the orienting of attention toward the target location.

Fourth, functional neuroimaging studies in humans have demonstrated strong functional overlap between regions of activation in parietal and frontal cortex during peripheral attention and saccadic eye movements. Figure 46.3 compares foci of activation for peripheral attention and saccadic eye movements across selected studies in the literature (Paus et al., 1993, 1995; Anderson et al., 1994; O'Driscoll et al., 1995; O'Sullivan et al., 1995; Petit et al., 1996, 1997; Sweeney et al., 1996; Luna et al., 1998) (see also color plate 31). These studies have explored the brain systems involved in visually guided, memory-guided, and conditionally guided (e.g., prelearned, cue-instructed) saccadic eye movements. Note that the overlap in parietal cortex is comparable to the one obtained with spatial working memory, whereas greater overlap is present in the precentral region. The precentral region contains the human homologue of FEF (Paus, 1996; Courtney et al., 1998). More anterior prefrontal regions (not shown) are active during memory-guided or conditional saccades (e.g., Sweeney et al., 1996; Petit et al., 1996). Corbetta and colleagues have recently compared in the same group of subjects regions of activations for attention and eye movements (Corbetta et al., 1998). Subjects were scanned either during a task in which attention was endogenously shifted to several sequential locations in order to detect visual probe stimuli, while fixation was centrally maintained, or during a task in which eye movement (and attention) shifts were performed toward the same locations. Figure 46.4 shows the functional anatomy of the two tasks in one subject after projection of the activity data on the surface

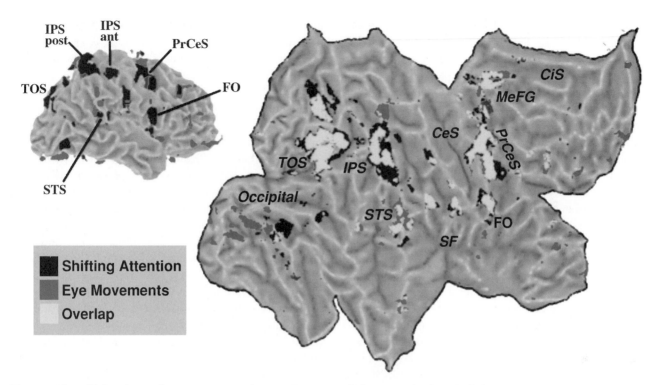

FIGURE 46.4 Shifts of spatial attention vs. oculomotor/attentional shifts in a single subject. fMRI activity projected on 3D and surface representation of the subject's own brain. Note precise localization of functional activity in relationship to sulcal and gyral landmarks. TOS = transverse occipital sulcus; IPS = intraparietal sulcus; STS = superior temporal sulcus; CeS = central sulcus; PrCeS = precentral sulcus; MeFG = medial frontal gyrus; CiS = cingulate sulcus; FO = frontal operculum. Note that the degree of overlap between attention and saccadic eye movement regions is much higher than in group data (cf. figure 46.3, right).

reconstruction of his own brain (see color plate 32). All regions active for eye movements, including the putative homologue of FEF (precentral sulcus region), supplementary eye field (SEF; medial frontal gyrus), and LIP/7a (intraparietal sulcus) were also active during the covert attention task. No region was uniquely active in one or the other condition, and the degree of overlap in each region across subjects was between 60 and 80%.

In summary, these data support a view by which control (source) attentional signals for directing the focus of processing toward a given visual field location may coincide with preparatory oculomotor signals to make a saccade toward the same location. However, one should be cautious in emphasizing this link between eye movements and spatial attention. It may turn out that, although the functional link between these two processes perhaps enjoys a privileged status, a similar functional relationship and sharing of neuronal machinery exists between spatial attention and any other system for the programming and execution of sensory controlled motor responses, such as reaching, grasping, and navigation. For instance, selective attention to an object for the purpose of reaching toward its location might correspond to premotor signals in areas involved in the control of reaching responses rather than eye movements. Several findings suggest this possibility.

In the macaque, the pattern of anatomical connectivity and the physiological properties of the neurons have led to a subdivision of the posterior parietal cortex into a number of areas (e.g., Andersen et al. 1990, 1997; Colby, Duhamel, and Goldberg, 1993; Colby, and Duhamel, 1996; Colby, 1998). Each of these areas is specialized both in terms of its dominant sensory input (e.g., visual vs. somatosensory), or combination of inputs, and its competence with respect to motor output (e.g., eye movements vs. reaching vs. grasping). In addition, each area has been shown to code spatial locations in a frame of reference that is most appropriate for the specific type of motor response being controlled (e.g., Colby, 1998). Likewise, a number of areas specialized with respect to different motor behaviors have been identified in premotor and prefrontal cortex (Kurata, 1994; Preuss, Stepniewska, and Kaas, 1996; Wise et al., 1997; Graziano and Gross, 1998). Functional modules in posterior parietal and frontal cortex, together with interconnected cortical and subcortical structures, work in concert to perform the relevant sensorimotor transformations required to control a specific motor behavior. One example of this functional frontoparietal interplay is represented by the LIP-FEF circuit that we considered previously. Other circuits have been described for the control of different types of movement, such as the one comprising area VIP in the intraparietal sulcus and area F4 (or ventral premotor) in the frontal lobe for the control of arm and head (mouth) reaching (e.g., Colby, Duhamel, and Goldberg, 1993; Fogassi et al., 1996; Gentilucci et al., 1988; Graziano, Hu, and Gross, 1997; Graziano and Gross, 1998) and the one comprising area AIP in the rostral intraparietal sulcus and frontal area F5 (rostral ventral premotor) for the control of grasping (e.g., Rizzolatti et al., 1988; Taira et al., 1990; Sakata and Taira, 1994; Jeannerod et al., 1995; Murata et al., 1996).

As noted previously, one prediction of the hypothesis that spatially selective attention is closely related to premotor signals in general, and not uniquely to oculomotor signals, is that control signals for attention should be carried by the activity of neurons implicated in reaching whenever a specific object in the field is selected in order to produce a reaching response toward its location. An indication that the relevance of a visual target is not uniquely coded by the activity of neurons in cortical networks for eye movements comes from recent experiments by Snyder and colleagues (Snyder, Batista, and Andersen, 1997, 1998). In these experiments, the monkey was required to produce either a saccade or a reach response toward a designated stimulus location. It was found that activity of intraparietal neurons specifically related to one or the other type of motor behavior was determined by the response being planned and executed (saccade vs. reach). Changing the motor plan toward a selected stimulus location from an eye vs. arm movement, without a change in the direction of attention, determined which neurons were more active prior to movement onset. This result indicates that the activity of these cells reflects the animal's intention to make a particular motor act, rather than a general attentional signal. If the activity were simply related to attention, then the activity should be indifferent to the type of movement actually performed (see Platt and Glimcher, 1997, for a related finding). More generally, this suggests that control signals reflecting the allocation of attention to visual field locations are not an exclusive prerogative of neurons involved in oculomotor behavior.

In accord with the idea that control signals for spatial attention are intrinsic to cortical networks other than those implicated in eye movements, lesion studies in monkeys have demonstrated contralesional attention deficit following damage to cortical regions implicated in other types of motor behaviors. For example, Rizzolatti, Matelli, and Pavesi (1983) showed that monkeys with lesions of area 6 in premotor cortex, an area known to be involved in reaching with the arm and the mouth,

had severe contralesional neglect for peripersonal but not far extrapersonal space.

Finally, there is some recent evidence in humans that the preparation of a manual reaching response, in the absence of eye movements, causes enhanced sensory processing of stimuli at the location selected for the movement. Deubel and Schneider (1998) required subjects to prepare and execute a reaching movement toward a cued target location, and also to discriminate alphanumeric characters presented at varying distances from the cued location just prior to, or simultaneously with, the onset of the movement (dual-task paradigm). They found that the discrimination of alphanumeric stimuli was optimal when their location coincided with the target location of the arm movement. One interpretation of this result is that the preparation of an arm movement toward a given visual field location yields enhanced perceptual processing at that location, similarly to what happens with saccadic eye movements.

The reviewed evidence is in line with several recent and less recent proposals emphasizing a fundamental functional link between mechanisms for the preparation and execution of overt motor actions and mechanisms for the orienting of covert attention in space (Neumann, 1987; Allport, 1987; Tassinari et al., 1987; Rizzolatti et al., 1987; Rizzolatti and Craighero, 1998).

Effects of spatial attention on object recognition mechanisms in the ventral visual system

We have noted that the frontoparietal cortical network may be the source of spatially selective modulations in the ventral visual system during object discrimination tasks performed at peripheral locations. In particular, many studies have demonstrated that the hemodynamic response to peripheral visual stimuli is enhanced when attention is directed toward them as compared to when attention is directed away from them, e.g., to the opposite visual field (see Heinze et al., 1994; Woldorff et al., 1997; Vandenberghe et al., 1996; Mangun et al., chapter 48 in this volume; Wojciulik, Kanwisher, and Driver 1998; Clark et al., 1997). The regions of activation in ventral extrastriate visual cortex include cortex near the collateral sulcus, fusiform, and parahippocampal gyri, which have been shown to be specialized for object feature analysis (shape, color, faces; e.g., Corbetta et al., 1991; Haxby et al., 1994). These hemodynamic modulations are spatially coincident with ERPs effects on the same tasks (Heinze et al., 1994; Woldorff et al., 1997). Hereinafter, candidate correlates of these effects at the single-cell level are considered.

Moran and Desimone (1985) were among the first to document the profound influence of spatial attention on the activity of cells in area V4 and the inferotemporal cortex. In their study, stimuli were simultaneously presented at two locations in the visual field and the monkey was instructed to perform a delayed match-to-sample task on the stimuli at one location while ignoring stimuli at the other location. One of the stimuli in a pair was selected to be an effective sensory stimulus for the cell when presented alone, whereas the other stimulus was selected to be an ineffective stimulus. In one condition both stimulus locations were confined to the RF of the recorded neuron, while in another condition one stimulus location was inside and the other was well outside of the RF under study. With both stimulus locations inside the RF, the critical comparison was between trials where the monkey attended to the location containing the effective stimulus and trials where the monkey attended to the location containing the ineffective stimulus. In both area V4 and IT cortex responses to the effective stimulus inside the RF were profoundly suppressed when attention was directed to the ineffective sensory stimulus. Suppressed responses to the effective sensory stimulus inside the RF were not observed in V4 when attention was directed to an ineffective stimulus outside the RF boundary (this was never the case in IT cortex due to the large RFs in this area).

This pattern of results has been confirmed by Luck and colleagues (1997) in a recent investigation of the effects of spatial attention on visual responses in areas V1, V2, and V4. As in the study of Moran and Desimone (1985), Luck's group had their monkeys attend to stimuli at one location in the visual field and ignore stimuli simultaneously presented at another location, in order to detect a deviant stimulus in a rapid temporal sequence of nontargets (figure 46.5A). Neurons in area V2 and V4 showed suppressed responses to an effective sensory stimulus presented inside their RF when the animal attended to an ineffective stimulus located within the same RF boundary (figure 46.5B). Suppression of responses to the effective stimulus inside the RF was almost absent in the same two areas when attention was directed to a location outside the RF border (figure 46.5C).

Overall, these findings suggest that spatial attention gates neuronal responses in the ventral visual system by suppressing activity related to irrelevant stimuli when they are located near relevant stimuli, but not when they are located far away from them. An intriguing implication of these findings is that competition between stimuli positioned far apart in opposite visual fields cannot be resolved at the level of the visual system, since even in inferotemporal cortex (the area with the largest RFs in the visual system) RFs do not cover the entire visual field. It should be noted, however, that other studies have reported substantial effects of directed spatial at-

tention on the response of neurons in areas V2 and V4 even in the absence of multiple competing stimuli inside the RF of the individual neuron (Motter, 1993; Connor et al., 1997). It is conceivable that under certain conditions effects of attention can be observed with a single stimulus inside the RF; nevertheless, it is also plausible that greater and more consistent effects are typically obtained by placing multiple stimuli within one RF boundary (see Treue and Maunsell, 1996, for a similar finding in the motion-sensitive areas MT and MST).

Of course, another question arises: Why have a number of single-unit recording experiments shown this predominant effect of attention within a restricted region of space when no similar spatial constraint is typical in psychophysical, ERPs, or brain imaging investigations in humans documenting robust effects of directed attention for stimuli located across opposite visual fields? There might be many potential explanations for this discrepancy, but one possibility is that the extracellular recording of the spiking activity of single neurons in visual cortex does not capture some critical neural codes reflecting the allocation of attention to spatial locations. For example, standard single-unit recordings would not detect systematic temporal correlations in the firing of neuronal populations within an area, while these might underlie important behavioral, surface electrical, or hemodynamic modulations related to attention.

A different type of neuronal modulation has been reported in ventral extrastriate visual cortex, whose characteristics match those of a spatially selective control signal (source signal). Luck and colleagues (1997) reported that the baseline activity of neurons in areas V2 and V4 was elevated when the animals were directing their attention to a location inside the RF, relative to when attention was directed outside the RF. Importantly, the baseline shift was greater when attention was aligned with the most sensitive portion of the RF and diminished progressively as attention was moved toward the RF border. This indicates that the spatial signal responsible for this effect has a spatial resolution higher than the size of a typical RF in these areas. This elevation of baseline firing was evident from the beginning of the trial (figure 46.5D)–i.e., prior to the onset of any task-relevant stimulus in the visual field–and persisted in all the intervals between stimulus presentations (figure 46.5E).

The sustained increase of baseline activity in areas V2 and V4 has the hallmarks of a control attentional signal by virtue of its spatial selectivity and independence from sensory input. It is also suggestively similar to the sustained activity recorded in LIP (Colby, Duhamel, and Goldberg, 1996) both during a spatial working memory task and a peripheral attention task. We have previously proposed that a frontoparietal cortical network in

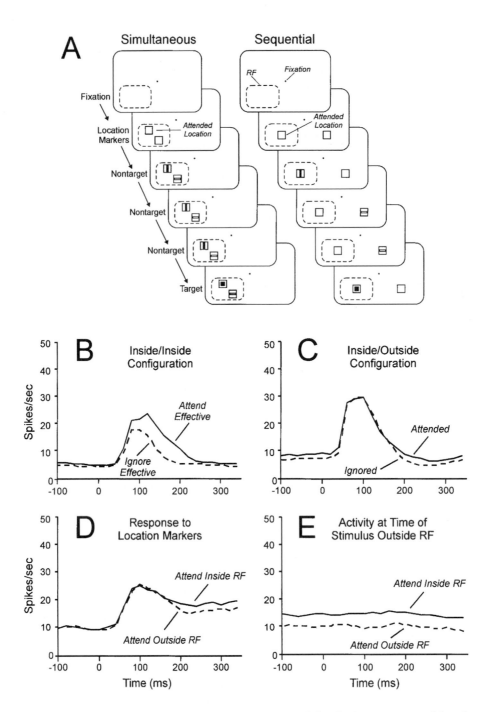

A

Simultaneous

Sequential

Fixation

Location Markers — Attended Location

Nontarget

Nontarget

Nontarget

Target

RF   Fixation

Attended Location

B Inside/Inside Configuration

Spikes/sec

Attend Effective

Ignore Effective

C Inside/Outside Configuration

Attended

Ignored

D Response to Location Markers

Spikes/sec

Attend Inside RF

Attend Outside RF

Time (ms)

E Activity at Time of Stimulus Outside RF

Attend Inside RF

Attend Outside RF

Time (ms)

humans, likely including regions homologous to LIP, is the source of spatially selective effects in the ventral visual system. A relatively straightforward prediction of this proposal is that sustained baseline effects in V2 and V4, as shown by Luck and colleagues (1997), should be abolished by transient deactivation with muscimol or other agents of regions involved in attentional control, e.g., LIP or FEF.

Some models have been developed to explain how selective (e.g., spatial) biasing signals may influence the neuronal response of neurons to attended and unattended objects. One such model is the biased competi-

tion model, which was inspired by the previous results obtained in areas V2, V4, and the inferotemporal cortex in the context of spatially selective attention tasks and other attention-related effects in these areas (Chelazzi et al., 1993, 1998; Chelazzi and Desimone, 1994; Desimone and Duncan, 1995; Luck et al., 1997). According to this model, objects in the visual field activate corresponding neural populations distributed across several cortical (and subcortical) visual structures. These neural populations are part of reciprocal inhibitory networks. As a consequence of this widespread architecture, object representations engage in competitive interactions.

FIGURE 46.5 Schematic description of the task and results from the study of Luck and colleagues (1997). (A) Example stimulus sequences in representative trial types. The two sets of displays illustrate simultaneous (left) and sequential (right) stimulus presentation, which were equally used for the recording of cells in the different conditions. In both cases the trial began with the monkey holding a response lever and fixating a target at the center of a computer monitor. Shortly after, location markers were shown, indicating the spatial locations where stimuli would be presented. According to special instruction trials, one location was relevant throughout a block of trials, while the other was irrelevant. The opposite was true in the subsequent block. The task of the animals was to signal with a lever release the onset of a target stimulus (a square) presented at the relevant location in a sequence of nontargets (rectangles), and to ignore stimuli presented at the irrelevant location. The spatial arrangement of the stimuli was varied systematically. In some cases (left) both stimulus locations were positioned within the RF of the recorded cell; in other cases (right) one stimulus location was positioned inside the RF while the other location was outside. In the former case, one stimulus inside the RF was selected to be effective at driving the cell's response when presented alone, while the second stimulus was selected to be ineffective. Note that the "inside/inside" and "inside/outside" stimulus configurations are depicted here for the simultaneous and sequential trials, respectively, although the opposite pairing of spatial configuration and temporal sequence was used as well. (B) Poststimulus histograms averaged over 29 V4 cells for effective and ineffective stimuli presented simultaneously inside the RF (left in A). The two curves compare responses to the RF stimuli when the location of the effective (solid line) or of the ineffective (dashed line) stimulus was attended. Activity was much higher when attention was directed to the effective stimulus in the pair. Using this inside/inside configuration, similar results were obtained with sequential stimulus presentation. (C) Poststimulus histograms averaged over 38 V4 cells showing response to RF stimulus during sequential presentation (right in A) as a function of attention. The solid line represents attention directed to the stimulus location inside the RF, and the dashed line represents attention directed to the stimulus location outside the RF. In this condition attention had no consistent effect on the population average sensory-driven response. A similar lack of modulation was obtained in the inside/outside configuration with simultaneous stimulus presentation. (D) Activity at the beginning of the trial for 40 V4 cells recorded with the inside/outside configuration and sequential stimulus presentation. Shortly after the onset of the location markers, i.e., before any task relevant stimulus was presented, baseline activity was higher when the animal's attention was directed to the stimulus location inside the RF compared to when attention was directed to the location outside the RF. (E) Activity of the same cells shown in D during the time periods in which a nontarget stimulus was presented outside the RF, indicating that the baseline shift persisted throughout the course of the trial.

These interactions are typically stronger when objects in the field activate nearby neural populations–for instance, when objects in the field are close to one another. Competitive interactions are influenced both by bottom-up, or stimulus-driven, factors, such as the relative contrast of the stimuli in the field (Reynolds, Pasternak, and Desimone, 1996), and by top-down feedback factors, such as the greater behavioral relevance of one stimulus over another, specified in working memory (Chelazzi et al., 1993, 1998; Luck et al., 1997). Two aspects of the results by Moran and Desimone (1985) and by Luck and colleagues (1997) are particularly consistent with the biased competition model. On the one hand, the model can explain why effects of directed attention are heavily constrained by spatial factors–i.e., the suppression of responses to an effective stimulus inside the RF of a neuron is mainly observed when attention is directed to a nearby location inside the same RF. This is due to the fact that competitive interactions are particularly strong among neurons whose RFs cover the same region of space. In turn, the reason for this is that the need for attentional mechanisms is related to the need to resolve the ambiguity when multiple stimuli impinge on a single RF, i.e., when they compete for the encoding capacity of a single neuron. On the other hand, the shift in baseline activity prior to stimulus onset in both areas V2 and V4 when the animal's attention is directed to the RF is consistent with the idea of a spatial signal that biases the competition in favor of the neural representation of stimuli at the attended location.

Conclusions

The ability to direct attention to extrapersonal locations in visual space is a critical biological function of higher organisms. Functional neuroimaging studies in humans and physiological recordings in awake behaving primates are beginning to elucidate the anatomical and physiological organization of brain systems mediating this function. In particular, a network of cortical regions that include the posterior parietal cortex and the frontal eye field is involved in generating neural signals that allow processing resources to be focused on one object of interest in the visual scene–although some evidence suggests the same frontoparietal network may play a more general role in the coordination of visual representations and visual awareness. Control signals for the allocation of attention in space may correspond to spatially selective premotor or working memory signals. Spatially selective source signals from the frontoparietal network bias neuronal activity in extrastriate visual areas involved in object analysis, and this is reflected in changes of baseline firing prior to stimulus onset and modulation of the sensory-evoked responses. The net effect of these changes is the amplification of neural signals representing stimuli at attended locations and the attenuation of neural signals representing stimuli at unattended locations. Future work will have to uncover through which routes control signals for spatially selective attention flow from frontoparietal to occipitotemporal extrastriate cortical areas, and through which cellular mechanisms they can affect processing of visual stimuli in the latter areas. However, the greatest conceptual and empirical challenge for the years to come will perhaps be to clarify the boundaries, or to delete them, between spatial attention, spatial working memory, and motor intention signals in the primate brain.

ACKNOWLEDGMENTS Preparation of this chapter was supported by NEI grant EY00379, The Charles A. Dana Foundation, and the McDonnell Center for Higher Brain Studies (MC) and by Human Frontier Science Program Organization (HFSPO) grant RG0136/97 and grants from Italian MURST and CNR (LC). We would like to thank Dr. Steve Petersen for suggestions and discussion on an early draft of the manuscript. We also thank Dr. Carol Colby for kindly providing figure 46.2, and Mr. Marco Veronese for helping preparing figure 46.5.

REFERENCES

ABRAMS, R. A., and R. S. DOBKIN, 1994. Inhibition of return: Effect of attentional cueing on eye movement latencies. *J. Exp. Psychol.: Hum. Percept. Perform.* 20:467–477.

ALLPORT, D. A., 1987. Selection for action: Some behavioural and neurophysiological considerations of attention and action. In *Perspectives on Perception and Action*, H. Heuer and A. F. Sanders, eds. Hillsdale, N.J.: Erlbaum, pp. 395–419.

ANDERSEN, R. A., C. ASANUMA, G. ESSICK, and R. M. SIEGEL, 1990. Corticocortical connections of anatomically and physiologically defined subdivisions within the inferior parietal lobule. *J. Comp. Neurol.* 296:65–113.

ANDERSEN, R. A., G. K. ESSICK, and R. M. SIEGEL, 1987. Neurons of area 7 activated by both visual stimuli and oculomotor behavior. *Exp. Brain. Res.* 67:316–322.

ANDERSEN, R. A., L. H. SNYDER, D. C. BRADLEY, and J. XING, 1997. Multimodal representation of space in the posterior parietal cortex and its use in planning movements. *Annu. Rev. Neurosci.* 20:303–330.

ANDERSON, T. J., I. K. JENKINS, D. J. BROOKS, M. B. HAWKEN, R. S. J. FRACKOWIACK, and C. KENNARD, 1994. Cortical control of saccades and fixation in man. *Brain* 117:1073–1084.

BARASH, S., R. M. BRACEWELL, L. FOGASSI, J. W. GNADT, and R. A. ANDERSEN, 1991. Saccade-related activity in the lateral intraparietal area. I. Temporal properties; comparison with area 7a. *J. Neurophysiol.* 66:1095–1108.

BARBAS, H., 1988. Anatomic organization of basoventral and mediodorsal visual recipient prefrontal regions in the rhesus monkey. *J. Comp. Neurol.* 276:313–342.

BASHINSKI, H. S., and V. R. BACHARACH, 1980. Enhancement of perceptual sensitivity as the result of selectively attending to spatial locations. *Percept. Psychophys.* 28:241–248.

BRUCE, C. J., and M. E. GOLDBERG, 1985. Primate frontal eye fields. I. Single neurons discharging before saccades. *J. Neurophysiol.* 53:603–635.

BUSHNELL, M. C., M. E. GOLDBERG, and D. L. ROBINSON, 1981. Behavioral enhancement of visual responses in monkey cerebral cortex. I. Modulation in posterior parietal cortex related to selective visual attention. *J. Neurophysiol.* 46:755–772.

CAVADA, C., and P. S. GOLDMAN-RAKIC, 1989. Posterior parietal cortex in rhesus monkey: II. Evidence for segregated corticocortical networks linking sensory and limbic areas with the frontal lobe. *J. Comp. Neurol.* 287:422–445.

CHAFEE, M. V., and P. S. GOLDMAN-RAKIC, 1998. Matching patterns of activity in primate prefrontal area 8a and parietal area 7ip during a spatial working memory task. *J. Neurophysiol.* 79:2919–2940.

CHELAZZI, L., M. BISCALDI, M. CORBETTA, A. PERU, G. TASSINARI, and G. BERLUCCHI, 1995. Oculomotor activity and visual spatial attention. *Behav. Brain. Res.* 71:81–88.

CHELAZZI, L., and R. DESIMONE, 1994. Responses of V4 neurons during visual search. *Soc. Neurosci. Abstr.* 20:434.6.

CHELAZZI, L., J. DUNCAN, E. K. MILLER, and R. DESIMONE, 1998. Responses of neurons in inferior temporal cortex during memory-guided visual search. *J. Neurophysiol.* 80:2918–2940.

CHELAZZI, L., E. K. MILLER, J. DUNCAN, and R. DESIMONE, 1993. A neural basis for visual search in inferior temporal cortex. *Nature* 363:345–347.

CLARK, V. P., R. PARASURAMAN, K. KEIL, R. KULANSKY, S. FANNON, J. M. MAISOG, L. G. UNGERLEIDER, and J. V. HAXBY, 1997. Selective attention to face identity and color studied with fMRI. *Hum. Brain Map.* 5:293–297.

COLBY, C. L., 1998. Action-oriented spatial reference frames in cortex. *Neuron* 20:15–24.

COLBY, C. L., and J.-R. DUHAMEL, 1996. Spatial representations for action in parietal cortex. *Cogn. Brain Res.* 5:105–115.

COLBY, C. L., J. R. DUHAMEL, and M. E. GOLDBERG, 1993. Ventral intraparietal area of the macaque: Anatomic location and visual response properties. *J. Neurophysiol.* 69:902–914.

COLBY, C. L., J. R. DUHAMEL, and M. E. GOLDBERG, 1996. Visual, presaccadic, and cognitive activation of single neurons in monkey lateral intraparietal area. *J. Neurophysiol.* 76:2841–2852.

CONNOR, C. E., D. C. PREDDIE, J. L. GALLANT, and D. C. VAN ESSEN, 1997. Spatial attention effects in macaque area V4. *J. Neurosci.* 17:3201–3214.

CONSTANTINIDIS, C., and M. A. STEINMETZ, 1996. Neuronal activity in posterior parietal area 7a during the delay periods of a spatial memory task. *J. Neurophysiol.* 76:1352–1355.

CORBETTA, M., E. AKBUDAK, T. E. CONTOURO, A. Z. SNYDER, J. M. OLLINGER, H. A. DRURY, M. R. LINENWEBER, S. E. PETERSEN, M. E. RAICHLE, D. C. VAN ESSEN, and G. L. SHULMAN, 1998. A common network of functional areas for attention and eye movements. *Neuron* 21:761–773.

CORBETTA, M., F. M. MIEZIN, S. DOBMEYER, G. L. SHULMAN, and S. E. PETERSEN, 1991. Selective and divided attention during visual discriminations of shape, color, and speed: Functional anatomy by positron emission tomography. *J. Neurosci.* 11:2383–2402.

CORBETTA, M., F. M. MIEZIN, G. L. SHULMAN, and S. E. PETERSEN, 1993. A PET study of visuospatial attention. *J. Neurosci.* 13:1202–1226.

CORBETTA, M., G. L. SHULMAN, F. M. MIEZIN, and S. E. PETERSEN, 1995. Superior parietal cortex activation during spatial attention shifts and visual feature conjunction. *Science* 270:802–805.

COURTNEY, S. M., L. PETIT, J. M. MAISOG, L. G. UNGERLEIDER, and J. V. HAXBY, 1998. An area specialized for spatial working memory in human frontal cortex. *Science* 279:1347–1351.

COURTNEY, S. M., L. G. UNGERLEIDER, K. KEIL, and J. V. HAXBY, 1996. Object and spatial visual working memory activate separate neural systems in human cortex. *Cereb. Cortex* 6:39–49.

COURTNEY, S. M., L. G. UNGERLEIDER, K. KEIL, and J. V. HAXBY, 1997. Transient and sustained activity in a distributed neural system for human working memory. *Nature* 386:608–611.

DESIMONE, R., 1996. Neural mechanisms for visual memory and their role in attention. *Proc. Natl. Acad. Sci. U.S.A.* 93:13494–13499.

DESIMONE, R., and J. DUNCAN, 1995. Neural mechanisms of selective visual attention. *Annu. Rev. Neurosci.* 18:193–222.

DEUBEL, H., and W. X. SCHNEIDER, 1996. Saccade target selection and object recognition: Evidence for a common attentional mechanism. *Vision Res.* 36:1827–1837.

DEUBEL, H., W. X. SCHNEIDER, and I. PAPROTTA, 1998. Selective dorsal and ventral processing: Evidence for a common attentional mechanism in reaching and perception. *Vis. Cogn.* 5:81–107.

DI PELLEGRINO, G., and S. P. WISE, 1991. A neurophysiological comparison of three distinct regions of the primate frontal lobe. *Brain* 114:951–978.

DI PELLEGRINO, G., and S. P. WISE, 1993. Visuospatial versus visuomotor activity in the premotor and prefrontal cortex of a primate. *J. Neurosci.* 13:1227–1243.

DOWNING, C. J., 1988. Expectancy and visual-spatial attention: Effects on perceptual quality. *J. Exp. Psychol.: Hum. Percept. Perform.* 14:188–202.

DRURY, H. A., D. C. VAN ESSEN, C. H. ANDERSON, C. W. LEE, T. A. COOGAN, and J. W. LEWIS, 1996. Computerized mappings of the cerebral cortex: A multiresolution flattening method and a surface-based coordinate system. *J. Cogn. Neurosci.* 8:1–28.

FOGASSI, L., V. GALLESE, L. FADIGA, G. LUPPINO, M. MATELLI, and G. RIZZOLATTI, 1996. Coding of peripersonal space in inferior premotor cortex (area F4). *J. Neurophysiol.* 76:141–157.

FUNAHASHI, S., C. J. BRUCE, and P. S. GOLDMAN-RAKIC, 1989. Mnemonic coding of visual space in the monkey's dorsolateral prefrontal cortex. *J. Neurophysiol.* 61:331–349.

FUNAHASHI, S., M. V. CHAFEE, and P. S. GOLDMAN-RAKIC, 1993. Prefrontal neuronal activity in rhesus monkeys performing a delayed anti-saccade task. *Nature* 365:753–756.

GENTILUCCI, M., L. FOGASSI, G. LUPPINO, M. MATELLI, R. CAMARDA, and G. RIZZOLATTI, 1988. Functional organization of inferior area 6 in the macaque monkey. I. Somatotopy and the control of proximal movements. *Exp. Brain Res.* 71:475–490.

GOLDBERG, M. E., and M. C. BUSHNELL, 1981. Behavioral enhancement of visual responses in monkey cerebral cortex. II. Modulation in frontal eye fields specifically related to saccades. *J. Neurophysiol.* 46:773–787.

GOLDBERG, M. E., C. L. COLBY, and J.-R. DUHAMEL, 1990. The representation of visuomotor space in the parietal lobe of the monkey. *Cold Spring Harbor Symp. Quant. Biol.* 55:729–739.

GOLDBERG, M. E., and R. H. WURTZ, 1972. Activity of superior colliculus in behaving monkey. II. Effect of attention on neuronal responses. *J. Neurophysiol.* 35:560–574.

GOTTLIEB, J. P., M. KUSUNOKI, and M. E. GOLDBERG, 1998. The representation of visual salience in monkey parietal cortex. *Nature* 391:481–484.

GRAZIANO, M. S. A., and C. G. GROSS, 1998. Spatial maps for the control of movement. *Curr. Opin. Neurobiol.* 8:195–201.

GRAZIANO, M. S., X. T. HU, and C. G. GROSS, 1997. Visuospatial properties of ventral premotor cortex. *J. Neurophysiol.* 77:2268–2292.

HAWKINS, H. L., M. G. SHAFTO, and K. RICHARDSON, 1988. Effects of target luminance and cue validity on the latency of visual detection. *Percept. Psychophys.* 44:484–492.

HAXBY, J. V., B. HORWITZ, L. G. UNGERLEIDER, J. M. MAISOG, P. PIETRINI, and C. L. GRADY, 1994. The functional organization of human extrastriate cortex: A PET–rCBF study of selective attention to faces and locations. *J. Neurosci.* 14:6336–6353.

HEINZE, H. J., G. R. MANGUN, W. BURCHERT, H. HINRICHS, M. SCHOLZ, T. F. MUENTE, A. GOES, M. SCHERG, S. JOHANNES, H. HUNDESHAGEN, M. S. GAZZANIGA, and S. A. HILLYARD, 1994. Combined spatial and temporal imaging of brain activity during visual selective attention in humans. *Nature* 372:543–546.

HOFFMAN, J. E., and B. SUBRAMANIAM, 1995. The role of visual attention in saccadic eye movements. *Percept. Psychophys.* 57:787–795.

JEANNEROD, M., M. A. ARBIB, G. RIZZOLATTI, and H. SAKATA, 1995. Grasping objects: The cortical mechanisms of visuomotor transformation. *Trends Neurosci.* 18:314–320.

JONIDES, J., E. E. SMITH, R. A. KOEPPE, E. AWH, S. MINOSHIMA, and M. A. MINTUN, 1993. Spatial working memory in humans as revealed by PET. *Nature* 363:623–625.

JONIDES, J., and S. YANTIS, 1988. Uniqueness of abrupt visual onset in capturing attention. *Percept. Psychophys.* 43:346–354.

KLEIN, R. M., 1980. Does oculomotor readiness mediate cognitive control of visual attention? In *Attention and Performance VIII*, R. S. Nickerson, ed. Hillsdale, N.J.: Erlbaum, pp. 259–276.

KODAKA, Y., A. MIKAMI, and K. KUBOTA, 1997. Neuronal activity in the frontal eye field of the monkey is modulated while attention is focused on to a stimulus in the peripheral visual field, irrespective of eye movement. *Neurosci. Res.* 28:291–298.

KOWLER, E., E. ANDERSON, B. DOSHER, and E. BLASER, 1995. The role of attention in the programming of saccades. *Vision Res.* 35:1897–1916.

KURATA, K., 1994. Information processing for motor control in primate premotor cortex. *Behav. Brain Res.* 61:135–142.

KUSTOV, A. A., and D. L. ROBINSON, 1996. Shared neural control of attentional shifts and eye movements. *Nature* 384:74–77.

LE, T. H., J. V. PARDO, and X. HU, 1998. 4 T-fMRI study of nonspatial shifting of selective attention: Cerebellar and parietal contributions. *J. Neurophysiol.* 79:1535–1548.

LUCK, S. J., L. CHELAZZI, S. A. HILLYARD, and R. DESIMONE, 1997. Neural mechanisms of spatial selective attention in areas V1, V2, and V4 of macaque visual cortex. *J. Neurophysiol.* 77:24–42.

LUMER, E. D., K. J. FRISTON, and G. REES, 1998. Neural correlates of perceptual rivalry in the human brain. *Science* 280:1930–1934.

LUNA, B., K. R. THULBORN, M. H. STROJWAS, B. J. MCCURTAIN, R. A. BERMAN, C. R. GENOVESE, and J. A. SWEENEY, 1998. Dorsal cortical regions subserving visually-guided saccades in humans: An fMRI study. *Cereb. Cortex* 8:40–47.

MAYLOR, E. A., and R. HOCKEY, 1985. Inhibitory components of externally controlled covert orienting in visual space. J. Exp. Psychol.: Human Percept. Perform. 11:777–787.

MESULAM, M. M., 1981. A cortical network for directed attention and unilateral neglect. *Ann. Neurol.* 10:309–315.

MESULAM, M.-M., 1990. Large-scale neurocognitive networks and distributed processing for attention, language, and memory. *Ann. Neurol.* 28:597–613.

MORAN, J., and R. DESIMONE, 1985. Selective attention gates visual processing in the extrastriate cortex. *Science* 229:782–784.

MOTTER, B. C., 1993. Focal attention produces spatially selective processing in visual cortical areas V1, V2, and V4 in the presence of competing stimuli. *J. Neurophysiol.* 70:909–919.

MURATA, A., V. GALLESE, M. KASEDA, and H. SAKATA, 1996. Parietal neurons related to memory-guided hand manipulation. *J. Neurophysiol.* 75:2180–2186.

NEUMANN, O., 1987. Beyond capacity: A functional view of attention. In *Perspectives on Perception and Action*, H. Heuer and A. F. Sanders, eds. Hillsdale, N.J.: Erlbaum, pp. 361–394.

NIKI, H., and M. WATANABE, 1976. Prefrontal unit activity and delayed response: Relation to cue location versus direction of response. *Brain Res.* 105:79–88.

NOBRE, A. C., G. N. SEBESTYEN, D. GITELMAN, M.-M. MESULAM, R. S. J. FRACKOWIAK, and C. D. FRITH, 1997. Functional localization of the system visuospatial attention using positron-emission tomography. *Brain* 120:515–533.

O'DRISCOLL, G. A., N. M. ALPERT, S. W. MATTHYSSE, D. L. LEVY, S. L. RAUCH, and P. S. HOLZMAN, 1995. Functional neuroanatomy of antisaccade eye movements investigated with positron emission tomography. *Proc. Natl. Acad. Sci. U.S.A.* 92:925–929.

O'SULLIVAN, E. P., I. H. JENKINS, L. HENDERSON, C. KENNARD, and D. J. BROOKS, 1995. The functional anatomy of remembered saccades: A PET study. *Neuroreport* 6:2141–2144.

OWEN, A. M., J. DOYON, M. PETRIDES, and A. C. EVANS, 1996. Planning and spatial working memory: A positron emission tomography study in humans. *Eur. J. Neurosci.* 8:353–364.

PAUS, T., 1996. Location and function of the human frontal eyefield: A selective review. *Neuropsychologia* 34:475–483.

PAUS, T., S. MARRETT, K. J. WORSLEY, and A. C. EVANS, 1995. Extraretinal modulation of cerebral blood flow in the human visual cortex: Implications for saccadic suppression. *J. Neurophysiol.* 74:2179–2183.

PAUS, T., M. PETRIDES, A. C. EVANS, and E. MEYER, 1993. Role of the human anterior cingulate cortex in the control of oculomotor, manual, and speech responses: A positron emission tomography study. *J. Neurophysiol.* 70:453–469.

PETERSEN, S. E., D. L. ROBINSON, and W. KEYS, 1985. Pulvinar nuclei of the behaving rhesus monkey: Visual responses and their modulation. *J. Neurophysiol.* 54:867–886.

PETIT, L., V. P. CLARK, J. INGEHOLM, and J. V. HAXBY, 1997. Dissociation of saccade-related and pursuit-related activation in human frontal eye fields as revealed by fMRI. *J. Neurophysiol.* 77:3386–3390.

PETIT, L., C. ORRSAUD, N. TZOURIO, F. CRIVELLO, A. BERTHOZ, and B. MAZOYER, 1996. Functional anatomy of a pre-

learned sequence of horizontal saccades in man. *J. Neurosci.* 16:3714–3726.

PETRIDES, M., and D. N. PANDYA, 1984. Projections to the frontal cortex from the posterior parietal region in the rhesus monkey. *J. Comp. Neurol.* 228:105–116.

PLATT, M. L., and P. W. GLIMCHER, 1997. Responses of intraparietal neurons to saccadic targets and visual distractors. *J. Neurophysiol.* 78:1574–1589.

POSNER, M. I., 1980. Orienting of attention. *Quart. J. Exp. Psychol.* 32:3–25.

POSNER, M. I., and Y. COHEN, 1984. Components of visual orienting. In *Attention and Performance X*, H. Bouma and D. Bouwhuis, eds. London: Erlbaum, pp. 531–556.

POSNER, M. I., and S. E. PETERSEN, 1990. The attention system of the human brain. *Annu. Rev. Neurosci.* 13:25–42.

POSNER, M. I., J. A. WALKER, F. J. FRIEDRICH, and R. D. RAFAL, 1984. Effects of parietal injury on covert orienting of attention. *J. Neurosci.* 4:1863–1874.

PREUSS, T. M., I. STEPNIEWSKA, and J. H. KAAS, 1996. Movement representation in the dorsal and ventral premotor areas of owl monkeys: A microstimulation study [published erratum]. *J. Comp. Neurol.* 371:649–676.

QUINTANA, J., and J. M. FUSTER, 1992. Mnemonic and predictive functions of cortical neurons in a memory task. *Neuroreport* 3:721–724.

RAFAL, R., R. EGLY, and D. RHODES, 1994. Effects of inhibition of return on voluntary and visually guided saccades. *Can. J. Exp. Psychol.* 48:284–300.

RAFAL, R. D., P. A. CALABRESI, C. W. BRENNAN, and T. K. SCIOLTO, 1989. Saccade preparation inhibits reorienting to recently attended locations. *J. Exp. Psychol.: Hum. Percept. Perform.* 15:673–685.

RAO, S. C., G. RAINER, and E. K. MILLER, 1997. Integration of what and where in the primate prefrontal cortex. *Science* 276:821–824.

REUTER-LORENZ, P. A., A. P. JHA, and J. N. ROSENQUIST, 1996. What is inhibited in inhibition of return? *J. Exp. Psychol.: Hum. Percept. Perform.* 22:367–378.

REYNOLDS, J., T. PASTERNAK, and R. DESIMONE, 1996. Attention increases contrast sensitivity of cells in macaque area V4. *Soc. Neurosci. Abstr.* 22:1197.

RIZZOLATTI, G., R. CAMARDA, L. FOGASSI, M. GENTILUCCI, G. LUPPINO, and M. MATELLI, 1988. Functional organization of inferior area 6 in the macaque monkey. II. Area F5 and the control of distal movements. *Exp. Brain Res.* 71:491–507.

RIZZOLATTI, G., and L. CRAIGHERO, 1998. Spatial attention: mechanisms and theories. In *Advances in Psychological Science:* Vol. 2, *Biological and Cognitive Aspects*, M. Sabourin, F. Craik, and M. Robert, eds. Hove: Psychology Press, pp. 171–198.

RIZZOLATTI, G., M. MATELLI, and G. PAVESI, 1983. Deficits in attention and movement following the removal of postarcuate (area 6) and prearcuate (area 8) cortex in macaque monkeys. *Brain* 106:655–673.

RIZZOLATTI, G., L. RIGGIO, I. DASCOLA, and C. UMILTA, 1987. Reorienting attention across the horizontal and vertical meridians: Evidence in favor of a premotor theory of attention. *Neuropsychologia* 25:31–40.

ROBINSON, D. L., E. M. BOWMAN, and C. KERTZMAN, 1995. Covert orienting of attention in macaques. II. Contributions of parietal cortex. *J. Neurophysiol.* 74:698–712.

ROBINSON, D. L., M. E. GOLDBERG, and G. B. STANTON, 1978. Parietal association cortex in the primate: Sensory

684   ATTENTION

mechanisms and behavioral modulations. *J. Neurophysiol.* 41:910–932.

ROBINSON, D. L., and S. E. PETERSEN, 1992. The pulvinar and visual salience. *Trends Neurosci.* 15:127–132.

SAKATA, H., and M. TAIRA, 1994. Parietal control of hand action. *Curr. Opin. Neurobiol.* 4:847–856.

SCHALL, J. D., and D. P. HANES, 1993. Neural basis of saccade target selection in frontal eye field during visual search. *Nature* 366:467–469.

SCHALL, J. D., D. P. HANES, K. G. THOMPSON, and D. J. KING, 1995a. Saccade target selection in frontal eye field of macaque. I. Visual and premovement activation. *J. Neurosci.* 15:6905–6918.

SCHALL, J. D., A. MOREL, D. J. KING, and J. BULLIER, 1995b. Topography of visual cortex connections with frontal eye field in macaque: Convergence and segregation of processing streams. *J. Neurosci.* 15:4464–4487.

SELEMON, L. D., and P. S. GOLDMAN-RAKIC, 1988. Common cortical and subcortical targets of the dorsolateral prefrontal and posterior parietal cortices in the rhesus monkey: Evidence for a distributed neural network subserving spatially guided behavior. *J. Neurosci.* 8:4049–4068.

SHELIGA, B. M., L. RIGGIO, and G. RIZZOLATTI, 1994. Orienting of attention and eye movements. *Exp. Brain Res.* 98:507–522.

SHELIGA, B. M., L. RIGGIO, and G. RIZZOLATTI, 1995. Spatial attention and eye movements. *Exp. Brain Res.* 105:261–275.

SHEPHERD, M., J. M. FINDLAY, and R. J. HOCKEY, 1986. The relationship between eye movements and spatial attention. *Quart. J. Exp. Psychol. A.* 38:475–491.

SMITH, E. E., and J. JONIDES, 1997. Working memory: A view from neuroimaging. *Cogn. Psychol.* 33:5–42.

SMITH, E. E., J. JONIDES, and R. A. KOEPPE, 1996. Dissociating verbal and spatial working memory using PET. Cereb. *Cortex* 6:11–20.

SMITH, E. E., J. JONIDES, R. A. KOEPPE, E. AWH, E. SCHUMACHER, and S. MINOSHIMA, 1995. Spatial versus object working memory: PET investigations. *J. Cogn. Neurosci.* 7:337–356.

SNYDER, L. H., A. P. BATISTA, and R. A. ANDERSEN, 1997. Coding of intention in the posterior parietal cortex. *Nature* 386:167–170.

SNYDER, L. H., A. P. BATISTA, and R. A. ANDERSEN, 1998. Change in motor plan, without a change in the spatial locus of attention, modulates activity in posterior parietal cortex. *J. Neurophysiol.* 79:2814–2819.

STEINMETZ, M. A., C. E. CONNOR, C. CONSTANTINIDIS, and J. R. MCLAUGHLIN, 1994. Covert attention suppresses neuronal responses in area 7a of the posterior parietal cortex. *J. Neurophysiol.* 72:1020–1023.

STEINMETZ, M. A., and C. CONSTANTINIDIS, 1995. Neurophysiological evidence for a role of posterior parietal cortex in redirecting visual attention. *Cereb. Cortex* 5:448–456.

SWEENEY, J. A., M. A. MINTUM, S. KWEE, M. B. WISEMAN, D. L. BROWN, D. R. ROSENBERG, and J. R. CARL, 1996. Positron emission tomography study of voluntary saccadic eye movement and spatial working memory. *J. Neurophysiol.* 75:454–468.

TAIRA, M., S. MINE, A. P. GEORGOPOULOS, A. MURATA, and H. SAKATA, 1990. Parietal cortex neurons of the monkey related to the visual guidance of hand movement. *Exp. Brain Res.* 83:29–36.

TALAIRACH, J., and P. TOURNOUX, 1988. *Co-planar Stereotaxic Atlas of the Human Brain.* New York: Thieme Medical Publishers.

TASSINARI, G., S. AGLIOTI, L. CHELAZZI, C. A. MARZI, and G. BERLUCCHI, 1987. Distribution in the visual field of the costs of voluntarily allocated attention and of the inhibitory after-effects of covert orienting. *Neuropsychologia* 25:55–71.

TASSINARI, G., S. AGLIOTI, L. CHELAZZI, A. PERU, and G. BERLUCCHI, 1994. Do peripheral non-informative cues induce early facilitation of target detection? *Vision Res.* 34:179–189.

THOMPSON, K. G., N. P. BICHOT, and J. D. SCHALL, 1997. Dissociation of visual discrimination from saccade programming in macaque frontal eye field. *J. Neurophysiol.* 77:1046–1050.

THOMPSON, K. G., D. P. HANES, N. P. BICHOT, and J. D. SCHALL, 1996. Perceptual and motor processing stages identified in the activity of macaque frontal eye field neurons during visual search. *J. Neurophysiol.* 76:4040–4055.

TIPPER, S. P., B. WEAVER, L. M. JERREAT, and A. L. BURAK, 1994. Object-based and environment-based inhibition of return of visual attention. *J. Exp. Psychol.: Hum. Percept. Perform.* 20:478–499.

TREISMAN, A., 1991. Search, similarity, and integration of features between and within dimensions. *J. Exp. Psychol.: Hum. Percept. Perform.* 17:652–676.

TREISMAN, A., 1996. The binding problem. *Curr. Opin. Neurobiol.* 6:171–178.

TREISMAN, A. M., and G. GELADE, 1980. A feature integration theory of attention. *Cogn. Psychol.* 12:97–136.

TREUE, S., and J. H. MAUNSELL, 1996. Attentional modulation of visual motion processing in cortical areas MT and MST. *Nature* 382:539–541.

ULLMAN, S., 1984. Visual routines. *Cognition* 18:97–159.

UNGERLEIDER, L. G., 1995. Functional brain imaging studies of cortical mechanisms for memory. *Science* 270:769–775.

VAN ESSEN, D. C., and H. A. DRURY, 1997. Structural and functional analyses of human cerebral cortex using a surface-based atlas. *J. Neurosci.* 17:7079–7102.

VAN VOORHIS, S., and S. HILLYARD, 1977. Visual evoked potentials and selective attention to points in space. *Percept. Psychophys.* 22:54–62.

VANDENBERGHE, R., J. DUNCAN, P. DUPONT, R. WARD, J. B. POLINE, G. BORMANS, J. MICHIELS, L. MORTELMANS, and G. A. ORBAN, 1997. Attention to one or two features in left or right visual field: A positron emission tomography study. *J. Neurosci.* 17:3739–3750.

VANDENBERGHE, R., P. DUPONT, B. DE BRUYN, G. BORMANS, J. MICHIELS, L. MORTELMANS, and G. A. ORBAN, 1996. The influence of stimulus location on the brain activation pattern in detection and orientation discrimination. A PET study of visual attention. *Brain* 119:1263–1276.

WISE, S. P., D. BOUSSAOUD, P. B. JOHNSON, and R. CAMINITI, 1997. Premotor and parietal cortex: Corticocortical connectivity and combinatorial computations. *Annu. Rev. Neurosci.* 20:25–42.

WOJCIULIK, E., N. KANWISHER, and J. DRIVER, 1998. Covert visual attention modulates face-specific activity in the human fusiform gyrus: fMRI study. *J. Neurophysiol.* 79:1574–1578.

WOLDORFF, M. G., P. T. FOX, M. MATZKE, J. L. LANCASTER, S. VEERASWAMY, F. ZAMARRIPA, M. SEABOLT, T. GLASS, J. H. GAO, C. C. MARTIN, and P. Jerabek, 1997. Retinotopic organization of early visual spatial attention effects as revealed by PET and ERPs. *Hum. Brain Map.* 5:280–286.

WURTZ, R. H., M. E. GOLDBERG, and D. L. ROBINSON, 1982. Brain mechanisms of visual attention. *Sci. Amer.* 246:124–135.

WURTZ, R. H., and C. W. MOHLER, 1976. Enhancement of visual responses in monkey striate cortex and frontal eye fields. *J. Neurophysiol.* 39:766–772.

47 The Operation of Selective Attention at Multiple Stages of Processing: Evidence from Human and Monkey Electrophysiology

STEVEN J. LUCK AND STEVEN A. HILLYARD

ABSTRACT Because of its finite computational resources, the human brain must process information selectively in a variety of domains. For example, we may limit processing to a subset of the many possible objects that could be perceived, a subset of the many possible memories that could be accessed, or a subset of the many possible actions that could be performed. Although the fundamental need for selective processing is present at each of these stages, there are important differences in the computations performed by different cognitive systems; hence it is likely that substantially different attentional mechanisms are responsible for selective processing at each stage. It has been difficult, however, to isolate the attentional mechanisms that operate in different cognitive systems, primarily because behavioral outputs typically reflect the combined effects of several stages of processing. In this chapter, we describe the application of electrophysiological techniques to the isolation of attentional operations at different stages of processing, including perception, working memory, and response selection.

During almost every waking moment, the human brain is confronted with a vast amount of information—thoughts, memories, and emotions—and innumerable sensory inputs from every modality. To avoid being overwhelmed by this cacophony, the brain relies on mechanisms of selective attention that limit processing to a subset of the available information. The resulting selectivity is easily observed in everyday human behavior: We generally focus our thoughts and conversations on a small number of topics at any given moment, and we typically notice and remember only a fraction of the objects and events we encounter. Moreover, because we have but two hands, two feet, and one mouth, our actions are typically directed toward a small number of tasks at any one time.

Although the effects of selective attention on behavior are ubiquitous, the internal mechanisms by which information is selected are just beginning to be understood. Indeed, the pervasiveness of selectivity is partly responsible for the difficulty of understanding how attention operates, because a given behavioral sign of selective attention could potentially reflect internal selectivity within any of the various cognitive subsystems that underlie a given behavior. Over the past 25 years, the techniques of cognitive neuroscience have played an increasingly important role in helping to analyze the level of processing at which information is selected and to understand the neural substrates of the selection process.

In this chapter, we focus on two fundamental and interrelated issues in the study of attention. The first issue is the classic "locus-of-selection" question, which asks whether attention operates at an early, perceptual stage or at a late, postperceptual stage. Previously, we have stressed the operation of attention at early stages (Hillyard et al., 1995), but here we discuss conditions under which attention operates at intermediate and late stages as well as at early stages. The second issue to be addressed in this chapter is the question of exactly why selective attention is needed at certain stages of processing. For many years, psychologists were satisfied with the proposal that cognitive processes were simply limited in capacity and that attention was used to allocate some sort of processing resource. But it is now possible to specify more exactly how selective attention may solve specific computational problems that arise in cognitive processing, such as the so-called "binding problem," which occurs when independently coded attributes of an object must be combined (Luck, Girelli, et al., 1997; Treisman, 1996).

STEVEN J. LUCK Department of Psychology, University of Iowa, Iowa City, Iowa
STEVEN A. HILLYARD Department of Neurosciences, University of California, San Diego, La Jolla, Calif.

Electrophysiological techniques

Several neuroscience techniques can be used to study attention, but in this chapter we focus primarily on event-related potentials (ERPs) in humans and single-unit recordings in monkeys. ERPs are voltage deflections that can be recorded on the scalp at the time of a stimulus, a response, or some other measurable event. These voltage deflections typically arise from summated postsynaptic potentials in the cerebral cortex that are passively conducted through the brain and skull to the scalp, where they can be recorded noninvasively from normal volunteers (reviewed in Hillyard and Picton, 1987). As illustrated in figure 47.1, the ERP waveform following a stimulus consists of several positive (P) and negative (N) deflections called "waves" or "components." The sequence of components following a stimulus reflects the sequence of neural processes triggered by the stimulus, beginning with early sensory processes and proceeding through decision- and response-related processes. The amplitude and latency of the successive peaks can be used to measure the time course of cognitive processing, and the distribution of voltage over the scalp can be used to estimate the neuroanatomical loci of these processes. ERPs have two main advantages over traditional behavioral measures in the context of attention research. First, they provide a continuous measure of processing between a stimulus and a response, making it possible to determine the stage or stages of processing that are influenced by attention. Second, ERPs provide a means of covertly measuring the processing of a stimulus—without requiring an overt response—which is very useful for assessing the processing of unattended stimuli. However, the spatial resolution of the ERP technique is limited, and so we also discuss data obtained from other human neuroimaging techniques and from recordings of single-unit activity in monkeys.

Multiple stages of selection

Across a wide variety of conditions, it can be shown that people are faster and more accurate at detecting attended stimuli than unattended stimuli. However, the origins of such effects have been debated since the 1950s, with some researchers arguing that attended stimuli are better perceived than unattended stimuli (the "early-selection" position) and others arguing that perceptual processing is unaffected by attention and that selective processing occurs only at postperceptual stages, such as working memory and response selection (the "late-selection" position). It is beyond debate that atten-

tion does sometimes operate at a late stage—after all, there are clearly occasions when an individual fully perceives a stimulus but chooses not to make an overt response to it. The burden of proof therefore rests on the shoulders of those who argue that attention operates at an early stage. As we discuss in the next section, neurophysiological studies have now conclusively demonstrated that attention operates at early stages as well, at least under some conditions. Thus, attention may oper-

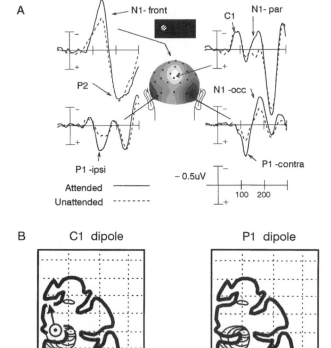

FIGURE 47.1 Stimuli and results from a typical ERP attention experiment (Clark and Hillyard, 1996). In experiments such as this, the subject fixates a central point and attends to either the left or right visual field. Stimuli are flashed to the left and right fields in a rapid, randomized sequence, and the subject responds to occasional targets embedded among frequently occurring nontargets in the attended field. (A) Grand average ERP waveforms from four different scalp sites, showing the C1, P1, and N1 components. The P1 and N1 components were larger for attended-location stimuli than for unattended-location stimuli, but the C1 component was unaffected by attention. The scalp map shows the distribution of voltage from 60–85 ms. In this time period, the C1 wave appears as a negative potential (indicated by light gray) at the midline, and the P1 wave appears as a positive potential (indicated by dark gray) at lateral occipital sites. (B) Estimates of the C1 and P1 dipole sources, projected onto coronal brain sections derived from the atlas of Talairach and Tournoux (1988). These best-fit dipoles were calculated from the scalp voltage distributions using the BESA algorithm (Scherg, 1990). (Reprinted with permission from Hillyard, Teder-Sälejärvi, and Münte, 1998.)

ate at either early or late stages of processing (or both), and the task for attention researchers has now shifted to determining what conditions lead to attentional selection at a given stage of processing.

We propose that a simple principle determines the stage at which attention operates: The presence or absence of attentional selection at a given stage of processing depends on the presence or absence of interference at that stage, which in turn depends on the stimuli and task. For example, consider a task in which red and green letters are presented individually at fixation at a rate of one letter per second, and the subjects are required to remember all the red letters, reporting them at the end of a 15-second trial block. The visual system could easily identify both the red letters and the green letters at this slow stimulus presentation rate; therefore, no selective processing of the red letters would be expected at the stage of perception. However, the limited capacity of working memory would make it difficult for most subjects to retain both the red and the green letters, so only the red letters would be selected for storage in working memory. In contrast, a very different pattern of selectivity would be expected if 14 green letters and 1 red letter were presented simultaneously in a densely packed array and the subject were required to report the identity of the red letter as quickly as possible. In this case, the memory load would be relatively modest, but the green letters might interfere with the perception of the red letter, thus necessitating a perceptual-level filtering of the green letters (i.e., early selection). Perceptual-level interference may also arise with individually presented stimuli under certain conditions, such as when the stimuli are presented at such low intensities that spontaneous neural noise becomes a significant source of interference (Hawkins et al., 1990).

By this account, the locus of selection is directly determined by the stage or stages of processing at which interference is present for a given stimulus-task combination (for a related account, see Lavie, 1995). Although this is a useful conceptualization of the locus-of-selection issue, it is difficult to test unless there is an independent means of determining the conditions under which interference will be present at a given stage. In the following sections, we describe conditions that would be expected to lead to interference at three coarsely defined stages of processing—namely, perception, working memory, and response selection.

Evidence for selection at the perceptual level

THE ONSET TIME OF SELECTIVE PROCESSING The application of the ERP technique to the locus-of-selection issue relies on straightforward logic: If attention operates at an early stage, then the early sensory-evoked ERP waves should be enhanced for attended stimuli relative to unattended stimuli, whereas if attention operates at a late stage, then only the later ERP waves should be affected. Several studies have used this logic in combination with variants of the experimental paradigm illustrated in figure 47.1A. In this paradigm, subjects fixate a central point while stimuli are flashed at predefined locations in the left visual field (LVF) and the right visual field (RVF). Subjects are instructed to attend to the LVF in some trial blocks and to the RVF in other trial blocks, and they are required to respond when they detect an infrequent target stimulus that occurs occasionally among the nontarget stimuli at the attended location. The stimuli are presented rapidly, making it difficult for the subjects to detect the targets without the use of focused attention. Under these conditions, numerous studies have shown that the initial P1 and N1 waves are larger in amplitude for stimuli presented at the attended location than for stimuli presented at the unattended location (reviewed in Hillyard, Vogel, and Luck, in press).

There are several reasons to believe that the modulation of P1 amplitude by spatial attention reflects a modulation of perceptual rather than postperceptual processing. First, the P1 component is an obligatory sensory response from the occipital cortex (see below) that is sensitive to stimulus factors such as contrast and stimulus position and is insensitive to cognitive factors (with the exception of spatial attention). Attentional modulations of this component are therefore most readily attributable to changes in sensory processing (Johannes et al., 1995; Wijers et al., 1997). Second, this effect typically begins 70–90 ms after stimulus onset, at which time visual information is only beginning to reach the object recognition areas of the inferotemporal cortex. Third, effects of this nature have been observed only in studies of spatial attention and have not been observed when attended and unattended stimuli are presented at the same location and differ in other stimulus dimensions such as color (Hillyard and Anllo-Vento, 1998). If attention operates after stimulus identification is complete, there would be no reason to expect that the dimension of spatial location would be treated any differently from other stimulus dimensions (e.g., see Bundesen, 1990), whereas a special mechanism for selection by location is entirely consistent with the topographically organized representations used in the early and intermediate stages of visual processing. Finally, equivalent P1 attention effects are observed regardless of the task-relevance of a stimulus. In particular, P1 amplitude modulations are observed both for targets and nontargets, and even for task-irrelevant "probe" stimuli that are occasionally flashed at the attended and unattended locations but do not resemble the task-relevant stimuli (Heinze et al., 1990; Luck, Fan, and Hillyard, 1993). Presumably, any attention effects that operate after a stimulus has been identified would be limited to task-relevant stimuli, because there would be little point in attending to a stimulus already identified as task-irrelevant. In contrast, any attention effects that occur before identification is complete must necessarily be insensitive to the identity of the stimulus. It should also be noted that results of this nature have been observed in the visual search and spatial cuing paradigms, which are frequently used to assess the behavioral effects of selective attention (Luck, Fan, and Hillyard, 1993; Luck and Hillyard, 1995; Luck et al., 1994; Mangun and Hillyard, 1991).

Neural Sites of Selective Attention   Although the P1 attention effect almost certainly represents a modulation of perceptual processing, it is not yet clear exactly which specific substages of perception are being modulated or which specific areas of visual cortex are subject to attentional control. To provide more specific information about the locus of selection within perception, recent studies have attempted to determine the neuroanatomical sources of the ERP attention effects and have recorded single-unit activity in specific areas of visual cortex in monkeys.

Recordings of ERPs from midline parieto-occipital scalp sites typically include a component called C1 that has an onset latency of 50–60 ms, which is even earlier than that of the P1 (see figure 47.1A). Two sources of evidence indicate that the C1 wave is generated in primary visual cortex (V1). First, as shown in figure 47.1B, dipole modeling procedures have indicated that the C1 scalp distribution is consistent with a generator source in area V1. Second, the scalp distribution and polarity of the C1 wave change as a function of stimulus position in the visual field, and these changes correspond closely to the known retinotopic projections of the upper versus lower visual fields upon the striate cortex within the calcarine fissure (Clark, Fan, and Hillyard, 1995; Mangun, Hillyard, and Luck, 1993). Several studies have found that the C1 wave is unaffected by spatial attention under conditions that lead to significant modulations of P1 amplitude (Clark and Hillyard, 1996; Gomez Gonzales et al., 1994; Mangun, Hillyard, and Luck, 1993), which indicates that the initial sensory response in V1 is not affected by attention [although attention may influence V1 at a later point in processing (see Aine, Supek, and George, 1995)]. In contrast, the neural generators of the P1 wave can be accurately modeled by dipoles in extrastriate cortical areas (figure 47.1B), and the effects of attention on the P1 wave suggest that spatial attention first

influences visual processing in extrastriate areas of visual cortex.

To assess the neural locus of the P1 attention effect more precisely, Heinze and colleagues (1994) conducted a study in which subjects performed a variant of the attention task shown in figure 47.1 during both an ERP recording session and a positron emission tomography (PET) session. The P1 attention effect was found to be associated with an increase in blood flow in the ventral occipital lobe in the posterior fusiform gyrus, and dipole modeling indicated that the scalp distribution of the P1 attention effect was consistent with a generator source in this region. Mangun and colleagues (1997) subsequently reported that both the P1 attention effect and the increase in fusiform blood flow are influenced similarly by task manipulations, thereby reinforcing the hypothesis that the two measures reflect the same underlying neural activity. A second area in the medial occipital gyrus also showed an effect of attention on blood flow. For stimuli presented in the lower visual field, however, Woldorff and colleagues (1997) observed increased blood flow and an associated P1 dipole in a dorsal extrastriate area of the occipital lobe, with a secondary focus in the fusiform gyrus. Although the specific areas affected by attention vary among the experiments, these combined PET and ERP data strongly indicate that early perceptual selection takes place in extrastriate visual cortex.

Converging evidence concerning the localization of attentional modulation was provided by a recent study in which single-unit activity was recorded from macaque monkeys while the animals performed a task similar to that shown in figure 47.1 (Luck, Chelazzi, et al., 1997). As shown in figure 47.2A, many neurons in area V4 exhibited larger responses to attended-location stimuli than to unattended-location stimuli. Figure 47.2B plots the difference in the response to the attended- and unattended-location stimuli, showing that the effect of attention began at 60 ms poststimulus, which is the same time as the beginning of the stimulus-evoked neural response. Thus, attention appears to operate as a preset filter that modulates the initial afferent volley of activity through area V4. In addition, as in the case of the P1 attention effect, this modulation of single-unit activity was identical for target and nontarget stimuli (see figure 47.2C). In contrast, no consistent effects of attention were observed in a parallel set of recordings from area V1, which is consistent with the lack of any attention effect for the C1 wave in ERP recordings. Together, the ERP, PET, and single-unit results provide compelling evidence that selective attention can modulate perceptual processing in extrastriate visual cortex, at least under cer-

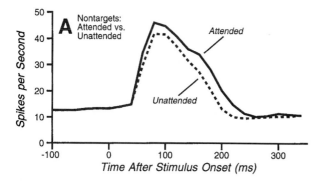

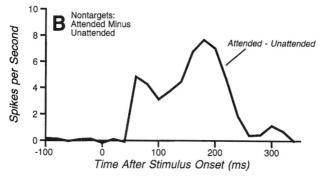

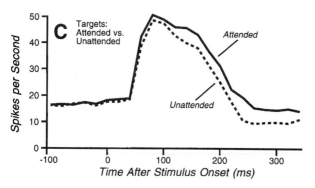

FIGURE 47.2 Single-unit responses recorded from area V4 in the study of Luck and co-workers (1997a). (A) Average post-stimulus histograms from 37 neurons that showed a significant difference in the response to an attended-location stimulus compared to an unattended-location stimulus. These responses were elicited by nontarget stimuli. (B) Difference between the responses to attended- and unattended-location stimuli. Note that this difference deviates from zero at approximately 60 ms, which is the same time as the onset of the sensory response. (C) Responses to target stimuli presented at the attended and unattended locations. (Adapted with permission from Luck, Chelazzi, et al., 1997.)

tain conditions (see also Connor et al., 1996; Moran and Desimone, 1985; Motter, 1993).

Conditions leading to early selection

As discussed above, we propose that attention will operate at a given stage of processing only when there is interference at that stage. Lavie and her colleagues have similarly argued that attention operates at an early stage

only under conditions of high perceptual load (Lavie, 1995; Lavie and Tsal, 1994). Consistent with these proposals, early attentional modulations of neural activity have been observed only when a significant perceptual load was imposed by requiring speeded responses, by using difficult-to-detect targets, by surrounding the target with competing nontarget stimuli, or by presenting the stimuli at a very rapid rate (e.g., see Luck, Fan, and Hillyard, 1993; Luck et al., 1994; Mangun and Hillyard, 1991). As detailed below, these are conditions that are likely to create perceptual-level interference and are thus likely to lead to perceptual-level attention effects. In particular, there are at least two different types of interference arising at the stage of perception that may be alleviated by selective attention. The first of these is interference among multiple objects, which can lead to binding errors (i.e., errors caused by incorrectly combining features that belong to different objects), and the second is interference from spontaneous neural activity.

THE BINDING PROBLEM The problem of correctly binding together the features of an object can arise at many stages of the nervous system, and one variant of this problem is illustrated in figure 47.3. This figure shows the responses of a set of four idealized V4 neurons that are selective for different features but have overlapping receptive fields. When a red horizontal bar is presented (figure 47.3A), the red-selective and horizontal-selective neurons are activated and the stimulus is coded correctly. Similarly, when a green vertical bar is presented (figure 47.3B), the green-selective and vertical-selective neurons are activated and the stimulus is again coded correctly. However, when the red horizontal and green vertical bars are presented simultaneously (figure 47.3C), all four neurons are activated and the neural coding becomes ambiguous; in particular, it is not possible to determine from these neurons whether the display contains a red horizontal bar and a green vertical bar or a green horizontal bar and a red vertical bar. In the terms used by Treisman and Schmidt (1982), the presence of multiple stimuli within the receptive fields of these cells may lead to "illusory conjunctions."

Luck, Girelli, and colleagues (1997) recently proposed an "ambiguity resolution theory" of attention, which postulates that ambiguity in neural coding can be resolved by an attentional mechanism that limits processing to a single object at any given moment. If the inputs from the other objects are momentarily suppressed, then the neurons that remain active must necessarily correspond to the attended object (figure 47.3D). The theory also proposes that such filtering will be necessary only under conditions that lead to ambiguous neural coding. For example, when an observer is required simply to de-

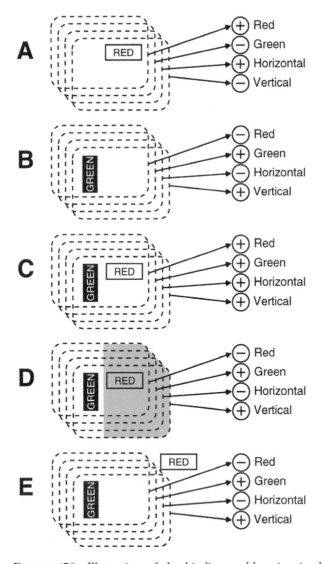

FIGURE 47.3 Illustration of the binding problem in visual cortex. The areas enclosed in broken lines represent the overlapping receptive fields of four neurons in area V4, each of which is selective for a different feature (red, green, horizontal, and vertical). A plus sign indicates that the neuron responds to the stimulus and a minus sign indicates no response. When only a single red horizontal bar is present (A), only the red-selective and horizontal-selective cells fire, and when only a single green vertical is present (B), only the green-selective and vertical-selective cells fire. However, when both bars are present simultaneously (C), all four cells fire and it is impossible to determine which features belong to the same object. This problem can be solved by an attentional mechanism that suppresses the responses to the unattended objects (indicated by the gray shading in D), such that the neural responses reflect only a single object. Importantly, the binding problem is not present when two objects are present but only one falls inside the receptive fields (E). In this case, the neurons unambiguously signal the features of the stimulus inside the receptive field.

tect the presence of red in a stimulus array, there is no ambiguity because the response of the red-selective neurons unambiguously signals the presence or absence of the color red, independently of the other objects in the display [as long as the colors of the objects are easily discriminable (see Treisman and Gormican, 1988)]. In addition, a neuron's responses are ambiguous only when multiple stimuli are presented inside its receptive field; when only a single object falls inside the receptive field, the neuron's response unambiguously codes the features of that object (figure 47.3E).

Evidence supporting this view of attention has been obtained in several single-unit recording studies (Chelazzi et al., 1993; Luck, Chelazzi, et al., 1997; Moran and Desimone, 1985; Treue and Maunsell, 1996), one of which is summarized in figure 47.4. Panel A of this figure shows the responses obtained from an individual neuron in area V4. When the monkey performed a simple fixation task, this neuron gave a large response to a blue vertical bar presented alone and a small response to a green horizontal bar presented alone. When the two stimuli were presented together and the monkey was instructed to attend to one of the two stimulus locations, the response of the cell was modulated by attention such that the response elicited by both stimuli presented simultaneously was similar to the response to the attended stimulus presented alone (figure 47.4B). In other words, when the monkey attended to the blue vertical bar, the response to the pair of bars was large, just like the response to the blue vertical bar presented alone; when the monkey attended to the green horizontal bar, the response to the pair of bars was small, as was the response to the green horizontal bar presented alone. Thus, attention appeared to filter out the contribution of the unattended stimulus.

Figure 47.4C shows the effects of attention averaged over a population of 29 neurons in area V4. Again, these neurons gave a larger response when attention was directed to an effective stimulus (i.e., a stimulus that elicited a large response regardless of attention) than to an ineffective stimulus (i.e., a stimulus that elicited a small response regardless of attention). As shown in figure 47.4D, however, this effect was eliminated when only one of the two stimuli was inside the receptive field and the other stimulus was outside the receptive field.

The effects of attention have been assessed in areas V1, V2, V4, and MT of the occipital lobe and also in inferotemporal cortex (Chelazzi et al., 1993; Luck, Chelazzi, et al., 1997; Moran and Desimone, 1985; Treue and Maunsell, 1996). In all of these areas, the results have suggested that strong attention-related modulations of sensory activity occur primarily when multiple stimuli are presented inside the classical excitatory receptive field (or so close to the receptive field that they

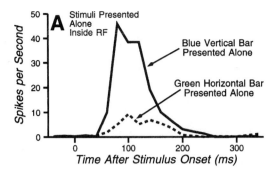

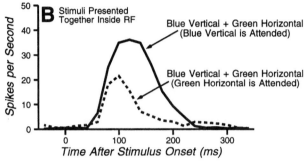

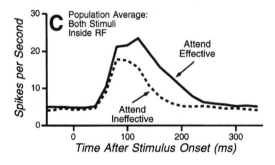

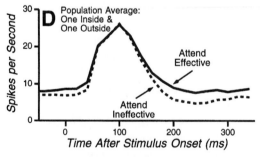

FIGURE 47.4 Single-unit responses recorded from area V4 in the study of Luck and co-workers (1997a). (A) Responses of a single neuron to a blue vertical bar and to a green horizontal bar, presented individually inside the receptive field. (B) Responses of the same neuron when the two stimuli are presented simultaneously inside the receptive field and attention is directed to the blue vertical stimulus in some trial blocks and to the green horizontal stimulus in other blocks. (C) Average response across 29 neurons when attention is directed to an effective or an ineffective stimulus when both are presented simultaneously inside the receptive field. (D) Average response across the same neurons when only one of the two stimuli is located inside the receptive field. (Adapted with permission from Luck, Chelazzi, et al., 1997.)

would be expected to indirectly influence the response of the cell). Receptive fields are so small in area V1 that it is virtually impossible for an animal to attend to one stimulus inside the receptive field and ignore another that is also inside the receptive field, and attention effects have only rarely been observed in this area (Motter, 1993). In area V2, receptive fields are only slightly larger, but attention effects have been observed in the subset of V2 cells with large enough receptive fields to contain both an attended and an unattended stimulus (Luck, Chelazzi, et al., 1997). In V4, most receptive fields are large enough to contain multiple stimuli, and two studies have found that the effects of attention are substantially larger when multiple stimuli are presented inside the receptive field (Luck, Chelazzi, et al., 1997; Moran and Desimone, 1985). A similar result has been reported for area MT (Treue and Maunsell, 1996). In inferotemporal cortex, the receptive fields are so large that it is difficult to place a stimulus outside the receptive field, and the majority of cells in this area exhibit large attention effects (Moran and Desimone, 1985). As will be discussed later, attention effects have sometimes been observed in extrastriate cortex in the absence of multiple stimuli inside the receptive field (Connor et al., 1996; Motter, 1993; Spitzer, Desimone, and Moran, 1988; Treue and Maunsell, 1995), but all studies that have compared multiple stimuli inside the receptive field to a single stimulus inside the receptive field have found substantially larger attention effects in the former condition. These results are consistent with the proposal that attention operates to resolve ambiguities in neural coding that arise when multiple stimuli influence the response of a neuron.

Two questions are often asked in the context of these results. First, how is it possible for a neuron to "know" when multiple stimuli are present inside its receptive field? The answer to this question is not yet known, but we assume that the local circuitry within each visual area contains the information necessary to determine—at least coarsely—when a potentially ambiguous stimulus configuration is present. Second, why is attentional filtering limited only to a subset of neurons? The answer to this question is relatively straightforward: There is a cost to throwing away information. For example, it appears that neurons in area V4 achieve color constancy by integrating wavelength information across broad areas of the visual field, and widespread filtering within V4 might impair color constancy. Everyday experience also supports the proposal of limited filtering, because we do not experience the sort of "tunnel vision" that would result if most of the visual scene were filtered at a given moment. Thus, it is reasonable to suppose that attention is used sparingly and

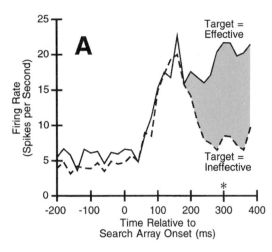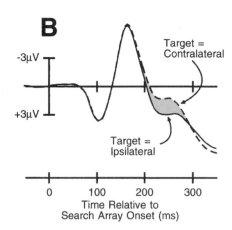

FIGURE 47.5 (A) Single-unit responses recorded from infero-temporal cortex in the study of Chelazzi and colleagues (1993), averaged over 22 neurons. Target and nontarget stimuli were presented simultaneously inside the receptive field, and the monkey was required to make a saccade toward the target (mean saccadic reaction time is indicated by the asterisk). In some trials, the target was an effective stimulus and the nontarget was an ineffective stimulus for the neuron being recorded, and in other trials, this was reversed. The neurons initially gave a large response whether the target was an effective or ineffective stimulus, but beginning around 175 ms poststimulus, the response became suppressed if the target was an ineffective stimulus. In other words, the cell initially responded to both stimuli, but eventually coded the features of the target exclusively. (B) Analogous ERP results from the study of Luck and colleagues (1997b). In this experiment, a distinctly colored target was embedded in an array of distractor items and the subject was required to press one of two buttons to indicate the target's shape. The ERP response was initially insensitive to the location of the target, but beginning around 175 ms, the response was more negative at electrode sites contralateral to the target compared to sites ipsilateral to the target; this effect is called the N2pc component (for N2-posterior-contralateral). (Adapted with permission from Luck, Girelli, et al., 1997.)

that neural responses are suppressed only when neural coding becomes ambiguous.

The short-latency attention effects shown in figure 47.4 were obtained when attention was precued to a location before stimulus onset, and similar but delayed effects are found when the location of the to-be-attended object is not known in advance. In visual search tasks, for example, it appears that neurons in extrastriate cortex initially provide a coarse preattentive coding of the entire visual field so that a potential target can be located, followed by the focusing of attention onto this item for complete identification. This is illustrated in an experiment reported by Chelazzi and colleagues (1993), in which monkeys were presented with two items simultaneously and were required to determine if either of them was a target item. As shown in figure 47.5A, when one of the stimuli was an effective stimulus and the other was an ineffective stimulus for the neuron being recorded, the neuron initially gave a large response. Beginning around 175 ms poststimulus, however, the neuron's firing became suppressed if the target was the ineffective stimulus but continued unabated if the target was the effective stimulus. In other words, after an initial preattentive period—during which the neuron simply signaled the presence of an effective stimulus—the neuron's output began to reflect only the properties of the target stimulus. As in the case of pre-

cued attention, these effects were larger when both stimuli were inside the receptive field.

An analogous set of results has been obtained in ERP recordings from human subjects (Luck, Girelli, et al., 1997). In particular, modulations of an occipital ERP component called the N2pc wave (shown in figure 47.5B) closely resemble the monkey single-unit suppression effect shown in figure 47.5A. In addition to having a similar outset time, the N2pc wave is affected by a variety of experimental manipulations in the same manner as the single-unit attention effects observed by Chelazzi and his colleagues (Chelazzi and Desimone, 1994; Chelazzi et al., 1993). Specifically, the N2pc component is larger for conjunction discrimination tasks than for feature detection tasks, is larger when a target is surrounded by nearby distractor items, and is larger when a simple feature must be localized than when it must simply be detected. Thus, in both human and nonhuman primates, one major role of attention is to resolve the ambiguous neural coding that occurs when multiple items are presented within a neuron's receptive field.

THE PROBLEM OF INTERNALLY GENERATED NOISE Despite the wide applicability of the ambiguity resolution theory, attention effects have also been observed under conditions that would not be expected to lead to ambiguous neural coding (Mangun and Hillyard, 1991;

694   ATTENTION

Motter, 1993; Spitzer, Desimone, and Moran, 1988). For example, attended stimuli have sometimes been found to elicit larger responses than unattended stimuli even though these stimuli were presented sequentially and at widely separated locations (Mangun and Hillyard, 1988; Motter, 1993). Such effects have been observed primarily when the stimuli were difficult to identify or when a limited amount of time was available for perceiving or responding to the stimuli. To explain these modulations of sensory responses, several researchers have proposed that attention operates like a sensory gain control, amplifying attended channels compared to unattended channels (Hawkins et al., 1990; Hillyard, Vogel, and Luck, in press; Treisman, 1964). It is important to note, however, that increasing the gain of an input source will not always lead to an improvement in perceptual performance, because both the signal and the noise contained in the input will be amplified. A gain control mechanism can be useful, however, when perceptual performance is limited by the brain's internal noise rather than by noise in the input. As an analogy, imagine listening to a high-fidelity musical recording through headphones in a quiet room. At low volumes, one's own breathing and heartbeat may make it difficult to hear the music clearly, and turning up the volume even slightly may significantly improve the clarity with which the music is heard. In contrast, imagine listening to a very poor recording at a moderate volume level. Owing to the noise in the input source, the music may be very difficult to perceive clearly, but turning up the volume provides no improvement because an increase in gain increases the noise as well as the signal. Thus, an attention-controlled sensory gain control mechanism would be useful whenever performance is limited by internal noise rather than by noise in the input source.

There are many experimental tasks in which a simple gain control mechanism would be useful. For example, when an observer is required to discriminate between two similar colors, any intrinsic variability in spontaneous neural activity may impair discrimination performance, and increasing the gain at an early stage in the system would minimize the effects of the spontaneous activity. Similarly, when an observer is asked to make a very rapid response, a decision must be made before the visual system has acquired much information about the stimulus, and internal noise could lead to erroneous responses. In addition, high rates of stimulus presentation may increase internal noise levels because the neural responses elicited by irrelevant stimuli may contribute noise during the processing of relevant stimuli, and a sensory gain control mechanism may again prove useful under such conditions. These are exactly the conditions under which gain control–like modulations of sensory

responses have been observed (e.g., Mangun and Hillyard, 1988; Mangun and Hillyard, 1991; Spitzer, Desimone, and Moran, 1988). Thus, it appears that attention plays at least two roles at the stage of perceptual processing—namely, resolving ambiguous neural coding by suppressing competing input sources and improving signal-to-noise ratios by controlling sensory gain.

Conditions leading to late selection

SELECTION IN VISUAL WORKING MEMORY   The term "working memory" refers to the temporary storage of information that can be manipulated according to task demands. Working memory has been divided into multiple subsystems, with a separate storage module for each sensory modality and a single central executive process that coordinates storage, manipulation, and retrieval for each module (see Baddeley, 1986). In this chapter, we concentrate on visual working memory, but similar principles apply to other types of working memory as well.

Working memory has at least two characteristics that make selective attention essential for its efficient operation. First, it is well known that the storage capacity of working memory is strictly limited, with a prototypical capacity of 7 ± 2 items in the domain of verbal working memory (Miller, 1956). The capacity of visual working memory is also quite small, with a limit of approximately 4 objects (Luck and Vogel, 1997). Consequently, it is important to store only the most relevant objects in working memory to avoid overloading its limited storage capacity. Second, the process of encoding an object into a durable form in working memory appears to be slow and resource-demanding. For example, Potter (1976) showed that subjects could identify pictures of complex, real-world scenes at very rapid rates of presentation (9 pictures per second), but they could not store the pictures in working memory at such rates. This result suggests that visual perception is typically much faster than working memory storage, and a selection process is therefore necessary to control which of the many perceived objects are stored in working memory.

Visual perception suffers from interference when many items are presented simultaneously at different locations, whereas working memory appears to be impaired when items are presented rapidly at a single location. These factors led us to propose that attention will begin to operate at the stage of perception in the former case and at the stage of working memory in the latter (Luck, Vogel, and Shapiro, 1996; Vogel, Luck, and Shapiro, in press). Evidence for this hypothesis has been derived from studies of the *attentional blink* phenomenon. When subjects view rapid sequences of stimuli, the

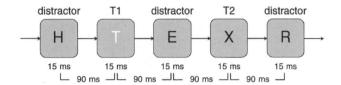

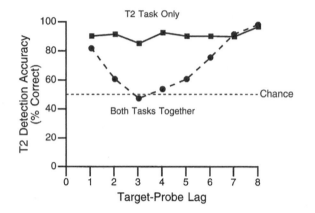

FIGURE 47.6 Stimuli and results from the attentional blink study of Raymond and colleagues (1992). Sequences of stimuli were presented rapidly at the fixation point, and at the end of each trial the subject reported the identity of the one letter that had been presented in white and indicated whether an X had been presented.

detection of a target is typically followed by a period of approximately 500 ms during which subsequent targets are missed; this impairment in the detection of subsequent targets is called the attentional blink because it is similar to the impairment that would occur if the first target triggered an eyeblink (Chun and Potter, 1995; Raymond, Shapiro, and Arnell, 1992; Shapiro, Raymond, and Arnell, 1994). As illustrated in figure 47.6A, for example, Raymond and colleagues (1992) presented subjects with rapid sequences of letters at the fixation point and asked the subjects to make two responses on each trial, the first to indicate the identity of the first target (T1, a white letter) and the second to indicate the presence or absence of the second target (T2, the letter X). In addition, a control condition was run in which subjects ignored T1 and reported only the presence or absence of T2. Figure 47.6B shows accuracy for detecting T2 as a function of the lag between T1 and T2. When the subjects were required to report both T1 and T2, T2 accuracy was severely impaired when T2 followed T1 by two to five items. However, when subjects were instructed to ignore T1, T2 accuracy was uniformly high at all lags, which indicates that the mere presence of T1 did not disrupt T2 performance. Thus, the allocation of attention to T1 resulted in a period of time during which T2 could not be reported (i.e., an attentional blink).

Initially, Raymond and colleagues (1992) suggested that the attentional blink reflects errors in the perceptual

processing of T2, but they and others have more recently proposed that the attentional blink reflects an impairment at the later stage of working memory (Chun and Potter, 1995; Shapiro, Raymond, and Arnell, 1994). In other words, the visual system can identify every item in the stimulus stream, but subjects cannot store T2 in working memory while they are busy trying to store T1, and the perceptual representation of T2 is therefore overwritten by the subsequently presented stimuli (see Giesbrecht and Di Lollo, in press). This hypothesis was recently tested in a series of electrophysiological experiments in which T2-elicited ERPs were recorded in the attentional blink paradigm (Luck, Vogel, and Shapiro, 1996; Vogel, Luck, and Shapiro, in press).

The most informative experiment focused on the N400 component, which is highly sensitive to the degree of mismatch between a word and a previously established semantic context (Kutas and Hillyard, 1980). For example, a large N400 would be elicited by the last word in the sentence, "He put the towels in the washing machine and added a cup of POPCORN," but not by the last word in the sentence, "He put the towels in the washing machine and added a cup of DETERGENT." Similar results are obtained in experiments using sequentially presented word pairs: A larger N400 is elicited by the second word if it deviates from the semantic context established by the first word [e.g., a larger N400 is elicited by the second word in lime-NICKEL than in lime-LEMON (see Kutas and Hillyard, 1989)]. Because a semantic context violation cannot be detected before the word's meaning has been assessed, the presence of a larger N400 component for a mismatching word indicates that the word has been identified to the point of lexical/semantic access. Therefore, the presence of a normal N400 component during the attentional blink period would provide strong evidence that words presented during the attentional blink are fully identified, even though the observer cannot accurately report them.

This prediction was tested in an attentional blink experiment in which T2 was a word that either matched or mismatched a semantic context established at the beginning of each trial. The results of this experiment are summarized in figure 47.7. Consistent with previous attentional blink experiments, T2 accuracy was impaired when T2 was the third item following T1 (lag 3) compared to when T2 was the first or seventh item following T1. In contrast, the N400 component was not suppressed during the attentional blink period, which indicates that the words were identified to the point of lexical/semantic access during this period, even though behavioral discrimination accuracy was substantially impaired. To demonstrate that the N400 component is actually sensitive to perceptual

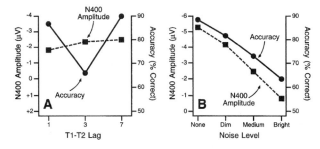

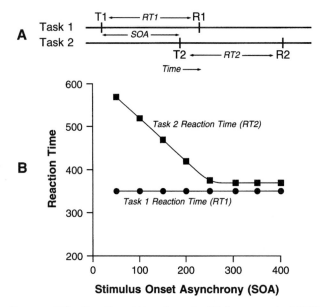

FIGURE 47.7 (A) N400 amplitude and T2 accuracy from the study of Vogel, Luck, and Shapiro (1998). When T2 was the third item after T1, T2 accuracy dropped dramatically, but there was no suppression of the N400 component. (B) Results from an additional experiment in which simultaneous visual noise was added to T2 and subjects were not required to report T1. As more noise was added, accuracy and N400 amplitude both declined, indicating that the N400 component is sensitive to manipulations of perceptual quality. (Data from Vogel, Luck, and Shapiro, in press. Copyright © 1998 by the American Psychological Association. Adapted with permission.)

FIGURE 47.8 Paradigm (A) and results (B) from a typical PRP experiment. On each trial, two targets are presented (T1 and T2), separated by a variable SOA. Independent responses are made to the two targets (R1 and R2), resulting in two reaction times on each trial (RT1 and RT2).

impairments, an additional experiment was conducted in which varying amounts of visual noise were added to the T2 stimulus, making it more difficult to perceive. This manipulation had a substantial influence on N400 amplitude, demonstrating that the N400 is quite sensitive to changes in perception. These results therefore provide strong evidence that attention operates at a postperceptual stage when stimuli are presented in a rapid sequence at a single location rather than being presented simultaneously at multiple locations.

To determine more precisely the stage at which processing is impaired during the attentional blink, an additional experiment was conducted to examine the P3 wave, which occurs after the N400 component and has been proposed to reflect the updating of working memory (Donchin, 1981). Unlike the N400 component, the P3 wave was found to be completely suppressed during the attentional blink period. This provides additional evidence for a role of attention in limiting the storage of information in working memory.

SELECTION DURING RESPONSE PROCESSING ERP recordings have also been used to examine even later stages of processing, such as the response selection processes that may be subject to attentional control when multiple responses must be made in a short period of time. For several decades, cognitive psychologists have studied this type of dual-task interference by means of the psychological refractory period (PRP) paradigm, which is illustrated in figure 47.8. In a typical PRP experiment, two targets (T1 and T2) are presented on a given trial, and the subjects is required to make a separate speeded response to each target. When the SOA be-

tween T1 and T2 is sufficiently long, the processing of T1 has completed before the processing of T2 begins, and no interference is observed. When the SOA is shortened, however, the processing of T1 interferes with the processing of T2, and the T2 response is delayed (McCann and Johnston, 1992; Welford, 1952). On the basis of behavioral experiments, Pashler (1994) has argued that this slowing of RTs is caused by interference at the stage of response selection, with minimal interference in perceptual or motor processes.

This proposal is consistent with the general model of attention presented here. Perceptual interference between T1 and T2 is not a plausible explanation for the slowed responses, because the basic PRP phenomenon is very robust even when the targets are very simple and are presented in different modalities. Similarly, interference in working memory is not a likely explanation because this task does not overload the storage capacity of working memory and because there are no masks that might overwrite the perceptual representations of the targets before they are encoded into working memory. Motor interference also seems unlikely, given that the responses are very simple and that the basic PRP effect is relatively insensitive to the similarity of the two motor responses (Pashler, 1994). Accordingly, the most likely stages for this interference would appear to be the intervening stages of target categorization (i.e., categorizing the stimuli according to the rules of the task) and response selection (i.e., mapping stimulus categories onto responses according to the rules of the task). To distinguish between these two possibilities, it is possible to examine the latency of the P3 wave, which can differentiate between stimulus categorization and response selection.

When a subject is instructed to discriminate between two or more stimulus categories, the P3 wave is typically larger for relatively improbable stimuli than for relatively probable stimuli (see review by Johnson, 1986). As an example, consider a task in which subjects view a sequence of names and must indicate whether each name is used for males or for females (e.g., John vs. Sue). If each name is presented once, but 90% of the total are male names and 10% are female names, then a larger P3 wave will be elicited by the female names. The P3 wave is thus sensitive to the probability of a task-defined category, not the probability of an individual stimulus. Accordingly, an effect of probability on P3 amplitude cannot occur until the subject has determined the task-defined category of the stimulus, and the latency of the P3 wave is therefore highly sensitive to the amount of time required to perceive and categorize a stimulus (McCarthy and Donchin, 1981). In contrast, P3 latency does not vary when the difficulty of response selection is manipulated (Kramer, Wickens, and Donchin, 1983; Magliero et al., 1984). Thus, P3 latency can be used as a relatively pure measure of the amount of time required to perceive and categorize a stimulus.

To test the hypothesis that the slowing of responses at short SOAs in the PRP paradigm reflects a delay in response selection, the P3 wave was examined in the paradigm illustrated in figure 47.9A (Luck, 1998). T1 was an outline square, and the subjects were required to press one of two buttons with one hand to indicate whether the square was red or green. T2 was a letter, and the subjects pressed one of two buttons with the other hand to indicate whether it was an X or an O. To elicit the probability-sensitive P3 wave, one of the two T2 alternatives was presented less frequently than the other (25% versus 75% of trials). The P3 wave was then isolated by constructing infrequent-minus-frequent difference waves. This subtraction eliminated any ERP activity that was unrelated to the probability of T2, including T1-elicited ERP activity. If the slowing of the response to T2 at short SOAs in the PRP paradigm is caused by interference in perception or categorization, then the latency of the P3 wave should also be delayed at short SOAs. In contrast, if the slowed RTs are caused by interference with response selection, then the P3 wave should not be delayed.

The results of this experiment are summarized in figure 47.9B. As in previous PRP experiments, the RT for T2 was significantly slowed at short SOAs. In contrast,

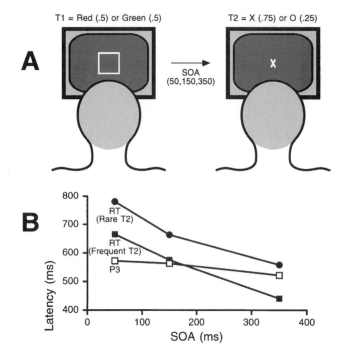

FIGURE 47.9 Stimuli (A) and results (B) from an experiment in which ERPs were recorded during a PRP task. On each trial, a red or green outline square was presented, followed by an X or an O, and subjects were required to make speeded responses to both stimuli. One of the T2 alternatives was presented less frequently than the other so that a robust P3 wave would be elicited. Reaction times decreased sharply as the SOA between T1 and T2 increased, and the same effect was seen for both rare and frequent T2 stimuli. In contrast, P3 latency decreased only slightly, indicating that the prolonged RTs observed at short SOAs are a consequence of interference at a relatively late stage of processing, probably response selection. (Adapted with permission from Luck, 1998.)

P3 latency was only slightly delayed at short SOAs, which indicates that the slowing in RT reflects interference at a stage that follows perception and categorization, presumably response selection. A follow-up experiment showed that manipulations of T2 luminance produced large changes in P3 latency, demonstrating the sensitivity of the P3 wave to manipulations of stimulus evaluation processes. Thus, it appears that the slowing of reaction time in the PRP paradigm is due primarily to delays in response selection, which is consistent with the model of Pashler (1994).

Conclusions

For several decades, cognitive psychologists have debated whether attention operates at an early stage or at a late stage, but it is now becoming clear that attention operates at both early and late stages (and at intermediate stages, as well). Moreover, attention researchers are now beginning to understand the specific reasons why attention may be necessary at a given stage under a given set of conditions. In this chapter, we have identified two computational problems—the binding problem and the problem of internally generated noise—that provide good explanations of why attention is necessary at the stage of visual perception under some conditions but not under others. We have also pointed out two key limitations at the stage of working memory—the limited storage capacity and the slowness of the storage process. Presumably, attention will operate at the stage of working memory whenever these two limitations may impair task performance. Finally, we have provided evidence that attention may sometimes be required at the stage of response selection, although it is not yet clear why it is not possible to select different responses in parallel. It seems likely that attention operates at other stages of processing in addition to those discussed here and that the coarsely defined stages described in this chapter can be subdivided more precisely. A major challenge for the future is to determine how these multiple attentional mechanisms operate in a coordinated manner to maintain unity of behavior (Posner and Petersen, 1990).

ACKNOWLEDGMENTS Preparation of this chapter was supported by grants from the National Institute of Mental Health (MH56877-01 and MH25594-24), the Human Frontier Science Program (RG0136), and the Office of Naval Research (N00014-93-I-0942).

REFERENCES

AINE, C. J., S. SUPEK, and J. S. GEORGE, 1995. Temporal dynamics of visual-evoked neuromagnetic sources: Effects of stimulus parameters and selective attention. *Int. J. Neurosci.* 80:79–104.

BADDELEY, A. D., 1986. *Working Memory.* Oxford: Clarendon.

BUNDESEN, C., 1990. A theory of visual attention. *Psychol. Rev.* 97:523–547.

CHELAZZI, L., and R. DESIMONE, 1994. Responses of V4 neurons during visual search. *Soc. Neurosci. Abstr.* 20:1054.

CHELAZZI, L., E. K. MILLER, J. DUNCAN, and R. DESIMONE, 1993. A neural basis for visual search in inferior temporal cortex. *Nature* 363:345–347.

CHUN, M. M., and M. C. POTTER, 1995. A two-stage model for multiple target detection in rapid serial visual presentation. *J. Exp. Psychol. Hum. Percept. Perform.* 21:109–127.

CLARK, V. P., S. FAN, and S. A. HILLYARD, 1995. Identification of early visually evoked potential generators by retinotopic and topographic analyses. *Hum. Brain Mapping* 2:170–187.

CLARK, V. P., and S. A. HILLYARD, 1996. Spatial selective attention affects early extrastriate but not striate components of the visual evoked potential. *J. Cogn. Neurosci.* 8:387–402.

CONNOR, C. E., J. L. GALLANT, D. C. PREDDIE, and D. C. VAN ESSEN, 1996. Responses in area V4 depend on the spatial relationship between stimulus and attention. *J. Neurophysiol.* 75:1306–1308.

DONCHIN, E., 1981. Surprise! . . . Surprise? *Psychophysiology* 18:493–513.

GIESBRECHT, B. L., and V. DI LOLLO, in press. Beyond the attentional blink: Visual masking by object substitution. *J. Exp. Psychol. Hum. Percept. Perform.*

GOMEZ GONZALES, C. M., V. P. CLARK, S. FAN, S. J. LUCK, and S. A. HILLYARD, 1994. Sources of attention-sensitive visual event-related potentials. *Brain Topography* 7:41–51.

HAWKINS, H. L., S. A. HILLYARD, S. J. LUCK, M. MOULOUA, C. J. DOWNING, and D. P. WOODWARD, 1990. Visual attention modulates signal detectability. *J. Exp. Psych. Hum. Percept. Perform.* 16:802–811.

HEINZE, H.-J., S. J. LUCK, G. R. MANGUN, and S. A. HILLYARD, 1990. Visual event-related potentials index focused attention within bilateral stimulus arrays. I. Evidence for early selection. *Electroencephalogr. Clin. Neurophysiol.* 75:511–527.

HEINZE, H.-J., G. R. MANGUN, W. BURCHERT, H. HINRICHS, M. SCHOLZ, T. F. MÜNTE, A. GÖS, M. SCHERG, S. JOHANNES, H. HUNDESHAGEN, M. S. GAZZANIGA, and S. A. HILLYARD, 1994. Combined spatial and temporal imaging of brain activity during visual selective attention in humans. *Nature* 372:543–546.

HILLYARD, S. A., and L. ANLLO-VENTO, 1998. Event-related brain potentials in the study of visual selective attention. *Proc. Natl. Acad. Sci. U.S.A.* 95:781–787.

HILLYARD, S. A., G. R. MANGUN, M. G. WOLDORFF, and S. J. LUCK, 1995. Neural systems mediating selective attention. In *The Cognitive Neurosciences*, M. S. Gazzaniga, ed. Cambridge, Mass.: MIT Press, pp. 665–681.

HILLYARD, S. A., and T. W. PICTON, 1987. Electrophysiology of cognition. In *Handbook of Physiology: Section 1. The Nervous System: Vol. 5. Higher Functions of the Brain, Part 2*, F. Plum, ed. Bethesda, Md.: Waverly Press, pp. 519–584.

HILLYARD, S. A., W. A. TEDER-SÄLEJÄRVI, and T. F. MÜNTE, 1998. Temporal dynamics of early perceptual processing. *Curr. Opin. Neurobiol.* 8:202–210.

HILLYARD, S. A., E. K. VOGEL, and S. J. LUCK, in press. Sensory gain control (amplification) as a mechanism of selective attention: Electrophysiological and neuroimaging evidence. *Philos. Trans. R. Soc. Lond. B. Biol. Sci.*

JOHANNES, S., U. KNALMANN, H. J. HEINZE, and G. R. MANGUN, 1995. Luminance and spatial attention effects on early visual processing. *Cogn. Brain Res.* 2:189–205.

JOHNSON, R., JR., 1986. A triarchic model of P300 amplitude. *Psychophysiology* 23:367–384.

KRAMER, A. F., C. D. WICKENS, and E. DONCHIN, 1983. An analysis of the processing requirements of a complex perceptual-motor task. *Hum. Factors* 25:597–621.

KUTAS, M., and S. A. HILLYARD, 1980. Event-related brain potentials to semantically inappropriate and surprisingly large words. *Biol. Psychol.* 11:99–116.

KUTAS, M., and S. A. HILLYARD, 1989. An electrophysiological probe of incidental semantic association. *J. Cogn. Neurosci.* 1:38–49.

LAVIE, N., 1995. Perceptual load as a necessary condition for selective attention. *J. Exp. Psychol. Hum. Percept. Perform.* 21:451–468.

LAVIE, N., and Y. TSAL, 1994. Perceptual load as a major determinant of the locus of selection in visual attention. *Percept. Psychophys.* 56:183–197.

LUCK, S. J., 1998. Sources of dual-task interference: Evidence from human electrophysiology. *Psychol. Sci.* 9:223–227.

LUCK, S. J., L. CHELAZZI, S. A. HILLYARD, and R. DESIMONE, 1997. Neural mechanisms of spatial selective attention in areas V1, V2, and V4 of macaque visual cortex. *J. Neurophysiol.* 77:24–42.

LUCK, S. J., S. FAN, and S. A. HILLYARD, 1993. Attention-related modulation of sensory-evoked brain activity in a visual search task. *J. Cogn. Neurosci.* 5:188–195.

LUCK, S. J., M. GIRELLI, M. T. MCDERMOTT, and M. A. FORD, 1997. Bridging the gap between monkey neurophysiology and human perception: An ambiguity resolution theory of visual selective attention. *Cogn. Psychol.* 33:64–87.

LUCK, S. J., and S. A. HILLYARD, 1995. The role of attention in feature detection and conjunction discrimination: An electrophysiological analysis. *Int. J. Neurosci.* 80:281–297.

LUCK, S. J., S. A. HILLYARD, M. MOULOUA, M. G. WOLDORFF, V. P. CLARK, and H. L. HAWKINS, 1994. Effects of spatial cuing on luminance detectability: Psychophysical and electrophysiological evidence for early selection. *J. Exp. Psychol. Hum. Percept. Perform.* 20:887–904.

LUCK, S. J., and E. K. VOGEL, 1997. The capacity of visual working memory for features and conjunctions. *Nature* 390:279–281.

LUCK, S. J., E. K. VOGEL, and K. L. SHAPIRO, 1996. Word meanings can be accessed but not reported during the attentional blink. *Nature* 382:616–618.

MAGLIERO, A., T. R. BASHORE, M. G. H. COLES, and E. DONCHIN, 1984. On the dependence of P300 latency on stimulus evaluation processes. *Psychophysiology* 21:171–186.

MANGUN, G. R., and S. A. HILLYARD, 1988. Spatial gradients of visual attention: Behavioral and electrophysiological evidence. *Electroencephalogr. Clin. Neurophysiol.* 70:417–428.

MANGUN, G. R., and S. A. HILLYARD, 1991. Modulations of sensory-evoked brain potentials indicate changes in perceptual processing during visual-spatial priming. *J. Exp. Psychol. Hum. Percept. Perform.* 17:1057–1074.

MANGUN, G. R., S. A. HILLYARD, and S. J. LUCK, 1993. Electrocortical substrates of visual selective attention. In *Attention and Performance XIV*, D. Meyer and S. Kornblum, eds. Cambridge, Mass.: MIT Press, pp. 219–243.

MANGUN, G. R., J. B. HOPFINGER, C. L. KUSSMAUL, E. M. FLETCHER, and H.-J. HEINZE, 1997. Covariations in ERP and PET measures of spatial selective attention in human extrastriate visual cortex. *Hum. Brain Mapping* 5:273–279.

MCCANN, R. S., and J. C. JOHNSTON, 1992. Locus of the single-channel bottleneck in dual-task interference. *J. Exp. Psychol. Hum. Percept. Perform.* 18:471–484.

MCCARTHY, G., and E. DONCHIN, 1981. A metric for thought: A comparison of P300 latency and reaction time. *Science* 211:77–80.

MILLER, G. A., 1956. The magical number seven, plus or minus two: Some limits on our capacity for processing information. *Psychol. Rev.* 63:81–97.

MORAN, J., and R. DESIMONE, 1985. Selective attention gates visual processing in the extrastriate cortex. *Science* 229:782–784.

MOTTER, B. C., 1993. Focal attention produces spatially selective processing in visual cortical areas V1, V2 and V4 in the presence of competing stimuli. *J. Neurophysiol.* 70:909–919.

PASHLER, H., 1994. Dual-task interference in simple tasks: Data and theory. *Psychol. Bull.* 116:220–244.

POSNER, M. I., and S. E. PETERSEN, 1990. The attention system of the human brain. *Annu. Rev. Neurosci.* 13:25–42.

POTTER, M. C., 1976. Short-term conceptual memory for pictures. *J. Exp. Psychol. Hum. Learn. Mem.* 2:509–522.

RAYMOND, J. E., K. L. SHAPIRO, and K. M. ARNELL, 1992. Temporary suppression of visual processing in an RSVP task: An attentional blink? *J. Exp. Psychol. Hum. Percept. Perform.* 18:849–860.

SCHERG, M., 1990. Fundamentals of dipole source potential analysis. In *Auditory Evoked Magnetic Fields and Potentials. Advances in Audiology VI*, F. Grandori, M. Hoke, and G. L. Romani, eds. Basel: Karger, pp. 40–69.

SHAPIRO, K. L., J. E. RAYMOND, and K. M. ARNELL, 1994. Attention to visual pattern information produces the attentional blink in rapid serial visual presentation. *J. Exp. Psychol. Hum. Percept. Perform.* 20:357–371.

SPITZER, H., R. DESIMONE, and J. MORAN, 1988. Increased attention enhances both behavioral and neuronal performance. *Science* 240:338–340.

TALAIRACH, J., and P. TOURNOUX, 1988. *Co-planar Stereotaxic Atlas of the Human Brain.* New York: Thieme Medical Publishers.

TREISMAN, A., 1996. The binding problem. *Curr. Opin. Neurobiol.* 6:171–178.

TREISMAN, A. M., 1964. Selective attention in man. *Br. Med. Bull.* 20:12–16.

TREISMAN, A., and S. GORMICAN, 1988. Feature analysis in early vision: Evidence from search asymmetries. *Psychol. Rev.* 95:15–48.

TREISMAN, A., and H. SCHMIDT, 1982. Illusory conjunctions in the perception of objects. *Cogn. Psychol.* 14:107–141.

TREUE, S., and J. H. R. MAUNSELL, 1995. Attentional modulation of direction-selective responses in the superior temporal sulcus of the macaque monkey. *Soc. Neurosci. Abstr.* 21:1759.

TREUE, S., and J. H. R. MAUNSELL, 1996. Attentional modulation of visual motion processing in cortical areas MT and MST. *Nature* 382:539–541.

VOGEL, E. K., S. J. LUCK, and K. L. SHAPIRO, in press. Electrophysiological evidence for a postperceptual locus of suppression during the attentional blink. *J. Exp. Psychol. Hum. Percept. Perform.*

WELFORD, A. T., 1952. The "psychological refractory period" and the timing of high speed performance—A review and a theory. *Br. J. Psychol.* 43:2–19.

WIJERS, A. A., J. J. LANGE, G. MULDER, and L. J. M. MULDER, 1997. An ERP study of visual spatial attention and letter target detection for isoluminant and nonisoluminant stimuli. *Psychophysiology* 34:553–565.

WOLDORFF, M. G., P. T. FOX, M. MATZKE, J. L. LANCASTER, S. VEERASWAMY, F. ZAMARRIPA, M. SEABOLT, T. GLASS, J. H. GAO, C. C. MARTIN, and P. JERABEK, 1997. Retinotopic organization of early visual spatial attention effects as revealed by PET and ERPs. *Hum. Brain Mapping* 5:280–286.

48 The Temporal Dynamics and Functional Architecture of Attentional Processes in Human Extrastriate Cortex

GEORGE R. MANGUN, AMISHI P. JHA, JOSEPH B. HOPFINGER, AND TODD C. HANDY

ABSTRACT   Attentional processes in healthy human visual cortex can be investigated using electrophysiological and functional neuroimaging approaches. Each of these methods provides a unique view of brain activity. Electrophysiological recordings provide information about the time course and functional properties of brain processes, while functional neuroimaging provides detailed information about the anatomy of such processes. Used in conjunction, these methods permit valuable cross-constraints to be placed on the interpretations that can be derived from either method used alone. Here we review the logic of how event-related potentials (ERPs) and functional neuroimaging using positron emission tomography (PET) or functional magnetic resonance imaging (fMRI) can be integrated and applied to studies of human attention. In so doing, we provide evidence about the time course and functional architecture of early spatial selection processes, including how early stages of visual cortical analysis are influenced by voluntary and reflexive attention, and by spatial working memory.

The human ability to focus one's mind on sensory input, motor output, or internal thought relies on the coordination of a distributed set of attentional systems within the brain. Systematic observation of patients suffering from neurological damage has identified many of the key brain structures involved in attentional control (e.g., Luria, 1973; Mesulam, 1981); and, over the past few decades, cognitive neuropsychological studies have revealed much about the elementary cognitive operations that are supported by major brain attention systems (e.g., Posner et al., 1984). In recent years, powerful new tools have been developed that permit the cognitive activity of the human brain to be measured in healthy individuals. In particular, electrophysiological recording (e.g., Luck and Hillyard, chapter 47, this volume) and hemodynamic imaging (e.g., Chelazzi and Corbetta,

chapter 46, this volume) of neural activity have proved highly effective in investigating attentional mechanisms. In this chapter, we focus on how the *integration* of these methods offers new insight into the temporal dynamics and functional anatomy of human attentional processes.

Integrating ERPs and functional neuroimaging

Event-related potentials (ERPs), which are recorded from the scalp, are signal-averaged voltage fluctuations that are time-locked to sensory, motor, or cognitive events. As a research tool, ERPs are unsurpassed in revealing the time course of neural activity associated with the ERP-eliciting event, and have been invaluable in the study of attention and attentional processes (for reviews, see Mangun, 1995; Mangun and Hillyard, 1995). One long-standing question in attention research, for example, concerns how early in the afferent processing stream can attention modulate sensory input. Asking this question, a number of studies have now demonstrated unequivocally that cortical sensory processing is modulated as a function of whether a stimulus occurs at an attended location (see Luck and Hillyard, chapter 47, this volume). Evidence from ERPs provided strong clues regarding the time course of early attentional selection; however, these scalp-recorded measures provided little information about the neuroanatomical loci at which attention exerted influence on stimulus analysis. Identification of the neuronal generators of these and other scalp-recorded ERPs could therefore be an important step toward the goal of describing the functional architecture of attentional circuitry in the human brain.

Unfortunately, inferences about the intracranial neural generators of scalp-recorded ERPs, termed inverse modeling, are difficult to make. The difficulty stems, in part, from the "inverse problem"–the fact that any specific pattern of electrical activity recorded at the scalp might arise from more than one unique configuration of electrical currents flowing within the volume of the head

GEORGE R. MANGUN   Center for Cognitive Neuroscience, Duke University, Durham, N.C.

AMISHI P. JHA   Brain Imaging and Analysis Center, Duke University, Durham, N.C.

JOSEPH B. HOPFINGER   Department of Psychology and Center for Neuroscience, University of California, Davis, Calif.

TODD C. HANDY   Department of Psychology and Center for Neuroscience, University of California, Davis, Calif.

and brain (e.g., Dale and Sereno, 1993; Zhang and Jewett, 1994). One possible means of mitigating the limitations in inverse modeling is to constrain the numbers of possible solutions by using prior knowledge of anatomy or physiology. We have introduced methods that experimentally integrate electrical and blood flow measures to provide additional information about the functional anatomy of attentional processes in visual cortex. The simple idea is that functional imaging using PET or fMRI can help to identify regions of the brain that are active during specific sensory, motor, or cognitive processes. Inverse electrical (or magnetic) modeling may thus be constrained, hence permitting tests of a limited set of possible generators for scalp-recorded ERPs.

In our original study using PET, we found that spatial selective attention to one-half of rapidly flashed (3 per second) bilateral symbol arrays activated extrastriate visual cortex (posterior fusiform gyrus) in the hemisphere contralateral to the attended stimuli (Heinze et al., 1994). These PET activations were then used to determine the possible locations and numbers of active areas in our task. Modeling was used to ask whether electrical activity within the brain regions defined by PET activations during spatial attention could possibly have yielded our ERP effects. We used the BESA (brain electric source analysis) method developed by Michael Scherg and his colleagues (see Scherg, 1992). BESA models the head as concentric spheres of different conductivity, and neural activity contributing to scalp-recorded ERPs as equivalent current dipoles. The BESA program permits one to specify a three-dimensional location within the volume of the spherical model head where a dipolar electric source is to be located, then allows calculation of the predicted voltage on the surface of the model head. Accordingly, we placed dipoles within the model head at the locations where PET indicated attention-related activations had occurred. We referred to these models as "seeded-forward solutions," because we placed (or seeded) the model neural sources (equivalent current dipoles) within the PET-defined brain loci. Using this approach, we argued that attention-related modulations of the sensory-evoked activity in visual cortex reflected changes in input processing in extrastriate visual cortex in the region of the posterior fusiform gyrus. Thus, for the first time, a cognitive operation (early attentional filtering) was localized both in time (80–130 ms poststimulus) and space (posterior fusiform gyrus) in the human brain.

Covariations in ERP and PET measures

Following up the study of Heinze and colleagues (1994), we investigated whether electrical (ERP) and blood flow

(PET) activations covaried across task manipulations (Mangun et al., 1997). The logic is that ERP and PET activities generated as the result of the same attentional processes should covary across conditions in which the allocation of spatial attention varies systematically. In order to vary the allocation of spatial attention, we manipulated *perceptual load*. Perceptual load has its conceptual roots in capacity theories of attention (see Kramer and Spinks, 1991). It follows from the notion that spatial attention can be likened to a limited-capacity resource that can be allocated to various spatial locations depending upon the perceptual demand created by the stimulus or task conditions (e.g., Lavie and Tsal, 1994; Lavie, 1995). Using ERPs, we have shown that perceptual load can affect the allocation of spatial attention at early stages of visual analysis (Handy and Mangun, in press). This suggests that as the perceptual load of a target item increases, more attentional resources are allocated to the spatial location of that target, leaving fewer residual resources for processing information in nontarget locations. Thus, manipulation of perceptual load offered a straightforward means of looking for covariations in ERP and PET measures of spatial attention.

In our study (Mangun et al., 1997), spatial attention effects were compared for a high-load condition similar to the symbol-matching task (see figure 48.1, top) used by Heinze and colleagues (1994), and for a lower load condition where subjects performed a simple luminance detection task. In the latter, "dot-detection" task, the target was a small dot stimulus (1 to 4 pixels, appearing anywhere within the area traversed by the symbols) whose onset was simultaneous with the symbol pairs. Lower perceptual load for the dot-detection task was demonstrated by a higher overall accuracy rate in behavioral performance in this condition relative to the more demanding symbol-matching task.

Independent of the specific task condition, focused attention to the left half of the arrays produced a PET activation in the right posterior fusiform gyrus, while attention to the right produced activation in the left posterior fusiform gyrus (figure 48.1). Additional activations in the contralateral middle occipital gyrus were also observed, but will not be discussed further here. Corresponding attention-related modulations of the P1 ERP component (110–140 ms) were observed over lateral occipital scalp regions contralateral to the attended hemifield. As the scalp voltage map of figure 48.1 indicates, the attention effect in the latency range of the P1 was sharply focused over scalp regions that overlie lateral extrastriate cortex, consistent with evidence from previous studies (e.g., Mangun, Hillyard, and Luck, 1993; Heinze et al., 1994).

However, of particular interest in this study was what differences, if any, would be observed as a function of perceptual load. Specifically, would the PET and ERP measures covary with the load-related manipulations of spatial attention? In order to address this question, the statistical interaction between the direction of attention (attend left vs. attend right) and task (symbol matching vs. dot detection) was evaluated. Attention effects in the fusiform gyri showed a statistically significant interaction of task and attention, with greater attentional activations during the difficult symbol-matching task than during the dot-detection task (figure 48.1). Importantly, this pattern was paralleled by the findings for the P1 ERP component, where the attention effect was significantly larger for symbol (high load) than for dot (low load) conditions (figure 48.1 shows the interaction in the P1). This covariation of the P1 attention effects and the fusiform gyrus PET activations can be interpreted as additional evidence that the P1 effect is actually generated in the fusiform gyrus, and converges with prior ERP data (e.g., Mangun and Hillyard, 1991) indicating an early locus of spatial attention effects on visual processing.

Mapping multiple attention-sensitive areas

The integration of ERPs and PET has helped to define the functional anatomy of early attentional modulation of stimulus inputs by providing evidence about the anatomical regions of the human brain in which attention can influence information processing. However, knowing, for example, that the posterior fusiform gyrus is activated by spatial attention tasks does not help us relate such activity to the current knowledge about the functional organization of the primate visual system derived from single-cell recordings in monkeys. That is, single-unit recordings in monkeys have identified numerous successive retinotopically organized maps (areas) of visual space in visual cortex (e.g., Felleman and Van Essen, 1991). These visual areas contain neurons that code different aspects of visual inputs, and thus it is important to identify which of these functionally defined visual areas can be influenced by attention and which cannot. In monkeys, these areas include maps for lower visual field regions projecting dorsally in the brain, beginning with V1 (striate cortex) and continuing with successive re-representations including V2 and V3 (second and third visual areas, respectively). For upper-field stimuli, the maps from V1 project ventrally toward inferotemporal lobe from V1 to V2, VP, and ventral V4 (V4v).

Functional neuroimaging is now being used to identify analogous visual cortical areas in humans, and the results are showing highly similar patterns of visual cortical organization between the macaque and human—despite critical differences in the underlying gross anat-

omy (e.g., Zeki et al., 1991; Engel et al., 1994; Sereno et al., 1995). In order to relate the PET activations reported above to these functionally defined visual areas, we have recently performed functional magnetic resonance imaging (fMRI) in single subjects. We first mapped the borders of the early visual areas (e.g., V1 and V2) in each of our subjects by stimulating the vertical and horizontal meridia of the visual field with a reversing checkerboard pattern. The activations in occipital cortex were then mapped onto anatomical templates that were derived from high-density anatomical scans of each subject (figure 48.2). The borders of V1, V2, VP, and V4v were identified as the locations where the visuotopic mappings reached either the vertical or horizontal meridian and reversed direction. Thereupon, the functionally defined visual areas were assigned using the "sign" method of Sereno and co-workers (1995).

During the same recording session, the subjects also performed the symbol-matching task used in the PET experiment discussed above, in which attention-related activations were found in both the fusiform and middle occipital gyri. Adapting the task to fMRI, subjects were instructed to attend to a location in one hemifield for a 16-s block; then in response to a visual arrow cue, they were required to switch attention to the other hemifield for 16 s. Attention was alternated between hemifields in this fashion for the duration of the ~4-min scanning period, with stimuli presented bilaterally at a rate of about three per second. Attention to upper- and lower-field stimuli was examined in separate scanning runs. Here, however, we discuss only the data for the upper visual field stimuli in order to compare the results directly with our prior PET (Heinze et al., 1994; Mangun et al., 1997) and fMRI (Mangun et al., 1998) studies. To identify which specific areas of cortex were modulated by attention, the functional scans from this task were coregistered with the anatomical templates described above, as shown in figure 48.2.

For the upper visual field stimuli, the attention-related fMRI activations were localized to the contralateral posterior lingual and fusiform gyri, and the inferior and middle occipital gyri. Although prior studies failed to identify the precise visual areas (e.g., V4v) generating these attentional modulations, the method of retinotopic mapping used in our study reveals that these extrastriate attentional activations occurred in areas V2, VP, and V4v, as can be seen by comparing the left and right halves of figure 48.2. In addition to providing key information about the stages of visual processing modulated by voluntary spatial attention, these data also provide important constraints for future dipole modeling of attention-sensitive ERP generators. That is, activations in separate visual cortical maps can now be modeled as

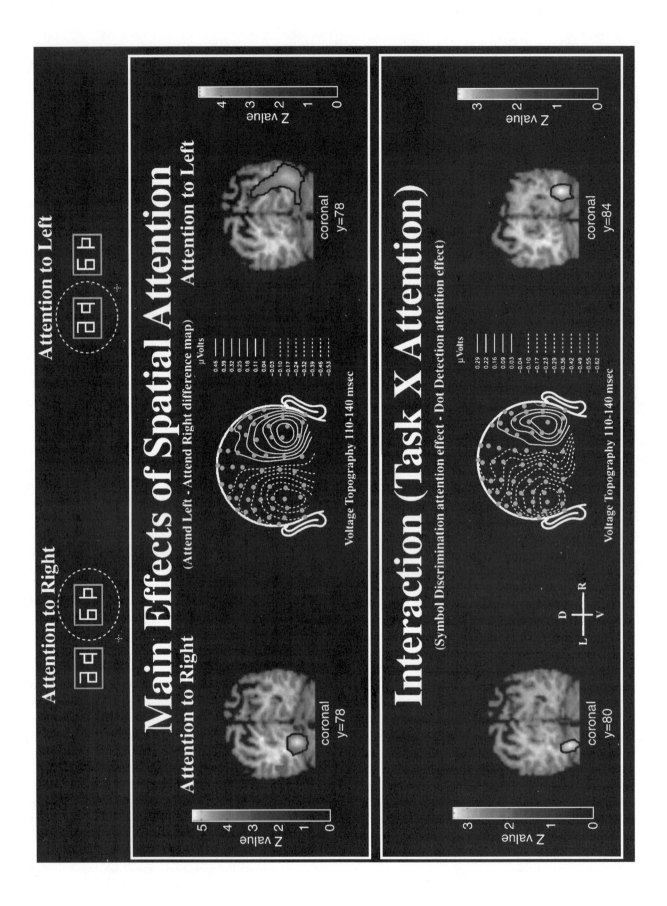

FIGURE 48.1 PET activations overlaid onto coronal sections of MRI scans, and scalp topographic voltage maps of attention effects. The task was to view bilaterally flashing stimulus arrays (top) and, while maintaining fixation on the cross-hairs, to covertly attend to either the right or left stimulus location (ignoring the opposite hemifield) in order to detect infrequent targets stimuli (matching symbols, in the symbol discrimination task; a small dot within the symbols in the dot-detection task). The main effects (collapsed across the perceptual load manipulation) of spatial selective attention (middle) included activations in the contralateral posterior fusiform (outlined in black). For example, attending to the right half of the arrays produced activations in the left occipital lobe (left of figure), while attending to the left produced activations in the right hemisphere (right of figure). (Note that the left hemisphere is on the left of each brain in the figure.) The ERP effect, shown in the center of the figure as a voltage topographic map over the period from 110–140 ms after stimulus onset, is the subtraction of the attend-left minus the attend-right voltage maps. The P1 attention effect is seen as the bilateral foci in each hemisphere. (Note that the apparently opposite polarity of the left and right hemisphere electrical effects is due to the direction of the subtraction; i.e., both foci actually represent contralateral enhancement of the positive polarity P1 component). At the bottom are shown the loci of brain activation where the attention effects interacted with the perceptual load manipulations. These fell within the posterior fusiform region. As predicted for a P1 effect generated in the posterior fusiform, the P1 effect also varied with perceptual load. Thus, there was a difference between the symbol and dot discrimination tasks in the amplitude of the P1 attention effect; this is shown in the difference map at bottom (P1 attention topographic map in the symbol condition, minus the map in the dot detection condition). Note that the P1 attention effect also showed a maximal difference as a function of perceptual load at the same occipital scalp loci that were found for the main effect of attention (compare bottom topographic map to top map). (Data adapted from Mangun et al., 1997.)

distinct electrical generators, rather than as a single neuroelectric source.

Reflexive orienting and spatial attention

So far, we have outlined the temporal dynamics of early attentional processing in the brain, as well as the neuroanatomical substrates underlying these effects in extrastriate visual cortex. However, our discussion has focused on *endogenous* attentional orienting–i.e., attentional processes that are under voluntary control. In this section, we turn to reflexive or *exogenous* attention (see Posner and Cohen, 1984). Unlike voluntary attention, which reflects the purposeful allocation of attention by a willing subject, reflexive attention is associated with external events that automatically "capture" attention, such as the abrupt or sudden onset of a transient visual stimulus (e.g., Yantis, 1996).

The fundamental differences between voluntary and reflexive attention have engendered speculation that re-

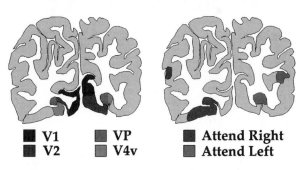

Visual Areas   Attentional Activations

■ V1   ■ VP   ■ Attend Right
■ V2   ■ V4v   ■ Attend Left

FIGURE 48.2 The visual activations from the meridian stimulation were used to determine the borders of the early occipital visual areas. One representative subject's functionally defined visual areas (V1, V2, VP, and V4v) are depicted on the left. The functionally defined visual areas are overlaid on anatomical templates for this subject that were constructed from anatomical MRI scans. On the right, the attentional activations in the same subject for the same slice are shown. The attentional activations occur in multiple visual areas including V2, VP, and V4v, as well as outside these areas in the inferior and middle occipital gyri.

flexive attention might be controlled–either wholly or in part–by neural mechanisms distinct from those involved in voluntary attention (e.g., Kustov and Robinson, 1996; Rafal, 1996; Robinson and Kertzman, 1995). However, whether the *effects* of voluntary versus reflexive attention on early visual processing are comparable remains an open question. That is, as shown above, voluntary visual-spatial attention involves a modification of cortical sensory processing, leading to a relative facilitation in visual processing in extrastriate visual cortex by 70–80 ms poststimulus (e.g., Eason, 1981; Heinze et al., 1994; Luck et al., 1994; Mangun and Hillyard, 1991; Van Voorhis and Hillyard, 1977). Are there, then, similar changes in the perceptual processing of visual stimuli as a result of reflexive shifts of attention?

Recently, we demonstrated that reflexive attention can indeed modulate early visual processing at the same neural locus as voluntary attention (Hopfinger and Mangun, 1998). In our study, targets were preceded by an uninformative flash (the cue) either at the same location (cued-location target) or at a location in the opposite hemifield (uncued-location target). Importantly, the subjects knew that the cue was completely uninformative of the location of the upcoming target, and therefore did not invoke any voluntary orienting in response to the cue. Two different cue-to-target inter-stimulus interval (ISI) ranges were used in order to measure the rapid and changing time course of reflexive attention. Both a short ISI of 34–234 ms and a long ISI of 576–766 ms were used; however, only the short ISI results are discussed here. In order to disentangle the brain responses to the

Reflexive Attention - Short ISI

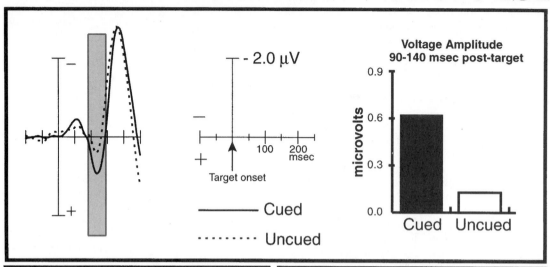

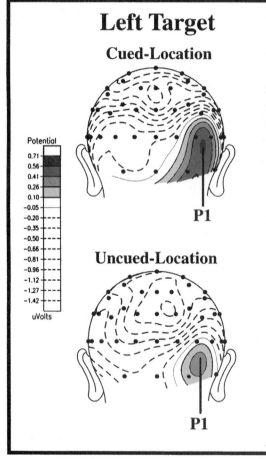

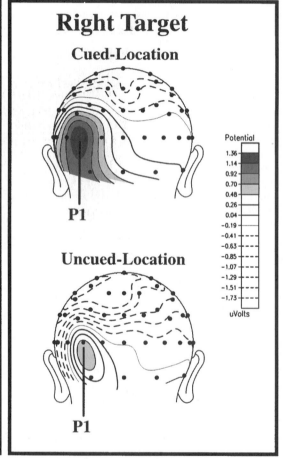

cue from those to the target, especially important for the short ISI condition, the Adjar filter developed by Woldorff (1993) was employed. This method estimates the contamination of an ERP by electrical potentials from prior or subsequent stimulus or response events, and permits the contamination to be removed.

Targets at a recently precued location elicited visual ERPs with significantly enhanced amplitudes compared to targets at an uncued location (figure 48.3, top). This enhancement was observed for the occipital P1 component. By investigating topographic voltage maps during the time period of the P1 component, it was

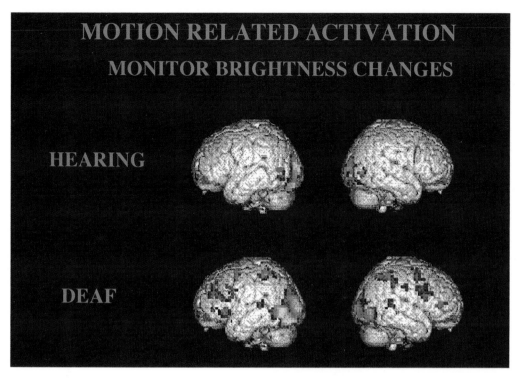

PLATE 1 Activation (fMRI, 1.5T) in normally hearing and congenitally deaf adults in response to visual motion.

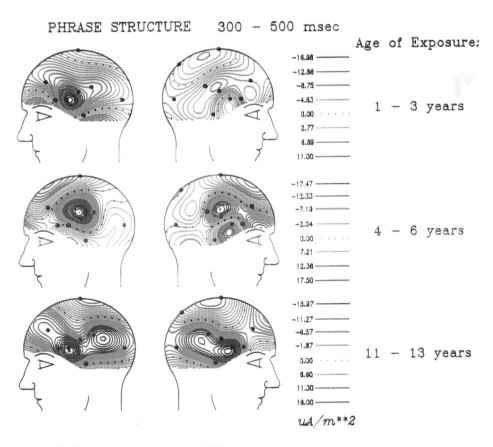

PLATE 2 Current source density (CSD) analyses of responses to grammatical anomalies (violations of phrase structure) in English. Early learners of English (1–3 years) display a left lateralized activation, but delays in age of exposure (4–13 years) are associated with bilateral activation.

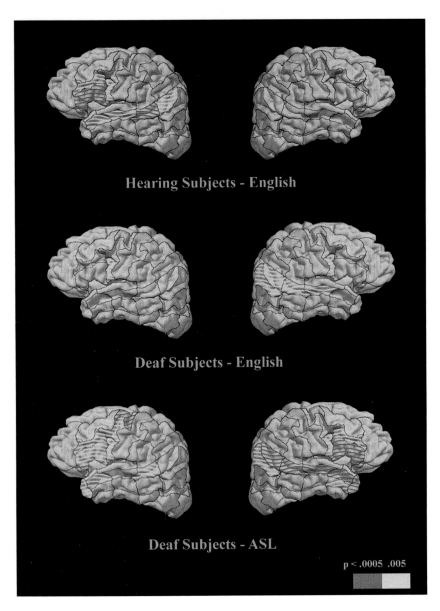

Hearing Subjects - English

Deaf Subjects - English

Deaf Subjects - ASL

p < .0005 .005

PLATE 3 Cortical areas showing increases in blood oxygenation on fMRI when normal hearing adults read English sentences (top), when congenitally deaf native signers read English sentences (middle), and when congenitally deaf native signers view sentences in their native sign language (American Sign Language).

CLOSED CLASS WORDS

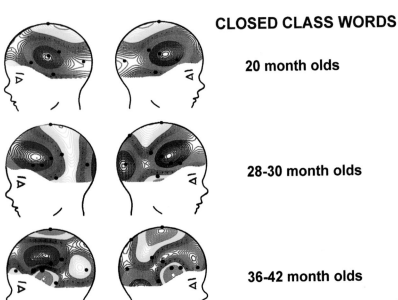

20 month olds

28-30 month olds

36-42 month olds

PLATE 4 Current source density (CSD) analyses of neural activity to closed-class words at 200 ms. The CSDs illustrate sinks [i.e., activity flowing into the head (purple)] and sources [i.e., activity flowing out of the head (orange)] at three age groups. Top: At 20 months the CSD shows sinks over both the left and the right hemispheres. Middle: At 28–30 months the CSD shows sinks that are bilateral but slightly more prominent over the right than the left hemisphere. Bottom: At 36–42 months the CSD shows a sink over left anterior regions.

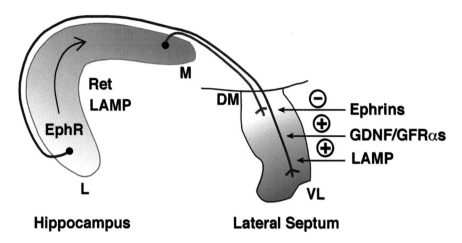

Hippocampus   **Lateral Septum**

PLATE 5 Regulation of topographic map formation in the hippocamposeptal projection. Medial (M) hippocampal neurons send their axons to the dorsomedial (DM) septal target, while the lateral (L) hippocampal neurons target the ventrolateral (VL) septum. The ligands located in the ventral lateral septum serve to restrict the medial hippocampal neurons (Eph receptor–positive, red) from innervating this region (ligand-positive, blue), which is topographically inappropriate for the medial neurons. However, the ligands allow the innervation of the ventral lateral septum by the lateral hippocampal neurons, because they express few Eph receptors (yellow). In addition to the Eph subfamily receptors and ligands, the GDNF receptor Ret is expressed in the hippocampal neurons, while the ligand-binding coreceptors GFRα1 and 2 are transcribed in the septum. The coreceptors are likely to trap GDNF and/or neurturin and thus serve as target-derived trophic factors for incoming hippocampal axons. Furthermore, both the hippocampal and the target neurons express LAMP, a homophilic cell adhesion molecule, which may serve to stabilize the connection between hippocampal axon terminals and the septal target cells.

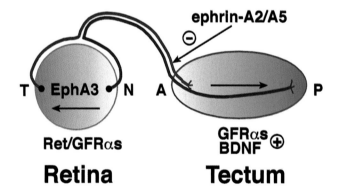

Retina   **Tectum**

PLATE 6 Specification of retinotectal topographic map. Temporal and nasal retinal ganglion neurons project to the anterior and posterior portions of the chick tectum (superior colliculus in mammals), respectively. The Eph receptor EphA3 is expressed in a nasal (N, low)–to–temporal (T, high) gradient in the retina. The Eph ligands ephrin-A2 and A5 are expressed in the tectum in an anterior (A, low)–to–posterior (P, high) gradient. The ligand gradient serves to repel/eliminate receptor-positive temporal axons. The extent of inhibition may be proportional to the extent of ligand-receptor interaction. In contrast, GDNF entrapped by its binding receptor GFRas and BDNF may serve as a positive guidance cue to promote the ingrowth of retinal axons in general.

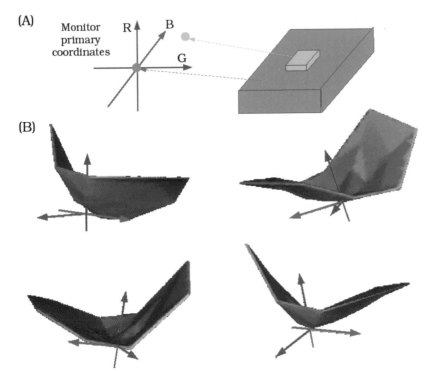

PLATE 7 A geometric description of colored stimuli that appear neither red nor green. (A) The test stimulus is a square patch shown on a uniform background. The background is plotted at the origin of the three-dimensional coordinate system. The test stimulus is represented in a three-dimensional coordinate system. The test stimulus is represented in a three-dimensional color space in terms of the intensities of the three display primaries relative to the background. The arrows on the three axes indicate the direction of increasing intensity. (B) A surface passing through red-green equilibrium stimuli is shown from four separate views. Stimuli represented on the surface appear blue, yellow, or achromatic. The surface is shaded with these colors to provide a rough guide about their color appearance. (From Chichilnisky and Wandell, in press.)

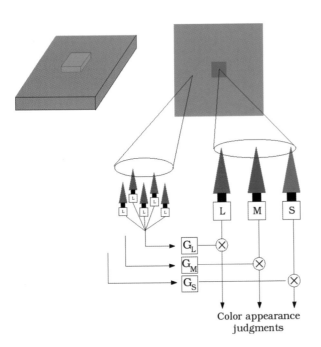

PLATE 8 Schematic of the von Kries model of adaptation. The stimuli are shown as a uniform background field and a small incremental test. Light from the background establishes the gain of the cone signals. Light from the test perturbs the cones. In this version of von Kries adaptation, only background photons absorbed in the L cones influence the gain of the L test signal, and incremental and decremental signals are treated the same. Neither of these assumptions is precisely correct (e.g., Chichilnisky and Wandell, 1996; Mausfeld and Niederee, 1993).

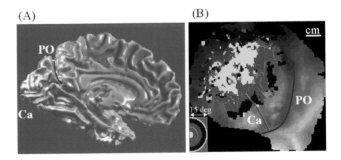

PLATE 9 Methods of visualizing the human brain. (A) A three-dimensional rendering of the gray/white boundary of a human brain is shown. The rendering was created by segmenting gray and white matter and creating a connected representation of the gray matter (Teo, Sapiro, and Wandell, 1997). This medial view shows the location of the calcarine (Ca) and parieto-occipital (PO) sulci. This image was created using software developed by R. Taylor in our laboratory. (B) Distances within the connected gray matter can be measured using Dijkstra's algorithm. From these distances, it is possible to create a flattened representation of the gray matter that minimizes the difference between distances measured along the curved gray matter surface and distances on the flattened representation. The underlying gray image represents the gray matter, shaded so that light and dark measure the position along the medial to lateral axis. The colored overlay shows the retinotopic organization with respect to distance from fixation (see the legend at the lower left). A description of the methods as well as software for segmenting and flattening can be obtained from the web site http://white.stanford.edu/wandell.html.

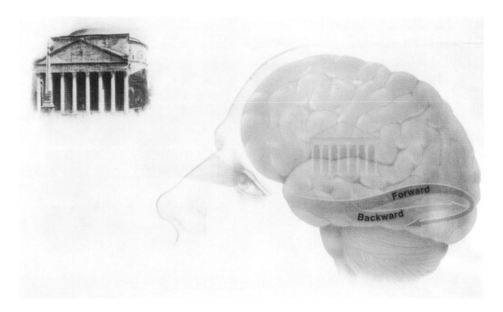

PLATE 10 Visual perception mainly relies on the forward, bottom-up flow of information. Image retrieval or imagery experience, in contrast, highlights the backward projections as an anatomical substrate of top-down mental operations. If an imagery task requires reconstruction of the detailed local geometry of the image (as in counting the columns in a memory of the Pantheon), backward signals from higher-order representations might reach topographically organized visual areas. This cartoon does not indicate that mental images are actual pictures in the brain; obviously, we cannot assume any homunculus in the brain who looks at the images. (Adapted from Miyashita, 1995; artwork by K. Sutliff.)

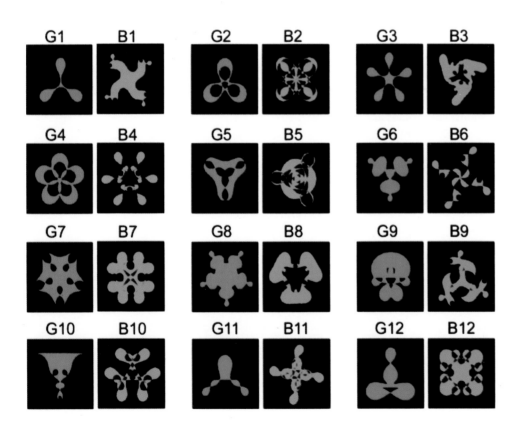

PLATE 11 Image retrieval task for monkeys. The pair-association with color switch (PACS) task uses twelve pairs of colored pictures. When one member of each pair is shown, trained monkeys can retrieve and choose the other member of the paired associates. The first pair consists of the picture G1 (green) and picture B1 (blue), the second pair consists of G2 and B2, and so on.

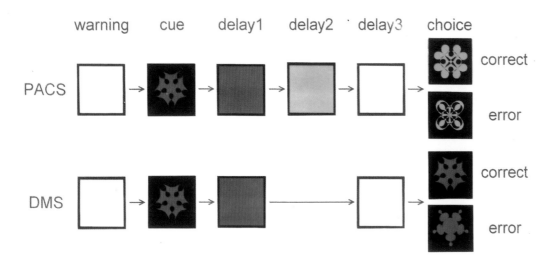

warning   cue   delay1   delay2   delay3   choice

PACS

correct

error

DMS

correct

error

PLATE 12 Sequence of events in the image retrieval task. Both PACS trials and DMS trials use the same color stimuli shown in figure 27.2. In each trial of the task, a cue stimulus is presented, and the monkey is rewarded when he chooses the correct choice stimulus. The correct choice stimulus is the paired associate of the cue in PACS trials and the cue itself in DMS trials. PACS trials and DMS trials were given randomly. Event sequence is the following: Warning, gray square for fixation (1 s in both trials); cue, one of 24 colored pictures (0.5 s); delay 1, fixation square the same color as the cue picture (2 s in PACS trials, 5 s in the DMS trials); delay 2, fixation square the same color as the paired associate of the cue picture (3 s in PACS trials); delay 3, fixation gray square (1 s in both trials); choice, a choice of two stimuli (1.2 s in both trials).

PLATE 13 Stimulus selectivity of the inferotemporal neuron (same as that in figure 27.4) is shown in different task periods (top, cue period; middle, delay 1; bottom, delay 3). The ordinate shows the mean discharge rate in each task period after the presentation of a cue stimulus; cue stimuli are labeled as "pair No." on the abscissa (G1 = green histogram bar in No.1; B1 = blue histogram bar in No.1; etc.). This neuron selectively responded to the cue stimulus G7 during the cue period. Note that the cue stimulus B7 does not elicit any response during the cue period and delay 1 in this neuron, but during delays 2 and 3 the same neuron became suddenly active.

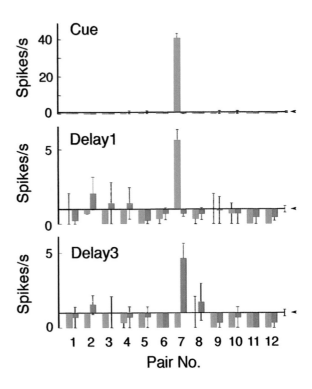

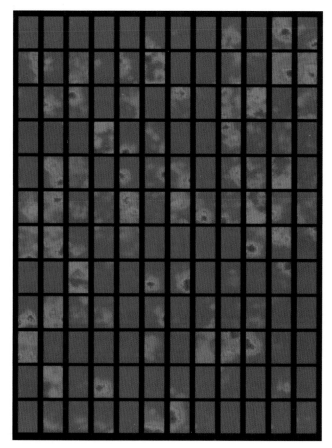

PLATE 25 Spatial firing distributions of 144 hippocampal place cells recorded simultaneously while the rat explored a 60 × 45-cm apparatus. Each panel represents the firing distribution of one cell. Red indicates high firing, dark blue indicates no firing. The 7 high rate cells are inhibitory interneurons, the rest are pyramidal cells. The spatial encoding by hippocampal cells is sufficiently robust that the animal's location in the apparatus can be predicted to within a few centimeters solely on the basis of the mean firing rate distributions and the activity of these cells over a 1-second window.

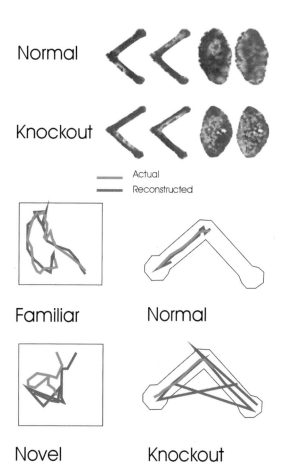

Normal

Knockout

—— Actual

—— Reconstructed

Familiar   Normal

Novel   Knockout

PLATE 26 The effect of blockade of synaptic plasticity on the robustness of the spatial signal in the hippocampus of a mouse. This mouse was engineered genetically to knock out the NMDA receptor selectively in region CA1 (Tsien, Huerta, and Tonegawa, 1996). Trajectory reconstruction is shown for normal and disrupted animals. This also is compared with trajectory reconstruction in normal rats during novel and familiar exposure to an environment. Accurate transmission of spatial information appears to require both experience and synaptic plasticity.

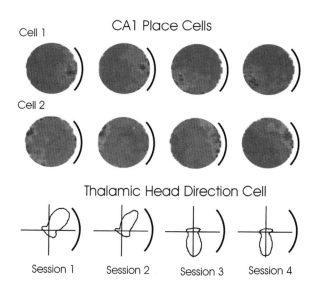

Cell 1

CA1 Place Cells

Cell 2

Thalamic Head Direction Cell

Session 1   Session 2   Session 3   Session 4

PLATE 27 Spontaneous rotation of hippocampal place cells and thalamic directional cells after disorientation.

PLATE 28 A patient with left hemispatial neglect from a recent frontoparietal stroke. He is not aware of the examiner approaching from the left side. Note the orienting bias toward his right ipsilesional side.

PLATE 29 A patient with Balint's syndrome, shown reaching for the handle of a screwdriver. Despite being able to report the object's identity and looking directly at it, he is not able to reach to its accurate location. When this patient was asked to reach for parts of his own body, he was able to do so easily and accurately, showing no evidence of a primary motor deficit or loss of coordination between an egocentric location and reaching.

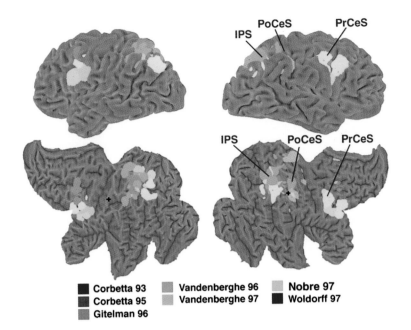

PLATE 30 Frontoparietal cortical network during peripheral visual attention. Common regions of activation across studies include the intraparietal (IPS), postcentral, and precentral sulcus (PrCeS). Foci of activity in each study were mapped onto 3D brain and 2D surface reconstruction of Visible Man brain atlas (Drury et al., 1996). The foci are spatially smoothed with a 10-mm radius filter to account for methodological differences across laboratories in entering the standard atlas space (Talairach and Tournoux, 1988; Van Essen and Drury, 1997).

PLATE 31 Peripheral attention vs. spatial working memory vs. saccadic eye movement across studies. 3D and surface reconstruction of right hemisphere of the Visible Man brain atlas. Left: Regions active for peripheral attention (red), regions active for spatial working memory (blue), and regions of overlap (magenta). Studies of attention are the same as those in figure 46.1; for studies of spatial working memory, see text. Note the remarkable overlap in parietal cortex, partial overlap in precentral region, and exclusive activation of prefrontal cortex (PFCx) for spatial working memory. Other anatomical abbreviations are as in figure 46.1. Right: Comparison between peripheral attention (red) and saccadic eye movements (green) (see text for list of studies). Note the strong overlap (yellow) in both parietal and precentral region. There is no activation in prefrontal cortex.

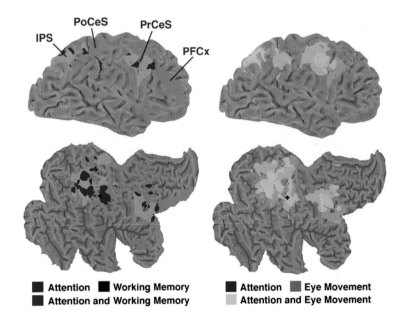

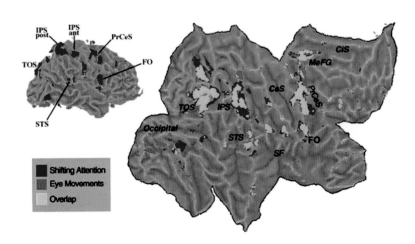

PLATE 32 Shifts of spatial attention vs. oculomotor/attentional shifts in a single subject. fMRI activity projected on 3D and surface representation of the subject's own brain. Note precise localization of functional activity in relationship to sulcal and gyral landmarks. TOS = transverse occipital sulcus; IPS = intraparietal sulcus; STS = superior temporal sulcus; CeS = central sulcus; PrCeS = precentral sulcus; MeFG = medial frontal gyrus; CiS = cingulate sulcus; FO = frontal operculum. Note that the degree of overlap between attention and saccadic eye movement regions is much higher than in group data (cf. figure 46.3, right).

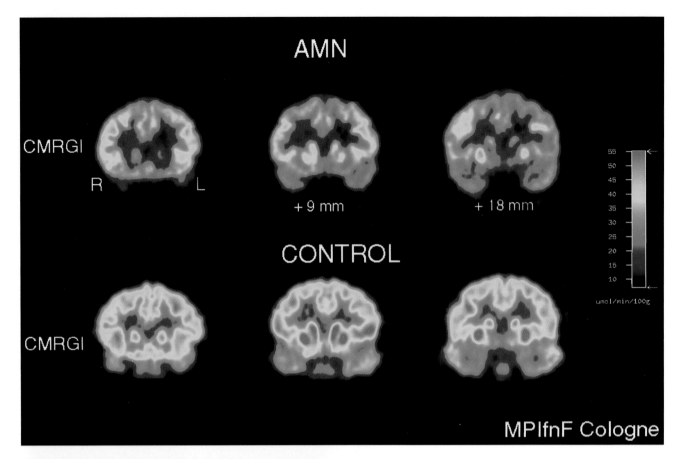

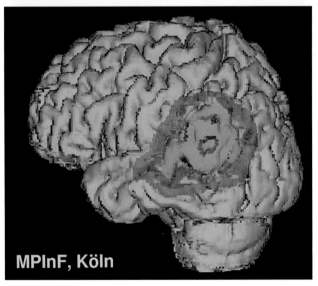

PLATE 33 FDG-PET–based coronal sections from anterior to posterior (left to right) through the brains of a patient with a shock-caused amnesic condition (Markowitsch et al., 1998) (top row) and a control subject (bottom row). Note the reduction in cerebral metabolism in widespread cortical and subcortical areas in the patient, compared with a control subject's brain at corresponding levels. A regions-of-interest analysis of the patient's regional cerebral glucose metabolism revealed that especially his temporal lobes and his thalami showed a more than 20% reduction compared with those of age-matched men. (Modified after figure 1 of Markowitsch et al., 1998.)

PLATE 34 Three-dimensional reconstruction of the left hemisphere revealing the tumor-caused brain damage (including the penumbra region) of a patient with major short-term memory impairments. The case has been described by Markowitsch and associates (1999).

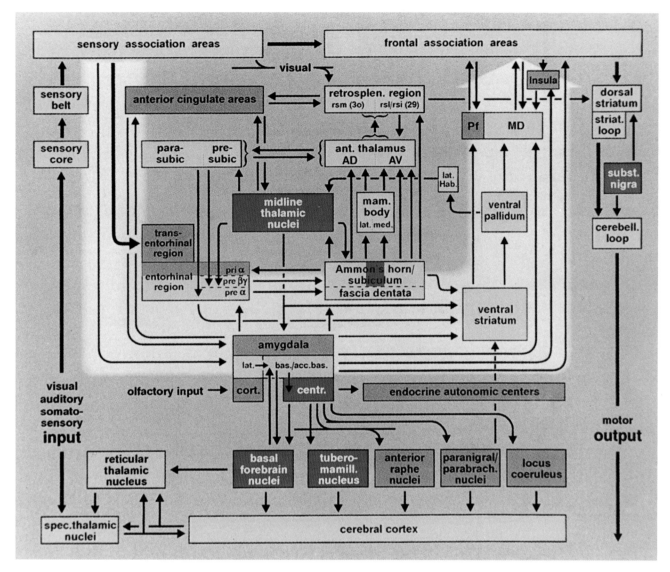

PLATE 35 The limbic loop and additional structures are shown in detail. The amygdala integrates exteroceptive sensory data with interoceptive stimuli from autonomic centers. A large number of amygdalar efferents terminate in nuclei, regulating endocrine and autonomic functions. In addition, the amygdala generates efferent connections to all nonthalamic nuclei that in a nonspecific manner project on the cerebral cortex. Abbreviations: ant. thalamus AD and AV = anterodorsal and anteroventral nuclei of the anterior thalamus; cerebell. loop = cerebellar loop; lat. Hab. = lateral habenula; lat., bas., acc. bas., cort., and centr. = lateral, basal, accessory-basal, cortical, and central amygdalar nuclei; mam. body lat. and med. = lateral and medial nuclei of the mamil- lary body; MD = mediodorsal thalamic nucleus; para-nigral/ parabrach. = paranigral and pigmented parabrachial nuclei; parasubic and presubic = parasubiculum and presubiculum; Pf = parafascicular nucleus; Pri-a, Pre-b, Pre-g, Pre-a = layers of the entorhinal region; retrosplen, region rsm (30) and rsl/rsi (29) = medial retrosplenial area (Brodmann's area 30) and lateral and intermediate retrosplenial areas (Brodmann's area 29) of the retrosplenial region; spec. thalamic nuclei = specific projection nuclei of the thalamus; striat. loop = striatal loop; subst. nigra = substantia nigra; tuberomamill. = tuberomamillary nucleus. (After figure 5 of Braak et al., 1996, with permission from Decker Periodicals and Dr. H. Braak.)

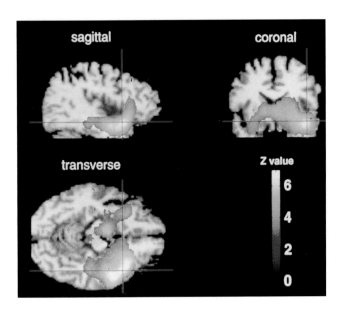

PLATE 36 Positron-emission-tomography (PET) representations of brain activations during ecphorizing affect-laden autobiographical memories (displayed on top of arbitrary magnetic resonance images of sagittal, coronal, and transverse brain images). The red cross-hair indicates the local maximum within the area of activation. The color bar indicates the Z statistics achieved. To obtain these activation patterns, PET activations during ecphorizing biographical information from an unknown individual were subtracted from those obtained during ecphorizing events from the tested subjects' own biography. Note that the activations are predominantly on the right. (Reproduced with permission from figure 2 of Fink et al., 1996.)

**Within Modality
(200-400 msec)**

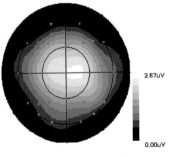

2.67uV

0.00uV

**Across Modality
(400-600 msec)**

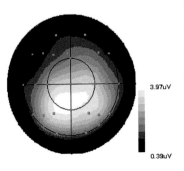

3.97uV

0.39uV

PLATE 37 Topographic maps illustrating the scalp distribution of the repetition effects illustrated in figure 56.1. Left panel: Distribution of the early (200–400 ms) within-modality effects. Right panel: Distribution of the late (400–600 ms) across modality effects. The latter effects have the more posterior distribution.

**Shallow Hit - New
(300-500 msec)**

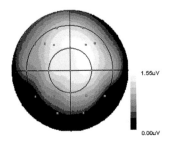

1.55uV

0.00uV

**Shallow Miss - New
(300-500 msec)**

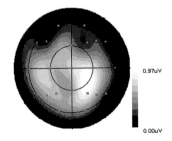

0.97uV

0.00uV

PLATE 38 Topographic maps of the differences between the ERPs to old and new words shown in figure 56.2, showing the distribution of the differences between 300 and 500 ms for recognized (hit) and unrecognized (miss) words, and between 500 and 800 ms for recognized deeply studied words.

**Deep Hit - New
(300-500 msec)**

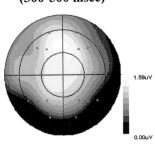

1.58uV

0.00uV

**Deep Hit - New
(500-800 msec)**

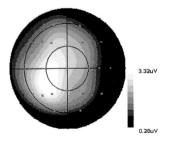

3.32uV

0.28uV

500-800 msec **800-1100 msec** **1100-1400 msec**

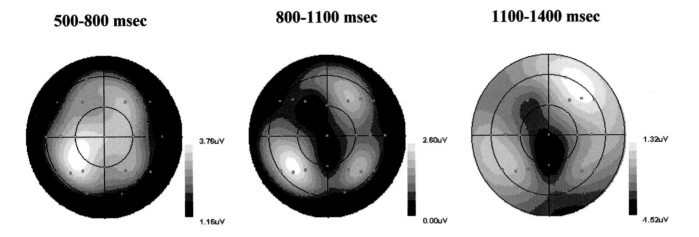

3.76uV

1.16uV

2.60uV

0.00uV

1.32uV

-1.52uV

PLATE 39 Topographic maps illustrating the scalp distribution of the differences between ERPs elicited by "recollected" words and words correctly classified as new for three consecutive regions of the waveforms (500–800, 800–1100, 1100–1400 ms poststimulus). Maxima corresponding to the left parietal and right frontal effects are clearly evident. The ERPs to recollected items were elicited by words that were either correctly recognized and assigned to their study context, or recognized and given a "remember" judgment in a "remember/know" task. (Data are from Mark and Rugg, 1998.)

400-700 msec **800-1100 msec** **1200-1500 msec**

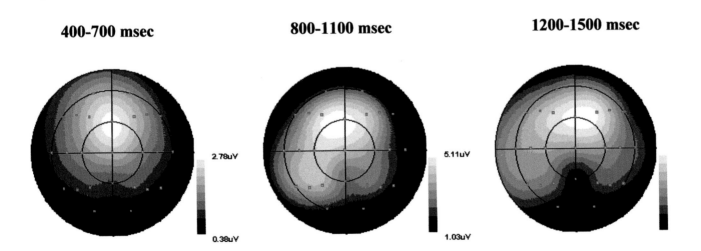

2.78uV

0.38uV

5.11uV

1.03uV

PLATE 40 Topographic maps illustrating the scalp distribution of the memory effects shown in figure 56.8. Each map depicts the differences between ERPs evoked by stems correctly completed with studied items, collapsed across the subsequent source judgment, and ERPs evoked by stems completed with unstudied items correctly endorsed as "new." Maps are shown for three latency regions, 400–700 ms, 800–1100 ms, and 1200–1500 ms.

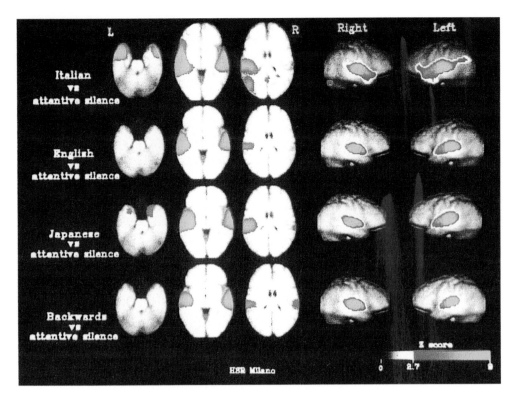

PLATE 41 Patterns of activation in a PET study measuring the activity in Italian speakers' brains while listening to Italian (mother tongue), English (second language), Japanese (unknown language), and backward Japanese (not a possible human language). There was a significant activation difference between Italian and English. In contrast, English and Japanese did not differ significantly. Japanese differed significantly from backward Japanese. (Adapted from Perani et al., 1996.)

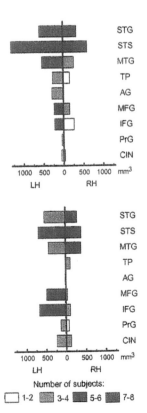

PLATE 42 Intersubject variability in the cortical representation of language is greater for the second than for the first language. Each bar represents an anatomical region of interest (left and right hemisphere). Its length represents the average active volume (in square millimeters) in that region. Its color reflects the number of subjects in which that region was active. (Adapted from Dehaene et al., 1997.)

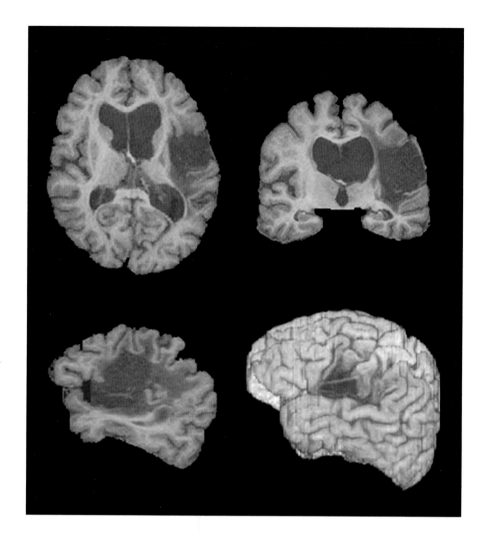

PLATE 43 This three-dimensional MRI reconstruction depicts the lesion in a patient with anomic aphasia and an apraxia of speech. The upper left image is a horizontal slice showing the left hemisphere lesion, while the upper right depicts a coronal section. (The images conform to radiologic convention, with the left hemisphere shown on the right side.) In the lower left is a sagittal section through the left hemisphere. The lower right image shows the 3D reconstruction of the brain with part of the lesion visible on the lateral surface of the left hemisphere.

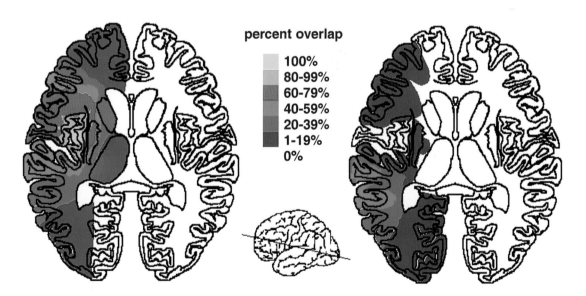

percent overlap

- 100%
- 80-99%
- 60-79%
- 40-59%
- 20-39%
- 1-19%
- 0%

PLATE 44 Lesion overlapping in 25 patients with apraxia of speech (left) and 19 patients without this disorder (right). All of the 25 patients with apraxia of speech have a lesion encompassing a small section of the insula, as shown in yellow, while the lesions of the 19 patients without apraxia of speech completely spare the same area.

A.

B.

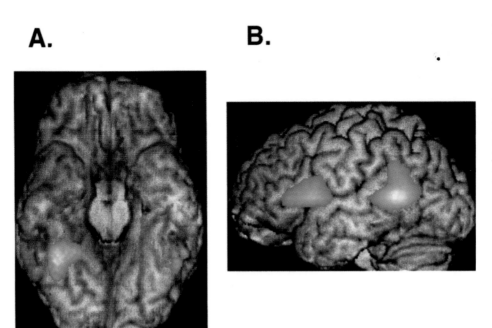

PLATE 45 (A) Ventral view of the brain showing regions in the temporal lobe more active when subjects retrieved information about object-associated color than object-associated action. (B) Lateral view of the left hemisphere showing regions more active when subjects retrieved information about object-associated action than object-associated color. (Adapted from Martin et al., 1995.)

A.　　　　　　　　**B.**

C.　　　　　　　　**D.**

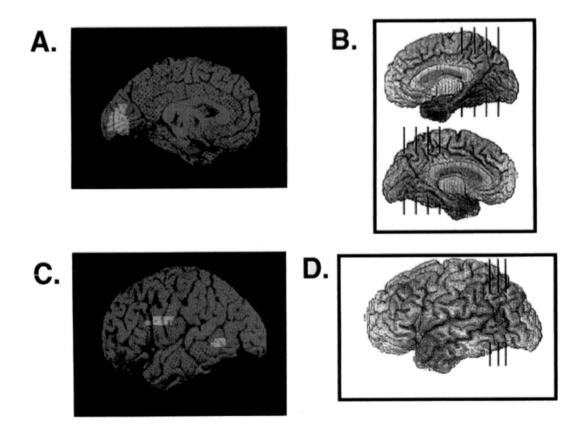

PLATE 46 (A) View of the medial surface of the left hemisphere showing the region of activation in the medial occipital lobe when subjects silently named drawings of animals relative to naming drawings of tools (adapted from Martin et al., 1996). (B) View of the medial surface of the left and right hemispheres showing the location of lesions in 28 subjects who had impaired recognition and naming of drawings of animals (adapted from Tranel, Damasio, and Damasio, 1997). (C) View of the lateral surface of the left hemisphere showing regions active in the premotor cortex and middle temporal gyrus when subjects silently named drawings of tools relative to naming drawings of animals (adapted from Martin et al., 1996). (D) View of the lateral surface of the left hemisphere showing the location of lesions in 8 subjects who had impaired recognition and naming of drawings of tools (adapted from Tranel, Damasio, and Damasio, 1997).

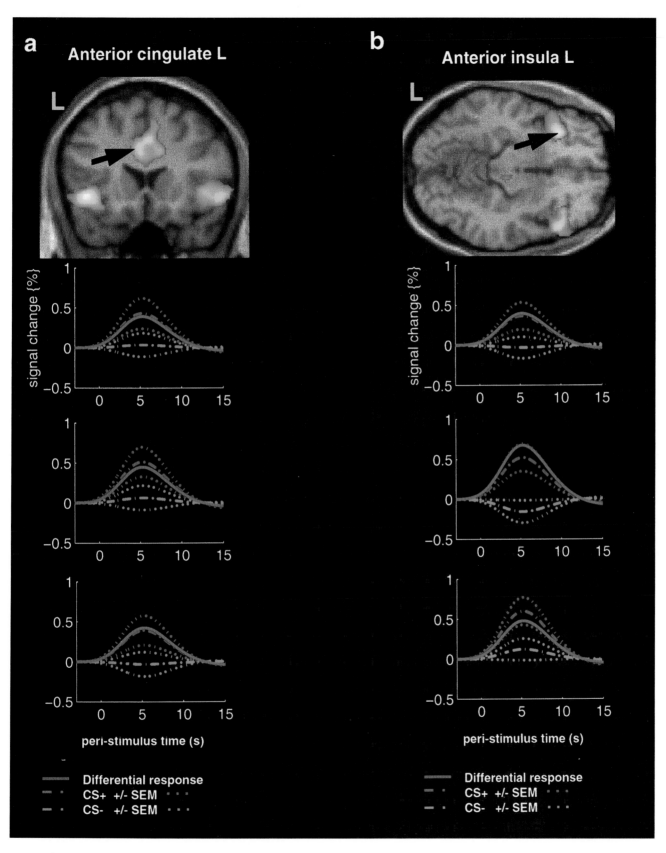

PLATE 47 Averaged single event responses during acquisition. The top of the figure shows the focus of significant differential activations (CS+ > CS–) in anterior cingulate (circled) and bilateral anterior insula superimposed on a structural MRI scan. At the bottom the peristimulus time plots for all 6 subjects are displayed with reference to differential cingulate responses. The plots show the fitted response +/– the standard error of the mean (SEM) for CS– (blue) and unpaired CS+ (red) events. Dashed lines correspond to mean responses, and dotted lines are SEM. Statistical inference is based on the difference between the two responses, which is shown in green.

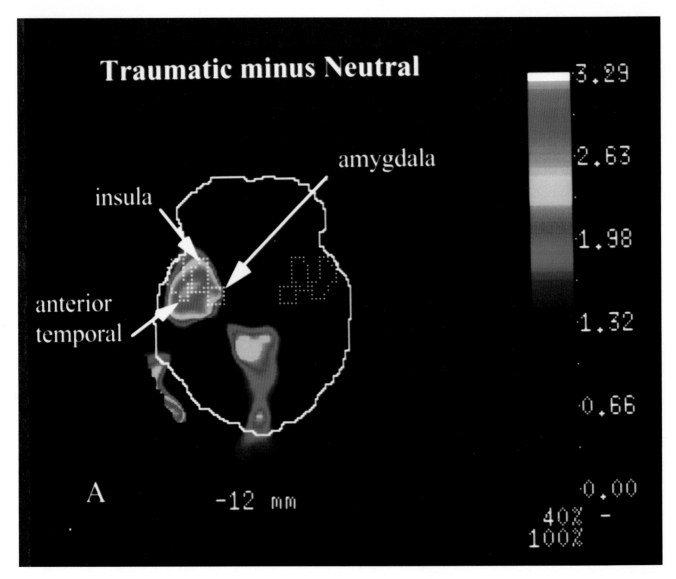

PLATE 48 Positron-emission-tomography statistical parametric map of regional cerebral blood flow during traumatic minus neutral personal imagery in eight subjects with post-traumatic stress disorder, displayed with a Sokoloff color scale in units of z score. White dashed outlines reflecting the boundaries of specified brain regions, as defined via a digitized version of the Talairach atlas, are superimposed for anatomical reference. Whole-brain slice outlines are demarcated with solid lines. The tranverse section shown is parallel and 12 mm inferior to the intercommissural plane. Top, anterior; bottom, posterior; right, left; left, right. (Rauch et al., 1996; reprinted with permission from *Archives of General Psychiatry*, vol. 53, no. 5, May 1996, p. 385; Copyright © American Medical Association.)

FIGURE 48.3   Top: Event-related potentials (ERPs) to lateralized target stimuli over the contralateral occipital scalp site where the P1 component was of maximum amplitude. The trace shown is averaged over left occipital site (OL) for right-field stimuli, and right occipital site (OR) for left-field stimuli. OL and OR are located midway between T5 and O1, and T6 and O2, respectively, of the International 10-20 system of electrode placement (Jasper, 1958). The shaded gray box indicates the P1 latency range (90–140 ms). For the short cue-to-target ISI condition, cued-location targets (solid line) elicited a significantly enhanced P1 component compared to uncued-location targets (dotted line). Bottom: Scalp topographic voltage maps, presented on rear view of the head and referenced to the right mastoid, showing attention effects at the peak of the P1 component (110–120 ms latency range). ERPs elicited by left visual field targets are presented on the left; ERPs elicited by right visual field targets are presented on the right. Cued-location targets (above) produced enhanced P1 peaks compared to uncued-location targets (below). The small black dots on each topographic map indicate the location of the electrodes. The positive maxima of each map are shaded. (Adapted from Hopfinger and Mangun, 1998.)

possible to see that the location of the maximal response at the scalp corresponding to the P1 component was highly similar for cued- versus uncued-location targets (figure 48.3, bottom). This pattern is consistent with the view that the same neural process was invoked in both cases, the primary difference being the strength of the response. The occipital P1 component represents the earliest stage of visual processing to be reliably modulated by *voluntary* spatial attention (e.g., Heinze et al., 1994; Mangun, 1995; Mangun and Hillyard, 1991). The present findings indicate that although separate control circuitry may be involved, reflexive attention leads to modulations at this same stage of visual cortical processing.

Working memory and spatial attention

In a voluntary attention task, attending to a specific location requires remembering–during the interval preceding a target–which location is task-relevant (i.e., where to attend). Spatial working memory refers to this ability to temporarily store and manipulate spatial information over brief periods of time. An area of increasing interest to researchers of both attention and memory is the possible relationship between spatial attention and spatial working memory processes. In this section, we discuss how the identification of cortical areas labile to modulation by spatial attention, as measured by ERPs and localized using functional neuroimaging, has provided novel insight into this issue.

Recent neuroimaging evidence suggests that there may be an overlap in the functional circuitry subserving spatial attention and spatial working memory. Frontal,

parietal, and extrastriate areas have been observed to be active during both of these cognitive operations (Jonides et al., 1993; McCarthy et al., 1996; Owen, Evans, and Petrides, 1996). In addition, recent behavioral studies have suggested that holding a location in working memory imparts a perceptual advantage to stimuli occurring there, something typically attributed to the benefits of selective attention. That is, when stimuli were presented to a location being maintained in working memory, they were responded to with greater speed and accuracy than when those stimuli were presented at other locations (Awh et al., 1998). Both the behavioral evidence and the neuroimaging evidence have led to the hypothesis that one maintains information about locations in working memory by selectively attending to those regions of space. If this is indeed true, then the activations observed in occipital cortex during spatial working memory tasks could be interpreted as analogous to those observed when subjects are required to selectively attend regions of space. We have tested this proposal using ERPs (Jha and Mangun, 1998).

As described above, voluntary spatial attention begins to affect visual processing as soon as 70–110 ms after the initial appearance of the stimulus, affecting the occipital P1 component–an especially well-understood attention-sensitive ERP (e.g., Mangun, 1995). If selective attention is involved in the maintenance of location information during spatial working memory, then the P1 component should be larger in amplitude for stimuli presented at a to-be-remembered location than for stimuli presented elsewhere. Additionally, if any such effects are found in the ERPs, it would be possible to ask whether the activity persisted throughout the period that working memory was maintained (the memory delay period). For example, if attention is required only for encoding the to-be-remembered location, attention-like modulations should be observed only for stimuli presented shortly after a memory cue, when encoding presumably takes place (Jones et al., 1995; Jones and Morris, 1992; Toms, Morris, and Foley, 1994).

To provide a measure of whether attention is involved in the maintenance of information in working memory, task-irrelevant probe stimuli were presented during the 4.8–5.3-s memory interval of a spatial working memory task. Subjects were informed that the probes were irrelevant to the task and were instructed not to respond to these stimuli. The probe followed the memory cue, with a stimulus onset asynchrony (SOA) of either 400–800 ms or 2600–3000 ms. Probe stimuli have been used in several studies of spatial attention as a means of sampling the distribution of attention, and have been found to elicit enhanced-amplitude P1 components when appearing at an attended location, even

ERP Responses to Probes

SHORT SOA
Lateral Occipital (OL/OR)

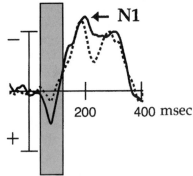

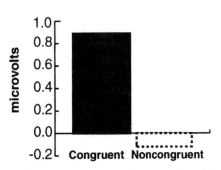

LONG SOA
Lateral Occipital (OL/OR)

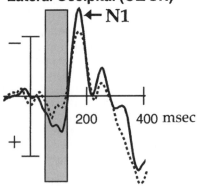

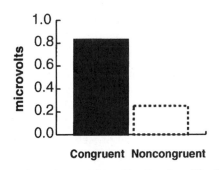

FIGURE 48.4 ERP responses to probe stimuli collapsed across the 6 possible probe locations. The contralateral ERP response is plotted for the lateral occipital electrode sites (OL/OR). The time range of the P50-100 effect is highlighted by shading. The *y*-axis is the microvolt value (range –2.0 to 2.0 microvolts) and the *x*-axis is the time epoch (0–400 ms). Probe onset is at the upright calibration bar. The P50-100 effect was larger for probes occurring at locations being held in working memory than when the probes occurred elsewhere in the visual field, and this was true at both SOAs. Below the ERPs are bar graphs depicting the microvolt value for the time period of the P50-100 effect for congruent and noncongruent probes.

when the probes are task-irrelevant (e.g., Heinze and Mangun, 1995).

Subjects were very accurate (90% correct, mean RT = 599 ms) in performing the memory task. Probe stimuli presented at the location congruent with the to-be-remembered location (congruent condition) elicited significantly ($p < .01$) larger occipital positive responses from the 50–100 ms latency than did probes at non-memorized (noncongruent condition) locations (figure 48.4). Because the relationship between this *spatial working memory effect,* and the *P1 attention effect* remains unclear at present, we will refer to the working memory effect using a polarity (P for positive polarity) and latency (50–100 ms range) nomenclature; that is, as the P50-100 effect. This P50-100 effect was observed both for probes presented at the short SOA and the long SOA. The P50-100 pattern is precisely that predicted for spatial attention focused on the memory location prior to the onset of the probe stimulus, and maintained there

throughout the delay period. Interestingly, there was also a significant amplitude enhancement in the N1 latency range from 160–180 msec.

To the extent that the P50-100 effect for spatial working memory reflects processes similar or identical to the P1 attention effect, the current ERP results suggest that the observed overlap in brain areas activated during spatial attention and spatial working memory tasks reflect a reliance on the same neural hardware. Previous single-unit studies of object working memory, for example, have suggested a similar relationship for object working memory and attention during visual search operations. That is, object working memory is needed to keep relevant object information active so that while many objects are in view, an attentional search for the relevant object will be facilitated (Chelazzi and Desimone, 1994; Chelazzi et al., 1993). A similar type of interdependence between working memory and attentional mechanisms may exist for spatial working memory.

Summary

In this chapter, we have reviewed a number of studies that investigated attentional and working memory processes using ERPs and functional neuroimaging. Both voluntary and reflexive attention were shown to modulate visual information processing at early stages. Holding a location in working memory also leads to changes in visual cortical processing, and in a manner that suggests a close relationship between spatial attention and spatial working memory during visual processing. Furthermore, these effects in visual cortex can be localized anatomically and related to functionally defined regions of extrastriate visual cortex using functional neuroimaging in combination with ERP recording. By integrating ERPs and functional imaging methods, the time course and functional anatomy of cognitive processes can be revealed with a higher resolution than has previously been possible. Although new methods are always, thankfully, lurking around the corner, the integration of electromagnetic and functional neuroimaging approaches will no doubt continue to reveal a unique view of the thinking human brain for the foreseeable future.

ACKNOWLEDGMENTS This research was supported by grants from the NIMH, NINDS, and HFSPO to G.R.M.. J.B.H. was supported by an NSF Fellowship, and A.P.J. was supported by an NIMH Fellowship. We gratefully acknowledge the contributions of M. Girelli, M. H. Buonocore, M. Soltani, H. Hinrichs, T. F. Münte, M. Scholz, W. Burchert, A. Gös, M. Scherg, H. Hundeshagen, S. Johannes, C. L. Kussmaul, M. S. Gazzaniga, S. A. Hillyard, and H. J. Heinze to portions of the research reviewed here.

REFERENCES

AWH, E., J. JONIDES, and P. A. REUTER-LORENZ, 1998. Rehearsal in spatial working memory. *J. Exp. Psychol.: Hum. Percept. Perform.* 24:780–790.

CHELAZZI, L., and R. DESIMONE, 1994. Responses of V4 neurons during visual search. *Soc. Neurosci. Abstr.* 20:1054.

CHELAZZI, L., E. K. MILLER, J. DUNCAN, and R. DESIMONE, 1993. A neural basis for visual search in inferior temporal cortex. *Nature* 363:345–347.

DALE, A., and M. SERENO, 1993. Improved localization of cortical activity by combining EEG and MEG with MRI cortical surface reconstruction: A linear approach. *J. Cogn. Neurosci.* 5:162–176.

EASON, R. G., 1981. Visual evoked potential correlates of early neural filtering during selective attention. *Bull. Psychonomic Soc.* 18:203–206.

EASON, R., M. HARTER, and C. WHITE, 1969. Effects of attention and arousal on visually evoked cortical potentials and reaction time in man. *Physiol. Behav.* 4:283–289.

ENGEL, S.A., D. E. RUMELHART, B. A. WANDELL, A. T. LEE, G. H. GLOVER, E. J. CHICHILNISKY, and M. N. SHADLEN, 1994. fMRI of human visual cortex. *Nature* 370:106.

FELLEMAN, D. J., and D. C. VAN ESSEN, 1991. Distributed hierarchical processing in the primate cerebral cortex. *Cereb. Cortex* 1:1–47.

HANDY, T. C., and G. R. MANGUN, in press. Attention and spatial selection: Electrophysiological evidence for modulation by perceptual load. *Percept. Psychophys.*

HEINZE, H. J., G. R. MANGUN, W. BURCHERT, H. HINRICHS, M. SCHOLZ, T. F. MÜNTE, A. GÖS, S. JOHANNES, M. SCHERG, H. HUNDESHAGEN, M. S. GAZZANIGA, and S. A. HILLYARD, 1994. Combined spatial and temporal imaging of spatial selective attention in humans. *Nature* 392:543–546.

HEINZE, H. J., and G. R. MANGUN, 1995. Electrophysiological signs of sustained and transient attention to spatial location. *Neuropsychologia* 33:889–908.

HOPFINGER, J. B., and G. R. MANGUN, 1998. Reflexive attention modulates processing of visual stimuli in human extrastriate cortex. *Psychol. Sci.* 9:441–447.

JASPER, H. H., 1958. The ten-twenty electrode system of the international federation. *Electroencephalogr. Clin. Neurophysiol.* 10:371–375.

JHA, A. P., and G. R. MANGUN, 1998. Neural basis of rehearsal in spatial working memory. *Soc. Neurosci. Abstr.* 24:506.

JONES, D., and N. MORRIS, 1992. Irrelevant speech and serial recall: Implications for theories of attention and working memory. *Scand. J. Psychol.* 33:221–229.

JONES, D., P. FARRAND, G. STUART, and N. MORRIS, 1995. Functional equivalence of verbal and spatial information in serial short-term memory. *J. Exp. Psychol.: Learn. Mem. Cogn.* 21:1008–1018.

JONIDES, J., E. E. SMITH, R. A. KOEPPE, E. AWH, S. MINOSHIMA, and M. A. MINTUN, 1993. Spatial working memory in humans as revealed by PET. *Nature* 363:623–625.

KRAMER, A. F., and J. SPINKS, 1991. Capacity views of human information processing. In *Handbook of Cognitive Psychophysiology: Central and Autonomic Nervous System Approaches*, J. R. Jennings and M. G. H. Coles, eds. New York: Wiley, pp. 179–249.

KUSTOV, A. A., and D. L. ROBINSON, 1996. Shared neural control of attentional shifts and eye movements. *Nature* 384:74–77.

LAVIE, N., 1995. Perceptual load as a necessary condition for selective attention. *J. Exp. Psychol.: Hum. Percept. Perform.* 21: 451–468.

LAVIE, N., and Y. TSAL, 1994. Perceptual load as a major determinant of the locus of visual selective attention. *Percept. Psychophys.* 56:183–197.

LUCK, S. J., S. A. HILLYARD, M. MOULOUA, M. G. WOLDORFF, V. P. CLARK, and H. L. HAWKINS, 1994. Effects of spatial cueing on luminance detectability: Psychophysical and electrophysiological evidence for early selection. *J. Exp. Psychol.: Hum. Percept. Perform.* 20:887–904.

LURIA, A. R., 1973. *The Working Brain.* New York: Penguin.

MANGUN, G. R., 1995. Neural mechanisms of visual selective attention. *Psychophysiology* 32:4–18.

MANGUN, G. R., and S. A. HILLYARD, 1991. Modulation of sensory-evoked brain potentials provide evidence for changes in perceptual processing during visual-spatial priming. *J. Exp. Psychol.: Hum. Percept. Perform.* 17:1057–1074.

MANGUN, G. R., and S. A. HILLYARD, 1995. Mechanisms and models of selective attention. In *Electrophysiology of Mind: Event-Related Brain Potentials and Cognition*, M. D. Rugg and M. G. H. Coles, eds. New York: Oxford, pp. 40–85.

MANGUN, G. R., S. A. HILLYARD, and S. J. LUCK, 1993. Electrocortical substrates of visual selective attention. In *Attention and Performance XIV*, D. Meyer and S. Kornblum, eds. Cambridge, Mass.: MIT Press, pp. 219–243.

MANGUN, G. R., J. B. HOPFINGER, C. L. KUSSMAUL, E. M. FLETCHER, and H. J. HEINZE, 1997. Covariations in ERP and PET measures of spatial selective attention in human extrastriate visual cortex. *Hum. Brain Mapping* 5:273–279.

MANGUN, G.R., M. H. BUONOCORE, M. GIRELLI, and A. JHA, 1998. ERP and fMRI measures of visual spatial selective attention. *Hum. Brain Mapping* 6:383–389.

MCCARTHY, G., A. PUCE, R. T. CONSTABLE, J. H. KRYSTAL, J. C. GORE, and P. GOLDMAN-RAKIC, 1996. Activation of human prefrontal cortex during spatial and nonspatial working memory tasks measured by functional MRI. *Cereb. Cortex* 6:600–611.

MESULAM, M.-M., 1981. A cortical network for directed attention and unilateral neglect. *Ann. Neurol.* 10:309–325.

OWEN, A. M., A. C. EVANS, and M. PETRIDES, 1996. Evidence for a two-stage model of spatial working memory processing within the lateral frontal cortex—A positron emission tomography study. *Cereb. Cortex* 6:31–38.

POSNER, M. I., and Y. COHEN, 1984. Components of visual orienting. *Attention and Performance X*, In H. Bouma and D. Bouwhis, eds. Hillsdale, N.J.: Erlbaum, pp. 531–554.

POSNER, M. I., J. A. WALKER, F. J. FRIEDRICH, and B. D. RAFAL, 1984. Effects of parietal injury on covert orienting of attention. *J. Neurosci.* 4:1863–1874.

RAFAL, R., 1996. Visual attention: Converging operations from neurology and psychology. In *Converging Operations in the Study of Visual Selective Attention*, A. F. Kramer, M. G. H.

Coles, and G. D. Logan, eds. Washington, DC: American Psychological Association, pp. 139–192.

ROBINSON, D. E., and C. KERTZMAN, 1995. Covert orienting of attention in macaques. III. Contributions of the superior colliculus. *J. Neurophysiol.* 74:713–721.

SERENO, M., A. DALE, J. REPPAS, K. KWONG, J. BELLIVEAU, B. BRADY, and R. TOOTELL, 1995. Borders of multiple visual areas in humans revealed by functional MRI. *Science* 268:889–893.

SCHERG, M., 1992. Functional imaging and localization of electromagnetic brain activity. *Brain Topography* 5:103–111.

TOMS, M., N. MORRIS, and P. FOLEY, 1994. Characteristics of visual interference with visuospatial working memory. *Br. J. Psychol.* 85:131–144.

WOLDORFF, M. G., 1993. Distortion of ERP averages due to overlap from temporally adjacent ERPs: Analysis and correction. *Psychophysiol.* 30:98–119.

VAN VOORHIS, S., and S. A. HILLYARD, 1977. Visual evoked potentials and selective attention to points in space. *Percept. Psychophys.* 22:54–62.

YANTIS, S., 1996. Attentional capture in vision. In *Converging Operations in the Study of Visual Selective Attention*, A. F. Kramer, M. G. H. Coles, and G. D. Logan, eds. Washington, DC: American Psychological Association, pp. 45–76.

ZEKI, S., J. WATSON, C. LUECK, K. FRISTON, C. KENNARD, and R. FRACKOWIAK, 1991. A direct demonstration of functional specialization in human visual cortex. *J. Neurosci.* 11:641–649.

ZHANG, Z., and D. L. JEWETT, 1994. Model misspecification detection by means of multiple generator errors, using the observed potential map. *Brain Topography* 7:29–40.

49 Networks of Attention

DAVID LABERGE

ABSTRACT   Attention is assumed to be expressed by the amplification of neural activity in particular clusters of cortical columns. The network that produces the expression of attention involves a neural amplification mechanism and structures that control this mechanism from both top-down and bottom-up directions. This chapter reviews recent neurobiological studies that indicate that attention-related neural activity increases in regions of the brain that correspond to the expressions, mechanisms, and controls of attention. These regions are distributed widely across the brain and are assumed to be interconnected by a triangular network, which produces activity simultaneously in these three regions when an attention event occurs.

The selective function of attention is assumed to be manifest in three main forms, according to one view (LaBerge, 1995a): simple selection, preparation, and maintenance. Simple selection is typically brief in duration, as in searching displays and reading words, and its immediate goal usually is the identification of the selected information. In preparatory attention, attention to a selected object, attribute, or spatial location is sustained over a preparatory period of time (e.g., between a cue and a target), and the goal is to respond more effectively to the anticipated stimulus event; this preparatory process often involves the imaging of the object or attribute. Maintenance attention refers to cases in which attention to a selected entity is sustained over a period of time, but the goal is the processing of the ongoing activity for its own sake; examples of this "appreciating" activity are tasting a wine, listening to music, and feeling sadness or joy.

The plan of this chapter is first to review the evidence regarding the following issues related to the selective operations of attention: (1) how attention carries out, or expresses, the selective operation in cortical columns; (2) discovering the brain structures that modulate the cortical expression of attention; and (3) determining the brain structures that control what is selected. Finally, a model will be described in which a triangular circuit interconnects the brain sites serving the expression, modulatory mechanism, and control operations that together are presumed to produce an attentional event.

DAVID LABERGE   Department of Cognitive Sciences, University of California, Irvine, Calif.

The expression of attention

The codes or representations that are activated into perceptions, images, ideas, feelings, and actions appear to reside within columns of the neocortex. It is commonly assumed that the cortex is organized in columnar fashion (Mountcastle, 1957; Szentágothai, 1975) and that the cognitive properties of brain function are produced not by single neurons but rather by the combined interactions of neurons within the columnar circuitry.

The selective property attention is presumed to be expressed by a positive difference between the activity levels in columns that code for the target and the activity levels in neighboring columns that code for other (distracting) objects. This difference in activity levels can be produced in three ways: by enhancement of the target site, by suppression (or decay) at the distractor site(s), or by both operations. Figure 49.1 presents a simplified schematic description of the average firing rates of

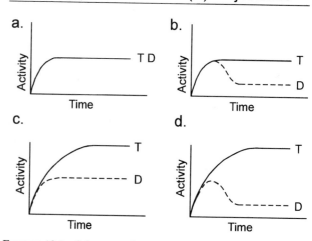

FIGURE 49.1   Schematic diagrams of three ways that selective attention to a target *T* presented near a distractor *D* can be expressed by activity in corresponding cortical columns (shown in b, c, and d). The stimulus-induced activity of both target and distractor sites is represented in a.

neurons in cortical columns coding a target item and a distractor item placed somewhere within the visual field.

In the early moments following display onset, cells in the column sites serving each item increase their activity in response to sensory input. If attention were directed to neither item or to both items, the trajectories would presumably take the form shown in figure 49.1a (with the attention-to-both case showing higher asymptotes and later declines). If one item becomes the target of attention, then the activities at the target and distractor sites diverge, and this divergence assumes one of the forms shown in figures 49.1b, c, and d. If attention to the target item is induced prior to the display (in the preparatory mode of attention), then the trajectory for the target in these three figures is displaced upward away from the trajectory for the distractor, and selective attention within the display undergoes a "head start."

In the psychological literature, selection by a target-enhancement operation has been implicitly assumed in the use of the metaphors of spotlight, zoom lens, capacity allocation, and gain, while the distractor-suppression operation has been implicit in the use of the terms filter, gate, and channel. Three psychological theories of selective attention, over two decades old, that embody either suppression or enhancement are represented schematically in figure 49.2. Figure 49.2a represents complete filtering of sensory input from distractors (Broadbent, 1958); figure 49.2b represents attenuated filtering of sensory input from distractors (Treisman, 1960); and figure 49.2c represents the enhancement of sensory input from the target (LaBerge and Samuels, 1974). The activity level at the target site in figures 49.2a and 49.2b is driven by retinal stimulation only, while in figure 49.2c it is also driven by internal, top-down sources.

Top-down influences on retina-driven activity apparently are carried by excitatory fibers by way of direct corticocortical projections or by way of indirect projections that synapse first in a thalamic nucleus (Jones, 1985; Salin and Bullier, 1995). These fibers apparently terminate mainly on excitatory neurons in cortical columns (Johnson and Burkhalter, 1996) where attention is expressed. Therefore, top-down selection would appear to be expressed predominantly by the enhancement of activity at the target site (or by decay of activity at the distractor sites) in extrastriate cortex. A theoretical description of bottom-up selection by distractor suppression, involving inhibitory influences within oculomotor mechanisms, is given elsewhere (LaBerge, 1995b, 1997b).

The mechanisms of attention

When target selection is characterized by an enhancement of activity in a specific set or cluster of cortical

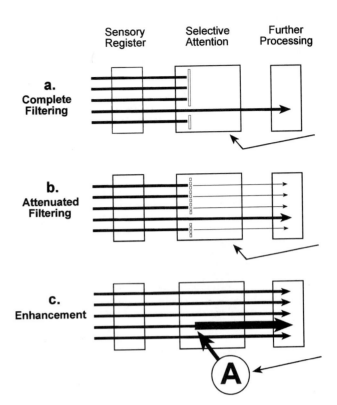

FIGURE 49.2   Schematic diagrams of selective attention operations according to some theories of attention in the psychological literature. (a) Complete suppression at distractor sites (Broadbent, 1958); (b) attenuated suppression at distractor sites (Treisman, 1960); (c) enhancement at the target site (LaBerge and Samuels, 1974). The arrows pointing from right to left represent controlling signals that select the part of the sensory input to be attended.

columns, where are the neural circuits that produce that enhancement? One possible location is within the cortical column itself, in which there exist a sufficient number of feedback connections to produce significant self-amplification (Douglas et al., 1995). Cortical self-amplifying circuits could be triggered or regulated by signals from sources outside the immediate cortical areas—for example, by fibers arising from the prefrontal cortex or from the thalamus.

Other possible locations of an amplifying circuit lie outside the cortical column. One possible external source of attentional amplification is the set of neuromodulatory cells in the brain stem and basal forebrain, whose axon fibers spread diffusely across large areas of cortex. These neuromodulatory centers regulate the state of wakefulness and states of alertness (Steriade, McCormick, and Sejnowski, 1993), which themselves are preconditions for states of attention. However, the distribution of these fibers to cortical columns is too diffuse to produce the differences in patterns of neural activity required for separation of target and distractor activities,

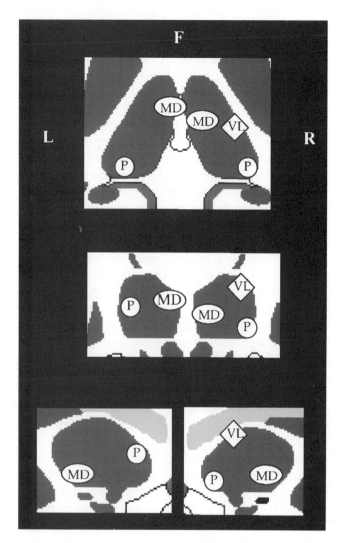

FIGURE 49.3 Activity increases indicated in three thalamic nuclei (pulvinar, mediodorsal, and ventrolateral) when a hard identification task was compared with both an easy identification task and a control task (right thalamus), and when the easy task was compared with a control task (left thalamus) (Liotti, Fox, and LaBerge, 1994).

particularly when they are spatially close in visual displays (e.g., figure 49.1).

Another possible external source of attentional amplification is the thalamus, which is known to contain circuits that reciprocally project to cortical columns in the form of thalamocortical loops. The thalamocortical loop receives axon fibers (at the relay neuron) from neurons in other brain areas (Conley and Raczkowsky, 1990; Ungerleider, Galkin, and Mishkin, 1983; Schiller, 1984), so that the thalamocortical loop may be driven directly by both bottom-up sources of sensory control (e.g., from V1 and superior colliculus) and top-down sources of voluntary control (from the prefrontal cortex).

The thalamus is connected reciprocally with virtually every area of cortex (Jones, 1985), and therefore tha-

lamic nuclei have the capability of influencing activity levels in any cortical area. Of particular interest in this chapter is the pulvinar nucleus, which projects reciprocally to visual areas in the occipital, temporal, parietal, and frontal lobes. In the human, the pulvinar is the largest nucleus of the thalamus, occupying approximately two-fifths of the thalamic volume. The proportional size of the pulvinar to the thalamus decreases from human to monkey, and in the cat the pulvinar is so small that it escapes labeling in many brain atlases. Within the primate pulvinar are four major divisions termed the *medial, lateral, inferior,* and *anterior* pulvinar (Jones, 1985).

The pathways of early visual processing in both cortex and superior colliculus interconnect with the pulvinar in a manner that preserves topographical relations, particularly with the inferior and lateral nuclei of the pulvinar (Burton and Jones, 1976; Petersen, Robinson, and Keys, 1985). In the posterior parietal areas, neurolabeling studies have shown connections from LIP and 7a to PuL and PuM and vice versa (Romanski et al., 1997; Schmahmann and Pandya, 1990). The PuM also connects reciprocally with lateral prefrontal areas (Romanski et al., 1997). The regions within PuM containing cells that connect to area 7a apparently overlap areas in PuL containing cells that connect with the lateral prefrontal area (Asanuma, Andersen, and Cowan, 1985) and with regions in the temporal lobe (Webster, Bachevalier, and Ungerleider, 1991). Therefore, reciprocal connections exist between parietal and temporal areas and the pulvinar, and also between lateral prefrontal areas and these pulvinar areas.

The neurons of the pulvinar form thalamocortical loops with the visual areas of the posterior cortex, and these neurons have well-defined receptive fields that are less than a degree in size near foveal center and increase in size as eccentricity increases (Bender 1981; Petersen, Robinson, and Keys, 1985). The size-eccentricity relationship of these pulvinar neuron receptive fields is quite similar to the size-eccentricity relationships of V1 and V2 cortical cells (Gattass, Gross, and Sandell, 1981). In view of the sensitivities of these neurons to small changes in visual locations of an object, it would not seem unreasonable to view pulvinar neurons as occupying a seventh layer of the visual cortex. This close relationship between thalamic neurons and cortical columns would appear to generalize to the rest of the neocortex.

The participation of the pulvinar in visual attention tasks has been proposed by several theories (e.g., LaBerge, 1990; LaBerge and Brown, 1989; Olshausen, Anderson, and Van Essen, 1993; Posner et al., 1988) and supported by the findings of a variety of neuroscience studies. Human patients with lesions in the posterior thalamus showed deficits in responding to cued and uncued locations of visual stimuli contralateral to the lesion, while showing no evidence of contralateral neglect (Rafal and Posner, 1987). Rafal and Posner interpret these findings as indicating an impairment in engaging attention at a new spatial location in contrast to the impairment in disengaging attention from a currently attended location, which is characteristic of the neglect syndrome typically produced by lesions in the posterior parietal areas (e.g., Posner et al, 1984). In monkeys, lesions in the pulvinar produce impairments in the attentional scanning of a visual display (Ungerleider and Christensen, 1979).

Single-cell studies indicate that pulvinar neurons increased their firing rates to a visual stimulus when that stimulus is a target of an impending eye movement or when the animal simply attends to it without a subsequent eye movement (Petersen, Robinson, and Keys, 1985). When microinjections of mucimol, a GABA agonist, were injected into the dorsal region of the medial pulvinar of monkeys, shifts of attention to the contralateral visual field were impaired in a spatial orienting task; injections of the GABA antagonist bicuilline into the same area facilitated shifts of attention to the contralateral visual field (Petersen, Robinson, and Morris, 1987).

A variety of PET studies of experiments with humans have shown activation of the pulvinar during visual attention tasks, and in an earlier review of the available evidence (LaBerge, 1990) it was proposed that the details of the thalamocortical circuit indicate that it embodies an algorithm that enhances firing in a target set of cortical cells while inhibiting firing in the surrounding set of cortical cells. Corbetta and colleagues (1991) used a task that focused attention in preparation for discriminating among an array of stimuli with respect to their shape, color, or velocity of movement, and found an increase in blood flow in the right thalamus during the velocity and shape conditions. Another PET study (LaBerge and Buchsbaum, 1990) used a task designed to strongly intensify the activity brain structures involved in selectively attending to a shape, by asking subjects to identify a briefly presented target shape *O* (versus a *C* or a zero) when the target was surrounded on all sides by eight similar characters (*G* and *Q*). The target display was presented in the same location during a block of trials (to the right or left of a central dot), and the 1400-ms interstimulus interval allowed time for the subject to increase preparatory attention to a level necessary to identify the briefly flashed target. The PET results showed a significant increase in the pulvinar, and it appeared that all of the increase was in the right pulvinar.

Using the same concentrated attention task of the LaBerge and Buchsbaum (1990) experiment (with a cue-target preparatory interval of 1600 ms), Liotti, Fox, and LaBerge (1994) added an easy task (the *O* surrounded by slanted lines) and a control task, and found a strong and significant increase in the right pulvinar for the hard task (see figure 49.3). Two other thalamic regions showed increases in activation when the hard condition was compared with the easy and control conditions. One activated thalamic region contained the mediodorsal nucleus, which connects strongly with the prefrontal cortex and also with the parietal cortex; this region was also activated in the Corbetta and colleagues (1991) study with shapes and in the Heinze and colleagues (1994) study in which subjects sustained focal attention on locations in the right visual field. The third thalamic region activated by the hard task in the Liotti, Fox, and LaBerge study was the ventrolateral nucleus, which connects with both the frontal areas and the basal ganglia. Corbetta and colleagues (1991) found activations in this region when subjects shifted attention toward the right in the right visual field. Thus three regions of the thalamus appear to be selectively active when humans are attending to visual shapes and their locations.

The Liotti, Fox, and LaBerge (1994) study also showed that increased activations in the three thalamic nuclei during the hard task are correlated with cortical regions that are directly connected with these three thalamic nuclei. Activations of the right pulvinar correlated with activations in the right and left fusiform gyrus; activations of the mediodorsal nucleus correlated with activations of the right ventrolateral prefrontal cortex; and activations of the right ventrolateral nucleus correlated with the right ventrolateral prefrontal cortex and the right head of the caudate nucleus of the basal ganglia. The prefrontal areas and the basal ganglia may control what will be attended to and how intensely. This issue will be addressed in the next section of this chapter concerned with the control of attention.

Other recent studies support the involvement of the thalamus in attention. Frith and Friston (1996) showed that the right midthalamus was activated when subjects were attending to sounds while ignoring visual stimuli. Morris, Friston, and Dolan (1997) found that increases in salience of emotionally expressive faces increased activation in the right pulvinar nucleus. Shulman and colleagues (1997) analyzed nine PET studies of visual processing, which included tasks of discrimination, search, language, memory, and imagery. Taken together, the nine tasks showed no common cortical regions of activations (outside of V1) but did show consistent activation in the thalamus and the cerebellum. In particular, the activated region of the right thalamus appeared to spread over several nuclei. The activations in the right and left thalamus were not correlated, suggesting that they serve different functions.

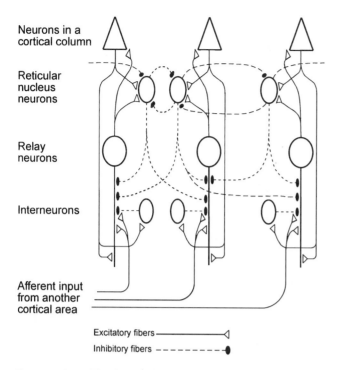

Neurons in a
cortical column

Reticular
nucleus
neurons

Relay
neurons

Interneurons

Afferent input
from another
cortical area

Excitatory fibers ————————▷
Inhibitory fibers ‑ ‑ ‑ ‑ ‑ ‑ ‑ ‑ ●

FIGURE 49.4   The thalamocortical circuit of virtually all cortical areas. Afferent fibers (e.g., from the frontal cortex) synapse
on dendrites of the relay cell near the soma, and axons of the
relay cells project mainly to middle layers of a cortical column.
Fibers from Layer 6 of the cortical column synapse mainly on
distal dendrites of the relay cells.

One way to determine the suitability of a proposed
mechanism for producing the expression of selective attention in cortical areas is to examine its circuitry and
then evaluate its potential for producing the output firing patterns that resemble one of the selection trajectories shown in figure 49.1.

THE STRUCTURE OF THE THALAMOCORTICAL CIR-
CUIT   Figure 49.4 shows a diagram of the types of
cells in the thalamic and cortical part of the circuit,
along with their known pattern of interconnections.
The only uncertainty about the connectivity concerns
whether the reticular nucleus projects its axons to relay
cells lying only within a thalamic column (e.g., Crick,
1984; Steriade, Domich, and Oakson, 1986), or to relay cells lying only in neighboring columns (e.g., Sherman and Koch, 1986), or to both (LaBerge, Carter, and
Brown, 1992). According to simulations of a network
model of the thalamocortical circuit (to be described
later in this section), all three patterns of connectivity
produce the mode of attentional expression shown in
figure 49.1D. Although almost all of the available cellular and connectivity knowledge about the thalamus
is based on the monkey, cat, and rat, it appears to be
relatively safe to extrapolate from monkey to human

because the monkey and human thalami show identical histochemical staining patterns (Hirai and Jones,
1989).

A thalamic nucleus is organized in a columnar manner, in the sense that the flow of impulses from an afferent input through a thalamic relay cell is segregated
from the impulses flowing through other thalamic relay
cells (Jones, 1985; Steriade, Jones, and Llinas, 1990).
The only known interactions between channels within
the thalamus occurs by means of the lateral inhibitory
links between cells of the reticular nucleus. Therefore, it
would seem that the separate channels of impulses from
thalamic inputs to thalamic outputs follow a precise local coding scheme (Jones, 1985).

Furthermore, the lateral inhibitory computations of
the reticular nucleus cells could be expected to sharpen
local gradients of neural activity across the cortical columns (in somewhat the same way that horizontal cells
enhance contrast in the retina), so that impulses that are
routed through the thalamus may serve to concentrate
neural activity spatially rather than to spread it. This
principle may hold generally for a cluster of input fibers
carrying a vector-coded representation, even considering that a typical thalamocortical axon spreads across a
2.0–2.5-mm diameter area within cortex (Kaske, Dick,
and Creutzfeldt, 1991) and that thalamocortical axons
terminating in primary visual, auditory, and somatosensory areas may be restricted to a 1–2-mm area (Ferster
and Levay, 1978; Gilbert and Wiesel, 1983). In contrast
to the isolation of thalamic columns (except for the local
lateral inhibitory connections in the reticular nucleus),
the columnar organization in the cortex is characterized
by extensive interconnections between neighboring columns (for a relevant review, see Toyama, 1988; Felleman and Van Essen, 1991), which enable activity in one
column to enhance as well as suppress activity in neighboring columns.

The remaining part of the circuit diagram of figure
49.4 concerns the reticular nucleus cells and the interneurons, both of which are inhibitory (Jones, 1985); the
reticular nucleus cells provide recurrent inhibition, and
the interneurons provide feedforward inhibition. In the
case of the reticular nucleus cells, the main axon fiber enters the main body of the thalamus, spreads its terminals
widely (Yen et al., 1985), and forms synapses not only
with relay cells but also with interneurons (Montero and
Singer, 1985). This pattern of connectivity enables reticular nucleus cells to reduce the inhibitory influence of
interneurons at the thalamic afferent input (Steriade,
Domich, and Oakson, 1986).

Often overlooked in circuit diagrams of cortical and
subcortical areas is the ubiquitous presence of axon terminals arising from nuclei in the brain stem and basal

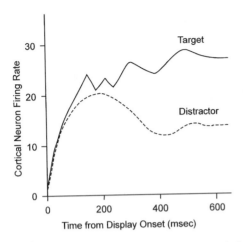

FIGURE 49.5 Simulated trajectories of target and distractor firing rates of cortical neurons, based on the network model of the thalamocortical circuit shown in figure 49.4. (Adapted from LaBerge, Carter, and Brown, 1992.)

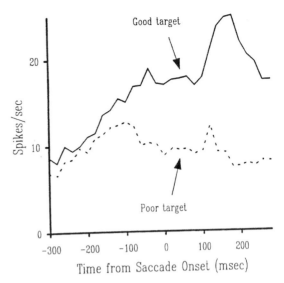

FIGURE 49.6 Trajectories of neural firing for the good (target) stimulus and the poor (distractor) stimulus. The animal produced a saccade to the target at time 0 (Chelazzi et al., 1993).

forebrain (Jones, 1985; Steriade, Jones, and Llinas, 1990). Neurotransmitter substances secreted by these axon terminals modulate in a diffuse manner both the synaptic connections between thalamic cells and the intrinsic membrane properties of cells that affect spontaneous firing and thereby influence states of sleep and arousal (McCormick, 1992).

Given the relatively well-known anatomical structure of the thalamic circuit, it is possible to determine by simulation methods whether the output of the thalamocortical circuit is suitable for producing the selective expression of attention in cortical columns. The results of one simulation study (LaBerge, Carter, and Brown, 1992) assumed that the input to the thalamocortical circuit represented sensory activations arising from a display containing a target item with adjacent distracting items on each side of it. Each item was represented by five columns of the kind shown in Figure 49.4, with two columns for the spaces between them. The simulations were carried out for each of the three variations of the thalamocortical circuit described earlier in this section. All three simulations produced the same pattern of selective trajectories for the target and distractor, which is the pattern shown in figure 49.1D.

An example of a more recent simulation of the thalamocortical network operation is shown in figure 49.5. The only modification of the network parameters of the first simulations was that the input from corticothalamic axons at the distal dendrites of the relay cell lowers the threshold of the cell instead of inducing it to fire (McCormick and Von Krosigk, 1992); thus there is an increase in the synaptic weight for the afferent input to the relay, with the consequence that the effect of incoming spikes from afferent axons synapsing near the

relay cell body are potentiated. The resulting selection trajectories were similar to those of the original simulation study, conforming to the expression pattern shown in figure 49.1D. The simulated trajectories of V4 cell activity, shown in figure 49.5, may be compared with the measurements of single-cell activity, shown in figure 49.6, of a monkey engaged in a selective attention task. The simulated trajectories of attentional selection show that small differences in firing rates between target and distractor top-down inputs can be magnified by a factor of at least 25 by the characteristics of the thalamocortical network.

The set of equations on which the simulation of the thalamocortical network is based contains 30 parameters, a fact which imposes severe difficulties on estimating parameters from empirical tests of the network. A different formulation of the thalamocortical network is based on equations containing only 11 parameters, of which 7 are fixed and 4 are free to vary (LaBerge, Carlson, and Williams, 1997); these equations can be solved by analytic methods, in contrast to the numerical method of simulation. This analytic model of the thalamocortical circuit produces pairs of trajectories that closely match the pattern of the pairs of trajectories generated by the network model (figure 49.5).

In evaluating the results of the present simulations, it should be noted that the finding that the thalamic network can greatly magnify a target-surround input difference by a large enhancement component with a relatively small suppression component does not prove that the thalamic network in fact operates in this manner. Rather, the simulation result has the status of an existence proof, which states that the thalamic circuit could instantiate a magnification of the target-surround contrast in the manner shown by Figure 49.1D. However, taken together with the PET evidence for thalamic activation (and some, e.g., Maunsell, 1995, but not all single-cell evidence, e.g., Moran and Desimone, 1985), the simulation of the thalamocortical network's operation supports the hypothesis that the thalamocortical circuit amplifies activity in cortical columns corresponding to the target of attention (relative to the activity in the surrounding columns) and thereby serves as a mechanism of the expression of attention.

The control of attention

The mechanism that produces the expression of attention in cortical columns, whether it be a thalamocortical circuit or a circuit intrinsic to a cluster of cortical columns, is unlikely to initiate the pattern of attentional activity by itself. Rather, the initiation of attentional activity in these mechanisms is presumed to be controlled by sources outside itself–for example, by afferent inputs from other cortical columns or by inputs from the superior colliculus (figure 49.4, bottom). The sources of control are commonly believed to be of two major types: bottom-up (exogenous, stimulus-driven) control and top-down (endogenous, goal-directed) control (for a review see Egeth and Yantis, 1997).

Much of the literature on attentional control is concerned with how the shifts of attention are controlled–in particular, how the shifts are triggered and how the shift process itself operates (i.e., what happens between the origin site of the shift and the destination site). Attentional control also operates after attention has shifted, to determine which of the alternative items in a display will be selected for the expression of attention and to determine the intensity and duration (dwell time) at the new locus of attention. What attention "does" for the organism (e.g., simple selection, preparation, and maintenance of neural activities) is a basic issue of this chapter, and the effects produced by the attention depend upon what happens during the time attention is being expressed, which takes place after the shift has been completed. Therefore, in this section of the chapter there will be more emphasis on the control of the expression of attention, rather than on the control of the shifting of attention.

BOTTOM-UP CONTROL OF ATTENTION   Bottom-up control of attention operates in two main ways: triggering shifts of attention (often termed attentional capture) and guiding attention to particular locations in the visual field. Examples of a stimulus that initiates a shift of at-

tention are a bar marker flashed near the location of an impending target object (Eriksen and Hoffman, 1972; Jonides, 1981) or the abrupt increase in luminance of a square located to the right or left of a central fixation point (e.g., Posner, 1980). It was proposed by Yantis and Jonides (1984) that these kinds of stimulus changes trigger shifts of attention because they share the property of an abrupt character of the stimulus onset.

Recently, Yantis (1996) proposed three categories of attentional capture: *strongly involuntary*, when a stimulus event captures attention when the subject is actively ignoring it; *weakly involuntary,* when an irrelevant stimulus event captures attention while the subject is not actively ignoring it; and when a subject actively searches for a particular *feature singleton.* Thus, whether or not a bottom-up sensory event will trigger an attention shift depends upon the momentary top-down control. A similar view of attentional capture is given in the guided search model of Wolfe (1994), in which attentional priorities in search are dependent jointly on bottom-up and top-down influences.

The display conditions that are less obligatory with respect to attentional shifts are feature singletons, which could be said to guide rather than trigger attentional shifts. Feature singletons have been described in the literature as items that appear to "pop out" during the search of an array of objects, by virtue of possessing a unique (and salient) feature, relative to the other items of the search array (Treisman and Gelade, 1980; Treisman and Gormican, 1988). The process by which an object defined by a unique feature is detected in these search tasks is described as a preattentive process, in contrast to the attentive process that is directed successively to item locations when the object is defined by a conjunction of features. Thus the feature singleton in an array of items first is detected, and then it guides the shift of attention to its location. According to Treisman's theory (Treisman, 1998), the simple features that constitute items in a search display are initially registered in parallel within separate feature maps, which are connected to a master map of location. Shifts of attention to location are carried out in the master map, and presumably only one shift is necessary when the target is defined by a feature singleton, whereas a succession of shifts to various item locations is required when the target is defined by a conjunction of features.

Thus, when an array of items is displayed (e.g., in a search task), the location map may be pictured as containing a set of activity peaks, each representing the initial registration of an item's location, with the activation of a feature singleton's location being higher than that of its neighboring items. This initial registration of object locations is preattentive, and has been described as "spatial indexing" in a model by Wright and Ward (1998). Preattentive registration of an object's location has also been described in terms of an "activity distribution" within a location module of the brain (LaBerge and Brown, 1989; LaBerge et al., 1997).

TOP-DOWN CONTROL OF ATTENTION   A changing sensory environment typically presents the system with an ongoing array of abrupt stimulus onsets and locally defined stimulus contrasts that operate as feature singletons. In order to respond effectively to this environmental flux, the system expresses attention to only a small part of this stimulus input. When a display of many objects is presented, the locations of those objects are presumed to be indexed spatially by individual peaks of activity distributions in a brain map, which is presumed to be located in parietal areas. The pattern of locations of these activity distributions is then projected to prefrontal areas that control attention to spatial locations, in particular the dorsolateral prefrontal area. A core premise of this chapter is that further processing in this and related frontal areas then determines which of these parietal activity distributions will be converted into an expression of attention by projecting to it, in the top-down direction, additional activation that is sustained for some minimal time.

Sites of top-down attentional control are presumed to underlie systems of working memory, in which (following the theory of Baddeley, 1995) two kinds of processes dominate: storage of information in a highly accessible form over a short period of time; and executive control, which governs encoding, retrieval, and commands for the expression of attention.

In the monkey prefrontal cortex, neurons that are active during the delays between a sample display and a test display appear to be clustered in anatomically distinct regions according to whether they are selectively responsive to spatial locations and the shape and color of objects (Wilson, O'Scalaidhe, and Goldman-Rakic, 1993), and to the identity of faces (O'Scalaidhe, Wilson, and Goldman-Rakic, 1997). Using PET measures with humans, Smith and Jonides (1997) indicated different working-memory systems for spatial, object, and verbal information.

The sustaining of information over a delay period would seem to be required in order to generate preparatory attention to an appropriate object or location prior to the appearance of a target. But keeping information in a state of high accessibility over a period of time does not imply that it is also generating an expression of preparatory attention: stated otherwise, the expectation for an upcoming event is not necessarily accompanied by an attentional preparation for the event (LaBerge,

1995b). The what, where, and when of an upcoming display of an object may be held in working memory involuntarily while simple selective attention may be directed elsewhere (Miller, Erickson, and Desimone, 1996), but attentional preparation to perceive that object is a voluntary act and interferes with attending elsewhere at the same time. This separation of expectancy and preparation in the attentional control process is consistent with the separate processes of information maintenance and executive control in theories of working memory.

The amount of attentional control (for simple selection as well as for preparation) and the amount of working memory load may vary somewhat independently in tasks, so that it would be expected that the neural circuitry underlying these components would be located in different sites of the frontal cortex. Owing to its action property, the command component of attentional control would seem to lie nearer the premotor areas than the memory component of control, but the two sets of circuits may be too close to show separated sites of activation in many PET and fMRI studies. However, attention-related activations have been shown in premotor areas in several PET studies (Corbetta et al., 1993; Haxby et al., 1994; Liotti, Fox, and LaBerge, 1994; Nobre et al., 1997). Additional research is needed to design tasks that allow a clearer separation of the frontal sites that underlie components of attentional control.

The triangular-circuit theory of attention

Under the first three major headings of this chapter are treatments of issues and evidence related to three different aspects of attention and the brain sites in which they are presumed to be located. At any moment while attention is being expressed, all three sites are presumed to be active by virtue of their interconnections. It has been proposed that the pattern by which these three sites are connected is a triangular circuit (LaBerge, 1995a, 1995b, 1997a, 1998).

Control areas of the prefrontal cortex send fibers to cortical columns where attention is expressed in the monkey inferotemporal area (Webster et al., 1994) and in the parietal area (Goldman-Rakic, Chafee, and Friedman, 1993), but another pathway of fibers also connects these prefrontal areas with these posterior cortical columns. The fibers in the other pathway connect with cells within the pulvinar, and cells in the pulvinar connect with the posterior cortical columns (Asanuma, Andersen, and Cowan, 1985; Romanski et al., 1997). Therefore, the two pathways that connect a prefrontal area of control with a cortical area of expression appear to form a triangular circuit.

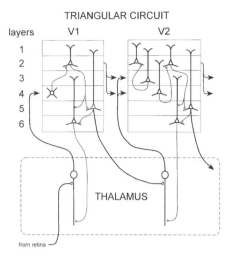

TRIANGULAR CIRCUIT

FIGURE 49.7 Schematic diagram of the triangular circuit connecting neurons of a V1 column with neurons of a V2 column. Direct connections arise from Layer 2 of V1 and terminate in middle layers of V2; indirect connections arise from Layer 5 of V1, synapse on a thalamic relay cell, and terminate in middle layers of V2. For simplicity of illustration, reticular nucleus neurons are not shown here.

The present theory assumes that the direct link within the triangular circuit functions primarily to select which columns of attentional expression shall be activated, and the indirect link through a thalamic nucleus functions to intensify activity in the selected columns. These two functions of selection and intensification, represented by each pathway within the triangular circuit, can be viewed as informational and modulatory aspects of attentional control, respectively. In order to clarify the way in which the triangular circuit separates the informational and modulatory aspects of signaling between cortical areas of attentional control and expression, we present a description of the general structure of the triangular circuit inferred from neurotracing studies. Most of the knowledge we have of cortical and thalamic circuitry has been obtained from studies of area V1 and its adjacent cortical areas, for example, V2. It is known that fibers from V1 cells synapse in the pulvinar nucleus of the thalamus (e.g., Ungerleider, Galkin, and Mishkin, 1983) and that these fibers arise from large pyramidal cells in Layer 5 and from smaller pyramidal cells in lower Layer 6 (Conley and Raczkowski, 1990). Relay neurons in the pulvinar project directly to neurons in area V2 (Jones, 1985), as well as to other visual areas in the posterior cortex (including area V1).

Figure 49.7 shows a schematic diagram of the direct (forward) fiber arising from Layer 2 of a V1 column and terminating in the middle layers of a V2 column. An indirect fiber connecting a V1 column with a V2 column arises from Layer 5 of a V1 column and terminates on a relay cell in the pulvinar, which in turn projects to the middle layers of a V2 column. (The indirect fibers that arise from lower Layer 6 are not shown here.)

The indirect connection between V1 and V2 that involves thalamic neurons appears to have properties that can enhance firing rates in V2 columns. Neurons in Layer 5 fire in bursts of a few spikes at rates at least as high as 250 Hz, with intraburst firing rates of approximately 15 Hz (Connors and Gutnick, 1990; Gray and McCormick, 1996); therefore, these neurons have the ability to drive their target neurons to high rates of firing. Axons of these intrinsically burst-firing cells synapse near the cell bodies of thalamic relay neurons, and this dendritic location provides a privileged position from which to drive the spike outputs of the relay neuron. The neurons arising from upper Layer 6, whose axon fibers have smaller diameters (and thus can be distinguished from those of Layer 5), synapse mostly at remote locations on the dendrite (Sherman and Koch, 1990). These (upper) Layer 6 neurons appear to function by lowering the threshold of the thalamic neuron to signals arriving at synapses near the cell body (McCormick and Von Krosigk, 1992). Therefore, the corticothalamic feedback loop involving Layer 6 neurons facilitates the synaptic efficacy of Layer 5 axons, and thereby potentiates the already strong effects of the bursting Layer 5 neurons on the relay neuron. These properties were incorporated into the network simulation of the thalamocortical circuit described earlier in this chapter, whose output trajectories are shown in figure 49.5.

Triangular circuits are assumed to exist within and between other cortical areas. Large Layer 5 fibers synapse near the relay cell body, and small Layer 6 fibers synapse at the distal locations on the relay cell dendrites for the auditory cortex (Ojima, 1994) and the prefrontal cortex (Schwartz, Dekker, and Goldman-Rakic, 1991). Because all regions of the cortex are connected with a nucleus of the thalamus, it seems highly probable that the triangular circuit exists wherever cortical columns in one area communicate with columns in another area. Samples of triangular circuits that are particularly relevant to attentional processing in the brain are shown in figure 49.8 (LaBerge, 1995a, 1995b). These proposed triangular circuits function to amplify corticocortical connections in both bottom-up and top-down directions, and it is conjectured that the enhancement operations provided by the thalamic part of the triangular circuit typically are stronger and of longer duration when the circuit involves top-down sources of activation than when it involves only bottom-up sources of activation (e.g., from abrupt onsets and feature singletons).

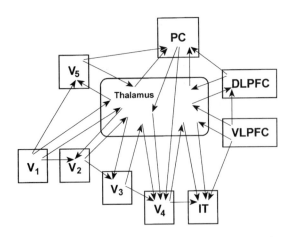

FIGURE 49.8 Some samples of the triangular circuits that are presumed to be involved in visual attention. The top-down triangular circuits serving visual attention are assumed to involve working memory circuits in the dorsolateral prefrontal cortex (DLPFC) for location and in the ventrolateral prefrontal cortex (VLPFC) for shape.

Direct connections from prefrontal areas of control to posterior areas are assumed to carry the signals that select the columns of attentional expression of perceptual events; therefore, this link in the triangular circuit is considered informational. One may question whether or not these fibers also carry the range of firing rates needed to induce varying degrees of intensity in the target columns; high rates of intensity can obscure the temporal properties of a signal train that is precisely tuned to choose the appropriate columns for attentional expression. Modulatory signaling of attentional control can be separated from the direct route serving informational signaling by means of the indirect route from prefrontal areas through the thalamus.

A triangular circuit of attention connecting the frontal, pulvinar, and parietal areas is illustrated schematically in figure 49.9. The frontal area (which may include premotor and prefrontal areas) is presumed to serve the storage and executive components of control (for a review of studies showing interconnections of parietal, prefrontal, and premotor areas see Selemon and Goldman-Rakic, 1988). In this example, a site in frontal cortex selects the site of attentional expression in columns of the parietal cortex and regulates the intensity of the cortical expression in these columns by means of the indirect connection through a thalamic nucleus. Since, in general, the posterior cortical areas code for perceptions and the anterior cortical areas code for actions, sites of attentional expression for actions are assumed to exist in the frontal area.

A metaphor for the operation of the triangular circuit of attention is the operation of a compact disc player (CD player). The CD player is assumed to contain a bank of thousands of discs (corresponding to column clusters in the cerebral cortex, which code memories of possible cognitive events). Selection of a disc occurs from the controlling hand (prefrontal/premotor cortex), which also adjusts the gain (thalamocortical circuit) of the disc. Discs may be initially activated bottom-up (from a fixed connection with the internet), but the disc is not heard unless the controlling hand turns up the gain for some minimum duration of time (LaBerge, 1997a, 1998).

CONTROL OF THE PREFRONTAL EXECUTIVE CONTROL The issue of the executive control of attention leads to the question of how the controlling operations of the frontal sites are themselves controlled. The thalamocortical loops in the frontal cortical areas (and not in the posterior cortical areas) are tonically inhibited by fibers from the basal ganglia (Alexander and Crutcher, 1990), specifically, from the substantia nigra (pars reticulata) and the globus pallidus (Ueki, 1983; Uno and Yoshida, 1975). The basal ganglia are directly connected with limbic areas and therefore provide a route by which motivational activities of the brain can influence action-related activities of the frontal cortex. Activity in the basal ganglia—for example, during working memory tasks (Levy et al., 1997) and concentrated preparatory attention tasks (Liotti, Fox, and LaBerge, 1994)—presumably results in the inhibition of inhibitory output fibers of the basal ganglia, so that the thalamic relay neurons receiving these fibers are released from the tonic inhibition of the basal ganglia and are free to activate columns of neurons in the frontal cortex within the thalamocortical loop (see figure 49.10). A more thorough discussion of the present view of basal ganglia control of frontal cortical columns is presented elsewhere (LaBerge, 1998), along with a diagram of the basal ganglia circuitry that connects with the triangular circuit of attention.

OPERATION OF THE TRIANGULAR CIRCUIT When the triangular circuit produces the expression of attention, it is presumed to be active over some minimum of time, and during this time interval activity flows repeatedly in both directions between the frontal control site and site of expression (figure 49.10). It is assumed that sustaining top-down activity directed to a site of attentional expression requires quasi-coincident detection of the top-down command and the resulting feedback from the site of expression. In somewhat the same manner, speaking aloud requires continuous feedback from hearing what is spoken, and when the time interval between the feedforward and feedback events is large, the act of speaking cannot be effectively sustained. Maintaining the appro-

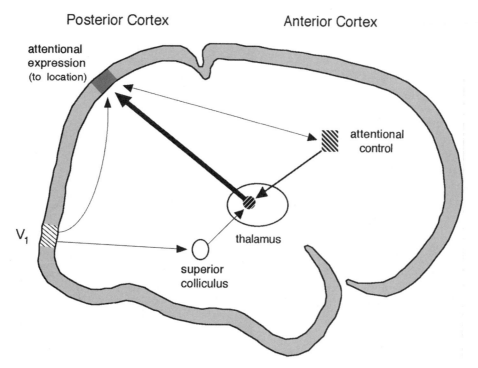

Posterior Cortex   Anterior Cortex

attentional
expression
(to location)

attentional
control

V₁

thalamus

superior
colliculus

FIGURE 49.9   A schematic example of a triangular circuit of attention, with the expression of attention in the parietal area, the control of attention in the frontal area (prefrontal and/or premotor area), and the amplification of attentional activity in the thalamic nucleus (pulvinar) serving the parietal area. An

abrupt stimulus onset is assumed to initiate brief parietal activity, regarded as an expression of orienting; prolonged parietal activity subsequently sustained (or initiated and sustained) by the top-down triangular circuit is regarded as an expression of attention.

priate timing between feedforward and feedback events within the triangular circuit of attention depends upon precise timing in frontal circuit activity, which is apparently affected strongly by the neurotransmitter fibers that pervade the frontal areas (e.g., Goldman-Rakic et al., 1992).

Attentional duration corresponds to the duration of cycling through the reciprocal triangular circuit of figure 49.10. Durations may be brief, as in the short dwell times during visual search, or long during preparatory attention for an upcoming target. A search display preattentively indexes locations of items by establishing small peaked activity distributions for each (regarded here as expressions of orienting), and then top-down attentional control selects one location after another by adding activity to the existing peak by means of a triangular circuit (see figure 49.9). The duration of top-down activity is presumed to be short for each location until a match is found, and then the triangular circuit sustains activity for a moderate duration. Similarly, when an abrupt onset of a luminance change indexes a location preattentively in the parietal location map and then in the frontal control map, attention is not considered to be expressed until the frontal map returns at least a moderate duration and intensity of activity through the triangular circuit to the parietal map.

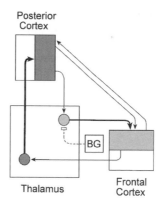

Posterior
Cortex

BG

Thalamus   Frontal
                  Cortex

FIGURE 49.10   Schematic diagram of reciprocal circuits connecting a site of attentional control with a site of attentional expression. Shading within rectangles represents levels of activity within a cortical column (dark is high, white is near-zero activity). Thalamic nuclei serving frontal cortical columns are tonically inhibited by fibers arising in the basal ganglia (BG); here the BG axon is shown to be disinhibited (by fibers from other brain areas), so that thalamic cells can increase activity in a frontal cortical column.

The circuit shown in figure 49.10 suggests two factors that contribute to the one-at-a-time property of attentional expressions. One factor is indicated by the activity contrast between a target column and neighboring columns, represented in figure 49.10 by the shading in the target column and the absence of shading in its neighboring column. At least some of the circuits responsible for the difference in column activations are the lateral inhibitory connections in the thalamic reticular nucleus (figure 49.4), which increase their inhibitory influence on neighboring columns as the activity in the target column increases. A second factor is the projection to the thalamic relay cell from the basal ganglia, which is selectively disinhibited in this example, while other thalamocortical loops serving other frontal columns are being tonically inhibited.

When reciprocal activity in a triangular circuit is intense, the resulting increased inhibition of neighboring columns of control provides protection from interruption by abrupt onsets of unattended stimuli, which normally activate these neighboring columns. This protective property is assumed to be mainly responsible for the longer detection times of uncued versus cued locations in visuospatial tasks. Thus the time to respond to an uncued probe stimulus can be used as a measure of the intensity of attention directed to the cued task (e.g., LaBerge, 1973).

Conclusions

A basic premise of this chapter is that the expression of attention in its manifestations of simple selection, preparation, and maintenance is produced by the intensification of neural activity in particular clusters of cortical columns. The expression of attention requires simultaneous activity in two other brain regions: the frontal areas, which control the selection and amplification commands; and the thalamus, which contains the amplification circuit mechanism. These brain sites of expression, mechanism, and control are assumed to be interconnected by a triangular circuit, and when simultaneous activity in the three sites is sufficiently prolonged and intense, it is conjectured that an attention state exists.

REFERENCES

ALEXANDER, G. E., and M. D. CRUTCHER, 1990. Functional architecture of basal ganglia circuits: Neural substrates of parallel processing. *Trends Neurosci.* 13:266–271.

ASANUMA, C., R. A. ANDERSEN, and W. M. COWAN, 1985. The thalamic relations of the caudal inferior parietal lobule and lateral prefrontal cortex in monkeys: Divergent cortical projections from cell clusters in the medial pulvinar nucleus. *J. Comp. Neurol.* 241:357–381.

BADDELEY, A., 1995. Working memory. In M. S. Gazzaniga, ed., *The Cognitive Neurosciences.* Cambridge, Mass.: MIT Press, pp. 755–764.

BENDER, D. B., 1981. Retinotopic organization of macaque pulvinar. *J. Neurophysiol.* 46:672–693.

BROADBENT, D. A., 1958. *Perception and Communication.* London: Pergamon Press.

BURTON, H., and E. G. JONES, 1976. The posterior thalamic region and its cortical projection in New World and Old World monkeys. *J. Comp. Neurol.* 168:249–301.

CHELAZZI, L., E. K. MILLER, J. DUNCAN, and R. DESIMONE, 1993. A neural basis for visual search in inferior temporal cortex. *Nature* 363:345–347.

CONLEY, M., and D. RACZKOWSKI, 1990. Sublaminar organization within layer V1 of the striate cortex in Galago. *J. Comp. Neurol.* 302:425–436.

CONNORS, B. W., and M. J. GUTNICK, 1990. Intrinsic firing patterns of diverse neocortical neurons. *Trends Neurosci.* 13:99–104.

CORBETTA, M., F. M. MIEZIN, S. DOBMEYER, G. L. SCHULMAN, and S. E. PETERSEN, 1991. Selective and divided attention during visual discrimination of shape, color, and speed: Functional anatomy by positron emission tomography. *J. Neurosci.* 11:2383–2402.

CORBETTA, M., F. M. MIEZIN, G. L. SHULMAN, and S. E. PETERSEN, 1993. A PET study of visuospatial attention. *J. Neurosci.* 13:1202–1226.

CRICK, F., 1984. The function of the thalamic reticular complex: The searchlight hypothesis. *Proc. Natl. Acad. Sci. U.S.A.* 81:4586–4590.

DOUGLAS, R. J., C. KOCH, M. MAHOWALD, K. A. MARTIN, and H. H. SUAREZ, 1995. Recurrent excitation in neocortical circuits. *Science* 269:981–985.

EGETH, H. E., and S. YANTIS., 1997. Visual attention: Control, representation, and time course. *Annu. Rev. Psychol.* 48:269–297.

ERIKSEN, C. W., and J. E. HOFFMAN, 1972. Temporal and spatial characteristics of selective encoding from visual displays. *Percept. Psychophys.* 12:201–204.

FELLEMAN, D. J., and D. C. VAN ESSEN, 1991. Distributed hierarchical processing in the primate cerebral cortex. *Cerebral Cortex* 1:1–47.

FERSTER, D., and S. LEVAY, 1978. The axonal arborization of lateral geniculate neurons in the striate cortex of the cat. *J. Comp. Neurol.* 182:923–944.

FRITH, C. D., and K. J. FRISTON, 1996. The role of the thalamus in "top-down" modulation of attention to sound. *Neuroimage* 4:210–215.

GATTASS, R., C. G. GROSS, and J. H. Sandell, 1981. Visuotopography of V2 in the macaque. *J. Comp. Neurol.* 21:5129–5139.

GILBERT, C. D., and T. N. WIESEL, 1983. Clustered intrinsic connections in cat visual cortex. *J. Neurosci.* 3:1116–1133.

GOLDMAN-RAKIC, P. S., M. CHAFEE, and H. FRIEDMAN, 1993. Allocation of function in distributed circuits. In T. Ono et al., eds., *Brain Mechanisms of Perception and Memory: From Neuron to Behavior.* New York: Oxford University Press, pp. 445–456.

GOLDMAN-RAKIC, P. S., M. S. LIDOW, J. F. SMILEY, and M. S. WILLIAMS, 1992. The anatomy of dopamine in monkey and human prefrontal cortex. *J. Neural Transm.* 36:163–177.

GRAY, C. M., and D. A. MCCORMICK, 1996. Chattering cells: Superficial pyramidal neurons contributing to the generation of synchronous oscillations in the visual cortex. *Science* 274:109–115.

HAXBY, J. V., B. HORWITZ, L. G. UNGERLEIDER, J. M. MAISOG, P. PIETRINI, and C. L. GRADY, 1994. The functional organization of human extrastriate cortex: A PET-rCBF study of selective attention to faces and locations. *J. Neurosci.* 14: 6336–6353.

HEINZE, H. J., G. R. MANGUN, W. BURCHERT, H. HINRICHS, M. SCHOLZ, T. F. MUENTE, A. GOES, M. SCHERG, S. JOHANNES, H. HUNDESHAGEN, M. S. GAZZANIGA, and S. A. HILLYARD, 1994. Combined spatial and temporal imaging of brain activity during visual selective attention in humans. *Nature* 372:543–546.

HIRAI, T., and E. G. JONES, 1989. A new parcellation of the human thalamus on the basis of histochemical staining. *Brain Res. Rev.* 14:1–34.

JOHNSON, R. R., and A. BURKHALTER, 1996. Microcircuitry of forward and feedback connections within rat visual cortex. *J. Comp. Neurol.* 368:383–398.

JONES, E. G., 1985. *The Thalamus.* New York: Plenum Press.

JONIDES, J., 1981. Voluntary versus automatic control over the mind's eye's movement. In J. B. Long and A. D. Baddeley, eds., *Attention and Performance IX.* Hillsdale, N.J.: Erlbaum, pp. 187–203.

KASKE, A., A. DICK, and O. D. CREUTZFELDT, 1991. The local domain for divergence of subcortical afferents to the striate and extrastriate visual cortex in the common marmoset: A multiple labeling study. *Exp. Brain Res.* 84:254–265.

LABERGE, D., 1973. Identification of the time to switch attention: A test of a serial and parallel model of attention. In S. Kornblum, ed., *Attention and Performance IV.* New York: Academic Press, pp. 50–64.

LABERGE, D., 1990. Thalamic and cortical mechanisms of attention suggested by recent positron emission tomographic experiments. *J. Cognit. Neurosci.* 2:358–372.

LABERGE, D., 1995a. Computational and anatomical models of selective attention in object identification. In M. Gazzaniga, ed., *The Cognitive Neurosciences.* Cambridge, Mass.: MIT Press.

LABERGE, D., 1995b. *Attentional Processing: The Brain's Art of Mindfulness.* Cambridge, MA: Harvard University Press.

LABERGE, D., 1997a. Attention, awareness, and the triangular circuit. *Conscious. Cogn.* 6:149–181.

LABERGE, D., 1997b. Attentional emphasis in visual orienting and resolving. In R. D. Wright, ed., *Visual Attention.* New York: Oxford University Press, pp. 417–459.

LABERGE, D., 1998. Attention as the intensification of cortical activity. *Rev. Neuropsychol.* 8:53–81.

LABERGE, D., and V. BROWN, 1989. Theory of attentional operations in shape identification. *Psychol. Rev.* 96:101–124.

LABERGE, D., and M. S. BUCHSBAUM, 1990. Positron emission tomographic measurements of pulvinar activity during an attention task. *J. Neurosci.* 10:613–619.

LABERGE, D., R. L. CARLSON, and J. K. WILLIAMS, 1997. Toward an analytic model of attention to visual shape. In A. A. J. Marley, ed., *Choice, Decision, and Measurement.* Mahwah, N.J.: Erlbaum, pp. 389–410.

LABERGE, D., R. L. CARLSON, J. K. WILLIAMS, and B. G. BUNNEY, 1997. Shifting attention in visual space: Tests of moving-spotlight models versus an activity-distribution model. *J. Exp. Psychol. Hum. Percept. Perform.* 23:1380–1392.

LABERGE, D., M. CARTER, and V. BROWN, 1992. A network simulation of thalamic circuit operations in selective attention. *Neural Computation* 4:318–331.

LABERGE, D., and J. SAMUELS, 1974. Toward a theory of automatic information processing in reading. *Cognit. Psychol.* 6: 293–323.

LEVY, R., H. R. FRIEDMAN, L. DAVACHI, and P. S. GOLDMAN-RAKIC, 1997. Differential activation of the caudate nucleus in primates performing spatial and nonspatial working memory tasks. *J. Neurosci.* 17:3870–3882.

LIOTTI, M., P. T. FOX, and D. LABERGE, 1994. PET measurements of attention to closely spaced visual shapes. *Soc. Neurosci. Abstr.* 20:354.

MAUNSELL, J. H. R., 1995. The brain's visual world: Representation of visual targets in cerebral cortex. *Science* 3:764–769.

MCCORMICK, D. A., 1992. Neurotransmitter actions in the thalamus and cerebral cortex and their role in neuromodulation of thalamocortical activity. *Prog. Neurobiol.* 39:337–388.

MCCORMICK, D. A., and M. VON KROSIGK, 1992. Corticothalamic activation modulates thalamic firing through glutamate "metabotropic" receptors. *Proc. Natl. Acad. Sci. U.S.A.* 89:2774–2778.

MILLER, E. K., C. A. ERICKSON, and R. DESIMONE, 1996. Neural mechanisms of visual working memory in prefrontal cortex of the macaque. *J. Neurosci.* 16:5154–5167.

MONTERO, V. M., and W. SINGER, 1985. Ultrastructural identification of somata and neural processes immunoreactive to antibodies against glutamic acid decarboxylase (GAD) in the dorsal lateral geniculate nucleus of the cat. *Exp. Brain Res.* 59:151–165.

MORAN, J., and R. DESIMONE, 1985. Selective attention gates visual processing in the extrastriate cortex. *Science* 229:782–784.

MORRIS, J. S., K. J. FRISTON, and R. J. DOLAN, 1997. Neural responses to salient visual stimuli. *Proc. R. Soc. Lond. B. Biol. Sci.* 264:769–775.

MOUNTCASTLE, V. B., 1957. Modality and topographic properties of single neurons of cat's somatic sensory cortex. *J. Neurophysiol.* 20:408–434.

NOBRE, A. C., G. N. SEBESTYEN, D. R. GITELMAN, M. M. MESULAM, R. S. FRACKOWIAK, and C. D. FRITH, 1997. Functional localization of the system for visuospatial attention using positron emission tomography. *Brain* 120:515–533.

OJIMA, H., 1994. Terminal morphology and distribution of corticothalamic fibers originating from layers 5 and 6 of cat primary auditory cortex. *Cerebral Cortex* 6:646–663.

OLSHAUSEN, B. A., C. H. ANDERSON, and D. C. VAN ESSEN, 1993. A neurobiological model of visual attention and invariant pattern recognition based on dynamic routing of information. *J. Neurosci.* 13:4700–4719.

O'SCALAIDHE, S. P., F. A. WILSON, and P. S. GOLDMAN-RAKIC, 1997. Areal segregation of face-processing neurons in prefrontal cortex. *Science* 278:1135–1138.

PETERSEN, S. E., D. L. ROBINSON, and W. KEYS, 1985. Pulvinar nuclei of the behaving rhesus monkey: Visual responses and their modulation. *J. Neurophysiol.* 54:867–886.

PETERSEN, S. E., D. L. ROBINSON, and J. D. MORRIS, 1987. Contributions of the pulvinar to visual spatial attention. *Neuropsychologia* 25:97–105.

POSNER, M. I., 1980. Orienting of attention. *Q. J. Exp. Psychol.* 32:3–25.

POSNER, M. I., S. E. PETERSEN, P. T. FOX, and M. E. RAICHLE, 1988. Localization of cognitive operations in the human brain. *Science* 240:1627–1631.

POSNER, M. I., J. A. WALKER, F. J. FRIEDRICH, and R. D. RAFAL, 1984. Effects of parietal injury on covert orienting of attention. *J. Neurosci.* 4:1863–1874.

RAFAL, R. D., and M. I. POSNER, 1987. Deficits in human visual spatial attention following thalamic lesions. *Proc. Natl. Acad. Sci. U.S.A.* 84:7349–7353.

ROMANSKI, L. M., M. GIGUERE, J. J. BATES, and P. S. GOLD-MAN-RAKIC, 1997. Topographic organization of medial pulvinar connections with the prefrontal cortex in the rhesus monkey. *J. Comp. Neurol.* 379:313–332.

SALIN, P.-A., and J. BULLIER, 1995. Corticocortical connections in the visual system: Structure and function. *Physiol. Rev.* 75:107–154.

SCHILLER, P. H., 1984. The superior colliculus and visual function. In *Handbook of Physiology*, sec. 1: The Nervous System, vol. 3: *Sensory Processes*, J. M. Brookhart and V. B. Mountcastle, eds. Bethesda, Md.: American Physiological Society, pp. 457–505.

SCHMAHMANN, J. D., and D. N. PANDYA, 1990. Anatomical investigation of projections from thalamus to posterior parietal cortex in the rhesus monkey: A WGA-HRP and fluorescent tracer study. *J. Comp. Neurol.* 295:299–326.

SCHWARTZ, M. L., J. J. DEKKER, and P. S. GOLDMAN-RAKIC, 1991. Dual mode of corticothalamic synaptic termination in the mediodorsal nucleus of the rhesus monkey. *J. Comp. Neurol.* 309:289–304.

SELEMON, L. D., and P. S. GOLDMAN-RAKIC, 1988. Common cortical and subcortical targets of the dorsolateral prefrontal and posterior parietal cortices in the rhesus monkey: Evidence for a distributed neural network subserving spatially guided behavior. *J. Neurosci.* 11:4049–4068.

SHERMAN, S. M., and C. KOCH, 1986. The control of retinogeniculate transmission in the mammalian lateral geniculate nucleus. *Exp. Brain Res.* 63:1–20.

SHERMAN, S. M., and C. KOCH, 1990. Thalamus. In G. M. Shepherd, ed., *The Synaptic Organization of the Brain*. New York: Oxford University Press.

SHULMAN, G. L., M. CORBETTA, R. L. BUCKNER, J. A. FIEZ, F. M. MIEZIN, M. E. RAICHLE, and S. E. PETERSEN, 1997. Common blood flow changes across visual tasks. I. Increases in subcortical structures and cerebellum but not in nonvisual cortex. *J. Cognit. Neurosci.* 9:624–647.

SMITH, E. E., and J. JONIDES, 1997. Working memory: A view from neuroimaging. *Cognit. Psychol.* 33:5–42.

STERIADE, M., L. DOMICH, and G. OAKSON, 1986. Reticularis thalami neurons revisited: Activity changes during shifts in states of vigilance. *J. Neurosci.* 6:68–81.

STERIADE, M., E. G. JONES, and R. R. LLINAS, 1990. *Thalamic Oscillations and Signaling*. New York: Wiley.

STERIADE, M., D. A. MCCORMICK, and T. J. SEJNOWSKI, 1993. Thalamocortical oscillations in the sleeping and aroused brain. *Science* 262:679–685.

SZENTÁGOTHAI, J., 1975. The "module-concept" in cerebral cortex architecture. *Brain Res.* 95:475–496.

TOYAMA, K., 1988. Functional connections of the visual cortex studied by cross-correlation techniques. In P. Rakic and W.

Singer, eds., *Neurobiology of Neocortex*. New York: Wiley, pp. 203–217.

TREISMAN, A., 1960. Contextual cues in selective listening. *Q. J. Exp. Psychol.* 12:242–248.

TREISMAN, A., 1998. The perception of features and objects. In R. D. Wright, ed., *Visual Attention*. New York: Oxford University Press, pp. 26–54.

TREISMAN, A., and G. GELADE, 1980. A feature integration theory of attention. *Cognit. Psychol.* 12:97–136.

TREISMAN, A., and S. GORMICAN, 1988. Feature analysis in early vision: Evidence from search asymmetries. *Psychol. Rev.* 95:15–48.

UEKI, A., 1983. The mode of nigro-thalamic transmission investigated with intracellular recording in the cat. *Exp. Brain Res.* 49:116–124.

UNGERLEIDER, L. G., and C. A. CHRISTIANSEN, 1979. Pulvinar lesions in monkeys produce abnormal scanning of a complex visual array. *Neuropsychologia* 17:493–501.

UNGERLEIDER, L. G., T. W. GALKIN, and M. MISHKIN, 1983. Visuotopic organization of projections from striate cortex to inferior and lateral pulvinar in rhesus monkey. *J. Comp. Neurol.* 217:137–157.

UNO, M., and M. YOSHIDA, 1975. Monosynaptic inhibition of thalamic neurons produced by stimulation of the pallidal nucleus in cats. *Brain Res.* 99:377–380.

WEBSTER, M. J., J. BACHEVALIER, and L. G. UNGERLEIDER, 1991. Subcortical connections of inferior temporal areas TE and TEO in macaques. *J. Comp. Neurol.* 335:73–91.

WILSON, F. A., S. P. O'SCALAIDHE, and P. S. GOLDMAN-RAKIC, 1993. Dissociation of object and spatial processing domains in primate prefrontal cortex. *Science* 260:1955–1958.

WOLFE, J. M., 1994. Guided search 2.0: A revised model of visual search. *Psychonomic Bull.* 1:202–238.

WRIGHT, R. D., and L. M. WARD, 1998. The control of visual attention. In R. D. Wright, ed., *Visual Attention*. New York: Oxford University Press, pp. 132–186.

YANTIS, S., 1996. Attentional capture in vision. In A. F. Kramer, M. G. H. Colegs, and G. D. Logan, eds., *Converging Operations in the Study of Visual Selective Attention*. Washington, D.C.: American Psychological Association, pp. 45–76.

YANTIS, S., and J. JONIDES, 1984. Abrupt visual onsets and selective attention: Evidence from visual search. *J. Exp. Psychol.: Hum. Percept. Perform.* 10:601–621.

YEN, C. G., M. CONLEY, S. H. C. HENDRY, and E. G. JONES, 1985. The morphology of physiologically identified GABAergic neurons in the somatic sensory part of the thalamic reticular nucleus in the cat. *J. Neurosci.* 5:2254–2268.

VI MEMORY

Introduction

ENDEL TULVING

Memory is the capacity of nervous systems to benefit from experience. It is a ubiquitous presence in all higher life forms. It takes many shapes, from simple to complex, from highly specific to most general, from trifling to fundamentally important. In its manifold expressions it is being observed, investigated, and measured in numerous organisms, at many different levels of analysis, from a variety of vantage points, and relying on many different approaches and techniques. It reaches its evolutionary culmination in human beings.

The study of memory has occupied the center stage of cognitive neuroscience since its inception. It continues to fascinate and frustrate large numbers of capable scientists. Novel findings are reported almost daily, yet the major insight gained from more than one hundred years of scientific study of memory may be the realization that the complexity of memory far exceeds anyone's imagination. It is clear that memory did not evolve for the convenience of the neuroscientist.

The nine chapters in the memory section of the second edition of *The Cognitive Neurosciences* provide summaries of and glimpses into some of the more active foci of contemporary cognitive neuroscience of memory. Six chapters deal solely or primarily with human memory, whereas three others focus on work done with nonhuman primates. Collectively, they illustrate the variety of methods and procedures used. These include electrical recording from single neurons in monkeys (chapters 50 and 51) and from multiple scalp sites in normal human subjects (chapter 56); the study of the effects of experimentally created lesions in monkeys (chapter 52) and the mnemonic consequences of brain damage resulting from disease or accident (chapters 53, 54, and 58); effects of psychoactive drugs (chapter 55); and functional neuroimaging of memory-related processes in healthy volunteers (chapters 57 and 58). The overarching concern in all these chapters is to gain insight into the neuronal substrates of behavioral and cognitive manifestations of learning and memory and into the nature of the relation between neural mechanisms and memory processes.

Because of the vast size and diversity of the domain, it simply is not possible to deal with memory as a whole. Nor is it possible to make any intelligent generalizations about it. Any claim about "memory" or "memory impairment" immediately requires clarification: About which kind of memory, memory task, memory process, or memory system are we talking? These terms define the major fault lines along which the whole of memory can be fractionated into more manageable components within which generalizability of factual statements and theoretical claims are more likely to be valid. The concepts represented by these terms have evolved from the observations made about memory at the level of observable behavior and reportable experience. Directly or indirectly, they provide the backdrop against which we seek to understand the relation between brain and behavior or between brain and mind.

This introduction to the section on memory describes the outlines of the conceptual framework within which much research on human memory is conducted and attempts to clarify some of the arcane terms that, although useful to insiders, frequently mystify outsiders. It touches on topics such as memory systems, memory tasks, memory processes, and conscious awareness in memory.

Memory systems

The concept of memory systems is one answer to the need to specify different "kinds" of memory. Different systems share certain basic features, such as some device or means of retaining the consequences of a current act of behavior or cognition, and they differ with respect to others, such as the functions they serve, their behavioral or cognitive manifestations, the principles of their operations, and the brain mechanisms involved in the operations.

The most fundamental division in memory deals with the distinction between behavior and thought. Many forms of learning and memory are expressed in behavior (doing something, carrying out a procedure), whereas others are expressed in thought (contemplating something, being cognizant of some mental contents). The behavioral kinds collectively are referred to as "procedural" memory; the ones expressed in thought are referred to as "cognitive" memory. Although the distinction is not a simple one, a rule of thumb that can be used for deciding how to classify any particular act

of memory consists in the answer to the question—can one hold in mind the *product* of the act of memory? An affirmative answer suggests that memory is cognitive; the negative answer means that it is procedural.

The distinction between procedural and cognitive holds very broadly for learning and memory in many species. Other terms have been used to designate them. Procedural memory has been called habit memory, non-declarative memory, and even implicit memory, although for many students of memory, implicit memory means something rather different than the broad category of learning and memory that is not cognitive. Cognitive memory has been called declarative memory, propositional memory, and also explicit memory, although, again, explicit memory does not really correspond to all forms of learning and memory that are not cognitive. The extensive, and sometimes undisciplined, use of different terms to designate the same underlying concepts is a continuing problem in the field.

Cognitive memory, which constitutes the lion's share of memory research with human subjects, can be further subdivided into four major categories, or "systems." They are (1) working memory, whose function is to hold information "on line" over short intervals of time while cognitive operations are performed on it; (2) the perceptual representation system, whose function is to mediate memory-based facilitation of perceptual identification of objects; (3) semantic memory, whose function is to mediate the acquisition and use of individuals' general knowledge of the world; and (4) episodic memory, whose function is to mediate conscious access to the personally experienced past.

The separability of the four systems from one another is widely if not universally accepted. The distinctions among them receive support from sharp dissociation between task performances that depend heavily on the different underlying systems in normal subjects and brain-damaged individuals, as well as from functional neuroimaging and psychopharmacological studies. Relevant evidence is discussed in many chapters in this section. Much of the research effort currently is directed at the refinement and elaboration of the taxonomic scheme, and at the identification and characterization of the many subdivisions of the major categories.

Tasks and processes

Cognitive memory in the laboratory is studied in segments of reality called *tasks*. A typical cognitive memory task consists of three stages: (1) presentation of some material to the subject, usually with instructions to "remember" it; (2) a retention interval during which the subject may engage in other (mental) activities; and (3) a test of the subject's knowledge of the originally presented material. The outcome of the test is expressed in terms of some measure of the subject's performance on the test. It is frequently but not necessarily a measure of how well the subject can reproduce originally presented material.

A great variety of cognitive memory tasks exists, defined in terms of a large number of possible variations in the specific features of the three stages of the task. Tasks can vary in the kinds and units of the material presented for learning and the specific parameters of the presentation, the length of the retention interval (which can range from seconds to years), the nature of the "interpolated" activities, and many other independent variables. An especially important feature of the task is the nature of the test. Tests also can vary widely with respect to the instructions that specify the subject's mission and the nature and type of cue information provided to guide and aid its execution.

Given this thumbnail sketch of the memory task, how are we to think about and describe, in general abstract terms, what happens when the subject is engaged in a cognitive memory task? For a long time in the history of learning and memory the dominant theoretical concept that provided the answer to this question was "association." During learning, associations were assumed to be formed, maintained in force, sometimes interfered with, and then expressed in behavior. The concept of association still is used in special situations, especially in studies of learning and memory with nonverbal subjects. In the mainstream cognitive psychology, however, some 30 to 40 years ago the associative paradigm was replaced by *information processing* as the general pretheoretical framework. This framework currently determines how most students of memory think and talk about the workings of memory.

The three sequential stages of the standard memory task correspond to three major memory processes of encoding, storage, and retrieval. The presentation of the to-be-remembered material is an event about which "information" is "encoded" into the memory "store." Usually, the material consists of discrete items (words, pictures, objects, faces, and simple sentences), and the presentation of each is a "miniature event" about which information is encoded into the store. During the retention interval, this information is maintained in the store as an "engram," and it may be "consolidated" or "recoded." *Consolidation* is thought of as a biologically determined autonomous process that runs its course independently of the interpolated activity, whereas *recoding* is an active psychological process that is shaped by the particulars of the interpolated activity. At the time of the test, the information "available" in the engram is "retrieved," or rendered "accessible." *Retrieval* means

use of stored information, and because stored information can be used in many different ways, the term retrieval is very broad and usually needs to be specified more precisely.

The concept of information runs through this pretheoretical processing framework like a red thread. It is useful to keep in mind, therefore, that neither *information* nor *process* can be defined readily. Information simply is the intangible, ineffable, unknown "stuff" that is somehow created, transferred, transformed, preserved ("processed") in the mind/brain, which, when appropriately "converted," determines behavior and conscious thought. Both information and process are "place-holder" concepts in contemporary cognitive sciences. They will be used until a better paradigm comes along. Even though they are not readily definable, the terms make abstract thought about the workings of the brain/mind possible and the doubts about how to best study it tolerable.

Conscious awareness in memory

The products of retrieval in all cognitive memory tasks are, in the first instance, expressed as mental experiences. They can be contemplated internally, in the absence of any overt behavior, and they can be "held in mind." It would be normal to expect, therefore, that the efforts to understand cognitive memory be directed at the study of the retrieval experience. For a long time in the history of the science of memory, however, this was not done. Subjects' memory performance invariably was measured in terms of behavioral indices of various kinds. The tacit assumption, seldom explicitly formulated, was that behavioral output in the memory test faithfully reflects the mental contents of what the individual has retrieved from memory. We now know that this assumption does not always hold.

Recently, the issue of individuals' conscious experiences that accompany the act of retrieval from the memory store has been shifted into a sharp focus, in two different ways. One distinguishes between "conscious" and "nonconscious" retrieval; the other, concerned solely with conscious retrieval, distinguishes between two forms of it. The first issue is dealt with under the heading of *explicit versus implicit* memory, the second under the heading of *remembering and knowing*, or *recollection and familiarity*. We consider them in turn.

Explicit and implicit memory

The first issue of consciousness in memory has to with the rememberer's awareness, at the time of the test, of the relation between the current experience (and activity) on the one hand, and the original learning or encoding episode on the other. In ordinary everyday-type of remembering, the relation is clearly felt: when the individual recollects a previous event, such as the study of some specific material in the first stage of the experiment, he or she also is fully aware that what he or she is experiencing has its origin in the earlier episode. The technical term that is used currently to refer to this kind of awareness at retrieval is *explicit* memory.

Explicit memory contrasts with *implicit* memory: retrieval of stored information in the *absence* of the awareness that the current behavior and experience have been influenced by a particular earlier happening. It is in this sense, and this sense only, that explicit memory is said to be "conscious," whereas implicit memory is "nonconscious." Consciousness refers to the awareness of the *relation between* the present thought (and action) and a *specific* previous thought (or action).

An important point to note is that the distinction between explicit and implicit memory is that between explicit and implicit *retrieval*–that is, the distinction applies only the final stage of our typical memory task. This is because there is no difference between explicit and implicit encoding, and there is, as yet, no known way to distinguish between explicit and implicit storage. For this reason among others, explicit and implicit memories do not qualify as memory "systems."

In memory experiments, explicit retrieval is effected by the instructions given to the subject at test: "Remember what you saw, or what you did, or what happened to you at some earlier time, in some place (such as the first stage of the experiment)?" Implicit retrieval, too, is experimentally effected by the instructions given to the subjects at the time of retrieval as to what they are to do. Many different forms of implicit memory tests exist and have been used, but they all have in common the fact that the subject *need not* think back to the first stage of the task, or to any other specific episode, to perform the task at a level that has benefited from the first stage. Thus, implicit memory satisfies the definition of memory–the individual benefits from experience, but he or she is unaware that he or she has done so.

It is important to note a complication: Explicit retrieval instructions do not necessarily guarantee that the responses made by the subject are accompanied by a sense of recollection, as they ideally would. Subjects' explicit memory performance may be influenced processes that support implicit retrieval. Nor do implicit instructions guarantee that retrieval occurs in the absence of recollection of the relevant encoding experience, as it ideally should. Purification of research designs aimed at reducing or eliminating such unwanted "contamination" of the desired type of retrieval by extraneous factors is an important part of research on explicit and implicit memory. Some of these issues are discussed in chapters 55, 56, and especially 58.

Many experiments, of many different kinds, have convincingly demonstrated the reality of the distinction between explicit and implicit memory. The major theoretical import of the discovery of these two forms of retrieval lies in the sharp distinction that they draw between overt behavior and the mental experience that accompanies such behavior. The subject's ability to produce a particular over-response, whose likelihood has been enhanced by a particular earlier event, may be identical in two tests. However, the mental experiences may be altogether different.

Remembering and knowing

The second issue of consciousness emerges in situations in which the awareness of the relation between the present experience and an earlier specific event is in fact present. It has to do with two different *kinds of awareness* that may accompany explicit memory retrieval. One is referred to as *remembering* or *recollection*, the other as *knowing* or *familiarity*. In explicit tests of recognition and recall, the subject may make a correct response not because he or she actually remembers or recollects the event of the item's earlier presentation, but rather because the recognition test item "looks familiar," or because he or she "simply knows" that the word he or she has just recalled was in the presented list. Because the subject is fully aware of the previous presentation episode of the material, he or she–usually correctly–attributes the feeling of familiarity or "knowing" to the episode.

The remembering/knowing or recollection/familiarity distinctions currently are subjects of lively interest to many memory researchers. Rugg and Allan (chapter 56) discusses the electrophysiological evidence for the distinction, and Squire and Knowlton (chapter 53) deal with the issue of how remembering and knowing are related to the amnesic syndrome and whether they are both dependent on the medial temporal lobes. Schacter and Curran (chapter 58) and Curran (chapter 55) also touch on the distinction. The major theoretical point, however, is that here, finally, we have an active area of research aimed at the essence of cognition: Conscious *mental experiences* that have been changed as a result of earlier experience-induced physical changes in the brain.

Other levels and species

Concepts such as encoding and retrieval, explicit and implicit memory, or remembering and knowing make good sense at the level of behavior and cognition of the whole individual, or the whole brain. They are less readily applicable to the study of memory-related events at the level of single neurons, in analyses of the kind described by Goldman-Rakic and associates and Erickson and colleagues in chapters 50 and 51, respectively. Although encoding and retrieval ultimately are rooted in neuronal activity, a single neuron cannot encode or retrieve anything. A neuron may "fire" differentially during the interval between the presentation of the target and the signal for the saccade in the oculomotor working-memory task used by Goldman-Rakic and colleagues, thus providing for a neat neuronal mechanism for holding information "on line" in the short-term memory "store." But although it is possible to think of this "on-line holding" mechanism as comparable in principle to "holding" information in the long-term "store," the parallel probably would not work. Retrieval–use of the "stored" information–has different meanings to the organism and is based on rather different operations, in the two situations. Similarly, a neuron may respond differentially to a stimulus when presented for the first time versus the second, as shown by the studies of Erickson and colleagues (chapter 51), and it is tempting to think of the difference as in some sense paralleling novelty versus familiarity detection, or even encoding and retrieval, at the level of the whole brain, but the two levels of analyses are too far apart to allow one to feel confident about such thoughts. A challenging task for neuroscience of memory is to determine to what extent such high-level phenomena as conscious recollection of the occurrence of an event depend on the differential activity of individual units, and to what extent they represent network-level happenings, or as yet unknown mechanisms, in the brain.

Similar thoughts apply to memory in nonhuman animals. A good deal of knowledge about memory, and especially about the neural basis of memory-based behavior, has been derived from work with other animals–nonhuman primates, rodents, birds, and others, all the way to insects, worms, and sea slugs. A major advantage of this work lies in the possibility of a greater range of surgical, chemical, and other material interventions in the normal brain activity.

Because memory capabilities, functions, and processes of any two species are always not only similar in some ways but also different in others, some of the methods, findings, and theoretical ideas about human memory have no direct parallels and no direct applicability to nonhuman animals. Thus, there are as yet no known means that could be used to separate implicit from explicit retrieval, or to distinguish between what animals remember and what they know, or what they

recollect and what they find merely familiar. Therefore, the important distinctions that shape thought about human memory cannot be transferred forthwith into the study of learning and memory in nonhuman animals. This simple fact also imposes certain limitations on the extent to which the findings from animal studies can be generalized to humans. When these limitations are kept in mind, however, and flat generalizations are avoided, study of memory in one species can be invaluable in providing useful information and offering inspiration to the study of memory in others. The basic structural similarity among the brains of all mammals, especially primates, cannot be gainsaid, and this structural similarity clearly implies *some* functional similarity as well. The challenging task is to identify exactly wherein the similarities lie.

Conclusion

This, then, is a brief description of the framework within which much of the neurocognitive research takes place. In one way or another, more or less directly, many empirical findings and most major theoretical ideas and debates involve memory processes, retrieval-related awareness, and memory systems. Study of amnesia and other forms of memory impairments, and theoretical disputes about it, revolve around issues of memory processes, memory awareness, and memory systems. Studies of functional neuroanatomy of memory, made possible by novel techniques such as positron emission tomography (PET) and functional magnetic resonance imaging (fMRI) are focused on memory processes, their interactions with the type of remembered material, and on differences between implicit and explicit retrieval.

The outsider who is not familiar with the field should gain some idea from this section about where cognitive neuroscience of memory stands at the turn of the millennium. The insider who knows what the situation was like only 5 years ago, when the first edition of *The Cognitive Neurosciences* appeared, should find that great changes have occurred since then. New techniques, such as the use of excitotoxic lesions, described by Murray (chapter 52), have produced data that, by past standards, can be regarded as revolutionary. New phenomena, such as "false remembering" discussed and dissected by Schacter and Curran (chapter 58), were not only unknown but also even largely unimaginable 5 years ago. Moreover, most everything that functional neuroimaging techniques (PET and fMRI) have revealed about human memory, as described and analyzed by Buckner (chapter 57), has been discovered in the last 5 years. Stress-related memory impairments and the real possibility that what were thought of as "psychogenic amnesias" have as real a physiological basis as "organic amnesias," discussed by Markowitsch (chapter 54), are newcomers on the memory scene. Even approaches that have been in use for a while, such as psychopharmacology (chapter 55), event-related potentials (chapter 56), single-unit recording (chapter 51), and the study of amnesic patients (chapter 53) have yielded new discoveries and fresh insights of a kind that attest genuine progress in the field.

These are exciting times in neurocognitive memory research. Happenings at the horizon point to the next 5 years being even more so.

50 Domain Specificity in Cognitive Systems

PATRICIA S. GOLDMAN-RAKIC, SÉAMAS P. Ó SCALAIDHE, AND MATTHEW V. CHAFEE

ABSTRACT The majority of organisms adapt to their environment largely through a process of natural selection of genetic variation. Humans, in addition, have evolved an extraordinary capacity to behave flexibly with respect to future consequences, in tandem with expansion of the prefrontal cortex. How do the new prefrontal regions relate to phylogenetically older sensory and motor areas? Are cognitive functions organized according to a different set of principles than those that govern sensory and motor areas? To address these questions, the authors examined how a cognitive process—working memory—is organized. Their research shows that the prefrontal cortex is organized into domain-specific regions based on anatomical connections with high-order sensory association areas. In addition to being consistent with anatomy, electrophysiology, and the effects of experimental lesions, the domain-specific hypothesis provides a sensible way for higher-order cognitive processes to evolve from nervous systems that respond largely on the basis of sensation and movement.

The majority of species respond to their environment in a stereotypical fashion determined by their evolutionary history and current stimulus milieu. For most organisms adaptability is a matter of selection of genetic variation within individuals, each of which responds to the environment in an unlearned and largely mindless fashion. Against this panorama of stimulus-driven organisms, there came a time in evolution when a member of the genus *Homo* became capable of verbal intelligence and unprecedented forethought. Which corresponding step was taken in the phylogenetic development of the brain? The mechanisms that enabled such an unparalleled capacity to behave adaptively with respect to future consequences coincided with the evolution of a greatly enlarged prefrontal cortex in primates in general and particularly in humans. In this chapter, we discuss recent work from our laboratory that explores, at the level of proximal causation, the functional organization of prefrontal areas involved in one of these abilities—working memory. In particular, we show that prefrontal mechanisms are constrained by content at the cellular, circuit, and areal levels determined by circuit relationships with the posterior association cortices. We begin with a review of the cellular underpinnings of these processes.

PATRICIA S. GOLDMAN-RAKIC and SÉAMAS P. Ó SCALAIDHE Section of Neurobiology, Yale University School of Medicine, New Haven, Conn.
MATTHEW V. CHAFEE Brain Science Center, VA Medical Center, Minneapolis, Minn.

Cellular specificity of the dorsolateral prefrontal cortex: The neuron's "memory field"

The human prefrontal cortex accounts for approximately one fourth of the cerebral surface and has been mapped by a variety of methods, including single-unit recording in nonhuman primates and functional imaging in both monkeys and humans. Single-neuron recording, however, is the only method currently capable of dissecting the neuronal elements involved in the working memory processes. We have applied this method in conjunction with performance on an oculomotor-delayed response (ODR) task, in which the location of a briefly presented visuospatial stimulus is maintained in working memory to provide guidance for subsequent saccadic eye movements (figure 50.1A, upper left). An essential feature of this task is that the item to be recalled has to be updated on every trial in analogous fashion to the moment-to-moment process of human mentation. Similar tasks have become paradigmatic for probing working memory both in animals and human imaging studies (figure 50.1C–E).

Prefrontal neurons with "memory fields" are particularly relevant to our discussion of cellular mechanisms. The concept of a memory field is based on the finding that a given prefrontal neuron increases its firing rate during the delay period of the ODR task only for specific spatial locations and this preference is constant across trials. For example, the neuron shown in the upper portion of figure 50.2 is activated consistently on every occasion that the monkey must recall a particular location. Further, in instances in which the firing of a neuron is not maintained throughout the delay and the activity falters, the animal is highly likely to make an error (Funahashi, Bruce, and Goldman-Rakic, 1989). The finding that neuronal firing is location specific and directly associated with accurate recall provides a dramatic example of a compartmentalized and constrained architecture for memory processing reminiscent of that observed in sensory systems. This is an important observation because it suggests that each neuron is dedicated to a specific type of information. Furthermore, individual neurons capable of holding specific visuospatial coordinates "on line" appear to be aggregated into a circumscribed region of prefrontal cortex. Within this region are columnar units defined by common visual-

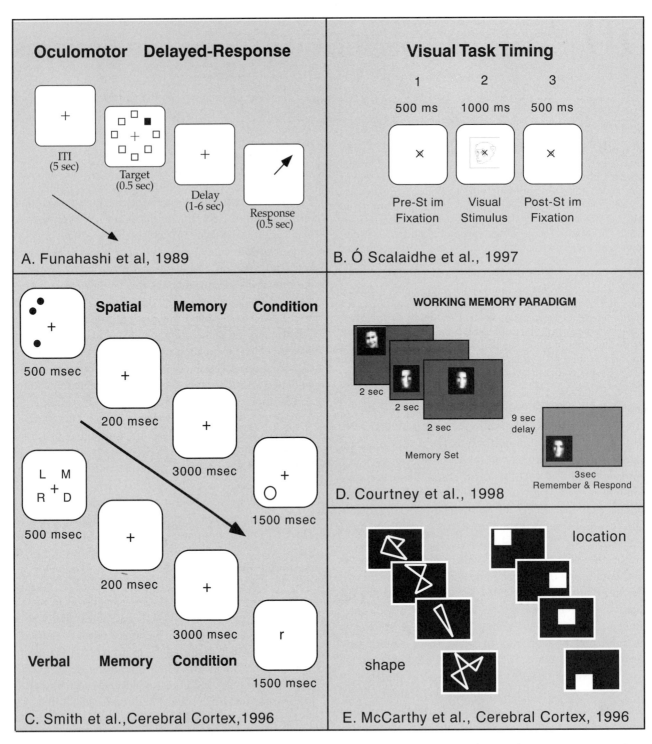

Oculomotor   Delayed-Response

ITI
(5 sec)

Target
(0.5 sec)

Delay
(1-6 sec)

Response
(0.5 sec)

A. Funahashi et al, 1989

Visual Task Timing

1   2   3

500 ms   1000 ms   500 ms

Pre-St im
Fixation

Visual
Stimulus

Post-St im
Fixation

B. Ó Scalaidhe et al., 1997

Spatial   Memory   Condition

500 msec

200 msec

3000 msec

1500 msec

L   M
 +
R   D

500 msec

200 msec

3000 msec

r

1500 msec

Verbal   Memory   Condition

C. Smith et al.,Cerebral Cortex,1996

WORKING MEMORY PARADIGM

2 sec

2 sec

2 sec

Memory Set

9 sec
delay

3sec
Remember & Respond

D. Courtney et al., 1998

location

shape

E. McCarthy et al., Cerebral Cortex, 1996

FIGURE 50.1 Common design of working memory paradigms as employed in studies of nonhuman primates (A and B) and humans (C–E). All tasks employ sequential presentation of the item or items to be recalled (shapes, letters, words, or markers of location), delay periods between items over which items must be recalled, and recall or response epochs.

spatial coordinates (Ó Scalaidhe and Goldman-Rakic, in press). Further, we have demonstrated that temporary inactivation of one or a few modules results in loss of on-line memory for particular target locations (Sawaguchi and Goldman-Rakic, 1991). These and other results provide strong evidence at a cellular level that neurons in dorsolateral areas 46 and 8A are dedicated by content–even at the level of specific visuospatial coordinates. The same neuron responds to the same location and guides the same directional response, trial after trial,

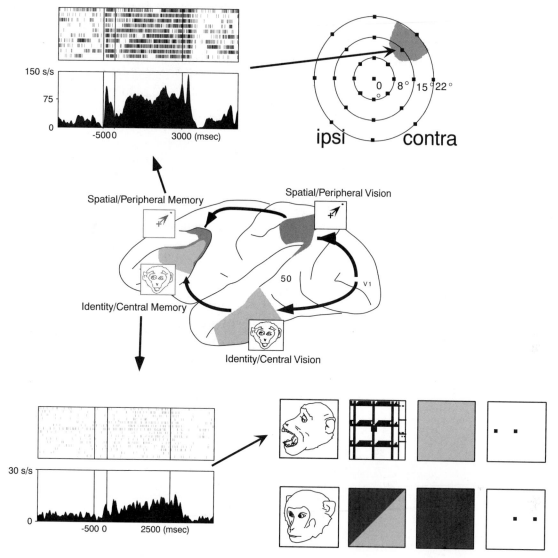

FIGURE 50.2 Multiple memory domains in the monkey prefrontal cortex. The dorsolateral area around the principal sulcus and anterior arcuate is important for spatial working memory, whereas the inferior convexity of the prefrontal cortex mediates identity working memory. *Upper*: The neuron shown was activated in the cue, delay, and saccade periods whenever the monkey had to respond to the target presented at the two most peripheral locations 45° above the horizontal meridian in the visual field contralateral to the recording electrode. The same neuron was not activated for any other targets during the delay period. The trial by trial rastergram shows neuronal activity with time in milliseconds represented on the ordinate axis for one location in the cell's memory field and the spike density function (sdf) represents the averaged activity across all trials (the scale of the sdf is in spikes per second). In both the rastergram and the spike density function, the first vertical line indicates onset of the visual cue, the second vertical line indicates offset of the visual cue and beginning of the delay period, and the third vertical line indicates offset of the central fixation point and the monkey's signal to make a saccade to the location of the previously presented cue. *Middle*: A lateral view of the monkey brain with the temporal lobe and parietal lobe visual streams and their extension into the prefrontal cortex. *Bottom*: A neuron activated in the delay whenever the stimulus was a picture of a particular face during a working memory task; the same neuron was unresponsive to other memoranda (another face, four color patterns, and two peripheral spots of light), or in relation to direction of response (13° left or right). Conventions are as in the upper panel, with the face and pattern stimuli presented foveally and signaling a 13° saccade to the left or right of the fixation point.

and each location in the visual field is represented by a cohort of neurons in the dorsolateral prefrontal cortex.

Although there are significant constraints on the information processing machinery of prefrontal cortex, this does not mean that a prefrontal neuron's sensory, mnemonic, and response-related activity is immutable. Within this modular architecture, mechanisms exist for plasticity in the neurons' responses to changing events. In particular, the memory fields of prefrontal cortex are subject to modulation by neurotransmitters, such as dopamine, serotonin, and the inhibitory neurotransmitter, gamma-amino-butyric acid (GABA). Examination of the memory fields of neurons in vivo shows that the mnemonic process can be sculpted by a combination of actions at the soma of a pyramidal cell (Rao, Williams, and Goldman-Rakic, 1999), by serotoninergic actions at the level of 5HT2 receptors on its proximal dendrite (Jakab and Goldman-Rakic, 1998), and by D1 dopaminergic action on the spines, which are the portion of the cell triggered by excitatory input (Williams and Goldman-Rakic, 1995). These studies show that physiologically realistic changes in the availability of dopamine or serotonin can alter dramatically the tuning of a "working memory" neuron and can either attenuate or enhance the response magnitude. By revealing basic mechanisms of neural plasticity, these findings have the potential to form the groundwork for a rational approach to drug design for cognitive enhancement in aging and in disease (Goldman-Rakic et al., 1996; Goldman-Rakic, 1997).

Network specificity: Neuronal activity patterns in macaque prefrontal and posterior parietal cortex during spatial working memory performance

The aforementioned data identify the dorsolateral prefrontal cortex as a critical element in a neural system that uses working memory to hold specific items of spatial in-

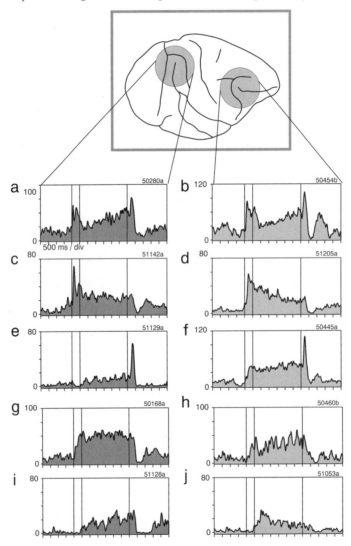

FIGURE 50.3 Similarity of delay period activity between single neurons in posterior parietal area 7ip (left column) and prefrontal area 8a (right column) during oculomotor-delayed response (ODR) performance. The spike density functions are as in the upper panel of figure 2 and represent the optimal location for each neuron. Delay period activity was observed in both areas in combination with greater bursts of activity during cue and saccade periods (a, b), during just the cue period (c, d), or the saccade period (e, f). Delay period activity without conspicuous bursts of activity also was seen during cue and saccade periods, beginning during the cue period (g, h), or after cue offset (i, j). All neuronal activity patterns were recorded from neurons in both cortical areas. (From Chafee and Goldman-Rakic, 1998.)

formation on line. Although Walker's area 46 and adjacent 8A have been identified specifically with this process, dissections of these broad areas undoubtedly will reveal further subspecializations consistent with how subregions of these areas receive distinct projections from posterior parietal cortex (Cavada and Goldman-Rakic, 1989). Further, recent results demonstrate that the neural system supporting working memory capacity cannot reside wholly within the prefrontal cortex but extends beyond it to involve and in fact require interactions with other cortical areas. Among these is the posterior parietal cortex, with which the dorsolateral prefrontal cortex is connected anatomically directly (Petrides and Pandya, 1984; Schwartz and Goldman-Rakic, 1984; Andersen, Asanuma, and Cowan, 1985; Barbas and Mesulam, 1985; Barbas, 1988; Cavada and Goldman-Rakic, 1989; Andersen et al., 1990a; Schall et al., 1995; Stanton, Bruce, and Goldberg, 1995; Tian and Lynch, 1996).

Previous single-unit recording studies of the prefrontal and parietal cortices have been carried out in separate studies of different animals, different methods, and different delay periods (Gnadt and Andersen, 1988; Andersen et al., 1990b; Colby, Duhamel, and Goldberg, 1996; Mazzoni et al., 1996; Snyder, Batista, and Andersen, 1997). To compare the nature and incidence of different neuron firing patterns, we have alternately recorded from prefrontal area 8A and parietal area LIP within the same hemisphere of the same animals. Recording from both areas in the same monkeys eliminates any confusion caused by individual differences between animals and methods that could be misinterpreted as differences between areas. Using this approach, we examined parietal and prefrontal neurons that significantly changed their firing rate during the cue, delay, or saccade periods of the ODR task (Chafee and Goldman-Rakic, 1998). Interestingly, task-related neuronal activities were remarkably similar in both areas. Cue period activity in the prefrontal and parietal cortices exhibited comparable spatial tuning and temporal duration characteristics, taking the form of phasic, tonic, or combined phasic/tonic excitation in both cortical populations. Neurons in both cortical areas exhibited sustained activity during the delay period, with nearly identical spatial tuning (26.8° in prefrontal and 26.3° in parietal). The various patterns of delay period activity—tonic, increasing, or decreasing, alone or in combination with phasic responses during cue or saccade periods—also were similar in both cortical areas (figure 50.3). Finally, similarities in the two populations extended to the proportion and spatial tuning of presaccadic and postsaccadic neuronal activity occurring in relation to the memory-guided saccade. Previous findings in the parietal cortex are in accord with this result (Gnadt and Andersen, 1988; Andersen et al., 1990b; Barash et al., 1991a; Barash et al., 1991b; Gnadt and Mays, 1995; Colby, Duhamel, and Goldberg, 1996; Mazzoni et al., 1996; Bracewell et al., 1996). They also are supported by 2-deoxyglucose studies of cortical metabolism in primates during working memory tasks (Friedman and Goldman-Rakic, 1994; figure 50.4). Therefore, numerous findings in nonhuman primates support and extend evidence for a faithful transmission of receptive field properties and virtually every other dimension of task-related activity observed when the parietal and prefrontal cortices are recruited to a common task. This striking similarity attests to the principal that information shared by a network of *association* areas, for example, a prefrontal region and a sensory association area with which it is connected, is domain specific.

Areal specificity: Multiple working memory domains in the prefrontal cortex

One of the major questions confronted by our field is that of how cortical function maps onto association cortex. In simple animals, such as most invertebrates, behavioral plasticity and learning reflect changes in sensory and motor neurons. A simple way to build a richer behavioral repertoire with more flexible responses to the environment would be for neurons connected, directly or transynaptically, to sensory receptors and motor effectors to mediate behavior in a flexible but still domain-specific fashion. For example, in the case of holding a stimulus on line, a neuron with visual selectivity could continue firing after the offset of the stimulus and thus mediate the memory of the recently seen object. In this last section, we review recent evidence, based on anatomical and physiological observations, that subregions of the dorsolateral prefrontal cortex may be organized according to informational domain and that each domain mediates on line processing (Goldman-Rakic, 1987).

To examine the issue of domain specificity, we have carried out a series of single-unit recordings from neurons in areas 12/45 that lie just below the principal sulcus on the inferior convexity of the prefrontal cortex (Wilson, Ó Scalaidhe, and Goldman-Rakic, 1993; Ó Scalaidhe, Wilson, and Goldman-Rakic, 1997). These areas were selected as likely candidates for processing nonspatial information—that is, color and form—because lesions of this area produce deficits on tasks requiring memory for the color or patterns of stimuli (Passingham, 1975; Mishkin and Manning, 1978) and the receptive fields of the neurons in this area, unlike those in areas 46 and 8 on the dorsolateral cortex, represent the fovea

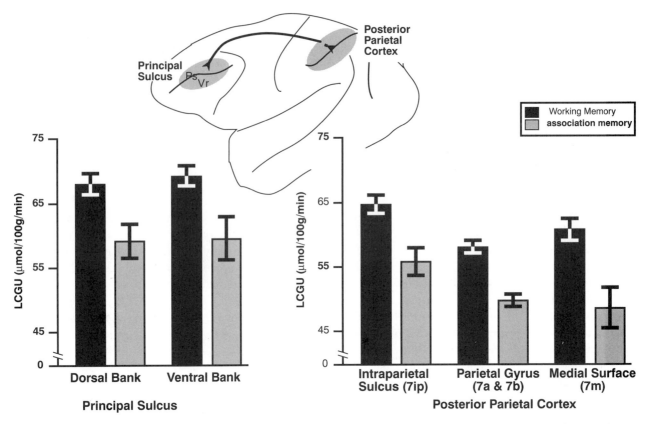

FIGURE 50.4   Mean local cerebral glucose utilization (LCGU) rates in the principal sulcus and posterior parietal cortices of monkeys performing spatial working memory and control (associative and sensorimotor) control tasks. Mean LCGU is enhanced in the working memory group (solid bars) by 15% or more compared with the same areas in monkeys performing the control tasks (hatched bars). The overlying schematic underscores the anatomical findings of Cavada and Goldman-Rakic (1989) showing the reciprocal connections between these two areas (Goldman-Rakic, Chafee, and Friedman, 1993).

(Suzuki and Azuma, 1983), the region of the retina specialized for the analysis of fine detail and color. Therefore, we used objects and faces as stimuli/memoranda and presented them centered on a point that the monkeys visually fixated, both in "picture" tasks (figure 50.1B) and delayed-response formats (figure 50.1A). Neurons were tested both with spatial and nonspatial tasks to determine whether the neurons had directional preferences, object/face preferences, or both. We discovered that the neurons in the inferior convexity are highly responsive to the sight of complex stimuli, such as pictures of faces or specific objects. Often, selective responses continued or began after the offset of the visual stimuli, in both trained and untrained monkeys, suggesting that delay-period activity reflects an intrinsic property of the neurons' responses. Neurons exhibiting selective neuronal activity for objects or faces are found disproportionately (objects) or almost exclusively (faces) in or around area 12 on the inferior convexity of the prefrontal cortex (figure 50.2, lower), beneath the principal sulcus, whereas neurons that responded selectively in the spatial tasks are concentrated in the dorsolateral cortical regions, where spatial processing has been observed in previous studies. The areas from which face or object selective neurons are recorded are connected directly with area TE in the inferotemporal cortex, which is a major component of the ventral pathway for object vision (Ungerleider and Mishkin, 1982) and an area rich in cells that respond to the features of visual stimuli, including faces (e.g., Gross, Rocha-Miranda, and Bender, 1972; Rolls and Baylis, 1986). These results suggest that attributes of an object or face related to its identity are processed separately from those dedicated to the analysis of spatial location. Further, the specialized circuits for maintaining the identity of objects and faces in Walker's areas 12 and 45 may process nonspatial information in a manner analogous to the mechanism by which area 46 mediates memory of visuospatial information.

Domain specificity of working memory function in human cognition

Considerable evidence for domain specificity can be found in the human imaging literature. Remarkably, fMRI and evoked potential recording studies of working memory for faces in humans show selective activation of an inferior region of the prefrontal cortex in the human brain that appears to correspond to the areas activated by object/face stimuli in the single-unit studies of monkeys (e.g., Courtney et al., 1997; Haxby et al., 1996; Kelley et al., 1998; Allison et al., in press). Working memory for the features of objects also engages anatomically lateral and inferior prefrontal regions (Adcock et al., 1996; Cohen et al., 1994; Courtney et al., 1996; Kelley et al., 1998; McCarthy et al., 1996). The Kelley study demonstrated, furthermore, that when verbal encoding is engaged, the left inferior prefrontal cortex is activated; when visual analysis is not aided by verbal encoding, right inferior prefrontal activation is observed; and when a task can be performed by both verbal and pictorial encoding, the inferior prefrontal areas of both areas are engaged. Hemispheric lateralization of response may depend on whether faces are encoded verbally; when temporal parameters discourage verbal labeling, right hemispheric localization prevails (Grady et al., 1995). Similarly, explicit verbal processing tasks, including word generation, naming objects, and word encoding tasks, consistently invariably activate inferior, insular, or anterior prefrontal regions in the left hemisphere (Kapur et al., 1994; Kapur et al., 1996; Raichle et al., 1994; Demb et al., 1995; Baker et al., 1996; Kelley et al., 1998; Fiez et al., 1996; Paulesu, Firth, and Frackowiak, 1993; Price, Wise, and Frackowiak, 1996). By contrast, the middle frontal gyrus, where area 46 is located, has been activated consistently as human subjects access visuospatial information from long-term storage or immediate experience through representation-based action (e.g., Baker et al., 1996; Gold et al., 1996; Goldberg et al., 1996; Nichelli et al., 1994; McCarthy et al., 1994; Owen, Evans, and Petrides, 1996; Smith, Jonides, and Koeppe, 1996; Sweeney et al., 1996). These findings indicate that, as in monkeys, domain specificity exists in humans. Indeed, the human brain contains a novel form of domain specificity–hemispheric specialization based on language.

Other studies (Owen et al., 1998) have failed to dissociate object and spatial working memory, and some, including our own, have shown overlapping right middle frontal activation for object and spatial processing. It perhaps is instructive that in both monkeys and humans, the best regional specialization for nonspatial stimuli has been observed when faces are used as stimuli (Ó Scalaidhe, Wilson, and Goldman-Rakic, 1997; Courtney et al., 1996; Haxby et al., 1996). There are a few factors that may explain this. First, faces have been of great ecological significance to both humans and rhesus monkeys, and therefore, neural responses to faces are likely to reflect the functional design of the nervous system. Second, faces, unlike many putatively nonspatial artificial stimuli, are spatially constrained with eyes, ears, nose, mouth, and hair in a fixed spatial relationship to each other. Unlike faces, letters, abstract figures, geometric figures, and computer-generated shapes can be encoded partly or largely by a spatial strategy (e.g., a set of parallel ellipses at a 45° angle). Many of these stimuli also lack characteristics of real objects, such as color, texture, and depth cues. With respect to the spatial system, the practically obligatory ecological relationship between spatial vision and movement (Goodale and Milner, 1992) suggests that the best isolation of spatial regions is seen by using visuo-movement tasks. Accordingly, the area most active in spatial working memory appears to be in and immediately anterior to the frontal eye fields both in macaque and human (Ó Scalaidhe and Goldman-Rakic, 1993; Courtney et al., 1998). The difficulty of interpreting negative findings notwithstanding, the functional architecture suggested by physiological and lesion studies in monkeys appears to be supported by findings from imaging studies in humans. The superior to inferior localization of spatial and object processing and the lateralization of verbal processing in imaging studies of human cognition support a multiple domain hypothesis of prefrontal functional architecture, which is based on network organization.

As to the remaining expanse of prefrontal areas, less is known. The evidence from recent studies of the medial wall and orbital surface indicate that these regions of the frontal lobe are compartmentalized similarly as to informational domain. The anatomical connections of the dorsomedial prefrontal cortex suggest that it is involved in high-order movement-related cognition (Dum and Strick, 1991). Baylis and colleagues and others have mapped a taste area in the caudolateral orbitofrontal cortex near an area concerned with olfaction (Baylis, Rolls, and Baylis, 1995; Tanabe, Ooshima, and Takagi, 1974; Carmichael and Price, 1995). Studies of orbital lesions in humans have revealed an autonomic pattern of deficits (Damasio, Tranel, and Damasio, 1991) as well as deficits in real world social contexts (Grattan et al., 1994; Eslinger, Grattan, and Geder, 1995). In addition to being domain specific, whether these prefrontal regions mediate on-line memory functions remains an issue for further investigation.

Conclusion

As aforementioned, neurophysiological and neuropsychological studies in nonhuman primates and functional imaging studies in humans demonstrate the organization of the prefrontal cortex into domains consonant with its anatomical connections. This suggests that organisms that primarily respond to sensory input and motor output may have developed the capacity to hold information on line by extending sensory responses to persist after the termination of sensory stimulation and thereby to flexibly instruct responses mediated by stored information, that is, information not available in the immediate stimulus environment. Ultimately, the elaboration of this process may have contributed to the human capability to behave independent of their immediate stimulus milieu and thereby to flexibly prepare for and think about future consequences of their actions.

ACKNOWLEDGMENTS This research was supported by NIMH grants MH44866 and MH38546 to P. S. Goldman-Rakic and by McDonnell Foundation fellowship JSMF 91-47 to S. P. Ó Scalaidhe.

REFERENCES

ADCOCK, R. A., R. T. CONSTABLE, J. C. GORE, and P. S. GOLDMAN-RAKIC, 1996. Functional magnetic resonance imaging of frontal cortex during performance of non-spatial associative memory tasks. *NeuroImage* 3:S526.

ALLISON, T., A. PUCE, D. D. SPENCER, and G. McCARTHY, in press. Electrophysiological studies of human face perception: I. Potentials generated in occipitotemporal cortex by face and non-face stimuli. *Cereb. Cortex.*

ANDERSEN, R. A., C. ASANUMA, and W. M. COWAN, 1985. Callosal and prefrontal associational projecting cell populations in area 7a of the macaque monkey: A study using retrogradely transported fluorescent dyes. *J. Comp. Neurol.* 232:443–455.

ANDERSEN, R. A., C. ASANUMA, G. ESSICK, and R. M. SIEGEL, 1990a. Corticocortical connections of anatomically and physiologically defined subdivisions within the inferior parietal lobule. *J. Comp. Neurol.* 296:65–113.

ANDERSEN, R. A., R. M. BRACEWELL, S. BARASH, J. W. GNADT, and L. FOGASSI, 1990b. Eye position effects on visual, memory, and saccade-related activity in areas LIP and 7a of Macaque. *J. Neurosci.* 10:1176–1196.

BAKER, S. C., C. D. FRITH, R. S. J. FRACKOWIAK, and R. J. DOLAN, 1996. Active representation of shape and spatial location in man. *Cereb. Cortex* 6:612–619.

BARASH, S., R. M. BRACEWELL, L. FOGASSI, J. W. GNADT, and R. A. ANDERSEN, 1991a. Saccade-related activity in the lateral intraparietal area I: Temporal properties; comparison with area 7a. *J. Neurophysiol.* 66:1095–1108.

BARASH, S., R. M. BRACEWELL, L. FOGASSI, J. W. GNADT, and R. A. ANDERSEN, 1991b. Saccade-related activity in the lateral intraparietal area: II. Spatial properties. *J. Neurophysiol.* 66:1109–1124.

BARBAS, H., 1988. Anatomic organization of basoventral and mediodorsal visual recipient prefrontal regions in the rhesus monkey. *J. Comp. Neurol.* 276:313–342.

BARBAS, H., and M.-M. MESULAM, 1985. Cortical afferent input to the principalis region of the rhesus monkey. *Neuroscience* 15:619–637.

BAYLIS, L. L., E. T. ROLLS, and G. C. BAYLIS, 1995. Afferent connections of the caudolateral orbitofrontal cortex taste area of the primate. *Neuroscience* 64:801–812.

BRACEWELL, R. M., P. MAZZONI, S. BARASH, and R. A. ANDERSEN, 1996. Motor intention activity in the macaque's lateral intraparietal area: II. Changes of motor plan. *J. Neurophysiol.* 76:1457–1464.

CARMICHAEL, S. T., and J. L. PRICE, 1995. Sensory and premotor connections of the orbital and medial prefrontal cortex of macaque monkeys. *J. Comp. Neurol.* 363:642–664.

CAVADA, C., and P. S. GOLDMAN-RAKIC, 1989. Posterior parietal cortex in rhesus monkey: II. Evidence for segregated corticocortical networks linking sensory and limbic areas with the frontal lobe. *J. Comp. Neurol.* 287:422–445.

CHAFEE, M. V., and P. S. GOLDMAN-RAKIC, 1998. Matching patterns of activity in primate prefrontal area 8a and parietal area 7ip neurons during a spatial working memory task. *J. Neurophysiol.* 79:2919–2940.

COHEN, J. D., S. D. FORMAN, T. S. BRAVER, B. J. CASEY, D. SERVAN-SCHREIBER, and D. C. NOLL, 1994. Activation of the prefrontal cortex in a nonspatial working memory task with functional *MRI. Hum. Brain Map* 1:293–304.

COLBY, C. L., J.-R. DUHAMEL, and M. E. GOLDBERG, 1996. Visual, presaccadic and cognitive activation of single neurons in monkey lateral intraparietal area. *J. Neurophysiol.* 76:2841–2852.

COURTNEY, S. M., L. G. UNGERLEIDER, K. KEIL, and J. V. HAXBY, 1996. Object and spatial visual working memory activate separate neural systems in human cortex. *Cereb. Cortex* 6:39–49.

COURTNEY, S. M., L. G. UNGERLEIDER, K. KEIL, and J. V. HAXBY, 1997. Transient and sustained activity in a distributed neural system for human working memory. *Nature* 386:608–611.

COURTNEY, S. M., L. PETIT, J. M. MAISOG, L. G. UNGERLEIDER, and J. V. HAXBY, 1998. An area specialized for spatial working memory in human frontal cortex. *Science* 279:1347–1351.

DAMASIO, A. R., D. TRANEL, and H. C. DAMASIO, 1991. Somatic markers and the guidance of behavior: Theory and preliminary testing. In *Frontal Lobe Function and Dysfunction*, H. S. Levin, H. M. Eisenberg, and A. L. Benton, eds. New York: Oxford University Press, pp. 217–229.

DEMB, J. B., J. E. DESMOND, A. D. WAGNER, C. J. VAIDYA, G. H. GLOVER, and J. D. E. GABRIELI, 1995. Semantic encoding and retrieval in the left inferior prefrontal cortex: A functional MRI study of task difficulty and process specificity. *J. Neurosci.* 15:5870–5878.

DUM, R. P., and P. L. STRICK, 1991. The origin of corticospinal projections from the premotor areas in the frontal lobe. *J. Neurosci.* 11:667–689.

ESLINGER, P. J., L. M. GRATTAN, and L. GEDER, 1995. Impact of frontal lobe lesions on rehabilitation and recovery from acute brain injury. *NeuroRehabilitation* 5:161–182.

FIEZ, J. A., E. A. RAIFE, D. A. BALOTA, J. P. SCHWARZ, M. E. RAICHLE, and S. E. PETERSEN, 1996. A positron emission tomography study of the short-term maintenance of verbal information. *J. Neurosci.* 16:808–822.

FRIEDMAN, H. R., and P. S. GOLDMAN-RAKIC, 1994. Coactivation of prefrontal cortex and inferior parietal cortex in working memory tasks revealed by 2DG functional mapping in the rhesus monkey. *J. Neurosci.* 14:2775–2788.

FUNAHASHI, S., C. J. BRUCE, and P. S. GOLDMAN-RAKIC, 1989. Mnemonic coding of visual space in the monkey's dorsolateral prefrontal cortex. *J. Neurophysiol.* 61:1–19.

GNADT, J. W., and R. A. ANDERSEN, 1988. Memory related motor planning activity in posterior parietal cortex of macaque. *Exp. Brain Res.* 70:216–220.

GNADT, J. W., and L. E. MAYS, 1995. Neurons in monkey parietal area LIP are tuned for eye-movement parameters in three-dimensional space. *J. Neurophysiol.* 73:280–297.

GOLD, J. M., K. F. BERMAN, C. RANDOLPH, T. E. GOLDBERG, and D. R. WEINBERGER, 1966. PET validation and clinical application of a novel prefrontal task. *Neuropsychology* 10:3–10.

GOLDBERG, T. E., K. F. BERMAN, C. RANDOLPH, J. M. GOLD, and D. R. WEINBERGER, 1996. Isolating the mnemonic component in spatial delayed response: A controlled PET ^{15}O-labeled water regional cerebral blood flow study in normal humans. *NeuroImage* 3:69–78.

GOLDMAN-RAKIC, P. S., 1987. Circuitry of primate prefrontal cortex and regulation of behavior by representational memory. In *Handbook of Physiology, The Nervous System, Higher Functions of the Brain*, F. Plum, ed. Bethesda, Md.: American Physiological Society, pp. 373–417.

GOLDMAN-RAKIC, P. S., 1997. Molecular mechanisms of neuronal communication in cognition. In *Molecular Mechanisms of Neuronal Communication*, K. Fuxe, T. Hokfelt, L. Olson, D. Ottoson, A. Dahlstrom, and A. Björklund, eds. Tarrytown, N.Y.: Elsevier Science, Inc., pp. 207–218.

GOLDMAN-RAKIC, P. S., C. BERGSON, L. MRZLJAK, and G. V. WILLIAMS, 1996. Dopamine receptors and cognitive function in nonhuman primates. In *The Dopamine Receptors*, K. A. Neve, and R. L. Neve, eds. Totowa, N.J.: Human Press, pp. 499–522.

GOLDMAN-RAKIC, P. S., M. CHAFEE, and H. FRIEDMAN, 1993. Allocation of function in distributed circuits. In *Brain Mechanisms of Perception and Memory: From Neuron to Behavior*, T. Ono, L. R. Squire, M. E. Raichle, D. I. Perrett, and M. Fukuda, eds. New York: Oxford University Press, pp. 445–456.

GOODALE, M. A., and A. D. MILNER, 1992. Separate visual pathways for perception and action. *Trends Neurosci.* 15:20–25.

GRADY, C. L., A. R. MCINTOSH, B. HORWITZ, J. M. MAISOG, L. G. UNGERLEIDER, M. J. MENTIS, P. PIETRINI, M. B. SCHAPIRO, and J. V. HAXBY, 1995. Age-related reductions in human recognition memory due to impaired encoding. *Science* 269:218–221.

GRATTAN, L. M., R. H. BLOOMER, F. X. ARCHAMBAULT, and P. J. ESLINGER, 1994. Cognitive flexibility and empathy after frontal lobe lesion. *Neuropsychiatr. Neuropsychol. Behav. Neurol.* 7:251–259.

GROSS, C. G., C. E. ROCHA-MIRANDA, and D. B. BENDER, 1972. Visual properties of neurons in inferotemporal cortex of the Macaque. *J. Neurophysiol.* 35:96–111.

HAXBY, J. V., L. G. UNGERLEIDER, B. HORWITZ, J. M. MAISOG, S. I. RAPPAPORT, and C. L. GRADY, 1996. Face encoding and recognition in the human brain: A PET-fMRI study. *Proc. Natl. Acad. Sci. U.S.A.* 93:922–927.

JAKAB, R. L., and P. S. GOLDMAN-RAKIC, 1998. 5-hydroxytryptamine$_{2A}$ serotonin receptors in the primate cerebral cortex: Possible site of action of hallucinogenic and antipsychotic drugs in pyramidal cell apical dendrites. *Proc. Natl. Acad. Sci. U.S.A.* 95:735–740.

KAPUR, S., F. I. M. CRAIK, E. TULVING, E. E. WILSON, S. HOULE, and G. BROWN, 1994. Neuroanatomical correlates of encoding in episodic memory; levels of processing effect. *Proc. Natl. Acad. Sci. U.S.A.* 91:2008–2011.

KAPUR, S., E. TULVING, R. CABEZA, A. R. MCINTOSH, S. HOULE, and F. I. M. CRAIK, 1996. The neural correlates of intentional learning of verbal materials: A PET study in humans. *Cogn. Brain Res.* 4:243–249.

KELLEY, W. M., F. M. MIEZIN, K. B. MCDERMOTT, T. L. BUCHNER, M. E. RAICHLE, N. J. COHEN, J. M. OLLINGER, E. AKBUDAK, T. E. CONTURO, A. Z. SNYDER, and S. E. PETERSON, 1998. Hemispheric specialization in human dorsal frontal cortex and medial temporal lobe for verbal and nonverbal memory encoding. *Neuron* 20:927–936.

MAZZONI, P., R. M. BRACEWELL, S. BARASH, and R. A. ANDERSEN, 1996. Motor intention activity in the macaque's lateral intraparietal area: I. Dissociation of motor plan from sensory memory. *J. Neurophysiol.* 76:1439–1456.

MCCARTHY, G., A. M. BLAMIRE, A. PUCE, A. C. NOBRE, G. BLOCH, F. HYDER, P. GOLDMAN-RAKIC, and R. G. SHULMAN, 1994. Functional magnetic resonance imaging of human prefrontal cortex activation during a spatial working memory task. *Proc. Natl. Acad. Sci. U.S.A.* 91:8690–8694.

MCCARTHY, G., A. PUCE, R. T. CONSTABLE, J. H. KRYSTAL, J. C. GORE, and P. S. GOLDMAN-RAKIC, 1996. Activation of human prefrontal cortex during spatial and object working memory tasks measured by functional MRI. *Cereb. Cortex* 6:600–611.

MISHKIN, M., and F. J. MANNING, 1978. Non-spatial memory after selective prefrontal lesions in monkeys. *Brain Res.* 143:313–323.

NICHELLI, P., J. GRAFMAN, P. PIETRINI, D. ALWAY, J. C. CARTON, and R. MILETICH, 1994. Brain activity in chess playing. *Nature* 369:191.

Ó SCALAIDHE, S. P., and P. S. GOLDMAN-RAKIC, 1993. Memory fields in the prefrontal cortex of the macaque. *Soc. Neurosci. Abs.* 19: 326.6.

Ó SCALAIDHE, S. P., and P. S. GOLDMAN-RAKIC, in press. Functional organization of prefrontal cortical columns. *Soc. Neurosci. Abst.*

Ó SCALAIDHE, S. P., F. A. W. WILSON, and P. S. GOLDMAN-RAKIC, 1997. Areal segregation of face-processing neurons in prefrontal cortex. *Science* 278:1135–1138.

OWEN, A. M., A. C. EVANS, and M. PETRIDES, 1996. Evidence for a two-stage model of spatial working memory processing with the lateral frontal cortex: A positron emission tomography study. *Cereb. Cortex* 6:31–38.

OWEN, A. M., C. E. STERN, R. B. LOOK, I. TRACEY, B. R. ROSEN, and M. PETRIDES, 1998. Functional organization of spatial and nonspatial working memory processing within the human lateral frontal cortex. *Proc. Natl. Acad. Sci. U.S.A.* 95:7721–7726.

PASSINGHAM, R. E., 1975. Delayed matching after selective prefrontal lesions in monkeys (*Macaca mulatta*). *Brain Res.* 92:89–102.

PAULESU, E., C. D. FRITH, and R. S. J. FRACKOWIAK, 1993. The neural correlates of the verbal component of working memory. *Nature* 362:342–345.

PETRIDES, M., and D. N. PANDYA, 1984. Projections to the frontal cortex from the posterior parietal region in the rhesus monkey. *J. Comp. Neurol.* 228:105–116.

PRICE, C. J., R. J. S. WISE, and R. S. J. FRACKOWIAK, 1996. Demonstrating the implicit processing of visually presented words and pseudowords. *Cereb. Cortex* 6:62–69.

RAICHLE, M. E., J. A. FIEZ, T. O. VIDEEN, A. K. MACLEOD, J. V. PARDO, P. T. FOX, and S. E. PETERSEN, 1994. Practice-related changes in human brain functional anatomy during non-motor learning. *Cereb. Cortex* 4:8–26.

RAO, S. G., G. V. WILLIAMS, and P. S. GOLDMAN-RAKIC, 1999. Isodirectional tuning of adjacent interneurons and pyramidal cells during working memory: Evidence for a microcolumnar organization in PFC. *J. Neurophysiol.* 81:1903–1916.

ROLLS, E. T., and G. C. BAYLIS, 1986. Size and contrast have only small effects on the responses to faces of neurons in the cortex of the superior temporal sulcus of the monkey. *Exp. Brain Res.* 65:38–48.

SAWAGUCHI, T., and P. S. GOLDMAN-RAKIC, 1991. D1 dopamine receptors in prefrontal cortex: Involvement in working memory. *Science* 251:947–950.

SCHALL, J. D., A. MOREL, D. J. KING, and J. BULLIER, 1995. Topography of visual cortex connections with frontal eye field in macaque: Convergence and segregation of processing streams. *J. Neurosci.* 15:4464–4487.

SCHWARTZ, M. L., and P. S. GOLDMAN-RAKIC, 1984. Callosal and intrahemispheric connectivity of the prefrontal association cortex in rhesus monkey: Relation between intraparietal and principal sulcal cortex. *J. Comp. Neurol.* 226:403–420.

SMITH, E. E., J. JONIDES, and R. A. KOEPPE, 1996. Dissociating verbal and spatial working memory using PET. *Cereb. Cortex* 6:11–20.

SNYDER, L. H., A. P. BATISTA, and R. A. ANDERSEN, 1997. Coding of intention in the posterior parietal cortex. *Nature* 386: 167–170.

STANTON, G. B., C. J. BRUCE, and M. E. GOLDBERG, 1995. Topography of projections to posterior cortical areas from the macaque frontal eye fields. *J. Comp. Neurol.* 353:291–305.

SUZUKI, H., and M. AZUMA, 1983. Topographic studies on visual neurons in the dorsolateral prefrontal cortex of the monkey. *Exp. Brain Res.* 53:47–58.

SWEENEY, J. A., M. A. MINTUN, M. B. KWEE, D. L. WISEMAN, D. R. BROWN, D. R. ROSENBERG, and J. R. CARL, 1996. Positron emission tomography study of voluntary saccadic eye movements and spatial working memory. *J. Neurophysiol.* 75:454–468.

TANABE, T., Y. OOSHIMA, and S. F. TAKAGI, 1974. An olfactory area in the prefrontal lobe. *Brain Res.* 80:127–130.

TIAN, J.-R., and J. C. LYNCH, 1996. Corticocortical input to the smooth and saccadic eye movement subregions of the frontal eye field in Cebus monkeys. *J. Neurophysiol.* 76:2755–2771.

UNGERLEIDER, L. G., and M. MISHKIN, 1982. Two cortical visual systems. In: *Analysis of Visual Behavior,* D. J. Ingle, M. A. Goodale, and R. J. W. Maunsfield, eds. Cambridge: MIT Press, pp. 549–586.

WILLIAMS, G. V., and P. S. GOLDMAN-RAKIC, 1995. Modulation of memory fields by dopamine D1 receptors in prefrontal cortex. *Nature* 376:572–575.

WILSON, F. A. W., S. P. Ó SCALAIDHE, and P. S. GOLDMAN-RAKIC, 1993. Dissociation of object and spatial processing domains in primate prefrontal cortex. *Science* 260:1955–1958.

51 Learning and Memory in the Inferior Temporal Cortex of the Macaque

CYNTHIA A. ERICKSON, BHARATHI JAGADEESH, AND ROBERT DESIMONE

ABSTRACT   The goal of visual processing is more than just to parse the pattern of active cones on the retina into representations of objects. Within the visual system, the neural representations of objects also are influenced strongly by experience and behavioral relevance, both of which involve cortical mechanisms for memory. In this chapter, the authors describe how object representations are modulated by both top-down mechanisms for working memory and bottom-up mechanisms for learned salience, processes that serve to extract behaviorally relevant objects out of cluttered scenes. Recent work also is described on long-term modification of object representations by associative memory, which serves to alter the neural representations of behaviorally relevant objects so that they reflect associations in time.

Pictures paint far more than a thousand words. Processing the huge quantities of raw data in a cluttered visual scene to recognize a particular object is profoundly difficult by machine but is accomplished rapidly and easily by our visual systems. The visual system takes a two-pronged approach to solving these computational problems. The first prong is an extremely effective mechanism for processing visual information. The second prong is concentration of processing resources on behaviorally relevant objects. These are both expressed in the transformation of visual information through successive stages of computation in the brain. In the highest stages of visual processing, the visual code reflects increasingly complex characteristics of the visual image, and the code is modified by influences not intrinsic to the visual stimulus, such as behavioral context, relevance, and experience.

The synthesis of these processes can be seen in the neuronal responses recorded in the inferior temporal (IT) cortex, at the end of the ventral, or "what" stream of visual processing (Gross, 1994). In this review, we focus on the portion of the IT cortex known as the perirhinal cortex. Although the perirhinal cortex shares many properties with surrounding cortices that also are con-

sidered part of the IT cortex, it appears to play an even greater role in mnemonic functions. Lesion studies in monkeys have shown that damage restricted to the perirhinal cortex cause memory impairment, including severe deficits of visual recognition (Gaffan, 1994; Meunier et al., 1993; Meunier et al., 1996; Murray and Mishkin, 1986; Suzuki et al., 1993; Zola-Morgan et al., 1989; Zola-Morgan et al., 1993) and association memory (Murray, Gaffan, and Mishkin, 1993).

Thus far, there is no evidence for a separate class of perirhinal neurons exclusively involved in "memory" functions. Rather, the mnemonic properties of perirhinal neurons exist simultaneously with their stimulus-selective properties. An example of stimulus selectivity for a representative perirhinal neuron is shown in figure 51.1. The histograms in the figure show the average responses of a neuron to complex color stimuli presented on a computer display while the monkey maintained fixation on a spot at the center of the display. The stimuli that elicit large responses should not be considered the "optimal" stimuli for the cell, in any sense. Although the cells in the posterior portion of the IT cortex may respond to identifiable stimulus features (Desimone et al., 1984; Tanaka, 1993), it often is difficult to identify a feature dimension that explains the selectivity of a neuron in perirhinal cortex for a given set of stimuli (Erickson and Jagadeesh, unpublished observations, 1998). However, the responses of perirhinal neurons can discriminate among complex sets of stimuli because the cells respond in a graded fashion to more than one stimulus. The difference in response between two different stimuli (e.g., the picture of the camel and the painting of the woman in figure 51.1) can be quite large.

The visual responses of many neurons in perirhinal cortex are modulated by the behavioral significance of the stimuli, which typically is established through experience. The major types of memory-related influences observed to affect the responses of perirhinal neurons are illustrated in figure 51.2. Some of these influences may require "top-down" feedback from other cortical areas, for example, cortical areas that mediate working memory. Feedback mechanisms may be the cause of

CYNTHIA A. ERICKSON, BHARATHI JAGADEESH, and ROBERT DESIMONE   Laboratory of Neuropsychology, National Institute of Mental Health, National Institutes of Health, Bethesda, Md.

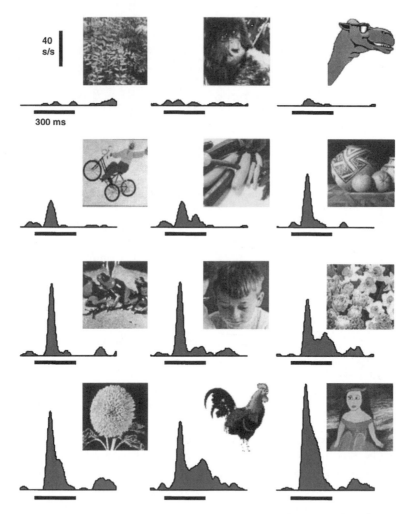

FIGURE 51.1 Example of stimulus selectivity in the perirhinal cortex. Response of a single neuron in the perirhinal cortex to presentation of 12 different complex visual images at the fovea while the monkey fixated on the screen. The histogram is generated by averaging the response of the neuron to multiple presentations of individual stimuli.

maintained activity during the delay period of working memory tasks in the IT cortex as well as enhanced responses when behaviorally relevant stimuli appear in a scene (see top two rows of figure 51.2). These influences, including delay activity, and biasing were discussed in the previous edition of this book (Desimone et al., 1995), and have been reported in several original studies, including Chelazzi and associates (1993) and Miller and colleagues (1993). Other mnemonic influences on perirhinal responses appear to be caused by "bottom-up" mechanisms, i.e. mechanisms that are intrinsic to extrastriate cortex itself. Repetition suppression as well as mechanisms for learned salience and associative memory are examples of processes that may be intrinsic to IT cortex (see bottom three rows of figure 51.2). Repetition suppression was discussed in the previous edition of this book (Desimone et al., 1995). In this review, we describe one example of top-down biasing of signals in the perirhinal cortex and compare and contrast that with bot-

tom-up mnemonic influences on perirhinal responses. These influences serve, in part, to extract behaviorally relevant objects from scenes and to "mold" the representations of objects to reflect meaningful associations. We have been able to identify the neural basis of some of these cognitive effects by recording the activity of single neurons in the perirhinal cortex while monkeys performed memory tasks designed to tax different aspects of visual memory.

Selection of relevant objects by means of top-down feedback mechanisms

A good example of how top-down feedback to perirhinal cortex may be used to select objects from a scene comes from studies using the visual search task (Chelazzi et al., 1993, 1998). In those studies, while the monkey maintained fixation, a cue stimulus was presented at the center of gaze, followed by a blank delay period. At the

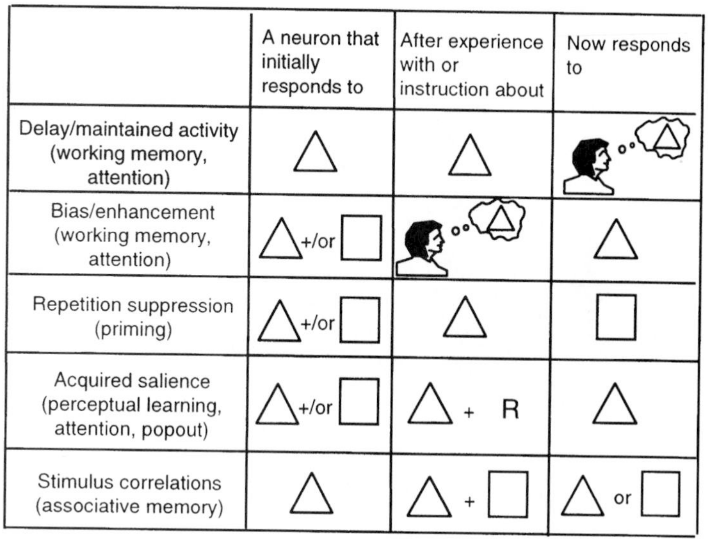

	A neuron that initially responds to	After experience with or instruction about	Now responds to
Delay/maintained activity (working memory, attention)	△	△	[person thinking △]
Bias/enhancement (working memory, attention)	△ +/or □	[person thinking △]	△
Repetition suppression (priming)	△ +/or □	△	□
Acquired salience (perceptual learning, attention, popout)	△ +/or □	△ + R	△
Stimulus correlations (associative memory)	△	△ + □	△ or □

FIGURE 51.2 Schematic diagram of memory mechanisms observed in temporal cortex. Delay/maintained activity and bias/enhancement are two examples of top-down processes discussed in the section on selection of relevant objects by means of top-down feedback mechanisms. Repetition suppression, a bottom-up process, refers to the reduction in response that occurs with repeated presentations of the same stimulus. Acquired salience and stimulus correlations also are examples of bottom-up processes, detailed in the section on selection of relevant objects by means of stimulus salience and the section on associative learning, respectively.

end of the delay, an array of two to five choice stimuli was presented peripherally, and the monkey was rewarded for making a saccadic eye movement to the target stimulus, that is, the choice stimulus that matched the cue stimulus (figure 51.3A). The identity and location of the target stimulus varied from trial to trial. The array was composed of one "good" stimulus (effective in driving the cell when presented alone) and one or more "poor" stimuli (ineffective in driving the cell when presented alone). Thus, one could compare the response to an array consisting of both good and poor stimulus on trials when the good stimulus was the target stimulus with the same array of stimuli when one of the poor stimuli was the target stimulus.

There were two critical time periods during the trial. The first was during the delay period, while the animal was gazing at a blank screen, preparing to find the target stimulus in the array. Most neurons showed higher activity during the delay after a good stimulus presented as a cue than after a bad stimulus presented as a cue. This activity could not have been merely a prolonged response to the cue stimulus because it also was higher during the period *preceding* the presentation of a good cue, if the animal expected it to occur. This was found in cases in which the same cue stimulus was used for a block of trials. Thus, the delay activity between presentation of the cue stimulus and choice array suggests a top-down, or feedback, bias in favor of neurons coding the relevant stimulus. In this situation, the delay activity in the perirhinal cortex is very similar to the stimulus-specific delay activity found in numerous studies of working memory in the prefrontal cortex (di Pellegrino and Wise, 1991; Fuster and Alexander, 1971; Kojima and Goldman-Rakic, 1982; Miller, Erickson, and Desimone, 1996; Wilson, Scalaidhe, and Goldman-Rakic, 1993).

The second critical period was when the choice array was presented. Within 150 to 200 ms of array onset, the responses of most neurons were determined almost exclusively by the target stimulus. If the target was the good stimulus, the response to the array was equal to the response to the good stimulus presented alone, whereas if the target was the poor stimulus, the response was suppressed almost to the level of response to the poor stimulus alone. Thus, the neurons responded as though only the target stimulus was present inside the receptive field. These effects occurred approximately 100 ms before the eye movement to the target stimulus was initiated. Overall, the results support a "biased competition" model of attention, according to which (1) objects in the visual field compete for representation in the cortex, and (2) this competition is biased in favor of the behaviorally relevant object by virtue of top-down feedback from structures involved in working memory. In the next section, we consider how relevant objects may be selected from a scene based on longer-term experience with that object.

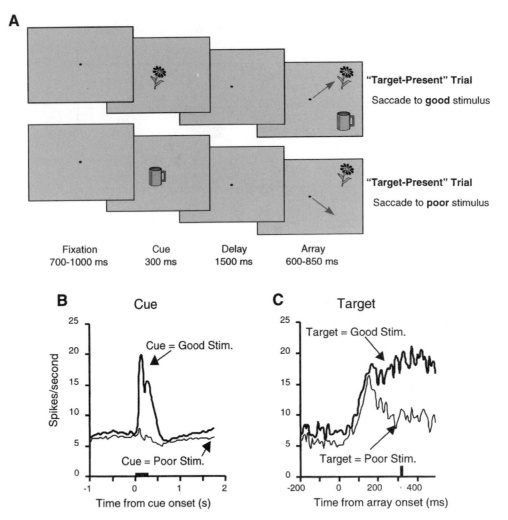

FIGURE 51.3 Responses of neurons in the inferior temporal (IT) cortex in a visual search task, with search arrays confined to the contralateral visual field. (A) Schematic representation of the task. A cue stimulus was presented at the start of the trial, followed by a delay, and then an array of stimuli. The array contained a target stimulus matching the cue stimulus, and the monkey was rewarded for making a saccade to it. On some trials, the cue-target was a good stimulus for the neuron (top row), and on other trials it was a poor stimulus for the neuron (bottom row). Relative locations of the good and poor stimulus in the array varied randomly from trial to trial. (B) Response of a population of 88 individually recorded IT neurons at the time of the cue stimulus presentation. Trials with a given cue stimulus were run in blocks. Neurons showed higher maintained activity both before and after the cue stimulus presentation on trials when the cue stimulus was a good stimulus for the neurons. (C) When the choice array was presented, the same neurons shown in (B) initially responded well, regardless of which stimulus was the target stimulus. By 170 ms after stimulus onset, responses diverged dramatically, depending on whether the target stimulus was the good or poor stimulus for the neuron. This target-selection effect occurred well in advance of the saccade to the target stimulus, indicated by the small vertical bar on the horizontal axis. (Adapted from Chelazzi et al., 1998.)

Selection of relevant objects by means of learned stimulus salience

Often, objects are selected from scenes even when we are not searching actively for them and have no prior expectation that they even will be present. For example, a bright red bird on a green tree immediately attracts attention, whereas a camouflaged brown sparrow in a brown field does not attract attention. This kind of salience generally is believed to reflect low-level processing and segmentation of visual scenes. In terms of the biased competition account, objects that differ from their backgrounds have a greater competitive advantage. However, the salience of an object also is affected by its relevance for behavior. Learned stimulus salience is acquired through experience with the object. For example, one's attention may be grabbed by the unexpected presence of one's spouse in a scene.

We tested for the kind of neural changes that may result from learned salience by repeatedly rewarding monkeys

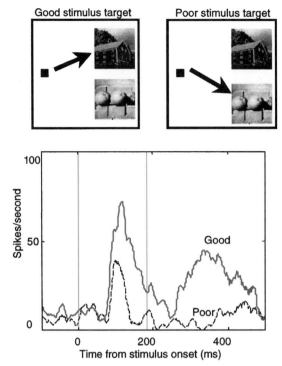

FIGURE 51.4 Responses from an individual neuron in the perirhinal cortex in a learned salience task. The array consisted of a good and a poor stimulus for the neuron (based on prior testing with individual stimuli), and the animal was rewarded for making an eye movement to the "positive" stimulus. Responses are shown for a block of trials in which the good stimulus was consistently the positive stimulus for the neuron (solid line) compared with a block of trials in which the poor stimulus was the positive stimulus for the neuron (dashed line).

for making a saccade to a target stimulus in an array. This task was similar to the visual search task described in the previous section, except that there was no cue at the start of the trial. The monkey simply had to learn through trial and error that making an eye movement to the target stimulus in the array led to reward and that making an eye movement to any other stimulus did not lead to a reward. As in the search task, the array consisted of one good stimulus and one poor stimulus for the neuron, determined by prior testing with each stimulus individually. Once the monkey had learned to select the target stimulus reliably, the association between stimulus and reward was reversed. Thus, the previously rewarded target stimulus became an irrelevant distracter, and the previous distracter now was associated with reward. For each neuron, we compared the neuron's responses to the scene when the good stimulus was the rewarded target stimulus versus when the poor stimulus was the rewarded target stimulus.

A representative neuron is illustrated in figure 51.4. In this figure, the solid line shows the response to the visual scene when the good stimulus was the behaviorally rele-

vant target stimulus, and the dashed line shows the response to the visual scene when the poor stimulus was the behaviorally relevant target stimulus. The monkey made the saccade to the target stimulus approximately 200 ms after stimulus onset, on average. Before the saccade occurs, the visual scene was identical in both conditions; the only difference was the behavioral relevance of the stimulus. The figure shows that when the good stimulus was the target stimulus, the response of the neuron remained high throughout the trial. However, when the poor stimulus was the target stimulus, the response to the same array was suppressed strongly. This difference ("target effect") occurred approximately 100 ms before the eye movement to the target stimulus was made.

The results in the learned salience task were very similar to those in the visual search task described previously except that there was no evidence for the differential "delay" activity found in the visual search task before the presentation of the array. In the learned salience task, the activity of neurons was the same before the presentation of the array, regardless of which stimulus was the target stimulus. This suggests that, unlike in the search task, there was no top-down feedback biasing activity in favor of the expected target in this task. Rather, we suggest that the bias in favor of the target resulted from a change in the competitive interactions between target and nontarget stimulus within the visual cortex itself.

Additional evidence in favor of the idea of a "bottom up" modification of the neurons' response to the scene, rather than the trial by trial influence of a top-down feedback selection process, came from examining data on error trials. On these trials, the animal selected and made an eye movement to a stimulus in the array, as on correct trials; however, on the error trials, the stimulus was not the one that had been paired repeatedly with reward. If the target effect were due to a selection mechanism actively modulating the responses of IT neurons, it still should have been found in the error trials, but linked to the stimulus that was selected by the animal rather than the stimulus that had been associated previously with reward. Instead, we found that there was no difference in response to the array, regardless of whether the good or poor stimulus was selected. The target effect simply was missing on the error trials. This suggests that the effects of learning failed to be expressed in neuronal responses in the IT cortex on these trials, and therefore, the information needed for a correct decision was not available to the animal.

To rule out conclusively the possibility of active feedback biasing IT activity in favor of the target stimulus and causing the target effect in the learned salience task, we conducted a control experiment. For this control, we trained the animals on 10 concurrent pairs of stimuli used in the choice arrays. We reasoned that 10 pairs should exceed the capacity of working memory and would prevent the animal from having any expectation of which target stimulus would appear on any given trial. The animal was trained on the 10 pairs during several weeks of training before the first recording session. Although this strategy precluded working memory, we nonetheless found the same target effect that we found in the first learned salience experiment–that is, the response to the array was determined by the target stimulus, the response to the nontarget being suppressed. This was strong evidence against active feedback and in favor of learning-induced changes in the extrastriate cortex itself.

MECHANISM OF LEARNED SALIENCE   In principle, the change in response to the scene might have resulted from a combination of two underlying mechanisms. The response to the pair could be enhanced when the good stimulus is the target, or the response to the pair could be suppressed when the poor stimulus is the target. To differentiate between these two possibilities, we examined changes in the neural response to the stimulus as the monkey learned to saccade to the target stimulus in return for the reward.

The change in neuronal response with training can be seen in figure 51.5. The average response in the time around the saccade is shown for a population of neurons, in the first 10 trials, when the monkey has just started learning the task, and in the last 10 trials, when the task is well learned. During this period, the percent of correct saccades (saccades to the rewarded target stimulus) increased from 55% to 89%. The average responses in the early trials and late trials are shown separately for responses to the scene when the good stimulus was the target stimulus and for scenes when the poor stimulus was the target stimulus. The response difference between trials in which the good stimulus is the target versus when the poor stimulus is the target is significant both early and late in the session. This difference grows in size as the monkey learns to do the task and the mechanism for that growth is increased suppression in the neuron's response to the good stimulus when the poor stimulus is the target. Thus, the main effect of the training was a suppression of responses to nontarget stimuli.

The hypothetical change in the cortical circuit occurring with training is shown in figure 51.6. In the diagram, the dark circles represent neurons that respond to the picture of the house but do not respond to the picture of the oranges, and the light circles represent neurons with the opposite stimulus preference. Before training, when the visual scene is shown, neurons that respond both to houses and oranges are active. After training, the house becomes

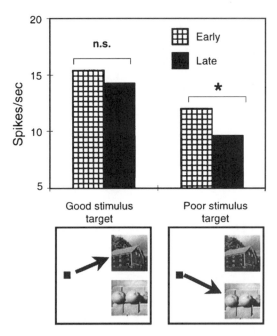

FIGURE 51.5   Response changes over trials during training session. Average in saccade interval (75 ms before saccade onset to 50 ms after saccade onset) for first 10 trials and last 10 trials for each stimulus set, when the good stimulus is the target stimulus or when the poor stimulus is the target stimulus. The difference in neural responses on early and late trials in the recording session was not significant for the good stimulus target trials. However, the difference between neural responses early and late in the recording session was significantly larger for the poor stimulus target trials ($P < .05$). Thus, responses to the good stimulus were suppressed increasingly as the poor stimulus was associated consistently with reward.

the behaviorally relevant stimulus, and the neurons that respond to the behaviorally irrelevant oranges are suppressed. If, however, the monkey is trained to saccade to the picture of oranges, the activity of those neurons remains high, but the neurons that respond to the house are suppressed. In either case, after training, the pattern of activity across the cortex selects the behaviorally relevant image from the scene.

If we look at the top panels in the figure, we see that the behaviorally relevant image is better represented in the scene because the neurons that represent the other image have been suppressed. Thus, this pattern of activity resembles that expected from traditional ideas of object salience; namely, the activity of neurons that represent the attention-grabbing objects in a visual scene is larger than that of neurons that represent less attention-grabbing objects.

Associative learning

In both the visual search task and the learned salience task, the responses of the neurons were modulated ac-

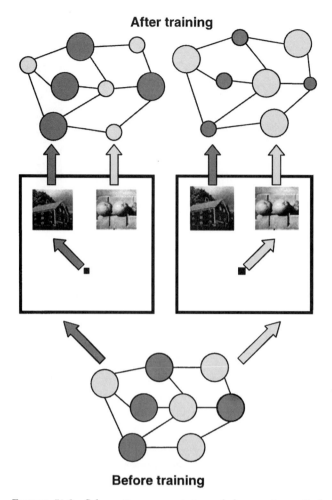

After training

Before training

FIGURE 51.6 Schematic representation of changes in cortical circuits with training. Each filled circle represents a neuron in perirhinal cortex, and the size of the circle represents the magnitude of the neuron's firing rate. Before learning, simultaneously presented stimuli in the visual field are represented by joint activity of neurons participating in the relevant neural representations, which engage in competitive (suppressive) interactions, indicated by the links between circles. As monkeys learn that one stimulus is behaviorally relevant, the neurons representing the target stimulus attain a competitive advantage, resulting in the exclusive representation of the target stimulus in the cortex.

cording to which stimulus was selected or rewarded, but the underlying stimulus selectivity of the neurons remained unchanged. This suggests that stimulus selectivity can be conserved during the other changes that come about as a result of attention or learning. Conversely, in the example neuron from the perirhinal cortex shown in figure 51.1, it is hard to imagine a set of visual features shared in common by all the stimuli that elicited good responses. This is typical of many neurons in the perirhinal cortex. Although high-level feature sets eventually may explain the pattern of stimulus-selective responses in this cortex, it also is possible that effective stimuli share more

abstract, or temporal, associations rather than visual features per se. For example, forks and plates commonly are associated with one another, but they do not resemble each other. If the responses of perirhinal neurons reflect these more abstract types of stimulus relationships, then the responses of the neurons may be determined, at least in part, by associative learning mechanisms.

Miyashita and colleagues examined the neural mechanisms that might underlie the formation of associations between pairs of stimuli in the neurons of the perirhinal cortex. Recordings were made from neurons in the perirhinal cortex and area TE while monkeys performed a paired-associate task similar to one used to test association learning in humans (Sakai and Miyashita, 1991; Higuchi and Miyashita, 1996; Miyashita et al., 1996). They found examples of neurons that responded best to both stimuli that were associated together behaviorally. Across the population of neurons, there was a small correlation between the neurons' selectivity for the sample stimuli and their selectivity for the associated choice stimuli. Two other groups, however, using different tasks, failed to find correlated responses to paired stimuli (Gochin et al., 1994; Sobotka and Ringo, 1993).

We designed a task in which stimuli were linked temporally and in which associated stimuli could be learned quickly, within a single recording session. In this task, the monkeys learned to discriminate between eight choice stimuli concurrently. The monkey was rewarded for releasing a bar to half the choice stimuli and for continuing to hold the bar for the other half of the stimuli. One second before the choice stimulus was presented; a predictor stimulus was presented briefly (figure 51.7).

Each choice stimulus was paired with a specific predictor stimulus for most of the trials. Occasionally, we presented mismatched stimulus pairs. Monkeys had longer response latencies on these trials, indicating that they had learned to associate the predictors with the choice stimuli, although they did not need to learn the associations to perform the task. We refer to this task as the "passive association task" because in contrast to the paired associate task used by Miyashita and colleagues, it does not require active memory for paired stimuli.

The responses of single neurons were recorded from the perirhinal cortex of these monkeys while they performed the association task with stimuli in which the monkeys were familiar after 1 or more days of previous training (familiar stimuli), as well as with stimuli that the monkey had never seen before that session (novel stimuli). Some neurons were found that responded best to images that had been paired together as predictor and choice (figure 51.8). Of course, these associations between preferred stimuli may have occurred by chance. To quantify the effects, we computed the correlation

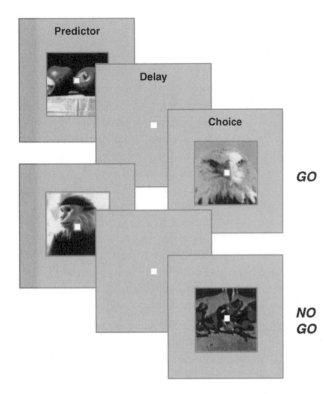

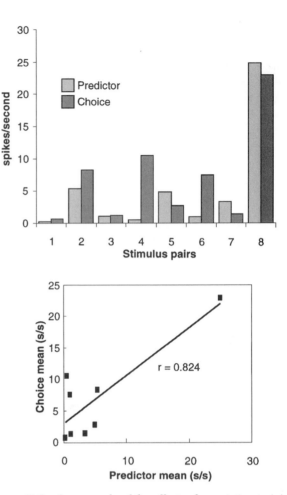

FIGURE 51.7   Schematic representation of an implicit association task. In this task, the monkeys initiated a trial by holding a bar and fixating a small spot, which they were required to fixate for the remainder of the trial. A predictor stimulus was then presented, followed, after a delay by a choice stimulus. The monkey was rewarded for releasing the bar on trials when the choice stimulus was a "go" stimulus and for holding the bar when the choice stimulus was a "no-go" stimulus.

FIGURE 51.8   An example of the effects of association training on responses to stimuli-paired stimuli. Each bar represents the average firing rate of this neuron to one stimulus. The largest responses were to the predictor-choice pair number 8. The association between responses to predictors and choices was measured by plotting the mean firing rate for each predictor stimulus against its paired choice stimulus and computing a correlation coefficient (r-value). In this case, the high r-value reflects the fact that the largest responses are to paired stimuli and smallest responses also are to paired stimuli.

between the responses to the paired predictor-choice stimuli for every neuron in the population. If there were no effects of learning, the average correlation should have been zero. We confirmed this by randomly shuffling the predictor-choice pairings and recalculating the correlations 1000 times. The actual correlations was not different from zero for the novel stimulus pairs but were significantly greater than zero (difference between the mean correlations, $r = 0.2$) for the familiar stimulus pairs. Thus, after 1 day of training, there is a small but measurable shift in the stimulus selectivity of the neurons, such that neurons tend to respond more similarly to stimuli that have been paired together. The fact that responses are not correlated on the first day of training, although the animals seem to have learned to associate the stimuli on the first day, suggests that the initial phase of associative learning involves structures outside the perirhinal cortex.

We observed the same basic finding in the visual discrimination task (described previously, as the multiple stimulus discrimination task) in which multiple pairs of stimuli were presented simultaneously on the screen and the monkey had to discriminate between the two stimuli. After the monkey had learned to discriminate between the images in the multiple pairs of stimuli after several weeks of training, the responses of the neurons to individual stimuli that had been paired together was tested, by presenting the stimuli at the fovea in a passive fixation task. The mean correlation between responses to stimuli that had paired together was significantly different from chance (mean correlation $= 0.2$, $n = 49$). This result suggests that temporal contiguity (the simultaneous presentation of images) may be sufficient to cause associations between individual stimuli to form. A critical factor may be the requirement that the animal respond separately to the different stimuli, so that it cannot treat them as a single compound stimulus.

In the versions of the associative learning task with both delayed and simultaneous presentation of the associated stimuli, the long-term changes found in the stimulus selectivity of the neurons most likely were caused by bottom-up, or intrinsic, mechanisms within the extrastriate cortex itself. However, in the version of the task with the delay between predictor and choice stimulus, we also found activity changes during the delay that may have been caused by active feedback from other structures.

DELAY ACTIVITY Many neurons exhibited stimulus-specific activity during the delay between the predictor and choice stimuli similar to what has been found in the delay period of the visual search task described in a previous section, as well as in the delay period in many previous studies of working memory (Colombo and Gross, 1994; Fuster and Jervey, 1981; Miller and Desimone, 1994; Miller, Li, and Desimone, 1991; Miller, Li, and Desimone, 1993). With novel stimuli, the magnitude of the delay activity was correlated significantly only with the responses to the predictor stimuli. The activity during the delay typically was higher after a good stimulus was used as a predictor than after a poor stimulus was used as a predictor (figure 51.9). The mean correlation between choice stimuli and the delay activity was not different from zero.

With familiar stimuli, the magnitude of delay activity was correlated with the responses to both the predictor and the choice stimuli. Thus, the relationship between the predictor stimulus and the delay activity was not different for the two experience conditions. However, the relationship between the choice stimulus and the delay activity was greater during testing with familiar stimuli than with novel stimuli. In some cases, a predictor stimulus that elicited a good response from a neuron would be followed by a high firing rate during the delay, ending with a good response to the associated choice stimulus. In these cases, the delay activity was associated not only with the stimulus that the animal had seen recently but also with the stimulus that the animal expected to see as a result of associative learning. Sakai and Miyashita (1991) also observed a correlation between delay activity and choice stimulus responses in the perirhinal cortex with familiar stimuli, although they did not test for correlations between predictor stimuli and the delay activity. We speculate that the delay activity resulting from feedback to the perirhinal cortex serves to increase the temporal proximity of predictor and choice activity and therefore may facilitate Hebbian changes in connectivity between neurons responding to the predictors and choices. These changes in functional connectivity may,

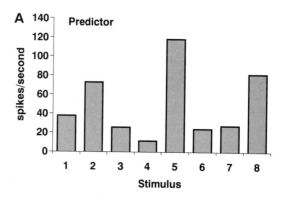

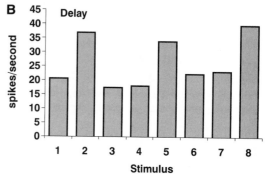

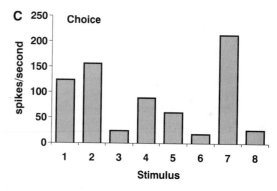

FIGURE 51.9 Example of delay activity correlated with the neuronal response to the predictor stimuli, in a neuron tested with novel predictor-choice pairs. By comparing the response during stimulus presentation (A) to the activity during the delay period (B), it can be seen that the magnitude of delay activity follows the preferences of the neuron for the predictor stimuli rather than the choice stimuli (C). This observation was confirmed by computing correlations between the mean firing rates to the stimuli and the activity during the delay period for stimulus pairs.

in turn, lead to the observed changes in stimulus selectivity after associative learning.

Conclusions

The goal of visual processing is more than the achievement of an accurate representation of the visual world. Rather, visual processing is in the service of behavior, and behavioral relevance plays a major role in how neurons in the perirhinal cortex represent visual stimuli. Because relevance typically is determined by memory and experience with stimuli, it therefore is not surprising that sensory processing and visual memory are intertwined in such a way that they are not easily distinguishable. Neurophysiological studies identify numerous long- and short-term changes in the way that neurons in the perirhinal cortex process visual information and, thus, changes in the way that the brain "sees."

ACKNOWLEDGMENTS This work is supported by NIMH IRP. The authors thank Sudi Shirazi, Amy Durham, and B. Kelly Changizi for their help with technical aspects of the experiments.

REFERENCES

CHELAZZI, L., J. DUNCAN, E. K. MILLER, and R. DESIMONE, 1998. Responses of neurons in inferior temporal cortex during memory-guided visual search. *J. Neurophysiol.* 80:2918–2940.

CHELAZZI, L., E. K. MILLER, J. DUNCAN, and R. DESIMONE, 1993. A neural basis for visual search in inferior temporal cortex. *Nature* 363:345–347.

COLOMBO, M., and C. G. GROSS, 1994. Responses of inferior temporal cortex and hippocampal neurons during delayed matching to sample in monkeys (*Macaca fascicularis*). *Behav. Neurosci.* 108:443–455.

DESIMONE, R., T. D. ALBRIGHT, C. G. GROSS, and C. BRUCE, 1984. Stimulus-selective properties of inferior temporal neurons in the macaque. *J. Neurosci.* 4:2051–2062.

DESIMONE, R., E. K. MILLER, L. CHELAZZI, and A. LUESCHOW, 1995. Multiple memory systems in the visual cortex. In *The Cognitive Neurosciences*. M.S. Gazzaniga, ed. Cambridge, Mass., MIT Press, pp. 475–486.

DI PELLEGRINO, G., and S. P. WISE, 1991. A neurophysiological comparison of three distinct regions of the primate frontal lobe. *Brain* 114:951–978.

FUSTER, J. M., and G. E. ALEXANDER, 1971. Neuron activity related to short-term memory. *Science* 173:652–654.

FUSTER, J. M., and J. P. JERVEY, 1981. Inferotemporal neurons distinguish and retain behaviorally relevant features of visual stimuli. *Science* 212:952–955.

GAFFAN, D., 1994. Dissociated effects of perirhinal cortex ablation, fornix transection and amygdalectomy: Evidence for multiple memory systems in the primate temporal lobe. *Exp. Brain Res.* 99:411–422.

GOCHIN, P. M., M. COLOMBO, G. A. DORFMAN, G. L. GERSTEIN, and C. G. GROSS, 1994. Neural ensemble coding in inferior temporal cortex. *J. Neurophysiol.* 71:2325–2337.

GROSS, C. G., 1994. How inferior temporal cortex became a visual area. *Cereb. Cortex* 4:455–469.

HIGUCHI, S., and Y. MIYASHITA, 1996. Formation of mnemonic neuronal responses to visual paired associates in inferotemporal cortex is impaired by perirhinal and entorhinal lesions. *Proc. Natl. Acad. Sci. U.S.A.* 93:739–743.

KOJIMA, S., and P. S. GOLDMAN-RAKIC, 1982. Delay-related activity of prefrontal neurons in rhesus monkeys performing delayed response. *Brain Res.* 248:43–49.

MEUNIER, M., J. BACHEVALIER, M. MISHKIN, and E. A. MURRAY, 1993. Effects on visual recognition of combined and separate ablations of the entorhinal and perirhinal cortex in rhesus monkeys. *J. Neurosci.* 13:5418–5432.

MEUNIER, M., W. HADFIELD, J. BACHEVALIER, and E. A. MURRAY, 1996. Effects of rhinal cortex lesions combined with hippocampectomy on visual recognition memory in rhesus monkeys. *J. Neurophysiol.* 75:1190–1205.

MILLER, E. K., and R. DESIMONE, 1994. Parallel neuronal mechanisms for short-term memory. *Science* 263:520–522.

MILLER, E. K., C. A. ERICKSON, and R. DESIMONE, 1996. Neural mechanisms of visual working memory in prefrontal cortex of the macaque. *J. Neurosci.* 16:5154–5167.

MILLER, E. K., L. LI, and R. DESIMONE, 1991. A neural mechanism for working and recognition memory in inferior temporal cortex. *Science* 254:1377–1379.

MILLER, E. K., L. LI, and R. DESIMONE, 1993. Activity of neurons in anterior inferior temporal cortex during a short-term memory task. *J. Neurosci.* 13:1460–1478.

MIYASHITA, Y., H. OKUNO, W. TOKUYAMA, T. IHARA, and K. NAKAJIMA, 1996. Feedback signal from medial temporal lobe mediates visual associative mnemonic codes of inferotemporal neurons. *Brain Res. Cogn. Brain Res.* 5:81–86.

MURRAY, E. A., P. GAFFAN, and M. MISHKIN, 1993. Neural substrates of visual stimulus-stimulus association in rhesus monkeys. *J. Neurosci.* 13:4549–4561.

MURRAY, E. A., and M. MISHKIN, 1986. Visual recognition in monkeys following rhinal cortical ablations combined with either amygdalectomy or hippocampectomy. *J. Neurosci.* 6:1991–2003.

SAKAI, K., and Y. MIYASHITA, 1991. Neural organization for the long-term memory of paired associates. *Nature* 354:152–155.

SOBOTKA, S., and J. L. RINGO, 1993. Investigation of long-term recognition and association memory in unit responses from inferotemporal cortex. *Exp. Brain Res.* 96:28–38.

SUZUKI, W. A., S. ZOLA-MORGAN, L. R. SQUIRE, and D. G. AMARAL, 1993. Lesions of the perirhinal and parahippocampal cortices in the monkey produce long-lasting memory impairment in the visual and tactual modalities. *J. Neurosci.* 13:2430–2451.

TANAKA, K., 1993. Neuronal mechanisms of object recognition. *Science* 262:685–688.

WILSON, F. A., S. P. SCALAIDHE, and P. S. GOLDMAN-RAKIC, 1993. Dissociation of object and spatial processing domains in primate prefrontal cortex. *Science* 260:1955–1958.

ZOLA-MORGAN, S., L. R. SQUIRE, D. G. AMARAL, and W. A. SUZUKI, 1989. Lesions of perirhinal and parahippocampal cortex that spare the amygdala and hippocampal formation produce severe memory impairment. *J. Neurosci.* 9:4355–4370.

ZOLA-MORGAN, S., L. R. SQUIRE, R. P. CLOWER, and N. L. REMPEL, 1993. Damage to the perirhinal cortex exacerbates memory impairment following lesions to the hippocampal formation. *J. Neurosci.* 13:251–265.

52 Memory for Objects in Nonhuman Primates

ELISABETH A. MURRAY

ABSTRACT The hippocampus has long been thought to be critical for memory, including memory for information about objects. However, recent research on nonhuman primates shows that another region within the medial temporal lobe, the rhinal cortex (i.e., entorhinal plus perirhinal cortex), is primarily responsible for object recognition and association. It specializes in storing knowledge about objects and may serve as the kernel of a system analogous to the semantic memory system in humans. The hippocampus and the amygdala make different, secondary contributions to object memory, associating objects with events and affective valences, respectively.

Selective cerebral lesions and disconnections have long been used to identify the brain structures necessary for object recognition and association. One persistent misconception holds that the hippocampus subserves object recognition memory. This view is based, in large part, on the memory impairment found in patient H.M., who, after surgery for relief of epilepsy, became profoundly amnesic. It initially was believed and often stated that damage to his hippocampus caused the amnesia, even though his ablation included several neighboring brain structures. In recent years, the "hippocampus" has been construed generally to include nearby structures, but the basic concept has remained the same. According to this view, a group of medial temporal lobe structures, specifically the hippocampus, entorhinal cortex, perirhinal cortex, and parahippocampal cortex (figure 52.1), together constitute a single functional system subserving object recognition. Indeed, it is held that this system underlies all declarative memory, and that the greater the damage to this unified system, the greater the deficit in declarative memory (Squire and Zola-Morgan, 1991; Zola-Morgan, Squire, and Ramus, 1994). It further has been proposed that the hippocampus, in particular, mediates associative memory in the declarative domain (Eichenbaum, Otto, and Cohen, 1992) and the consolidation of information into long-term memory (Squire, Shimamura, and Amaral, 1989). In this chapter, a differ-ent view is presented, based in part on a new method for making experimental lesions in nonhuman primates.

The use of excitotoxins, together with a stereotaxic surgical approach guided by magnetic resonance imaging (MRI), has proven to be particularly useful in studying the neural basis of object recognition and association. Magnetic resonance imaging and excitotoxins provide greater accuracy and selectivity, respectively. The former allows the direct visualization of a given structure and the accurate placement of lesion sites tailored to each subject. The latter can damage deep structures in relative isolation from superficial ones and spare fibers passing nearby or through the site of the lesion. For example, in the case of the amygdala, it is clear that traditional aspiration removal not only produces cell loss in the amygdala, as intended, but also transects efferent fibers arising from neurons located in the nearby entorhinal cortex, the perirhinal cortex, and area TE (Murray, 1992; Goulet, Doré, and Murray, 1998). Thus, the older method produces inadvertent damage, causing dysfunction in all three cortical fields.

Experiments employing the newer method show that rather than operating as a single functional unit, components of the medial temporal lobe make independent and dissociable contributions to object recognition and associative memory. One key finding is that certain types of sensory information, especially different aspects of information about objects, can be associated with one another *and* consolidated into long-term memory in the absence of the hippocampus. Thus, the hippocampus is not an obligatory part of either the associative or the information storage networks operating in the medial temporal lobe. This realization has, of course, led to a reconsideration of the function of the hippocampus, as well as the other major components of the medial temporal lobe.

Object recognition memory

The tasks most commonly employed to evaluate object recognition in monkeys are delayed nonmatching-to-sample (DNMS) and delayed matching-to-sample (DMS). In a typical DNMS task, the monkey sees a

ELISABETH A. MURRAY Laboratory of Neuropsychology, National Institute of Mental Health, National Institutes of Health, Bethesda, Md.

753

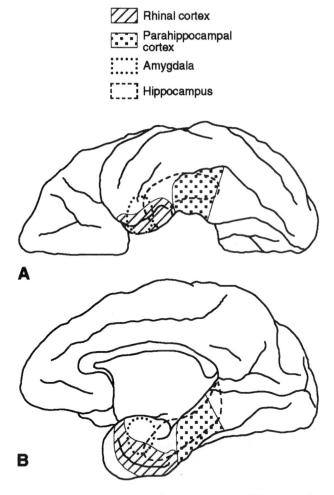

Rhinal cortex

Parahippocampal cortex

Amygdala

Hippocampus

A

B

FIGURE 52.1 Schematic diagrams of ventral (A) and medial (B) views of macaque brain hemisphere showing the locations and extents of various medial temporal lobe structures. The amygdala and the hippocampus are buried deep within the temporal lobe, whereas the rhinal (i.e., entorhinal and perirhinal) cortex and the parahippocampal cortex are located on the surface of the brain.

sample object, which it displaces to retrieve a food reward hidden underneath. After a brief interval, the monkey is allowed to choose between the sample and some different object. In DNMS tasks, the monkey must choose that "different" object to obtain another food reward; in DMS tasks, it must choose the sample object. Recognition abilities can be assessed by lengthening the interval between sample presentation and choice test or increasing the number of to-be-remembered items, or both. There are many variations of the matching tasks. In the following experiments, the task is administered with novel objects on each trial. Thus, at the choice test, the question for the monkey is "which item have you seen before?" For the purposes of the present discussion, it is this judgment, a "judgement of prior occurrence" (Brown, 1996), that we mean by *recognition*.

Using the aforementioned modern lesion techniques, one can conclude that the hippocampus plays a very limited, and probably dispensable, role in object recognition. Monkeys with combined, selective lesions of the amygdala and hippocampus perform as well as unoperated controls on tests of visual recognition (figure 52.2A), even when delay intervals as long as 40 minutes intervene between sample presentation and choice test (Murray and Mishkin, 1998). Surprisingly, in these same operated monkeys, there was a significant positive correlation between the extent of damage to the hippocampus and DNMS task performance, suggesting that the greater the hippocampal damage, the *better* the recognition (figure 52.2B). This result is in direct contrast to expectations based on studies using aspiration lesions. In those studies, combined removal of the amygdala and the hippocampus was found necessary to produce a severe object recognition impairment in monkeys (Mishkin, 1978; Zola-Morgan, Squire, and Mishkin, 1982; Saunders, Murray, and Mishkin, 1984; Murray and Mishkin, 1984), and it was believed that aspiration or radiofrequency lesions of the hippocampus alone yielded a significant impairment in visual recognition as well (Zola-Morgan, Squire, and Ramus, 1994). The present view does not deny the hippocampus a contribution to stimulus recognition per se, under some circumstances. However, the results of Murray and Mishkin (1998) show conclusively that its contribution must be minor and probably is indirect.

In contrast to selective, excitotoxic lesions of the amygdala and the hippocampus, which fail to disrupt visual recognition, removal of the rhinal cortex (i.e., the entorhinal and perirhinal cortex, cortical fields that lie ventrally subjacent to the amygdala and the rostral third of the hippocampus) yields a severe deficit (Meunier et al., 1993; Eacott, Gaffan, and Murray, 1994). Monkeys that have sustained removal of the rhinal cortex perform at near chance levels when given recognition choice tests only 60 seconds or so after presentation of the sample stimulus. The same region appears to be critical for tactual recognition as well (Suzuki et al., 1993). Thus, within the medial temporal lobe, damage to the entorhinal and perirhinal cortical fields is both necessary and sufficient to produce the severe impairments in visual recognition.

The perirhinal cortex plays a particularly central role in visual recognition. There is widespread agreement that, of the medial temporal lobe structures under discussion, damage to this region produces the most devastating effects on visual recognition (Horel et al., 1987; Meunier et al., 1993; Leonard et al., 1995). Nevertheless, it seems likely that two additional regions, the entorhinal cortex and area TE (von Bonin and Bailey, 1947), also

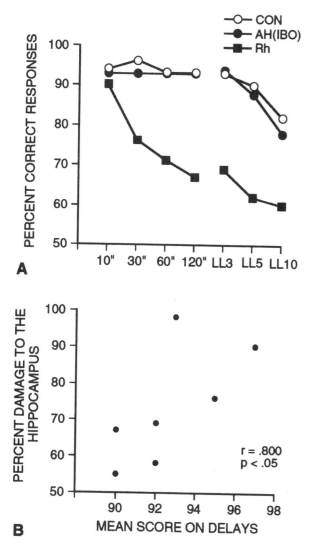

A

B

FIGURE 52.2   Effects on visual recognition, as measured by the delayed nonmatching-to-sample task, of selective, excitotoxic lesions of the amygdala and hippocampus vs. lesions of the rhinal cortex. (A) Curves on the left show the effect of imposition of increasingly longer delays (10–120 s) between sample presentation and choice test, whereas curves on the right show the results of testing with lists of 3, 5, or 10 items. Note that for the list-length testing, the delay for each item in the list is, approximately, the product of 20 s times the length of the list. *Abbreviations:* CON, unoperated controls ($N = 7$; from Meunier et al., 1993, and Murray and Mishkin, 1998, combined); AH (IBO), monkeys ($N = 7$) with excitotoxic lesions of the amygdala and hippocampus (Murray and Mishkin, 1998); Rh, monkeys ($N = 7$) with aspiration removals of the rhinal cortex (Meunier et al., 1993). (B) Correlation of the extent of damage to the hippocampus with the scores on the delay portion (i.e., the 3 longer delays) of the recognition performance test for monkeys with excitotoxic lesions of the amygdala and hippocampus (Murray and Mishkin, 1998). There was a significant positive correlation, suggesting that the greater the damage to the hippocampus, the *better* the recognition. There were no negative correlations of performance test scores with damage to any structure involved in the lesion, namely the amygdala, the entorhinal cortex, the perirhinal cortex, or the subicular complex.

contribute. Three findings point to this conclusion: (1) combined entorhinal plus perirhinal cortex removal yields a greater deficit than that seen after removal of either region alone (Meunier et al., 1993); (2) combined removal of the perirhinal cortex plus area TE (see group "TE," Mishkin, 1982) likewise produces a greater deficit than does removal of either region alone (Buckley, Gaffan, and Murray, 1997); and (3) neither combined lesions in (1) or (2) yields as great an impairment as that observed after either combined amygdala and hippocampal removals, made by aspiration (Mishkin, 1978) or combined amygdala plus rhinal cortex lesions (Murray and Mishkin, 1986). As mentioned earlier, amygdala removal by aspiration causes indirect damage to the neighboring cortical fields by interrupting fiber pathways near the amygdala. Thus, the most parsimonious explanation for finding (3) is that aspiration lesions of the amygdala produced a combination of direct and indirect damage to the rhinal cortex and area TE, rostrally, which, together with the direct damage to portions of the rhinal cortex, caudally, caused the most severe impairments in visual object recognition. Finally, although another region, namely the parahippocampal cortex (areas TF and TH [von Bonin and Bailey, 1947]), has been designated by some investigators (Squire and Zola-Morgan, 1991) as part of the "medial temporal lobe memory system," experimental evidence shows that this region is unlikely to contribute to either visual or tactual recognition. Removal of the parahippocampal cortex alone yields no impairment on trial-unique visual DNMS (Ramus, Zola-Morgan, and Squire, 1994), and removal of the parahippocampal cortex together with the hippocampus has no effect on tactual DNMS (Murray and Mishkin, 1984).

Object association memory

The central nervous system not only supports recognition of objects, it also can "map" or "associate" objects with other objects or information from other modalities. Recent evidence indicates that many of the same areas that underlie object recognition also contribute to the obligate neural network for object association memory.

An early indication that the ventromedial temporal cortex, namely the entorhinal and perirhinal cortex, might be important for the long-term memory of object associations came from a study in which monkeys were required to learn visual stimulus–stimulus associations, or paired associates (Murray et al., 1993). Trials took the form "If sample *A*, then choose *X* but not *Y* on the choice test; and if sample *B*, then choose *Y* but not *X*." Monkeys were trained preoperatively on a set of 10 paired associates. Combined removals (by aspiration) of the amygdala and the hippocampus, which included some of the underlying entorhinal and perirhinal cortex, had a profound effect on both the retention of preoperatively learned paired associates and on the rate of learning of new ones of the same type (Murray, Gaffan, and Mishkin, 1993). By contrast, removals of the amygdala plus the subjacent cortex had a much milder effect on retention, and removal of the hippocampus plus the subjacent cortex had virtually no effect on retention. Furthermore, neither the amygdala nor the hippocampal removal significantly disrupted the learning of new visual paired associates (figure 52.3). These data argue strongly against the idea that the hippocampus is critical for associative memory and for the consolidation of long-term memory about objects. Removals of the rhinal cortex (figure 52.3) cause impairments in new learning comparable to those caused by aspiration lesions of the amygdala plus the hippocampus. Thus, it appears that paired-associate learning, like recognition memory, depends on the entorhinal and perirhinal cortex, and not on the amygdala and the hippocampus, either separately or together (see also Buckley and Gaffan, 1998).

Another recent finding implicates the rhinal cortex in associative mechanisms even more directly. In 1991, Sakai and Miyashita reported "pair-coding" neurons in the inferior temporal cortex of monkeys trained on a paired-associate learning task. These cells showed responses of similar magnitude to separate presentations of certain paired associates but not to other stimuli or other pairs. The probability of this phenomenon occurring by chance is extremely low, so this kind of activity likely reflects information storage. Higuchi and Miyashita (1996) studied the effect of rhinal cortex ablation on pair coding in the following way. Monkeys with transection of the anterior commissure were trained on several pairs of visual stimulus–stimulus associations. After the monkeys had learned a set of stimulus–stimulus associations, the activity of cells in the inferior temporal cortex (the portion lateral to the rhinal cortex) was recorded, and, as expected based on the original study by Sakai and Miyashita (1991), pair-coding neurons were found. The monkeys then received a unilateral excitotoxic lesion of the rhinal cortex and were retrained on the original stimulus–stimulus associations and on a new set of associations as well. Finally, single units were recorded in the same region as for the prelesion control. Although neurons responded selectively to the visual stimuli in both the preoperatively and postoperatively learned sets, there was no evidence of pair coding for either set. Thus, consistent with the evidence from ablation studies, it appears that the rhinal cortex is critical for the emergence and maintenance of the mechanisms that underlie the learning and retention of visual stimulus–stimulus as-

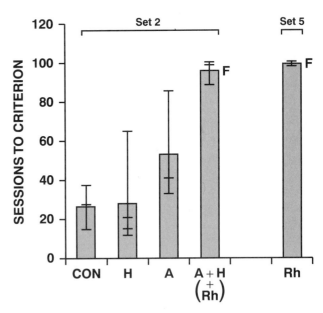

FIGURE 52.3 Postoperative learning of a set of 10 visual paired associates (Murray, Gaffan, and Mishkin, 1993). The height of the bar indicates group mean sessions to learn. Vertical lines indicate the range of scores in each group, and small horizontal hatch marks denote scores of individual monkeys. Note that the monkeys with removal of the rhinal cortex were unable to attain criterion within the training limit of 100 sessions, as were two of the three monkeys with combined removals of the amygdala and the hippocampus that included some of the underlying rhinal cortex. *Abbreviations:* CON, unoperated control monkeys ($N = 3$); H, monkeys ($N = 4$) with aspiration removals of the hippocampal formation plus subjacent cortex; A, monkeys ($N = 3$) with aspiration removals of the amygdala plus subjacent cortex; A + H (+ Rh), monkeys ($N = 3$) with combined aspiration removals of the amygdala and hippocampus that included the subjacent cortex; Rh, monkeys ($N = 2$) with aspiration removals of the rhinal cortex. These animals had served as controls in the main part of the experiment (set 2); set 2, first set of visual paired associates that was learned entirely postoperatively; set 5, fifth set of paired associates; this was the first set learned entirely postoperatively for the group with rhinal cortex lesions. F, failed to attain criterion in the training limit of 100 sessions.

sociations. Higuchi and Miyashita (1996) suggested that the neurons projecting from the rhinal cortex "back" to visual sensory area TE were the critical element of the associative mechanism that had been disrupted.

Because the perirhinal cortex, in particular, is in receipt of sensory inputs from several higher-order modality-specific cortical fields (Suzuki and Amaral, 1994), it is a candidate region for associating together the different sensory qualities of individual objects (figure 52.4). Although an earlier study had suggested that the amygdala was responsible for this type of cross-modal association (Murray and Mishkin, 1985; Murray, 1990), preliminary evidence suggests that the rhinal cortex, rather than the amygdala, is the critical substrate (Goulet and Murray,

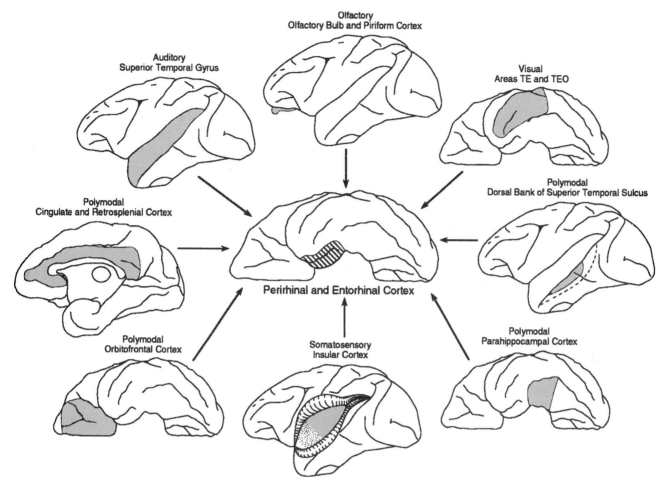

FIGURE 52.4   Schematic diagram showing sources of cortical afferent inputs to the rhinal (i.e., perirhinal and entorhinal) cortex. Note that this region receives sensory inputs from both modality-specific cortical fields (e.g., areas TE and TEO) as well as from polymodal regions (e.g., orbitofrontal cortex). (Adapted from Suzuki, 1996.)

1995). This picture emerges from a study in which monkeys were required to perform a cross-modal DNMS task administered with tactual sample objects (i.e., sample objects presented in the dark) and visual choices (i.e., sample and other objects presented for choice in the light; the choice was known to be guided by vision because the first object touched was scored as the monkey's response). Monkeys were trained to perform this cross-modal tactual-to-visual version of a DNMS task with a fixed set of 40 objects that differed widely in size, shape, texture, and compressibility. As shown in figure 52.5, removal of the anterior portion of the rhinal cortex (the portion underlying the amygdala) but not selective lesions of the amygdala made with the excitotoxin ibotenic acid consistently produced impairments on this task (Goulet and Murray, 1995; Malkova and Murray, 1996). Similarly, removal of the rhinal cortex yields a deficit on a cross-modal task in which the flavor of a food item (including both olfactory and gustatory cues) served to indicate which one of two visual objects should

be chosen (Parker and Gaffan, 1998a), and, in yet another study, removal of the amygdala plus an underlying portion of the rhinal cortex was found to yield an impairment on a task in which auditory cues served to instruct visual choices (Murray and Gaffan, 1994). Thus, in contrast with the earlier idea that the amygdala might mediate cross-modal stimulus–stimulus associations, it appears that this function can be identified as belonging instead to the rhinal cortex. As was the case for another type of object-based associative memory, namely visual paired associates, the hippocampus is not necessary for retention of cross-modal tactual-visual associations (Murray and Mishkin, 1985; Goulet and Murray, unpublished data, 1995).

Taken together, these studies strongly suggest that the rhinal cortex plays a central role in stimulus–stimulus association. Although the rhinal cortex is critical for the formation of new memories involving objects, it is not necessarily the site of storage of those memories. Current models of information storage suggest that stimulus

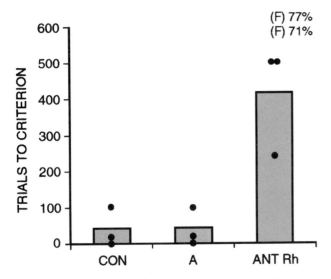

FIGURE 52.5 Postoperative relearning of tactual-to-visual cross-modal DNMS tasks (Goulet and Murray, 1995). These scores were obtained after an initial postoperative assessment on the same cross-modal task and after retraining on both intramodal versions (visual and tactual) of DNMS tasks. Filled circles show the scores of individual monkeys. *Abbreviations:* CON, unoperated control monkeys; A, monkeys with excitotoxic lesions of the amygdala; ANT Rh, monkeys with removals of the anterior portion of the rhinal cortex; F, failed to attain criterion in the training limit of 500 trials; numerals indicate the percent correct responses over final 100 trials.

representations are distributed widely throughout the neocortex, and it has been suggested that the projections from the entorhinal and perirhinal cortex back to modality-specific neocortical fields may provide a mechanism enabling this distributed long-term storage. Instead, the mnemonic contribution of the rhinal cortex may be characterized best as one of object identification, part of the process through which the visual, tactual, gustatory, olfactory, auditory, and perhaps motion properties of individual objects, as appropriate, are linked together, and through which environmental stimuli are invested with meaning. The rhinal cortex thus can be viewed as the kernel of a system for storing knowledge about objects, analogous to the semantic memory system in humans (Murray, 1996; Parker and Gaffan, 1998b; Murray, Malkova, and Goulet, 1998).

Is the medial temporal lobe a functionally homogeneous neural network?

As indicated previously, the prevailing view of medial temporal lobe function dictates that the hippocampus, the entorhinal cortex, the perirhinal cortex, and the parahippocampal cortex function collectively in memory. These structures are proposed to operate together as a single functional system supporting declarative mem-

ory (Squire and Zola-Morgan, 1991; Zola-Morgan, Squire, and Ramus, 1994). However, taken to its extreme, which holds that all parts of the medial temporal lobe contribute equally to all of its information-processing functions, this notion contradicts one of the most fundamental principles in biology: the relationship between structure and function. In addition, there are several findings in nonhuman primates that provide clear evidence that different parts of the medial temporal lobe subserve different functions. For example, there are several tests of object memory that are disrupted severely by damage to the rhinal cortex yet are unaffected by damage to the hippocampus. Many of these findings, summarized in table 52.1, have been outlined in earlier sections of this chapter. However, there are several additional findings that are worthy of mention. For example, Gaffan (1994a) has reported that lesions of the perirhinal cortex produce severe impairments on DNMS tasks with scenes but fail to affect spatial reversal learning; conversely, fornix transection disrupts spatial reversal learning but produces only mild effects on a DNMS task (table 52.1). Furthermore, hippocampal lesions yield a temporally limited effect on retrograde memory, disrupting the storage of recently but not remotely learned object discrimination problems (Zola-Morgan and Squire, 1990). By contrast, rhinal cortex removals yield a temporally extensive effect (Thornton, Rothblat, and Murray, 1997), one extending much longer before surgery (at least 16 weeks) than that reported to follow hippocampal removal (8 weeks). Finally, Meunier, Hadfield, and colleagues (1996) found, paradoxically, that ablations of the rhinal cortex, when combined with removal of the hippocampus plus the subjacent parahippocampal cortex (areas TF/TH), yield a recognition deficit that is *less* severe than that which follows rhinal cortex ablation alone. Possible reasons for this outcome are provided elsewhere (Meunier, Hadfield, et al., 1996). Regardless, this finding directly refutes the idea that the medial temporal lobe structures are working together as a single functional unit. Instead, it seems that these structures may interact competitively in information processing (for examples in rodents, see Gallagher and Holland, 1992; McDonald and White, 1995; Matthews and Best, 1995; Bussey et al., 1998).

Neuropsychological studies carried out in rodents have identified dissociations of function among medial temporal lobe structures that parallel those just described in monkeys. Thus, visual recognition is affected little by amygdala plus hippocampal damage in rats (Mumby, Wood, and Pinel, 1992) but is affected greatly by damage to the rhinal cortex (Mumby and Pinel, 1994). Consistent with the foregoing, rhinal cortex damage also has marked effects on olfactory recognition

TABLE 52.1
Summary of selected studies in the literature contrasting the effects of rhinal cortex damage and hippocampal damage on various types of learning and memory

Task	Damage to the Hippocampal System*	Damage to the Rhinal Cortex	References
Visual recognition	−	+++	Meunier et al., 1993; Murray and Mishkin, 1998
Tactual recognition)	−	+++	Murray and Mishkin, 1984; Suzuki et al., 1993
Visual-visual associations	−	+++	Murray et al., 1993; Buckley and Gaffan, 1998
Tactual-visual associations	−	+++	Murray and Mishkin, 1985; Goulet and Murray, 1995
DNMS with scenes	+	+++	Gaffan, 1994a
Spatial reversal learning	+	−	Gaffan, 1994a; Jones and Mishkin, 1972; Murray, Baxter, and Gaffan, 1998
Spatial scene learning	++	++	Murray, Baxter, and Gaffan, 1998
Retrograde memory for object discriminations	Temporally limited effect	Temporally extensive effect	Zola-Morgan and Squire, 1991; Thornton, Rothblat, and Murray, 1997

Number of plus signs (+, range, 1–3) indicates severity of effect; dash (−) indicates no effect.

*_Hippocampal system_ is defined as the hippocampal formation (hippocampus proper, dentate gyrus, subicular complex) plus fornix.

(Otto and Eichenbaum, 1992). Furthermore, stimulus–stimulus paired associates–in this case, olfactory paired associates–are disrupted by rhinal cortex damage but not by hippocampal damage (Bunsey and Eichenbaum, 1993; Eichenbaum and Bunsey, 1995). Indeed, selective hippocampal damage produces a facilitation in performance on this task. Although these latter studies often differ from those used in monkeys in the sensory modality examined and in the details of the test procedures, they lend general support to the idea that there are multiple functional subdivisions within the medial temporal lobe. In noting the independent contributions of the medial temporal lobe structures to memory, I do not mean to imply that these closely interconnected structures operate in complete isolation from each other, as different "memory systems." To the contrary, the structures appear to work together in mediating information storage. The next section addresses additional functional specializations of medial temporal lobe structures and considers the interactions among these structures.

Specializations within the medial temporal lobe

If the amygdala, the hippocampus, and the rhinal cortex are making independent contributions to memory, as the data suggest, how are we to apprehend their respective contributions?

LINKING OBJECTS WITH AFFECTIVE VALENCES, PLACES, AND EVENTS Although there is scant evidence available from the study of nonhuman primates, a wealth of data from rodents suggests that the amygdala is critical for eliciting the appropriate emotions in response to environmental stimuli (see chapter 74 of this volume) and for associating the values of particular reinforcers with stimuli (Cador, Robbins, and Everitt, 1989; Hiroi and White, 1991; Hatfield et al., 1996). Consistent with this idea, selective excitotoxic amygdala damage in monkeys disrupts the normal pattern of emotional responses to objects (Meunier, Bachevalier, et al., 1996) and also disrupts the ability of monkeys to associate the values of particular reinforcers with objects (Malkova, Gaffan, and Murray, 1997).

In addition to being endowed with affective qualities, objects can be embedded in the context of places and events. Putting aside, for the sake of discussion, the commonly held view that the hippocampus functions primarily in spatial memory and spatial navigation generally (for review, see O'Keefe and Nadel, 1978; Eichenbaum, Otto, and Cohen, 1994), some evidence suggests that the hippocampus is needed specifically for learning how to move to particular locations demarcated by objects in the environment. Removal of the perirhinal cortex or of the rhinal cortex does not disrupt place reversal learning (Gaffan, 1994a; Murray, Baxter, and Gaffan, 1998), which is not dependent on the identification of objects in the environment. By contrast, transection of the fornix (Gaffan, 1994a) and aspiration removal of the hippocampus plus the subjacent parahippocampal cortex (Jones and Mishkin, 1972) do disrupt this "nonobject" kind of spatial learning. On another type of spatial memory task, one that requires monkeys to learn about locations within complex two-dimensional (2-D) scenes, lesions of either the rhinal cortex or the hippocampus disrupt the rate at which monkeys learn (Murray, Baxter, and Gaffan, 1998) (see figure 52.6). In the nonobject

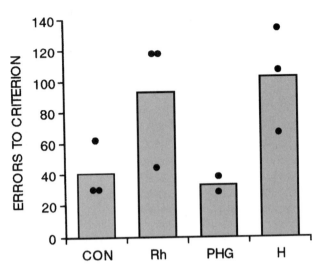

FIGURE 52.6 Postoperative learning of spatial scenes (Murray, Baxter, and Gaffan, 1998). The height of the bars shows the group mean errors to criterion averaged across 3 sets consisting of 8 scenes each. Filled circles show the scores of individual monkeys. *Abbreviations:* CON, unoperated control monkeys; Rh, monkeys with removals of the rhinal cortex; PHG, monkeys with removals of the parahippocampal cortex (areas TF and TH); H, monkeys with excitotoxic lesions of the hippocampus. Groups Rh and H are significantly impaired.

spatial task, identical gray plaques typically mark the relevant locations, and information concerning object identification is irrelevant. In the "object-based" spatial task, the relevant locations are presumably identified by their relative distance from particular objects, which also comprise part of the scene. It is tempting to speculate on this basis that the rhinal cortex is necessary for spatial memory only to the extent that "object" processing is involved in that spatial memory. Thus, in tasks such as place reversal learning, in which a "place" is specified by an egocentric frame of reference, the rhinal cortex likely would be unnecessary. In tasks such as spatial scene learning, in which reaching or navigation to a "place" is achieved relative to a particular object or set of objects, the rhinal cortex likely would be critical.

As for event memory, theories of hippocampal function predict that this region might be important for event memory as well as spatial memory. Episodic memory is a term meant to capsulize the information concerning "what," "where," and "when" of particular events. (For present purposes, "event" memory and "episodic" memory are used interchangeably, but it should be noted that not all investigators agree with this view.) Humans with damage to structures in the medial temporal lobe, including patients with damage largely restricted to the hippocampal formation, have impairments in event memory; the deficit is considered the core feature of the amnesic syndrome. Thus, hippocampal damage is be-

lieved to produce an impairment in event memory, but this represents only a subset of the broader disruption of declarative memories more generally (e.g., Hamann and Squire, 1995). Gaffan (1994b) has proposed that the learning of spatial scenes constitutes an analog of episodic memory in monkeys.

In short, it appears that the rhinal cortex is critical for knowledge about objects, the hippocampus for knowledge about places and events, and the amygdala for linking object, event, or place information with affective valence. Thus, the medial temporal lobe system might be organized in a hierarchical fashion, with the rhinal cortex providing an initial stage of processing involving object recognition, association, and identification. In later stages, already processed information about objects would be linked with events or affective valences by the hippocampus and amygdala, respectively. If so, we might expect that, to the extent that the later stages of processing require knowledge about objects, damage to the rhinal cortex would disrupt storage of information linking objects with events and affective valence.

There presently are few direct tests of this model. As we already have seen, storage of "fact" information about objects is severely disrupted by damage to the rhinal cortex (Murray, Gaffan, and Mishkin, 1993; Goulet and Murray, 1995; Parker and Gaffan, 1998a) yet appears to proceed normally in the absence of the hippocampus and the amygdala (Murray, Gaffan, and Mishkin, 1993; Murray and Mishkin, 1985; Goulet and Murray, 1995). Object recognition likewise depends on the rhinal cortex (Meunier et al., 1993; Eacott, Gaffan, and Murray, 1994) rather than on the amygdala and the hippocampus (Murray and Mishkin, 1998; cf. Alvarez, Zola-Morgan, and Squire, 1995). In support of the idea that later stages of processing are dependent on earlier ones, Gaffan and Parker (1996) have found that disconnection of the perirhinal cortex from the fornix disrupts learning of an "object-in-place" task, in which monkeys are required to learn object discriminations embedded in complex 2-D scenes. It already has been shown that the fornix provides an advantage in just this type of learning. Thus, the finding indicates that the hippocampal system is indeed dependent on inputs from the perirhinal cortex for performance on this task.

In addition to the findings from monkeys, some evidence from clinical studies also is consistent with the model outlined. Indeed, others (Tulving and Markowitsch, 1998; Mishkin et al., 1997) have presented similar models to the one proposed here, based in part on findings from amnesic patients. Aggleton and Shaw (1996) have reported that, among amnesic patients, those with damage restricted to the hippocampal/fornix system appear to have minimal recognition deficits, whereas those with damage outside these regions, or in addition to these regions, have greater recognition impairments. In addition, Vargha-Khadem and colleagues (1997) found that patients who had sustained hippocampal damage (with sparing of most of the surrounding cortex) early in life were able to acquire a large amount of factual information and general knowledge about the world, despite their profound deficits in event memory. In agreement with the findings of Aggleton and Shaw, preliminary evidence suggests that these same patients are quite good at stimulus recognition (Mishkin et al., 1997). Moreover, semantic knowledge has been reported to be disrupted by damage to the ventromedial temporal cortex (Hodges et al., 1992; Kapur et al., 1994). Thus, some clinical data support the view that the rhinal and neighboring temporal cortex subserve "fact" memory, object-based information processing, and semantic knowledge, whereas the hippocampus underlies episodic or event memory. This view is countered by the findings of Squire and colleagues, who report that amnesic patients of mixed etiology have deficits in fact memory that are commensurate with their deficits in event memory (Hamann and Squire, 1995) and that amnesic patients with restricted damage to the hippocampus are significantly impaired in recognition (Reed and Squire, 1997). Additional studies need to be conducted before we can draw firm conclusions regarding the proposed hierarchical organization of memory.

ACKNOWLEDGMENTS The author thanks M. G. Baxter, T. J. Bussey, E. Tulving, and S. P. Wise, who kindly provided valuable comments on an earlier version of the chapter. This work is supported by the NIMH-IRP.

REFERENCES

AGGLETON, J. P., and C. SHAW, 1996. Amnesia and recognition memory: A re-analysis of psychometric data. *Neuropsychologia* 34:51–62.

ALVAREZ, P., S. ZOLA-MORGAN, and L. R. SQUIRE, 1995. Damage limited to the hippocampal region produces long-lasting memory impairment in monkeys. *J. Neurosci.* 15:3796–3807.

BROWN, M. W., 1996. Neuronal responses and recognition memory. *Semin. Neurosci.* 8:23–32.

BUCKLEY, M. J., and D. GAFFAN, 1998. Perirhinal cortex ablation impairs configural learning and paired-associate learning equally. *Neuropsychologia* 36:535–546.

BUCKLEY, M. J., D. GAFFAN, and E. A. MURRAY, 1997. Functional double dissociation between two inferior temporal cortical areas: perirhinal cortex versus middle temporal gyrus. *J. Neurophysiol.* 77:587–598.

BUNSEY, M., and H. EICHENBAUM, 1993. Critical role of the parahippocampal region for paired-associate learning in rats. *Behav. Neurosci.* 107:740–747.

BUSSEY, T. J., E. C. WARBURTON, J. P. AGGLETON, and J. L. MUIR, 1998. Fornix lesions can facilitate acquisition of the transverse patterning task: A challenge for "configural" theories of hippocampal function. *J. Neurosci.* 18:1622–1631.

CADOR, M., T. W. ROBBINS, and B. J EVERITT, 1989. Involvement of the amygdala in stimulus-reward associations: Interaction with the ventral striatum. *Neuroscience* 30:77–86.

EACOTT, M. J., D. GAFFAN, and E. A. MURRAY, 1994. Preserved recognition memory for small sets, and impaired stimulus identification for large sets, following rhinal cortex ablations in monkeys. *Eur. J. Neurosci.* 6:1466–1478.

EICHENBAUM, H., and M. BUNSEY, 1995. On the binding of associations in memory: Clues from studies on the role of the hippocampal region in paired-associate learning. *Curr. Dir. Psychol. Sci.* 4:19–23.

EICHENBAUM, H., T. OTTO, and N. J. COHEN, 1992. The hippocampus—What does it do? *Behav. Neural Biol.* 57:2–36.

EICHENBAUM, H., T. OTTO, and N. J. COHEN, 1994. Two functional components of the hippocampal memory system. *Behav. Brain Sci.* 17:449–472.

GAFFAN, D., 1994a. Dissociated effects of perirhinal cortex ablation, fornix transection and amygdalectomy: Evidence for multiple memory systems in the primate temporal lobe. *Exp. Brain Res.* 99: 411–422.

GAFFAN, D., 1994b. Scene-specific memory for objects: A model of episodic memory impairment in monkeys with fornix transection. *J. Cogn. Neurosci.* 6:305–320.

GAFFAN, D., and A. PARKER, 1996. Interaction of perirhinal cortex and the fornix-fimbria in primate memory: Memory for objects and object-in-place memory. *J. Neurosci.* 16:5864–5869.

GALLAGHER, M., and P. C. HOLLAND, 1992. Preserved configural learning and spatial learning impairment in rats with hippocampal damage. *Hippocampus.* 2:81–88.

GOULET, S., F. Y. DORÉ, and E. A. MURRAY, 1998. Aspiration lesions of the amygdala disrupt the rhinal corticothalamic projection system in rhesus monkeys. *Exp. Brain Res.* 119:131–140.

GOULET, S., and E. A. MURRAY, 1995. Effects of lesions of either the amygdala or anterior rhinal cortex on crossmodal DNMS in rhesus macaques. *Soc. Neurosci. Abs.* 21:1446.

HAMANN, S. B., and L. R. SQUIRE, 1995. On the acquisition of new declarative knowledge in amnesia. *Behav. Neurosci.* 109:1027–1044.

HATFIELD, T., J. HAN, M. CONLEY, M. GALLAGHER, and P. HOLLAND, 1996. Neurotoxic lesions of basolateral, but not central, amygdala interfere with Pavlovian second-order conditioning and reinforcer devaluation effects. *J. Neurosci.* 16:5256–5265.

HIGUCHI, S., and Y. MIYASHITA, 1996. Formation of mnemonic neuronal responses to visual paired associates in ferotemporal cortex is impaired by perirhinal and entorhinal cortex lesions. *Proc. Natl. Acad. Sci. U.S.A.* 93:739–743.

HIROI, N., and N. M. WHITE, 1991. The lateral nucleus of the amygdala mediates expression of the amphetamine-produced conditioned place preference. *J. Neurosci.* 11:2107–2116.

HODGES, J. R., K. PATTERSON, S. OXBURY, and E. FUNNELL, 1992. Semantic dementia: Progressive fluent aphasia with temporal lobe atrophy. *Brain* 115:1783–1806.

HOREL, J. A., D. E. PYTKO-JOINER, M. L. VOYTKO, and K. SALSBURY, 1987. The performance of visual tasks while segments of the inferotemporal cortex are suppressed by cold. *Behav. Brain Res.* 23:29–42.

JONES, B., and M. MISHKIN, 1972. Limbic lesions and the problem of stimulus–Reinforcement associations. *Exp. Neurol.* 36:362–377.

KAPUR, N., D. ELLISON, A. J. PARKIN, N. M. HUNKIN, E. BURROWS, S. A. SAMPSON, and E. A. MORRISON, 1994. Bilateral temporal lobe pathology with sparing of medial temporal lobe structures: Lesion profile and pattern of memory disorder. *Neuropsychologia* 32:23–38.

LEONARD, B. W., D. G. AMARAL, L. R. SQUIRE, and S. ZOLA-MORGAN, 1995. Transient memory impairment in monkeys with bilateral lesions of the entorhinal cortex. *J. Neurosci.* 15:5637–5659.

MALKOVA, L., D. GAFFAN, and E. A. MURRAY, 1997. Excitotoxic lesions of the amygdala fail to produce impairment in visual learning for auditory secondary reinforcement but interfere with reinforcer devaluation effects in rhesus monkeys. *J. Neurosci.* 17:6011–6020.

MALKOVA, L., and E. A. MURRAY, 1996. Effects of partial versus complete lesions of the amygdala on crossmodal associations in cynomolgus monkeys. *Psychobiology* 24:255–264.

MATTHEWS, D. B., and P. J. BEST, 1995. Fimbria/fornix lesions facilitate the learning of a nonspatial response task. *Psychonomic Bull. Rev.* 2:113–116.

MCDONALD, R. J., and N. M. WHITE, 1995. Information acquired by the hippocampus interferes with acquisition of the amygdala-based conditioned-cue preference in the rat. *Hippocampus* 5:189–197.

MEUNIER, M., J. BACHEVALIER, M. MISHKIN, and E. A. MURRAY, 1993. Effects on visual recognition of combined and separate ablations of the entorhinal and perirhinal cortex in rhesus monkeys. *J. Neurosci.* 13:5418–5432.

MEUNIER, M., J. BACHEVALIER, E. A. MURRAY, L. MALKOVA, and M. MISHKIN, 1996. Effects of aspiration vs. neurotoxic lesions of the amygdala on emotional reactivity in rhesus monkeys. *Soc. Neurosci. Abs.* 22:1862.

MEUNIER, M., W. HADFIELD, J. BACHEVALIER, and E. A. MURRAY, 1996. Effects of rhinal cortex lesions combined with hippocampectomy on visual recognition memory in rhesus monkeys. *J. Neurophysiol.* 75:1190–1205.

MISHKIN, M., 1978. Memory in monkeys severely impaired by combined but not by separate removal of amygdala and hippocampus. *Nature* 273:297–298.

MISHKIN, M., 1982. A memory system in the monkey. *Philos. Trans. R. Soc. Lond. B Biol. Sci.* 298:83–95.

MISHKIN, M., W. A. SUZUKI, D. G. GADIAN, and F. VARGHA-KHADEM, 1997. Hierarchical organization of cognitive memory. *Philos. Trans. R. Soc. Lond. B Sci.* 352:1461–1467.

MUMBY, D. G., and J. P. J. PINEL, 1994. Rhinal cortex lesions and object recognition in rats. *Behav. Neurosci.* 108:11–18.

MUMBY, D. G., E. R. WOOD, and J. P. J. PINEL, 1992. Object-recognition memory is only mildly impaired in rats with lesions of the hippocampus and amygdala. *Psychobiology* 20:18–27.

MURRAY, E. A., 1990. Representational memory in nonhuman primates. In *Neurobiology of Comparative Cognition*, R. P. Kesner and D. S. Olton, eds. Hillsdale, N.J.: Lawrence Erlbaum Associates, pp. 127–155.

MURRAY, E. A., 1992. Medial temporal lobe structures contributing to recognition memory: The amygdaloid complex versus the rhinal cortex. In *The Amygdala: Neurobiological Aspects of Emotion, Memory, and Mental Dysfunction,* J. P. Aggleton, ed. New York: Wiley-Liss, pp. 453–470.

MURRAY, E. A., 1996. What have ablation studies told us about the neural substrates of stimulus memory? *Semin. Neurosci.* 5:10–20.

MURRAY, E. A., M. G. BAXTER, and D. GAFFAN, 1998. Monkeys with rhinal cortex damage or neurotoxic hippocampal lesions are impaired on spatial scene learning and object reversals. *Behav. Neurosci.* 112:1291–1303.

MURRAY, E. A., and D. GAFFAN, 1994. Removal of the amygdala plus subjacent cortex disrupts the retention of both intramodal and crossmodal associative memories in monkeys. *Behav. Neurosci.* 108:494–500.

MURRAY, E. A., D. GAFFAN, and M. MISHKIN, 1993. Neural substrates of visual stimulus-stimulus association in rhesus monkeys. *J. Neurosci.* 13:4549–4561.

MURRAY, E. A., L. MALKOVA, and S. GOULET, 1998. Crossmodal associations, intramodal associations, and object identification. In *Comparative Neuropsychology,* A. D. Milner, ed. Oxford: Oxford University Press, pp. 51–69.

MURRAY, E. A., and M. MISHKIN, 1984. Severe tactual as well as visual memory deficits follow combined removal of the amygdala and hippocampus in monkeys. *J. Neurosci.* 4:2565–2580.

MURRAY, E. A., and M. MISHKIN, 1985. Amygdalectomy impairs crossmodal association in monkeys. *Science* 228:604–606.

MURRAY, E. A., and M. MISHKIN, 1986. Visual recognition in monkeys following rhinal cortical ablations combined with either amygdalectomy or hippocampectomy. *J. Neurosci.* 6:1991–2003.

MURRAY, E. A., and M. MISHKIN, 1998. Object recognition and location memory in monkeys with excitotoxic lesions of the amygdala and hippocampus. *J. Neurosci.* 18:6568–6582.

O'KEEFE, J., and L. NADEL, 1978. *The Hippocampus as a Cognitive Map,* 1st ed. Oxford: Clarendon Press.

OTTO, T., and H. EICHENBAUM, 1992. Complementary roles of the orbital prefrontal cortex and the perirhinal-entorhinal cortices in an odor-guided delayed-nonmatching-to-sample task. *Behav. Neurosci.* 106:762–775.

PARKER, A., and D. GAFFAN, 1998a. Lesions of the primate rhinal cortex cause deficits in flavour-visual associative memory. *Behav. Brain Res.* 93:99–105.

PARKER, A., and D. GAFFAN, 1998b. Memory systems in primates: Episodic, semantic, and perceptual learning. In *Comparative Neuropsychology,* A. D. Milner, ed. Oxford: Oxford University Press, pp. 109–126.

RAMUS, S. J., S. ZOLA-MORGAN, and L. R. SQUIRE, 1994. Effects of lesions of perirhinal cortex or parahippocampal cortex on memory in monkeys. *Soc. Neurosci. Abs.* 20:1074.

REED, J. M., and L. R. SQUIRE, 1997. Impaired recognition memory in patients with lesions limited to the hippocampal formation. *Behav. Neurosci.* 111:667–675.

SAKAI, K., and Y. MIYASHITA, 1991. Neural organization for the long-term memory of paired associates. *Nature* 354:152–155.

SAUNDERS, R. C., E. A. MURRAY, and M. MISHKIN, 1984. Further evidence that amygdala and hippocampus contribute equally to recognition memory. *Neuropsychologia* 22:785–796.

SQUIRE, L. R., A. P. SHIMAMURA, and D. G. AMARAL, 1989. Memory and the hippocampus. In *Neural Models of Plasticity,* J. Byrne, W. Berry, eds., New York: Academic Press, pp. 208–239.

SQUIRE, L. R., and S. ZOLA-MORGAN, 1991. The medial temporal lobe memory system. *Science* 253:1380–1386.

SUZUKI, W. A., 1996. Neuroanatomy of the monkey entorhinal, perirhinal and parahippocampal cortices: Organization of cortical inputs and interconnections with amygdala and striatum. *Semin. Neurosci.* 8:3–12.

SUZUKI, W. A., and D. G. AMARAL, 1994. Perirhinal and parahippocampal cortices of the macaque monkey: Cortical afferents. *J. Comp. Neurol.* 350:497–533.

SUZUKI, W. A., S. ZOLA-MORGAN, L. R. SQUIRE, and D. G. AMARAL, 1993. Lesions of the perirhinal and parahippocampal cortices in the monkey produce long-lasting memory impairment in the visual and tactual modalities. *J. Neurosci.* 13:2430–2451.

THORNTON, J. A., L. A. ROTHBLAT, and E. A. MURRAY, 1997. Rhinal cortex removal produces amnesia for preoperatively learned discrimination problems but fails to disrupt postoperative acquisition and retention in rhesus monkeys. *J. Neurosci.* 17:8536–8549.

TULVING, E., and H. J. MARKOWITSCH, 1998. Episodic and declarative memory: role of the hippocampus. *Hippocampus* 8:198–204.

VARGHA-KHADEM, F., D. G. GADIAN, K. E. WATKINS, A. CONNELLY, W. VAN PAESSCHEN, and M. MISHKIN, 1997. Differential effects of early hippocampal pathology on episodic and semantic memory. *Science* 277:376–380.

VON BONIN, G., and P. BAILEY, 1947. *The Neocortex of Macaca Mulatta*. Urbana: University of Illinois Press.

ZOLA-MORGAN, S., and L. R. SQUIRE, 1990. The primate hippocampal formation: Evidence for a time-limited role in memory storage. *Science* 250:288–290.

ZOLA-MORGAN, S., L. R. SQUIRE, and M. MISHKIN, 1982. The neuroanatomy of amnesia: Amygdala-hippocampus versus temporal stem. *Science* 218:1337–1339.

ZOLA-MORGAN, S., L. R. SQUIRE, and S. J. RAMUS, 1994. Severity of memory impairment in monkeys as a function of locus and extent of damage within the medial temporal lobe memory system. *Hippocampus* 4:483–495.

53 The Medial Temporal Lobe, the Hippocampus, and the Memory Systems of the Brain

LARRY R. SQUIRE AND BARBARA J. KNOWLTON

ABSTRACT   This chapter focuses on the memory systems of the brain, a continuing major theme in behavioral and cognitive neuroscience. One major topic is conscious declarative memory, which depends on the medial temporal lobe and its interaction with the neocortex. Another major topic is retrograde amnesia. The facts about retrograde amnesia provide the key evidence for a lengthy process of reorganization and stabilization within declarative memory that begins after learning has been completed. A related topic concerns how the anatomical components of the medial temporal lobe, including the hippocampus itself, might contribute differently to declarative memory. Another topic centers on the distinction between remembering and knowing. This distinction, which concerns two forms of declarative memory, is of interest because it provides one of the best methods for assessing episodic and semantic memory function in humans. Finally, new information is available about several forms of nondeclarative memory, including the phenomenon of priming, skill and habit learning, artificial grammar learning, category learning, and classical conditioning. New lesion studies and functional neuroimaging studies are illuminating the nature and organization of these forms of memory.

Declarative versus nondeclarative memory

The distinction between declarative (explicit) and nondeclarative (implicit) memory continues as a major theme in behavioral and cognitive neuroscience. This distinction is based on converging evidence from studies of experimental animals, neurological patients, and normal individuals (Schacter and Tulving, 1994; Squire and Zola, 1996). Declarative memory refers to memories for facts and events that are recollected consciously. This type of memory depends on the integrity of medial temporal lobe structures, including the hippocampus, as well as midline diencephalic nuclei. Nondeclarative memory is expressed through performance without any requirement

LARRY R. SQUIRE   Department of Psychiatry and Neurosciences, University of California at San Diego, and Department of Veterans Affairs, San Diego, Calif.
BARBARA J. KNOWLTON   Department of Psychology, University of California, Los Angeles, Calif.

for conscious memory content. Nondeclarative memory is independent of the medial temporal lobe and diencephalic structures that support declarative memory. Nondeclarative memory is not a single entity but rather describes a collection of abilities: memory for skills and habits, simple forms of conditioning, and priming.

Describing the properties of declarative and nondeclarative memory independently of their neuroanatomy is an important goal. Declarative memory is well suited for storing information about single events. The knowledge is flexible and applied readily to novel situations. In general, nondeclarative memory is inflexible and bound to the learning situation. Unlike declarative memories, nondeclarative memories cannot be accessed readily by response systems that did not participate in the original learning (Eichenbaum, Mathews, and Cohen, 1989; Reber, Knowlton, and Squire, 1996; Saunders and Weiskrantz, 1989).

Retrograde amnesia

The brain system that supports declarative memory has only a temporary role in the formation of long-term memory. Retrograde amnesia, the loss of memories that were acquired before the onset of amnesia, usually is graded temporally so that recent memories are more impaired than remote memories (Ribot, 1881). Retrograde amnesia sometimes can be ungraded and extensive, as in conditions such as encephalitis and head trauma, when damage typically occurs beyond the brain system that supports declarative memory (e.g., Damasio et al., 1985; Cermak and O'Connor, 1983; Reed and Squire, 1998). Nevertheless, in patients with restricted damage to the CA1 zone of the hippocampus proper, such as patient R.B. (Zola-Morgan, Squire, and Amaral, 1986) and patient G.D. (Rempel-Clower et al., 1996), retrograde amnesia is brief, perhaps covering 1 or 2 years at most. Other patients with more complete damage to the hippocampal formation also have temporally limited

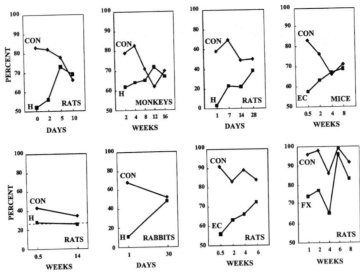

FIGURE 53.1 The panels show all the studies through 1998 in which an equivalent amount of training was given at each of two or more times before hippocampal formation damage, and retention was assessed shortly after surgery. The eight studies involve eight different tasks and four species. In each case, the data show the performance of control (CON) and operated animals (H = hippocampus, EC = entorhinal cortex, FX = fornix) as a function of the interval between training and surgery. Control animals typically exhibited forgetting as the interval between training and surgery increased. In seven of the eight studies, operated animals exhibited temporally graded retrograde amnesia. They were impaired at retaining material they had learned recently, but they retained re-motely learned material as well as control animals. In addition, the operated animals typically retained remotely learned material better than recently learned material. In the lower left panel, both groups of operated animals performed at chance levels (dotted line), which could have obscured a temporal gradient of amnesia if one were present. From left to right, beginning on the top row, the studies are by Winocur (1990); Zola-Morgan and Squire (1990); Kim and Fanselow (1992); Cho and associates (1993); Bolhuis and associates (1994); Kim and colleagues (1995); Cho and Kesner (1996); and Wiig and coworkers (1996). (From Milner, Squire, and Kandel, 1998. Reprinted with permission of Cell Press.)

retrograde amnesia (Reed and Squire, 1998), but graded loss of memory can extend back a decade or more (Rempel-Clower et al., 1996).

Because the study of human retrograde amnesia is based almost entirely on findings from retrospective tests, the clearest evidence about retrograde amnesia gradients comes from studies using experimental animals, where the delay between initial learning and a lesion can be manipulated directly (figure 53.1). These studies make three important points: (1) temporal gradients of retrograde amnesia can occur within long-term memory (i.e., retrograde amnesia does not reflect simply the vulnerability of a short-term memory that has not yet been converted into a long-term memory); (2) after a lesion, remote memory can be retained better than recent memory; and (3) lesions can spare weak memories while disrupting strong ones. To illustrate these three points, consider the case of rabbits given trace eyeblink conditioning. Trace conditioning is a variant of classical conditioning in which the conditioned stimulus (CS), such as a tone, is presented and terminated, and then a short interval is imposed before the presentation of the unconditioned stimulus (US). In normal rabbits, forgetting occurs gradually after training; thus, retention of the conditioned response is much poorer 30 days after training than after only 1 day. Nevertheless, complete aspiration of the hippocampus 1 day after training abolished the strong 1-day-old memory, whereas the same lesion made 30 days after training had no effect on the weaker, 30-day-old memory (Kim, Clark, and Thompson, 1995; figure 53.1).

The results from experimental animals provide evidence for a gradual process of reorganization and stabilization in the neocortex whereby long-term memory eventually becomes independent of the medial temporal lobe. The medial temporal lobe is the target of highly processed information originating from a variety of cortical regions, and it returns projections to these same cortical regions. The hippocampal formation may direct a process of reorganization in the neocortex by gradually binding together the multiple, geographically separate cortical regions that together store memory for a whole event (Alvarez and Squire, 1994; Squire and Alvarez, 1995; McClelland, McNaughton, and O'Reilly, 1995). The lengthy time period required by this process suggests that morphological growth and change may be required at the synapses within the corticocortical projections that comprise a representation.

There is precedent for gradual changes in neuronal morphology occurring as the result of behavioral experience. Specifically, gradual morphological changes can occur in visual cortical neurons as the result of a small retinal lesion. These changes serve to reduce the size of the visual scotoma and are likely driven by continuing sensory input (Darian-Smith and Gilbert, 1994). To explain why this long process occurs in the organization of long-term memory, McClelland and associates (1995) suggested on computational grounds that the hippocampal system itself can learn specific instances rapidly but that information can be incorporated into the neocortex only gradually. The gradual incorporation of information into neocortex minimizes disruption of existing knowledge structures. Much more needs to be learned about this gradual process. Interestingly, measured against life span, a 30-day gradient of retrograde amnesia in a mouse or rat is equivalent to a gradient of a few years in a human. Whether such a comparison is meaningful must await parametric studies of retrograde amnesia in experimental animals and the identification of which task factors can influence the severity and extent of retrograde amnesia.

Components of the medial temporal lobe memory system

Studies with monkeys and humans have identified the brain structures within the medial temporal lobe that are important for declarative memory. These structures are the hippocampus, the entorhinal cortex, the parahippocampal cortex, and the perirhinal cortex (figure 53.2). The amygdala, although critical for aspects of emotional learning (Davis, 1994; LeDoux, 1996) and for the enhancement of declarative memory by emotion (Adolphs et al., 1997), is not critical for declarative memory itself (Zola-Morgan, Squire, and Amaral, 1989).

The question whether these medial temporal lobe structures play different roles in declarative memory follows naturally from the fact that anatomical connections from different parts of the neocortex enter the medial temporal lobe at different points (Suzuki and Amaral, 1994a, b). For example, the visual association cortex, including area TE, projects more strongly to the perirhinal cortex than to the parahippocampal cortex, whereas the parietal cortex projects to the parahippocampal cortex but not to the perirhinal cortex.

The evidence from monkeys and humans at first might seem to count against the idea that the different structures of the medial temporal lobe have distinct functions. The data are that the severity of memory impairment increases as more components of the medial

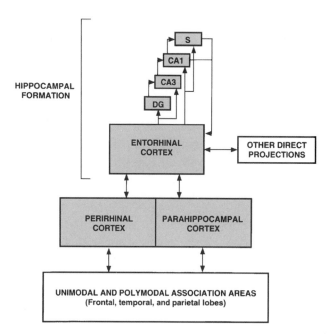

FIGURE 53.2 Schematic view of the medial temporal lobe memory system. The entorhinal cortex is a major source of projections to the hippocampal region (which includes the dentate gyrus, the cell fields of the hippocampus proper, and the subicular complex). Nearly two thirds of the cortical input to the entorhinal cortex originate in the adjacent perirhinal and parahippocampal cortices, which in turn receive projections from unimodal and polymodal areas in the frontal, temporal, and parietal lobes. The entorhinal cortex also receives other direct inputs from the orbital frontal cortex, the insular cortex, the cingulate cortex, and the superior temporal gyrus. All these projections are reciprocal. (From Squire and Zola, 1996. Copyright 1996 National Academy of Sciences, U.S.A.)

temporal lobe are damaged (Rempel-Clower et al., 1996; Zola-Morgan, Squire, and Ramus, 1994). However, these findings are compatible with the idea that different components of the medial temporal lobe contribute to memory in different ways. As damage increases, fewer strategies may be available for storing memory, resulting in more severe memory impairment.

Direct comparisons of the separate effects of perirhinal and parahippocampal lesions suggest that these structures may play distinct roles, as the neuroanatomical findings first suggested. Visual recognition memory appears to be more dependent on the perirhinal cortex than the parahippocampal cortex (Squire and Zola, 1996), whereas spatial memory appears to be more dependent on the parahippocampal cortex than the perirhinal cortex (Malkova and Mishkin, 1997; Parkinson, Murray, and Mishkin, 1988; Teng, Squire, and Zola, 1997).

There also has been interest in which, if any, memory functions can be identified that are specific for the hippocampus. Anatomically, the hippocampus lies at the end of the medial temporal lobe system and is a recipient of convergent projections from each of the structures that precedes it in the hierarchy (figure 53.2). This arrangement has suggested to some that the hippocampus has a special role in memory tasks that depend especially on relating or combining information from multiple sources, such as spatial information or information about specific events, as opposed to factual knowledge (Mishkin et al., 1997; Nadel, 1991; Eichenbaum, Otto, and Cohen, 1994). These possibilities are active topics of investigation. Three observations seem warranted at this point.

First, it is clear that animals with neurotoxic damage limited to the hippocampus are impaired at nonspatial memory tasks (Bunsey and Eichenbaum, 1996). Spatial tasks are simply a good example of the large category of declarative memory abilities that are impaired after hippocampal damage (Squire, 1992). Second, in monkeys and humans, damage limited to the hippocampal region (hippocampus, dentate gyrus, and subicular complex) impairs simple tasks of recognition memory (Reed and Squire, 1997; Zola et al., 1998). For example, monkeys with circumscribed, radiofrequency lesions of the hippocampal region were impaired in the visual paired-comparison task (Zola et al., 1998). This task measures familiarity for recent stimuli by taking advantage of the natural (untrained) tendency that monkeys have to look longer at novel pictures than familiar pictures. Third, formal tests suggest that amnesic patients with hippocampal region damage have difficulty learning new facts just as they have difficulty learning about new events (Hamann and Squire, 1995; also see Squire and Zola, 1998).

These considerations suggest that the hippocampal region is important for both spatial and nonspatial memory, for both recognition memory and recall, and for both fact and event memory. This is, in fact, the impression that one gains through study of amnesic patients like R.B. and G.D., who had bilateral damage limited to the CA1 region of the hippocampus. If the hippocampus has some unique function that can be detected in behavioral measures, then there should be some memory task that G.D. and R.B. would have performed as poorly as patients with CA1 damage plus damage to other medial temporal lobe structures (e.g., the well-studied amnesic patient H.M. [Scoville and Milner, 1957]). However, G.D. and R.B. appeared simply to be less severely affected than patients like H.M. One possibility is that the hippocampus makes a unique contribution to declarative memory, but that this contribution will become clear only when the intrinsic circuitry of the hippocampus is better understood computationally. Another possibility is that the hippocampus, as the result of its placement at the end of the processing hierarchy of the medial temporal lobe (figure 53.2), combines and ex-

tends the functions of the structures that are positioned earlier in the hierarchy. In this view, the hippocampus supports and extends the operations of the structures that send projections to it, and studies of lesions and behavior would not reveal deficits unique to the hippocampus that could not also be observed by damaging the perirhinal cortex, the parahippocampal cortex, or the entorhinal cortex.

The distinction between remembering and knowing

When an item evokes a conscious recollection that includes specific information about the item and the context in which the item was learned, a subject is said to "remember" (R). When a subject is confident an item is familiar and was seen before, but is unable to remember anything about the item in its original learning context, the subject is said to experience "knowing" (K) (Tulving, 1985). In some respects, the distinction between remembering and knowing is similar to the distinction between declarative and nondeclarative memory, and R and K responses can be dissociated in a number of ways that are reminiscent of that distinction (Gardiner and Parkin, 1990). However, recent work shows that both R and K responses are impaired in amnesia (Knowlton and Squire, 1995; figure 53.3; Kroll, Yonelinas, and Knight, 1997). Accordingly, the evidence suggests that remembering and knowing are two different expressions of declarative memory.

In another study, event-related potentials (ERPs) from recently presented items that elicited R responses were similar to ERPs from recently presented items that elicited K responses until 500 ms after each item was presented (Smith, 1993). However, items that were endorsed as having been presented before (i.e., all the items that received either R or K responses) could be distinguished from items that were endorsed as new items beginning approximately 350 ms after item presentation. Smith (1993) suggested that both R and K responses result from a common process of recollection dependent on declarative memory. The distinction between R and K responses then arises from a postrecollective process, when subjects attend to the products of their retrieval efforts.

The nature of this postrecollective component of memory has been described in a number of ways. Tulving (1989) originally described remembering and knowing as measuring episodic and semantic memory, respectively. Items that are "remembered" after a short study-test delay are likely to become merely "known" after a long delay, and this transition has been likened to the transition between episodic and semantic memory (Conway et al., 1997).

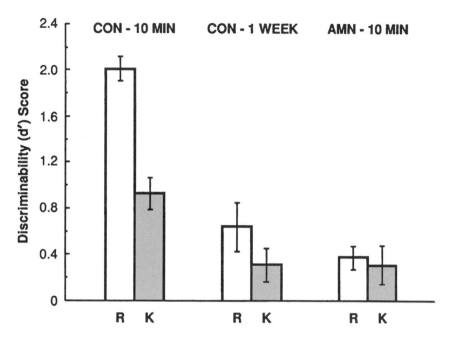

FIGURE 53.3   Recognition memory (measured by d', discriminability) for test items labeled *remember* (R; open bars) or *know* (K; closed bars) by amnesic patients (AMN) and two control groups (CON). The amnesic patients ($n = 13$) were tested 10 minutes after the study phase, and the control groups were tested 10 minutes ($n = 14$) or 1 week after the study phase ($n = 11$). For amnesic patients, the accuracy of both R responses and K responses were impaired. Brackets show standard errors of the mean. (From Knowlton and Squire, 1995.)

This line of thinking leads to the idea that although remembering and knowing are both forms of declarative memory, they nevertheless can be distinguished in a fundamental way. Whereas both remembering and knowing are dependent on the medial temporal lobe and diencephalic brain structures that support declarative memory, remembering depends additionally on the frontal lobes (Schacter, Harbluk, and McLachlan, 1984; Janowsky, Shimamura, and Squire, 1989). In one study, elderly individuals were impaired in remembering (i.e., making accurate R responses) in proportion to the extent that they exhibited neuropsychological signs of frontal lobe dysfunction (Parkin and Walter, 1992).

One critical component of "remember" judgments seems to be the availability of source memory. Individuals often describe an item as "remembered" because they have a specific memory of the learning context for that item. They remember the source of the item. Source memory is sensitive to frontal lobe damage (Schacter, Harbluk, and McLachlan, 1984; Janowsky, Shimamura, and Squire, 1989), consistent with the idea that remember "judgments" depend on the integrity of the frontal lobes. However, remember judgments are not fully equivalent to source judgments, broadly defined, because even when individuals recognize an item by familiarity (a "know" response), they still are indicating in their endorsement of the item that they believe the items were presented during the study phase. Thus, remem-

bering and knowing both require knowledge that a test item was encountered recently in the study context, but remembering additionally requires that specific information be available about a particular moment in recent time when the item was encountered.

Nondeclarative memory

PRIMING   Priming refers to the enhanced ability to identify or produce a stimulus as a result of its recent presentation. The first encounter with an item results in a representation of that item, which then allows it to be processed more efficiently than items that were not encountered recently. Priming is not merely the activation of previously existing representations because priming can occur for novel material, including orthographically illegal nonwords such as KHSF (Keane et al., 1995b; Hamann and Squire, 1997) and for newly associated word pairs (Gabrieli et al., 1997; Poldrack and Cohen, 1997). Some of the best evidence that priming is a distinct form of memory comes from the finding that amnesic patients exhibit intact priming (see Schacter, Chiu, and Ochsner, 1993, for a review).

The dissociation between intact priming and impaired recognition memory in amnesic patients is particularly compelling. One study investigated priming in a patient who is so severely amnesic that he exhibits no detectable declarative memory (Hamann and Squire, 1997). Patient

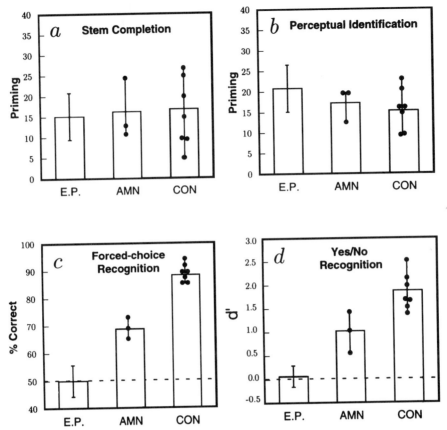

FIGURE 53.4   Performance on four different memory tests after studying 24 simple English words. (A) Stem completion priming. Six priming tests were given to the severely amnesic patient E.P., other less severely affected amnesic patients (AMN, $n = 3$), and normal controls (CON, $n = 7$). Priming scores were calculated as percentage correct for studied items minus percentage correct for nonstudied items. (B) Perceptual identification priming. Twelve tests were given to all participants. Priming scores were calculated as percentage of correct identifications of studied items minus percentage of correct identifications of nonstudied items. (C) Two-alterna-tive, forced-choice recognition. Percentage correct across six tests for each participant. (D) Yes–no recognition. Discrimination accuracy (d') is shown across six tests for each participant. Percentage correct scores (hits plus correct rejections) were 52%, 65%, and 81% for E.P., AMN patients, and CON participants, respectively. Brackets for E.P. indicate the standard error of the mean; the data points for AMN and CON groups indicate individual participant means across all the tests. Dashed lines indicate chance performance. (From Hamann and Squire, 1997.)

E.P. sustained complete bilateral damage to the medial temporal lobe as the result of herpes simplex encephalitis. Two tests of priming were given–perceptual identification of words and word-stem completion. Two parallel tests of recognition memory for words were also given–two-alternative forced-choice and yes–no recognition. Each test was given 6 to 12 times to obtain a robust measure of performance. The result: E.P. performed entirely normally on the two priming tests but performed at chance on the recognition tests (figure 53.4). These results support the idea that priming depends on brain structures independent of the medial temporal lobe memory system. In addition, the fact that E.P. performed at chance on the recognition tests shows that he was unable to benefit his recognition performance by using the information available to him from priming.

The anatomical locus of perceptual priming appears to be in posterior neocortex. Positron emission tomography (PET) and functional magnetic resonance imaging (fMRI) studies have shown that primed items result in less activation in the posterior neocortex than do unprimed items (Schacter and Buckner, 1998). For example, in a word-stem completion task, volunteers showed reduced activation of the right posterior cortex while completing stems of words that had been presented recently, for example, study BRIDE, complete BRI__ (Squire et al., 1992). This decrease in activation likely reflects a decrease in the resources required to process material when it recurs because the material left a trace in the visual pathways after its first presentation.

Two patients with unilateral extrastriate lesions have been identified who performed poorly on visual perceptual priming tasks, but who exhibited intact recognition memory for the same stimuli (Gabrieli et al., 1995; Keane et al., 1995a). These patients also exhibited intact nonvisual priming and intact semantic priming. This dissociation of priming and recognition memory provides further support for the idea that these two forms of memory depend on different brain systems. The patients may have achieved normal recognition memory performance by accessing different information than is used to support priming. Whereas perceptual priming depends on the visual features of the stimulus items, recognition memory could draw on phonetic or semantic information that was established in parallel with and independently of information about visual features.

SKILLS AND HABITS   The learning of motor, perceptual, and cognitive skills is largely nondeclarative in some circumstances, as evidenced by the fact that amnesic patients can learn some skills at an entirely normal rate. In one study, amnesic patients and control subjects performed a serial reaction-time task (Nissen and Bullemer, 1987) in which they responded successively to a sequence of four illuminated spatial locations. The task was to press one of four keys as rapidly as possible as soon as the location above that key was illuminated. Amnesic patients and normal subjects successfully learned a repeating sequence of locations, as indicated by gradually decreasing reaction times for key presses as the sequence repeated itself. When the sequence was changed, reaction times increased again. Amnesic patients learned the sequence even when they had little or no declarative knowledge of it, as measured by four different tests of declarative knowledge (Reber and Squire, 1994).

In a second study, the distinction between procedural knowledge for the sequence and declarative knowledge for the sequence was established in a different way. Amnesic patients received extended practice on a sequence (1200 trials), and control subjects were given no practice but attempted to memorize the sequence during a brief period of 60 observation trials (Reber and Squire, 1998). The result: control subjects answered questions about the sequence better than the amnesic patients, but the amnesic patients exhibited better nondeclarative knowledge of the sequence than the controls, as measured by their improved reaction times while performing the task.

Neuropsychological studies of skill learning point to the involvement of the neostriatum in many of the tasks. Patients with striatal damage, including patients with Huntington's disease or Parkinson's disease, are impaired at acquiring perceptuomotor skills (see Salmon and Butters, 1995, for a review). Functional neuroimaging also has implicated the neostriatum in the serial reaction-time task (Doyon et al., 1996; Grafton, Hazeltine, and Ivry, 1995; Hazeltine, Grafton, and Ivry, 1997; Rauch et al., 1997).

Habit learning refers to stimulus-response–based associations that are formed gradually and independently of declarative memory for the training episode (Mishkin, Malamut, and Bachevalier, 1984). In experimental animals, there is strong evidence that the neostriatum is essential for habit learning (White, 1997). To study habit learning in humans requires thwarting the tendency to memorize the structure of the task by using declarative memory. For example, in the win-stay radial-arm maze task, rats gradually learn the habit of entering a lit arm across many trials. However, humans could learn to enter a lit arm in a single trial by acquiring the declarative fact "light signals food."

We developed a task in which the probabilistic nature of what was to be learned made a declarative memorization strategy ineffective (Knowlton, Squire, and Gluck, 1994). Information learned on single trials is not nearly as useful as information abstracted across many trials. The task was presented to subjects as a weather prediction game in which a series of cues appear on a computer screen, and the subject must guess on each trial whether the cues predict sunshine or rain (figure 53.5). Subjects receive feedback on every trial, and memorization is minimized by requiring subjects to respond within 5 seconds. Although subjects often report that they are simply guessing, they nevertheless show evidence of learning. They begin the task performing at chance (50% correct), and they end up after 50 trials choosing the most associated outcome approximately 70% of the time.

As is the case with habit learning tasks studied in experimental animals, the medial temporal lobe memory system is not necessary for this type of learning. Amnesic patients were able to learn normally across the first 50 trials of this task (Knowlton, Squire, and Gluck, 1994). Further evidence that the probabilistic classification task is an example of habit learning is provided by the fact that patients with Parkinson's disease exhibited significant impairment on this task. In fact, a double dissociation was found between amnesic patients and Parkinson patients. Amnesic patients learned the task but then could not answer questions about the nature of the task and what they had done. Parkinson patients failed to learn the task but were normal at answering questions about the test episode (Knowlton, Mangels, and Squire, 1996; figure 53.6). These data provide evidence for the existence of a neostriatal habit learning system in humans.

ARTIFICIAL GRAMMAR LEARNING   In an artificial grammar learning task, subjects are presented with a

FIGURE 53.5 Appearance of the computer screen at the beginning of the probabilistic classification task. The four cues are shown along with the sun and rain icons. On each trial, one, two, or three of these cues were presented side by side (in 1 of the 14 possible combinations), and individuals predicted whether the outcome would be sunshine or rain by pressing one of two keys. Feedback was provided immediately to signal a correct or incorrect response. A particular cue was associated with the outcome sunshine either 75%, 57%, 43%, or 25% of the time, and thus either 25%, 43%, 57%, or 75% of the time with the other outcome (rain). For each person in the study, the four cues were randomly assigned one of these probabilities. Testing proceeded for 50 trials. (From Knowlton, Squire, and Gluck, 1994.)

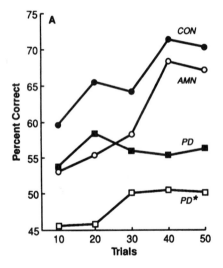
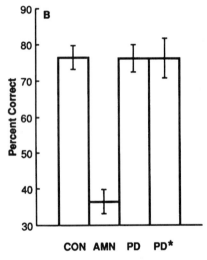

FIGURE 53.6 (A) Performance on the probabilistic classification task by controls (CON, $n = 15$), amnesic patients (AMN, $n = 12$), patients with Parkinson's disease (PD, $n = 20$), and a subgroup of the PD patients with the most severe symptoms (PD*, $n = 10$). None of the groups performed significantly above chance levels (50% correct) on the first block of 10 trials. The controls and amnesic patients gradually learned the cue–outcome associations during 50 trials. The PD patients exhibited no measurable learning across 50 trials. (B) Performance on a declarative memory task that asked about the testing episode. Both PD and PD* groups exhibited entirely normal declarative memory for facts about the testing episode, despite their poor performance on the classification task itself. In contrast, the amnesic patients exhibited a severe impairment in declarative memory for the testing episode but normal performance on the classification test. Brackets show standard errors of the mean. (Reprinted with permission from Knowlton, Mangels, and Squire, 1996. Copyright 1996 American Association for the Advancement of Science.)

series of letter strings that are formed according to a finite-state rule system like the one in figure 53.7. After viewing these letter strings, subjects are told for the first time that the letter strings were formed according to a set of rules and that their task is to decide for a new set of letter strings whether each one is formed by the same set of rules. Even though subjects typically report that they are simply guessing, they are able to classify new letter strings as "grammatical" or "nongrammatical" significantly above chance (see Reber,

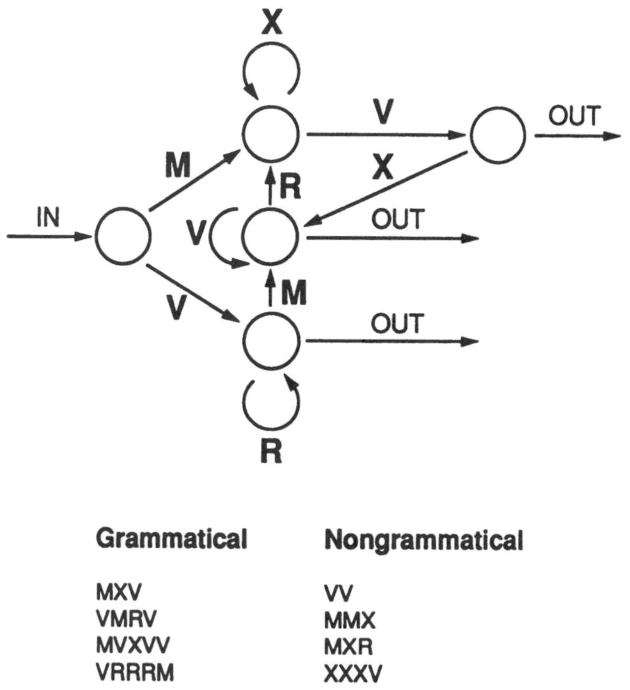

Grammatical

MXV
VMRV
MVXVV
VRRRM

Nongrammatical

VV
MMX
MXR
XXXV

FIGURE 53.7 Artificial grammar learning. Letter strings are generated from a finite state rule system. Grammatical letter strings are formed by traversing the diagram from the in arrow to the out arrows, adding a letter at each transition from one node to the next. Nongrammatical letter strings are formed by introducing an error into a grammatical letter string. (From Knowlton and Squire, 1994.)

1989, for a review). Interestingly, amnesic patients classify items as grammatical or nongrammatical as well as normal subjects, despite being impaired at recognizing the letter strings that were used during training (Knowlton, Ramus, and Squire, 1992; Knowlton and Squire, 1994; 1996; figure 53.8).

The information that is acquired nondeclaratively in an artificial grammar learning task initially was assumed to be some veridical portion of the actual rule system that was used to form the exemplars. However, grammatical and nongrammatical letter strings differ in other ways besides their adherence to grammatical rules. For example, test letter strings that are grammatical are more likely to be composed of letter bigrams and trigrams (chunks) that appeared frequently in the training exemplars than are nongrammatical letter strings. In this sense, grammatical letter strings are considered to have a higher "chunk strength" than nongrammatical items. It turns out that subjects are likely to endorse as grammatical those test items with high chunk strength, regardless of whether the items follow grammatical rules. This finding demonstrates that the information learned about an artificial grammar includes very simple, concrete associations between features of the training items and the test

items (Knowlton and Squire, 1994; Servan-Schreiber and Anderson, 1990).

It also is true that subjects are able to transfer some knowledge about an artificial grammar to letter strings composed of entirely new letters, and they can even accomplish a change in sensory modality from training to testing (Altmann, Dienes, and Goode, 1995). Thus, it appears that subjects are able to learn some abstract information about the artificial grammar, which then allows them to transfer their knowledge to new test items that differ in surface structure. The question of whether learning on this task is abstract or concrete is orthogonal to the question of whether this learning is declarative or nondeclarative. Amnesic patients and normal subjects appear to exhibit the same sensitivity to chunk strength, and they both transfer to stimuli formed using new letters (Knowlton and Squire, 1996). Thus, both abstract and concrete information can be learned nondeclaratively.

Patients with basal ganglia dysfunction can accomplish artificial grammar learning (Knowlton et al., 1996; Reber and Squire, in press). The fact that much of artificial grammar learning is based on concrete, item-specific information about bigrams and trigrams raises the possibility that this type of learning could resemble priming or perceptual learning. For example, it was shown that subjects trained on an artificial grammar are able to perceive grammatical letter strings at a shorter exposure duration than nongrammatical letter strings, demonstrating that the grammatical letter strings enjoy enhanced perceptual fluency (Buchner, 1994). If so, artificial grammar learning may depend on changes within the neocortex.

CATEGORY LEARNING After exposure to several exemplars of a category, subjects are able to classify new items according to whether they are members of that category. In addition, subjects identify the prototype, or central tendency of the category, as a member of the learned category more readily than the items used during training, even when the prototype itself was not presented during training. Such findings originally were interpreted as showing that subjects abstract a prototype from the training exemplars and use the abstracted prototype to classify new items. However, computational work has shown that superior classification of prototypes also occurs when nothing is stored except the characteristics of individual exemplars (Medin and Schaffer, 1978). The prototype usually is similar to a large number of the training items so that it would be strongly endorsed if subjects were making their judgments by making comparisons between each test item and the exemplars stored in memory.

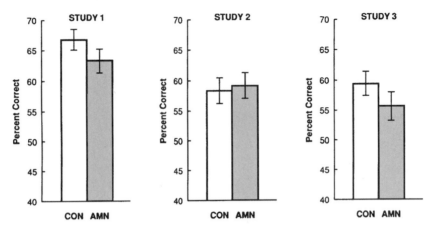

FIGURE 53.8   The results of three separate studies showing normal performance of amnesic patients (AMN) compared with control subjects (CON) on classification tasks based on ar-tificial grammars. Brackets show standard error of the mean. (From Knowlton, Ramus, and Squire, 1992, and Knowlton and Squire, 1994.)

The matter of whether category learning depends on abstracting a prototype or whether it is exemplar based is orthogonal to the issue of whether category learning is declarative or nondeclarative. Support for the idea that category learning is nondeclarative comes from the finding that amnesic patients are able to classify items according to a learned category, despite a severe deficit in recognizing the items that were used to train the category (Knowlton and Squire, 1993). The task was similar to one developed by Posner and Keele (1968). Amnesic patients and control subjects were shown a series of dot patterns formed by distorting a randomly generated pattern that was defined arbitrarily as the prototype of the category. Having seen a series of dot patterns, all of which were distortions of an underlying prototype, subjects then were able to discriminate new dot patterns that belonged to the training category from other dot patterns that did not (figure 53.9). Amnesic patients performed the same as control subjects, even though the patients were severely impaired at recognizing which dot patterns had been presented for training. These data demonstrate that category-level knowledge can be acquired nondeclaratively. Moreover, if category-level knowledge is exemplar based, then it is independent of the exemplar-based information used to support recognition memory.

A challenge to the notion that classification and recognition arise from independently acquired sources of knowledge comes from computational work showing how the performance of amnesic patients could depend on a single knowledge base. The key idea is that the function relating exemplar knowledge and classification performance is nonlinear. If a little exemplar knowledge is all that is needed to achieve near-normal classification performance, then amnesic patients could perform nearly

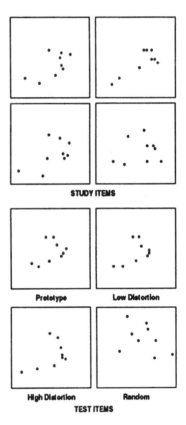

FIGURE 53.9   Examples of the 40 study items and 84 test items used to assess category learning of dot patterns. The study items were all distortions of a prototype dot pattern that was not presented. The test items were new dot patterns, either presentations of the prototype ($n = 4$), low distortions of the prototype ($n = 20$), high distortions of the prototype ($n = 20$), or random dot patterns ($n = 40$). (From Squire and Knowlton, 1995. Copyright 1995 National Academy of Sciences, U.S.A.)

normally on category learning, despite having impaired exemplar knowledge as assessed by recognition memory (Nosofsky and Zaki, 1998).

This possibility has been addressed in two ways. First, amnesic patients and patients with Parkinson's disease demonstrated a double dissociation between classification performance and recognition memory on the probabilistic classification task (figure 53.6). This finding shows that, for this task, knowledge stores appear to be independent. Classification is not simply easier than recognition because the patients with Parkinson's disease actually found classification more difficult than recognition (Knowlton et al., 1996).

Another way to test the independence of classification and recognition is to test the category-learning abilities of a patient who has no detectable declarative memory capacity. If normal category learning occurs in such a patient, then classification performance must be based on nondeclarative knowledge. This set of requirements was met with the severely amnesic patient E.P. (Squire and Knowlton, 1995). After viewing 40 different dot patterns, he classified new dot patterns as well as normal subjects (figure 53.10). Six different tests were given to obtain a robust performance measure. Despite his intact ability to classify new dot patterns, he failed to recognize a single dot pattern as familiar after it had been presented 40 times consecutively. This recognition test also was repeated six different times. It is not clear how to explain these results except to suppose that learning about categories can occur independently of declarative memory.

Category learning, like artificial grammar learning, may resemble priming effects with respect to the importance of perceptual fluency. Categorical dot patterns presented at test are similar to previously viewed patterns and therefore may be processed more rapidly and less effortfully than noncategorical patterns. Accordingly, the prototype of the trained category would benefit the most from perceptual fluency because it should be similar to a larger number of training items than any other individual dot pattern. Similarly, dot patterns that resemble the prototype should benefit more from perceptual fluency than random dot patterns. Neuroimaging data support this idea (Reber, Stark, and Squire, 1998). Volunteers studied 40 dot patterns that were distortions of an underlying prototype and then, while fMRI data were collected, they made yes–no category judgments about new dot patterns. Posterior occipital cortex (areas 17/18) exhibited less activity during processing of the categorical patterns than during processing of noncategorical patterns. This result suggests that category learning and perceptual priming may be based on similar mechanisms. That is, decreased activity in the posterior cortex may occur not only when a stimulus is repeated a second time but also when a stimulus is presented that is similar to one seen earlier.

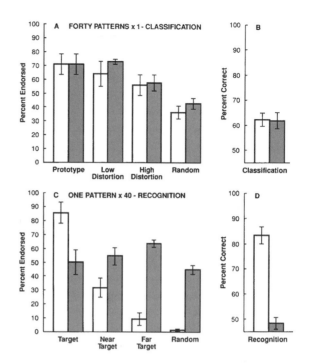

FIGURE 53.10 Performance on parallel tasks of categorization and recognition memory by the severely amnesic patient E.P. and control subjects. All subjects were tested six times on both tests. Brackets show standard errors of the mean. (A) Categorization. Classification of 84 novel dot patterns 5 minutes after studying 40 different training patterns that were distortions of a prototype dot pattern. Control subjects ($n = 4$, open bars) and E.P. (closed bars) performed similarly, endorsing test items as a function of how closely they resembled the prototype of the training category. There were four types of test items (4 prototypes, 20 low distortions, 20 high distortions, and 40 random dot patterns). (B) Overall percentage correct scores for classification. E.P. performed as well as control subjects at categorization. (C) Recognition. Recognition memory 5 minutes after 40 presentations of the same prototype dot pattern. The recognition test was structured identically to the categorization test (A), and only the instructions differed—that is, recognition instead of classification. Thus, at test there were 4 presentations of the prototype target pattern, 20 near targets, 20 far targets, and 40 random patterns. (D) Overall percentage correct scores for recognition. Correct responses consisted of endorsements of the training pattern (the 4 targets) and rejections of the other 80 patterns. E.P. performed at chance. (From Squire and Knowlton, 1995.)

CLASSICAL CONDITIONING Classical conditioning is an extensively studied example of simple associative learning and, in its simplest form, is a quintessential example of nondeclarative memory. The best studied paradigm, delay conditioning of the eyeblink response (conditioned stimulus = tone; unconditioned stimulus = airpuff to the eye) is reflexive and automatic and depends solely on structures below the forebrain, including the cerebellum and associated brainstem circuitry (Thompson and Krupa, 1994). Amnesic patients also exhibit intact

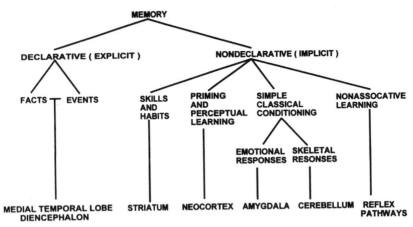

FIGURE 53.11   A taxonomy of mammalian long-term memory systems. The taxonomy lists the brain structures thought to be especially important for each form of declarative and nondeclarative memory. In addition to its central role in emotional learning, the amygdala is able to modulate the strength of both declarative and nondeclarative memory. (From Squire and Zola, 1996.)

acquisition and retention of delay eyeblink conditioning (Daum and Ackerman, 1994; Gabrieli et al., 1995).

In trace conditioning, an interval is interposed between the CS and the US. This form of conditioning requires the hippocampus in both rabbits (Solomon et al., 1986) and humans (McGlinchey-Berroth et al., 1997). Studies of elderly normal subjects (mean age = 67 years) given differential eyeblink conditioning (CS+ vs. CS–) suggest that trace conditioning is hippocampus dependent because it requires the acquisition and retention of conscious knowledge during the course of the conditioning session (Clark and Squire, 1998). Only subjects who became aware of the CS–US relationship acquired differential trace conditioning. The correlation between measures of awareness taken after trace conditioning and conditioning performance itself was $r = 0.74$ and $r = 0.69$ for two different trace-conditioning tasks. In contrast, in two tasks of delay conditioning, awareness bore no relationship to conditioning performance ($r = 0.10$ and $r = 0.16$).

Trace conditioning is dependent on the cerebellum as well as the hippocampus (Woodruff-Pak, Lavond, and Thompson, 1985). Thus, a nondeclarative learning circuit in the cerebellum presumably is required for the generation of the conditioned response. Trace conditioning likely requires the hippocampus (and an interaction between hippocampus and neocortex) because the existence of the trace interval makes it difficult for the cerebellum to process the CS and US in an automatic way. With the help of the hippocampus, the neocortex may develop a representation of the temporal relationship between the stimuli, which then can be available to the cerebellum in a format that the cerebellum can use.

Conclusion

It presently is possible to link particular brain regions and systems to particular kinds of memory (figure 53.11). Unlike declarative memory, nondeclarative memory does not depend on a single brain system. These different forms of nondeclarative memory have different properties and different functions. A common thread is their independence from declarative memory and the fact that they are nonconscious. As the functional neuroanatomy of memory is becoming better understood, it should become possible to discover where and how plasticity is occurring in the different circuits that comprise each memory system. This information also would illuminate a number of long-standing systems-level questions about memory: (1) What is a memory system? (2) How independent are the systems from each other? and (3) When memory loss occurs, is the information simply inaccessible or has it been erased?

REFERENCES

ADOLPHS, R., L. CAHILL, R. SCHUL, and R. BABINSKY, 1997. Impaired declarative memory for emotional material following bilateral amygdala damage in humans. *Learn. Mem.* 291–300.

ALTMANN, G. T. M., Z. DIENES, and A. GOODE, 1995. Modality independence of implicitly learned grammatical knowledge. *J. Exp. Psychol. Learn. Mem. Cogn.* 21:899–912.

ALVAREZ, P., and L. R. SQUIRE, 1994. Memory consolidation and the medial temporal lobe: A simple network model. *Proc. Natl. Acad. Sci. U.S.A.* 91:7041–7045.

BOLHUIS, J. J., C. A. STEWART, and E. M. FOREST, 1994. Retrograde amnesia and memory reactivation in rats with ibotenate lesions to the hippocampus or subiculum. *Q. J. Exp. Psychol.* 47:129–150.

BUCHNER, A., 1994. Indirect effects of synthetic grammar learning in an identification task. *J. Exp. Psychol. Learn. Mem. Cogn.* 20:550–566.

BUNSEY, M., and H. EICHENBAUM, 1996. Conservation of hippocampal memory function in rats and humans. *Nature* 379:255–257.

CERMAK, L. S., and M. O'CONNOR, 1983. The anterograde and retrograde retrieval ability of a patient with amnesia due to encephalitis. *Neuropsychologia* 19:213–224.

CHO, Y. H., D. BERACOCHEA, and R. JAFFARD, 1993. Extended temporal gradient for the retrograde and anterograde amnesia produced by ibotenate entorhinal cortex lesions in mice. *J. Neurosci.* 13:1759–1766.

CHO, Y. H., and R. P. KESNER, 1996. Involvement of entorhinal cortex or parietal cortex in long-term spatial discrimination memory in rats: Retrograde amnesia. *Behav. Neurosci.* 110:436–442.

CLARK, R. E., and L. R. SQUIRE, 1998. Classical conditioning and brain systems: A key role for awareness. *Science* 280:77–81.

CONWAY, M. A., J. M. GARDINER, T. J. PERFECT, S. J. ANDERSON, and G. M. COHEN, 1997. Changes in memory awareness during learning: The acquisition of knowledge by psychology undergraduates. *J. Exp. Psych. Gen.* 126:393–413.

DAMASIO, A. R., P. J. ESLINGER, H. DAMASIO, G. W. VAN HOESEN, and S. CORNELL, 1985. Multimodal amnesic syndrome following bilateral temporal and basal forebrain damage. *Arch. Neurol.* 42:252–259.

DARIAN-SMITH, C., and C. D. GILBERT, 1994. Axonal sprouting accompanies functional reorganization in adult cat striate cortex. *Nature* 354:152–155.

DAUM, I., and H. ACKERMAN, 1994. Frontal-type memory impairment association with thalamic damage. *Int. J. Neurosci.* 77:187–198.

DAVIS, M., 1994. The role of the amygdala in emotional learning. *Int. Rev. Neurobiol.* 36:225–266.

DOYON, J., A. M. OWEN, M. PETRIDES, V. SZIKLAS, and A. C. EVANS, 1996. Functional anatomy of visuomotor skill learning in human subjects examined with positron emission tomography. *Eur. J. Neurosci.* 8:637–648.

EICHENBAUM, H., P. MATHEWS, and N. J. COHEN, 1989. Further studies of hippocampal representation during odor discrimination learning. *Behav. Neurosci.* 103:1207–1216.

EICHENBAUM, H., T. OTTO, and N. J. COHEN, 1994. Two functional components of the hippocampal memory system. *Behav. Brain Sci.* 17:449–518.

GABRIELI, J. D. E., D. A. FLEISCHMAN, M. M. KEANE, S. L. REMINGER, and F. MOREL, 1995. Double dissociation between memory systems underlying explicit and implicit memory in the human brain. *Psychol. Sci.* 6:76–82.

GABRIELI, J. D. E., M. M. KEANE, M. ZARELLA, and R. A. POLDRACK, 1997. Preservation of implicit memory for new associations in global amnesia. *Psychol. Sci.* 8:326–329.

GARDINER, J. M., and A. J. PARKIN, 1990. Attention and recollective experience in recognition memory. *Mem. Cogn.* 18:579–583.

GRAFTON, S. T., E. HAZELTINE, and R. IVRY, 1995. Functional mapping of sequence learning in normal humans. *J. Cogn. Neurosci.* 7:497–510.

HAMANN, S. B., and L. R. SQUIRE, 1995. On the acquisition of new declarative knowledge in amnesia. *Behav. Neurosci.* 109:1027–1044.

HAMANN, S. B., and L. R. SQUIRE, 1997. Intact perceptual memory in the absence of conscious memory. *Behav. Neurosci.* 111:850–854.

HAZELTINE, E., S. T. GRAFTON, and R. IVRY, 1997. Attention and stimulus characteristics determine the locus of motor sequence encoding: A PET study. *Brain* 120:123–140.

JANOWSKY, J. S., A. P. SHIMAMURA, and L. R. SQUIRE, 1989. Source memory impairment in patients with frontal lobe lesions. *Neuropsychologia* 27:1043–1056.

KEANE, M. M., J. D. E. GABRIELI, H. C. MAPSTONE, K. A. JOHNSON, and S. CORKIN, 1995a. Double dissociation of memory capacities after bilateral occipital-lobe or medial temporal-lobe lesions. *Brain* 118:1129–1148.

KEANE, M. M., J. D. E. GABRIELI, J. S. NOLAND, and S. I. MCNEALY, 1995b. Normal perceptual priming of orthographically illegal nonwords in amnesia. *J. Int. Neuropsychol. Soc.* 1:425–433.

KIM, J. J., R. E. CLARK, and R. F. THOMPSON, 1995. Hippocampectomy impairs the memory of recently, but not remotely, acquired trace eyeblink conditioned responses. *Behav. Neurosci.* 109:195–203.

KIM, J. J., and M. S. FANSELOW, 1992. Modality-specific retrograde amnesia of fear. *Science* 256:675–677.

KNOWLTON, B. J., J. A. MANGELS, and L. R. SQUIRE, 1996. A neostriatal habit learning system in humans. *Science* 273:1399–1402.

KNOWLTON, B. J., S. J. RAMUS, and L. R. SQUIRE, 1992. Intact artificial grammar learning in amnesia: Dissociation of classification learning and explicit memory for specific instances. *Psychol. Sci.* 3:172–179.

KNOWLTON, B. J., and L. R. SQUIRE, 1993. The learning of natural categories: Parallel memory systems for item memory and category-level knowledge. *Science* 262:1747–1749.

KNOWLTON, B. J., and L. R. SQUIRE, 1994. The information acquired during artificial grammar learning. *J. Exp. Psychol. Learn. Mem. Cogn.* 20:79–91.

KNOWLTON, B. J., and L. R. SQUIRE, 1995. Remembering and knowing: Two different expressions of declarative memory. *J. Exp. Psychol. Learn. Mem. Cogn.* 21:699–710.

KNOWLTON, B., and L. R. SQUIRE, 1996. Artificial grammar learning depends on implicit acquisition of both rule-based and exemplar-based information. *J. Exp. Psychol. Learn. Mem. Cogn.* 22:169–181.

KNOWLTON, B. J., L. R. SQUIRE, and M. GLUCK, 1994. Probabilistic classification learning in amnesia. *Learn. Mem.* 1:106–120.

KNOWLTON, B. J., L. R. SQUIRE, J. S. PAULSEN, N. SWERDLOW, M. SWENSON, and N. BUTTERS, 1996. Dissociations within nondeclarative memory in Huntington's disease. *Neuropsychology* 10:538–548.

KROLL, N. E. A., A. P. YONELINAS, and R. T. KNIGHT, 1992. The contribution of recollection and familiarity to recognition memory in normals and amnesics. *Soc. Neurosci. Abs.* 23:1580.

LEDOUX, J. E., 1996. *The Emotional Brain.* New York, Simon and Schuster.

MALKOVA, L., and M. MISHKIN, 1997. Memory for the location of objects after separate lesions of the hippocampus and parahippocampal cortex in rhesus monkeys. *Soc. Neurosci. Abs.* 23:12.

MCCLELLAND, J. L., B. L. MCNAUGHTON, and R. C. O'REILLY, 1995. Why there are complementary learning systems in the hippocampus and neocortex: Insights from the successes and failures of connectionist models of learning and memory. *Psychol. Rev.* 102:419–457.

McGlinchey-Berroth, R., M. C. Carrillo, J. D. E. Gabrieli, C. M. Brawn, and J. F. Disterhoft, 1997. Impaired trace eyeblink conditioning in bilateral, medial-temporal lobe amnesia. *Behav. Neurosci.* 111:873–882.

Medin, D. L., and M. M. Schaffer, 1978. Context theory of classification learning. *Psychol. Rev.* 85:207–238.

Milner, B., L. R. Squire, and E. R. Kandel, 1998. Cognitive neuroscience and the study of memory. *Neuron* 20:445–468.

Mishkin, M., B. Malamut, and J. Bachevalier, 1984. Memories and habits: Two neural systems. In *Neurobiology of Learning and Memory*, G. Lynch, J. L. McGaugh, and N. M. Weinberger, eds. New York, Guilford, pp. 65–77.

Mishkin, M., W. A. Suzuki, D. G. Gadian, and F. Vargha-Khadem, 1997. Hierarchical organization of cognitive memory. *Philos. Trans. R. Soc. Lond. B Sci.* 352:1461–1467.

Nadel, L., 1991. The hippocampus and space revisited. *Hippocampus* 1:221–229.

Nissen, M. J., and P. Bullemer, 1987. Attentional requirements of learning: Evidence from performance measures. *Cogn. Psychol.* 19:1–32.

Nosofsky, R., and Zaki, S., 1998. Dissociations between categorization and recognition in amnesics and normals: An exemplar-based interpretation. *Psychol. Sci.* 9:247–255.

Parkin, A. J., and B. M. Walter, 1992. Recollective experience, normal aging, and frontal dysfunction. *Psychol. Aging* 7:290–298.

Parkinson, J. K., E. A. Murray, and M. Mishkin, 1988. A selective mnemonic role for the hippocampus in monkeys: Memory for the location of objects. *J. Neurosci.* 8:4159–4167.

Poldrack, R. A., and N. J. Cohen, 1997. Priming of new associations in reading time: What is learned? *Psychonomic Bull. Rev.* 4:398–403.

Posner, M. I., and S. W. Keele, 1968. On the genesis of abstract ideas. *J. Exp. Psychol.* 77:353–363.

Rauch, S. L., P. J. Whalen, C. R. Savage, T. Curran, A. Kendrick, H. D. Brown, G. Bush, H. C. Breiter, and B. R. Rosen, 1997. Striatal recruitment during an implicit sequence learning task as measured by functional magnetic resonance imaging. *Hum. Brain Mapping* 5:124–132.

Reber, A. S., 1989. Implicit learning and tacit knowledge. *J. Exp. Psychol. Gen.* 118:219–235.

Reber, P. J., B. J. Knowlton, and L. R. Squire, 1996. Dissociable properties of memory systems: Differences in the flexibility of declarative and nondeclarative knowledge. *Behav. Neurosci.* 110:861–871.

Reber, P. J., and L. R. Squire, 1994. Parallel brain systems for learning with and without awareness. *Learn. Mem.* 2:1–13.

Reber, P. J., and L. R. Squire, 1998. Encapsulation of implicit and explicit memory in sequence learning. *J. Cogn. Neurosci.* 10:248–263.

Reber, P. J., and L. R. Squire, in press. Intact learning of artificial grammars and intact category learning by patients with Parkinson's disease. *Behav. Neurosci.*

Reber, P. J., C. E. L. Stark, and L. R. Squire, 1998. Cortical areas supporting category learning identified using fMRI. *Proc. Natl. Acad. Sci. U.S.A.* 95:747–750.

Reed, J. M., and L. R. Squire, 1998. Retrograde amnesia for facts and events: Findings from four new cases. *J. Neurosci.* 18:3943–3954.

Reed, J. M., and L. R. Squire, 1997. Impaired recognition memory in patients with lesions limited to the hippocampal formation. *Behav. Neurosci.* 111:667–675.

Rempel-Clower, N. L., S. M. Zola, L. R. Squire, and D. G. Amaral, 1996. Three cases of enduring memory impairment following bilateral damage limited to the hippocampal formation. *J. Neurosci.* 16:5233–5255.

Ribot, T. 1881. *Les Maladies de la Memoire* [English translation: *Diseases of Memory*]. New York: Appleton-Century-Crofts.

Salmon, D. P., and N. Butters, 1995. Neurobiology of skill and habit learning. *Curr. Opin. Neurobiol.* 5:184–190.

Saunders, R. C., and L. Weiskrantz, 1989. The effects of fornix transection and combined fornix transection, mammillary body lesions and hippocampal ablations on object-pair association memory in the rhesus monkey. *Behav. Brain Res.* 35:85–94.

Schacter, D. L., and R. L. Buckner, 1998. Priming and the brain. *Neuron* 20:185–195.

Schacter, D. L., C. Y. Chiu, and K. N. Ochsner, 1993. Implicit memory: A selective review. *Annu. Rev. Neurosci.* 16:159–182.

Schacter, D. L., J. L. Harbluk, and D. R. McLachlan, 1984. Retrieval without recollection: An experimental analysis of source amnesia. *J. Verbal Learn. Verbal Behav.* 23:593–611.

Schacter, D. L., and E. Tulving, 1994. *Memory Systems 1994*. Cambridge, Mass.: MIT Press.

Scoville, W. B., and B. Milner, 1957. Loss of recent memory after bilateral hippocampal lesions. *J. Neurol. Neurosurg. Psychiatry* 20:11–21.

Servan-Schreiber, E., and J. R. Anderson, 1990. Learning artificial grammars with competitive chunking. *J. Exp. Psychol. Learn. Mem. Cogn.* 16:592–608.

Smith, M. E., 1993. Neurophysiological manifestations of recollective experience during recognition memory judgments. *J. Cogn. Neurosci.* 5:1–13.

Solomon, P. R., E. R. Vander Schaaf, R. F. Thompson, and D. J. Weiz, 1986. Hippocampus and trace conditioning of the rabbit's classically conditioned nictitating membrane response. *Behav. Neurosci.* 100:729–744.

Squire, L. R., 1992. Memory and the hippocampus: A synthesis from findings with rats, monkeys, and humans. *Psychol. Rev.* 99:195–231.

Squire, L. R., and P. Alvarez, 1995. Retrograde amnesia and memory consolidation: A neurobiological perspective. *Curr. Opin. Neurobiol.* 5:169–177.

Squire, L. R., and B. J. Knowlton, 1995. Learning about categories in the absence of memory. *Proc. Natl. Acad. Sci. U.S.A.* 92:12470–12474.

Squire, L. R., J. G. Ojemann, F. M. Miezin, S. E. Peterson, T. O. Videen, and M. E. Raichle, 1992. Activation of the hippocampus in normal humans: A functional anatomical study of memory. *Proc. Natl. Acad. Sci. U.S.A.* 89:1837–1841.

Squire, L. R., and S. M. Zola, 1996. Structure and function of declarative and nondeclarative memory systems. *Proc. Natl. Acad. Sci. U.S.A.* 93:13515–13522.

Squire, L. R., and S. Zola, 1998. Episodic memory, semantic memory, and amnesia. *Hippocampus* 8:205–211.

Suzuki, W. A., and D. G. Amaral, 1994a. Perirhinal and parahippocampal cortices of the Macaque monkey: Cortical afferents. *J. Comp. Neurol.* 350:497–533.

Suzuki, W. A., and D. G. Amaral, 1994b. Topographic organization of the reciprocal connections between the monkey entorhinal cortex and the perirhinal and parahippocampal cortices. *J. Neurosci.* 14:1856–1877.

TENG, E., L. R. SQUIRE, and S. ZOLA, 1997. Different memory roles for the parahippocampal and perirhinal cortices in spatial reversal. *Soc. Neurosci. Abs.* 23:12.

THOMPSON R. F., and D. J. KRUPA, 1994. Organization of memory traces in the mammalian brain. *Annu. Rev. Neurosci.* 17:519–550.

TULVING, E., 1985. How many memory systems are there? *Am. Psychol.* 40:385–398.

TULVING, E., 1989. Remembering and knowing the past. *Ami. Sci.* 77:361–367.

WHITE, N. M. 1997. Mnemonic functions of the basal ganglia. *Curr. Opin. Neurobiol.* 7:164–169.

WIIG, K. A., COOPER, and M. F. BEAR, 1996. Temporally graded retrograde amnesia following separate and combined lesions of the perirhinal cortex and fornix in the rat. *Learn. Mem.* 3:305–312.

WINOCUR, G., 1990. Anterograde and retrograde amnesia in rats with dorsal hippocampal or dorsomedial thalamic lesions. *Behav. Brain Res.* 38:145.

WOODRUFF–PAK, D. S., D. G. LAVOND, and R. F. THOMPSON, 1985. Trace conditioning: Abolished by cerebellar nuclear lesions but not lateral cerebellar cortex aspirations. *Brain Res.* 348:249–260.

ZOLA, S. M., E. TENG, R. E. CLARK, L. STEFANACCI, E. A. BUFFALO, and L. R. SQUIRE, 1998. Impaired recognition memory and simple discrimination learning in monkeys following lesions limited to the hippocampal region made by radio frequency, ischemia, or ibotenic acid. *Soc. Neurosci. Abs.* 24:17.

ZOLA-MORGAN, S., and L. R. SQUIRE, 1990. The primate hippocampal formation: Evidence for a time-limited role in memory storage. *Science* 250:288–290.

ZOLA-MORGAN, S., L. R. SQUIRE, and D. G. AMARAL, 1986. Human amnesia and the medial temporal region: Enduring memory impairment following a bilateral lesion limited to field CA1 of the hippocampus. *J. Neurosci.* 6:2950–2967.

ZOLA-MORGAN, S., L. R. SQUIRE, and D. G. AMARAL, 1989. Lesions of the hippocampal formation but not lesions of the fornix or the mammillary nuclei produce long-lasting memory impairment in monkeys. *J. Neurosci.* 9:898–913.

ZOLA-MORGAN, S., L. R. SQUIRE, and S. J. RAMUS, 1994. Severity of memory impairment in monkeys as a function of locus and extent of damage within the medial temporal lobe memory systems. *Hippocampus* 4:483–495.

54 The Anatomical Bases of Memory

HANS J. MARKOWITSCH

ABSTRACT Memory is a basic function for survival of the individual and the species. Its functions are represented in an extensive number of brain structures. Successful storage of information in memory depends on a number of associated functions, among which emotional embedding is of special importance. The combined application of modern neuroradiological, neuropsychological, and neurological methods, which allow the in vivo study of the healthy as well as of the damaged brain, has resulted in a degree of functional localization that was unpredictable until recently. Psychological insights into classification of memory along the dimensions of time (short-term memory, long-term memory) and contents (episodic memory, knowledge, procedural memory, priming) and the formulation of neuropsychological mechanisms of information transfer, storage, and retrieval have resulted in the specification of both essential and supportive structural conglomerates or combinations that underlie the acquisition, storage, and retrieval of memory. The division between short-term and long-term memory continues to be useful. Short-term memory depends mainly on cortical association regions, particularly within prefrontal and parietal areas. The transfer of episodes and facts for long-term storage in cortical networks depends on the limbic system. Primed information is processed, and probably stored, in unimodal cortical regions, and procedural information is processed, and probably stored, in subcortical areas—in particular, the basal ganglia and the cerebellar structures. Retrieval of information concerning facts and episodes engages frontotemporopolar regions asymmetrically: The left hemisphere dominates retrieval of facts, and the right hemisphere dominates retrieval of episodes.

Contrary to some traditional views, there is little doubt that memory is represented in many widely distributed areas of the brain. This statement is based not only on the existence of multiple forms of memories and on the likely physiological processes of information transmission by means of cellular processes, but also on the complexity of the mnestic information itself. Memorizing information usually is an active and complex process that may include attentive and emotional factors and that depends on the constellations and availability of essential and supporting variables. Nevertheless, it is possible to specify, to a certain degree, anatomical bases of the acquisition and retrieval of various kinds of information in the mammalian and human brain.

The selection of topics covered in this chapter is based on two primary considerations: What is basic to memory, and wherein lie the advances? The basics are given by the organization of memory along the time-related sequence of information processing: acquisition, encoding and consolidation, storage, and retrieval. The advances come primarily from insights obtained by interdisciplinary approaches, including the fields of neurobiology and psychiatry. The more normal findings are the more controversial as well: Are different brain structures involved in information encoding and retrieval? Are there similarities between environmentally induced psychic (psychogenic) forms of amnesia and forms with a clear, measurable anatomical basis? Is memory consolidation time-limited and, if so, what are the limits, and do they depend on the content of the information?

Methods and concepts

As in all fields of science, a discussion of the anatomy of memory also depends on individual points of view of the brain and its evolution and workings. The basic assumptions adopted here include the notions of a common blueprint of neural organization among mammalian species and especially among primates, greater diversity of human memory than that of other species, mnestic information processing nearly everywhere in the brain, and greater centrality of some brain regions than others for collecting, evaluating, storing, and transmitting the information.

The study of brain/memory relations has grown tremendously in the past few years, owing mainly to the expansion in methods used and increase in the species studied. Basic mechanisms of information transfer are investigated in invertebrates with as simple nervous systems as the mushroom bodies of flies or bees (Connolly et al., 1997), and methods currently employed range from electrophysiological recordings through the study of brain-damaged individuals with neuropsychological tests, to the combination of brain imaging and neuromonitoring methods in normal human individuals (Mangun, 1997). This wide spectrum has resulted in a far more complex but much more integrated view of mnestic information processing than propagated in previous times (Lashley, 1950).

A considerable impetus for a refined analysis of brain/memory interrelations was provided by various

HANS J. MARKOWITSCH Physiological Psychology, University of Bielefeld, Bielefeld, Germany

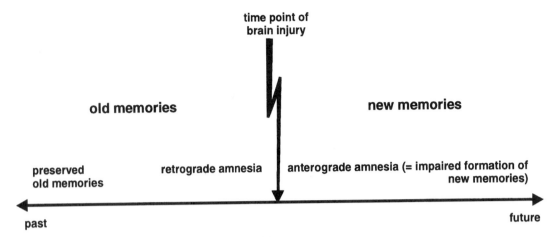

FIGURE 54.1 Possible consequences of brain injury on old and new memories.

proposals of the existence of different content-based memory systems (episodic memory, semantic memory) that augmented the time-related organization of memory. These systems, therefore, constitute a pivotal point in the following discussion. The other major classificatory dimension, exemplified in terms such as short-term memory and long-term memory, can create uncertainties because of lack of agreement among different researchers. Thus, for some, short-term memory encompasses hours, for others minutes, and still for others seconds. In this chapter, short-term memory is assumed to cover time periods of seconds to a few minutes at most, and long-term memory is everything beyond. In addition, work with brain-damaged patients has made another distinction necessary, namely that between memories acquired before brain injury (old or retrograde memories) and memories acquired thereafter (new or anterograde memories) (figure 54.1).

Because the contents-specific subdivisions of memory are of more recent origin, they tend to be more controversial. The discussion in this chapter relies on Tulving's terms (see his chapter), because his classification seems to correspond closely to observations of selective memory loss in patients with different forms of brain damage.

Briefly, long-term memory is subdivided into episodic memory, the knowledge system (frequently named "semantic memory"), procedural memory, and priming. Episodic memory is event or autobiographical memory—that is, memory for context-embedded events of one's own past. The knowledge system refers to context-free facts, procedural memory to various (perceptual, motor, cognitive) skills, and priming to enhanced probability of reidentifying of previously perceived stimuli (or, for conceptual priming, stimuli from a previously encountered set or category).

Amnesia and functional localization

Insights into the processing of memory by the brain traditionally were derived from patients (or animals) with brain lesions. Indeed, memory disorders belong to the most common consequences of brain damage. For a long time, and in the neurological literature until quite recently, the failure or lack of memory was simply termed "amnesia." A single gross distinction was made between global amnesiacs and demented patients. Demented patients were amnesic, but they additionally had marked changes in personality (e.g., patients with Alzheimer's disease). Amnesiacs were seen as having preserved intelligence and short-term memory but impaired long-term memory. This simple dichotomy has been replaced with more complex classificatory schemes because clinical research has produced an overwhelming number of case reports on patients with rather special types of memory impairment. Some patients are labeled amnesiacs when their sole mnestic inability has to do with naming contemporary celebrities (Lucchelli, Muggia, and Spinnler, 1997). Table 54.1 gives some examples of the varieties of amnesia.

The partitioning of amnesia was accompanied by a partitioning of brain loci associated with each form, bringing back the question of functional localization. It is trivial to say that no brain structure acts on its own but rather depends on its inflow and outflow for successful functioning. The popular concept of "disconnection syndrome," which was created some time ago, describes the interruption of a function or ability after focal brain damage without any need to assume that the impaired function or ability was actually "situated" in the damaged area. Nevertheless, one still discerns a strong tendency in the literature to relate specific functions to specific brain regions, a practice that probably is respon-

TABLE 54.1

TABLE 54.1

Examples of amnesic states

Anterograde amnesia	The failure to store new memories long-term
Retrograde amnesia	The failure to retrieve (or ecphorize) old memories
Transient global amnesia	Anterograde (and possibly, although to a lesser degree, retrograde) amnesia for a time period of 1 day or less
Psychogenic amnesia	Retrograde amnesia without (obvious) brain damage, usually as a consequence of strong psychic pressure(s)
Functional amnesia	Retrograde (and in rare instances, also anterograde) amnesia of differing, but at least partly psychic, origin
Topographical amnesia	Inability to remember or retrieve loci in space
Color amnesia	Inability to remember or retrieve the names of colors
Autotopagnosia	An orientation disturbance for the own body or parts of it
Anomia	Inability to remember or retrieve names
Anosognosia	Inability to recognize own illness-dependent functional losses
Reduplicative paramnesia	The phenomenon of being convinced that a person, a place, or an object exists twice
Prosopagnosia	Inability to recognize faces

sible for a good deal of confusion in the field. All serious students of memory pathology would do well to pay careful attention to Chow's (1967) caveats on interpreting interdependencies between the brain and behavior. He proposed that "if a brain lesion fails to affect a learning task, it cannot be stated that this part of the brain is unimportant in normal animals. Second, if the lesion does influence performance of the task, it does not necessarily mean that it is the only neural structure involved. Third, the aim of the ablation methods is in a way never attainable, for it throws away the object (a region of the brain) one wishes to study" (p. 708).

Brain damage and memory

Following are examples of relations between brain damage and aspects of memory. The emphasis is on anatomical networks that are important for different aspects of memory (Mesulam, 1998).

Most of our knowledge on brain/memory interrelations stems from the careful anatomical and neuropsychological study of brain-damaged patients. Modeling of human brain damage by inducing brain lesions in animals has provided additional or confirmatory insights. From the earliest days of scientific brain research, observations of behavioral alterations of brain damaged subjects have constituted nature's teaching book (Markowitsch, 1992). For the field of memory, some kinds of brain damage that occurred regularly as a consequence of a disease process served to establish the basis for functional localization. The Korsakoff syndrome is one of these disease processes that is accompanied regularly by severe memory deterioration, although patients' general intelligence may be largely preserved. The anatomical basis of the syndrome—degeneration of diencephalic nuclei, the mamillary bodies, and the medial thalamic region—already was suspected

around the turn of the 19th century, and this view generally has been confirmed (Mair, Warrington, and Weiskrantz, 1979), leading to the creation of the concept of "medial diencephalic amnesia."

Another impetus for the study of amnesia came from therapeutically induced brain surgery. H.M., the most intensely studied patient, received in 1953 a bilateral resection of major portions of his medial temporal lobes with the consequence of persistent anterograde amnesia (Scoville and Milner, 1957). Again, the historical roots of memory's connection with the hippocampus and the surrounding structures can be traced back to the earliest days of our science (von Bechterew, 1900; Markowitsch, 1992). The study of the hippocampus and memory has continued relentlessly to this day. The most recent observations have pointed to a special role of the hippocampal formation in episodic memory acquisition (Vargha-Khadem et al., 1997). The set of cases with this form of pathology is named "medial temporal lobe amnesia."

More recently, damage to regions in the basal forebrain, usually caused by rupture of the anterior communicating artery, also was found to result in amnesia (Damasio et al., 1985), giving rise to the concept of "basal forebrain amnesia."

What unifies the different forms of amnesia is the fact that all of the damaged regions belong to the limbic system, or at least to its "expanded" form (Nauta, 1979). Consequently, the limbic system can be seen as playing a crucial role in memory processing—a conclusion that also makes good sense from an evolutionary point of view (Markowitsch, 1999). The limbic system, originally called the smell brain or rhinencephalon (Herz and Engen, 1996), was critical for survival of the individual and the species at early stages in evolution. Later, it served in more general ways for the binding and preservation of emotions and memories (Papez, 1937; Markowitsch, 1994).

Nonlimbic structures have had a less clear-cut role in memory. Damage to neocortical regions was seen as causing either quite restricted forms of amnesia, such as an inability to remember or retrieve names or faces (e.g., Reinkemeier et al., 1997), or—in its more widely spread form, as in Alzheimer's disease—a general intellectual decline, including that in memory. The memory decline in Alzheimer's disease typically is more complete than in amnesia because it also is affected by cortical damage and includes impairment in short-term memory (Belleville, Peretz, and Malenfant, 1996), anterograde and retrograde, episodic and semantic memory (Beatty et al., 1988; Brustrom and Ober, 1996; Daum et al., 1996; Greene, Baddeley, and Hodges, 1996). Depending on the particular combination of damaged cortical surfaces, the patterns of symptoms may shift somewhat, and amnesia is nearly always the core deficit. Pick's disease or frontotemporal dementia represents another example in this category (Knopman et al., 1989; Neary and Snowden, 1996). It must be mentioned, however, that many forms of cortical dementia, and especially Alzheimer's disease, include damage to limbic structures as well, above all of those including and surrounding the hippocampus (Braak and Braak, 1997). Therefore, it seems logical that Hassing and Bäckman (1997) found that cortical dementia diseases particularly affected the ability to transfer information from temporary to permanent storage.

Damage to nonlimbic subcortical structures causes other syndrome pictures in which memory complaints occur less frequently and are less severe. However, again stimulated by the appearance of contents-based memory subdivisions, investigations during the past decade have begun to reveal close relations between severe procedural memory impairments and Parkinson's disease and Huntington's chorea. Conventional neurology had regarded both diseases (and more generally, damage to the basal ganglia) as resulting in major motor impairments, rigidity, tremor, and akinesia for parkinsonism, and choreiform movements for Huntington's chorea—this despite the fact that it was known that (for both forms) progression of the disease process may lead to dementia ("subcortical dementia," "frontostriatal dementia"; Darvesh and Freedman, 1996; Bäckman et al., 1997). Paralleling the effects of basal ganglia damage, damage to the cerebellum also has been found to result in procedural memory impairments.

To complete this short overview, cortical regions surrounding primary sensory regions, especially the belt zones of unimodal nonprimary cortices, are coming to be seen as controlling priming forms of memory (Nielsen-Bohlman et al., 1997; Ochsner, Chiu, and Schacter, 1994; Seeck et al., 1997). However, a study by Zhang, Begleiter, and Porjesz (1997), which recorded event-related potentials associated with priming of visual and verbal material, found, for normal subjects, the expected occipitotemporal activation (bilaterally, with some preponderance to the right) for the visual but not the word material. For the word material, a frontal activation (current source analysis), together with some less prominent posterior sources, was observed. Thus, as far as priming is concerned, data that would allow firm inferences and would include all modalities still are lacking (but see chapter 58).

Brain structures implicated in information acquisition, storage, and retrieval

Processing of information usually is induced by environmental stimulation but also may be created internally, that is, from within the brain. For both ways, the principles of divergence and convergence regulate information transmission, distribution, and focusing. Most of the information is transferred from the peripheral sensory (recipient) organs by means of subcortical nuclei to cortical areas. Immediate processing of received information is referred to as working memory (see chapter 50) and is regarded to occur cortically as well, with prefrontal and parietal regions participating. Long-term memory has been more difficult to localize or to correlate with brain regions because both its processing and storage are more diverse. The transfer from short-term to long-term storage probably is the most delicate stage and is related widely to an agglomerate of subcortical and allocortical structures, named the limbic system. Following is an overview of regional networks involved in information encoding, storage, and retrieval. Kornhuber's scheme (figure 54.2) provides an instructive and easy-to-follow model of a possible brain circuitry engaged in information transmission from sensory input to final storage as engram. An added strength of the scheme is that it points to the importance of motivational and emotional factors for memory processing.

AFFECT AND MEMORY Affect is an important dimension for memory-encoding storage and retrieval, and many patients with memory problems have problems in affect as well. Certain structures within the limbic system, especially the septum and the amygdala, stand out against most of the others when it comes to affective information modulation. The amygdala (1) is connected with the hippocampus and (2) represents one of three components of the so-called basolateral limbic circuit (Sarter and Markowitsch, 1985). Damage to the amygdala results in a flattening of emotions (similar to

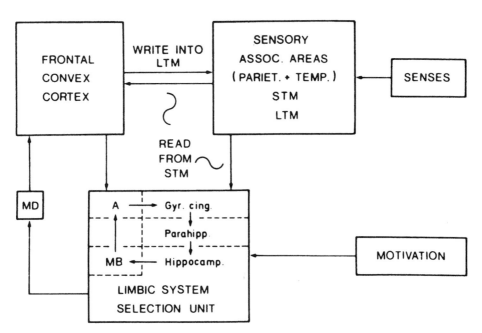

FIGURE 54.2   Kornhuber's (1988) scheme of memory processing emphasizes the posterior association areas of the cerebral cortex as involved in short-term memory (STM) processing, the limbic system (Papez circuit) as involved in the transmission of information from short-term to long-term memory (LTM), and the cortical regions are assumed to basically be the storage places of successfully formed engrams. Interpreting this model liberally, it can be assumed that information enters the brain via the senses, that largely internally created motivational and emotional stimuli interact with the preprocessed sensory information within the "limbic system selection unit," and that information which "harmonizes" or "synchronizes" with the motivational/emotional state of the organism and which can be further synchronized or associated with already existing (and matching) engrams is transmitted for permanent storage. Note that this scheme (1) holds principally only for episodic memories, (2) says nothing about information retrieval, and (3) gives a very important role to the thalamic mediodorsal nucleus (Markowitsch, 1988). *Abbreviations*: A, anterior thalamic nucleus; Gyr cing, cingulate gyrus; Hippocamp, hippocampus; MB, mammillary body; MD, mediodorsal thalamic nucleus; Parahipp, parahippocampal region. (Reproduced from figure 4 of Kornhuber, 1988, with permission.)

that seen in the Klüver-Bucy syndrome, which occurs after amygdaloid and some additional temporal lobe damage); patients with bilateral amygdala damage may no longer be able to differentiate successfully between relevant and irrelevant information. They consequently fail to successfully encode pertinent new material (Cahill et al, 1995; Markowitsch et al., 1994). Similar deficits may occur after septal damage, which seems to lead to an exaggerated affective engagement that also blurs successful information discrimination and selection (von Cramon and Markowitsch, in press; von Cramon, Markowitsch, and Schuri, 1993).

The basolateral thalamic circuit, composed of the amygdala, the mediodorsal nucleus, and area subcallosa (figure 54.3) most likely supports the action of the Papez circuit by controlling and selecting information of major relevance to the organism. In this sense, it feeds the motivational–emotional content into Kornhuber's Limbic System Selection Unit (figure 54.2). Interruption of this loop may occur after capsular genu infarcts and results in profound memory disturbances (Markowitsch et al., 1990) that have been interpreted as "contextual amne-

sia" (Schnider et al., 1996). A somewhat more extended circuit for mood regulation was proposed by Soares and Mann (1997), who included striatal and ventral pallidar structures and the cerebellum as well.

There also is some evidence that altered affective states that may be caused by prolonged stress or by the appearance of a major stress event reminding a person of a similar one experienced previously (e.g., a life-threatening situation) may change the brain's biochemistry—release and binding of glucocorticoids or of gamma amino butyric acid (GABA) agonists—and may result in an inability to successfully store new information: the mnestic block syndrome (Markowitsch, 1997a; Markowitsch et al., 1998; Sapolsky, 1996). In a few instances, even permanent brain damage in the hippocampus has been found as the likely result of such stressful events (Bremner et al., 1995, 1997).

Of the relevant cases that have been reported, that of a young man who for approximately 8 months lost his ability to form new memories for permanent storage is most interesting (Markowitsch et al., 1998). The patient had seen a fire in his house, and this event seems to have

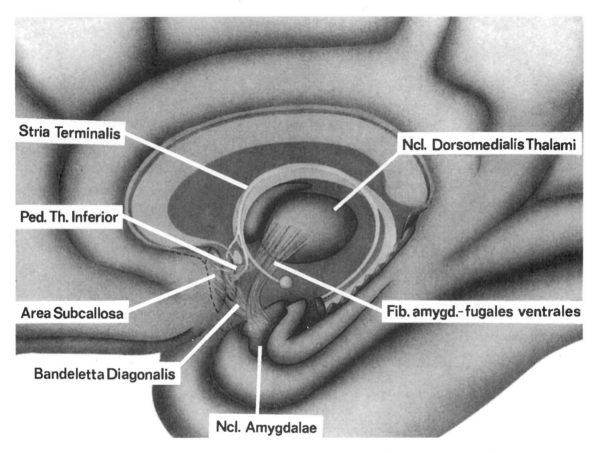

Stria Terminalis

Ped. Th. Inferior

Area Subcallosa

Bandeletta Diagonalis

Ncl. Dorsomedialis Thalami

Fib. amygd.-fugales ventrales

Ncl. Amygdalae

FIGURE 54.3   The basolateral limbic circuit. Amygdala, mediodorsal thalamic nucleus, and area subcallosa are linked with each other by distinct fiber projections, namely the ventral amygdalofugal pathway, the inferior thalamic peduncle, and the bandeletta diagonalis. Additionally mentioned is the stria terminalis, which connects the amygdala and the hypothalamus. (Reproduced from figure 5.3 of von Cramon, 1992, with permission.)

induced a shock (mnestic block) condition resulting in anterograde and partial (for the past 6 six years of his life) retrograde memory loss. When he was 4 years old, the patient had seen a man burning to death in his car. Although conventional neuroradiological investigations failed to show any deviations from normal, an FDG-PET (positron emission tomography with [18]fluorodeoxyglucose) revealed major hypometabolic in zones of the medial and anterolateral temporal cortex and the medial diencephalon (figure 54.4; see color plate 33). The hypometabolic zones can be assumed to correspond to the mnestic deficits.

MEMORY ACQUISITION   Memory acquisition usually is divided into the sensory uptake of information, its initial encoding, and further consolidation. Of these time-related subdivisions, sensory uptake is easiest to specify because it refers simply to the engagement of the appropriate sensory receptors, for example, rods and cones in the retina and hair cells in the cochlea, and to the further transmission up to the cortex. There is some controversy as to whether memory encoding and memory consoli-

dation should be viewed as separate processes or whether they in fact constitute a single one (Cermak, 1989, 1997). Usually, however, encoding is viewed as the more initial part of information transmission and consolidation as the more advanced part.

Baddeley (1997) has discussed elaborately the separability of the short-term and long-term memory systems. Although he appeared to be inclined to assume their separation, he did not settle the issue but instead introduced his more complex (multicomponent) working memory model that might be seen as a replacement of the short-term memory system but still adheres to the basic dichotomy. Because this chapter deals with the neuroanatomy of memory and—as also is acknowledged by Baddeley (1997)—especially cases with brain damage, which speak for the existence of a short-term and a long-term store that "could be separately and differentially impaired in different types of patient" (p. 48), the following arguments are based on assuming their existence (see also confirmatory evidence obtained under amytal injection in epileptic patients, Rouleau et al., 1989).

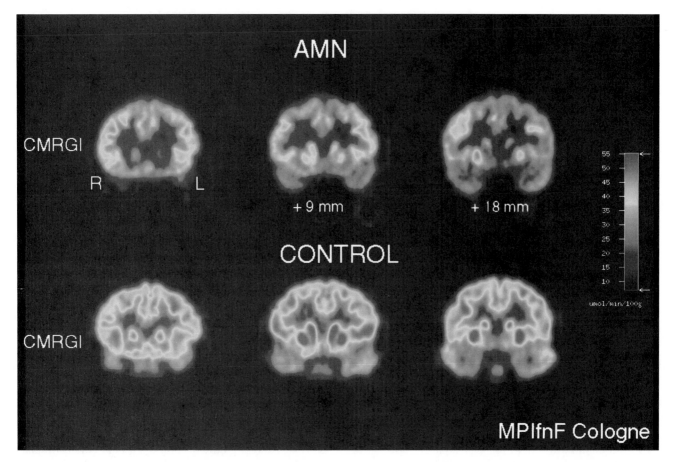

FIGURE 54.4 FDG-PET–based coronal sections from anterior to posterior (left to right) through the brains of a patient with a shock-caused amnesic condition (Markowitsch et al., 1998) (top row) and a control subject (bottom row). Note the reduction in cerebral metabolism in widespread cortical and subcortical areas in the patient, compared with a control subject's brain at corresponding levels. A regions-of-interest analysis of the patient's regional cerebral glucose metabolism revealed that especially his temporal lobes and his thalami showed a more than 20% reduction compared with those of age-matched men. (Modified after figure 1 of Markowitsch et al., 1998.)

While at first seen as outstandingly exceptional, the number of reported cases with selective short-term memory impairments is increasing (Butterworth, Cipolotti, and Warrington, 1996; Markowitsch et al., in press; Shallice and Warrington, 1970). Usually, the damage is found in the angular gyrus region of the left parietal cortex (figure 54.5; see color plate 34), which indicates that this cortical area is involved centrally in short-term memory processing and therefore in the initial level of information acquisition. Especially revealing are the results from dynamic imaging studies that suggest a role of laterodorsal prefrontal regions in working memory (Casey et al., 1995; Manoach et al., 1997). ("Working memory" can be defined as a system for temporarily holding and manipulating information; Baddeley, 1997.) Consequently, it seems reasonable to assume that both anterior and posterior parts of the association cortex are engaged in the temporary or transient storage of information.

This statement, however, has to be qualified further by reserving it for those forms of information that are ac-quired explicitly or consciously, that is, as episodic memories. For the other forms of information, a more gradual acquisition process, along the lines of Craik and Lockhart's (1972) depth of processing idea, may be assumed to exist. For these forms, which may include conditioning, cerebellar, amygdaloid, and also various cerebral cortical regions, have been named as relevant (e.g., Knowlton, Mangels, and Squire, 1996; Squire, Knowlton, and Musen, 1993; Thompson and Kim, 1996).

MEMORY TRANSFER   The most important part of information processing is its transfer into long-term memory. In Kornhuber's model (figure 54.2), it is assumed that the so-called Limbic System Selection Unit reads the information from the short-term store and selects appropriate portions for transfer into the long-term store. This idea of the limbic system being the central processor for information transfer has a long tradition. Its forefathers may be seen in Papez (1937) and Hebb (1949). Papez

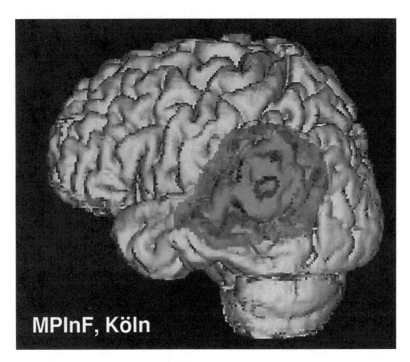

FIGURE 54.5 Three-dimensional reconstruction of the left hemisphere revealing the tumor-caused brain damage (including the penumbra region) of a patient with major short-term memory impairments. The case has been described by Markowitsch and associates (in press).

had the idea of a circuit within limbic structures, named Papez circuit after him (figures 54.6 and 54.7), and Hebb assumed that information has to circulate within certain brain regions before being transferred for long-term storage.

Although the term *limbic system* is somewhat unclear and is defined differently by differing authors (see Markowitsch, 1999), there is general agreement with respect to its core structures. As aforementioned (see section on brain damage and memory), the region of the medial temporal lobe (which contains the hippocampal formation), the region of the medial diencephalon (including the medial thalamic and the mamillary nuclei), and possibly also the basal forebrain region are included. A number of strong and in part bidirectional fiber bundles interconnect the structures of all three regions (cf. figure 54.6). This arrangement brings up the question of whether the aforementioned three regional systems should be regarded as a unity or as three separable blocks. Squire (1995) suggested that the temporal and the diencephalic blocks probably constitute a single memory system and that evidence for different functional contributions may be difficult to demonstrate.

From an anatomical point of view, it seems justified to embed them and even a number of additional structures in one major memory processing system. Braak and colleagues (1996) have delineated an extensive scheme that represents the components of such an all-inclusive cir-

cuitry (figure 54.8; see color plate 35). It seems likely, however, that even the original regional systems (medial temporal, medial diencephalic, basal forebrain) make different functional contributions. Again, the anatomy can be drawn on to make this suggestion: the mediodorsal nucleus is interconnected most intensely with the prefrontal cortex, the basal forebrain has numerous cholinergic connections with widespread cortical regions, and the hippocampal region is associated widely with the temporal cortex. Insight, the tendency to confabulate, retrograde amnesia, conscious reflection, affective involvement, time perception, and susceptibility to interference are examples of the kinds of features that may differ between the three regional blocks (von Cramon, Markowitsch, and Schuri, 1993; Markowitsch, von Cramon, and Schuri, 1993; Vargha-Khadem et al., 1997).

Nevertheless, bilateral and largely complete damage to the major components (including pathways) of the medial temporal and the medial diencephalic system usually results in persistent amnesia. Each of these structures therefore can be thought of as representing a bottleneck structure through which information has to pass for successful consolidation. Bilateral damage to any of these structures typically results in a disconnection syndrome, which is termed amnesia. There are, however, some exceptions to this inability that question the universal involvement of the limbic system in (episodic) memory transfer. Patient H. M., for example, learned

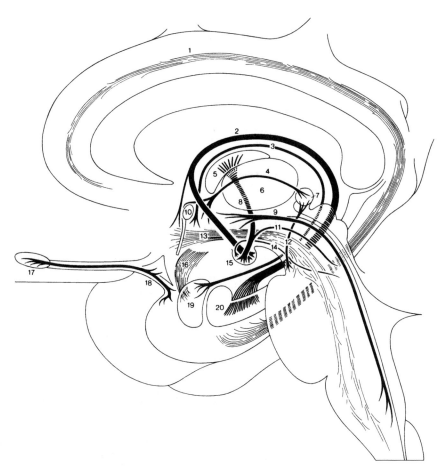

FIGURE 54.6 The major pathways of the limbic system and the rhinencephalon. 1, cingulum; 2, fornix; 3, stria terminalis; 4, stria medullaris thalami; 5, nucleus anterior thalami; 6, nucleus medialis thalami; 7, nuclei habenulae; 8, tractus mammillothalamicus; 9, fasciculus longitudinalis dorsalis; 10, commissura anterior; 11, tractus mammillotegmentalis; 12, tractus habenulointerpeduncularis; 13, fasciculus telencephalicus medialis; 14, pedunculus corporis mammillaris; 15, corpus mammillare; 16, ansa peduncularis; 17, bulbus olfactorius; 18, stria olfactoria lateralis; 19, corpus amygdaloideum; 20, hippocampus. (Reproduced from figure 191 of Nieuwenhuys, Voogt, and van Huizen, 1988, with permission.)

the shooting of President Kennedy, the death of his parents, or a melody he loved. These exceptions and some additional arguments have led some researchers to postulate the existence of a nonlimbic, neocortical memory encoding system that is, however, slow and quite limited in its capacity to result in permanent information storage and that also seems to be more prone to encoding of frequently repeated facts than of episodes (Kapur, 1994; McClelland, 1994).

Memory storage

There is little concrete evidence concerning the actual storage of information in the human brain. Animal research indicates that successful information acquisition is correlated with changes in neuronal morphology: synaptic enlargement, dendritic spine growth, expansion of the neuropil, and the like. (Before successful acquisition and morphological alterations, bioelectrical changes such as long-term potentiation/depression may represent the encoding/consolidation processes.) Furthermore, the evidence of successful retrieval of old information in patients with complete bilateral damage of one of the limbic bottleneck structures assumed to transfer information for long-term storage suggests that none of these (e.g., medial thalamus, hippocampal region) is a long-term memory storage place. Instead, frequently proposed loci for long-term storage of information are the cerebral cortical areas and especially the association or polymodal regions–Kornhuber's scheme (figure 54.2) is an example (Eichenbaum, 1997).

Although it is quite likely that the cerebral cortex is indeed the major storage place for the episodic as well as for the knowledge and the priming systems (neuronal capacity alone favors it [Schaefer, 1960] and also the apparent trace decay in patients with widespread cortical damage [e.g., patients with Alzheimer's disease]), it still is unknown whether singular neuronal modules or

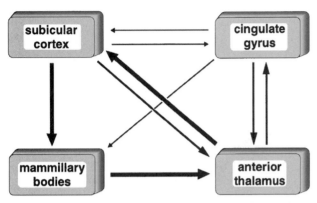

FIGURE 54.7 The Papez circuit interconnecting the hippo-campal formation by means of the (postcommissural) fornix to the mammillary bodies, these by means of the mammillothalamic tract (or tractus Vicq d'Azyr) to the anterior thalamus; the anterior thalamus with its cortical projection targets reaches the cingulate gyrus, and the subicular part of the hippocampal formation, and the cingulum fibers in addition project back from the cingulate gyrus into the hippocampal formation. (The precommissural fornix in addition provides a bidirectional connection between the hippocampal formation and the basal forebrain.) (Adapted from Irle and Markowitsch, 1982.)

widespread neuronal networks represent particular bits of information. It is not even known in which form and complexity (e.g., singular bits, large-scale agglomerates) an event or item is represented or whether glial cells also might play a role in representation. Furthermore, it is an unsolved question whether cortical regions alone are able to represent an event or whether they might need assistance by emotion-coding regions such as the amygdala or the septum.

Here, it is assumed that information is represented in widespread networks (Abeles, 1992; Bartlett and John, 1973; Fuster, 1997) that nevertheless may have a modular organization (Szentagothai, 1983) as their basis. For the storage of procedural memories, components within the basal ganglia and the cerebellum most likely are relevant. Squire and associates (1993) assumed that storage of skills and habits might occur "at the synapses between cortical neurons and neurons in the neostriatum" (p. 482) (see also Knowlton, Mangels, and Squire, 1996).

MEMORY RETRIEVAL Memory retrieval refers to the use of available stored information. In fact, as pointed out by Tulving (1983) and also evident from the results on "false memories" (Loftus, 1998), environmental conditions determine to a considerable degree the retrieval of information. Tulving (1983) therefore reintroduced the term "ecphory" to describe the process by which retrieval cues interact with stored information so that an image or a representation of the information in question appears. One question is whether in the normal (non-damaged) brain, the retrieval of information occurs in-

dependent of the encoding regions (limbic system) or activates them as well. Because every form of retrieval necessarily leads to simultaneous re-encoding of the just-retrieved information, dynamic imaging studies up to now could not solve this question (e.g., Fink et al., 1996).

A number of findings (e.g., ecphory under hypnosis, ecphory with strong retrieval cues) demonstrates that the nervous system has stored enormous amounts of information of which only minor parts are constantly available without appropriate retrieval cues. The idea that the recall of information may depend on brain regions other than those involved in long-term transfer is a recent one, having arisen only in the last decade. It was prompted by clinical observations of patients with focal brain damage outside of the classical limbic regions who had lost old memories, but who had a preserved ability to successfully form new memories (Kapur et al., 1992; Markowitsch et al., 1993; O'Connor et al., 1992). Shortly thereafter, Tulving and coworkers (1994) formulated their HERA-model (HERA = Hemispheric-Encoding-Retrieval-Asymmetry) on the basis of PET results in normal subjects. They proposed a differentially more prominent left-hemispheric prefrontal activation for memory encoding and a differentially more prominent right-hemispheric one for retrieval. Episodic memories of a more emotional content and of yearlong remoteness have been found to engage temporopolar regions to an even higher extent than prefrontal ones (Fink et al., 1996; Markowitsch, 1997b; Markowitsch, Thiel, et al., 1997) (figure 54.9; see color plate 36).

A combination of inferolateral prefrontal and temporopolar regions consequently was assumed to trigger the retrieval of stored old memories. (Thompson-Schill et al., 1997, made the suggestion that it might not be retrieval per se, but the selection among competing alternatives.) For patients with normal left-hemispheric language representation, it was proposed that mainly right-hemispheric (but also some left-hemispheric) damage of this regional combination results in profound retrograde amnesia for episodic (autobiographical) material (Markowitsch, 1995); the reverse pattern with mainly left-hemispheric damage should result in retrograde amnesia for information of the knowledge system. This hypothesis essentially was confirmed by results from brain-damaged patients (e.g., Calabrese et al., 1996; De Renzi, Liotti, and Nichello, 1987; Kroll et al., 1997).

A special form of the mnestic block syndrome also may occur in memory recall: Patients with psychogenic or functional amnesia (De Renzi et al., 1997) have a block to retrieve stored information of autobiographical character without corresponding brain

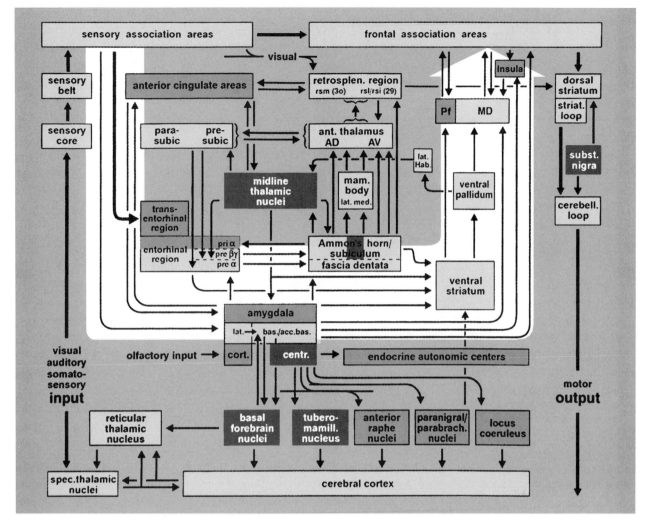

FIGURE 54.8 The limbic loop and additional structures are shown in detail. The amygdala integrates exteroceptive sensory data with interoceptive stimuli from autonomic centers. A large number of amygdalar efferents terminate in nuclei, regulating endocrine and autonomic functions. In addition, the amygdala generates efferent connections to all nonthalamic nuclei that in a nonspecific manner project on the cerebral cortex. *Abbreviations*: ant. thalamus AD and AV = anterodorsal and anteroventral nuclei of the anterior thalamus; cerebell. loop = cerebellar loop; lat. Hab. = lateral habenula; lat., bas., acc. bas., cort., and centr. = lateral, basal, accessory-basal, cortical, and central amygdalar nuclei; mam. body lat. and med. = lateral and medial nuclei of the mamil- lary body; MD = mediodorsal thalamic nucleus; paranigral/ parabrach. = paranigral and pigmented parabrachial nuclei; parasubic and presubic = parasubiculum and presubiculum; Pf = parafascicular nucleus; Pri-α, Pre-β, Pre-γ, Pre-α = layers of the entorhinal region; retrosplen, region rsm (30) and rsl/ rsi (29) = medial retrosplenial area (Brodmann's area 30) and lateral and intermediate retrosplenial areas (Brodmann's area 29) of the retrosplenial region; spec. thalamic nuclei = specific projection nuclei of the thalamus; striat. loop = striatal loop; subst. nigra = substantia nigra; tuberomamill. = tuberomamil- lary nucleus. (After figure 5 of Braak et al., 1996, with permis- sion from Decker Periodicals and Dr. H. Braak.)

damage (Markowitsch, 1996). PET results from a case reported by Markowitsch, Fink, and colleagues (1997) suggest, however, that their brain function may deviate from that of nonamnesic (normal) individuals and may show a brain activation pattern that indicates that such patients indeed fail to ecphorize bio- graphical material because their brain does not en- gage the proper right-hemispheric frontotemporal trigger structures.

Conclusions

In relation to what was known about the anatomy of memory 5 years ago, it seems reasonable to propose that the basic framework has not been changed. Thus, the differentiation between short- and long-term memory and that between content-based memory subdivisions still motivates questions of functional anatomy, and the study of memory impairment caused by brain damage

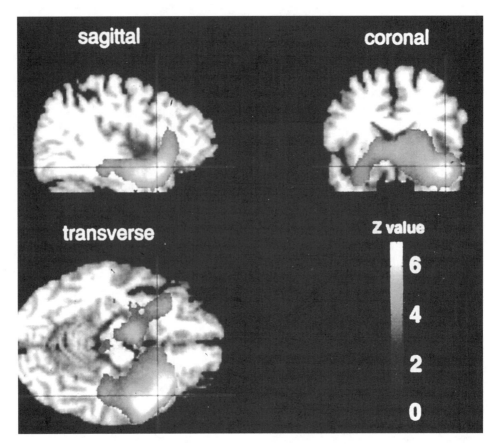

FIGURE 54.9 Positron-emission-tomography (PET) representations of brain activations during ecphorizing affect-laden autobiographical memories (displayed on top of arbitrary magnetic resonance images of sagittal, coronal, and transverse brain images). The red cross-hair indicates the local maximum within the area of activation. The color bar indicates the Z statistics achieved. To obtain these activation patterns, PET activations during ecphorizing biographical information from an unknown individual were subtracted from those obtained during ecphorizing events from the tested subjects' own biography. Note that the activations are predominantly on the right. (Reproduced with permission from figure 2 of Fink et al., 1996.)

also follows these dimensions. What is new is the enormous expansion of converging data obtained with functional imaging studies and by descriptions of single cases (see, e.g., the newly established journal *Neurocase*, which specializes on single cases). Furthermore, there currently is a much higher degree of convergence from a wider range of disciplines than a few years ago. For example, the biologically oriented psychiatry recently has provided a lot of evidence for brain changes that are related to observed memory impairments. Similarities between environmentally related ("psychic") and organically caused brain changes and amnesia are documented increasingly. Animal research is supportive in this endeavor from various perspectives.

The medial temporal lobe still is in the center of memory research. Questions concern the contributions of individual regions—for example, the hippocampus proper or the entorhinal cortex—in information processing; here research with nonhuman animals is used to unravel the microcircuitry of the kind that patient studies usually cannot provide (Murray, 1996). Also, direct injections of neuroactive drugs are used to attack questions such as that on the independence of time-related memory subsystems (Izquierdo et al., 1998). Time and the hippocampus is another issue that is hotly debated: What is the duration of consolidation and how necessary is the hippocampus for long-term retrieval of information? Although much evidence speaks for a time-limited role of the hippocampal region (Knowlton and Fanselow, 1998), exceptionally more extreme positions have recently been proposed (Moscovitch and Nadel, 1998). Finally, the role of the hippocampal formation for different subsystems of content-related memory (episodic vs. semantic memory) is in dispute (Vargha-Khadem et al., 1997; Tulving and Markowitsch, 1998).

The representation of memory in the human brain (as well as its loss—forgetting) remains one of the major riddles of neuroscience. Unraveling the circuits, networks and neurophysiological actions involved in the processes of information input and output helps to identify the brain's mechanisms for information storage. A disclosure of the relevant structures and fiber tracts engaged in information transfer also helps to select methods for treatment of memory disorders after brain damage. The detection of commonalities and differences in memory disturbances after various forms of focal brain damage elucidates the degree to which brain regions work in a modular and complementing form and to what degree they are part of a common network whose damage at one point leads to disconnection and major memory failure. The combined application of modern neuropsychological, neurological, and neuroradiological methods provides opportunities in this endeavor that would have been classified science fiction even a few years ago.

ACKNOWLEDGMENTS This work was supported by grants from the German Research Council (DFG; Ma 795/24-1+2, Ma 795/27-1, and He 21/1).

REFERENCES

ABELES, M., 1992. *Corticonics*. Cambridge, U.K.: Cambridge University Press.

BÄCKMAN, L., T.-B. ROBINS-WAHLIN, A. LUNDIN, N. GINOVART, and L. FARDE, 1997. Cognitive deficits in Huntington's disease are predicted by dopaminergic PET markers and brain volumes. *Brain* 120:2207–2217.

BADDELEY, A., 1997. *Human Memory: Theory and Practice*, revised ed. Hove, U.K.: Psychology Press.

BARTLETT, F., and E. R. JOHN, 1973. Equipotentiality quantified: The anatomical distribution of the engram. *Science* 181:764–767.

BEATTY, W. W., D. P. SALMON, N. BUTTERS, W. C. HEINDEL, and E. L. GRANHOLM, 1988. Retrograde amnesia in patients with Alzheimer's disease or Huntington's disease. *Neurobiol. Aging* 9:181–186.

BECHTEREW, W. VON, 1900. Demonstration eines Gehirnes mit Zerstörung der vorderen und inneren Theile der Hirnrinde beider Schläfenlappen. *Neurol. Zentralbl.* 19:990–991.

BELLEVILLE, S., I. PERETZ, and D. MALENFANT, 1996. Examination of the working memory components in normal aging and in dementia of the Alzheimer type. *Neuropsychologia* 34:195–207.

BRAAK, H., and E. BRAAK, 1997. Frequency of stages of Alzheimer-related lesions in different age categories. *Neurobiol Aging* 18:351–357.

BRAAK, H., BRAAK, E., YILMAZER, D., and J. BOHL, 1996. Functional anatomy of human hippocampal formation and related structures. *J. Child Neurol.* 11:265–275.

BREMNER, J. D., P. RANDALL, T. M. SCOTT, R. A. BRONEN, J. P. SEIBYL, S. M. SOUTHWICK, R. C. DELANEY, G. MCCARTHY, D. S. CHARNEY, and R. B. INNIS, 1995. MRI-based measurement of hippocampal volume in patients with combat-related posttraumatic stress disorder. *Am. J. Psychiat.* 152: 973–981.

BREMNER, J. D., P. RANDALL, E. VERMETTEN, L. STAIB, R. A. BRONEN, C. MAZURE, S. CAPELLI, G. MCCARTHY, R. B. INNIS, and D. S. CHARNEY, 1997. Magnetic resonance imaging-based measurement of hippocampal volume in posttraumatic stress disorder related to childhood physical and sexual abuse–a preliminary report. *Biol. Psychiat.* 41: 23–32.

BRUSTROM, J. E., and B. A. OBER, 1996. Source memory for actions in Alzheimer's disease. *Aging, Neuropsychology, and Cognition* 3:56–66.

BUTTERWORTH, B., L. CIPOLOTTI, and E. K. WARRINGTON, 1996. Short-term memory impairment and arithmetical ability. *Q. J. Exp. Psychol.* 49A:251–262.

CAHILL, L., R. BABINSKY, H. J. MARKOWITSCH, and J. L. MCGAUGH, 1995. Involvement of the amygdaloid complex in emotional memory. *Nature* 377:295–296.

CALABRESE, P., H. J. MARKOWITSCH, H. F. DURWEN, B. WIDLITZEK, M. HAUPTS, B. HOLINKA, and W. GEHLEN, 1996. Right temporofrontal cortex as critical locus for the ecphory of old episodic memories. *J. Neurol. Neurosurg. Psychiatr.* 61:304–310.

CASEY, B. J., J. D. COHEN, P. JEZZARD, R. TURNER, D. C. NOLL, R. J. TRAINOR, J. GIEDD, D. KAYSEN, L. HERTZPANNIER, and J. L. RAPOPORT, 1995. Activation of prefrontal cortex in children during a nonspatial working memory task with functional MRI. *Neuroimage* 2:221–229.

CERMAK, L. S., 1989. Encoding and retrieval deficits of amnesic patients. In *Integrating Theory and Practice in Clinical Neuropsychology*, E. Perecman, ed. Hillsdale, N.J.: Lawrence Erlbaum, pp. 139–154.

CERMAK, L. S., 1997. A positive approach to viewing processing deficit theories of amnesia. *Memory* 5:89–98.

CHOW, K. L., 1967. Effects of ablation. In *The Neurosciences*, G.C. Quarton, T. Melnechuk, and F.O. Schmitt, eds. New York: Rockefeller University Press, pp.705–713.

CONNOLLY, J. B., I. J. H. ROBERTS, J. D. ARMSTRONG, K. KAISER, M. FORTE, T. TULLY, and C. J. O'KANE, 1997. Associative learning disrupted by impaired GS signaling in Drosophila mushroom bodies. *Science* 274:2104–2107.

CRAIK, F. I. M., and R. S. LOCKHART, 1972. Levels of processing: A framework for memory research. *J. Verb. Learn. Verb. Behav.* 11:671–684.

DAMASIO, A. R., N. R. GRAFF-RADFORD, P. J. ESLINGER, H. DAMASIO, and N. KASSELL, 1985. Amnesia following basal forebrain lesions. *Arch. Neurol.* 42:263–271.

DARVESH, S., and M. FREEDMAN, 1996. Subcortical dementia: A neurobehavioral approach. *Brain Cogn.* 31:230–249.

DAUM, I., G. RIESCH, G. SARTORI, and N. BIRBAUMER, 1996. Semantic memory impairment in Alzheimer's disease. *J. Clin. Exp. Neuropsychol.* 18:648–665.

DE RENZI, E., M. LIOTTI, and P. NICHELLI, 1987. Semantic amnesia with preservation of autobiographic memory: A case report. *Cortex* 23:575–597.

DE RENZI, E., F. LUCCHELLI, S. MUGGIA, and H. SPINNLER, 1997. Is memory without anatomical damage tantamount to a psychogenic deficit? The case of pure retrograde amnesia. *Neuropsychologia* 35:781–794.

EICHENBAUM, H., 1997. To cortex: Thanks for the memories. *Neuron* 19:481–484.

FINK, G. R., H. J. MARKOWITSCH, M. REINKEMEIER, T. BRUCKBAUER, J. KESSLER, and W.-D. HEISS, 1996. A PET-study of autobiographical memory recognition. *J. Neurosci.* 16:4275–4282.

FUSTER, J. M., 1997. Network memory. *TINS* 20:451–459.

GREENE, J. D. W., A. D. BADDELEY, and J. R. HODGES, 1996. Analysis of the episodic memory deficit in early Alzheimer's disease: Evidence from the doors and people test. *Neuropsychologia* 34:537–551.

HASSING, L., and L. BÄCKMAN, 1997. Episodic memory functioning in population-based samples of very old adults with Alzheimer's disease and vascular dementia. *Dementia Geriatr. Cogn. Disord.* 8:376–383.

HEBB, D. O., 1949. *The Organization of Behavior.* New York, Wiley.

HERZ, R. S., and T. ENGEN, 1996. Odor memory: Review and analysis. *Psychon. Bull. Rev.* 3:300–313.

IRLE, E., and H. J. MARKOWITSCH, 1982. Connections of the hippocampal formation, mamillary bodies, anterior thalamus and cingulate cortex: A retrograde study using horseradish peroxidase in the cat. *Exp. Brain Res.* 47:79–94.

IZQUIERDO, I., D. M. BARROS, T. MELLO E SOUZA, M. M. DE SOUZA, and L. A. IZQUIERDO, 1998. Mechanisms for memory types differ. *Nature* 393:635–636.

KAPUR, N., 1994. Remembering Norman Schwarzkopf: Evidence for two distinct long-term fact learning mechanisms. *Cogn. Neuropsychol.* 11:661–660.

KAPUR, N., D. ELLISON, M. P. SMITH, D. L. MCLELLAN, and E. H. BURROWA, 1992. Focal retrograde amnesia following bilateral temporal lobe pathology. *Brain* 115:73–85.

KNOPMAN, D. S., K. J. CHRISTENSEN, L. J. SCHUT, R. E. HARBAUGH, T. REEDER, T. NGO, and W. FREY, 1989. The spectrum of imaging and neuropsychological findings in Pick's disease. *Neurology* 39:362–368.

KNOWLTON, B. J., and M. S. FANSELOW, 1998. The hippocampus, consolidation and on-line memory. *Curr. Opin. Neurobiol.* 8:293–296.

KNOWLTON, B. J., J. A. MANGELS, and L. R. SQUIRE, 1996. A neostriatal habit learning systems in humans. *Science* 273:1399–1402.

KORNHUBER, H. H., 1988. The human brain: From dream and cognition to fantasy, will, conscience, and freedom. In *Information Processing by the Brain*, H. J. Markowitsch, ed. Toronto: Huber, pp. 241–258.

KROLL, N. E. A., H. J. MARKOWITSCH, R. KNIGHT, and D. Y. VON CRAMON, 1997. Retrieval of old memories–The temporo-frontal hypothesis. *Brain* 120:1377–1399.

LASHLEY, K.S., 1950. In search of the engram. *Soc. Exp. Biol. Symposium* 4:454–482.

LOFTUS, E. F., 1998. Creating false memories. *Sci. Am.* 277:70–75.

LUCCHELLI, F., S. MUGGIA, and H. SPINNLER, 1997. Selective proper name anomia: A case involving only contemporary celebrities. *Cogn. Neuropsychol.* 14:881–890.

MAIR, W. G. P., E. K. WARRINGTON, and L. WEISKRANTZ, 1979. Memory disorder in Korsakoff psychosis: A neuropathological and neuropsychological investigation of two cases. *Brain* 102:749–783.

MANGUN, G. R., 1997. Viewing the human brain in real time: Integrating electromagnetic and hemodynamic measures. *IBRO News* 25:10–11.

MANOACH, D. S., G. SCHLAUG, B. SIEWERT, D. G. DARBY, B. M. BLY, A. BENFIELD, R. R. EDELMAN, and S. WARACH, 1997. Prefrontal cortex fMRI signal changes are correlated with working memory load. *Neuroreport* 8:545–549.

MARKOWITSCH, H. J., 1988. Diencephalic amnesia: A reorientation towards tracts? *Brain. Res. Rev.* 13:351–370.

MARKOWITSCH, H. J., 1992. *Intellectual Functions and the Brain: An Historical Perspective.* Toronto: Hogrefe & Huber.

MARKOWITSCH, H. J., 1994. Effects of emotion and arousal on memory processing by the brain. In *Memory, Learning and the Brain*, J. Delacour, ed. Singapore: World Scientific Pub. Co., pp. 210–240.

MARKOWITSCH, H. J., 1995. Which brain regions are critically involved in the retrieval of old episodic memory? *Brain Res. Rev.* 21:117–127.

MARKOWITSCH, H. J., 1996. Organic and psychogenic retrograde amnesia: Two sides of the same coin? *Neurocase* 2:357–371.

MARKOWITSCH, H. J., 1997a. Varieties of memory: Systems, structures, mechanisms of disturbance. *Neurol. Psychiatr. Brain Sci.* 5:37–56.

MARKOWITSCH, H. J., 1997b. The functional neuroanatomy of episodic memory retrieval. *TINS* 20:557–558.

MARKOWITSCH, H. J., 1999. The limbic system. In *The MIT Encyclopedia of Cognitive Science*, R. Wilson and F. Keil, eds. Cambridge, Mass., MIT Press, pp. 470–472.

MARKOWITSCH, H. J., P. CALABRESE, M. HAUPTS, H. F. DURWEN, J. LIESS, and W. GEHLEN, 1993. Searching for the anatomical basis of retrograde amnesia. *J. Clin. Exp. Neuropsychol.* 15:947–967.

MARKOWITSCH, H. J., P. CALABRESE, M. WÜRKER, H. F. DURWEN, J. KESSLER, R. BABINSKY, D. BRECHTELSBAUER, L. HEUSER, and W. GEHLEN, 1994. The amygdala's contribution to memory–A PET-study on two patients with Urbach-Wiethe disease. *Neuroreport* 5: 1349–1352.

MARKOWITSCH, H. J., D. Y. VON CRAMON, E. HOFMANN, D.-D. SICK, and P. KINZLER, 1990. Verbal memory deterioration after unilateral infarct of the internal capsule in an adolescent. *Cortex* 26:597–609.

MARKOWITSCH, H. J., D. Y. VON CRAMON, and U. SCHURI, 1993. Mnestic performance profile of a bilateral diencephalic infarct patient with preserved intelligence and severe amnesic disturbances. *J. Clin. Exp. Neuropsychol.* 15:627–652.

MARKOWITSCH, H. J., G. R. FINK, A. I. T. THÖNE, J. KESSLER, and W.-D. HEISS, 1997. Persistent psychogenic amnesia with a PET-proven organic basis. *Cogn. Neuropsychiatr.* 2: 135–158.

MARKOWITSCH, H. J., E. KALBE, J. KESSLER, H.-M. VON STOCKHAUSEN, M. GHAEMI, and W.-D. HEISS, in press. Short-term memory deficit after focal parietal damage. *J. Clin. Exp. Neuropsychol.*

MARKOWITSCH, H. J., J. KESSLER, C. VAN DER VEN, G. WEBER-LUXENBURGER, and W.-D. HEISS, 1998. Psychic trauma causing grossly reduced brain metabolism and cognitive deterioration. *Neuropsychologia* 36:77–82.

MARKOWITSCH, H. J., A. THIEL, J. KESSLER, and W.-D. HEISS, 1997. Ecphorizing semi-conscious episodic information via the right temporopolar cortex–A PET study. *Neurocase* 3:445–449.

MCCLELLAND, J. L., 1994. The organization of memory: A parallel distributed processing perspective. *Rev. Neurol.* 150: 570–579.

MESULAM, M., 1998. From sensation to cognition. *Brain* 121:1013–1052.

MOSCOVITCH, M., and L. NADEL, 1998. Consolidation and the hippocampal complex revisited; in defense of the multiple-trace model. *Curr. Opin. Neurobiol.* 8:297–300.

MURRAY, E. A., 1996. What have ablation studies told us about the neural substrates of stimulus memory? *Semin. Neurosci.* 8:13–22.

NAUTA, W. J. H., 1979. Expanding borders of the limbic system concept. In *Functional Neurosurgery*, T. Rasmussen and R. Marino, eds. New York: Raven Press, pp. 7–23.

NEARY, D., and J. SNOWDEN, 1996. Fronto-temporal dementia: Nosology, neuropsychology, and neuropathology. *Brain Cogn.* 31:176–187.

NIELSEN-BOHLMAN, L., M. CIRANNI, A. P. SHIMAMURA, and R. T. KNIGHT, 1997. Impaired word-stem priming in patients with temporal-occipital lesions. *Neuropsychologia* 35:1087–1092.

NIEUWENHUYS, R., J. VOOGT, and C. VAN HUIZEN, 1988. *The Human Central Nervous System: A Synopsis and Atlas*, 3rd ed. Berlin: Springer.

OCHSNER, K. N., C.-Y. P. CHIU, and D. L. SCHACTER, 1994. Varieties of priming. *Curr. Opin. Neurobiol.* 4:189–194.

O'CONNOR, M., N. BUTTERS, P. MILIOTIS, P. ESLINGER, and L. S. CERMAK, 1992. The dissociation of anterograde and retrograde amnesia in a patient with herpes encephalitis. *J. Clin. Exp. Neuropsychol.* 14:159–178.

PAPEZ, J. W., 1937. A proposed mechanism of emotion. *Arch. Neurol. Psychiatr.* 38:725–743.

REINKEMEIER, M., H. J. MARKOWITSCH, B. RAUCH, and J. KESSLER, 1997. Memory systems for people's names: A case study of a patient with deficits in recalling, but not learning people's names. *Neuropsychologia* 35:677–684.

ROULEAU, I., R. LABRECQUE, J.-M. SAINT-HILAIRE, B. CARDU, and N. GIARD, 1989. Short-term and long-term memory deficit following intracarotid amytal injection: Further support for the memory consolidation hypothesis. *Brain Cogn.* 11:167–185.

SAPOLSKY, R. M., 1996. Stress, glucocorticoids, and damage to the nervous system: The current state of confusion. *Stress* 1:1–19.

SARTER, M., and H. J. MARKOWITSCH, 1985. The amydala's role in human mnemonic processing. *Cortex* 21:7–24.

SCHAEFER, E. 1960. Das menschliche Gedächtnis als Informationsspeicher. *Elektron. Rundsch.* 14:79–84.

SCHNIDER, A., K. GUTBROD, C. W. HESS, and G. SCHROTH, 1996. Memory without context: Amnesia with confabulations after infarction of the right capsular genu. *J. Neurol. Neurosurg. Psychiatr.* 61:186–193.

SCOVILLE, W. B., and B. MILNER, 1957. Loss of recent memory after bilateral hippocampal lesions. *J. Neurol. Neurosurg. Psychiatr.* 20:11–21.

SEECK, M., N. MAINWARING, M. D. COSGROVE, H. BLUME, D. DUBUISSON, M. M. MESULAM, and D. L. SCHOMER, 1997. Neurophysiologic correlates of implicit face memory in intracranial visual evoked potentials. *Neurology* 49:1312–1316.

SHALLICE, T., and E. K. WARRINGTON, 1970. Independent functioning of the verbal memory stores: A neuropsychological study. *Q. J. Exp. Psychol.* 22:261–273.

SOARES, J.C., and J. J. MANN, 1997. The functional neuroanatomy of mood disorders. *J. Psychiatr. Res.* 31:393–432.

SQUIRE, L. R., 1995. Biology of memory. In *Comprehensive Textbook of Psychiatry*, H. Kaplan and B. J. Sadock, eds. Baltimore, Md.: Williams and Wilkins, pp. 317–328.

SQUIRE, L. R., B. KNOWLTON, and G. MUSEN, 1993. The structure and organization of memory. *Annu. Rev. Psychol.* 44:453–495.

SZENTÁGOTHAI, J., 1983. The modular architectonic principle of neural centers. *Rev. Physiol.* 98:11–61.

THOMPSON, R. F., and J. J. KIM, 1996. Memory systems in the brain and localization of memory. *Proc. Natl. Acad. Sci. U.S.A.* 93:13428–13444.

THOMPSON-SCHILL, S. L., M. D'ESPOSITO, A. K. AGUIRRE, and M. J. FARAH, 1997. Role of left inferior prefrontal cortex in retrieval of semantic knowledge: A reevaluation. *Proc. Natl. Acad. Sci. U.S.A.* 94:14792–14797.

TULVING, E., 1983. *Elements of Episodic Memory*. Cambridge, U.K.: Cambridge University Press.

TULVING, E., S. KAPUR, F. I. M. CRAIK, M. MOSCOVITCH, and S. HOULE, 1994. Hemispheric encoding/retrieval asymmetry in episodic memory: Positron emission tomography findings. *Proc. Natl. Acad. Sci. U.S.A.* 91:2016–2020.

TULVING, E., and H. J. MARKOWITSCH, 1998. Episodic and declarative memory: Role of the hippocampus. *Hippocampus* 8:198–204.

VARGHA-KHADEM, F., D. G. GADIAN, K. E. WATKINS, A. CONNELLY, W. VAN PAESSCHEN, and M. MISHKIN, 1997. Differential effects of early hippocampal pathology on episodic and semantic memory. *Science* 277:376–380.

VON CRAMON, D. Y., and H. J. MARKOWITSCH, in press. *The Septal Region and Human Memory*. New York: Springer.

VON CRAMON, D.Y., H. J. MARKOWITSCH, and U. SCHURI, 1993. The possible contribution of the septal region to memory. *Neuropsychologia* 31:1159–1180.

ZHANG, X. L., H. BEGLEITER, and B. PORJESZ, 1997. Do chronic alcoholics have intact implicit memory? An ERP study. *Electroenceph. Clin. Neurophysiol.* 103:457–473.

55 Psychopharmacological Approaches to Human Memory

H. VALERIE CURRAN

ABSTRACT A range of psychoactive drugs affect memory, often impairing some aspects of memory while sparing others. Such drugs therefore can provide useful tools for exploring the neurochemical bases of memory and memory disorders. This chapter provides an overview of research on the psychopharmacology of human memory. It looks at why studies of the effects of drugs on memory are theoretically relevant before presenting a summary of the mnemonic effects of the two most widely studied classes of drugs–cholinergic compounds and benzodiazepine receptor ligands. Areas of controversy are discussed, focussing on the degree to which the specific memory effects of psychoactive drugs can be distinguished from their nonmemory effects. These issues also are considered in discussing drug treatments aimed at ameliorating cognitive dysfunction in Alzheimer's disease.

Psychopharmacology is the study of the psychological effects of "psychoactive drugs"–drugs that act on the central nervous system. By using pharmacological knowledge of how a particular drug affects neurotransmitters, psychopharmacologists aim to relate brain chemistry to psychological changes induced by a drug.

The second half of the 20th century has seen a rapid development of new psychoactive drugs. These include many new therapeutic agents used to treat psychological disorders such as depression (e.g., fluoxetine [Prozac]), anxiety (e.g., alprazolam [Xanax]), or schizophrenia (e.g., clozapine [Clozaril]). They also include drugs that can help to slow down cognitive decline in progressive dementia like Alzheimer's disease (AD). Many other psychoactive drugs are used recreationally rather than therapeutically, and these include legal drugs, such as alcohol and nicotine, as well as various illegal substances.

There is a reciprocal interaction between the development and use of drugs for therapeutic purposes and the use of drugs as tools to understand the basis of the mind and mental disorders. This interaction is central to research on the psychopharmacology of memory. A range of psychoactive drugs affects memory, often impairing some aspects of memory while sparing other aspects. Because new drugs are developed with ever-increasing

H. VALERIE CURRAN   Clinical Health Psychology, University College London, London, U.K.

specificity in terms of their neurochemical actions, researchers have a wider pharmacological tool kit with which to explore memory.

Studies of drug-induced amnesia have certain methodological advantages over studies of amnesia in brain-damaged patients. Drugs can be used to induce an amnesia that is temporary and reversible; the degree of amnesia can be manipulated by using different dose levels. By using a placebo condition (i.e., giving a chemically inert substance), each participant can act as their own control. In studies of brain damage, the effects of lesions in different brain areas necessarily involve comparisons between different patients; in psychopharmacological studies, the effects of several different treatments can be examined in the same person. Because healthy people often are the participants in such research, sample sizes can be large enough to create a powerful study. Characteristics of volunteers, such as age, psychopathology, or organic state, also can be varied.

Although these methodological advantages are present, psychopharmacological studies of memory also have certain disadvantages, many of which relate to the lack of specificity of the pharmacological compounds that currently are available. Most drugs have a diffuse effect on the brain, and there is no drug that *only* affects memory. Some drugs produce sedation, and this can have knock-on effects on performance of a wide range of tasks. Therefore, one issue addressed later in this chapter is that of *specificity* of amnestic effects of drugs.

There are some clinical circumstances in which drug-induced amnesia is viewed positively. Anesthesiologists value drugs that induce amnesia because they want to ensure that patients have no recollection of events during their operation. More recently, there has been renewed interest in studies of drugs and memory during anesthesia as a way of studying the role of consciousness in memory (Andrade, 1996). When patients are anesthetized fully and therefore thought to be unconscious, researchers have sought to determine whether they can remember anything from their operation despite global anesthesia. In general, there is more evidence of a degree of preserved memory when implicit rather than explicit memory tests are used, although findings overall have been conflicting (Ghoneim and Block, 1997).

Drug studies clearly are critical in the development of new pharmacological treatments aimed at ameliorating organic cognitive dysfunctions. To date, researchers have been more successful in creating amnesia with drugs than they have in finding compounds that enhance memory in organic disorders. However, we can learn from memory-impairing drugs: If by inhibiting a neurotransmitter a drug impairs memory, it may be that a drug designed to stimulate that neurotransmitter will enhance memory. A few "antidementia" drugs have been shown to slow the rate of cognitive deterioration in some patients with AD, and this has fired hope that new, more effective treatments soon may be discovered.

Memory and pharmacology: The theoretical context

Many drugs have differential effects on performance on different memory tasks, and thus, drugs can allow us to draw dissociations between different aspects of memory. In this way, they can be complimentary to research with brain-damaged people or research showing functional or developmental dissociations (Nyberg and Tulving, 1996). Drugs known to have particular effects on a neurotransmitter can be used as chemical probes to study the functional role of that neurotransmitter in memory. For example, we know that in AD, postmortem brains show a marked depletion in one neurotransmitter—acetylcholine (ACh)—as well as less marked depletions in several other of the estimated 50+ neurotransmitters in the brain. To examine what role ACh plays in memory, many researchers have given a drug that blocks the action of ACh in normal, healthy subjects (Kopelman and Corn, 1988). The pattern of memory impairments induced by the drug is then compared with that seen in AD.

Another example stems from the robust amnestic effects of a group of drugs called benzodiazepines, which have well-known commercial names like Valium (diazepam), Xanax (alprazolam), and Halcion (triazolam). Thirty years after the discovery of these drugs, specific benzodiazepine receptors were identified in the brain. These receptors are found in greatest concentrations in the cerebral cortex and limbic system (including the hippocampus and the amygdala), areas that neuropsychology has long implicated in memory. Why we all should have benzodiazepine receptors regardless of whether we have ever taken a benzodiazepine is an intriguing question. It suggests that there must be a natural substance (an endogenous ligand) that binds to those receptors, and that such natural ligands play a role in the normal regulation of memory processes. Thus, benzodiazepines have been useful not only as tools to study pharmaco-

logical amnesia, but also in providing a potential keyhole on the brain's natural chemistry.

The mood-altering properties of psychoactive drugs also can offer tools in looking at the relation between mood and memory. For example, an elegant series of studies by Cahill and associates (1995) has shown that one drug, propanalol (which blocks beta-adrenergic receptors) impaired normal subjects' recall of emotionally arousing (but not neutral) elements of a story. Using the same task with two patients who had bilateral damage to the amygdala, they found a similar pattern of memory for the emotional and neutral story elements. Together with evidence that the neurotransmitter, noradrenaline, is released in the rat amygdala in response to learning to avoid an aversive stimulus, Cahill and colleagues suggest that their findings imply that adrenergic function in the amygdala mediates memory for emotional material. It also might be suggested that noradrenergic function mediates arousal or attentional function rather than memory. Nevertheless, these studies illustrate how neuropsychological and psychopharmacological studies can be used in parallel in research on memory.

CHOLINERGICS AND BENZODIAZEPINES Psychopharmacological studies have researched two classes of drugs far more than any others: cholinergics and benzodiazepines (BDZs). Interest in cholinergic drugs was stimulated by the cholinergic hypothesis of AD after observations of marked cholinergic depletion in the brains of patients with this devastating disease. Thus, cholinergic drugs have been the most frequently explored pharmacological strategy in terms of enhancing memory in AD. Further, drugs such as scopolamine (hyoscine), which act as cholinergic blockers, are used to study the functional role of ACh in memory.

Since the original work of Drachman and Leavitt (1974), the amnestic effects of this drug have been studied extensively, and scopolamine was put forward as a "pharmacological model" of AD (Weingartner, 1985). Scopolamine is a selective antagonist at muscarinic ACh receptors, which at high doses also acts an antagonist at nicotinic receptors. Its effects can be attenuated if not fully reversed also by giving an agonist like physostigmine or arecoline. Scopolamine's effects only partially parallel the memory deficits observed in AD. The drug does not mimic the extensive retrograde memory loss or the range of working memory impairments seen in AD. Despite this, the "scopolamine model" remains widely used currently in early tests of potential cognitive enhancing drugs on the basis that if a drug can reverse or ameliorate the temporary amnesia induced in healthy volunteers by scopolamine, it may be effective in the cholinergic depletion of AD.

The amnestic effects of benzodiazepines, initially recognized by anesthetists, were less welcome for the millions who took these drugs on a daily basis for anxiety disorders or insomnia. It was suggested that the administration of benzodiazepines to normal, healthy subjects may provide a useful model of Korsakoff's disease (Weingartner, 1985), although these drugs do not produce the retrograde impairments seen in this disease.

Benzodiazepines act by means of specific benzodiazepine receptors and facilitate the transmission of gamma-aminobutyric acid (GABA), the major inhibitory neurotransmitter in the brain. Like diazepam, lorazepam, and 30 or more similar compounds, BZDs act as agonists at the $GABA_A$-BDZ receptor (the single term benzodiazepine used here refers to these full agonists). A benzodiazepine antagonist such as flumazenil can block the same benzodiazepine receptor. Compounds also exist that have opposite effects to benzodiazepines at the same receptor—beta-carbolines act as inverse agonists to inhibit the transmission of GABA. Several other compounds act as partial agonists, binding to the receptor but producing less effect than full agonists.

Anterograde "amnesia" is a consistent finding from volunteer studies of single doses of a benzodiazepine or scopolamine: Information presented after the drug is administered is poorly remembered. In contrast, no study has found objective evidence of retrograde impairments of memory: Information acquired before drug administration is retained intact. These drugs therefore impede the acquisition of new information. The degree and duration of anterograde amnesia depends on several factors (dosage and route of administration; the memory assessments used; the times postdrug at which information is presented and retrieval is required; characteristics of the subject population tested; for the benzodiazepines, the particular benzodiazepine taken). Although there is considerable variation between studies in these factors, the relatively large number of studies carried out to date allows some generalizations to be drawn out.

In general, tasks requiring remembering a few items for a period of seconds (e.g., digit span, block span) are unaffected by benzodiazepines or scopolamine. In more complex tasks in which information is manipulated while it is retained, benzodiazepine- and scopolamine-induced deficits are found (Kopelman and Corn, 1988; Broks et al., 1988). On the whole, the evidence points to a reduction in the speed with which information is processed rather than qualitative effects on components of working memory. For example, error rates generally are affected much less than response times (Rusted, 1994).

There is considerable debate among cognitive psychologists about how to characterize long-term remembering in terms of systems, processes and functions, and a parallel debate about what common terminology we might use to describe memory or the dissociations found in performance on memory tasks. Although psychopharmacological dissociations are relevant to this debate, the debate itself is not within the remit of the present chapter. For discussing drug effects on memory, Tulving's memory systems account (Tulving, 1985; Tulving and Schacter, 1990) is used because it most neatly embraces current findings.

A consistent and robust finding is that benzodiazepines and scopolamine impair performance on tasks that place demands on episodic memory. This impairment clearly is dose dependent. Overall, when direct or explicit assessments of memory are used, the experimental manipulations that affect the performance of normal (nondrugged) participants produce a broadly parallel pattern of influences on the performance of participants administered single doses of benzodiazepines. Thus, if subjects are required to process information at different depths, from the relatively superficial (e.g., deciding whether a word is in capital letters or in small case) to the relatively deep (e.g., deciding whether a word belongs to a particular semantic category), benzodiazepines result in fewer words being subsequently recalled but the pattern of recall is the same as normal (i.e., deeper levels of encoding lead to better recall) (Curran et al., 1988; Bishop and Curran, 1995). Rehearsal effects are normal with benzodiazepines, and after acquisition, forgetting rate is not affected by benzodiazepines or scopolamine (Kopelman and Corn, 1988). Further, benzodiazepines do not increase susceptibility to interference when initial acquisition levels on drug and placebo are matched (Gorissen, Curran, and Ehling, 1998).

Many pharmacological studies have used verbal learning tasks to "assess" episodic memory, often implicitly assuming a one-to-one relationship between a task and the episodic memory system. However, many verbal learning tasks are only minimally episodic in nature and performance depends on other memory systems, such as working memory and semantic memory. As Wheeler and colleagues (1997) discuss in their comprehensive review, the essence of episodic memory is enabling "mental time travel"–the capacity to remember in the sense of re-experiencing events in subjective time. Thus "episodic recollection is infused with autonoetic awareness of one's existence in subjective time" (Wheeler, Stuss, and Tulving, 1997, p. 349). Experiential approaches using the remember–know paradigm (Tulving, 1985; Gardiner and Java, 1993) are increasingly giving support to a distinction between "remembering" in the sense of re-experiencing as a participant in an event and "knowing" in the sense of a personally detached observer of an event.

Using the "remember–know" recognition paradigm, two studies have shown that "remember" responses are reduced by benzodiazepines (Curran et al., 1993; Bishop and Curran, 1995). However, "know" responses are not reduced (and can be somewhat increased) by these drugs. This pattern of drug effects parallels that on other tasks tapping episodic and semantic memory, supporting the notion that "know" responses tap semantic memory. Retrieval of well-established (semantic) knowledge generally is intact after drug administration (Ghoneim and Mewaldt, 1990; Polster, 1993). For example, verbal fluency is unaffected by drugs, and in sentence verification tasks, error rates are not increased although drugs often increase the time to complete the task. Further, conceptual priming in category generation tasks is intact following administration of benzodiazepines and scopolamine even though subjects' explicit recall of studied category exemplars showed marked impairment (Bishop and Curran, 1998). Taken as a whole, these findings therefore provide evidence that episodic and semantic memory can be dissociated pharmacologically.

The contents of episodic and semantic memory are directly accessible to consciousness—we can bring to mind both personal episodes and impersonal facts. In contrast, procedural memory is expressed indirectly through skilled performance. Benzodiazepines do not affect procedural learning in perceptual-learning tasks (e.g., mirror reading) or in anagram-solving tasks (Ghoneim and Mewaldt, 1990). In tasks that have a significant motor response component or where speed of reaction time is critical (e.g., pursuit rotor, serial reaction time), a drug effect may be found, but this usually is a general slowing of performance that relates to the drug's sedative effect (Nissen et al., 1987; Curran, 1991). Critically, learning *curves* on drugs tend to parallel those on placebo.

Tasks assessing procedural memory in these ways are indirect tests of memory—remembering is inferred from changes in the performance of a skill. Another kind of indirect test of memory includes what is usually termed "priming": the influence of prior exposure on subsequent performance. As already noted, there is some evidence that conceptual priming is intact after administration of benzodiazepines and scopolamine. Perceptual priming studies with drugs have produced an intriguing finding that one benzodiazepine, lorazepam, produces impairments on standard tasks tapping perceptual priming (e.g., word-stem, word-fragment, and degraded picture identification). Even though benzodiazepines as a class are chemically very similar and all produce impairments on explicit memory tasks, a range of other benzodiazepines (alprazolam, triazolam, diazepam, oxazepam, midazolam), as well as scopolamine, leave perceptual priming intact.

Originally noted by Brown and associates (1989), the effect of lorazepam on perceptual priming has been replicated and extended by several groups of researchers (Knopman, 1991; Curran and Gorenstein, 1993; Vidailhet et al., 1994; Stewart et al., 1996). Task purity criticisms can be applied to some earlier studies on the grounds that explicit impairments contaminated performance on the "implicit" task. However, these could not explain findings of several studies that compared lorazepam with another drug (a different benzodiazepine or scopolamine) that produced the same degree of impairment on an explicit task but showed only that lorazepam impaired perceptual priming (e.g., Sellal et al., 1992; Bishop, Curran, and Lader, 1996). Vidailhet and colleagues (1996) used Jacoby's "process dissociation procedure" (Jacoby, 1991) to examine perceptual priming effects of diazepam and lorazepam. Although findings overall were not clear-cut, when the deleterious effect of the two benzodiazepines on conscious uses of memory were matched carefully, only lorazepam impaired the automatic use of memory. Using experimental manipulations in accordance with Schacter's retrieval intentionality criterion, we found that lorazepam impaired word-stem completion and this effect was attenuated by coadministration of the benzodiazepine antagonist, flumazenil (Bishop and Curran, 1995). One could speculate that there is a second population of benzodiazepine receptors, perhaps concentrated in occipital areas, to which lorazepam and flumazenil bind but not other benzodiazepine receptor ligands. Benzodiazepine receptor subtypes have been identified but their functional significance is not known.

Thus, although all benzodiazepines produce impairments of episodic memory, one benzodiazepine, lorazepam, impairs perceptual priming. Because this one benzodiazepine is qualitatively different from others in its effects, this lends support to the notion of perceptual representation systems that are distinct from other memory systems (Tulving and Schacter, 1990).

SPECIFICITY OF DRUG EFFECTS ON MEMORY   An ongoing debate in research on the psychopharmacology of memory centers on the specificity of drug effects on memory. At a psychological level, there is the question of how much a drug's apparent effects on memory can be seen as by-products of its effects on arousal or attentional functions. At a pharmacological level, there is the question of the overlap in patterns of memory effects of drugs with differing pharmacological actions.

Memory and arousal

Benzodiazepines and scopolamine produce dose-related reductions in arousal, and this may contribute to decrements in performance on tasks tapping episodic memory. How can specific mnemonic effects of drugs be differentiated from their effects on arousal? Five main approaches are summarized in table 55.1. For example, one way of dissociating sedation and amnesia would be to show that tolerance over repeated doses of BZDs builds up differentially to the two effects. Tolerance reflects neuronal adaptation to a drug whereby the same dose has less of an effect over repeated use. A general finding is that tolerance develops to drugs' sedative effects fairly quickly, but tolerance to amnestic effects develops over much longer time periods and may not develop fully after several years. Another way of dissociating memory and arousal is to demonstrate differential dose-response curves on the two measures (Weingartner et al., 1995; Smirne et al., 1989).

In a number of studies, benzodiazepine antagonists *and* agonists were given to see whether there is differential reversal of amnestic and sedative effects by an antagonist. On the whole, studies with flumazenil have produced an inconsistent pattern of results as different agonist/antagonist dosages as well as different procedures have been used. A fair conclusion probably is that sedative and attentional effects are reversed more easily, and at lower antagonist doses, than amnestic effects. However, another method of dissociation has been to show that different drugs may produce the same effect on sedation but different effects on memory, or vice versa. For example, in a comparison of the effects of a sedative antihistamine (diphenhydramine) with scopolamine and the benzodiazepine lorazepam, 50 mg of the antihistamine produced similar sedation levels to scopolamine and lorazepam (Curran et al., 1998). However, unlike scopolamine and the benzodiazepine, it did not produce any impairment on a task tapping episodic memory (continuous word recognition). Event-related potentials (ERPs) also were recorded and showed that all three drugs affected earlier components of ERPs sim-

ilarly, whereas later components such as P_{300} were affected more by scopolamine and lorazepam than the antihistamine.

Psychopharmacologists would welcome drugs that had a range of memory and arousal effects (improving as well as impairing) that would enable double-dissociations to be drawn. However, taken together, results from studies assessing co-occurrence of sedative and memory effects in these different ways provide strong evidence that benzodiazepines and scopolamine have specific effects on memory over and above their sedative effects.

Memory and attention

It could be argued that drugs might reduce attentional resources and thereby impede encoding of information. Gorissen and Ehling (1998) carried out two experiments in which participants were given dual tasks. They performed a visual discrimination task of varying levels of complexity concurrently with a paired-associate learning task. The benzodiazepine diazepam (15 mg) impaired subsequent recall of paired associates, but the level of impairment did not interact with the level of complexity of the visual discrimination task. Although dividing attention did reduce people's memory performance, it was no more disruptive to those given diazepam than to those given placebo. This suggests that reduced attentional resources cannot account for the amnestic effects of benzodiazepines.

The issue of whether amnestic effects are related to impaired attentional functions is a particularly heated debate in the scopolamine literature (Broks et al., 1988; Kopelman and Corn, 1988; Lawrence and Sahakian, 1995). Having concluded from her earlier elegant studies using dual-task paradigms that scopolamine produced impairments of the central executive component of working memory, Rusted (1994) argues that this is not sufficient to explain the drug's effects on attention and

TABLE 55.1

Methods for dissociating drugs' specific effects on memory (M) from their effects on arousal (A)

Method	Typical Findings	Examples
Differential tolerance to drug's arousal and memory effects over repeated dosing	Tolerance to sedation develops before tolerance to memory effects	Ghoneim et al., 1981; Curran et al., 1994; Tata et al., 1994
Differential dose response curves for arousal and amnestic effects	M and A effects show different dose-response curves	Weingartner et al., 1995; Smirne et al., 1989
Differential reversal of agonist effects on A and by antagonist	Variable—depends on ratio of doses of agonist and antagonist	Hommer, Weingartner, and Breier, 1993; Curran and Birch, 1991
Equate effects on A and show differential effects on M	Different drugs produce same A effects but different M effects	Curran, Schiffano, and Lader, 1991; Curran et al., 1998
Statistical (e.g., covariance)	Covariance of arousal measures leaves significant memory impairment	See reviews: Ghoneim and Mewaldt, 1990; Curran, 1991

memory. Impairment of a unitary resource allocator like the central executive would mean that attentional and memory impairments should occur together, and as Rusted shows, this clear correspondence is not often found in studies of scopolamine. Attention is an umbrella term and it may be that different neurobiological systems mediate different aspects of attention. Studies in which a range of attentional tasks have been used show that scopolamine has effects on some but not other aspects of attentional functions (Broks et al., 1988). Indeed, there is increasing evidence for the role of the catecholamines, especially noradrenaline, in attentional processing (Robbins and Everitt, 1995; Coull et al., 1995). A similar issue of "umbrella terms" also arises with the conceptually ill-defined but psychopharmacologically necessary concept of arousal. Different measures of arousal often bear little relationship to each other, and Robbins and Everitt (1995) argue that different aspects of arousal are mediated by different neurotransmitter systems.

Memory: Pharmacological specificity

As we have seen, the cholinergic blocker scopolamine produces a profile of memory effects that are broadly similar to benzodiazepines. Despite the different pharmacological actions of these compounds, their amnestic effects have proved difficult to differentiate. Two main differences have been noted. First, scopolamine differs from one benzodiazepine (lorazepam) because it does not impair perceptual priming. Second, patients with AD show an increased sensitivity to the detrimental effects of anticholinergics such as scopolamine but no increased sensitivity to benzodiazepines like lorazepam (Sunderland et al., 1986). However, similarities are more pervasive, with both scopolamine and benzodiazepines producing marked anterograde impairments of episodic memory while leaving semantic, procedural, and working memory relatively intact. This similarity in effects may reflect a common neuropharmacological action because GABA inhibition influences cholinergic projection pathways (GABA-ergic mechanisms may inhibit cholinergic activity in the cortex by means of interaction at the level of the basal forebrain). In research with rats, one study showed that injection of a benzodiazepine into the medial septum reduced ACh release in the hippocampus by 50%, whereas injecting the benzodiazepine antagonist flumazenil increased hippocampal ACh release by 95% (Imperato et al., 1994). These kinds of studies are beginning to reveal the interaction between different neurotransmitters and neuromodulators in memory (see McGaugh and Cahill, 1997). Inhibition of long-term potentiation (LTP) in the hippocampus may be a common neuropharmacological effect of benzodiazepines and scopolamine.

PHARMACOLOGICAL STRATEGIES FOR ENHANCING MEMORY FUNCTION In terms of strategies for enhancement of memory, the largest effort is directed toward the development of treatments for AD. Although several neurotransmitters have been implicated in AD (for review, see Curran and Kopelman, 1996), cholinergic depletion still is the most well-documented neurochemical loss, and much effort has focused on compounds designed to correct or moderate this cholinergic deficit. The most widely discussed strategy has been to inhibit the enzyme acetylcholinesterase (AChE). Acetylcholinesterase inhibitors prevent the hydrolysis of synaptically released ACh and therefore increase the efficiency of cholinergic transmission. Tacrine (tetrahydroaminoacridine) was the first antidementia drug to be given approval by the U. S. Food and Drug Administration (FDA), followed by two other AchE inhibitors, donepezil hydrochloride ("Aricept") and rivastigmine.

Both tacrine and donepezil have modest effects of slowing down the rate of cognitive deterioration over time in patients with mild to moderate AD. Side effects can be problematic, and only a proportion of patients show cognitive improvement with treatment (Knopman, 1995). There is substantial clinical heterogeneity in patients meeting diagnostic criteria for AD and various "subtypes" of AD have been suggested on the bases of neuropathological or cognitive variations (Richards, 1997). It is possible that different clinical subgroups show a different response to different pharmacological treatments.

It is not clear to what extent these drugs produce any specific improvement in memory functions. Sahakian and associates (1993) showed that tacrine improved choice reaction time and improved performance on a task in which patients learned to follow a simple rule and then reverse this rule. However, it had no effect compared with placebo on any memory task, leading Sahakian and colleagues to argue that tacrine improved attentional functions and to suggest that the cholinergic system is implicated in the control of attentional rather than memory processes.

Cholinergic agonists like nicotine increase the effect of ACh either directly or by sensitizing the receptor site. There is evidence that AD is associated with a reduced number of nicotinic cholinergic receptors and that tacrine increases the number of nicotinic cholinergic receptors in patients with AD (Nordberg et al., 1992). Subcutaneous nicotine improves AD patients' speed of information processing but does not affect performance on memory tasks (Lawrence and Sahakian, 1995), again suggesting that the cholinergic system is involved in attentional rather than memory function.

Evidence from animal studies has implicated nerve growth factor (NGF) as a possible mediator of cholinergic depletion in AD (when NGF is given to animals, cholinergic function is increased). Other approaches have shown some promise in AD, such as estrogen therapy in postmenopausal women and Vitamin E. A range of noncholinergic techniques currently are being explored, including vasodilators, so-called "nootropics"–putative cognitive enhancers like piracetam, and a range of other compounds (e.g., neuropeptides, opiate antagonists, benzodiazepine inverse agonists). There also are neurotropic agents such as oligonucleotides that are intended to modify biosynthetic pathways involved in generation of AD pathology. Whether any of these agents have potential to improve cognitive function in AD is not yet known.

Conclusions

This chapter has focused mainly on drugs that impair memory and mainly on the most widely studied drugs, benzodiazepines and scopolamine. Studies of noradrenergic drugs have shown effects on arousal and attention rather than memory. At least 50 neurotransmitters probably exist, although most drugs act on just a few of these, and we are only beginning to explore the complexities of memory's neurochemistry. A large body of animal research has implicated the glutamatergic N-methyl-d-aspartate (NMDA) receptor in memory. In humans, the NMDA receptor antagonist, ketamine, produces memory and attentional impairments (as well as unpleasant psychotic-like symptoms) (Malhotra et al., 1996).

Psychopharmacologists studying memory are reliant on their tools–the chemical probes that are available, and at present, many of these have diffuse effects. Ever more specific pharmacological agents are being produced that will greatly aid researchers to tease apart the neurochemical substrates of memory. The use of radiolabeled drugs in imaging studies are already allowing delineation of receptors in the living brain, and this may provide a means of assessing abnormalities in receptor populations in neurological and psychiatric disorders. A drug and placebo also can be administered during functional imaging and this allows drug-induced changes in activation to be monitored during performance of a memory task (Fletcher et al., 1996). Psychopharmacology will progress enormously given refinements in both the drugs available and the techniques for studying their effects.

REFERENCES

ANDRADE, J., 1996. Investigations of hypesthesia: Using anesthetics to explore relationships between consciousness, learning and memory. *Conscious. Cogn.* 5:562–580.

BISHOP, K., and H. V. CURRAN, 1995. Psychopharmacological analysis of implicit and explicit memory: A study with lorazepam and the benzodiazepine antagonist, flumazenil. *Psychopharmacology* 121:267–278.

BISHOP, K., and H. V. CURRAN, 1998. An investigation of the effects of benzodiazepine receptor ligands and of scopolamine on conceptual priming. *Psychopharmacology* 140:345–353.

BISHOP, K. I., H. V. CURRAN, and M. LADER, 1996. Do scopolamine and lorazepam have dissociable effects on human memory systems? A dose-response study with normal volunteers. *Exp. Clin. Psychopharmacol.* 4:292–299.

BROKS, P., G. PRESTON, M. TRAUB, P. POPPLETON, C. WARD, and S. M. STAHL, 1988. Modelling dementia: Effects of scopolamine on memory and attention. *Neuropsychologia* 26:685–700.

BROWN, M. W., J. BROWN, and J. BOWES, 1989. Absence of priming coupled with substantially preserved recognition in lorazepam induced amnesia. *Q. J. Exp. Psychol.* 41A:599–617.

CAHILL, L., R. BABINSKY, H. J. MARKOVITSCH, and J. L. McGAUGH, 1995. The amygdala and emotional memory. *Nature* 377:295–296.

COULL, J. T., B. J. SAHAKIAN, H. C. MIDDLETON, A. H. YOUNG, S. B. PARK, R. H. McSHANE, P. J. COWEN, and T. W. ROBBINS, 1995. Differential effects of clonidine, haloperidol, diazepam and tryptophan depletion on focussed attention and attentional search. *Psychopharmacology* 121:222–230.

CURRAN, H. V., 1991. Benzodiazepines, memory and mood: A review. *Psychopharmacology* 105:1–8.

CURRAN, H. V., and B. BIRCH, 1991. Differentiating the sedative and amnestic effects of benzodiazepines: A study with midazolam and the benzodiazepine antagonist, flumazenil. *Psychopharmacology* 103:519–523.

CURRAN, H. V., A. BOND, G. O'SULLIVAN, M. BRUCE, I. MARKS, P. LELLIOT, P. SHINE, and M. LADER, 1994. Memory functions, alprazolam and exposure therapy: A controlled longitudinal study of patients with agoraphobia and panic disorder. *Psychol. Med.* 24:969–976.

CURRAN, H. V., and C. GORENSTEIN, 1993. Differential effects of lorazepam and oxazepam on priming. *Int. Clin. Psychopharmacol.* 8:37–42.

CURRAN, H. V., J. GARDINER, R. JAVA, and D. J. ALLEN, 1993. Effects of lorazepam on recollective experience in recognition memory. *Psychopharmacology* 110:374–378.

CURRAN, H. V., and M. D. KOPELMAN, 1996. The cognitive psychopharmacology of Alzheimer's disease. In *The Neuropsychology of Alzheimer's Disease*, R.G. Morris, ed. Oxford: Oxford University Press.

CURRAN, H. V., P. POOVIBUNSUK, J. DALTON, and M. H. LADER, 1998. Differentiating the effects of centrally acting drugs on arousal and memory: An event-related potential study of scopolamine, lorazepam and diphenhydramine. *Psychopharmacology* 135:27–36.

CURRAN, H. V., F. SCHIFFANO, and M. H. LADER, 1991. Models of memory dysfunction? A comparison of the effects of scopolamine and lorazepam on memory, psychomotor performance, and mood. *Psychopharmacology* 103:83–90.

CURRAN, H. V., W. SCHIWY, F. EVES, P. SHINE, and M. LADER, 1988. A "levels of processing" study of the effects of benzodiazepines on human memory. *Human Psychopharmacology* 3:21–25.

DRACHMAN, D. A., and J. LEAVITT, 1974. Human memory and the cholinergic system. *Arch. Neurol.* 30:113–121.

FLETCHER, P. C., C. D. FRITH, P. M. GRASBY, K. J. FRISTON, and R. J. DOLAN, 1996. Local and distributed effects of apomorphine on fronto-temporal function in acute unmedicated schizophrenics. *J. Neurosci.* 16:7055–7062.

GARDINER, J. M., and R. I. JAVA, 1993. Recognition memory and awareness: An experiential approach. *Eur. J. Cogn. Psychol.* 5(3):337–346.

GHONEIM, M. M., and R. I. BLOCK, 1997. Learning and memory during general anesthesia: An update. *Anesthesiology* 87:387–410.

GHONEIM, M. M., and S. P. MEWALDT, 1990. Benzodiazepines and human memory: A review. *Anesthesiology* 72:926–938.

GHONEIM, M. M., S. P. MEWALDT, J. L. BERIE, and V. HINRICHS, 1981. Memory and performance effects of single and 3 week administration of diazepam. *Psychopharmacology* 73:147–151.

GORISSEN, M. E. E., H. V. CURRAN, and P. A. EHLING, 1998. Proactive interference and temporal context encoding after diazepam intake. *Psychopharmacology* 138:334–343.

GORISSEN, M. E. E., and P. A. EHLING, 1998. Dual task performance after diazepam intake: Can resource depletion explain the benzodiazepine-induced amnesia? *Psychopharmacology* 138:354–361.

HOMMER, D., H. WEINGARTNER, and A. BREIER, 1993. Dissociation of benzodiazepine-induced amnesia from sedation by flumazenil. *Psychopharmacology* 112:455–460.

IMPERATO, A., L. DAZZI, M. C. OBINU, G. L. GESSA, and G. BIGGIO, 1994. The benzodiazepine receptor antagonist flumazenil increases acetylcholine release in rat hippocampus. *Brain Res.* 647:167–171.

JACOBY, L. L., 1991. A process dissociation framework: Separating automatic from intentional use of memory. *J. Memory Language* 30:513–541.

KNOPMAN, D., 1991. Unaware learning versus preserved learning in pharmacologic amnesia: Similarities and differences. *J. Exp. Psychol. Learn. Mem. Cogn.* 17:1017–1029.

KNOPMAN, D., 1995. Tacrine in Alzheimer's disease: A promising first step. *Neurologist* 1:86–94.

KOPELMAN, M. D., and T. H. CORN, 1988. Cholinergic "blockade" as a model for cholinergic depletion. *Brain* 111:1079–1110.

LAWRENCE, A. D., and B. J. SAHAKIAN, 1995. Alzheimer disease, attention and the cholinergic system. *Alzheimer Dis. Assoc. Disord.* 9(S2):43–49.

MALHOTRA, A. K., D. A. PINALS, H. WEINGARTNER, K. SIROCCO, C. D. MISSAR, D. PICKAR, and A. BREIER, 1996. NMDA receptor function and human cognition: The effects of ketamine in healthy volunteers. *Neuropsychopharmacology* 14:301–307.

MCGAUGH, J. L., and L. CAHILL, 1997. Interaction of neuromodulatory systems in modulating memory storage. *Behav. Brain Res.* 83:31–38.

NISSEN, M. J., D. S. KNOPMAN, and D. L. SCHACTER, 1987. Neurochemical dissociations of memory systems. *Neurology* 37:789–794.

NORDBERG, A., A. LILJA, H. LUNDQVIST, P. HARTVIG, K. AMBERLA, and M. VIITANEN, 1992. Tacrine restores cholinergic nicotinic receptors and glucose metabolism in Alzheimer patients as visualised by positron emission tomography. *Neurobiol. Aging* 13:747–758.

NYBERG, L., and E. TULVING, 1996. Classifying human long-term memory: Evidence from converging dissociations. *Eur. J. Cogn. Psychol.* 8:163–183.

POLSTER, M. R., 1993. Drig-induced amnesia: Implications for cognitive neuropsychological investigations of memory. *Psychol. Bull.* 114:477–493.

RICHARDS, M., 1997. Neurobiological treatment of Alzheimer's disease. In *The Cognitive Neuropsychology of Alzheimer's Disease*, R. G. M. Morris, ed. Oxford: Oxford University Press, pp. 327–342.

ROBBINS, T. W., and B. J. EVERITT, 1995. Arousal systems and attention. In *The Cognitive Neurosciences*, M. Gazzaniga, ed. Cambridge, Mass.: MIT Press, pp. 703–725.

RUSTED, J. M., 1994. Cholinergic blockade: Are we asking the right questions? *J. Psychopharmacol.* 8:54–59.

SAHAKIAN, B. J., A. M. OWEN, N. J. MORANT, S. A. EAGGER, et al., 1993. Further analysis of the cognitive effects of tetrahydroaminoacridine (THA) in Alzheimer's disease: Assessment of attentional and mnemonic function using CANTAB. *Psychopharmacology* 110:395–410.

SELLAL, F., J. M. DANION, F. KAUFFMANN-MULLER, D. GRANGE, J. L. IMBS, M. VAN DER LINDEN, and L. SINGER, 1992. Differential effects of diazepam and lorazepam on repetition priming in healthy volunteers. *Psychopharmacology* 108:371–379.

SMIRNE, S., L. FERINI-STRAMBI, R. PIROLA, O. TANCREDI, M. FRANCESCHI, P. PINTO, and S. R. BAREGGI, 1989. Effects of flunitrazepam on cognitive functions. *Psychopharmacology* 98:251–256.

STEWART, S. H., G. F. RIOUX, J. F. CONNOLLY, et al., 1996. Effects of oxazepam and lorazepam on implicit and explicit memory: Evidence for possible influences of time course. *Psychopharmacology* 128:139–149.

SUNDERLAND, T., P. TARIOT, H. WEINGARTNER, D. MURPHY, P. A. NEWHOUSE, E. A. MUELLER, and R. M. COHEN, 1986. Anticholinergic challenge in Alzheimer patients: A controlled dose-response study. *Progr. Neuropsychopharmacol. Biol. Psychiatry* 10:599–610.

TATA, P. R., J. ROLLINGS, M. COLLINS, A. PICKERING, and R. R. JACOBSON, 1994. Lack of cognitive recovery following withdrawal from long-term benzodiazepine use. *Psychol. Med.* 24:203–213.

TULVING, E., 1985. How many memory systems are there? *Am. Psychologist* 40:385–398.

TULVING, E., and D. L. SCHACTER, 1990. Priming and human memory systems. *Science* 247:301–306.

VIDAILHET, P., J. M. DANION, F. KAUFFMANN-MULLER, D. GRANGE, A. GIERSCH, M. VAN DER LINDEN, and J. L. IMBS, 1994. Lorazepam and diazepam effects on memory acquisition in priming tests. *Psychopharmacology* 115:397–406.

VIDAILHET, P., M. KAZES, J. M. DANION, F. KAUFFMANN-MULLER, and D. GRANGE, 1996. Effects of lorazepam and diazepam on conscious and automatic memory processes. *Psychopharmacology* 127:63–72.

WEINGARTNER, H., 1985. Models of memory dysfunctions. *Ann. N.Y. Acad. Sci.* 444:359–369.

WEINGARTNER, H. J., K. SIROCCO, R. RAWLINGS, E. JOYCE, and D. HOMMER, 1995. Dissociations in the expression of the sedative effects of triazolam. *Psychopharmacology* 119:27–33.

WHEELER, M. A., D. T. STUSS, and E. TULVING, 1997. Toward a theory of episodic remembering: The frontal lobes and autonoetic consciousness. *Psychol. Bull.* 121:331–354.

56 Memory Retrieval: An Electrophysiological Perspective

MICHAEL D. RUGG AND KEVIN ALLAN

ABSTRACT Event-related potential (ERP) studies of indirect and direct memory tasks have identified retrieval-related neural activity that onsets at approximately 200 to 250 ms post-stimulus. This activity is sensitive to variables that selectively influence item-specific implicit (unaware) memory and differs in its scalp distribution from neural activity engaged during the retrieval of explicit (aware) memories. These findings support the view that implicit memory and explicit memory engage distinct retrieval processes and give insights into their relative timing. Other studies, contrasting ERPs elicited by items that were explicitly recognized on the basis of "recollection" or "familiarity," have failed to find evidence in favor of the idea that these two kinds of memory are supported by qualitatively different processes. The findings from these studies indicate, however, that multiple processes support recollection. Whereas some of these processes support the retrieval of information from episodic memory, other, "postretrieval" processes are required to make the products of retrieval available to current behavioral goals.

In this chapter, studies employing event-related brain potentials to investigate the neural correlates of human memory are reviewed. Because event-related potential (ERP) studies of memory published before 1995 are already the subject of comprehensive reviews (Johnson, 1995; Rugg, 1995a, b), these studies are not discussed in any detail in this chapter. We focus on the area–item-specific long-term memory retrieval–in which progress since 1994 has been both substantial and cumulative, leaving aside topics such as encoding, working memory, and semantic memory, where, at the time of writing, there is little to be added to the content of the reviews just cited.

Event-related potentials and memory

Event-related potentials represent scalp-recorded changes in brain electrical activity (electroencephalogram [EEG]) time-locked to some definable event. The magnitude of these changes is small compared with the amplitude of the "background" EEG. ERP waveforms

MICHAEL D. RUGG and KEVIN ALLAN Institute of Cognitive Neuroscience, University College London, London, U.K.

with satisfactory signal-to-noise ratios are obtained by averaging the EEG samples obtained on a number of trials (typically, 20–50) belonging to the same experimental condition. ERP waveforms thus represent estimates of time-locked neural activity elicited by stimuli belonging to different experimental conditions (see Kutas and Dale, 1998, and Rugg and Coles, 1995a, for introductions to the ERP technique).

ERPs are useful for studying memory for a number of reasons. First, neural activity associated with stimulus processing can be measured with a temporal resolution in the millisecond range. Thus, upper-bound estimates of the time required by the nervous system to discriminate between different classes of item (e.g., old and new words in a recognition memory test) can be made directly. This level of temporal resolution is presently unattainable with functional neuroimaging techniques such as positron emission tomography (PET) and functional magnetic resonance imaging (fMRI). A second benefit of the ERP technique, central to the research reviewed subsequently, is that ERP waveforms can be formed "off-line," after the experimental trials have been sorted into different conditions according to the subject's behavior. Thus, it is easy to compare records of brain activity associated with different classes of response to the same experimental items (e.g., hits vs. misses, or false alarms vs. correct rejections).

Finally, ERPs can be used to investigate whether different experimental conditions engage functionally dissociable cognitive processes. This application of ERPs rests on the assumption that if two experimental conditions are associated with qualitatively different patterns of scalp electrical activity, this usually signifies the engagement of at least partially nonoverlapping neural and, thus, functional processes (Rugg and Coles, 1995b). In the following research, the analysis of the spatial distribution (the "scalp topography") of ERP effects occupies a central place; when two topographies differ, we take this to mean that the cognitive processes engaged in the respective experimental conditions are not identical.

Event-related potentials and memory retrieval

Studies employing ERPs to investigate memory retrieval have shared a common logic. Event-related potential waveforms are obtained during memory tests for two or more classes of test item. Items may be defined *a priori* (e.g., previously studied vs. unstudied) or classified according to behavior (e.g., recognition hit vs. false alarm). Differences between the ERPs elicited by different classes of test items are taken to represent the neural correlates of the memory processes engaged to a greater extent by one class of item than another.

Theoretical background

There have been numerous proposals about how memory for specific events is fractionated. Perhaps the most widely accepted fractionation is between explicit (aware) and implicit (unaware) memory. This distinction is supported by findings (see Moscovitch, Vriezen, and Gottstein, 1993, for review) demonstrating that implicit memory, as assessed by performance on "indirect" memory tests (when memory for study items is incidental to task performance and expressed through "priming" effects such as facilitation of reaction time or identification accuracy), can be normal or near normal in amnesic patients exhibiting severe impairments on the "direct" memory tests of recognition and recall. The distinction receives further support from the many studies with healthy participants in which dissociations between direct and indirect test performance have been reported (see Roediger and McDermott, 1993, for review). Findings from neuropsychological and normal studies suggest that implicit memory may further fractionate into "data-driven" and "conceptually-driven" components (Roediger and McDermott, 1993). Data-driven implicit memory reflects processing overlap at early, presemantic processing stages, as evidenced by its relative insensitivity to the degree of semantic processing accorded study items and its sensitivity to the perceptual similarity of study and test items. Conceptually-driven implicit memory is a consequence of processing overlap at the semantic level and shows the reverse pattern of sensitivity to semantic and perceptual variables.

A second and more controversial memory fractionation is between two different forms of explicit memory—familiarity and recollection (episodic retrieval). According to the proponents of "dual process" models (Jacoby and Dallas, 1981; Jacoby and Kelley, 1992; Mandler, 1980; Richardson-Klavehn, Gardiner, and Java, 1996), these two forms of memory represent qualitatively different ways in which a retrieval cue can access information about a past episode. In the case of recollection, the information includes contextual details of the learning episode and is accompanied by the phenomenological experience of having brought back to mind ("remembering") a specific past event. When memory is based on familiarity, information about the context in which the test item was encoded, and the phenomenal experience of remembering (in the sense defined previously) are both absent.

Event-related potentials and implicit memory

As has been noted previously (Rugg 1995a, b), the identification of an electrophysiological correlate of implicit memory requires more than the mere demonstration that ERPs vary in an indirect memory test according to the study status of the items (e.g., old vs. new). It also is necessary to show that the ERP effect does not reflect "incidental" or "involuntary" explicit memory (Bowers and Schacter, 1990). Because of the difficulty of satisfying this requirement, one of us (Rugg, 1995a, b) argued that despite the large number of studies demonstrating the sensitivity of ERPs to item repetition in indirect memory tests, it was not possible to conclude that any aspect of these "ERP repetition effects" reflected implicit memory. One way around this impasse is to employ experimental manipulations known to have dissociative effects on implicit and explicit memory. The demonstration that an ERP memory effect is modulated by the same variables that selectively influence behavioral manifestations of implicit memory makes it unlikely that the effect is a reflection of explicit memory for the test items.

One such variable is presentation modality. As assessed on a variety of indirect tasks, implicit memory is weaker when study and test items are presented in different sensory modalities than when the modality is held constant (Roediger and McDermott, 1993). Therefore, it is noteworthy that the effects of repetition within modality (visual–visual) and across modality (auditory–visual) on ERPs elicited by visually presented words differ markedly (Rugg and Nieto-Vegas, unpublished data; figure 56.1). Although visual–visual repetition gave rise to the "standard" ERP repetition effect—a widespread, positive-going shift that onsets approximately 250 ms poststimulus—auditory–visual repetition resulted in the absence of the early part of this effect. As illustrated in figures 56.1 and 56.2 (see color plate 37) even when repetition was immediate, within- and across-modality repetition effects differed in their magnitudes and scalp topographies.

These findings point to the existence of neural activity occupying a latency region of approximately 200 to

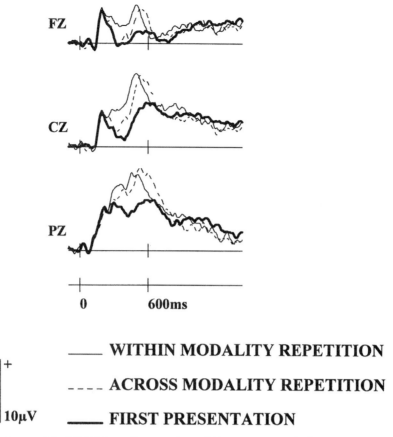

FZ

CZ

PZ

0   600ms

+

10μV

—— WITHIN MODALITY REPETITION

- - - - ACROSS MODALITY REPETITION

—— FIRST PRESENTATION

FIGURE 56.1   Event-related potentials (ERPs) from Rugg and Nieto-Vegas (unpublished data), illustrating the effects of immediate word repetition within and across modality on ERPs to visually presented words. ERPs are shown from mid-frontal (Fz), mid-central (Cz), and mid-parietal (Pz) electrodes. The task requirement was to respond to occasional animal name "targets." Modality-dependent repetition effects are prominent from approximately 200 to 400 ms poststimulus.

400 ms poststimulus that is both repetition and modality sensitive. This effect seems likely to reflect the modulation of perceptual processes contributing to data-driven implicit memory for words and word-like stimuli. This proposal receives support from the finding (Doyle, Rugg, and Wells, 1997) that "formal" priming (e.g., SCAN-SCANDAL), nonword repetition (e.g., BLINT-BLINT), and word repetition all have similar effects on ERPs in the latency range occupied by the modality-sensitive effects illustrated in figure 56.1. Event-related potential findings analogous to those of Rugg and Nieto-Vegas (unpublished data) were also described by Paller and associates (Paller, Kutas, and McIsaac, 1998; Paller and Gross, 1998), who employed manipulations of item presentation format, rather than modality, to identify ERP correlates of data-driven implicit memory. In sum, these observations suggest that ERP repetition effects may reflect the functioning of the domain-specific "perceptual representation systems" proposed by Tulving and Schacter (Tulving and Schacter, 1990; Schacter, 1994) to underlie data-driven priming.

The neural correlates of implicit memory can also be investigated in direct memory tests by contrasting ERPs elicited by studied items that are misclassified as new (misses) with those elicited by correctly classified new items. On the assumption that studied items are "missed" when they fail to elicit explicit memory, differences between these two classes of ERPs represent neural correlates of implicit memory retrieval. This approach has two advantages over studies that investigate implicit memory with indirect memory tests. First, the problem of "contamination" by explicit memory is minimal; the critical items are those that were not remembered explicitly at the time the ERPs were recorded. Second, the approach allows the neural correlates of implicit and explicit memory to be contrasted in one and the same test. This is important because almost all studies that have sought to dissociate brain activity associated with implicit and explicit memory have contrasted findings from direct and indirect tests. Because memory retrieval is intentional on direct tests but unintentional on indirect tests, such

Within Modality
(200–400 msec)

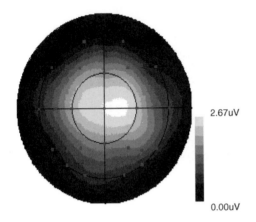

2.67uV

0.00uV

Across Modality
(400–600 msec)

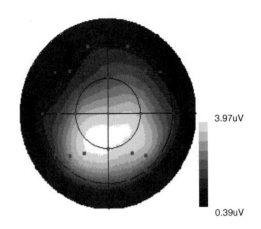

3.97uV

0.39uV

FIGURE 56.2   Topographic maps illustrating the scalp distribution of the repetition effects illustrated in figure 56.1. Left panel: distribution of the early (200–400 ms) within-modality effects. Right panel: distribution of the late (400–600 ms) across modality effects. The latter effects have the more posterior distribution.

A

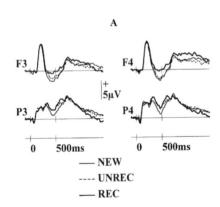

F3   F4

$|^{+}_{5\mu V}$

P3   P4

0   500ms   0   500ms

— NEW

---- UNREC

— REC

B

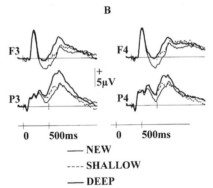

F3   F4

$|^{+}_{5\mu V}$

P3   P4

0   500ms   0   500ms

— NEW

---- SHALLOW

— DEEP

FIGURE 56.3   Event-related potentials (ERPs) from Rugg and associates (1998b), shown for lateral frontal (F3, F4) and parietal (P3, P4) sites. (A) Waveforms elicited by correctly rejected new items (new), and by recognized (rec) and unrecognized (unrec) old items. Note the similarity at the parietal sites of the early differences between the ERPs to new items and those to each class of old item. (B) Waveforms elicited by correctly rejected new items, and recognized items accorded either deep or shallow study.

studies confound retrieval intentionality with type of memory.

Event-related potentials elicited by recognition "misses" were investigated by Rugg, Mark, and colleagues (1998). Participants studied a series of words under either "deep" (sentence generation) or "shallow" (alphabetic judgment) conditions and subsequently were tested for their recognition memory of these words. Although more than 90% of the deeply studied words were recognized, this was true for only 50% of the shallowly studied items, permitting ERPs of equivalent signal quality to be formed for shallow "hits" and shallow "misses." At central and parietal electrode locations, the ERPs to

hits and misses were both more positive-going than were those to correct rejections. At frontal sites, by contrast, only the ERPs to hits differed from those to new items (figure 56.3A). Furthermore, as shown in figure 56.3B, up to approximately 500 ms poststimulus, a very similar ERP modulation was found in the ERPs from parietal electrodes that were elicited by deeply studied test items. Thus, "shallow misses," "shallow hits," and "deep hits" were all associated with a posteriorly distributed positive-going memory effect between approximately 300 to 500 ms poststimulus.

These findings suggest that ERPs detect neural activity associated with implicit memory for recently experi-

**Shallow Hit - New
(300-500 msec)**

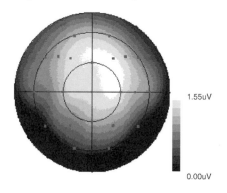

1.55uV

0.00uV

**Shallow Miss - New
(300-500 msec)**

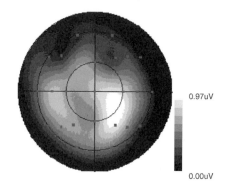

0.97uV

0.00uV

**Deep Hit - New
(300-500 msec)**

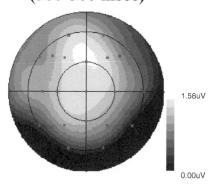

1.58uV

0.00uV

**Deep Hit - New
(500-800 msec)**

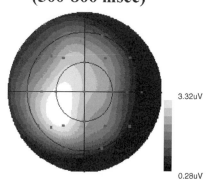

3.32uV

0.28uV

FIGURE 56.4   Topographic maps of the differences between the ERPs to old and new words shown in figure 56.2, showing the distribution of the differences between 300 and 500 ms for recognized (hit) and unrecognized (miss) words, and between 500 and 800 ms for recognized deeply studied words.

enced words and that this activity is neuroanatomically dissociable from that associated with explicit memory (figure 56.4; see color plate 38). Thus, when task factors are held constant, these two forms of memory nonetheless can be dissociated neurophysiologically.

In summary, the view (Rugg, 1995a, b) that there are no convincing examples of ERP correlates of implicit memory no longer seems tenable. Event-related potential repetition effects in indirect tasks are sensitive to the degree of perceptual match between study and test items, mimicking the sensitivity of data-driven implicit memory to this variable. Furthermore, there is evidence that ERPs detect neural activity that is sensitive to the repetition of items for which recognition failed. An important remaining question is whether these different putative neural correlates of implicit memory reflect the activity of a common neural population.

Recollection versus familiarity

As already noted, the proposal that two functionally distinct forms of memory–recollection and familiarity–support recognition memory is controversial. Although support for this view has been claimed on the basis of behavioral findings from studies of both healthy (Jacoby, 1991; Jacoby and Dallas, 1981; Yonelinas, 1994) and amnesic (Verfaille and Treadwell, 1993) participants, the claims have been challenged on the grounds that the findings can be accommodated within models of recognition memory that posit only a single process (Knowlton and Squire, 1995; Mulligan and Hirshman, 1997).

The question of whether recognition memory is supported by one or two processes has been addressed in a number of ERP studies, employing a variety of operational definitions of familiarity and recollection. In all

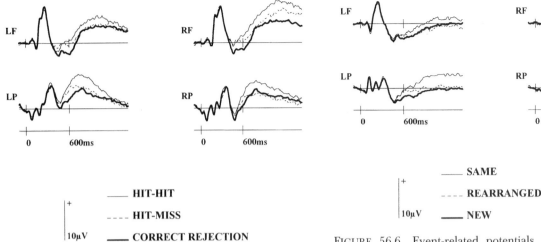

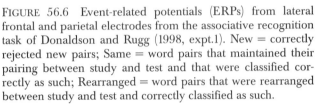

_____ SAME

- - - - REARRANGED

_____ NEW

FIGURE 56.6 Event-related potentials (ERPs) from lateral frontal and parietal electrodes from the associative recognition task of Donaldson and Rugg (1998, expt.1). New = correctly rejected new pairs; Same = word pairs that maintained their pairing between study and test and that were classified correctly as such; Rearranged = word pairs that were rearranged between study and test and correctly classified as such.

_____ HIT-HIT

- - - - HIT-MISS

_____ CORRECT REJECTION

FIGURE 56.5 Data from Wilding and Rugg (1996, expt. 2) illustrating ERPs from lateral frontal and parietal electrodes elicited during a source memory test by words correctly classified as new (correct rejections), recognized and assigned to the incorrect study context (hit-miss), or recognized and assigned to the correct study context (hit-hit).

studies, test items were segregated according to whether they were recollected or recognized on the basis of familiarity alone. If ERP memory effects (i.e., the differences between ERPs to recognized and to new items) elicited by the two classes of item are topographically distinct, this would lend support to the view that recollection and familiarity are supported by functionally distinct cognitive operations. By contrast, single-process models would receive support from the finding that differences between the memory effects are quantitative only.

One way to operationalize the distinction between recollection and familiarity is with a test of source memory. In such tests, participants study a series of items in one context or another. At test, they discriminate studied from unstudied items (yes/no recognition), and in addition, they categorize recognized items according to their study context. According to proponents of the dual-process framework (Jacoby, 1991), trials on which source memory is successful involve recollection of the study episode, whereas trials on which recognition is accurate but memory for source is not are likely to be based solely on familiarity. Thus, the relative proportions of trials associated with each form of memory should vary according to whether source memory is successful or unsuccessful. If recollection and familiarity have distinct neural correlates, the scalp distributions of ERPs elicited by recognized items should vary according to the accuracy of the source judgment.

Wilding and colleagues reported two studies in which ERPs associated with accurate and inaccurate source

memory were contrasted. In their first study (Wilding, Doyle, and Rugg, 1995), the source attribute was sensory modality; in the second study (Wilding and Rugg, 1996), it was speaker voice. In both cases, memory effects were larger for recognized items that were assigned correctly to their study context, but in neither case was there evidence that the effects differed qualitatively (figure 56.5).

Similar findings were reported by Donaldson and Rugg (1998), who investigated the ERP correlates of associative recognition. Participants performed recognition judgments on word pairs that were new, representations of pairs studied in a preceding study task, or re-pairings of study items. Donaldson and Rugg assumed that words that maintained their pairing between study and test (*same* pairs) would be more likely to elicit recollection than rearranged pairs, a high proportion of which would be recognized exclusively on the basis of familiarity (Yonelinas, 1997). As illustrated in figure 56.6, ERP memory effects were markedly larger when elicited by same versus rearranged pairs. However, there was no evidence that the effects elicited by the rearranged pairs differed qualitatively from those elicited by the same pairs.

The findings reviewed previously (see also Wilding and Rugg, 1997) offer little support for dual process models of recognition memory. Rather, the findings support the view (Johnson, Hashtroudi, and Lindsay, 1993; Mulligan and Hirshman, 1997) that recognition based on "familiarity" depends on the same processes as those that support recollection and is better conceived of as impoverished recollection rather than an independent

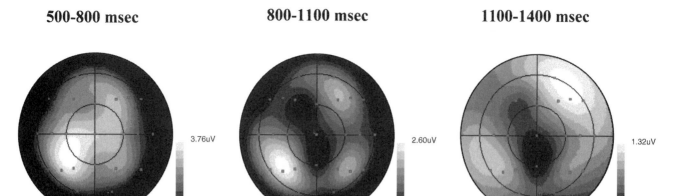

500-800 msec **800-1100 msec** **1100-1400 msec**

3.76uV   2.60uV   1.32uV

1.16uV   0.00uV   4.62uV

FIGURE 56.7   Topographic maps illustrating the scalp distribution of the differences between ERPs elicited by "recollected" words and words correctly classified as new for three consecutive regions of the waveforms (500–800, 800–1100, 1100–1400 ms poststimulus). Maxima corresponding to the left parietal and right frontal effects are clearly evident. The ERPs to recollected items were elicited by words that were either correctly recognized and assigned to their study context, or recognized and given a "remember" judgment in a "remember/know" task. (Data are from Mark and Rugg, 1998.)

basis for recognition. This conclusion is tempered by the possibility that these negative findings reflect the insensitivity of ERPs to the neural activity supporting familiarity, rather than the inadequacy of dual-process models.

The foregoing conclusion also should be qualified in light of the findings from two studies in which a dissociation between the neural correlates of recollection and familiarity may have been obtained. Düzel and colleagues (1997) employed the "Remember/Know" procedure (Tulving, 1985) to distinguish between trials on which recognition was associated with the presence or absence of a "recollective experience." Düzel and associates (1997) reported that ERPs elicited by recognized words endorsed as remembered or known differed in their scalp distributions from approximately 300 to 1000 ms poststimulus. These findings suggest that recollection and familiarity indeed may be electrophysiologically dissociable. For two reasons, however, this conclusion should be considered tentative. First, the number of trials forming the ERPs to old words assigned a "know" judgment was very low in some participants, raising concerns about signal quality. Second, the claim of differing scalp topographies for the ERPs associated with remember and know judgments was made in the absence of appropriate statistical analysis (McCarthy and Wood, 1985).

The second study to suggest that familiarity and recollection can be dissociated electrophysiologically is that of Rugg, Mark, and coworkers (1998) described in the previous section. As shown in figure 56.3, between approximately 300 and 500 ms poststimulus, ERPs from frontal electrodes were more positive-going for recognized old words than they were for correctly rejected and missed items. Unlike the prominent memory effects arising after approximately 500 ms, this frontal effect was insensitive to depth of study processing. These findings therefore provide evidence for two qualitatively distinct patterns of neural activity associated with successful recognition, only one of which is sensitive to depth of study processing. If depth of processing exerts its effects exclusively through recollection (Gardiner, Java, and Richardson-Klavehn, 1996), the ERP findings suggest that familiarity and recollection have distinct neural correlates. Unfortunately, it is unlikely that depth of processing does dissociate recollection and familiarity (Toth, 1996; Yonelinas et al., 1998), leaving the interpretation of these ERP findings uncertain.

In summary, recent ERP findings provide, at best, only weak support for dual-process models of recognition memory. It appears, however, that although ERP memory effects may not dissociate two bases for recognition memory, the effects are sensitive to more than just whether a test item is old or new and index instead the amount of information that can be retrieved about the context in which an old item was experienced. Thus, ERP memory effects appear to reflect cognitive operations associated with the recollection of recently experienced episodes (episodic memory). In the next section, we assess this proposal in more detail, and address the question of whether the cognitive operations supporting recollection can be dissociated neurally and functionally.

Event-related potentials and recollection

As is evident from figures 56.5 and 56.7 (see color plate 39), the ERP memory effects associated with successful recollection are manifest as at least two positive-going modulations of the waveform, dissociable on both temporal and neuroanatomical criteria (see also Allan, Wilding, and Rugg, 1998). One of these modulations (the "left parietal effect") onsets at approximately 400 to 500 ms, is maximal over the left parietal scalp, and typically has a duration of approximately 500 ms. The other modulation (the "right frontal effect") onsets at about the same time or a little later, is maximal over the right frontal scalp, and is considerably more sustained over time.

The proposal that the left parietal effect is an electrophysiological correlate of recollection fits well with the findings of previous research investigating the ERP correlates of recognition memory (Rugg, 1995a,b; Allan, Wilding, and Rugg, 1998). The proposal receives additional support from studies (Düzel et al., 1997; Johnson et al., 1997) in which the ERP correlates of "false recollection" (Roediger and McDermott, 1995) were investigated. This term refers to the tendency of participants to make a "false alarm" response to unstudied associates of study items and to endorse such responses as "remembered." This tendency is believed to depend on the same processes that support "true" recollection (Schacter et al., 1996). Düzel and associates (1997) and Johnson and colleagues (1997) found that in contrast to the ERPs elicited by false alarms to items that are not associates of study words, the ERPs to falsely recollected items elicited prominent left parietal effects, comparable in magnitude to the effects elicited by items correctly endorsed as old.

The right frontal effect appears to be most prominent in tasks that require more than simple old/new recognition judgments and first came to light in the study of source memory by Wilding and Rugg (1996; see figure 56.5). The effect was also found in the associative recognition task of Donaldson and Rugg (1998; see figure 56.6), in the Remember/Know task (Rugg, Schloerscheidt, and Mark, 1998; Düzel et al., 1997) and, in a much attenuated form, in a study of old/new recognition (Allan and Rugg, 1997a).

The differing spatiotemporal characteristics of the left parietal and right frontal effects suggest that they reflect distinct cognitive operations. Wilding and Rugg (1996) proposed that these operations involve the retrieval of item and contextual information from memory–operations supported by the "medial temporal lobe memory system" (Squire, 1992)–and processing the products of retrieval to generate an episodic representation capable of supporting accurate source discrimination–operations held to be dependent on the prefrontal cortex (Squire, Knowlton, and Musen, 1993). Wilding and Rugg (1996) linked the left parietal effect to the first of these operations and the right frontal effect with the second, "postretrieval," operation.

By linking the left parietal effect to retrieval operations supported by the medial temporal lobe, Wilding and Rugg (1996) did not mean to imply that the effect directly reflected neural activity in these regions. Indeed, current evidence suggests that hippocampal activity makes, at best, a very modest contribution to scalp-recorded potentials (Rugg, 1995c). A more likely possibility is that the left parietal effect reflects changes in cortical activity resulting from the corticohippocampal interactions that have been proposed to underlie episodic memory retrieval (McClelland, McNaughton, and O'Reilly, 1995). This hypothesis about the neural origins of the left parietal effect is consistent with the findings of a PET study of depth of processing effects on recognition memory (Rugg et al., 1997; Rugg, Walla, et al., 1998). Relative to the recognition of shallowly studied items, recognition of deeply studied items was associated with activation not only in the left hippocampal formation, but also in an extensive region of the cortex of the left hemisphere, including frontal, temporal, and parietal areas.

The proposal that the right frontal effect reflects cognitive operations associated with "post-retrieval" processing receives support from both functional and neuroanatomical evidence. The idea that the products of memory retrieval are subjected to such operations as "monitoring" or "evaluation," and that the need for such operations varies with task demands, is central to some models of memory retrieval (Koriat and Goldsmith, 1996). The nature of the memory impairments that follow lesions of the prefrontal cortex suggests that these impairments reflect, in part, the disruption of postretrieval processing (Shallice, 1988).

The scalp distribution (figure 56.7) of the right frontal effect suggests that its generator is located within right prefrontal cortex. This hypothesis receives support from the findings of studies of memory retrieval using PET and fMRI, which have demonstrated consistently that episodic memory retrieval is associated with activation of right dorsolateral and anterior prefrontal cortex (Fletcher, Frith, and Rugg, 1997). The hypothesis receives further support from functional neuroimaging studies showing that the activity of this region is greater when recognition memory test items elicit successful retrieval than when they do not (Buckner et al., 1998a; Rugg et al., 1996; Rugg, Fletcher, et al., 1998; but see also Buckner et al., 1998b; Kapur et al., 1995; Nyberg et al., 1995).

Thus far, the experiments described in this section have all investigated the ERP correlates of recollection by employing "copy" cues to elicit the retrieval of episodic memories. It is, of course, also possible to elicit memory retrieval with cues that provide only an incomplete specification of study items. One such task is wordstem cued recall, in the simplest version of which participants are required to retrieve study words in response to three letter (stem) cues (e.g., MOTEL > MOT___). The ERP correlates of recollection engendered by such cues differ from those found with copy cues (Allan, Doyle, and Rugg, 1996; Allan and Rugg, 1997a, b). These studies all employed the same basic test procedure: A series of stems were presented, only a proportion of which corresponded to study items. Participants attempted to retrieve a study word in response to each stem and, following a response cue, provided a study word if they could or gave the first word to come to mind. Crucially, participants also judged whether each completion belonged to the study list, making it possible to separate recalled study items according to whether recall was implicit (associated with the judgment that the item had *not* appeared at study) or accompanied by explicit memory for the study presentation (associated with a positive judgment; see Jacoby, Toth, and Yonelinas, 1993, and Jacoby, 1998, for discussion of the explicit/implicit distinction in cued recall).

The basic finding from these studies is illustrated in figure 56.8, which contrasts waveforms elicited by stems completed with explicitly retrieved study words and unstudied items. The ERPs to the stems corresponding to the studied items show a positive-going ERP modulation that onsets at approximately 300 ms and continues until the end of the recording epoch. Figure 56.9 (see color plate 40) shows that the scalp distribution of these memory effects evolves from an initial anterior midline focus to include a left temporoparietal maximum, before shifting back to a (right) anterior focus. These effects seem likely to be a relatively pure reflection of episodic memory because they are absent in ERPs elicited by stems completed with falsely recognized unstudied items and in ERPs elicited by correct completions wrongly judged

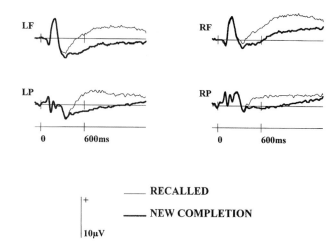

FIGURE 56.8 Event-related potentials (ERPs) from lateral frontal and parietal electrodes elicited by word stems in the study of Allan and Rugg (1997b). ERPs are shown for stems correctly completed with items judged to have been shown at study, collapsed across a subsequent source (study list) judgment (recalled), and for stems completed with unstudied items correctly endorsed as "new" (new completion).

to be unstudied (Allan, Doyle, and Rugg, 1996). This proposal is strengthened by the findings of Allan and Rugg (1997b). Employing a source procedure, they reported that the scalp distribution of the memory effects for correctly completed stems assigned to their correct encoding context was indistinguishable from the distribution of the effects elicited by stems attracting an incorrect source judgment. This finding suggests that, as far as can be detected from the scalp, the same memory processes supported retrieval of the study item and its encoding context.

The findings from the cued recall studies described previously are important for two reasons. First, they

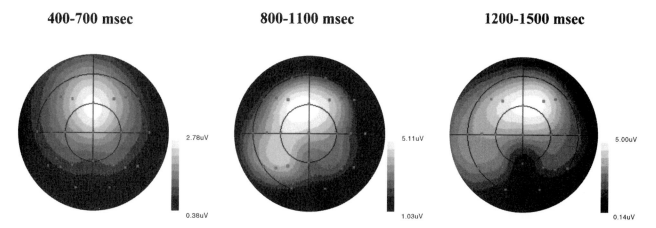

FIGURE 56.9 Topographic maps illustrating the scalp distribution of the memory effects shown in figure 56.8. Each map depicts the differences between ERPs evoked by stems correctly completed with studied items, collapsed across the subsequent source judgment, and ERPs evoked by stems completed with unstudied items correctly endorsed as "new." Maps are shown for three latency regions, 400–700 ms, 800–1100 ms, and 1200–1500 ms.

indicate that recollection is associated with more than one pattern of ERP memory effects. Although the effects from cued recall appear to include contributions from the generators of the left parietal and right frontal effects discussed previously, the cued recall effects are distributed more diffusely over the scalp than are the effects elicited by copy cues (Allan and Rugg, 1997a). Second, the findings show that the left parietal effect is not necessarily the earliest electrophysiological sign of successful memory retrieval. In cued recall, the earliest such sign takes the form of a bilaterally distributed effect over the frontal scalp (figure 56.9). Similar findings have been reported in other studies (figure 56.4; Rugg, Mark, et al., 1998; Tendolkar, Doyle, and Rugg, 1997; Schloerscheidt and Rugg, 1997).

Together, the findings reviewed in this section indicate that recollection–the bringing to mind of aspects of a prior episode–is associated with a pattern of neural activity that varies in its scalp distribution over the first two seconds or so following the presentation of a retrieval cue. Although part of this activity (e.g., that reflected by the left parietal effect) appears to be engaged in an obligatory fashion when a test item engenders recollection, other activity appears to be more task dependent.

By identifying the structures responsible for generating recollection-related ERP effects and specifying their functional significance, it will be possible to shed further light on the mechanisms by which retrieval cues engender recollection and the means by which representations of prior experiences can be used to guide behavior.

ACKNOWLEDGMENTS The authors' research was supported by the Wellcome Trust, the Medical Research Council, and the Biotechnology and Biological Sciences Research Council. The authors thank David I. Donaldson for his comments on a draft of this chapter.

REFERENCES

ALLAN, K., M. C. DOYLE, and M. D. RUGG, 1996. An event-related potential study of word-stem cued recall. *Cogn. Brain Res.* 4:251–262.

ALLAN, K., and M. D. RUGG, 1997a. An event-related potential study of explicit memory on tests of word-stem cued recall and recognition memory. *Neuropsychologia* 35:387–397.

ALLAN, K., and M. D. RUGG, 1997b. Electrophysiological correlates of cued episodic retrieval. *Neuroimage* 5:S613.

ALLAN, K., E. L. WILDING, and M. D. RUGG, 1998. Electrophysiological evidence for dissociable processes contributing to recollection. *Acta Psychologica* 98:231–252.

BOWERS, J. S., and D. L. SCHACTER, 1990. Implicit memory and test awareness. *J. Exp. Psychol. Learn. Mem. Cogn.* 16:404–416.

BUCKNER, R.L., W. KOUTSAAL, D. L. SCHACTER, A. D. WAGNER, and B. R. ROSEN, 1998a. Functional-anatomic study of episodic memory using fMRI: I. Retrieval effort versus retrieval success. *Neuroimage* 7:151–162.

BUCKNER, R.L., W. KOUTSAAL, D. L. SCHACTER, A. M. DALE, M. ROTTE, and B. R. ROSEN, 1998b. Functional-anatomic study of episodic memory using fMRI: II. Selective averaging of event-related fMRI trials to test the retrieval success hypothesis. *Neuroimage* 7:163–175.

DONALDSON, D. I., and M. D. RUGG, 1998. Recognition memory for new associations: Electrophysiological evidence for the role of recollection. *Neuropsychologia* 36:377–395.

DOYLE, M. C., M. D. RUGG, and T. WELLS, 1997. A comparison of the electrophysiological effects of formal and repetition priming. *Psychophysiology* 33:132–147.

DÜZEL, E., A. P. YONELINAS, G. R. MANGUN, H. J. HEINZE, and E. TULVING, 1997. Event-related brain potential correlates of two states of conscious awareness in memory. *Proc. Natl. Acad. Sci. U.S.A.* 94:5973–5978.

FLETCHER, P.C., C. D. FRITH, and M. D. RUGG, 1997. The functional neuroanatomy of episodic memory. *Trends Neurosci.* 20:213–218.

GARDINER, J. M., R. I. JAVA, and A. RICHARDSON-KLAVEHN, 1996. How level of processing really influences awareness in recognition memory. *Can. J. Exp. Psychol.* 50:114–122.

JACOBY, L. L., 1991. A process dissociation framework: Separating automatic from intentional uses of memory. *J. Mem. Lang.* 30:513–541.

JACOBY, L. L., 1998. Invariance in automatic influences of memory: Toward a user's guide for the process-dissociation procedure. *J. Exp. Psychol. Learn. Mem. Cogn.* 24:3–26.

JACOBY, L. L., and M. DALLAS, 1981. On the relationship between autobiographical memory and perceptual learning. *J. Exp. Psychol. Gen.* 3:306–340.

JACOBY, L. L., and C. KELLEY, 1992. Unconscious influences of memory: Dissociations and automaticity. In *The Neuropsychology of Consciousness*, A. D. Milner and M. D. Rugg, eds. London: Academic Press, pp. 201–233.

JACOBY, L. L., J. P. TOTH, and A. P. YONELINAS, 1993. Separating conscious and unconscious influences of memory: Measuring recollection. *J. Exp. Psychol. Gen.* 122:139–154.

JOHNSON, M. K., S. HASHTROUDI, and D. S. LINDSAY, 1993. Source monitoring. *Psychol. Bull.* 114:3–28.

JOHNSON, M. K., S. F. NOLDE, M. MATHER, J. KOUNIOS, D. L. SCHACTER, and T. CURRAN, 1997. The similarity of brain activity associated with true and false recognition memory depends on test format. *Psychol. Sci.* 8:250–257.

JOHNSON, R., 1995. Event-related potential insights into the neurobiology of memory systems. In *Handbook of Neuropsychology, Vol. 10*, J. C. Boller and J. Grafman, eds. Amsterdam: Elsevier, pp. 135–164.

KAPUR, S., F. I. M. CRAIK, C. JONES, G. M. BROWN, S. HOULE, and E. TULVING, 1995. Functional role of the prefrontal cortex in retrieval of memories–A PET study. *Neuroreport* 14:1880–1884.

KNOWLTON, B. J., and L. R. SQUIRE, 1995. Remembering and knowing: Two different expressions of declarative memory. *J. Exp. Psychol. Learn. Mem Cogn.* 21:699–710.

KORIAT, A., and M. GOLDSMITH, 1996. Monitoring and control processes in the strategic regulation of memory accuracy. *Psychol. Rev.* 103:490–517.

KUTAS, M., and A. DALE, 1998. Electrical and magnetic readings of mental functions. In *Cognitive Neuroscience*, M. D. Rugg, ed. Hove, U.K.: Psychology Press, pp. 197–242.

MANDLER, G., 1980. Recognising: The judgment of previous occurrence. *Psychol. Rev.* 87:252–271.

MARK, R. E., and M. D. RUGG, 1998. Age effects on brain activity associated with episodic memory retrieval: An electrophysiological study. *Brain* 121:861–873.

MCCARTHY, G., and C. C. WOOD, 1985. Scalp distributions of event-related potentials: An ambiguity associated with analysis of variance models. *Electroencephalogr. Clin. Neurophysiol.* 62:203–208.

MCCLELLAND, J. L., B. L. MCNAUGHTON, and R. C. O'REILLY, 1995. Why are there complementary learning systems in the hippocampus and neocortex: Insights from the successes and failures of connectionist models of learning and memory. *Psychol. Rev.* 102:419–457.

MOSCOVITCH, M., E. VRIEZEN, and J. GOTTSTEIN, 1993. Implicit tests of memory in patients with focal lesions or degenerative brain disorders. In *The Handbook of Neuropsychology, Vol. 9*. H. Spinnler and J. Boller, eds. Amsterdam: Elsevier, pp. 133–178.

MULLIGAN, N. W., and E. HIRSHMAN, 1997. Measuring the bases of recognition memory: An investigation of the process-dissociation framework. *J. Exp. Psychol. Learn. Mem. Cogn.* 23:280–304.

NYBERG, L., E. TULVING, R. HABIB, L.-G. NILSSON, S. KAPUR, S. HOULE, R. CABEZA, and A. R. MCINTOSH, 1995. Functional brain maps of retrieval mode and recovery of episodic information. *Neuroreport* 7:249–252.

PALLER, K. A., and M. GROSS, 1998. Brain potentials associated with perceptual priming versus explicit remembering during the repetition of visual word-form. *Neuropsychologia* 36:559–571.

PALLER, K. A., M. KUTAS, and H. K. MCISAAC, 1998. An electrophysiological measure of priming of visual word-form. *Conscious. Cogn.* 7:54–66.

RICHARDSON-KLAVEHN, A., J. M. GARDINER, and R. I. JAVA, 1996. Memory: Task dissociations, process dissociations and dissociations of consciousness. In *Implicit Cognition*, G. Underwood, ed. Oxford, U.K.: Oxford University Press, pp. 85–158.

ROEDIGER, H. L., and K. B. MCDERMOTT, 1993. Implicit memory in normal human subjects. In *The Handbook of Neuropsychology, Vol. 9*, H. Spinnler and J. Boller, eds. Amsterdam: Elsevier, pp. 63–131.

ROEDIGER, H. L., and K. B. MCDERMOTT. 1995. Creating false memories–Remembering words not presented in lists. *J. Exp. Psychol. Learn. Mem. Cogn.* 21:803–814.

RUGG, M. D., 1995a. ERP studies of memory. In *Electrophysiology of Mind: Event-Related Brain Potentials and Cognition*, M. D. Rugg and M. G. H. Coles, eds. Oxford, U.K.: Oxford University Press, pp. 132–170.

RUGG, M. D., 1995b. Event-related potential studies of human memory. In *The Cognitive Neurosciences*, M.S. Gazzaniga, ed. Cambridge, Mass.: MIT Press, pp. 1341–1356.

RUGG, M.D., 1995c. Cognitive event-related potentials: Intracranial and lesion studies. In *Handbook of Neuropsychology, Vol. 10*, J. C. Baron and J. Grafman, eds. Amsterdam: Elsevier, pp. 165–186.

RUGG, M. D., and M. G. H. COLES, 1995a. *Electrophysiology of Mind: Event-Related Brain Potentials and Cognition*. Oxford, U.K.: Oxford University Press.

RUGG, M. D., and M. G. H. COLES, 1995b. The ERP and cognitive psychology: Conceptual issues. In *Electrophysiology of Mind: Event-Related Brain Potentials and Cognition*, M. D.

Rugg and M. G. H. Coles, eds. Oxford, U.K.: Oxford University Press, pp. 27–39.

RUGG, M.D., P. C. FLETCHER, K. ALLAN, C. D. FRITH, R. S. J. FRACKOWIAK, and R. J. DOLAN, 1998. Neural correlates of memory retrieval during recognition memory and cued recall. *Neuroimage* 8:262–273.

RUGG, M.D., P. C. FLETCHER, C. D. FRITH, R. S. J. FRACKOWIAK, and R. J. DOLAN, 1996. Differential activation of the prefrontal cortex in successful and unsuccessful memory retrieval. *Brain* 119:2073–2083.

RUGG, M.D., P. C. FLETCHER, C. D. FRITH, R. S. J. FRACKOWIAK, and R. J. DOLAN, 1997. Brain regions supporting intentional and incidental memory: A PET study. *Neuroreport* 8:1283–1287.

RUGG, M.D., R. E. MARK, P. WALLA, E. M. SCHLOERSCHEIDT, C. S. BIRCH, and K. ALLAN, 1998. Dissociation of the neural correlates of implicit and explicit memory. *Nature* 392:595–598.

RUGG, M. D., A. M. SCHLOERSCHEIDT, and R. E. MARK, 1998. An electrophysiological comparison of two indices of recollection. *J. Mem. Lang.* 39:47–69.

RUGG, M. D., P. WALLA, E. M. SCHLOERSCHEIDT, P. C. FLETCHER, C. D. FRITH, and R. J. DOLAN, 1998. Neural correlates of depth of processing effects on recollection: Evidence from brain potentials and PET. *Exp. Brain Res.* 123:18–23.

SCHACTER, D. L., 1994. Priming and multiple memory systems: Perceptual mechanisms of implicit memory. In *Memory Systems 1994*, D. L. Schacter and E. Tulving, eds. Cambridge, Mass.: MIT Press, pp. 233–268.

SCHACTER, D. L., E. REIMAN, T. CURRAN, L. S. YUN, D. BANDY, K. B. MCDERMOTT, and H. L. ROEDIGER, 1996. Neuroanatomical correlates of veridical and illusory recognition memory–Evidence from positron emission tomography. *Neuron* 17:267–274.

SCHLOERSCHEIDT, A. M., and M. D. RUGG, 1997. Recognition memory for words and pictures: An event-related potential study. *Neuroreport* 8:3281–3285.

SHALLICE, T., 1988. *From neuropsychology to mental structure*. Cambridge, U.K.: Cambridge University Press.

SQUIRE, L. R., 1992. Memory and hippocampus: A synthesis from findings with rats, monkeys and humans. *Psychol. Rev.* 99:195–231.

SQUIRE, L. R., B. KNOWLTON, and G. MUSEN, 1993. The structure and organization of memory. *Annu. Rev. Psychol.* 44:453–495.

TENDOLKAR, I., M. C. DOYLE, and M. D. RUGG, 1997. An event-related potential study of retroactive interference in memory. *Neuroreport* 8:501–506.

TOTH, J. P., 1996. Conceptual automaticity in recognition memory: Levels of processing effects on familiarity. *Can. J. Exp. Psychol.* 50:123–138.

TULVING, E., 1985. Memory and consciousness. *Can. Psychologist* 26:1–12.

TULVING, E., and D. L. SCHACTER, 1990. Priming and human memory systems. *Science* 247:301–306.

VERFAELLIE, M., and J. R. TREADWELL, 1993. The status of recognition memory in amnesia. *Neuropsychology* 7:5–13.

WILDING, E. L., M. C. DOYLE, and M. D. RUGG, 1995. Recognition memory with and without retrieval of context: An event-related potential study. *Neuropsychologia* 33:743–767.

WILDING, E. L., and M. D. RUGG, 1996. An event-related potential study of recognition memory with and without retrieval of source. *Brain* 119:889–906.

WILDING, E. L., and M. D. RUGG, 1997. Event-related potentials and the recognition memory exclusion task. *Neuropsychologia* 35:119–128.

YONELINAS, A. P., 1994. Receiver-operating characteristics in recognition memory: evidence for a dual-process model. *J. Exp. Psychol. Learn. Mem. Cogn.* 20:1341–1354.

YONELINAS, A. P., 1997. Recognition memory ROCs for item and associative information: The contribution of recollection and familiarity. *Mem. Cogn.* 25:747–763.

YONELINAS, A. P., N. E. A. KROLL, I. DOBBINS, and M. LAZZARA, 1998. Recollection and familiarity deficits in amnesia: Convergence of remember/know, process dissociation and ROC data. *Neuropsychology* 12:323–339.

57 Neuroimaging of Memory

RANDY L. BUCKNER

ABSTRACT Human functional neuroimaging based on positron emission tomography (PET) and functional magnetic resonance imaging (fMRI) provides a powerful means of linking neural level description of brain function and memory. In this chapter, the bases of these neuroimaging methods are discussed, along with three distinct sets of findings linking memory-related cognitive processes to brain activity. (1) Memory encoding activates specific posterior prefrontal regions (near Brodmann areas 44/6 and 44/45) that act interdependently with medial temporal regions to promote memory formation. The laterality of activity within these regions is modulated by the kinds of materials being memorized; verbal materials almost always have activated left-lateralized cortex and nonverbal materials have activated either left- or right-lateralized cortex, depending on the specific encoding task. (2) Repetition of items that results in priming is accompanied by activity reductions in brain areas activated during a task. These reductions can be found in both perceptual and higher-level brain areas, depending on which task components are facilitated through repetition. (3) Explicit attempts to remember the past are associated with increases in anterior prefrontal activity (near Brodmann area 10) that generalize across stimulus type and exact test format. Such investigations suggest that anterior prefrontal areas may participate in processes associated with monitoring of the retrieval attempt. Taken collectively, these three sets of findings illustrate how neuroimaging methods can be applied to elucidate questions about human memory, complementing and extending data derived from other methods.

A primary challenge for the cognitive neuroscience of human memory is the development and application of methods that link mnemonic processes with their underlying neural bases. Providing one kind of link, functional neuroimaging methods offer a means to visualize brain areas active during cognitive operations in awake, healthy humans. By monitoring changes in blood properties correlated with neuronal activity, these methods enable measurement of localized changes in brain function (Posner and Raichle, 1994). In their most technically refined forms, these methods presently allow noninvasive imaging of single trials in memory tasks with a spatial resolution of a few millimeters. This chapter focuses on these and other aspects of how functional neuroimaging methods are

RANDY L. BUCKNER   Departments of Psychology, Anatomy and Neurobiology, and Radiology, Washington University, St. Louis, Mo.

being applied to the study of human memory. The basic properties and limitations of commonly used methods are presented, followed by a description of recent findings.

What can neuroimaging methods tell us about memory?

Cognitive neuroscientific inquiry into human memory seeks to understand how brain activity is modified by experience and to further understand how these modifications influence future information processing. In nonhuman primates and other animals, single-unit activity of neurons or populations of neurons can be recorded directly. In humans, however, these procedures are too invasive to perform other than in the context of brain surgery. We must, therefore, seek alternative methods to characterize neuronal changes relating to memory.

Functional neuroimaging techniques (PET and fMRI) provide one set of alternatives and are able to measure indirectly net neuronal changes within the human brain (Posner and Raichle, 1994; Roland, 1993). PET and fMRI both take advantage of a fortuitous physiologic property: When a region of the brain increases activity, blood flow to that region increases. By injecting into the blood stream radiolabeled isotopes that can be detected by PET scanners, PET allows visualization of blood flow changes relating to neural activity. Functional MRI, which has been applied only widely in the past 5 years, similarly visualizes neural activity indirectly through blood property changes that affect the magnetic signal to which MRI images are sensitive (Kwong et al., 1992).

Several empirical observations suggest that the signals detected by PET and fMRI are valid measurements of local changes in neuronal activity. First, studies of visual cortex activation in relation to well-understood retinotopic organization have repeatedly demonstrated predictable activation patterns (Fox et al., 1995; DeYoe et al., 1996; Sereno et al., 1995) and suggest a current practical resolution of approximately 3 to 6 mm (Engel et al., 1997). Resolution at this level can map areas within broad regions of cortex, such as separate areas within prefrontal or occipital cortex, or can distinguish between

817

the amygdala and hippocampal formation, but would not be expected to resolve the columnar organization within a functional area. Second, fMRI signal change tracks neuronal activity temporally. When prolonged or multiple visual stimuli have been presented to subjects, the fMRI signal summates across the separate (Dale and Buckner, 1997) and continuous (Boynton et al., 1996) evoked neuronal events, as would be predicted for a measurement linked to neuronal activity. Neuroimaging methods also have demonstrated reliability across independent subject groups and even imaging modality (e.g., PET compared with fMRI; Ojemann et al., 1998; Clark et al., 1996). However, despite their many advantages, these methods do come with limitations.

It is unlikely that PET or currently applied fMRI provides much information about local physiologic properties (e.g., whether net activity changes reflect inhibitory or excitatory synapses, or the relative combinations of the two). In this regard, studies with current functional neuroimaging methods likely yield information about net changes in activity (both excitatory and inhibitory) within brain regions spanning several millimeters of the cortex. Furthermore, changes in blood flow in response to neuronal activity are revealed on a temporal scale far longer than the neuronal activity itself (Raichle, 1987; Rosen, Buckner, and Dale, 1998); for a brief sensory event lasting fractions of a second, blood properties change over a 10- to 12-s period. This temporal "blurring" of the signal provides a limitation, but perhaps not as severe as one might imagine. For example, changes in neural activity associated with individual trials of a task can be observed (Buckner et al., 1996). Richter and associates (1997), in a dramatic demonstration of fMRI temporal resolution and sensitivity, captured brain activity associated with a single momentary cognitive act of mentally rotating a stimulus, without averaging over events. Functional MRI methods also have taken advantage of the reliable timing of the evoked blood flow signal to demonstrate temporal resolution at the subsecond level (Menon et al., 1998; Rosen, Buckner, and Dale, 1998).

Beyond basic technical considerations, one also must consider issues related to the practical application of neuroimaging techniques to questions about higher human brain function. Namely, how can a set of tasks and the trials within the tasks be constructed to disentangle brain-based cognitive operations? The basic paradigm construct most commonly used is to have subjects engage one task for a period of time (perhaps a verbal memory retrieval task) and then contrast that with periods of time where subjects perform a reference task (perhaps a matched task involving many of the same components, but lacking a memory retrieval demand).

The logic of such a paradigm assumes that brain activity changes between the two task states and correlates selectively with the manipulated memory retrieval demands. More recently, paradigms that isolate individual trials of memory tasks have been developed—so-called "event-related" procedures (Rosen, Buckner, and Dale, 1998). These procedures allow experimenters to contrast activity associated with different trial types, much like electroencephalogram (EEG) and magnetoencephalogram (MEG) data are analyzed (see chapter 56).

Within both of these paradigm constructs, a significant challenge arises from the uncertainty surrounding how to design tasks that can isolate component processes involved with memory. Although no sure answer can be given here, two basic points are worth making. First, because there is uncertainty, no single study reveals a complete picture. Commonalties across groups of studies should be used to identify convergent findings. Second, it is essential to consider exactly what a subject is performing during the task period or trial being imaged. Memory is an odd entity in this regard. The essence of memory is how task performance at one point in time influences performance at another point in time. Key memory processes associated with storage and learning extend over time. Neuroimaging methods, however, likely only reveal neural correlates of the subset of memory processes associated with acute changes in activity that occur when tasks are being performed. That is, PET and fMRI measurements reflect what a subject is doing at the time of imaging. Such performance may influence learning or benefit from learning, but the snapshot of brain activity provided most likely reflects active information processing associated with task performance and immediate task goals. Memory processes set into motion by the active information processing, but not revealed in terms of acute net changes in neural activity, go undetected. These methods are thus unlike those based on patients with lesions that provide information about processes of any sort that are affected by a loss of a brain region.

Following, three separate areas in which insights about human memory function have been gained through neuroimaging studies are discussed with key points summarized in italics (for additional reviews, see Buckner and Tulving, 1995; Cabeza and Nyberg, 1997; Fletcher, Frith, and Rugg, 1997; Schacter and Buckner, 1998; Ungerleider, 1995).

Episodic memory encoding

A prime example of how neuroimaging has been applied to study human memory arises in explorations of episodic encoding. Memory encoding occurs when information processing leads to memories (and presumably neuronal changes) that endure over time. Daniel Schacter described encoding as "a special way of paying attention to ongoing events that has a major impact on subsequent memory for them" (Schacter, 1996). These processes may be engaged when subjects *intentionally* attempt to remember new materials or when information processing, by means of the kind of task a subject engages, *incidentally* encourages memorization of new materials (Craik and Lockhart, 1972; Craik and Tulving, 1975). Functional neuroimaging studies suggest that both intentional and incidental episodic encoding may depend on common functional changes in brain activity in prefrontal cortex. The data further suggest that frontally mediated processes may involve strategic and volitional aspects of encoding that act interdependently with medial temporal regions to promote memory formation.

FUNCTIONAL-ANATOMIC CORRELATES OF EPISODIC ENCODING   An early illustration of a prototypic incidental encoding study is provided by Kapur and colleagues (1994). In their study, subjects decided whether visually presented words represented entities that were either living or nonliving. This meaning-based (or "deep") word-processing task led to high incidental encoding as evidenced by 75% correct recognition on a later memory test. Positron-emission tomography imaging data contrasting this deep encoding task to a second, poorer encoding task (57% correct recognition) demonstrated robust activation of multiple prefrontal regions. Of importance, this effect was mediated by subject-initiated strategies. Across all encoding conditions, the same items (by means of counterbalancing) were presented. The goals of the subject across conditions mediated participation of left prefrontal regions and facilitated memory encoding.

This basic finding has been replicated and extended with fMRI. Gabrieli and colleagues (Demb et al., 1995; Gabrieli et al., 1996) and Wagner and associates (1998b) have explored another incidental encoding task using fMRI, in which participants decide whether words are abstract (e.g., hope) or concrete (e.g., tree). Significant left prefrontal activation was noted in each of these studies. Demb and associates (1995) further demonstrated that prefrontal activity changes are selective to the kinds of processes that promote encoding and not due to secondary factors such as task difficulty or time on task. In their study, subjects made a difficult surface judgment about the words that took longer to complete than the meaning-based "deep" encoding task. Despite the longer time to respond, minimal activity change was noted for left prefrontal cortex and memory performance was poor. Furthermore, *intentional* memorization

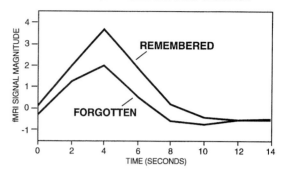

FIGURE 57.1   One example of the association between posterior prefrontal cortex activity and memory encoding is displayed (adapted from Wagner et al., 1998b). The graph shows an fMRI signal change for a left prefrontal region during a verbal semantic classification task. The signal is shown separately for those words later remembered versus those words later forgotten. A clear difference is apparent: Increased activity predicts whether the word will be remembered or forgotten, suggesting a link between processing within left prefrontal cortex and effective verbal memory encoding.

of verbal materials has activated similar left prefrontal regions (Kapur et al., 1996; Kelley et al., 1998), suggesting, as would be predicted from behavioral studies (Craik and Tulving, 1975), that both kinds of encoding task lead to engagement of common underlying processes and brain systems.

Illustrating the variety of manners in which neuroimaging studies may be conducted, procedures for sorting fMRI data post hoc based on subject performance provide yet another link between processing associated with left prefrontal cortex and long-term memory encoding. Using event-related fMRI, Wagner and colleagues (1998b) sorted words presented during a deep encoding task by whether the words were remembered subsequently or forgotten on a later recognition test (similar to many event-related potential (ERP) studies; Halgren and Smith, 1987; Paller, 1990). Left prefrontal regions hypothesized to be involved in memory encoding via direct manipulations of encoding operations (Kapur et al., 1996) were most active for those words that would be subsequently remembered (figure 57.1). In essence, neuroimaging measurements of specific left prefrontal brain regions could predict—on average—the level of encoding associated with individual words. The conclusion across all these neuroimaging studies is that *the left prefrontal cortex is active when subjects engage verbal processing tasks that lead to encoding.* Figure 57.2 illustrates this convergence.

It is not, however, likely that left prefrontal regions participate exclusively to promote memory encoding. Quite to the contrary, it appears more reasonable that

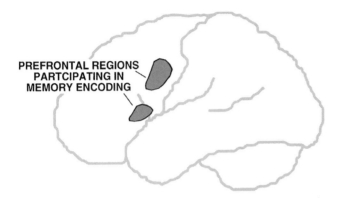

PREFRONTAL REGIONS
PARTCIPATING IN
MEMORY ENCODING

FIGURE 57.2 A schematic of the left hemisphere shows convergence across a number of studies in which verbal episodic memory encoding has been examined (shaded region). Multiple distinct regions of the posterior left prefrontal cortex are consistently active during verbal memory encoding.

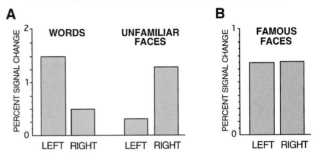

LATERALITY OF PREFRONTAL ACTIVITY DURING ENCODING IS AFFECTED BY THE MATERIAL TYPE BEING MEMORIZED

LATERALITY OF PREFRONTAL REGION

FIGURE 57.3 Data from Kelley and colleagues (1998a, b) demonstrate that lateralization of posterior prefrontal cortex activity during episodic memory encoding can be influenced by the kind of materials being memorized. (A) In their study, verbal materials (words) activated left prefrontal cortex while nonverbal materials (unfamiliar faces) activated right prefrontal cortex (but see also Grady et al., 1995; Haxby et al., 1996). (B) Left prefrontal participation in encoding can be manipulated by increasing the verbal content associated with a stimulus, as shown by the increase in left prefrontal activity when famous faces (e.g., Bill Clinton) are presented, which allow for a verbal referent.

their processing contributions surround active verbal (and perhaps certain forms of nonverbal) information processing that can, as a byproduct, yield activity changes that result in enduring memories. A number of data support this position. Many verbal processing tasks that occur without any instruction to form new memories (or even in the context of a memory study) activate these left prefrontal regions, as noted for several of the aforementioned studies. These kinds of tasks incidentally promote memorization of the words encountered (Tulving et al., 1994). Similarly, a number of verbal working memory tasks have activated these left prefrontal regions (for reviews, see Smith and Jonides, 1997). At the farthest extreme, direct comparisons between intentional verbal encoding and verbal tasks designed to isolate memory retrieval processes have produced similar left prefrontal activations (Buckner and Koutstaal, 1998). The inevitable conclusion is that elaborate verbal processing in a broad range of contexts can activate multiple regions in inferior and dorsal prefrontal cortex and promote memory encoding. This may be the neural basis of "deep" encoding. *Certain forms of elaborate information processing engaged to solve task demands in the present use left prefrontal regions and, as a byproduct, set into motion the cascade of events that leads to memory formation.*

HEMISPHERIC ASYMMETRIES A debated topic has been whether the left prefrontal cortex is associated broadly with processing changes related to episodic encoding or for only a subset of operations relating to verbal materials. On one side of the debate, neuropsychological findings often have found asymmetries in relation to the kinds of materials being processed, the left hemisphere associated more with verbal materials and the right with nonverbal materials. Although such ideas provide only heuristic distinctions, they nonetheless predict against a general left-lateralized set of regions for all memory-encoding operations. On the other side, initial neuroimaging studies found almost exclusively left greater than right activity in relation to memory encoding. Based on these neuroimaging data, Tulving and colleagues (1994) formulated an influential model about hemispheric asymmetry in relation to memory function. As part of their model, they postulated that left prefrontal regions are involved in encoding information to the extent that right prefrontal regions are not, at least in so far as verbal information is concerned. The eight initial studies on which they based their model all involved encoding of verbal materials. An open question has been whether left prefrontal regions participating in encoding would generalize to all nonverbal materials or whether neuropsychological findings would predict hemispheric lateralization.

Recent fMRI data suggest that the materials being memorized influence the laterality of the prefrontal areas engaged during encoding. Supporting this possibility, Kelley and associates (1998a) showed that intentional memorization of words activates the left prefrontal cortex whereas memorization of unfamiliar faces (which lack a verbal referent) activates a homologous right frontal region with minimal left frontal activity (figure 57.3). In a further study (Kelly et al., 1998b), they showed that adding a verbal tag associated with the faces additionally activates the left prefrontal cortex in a region similar to that activated by words. This latter finding was demonstrated by contrasting encoding of nameable famous faces (e.g., Bill Clinton) with unfamiliar faces. Unfamiliar faces activated the unilateral right frontal cortex, whereas nameable famous faces activated the bilateral frontal cortex. The complete interpretation of these findings is complicated by additional studies that have shown bilateral or left-lateralized changes associated with face encoding (Grady et al., 1995; Haxby et al., 1996). However, the presence of studies in which right-lateralized prefrontal regions are sufficient for effective memory encoding argues strongly against the idea that a general encoding operation can be performed only by the left prefrontal cortex. It is more likely that *multiple left and right prefrontal regions participate in memory encoding dependent on the exact materials and/or encoding strategies that certain classes of materials may tend to encourage.* Prefrontal participation in episodic memory encoding appears to be domain specific.

MEDIAL TEMPORAL CONTRIBUTIONS TO MEMORY ENCODING   As is well established from human lesion and primate studies, the integrity of the medial temporal lobe is important for the long-term formation of certain kinds of memories (Cohen and Eichenbaun, 1993; Corkin, 1984; Squire, 1992). A puzzle has existed in the neuroimaging field because there have been only sporadic findings of medial temporal lobe involvement in PET and fMRI studies of encoding. Most notably, effective incidental encoding tasks often have failed to detect differential activation in these regions compared with less effective encoding tasks (Buckner and Koutstaal, 1998; Fletcher et al., 1995; Kapur et al., 1994). This has led to past conclusions that functional neuroimaging may be unable to detect reliably the role of medial temporal regions, specifically the hippocampal formation, in memory encoding (Buckner and Koutstaal, 1998; Fletcher, Frith, and Rugg, 1997). However, there also have been several reports of hippocampal involvement in encoding when novel, visual scenes or faces are presented and contrasted with repeated (familiar) stimuli or scrambled meaningless forms (Gabrieli et al., 1997; Grady et al., 1995; Haxby et al., 1996; Stern et al., 1996; Tulving et al., 1996). Across these studies and those that followed, an important (but not completely predictive) variable for activating the hippocampal formation has been the status of the cue (e.g., type, familiarity, and its context). Martin and colleagues (1997), for example, found that the kind of stimulus presented (e.g., word vs. nonsense noise pattern) dictated the level of hippocampal activity. Similarly, Kelley and associates (1998a) noted clear asymmetry of hippocampal formation activation; words activated the left, and faces activated the right. Dolan and Fletcher (1997) found that word pairs differentially

activated the hippocampal formation dependent on the familiarity and prior manner in which they had been associated (paired).

These findings are complicated by several studies yielding null results and a few that have shown modulation of hippocampal formation activity change in relation to task instructions (Kelley et al., 1998a). Nonetheless, the aforementioned studies suggest a reasonably consistent pattern of medial temporal lobe activation, often including the hippocampal formation, when cues are presented that elicit memory encoding. A working hypothesis derived from the neuroimaging data, which is similar to ideas expressed previously based on neuropsychological data (Moscovitch, 1992), is that *strategic frontally mediated processes act interdependently with more cue-driven participation of medial temporal regions to promote memory formation* (see also Schacter et al., 1996; see chapter 56 for a related idea in terms of memory retrieval). Participation of both regions is critical. Task situations that do not activate prefrontal regions tend not to promote long-term memory encoding. Conceptualized in functional terms, the hypothesis is that to encode a memory in a consciously accessible form, it is necessary to involve prefrontal-mediated pathways that participate in high-level representation of the information as well as medial temporal systems that may be necessary for long-term integration or binding of the information (Buckner et al., 1999).

One immediate objection to such an idea may be that frontal lesions often do not significantly impair memory encoding. Here may lie one of the great overstatements of memory research. Left frontal lesions that damage the prefrontal regions commonly activated by memory-encoding tasks cause aphasia and related disturbances of language (Buckner and Tulving, 1995). Contributions that these regions make to memory encoding may have been downplayed previously because of their interdependent roles in active verbal processing and speech production. That is, secondary deficits (e.g., memory encoding) may be overshadowed by their more immediately present symptoms (e.g., production aphasia). Neuroimaging data encourage us to reconsider the important roles prefrontal regions play in episodic memory encoding.

Implicit memory (priming)

Implicit memory refers to any nonconscious influence of past experience on current performance or behavior (Roediger and McDermott, 1993; Schacter, 1987a). Relevant to this chapter, exploration of human neural correlates of implicit memory is an area in which neuroimaging has been influential in providing insight. In particular, a large number of studies have focussed on

A. BEHAVIORAL DATA   B. PET DATA FROM VISUAL CORTEX

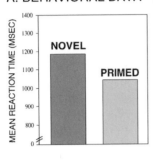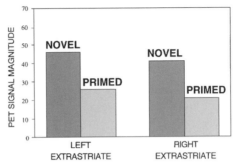

FIGURE 57.4 Repeating an item within a task leads to decreases in reaction time (A) that correlate with decreases in specific brain areas (B). The change in neural activity in (B) is likely a correlate of repetition priming. (Adapted from Buckner et al., 1995.)

a subset of implicit memory phenomenon referred to as *priming*. Priming occurs when the ability to identify or produce an item is changed as a result of a specific prior encounter with the item (Tulving and Schacter, 1990). The prototypical experimental task eliciting priming involves presenting items on at least two separate occasions and asking how the presence of the item on the first occasion influences performance measures taken during the presentation of the item on subsequent occasions. Most typically, performance during the repeated exposures is faster or the response is biased (e.g., seeing the word "house" on one occasion speeds the reading of the word "house" on a later occasion).

FUNCTIONAL-ANATOMIC CORRELATES OF PRIMING Functional-anatomic exploration of priming began with a series of PET studies by Petersen and colleagues (Buckner et al., 1995; Squire et al., 1992) in which subjects were exposed to words (e.g., course) and then asked to generate completions to word-stems (e.g., cou___). Priming was manifest in an increased likelihood that subjects would respond with the study words as compared with the situation where no relevant study words had been presented. Subjects were not instructed to refer to the earlier study lists, yet the primed exposure had implicitly influenced performance. In terms of brain activity, measurements indicated that visual extrastriate regions active during word completion were less active if prior exposure to related words primed performance. Combined with the behavioral observation that primed word completions were produced faster than nonprimed words, the data revealed a neural correlate of priming: *perceptual processing of a stimulus is more efficient after exposure to that stimulus, producing quicker response and requiring less net neural activity in brain areas actively processing perceptual information.*

Activity reductions in extrastriate cortical regions in relation to priming have generalized to a number of different tasks using varied visual stimulus types, including word-stems (Backman et al., 1997; Schacter et al., 1996), word fragments (Blaxton et al., 1996), and visual objects (Buckner et al., 1998a) (figure 57.4). Moreover, examination of the anatomic locations of the priming-related reductions for words and objects indicates that higher-level visual areas are most affected while early visual areas falling at or near the striate cortex are least affected. The data thus suggest that *priming-related activity reductions manifest in an anatomically specific manner, with only a subset of active brain areas modulating in response to prior stimulus exposure* (figure 57.5; Buckner et al., 1998a).

Although anatomic specificity is present, priming-related activity reductions are not limited to perceptual processing areas. Raichle and associates (1994) explored item repetition across a word generation task requiring semantic access. Subjects generated verbs for nouns and then were exposed to many repetitions of the same nouns. They found robust decreases in left prefrontal areas associated with increasing task facilitation across the many item repetitions. Gabrieli and colleagues (Demb et al., 1995; Gabrieli et al., 1996) examined direct-item repetition after a single exposure in a semantic decision task. Subjects viewed words and decided whether the words were abstract or concrete. Functional MRI data revealed that repetition again was correlated with reduced activation in left prefrontal regions. Thus, *priming effects can be observed in higher-order brain regions when appropriate task processes overlap across item repetitions* (Schacter and Buckner, 1998).

Neuroimaging studies of human priming also provide a point of contact for nonhuman primate studies of memory, allowing insight into single-unit neural activity changes that might underlie the PET and fMRI effects

BRAIN AREAS AFFECTED BY PRIMING ARE ANATOMICALLY SELECTIVE

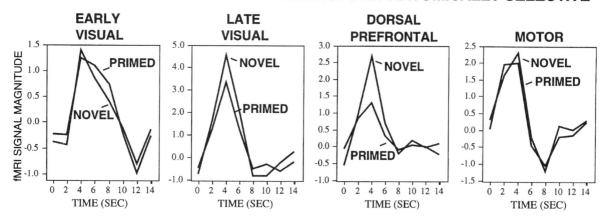

FIGURE 57.5 Priming-related activity reductions are anatomically specific. Functional MRI signal changes across distributed regions of cortex for an object decision task in which items were repeated (primed) or novel. Brain areas within midlevels of the processing hierarchy (late visual and prefrontal) demonstrate decreased activity in relation to item repetition, whereas earlier visual areas and output motor areas show minimal or no effects of prior item exposure.

(Ungerleider, 1995; Wiggs and Martin, 1998). For example, Miller and Desimone (1994) presented sequences of objects to monkeys, one object at a time. The monkeys' task was to detect a target object identified before the sequence. Secondary to the task, presentation of some of the objects (nontarget objects) was repeated. Net reductions in single-unit activity in the inferotemporal cortex were observed for repeated nontarget objects, similar to repetitions of objects in humans (Buckner et al., 1998a). Moreover, the signal reductions in fMRI and the reductions in single-unit spike activity both rebound (return to near baseline levels) when new items are presented. Thus, the observations in both humans and monkeys suggest item repetition can be associated with a stimulus-specific reduction in activity as would be expected for a neural mechanism underlying behavioral repetition priming effects.

THE CONCEPT OF STIMULUS NOVELTY A number of studies have examined neural correlates of item repetition in the context of asking questions about the fate of novel versus repeated stimuli. These studies suggest the possibility that there exist certain processes to deal with unexpected or novel stimuli (Tulving et al., 1996). Novel stimuli demand the most elaborate and flexible processing because they either are not currently anticipated or do not have a preexisting representation. Critical to this chapter, novelty phenomena share many of the same properties as repetition priming: A differential response is being assessed for novel stimuli compared with repeated stimuli. It therefore is worth flushing out similarities and differences between the two concepts.

The concept of novelty subsumes at least two separable effects. One is the possibility of a signal or a response that indicates a stimulus is novel–independent of the specific stimulus. Activity in a population of neurons conveying this kind of "novelty signal" would be expected to modulate during the presentation of a large class of novel stimuli. Such activity could aid in the detection of novelty, but would not participate directly in the perception of the novel object. Another kind of effect would be stimulus specific and manifest as a change in activity in those neurons differentially responsive to the specific stimulus repeating. The former refers to a more global signal that could serve to orient or modulate brain systems, whereas the latter relates to the underlying codes used to identify or process a specific stimulus that may change with experience.

Unfortunately, PET and fMRI data are noncommittal as to which of these two kinds of effect cause the modulations discussed. Visual extrastriate activity reductions, for example, might originate because novel stimuli trigger an enhancement of visual pathways being used to extract visual characteristics of a stimulus independent of the specific stimulus being presented or, alternatively, may reflect decreased (or tuned) activity in neurons coding the specific stimulus in question. The reason for the lack of information is that neuroimaging techniques do not provide information about the responses of specific neurons to specific stimuli. Driven largely by the similarity between human priming-related activity reductions and single-unit studies in monkeys, it seems most likely that the effect is specific to the stimulus and reflects an underlying tuning of cells responsive to novel as compared with repeated stimuli (Desimone et al., 1995).

Miller, Li, and Desimone (1991) suggested, based on single-unit studies, that certain classes of neurons may "function as adaptive mnemonic 'filters' that preferentially pass information about new, unexpected, or not recently seen stimuli." The same process may be at work in humans and reflect the direct relation between priming and novelty phenomena. When priming is discussed, the immediate effects of neural tuning on performance for items are the focus; when novelty phenomena are discussed, the consequences of the more extensive processing for novel items are the focus, which may include better encoding of the item into long-term memory.

Explicit memory retrieval

Explicit memory, by contrast to implicit memory, is manifest in tasks where there is an intentional attempt to retrieve information from the past. Attempting to remember what one ate for breakfast or where the car is parked are examples of explicit retrieval. In the experimental laboratory, the process of explicit retrieval can be reduced to a study and test procedure in which a subject is instructed during a test to remember words from an earlier study list. To perform such a task, a subject explicitly attempts to remember the past.

FUNCTIONAL-ANATOMIC CORRELATES OF RETRIEVAL ATTEMPT   A clear illustration of the presence and effects of explicit retrieval attempt is exemplified in the comparison of two variants of the word-stem completion task. In the implicit variant discussed earlier in this chapter, priming was the focus. Subjects were instructed to complete word-stems with the first word that came to mind. Subjects were not encouraged to retrieve the earlier study words. One can study explicit retrieval attempts by presenting subjects with word-stems, of the same kind used in the implicit tasks, and asking them to use these as cues to recover the words from a specific previously studied list. The goal of the task is changed from generating any word to generating words associated with a specific prior study episode.

With such instructions, two performance changes are evident. First, subjects complete more cues with earlier study words than would be obtained with priming instructions. Thus, *attempting* to retrieve is associated with generating information from the past more readily than would spontaneously occur by way of implicit processes. Second, subjects tend to take longer to complete the word cues. Thus, unlike implicit retrieval processes that tend to have decreased reaction times, explicit retrieval processes tend to have increased reaction times; explicit retrieval attempt has a processing cost.

Correlated with these behavioral changes, functional neuroimaging studies have demonstrated consistently

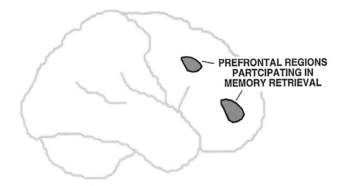

FIGURE 57.6 Explicitly attempting to remember an item from the recent past activates anterior prefrontal cortex (most often right > left). A schematic of the right hemisphere shows convergence across a large number of PET and fMRI studies that have examined explicit retrieval tasks. Note that the location of this anterior prefrontal region is not homologous to the left and right prefrontal regions associated with memory encoding.

that *the anterior prefrontal cortex, near Brodmann area 10, increases activity when subjects attempt to retrieve information from a specific study episode.* The finding has generalized across a wide range of tasks spanning both recognition and recall, using various kinds of experimental materials, including words, pictures of faces, and objects (Buckner, 1996; figure 57.6). The consistent observation of prefrontal activation and the tendency toward right greater than left lateralization led Tulving and colleagues (1994) to suggest that there is preferential involvement of right prefrontal cortex during conscious attempts to remember the past. This important observation provides a useful heuristic, but it should be noted that the areas tending to show differential activation during retrieval (which localize to anterior prefrontal cortex) often occur concurrently with either bilateral or left-lateralized activations in the posterior prefrontal cortex. Attempting to explicitly retrieve information from a specific study episode additionally recruits the anterior prefrontal cortex at or near Brodmann area 10 (sometimes bilateral but often right > left) (Buckner, 1996; Petrides, Alivisatos, and Evans, 1995).

What role do these anterior prefrontal areas play in retrieval attempt? The answer is not obvious because the behavior of these regions has not been predicted well by many of our preconceived notions of how we go about retrieving information. For example, certain prefrontal areas activated in neuroimaging studies may play a role in the effortful aspects of retrieval attempt (Schacter et al., 1996; Squire, 1992). Situations in which past events come to mind readily have shown less activity within more posterior left prefrontal brain areas compared with situations in which retrieval is more demanding (as measured by reaction times) (Buckner et al., 1998c; Schacter et al., 1996), suggesting that these prefrontal areas correlate with overall effort. However, activity *within anterior prefrontal regions near Brodmann area 10,* if anything, shows the opposite pattern being most active when retrieval effort is minimal (Buckner et al., 1998c). Thus, the quantitative amount of "effort"—or time on task—does not appear to predict participation of anterior prefrontal cortex in retrieval attempt.

Other ideas, such as the possibility that anterior prefrontal areas participate in the successful retrieval of past information (Rugg et al., 1996), have been suggested and also met with mixed success (Buckner et al., 1998a; Buckner et al., 1998b; Kapur et al., 1995; Nyberg et al., 1995; Wagner et al., 1998a). The collective PET and fMRI data currently suggest that *anterior prefrontal activity increases with the attempt to remember and, under certain circumstances, is unaffected by the history of the stimulus being operated on (whether it is old or new).* Such a pattern is exactly opposite to that observed for the priming related reductions discussed earlier, which are present independent of the intentions of the subject and correlate with the history of a stimulus.

A final idea, which presently appears to be the forerunner, is that the anterior regions play a role in monitoring the retrieval attempt or evaluating the products of a retrieval attempt. Event-related potential studies have noted that prefrontal scalp signatures of remembering may occur relatively late (see chapter 56), a finding that has a rough correlate in event-related fMRI studies (Buckner et al., 1998b; Schacter et al., 1997). Moreover, working memory studies that place extensive demands on task monitoring sometimes activate these anterior prefrontal regions (MacLeod et al., 1998; Petrides, Alivisatos, and Evans, 1995), suggesting that they likely participate in a fairly generic set of high-level monitoring processes. For incompletely understood reasons, these processes are almost ubiquitously active during the attempt to retrieve information from long-term memory. Moreover, these processes are sensitive to subject-initiated strategies (Wagner et al., 1998a), suggesting that their involvement is dependent on volitional, rather than obligatory, monitoring processes.

It also is worthwhile to consider why we are so dumbfounded by the role of these prefrontal regions in memory processes. We can demonstrate reliably their participation in explicit retrieval processes, suggesting that we have some experimental control over their behavior. However, our many theories and ideas about what it is we are doing when information is retrieved from memory have provided little guidance to hone in on their more specific processing contributions. Current theoretical concepts such as that of retrieval effort and

success cannot account for the available data. This may well be progress. In time we likely will be able to explain why anterior prefrontal areas are activated so consistently during explicit retrieval tasks, which, in turn, will help us to better understand the process of retrieval itself. The functional neuroimaging results to date, which currently are somewhat phenomenological in nature, will drive us to new theoretical ideas about memory in the future. To borrow a quote from Desimone and colleagues (1995), "Neuroscience is sometimes like the game-show 'Jeopardy': It provides answers and the trick is to figure out the right questions." Activation of the anterior prefrontal cortex during explicit retrieval attempts is such an instance.

Conclusions

Human memory encompasses a remarkably complex set of functions that are intertwined intimately with information processing occurring in the here and now. Functional neuroimaging techniques (such as PET and fMRI) provide one source of data helping to elucidate how local changes in net brain activity relate to normal human memory processes. The studies surveyed in this chapter point us toward several conclusions worth reemphasizing. These conclusions represent testable hypotheses about how the brain participates in memory function. They currently are supported by a number of studies in the literature and are able to provide targets for further explorations, helping us to build a cognitive neuroscience of human memory.

1. Posterior dorsal and inferior prefrontal areas are active when subjects engage processing tasks that lead to effective episodic encoding of information, independent of whether these tasks are engaged intentionally by the subject or incidentally.

2. The materials being memorized or the kinds of strategies that the materials being memorized encourage influence laterality of prefrontal areas active during episodic encoding.

3. Strategic frontally mediated processes act interdependently with participation of medial temporal regions to promote memorization of information into a consciously accessible form.

4. Perceptual processing of a stimulus is more efficient after exposure to that stimulus, producing a quicker response (priming) and requiring less net neural activity in a subset of active brain areas.

5. The anterior prefrontal cortex, near Brodmann area 10, increases activity when subjects attempt to consciously retrieve information from a specific study episode.

REFERENCES

BACKMAN, L., O. ALMKVIST, J. ANDERSSON, A. NORDBERG, B. WINBALD, R. REINECK, and B. LANGSTROM, 1997. Brain activation in young and older adults during implicit and explicit retrieval. *J. Cogn. Neurosci.* 9:378–391.

BLAXTON, T. A., S. BOOKHEIMER, T. A. ZEFFIRO, C. M. FIGLOZZI, W. D. GAILLARD, and W. H. THEODORE, 1996. Functional mapping of human memory using PET: Comparisons of conceptual and perceptual tasks. *Can. J. Exp. Psychol.* 50:42–56.

BOYNTON, G. M., S. A. ENGEL, G. H. GLOVER, and D. J. HEEGER, 1996. Linear systems analysis of functional magnetic resonance imaging in human V1. *J. Neurosci.* 16:4207–4221.

BUCKNER, R. L., 1996. Beyond HERA: Contributions of specific prefrontal brain areas to long-term memory retrieval. *Psychonom. Bull. Rev.* 3:149–158.

BUCKNER R. L., J. GOODMAN, M. BUROCK, M. ROTTE, M. KOUTSTAAL, D. L. SCHACTER, B. ROSEN, and A. M. DALE, 1998a. Functional-anatomic correlates of object priming in humans revealed by rapid presentation event-related fMRI. *Neuron* 20:285–296.

BUCKNER, R. L., W. M. KELLEY, and S. E. PETERSEN, 1999. Frontal cortex contributes to human memory formation. *Nature Neurosci.* 2:1–4.

BUCKNER, R. L., and W. KOUTSTAAL, 1998. Functional neuroimaging studies of encoding, priming, and explicit memory retrieval. *Proc. Natl. Acad. Sci. U.S.A.* 95:891–898.

BUCKNER, R. L., W. KOUTSTAAL, D. L. SCHACTER, A. M. DALE, M. R. ROTTE, and B. R. ROSEN, 1998b. Functional-anatomic study of episodic retrieval: II. Selective averaging of event-related fMRI trials to test the retrieval success hypothesis. *Neuroimage* 7:163–175

BUCKNER, R. L., W. KOUTSTAAL, D. L. SCHACTER, A. D. WAGNER, and B. R. ROSEN, 1998c. Functional-anatomic study of episodic retrieval using fMRI: I. Retrieval effort versus retrieval success. *Neuroimage* 7:151–162

BUCKNER, R. L., S. E. PETERSEN, J. G. OJEMANN, F. M. MIEZIN, L. R. SQUIRE, and M. E. RAICHLE, 1995. Functional anatomical studies of explicit and implicit memory retrieval tasks. *J. Neurosci.* 15:12–29.

BUCKNER, R. L., M. E. RAICHLE, F. M. MIEZIN, and S. E. PETERSEN, 1996. Functional anatomic studies of memory retrieval for auditory words and visual pictures. *J. Neurosci.* 16:6219–6235.

BUCKNER, R.L., and E. TULVING, 1995. Neuroimaging studies of memory: Theory and recent PET results. In: *Handbook of Neuropsychology,* Vol. 10, F. Boller and J. Grafman, eds. Amsterdam: Elsevier, pp. 439–466.

CABEZA, R., and L. NYBERG, 1997. Imaging cognition: An empirical review of PET studies with normal subjects. *J. Cogn. Neurosci.* 9:1–26.

CLARK, V. P., K. KEIL, M. MAISOG, S. COURNEY, L. G. UNGERLEIDER, and J. V. HAXBY, 1996. Functional magnetic resonance imaging of human visual cortex during face matching: A comparison with positron emission tomography. *Neuroimage* 4:1–15.

COHEN, N. J., and H. EICHENBAUN, 1993. *Memory, Amnesia, and the Hippocampal System.* Cambridge, Mass.: MIT Press.

CORKIN, S., 1984. Lasting consequences of bilateral medial temporal lobe lobectomy: Clinical course and experimental findings in H.M. *Semin. Neurol.* 4:249–259.

CRAIK, F. I. M., and R. S. LOCKHART, 1972. Levels of processing: A framework for memory research. *J. Verb. Learn. Verb. Behav.* 11:671–684.

CRAIK, F. I. M., and E. TULVING, 1975. Depth of processing and the retention of words in episodic memory. *J. Exp. Psychol. Gen.* 104:168–294.

DALE, A. M., and R. L. BUCKNER, 1997. Selective averaging of rapidly presented individual trials using fMRI. *Hum. Brain Mapping* 5:329–340.

DEMB, J. B., J. E. DESMOND, A. D. WAGNER, C. J. VAIDYA, G. H. GLOVER, and J. D. E. GABRIELI, 1995. Semantic encoding and retrieval in the left inferior prefrontal cortex: A functional MRI study of task difficulty and process specificity. *J. Neurosci.* 15:5870–5878.

DESIMONE, R., E. K. MILLER, L. CHELAZZI, and A. LUESCHOW, 1995. Multiple memory systems in the visual cortex. In: *The Cognitive Neurosciences*, M. S. Gazzaniga, ed. Cambridge, Mass.: MIT Press, pp. 475–486.

DEYOE, E. A., G. J. CARMAN, P. BANDETTINI, S. GLICKMAN, J. WIESER, R. COX, D. MILLER, and J. NEITZ, 1996. Mapping striate and extrastriate visual areas in human cerebral cortex. *Proc. Natl. Acad. Sci. U.S.A.* 93:2382–2386.

DOLAN, R. J., and P. C. FLETCHER, 1997. Dissociating prefrontal and hippocampal function in episodic memory encoding. *Nature* 388:582–585.

ENGEL, S. A., G. H. GLOVER, and B. A. WANDELL, 1997. Retinotopic organization in human visual cortex and the spatial precision of functional MRI. *Cereb. Cortex* 7:181–192.

FLETCHER, P. C., C. D. FRITH, P. M. GRASBY, T. SHALLICE, R. S. J. FRACKOWIAK, and R. J. DOLAN, 1995. Brain systems for encoding and retrieval of auditory-verbal memory: An in vivo study in humans. *Brain* 118:401–406.

FLETCHER, P. C., C. D. FRITH, and M. D. RUGG, 1997. The functional neuroanatomy of episodic memory. *Trends Neurosci.* 20:213–223.

FOX, P. T., F. M. MIEZIN, J. M. ALLMAN, D. C. VAN ESSEN, and M. E. RAICHLE, 1987. Retinotopic organization of human visual cortex mapped with positron emission tomography. *J. Neurosci.* 7:913–922.

GABRIELI, J. D., J. B. BREWER, J. E. DESMOND, and G. H. GLOVER, 1997. Separate neural bases of two fundamental memory processes in the human medial temporal lobe. *Science* 276:264–266.

GABRIELI, J. D. E., J. E. DESMOND, J. B. DEMB, A. D. WAGNER, M. V. STONE, C. J. VAIDYA, and G. H. GLOVER, 1996. Functional magnetic resonance imaging of semantic memory processes in the frontal lobes. *Psychol. Sci.* 7:278–283.

GRADY, C. L., A. R. MCINTOSH, B. HORWITZ, J. M. MAISOG, L. G. UNGERLEIDER, M. J. MENTIS, P. PIETRINI, M. B. SCHAPIRO, and J. V. HAXBY, 1995. Age-related reductions in human recognition memory due to impaired encoding. *Science* 269:218–221.

HALGREN, E., and M. E. SMITH, 1987. Cognitive evoked potentials as modulatory processes in human memory formation and retrieval. *Hum. Neurobiol.* 6:129–139.

HAXBY, J. V., L. G. UNGERLEIDER, B. HORWITZ, J. M. MAISOG, S. L. RAPOPORT, and C. L. GRADY, 1996. Face encoding and recognition in the human brain. *Proc. Natl. Acad. Sci. U.S.A.* 93:922–927.

KAPUR, S., F. I. M. CRAIK, C. JONES, G. M. BROWN, S. HOULE, and E. TULVING, 1995. Functional role of the prefrontal cortex in retrieval of memories: A PET study. *Neuroreport* 6:1880–1884.

KAPUR, S., F. I. M. CRAIK, E. TULVING, A. A. WILSON, S. HOULE, and G. M. BROWN, 1994. Neuroanatomical correlates of encoding in episodic memory: Levels of processing effects. *Proc. Natl. Acad. Sci. U.S.A.* 91:2008–2011.

KAPUR, S., E. TULVING, R. CABEZA, A. R. MCINTOSH, S. HOULE, and F. I. M. CRAIK, 1996. The neural correlates of intentional learning of verbal materials: A PET study in humans. *Cogn. Brain Res.* 4:243–249.

KELLEY, W. M., R. L. BUCKNER, F. M. MIEZIN, N. J. COHEN, M. E. RAICHLE, and S. E. PETERSEN, 1998b. Encoding of famous and nonfamous faces using fMRI. *Soc. Neurosci. Abstr.* 24:760.

KELLEY, W. M., F. M. MIEZIN, K. B. MCDERMOTT, et al., 1998a. Hemispheric specialization in human dorsal frontal cortex and medial temporal lobe for verbal and nonverbal encoding. *Neuron* 20:927–936.

KWONG, K. K., J. W. BELLIVEAU, D. A. CHESLER, et al., 1992. Dynamic magnetic resonance imaging of human brain activity during primary sensory stimulation. *Proc. Natl. Acad. Sci. U.S.A.* 89:5675–5679.

MACLEOD, A. K., R. L. BUCKNER, F. M. MIEZIN, S. E. PETERSEN, and M. E. RAICHLE, 1998. Right anterior prefrontal cortex activation during semantic monitoring and working memory. *Neuroimage* 7:41–48.

MARTIN, A., C. L. WIGGS, and J. WEISBERG, 1997. Modulation of human medial temporal lobe activity by form, meaning, and experience. *Hippocampus* 7:587–593.

MILLER, E. K., and R. DESIMONE, 1994. Parallel neuronal mechanisms for short-term memory. *Science* 263:520–522.

MILLER, E. K., L. LI, and R. DESIMONE, 1991. A neural mechanism for working and recognition memory in inferior temporal cortex. *Science* 254:1377–1379.

MOSCOVITCH, M., 1992. Memory and working-with-memory: A component process model based on modules and central systems. *J. Cogn. Neurosci.* 4:257–267.

NYBERG, L., E. TULVING, R. HABIB, L.-R. NILSSON, S. KAPUR, S. HOULE, R. CABEZA, and A.R. MCINTOSH, 1995. Functional brain maps of retrieval mode and recovery of episodic information. *Neuroreport* 7:249–252.

OJEMANN, J. G., R. L. BUCKNER, E. AKBUDAK, A. Z. SNYDER, J. M. OLLINGER, R. C. MCKINSTRY, B. R. ROSEN, S. E. PETERSEN, M. E. RAICHLE, and T. E. CONTURO, 1998. Functional MRI studies of word stem completion: Reliability across laboratories and comparison to blood flow imaging with PET. *Hum. Brain Mapp.* 6:203–215.

PALLER, K. A., 1990. Recall and stem-completion priming have different electrophysiological correlates and are modified differentially by directed forgetting. *J. Exp. Psychol. Learn. Mem. Cogn.* 16:1021–1032.

PETRIDES, M., B. ALIVISATOS, and A. C. EVANS, 1995. Functional activation of the human ventrolateral frontal cortex during mnemonic retrieval of verbal information. *Proc. Natl. Acad. Sci. U.S.A.* 92:5803–5807.

POSNER, M. I., and M. E. RAICHLE, 1994. *Images of Mind*. New York: Scientific American Books.

RAICHLE, M. E., 1987. Circulatory and metabolic correlates of brain function in normal humans. In *The Handbook of Physiology: Section 1. The Nervous System: Vol. V. Higher Functions of the Brain: Pt. 1,* F. Plum and V. Mountcastle, eds. Bethesda, Md.: American Physiological Association, pp. 643–674.

RAICHLE, M. E., J. A. FIEZ, T. O. VIDEEN, A.-M. K. MACLOED, J. V. PARDO, P. T. FOX, and S. E. PETERSEN, 1994. Practice-related changes in human brain functional anatomy during nonmotor learning. *Cereb. Cortex* 4:8–26.

RICHTER, W., K. UGURBIL, A. GEORGOPOLOUS, and S.-G. KIM, 1997. Time-resolved fMRI of mental rotation. *Neuroreport* 8:3697–3702.

ROEDIGER, H. L., III, and K. B. MCDERMOTT, 1993. Implicit memory in normal human subjects. In *Handbook of Neuropsychology,* Vol. 8, F. Boller and J. Grafman, eds. Amsterdam: Elsevier, pp. 63–131.

ROLAND, P. E., 1993. *Brain Activation*. New York: Wiley-Liss.

ROSEN, B. R., R. L. BUCKNER, and A. M. DALE, 1998. Event related fMRI: Past, present, and future. *Proc. Natl. Acad. Sci. U.S.A.* 95:773–780.

RUGG, M. D., 1995. ERP studies of memory. In *Electrophysiology of Mind: Event-Related Brain Potentials and Cognition,* M. D. Rugg and M. G. H. Coles, eds. Oxford: Oxford University Press.

RUGG, M. D., P. C. FLETCHER, C. D. FRITH, R. S. J. FRACKOWIAK, and R. J. DOLAN, 1996. Differential response of the prefrontal cortex in successful and unsuccessful memory retrieval. *Brain* 119:2073–2083.

SCHACTER, D. L., 1987a. Implicit memory: History and current status. *J. Exp. Psychol. Learn. Mem. Cogn.* 13:501–518.

SCHACTER, D. L., 1987b. Memory, amnesia, and frontal lobe dysfunction. *Psychobiology* 15:21–36.

SCHACTER, D. L., 1996. *Searching for Memory*. New York: Basic Books.

SCHACTER, D. L., N. M. ALPERT, C. R. SAVAGE, S. L. RAUCH, and M. S. ALBERT, 1996. Conscious recollection and the human hippocampal formation: Evidence from positron emission tomography. *Proc. Natl. Acad. Sci. U.S.A.* 93:321–325.

SCHACTER, D. L., and R. L. BUCKNER, 1998. Priming and the brain. *Neuron* 20:185–195.

SERENO, M. I., A. M. DALE, J. B. REPPAS, K. K. KWONG, J. W. BELLIVEAU, T. J. BRADY, B. R. ROSEN, and R. B. H. TOOTELL, 1995. Borders of multiple visual areas in humans revealed by functional magnetic resonance imaging. *Science* 268:889–893.

SMITH, E. E., and J. JONIDES, 1997. Working memory: A view from neuroimaging. *Cogn. Psychol.* 33:5–42.

SQUIRE, L. R., 1992. Memory and the hippocampus: A synthesis from findings with rats, monkeys, and humans. *Psychol. Rev.* 99:195–231.

SQUIRE, L. R., J. G. OJEMANN, F. M. MIEZIN, S. E. PETERSEN, T. O. VIDEEN, and M. E. RAICHLE, 1992. Activation of the hippocampus in normal humans: A functional anatomical study of memory. *Proc. Natl. Acad. Sci. U.S.A.* 89:1837–1841.

STERN, C. E., S. CORKIN, R. G. GONZALEZ, A. R. GUIMARAES, J. R. BAKER, P. J. JENNINGS, C. A. CARR, R. M. SUGIURA, V. VEDANTHAM, and B. R. ROSEN, 1996. The hippocampal formation participates in novel picture encoding: Evidence from functional magnetic resonance imaging. *Proc. Natl. Acad. Sci. U.S.A.* 93:8660–8665.

TULVING E., S. KAPUR, F.I.M. CRAIK, M. MOSCOVITCH, and S. HOULE, 1994. Hemispheric encoding/retrieval asymmetry in episodic memory: Positron emission tomography findings. *Proc. Natl. Acad. Sci. U.S.A.* 91:2016–2020.

TULVING, E., H. J. MARKOWITSCH, F. I. M. CRAIK, R. HABIB, and S. HOULE, 1996. Novelty and familiarity activations in PET studies of memory encoding and retrieval. *Cereb. Cortex* 6:71–79.

TULVING, E., and D. L. SCHACTER, 1990. Priming and human memory systems. *Science* 247:301–306.

UNGERLEIDER, L. G., 1995. Functional brain imaging studies of cortical mechanisms for memory. *Science* 270:769–775.

WAGNER, A. D., J. E. DESMOND, G. H. GLOVER, and J. D. E. GABRIELI, 1998a. Prefrontal cortex and recognition memory: fMRI evidence for context-dependent retrieval processes. *Brain* 121:1985–2002.

WAGNER, A. D., D. L. SCHACTER, M. ROTTE, W. KOUTSTAAL, A. MARIL, A. M. DALE, B. R. ROSEN, and R. L. BUCKNER, 1998b. Left prefrontal and temporal lobe activation during human encoding is associated with whether experiences are remembered or forgotten. *Science* 281:1188–1191.

WIGGS, C. L., and A. MARTIN, 1998. Properties and mechanisms of perceptual priming. *Curr. Opin. Neurobiol.* 8:227-233.

58 Memory without Remembering and Remembering without Memory: Implicit and False Memories

DANIEL L. SCHACTER AND TIM CURRAN

ABSTRACT Cognitive neuroscience analyses of memory typically rely on experimental paradigms in which participants are asked to remember facts or events presented earlier in the experiment. Here we consider two phenomena of memory that do not involve conscious recollections of previous experiences: implicit memory, the nonconscious influence of a past event on subsequent performance, and false memory, the conscious recollection of an event that never happened. We consider neuropsychological and neuroimaging evidence from four different types of implicit memory phenomena: priming, artificial grammar learning, category learning, and sequence learning. Different brain systems are involved in explicit and implicit memory, and subtypes of implicit memory appear to engage some shared and some distinct mechanisms. We then consider similar kinds of evidence concerning the phenomenon of false recognition–the mistaken conviction that a novel item was encountered previously–that supports a distinction between memory for general similarity or gistlike information on one hand and recollection of specific details on the other. We conclude by considering possible parallels and connections between implicit memory and false memory.

The topics of this chapter–implicit memory and false memory–are relative newcomers to the landscape of memory research. As noted by Schacter (1995a) in the first edition of this volume, the term *implicit memory* had been introduced to the field barely a decade earlier (Graf and Schacter, 1985; Schacter, 1987). Implicit memory occurs when subjects are exposed to target information and are later influenced by that information even when they cannot recollect it consciously. As stated in Schacter (1987, p. 501), "Implicit memory is revealed when previous experiences facilitate performance on a task that does not require conscious or intentional recollection of those experiences." By contrast, explicit memory "is revealed when performance on a task requires conscious recollection of previous experiences." Schacter (1995a) summa-

rized the historical development of implicit memory research, considered methodological issues surrounding such research, and reviewed the characteristics of implicit memory that had been revealed by cognitive studies of normal memory and by neuropsychological investigations of amnesic patients. Whereas relatively little was known about the neural correlates of implicit memory when Schacter's (1995a) chapter was written, a great deal more has been learned during the past few years, mainly from neuroimaging studies and from research with an increasing variety of patient populations. In this chapter we review these recent developments in implicit memory research.

We also consider an even more recent addition to the research agenda of cognitive neuroscience: investigations concerning false memory. The term *false memory* refers to a conscious "recollection" of an event that never happened. False memories are important theoretically because they provide support for the idea that remembering is a fundamentally constructive process, rather than a literal replaying of past events. Cognitive psychologists have known for many years that memory is subject to various kinds of errors, biases, and distortions, dating to the publication of Bartlett's (1932) pioneering work and even earlier (for historical reviews, see Roediger, 1996; Schacter, 1995b). However, cognitive research on phenomena of constructive remembering, memory distortion, and false memory has been revived recently, stimulated in part by debates and discussions concerning false and recovered memories of childhood trauma (see, for example, Conway, 1997). This rise has been paralleled by a new wave of cognitive neuroscience studies concerning false memories that, during the past few years, has begun to provide insights into the brain processes that underlie constructive memory phenomena (Schacter, Norman, and Koutstaal, 1998). Here we summarize and assess some of the major developments.

Although implicit memory and false memory may appear to be entirely unrelated domains of study, we find it

DANIEL L. SCHACTER Department of Psychology, Harvard University, Cambridge, Mass.
TIM CURRAN Department of Psychology, Case Western Reserve University, Cleveland, Ohio

interesting to consider them together, for two reasons. First, whereas traditional studies of memory are linked by a common feature–subjects recall or recognize what has been presented to them previously in an experiment –neither implicit memory nor false memory involves remembering events that occurred previously. We find it intriguing to consider what we have learned about accurate recollections of past experiences by studying memory without remembering and remembering events that never happened. Second, we believe that there are some points of theoretical contact between studies of implicit memory and false memory, which we touch on briefly in our concluding section.

Implicit memory

Although observations concerning what we now call implicit memory have a long history (see Schacter, 1987), during the 1960s and 1970s–and especially during the early 1980s–systematic experimental evidence began to accumulate indicating that effects of prior experiences could be expressed without, and dissociated from, intentional or conscious recollection. The terms *implicit* and *explicit memory* were put forward in an attempt to capture and describe essential features of the observed dissociations (for a related distinction between declarative and nondeclarative memory, see Squire, 1994).

The term "implicit memory" subsumes various different types of phenomena, and we do not attempt to comprehensively review all of them here (for review and discussion, see Roediger and McDermott, 1993; Salmon and Butters, 1995; Schacter and Buckner, 1998b; Stadler, 1997; Wiggs and Martin, 1998). Instead we focus on recent studies concerned with four different phenomena of implicit memory: priming, artificial grammar learning, category learning, and sequence learning.

PRIMING   Priming refers to a change in the ability to identify or produce an item as a result of a particular prior encounter with the item (Schacter and Buckner, 1998b; Tulving and Schacter, 1990). Priming is assessed with tests in which subjects attempt to identify briefly flashed stimuli–complete words, stems, or fragments–with the first word that comes to mind, or produce items from a category in response to a category cue. Data concerning the cognitive and behavioral properties of priming effects on these and related tests have been summarized in several comprehensive reviews (Roediger and McDermott, 1993; Schacter, Chiu, and Ochsner, 1993; Tenpenny, 1995).

Insights into the brain systems involved in priming were provided initially by studies of amnesic patients. Beginning with the pioneering studies of Warrington and Weiskrantz (1974), a variety of studies have shown that amnesic patients with damage to medial temporal and diencephalic brain regions, as well as severe deficits in explicit memory, nonetheless often show normal priming effects. Intact priming in amnesia has been shown for both visual information (Graf, Squire, and Mandler, 1984) and auditory information (Schacter, Church, and Treadwell, 1994), for nonsense words (Keane et al., 1995) and novel objects (Schacter, Cooper, and Treadwell, 1993), for various types of conceptual information (Carlesimo, 1994), and under conditions in which explicit memory does not exceed chance levels (Hamann and Squire, 1997).

Amnesic patients do not, however, always show normal priming effects. When priming is based on general information about a familiar word or object, amnesics typically show intact priming (for discussion of this point, see Ostergaard and Jernigan, 1993; Hamann, Squire, and Schacter, 1995). But several studies have shown that amnesics sometimes exhibit impaired priming when the priming effects depend on highly specific information about the pairing of unrelated words (Schacter and Graf, 1986; Shimamura and Squire, 1989) or the exact perceptual details of previously presented words (Kinoshita and Wayland, 1993; Schacter, Church, and Bolton, 1995). Nonetheless, conditions exist in which amnesics can show priming for specific pairing of unrelated items (Gabrieli et al., 1997) and perceptual details of recently studied words (Vaidya et al., in press). Although the relation between priming based on general versus specific features of a word or object is not well understood (for data and discussion, see Curran, Schacter, and Bessenhoff, 1996; Tenpenny, 1995), studies by Marsolek and colleagues have delineated a number of experimental conditions in which priming based on general information is mediated primarily by the left hemisphere whereas priming based on specific information appears to be based primarily on the right hemisphere (e.g., Marsolek, Kosslyn, and Squire, 1992; Marsolek, Schacter, and Nicholas, 1996).

Recent studies using neuroimaging techniques have provided additional insights into brain regions that are associated with priming effects. Several studies using positron emission tomography (PET) and functional magnetic resonance imaging (fMRI) have shown that perceptually based visual priming is accompanied by reduced activity in posterior extrastriate regions that have previously been implicated in visual word and object processing (Buckner et al., 1998; Schacter, Alpert, et al., 1996; Squire et al., 1992; for review, see Schacter and Buckner, 1998a; Wiggs and Martin, 1998). These studies complement findings reported by Gabrieli and colleagues (1995) that perceptual priming is absent in a patient with damage to right extrastriate cortex. Thus the imaging and neuropsychological data converge on the conclusion that posterior cortical regions play an important role in perceptually based priming effects.

Neuroimaging studies also indicate that conceptually based priming effects are accompanied by reduced activity in prefrontal cortex (Buckner et al., 1998; Demb et al., 1995). As Schacter and Buckner (1998a) point out, it is too simplistic to equate perceptual priming with reduced activity in posterior areas and conceptual priming with reduced activity in more anterior reductions. Nonetheless, the consistent finding of priming-related reductions in various cortical areas that are typically not damaged in amnesic patients fits well with the more general conclusion that such areas make an important contribution to various kinds of priming effects (for an electrophysiological index of implicit memory that may be related to priming, see Rugg et al., 1998).

A persisting issue in neuroimaging studies of priming concerns whether priming-related changes in blood flow are produced by nonconscious, implicit expressions of memory or whether they are related to "contamination" from voluntary or involuntary explicit memory (for extensive discussion of this issue, see Schacter and Buckner, 1998a). For instance, in an early study of priming on a word stem completion test by Squire and colleagues (1992), priming-related extrastriate blood flow reductions were accompanied by a priming-related increase in right parahippocampal gyrus. Because levels of explicit memory were quite high under the particular conditions used in this experiment, Squire and colleagues (1992) and Schacter, Alpert, and colleagues (1996) noted that the right parahippocampal activation might reflect voluntary or involuntary explicit memory for previously studied words. Schacter, Alpert, and colleagues (1996) tested this idea by using an encoding task that produced low levels of explicit memory. They found a priming-related extrastriate blood flow reduction together with no evidence of parahippocampal activation, thus supporting the idea that the parahippocampal activation observed by Squire and colleagues (1992) reflected contamination from explicit memory.

More recently, Beauregard and colleagues (1998) reported evidence of hippocampal activation during priming of a semantic-category decision task, following a subliminal encoding task that produced little or no evidence of explicit memory. Although intriguing, interpretation of this finding is difficult because of the presence of several key confoundings in the study. Evidence for hippocampal activation emerged from comparison of a primed semantic category decision condition and a nonprimed semantic-category decision task. Unfortunately, the two conditions differed in many ways: In the primed condition subjects decided whether previously studied words belonged to the category of "animals," and in the unprimed condition they decided whether an entirely different set of words belonged to the category of "tools"; the order of primed and unprimed scans was not counterbalanced; and because of the different item sets used in the primed and unprimed scans, there were more "yes" responses required in the primed than the unprimed scans. In view of these serious methodological problems, further studies will be needed to evaluate the possibility that hippocampal activation is linked to implicit memory.

ARTIFICIAL GRAMMAR LEARNING   Reber (1967) developed an artificial-grammar-learning task in which subjects are exposed to seemingly random consonant strings that, unbeknownst to them, were generated from a complex set of rules (an "artificial grammar"). After viewing a list of grammatical stimuli, subjects are able to discriminate between grammatical and nongrammatical strings despite their limited ability to articulate the information upon which their judgments are based. Reber (1967) first coined the term "implicit learning" to describe this ability to learn complex information in the absence of awareness (reviewed by Reber, 1989). In contrast to implicit memory, which primarily emphasizes limited awareness and/or intention during retrieval, implicit learning primarily emphasizes limited awareness/intention during encoding (Buchner and Wippich, 1997; Stadler and Roediger, 1997).

Reber (1967, 1989) originally maintained that subjects in an artificial-grammar-learning experiment develop an abstract representation of the rules that comprise the grammar. In contrast, episodic accounts maintain that subjects learn by storing individual exemplars (Vokey and Brooks, 1992; Whittlesea and Dorken, 1993). Episodic theories can account for subjects' ability to classify grammatical, but nonstudied, strings correctly by positing that judgments are based on the global similarity between the test item and stored exemplars (e.g., Hintzman, 1986). Grammatical test items will tend to be more similar to encoded exemplars than nongrammatical items, so subjects will be more likely to classify grammatical items accordingly.

The debate over abstractionist and episodic theories will not be settled here (see Dienes and Berry, 1997; Neal and Hesketh, 1997; and accompanying commentaries), but one possible resolution is that implicit learning leads to abstract representation whereas explicit learning results in exemplar storage. Amnesic patients can learn to make grammaticality judgments as accurately as control subjects, despite their recognition impairment for studied exemplars (Knowlton, Ramus, and

Squire, 1992; Knowlton and Squire, 1994, 1996). Knowlton, Ramus, and Squire (1992) originally concluded that normal grammaticality judgments indicated spared implicit abstraction and that poor recognition performance indicated impaired exemplar memory. More recently, Knowlton and Squire (1996) have argued for both abstract and exemplar-specific implicit learning. Exemplar-specific implicit learning was inferred from amnesic patients' normal sensitivity to the frequency of letter bigrams and trigrams (chunks) that were in the original training set. Abstract implicit learning was inferred from amnesic patients' normal ability to transfer learning across physical changes in the letters entered into the grammar (though letter-set transfer is not universally agreed to demand an abstract representation; Neal and Hesketh, 1997; Whittlesea and Dorken, 1993). Reber has recently concurred that implicit learning can result in both abstract and episodic representations (Reber, Allen, and Reber, in press).

Currently, there is no evidence to link grammar learning directly to particular neural mechanisms beyond the data from amnesic patients indicating that medial temporal regions are not necessary for such learning to occur. Unlike other implicit learning tasks (described in the following subsections), patients with Huntington's disease (HD, Knowlton et al., 1996) and Parkinson's disease (PD, Reber and Squire, in press) show normal artificial grammar learning, so the striatum (which is typically damaged in such patients) does not appear to make a critical contribution.

CATEGORY LEARNING Other evidence for priming-like effects has been documented in a task that is conceptually similar to artificial grammar learning. Artificial grammar learning can be considered to be a special case of category learning in that subjects are required to judge whether individual stimuli (e.g., consonant strings) are members of a larger class (e.g., a grammar). Parkinson's disease patients (Reber and Squire, in press) as well as patients with amnesia (Knowlton and Squire, 1995; Knowlton, Squire, and Gluck, 1994) show normal category learning in a task that requires subjects to decide if novel dot patterns belong to the same category as a set of training patterns (following Posner and Keele, 1968). A recent fMRI experiment suggests that processing of categorical dot patterns elicits less posterior, occipital activation than does processing of noncategorical patterns (Reber, Stark, and Squire, 1998). Thus perceptual categorization may involve mechanisms similar to those that support perceptual priming.

Another form of implicit category learning has been demonstrated with probabilistic categorization tasks. These classification tasks require subjects to predict which of two outcomes (e.g., sunshine or rain) will follow particular cue combinations (e.g., combinations of 1 to 4 geometric symbols). The cues are probabilistically predictive of outcomes, so that subjects' predictive accuracy increases with training. As observed for learning artificial grammars and novel dot patterns, amnesic patients show normal classification learning (Knowlton, Gluck, and Squire, 1994; Knowlton, Mangels, and Squire, 1996; Reber, Knowlton, and Squire, 1996). Unlike these other forms of categorical learning, probabilistic classification learning is impaired in patients with PD (Knowlton, Mangels, and Squire, 1996) and HD (Knowlton et al., 1996).

Impaired performance in HD and PD patients is most often attributed to striatal neuropathology. Willingham (in press) has suggested that the striatum (along with the supplementary motor area) enables the learning of repeated response sequences, but such information does not appear to be learned in the probabilistic classification task. However, primary and secondary effects of PD and HD can be more widespread, with frontal impairments especially prevalent (Jacobs, Stern, and Mayeux, 1996), so any cognitive/behavioral deficits found in these disorders can only be tentatively linked to striatal dysfunction. Understanding why PD and HD patients perform more proficiently on some categorical learning tasks than others, as well as understanding the precise neuropathology responsible for their classification deficit, remains an important goal for future research.

SEQUENCE LEARNING Implicit sequence learning is another task that, like probabilistic classification learning, requires subjects to learn associations between multiple cues and outcomes, and it has been more clearly linked to the striatum. Implicit sequence learning has been primarily studied with the serial reaction time (SRT) task (Nissen and Bullemer, 1987). Subjects typically view a stimulus moving across different visual locations and press location-corresponding response keys as quickly as possible. Normal subjects (e.g., Curran and Keele, 1993; Reed and Johnson, 1994; Stadler, 1995; Willingham, Nissen, and Bullemer, 1989) and patients with amnesia (e.g., Curran, 1997a; Nissen and Bullemer, 1987; Reber and Squire, 1994) show improved performance when stimulus locations follow a repeating pattern, compared to conditions in which stimulus locations are randomly determined. This form of learning does not depend on explicit knowledge (for contrary views, see Perruchet and Amorim, 1992; Shanks and St. John, 1994). SRT learning is impaired in both patients with PD (e.g., Jackson et al., 1995) and patients with HD (e.g., Willingham and Koroshetz, 1993).

Impaired sequence learning in PD and HD patients suggests a striatal contribution that has been confirmed by SRT studies using PET (Berns, Cohen, and Mintun, 1997; Grafton, Hazeltine, and Ivry, 1995; Hazeltine, Grafton, and Ivry, 1997; Rauch et al., 1995) and fMRI (Rauch et al., 1998, 1997). These studies additionally have identified learning-related changes in primary motor cortex, supplementary motor areas, premotor cortex, thalamus, parietal cortex, and occipital cortex (for reviews, see Curran, 1997b; Keele et al., 1998). The distribution of learning-related activity suggests that SRT learning involves changes in perceptual and motor areas that subserve visually guided movement. This observation is conceptually similar to our previous conclusion that visual priming is accompanied by reduced activity in posterior extrastriate regions implicated in visual word and object processing. Generally, implicit learning and memory appear to involve changes in information processing systems that normally contribute to task performance. However, whereas priming typically leads to decreased activity in implicated areas, sequence learning most often leads to increases in activity. Ungerleider (1995) has previously noted this apparent contradiction, and has suggested that early stages of perceptual-motor learning may involve activity decreases followed by increases in later stages. Across the temporal course of SRT learning, thalamic activity initially decreases, then later increases (Rauch et al., 1998). Rauch and colleagues hypothesize that these effects reflect input from distinct striatal circuits that, respectively, suppress and enhance thalamic activity. Further understanding of the functional significance of learning-related increases and decreases in activity will depend on more detailed temporal information as well as better understanding of the neurophysiology of implicated areas.

The precise functional anatomy of sequence learning depends on the nature of the information that is learned. For example, under otherwise identical conditions, PET experiments have shown that learning-related brain areas differ between visuospatial sequences (Grafton, Hazeltine, and Ivry, 1995) and color sequences (Hazeltine, Grafton, and Ivry, 1997). Based on these PET results as well as behavioral experiments indicating both independent (Mayr, 1996) and interdependent (Schmidtke and Heuer, 1997) learning effects when stimulus/response characteristics of sequences are varied, Keele and colleagues (1998) suggested the existence of two distinct sequence learning systems (cf. Curran and Keele, 1993). An implicit dorsal system learns response-based sequences within a given stimulus modality (e.g., visuospatial, color, auditory). A ventral system can learn cross-dimensional sequences (e.g., sequences composed of a combination of visual and auditory signals; Schmidtke and Heuer, 1997)

in either an implicit or explicit manner. Keele and colleagues also hypothesize that the ventral cross-dimensional system may be better able to learn complex, higher-order associations between multiple stimuli (cf. Curran, 1997a) than the dorsal unidimensional system. Both systems are hypothesized to depend on a striatal switching function (Hayes et al., 1998) that controls access to learned sequence chunks (cf. Stadler, 1995).

False memory

We now turn our attention from nonconscious influences of past experiences to those situations in which people consciously recollect experiences that never occurred.

When we use such phrases as "false memory," "illusory memory," or "remembering events that never happened," what exactly do we mean? At one extreme, consider the case of a patient who reports a detailed recollection of having served as an officer in Vietnam and describes vividly war episodes in which he acted heroically to save lives—even though government records show that the patient never went to Vietnam. The patient has produced a confabulation, and there can be little doubt that his subjectively compelling recollective experience deserved to be called a false or illusory memory. At another extreme, however, consider a participant in a recognition memory experiment who has studied a list of words and makes old/new judgments about previously studied words and novel words that are unrelated to studied items. Most participants will say "old" to at least a few new words—that is, they will commit a few false alarms. The participant is claiming memory for an event that never happened (i.e., seeing a word in a list even though it was never presented) and so in some sense is exhibiting a false or illusory memory. However, most researchers would probably be reluctant to apply these labels here, because false alarms to unrelated words are relatively infrequent, tend not to be accompanied by strong subjective convictions that the information was previously encountered, and are often viewed as providing estimates of guessing biases.

In most research settings, the phenomena that have been cited as evidence of "false memories" generally fall somewhere between the two extremes of detailed confabulation on the one hand and the more innocuous false alarm to a novel word on the other. Here we focus on the phenomenon of *false recognition*, which occurs when subjects are shown novel items (e.g., words or pictures) and incorrectly claim to have encountered them earlier in the experiment (for review and discussion of confabulation and related kinds of false recall, see Moscovitch, 1995; Schacter, Norman, and Koutstaal, 1998).

False recognition is typically inferred from "old" responses to novel items that are in some way related (conceptually or perceptually) to previously studied items–that is, false alarms above and beyond the "baseline" level of false alarms to unrelated novel items noted in the preceding paragraph, (cf. Roediger and McDermott, 1995; Underwood, 1965).

False recognition has been studied experimentally since the classic work of Underwood (1965), which used a continuous recognition paradigm in which subjects make old/new decisions about previously studied words, new words preceded by an associated word (related lures), and new words that are not preceded by an associated word (unrelated lures). False recognition in this paradigm takes the form of a small increase in false alarms to related lures compared to unrelated lures. More recent research has shown that stronger false recognition effects can be obtained when participants study large numbers of items that are conceptually or perceptually similar to a novel test item (e.g., Shiffrin, Huber, and Marinelli, 1995).

Roediger and McDermott (1995) provided an especially striking demonstration of robust false recognition. They modified and extended a procedure developed initially by Deese (1959) in which subjects hear lists of associated words (e.g., *candy, sour, sugar, bitter, good, taste, tooth*, etc.) that all converge on a nonpresented "theme word" or false target (e.g., *sweet*). Roediger and McDermott reported exceptionally high levels of false recognition (e.g., 80%) to the theme words. The level of false recognition responses was indistinguishable from the hit rate to studied items, and false recognitions were accompanied by high confidence and a sense of detailed recollection. Subsequent studies have delineated various characteristics of this powerful false recognition effect (e.g., Mather, Henkel, and Johnson, 1997; McDermott, 1997; Norman and Schacter, 1997; Payne et al., 1996; Robinson and Roediger, 1997).

FALSE RECOGNITION AND AMNESIC PATIENTS Neuropsychological evidence concerning the basis of robust false recognition has been provided by several recent studies of amnesic patients. Using the Deese/Roediger-McDermott procedure, Schacter, Verfaellie, and Pradere (1996) found that, not surprisingly, amnesic patients with damage to either the medial temporal region (i.e., anoxia, encephalitis) or the diencephalic regions (i.e., Korsakoff patients) showed significantly reduced levels of true recognition compared to matched controls: Amnesics made fewer hits to studied items and more false alarms to unrelated lure words than did control subjects. But despite making more false alarms to unrelated lures, amnesic patients made significantly fewer false alarms to semantically related lure words; that is, they

showed a smaller false recognition effect than did controls.

These findings have recently been extended to the domain of perceptual false recognition: After studying lists of perceptually related words (e.g., *lake, fake, sake*), amnesic patients committed fewer false recognition errors to perceptually related lure words (e.g., *rake*) than did controls (Schacter, Verfaellie, and Anes, 1997). Similarly, Koutstaal and colleagues (in press) examined false recognition of abstract visual patterns in amnesic patients, using a prototype recognition procedure that is similar in some respects to the paradigms used in category learning experiments described earlier. Koutstaal and colleagues found robust false recognition to prototypes in control subjects, together with significantly reduced false recognition of prototypes in amnesic patients.

The overall pattern of results from the foregoing studies indicates that the medial temporal/diencephalic regions that are damaged in amnesic patients, which have long been linked to veridical recognition, are also involved in false recognition. Specifically, it has been proposed (Schacter, Verfaellie, and Pradere, 1996; Schacter, Norman, and Koutstaal, 1998) that medial temporal areas are involved in the encoding and/or retrieval of semantic and perceptual-gist information (Brainerd, Reyna, and Kneer, 1995) or global-similarity information (Hintzman and Curran, 1994) that supports robust false recognition. Amnesia typically reduces false recognition by impairing this proposed mechanism, but the false recognition rate of amnesic patients can exceed that of control subjects when experimental conditions are created that increase control subjects' episodic memory for actually studied words, thus allowing them–but not amnesic patients–to suppress their false recognition responses (Schacter, Verfaellie, and colleagues, 1998; cf. Brainerd, Reyna, and Kneer, 1995).

A related line of studies has examined false recognition in amnesic patients using a procedure, introduced by Underwood and Zimmerman (1973) and developed further by Reinitz and his colleagues (e.g., Reinitz and Demb, 1994), that produces "memory conjunction errors." In this paradigm, conjunction false alarms occur when subjects incorrectly claim to have studied lure words (e.g., *handgun*) that are formed by recombining features of studied compound words (e.g., *handstand, shotgun*); similar effects have been observed when features of faces or of nonsense syllables are recombined after study. Reinitz, Verfaellie, and Milberg (1996) found that control subjects made more "old" responses to previously studied compound words than to conjunction lures. Amnesic patients, by contrast, made similar numbers of "old" responses to the two types of items: Amnesics made fewer "old" responses to studied words than did controls, and made comparable numbers of false alarms to conjunction lures.

Kroll and colleagues (1996) used similar procedures in experiments that included patients with left or right hippocampal damage, reporting that patients with left but not right hippocampal damage showed elevated rates of memory conjunction errors to recombined words, whereas both patient groups showed higher levels of conjunction errors than did controls with recombined faces. Kroll and colleagues (1996) suggested that hippocampal lesions interfere with binding features of an episode into a cohesive representation.

FALSE RECOGNITION IN NONAMNESIC PATIENTS Several recent case studies have shown dramatic increases of false recognition in patients with lesions to various aspects of the frontal lobes. For instance, Parkin and colleagues (1996) reported elevated false recognition in a patient who had suffered a ruptured anterior communicating artery aneurysm that produced left frontal lobe atrophy. False recognition of nonpresented materials was accompanied by high confidence, but was nearly eliminated when lure items were perceptually dissimilar to studied items.

In a case study similar to the foregoing reports, we found extremely high levels of false recognition to words, nonsense syllables, pictures, and sounds in a patient (B. G.) who had suffered an infarction to the right frontal lobe (Curran et al., 1997; Schacter, Curran, et al., 1996). As with Parkin and colleagues' patient J. B., however, false recognition in patient B. G. was reduced when lure items did not share the general features of studied items. Thus, for example, after studying pictures of animate objects from various categories, B. G. made frequent false alarms to novel pictures from studied categories, but virtually never made false alarms to pictures of animals (Schacter, Curran, et al., 1996). Subsequent experiments showed that false recognition in patient B. G. could also be reduced by requiring him to make encoding judgments that resulted in detailed recollections of studied items (Curran et al., 1997). The overall pattern of results suggests that when making recognition judgments, patient B. G. (like patient J. B.) relies excessively on general similarities between study and test items unless he is provided with an encoding task that promotes the accessibility of item-specific information.

Studies of split-brain patients also highlight the distinction between general similarity and item-specific information. A series of experiments has shown that the left hemisphere is often prone to false recognition based on conceptual or perceptual similarity between lure items and previously studied information—words, faces, visual patterns, or scenes—whereas the right hemisphere tends to respond "old" only when study and test items are identical (Metcalfe, Funnell, and Gazzaniga, 1995). Finally, several recent studies have shown that older adults are often more prone to false recognition based on general similarity or gist information than are younger adults (for review, see Schacter, Koutstaal, and Norman, 1997).

NEUROIMAGING OF FALSE RECOGNITION Only a handful of studies have examined false recognition with neuroimaging techniques, mainly using the Deese/Roediger-McDermott semantic associates paradigm. The general conclusion from studies using PET (Schacter, Reiman, et al., 1996), fMRI (Schacter, Buckner, et al., 1997), and ERPS (Duzel et al., 1997; Johnson et al., 1997) is that the same or similar patterns of brain activity are observed during true and false recognition, with some small differences occurring under particular experimental conditions. More specifically, differences between true and false recognition have been reported when true and false targets are tested in separate "blocks," with PET data indicating greater activation in the left superior temporal gyrus during true than false recognition and trends for more anterior prefrontal regions during false than true recognition (Schacter, Reiman, et al., 1996), fMRI data indicating greater right anterior frontal activity during false than true recognition (Schacter, Buckner, et al., 1997), and ERP data indicating differences between true and false recognition in frontal and left temporoparietal electrode sites (Johnson et al., 1997). However, when true and false targets are randomly intermixed during recognition testing, as can be done with ERPs and "event-related" fMRI, no significant differences in brain activity underlying true and false recognition have been reported (Duzel et al., 1997; Johnson et al., 1997; Schacter, Buckner, et al., 1997).

One other notable finding to emerge from neuroimaging studies concerns the time course of brain activation. Using event-related fMRI, Schacter, Buckner, and colleagues (1997) reported that anterior prefrontal regions showed a delayed onset of activity in comparison to all other regions that were activated during true and false recognition. Schacter, Buckner, and colleagues (1997) suggested that anterior prefrontal areas might be involved in postretrieval monitoring activities, which in turn may be related to criterion-setting processes that play an important role in false recognition (see Johnson et al., 1997; Schacter, Norman, and Koutstaal, 1998).

Conclusions

The research we have considered in this chapter indicates that neuropsychological evidence from various patient populations and neuroimaging studies of healthy volunteers are beginning to illuminate the neural underpinnings of the two phenomena we have characterized as "paradoxical": implicit memory and false memory. Having considered the two separately, we now conclude by asking about possible connections between them.

One theme that occupies a prominent place in both literatures concerns the contrast between memory for general or gist information on one hand versus memory for specific exemplars or items on the other. In studies of priming, for example, it has been suggested that priming of generic or abstract representations may depend on different mechanisms than does priming specific perceptual features (cf., Curran, Schacter, and Bessenhoff, 1996; Marsolek, Kosslyn, and Squire, 1992; Marsolek, Schacter, and Nicholas, 1996). Studies of artificial grammar learning and category learning have also been concerned with the distinction between abstract and exemplar-based learning (e.g., Knowlton and Squire, 1996; Reber, Allen, and Reber, in press). In studies of false memories, the idea that false recall and recognition reflect the influences of gist or general similarity information, whereas veridical recall and recognition reflect the influence of item-specific information, has assumed central stage (e.g., Brainerd, Reyna, and Kneer, 1995; Curran et al., 1997; Payne et al., 1996; Schacter, Norman, and Koutstaal, 1998). To what extent is the gist or general similarity information that drives false memories the same as or similar to the generic or abstract information that underlies certain kinds of implicit memory effects? Earlier we reviewed data indicating that amnesic patients typically show normal priming effects after studying familiar words. Yet we also considered evidence that amnesic patients exhibit decreased gist-based false recognition after studying lists of semantically related words (Schacter, Verfaellie, and Pradere, 1996) or perceptually related words (Schacter, Verfaellie, and Anes, 1997). These kinds of findings suggest that priming and false recognition are based, at least in part, on different underlying mechanisms. Likewise, we noted recent evidence indicating that amnesic patients show reduced false recognition of visual prototypes (Koutstaal et al., in press), even though other studies have documented normal implicit prototype learning in amnesics (Knowlton and Squire, 1993). These findings, too, suggest possible differences between the mechanisms that support false recognition and implicit learning of prototypes.

To link the two domains of research more tightly, it will be necessary to carry out studies in which implicit and explicit measures of true and false memories are examined within a single experiment. Some evidence of this kind already exists. As noted earlier, in their study of memory conjunction errors Reinitz, Verfaellie, and Milberg found that control subjects made more "old" responses to previously studied words than to conjunction lures, whereas amnesic patients made similar numbers of "old" responses to the two types of items. In addition to this explicit recognition test, however, Reinitz, Verfaellie, and Milberg (1996) also examined priming of studied compound words and recombined items using a perceptual identification test, where subjects tried to identify briefly flashed stimuli. On this implicit measure, both amnesic patients and controls showed more priming for studied than recombined words, and there were no between-group differences in the magnitude of priming. Thus, even though amnesics showed no discrimination between studied items (true memories) and conjunction lures (false memories) on an explicit measure, they did show significant (and normal) levels of discrimination between the two on an implicit measure.

McDermott (1997) has also reported relevant data. In her experiments, subjects initially studied the Deese/Roediger-McDermott semantic associate lists, and were then given a stem completion test in which they provided the first word that came to mind in response to stems that could be completed with studied words, related lures, or unrelated items. She found that subjects showed significant "false priming" for the nonpresented semantic associates: When given a stem that could be completed with a nonpresented semantic associate, subjects provided the related false target at greater than baseline levels (e.g., after studying *candy, sour, sugar, bitter*, and related associates, when given the word stem "swe__," subjects were primed to respond with *sweet*). Would such effects also be observed to the same extent in amnesic patients who, as reported by Schacter, Verfaellie, and Pradere (1996), show reduced false recognition of semantic associates on explicit measures? Experiments that address such questions should help to clarify the relations between the intriguing phenomena of implicit memory and false memory that have, perhaps paradoxically, enriched our understanding of what it means to remember experiences that really did happen.

ACKNOWLEDGMENTS The writing of this chapter was supported by National Institute on Aging grant AG08441 and a grant from the Human Frontiers Science Program.

REFERENCES

BARTLETT, F. C., 1932. *Remembering*. Cambridge, U.K.: Cambridge University Press.

BEAUREGARD, M., D. GOLD, A. C. EVANS, and H. CHERTKOW, 1998. A role for the hippocampal formation in implicit memory: A 3-D PET study. *Neuroreport* 9:1867–1873.

BERNS, G. S., J. D. COHEN, and M. A. MINTUN, 1997. Brain regions responsive to novelty in the absence of awareness. *Science* 276:1272–1275.

BRAINERD, C. J., V. F. REYNA, and R. KNEER, 1995. False-recognition reversal: When similarity is distinctive. *J. Mem. Lang.* 34:157–185.

BUCHNER, A., and W. WIPPICH, 1997. Differences and commonalities between implicit learning and implicit memory. In *Handbook of Implicit Learning*, M. A. Stadler and P. A. Frensch, eds. Thousand Oaks, CA: Sage, pp. 3–46.

BUCKNER, R., J. GOODMAN, M. BUROCK, M. ROTTE, W. KOUTSTAAL, D. SCHACTER, B. ROSEN, and A. DALE, 1998. Functional-anatomic correlates of object priming in humans revealed by rapid presentation event-related fMRI. *Neuron* 20:285–296.

CARLESIMO, G. A., 1994. Perceptual and conceptual priming in amnesic and alcoholic patients. *Neuropsychologia* 32:903–921.

CONWAY, M. A., ed, 1997. *Recovered Memories and False Memories.* Oxford, U.K.: Oxford University Press.

CURRAN, T., 1997a. Higher-order associative learning in amnesia: Evidence from the serial reaction time task. *J. Cognit. Neurosci.* 9:522–533.

CURRAN, T., 1997b. Implicit sequence learning from a cognitive neuroscience perspective: What, how, and where? In *Handbook of Implicit Learning*, M. A. Stadler and P. A. Frensch, eds. Thousand Oaks, Calif.: Sage, pp. 365–400.

CURRAN, T., and S. W. KEELE, 1993. Attentional and nonattentional forms of sequence learning. *J. Exp. Psychol. Learn. Mem. Cogn.* 19:189-202.

CURRAN, T., D. L. SCHACTER, and G. BESSENHOFF, 1996. Visual specificity effects on word stem completion: Beyond transfer appropriate processing? *Can. J. Exp. Psychol.* 50:22–33.

CURRAN, T., D. L. SCHACTER, K. A. NORMAN, and L. GALLUCCIO, 1997. False recognition after a right frontal lobe infarction: Memory for general and specific information. *Neuropsychologia* 35:1035–1049.

DEESE, J., 1959. On the prediction of occurrence of particular verbal intrusions in immediate recall. *J. Exp. Psychol.* 58:17–22.

DEMB, J. B., J. E. DESMOND, A. D. WAGNER, C. J. VAIDYA, G. H. GLOUER, and J. D. E. GABRIELI, 1995. Semantic encoding and retrieval in the left inferior prefrontal cortex: A functional MRI study of task difficulty and process specificity. *J. Neurosci.* 15:5870–5878.

DIENES, Z., and D. BERRY, 1997. Implicit learning: Below the subjective threshold. *Psychol. Bull. Rev.* 4:3–23.

DUZEL E., A. P. YONELINAS, G. R. MANGUN, H. J. HEINZE, and E. TULVING, 1997. Event-related brain potential correlates of two states of conscious awareness in memory. *Proc. Natl. Acad. Sci. U.S.A.* 94:5973–5978.

GABRIELI, J. D. E., D. A. FLEISCHMAN, M. M. KEANE, S. L. REMINGER, and F. MORRELL, 1995. Double dissociation between memory systems underlying explicit and implicit memory in the human brain. *Psychol. Sci.* 6:76–82.

GABRIELI, J. D. E., M. M. KEANE, M. M. ZARELLA, and R. A. POLDRACK, 1997. Preservation of implicit memory for new associations in global amnesia. *Psychol. Sci.* 8:326–329.

GRAF, P., and D. L. SCHACTER, 1985. Implicit and explicit memory for new associations in normal subjects and amnesic patients. *J. Exp. Psychol. Learn. Mem. Cogn.* 11:501–518.

GRAF, P., L. R. SQUIRE, and G. MANDLER, 1984. The information that amnesic patients do not forget. *J. Exp. Psychol. Learn. Mem. Cogn.* 10:164–178.

GRAFTON, S. T., E. HAZELTINE, and R. IVRY, 1995. Functional mapping of sequence learning in normal humans. *J. Cognit. Neurosci.* 7:497–510.

HAMANN, S. B., and L. R. SQUIRE, 1997. Intact perceptual memory in the absence of conscious memory. *Behav. Neurosci.* 111:850–854.

HAMANN, S. B., L. R. SQUIRE, and D. L. SCHACTER, 1995. Perceptual thresholds and priming in amnesia. *Neuropsychology* 9:1–13.

HAYES, A. E., M. C. DAVIDSON, S. W. KEELE, and R. D. RAFAL, 1998. Toward a functional analysis of the basal ganglia. *J. Cognit. Neurosci.* 10:178–198.

HAZELTINE, E., S. T. GRAFTON, and R. IVRY, 1997. Attention and stimulus characteristics determined the locus of motor sequence encoding. A PET study. *Brain* 120:123–140.

HINTZMAN, D. L., 1986. "Schema abstraction" in a multiple-trace memory model. *Psychol. Rev.* 93:411–428.

HINTZMAN, D. L., and T. CURRAN, 1994. Retrieval dynamics of recognition and frequency judgments: Evidence for separate processes of familiarity and recall. *J. Mem. Lang.* 33:1–18.

JACKSON, G. M., S. R. JACKSON, J. HARRISON, L. HENDERSON, and C. KENNARD, 1995. Serial reaction time learning and Parkinson's disease: Evidence for a procedural learning deficit. *Neuropsychologia* 33:577–593.

JACOBS, D. M., Y. STERN, and R. MAYEUX, 1996. Dementia in Parkinson disease, Huntington disease, and other degenerative conditions. In *Behavioral Neurology and Neuropsychology*, T. E. Feinberg and M. J. Farah, eds. New York: McGraw-Hill, pp. 579–587.

JOHNSON, M. K., S. F. NOLDE, M. MATHER, J. KOUNIOS, D. L. SCHACTER, and T. CURRAN, 1997. Test format can affect the similarity of brain activity associated with true and false recognition memory. *Psychol. Sci.* 8:250–257.

KEANE, M. M., J. D. E. GABRIELI, J. S. NOLAND, and S. I. MCNEALY, 1995. Normal perceptual priming of orthographically illegal nonwords in amnesia. *J. Intl. Neuropsych. Soc.* 5:425–433.

KEELE, S. W., R. B. IVRY, E. HAZELTINE, U. MAYR, and H. HEUER, 1998. *The cognitive and neural architecture of sequence representation* (Technical Report 98–03). Institute of Cognitive and Decision Sciences, University of Oregon, Eugene.

KINOSHITA, S., and S. V. WAYLAND, 1993. Effects of surface features on word-fragment completion in amnesic subjects. *Am. J. Psychol.* 106:67–80.

KNOWLTON, B. J., M. A. GLUCK, and L. R. SQUIRE, 1994. Probabilistic classification learning in amnesia. *Learn. Mem.* 1:106–120.

KNOWLTON, B. J., J. A. MANGELS, and L. R. SQUIRE, 1996. A neostriatal habit learning system in humans. *Science* 273:1399–1402.

KNOWLTON, B. J., S. J. RAMUS, and L. R. SQUIRE, 1992. Intact artificial grammar learning in amnesia: Dissociation of classification learning and explicit memory for specific instances. *Psychol. Sci.* 3:172–179.

KNOWLTON, B. J., and L. R. SQUIRE, 1993. The learning of categories: Parallel brain systems for item memory and category level knowledge. *Science* 262:1747–1749.

KNOWLTON, B. J., and L. R. SQUIRE, 1994. The information acquired during artificial grammar learning. *J. Exp. Psychol. Learn. Mem. Cogn.* 20:79–91.

KNOWLTON, B. J., and L. R. SQUIRE, 1995. Learning about categories in the absence of memory. *Proc. Natl. Acad. Sci. U.S.A.* 92:12470–12474.

KNOWLTON, B. J., and L. R. SQUIRE, 1996. Artificial grammar learning depends on implicit acquisition of both abstract and exemplar-specific knowledge. *J. Exp. Psychol. Learn. Mem. Cogn.* 22:169–181.

KNOWLTON, B. J., L. R. SQUIRE, and M. A. GLUCK, 1994. Probabilistic classification learning in amnesia. *Learn. Mem.* 1:106–120.

KNOWLTON, B. J., L. R. SQUIRE, J. S. PAULSEN, N. R. SWERDLOW, M. SWENSON, and N. BUTTERS, 1996. Dissociations within nondeclarative memory in Huntington's disease. *Neuropsychology* 10:538–548.

KOUTSTAAL, W., D. L. SCHACTER, M. VERFAELLIE, C. J. BRENNER, and E. M. JACKSON, in press. Perceptually based false recognition of novel objects in amnesics: Effects of category size and similarity to category prototypes. *J. Cognit. Neurosci.*

KROLL, N. E. A., R. T. KNIGHT, J. METCALFE, E. S. WOLF, and E. TULVING, 1996. Cohesion failure as a source of memory illusions. *J. Mem. Lang.* 35:176–196.

MARSOLEK, C. J., S. M. KOSSLYN, and L. R. SQUIRE, 1992. Form-specific visual priming in the right cerebral hemisphere. *J. Exp. Psychol. Learn. Mem. Cogn.* 18:492–508.

MARSOLEK, C. J., D. L. SCHACTER, and C. Nicholas, 1996. Form-specific visual priming for new associations in the right cerebral hemisphere. *Mem. Cogn.* 24:539–556.

MATHER, M., L. A. HENKEL, and M. K. JOHNSON, 1997. Evaluating characteristics of false memories: Remember/know judgments and memory characteristics questionnaire compared. *Mem. Cogn.* 25:826–837.

MAYR, U., 1996. Spatial attention and implicit sequence learning: Evidence for independent learning of spatial and nonspatial sequences *J. Exp. Psychol. Learn. Mem. Cogn.* 22:350–364.

MCDERMOTT, K., 1997. Priming on perceptual implicit memory test can be achieved through presentation of associates. *Psychon. Bull. Rev.* 4:582–586.

METCALFE, J., M. FUNNELL, and M. S. GAZZANIGA, 1995. Right-hemisphere memory superiority: Studies of a split-brain patient. *Psychol. Sci.* 6:157–164.

MOSCOVITCH, M., 1995. Confabulation. In *Memory Distortion: How Minds, Brains, and Societies Reconstruct the Past*, D. L. Schacter, J. T. Coyle, G. D. Fischbach, M. M. Mesulam, and L. E. Sullivan, eds. Cambridge, Mass.: Harvard University Press, pp. 226–254.

NEAL, A., and B. HESKETH, 1997. Episodic knowledge and implicit learning. *Psychol. Bull. Rev.* 4:24–37.

NISSEN, M. J., and P. BULLEMER, 1987. Attentional requirements of learning: Evidence from performance measures. *Cognit. Psychol.* 19:1–32.

NORMAN, K. A., and D. L. SCHACTER, 1997. False recognition in young and older adults: Exploring the characteristics of illusory memories. *Mem. Cogn.* 25:838–848.

OSTERGAARD, A. L., and T. L. JERNIGAN, 1993. Are word priming and explicit memory mediated by different brain structures? In *Implicit Memory: New Directions in Cognitive, Development, and Neuropsychology*, P. Graf and M. E. J. Masson, eds. Hillsdale, N. J.: Erlbaum, pp. 327–349.

PARKIN, A. J., C. BINDSCHAEDLER, L. HARSENT, and C. METZLER, 1996. Pathological false alarm rates following damage to the left frontal cortex. *Brain Cogn.* 32:14–27.

PAYNE, D. G., C. J. ELIE, J. M. BLACKWELL, and J. S. NEUSCHATZ, 1996. Memory illusions: Recalling, recognizing, and recollecting events that never occurred. *J. Mem. Lang.* 35:261–285.

PERRUCHET, P., and M. AMORIM, 1992. Conscious knowledge and changes in performance in sequence learning: Evidence against dissociation. *J. Exp. Psychol. Learn. Mem. Cogn.* 18:785–800.

POSNER, M. I., and S. W. KEELE, 1968. On the genesis of abstract ideas. *J. Exp. Psychol.* 77:353–363.

RAUCH, S. L., C. R. SAVAGE, H. D. BROWN, T. CURRAN, N. M. ALPERT, A. KENDRICK, A. J. FISCHMAN, and S. M. KOSSLYN, 1995. A PET investigation of implicit and explicit sequence learning. *Hum. Brain Mapping* 3:271–286.

RAUCH, S. L., P. J. WHALEN, T. CURRAN, S. MCINERNEY, S. HECKERS, and C. R. SAVAGE, 1998. Thalamic deactivation during early implicit sequence learning: A functional MRI study. *Neuroreport* 9:865–870.

RAUCH, S. L., P. J. WHALEN, C. R. SAVAGE, T. CURRAN, A. KENDRICK, H. D. BROWN, G. BUSH, H. C. BREITER, and B. R. ROSEN, 1997. Striatal recruitment during an implicit sequence learning task as measured by functional magnetic resonance imaging. *Hum. Brain Mapping* 5:124–132.

REBER, A. S., 1967. Implicit learning of artificial grammars. *J. Verb. Learn. Verb. Behav.* 6:855–863.

REBER, A. S., 1989. Implicit learning and tacit knowledge. *J. Exp. Psychol. Gen.* 118:219–235.

REBER, A. S., R. ALLEN, and P. J. REBER, in press. Implicit and explicit learning. In *The Nature of Cognition*, R. J. Sternberg, ed. Cambridge, Mass.: MIT Press.

REBER, P. J., B. J. KNOWLTON, and L. R. SQUIRE, 1996. Dissociable properties of memory systems: Differences in the flexibility of declarative and nondeclarative knowledge. *Behav. Neurosci.* 110:861–871.

REBER, P. J., and L. R. SQUIRE, 1994. Parallel brain systems for learning with and without awareness. *Learn. Mem.* 1:217–229.

REBER, P. J., and L. R. SQUIRE, in press. Intact learning of artificial grammars and intact category learning by patients with Parkinson's disease. *Behav. Neurosci.*

REBER, P. J., C. E. STARK, and L. R. SQUIRE, 1998. Cortical areas supporting category learning identified using functional MRI. *Proc. Natl. Acad. Sci. U.S.A.* 95:747–750.

REED, J., and P. JOHNSON, 1994. Assessing implicit learning with indirect tests: Determining what is learned about sequence structure *J. Exp. Psychol. Learn. Mem. Cogn.* 20:585–594.

REINITZ, M. T., and J. B. DEMB, 1994. Implicit and explicit memory for compound words. *Mem. Cog.* 22:687–694.

REINITZ, M. T., M. VERFAELLIE, and W. P. MILBERG, 1996. Memory conjunction errors in normal and amnesic subjects. *J. Mem. Lang.* 35:286–299.

ROBINSON, K. J., and H. L. ROEDIGER III, 1997. Associative processes in false recall and false recognition. *Psychol. Sci.* 8:231–237.

ROEDIGER, H. L., III., 1996. Memory illusions. *J. Mem. Lang.* 35:76–100.

ROEDIGER, H. L., III, and K. B. MCDERMOTT, 1993. Implicit memory in normal human subjects. In *Handbook of Neuropsychology*, vol. 8, H. Spinnler and F. Boller, eds. Amsterdam: Elsevier, pp. 63–131.

ROEDIGER, H. L., III, and K. B. MCDERMOTT, 1995. Creating false memories: Remembering words not presented in lists. *J. Exp. Psychol. Learn. Mem. Cogn.* 21:803–814.

RUGG, M. D., R. E. MARK, P. WALLA, A. M. SCHLOER-
SCHEIDT, C. S. BIRCH, and K. ALLAN, 1998. Dissociation of
the neural correlates of implicit and explicit memory. *Nature*
392:595–598.

SALMON, D. P., and N. BUTTERS, 1995. Neurobiology of skill
and habit learning. *Curr. Opin. Neurobiol.* 5:184–190.

SCHACTER, D. L., 1987. Implicit memory: History and current
status. *J. Exp. Psychol. Learn. Mem. Cogn.* 13:501–518.

SCHACTER, D. L., 1995a. Implicit memory: A new frontier
for cognitive neuroscience. In *The Cognitive Neurosciences*,
M. S. Gazzaniga, ed. Cambridge, Mass.: MIT Press, pp.
815–824.

SCHACTER, D. L., 1995b. Memory distortion: History and current status. In *Memory Distortion: How Minds, Brains and Societies Reconstruct the Past*, D. L. Schacter, J. T. Coyle, G. D.
Fischbach, M. M. Mesulam, and L. E. Sullivan, eds. Cambridge, Mass.: Harvard University Press, pp. 1–43.

SCHACTER, D. L., N. M. ALPERT, C. R. SAVAGE, S. L. RAUCH,
and M. S. ALBERT, 1996. Conscious recollection and the human hippocampal formation: Evidence from positron emission tomography. *Proc. Natl. Acad. Sci. U.S.A.* 93:321–325.

SCHACTER, D.L. and R. L. BUCKNER, 1998a. On the relations
among priming, conscious recollection, and intentional retrieval: Evidence from neuroimaging research. *Neurobiol.
Learn. Mem.* 70:284–303.

SCHACTER, D. L., and R. L. BUCKNER, 1998b. Priming and the
brain. *Neuron* 20:185–195.

SCHACTER, D. L., R. L. BUCKNER, W. KOUTSTAAL, A. M.
DALE, and B. R. ROSEN, 1997. Late onset of anterior prefrontal activity during retrieval of veridical and illusory
memories: A single trial fMRI study. *Neuroimage* 6:259–
269.

SCHACTER, D. L., C. Y. P. CHIU, and K. N. OCHSNER, 1993.
Implicit memory: A selective review. *Annu. Rev. Neurosci.*
16:159–182.

SCHACTER, D. L., B. CHURCH, and E. BOLTON, 1995. Implicit
memory in amnesic patients: Impairment of voice-specific
priming. *Psychol. Sci.* 6:20–25.

SCHACTER, D. L., B. CHURCH, and J. TREADWELL, 1994. Implicit memory in amnesic patients: Evidence for spared auditory priming. *Psychol. Sci.* 5:20–25.

SCHACTER, D. L., L. A. COOPER, and J. TREADWELL, 1993.
Preserved priming of novel objects across size transformation in amnesic patients. *Psychol. Sci.* 4:331–335.

SCHACTER, D. L., T. CURRAN, L. GALLUCCIO, W. MILBERG,
and J. BATES, 1996. False recognition and the right frontal
lobe: A case study. *Neuropsychologia* 34:793–808.

SCHACTER, D. L., and P. GRAF, 1986. Preserved learning in
amnesic patients: Perspectives on research from direct priming. *J. Clin. Exp. Neuropsych.* 8:727–743.

SCHACTER, D. L., W. KOUTSTAAL, and K. A. NORMAN, 1997.
False memories and aging. *Trends Neurosci.* 1:229–236.

SCHACTER, D. L., K. A. NORMAN, and W. KOUTSTAAL, 1998.
The cognitive neuroscience of constructive memory. *Annu.
Rev. Psychol.* 49:289–318.

SCHACTER, D. L., E. REIMAN, T. CURRAN, L. S. YUN, D.
BANDY, K. B. MCDERMOTT, and H. L. ROEDIGER III, 1996.
Neuroanatomical correlates of veridical and illusory recognition memory: Evidence from positron emission tomography. *Neuron* 17:267–274.

SCHACTER, D. L., M. VERFAELLIE, and M. D. ANES, 1997. Illusory memories in amnesic patients: Conceptual and perceptual false recognition. *Neuropsychology* 11:331–342.

SCHACTER, D. L., M. VERFAELLIE, M. D. ANES, and C. A.
RACINE, 1998. When true recognition suppresses false recognition: Evidence from amnesic patients. *J. Cognit. Neurosci.* 10:668–679.

SCHACTER, D. L., M. VERFAELLIE, and D. PRADERE, 1996.
The neuropsychology of memory illusions: False recall
and recognition in amnesic patients. *J. Mem. Lang.* 35:319–
334.

SCHMIDTKE, V., and H. HEUER, 1997. Task integration as a factor in secondary-task effects on sequence learning. *Psychol.
Res./Psychol. Forsch.* 60:53–71.

SHANKS, D. R., and M. F. ST. JOHN, 1994. Characteristics of
dissociable human learning systems. *Behav. Brain Sci.* 17:
367–447.

SHIFFRIN, R. M., D. E. HUBER, and K. MARINELLI, 1995.
Effects of category length and strength on familiarity in
recognition. *J. Exp. Psychol. Learn. Mem. Cogn.*, 21:267–287.

SHIMAMURA, A. P., and L. R. SQUIRE, 1989. Impaired priming
of new associations in amnesia. *J. Exp. Psychol. Learn. Mem.
Cogn.* 15:721–728.

SQUIRE, L. R., 1994. Declarative and nondeclarative memory:
Multiple brain systems supporting learning and memory. In
Memory Systems, 1994, D. L. Schacter and E. Tulving, eds.
Cambridge, Mass.: MIT Press, pp. 203–231.

SQUIRE, L. R., J. G. OJEMANN, F. M. MIEZIN, S. E. PE-
TERSEN, T. O. VIDEEN, and M. E. RAICHLE, 1992. Activation of the hippocampus in normal humans: A functional
anatomical study of memory. *Proc. Natl. Acad. Sci. U.S.A.* 89:
1837–1841.

STADLER, M. A., 1995. Role of attention in implicit learning *J.
Exp. Psychol. Learn. Mem. Cogn.* 21:674–685.

STADLER, M. A., 1997. Distinguishing implicit and explicit
learning. *Psychol. Bull. Rev.* 4:56–62.

STADLER, M. A., and H. L. ROEDIGER III, 1997. The question
of awareness in research on implicit learning. In *Handbook of
Implicit Learning*, M. A. Stadler and P. A. Frensch, eds. Thousand Oaks, Calif.: Sage, pp. 47–104.

TENPENNY, P. L., 1995. Abstractionist versus episodic theories
of repetition priming and word identification. *Psychon. Bull.
Rev.* 2:339–363.

TULVING, E., and D. L. SCHACTER, 1990. Priming and human
memory systems. *Science* 247:301–306.

UNDERWOOD, B. J., 1965. False recognition produced by implicit verbal responses. *J. Exp. Psychol.* 70:122–129.

UNDERWOOD, B. J., and J. ZIMMERMAN, 1973. The syllable as
a source of error in multisyllable word recognition. *J. Verb.
Learn. Verb. Behav.* 12:701–706.

UNGERLEIDER, L., 1995. Functional brain imaging studies of
cortical mechanisms for memory. *Science* 270:769–775.

VAIDYA, C. J., J. D. E. GABRIELI, M. VERFAELLIE, D. A.
FLEISCHMAN, and N. ASKARI, 1998. Font-specific priming
following global amnesia and occipital-lobe damage. *Neuropsychology* 12:183–192.

VOKEY, J. R., and L. R. BROOKS, 1992. Salience of item knowledge in learning artificial grammars. *J. Exp. Psychol. Learn.
Mem. Cogn.* 18:328–344.

WARRINGTON, E. K., and L. WEISKRANTZ, 1974. The effect of
prior learning on subsequent retention in amnesic patients.
Neuropsychologia 12:419–428.

WHITTLESEA, B. W. A., and M. D. DORKEN, 1993. Incidentally, things in general are particularly determined: An epi-
sodic-processing account of implicit learning. *J. Exp. Psychol.
Gen.* 122:277–248.

WIGGS, C. L., and A. MARTIN, 1998. Properties and mechanisms of perceptual priming. *Curr. Opin. Neurobiol.* 8:227–233.

WILLINGHAM, D. B., 1998. A neuropsychological theory of motor skill learning. *Psychol. Rev.* 105:558–584.

WILLINGHAM, D. B., and W. J. KOROSHETZ, 1993. Evidence for dissociable motor skills in Huntington's disease patients. *Psychobiology* 21:173–182.

WILLINGHAM, D. B., M. J. NISSEN, and P. BULLEMER, 1989. On the development of procedural knowledge. *J. Exp. Psychol. Learn. Mem. Cogn.* 15:1047–1060.

VII LANGUAGE

Introduction

WILLEM J. M. LEVELT

Language evolved as the species-specific communication system of *homo sapiens*. Although its evolutionary history will always remain intractable, it is reasonable to suppose that a major selective pressure derived from the need to maintain coherence in ever-growing cooperative clans. Our closest relatives in nature, the old world primates, achieve this bonding largely by grooming and, as Dunbar (1996) has shown, the amount of time spent on grooming indeed increases rapidly with group size across primate species. Bonding-by-grooming, however, becomes impractical for the much larger clan size that is typical of a human hunter-gatherer society. Clearly, language can serve this function of social bonding and much more. It is particularly well designed for communication in a society of individuals that have a "theory of mind" (Premack and Woodruff, 1978). When interactants mutually interpret their behaviors as proceeding from beliefs, wishes, hopes, and the like, as is the case in human societies only (Tomasello and Call, 1997), it is certainly useful to have a communicative system that can express such recursive attributions as "A believes that B knows X." But it is a vain hope to *predict* the design of natural languages from the evolutionary pressures that must have shaped it. More is known about which areas of the primate brain were engaged to serve these new communicative functions. This is, first of all, the old call system, which is one of phonation. It involves the caudal midbrain structures and is expressive of the animal's emotions (Müller-Preuss and Ploog, 1983). Neocortical control is restricted to input from the (limbic) anterior cingulate gyrus. This evolutionary old system is still involved in the modulation of vocal fold activity during speech, in particular intonation, which remains highly expressive of emotion. However, in our species phonation is clearly under neocortical control: We can sing and we can feign emotion in speech. The same is true for the new supralaryngeal system. It modulates phonation in the time-frequency domain, i.e., it controls articulation. MacNeilage (1998) outlines the evolutionary precursors of this syllabic, articulatory system. Its evolution corresponds to further specialization of the face area in the primary motor cortex and to a vast expansion of supplementary and premotor cortices. At the same time, left temporal lobe areas adjacent to the primary auditory cortex became more specialized for the storage of phonological codes. Various left-hemisphere perisylvian areas (temporal, parietal, insular, frontal) became involved with the complexities of linguistic processing, ranging from semantic to syntactic, morphological, phonological, and phonetic analysis and synthesis. But evolution did not prepare us for reading. It is, in fact, an unexplained accident that most of us can learn to read. The skill is obviously parasitical on the reader's pre-existing linguistic and visual competence, but the specifics of grapheme-to-phoneme mapping (in alphabetic systems) requires the engagement of cortical structures that did not evolve for that purpose and that may vary from learner to learner. Given this biologically secondary status of reading, it is at least remarkable that the large majority of language-related brain-imaging studies involve printed, not spoken language as input.

The aim of this Language section is to review major relations between the functional and the neural architecture of language. The functional architecture of language use, i.e., its organization as a behavioral system, is the domain of psycholinguistics. Traditionally, the field is partitioned as the study of language production (speaking, signing), language comprehension, the development of these skills (language acquisition), and the study of their disorders. This schema is also followed in the present section. In their chapter on language production, Indefrey and Levelt relate the functional architecture of the process of speaking, in particular the generation of spoken words, to a wide range of recent imaging results. Language comprehension, always the more active field of research, is covered by two chapters. The first one, by Norris and Wise, deals with accessing words from auditory or visual input and relates the functional organization of word recognition to the neural architecture involved. The second one, by Brown, Hagoort, and Kutas, reviews the neurophysiology and hemodynamics of postlexical processing, i.e., the integration of words in their larger syntactic and se-

mantic context during sentence processing. Two further chapters are dedicated to the acquisition of linguistic skills. Mehler and Christophe discuss the initial stage, the infant's discovery of the sound structure of the single or multiple languages with which it is confronted. Stromswold reviews the further maturation of linguistic skills, both normal and disordered, from the perspective of the human brain's predisposition for language. Both chapters consider in some detail the neural architecture that supports this rapid buildup of linguistic competence. The final pair of chapters is dedicated to language disorders. Saffran, Dell, and Schwartz review recent computational accounts of the major aphasic disorders: Can aphasic syndromes be modeled by "damaging" the normal computational architecture? In their chapter, Dronkers, Redfern, and Knight discuss language disorders from the perspective of the damaged cortical structures involved. Their "triangulation" approach requires a detailed analysis of functional components combined with a substantial database of brain and behavioral patient data.

Together, these seven chapters provide optimal coverage of the cognitive neuroscience of language. But the coverage is, by no means, intended to be comprehensive. Not only is the literature, including such a classical source as Caplan's (1992) book, already vast, but the recent volcanic eruption of imaging studies of language use is transforming the field in ways that will become fully apparent only after the first dust has settled. Meanwhile, the best coverage of the field can be found in Stemmer and Whitacker (1998) and Brown and Hagoort (1999).

REFERENCES

BROWN, C., and P. HAGOORT (eds.), 1999. *Neurocognition of Language.* Oxford: Oxford University Press.

CAPLAN, D., 1992. *Language: Structure, Processing, and Disorders.* Cambridge, Mass.: MIT Press.

DUNBAR, R., 1996. *Grooming, Gossip, and the Evolution of Language.* London: Faber and Faber.

MACNEILAGE, P. F., 1998. The frame/content theory of evolution of speech production. *Behav. Brain Sci.* 21:499–511.

MÜLLER-PREUSS, P., and D. PLOOG, 1983. Central control of sound production in mammals. In *Bioacoustics–A Comparative Study,* B. Lewis, ed. London: Academic Press, pp. 125–146.

PREMACK, D., and G. WOODRUFF, 1978. Does the chimpanzee have a theory of mind? *Behav. Brain Sci.* 1:515–526.

STEMMER, B., and H. A. WHITACKER (eds.), 1998. *Handbook of Neurolinguistics.* San Diego: Academic Press.

TOMASELLO, M., and J. CALL, 1997. *Primate Cognition.* Oxford: Oxford University Press.

59 The Neural Correlates of Language Production

PETER INDEFREY AND WILLEM J. M. LEVELT

ABSTRACT   This chapter reviews the findings of 58 word production experiments using different tasks and neuroimaging techniques. The reported cerebral activation sites are coded in a common anatomic reference system. Based on a functional model of language production, the different word production tasks are analyzed in terms of their processing components. This approach allows a distinction between the core process of word production and preceding task-specific processes (lead-in processes) such as visual or auditory stimulus recognition. The core process of word production is subserved by a left-lateralized perisylvian/thalamic language production network. Within this network there seems to be functional specialization for the processing stages of word production. In addition, this chapter includes a discussion of the available evidence on syntactic production, self-monitoring, and the time course of word production.

In reading the neuroscience literature on language production, one might infer that producing language simply means producing words. Neuroimaging studies of language production typically require subjects to generate (silently) words in response to other words (as in verb generation)—words of a particular semantic category, names of depicted objects, words beginning with a particular phoneme (or letter), and the like. Such studies have provided a wealth of information on the neurophysiology of lexical access, but they should not obscure our perspective on the larger speech production process. Speaking is, after all, our most complex cognitive-motor skill, designed by evolution to support communication in large clans of *homo sapiens*. A vast network of brain structures, both cortical and subcortical, contributes to the high-speed generation of utterances in never-identical communicative settings. It also generates the ever-babbling internal speech, speech whose representational functions are still fallow research territory.

In this chapter, therefore, we begin with a summary outline of the functional organization of speaking, laying out the processing components involved, including grammatical encoding, phonological encoding, and self-monitoring. These components then offer a structure for

the subsequent review of neuroimaging studies, most of them word production studies.

The functional organization of language production

The interactive generation of utterances in conversation, the evolutionary basic setting for language use, involves a multicomponent processing system. It can map communicative intentions onto articulatory gestures, which in turn produce the auditory signals from which the interlocutor can derive or recognize these intentions. Figure 59.1 diagrams the major processing components involved (roughly as defined in Levelt, 1989). Although the modeling of component processes and their interaction still differs substantially among theories of language production (see, in particular, the BBS commentaries to Levelt, Roelofs, and Meyer, 1999), there is reasonable consensus about the major components involved in the generation of speech.

It makes both functional and neuropsychological sense to partition these components as follows. There is, on the one hand, a rhetorical/semantic/syntactic system. It decides on the communicatively effective information to express, puts it in terms of linguistically expressible conceptual structures ("messages"), whereupon these messages trigger the generation of ordered lexicosyntactic structures ("surface structures"). On the other hand, there is also a phonological/phonetic system whose aim it is to generate the appropriate articulatory shape for these surface structures. Both systems have access to a huge mental lexicon. The rhetorical/semantic/syntactic system has, in addition, access to communicatively relevant perceptual and memory systems which represent the speaker's external and internal world. The form-generating system has access to a mental syllabary. Let us now turn to the processing components in slightly more detail.

CONCEPTUAL PREPARATION   In preparing a message for expression, we exercise our social and rhetorical competence. An effective utterance will mind the knowledge state of the listener, the intention to be realized, the

PETER INDEFREY and WILLEM J. M. LEVELT   Max Planck Institute for Psycholinguistics, Nijmegen, The Netherlands

845

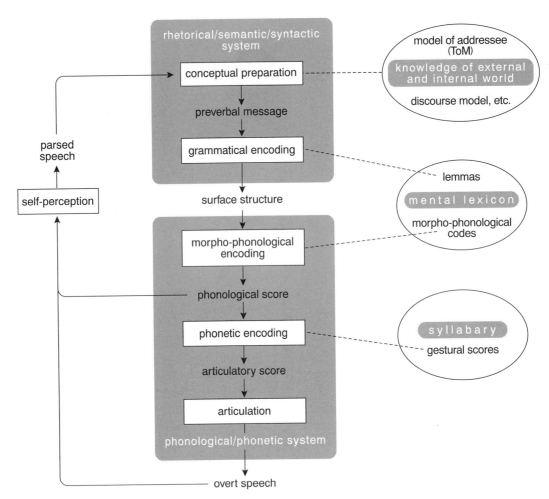

FIGURE 59.1 Framework of processing components involved in speech production. (From Levelt, 1999.)

achieved state of discourse, the attentional focus of the interlocutor, and so on (Clark, 1996). Conceptual preparation capitalizes on our "theory of mind" skills—the ability to estimate an interlocutor's state of relevant beliefs and desires (Premack and Premack, 1995). All this is subsumed under *macroplanning* (Butterworth, 1980; Levelt, 1989). One important aspect of macroplanning is "linearization"—deciding what to say first, what to say next, etc. (Levelt, 1981). This involves both rhetorical decisions about how to guide the listener's attention and efficient management of working memory.

There is, in addition, *microplanning*. To be expressible in language, a conceptual structure must be in a special, "propositional" format. Visual images, musical patterns, and motor images are typically in a different representational format. If they are to be expressed linguistically, they must be recoded. This recoding is flexible, and dependent on the communicative goals. The same visual image of a sheep and a goat juxtaposed can be expressed as "there is a sheep, and a goat to the right of it" or "there is a goat, and a sheep to the left of it" (and in

many other ways). This phenomenon, called *perspective taking*, is not limited to the recoding of visual representations (cf. Levelt, 1996; Clark, 1997). The terminal elements in the propositional format must be *lexical concepts*, concepts for which there are words in the language. The choice of lexical concept is an important aspect of perspective taking. There are always multiple ways to refer to the same entity: The *animal/dog/labrador frightened me* or *the interval/consonant/fifth is out of place here*. Perspective taking is ubiquitous in language production. As speakers, we are continuously mediating between visual, motor, person, etc., imagery systems and semantic systems of lexical concepts. This mediation is under the pressure of communicative effectiveness. It wouldn't be surprising if conceptual preparation turns out to be a widely distributed cerebral affair.

GRAMMATICAL ENCODING The lexical concepts that are activated in constructing a message for expression trigger the retrieval of *lemmas* from the mental lexicon. These are syntactic words, characterized by a syntactic frame. There is a lemma for each lexical concept and for all function words. Syntactic word frames specify, among other things, how semantic arguments in the message (such as theme or recipient) should be mapped onto syntactic functions (such as direct or indirect object). In *Sally gave Peter a bike*, the recipient of Sally's giving is Peter and the theme is a bike. The syntactic frame of *give* moves the corresponding lemmas into indirect and direct object position, respectively. The syntactic frames of selected lemmas (verbs, nouns, etc.) combine and recombine to build a syntactic pattern for the message as a whole, a "surface structure." Surface structures are *incrementally* created. As soon as a first lemma is selected, syntactic construction is initiated, and it keeps going as further lemmas become available. These processes are typically disturbed in agrammatic patients.

MORPHOPHONOLOGICAL ENCODING   A first major step in the generation of the articulatory shape of an utterance involves the creation of phonological words and phrases and the generation of intonational phrases. A core process here is the retrieval of phonological codes. Once selected, a lemma activates the phonological codes of each of its morphemes. For instance, after selection of the noun lemma *postbox*, the codes for each of its morphemes *post* and *box* are activated: /pəʊst/, /bɒks/. Most neuroimaging work in word production involves monomorphemic words and hence reveals nothing about the production of complex morphology.

Accessing a word's or morpheme's phonological code is no trivial matter, neuropsychologically speaking. Anomic disorders, for instance, are often blockades of phonological access with preserved access to syntactic information. Badecker, Miozzo, and Zanuttini (1995), for instance, reported the case study of an Italian anomic patient who is unable to name any picture, but in all cases knows the gender of the target word. Gender is a syntactic word property, encoded in the lemma. Jescheniak and Levelt (1994) have shown that the "word-frequency effect" (i.e., picture naming is slower when the name is a low-frequency word than when it is a high-frequency word) emerges during the retrieval of a word's phonological code. It does not arise at the level of lemma selection. Clearly, there is a dedicated system involved in the storage and retrieval of phonological codes.

The primary use of phonological codes is the generation of syllabic structure. The domain of syllabification is the phonological word. Syllabification doesn't respect lexical boundaries. In the phrase *I understand it*, the syllabification becomes *I un-der-stan-dit*, where the last syllable *(dit)* straddles a lexical boundary; *understandit* is a single phonological word. Syllabification also depends on inflection—*un-der-stand, un-der-stands, un-der-*

stan-ding—it is a highly context-dependent process. Most probably, a word's syllabification is not stored in its phonological code. The incremental syllabification of phonological words in connected speech is an independent computational process (cf. Levelt, Roelofs, and Meyer, 1999, for a detailed theory of phonological word formation).

As the surface structure expands, the speaker also composes larger phonological units. One such unit is the *phonological phrase*. It is a metrical unit. It tends to start right after the lexical head of a surface phrase (i.e., right after the noun of a noun phrase, or right after the main verb in a verb phrase), and it leads up to include the next lexical head. Here is such a metrical grouping: *the fellow/that I sought/was standing/near the table/*. Within a phonological phrase, there is so-called nuclear stress on the lexical head word.

Phonological phrases combine into smaller or larger *intonational phrases*. These are sense units that are characterized by their intonation contour. The whole of the example sentence above can be cast as a single intonational phrase. Pitch movement will then lead up to the *nuclear tone*, which consists of a pitch accent on the first syllable of *table (ta-)*, followed by a boundary tone on the last syllable of the phrase *(-ble)*. Falling boundary tones suggest completion, whereas rising boundary tones invite continuation either on the part of the speaker or on the part of the interlocutor. The ultimate output of morphophonological encoding is called the *phonological score* (in analogy to a musical score).

PHONETIC ENCODING   The incremental generation of metrically grouped and pitch-marked phonological syllables is closely followed by the generation of gestural patterns for these syllables in their larger context. It is largely unknown what kind of processing mechanism creates these gestural scores. The system must be generative in that speakers can produce syllables that they never produced before (in reading nonsense words for instance). Still, it appears from language statistics that speakers of English or Dutch do some 85% of their speaking with no more than 500 different syllables (out of more than 12,000 different syllables; cf. Schiller et al., 1996). In these languages, speakers hardly ever produce an entirely new syllable. Also, many languages (such as Mandarin Chinese) have no more than a few hundred different syllables. Hence, it is reasonable to assume that these highly overused articulatory routines are stored somewhere in the brain, and the premotor cortex is a good candidate (cf. Rizzolatti and Gentilucci, 1988). This repository of gestural scores is called the *mental syllabary* (Levelt, 1992). The generated gestural pattern for an utterance is called the *articulatory* or *gestural score*.

ARTICULATION   Whatever the origin of the articulatory score, it is ultimately executed by the laryngeal and supralaryngeal systems. These are under the control of the larynx and face area of the somatosensory cortex, caudal midbrain structures, and cerebellum. Articulatory execution is quite flexible. The same articulatory target can often be realized in different ways. The system tends to minimize effort, given the prevailing physical contingencies. It is, for instance, possible to speak intelligibly with food or even a pipe in the mouth. Articulation is our most sophisticated motor system. It is normal to produce some 12 speech sounds (consonants, vowels) per second, and this involves control over some 100 different muscles. This masterpiece is achieved by concurrent, overlapping execution of articulatory gestures (Liberman, 1996).

SELF PERCEPTION, MONITORING, AND REPAIR   Speakers are their own listeners. Whether listening to one's own speech or listening to somebody else's speech, the same superior temporal lobe structures are activated (McGuire, Silbersweig, and Frith, 1996, Price, Wise, et al., 1996). This feedback is one way for the speaker to exercise some degree of output control. For instance, we immediately adapt the loudness of our speech to the prevailing noise in our speech environment. We also tend to correct obvious or disturbing output errors or infelicities. This self-monitoring, however, is not based solely on the feedback of overt speech. We can also monitor our internal speech and catch an error before the word is (fully) pronounced (as in: *we can go straight to the* ye-, *to the* orange *node*, where the almost-error here is *yellow*). What is this internal speech? As Wheeldon and Levelt (1995) have experimentally argued, it's likely that what we monitor for in internal speech is the phonological score, i.e., the output of morphophonological encoding.

This bird's eye view of the speaker's functional organization provides us with the further layout of this chapter. We first discuss the many neuroimaging studies in word production. In that discussion, we are guided by a stage theory of word production, as diagrammed in figure 59.1. Following that, we turn to the few studies of grammatical encoding and to some studies of internal speech and self-monitoring.

Producing words: A task analysis

In neuroimaging studies of word production, we encounter a rich variety of tasks—verb generation, noun generation, picture naming, word reading, word repetition, generating words starting with a particular letter, and the like. The choice of experimental tasks and controls demonstrates both inventiveness and ingenuity, but may also carry with it some degree of arbitrariness. Subtraction studies, in particular, are based on a difference logic that requires a componential analysis of the functional organization involved in the experimental and control tasks. It is rare, however, that such a componential analysis is independently performed and tested—say, by way of reaction time studies. Pending such task analyses, the present review can provide only a theoretical handle, presenting a componential analysis of normal word production based on the theoretical framework in figure 59.1. A fuller, comprehensive account of that functional word production theory can be found in Levelt, Roelofs, and Meyer (1999).

The left panel of figure 59.2 represents the components—the "core processes"—involved in word production, as derived from figure 59.1. As far as word production is concerned, the core aspect of conceptual preparation is to map some state of affairs onto a lexical concept. The state of affairs can be a perceptual image (as in picture naming), the image of an activity (as in verb generation), and so forth. In all cases we find perspective taking—a decision on the type of lexical concept that is apparently wanted in the experimental task. (For instance, one must decide whether to name an object by its basic level term, such as *dog* in normal picture naming, or to use a superordinate term, such as *animal* in a semantic categorization task.) The grammatical encoding aspect of word production is lemma access—selecting the appropriate syntactic word. It is at this step that the word's syntactic properties, such as gender, mass/count noun, syntactic argument structure, etc., become available. There are two major aspects to morphophonological encoding, now distinguished in figure 59.2. The first one, morphological encoding, provides access to the word's morphological structure and the phonological codes of each morpheme. For the monomorphemic words used in almost all neuroimaging studies, this stage is just accessing the word's phonological code. An important independent variable here, affecting just this stage, is word/morpheme frequency. The second one, phonological encoding proper, is the incremental construction of the phonological word and in particular the word's syllabification in context. This is probably the word representation figuring in internal speech. It may be (but need not be) the end stage in silent word generation tasks. The next component, phonetic encoding, provides a gestural or articulatory score for the word. It is likely that highly practiced syllabic motor routines are accessed at this stage. In the final stage of word production, the constructed or retrieved gestural score is executed by the articulatory apparatus, resulting in an overt acoustic signal, the spoken word. In all nonsilent word generation tasks

Tasks	(silent) Picture naming	(silent) Verb or Noun generation	(silent) Reading	(silent) Pseudoword reading	(silent) Generation from initial letters	(delayed) Word repetition
Lead-in Processes	visual object recognition	visual or auditory word recognition, visual imagery, retrieving associated actions from LTM, word association	visual word recognition	visual grapheme recognition, conversion of graphemic to phonological code	retrieving and "reading" orthographic word patterns some semantic processing	auditory word perception or audio-phonological parsing, (articulatory loop rehearsal)
Core processes						
conceptual preparation	✓	✓	?		?	
lexical concept						
lexical selection	✓	✓	?		✓	(✓)
lemma						
phonological code retrieval	✓	✓	✓		✓	(✓)
phonological code						
phonological encoding	✓	✓	✓	✓	✓	✓
phonological word						
phonetic encoding	(✓)	(✓)	(✓)	(✓)	(✓)	✓
gestural score						
articulation	(✓)	(✓)	(✓)	(✓)	(✓)	✓
spoken word						

FIGURE 59.2 Core processing stages in the production of words and the involvement of core and lead-in processes in various word production tasks. A check mark indicates involvement of the component process in the task. A check mark in parentheses indicates that the component's involvement depends on details of the task. Phonetic encoding and articulation, for instance, are involved in overt, but not in silent word production tasks.

there is auditory feedback, triggering the speaker's normal word perception system. But there is feedback in silent word generation too, probably from the level of phonological word encoding.

The subsequent columns of figure 59.2 present a tentative analysis of the various word production tasks reviewed in this chapter. In particular, these columns mark the core processing components that are probably involved in these tasks. This aspect of the task analysis is relatively straightforward (though not at all inviolable). Much more problematic is the analysis of what we call

the task's "lead-in." Different tasks enter the componential structure depicted in the left panel at different levels. In picture naming, for instance, the task enters the componential hierarchy from the very top component, conceptual preparation. The lead-in process is visual object recognition, which provides an object percept as input to conceptual preparation. Compare this to pseudoword reading. Here the hierarchy is probably entered at the level of phonological encoding–there is no accessing of a syntactic word or of a word's phonological code, but there is syllabification. The lead-in process is visual orthographic analysis, some kind of bottom-up grapheme-to-phoneme mapping, which provides the ordered pattern of phonemes as input to syllabification. These lead-in processes are the real bottleneck for neuroimaging studies in word production. They are usually easily invented but ill-understood; still, they always contribute essentially to the neuroimaging results. Without serious behavioral research, one can only speculate at the processes involved in most task lead-ins. The top row of the columns in figure 59.2 provides some hunches about the lead-in processes involved in the various neuroimaging studies of word production. Here, we discuss just seven of them.

Picture naming   Here the lead-in process is visual object recognition. It is the best understood lead-in process. Still, many variables are to be controlled, including visual complexity, perspectival orientation of the object, color versus black-and-white, and, of course, object category. All core components of word production are involved in picture naming.

Verb generation   This task also involves all core components of word production, but the lead-in process is ill-understood (cf. Indefrey, 1997). The subject sees or hears a noun, which triggers a visual or auditory word recognition process. If the noun is a concrete one, the subject will probably generate a visual image; and, under the perspective of the task, that image activates one or more associated actions in long-term memory. These, then, guide the further conceptual preparation. When the noun is abstract, long-term memory may be accessed without visual imagery. But there are possible shortcuts, too. A perceived noun may directly activate a verbal concept or even a verb lemma by sheer association, as in *knife–cut*.

Noun generation   The typical task here is to present a semantic category, such as "jobs" or "tools" or "animals," and the subject is asked to generate as many exemplars as possible. It is a so-called "word fluency" task. The lead-in process may involve something as complicated as an imaginary tour, such as mentally touring a zoo, or it may be a much lower-level process, such as word association. And the subject's strategy may differ rather drastically for different semantic categories. But it is quite likely that, at least from lexical selection on, all core processes of word generation are involved.

Generating words from beginning letter(s)   The lead-in process is quite enigmatic. The letter "*a*" is a preferred stimulus. Like most other letters, it does not represent a unique phoneme in English, and the task probably capitalizes on visual word imagery. We can apparently retrieve orthographic word patterns beginning with "*a*." The same holds for so-called "stem completion"–transforming a word-beginning like "*gre-*" to its completed form "*green*." These visually imaged patterns are then "read," occasionally involving some semantic activation. From there on, we are back to the core process, somewhere beginning at morphological or phonological encoding.

Word repetition   The subject repeats a heard word. The lead-in process involves auditory word recognition, at least to some extent. We can repeat words we don't understand (and nonwords for that matter); hence it suffices to have the phonological parse of the word. From there, the core process can be triggered at the level of phonological encoding (we must syllabify the word). Still, the lead-in process may be a lot richer, involving activation of the full lexical concept. In delayed word repetition tasks, an "articulatory loop" is involved–the subject rehearses the word during the delay.

Word reading   The lead-in process is visual word recognition, which is complicated enough by itself. The core process may start at the low level of phonological encoding, from the set of activated phonemes (the phonological route); or it may start all the way up from the activated lexical concept (the semantic route). The strategy may differ from subject to subject, even from word to word.

Pseudoword reading   Here, only the phonological route is available after the visual lead-in process. Although nonwords can have morphology (as in "*Jabberwocky*"), that was never the case in the tasks reviewed here. Hence, phonological encoding is the first core process in a pseudoword reading task.

In the following we will, to the best of our abilities, acknowledge the components involved in both the experimental word production tasks and their controls. But given the present state of the art, this is not always possible.

Cerebral localizations for word production–A meta-analysis

Research on brain regions involved in word production has been carried out with a wide variety of techniques. Among these are the study of brain lesions, direct cortical electrical stimulation, cortical stimulation by means of implanted subdural electrode grids, recording and source localization of event-related electrical and magnetic cortical activity (ERP, MEG, subdural electrode grids, single-cell recordings), and measurement of regional cerebral metabolic and blood flow changes (PET, fMRI). Clearly, these techniques have contributed to our present knowledge on the neural substrates of single word production in different ways. Take cortical stimulation for example. Usually applied in the context of impending surgical interventions, cortical stimulation has provided evidence on loci which, when temporarily inactivated, impair word production–i.e., loci that are in some way necessary for the production process. But this technique is applied only to locations where language-related sites are suspected and then only to the limited part of the cortex that is exposed. In contrast, PET and fMRI can, in principle, reveal all areas that are more strongly activated during word production–including areas that may not be essential to the process and/or those whose impairment leads to no detectable difference in performance. ERP and MEG have provided preliminary insights in the temporal course of cortical activations. The sources of event-related electrical or magnetic activations can be localized. There are, however, limitations inherent in the mathematical procedures involved, so that, at present, the spatial information provided by these methods is considered less reliable. Due to the nature of the signal, subcortical structures are largely invisible to electrophysiological methods.

The purpose of this section is to combine the evidence provided by all these techniques and to give an overview of the localization (and to some extent the temporal order) of cerebral activations during word production. Furthermore, we will try to identify the neural substrates of the different processing components laid out in the previous section. To this end, we analyze the data reported in a large number of studies according to the following heuristic principle: If, for a given processing component, there are subserving brain regions, then these regions should be found active in all experimental tasks sharing the processing component, whatever other processing components these tasks may comprise. In addition, the region(s) should not be active in experimental tasks that do not share the component.

This approach allows for the isolation of processing components between studies even if isolation within single studies is not possible due to the difficulty in controlling for lead-in processes. Nevertheless, four conditions must be met. First, the processing components must be independently defined, so that their absence or presence can be evaluated for every experiment by applying the same criteria (which may differ from the author's criteria). Second, the task and control conditions must be heterogeneous enough across different experiments to ensure that a specific processing component is the only shared component. Third, the task and control conditions must be heterogeneous enough across different experiments to ensure that for every processing component there is a different set of tasks that share the component. Fourth, the data base must be large, comprising enough experiments for a reliable identification of activations typically found for the different tasks. For word production these requirements seem to be sufficiently met, considering that word production tasks have been among the most frequently applied language tasks in neurocognitive research.

PROCEDURE We analyzed the cerebral localization data from 58 word production experiments (table 59.1). Our focus was on the core process of word production; thus, we excluded experiments reporting enhanced cerebral activations during word production tasks relative to control tasks that comprised most or all of the word production process–reading aloud, for example (Petersen et al., 1989; Raichle et al., 1994; Buckner, Raichle, and Petersen, 1995; Snyder et al., 1995; Fiez et al., 1996; Abdullaev and Posner, 1997), or object naming (Martin et al., 1995). Nor did our approach allow for inclusion of experiments or task comparisons focusing on the relative strengths of components of the word production process–comparisons of reading regularly spelled versus irregularly spelled words, for example (Herbster et al., 1997). Activations of these two tasks relative to baseline, however, were included. It was assumed throughout that the reported activation foci reflected true increases during the tasks rather than decreases during the baseline conditions.

Combining data from different techniques made it necessary to find a common term for cerebral localizations observed in relation to certain tasks. Since the majority of experiments employed PET or fMRI, we will use the terms "activations" or "activated areas," extending that usage to EEG and MEG sources and to sites where cortical stimulation or lesions interfere with certain functions. We are aware that, for the latter case, one can at best infer that such locations are "active" in normal functioning.

The double reference system for anatomical localizations adopted here was used in order to capture data on the localization of cerebral activations stemming from methods with different resolution. On a gross level, comparable to a high degree of filtering, the reported loci were coded in a descriptive reference system dividing the cerebral lobes into two or three rostrocaudal or mediolateral segments of roughly equal size. Activations of cingulate, insula, and cerebellum were only differentiated in left and right. The segment labels were defined in terms of Talairach coordinates as given in table 59.2 (top).

Task	Authors, methods, control conditions			
Picture naming aloud	Ojemann (1983) Cortical/thalamic stimulation	Ojemann et al. (1989) Cortical stimulation	Schäffler et al. (1993) Cortical stimulation	Crone et al. (1994) Subdural grid
	Haglund et al. (1994) Cortical stimulation	Salmelin et al. (1994) MEG	Abdullaev & Melnichuk (1995) Single-cell recordings, blank screen	
	Bookheimer et al. (1995) PET, nonsense drawings	Damasio et al. (1996) Lesion data	Damasio et al. (1996) PET, "faces," up/down	Levelt et al. (1998) MEG
Picture naming silent	Bookheimer et al. (1995) PET, nonsense drawings	Martin et al. (1996) PET, nonsense objects	Price, Moore, et al. (1996) PET, objects, "yes"	
Word generation silent, verbs	Wise et al. (1991) PET, rest	Crivello et al. (1995) PET, rest	Poline et al. (1996) PET, rest	Warburton et al. (1996) Exp. 1B, 2B+C, 3A (4) PET, rest
Word generation silent, nouns	Warburton et al. (1996) PET, rest	Paulesu et al. (1997) fMRI, rest		
Generation from initial letter(s)	Aloud: Buckner, Raichle, & Petersen (1995) PET, silent fixation		Silent: Paulesu et al. (1997) fMRI, rest	
Word reading aloud	Ojemann (1983) Cortical stimulation	Howard et al. (1992) PET, false fonts, "crime"	Sakurai et al. (1992) PET, fixation	Sakurai et al. (1993) PET, fixation
	Price et al. (1994) PET, false fonts, "ab-/present"	Bookheimer et al. (1995) PET, nonsense drawings	Price, Moore, & Frackowiak (1996) PET, rest	
	Gordon et al. (1997) Cortical stimulation	Herbster et al. (1997) Regular and irregular words (2) PET, letter strings, "hiya"		Rumsey et al. (1997) PET, fixation
Word reading silent	Petersen et al. (1989) PET, fixation	Petersen et al. (1990) PET, fixation	Bookheimer et al. (1995) PET, nonsense drawings	Menard et al. (1996) PET, xxXxx
	Price, Moore, & Frackowiak (1996) PET, rest	Beauregard et al. (1997) Concrete, abstract, emotional words (3) PET, word reading instructions + fixation		Hagoort et al. (1999) PET, fixation
Pseudoword reading aloud	Sakurai et al. (1993) PET, fixation	Indefrey et al. (1996) PET, false font strings	Herbster et al. (1997) PET, letter strings, "hiya"	Rumsey et al. (1997) PET, fixation
Pseudoword reading silent	Petersen et al. (1990) PET, fixation	Fujimaki et al. (1996) MEG	Hagoort et al. (1999) PET, fixation	
Word repetition aloud	Petersen et al. (1989) PET, silent listening	Howard et al. (1992) PET, reversed words, "crime"		Crone et al. (1994) Subdural grid
	Price et al. (1996b) PET, rest	Gordon et al. (1997) Cortical stimulation		
Pseudoword repetition silent	Warburton et al. (1996) PET, rest			

More detailed anatomical references were additionally coded on a finer level in terms of gyri and subcortical structures following Talairach and Tournoux (1988). At this level, cingulate, insular, and cerebellar activations were further differentiated descriptively (table 59.2, bottom). In this way, it was possible to capture the fact that a PET activation focus reported as, for example, left inferior temporal gyrus, BA 37, would be consistent with electrophysiological data reporting a posterior temporal source localization or with patient data reporting a left posterior temporal lesion. Note that the sum of activations on the detailed level does not equal the number of activations on the gross level. A location, for example, that was reported as posterior temporal would be marked only on the gross level. Conversely, two posterior temporal locations in the superior and middle temporal gyrus were marked as such on the detailed level but only once on the gross level.

The studies included in this meta-analysis were not given any weights reflecting reliability differences due to design or size. This means that a certain degree of overlap of activations between studies was considered meaningful, but should not be interpreted as statistically significant. Nonetheless, the notion of "meaningfulness" was not totally arbitrary, but based on the following quasi-statistical estimate: At the gross level of description, there were on average 6.5 activation sites reported per experiment. Given that on this level of description

there were 28 regions of interest, any particular region had a chance of less than one-fourth to be reported as activated if reports were randomly distributed over regions. At the finer level of description, the average number of reported activation sites per experiment was 8.8 and there were 104 regions of interest; thus each had a chance of less than one-tenth to be reported as activated. Assuming these probabilities, the chance level for a region to be reported as activated in a number of studies was given by a binomial distribution. We rejected the possibility that the agreement of reports about a certain region was coincidental if the chance level was less than 10%. At the finer level of description, this corresponded to minimally two reported activations for regions covered by less than six experiments, minimally three reported activations for regions covered by six to eleven experiments, and so forth (4 out of 12–18; 5 out of 19–25; 6 out of 26–32). Note that for regions covered by many experiments a relatively smaller number of positive reports was required to be above chance (comparable to the fact that getting a 6 five times with ten dice throws is less likely than getting one 6 with two dice throws). But this criterion does not mean that atypical findings of activations in any single study are necessarily coincidental. In most cases, the number of experiments *not* reporting activations was not sufficient to consider a region as inactive at the chosen error probability level. Rare observations do not,

TABLE 59.2
Definition of descriptive anatomical labels

Subdivisions of cortical lobes at grosser level of description			
Frontal		**Temporal**	
Anterior	$y > 34$	Anterior	$y > -7$
Posterior	$34 \geq y \geq 0$	Mid	$-7 \geq y \geq -38$
Motor (approx.)	$y < 0$	Posterior	$y < -38$
Parietal		**Occipital**	
Sensory (approx.)	$y > -23$	Medial	$x \leq |25|$
Anterior	$-23 \geq y \geq -48$	Lateral	$x > |25|$
Posterior	$y < -48$		

Subdivisions of cingulum, insula, and cerebellum at finer level of description			
Cingulum		**Insula**	
Anterior	$y > 12$	Anterior	$y > 0$
Mid	$12 \geq y \geq -24$	Posterior	$y \leq 0$
Posterior	$y < -24$		
Cerebellum			
Medial	$x \leq |20|$		
Lateral	$x > |20|$		

therefore, exclude the possibility that a region is active. They may, for example, reflect smaller activations that are only detectable with refined techniques or better scanning devices.

A second, related point is that the nature of the data does not allow for an interpretation in terms of relative strengths of activations of certain areas. It is known that parameters such as item duration and frequency strongly influence the resulting pattern of activations (Price et al., 1994; Price, Moore, and Frackowiak, 1996). It is thus possible that areas are more frequently found active in some tasks, because their "typical" item durations and frequencies are higher or lower than in other tasks. It seems wise not to overinterpret the data, given that there is a considerable variability of these parameters across the studies of our data base; also, the interactions of these parameters with other experimental factors are largely unknown.

LEAD-IN PROCESSES   According to our task analysis, nonshared activations in picture naming and word generation (table 59.3, first two columns) cannot be related to the core process of word production. The two tasks differ not only with respect to their lead-in processes but also with respect to the processes of phonetic encoding and articulation, given that word generation was performed silently in all experiments of the data set, whereas the majority of picture naming experiments involved overt articulation with silent control tasks (see table 59.1). Hence, to study the lead-in processes of picture naming, we must take into account activations that were specific for picture naming when compared to word generation and at the same time were not specific for overt (in contrast to silent) naming in general (table 59.3, last two columns). Although such lead-in activations were fairly numerous, we cover only the two most conspicuous sets here.

Six regions were reported as activated during word generation but rarely activated during picture naming: the left anterior superior frontal gyrus, the right anterior insula, the right mid superior and middle temporal gyri, the left caudate nucleus, and the right thalamus. While activations of the left anterior frontal and middle temporal gyri, right anterior insula, and left caudate seem to be specifically related to lead-in processes of word generation (see also Fiez, Raichle, and Petersen, 1996), the case is different for the right mid superior temporal gyrus and the right thalamus, which are also found in word reading.

Ten regions were activated during picture naming but not or only rarely during word generation: the left anterior insula, the left posterior inferior temporal and fusiform gyri, the medial occipital lobe bilaterally, the right caudate nucleus, the left midbrain, and the medial and right lateral cerebellum (see, however, Fiez and Raichle, 1997, for evidence on right cerebellar activations in word generation when directly compared with word reading or picture naming). Five of these—the left anterior insula, the left posterior fusiform gyrus, the left and right medial occipital lobe, and the right medial cerebellum—were also found active in word reading, suggesting an involvement in visual processing, the principal lead-in component of picture naming and reading. Taking into account that activations of the posterior fusiform gyrus or the insula were not reported for pseudoword reading, it seems that these two areas may play a role at later visual processing stages, such as the retrieval of visual word forms or object patterns (cf. Sergent, Ohta, and MacDonald, 1992). In contrast, medial occipital activations observed during word and pseudoword reading are demonstrably due to the processing of nonlinguistic visual features of word-like stimuli, such as string length (Beauregard et al., 1997; Indefrey et al., 1997).

THE CORE PROCESS OF WORD PRODUCTION   According to our task analysis, picture naming and word generation are the two tasks that include all components of word production. The set of regions reported as activated for both tasks (table 59.3, first two columns) can be considered as being related to the core process of word production up to and including phonological encoding. This word production network is strictly left-lateralized, and consists of the posterior inferior frontal gyrus (Broca's area), the mid superior and middle temporal gyri, the posterior superior and middle temporal gyri (Wernicke's area), and the left thalamus.

By taking into account further tasks that enter the word production process at different stages, we now attempt to identify the subprocesses to which these regions are particularly sensitive.

Conceptual preparation and lexical selection   The activation of a lexical concept and the subsequent selection of the corresponding lemma are processes that are shared by picture naming and word generation but not necessarily by word reading. The synopsis of reported results yielded one area within the word production network—the mid segment of the left middle temporal gyrus—that has been found activated during picture naming and word generation, but less so during word reading. This area is the best candidate for a neural correlate of conceptual and/or lexical selection processes in word production. The mid part of the left middle temporal gyrus has been found as part of a "common semantic system" in a study (Vandenberghe et al., 1996) involving word and object stimuli. This finding is compatible with a role of this region in conceptual

TABLE 59.3
Synopsis of cerebral localizations for word production tasks*

Task		Picture naming	Word generation	Word reading	Pseudo-word reading	Word generation from initial letter(s)	Word repetition	Pseudo-word repetition	All tasks aloud/ silent control	All tasks silent or aloud control
No. of studies		14	9	20	7	2	5	1	25	33
Temporal										
R	Anterior	1/9						1/1		2/32
	GTs	1/9						1/1		2/32
	GTm									
	GTi									
	Mid	2/9	**7/9**	5/18	**4/7**		2/3	1/1	**10/16**	11/32
	GTs	1/9	**5/9**	**5/18**	3/7		**2/3**	1/1	**10/16**	**7/32**
	GTm		6/9	2/18			1/3		3/16	6/32
	GTi									
	GF			1/18	1/7				1/16	1/32
	Gh	1/9								1/32
	Posterior	2/9		5/18	1/7		1/3		4/16	5/32
	GTs			2/18	1/7		1/3		2/16	2/32
	GTm			1/18	1/7					2/32
	GTi			2/18					2/16	
	GF	2/9		2/18					1/16	3/32
	GL			1/18						1/32
L	Anterior	**5/12**	1/9	2/18					4/18	5/33
	GTs	**5/12**	1/9	1/18					**4/18**	4/32
	GTm	1/12							1/18	
	GTi	1/12		1/18					1/18	1/32
	Mid	9/13	**6/9**	**13/20**	**5/7**		3/5	1/1	**17/23**	20/33
	GTs	6/13	3/9	10/20	5/7		3/5	1/1	17/23	11/33
	GTm	5/13	5/9	4/20	2/7		2/5		6/23	12/33
	GTi	1/12		1/20						2/33
	GF	2/11		4/20					2/21	5/33
	Gh	1/10		1/20						2/33
	Posterior	**11/12**	6/9	17/20	2/7		3/5	1/1	17/22	23/33
	GTs	6/12	4/9	6/20			3/5		12/22	7/33
	GTm	4/12	4/9	5/20					**5/22**	8/33
	GTi	3/11	1/9	3/18	1/7			1/1	3/18	6/33
	GF	3/10	1/9	**7/18**					3/18	**8/33**
	GL			2/18	1/7					3/33

(*continued*)

TABLE 59.3 *Continued*

Task	Picture naming	Word generation	Word reading	Pseudo-word reading	Word generation from initial letter(s)	Word repetition	Pseudo-word repetition	All tasks aloud/ silent control	All tasks silent or aloud control
No. of studies	14	9	20	7	2	5	1	25	33
Frontal									
R Anterior		1/9	1/18						2/32
GFs									
GFm		1/9							1/32
GFi			1/18						1/32
GFd, GO									
Posterior	3/6	3/9	1/18	1/7				3/14	5/32
GFs									
GFm		2/9							2/32
GFi	1/5	2/9	1/18	1/7				2/14	3/32
GR, Gs									
Motor	2/6	**5/9**	5/18	3/7		2/3		**10/14**	7/32
ventral GPrC	1/6		**4/18**	2/7		**2/3**		**8/14**	1/32
dorsal GPrC	1/6		3/18	1/7				3/14	2/32
SMA		**5/9**	**4/18**			**2/3**		**5/14**	6/32
L Anterior		3/9	3/18						6/32
GFs		3/9	1/18						4/32
GFm		2/9	1/18						3/32
GFi		1/9							1/32
GFd, GO		1/9	1/18						2/32
Posterior	**8/10**	**9/9**	**11/20**	3/7	2/2	2/5	1/1	**14/22**	**22/32**
GFs	1/8	2/9				1/5		2/20	2/32
GFm	2/8	**4/9**	4/20					1/20	**9/32**
GFi	**5/9**	**9/9**	**9/20**	**3/7**	**2/2**	1/5	1/1	**11/21**	**18/32**
GR, Gs									
Motor	**5/10**	7/9	7/20	3/7		2/5	1/1	**13/22**	**12/32**
ventral GPrC	4/10	1/9	**6/20**	3/7		**2/5**	1/1	**11/22**	6/32
dorsal GPrC	2/9	1/9	3/18			1/4		**5/18**	2/32
SMA	2/6	**7/9**	4/18	1/7		1/4		8/15	**8/32**
Insula									
R		5/9	3/18	1/7		1/3	1/1	3/13	8/32
anterior		5/9	2/18	1/7		1/3	1/1	2/13	**8/32**
posterior			1/18			1/3		2/13	
L	3/6	1/9	6/18		1/1	2/3	1/1	**6/13**	8/32
anterior	**3/6**	1/9	**6/18**		1/1	**2/3**	1/1	**6/13**	**8/32**
posterior									

TABLE 59.3 *Continued*

Task	Picture naming	Word generation	Word reading	Pseudo-word reading	Word generation from initial letter(s)	Word repetition	Pseudo-word repetition	All tasks aloud/ silent control	All tasks silent or aloud control
No. of studies	14	9	20	7	2	5	1	25	33
Parietal									
R Sensory	1/7		3/18	1/7		1/3		5/14	1/32
ventral GPoC dorsal GPoC	1/7		3/15	1/7		1/3		**5/11**	1/32
Anterior			2/18					1/14	1/32
LPi LPs PCu			2/15					1/11	1/32
Posterior	3/7		3/18	1/7				4/14	3/32
LPi									
LPs	1/7			1/7					2/32
Gsm	1/7							1/11	
Ga	1/7							1/11	
PCu			1/15						1/32
L Sensory	3/9		5/20	1/7		1/4		**8/19**	2/32
ventral GPoC dorsal GPoC	**3/9**		**5/17**	1/7		1/4		**8/16**	2/32
Anterior	2/9		3/20					3/19	2/32
LPi LPs PCu	2/9		3/17					3/16	2/32
Posterior	3/8	2/9	4/20					5/18	4/32
LPi									
LPs									
Gsm	1/7	1/9	1/17					2/15	1/32
Ga	1/6	1/9	1/17					2/14	1/32
PCu									
Cingulum									
R		1/9	2/18	2/7				1/13	4/32
anterior		1/9	2/18					1/13	2/32
mid				2/7					2/32
posterior				1/7					1/32
L	2/6	3/9	5/18	**4/7**				5/13	9/32
anterior	2/6	2/9	**4/18**					3/13	5/32
mid			2/18	**4/7**				2/13	4/32
posterior		1/9	1/18	1/7					3/32

(*continued*)

TABLE 59.3 *Continued*

Task	Picture naming	Word generation	Word reading	Pseudo-word reading	Word generation from initial letter(s)	Word repetition	Pseudo-word repetition	All tasks aloud/silent control	All tasks silent or aloud control
No. of studies	14	9	20	7	2	5	1	25	33
Occipital									
R Medial	**4/6**		7/18	3/7		1/3		7/13	8/32
Sca						1/3			1/30
Cu				1/7		1/3		1/8	1/30
GL			5/15	1/7				1/8	5/30
GF			2/15					1/8	1/30
Lateral	1/6		3/18	1/7				4/13	1/32
GOs,m,i			1/15						1/30
L Medial	**5/6**	1/9	**8/18**	4/7				8/13	11/32
Sca	2/3	1/9	1/15					1/10	3/30
Cu				1/7				1/10	
GL	1/3		**5/15**	2/7				2/10	**6/30**
GF	1/3		2/15	1/7				3/10	1/30
Lateral	2/6	1/9	6/18	1/7				3/13	7/32
GOs,m,i	1/3		4/15						5/30
Subcortical structures									
R Caudate	**2/5**	1/9						1/12	2/31
NL	1/4	1/9	2/18					2/11	2/31
Thalamus	1/5	**4/9**	5/18	1/7		1/3		**6/12**	**6/31**
Hypothalamus									
Midbrain	1/4	1/9	1/18					2/11	1/31
Hippocampus									
L Caudate	1/4	3/9	1/18					1/12	4/31
NL	1/4	2/9	**4/18**					1/11	**6/31**
Thalamus	**4/5**	**6/9**	5/18	2/7	1/1	1/3		**9/12**	**10/31**
Hypothalamus									
Midbrain	2/4	1/9	2/18					2/11	3/31
Hippocampus	1/4		2/18					1/11	2/31
Cerebellum									
R	**3/4**	1/9	7/18	3/7		1/3		**8/11**	7/31
medial	**2/4**	1/8	**4/16**	3/6		1/3		**7/9**	4/30
lateral	**3/4**	1/8	3/16	2/6				**3/9**	**6/30**
L	2/4	2/9	3/18	**4/7**		1/3		**7/11**	5/31
medial	2/4		2/16	2/6		1/3		**5/9**	2/30
lateral	1/4	1/8	2/16	**3/6**				**5/9**	2/30

*The number of activations reported for a region is given in proportion to the number of studies covering it. Relative cell frequencies exceeding the error probability threshold of $p < .1$ are printed in bold. Data were collapsed with respect to overt versus silent responses in the last two columns. Aloud tasks with aloud control conditions are grouped with silent tasks.

Key: Except for SMA (= supplementary motor area), the abbreviations of gyri and subcortical structures follow Talairach and Tournoux (1988): GFs, GFm, GFi = superior, middle, and inferior frontal gyrus; GFd = medial frontal gyrus; GO = orbital gyri; GR = gyrus rectus; Gs = gyrus subcallosus; GPrC = precentral gyrus; GTs, GTm, GTi = superior, middle, and inferior temporal gyrus; GF = fusiform gyrus; Gh = parahippocampal gyrus; GL = lingual gyrus; GpoC = postcentral gyrus; LPs, LPi = superior and inferior parietal lobule; PCu = precuneus; Gsm = supramarginal gyrus; Ga = angular gyrus; Sca = calcarine sulcus; Cu = cuneus; GOs, GOm, GOi = superior, middle, and inferior occipital gyri; NL = lenticular nucleus.

processing. It should, however, be kept in mind that the activation of a lexical concept for word production is only one very specific conceptual process among many other conceptual-semantic processes. It is, more precisely, to be distinguished from the semantically guided search processes in word generation (possibly subserved by anterior frontal regions), as well as from prelinguistic conceptual processes involved in object recognition and categorization [possibly subserved by the ventral temporal lobe and a heterogeneous set of category-specific regions (cf. Martin et al., 1995, 1996; Damasio et al., 1996; Beauregard et al., 1997)]. As far as the core process of word production is concerned, these conceptual processes are to be considered as lead-in processes.

Phonological code retrieval Lexical word form retrieval takes place in picture naming, word generation, and word reading, but not in pseudoword reading. This pattern is found in the reports on activations of the left posterior superior and middle temporal gyri, i.e., Wernicke's area, and the left thalamus. The posterior superior temporal lobe has also been found active during word comprehension (Price, Wise, et al., 1996). It is thus conceivable that a common store of lexical word form representations is accessed in word production and comprehension.

Phonological encoding All tasks, including word repetition and pseudoword reading, involve the production of phonological words. Neural structures subserving this process should consequently be found active throughout. No region fulfills this requirement perfectly, but the left posterior inferior frontal gyrus (Broca's area) and the left mid superior temporal gyrus come very close. Both regions just miss our criterion for a meaningful number of activations in tasks for which there are only few studies in the data set (word repetition, word generation from initial letters). Cabeza and Nyberg (1997) reviewed one repetition and two reading aloud experiments with Broca's area as the only active region in common. According to our task analysis, the only common processing component was indeed phonological encoding.

Broca's area has been observed to be active not only during explicit but also during implicit processing of pseudowords (performing a feature detection task; Frith et al., 1995; Price, Wise, and Frackowiak, 1996). The left mid superior temporal gyrus, however, was not found active in these studies, which may indicate a functional difference between the two areas within nonlexical phonological processing.

Broca's area is, furthermore, known to be activated in tasks involving phonological processing in language comprehension (Démonet et al., 1992,1996; Zatorre et al., 1992; Fiez and Raichle, 1997). The common denom-inator of these observations and the activation of Broca's area in language production seems to be that this region is a nonlexical phonological processor.

Price and Friston (1997) presented a statistical method–conjunction analysis–to isolate common processing components between different experiments. They used this method to identify a processing component, which they called phonological retrieval, across four word production experiments. The following areas were reported to be related to this processing component: the left posterior basal temporal lobe BA 37 (this area corresponds to the fusiform gyrus in our terminology), the left frontal operculum, the left thalamus, and the midline cerebellum. Given that "phonological retrieval" according to our analysis corresponds to the two processing stages of phonological code retrieval *and* phonological encoding, the observed activations of the left thalamus and the left frontal operculum are in good agreement with the results we obtained here on the basis of a large number of reported experiments. The other two areas according to our analysis subserve a high-level visual lead-in process and the articulatory process. Price and Friston (1997) assume these processes to be shared by the control conditions (viewing objects or strings of false fonts and saying "yes" to every stimulus), leaving only "phonological retrieval" as the common component of all task-control contrasts. It should, however, be noted that this assumption holds only if the contributions of these task components are constant in the active task and the baseline task. The authors themselves point out that this core assumption of the cognitive subtraction paradigm is problematic. Visual and motor-related activations have been observed to be modulated (e.g., by attention or response selection) in active relative to passive tasks (Friston et al., 1996; see also Shulman et al., 1997, for medial cerebellar activations in controlled motor response tasks). It is therefore not excluded that activations related to visual and articulatory processing were equally enhanced in all four active tasks and consequently not filtered out by the conjunction statistics.

Phonetic encoding and articulation Activations related to the production of the abstract articulatory program and its execution should be found in tasks with overt pronunciation and silent control conditions, but not in silent tasks or in tasks where articulation has been controlled for (table 59.3, last two columns). All aloud tasks with silent controls led to activations of primary motor and sensory areas, i.e., the right and left ventral (and, to some extent, dorsal) precentral gyri and the right and left ventral postcentral gyri; but in the group of silent or controlled aloud tasks, such activations were rarely reported. This finding was expected, since these areas are known to be involved in the sensorimotor aspects of articulation. Hence, it provides independent validation for our analysis procedure. It can also be concluded that output control conditions such as saying the same word to every stimulus cancel out these sensorimotor activations effectively.

Further regions typically found in aloud but not in silent tasks were the left anterior superior temporal gyrus, the right SMA, and the left and medial cerebellum. The dissociation in cerebellar activity, with left and medial parts being closely linked to motor output, confirms an observation by Shulman and colleagues (1997); it is also discussed in a comprehensive review of cerebellar activations by Fiez and Raichle (1997).

Our survey shows a complex pattern of reports on left anterior temporal and SMA activations. Both regions are related to overt pronunciation, but seem to be task-sensitive as well. While the temporal area is most frequently reported in overt picture naming, SMA activations (left and right) seem to be rare in this task. Also, SMA activations, though more frequent for aloud tasks, are observed to some extent in silent tasks as well. The latter is not restricted to silent word production, but is also found in tasks involving verbal working memory or nonverbal imagination of movements (for a discussion, see Fiez and Raichle, 1997). It may be concluded that the SMA is in some complex way related to motor planning and imagination of articulation. Given that the instructions in what we have designated silent tasks ranged from mere "viewing" to "thinking" to silent "mouthing" of responses, it is not difficult to understand that the SMA involvement may vary to a great extent between tasks.

SUMMARY The word production network that has been identified on the basis of a substantial number of experiments makes sense. It is largely identical with the set of regions found to be necessary for picture naming in direct cortical stimulation studies. Given that these comprised but a minority of the experiments analyzed and furthermore concentrated on a single task, this is not a trivial result. It means that the neuroimaging studies, despite their heterogeneity of methods and tasks, captured the essential processes of word production. It also means that the cerebral structures subserving these processes can be successfully distinguished from the large number of cerebral activations related to task-specific and experiment-specific processes by an appropriate meta-analysis procedure. On the other hand, neither the network as a whole nor any single region was found activated in all experiments. There are a number of reasons for this. First, weaker activations may have been overlooked or not reported. In general, the statistical thresholds applied in neuroimaging experiments tend to be conservative; moreover, some authors may have focused on robust findings, applying very strict statistical thresholds that rendered minor activations insignificant. There also was a tendency toward fewer activations in older studies, where the technology could not reliably detect as many activations. Second, although we focused on experiments with low-level control conditions, so that the word production process itself would not be obscured, we could not confidently eliminate this obscuring in all cases. Stereotype overt responses (for instance, a "yes" response on all trials) may be retrieved from an articulatory buffer, but may also be normally produced (as is the case with meaningful response alternatives, such as saying "up" or "down" depending on the orientation of the stimulus object in the baseline task)—thereby taking away at least part of the activations due to core word production processes. Considering these points, it would have been misleading to apply the above heuristic principle to every single experiment rather than to sets of experiments using similar tasks, as we have done here.

The time course of word production

TIME WINDOWS FOR COMPONENT PROCESSES Every processing stage of word production takes time. Furthermore, as the above analysis suggests, cortical areas involved in word production are specialists for certain processing components. Activations in these regions should, therefore, have temporal properties that are compatible with the durations of the different processing stages. Table 59.4 summarizes the small number of studies that, to date, have provided timing information related to cortical areas involved in word production. We compare these data with estimates for the processing stages in picture naming given by Levelt and colleagues (1998) based on work by Thorpe, Fize, and Marlot (1996), Levelt and colleagues (1991), Roelofs (1997), Wheeldon and Levelt (1995), and Van Turennout, Hagoort, and Brown (1997, 1998).

It is estimated that visual and conceptual processing are accomplished within the first 150 ms, and lexical selection within 275 ms from picture onset. As identified in the previous section, the corresponding cortical sites were the medial occipital lobe (bilaterally), the left medial posterior temporal lobe for visual processing, and the mid segment of the left middle temporal gyrus for conceptual preparation and lexical selection. The time windows given for occipital activations in table 59.4 are in good agreement with what is assumed for early visual processing. Inferior posterior temporal activations during reading also seem to occur

TABLE 59.4
*Time course of word production in relation to anatomical regions**

Task		Picture naming aloud			Word reading silent	Pseudoword reading silent	Word repetition aloud
Studies		Crone et al. (1994)	Salmelin et al. (1994)	Levelt et al. (1998)	Salmelin et al. (1996)	Fujimaki et al. (1996)	Crone et al. (1994)
		Subdural grid	MEG	MEG	MEG	MEG	Subdural grid
Occipital R	medial		0–200	0–275	100–200		
	lateral			0–275			
L	medial			0–275	100–200		
	lateral			0–275			
Parietal R	posterior		200–400 (Ga)	150–275 (Gsm)		>400 (cingulum)	
	anterior					>400 (cingulum)	
	sensory			400–600			
L	posterior		200–400 (Ga)				
	anterior						
	sensory			400–600			
Temporal R	posterior				100–200 (GTi)	<400	
	mid		300–500 (GTs)				
	anterior						
L	posterior	300–600 (GTs,Tm)	200–400 (GTs)	275–400 (GTs)	100–200 (GTi) 200–400 (GTs,GTm)		
	mid	600–900 (GTs)		275–400 (GTs)	200–400 (GTs,GTm)	<400	300–900 (GTs)
	anterior						
Frontal R	motor		500–600		200–400		
	posterior		200–400				
	anterior						
L	motor		500–600				
	posterior	300–900 (GFi)	200–400				600–900 (GFi)
	anterior						

*Time intervals are given in milliseconds; additional anatomical information is given in parentheses. Ga = angular gyrus; Gsm = supramarginal gyrus; GTs, GTm = superior, middle temporal gyrus; GFi = inferior frontal gyrus.

in this time window (Salmelin et al., 1996). Instead of the expected middle temporal activation site, however, both Salmelin and colleagues (1994) and Levelt and colleagues (1998) identified dipoles in posterior parietal regions, which have not been found active in PET studies.

Lexical phonological code retrieval and phonological encoding are estimated to take place between 275 and

400 ms. The corresponding cortical sites identified above were the left posterior superior and middle temporal gyri for accessing the form code, as well as the left posterior inferior frontal gyrus and the left mid superior temporal gyrus for phonological encoding. The time windows given in table 59.4 clearly support an involvement of Wernicke's area in word form retrieval. Further support comes from a study by Kuriki and colleagues (1996) reporting a time window of 210–410 ms in this region during a phonological matching task on syllabograms. The situation is less clear for phonological encoding, where both supporting and disagreeing time windows have been found for Broca's area and the mid segment of the left superior temporal lobe. The available data on the time course of word production thus support the localization studies with respect to lead-in processes and word form access. They are consistent with respect to phonological encoding, but raise doubt with respect to the cortical sites related to conceptual preparation and lemma access in word production.

INTEGRATING SPATIAL AND TEMPORAL INFORMATION Taking into account both the results of the previous section and the present data on the time course of word production, the following (tentative) picture of the spatial and temporal flow of activation in word production has emerged: In picture naming and probably also in word generation from visual stimuli (see Abdullaev and Posner, 1997) visual and conceptual lead-in processes involving occipital, ventrotemporal, and anterior frontal regions converge within 275 ms from stimulus onset on a lexical concept to be expressed. In addition, the best-fitting lexical item is selected within this period. The middle part of the left middle temporal gyrus may be involved in this conceptually driven lexical selection process. Within the following 125 ms, the activation spreads to Wernicke's area, where the lexically stored phonological code of the word is retrieved, and this information is relayed anteriorly to Broca's area and/or the left mid superior temporal lobe for post-lexical phonological encoding. Within another 200 ms, the resulting phonological word is phonetically encoded (with possible contributions of SMA and cerebellum to this or additional motor planning processes) and sensorimotor areas involved in articulation become active.

Syntactic production

Research on the neural correlates of syntactic processing has mainly concentrated on syntactic comprehension. Regions in and around Broca's area have been most frequently identified as being related to syntactic processing (Stowe et al., 1994; Indefrey et al., 1996;

Just et al., 1996; Stromswold et al., 1996). Caplan, Hildebrandt, and Makris (1996), on the other hand, did not find a significant difference in syntactic comprehension of agrammatic patients between anterior and posterior sylvian lesion sites in a thorough study involving a range of syntactic constructions. Just and colleagues (1996), too, found Wernicke's area (as well as the right-sided homologs of Broca's and Wernicke's area) to be sensitive to syntactic complexity. Two studies (Mazoyer et al., 1993; Dronkers et al., 1999) suggested a role for the left anterior superior temporal lobe in syntactic processing. The pseudoword sentence repetition task of Indefrey and colleagues (1996) comprised a syntactic production component in addition to syntactic parsing, and the resulting activation focus was more rostrodorsally located (border of Broca's area and the adjacent middle frontal gyrus, BA 9) than the foci identified in pure comprehension tasks. Direct electrical stimulation of a similar site was found by Ojemann (1983) to interfere with the grammatically correct repetition of sentences. In the latter study, however, a number of perisylvian stimulation sites yielded the same effect, so that at present there is no real evidence for cortical areas specifically subserving syntactic production.

Self-monitoring

Self-monitoring (see figure 59.1) involves an *external loop*, taking as input the acoustic speech signal of the speaker's own voice, and an *internal loop*, taking as input the phonological score—i.e., the output of phonological encoding. The most economical assumption is that both loops enter the processing pathway that is used for normal speech comprehension (Levelt, 1989).

EXTERNAL LOOP There is evidence that hearing one's own voice while speaking induces the same temporal lobe activations as listening to someone else's voice (McGuire, Silbersweig, and Frith, 1996; Price, Wise, et al., 1996). McGuire, Silbersweig, and Frith, furthermore, were able to induce additional bilateral superior temporal activations by distorting the subjects' feedback of their own voices or presenting the subjects with alien feedback while they spoke. These results show that just as in listening to other people's speech (Démonet et al., 1992; Zatorre et al., 1992) attentional modulation of the activity of the temporal cortices in self-monitoring is possible.

INTERNAL LOOP McGuire and colleagues (1996) also provided some evidence that internal monitoring, too, makes use of a cortical area involved in speech perception—more precisely, the left posterior superior temporal lobe. This area showed stronger activation (together with motor areas) when subjects imagined hearing another person's voice than when they spoke silently to themselves. It is not implausible that the observed blood flow increase was due to an attentional modulation of internal self-monitoring, although other explanations are possible as well.

Conclusion

Speaking involves substantially more than merely producing words. The recent neuroscience literature on speech production reviewed in this chapter is limited owing to its emphasis on word production. But this may well be a transient state of affairs. After all, the wealth of data that enabled the present meta-analysis derives from no more than a decade or so of neuroimaging research. We have an emerging picture now of the cerebral network that underlies the production of words. A crucial ingredient of this meta-analysis is the explicit, detailed functional theory of word production. It provided us with the framework for a componential task analysis and with time frame estimates for the component processes. No doubt, the same approach, applied to other aspects of speaking, will eventually lead to similar progress.

REFERENCES

ABDULLAEV, Y. G., and K. V. MELNICHUK, 1995. Neuronal activity of human caudate nucleus in cognitive tasks. *Technical Report* 95-09. University of Oregon.

ABDULLAEV, Y. G., and M. I. POSNER, 1997. Time course of activating brain areas in generating verbal associations. *Psychol. Sci.* 8:56–59.

BADECKER, W., M. MIOZZO, and R. ZANUTTINI, 1995. The two-stage model of lexical retrieval: Evidence from a case of anomia with selective preservation of grammatical gender. *Cognition* 57:193–216.

BEAUREGARD, M., H. CHERTKOW, D. BUB, S. MURTHA, R. DIXON, and A. EVANS, 1997. The neural substrate for concrete, abstract, and emotional word lexica: A positron emission tomography study. *J. Cogn. Neurosci.* 9:441–461.

BOOKHEIMER, S. Y., T. A. ZEFFIRO, T. BLAXTON, W. GAILLARD, and W. THEODORE, 1995. Regional cerebral blood flow during object naming and word reading. *Hum. Brain Map.* 3:93–106.

BUCKNER, R. L., M. E. RAICHLE, and S. E. PETERSEN, 1995. Dissociation of human prefrontal cortical areas across different speech production tasks and gender groups. *J. Neurophysiol.* 74:2163–2173.

BUTTERWORTH, B., 1980. Evidence from pauses in speech. In *Language Production, Vol. 1. Speech and Talk*, B. Butterworth, ed. London: Academic Press, pp. 155–176.

CABEZA, R., and L. NYBERG, 1997. Imaging cognition: An empirical review of PET studies with normal subjects. *J. Cogn. Neurosci.* 9:1–26.

CAPLAN, D., N. HILDEBRANDT, and N. MAKRIS, 1996. Location of lesions in stroke patients with deficits in syntactic processing in sentence comprehension. *Brain* 119: 933–949.

CLARK, E. V., 1997. Conceptual perspective and lexical choice in acquisition. *Cognition* 64:1–37.

CLARK, H., 1996. *Using Language.* Cambridge: Cambridge University Press.

CRIVELLO, F., N. TZOURIO, J. B. POLINE, R. P. WOODS, J. C. MAZZIOTTA, and B. MAZOYER, 1995. Intersubject variability in functional neuroanatomy of silent verb generation: Assessment by a new activation detection algorithm based on amplitude and size information. *Neuroimage* 2:253–263.

CRONE, N. E., J. HART, JR., D. BOATMAN, R. P. LESSER, and B. GORDON, 1994. Regional cortical activation during language and related tasks identified by direct cortical electrical recording. Paper presented at the Academy of Aphasia.

DAMASIO, H., T. J. GRABOWSKI, D. TRANEL, R. D. HICHWA, and A. R. DAMASIO, 1996. A neural basis for lexical retrieval. *Nature* 380:499–505.

DÉMONET, J.-F., F. CHALET, S. RAMSET, D. CARDEBAT, J.-L. NESPOULOUS, R. WISE, A. RASCOL, and R. FRACKOWIAK, 1992. The anatomy of phonological and semantic processing in normal subjects. *Brain* 115:1753–1768.

DÉMONET, J.-F., J. A. FIEZ, E. PAULESU, S. E. PETERSEN, and R. J. ZATORRE, 1996. PET studies of phonological processing: A critical reply to Poeppel. *Brain Lang.* 55:352–379.

DRONKERS, N. F., D. P. WILKINS, R. D. VAN VALIN, JR., B. B. REDFERN, and J. J. JAEGER, 1999. Cortical areas underlying the comprehension of grammar. Submitted.

FIEZ, J. A., and M. E. RAICHLE, 1997. Linguistic processing and the cerebellum: Evidence from clinical and positron emission tomography studies. *Neurobiology* 41:233–254.

FIEZ, J. A., M. E. RAICHLE, D. A. BALOTA, P. TALLAL, and S. E. PETERSEN, 1996. PET activation of posterior temporal regions during auditory word presentation and verb generation. *Cereb. Cortex* 6:1–10.

FIEZ, J. A., M. E. RAICHLE, and S. E. PETERSEN, 1996. Use of positron emission tomography to identify two pathways used for verbal response selection. In *Developmental Dyslexia: Neural, Cognitive, and Genetic Mechanisms*, C. Chase, G. Rosen, and G. Sherman, eds. Timonium, Md.: York Press, pp. 227–258.

FRISTON, K. J., C. J. PRICE, P. FLETCHER, C. MOORE, R. S. J. FRACKOWIAK, and R. J. DOLAN, 1996. The trouble with cognitive subtraction. *NeuroImage* 4:97–104

FRITH, C. D., K. J. FRISTON, P. F. LIDDLE, and R. S. J. FRACKOWIAK, 1991. A PET study of word finding. *Neuropsychologia* 29:1137–1148.

FUJIMAKI, N., Y. HIRATA, S. KURIKI, and H. NAKAJIMA, 1996. Event-related magnetic fields during processing of readable and unreadable character strings. In *Visualization of Information Processing in the Human Brain: Recent Advances in MEG and Functional MRI* (EEG Suppl. 47), I. Hashimoto, Y. C. Okada, and S. Ogawa, eds. Amsterdam: Elsevier Science B. V., pp. 219–229.

GORDON, B., D. BOATMAN, N. E. CRONE, and P. LESSER, 1997. Multi-perspective approaches to the cortical representation of speech perception and production: Electrical cortical stimulation and electrical cortical recording. In *Speech Production: Motor Control, Brain Research and Fluency Disorders*, W. Hulstijn, H. E. M. Peters, and P. H. H. M. Van Lieshout, eds. Amsterdam: Elsevier Science B. V., pp. 259–268.

HAGLUND, M. M., M. S. BERGER, M. SHAMSELDIN, E. LETTICH, and G. A. OJEMANN, 1994. Cortical localization of temporal lobe language sites in patients with gliomas. *Neurosurgery* 34:567–576.

HAGOORT, P, P. INDEFREY, C. BROWN, H. HERZOG, H. STEINMETZ, and R. J. SEITZ, 1999. The neural circuitry involved in the reading of German words and pseudowords: A PET study. In preparation.

HERBSTER, A. N., M. A. MINTUN, R. D. NEBES, and J. T. BECKER, 1997. Regional cerebral blood flow during word and nonword reading. *Hum. Brain Map.* 5:84–92.

HOWARD, D., K. PATTERSON, R. WISE, W. D. BROWN, K. FRISTON, C. WEILLER, and R. FRACKOWIAK, 1992. The cortical localization of the lexicons: Positron emission tomography evidence. *Brain* 115:1769–1782.

INDEFREY, P., 1997. PET research in language production. In *Speech Production: Motor Control, Brain Research and Fluency Disorders*, W. Hulstijn, H. E. M. Peters, and P. H. H. M. Van Lieshout, eds. Amsterdam: Elsevier Science B. V., pp. 269–278.

INDEFREY P., P. HAGOORT, C. BROWN, H. HERZOG, and R. SEITZ, 1996. Cortical activation induced by syntactic processing: A [15O]-butanol PET study. *NeuroImage* 3:S442

INDEFREY, P., A. KLEINSCHMIDT, K.-D. MERBOLDT, G. KRÜGER, C. BROWN, P. HAGOORT, and J. FRAHM, 1997. Equivalent responses to lexical and nonlexical visual stimuli in occipital cortex: A functional magnetic resonance imaging study. *NeuroImage* 5:78–81.

JESCHENIAK, J. D., and W. J. M. LEVELT, 1994. Word frequency effects in speech production: Retrieval of syntactic information and of phonological form. *J. Exp. Psychol.: Learn. Mem. Cogn.* 20:824–843.

JUST, M. A., P. A. CARPENTER, T. A. KELLER, W. F. EDDY, and K. R. THULBORN, 1996. Brain activation modulated by sentence comprehension. *Science* 274:114–116.

KURIKI, S., Y. HIRATA, N. FUJIMAKI, and T. KOBAYASHI, 1996. Magnetoencephalographic study on the cerebral neural activities related to the processing of visually presented characters. *Cogn. Brain Res.* 4:185–199.

LEVELT, W. J. M., 1981. The speaker's linearization problem. *Phil. Trans. R. Soc. B* 295:305–315.

LEVELT, W. J. M., 1989. *Speaking: From Intention to Articulation.* Cambridge, Mass.: MIT Press.

LEVELT, W. J. M., 1992. Accessing words in speech production: Stages, processes and representations. *Cognition* 42:1–22.

LEVELT, W. J. M., 1996. Perspective taking and ellipsis in spatial descriptions. In *Language and Space*, P. Bloom, M. A. Peterson, L. Nadel, and M. F. Garrett, eds. Cambridge, Mass.: MIT Press, pp. 77–107.

LEVELT, W. J. M., 1999. Language production: A blueprint of the speaker. In *Neurocognition of Language,* C. Brown and P. Hagoort, eds. Oxford: Oxford University Press.

LEVELT, W. J. M., P. PRAAMSTRA, A. S. MEYER, P. HELENIUS, and R. SALMELIN, 1998. An MEG study of picture naming. *J. Cogn. Neurosci.* 10:553–567.

LEVELT, W. J. M., A. ROELOFS, and A. S. MEYER, 1999. A theory of lexical access in speech production. *Behav. Brain Sci.* 22:1–38.

LEVELT, W. J. M., H. SCHRIEFERS, D. VORBERG, A. S. MEYER, TH. PECHMANN, and J. HAVINGA, 1991. The time course of lexical access in speech production: A study of picture naming. *Psychol. Rev.* 98:122–142.

LIBERMAN, A., 1996. *Speech: A Special Code.* Cambridge, Mass.: MIT Press.

MARTIN, A., J. V. HAXBY, F. M. LALONDE, C. L. WIGGS, and L. G. UNGERLEIDER, 1995. Discrete cortical regions associated with knowledge of color and knowledge of action. *Science* 270:102–105.

MARTIN, A., C. L. WIGGS, L. G. UNGERLEIDER, and J. V. HAXBY, 1996. Neural correlates of category-specific knowledge. *Nature* 379:649–652.

MAZOYER, B. M., N. TZOURIO, V. FRAK, A. SYROTA, N. MURAYAMA, O. LEVRIER, G. SALAMON, S. DEHAENE, L. COHEN, and J. MEHLER, 1993. The cortical representation of speech. *J. Cogn. Neurosci.* 5:467–479.

MCGUIRE, P. K., D. A. SILBERSWEIG, and C. D. FRITH, 1996. Functional neuroanatomy of verbal self-monitoring. *Brain* 119:101–111.

MCGUIRE, P. K., D. A. SILBERSWEIG, R. M. MURRAY, A. S. DAVID, R. S. J. FRACKOWIAK, and C. D. FRITH, 1996. Functional anatomy of inner speech and auditory verbal imagery. *Psychol. Med.* 26:29–38.

MENARD, M. T., S. M. KOSSLYN, W. L. THOMPSON, N. M. ALPERT, and S. L. RAUCH, 1996. Encoding words and pictures: A positron emission tomography study. *Neuropsychologia* 34:185–194.

OJEMANN, G. A., 1983. Brain organization for language from the perspective of electrical stimulation mapping. *Behav. Brain Sci.* 2:189–230.

OJEMANN, G., J. OJEMANN, E. LETTICH, and M. BERGER, 1989. Cortical language localization in left, dominant hemisphere. An electrical mapping investigation in 117 patients. *J. Neurosurg.* 71:316–326.

PAULESU, E., B. GOLDACRE, P. SCIFO, S. F. CAPPA, M. C. GILARDI, I. CASTIGLIONI, D. PERANI, and F. FAZIO, 1997. Functional heterogeneity of left inferior frontal cortex as revealed by fMRI. *NeuroReport* 8:2011–2016.

PETERSEN, S. E., P. T. FOX, M. I. POSNER, M. MINTUN, and M. E. RAICHLE, 1989. Positron emission tomographic studies of the processing of single words. *J. Cogn. Neurosci.* 1:153–170.

PETERSEN, S. E., P. T. FOX, A. Z. SNYDER, and M. E. RAICHLE, 1990. Activation of extrastriate and frontal cortical areas by visual words and word-like stimuli. *Science* 249:1041–1044.

POLINE, J-B., R. VANDENBERGHE, A. P. HOLMES, K. J. FRISTON, and R. S. J. FRACKOWIAK, 1996. Reproducibility of PET activation studies: Lessons from a multi-center European experiment. EU concerted action on functional imaging. *Neuroimage* 4:34–54.

PREMACK, D., and A. J. PREMACK, 1995. Origins of human social competence. In *The Cognitive Neurosciences*, M. Gazzaniga, ed. Cambridge, Mass.: MIT Press, 205–218.

PRICE, C. J., and K. J. FRISTON, 1997. Cognitive Conjunction: A new approach to brain activation experiments. *Neuroimage* 5:261–270.

PRICE, C. J., C. J. MOORE, and R. S. J. FRACKOWIAK, 1996. The effect of varying stimulus rate and duration on brain activity during reading. *Neuroimage* 3:40–52.

PRICE, C. J., C. J. MOORE, G. W. HUMPHREYS, R. S. J. FRACKOWIAK, and K. J. FRISTON, 1996. The neural regions sustaining object recognition and naming. *Proc. R. Soc. Lond. B* 263:1501–1507.

PRICE, C. J., R. J. S. WISE, and R. S. J. FRACKOWIAK, 1996. Demonstrating the implicit processing of visually presented words and pseudowords. *Cereb. Cortex* 6:62–70.

PRICE, C. J., R. J. S. WISE, E. A. WARBURTON, C. J. MOORE, D. HOWARD, K. PATTERSON, R. S. J. FRACKOWIAK, and K. J. FRISTON, 1996. Hearing and saying. The functional neuro-anatomy of auditory word processing. *Brain* 119:919–931.

PRICE, C. J., R. J. S. WISE, J. D. G. WATSON, K. PATTERSON, D. HOWARD, and R. S. J. FRACKOWIAK, 1994. Brain activity during reading. The effects of exposure duration and task. *Brain* 117:1255–1269.

RAICHLE, M. E., J. A. FIEZ, T. O. VIDIAN, A.-M. K. MACLEOD, J. V. PARDI, P. T. FOX, and S. E. PETERSEN, 1994. Practice-related changes in human brain functional anatomy during nonmotor learning. *Cereb. Cortex* 4:8–26.

RIZZOLATTI, G., and M. GENTILUCCI, 1988. Motor and visual-motor functions of the premotor cortex. In *Neurobiology of Motor Cortex*, P. Rakic and W. Singer, eds. Chichester: Wiley.

ROELOFS A., 1997. The WEAVER model of word-form encoding in speech production. *Cognition* 64:249–284.

RUMSEY, J. M., B. HORWITZ, B. C. DONOHUE, K. NACE, J. M. MAISOG, and P. ANDREASON, 1997. Phonological and orthographic components of word recognition. A PET-rCBF study. *Brain* 120:739–759.

SAKURAI, Y., T. MOMOSE, M. IWATA, T. WATANABE, T. ISHIKAWA, and I. KANAZAWA, 1993. Semantic process in kana word reading: Activation studies with positron emission tomography. *NeuroReport* 4:327–330.

SAKURAI, Y., T. MOMOSE, M. IWATA, T. WATANABE, T. ISHIKAWA, K. TAKEDA, and I. KANAZAWA, 1992. Kanji word reading process analyzed by positron emission tomography. *NeuroReport* 3:445–448.

SALMELIN, R., R. HARI, O. V. LOUNASMAA, and M. SAMS, 1994. Dynamics of brain activation during picture naming. *Nature* 368:463–465.

SALMELIN, R., E. SERVICE, P. KIESILÄ, K. UUTELA, and O. SALONEN, 1996. Impaired visual word processing in dyslexia revealed with magnetoencephalography. *Ann. Neurol.* 40:157–162.

SCHÄFFLER, L., H. O. LÜDERS, D. S. DINNER, R. P. LESSER, and G. J. CHELUNE, 1993. Comprehension deficits elicited by electrical stimulation of Broca's area. *Brain* 116:695–715.

SCHILLER, N., A. S. MEYER, H. BAAYEN, and W. J. M. LEVELT, 1996. A comparison of lexeme and speech syllables in Dutch. *J. Quant. Linguistics* 3:8–28.

SERGENT, J., S. OHTA, and B. MACDONALD, 1992. Functional neuroanatomy of face and object processing: A position emission tomography study. *Brain* 115:15–36.

SHULMAN, G. L., M. CORBETTA, R. L. BUCKNER, J. A. FIEZ, F. M. MIEZIN, M. E. RAICHLE, and S. E. PETERSEN, 1997. Common blood flow changes across visual tasks: I. Increases in subcortical structures and cerebellum but not in nonvisual cortex. *J. Cogn. Neurosci.* 9:624–647.

SNYDER, A. Z., Y. G. ABDULLAEV, M. I. POSNER, and M. E. RAICHLE, 1995. Scalp electrical potentials reflect regional cerebral blood flow responses during processing of written words. *Proc. Natl. Acad. Sci. U.S.A.* 92:1689–1693.

STOWE, L. A., A. A. WIJERS, A. T. M. WILLEMSEN, E. REULAND, A. M. J. PAANS, and W. VAALBURG, 1994. PET studies of language: An assessment of the reliability of the technique. *J. Psycholinguist. Res.* 23:499–527.

STROMSWOLD, K., D. CAPLAN, N. ALPERT, and S. RAUCH, 1996. Localization of syntactic comprehension by positron emission tomography. *Brain Lang.* 52:452–473.

TALAIRACH, J., and P. TOURNOUX, 1988. *Co-planar Stereotaxic Atlas of the Human Brain.* Stuttgart, New York: Georg Thieme Verlag.

THORPE, S., D. FIZE, and C. MARLOT, 1996. Speed of processing in the human visual system. *Nature* 381:520–522.

VANDENBERGHE, R., C. PRICE, R. WISE, O. JOSEPHS, and R. S. J. FRACKOWIAK, 1996. Functional anatomy of a common semantic system for words and pictures. *Nature* 383:254–256.

VAN TURENNOUT, M., P. HAGOORT, and C. M. BROWN, 1997. Electrophysiological evidence on the time course of semantic and phonological processes in speech production. *J. Exp. Psychol.: Learn. Mem. Cogn.* 23:787–806.

VAN TURENNOUT, M., P. HAGOORT, and C. M. BROWN, 1998. Brain activity during speaking: From syntax to phonology in 40 milliseconds. *Science* 280:572–574.

WARBURTON, E., R. J. S. WISE, C. J. PRICE, C. WEILLER, U. HADAR, S. RAMSET, and R. S. J. FRACKOWIAK, 1996. Noun and verb retrieval by normal subjects. Studies with PET. *Brain* 119:159–179.

WHEELDON, L. R., and W. J. M. LEVELT, 1995. Monitoring the time course of phonological encoding. *J. Mem. Lang.* 34:311–334.

WISE, R., F. CHOLLET, U. HADAR, K. FRISTON, E. HOFFNER, and R. S. J. FRACKOWIAK, 1991. Distribution of cortical neural networks involved in word comprehension and word retrieval. *Brain* 114:1803–1817.

ZATORRE, R. J., A. C. EVANS, E. MEYER, and A. GJEDDE, 1992. Lateralization of phonetic and pitch discrimination in speech processing. *Science* 256:846–849.

60 The Study of Prelexical and Lexical Processes in Comprehension: Psycholinguistics and Functional Neuroimaging

DENNIS NORRIS AND RICHARD WISE

ABSTRACT   Here we review the functional neuroimaging literature relating to prelexical auditory and visual processes. We relate neuroimaging work to current psychological models of word perception and discuss some of the problems inherent in the use of the standard subtractive method in this area. The signal returned by cortex associated with speech perception is large, which makes the techniques sensitive to the study of prelexical processes. The major regions involved are primary and association auditory and visual cortices of both hemispheres. The results of the neuroimaging work are shown to be consistent with other studies using ERP and MEG.

Functional neuroimaging of prelexical and lexical processes: Introduction

Over the past decade, a number of functional neuroimaging papers have been published on language activation studies. Studies with positron emission tomography (PET) have predominated, although the number of functional magnetic resonance imaging (fMRI) studies is increasing. Both techniques rely on the rise in regional cerebral blood flow (rCBF) that accompanies a net increase in local synaptic activity. PET activation studies are based on the accumulation of regional tissue counts after the intravenous bolus infusion of radiolabeled water ($H_2{}^{15}O$) (Mazziotta et al., 1985). The signal in the most commonly used fMRI technique, the BOLD (blood oxygenation level–dependent) image contrast, originates from an increase in the oxyhemoglobin:deoxyhemoglobin ratio on the venous side of the local intravascular compartment of the tissue being sampled; a transient increase in local synaptic activity is associated

DENNIS NORRIS   Medical Research Council Cognition and Brain Sciences Unit, Cambridge
RICHARD WISE   Medical Research Council Cyclotron Unit and Imperial College School of Medicine, Hammersmith Hospital, London

with an increase in rCBF in excess of the rise in oxygen consumption, with greater oxygen saturation of venous blood (Thulborn, 1998). Emphasizing the source of the signal in functional neuroimaging acknowledges one of the two major limitations of these techniques in the study of prelexical (and other) processes: Changes in nutrient blood flow occur over many hundreds of milliseconds whereas many of the underlying electrochemical events are complete in tens of milliseconds. The limited temporal resolution of functional neuroimaging (thousands of milliseconds with fMRI; and, with PET, neural transients have to be summed over 15–30 seconds) is also confounded by limited spatial resolution. Even the theoretical resolving power of MRI (1–2 mm) may be misleading, as the signal comes from the intravascular compartment, possibly a little distant from the local neural system under investigation. The signal from PET, the tissue concentration of $H_2{}^{15}O$, more directly signals where events are occurring, but the physics associated with this technique, and the smoothing required in image analysis, means that it is difficult to resolve separate peaks of activation that are less than 5 mm apart. It is possible to overcome the problem of temporal resolution when studying some functional systems, such as visual attention, by combining neuroimaging and electrophysiological techniques to relate a component of an event-related potential to an activated region on a PET/fMRI image (Heinze et al., 1994). The spatial resolution results in an "activation" that is the net change in activity of many millions of synapses.

Using modern PET cameras it is possible to do a 12–16 scan activation study in under two hours with a radiation exposure acceptable to radiation advisory committees. An fMRI study of comparable duration, with no exposure to ionizing radiation, typically allows ten times the number of measurements, although fMRI has its own problems: relatively low sensitivity, susceptibility to movement artifacts because of the higher spatial resolution, and the sheer volume of data that is acquired.

Although the limitations of functional neuroimaging restrict the ability to address many issues of interest to psychologists and psycholinguists, relating behavioral observations to human brain structure and physiology is one of the more important bridges to cross in cognitive neuroscience. This chapter reviews currently available data on sublexical and lexical processing of both spoken and written language and considers the success (or otherwise) of functional neuroimaging and electrophysiological studies when addressing psychological theories of prelexical processing. The brain regions involved are the primary and association auditory and visual cortices. One of the challenges in such studies has been to demonstrate lateralized activations, as it soon became evident from the earliest PET studies that the perception of heard and seen words produced very symmetrical activations in auditory and visual cortices, respectively, in terms of both peak and extent.

The subtractive method and language

The standard functional neuroimaging paradigm is the subtractive method. Ideally, two tasks are chosen which differ only in their demands on a single process. Subtraction of images obtained during the performance of both tasks identifies the brain area(s) responsible for that process. Effective application of this method needs a good cognitive model of the processes under study and a detailed analysis of the tasks. An a priori hypothesis about how the cognitive model might be implemented neurally will also considerably enhance the interpretation of the results.

Even if all of these prerequisites were met, any attempt to apply the subtractive method to language processing to isolate a specific stage of linguistic processing faces considerable technical and theoretical problems. The early stages of language processing are highly automatic and overlearned, so it is difficult or impossible to devise tasks that make listeners or readers process input to one level and no further. Consider the problem of trying to force spoken input to be processed up to, but not including the lexical level. The obvious comparison here would be between words and nonwords. However, all current theories of spoken word recognition assume that nonwords will activate a number of partially matching candidate words to some level. The best we can do is hope that nonwords produce less lexical activation than words. To compound the problem, once input is processed to the lexical level, it is likely also to be processed semantically and possibly even interpretively. So, words

will also activate semantic areas while nonwords will activate lexical areas (at least). Unfortunately, subtracting word and nonword processing is not going to have the desired effect of isolating areas responsible for a specifically lexical level of processing. This may explain why at least two PET studies have failed to find any differences between words and nonlexical stimuli. Hirano and colleagues (1997) compared normal Japanese sentences with the same sentences played in reverse. Fiez and colleagues (1996) compared words with nonwords. Neither study found differences.

Models

The central focus of cognitive models of both spoken and written word recognition has been the lexical access process itself. Theories like the interactive activation models of McClelland and Rumelhart (1981) and Grainger and Jacobs (1996) in the visual domain, and TRACE (McClelland and Elman, 1986), Shortlist (Norris, 1994), and Cohort (Marslen-Wilson and Welsh, 1978) in the spoken domain have all concentrated on explaining how orthographic or phonological representations make contact with lexical representations. These models differ in important respects (for example, TRACE is interactive while Shortlist is bottom-up); however, with the exception of the Cohort model, each of these theories assumes that lexical access involves a process of competition between simultaneously activated lexical candidates. Visual or spoken input results in the activation of a number of matching, or partially matching, lexical candidates that compete with each other by means of lateral inhibition until a single winning candidate emerges. In the case of spoken input, the competition process also performs the essential task of parsing continuous input (in which word boundaries are generally not marked) into a sequence of words. The principle of competition now has extensive empirical support in the case of both spoken (e.g., McQueen, Norris, and Cutler, 1994) and visual input (e.g., Andrews, 1989; Forster and Taft, 1994). So, there is widespread agreement among models in terms of the broad characterization of lexical access. There is much less of a consensus about prelexical processing. In reading there is unanimity over the importance of letters in prelexical processing, but much less certainty about the nature of any intermediate orthographic representations (e.g., Raap, 1992; Perea and Carreiras, 1998, on syllables) or whether phonological representations play a role in lexical access (e.g., van Orden, 1987; Lesch and Pollatsek, 1998).

In speech, most models largely follow a standard linguistic hierarchy and have stages of acoustic, phonetic, phonemic, and phonological analysis, although not all models have all stages. For example, TRACE adopts a very conventional linguistic approach with levels corresponding to features and phonemes. However, TRACE has no phonological representation of metrical structure such as mora, syllable, or foot. Shortlist (Norris et al., 1997) assumes that metrical information must be available, but it too does not specify an explicit prelexical stage of phonological processing. In fact, although Shortlist accesses the lexicon via phonemic representations, this is really a matter of implementational convenience rather than a result of a commitment to a phonemic level of representation.

The existence of a strictly phonemic level of processing has been questioned in both the linguistic and the psycholinguistic literature. Some linguistic frameworks, such as underspecification theory (cf. Archangeli, 1984; Kiparski, 1985; Pulleyblank, 1983), have no role for the a phonemic level of representation. In psychology, Lahiri and Marslen-Wilson (1991) have argued that the work usually attributed to a phonemic level can be accomplished by a level of featural representation instead. Marslen-Wilson and Warren (1994) have argued that phonemic and phonological representations are constructed postlexically (but see Norris, McQueen, and Cutler, in press). Other authors have argued that the syllable is the most important prelexical level of representation (Mehler, 1981) and that phonemes play only a secondary role. It should be clear from this that psycholinguists cannot yet offer a definitive cognitive account of prelexical processes and representations. Indeed, determining exactly what those processes and representations are is one of the central goals of current psycholinguistic research.

Implementation

Even when we seem to be asking very simple questions about large-scale architectural issues, questions of implementation can significantly alter the kind of conclusions we might draw from an imaging study. Consider the problem of identifying areas responsible for auditory and "phonological" processing. In the imaging literature this has been approached by comparing speech (in either active or passive listening tasks) with "nonspeech" stimuli such as tones (Demonet et al., 1992, 1994; Binder et al., 1996), noise bursts (Zatorre et al., 1992), or signal-correlated noise (Mummery et al., in press). The assumption behind these studies is that the nonspeech stimuli will not activate the areas responsible for phonological processing. But both "nonspeech" and speech should be fully processed by acoustic areas. The output from these areas must then be passed on to the "phonological" areas. Unless the auditory areas are designed to prevent nonspeech signals from being passed on to the

phonological system, the phonological system will receive at least some input. Intuitively, of course, it seems that speech should engage the phonological areas much more than nonspeech. But this needn't be the case, certainly not for the early stages of phonological or phonetic processing. It is only once some part of the speech processing system has tried, and then failed, to categorize the input into a form appropriate for further speech analysis that subsequent areas will not receive an input. As we all know, trying to do something we can't do can be much harder than doing something we can do. We can see this kind of problem in a very extreme form in the Auditory Image Model proposed by Patterson, Allerhand, and Giguere (1995). In this model of early auditory processing there is a component designed to deal with periodic signals. When given periodic signals, it produces a clean stabilized image of the input, revealing the fine structure of the periodic signal. With aperiodic signals, this stage produces noise. Depending on the details of the neural implementation, this component could do less work when analyzing the periodic signals it is specialized for than when attempting to analyze aperiodic signals. However, we should bear in mind that it is not at all clear how a hemodynamic response on a scan relates to apparent task "difficulty." Furthermore, even connectionist models are not attempts to faithfully capture the architecture of inhibitory and excitatory neural subsystems. For example, inhibitory and excitatory synapses both consume energy, and a "deactivation" (reduction in local blood flow) on an image reflects a net reduction of synaptic activity in a region with many polysynaptic pathways.

At least some of these issues might be profitably approached by correlational methods. Instead of contrasting speech and nonspeech, one could vary the strength of a particular speech property (while keeping the signal relatively unchanged acoustically). Therefore, a subject may be required to listen to acoustic or visual signals that vary along one of a number of dimensions, and the changing response of a brain region correlated with this varying input. This technique is being applied in terms of the rate of presentation of stimuli, or by using psychological variables such as word imagability or frequency, and the same strategy can be used for the physical properties of an input signal. These techniques can explore the natural processing of the stimuli without the need to make A – B subtractions between two more or less metalinguistic tasks.

Tasks

The processing of heard words is a function of primary and association auditory cortex; and similarly, seen words activate striate and prestriate cortex (figure 60.1A,B). One

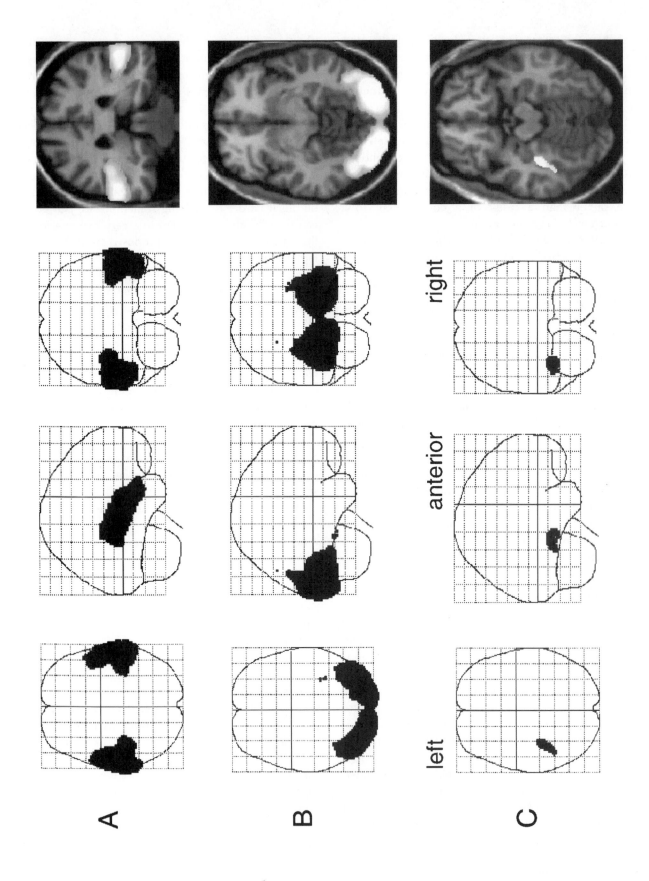

FIGURE 60.1 The first three columns show the orthogonal projections of the brain created by the image data analysis program (SPM96–Wellcome Department of Cognitive Neurology) (Friston et al., 1995a,b): Left = axial; middle = saggital; right = coronal. The orientation (left/right/anterior) is shown on the bottom row of images. In the fourth column are activations displayed on selected slices of the MRI template available in SPM96. The threshold was set at $p < .05$, corrected for analysis of the whole brain volume. (A) Twelve normal subjects listening to single words contrasted with seeing the same words. There are bilateral, symmetrical, extensive DLTC activations. In the coronal MRI slice, the activations are seen to run mediolaterally along Heschl's gyrus. (B) As (A), but now seeing single words has been contrasted with hearing words. There are bilateral, symmetrical, extensive posterior striate/prestriate activations. In the axial MRI slice, the activations are seen to extend toward the occipitotemporal junction. As only foveal vision is used to read singe words, striate cortex subserving parafoveal and peripheral retinal vision has not been activated. (C) Three experiments with six normal subjects in each (eighteen subjects in all), in which seen and heard word imagability was varied. Words of higher imagability produced greater activity in left ventral temporal cortex (the fusiform gyrus). Both the peak and extent of this imagability effect were much smaller than observed in (A) and (B). It is a feature of all functional imaging experiments on lexical semantic processes, in a temporal lobe region thought to be a major site for the representations of semantic knowledge, that the signal is small relative to prelexical processes.

---

noticeable feature is that they return a strong signal, even when the stimuli are "passively" perceived. Although many neuroimaging studies to date have been concerned with lexical–semantic processes, the signal obtained in ventral temporal regions is smaller, both in terms of extent and peak activity (figure 60.1C). Therefore, anatomically constrained, strongly activated prelexical systems are potentially easier to study with functional neuroimaging than lexical–semantic and syntactic language systems.

Imaging studies have generally adopted standard psycholinguistic tasks. For example, a popular task in imaging studies has been phoneme monitoring, in which listeners are required to press a button when they hear a particular phoneme in the input. This task is employed as a way of engaging "phonological[1]" processing, and has been compared with passive listening (Zatorre et al., 1992, 1996) or monitoring for changes in the pitch of pure tones (Demonet et al., 1992, 1994). However, from a psycholinguistic standpoint, the most significant observation about the phoneme monitoring task is that it can be performed only by listeners who have been taught to read an alphabetic script (Read et al., 1986). Illiterates, for example, are unable to perform phoneme monitoring, or most other tasks involving explicit segmentation. In other words, phoneme monitoring makes cognitive demands over and above those required by normal speech perception. This fact has long been recognized

by psycholinguists and is an important feature of the most recent psychological model of phoneme monitoring and phonetic judgments (Norris, McQueen, and Cutler, in press).

Interpretation of phoneme monitoring studies therefore has to be tempered with the possibility that the results may tell us as much about the structures involved in performing a particular metalinguistic task as they do about speech perception itself. However, it can still be a valuable cognitive task as, in almost all psycholinguistic accounts, phoneme monitoring is assumed to tap into the products of the normal speech recognition process at some level. However, the use of phoneme monitoring to tap into speech processing is logically very different from its use in an imaging study if the intention is that the task should engage normal phonemic/phonetic processing. If we find that a particular brain area activates only when performing an explicit metalinguistic task, like phoneme monitoring, we have no evidence that this area is directly involved in the normal phonetic or phonological processing of speech. The area could be responsible solely for interrogating the normal speech recognition systems in order to generate a response in this particular task.

Interestingly, much of the data showing specifically left-hemisphere activation comes from a comparison of metalinguistic, or active, tasks, with passive listening (Zatorre et al., 1992; Demonet et al., 1994). There tends to be more left-hemisphere activation with active listening. A similar pattern also emerges in a MEG study (Poeppel et al., 1996) where active discrimination of a voicing contrast (/bæ/ and /dæ/ vs. /pæ/ and /tæ/) led to an increase in M100 amplitude in the left hemisphere and a decrease in the right as compared to a passive listening condition.

Note that one interpretation of the imaging data on phoneme monitoring and other active listening tasks is suggested by Fiez and colleagues (1995). Possibly, the increased attentional demands of these tasks lead to increased activation in normal speech processing areas relative to passive listening tasks. This would be consistent with ERP and MEG studies of auditory processing that have found increased activation in the auditory areas contralateral to the attended ear (Näätänen, 1990; Woldorff, Hackley, and Hillyard, 1991; Woldorff and Hillyard, 1991; Woldorff et al., 1993). However, any cognitive model still needs to account for the behavior of illiterates and assume that there is some process responsible for the metalinguistic phonemic judgment, which should presumably result in brain activation itself.

We can see some evidence of activation of other brain areas involved in phoneme monitoring in the studies by Zatorre and colleagues (1992, 1996), who found activation of visual cortex, and by Demonet and colleagues (1994), who found activation of the left fusiform gyrus. Possibly, this is related to the fact that phoneme monitoring is known to be influenced by orthographic factors (Dijkstra, Roeloffs, and Fieuws, 1995; see also Donnenwerth-Nolan, Tanenhaus, and Seidenberg, 1981; Seidenberg and Tanenhaus, 1979). However, perhaps the most worrying feature of studies comparing active and passive listening tasks is that passive listening is more than likely to involve completely normal phonetic/phonemic processing. What these studies may well have done is to design tasks that factor out normal speech processing and highlight the brain areas involved specifically in the metalinguistic tasks. Indeed, Zatorre and co-workers (1996) acknowledge that passive listening would engage an important automatic component of phonetic processing and may involve essentially full semantic processing.

Acoustic–phonetic and phonemic processes

It is hard to know exactly where, if at all, to place a boundary between acoustic and phonetic processing. One could define phonetic processing as being concerned with extraction of specifically linguistic features such as place and manner of articulation of consonants. Acoustic processing would then be defined as those characteristics, such as loudness and frequency, that are not of direct linguistic significance. Architecturally, however, there is no a priori reason why a particular phonetic feature should not computed by the same brain areas responsible for acoustic analysis rather than some later, purely linguistic, stage. Indeed, many animal studies show that primary auditory cortex is sensitive to complex acoustic features that, in humans, might well be considered to be phonetic. A great deal of work has shown that the primary auditory cortex of a number of different species produces a change in response at voice onset times analogous to the human category boundary between voiced and unvoiced consonants (e.g., Eggermont, 1995; Sinex, McDonald, and Mott, 1991; Steinschneider et al., 1995). Recently, Ohl and Scheich (1997) have shown that the primary auditory cortex of gerbils is organized in a manner that is sensitive to the difference between the first and second formant frequencies of vowels, an important factor in human classification of vowels (Peterson and Barney, 1952). In a nonlinguistic species, presumably, these features must be acoustic, and not phonetic. In humans, too, we should probably not be surprised to find such features processed by auditory cortex rather than some later, specifically linguistic, stage of phonetic or phonemic processing. As we will see later, the idea that much phonetically significant processing takes place in primary auditory cortex also receives support from many human studies, especially those using ERP and MEG.

Although studies using PET and fMRI have been directed at identifying particular stages of phonetic or phonological processing, other work has addressed more detailed questions about differences in processing within individual stages of linguistic analysis. For example, how does processing differ between vowels and consonants or even between different vowels? Much of this work has used ERP, MEG, or even direct cortical stimulation.

Boatman and colleagues (1997) examined the effects of direct cortical electrical interference on consonant and vowel discrimination using implanted subdural electrode arrays. With electrical interference, consonant discrimination was impaired at one electrode site in each patient on the superior temporal gyrus of the lateral left perisylvian cortex. Without electrical interference, consonant–vowel discrimination was intact and vowel and tone discrimination remained relatively intact when tested with electrical interference at the same site. Rather interestingly, the crucial sites were located differently in different patients. This suggests that within these anatomical areas there are individual differences in the details of functional localization. Such differences could reflect either innate structural differences or different outcomes of a learning process.

Given the considerable crosslinguistic variation in phonemic inventories, both in the number and the nature of the phonemic categories, learning must play some role in the establishment of phonemic categories. Using both ERPs and magnetoencephalographic recordings, Näätänen and colleagues (1997) compared processing of vowels by Finnish and Estonian listeners. They measured both the electrical (MMN) and the magnetic mismatch negativity (MMNM or magnetic mismatch field: MMF) response to a set of four vowels. For the Estonian listeners, the four vowels all corresponded to prototypical Estonian vowels. For the Finnish listeners, only three of the four vowels corresponded to prototypical vowels in their language. Listeners were presented with the phoneme /e/ and, infrequently, with one of the other three vowels to elicit a mismatch response. For the Finnish listeners, there was a much larger mismatch negativity when the infrequent vowel was the Finnish /ö/ than when it was a nonprototypical vowel (the Estonian /õ/), even though the /õ/ is actually more dissimilar to the /e/ phoneme in terms of formant structure. Estonian listeners showed large mismatch responses to both /ö/ and /õ/. In contrast to this phonemically determined response in the MMN amplitude, MMN latency was a function solely of the degree of acoustic dissimilarity of the infrequent stimulus. For the Finnish listeners the magnetic mismatch neg-activity (MMNM) response was larger in the left hemisphere than the right when the infrequent phoneme was a Finnish prototype vowel. In the left hemisphere the MMNM originated in the auditory cortex, but in the right hemisphere the responses were not strong enough to reliably localize the source of the response.

Other studies have examined the neuromagnetic responses N100m (or N1m or M100), P200m, and SF (sustained field), which are the magnetic analogs of the electrical responses N100, P200, and SP (sustained potential). By combining MEG and MRI, the source of the N100m evoked by pure tones is known to lie on the surface of the Heschl gyri, which include primary auditory cortex (Pantev et al., 1990).

Poeppel and colleagues (1997) measured the N100m response to vowels varying in pitch and to pure tones. The N100m dipole localizations in supratemporal auditory cortex were the same for vowels and pure tones. They found no differences in N100m amplitude due to vowel type or pitch. However, response latency was influenced by vowel type but not by pitch. Response latency thus appears to be sensitive to vowel type, but not to pitch. This suggests that processing in supratemporal auditory cortex is already extracting pitch-invariant phonetic properties. Aulanko and colleagues (1993) used the syllables /bæ/ and /gæ/ in a mismatch paradigm where the syllables were synthesized on 16 different pitches. They also found that MMNM responses (localized to the supratemporal auditory cortex) were maintained despite the variations in pitch. In another MEG study Diesch and co-workers (1996) looked at dipole localizations of N100m and SF deflection in response to the German vowels /a/, /æ/, /u/, /i/, and /ø/. Here, too, there was considerable intersubject variability in the locations of the sources, but the ordering of the distances between N100m and SF equivalent dipole locations was much more systematic and could be interpreted as reflecting distances in vowel space or featural representations of the vowels.

Listening to words

In imaging studies, listening to words without an explicit task demand produces strong activations in bilateral dorsolateral temporal cortex (DLTC) that is both extensive and symmetrical (figure 60.1A; see Petersen et al., 1988; Wise et al., 1991; Binder et al., 1994). This symmetry seems to be at odds with the "dominance" of the left hemisphere for heard word perception; psychophysical and psychological evidence suggests that the temporal resolution required for analysis of the rapid frequency transitions associated with consonants (occurring over < 50 ms) is dependent on a neural system lateralized to the left hemisphere (for review, see Fitch, Miller, and Tallal, 1997).

It has been suggested that the more constant acoustic features of words, such as vowel sounds, might be analyzed by the right hemisphere (Studdert-Kennedy and Shankweiler, 1970). However, Lund and colleagues (1986) found that left-hemisphere lesions, mainly located in Wernicke's area, tended to disrupt vowel perception whereas none of their patients with lesions in the corresponding area of the right hemisphere had perceptual problems.

Speech perception is robust, even when the sounds are distorted in a variety of ways (e.g., Miller, 1951; Plomp and Mimpen, 1979). No single cue seems to determine the comprehensibility of speech and a listener uses a range of acoustic features, which may explain why word deafness (agnosia for speech in the absence of aphasia) usually occurs only after bilateral lesions of dorsolateral temporal cortex (DLTC) (Buchman et al., 1986; Polster and Rose, 1998). Therefore, it is to be expected that acoustic processing of speech input should involve the DLTC of both hemispheres.

Using a parametric design, where the rate of hearing single words was varied between 0 and 90 words per minute (wpm), one PET study distinguished regions in left and right DLTC that showed an approximately linear relationship between activity and rate from a single region, in the left posterior superior temporal gyrus (postDLTC), where activity was close to maximal at 10 wpm (Price et al., 1992). This study set a precedent for inferring a difference in processing from the shape of the activity-input curve. It is true that another study—one using fMRI to investigate left and right primary auditory cortex (PAC) and postDLTC—did not reproduce this original result (Dhankar et al., 1997); but this may be because the preeminent interest in left postDLTC (the core of "classic" Wernicke's area) may be misplaced. It has become apparent from a number of imaging studies that the DLTC anterior to PAC (midDLTC) is central to the acoustic and phonological processing of heard words. Three studies (Zatorre et al., 1992; Demonet et al., 1992, 1994) have contrasted phoneme monitoring in syllables or nonwords with decisions on the pitch of stimuli (syllables or tones). All three studies identified bilateral midDLTC, although activation on the left was greater than on the right for the detection of speech sounds. This emphasis on midDLTC, and not postDLTC, in the prelexical processing of words is also evident in the fMRI study of Binder and co-workers (1996).

Although neurologists generally attribute a central role in speech perception to Wernicke's area, support for this from functional neuroimaging is mixed. Fiez and colleagues (1996) and Petersen and colleagues

(1988, 1989) all found activation of Wernicke's area (Brodmann's area 22 close to the temporoparietal junction) when comparing passive word listening with fixation. Interestingly, Fiez and co-workers (1996) also found no differences between words and nonwords. They acknowledge that this could be due to phonological analysis, lexical activation, or perhaps to phonological storage. However, Fiez and colleagues (1995) and Zatorre and colleagues (1992) failed to find temporoparietal activation, even though Fiez's group examined both active and passive listening tasks, and did find temporoparietal activation when comparing listening to tones with a fixation task. Binder and co-workers (1996) demonstrated that activation in the left planum temporale was similar for tones and words, and there was greater activity for tones in an explicit task on the stimuli. However, as we have discussed, a response to nonlinguistic stimuli does not preclude the possibility that a region is specialized for a linguistic purpose.

As noted, midDLTC asymmetry in studies using phoneme monitoring may reflect modulation of DLTC activity by attentional processes rather than "dominance" of the left temporal lobe in prelexical processing. A contrast of "passive" listening to words with listening to signal-correlated noise (SCN—acoustically complex sounds without the periodicity of words) demonstrated symmetry of DLTC function: The rates of hearing both words and SCN correlated with cerebral activity in PAC and adjacent periauditory cortex of both hemispheres, and correlations specific to words were located symmetrically in left and right midDLTC (Mummery et al., in press). Frontal activations were absent. Although it cannot be inferred that symmetrical PET activations imply symmetrical processing functions, these results do support single-case studies suggesting that the DLTC of both hemispheres is involved in the acoustic *and* phonological processing of words (Praamstra et al., 1991).

Another, more natural demand on auditory attention is made when a subject has to "stream out" a particular source of speech in a noisy environment, the usual example cited being the cocktail party. Auditory stream segregation (Bregman, 1989) is open to investigation with functional neuroimaging, although no studies, to the authors' knowledge, have as yet been published. However, the effects of another source of speech sounds, one's own voice, has been investigated. Attention to one's own articulated output will be variable, depending on how carefully a speaker wishes to use on-line, post-articulatory self-monitoring in the detection and correction of a wide range of potential speech errors (Levelt, 1989). It is assumed that the same processors that analyze the speech of others are used to monitor one's own voice. This has been confirmed by a number of PET studies (Price et al.,

1996; McGuire et al., 1996). However, studies in humans and monkeys with single-cell recordings have demonstrated modulation of temporal cortical activity by phonation/articulation (Müller-Preuss and Ploog, 1981; Creutzfeldt, Ojemann, and Lettich, 1989). Figure 60.2 demonstrates a comparable result at the local systems level in a PET study that investigated variable rates of listening and repeating in normal subjects. When listening, each subject heard word doublets, with each word heard a second time after an interval of 500 ms. Therefore, during both the listening and repeating conditions the subjects heard the same word twice, although in the former both words of each pair came via headphones while in the latter the second word of each pair was the subject's own voice. During repeating, particularly at high rates, the articulated output must be discriminated from the stimuli so as not to interfere with the acoustic and phonological analysis of the latter. When activity in left periauditory cortex was plotted against the rate of hearing words during both the listening and repeating tasks, there was some separation of the curves (figure 60.2A); but when plotted against the rate of hearing the stimuli alone (figure 60.2B), there was no evidence of modulation (i.e., suppression) of the response to the stimuli by articulation. The small additional contribution of own voice to activity may be explained by a general reduction of attention to this source of sound, and by the attenuation of the higher tones of own voice because of transmission to the middle ear by bone conduction. In contrast, the same activity-rate plots show suppression of activity in response to the stimuli in left midDLTC by articulation (figure 60.2C and D), the physiological expression of auditory streaming during repeating. Post-articulatory self-monitoring is likely to be minimal when repeating single words. Manipulating the complexity of speech output could be used to test the hypothesis that varying the demand on post-articulatory self-monitoring correlates with activity in left midDLTC, which would confirm modulation of activity in this region by attention towards one's own speech output.

A further study has assessed the modulation of DLTC activity by articulation (Paus et al., 1996). Subjects whispered syllables at rates varying from 30 to 150 per minute (any residual sound from the subject's larynx was masked by white noise), and increasing motor activity was associated with an increase in activity in the left planum temporale and left posterior perisylvian cortex, attributed to motor-to-sensory discharges. Such discharges may allow listeners to rapidly segregate their own articulations from the simultaneous speech of others.

So far, two activity-rate responses have been recorded in DLTC in response to hearing single words. The first reaches a maximum at relatively low rates of

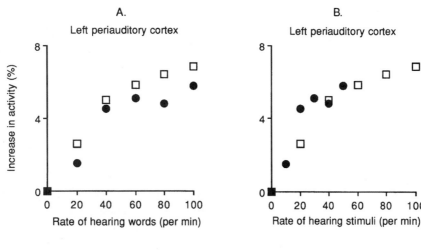

A.
Left periauditory cortex

B.
Left periauditory cortex

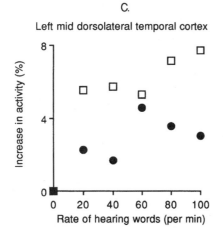

C.
Left mid dorsolateral temporal cortex

D.
Left mid dorsolateral temporal cortex

FIGURE 60.2   (A) The percentage increase of activity (regional cerebral blood flow) plotted against the rate of hearing words during listening (open squares) and repeating (closed circles) in left periauditory cortex. The baseline activity (closed square) was measured when the subjects were expecting to hear stimuli but received none during the period of data acquisition. During the listening task the words were heard as doublets (each word was repeated after a delay of 500 ms); during repeating the stimulus words were only heard once, but the rate of hearing words was the same as that in the listening task, as the subjects heard their articulated responses. The response curves showed activity to be a little less during repeating than listening, but this did not reach significance. (B) The same plot as (A), but the ordinate is the rate of hearing stimuli; therefore,

during repeating the range is half that during repeating, as hearing own voice is excluded in this analysis. Activity in response to external input is approximately matched in the two conditions–the slightly greater activity associated with repeating reflects a small contribution from own voice. (C) The same plot as in (A), but for left midDLTC. There was a significantly lower activity ($p < .05$, corrected for analysis of the whole brain volume) for repeating compared to listening. (D) The same plot as (B): Activity was modulated (suppressed) by articulation, so that net synaptic activity was reduced even in response to the external stimuli. This demonstrates an overall reduction of responsiveness of this local neural system, interpreted as a "focusing" of prelexical processing on the stimuli and not the articulated output.

word presentation and there is little increase in activity for higher rates of hearing words (figure 60.3); this was the response reported by Price and colleagues (1992) in left postSTG and approximately describes the behavior of left midDLTC in figure 60.2C. The second is one of increasing, if progressively diminishing, activity up to a rate of ~90–100 wpm, seen in left periauditory cortex in figure 60.2A; but at higher rates activity diminishes (figure 60.3), as observed by Dhankar and colleagues (1997). Cortical responses are dependent on both the

local neural architecture and those of subcortical structures that directly or indirectly (via polysynaptic pathways) project to DLTC. All neural systems have a refractory period after receiving an input, during which time further input cannot be processed. The curves in figure 60.3 originate from the behavior of the local neural subsystem plus or minus its interaction with other local (cortical and subcortical) subsystems. The shape of these, and other, response curves in DLTC could be subjected to signal modeling; although these models

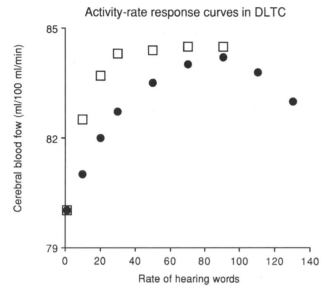

Activity-rate response curves in DLTC

FIGURE 60.3   A representation of the two types of activity-rate responses (open squares and closed circles) in DLTC so far reported in the literature.

will inevitably be simplifications, analyses of response curves is potentially a powerful way of observing neuromodulation and rapidly or slowly evolving neural plasticity. Thus, instead of subtraction analysis between observations made in two behavioral states to decide whether a local system is "on" or "off," parametric designs with a varying input could be used to observe changes in the response curves of cortical and subcortical subsystems: for example, when the subject is or is not attending to the stimuli; during the course of learning/habituating to an executive task on the stimuli; and, translating into clinical research, during the course of recovery following a stroke, either occurring naturally or as the result of a particular therapy, in perilesional or remote cortex. The relatively high signal:noise ratio in functional images of the prelexical systems of DLTC make these good candidates for such research.

Seeing words: PET and fMRI studies

It has been known for more than a century that normal subjects can recognize single words as fast as single letters (Cattel, 1886). Therefore, the letters of a written word are perceived in parallel, and are not processed serially. The neuropsychological literature explains the alexia accompanying left occipital lesions in terms of impaired letter form discrimination, parallel letter identification, whole word form recognition, or visual attentional processes (for review, see Behrmann, Plaut, and Nelson, in press). The resulting "pure alexia" is associated with an increase in reaction time as the number of letters in a word increases (the word length effect).

Acuity in discerning a word's constituent letters is dependent on foveal vision, which extends 1° to either side of fixation. Acuity in parafoveal vision, extending 5° to either side of fixation, rapidly declines with greater distance from fixation. Nevertheless, vision from this part of the retina provides important information about the overall shape and length of words (Rayner and Bertera, 1979). It has been determined that the spatial extent of a subject's perceptual span during reading is asymmetric; it covers only 3–4 characters to the left but 12–15 characters to the right for a left-to-right reader (McConkie and Rayner, 1975), with presumably the opposite asymmetry for readers of Arabic, Farsee, and Hebrew. There is also a temporal component, with the duration of fixation on an individual word within a text lasting ~250 ms. A saccade, ending 7–9 characters to the right, moves the fixation point to the viewing point of the next word. In this way, text information is acquired rapidly, without discontinuities and the need for regressive saccades to fill in perceptual gaps.

Reduced right foveal/parafoveal visual information impairs text reading ("hemianopic" alexia; Zihl, 1995), and eye movement recordings have shown this to be due to disorganization of the spatial and temporal components of the perceptual span: Saccades may be too short or long, with frequent regressive saccades to fill in perceptual gaps. Text reading speed correlates with the number of degrees of sparing of the 5° of right foveal/parafoveal vision.

It is probable that there is no clear clinical division between the psychophysicists' "hemianopic" alexia and the neuropsychologists' "pure" alexia, and it is varying proportions of impairments in perceptual and temporal span, letter identification, and attentional processes that result in the slow reading of any particular patient. As both conditions accompany left occipital infarcts, the exact distribution of the lesion must affect one of two prelexical neural systems involved in perceiving text: one responsible for letter and whole word identification, and the other for rightward-directed attention (for European languages) controlling reading saccades. Functional neuroimaging studies have shown that the perception of letter strings and words activate posterior striate cortex (the receptive field for foveal vision) and prestriate cortex (Petersen et al., 1990; Rumsey et al., 1997; Price, Wise, and Frackowiak, 1996). As observed with auditory cortex, there is no evidence for asymmetry, although only left occipital lesions result in alexia. However, global alexia, which includes an inability to recognize single letters, usually occurs only when a left occipital lesion is accompanied by disconnection of right striate/prestriate cortex from the mirror regions on the left (Binder and Mohr, 1992). The presence of a complete, macular-

left   right

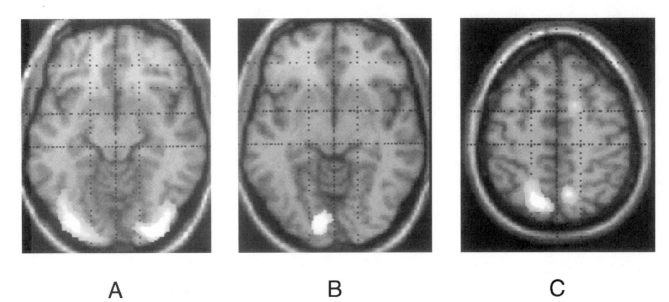

A   B   C

FIGURE 60.4 Activations coregistered onto axial MRI slices from the SPM96 template (the coordinate marks are in red). (A) Viewing single words, as in figure 60.1B. (B) Reading across horizontal word arrays (3 and 5 words) contrasted with viewing single words at the same rate, coregistered onto an MRI axial image 16 mm dorsal to the image in (A). This subtraction reveals the activation in the representation of right parafoveal space in the left striate cortex, demonstrating the way that visual attention during text reading modulates activity in V1. (C) The same behavioral contrast as in (B), but 55 mm dorsal to the plane depicted in (B). This shows bilateral PPC and right FEF activations associated with the planning and generation of forward saccades during reading across horizontal arrays of words.

splitting hemianopia (with no visual information about letter/word form reaching the left striate cortex) does not preclude the ability to read single words; therefore, orthographic information can be processed in the right occipital lobe sufficient to support reading once the information is transferred to the left hemisphere via the corpus callosum.

The neural system for letter and word identification is shown in figures 60.1B and 60.4A. It has been shown that activity in these regions increases with increasing rate or duration of seeing single words (Price, Moore, and Frackowiak, 1996). Petersen and co-workers (1990) demonstrated that most of this cortex responded similarly to words, letter strings, and letter-like symbols, with the exception of a region in left prestriate cortex which responded only to words and pronounceable nonwords; they concluded that this was the location of the visual whole word form system. Subsequently, in a study of different design, Howard and colleagues (1992) located the word form system in the left posterior temporal lobe. This sharp phrenological distinction, on the basis of contrasts on observations made during two behavioral conditions, may be misleading, and it is unlikely that the more central "black boxes" of information processing models of language are represented as anatomically discrete cortical regions; realization of vi-sual word form is perhaps better viewed as a distributed system between left prestriate and left posterior temporal cortex.

The neural system involved in word identification by controlling attention and eye movements across text is shown in figure 60.4B,C. This involves left striate cortex (V1, in the depth of the calcarine sulcus) receiving information from right parafoveal visual space (for left-to-right readers) (figure 60.4B), and posterior parietal cortex (PPC) and the frontal eye fields (FEF, right $\gg$ left) (figure 60.4C). Activity in these regions is not affected by the rate of presentation of single words, but is apparent when contrasting reading across horizontal arrays of words with reading single words presented at the same rate. PPC and FEF activations are apparent in other studies that have investigated directed visual attention (Corbetta, 1998). The parafoveal V1 activation is consistent with visual attention's being directed to the right of fixation when reading text left-to-right, and is a demonstration that visual attentional processes, at least during text reading, may modulate activity at the level of primary visual cortex. This is in contrast to the combined PET and event-related potential studies which have suggested that attention directed toward objects in visual space normally acts at the level of prestriate cortex (for example, see Heinze et al., 1994).

Conclusions

Much of the functional neuroimaging of language has been involved with responses in multimodal association cortex, which has on occasion been bedeviled by inconsistency of results across studies and debates about whether activations directly reflect language processing itself or represent a parallel process, such as working memory, involved in the performance of the tasks being used. Prelexical processes return stronger signals, and manipulating any one of a number of the physical properties of seen or heard verbal input, with or without the explicit attention of the subject, is an approach that has yet to be fully exploited. One of the more interesting applications will be to show changes in physiological responses over a series of scans in the same individual, particularly in relation to clinical questions directed at the processes underlying stroke recovery and post surgical adaptations to a cochlear implant (Okazawa et al., 1996).

NOTE

1. Note that in the imaging literature the term "phonological" is used to cover a far broader range of processes than simply the phonological component of spoken word recognition. In general, imaging studies of phonological processing have examined a range of tasks involving the manipulation and storage of phonological representations. Very little of this work can claim to have identified specifically linguistic areas of phonological processing (see Poeppel, 1996, for a critique of this work). The choice of tasks in this work often makes it difficult to relate imaging studies to standard distinctions in either the cognitive or linguistic literature.

REFERENCES

ANDREWS, S., 1989. Frequency and neighborhood effects on lexical access: Activation or search? *J. Exp. Psychol.: Learn. Mem. Cogn.* 15:802–814.

ARCHANGELI, D., 1984. *Underspecification in Yawelmani Phonology.* Doctoral dissertation, Cambridge, Mass.: MIT Press.

AULANKO, R., R. HARI, O. V. LOUNASMAA, R. NÄÄTÄNEN, and M. SAMS, 1993. Phonetic invariance in the human auditory cortex. *Neuroreport* 30:1356–1358.

BEHRMANN, M., D. C. PLAUT, and J. NELSON, in press. A meta-analysis and new data supporting an interactive account of postlexical effects in letter-by-letter reading. *Cogn. Psychol.*

BINDER, J. R., J. A. FROST, T. A. HAMMEKE, S. M. RAO, and R. W. COX, 1996. Function of the left planum temporale in auditory and linguistic processing. *Brain* 119:1239–1247.

BINDER, J. R., and J. P. MOHR, 1992. The topography of callosal reading pathways. A case-control analysis. *Brain* 115:1807–1826.

BINDER, J. R., S. M. RAO, T. A. HAMMEKE, F. Z. YETKIN, A. JESMANOWICZ, P. BADETTINI, E. WONG, L. ESTKOWSKI, M.

GOLDSTEIN, V. HAUGHTON, and J. HYDE, 1994. Functional magnetic resonance imaging of human auditory cortex. *Ann. Neurol.* 35:662–672.

BOATMAN, D., C. HALL, M. H. GOLDSTEIN, R. LESSER, and B. GORDON, 1997. Neuroperceptual differences in consonant and vowel discrimination: As revealed by direct cortical electrical interference. *Cortex* 33:83–98.

BREGMAN, A. S., 1990. *Auditory Scene Analysis: The Perceptual Organization of Sound.* Cambridge, Mass.: MIT Press.

BUCHMAN, A. S., D. C. GARRON, J. E. TROST-CARDAMONE, M. D. WICHTER, and M. SCHWARTZ, 1986. Word deafness: One hundred years later. *J. Neurol. Neurosurg. Psychiat.* 49:489–499.

CATTEL, J. M., 1886. The inertia of the eye and brain. *Brain* 8:295–312.

CORBETTA, M., 1998. Frontoparietal cortical networks for directing attention and the eyes to visual locations: Identical, independent, or overlapping neural systems? *Proc. Natl. Acad. Sci. U.S.A.* 95:831–838.

CREUTZFELDT, O., G. OJEMANN, and E. LETTICH, 1989. Neuronal activity in the human lateral temporal lobe. II. Responses to the subject's own voice. *Exp. Brain Res.* 77:476–489.

DEMONET, J. F., F. CHOLLET, S. RAMSAY, D. CARDEBAT, J. L. NESPOULOUS, R. WISE, A. RASCOL, and R. FRACKOWIAK, 1992. The anatomy of phonological and semantic processing in normal subjects. *Brain* 115:1753–1768.

DEMONET, J. F., C. PRICE, R. WISE, and R. FRACKOWIAK, 1994. A PET study of cognitive strategies in normal subjects during language tasks. Influence of phonetic ambiguity and sequence processing on phoneme monitoring. *Brain* 117:671–682.

DHANKAR, A., B. E. WEXLER, R. K. FULBRIGHT, T. HALWES, A. M. BLAMIRE, and R. G. SHULMAN, 1997. Functional magnetic resonance imaging assessment of the human brain auditory cortex response to increasing word presentation rates. *J. Neurophysiol.* 77:476–483.

DIESCH, E., C. EULITZ, S. HAMPSON, and R. ROSS, 1996. The neurotopography of vowels as mirrored by evoked magnetic field measurements. *Brain Lang.* 53:143–168.

DIJKSTRA, T., A. ROELOFS, and S. FIEUWS, 1995. Orthographic effects on phoneme monitoring. *Can. J. Exp. Psychol.* 49:264–271.

DONNENWERTH–NOLAN, S., M. K. TANENHAUS, and M. S. SEIDENBERG, 1981. Multiple code activation in word recognition: Evidence from rhyme monitoring. *J. Exp. Psychol.: Hum. Learn. Mem.* 7:170–180.

EGGERMONT, J. J., 1995. Representation of a voice onset time continuum in primary auditory cortex of the cat. *J. Acoust. Soc. Am.* 98:911–920.

FIEZ, J. A., M. E. RACHLIE, D. A. BALOTA, P. TALLAL, and S. E. PETERSEN, 1996. PET activation of posterior temporal regions during auditory word presentation and verb generation. *Cereb. Cortex* 6:1–10.

FIEZ, J. A., M. E. RACHLIE, F. M. MEIZIN, S. E. PETERSEN, P. TALLAL, and W. F. KATZ, 1995. PET studies of auditory and phonological processing: Effects of stimulus characteristics and task demands. *J. Cogn. Neurosci.* 7:357–375.

FITCH, R. H., S. MILLER, and P. TALLAL, 1997. Neurobiology of speech perception. *Annu. Rev. Neurosci.* 20:331–353.

FORSTER, K. I., and M. TAFT, 1994. Bodies, antibodies, and neighborhood density effects in masked form priming. *J. Exp. Psychol.: Learn. Mem. Cognit.* 20:844–863.

FRISTON, K. J., J. ASHBURNER, C. D. FRITH, J.-B. POLINE, J. D. HEATHER, and R. S. J. FRACKOWIAK, 1995a. Spatial registration and normalization of images. *Hum. Brain Mapp.* 2:165–188.

FRISTON, K. J., A. P. HOLMES, K. J. WORSLEY, J.-B. POLINE, C. D. FRITH, and R. S. J. FRACKOWIAK, 1995b. Statistical parametric maps in functional imaging: A general linear approach. *Hum. Brain Mapp.* 2:189–210.

GRAINGER, J., and A. M. JACOBS, 1996. Orthographic processing in visual word recognition: A multiple read-out model. *Psychol. Rev.* 103:674–691.

HEINZE, H. J., G. R. MANGUN, W. BURCHERT, H. HINRICHS, M. SCHOLZ, T. F. MÜNTE, A. GOS, M. SCHERG, S. JOHANNES, H. HUNDESHAGEN, M. S. GAZZANIGA, and S. A. HILLYARD, 1994. Combined spatial and temporal imaging of brain activity during visual selective attention in humans. *Nature* 372:543–546.

HIRANO, S., Y. NAITO, H. OKAZAWA, H. KOJIMA, I. HONJO, K. ISHIZU, Y. YENOKURA, Y. NAGAHAMA, H. FUKUYAMA, and J. KONISHI, 1997. Cortical activation by monaural speech sound stimulation demonstrated by positron emission tomography. *Exp. Brain Res.* 113:75–80.

HOWARD, D., K. PATTERSON, R. WISE, W. D. BROWN, K. FRISTON, C. WEILLER, and R. FRACKOWIAK, 1992. The cortical localization of the lexicons. *Brain* 115:1769–1782.

KIPARSKI, P., 1985. Some consequences of lexical phonology. *Phonology Yearbook* 2:85–138.

LAHIRI, A., and W. MARSLEN-WILSON, 1991. The mental representation of lexical form: A phonological approach to the recognition lexicon. *Cognition* 38:245–294.

LESCH, M. F., and A. POLLATSEK, 1998. Evidence for the use of assembled phonology in accessing the meaning of printed words. *J. Exp. Psychol.: Learn. Mem. Cognit.* 24:573–592.

LEVELT, W. J. L., 1989. *Speaking: From Intention to Articulation.* Cambridge, Mass.: MIT Press.

LUND, E., P. E. SPLIID, E. ANDERSEN, and M. BOJSEN-MOLLER, 1986. Vowel perception: A neuroradiological localization of the perception of vowels in the human cortex. *Brain Lang.* 29:191–211.

MCCLELLAND, J. L., and J. L. ELMAN, 1986. The TRACE model of speech perception. *Cogn. Psychol.* 18:1–86.

MCCLELLAND, J. L., and D. E. RUMELHART, 1981. An interactive activation model of context effects in letter perception: 1. An account of the basic findings. *Psychol. Rev.* 88:375–407.

MCCONKIE, G., and K. RAYNER, 1975. The span of the effective stimulus during a fixation in reading. *Percept. Psychophys.* 17:578–586.

MCGUIRE, P. K., D. A. SILBERSWEIG, and C. D. FRITH, 1996. Functional anatomy of verbal self-monitoring. *Brain* 119:907–917.

MCQUEEN, J. M., D. NORRIS, and A. CUTLER, 1994. Competition in spoken word recognition: Spotting words in other words. *J. Exp. Psychol.: Learn. Mem. Cognit.* 20:621–638.

MARSLEN-WILSON, W., and P. WARREN, 1994. Levels of perceptual representation and process in lexical access: Words, phonemes, and features. *Psychol. Rev.* 101:653–675.

MARSLEN-WILSON, W. D., and A. WELSH, 1978. Processing interactions and lexical access during word recognition in continuous speech. *Cogn. Psychol.* 10:29–63.

MAZZIOTTA, J. C., S.-C. HUANG, M. E. PHELPS, R. E. CARSON, N. S. MACDONALD, and K. MAHONEY, 1985. A noninvasive positron computed tomography technique using oxygen-15 labeled water for the evaluation of neurobehavioral task batteries. *J. Cereb. Blood Flow Metab.* 5:70–78.

MEHLER, J., 1981. The role of syllables in speech processing: Infant and adult data. *Phil. Trans. R. Soc. Lond.* B 295:333–352.

MILLER, G. A., 1951. *Language and Communication.* New York: McGraw–Hill.

MÜLLER-PREUSS, P., and D. PLOOG, 1981. Inhibition of auditory cortical neurons during phonation. *Brain Res.* 215:61–76.

MUMMERY C. J., S. K. SCOTT, J. ASHBURNER, and R. J. S. WISE, in press. Functional neuroimaging of speech perception in six normal and two aphasic subjects. *J. Acoust. Soc. Am.*

NÄÄTÄNEN, R., 1990. The role of attention in auditory information processing as revealed by event-related potentials and other brain measures of cognitive function. *Behav. Brain Sci.* 13:201–288.

NÄÄTÄNEN, R., A. LEHTOKOSKI, M. LENNES, M. CHEOUR, M. HUOTILAINEN, A. IIVONEN, M. VAINIO, P. ALKU, R. J. ILMONIEMI, A. LUUK, J. ALLIK, J. SINKKONEN, and K. ALHO, 1997. Language-specific phoneme representations revealed by electric and magnetic brain responses. *Nature* 385:432–434.

NORRIS, D. G., 1994. Shortlist: A connectionist model of continuous speech recognition. *Cognition* 52:189–234.

NORRIS, D., J. M. MCQUEEN, and A. CUTLER, in press. Merging information in speech recognition: Feedback is never necessary. *Behav. Brain Sci.*

NORRIS, D., J. M. MCQUEEN, A. CUTLER, and S. BUTTERFIELD, 1997. The possible-word constraint in the segmentation of continuous speech. *Cogn. Psychol.* 34:191–243.

OHL, F. W., and H. SCHEICH, 1997. Orderly cortical representation of vowels based on formant interaction. *Proc. Natl. Acad. Sci. U.S.A.* 94:9440–9444.

OKAZAWA, H., Y. NAITO, Y. YONEKURA, N. SADATO, S. HIRANO, S. NISHIZAWA, Y. MAGATA, K. ISHIZU, N. TAMAKI, I. HONJO, and J. KONISHI, 1996. Cochlear implant efficiency in pre- and postlingually deaf subjects. A study with $H_2{}^{15}O$ and PET. *Brain* 119:1297–1306.

PANTEV, C., M. HOKE, K. LEHNERTZ, B. LUTKENHONER, G. FAHRENDORF, and U. STOBER, 1990. Identification of sources of brain neuronal activity with high spatiotemporal resolution through combination of neuromagnetic source localization (NMSL) and magnetic resonance imaging (MRI). *Electroencephalogr. Clin. Neurophysiol.* 75:173–184.

PATTERSON, R. D., M. H. ALLERHAND, and C. GIGUERE, 1995. Time-domain modelling of peripheral auditory processing: A modular architecture and a software platform. *J. Acoust. Soc. Am.* 98:1890–1894.

PAUS, T., D. W. PERRY, R. J. ZATORRE, K. J. WORSLEY, and A. C. EVANS, 1996. Modulation of cerebral blood flow in the human auditory cortex during speech: Role of motor-to-sensory discharges. *Eur. J. Neurosci.* 8:2236–2246.

PEREA, M., and M. CARREIRAS, 1988. Effects of syllable frequency and syllable neighborhood frequency in visual word recognition. *J. Exp. Psychol.: Hum. Perf. Cognit.* 24:134–144.

PETERSEN, S. E., P. T. FOX, M. I. POSNER, M. MINTUN, and M. E. RAICHLE, 1988. Positron emission tomographic studies of the cortical anatomy of single-word processing. *Nature* 331:585–589.

PETERSEN, S. E., P. T. FOX, M. I. POSNER, M. MINTUN, and M. E. RAICHLE, 1989. Positron emission tomography studies of the processing of single worlds. *J. Cogn. Neurosci.* 1:153–170.

PETERSEN, S. E., P. T. FOX, A. Z. SNYDER, and M. E. RAICHLE, 1990. Activation of extrastriate and frontal cortical areas by words and word-like stimuli. *Science* 249:1041–1044.

PETERSON, G. E., and H. L. BARNEY, 1952. Control methods used in the study of vowels. *J. Acoust. Soc. Am.* 24:175–184.

PLOMP, R., and A. M. MIMPEN, 1979. Speech-reception threshold for sentences as a function of age and noise. *J. Acoust. Soc. Am.* 66:1333–1342.

POEPPEL, D., 1996. A critical review of PET studies of phonological processing. *Brain Lang.* 55:317–351.

POEPPEL, D., E. YELLIN, C. PHILLIPS, T. P. L. ROBERTS, H. A. ROWLEY, K. WEXLER, and A. MARANTZ, 1996. Task-induced asymmetry of the auditory evoked M100 neuromagnetic field elicited by speech sounds. *Cogn. Brain Res.* 4:231–242.

POEPPEL, D., C. PHILLIPS, E. YELLIN, H. A. ROWLEY, T. P. ROBERTS, and A. MARANTZ, 1997. Processing of vowels in supratemporal auditory cortex. *Neurosci. Lett.* 221:145–148.

POLSTER, M. R., and S. B. ROSE, 1998. Disorders of auditory processing: Evidence for modularity in audition. *Cortex* 34:47–65.

PRAAMSTRA, P., P. HAGOORT, B. MAASEN, and T. CRUL, 1991. Word deafness and auditory cortical function. A case history and hypothesis. *Brain* 114:1197–1225.

PRICE, C. J., C. J. MOORE, and R. S. J. FRACKOWIAK, 1996. The effect of varying stimulus rate and duration on brain activity during reading. *Neuroimage* 3:40–52.

PRICE, C. J., R. J. S. WISE, and R. S. J. FRACKOWIAK, 1996. Demonstrating the implicit processing of visually presented words and pseudowords. *Cereb. Cortex* 6:62–70.

PRICE, C., R. WISE, S. RAMSAY, K. FRISTON, D. HOWARD, K. PATTERSON, and R. FRACKOWIAK, 1992. Regional response differences within the human auditory cortex when listening to words. *Neurosci. Lett.* 146:179–182.

PRICE, C., R. J. S. WISE, E. A. WARBURTON, C. J. MOORE, D. HOWARD, K. PATTERSON, R. S. J. FRACKOWIAK, and K. J. FRISTON 1996. Hearing and saying. The functional neuroanatomy of auditory word processing. *Brain* 119:919–931.

PULLEYBLANK, D., 1983. *Tone in Lexical Phonology.* Doctoral dissertation, Cambridge, Mass.: MIT.

RAYNER, K., and J. H. BERTERA, 1979. Reading without a fovea. *Science* 206:468–469.

RAAP, B. C., 1992. The nature of sublexical orthographic organization: The bigram-trough hypothesis examined. *J. Mem. Lang.* 31:33–53.

READ, C. A., Y. ZHANG, H. NIE, and B. DING, 1986. The ability to manipulate speech sounds depends on knowing alphabetic reading. *Cognition* 24:31–44.

RUMSEY, J. M., B. HORWITZ, B. C. DONOHUE, K. NACE, J. M. MAISOG, and P. ANDREASON, 1997. Phonological and orthographic components of word recognition. A PET-rCBF study. *Brain* 120:739–759.

SEIDENBERG, M. S., and M. K. TANENHAUS, 1979. Orthographic effects on rhyming. *J. Exp. Psychol.: Hum. Learn. Mem.* 5:546–554.

SINEX, D. G., L. P. MCDONALD, and J. B. MOTT, 1991. Neural correlates of nonmonotonic temporal acuity for voice onset time. *J. Acoust. Soc. Am.* 90:2441–2449.

STEINSCHNEIDER, M., C. E. SCHROEDER, J. C. AREZZO, and H. G. VAUGHAN JR, 1995. Physiologic correlates of the voice onset time boundary in primary auditory cortex (A1) of the awake monkey: Temporal response patterns. *Brain Lang.* 48:326–340.

STUDDERT-KENNEDY, M., and D. SHANKWEILER, 1970. Hemispheric specialization for speech perception. *J. Acoust. Soc. Am.* 48:579–594.

THULBORN, K. R., 1998. A BOLD move for fMRI. *Nature Med.* 4:155–156.

VAN ORDEN, G. C., 1987. A ROWS is a ROWS: Spelling, sound, and reading. *Mem. Cognit.* 15:181–198.

WISE, R., F. CHOLLET, U. HADAR, K. FRISTON, E. HOFFNER, and R. FRACKOWIAK, 1991. Distribution of cortical neural networks involved in word comprehension and word retrieval. *Brain* 114:1803–1817.

WOLDORFF, M. G., C. C. GALLEN, S. A. HAMPSON, S. A. HILLYARD, C. PANTEV, D. SOBEL, and F. E. BLOOM, 1993. Modulation of early sensory processing in human auditory cortex during auditory selective attention. *Proc. Natl. Acad. Sci. U.S.A.* 90:8722–8726.

WOLDORFF, M. G., S. A. HACKLEY, and S. A. HILLYARD, 1991. The effects of channel-selective attention on the mismatch negativity wave elicited by deviant tones. *Psychophysiology* 28:30–42.

WOLDORFF, M. G., and S. A. HILLYARD, 1991. Modulation of early auditory processing during selective listening to rapidly presented tones. *Electroencephalogr. Clin. Neurophysiol.* 79:170–191.

ZATORRE, R. J., A. C. EVANS, E. MEYER, and A. GJEDDE, 1992. Lateralization of phonetic and pitch discrimination in speech processing. *Science* 256:846–849.

ZATORRE, R. J., E. MEYER, A. GJEDDE, and A. C. EVANS, 1996. PET studies of phonetic processing of speech: Review, replication, and reanalysis. *Cereb. Cortex* 6:21–30.

ZIHL, J., 1995. Eye movement patterns in hemianopic dyslexia. *Brain* 118:891–912.

61 Postlexical Integration Processes in Language Comprehension: Evidence from Brain-Imaging Research

COLIN M. BROWN, PETER HAGOORT, AND MARTA KUTAS

ABSTRACT Language comprehension requires the activation, coordination, and integration of different kinds of linguistic knowledge. This chapter focuses on the processing of syntactic and semantic information during sentence comprehension, and reviews research using event-related brain potentials (ERPs), positron emission tomography (PET), and functional magnetic resonance imaging (fMRI). The ERP data provide evidence for a number of qualitatively distinct components that can be linked to distinct aspects of language understanding. In particular, the separation of meaning and structure in language is associated with different ERP profiles, providing a basic neurobiological constraint for models of comprehension. PET and fMRI research on sentence-level processing is at present quite limited. The data clearly implicate the left perisylvian area as critical for syntactic processing, as well as for aspects of higher-order semantic processing. The emerging picture indicates that sets of areas need to be distinguished, each with its own relative specialization.

In this chapter we discuss evidence from cognitive neuroscience research on sentence comprehension, focusing on syntactic and semantic integration processes. The integration of information is a central feature of such higher cognitive functions as language, where we are obliged to deal with a steady stream of a multitude of information types. Understanding a written or spoken sentence requires bringing together different kinds of linguistic and nonlinguistic knowledge, each of which provides an essential ingredient for comprehension. One of the core tasks that faces us, then, is to construct an integrated representation. For example, if a listener is to understand an utterance, then at least the following processes need to be successfully completed: (a) recognition of the signal as speech (as opposed to some other kind of noise), (b) segmentation of the signal into constituent parts, (c) access to the mental lexicon based on

the products of the segmentation process, (d) selection of the appropriate word from within a lexicon containing some 30,000 or more entries, (e) construction of the appropriate grammatical structure for the utterance up to and including the word last processed, and (f) ascertaining the semantic relations among the words in the sentence. Each of these processes requires the activation of different kinds of knowledge. For example, segmentation involves phonological knowledge, which is largely separate from, for instance, the knowledge involved in grammatical analysis. But knowledge bases like phonology, word meaning, and grammar do not, on their own, yield a meaningful message. While there is no question that integration of these (and other) sources of information is a prerequisite for understanding, considerable controversy surrounds the details.

Which sources of knowledge actually need to be distinguished? Is the system organized into modules, each operating within a representational subdomain and dealing with a specific subprocess of comprehension? Or are the representational distinctions less marked or even absent? What is the temporal processing nature of comprehension? Does understanding proceed via a fixed temporal sequence, with limited crosstalk between processing stages and representations? Or is comprehension the result of more or less continuous interaction among many sources of linguistic and nonlinguistic knowledge? These questions, which are among the most persistent in language research, are now gaining the attention of cognitive neuroscientists. This is an emerging field, with a short history. Nevertheless, progress has been made, and we present a few specific examples in this chapter.

A cognitive neuroscience approach to language might contribute to language research in several ways. Neurobiological data can, in principle, provide evidence on the representational levels that are postulated by different language models–semantic, syntactic, and so on (see the section on PET/fMRI). Neurobiological data can

COLIN M. BROWN and PETER HAGOORT Neurocognition of Language Processing Research Group, Max Planck Institute for Psycholinguistics, Nijmegen, The Netherlands
MARTA KUTAS Department of Cognitive Science, University of California, San Diego, Calif.

reveal the temporal dynamics of comprehension, crucial for investigating the different claims of sequential and interactive processing models (see the sections on the N400 and the P600/SPS). And, by comparing brain activity within and between cognitive domains, neurobiological data can also speak to the domain-specificity of language. It is, for example, a matter of debate whether language utilizes a dedicated working-memory system or a more general system that subserves other cognitive functions as well (see the section on slow brain-potential shifts).

Postlexical syntactic and semantic integration processes

In this chapter we focus specifically on what we refer to as postlexical syntactic and semantic processes. We do not discuss the processes that precede lexical selection (see Norris and Wise, chapter 60, for this subject), but rather concern ourselves with processes that follow word recognition. Once a word has been selected within the mental lexicon, the information associated with this word needs to be integrated into the message-level representation that is the end product of comprehension. If this integration is to be successful, both syntactic and semantic analyses need to be performed.

At the level of syntax, the sentence needs to be parsed into its constituents, and the syntactic dependencies among constituents need to be specified (e.g., What is the subject of the sentence? Which verbs are linked with which nouns?). At the level of semantics, the meaning of an individual word needs to be merged with the representation that is being built up of the overall meaning of the sentence, such that thematic roles like agent, theme, and patient can be ascertained (e.g., Who is doing what to whom?). These syntactic and semantic processes lie at the core of language comprehension. Although words are indispensable bridges to understanding, it is only in the realm of sentences (and beyond in discourses) that they achieve their full potential to convey rich and varied messages.

The field of language research lacks an articulated model of how we achieve (mutual) understanding. This lack is not too surprising when we consider the problems that confront us in devising a theory of meaning for natural languages, let alone the difficulties attendant on combining such a representational theory with a processing model that delineates the comprehension process at the millisecond level. However understandable, the lack of an overall model has meant that the processes involved in meaning integration at the sentential level have received scant experimental attention. The one area in which quite specific models of the relationship between semantic representations and on-line language processing have been proposed is the area of parsing research. Here, a major concern has been to assess the influence of semantic representations on the syntactic analysis of sentences, with a particular focus on the moments at which integration between meaning and structure occurs (cf. Frazier, 1987; Tanenhaus and Trueswell, 1995). Research in this area has concentrated on the on-line resolution of sentential-syntactic ambiguity (e.g., "The woman sees the man with the binoculars." Who is holding the binoculars?). The resolution of this kind of ambiguity speaks to the separability of syntax and semantics, as well as to the issue of sequential or interactive processing. The prevailing models in the literature can be broadly separated into autonomist and interactive accounts.

In *autonomous approaches*, a separate syntactic knowledge base is used to build up a representation of the syntactic structure of a sentence. The prototypical example of this approach is embodied in the Garden-Path model (Frazier, 1987), which postulates that an intermediate level of syntactic representation is a necessary and obligatory step during sentence processing. This model stipulates that nonsyntactic sources of information (e.g., message-level semantics) cannot affect the parser's initial syntactic analysis (see also Frazier and Clifton, 1996; Friederici and Mecklinger, 1996). Such sources come into play only after a first parse has been delivered. When confronted with a sentential-syntactic ambiguity, the Garden-Path model posits principles of economy, on the basis of which the syntactically least complex analysis of the alternative structures is chosen at the moment the ambiguity arises. If the chosen analysis subsequently leads to interpretive problems, this triggers a syntactic reanalysis.

In the most radical *interactionist approach*, there are no intermediate syntactic representations. Instead, undifferentiated representational networks are posited, in which syntactic and semantic information emerge as combined constraints on a single, unified representation (e.g., Bates et al., 1982; Elman, 1990; McClelland, St. John, and Taraban, 1989). In terms of the processing nature of the system, comprehension is described as a fully interactive process, in which all sources of information influence the ongoing analysis as they become available.

A third class of models sits somewhere in between the autonomous and radical interactionist approaches. In these so-called *constraint-satisfaction models*, lexically represented information (such as the animacy of a noun or the transitivity of a verb) but also statistical information about the frequency of occurrence of a word or of syntactic constructions play a central role (cf. MacDonald, Pearlmutter, and Seidenberg, 1994; Spivey-Knowlton and Sedivy, 1995). The approach emphasizes the interactive nature of comprehension, but does not exclude the existence of separate representational levels as a matter of principle. Comprehension is seen as a competition among alternatives (e.g., multiple parses), based on both syntactic and nonsyntactic information. In this approach, as in the more radical interactive approach, sentential-syntactic ambiguities are resolved by the immediate interaction of lexical-syntactic and lexical-semantic information, in combination with statistical information about the relative frequency of occurrence of particular syntactic structures, and any available discourse information, without appealing to an initial syntax-based parsing stage or a separate revision stage (cf. Tanenhaus and Trueswell, 1995).

Although we have discussed these different models in the light of sentential-syntactic ambiguity resolution, their architectural and processing assumptions hold for the full domain of sentence and discourse processing. Clearly, the representational and processing assumptions underlying autonomous and (fully) interactive models have very different implications for an account of language comprehension. We will return to these issues after giving an overview of results from the brain-imaging literature on syntactic and semantic processes during sentence processing.

Before discussing the imaging data, a few brief comments on the sensitivity and relevance for language research of different brain-imaging methods are called for. The common goal in cognitive neuroscience is to develop a model in which the cognitive and neural approaches are combined, providing a detailed answer to the very general question of where and when in the brain what happens. Methods like event-related brain potentials (ERPs), positron emission tomography (PET), and functional magnetic resonance imaging (fMRI) are not equally revealing or relevant in this respect. In terms of the temporal dynamics of comprehension, only ERPs (and their magnetic counterparts from magnetoencephalography, MEG) can provide the required millisecond resolution (although recent developments in noninvasive optical imaging indicate that near-infrared measurements might approach millisecond resolution; cf. Gratton, Fabiani, and Corballis, 1997). In contrast, the main power of PET and fMRI lies in the localization of brain areas involved in language processing (although recent advances in neuronal source-localization procedures with ERP measurements are making this technique more relevant for localizational issues; cf. Kutas, Federmeier, and Sereno, 1999). Recent analytic developments in PET and fMRI research further indicate that information on effective connectivity in the brain (i.e., the influence that one neuronal system exerts over an-

other) might begin to constrain our models of the language system (cf. Büchel, Frith, and Friston, 1999; Friston, Frith, and Frackowiak, 1993). However, localization as such does not reveal the nature of the activated representations: The hemodynamic response is a quantitative measure that does not of itself deliver information on the nature of the representations involved. The measure is maximally informative when separate brain loci can be linked, via appropriately constraining experimental conditions, with separate representations and processes. A similar situation holds for the ERP method: The polarity and scalp topography of ERP waveforms can, in principle, yield qualitatively different effects for qualitatively different representations and/or processes, but only appropriately operationalized manipulations will make such effects interpretable (cf. Brown and Hagoort, 1999; Osterhout and Holcomb, 1995). In short, whatever the brain-imaging technique being used, the value of the data critically depends on its relation to an articulated cognitive-functional model.

Cognitive neuroscience investigations of postlexical integration

EVENT-RELATED BRAIN POTENTIAL MANIFESTATIONS OF SENTENCE PROCESSING Space limitations rule out an introduction on the neurophysiology and signal-analysis techniques of event-related brain potentials (see Picton, Lins, and Scherg, 1995, for a recent review). It is, however, important to bear in mind that, owing to the signal-to-noise ratio of the EEG signal, one cannot obtain a reliable ERP waveform in a standard language experiment without averaging over at least 20–30 different tokens within an experimental condition. Thus, when we speak of the ERP elicited by a particular word in a particular condition, we mean the electrophysiological activity averaged over different tokens of the same type.

Within the realm of sentence processing, four different ERP profiles have been related to aspects of syntactic and semantic processing: (1) A transient negativity over left-anterior electrode sites (labeled the left-anterior negativity, LAN) that develops in the period roughly 200–500 ms after word onset. The LAN has been related not only to the activation and processing of syntactic word-category information, but also to more general processes of working memory. (2) A transient bilateral negativity, labeled the N400, that develops between 200 and 600 ms after word onset; the N400 has been related to semantic processing. (3) A transient bilateral positivity that develops in the period between 500 and 700 ms. Variously labeled the syntactic positive shift (SPS) or the P600, this positivity has been related to syntactic processing. (4) A slow positive shift over the front of the head, accumulating across the span of a sentence, that has been related to the construction of a representation of the overall meaning of a sentence. Let us discuss each of these ERP effects in turn.

Left-anterior negativities The LAN is a relative newcomer to the set of language-related ERP effects. Both its exact electrophysiological signature and its functional nature are still under scrutiny. Some researchers have suggested that the LAN is related to early parsing processes, reflecting the assignment of an initial phrase structure based on syntactic word-category information (Friederici, 1995; Friederici, Hahne, and Mecklinger, 1996). Other researchers propose that a LAN is a reflection of working-memory processes during language comprehension, related to the activity of holding a word in memory until it can be assigned its grammatical role in a sentence (Kluender and Kutas, 1993a,b; Kutas and King, 1995). Clearly more research is called for to decide between these quite separate views. One of the pending issues is the uniformity of the LAN. There is variability in both its topography and latency. It is possible, therefore, that more than one LAN exists (some researchers distinguish between an early left-anterior negativity and a later left-anterior negativity; cf. Friederici, 1995), with different functional interpretations.

An example of a left-anterior negativity is given in figure 61.1 (from work by Kluender and Münte, 1999), in which a preferred and a nonpreferred version (at least in standard Northern German dialects) of a so-called wh-movement is contrasted. The particular wh-movement under investigation is the displacement of the direct object of a verb that occurs when a declarative sentence is transformed into a question-sentence–e.g., the transformation of the declarative "The cautious physicist has stored the data on a diskette" into the question-sentence "What has the cautious physicist stored on a diskette?" In the declarative sentence, *the data* is the direct object of its immediately preceding verb. In the question-sentence, *the data* has been replaced by the interrogative pronoun *what*, which, moreover, has been moved to the beginning of the sentence. (This is, therefore, an instance of wh-movement, where *wh* is a shorthand notation for the category of interrogative words, such as *what, who, which*, etc.) Although *the data* no longer appears in the question-sentence, syntactically speaking, the wh-element *what* is extracted from the direct-object position to sentence-initial position, leaving a trace after *stored* (i.e., "What$_i$ has the cautious physicist stored ____$_i$ on a diskette?"). This trace is presumed to co-index the empty syntactic position after *stored* in the question-sentence with the pronoun *what* in sentence-initial position.

The comparison in the figure concerns a preferred and a nonpreferred wh-movement in standard Northern German dialect. The nonpreferred movement elicited a focal left-anterior negativity. This result is particularly interesting because it adds to the set of syntactic phenomena that have been associated with left-anterior negativities. The effect that Kluender and Münte obtained is incompatible with an interpretation in terms of a violation of expected syntactic word-category information: The word that elicits the LAN effect does not violate category constraints. One hypothesis is that the effect is reflecting a disruption in the primary parsing process of working out the co-index relationship that is indicated by the first part of the wh-question, with a concomitant sudden increase in working-memory load.

The N400 component Of all the ERP effects that have been related to language, the N400 is the most firmly established component (Kutas and Hillyard, 1980). This negative-polarity potential with a maximal amplitude at approximately 400 ms after stimulation onset is, as a rule, elicited by any meaningful word (especially nouns, verbs, and adjectives, sometimes referred to as open-class words) presented either in isolation, in word-word contexts (e.g., priming paradigms) or in sentences. The effect starts some 200–250 ms after word onset and can last for some 200–300 ms; it is widely distributed over the scalp, with a tendency toward greater amplitudes over more central and posterior electrode sites. Although originally demonstrated for sentence-final words that violate the semantic constraints of sentences (e.g., "The woman spread her toast with hypotheses"), more than 15 years of research has demonstrated that this component is not a simple incongruity detector; rather, it is a sensitive manifestation of semantic processing during on-line comprehension (for reviews see Kutas and Van Petten, 1994; Osterhout and Holcomb, 1995). An example of this sensitivity is given in figure 61.2, which shows the ERP waveform elicited by two visually presented words that differ in the extent of their semantic fit with preceding discourse. In this experiment subjects read sentences for comprehension, without having to perform any extraneous task. (This is an advantage of the ERP method compared to the reaction-time method, where one must always consider additional processes, such as lexical decision, due to the external task.) Subjects were presented with a short discourse followed by one of two sentences containing a critical word. The critical word was entirely acceptable within the restricted context of the final sentence itself, but in one case the critical word did not match the message-level meaning set up by the preceding discourse. For example:

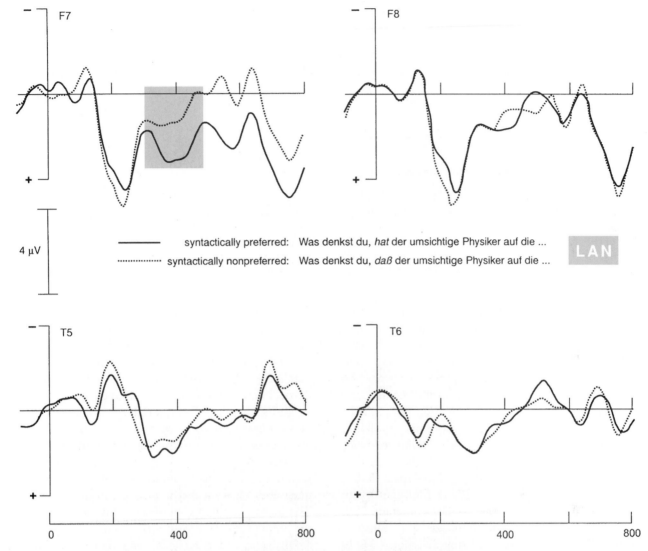

FIGURE 61.1 Grammatical movement effect. The solid line represents the average ERP waveform for a grammatically preferred continuation. The dotted line represents the average waveform for the grammatically nonpreferred continuation. Preferred sentence (critical word in italics, to which the ERP waveform is time-locked): "Was denkst du, *hat* der umsichtige Physiker auf die Diskette gespeichert?" (literally translated: "What think you, has the cautious physicist on the disk stored?"). Nonpreferred sentence: "Was denkst du, *daß* der umsichtige Physiker auf die Diskette gespeichert hat?" (literal translation: "What think you, that the cautious physicist on the disk stored has?"). In wh-question sentences in Northern German dialects, the complementizer *daß* at the beginning of an embedded clause is less preferred in combination with the movement of direct objects to sentence-initial position. Four electrode positions are shown, two over left- and right-anterior sites, and two over left and right temporal sites. Negative polarity is plotted upward, in microvolts. (Data from Kluender and Münte, 1999.)

Discourse: "As agreed upon, Jane was to wake her sister and her brother at 5 o'clock. But the sister had already washed herself, and the brother had even got dressed."
Normal continuation: "Jane told the brother that he was exceptionally *quick* today."
Anomalous continuation: "Jane told the brother that he was exceptionally *slow* today."

As figure 61.2 shows, both words (*quick, slow*) elicit the N400 component, with an onset at about 200–250 ms. This underscores the general observation that each meaningful word in a sentence elicits an N400. The difference in the match between the meaning of the critical word and the meaning of the discourse emerges as a difference in the overall amplitude of the N400, with the mismatching word eliciting the largest amplitude. The amplitude difference is referred to as the N400 effect. Clearly, this N400 effect can emanate only from an attempt to integrate the meaning of the critical word within the discourse. This testifies both to the semantic sensitivity of the N400 and to the integrational processes

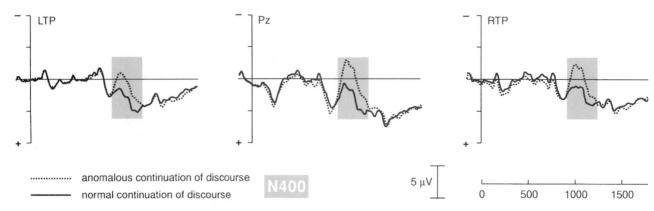

FIGURE 61.2   Discourse-semantic N400 effect. The solid line represents the average ERP waveform for the normal continuation of the discourse, and the dotted line for the anomalous continuation. In the figure, the potential elicited by the critical word starts at 600 ms, and is preceded and followed by the po-tentials elicited by the word before and after the critical word. Three electrode positions are shown: one over the posterior midline of the scalp (Pz), and one each on left and right lateral temporal-posterior sites (LTP and RTP). (Data from Van Berkum, Hagoort, and Brown, 1999.)

that are manifest in modulations of N400 amplitude (see also St. George, Mannes, and Hoffman, 1994, 1997). Note, moreover, that the onset latency of the effect reveals that these high-level processes are already operative within some 200 ms of the word's occurrence. The very early moment at which high-level discourse information is modulating the comprehension process is less readily compatible with strictly sequential models, in which lower-level analyses have to be completed before higher levels of information can affect comprehension.

For present purposes a synopsis of five main findings on the N400 suffices to exemplify its relevance for the study of postlexical processes: (1) The amplitude of the N400 is inversely related to the cloze probability of a word in sentence context. The better the semantic fit between a word and its context, the smaller the amplitude of the N400. (2) This inverse relationship holds for single-word, sentence, and discourse contexts. (3) The amplitude of the N400 varies with word position. Open-class words at the beginning of a sentence elicit larger negativities than open-class words in later positions. This most likely reflects the incremental impact of semantic constraints throughout the sentence. (4) The elicitation of the N400 is independent of input modality—naturally produced connected speech, sign language, or slow and fast visual stimulation. (5) Grammatical processes typically do not directly elicit larger N400s, although difficulty in grammatical processing subsequently gives rise to N400 activity in some cases.

On the basis of these findings it is by now widely accepted that, within the domain of language comprehension, the elicitation of the N400 and the modulations in N400 amplitude are indicative of the involvement of semantic representations and of differential semantic processing during on-line language comprehension. Note

that the claim is not that the N400 is a language-specific component (i.e., modulated solely by language-related factors); rather, in the context of language processing, N400 amplitude variation is linked to lexical and message-level semantic information. In terms of the functional interpretation of the N400 effect, it has been suggested that the effect is a reflection of lexical integration processes. After a word has been activated in the mental lexicon, its meaning has to be integrated into a message-level conceptual representation of the context within it occurs. The hypothesis is that it is this meaning-integration process that is manifest in the N400 effect. The more difficult the integration process is, the larger the amplitude of the N400 (Brown and Hagoort, 1993, 1999; Kutas and King, 1995; Osterhout and Holcomb, 1992).

The P600, or syntactic positive shift (SPS)   The P600/SPS, which is of more recent origin, was first reported as a response to syntactic violations in sentences (Hagoort, Brown, and Groothusen, 1993; Osterhout and Holcomb, 1992). For example, in the sentence "The spoilt child throw the toy on the ground," the grammatical number marking on the verb *throw* does not agree with the fact that the grammatical subject of the sentence (i.e., the *spoilt child*) is singular. This kind of agreement error elicits a positive shift that starts at approximately 500 ms after the violating word (in this case *throw*) has been presented. The shift can last for more than 300 ms, and is widely distributed over the scalp, with posterior maxima. Since its discovery in the early nineties, the P600/SPS has been observed in a wide variety of syntactic phenomena (see Osterhout, McLaughlin, and Bersick, 1997, for a recent overview). In the realm of violations, it has been shown that the P600/SPS is elicited by violations of

(a) constraints on the movement of sentence constituents (e.g., "What was a proof *of* criticized by the scientist?"), (b) phrase structure rules (e.g., "The man was upset by the emotional rather *response* of his employer"), (c) verb subcategorization (e.g., "The broker persuaded *to* sell the stock"), (d) subject–verb number agreement (as in the above example), (e) reflexive-antecedent gender agreement (e.g., "The man congratulated *herself* on the promotion"), and (f) reflexive-antecedent number agreement (e.g., "The guests helped *himself* to the food").

It should be noted that these violations involve very different aspects of grammar. The fact that in each instance a P600/SPS is elicited points toward the syntactic sensitivity of the component. At the same time the heterogeneity of syntactic phenomena associated with the P600/SPS raises questions about exactly what the component is reflecting about the language process. We will return to this issue after presenting further evidence on the sensitivity of the P600/SPS.

The P600/SPS is not restricted to the visual modality, but is also observed for naturally produced connected speech (Friederici, Pfeifer, and Hahne, 1993; Hagoort and Brown, in press; Osterhout and Holcomb, 1993). Furthermore, it has been demonstrated that the P600/SPS is not a mere violation detector. In fact, it can be used to investigate quite subtle aspects of parsing, such as are involved in the resolution of sentential-syntactic ambiguity. For example, in the written sentence "The sheriff saw the cowboy and the Indian spotted the horse in the canyon," the sentence is syntactically ambiguous until the verb *spotted*. The ambiguity is between a conjoined noun-phrase reading of *the cowboy and the Indian*, and a reading in which *the Indian* is the subject of a second clause, thereby signaling a sentence conjunction. At the verb *spotted* this ambiguity is resolved in favor of the second-clause reading. It has been suggested in the parsing literature that the conjoined noun-phrase analysis results in a less complex syntactic structure than the sentence-conjunction analysis. Furthermore, as we noted above, it has been claimed that the parser operates economically, such that less complex syntactic analyses are preferred over more complex ones. This would imply that during the reading of the ambiguous example sentence, subjects would experience difficulty in parsing the sentence at the verb *spotted*, despite the fact that in terms of its meaning and in terms of the grammatical constraints of the language, the sentence is perfectly in order. This difficulty should become apparent in a comparison with the same sequence of words in which the ambiguity does not arise, and in which the sentence-conjunction reading is the only option, due to the inclusion of an appropriately placed comma: "The sheriff saw the cowboy, and the Indian spotted the

horse in the canyon." Note that this particular disambiguation obviously only holds for the visual modality.

When we compare the waveform elicited by the critical written verb *spotted* in the ambiguous sentence to that elicited by the same verb in the control sentence, a P600/SPS is seen in the ambiguous sentence. This is shown in figure 61.3, which depicts the ERP waveform, over four representative electrode sites, for the verb *spotted* in the ambiguous and nonambiguous sentence, preceded and followed by one word. This finding demonstrates that the P600/SPS does not depend on grammatical violations for its elicitation. The component can reflect on-line sentence-processing operations related to the resolution of sentential-syntactic ambiguity. Interestingly, the more frontal scalp distribution of the P600/SPS to sentential-syntactic ambiguity resolution differs from the predominantly posterior distribution elicited by syntactic violations. It might be the case, therefore, that there is more than one positive shift under the general heading of P600/SPS (cf. Brown and Hagoort, 1998; Hagoort and Brown, in press).

Given the sensitivity of the P600/SPS to processes related to the resolution of syntactic ambiguity, it is a good tool with which to investigate the impact of lexical-semantic and higher-order (e.g., discourse) meaning representations on parsing. The impact of semantic information during sentence processing is one of the issues that we raised earlier on the processing nature of the parser. Namely, can nonsyntactic knowledge immediately contribute to sentential-syntactic analysis, or is a first-pass structural analysis performed on the basis of only syntactic knowledge? So, in the written sentence "The helmsman repairs the mainsail and the skipper varnishes the mast after the storm," the same syntactic ambiguity is present as in the cowboy-and-Indian example. But since the meaning of the verb *repair* is compatible only with inanimate objects, a noun-phrase conjunction of *the mainsail and the skipper* can be excluded on semantic grounds (i.e., the helmsman cannot repair the skipper). Nevertheless, parsing models claiming that the first-pass structural assignment is based solely on syntactic information maintain that the conjoined noun-phrase analysis will be initially considered, and preferred over a sentence-conjunction analysis. This claim has been assessed by investigating the ERP waveform to the verb *repair* in the ambiguous sentence and a nonambiguous control (again realized by appropriately inserting a comma, in this case after *the mainsail*). The results were clear: No difference was seen between the unpunctuated ambiguous and the punctuated nonambiguous sentences (cf. Hagoort, Brown, Vonk, and Hoeks, 1999). This indicates that the semantic information carried by the verb *was* immediately used to

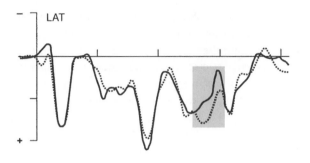

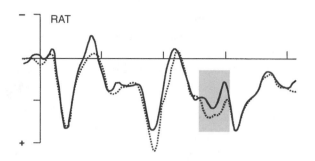

2 µV | ———— syntactically unambiguous: The sheriff saw the cowboy, and the indian spotted the horse in the canyon.
| ········ syntactically ambiguous: The sheriff saw the cowboy and the indian spotted the horse in the canyon.

SPS

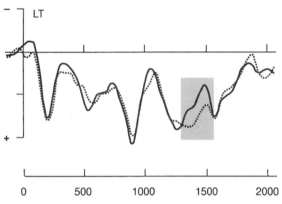

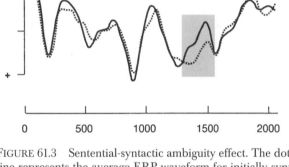

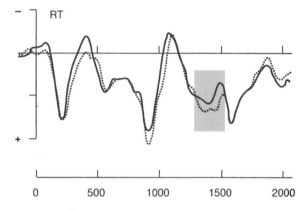

FIGURE 61.3 Sentential-syntactic ambiguity effect. The dotted line represents the average ERP waveform for initially syntactically ambiguous sentences. At the point of disambiguation (at 686 ms) the sentence continued with a grammatically correct but nonpreferred reading. The solid line represents the control condition, in which unambiguous versions of the same nonpreferred structures were presented. In the figure, the critical word is preceded and followed by one word. The region within which the P600/SPS developed is shaded. Four electrode positions are shown, two over left- and right-anterior temporal sites, and two over left and right temporal sites. (From Brown and Hagoort, 1999. © 1999 Cambridge University Press.)

constrain the ongoing analysis, and thus argues against models that propose an autonomous first-pass structural analysis.

The functional interpretation of the P600/SPS has not yet been fully clarified. Some researchers claim that the late positivity is a member of the P300 family–namely, the so-called P3b component (Coulson, King, and Kutas, 1998; Gunter, Stowe, and Mulder, 1997; but see Osterhout et al., 1996). Other researchers have suggested that the P600/SPS is a reflection of specifically grammatical processing, related to (re)analysis processes that occur whenever the parser is confronted with a failed or nonpreferred syntactic analysis (Friederici and Mecklinger, 1996; Hagoort, Brown, and Groothusen, 1993; Osterhout, 1994; Münte, Matzke, and Johannes, 1997). Note that this position does not necessarily entail any commitment to the language specificity of the component. Rather, the claim advanced by Hagoort, Brown, and Groothusen (1993) and Osterhout (1994) is

that, within the domain of sentence processing, the P600/SPS is a manifestation of processes that can be directly linked to the grammatical properties of language (cf. Osterhout et al., 1996; Osterhaut and Hagoort, 1999).

The issue of the functional characterization of the P600/SPS clearly stands to benefit from other areas of brain-imaging research. In particular, localizational techniques such as PET and fMRI could provide crucial information on the commonalities and divergences in the neural circuitry underlying the P600/SPS and the P300.

Despite our still incomplete understanding of the functional nature of the P600/SPS, one important fact already stands out–namely, this component is electrophysiologically distinct from the N400, implying at least a partial separation in the neural tissue that underlies the two components. These electrophysiological findings are therefore directly relevant for the question

Good comprehenders

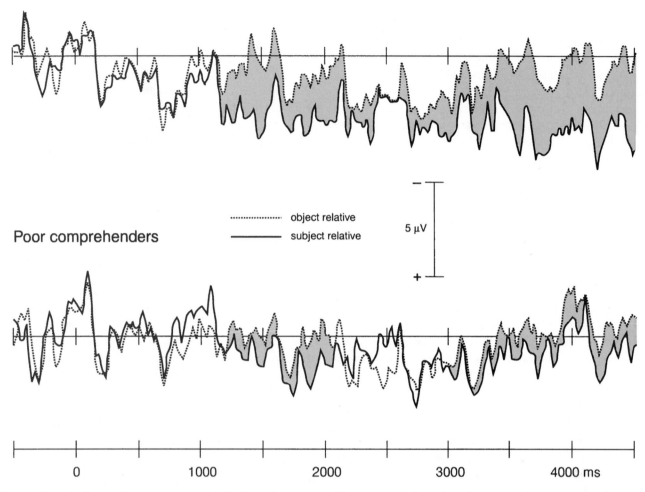

Poor comprehenders

.... object relative
——————— subject relative

5 μV

| | | | | | | | | |
0   1000   2000   3000   4000 ms

FIGURE 61.4 Differential comprehension skill effect. Average ERP waveforms recorded at one left-frontal electrode site for object-relative (dotted line) and subject-relative (solid line) sentences, for a group of 12 good and 12 poor comprehenders. Waveforms are aligned on the first word of each sentence type. The shaded regions indicate areas of statistically significant difference between the two sentence types. (From King and Kutas, 1995. ©1995 MIT Press.)

of the possible separation in the brain of syntactic and semantic knowledge. Sentence-processing models that conflate the processing and/or representational distinctions between syntax and semantics (e.g., McClelland, St. John, and Taraban, 1989) cannot account for these findings.

Slow shifts Language processing beyond the level of the individual word is revealed in ERPs averaged across clauses and sentences (see Kutas and King, 1995). These slow potentials show systematic variation in a variety of sentence types, none of which has to contain any violation. Kutas and King have identified several such slow potentials with different distributions over the left and right side of the head. Of particular relevance is their finding of an ultraslow frontal positivity which has been hypothesized to reflect the linking of

information in working and long-term memory during the creation of a message-level representation of a sentence.

An example of such a slow frontal-positivity from the work of King and Kutas (1995) is shown in figure 61.4. This effect was elicited by the relative processing difficulty of so-called object-relative sentences, compared to subject-relative sentences. In an object-relative sentence, e.g., "The reporter who the senator harshly attacked admitted the error," the subject of the main clause (*The reporter*) is the object of the relative-clause verb (*attacked*). Such sentences have consistently been shown to be much harder to process than subject-relative sentences, where the subject of the main clause is also the subject of the relative clause (e.g., "The reporter who harshly attacked the senator admitted the error"). This processing difficulty is attributed to the greater working-memory demands of object-relative sentences, where information has to be maintained in memory over longer stretches of time than for subject-relative sentences.

The figure shows separate pairs of waveforms for two groups of subjects–those with high language comprehension scores and those with low scores. This separation in two groups of subjects is informative because differences in comprehension performance have been linked to differences in working-memory capacity (e.g., King and Just, 1991). Two aspects are particularly noteworthy in these data. First, the waveforms for the object-relative sentences diverge from the slow-frontal positive shift for the subject-relative sentences at the first possible moment of working-memory load difference, i.e., when the second noun-phrase (*the senator*) had to be added to working memory. Second, there are substantial processing differences as a function of comprehension skill and hence, by hypothesis, of working-memory capacity. The slow positivity is present only in the good comprehenders, for whom the increased memory demands of the object-relative sentences emerge as a negative-going deflection from the slow positivity that is characteristic of the subject-relative sentences. In contrast, the poor comprehenders show basically the same ERP profile for the two types of sentences, both being as negative as the waveform elicited by the object-relative sentences in the good comprehenders. It would seem that the poor comprehenders are already maximally taxed by having to cope with any kind of embedded clause.

This finding of differential effects for readers with differing degrees of comprehension skills bears on the question of whether language uses a dedicated working-memory system or draws upon a general system shared by other cognitive functions (Caplan and Waters, in press). A systematic investigation of the (non)linguistic variables that modulate the slow-potential shift will be of direct relevance for this issue. More generally, the finding of long-lasting potentials linked to sentence processing opens the way for investigating the more sustained and incremental effects that wax and wane over the course of an entire sentence.

Summary We have discussed several qualitatively distinct ERP components that can be reliably linked to distinct aspects of language comprehension. On the basis of their different electrophysiological profiles, we can conclude that nonidentical brain systems underlie the various aspects of linguistic processing that are manifest in these different components. This provides a neurobiological constraint for models of language comprehension–models that will need to account for these different patterns of ERP effects.

An important working hypothesis concerns how the basic distinction of meaning and structure in language is linked to the N400 and the P600/SPS. Research that has used these components to address the basic processing nature of parsing has yielded evidence that is incompatible with strict autonomous characterizations of sentence processing. Furthermore, slow potential shifts that develop over entire clauses and sentences have been linked to integrational processes at the message level, and have demonstrated considerable effects of between-subject working memory differences.

At the temporal level, the millisecond resolution of the electrophysiological signal provides a dynamic picture of the ongoing comprehension process. Different language-related ERP effects are observed to arise at different moments and to persist for differing stretches of time. Within some 200 ms after stimulation, processes related to lexical meaning and integration emerge in the ERP waveform. Some researchers argue that syntactic processes can be seen preceding and partly overlapping with this early onset (cf. LAN effects). Processes related to modifying the ongoing syntactic analysis can be seen at some 500 ms in the ERP waveform. Various co-occurrences of LAN, N400, and P600/SPS effects have been reported, in ways that can be sensibly linked to the on-line comprehension process (e.g., N400 semantic processing effects as a consequence of preceding P600/SPS syntactic processing effects).

LESION AND HEMODYNAMIC DATA ON BRAIN AREAS INVOLVED IN SENTENCE PROCESSING In the previous section we discussed the relevance of ERP data for models of sentence comprehension. The processing of syntactic ambiguities has been a major testing ground for such models. The classical lesion studies and the more recent PET/fMRI studies on sentence comprehension have a slightly different focus. These studies attempt to determine areas that are involved in sentence processing, or to isolate and localize a specific subcomponent of sentence comprehension. This aim is independent of the issue of whether and when different processing components influence each other during sentence comprehension.

Until fairly recently most of the evidence on the neural circuitry of sentence processing came from lesion studies. One of the central issues in this work has been the identification of areas involved in the computation of syntactic structure during language comprehension. The general picture that has emerged from this research is complicated (for a more extensive overview, see Hagoort, Brown, and Osterhout, 1999). Despite the classical association between Broca's area and syntactic functions (e.g., Caramazza and Zurif, 1976; Heilman and Scholes, 1976; Von Stockert and Bader, 1976; Zurif, Caramazza, and Myerson, 1972), detailed lesion analyses have made it doubtful that lesions restricted to this area result in lasting syntactic deficits (e.g., Mohr et al., 1978). More recent analyses confirm that the left perisylvian cortex is critically involved in both parsing and syntactic encoding. Within this large cortical area it has been difficult to pinpoint a more restricted area that is crucial for syntactic processing. One reason is that lesions in any one part of this cortex can result in syntactic deficits (Caplan, Hildebrandt, and Makris, 1996; Vanier and Caplan, 1990). Moreover, the left anterior-temporal cortex, which has classically not been associated with any particular linguistic function, nonetheless appears to be consistently associated with syntactic deficits (Dronkers et al., 1994). This area is claimed to be involved in morphosyntactic processing, in addition to other areas in the left perisylvian cortex.

The lesion data thus suggest that it is impossible to single out one brain area that is dedicated to syntactic processing. There are at least two reasons for this complicated picture. One is that within the perisylvian cortex, individual variation in the neural circuitry for higher-order language functions might be substantially larger than for functions subserved by the primary sensorimotor cortices (cf. Bavelier et al., 1997; Ojemann, 1991). In addition, the wide variety of "syntactic" manipulations across studies makes it difficult to pinpoint the causal factors underlying the reported variation in brain areas. It is important to keep in mind that the areas involved in parsing (i.e., comprehension) are not necessarily the same as those involved in grammatical encoding (i.e., production), and that processing of word-category information or morphosyntactic features is different from establishing the syntactic dependencies among constituents. While all of these involve syntactic processing at some level, they clearly refer to very different aspects of syntactic processing. Comparing results across studies therefore requires an appreciation of the different syntactic manipulations employed.

Hemodynamic studies So far, PET and fMRI studies on language comprehension have largely focused on single word processing. Very few studies investigated integration processes at the sentence level or beyond (Bavelier et al., 1997; Caplan, Alpert, and Waters, 1998; Indefrey et al., 1996; Mazoyer et al., 1993; Nichelli et al., 1995; Stowe et al., 1994; Stromswold et al., 1996). In all but one of these (Mazoyer et al., 1993), the sentences were presented visually.

Two studies tried to isolate activations related to sentence-level processes from lower-level verbal processing, such as the reading of consonant strings (Bavelier et al., 1997) and single word comprehension (Mazoyer et al., 1993). The very nature of the comparisons in these studies makes it difficult to distinguish between sentence-level activations related to prosody, syntax, and sentence-level semantics.

The remaining brain-imaging studies on sentence processing were aimed at isolating the syntactic processing component (Caplan, Alpert, and Waters 1998; Indefrey et al., 1996; Just et al., 1996; Stowe et al., 1994; Stromswold et al., 1996). Although these different studies show non-identical patterns of activation, all five report activation in the left inferior-frontal gyrus, including Broca's area.

Four studies manipulated the syntactic complexity of the sentence materials (Caplan, Alpert, and Waters, 1998; Just et al., 1996; Stowe et al., 1994; Stromswold et al., 1996). For instance, Stromswold et al. (1996) compared sentences that were similar in terms of their propositional content, but differed in syntactic complexity. In one condition sentences with center-embedded structures were presented (e.g., "The juice that the child spilled stained the rug"). The other condition consisted of sentences with right-branching structures (e.g., "The child spilled the juice that stained the rug"). The former structures are notoriously harder to process than the latter. A direct comparison between the structurally complex (center-embedded) and the less complex sentences (right-branching) resulted in activation of Broca's area, particularly in the pars opercularis.

Caplan, Alpert, and Waters (1998) performed a partial replication of this study. They also observed increased activation in Broca's area for the center-embedded sentences. However, although the activation was in the pars opercularis, the blood flow increase was more dorsal and more anterior than in the previous study. Factors related to subject variation between studies may account for this regional activation difference within Broca's area.

In contrast to the other studies on syntactic processing (Caplan, Alpert, and Waters, 1998; Just et al., 1996; Stowe et al., 1996; Stromswold et al., 1996), the critical comparisons in the Indefrey study were not between conditions that differed in syntactic complexity, but rather those that did and did not require syntactic computations. Subjects were asked to read sentences consisting of pseudowords and function words in German [e.g., "(Der Fauper) (der) (die Lüspeln) (febbt) (tecken) (das Baktor)"]. Some of the sentences contained a syntactic error (e.g., *tecken*, a number agreement error with respect to the singular subject *Fauper*). In one condition, subjects were asked to detect this error (parsing) and to produce the sentence in its correct syntactic form ("Der Fauper, der die Lüspeln febbt, teckt das Baktor"). The latter task requires grammatical encoding in addition to parsing. In another condition, subjects were only asked to judge the grammaticality of the input string as they read it out. In a third condition, they were asked to make phonological acceptability judgments for the same pseudowords and function strings, presented without syntactic structure and with an occasional element that violated the phonotactic constraints of German. The experimental conditions were contrasted with a control condition in which subjects were asked to read out unstructured strings of the same pseudowords and function words used in the other conditions. All three syntactic conditions (including the syntactic error detection) were associated with activation of the inferior frontal sulcus between dorsal Broca's area and adjacent parts of the middle frontal gyrus. Both acceptability judgment tasks (syntactic and phonological) showed activation in bilateral anterior inferior frontal areas, as well as in the right hemisphere homologue of Broca's area. These results suggest that the right hemisphere activation that has also been found by others (Just et al., 1996; Nichelli et al., 1995) might reflect error detection. The syntactic processing component that is common across studies seems to be subserved by the left frontal areas.

The first fMRI study at 4 tesla on sentence processing was performed by Bavelier and colleagues (1997). They compared activations due to sentence reading with the activations induced by consonant strings presented like the sentences. Although the design does not allow the isolation of different sentence-level components (e.g., phonological, syntactic, and semantic processing), it nevertheless contains a number of relevant results. Overall, activations were distributed throughout the left perisylvian cortex, including the classical language areas (Broca's area, Wernicke's area, angular gyrus, and supramarginal gyrus). Other parts of the perisylvian cortex were also activated, such as left prefrontal areas and the left anterior-temporal lobe. At the individual subject level, these activations were in several small and distributed patches of cortex. In other visual but nonlanguage tasks, local activations were much less patchy, i.e., containing more contiguous activated voxels than the activations during visual sentence reading. Moreover, the precise pattern of activations varied substantially across individuals. For instance, the activations in Broca's area varied significantly in the precise localization with respect to an individual's main sulci.

If this patchy pattern of activations and the substantial differences across subjects during sentence reading reflect a basic difference between the neural organization of linguistic integration processes and the neural organization of sensory processing, this might in part explain the inconsistency of the lesion and brain-imaging data on sentence-level processing.

Conclusion The data indicate that syntactic processing is based on the concerted action of a number of different areas, each with its own relative specialization. These rela-

tive specializations may include memory requirements for establishing long-distance structural relations, the retrieval of lexical-syntactic information (word classes, such as nouns and verbs; grammatical gender; argument structure; etc.), the use of implicit knowledge of the structural constraints in a particular language to group words into well-formed utterances, and so on. All these operations are important ingredients of syntactic processing. At the same time, they are quite distinct and hence unlikely to be the province of one and the same brain area. The same conclusions apply, *mutatis mutandis*, to semantic integration processes.

In light of the available evidence, it can be argued that sets of areas in the left perisylvian cortex, each having its own relative specialization, contribute to syntactic processing and to important aspects of higher-order semantic processing. Exactly what these specializations are needs to be determined in studies that successfully isolate the relevant syntactic and semantic variables, as specified in articulated cognitive models of listening and reading. In addition, there appears to be restricted but nonetheless salient individual variation in the organization of the language processing networks in the brain, which adds to the complexity of determining the neural architecture of sentence processing (cf. Bavelier et al., 1997).

Broca's area has been found to be especially sensitive to the processing load involved in syntactic processing. It thus might be a crucial area for keeping the output of structure-building operations in a temporary buffer (working memory). The left temporal cortex, including anterior portions of the superior-temporal gyrus is presumably involved in morphosyntactic processing (Dronkers et al., 1994; Mazoyer et al., 1993). The retrieval of lexical-syntactic information, such as word class, supposedly involves the left frontal and left temporal regions (Damasio and Tranel, 1993; Hillis and Caramazza, 1995).

Although lesion and PET/fMRI studies on sentence comprehension have not yet reached the sophistication of bearing results with clear implications for our functional models of parsing and other sentence-level integration processes, they have begun to demarcate the outlines of the neural circuitry involved. Moreover, these studies have raised a number of important issues that have to be dealt with in future studies on the cognitive neuroscience of language. Prime among them is the issue of individual variation.

Cognitive neuroscience research on language comprehension: The next millennium

The ERP work offers us a rich collection of potentials that can be fruitfully related to language comprehension, providing important constraints on the architecture and mechanisms of the language system. The PET and fMRI research on sentence processing has complemented the lesion work, further delimiting language-related areas in the brain. At the very least, we have a solid basis on which to continue building a cognitive neuroscience research program on language understanding. However, various challenges still lie ahead, two of which we briefly mention here.

First, an appreciation of the differences between the various brain-imaging methods has led to the view that cognitive neuroscience research must bring together the more temporally and spatially sensitive research tools. In fact, it is becoming something of a dogma that ERP/MEG, PET, and fMRI measurements should be combined, preferably in the same experiment. However, a note of caution is called for here: We have, as yet, very little understanding of how the electrophysiological and the hemodynamic signals are related. Without such knowledge, it is difficult to ascertain in what way a particular component of the ERP/MEG signal relates to a hemodynamic response in a specific area of the brain and vice versa. Therefore, any response to the call for a spatiotemporal integrative approach is, at present, more a promise for the future than an actual, substantive research program. For the moment, cognitive neuroscience research on language mirrors the standard methodological division in the brain-imaging field, with separate experiments with ERP and/or MEG methodology, and others with PET or fMRI. Much basic research is needed before it will be clear whether a meaningful (as opposed to a mere technical) marriage of electromagnetic and hemodynamic approaches is possible (see for further discussion Rugg, 1999).

A second issue concerns the PET and fMRI work on sentence processing. Most PET and fMRI language researchers have, perhaps understandably, steered clear of the complexities of integrational processes during comprehension; however, the field needs a concerted effort in this area. Language understanding entails much more than word recognition, and we must expand our knowledge of the neural architecture to include the circuitry involved in postlexical integration. A particular challenge for PET and fMRI work will be to implement research that does justice to the elegance and richness of human language.

ACKNOWLEDGMENTS We thank Robert Kluender, Pim Levelt, Jacques Mehler, Tom Münte, and Richard Wise for helpful comments, and Inge Doehring for graphical assistance. Colin Brown and Peter Hagoort are supported in part by grant 400-56-384 from the Netherlands Organization for Scientific Research. Marta Kutas is supported in part by grants HD22614, AG08313, MH52893.

REFERENCES

BATES, E., S. MCNEW, B. MACWHINNEY, A. DEVESCOVI, and S. Smith, 1982. Functional constraints on sentence processing: A cross-linguistic study. *Cognition* 11:245–299.

BAVELIER, D., D. CORINA, P. JEZZARD, S. PADMANABHAN, V. P. CLARK, A. KARNI, A. PRINSTER, A. BRAUN, A. LALWANI, J. P. RAUSCHECKER, R. TURNER, and H. NEVILLE, 1997. Sentence reading: A functional MRI study at 4 tesla. *J. Cogn. Neurosci.* 9:664–686.

BROWN, C. M., and P. HAGOORT, 1993. The processing nature of the N400: Evidence from masked priming. *J. Cogn. Neurosci.* 5:34–44.

BROWN, C. M., and P. HAGOORT, 1999. On the electrophysiology of language comprehension: Implications for the human language system. In *Architectures and Mechanisms for Language Processing*, M. Crocker, M. Pickering, and C. Clifton, eds. Cambridge: Cambridge University Press, pp. 213–237.

BÜCHEL, C., C. FRITH, and K. FRISTON, 1999. Functional integration: Methods for assessing interactions among neuronal systems using brain imaging. In *Neurocognition of Language*, C. M. Brown and P. Hagoort, eds. Oxford: Oxford University Press, pp. 337–358.

CAPLAN, D., N. ALPERT, and G. WATERS, 1998. Effects of syntactic structure and propositional number on patterns of regional cerebral blood flow. *J. Cogn. Neurosci.* 10:541–552.

CAPLAN, D., N. HILDEBRANDT, and N. MAKRIS, 1996. Location of lesions in stroke patients with deficits in syntactic processing in sentence comprehension. *Brain* 199:933–949.

CAPLAN, D., and G. WATERS, in press. Verbal working memory and sentence comprehension. *Brain Behav. Sci.*

CARAMAZZA, A., and E. B. ZURIF, 1976. Dissociation of algorithmic and heuristic processes in language comprehension: Evidence from aphasia. *Brain Lang.* 3:572–582.

COULSON, S., J. W. KING, and M. KUTAS, 1998. Expect the unexpected: Event-related brain response to morphosyntactic violations. *Lang. Cogn. Proc.* 13:21–58.

DAMASIO, A. R., and D. TRANEL, 1993. Verbs and nouns are retrieved from separate neural systems. *Proc. Natl. Acad. Sci. U.S.A.* 90:4957–4960.

DRONKERS, N. F., D. P. WILKINS, R. D. VAN VALIN, JR., B. B. REDFERN, and J. J. JAEGER, 1994. A reconsideration of the brain areas involved in the disruption of morphosyntactic comprehension. *Brain Lang.* 47:461–463.

ELMAN, J. L., 1990. Representation and structure in connectionist models. In *Cognitive Models of Speech Processing: Psycholinguistic and Computational Perspectives*, G. T. M. Altmann, ed. Cambridge, Mass.: MIT Press, pp. 345–382.

FRAZIER, L., 1987. Sentence processing: A tutorial review. In *The Psychology of Reading, Attention and Performance XII*, M. Coltheart, ed. Hillsdale, N.J.: Lawrence Erlbaum, pp. 559–586.

FRAZIER, L., and C. CLIFTON, 1996. *Construal*. Cambridge, Mass.: MIT Press.

FRIEDERICI, A. D., 1995. The time course of syntactic activation during language processing: A model based on neuropsychological and neurophysiological data. *Brain Lang.* 50:259–281.

FRIEDERICI, A. D., A. HAHNE, and A. MECKLINGER, 1996. Temporal structure of syntactic parsing: Early and late event-related brain potential effects elicited by syntactic anomalies. *J. Exp. Psychol.: Learn. Mem. Cognit.* 22:1219–1248.

FRIEDERICI, A. D., and A. MECKLINGER, 1996. Syntactic parsing as revealed by brain responses: First-pass and second-pass parsing processes. *J. Psycholinguistic Res.* 25:157–176.

FRIEDERICI, A. D., E. PFEIFER, and A. HAHNE, 1993. Event-related brain potentials during natural speech processing: Effects of semantic, morphological and syntactic violations. *Cogn. Brain Res.* 1:183–192.

FRISTON, K., C. FRITH, and R. S. J. FRACKOWIAK, 1993. Time-dependent changes in effective connectivity measured with PET. *Hum. Brain Mapp.* 1:69–80.

GRATTON, G., M. FABIANI, and P. M. CORBALLIS, 1997. Can we measure correlates of neuronal activity with non-invasive optical methods? In *Optical Imaging of Brain Function and Metabolism II*, A. Villringer and U. Dirnagl, eds. New York: Plenum Press, pp. 53–62.

GUNTER, T. C., L. A. STOWE, and G. M. MULDER, 1997. When syntax meets semantics. *Psychophysiol.* 34:660–676.

HAGOORT, P., and C. M. BROWN, in press. Semantic and syntactic ERP effects of listening to speech compared to reading. *Neuropsychologia.*

HAGOORT, P., C. M. BROWN, and J. GROOTHUSEN, 1993. The syntactic positive shift (SPS) as an ERP-measure of syntactic processing. *Lang. Cogn. Proc.* 8:439–483.

HAGOORT, P., C. M. BROWN, and L. OSTERHOUT, 1999. The neurocognition of syntactic processing. In *Neurocognition of Language*, C. M. Brown and P. Hagoort, eds. Oxford: Oxford University Press, pp. 273–316.

HAGOORT, P., C. M. BROWN, W. VONK, and J. HOEKS, 1999. Manuscript in preparation.

HEILMAN, K. M., and R. J. SCHOLES, 1976. The nature of comprehension errors in Broca's conduction and Wernicke's aphasics. *Cortex* 12:258–265.

HILLIS, A. E., and A. CARAMAZZA, 1995. Representation of grammatical knowledge in the brain. *J. Cogn. Neurosci.* 7:397–407.

INDEFREY, P., P. HAGOORT, C. M. BROWN, H. HERZOG, and R. J. SEITZ, 1996. Cortical activation induced by syntactic processing: A [15O]-butanol PET study. *NeuroImage* 3:S442.

JUST, M. A., P. A. CARPENTER, T. A. KELLER, W. F. EDDY, and K. R. THULBORN, 1996. Brain activation modulated by sentence comprehension. *Science* 274:114–116.

KING, J. W., and M. A. JUST, 1991. Individual differences in syntactic processing: The role of working memory load. *J. Mem. Lang.* 30:580–602.

KING, J. W., and M. KUTAS, 1995. Who did what and when? Using word- and clause-related ERPs to monitor working memory usage in reading. *J. Cogn. Neurosci.* 7:378–397.

KLUENDER, R., and M. KUTAS, 1993a. The interaction of lexical and syntactic effects in the processing of unbounded dependencies. *Lang. Cogn. Proc.* 8:573–633.

KLUENDER, R., and M. KUTAS, 1993b. Bridging the gap: Evidence from ERPs on the processing of unbounded dependencies. *J. Cogn. Neurosci.* 2:196–214.

KLUENDER, R., and T. F. MÜNTE, 1999. Wh-strategies in German: The influence of universal and language-specific variation on the neural processing of wh-questions. In preparation.

KUTAS, M., K. D. FEDERMEIER, and M. I. SERENO, 1999. Current approaches to mapping language in electromagnetic space. In *Neurocognition of Language*, C. M. Brown and P. Hagoort, eds. Oxford: Oxford University Press, pp. 359–392.

KUTAS, M., and S. A. HILLYARD, 1980. Reading senseless sentences: Brain potentials reflect semantic incongruity. *Science* 207:203–205.

KUTAS, M., and J. W. KING, 1995. The potentials for basic sentence processing: Differentiating integrative processes. In *Attention and Performance XVI: Information Integration in Perception and Communication*, T. Inui and J. McClelland, eds. Cambridge, Mass.: MIT Press, pp. 501–546.

KUTAS, M., and C. VAN PETTEN, 1994. Psycholinguistics electrified: Event-related brain potential investigations. In *Handbook of Psycholinguistics*, M. Gernsbacher, ed. New York: Academic Press, pp. 83–144.

MACDONALD, M. A., N. J. PEARLMUTTER, and M. S. SEIDENBERG, 1994. The lexical nature of syntactic ambiguity resolution. *Psych. Rev.* 101:676–703.

MAZOYER, B., N. TZOURIO, V. FRAK, A. SYROTA, N. MURAYAMA, O. LEVRIER, G. SALAMON, S. DEHAENE, L. COHEN, and J. MEHLER, 1993. The cortical representation of speech. *J. Cogn. Neurosci.* 5:467–479.

MCCLELLAND, J. L., M. ST. JOHN, and R. TARABAN, 1989. Sentence comprehension: A parallel distributed processing approach. *Lang. Cogn. Proc.* 4:287–335.

MOHR, J. P., M. S. PESSIN, S. FINKELSTEIN, H. H. FUNKENSTEIN, G. W. DUNCAN, and K. R. DAVIS, 1978. Broca aphasia: Pathologic and clinical. *Neurology* 28:311–324.

MÜNTE, T. F., M. MATZKE, and S. JOHANNES, 1997. Brain activity associated with syntactic incongruities in words and pseudo-words. *J. Cogn. Neurosci.* 9:300–311.

NICHELLI, P., J. GRAFMAN, P. PIETRINI, K. CLARK, K. Y. LEE, and R. MILETICH, 1995. Where the brain appreciates the moral of a story. *NeuroReport* 6:2309–2313.

OJEMANN, G., 1991. Cortical organization of language and verbal memory based on intraoperative investigation. *Prog. Sens. Physiol.* 12:193–210.

OSTERHOUT, L., 1994. Event-related brain potentials as tools for comprehending sentence comprehension. In *Perspectives on Sentence Processing*, C. Clifton, L. Frazier, and K. Rayner, eds. Hillsdale, N.J.: Erlbaum, pp. 15–44.

OSTERHOUT, L., and P. HAGOORT, 1999. A superficial resemblance does not necessarily mean you are part of the family: Counterarguments to Coulson, King, and Kutas (1998) in the P600/SPS-P300 debate. *Lang. Cogn. Proc.* 14:1–14.

OSTERHOUT, L., and P. J. HOLCOMB, 1992. Event-related brain potentials elicited by syntactic anomaly. *J. Mem. Lang.* 31:785–806.

OSTERHOUT, L., and P. J. HOLCOMB, 1993. Event-related potentials and syntactic anomaly: Evidence of anomaly detection during the perception of continuous speech. *Lang. Cogn. Proc.* 8:413–437.

OSTERHOUT, L., and P. J. HOLCOMB, 1995. Event-related potentials and language comprehension. In *Electrophysiology of Mind: Event-Related Brain Potentials and Cognition*, M. D. Rugg and M. G. H. Coles, eds. New York: Oxford University Press, pp. 171–215.

OSTERHOUT, L., R. MCKINNON, M. BERSICK, and V. COREY, 1996. On the language-specificity of the brain response to syntactic anomalies: Is the syntactic positive shift a member of the P300 family? *J. Cogn. Neurosci.* 8:507–526.

OSTERHOUT, L., J. MCLAUGHLIN, and M. BERSICK, 1997. Event-related brain potentials and human language. *Trends Cogn. Sci.* 1:203–209.

PICTON, T. W., O. G. LINS, and M. SCHERG, 1995. The recording and analysis of event-related potentials. In *Handbook of Neuropsychology*, Vol. 10, F. Boller and J. Grafman, eds. Amsterdam: Elsevier, pp. 3–73.

RUGG, M., 1999. Functional neuroimaging in cognitive neuroscience. In *Neurocognition of Language*, C. M. Brown and P. Hagoort, eds. Oxford: Oxford University Press, pp. 15–36.

SPIVEY-KNOWLTON, M. J., and J. C. SEDIVY, 1995. Resolving attachment ambiguities with multiple constraints. *Cognition* 55:227–267.

ST. GEORGE, M., S. MANNES, and J. E. HOFFMAN, 1994. Global semantic expectancy and language comprehension. *J. Cogn. Neurosci.* 6:70–83.

ST. GEORGE, M., S. MANNES, and J. E. HOFFMAN, 1997. Individual differences in inference generation: An ERP analysis. *J. Cogn. Neurosci.* 9:776–787.

STOWE, L. A., A. A. WIJERS, A. T. M. WILLEMSEN, E. REULAND, A. M. J. PAANS, and W. VAALBURG, 1994. PET-studies of language: An assessment of the reliability of the technique. *J. Psycholinguistic Res.* 23:499–527.

STROMSWOLD, K., D. CAPLAN, N. ALPERT, and S. RAUCH, 1996. Localization of syntactic comprehension by positron emission tomography. *Brain Lang.* 52:452–473.

TANENHAUS, M. K., and J. C. TRUESWELL, 1995. Sentence comprehension. In *Handbook of Perception and Cognition, Vol. 11: Speech, Language, and Communication*, J. Miller and P. Eimas, eds. New York: Academic Press, pp. 217–262.

VAN BERKUM, J. J. A., P. HAGOORT, and C. M. BROWN, in press. Semantic integration in sentences and discourse: Evidence from the N400. *J. Cogn. Neurosci.*

VANIER, M., and D. CAPLAN, 1990. CT-scan correlates of agrammatism. In *Agrammatic Aphasia: A Cross-Language Narrative Source Book*, L. Menn and L. K. Obler, eds. Amsterdam: John Benjamins, pp. 37–114.

VON STOCKERT, T. R., and L. BADER, 1976. Some relations of grammar and lexicon in aphasia. *Cortex* 12:49–60.

ZURIF, E. B., A. CARAMAZZA, and R. MYERSON, 1972. Grammatical judgments of agrammatic aphasics. *Neuropsychologia* 10:405–417.

62 Acquisition of Languages: Infant and Adult Data

JACQUES MEHLER AND ANNE CHRISTOPHE

ABSTRACT This chapter advocates a multidimensional approach to the issues raised by language acquisition. We bring to bear evidence from several sources–experimental investigations of infants, studies of bilingual infants and adults, and data from functional brain-imaging–to focus on the problem of early language learning. At bottom, we believe that our understanding of development and knowledge attainment requires the joint study of the initial state, the stable state, and the mechanisms that constrain the timetables of learning. And we are persuaded that such an approach must take into account data from many disciplines.

What advantage can a newborn infant draw from listening to speech? Possibly none, as was thought not so long ago (Mehler and Fox, 1985). But now we conjecture that the speech signal furnishes information about the structure of the mother tongue (see Christophe et al., 1997; Gleitman and Wanner, 1982; Mazuka, 1996; Mehler and Christophe, 1995). This position, dubbed the "phonological bootstrapping" hypothesis (Morgan and Demuth, 1996a), reflects an increasing tendency in language acquisition research (Morgan and Demuth, 1996b; Weissenborn and Höhle, 1999)–namely, that language acquisition starts very early and that a purely phonological analysis of the speech signal (a surface analysis) gives information about the grammatical structure of the language.

Phonological bootstrapping rests on the idea that language is a species-specific ability, the product of a "language organ" specific to human brains. Hardly new, this view has been advocated by psychologists, linguists, and neurologists since Gall (1835). Lenneberg (1967) initially provided much evidence for the biological foundations of language, evidence that has been corroborated by other research programs (for review, see Mehler and Dupoux, 1994; Pinker, 1994). Human brains appear to have specific neural structures, part of the species endowment, that mediate the grammatical systems of language. Noam Chomsky (1988) proposed conceiving of the "knowledge of language" that newborns bring to the task of acquiring a language in terms of principles and parameters–universal principles that are common to all human languages and parameters that elucidate the diversity of natural languages (together, then, principles and parameters constitute Universal Grammar). Parameters are set through experience with the language spoken in the environment (for a different opinion about how species-specific abilities may be innately specified, see Elman et al., 1996).

In this chapter, we first present experimental results with infants to illustrate the phonological bootstrapping approach. We then examine how word forms can be learned. Finally, we discuss studies of the cortical representation of languages in bilingual adults, who, by being bilingual, exhibit the end result of a special (though frequent) language-learning case. The structure of this chapter illustrates an unconventional view of development. Given the task of presenting language acquisition during the first year of life, why do we include studies on the representation of languages in adult bilinguals? We do so in the belief that development is more than the study of change in developing organisms. To devise an adequate theory of how an initial capacity turns into the full-fledged adult capacity, we need a good description of both endpoints. In addition, considering both endpoints together while focusing on the problem of development is a good research strategy, one that has increased our understanding of language acquisition.

Phonological bootstrapping

In our chapter in the first edition of this book, (Mehler and Christophe, 1995), we started from the fact that many babies are exposed to more than one language–languages that must be kept separate in order to avoid confusion. We reviewed a number of studies that illustrate such babies' ability to discriminate between languages. The picture that emerged was that, from birth onward, babies are able to distinguish their mother tongue from foreign languages (Bahrick and Pickens, 1988; Mehler et al., 1988); moreover, they show a preference for their mother tongue (Moon, Cooper, and Fifer,

JACQUES MEHLER and ANNE CHRISTOPHE Laboratoire de Sciences Cognitives et Psycholinguistique, Ecole des Hautes Etudes en Sciences Sociales, CNRS, UMR 8554, Paris, France

897

1993). Both these facts hold when speech is low-pass–filtered, preserving only prosodic information (Dehaene-Lambertz and Houston, 1998; Mehler et al., 1988). In addition, after reanalyzing our data (from Mehler et al., 1988), we noticed a developmental trend between birth and 2 months of age: Whereas newborns discriminated between two foreign languages, 2-month-olds did not. More recent data confirm this developmental trend. Thus, Nazzi, Bertoncini, and Mehler (1999) showed that French newborns could discriminate filtered sentences in English and Japanese; and Christophe and Morton (1998) showed that, while English 2-month-olds do not react to a change from French to Japanese (using unfiltered sentences), they do discriminate between English and Japanese in the same experimental setting. A possible interpretation of this counterintuitive result is that, while newborns attempt to analyze every speech sample in detail, 2-month-olds have gained enough knowledge of their mother tongue to be able to filter out utterances from a foreign language as irrelevant. As a consequence, they do not react to a change from one foreign language to another. This takes place when the infant is about 2 months old, and thus marks one of the earliest reorganizations of the perceptual responses as a result of exposure to speech.

When Mehler and colleagues (1996) proposed a framework to explain babies' ability to discriminate languages, they began with two facts: first, that babies discriminate languages on the basis of prosodic properties and, second, that vowels are salient features for babies (see Bertoncini et al., 1988; Kuhl et al., 1992). They conjectured that babies construct a grid-like representation containing only vowels. Such a representation would facilitate the discrimination of the language pairs reported. Indeed, the pairs invariably involved *distant* languages. In addition, it predicts that infants should have most difficulty discriminating languages having similar prosodic/rhythmic properties. It is assumed that the vowel grid represents the languages of the world as clusters around discrete positions in the acoustic space.

Nazzi, Bertoncini, and Mehler (1998) began to test some predictions of this framework. First, they showed that French newborns fail to discriminate English and Dutch filtered sentences. English and Dutch share a number of prosodic properties (complex syllables, vowel reduction, similar word stress) and both are "stress-timed"; they should therefore receive similar grid-like representations. The authors also investigated the question of whether languages receiving similar grid representation would be grouped into one single category—a language family or class. To that end, they selected four languages falling into two language classes: Dutch and English (stress-timed), and Spanish and Italian (syllable-timed). They presented infants with a mixture of filtered sentences from two different languages. When habituated to sentences in Dutch and English, infants responded to a change to sentences in Spanish and Italian, and vice versa. In contrast, when habituated to English and Spanish and tested with Dutch and Italian, infants failed to discriminate. (Note: All the possible interlanguage class combinations were used.) Infants reacted only if a change of language class had taken place (see figure 62.1). These experiments suggest that infants spontaneously classify languages into broad classes or rhythmic-prosodic families, as hypothesized.

So now we know that some languages are more similar than others, even for babies. How can we learn more about the metric underlying perceptual judgments? Two lines of research have allowed us to investigate the perceptual space. One of these exploits adaptation to time-compressed speech (artificially accelerated speech, which is about twice as fast as normal speech). Subjects are asked to listen to and comprehend compressed sentences. Comprehension is initially rather poor; but subjects habituate to compressed speech, and their performance improves after listening to a few sentences (Mehler et al., 1993). Dupoux and Green (1997) observed that adaptation resists speaker change, demonstrating that adaptation takes place at a relatively abstract level. However, Altmann and Young (1993) reported adaptation to compressed speech in sentences composed of nonwords, showing that lexical access is not necessary for adaptation. Similarly, Pallier and colleagues (1998) found that monolingual Spanish subjects listening to Spanish compressed sentences benefit from previous exposure to highly compressed Catalan, a language that they were unable to understand. The same pattern of results was observed when monolingual British subjects were exposed to highly compressed Dutch. Pallier and colleagues (1998) also reported that French-English bilinguals showed no transfer of adaptation from French to English, or vice-versa, again demonstrating that comprehension contributes, at best, very little to adaptation.

These results were interpreted in terms of the phonological (prosodic and rhythmical) similarity of the adapting and the target languages. Phonologically similar languages, such as Catalan and Spanish or English and Dutch, show transfer of adaptation from one member of the pair to the other; however, adaptation to French or English, two phonologically dissimilar languages, does not transfer from one to the other. Sebastian-Gallés, Dupoux, and Costa (in press) extended these findings by adapting Spanish subjects to Spanish, Italian, French, Greek, English, or Japanese sentences. Sebastian-Gallés and colleagues replicated and extended the findings by

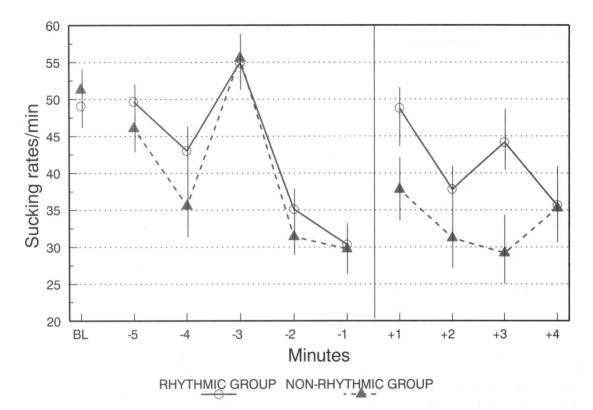

RHYTHMIC GROUP   NON-RHYTHMIC GROUP
      ─○─   ─▲─

FIGURE 62.1   Results of a nonnutritive sucking experiment: Auditory stimulation is presented contingently upon babies' high-amplitude sucks on a blind dummy. After a baseline period without stimulation, babies hear sentences from one category until they reach a predefined habituation criterion. They are then switched to sentences from the second category. The graph displays sucking-rate averages for 32 French newborns for the baseline period, 5 minutes before the change in stimulation, and 4 minutes after the change. The rhythmic group was switched from a mixture of sentences taken from two stress-timed languages (Dutch and English) to a mixture of sentences from two syllable-timed languages (Spanish and Italian), or vice versa. The nonrhythmic group also changed languages, but in each phase of the experiment there were sentences from one stress-timed and one syllable-timed language (e.g., Spanish and English, then Italian and Dutch). Infants from the rhythmic group reacted significantly more to the change of stimulation than infants from the nonrhythmic group, indicating that only those in the rhythmic group were able to form a category with the habituation sentences and notice a change in category (syllable-timed vs. stress-timed). (Adapted from Nazzi, Bertoncini, and Mehler, 1998.)

Pallier and co-workers; in particular, they observed that Greek, which shares rhythmic properties with Spanish but has little lexical overlap, is very efficient in promoting adaptation to Spanish. These authors concluded that the technique of time-compressed speech can serve as a tool to explore the grouping of languages into classes. Another technique being assessed as a tool to study the metric of natural languages is speech resynthesis—a procedure that makes it possible to selectively preserve some aspects of the original sentences, such as phonemes, phonotactics, rhythm, and intonation (see Ramus and Mehler, 1999). It is too early to relate these early categorizations of languages with the language classifications proposed by comparative linguists and biologists (see Cavalli-Sforza, 1991; Renfrew, 1994).

So far, we have seen that the languages of the world can be organized on a metric; that is, some languages are more distant than others. This metric could be discrete, like the one Miller and Nicely (1955) proposed for phonemes—a space structured by a finite number of dimensions (e.g., the parameters within the principles-and-parameters theory). Or it could be a continuous space, without structure, with as many dimensions as there are languages. Mehler and colleagues (1996) claimed that the first option should be correct because the metric of languages, the underlying structure, could aid in acquisition. The way a language sounds (i.e., its phonological information) would help infants to discover some properties of their native language and allow them to start the process of acquisition. This is a kind of phonological bootstrapping.

One recent proposal (Nespor, Guasti, and Christophe, 1996) illustrates how phonological information may bootstrap the acquisition of syntax. Languages vary as to the way words are organized in sentences. Either complements follow their heads, as in English or Italian (e.g., *He reads the book*, where *book* is the complement of *read*), or they precede their heads, as in Turkish or Japanese (e.g., *KitabI yazdim* [*The-book I-read*]). This structural property possesses a prosodic correlate: In head-initial languages like English, prominence falls at the end of phonological phrases (small prosodic units, e.g., *the big book*), but in head-final languages like Turkish, prominence falls at the beginning of phonological phrases. Therefore, if babies can hear whether prominence falls at the beginning or end of phonological phrases, they can decipher their language's word order. Infants could understand some structural aspects before they learn words (see Mazuka, 1996, for a discussion). They could use their knowledge of the typical order of words in their mother tongue to guide the acquisition of word meanings (e.g., see Gleitman, 1990).

If babies are to use prosodic information to determine the word order of their language, they should first be able to perceive the prosodic correlates of word order. In order to test the plausibility of this hypothesis, Christophe and colleagues (1999) compared two languages that differ on the head-direction parameter, but have otherwise similar prosodic properties: French and Turkish. Both languages have word-final stress, fairly simple syllabic structure through resyllabification, and no vowel reduction. Matched sentences in the two languages were constructed such that they had the same number of syllables, and their word boundaries and phonological phrase boundaries fell in the same places. Only prominence within phonological phrases distinguished these sentences. They were read naturally by native speakers of French and Turkish. And, in order to eliminate phonemic information while preserving prosodic information, the sentences were resynthesized so that all vowels were mapped to schwa and consonants by manner of articulation (stops, fricatives, liquids, etc.). The prosody of the original sentences was copied onto the resynthesized sentences. An initial experiment showed that 2-month-old French babies were able to distinguish between these two sets of sentences (see also Guasti et al., in press). This result suggests that babies are able to perceive the prosodic correlate of word order well before the end of the first year of life (although additional control experiments are needed to rule out alternative explanations). As they stand, the findings support the notion that babies determine the word order of their language before the end of the first year of life–about the time that lexical and syntactic acquisition begins.

This proposal is an example of how purely phonological information (in that case, prosodic information) directly gives information about syntax. Languages differ not only in syntax, but in their phonological properties as well; and babies may learn about these properties of their mother tongue early in life. (The alternative is that children learn the phonology of a language when they learn its lexicon, after age 1). In fact, recent experiments have shown that the adult speech processing system is shaped by the phonological properties of the native language (e.g., Cutler and Otake, 1994; Otake et al., 1996; see Pallier, Christophe, and Mehler, 1997, for a review). For instance, Dupoux and his colleagues examined Spanish and French adult native speakers' processing of stress information (stress is contrastive in Spanish: *BEbe* and *beBE* are different words, meaning "baby" and "drink," respectively; in French stress is uniformly word-final). They used an ABX paradigm where subjects listened to triplets of pseudowords and had to decide whether the third one was like the first or like the second one (Dupoux et al., 1997). They observed that French native speakers were almost unable to make the correct decision when stress was the relevant factor (e.g., *VAsuma, vaSUma, VAsuma*, correct answer first item), whereas Spanish speakers found it as straightforward to monitor for stress as to monitor for phonetic content. In addition, Spanish speakers found it very hard to base their decision on phonemes when stress was an irrelevant factor (e.g., *VAsuma, faSUma, vaSUma*, correct answer first item), whereas French speakers happily ignored the stress information. In another set of experiments, Dupoux and colleagues investigated the perception of consonant clusters and vowel length in French and Japanese speakers (Dupoux et al., in press). In French, consonant clusters are allowed but vowel length is irrelevant, while in Japanese, consonant clusters are not allowed and vowel length is relevant. They observed that Japanese speakers were at chance level in an ABX task when the presence of a consonant cluster was the relevant variable (e.g., *ebzo, ebuzo, ebuzo*, correct answer second item), whereas they performed very well when they had to base their decision on vowel length (e.g., *ebuzo, ebuuzo, ebuzo*, correct answer first item). In contrast, French speakers showed exactly the reverse pattern of performance (see figure 62.2).

All these results suggest that adult speakers of a language listen to speech through the filter of their own phonology. Presumably, they represent all speech sounds with a sublexical representation that is most adequate for their mother tongue, but inadequate for foreign languages. How and when do babies learn about such phonological aspects of their mother tongue? Although we still lack experimental results on this topic, we conjecture that babies must stabilize the correct sublexical representation for their mother tongue sometime during the first year of life. Thus, when they start acquiring a lexicon toward the end of their first year, they may directly establish lexical representations in a format that is most suitable to their mother tongue. Consistent with this view, evidence is emerging that the representations in adults' auditory in-

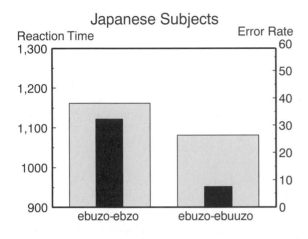

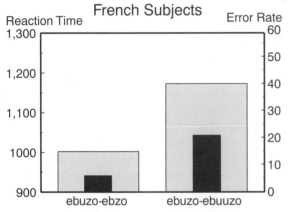

FIGURE 62.2 Reaction times (in gray) and error rates (in black) to ABX judgments in French and Japanese subjects on a vowel length contrast and on an epenthesis contrast. (Adapted from Dupoux et al., 1999.)

put lexicon depend on the phonological properties of the native language (Pallier, Sebastian-Gallés, and Colome, 1999).

Here we have discussed one particular kind of phonological bootstrapping, whereby the way a language sounds gives information as to its abstract structure (such as the head-direction parameter, or the kind of sublexical representation it uses). Phonological information may help bootstrap acquisition in other ways (Morgan and Demuth, 1996a): For instance, prosodic boundary information may help parse a sentence (e.g., Morgan, 1986); prosodic and distributional information may help reveal word boundaries (e.g., Christophe and Dupoux, 1996; Christophe et al., 1997); and phonological information may help to categorize words (see Morgan, Shi, and Allopenna, 1996). This is not to imply that everything about language can be learned through a purely phonological analysis of the speech signal during the first year of life and before anything else has been learned. Of course this is not the case. For instance, although we argued that some syntactic properties may be cued by prosodic correlates (e.g., the head-direction parameter), we

do not claim that prosody contains traces for *all* syntactic properties. But if the child can discover only a few basic syntactic properties from such traces, learning is made easier. The number of possible grammars diminishes by half with each parameter that is set (for binary parameters). As a consequence, the first parameter that is set eliminates the largest number of candidate grammars (see Fodor, 1998; Gibson and Wexler, 1994; Tesar and Smolensky, 1998, for discussions about learnability). In other words, a purely phonological analysis may *bootstrap* the acquisition process but not solve it entirely. Fernald and McRoberts (1996) also discussed the potential help of prosody in bootstrapping syntactic acquisition: They criticized this approach on the grounds that the proportion of syntactic boundaries reliably cued by prosodic cues (pauses, lengthening, etc.) is not high. Some syntactic boundaries are not marked and some cues appear in inadequate positions. If so, children may often think that a syntactic boundary is present when none is and posit erroneous grammars. This argument holds only if one assumes that children use prosodic boundaries to parse every sentence they hear. Infants' brains may instead keep statistical tabs established on the basis of prosody and use such information to learn something about their language. For instance, they may tally the most frequent syllables at prosodic edges, in which case they find the function words and morphemes of their language at the top of the list. In that view, it does not matter very much if prosodic boundaries do not correlate perfectly with syntactic boundaries.

Learning words

Learning the syntax and phonology of their native language is not all babies have to do to acquire a functioning language. They also have to learn the lexicon—an arbitrary collection of word forms and their associated meanings (word forms respect the phonology of the language, but there is no systematic relationship between form and meaning). Experimental work shows that babies start to know the meaning of a few words at about 1 year of age (Oviatt, 1980; Thomas et al., 1981), and this is consistent with parental report. Mehler, Dupoux, and Segui (1990) argued that infants must be able to segment and store word forms in an appropriate language-specific representation before the end of the first year of life in order to be ready for the difficult task of linking word forms to their meaning (Gleitman and Gleitman, 1997). Recent experiments by Peter Jusczyk and colleagues supported this view by showing that babies are able to extract word forms from the speech stream and remember them by about 8 months of age. Jusczyk and Aslin (1995) showed that 7.5-month-olds attended less to new words than to "familiar" words–i.e., isolated monosyllabic words with which they had been familiarized in the context of whole sentences. This result was later replicated with multisyllabic words, indicating that babies of this age have at least some capacity to extract word-like units from continuous speech (Jusczyk, Houston, and Newsome, in press). These word forms are not forgotten immediately afterwards. When 8-month-olds were repeatedly exposed to recorded stories at home then brought into the lab a week later, they exhibited a listening preference to words that frequently occurred in these stories (Jusczyk and Hohne, 1997).

How do babies extract word forms from the speech stream? This area of research has exploded since our last version of this chapter, and we now have a reasonably good view of what babies might do. Babies may exploit distributional regularities (i.e., segments belonging to a word tend to cohere). Brent and Cartwright (1996) showed that an algorithm exploiting these cues could recover a significant number of words from unsegmented input. In addition, Morgan (1994) demonstrated that 8-month-old babies exploited distributional regularity to package unsegmented strings of syllables (see also Saffran, Aslin, and Newport, 1996). Babies may also exploit the phonotactic regularities of the language, such as the fact that some strings of segments occur only at the beginning or at the end of words. Babies may learn about these regularities by examining utterance boundaries, then use these regularities to find word boundaries (Brent and Cartwright, 1996; Cairns et al., 1997). Interestingly, Friederici and Wessels (1993) showed that at 9 months, babies are already sensitive to the phonotactic regularities of their native language (see also Jusczyk, Cutler, and Redanz, 1993; Jusczyk, Luce, and Charles-Luce, 1994).

Next, babies may rely on their knowledge of the typical word shapes of their language. Anne Cutler and her colleagues extensively explored a well-known example of such a strategy in English. Cutler's metrical segmentation strategy relies on the fact that English content words predominantly start with a strong syllable (containing a full vowel, as opposed to a weak syllable containing a reduced vowel). Adult English-speaking listeners make use of this regularity when listening to faint speech or when locating words in nonsense syllable strings (e.g., Cutler and Butterfield, 1992; McQueen, Norris, and Cutler, 1994). Importantly, 9-month–old American babies prefer to listen to lists of strong–weak words (bisyllabic words in which the first syllable is strong and the second weak) than to lists of weak–strong words (Jusczyk, Cutler, and Redanz, 1993). In addition, Peter Jusczyk and his colleagues showed, in a recent series of experiments, that babies of about 8 months find it easier to segment

strong–weak (SW) words than weak–strong (WS) words from passages (Jusczyk, Houston, and Newsome, in press).

Finally, babies may rely on prosodic cues to perform an initial segmentation of continuous speech. Prosodic units roughly corresponding to phonological phrases (small units containing one or two content words plus some grammatical words or morphemes) were shown to be available to adult listeners (de Pijper and Sanderman, 1994), and presumably to babies as well (Christophe et al., 1994; Gerken, Jusczyk, and Mandel, 1994; see also Morgan, 1996; Fisher and Tokura, 1996, for evidence that prosodic boundary cues have robust acoustic correlates in infant-directed speech). These prosodic units would not allow babies to isolate every word; however, they would provide a first segmentation of the speech stream and restrict the domain of operation of other strategies (e.g., distributional regularities). In addition, prosodic units possess the interesting property that they derive from syntactic constituents (in a nonisomorphic fashion; see Nespor and Vogel, 1986); as a consequence, function words and morphemes tend to occur at prosodic edges. Therefore, infants may keep track of frequent syllables at prosodic edges, and the most frequent will correspond to the function words and morphemes in their language. Actually, LouAnn Gerken and her colleagues showed that 11-month-old American babies reacted to the replacement of function words by nonwords, indicating that they already knew at least some of the English function words (Gerken, 1996; and Shafer et al., 1998). Once babies have identified the function words of their native language, they may "strip" syllables homophonous to function words from the beginning and end of prosodic units; the remainder can then be treated as one or several content words.

This area of research illustrates particularly well the advantages of studying adults and babies simultaneously. For instance, the fact that English speakers rely on the predominant word pattern of English to perform lexical segmentation was first shown for adult subjects; this result was then extended to babies between 8 and 12 months of age. Reciprocally, the use of prosody to hypothesize word or syntactic boundaries was first advocated to solve the acquisition problem, and is now being fruitfully studied in adults (e.g., Warren et al., 1995).

The bilingual brain

We have argued that the speech signal provides fairly useful hints to isolate some basic properties of one's maternal language. There is, however, a situation that presents the infant with incompatible evidence; that is, sometimes two languages are systematically presented at the same time in the environment. But this apparently insurmountable problem is readily solved by every child raised in a multilingual society—no important delay in language acquisition has been reliably documented. We have to provide a model of language acquisition that can account for that.

Bosch and Sebastian-Gallés (1997) have shown that at 4 months bilingual Spanish/Catalan babies already behave differently than do monolingual controls of either language. These investigators showed that monolingual babies orient faster to their mother tongue (Spanish for half of the babies and Catalan for the other half) than to English. In contrast, bilingual babies orient to Spanish or Catalan significantly more slowly than to English. In more recent and still unpublished work, these authors show that the bilingual infants can discriminate between Spanish and Catalan, indicating that confusion cannot be adduced to explain the above results. Needing to keep the languages separate, bilingual infants might be performing more fine-grained analyses of both Spanish and Catalan, and hence need more processing time.

Does the bilingual baby become equally competent in both languages? To answer this question, we have to study adult bilinguals. Pallier, Bosch, and Sebastian-Gallés (1997) studied Spanish/Catalan bilinguals who learned to speak Catalan and Spanish before the age of 4 (although one language was always dominant—the one spoken by both parents). Whereas Spanish has only one /e/ vowel, Catalan has two, an open and a closed /e/. Pallier and colleagues showed that the Spanish-dominant speakers could not correctly perceive the Catalan vocalic contrast, even though they had had massive exposure to that language and spoke it fluently. Had these subjects been exposed to both languages in the crib, would they have learned both vowel systems? Behavioral studies are not yet readily available.

In the remainder of this section, we will review what brain-imaging techniques can tell us about language representation in bilingual adults. Mazoyer and colleagues (1993) explored brain activity in monolingual adults who were listening to stories in their maternal tongue (French) or in an unknown foreign language (Tamil). Listening to French stories activated a large left hemisphere network including parts of the prefrontal cortex and the temporal lobes—a result that is congruent with the standard teachings of neuropsychology.[1] In contrast, the activation for Tamil was restricted to the midtemporal areas in both the left and right hemispheres. Was the left hemisphere of the French subjects activated by French because it was their mother tongue or because French, in contrast to Tamil, was a language they understood? Perani and colleagues (1996) investigated native Italians with moderate-to-good English comprehension. When

Italians were listening to Italian, they exhibited the same pattern of activation as that reported in the Mazoyer study. Italians listening to and understanding English displayed a weak symmetrical right-hemisphere and left-hemisphere activation. Surprisingly, they displayed a similar activation when listening to stories in Japanese, a language they did not understand.[2] Comparing the cortical activation to English and Japanese ought to have uncovered the cortical areas dedicated to processing the words, syntax, and semantics of English. Figure 62.3 (see color plate 41) illustrates the fact that our expectation was not fulfilled.

How can we explain this failure? It seems unlikely that natural languages should yield comparable activation regardless of comprehension. An alternative account is that the native language yields the same cortical structures in every volunteer while a second language "shows greater inter-individual variability and therefore fails to stand out when averaged across subjects." Dehaene and colleagues (1997) used fMRI to explore this possible explanation. They examined eight French volunteers who had a fair understanding of English comparable in proficiency to the bilinguals tested by Perani and co-workers. The French volunteers listened to French or English stories and backward speech in alternation. When listening to French, their mother tongue, they all showed more activity in and around the left superior temporal sulcus. But when they listened to English, left and right cortical activation was highly variable among subjects (see figure 62.4; color plate 42). This result may reflect the fact that a second language may be learned in a number of different ways (e.g., through explicit tuition or more naturally), and hence the end result may vary from one individual to the next. To assess this, we need to examine the cortical representation of the second language when it was learned in a natural setting during childhood.

Perani and colleagues (1998) tried to explore these issues by testing two groups of highly proficient bilinguals. The first were Spanish/Catalan bilinguals who had acquired their second language between ages 2 and 4 and appeared to be equally proficient in both of their languages (but see Pallier, Bosch, and Sebastian-Gallés, 1997, who tested the same population of subjects). The second were Italians who had learned English after the age of 10 and had attained excellent performance. The main finding of this PET study was that the cortical representations of the two languages were very similar (for both groups of high-proficiency bilinguals), and significantly different from that in low-proficiency bilinguals. This study suggests that proficiency is more important than age of acquisition as a determinant of cortical representation of the second language, at least in bilinguals

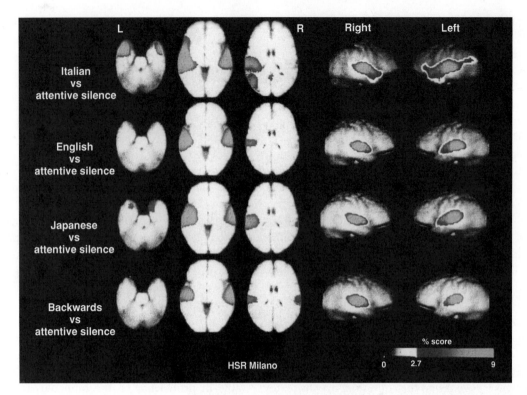

FIGURE 62.3 Patterns of activation in a PET study measuring the activity in Italian speakers' brains while listening to Italian (mother tongue), English (second language), Japanese (unknown language), and backward Japanese (not a possible human language). There was a significant activation difference between Italian and English. In contrast, English and Japanese did not differ significantly. Japanese differed significantly from backward Japanese. (Adapted from Perani et al., 1996.)

who speak languages that are historically, lexically, and syntactically reasonably close (even though there are phonological differences). All these studies investigated the cortical activation while *listening* to speech. What happens for speech *production*?

Kim and colleagues (1997) investigated a kind of speech production situation: They used fMRI with bilingual volunteers who were silently speaking in either of their languages. They tested bilingual volunteers who mastered their second language either early or late in life (the languages involved in the study were highly varied). They found that the first and second languages have overlapping representation in Broca's area in early learners whereas these representations are segregated in late learners. In contrast, both languages overlap over Wernicke's area regardless of age of acquisition. However, only age of acquisition and not proficiency was controlled; thus it is difficult to evaluate their separate contribution. As Perani and colleagues have indicated, there is a negative correlation between age of acquisition and proficiency (Johnson and Newport, 1989).

How can we harmonize the picture we get from the brain imaging studies with behavioral results? Even with very proficient bilinguals, it has been shown that the languages are not equivalent: People behave as natives in their dominant language and do not perform perfectly well in the other language. This has been shown for phonetic perception (Pallier, Bosch, and Sebastian-Gallés, 1997), sublexical representations (Cutler et al., 1989; 1992), grammaticality judgments (Weber-Fox and Neville, 1996), and speech production (Flege, Munro, and MacKay, 1995). Possibly, the fact that the cortical representations for the first and second languages tend to span overlapping areas with increased proficiency cannot be taken to mean equivalent competence. As Perani and colleagues state:

A possible interpretation of what brain imaging is telling us is that in the case of low proficiency individuals, the brain is recruiting multiple, and variable, brain regions, to handle as far as possible the dimensions of the second language, which are different from the first language. As proficiency increases, the highly proficient bilinguals use the same neural machinery to deal with the first and the second languages. However, this anatomical overlap cannot exclude that this brain network is using the linguistic structures of the first language to assimilate less than perfectly the dimensions of the second language.

Another inconsistency will have to be explained in future work. We know from several studies (e.g., Cohen et al., 1997; Kaas, 1995; Rauschecker, 1997; Sadato et al., 1996) that changing the nature and distribution of sen-

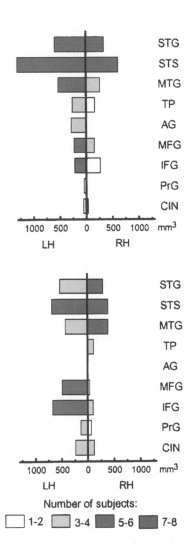

Number of subjects:

☐ 1-2 ☐ 3-4 ☐ 5-6 ■ 7-8

FIGURE 62.4   Intersubject variability in the cortical representation of language is greater for the second than for the first language. Each bar represents an anatomical region of interest (left and right hemisphere). Its length represents the average active volume (in square millimeters) in that region. Its color reflects the number of subjects in which that region was active. (Adapted from Dehaene et al., 1997.)

sory input can result in important modifications of the cortical maps, even in adult organisms. However, people do not reach native performance in a second language, despite massive exposure, training, and motivation. Can we reconcile cortical plasticity with behavioral rigidity?

Yet another area in great need of more research is the functional significance of activation maps in general. Consider the work by Neville and her colleagues on the representation of American Sign Language (ASL) in deaf and hearing native signers. These authors carried out an fMRI study and showed that ASL is bilaterally represented in both populations while written English is basically represented in the left hemisphere of the hearing signers (who were also native speakers of English). Hickok, Bellugi, and Klima (1996) studied 23 native

speakers of ASL with unilateral brain lesions and found clear and convincing evidence for a left-hemispheric dominance, much like the one found in speakers of natural languages. This leaves us in a dilemma: Either we assert that it is not easy to draw functional conclusions from activation maps, and/or we have to posit that ASL is not a natural language.

Mapping the higher cognitive functions to neural networks is an evolving skill. In the near future, we expect to witness a trend toward a more exhaustive study of a given function in a single subject. For instance, each volunteer could be tested several times to investigate in detail how language competence is organized and represented in his/her cortex. This should help us to elucidate several of the seemingly paradoxical findings we reported above. However things evolve, it is clear that when we understand these issues in greater depth, we will be able to make gigantic leaps in our understanding of development.

Conclusion

We have presented data drawn from experimental psychology, infant psychology, and brain-imaging to propose another way of addressing the study of development—this, to illustrate an approach to the study of development now gaining in support. By bringing together some of the areas that jointly clarify how the human mind gains access to language, logic, mathematics, and other such recursive systems, we can begin to answer several fundamental questions: (1) Why is the acquisition of some capacities possible for human brains and not for the brains of other higher vertebrates? (2) Are there skills that can be acquired more naturally and with a better outcome before a certain age? (3) Does the acquisition of some skill facilitate the acquisition of similar skills in older organisms—those who would normally show little disposition to learn "from scratch"? The need to answer such questions is the essence of many developmental research programs. The fact that questions like these are being asked has implications for the cognitive psychologist and cognitive neuroscience. Cognitive psychologists are becoming increasingly aware that they must conceive of development as a critical aspect of cognitive neuroscience. If, for instance, there are time schedules to naturally learn certain skills, the joint study of the time course of development and the concurrent maturation of neural structures may tell us which neural structures are responsible for the acquisition of which capacities. Coupled with brain-imaging and neuropsychological data, these facts may help us to understand better the mapping between neural structure and cognitive function. One may call such a study the "neuropsychology of the normal."

In concluding, we dispute the notion that the acquisition of mental abilities can be sufficiently studied by looking only at growing children. We suggest that to understand the mechanisms responsible for change, one must first specify the normal envelope of stable states and the species-specific endowment; then we can go on to develop a theory of acquisition that accounts for the mapping from the initial to the stable state. Many different disciplines will have to participate in achieving this goal. Neuroscience has made many discoveries that are essential to the understanding of development; in particular, brain-imaging studies may bring in a new perspective to the research of growth and development. Thus, rather than making the study of development an autonomous part of cognition, we conceive of it as a unique source of information that should be an integral component of cognitive psychology.

ACKNOWLEDGMENTS   We wish to thank the Human Frontiers Science Programme, Human Capital and Mobility Programme, the Direction de la Recherche, des Etudes, et de la Technologie, and the Franco-Spanish grant.

NOTES

1. There are some areas–e.g., the anterior poles of the temporal lobes and Brodmann 8–that had not often been related to language processing by classical neuropsychology.
2. Interestingly, the left inferior frontal gyrus, the left midtemporal gyrus, and the inferior left parietal lobule were more active when subjects were listening to Japanese compared to backward Japanese. These activations could mirror the subjects' attempt to store the input as meaningless phonological information in auditory short-term memory (see Paulesu, Frith, and Frackowiak, 1993). Perani and colleagues observed that the left middle temporal gyrus activation appeared only when subjects were listening to speech, regardless of whether they understood the stories, but not when listening to backward speech, an unnatural stimulus. The authors suggest that the left middle temporal gyrus is highly attuned to the processing of the sound patterns of any natural language.

REFERENCES

ALTMANN, G. T. M., and D. H. YOUNG, 1993. Factors affecting adaptation to time–compressed speech. Paper presented at the Eurospeech 9, Berlin.

BAHRICK, L. E., and J. N. PICKENS, 1988. Classification of bimodal English and Spanish language passages by infants. *Infant Behav. Dev.* 11:277–296.

BERTONCINI, J., R. BIJELJAC-BABIC, P. W. JUSCZYK, L. KENNEDY, and J. MEHLER, 1988. An investigation of young infants' perceptual representations of speech sounds. *J. Exp. Psychol.* 117:21–33.

BOSCH, L., and N. SEBASTIAN-GALLÉS, 1997. Native-language recognition abilities in four-month–old infants from monolingual and bilingual environments. *Cognition* 65:33–69.

BRENT, M. R., and T. A. CARTWRIGHT, 1996. Distributional regularity and phonotactic constraints are useful for segmentation. *Cognition* 61:93–125.

CAIRNS, P., R. SHILLCOCK, N. CHATER, and J. LEVY, 1997. Bootstrapping word boundaries: A bottom-up corpus-based approach to speech segmentation. *Cogn. Psychol.* 33:111–153.

CAVALLI-SFORZA, L. L., 1991. Genes, people and languages. *Scientific American* 265:104–110.

CHOMSKY, N., 1988. *Language and Problems of Knowledge*: Cambridge, Mass.: MIT Press.

CHRISTOPHE, A., and E. DUPOUX, 1996. Bootstrapping lexical acquisition: The role of prosodic structure. *Linguistic Rev.* 13:383–412.

CHRISTOPHE, A., E. DUPOUX, J. BERTONCINI, and J. MEHLER, 1994. Do infants perceive word boundaries? An empirical study of the bootstrapping of lexical acquisition. *J. Acoust. Soc. Amer.* 95:1570–1580.

CHRISTOPHE, A., M. T. GUASTI, M. NESPOR, E. DUPOUX, and B. VAN OOYEN, 1997. Reflections on phonological bootstrapping: Its role for lexical and syntactic acquisition. *Lang. Cogn. Processes* 12:585–612.

CHRISTOPHE, A., M. T. GUASTI, M. NESPOR, E. DUPOUX, and B. VAN OOYEN, 1999. Prosodic structure and syntactic acquisition: The case of the head-complement parameter. In preparation.

CHRISTOPHE, A., and J. MORTON, 1998. Is Dutch native English? Linguistic analysis by 2-month-olds. *Dev. Sci.* 215–219.

COHEN, L. G., P. CELNIK, A. PASCUAL-LEONE, B. CORWELL, L. FALZ, J. DAMBROSIA, M. HONDA, N. SADATO, C. GERLOFF, M. D. CATALA, and M. HALLETT, 1977. Functional relevance of cross-modal plasticity in blind humans. *Nature* 389:180–183.

CUTLER, A., and S. BUTTERFIELD, 1992. Rhythmic cues to speech segmentation: Evidence from juncture misperception. *J. Mem. Lang.* 31:218–236.

CUTLER, A., J. MEHLER, D. NORRIS, and J. SEGUI, 1989. Limits on bilingualism. *Nature* 320:229–230.

CUTLER, A., J. MEHLER, D. NORRIS, and J. SEGUI, 1992. The monolingual nature of speech segmentation by bilinguals. *Cogn. Psychol.* 24:381–410.

CUTLER, A., and T. OTAKE, 1994. Mora or phoneme: Further evidence for language-specific listening. *J. Mem. Lang.* 33:824–844.

DEHAENE, S., E. DUPOUX, J. MEHLER, L. COHEN, E. PAULESU, D. PERANI, P.-F. VAN DE MOORTELE, S. LÉHERICY, and D. LEBIHAN, 1997. Anatomical variability in the cortical representation of first and second languages. *Neuroreport* 8:3809–3815.

DEHAENE-LAMBERTZ, G., and D. HOUSTON, 1998. Faster orientation latency toward native language in two-month-old infants. *Lang. Speech* 41:21–43.

DE PIJPER, J. R., and A. A. SANDERMAN, 1994. On the perceptual strength of prosodic boundaries and its relation to suprasegmental cues. *J. Acoust. Soc. Amer.* 96:2037–2047.

DUPOUX, E., and K. GREEN, 1997. Perceptual adjustment to highly compressed speech: effects of talker and rate changes. *J. Exp. Psychol.: Human Percept. Perform.* 23:914–927.

DUPOUX, E., K. KAKEHI, Y. HIROSE, C. PALLIER, S. FITNEVA, and J. MEHLER, in press. Epenthetic vowels in Japanese: A perceptual illusion. *J. Mem. Lang.*

DUPOUX, E., C. PALLIER, N. SEBASTIAN-GALLÉS, and J. MEHLER, 1997. A destressing "deafness" in French? *J. Mem. Lang.* 36:406–421.

ELMAN, J. L., E. A. BATES, M. H. JOHNSON, A. KARMILOFF–SMITH, D. PARISI, and K. PLUNKETT, 1996. *Rethinking Innateness: A Connectionist Perspective on Development.* Cambridge, Mass.: MIT Press.

FERNALD, A., and G. MCROBERTS, 1996. Prosodic bootstrapping: A critical analysis of the argument and the evidence. In *Signal to Syntax: Bootstrapping from Speech to Grammar in Early Acquisition*, J. L. Morgan and K. Demuth, eds. Mahwah, N.J.: Lawrence Erlbaum, pp. 365–388.

FISHER, C., and H. TOKURA, 1996. Prosody in speech to infants: Direct and indirect acoustic cues to syntactic structure. In *Signal to Syntax: Bootstrapping from Speech to Grammar in Early Acquisition*, J. L. Morgan and K. Demuth, eds. Mahwah, N.J.: Lawrence Erlbaum, pp. 343–363.

FLEGE, J. E., M. J. MUNRO, and I. R. A. MACKAY, 1995. Factors affecting strength of perceived foreign accent in a second language. *J. Acoust. Soc. Amer.* 97:3125–3134.

FODOR, J. D., 1998. Unambiguous triggers. *Linguistic Inquiry* 29.

FRIEDERICI, A. D., and J. M. I. WESSELS, 1993. Phonotactic knowledge of word boundaries and its use in infant speech perception. *Percept. Psychophysics* 54:287–295.

GALL, F. J., 1835. *Works: On the Function of the Brain and Each of Its Parts.* Boston: March Capon and Lyon.

GERKEN, L., 1996. Phonological and distributional information in syntax acquisition. In *Signal to Syntax: Bootstrapping from Speech to Grammar in Early Acquisition*, J. L. Morgan and K. Demuth, eds. Mahwah, N.J.: Lawrence Erlbaum, pp. 411–425.

GERKEN, L., P. W. JUSCZYK, and D. R. MANDEL, 1994. When prosody fails to cue syntactic structure: 9-month-olds' sensitivity to phonological versus syntactic phrases. *Cognition* 51:237–265.

GIBSON, E., and K. WEXLER, 1994. Triggers. *Linguistic Inquiry* 25:407–454.

GLEITMAN, L., 1990. The structural sources of verb meanings. *Language Acquisition* 1:3–55.

GLEITMAN, L., and H. GLEITMAN, 1997. What is a language made out of? *Lingua* 100:29–55.

GLEITMAN, L., and E. WANNER, 1982. The state of the state of the art. In *Language Acquisition: The State of the Art*, E. Wanner and L. Gleitman, eds. Cambridge: Cambridge University Press, pp. 3–48.

GUASTI, M. T., M. NESPOR, A. CHRISTOPHE, and B. VAN OOYEN, in press. Pre-lexical setting of the head complement parameter through prosody. In *Signal to Syntax II: Approaches to Bootstrapping in Early Language Development.* J. Weissenborn and B. Höhle, eds. Amsterdam/Philadelphia: John Benjamins.

HICKOK, G., U. BELLUGI, and E. S. KLIMA, 1996. The neurobiology of sign language and its implications for the neural basis of language. *Nature* 381:699–702.

JOHNSON, J. S., and E. L. NEWPORT, 1989. Critical period effects in second language learning: The influence of maturational state on the acquisition of English as a second language. *Cogn. Psychol.* 21:60–99.

JUSCZYK, P. W., and R. N. ASLIN, 1995. Infants' detection of the sound patterns of words in fluent speech. *Cogn. Psychol.* 29:1–23.

JUSCZYK, P. W., A. CUTLER, and N. J. REDANZ, 1993. Infants' preference for the predominant stress patterns of English words. *Child Dev.* 64:675–687.

JUSCZYK, P. W., and E. A. HOHNE, 1997. Infants' memory for spoken words. *Science* 277:1984–1986.

JUSCZYK, P. W., D. M. HOUSTON, and M. NEWSOME, in press. The beginnings of word segmentation in English-learning infants. *Cogn. Psychol.*

JUSCZYK, P. W., P. A. LUCE, and J. CHARLES-LUCE, 1994. Infants' sensitivity to phonotactic patterns in the native language. *J. Mem. Lang.* 33:630–645.

KAAS, J. H., 1995. The reorganization of sensory and motor maps in adult mammals. In *The Cognitive Neurosciences*, M. S. Gazzaniga, ed. Cambridge, Mass.: MIT Press, pp. 51–72.

KIM, K. H. S., N. R. RELKIN, K. M. LEE, and J. HIRSCH, 1997. Distinct cortical areas associated with native and second languages. *Nature* 388:171–174.

KUHL, P. K., K. A. WILLIAMS, F. LACERDA, K. N. STEVENS, and B. LINDBLOM, 1992. Linguistic experience alters phonetic perception in infants by 6 months of age. *Science* 255:606–608.

LENNEBERG, E., 1967. Biological Foundations of Language. New York: Wiley.

MAZOYER, B. M., S. DEHAENE, N. TZOURIO, V. FRAK, N. MURAYAMA, L. COHEN, O. LÉVRIER, G. SALAMON, A. SYROTA, and J. MEHLER, 1993. The cortical representation of speech. *J. Cogn. Neurosci.* 5:467–479.

MAZUKA, R., 1996. How can a grammatical parameter be set before the first word? In *Signal to Syntax: Bootstrapping from Speech to Grammar in Early Acquisition*, J. L. Morgan and K. Demuth, eds. Mahwah, N.J.: Lawrence Erlbaum, pp. 313–330.

MCQUEEN, J. M., D. NORRIS, and A. CUTLER, 1994. Competition in spoken word recognition: Spotting words in other words. *J. Exp. Psychol.: Learn. Mem. Cognit.* 20:621–638.

MEHLER, J., and A. CHRISTOPHE, 1995. Maturation and learning of language in the first year of life. In *The Cognitive Neurosciences*, M. S. Gazzaniga, ed. Cambridge, Mass.: MIT Press, pp. 943–954.

MEHLER, J., and E. DUPOUX, 1994. *What infants know.* Cambridge, Mass.: Basil Blackwell.

MEHLER, J., E. DUPOUX, T. NAZZI, and G. DEHAENE-LAMBERTZ, 1996. Coping with linguistic diversity: The infant's viewpoint. In *Signal to Syntax: Bootstrapping from Speech to Grammar in Early Acquisition*, J. L. Morgan and K. Demuth, eds. Mahwah, N.J.: Lawrence Erlbaum, pp. 101–116.

MEHLER, J., E. DUPOUX, and J. SEGUI, 1990. Constraining models of lexical access: the onset of word recognition. In *Cognitive Models of Speech Processing: Psycholinguistic and Computational Perspectives*, G. T. M. Altmann, ed. Cambridge Mass: MIT Press, pp. 263–280.

MEHLER, J., and R. FOX (eds.), 1985. *Neonate Cognition: Beyond the Blooming, Buzzing Confusion.* Hillsdale N.J.: Lawrence Erlbaum.

MEHLER, J., P. W. JUSCZYK, G. LAMBERTZ, G. HALSTED, J. BERTONCINI, and C. AMIEL-TISON, 1988. A precursor of language acquisition in young infants. *Cognition* 29:143–178.

MEHLER, J., N. SEBASTIAN-GALLÉS, G. ALTMANN, E. DUPOUX, A. CHRISTOPHE, and C. PALLIER, 1993. Understanding compressed sentences: The role of rhythm and meaning. *Ann. N.Y. Acad. Sci.* 682:272–282.

MILLER, G. A., and P. W. NICELY, 1955. An analysis of perceptual confusions among some English consonants. *J. Acoust. Soc. Amer.* 27:338–352.

MOON, C., R. COOPER, and W. FIFER, 1993. Two-day-olds prefer their native language. *Infant Behav. Dev.* 16:495–500.

MORGAN, J., 1996. Phonological bootstrapping in early acquisition: The importance of starting small versus starting 'sharp.' Paper presented at How to Get into Language: Approaches to Bootstrapping in Early Language Development, Potsdam, Germany.

MORGAN, J. L., 1986. *From Simple Input to Complex Grammar.* Cambridge, Mass.: MIT Press.

MORGAN, J. L., 1994. Converging measures of speech segmentation in preverbal infants. *Infant Behav. Dev.* 17:389–403.

MORGAN, J. L., and K. DEMUTH, 1996a. Signal to syntax: An overview. In *Signal to Syntax: Bootstrapping from Speech to Grammar in Early Acquisition,* J. L. Morgan and K. Demuth, eds. Mahwah, N.J.: Lawrence Erlbaum, pp. 1–22.

MORGAN, J. L., and K. DEMUTH (eds.), 1996b. *Signal to Syntax: Bootstrapping from Speech to Grammar in Early Acquisition.* Mahwah, N.J.: Lawrence Erlbaum.

MORGAN, J. L., R. SHI, and P. ALLOPENNA, 1996. Perceptual bases of rudimentary grammatical categories: Toward a broader conceptualization of bootstrapping. In *Signal to Syntax: Bootstrapping from Speech to Grammar in Early Acquisition,* J. L. Morgan and K. Demuth, eds. Mahwah, N.J.: Lawrence Erlbaum, pp. 263–283.

NAZZI, T., J. BERTONCINI, and J. MEHLER, 1998. Language discrimination by newborns: Towards an understanding of the role of rhythm. *J. Exp. Psychol.: Human Percept. Perform.* 24:1–11.

NESPOR, M., M. T. GUASTI, and A. CHRISTOPHE, 1996. Selecting word order: The rhythmic activation principle. In *Interfaces in Phonology,* U. Kleinhenz, ed. Berlin: Akademie Verlag, pp. 1–26.

NESPOR, M., and I. VOGEL, 1986. *Prosodic Phonology.* Dordrecht: Foris.

OTAKE, T., K. YONEYAMA, A. CUTLER, and A. VAN DER LUGT, 1996. The representation of Japanese moraic nasals. *J. Acoust. Soc. Amer.* 100:3831–3842.

OVIATT, S. L., 1980. The emerging ability to comprehend language: An experimental approach. *Child Dev.* 51:97–106.

PALLIER, C., L. BOSCH, and N. SEBASTIAN-GALLÉS, 1997. A limit on behavioral plasticity in vowel acquisition. *Cognition* 64:B9–B17.

PALLIER, C., A. CHRISTOPHE, and J. MEHLER, 1997. Language-specific listening. *Trends Cogn. Sci.* 1:129–132.

PALLIER, C., N. SEBASTIAN-GALLÉS, and A. COLOME, 1999. The use of phonological code in auditory repetition priming. In preparation.

PALLIER, C., N. SEBASTIAN-GALLÉS, E. DUPOUX, A. CHRISTOPHE, and J. MEHLER, 1998. Perceptual adjustment to time-compressed speech: A cross-linguistic study. *Mem. Cognit.* 26:844–851.

PAULESU, E., C. D. FRITH, and R. S. J. FRACKOWIAK, 1993. The neural correlates of the verbal component of working memory. *Nature* 362:342–345.

PERANI, D., S. DEHAENE, F. GRASSI, L. COHEN, S. F. CAPPA, E. DUPOUX, F. FAZIO, and J. MEHLER, 1996. Brain processing of native and foreign languages. *Neuroreport* 7:2349–2444.

PERANI, D., E. PAULESU, N. SEBASTIAN-GALLÉS, E. DUPOUX, S. DEHAENE, V. BETTINARDI, S. F. CAPPA, J. MEHLER, and F. FAZIO, 1998. The bilingual brain: Proficiency and age of acquisition of the second language. *Brain* 121:1849–1852.

PINKER, S., 1994. *The Language Instinct.* London: Penguin Books.

RAMUS, F., and J. MEHLER, 1999. Language identification with suprasegmental cues: A study based on speech resynthesis. *J. Acoust. Soc. Amer.* 105:512–521.

RAUSCHECKER, J. P., 1997. Mechanisms of compensatory plasticity in cerebral cortex. In *Brain Plasticity: Advances in Neurology, Vol. 7,* H.-J. Freund, B. A. Sabel, and O. W. Witte, eds. Philadelphia: Lippincott-Raven, pp. 137–146.

RENFREW, C., 1994. World linguistic diversity. *Scientific American* 270:116–123.

SADATO, N., A. PASCUAL-LEONE, J. GRAFMAN, V. IBANEZ, M. P. DELBER, G. DOLD, and M. HALLETT, 1996. Activation and the primary visual cortex by Braille reading in blind subjects. *Nature* 380:526–528.

SAFFRAN, J. R., R. N. ASLIN, and E. L. NEWPORT, 1996. Statistical learning by 8-month-old infants. *Science* 274:1926–1928.

SEBASTIAN-GALLÉS, N., E. DUPOUX, and A. COSTA, in press. Adaptation to time-compressed speech: Phonological determinants. *Percept. Psychophys.*

SHAFER, V. L., D. W. SHUCARD, J. L. SHUCARD, and L. GERKEN, 1998. An electrophysiological study of infants' sensitivity to the sound patterns of English speech. *J. Speech, Lang., Hear. Res.* 41(4):874–886.

TESAR, B., and P. SMOLENSKY, 1998. Learnability in optimality theory. *Linguistic Inq.* 29(2):229–268.

THOMAS, D. G., J. J. CAMPOS, D. W. SHUCARD, D. S. RAMSEY, and J. SHUCARD, 1981. Semantic comprehension in infancy: A signal detection analysis. *Child Dev.* 52:798–803.

WARREN, P., F. NOLAN, E. GRABE, and T. HOLST, 1995. Postlexical and prosodic phonological processing. *Lang. Cogn. Processes,* 10:411–417.

WEBER-FOX, C. M., and H. J. NEVILLE, 1996. Maturational constraints on functional specializations for language processing: ERP and behavioral evidence in bilingual speakers. *J. Cogn. Neurosci.* 8:231–256.

WEISSENBORN, J., and B. HÖHLE (eds.), 1999. *From Signal to Syntax, II: Approaches to Bootstrapping in Early Language Development.* Amsterdam: John Benjamins.

63 The Cognitive Neuroscience of Language Acquisition

KARIN STROMSWOLD

ABSTRACT This chapter reviews findings from several research areas–normal language acquisition, learnability theory, developmental and acquired language disorders, and language acquisition after the critical period–indicating that the ability to acquire language is the result of innate brain mechanisms. It is possible that infants' brains are predisposed to perceive categorically such stimuli as phonemes, words, syntactic categories, and phrases, and this predisposition allows children to acquire language rapidly and with few errors.

Because the ability to learn a language is a uniquely human ability, language acquisition is an important topic in cognitive neuroscience. Perhaps the most fundamental question about language and language acquisition is the extent to which the ability to learn language is the result of innate mechanisms or predispositions (henceforth referred to as innate abilities). Innate abilities often share certain characteristics. An innate ability is usually present in all normal individuals. Its acquisition tends to be uniform and automatic, with all normal individuals going through the same stages at the same ages, without specific instruction. There may be a critical period for successful acquisition. The ability is likely to be functionally and anatomically autonomous or modular. Finally, the trait may be heritable.

Although these characteristics are by no means definitive, they can be used to evaluate traits that may be innate. Consider, for example, the ability to walk and the ability to knit. The ability to walk exhibits most of the hallmarks of innate abilities, and is presumably innate; but the ability to knit exhibits few of these hallmarks, and is presumably not innate. If children's brains are innately predisposed to learn language, then given adequate exposure to language, all children with normal brains should, without instruction, learn language in a relatively uniform way, just as normal vision develops given adequate exposure to visual stimuli (Hubel and Wiesel, 1970). But if the ability to learn language is not innate, instruction may be necessary, the course of acquisition may vary greatly from person to person (per-

haps as a function of the quality of instruction), and there may be no critical period for acquisition.

Even if the ability to learn language is the result of innate mechanisms and predispositions, another question remains: Are these mechanisms specific to language and language acquisition (e.g., Chomsky, 1981, 1986; Pinker, 1994) or are they also involved in tasks and abilities that are not linguistic (e.g., Karmiloff-Smith, 1991; Elman et al., 1996)? If the ability to acquire language is the result of innate mechanisms used solely for language and language acquisition, language may be functionally and anatomically autonomous or modular from other abilities, in which case developmental and acquired lesions may specifically impair or spare the ability to learn language. Conversely, if general-purpose mechanisms are involved in language acquisition, we would not expect to find evidence of the functional or anatomical modularity of language or language acquisition.

Language development

LINGUISTICS AND THE UNIVERSAL FEATURES OF LANGUAGE Superficially, learning to talk differs from learning to walk in that children are capable of learning many different languages, but just one basic walk. If children really are predisposed to learn all human languages, then all languages must be fundamentally the same. In fact, linguists have discovered that, although some languages seem to differ radically from other languages (e.g., Turkish and English), in essential ways all human languages are remarkably similar to one another (Chomsky, 1981, 1986; Croft, 1990).

Generative linguists usually assume that language involves rules and operations that have no counterparts in nonlinguistic domains and that the ability to use and acquire language is part of our innate endowment. For example, within principles-and-parameters (P&P) generative theory (Chomsky, 1981, 1986), all languages are said to share a common set of grammatical principles. Differences among languages result from the different parametric values chosen for those principles. According to P&P theory, at some level, children are born knowing

KARIN STROMSWOLD Department of Psychology and Center for Cognitive Science, Rutgers University, New Brunswick, N.J.

909

the principles that are universal to all languages (Universal Grammar); thus, to learn a particular language, all they must do is learn the vocabulary and parametric settings of that language. Similarly, within another generative linguistic theory—optimality theory (OT)—the same universal constraints operate in all languages, and languages differ merely in the ranking of these constraints (Prince and Smolensky, 1993). According to OT, children are born "knowing" the universal constraints; thus, to learn a particular language, all children must do is learn the vocabulary and ranking of constraints for that language (Tesar and Smolensky, 1996). Linguists working within the functionalist tradition (e.g., Foley and Van Valin, 1984) are more likely to assume that language shares properties with nonlinguistic abilities, and that operations used in language acquisition are used in other, nonlinguistic domains (e.g., Bates and MacWhinney, 1982; Budwig, 1995; Van Valin, 1991).

UNIFORMITY IN LANGUAGE ACQUISITION   Within a given language, the course of language acquisition is remarkably uniform (Brown, 1973).[1] Most children say their first referential words at 9 to 15 months (Morley, 1965; Benedict, 1979; Fenson et al., 1994; Huttenlocher and Smiley, 1987), and for the next 6–8 months, children typically acquire single words fairly slowly until they have acquired approximately 50 words. For most children acquiring English, the majority of their first 50 words are labels for objects (e.g., *cookie, mother, father, bottle*) with a few action verbs (*eat, come, go*), social terms (*good-bye, hello*), and prepositions (*up, down*) rounding out the list (Nelson, 1973; Bates et al., 1994; Benedict, 1979). Once children have acquired 50 words, their vocabularies often increase rapidly (e.g., Reznick and Goldfield, 1992; Benedict, 1979; Mervis and Bertrand, 1995), expanding by 22 to 37 words per month (Benedict, 1979; Goldfield and Reznick, 1990).

At around 18 to 24 months, children learning morphologically impoverished languages such as English begin combining words to form two-word utterances such as *want cookie, play checkers,* and *big drum* (Brown, 1973). During this two-word stage, the vast majority of children's utterances are legitimate portions of sentences in the language they are learning. Thus, in English—a language that has restricted word order—children will say *want cookie* but not *cookie want* (Brown, 1973) and *he big* but not *big he* (Bloom, 1990). Children acquiring such morphologically impoverished languages gradually begin to use sentences longer than two words; but for several months, their speech often lacks phonetically unstressed functional category morphemes such as determiners, auxiliary verbs, and verbal and nominal inflectional endings (Brown, 1973; Mills, 1985; Schieffelin,

1985). Representative utterances during this period include *Sarah want cookie, Where Humpty Dumpty go?*, and *Adam write pencil*. Children's early speech is often described as "telegraphic" (Brown, 1973) because it resembles the way adults speak when words are at a premium, as in a telegram. Gradually, omissions become rarer until children are between three and four years old, at which point the vast majority of English-speaking children's utterances are completely grammatical (Stromswold, 1990a,b, 1994b). Children who are acquiring languages like Turkish, which have rich, regular, and perceptually salient morphological systems, generally begin to use functional category morphemes at a younger age than children acquiring morphologically poor languages (Aksu-Koc and Slobin, 1985; Berman, 1986; Peters, 1995). For example, in striking contrast to the telegraphic speech of English-speaking children, Turkish-speaking children often begin to produce morphologically complex words before they begin to use multiword utterances (Aksu-Koc and Slobin, 1985).[2]

Within a given language, children master the syntax (grammar) of their language in a surprisingly similar manner (Brown, 1973). For example, children acquire the 14 grammatical morphemes of English in essentially the same order (Brown, 1973; deVilliers and deVilliers, 1973). Similarly, all 15 of the children I studied acquired the 20-odd English auxiliary verbs in essentially the same order (Stromswold, 1990a). The order in which these 15 children acquired complex constructions—questions, negative constructions, passives, datives, exceptional-case–marking constructions, embedded sentences, preposition-stranding constructions, causative constructions, small clause constructions, verb-particle constructions, and relative clauses constructions—was also extremely regular (Stromswold, 1988, 1989a,b, 1990a,b, 1992, 1994b, 1995; Stromswold and Snyder, 1995; Snyder and Stromswold, 1997). Finally, to a remarkable degree, within and across languages, children make certain types of mistakes and not others.

ACQUISITION OF SYNTACTIC CATEGORIES   In order to acquire their language, children must not only learn the meanings of words like *cat* and *eat*, they must also learn that words like *cat* are nouns and words like *eat* are verbs. That is, they must learn the categorical membership of words. This is critical because whether a syntactic or morphological rule applies to a particular word depends on its categorical membership, not on its meaning. Consider, for example, the sentence *Linus cratomizes Lucy:* Any speaker of English automatically knows that *Linus* is the grammatical subject of the sentence (because, within an intonational clause, it is in preverbal position), *Lucy* is the grammatical object (because it is in postverbal position), and the nonsense word *cratomize* is a lexical verb. Even without knowing what *cratomize* means, an English speaker automatically knows that its progressive form is *cratomizing* and that its past tense form is *cratomized*; that *do*-support is required to ask a standard matrix question (e.g., *Did Linus cratomize Lucy?* and not *Cratomized Linus Lucy?*[3] or *Linus cratomized Lucy?*) or negate an utterance (e.g., *Linus didn't cratomize Lucy* and not *Linus cratomized not Lucy, *Linus not cratomized Lucy*); and that the grammatical subject precedes rather than follows *cratomize* in simple declarative utterances (e.g., *Linus cratomizes Lucy* and not *cratomizes Linus Lucy*). The fact that English speakers know the syntactic and morphological behavior of *cratomize* without having the slightest idea what *cratomize* means demonstrates that categorical membership and not meaning determines syntactic and morphological behavior. A central question in the field of language acquisition is how children learn the categorical membership of words. For adults, the answer is simple. Even from the single sentence *Linus cratomizes Lucy,* adults recognize that cratomize is clearly a verb—it appears after the grammatical subject *Linus* and before the object *Lucy*, has the third-person verbal inflection *-s*, and exhibits other verb-like properties. The answer is much trickier for children.

How do children learn which words are verbs if they don't know what properties are typical of verbs? And how can they learn the properties of verbs if they don't know which words are verbs? One simple possibility is that every verb in every human language shares some readily accessible property for which children are innately predisposed to look. Unfortunately, no such property seems to exist. Instead, infants probably rely on a combination of cues—prosodic, semantic, and correlational—to learn which words are nouns and which are verbs (Pinker, 1987). Infants may, for example, use prosodic cues such as changes in fundamental frequency and lengthening to help determine where major clausal and phrasal boundaries are. Combined with knowledge of the universal properties of clauses and phrases (e.g., that verbs are contained within verb phrases and sentential clauses contain noun phrases and verb phrases), this could help children learn which words are verbs (Jusczyk et al., 1992; Jusczyk and Kemler Nelson, 1996; Morgan and Demuth, 1996). Infants might also set up an enormous correlation matrix in which they record all of the behaviors associated with words; in that case, categories are the result of children noticing that certain behaviors tend to be correlated. Thus, having noticed that certain words often end in *-ing, -ed*, or *-s*, frequently occur in the middle of sentences, and rarely appear in the beginning of a sentence, children sort out these words as a verb category (see Maratsos and Chalkley, 1981). The problem with the notion of a simple, un-constrained, and unbiased correlational learner is the infinite number of correlations that children must consider, most of which will never appear in any language (Pinker, 1984, 1987). If infants are born "knowing" that, in language, objects are expressed by nouns, physical actions by verbs, and attributes by adjectives, infants could infer that words referring to physical objects are nouns, words referring to actions are verbs, and words referring to attributes are adjectives. They could learn the properties of nouns and verbs from these semantically prototypical cases, a process often referred to as "semantic bootstrapping" (see Pinker, 1984, 1987).

ACQUISITION OF AUXILIARY AND LEXICAL VERBS
The paradox of syntax acquisition is this: Unless children basically know what they have to learn before they begin, they cannot successfully learn the grammar of their language. However, even if it is demonstrated that children do indeed have innate mechanisms for learning the categorical membership of words, it is possible that such mechanisms are not specifically linguistic (for one such proposal, see Elman et al., 1996). To examine this proposition, we can look at the acquisition of auxiliary verbs and lexical verbs.

The acquisition of English auxiliary and lexical verbs is a particularly good test case because the two types of verbs are semantically, syntactically, and lexically similar; that is, a learner who has no knowledge of auxiliary and lexical verbs (i.e., a simple, unbiased correlational learner) is almost certain to confuse the two types of verbs. For many auxiliaries there is a lexical verb counterpart with an extremely similar meaning—e.g., the pairs *can/is able to, will/is going to,* and *must/have to*). Auxiliary and lexical verbs are syntactically similar in that both types often take verbal endings, follow subject noun phrases, and lack the grammatical properties of nouns, adjectives, and other syntactic categories. Moreover, auxiliary and lexical verbs typically have identical forms (e.g., copula and auxiliary forms of *be*, possessive and auxiliary forms of *have*, lexical verb and auxiliary forms of *do*). The remarkable degree of similarity can be appreciated by comparing pairs of sentences such as *he is sleepy* and *he is sleeping, he has cookies* and *he has eaten cookies*, and *he does windows* and *he does not do windows*.

The syntactic and morphological behavior of auxiliaries is extremely complex, and there are no obvious non-linguistic correlates for this behavior to aid in learning (Stromswold, 1990a). Without innate, specifically linguistic mechanisms, how could children correctly identify the 99 unique strings of auxiliaries that are acceptable in English from among ~23! (2.59×10^{22}) unique strings of English auxiliaries?[4] Descriptively, the basic restrictions on auxiliaries can be summarized as follows:

AUX →

(Modal) (*have -en*) (progressive *be -ing*) (passive *be -en*)

Any or all of the auxiliaries are optional, but if they are present, they must occur in the above order. In addition, each auxiliary requires that the succeeding verb be of a certain form. Modal auxiliaries (e.g., *can, will, might*) require that the succeeding verb be an infinitival form (e.g., *eat*), perfect *have* requires that the succeeding verb be a perfect participle (e.g., *eaten*), progressive *be* requires that the succeeding verb be a progressive participle (e.g., *eating*), and passive *be* requires that the main verb be a passive participle (e.g., *eaten*). In addition, the first verbal element must be tensed in a matrix clause. Finally, matrix questions and negative statements are formed by inverting or negating the first auxiliary. If no auxiliary is present, *do*-support is required (see Stromswold, 1990a, and Stromswold, 1992, for additional restrictions and complications). Lexical and auxiliary verbs pose a serious learnability question (Baker, 1981; Pinker, 1984; Stromswold, 1989a, 1990a, 1992): How can children distinguish between auxiliary and lexical verbs before they learn the behavior of the two types of verbs, and how do children learn the two types of verbs' behaviors before they can distinguish between them?

If children don't distinguish between auxiliary and lexical verbs, they will generalize what they learn about one type of verb to the other type of verb. This will result in rapid learning. It will also lead children to make errors that can be set right only by negative evidence (information that a particular construction is ungrammatical). Unfortunately, parents don't seem to provide usable negative evidence (Brown and Hanlon, 1970; Marcus, 1993). Thus, if children do not distinguish between auxiliaries and lexical verbs, they are destined to make certain types of inflectional errors (e.g., **I aming go, *I musts eat*) and combination errors involving multiple lexical verbs (e.g., **I hope go Disneyland*), negated lexical verbs (e.g., **I eat not cookies*), lone auxiliaries (e.g., **I must coffee*), and unacceptable combinations of auxiliaries (e.g., **I may should go*). They will also make word order errors, scrambling the order of lexical verbs and auxiliaries (e.g., **I go must*), scrambling the order of auxiliaries (e.g., **He have must gone*), and incorrectly inverting lexical verbs (e.g., *eats he meat?*). If, on the other hand, children have innate predispositions that allow them to distinguish between auxiliary and lexical verbs, they will not make these errors.

In order to test whether English-speaking children distinguish between auxiliary and lexical verbs, I searched the transcripts of 14 children's speech, examining by hand more than 66,000 utterances that contained auxiliaries (Stromswold, 1989a, 1990a). I found that the chil-

dren acquired the auxiliary system with remarkable speed and accuracy. In fact, I found no clear examples of the types of inflectional errors, combination errors, or word order errors they would have made if they confused auxiliary and lexical verbs. Thus, children seem to have innate, specifically linguistic mechanisms that allow them to distinguish between auxiliary and lexical verbs.

ERRORS, INSTRUCTION, AND THE AUTOMATICITY OF LANGUAGE   One of the hallmarks of innate abilities is that they can be acquired without explicit instruction. This seems to be true for language. Parents do correct their children when they make errors that affect the meaning of utterances, but they do not reliably correct grammatical errors (Brown and Hanlon, 1970; Marcus, 1993). And even when parents do try to correct grammatical errors, their efforts are often in vain (McNeill, 1966). Furthermore, correction is not necessary for lexical and syntactic acquisition because some children who are unable to speak (and hence cannot be corrected by their parents) have normal receptive language (Stromswold, 1994a). If teaching and correction are necessary for language development, it should not be possible for children to have impaired production and intact comprehension. I have studied the language acquisition of a young child who is unable to speak. Despite the fact that he had essentially no expressive language (he could say only a handful of phonemes), his receptive language was completely intact. At age 4, he was able to distinguish between reversible active and passive sentences (correctly distinguishing the meanings conveyed by sentences such as *The dog bit the cat, The cat bit the dog, The dog was bitten by the cat,* and *The cat was bitten by the dog*) and to make grammaticality judgments (e.g., correctly recognizing that *What can Cookie Monster eat?* is grammatical whereas **What Cookie Monster can eat?* is not) (see Stromswold, 1994a).

Children learn language quickly, never making certain types of errors that seem very reasonable (e.g., certain types of auxiliary errors). But as Pinker (1989) points out, children are not perfect: They do make certain types of errors. They overregularize inflectional endings, saying *eated* for *ate* and *mouses* for *mice* (Pinker, 1989). They make lexical errors, sometimes passivizing verbs such as *die* that do not passivize (e.g., *He get died*; from Pinker, 1989). They also make certain types of syntactic errors, such as using *do*-support when it is not required (e.g., *Does it be around it?* and *This doesn't be straight*; Stromswold, 1990b, 1992) and failing to use *do*-support when it is required (e.g., *What she eats?* Stromswold, 1990a, 1994b). What do these errors tell us? First, they confirm that children use language productively and are not merely repeating what they hear their parents say because parents do not use these unacceptable forms (Pinker, 1989). These errors may also provide an insight into the peculiarities of languages. For example, children's difficulty with *do*-support suggest that *do*-support is not part of universal grammar, but rather is a peculiar property of English (Stromswold, 1990a,b, 1994b).

Finally, these errors may provide insight into the types of linguistic categories that children are predisposed to acquire. Consider, for example, the finding that children overregularize lexical *be, do,* and *have,* but they never overregularize auxiliary *be, do,* and *have* (Stromswold, 1989a, 1990a, in press-a). The fact that children say sentences like **She beed happy* but not **She beed smiling* indicates that children not only distinguish between auxiliary verbs and lexical verbs, but they treat the two types of verbs differently. What kind of innate learning mechanism could result in children's overregularizing lexical verbs but not the homophonous auxiliaries? One possibility is that children have innate learning mechanisms that specifically cause them to treat auxiliary and lexical verbs differently. Unfortunately, there are problems with this explanation. Although many languages contain words that are semantically and syntactically similar to English auxiliaries (Steele, 1981), and all languages are capable of making the semantic and syntactic distinctions that in English are made by auxiliaries, some languages either lack auxiliaries (instead making use of inflectional affixes) or make no distinction between auxiliaries and lexical verbs. Given that not all languages contain easily confused auxiliary verbs and lexical verbs, the existence of a specific innate mechanism for making this distinction seems unlikely. In addition, hypothesizing a specific innate mechanism has little explanatory power—it explains nothing beyond the phenomena that led us to propose its existence.

Alternatively, children's ability to distinguish between auxiliary and lexical verbs might reflect a more general ability to distinguish between functional categories (determiners, auxiliaries, nominal and verbal inflections, pronouns, etc.) and lexical categories (nouns, verbs, adjectives, etc.). Lexical categories are promiscuous: They freely admit new members (*fax, modem, email,* etc.) and the grammatical behavior of one member of a lexical category can fairly safely be generalized to another member of the same lexical category. Functional categories are conservative: New members are not welcome and generalizations, even within a functional category, are very dangerous (see Stromswold, 1990a, 1994c). Innate mechanisms that specifically predispose children to distinguish between lexical and functional categories have a number of advantages over a specific mechanism for auxiliary and lexical verbs. Unlike the auxiliary/lexical verb distinction, the lexical/functional category distinction is found in all human languages; thus, mechanisms that predispose children to distinguish between lexical categories and functional categories are better candidates, a priori, for being innate. In addition, research on speech errors (e.g., Garrett, 1976), neologisms (Stromswold, 1994c), parsing (e.g., Morgan and Newport, 1981), linguistic typology (e.g., Croft, 1990), aphasia (e.g., Goodglass, 1976), and developmental language disorders (e.g., Guilfoyle, Allen, and Moss, 1991) as well as findings from event-related potentials (Neville, 1991; Holcomb, Coffey, and Neville, 1992; Neville et al., 1993; Neville, 1995; Neville, Mills, and Lawson, 1992) and functional magnetic resonance imaging (Neville et al., 1994) all point to the importance of the lexical/functional distinction.

Innate mechanisms that predispose children to distinguish between lexical and functional categories would also help them to distinguish between auxiliary and lexical verbs, as well as pronouns and nouns, determiners and adjectives, verbal stems and verbal inflections, and other pairs of lexical and functional categories. If these innate mechanisms predispose children to distinguish between syntactic categories that allow for free generalization (lexical categories) and those that do not (functional categories), this would explain why children overregularize lexical *be, do,* and *have* but not auxiliary *be, do,* and *have.* It would also help explain why children are able to learn language so rapidly and with so few errors; that is, such a learning mechanism would permit children to generalize only where it is safe to do so (i.e., within a lexical category). Computationally, the difference between lexical and functional categories might be expressed as the difference between rule-based generalizations and lists, or within a connectionist framework, between network architectures that have different degrees and configurations of connectivity (see Stromswold, 1994c).

Role of linguistic input and critical periods in language acquisition

PIDGINS   The uniformity of language development under normal conditions could be due to biological or environmental processes. One way to investigate the relative roles of biological and environmental factors is to investigate the linguistic abilities of children whose early language environments are suboptimal. Studies of creolization provide compelling evidence that human children are innately endowed with the ability to develop a very specific kind of language even when they receive minimal input. Creolization may occur, for example, when migrant workers who speak a variety of languages must work together and their only common language is a simplified pidgin of another, dominant language. Pidgins typically consist of fixed phrases and pantomimes and can express only basic needs and ideas. Bickerton (1981, 1984), studying the language of second-generation pidgin speakers (i.e., the children of pidgin speakers), has found that they use a creolized language that is much richer than their parents' pidgin. For example, the creolized language of second-generation pidgin speakers includes embedded and relative clauses, aspectual distinctions, and consistent word order, despite the absence of such features in the input (pidgin) language (Bickerton, 1981, 1984). Thus, second-generation pidgin speakers "invent" a language that is more complex than the pidgin language to which they are exposed.

HOMESIGN How minimal can the input be? Although children who hear only pidgin languages have impoverished input, there are even more extreme situations of language deprivation. Consider deaf children born to hearing parents who do not use or expose their infants to sign language but otherwise provide normal care (i.e., their parents neither abuse nor neglect them). Such children are deaf isolates—they receive essentially no linguistic input. Deaf isolates offer us a fascinating picture of the limits of the innate endowment to create language, and hence a glimpse at the early unfolding of language in all infants. As infants and toddlers, deaf isolates seem to achieve the same early-language milestones as hearing children. Right on schedule, at around 6–8 months, deaf isolates begin to "babble"—they make hand motions analogous to the spoken babbling of hearing babies. They invent their first signs at about the same age that hearing children produce their first words. They even begin to form short phrases with these signs, also on a comparable schedule to hearing children (Goldin-Meadow and Mylander, 1984, 1998; Morford, 1996). Thus, these early linguistic milestones are apparently able to unfold even without linguistic input. Preliminary research on older deaf isolates indicates that their gestural communication systems are more sophisticated than those used by young deaf isolates, although even their systems do not exhibit the complexity of natural sign languages (Coppola et al., 1998).

The ability to learn language appears to be the result of innate processes; however, childhood language exposure is necessary for normal language development, just as the ability to see is innate but visual stimulation is necessary for normal visual development (Hubel and Wiesel, 1970). The hypothesis that exposure to language must occur by a certain age in order for language to be acquired normally is called the critical (or sensitive) period hypothesis. The critical period for language acquisition is generally believed to coincide with the period of great neural plasticity and is often thought to end at or sometime before the onset of puberty (see Lenneberg, 1967).

WILD CHILDREN Skuse (1984a,b) reviewed nine well-documented cases of children who had been raised under conditions of extreme social and linguistic deprivation for 2.5 to 12 years. All of these cases involved grossly impoverished environments, frequently accompanied with malnourishment and physical abuse. At the time of discovery, the children ranged in age from 2.5 years to 13.5 years, had essentially no receptive or expressive language, and were globally retarded in nonlinguistic domains. The six children who eventually acquired normal or near-normal language function were all discovered by age 7 and had no signs of brain damage. Of the three children who remained language-impaired, one was discovered at age 5 but had clear evidence of brain damage (Davis, 1940, 1947) and one was discovered at age 3.5 but had organic abnormalities not attributable to extreme deprivation (Skuse, 1984a). Genie, the third child with persistent linguistic impairments, is remarkable both for having the most prolonged period of deprivation (12 years) and, at almost 14 years of age, for being the oldest when discovered (Curtiss, 1977). Neuropsychological testing suggests that Genie does not have the expected left hemisphere lateralization for language. It is tempting to conclude that Genie's failure to acquire normal language and her anomalous lateralization of language function are both the result of her lack of exposure to language prior to the onset of puberty; however, it is possible that cortical anomalies in the left hemisphere are the cause of her anomalous lateralization and her failure to acquire language (Curtiss, 1977).

DEAF ISOLATES As Curtiss (1977, 1989) points out, it is impossible to be certain that the linguistic impairment observed in children such as Genie are the result of linguistic isolation, and not the result of social and physical deprivation and abuse. Curtiss (1989) has described the case of Chelsea, a hearing-impaired woman who had essentially no exposure to language until age 32. Unlike Genie, Chelsea did not experience any social or physical deprivation. Chelsea's ability to use language (particularly syntax) is at least as impaired as Genie's, an observation consistent with the critical period hypothesis (Curtiss 1989). To test whether there is a critical period for first language acquisition, Newport and colleagues (Newport, 1990) have studied the signing abilities of deaf people whose first exposure to American Sign Language (ASL) was at birth (native signers), before age 6 (early signers), or after age 12 (late signers). Consistent with the critical period hypothesis, even after 30 years of using ASL, on tests of morphology and complex syntax, native signers outperform early signers, who in turn outperform late signers (Newport, 1990).

SECOND LANGUAGE ACQUISITION   To test whether there is a critical period for second language acquisition, Johnson and Newport (1989) studied the English abilities of native speakers of Korean or Chinese who first became immersed in English between the ages of 3 and 39. For subjects who began to learn English before puberty, age of English immersion correlated extremely highly with proficiency with English syntax and morphology, whereas no significant correlation was found for subjects who began to learn English after puberty (Johnson and Newport, 1989).

Evidence from studies of children such as Genie, deaf isolates, and people who acquire a second language suggests that the ability to acquire language diminishes with age. Other research has shown that complete language recovery rarely occurs if a left hemisphere lesion occurs after age 5 and substantial recovery rarely occurs if a lesion is acquired after the onset of puberty. Moreover, subtle tests of linguistic abilities reveal that native fluency in a language is rarely attained if one's first exposure to that language occurs after early childhood and competence in a language is rarely attained if first exposure occurs after the onset of puberty. This is consistent with Hubel and Wiesel's (1970) finding that normal visual development requires visual stimuli during a critical period of neural development and suggests that neural fine-tuning is a critical to normal language acquisition–a fine-tuning that can occur only with exposure to language during a certain time period.

Language acquisition and brain development

We have argued that the ability to learn language is the result of innate, language-specific learning mechanisms. And we have investigated the extent to which normal language development depends on receiving appropriate linguistic input during a critical window of cognitive (and presumably neuronal) development. Here we review the neurobiological evidence supporting the idea that language is the result of innate, language-specific learning mechanisms.

DEVELOPMENT OF LANGUAGE REGIONS OF THE BRAIN   Lenneberg (1967) notwithstanding, the language areas of the human brain appear to be anatomical and functionally asymmetrical at or before birth. Anatomically, analyses of fetal brains reveal that the temporal plane is larger in the left hemisphere than in the right hemisphere (Wada, Clarke, and Hamm, 1975).[5] Development of the cortical regions that subserve language in the left hemisphere consistently lags behind the development of the homologous regions in the right hemisphere. The right temporal plane appears during the thirtieth gestational week, while the left temporal plane appears about 7–10 days later (Chi, Dooling, and Gilles, 1977). Even in infancy, dendritic development in the region around Broca's area on the left lags behind that found in the homologous region on the right (Scheibel, 1984). Event-related potential (ERP) and dichotic listening experiments suggest that the left hemisphere is differentially sensitive for speech from birth (for a review, see Mehler and Christophe, 1995).

Relatively few studies have investigated the neural bases of lexical or syntactic abilities in neurologically intact children. Among these is the work of Molfese and colleagues (Molfese, 1990; Molfese, Morse, and Peters, 1990), who taught infants as young as 14 months labels for novel objects, then compared the ERPs when the objects were paired with correct and incorrect verbal labels. A late-occurring response was recorded in the left hemisphere electrode sites when the correct label was given but not when an incorrect label was given. Similarly, an early-occurring response was recorded bilaterally in the frontal electrodes when the correct label was given, but not when an incorrect label was given. In recent work, Mills, Coffey-Corina, and Neville (1997) recorded the ERPs when children between 13 to 20 months of age listened to words meanings they knew, words whose meanings they did not know, and backward words. They found that the ERPs differed as a function of meaning within 200 ms of word onset. Between 13 and 17 months, the ERP differences for known versus unknown words were bilateral and widely distributed over anterior and posterior regions. By 20 months, the differences were limited to left temporal and parietal regions.

In another ERP study, Holcomb, Coffey, and Neville (1992) found no clear evidence prior to age 13 of the normal adult pattern of greater negativity in the left hemisphere for semantically plausible sentences (e.g., *We baked cookies in the oven*) and greater negativity in the right hemisphere for semantically anomalous sentences (e.g., *Mother wears a ring on her school*). In addition, the negative peak associated with semantic anomalies (the N400) was later and longer in duration for younger subjects than older subjects. Holcomb, Coffey, and Neville (1992) also found evidence that the normal adult pattern of a left anterior N280 waveform associated with functional category words and a bilateral posterior N350 waveform associated with lexical category words (Neville, Mills, and Lawson, 1992) does not develop until around puberty. Four-year-old children typically have N350 response to both lexical and functional words. By 11 years of age, the N350 is greatly reduced or absent for functional category words. It isn't until approximately 15 years of age that functional category words result in a clear N280 response with adult-like distribution

(Holcomb, Coffey, and Neville, 1992). In summary, simple linguistic stimuli (e.g., lexical words) appear to evoke similar types of electrical activity in young children's and adult brains; but for more complicated linguistic stimuli involving grammatical aspects of language, children's ERPs may not closely resemble adult ERPs until around puberty. That the critical period for language acquisition (especially syntax) ends at approximately the same age that children develop adult-like ERPs for grammatical aspects of language is intriguing. It is also suggestive, raising the possibility that once adult-like neural pathways and operations are acquired, neural plasticity is so greatly reduced that the ability to acquire all but the most rudimentary aspects of syntax is lost.

MODULARITY OF LANGUAGE ACQUISITION With some notable exceptions, most of what is known about the relationship between brain development and lexical and syntactic development has come from studying language acquisition by children who have developmental syndromes or brain lesions. If, as was argued earlier, language acquisition involves the development of specialized structures and operations having no counterparts in nonlinguistic domains, then it should be possible for a child to be cognitively intact and linguistically impaired or to be linguistically intact and cognitively impaired. But if language acquisition involves the development of the same general symbolic structures and operations used in other cognitive domains, then dissociation of language and general cognitive development should be impossible. Recent studies suggest that language development is selectively impaired in some children with specific language impairment (SLI) and selectively spared in children who suffer from disorders such as Williams syndrome.

Specific language impairment SLI encompasses developmental disorders characterized by severe deficits in the production and/or comprehension of language that cannot be explained by hearing loss, mental retardation, motor deficits, neurological or psychiatric disorders, or lack of exposure to language. Because SLI is a diagnosis of exclusion, SLI children are a very heterogeneous group. This heterogeneity can and does affect the outcome of behavioral and neurological studies, with different studies of SLI children frequently reporting different results depending on how SLI subjects were chosen. The exact nature of the etiology of SLI remains uncertain (for a review, see Leonard, 1998; Stromswold, 1997), with proposals including impoverished or deviant linguistic input (Cramblit and Siegel, 1977; Lasky and Klopp, 1982), transient, fluctuating hearing loss (Bishop and Edmundson,

1986; Gordon, 1988; Gravel and Wallace, 1992; Teele et al., 1990), impairment in short-term auditory memory (Graham, 1968, 1974; Rapin and Wilson, 1978), impairment in auditory sequencing (Efron, 1963; Monsee, 1961), impairment in rapid auditory processing (Tallal and Piercy, 1973a,b, 1974), general impairment in sequencing (Poppen et al., 1969), general impairment in rapid sensory processing (Tallal, 1990), general impairment in representational or symbolic reasoning (Johnston and Weismer, 1983; Kahmi, 1981; Morehead and Ingram, 1973), general impairment in hierarchical planning (Cromer, 1983), impairments in language perception or processing [e.g., the inability to acquire aspects of language that are not phonologically salient (Leonard, 1989, 1994; Leonard, McGregor, and Allen, 1992)], impairments in underlying grammar [e.g., the lack of linguistic features such as tense and number (Crago and Gopnik, 1994; Gopnik, 1990a,b; Gopnik and Crago, 1991), the inability to use government to analyze certain types of syntactic relations (van der Lely, 1994), and the inability to form certain types of agreement relations (Clahsen, 1989, 1991; Rice, 1994)], or some combination thereof. Some researchers have even suggested that SLI is not a distinct clinical entity, and that SLI children just represent the low end of the normal continuum in linguistic ability (Johnston, 1991; Leonard, 1991).

At the neural level, the cause of SLI is also uncertain. Initially, it was theorized that children with SLI had bilateral damage to the perisylvian cortical regions that subserve language in adults (Bishop, 1987). Because SLI is not a fatal disorder and people with SLI have normal life spans, to date, only one brain of a possible SLI child has come to autopsy. Post-mortem examination of this brain revealed atypical symmetry of the temporal planes and a dysplastic microgyrus on the interior surface of the left frontal cortex along the inferior surface of the sylvian fissure (Cohen, Campbell, and Yaghmai, 1989), findings similar to those reported in dyslexic brains by Geschwind and Galaburda (1987). It is tempting to use the results of this autopsy to argue—as Geschwind and Galaburda (1987) have for dyslexia—that SLI is the result of subtle anomalies in the left perisylvian cortex. However, the child whose brain was autopsied had a performance IQ of just 74 (verbal IQ 70); hence the anomalies noted on autopsy may be related to the child's general cognitive impairment rather than to her language impairment.

Computed tomography (CT) and magnetic resonance imaging (MRI) scans of SLI children have failed to reveal the types of gross perisylvian lesions typically found in patients with acquired aphasia (Jernigan et al., 1991; Plante et al., 1991). But CT and MRI scans have revealed that the brains of SLI children often fail to exhibit the normal pattern in which the left temporal plane is larger than the right (Jernigan et al., 1991; Plante, 1991; Plante, Swisher, and Vance, 1989; Plante et al., 1991). Examinations of MRI scans have revealed that dyslexics are more likely to have additional gyri between the postcentral sulcus and the supramarginal gyrus than are normal readers (Leonard et al., 1993). Jackson and Plante (1997) recently performed the same type of gyral morphology analyses on MRI scans of 10 SLI children, their parents, 10 siblings, and 20 adult controls.[6] For the control group, 23% of the hemispheres showed an intermediate gyrus, whereas 41% of the hemispheres for SLI family members (probands, their siblings, and parents combined) showed an intermediate gyrus. However, affected family members did not appear to be more likely to have an intermediate gyrus than unaffected members. Clark and Plante (1995) compared the morphology of Broca's area in parents of SLI children and adult controls. Overall, parents of SLI children were no more likely to have an extra sulcus in the vicinity of Broca's area. However, parents with documented language impairments were more likely to have an extra sulcus than unaffected parents.

A number of researchers have studied the functional characteristics of SLI children's brains. Data from dichotic listening experiments (e.g., Arnold and Schwartz, 1983; Boliek, Bryden, and Obrzut, 1988; Cohen et al., 1991) and ERP experiments (e.g., Dawson et al., 1989) suggest that at least some SLI children have aberrant functional lateralization for language, with language present either bilaterally or predominantly in the right hemisphere. Single photon emission computed tomography (SPECT) studies of normal and language-impaired children have revealed hypoperfusion in the inferior frontal convolution of the left hemisphere (including Broca's area) in two children with isolated expressive language impairment (Denays et al., 1989), hypoperfusion of the left temporoparietal region and the upper and middle regions of the right frontal lobe in nine of twelve children with expressive and receptive language impairment (Denays et al., 1989), and hypoperfusion in the left temporofrontal region of language-impaired children's brains (Lou, Henriksen, and Bruhn, 1990).

Courchesne and colleagues (1989) did not find any differences in ERP amplitude or latency between SLI adolescents and adults and age-matched controls. But in a subsequent study of school-age SLI children (Lincoln et al., 1995), they found that normal age-matched controls exhibited the normal pattern of larger amplitude N100s for more intense auditory stimuli intensity, while SLI subjects did not exhibit that pattern. This finding suggests the possibility of some abnormality in the auditory cortex of SLI children. Neville and colleagues (1993) compared the ERPs of SLI children and normal age-matched controls for three tasks. In the first task, subjects pressed a button when they detected 1000-Hz tones among a series of 2000-Hz tones. In the second task, subjects were asked to detect small white rectangles among a series of large red squares. In the third task, children read sentences one word at a time and judged whether or not the sentences were semantically plausible (half of the sentences ended with a semantically appropriate word and half ended with a semantically inappropriate word). Overall, for the auditory monitoring task, the SLI children's ERPs did not differ from those of the control children. However, when the SLI children were divided into groups according to their performance on Tallal and Piercy's (1973a,b) auditory processing task, children who performed poorly on that task exhibited reduced-amplitude ERP waves over the anterior portion of the right hemisphere together with greater latency for the N140 component. In general, the SLI children had abnormally large N400s on the sentence task. As is typically seen with adults, the normal children's N400s for closed-class words were larger over the anterior left hemisphere than the anterior right hemisphere. However, the SLI children with the greatest morphosyntactic deficits did not exhibit this asymmetry.[7]

Despite decades of intensive and productive research on SLI, a number of fundamental questions about SLI remain unanswered. Researchers disagree about the etiology of SLI at a neural or cognitive level, and offer proposals ranging from a specific impairment in a circumscribed aspect of abstract linguistics to general cognitive/processing impairments due to environmental causes. Even among researchers who believe that SLI specifically affects linguistic competence, there is disagreement about what aspect of the underlying grammar is impaired. Furthermore, numerous studies have revealed that many (if not most) children with SLI exhibit nonlinguistic deficits, although some researchers argue that these nonlinguistic deficits are secondary to their primary linguistic impairments (for a review, see Leonard, 1998). A first step in seeking answers to these questions is to study more homogeneous subgroups of children diagnosed with SLI.[8] In summary, although generally consistent with the hypothesis of a specific module for language and language acquisition, the emerging picture of SLI is not as "clean" as modularists might hope: SLI children are a heterogeneous group, and many (perhaps all) are not perfectly intact but for a damaged language module.

Williams syndrome Although mental retardation generally results in depression of language function (Rondal, 1980), researchers have reported that some mentally retarded children have remarkably intact language. This condition has been reported in some children with hydrocephalus (Swisher and Pinsker, 1971), Turner's syndrome (Yamada and Curtiss, 1981), infantile hypercalcemia or Williams syndrome (Bellugi et al., 1992), and mental retardation of unknown etiology (Yamada, 1990).

Williams syndrome (WS) is a rare (1 in 25,000) genetic disorder involving deletion of portions of chromosome 7 around and including the elastin gene (Ewart et al., 1993a,b). People with WS often have particularly extreme dissociation of language and cognitive functions (Bellugi et al., 1992). Hallmarks of WS include microcephaly with a "pixie-like" facial appearance, general mental retardation with IQs typically in the 40s and 50s, delayed onset of expressive language, and "an unusual command of language combined with an unexpectedly polite, open and gentle manner" by early adolescence (Von Arman and Engel, 1964). In a recent study, the MacArthur Communicative Development Inventory (a parental report measure) was used to assess the earliest stages of language development for children with WS and children with Down syndrome (DS). This study revealed that WS and DS children were equally delayed in the acquisition of words, with an average delay of 2 years for both groups (Singer Harris et al., 1997). WS and DS children who had begun to combine words (mean age 46 months) did not differ significantly in language age (mean ages 23.7 months and 21 months, respectively). However, compared to the DS children, these older WS children had significantly higher scores on grammatical complexity measures and on mean length of utterance for their longest three sentences (Singer Harris et al., 1997). The gap in linguistic abilities of WS and DS children increases with age (Bellugi, Wang, and Jernigan, 1994). Although adolescents with WS use language that is often deviant for their chronological age and do poorly on many standardized language tests, they have larger vocabularies than do children of equivalent mental ages and speak in sentences that are syntactically and morphologically more complex and well-formed. In addition, WS adolescents and adults demonstrate good metalinguistic skills, such as the ability to recognize an utterance as ungrammatical and to respond in a contextually appropriate manner (Bellugi et al., 1992).

Volumetric analyses of MRI scans indicate that compared to normal brains, cerebral volume and cerebral gray matter of WS brains are significantly reduced in size and the neocerebellar vermal lobules are increased in size, with paleocerebellar vermal regions of low-normal size (Jernigan and Bellugi, 1994; Jernigan et al., 1993; Wang et al., 1992). To date only one WS brain

has come to autopsy (Galaburda et al., 1994). This brain had extensive cytoarchitectural abnormalities, including exaggeration of horizontal abnormalities within layers (most striking in area 17 of the occipital lobe), increased cell density throughout the brain, and abnormally clustered and oriented neurons. In addition, although the frontal lobes and most of the temporal lobes were relatively normal in size, the posterior forebrain was much smaller than normal. Galaburda and colleagues interpreted these findings as evidence of developmental arrest between the end of the second trimester and the second year of life. They further suggested that these findings may be related to hypercalcemia found in WS. Alternatively, elastin may have a direct, but hitherto undiscovered, neurodevelopmental function, in which case the macroscopic and microscopic abnormalities may be associated with the decreased levels of elastin in WS.

Early studies revealed that, although auditory ERPs for WS adolescents are similar in morphology, distribution, sequence, and latency to those of age-matched controls, WS adolescents display large-amplitude responses even at short interstimulus intervals, suggesting hyperexcitability of auditory mechanisms at the cortical level with shorter refractory periods (Neville, Holcomb, and Mills, 1989; Neville, Mills, and Bellugi, 1994). When WS subjects listened to spoken words, their ERPs had grossly abnormal morphology not seen in normal children at any age (Neville, Mills, and Bellugi, 1994). In contrast, the morphology of their ERPs for visually presented words was normal. Compared with normal subjects, WS subjects had larger priming effects for auditorily presented words, but priming effects for visually presented words were normal or smaller than those observed for normal subjects (Neville, Mills, and Bellugi, 1994). These results suggest that WS subjects' relative sparing of language function is related to hypersensitivity to auditorily presented linguistic material. To date no PET or SPECT studies of WS children have been reported. It will be interesting to learn from such studies whether it is the classically defined language areas in general or just primary auditory cortex in WS brains that become hyperperfused in response to auditory linguistic stimuli. In summary, although generally consistent with the hypothesis of specific module for language and language acquisition, the emerging picture of WS is not as "clean" as modularists might hope: Although WS adolescents and adults have better linguistic abilities than others with comparable IQs, their language is far from perfect and the mechanisms they use for language acquisition may not be the same as those used by normal children (see, for example, Karmiloff-Smith et al., 1997, 1998; Stevens and Karmiloff-Smith, 1997).

GENETIC BASIS OF LANGUAGE If the acquisition of language is the result of specialized structures in the brain and these linguistically specific structures are coded for by information contained in the genetic code, one might expect to find evidence for the heritability of language (see Pinker and Bloom, 1990; Ganger and Stromswold, 1998). But if language acquisition is essentially the result of instruction and involves no specifically linguistic structures, one should find no evidence of genetic transmission of language.

Familial aggregation studies A comprehensive review of family aggregation studies, sex ratio studies, pedigree studies, commingling studies, and segregation studies of spoken language disorders reveals that spoken language disorders have a strong tendency to aggregate in families (Stromswold, 1998). Stromswold (1998) reviewed 18 family aggregation studies of spoken language impairment (see table 63.1). In all seven studies that collected data for both probands and controls, the incidence of positive family history was significantly greater for probands than controls.[9] In these seven studies, the reported incidence of positive family history for probands ranged from 24% (Bishop and Edmundson, 1986) to 78% (van der Lely and Stollwerck, 1996), with a mean incidence of 46% and a median incidence of 35%.[10] For controls, positive family history rates ranged from 3% (Bishop and Edmundson, 1986) to 46% (Tallal, Ross, and Curtiss, 1989a), with a mean incidence of 18% and a median incidence of 11%.

Of all the studies of family aggregation Stromswold (1998) reviewed, eleven reported the percentage of probands' relatives who were impaired. For probands, the percentage of family members who were impaired ranged from 20% (Neils and Aram, 1986) to 42% (Tallal, Ross, and Curtiss, 1989a), with a mean impairment rate of 28% and median impairment rate of 26%. For controls, the percentage of family members who were impaired ranged from 3% (Neils and Aram, 1986) to 19% (Tallal, Ross, and Curtiss, 1989a), with a mean impairment rate of 9% and a median impairment rate of 7%. The incidence of impairment was significantly higher among proband relatives than control relatives in seven of the eight studies that made such a comparison.

Although data on familial aggregation suggest that some developmental language disorders have a genetic component, it is possible that children with language-impaired parents or siblings are more likely to be linguistically impaired themselves because they are exposed to deviant language (the deviant linguistic environment hypothesis, DLEH). Some studies have reported that mothers are more likely to use directive speech and less likely to use responsive speech when talking to their language-

impaired children than are mothers speaking to normal children (e.g., Conti-Ramsden and Friel-Patti, 1983; Conti-Ramsden and Dykins, 1991). However, children's language impairments may cause mothers to use simplified speech, rather than vice versa. That is, mothers of language-impaired children may use directive speech because they cannot understand their impaired children and their impaired children do not understand them if they use more complicated language. Furthermore, although within a fairly wide range, linguistic environment may have little or no effect on language acquisition by normal children (e.g., Heath, 1983), genetics and environment may exert a synergistic effect in children who are genetically at risk for developing language disorders. Such children may be particularly sensitive to subtly impoverished linguistic environments.

Despite the DLEH prediction that the most severely impaired children should come from families with the highest incidence of language impairments, Byrne, Willerman, and Ashmore (1974) found that children with profound language impairments were less likely to have positive family histories of language impairment than children with moderate language impairments. Similarly, Tallal and colleagues (1991) found no differences in the language abilities of children who did and did not have a positive family history of language disorders. According to the DLEH, the deficits exhibited by language-impaired children result from "copying" the ungrammatical language of their parents. Therefore, the DLEH predicts that language-impaired children should have the same type of impairment as that of their relatives. However, Neils and Aram (1986) found that 38% of parents with a history of a speech and language disorder said that their disorder differed from their children's disorder. According to the DLEH, parents with a history of spoken language impairment who are no longer impaired should be no more likely to have language-impaired children than parents with no such history. But Neils and Aram (1986) found that a third of the probands' parents who had a history of a spoken language disorder did not suffer from the disorder as adults. The DLEH predicts that all children with SLI should have at least one close relative with a language impairment; however, in the studies reviewed, an average of 58% of the language-impaired children had no first-degree relatives with impairments. If the DLEH is correct, birth order might affect the likelihood that a child will exhibit a language disorder. But birth order apparently affects neither the severity nor the likelihood of developing language disorders (see Tomblin, Hardy, and Hein, 1991). In our society, mothers typically have the primary responsibility for child-rearing; hence the DLEH predicts that the correlation of language status

TABLE 63.1
Family aggregation studies of spoken language disorders

Study	Sample Size	Other Family Diagnoses	Positive Family History	Frequency of Impairment among Relatives (Proband vs. Control)
Ingram (1959)	75 probands	None	24% parental history 32% sibling history	N/A
Luchsinger (1970)	127 probands	None	36% probands	N/A
Byrne, Willerman, & Ashmore (1974)	18 severely impaired 20 moderately impaired	None	17% "severe" probands 55% "moderate" probands**	N/A
Neils & Aram (1986)	74 probands 36 controls	Dyslexia Stuttering Articulation	46% 1st-degree proband 8% 1st-degree controls****	20% vs. 3% all relatives ***
Bishop & Edmundson (1987)	34 probands 131 controls	None (for strict criteria)	24% 1st-degree proband 3% 1st-degree control****	N/A
Lewis, Ekelman, & Aram (1989)	20 probands 20 controls	Dyslexia Stuttering LD	N/A	Any: 12% vs. 2% all relatives**** 26% vs. 5% 1st-degree relatives*** SLI: 9% vs. 1% all relatives****
Tallal, Ross, & Curtiss (1989a)	62 probands 50 controls	Dyslexia LD School problems	77% 1st-degree proband 46% 1st-degree control**	42% vs. 19% 1st-degree relatives***
Tomblin (1989)	51 probands 136 controls	Stuttering Articulation	53% 1st-degree probands Controls: N/A	23% vs. 3% 1st-degree relatives****
Haynes & Naido (1991)	156 probands	None	54% all probands 41% 1st-degree probands	28% proband parents 18% proband sibs
Tomblin, Hardy, & Hein (1991)	55 probands 607 controls	None	35% probands 17% controls***	N/A
Whitehurst et al. (1991)	62 probands 55 controls	Speech Late talker School problems	N/A	Any: 24% vs. 16% 1st-degree relatives Speech: 12% vs. 8% 1st-degree relatives Late-talker: 12% vs. 7% 1st-degree relatives School probs.: 7% vs. 5% 1st-degree relatives
Beitchman, Hood, & Inglis (1992)	136 probands 138 controls	Dyslexia LD Articulation	47% vs 28% all relatives *** 34% vs. 11% 1st-degree ****	Multiple affected relatives: 19% vs. 9%*
Lewis (1992)	87 probands 79 controls	Dyslexia LD Stuttering Hearing loss	N/A	LI: 15% vs. 2% all relatives**** 32% vs. 5% 1st-degree relatives***** Dyslexia: 3% vs. 1% all relatives**** 6% vs. 3% 1st-degree relatives LD: 3% vs. 1% all relatives**** 6% vs. 1% 1st-degree relatives*

TABLE 63.1 *Continued*

Study	Sample Size	Other Family Diagnoses	Positive Family History	Frequency of Impairment among Relatives (Proband vs. Control)
Tomblin & Buckwalter (1994)	26 probands	None	42% 1st-degree	Overall: 21% Mother: 15% Father: 40% Sister: 6%, Brother: 24%
Lahey & Edwards (1995)	53 probands	Learning problems	60% 1st-degree	Overall: 26% Mother: 26% Father: 22% Siblings: 29%

Rice, Rice, & Wexler (1996)	31 probands
	 67 controls
		Reading
		 Spelling
		 Learning
			N/A	Any: 18% vs. 9% all relatives***
				    26% vs. 13% 1st-degree relatives **
				 LI: 15% vs. 6% all relatives***
				    22% vs. 7% 1st-degree relatives***
				 Other: 7% vs. 5% all relatives
				    12% vs. 9% 1st-degree relatives

Tomblin (1996)	534 probands 6684 controls		29% probands 11% controls****	
van der Lely & Stollwerck (1996)	9 probands 49 controls	Reading or writing	78% 1st-degree probands 29% 1st-degree controls **	Overall: 39% vs. 9% **** Mothers: 33% vs. 2% *** Fathers: 38% vs. 8%* Sisters: 40% vs. 8%* Brothers: 44% vs. 19%

* $p < .05$; ** $p < .01$; *** $p < .001$, **** $p < .0001$; Significance tests are for one-tailed tests.
SLI = Specific Language Impairment, LI = Speech or Language Impairment; LD = Learning Disability.
Adapted from Stromswold (1998).

should be greatest between mother and child. Contrary to this prediction, Tomblin (1989) found that among the family relations he studied (i.e., mother–child, father–child, male sibling–child, female sibling–child), the relationship was weakest between mother and child. Other studies that measured the ratio of impaired fathers to impaired mothers also report contra-DLEH results: The father:mother ratio has been reported as 2.7:1 (Tomblin and Buckwalter, 1994), 1.4:1 (Neils and Aram, 1986), and approximately 1:1 (Tallal, Ross, and Curtiss, 1989b; Whitehurst et al., 1991; Lewis, 1992).

Twin studies The influences of environmental and genetic factors on language disorders can be teased apart by comparing the concordance rates for language impairment in monozygotic (MZ) and dizygotic (DZ) twins. MZ and DZ twins share the same pre- and postnatal environment. Thus, if the concordance rate for a particular trait is greater for MZ than DZ twins, it probably reflects the fact that MZ twins share 100% of their genetic material while DZ twins share, on average, just 50% of their genetic material (for a review, see Eldridge, 1983). Stromswold (1996, in press-b) reviewed five studies that examined the concordance rates for written language disorders and four studies that examined the concordance rates for spoken

language disorders (see tables 63.2 and 63.3). In all nine studies, the concordance rates for MZ twin pairs were greater than those for DZ twin pairs, with the differences being significant in all but one study (Stevenson et al., 1987). In these studies concordance rates ranged from 100% (Zerbin-Rudin, 1967) to 33% (Stevenson et al., 1987) for MZ twins, and from 61% (Tomblin and Buckwalter, 1995) to 29% (Stevenson et al., 1987) for DZ twins.[11]

The studies Stromswold reviewed included 212 MZ and 199 DZ twins pairs in which at least one member of the pair had a written language disorder, for concordance rates of 74.9% for MZ twins and 42.7% for DZ twins ($z = 6.53$, $p < .00000005$). The studies included 188 MZ and 94 DZ twin pairs in which at least one member of the twin pair had a spoken language disorder, for concordance rates of 84.3% for MZ twins and 52.0% for DZ twins ($z = 5.14$, $p < .00000025$). Overall, the studies included 400 MZ twin pairs and 293 DZ twin pairs, for concordance rates of 79.5% for MZ twins and 45.8% for DZ twins ($z = 8.77$, $p < .00000005$).

The finding that concordance rates were significantly greater for MZ than for DZ twins indicates that genetic factors play a significant role in the development of language disorders. The overall concordance rates for written and spoken language disorders are reasonably similar, with

TABLE 63.2

Concordance rates for twins with written language disorders

Study	Twin Pairs	Diagnosis	Proband Concordance
Zerbin-Rubin (1967)	17 MZ 33 DZ	Word blindness	100% MZ vs. 50% DZ***
Bakwin (1973)	31 MZ 31 DZ	Dyslexia	Overall: 91% MZ vs. 45% DZ*** Male: 91% MZ vs. 59% DZ* Female: 91% MZ vs. 15% DZ****
Matheny, Dolan, & Wilson (1976)	17 MZ 10 DZ	Dyslexia or academic problems	86% MZ vs. 33% DZ
Stevenson et al. (1987)	18 MZ † 30 DZ†	Reading and spelling retardation (Neale & Schonell tests)	Neale reading: 33% MZ vs. 29% DZ Schonell reading: 35% MZ vs. 31% DZ Spelling: 50% MZ vs. 33% DZ
DeFries & Gillis (1993)	133 MZ 98 DZ	Dyslexia (PIAT scores)	66% MZ vs. 43% DZ***
Overall††	212 MZ 199 DZ		74.9% MZ vs. 42.7% DZ****

Significance tests are one-tailed tests comparing concordance rates for MZ and DZ twins: * $p < .05$; ** $p < .01$; *** $p < .001$, **** $p < .0001$.

† Number of pairs of twins varied according to diagnosis.

†† Overall rates include data for Stevenson and colleagues' "Schonell reading retarded" group.

Tests: PIAT (Peabody Individual Achievement Test); Word Recognition Reading (Dunn and Markwardt, 1970); Schonell Reading and Spelling Tests (Schonell and Schonell, 1960); Neale Reading Test (Neale, 1967).

Adapted from Stromswold (in press-b).

TABLE 63.3

Concordance rates for twins with spoken language disorders

Study	Twin Pairs	Diagnosis	Proband Concordance
Lewis & Thompson (1992)	32 MZ† 25 DZ†	Received speech or language therapy	Any disorder: 86% MZ vs. 48% DZ** Articulation: 98% MZ vs. 36% DZ**** LD: 70% MZ vs. 50% DZ Delayed speech: 83% MZ vs. 0% DZ*
Tomblin & Buckwalter (1994)	56 MZ 26 DZ	SLI (questionnaire to speech pathologists)	89% MZ vs. 55% DZ**
Bishop, North, & Dolan (1995)	63 MZ 27 DZ	SLI (by test scores)	Strict criteria: 70% MZ vs. 46% DZ* Broad criteria: 94% vs. 62% DZ**
Tomblin & Buckwalter (1995)	37 MZ 16 DZ	SLI (composite score >1 SD below mean)	96% MZ vs. 61% DZ**
Overall†	188 MZ 94 DZ		84.3% MZ vs. 52.0% DZ ****

Significance tests are one-tailed tests: * $p < .05$; ** $p < .01$; *** $p < .001$, **** $p < .0001$.

LD = Learning Disorder.

† Overall rates include data for Lewis and Thompson's "any diagnosis" group and Bishop and colleagues' strict criteria group.

Adapted from Stromswold (in press-b).

concordance rates for spoken language disorders being approximately 10 percentage points higher than the rates for written language disorders. However, the fact that the difference between MZ and DZ concordance rates was very similar for written and spoken language disorders is consistent with the hypothesis that genetic factors play an equal role in both types of impairments.

Modes of transmission In a recent review of behavioral genetic studies of spoken language disorders, Stromswold (1998) concluded that most familial language disorders are the product of complex interactions between genetics and environment. In rare cases, however, language disorders may have a single major locus. For example, researchers have reported a number of kindred with extremely large numbers of severely affected family members (e.g., Arnold, 1961; Gopnik, 1990; Hurst et al., 1990; Lewis, 1990) in which transmission seems to be autosomal-dominant with variable rates of expressivity and penetrance. When Samples and Lane (1985) performed a similar analysis on a family in which six of six siblings had a severe developmental language disorder, they concluded that the mode of transmission in that family was a single autosomal recessive gene. If there are multiple modes of transmission for SLI, as the above results seem to indicate, SLI is probably genetically heterogeneous, just as dyslexia appears to be genetically heterogeneous.

The final—and most definitive—method for determining whether there is a genetic basis for familial language disorders is to determine which gene (or genes) is responsible for the language disorders found in these families. Typically, this is done by using linkage analysis techniques to compare the genetic material of language-impaired and normal family members, thereby allowing researchers to determine how the genetic material of affected family members differs from that of unaffected members. Linkage analyses of dyslexic families suggest that written language disorders are genetically heterogeneous (Bisgaard et al., 1987; Smith et al., 1986), with different studies revealing involvement of chromosome 15 (Smith et al., 1983; Pennington and Smith, 1988), the HLA region of chromosome 6 (Rabin et al., 1993), and the Rh region of chromosome 1 (Rabin et al., 1993). Froster and colleagues (1993) have reported a case of familial speech retardation and dyslexia that appears to be caused by a balanced translocation of the short arm of chromosome 1 and the long arm of chromosome 2. Recently, Fisher and colleagues (1998) conducted the first linkage analyses for spoken language disorders, performing genome-wide analyses of the genetic material of the three-generation family studied by Gopnik (1990a) and Hurst and colleagues (1990). They determined that the impairments exhibited by members of this family

are linked to a small region on the long arm of chromosome 7, confirming autosomal dominant transmission with near 100% penetrance. However, it is important to note that in addition to the grammatical deficits described by Gopnik (1990a), affected members of this family also suffer from orafacial dyspraxia and associated speech disorders (see Hurst et al., 1990; Fisher et al., 1998). We cannot, therefore, conclude that the identified region of chromosome 7 necessarily contains a gene or genes specific to language. Clearly, linkage studies must be performed on other families whose deficits are more circumscribed.

At least three distinct relationships could obtain between genotypes and behavioral phenotypes. It is possible (albeit unlikely) that there is a one-to-one relationship between genotypes and phenotypes, with each genotype causing a distinct type of language disorder. Alternatively, there might be a one-to-many mapping between genotypes and phenotypes, with a single genetic disorder resulting in many behaviorally distinct types of language disorders. For example, one MZ twin with a genetically encoded articulation disorder might respond by refusing to talk at all, whereas his cotwin with the same genotype might speak and make many articulation errors. Finally, there may be a many-to-one mapping between genotypes and phenotypes, with many distinctive genetic disorders resulting in the same type of linguistic disorder. For example, SLI children who frequently omit grammatical morphemes (see Leonard, 1998; Stromswold, 1997) might do so because they suffer from an articulation disorder such as dyspraxia which causes them to omit grammatical morphemes that are pronounced rapidly, because they have difficulty processing rapid auditory input such as unstressed, short-duration grammatical morphemes or because they have a syntactic deficit.

Although a single genotype may result in different linguistic profiles and, conversely, different genotypes may result in very similar profiles, researchers should attempt to limit behavioral heterogeneity. Doing so will increase the likelihood of identifying specific genotypes associated with specific types of linguistic disorders. And such focused research would help answer the fundamental question: Is the ability to learn language the result of genetically encoded, linguistically specific operations?

RECOVERY FROM ACQUIRED BRAIN DAMAGE Lesions acquired during infancy typically result in relatively transient, minor linguistic deficits, whereas similar lesions acquired during adulthood typically result in permanent, devastating language impairments (see, for example, Guttman, 1942; Lenneberg, 1967; but see Dennis, 1997, for a critique).[12] The generally more optimistic prognosis for injuries acquired during early childhood may reflect the fact that less neuronal pruning has occurred in young brains (Cowan et al., 1984), and that the creation of new synapses and the reactivation of latent synapses is more likely in younger brains (Hutten-locher, 1979). Language acquisition after childhood brain injuries typically has been attributed either to recruitment of brain regions adjacent to the damaged peri-sylvian language regions in the left hemisphere or to recruitment of the topographically homologous regions in the undamaged right hemisphere. According to Lenneberg (1967), prior to puberty, the right hemisphere can completely take over the language functions of the left hemisphere. The observation that infants and toddlers who undergo complete removal of the left hemisphere acquire or recover near-normal language suggests that the right hemisphere can take over *most* of the language functions of the left hemisphere provided the transfer of function happens early enough (Byrne and Gates, 1987; Dennis, 1980; Dennis and Kohn, 1975; Dennis and Whitaker, 1976; Rankin, Aram, and Horwitz, 1981; but see Bishop, 1983, for a critique). Because few studies have examined the linguistic abilities of children who undergo left hemispherectomy during middle childhood, the upper age limit for hemispheric transfer of language is unclear. Right-handed adults who undergo left hemispherectomy typically become globally aphasic with essentially no recovery of language (e.g., Crockett and Estridge, 1951; Smith, 1966; Zollinger, 1935). The observation that a right-handed 10-year-old (Gardner et al., 1955) and a right-handed 14-year-old (Hillier, 1954) who underwent left hemispherectomy suffered from global aphasia with modest recovery of language function suggests that hemispheric transfer of language function is greatly reduced but perhaps not completely eliminated by puberty.

Studies revealing that left hemisphere lesions are more often associated with (subtle) syntactic deficits than are right hemisphere lesions (Aram et al., 1985; Aram, Ekelman, and Whitaker, 1986; Byrne and Gates, 1987; Dennis, 1980; Dennis and Kohn, 1975; Dennis and Whitaker, 1976; Kiessling, Denckla, and Carlton, 1983; Rankin, Aram, and Horwitz, 1981; Thal et al., 1991; Woods and Carey, 1979) call into question the complete equipotentiality of the right and left hemispheres for language, and suggest that regions in the left hemisphere may be uniquely suited to acquire syntax. It should be noted, however, that some studies have not found greater syntactic deficits with left than right hemisphere lesions (e.g., Basser, 1962; Feldman et al., 1992; Levy, Amir, and Shalev, 1992). These studies may have included children whose lesions were smaller (Feldman et al., 1992) or in different locations than those in studies in which a hemi-

spheric difference for syntax was found. Bates and colleagues (1997) have examined early language acquisition in children who suffered unilateral brain injuries prior to 6 months of age. Parents of 26 children (16 with left hemisphere lesions, 10 with right hemisphere lesions) between the ages 10 and 17 months completed the MacArthur Communicative Development Inventory. According to parental report, overall, children with brain injuries had smaller vocabularies than normal children.[13] Consistent with Mills, Coffey-Corina, and Neville's (1997) ERP findings that the right hemisphere is particularly crucial in the perception of unknown words by children between 13 and 20 months of age, children with right hemisphere lesions had smaller expressive vocabularies and used fewer communicative gestures than children with left hemisphere lesions (Bates et al., 1997). Parental report for 29 children (17 with left hemisphere lesions, 12 with right hemisphere lesions) between 19 and 31 months of age generally revealed that children with left hemisphere lesions had more limited grammatical abilities than children with right hemisphere lesions (Bates et al., 1997). This was particularly true for children with left temporal lesions. Bates and colleagues also compared the mean length of utterance (MLU) in free speech samples for 30 children (24 with left-hemisphere lesions, 6 with right hemisphere lesions) between the ages of 20 and 44 months. Consistent with the parental report results, children with left hemisphere lesions had lower MLUs than children with right hemisphere lesions. MLUs for children with left temporal lesions were especially depressed compared to children without left temporal injuries.

In children who suffer from partial left hemisphere lesions rather than complete left hemispherectomies, language functions could be assumed by adjacent undamaged tissues within the left hemisphere or by homotopic structures in the intact right hemisphere. Results of Wada tests (in which lateralization of language is determined by testing language function when each hemisphere is temporarily anesthetized) indicate that children with partial left hemisphere lesions often have language represented bilaterally or in the right hemisphere (Mateer and Dodrill, 1983; Rasmussen and Milner, 1977). However, one ERP study suggests that children with partial left hemisphere lesions are more likely to have language localized in the left hemisphere than the right hemisphere (Papanicolaou et al., 1990). There are a number of possible reasons for this discrepancy, including differences in the types of linguistic tasks used in the ERP and Wada studies and possible differences in sizes and sites of left hemisphere lesions in the children studied. In addition, it is possible that the discrepancy is due to the fact that most of the children in the ERP study acquired their lesions after age 4. Furthermore, the extent to which any of the children in the ERP study ever exhibited signs of language impairment is unclear.

Despite disagreement about the details of language recovery after postnatally acquired left hemisphere lesions, the following generalizations can be made (but see Dennis, 1997). Behaviorally, the prognosis for recovery of language is generally better for lesions acquired at a young age, and syntactic deficits are among the most common persistent deficits. If a lesion is so large that little or no tissue adjacent to the language regions of the left hemisphere remains undamaged, regions of the right hemisphere (presumably homotopic to the left hemisphere language areas) can be recruited for language. The essentially intact linguistic abilities of children with extensive left hemisphere lesions are particularly remarkable when contrasted with the markedly impaired linguistic abilities of SLI children who have minimal evidence of neuropathology on CT or MRI scans. Perhaps the reason for this curious finding is that, although SLI children's brains are not deviant on a macroscopic level, SLI brains may have pervasive, bilateral microscopic anomalies such that no normal tissue can be recruited for language function. One piece of data that supports this hypothesis is found in the results of an autopsy performed on a boy who suffered a severe cyanotic episode at 10 days of age. This child subsequently suffered from pronounced deficits in language comprehension and expression until his death (from mumps and congenital heart disease) at age 10. Autopsy revealed that the boy had bilateral loss of cortical substance starting at the inferior and posterior margin of the central sulci and extending backward along the course of the insula and sylvian fissures for 8 cm on the left side and 6 cm on the right side (Landau, Goldstein, and Kleffner, 1960). Perhaps this child did not "outgrow" his language disorder because these extensive bilateral lesions left no appropriate regions that could be recruited for language.

Summary

Evidence from normal and abnormal language acquisition suggests that innate mechanisms allow children to acquire language. Given adequate early exposure to language, children's language development proceeds rapidly and fairly error-free, despite little or no instruction. The brain regions that permit this development seem to be functionally and anatomically distinct at birth, and may correspond to what linguists call Universal Grammar. To account for the fact that mastery of a particular language does not occur without exposure to that language during infancy or early childhood, it is possible that the neural fine-tuning associated with learning a language's particular parameters must take place during a period of high neural plasticity. There is some evidence to suggest that the structures and operations involved in language are at least partially anatomically and functionally modular and apparently have no nonlinguistic counterparts. One possibility is that children have innate mechanisms that predispose them to perceive categorically linguistic stimuli such as phonemes, words, syntactic categories, and phrases and exposure to these types of linguistic stimuli facilitates the neural fine-tuning necessary for normal language acquisition. For example, some innate mechanisms might predispose children to assume that certain types of meanings and distinctions are likely to be conveyed by morphemes. Also, some innate mechanisms might specifically predispose children to distinguish between syntactic categories that allow for free generalization (lexical categories) and those that do not (functional categories). These innate mechanisms may allow children's brains to solve the otherwise intractable induction problems that permeate language acquisition.

In the future, fine-grained linguistic analyses of the speech of language-impaired children may be used to distinguish between different types of SLI. Linkage studies of SLI may tell us which genes code for the brain structures that are necessary for language acquisition. MRI's exquisite sensitivity to white matter/gray matter distinctions means that MRI could be used to look for more subtle defects associated with developmental language disorders, including subtle disorders arising from neuronal migration or dysmyelinization (Barkovich and Kjos, 1992; Edelman and Warach, 1993). Furthermore, the correlation between myelinization and development of function (Smith, 1981) means that serial MRIs of normal children, SLI children, and WS children could shed light on the relationship between brain maturation and normal and abnormal language development. Finally, functional neuroimaging techniques such as ERP, PET, and fMRI may help to answer questions about the neural processes that underlie language and language acquisition in normal children, SLI children, WS children, children with left hemisphere lesions, and children who are exposed to language after the critical period.

ACKNOWLEDGMENTS Preparation of this chapter was supported by a Merck Foundation Fellowship in the Biology of Developmental Disabilities and a Johnson & Johnson Discovery Award. I am grateful to Willem Levelt for his support during the writing of this chapter and to Anne Christophe, Steve Pinker, and Myrna Schwartz for their comments on earlier drafts. A similar chapter will appear in E. Lepore and Z. Pylyshyn (eds.), *What Is Cognitive Science?* Oxford: Basil Blackwell.

NOTES

1. Children differ dramatically in the rate of acquisition. For example, Brown (1973) and Cazden (1968) investigated when three children mastered the use of 14 grammatical

morphemes. Although all three children eventually obtained competence in the use of the third-person singular verbal inflection -s (as in *he sings*) and all three reached this point after they achieved adult-like performance on plurals and possessives, one of the children reached competence at 2;3 (2 years and 3 months), one at 3;6, and one at 3;8. Similar findings concerning individual differences have been found in the rate of acquisition of questions (Stromswold, 1988, 1995) and auxiliaries (Stromswold, 1990a,b) as well as datives, verb particles, and related constructions (Snyder and Stromswold, 1997; Stromswold, 1989a,b). A number of studies have also reported that children's vocabulary development can vary greatly in both rate and style (e.g., Nelson, 1973; Goldfield and Reznick, 1990).

2. Although the observation that the pattern of acquisition varies depending on the structure of the language is consistent with functionalist accounts of language acquisition (e.g., MacWhinney, 1987), such observations can be accounted for within generative theories if one makes the assumption that children must receive a certain amount of positive data from the input in order to set parameters (for P&P) or rank constants (for OT).

3. Throughout this chapter, ungrammatical sentences are indicated with an asterisk (*).

4. There are 23! logically possible unique orders of all 23 auxiliaries. The total number of orders including sets with fewer than 23 auxiliaries is considerably bigger. Because the 23! term is the largest term in the summation, it serves as a lower bound for the number of unique orders and suffices as an estimation of the number of orders.

5. The mere existence of cerebral asymmetries does not prove that there is an innate basis for language, as other mammals also exhibit such asymmetries.

6. Fifteen of the 20 parents and 4 of the 10 siblings had language deficits. The controls had no personal or family history of language impairment or delay.

7. These were not, however, the same children who did poorly on Tallal and Piercy's (1973a,b) auditory processing task.

8. Clinicians and researchers generally agree that considerable diversity exists in the behavioral profiles and manifestations of children diagnosed with SLI and that it is important to distinguish between various subtypes of SLI. However, no system for classifying subtypes of SLI is generally accepted (Stromswold 1997).

9. The term "proband" refers to an affected individual through whom a family is brought to the attention of an investigator.

10. The variance is due in large part to what was counted as evidence of language impairment in families. As indicated in table 63.1, some studies considered family members to be affected only if they suffered from a spoken language disorder, whereas other studies counted as affected any family members having a history of dyslexia, nonlanguage learning disabilities, or school problems.

11. In this chapter, all concordance rates are for proband-wise concordance rates. Proband-wise concordance rates are calculated by taking the number of affected individuals in concordant twin pairs (i.e., twin pairs where both twins are affected) and dividing this number by the total number of affected individuals.

12. In a recent review of research on children whose brain injuries occurred after the onset of language acquisition,

Dennis (1997) argues that the prognosis is no better for children than adults once the etiology of the brain injury is taken into account.

13. Bates and colleagues (1997) report large variance in language abilities among their lesioned subjects, with some of the children's language being at the high end of the normal and other children suffering from profound impairments. This probably reflects, at least in part, variations in the size and sites of the lesions among their subjects.

REFERENCES

AKSU-KOC, A. A., and D. I. SLOBIN, 1985. The acquisition of Turkish. In *The Crosslinguistic Study of Language Acquisition,* Vol. 1, D. I. Slobin, ed. Hillsdale, N.J.: Erlbaum, pp. 839–880.

ARAM, D. M., B. L. EKELMAN, D. F. ROSE, and H. A. WHITAKER, 1985. Verbal and cognitive sequelae of unilateral lesions acquired in early childhood. *J. Clin. Exp. Neuropsychol.* 7:55–78.

ARAM, D. M., B. L. EKELMAN, and H. A. WHITAKER, 1986. Spoken syntax in children with acquired unilateral hemisphere lesions. *Brain Lang.* 27:75–100.

ARNOLD, G. E., 1961. The genetic background of developmental language disorders. *Folia Phoniatr.* 13:246–254.

ARNOLD, G., and S. SCHWARTZ, 1983. Hemispheric lateralization of language in autistic and aphasic children. *J. Autism Dev. Disorders* 13:129–139.

BAKER, C. L., 1981. Learnability and the English auxiliary system. In *The Logical Problem of Language Acquisition*, C. L. Baker and J. J. McCarthy, eds. Cambridge, Mass.: MIT Press, pp. 297–323.

BAKWIN, H., 1973. Reading disabilities in twins. *Dev. Med. Child Neurol.* 15:184–187.

BARKOVICH, A. J., and B. O. KJOS, 1992. Grey matter heterotopias: MR characteristics and correlation with developmental and neurological manifestations. *Radiology* 182:493–499.

BASSER, L. S., 1962. Hemiplegia of early onset and faculty of speech, with special reference to the effects of hemispherectomy. *Brain* 85:427–460.

BATES, E., and B. MACWHINNEY, 1982. Functionalist approaches to grammar. In *Language Acquisition: The State of the Art*, L. Gleitman and E. Wanner, eds. Cambridge: Cambridge University Press.

BATES, E., V. MARCHMAN, D. THAL, L. FENSON, P. DALE, J. S. REZNICK, J. REILLY, and J. HARTUNG, 1994. Developmental and stylistic variation in the composition of early vocabulary. *J. Child Lang.* 21:85–124.

BATES, E., D. THAL, D. TRAUNER, J. FENSON, D. ARAM, J. EISELE, and R. NASS, 1997. From first words to grammar in children with focal brain injury. *Dev. Neuropsychol.* 13(3):275–343.

BAVALIER, D., D. CORINA, P. JEZZARD, V. CLARK, A. KARNI, A. LALWANI, J. P. RANSCHECKER, A. BRAUN, R. TURNER, and H. J. NEVILLE, 1998. Hemispheric specialization for English and ASL: Left invariance–right variability. *Neuroreport* 9:1537–1542.

BEITCHMAN, J. H., J. HOOD, and A. INGLIS, 1992. Familial transmission of speech and language impairment: A preliminary investigation. *Can. J. Psychiatry* 37(3):151–156.

BELLUGI, U., A. BIRHLE, H. NEVILLE, T. L. JERNIGAN, and S. DOHERTY, 1992. Language, cognition, and brain organization in a neurodevelopmental disorder. In *Developmental Behavioral Neuroscience*, M. Gunnar and C. Nelson, eds. Hillsdale, N.J.: Lawrence Erlbaum, pp. 201–232.

BELLUGI, U., P. P. WANG, and T. L. JERNIGAN, 1994. Williams syndrome: An usual neuropsychological profile. In *Atypical Cognitive Deficits in Developmental Disorders: Implications for Brain Function*, S. H. Bronman and J. Grafman, eds. Hillsdale, N.J.: Lawrence Erlbaum, pp. 23–56.

BENEDICT, H., 1979. Early lexical development: Comprehension and production. *J. Child Lang.* 6:183–200.

BERMAN, R. A., 1986. A crosslinguistic perspective: Morphology and syntax. In *Language Acquisition*, 2d Ed., P. Fletcher and M. Garman, eds. Cambridge: Cambridge University Press, pp. 429–447.

BICKERTON, D., 1981. *Roots of Language.* Ann Arbor, Mich.: Karoma.

BICKERTON, D., 1984. The language biprogram hypothesis. *Behav. Brain Sci.* 7:173–221.

BISGAARD, M., H. EIBERG, N. MOLLER, E. NIEBUHR, and J. MOHR, 1987. Dyslexia and chromosome 15 heteromorphism: Negative lod score in a Danish material. *Clin. Genetics* 32:118–119.

BISHOP, D. V. M., 1983. Linguistic impairment after left hemidecortication for infantile hemiplegia: A reappraisal. *Quart. J. Exp. Psychol.* 35A:199–207.

BISHOP, D. V. M., 1987. The causes of specific developmental language disorder ("developmental dysphasia"). *J. Child Psychol. Psychiatry* 28:1–8.

BISHOP, D. V. M., and A. EDMUNDSON, 1986. Is otitis media a major cause of specific developmental language disorders? *Brit. J. Disorders Commun.* 21:321–338.

BISHOP, D. V. M., T. NORTH, and C. DONLAN, 1995. Genetic basis of specific language impairment: Evidence from a twin study. *Dev. Med. Child Neurol.* 37:56–71.

BLOOM, P., 1990. Syntactic distinctions in child language. *J. Child Lang.* 17:343–355.

BOLIEK, C.A., M. P. BRYDEN, and J. E. OBRZUT, 1988. Focused attention and the perception of voicing and place of articulation contrasts with control and learning-disabled children. Paper presented at the 16th Annual Meeting of the International Neuropsychological Society, January 1988.

BROWN, R., 1973. *A First Language: The Early Stages.* Cambridge, Mass.: Harvard University Press.

BROWN, R., and C. HANLON, 1970. Derivational complexity and order of acquisition in child speech. In *Cognition and the Development of Language*, J. R. Hayes, ed. New York: Wiley.

BUDWIG, N., 1995. *A Developmental-Functionalist Approach to Language.* Mahwah, N.J.: Erlbaum.

BYRNE, B. M., L. WILLERMAN, and L. L. ASHMORE, 1974. Severe and moderate language impairment: Evidence for distinctive etiologies. *Behav. Genetics* 4:331–345.

BYRNE, J. M., and R. D. GATES, 1987. Single-case study of left cerebral hemispherectomy: Development in the first five years of life. *J. Clin. Exp. Neuropsychol.* 9:423–434.

CAZDEN, C., 1968. The acquisition of noun and verb inflections. *Child Dev.* 39:433–448.

CHI, J. G., E. C. DOOLING, and F. H. GILLES, 1977. Left-right asymmetries of the temporal speech areas of the human brain. *Arch. Neurol.* 34:346–348.

CHOMSKY, N., 1981. *Lectures on Government and Binding.* Dordrecht, Holland: Foris.

CHOMSKY, N., 1986. *Knowledge of Language: Its Nature, Origin and Use.* New York: Praeger.

CLAHSEN, H., 1989. The grammatical characterization of developmental dysphasia. *Linguistics* 27(5):897–920.

CLAHSEN, H., 1991. *Child Language and Developmental Dysphasia: Linguistic Studies of the Acquisition of German.* Philadelphia, Pa.: J. Benjamins Publishing Company.

CLARK, M., and E. PLANTE, 1995. Morphology in the inferior frontal gyrus in developmentally language-disordered adults. Paper presented at the Conference on Cognitive Neuroscience, San Francisco.

COHEN, H., C. GELINAS, M. LASSONDE, and G. GEOFFROY, 1991. Auditory lateralization for speech in language-impaired children. *Brain Lang.* 41:395–401.

COHEN, M., R. CAMPBELL, and F. YAGHMAI, 1989. Neuropathological abnormalities in developmental dysphasia. *Ann. Neurol.* 25:567–570.

CONTI-RAMSDEN, G., and J. DYKINS, 1991. Mother-child interactions with language-impaired children and their siblings. *Brit. J. Disorders Commun.* 26:337–354.

CONTI-RAMSDEN, G., and S. FRIEL-PATTI, 1983. Mothers' discourse adjustments with language-impaired and non–language-impaired children. *J. Speech Hearing Disorders* 48: 360–367.

COPPOLA, M., A. SENGHAS, E. L. NEWPORT, and T. SUPALLA, 1998. *The Emergence of Grammar: Evidence from Family-Based Gesture Systems in Nicaragua.* University of Rochester, unpublished manuscript.

COURCHESNE, E., A. LINCOLN, R. YEUNG-COURCHESNE, R. ELMASIAN, and C. GRILLON, 1989. Pathophysiological finding in nonretarded autism and receptive developmental language disorder. *J. Autism Dev. Disorders* 19:1–17.

COWAN, W. M., J. W. FAWCETT, D. D. O'LEARY, and B. B. STANFIELD, 1984. Regressive events in neurogenesis. *Science* 225:1258–1265.

CRAGO, M. B., and M. GOPNIK, 1994. From families to phenotypes: Theoretical and clinical implications of research into the genetic basis of specific language impairment. In *Specific Language Impairments in Children*, R. V. Watkins and M. L. Rice, eds. Baltimore, Md.: Paul H. Brookes, pp. 35–52.

CRAMBLIT, N., and G. SIEGEL, 1977. The verbal environment of a language-impaired child. *J. Speech Hearing Disorders* 42: 474–482.

CROCKETT, H. G., and N. M. ESTRIDGE, 1951. Cerebral hemispherectomy. *Bull. L.A. Neurol. Soc.* 16:71–87.

CROFT, W., 1990. *Typology and Universals.* New York: Cambridge University Press.

CROMER, R., 1983. Hierarchical planning disability in the drawings and constructions of a special group of severely aphasic children. *Brain Cognit.* 2:144–164.

CURTISS, S., 1977. *Genie: A Psycholinguistic Study of a Modern Day "Wild Child."* New York: Academic Press.

CURTISS, S., 1989. The independence and task-specificity of language. In *Interaction in Human Development*, A. Bornstein and J. Bruner, eds. Hillsdale, N.J.: Erlbaum, pp. 105–137.

DAVIS, K., 1940. Extreme social isolation of a child. *Amer. J. Sociol.* 45:554–565.

DAVIS, K., 1947. Final note on a case of extreme isolation. *Amer. J. Sociol.* 52:432–437.

DAWSON, G., C. FINLEY, S. PHILLIPS, and A. LEWY, 1989. A comparison of hemispheric asymmetries in speech-related brain potentials of autistic and dysphasic children. *Brain Lang.* 37:26–41.

DEFRIES, J. C., D. W. FULKER, and M. C. LABUDA, 1987. Evidence for a genetic aetiology in reading disability of twins. *Nature* 329:537–539.

DEFRIES, J. C., and J. J. GILLIS, 1993. Genetics of reading disability. In *Nature, Nurture, and Psychology*, R. Plomin and G. E. McClearn, eds. Washington, D.C.: American Psychological Association, pp. 121–145.

DENAYS, R., M. TONDEUR, M. FOULON, F. VERSTRAETEN, H. HAM, A. PIEPSZ, and P. NOEL, 1989. Regional brain blood flow in congenital dysphasia studies with technetium-99M HM–PAO SPECT. *J. Nuclear Med.* 30:1825–1829.

DENNIS, M., 1980. Capacity and strategy for syntactic comprehension after left or right hemidecortication. *Brain Lang.* 10:287–317.

DENNIS, M., 1997. Acquired disorders of language in children. In *Behavioral Neurology and Neuropsychology*, T. E. Feinberg and M. J. Farah, eds. New York: McGraw Hill, pp. 737–754.

DENNIS, M., and B. KOHN, 1975. Comprehension of syntax in infantile hemiplegics after cerebral hemidecortication: Left hemisphere superiority. *Brain Lang.* 2:475–486.

DENNIS, M., and H. A. WHITAKER, 1976. Language acquisition following hemi-decortication: Linguistic superiority of the left over the right hemisphere. *Brain Lang.* 3:404–433.

DEVILLIERS, J., and P. DEVILLIERS, 1973. A cross-sectional study of the acquisition of Grammatical morphemes in child speech. *J. Psycholinguistic Res.* 2:267–278.

EDELMAN, R. R., and S. WARACH, 1993. Magnetic resonance imaging (Part 1). *New Eng. J. Med.* 328:708–716.

EFRON, R., 1963. Temporal perception, aphasia, and deja vu. *Brain* 86:403–424.

ELDRIDGE, R., 1983. Twin studies and the etiology of complex neurological disorders. In *Genetic Aspects of Speech and Language Disorders*, C. L. Ludlow and J. A. Cooper, eds. New York: Academic Press, pp. 109–120.

ELMAN, J., E. BATES, M. JOHNSON, A. KARMILOFF-SMITH, D. PARISI, and K. PLUNKETT, 1996. *Rethinking Innateness: A Connectionist Perspective on Development*. Cambridge, Mass.: MIT Press.

EWART, A. K., C. A. MORRIS, D. ATKINSON, J. WIESHAN, K. STERNES, P. SPALLONE, A. D. STOCK, M. LEPPERT, and M. T. KEATING, 1993a. Hemizygosity at the elastin locus in a developmental disorder: Williams syndrome. *Nature Genetics* 5:11–16.

EWART, A. K., C. A. MORRIS, G. J. ENSING, J. LOKER, C. MOORE, M. LEPPERT, and M. KEATING, 1993b. A human vascular disorder, supravalvular aortic stenosis, maps to chromosome 7. *Proc. Natl. Acad. Sci.* 90(8):3226–3230.

FELDMAN, H., A. L. HOLLAND, S. S. KEMP, and J. E. JANOSKY, 1992. Language development after unilateral brain injury. *Brain Lang.* 42:89–102.

FENSON, L., P. S. DALE, J. S. REZNICK, E. BATES, D. J. THAL, and S. J. PETHICK, 1994. Variability in early communicative development. *Monographs Soc. Res. Child Dev.* 59(242).

FISHER, S. E., F. VARGHA-KHADEM, K. E. WATKINS, A. P. MONACO, and M. E. PEMBREY, 1998. Localization of a gene implicated in a severe speech and language disorder. *Nature Genetics* 18:168–170.

FOLEY, W., and R. VAN VALIN, 1984. *Functional Syntax and Universal Grammar*. Cambridge: Cambridge University Press.

FROSTA, H., G. SCHULTE-KORNE, J. HEBEBRAND, and H. REMSCHNOIDT, 1993. Cosegregation of balanced translocation (1,2) with retarded speech development and dyslexia. *Lancet* 342:178–190.

FUNDUDIS, T., I. KOLVIN, and G. GARSIDE, 1979. *Speech Retarded and Deaf Children*. London: Academic Press.

GALABURDA, A. M., P. R. WANG, U. BELLUGI, and M. ROSSEN, 1994. Cytoarchitectonic anomalies in a genetically based disorder: Williams syndrome. *Neuroreport* 5:753–757.

GANGER, J., and K. STROMSWOLD, 1998. The innateness, evolution and genetics of language. *Human Biol.* 70:199–213.

GARDNER, W. J., L. J. KARNOSH, C. C. MCCLURE, and A. K. GARDNER, 1955. Residual function following hemispherectomy for tumour and for infantile hemiplegia. *Brain* 78:487–502.

GARRETT, M., 1976. Syntactic processes in sentence production. In *New Approaches to Language Mechanisms*, R. Wales and E. Walker, eds. Amsterdam: North-Holland.

GESCHWIND, N., and A. GALABURDA, 1987. *Cerebral Lateralization: Biological Mechanisms, Associations, and Pathology*. Cambridge, Mass.: MIT Press.

GOLDFIELD, B. A., and J. S. REZNICK, 1990. Early lexical acquisition: Rate, content and vocabulary spurt. *J. Child Lang.* 17:171–184.

GOLDIN-MEADOW, S., and C. MYLANDER, 1984. Gestural communication in deaf children: The effects and non-effects of parental input on early language development. *Monographs Soc. Res. Child Dev.* 49:1–121.

GOLDIN-MEADOW, S., and C. MYLANDER, 1998. Spontaneous sign systems created by deaf children in two cultures. *Nature* 391:279–281.

GOODGLASS, H., 1976. Agrammatism. In *Perspectives in Neurolinguistics and Psycholinguistics*, H. Whitaker and H. Whitaker, eds. New York: Academic Press.

GOPNIK, M., 1990a. Feature-blind grammar and dysphasia. *Nature* 344:715.

GOPNIK, M., 1990b. Feature blindness: A case study. *Lang. Acquisition* 1:139–164.

GOPNIK, M., and M. B. CRAGO, 1991. Familial aggregation of a developmental language disorder. *Cognition* 39:1–50.

GORDON, A. G., 1988. Some comments on Bishop's annotation "Developmental dysphasia and otitis media." *J. Child Psychol. Psychiatry* 29:361–363.

GRAHAM, N. C., 1968. Short term memory and syntactic structure in educationally subnormal children. *Lang. Speech* 11:209–219.

GRAHAM, N. C., 1974. Response strategies in the partial comprehension of sentences. *Lang. Speech* 17:205–221.

GRAVEL, J. S., and I. F. WALLACE, 1992. Listening and language at 4 years of age: Effects of early otitis media. *J. Speech Hearing Res.* 35:588–595.

GUILFOYLE, E., S. ALLEN, and S. MOSS, 1991. Specific language impairment and the maturation of functional categories. Paper presented at the 16th Annual Boston University Conference on Language Development, October 19, 1991.

GUTTMAN, E., 1942. Aphasia in children. *Brain* 65:205–219.

HAYNES, C., and S. NAIDO, 1991. *Children with Specific Speech and Language Impairment*. London: MacKeith Press.

HEATH, S. B., 1983. *Ways with Words: Language, Life and Work in Communities and Classrooms*. New York: Cambridge University Press.

HILLIER, W. F., 1954. Total left cerebral hemispherectomy for malignant glioma. *Neurology* 4:718–721.

HOLCOMB, P. J., S. A. COFFEY, and H. J. NEVILLE, 1992. Visual and auditory sentence processing: A developmental analysis using event-related brain potentials. *Dev. Neuropsychol.* 8:203–241.

HUBEL, D., and T. WIESEL, 1970. The period of susceptibility to the physiological effects of unilateral eye closure in kittens. *J. Physiol.* 206:419–436.

HURST, J. A., M. BARAITSER, E. AUGER, F. GRAHAM, and S. NORELL, 1990. An extended family with a dominantly inherited speech disorder. *Dev. Med. Child Neurol.* 32:347–355.

HUTTENLOCHER, J., and P. Smiley, 1987. Early word meanings: The case of object names. *Cogn. Psychol.* 19:63–89.

HUTTENLOCHER, P. R., 1979. Synaptic density in human frontal cortex–Developmental changes and effects of aging. *Brain Res.* 163:195–205.

INGRAM, T. T. S., 1959. Specific developmental disorders of speech in childhood. *Brain* 82:450–467.

JACKSON, T., and E. PLANTE, 1997. Gyral morphology in the posterior sylvian regions in families affected by developmental language disorders. *Neuropsychol. Rev.* 6:81–94.

JERNIGAN, T. L., and U. BELLUGI, 1994. Neuroanatomical distinctions between Williams and Down syndrome. In *Atypical Cognitive Deficits in Developmental Disorders: Implications for Brain Function*, S. H. Bronman and J. Grafman, eds. Hillsdale, N.J.: Erlbaum, pp. 57–66.

JERNIGAN, T. L., U. BELLUGI, E. SOWELL, S. DOHERTY, and J. HESSELINK, 1993. Cerebral morphological distinctions between Williams and Down syndromes. *Arch. Neurol.* 50:186–191.

JERNIGAN, T. L., J. R. HESSELINK, E. SOWELL, and P. A. TALLAL, 1991. Cerebral structure on magnetic resonance imaging in language-impaired and learning-impaired children. *Arch. Neurol.* 48:539–545.

JOHNSON, J., and E. NEWPORT, 1989. Critical period effects in second language learning: The influence of maturational state on the acquisition of English as a second language. *Cogn. Psychol.* 21:60–99.

JOHNSTON, J., and S. WEISMER, 1983. Mental rotation abilities in language-disordered children. *J. Speech Hearing Res.* 26:397–403.

JOHNSTON, J. R., 1991. The continuing relevance of cause: A reply to Leonard's "Specific language impairment as a clinical category." *Lang. Speech Hearing Serv. Schools* 22:75–79.

JUSCZYK, P. W., K. HIRSCH-PASEK, D. KEMLER NELSON, and L. J. KENNEDY, 1992. Perception of acoustic correlates of major phrasal units by young infants. *Cogn. Psychol.* 24:252–293.

JUSCZYK, P. W., and D. G. KEMLER NELSON, 1996. Syntactic units, prosody, and psychological reality in infancy. In *Signal to Syntax: Bootstrapping from Speech to Grammar in Early Acquisition*, K. Demuth and J. L. Morgan, eds. Mahwah, N.J.: Erlbaum, pp. 389–408.

KAHMI, A., 1981. Nonlinguistic symbolic and conceptual abilities in language-impaired and normally developing children. *J. Speech Hearing Res.* 24:446–453.

KARMILOFF-SMITH, A., 1991. *Beyond Modularity.* Cambridge, Mass.: MIT Press.

KARMILOFF-SMITH, A., J. GRANT, I. BERTHOUD, M. DAVIES, P. HOWLIN, and O. UDWIN, 1997. Language and Williams syndrome: How intact is "intact"? *Child Dev.* 68(2):246–262.

KARMILOFF-SMITH, A., L. K. TYLER, K. VOICE, K. SIMS, O. UDWIN, P. HOWLIN, and M. DAVIES, 1998. Linguistic dissociations in Williams syndrome: Evaluating receptive syntax in on-line and off-line tasks. *Neuropsychologia* 36:343–351.

KIESSLING, L. S., M. B. V. DENCKLA, and M. CARLTON, 1983. Evidence for differential hemispheric function in children with hemiplegic cerebral palsy. *Dev. Med. Child. Neurol.* 25:727–734.

LAHEY, M., and J. EDWARDS, 1995. Specific language impairment: Preliminary investigation of factors associated with family history and with patterns of language performance. *J. Speech Hearing Res.* 38:643–657.

LANDAU, W. M., R. GOLDSTEIN, and F. R. KLEFFNER, 1960. Congenital aphasia: A clinicopathological study. *Neurology* 10:915–921.

LASKY, E., and K. KLOPP, 1982. Parent-child interactions in normal and language-disordered children. *J. Speech Hearing Disorders* 47:7–18.

LENNEBERG, E. H., 1967. *Biological Foundations of Language.* New York: John Wiley and Sons.

LEONARD, C. M., K. VOELLER, L. LOMBARDINO, M. MORRIS, G. HYND, A. ALEXANDER, H. ANDERSON, M. GAROFALAKIS, J. HONEYMAN, J. MAO, O. AGEE, and E. STAAB, 1993. Anomalous cerebral structure in dyslexia revealed with magnetic resonance imaging. *Arch. Neurol.* 50:461–469.

LEONARD, L., 1998. *Children with Specific Language Impairment.* Cambridge, Mass.: MIT Press.

LEONARD, L. B., 1989. Language learnability and specific language impairment in children. *Appl. Psycholinguistics* 10:179–202.

LEONARD, L. B., 1991. Specific language impairment as a clinical category. *Lang. Speech Hearing Serv. Schools* 22:66–68.

LEONARD, L. B., 1994. Some problems facing accounts of morphological deficits in children with specific language impairments. In *Specific Language Impairments in Children*, R. V. Watkins and M. L. Rice, eds. Baltimore, Md.: Paul H. Brookes, pp. 91–106.

LEONARD, L. B., K. K. MCGREGOR, and G. D. ALLEN, 1992. Grammatical morphology and speech perception in children with specific language impairment. *J. Speech Hearing Res.* 35:1076–1085.

LEVY, Y., N. AMIR, and R. SHALEV, 1992. Linguistic development of a child with congenital localised L.H. lesion. *Cogn. Neuropsychol.* 9:1–32.

LEWIS, B. A., 1990. Familial phonological disorders: Four pedigrees. *J. Speech Hear. Disorders* 55:160–170.

LEWIS, B. A., 1992. Pedigree analysis of children with phonology disorders. *J. Learning Disabilities* 25(9):586–597.

LEWIS, B. A., B. L. EKELMAN, and D. M. ARAM, 1989. A familial study of severe phonological disorders. *J. Speech Hearing Res.* 32:713–724.

LEWIS, B. A., and L. A. THOMPSON, 1992. A study of developmental speech and language disorders in twins. *J. Speech Hearing Res.* 35:1086–1094.

LINCOLN, A., E. COURCHESNE, L. HARMS, and M. ALLEN, 1995. Sensory modulation of auditory stimuli in children with autism and receptive developmental language disorder: Event-related brain potential evidence. *J. Autism Dev. Disorders* 25:521–539.

LOCKE, J. L., and P. L. MATHER, 1989. Genetic factors in the ontogeny of spoken language: Evidence from monozygotic and dizygotic twins. *J. Child Lang.* 16:553–559.

LOU, H. D., L. HENRIKSEN, and P. BRUHN, 1990. Focal cerebral dysfunction in developmental learning disabilities. *Lancet* 335:8–11.

LUCHSINGER, R., 1970. Inheritance of speech deficits. *Folia Phoniatrica* 22:216–230.

MACWHINNEY, B., 1987. The competition model. In *Mechanisms in Language Acquisition*, B. MacWhinney, ed. Hillsdale, N.J.: Erlbaum, pp. 249–308.

MARATSOS, M., and M. CHALKLEY, 1981. The internal language of children's syntax: The ontogenesis and representation of syntactic categories. In *Children's Language*, Vol. 2, K. Nelson, ed. New York: Gardner Press.

MARCUS, G. F., 1993. Negative evidence in language acquisition. *Cognition* 46(1):53–85.

MARTIN, J. A., 1981. *Voice, Speech and Language in the Child: Development and Disorder.* New York: Springer.

MATEER, C. A., and C. B. DODRILL, 1983. Neuropsychological and linguistic correlates of atypical language lateralization: Evidence from sodium amytal studies. *Human Neurobiol.* 2:135–142.

MATHENY, A. P., A. B. DOLAN, and R. S. WILSON, 1976. Twins with academic learning problems: Antecedent characteristics. *Amer. J. Orthopsychiatry* 46(3):464–469.

MCNEILL, D., 1966. Developmental psycholinguistics. In *The Genesis of Language*, F. Smith and G. Miller, eds. Cambridge, Mass.: MIT Press.

MEHLER, J., and A. CHRISTOPHE, 1995. Maturation and learning of language in the first year of life. In *The Cognitive Neurosciences*, M. S. Gazzaniga, ed. Cambridge, Mass.: MIT Press, pp. 943–954.

MERVIS, C. B., and J. BERTRAND, 1995. Early lexical acquisition and the vocabulary spurt: A response to Goldfield and Reznick. *J. Child Lang.* 22:461–468.

MILLS, A., 1985. The acquisition of German. In *The Crosslinguistic Study of Language Acquisition*, Vol. 1, D. I. Slobin, ed. Hillsdale, N.J.: Lawrence Erlbaum, pp. 141–254.

MILLS, D. L., S. COFFEY-CORINA, and H. J. NEVILLE, 1997. Language comprehension and cerebral specialization from 13 to 20 months. *Dev. Neuropsychol.* 13(3):397–445.

MOLFESE, D. L., 1990. Auditory evoked responses recorded from 16-month old human infants to words they did and did not know. *Brain Lang.* 36:345–363.

MOLFESE, D. L., P. A. MORSE, and C. J. PETERS, 1990. Auditory evoked responses to names for different objects: Cross-modal processing as a basis for infant language acquisition. *Dev. Psychol.* 26(5):780–795.

MONSEE, E. K., 1961. Aphasia in children. *J. Speech Hearing Disorders* 26:83–86.

MOREHEAD, D., and D. INGRAM, 1973. The development of base syntax in normal and linguistically deviant children. *J. Speech Hearing Res.* 16:330–352.

MORFORD, J. P., 1996. Insights to language from the study of gesture: A review of research on the gestural communication of non-signing deaf people. *Lang. Commun.* 16(2):165–178.

MORGAN, J. L., and K. DEMUTH (eds.), 1996. *Signal to Syntax: Bootstrapping from Speech to Grammar in Early Acquisition.* Hillsdale, N.J.: Erlbaum.

MORGAN, J., and E. NEWPORT, 1981. The role of constituent structure in the induction of an artificial language. *J. Verbal Learning Verbal Behav.* 20:67–85.

MORLEY, M., 1965. *The Development and Disorders of Speech in Children.* Edinburgh: E&S Livingstone.

NEILS, J., and D. M. ARAM, 1986. Family history of children with developmental language disorders. *Percept. Motor Skills* 63:655–658.

NELSON, K., 1973. Structure and strategy in learning to talk. *Monographs Soc. Res. Child Dev.* 38.

NEVILLE, H. J., 1991. Neurobiology of cognitive and language processing: Effects of early experience. In *Brain Maturation and Cognitive Development*, K. Gibson and A. Petersen, eds. New York: Aldine de Gruyter, pp. 355–380.

NEVILLE, H. J., 1995. Developmental specificity in neurocognitive development in humans. In *The Cognitive Neurosciences*, M. S. Gazzaniga, ed. Cambridge, Mass.: MIT Press, pp. 219–231.

NEVILLE, H., S. COFFEY, P. HOLCOMB, and P. TALLAL, 1993. The neurobiology of sensory and language processing in language-impaired children. *J. Cogn. Neurosci.* 5:235–253.

NEVILLE, H. J., P. J. HOLCOMB, and D. M. MILLS, 1989. Auditory sensory and language processing in Williams syndrome: An ERP study. Paper presented at the International Neuropsychological Society, January 1989.

NEVILLE, H. J., D. L. MILLS, and U. BELLUGI, 1994. Effects of altered auditory sensitivity and age of language acquisition on the development of language-relevant neural systems: Preliminary studies of Williams syndrome. In *Atypical Cognitive Deficits in Developmental Disorders: Implications for Brain Function*, S. H. Bronman and J. Grafman, eds. Hillsdale, N.J.: Erlbaum, pp. 67–83.

NEVILLE, H. J., D. L. MILLS, and D. S. LAWSON, 1992. Fractionating language: Different neural subsystems with different sensitive periods. *Cerebral Cortex* 2(3):244–258.

NEWPORT, E., 1990. Maturational constraints on language learning. *Cogn. Sci.* 14:11–28.

PAPANICOLAOU, A. C., A. DISCENNA, L. GILLESPIE, and D. ARAM, 1990. Probe-evoked potential finding following unilateral left-hemisphere lesions in children. *Arch. Neurol.* 47:562–566.

PAULS, D. L., 1983. Genetic analysis of family pedigree data: A review of methodology. In *Genetic Aspects of Speech and Language Disorders*, C. L. Ludlow and J. A. Cooper, eds. New York: Academic Press, pp. 139–148.

PENNINGTON, B., and S. SMITH, 1988. Genetic influences on learning disabilities: An update. *J. Consult. Clin. Psychol.* 56:817–823.

PETERS, A. M., 1995. Strategies in the acquisition of syntax. In *The Handbook of Child Language*, P. Fletcher and B. MacWhinney, eds. Oxford: Basil Blackwell, pp. 462–483.

PINKER, S., 1984. *Language Learnability and Language Development.* Cambridge, Mass.: Harvard University Press.

PINKER, S., 1987. The bootstrapping problem in language acquisition. In *Mechanisms of Language Acquisition*, B. MacWhinney, ed. Hillsdale, N.J.: Erlbaum, pp. 399–441.

PINKER, S., 1989. *Learnability and Cognition: The Acquisition of Argument Structure.* Cambridge, Mass.: MIT Press.

PINKER, S., 1994. *The Language Instinct: How the Mind Creates Language.* New York: Morrow.

PINKER, S., and P. BLOOM, 1990. Natural language and natural selection. *Behav. Brain Sci.* 13:707–784.

PLANTE, E., 1991. MRI findings in the parents and siblings of specifically language-impaired boys. *Brain Lang.* 41:67–80.

PLANTE, E., L. SWISHER, and R. VANCE, 1989. Anatomical correlates of normal and impaired language in a set of dizygotic twins. *Brain Lang.* 37:643–655.

PLANTE, E., L. SWISHER, R. VANCE, and S. RAPSAK, 1991. MRI findings in boys with specific language impairment. *Brain Lang.* 41:52–66.

POPPEN, R., J. STARK, J. EISENSON, T. FORREST, and G. WERTHHEIM, 1969. Visual sequencing performance of aphasic children. *J. Speech Hearing Res.* 12:288–300.

PRINCE, A., and P. SMOLENSKY, 1993. *Optimality Theory.* Cognitive Science Technical Report: Rutgers University and University of Colorado.

RABIN, M., X. L. WEN, M. HEPBURN, H. A. LUBS, E. FELDMAN, and R. DUARA, 1993. Suggestive linkage of developmental dyslexia to chromosome 1p34–p36. *Lancet* 342:178.

RANKIN, J. M., D. M. ARAM, and S. J. HORWITZ, 1981. Language ability in right and left hemiplegic children. *Brain Lang.* 14:292–306.

RAPIN, I., and B. C. WILSON, 1978. Children with developmental language disability: Neuropsychological aspects and assessment. In *Developmental Dysphasia*, M. A. Wyke, ed. London: Academic Press, pp. 13–41.

RASMUSSEN, T., and B. MILNER, 1977. The role of early left-brain injury in determining lateralization of cerebral speech functions. *Ann. N.Y. Acad. Sci.* 299:335–369.

REZNICK, J. S., and B. A. GOLDFIELD, 1992. Rapid change in lexical development in comprehension and production. *Dev. Psychol.* 28:406–413.

RICE, M. L., 1994. Grammatical categories of children with specific language impairments. In *Specific Language Impairments in Children*, R. V. Watkins and M. L. Rice, eds. Baltimore, Md.: Paul H. Brookes, pp. 69–90.

RICE, M. L., K. R. HANEY, and K. WEXLER, 1998. Family histories of children with extended optional infinitives. *J. Speech Hearing Res.* 41:419–432.

ROBINSON, R. J., 1987. The causes of language disorder: An introduction and overview. In *Proceedings of the First International Symposium on Specific Speech and Language Disorders in Children*. London: AFASIC.

RONDAL, J., 1980. Language delay and language difference in moderately and severely retarded children. *Special Ed. Can.* 54:27–32.

SAMPLES, J., and V. LANE, 1985. Genetic possibilities in six siblings with specific language learning disorders. *Asha* 27:27–32.

SCHEIBEL, A. B., 1984. A dendritic correlate of human speech. In *Cerebral Dominance: The Biological Foundations*, N. Geschwind and A. M. Galaburda, eds. Cambridge, Mass.: Harvard University Press.

SCHIEFFELIN, B. B., 1985. The acquisition of Kaluli. In *The Crosslinguistic Study of Language Acquisition*, Vol. 1, D. I. Slobin, ed. Hillsdale, N.J.: Lawrence Erlbaum, pp. 525–594.

SILVA, P. A., S. WILLIAMS, and R. MCGEE, 1987. Early language delay and later intelligence, reading and behavior problems. *Dev. Med. Child Neurol.* 29:630–640.

SINGER HARRIS, N. G., U. BELLUGI, E. BATES, W. JONES, and M. ROSSEN, 1997. Contrasting profiles of language development in children with Williams and Down syndromes. *Dev. Neuropsychol.* 13(3):345–370.

SKUSE, D. H., 1984a. Extreme deprivation in early childhood. I: Diverse outcomes for 3 siblings from an extraordinary family. *J. Child Psychol. Psychiatry* 25:523–541.

SKUSE, D. H., 1984b. Extreme deprivation in early childhood. II: Theoretical issues and a comparative review. *J. Child Psychol. Psychiatry* 25:543–572.

SLOBIN, D. (ed.), 1985. *The Crosslinguistic Study of Language Acquisition,* Vols. 1–2. Hillsdale, N.J.: Erlbaum.

SMITH, A., 1966. Speech and other functions after left dominant hemispherectomy. *J. Neurol. Neurosurg. Psychiatry* 29:467–471.

SMITH, J. F., 1981. Central nervous system. In *Paediatric Pathology*, C. L. Berry, ed. Berlin: Springer Verlag, pp. 147–148.

SMITH, S., B. PENNINGTON, P. FAIN, W. KIMBERLING, and H. LUBS, 1983. Specific reading disability: Identification of an inherited form through linkage analysis. *Science* 219:1345–1347.

SMITH, S., B. PENNINGTON, W. KIMBERLING, P. FAIN, P. ING, and H. LUBS, 1986. Genetic heterogeneity in specific reading disability (Abstract 500). *Amer. J. Clin. Genetics* 39:A169.

SNYDER, W., and K. STROMSWOLD, 1997. The structure and acquisition of English dative constructions. *Linguistic Inquiry* 28:281–317.

STEELE, S., 1981. *An Encyclopedia of AUX: A Study in Cross-Linguistic Equivalence.* Cambridge, Mass.: MIT Press.

STEVENS, T., and A. KARMILOFF-SMITH, 1997. Word learning in a special population: Do individuals with Williams syndrome obey lexical constraints? *J. Child Lang.* 24:737–765.

STEVENSON, J., P. GRAHAM, G. FREDMAN, and V. MC-LOUGHLIN, 1987. A twin study of genetic influences on reading and spelling ability and disability. *J. Child Psychol. Psychiatry* 28:229–247.

STROMSWOLD, K., 1988. Linguistic representations of children's *wh*-questions. *Papers Reports Child Lang.* 27:107–114.

STROMSWOLD, K., 1989a. How conservative are children? *Papers Reports Child Lang.* 28:148–155.

STROMSWOLD, K., 1989b. Using naturalistic data: Methodological and theoretical issues (or How *not* to lie with naturalistic data). Paper presented at the 14th Annual Boston University Child Language Conference, October 13–15, 1989.

STROMSWOLD, K., 1990a. Learnability and the acquisition of auxiliaries. Unpublished Ph.D. dissertation. Available through MIT's *Working Papers in Linguistics.*

STROMSWOLD, K., 1990b. The acquisition of language-universal and language-specific aspects of tense. Paper presented at the 15th Boston University Child Language Conference, October 19–21, 1990.

STROMSWOLD, K., 1992. Learnability and the acquisition of auxiliary and copula *be.* In *ESCOL '91.* Columbus, Ohio: Ohio State University.

STROMSWOLD, K., 1994a. Language comprehension without language production: Implications for theories of language acquisition. Paper presented at the 18th Boston University Conference on Language Development. January 1994.

STROMSWOLD, K., 1994b. The nature of children's early grammar: Evidence from inversion errors. Paper presented at the 1994 Linguistic Society of America Conference, January 1994. Boston, Massachusetts.

STROMSWOLD, K., 1994c. Lexical and functional categories in language and language acquisition. Rutgers University Manuscript.

STROMSWOLD, K., 1995. The acquisition of subject and object *wh*-questions. *Lang. Acquisition* 4:5–48.

STROMSWOLD, K., 1996. The genetic basis of language acquisition. In *Proceedings of the 20th Annual Boston University Conference on Language Development*, Vol. 2. Somerville, Mass.: Cascadilla Press, pp. 736–747.

STROMSWOLD, K., 1997. Specific language impairments. In *Behavioral Neurology and Neuropsychology*, T. E. Feinberg and M. J. Farah, eds. New York: McGraw-Hill, pp. 755–772.

STROMSWOLD, K., 1998. The genetics of spoken language disorders. *Human Biol.* 70:297–324.

STROMSWOLD, K., in press-a. Formal categories in language: Evidence from regularization errors in acquisition. *Lang. Cogn. Processes.*

STROMSWOLD, K., in press-b. The heritability of language: A review of twin and adoption studies. *Language.*

STROMSWOLD, K., and W. SNYDER, 1995. Acquisition of datives, particles, and related constructions: Evidence for a parametric account. In *Proceedings of the 19th Annual Boston University Conference on Language Development*, Vol. 2, D. MacLaughlin and S. McEwen, eds. Somerville, Mass.: Cascadilla Press, pp. 621–628.

SWISHER, L. P., and E. J. PINSKER, 1971. The language characteristics of hyperverbal hydrocephalic children. *Dev. Child Neurol.* 13:746–755.

TALLAL, P., 1990. Fine-grained discrimination deficits in language-learning impaired children are specific neither to the auditory modality nor to speech perception. *J. Speech Hearing Res.* 33:616–621.

TALLAL, P., and M. PIERCY, 1973a. Defects of non-verbal auditory perception in children with developmental dysphasia. *Nature* 241:468–469.

TALLAL, P., and M. PIERCY, 1973b. Developmental aphasia: Impaired rate of non-verbal processing as a function of sensory modality. *Neuropsychologia* 11:389–398.

TALLAL, P., and M. PIERCY, 1974. Developmental aphasia: Rate of auditory processing as a selective impairment of consonant perception. *Neuropsychologia* 12:83–93.

TALLAL, P., R. ROSS, and S. CURTISS, 1989a. Familial aggregation in specific language impairment. *J. Speech Hearing Disorders* 54:167–173.

TALLAL, P., R. ROSS, and S. CURTISS, 1989b. Unexpected sex-ratios in families of language/learning impaired children. *Neuropsychologia* 27:987–998.

TALLAL, P., J. TOWNSEND, S. CURTISS, and B. WULFECK, 1991. Phenotypic profiles of language-impaired children based on genetic/family history. *Brain Lang.* 41:81–95.

TEELE, D. W., J. O. KLEIN, C. CHASE, P. MENYUK, and B. A. ROSNER, 1990. Otitis media in infancy and intellectual ability, school achievement, speech, and language at age 7 years. *J. Infect. Diseases* 162:685–694.

TESAR, B., and P. SMOLENSKY, 1996. *Learnability in Optimality Theory* (Technical Report JHU-CogSci 96-2): Johns Hopkins University.

THAL, D. J., V. MARCHMAN, J. STILES, D. ARAM, D. TRAUNER, R. NASS, and E. BATES, 1991. Early lexical development in children with focal brain injury. *Brain Lang.* 40:491–527.

TOMBLIN, J. B., 1989. Familial concentrations of developmental language impairment. *J. Speech Hearing Disorders* 54:287–295.

TOMBLIN, J. B., 1996. The big picture of SLI: Results of an epidemiologic study of SLI among kindergarten children. Paper read at Symposium on Research in Child Language Disorders at Madison, Wisconsin.

TOMBLIN, J. B., and P. R. BUCKWALTER, 1994. Studies of genetics of specific language impairment. In *Specific Language Impairments in Children*, R. V. Watkins and M. L. Rice, eds. Baltimore, Md.: Paul H. Brookes, pp. 17–34.

TOMBLIN, J. B., and P. R. BUCKWALTER, 1995. *The Heritability of Developmental Language Impairment among Twins*, University of Iowa, unpublished manuscript.

TOMBLIN, J. B., J. C. HARDY, and H. A. HEIN, 1991. Predicting poor-communication status in preschool children using risk factors present at birth. *J. Speech Hearing Res.* 34:1096–1105.

VAN DER LELY, H. K. J., 1994. Canonical linking rules: Forward versus reverse linking in normally developing and specifically language-impaired children. *Cognition* 51(1):29–72.

VAN DER LELY, H., and K. STOLLWERCK, 1996. A grammatical specific language impairment in children: An autosomal dominant inheritance? *Brain Lang.* 52:484–504.

VAN VALIN, JR., R., 1991. Functionalist linguistic theory and language acquisition. *First Language* 11:7–40.

VON ARMAN, G., and P. ENGEL, 1964. Mental retardation related to hypercalcaemia. *Dev. Med. Child Neurol.* 6:366–377.

WADA, J. A., R. CLARKE, and A. HAMM, 1975. Cerebral hemispheric asymmetry in humans. *Arch. Neurol.* 32:239–246.

WANG, P. P., J. R. HESSELINK, T. L. JERNIGAN, S. DOHERTY, and U. BELLUGI, 1992. The specific neurobehavioral profile of Williams syndrome is associated with neocerebellar hemispheric preservation. *Neurology* 42:1999–2002.

WHITEHURST, G. J., D. S. ARNOLD, M. SMITH, J. E. FISCHEL, C. J. LONIGAN, and M. C. VALDEZ-MENCHACHA, 1991. Family history in developmental expressive language delay. *J. Speech Hearing Res.* 34:1150–1157.

WOODS, B. T., and S. CAREY, 1979. Language deficits after apparent clinical recovery from childhood aphasia. *Ann. Neurol.* 6:405–409.

YAMADA, J., 1990. *Laura: A Case for the Modularity of Language.* Cambridge, Mass.: MIT Press.

YAMADA, J., and S. CURTISS, 1981. The relationship between language and cognition in a case of Turner's syndrome. *UCLA Working Papers Cogn. Linguistics* 3:93–115.

ZERBIN-RUDIN, E., 1967. Congenital word blindness. *Bull. Orton Soc.* 17:47–54.

ZOLLINGER, R., 1935. Removal of left cerebral hemisphere. Report of a case. *Arch. Neurol. Psychiatry* 34:1055–1064.

64 Computational Modeling of Language Disorders

ELEANOR M. SAFFRAN, GARY S. DELL, AND MYRNA F. SCHWARTZ

ABSTRACT Computational modeling of aphasia and related language disorders is a relatively new aspect of cognitive neuroscience. This chapter reviews three recent models that represent different domains and architectures: a model of aphasic sentence comprehension based on a hybrid/symbolic connectionist architecture (Haarmann, Just, and Carpenter, 1997), a localist connectionist model of lexical access by aphasic speakers (Dell et al., 1997), and a parallel-distributed processing model of deep dyslexia (Plaut and Shallice, 1993). The models share the key assumption that the complexities of language disorders emerge from the processes that underlie normal performance. Each model processes information by spreading activation and attributes pathological symptoms to lesions in the mechanisms that shape activation patterns. The models give a good account of several basic phenomena in language pathology, including variation in symptom patterns with severity of damage, the graded, probabilistic nature of errors, and relationships among error types. Although the models have made good progress in simulating the behavioral data associated with aphasia, they do not, as yet, speak to the brain-behavior mapping for language.

Over the course of the past decade, the modeling of cognitive processes has shifted from the "box-and-arrow" information flow diagram toward a more computational approach. Computational modeling offers a number of advantages: (1) The model must be translated into a computer program, forcing theorists to be explicit about their theoretical assumptions; (2) it is possible to run experiments in the form of simulations, allowing for a determination of a model's descriptive adequacy and an understanding of the mechanisms by which it accommodates or fails to accommodate the data; (3) simulations occur over time, providing the opportunity to examine dynamic aspects of processing that were difficult to capture in flow diagram models; (4) and there is the hope of simulating the architecture of real networks of neurons, a long-range goal currently far from realization.

ELEANOR M. SAFFRAN Center for Cognitive Neuroscience, Temple University School of Medicine, Philadelphia, Pa.

GARY S. DELL Beckman Institute, University of Illinois at Urbana-Champaign, Urbana, Ill.

MYRNA F. SCHWARTZ Moss Rehabilitation Research Institute, Philadelphia, Pa.

Although most computational modeling has been concerned with normal cognitive processes, there is an increasing effort to perturb these models in ways that simulate the pathologies produced by damage to the brain. Lesioning the model—weakening connections, deleting units, increasing noise or the rate of decay of activation—generates abnormal response patterns. The effort to simulate actual behavior patterns associated with brain damage provides another means of testing the validity of the model, and, perhaps, a source of new insights into the pathological condition.

In this chapter, we examine several attempts to lesion computational models of language processing to simulate the language deficits of aphasics. To provide an indication of the range of approaches and empirical domains, we consider three different types of models, each concerned with a different aspect of language behavior. The first is the simulation of sentence comprehension impairments on a hybrid symbolic/connectionist model developed by Just and Carpenter and their colleagues (Just and Carpenter, 1992; Haarmann, Just, and Carpenter, 1997). In the symbolic approach, an early development in computational modeling (e.g., Anderson, 1983), rules are instantiated as procedures: If input A satisfies condition X, then transform A to B. The sentence comprehension model effects such transformations by transmitting activation from one node to another, as in connectionist networks; the amount of activation available to the comprehension system is a critical component of the model. Next we present simulations of disordered picture naming on the localist connectionist model of word retrieval developed by Dell and his colleagues (Dell, 1986; Dell and O'Seaghdha, 1991; Dell et al., 1997). The model employs activation flow from semantic to phonological levels of representation to simulate lexical retrieval. It is a localist model in that each informational element (semantic feature, lexical unit, phoneme) is represented as a unitary node. The connections between units are determined a priori and hardwired into the model. The localist approach is distinguished from the third model we present, which is a parallel-distributed processing (PDP) model of reading. This model, developed by Plaut and Shallice

(1993; Hinton and Shallice, 1991), addresses the phenomena that distinguish the acquired reading disorder known as deep dyslexia. This model has two salient features: (1) Representations are distributed in that, except for input and output units, a single node does not encode a particular unit of information; (2) connections are not hardwired, but random to begin with and modified over the course of learning trials. In addition to describing the models and comparing the results of simulations to the behavior patterns associated with the relevant disorders, we consider both the achievements and the limitations of each approach.

Sentence comprehension: A hybrid (symbolic/connectionist) model

Sentence comprehension is a complex process. It involves perceiving the successive words in the sentence, retrieving semantic and syntactic specifications for these words, assembling syntactic structure, and integrating lexical and syntactic information to yield a semantic and ultimately pragmatic interpretation. There have been attempts to model the process in its entirety using a localist framework (e.g., Cottrell, 1985), as well as efforts to build PDP models that focus on its syntactic (e.g., Elman, 1991) or semantic (e.g., McClelland, St. John, and Taraban, 1989) aspects. The model we examine here represents an attempt to deal with the sentence comprehension process as a whole. This model, described by Haarmann, Just, and Carpenter (1997)–henceforth HJC–is the most recent version of the CAPS/CC READER model developed by Just and Carpenter (1992) and their colleagues.

The model instantiates a capacity theory of individual differences in sentence comprehension. Support for this theory comes from the reading span task (Daneman and Carpenter, 1980), in which subjects are required to read a set of unrelated sentences and, in addition, to hold the last word of each sentence in memory. Subjects with high and low word spans, as assessed by the number of terminal words they were able to report, performed differently on sentence comprehension measures; in particular, differences between high and low span subjects increased as a function of syntactic complexity (e.g., Just and Carpenter, 1992). These findings motivated the assumption that there is a fixed working memory capacity for language processing that differs across individuals; subjects with high spans, as measured by the reading span task, have greater capacity than those with low spans.

The range of individual differences that HJC sought to account for includes the effects of brain damage on language function, which in most cases involve deficits in sentence comprehension. The variables that ad-versely affect sentence understanding in aphasia include the following (see accompanying box):

i. Semantic reversibility, or the absence of semantic constraints on thematic role assignment [the sentence in (1b) is reversible, whereas (1a) is not]. Aphasics often perform better on nonreversible sentences, indicating that they are placing significant weight on semantic constraints.

ii. Syntactic complexity, which includes factors such as noncanonical order of the noun phrases [compare (1b) and (1c), where the agent-patient order typical of English sentences applies in (1b) but not in the passive sentence (1c)]. Aphasics tend to do better on sentences with canonical word order.

iii. The occurrence of intervening words between a noun phrase and the information required to assign it a thematic role [compare (1b) and the object relative construction in (1d)].[1]

iv. An increase in the number of noun arguments and/or verbs, as in the dative construction (1e) and in sentences with multiple clauses (1f).

While these variables have been most extensively studied in patients with syntactic deficits in production (agrammatic aphasics), sensitivity to these factors is also evident in data for groups of unselected aphasics. For example, Caplan and Hildebrandt (1988) found that aphasic performance over a range of reversible sentence types decreases over the constructions exemplified in (1b)–(1f), except that datives (1e) are generally easier than object relatives (1d).

1a.	The dog buried the bone.
1b.	The cat chased the dog.
1c.	The dog was chased by the cat.
1d.	The dog that the cat chased was black.
1e.	The elephant showed the giraffe the tiger.
1f.	The elephant that the giraffe pushed kicked the tiger.

One conclusion that has been drawn from such findings is that a unitary impairment underlies the sentence comprehension deficits of aphasics. Two causal factors proposed by a number of investigators are time and capacity. The concern with timing reflects the consideration that comprehension entails coactivation of the successive elements of the sentence at some level of representation. If processing is slowed, so that information cannot be maintained over the span of the sentence, comprehension is likely to break down. A decrease in processing rate is the explicit focus of computational models of aphasic sentence comprehension proposed by Gigley (1983) and by Haarmann and Kolk (1991), and has been implicated in other accounts of aphasic performance (e.g., Swinney et al., 1996). Timing and capacity are interrelated in the account of aphasic sentence comprehension that HJC instantiated in their computational model. Other capacity-based accounts are presented in Blackwell and Bates (1995) and Frazier and Friederici (1991).

HJC assume that aphasics have insufficient verbal working memory capacity to sustain normal comprehension performance. This assumption follows from an earlier study by Miyake, Carpenter, and Just (1994), who demonstrated that speeding up presentation time [using the rapid serial visual presentation (RSVP) paradigm], elicited aphasic-like performance patterns in normal subjects. Although these subjects performed at higher levels than aphasics, their behavior across sentence types replicated the effects of syntactic complexity and verb and argument number that emerged in Caplan and Hildebrandt's (1988) studies of aphasics. One consequence of speeded presentation under RSVP is that less processing time can be dedicated to each element, effectively limiting the buildup of activation; the effect is therefore similar to that of lowering capacity. On the basis of their results in normal subjects, Miyake and colleagues argued that reduction in working memory capacity underlies the sentence comprehension deficits of aphasics. Citing Caplan and Hildebrandt's finding that aphasics' comprehension performance was highly correlated with the overall severity of the language impairment, Miyake and co-workers reasoned that severity was a reflection of decreased capacity.

The model combines features of symbolic production-action and connectionist models. The production-action feature is the instantiation of a procedural memory that embodies a set of rules (e.g., Anderson, 1983). When the conditions for a particular procedure are met, the appropriate operation is executed by means of activation flow, in the manner of connectionist models. For example, the occurrence of a preposition (e.g., *to, by*) signals the beginning of a prepositional phrase, indicating that a noun phrase must follow. When a node signifying the identification of a preposition has been activated, activation flows to the node that represents the syntactic constituent "noun phrase complement." This structure is then integrated into the syntactic structure for the sentence. The flow of activation does not occur all at once but over a number of time steps, as in connectionist networks. Figure 64.1 provides an overview of the HJC model. Note that the model includes a lexical component, which provides access to the semantic and syntactic properties of the words in the sentence; a parser, which constructs a hierarchical phrase tree along the lines of X-bar grammar (e.g., Jackendoff, 1977); and a

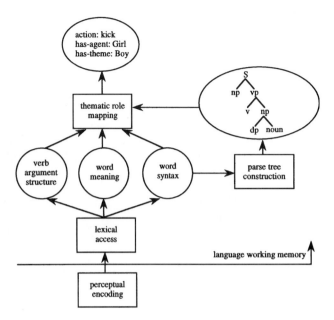

FIGURE 64.1 Overview of the HJC model. (Adapted from Haarmann, Just, and Carpenter, 1997.)

thematic role component, which utilizes lexical syntactic information–together with the output of the parser–to map noun phrase constituents onto the roles specified by the verb(s) in the sentence (e.g., agent, patient, goal). The components of the model operate in parallel. Sentence comprehension is assessed by examining the activation levels of the filled thematic role slots.

Verbal working memory capacity in this model is defined in terms of activation. The model's core assumption is that activation is a limited resource that is used both to perform linguistic operations and to maintain the products in an active form for further processing. The model does not distinguish between processing and maintenance functions: If processing operations require more capacity, less is available for maintenance, and vice versa. An activation shortage can arise when storage and processing exceed capacity, in which case "the activations that are associated with individual working memory elements and with individual propagation amounts are scaled down so that the total activation (i.e., the capacity) is allocated. . . . This results in both forgetting and slower processing." (Haarmann, Just, and Carpenter, 1997, p. 87)

The underlying principle is that aphasic disorders arise from a pathological reduction in working memory. The degree of severity of the aphasic deficit varies with the amount of reduction. The model predicts (i) a syntactic complexity effect and (ii) an interaction between syntactic complexity and the extent to which working memory capacity is decreased below normal levels. The assignment of thematic roles is especially capacity-demanding,

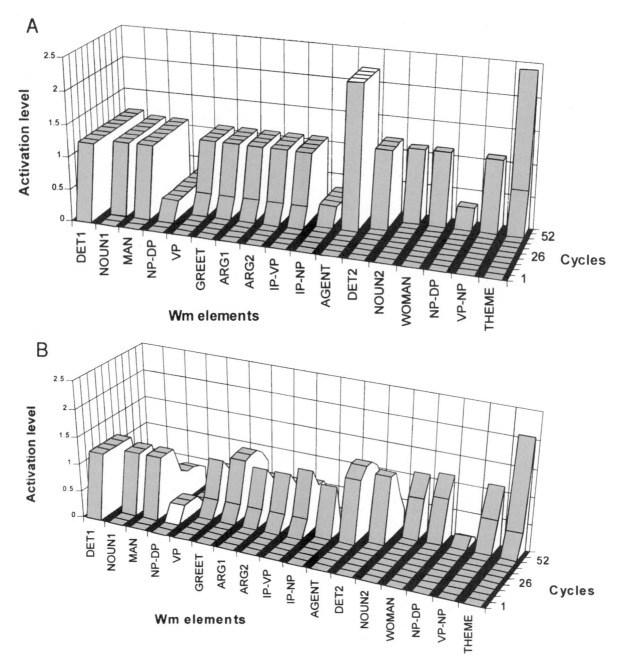

FIGURE 64.2 Example of the HJC model's processing of a sentence with high (above) and low capacity: Activation level for elements in working memory as a function of time cycles for the sentence, "The man greets the woman." (Reprinted with permission from Haarmann, Just, and Carpenter, 1997.)

which may account for the vulnerability of this process in aphasia (e.g., Linebarger, Schwartz, and Saffran, 1983).

In simulations, the model required a working memory capacity equal to 30 to achieve perfect comprehension over a range of sentence types. To simulate aphasic comprehension, HJC decreased capacity below that level. This reduction has an impact on processing as well as the ability to maintain information over the course of the sentence. Figure 64.2 illustrates the model's processing of an active sentence under high (capacity = 30) and

low working memory (capacity = 10) conditions. It is evident that, although the activation of elements at the beginning of the sentence remains high in the case of the high-capacity simulation, earlier elements decay over time under the low-capacity condition. In the latter case, the level of thematic role binding does not achieve threshold (set at an activation level of 2) for either agent or theme, and comprehension fails.

To examine the model's ability to simulate aphasic performance, HJC tested its comprehension of a range of

TABLE 64.1
Sentence types used by Caplan and colleagues (1985)*

Sentence Types
Active (A)
The rat hit the dog.
Passive (P)
The rat was hit by the dog.
Cleft-subject (CS)
It was the rat that hit the dog.
Cleft-object (CO)
It was the rat that the dog hit.
Dative (D)
The rat gave the dog to the cow.
Dative passive (DP)
The rat was given to the dog by the cow.
Conjoined (C)
The rat hit the dog and kissed the cow.
Right-branching subject relative or object-subject relative (OS)
The rat hit the dog that kissed the cow.
Center-embedded object relative or subject-object relative (SO)
The rat that the dog hit kissed the cow.

*Table taken from Haarmann, Just, and Carpenter, 1997.

sentence types with working memory capacity set at half the optimal level (15). The sentence types (see table 64.1) were those used in Caplan and Hildebrandt's (1988) study of aphasic comprehension (and by Caplan, Baker, and Dehaut, 1985). Figure 64.3 compares the simulation data to the performance of Caplan and Hildebrandt's aphasics. For the most part, the simulations capture the order of difficulty in the aphasic data, as well as the effect of severity of the aphasic impairment. Additional simulations carried out by HJC included an examination of performance on

actives and passives at two different levels of capacity reduction. The relative difficulty of passives increased under both manipulations. The capacity reduction effect accords with data reported for agrammatic aphasics at different severity levels (see Kolk and van Grunsven, 1985).

The simulations reveal that the model is reasonably successful in capturing the relative difficulty of sentence types, as assessed by the average performance of a heterogeneous group of aphasics, as well as the performance of normals under RSVP. To our knowledge, this is the only computational model that attempts to deal with effects of syntactic complexity in both normals and aphasics. Another strength of the model is that it provides a simple account of variability in performance, both within each group of subjects and between groups. At a more general level, Just and colleagues deserve credit for tackling a very complex problem with empirical data and computational techniques that integrate major perspectives in cognitive science: linguistic theory, production systems, and connectionism.

However, there are reasons to question the model's basic assumption that comprehension patterns in aphasic subjects reflect capacity limitations (see Martin, 1995; Caplan and Waters, 1995; and the response by Miyake, Carpenter, and Just, 1995). It may be that the problem lies not in capacity per se, but in the inefficiency of particular operations. Some aphasic patients have more difficulty with lexical processing than others, some are more affected by padding sentences with extra material (Schwartz et al., 1987), and some rely very heavily on semantic constraints (Saffran, Schwartz, and Linebarger, 1998). The greater the severity of the language impairment, the more likely that the patient has multiple deficits. As a result of such deficits, aphasics may devote capacity to the impaired domains, diminishing the resources available for processing and maintaining sentential information in memory. This formulation salvages

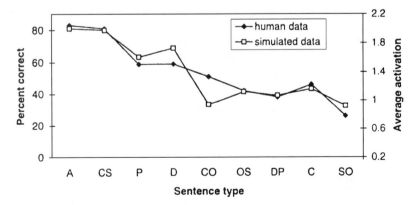

FIGURE 64.3 Data on aphasic sentence composition from Caplan and Hildebrandt (1988) and simulated data from the HJC model. AZ, active; CS, cleft-subject; P, passive; D, dative; CO, cleft-object; OS, object-subject relative; C, conjoined; DP, dative passive; SO, subject-object relative. (Reprinted with permission from Haarmann, Just, and Carpenter, 1997.)

the assumption of a common pool of resources that is central to HJC's approach, while acknowledging that the source of the deficit may vary from one patient to another. However, the possibility that specific deficits are the direct cause of patients' failure on the more difficult sentences cannot be excluded. In view of this possibility, simulating the performance of a heterogeneous group of aphasics does not constitute a particularly strong test of the model. A more rigorous test would involve an attempt to simulate individual patients' performance levels across a range of sentence types.

There are also experimental data that challenge the core assumptions of the model. Rochon and her colleagues have examined sentence processing in patients with Alzheimer's disease, whose reading spans, as assessed by the Daneman and Carpenter (1980) measure, are limited to one or two items (Rochon, Waters, and Caplan, 1994). These patients show little effect of the syntactic complexity factors that impede aphasic comprehension, although they are adversely affected by increasing the number of propositions in the sentence.

Finally, the model is incomplete in that it fails to deal with effects of semantic constraints on comprehension. These influences have emerged in studies of normal comprehension (e.g., MacDonald, Pearlmutter, and Seidenberg, 1994), as well as in the effects of semantic reversibility on aphasic performance (e.g., Caramazza and Zurif, 1976). The force of these constraints is dramatically evident in patients' insensitivity to assertions that violate them. Saffran, Schwartz, and Linebarger (1998) demonstrated that aphasics were only 57 percent correct in judging the plausibility of simple active sentences that contained semantic incongruities (e.g., The children frightened the movie). This effect emerged in patients whose performance was highly sensitive to syntactic complexity, as well as in those who showed little influence of this factor. In normals, King and Just (1991) found that high span subjects were more likely to show semantic influences than low span subjects, suggesting that the interaction between syntax and semantics requires working memory capacity (Just and Carpenter, 1992). If aphasics are considered to have less capacity than low span normals, they should not demonstrate this interaction. Alternatively, the semantic effect may have a different locus in the aphasics. In either case, it is clear that the model in its current form fails to account for this salient aspect of aphasic comprehension.

Lexical retrieval in picture naming: An interactive activation model

To a first approximation, one can conceptualize the production of a sentence as comprehension in reverse. The speaker's task is to formulate a message that specifies the thematic content of the sentence, select the words and syntactic form (phrase structure) suitable to express this content, order the words in a manner dictated by the phrase structure, and encode this in a phonetic form for articulation.

It occasionally happens in normal speech that something goes awry and the wrong word is uttered, or the right word is uttered at the wrong time or with the wrong pronunciation. Close study of these sorts of speech errors has given rise to an influential theory of production that incorporates two informationally encapsulated stages of lexical retrieval (Fay and Cutler, 1977; Fromkin, 1971; Garrett, 1975; Levelt, 1989; Levelt, Roelofs, and Meyer, 1998). The first stage is controlled by a structure that represents sentence meaning and that is sensitive to the semantic-syntactic properties of words and not to their phonological form. The second stage is controlled by a structure that represents surface phrasal geometry and that is responsive only to the phonological properties of words. The controlling structures may be characterized as frames containing slots that specify and receive the retrieved lexical content (Bock and Levelt, 1994; Dell, 1986; Garrett, 1975; MacKay, 1972; Shattuck-Hufnagel, 1979).

Most theoretical accounts of impaired word retrieval in aphasia similarly separate semantic and phonological stages of retrieval (Butterworth, 1989; Caramazza, 1988; Ellis, 1985; Garrett, 1984; Saffran, 1982; Schwartz, 1987). Aphasics produce errors in both connected speech and single word tasks, and many of their errors, like those of normals, are related to the target in meaning (semantic errors, like dog for cat or form (formal errors like mat for cat; neologisms like dat for cat) (Buckingham, 1980). Patients can be categorized according to whether their errors are mostly of one type or another.

The claim that the stages of word retrieval are informationally encapsulated, hence modular, has not gone unchallenged. Interactive activation models have been proposed as alternative accounts of lexical retrieval in normality (Dell, 1986; Dell and Reich, 1981; Harley, 1984; Houghton, 1990; Stemberger, 1985) and pathology (Dell et al., 1997; Ellis, 1985; Martin and Saffran, 1992; Martin et al., 1994; Schwartz et al., 1994; Wilshire and McCarthy, 1996). The hallmark of interactive activation models is their nonmodularity. Because activation spreads continuously and bidirectionally, early stages of processing are influenced by information from later stages, and vice versa (McClelland and Rumelhart, 1981).

Do semantic and phonological information sources interact during word retrieval? There is evidence both pro and con. Although most word substitution errors

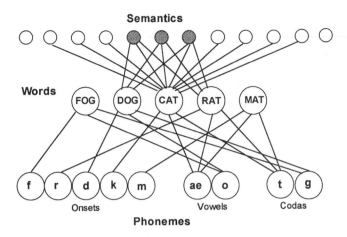

FIGURE 64.4 The DSMSG model. Only the features of the target "cat" are shown. (Reprinted with permission from Dell et al., 1997.)

bear either a semantic or phonologic relation to the target, the frequency of mixed (semantic + phonologic) word substitution errors (e.g., *rat* for *cat*) is significantly higher, for both normals and aphasics, than what would be expected if semantic and phonological factors were associated with strict serially ordered modular processes (Dell and Reich, 1981; Harley, 1984; Martin, Weisberg, and Saffran, 1989; Martin et al., 1996). But whereas the mixed error evidence is consistent with interaction (see, however, Levelt, Roelofs, and Meyer, 1999), experiments on the time course of semantic and phonological retrieval in lexical access show conclusively that the interaction, if it exists at all, must be limited. At the earliest points, processing appears to be exclusively semantic; however, just prior to articulation, the retrieval of phonological information completely dominates that of semantic information (Dell and O'Seaghdha, 1991; Levelt et al., 1991; Peterson and Savoy, 1998; Schriefers, Meyer, and Levelt, 1990).

The DSMSG model [from Dell, Schwartz, Martin, Saffran, and Gagnon (1997)] is a spreading activation model of retrieval in which interactivity is combined with a two-stage selection process (see also Dell and O'Seaghdha, 1991). In effect, this model represents a compromise between strictly modular accounts (e.g., Levelt et al., 1991) and more fully interactive ones (e.g., Harley, 1984; Stemberger, 1985).

Like other interactive activation models of lexical processing, the DSMSG model has lexical knowledge represented in a layered network of units or nodes. Nodes are not repositories for stored information, but rather simple, neuron-like devices that collect, summate, and transmit activation. An important distinction among connectionist models is whether they use a local or distributed style of representation. In localist models, nodes

stand in one-to-one correspondence with psychologically meaningful properties. Such is the case in the DSMSG model, where the top level in the network represents semantic features, the middle level represents known words, and the bottom level represents phonemes (figure 64.4).

All connections in the DSMSG model are excitatory and bidirectional. Each node's activation level is a positive real number, determined by a linear activation updating function that includes a decay factor (q) and normally distributed noise. All connections in the model have the same weight (designated by p), meaning that for any two connected nodes i and j, node i transmits a proportion p of its activation to node j at each time step. The values of p and q are preset; there is no learning in this model.

In addition to the activation updating function, there are external sources of activation that influence a node's level of activation. At the outset of a trial, external activation is applied to the semantic features that correspond to the target (here designated as *cat*). Activation is allowed to spread freely for a specified number of time steps (n), whereupon the most highly activated word node is selected. This is the first of two selection steps; it entails linking the word node to a syntactic frame (a single noun frame, in the case of naming) and giving it an external boost of activation. Activation continues to spread for another n time steps. This is followed by step-2 selection, in which the most activated onset, vowel, and coda phonemes are linked to their respective slots in the phonological frame (a CVC–or consonant-vowel-consonant–frame, in this model) and their activation levels are boosted. This ends the trial. If the model selects *cat* at step 1 and /k/, /æ/ and /t/ at step 2, it has performed correctly. Otherwise it has made an error.

Mis-selections at step 1 can give rise to semantic, formal, mixed, or unrelated errors. Semantic errors (*dog* for *cat*) are encouraged by the overlap in semantic features (see figure 64.4). Formal errors (*mat* for *cat*) are encouraged by bottom-up feedback from the primed phonemes (/æ/, /t/). Mixed competitors (*rat* for *cat*) benefit from both top-down and bottom-up activation. Unrelated competitors (*fog* for *cat*) benefit from neither of these, but in a noisy system, they will sometimes be selected, thereby creating unrelated errors. Mis-selections at step 2 primarily give rise to neologisms (*dat* for *cat*), but word errors may also arise at this step, when the substituted phoneme happens to create another word (*rat*; *mat*).

The frequency with which the model makes various types of error is in large measure determined by its network structure. Dell and colleagues used a very small network, but they made sure that its structure resembled the error opportunities of the English lexicon, as used in naming experiments. The error opportunities associated with a lexicon are the distribution of errors that would occur if output consisted of random phonologically legal strings. Thus, the model affords many opportunities for neologisms, unrelated words, and formals, and fewer opportunities for semantic and mixed. This plays an important role in the simulation of the aphasics' data, as will be seen.

In their first simulation, Dell and colleagues fit the model to the performance of normal speakers (controls) performing the 175-item Philadelphia Naming Test (PNT) (Roach et al., 1996). Both the controls and the model were correct on a very high proportion of the trials; and when they erred, they made mostly semantic and mixed errors (see table 64.2).

The Dell group then sought to model the data from 21 aphasic patients who performed the same picture naming task. These patients included a variety of fluent aphasic types (Wernicke's, anomics, conduction, and transcortical sensory). To simulate the data from aphasic namers, they concentrated on two parameters of the model: *p* and *q*. Reducing the setting of *p* (weakening connections) or raising the setting of q (increasing decay) both cause the model to make more errors. Activation levels get small and noise has a greater influence. At moderately deviant settings of *p* or *q*, the model is correct on about 20–80% of trials. At more deviant settings the model's performance is completely dominated by noise, which means that the output consists primarily of the high opportunity errors (neologisms, unrelateds, and, to some extent, formals). This was also true in the data: neologisms, formals, and unrelateds increase as correctness decreases, but semantic and mixed errors do not. The model explains this fact in terms of opportunities for errors and the increasing role this plays as severity increases.

The combination of variation in severity and type of lesion (*p* or *q*) allows the model to simulate dissociations between patients who produce mostly semantic errors and those whose errors are mostly phonological. In the model, reduced connection strength (*p* lesion) diminishes the extent to which different levels of representation are consistent with one another. This promotes what the Dell group called "stupid" errors: nonwords and unrelated word errors. In contrast, *q* lesions promote "smart errors": semantic, mixed, and formal. Decay lesions that are not severe lead to patterns in which nearly all errors have a semantic component. Severe lesions in connection weight (*p*) produce a mostly phonological pattern. Combinations of *p* and *q* lesions produce intermediate patterns.

To model patient data, Dell and colleagues chose the best matching values of *p* and *q* for each patient. Table 64.2 shows the fits for three modeled patients, two who perform at the same level of correctness, but with different error patterns (L.H. and I.G.), and an additional patient whose naming is more severely disrupted (G.L.). I.G.'s primarily semantic pattern (9% semantic; 2% neologism) was closely fit by a pure decay lesion. L.H.'s more phonological pattern (3% semantic; 15% neologism) was closely fit by a pure strength lesion. G.L.'s pattern illustrates the tendency for the more severe patients to have more errors in categories with large numbers of error opportunities and the model's ability to fit that pattern. Across all 21 patients, the fit between the model and patients was good, and much better than the fit for error patterns generated at random. This is important, because it shows that there are many response patterns that cannot be simulated well by varying *p* and *q*.

The Dell group presented other evidence to support the model's characterization of the patients. For example, several patients were modeled again at a later date, when their level of correctness on the PNT had improved; and the fits were, once again, good. More importantly, the model's account of a given patient remained constant over time: If the naming profile at time 1 was best fit by a decay lesion, so too was the profile at time 2. Where substantial improvement had occurred between time 1 and time 2, this was reflected in the movement of the affected parameter closer to the normal value. This demonstrates that the original characterization of the deficit was reliable and stable. It also supports a restitution account of recovery over a compensation account: Recovery is the movement of pathological parameters toward normal values.

The DSMSG model represents the first effort to model both normal language data and data sets from a large number of individual aphasic patients (see Bates

TABLE 64.2
PNT naming data and predictions of the model

Patient Parameters	Response Types						
	Correct	Semantic	Formal	Nonword	Mixed	Unrelated	RMSD*
Normal controls: $p = .1$, $q = .5$							
Obtained	.97	.01	.00	.00	.01	.00	
Predicted	.97	.02	.00	.00	.01	.00	
L.H.: $p = .0057$, $q = .5$							
Obtained	.69	.03	.07	.15	.01	.02	
Predicted	.69	.07	.06	.14	.01	.03	.018
I.G.: $p = .1$, $q = .86$							
Obtained	.69	.09	.05	.02	.03	.01	
Predicted	.73	.13	.04	.05	.04	.01	.027
G.L.: $p = .079$, $q = .85$							
Obtained	.28	.04	.21	.30	.03	.09	
Predicted	.27	.11	.20	.29	.03	.10	.030

*RSMD is the root mean square deviation between the six patient and model proportions.

et al., 1991; Plaut et al., 1996, for other attempts to model individuals). In doing so, it casts new light on some long-standing issues. On the question of the relation between normal and aphasic speech, for example, the work of Dell and colleagues, like that of Haarmann and colleagues (1997), suggests that aphasic error patterns reflect deviant values of parameters of the normal system. And it assigns new importance to the severity dimension by linking the errors of more severe patients to the opportunities afforded by the structure of the lexicon.

The parameters manipulated in the model are not specific to semantic nodes or phonologic nodes; that is, Dell and colleagues hypothesize global rather than local deficits. Nevertheless, at particular values of these parameters, the model can achieve selective promotion of one type of error over another. This raises the question of whether it is ever necessary to postulate local impairments to semantic or phonologic nodes or connections. At this point, one would have to answer yes. First, such local impairments still provide the best account for certain consistencies in performance patterns across tasks (e.g., Caramazza, 1988). Furthermore, the DSMSG model cannot handle certain pure naming error patterns, and there is evidence that such patterns do exist. For example, there are patients exhibiting low levels of correctness with purely semantic errors (Caramazza and Hillis, 1990; Hillis and Caramazza, 1995; Hillis et al., 1990) or purely phonological errors (Caplan, Vanier, and Baker, 1986). Based on these lines of evidence, it may be necessary to reconsider the model's globality as-

sumption in the model, that is, the notion that parameter alterations affect all layers of the network equally.

Apart from this, the most serious weaknesses in the model have to do with its simplicity. In its present form, the model cannot deal with the precise character of phonological errors (e.g., how target and error overlap in phonemic content and metrical and syllabic structure), or with the influence of word length and frequency, or with perseverated responses and "no response" trials. It also makes no allowance for variations in response time. Dealing with these issues will require considerable expansion of the model, both with respect to its vocabulary and to its representational and processing assumptions. It remains to be seen whether the model's fundamental assumptions about constrained interactivity within a two-step retrieval process can survive these modifications.

A parallel distributed processing approach to deep dyslexia

There can be little doubt that PDP approaches have been increasingly influential in cognitive neuropsychology (see, e.g., Farah, 1994). However, for various reasons, PDP models of language pathology have addressed single-word reading rather than spoken language production and comprehension. Consequently, these models are more properly described as models of dyslexia than aphasia. Here, we present some of the facts associated with a particular dyslexia symptom complex, deep dyslexia; then we discuss the PDP framework generally and illustrate its application to this disorder by presenting a specific model (Plaut and Shallice, 1993).

As with other acquired dyslexias, deep dyslexia is characterized by the nature of the patients' errors when reading aloud (e.g., Coltheart, Patterson, and Marshall, 1980; Marshall and Newcombe, 1966). The defining error for deep dyslexia is the semantic error. A patient reads NIGHT as "sleep" or BLOWING as "wind." (All examples are taken from Plaut and Shallice, 1993.) In addition to semantic errors, patients also make visual errors ("sandals" for SCANDAL), and the visual and semantic influences on errors sometimes combine as in mixed visual-semantic errors (SHIRT–"skirt") or visual-then-semantic errors (SYMPATHY–"orchestra"). In addition to these error types, deep dyslexia is associated with difficulty in reading function words, verbs, and, in general, words that are low in concreteness. Reading nonwords aloud is particularly hard for these patients.

This combination of symptoms presents a theoretical puzzle. What functional system is damaged? The occurrence of both semantic and visual errors suggests different kinds of damage in the mapping from orthography to meaning. At the same time, the inability to read nonwords must reflect trouble in visual to phonological mappings. Adding to the mix are the interactions among visual and semantic errors, and the effects of concreteness. Finally, there is considerable variability among patients. For example, not all of the patients who make semantic errors make visual errors. In sum, it is a challenge to come up with a theory of deep dyslexia that follows naturally from a functional analysis of reading and does not resort to unmotivated assumptions (e.g., assuming that there are several deficits that happen to co-occur for random or unspecified anatomical reasons). Providing such a theory was the goal of Plaut and Shallice (1993), whose work we present here. However, before we turn directly to their model, it is useful to review some principles of PDP models and how they might be used in neuropsychology.

Parallel distributed processing is a framework–that is, a set of pretheoretical assumptions about what theories should be like–rather than a theory. As with the other computational approaches described here, the PDP framework assumes that processing occurs through spreading activation among simple units in a network. In contrast to the other approaches, however, the units are quite neuron-like. Each unit's activation level is a nonlinear–typically sigmoidal–function of its input. This input is the sum of signals sent from neighboring activated units through weighted excitatory or inhibitory connections. Critically, these weights are set by training the network in the mapping required for the task. In the case of reading and reading aloud, orthographic representations need to be mapped to representations of meaning and phonology. So, a PDP reading model would be trained by presenting words to the network, one at a time, each word corresponding to patterns of activation in an input orthographic layer, and in output (semantic or phonological) layers. Connection weights would then be altered by a learning algorithm (e.g., backpropagation; see Rumelhart, Hinton, and Williams, 1986) with the effect that later presentation of that word's orthography would be more likely to produce the correct output semantic or phonological patterns.

The PDP framework's emphasis on learning the connection weights has two important consequences. First, the learning techniques that are employed develop distributed representations. In a reading model, for example, each word comes to be associated with a great many units and connections. Damage to the network–loss of units and connections, or noise added to connections–does not, therefore, necessarily lead to all-or-none loss of particular words. Performance is, instead, graded. A particular word might be correctly read under some circumstances, and incorrectly under other circumstances. Moreover, incorrect responses would be expected to resemble correct ones to varying extents. Because language pathology exhibits exactly this kind of graded performance, distributed representations have much to recommend them as accounts of aphasia and dyslexia. Another key aspect of distributed representations is that units and connections are shared among similar words. So, in a model of dyslexia, damage to a single unit or connection has ramifications for the processing of several similar words. By varying the number and location of damaged components, one can create losses of varying degrees of specificity within the vocabulary, offering a potential account of category specific losses in patients (e.g., Hinton and Shallice, 1991). In addition, if a model allows for interaction among the processing layers (which Plaut and Shallice's model does), there is the potential that damage at one layer (e.g., a semantic layer in a reading model) will create effects that reflect knowledge from other layers (e.g., visual errors; Hinton and Shallice, 1991).

The second consequence of the PDP framework's learning assumption is that learning, damage, and recovery can be understood as different manifestations of the same process (Plaut, 1996). Learning is adaptive weight change; damage is counteradaptive change to those weights; and recovery, insofar as it occurs, is relearning or further adaptive weight change. This potential to offer a theory of recovery and loss of function is a great strength of the PDP approach to neuropsychological deficits.

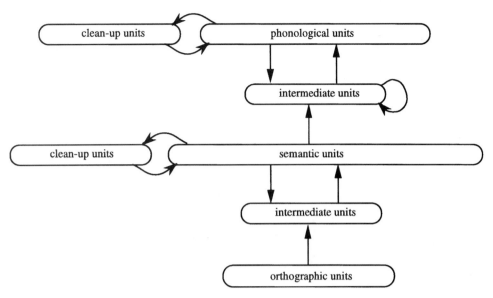

FIGURE 64.5 Architecture of a deep dyslexia model. (Redrawn from Plaut and Shallice, 1993.)

In general, the PDP framework gives the neuropsychologist a different perspective on the functional modularity of cognitive systems, and on the relation between functional modules, error types, and the actual location of damage (Farah, 1994). PDP models certainly look a lot different from the standard box-and-arrow diagrams. However, we agree with Plaut and Shallice (1993) that one should not view these models as strict alternatives to box-and-arrow models, but rather as an "elaboration" (p. 383) of them, one that identifies the computations associated with each box and each arrow more fully.

Plaut and Shallice (1993) actually implemented several models of dyslexia. Starting with a related model by Hinton and Shallice (1991), they systematically varied model characteristics including the model's architecture (i.e., what particular levels of representation and connections are assumed), its learning algorithm, and the reading task (whether the model must assign meanings to words, or must also be capable of producing their phonological forms). In general, the models exhibited roughly similar behavior, and so we describe just one of them, the final one presented.

Figure 64.5 presents the architecture of the model. The network's task is to generate the semantics of a word from orthographic input, and to generate the phonological representation corresponding to that semantics. In short, the network must understand a word and then pronounce it. Notice that this model is not allowing for any direct mapping from orthography to phonology, in keeping with most theorists' view that deep dyslexics are unable to use phonology in reading for meaning.

(The absence of this mapping in the network enables it to simulate the patients' near total failure in reading nonwords.) There were three network levels with explicit a priori representations: orthographic, semantic, and phonological. The orthographic input layer contained 32 units, 8 for each of four letter positions. Each letter corresponded to a pattern of activation (1s and 0s) across the 8 units in each position. At the semantic level, there were 98 units, each representing a feature such as "hard" or "has-legs." Crucially, concrete words (e.g., COAT) had more features (18.2) than abstract words (e.g., PLAN; 4.7 features). The phonological level used localist representations of phonemes associated with slots similar to the DSMSG model. The other layers of units shown in the figure were not associated with any a priori representation. Instead they developed through learning. Intermediate units mapped from one explicit representation to another and clean-up units mapped from explicit representations to themselves.

Each arrow in the figure indicates connections that are learned. Initially, the network was trained to generate the semantics for each orthographic word, and then later to create the phonology from the semantic patterns. The learning algorithm was backpropagation, which is a technique for training networks to generate target patterns at certain layers (here, semantics and phonology) by changing weights in response to error feedback. A critical feature of the model is that the flow of activation is recurrent or interactive. Like the DSMSG model, activation at later levels can influence earlier ones. Also, in the dyslexia model, levels feed to themselves either directly or through clean-up units.

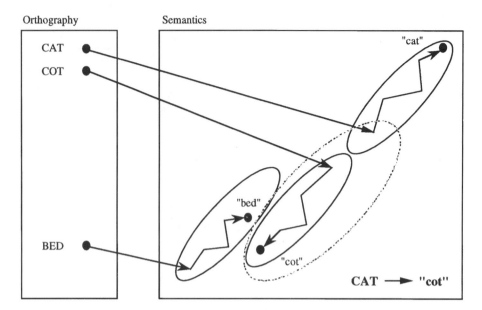

FIGURE 64.6 How damage at the semantic level can cause visual errors. Ovals are attractor basins, and the larger dotted oval represents a basin after damage. (Redrawn from Plaut and Shallice, 1993.)

The recurrent connections in the model allow it to develop *attractors*. To understand this concept, one must first conceive of model layers such as the semantic or phonological layer as multidimensional spaces. Each unit's activation is a dimension in this space, and hence a pattern of activation corresponds to a point in the space. When a word is presented to the orthographic level, activation spreads through intermediate units to the semantic level. The initial pattern of activation at the semantic level–a point in semantic space–then changes over time as activation circulates among the semantic, intermediate, and clean-up units. Eventually, the activation stops changing or settles, and it is this meaning that is assigned to the word. After training, familiar meanings correspond to settling points or attractors in semantic space. Points corresponding to unfamiliar meanings will tend to move to the nearest familiar meaning, defining *attractor basins*. For example, suppose that the meaning of CAT is (*feline, pet, furry, animal*). When CAT is presented to the model, the initial activation pattern might be (*feline, pet, animal, nonfurry*). However, because the model knows of no nonfurry felines, the activation quickly goes to the CAT-meaning attractor by switching nonfurry to furry. The phonological level has analogous attractor basins, ones that direct phonological output to familiar pronunciations.

The model's ability to simulate the co-occurrence of error types in deep dyslexia comes from its use of attractors. Plaut and Shallice lesioned their model by randomly removing varying percentages of connections (5–70%) in particular network locations, with the result that the model then produced errors. All of the

lesion locations, except for one that produced few errors, were associated with the basic error types in deep dyslexia: semantic, visual, mixed-visual-semantic, and unrelated errors (including some visual-then-semantic). Let us first consider the striking finding that lesions in the semantic areas produce visual as well as semantic errors.

Connectionist learning models generally find it difficult to learn arbitrary mappings, such as the relation between a word's orthography and its meaning. It is more natural for a model to want to map similar inputs, such as CAT and COT, onto similar outputs. However, because CAT and COT are unrelated in meaning, this is not possible. The potential to develop attractors in these models alleviates the difficulty. Figure 64.6 (derived from Hinton and Shallice, 1991; Plaut and Shallice, 1993) shows how this happens. As a word is read, its initial semantic representation, which is determined by the bottom-up connections only, is somewhat off of the correct one. The deviation reflects a tendency for the model to make initial semantic representations of visually similar words be similar. So, CAT's and COT's initial semantic representations would be close. However, CAT and COT exist in different attractor basins; thus, once the recurrent feedback and clean-up connections begin influencing the pattern, the semantic patterns for CAT and COT drift to their correct attractors. In short, the model learns to build large attractors in semantic space and to exploit them to simplify the initial mapping from the orthography to the semantics as much as possible. Given this mechanism, it is easy to see how both semantic and visual errors happen when the network is damaged. Damage changes the attractor basins. If the attractor basin for COT changes to include that for the semantic neighbor, BED, one gets semantic errors. Other changes, particularly those at the edge of a basin far from the attractor point itself, can lead to visual errors. This is illustrated in figure 64.6, which shows how, after damage, the basin for COT expands to include the visual neighbor CAT. Because all of the lesion locations are associated with roughly the same kinds of errors, one also gets semantic errors when there is damage to visual levels. In general, the similarity of error patterns across lesion locations reflects the interactive nature of the model: The activation pattern at a particular level is influenced by that of many other levels.

Plaut and Shallice also showed that their model mimicked patients by producing combinations of visual and semantic influences on errors. For example, it made mixed visual-semantic errors. The rates of these errors for abstract words were at least three times greater than what the rate would be if semantic and visual effects were independent, for all lesion locations. So, like the DSMSG model, there is a true mixed error effect. In the deep dyslexia model, it arises because attractors are sensitive to both semantic and visual information. Words that are similar in both respects, such as RAT and CAT, would have basins that are especially close. The model also produced visual-then-semantic errors, such as PLAN→(flan)→"tart." These occur when the semantics of FLAN is present at the semantic level (a visual error), but because the FLAN pattern is corrupted, it is subject to error when it is transmitted to the phonological level for output.

Aside from the basic types of reading errors, the model also exhibited the effects of concreteness shown by some deep dyslexic patients. Because concrete words have a richer semantics, some of the lesion types, those involving direct (e.g., orthography-to-intermediate) rather than recurrent pathways, lead to better performance with concrete words. Importantly, the model produced a key interaction found in the patients: Abstract words are associated with visual errors (41.4% of errors are visual and 6.4% are semantic) while concrete words have a higher proportion of semantic errors (36.4% visual and 32.3% semantic). The richer semantics of concrete words allows them to benefit more from constraints among the semantic features (via connections to and from the semantic clean-up units). Consequently, damage to direct pathways from orthography to semantics has a more deleterious effect on abstract than concrete words.

In general, Plaut and Shallice's deep dyslexia model provides a compelling account of the error pattern in deep dyslexia, one that allows us to understand how these patterns arise through learning in neural systems. Like the other models we have presented, however, it has its limitations. Because PDP models learn, their behavior must reflect the set of trained items. The deep dyslexia models–and PDP models of linguistic processes in general–use a small number of words and employ particular assumptions about their semantics. This leads to two kinds of limitations. First, the actual vocabularies used by Plaut and Shallice prohibited investigation of other aspects of deep dyslexia such as patients' difficulties with certain syntactic classes and their morphological errors. However, a more fully developed model might accommodate these findings through the mechanisms responsible for concreteness and mixed error effects. The second limitation is that the model is not able to provide quantitatively accurate accounts of the error patterns of individual patients. Although it is possible to attribute this to characteristics of the training set and other convenience assumptions, such an attribution requires a solid understanding of the distinction between the implemented models and the theory. Such understanding is difficult to achieve within the PDP framework (or other computational modeling frameworks for that matter). The patients that would be the most difficult for the model to fit would be those whose reading errors are overwhelmingly semantic (e.g., Caramazza and Hillis, 1990). The model's basic nature is to create both visual and semantic errors. In this way, the deep dyslexia model shares a failing with the DSMSG model.

Some comparisons among the models

The three models that we have discussed share key features. Each processes information by spreading activation and attributes pathological symptoms to quantitative variation in the mechanisms that shape activation patterns. Each offers a simple way to lesion the model, and the complexities of pathological language emerge from the processes that underlie normal performance. That is, the lesions really just exaggerate tendencies that were there to begin with. In the HJC model, aphasics' difficulties with passives and three-argument sentences are rooted in the way that these sentences are normally understood. For the DSMSG model, aphasic naming errors patterns represent intermediate states between the normal error pattern and a completely random pattern determined by the opportunities afforded by the lexicon. Plaut and Shallice's reading model develops a landscape of attractor basins based on visual, semantic, and phonological properties of words; dyslexic errors result from perturbations of this landscape.

Despite these similarities, the three modeling efforts contrast in several ways. Importantly, each has a different view of what brain damage corresponds to. To a large extent, the theory of damage derives from the basic architecture of the model. For the HJC architecture, which was initially developed to explain individual differences in sentence processing and working memory, it is only natural to extend the hypothesized mechanism for individual differences–capacity limitations–to aphasia. The resulting model effectively links these research areas. The damage mechanism in the DSMSG model–altering spreading activation parameters–is, in part, dictated by it localist connectionist architecture. The alternative of removing units and connections would simply lead to the wrong behavior. Patients would never be able to say some words and always be able to say others. The PDP architecture does not have this limitation. Because representations are distributed, lesions involving the removal of units and connections lead to graded, probabilistic performance. These lesions are more biologically realistic, and thus PDP models offer more potential for links to neural processes than the other architectures.

Another important difference among the models concerns the target data. Dell and colleagues sought to match individual patient data, while the Haarmann group and Plaut and Shallice were modeling general syndromes rather than patients. This distinction echoes a major controversy in neuropsychology: Should one focus on single-cases or do studies comparing groups of patients in different diagnostic categories? Ideally, a model should both be able to explain the individual variation and lead to theoretically motivated grouping of patients.

Conclusions

Aphasiology as a branch of cognitive neuroscience has relied heavily on the study of unusual cases–patients who exhibit relatively pure functional dissociations. Comparison among such patients has played an important role in identifying the structure of the language processing system. Now, with the advent of computational models, the relevance of aphasia to cognitive neuroscience has broadened. In addition to providing more specific descriptions of the "boxes and arrows," the models allow us to explain the graceful degradation (and even recovery) of performance after brain damage, and the variation among patients and between patients and normals.

Despite these accomplishments, computational models of aphasia have a long way to go. Each model has the specific limitations that we mentioned in their ability to explain the output error performance of patients. To this, we would add that the models, as currently developed, do not relate themselves to the temporal dynamics of processing leading up to the output. They have not, for example, been applied to response time (e.g., Levelt, Roelofs, and Meyer, 1999) or event-related potential data (e.g., Swaab, Brown, and Hagoort, 1997).

In addition to the models' empirical limitations, the theories behind the existing models are seriously under-developed in two respects. First, there is the problem of meaning. Language is a mapping between utterances and meanings. We have some solid ideas about the units and structures of utterances, and the existing models make good use of this knowledge. However, our understanding of the semantic representations of words and sentences is less fully developed, and consequently the models have less to work with. The models dealing with words use somewhat arbitrary representations of features to represent word meaning. The sentence processing model assigns each word a core meaning, which is activated when the word is processed. But these representations are not decomposed into features, and there is no provision for shifting meaning as a function of context. While new meanings are created when the thematic role component binds noun arguments to a verb, these representations simply consist of the specified roles (e.g., agent) and the noun fillers, along with the verb. So, for example, in figure 64.1, assigning GIRL the role of KICKER does not alter the representation of GIRL. Until we gain a better understanding of semantic representations, computational modeling of aphasia will be severely hampered.

The second undeveloped area concerns the models' ties to the brain. One reason that aphasia is of interest is that it allows for inferences about the brain-behavior mapping for language. At present, computational models of aphasia have had little to say about this mapping, aside from statements that link the model as a whole to well-known language areas (e.g., left posterior language regions for the DSMSG model). This, we expect, will soon change. Not only will the models be used to interpret functional imaging and lesion location data, but they ultimately will be able to make predictions about such data. If a model provides an effective functional explanation of language behavior, which the models that we have discussed here are beginning to do, there is no reason why it should not offer insight into neural mechanisms.

NOTE

1. In both (1c) and (1d), generative grammar postulates the movement of noun arguments from their base positions in the sentence, such that processing involves linkage of the argument to a trace inserted at the moved location. Some investigators have suggested that traces are a source of difficulty for aphasics (e.g., Grodzinsky, 1990).

ACKNOWLEDGMENTS This research was supported by NIH DC-00191 and DC-01924, and NSF SBR 93-19368. The authors thank Peter Hagoort for helpful comments and Linda May for work on the manuscript.

REFERENCES

ANDERSON, J. R., 1983. *The Architecture of Cognition.* Cambridge, Mass.: Harvard University Press.

BATES, E., J. McDONALD, B. MacWHINNEY, and B. APPELBAUM, 1991. A maximum likelihood procedure for the analysis of group and individual data in aphasia research. *Brain Lang.* 40:231–265.

BLACKWELL, A., and E. BATES, 1995. Inducing agrammatic profiles in normals: Evidence for the selective vulnerability of morphology under cognitive resource limitation. *J. Cogn. Neurosci.* 7:228–257.

BOCK, J. K., and W. J. M. LEVELT, 1994. Language production: Grammatical encoding. In *Handbook of Psycholinguistics*, M. Gernsbacher, ed. San Diego, Calif.: Academic Press, pp. 945–984.

BUCKINGHAM, H. W., 1980. On correlating aphasic errors with slips of the tongue. *Appl. Psycholinguistics* 1:199–200.

BUTTERWORTH, B., 1989. Lexical access in speech production. In *Lexical Representation and Process*, W. Marslen-Wilson, ed. Cambridge, Mass.: MIT Press.

CAPLAN, D., C. BAKER, and F. DEHAUT, 1985. Syntactic determinants of sentence comprehension in aphasia. *Cognition* 21:117–175.

CAPLAN, D., and N. HILDEBRANDT, 1988. *Disorders of syntactic comprehension.* Cambridge, Mass.: MIT Press.

CAPLAN, D., M. VANIER, and C. BAKER, 1986. A case study of reproduction conduction aphasia I: Word production. *Cogn. Neuropsychol.* 3:99–128.

CAPLAN, D., and G. S. WATERS, 1995. Aphasic disorders of syntactic comprehension and working memory capacity. *Cogn. Neuropsychol.* 12:637–650.

CARAMAZZA, A., 1988. Some aspects of language processing revealed through the analysis of acquired aphasia: The lexical system. *Ann. Rev. Neurosci.* 11:395–421.

CARAMAZZA, A., and A. HILLIS, 1990. Where do semantic errors come from? *Cortex* 26:95–122.

CARAMAZZA, A., and E. G. ZURIF, 1976. Dissociation of algorithmic and heuristic processes in sentence comprehension: Evidence from aphasia. *Brain Lang.* 3:572–582.

COLTHEART, M., K. E. PATTERSON, and J. L. MARSHALL (eds.), 1980. *Deep Dyslexia.* London: Routledge and Kegan Paul.

COTTRELL, G. W., 1985. Implications of connectionist parsing for aphasia. *Proc. 9th SCAMC.*

DANEMAN, M., and P. A. CARPENTER, 1980. Individual differences in working memory and reading. *J. Verbal Mem. Verbal Behav.* 19:450–466.

DELL, G. S., 1986. A spreading activation theory of retrieval in language production. *Psychol. Rev.* 93:283–321.

DELL, G. S., and P. G. O'SEAGHDHA, 1991. Mediated and convergent lexical priming in language production: A comment on Levelt et al. *Psychol. Rev.* 98:604–614.

DELL, G. S., and P. A. REICH, 1981. Stages in sentence production: An analysis of speech error data. *J. Verbal Learn. Verbal Behav.* 20:611–629.

DELL, G. S., M. F. SCHWARTZ, N. MARTIN, E. M. SAFFRAN, and D. A. GAGNON, 1997. Lexical access in aphasic and nonaphasic speakers. *Psychol. Rev.* 104:801–838.

ELLIS, A. W., 1985. The production of spoken words. In *Progress in the Psychology of Language*, Vol. 2, A. W. Ellis, ed. London: Erlbaum, pp. 107–145.

ELMAN, J. L., 1991. Distributed representations, simple recurrent networks, and grammatical structure. *Machine Learning* 7:195–225.

FARAH, M. J., 1994. Neuropsychological inference with an interactive brain: A critique of the "locality" assumption. *Behav. Brain Sci.* 17:43–104.

FAY, D., and A. CUTLER, 1977. Malapropisms and the structure of the mental lexicon. *Linguistic Inquiry* 8:505–520.

FRAZIER, L., and A. D. FRIEDERICI, 1991. On deriving properties of agrammatic comprehension. *Brain Lang.* 40:51–66.

FROMKIN, V. A., 1971. The non-anomalous nature of anomalous utterances. *Language* 47:27–52.

GARRETT, M. F., 1975. The analysis of sentence production. In *The Psychology of Learning and Motivation*, G. H. Bower, ed. San Diego, Calif.: Academic Press, pp. 133–175.

GARRETT, M., 1984. The organization of processing structure of language production: Application to aphasic speech. In *Biological Perspectives on Language*, D. Caplan, A. Lecours, and A. Smith, eds. Cambridge, Mass.: MIT Press.

GIGLEY, H. M., 1983. HOPE — AI and the dynamic process of language behavior. *Cognit. Brain Theory* 6:39–88.

GRODZINSKY, Y., 1990. *Theoretical Perspectives on Language Deficits.* Cambridge, Mass.: MIT Press.

HAARMANN, H. J., M. A. JUST, and P. A. CARPENTER, 1997. Aphasic sentence comprehension as a resource deficit: A computational approach. *Brain Lang.* 59:76–120.

HAARMANN, H. J., and H. H. J. KOLK, 1991. A computer model of the temporal course of agrammatic sentence understanding: The effects of variation in severity and sentence complexity. *Cogn. Sci.* 15:49–87.

HARLEY, T. A., 1984. A critique of top-down independent levels models of speech production: Evidence from non-plan-internal speech errors. *Cogn. Sci.* 8:191–219.

HILLIS, A. E., and A. CARAMAZZA, 1995. Representation of grammatical categories of words in the brain. *J. Cogn. Neurosci.* 7:396–407.

HILLIS, A. E., B. RAPP, D. ROMANI, and A. CARAMAZZA, 1990. Selective impairment of semantics in lexical processing. *Cogn. Neuropsychol.* 7:191–243.

HINTON, G. E., and T. SHALLICE, 1991. Lesioning an attractor network: Investigations of acquired dyslexia. *Psychol. Rev.* 98:74–95.

HOUGHTON, G., 1990. The problem of serial order: A neural network memory of sequence learning and recall. In *Current Research in Natural Language Generation*, R. Dale, C. Mellish, and M. Zock, eds. London: Academic Press.

JACKENDOFF, R. S., 1977. *X-Bar Syntax: A Study of Phrase Structure.* Cambridge, Mass.: MIT Press.

JUST, M. A., and P. A. CARPENTER, 1992. A capacity theory of comprehension: Individual differences in working memory. *Psychol. Rev.* 99:122–149.

KING, J., and M. A. JUST, 1991. Individual differences in syntactic processing: The role of working memory. *J. Mem. Lang.* 30:580–602.

KOLK, H. H. J., and M. M. F. VAN GRUNSVEN, 1985. Agrammatism as a variable phenomenon. *Cogn. Neuropsychol.* 2:347–384.

LEVELT, W. J. M., 1989. *Speaking: From Intention to Articulation.* Cambridge, Mass.: MIT Press.

LEVELT, W. J. M., A. ROELOFS, and A. S. MEYER, 1999. A theory of lexical access in speech production. *Behav. Brain Sci.* 22:1–38.

LEVELT, W. J. M., H. SCHRIEFERS, D. VORBERG, A. S. MEYER, T. PECHMANN, and J. HAVINGA, 1991. The time course of lexical access in speech production: A study of picture naming. *Psychol. Rev.* 98:122–142.

LINEBARGER, M. C., M. F. SCHWARTZ, and E. M. SAFFRAN, 1983. Sensitivity to grammatical structure in so-called agrammatic aphasics. *Cognition* 13:641–662.

MACDONALD, M. C., N. J. PEARLMUTTER, and M. S. SEIDENBERG, 1994. The lexical nature of syntactic ambiguity resolution. *Psychol. Rev.* 101:676–703.

MACKAY, D. G., 1972. The structure of words and syllables: Evidence from errors in speech. *Cogn. Psychol.* 3:210–227.

MARSHALL, J. C., and F. NEWCOMBE, 1966. Syntactic and semantic errors in paralexia. *Neuropsychologia* 4:169–176.

MARTIN, N., G. S. DELL, E. M. SAFFRAN, and M. F. SCHWARTZ, 1994. Origins of paraphasias in deep dysphasia: Testing the consequence of a decay impairment of an interactive spreading activation model of lexical retrieval. *Brain Lang.* 47:609–660.

MARTIN, N., D. A. GAGNON, M. F. SCHWARTZ, G. S. DELL, and E. M. SAFFRAN, 1996. Phonological facilitation of semantic errors in normal and aphasic speakers. *Lang. Cogn. Processes* 11:257–282.

MARTIN, N., and E. M. SAFFRAN, 1992. A computational account of deep dysphasia: Evidence from a single case study. *Brain Lang.* 43:240–274.

MARTIN, N., R. W. WEISBERG, and E. M. SAFFRAN, 1989. Variables influencing the occurrence of naming errors: Implications for a model of lexical retrieval. *J. Mem. Lang.* 28:462–485.

MARTIN, R. C., 1995. Working memory doesn't work: A critique of Miyake et al.'s capacity theory of aphasic comprehension. *Cogn. Neuropsychol.* 12:623–636.

MCCLELLAND, J. L., M. ST. JOHN, and R. TARABAN, 1989. Sentence comprehension: A parallel distributed processing approach. *Lang. Cogn. Processes* 4:287–335.

MCCLELLAND, J. L., and D. E. RUMELHART, 1981. An interactive activation model of context effects in letter perception: Part 1. An account of basic findings. *Psychol. Rev.* 88:375–407.

MIYAKE, A., P. A. CARPENTER, and M. A. JUST, 1994. A capacity approach to syntactic comprehension disorders: Making normal adults perform like aphasics. *Cogn. Neuropsychol.* 11:671–717.

MIYAKE, A., P. A. CARPENTER, and M. A. JUST, 1995. Reduced resources and specific impairments in normal and aphasic sentence comprehension. *Cogn. Neuropsychol.* 12:651–679.

PETERSON, R. R., and P. SAVOY, 1998. Lexical selection and phonological encoding during language production: Evidence for cascaded processing. *J. Exp. Psychol.: Learning Mem. Cognit.* 24:539–557.

PLAUT, D., 1996. Relearning after damage in connectionist networks: Toward a theory of rehabilitation. *Brain Lang.* 52:25–82. Special issue on cognitive approaches to rehabilitation and recovery in aphasia.

PLAUT, D. C., J. L. MCCLELLAND, M. S. SEIDENBERG, and K. E. PATTERSON, 1996. Understanding normal and impaired word reading: Computational principles in quasi-regular domains. *Psychol. Rev.* 103:56–115.

PLAUT, D. C., and T. SHALLICE, 1993. Deep dyslexia: A case study of connectionist neuropsychology. *Cogn. Neuropsychol.* 10:377–500.

ROACH, A., M. F. SCHWARTZ, N. MARTIN, R. S. GREWAL, and A. BRECHER, 1996. The Philadelphia Naming Test: Scoring and rationale. *Clin. Aphasiol.* 24:121–133.

ROCHON, E., G. S. WATERS, and D. CAPLAN, 1994. Sentence comprehension in patients with Alzheimer's disease. *Brain Lang.* 46:329–349.

RUMELHART, D. E., G. E. HINTON, and R. J. WILLIAMS, 1986. Learning internal representations by error propagation. In *Parallel Distributed Processing: Explorations in the Microstructure of Cognition*, Vol. 1, D. E. Rumelhart and J. L. McClelland, eds. Cambridge, Mass.: MIT Press, pp. 318–364.

SAFFRAN, E. M., 1982. Neuropsychological approaches to the study of language. *Brit. J. Psychol.* 73:317–337.

SAFFRAN, E. M., M. S. SCHWARTZ, and M. C. LINEBARGER, 1998. Semantic influences on thematic role assignment: Evidence from normals and aphasics. *Brain Lang.* 62:255–297.

SCHRIEFERS, H., A. S. MEYER, and W. J. M. LEVELT, 1990. Exploring the time-course of lexical access in production: Picture-word interference studies. *J. Mem. Lang.* 29:86–102.

SCHWARTZ, M. F., 1987. Patterns of speech production deficit within and across aphasia syndromes: Applications of a psycholinguistic model. In *The Cognitive Neuropsychology of Language*, M. Coltheart, R. Job, and G. Sartori, eds. Hillsdale, N.J.: Erlbaum, pp. 163–200.

SCHWARTZ, M. F., M. C. LINEBARGER, E. M. SAFFRAN, and D. S. PATE, 1987. Syntactic transparency and sentence interpretation in aphasia. *Lang. Cogn. Processes* 2:85–113.

SCHWARTZ, M. F., E. M. SAFFRAN, D. BLOCH, and G. S. DELL, 1994. Disordered speech production in aphasic and normal speakers. *Brain Lang.* 47:52–88.

SHATTUCK-HUFNAGEL, S., 1979. Speech errors as evidence for a serial-order mechanism in sentence production. In *Sentence Processing: Psycholinguistic Studies Presented to Merrill Garrett*, W. E. Cooper and E. C. T. Walker, eds. Hillsdale, N.J.: Erlbaum, pp. 295–342.

STEMBERGER, J. P., 1985. An interactive activation model of language production. In *Progress in the Psychology of Language*, Vol. 1, A. W. Ellis, ed. Hillsdale, N.J.: Erlbaum, pp. 143–186.

SWAAB, T., C. BROWN, and P. HAGOORT, 1997. Spoken sentence comprehension in aphasia: Event-related potential evidence for a lexical integration deficit. *J. Cogn. Neurosci.* 9:39–66.

SWINNEY, D., E. ZURIF, P. PRATHER, and T. LOVE, 1996. Neurological distribution of processing resources underlying language comprehension. *J. Cogn. Neurosci.* 8:174–184.

WILSHIRE, C. E., and R. A. MCCARTHY, 1996. Experimental investigations of an impairment in phonological encoding. *Cogn. Neuropsychol.* 13:1059–1098.

65 The Neural Architecture of Language Disorders

NINA F. DRONKERS, BRENDA B. REDFERN, AND ROBERT T. KNIGHT

ABSTRACT   Traditional models of language processing in the brain presume certain functions for Broca's area, Wernicke's area, and the fiber tracts that connect them. These descriptions have served a useful clinical purpose over the last century, but recent advances in the study of language and in structural and functional neuroimaging have found them somewhat insufficient. This chapter discusses findings from our work with aphasic patients examining the relationship between specific speech and language disorders and the lesions underlying these deficits. It is shown that traditional language areas may serve somewhat different functions than originally described, and that the identification of more specific deficits and their neuroanatomic correlates can lead to more informative mapping of language functions in the brain.

Much has been written about the behavioral deficits observed in the various types of aphasia, or language disorders, that arise from injury to the brain. Some describe the clinical manifestations of the disorders, others, the implications for theories of normal language processing. In this chapter, we discuss the brain areas that have been associated with these disorders and the current neurological model of language processing that was derived from these patient studies. We begin with a review of the clinical observations of Broca and Wernicke–observations that laid the foundation for how most clinicians and neuroscientists believe the brain processes language. We provide some basic information about the three aphasias that are most pertinent to this model and show how these descriptions have changed since they were first presented more than 100 years ago. Finally, we present our view of the organization of language in the brain by reviewing what we have learned from our patients with aphasia. We review the speech and language deficits we have studied and the correlations we have found with the brain areas that were destroyed by these patients' injuries. With these more recent data, we hope to provide some suggestions for expanding current models concerning the neural architecture of language disorders.

NINA F. DRONKERS and BRENDA B. REDFERN   VA Northern California Health Care System and University of California, Davis, Calif.
ROBERT T. KNIGHT   University of California, Berkeley, Calif.

The classical theory

In the late 1700s, the simple observation of a 14-year-old formed the basis of a theory concerning the neural mechanisms of language. At that time, Franz Joseph Gall noticed that some of his more articulate friends also had markedly protruding eyeballs. He reasoned that the areas of the brain behind both eyes must have grown larger to accommodate the superior language skills of his friends and were thus pushing the eyeballs forward. With this, Gall instigated the popular practice of phrenology in which bumps on the head were related to enhanced "faculties" of the mind. Even after the phrenology fervor had subsided, many scholarly societies still debated whether speech resided in the frontal lobes.

It was in this context that (Pierre) Paul Broca, a surgeon with an interest in anthropology, saw a patient with an infected leg and a right hemiparesis who also had lost the capability of speech. The patient, whose name was Leborgne, could only utter the single syllable, "tan," which he used each time he initiated speech. Broca thought the patient understood most of what was said to him and thus presented as the perfect case to prove Gall's theory of speech in the frontal lobes. As it happened, the patient died a few days later and Broca was able to view the brain at autopsy. Indeed, a lesion was found in the frontal lobe on the posterior surface of the third frontal gyrus on the left side (Broca, 1861), the area later referred to as "Broca's area" (figure 65.1). Broca also noted softening as far posterior as the parietal operculum; but since he was only looking for involvement of the frontal lobes, this observation was deemed less important. In order to preserve the brain for posterity, it was never cut, and the extent of the lesion medially or posteriorly was not known until a century later (Signoret et al., 1984). By that time, the notion that the frontal lobes were involved in speech was firmly set.

Broca believed that Leborgne's deficits affected only his articulation abilities, not his language; hence he termed the deficit "aphemia," not "aphasia." Later, he published another, very similar case, also with a right

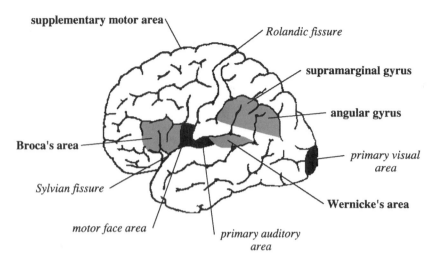

FIGURE 65.1   Lateral view of the left hemisphere with some of the brain areas implicated in language labeled in boldface.

hemiparesis and a lesion in the left frontal lobe. Two years later, he had accumulated six more cases, none of which came to autopsy, but all of which had a right hemiparesis. By 1865, Broca realized that the co-occurrence of the right hemiparesis and the speech deficit was beyond coincidental and concluded that it was the *left* frontal lobe, at least in right-handers, that controlled the ability for speech.

Not long thereafter, Carl Wernicke, a 26-year-old physician, described another type of language problem. He had examined two patients with profound deficits in understanding spoken language. Their speech, though perfectly fluent, was incomprehensible and riddled with nonsense words that did not exist in German. Wernicke examined the brain of one of these patients and found a lesion in the posterior part of the superior temporal gyrus, posterior to primary auditory cortex (figure 65.1). The lesion of the other patient was assumed to be in the same place. He associated this region (later termed "Wernicke's area") with the storage of "the auditory memory for words." Wernicke believed that comprehension deficits were caused by the loss of these memories, while the distorted output was due to the inability to monitor self-spoken auditory images (Wernicke, 1874).

By documenting this second type of language disorder, Wernicke provided a formal distinction between two components of language, firmly departing from previous phrenological notions that language was a single entity, localizable in one brain region. With the addition of this new aphasia, differences were drawn between the "expressive" aphasia of Broca and the "receptive" aphasia described by Wernicke. Though these terms are now considered somewhat imprecise, the differentiation was an important one for its time and set aphasiologists to

thinking about what other components of the language system could be affected by brain injury.

Wernicke made another important contribution to the study of brain and language. He detailed an impressive theory establishing the notion of brain centers and the connections between them. He believed that auditory memories, first evoked in the posterior superior temporal gyrus, were then passed on to Broca's area where they were prepared for articulation. He thereby predicted another type of aphasia, "conduction" aphasia, caused by lesions to the pathway *between* these centers, resulting in an interruption of the transmission of linguistic information from Wernicke's area to anterior speech areas. The result would be a disruption in verbal production, since auditory word images evoked in Wernicke's area would be cut off from articulatory mechanisms in the frontal lobe.

This "connectionist" approach, as it came to be called (not to be confused with the "connectionism" of today's models), became extremely popular. Though it underwent a period of disfavor in later years, it returned to popularity with the work of Norman Geschwind. In his influential paper, "Disconnexion syndromes in animals and man" (Geschwind, 1965), he presented and explained several behavioral deficits in terms of the lesions in major centers and the disconnections between them. For the study of aphasia, he assimilated the most current information from behavioral neurology, psychology, and linguistics and formulated a working model of the neural mechanisms of language (see Geschwind, 1970). This model assumed the involvement of Wernicke's area in language comprehension and that of Broca's area for articulation and possibly in assisting in the grammatical organization of language. Geschwind also identified the arcuate fasciculus as the fiber pathway that should con-

BOX 65.1
Spontaneous speech examples from patients with Broca's and Wernicke's aphasia on a picture description task

Patient WR (Broca's aphasia)

> "O, yeah. Det's a boy an' a girl ... an' ... a ... car ... house ... light po' (pole). Dog an' a ... boat. 'N det's a ... mm ... a ... coffee, an' reading. Det's a ... mm ... a ... det's a boy ... fishin'." (Elapsed time: 1 min, 30 s)

Patient OB (Wernicke's aphasia)

> "Ah, yes, it's, ah ... several things. It's a girl ... uncurl ... on a boat. A dog ... 'S is another dog ... uh–oh ... long's ... on a boat. The lady, it's a young lady. An' a man. They were eatin'. 'S be place there. This ... a tree! A boat. No, this is a.... It's a house. Over in here ... a cake. An' it's, it's alot of water. Ah, all right. I think I mentioned about that boat. I noticed a boat being there. I did mention that before.... Several things down, different things down ... a bat ... a cake ... you have a...." (Elapsed time: 1 min, 20 s)

nect Wernicke's and Broca's areas as it passes through the parietal lobe. Lesions to it would presumably cause a disconnection of these two areas, resulting in the repetition deficit so characteristic of conduction aphasia, the other type of aphasia predicted by Wernicke more than a century ago.

Current descriptions of the aphasias

Current descriptions of aphasic deficits have modified Broca's and Wernicke's definitions considerably. Recall that Broca considered the deficit in his patients to be exclusively in articulation. He was confident that his patients understood everything said to them. Wernicke viewed his patients' problem as one in the storage of "the auditory memory for words." He believed that the loss of these memories resulted in the comprehension deficit, while an inability to monitor self-spoken auditory images resulted in his patients' distorted output. Today, we describe the main aphasias in a somewhat different way.

BROCA'S APHASIA   The most striking characteristic of Broca's aphasia is the slow and effortful speech and the lack of grammatical markers in language production. Utterances are produced in a telegraphic or agrammatic style, with patients relying mostly on high-frequency content words and omitting the smaller function words that convey mostly grammatical information (see box 65.1.) Repetition is impaired in the same fashion as their spontaneous speech. Word-finding is also impaired and contributes to the difficulty in production.

Patients with a more severe form of Broca's aphasia can produce nothing more than recurring utterances– syllables, words, or phrases repeated again and again

(e.g., "/tono tono/," "yes, yes," "Sweet sweetie, I miss sweet sweetie")–like Leborgne's "tan." Patients with a milder Broca's aphasia tend to produce sentences and phrases that contain some grammatical organization. However, some aphasia batteries will not recognize a patient as a Broca's aphasic unless there is a complete absence of such structures in the patient's spontaneous speech.

Patients with Broca's aphasia were long thought to have intact language comprehension. This is clearly not the case. Although these patients appear to follow conversations with little difficulty, careful testing reveals that complex grammatical structures requiring the manipulation of grammatical information or the processing of grammatical rules elude them. Thus, the sentence "The boy kissed the girl" may be understood perfectly, while the more complex sentence "The girl was kissed by the boy" may not, though their meanings are identical. There is much debate as to the nature of this phenomenon–whether it is due to a central syntactic processing deficit or to an attentional or working memory disorder, and whether this deficit is associated with Broca's area. No doubt this debate will continue for years to come, as syntax is a critical part of human language, conceivably comprising the fundamental difference between our communication system and those of other species.

Speech deficits such as *dysarthria* and *apraxia of speech* frequently accompany Broca's aphasia. Dysarthria is the inability to control the muscles of articulation. Speech sounds are systematically distorted such that all of the patient's utterances sound similarly weak and flaccid or spastic, depending on the type of dysarthria. Apraxia of speech is an articulatory programming disorder that produces errors that, while inconsistent, approximate the target word (e.g., saying /yawyer/ for "lawyer" or /chookun/ for "cushion"). These disorders also contribute to the fluency deficits of patients with Broca's aphasia and must be distinguished from the aphasia itself.

WERNICKE'S APHASIA Patients with Wernicke's aphasia have a deep disruption in their ability to use language to express their ideas. Whereas Broca's aphasics can participate in a conversation and get most of its meaning, Wernicke's aphasics can understand very little of what is said and contribute less in return. Again, there is considerable range in these characteristics, with some patients communicating some linguistic information and others producing only jargon, or meaningless sounds.

Patients with Wernicke's aphasia score poorly on tests of auditory and reading comprehension. In severe cases, their ability to understand even single words is compromised. Comprehension of sentences and phrases is even more impaired. The spontaneous speech of Wernicke's aphasic patients is very fluid, quite the opposite of the halting and telegraphic style of Broca's aphasia (see box 65.1). Sentences appear to be well-formed but are often riddled with *paraphasias*, words that are substituted for the intended word. If one did not speak the patient's language, one would be unable to detect anything particularly wrong, the speech output being so fluent. Word retrieval on confrontation naming tasks is severely impaired. Patients with Wernicke's aphasia not only have difficulty in finding the correct word but often cannot recognize the correct name even when it is offered to them.

CONDUCTION APHASIA The hallmark of conduction aphasia is the repetition deficit in contrast to relatively preserved comprehension. Patients with conduction aphasia can repeat single words and short high-frequency sentences (e.g., "He is not coming back") fairly easily. Longer sentences, or those that might occur less frequently in normal language (e.g., "The pastry cook was elated"), are far more difficult for conduction aphasics. In contrast, their auditory comprehension is relatively intact, even demonstrating their understanding of a sentence they were just unable to repeat.

Other aphasias include *global aphasia* (in which language is very severely impaired, yielding something of a combination of Broca's and Wernicke's aphasia), *anomic aphasia* (in which a word-finding problem is the most significant impairment), and the *transcortical aphasias* (in which repetition is spared). Clinically, these aphasias are seen very often, but are less relevant to our discussion and will be treated cursorily. More detailed descriptions can be found in clinical reference books such as Benson

and Ardila (1996), Goodglass (1993), and Goodglass and Kaplan (1972).

Does the classical theory explain these disorders?

Since Broca's and Wernicke's observations, converging evidence from several other sources has emerged to support some of their claims. For example, Broca's important distinction between left and right hemisphere contributions to speech continued to find support through numerous lateralization studies, including those with split brain patients, and those using dichotic listening and visual half field testing. In addition, observations of aphasic patients confirmed that the aphasia of 90–98% of right-handed patients was caused by left hemisphere lesions. The work of Rasmussen and Milner (1977) also demonstrated that 95% of right-handed patients undergoing Wada testing for epilepsy surgery became temporarily aphasic after injection of the anesthetic into the left internal carotid artery feeding the left cerebral hemisphere. Furthermore, Penfield and Roberts (1959) found that electrical stimulation to the left hemisphere of the brain caused aphasia-like symptoms more often than right hemisphere stimulation.

But evidence about the localization of language and speech *within* the left hemisphere has been less well substantiated. For the most part, the classical model is successful at describing patients' disorders and in predicting the brain areas that are compromised. However, there are numerous occasions on which the model fails. Some examples from our own clinic may help to illustrate this point.

Patient JC has a large frontal lobe lesion encompassing Broca's area and areas anterior and superior to it, extending deep into underlying white matter (figure 65.2). Traditional theory would predict that this patient should have a Broca's aphasia, producing short telegraphic sentences consisting mostly of high-frequency content words and few function words (prepositions, conjunctions, etc.), with impaired comprehension for complex grammatical constructions (embedded clauses, passive voice, etc.). Though JC's speech is slow and effortful, the sentences he produces are perfectly grammatical and contain numerous examples of complex constructions. In addition, his language comprehension is virtually unaffected. Another patient, JH, does have a persisting Broca's aphasia with the symptoms just described, but his lesion completely spares Broca's area.

As for Wernicke's area, patient MC has a lesion encompassing Wernicke's area and should have impaired comprehension and a Wernicke's aphasia. Instead, this patient has intact auditory comprehension and the repetition deficit typical of conduction aphasia. Patient OB

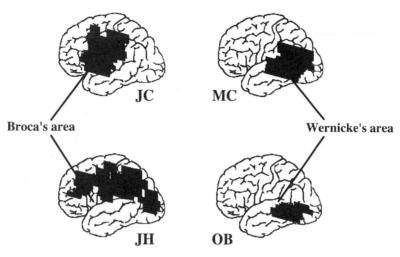

FIGURE 65.2   Top: Computer-reconstructed lesions of two patients, one with a lesion involving Broca's area (patient JC) and one with a lesion in Wernicke's area (patient MC). Neither of these patients was classified with the Broca's and Wernicke's aphasia predicted by traditional theory. Bottom: Two patients who do classify with a Broca's aphasia (patient JH) and a Wernicke's aphasia (patient OB). Neither of these patients has a lesion in Broca's or Wernicke's areas, respectively.

has a dense Wernicke's aphasia with severely impaired comprehension and conversation littered with paraphasic errors. His lesion should include Wernicke's area. But it doesn't. In fact, his lesion spares Wernicke's area and instead involves the middle temporal gyrus and underlying white matter.

None of these patients is left-handed or multilingual; nor does any have an early neurological or medical problem that might have caused a reorganization of language functions in their brains. Moreover, these patients are not isolated examples. Even after Broca's historic paper, numerous cases were presented that refuted Broca's claim (e.g., Charcot cited in Finger, 1994; Bateman, 1870; Brown-Sequard, 1877; Marie, 1906; Moutier, 1908). Several found patients with lesions to Broca's area who had no Broca's aphasia at all or patients with Broca's aphasia and no lesion in Broca's area. Even the renowned neurosurgeon Wilder Penfield was reported to have completely removed Broca's area with no persisting speech or language impairments. Mohr (1976) did an extensive review of the literature on Broca's area and Broca's aphasia and found that it takes a much larger lesion than Broca described to produce a persisting Broca's aphasia. Other studies have looked at the relationship between Broca's area and Broca's aphasia and Wernicke's area and Wernicke's aphasia, with most finding a far-from-perfect correlation (e.g., Basso et al., 1985; Bogen and Bogen, 1976; Dronkers, Redfern, and Ludy, 1995; Mazzocchi and Vignolo, 1979; Murdoch et al., 1986). Why does the model fail so often?

One reason the model is often inadequate is that it oversimplifies the richness and complexity of language. Language is more than just speaking and listening; it consists of complex rules that govern the way we combine sounds and signs into words and sentences to express thoughts to other human beings who share the same set of rules. At the very least, it involves retrieving words that label concepts, retrieving and applying the grammatical constraints that convey the relationships between the words, preparing the words for articulation, attaching the appropriate intonational patterns and social rules particular to the situation, and then producing the utterance through speech or signed gestures. The field of linguistics is entirely dedicated to studying the intricacies of this complex system, to an extent that could never have been appreciated in Broca's or Wernicke's time.

Second, many studies have attempted to localize behaviors that were not stable. It is now known that in patients with acute Broca's aphasia in the first few weeks after injury, the condition often evolves into a milder form of language impairment, where the deficit is largely one of word-finding. In patients with acute Wernicke's aphasia, the condition almost always evolves into a milder conduction aphasia or anomic aphasia. These early deficits are most likely influenced by the effects of the lesion on neighboring or connected brain regions and do not accurately reflect the deficits caused by lesions to these areas. In our opinion, this lesion–deficit correlation must wait until the behavior has stabilized.

Finally, aphasiologists have never agreed on what we are trying to localize. Broca thought it was the faculty of articulation that resided in Broca's area; later in history, it was syntax. In fact, Broca's aphasia is a *syndrome*, a cluster of aphasia deficits that collectively form a pattern. Patients with Broca's aphasia have numerous

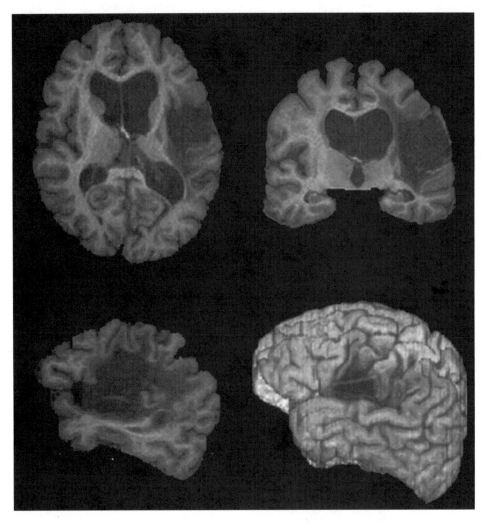

FIGURE 65.3 This three-dimensional MRI reconstruction depicts the lesion in a patient with anomic aphasia and an apraxia of speech. The upper left image is a horizontal slice showing the left hemisphere lesion, while the upper right depicts a coronal section. (The images conform to radiologic convention, with the left hemisphere shown on the right side.) In the lower left is a sagittal section through the left hemisphere. The lower right image shows the 3D reconstruction of the brain with part of the lesion visible on the lateral surface of the left hemisphere.

problems: They are impaired in articulatory agility, word-finding, repetition, and comprehension for complex grammatical structures. Realistically, it makes little sense to suppose that all of these behaviors would be located in one area of the brain. Instead, we find that looking for brain areas associated with more specific components of the speech and language process results in far more reliable correlations. We illustrate this point in the following section.

Recent contributions

Over the last several years, we have looked closely at the specific deficits in our aphasic patients and evaluated these in parallel with a careful analysis of lesion sites. Owing to the large number of aphasic patients at our fa-

cility, we have been able to impose several controls on our studies. First, all of the patients we study have suffered a single cerebral infarction (stroke) with no previous neurologic or psychiatric history that might influence their results. All are right-handed, native English-speaking, and have normal or corrected-to-normal vision and hearing. All speech and language testing is performed at least one year after the stroke to ensure that the deficits are stable and persisting. Each patient has undergone CT or MR imaging at least 3 weeks postonset so that the boundaries of the lesion can be clearly discerned and reliably reconstructed. Most cases are imaged close to the time of testing, and on some patients, we have also obtained 3D MRIs (figure 65.3; see also color plate 43). Patients' lesions are reconstructed onto templates and entered into a microcomputer running

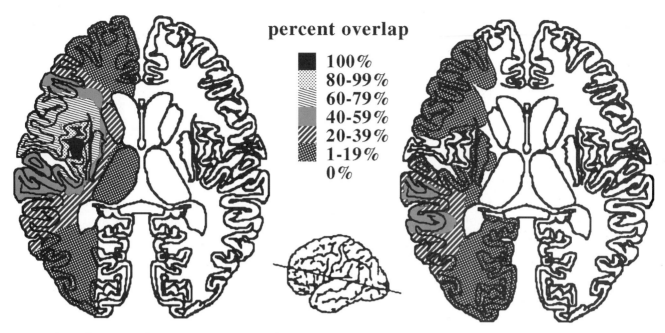

percent overlap

- 100%
- 80-99%
- 60-79%
- 40-59%
- 20-39%
- 1-19%
- 0%

FIGURE 65.4   Lesion overlapping in 25 patients with apraxia of speech (left) and 19 patients without this disorder (right). All of the 25 patients with apraxia of speech have a lesion encompassing a small section of the insula, as shown in yellow, while the lesions of the 19 patients without apraxia of speech completely spare the same area.

software developed at our facility (Frey et al., 1987). Patients who exhibit similar deficits are grouped together and their lesions overlapped by the computer to reveal any common areas of infarction. In this way, lesion locations can be determined that are shared by all patients exhibiting the same disorder.

We have accumulated substantial behavioral and imaging data on more than 100 patients, each of whom met all of these criteria. In our first test of this analysis, we examined 12 right-handed chronic patients with a persisting Broca's aphasia and overlapped their lesions to see if Broca's area was involved in all cases, as predicted by traditional theory (Dronkers et al., 1992). It was not. Two cases had lesions that completely spared Broca's area, even though their aphasia was classified as Broca's with a standardized aphasia battery. In addition, we found ten other patients with lesions in Broca's area who had no Broca's aphasia at all, confirming Mohr's finding. Most of these were mildly anomic, and one was a conduction aphasic with a large posterior lesion extension. Thus, we received our first confirmation that the classical model would not be able to explain all of our patients' language deficits.

Yet the lesion overlapping of the Broca's aphasics did yield a consistent relationship. All of the patients with Broca's aphasia, even those without lesions to Broca's area, had a lesion that encompassed part of the insula, the island of cortex deep within the cerebral hemispheres. This led us to explore whether this area might

be the critical area for Broca's aphasia, much as Marie (1906) had once suggested. In fact, we found numerous patients with lesions in this area of the insula who did not have a Broca's aphasia, but did have an apraxia of speech in common. This disorder is believed to be a deficit in planning the movements necessary for speech, with patients producing inconsistent errors that are phonemically similar to the target word. We found that when we overlapped the lesions of 25 patients who were diagnosed with this disorder, all had involvement of a discrete area of the superior tip of the precentral gyrus of the insula (Dronkers, 1996; see figure 65.4). To be certain that the finding was not artifact, we also overlapped the lesions of 19 patients without apraxia of speech and found that their lesions covered nearly as large an area within the left cerebral hemisphere, but completely spared the part of the precentral gyrus that was lesioned in all of the patients with the disorder (figure 65.4; see also color plate 44). This clear dissociation led us to link this new functional area with this articulatory planning deficit.

With regard to Broca's aphasia, apraxia of speech is a disorder that nearly always occurs in patients with this type of aphasia. Thus, it is not surprising to find that the same area of the precentral gyrus of the insula that was lesioned in all of the patients with apraxia of speech was also lesioned in the patients with Broca's aphasia. Even if we overlap the lesions of patients with a milder, but still Broca-like aphasia, we find that these patients also have lesions in the same area of the insula, and all have an apraxia of speech. Are we saying that this spot on the precentral gyrus of the insula is the new Broca's area? No. We are merely saying that apraxia of speech is one of the central deficits of patients with Broca's aphasia, and this particular behavior is likely caused by lesions to this specific area of the insula.

Another problem of Broca's aphasic patients is in sentence comprehension, particularly for complex grammatical constructions. We have found that patients with lesions to the anterior portion of the superior temporal gyrus have difficulty in processing sentences, particularly those with complex grammatical constructions (Dronkers et al., 1994). This area has rich connections to the hippocampus and may be involved in recruiting memory mechanisms that contribute to the processing of longer and more complex sentences. Other studies have also implicated this area in sentence processing with PET and fMRI technology (Bevalier et al., 1997; Mazoyer et al., 1993). Not surprisingly, this is also an area lesioned in many patients with persisting Broca's aphasia. This is not to say that this area is involved exclusively in sentence comprehension. Language processing at the sentence level is extremely complex and undoubtedly involves numerous brain regions and co-processes.

A feature of more severe Broca's aphasia is that of "recurring utterances," those phrases that are involuntarily produced each time the patient attempts to speak. Here again, we find that Broca's aphasic patients with this characteristic share a common lesion (Dronkers, Redfern, and Shapiro, 1993). Specifically, all had lesions that severed the arcuate fasciculus in a region of the brain where the fibers of this important tract bundle together and ascend out of the temporal lobe to pass over the ventricles. This fiber bundle is susceptible to injuries in the deep parietal region, as even small strokes can completely bisect it, disrupting the transmission of information generated in posterior language zones to more anterior motor speech areas. Classical theory predicts that lesions to this fiber tract would result in repetition deficits. Instead, patients with this lesion cannot speak at all, much less repeat. Aphasic patients without this lesion are not impaired in this way.

Thus we see that trying to associate Broca's aphasia to any one area is futile since this aphasia type is, in reality, a syndrome complex consisting of many different individual deficits. Instead, each specific problem may be related to particular brain areas that subserve specialized functions. The fact that it takes such a large lesion to produce a persisting Broca's aphasia tells us that this lesion must encompass several different brain areas in order to

capture all the structures involved in processing the different aspects of language that are disrupted in this syndrome.

With regard to Broca's area, we feel that a more conservative conclusion should be drawn concerning its function. Given that neurosurgical resection and other injuries to Broca's area result in only a passing motor speech deficit, it may be more reasonable to attribute a limited role specifically in articulation to this region, much as Broca himself had originally done. The location of this area, neighboring on motor face cortex in the primary motor strip, makes it a perfect candidate as a motor association area dedicated to the motor control of the speech musculature. It is likely that in our quest to associate deficits in higher linguistic functions to Broca's aphasia, we may have inadvertently assigned too great a responsibility to Broca's area. Another possibility is that it (or neighboring regions) may play a role in working memory for linguistic material (Stromswold et al., 1996) or function as part of an articulatory loop (Paulesu, Frith, and Frackowiak, 1993), as some recent PET studies have suggested.

This is also true of Wernicke's aphasia and the role we attribute to Wernicke's area. We have found that of seven patients with a persisting Wernicke's aphasia in our group of more than 100 chronic left hemisphere aphasic stroke patients, only five have lesions in Wernicke's area (Dronkers et al., 1995). Seven additional patients have lesions in Wernicke's area with no persisting Wernicke's aphasia. Others have found such discrepancies, as well (Basso et al., 1985). In fact, there is quite a bit of disagreement as to where Wernicke's area is (Bogen and Bogen, 1976), since Wernicke himself had no autopsy data on his first patient and the second patient was reportedly demented, with numerous other neuropathological findings.

We have found that, as in Broca's aphasia, it takes a larger lesion encompassing areas outside of Wernicke's area to produce a persisting Wernicke's aphasia. Most of our chronic Wernicke's aphasics have large temporal lobe lesions with total destruction of the posterior half of the middle temporal gyrus, and all have significant involvement of the underlying white matter. Patients with smaller temporal lobe lesions tend to have transient Wernicke's aphasia which resolves to a milder aphasia type within the first year of recovery. Interestingly, these smaller lesions can be anywhere within the posterior half of the temporal lobe and still produce a Wernicke-like aphasia for the first few months. Thereafter, the network of semantic information that resides in the posterior temporal lobe is apparently able to compensate for the hole in its web, with the patient recovering to a milder residual deficit.

With regard to Wernicke's area itself, we find that lesions there lead to the repetition deficits characteristic of chronic conduction aphasia (Dronkers et al., 1998) and not to a persisting Wernicke's aphasia. These patients have difficulty in holding the sentence in echoic memory and repeating these sentences verbatim, but have little difficulty in understanding the meaning of the sentence. They also have trouble deciding whether two words rhyme, particularly when orthographic or semantic cues cannot be used to make the decision (e.g., when the ends of the words do not share the same spelling or when the words are nonsense words with no meaning). Apparently, the echoic trace is lost, preventing patients from hanging onto the sounds of these words, making rhyme judgments difficult and verbatim repetitions of low-frequency phrases nearly impossible. Other work also points to the involvement of the superior temporal gyrus in the perception and immediate store of auditory information (Damasio and Damasio, 1980), while more complicated semantic processing involves larger temporal regions.

Conclusion

In sum, the earlier aphasiologists identified several key areas in the brain that they thought related to speech and language. Our analysis, with more modern tools and assessments, suggests a somewhat different role for these key areas than has been assumed over the years. Our findings indicate that Broca's area is not related to "speechlessness" as Broca claimed, nor necessarily to grammatical processing, as later psycholinguists believed. Its precise role remains to be seen, and current functional neuroimaging may help to cast some light on this issue (see Brown, Hagoort, and Kutas, this volume). Wernicke's area seems to be related more to echoic rehearsal than to "language comprehension," and the arcuate fasciculus to carrying all types of utterances forward to motor speech areas, not just those that need repeating.

Still, the observations of Broca and Wernicke have pointed us in the right direction toward understanding language and the brain. After all, Broca said the posterior inferior frontal gyrus was related to "the faculty of articulate language" and it is clear that frontal areas do contribute to speech output. Wernicke thought the posterior superior temporal gyrus responsible for language comprehension. Though there is some controversy regarding the role of that particular gyrus, it is generally accepted that the temporal lobe is critical for the storage and retrieval of words and their meanings.

In our view, temporal association cortex, in particular, the middle temporal gyrus, is the region of the brain that is most involved with the core components of language.

Lesions to this general area cause the most profound language deficits, as can be seen in our severe Wernicke's aphasic patients. These individuals demonstrate how destruction of large amounts of temporal cortex with extensive white matter damage can lead to permanent loss of important language functions and the effective use of language in both production and comprehension. Small lesions lead to temporary loss, as though the network is able to reorganize itself if the damage is not too extensive. Localization of specific functions within this temporal lobe network will most likely never be possible since it is built on individual experiences that differ from person to person.

On the other hand, there are speech and language mechanisms that are highly localizable, as our work with articulatory planning and echoic memory has indicated. It must be kept in mind that such functions represent input, output, or support mechanisms for the language system and thus would not be expected to vary greatly across individuals. The function of the arcuate fasciculus in transferring information between language areas should therefore also be consistent. The role of the anterior superior temporal gyrus in sentence comprehension also seems to be consistent across patients, but again, is most likely an area that provides support to a very complex process. Brain regions that contribute to such cognitive functions as attention, memory, working memory, and executive control certainly also play their roles in supporting the processes of language.

Finally, in evaluating the validity of the classical model, we must keep in mind how it was derived. Recall that Broca was very interested in whether Gall's idea of language in the frontal lobe could still be supported, even after other phrenological relationships were discarded. When he examined the brain of Leborgne, he was specifically looking for a lesion in the frontal lobes. When he found one, he took it as immediate confirmation of Gall's theory, even though he never cut the brain to see how extensive the damage was. In addition, Broca's patient had apparently suffered numerous strokes and it was never clear which one had led to his "speechlessness." Ironically, such a patient would never be included in today's localization studies. Broca's second patient also had a deeper frontal lobe lesion, though Broca considered only the posterior inferior frontal gyrus to be of importance. His subsequent cases were rarely autopsied, only assumed to have the same lesion.

Wernicke's cases are no more convincing by today's standards. One was demented, with widespread neuropathological changes, while the other patient recovered within weeks and was never autopsied. While many subsequent cases provided support for Broca's and

Wernicke's claims, many were also found to refute them. In fact, the Wernicke model fell out of favor for most of the century and was replaced with numerous other theories. It was not until Geschwind revived the model in the 1960s that it was again brought into vogue.

The last century has seen a blossoming of interest in the neural mechanisms of language and great changes in how these functions are investigated. New technologies and a better understanding of the behaviors we are trying to localize have merged to offer us some necessary modifications to the classical theory. The classical language areas may indeed contribute to language processing, but may do so in slightly different ways. It is also clear that other brain areas besides Broca's area, Wernicke's area, and the arcuate fasciculus can contribute to language processing. Some of these areas determined by lesion analysis include the insula, the anterior superior temporal gyrus, and a larger swath of temporal cortex than previously thought. These modifications do not belittle the older model in any way; they merely offer us the opportunity to improve upon it and to come to a better understanding of the areas involved in speech and language.

ACKNOWLEDGMENTS   This work was supported by the Department of Veterans Affairs and the National Institute of Neurological Disorders and Stroke.

REFERENCES

BASSO, A., A. R. LECOURS, S. MORASCHINI, and M. VANIER, 1985. Anatomoclinical correlations of the aphasias as defined through computerized tomography: Exceptions. *Brain Lang.* 26:201–229.

BATEMAN, F., 1870. *On Aphasia.* London: Churchill.

BENSON, D. F., and A. ARDILA, 1996. *Aphasia: A Clinical Perspective.* New York: Oxford University Press.

BEVALIER, D., D. CORINA, P. JEZZARD, S. PADMANABHAN, V. P. CLARK, A. KARNI, A. PRINSTER, A. BRAUN, A. LALWANI, J. P. RAUSCHECKER, R. TURNER, and H. NEVILLE, 1997. Sentence reading: A functional MRI study at 4 tesla. *J. Cogn. Neurosci.* 9(5):664–686.

BOGEN, J. E., and G. M. BOGEN, 1976. Wernicke's region—Where is it? *Ann. N.Y. Acad. Sci.* 280:834–843.

BROCA, P., 1861. Perte de la parole, remollissement chronique et destruction partielle du lobe anterieur gauche du cerveau. *Bull. Soc. Anthropol.* 2:235–238.

BROWN-SEQUARD, C. E., 1877. Aphasia as an effect of brain-disease. *J. Med. Sci.* 63:209–225.

DAMASIO, H., and A. DAMASIO, 1980. The anatomical basis of conduction aphasia. *Brain* 103:337–350.

DRONKERS, N. F., 1996. A new brain region for coordinating speech articulation. *Nature* 384:159–161.

DRONKERS, N. F., B. B. REDFERN, and J. K. SHAPIRO, 1993. Neuroanatomic correlates of production deficits in severe Broca's aphasia. *J. Clin. Exp. Neuropsychol.* 15(1): 59–60.

DRONKERS, N. F., B. B. REDFERN, C. LUDY, and J. BALDO, 1998. Brain regions associated with conduction aphasia and echoic rehearsal. *J. Intl. Neuropsychol. Soc.* 4(1):23–24.

DRONKERS, N. F., B. B. REDFERN, and C. A. LUDY, 1995. Lesion localization in chronic Wernicke's aphasia. *Brain Lang.* 51(1):62–65.

DRONKERS, N. F., J. K. SHAPIRO, B. REDFERN, and R. T. KNIGHT, 1992. The role of Broca's area in Broca's aphasia. *J. Clin. Exp. Neuropsychol.* 14:52–53.

DRONKERS, N. F., D. P. WILKINS, B. B. REDFERN, J. R. VAN VALIN, and J. J. JAEGER, 1994. A reconsideration of the brain areas involved in the disruption of morphosyntactic comprehension. *Brain Lang.* 47(3):461–463.

FINGER, S., 1994. *Origins of Neuroscience.* New York: Oxford University Press.

FREY, R. T., D. L. WOODS, R. T. KNIGHT, D. SCABINI, and C. CLAYWORTH, 1987. Defining functional areas with averaged CT scans. *Soc. Neurosci.* 13:1266.

GESCHWIND, N., 1965. Disconnexion syndromes in animals and man. *Brain* 88:237–294.

GESCHWIND, N., 1970. The organization of language and the brain. *Science* 170:940–944.

GOODGLASS, H., 1993. *Understanding Aphasia.* San Diego: Academic Press.

GOODGLASS, H., and E. KAPLAN, 1972. *The Assessment of Aphasia and Related Disorders.* Philadelphia: Lea and Febiger.

MARIE, P., 1906. Revision de la question de l'aphasie: La troisieme circonvolution frontale gauche ne joue aucun role special dans la fonction du langage. *Semaine Medicale* 26:241–247.

MAZOYER, B. M., N. TZOURIO, V. FRAK, A. SYROTA, N. MURAYAMA, O. LEVRIER, G. SALAMON, S. DEHAENE, L. COHEN, and J. MEHLER, 1993. The cortical representation of speech. *J. Cogn. Neurosci.* 5(4):467–479.

MAZZOCCHI, F., and L. A. VIGNOLO, 1979. Localization of lesions in aphasia: Clinical CT-scan correlations in stroke patients. *Cortex* 15:627–654.

MOHR, J. P., 1976. Broca's area and Broca's aphasia. In *Studies in Neurolinguistics*, Vol. 1, H. Whitaker and H. Whitaker, eds. New York: Academic Press, pp. 201–233.

MOUTIER, F., 1908. *L'aphasie de Broca.* Paris: Steinheil.

MURDOCH, B. E., R. J. AFFORD, A. R. LING, and B. GANGULEY, 1986. Acute computerized tomographic scans: Their value in the localization of lesions and as prognostic indicators in aphasia. *J. Commun. Disorders* 19: 311–345.

PAULESU, E., C. D. FRITH, and R. S. J. FRACKOWIAK, 1993. The neural correlates of the verbal component of working memory. *Nature* 362:342–345.

PENFIELD, W., and L. ROBERTS, 1959. *Speech and Brain Mechanisms.* Princeton, New Jersey: Princeton University Press.

RASMUSSEN, T., and B. MILNER, 1977. The role of early left-brain injury in determining lateralization of cerebral speech functions. *Ann. N.Y. Acad. Sci.* 229:355–369.

SIGNORET, J., P. CASTAIGNE, F. LEHRMITTE, R. ABELANET, and P. LAVOREL, 1984. Rediscovery of Leborgne's brain: Anatomical description with CT scan. *Brain Lang.* 22:303–319.

STROMSWOLD, K., D. CAPLAN, N. ALPERT, and S. RAUCH, 1996. Localization of syntactic comprehension by positron emission tomography. *Brain Lang.* 52:452–473.

WERNICKE, C., 1874. *Der aphasische Symptomencomplex.* Breslau: Kohn and Weigert.

VIII HIGHER COGNITIVE FUNCTIONS

Introduction

STEPHEN M. KOSSLYN AND EDWARD E. SMITH

In this section we consider examples of cognitive abilities that are often characterized as higher brain functions, as distinct from lower brain functions. Functions like those involved in early perception and motor control are considered "lower," while those involved in reasoning and problem solving are considered to be "higher." Lower functions often appear to rest on a relatively small collection of processes. And these processes perform a small number of specific operations, interact in straightforward ways, and operate in the same way over a wide range of different "contents" (specific information). For example, low-level perceptual processes operate the same way whether we see a shoe being tied or watch a movie of a horse stepping on a snake. In contrast, higher functions rely on relatively large numbers of processes, and these processes may themselves have complex internal structures. Moreover, their interactions are rarely straightforward, and their operations can vary for different contents. For example, when reasoning about relative quantities, the strategies we use may depend, in part, on the actual quantities involved. Asked to multiply two single-digit numbers, we may rely on rote memorization; but if asked to multiply two double-digit numbers, we may visualize them, rehearse their names, and use various strategies to keep partial results in mind while proceeding. Higher functions are often organized hierarchically, the more complex ones drawing on collections of more fundamental (and simpler) ones. And these more complex functions may have "emergent" properties–properties that cannot be predicted based on simple interactions among simpler functions.

The characteristics of higher functions imply that such functions will be difficult to understand. In many cases, we may not *fully* understand higher cognitive functions until we understand the more basic lower-level functions that they invoke. Nevertheless, it is erroneous to assume that we cannot begin to understand higher cognitive functions until we have understood simpler, lower-level ones. Cognitive researchers need not sit on their hands, waiting patiently until neuroscientists have worked out the details of low-level processing. This would be like saying that we cannot understand visual cortex until we have understood how the retina operates in detail (an argument actually advanced in the 1950s). There are many reasons to move ahead now, and study how the brain gives rise to cognition: (1) We will never understand *which* elementary processes contribute to cognition unless we study cognition; (2) we will never understand *how* processes interact during cognition unless we study cognition; and (3) we may never understand *all* of the functions of low-level processes unless we study their role in higher cognitive functions. Consider the study of building materials and architecture, for example. We must study the properties of bricks, boards, and so on if we want to understand the details of building construction; but if we don't study architecture, we will never understand why particular buildings are constructed the way they are. Moreover, by studying architecture, we are led to ask about specific properties of the material themselves—why, for instance, steel is necessary in some buildings and what properties of bricks make them useful for defining arches over doorways.

The chapters presented in this section illustrate these points well. Farah reviews evidence that mental imagery draws on processes used in like-modality perception. Farah shows that imagery can be understood in part by considering the roles of specific brain structures in perception and memory. Kosslyn and Thompson extend this general theme, providing a theory of such interactions (and maintaining that imagery actually plays a role in ordinary perception) and arguing that motor processes are invoked in mental imagery. Thus, we see in these two chapters examples of how our understanding of lower-level processes informs our understanding of higher cognitive functions, and also how the study of higher cognitive functions provides insights and hypotheses about the possible roles of lower-level processes. Dehaene takes this theme in a different direction, offering a particularly dramatic example of how low-level processes can contribute to high-level ones—i.e., mathematics. He discusses evidence that a "number line" representation exists in the interparietal sulcus. Apparently, when exercising an abstract ability like arithmetic, we humans invoke spatial representations, much like those involved in some forms of mental imagery. Ivry and Fiez echo the general theme that low-level processes can best

be understood by their roles in high-level functions. They review evidence that the cerebellum, long characterized as the "slave of the cerebral cortex," plays important roles in attention and cognition. They show that the functions of this complex structure can be understood only by considering its possible roles in different aspects of cognition.

The next three chapters shift the substantive focus to categories and concepts, but maintain the emphasis on explaining higher-level functions in terms of lower-level ones. Smith and Jonides review evidence for multiple ways of assigning an object to a category, each method being characterized by the lower-level mechanisms it recruits. As one example, Smith and Jonides provide neuroimaging evidence that rule-based categorization relies extensively on working memory, as witnessed by the activation of working-memory circuitry when subjects categorize novel objects by an explicit rule. The chapters by Martin, Ungerleider, and Haxby and by Caramazza deal with the conceptual knowledge involved in categorization. Using neuroimaging evidence from normal subjects, Martin, Ungerleider, and Haxby suggest that information about an object is represented in the brain as a distributed network of discrete cortical regions. Furthermore, within this cortical network, the features that define an object are stored close to the primary sensory and motor areas that were active when information about the object was acquired. (For example, information about the typical color of an object is stored close to color-perception areas.) Thus the organization of higher-level conceptual knowledge likely parallels the organization of low-level sensory systems—a remarkable example of the proposition that higher-level cortical function is based on lower-level principles. Caramazza's chapter also deals with the cortical representation of conceptual knowledge, although his focus is on studies of category-specific deficits observed in neurological patients (e.g., a selective deficit in knowledge about fruits and vegetables). He reviews the evidence that such deficits can be understood in terms of the distinction between perceptual and functional knowledge; but, finding this evidence wanting in several respects, he proposes alternative models of category-specific deficits. Importantly, some of these alternative models, like the perceptual/functional one, posit that conceptual knowledge can be understood in terms of lower-level features.

The final chapter in this section deals with the highest-level function covered here, namely, decision making. In particular, Tranel, Bechara, and Damasio focus on the interaction between decision making and affect. These authors review a specific hypothesis about this interaction, the somatic marker hypothesis, which proposes that certain structures in prefrontal cortex use associations between aspects of the task and internal affective states to guide decision making. Much of the evidence for the hypothesis comes from studies of impaired decision making by neurological patients with selective damage to key prefrontal areas. Because the affective states involved can be equated with signals from bioregulatory responses, the work again shows the utility of grounding the study of higher-level neural functioning in what is known about lower-level processes.

66 The Neural Bases of Mental Imagery

MARTHA J. FARAH

ABSTRACT The mind's eye was once shunned by psychologists as too subjective, too mentalistic a phenomenon for scientific study. In the 1970s imagery became an active research area, thanks to the concepts and methods of cognitive psychology, and we are now in the process of exploring its neural bases. This chapter reviews research with focally brain-damaged patients and with functional neuroimaging in normal subjects—research aimed at understanding the brain mechanisms underlying mental imagery. The view emerging from these studies is that many of the same modality-specific cortical areas activated by stimuli in visual perception are also activated by higher-order brain regions in imagery, including spatially mapped regions of occipital cortex. There is also evidence for a distinct image generation mechanism, required for the top-down generation of images from memory but not for bottom-up perception.

What color are the stars on the American flag? To answer this question, very likely you called up a mental image of the flag in your "mind's eye," and "saw" that the stars are white. The mind's eye was once dismissed by psychologists as too subjective, too mentalistic a phenomenon for scientific study (cf. Skinner, 1978), but the development of the information-processing framework within cognitive psychology made mental imagery scientifically tractable. Early pioneers of imagery research devised many elegant and ingenious experimental paradigms to demonstrate the distinction between imagery and verbal thought, and to characterize imagery in objective information-processing terms (e.g., Kosslyn, 1980; Paivio, 1971; Shepard, 1978). Two schools of thought concerning imagery developed, giving rise to the so-called imagery debate.

The imagery debate

Starting in the late 1970s, two related issues concerning imagery emerged. (1) Does mental imagery involve some of the same representations normally used during visual perception, or does imagery involve only more abstract, post-perceptual representations? (For a more explicit discussion, cf. Finke, 1980; Shepard, 1978.) (2) Do mental images have a spatial, or array-like, format,

MARTHA J. FARAH Department of Psychology, University of Pennsylvania, Philadelphia, Pa.

or are they propositional (symbolic or language-like) in format? Much of Kosslyn's research was aimed at addressing this issue (cf. Kosslyn, 1980). The two issues are, in principle, independent, although given the fact that much of visual representation is array-like (e.g., Maunsell and Newsome, 1987), they are closely related.

Despite their straightforward, empirical nature, these issues proved difficult to settle using the experimental methods of cognitive psychology. Consider the classic image scanning experiments of Kosslyn (e.g., Kosslyn, Ball, and Reiser, 1978) for example. Kosslyn and associates instructed subjects to focus their attention on one part of an image, then move it continuously, as quickly as possible, to some other part of the image. They found that the time taken to scan between the two locations was directly proportional to their metric separation, just as if subjects were scanning across a perceived stimulus. This finding follows naturally from the view that images share representations with visual percepts, and that these representations have a spatial format. However, not all psychologists agreed with this interpretation. Various types of alternative explanations were proposed— explanations that accounted for the scanning findings (and many others) without hypothesizing shared representations for imagery and perception or a spatial format for imagery. These alternative explanations are discussed in detail by Farah (1988) as motivation for turning to neuropsychological evidence. Two examples are mentioned briefly here.

Pylyshyn (1981) suggested that subjects in imagery experiments take their task to be simulating the use of visual-spatial representations; hence, with their tacit knowledge of the functioning of their visual system, subjects are able to perform this simulation using nonvisual representations. Intons-Peterson (1983) suggested that subjects in imagery experiments may be responding to experimenters' expectations; in fact, she has shown that at least certain aspects of the data in imagery experiments can be shaped by the experimenters' preconceptions. Perhaps less plausible than the hypothesis that images are modality-specific visual representations and hence intrinsically spatial in format, these accounts have proved difficult to rule out. In fact, Anderson (1978) has argued that no behavioral data (i.e., sets of stimulus inputs paired with subjects' responses to those stimuli and the latencies of the responses) can ever distinguish alternative, nonvisual, theories of imagery from the visual-spatial theories.

One way out of this impasse is to turn to neuropsychological data, which are immune to many of the alternative explanations that plague the behavioral data (Farah, 1988). The methods of cognitive neuroscience, including lesion studies and functional neuroimaging studies, have the potential to be more decisive on the imagery debate because they provide more direct evidence on the internal processing stages intervening between stimulus and response in imagery experiments.

The brain bases of mental images: Modality-specificity and format

The studies relevant to the two issues of the imagery debate—are images visual, and do they have a spatial format?—include studies of brain-damaged subjects as well as measures of regional brain activity in normal subjects.

STUDIES OF BRAIN-DAMAGED PATIENTS If forming a mental image consists of activating cortical visual representations, then patients with selective impairments of visual perception should manifest corresponding impairments in mental imagery. This is often the case. For example, DeRenzi and Spinnler (1967) investigated various color-related abilities in a large group of unilaterally brain-damaged patients. They found an association between impairment on color vision tasks, such as the Ishihara test of color blindness, and on color imagery tasks, such as verbally reporting the colors of common objects from memory. Beauvois and Saillant (1985) studied the imagery abilities of a patient with a visual-verbal disconnection syndrome. The patient could perform purely visual color tasks (e.g., matching color samples) and purely verbal color tasks (e.g., answering questions such as "What color is associated with envy?"), but could not perform tasks in which a visual representation of color had to be associated with a verbal label (e.g., color naming). When the patient's color imagery was tested purely visually, she did well, easily selecting the color sample that represented the color of an object depicted in black-and-white,. However, when the equivalent problems were posed verbally (e.g., "What color is a peach?"), she did poorly. In other words, mental images interacted with other visual and verbal task components as if they were visual representations. De Vreese (1991) reported two cases of color imagery impairment: One patient had left occipital damage and displayed the same type of visual-verbal disconnection as the patient just described, and the other had bilateral occipital dam-

age and displayed parallel color perception and color imagery impairments.

In another early study documenting the relations between imagery and perception, Bisiach and Luzzatti (1978) found that patients with hemispatial neglect for visual stimuli also neglected the contralesional sides of their mental images. Their two right-parietal–damaged patients were asked to imagine a well-known square in Milan, as shown in figure 66.1. When they were asked to describe the scene from vantage point A in the figure, they tended to name more landmarks on the east side of the square (each marked with a lowercase a in figure 66.1); that is, they named the landmarks on the right side of the imagined scene. When they were asked to imagine the square from the opposite vantage point, marked B on the map, they reported many of the landmarks previously omitted (because these were now on the right side of the image) and omitted some of those previously reported.

Levine, Warach, and Farah (1985) studied the roles of the "two cortical visual systems" (Ungerleider and Mishkin, 1982) in mental imagery, with a pair of patients. Case 1 had visual disorientation following bilateral parieto-occipital damage, and case 2 had visual agnosia following bilateral inferior temporal damage. We found that the preserved and impaired aspects of visual imagery paralleled the patients' visual abilities: Case 1 could neither localize visual stimuli in space nor accurately describe the locations of familiar objects or landmarks from memory. However, he was good at both perceiving object identity from appearance and describing object appearance from memory. Case 2 was impaired at perceiving object identity from appearance and describing object appearance from memory, but was good at localizing visual stimuli and at describing their locations from memory.

Farah and associates (1988) carried out more detailed testing on the second patient. We adapted a large set of experimental paradigms from the cognitive psychology literature—paradigms that had been used to argue either for the visual nature of imagery (the "picture-in-the-head" imagery) or for its more abstract spatial nature. Our contention was that both forms of mental imagery exist, contrary to much of the research in cognitive psychology aimed at deciding which of the two characterizations was correct. On the basis of the previous study, we conjectured that the patient with the damaged ventral temporo-occipital system would fail cognitive psychology's so-called visual imagery tasks but would have no problem with so-called spatial imagery tasks owing to his intact dorsal parieto-occipital system.

The visual imagery tasks included imagining animals and reporting whether they had long or short tails,

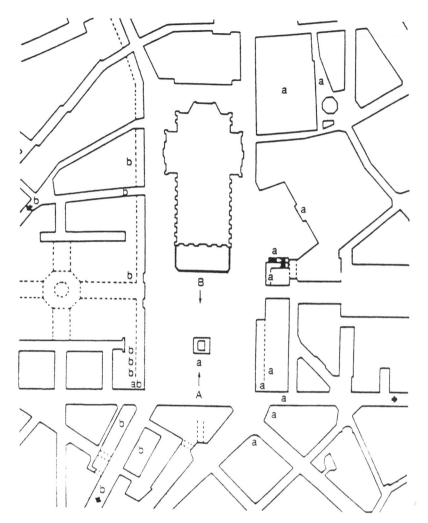

FIGURE 66.1   Map of the Piazza del Duomo in Milan. A and B are the two positions from which patients were asked to imagine viewing the piazza; a and b are the respective landmarks the patients recalled from each imagined position.

imagining common objects and reporting their colors, and imagining triads of states within the U.S.A. and reporting which two are most similar in outline shape. The spatial imagery tasks included such mental image transformations as mental rotation, scanning and size scaling, and imagining triads of shapes and reporting which two are closest to one another. The patient was impaired relative to control subjects at the visual-pattern-color imagery tasks, but entirely normal at the spatial imagery tasks.

Although the foregoing studies implicate modality-specific visual representations in imagery, they are either ambiguous as to the level of visual representation involved, or they implicate relatively high-level representation in the temporal and parietal lobes. In a recent study, Farah, Soso, and Dasheiff (1992) examined the role of the occipital lobe in mental imagery. If mental imagery consists of activating relatively early representa-

tions in the visual system, at the level of the occipital lobe, then it should be impossible to form images in regions of the visual field that are blind owing to occipital lobe destruction. This predicts that patients with homonymous hemianopia should have a smaller maximum image size, or visual angle of the mind's eye. The maximum image size can be estimated using a method developed by Kosslyn (1978): Subjects are asked to imagine walking toward objects of different sizes and report the distance at which the image just fills their mind's eye's visual field and is about to "overflow." The trigonometric relation between the distance, object size, and visual angle can then be used to solve for the visual angle.

We were fortunate to encounter a very high-functioning, educated young woman who could perform the rather demanding task of introspecting on the distance of imagined objects at overflow. In addition, she could serve as her own control because she was about to

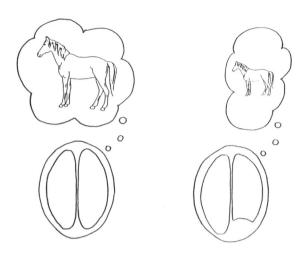

"I can get to within 15 feet
of the horse in my imagination
before it starts to overflow"

"The horse starts to overflow
at an imagined distance of
about 35 feet"

FIGURE 66.2   The effects of occipital lobectomy on the maximal mental image size of case MGS.

undergo unilateral occipital lobe resection for treatment of epilepsy. We found that the size of her biggest possible image was reduced after surgery, as represented in figure 66.2. Furthermore, by measuring maximal image size in the vertical and horizontal dimensions separately, we found that only the horizontal dimension of her imagery field was significantly reduced. These results provide strong evidence for the use of occipital visual representations during imagery.

The results from brain-damaged patients are generally consistent with the hypothesis that mental imagery involves representations within the visual system proper, including relatively early representations in the occipital lobe known to be spatial in format. But there are discrepant findings, as well. Goldenberg, Mulbacher, and Nowack (1995) described a case of cortical blindness following bilateral occipital lobe lesions; the patient performed well on some, but not all, imagery tasks, suggesting that occipital cortex may not be necessary for mental imagery. This patient did, however, retain some small islands of intact occipital cortex, and eventually recovered vision in the sectors of the visual field corresponding to the preserved cortex. Thus it is possible that this occipital cortex was also subserving her mental imagery.

More clear-cut cases of perceptual impairment with preserved imagery involve patients with agnosia. An apperceptive agnosic patient has been found to perform well on imagery tasks despite a perceptual impairment so severe that the patient could not reliably distinguish squares and circles (Servos and Goodale, 1995). Behrmann, Moscovitch, and Winocur (1994) and Bartolomeo

and colleagues (1998) describe associative agnosic patients who demonstrate good visual mental imagery abilities.

On the face of things, these observations conflict with the hypothesis that imagery and visual perception share representations. Of course, if we accept the alternative hypothesis—that imagery does not share representations with perception—the evidence of parallel impairments in imagery and perception is equally confounding. Is there some way to accommodate both the associations and the dissociations between imagery and perception?

One possibility is that there are general visual representations common to imagery and perception, in which case damage would generate associated impairments and disconnection from afferent perceptual inputs would generate the dissociations occasionally observed. In the light of this possibility, it is interesting that the MRI of the agnosic studied by Bartolomeo and associates (1998) shows predominantly white matter damage, undercutting intact visual association cortex (see their figure 1). A related possibility concerns damage to relatively early levels of cortical visual processing. Assume the damaged representations are among those shared by imagery and perception, not purely perceptual afferents, and consider the impact of interrupting processing at this stage: When the flow of processing is bottom-up or afferent, as in perception, the impact will be large because the majority of visual representations cannot be accessed. In contrast, when the flow of processing is top-down or efferent, as in imagery, the impact will be smaller because just a minority of the representations normally activated in imagery are unavailable. This possibility seems relevant in cases with evidence of early damage, such as apperceptive agnosia or the associative agnosic of Behrmann, Moscovitch, and Winocur (1994), whose perceptual impairment was evident on such low-level visual tasks as segmenting overlapping figures. A final possibility, which may interact with the previous one, concerns individual differences in imagery ability. Given that people differ in how fully they engage their early visual representations when generating mental images (see Farah and Peronnet, 1989), some people's mental imagery ability may be more susceptible to early visual system damage than others. The same hypothetical lesion in visual association cortex might interfere with one person's imagery, whereas an individual whose imagery was confined to higher levels of association cortex might be unaffected.

To conclude, in most (but not all) cases of selective visual impairments following damage to the cortical visual system, patients manifest qualitatively similar impairments in mental imagery and perception. Spatial attention impairments for the left side of the visual scene also affect the left side of mental images. Central impairments of color perception tend to co-occur with impairments of color imagery. Higher-order impairments of visual spatial orientation sparing visual object recognition (and the converse) are associated with impairments of spatial imagery sparing imagery for object appearance (and the converse). Finally, hemianopia resulting from surgical removal of one occipital lobe is associated with a corresponding loss of half the mind's eye's visual field.

Two conclusions follow from these findings. First, at least some modality-specific cortical representations perform "double duty," supporting both imagery and perception. Second, those representations are functioning in analogous ways, specialized for the same kinds of visual or spatial information in both perception and imagery. Let us now turn to a different source of evidence on the relation between imagery and perception.

BRAIN IMAGING STUDIES IN NORMAL SUBJECTS
Starting in the mid-1980s, regional brain activity during mental imagery has been monitored in normal subjects using a variety of techniques. The earliest work in this vein was done with single photon emission computed tomography (SPECT). Roland and Friberg (1985) examined patterns of regional blood flow while subjects performed three different cognitive tasks, one of which was to visualize a walk through a familiar neighborhood, making alternate left and right turns. In this task (unlike the other tasks) blood flow indicated activation of the posterior regions of the brain, including visual cortices of the parietal and temporal lobes. These results are therefore consistent with the general hypothesis that mental imagery is a function of visual cortical areas. But they failed to support the more specific hypothesis of early, occipital involvement, due, at least partly, to incomplete monitoring of occipital cortex in this study.

Goldenberg and his colleagues (e.g., Goldenberg et al., 1987, 1989a,b, 1991, 1992) performed a series of blood flow studies of mental imagery using SPECT. Using very elegant experimental designs, they inferred which brain areas were activated by mental imagery. In these experiments, imagery tasks were closely matched with control tasks involving many of the same processing demands except for the mental imagery per se. Thus, for example, one imagery task was the memorization of word lists using an imagery mnemonic while its control task was memorization without imagery (Goldenberg et al., 1987). Another task involved answering questions of equal difficulty, which either did (e.g., "What is darker green, grass or a pine tree?") or did not (e.g., "Is the Categorical Imperative an ancient grammatical form?") require mental imagery (Goldenberg et

al., 1989a). In all of these studies, visual imagery was found to be associated with occipital and temporal activation. It is possible that the greater parietal involvement observed by Roland and colleagues (Roland and Friberg, 1985; Roland et al., 1987) is related to the need to represent spatial aspects of the environment in their mental walk task [cf. the findings of Farah and colleagues (1988) on dissociable visual and spatial mental imagery].

A study by Charlot and co-workers (1992) used SPECT while subjects generated and scanned images in the classic cognitive psychology image scanning paradigm developed by Kosslyn's group (1978). These authors also found activation of visual association cortex, including occipital cortex.

In general, the findings with SPECT are consistent with those of work with patients, showing visual cortical activity associated with mental imagery. Of greatest interest, perhaps, is the pronounced and consistent activation of occipital cortex observed in these studies. This suggests that imagery involves spatially mapped visual representations.

Event-related potentials (ERPs) have also been used to address the question of whether visual mental imagery has a visual locus in the brain. In one study, Farah and colleagues (1988) used ERPs to map out, in space and in time, the interaction between mental imagery and concurrent visual perception. We found that imagery affected the ERP to a visual stimulus early in stimulus processing—within the first 200 ms. This implies that imagery involves visual cortical regions that are normally activated in early visual perception. The visual ERP component that is synchronized with the effect of imagery, the N1, is believed to originate in areas 18 and 19, implying a relatively early extrastriate locus for imagery in the visual system. Interpolated maps of the scalp-recorded ERPs were also consistent with this conclusion.

A second series of studies (Farah et al., 1989) took a very different approach to localizing imagery in the brain using ERP methods. Rather than observing the interaction between imagery and concurrent perception, we simply asked subjects to generate a mental image from memory, in response to a visually presented word. By subtracting the ERP to the same words when no imagery instructions were given from the ERP when subjects were imaging, we obtained a relatively pure measure of the brain electrical activity that is synchronized with the generation of a mental image. Again, we constructed maps of the scalp distribution of the ERP imagery effect in order to determine whether the maxima lay over modality-specific visual perceptual areas. Despite the very different experimental paradigm, we found a highly similar scalp distribution to the previous experiment, clearly implicating visual areas. When the experiment was repeated using auditory word presentation, the same visual scalp topography was obtained. Control experiments showed that the imagery effects in these experiments were not due to the cognitive effort expended by subjects when imaging (as opposed to imagery per se), or to eye movements.

Farah and Peronnet (1989) reported two studies in which subjects who rated their imagery as relatively vivid showed a larger occipital ERP imagery effect when generating images than subjects who claimed to be relatively poor imagers. This result, which we then replicated under slightly different conditions, suggests that some people are more able to efferently activate their visual systems than others, and that such people experience especially vivid imagery.

A different study (Uhl et al., 1990) used scalp-recorded DC shifts to localize brain activity during imagery for colors, faces, and maps. Following transient positive deflections of the kind observed by Farah's group (1989), a sustained negative shift was observed over occipital, parietal, and temporal regions of the scalp. Consistent with the different roles of the two cortical visual systems, the effect was maximal over parietal regions during map imagery, and maximal over occipital and temporal regions during face and color imagery.

With the advent of PET, the spatial localization of cognitive neuroimaging improved greatly, and researchers soon applied this technique to experiments on imagery. In an early study, Roland and co-workers (1987) repeated their mental walk task with PET, again finding only higher-order visual association cortices activated. In subsequent years, Roland and colleagues conducted a number of simple experiments intended to map the neural substrates of imagery, without observing reliable occipital activation (Roland and Gulyas, 1994).

Kosslyn and colleagues (1993) also used PET to localize imagery, obtaining results more consistent with the data from focally lesioned patients (cf. Farah et al., 1992) and the preponderance of neuroimaging studies so far reviewed. In the first two of their experiments, subjects viewed grids in which block letters were either present or to be imagined, and judged whether an X occupying one cell of the grid fell on or off the letter. Comparisons between imagery and relevant baseline conditions showed activation of many brain areas, including occipital visual cortex. In a third experiment, subjects generated either large or small images of letters of the alphabet with eyes closed; then the researchers directly compared the two imagery conditions. They found that the large images activated relatively more anterior parts of visual cortex than the small ones, consistent with the known mapping of the visual field onto primary visual cortex. A later study (Kosslyn et al., 1995) also found that occipital patterns of activation varied according to image size in a way that is consistent with the anatomy of primary visual cortex. Other PET studies of imagery have agreed with these studies insofar as occipital cortex was activated, but have disagreed as to whether primary visual cortex is involved (e.g., Mellet et al., 1995, 1996).

Recently, functional magnetic resonance imaging (fMRI) has allowed researchers to obtain blood flow–based images of function with good temporal as well as spatial resolution. The earliest study to exploit these qualities for the study of mental imagery (Le Bihan et al., 1993) measured brain activity in primary visual cortex as subjects alternately viewed flashing patterns and imagined them. The results for one subject, as shown in figure 66.3, provide a striking demonstration of the involvement of primary visual cortex in mental imagery as well as in perception.

D'Esposito and colleagues (1997) measured regional activity throughout the brain with fMRI while subjects performed the image generation task of Farah and co-workers (1989): either passively listening to words or generating mental images of the words' referents. We found temporo-occipital activation, extending further into occipital cortex for some subjects than for others, but in no case reaching primary visual cortex.

Perhaps not surprisingly, there are differences in the conclusions that can be drawn from the studies reviewed here, which varied in their imaging techniques and cognitive tasks. Nevertheless, some generalizations can be made. In almost every study, mental imagery activates modality-specific visual cortical areas, including spatially mapped regions of occipital association cortex.

THE IMAGERY DEBATE REVISITED In Anderson's (1978) discussion of the intrinsic ambiguities of behavioral data for resolving the imagery debate, he suggested that physiological data might someday provide a decisive answer. Just two decades later, that day may have arrived. There is much more to find out and some current conclusions doubtless need revision; nevertheless, we can point to a body of converging evidence that supports the modality-specific visual nature of mental images, suggesting that at least some of their neural substrates have a spatial representational format. That is, damage to visual areas representing such specialized stimulus properties as color, location, and form results in the loss of these properties in mental imagery. Spatially delimited impairments of visual attention and of visual representation are accompanied by corresponding impairments in imagery. Psychophysiological studies using blood flow imaging methods and ERPs

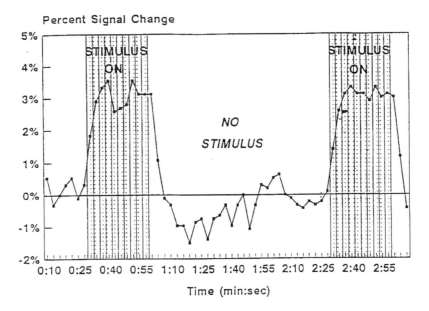

Percent Signal Change

Time (min:sec)

→ Visual Striate Cortex

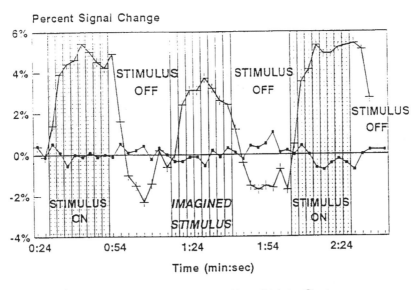

Percent Signal Change

Time (min:sec)

+ Visual Striate Cortex → Non Striate Cortex

FIGURE 66.3 Plot of activity over time in primary visual cortex measured by MRI, as a function of the subject's activity. Upper panel: The subject was resting between two real visual stimuli. Lower panel: The subject imagined the stimuli between actual stimulus presentations.

have operationalized imagery in a wide variety of ways; these include instructions to take a mental walk, imagery mnemonics, general knowledge questions about the appearances of familiar objects, the effect of imagery on concurrent perception, instructions to image common objects, self-reported individual differences in vividness of imagery, and judgments about imagined letters of the alphabet. Across all of these superficially different tasks, indices of regional brain activity implicate modality-specific visual cortex in mental imagery.

Image generation

During visual perception, the stimulus initiates a cascade of processing. Beginning at the retina, this processing passes through various intermediate representations in the LGN and occipital cortex that roughly preserve the spatial mapping of the retina, then culminates with relatively abstract representations of object appearance and location in temporal and parietal cortices. The evidence just reviewed suggests that, during imagery, the direction of information flow is reversed, and some of the intermediate, spatially mapped, representations are reactivated by higher-level mechanisms rather than by a stimulus. The process of activating visual representations top-down rather than bottom-up is known as image generation.

An important difference between perception and imagery concerns the automaticity of the processes involved. One cannot see a familiar object and fail to recognize it. But one can think about familiar objects without inexorably calling to mind a visual mental image. This suggests that the activation of spatially mapped visual cortical regions from memory requires the intervention of a separate, attention-demanding process, needed for image generation but not for visual perception and object recognition.

Farah (1984) reviewed the neurological literature on imagery impairments and identified a set of cases in which perception was grossly intact. In subsequent years, a small number of additional cases of selectively impaired imagery have been reported (e.g., Farah, Levine, and Calvanio, 1988; Goldenberg, 1992; Grossi, Orsini, and Modafferi, 1986; Riddoch, 1990), as well as similar but weaker dissociations in subgroups of patients in group studies (Bowers et al., 1991; Goldenberg, 1989; Goldenberg and Artner, 1991; Stangalino, Semenza, and Mondini, 1995). On the face of things, the preservation of perceptual abilities in the context of impaired imagery is consistent with the existence of a distinct image generation process.

Goldenberg and Artner (1991) propose an alternative possibility—that image generation requires higher-quality visual representations than normal perception—and show that patients with an apparent image generation deficit perform poorly on subtle visual discriminations (e.g., between a bear with pointy ears and a bear with rounded ears). At a very general level, one can view these alternatives as mutually compatible. Image generation may be just the additional visual processing that is needed for difficult perceptual tasks when, for example, one forms a search image or, in the case of the study at hand, visualizes a bear from memory to check its ears.

The localization of mental image generation has been a controversial topic. Although mental imagery was for many years assumed to be a function of the right hemisphere, Ehrlichman and Barrett (1983) pointed out that there was no direct evidence for this assumption. Farah (1984) noted a trend in the cases she reviewed for left posterior damage. Later, she suggested that the left temporo-occipital area may be critical (Farah et al., 1988). The recent focally damaged cases mentioned above (Farah et al., 1988; Goldenberg, 1992; Grossi, Orsini, and Modafferi, 1986; Riddoch, 1990) have supported this suggestion, as have the group studies to varying degrees (most clearly Goldenberg and Artner, 1991; Stangalino, Semenza, and Mondini, 1995). The rarity of cases of image generation deficit suggests that this function may not be strongly lateralized in most people; however, when impairments are observed after focal unilateral damage, the left or dominant hemisphere is implicated.

This conclusion is supported by the majority of neuroimaging studies, although exceptions exist. Interested readers may consult my review article (Farah, 1995) on image generation for the neuroimaging evidence as of the mid-1990s concerning the role of left temporo-occipital cortex in image generation (see also D'Esposito et al., 1997).

Conclusions

What neural events underlie the generation of a visual mental image? Over the past fifteen years a variety of cognitive neuroscience methods have been brought to bear on this question, and a reasonably consistent answer seems to be emerging. Mental imagery is believed to be the efferent, or top-down, activation of some subset of the brain's visual areas. In other words, at least some of our cortical visual areas are used both for imagery and perception. Furthermore, these areas subserve the same types of representational functions in both cases, carrying information specifically about color, shape, spatial location, and so on.

Some of the visual areas implicated in imagery, by both lesion and imaging studies, are known to be spatially mapped. This finding provides evidence for the spatial nature of image representation, in contrast to the view that imagery is a propositional, or language-like, mode of representation. Finally, the existence of a distinct mechanism for image generation, one separate from the processes needed for normal bottom-up perception, is supported by dissociations between imagery and perception in brain-damaged patients. The evidence from patients strongly implicates a left temporo-occipital localization for this process; neuroimaging data are mixed, but generally support this conclusion.

ACKNOWLEDGMENTS The writing of this chapter was supported by NIH grants R01-NS34030, R01-AG14082, and K02-AG0056.

REFERENCES

ANDERSON, J. R., 1978. Arguments concerning representation for mental imagery. *Psychol. Rev.* 85:249–277.

BARTOLOMEO, P., A. C. BACHOUD-LEVI, B. DE GELDER, G. DENES, G. DALLA BARBA, P. BRUGIERES, and J. D. DEGOS, 1998. Multiple-domain dissociation between impaired visual perception and preserved mental imagery in a patient with bilateral extrastriate lesions. *Neuropsychologia* 36:239–249.

BARTOLOMEO, P., P. D'ERME, and G. GAINOTTI, 1994. The relationship between visuospatial and representational neglect. *Neurology* 44:1710–1714.

BEAUVOIS, M. F., and B. SAILLANT, 1985. Optic aphasia for colours and colour agnosia: A distinction between visual and visuo-verbal impairments in the processing of colours. *Cogn. Neuropsychol.* 2:1–48.

BEHRMANN, M., M. MOSCOVITCH, and G. WINOCUR, 1994. Intact visual imagery and impaired visual perception in a patient with visual agnosia. *J. Exp. Psychol.: Human Percept. Perform.* 30:1068–1087.

BISIACH, E., and C. LUZZATTI, 1978. Unilateral neglect of representational space. *Cortex* 14:129–133.

BOWERS, D., L. X. BLONDER, T. FEINBERG, and K. M. HEILMAN, 1991. Differential impact of right and left hemisphere lesions on facial emotion and object imagery. *Brain* 114:2593–2609.

CHARLOT, V., N. TZOURIO, M. ZILBOVICIUS, B. MAZOYER, and M. DENIS, 1992. Different mental imagery abilities result in different regional cerebral blood flow activation patterns during cognitive tasks. *Neuropsychologia* 30:565–580.

D'ESPOSITO, M., J. A. DETRE, G. K. AGUIRRE, M. STALLCUP, D. C. ALSOP, L. J. TIPPET, and M. J. FARAH, 1997. A functional MRI study of mental image generation. *Neuropsychologia* 35:725–730.

DERENZI, E., and H. SPINNLER, 1967. Impaired performance on color tasks in patients with hemispheric lesions. *Cortex* 3:194–217.

DE VREESE, L. P., 1991. Two systems for colour-naming defects: Verbal disconnection vs. colour imagery disorder. *Neuropsychologia* 29:1–18.

EHRLICHMAN, H., and J. BARRETT, 1983. Right hemisphere specialization for mental imagery: A review of the evidence. *Brain Cognit.* 2:39–52.

FARAH, M. J., 1984. The neurological basis of mental imagery: A componential analysis. *Cognition* 18:245–272.

FARAH, M. J., 1988. Is visual imagery really visual? Overlooked evidence from neuropsychology. *Psychol. Rev.* 95:307–317.

FARAH, M. J., 1995. Current issues in the neuropsychology of mental image generation. *Neuropsychologia* 33:1445–1471.

FARAH, M. J., K. L. HAMMOND, D. N. LEVINE, and R. CALVANIO, 1988. Visual and spatial mental imagery: Dissociable systems of representation. *Cogn. Psychol.* 20:439–462.

FARAH, M. J., D. N. LEVINE, and R. CALVANIO, 1988. A case study of mental imagery deficit. *Brain Cognit.* 8:147–164.

FARAH, M. J., and F. PERONNET, 1989. Event-related potentials in the study of mental imagery. *J. Psychophysiol.* 3:99–109.

FARAH, M. J., F. PERONNET, M. A. GONON, and M. H. GIARD, 1988. Electrophysiological evidence for a shared representational medium for visual images and percepts. *J. Exp. Psychol.* 117:248–257.

FARAH, M. J., F. PERONNET, L. L. WEISBERG, and M. A. MONHEIT, 1989. Brain activity underlying mental imagery: Event-related potentials during image generation. *J. Cogn. Neurosci.* 1:302–316.

FARAH, M. J., M. J. SOSO, and R. M. DASHEIFF, 1992. The visual angle of the mind's eye before and after unilateral occipital lobectomy. *J. Exp. Psychol.: Human Percept. Perform.* 18:241–246.

FINKE, R. A., 1980. Levels of equivalence in imagery and perception. *Psychol. Rev.* 87:113–132.

GOLDENBERG, G., 1989. The ability of patients with brain damage to generate mental visual images. *Brain* 112:305–325.

GOLDENBERG, G., 1992. Loss of visual imagery and loss of visual knowledge–A case study. *Neuropsychologia* 30:1081–1099.

GOLDENBERG, G., and C. ARTNER, 1991. Visual imagery and knowledge about the visual appearance of objects in patients with posterior cerebral artery lesions. *Brain Cognit.* 15:160–186.

GOLDENBERG, G., W. MULBACHER, and A. NOWACK, 1995. Imagery without perception–A case study of anosognosia for cortical blindness. *Neuropsychologia* 33:1373–1382.

GOLDENBERG, G., I. PODREKA, M. STEINER, P. FRANZEN, and L. DEECKE, 1991. Contributions of occipital and temporal brain regions to visual and acoustic imagery–A spect study. *Neuropsychologia* 29:695–702.

GOLDENBERG, G., I. PODREKA, M. STEINER, and K. WILLMES, 1987. Patterns of regional cerebral blood flow related to memorizing of high and low imagery words: An emission computer tomography study. *Neuropsychologia* 25:473–486.

GOLDENBERG, G., I. PODREKA, M. STEINER, K. WILLMES, E. SUESS, and L. DEECKE, 1989a. Regional cerebral blood flow patterns in visual imagery. *Neuropsychologia* 27:641–664.

GOLDENBERG, G., I. PODREKA, F. UHL, M. STEINER, K. WILLMES, and L. DEECKE, 1989b. Cerebral correlates of imagining colours, faces and a map–I. Spect of regional cerebral blood flow. *Neuropsychologia* 27:1315–1328.

GOLDENBERG, G., M. STEINER, I. PODREKA, and L. DEECKE, 1992. Regional cerebral blood flow patterns related to verification of low- and high-imagery sentences. *Neuropsychologia* 30:581–586.

GROSSI, D., A. ORSINI, and A. MODAFFERI, 1986. Visuoimaginal constructional apraxia: On a case of selective deficit of imagery. *Brain Cognit.* 5:255–267.

INTONS-PETERSON, M. J., 1983. Imagery paradigms: How vulnerable are they to experimenters' expectations? *J. Exp. Psychol.: Human Percept. Perform.* 9:394–412.

KOSSLYN, S. M., 1978. Measuring the visual angle of the mind's eye. *Cogn. Psychol.* 10:356–389.

KOSSLYN, S. M., 1980. *Image and Mind.* Cambridge, Mass.: Harvard University Press.

KOSSLYN, S. M., N. M. ALPERT, W. L. THOMPSON, V. MALJKOVIC, S. WEISE, C. CHABRIS, S. E. HAMILTON, S. L. RAUCH, and F. S. BUONANNO, 1993. Visual mental imagery activates topographically organized visual cortex: PET investigations. *J. Cogn. Neurosci.* 5:263–287.

KOSSLYN, S. M., T. M. BALL, and B. J. REISER, 1978. Visual images preserve metric spatial information: Evidence from studies of image scanning. *J. Exp. Psychol.: Human Percept. Perform.* 4:47–60.

KOSSLYN, S. M., W. L. THOMPSON, I. J. KIM, and N. M. ALPERT, 1995. Topographical representations of mental images in primary visual cortex. *Nature* 378:496–498.

LE BIHAN, D., R. TURNER, T. A. ZEFFIRO, C. A. CUENOD, P. JEZZARD, and V. BONNEROT, 1993. Activation of human primary visual cortex during visual recall: A magnetic resonance imaging study. *Proc. Natl. Acad. Sci.* 90:11802–11805.

LEVINE, D. N., J. WARACH, and M. J. FARAH, 1985. Two visual systems in mental imagery: Dissociation of 'What' and 'Where' in imagery disorders due to bilateral posterior cerebral lesions. *Neurology* 35:1010–1018.

MAUNSELL, J. H. R., and W. T. NEWSOME, 1987. Visual processing in monkey extrastriate cortex. *Annu. Rev. Neurosci.* 10:363–401.

MELLET, E., N. TZOURIO, F. CRIVELLO, M. JOLIOT, M. DENIS, and B. MAZOYER, 1996. Functional anatomy of spatial mental imagery generated from verbal instructions. *J. Neurosci.* 16:6504–6512.

MELLET, E., M. TZOURIO, M. DENIS, and B. MAZOYER, 1995. A Positron Emission Topography study of visual and mental spatial exploration. *J. Cogn. Neurosci.* 7:433–445.

PAIVIO, A., 1971. *Imagery and Verbal Processes.* New York: Holt, Rinehart, and Winston.

PYLYSHYN, Z. W., 1981. The imagery debate: Analogue media versus tacit knowledge. *Psychol. Rev.* 88:16–45.

RIDDOCH, M. J., 1990. Loss of visual imagery: A generation deficit. *Cogn. Neuropsychol.* 7:249–273.

ROLAND, P. E., L. ERIKSSON, A. STONE-ELANDER, and L. WIDEN, 1987. Does mental activity change the oxidative metabolism of the brain? *J. Neurosci.* 7:2373–2389.

ROLAND, P. E., and L. FRIBERG, 1985. Localization of cortical areas activated by thinking. *J. Neurophysiol.* 53:1219–1243.

ROLAND, P. E., and B. GULYAS, 1994. Visual imagery and visual representation. *Trends Neurosci.* 17:281–287; discussion 294–297.

SERVOS, P., and M. A. GOODALE, 1995. Preserved visual imagery in visual form agnosia. *Neuropsychologia* 33:1383–1394.

SHEPARD, R. N., 1978. The mental image. *Amer. Psychologist* 33:125–137.

SKINNER, B. F., 1978. Why I am not a cognitive psychologist. In *Reflections on Behaviorism and Society*, Englewood Cliffs, N.J.: Prentice Hall.

STANGALINO, C., C. SEMENZA, and S. MONDINI, 1995. Generating visual mental images: Deficit after brain damage. *Neuropsychologia* 33:1473–1483.

UHL, F., G. GOLDENBERG, W. LANG, G. LINDINGER, M. STEINER, and L. DEECKE, 1990. Cerebral correlates of imagining colours, faces and a map–II. Negative cortical DC potentials. *Neuropsychologia* 28:81–93.

UNGERLEIDER, L. G., and M. MISHKIN, 1982. Two cortical visual systems. In *Analysis of Visual Behavior*, D. J. Ingle, M. A. Goodale, and R. J. W. Mansfield, eds. Cambridge, Mass.: MIT Press.

67 Shared Mechanisms in Visual Imagery and Visual Perception: Insights from Cognitive Neuroscience

STEPHEN M. KOSSLYN AND WILLIAM L. THOMPSON

ABSTRACT   A confluence of behavioral, lesion-deficit, and neuroimaging data has shown that visual mental imagery and visual perception rely on some common brain mechanisms. However, other data show that the two do not recruit identical systems. In this chapter we characterize the information-processing roles of the mechanisms shared by visual imagery and perception. Then we use the theory to examine apparent disparities and inconsistencies in the neuroimaging literature and to consider different ways in which visual mental images can arise.

Mental imagery has long been thought to share mechanisms with like-modality perception. If so, we can take advantage of the rich literature on perception when theorizing about mental imagery. In fact, three classes of findings indicate that the two functions draw on some of the same mechanisms (for reviews, see Craver-Lemley and Reeves, 1987, 1992; Farah, 1988; Finke, 1989; Kosslyn, 1994; Shepard and Cooper, 1982). One class of findings has focused on behavioral phenomena. For example, following long tradition (e.g., Perky, 1910; Segal and Fusella, 1970), Craver-Lemley and Reeves (1987) demonstrated that visual perceptual acuity may be diminished when subjects visualize a pattern that overlaps with a perceptual stimulus. In addition, Finke, Johnson, and Shyi (1988), Intraub and Hoffman (1992), and Johnson and Raye (1981) showed that subjects may not be able to distinguish clearly between actually perceiving a stimulus versus simply "seeing" it in imagination. Moreover, Demarais and Cohen (in press) showed that people make more horizontal than vertical eye movements when "inspecting" a horizontal array in an image, but more vertical than horizontal eye movements when inspecting a vertical array in an image. A second class of findings includes many reports that brain damage causes parallel impairments in imagery and perception. For instance, patients whose unilateral visual neglect causes them to ignore half of perceptual space also ignore that same half of "representational space" during imagery (Bisiach and Luzzatti, 1978); and the inability of some brain-damaged patients to recognize faces is accompanied by a similar inability to visualize faces (Shuttleworth, Syring, and Allen, 1982). Yet a third class of findings focuses on similarities in the brain areas that are activated during imagery and perception. Goldenberg and colleagues (1989), for example, used single photon emission computed tomography (SPECT) to examine differences in brain events when subjects evaluated the veracity of sentences with and without imagery, and reported an increase in blood flow in posterior visual areas of the brain during imagery. Similar effects during visual imagery were found by Farah and colleagues (1988), who recorded evoked potentials over the posterior scalp. Roland and associates (1987) also report activation in visual areas during visual imagery tasks [although not in the posterior regions found by Goldenberg et al. (1989), Kosslyn et al. (1993), and others; for reviews, see Roland and Gulyas (1994) and accompanying commentaries, as well as Kosslyn et al. (1995b) and Thompson and Kosslyn (in press)].

Other findings, however, paint a more complex picture. For example, two groups (Behrmann, Winocur, and Moscovitch, 1992; Jankowiak et al., 1992) report cases of brain-damaged patients whose imagery is intact in spite of impaired perceptual abilities, and Farah (1984) reviews reports of patients who had impaired imagery abilities in the face of intact perceptual abilities. These observations clearly show that only some of the same processes are recruited during both imagery and perception. Such findings are unsurprising, given that imagery relies on previously organized and stored information whereas perception requires on-the-spot computations, including figure–ground segregation, recognition, and identification. Thus, imagery relies on top-down mechanisms that may not be necessary in all perception, and perception relies on bottom-up mechanisms that may not be used in many imagery tasks.

STEPHEN M. KOSSLYN and WILLIAM L. THOMPSON   Department of Psychology, Harvard University, Cambridge, Mass.

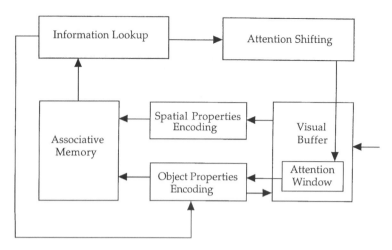

FIGURE 67.1 Six subsystems shared by visual imagery and perception.

Nevertheless, visual imagery and perception appear to share a core set of processes. Here, we begin by describing a positron emission tomography (PET) study that examined brain areas shared by visual mental imagery and high-level visual perception. The theory developed by Kosslyn (1994) is then drawn upon to characterize the roles of the shared processes. Following this, we use this theory to help us offer possible explanations for divergent results in the neuroimaging literature. Finally, we consider how the system may give rise to alternative types of imagery that may be used in different types of tasks.

Imagery and perception: Shared brain areas

Kosslyn, Thompson, and Alpert (1997) investigated the commonalities and differences in brain activation during visual imagery and visual perception. In order to show the strength of our analysis, we examined two tasks that appear, on the surface, to be very different. The perceptual task required the participants to judge whether words named line drawings of objects. In the baseline condition, the objects were shown from typical, or canonical, viewpoints, in which case recognition and identification should be accomplished in a straightforward manner. In the comparison condition, the objects were shown from atypical, or noncanonical, viewpoints. In this case, objects would not be recognized immediately, but only after more detailed processing had occurred. We predicted that in this condition the first encoding would be used to generate a hypothesis as to the identity of the object. This hypothesis would then be tested using mechanisms of top-down search. In order to decide whether the word did, in fact, name the pictured object, stored information representing specific properties of the candidate object would be accessed, then attention

would be directed to the place where a distinctive property should be found and additional information would be encoded. If the sought property is located, it would support the hypothesis, allowing a decision to be made (for additional details, see Kosslyn, 1994).

More specifically, the theory predicts that when one identifies an object from a noncanonical, rather than a canonical, viewpoint, the brain areas that implement certain subsystems would become more strongly activated. All of these subsystems would be used during an additional encoding cycle, when one seeks a distinctive property of the hypothesized object. Kosslyn and coworkers (1994) in fact found more activation in a network of brain regions when subjects judged the identities of objects portrayed from noncanonical viewpoints (the anatomical predictions were based on prior research findings, principally using nonhuman primates; for reviews, see Felleman and Van Essen, 1991; Kosslyn, 1994; Maunsell and Newsome, 1987; Ungerleider and Mishkin, 1982; Van Essen and Maunsell, 1983; Van Essen, 1985). Our interpretation of the findings rests on the following characterization of the subsystems used to recognize and identify objects (see figure 67.1).

VISUAL BUFFER   If supplementary information must be registered in order to identify an object perceived from a noncanonical point of view, we predict activation in a subsystem we call the "visual buffer." This structure plays a key role in figure–ground segregation and should be recruited more often if additional parts or properties must be encoded. The visual buffer is composed of a set of topographically organized brain areas, with "earlier" areas (e.g., Areas 17 and 18) providing the highest spatial resolution. Neurons in Areas 17 and 18 are characterized by smaller receptive fields than those in "later" areas (e.g., Area V4), so earlier areas can represent spatial variations that cannot be resolved by later areas. Earlier areas must therefore be drawn upon to represent high-resolution visual stimuli.

OBJECT-PROPERTIES ENCODING Activation was also observed in areas responsible for encoding object properties (e.g., shape or color) and matching them to stored visual memories. The object-properties-encoding subsystem we posit relies on the middle and inferior temporal gyri of humans (e.g., see Bly and Kosslyn, 1997; Gross et al., 1984; Kosslyn et al., 1994; Levine, 1982; Tanaka et al., 1991; Sergent, Ohta, and MacDonald, 1992; Sergent et al., 1992; Haxby et al., 1991; Ungerleider and Haxby, 1994; Ungerleider and Mishkin, 1982). *Recognition* occurs when a visual input matches a stored visual memory in this structure; when an object is recognized, one knows that it has been seen before.

SPATIAL-PROPERTIES ENCODING Spatial properties (e.g., location and size) are encoded at the same time as object properties. This subsystem relies on the posterior parietal lobes; thus, if additional parts and their spatial relations must be encoded in the noncanonical condition, we also expected additional activation in this region (e.g., Andersen, 1987; Andersen, Essick, and Siegel, 1985; Corbetta et al., 1993; Ungerleider and Haxby, 1994; Ungerleider and Mishkin, 1982). Such activation was in fact observed.

ASSOCIATIVE MEMORY Information carried by the pathways that register spatial and object properties must converge somewhere in the brain; both object and spatial properties furnish information useful for object identification (in addition, people can remember the particular locations of objects, which itself suggests that the two streams are conjoined at some point in processing). In fact, Felleman and Van Essen (1991) review findings that suggest several sites of convergence of the two pathways. We thus propose an "associative memory" subsystem that combines information from the two types of properties and compares this information to stored multimodal and amodal representations. We hypothesize that this structure is implemented by cortex in Area 19 and the angular gyrus (for evidence, see Kosslyn, Thompson, and Alpert, 1995). When input matches a stored representation here, the stimulus has been *identified*. When an object is identified, one has access to information associated with it, such as its name and categories to which it belongs. Thus, recognition arises when modality-specific representations are activated, whereas identification arises when multimodal and amodal representations are activated. (Consider, for example, what happens when you see someone and know

that you know her, but you can recall neither her name nor the context in which you met. This is an example of recognition without identification.) If the identity and location of distinctive parts are looked up, then encoded in the noncanonical but not the canonical condition, we should find more activation in the neural structures that implement this system. And in fact, such observation was observed.

INFORMATION LOOKUP If the input does not exactly match a stored representation in the object-properties–encoding subsystem, then the closest match may be treated as a hypothesis. When this occurs, additional information about the candidate object is gathered. We propose that an "information lookup" subsystem actively seeks supplementary information from stored memories, which permits the search for distinct properties. This subsystem, like all the others, is always operating, but operates more or less vigorously in different situations. If a stimulus is recognized confidently, the output from the object-properties–encoding subsystem will strongly activate a single representation in associative memory, so the information lookup subsystem does not run to completion. But if a poor match is found, no single stored representation is fully activated. In this case, the representation in associative memory that is most strongly activated following the tentative recognition will be accessed, and associated information (such as a particular mark or prominent part of an object) will be sought in top-down search. This subsystem relies on tissue in the dorsolateral prefrontal cortex, and plays a role in "working memory" (for supporting evidence, see Kosslyn, Thompson, and Alpert, 1995; cf. Goldman-Rakic, 1987).

ATTENTION SHIFTING Finally, we posit an "attention shifting" subsystem that changes the focus of one's attention to the possible location of a distinctive property or characteristic, allowing such a characteristic to be encoded. This subsystem relies on a network that includes the frontal eye fields, superior colliculus, and superior posterior parietal lobes, in addition to other regions (see Corbetta et al., 1993; LaBerge and Buchsbaum, 1990; Mesulam, 1981; Posner and Petersen, 1990). In addition to shifting the locus of attention, this subsystem primes the representation of the sought part or property in the object-properties–encoding subsystem. Such priming allows the system to encode the sought part or property more easily (for evidence of such priming in perception, see Kosslyn, 1994, pp. 287–289; McDermott and Roediger, 1994). If more parts or properties are encoded in the noncanonical than the canonical condition, then the neural structures that implement these processes should be more strongly activated in the noncanonical condition. We found activation in many of the structures used in attention.

We have summarized the functions of each subsystem as they are used in visual object identification, but each subsystem could also play a role in visual mental imagery. For example, consider the imagery task used by Kosslyn and colleagues (1993; experiment 2). Superficially, the task seems completely different from the object identification task; no objects are shown and name verification is not required. Instead, in the baseline condition the subjects see a lowercase letter followed by a 4×5 grid that contains an X probe in one cell. The subjects are merely told to respond when they have seen the grid. During the imagery condition, the same stimuli appear, but now the subjects are told that the lowercase letter is a cue to visualize the corresponding (previously learned) uppercase letter within the grid. Subjects must then decide whether the X would fall on a portion of the uppercase letter if the letter were in fact in the grid, or whether the X would fall in a cell not occupied by the letter. This task was designed by Podgorny and Shepard (1978) and employed by Kosslyn and co-workers (1988, 1993) to study the process of generating an image in short-term memory on the basis of information stored in long-term memory.

Given the evidence that imagery shares mechanisms with like-modality perception, it is reasonable to ask how the six functions schematized in figure 67.1 could come into play when a visual mental image is generated. The process of generating an image of an uppercase letter would begin when the information lookup subsystem retrieves a description of the letter's shape (which includes details about its parts and their locations) from associative memory. The attention-shifting subsystem shifts attentional focus to the location where the first segment should be placed, in the same way that one would attend to the possible location of a distinctive part during top-down hypothesis testing in perception. In imagery, however, the image must be generated at the location. According to our theory, forming a visual mental image relies on the mechanism that primes the representation (in the object-properties–encoding subsystem) of an expected object or part during perception. However, in imagery this priming is so strong that the shape itself is reconstructed in the visual buffer (see Kosslyn, 1994, for a review of the possible underlying anatomy, physiology, and computational mechanisms). That is, the anticipation of perceiving the object is so strong that an image of the object is imposed on the visual buffer. At least in the monkey, visual long-term memories are not stored in a topographically organized form, but rather are coded in columns that specify relatively abstract

properties (e.g., see Fujita et al., 1992). Thus, reconstructing the geometric layout of a shape requires "unpacking" the stored information and reconstructing the shape in lower-level, topographically organized areas. Imagery serves to make explicit the implicit spatial properties of an object.

Once the visual buffer contains the image of the first segment, the process is repeated for the second segment. In this case, the description of the letter is again accessed, attention is shifted appropriately, and another part is added. This view, then, predicts that parts are added to an image sequentially. And, in fact, in the grid-and-X task (Kosslyn et al., 1988), people judged X marks fastest if they fell on the first segment that is typically drawn, next fastest on the second segment, and so forth. This ordering of times was not observed when the image was formed before the X mark was presented, or when the subjects actually saw a dim uppercase letter in the grid. The ordering of times is as expected if segments are generated one segment at a time, and more segments had to be generated before "later" segments were included in the image.

According to this theory, once an image is generated (i.e., a pattern of activation is imposed in the visual buffer), further processing occurs in the same way that it occurs during perception: The object and spatial properties are encoded, then patterns and properties can be identified and spatial relations computed. Thus, for example, one can visualize the uppercase version of the first letter of the alphabet and "see" that there is a triangular shape enclosed in it, even though one had never explicitly considered this before. Similarly, one can visualize the word TREE in lowercase letters, and "see" that the last letter is not as high as the first.

We analyzed the PET data from the grids imagery task and picture verification task together, and we observed which areas were activated in both experimental conditions more than in both baseline conditions; by combining the conditions in this way, we could determine where activation generalized over both sets of conditions. As figure 67.2 shows, the areas activated in common by the perception and imagery tasks are easily organized according to the scheme outlined in figure 67.1. First, we discovered activation in left Area 18, a topographically organized region that implements part of the visual buffer. Second, we discovered common sites of activation in regions that implement the object-properties–encoding subsystem, in particular a left occipito-temporal area that included portions of the middle temporal gyrus and the right lingual gyrus. Third, we discovered common sites of activation in regions that implement the spatial-properties–encoding subsystem, namely, bilateral activation in the inferior parietal lobes.

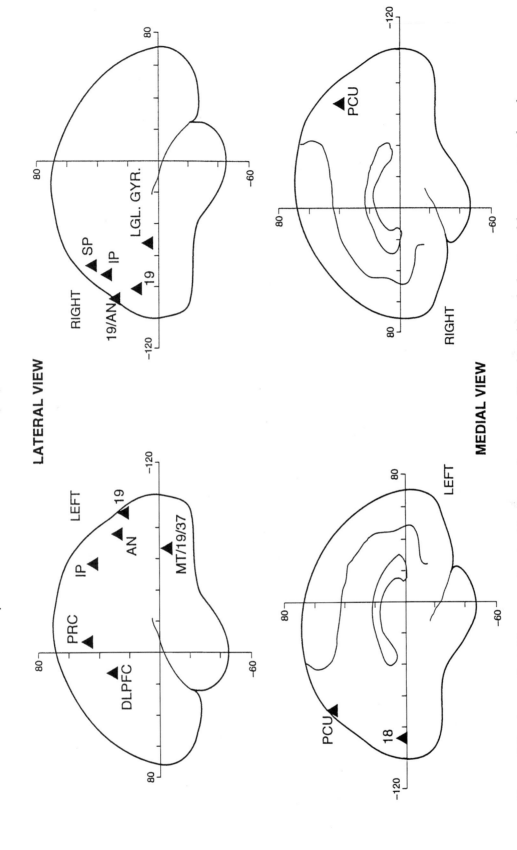

(IMAGERY + NONCANONICAL) - (IMAGEBASE + CANONICAL)

LATERAL VIEW

MEDIAL VIEW

FIGURE 67.2   Areas activated in common by visual imagery and visual perception. The panels on the left illustrate the left hemisphere, and those on the right, the right hemisphere. The top panels illustrate the lateral surface, and the bottom, the medial surface. Triangles indicate the location of the most activated voxel in an area, with a Z value greater than 3.1. (From Kosslyn, Thompson, and Alpert, 1997.)

979

Fourth, we found common activation in regions that we hypothesize to implement associative memory. In the left hemisphere, two distinct points were detected, one in the angular gyrus and the other in Area 19; in the right hemisphere, two areas of activation in Area 19 (one merging into the angular gyrus) emerged. Some of these regions are very near to areas reported by Kosslyn, Thompson, and Alpert (1995), who provided evidence that such activation reflects the operation of associative memory. Fifth, we discovered activation in areas that have been taken to implement the information lookup subsystem, specifically in the dorsolateral prefrontal cortex. The lateralization to the left would be predicted if this region has a particular specialization for seeking information about "categorical" spatial relations (cf. Kosslyn et al., 1995a, 1998). Sixth, activation was also observed in areas that implement attention-shifting processes, namely the bilateral precuneus and the right superior parietal lobe (cf. Corbetta et al., 1993).

In short, the results are easily interpreted within the context of the theory. Nevertheless, some unpredicted points of activation were also discovered. In particular, there was common activation in the left precentral gyrus, an area that Decety and colleagues (1994) have taken to be involved in motor-related imagery. Thus it is possible that motor processes may be involved in both types of tasks described here. However, a more straightforward interpretation is that this finding reflects activation in the frontal eye fields. Paus (1996) reviews the blood flow and lesion study literature and deduces that the most likely locus of human frontal eye fields is the most caudal part of superior frontal sulcus, very near the precentral sulcus. However, this inference diverges with the long-held view that Brodmann's Area 8 contains the human frontal eye fields; thus, the issue is best left open at present.

Finally, given the double dissociation between imagery and perception, we also asked which areas were more activated in one task than the other. Two areas in the right hemisphere, the middle temporal gyrus and the orbitofrontal cortex, were more activated in perception than imagery. In contrast, five areas were more activated in imagery than perception—two in the left inferior parietal lobe, the right superior parietal lobe, Area 19, and an area that included parts of Area 19 and the angular gyrus. Thus, a total of 21 areas were activated, with two-thirds of them activated in common by imagery and perception. If more areas are activated solely by imagery than perception than vice versa, we would expect to find more cases of brain-damaged patients who have disrupted imagery without disrupted perception than vice versa, which appears to be the case.

Resolving disparate results

A major issue currently debated within the neuroimaging literature is whether early visual cortex is activated during imagery. The theory that we have outlined leads us to expect images to rely on topographically organized areas in the occipital lobe, the site of the visual buffer. Some studies have even found activation in the first cortical visual area (known as Area V1, Area 17, primary visual cortex, striate cortex, and Area OC) when subjects close their eyes and visualize objects (e.g., Chen et al., 1996, 1998; Damasio et al., 1993; Kosslyn et al., 1993; Kosslyn et al., 1995b, 1996, 1999; LeBihan et al., 1993; Menon et al., 1993; Putz et al., 1996; Sabbah et al., 1995). Other studies have not found such activation (e.g., Charlot et al., 1992; Fletcher et al., 1995; Roland and Gulyas, 1994; Roland et al., 1987; Mellet et al., 1993, 1995, 1996). Because it is often difficult to be certain whether activation is in Area 17 or 18, and both areas implement high-resolution components of the visual buffer, we find it convenient to group them together under the rubric of medial occipital cortex (MOC).

Studies in which activation in the earliest visual areas is observed often require subjects to generate high-resolution images (but also vary in other ways, for instance, by having resting baseline conditions; see Kosslyn et al., 1995b). Sharper, more vivid images would result when neurons in earlier visual areas are recruited; these areas preserve finer spatial variations than do those in later areas. Thus, one possible explanation for the divergent findings is that MOC is engaged only when one must represent objects in high-resolution images. This account makes sense if it requires more effort to generate high-resolution images than to generate low-resolution images; thus, one would not form a high-resolution image unless performance of the task demands it.

If this account is true, we would predict that patterns requiring higher resolution would be more difficult to visualize than similar patterns requiring a lower degree of resolution. Kosslyn, Sukel, and Bly (1999) tested this hypothesis by asking subjects either to view or visualize displays that featured four quadrants, with each quadrant containing a pattern made up of a set of stripes. In two experiments, one of the displays featured only relatively narrow stripes, whereas another display featured only relatively thick stripes. High resolution is required to resolve narrow stripes, whereas only low resolution is necessary to resolve thick stripes. The task required the subjects to compare sets of stripes in different quadrants, then decide which set was longer, had more separation between the stripes, was tilted more, or was wider. When the participants visualized the displays, they required more time to compare high-resolution patterns than low-resolution patterns; however, when the subjects actually perceived the displays, both high- and low-resolution, they compared the patterns equally easily. This result is in line with the notion that greater effort is required to generate high-resolution images. Furthermore, the third experiment in the series furnished strong support for the inference that imagery was indeed used in this task. In this experiment, the stimuli in one condition were four oblique sets of stripes (one per quadrant) and those in another condition were four vertical or horizontal sets of stripes (one per quadrant). During both perception and imagery, subjects made more errors when they compared oblique stimuli; and in imagery, they also required more time for the oblique stimuli. The stimuli were in fact identical except for orientation (and the orientation judgment was replaced, and thus orientation per se did not figure in the comparisons). This "oblique effect" has been well documented in perception (Appelle, 1972), but few outside the field of vision research are aware of it. Thus, it is highly unlikely that subjects were merely responding to experimenter demands or tacit knowledge in producing this effect; rather, this finding is good evidence that imagery and perception draw on common mechanisms.

Thompson and Kosslyn (in press) reviewed all available neuroimaging studies of imagery with a view to discovering the conditions in which different neural structures are invoked during imagery. The review revealed that, of the 42 studies where Areas 17 and 18 were examined, 25 reported activation in at least one of those areas. Based on these findings, Thompson and Kosslyn performed a meta-analysis in which each study was coded for various characteristics, which served as independent variables in the analysis. The dependent variable was a binary code expressing the presence or absence of MOC activation. These values were regressed onto the independent variables. This analysis revealed that the strongest predictor of MOC activation was the requirement to use high-resolution imagery.

Further consideration of the theory outlined in figure 67.1 suggests another possible, but not exclusive, account for the disparate reports of MOC activation. We note that in the monkey, the efferent connections from the inferior temporal lobe to the medial occipital lobe are diffuse; they are not point-for-point backward projections that mirror the afferent connections (e.g., Douglas and Rockland, 1992). To form an image, however, the feedback from higher-level areas need not necessarily define a precise image, mapping point-for-point from stored memories to the visual buffer. Rather, this feedback could serve to define an "attractor" in the visual buffer, which in turn causes activity to be organized in particular ways (cf. Hinton and Shallice, 1991).

If so, the system should operate more effectively if there is random "noise" in the areas that implement the visual buffer, noise that can be amplified and organized in accordance with feedback. The analogous case is listening to white noise and hearing voices or melodies within it; the same kinds of mechanisms presumably amplify and organize selected aspects of the noise. This idea led us to notice a previously overlooked aspect of the neuroimaging literature on visual imagery: In many studies in which subjects were reported to be blindfolded or tested in pitch-dark conditions, there was a failure to find activation of MOC during imagery. It is possible that even a small amount of diffuse light coming in from closed eyelids is sufficient to provide enough activation for top-down processes to amplify and augment it. Future studies will need to be designed to test this hypothesis directly.

Types of imagery

The system outlined in figure 67.1 could operate in more than one way, and there is reason to believe that the subsystems function differently in different tasks. For example, when Mellet and colleagues (1995) contrasted perception and imagery, their study yielded results very dissimilar to ours. Their experiment required subjects to use mental imagery to scan a map of an island or actually to look at and scan the map. When imagery and perception were directly compared, more activation was present in perception bilaterally in primary visual cortex, the superior occipital gyrus, the inferior occipital gyrus, the cuneus, the fusiform/lingual gyri, and superior parietal cortex. Many of these areas may be particularly involved in visual search. Conversely, more activation was found in imagery than perception bilaterally in the superior temporal and precentral gyri, as well as in the left dorsolateral prefrontal cortex (DLPFC), inferior frontal cortex, and in the supplementary motor area, anterior cingulate, median cingulate, and cerebellar vermis. In addition, Mellet and co-workers were not able to detect any activation in Areas 17 or 18 during the imagery task. These results suggest that the imagery task was performed using spatial representations (possibly in conjunction with motor processes), which rely on only part of the system outlined in figure 67.1.

In more recent work, Mellet and colleagues (1996) used a different type of spatial task, and again found no evidence of MOC activation in imagery. In this case, the subjects' task was to listen to a series of spatial directions, which were to be used to generate a mental image of a multi-armed object. The parts of the object were distinguished only by their direction and relative length, both of which are spatial properties. Roland and colleagues

(1987; see also Roland and Friberg, 1985), also using spatial directions, did not detect any MOC activation when they asked subjects to imagine walking along a path, making left or right turns at each junction. Again, areas that implement spatial and attentional processing were activated in these studies.

To make sense of these various findings, it is useful to consider three different types of imagery. First, there is the type of imagery used by Mellet and colleagues (1996) and Roland and colleagues (1987). Such imagery appears to be based on the mental representation of spatial relations, rather than that of shapes, textures, or colors. Within the scheme outlined in figure 67.1, this type of processing would invoke neither the visual buffer nor the object-properties–encoding subsystem; but it would activate the rest of the system, which is implemented in the posterior parietal lobes, DLPFC, and the angular gyrus/Area 19 as well as various areas that allocate attention. In addition, processing of this kind may often make use of motor processes (e.g., see Berthoz, 1996; Jeannerod et al., 1995). It is not clear to us that visual imagery is actually used in these sorts of situations. If there is a visual image (i.e., a pattern of activation in topographically organized areas), it may simply be epiphenomenal, not actually contributing to the information processing necessary to perform the task. If so, it is not surprising that little cerebral blood flow is associated with such visual image representations.

Second, there is a "figural imagery"–a type of imagery that relies on cortex situated in the inferior temporal lobes [this is different from the processing of spatial representations, as Mellet et al. (1996) have also suggested]. Figural imagery occurs only when a low-resolution topographic image is generated from the activation of stored representations of shapes and other object properties. Such representations arise in the posterior portions of inferior temporal cortex. There is some evidence in the literature that the region may, at least in monkey cortex, contain coarsely organized topographic areas (for an overview, see Felleman and Van Essen, 1991; see also DeYoe et al., 1994). The high-resolution components of the visual buffer need not be activated for such imagery to occur; however, DLPFC, the angular gyrus/Area 19, and areas that drive attentional processing should be recruited. These ideas fit well with results reported by Fletcher and colleagues (1995). In this PET experiment, participants were asked to remember and later recall concrete and abstract words. No activation was detected in MOC during recall of concrete words, which was assumed to induce imagery (e.g., see Paivio, 1971). However, the right superior temporal and fusiform gyri were activated (and activation was also observed in the left anterior cingulate and the precuneus). This task did not re-

quire high-resolution images; hence subjects may have formed only the minimal images needed to serve as memory prompts–which did not include details.

Levine, Warach, and Farah (1985) report a double dissociation that makes sense in light of this distinction between spatial representation and figural imagery. One patient who had damage to the parietal lobes was able to visualize objects but not spatial relations; in contrast, another patient had damage to the temporal lobes, and was able to mentally represent spatial relations but not objects.

Finally, we posit a third type of processing, which we call "depictive imagery." This type of imagery, which relies on high-resolution representations in MOC, allows one to reorganize, reinterpret, or compare shapes. This type of imagery–the focus of this chapter–corresponds to what most people seem to mean when they say they are "seeing with the mind's eye."

Pure forms of these three types of processing may be relatively rare. We note, for instance, that the temporal/fusiform/lingual gyrus area seems to be activated in at least three of the studies that used spatial tasks (Charlot et al., 1992; Mellet et al., 1995; Roland and Friberg, 1985). Indeed, visual imagery may often be supplemented by linguistic representations, as well as other forms of imagery (e.g., motor and auditory).

Conclusions

Two major conclusions can be drawn from this review: First, many common neural processes underlie perception and depictive imagery. Second, the type of processing used depends on the task at hand. This last point is worth underlining: Many tasks in the neuroimaging imagery literature have not been specifically designed to tap a particular type of imagery processing. In fact, many of the tasks do not permit a clear appraisal of the type of processing that has occurred because they do not require subjects to produce a response. Given the complex nature of imagery and its component processes, it is clear that great care must be given to task design, with the aim of inducing a specific mode of operation of the system.

ACKNOWLEDGMENTS This report was supported by NIA Grant 5 R01 AG12675-03. Preparation was also supported by the Collège de France.

REFERENCES

ANDERSEN, R. A., 1987. Inferior parietal lobule function in spatial perception and visuomotor integration. In *Handbook of Physiology, Sect. 1: The Nervous System, Vol. 5: Higher Functions of the Brain*, F. Plum, ed. Bethesda, Md.: American Physiological Society, pp. 483–518.

ANDERSEN, R. A., G. K. ESSICK, and R. M. SIEGEL, 1985. Encoding of spatial location by posterior parietal neurons. *Science* 230:456–458.

APPELLE, S., 1972. Perception and discrimination as a function of stimulus orientation: The "oblique effect" in man and animals. *Psychol. Bull.* 89:266–273.

BEHRMANN, M., G. WINOCUR, and M. MOSCOVITCH, 1992. Dissociation between mental imagery and object recognition in a brain-damaged patient. *Nature* 359:636–637.

BERTHOZ, A., 1996. The role of inhibition in the hierarchical gating of executed and imagined movements. *Cogn. Brain Res.* 3:101–113.

BISIACH, E., and C. LUZZATTI, 1978. Unilateral neglect of representational space. *Cortex* 14:129–133.

BLY, B. M., and S. M. KOSSLYN, 1997. Functional anatomy of object recognition in humans: Evidence from positron emission tomography and functional magnetic resonance imaging. *Curr. Opin. Neurol.* 10:5–9.

CHARLOT, V., N. TZOURIO, M. ZILBOVICIUS, B. MAZOYER, and M. DENIS, 1992. Different mental imagery abilities result in different regional cerebral blood flow activation patterns during cognitive tests. *Neuropsychologia* 30:565–580.

CHEN, W., T. KATO, X.-H. ZHU, S. OGAWA, D. W. TANK, and K. UGURBIL, 1998. Human primary visual cortex and lateral geniculate nucleus activation during visual imagery. *NeuroReport* 9:3669–3674.

CHEN, W., T. KATO, X.-H. ZHU, S. OGAWA, and K. UGURBIL, 1996. Primary visual cortex activation during visual imagery in human brain. A fMRI mapping study. *NeuroImage* 3:S204.

CORBETTA, M., F. M. MIEZEN, G. L. SCHULMAN, and S. E. PETERSEN, 1993. A PET study of visuospatial attention. *J. Neurosci.* 13:1202–1226.

CRAVER-LEMLEY, C., and A. REEVES, 1987. Visual imagery selectively reduces vernier acuity. *Perception* 16:533–614.

CRAVER-LEMLEY, C., and A. REEVES, 1992. How visual imagery interferes with vision. *Psychol. Rev.* 99:633–649.

DEMARAIS, A. M., and B. H. COHEN, in press. Evidence for image-scanning eye movements during transitive inference. *Biol. Psychol.*

DAMASIO, H., T. J. GRABOWSKI, A. DAMASIO, D. TRANEL, L. BOLES-PONTO, G. L. WATKINS, and R. D. HICHWA, 1993. Visual recall with eyes closed and covered activates early visual cortices. *Soc. Neurosci. Abstr.* 19:1603.

DECETY, J., D. PERANI, M. JEANNEROD, V. BETTINARDI, B. TADARY, R. WOODS, J. C. MAZZIOTTA, and F. FAZIO, 1994. Mapping motor representations with PET. *Nature* 371:600–602.

DEYOE, E. A., D. J. FELLEMAN, D. C. VAN ESSEN, and E. MCCLENDON, 1994. Multiple processing streams in occipitotemporal visual cortex. *Nature* 371:151–154.

DOUGLAS, K. L., and K. S. ROCKLAND, 1992. Extensive visual feedback connections from ventral inferotemporal cortex. *Soc. Neurosci. Abstr.* 18:390.

FARAH, M. J., 1984. The neurological basis of mental imagery: A componential analysis. *Cognition* 18:245–272.

FARAH, M. J., 1988. Is visual imagery really visual? Overlooked evidence from neuropsychology. *Psychol. Rev.* 95:307–317.

FARAH, M. J., F. PERONNET, M. A. GONON, and M. H. GIRARD, 1988. Electrophysiological evidence for a shared representational medium for visual images and visual percepts. *J. Exp. Psychol.* 117:248–257.

FELLEMAN, D. J., and D. C. VAN ESSEN, 1991. Distributed hierarchical processing in primate cerebral cortex. *Cereb. Cortex* 1:1–47.

FINKE, R. A., 1989. *Principles of Mental Imagery.* Cambridge, Mass.: MIT Press.

FINKE, R. A., and R. N. SHEPARD, 1986. Visual functions of mental imagery. In *Handbook of Perception and Human Performance*, K. R. Boff, L. Kaufman, and J. P. Thomas, eds. New York: Wiley-Interscience, pp. 37-1–37-55.

FINKE, R. A., M. K. JOHNSON, and G. C.-W. SHYI, 1988. Memory confusions for real and imagined completions of symmetrical visual patterns. *Mem. Cognit.* 16:133–137.

FLETCHER, P. C., C. D. FRITH, S. C. BAKER, T. SHALLICE, R. S. J. FRACKOWIAK, and R. J. DOLAN, 1995. The mind's eye–Precuneus activation in memory-related imagery. *NeuroImage* 2:195–200.

FUJITA, I., K. TANAKA, M. ITO, and K. CHENG, 1992. Columns for visual features of objects in monkey inferotemporal cortex. *Nature* 360:343–346.

GOLDENBERG, G., I. PODREKA, M. STEINER, K. WILLMES, E. SUESS, and L. DEECKE, 1989. Regional cerebral blood flow patterns in visual imagery. *Neuropsychologia* 27:641–664.

GOLDMAN-RAKIC, P. S., 1987. Circuitry of primate prefrontal cortex and regulation of behavior by representational knowledge. In *Handbook of Physiology, Sect. 1: The Nervous System, Vol. 5: Higher Functions of the Brain*, F. Plum and V. Mountcastle, eds. Bethesda, Md.: American Physiological Society, pp. 373–417.

GROSS, C. G., R. DESIMONE, T. D. ALBRIGHT, and E. L. SCHWARTZ, 1984. Inferior temporal cortex as a visual integration area. In *Cortical Integration*, F. Reinoso-Suarez and C. Ajmone-Marsan, eds. New York: Raven Press, pp. 291–315.

HAXBY, J. V., C. L. GRADY, B. HOROWITZ, L. G. UNGERLEIDER, M. MISHKIN, R. E. CARSON, P. HERSCOVITCH, M. B. SCHAPIRO, and S. I. RAPOPORT, 1991. Dissociation of object and spatial visual processing pathways in human extrastriate cortex. *Proc. Natl. Acad. Sci. U.S.A.* 88:1621–1625.

HINTON, G. E., and T. SHALLICE, 1991. Lesioning an attractor network: Investigations of acquired dyslexia. *Psychol. Rev.* 98:74–95.

INTRAUB, H., and J. E. HOFFMAN, 1992. Reading and visual memory: Remembering scenes that were never seen. *Amer. J. Psychol.* 105:101–114.

JANKOWIAK, J., M. KINSBOURNE, R. S. SHALEV, and D. L. BACHMAN, 1992. Preserved visual imagery and categorization in a case of associative visual agnosia. *J. Cogn. Neurosci.* 4:119–131.

JEANNEROD, M., M. A. ARBIB, G. RIZZOLATTI, and H. SAKATA, 1995. Grasping objects: The cortical mechanisms of visuomotor transformation. *Trends Neurosci.* 18:314–320.

JOHNSON, M. K., and C. L. RAYE, 1981. Reality monitoring. *Psychol. Rev.* 88:67–85.

KOSSLYN, S. M., 1994. *Image and Brain: The Resolution of the Imagery Debate.* Cambridge, Mass.: MIT Press.

KOSSLYN, S. M., N. M. ALPERT, W. L. THOMPSON, C. F. CHABRIS, S. L. RAUCH, and A. K. ANDERSON, 1994. Identifying objects seen from different viewpoints: A PET investigation. *Brain* 117:1055–1071.

KOSSLYN, S. M., N. M. ALPERT, W. L. THOMPSON, V. MALJKOVIC, S. B. WEISE, C. F. CHABRIS, S. E. HAMILTON, S. L. RAUCH, and F. S. BUONANNO, 1993. Visual mental imagery activates topographically organized visual cortex: PET investigations. *J. Cogn. Neurosci.* 5:263–287.

KOSSLYN, S. M., C. B. CAVE, D. PROVOST, and S. VON GIERKE, 1988. Sequential processes in image generation. *Cognit. Psychol.* 20:319–343.

KOSSLYN, S. M., V. M. MALJKOVIC, S. E. HAMILTON, G. HOR-
WITZ, and W. L. THOMPSON, 1995a. Two types of image
generation: Evidence for left and right hemisphere processes. *Neuropsychologia* 33:1485–1510.

KOSSLYN, S. M., A. PASCUAL-LEONE, O. FELICIAN, S. CAM-
POSANO, J. P. KEENAN, W. L. THOMPSON, G. GANIS, K. E.
SUKEL, and N. M. ALPERT, 1999. The role of Area 17 in vi-
sual imagery: Convergent evidence from PET and rTMS.
Science 284:167–170.

KOSSLYN, S. M., K. E. SUKEL, and B. M. BLY, 1999. Squinting
with the mind's eye: Effects of stimulus resolution on imagi-
nal and perceptual comparisons. *Mem. Cognit.* 27:276–287.

KOSSLYN, S. M., W. L. THOMPSON, D. R. GITELMAN, and
N. M. ALPERT, 1998. Neural systems that encode categori-
cal versus coordinate spatial relations: PET investigations.
Psychobiology 26:333–347.

KOSSLYN, S. M., W. L. THOMPSON, I. J. KIM, and N. M. AL-
PERT, 1995b. Topographical representations of mental images in primary visual cortex. *Nature* 378:496–498.

KOSSLYN, S. M., W. L. THOMPSON, and N. M. ALPERT, 1995.
Identifying objects at different levels of hierarchy: A
positron emission tomography study. *Hum. Brain Map.* 3:
107–132.

KOSSLYN, S. M., W. L. THOMPSON, I. J. KIM, S. L. RAUCH, and
N. M. ALPERT, 1996. Individual differences in cerebral
blood flow in area 17 predict the time to evaluate visualized
letters. *J. Cogn. Neurosci.* 8:78–82.

KOSSLYN, S. M., W. L. THOMPSON, and N. M. ALPERT, 1997.
Neural systems shared by visual imagery and visual perception: A positron emission tomography study. *NeuroImage*
6:320–334.

LABERGE, D., and M. S. BUCHSBAUM, 1990. Positron emission
tomography measurements of pulvinar activity during an attention task. *J. Neurosci.* 10:613–619.

LEBIHAN, D., R. TURNER, T. A. ZEFFIRO, C. CUÉNOD, P. JEZ-
ZARD, and V. BONNEROT, 1993. Activation of human primary
visual cortex during visual recall: A magnetic resonance imaging study. *Proc. Natl. Acad. Sci.* 90:11802–11805.

LEVINE, D. N., 1982. Visual agnosia in monkey and man. In
Analysis of Visual Behavior, D. J. Ingle, M. A. Goodale, and R.
J. W. Mansfield, eds. Cambridge, Mass.: MIT Press, pp.
629–670.

LEVINE, D. N., J. WARACH, and M. J. FARAH, 1985. Two visual
systems in mental imagery: Dissociation of 'what' and
'where' in imagery disorders due to bilateral posterior cerebral lesions. *Neurology* 35:1010–1018.

MAUNSELL, J. H. R., and W. T. NEWSOME, 1987. Visual processing in monkey extrastriate cortex. *Annu. Rev. Neurosci.*
10:363–401.

MCDERMOTT, K. B., and H. L. ROEDIGER, 1994. Effects of imagery on perceptual implicit memory tests. *J. Exp. Psychol.:
Learn. Mem. Cognit.* 20:1379–1390.

MELLET, E., N. TZOURIO, F. CRIVELLO, M. JOLIOT, M. DENIS,
and B. MAZOYER, 1996. Functional anatomy of spatial mental imagery generated from verbal instructions. *J. Neurosci.*
16:6504–6512.

MELLET, E., N. TZOURIO, M. DENIS, and B. MAZOYER, 1995.
A positron emission tomography study of visual and mental
spatial exploration. *J. Cogn. Neurosci.* 7:433–445.

MELLET, E., N. TZOURIO, U. PIETRZYK, L. RAYNAUD, M. DE-
NIS, and B. MAZOYER, 1993. Visual perception versus men-
tal imagery: A PET activation study. *J. Cereb. Blood Flow
Metab.* 13(Suppl. 1):S563.

MENON, R., S. OGAWA, D. W. TANK, J. ELLERMANN, H.
MERKELE, and K. UGURBIL, 1993. Visual mental imagery
by functional brain MRI. In *Functional MRI of the Brain*, D.
L. Bihan, R. Turner, M. Mosley, and J. Hyde, eds.
Arlington, Va.: Society of Magnetic Resonance in Medi-
cine, p. 252.

MESULAM, M.-M., 1981. A cortical network for directed attention and unilateral neglect. *Ann. Neurol.* 10:309–325.

PAIVIO, A., 1971. *Imagery and Verbal Processes.* New York: Holt,
Rinehart and Winston.

PAUS, T., 1996. Location and function of the human frontal eye
field: A selective review. *Neuropsychologia* 34:475–483.

PERKY, C. W., 1910. An experimental study of imagination.
Amer. J. Psychol. 21:422–452.

PODGORNY, P., and R. N. SHEPARD, 1978. Functional representations common to visual perception and imagination. *J
Exp. Psychol.: Hum. Percept. Perform.* 4:21–35.

POSNER, M. I., and S. E. PETERSEN, 1990. The attention system
of the human brain. *Annu. Rev. Neurosci.* 13:25–42.

PUTZ, B., S. MIYAUCHI, Y. SASAKI, R. TAKINO, M. OHKI, and
J. OKAMOTO, 1996. *NeuroImage* 3:S215.

ROLAND, P. E., and L. FRIBERG, 1985. Localization of cortical
areas activated by thinking. *J. Neurophysiol.* 53:1219–1243.

ROLAND, P. E., and B. GULYAS, 1994. Visual imagery and visual representation. *Trends Neurosci.* 17:281–296 (with commentaries).

ROLAND, P. E., L. ERIKSON, S. STONE-ELANDER, and L.
WIDEN, 1987. Does mental activity change the oxidative metabolism of the brain? *J. Neurosci.* 7:2373–2389.

SABBAH, P., G. SIMOND, O. LEVRIER, M. HABIB, V. TRABAUD,
N. MURAYAMA, B. MAZOYER, J. F. BRIANT, C. RAYBAUD,
and G. SALAMON, 1995. Functional magnetic resonance imaging at 1.5 T during sensorimotor and cognitive task. *Eur.
Neurol.* 35:131–136.

SEGAL, S. J., and V. FUSELLA, 1970. Influence of imaged pictures and sounds on detection of visual and auditory signals.
J. Exp. Psychol. 83:458–464.

SERGENT, J., S. OHTA, and B. MACDONALD, 1992. Functional
neuroanatomy of face and object processing: A positron
emission tomography study. *Brain* 115:15–36.

SERGENT, J., E. ZUCK, M. LEVESQUE, and B. MACDONALD,
1992. Positron emission tomography study of letter and object processing: Empirical findings and methodological considerations. *Cereb. Cortex* 2:68–80.

SHEPARD, R. N., and L. R. COOPER, 1982. *Mental Images and
Their Transformations.* Cambridge, Mass.: MIT Press.

SHUTTLEWORTH, E. C., V. SYRING, and N. ALLEN, 1982. Further observations on the nature of prosopagnosia. *Brain
Cognit.* 1:302–332.

TANAKA, K., H. SAITO, Y. FUKADA, and M. MORIYA, 1991.
Coding visual images of objects in the inferotemporal cortex
of the macaque monkey. *J. Neurophysiol.* 66:170–189.

THOMPSON, W. L., and S. M. KOSSLYN, in press. Neural systems activated during visual mental imagery: A review and
meta-analyses. In *Brain Mapping II: The Systems*, A. W. Toga
and J. C. Mazziotta, eds. San Diego: Academic Press.

UNGERLEIDER, L. G., and J. V. HAXBY, 1994. 'What' and
'Where' in the human brain. *Curr. Opin. Neurol.* 4:157–
165.

UNGERLEIDER, L. G., and M. MISHKIN, 1982. Two cortical vi-
sual systems. In *Analysis of Visual Behavior*, D. J. Ingle, M. A.
Goodale, and R. J. W. Mansfield, eds. Cambridge, Mass.:
MIT Press, pp. 549–586.

Van Essen, D. C., 1985. Functional organization of primate visual cortex. In *Cerebral Cortex*, A. Peters and E. G. Jones, eds. New York: Plenum Press, pp. 259–329.

Van Essen, D. C., and J. H. Maunsell, 1983. Hierarchical organization and functional streams in the visual cortex. *Trends Neurosci.* 6:370–375.

68 Cerebral Bases of Number Processing and Calculation

STANISLAS DEHAENE

ABSTRACT   What is the cerebral basis of the human competence for mathematics? Cognitive neuroscientists have begun to address this issue in the small domain of elementary arithmetic. Chronometric experiments indicate that the human brain comprises an analogical representation of numbers, in which numerical quantities are internally manipulated as points on a mental "number line." Neuropsychological studies of number processing indicate that this representation is distributed in the two hemispheres and point to inferior parietal cortex as its dominant site. The intraparietal network may provide a category-specific semantic representation of numerical quantities. Recent neuroimaging experiments confirm that this area is specifically activated when normal subjects manipulate numbers, regardless of the particular notations used to convey them.

Mental arithmetic is a basic ability of the human brain. In daily life, we encounter numbers in a wide variety of situations: We punch phone numbers, check our change, balance our bank accounts, take a train, check our driving speed; and, sometimes, we even plan or analyze scientific experiments. Of the content words of language, number words are among the most frequent: In English, we utter the word "one" once in every 70 words, and the word "two" once in every 600 words (Dehaene and Mehler, 1992; frequencies are comparable in other languages). Arguably, numbers are one of humanity's most important cultural inventions, without which science or society as we know it would never have seen the light of day.

In recent years, experimental studies have begun to address an age-old puzzle–the origins of the human mind's competence for mathematics. Using the methods of cognitive neuroscience, we can now ask what internal representations are used to manipulate numbers mentally, when and how they develop, and what brain areas are involved. Space precludes an exhaustive description of cognitive neuroscience studies of numeracy (but see Campbell, 1992; Dehaene, 1997; Dehaene and Cohen, 1995); rather, this chapter focuses on two issues–category specificity and modularity–issues of general inter-

STANISLAS DEHAENE   INSERM U. 334, Service Hospitalier Frédéric Joliot, CEA/DRM/DSV, Orsay, France

est in cognitive neuroscience that have been addressed in the specific domain of numbers.

Category specificity refers to the hypothesis that different domains of knowledge–such as knowledge of animals, foods, actions, or objects–are subserved by dedicated mental processes, even by specific brain circuits. I have argued that the number domain provides a remarkable example of a biologically determined, category-specific domain of knowledge (Dehaene, Dehaene-Lambertz, and Cohen, 1998). Supporting evidence has accrued from multiple converging fields of research, including animal, infant, and adult human psychology, as well as lesion studies and brain imaging. This empirical evidence suggests that humans and animals possess a specific, biologically determined ability to attend to small numbers of objects or events in their environment. In humans, an internal representation of numerical quantities develops very rapidly in the first year of life; and, later in life, this representation underlies our ability to learn symbols for numbers and to perform simple calculations. It is specifically associated with neural circuitry in the inferior parietal lobule. Brain damage to these circuits can cause highly specific impairments in the representation and manipulation of numbers.

Arguably, then, biological evolution has internalized in our brains a dedicated cerebral system for number, comparable to the specialized cerebral devices that subserve color or stereo vision, auditory localization, or visuomotor transformations. Such a "number sense" is obviously useful to survival: It helps us make sense of a world composed, at the scale in which we live, largely of discrete objects forming sets whose combinations follow the rules of arithmetic.

The hypothesis of a dedicated brain system for quantity knowledge is superficially reminiscent of Gall and Spurzheim's phrenology. In phrenological diagrams, all knowledge of numbers and mathematics was attributed to a specific brain convolution. Of course, the present claim is quite different. According to the hypothesis developed here, the internal representation of numerical quantities, which is putatively linked to cortical tissue within the intraparietal sulcus, is not the only repository

987

of arithmetic knowledge in our brains. Rather, it is assumed to be associated with a highly specific and limited mode of representation and manipulation of numbers, in the form of abstract quantities laid down on an analogical number line. Chronometric and neuropsychological studies indicate that the quantity representation is by no means the only internal code that humans use to manipulate numbers. Multiple representations, supported by a distributed cortical and subcortical network, underlie our ability to understand, produce, and mentally manipulate numbers in various formats, including arabic numerals (e.g., 32) and number words ("thirty-two"). Even extremely simple calculations, such as producing the result of 3 – 1, involve the coordination of multiple brain areas within a complex cognitive architecture.

This is the second key concept of cognitive neuroscience to which the study of numerical cognition has strongly contributed—the *modularity of the cognitive architecture* for verbal and nonverbal processing. Numbers constitute a small domain of language, with its own lexicon of thirty-some words, its restricted syntax, and its easily defined semantics. Fine-grained studies of number production, comprehension, and calculation tasks have provided strong evidence for a modular organization at each of these levels.

Number processing in normal subjects

Moyer and Landauer (1967) first characterized the semantic representation of numerical quantities in human adults. They presented subjects with pairs of arabic digits, such as 3:4, and asked them to indicate which number was larger (or smaller). Response times and error rates were strikingly affected by number size and number distance (figure 68.1). As the numbers to be compared represented closer and closer quantities (e.g., 2:8 vs. 4:5), the subjects' responses became increasingly slower and more error-prone. And when distance was kept constant, increasingly larger quantities again resulted in increasingly slower responses and larger error rates. Performance in comparing two numbers was determined by a Weber fraction, similar to that found when subjects have to compare physical parameters such as object size, line length, or tone height. Yet the number stimuli were presented in a symbolic notation, arabic numerals, whose surface form is largely arbitrary, conveying no information about number meaning. The distance effect suggested that subjects were converting the input numerals to an internal continuum, a mental "number line," and were performing a psychophysical comparison on this internal representation rather than on the surface form of the numbers.

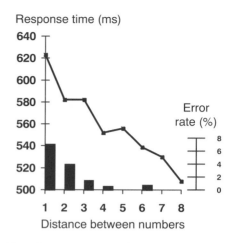

FIGURE 68.1 Distance effect: the amount of time it takes to decide which of two digits is larger is inversely related to the distance between them. Error rates show a similar trend. (Redrawn from Moyer and Landauer, 1967.)

Subsequent work largely confirmed the hypothesis of an internal conversion to a notation-independent analogical representation of quantity. Buckley and Gillman (1974) measured the time to compare numbers that were conveyed either by arabic numerals or by the numerosity of dot patterns. Performance was remarkably similar, driven in both cases by numerical distance and size effects. In later work, parallel performance patterns were found when subjects compared arabic numerals and number words in various languages (Dehaene, 1996; Tzeng and Wang, 1983). Obviously, the mental representation on which subjects based their comparative judgments abstracted away from the symbolic surface form of the numerals and encoded their quantitative meaning only. A continuous distance effect was found even when subjects compared two-digit numerals. The two-digit number comparison results indicated that subjects did not rely on a digit-by-digit analysis of decades and units, but rather performed a holistic evaluation of numerical quantity (Dehaene, Dupoux, and Mehler, 1990; Hinrichs, Yurko, and Hu, 1981).

Beyond the number comparison task, chronometric experiments with various number processing and calculation tasks have revealed ubiquitous number size and distance effects, indicating that the quantity representation plays a pivotal role in numerical cognition. For instance, in a same–different judgment task (Dehaene and Akhavein, 1995; Duncan and McFarland, 1980), subjects were shown a pair of numbers, such as 2:5, and asked to say whether or not the two numbers were the same, responding as fast as they could. Conceivably, subjects can respond on the basis of visual similarity alone. Thus, in one version of the task, subjects were actually encouraged to rely on such a superficial visual analysis: They were asked to respond "different" to such pairs as "2:two," in which the numbers are numerically identical but physically different. Nonetheless, response times were always affected by a distance effect. When subjects responded "different," their responses were slower when the pair comprised two numbers that were numerically close (e.g., 2 and 3) than when it comprised two very different numbers (e.g., 2 and 8). Obviously, subjects could not prevent a mental conversion from digital symbols to the corresponding quantities.

Size and distance effects are also obvious when subjects calculate (Ashcraft and Battaglia, 1978). The time to perform an internal addition or multiplication operation varies considerably with the size of the numbers involved. Problems with small numbers, such as $2 + 3$ or 3×2, are solved much faster than problems with large numbers such as $6 + 8$ or 6×8. Of course, the greater practice we have with small arithmetic facts may contribute to this effect. The distance effect in calculation verification, however, cannot be explained by practice. When subjects are asked to verify whether an operation is true or false (e.g., $3 \times 6 = 72$?), responses are increasingly faster as the proposed result gets more distant from the true result of the operation. As with number comparison, number size and distance effects in calculation are similar whether numbers are presented as arabic digits or as number words, even though small but systematic differences seem to be found (for discussion, see Brysbaert, Fias, and Noel, 1998; Campbell, 1994; Noel, Fias, and Brysbaert, 1997; Vorberg and Blankenberger, 1993).

Hemispheric distribution of number processing abilities

While the existence of a mental representation of quantity has been known since the 1970s, cognitive neuropsychological studies have only recently begun to investigate the cerebral organization of number processing in the human brain. Perhaps the simplest question we can ask is, what is the hemispheric distribution of number processing abilities? Do both hemispheres have access to the quantity representation, and can both hemispheres calculate? This question has been examined in patients with callosal lesions. The corpus callosum is a large bundle of fibers that connects the two cerebral hemispheres. When it is lesioned or surgically sectioned, the cognitive abilities of each hemisphere can be assessed (Sperry, 1968). Numerical abilities were tested in a series of experiments initially performed with surgical split-brain cases (Gazzaniga and Hillyard, 1971; Gazzaniga and Smylie, 1984; Seymour, Reuter-Lorenz, and Gazzaniga, 1994). These results were recently replicated and extended in a study

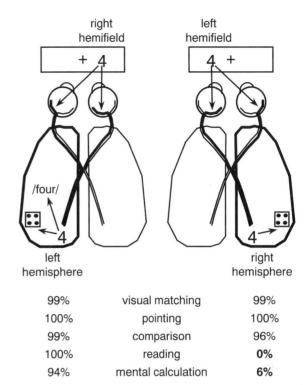

99%	visual matching	99%
100%	pointing	100%
99%	comparison	96%
100%	reading	**0%**
94%	mental calculation	**6%**

FIGURE 68.2 Split-brain patients provide evidence about the hemispheric distribution of number-processing abilities (Cohen and Dehaene, 1996). When digits are presented in the right visual hemifield, hence contacting only the left hemisphere, the patient can perform any number processing task with them, including visual recognition, pointing to the digit in a random array, larger–smaller comparison, reading, and calculation. Thus, the left hemisphere contains visual, verbal, and quantity representations of numbers. But when digits are presented in the left hemifield, hence contacting only the right hemisphere, the patient may still recognize, point to, or compare them, but fails to read them or calculate with them. Although the right hemisphere has access to visual and quantity representations, it seems to lack a verbal representation of numbers as well as procedures for exact calculation. (Data from patient JW; Gazzaniga and Smylie, 1984; Seymour, Reuter-Lorenz, and Gazzaniga, 1994.)

of a patient who suffered a posterior callosal lesion in adulthood (Cohen and Dehaene, 1996). In both sets of experiments, digits were flashed in either the left or the right hemifield, thus contacting only the contralateral hemisphere, and the patients were asked to perform number processing tasks of varying complexity with them (figure 68.2).

An important conclusion of these experiments is that both hemispheres can process digits and quantities. When two digits are presented simultaneously *within* the same hemifield, split-brain patients experience no difficulty deciding whether they are the same or different (while their disconnection renders them completely unable to compare two digits *across* the two hemifields). Hence, both hemispheres can analyze digit shapes. Furthermore, both hemispheres can also point to the larger digit (or to the smaller), and both can classify digits or even two-digit numbers as larger or smaller than some reference. Hence, both hemispheres seem to possess a quantity representation of numbers.

The conclusions drawn from split-brain studies are sometimes questioned, either because some pathways for interhemispheric communication may remain functional, or because the patients may have had an abnormal cerebral organization to begin with. In the present case, however, both arguments can be refuted. First, it is true that the surgical-split cases (Gazzaniga and Smylie, 1984; Seymour, Reuter-Lorenz, and Gazzaniga, 1994) had an intact anterior commissure, and that the patient reported by Cohen and Dehaene (1996) had an infarct affecting only the posterior part of the corpus callosum. But the fact that the patients were at chance level when asked to compare arabic digits *across* the two hemifields offers clear evidence that the remaining pathways were not sufficient for the transmission of numerical information. Hence, their excellent performance when both stimuli were within the left hemifield cannot be attributed to transfer to the left hemisphere. The sharp dissociation between excellent within-hemifield performance and chance-level across-hemifield performance, indicating disrupted interhemispheric transmission, supports the hypothesis that both hemispheres can compare numbers. Second, while the patients studied by Gazzaniga and colleagues suffered from life-long neurological impairments, the patient studied by Cohen and Dehaene was neurologically normal prior to suffering a callosal lesion. Yet the number comparison results were identical in both cases. Hence, the ability of both hemispheres for number comparison does not seem to be an artifact of abnormal initial brain reorganization.

In only one callosal patient (to date) have the response times been recorded during the number comparison task and the distance effect analyzed (Cohen and Dehaene, 1996). A normal distance effect was observed in both hemispheres, with no significant difference in effect size between the two hemispheres. This suggests that the quantity representations of the left and right hemispheres may have similar characteristics. However, more evidence is needed before this point can be firmly accepted.

There are, however, at least two striking differences between the numerical abilities of the left and the right hemispheres. First, digits presented to the left hemisphere can be named normally by the patients, but digits presented to the right hemisphere cannot. This is in keeping with the well-known lateralization of speech production abilities to the left hemisphere. Second, split-brain patients can calculate only with digits presented to

their left hemisphere. When digits are presented to their right hemisphere, the patients fail with operations as simple as adding 2, multiplying by 3, subtracting from 10, or dividing by 2. This is the case even when they merely have to point to the correct result among several possible results, or to indicate nonverbally whether a proposed result is correct or not. The only calculation ability that seems to be available to an isolated right hemisphere, at least occasionally, is approximation. A patient might not be able to decide whether $2 + 2$ makes 4 or 5, but might still easily notice that $2 + 2$ cannot make 9 (Cohen and Dehaene, 1996; Dehaene and Cohen, 1991).

Modular dissociations in brain-lesioned patients

Detailed single-case studies of patients with various cerebral lesions have indicated that the fractionation of calculation skills in neuropsychological cases is much greater than that seen in split-brain cases alone. The number processing skills of a normally educated adult include the ability to

read, write, produce, or comprehend numerals in both arabic (e.g., 12) and verbal ("twelve") formats, thus implying both lexical (single-word) and syntactic (multiple-word) processes;
convert numbers in these various formats to internal quantities, and vice-versa;
compute single-digit addition, subtraction, multiplication, and division operations;
coordinate several such elementary operations to solve a complex, multidigit arithmetic problem.

Most if not all of these abilities have been found to dissociate in brain-lesioned patients, often in a highly specific manner, indicating that there must be partially specific cerebral circuits associated with each of them.

As a detailed example, let us consider the case of patient HY (McCloskey, Sokol, and Goodman, 1986). When attempting to read an arabic numeral aloud, HY often erred, for instance, reading 5 as "seven" and 29 as "forty-nine." A careful analysis indicated that reading errors stemmed from a highly restricted impairment, affecting only one particular cognitive component of the processing chain that converts written arabic numerals into spoken words. First, HY could still decide which of two arabic numerals was the largest. She could also match an arabic digit to a written number word, verify written calculations, or select a number of poker chips corresponding to a given arabic numerals. Thus, identification of digits and access to quantity information were preserved. This narrowed down the reading deficit to an impairment at the level of producing spoken words. Indeed, McCloskey and his colleagues showed that, in a variety of tasks, HY was much more impaired when he had to produce the numerical answers aloud than when he had to write them down as arabic digits. For instance, when asked the number of eggs in a dozen, HY wrote 12 but said "sixteen."

A careful analysis of HY's number production errors revealed strong regularities. The vast majority of errors were substitutions of one number word for another, keeping the grammatical structure of the number intact. Not all substitutions were equally permissible. When the number fell between 1 and 9, so did HY's erroneous response. The categories of teens (10 to 19) and decades (20 to 90) was also respected. In the final analysis, the deficit could be explained by a highly selective impairment in selecting the appropriate number word in the output lexicon. When reading "15," for instance, the patient prepared to read aloud the fifth element of the teens category (eleven, twelve, thirteen, fourteen, *fifteen*), but he mistakenly selected, say, the eighth element *eighteen* instead. Only minor details of the word substitutions remained unexplained by this hypothesis (Campbell and Clark, 1988; Sokol, Goodman-Schulman, and McCloskey, 1989).

A wide variety of similar highly specific deficits of number processing have now been reported (Cipolotti and Butterworth, 1995; Cipolotti, Warrington, and Butterworth, 1995; Dehaene and Cohen, 1995; McCloskey, 1992). Most importantly, at virtually all levels of processing, dissociations have been observed between numbers and the rest of language, suggesting an amazing degree of modularity in the human brain. For instance, at the visual identification level, pure alexic patients who fail to read words often show a largely preserved ability to read and process digits (Cohen and Dehaene, 1995; Déjerine, 1891, 1892). Conversely, a case of impaired number reading with preserved word reading is on record (Cipolotti, Warrington, and Butterworth, 1995). In the writing domain, severe agraphia and alexia may be accompanied by a fully preserved ability to write and read arabic numbers (Anderson, Damasio, and Damasio, 1990). Finally, within the speech production system, patients who suffer from random phoneme substitutions, resulting in the production of an incomprehensible jargon, may produce jargon-free number words (Cohen, Verstichel, and Dehaene, 1998; Geschwind, 1965).

Selective impairments of the quantity representation

The aforementioned deficits concerned the processing of numerical symbols. But do some cases qualify as selective impairments of the semantic quantity representation

of numbers? Laurent Cohen and I have proposed that patients with inferior parietal lesions and Gerstmann-type acalculia suffer from a category-specific impairment of the semantic representation and manipulation of numerical quantities (Dehaene and Cohen, 1995, 1997). From the beginning of this century, it has been known that parietal lesions, usually in the dominant hemisphere, can cause calculation deficits. Gerstmann (1940) reported the frequent co-occurrence of agraphia, acalculia, finger agnosia, and left–right confusion in parietal cases, a tetrad of deficits referred to as Gerstmann's syndrome (although the elements of the syndrome are now know to be dissociable; see Benton, 1992). The lesions that cause acalculia of the Gerstmann type are typically centered on the portion of the intraparietal sulcus that sits immediately behind the angular gyrus (Brodmann's area 39; see figure 68.3). In many cases, the deficit can be extremely incapacitating. Patients may fail to compute operations as simple as $2 + 2$, $3 - 1$, or 3×9. Several characteristics indicate that the deficit arises at a rather abstract level of processing. First, patients may remain fully able to comprehend and to produce numbers in all formats. Second, they show the same calculation difficulties whether the problem is presented to them visually or auditorily, and whether they have to respond verbally or in writing, or even merely have to decide whether a proposed operation is true or false. Thus, the calculation deficit is not due to an inability to identify the numbers or to produce the operation result.

Cohen and I, however, also believe that the patients' impairment is not best described as a specific deficit of calculation only ("anarithmetia" or "acalculia proper"). On the one hand, some calculation processes may remain preserved. Patient MAR, for instance (Dehaene and Cohen, 1997), remained able to retrieve simple multiplication results, such as $2 \times 3 = 6$ or $3 \times 9 = 27$, which he knew by rote. He was very specifically impaired with calculations that were not stored in rote memory and required an internal quantity manipulation, even if it was as simple as $3 - 1$ (he stated that this equaled 7). On the other hand, tasks that require a quantitative understanding of numbers, but are not typically associated with calculation per se, can be impaired in Gerstmann's syndrome patients. Patient MAR could not decide which number fell between 2 and 4 (number bisection task), even though he knew what letter fell between B and D, or what month fell between February and April. MAR also exhibited a discrete difficulty in number comparison, occasionally stating, for instance, that 5 was larger than 6.

The latter deficit suggests that MAR's understanding of the number line was impaired. Indeed, Cohen and I have suggested that inferior parietal cortex holds the

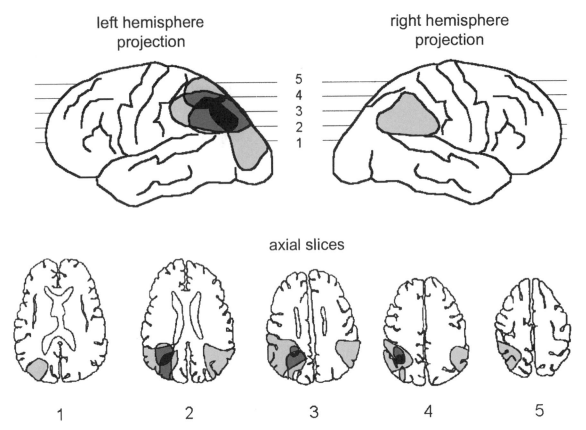

left hemisphere
projection

right hemisphere
projection

5
4
3
2
1

axial slices

1   2   3   4   5

FIGURE 68.3 Overlapping lesions of five patients with Gerst-mann's syndrome. All patients showed severe deficits in the comprehension and mental manipulation of numbers. The le-sions overlap deep in the inferior lobule, in the vicinity of the intraparietal sulcus. (Redrawn from Dehaene and Cohen, 1997; Takayama et al., 1994.)

internal analogical representation of numerical quanti-ties. Damage to this region causes calculation deficits only if the requested calculations call for internal ma-nipulation of quantities, and not if the task merely in-volves the retrieval of rote arithmetic facts from verbal memory. Typically, then, subtraction and number bi-section are severely impaired, while simple multiplica-tion may be relatively preserved. The fact that interval bisection is affected only in the number domain, but not in the domain of the alphabet, months, or days of week, gives direct evidence that the deficit can be cate-gory-specific and not just task-specific.

A simple model of number processing circuits

Based on the variety of number-processing deficits that can be observed in patients, Laurent Cohen and I have proposed a tentative model of the cerebral circuits impli-cated in calculation and number processing: the *triple-code model* (see figure 68.4; Dehaene, 1992; Dehaene and Cohen, 1995). Initially developed as a purely cognitive model of the different types of representations involved in various number-processing tasks, this model also aims to explain chronometric data from normal subjects (De-haene, 1992). A later version (Dehaene and Cohen, 1995) made specific proposals as to the putative cerebral substrates of these representations.

Functionally, the model rests on three fundamental hypotheses:

1. Numerical information can be manipulated men-tally in three formats: an analogical representation of quantities, in which numbers are represented as distribu-tions of activation on the number line; a verbal format, in which numbers are represented as strings of words (e.g., thirty-seven); and a visual Arabic number form representation, in which numbers are represented as a string of digits (e.g., 37).

2. Transcoding procedures allow information to be translated directly from one code to the other. For in-stance, the model supposes that one can mentally con-vert an arabic digit to the corresponding number word (from 3 to three) nonsemantically, without passing through the semantic representation of the quantity three. This hypothesis distinguishes the triple-code model from other modular models of number process-ing (e.g., McCloskey, Macaruso, and Whetstone, 1992)

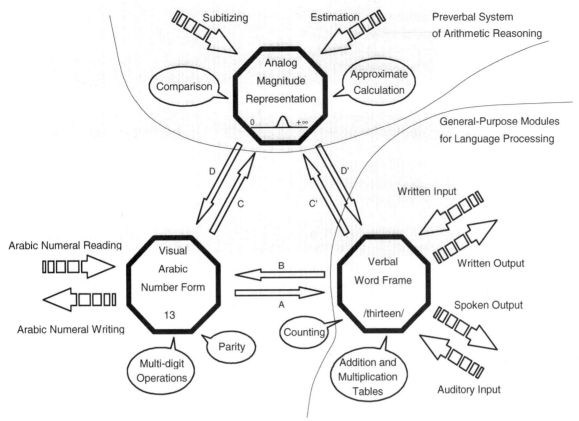

FIGURE 68.4 Functional architecture of the triple-code model of number processing. The three cardinal representations of numbers are represented by octagons. Direct input and output pathways to and from these representations are represented by thick arrows, while thin arrows represent the six possible transcoding pathways that link them. Specific processes putatively attached to a given level of representation are denoted by balloons. (Redrawn from Dehaene, 1992.)

and is more in line with multiple-route models of word processing. Recently, this aspect of the model has received strong support from the observation of patients who cannot convert directly from arabic to verbal numerals (e.g., cannot read arabic digits aloud), but can still convert back-and-forth between these representations and the corresponding quantities (Cipolotti and Butterworth, 1995; Cohen and Dehaene, 1995).

3. Each number-processing task is assumed to rest on a fixed set of input and output codes. For instance, number comparison is postulated to rely on numbers coded as quantities on the number line. Likewise, the model postulates that multiplication tables are memorized as verbal associations between numbers represented as a string of words; that subtraction, an operation that is not memorized by rote verbal learning, calls heavily on the quantity representation; and that multidigit operations are often performed mentally using the visual arabic code and a spatially laid-out representation of the aligned digits.

Neuropsychological observations have enabled us to flesh out the model and to associate tentative anatomical

circuits to each function. Cohen and I speculate that the inferior occipitotemporal sectors of both hemispheres are involved in the visual identification processes that give rise to the arabic number form; that the left perisylvian areas are implicated in the verbal representations of numbers (as with any other string of words); and, most crucially, that the inferior parietal areas of both hemispheres are involved in the analogical quantity representation.

Note that the redundant representation of the visual and quantity codes in the left and right hemispheres can explain why, in callosal patients, number comparison remains feasible by both hemispheres (Cohen and Dehaene, 1996; Seymour, Reuter-Lorenz, and Gazzaniga, 1994). This bilaterality assumption does seem to raise a problem for interpreting acalculia cases, however. If there is a bilateral quantity representation, why does a *unilateral* inferior parietal lesion suffice to impair quantity manipulation in Gerstmann syndrome patients? Lesion data clearly indicate that, although the right hemisphere contains a representation of quantity (and although the right inferior parietal cortex is strongly activated during calculation), only a left-lateralized lesion, in

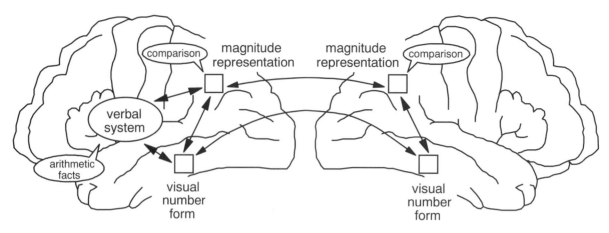

FIGURE 68.5 A schematic diagram of the anatomical substrates of the triple-code model of number processing. (Redrawn from Dehaene and Cohen, 1995.)

subjects with normal hemispheric dominance, causes acalculia of the Gerstmann type.

In spite of the superficial paradox, the triple-code model can explain this result. According to the model, only the left hemisphere has access to the verbal code and to the calculation abilities that depend on it. In the case of a unilateral left inferior parietal lesion, the model therefore predicts that the right-hemispheric parietal quantity representation, although intact, will be functionally disconnected from the left-hemispheric language system (see figure 68.5). Hence, such patients may remain largely able to compare number and perform other manipulations of pure quantities (this was the case with patient MAR, who was largely above chance in number comparison). Yet, according to the model, they are not able to use this quantity knowledge to guide arithmetic fact retrieval and number production, hence their striking deficit in simple arithmetic. The same argument also explains why the right hemisphere of callosal patients cannot read numbers aloud nor calculate with them. Only further research will tell whether this account of the special role of left parietal lesions in acalculia cases is valid. It should also help us grasp a better understanding of the respective roles of the left and right inferior parietal areas in number processing.

Brain imaging of calculation

Functional brain-imaging techniques now provide new tests of the organization of cognitive processes, including calculation processes. In itself, information about cerebral localization is not particularly interesting to cognitive scientists. Once a specific brain area has been localized, however, it becomes possible to ask some fruitful questions: What are the parameters that make it more or less active? What tasks is it responsive to? And what aspects of the stimulus, task, or response do *not* affect its state of activity? With dynamic methods such as electro- or magnetoencephalography, it is also possible to record how quickly and for how long a region activates. In all these respects, the triple-code model makes specific predictions. Most critically, it predicts that the left and right inferior parietal areas should be active during various quantitative number-processing tasks, and that their activation should depend purely on quantitative parameters such as number size and numerical distance, but not on input or output modality nor on the notation used for numbers.

Roland and Friberg (1985) were the first to monitor blood flow changes during calculation as opposed to rest. When subjects repeatedly subtracted 3 from a given number, activation increased bilaterally in inferior parietal and prefrontal cortex. These locations have been confirmed using fMRI (Burbaud et al., 1995; Rueckert et al., 1996). Because the serial subtraction task imposes a heavy load on working memory, it was not clear whether any of these activations were specifically related to number processing. However, experiments using simpler tasks have confirmed that the inferior parietal area seems to play a specific role involved in number processing. In a positron emission tomography study of multiplication and comparison of digit pairs, with little or no working memory component, my colleagues and I again found bilateral parietal activation confined to the intraparietal region (Dehaene et al., 1996). This confirmed results obtained with a coarser resolution EEG method (Inouye et al., 1993) as well as with single-unit recordings in neurological patients (Abdullaev and Melnichuk, 1996).

While these studies indicate that the left and right inferior parietal areas are active and presumably play an important role in calculation tasks, they do not establish the exact nature of their contribution. The triple-code model, however, makes the specific prediction that the inferior parietal cortex activation reflects the operation of an abstract quantity system independent of input and output modalities. Recently, my colleagues and I have begun to test this prediction.

In one study, we used high-density recordings of event-related potentials (ERPs) during a number comparison task to study the cerebral basis of the distance effect. An additive-factor design was used in which three factors were varied: number notation (arabic or verbal), numerical distance (close or far pairs), and response hand (right or left). The results revealed that inferior parietal activity was modulated by the numerical distance separating the numbers to be compared, but not by the notation used to present them (Dehaene et al., 1996). Notation did have a significant effect on the N1 wave, around 150 milliseconds after the visual presentation of the stimuli, indicating bilateral processing for arabic digits, but unilateral left-hemispheric processing for visual number words (in agreement with the triple-code model). By about 200 ms, however, ERPs were dominated by a parietal distance effect with a significant lateralization to the right, and without further influence of notation. Dipole models indicated that the scalp-recorded distance effect could be modeled by two bilateral dipoles located deep within the inferior parietal lobule, with the right-hemispheric dipole showing stronger activation than the left. The response hand effect, which emerged as early as 250 ms after the stimulus, provided an upper bound on the duration of the numerical comparison process.

A similar ERP study of number multiplication (Kiefer and Dehaene, 1997) showed that inferior parietal activity lasts longer during multiplication of two large digits than during multiplication of two small digits—again, regardless of the modality of presentation of the operands (auditory or visual). The main difference with the previous study of number comparison was that the ERP effects, though always bilateral, were stronger over the left inferior parietal area during multiplication, but stronger over the right parietal area during number comparison.

Recently, my colleagues and I replicated this modulation by task demands using fMRI (Chochon et al., 1999). We alternated 36-second blocks during which either single letters or single digits were flashed in the center of a screen. During the letter blocks, the subjects mentally named the letters. This served as a control for the various arithmetic tasks used during the digit blocks. On different runs, subjects were asked to name the digits, to compare them with 5, to multiply them by 3, or to subtract them from 11. In all subjects, fMRI identified a bilateral network that was very clearly pinpointed to the banks of the middle segment of the intraparietal sulcus (figure 68.6), in a location in excellent agreement with the result of lesion studies in Gerstmann's syndrome (figure 68.3). Importantly, however, the size and lateralization of this parietal activation was modulated by task demands. Relative to letter reading, digit comparison yielded greater activity in the right inferior parietal area, multiplication greater activity in the left parietal area, and subtraction a bilateral increase. In agreement with the hypothesis of a nonsemantic direct naming route, however, digit naming in itself did not significantly activate the parietal areas, although a small activation of the right intraparietal cortex was occasionally seen in some subjects.

Number: A biological determined category of knowledge?

In summary, number processing constitutes a remarkable example of the power of the cognitive neuroscience approach, in which a combination of methodologies borrowed from cognitive psychology, neuropsychology, and brain imaging is brought to bear on a single problem. Based on the converging evidence just reviewed, the following working hypotheses can be formulated:

1. The human brain contains an analogical representation of numerical quantities, which can be likened to a mental "number line." This representation is independent of, and common to, the multiple input and output notation systems we use to communicate numbers, such as words or arabic digits. It is subject to distance and magnitude effects.

2. Both the left and the right hemisphere have access to the mental representation of numerical quantity.

3. Lesions of the intraparietal cortex in the dominant hemisphere yield a specific impairment in the mental manipulation of quantities, particularly evident in subtraction and number bisection tasks.

4. The left and right intraparietal cortices are active when normal subjects perform simple calculation tasks. The strength, duration, and lateralization of their activation depends on the nature and difficulty of the operation involved, which in turn is related to the size and numerical distance of the numbers involved. It does not, however, depend on the modality or notation in which the numbers are presented.

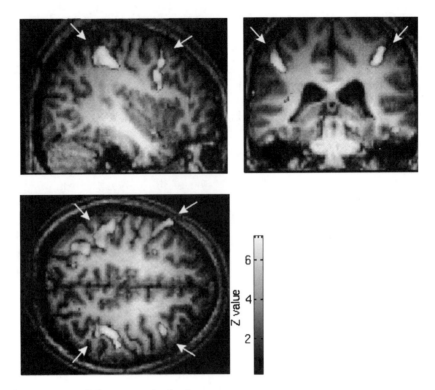

FIGURE 68.6 Bilateral activations of the intraparietal sulcus, postcentral sulcus, and prefrontal areas during single-digit subtraction in a single subject. (Data from Chochon et al., 1999.)

Empirical findings lend support to the hypothesis that some neural circuits within intraparietal cortex include a partially prewired, biologically determined representation of numerical quantities, a category-specific system innately biased toward acquiring and manipulation information about numbers. In that respect, several details of the data should be mentioned, although space precludes a more thorough discussion of these topics (see Dehaene, 1997; Dehaene, Dehaene-Lambertz, and Cohen, 1998; Gallistel and Gelman, 1992). First, nonhuman primates, as well as other species such as rats, pigeons, or dolphins, exhibit remarkable capacities for extracting and manipulating numerosities. Furthermore, like humans, they are sensitive to numerical distance and size effects, suggesting that their numerical abilities may be phylogenetically related to ours, and are not merely superficially analogous. This supports the idea that our brains may have incorporated a dedicated representation of numbers in the course of evolution. Second, preverbal human infants also show remarkable number-processing abilities prior to schooling, supporting the autonomous emergence of a dedicated "number sense" during early development. Third, there are cases of developmental calculation deficits–highly specific, modular deficits of number processing, plausibly related to early brain damage–that leave intact other semantic

processing abilities. This supports the existence of a dedicated brain circuit specifically prepared to acquire elementary arithmetic and whose lesion largely abolishes the acquisition of numeracy. Fourth, the specific role of the intraparietal cortex in calculation in adult humans seems to be universal and largely independent of the culture, education, or number notation system acquired by the individual. Hence, acalculia in the context of Gerstmann's syndrome is found with similar lesion sites in patients from various countries and cultures, and intraparietal activations during calculation have been seen in subjects from various countries.

While this converging evidence certainly supports the notion of a dedicated, category-specific cerebral circuit for number sense, the final validation of this concept will have to await the acquisition of important new data. There are several loose ends to the demonstration that intraparietal cortex is the seat of a specialized, biologically determined representation of number. It seems, therefore, quite appropriate that this chapter should end with a list of open questions for further research to address:

• Is a specific region of the human intraparietal cortex entirely specialized for number processing, or is there some overlap with areas involved in spatial representation, attentional displacements, hand movements, and/ or mental rotation tasks?

• Is a homolog of human intraparietal cortex active in animals during number processing tasks? If so, what is its architecture and what are its single-cell properties?

• Is intraparietal cortex active during infancy and does it underlie infants' abilities for elementary arithmetic?

• How are the cerebral circuits for number processing modified as children acquire the formal rules of arithmetic? How is numerical expertise reflected in the organization of intraparietal cortex?

We can hope that in the upcoming years we will begin to answer these questions, and hence begin to understand how the human brain gives rise to what is perhaps its most extraordinary feat–mathematics.

REFERENCES

ABDULLAEV, Y. G., and K. V. MELNICHUK, 1996. Counting and arithmetic functions of neurons in the human parietal cortex [abstr.]. *NeuroImage* 3:S216.

ANDERSON, S. W., A. R. DAMASIO, and H. DAMASIO, 1990. Troubled letters but not numbers: Domain specific cognitive impairments following focal damage in frontal cortex. *Brain* 113:749–766.

ASHCRAFT, M. H., and J. BATTAGLIA, 1978. Cognitive arithmetics: Evidence for retrieval and decision processes in mental addition. *J. Exp. Psychol.: Hum. Learn. Mem.* 4:527–538.

BENTON, A. L., 1992. Gerstmann's syndrome. *Arch. Neurol.* 49:445–447.

BRYSBAERT, M., W. FIAS, and M.-P. NOËL, 1998. The Whorfian hypothesis and numerical cognition: Is "twenty-four" processed in the same way as "four-and-twenty"? *Cognition* 66:51–77.

BUCKLEY, P. B., and C. B. GILLMAN, 1974. Comparison of digits and dot patterns. *J. Exp. Psychol.* 103:1131–1136.

BURBAUD, P., P. DEGREZE, P. LAFON, J. M. FRANCONI, B. BOULIGAND, B. BIOULAC, J. M. CAILE, and M. ALLARD, 1995. Lateralization of prefrontal activation during internal mental calculation: A functional magnetic resonance imaging study. *J. Neurophysiol.* 74:2194–2200.

CAMPBELL, J. I. D., 1992. *The Nature and Origins of Mathematical Skills.* Amsterdam: Elsevier.

CAMPBELL, J. I. D., 1994. Architectures for numerical cognition. *Cognition* 53:1–44.

CAMPBELL, J. I. D., and J. M. CLARK, 1988. An encoding complex view of cognitive number processing: Comment on McCloskey, Sokol & Goodman (1998). *J. Exp. Psychol.: Gen.* 117:204–214.

CHOCHON, F., L. COHEN, P. F. VAN DE MOORTELE, and S. DEHAENE, 1999. Differential contributions of the left and right inferior parietal lobules to number processing. Submitted.

CIPOLOTTI, L., and B. BUTTERWORTH, 1995. Toward a multiroute model of number processing: Impaired number transcoding with preserved calculation skills. *J. Exp. Psychol.: Gen.* 124:375–390.

CIPOLOTTI, L., E. K. WARRINGTON, and B. BUTTERWORTH, 1995. Selective impairment in manipulating arabic numerals. *Cortex* 31:73–86.

COHEN, L., and S. DEHAENE, 1995. Number processing in pure alexia: The effect of hemispheric asymmetries and task demands. *NeuroCase* 1:121–137.

COHEN, L., and S. DEHAENE, 1996. Cerebral networks for number processing: Evidence from a case of posterior callosal lesion. *NeuroCase* 2:155–174.

COHEN, L., P. VERSTICHEL, and S. DEHAENE, 1998. Neologistic jargon sparing numbers: A category-specific phonological impairment. *Cogn. Neuropsychol.* 14:1029–1061.

DEHAENE, S., 1992. Varieties of numerical abilities. *Cognition* 14:1–42.

DEHAENE, S., 1996. The organization of brain activations in number comparison: Event-related potentials and the additive-factors methods. *J. Cogn. Neurosci.* 8:47–68.

DEHAENE, S., 1997. *The Number Sense.* New York: Oxford University Press.

DEHAENE, S., and R. AKHAVEIN, 1995. Attention, automaticity and levels of representation in number processing. *J. Exp. Psychol.: Learn. Mem. Cognit.* 21:314–326.

DEHAENE, S., and L. COHEN, 1991. Two mental calculation systems: A case study of severe acalculia with preserved approximation. *Neuropsychologia* 29:1045–1074.

DEHAENE, S., and L. COHEN, 1995. Towards an anatomical and functional model of number processing. *Math. Cognit.* 1:83–120.

DEHAENE, S., and L. COHEN, 1997. Cerebral pathways for calculation: Double dissociation between rote verbal and quantitative knowledge of arithmetic. *Cortex* 33:219–250.

DEHAENE, S., G. DEHAENE-LAMBERTZ, and L. COHEN, 1998. Abstract representation of numbers in the animal and human brain. *Trends Neurosci.* 21:355–361.

DEHAENE, S., E. DUPOUX, and J. MEHLER, 1990. Is numerical comparison digital: Analogical and symbolic effects in two-digit number comparison. *J. Exp. Psychol.: Hum. Percept. Perf.* 16:626–641.

DEHAENE, S., and J. MEHLER, 1992. Cross-linguistic regularities in the frequency of number words. *Cognition* 43:1–29.

DEHAENE, S., N. TZOURIO, V. FRAK, L. RAYNAUD, L. COHEN, J. MEHLER, and B. MAZOYER, 1996. Cerebral activations during number multiplication and comparison: A PET study. *Neuropsychologia* 34: 1097–1106.

DÉJERINE, J., 1891. Sur un cas de cécité verbale avec agraphie suivi d'autopsie. *Mem. Soc. Biol.* 3:197–201.

DÉJERINE, J., 1892. Contribution à l'étude anatomo-pathologique et clinique des differentes variétés de cécité verbale. *Mem. Soc. Biol.* 4:61–90.

DUNCAN, E. M., and C. E. MCFARLAND, 1980. Isolating the effects of symbolic distance and semantic congruity in comparative judgments: An additive-factors analysis. *Mem. Cognit.* 8:612–622.

GALLISTEL, C. R., and R. GELMAN, 1992. Preverbal and verbal counting and computation. *Cognition* 44:43–74.

GAZZANIGA, M. S., and S. A. HILLYARD, 1971. Language and speech capacity of the right hemisphere. *Neuropsychologia* 9:273–280.

GAZZANIGA, M. S., and C. E. SMYLIE, 1984. Dissociation of language and cognition: A psychological profile of two disconnected right hemispheres. *Brain* 107:145–153.

GERSTMANN, J., 1940. Syndrome of finger agnosia disorientation for right and left agraphia and acalculia. *Arch. Neurol. Psychiatry* 44:398–408.

GESCHWIND, N., 1965. Disconnection syndromes in animals and man. *Brain* 88:237–294.

HINRICHS, J. V., D. S. YURKO, and J. M. HU, 1981. Two-digit number comparison: Use of place information. *J. Exp. Psychol.: Hum. Percept. Perf.* 7:890–901.

INOUYE, T., K. SHINOSAKI, A. IYAMA, and Y. MATSUMOTO, 1993. Localisation of activated areas and directional EEG patterns during mental arithmetic. *Electroenceph. Clin. Neurophysiol.* 86:224–230.

KIEFER, M., and S. DEHAENE, 1997. The time course of parietal activation in single-digit multiplication: Evidence from event-related potentials. *Math. Cognit.*, 3:1–30.

MCCLOSKEY, M., P. MACARUSO, and T. WHETSTONE, 1992. The functional architecture of numerical processing mechanisms: Defending the modular model. In *The Nature and Origins of Mathematical Skills*, J. I. D. Campbell, ed. Amsterdam: Elsevier, pp. 493–537.

MCCLOSKEY, M., S. M. SOKOL, and R. A. GOODMAN, 1986. Cognitive processes in verbal-number production: Inferences from the performance of brain-damaged subjects. *J. Exp. Psychol.: Gen.* 115:307–330.

MOYER, R. S., and T. K. LANDAUER, 1967. Time required for judgements of numerical inequality. *Nature* 215:1519–1520.

NOEL, M. P., W. FIAS, and M. BRYSBAERT, 1997. About the influence of the presentation format on arithmetic fact retrieval processes. *Cognition* 63:325–374.

ROLAND, P. E., and L. FRIBERG, 1985. Localization of cortical areas activated by thinking. *J. Neurophysiol.* 53:1219–1243.

RUECKERT, L., N. LANGE, A. PARTIOT, I. APPOLLONIO, I. LITVAR, D. LeBIHAN, and J. GRAFMAN, 1996. Visualizing cortical activation during mental calculation with functional MRI. *NeuroImage* 3:97–103.

SEYMOUR, S. E., P. A. REUTER-LORENZ, and M. S. GAZZANIGA, 1994. The disconnection syndrome: Basic findings reaffirmed. *Brain* 117:105–115.

SOKOL, S. M., R. GOODMAN-SCHULMAN, and M. MCCLOSKEY, 1989. In defense of a modular architecture for the number-processing system: Reply to Campbell and Clark. *J. Exp. Psychol.: Gen.* 118:105–110.

SPERRY, R. W., 1968. Mental unity following surgical disconnection of the cerebral hemispheres. In *The Harvey Lectures*, 62. New York: Academic Press.

TAKAYAMA, Y., M. SUGISHITA, I. AKIGUCHI, and J. KIMURA, 1994. Isolated acalculia due to left parietal lesion. *Arch. Neurol.* 51:286–291.

TZENG, O. J. L., and W. WANG, 1983. The first two R's. *Amer. Scientist* 71:238–243.

VOBERG, D., and S. BLANKENBERGER, 1993. Mentale Repräsentation von Zahlen. *Sprache Kogn.* 12:98–114.

69 Cerebellar Contributions to Cognition and Imagery

RICHARD B. IVRY AND JULIE A. FIEZ

ABSTRACT The cerebellum has traditionally been viewed as an integral part of the motor system. However, recent anatomical, neuropsychological, and neuroimaging work indicates that this subcortical structure may contribute to cognitive processing in a substantive manner. A number of different theoretical frameworks for understanding cerebellar involvement in cognition have been developed. These include functional hypotheses that have emphasized diverse ideas ranging from an essential role for the cerebellum in the control of attention, error detection and learning, internal control of timing, or covert action and imagery. This chapter outlines the principal sources of motivation for this mini-revolution and reviews the evidence in support of these theoretical conjectures.

A decade ago, the inclusion of a chapter on the cerebellum in a section on "Thought and Imagery" would have seemed preposterous. The cerebellum has traditionally been viewed as an integral part of the motor system, with functional descriptions referring to its role in the coordination of skilled movement, motor learning, and the control of balance. Cognitive psychologists have tended to overlook the study of such processes, perhaps because movements are assumed to be built on reflexive units, subserved by dedicated systems that involve few of the kinds of representational capabilities characteristic of cognitive systems. Nonetheless, action systems have recently garnered increased interest in cognitive psychology as researchers recognize that the essence of a complex processing system is to allow an organism to act in a flexible and efficient manner.

As part of these developments, interest in the cerebellum has exploded in the past decade. Much of the work here continues in the motor tradition, especially that in the computational and neurophysiological literatures. However, the view that the domain of cerebellar function can be understood within the relatively narrow framework of motor control and learning is undergoing some serious challenges. Some of the new hypotheses are extensions of functional accounts of the cerebellum's role in motor control, based on the idea that certain

computations originally evolved for controlling action may have been co-opted into other contexts. Other hypotheses are divorced from the motor domain, building on the idea that this massive structure may contribute in a heterogeneous manner to a number of distinct cognitive systems.

Here, we review the evidence motivating this revolution and provide an overview of the different functional hypotheses proposed to account for how the cerebellum might contribute to the executive operations of a sophisticated cognitive system. Given that this paradigm shift is truly in its infancy, our evaluation of the evidence is tempered. We seek to maintain the appropriate level of skepticism demanded by science while avoiding the temptation to suffocate, prematurely, the ideas that may provide the seeds for novel conceptualizations of the relationship between the brain and behavior.

Evidence indicating a role for the cerebellum in higher cognition

The hypothesis that the cerebellum might be involved in higher level cognition did not spring, Athene-like, from the head of Zeus. Over the past century, there have been scattered proposals suggesting that a strictly motoric view might be limited (see review in Schmahmann, 1997). Some of these early hypotheses were inspired by Piagetian ideas emphasizing the link between action and knowledge; others derived from observations regarding the link between the cerebellum and certain autonomic functions. These ideas, however, failed to take hold, in part because the experimental evidence in support of these somewhat radical notions was minimal at best. Moreover, simple clinical observation was sure to exert a powerful bias: Patients or animals with cerebellar lesions exhibit pronounced deficits in motor control. Any coexisting disorders of autonomic function, emotion, or higher mental thought were clearly minimal in contrast to the severe problems in coordination.

New perspectives on cerebellar function are closely linked to the emergence of cognitive neuroscience as an interdisciplinary enterprise. In this section, we briefly

RICHARD B. IVRY Department of Psychology, University of California, Berkeley, Calif.
JULIE A. FIEZ Department of Psychology, University of Pittsburgh, Pittsburgh, Pa.

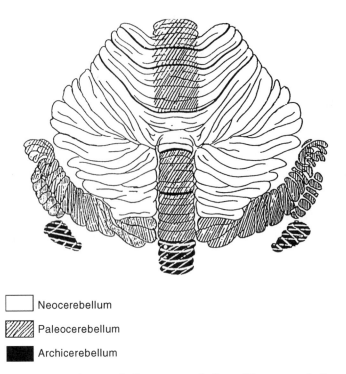

☐ Neocerebellum

▨ Paleocerebellum

■ Archicerebellum

FIGURE 69.1 Schematic drawing of the monkey cerebellum indicating the relative proportion of the three major subdivisions—the archicerebellum, the paleocerebellum, and the neo-cerebellum. The neocerebellum has undergone tremendous expansion in primates, paralleling similar evolutionary developments in the frontal lobes.

review some of the anatomical, behavioral, and imaging findings that have motivated researchers to propose extensions of the domain of cerebellar function beyond motor control. These results set the stage for the next section, in which we evaluate various functional hypotheses of how the cerebellum may contribute to cognition.

ANATOMICAL CONSIDERATIONS The cerebellum has long fascinated neuroanatomists. While it constitutes about 10% of the total mass of the central nervous system in humans, it contains more than 50% of all the neurons. The cerebellar cortex is traditionally divided into three subregions—the archicerebellum, the paleocerebellum, and the neocerebellum (figure 69.1). The latter region, especially the more lateral zones that constitute the cerebellar hemispheres, would seem to provide the essential anatomical substrate for influencing cognition. This region has undergone tremendous expansion in primates (Leiner, Leiner, and Dow, 1986). The primary input to the cerebellar hemispheres comes from the pontine nuclei. Labeling methods demonstrate that these brainstem nuclei are innervated by both ascending and descending fibers. Of particular interest is the fact that the descending corticopontine fibers not only originate in motor and premotor areas, but are also found in parietal, temporal, and prefrontal cortices (Schmahmann and Pandya, 1997).

The output from the cerebellum also suggests that this structure is part of a network that extends beyond the "motor" system. All cerebellar output originates in the deep cerebellar nuclei. Most prominent in humans, indeed, accounting for more than 90% of all nuclear cells, is the dentate nucleus. Using a transneuronal retrograde tracing technique, Middleton and Strick (1994, 1997) demonstrated that the output from the dentate nuclei is linked with motor, premotor, and prefrontal cortex via segregated thalamic relays. Thus, the cerebellum is not just receiving input from distributed cortical regions; it also has the prerequisite connections for influencing the kinds of functions associated with prefrontal cortex. It should be noted that there have been no systematic quantitative studies comparing the distribution of cerebellar projections to motor, premotor, and prefrontal areas, and little effort has been made to ascertain whether the cerebellum projects to more medial aspects of prefrontal cortex. The emphasis to date has been on establishing the existence of cerebello-prefrontal pathways.

Studies of the neuropathology associated with certain psychiatric disorders also suggest a cerebellar role in cognition and emotion. In vivo structural MR studies have shown that cerebellar pathology, especially in neocerebellar regions, appears to be a consistent feature of autism (Courchesne, Townsend, and Saitoh, 1994; but see Bauman, Filipek, and Kemper, 1997), as post-mortem histological analyses suggest (Ritvo et al., 1986). More recent studies have also shown pathology in non-cerebellar structures, including the brainstem, limbic regions, the corpus callosum, and the parietal lobes (see Courchesne, 1997). Thus, the question as to whether there is a causal link between the cerebellar pathology and autism remains open. Nonetheless, the fact that cerebellar anatomy is consistently abnormal in autism is provocative, given that coordination problems are not generally associated with this disorder. There are also reports of cerebellar abnormalities in the brains of schizophrenics (Katsetos, Hyde, and Herman, 1997).

PERFORMANCE OF CEREBELLAR PATIENTS ON NEUROPSYCHOLOGICAL TESTS A more direct assay on the role of the cerebellum in cognition comes from neuropsychological studies of patients with either focal or diffuse cerebellar damage. The evidence is mixed on the basis of assessments using standardized batteries from clinical neuropsychology (see review by Daum and Ackermann, 1997). In general, patients with lesions restricted to the cerebellum perform within the normal range on IQ tests. It is difficult to compare their performance to normal subjects since the latter are selected in order to match the patients in terms of IQ. Nonetheless, group studies from three different laboratories have found that the patients score in the normal range when given either the complete Wechsler Adult Intelligence Scale or subtests of this instrument (Daum et al., 1993; Dimitrov et al., 1996; Mangels, Ivry, and Shimizu, 1998).

Daum and colleagues (1993) report one of the most comprehensive studies to date. Their study included nineteen patients: In thirteen patients the damage was restricted to the cerebellum, and in six the damage extended to brainstem structures (e.g., olivopontocerebellar atrophy). The patients were given an extensive battery of tests designed to assess frontal lobe function, verbal memory, and visuospatial memory. The performance of the cerebellar-only group was comparable to that of age-, IQ-, and mood-matched control subjects. In contrast, the patients with cerebellar plus brainstem damage performed more poorly than the control and cerebellar-only groups on the various measures. This pattern is evident in related studies (Appollonio et al., 1993). Performance on neuropsychological tests appears to decline as atrophic processes become more advanced, and may well reflect the involvement of noncerebellar structures (Kish et al., 1994).

A number of researchers have borrowed experimental tasks from cognitive psychology to explore specific domains of performance by patients with cerebellar lesions. These studies have shown that these patients may perform poorly even when the tasks minimize motor requirements. For instance, cerebellar patients have difficulty in generating a list of words that begin with a target letter (Appollonio et al., 1993; Mangels, Ivry, and

Shimizu, 1998) or in learning arbitrary associations between different semantic categories (Bracke-Tolkmitt et al., 1989). Results from such testing have been used to provide support for various functional theories of the cerebellum, as we discuss in greater detail below. It should be noted that the interpretation of the findings is often a matter of debate, since many of the tasks involve a number of component operations and similar abnormal performance can be observed in a variety of groups with cortical lesions (Daum and Ackermann, 1997). For instance, impaired performance on tasks associated with the frontal lobes may not be directly related to cerebellar function, but rather may be secondary to changes in cortical processing that arise indirectly from cerebellar pathology.

NEUROIMAGING Neuroimaging data have probably provided the greatest impetus for the cerebellar cognitive revolution. A large body of literature has convincingly demonstrated that changes in metabolic activity in the cerebellum are not simply correlated with the extent of overt motor behavior (for a review of visual studies, see Shulman et al., 1997). Indeed, it is almost harder to find a study using subtractive logic that does not identify a cerebellar locus of activity than one in which the cerebellum appears silent.

Consider the widely cited language studies of Petersen and colleagues (Petersen et al., 1989; Raichle et al., 1994). One contrast sought to identify neural structures associated with the analysis of semantics. On each trial, subjects were presented with a single word, a common noun. In the control condition, they simply had to read the stimulus word aloud. In the experimental condition, they were required to generate a semantic associate of the stimulus word, in particular, a verb associate. For example, for a target word *apple*, an appropriate response might be "peel" or "throw" or "eat." Thus, the perceptual demands were identical in the two conditions–read a single word; and, motorically, the subjects articulated a single word on each trial. Nonetheless, activation in the right cerebellar cortex was significantly greater in the generate condition than in the control condition.

Initially, the cerebellar activation sites were reported with relatively little discussion, reflecting the fact that the existing literature offered scant basis for interpreting these results. But as these serendipitous results turned up across a range of imaging studies, they began to invite attention. Several recent studies have focused specifically on the cerebellum, with a view to identifying task domains that produce signal changes in this subcortical structure. For example, Kim, Ugurbil, and Strick (1994) used a 4-tesla magnet in a functional MRI study to focus on activation in the dentate nucleus. This structure showed greater activation during a difficult problem-solving task, even though the subjects were actually producing less overt movement in this condition compared to a control condition involving an easy problem-solving task. Other fMRI researchers have hypothesized that cerebellar activation may be related to attention shifting (Allen et al., 1997), memory rehearsal (Desmond et al., 1997), and sensory exploration (Gao et al., 1996).

Functional hypotheses

While the evidence just reviewed is intriguing, the cognitive neuroscience community has yet to reach consensus on how (and even if) the cerebellum contributes to higher cognition. Many of the behavioral tasks used in neuropsychological studies are quite complex and the observed deficits are open to a variety of interpretations. Neuroimaging techniques such as PET and fMRI offer powerful tools for addressing questions of anatomy but, to date, have been of limited value for developing functional accounts of the metabolic changes. In this section, we review some of the functional hypotheses that have been proposed for how the cerebellum contributes to cognition. Our review here is selective. Our criterion was twofold. First, we focus on those that have been articulated with sufficient clarity to allow empirical evaluation. Second, in keeping with the spirit of this section of the volume, we emphasize hypotheses that are most relevant to the study of thought and imagery.

MENTAL COORDINATION AND THE CONTROL OF ATTENTION   Theories of the cerebellum and cognition are generally grounded in the belief that, over the course of evolution, the functional capabilities of this subcortical structure have come to extend beyond a more restricted motor domain. In their seminal paper, Leiner, Leiner, and Dow (1986) offered the conjecture that the highly evolved cerebellum of primates plays a central role in mental coordination, analogous to its role in motor coordination. The idea here, although somewhat vague, is that the cerebellum ensures that processing in distributed regions of the central nervous system is coordinated in order to allow efficient and skilled thought, in much the same way the cerebellum apparently contributes to the control of skilled action.

One relatively specific variant of this hypothesis is that the cerebellum is important for orienting attention (for reviews, see Courchesne and Allen, 1997; Akshoomoff, Courchesne, and Townsend, 1997). Attentional functions have been attributed to numerous brain structures (see Posner and Petersen, 1990), and considerable effort has been devoted to identifying the specific contributions of these structures. According to Courchesne

and colleagues, the cerebellar contribution to attentional functions is to rapidly prime task-relevant systems in order to enhance neural responsiveness. This anticipatory effect is assumed to be multimodal. Indeed, the fact that cerebellar neurons are responsive to auditory, visual, somatosensory, and perhaps even affective input, provides one of the main sources of motivation for this theory. The cerebellum is not necessarily the locus of the attentional commands. Rather, the cerebellum ensures that attentional commands are implemented in a rapid and coordinated manner. Thus, cerebellar lesions are not expected to produce dramatic attentional deficits such as neglect, but only to make shifts of attention slower and more effortful.

Evidence in support of the attention hypothesis comes from behavioral, electrophysiological, and neuroimaging studies (Akshoomoff, Courchesne, and Townsend, 1997). A series of studies have compared various patient groups on two monitoring tasks—a control task in which attention remains focused on a single dimension and an experimental task in which attention must be rapidly shifted between two dimensions. In both tasks, subjects are presented with a series of auditory and visual stimuli. On each dimension, one value is designated the target (e.g., red and high pitch) and one value is designated the distractor (e.g., green and low pitch). On the focused-attention task, subjects are instructed to respond to every target on a designated dimension, either color or pitch. On the divided-attention task, subjects alternate between the two dimensions, first responding to the color target, then the pitch target, then the color target, etc. (see figure 69.2).

Compared to control subjects, patients with cerebellar lesions, either associated with autism (Akshoomoff and Courchesne, 1992) or due to acquired cerebellar pathology (Courchesne et al., 1994), show a selective impairment on the divided-attention condition. For both groups, the deficit is evident only when the interval between successive targets is relatively short (e.g., less than 2.5 s). This is consistent with the idea that the cerebellum does not provide the attentional instructions, but rather ensures that such instructions are implemented rapidly (see also Townsend, Harris, and Courchesne, 1996). Importantly, the patients' performance is similar to controls on the focused-attention task regardless of whether the targets occur in rapid succession or are widely spaced in time. This dissociation would suggest that the problem is not motoric since the movement requirements are identical in the two tasks. Evoked potentials to the missed targets are comparable to ignored distractors, confirming that in such situations, the participants have failed to shift attention at the time of target presentation (Akshoomoff and Courchesne, 1994).

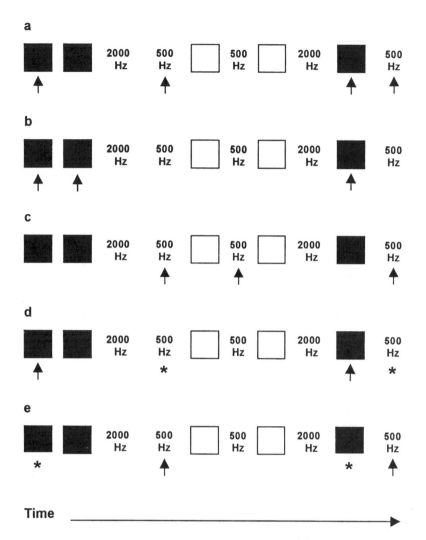

Time

FIGURE 69.2 Attention tasks developed by Courchesne and colleagues to examine the cerebellar role in shifting attention. A stream of tones and colored patches is presented. In the divided-attention condition (a), subjects alternately responded to targets on the two dimensions and the inter-target interval was varied. In the focused-attention conditions, subjects responded only to the visual targets (b) or to the au-ditory targets (c). In the Go/No-go version of the tasks, subjects alternated between the two dimensions, but responded only to targets on the visual (d) or the auditory (e) dimension. Patients with cerebellar lesions show a significant improvement in the Go/No-go version, despite the fact that the attention-switching demands are similar to those of the divided-attention condition.

While the attention hypothesis is intriguing, three other laboratories have failed to find a deficit in the performance of cerebellar patients on a visual selective-attention task that requires rapid orienting between spatial positions (Dimitrov et al., 1996; Helmuth, Ivry, and Shimizu, 1997; Yamaguchi, Tsuchiya, and Kobayashi, 1998). One possible account of this discrepancy is based on the idea that the deficits observed on the divided-attention task in the studies of Courchesne's lab reflect a more generic resource problem, one that is indirectly related to the motor problems of the cerebellar patients. The divided-attention task is considerably more difficult than the focused-attention task. In fact, many of the participants, both patients and controls, are near ceiling in the latter condition. Perhaps the patients have to devote

more processing resources to monitoring their key presses, a problem that causes them to miss rapidly appearing targets in the divided-attention condition. Motor control is certainly effortful for patients with cerebellar lesions, both in initiating and in terminating a movement.

Ravizza and Ivry (1998) have recently tested this hypothesis with a simple variant of the divided-attention task. In this version, subjects were again instructed to switch back and forth between the two dimensions following the detection of a target. However, they were to make overt responses to the targets on just one of the two dimensions. Targets on the other dimension simply required a covert shift of attention. With this design, the number of attentional shifts was equated in the two-response and one-response versions of the divided-attention task. However, the rapid shifts in the latter condition never came on the heels of an overt response, ensuring that resources would not be diverted due to the production and termination of a preceding response. Ravizza and Ivry replicated the cerebellar deficit on the divided-attention condition when responses were required to targets on both dimensions. However, when overt responses were required on just one dimension, the patients with cerebellar lesions showed a large improvement, reaching performance levels comparable to those of control subjects. Thus, these results cast doubt on the hypothesis that cerebellar lesions disrupt attentional orienting, and suggest that the patients' deficits may be indirectly related to problems in motor control.

A sensory variant of the coordination and attention theoretical framework comes from the work of Bower and associates (see Bower, 1997), who have recently promoted the hypothesis that the emphasis on the cerebellum as a motor structure is somewhat misguided. Rather, they argue that the fundamental characterization of the cerebellum should focus on its role in sensory exploration. The intimate links of the cerebellum with motor systems reflect the fact that animals, especially humans, use somatosensory information as a way to gain knowledge about the environment and manipulate objects.

This theory does not posit a necessary role for the cerebellum in primary sensory or cognitive functions. Rather, the cerebellum is viewed as a support system, facilitating the efficiency with which sensory systems (especially the somatosensory system) acquire information. Gao and colleagues (1996) tested this hypothesis in a recent fMRI study. Activity in the dentate nucleus was monitored while subjects performed a series of tasks involving both active and passive manual exploration. In one experiment, subjects were asked to successively manipulate a series of unseen objects. In one condition, they simply picked up the objects, then placed them down. In the other condition, they had to pick up the objects, then judge if they matched a target object. Dentate activation was considerably greater in the discrimination condition. Similarly, the dentate was more active when various textured surfaces were passively moved across the subjects' stationary fingers if the subjects were required to evaluate the textures.

The sensory exploration idea is intriguing. While it has currently been applied to the somatosensory domain, Bower (1997) suggests the hypothesis may be more general. In one sense, this hypothesis is similar to the attention-shifting hypothesis outlined above. However, the cerebellum need not be viewed as essential for directing the focus of attention, nor for implementing these shifts in a coordinated fashion. Rather, the focus of attention may be guided by noncerebellar structures, while the cerebellum contributes by ensuring that the selected information is processed with maximal efficiency to satisfy current task demands (see also Courchesne and Allen, 1997). A current weakness with this hypothesis is that, at present, there are minimal supportive data from patient studies. Somatosensory and proprioceptive functions are not generally assumed to be disturbed in patients with cerebellar lesions, although the examination of these functions has been rather crude.

ERROR DETECTION AND LEARNING   A different focus of the role of the cerebellum in cognition is based on the idea that this structure operates as an important source of feedback, monitoring movement and thought in order to modify ongoing behavior, then using this information to alter future performance. This theoretical perspective draws upon the motor learning literature to explain cerebellar involvement in learning certain types of cognitive tasks, particularly those that improve with practice. These tasks include the verb-generation task described above, puzzle tasks in which the goal is to solve a puzzle in as few moves as possible while observing constraints on how the pieces can be positioned (e.g., the Tower of Hanoi), and motor sequence and trajectory learning tasks. Across these and related tasks, neuroimaging studies have demonstrated that cerebellar activity is high during initial performance of the task, that activity decreases as performance becomes more skilled and accurate, and that shifts in cortical activity co-occur with changes in cerebellar activity (e.g., Raichle et al., 1994).

Many of the cognitive tasks associated with cerebellar activation and practice-dependent changes are quite complicated, and thus the cerebellar activation can be interpreted in many ways. The cerebellar changes could reflect a correlation with learning, rather than a causal involvement. Some support for a causal relationship comes from converging neuropsychological studies. For each of the general tasks described above, impaired acquisition of skilled performance has been demonstrated in subjects with cerebellar damage or atrophy, though not all of the findings have been replicated.

The idea that the cerebellum is involved in the detection and correction of errors offers a potential causal link between on-line performance and learning. At the center of this idea in the motor domain is evidence that the cerebellum modifies output in the face of unexpected perturbations or sensory input. For instance, it has been hypothesized that during locomotion, corticocerebellar signals provide an efference copy of corticospinal motor commands that can be compared with afferent information provided by spinocerebellar circuits (Kawato and Gomi, 1992). When a mismatch is detected, descending output from the cerebellar nuclei allows for rapid, on-line adjustments in the motor patterns without requiring extensive cortical intervention. Moreover, the error signals generated when the movement is perturbed are then used to modify the production of similar movements in the future (Gilbert and Thach, 1977). Similar ideas form the basis of computational models of the cerebellum's role in simple associative learning tasks such as eyeblink conditioning (reviewed in Thompson, 1988). Unexpected aversive stimuli such as an airpuff are assumed to provide an error signal in the cerebellum, modifying the animal's behavior so that it will make an anticipatory blink in the future when presented with the same context.

The cognitive generalization of this hypothesis implicitly assumes that the cerebellum has evolved so that it can now provide a more generic error-correction role, modifying internal thought in addition to external movement. Canavan and his colleagues (Bracke-Tolkmitt et al., 1989; Canavan et al., 1994) reported severe deficits on a conditional learning task in which the subjects had to learn the correct mapping between colored shapes and arbitrary verbal labels. The subjects were given no explicit instructions; rather, learning was solely through trial and error, with the experimenter indicating whether a response was correct or not after each trial. Fiez and colleagues (1992) report a case study of a patient who suffered a large infarct in the posterior and inferior region of the right cerebellar hemisphere. On standardized neuropsychological assessment, this patient's performance clearly indicated superior overall cognitive function. Yet the patient's performance on relatively simple verbal discrimination tasks, again involving trial-and-error learning, was extremely poor. Moreover, on a variety of tasks, he failed to use explicit verbal feedback from the experimenter to modify his responses. The same patient also failed to learn and perform the verb-generation task normally. Specifically, he produced a large number of inappropriate, but semantically related responses (e.g., producing "old" as a synonym for "garbage").

The dissociation between this patient's overall intelligence and his performance on these seemingly simple tasks is quite striking. It is not clear, however, whether these results provide strong support for the error-correction hypothesis. Issues remain, at least in part, because no explicit models have been developed to explain how error-correction would be implemented in a cognitive task; thus it is hard to evaluate whether some of the patient's difficulties fit within an error-detection framework. For example, the patient performed poorly in judging whether two words were synonyms and in identifying whether common words were nouns or verbs. Since we can assume that he was, or had been, familiar with these words in the past, these deficits may indicate a disruption of semantic knowledge rather than an inability to make use of current error signals (and, indeed, he was given no feedback on such tests). A second issue is that of reproducibility. Helmuth and associates (1997) failed to replicate these findings in a group study of patients with focal cerebellar lesions. On the trial-and-error verbal discrimination task, these patients showed comparable learning functions across blocks of trials as age-matched control subjects. Similarly, on a speeded semantic generation task, the patients, while slower than controls, showed similar improvements over successive blocks.

Related to the ideas of both error detection and attention is the notion that the cerebellum may best be characterized as a predictive device, a neural structure that is specialized to make anticipatory adjustments (e.g., Courchesne and Allen, 1997; Paulin, 1997). For instance, through experience, a particular sensory context or internal state could become associated with a particular motor response or adjustment of the internal state. Eventually, the occurrence of a specific context could trigger the occurrence of a specific external or internal response; this procedure could be applied iteratively in order to produce a temporal sequence of internal events or overt responses. Models such as these emphasize the dynamic properties of cerebellar function (Raymond, Lisberger, and Mauk, 1996). A consistent feature of cerebellar theories is the focus on this system as performing predictive functions–the ability to anticipate forthcoming information and ensure that actions correctly anticipate changes in the environment.

GENERALIZED TIMING FUNCTION   A specific variant of the prediction idea is that the cerebellum operates as an internal timing system, providing the precise representation of temporal information across a range of tasks (Ivry and Keele, 1989; reviewed in Ivry, 1997). The timing hypothesis originates in an analysis of the motor control deficits observed in animals and patients with cerebellar lesions. Cerebellar symptoms such as intentional tremor and hypermetria can be interpreted as resulting from the disorganization of the temporal pattern between agonist and antagonist muscles during rapid movements (Hore, Wild, and Diener, 1991). When asked to produce periodic movements, patients with cerebellar lesions exhibit a large increase in variability, and this increase is associated with central control processes regulating the timing of central motor commands (Ivry and Keele, 1989; Ivry, Keele, and Diener, 1988; Franz, Ivry, and Helmuth, 1996).

The timing deficits for these patients extend beyond the motor domain, being manifest in a variety of perceptual tasks that require the precise representation of temporal information. This temporal processing deficit has been found on perceptual tasks across different sensory modalities including audition (Ivry and Keele, 1989; Mangels, Ivry, and Shimizu, 1998), vision (Ivry and Diener, 1991; Nawrot and Rizzo, 1995), and somatosensation (Grill et al., 1994). A recent speech perception study provides an especially compelling demonstration of the importance of the cerebellum in temporal processing (Ackermann et al., 1997). Patients with cerebellar dysarthria, a difficulty in speech articulation, were unable to discriminate speech sounds that differed solely in the duration of an intersyllabic silent period (figure 69.3), yet performed comparably to control subjects for sounds that had different spectral cues.

Again, one might suppose a generalization of function over the course of evolution: A form of representation that evolved as part of a limited task domain might become accessible for the performance of other tasks that can exploit this specialization (Rozin, 1976). Within the framework of the timing hypothesis, the cerebellum must be critical for tasks that require precise timing, whether or not they are motoric. This hypothesis also provides a parsimonious account of the task domain of the cerebellum in learning, namely, when the response requires the representation of the temporal relationships between different stimuli or stimuli and responses. In eyeblink conditioning, for example, the learned response is adaptive only when it occurs at the right point in time, that is, when the animal has extracted the precise timing between the conditioning and unconditioned stimuli (Ivry and Keele, 1989). Without the cerebellar cortex, the association may be formed, but it loses its adaptive value, as evidenced by the fact that the animal no longer blinks when the aversive stimulus is presented (Perrett, Ruiz, and Mauk, 1993; Anderson and Keifer, 1997).

The research in this area has focused on tasks that impose real-time processing demands, and the corresponding computational models here have focused on how metrical temporal information might be represented in the cerebellar cortex (e.g., Buonomano and Mauk, 1994; Fiala, Grossberg, and Bullock, 1996). The representation of the temporal information is a central component of much of our perceptual experience and a prerequisite for skilled behavior. Consider the frog by the river gathering up an evening meal of flies, or the basketball player looking to pass the ball to a teammate who is moving toward the basket. Anticipating the future position of a moving stimulus and coordinating the multilimb gestures required to interact with that stimulus re-

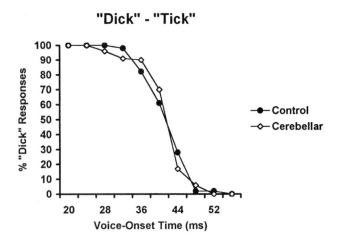

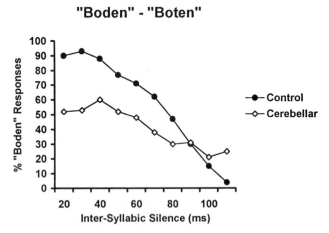

FIGURE 69.3   Identification functions for two speech continua in control subjects and patients with bilateral cerebellar lesions. For the tick–dick continuum, the voice-onset time was varied in steps of 10 ms. This change in the timing between voicing and the release of the stop consonant produces both temporal and spectral changes. For the boten–boden continuum, a silent interval was inserted between the syllables, thus providing only a temporal cue. The patients showed poor discrimination performance in this condition. (Adapted from Ackermann et al., 1997.)

quires extremely precise timing. The cerebellum appears to be an exquisite device for this form of dynamic processing, and its manifestation in both perception and action reflects the intimate links between these domains that are required for skilled behavior.

As currently articulated, the conceptualization of a cerebellar timing system is limited to the relatively narrow temporal range that might be relevant for the control of coordinated movement. Here again, the motivation is based on an evolutionary perspective. An internal timing system likely emerged from a system that had access to information that contained temporal regularities. A candidate here would be the pattern generated by a locomoting organism (be it terrestrial, arial, or aquatic). While locomotion signals might be generated by relatively simple spinal mechanisms, a hierarchical control system might be essential for endowing flexibility as well as for producing corrections in response to unexpected perturbations (Arshavsky, Gelfand, and Orlovsky, 1983). Perhaps the cerebellar timing system took root in this manner and the temporal extent of the cerebellum is constrained by its links to locomotion cycles.

The timing hypothesis is a narrower, more specific statement of how the cerebellum might be viewed as a predictive device. It is possible that a cerebellar timing function is simply one manifestation of a more general predictive capability (Ivry and Keele, 1989; Courchesne and Allen, 1997; Bower, 1997). On the other hand, in many situations, animals need to anticipate future events that do not require precise detail of the temporal structure of the series of intervening events. For example, the temporal requirements for knowing when to move on to a new foraging patch or when a signal light will change to green are quite different from that needed to anticipate when to swing a tennis racquet in order to serve a tossed tennis ball. And in other situations such as anticipating the next move in a chess game, skilled performance requires a predictive capability, but one that has essentially no temporal requirements. It remains to be seen whether the cerebellum contributes to tasks that entail prediction in this more generic sense. The timing hypothesis predicts that the cerebellum will not play a role in such tasks since its domain is assumed to be limited to tasks requiring a particular form of computation, the representation of the temporal relations between events.

IMAGERY, COVERT ACTION, AND WORKING MEMORY As reviewed above, the neuropsychological record is mixed regarding some of the more cognitive interpretations of cerebellar function. Nonetheless, there remains the challenge of interpreting the consistent finding of cerebellar activation in imaging studies, even when motor demands are equated in the experimental and control tasks. One hypothesis is based on the observation that there is a correlation between task difficulty and the degree of cerebellar activation (Ivry, 1997). Across a wide range of studies, metabolic activity in the cerebellum is most pronounced for the more difficult condition when pairs of tasks are compared.

It is, of course, necessary to operationalize "difficulty." One metric is based simply on the number of possible responses afforded by a situation: Tasks associated with a large number of possible responses are more difficult than those associated with a small number of possible responses. For example, in the language study of Pe-

tersen and colleagues (1989), there are more possible responses in the generate condition in which subjects must generate a semantic associate to the stimulus word compared to the control condition in which the subjects simply have to repeat the stimulus word. Similarly, in the difficult problem-solving condition of another study (Gao et al., 1996), there were four possible moves on each trial compared to just one in the easy condition. Perhaps the cerebellum is involved in the preparation and planning of candidate responses. The increased cerebellar activation in "difficult" conditions might reflect the parallel preparation of all the possible responses. By engaging in response preparation prior to completion of response selection, the system is able to respond in a more rapid manner. This hypothesis is in accord with the documented deficits in reaction time associated with cerebellar lesions (Meyer-Lohmann, Hore, and Brooks, 1977; Spidalieri, Busby, and Lamarre, 1983).

While this response preparation hypothesis can account for many of the imaging results, there are some notable exceptions. In a stem completion task (e.g., say "cougar" after seeing the stem "cou___"), cerebellar activation was found to be greater when there were few possible completions for the target stem than when there were many (Desmond, Gabrieli, and Glover, 1998). This result is the opposite of what one would predict based on the response preparation hypothesis. Another intriguing exception comes from a study comparing phonological and visual judgments of letters (Sergent et al., 1992). On each trial, a single letter was presented in the center of the screen, oriented either normally or mirror-reversed. In one condition, subjects judged the orientation, pressing one button if the stimulus was in its normal orientation and another if the stimulus was mirror-reversed. In a second condition, the same stimuli were presented, but now the judgment was based on whether or not the stimulus contained a target phoneme, the sound "ee" (as in B, D, or T). The tasks appeared to be of equal difficulty, both by the response alternative metric described above (two per trial) and by the fact that reaction times were comparable, with the phonological task taking slightly more time. Nonetheless, cerebellar activation was more pronounced in the orientation task.

An alternative view of the response preparation hypothesis is that response preparation and related action-related processes are essential to the critical cognitive operations required for these tasks. For instance, it is likely that imagery, in the form of mental rotation, is required for performing letter orientation judgments. A number of other neuroimaging studies have implicated the cerebellum in imagery tasks, especially when the task requires imagining motoric gestures. Compared to baseline conditions involving rest, cerebellar activation is found when people imagine hitting a tennis ball (Decety et al., 1990) and when people perform either active or imagined hand gestures (Peter Fox, personal communication). Parsons and Fox (1998) report that cerebellar activation can occur even when subjects are not instructed to imagine movements. In their task, subjects were required to discriminate between line drawings of left and right hands shown from different perspectives. Based upon data from behavioral studies, it appears that subjects make these judgments by imagining they are moving their own hands to match the orientation of the stimulus hand.

Many verbal tasks may engage an articulatory form of imagery. For example, a key component of Baddeley's (1992) influential model of working memory entails a process by which linguistic information is actively maintained over short delays via covert (silent) articulatory rehearsal. The imaging literature suggests that the cerebellum may be an essential component of this rehearsal system. For example, increased blood flow is observed in the cerebellum when subjects are required to maintain five words over a 40-s delay interval (Fiez et al., 1996), or when they must decide whether each letter in a sequence is the same as the letter presented two trials previously, the so-called "two-back" task (Awh et al., 1996). It is important to note that task-related activation here, and in all of the imagery studies cited above, is not limited to the cerebellum. Meta-analyses indicate that the cerebellum, supplementary motor area (SMA), and Broca's area are active during verbal, but not spatial, working memory tasks, whereas regions such as dorsolateral prefrontal cortex are active during both verbal and spatial working memory tasks (figure 69.4; see also Fiez et al., 1996). This selective activation has led to the hypothesis that SMA, Broca's area, and the cerebellum comprise the neural basis of an articulatory rehearsal system (Awh et al., 1996; Fiez et al., 1996; Paulesu, Frith, and Frackowiak, 1993).

In evaluating the cerebellar contributions to imagery, one issue is whether its contributions to imagined movement are identical to its contributions to real movement. In terms of articulatory rehearsal, for instance, it may contribute to motoric aspects of internal speech representation in much the same way that it contributes to overt speech production. This hypothesis is consistent with behavioral evidence showing links between overt and covert articulation; for example, the number of items that subjects can maintain in working memory is correlated with the amount of time it takes to say them aloud (Baddeley, Thomson, and Buchanan, 1975). However, the observation of load-effects on cerebellar activation argues against overly simplistic interpretations of

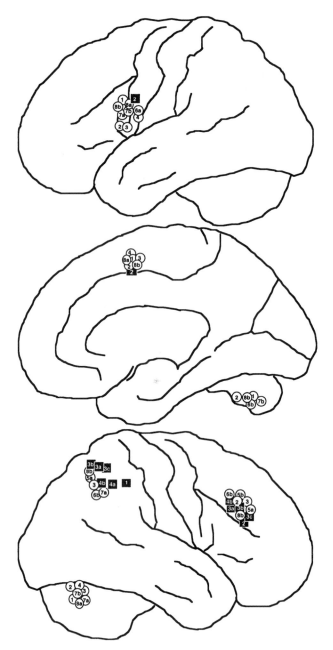

FIGURE 69.4   The loci of peak activation associated with verbal working memory tasks (open circles) and spatial working memory tasks (filled squares) are plotted from a number of different PET studies. Broca's area in the left hemisphere, supplementary motor cortex in the superior medial cortex, and the medial and right lateral cerebellum are typically activated in verbal working memory but not spatial working memory tasks. Other areas, such as the right dorsolateral prefrontal cortex and the right inferior parietal cortex are activated by both verbal working memory and spatial working memory tasks. Verbal working memory coordinates drawn from (1) Awh et al., 1996; (2) Fiez et al., 1996; (3) Jonides et al., 1998; (4) Paulesu et al., 1993; (5) Petrides et al., 1993; (6) Salmon et al., 1996; (7) Schumacher et al., 1996;(8) Smith, Jonides, and Koeppe, 1996. Spatial working memory coordinates drawn from (1) Courtney et al., 1996; (2) Goldberg et al., 1996; (3) Owen et al., 1996; (4) Smith, Jonides, and Koeppe, 1996.

the relationship between real and imagined movement. As a control condition in studies of verbal working memory, subjects have been asked to internally rehearse relatively simple material that does not impose a memory load (e.g., count from 1 to 5 repeatedly or silently repeat a single letter). Cerebellar activation is greater in the experimental working memory condition than in these rehearsal conditions (Fiez et al., 1996; Desmond et al., 1997; Awh et al., 1996). Furthermore, cerebellar activation has been found to be higher in direct comparisons of high- versus low-load conditions (Desmond et al., 1997). While some of the changes in cerebellar activation reflect increases in areas active during both simple rehearsal and working memory tasks, others reflect the recruitment of areas that are not significantly active during simple rehearsal.

Viewing cerebellar contributions to verbal working memory from a more motoric perspective need not reduce its cognitive importance. A breakdown in the articulatory rehearsal system could have widespread consequences. Consider, for example, that verbal working memory is central to our ability to perform tasks that range from solving mathematical equations to comprehending sentence clauses. Furthermore, articulatory rehearsal and recoding have been associated with many other language tasks outside the domain of verbal working memory, such as speech recognition and the generation of word phonology. This may explain cerebellar activation in verbal fluency, stem completion, and verb generation tasks. Successful production of correct responses for these tasks may involve the ability to retrieve and maintain potential responses using a covert articulatory process (Desmond, Gabrieli, and Glover, 1998). There is also limited but provocative evidence implicating cerebellar dysfunction in developmental dyslexia (Fawcett, Nicolson, and Dean, 1996). Perhaps an inability to engage in fluent covert articulation interferes with the development of salient phonological representations. Without such codes, children are likely to have severe problems in acquiring reading skills (Liberman and Shankweiler, 1991).

Conclusions

As reviewed in this chapter, the cerebellum has stepped out from the shadows of its traditional role as part of the motor system, essential for the control of fine movement and balance. Patient, imaging, and modeling studies have brought the study of cerebellar function into the mainstream of cognitive neuroscience, with researchers hypothesizing links to attention, learning, memory, language, and thought. We have reviewed a diverse set of literatures here, seeking to identify the principal sources

of motivation for this mini-revolution and outlining some of the recent theoretical conjectures.

In general, we have adopted a somewhat skeptical perspective, seeking convergence from anatomical, neuropsychological, and neuroimaging studies for the proper evaluation of the various functional hypotheses that have been developed over the past decade. We do not intend this skepticism to be taken as an attempt to dismiss these hypotheses. It is essential to maintain an open mind as researchers develop experiments that will allow strong inference and seek theoretical accounts that may integrate various hypotheses. At the same time, the conservative nature of evolutionary processes leads us to expect that there will be some continuity between the contributions of the cerebellum to motor control and the contribution of this structure to language and thought.

ACKNOWLEDGMENTS This work was supported by Grants NS-30256 and NS-17778 from the National Institute of Health and IRI-9720350 from the National Science Foundation. The authors are grateful to Eliot Hazeltine, Steve Keele, Susan Ravizza, and Steven Kosslyn for their comments and to Kristi Hiatt for her help in preparing this chapter.

REFERENCES

ACKERMANN, H., S. GRABER, I. HERTRICH, and I. DAUM, 1997. Categorical speech perception in cerebellar disorders. *Brain Lang.* 60:323–331.

AKSHOOMOFF, N. A., and E. COURCHESNE, 1992. A new role for the cerebellum in cognitive operations. *Behav. Neurosci.* 106(5):731–738.

AKSHOOMOFF, N. A., and E. COURCHESNE, 1994. ERP evidence for a shifting attention deficit in patients with damage to the cerebellum. *J. Cogn. Neurosci.* 6:388–399.

AKSHOOMOFF, N. A., E. COURCHESNE, and J. TOWNSEND, 1997. Attention coordination and anticipatory control. *Intl. Rev. Neurobiol.* 41:575–598.

ALLEN, G., R. B. BUXTON, E. C. WONG, and E. COURCHESNE, 1997. Attentional activation of the cerebellum independent of motor involvement. *Science* 275:1940–1943.

ANDERSON, C. W., and J. KEIFER, 1997. The cerebellum and red nucleus are not required for in vitro classical conditioning of the turtle abducens nerve response. *J. Neurosci.* 17(24):9736–9745.

APPOLLONIO, I. M., J. GRAFMAN, V. SCHWARTZ, S. MASSAQUOI, and M. HALLETT, 1993. Memory in patients with cerebellar degeneration. *Neurology* 43:1536–1544.

ARSHAVSKY, Y. I., I. M. GELFAND, and G. N. ORLOVSKY, 1983. The cerebellum and control of rhythmical movements. *Trends Neurosci.* 10:417–422.

AWH, E., J. JONIDES, E. E. SMITH, E. H. SCHUMACKER, R. KOEPPE, and S. KATZ, 1996. Dissociation of storage and rehearsal in verbal working memory: Evidence from PET. *Psychol. Sci.* 7:25–31.

BADDELEY, A. D., 1992. Working memory. *Science* 255:556–559.

BADDELEY, A. D., N. THOMSON, and M. BUCHANAN, 1975. Word length and the structure of short-term memory. *J. Verbal Learn. Verbal Behav.* 14:575–589.

BAUMAN, M. L., P. A. FILIPEK, and T. L. KEMPER, 1997. Early infantile autism. *Intl. Rev. Neurobiol.* 41:367–386.

BOWER, J. M., 1997. Control of sensory data acquisition. *Intl. Rev. Neurobiol.* 41:489–513.

BRACKE-TOLKMITT, R., A. LINDEN, A. G. M. CANAVAN, B. ROCKSTROH, E. SCHOLZ, K. WESSEL, and H.-C. DIENER, 1989. The cerebellum contributes to mental skills. *Behav. Neurosci.* 103(2):442–446.

BUONOMANO, D. V., and M. MAUK, 1994. Neural network model of the cerebellum: Temporal discrimination and the timing of motor responses. *Neural Computation* 6(1):38–55.

CANAVAN, A. G. M., R. SPRENGELMEYER, H.-C. DIENER, and V. HOMBERG, 1994. Conditional associative learning is impaired in cerebellar disease in humans. *Behav. Neurosci.* 108(3):475–485.

COURCHESNE, E., 1997. Brainstem, cerebellar and limbic neuroanatomical abnormalities in autism. *Curr. Opin. Neurobiol.* 7(2):269–278.

COURCHESNE, E., and G. ALLEN, 1997. Prediction and preparation, fundamental functions of the cerebellum. *Learn. Mem.* 4:1–35.

COURCHESNE, E., J. TOWNSEND, and O. SAITOH, 1994. The brain in infantile autism: Posterior fossa structures are abnormal. *Neurology* 44(2):214–223.

COURCHESNE, E., J. TOWNSEND, N. A. AKSHOOMOFF, O. SAITOH, R. YEUNG-COURCHESNE, A. J. LINCOLN, H. E. JAMES, R. H. HAAS, L. SCHREIBMAN, and L. LAU, 1994. Impairment in shifting attention in autistic and cerebellar patients. *Behav. Neurosci.* 108:848–865.

COURTNEY, S. M., L.G. UNGERLEIDER, K. KEIL, and J.V. HAXBY, 1996. Object and spatial visual working memory activate separate neural systems in human cortex. *Cerebral Cortex* 6, 39–49.

DAUM, I., and H. ACKERMANN, 1995. Cerebellar contributions to cognition. *Behav. Brain Res.* 67:201–210.

DAUM, I., and H. ACKERMANN, 1997. Neuropsychological abnormalities in cerebellar syndromes–fact or fiction? *Intl. Rev. Neurobiol.* 41:455–471.

DAUM, I., H. ACKERMANN, M. M. SCHUGENS, C. REIMOLD, J. DICHGANS, and N. BIRBAUMER, 1993. The cerebellum and cognitive functions in humans. *Behav. Neurosci.* 107(3):411–419.

DECETY, J., H. SJOHOLM, E. RYDING, G. STENBERG, and D. H. INGVAR, 1990. The cerebellum participates in mental activity: Tomographic measurements of regional cerebral blood flow. *Brain Res.* 535:313–317.

DESMOND, J. E., J. D. E. GABRIELI, A. D. WAGNER, B. L. GINIER, and G. H. GLOVER, 1997. Lobular patterns of cerebellar activation in verbal working-memory and finger-tapping tasks as revealed by functional MRI. *J. Neurosci.* 17(24):9675–9685.

DESMOND, J. E., J. D. E. GABRIELI, and G. H. GLOVER, 1998. Dissociations of frontal and cerebellar activity in a cognitive task: Evidence for a distinction between selection and search. *Neuroimage* 7:368–376.

DIMITROV, M., J. GRAFMAN, P. KOSSEFF, J. WACHS, D. ALWAY, J. HIGGINS, I. LITVAN, J.-S. LOU, and M. HALLETT, 1996. Preserved cognitive processes in cerebellar degeneration. *Behav. Brain Res.* 79:131–135.

FAWCETT, A. J., R. I. NICOLSON, and P. DEAN, 1996. Impaired performance of children with dyslexia on a range of cerebellar tasks. *Ann. Dyslexia* 46:259–283.

FIALA, J. C., S. GROSSBERG, and D. BULLOCK, 1996. Metabotropic glutamate receptor activation in cerebellar Purkinje cells as substrate for adaptive timing of the classically conditioned eye-blink response. *J. Neurosci.* 16(11):3760–3774.

FIEZ, J. A., S. E. PETERSEN, M. K. CHENEY, and M. E. RAICHLE, 1992. Impaired nonmotor learning and error detection associated with cerebellar damage: A single-case study. *Brain* 115:155–178.

FIEZ, J., E. RAIFE, D. BALOTA, J. SCHWARZ, M. RAICHLE, and S. PETERSEN, 1996. A positron emission tomography study of the short-term maintenance of verbal information. *J. Neurosci.* 16:808–822.

FRANZ, E. A., R. B. IVRY, and L. L. HELMUTH, 1996. Reduced timing variability in patients with unilateral cerebellar lesions during bimanual movements. *J. Cogn. Neurosci.* 8(2):107–118.

GAO, J.-H., L. M. PARSONS, J. M. BOWER, J. XIONG, J. LI, and P. T. FOX, 1996. Cerebellum implicated in sensory acquisition and discrimination rather than motor control. *Science* 272:545–547.

GILBERT, P. F. C., and W. T. THACH, 1977. Purkinje cell activity during motor learning. *Brain Res.* 128:309–328.

GOLDBERG, T. E., K. F. BERMAN, C. RANDOLPH, J. M. GOLD, and D. R. WEINBERGER, 1996. Isolating the mnemonic component in spatial delayed response: A controlled PET ^{15}O-labeled water regional cerebral blood flow study in normal humans. *Neuroimage* 3:69–78.

GRILL, S. E., M. HALLETT, C. MARCUS, and L. MCSHANE, 1994. Disturbances of kinaesthesia in patients with cerebellar disorders. *Brain* 117(6):1433–1447.

HELMUTH, L. L., R. B. IVRY, and N. SHIMIZU, 1997. Preserved performance by cerebellar patients on tests of word generation, discrimination learning, and attention. *Learn. Mem.* 3:456–474.

HORE, J., B. WILD, and H. C. DIENER, 1991. Cerebellar dysmetria at the elbow, wrist, and fingers. *J. Neurophysiol.* 65(3):563–571.

IVRY, R. B., 1997. Cerebellar timing systems. *Intl. Rev. Neurobiol.* 41:555–573.

IVRY, R. B., and H. C. DIENER, 1991. Impaired velocity perception in patients with lesions of the cerebellum. *Cogn. Neurosci.* 3(4):355–366.

IVRY, R. B., S. W. KEELE, and H. C. DIENER, 1988. Dissociation of the lateral and medial cerebellum in movement timing and movement execution. *Exp. Brain Res.* 73(1):167–180.

IVRY, R. B., and S. W. KEELE, 1989. Timing functions of the cerebellum. *J. Cogn. Neurosci.* 1(2):136–152.

JONIDES, J., E. H. SCHUMACHER, E. E. SMITH, R. A. KOEPPE, E. AWH, P. A. REUTER-LORENZ, C. MARSHUETZ, and C. R. WILLIS, 1998. The role of parietal cortex in verbal working memory. *J. Neurosci.* 18:5026–5034.

KATSETOS, C. D., T. M. HYDE, and M. M. HERMAN, 1997. Neuropathology of the cerebellum in schizophrenia–An update: 1996 and future directions. *Biol. Psychiatry* 42(3):213–224.

KAWATO, M., and H. GOMI, 1992. A computational model of four regions of the cerebellum based on feedback-error learning. *Biol. Cybern.* 68(2):95–103.

KIM, S.-G., K. UGURBIL, and P. L. STRICK, 1994. Activation of a cerebellar output nucleus during cognitive processing. *Science* 265:949–951.

KISH, S. J., M. EL-AWAR, D. STUSS, J. NOBREGA, R. CURRIER, J. F. AITA, L. SCHUT, H. Y. ZOGHBI, and M. FREEDMAN, 1994. Neuropsychological test performance in patients with dominantly inherited spinocerebellar ataxia: Relationship to ataxia severity. *Neurology* 44:1738–1746.

LEINER, H. C., A. L. LEINER, and R. S. DOW, 1986. Does the cerebellum contribute to mental skills? *Behav. Neurosci.* 100:443–454.

LIBERMAN, I. Y., and D. SHANKWEILER, 1991. Phonology and beginning reading: A tutorial. In *Learning to Read: Basic Research and Its Implications*, L. Rieben and C. A. Perfetti, eds. Hillsdale, N.J.: Lawrence Erlbaum, pp. 213–227.

MANGELS, J. A., R. B. IVRY, and N. SHIMIZU, 1998. Dissociable contributions of the prefrontal and neocerebellar cortex to time perception. *Cogn. Brain Res.* 7:15–39.

MEYER-LOHMANN, J., J. HORE, and V. B. BROOKS, 1977. Cerebellar participation in generation of prompt arm movements. *J. Neurophysiol.* 40(5):1038–1050.

MIDDLETON, F. A., and P. L. STRICK, 1994. Anatomical evidence for cerebellar and basal ganglia involvement in higher cognitive function. *Science* 266:458–461.

MIDDLETON, F. A., and P. L. STRICK, 1997. Cerebellar output channels. *Intl. Rev. Neurobiol.* 41:61–82.

NAWROT, M., and M. RIZZO, 1995. Motion perception deficits from midline cerebellar lesions in human. *Vision Res.* 35(5):723–731.

OWEN, A., A. C. EVANS, and M. PETRIDES, 1996. Evidence for a two-stage model of spatial working memory processing within the lateral frontal cortex: A positron emission tomography study. *Cereb. Cortex* 6:31–38.

PARSONS, L. M., and P. T. FOX, 1998. The neural basis of implicit movements used in recognizing hand shape. *Cogn. Neuropsychol.* 15(6–8):583–615.

PAULESU, E., C. D. FRITH, and R. S. J. FRACKOWIAK, 1993. The neural correlates of the verbal component of working memory. *Nature* 362:342–345.

PAULIN, M. G., 1997. Neural representations of moving systems. *Intl. Rev. Neurobiol.* 41:516–533.

PERRETT, S. P., B. P. RUIZ, and M. D. MAUK, 1993. Cerebellar cortex lesions disrupt learning-dependent timing of conditioned eyelid responses. *J. Neurosci.* 13(4):1708–1718.

PETERSEN, S. E., P. T. FOX, M. I. POSNER, M. MINTUN, and M. E. RAICHLE, 1989. Positron emission tomographic studies of the processing of single words. *J. Cogn. Neurosci.* 1:153–170.

PETRIDES, M., B. ALVISATOS, E. MEYER, and A. C. EVANS, 1993. Functional activation of the human frontal cortex during the performance of verbal working memory tasks. *Proc. Natl. Acad. Sci. U.S.A.* 90:878–882.

POSNER, M. I., and S. J. PETERSEN, 1990. The attention system of the human brain. *Annu. Rev. Neurosci.* 13:25–42.

RAICHLE, M. E., J. A. FIEZ, T. O. VIDEEN, and A. K. MACLEOD, 1994. Practice-related changes in human brain functional anatomy during nonmotor learning. *Cereb. Cortex* 4(1):8–26.

RAVIZZA, S. M., and R. B. IVRY, 1998. Comparison of the cerebellum and basal ganglia in shifting attention. Presented at the 5th Annual Meeting of the Cognitive Neuroscience Society. San Francisco, Calif.

RAYMOND, J. L., S. G. LISBERGER, and M. D. MAUK, 1996. The cerebellum: A neuronal learning machine? *Science* 272(5265):1126–1131.

RITVO, E. R., B. J. FREEMAN, A. B. SCHEIBEL, T. DUONG, H. ROBINSON, D. GUTHRIE, and A. RITVO, 1986. Lower Purkinje cell counts in the cerebella of four autistic subjects: Initial findings of the UCLA–NSAC Autopsy Research Report. *Am. J. Psychiatry* 143(7):862–866.

ROZIN, P., 1976. The evolution of intelligence and access to the cognitive unconscious. In *Progress in Psychobiology and Physiological Psychology*, Vol. 6, J. M. Sprague and A. N. Epstein, eds. New York: Academic Press, pp. 245–280.

SALMON, E., M. VAN DER LINDEN, F. COLLETTE, G. DELFIORE, P. MAQUET, C. DEGUELDRE, A. LUXEN, and G. FRANCK, 1996. Regional brain activity during working memory tasks. *Brain* 119:1617–1625.

SCHMAHMANN, J. D., 1997. *The Cerebellum and Cognition.* San Diego: Academic Press. (Also published as special edition of *Int. Rev. Neurobiol.* 41.)

SCHMAHMANN, J. D., and D. N. PANDYA, 1997. The cerebrocerebellar system. *Int. Rev. Neurobiol.* 41:31–60.

SCHUMACHER, E. H., E. LAUBER, E. AWH, J. JONIDES, E. E. SMITH, and R. A. KOEPPE, 1996. PET evidence for an amodal verbal working memory system. *Neuroimage* 3:79–88.

SERGENT, J., E. ZUCK, M. LÉVESQUE, and B. MACDONALD, 1992. Positron emission tomography study of letter and object processing: Empirical findings and methodological considerations. *Cereb. Cortex* 2(1):68–80.

SHULMAN, G. L., M. CORBETTA, R. L. BUCKNER, J. A. FIEZ, F. M. MIEZEN, M. E. RAICHLE, and S. E. PETERSEN, 1997. Common blood flow changes across visual tasks: I. Increases in subcortical structures and cerebellum but not in nonvisual cortex. *J. Cogn. Neurosci.* 9(5):624–647.

SMITH, E. E., J. JONIDES, and R. A. KOEPPE, 1996. Dissociating verbal and spatial working memory using PET. *Cereb. Cortex* 6:11–20.

SPIDALIERI, G., L. BUSBY, and Y. LAMARRE, 1983. Fast ballistic arm movements triggered by visual, auditory, and somesthetic stimuli in the monkey: II. Effects of unilateral dentate lesion on discharge of precentral cortical neurons and reaction time. *J. Neurophysiol.* 50(6):1359–1379.

THOMPSON, R., 1988. Neural mechanisms of classical conditioning in mammals. *Phil. Trans. R. Soc. Lond. [Biol.]* 329: 161–170.

TOWNSEND, J., N. S. HARRIS, and E. COURCHESNE, 1996. Visual attention abnormalities in autism: Delayed orienting to location. *J. Intl. Neuropsychol. Soc.* 2(6):541–550.

YAMAGUCHI, S., H. TSUCHIYA, and S. KOBAYASHI, 1998. Visuospatial attention shift and motor responses in cerebellar disorders. *J. Cogn. Neurosci.* 10(1):95–107.

70 The Cognitive Neuroscience of Categorization

EDWARD E. SMITH AND JOHN JONIDES

ABSTRACT   Behavioral work on categorization has proposed three different categorization procedures–classification by rule, by stored exemplars, and by prototype–and has often assumed that just one of these procedures underlies all acts of categorization. In this chapter, we use findings from cognitive neuroscience to argue that all three procedures are used in categorization and, further, that the three procedures have different neural bases. We discuss evidence from two kinds of studies. The first kind involves neuropsychological experiments with amnesic patients, and deals with the contrast between exemplars and prototypes. These studies indicate that amnesic patients can use implicit representations–presumably prototypes–in categorization tasks in which normal subjects use explicit exemplars. The second kind of study involves neuroimaging normal subjects while they perform categorization tasks that encourage the use of either rules or exemplars. These experiments indicate that rule use involves at least some neural circuits that are distinct from those involved in categorization by exemplars.

CATEGORIZATION PROCEDURES   We routinely+ divide the world into categories–a particular wooden configuration is perceived as a *chair*, a particular assemblage of body parts as a *dog*, and so on. Categorization greatly reduces the amount of information we have to process, and allows us to draw inferences about imperceptible properties (e.g., "If it's a dog, it may bark when provoked"). Categorization may be what makes possible human perception, memory, communication, and thought as we know it.

To categorize some test object "x" is to come to treat it as an instance of some category (a nonarbitrary class of objects). How do people do this? Presumably, we have some mental representations of various categories and procedures for deciding which of these mental representations provides the best fit for object x (Smith, 1995). In this chapter, we focus on categorization procedures themselves (as opposed to mental representations of categories). In particular, we consider three categorization procedures that have been widely studied in cognitive science, in order to see what recent findings in cognitive neuroscience can tell us about these procedures.

EDWARD E. SMITH and JOHN JONIDES   Department of Psychology, University of Michigan, Ann Arbor, Mich.

The three categorization procedures of interest can be roughly characterized in the following way (after Smith, Patalano, and Jonides, 1998). In deciding whether a test object belongs to a particular category, one may

1. determine whether the test object fits a rule that defines the category ("rule application");
2. determine the similarity of the test object to one or more remembered exemplars of the category ("exemplar similarity"); or
3. determine the similarity of the test object to a prototype of the category ("prototype similarity").

One issue arising from the extensive study of these procedures is central: Do people use a variety of categorization procedures? Or is all (or most) human categorization based on a single procedure? In its currently popular form the latter possibility involves the following reasoning: Categorization is always based on exemplar similarity; hence, what appear to be cases of rule application and prototype similarity can be shown, under more intensive analyses, to involve an exemplar-similarity procedure (Estes, 1994; Nosofsky, 1992a,b). We refer to this approach as the "unitary view." The obvious alternative is the "multiple view"–that all three procedures are widely used in categorization. Among those who argue for multiple procedures, the major issues concern the nature of these mechanisms: What component processes are involved and how do they differ for the different procedures?

CONSTRAINTS   FROM   COGNITIVE   NEUROSCIENCE
Purely behavioral studies may be limited in what they can tell us about the question of unitary versus multiple categorization mechanisms. Most behavioral experiments on this issue have produced results that fit better with exemplar- rather than prototype-based mathematical models; however, this may be because exemplar models contain more information (they contain representations of *all* relevant exemplars, whereas prototype models discard much of this information). Also, while quantitative modeling favors exemplar models, some qualitative considerations favor prototype models (e.g.,

1013

Smith, 1995). Thus, there is a clear need to consider another kind of evidence about categorization; for this reason, we turn to more neurologically based research.

Findings from cognitive neuroscience can contribute both to the general issue of unitary versus multiple categorization procedures and to specific issues about component processes. In this chapter, we consider two cases of such contributions from cognitive neuroscience. In the first section, we focus on exemplar-similarity and prototype-similarity procedures, and we consider evidence from amnesic patients in categorization tasks. Such patients should have serious difficulty in learning exemplars of new categories, and consequently their performance in categorization tasks can be revealing about an exemplar mechanism. If categorization is based solely on similarity to remembered exemplars, then amnesics' performance should be very poor compared to that of normals; but if categorization can be accomplished by other means, amnesics' performance might be normal in some cases.

In the second section, we focus on the contrast between exemplar similarity and rule application. Again, we consider some evidence from neuropsychology, noting how different kinds of patients perform in different kinds of tasks. Here, however, we concentrate on neuroimaging studies that attempt to show that different neural processes are involved when people categorize the same objects by different procedures.

Throughout, the studies that we review involve artificial categories (e.g., categories of dot patterns or imaginary animals) rather than natural categories (e.g., dogs or hammers). We emphasize artificial categories because of our concern with categorization procedures: Artificial categories maximize the chances that the categorization procedure of interest is employed. In seeking to determine if rule application is ever employed, one will do better to create, for example, a set of imaginary animals conforming to a novel rule instead of trusting that some particular natural category is, in fact, based on a rule.

Exemplars, prototypes, and categorization by amnesic patients

LOGIC OF THE RESEARCH It is useful to begin by fleshing out the two procedures of interest. To illustrate paradigmatic cases of exemplar- and prototype-similarity procedures, consider a situation in which a dermatologist must decide whether a particular skin lesion is an instance of disease Y.

Assuming the dermatologist has seen many patients, she will likely have stored in long-term memory numerous exemplars of various skin diseases. She may then note that the current lesion is very similar to stored exemplars of disease Y, and on this basis categorize the current lesion as an instance of Y. The sequence of processes presumably includes

1. retrieval of stored exemplars (of various disease categories) that are similar to the current lesion (the test object); and

2. selection of that category whose retrieved exemplars are (by some measure) most similar to the test object.

Note that if the exemplars retrieved in stage 1 all belong to the same category, then the selection process of stage 2 is trivial (or nonexistent). But if the exemplars retrieved in stage 1 belong to different categories, then stage 2 requires a systematic choice process (see, e.g., Estes, 1994; Nosofsky, 1992a,b).

Categorization based on prototype similarity is somewhat different. We assume that, as a consequence of seeing numerous patients, our dermatologist has abstracted from the individual cases a prototype of each relevant skin disease. This prototype is some measure of central tendency of lesions within a disease category–perhaps an average over the dimensions of shape, texture, and color, or the modal values on these dimensions. In any event, our dermatologist might note that the current lesion is more similar to the prototype of disease Y than it is to rival prototypes, and on this basis categorize the current lesion as an instance of Y. The sequence of processes presumably includes

1. retrieval of prototypes (of various disease categories) that are similar to the current lesion; and

2. selection of that category whose prototype is most similar to the test object.

In behavioral research we find numerous studies that directly contrast exemplar similarity and prototype similarity in specific categorization tasks (see Estes, 1994, for a partial review). Typically, the tasks require normal subjects to learn and subsequently use some artificial categories–say, two categories of dot patterns, or schematic faces. The researchers develop quantitative models of exemplar-similarity and prototype-similarity procedures, then determine which model provides a better fit to the data on category learning and use. As previously noted, many of these studies have favored exemplar-similarity models, so much so as to suggest that categorization with novel categories is always done by exemplar similarity (this is the unitary view). Importantly, these studies have frequently bolstered their case for exemplar-based categorization by showing that the representations assumed for categorization can also be invoked to explain performance on tests of recognition memory. That is, an experiment may require subjects to learn the instances of two novel categories of visual patterns, then test the subjects both on categorization with novel items and on recognition of the originally learned instances. One can then use modeling techniques to show that the same representations are involved both in categorization and long-term recognition memory (e.g., Nosofsky and Zaki, 1998; Shin and Nosofsky, 1992).

The link between categorization and recognition memory indicates that the memory representations involved are *explicit.* That is, the representations contain information about the context in which the item occurred, and may also permit conscious recollection of the item. These characteristics of explicit representations provide a basis for responding in tasks like recall and recognition. All of this is in contrast to *implicit* representations, which can provide a basis for performance changes but cannot be intentionally reinstated (see, e.g., Bower, 1998; Schacter, 1989).

This is where neuropsychology enters the picture. One of the best documented sets of findings in the field involves amnesic patients: Amnesics with damage either to medial-temporal–lobe or diencephalic structures have difficulty committing new information to explicit memory (see Squire, 1992, for a review). Amnesics should therefore have difficulty employing the exemplar-similarity procedure in learning and using novel categories, since the exemplars involved are presumably part of explicit memory. Under the unitary view that all categorization is based on exemplar similarity, amnesics should perform poorly in *all* tasks that require the learning and use of novel categories. Under the multiple-procedures view, however, amnesics should perform poorly in those categorization tasks that elicit an exemplar-similarity procedure, but they may perform normally on tasks that recruit other procedures, as long as these other procedures place a minimal load on explicit memory. Prototype similarity might be such an "other" procedure. These ideas were tested in the studies described in the following section.

AMNESIC PERFORMANCE IN CATEGORIZATION TASKS
Using the above logic, Kolodny (1994) compared normal controls and a group of medial-temporal–lobe and Korsakoff's amnesics on two different categorization tasks. One task involved paintings and presumably elicited an exemplar-similarity procedure, whereas the other task involved dot patterns and presumably triggered prototype similarity.

Consider first the dot-pattern task. In a *learning phase*, subjects were presented a sequence of dot patterns and were informed in which of three categories each pattern belonged. Every pattern, which contained nine dots, was generated by statistically distorting one of three proto-type patterns. In a subsequent *test phase*, the subjects were presented the learned patterns plus novel ones, then asked to indicate the appropriate category for each one. This kind of task has been widely used in categorization studies with normal subjects, and performance on the task has typically been interpreted in terms of prototype similarity (e.g., Posner and Keele, 1968; Homa, Sterling, and Trepel, 1981). Following the categorization task, subjects were shown patterns they had categorized as well as completely novel ones, then were asked to decide which ones were "old" and which "new"; this is a recognition test of explicit memory.

The paintings task was similar in structure: a learning phase, followed by a test phase that involved learned and novel items, followed by a recognition task. But now the items were Renaissance paintings, and categorization required the subjects to learn which paintings were done by the same artist. Prior research indicated that categorization in this task was based on exemplar similarity; indeed, paintings done by the same painter were sufficiently dissimilar that it is difficult even to generate a plausible prototype for each artist (Hartley and Homa, 1981).

The results for the paintings task were exactly what one would expect if categorization were mediated by exemplar similarity. Amnesics performed far worse than normal controls during both the training and test phases of categorization. Indeed, amnesic categorization performance did not differ significantly from chance. As corroborating evidence that the control/amnesic difference in categorization was mediated by an underlying difference in retrieval from explicit long-term memory, amnesics performed more poorly than normals on the recognition memory test. There is, then, a clear connection between explicit memory and categorization of novel items, just as has been found in the studies with normals, and all of this is in keeping with an exemplar-similarity procedure.

The results are very different for the task involving dot patterns. Here, amnesics performed as well as normal controls during both the training and test phases of categorization. This suggests that categorization was based on a mechanism other than exemplar similarity. This suggestion is strengthened by the results on the recognition memory test, on which amnesics performed more poorly than normals. In the dot-pattern task, then, there is a dissociation between memory and categorization, with amnesics being impaired on the former but normal on the latter. The magnitude of this dissociation is striking, as amnesic patients achieved their normal categorization while performing at chance on the memory test. It therefore seems highly likely that a mechanism other than explicit exemplar similarity was involved in the categorization of dot patterns.[1]

A report by Squire and Knowlton (1995) contains even more dramatic evidence for a dissociation between categorization and explicit memory (see also Knowlton and Squire, 1993). These researchers worked with a severely amnesic patient E.P. who, according to standard tests, has virtually no capacity for explicit memory (unlike the patients in the preceding study, who scored above chance on recognition memory for paintings). But despite his complete loss of memory, E.P. is normal on the categorization of dot patterns. In one study, E.P. and a group of normal controls were presented a series of dot patterns during a training phase; all patterns were distortions of the same prototype. In a test phase, E.P. and the controls were presented novel patterns, which included the prototype itself, distortions relatively similar to the prototype ("low distortions"), distortions relatively dissimilar to the prototype ("high distortions"), and random dot patterns. The subjects' task was to decide which of these test patterns belonged to the same category as that exemplified in the training phase. As in prior studies with normal subjects, the controls gave their highest ratings ("Yes, it's a member of the category") to the prototype, next highest to the low distortions, and next to the high distortions, giving their lowest rating to the random patterns. E.P. did the same, and to the same degree. There were no significant differences between E.P.'s gradient of categorization and that of the normals.

This is only half the dissociation between categorization and memory. E.P. and the normal controls were also given an extremely simple recognition-memory test. A single dot pattern was presented 40 times in succession, and 5 minutes later subjects were given a recognition test in which they had to decide whether each pattern presented was the memory pattern or not. Unsurprisingly, control subjects were almost perfect on this test. But E.P. performed at chance. Thus E.P. completely failed the simplest test of explicit memory, but was perfectly normal on a categorization test with the same kind of stimuli. Clearly, E.P.'s categorization performance cannot be based on explicit memory, hence not on an (explicit) exemplar-similarity procedure. There must be some other procedure in use.

PROTOTYPES AND EXPLICIT VERSUS IMPLICIT MEMORY   On the face of it, that other procedure would likely be prototype similarity. For one thing, prior work suggests that the categorization of dot patterns is accomplished by a prototype-similarity mechanism (e.g., Posner and Keele, 1968; Homa, Sterling, and Trepel, 1981; but see Shin and Nosofsky, 1992). Another point is that prototype similarity makes minimal demands on long-term explicit memory. Because the dot patterns are pre-

sented every few seconds during the training phase, subjects can extract a prototype simply by holding in working memory (which is spared in amnesia) the measure of central tendency they have extracted thus far, combining it with the next item to form a new prototype. But there is a problem with the claim that prototype similarity is the mechanism operative in the dot-pattern categorization tasks of the preceding studies. Subjects would have to store the prototype in long-term memory between the training and test phases (usually, a matter of minutes), as well as during the test phase (again, a matter of minutes). However, patient E.P., who cannot store a single item for minutes, performs normally on dot-pattern categorization.

There are a couple of possible solutions to this dilemma. One is that the categorization procedure that E.P. and other amnesic patients use is not prototype similarity, but some more primitive procedure that has been spared in amnesia. The only such primitive procedure in sight is a simple mechanism that forms associations between stimulus cues and categories in a manner analogous to classical conditioning. Amnesic subjects might, for example, learn to associate a set of dots in a certain region with category A. This kind of associative mechanism has been used to explain performance in probabilistic categorization tasks, tasks in which the features of objects are only probabilistically related to categorization. In such tasks, amnesics again sometimes perform as well as normals (e.g., Knowlton, Squire, and Gluck, 1994). However, it seems unlikely that the associative mechanism that underlies probabilistic categorization is involved in dot-pattern categorization, since there is a dissociation between the two tasks. Parkinson's patients are impaired in the probabilistic categorization task, yet perform normally on dot-pattern categorization. Hence, two different categorization mechanisms may be involved in the two tasks (Reber and Squire, 1997).[2]

So what procedure is used in dot-pattern categorization? Perhaps the abstraction and use of prototypes requires only implicit, not explicit, memory; consequently, amnesic patients may be able to use an implicit prototype for categorization purposes (which, of course, would not work for recognition). What would an implicit prototype contain? Likely, it would represent the central tendencies of the items presented (like an explicit prototype), but not associations with context (unlike an explicit prototype) (e.g., Bower, 1998). The establishment of such contextual associations is at least part of what distinguishes explicit from implicit representations, and this process requires an intact medial-temporal–diencephalic system.[3]

CONCLUSIONS   What can we conclude about categorization procedures from this line of work? First, at least in some tasks, categorization need not be based on explicit memory. Because exemplar similarity has been tied to explicit memory in experiments with normal subjects, it follows that categorization need not be based on exemplar similarity. In contrast, there *are* tasks in which categorization performance is tied to explicit memory (e.g., the paintings task used by Kolodny, 1994), and in such cases exemplar similarity seems the most plausible account of categorization. Thus, in contrast to the unitary view, there appears to be more than one mechanism of categorization, and at least one of these mechanisms is spared in amnesia. The best guess about the spared mechanism is that it is prototype similarity, with the prototypes involved being implicit representations. These conclusions are in rough agreement with conclusions drawn by Knowlton, Squire, and their co-workers.[4]

Exemplars, rules, and categorization by normal subjects

LOGIC OF THE RESEARCH We turn now to a second line of research on categorization procedures, one that focuses on the contrast between exemplar similarity and rule application, and involves the neuroimaging of normal subjects as well as the behavioral study of neurological patients. We have already characterized the exemplar-similarity procedure, and it is useful to do the same for rule application. Returning to our dermatologist, suppose she knows the additive rule: If the lesion has a sufficient number of the following features—elliptic shape, bumpy texture, reddish-brown coloring, etc.— then disease Y is indicated. If the dermatologist applies this rule in making her diagnosis (categorization), presumably she will engage in the following sequence of processes (after Smith, Patalano, and Jonides, 1998):

1. selectively attend to each critical attribute of the test object (e.g., the shape, texture, and color of the lesion);
2. for each attended-to attribute, determine whether the perceptual information instantiates the value specified in the rule (e.g., "Is this color reddish-brown"?); and
3. amalgamate the outcomes of stage 2 so as to determine the final categorization.

The first stage involves selective attention, the second involves the perceptual instantiation of abstract conditions, and the third requires the working-memory operations of storing and combining information.

Given this characterization of rule application and our previous one of exemplar similarity, we can now consider how data from cognitive neuroscience can be used to determine if the putative mechanisms are distinct, as well as the nature of their component processes. One approach is to look for dissociations between the pro-

cesses of interest in different patient populations; for example, brain damage in frontal regions may lead to a deficit in tasks requiring rule application, but not in tasks requiring exemplar similarity. We will briefly consider such neuropsychological evidence. A second approach is to use neuroimaging techniques to compare categorization based on rule application versus that based on exemplar similarity. This approach allows us to determine the neural regions activated in a particular categorization procedure, and then to use what is known about the functionality of the activated regions to infer the processes involved in the categorization procedure. We will review a PET study that embodies this approach.

NEUROLOGICAL PATIENT PERFORMANCE ON CATEGORIZATION TASKS What neural regions are involved in the application of rules? For years, the best guess has been frontal regions, particularly the dorsolateral prefrontal cortex (DLPFC). One source of suggestive evidence comes from clinical observations of patients with selective frontal lesions. Such patients seem to be particularly deficient in complex tasks, like planning and decision making, and some of this deficiency is thought to arise from the patients' inability to follow explicit rules (e.g., Luria, 1969). A second line of evidence comes from experiments that demonstrate that frontal-lobe patients, particularly those with DLPFC damage, have difficulty in a categorization task that requires the use of explicit rules, the Wisconsin Card Sort task. In this task, on each trial a card is presented that contains geometric forms, the forms varying from card to card with respect to number, shape, size, and background shading. The subjects must first learn which of the four attributes to use as a basis for sorting the cards; and, once they have learned this, the experimenter switches the relevant attribute, so subjects must now discover the new critical attribute. The basic finding is that frontal-lobe patients are relatively normal in learning the initial rule, but are impaired in shifting to a new rule when the experimenter switches relevant attributes (e.g., Milner, 1964).

This finding has frequently been interpreted in terms of deficient use of rules, but a related explanation may be more plausible. The frontal-lobe patients' major deficit may be in *switching* between rules rather than in *applying* them. Indeed, frontal-lobe patients may be deficient in switching their attention between *any* two mental processes. Support for this interpretation comes from studies showing that patients with DLPFC lesions are selectively impaired in switching between two simple tasks (e.g., sorting by color versus sorting by shape), even when compared to neurological patients who have lesions in other parts of frontal cortex (Rubenstein, Evans, and

Meyer, 1994). Further evidence that the DLPFC is involved in switching internal attention comes from neuroimaging studies with normal subjects. While having their brains scanned by functional magnetic resonance imaging (fMRI), subjects were required to perform categorization and mental-rotation tasks concurrently, or to perform each task alone. When doing both tasks concurrently, and hence switching back and forth between them, DLPFC was activated; when the tasks were performed alone, and hence no switching was required, there was no activation in DLPFC (D'Esposito et al., 1995). So it may be that the DLPFC is involved in rule-based categorization to the extent the task requires switching attention between mental processes. Such attention switching is bound to occur when the rule involves multiple attributes. For one thing, the categorizer must switch attention between attributes; for another, the categorizer must remember the outcomes of attributes already tested while interrogating the remaining attributes, and this too may require switching of attention.

If we assume that the DLPFC is involved in many cases of rule application while medial-temporal–lobe and diencephalic structures mediate exemplar similarity, the stage is set for a possible neuropsychological double dissociation between the two categorization procedures; for example, an experiment that tests DLPFC and medial-temporal–lobe patients in two categorization tasks–one that recruits primarily rule application and one that rests on exemplar similarity. To our knowledge, no such attempt at a double dissociation has been published.

A NEUROIMAGING CONTRAST BETWEEN RULE APPLICATION AND EXEMPLAR SIMILARITY   To obtain stronger evidence for a distinction between rule application and exemplar similarity, we had normal subjects perform either a rule- or exemplar-based categorization task while having their brains imaged by positron emission tomography (PET). The categorization tasks (adapted from prior work by Allen and Brooks, 1991) required subjects to learn to sort pictures of artificial animals–exemplified in figure 70.1–into two categories. Two different groups of subjects were tested, one induced to categorize the animals by rule, the other induced to categorize the very same animals on the basis of remembered examples.

Both groups went through a training and a test phase. During training, subjects in the rule group learned to sort the ten animals into the two equal-sized categories by applying an explicit rule. The rule stated that an animal was from one of the categories if it had at least three of five critical features. For example: "An animal is from Venus if at least three of the following five are true: an-

FIGURE 70.1   Examples of artificial animals used in the PET studies of rule-based versus memory-based categorization.

tennae ears, curly tail, hoofed feet, beak, and long neck. Otherwise, it is from Saturn." After training, rule subjects participated in a test phase while being scanned by PET. Only novel animals were presented, and subjects continued to categorize by the training rule. The memory group had comparable training and test phases. During training, subjects learned to sort the ten animals into the appropriate categories, relying totally on their memory for previous categorizations (feedback was given during training, so subjects could remember to which category each animal belonged). During the test phase, again subjects had to categorize novel animals while being scanned by PET. But memory subjects presumably based their decisions about the test animals on similar exemplars they learned during training (this is the conclusion supported by the behavioral findings of Allen and Brooks, 1991).

Before considering the PET data, it is useful to look at the behavioral data in the test phase, to provide corroborating evidence that the rule and memory groups were indeed using two different categorization procedures. Two kinds of test items were of particular importance: (1) a test animal that, according to the rule, was a member of one category, say Venus, and also was extremely similar to a learned item known to be a member of Venus; and (2) a test animal that, according to the rule, was a member of one category, say Venus, but also was extremely similar to a learned item known to be a member of the other category, Saturn. Thus, for type 1 items, both rule application and exemplar similarity should yield the same categorization, whereas the two procedures should yield different decisions for type 2 items. Subjects showed exactly this pattern—rule and memory subjects agreed on the dominant categorization of type 1 items, but not on type 2 items. With regard to the latter, rule subjects categorized 71% of type 2 items according to the rule, whereas memory subjects categorized 76% of type 2 items in terms of similarity to learned exemplars (which goes against the rule). These behavioral data therefore show the expected dissociation between rule application and exemplar similarity. Do the imaging data show such a dissociation as well?

The PET data obtained during the test phase should reflect neural differences between rule application and exemplar similarity. To aid in interpreting the PET data for categorization, subjects in both the rule and memory groups also performed a control task while being scanned. In this control condition, subjects simply looked at each presented animal and arbitrarily made one of two responses. The results obtained during this control task were subtracted from those obtained during the categorization tasks to remove activations due to noncategorization processes (e.g., perceptual and response processes; see Posner et al., 1988).

The subtraction images revealed numerous areas of significant activation, all of which are presented schematically in figure 70.2. The cortical areas are labeled on the schematic using Brodmann numbers, whereas cerebellar regions are designated by Cb. The finding most evident in the schematic is that of a dissociation: Of the twenty-three areas activated across both conditions, fourteen were activated solely in the rule condition. Of the remaining nine areas, seven were active in both conditions, and only two were active in the memory condition alone.[5]

Among the areas distinct to the rule condition, some are of particular significance because of what is known about their functionality. These include two areas in bilateral superior parietal cortex (Brodmann area, or BA, 7), one area in right-hemisphere DLPFC (BA 46), and three areas in bilateral supplementary motor cortex (BA 6). The superior parietal region is known to be involved in selective attention to spatial positions. Thus, studies with human neurological patients show that damage to this parietal region is associated with impairments in spatial, selective attention (Posner and Dehaene, 1994). As we noted earlier, spatial selective attention should

have been involved in rule application, because subjects had to selectively attend to the location of each relevant attribute. The DLPFC activation also fits with rule use. Earlier, we reviewed evidence that this region is activated in a task that requires changing rules, and shifting between the different attributes might be comparable to shifting rules. Finally, the three premotor activations are routinely found in imaging studies of working memory (Smith and Jonides, 1997), and, as previously argued, categorization based on a multi-attribute rule requires the involvement of working memory. Thus, what is known about the functions of these rule-distinct areas fits well with prior conceptions of what is involved in rule application.

There were seven areas of activation common to both rule and memory groups. These include five areas in the visual cortex (one in left BA 17, one in left and one in right BA 18, one in left BA 18/37, and one in right BA 19) and two areas in the right cerebellum. We have no interpretation of the functions of the cerebellar areas, but there are a number of possibilities for the functions of the occipital activations. One possibility is that some automatic exemplar retrieval occurred even in the rule condition (because the test items were similar to the training animals), and the occipital activations reflect this retrieval of visual memories. A second possibility is that both categorization conditions required a fuller perceptual analysis of the test animals than did the control condition, and this additional analysis is the source of the occipital activations. And a third possibility is that, given that the occipital areas were only *roughly* in the same locations for the rule and memory conditions, they may be the result of different kinds of perceptual processing in each condition (e.g., perceptual testing of rule-relevant attributes in the rule condition versus retrieval of visual memories in the memory condition).

The two areas active only in the memory condition were in visual cortex (left BA 18) and the left cerebellum. Because these areas are in regions in which common rule and memory areas were also found, it seems unlikely that the two areas reflect novel cognitive processes. More likely, they may fit with one of the three possibilities discussed in the preceding paragraph.

In sum, the PET results show a dissociation between the neural regions activated in the rule and memory conditions, and the rule-distinct areas may mediate mechanisms unique to rule use, namely selective attention and working memory.

Concluding remarks

Our PET results indicate that different neural mechanisms underlie rule application and exemplar similarity.

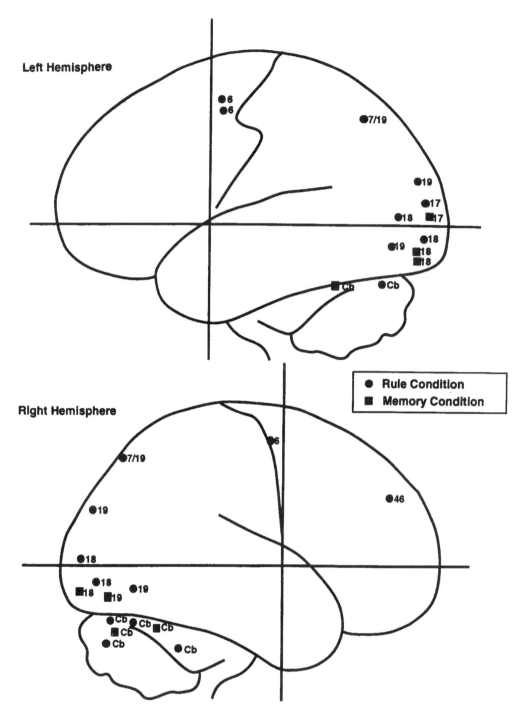

FIGURE 70.2   The marked areas on the left and right lateral surfaces of the cortex denote regions of significant activation in the rule- and memory-condition subtraction images. Circles designate the rule condition, squares the memory condition; numbers designate Brodmann areas, and Cb designates cere-bellum. The only active regions that are not visible from this perspective are left BA 32 (memory condition only) and right thalamus (rule condition only). (Adapted from Smith, Pata-lano, and Jonides, 1998.)

This distinction between procedures is also supported by the neuropsychological evidence that we reviewed, though that evidence is considerably less diagnostic than the PET findings. All things considered, the evidence from cognitive neuroscience supports the cognitive dis-

tinction between rule application and exemplar similarity as categorization mechanisms. Earlier, we showed com-parable evidence for a distinction between exemplar sim-ilarity and prototype similarity. Putting this together, we have support for three different categorization procedures, which argues against the unitary view of categorization and for the multiple-procedures view.

In addition, the various studies tell us something about the processes involved in the three categorization procedures. The poor performance of amnesic patients on a task that clearly requires exemplar retrieval (the paintings task) indicates that the heart of this procedure is retrieval from explicit, long-term memory. This proposal is consistent with the PET findings showing that most of the activation during memory-based categorization is in the posterior part of the brain, where visual memories are presumably stored. The good performance of amnesics on tasks that seem to require prototype similarity (dot-pattern categorization) indicates that, whatever the component processes involved in this procedure, the representations are implicit. And, finally, the PET findings obtained during rule-based categorization indicate that the processes involved in rule application include selective attention and working memory.

Finally, we note that while we have focused on procedures of categorization, much of the neural activation mediating any act of categorization is determined by the contents of the categories, i.e., by *what* is been categorized, not just *how* it is categorized. For example, in our PET study, we might have used verbal descriptions of the imaginary animals instead of pictures–and likely would have found less activation in occipital regions and more in language areas in both the rule and memory conditions. Similarly, neuroimaging studies of dot-pattern categorization show activation in occipital areas, areas that are known to be involved in the initial encoding of visual-spatial information (Reber, Stark, and Squire, 1998).

Content effects have also been obtained in neuroimaging studies of natural categories. In some experiments, subjects are first told the name of a target category (e.g., *vegetable*), and then decide whether named test objects (e.g., lettuce, apple) are instances of the target category. Activation is routinely observed in the left-hemisphere angular gyrus, known to be involved in the processing of linguistic information (e.g., Grossman, Robinson, and Jaggi, 1996). In other studies, the same kind of categorization task is used, but the test items are presented pictorially rather than verbally (e.g., Kosslyn, Alpert, and Thompson, 1995). Now activation is observed in occipital cortex, not in the angular gyrus. Thus, while the categorization procedure is presumably the same in these verbal and visual tasks–prototype or exemplar similarity (e.g., Smith, 1995)–the activation patterns vary in predictable fashion with the kind of information being categorized. A true understanding of the neural bases of categorization, then, must consider both the content of the representations and the procedures that operate on them.

ACKNOWLEDGMENTS Preparation of this paper, and some of the research reported here, was supported by grants from the National Institute on Aging and the Office of Naval Research.

NOTES

1. A dissociation between performance in categorization and recognition memory tasks has often been taken as strong evidence that different processes are involved in the two tasks. But insightful analyses by Nosofsky and Zaki (1998) challenge the evidentiary status of such dissociations. Essentially, these authors demonstrate that such a dissociation could arise if: (1) categorization is based on exemplar similarity, and hence both tasks involve the same memory representations; (2) the categorization task requires a less demanding memory discrimination than does the memory task; and (3) the amnesics have diminished memory capacity (which they surely do). Kolodny's (1994) specific dissociation between dot-pattern categorization and memory might not survive Nosofsky and Zaki's critique. However, the study of amnesic patient E.P. (Squire and Knowlton, 1995; Knowlton and Squire, 1993) would survive this critique (as noted by Nosofsky and Zaki themselves), presumably because the recognition memory task involved was extremely easy.

2. Nosofsky and Zaki's (1998) distrust of dissociations (see note 1) applies here as well. However, the dissociation at issue– that between probabilistic categorization and dot-pattern categorization–is unlikely to hinge on the two tasks' having differential memory requirements. But the dissociation could arise if (1) categorization is based on prototype similarity in both tasks; (2) the extent to which test objects were more similar to one category prototype than the other was greater in the dot-pattern than the probabilistic-categorization task, and hence the decision was more difficult in the probabilistic-categorization task; and (3) Parkinson's patients are impaired in making similarity-based decisions, and hence performed less well in probabilistic categorization.

3. Since we have raised the specter of an implicit prototype, what about the possibility that amnesics rely on implicit exemplars when categorizing dot patterns? At least two reasons argue against the latter possibility. First, if categorization can be based on exemplars, why didn't the amnesic subjects in Kolodny's (1994) experiment use such exemplars to perform normally on the paintings task? This task almost certainly requires exemplar-based categorization, yet amnesic performance on it was at chance, suggesting that the exemplars involved had to be explicitly represented. Second, as noted earlier, there is some independent evidence that the categorization of dot patterns is done by a prototype (e.g., Homa, Sterling, and Trepel, 1981).

4. Ashby, Alfonso-Reese, and Turken (1998) have also proposed distinct neural systems for explicit and implicit categorization mechanisms, but they identify the explicit system only with rule application.

5. Each area of activation contains a peak–a point of greatest change in activation within the area–that can be specified in

an x,y,z-coordinate system. An area of activation found in the rule condition is considered "common" to an area found in the memory condition if the peaks of the two areas differ by less than 10 mm–the approximate spatial resolution of PET–on each coordinate.

REFERENCES

ALLEN, S. W., and L. R. BROOKS, 1991. Specializing the operation of an explicit rule. *J. Exp. Psychol.: Gen.* 120:3–19.

ASHBY, F.G., L. A. ALFONSO-REESE, A. U. TURKEN, and E. M. WALDRON, 1998. A neuropsychological theory of multiple systems in category learning. *Psychol. Rev.* 105:442–481.

BOWER, G. H., 1998. An associative theory of implicit and explicit memory. In *Theories of Memory II*, M. A. Conway, S. E. Gathercole, and C. Cornoldi, eds. East Sussex: Psychology Press, pp. 25–60.

D'ESPOSITO, M., J. DETRE, D. C. ALSOP, R. K. SHIN, S. ATLAS, and M. GROSSMAN, 1995. The neural basis of the central executive system of working memory. *Nature* 378:279–281.

ESTES, W. K., 1994. *Classification and Cognition*. New York: Oxford University Press.

GROSSMAN, M., K. ROBINSON, and J. JAGGI, 1996. The neural basis for semantic memory: Converging evidence from Alzheimer's disease. *Brain Lang.* 55:96–98.

HARTLEY, J., and D. HOMA, 1981. Abstraction of stylistic concepts. *J. Exp. Psychol.: Hum. Learn. Mem.* 7:33–46.

HOMA, D., S. STERLING, and L. TREPEL, 1981. Limitations of exemplar-based generalization and the abstraction of categorical information. *J. Exp. Psychol.: Hum. Learn. Mem.* 7:418–439.

KNOWLTON, B. J., and L. R. SQUIRE, 1993. The learning of categories: Parallel brain systems for item memory and category knowledge. *Science* 262:1747–1749.

KNOWLTON, B. J., L. R. SQUIRE, and M. A. GLUCK, 1994. Probabilistic classification learning in amnesia. *Learn. Mem.* 1:106–120.

KOLODNY, J. A., 1994. Memory processes in classification learning: An investigation of amnesic performance in categorization of dot patterns and artistic styles. *Psychol. Sci.* 5:164–169.

KOSSLYN, S. M., H. M. ALPERT, and W. L. THOMPSON, 1995. Identifying objects at different levels of hierarchy: A position emission tomography study. *Hum. Brain Map.* 3:107–132.

LURIA, A. R., 1969. Frontal lobe syndromes. In *Handbook of Clinical Neuropsychology*, Vol. 2, P. J. Vinken and G. W. Bruyn, eds. Amsterdam: North Holland.

MILNER, B., 1964. Some effects of frontal lobectomy in man. In *The Frontal Granular Cortex and Behavior*, J. M. Warren and K. Akert, eds. New York: McGraw-Hill.

NOSOFSKY, R. M., 1992a. Exemplar-based approach to relating categorization, identification, and recognition. In *Multidimensional Models of Perception and Cognition*, F. G. Ashby, ed. Hillsdale, N.J.: Lawrence Erlbaum, pp. 363–393.

NOSOFSKY, R. M., 1992b. Exemplars, prototypes, and similarity rules. In *From Learning Theory to Connectionist Theory: Essays in Honor of William K. Estes*, Vol. 1, A. F. Healy, S. M. Kosslyn, and R. M. Shiffrin, eds. Hillsdale, N.J.: Lawrence Erlbaum, pp. 149–168.

NOSOFSKY, R. M., and S. R. ZAKI, 1998. Dissociations between categorization and recognition. *Psychol. Sci.*, 9:247–255.

POSNER, M. I., and S. DEHAENE, 1994. Attentional networks. *Trends Neurosci.* 17:75–79.

POSNER, M. I., and S. W. KEELE, 1968. On the genesis of abstract ideas. *J. Exp. Psychol.* 77:353–363.

POSNER, M. I., S. E. PETERSEN, P. T. FOX, and M. E. RAICHLE, 1988. Localization of cognitive functions in the human brain. *Science* 240:1627–1631.

REBER, P. J., and L. R. SQUIRE, 1997. Implicit learning in patients with Parkinson's disease. Poster presented at the 38th Annual Meeting of the Psychonomic Society. Philadelphia, Pa.

REBER, P. J., C. E. L. STARK, and L. R. SQUIRE, 1998. Cortical areas supporting category learning identified using functional MRI. *Proc. Natl. Acad. Sci. U.S.A.* 95:747–750.

RUBENSTEIN, J., J. E. EVANS, and D. E. MEYER, 1994. Task switching in patients with prefrontal cortex damage. Paper presented at the annual meeting of the Cognitive Neuroscience Society, San Francisco, Calif.

SCHACTER, D. L., 1989. Memory. In *Foundations of Cognitive Science*, M. I. Posner, ed. Cambridge, Mass.: MIT Press, pp. 683–726.

SHIN, H. J., and R. M. NOSOFSKY, 1992. Similarity-scaling studies of "dot-pattern" classification and recognition. *J. Exp. Psychol.: Gen.* 121:278–304.

SMITH, E. E., 1995. Concepts and categorization. In *Invitation to Cognitive Science*, Vol. 3: *Thinking* (2d Ed.), E. E. Smith and D. Osherson, eds. Cambridge, Mass.: MIT Press.

SMITH, E. E., and J. JONIDES, 1997. Working memory: A view from neuroimaging. *Cogn. Psychol.* 33:5–42.

SMITH, E. E., A. PATALANO, and J. JONIDES, 1998. Alternative strategies of categorization. *Cognition* 65:167–196.

SQUIRE, L. R., 1992. Memory and the hippocampus: A synthesis from findings with rats, monkeys, and humans. *Psychol. Rev.* 99:195–231.

SQUIRE, L. R., and B. J. KNOWLTON, 1995. Learning about categories in the absence of memory. *Proc. Natl. Acad. Sci. U.S.A.* 92:12470–12474.

71 Category Specificity and the Brain: The Sensory/Motor Model of Semantic Representations of Objects

ALEX MARTIN, LESLIE G. UNGERLEIDER, AND JAMES V. HAXBY

ABSTRACT The semantic representation of an object is composed of stored information about the features and attributes defining that object, including its typical form, color, motion, and the motor movements associated with its use. Evidence from functional brain imaging studies of normal individuals indicates that this information is represented in the brain as a distributed network of discrete cortical regions. Within this network the features that define an object are stored close to the primary sensory and motor areas that were active when information about that object was acquired. Thus, the organization of semantic information parallels the organization of the sensory and motor systems in the primate brain. This organizational scheme provides a basis for understanding category-specific disorders of knowledge resulting from focal brain damage based on the premise that the distinction between members of different categories of objects, such as animals and tools, is dependent on access to information about different types of features. Storage of information about such features as form, color, motion, and object use–associated motor movements in separate regions of the brain may provide innately determined, neurobiologically plausible mechanisms that function in the service of referential meaning.

One of the most puzzling and intriguing consequences of focal brain injury is a category-specific disorder of knowledge—a selective difficulty naming and retrieving information about objects from a single semantic category. Reports of such patients have appeared in the clinical literature for more than 100 years (for review see Nielsen, 1958), but it is mostly in the past 10 to 15 years that significant progress has been made in understanding these category-specific effects. This progress is due largely to the seminal work of Elizabeth Warrington and her colleagues in the mid-1980s (Warrington and McCarthy, 1983, 1987; Warrington and Shallice, 1984), the ever-increasing number of careful case studies and theoretical analyses that followed (e.g., Allport, 1985; Damasio, 1989, 1990; Farah and McClelland, 1991; Farah, Mc-

Mullen, and Meyer, 1991; Hillis and Caramazza, 1991; Humphreys and Riddoch, 1987; Saffran and Schwartz, 1994; Shallice, 1988), and, more recently, functional brain-imaging studies of normal individuals.

This chapter focuses on functional brain-imaging studies of semantic object processing and on category-specific effects using positron emission tomography (PET) and functional magnetic resonance imaging (fMRI). Although these studies are in their infancy, the available evidence suggests that the study of object recognition and object naming can provide us with a window into the much broader issue of how information is stored and organized in the cerebral cortex.

In 1988, Petersen, Posner, Raichle, and colleagues published the first report on the functional neuroanatomy of semantic processing in the normal human brain (Petersen et al., 1988). Using PET, they presented single words (concrete nouns; e.g., "cake") and asked their subjects to generate a word denoting a use associated with the noun (e.g., "eat"). Comparison of activity recorded during this scan with activity recorded while the subjects simply read the words revealed activity in left lateral prefrontal cortex (Brodmann area, BA 47). Activation of left prefrontal cortex was found regardless of whether the words were presented visually or auditorily (in which case the subjects orally repeated the presented nouns to serve as the baseline), thus strengthening the authors' conclusion of an association between left prefrontal cortex and semantics.

This was an extremely important study because it demonstrated the power of O15 PET and the subtraction method for isolating distinct regions of the brain associated with specific cognitive processes. However, there were two main problems with their conclusion concerning semantics. First, linguistic and cognitive models posit that the meaning of a concrete noun is not unitary, but rather is composed of parts—specifically, knowledge about the physical and functional properties of the object. As such, meaning in the brain has been viewed as a

ALEX MARTIN, LESLIE G. UNGERLEIDER, and JAMES V. HAXBY National Institute of Mental Health, Laboratory of Brain and Cognition, Bethesda, Md.

1023

distributed system, involving many brain regions (e.g., Damasio, 1989). Second, even if semantic networks were confined to a single region, the neuropsychological evidence suggested that the critical area would be the left temporal, not the left frontal, lobe (e.g., Cappa, Cavallotti, and Vignolo, 1981; Hart and Gordon, 1990).

Thus, motivated by these issues, we began to explore the functional neuroanatomy of object semantics in the normal brain using PET. Specifically, we sought to determine whether information about the attributes and features that define an object is stored in the sensory and motor systems that were active during initial learning about that object. This hypothesis, which we call the *sensory/motor model of semantic knowledge* (Martin, 1998), has a long history in behavioral neurology. In fact, turn-of-the-century neurologists commonly assumed that the concept of an object (i.e., its representation) was composed of information about that object learned through direct sensory experience (e.g., Broadbent, 1878; Lissauer, 1890; Freud, 1891; Lewandowsky, 1908, translated in Davidoff and Fodor, 1989).

Retrieving information about object attributes

Given this framework, the critical question was: What object features should be studied? We decided on color and action because there is considerable evidence suggesting that the perception of these features, and knowledge about these features, can be differentially impaired following focal damage to the human brain. For example, acquired color blindness, or achromatopsia, can occur from a lesion of the ventral surface of the occipital lobes (e.g., Damasio et al., 1980; Vaina, 1994; Zeki, 1990), and PET and fMRI studies of normal individuals have confirmed selective activation of this region (specifically, the fusiform gyrus and collateral sulcus in the occipital lobe) during color perception (e.g., Corbetta et al., 1990; Sakai et al., 1995; Zeki et al., 1991). In contrast, a more dorsally located lesion, in the region of the lateral occipital gyrus (located at the border of occipital, temporal, and parietal lobes), can result in impaired motion perception, or akinetopsia (e.g., Zeki, 1991; Zihl et al., 1991; Vaina, 1994), and this location was subsequently confirmed by functional brain-imaging studies of normal subjects (e.g., Beauchamp, Cox, and DeYoe, 1997; Corbetta et al., 1990; Zeki et al. 1991; Watson et al., 1993).

In addition, focal lesions can result in selective deficits in retrieving information about object-associated color and object-associated motion. There are, for example, patients with color agnosia who can neither retrieve the name of a color typically associated with an object nor choose from among a set of colors the one commonly

associated with a specific object (e.g., De Vreese, 1991; Luzzatti and Davidoff, 1994), and other patients have been described with a selective deficit in retrieving verbs (e.g., Caramazza and Hillis, 1991; Damasio and Tranel, 1993). Although the behavioral dissociations exhibited by these patients could be remarkably focal, their brain lesions were not. As a result, the locations of the regions which, when damaged, produced these deficits could not be precisely defined, aside from the suggestion that color agnosias were most commonly associated with damage to the posterior region of the left temporal lobe (see Damasio, Tranel, and Damasio, 1989, for review), whereas verb-generation deficits most commonly were seen in association with damage in and around Broca's area. However, the lesions in these patients often extended posteriorly to include perisylvian cortex (see Gainotti et al., 1995, for review).

The paradigm we used was straightforward. Subjects were presented with black and white line drawings of objects. During one PET scan they named the object, during another scan they retrieved a single word denoting a color commonly associated with the object, and during a third scan they retrieved a single word denoting an action commonly associated with the object. For example, subjects shown a picture of a child's wagon would respond "wagon," "red," and "pull" during the different PET scanning conditions. This last condition is the same as the verb-generation task developed by Petersen, Posner, and colleagues, discussed above.

In agreement with Petersen and co-workers (1988), retrieving object attribute information activated the left lateral prefrontal cortex, over and above that seen for object naming. However, this prefrontal activity did not vary as a function of the type of information subjects retrieved. Rather, the activation was similar for the color and action retrieval conditions, and hence consistent with the idea that left lateral prefrontal cortex is critically involved in retrieval from semantic memory (e.g., Gabrieli, Poldrack, and Desmond, 1998). In contrast, other brain regions were differentially active depending on the type of information retrieved. Importantly, behavioral data collected during the scans (voice response times) confirmed that the color and action retrieval tasks were equally difficult to perform. As a result, differences in pattern of cortical activity associated with these tasks could be attributed to differences in the type of information that the subjects retrieved, rather than to differences in the ease of retrieving the information.

Relative to action verbs, generating color words activated the ventral region of the temporal lobes bilaterally, including the fusiform and inferior temporal gyri, approximately 2–3 cm anterior to regions known to be active during color perception (figure 71.1A; see also color plate

A.

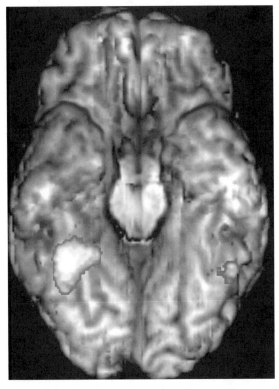

B.

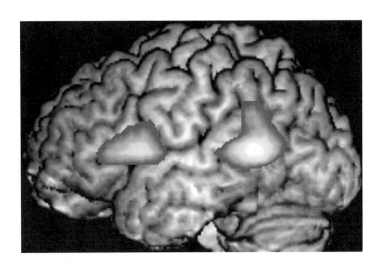

FIGURE 71.1   (A) Ventral view of the brain showing regions in the temporal lobe more active when subjects retrieved information about object-associated color than object-associated action. (B) Lateral view of the left hemisphere showing regions more active when subjects retrieved information about object-associated action than object-associated color. (Adapted from Martin et al., 1995.)

45). In contrast, action word generation was associated with a broader pattern of activation that included the classic language zones (left inferior frontal cortex–Broca's area–and the posterior aspect of the left superior temporal gyrus–Wernicke's area) and the posterior region of the left middle temporal gyrus (figure 71.1B; see also color plate 45).[1] The middle temporal activation was located approximately 1–2 cm anterior to the regions active during the motion perception, based on previous PET findings. Thus, retrieving information about specific object attributes activated brain regions proximal to the areas that mediate perception of those attributes.

Replication and converging evidence

COLOR   There are now three additional studies reporting an association between the retrieval of object color information and activation of the ventral region of the posterior temporal lobes. In one experiment, subjects generated color words in response to written names of objects, rather than to object pictures (Martin et al., 1995). In

another study, color word generation to pictures of objects was contrasted with generating a color word based on a recently learned, novel, object–color association (Wiggs, Weisberg, and Martin, in press). In a third study, color word generation was evaluated in relation to color naming and color perception (Chao and Martin, 1999). In each study, generating the name of a color commonly associated with an object activated the same region of the ventral temporal cortex, bilaterally in three of the four investigations, located anterior and lateral to the occipital areas active during color perception (figure 71.2A).

Additional evidence that this region may be the site where object-associated color information is stored comes from a PET study of individuals with color-word synesthesia (Paulesu et al., 1995). These individuals, who experience vivid colors when hearing words, showed activity in the left ventral temporal lobe when listening to single words (concrete nouns), whereas normal subjects did not. Moreover, the region active in the synesthetes when they heard words and experienced colors was the same area active when normal subjects retrieved object

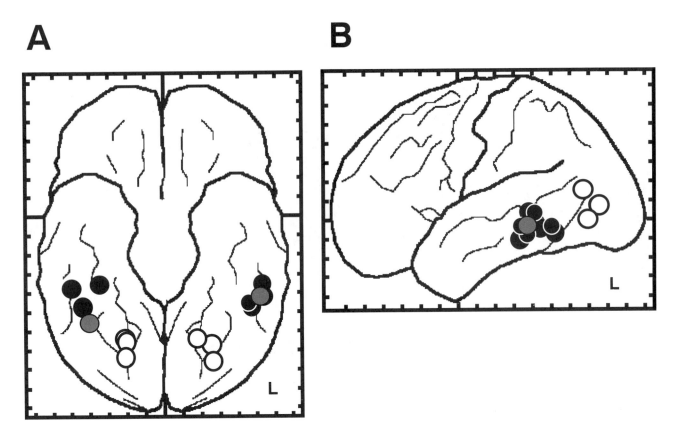

FIGURE 71.2 (A) Summary of findings suggesting that color information is stored in the ventral temporal lobe, anterior to the regions that mediate color perception. White circles show the location of regions active during color perception (Corbetta et al., 1990; Sakai et al., 1995; Zeki et al., 1991); black circles show the location of regions in the ventral temporal lobes active when subjects generated color words (Martin et al., 1995, two studies; Wiggs, Weisberg, and Martin, 1999; Chao and Martin, 1999); the gray circle on the left hemisphere shows the location of the region active when color-word synesthetes experienced color imagery (Paulesu et al., 1995); the gray circle on the right hemisphere shows the location of the region active in normal subjects during a color imagery task

(Howard et al., 1998). (B) Summary of findings suggesting that motion information is stored in the middle temporal gyrus, anterior to the regions that mediate motion perception. White circles show the location of regions active during motion perception (Corbetta et al., 1990; Watson et al., 1993; Zeki et al., 1991); black circles show the location of the area in the left middle temporal gyrus active when subjects generated action words (Fiez et al., 1996; Martin et al., 1995, two studies; Warburton et al., 1996, four studies; Wise et al., 1991); the gray circle shows the location of activity in the left middle temporal gyrus from an analysis of the pooled data from verb generation experiments conducted at 12 centers participating in the European Union collaborative study (Poline et al., 1996).

color information (figure 71.2A). Thus, the vivid experience of color imagery automatically elicited by auditory stimulation in the synesthetes and the effortful retrieval of information about object color by normal individuals activated a similar region of ventral temporal cortex.

Interestingly, although the word-color synesthesia subjects experienced color when they heard words, they did not show activation in ventral occipital cortex. This finding is in accord with studies in normal subjects of color perception that also evaluated color word (Chao and Martin, 1999) and color imagery generation (Howard et al., 1998)—studies that found activation in the ventral temporal lobe, but not in regions of the occipital cortex active when colors were perceived. These findings, coupled with reports of intact color imagery in an achromatopsic patient (Shuren et al., 1996) and impaired color

imagery in a patient with intact color perception (De Vreese, 1991; case II), suggest that information about object color is stored in the ventral temporal lobe, and that the critical site is close to, but does not include, the areas in occipital cortex that selectively respond to the presence of color.

ACTION There are at least a dozen studies in the literature that have used the action word generation task. As with studies of color word generation, the results have been remarkably consistent. The stimuli used in these studies have included pictures of objects, words presented visually, and words presented auditorily. Subjects have responded aloud in some studies, and silently in others; and they have been required to produce a single response to each item in some studies, and multiple responses to each item in others. Nevertheless, retrieving information about object-associated action has consistently activated the left middle temporal gyrus, anterior to the region commonly activated during motion perception (figure 71.2B). Moreover, direct electrical stimulation of this region produced greater disruption of action naming than object naming (Corina et al., 1998). Thus, the posterior region of the left middle temporal gyrus appears to be a critical site for storing information about object-associated motion.

Taken together, the findings provide clear and compelling evidence against the idea that information about object attributes and features is stored in a single region of the brain. Rather, these data suggest that this information is distributed throughout the cerebral cortex, and that information about different features is stored in different regions. In addition, the locations of the sites are not distributed randomly, but rather follow a specific plan that parallels the organization of sensory systems, and perhaps motor systems, as well. Thus, within this view, information about object features and attributes such as form, color, and motion would be stored within the processing streams active when that information was acquired, but downstream from (i.e., anterior to) the regions that mediate perception of those attributes.

Automatic activation of semantic object representations

In requiring subjects to focus attention on their knowledge (i.e., stored information) about different object attributes, these findings showed an association with activity in different regions of the posterior temporal lobe. These findings were therefore similar to studies showing modulation of activity in different regions of occipital cortex when subjects attended to different, physically present, features of a stimulus such as its color and motion (e.g., Corbetta et al., 1990). The difference was that in the word generation and imagery studies, attention was paid to stored information about these attributes, rather than to visual properties of the stimulus.

However, as noted earlier, a defining characteristic of patients with category-specific deficits is that they have trouble naming particular types of objects. This finding, in turn, is in accord with models of object naming in which access to stored information about the object is necessary to name it (e.g., Glaser, 1992; Humphreys, Riddoch, and Quinlan, 1988). Simply put, there is no way to get from the lower-order processing of the physically presented object to the object's name without activating prior knowledge about that object. Therefore, a number of investigators have asked whether one could

find evidence for automatic activation of semantic representations during object naming.

The strategy used in these investigations was similar to the word-generation studies reviewed above. The main idea was to try to identify different patterns of activation by pitting different categories against each other. Now, however, instead of focusing attention on information about different attributes, subjects simply named objects from different categories during different brain-imaging scans.

The categories most commonly investigated have been animals (primarily four-legged mammals) and manipulable man-made objects such as tools and utensils. As with the choice of color and action attributes, this choice was motivated by the clinical literature. Specifically, some patients have been described with selective deficits in naming and retrieving information about animals (and often other living things) and others with selective deficits concerning tools (and often other man-made objects), and these are the most common categories affected in patients with category-specific disorders (see Saffran and Schwartz, 1994, for review). One idea as to why this dissociation occurs is based on an argument initially advanced by Warrington and her colleagues (Warrington and McCarthy, 1987): Recognition and naming of individual animals may depend on access to stored information about visual form, whereas recognition and naming of individual tools may depend on access to stored information about function. In fact, as demonstrated by Farah and McClelland (1991), these relationships are evident in standard dictionary definitions. For example, the word *camel* is defined by what it looks like–specifically, as being large, having a humped back, a long neck, and large feet; the word *wrench*, however, is defined by its function–specifically as being used for holding and turning other objects (cf. *Webster's New World Dictionary*, 3d edition, 1988).

Thus the central idea is that we need to utilize information about relatively subtle differences in visual form to distinguish one four-legged animal from another. We know animals, and we distinguish among them by their physical features–primarily shape and, to a lesser extent, color and pattern (consider, for example, the difference between a leopard, a tiger, and a jaguar, or between a horse, a donkey, and a zebra). But tools are different. Although tools clearly have different shapes, and there is certainly a relationship between their form and function, the relationship between a tool's physical shape and its name is simply not as tightly constrained as the relationship between the physical shape of an animal and its name. Thus, for animals, there is an invariant relationship between name and form, whereas for tools there is an invariant relationship between name and function.

An important point to be addressed, then, is the meaning of "function" in the present context. In some formulations the term *function* is used to designate a large number of characteristics concerned with an object's use. As such, the information is characterized as more "abstract," "conceptual," "verbal," and "semantic" than the visual form–based information needed to distinguish among animals (e.g., Riddoch and Humphreys, 1987; and see discussion in Tyler and Moss, 1997). In contrast, the position proposed here is that the information about object function needed to support tool recognition and naming is information about the patterns of visual motion and patterns of motor movements associated with the actual use of the object. As such, this information is as dependent on sensory experience as is information about the visual form. The difference is that functional information is derived from motor movements, and visual processing of motion, rather than visual processing of form.

In our first study we asked subjects to silently name line drawings of real objects, each presented for a brief period of time (180 ms) (Martin et al., 1996). For one scan the objects were four-legged animals, and for another the objects were common tools and utensils. Subjects also attended to visual noise patterns, and stared at novel, nonsense objects during other scans to provide baselines. First, as expected, relative to viewing nonsense objects, naming real objects was associated with activity in the left inferior frontal lobe (i.e., Broca's area), thus indicating that the subjects named the objects to themselves, as instructed. In addition, naming animals and naming tools both produced strong, bilateral activity in the posterior region of the fusiform gyrus of the temporal lobe, greater on the left than on the right. This failure to find category-related differences in the ventral temporal lobe was somewhat problematic, and we will revisit this issue.

In addition to these regions that were active during both animal and tool naming, other brain regions were differentially activated by animal and tool naming. First, naming tools was associated with activity in the left middle temporal gyrus, in the same region that was active in the previously discussed action verb generation studies. Tool naming was also associated with activity in the left premotor cortex, in the same region active when subjects imagined grasping objects with their dominant hand (Decety et al., 1994). Taken together, these findings were consistent with the idea that identifying individual tools was dependent on accessing information about object-associated patterns of visual motion, stored in the posterior region of the left middle temporal gyrus, and accessing information about object-associated patterns of motor movements stored in left premotor cortex (Martin et al., 1996).

In contrast, relative to naming tools, naming animals was associated with activation of medial occipital cortex. This activation was bilateral, but stronger on the left than the right. We suggested that this occipital activity reflected top-down activation, which would occur whenever information about visual features is needed to distinguish between category members. Thus, there were two parts to this argument. First, that animals are defined by their physical form, and that in order to name them we need to gain access to this stored-form information. Second, when the differences between members of a category are determined by relatively subtle differences in form (as in the previously mentioned animal examples), the occipital cortex is brought into play to help to visualize (image) these differences. Thus, the second part of the argument was the same as the idea proposed by Kosslyn (e.g., Kosslyn, Thompson, and Alpert, 1995; Kosslyn et al., 1995) with regard to involvement of occipital cortex in visual imagery tasks that require imaging fine details of an object or scene. But while in Kosslyn's tasks subjects are explicitly asked to create and manipulate an image, in this formulation the image would be generated automatically, and often outside of awareness (and see Shulman et al., 1997, for additional evidence for top-down modulation of medial occipital cortex associated with other types of visual processing tasks).

Replication and converging evidence

RECOGNITION OF ANIMALS AND THE MEDIAL OCCIPITAL CORTEX Of course, the alternative, and more straightforward interpretation of the medial occipital activation when naming animals is that it reflects differences in the visual complexity of the stimuli. Under this view, pictures of animals produce greater activity in medial occipital cortex because the line drawings depicting these objects were more visually complex than the line drawings depicting tools. Similarly, a patient could have greater difficulty naming animals than tools because the pictures are more visually complex, and less familiar, than pictures of tools and other manipulable objects, such as kitchen utensils (see Gaffan and Heywood, 1993; Stewart, Parkin, and Hunkin, 1992, for supportive data; Farah, Meyer, and McMullen, 1996, for counter-evidence). Therefore, we attempted to rule out stimulus differences in visual complexity by transforming each of the object pictures to a silhouette, thereby eliminating differences between animal and tool pictures with regard to internal visual detail. This transformation produced a modest slowing of naming speed and increased errors, but importantly, eliminated the speed and accuracy advantage for tool naming relative to animal naming found in the study using line drawn stimuli.

Silent naming of the object silhouettes produced the same differential patterns of activation for animal and tool naming found in the first study, including greater activation of the left medial occipital region when naming animals than when naming tools (Martin et al., 1996). Greater medial occipital activation for animal than tool stimuli was also reported by Perani and colleagues (1995) using a semantic, exemplar match paradigm, and by Damasio and colleagues (1996) using an object naming task. Thus, these findings were more consistent with a top-down explanation than with a bottom-up explanation for the association of medial occipital activation and naming pictures of animals.

Additional, and more direct, evidence for the differential patterns of activation associated with identifying and naming animals and tools comes from a recent study of patients with category-specific knowledge disorders. Tranel, Damasio, and Damasio (1997) identified 28 individuals with focal brain lesions that had impaired recognition and naming of animal pictures. Unlike the patients in their previous report (Damasio et al., 1996) of category-specific naming, but not knowledge, disorders, the patients included in the 1997 study failed to provide evidence of intact knowledge about the stimuli they could not name. For example, they were unable to provide accurate, detailed descriptions of the items, thus suggesting that they had a semantic, category-specific deficit. Each of the 28 patients had a lesion that included the medial aspect of the occipital lobe. In 14 of the cases, the lesion was lateralized to the left hemisphere; in the remaining cases, the lesion was lateralized to the right. These were not the first cases with unilateral occipital lesions and category-specific disorders. For example, Nielsen (1958) described six patients with what he termed a selective agnosia for animate objects, all of whom had unilateral occipital lesions, mostly on the left. Thus the functional brain imaging studies of normal subjects and studies of patients with focal brain lesions provide converging evidence that the medial occipital cortex is more involved in recognizing and naming animals than tools (figure 71.3A,B; see also color plate 46), and that its role in mediating this ability is not easily attributed to bottom-up processing of stimulus characteristics.

RECOGNITION OF TOOLS AND THE LEFT MIDDLE TEMPORAL GYRUS The Tranel, Damasio, and Damasio (1997) study also identified eight patients with impaired recognition and naming of tools. The lesions in those patients all included the posterior region of the left middle temporal gyrus, in nearly the same region active during tool naming, and action word generation (figure 71.3C,D). Thus, these patients provided converging evidence that the left posterior middle temporal gyrus is necessary for naming tools, but not animal pictures. In addition, in a PET study of verbal fluency to orally presented category cues, Mummery and colleagues (1996) found activation of this same region of the left middle temporal gyrus when normal subjects simply generated the names of tools and other manipulable objects, such as weapons and toys, relative to generating the names of animals, vegetables, and fruits. Therefore, these studies provide additional evidence consistent with the idea that this region of the left temporal lobe may be where information about object associated motion is stored.

RECOGNITION OF TOOLS AND LEFT PREMOTOR CORTEX Although the Tranel, Damasio, and Damasio (1997) study did not identify patients with anterior lesions, there are reports of at least five patients with lesions that included the left frontal lobe who were more impaired with man-made objects than animals (reviewed in Gainotti et al., 1995). However, as is common with patients with category-specific disorders, the lesions were large, and included the left parietal lobe (all five cases), as well as the left temporal lobe (three of five cases). Therefore, although consistent with the idea that the left premotor region may be involved in naming and knowing about tools, these cases do not provide evidence for the specific involvement of left premotor cortex.

Supportive evidence, however, has been provided by other functional brain imaging studies. Activation of the left premotor site associated with naming tools, but not animals, was found when subjects imagined grasping objects with their right hand (Decety et al., 1994; Grafton et al., 1996), imagined performing a sequence of joystick movements with their right hand (Stephan et al., 1995; activation of the left middle temporal gyrus was also reported in this study), and silently generated action words to pictures of tools (Grafton et al., 1997) (figure 71.4).

Interestingly, studies by Rizzolatti and colleagues have identified neurons in the inferior region of monkey premotor cortex (area F5) that respond both during the execution of a movement, and when observing the movement performed by others. These and related findings have led to the suggestion that these neurons represent observed action, and form the basis for the understanding of motor events (Rizzolatti et al., 1996a). Thus, it may be that the left premotor region identified in the above-noted functional brain imaging studies carries out a similar function—specifically, storing information about the patterns of motor movements associated with the use of an object. If so, the fact that naming tools, but not animals, activates this region further

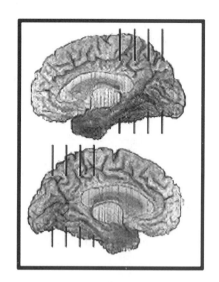

A.

B.

C.

D.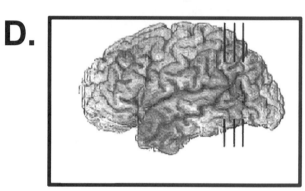

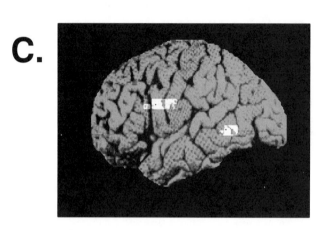

FIGURE 71.3   (A) View of the medial surface of the left hemisphere showing the region of activation in the medial occipital lobe when subjects silently named drawings of animals relative to naming drawings of tools (adapted from Martin et al., 1996). (B) View of the medial surface of the left and right hemispheres showing the location of lesions in 28 subjects that had impaired recognition and naming of drawings of animals (adapted from Tranel, Damasio, and Damasio, 1997). (C) View of the lateral surface of the left hemisphere showing regions active in the premotor cortex and middle temporal gyrus when subjects silently named drawings of tools relative to naming drawings of animals (adapted from Martin et al., 1996). (D) View of the lateral surface of the left hemisphere showing the location of lesions in 8 subjects that had impaired recognition and naming of drawings of tools (adapted from Tranel, Damasio, and Damasio, 1997).

suggests that this information is automatically accessed when manipulable objects are identified. Indeed, while some neurons in monkey F5 responded when movements were observed, other neurons responded as soon as a graspable object was visually presented (see Jeannerod et al., 1995 for review).

Posterior temporal cortex revisited: The representation of object form and motion

As noted previously, in the study by Martin and colleagues (1996), the ventral region of the posterior temporal lobe was activated bilaterally, and to an equal extent by animal and tool naming. Perani and associates (1995) also reported activity in the ventral temporal region for both animals and tools; but again, this region

was not differentially involved in processing objects from one category or the other. These findings were problematic for two reasons. First, if greater activation of the medial occipital lobe when naming animals than tools results from top-down modulation, there should be differentiation more anteriorly in the ventral object-processing stream to drive this process. If there is no anterior site that responds more during animal than tool naming, then where is the top-down influence originating from? Second, although, as reviewed above, there have been reports of patients with unilateral occipital lesions that had category-specific impairment for animals and other animate or living objects, many other cases have had lesions confined to the temporal lobes, often as a result of herpes encephalitis (see Ferreira, Giusiano, and Poncet, 1997, for recent cases; and see Gainotti et

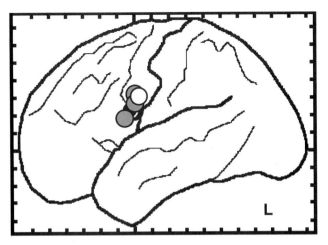

FIGURE 71.4 Summary of findings suggesting that information about patterns of motor movements associated with the use of objects is stored in left premotor cortex. Black circles show the location of regions active when subjects silently named line drawings and silhouettes of tools relative to naming animals (Martin et al., 1996). The white circle shows the location of the region active when subjects silently generated action words in response to pictures of tools (Grafton et al., 1997). Gray circles show locations active when subjects imagined grasping objects with their right hand (Decety et al., 1994; Grafton et al., 1997), and imagined a sequence of joystick movements (Stephan et al., 1995).

al., 1995, for review). The functional brain imaging data indicated that the posterior region of the middle temporal gyrus was selectively involved in recognizing and naming tools, and the human lesion data showed that a lesion in this region could produce a category-specific deficit for tools (Tranel, Damasio, and Damasio, 1997). However, the functional brain imaging data have not identified a region of the temporal lobe selectively involved in processing and knowing about animals, even though the human lesion data suggest that such a region, or regions, should be found.

One possibility is that this discrepancy between the functional brain imaging and lesion data is a result of the limited spatial resolution of PET. Perhaps there is a consistent category-related topology in the ventral region of the temporal lobe, but the sites are situated too close to one another to be visualized by PET. Evidence in support of this idea has been provided by studies of epileptic patients with chronically implanted electrodes, and fMRI studies of normal subjects. These studies have identified relatively small regions in the ventral temporal lobe that selectively respond to the presentation of different types of stimuli, such as human faces (e.g., Allison et al., 1994; Haxby et al., 1997; Kanwisher, McDermott, and Chun, 1997; McCarthy et al., 1997; Puce et al., 1995), letters (Allison et al., 1994; Puce et al., 1995; Polk and Farah, 1998), houses (Haxby et al.,

1997), chairs (Ishai et al., 1997), and representations of the local visual environment (Epstein and Kanwisher, 1998).

The most consistent finding has been the selective activation of the more lateral aspect of the fusiform gyrus, usually stronger on the right than on the left, in response to human faces. In addition, using fMRI, Haxby and colleagues have found that whereas the lateral fusiform is more responsive to faces, the more medial aspect of the fusiform gyrus is more responsive to pictures of houses (Haxby et al., 1997; Ishai et al., 1997). This topological arrangement was highly consistent across subjects, variation in stimuli (i.e., photographs and line drawings), and task (passive viewing, delayed match to sample). Moreover, a similar, highly consistent topology in the fusiform gyrus has also been revealed for the processing of animals and tools across several different paradigms (passive viewing, delayed match to sample, and naming) (Chao et al., 1998a,b).

First, pictures of animals produced a robust response in essentially the same region activated by human faces (i.e., lateral fusiform gyrus, bilaterally), regardless of whether the animal's face was visible or not (Chao et al., 1998b). Second, in contrast to human faces, animal pictures also elicited weaker, yet significant, bilateral activity in the more medial aspect of the fusiform gyrus that responded most strongly to houses; faces, in contrast, produced essentially no activity in this region.[2] Third, relative to animals, tools were associated with greater activation of the more medial aspect of the fusiform gyrus that overlapped with, but was not identical to, the medial fusiform region most responsive to houses (Chao et al., 1998a).

Therefore, in contrast to the PET data, fMRI revealed distinct and consistent patterns of activity for animals and tools in the ventral region of the temporal lobe, bilaterally. Viewing, matching, and naming pictures of animals were associated with stronger activation of the lateral aspect of the fusiform gyrus than was performing these tasks with pictures of tools, whereas tools produced greater activity in the more medial aspect of the fusiform gyrus than did animals.

It is important to note, however, that in these studies no area was identified that responded exclusively to one class of objects and not others. Rather, each object type activated a relatively broad region of the fusiform gyrus (albeit more narrowly for faces), but the peaks of these activations were centered on different parts of the fusiform gyrus. Therefore, rather than being organized by object category, per se, this pattern of results was more consistent with the idea that this cortex is tuned to different object features that members of a category have in common. The nature of these features remain to be determined. However, because the fusiform gyrus is part of the ventral, object-processing stream, a likely possibility is that this region may be tuned to features of object form. Thus, information about object form may be stored in the fusiform gyrus and other regions of ventral temporal cortex, downstream from the regions of occipital cortex that mediate form perception. Moreover, this cortex may have a consistent topological arrangement based on stored features of form shared by objects in the same category (i.e., faces, houses, animals, tools).

Animals and tools were also associated with activations of neighboring regions. Consistent with the PET data, tools were associated with activity in the middle temporal gyrus in most subjects, stronger on the left than on the right (i.e., the same region active when subjects retrieve action verbs). Animals and faces, however, were associated with activation in the superior temporal sulcus (STS) in about half the subjects, usually stronger on the right than on the left (also reported by Kanwisher, McDermott, and Chun, 1997).

Single-cell recording studies in awake monkeys have shown activity in STS when the monkeys were viewing faces and face components, and when the monkeys observed motion of people and other monkeys (see Desimone, 1991, for review). Consistent with these findings, human brain imaging studies have revealed STS activity when viewing faces (Kanwisher, McDermott, and Chun, 1997), viewing mouth and eye movements (Puce et al., 1998), and when observing human movements (Bonda et al., 1996; Rizzolatti et al., 1996b). Thus it may be that the STS is involved not only in the perception of biological motion, but also in storing information about biological motion, perhaps in different parts of this region. If so, the fact that viewing animals and faces activates a portion of STS suggests that this information may be necessary, or at least available, to support processing of these stimuli. Similarly, the consistent finding of left middle temporal gyrus activity in response to pictures of tools suggests that information about motion properties of nonbiological objects may be stored in this region of the temporal lobe.

Finally, as was the case for the ventral temporal lobe, the lateral temporal cortex may not be organized by object category, per se, but rather may be tuned to different object features that members of a category have in common. Again, although the nature of these features remain to be determined, the proximity of these activations to the more posterior motion processing areas suggests that this region may be tuned to features of object motion. Yet-to-be-determined properties associated with biological motion produce activity centered around the STS, whereas properties of man-made object–associated motion produce activity centered around the middle temporal gyrus and inferior temporal sulcus (figure 71.5).

Summary: Multiple, distinct regions for processing and storing information about object attributes

Studies of patients with focal cortical lesions and the findings from functional brain imaging of the intact human brain provide converging evidence for the idea that recognition and naming of different types, or classes, of objects, such as animals and tools, are associated with different networks of discrete cortical regions. Tasks dependent on identifying and naming pictures of animals are associated with activity in the more lateral aspect of the fusiform gyrus, medial occipital cortex, and STS. These activations may be related to the automatic activation of stored information about object form, visual detail, and biological motion, respectively. In contrast, identifying and processing pictures of tools were associated with activation of the more medial aspect of the fusiform gyrus, left middle temporal gyrus, and left premotor cortex; and these sites may be related to the automatic activation of stored information about object form, nonbiological motion, and object use–associated motor movements, respectively.

The important point here is that regardless of the functions or computations ultimately attributed to these regions, these data suggest that the proper level of analysis for understanding semantic object representations is at the level of features, not at the level of whole-object concepts like animals and tools (for an alternative view, see Caramazza and Shelton, 1998, and Caramazza, this volume).

Finally, although much of the evidence reviewed here concerns processing of pictures of objects, it is assumed that these networks will be active regardless of the physical characteristics of the stimulus (picture or word) or modality of presentation (visual or auditory).

Conclusion: Semantic primitives

If there is one aspect of a semantic system that invites consensus, it is that the system must be productive. And, in order to be productive, it must be compositional (e.g., Fodor and Lepore, 1996). In this chapter we have reviewed evidence that suggests what some of those components may be. These components can be thought of as prelexical, semantic primitives for processing and storing information about form, color, motion, and movement (Martin, 1998). This list is not meant to be exhaustive. A good case could be made for other semantic primitives concerned with space, time, number, and

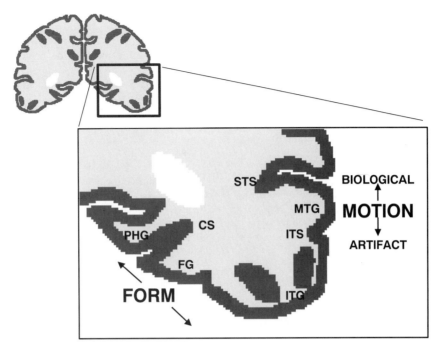

FIGURE 71.5 Schematic representation of posterior temporal cortex proposed to be tuned to features of object form (ventral surface) and motion (lateral surface) shared by members of a category. It is assumed that information is stored in this region according to some as-yet undetermined, but probably innate, properties. It is further assumed that this region would be ac-tive in support of object identification, regardless of stimulus format (object or word) or modality of input. PHG, parahip-pocampal gyrus; CS, collateral sulcus; FG, fusiform gyrus; ITG, inferior temporal gyrus; ITS, inferior temporal sulcus; MTG, middle temporal gyrus; STS, superior temporal sulcus.

affective valence. These should be thought of as innately determined, neurobiologically plausible mechanisms that function in the service of meaning. Such a scheme, on the level of features and attributes, provides us with combi-natorial power out of which different, and finer shades of meaning can be created.

NOTES

1. Re-analysis of the initial study by Petersen and colleagues (1988) indicated that the posterior region of the left middle temporal gyrus was active during their verb generation con-dition. This activation was not reported because it was be-low the threshold for statistical significance. Subsequent studies of verb generation by these investigators showed ro-bust activation of the left middle temporal region when the rate of stimulus presentation was slowed from 1 per second (used in Petersen et al., 1988) to 1 per 1.5 seconds, thus giv-ing subjects more time to retrieve each verb (see Raichle et al., 1994, and Fiez et al., 1996).
2. The differential patterns of activity in the lateral and medial fusiform gyrus in response to pictures of animals and hu-man faces may provide a clue to why patients can present with a selective deficit for faces, and not other types of ob-jects such as animals. It is not because the lateral region of the fusiform gyrus processes only faces; rather, it is because faces, as stimuli, are more focally represented than other classes of objects. Thus, when the lateral fusiform is dam-aged, face processing suffers to a greater extent than the processing of other object types.

REFERENCES

ALLISON, T., G. MCCARTHY, A. NOBRE, A. PUCE, and A. BELGER, 1994. Human extrastriate visual cortex and the per-ception of faces, words, numbers, and colors. *Cereb. Cortex* 5: 544–554.

ALLPORT, D. A., 1985. Distributed memory, modular sub-systems and dysphasia. In *Current Perspectives in Dysphasia*, S.K. Newman and R. Epstein, eds. Edinburgh.: Churchill Livingston, pp. 32–61.

BEAUCHAMP, M. S., R. W. COX, and E. A. DEYOE, 1997. Graded effects of spatial and featural attention on human area MT and associated motion processing areas. *J. Neuro-physiol.* 78:516–520.

BONDA, E., M. PETRIDES, D. OSTRY, and A. EVANS, 1996. Specific involvement of human parietal systems and the amygdala in the perception of biological motion. *J. Neurosci.* 16:3737–3744.

BROADBENT, W. H., 1878, 1879. A case of peculiar affection of speech with commentary. *Brain* 1:484–503.

CAPPA, S., G. CAVALLOTTI, and L. A. VIGNOLO, 1981. Phone-mic and lexical errors in fluent aphasia: Correlation with le-sion site. *Neuropsychologia* 19:171–177.

CARAMAZZA, A., and A. E. HILLIS, 1991. Lexical organiza-tion of nouns and verbs in the brain. *Nature* 349: 788–790.

CARAMAZZA, A., and J. R. SHELTON, 1998. Domain specific knowledge systems in the brain: The animate–inanimate distinction. *J. Cogn. Neurosci.* 10:1–34.

CHAO, L. L., J. V. HAXBY, F. M. LALONDE, L. G. UNGERLEIDER, and A. MARTIN, 1998a. Pictures of animals and tools differentially engage object-related and motion-re-lated brain regions. *Soc. Neurosci. Abstr.* 24:1507.

CHAO, L. L., and A. MARTIN, 1999. Cortical representation of perception, naming, and knowledge of color. *J. Cogn. Neurosci.* 11:25–35.

CHAO, L. L, A. MARTIN, F. M. LALONDE, L. G. UNGERLEIDER, and J. V. HAXBY, 1998b. Faces, animals, and animals with obscured faces elicit similar fMRI activation in the ventral object vision pathway. *Neuroimage Abstr.* 7:5350.

CORBETTA, M., F. M. MIEZIN, S. DOBMEYER, G. L. SHULMAN, and S. E. PETERSEN, 1990. Attentional modulation of neural processing of shape, color, and velocity in humans. *Science* 248:1556–1559.

CORINA, D. P., G. OJEMANN, L. POST, and E. LETTICH, 1998. Neural representation for naming objects and actions: Evidence from cortical stimulation mapping. [abstr.]. *J. Cogn. Neurosci.* supplement, p. 130.

DAMASIO, A. R., 1989. Time locked multiregional retroactivation: A systems level proposal for the neural substrates of recall and recognition. *Cognition* 33:25–62.

DAMASIO, A. R., 1990. Category-related recognition deficits as a clue to the neural substrates of knowledge. *Trends Neurosci.* 13:95–98.

DAMASIO, A. R., and D. TRANEL, 1993. Nouns and verbs are retrieved with differently distributed neural systems. *Proc. Natl. Acad. Sci. U.S.A.* 90:4957–4960.

DAMASIO, A. R., D. TRANEL, and H. DAMASIO. 1989. Disorders of visual recognition. In *Handbook of Neuropsychology*, Vol. 2, F. Boller and J. Grafman, eds. Amsterdam: Elsevier, pp. 317–332.

DAMASIO, A., T. YAMADA, H. DAMASIO, J. CORBETT, and J. MCKEE, 1980. Central achromatopsia: Behavioral, anatomic, and physiologic aspects. *Neurology* 30:1064–1071.

DAMASIO, H., T. J. GRABOWSKI, D. TRANEL, R. D. HICHWA, and A. R. DAMASIO, 1996. A neural basis for lexical retrieval. *Nature* 380:499–505.

DAVIDOFF, J., and G. FODOR, 1989. An annotated translation of Lewandowsky (1908). *Cogn. Neuropsychol.* 6:165–177.

DE VREESE, L. P., 1991. Two systems for colour-naming defects: Verbal disconnection vs. colour imagery disorder. *Neuropsychologia* 29:1–18.

DECETY, J., D. PERANI, M. JEANNEROD, V. BETTINARDI, B. TADARY, R. WOODS, J. C. MAZZIOTTA, and F. FAZIO, 1994. Mapping motor representations with positron emission tomography. *Nature* 371:600–602.

DESIMONE, R., 1991. Face-selective cells in the temporal cortex of monkeys. *J. Cogn. Neurosci.* 3:1–8.

EPSTEIN, R., and N. KANWISHER, 1998. A cortical representation of the local environment. *Nature* 392:598–601.

FARAH, M. J., and J. L. MCCLELLAND, 1991. A computational model of semantic memory impairment: Modality specificity and emergent category specificity. *J. Exp. Psychol.* 120:339–357.

FARAH, M. J., P. A. MCMULLEN, and M. M. MEYER, 1991. Can recognition of living things be selectively impaired? *Neuropsychologia* 29:185–193.

FARAH, M. J., M. M. MEYER, and P. A. MCMULLEN, 1996. The living/nonliving dissociation is not an artifact: Giving an a priori implausible hypothesis a strong test. *Cogn. Neuropsychol.* 13:137–154.

FERREIRA, C. T., B. GIUSIANO, and M. PONCET, 1997. Category-specific anomia: Implication of different neural networks in naming. *NeuroReport* 8:1595–1602.

FIEZ, J. A., M. E. RAICHLE, D. A. BALOTA, P. TALLAL, and S. E. PETERSEN, 1996. PET activation of posterior temporal regions during auditory word presentation and verb generation. *Cereb. Cortex* 6:1–10.

FODOR, J., and E. LEPORE, 1996. The red herring and the pet fish: Why concepts can't be prototypes. *Cognition* 58:253–270.

FREUD, S., 1891. *On Aphasia.* English translation by E. Stengel, 1953. New York: International Universities Press.

GABRIELI, J. D. E., R. A. POLDRACK, and J. E. DESMOND, 1998. The role of left prefrontal cortex in language and memory. *Proc. Natl. Acad. Sci. U.S.A.* 95:906–913.

GAFFAN, D., and C. A. HEYWOOD, 1993. A spurious category-specific visual agnosia for living things in normal human and nonhuman primates. *J. Cogn. Neurosci.* 5:118–128.

GAINOTTI, G., M. C. SILVERI, A. DANIELE, and L. GIUSTOLISI, 1995. Neuroanatomical correlates of category-specific semantic disorders: A critical survey. *Memory* 3:247–264.

GLASER, W. R., 1992. Picture naming. *Cognition* 42:61–105.

GRAFTON, S. T., M. A. ARBIB, L. FADIGA, and G. RIZZOLATTI, 1996. Localization of grasp representations in humans by PET: 2. Observation compared with imagination. *Exp. Brain Res.* 112:103–111.

GRAFTON, S. T., L. FADIGA, M. A. ARBIB, and G. RIZZOLATTI, 1997. Premotor cortex activation during observation and naming of familiar tools. *NeuroImage* 6:231–236.

HART, J., and B. GORDON, 1990. Delineation of single-word semantic comprehension deficits in aphasia, with anatomical correlation. *Ann. Neurol.* 27:226–231.

HAXBY, J. V., A. MARTIN, V. P. CLARK, E. HOFFMAN, J. SCHOUTEN, and L. G. UNGERLEIDER, 1997. The processing of faces, inverted faces, and other objects in the ventral object vision pathway. *NeuroImage* 5:S4.

HILLIS, A. E., and A. CARAMAZZA, 1991. Category-specific naming and comprehension impairment: A double dissociation. *Brain* 114:2081–2094.

HOWARD, R. J., D. H. FFYTCHE, J. BARNES, D. MCKEEFRY, Y. HA, P. W. WOODRUFF, E. T. BULLMORE, A. SIMMONS, S. C. R. WILLIAMS, A. S. DAVID, and M. BRAMMER, 1998. The functional anatomy of imagined and perceived colour. *NeuroReport* 9:1019–1023.

HUMPHREYS, G. W., and M. J. RIDDOCH, 1987. On telling your fruit from vegetables: A consideration of category-specific deficits after brain damage. *Trends Neurosci.* 10:145–148.

HUMPHREYS, G. W., M. J. RIDDOCH, and P. T. QUINLAN, 1988. Cascade processes in picture identification. *Cogn. Neuropsychol.* 5:67–103.

ISHAI, A., L. G. UNGERLEIDER, A. MARTIN, J. M. MAISOG, and J. V. HAXBY, 1997. fMRI reveals differential activation in the ventral object vision pathway during the perception of faces, houses, and chairs. *NeuroImage* 5:S149.

JEANNEROD, M., M. A. ARBIB, G. RIZZOLATTI, and H. SAKATA, 1995. Grasping objects: The cortical mechanisms of visuomotor transformation. *Trends Neurosci.* 18:314–320.

KANWISHER, N., J. MCDERMOTT, and M. M. CHUN, 1997. The fusiform face area: A module in human extrastriate cortex specialized for face perception. *J. Neurosci.* 17:4302–4311.

KOSSLYN, S. M., W. L. THOMPSON, and N. M. ALPERT, 1995a. Neural systems shared by visual imagery and visual perception: A positron emission tomography study. *NeuroImage* 6:320–334.

KOSSLYN, S. M., W. L. THOMPSON, I. J. KIM, and N. M. ALPERT, 1995b. Topographical representations of mental images in primary visual cortex. *Nature* 378:496–498.

LISSAUER, H., 1890, 1988. A case of visual agnosia with a contribution to theory (translated by M. Jackson). *Cogn. Neuropsychol.* 5:157–192.

LUZZATTI, C., and J. DAVIDOFF, 1994. Impaired retrieval of object colour knowledge with preserved colour naming. *Neuropsychologia* 32:933–950.

MARTIN, A., 1998. The organization of semantic knowledge and the origin of words in the brain. In *The Origins and Diversification of Language. Memoirs of the California Academy of Sciences*, No. 24, N. G. Jablonski and L. C. Aiello, eds. San Francisco: California Academy of Sciences, pp. 69–88.

MARTIN, A., J. V. HAXBY, F. M. LALONDE, C. L. WIGGS, and L. G. UNGERLEIDER, 1995. Discrete cortical regions associated with knowledge of color and knowledge of action. *Science* 270:102–105.

MARTIN, A., C. L. WIGGS, L. G. UNGERLEIDER, and J. V. HAXBY, 1996. Neural correlates of category-specific knowledge. *Nature* 379:649–652.

MCCARTHY, G., A. PUCE, J. C. GORE, and T. ALLISON, 1997. Face-specific processing in the human fusiform gyrus. *J. Cogn. Neurosci.* 9:605–610.

MUMMERY, C. J., K. PATTERSON, J. R. HODGES, and R. S. J. WISE, 1996. Generating 'tiger' as an animal name or a word beginning with T: Differences in brain activation. *Proc. R. Soc. Lond. B* 263:989–995.

NIELSEN, J. M., 1958. *Memory and Amnesia.* Los Angeles: San Lucas Press.

PAULESU, E., J. HARRISON, S. BARON-COHEN, J. D. G. WATSON, L. GOLDSTEIN, J. HEATHER, R. S. J. FRACKOWIAK, and C. D. FRITH, 1995. The physiology of coloured hearing: A PET activation study of colour-word synaesthesia. *Brain* 118:661–676.

PERANI, D., S. F. CAPPA, V. BETTINARDI, S. BRESSI, M. GORNO-TEMPINI, M. MATARRESE, and F. FAZIO, 1995. Different neural systems for the recognition of animals and man-made tools. *NeuroReport* 6:1637–1641.

PETERSEN, S. E., P. T. FOX, M. I. POSNER, M. MINTUN, and M. E. RAICHLE, 1988. Positron emission tomographic studies of the cortical anatomy of single-word processing. NATURE 331:585–589.

POLINE, J.-B., R. VANDENBERGHE, A. P. HOLMES, K. J. FRISTON, and R. S. J. FRACKOWIAK, 1996. Reproducibility of PET activation studies: Lessons from a multi-center European experiment, EU concerted action on functional imaging. *NeuroImage* 4:34–54.

POLK, T. A., and M. J. FARAH, 1998. The neural development and organization of letter recognition: Evidence from functional neuroimaging, computational modeling, and behavioral studies. *Proc. Natl. Acad. Sci. U.S.A.* 95: 847–852.

PUCE, A., T. ALLISON, M. ASGARI, J. C. GORE, and G. MCCARTHY, 1995. Differential sensitivity of human visual cortex to faces, letterstrings, and textures. *J. Neurosci.* 16:5205–5215.

PUCE, A., T. ALLISON, S. BENTIN, J. C. GORE, and G. MCCARTHY, 1998. Temporal cortex activations in humans viewing eye and mouth movements. *J. Neurosci.* 18:2188–2199.

RAICHLE, M. E., J. A. FIEZ, T. O. VIDEEN, M. K. MACLEOD, J. V. PARDO, P. T. FOX, and S. E. PETERSEN, 1994. Practice-related changes in human brain functional anatomy during nonmotor learning. *Cereb. Cortex* 4:8–26.

RIDDOCH, M. J., and G. W. HUMPHREYS, 1987. Visual object processing in optic aphasia: A case of semantic access agnosia. *Cogn. Neuropsychol.* 4:131–186.

RIZZOLATTI, G., L. FADIGA, V. GALLESE, and L. FOGASSI, 1996a. Premotor cortex and the recognition of motor actions. *Cogn. Brain Res.* 3:131–141.

RIZZOLATTI, G., L. FADIGA, M. MATELLI, V. BETTINARDI, E. PAULESU, D. ERANI, and F. FAZIO, 1996b. Localization of grasp representations in humans by PET: 1. Observation versus execution. *Exp. Brain Res.* 111:246–252.

SAFFRAN, E. M., and M. F. SCHWARTZ, 1994. Of cabbages and things: Semantic memory from a neuropsychological perspective–a tutorial review. In *Attention and Performance XV*, C. Umilta and M. Moscovitch, eds. Cambridge, Mass.: MIT Press, pp. 507–536.

SAKAI, K., E. WATANABE, Y. ONODERA, I. UCHIDA, H. KATO, E. YAMAMOTO, H. KOIZUMI, and Y. MIYASHITA, 1995. Mapping of the human colour centre with echo-planar magnetic resonance imaging. *Proc. R. Soc. Lond. B* 261:89–98.

SHALLICE, T., 1988. *From Neuropsychology to Mental Structure.* New York: Cambridge University Press.

SHULMAN, G. L., M. CORBETTA, R. BUCKNER, M. E. RAICHLE, J. FIEZ, F. M. MIEZIN, and S. E. PETERSEN, 1997. Top-down modulation of early sensory cortex. *Cereb. Cortex* 7:193–206.

SHUREN, J. E., T. G. BROTT, B. K. SCHEFFT, and W. HOUSTON, 1996. Preserved color imagery in an achromatopsic. *Neuropsychologia* 34:485–489.

STEPHAN, K. M., G. R. FINK, R. E. PASSINGHAM, D. SILBERSWEIG, A. O. CEBALLOS-BAUMANN, C. D. FRITH, and R. S. J. FRACKOWIAK, 1995. Functional anatomy of the mental representation of upper extremity movements in healthy subjects. *J. Neurophysiol.* 73:373–386.

STEWART, F., A. J. PARKIN, and N. M. HUNKIN, 1992. Naming impairments following recovery from herpes simplex encephalitis: Category specific? *Quart. J. Exp. Psychol.* 44A:261–284.

TRANEL, D., H. DAMASIO, and A. R. DAMASIO, 1997. A neural basis for the retrieval of conceptual knowledge. *Neuropsychologia* 35:1319–1328.

TYLER, L. K., and H. E. MOSS, 1997. Functional properties of concepts: Studies of normal and brain-damaged patients. *Cogn. Neuropsychol.* 14:511–545.

VAINA, L. M., 1994. Functional segregation of color and motion processing in the human visual cortex: Clinical evidence. *Cereb. Cortex* 5:555–572.

WARBURTON, E., R. S. J. WISE, C. J. PRICE, C. WEILLER, U. HADAR, S. RAMSAY, and R. S. J. FRACKOWIAK, 1996. Noun and verb retrieval by normal subjects studied with PET. *Brain* 119:159–179.

WARRINGTON, E. K., and R. MCCARTHY, 1983. Category specific access dysphasia. *Brain* 106:859–878.

WARRINGTON, E. K., and R. MCCARTHY, 1987. Categories of knowledge: Further fractionation and an attempted integration. *Brain* 110:1273–1296.

WARRINGTON, E. K., and T. SHALLICE, 1984. Category-specific semantic impairments. *Brain* 107:829:854.

WATSON, J. D. G., R. MYERS, R. S. J. FRACKOWIAK, J. V. HAJNAL, R. P. WOODS, J. C. MAZZIOTTA, S. SHIPP, and S. ZEKI, 1993. Area V5 of the human brain: Evidence from a combined study using positron emission tomography and magnetic resonance imaging. *Cereb. Cortex* 3:79–94.

WIGGS, C. L., J. A. WEISBERG, and A. MARTIN, in press. Neural correlates of semantic and episodic memory retrieval. *Neuropsychologia.*

WISE, R., F. CHOLLET, U. HADAR, K. FRISTON, E. HOFFNER, and R. FRACKOWIAK, 1991. Distribution of cortical neural networks involved in word comprehension and word retrieval. *Brain* 114:1803–1817.

ZEKI, S., 1990. A century of cerebral achromatopsia. *Brain* 113:1721–1777.

ZEKI, S., 1991. Cerebral akinetopsia (visual motion blindness). *Brain* 114:811–824.

ZEKI, S., J. D. G. WATSON, C. J. LUECK, K. J. FRISTON, C. KENNARD, and R. S. J. FRACKOWIAK, 1991. A direct demonstration of functional specialization in human visual cortex. *J. Neurosci.* 11: 641–649.

ZIHL, J., D. VON CRAMON, N. MAI, and C. H. SCHMID, 1991. Disturbance of movement vision after bilateral posterior brain damage. *Brain* 114:2235–2252.

72 The Organization of Conceptual Knowledge in the Brain

ALFONSO CARAMAZZA

ABSTRACT Theories of how conceptual knowledge is organized in the brain are evaluated. Three types of evidence are considered: the patterns of cognitive disorders following brain injury, computer simulations of these disorders, and functional neuroimaging results. However, the focus is on the neuropsychological evidence. The results show that the categories of animals, fruits and vegetables, artifacts, and body parts can each be damaged or spared selectively. It is argued that this pattern of dissociations and other aspects of these patients' performance are incompatible with theories that propose that conceptual knowledge is organized into several modality-specific subsystems. The proposal is made that conceptual knowledge is organized into broad domains of knowledge reflecting evolutionary adaptations.

How is conceptual knowledge organized in the brain? What are the principles that govern its organization? Various proposals have been made. The most widely adopted principle is that conceptual knowledge is distributed over several modality-specific subsystems. On this view, the visual properties of an object are represented in a visual semantic subsystem, its auditory properties (e.g., its characteristic sounds) in an auditory semantic subsystem, its action properties in an action semantic subsystem, and so on (see, for example, Allport, 1985). I will refer to this principle as the "modality-specific principle." Another proposal is that what determines the organization of conceptual knowledge is the relative strengths of the associations among the properties that characterize an object, irrespective of their sensory/motor content (see, for example, Caramazza et al., 1990; Riddoch et al., 1988). On this view, properties that are highly correlated (e.g., having a particular shape and a particular function) will tend to be processed together and are likely to be represented in close proximity in the brain. I will refer to this principle as the "correlated-structure principle." A radically different proposal is that conceptual knowledge is organized into several broad domains (Caramazza and Shelton, 1998). The determining principle here is an evolutionary one: It is assumed that evolutionary pressures resulted in dedicated brain mechanisms for processing specific classes of objects (Gelman, 1990; Premack, 1990; Hauser, 1997). Plausible candidates are the categories of conspecifics, animals, and plant life (and perhaps artifacts[1]). I will refer to this principle as the "domain-specific principle."

These principles are not mutually exclusive. It is possible that more than one principle is at play in determining the organization of knowledge in the brain. For example, it could turn out that the organization of conceptual knowledge is determined both by the domain-specific and the correlated-structure principles. However, extant proposals have tended to favor one or another principle to the exclusion of others. In this chapter I review the major theories of conceptual representation that have resulted from the adoption of these principles, and the empirical evidence that has been adduced in their support. I focus primarily on a widely held theory that is based on the modality-specific principle. I show that, despite its popularity, the theory is not well supported by empirical evidence. Alternative accounts based on the correlated-structure principle and the domain-specific principle will be considered briefly.

Three types of evidence have been used to inform theories of conceptual organization in the brain: the patterns of cognitive disorders following brain injury, computer simulations of these disorders, and functional neuroimaging results. However, most of the evidence to date consists of the patterns of dissociations of functions observed in brain-damaged patients. Two neuropsychological phenomena have been especially important in this regard: modality-specific and category-specific naming/comprehension disorders. Accordingly, this discussion of the organization of conceptual knowledge focuses primarily on the implications from the neuropsychological evidence, but will also briefly consider the computational modeling and functional neuroimaging evidence.

Modality-specific semantics

The idea that semantics is not a unitary system but a collection of modality-specific subsystems has recently emerged as the dominant view in the cognitive

ALFONSO CARAMAZZA Department of Psychology, Harvard University, Cambridge, Mass.

neurosciences. In its original formulation, theories of modality-specific semantics distinguished between visual and verbal semantic subsystems (e.g., Beauvois, 1982; Paivio, 1971; Warrington, 1975). More recent formulations (e.g., Allport, 1985; Shallice, 1987) have included other modality-specific subsystems. But the core components of the theory are the visual and the functional/associative subsystems: The visual semantic subsystem stores information about the visual properties of objects (e.g., cars have wheels; donkeys have legs) and the functional/associative semantic subsystem stores information about the uses of objects, where they might be found, and other nonsensory properties (e.g., birds lay eggs; chairs are for sitting; whales live in water). I will refer to this theory of the organization of conceptual knowledge in the brain as the "sensory/functional theory" (SFT).

NEUROPSYCHOLOGICAL EVIDENCE: MODALITY-SPECIFIC NAMING DISORDERS Modality-specific naming disorders played an important role in the original formulation of the SFT but have since been given less emphasis. The relevant observation is the following: There are neurological patients who show greater difficulty in naming objects presented in one modality relative to other modalities. The classical form of the disorder is known as optic aphasia—a selective disturbance in naming visually presented objects despite intact visual processes and intact ability to name objects presented in other modalities. These patients typically present with left occipital cortical and subcortical lesions extending to the posterior part of the corpus callosum, effectively disconnecting the left hemisphere from visual input. A number of patients have been described with this general profile of performance and brain lesions (e.g., Coslett and Saffran, 1989; Hillis and Caramazza, 1995; Lhermitte and Beauvois, 1973).

Beauvois (1982; see also Shallice, 1987) interpreted the modality-specific dissociation in such patients as reflecting a disconnection between intact visual and verbal *semantic* subsystems. The verbal semantic subsystem was assumed to be intact because optic aphasics produce language normally, show normal ability to understand spoken words, and can name normally in response to verbal definitions. The visual semantic subsystem was assumed to be intact because the patients are supposedly able to mime the use of objects they cannot name. The latter performance was also taken as an indication that access to visual semantics from visual inputs was normal. Thus, optic aphasia could be construed as providing evidence for modality-specific semantics. Other types of modality-specific naming/semantic deficits have similarly been interpreted as support for a modality-specific, multiple semantics theory (e.g., McCarthy and

Warrington, 1988). However, it has been argued that the existence of modality-specific anomias does not require postulating distinct semantic subsystems. These disorders are more plausibly and parsimoniously explained as reflecting a partial disconnection between modality-specific *structural* descriptions of objects and a modality-neutral, unitary semantic system (for detailed discussion see Caramazza et al., 1990; see also Rapp, Hillis, and Caramazza, 1993; Riddoch et al., 1988). Thus, the evidence from modality-specific naming deficits does not distinguish between multiple (modality-specific) and unitary semantics theories and will not be discussed further here.

NEUROPSYCHOLOGICAL EVIDENCE: SEMANTIC CATEGORY-SPECIFIC DISORDERS The more intriguing result bearing on the organization of conceptual knowledge in the brain is the existence of semantic category–specific deficits.[2] These deficits are characterized by the disproportionate impairment (or sparing) of a semantic category. For example, a patient might have severe difficulties in naming living things but relatively preserved ability in naming all other objects. The importance of the existence of these deficits for informing theories of the organization of conceptual knowledge in the brain was first forcefully emphasized by Elizabeth Warrington and her collaborators, who also reported the first thoroughly investigated cases of such deficits. Warrington, Shallice, and McCarthy reported a series of patients who were disproportionately impaired either in naming and recognizing living things (Warrington and Shallice, 1984) or nonliving things (Warrington and McCarthy, 1983, 1987). Since these seminal reports, many other cases of category-specific deficits have been reported. Most reports have concerned the disproportionate impairment of living things in patients with neurological disease affecting the inferior temporal lobe (e.g., Basso, Capitani, and Laiacona, 1988; DeRenzi and Lucchelli, 1994; Silveri and Gainotti, 1988; see Gainotti et al., 1995, for review). However, there are also reports of disproportionate impairment of nonliving things (e.g., Hillis and Caramazza, 1991; Sacchett and Humphreys, 1992). Although these contrasting patterns of deficits would seem to provide prima facie evidence for some type of categorical organization of conceptual knowledge in the brain, Warrington and her collaborators argued, instead, that they provide evidence for a modality-specific organization of the semantic system.

The phenomenon of category-specific deficits could be used to inform claims about the organization of conceptual knowledge only if it could be demonstrated that (at least some of) these deficits concern the semantic system and not merely perceptual processes involved in recognizing objects or output processes involved in lexical selection. This condition is easily met by a number of well-studied cases (e.g., Lambon-Ralph et al., 1998; Samson, Pillon, and De Wilde, 1998). The performance of patient EW (Caramazza and Shelton, 1998) is typical of such cases.[3]

A 72-year-old woman at the time of testing (in 1996), EW had suffered (in 1988) a left cerebral vascular accident involving the left posterior frontal and parietal lobes. When she was first tested in our laboratory, she was only mildly aphasic but demonstrated difficulties naming the animals in a screening test for aphasia. Detailed investigation of her naming and comprehension abilities documented a highly selective deficit for animals. In naming the Snodgrass–Vanderwart (1980) pictures, she named all fruits and vegetables correctly (24/24) and 109/118 (92%) items in various artifact categories (tools, furniture, etc.). However, she was able to name only 16/47 (34%) animals. Her difficulties with animals could not be attributed to such factors as frequency, familiarity, or visual complexity (Funnell and Sheridan, 1992; Stewart, Parkin, and Hunkin, 1992).

EW's difficulties in processing animals were not restricted to naming. She was also severely impaired in distinguishing real from unreal animals (chimeras) and in deciding which of two heads or parts of an object went with a body. In both tasks she was severely impaired with animals (object decision: 60% correct; part decision: 70% correct) but performed normally with artifacts. Her difficulties also extended to the comprehension of property statements (e.g., a horse has four legs). Collapsing across several attribute judgment tasks, EW performed very poorly with animals (425/601; 70.7% correct) but normally with artifacts (434/445; 97.5% correct). The fact that EW's difficulties in processing the category of animate objects were observed in naming tasks, object decision tasks, and property judgment tasks invites the inference that the functional locus of the damage is at the level of the semantic system—the only component that is shared across all three tasks. Thus, we can conclude that EW has a category-specific *semantic* deficit, and we can proceed to explore the implication of this conclusion (and similar conclusions for related cases) for theories of the organization of conceptual knowledge.

Semantic category-specific deficits How can category-specific semantic deficits be construed as support for the SFT? The argument is not straightforward and depends on crucial assumptions about the relative importance of visual and functional/associative properties in determining the meaning of living and nonliving things. These assumptions are that visual properties are more important than functional/associative properties in determining the meaning of living things and that functional/associative properties are more important than visual properties in determining the meaning of nonliving things. That is, it is assumed that our ability to distinguish among living things depends far more on our knowledge of the visual attributes of the members of the category than on our knowledge of their functional/associative properties. Similarly, it is assumed that we distinguish among the members of nonliving things primarily through our knowledge of their functional/associative properties. Given these assumptions, selective damage to the visual semantic subsystem would be expected to result in disproportionate impairment for the category of living things, while selective damage to the functional/associative semantic subsystem would result in disproportionate impairment for the category of nonliving things. Thus, the SFT could in principle account for the occurrence of category-specific deficits. However, these deficits would have to take a particular form. The types of category-specific deficits that are expected to occur should not strictly honor folk taxonomic boundaries (e.g., impairment restricted only to animals). Rather, the deficits should involve clusters of categories reflecting the relative importance for each category of the damaged modality-specific subsystem. For example, damage to the visual semantic subsystem should result in impairment of all categories for which visual information plays an important role distinguishing among their members (e.g., on some accounts this will include at least animals, fruits and vegetables, and musical instruments).

The SFT also makes a highly specific prediction. Since category-specific deficits are the result of selective damage to one of the modality-specific semantic subsystems—the visual or the functional/associative subsystems for living and nonliving things, respectively—it follows that these deficits should be associated with disproportionate impairment for either visual or functional/associative knowledge. In other words, the SFT predicts that category-specific deficits for living things should co-occur with disproportionate difficulty for the visual attributes of objects, and that selective deficits for nonliving things should co-occur with disproportionate impairment for the functional/associative properties of objects. A corollary of this prediction is that damage to either the visual or the functional/associative semantic subsystem must result in selective difficulties for living or nonliving things, respectively. In other words, the SFT predicts a necessary co-occurrence of impairments for kinds of information (visual or functional/associative) and types of semantic categories (living and nonliving).

The early accounts of category-specific deficits seemed to confirm the expectations derived from the

SFT. These reports appeared to confirm both the prediction that category-specific deficits involve clusters of categories defined by their dependence on a particular type of information (e.g., visual properties) and the prediction that selective deficits for living things are associated with disproportionate difficulty for the visual properties of objects. A recent review of semantic category–specific deficits concluded that the forms of this disorder support the SFT (Saffran and Schwartz, 1994). However, critical scrutiny of the early reports and the results of tightly controlled recent investigations cast serious doubt on this conclusion (see Caramazza and Shelton, 1998, for detailed review).

What are the categories of category-specific deficits? Although the early cases of category-specific deficit were characterized as disorders of either the category of living things or nonliving things, the actual pattern of impaired and spared categories was more complex than a simple living/nonliving dichotomy. One of the paradigm cases of category-specific deficit for living things–JBR (Warrington and Shallice, 1984)–was also impaired in processing the categories of foods, musical instruments, precious stones, diseases, cloths, and metals. Other patients have shown similarly complex configurations of category deficits. For example, a number of patients have been shown to be impaired in processing living things and foods (e.g., De Renzi and Lucchelli, 1994; Sheridan and Humphreys, 1993; Silveri and Gainotti, 1988), and others in processing living things and musical instruments (e.g., Silveri and Gainotti, 1988).[4]

Warrington and Shallice interpreted this pattern of co-occurrence of category deficits as reflecting damage to a semantic subsystem that is important for distinguishing among members of the affected categories. That is, the co-occurrence of impairments for the categories of living things, musical instruments, and foods is assumed to reflect the fact that visual properties are especially important in distinguishing among the members of these categories, whereas functional/associative attributes are especially important in distinguishing among the members of the spared categories (e.g., tools, furniture, vehicles, etc.). On this view, damage to the visual semantic subsystem would result in impairment of the categories of animals and plant life as well as musical instruments and foods (and other categories that are similarly dependent on visual properties).

There are two problems with this conclusion. One problem is that it is not obvious that the observed association of category-specific deficits is explicable by postulating damage to the visual semantic subsystem. That is, it is not obvious that visual as opposed to functional/associative attributes are more important for distinguishing among members of the categories of musical instruments and foods (think of what distinguishes scrambled eggs from hamburgers or pianos from drums, piccolos, and violins). Nor is there independent empirical confirmation for this contention. More problematic for the SFT is the fact that category-specific deficits dissociate along lines that are not expected from the claim that the deficits reflect damage to a common semantic subsystem. There are reports of patients with category-specific deficits for animals (and fruits and vegetables, in some cases) but not foods (Hart and Gordon, 1992; case P.S.: Hillis and Caramazza, 1991; Laiacona, Barbarotto, and Capitani, 1993); there are patients who are impaired in naming foods but not animals (case J.J.: Hillis and Caramazza, 1991); there are patients who are impaired for the categories of animals and foods but not musical instruments (De Renzi and Lucchelli, 1994); and so on. And there are even finer-grained dissociations of category-specific deficits. For example, there are now several reports that show that the categories of animals and of fruits and vegetables can be damaged independently of each other (Caramazza and Shelton, 1998; Farah and Wallace, 1992; Hillis and Caramazza, 1991; Hart, Berndt, and Caramazza, 1985; Hart and Gordon, 1992). Thus the claim that certain semantic categories are damaged together because of their common dependence on a modality-specific semantic subsystem is not supported.

Is there a necessary dependence between type of semantic category-specific deficit and subtype of semantic information that is damaged? The core empirical prediction of the SFT is that selective deficit for living things necessarily co-occurs with disproportionate impairment for the visual attributes of objects (Farah and McClelland, 1991; Gainotti and Silveri, 1996). Early reports of cases of category-specific deficits seemed to confirm this expectation. Patients with category-specific deficits for living things were also reported to be disproportionately impaired in processing the visual attributes of objects (e.g., Basso, Capitani, and Laiacona, 1988; Farah et al., 1989; Silveri and Gainotti, 1988). However, these studies have been criticized on methodological grounds (see Caramazza and Shelton, 1998). For example, Farah and coworkers reported a patient with a category-specific deficit for living things who performed more poorly in verifying property statements concerning visual (e.g., ducks have long ears) than functional/associative attributes (e.g., roses are given on Valentine's Day). Furthermore, this effect was more marked for living than nonliving things. However, inspection of the data shows that normal subjects were also disproportionately worse with the visual attributes of living things.

TABLE 72.1

Percent correct performance for visual and functional/associative property judgments by patients with category-specific deficits for living things

Patient	Living		Nonliving	
	Visual	Functional	Visual	Functional
EW (Caramazza and Shelton, 1998)	67	74	96	99
GR (Laiacona, Barbarotto, and Capitani, 1993)	55	58	91	84
FM (Laiacona, Barbarotto, and Capitani, 1993)	73	69	96	96
JEN (Samson et al., 1998)	42	51	75	83
DB (Lambon-Ralph et al., 1998)	69	69	100	100
RC (Moss et al., 1998)	69	70	79	90

Far more problematic for the SFT are recent reports showing that patients with category-specific deficits for living things are equally impaired in processing visual and functional/associative attributes when these are matched for difficulty (Caramazza and Shelton, 1998; Laiacona, Barbarotto, and Capitani, 1993; Laiacona, Capitani, and Barbarotto, 1997; Lambon-Ralph et al., 1998; Moss et al., 1998; Samson, Pillon, and De Wilde, 1998). There are now at least eight patients with category-specific deficits for living things who have been tested with property judgment tasks in which the difficulty levels of the visual and functional/associative attribute judgments have been equated. In all cases, no difference was observed between visual and functional/associative attribute conditions. A summary of the performance of some of these cases is shown in table 72.1.

Equally problematic for the SFT is the recent observation that patients with disproportionate difficulties in processing visual attributes of objects do not show greater impairment for the category of living things (Coltheart et al., 1998; Lambon-Ralph et al., 1998). For example, in a word-to-definition matching task, patient IW (Lambon-Ralph et al., 1998) was far worse at matching definitions that stressed perceptual attributes than those that stressed functional/associative attributes (46% versus 79%, respectively). However, in various naming tasks involving several hundred items all together, she performed better or equally well with the category of living than the category of nonliving things (42% versus 33% correct, respectively).

None of the major predictions derived from the SFT has received empirical confirmation: (1) The pattern of attested semantic category–specific deficits does not conform with the expectation that certain semantic categories should always be impaired (or spared) together; (2) category-specific deficits for living things are not associated with disproportionate impairment for visual attributes of objects; and (3) selective deficit for visual attributes is not associated with disproportionate impairment for the category of living things. And there is reason to be skeptical about the truth of this theory's assumption about the relative importance of visual and functional/associative properties in distinguishing between living and nonliving things, respectively. The empirical justification for this claim was provided by Farah and McClelland (1991), who had subjects count the number of visual and functional attributes in dictionary definitions of living things and nonliving things. They found that the ratio of visual to functional/associative attributes is much larger for living than nonliving things. However, the instructions given to subjects had the effect of excluding from the count of functional/associative properties of living things such attributes as "carnivore" and "lives in desert regions." When instructions allow subjects to count such attributes, the ratios of visual to functional/associative properties for living and nonliving things are roughly equal (Caramazza and Shelton, 1998).

Computational modeling   Computational modeling does not provide empirical support for cognitive or neural theories. However, it can provide existence proofs of the viability of complex theories. Farah and McClelland developed a computational model of semantic memory consisting of separate visual and functional/associative subsystems. Their model implemented the assumptions made by the SFT–the ratio of visual to functional/associative attributes was larger for living than nonliving things. When the visual component was damaged selectively, the system performed more poorly in "naming" living than nonliving things. The reverse dissociation was obtained when the functional/associative component was damaged selectively. Furthermore, it was found that damage to one of the modality-specific semantic subsystems (e.g., the visual semantic component) resulted in greater impairment for the properties associated with that modality (visual properties) but also with some impairment for the properties associated with the spared semantic subsystem (functional/associative properties). Thus, this model provides an existence proof that category-like effects can be obtained even when there is no underlying categorical organization in the system. However, this demonstration merely establishes that if information is segregated in such a way that one part is more important for one category than for another, then it is possible to damage part of the information so as to produce disproportionate consequences for one category over another. The value of this demonstration specifically for the SFT (as opposed to any theory that assumes some type of correlation between property types and categories) is that damage to the visual component resulted in greater impairment for the visual attributes of living than nonliving things. But, as we have seen, there is no reliable evidence that category-specific deficits for living things are associated with disproportionate impairment for the visual attributes of objects.

Neuroimaging results Martin (1998) has interpreted the results of several neuroimaging studies as providing support for a modality-based organization of conceptual knowledge. Two studies in particular are relevant to his argument. In one PET study, Martin and his collaborators (Martin et al., 1995) asked subjects to retrieve either the color (e.g., red) or an action (e.g., pull) typically associated with an object (e.g., wagon). They found that retrieving the color of objects led to the activation of the inferior region of the temporal lobe whereas retrieving actions associated with objects led to activation of a more superior region of the temporal lobe. Intriguingly, these areas are close to areas known to mediate color and motor perception, respectively. In another PET study, Martin and associates (Martin et al., 1996) asked subjects to name pictures of animals and tools. They found that naming tools (relative to animals) activated a region of the left temporal lobe similar to that activated by action naming in their earlier experiment. They also found that tool naming activated a region of the left premotor cortex that corresponds roughly to an area that is activated during imaging of actions (Decety et al., 1994). Animal naming (relative to tools) activated the inner surface of occipital cortex, bilaterally (see also Perani et al., 1995).

The results of these studies suggest that brain areas closely associated with modality-specific processing (vision and action) are differentially involved in processing animate objects and artifacts. These are very interesting results. However, they do not require us to adopt a modality-specific theory of *semantics*. The results might only be telling us something about processing differences at the level of visual structural descriptions of objects and the imagery of action. In support of the latter interpretation of the PET results obtained by Martin and collaborators, we note that patients with category-specific semantic deficits for living things tend to have lesions involving temporolimbic structures, inferotemporal areas, or posterior frontal/parietal areas and not the occipital cortex. And there is no reliable evidence that category-specific semantic deficits result from damage to modality-specific semantic subsystems. Further support for this interpretation is provided by the results of a study by Tranel, Damasio, and Damasio (1997), who found that patients with right occipital lesions have disproportionate difficulties recognizing pictured animals but are otherwise supposedly unimpaired at the conceptual level. In other words, the occipital lobes may be important in processing the visual structural representations of objects and not their conceptual content.

The correlated-structure principle

The SFT is not the only reductionist account that can be given for the existence of semantic category–specific deficits. In other words, we do not have to assume a modality-based organization of conceptual knowledge in the brain for category-specific effects to "emerge" from a noncategorically organized conceptual system. For example, given certain assumptions about the structure of concepts (see S. Gelman and Coley, 1990; Keil, 1989; Rosch, 1973, 1975) and given the assumption that highly correlated properties are represented near each other in the brain, we can account for the existence of category-specific deficits. The following assumptions are sufficient: (1) The members of natural-kind categories (e.g., animals, plant life) share many more properties in common than do the members of artifact categories; (2) attributes are not distributed uniformly across objects but vary considerably in their likelihood of co-occurrence; (3) the attributes of natural-kind objects are more highly intercorrelated than the attributes of artifacts, but the latter can also be highly intercorrelated; and (4) highly correlated properties tend to cluster together in the brain. Given these assumptions, the semantic properties of natural-kind objects are highly likely to be found near each other and hence are more likely to be damaged together.

The Organized Unitary Content Hypothesis (OUCH) is one instantiation of these principles (Caramazza et al., 1990), but there are various other possibilities (e.g., see Devlin et al., 1998; Durrant-Peatfield, Moss, and Tyler, 1998). The core assumption in OUCH is that conceptual space is "lumpy." That is, it is assumed that semantic properties are not distributed uniformly across categories, but tend to cluster together, independently of their modality. For example, objects that are capable of a particular type of motion are likely to be made of certain kinds of stuff (substance, texture, color), to have particular odors, to have particular shapes, and to be found in particular types of environments (think of chicken or elephant). Similarly, objects that are shaped like a hammer and are not capable of biological motions tend to be made of certain kinds of stuff (metals, plastics, wood), to have particular odors, and to be found in particular types of environments. In other words, the lumpiness of semantic space reflects in part the distinction between natural kinds and artifacts. Brain damage that affects one of the lumpy regions of semantic space would result in category-like effects.

OUCH (and similar models) can account for the fact that living and nonliving things can be damaged independently of each other. It also naturally accounts for the fact that category-specific deficits are not associated with selective impairment to a modality-defined type of knowledge. Thus, the model is generally consistent with the major neuropsychological observations on record. However, it is silent on whether finer-grained dissociations are possible and what form they might take. To be sure, it is not unreasonable to assume that animals should dissociate from fruits and vegetables because the two classes of objects share few attributes. But such expectations are based on simple intuition and not on an articulated set of claims about the structure of semantic space. This does not mean that it is impossible to make progress in specifying such structure; but until such steps are taken, it is not possible to subject the theory to serious empirical test. Nonetheless, the correlated-structure principle for the organization of conceptual knowledge in the brain remains a viable candidate, albeit without direct empirical support at this time.

The domain-specific principle

As already noted, the existence of category-specific deficits would seem to provide prima facie evidence for some type of categorical organization of conceptual knowledge. But what might the categories of such a categorical organization be? Are "vehicles" and "animals" semantic categories for the purposes of this theory? And what about "European cars," "airplanes," "aquatic animals," "furniture," and "objects typically found in a house"? Is any one of these the right sort of category for the organization of conceptual knowledge in the brain? A theory that would advocate a categorical organization of conceptual knowledge would have to articulate the nature of the categories and provide independent motivation for the proposed set of categories.

Caramazza and Shelton (1998) have argued that evolutionary pressures resulted in specialized neural mechanisms for perceptually *and* conceptually distinguishing specific kinds of objects, leading to the categorical organization of knowledge in the brain (e.g., R. Gelman, 1990; Premack, 1990). The range of categories that can be subsumed under this principle is very narrow—it is restricted to categories of objects whose rapid and accurate classification would have led to survival and reproductive advantages. Plausible candidates are the categories of conspecifics, animals, and plant life (and perhaps artifacts). The fitness value of specific adaptations for recognizing and responding to these types of objects would seem to be uncontroversial: Animals are potential predators and a source of food, plants are a source of food and medication, and conspecifics are a source of nurturance and protection. Thus, the domain-specific assumption provides a principled motivation for restricting the categories of category-specific deficits (or selective sparing) to the categories of conspecifics, animals, and plant life (fruits and vegetables). In this framework, cases of category-specific deficit for nonliving things are actually cases of selective sparing of the evolutionarily defined categories of conspecifics, animals, and plant life (but see Hauser, 1997, for the possibility that artifacts should be accorded a comparably evolutionarily important status).

What evidence can we adduce in support of this claim? The evidence is indirect. It consists of the patterns of categories involved in category-specific semantic deficits. Earlier, we noted that there are finer-grained, category-specific deficits than the simple dichotomy living/nonliving things. Various dissociations have been reported. A summary of the dissociations involving animals, fruits and vegetables, and artifacts is shown in table 72.2. The most clearly documented cases concern the category of animals. Patient EW, whose performance was described earlier, is selectively impaired in processing animals. This pattern of performance contrasts with that of another patient, JJ (Hillis and Caramazza, 1991), who was shown to have a severe impairment in processing all categories tested but animals. Another category that can be damaged selectively is that of fruits and vegetables (plant life?). There are reports of selective impairment of this category (Farah and Wallace, 1992; Hart, Berndt, and Caramazza, 1985) and of its selective impairment relative to the category of animals (Hillis and Caramazza, 1991). These cases of disproportionate impairment of fruits and vegetables contrast with cases of selective sparing relative to the category of animals (Caramazza and Shelton, 1998; Hart and Gordon, 1992). Finally, there are various reports of selective deficit (e.g., Dennis, 1976; Goodglass and

TABLE 72.2
Selected cases of category-specific deficits

Living		Nonliving	
Animals	Fruits and vegetables	Artifacts	Examples of Case Reports
✓	✓		Warrington and Shallice (1984), Silveri and Gainotti (1988)
		✓	Warrington and McCarthy (1983), Sheridan and Humphreys (1993)
✓			Hart and Gordon (1992), Caramazza and Shelton (1998)
	✓	✓	Hillis and Caramazza (1991)
	✓		Hart, Berndt, and Caramazza (1985), Farah and Wallace (1992)
✓		✓	Not observed

✓ = Disproportionate impairment.

Budin, 1988) or sparing (e.g., Goodglass and Wingfield, 1993; Shelton, Fouch, and Caramazza, 1998) of body parts, which might reflect the autonomy of conceptual knowledge of conspecifics.

The pattern of category-specific deficits reviewed here conforms well with expectations derived from the domain-specific hypothesis. The categories for which there is reliable evidence of selective deficit (or sparing) are precisely those that might be considered to be evolutionarily important—those classes of objects for which it can plausibly be argued that their rapid and accurate recognition would have fitness value. The animate/inanimate distinction certainly satisfies this criterion. And there is converging evidence from the developmental literature that this distinction is especially salient in very young infants. There are compelling results showing that very young infants can easily distinguish between biological and nonbiological motion and can distinguish self-initiated from caused motion (Bertenthal, 1993; Spelke, Phillips, and Woodward, 1995). Furthermore, there is evidence that young infants can easily distinguish between animals and visually similar artifacts, indicating that they can make the global differentiation animate/inanimate before they can identify individual animals or artifacts (Mandler, 1992).

Conclusion

Neuropsychological and neuroimaging results are beginning to provide the foundations on which to base empirically testable proposals about the organization of conceptual knowledge in the brain. The available results do not support the view that conceptual knowledge is organized into modality-specific semantic subsystems. The major evidence against this view is provided by the patterns of category-specific semantic deficits. These deficits can be quite discrete, involving fairly narrow semantic categories such as animals, body parts, or fruits and vegetables. Furthermore, patients with category-specific deficits involving these categories are not also disproportionately impaired for the visual attributes of objects, contrary to a core prediction of modality-specific semantic theories. These results are consistent with unitary, modality-neutral semantic accounts. And they encourage the view that the conceptual system consists of domain-specific structures reflecting evolutionary adaptations.

ACKNOWLEDGMENTS The preparation of this chapter was supported in part by grant NS22201.

NOTES

1. I do not discuss number concepts here. However, it is not implausible that number concepts are organized as a separate domain of knowledge (see Dehaene, 1997; Hauser, 1997).
2. Note the distinction between "semantic category–specific deficits" and "category-specific semantic deficits." The former, the semantic category–specific deficits, refers to deficits that are restricted to a semantic category (as opposed to, say, a grammatical category) but do not necessarily involve damage to the semantic system (but they could, of course). That is, they could simply involve deficits restricted to lexical access or to object recognition for a particular semantic category. Because in this chapter I only consider deficits involving semantic categories, I drop the modifier "semantic," accepting as understood the fact that "category-specific" deficits refers to deficits restricted to one or another semantic category. By contrast, "category-specific semantic" deficit refers to a deficit that is restricted to a semantic category *and* the damage is at the level of the semantic system.
3. By claiming that EW's performance is typical of certain patients with category-specific deficits, I do not mean to imply that the patients have the same neurological or cognitive

deficit. I mean only that these patients can all be shown to have at least a semantic deficit in addition to whatever other deficits their particular form of brain damage might have produced. Patient classification for the purpose of cognitive research remains controversial (see Caramazza, 1986).

4. Caution should be exercised in interpreting the early cases of category-specific deficit. Funnell and Sheridan (1992) and Stewart, Parkin, and Hunkin (1992) have shown that semantic categories can vary considerably in terms of the familiarity and visual complexity of their members. And since these factors are important determinants of recognition/naming performance, the interpretation of performance differences across categories is legitimate only if the contribution of these factors is taken into consideration. Unfortunately, not all studies have systematically controlled these factors. Consequently, we cannot be sure that all putative cases of category-specific deficit are "true" cases of selective deficit of a semantic category.

REFERENCES

ALLPORT, D. A., 1985. Distributed memory, modular subsystems and dysphasia. In *Current Perspectives in Dysphasia*, S. K. Newman and R. Epstein, eds. Edinburgh: Churchill Livingstone, pp. 32–60.

BASSO, A., E. CAPITANI, and M. LAIACONA, 1988. Progressive language impairment without dementia: A case with isolated category specific semantic defect. *J. Neurol. Neurosurg. Psychiatry* 51:1201–1207.

BEAUVOIS, M.-F., 1982. Optic aphasia: A process of interaction between vision and language. *Phil. Trans. R. Soc. Lond. B* 298:35–47.

BERTENTHAL, B. I., 1993. Infants' perception of biomechanical motions: Intrinsic image and knowledge-based constraints. In *Visual Perception and Cognition in Infancy. Carnegie Mellon Symposia on Cognition*, C. Granrud, ed. Hillsdale, N.J.: Lawrence Erlbaum Associates, pp. 175–214.

CARAMAZZA, A., 1986. On drawing inferences about the structure of normal cognitive systems from the analysis of patterns of impaired performance: The case for single-patient studies. *Brain Cognit.* 5:41–66.

CARAMAZZA, A., A. E. HILLIS, B. C. RAPP, and C. ROMANI, 1990. The multiple semantics hypothesis: Multiple confusions? *Cogn. Neuropsychol.* 7:161–189.

CARAMAZZA, A., and J. R. SHELTON, 1998. Domain-specific knowledge systems in the brain: The animate–inanimate distinction. *J. Cogn. Neurosci.* 10:1–34.

COLTHEART, M., L. INGLIS, L. CUPPLES, P. MICHIE, A. BATES, and B. BUDD, 1998. A semantic subsystem specific to the storage of information about the visual attributes of animate and inanimate objects. *Neurocase* 4:353–369.

COSLETT, H. B., and E. M. SAFFRAN, 1989. Preserved object recognition and reading comprehension in optic aphasia. *Brain* 112:1091–1110.

DECETY, J. D., D. PERANI, M. JEANNEROD, V. BETTINARDI, B. TADARY, R. WOODS, J. C. MAZZIOTTA, and F. FAZIO, 1994. Mapping motor representations with positron emission tomography. *Nature* 371:600–602.

DEHAENE, S., 1997. *The Number Sense: How the Mind Creates Mathematics*. New York: Oxford University Press.

DENNIS, M., 1976. Dissociated naming and locating of body parts after left anterior temporal lobe resection: An experimental case study. *Brain Lang.* 3:147–163.

DE RENZI, E., and F. LUCCHELLI, 1994. Are semantic systems separately represented in the brain? The case of living category impairment. *Cortex* 30:3–25.

DEVLIN, J. T., L. M. GONNERMAN, E. S. ANDERSEN, and M. S. SEIDENBERG, 1998. Category-specific semantic deficits in focal and widespread brain damage: A computational account. *J. Cogn. Neurosci.* 10:77–94.

DURRANT-PEATFIELD, M., H. E. MOSS, and L. K. TYLER, 1998. The emergence of categories in a damaged PDP system. Paper presented to the Meeting of the Cognitive Neuroscience Society, San Francisco, April, 1998.

FARAH, M. J., and J. L. MCCLELLAND, 1991. A computational model of semantic memory impairment: Modality specificity and emergent category specificity. *J. Exp. Psychol.: Gen.* 120:339–357.

FARAH, M. J., K. M. HAMMOND, Z. MEHTA, and G. RATCLIFF, 1989. Category-specificity and modality-specificity in semantic memory. *Neuropsychologia* 27:193–200.

FARAH, M. J., and M. A. WALLACE, 1992. Semantically-bounded anomia: Implications for the neural implementation of naming. *Neuropsychologia* 30:609–621.

FUNNELL, E., and J. S. SHERIDAN, 1992. Categories of knowledge? Unfamiliar aspects of living and nonliving things. *Cogn. Neuropsychol.* 9:135–153.

GAINOTTI, G., and M. C. SILVERI, 1996. Cognitive and anatomical locus of lesion in a patient with a category-specific semantic impairment for living beings. *Cogn. Neuropsychol.* 13:357–389.

GAINOTTI, G., M. C. SILVERI, A. DANIELE, and L. GIUSTOLISI, 1995. Neuroanatomical correlates of category-specific semantic disorders: A critical survey. In *Semantic Knowledge and Semantic Representations. Memory*, Vol. 3, Issues 3 and 4, R. A. McCarthy, ed. Hove: Lawrence Erlbaum Associates, pp. 247–264.

GELMAN, R., 1990. First principles organize attention to and learning about relevant data: Number and the animate–inanimate distinction as examples. *Cogn. Sci.* 14:79–106.

GELMAN, S., and J. D. COLEY, 1990. The importance of knowing a dodo is a bird: Categories and inferences in 2-year–old children. *Dev. Psychol.* 26:796–804.

GOODGLASS, H., and C. BUDIN, 1988. Category- and modality-specific dissociations in word-comprehension and concurrent phonological dyslexia: A case study. *Neuropsychologia* 26:67–78.

GOODGLASS, H., and A. WINGFIELD, 1993. Selective preservation of a lexical category in aphasia: Dissociations in comprehension of body parts and geographical place names following focal brain lesion. *Memory* 1:313–328.

HART, J., R. S. BERNDT, and A. CARAMAZZA, 1985. Category-specific naming deficit following cerebral infarction. *Nature* 316:439–440.

HART, J., and B. GORDON, 1992. Neural subsystems for object knowledge. *Nature* 359:60–64.

HAUSER, M. D., 1997. Artifactual kinds and functional design features: What a primate understands without language. *Cognition* 64:285–308.

HILLIS, A. E., and A. CARAMAZZA, 1991. Category-specific naming and comprehension impairment: A double dissociation. *Brain* 114:2081–2094.

HILLIS, A. E., and A. CARAMAZZA, 1995. Cognitive and neural mechanisms underlying visual and semantic processing: Implications from "optic aphasia." *J. Cogn. Neurosci.* 7:457–478.

KEIL, F. C., 1989. *Concepts, Kinds, and Cognitive Development.* Cambridge, Mass.: MIT Press.

LAIACONA, M., R. BARBAROTTO, and E. CAPITANI, 1993. Perceptual and associative knowledge in category specific impairment of semantic memory: A study of two cases. *Cortex* 29:727–740.

LAIACONA, M., E. CAPITANI, and R. BARBAROTTO, 1997. Semantic category dissociations: A longitudinal study of two cases. *Cortex* 33:441–461.

LAMBON-RALPH, M. A., D. HOWARD, G. NIGHTINGALE, and A. W. ELLIS, 1998. Are living and nonliving category-specific deficits causally linked to impaired perceptual or associative knowledge? Evidence from a category-specific double dissociation. *Neurocase* 4:311–337.

LHERMITTE, F., and M.-F. BEAUVOIS, 1973. A visual-speech disconnexion syndrome. Report of a case with optic aphasia, agnosic alexia and color agnosia. *Brain* 96:695–714.

MANDLER, J. M., 1992. How to build a baby: II. Conceptual primitives. *Psychol. Rev.* 99:587–604.

MARTIN, A., 1998. The organization of semantic knowledge and the origin of words in the brain. In *The Origins and Diversification of Language*, N. G. Jablonski and L. C. Aiello, eds. San Francisco: California Academy of Sciences, pp. 69–88.

MARTIN, A., J. V. HAXBY, F. M. LALONDE, C. L. WIGGS, and L. G. UNGERLEIDER, 1995. Discrete cortical regions associated with knowledge of color and knowledge of action. *Science* 270:102–105.

MARTIN, A., C. L. WIGGS, L. G. UNGERLEIDER, and J. V. HAXBY, 1996. Neural correlates of category-specific knowledge. *Nature* 379:649–652.

MCCARTHY, R. A., and E. K. WARRINGTON, 1988. Evidence for modality-specific meaning systems in the brain. *Nature* 334:428–430.

MOSS, H. E., L. K. TYLER, M. DURRANT-PEATFIELD, and E. M. BUNN, 1998. Two eyes of a see-through: Impaired and intact semantic knowledge in a case of selective deficit for living things. *Neurocase* 4:291–310.

PAIVIO, A., 1971. *Imagery and Visual Processes.* New York: Holt, Rinehart and Winston.

PERANI, D., S. F. CAPPA, V. BETTINARDI, S. BRESSI, M. GORNO-TEMPINI, M. MATARRESE, and F. FAZIO, 1995. Different neural systems for the recognition of animals and man-made tools. *NeuroReport* 6:1637–1641.

PREMACK, D., 1990. The infant's theory of self-propelled motion. *Cognition* 36:1–16.

RAPP, B., A. E. HILLIS, and A. CARAMAZZA, 1993. The role of the representations in cognitive theory: More on multiple semantics and the agnosias. *Cogn. Neuropsychol.* 10:235–249.

RIDDOCH, M. J., G. W. HUMPHREYS, M. COLTHEART, and E. FUNNELL, 1988. Semantic systems or system? Neuropsychological evidence re-examined. *Cogn. Neuropsychol.* 5:3–25.

ROSCH, E., 1973. On the internal structure of perceptual and semantic categories. In *Cognitive Development and the Acquisition of Language*, T. E. Moore, ed. New York: Academic Press, pp. 111–144.

ROSCH, E., 1975. Cognitive representations of semantic categories. *J. Exp. Psychol.: Gen.* 104:192–233.

SACCHETT, C., and G. W. HUMPHREYS, 1992. Calling a squirrel a squirrel but a canoe a wigwam: A category-specific deficit for artefactual objects and body parts. *Cogn. Neuropsychol.* 9:73–86.

SAFFRAN, E. M., and M. F. SCHWARTZ, 1994. Of cabbages and things: Semantic memory from a neuropsychological perspective–A tutorial review. In *Attention and Performance 15: Conscious and Nonconscious Information Processing*, C. Umilta and M. Moscovitch, eds. Cambridge, Mass.: MIT Press, pp. 507–536.

SAMSON, D., A. PILLON, and V. DE WILDE, 1998. Impaired knowledge of visual and non-visual attributes in a patient with a semantic impairment for living entities: A case of a true category-specific deficit. *Neurocase* 4:273–289.

SHALLICE, T., 1987. Impairments of semantic processing: Multiple dissociations. In *The Cognitive Neuropsychology of Language*, M. Coltheart, G. Sartori, and R. Job, eds. London: Lawrence Erlbaum Associates, pp. 111–127.

SHELTON, J. R., E. FOUCH, and A. CARAMAZZA, 1998. The selective sparing of body part knowledge: A case study. *Neurocase* 4:339–350.

SHERIDAN, J., and G. W. HUMPHREYS, 1993. A verbal-semantic category-specific recognition impairment. *Cogn. Neuropsychol.* 10:143–184.

SILVERI, M. C., and G. GAINOTTI, 1988. Interaction between vision and language in category-specific impairment. *Cogn. Neuropsychol.* 5:677–709.

SNODGRASS, J. G., and M. VANDERWART, 1980. A standardized set of 260 pictures: Norms for name agreement, image agreement, familiarity and visual complexity. *J. Exp. Psychol.: Hum. Learn. Mem.* 6:174–215.

SPELKE, E. S., A. PHILLIPS, and A. L. WOODWARD, 1995. Infants' knowledge of object motion and human action. In *Causal Cognition: A Multidisciplinary Debate*, D. Sperber, D. Premack, and A. J. Premack, eds. New York: Clarendon Press/Oxford University Press, pp. 44–78.

STEWART, F., A. J. PARKIN, and N. M. HUNKIN, 1992. Naming impairments following recovery from herpes simplex encephalitis: Category-specific? *Quart. J. Exp. Psychol.* 44A: 261–284.

TRANEL, D. H., H. DAMASIO, and A. R. DAMASIO, 1997. A neural basis for the retrieval of conceptual knowledge. *Neuropsychologia* 35:1319–1328.

WARRINGTON, E. K., 1975. The selective impairment of semantic memory. *Quart. J. Exp. Psychol.* 27:187–199.

WARRINGTON, E. K., and R. MCCARTHY, 1983. Category specific access dysphasia. *Brain* 106:859–878.

WARRINGTON, E. K., and R. MCCARTHY, 1987. Categories of knowledge: Further fractionations and an attempted integration. *Brain* 110:1273–1296.

WARRINGTON, E. K., and T. SHALLICE, 1984. Category specific semantic impairments. *Brain* 107:829–854.

73 Decision Making and the Somatic Marker Hypothesis

DANIEL TRANEL, ANTOINE BECHARA, AND ANTONIO R. DAMASIO

ABSTRACT How do we make decisions, simple or complicated? Which neural structures are important for decision making? Why do we sometimes make decisions that are favorable to us and sometimes decide against our best interests? Why do some individuals have a proclivity for bad decision making? These are just a few of the pressing questions regarding decision making–questions that are finally being asked within the compass of cognitive neuroscience.

We have been investigating the neural basis of decision making by using a theoretical framework known as the *somatic marker hypothesis*. The framework proposes that decision making is dependent on signals from bioregulatory responses–those responses that are aimed at maintaining homeostasis and ensuring survival. The highest level of such responses includes emotions and feelings. We have studied both normal individuals and neurological patients whose decision making is profoundly impaired following damage to various sectors of the central nervous system (including the ventromedial prefrontal region, the right somatosensory and insular cortices, and the amygdala) and to the peripheral nervous system. Neuropsychological and psychophysiological experiments in these patients have yielded intriguing new insights into the neural architectures required for decision making. A surprising conclusion from our work is that too little emotion has profoundly deleterious effects on decision making; in fact, too little emotion may be just as bad for decision making as excessive emotion has long been considered to be. Our work indicates that individuals utilize bioregulatory responses, including emotions and feelings, to guide decision making in several important ways, both consciously and nonconsciously.

Emotion and the somatic marker hypothesis

BACKGROUND Throughout the history of neuropsychology, the psychological capacities associated with the prefrontal region of the brain have remained enigmatic and elusive. However, the special significance of this region has long been linked to the idea that it provides the neural substrate for a collection of higher-order capacities such as planning, reasoning, self-awareness, empathy, emotional modulation, and especially, decision making (cf. Benton, 1991). Also, the portion of the prefrontal region formed by the orbital and lower mesial sectors ("ventromedial") has been considered by some to be the neural basis for "personality." Over the past century, a number of case studies supported this idea, as investigators called attention to the oftentimes bizarre development of abnormal social behavior following prefrontal brain injury (e.g., Damasio, 1979; Damasio and Anderson, 1993; H. Demasio et al., 1994; Eslinger and Damasio, 1985; Stuss and Benson, 1986). The affected patients had a number of features in common: inability to organize future activity and hold gainful employment, diminished capacity to respond to punishment, and tendencies to present an unrealistically favorable view of themselves and to display inappropriate emotional reactions. Making this profile all the more puzzling was the fact that most of these patients retained normal intelligence, language, memory, and perception.

This personality profile bears some striking similarities to that characterized in clinical psychology and psychiatry as *psychopathic* (or *sociopathic*) (American Psychiatric Association, 1994). In fact, we have designated this condition as "acquired sociopathy," thereby emphasizing the fact that prefrontal injured patients have many personality manifestations that are highly reminiscent of those associated with sociopathy (Damasio, Tranel, and Damasio, 1990, 1991; Tranel, 1994). The qualifier "acquired" signifies that in the brain-damaged patients, the condition follows the onset of brain injury, and occurs in persons whose personalities and social conduct were previously normal. Patients with acquired sociopathy are inclined to engage in decisions and behaviors that have repeated negative consequences for their well-being. The patients are usually not destructive and harmful to others, a feature that tends to distinguish the acquired form of the disorder from the standard developmental form. However, they repeatedly select courses of action that are not in their best interests in the long run. They act as though they have lost the ability to ponder different courses of action and then select the one that promises the best blend of short- and long-term benefit. They have difficulty planning and organizing their lives: They cannot

DANIEL TRANEL, ANTOINE BECHARA, and ANTONIO R. DAMASIO Department of Neurology, Division of Behavioral Neurology and Cognitive Neuroscience, University of Iowa College of Medicine, Iowa City, Iowa

plan their work and they make poor decisions about friends, business associates, and assorted activities. In short, the choices these patients make are neither personally advantageous nor socially adequate. And of particular importance, the choices are very different from the kinds of choices the patients were capable of before the onset of their brain injury.

THE SOMATIC MARKER HYPOTHESIS One observation was key to the development of the somatic marker hypothesis: Although patients with ventromedial prefrontal damage were capable of performing normally on nearly every neuropsychological test they were asked to take, and obviously had preserved conventional intellectual functions, their ability to express emotion and experience feeling relative to complex personal and social situations, for example, as in the expression and experience of embarrassment, was compromised. Given that primary disturbances of intellect, memory, language, attention, or working memory could not explain the bizarre changes in social conduct and decision making typical of these patients, we proposed that deficits in bioregulatory responses might provide a plausible explanation (Damasio, Tranel, and Damasio, 1990, 1991; Damasio, 1994, 1995a,b, 1996). In brief, we can describe the *somatic marker hypothesis* as follows:

1. Certain structures in prefrontal cortex are required in order to learn associations between various classes of complex (higher-order) stimuli and various internal states of the organism (such as emotions) usually experienced in conjunction with those classes of stimuli. These internal states are represented in the brain as transient changes in patterns of activity in somatosensory maps of a large collection of structures, from the brain stem and hypothalamus to the cerebral cortex. We refer to these states as "somatic" (meaning all components of the soma, including the musculoskeletal, the visceral, and the internal milieu).

2. When a situation from a particular class of complex stimuli recurs in one's ongoing experience, systems in the ventromedial prefrontal region—those that previously acquired the association between that class of stimuli and a certain class of somatic states—trigger the reactivation of the somatosensory pattern depicting the appropriate somatic state. This can be achieved by two routes—a *body loop* or an *as-if-body loop*. In the body loop, the soma actually changes in response to the activation, and signals of those changes are relayed back to somatosensory maps; in the as-if-body loop, the reactivation signals are relayed directly to somatosensory maps, bypassing the body and prompting the appropriate pattern of activation in the somatosensory structures. Moreover,

each of these mechanisms—the body loop and the as-if-body loop—may operate either overtly (consciously) or covertly (nonconsciously).

3. With regard to reasoning and decision making, the reactivation of the somatosensory pattern appropriate to a given situation, concurrent with evocation of pertinent factual knowledge, operates to constrain the reasoning and decision-making space via a qualification mechanism. That is, when the somatosensory pattern image is juxtaposed both to the images prompting the somatic state and those depicting potential outcomes, the somatosensory pattern *marks* outcomes as good or bad. When it operates covertly, the somatic marker constitutes a nonconscious biasing signal that facilitates appetitive or avoidance behavior. When it operates overtly, the somatic marker process serves as an incentive or deterrent.

4. Patterns of somatosensory activity can also facilitate attention and working memory, thereby influencing the decision-making process indirectly.

5. The mechanisms described in steps 3 and 4 facilitate logical reasoning.

A NEURAL NETWORK FOR SOMATIC MARKERS We have proposed that the ventromedial prefrontal cortices hold records of temporal conjunctions of activity in various neural units (e.g., sensory cortices, limbic structures), arriving from both external and internal stimuli. They do so in the form of convergence zones (Damasio, 1989a,b). The records hold signals from simultaneously active neural regions, which, as a set, define particular situations. A key output of ventromedial convergence zones is to autonomic effectors, as follows: When aspects of a particular exteroceptive-interoceptive conjunction are reprocessed (nonconsciously or consciously), activation is signaled to ventromedial prefrontal cortices, which in turn activate somatic effectors in structures such as the amygdala, hypothalamus, and brainstem nuclei. In essence, there is an attempt to reconstruct the kind of somatic state that belonged to the original conjunction as learned and modified by experience. The reconstituted somatic state is then signaled to cortical and subcortical somatosensory structures, whence it triggers either a covert process modifying appetitive/aversive behavior or a conscious perception in the form of a *feeling*.

Anatomically, the ventromedial prefrontal cortices are well suited for their role as dispositional convergence zones.[1] They receive projections from all sensory modalities, directly or indirectly (Chavis and Pandya, 1976; Jones and Powell, 1970; Pandya and Kuypers, 1969; Potter and Nauta, 1979). They project to central autonomic effectors (Nauta, 1971), which have, in turn, a physiological influence on visceral control (Hall, Livingston, and Bloor, 1977). They also have extensive two-way connections with the amygdala and hippocampus (Amaral and Price, 1984; Goldman-Rakic, Selemon, and Schwartz, 1984; Porrino, Crane, and Goldman-Rakic, 1981; Van Hoesen, Pandya, and Butters, 1972, 1975). In short, the ventromedial prefrontal cortices receive signals regarding multiple-site representations of scenarios of complex situations from early sensory cortices, and they also receive signals from somatosensory cortices and bioregulatory structures. They can originate signals to bioregulatory structures including the amygdala, hypothalamus, and brainstem nuclei.

To summarize, the anatomical systems network required for somatic markers includes the following: (1) Ventromedial prefrontal cortices containing convergence zones that record associations between the dispositions that represent (a) classes of complex situations and (b) somatic states prepotently associated with such complex situations; (2) central autonomic effectors, including the amygdala, capable of activating somatic responses in the viscera, vascular bed, endocrine system, and nonspecific neurotransmitter systems; (3) somatosensory and insular cortices and their associated two-way projections. Later in this chapter, we describe a systematic investigation of many of the components of the somatic marker neural network.

Consider, for example, a complex social scenario requiring certain decisions and courses of action, say, a tense faculty meeting concerning promotions and work assignments. Dispositions are activated in higher-order association cortices, leading to the recall of pertinent facts and related knowledge. The contingent ventromedial prefrontal linkages are activated concurrently, leading to activation of the emotional disposition apparatus—the amygdala, ventral striatum, cingulate, insular cortex, and so forth. The net result is a reconstruction of a previously learned factual–emotional set. In other words, the somatosensory pattern evoked by a particular situation is co-displayed with factual knowledge pertinent to the situation. With respect to decision making, the key idea is that the somatosensory pattern operates to constrain the process of reasoning over multiple options and multiple future outcomes. Images of future scenarios are marked, and thus "qualified" or "judged," by the juxtaposed images of the somatic state. In a complex decision-making space, this process greatly facilitates the operation of logical reasoning. Somatic markers allow certain option–outcome pairs to be rapidly endorsed or rejected, rendering the decision-making space more manageable for a subsequent cost–benefit analysis based on overt logical reasoning. In situations with a high degree of uncertainty as to the future and/or which course of action is optimal, the constraints imposed by somatic markers allow individuals to decide efficiently within reasonable time intervals. This would apply to many complex social situations, and to the on-line navigation required therein.

In the absence of somatic markers, response options and outcomes become more or less equalized. Subjects may then resort to a strategy of deciding on an option based on extremely slow and laborious logic operations over many potential alternatives, themselves lacking somatic markers, and hence fail to take affectively salient previous experience into account. As a consequence, decision making may fail to be timely, accurate, and propitious. Another possible consequence of missing somatic markers is that decision making may become random or impulsive. Such manifestations, as it seems, are precisely what one sees in the real-world behavior of patients with damage to ventromedial prefrontal cortices.

WHY IS EMOTION IMPORTANT? Before turning to a description of recent work and to the testing of various aspects of the somatic marker hypothesis, let us briefly comment on why we consider emotion a crucial ingredient in the process of reasoning and decision making. Situations involving personal and social matters are typically, and powerfully, associated with reward and punishment, with pleasure and pain—in short, with the regulation of homeostatic states as expressed by emotions and feelings. So, assuming the brain owns a mechanism for selecting good from bad responses in social situations, we suggest that this mechanism was co-opted for behavioral guidance, even though, strictly speaking, it falls outside the purview of social cognition. Whether or not they are perceived consciously in the form of feelings, somatic markers provide the "go," "stop," and "turn" signals needed for much decision making and planning, even in regard to highly abstract topics.

Testing the somatic marker hypothesis

SOMATIC RESPONSES TO EMOTIONALLY CHARGED STIMULI The somatic marker hypothesis predicts that patients with ventromedial prefrontal dysfunction would fail to generate somatic responses to emotionally charged stimuli. That is, we contend that the ventromedial prefrontal region is pivotal to the reactivation of somatic states normally associated with powerful emotional stimuli in the course of an individual's learning experience; hence, damage to this region should attenuate or abolish such somatic responses. We tested this prediction in the following experiments (Damasio, Tranel, and Damasio, 1990, 1991; Tranel, 1994).

Three groups of subjects were tested: (1) ventromedial prefrontal, comprising five subjects with bilateral

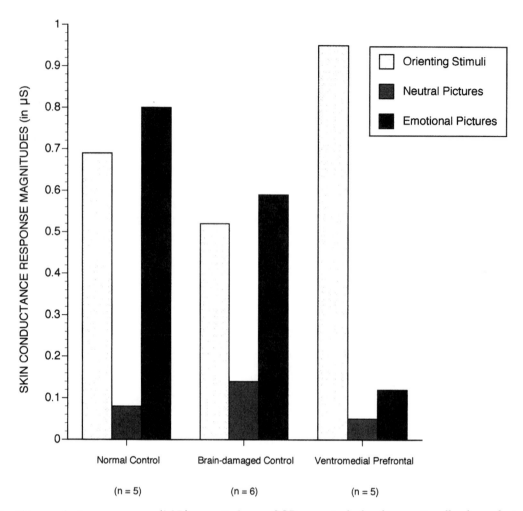

FIGURE 73.1 Skin conductance response (SCR) magnitudes to orienting stimuli, neutral pictures, and emotionally charged pictures in normal controls, brain-damaged controls, and ventromedial prefrontal subjects. There were no significant differences between the groups in the SCR magnitude for the orienting stimuli. In the ventromedial prefrontal group, the SCR magnitude for the emotionally charged pictures was severely abnormal. Statistically, it is (1) not different from this group's SCR magnitude for the neutral pictures and (2) significantly lower than the SCRs produced by the normal and brain-damaged controls to the emotionally charged pictures.

ventromedial prefrontal damage and acquired impairments in social conduct and decision making; (2) brain-damaged controls, comprising six subjects with lesions outside the ventromedial prefrontal sector and lacking acquired defects in decision making; (3) normal controls, comprising five individuals having no history of neurological or psychiatric disease. The three groups were of comparable age and education. The subjects were shown two types of visual stimuli: *targets*–pictures of emotionally charged stimuli such as mutilations and nudes; *nontargets*–pictures of emotionally neutral stimuli such as farm scenes and abstract patterns. The dependent measure was the skin conductance response (SCR), a highly sensitive index of autonomic responsivity, especially in regard to emotional stimuli (see Tranel, in press, for a review).

Before showing subjects the target and nontarget pictures, we determined that they were all capable of generating SCRs to basic physical stimuli (e.g., a loud noise or deep breath), thereby ruling out the possibility that unresponsiveness to the pictures could be attributed to a general, nonspecific lack of autonomic response. For the experiment proper, we compared the three groups in terms of their average SCRs to the target versus nontarget pictures. Both the normal and brain-damaged control groups displayed large-amplitude SCRs to the targets, and little or no response to the nontargets (figure 73.1). The ventromedial prefrontal subjects, by contrast, generated almost no response to the targets, and completely failed to show the standard target–nontarget SCR difference, despite the fact that their ability to generate SCRs to basic physical stimuli was intact.

The findings from these experiments are consistent with our prediction from the somatic marker hypothesis, and we have interpreted them as evidence that patients with bilateral ventromedial prefrontal damage have lost the ability to generate normal somatic responses to emotionally charged stimuli. We believe, furthermore, that this defect is a key component of the explanation as to why the real-world social behavior of these patients is so impaired.

The Gambling Task   We have also approached the testing of the somatic marker hypothesis by developing a card game (the Gambling Task) in which the goal is to maximize profit on a loan of play money—a game in which response selection is guided by various schedules of immediate reward and delayed punishment (Bechara et al., 1994). The motivation for developing this task came from the well-replicated finding that many patients with prefrontal damage do not demonstrate impairments on conventional neuropsychological procedures, even quintessential "executive function" or "frontal lobe" tasks such as the Wisconsin Card Sorting Test, the Trail-Making Test, and the Tower of Hanoi (see Tranel, Anderson, and Benton, 1994, for review). The Gambling Task provides a closer analog to real-world decision making, inasmuch as it makes unpredictable rewards and punishments a more explicit aspect of the situation, and requires subjects to forgo short-term benefit for long-term gain. Patients with bilateral ventromedial prefrontal lobe lesions show a reliable pattern of disadvantageous responding on the Gambling Task, even when they are retested again and again over various intervals of time (Bechara et al., 1994). The principal findings are summarized below.

In the Gambling Task, subjects sit in front of four decks of cards equal in appearance and size, and are given a $2000 loan of money (facsimile U.S. bills). The subjects are told that the game requires a long series of card selections, one card at a time, from any of the four decks, until they are told to stop. After turning each card, the subjects receive some money (the amount is announced only after the turning, and it varies from deck to deck). After turning certain of the cards, however, the subjects are both given money and asked to pay a penalty (again, the amount is announced only after the card is turned, and it varies from deck to deck and from position to position within a given deck, according to a schedule unknown to the subjects). The subjects are told that the goal of the task is to maximize their profit, and that they are free to switch from any deck to another, at any time, and as often as they wish. Subjects are not told ahead of time how many card selections will be made in all (the task is stopped after 100 selections).

Turning any card from deck A or deck B yields $100; turning any card from deck C or deck D yields $50. However, the ultimate future yields of the decks vary, because the penalty amounts are higher in the high-paying decks (A and B), and lower in the low-paying decks (C and D). In fact, the task is rigged so it is better to select from decks C and D over the long haul. Decks A and B are disadvantageous because they cost the subject in the long run; decks C and D are advantageous because they result in an overall gain to the subject in the long run.

In our study (Bechara et al., 1994), we investigated the performances of three groups of subjects on the Gambling Task: (1) ventromedial prefrontal, comprising six subjects with bilateral ventromedial prefrontal lesions and abnormal real-world decision making; (2) brain-damaged controls, comprising six subjects with lesions outside the ventromedial prefrontal region and lacking decision-making deficits; and (3) normal controls, comprising 44 subjects free of neurological or psychiatric disease. The three groups were age- and education-matched. To determine what would happen to performance when the task was repeated over time, we retested the ventromedial prefrontal subjects and five normal controls at follow-up intervals of 1 and 6 months.

To evaluate performance on the Gambling Task, we subdivided the 100 card selections into 5 discrete blocks of 20 each; and for each block, we calculated the number of selections for decks A and B (disadvantageous) and the number of selections for decks C and D (advantageous). The results are presented graphically in figure 73.2, broken down as a function of group, block, and deck type. As the task progressed, normal and brain-damaged controls gradually shifted their selections toward the good decks (C and D), and away from the bad decks (A and B). By the last two blocks (trials 61–100), in fact, the subjects were choosing almost exclusively from the good decks. In sharp contrast, ventromedial prefrontal subjects failed to demonstrate this shift in behavior. In all but one trial block, they selected more cards from the bad decks, and fewer from the good decks; on blocks 4 and 5, they reliably selected more frequently from the disadvantageous decks, which is a strikingly different pattern than that produced by the control subjects. A 3 (group) $\times$ 2 (deck) $\times$ 5 (block) ANOVA on these data showed significant interactions between deck and group ($F_{(2,53)} = 20.78$, $p < .0001$) and between deck and block ($F_{(4,212)} = 12.58$, $p < .0001$); also, the three-way interaction was significant ($F_{(8,212)} = 2.69$, $p < .01$). Together, these outcomes reflect the fact that as the task progressed, both control groups showed a strong shift away from the bad decks and toward the good decks, whereas the ventromedial prefrontal group failed to shift their behavior toward more advantageous responding, and in fact, persisted reliably with the bad decks during the last 40 trials of the session.

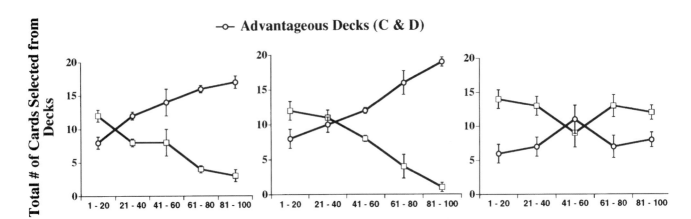

Normal Control (N=44)   Brain-damaged Control (N=6)   Ventromedial Prefrontal (N=6)

–□– **Disadvantageous Decks (A & B)**

–○– **Advantageous Decks (C & D)**

Total # of Cards Selected from Decks

Order of Card Selection from the 1st to the 100th Trial

FIGURE 73.2   Card selections on the Gambling Task as a function of group (normal control, brain-damaged control, and ventromedial prefrontal), deck type (disadvantageous versus advantageous), and trial block. The two control groups gradually shifted their response selections toward the advantageous decks, and this tendency became stronger as the game went on. The ventromedial prefrontal subjects did not make a reliable shift, and continued to opt for the disadvantageous decks even during the latter stages of the game, when controls had almost completely abandoned choosing from the bad decks.

A follow-up study showed that the performances of the ventromedial prefrontal subjects did not improve over time; they performed in a similar defective manner (disadvantageous responding) at both 1-month and 6-month follow-up epochs. The performances of the control subjects did improve over time, as the subjects retained their learning from the first session, and avoided the bad decks even earlier in the game than they had in the original go-round.

ANTICIPATORY PSYCHOPHYSIOLOGICAL RESPONSES Our next experiment in this series of studies involved adding a psychophysiological dependent variable to the Gambling Task paradigm, in order to assess somatic state activation during the task (Bechara et al., 1996b). Specifically, we measured skin conductance responses during the task, as follows.

We studied two groups of subjects: (1) ventromedial prefrontal, comprising seven subjects with bilateral ventromedial prefrontal lesions and real-world decision-making deficits, and (2) normal controls, comprising twelve neurologically and psychiatrically healthy individuals who were age- and education-matched to the ventromedial subjects.

The psychophysiological measure was skin conductance responding (SCR), which was recorded while subjects performed the Gambling Task. Equipment,

recording, and scoring procedures were as described in some of our other work (e.g., Tranel and Damasio, 1989, 1994). Skin conductance electrodes were attached, then the subject was seated in front of a table on which the four decks of cards were placed. The decks were in close proximity to the subject, to minimize the motor response demand required for the subject to reach out and select a card. One experimenter sat across from the subject and administered the task. The subject was instructed to select a card from one of the decks, whenever a second experimenter (who was monitoring the polygraph record) gave the signal to "go." The subject was not allowed to respond again until the signal was again delivered. This format allowed us to identify precisely each SCR generated in association with a specific card from a specific deck. Approximately 15 seconds elapsed between card turns.

Three types of SCRs generated during the task were defined: (1) *reward* SCRs, defined as the SCRs generated after the subject had turned cards for which there was a reward and no penalty; (2) *punishment* SCRs, defined as the SCRs generated after the subject had turned cards for which there was a reward followed immediately by a penalty; and (3) *anticipatory* SCRs, defined as the SCRs generated immediately *prior to* the point at which the subject turned a card from any given deck, i.e., during the time period the subject was pondering from which deck to choose. The time window for the onset of reward and

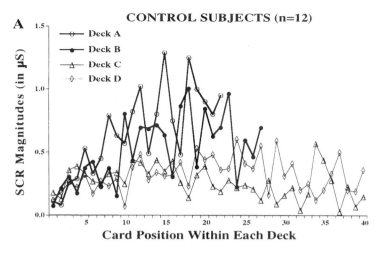

CONTROL SUBJECTS (n=12)

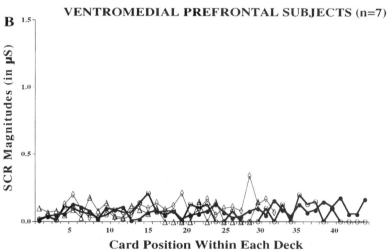

VENTROMEDIAL PREFRONTAL SUBJECTS (n=7)

FIGURE 73.3   Anticipatory SCR magnitudes as a function of group, deck, and card position within each deck: (A) control subjects; (B) ventromedial prefrontal subjects. While pondering from which deck to choose, control subjects gradually began generating high-amplitude SCRs to the disadvantageous decks (A and B), but not to the advantageous decks (C and D). The ventromedial prefrontal subjects showed no such anticipatory SCRs.

punishment SCRs was within 4 seconds after receipt of feedback information (e.g., "You have won $500"). SCRs generated during the time between completion of the money exchange and the next card selection were considered anticipatory SCRs.

Both ventromedial prefrontal and control subjects generated SCRs in reaction to reward and punishment.[2] However, as they became experienced with the task, controls also began to generate SCRs *prior to* the selection of some cards (figure 73.3A). The ventromedial prefrontal subjects entirely failed to generate such anticipatory SCRs (figure 73.3B). A statistical analysis indicated that controls generated anticipatory SCRs in relation to decks A and B (the disadvantageous decks) which were higher than those generated in relation to decks C and D (advantageous decks); no such difference was evident in the ventromedial prefrontal subjects.

Analyses of the reward and punishment SCRs revealed only an effect of the decks (punishment SCRs generated in association with deck B, which has the highest magnitude of punishment, were higher than those for deck A; figure 73.4). There were no statistically significant between-group differences in the reward and punishment SCRs (although controls did tend to produce marginally larger SCRs for most of the decks). Further inspection of the results indicated that the anticipatory SCRs generated by controls (1) developed over time, i.e., the subjects began to respond, and responded more systematically, after selecting several cards from each deck, thereby encountering several instances of reward and punishment; and (2) became more pronounced prior to the selection of cards from the disadvantageous decks (A and B). No such SCRs were evident in the ventromedial prefrontal subjects (figures 73.3 and 73.4).

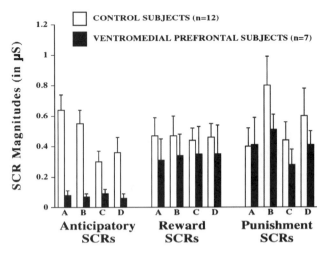

CONTROL SUBJECTS (n=12)

VENTROMEDIAL PREFRONTAL SUBJECTS (n=7)

FIGURE 73.4 Anticipatory, reward, and punishment SCR magnitudes for control subjects and ventromedial prefrontal subjects. The groups did not differ from one another in their reward and punishment SCRs; and as expected, SCRs were largest to the deck with the highest magnitude of punishment (deck B). However, there was a striking group difference for the anticipatory SCRs. Such responses were virtually absent in the ventromedial prefrontal subjects; in the control subjects, there were large-amplitude anticipatory SCRs for the disadvantageous decks (A and B).

In sum, after a number of trials, control subjects began to generate SCRs prior to their card selections, even while they pondered from which deck to choose. Ventromedial prefrontal subjects never showed such anticipatory responses. We have interpreted these results to indicate that the absence of anticipatory SCRs in the ventromedial patients is a physiological correlate for their insensitivity to future outcomes. This interpretation is compatible with the idea that these subjects fail to activate biasing signals which would serve as value markers in the distinction between choices with good or bad future outcomes. We have reasoned further that these signals also participate in the enhancement of attention and working memory relative to representations pertinent to the decision-making process. Further still, as noted in our sketch of the somatic marker hypothesis, we contend that such signals hail from bioregulatory machinery which sustains somatic homeostasis and can be expressed in emotion and feeling.

SOMATIC MARKERS CAN BE COVERT The somatic marker hypothesis holds that somatic markers can operate either covertly or overtly. To begin testing this aspect of the proposal, we explored the notion that the overt reasoning used to decide advantageously in a complex situation is actually *preceded* by a nonconscious biasing step, one whose results would not be available to consciousness and uses neural systems other than those that support declarative (conscious) knowledge (Bechara et al., 1997a).

In this study, six subjects with ventromedial prefrontal damage and decision-making defects and ten normal controls of comparable age and education performed the Gambling Task. Behavioral (task performance), psychophysiological (SCRs), and self-report measures were obtained in parallel. The self-report data were used to judge whether subjects had developed a conscious notion of how the game worked, on which basis we divided the task into four "knowledge periods." To do this, we interrupted the task briefly after each subject had made 20 card selections, then asked the subject to respond to the following prompts: (1) "Tell me all you know about what is going on in this game"; and (2) "Tell me how you feel about this game." The prompts were repeated at 10-card intervals for the remainder of the task.

After sampling from all four decks, and before encountering any punishments, subjects tended to prefer decks A and B, and no anticipatory SCRs were evident. We defined this as the *pre-punishment* period. After encountering some punishments in decks A and B, the normal subjects began to generate anticipatory SCRs to these decks (as described previously in Bechara et al., 1996b). During this period, though, none of the subjects had any notion as to what was happening in the task, as judged from their self-reports. We defined this as the *pre-hunch* period. Roughly halfway through the task (by about card 50), the normal subjects began to express a "hunch" that decks A and B were less favorable and more risky, and they generated anticipatory SCRs when pondering whether to select a card from the A or B decks. We termed this the *hunch* period. The balance of the task we termed the *conceptual* period, during which most of the normal subjects (seven of ten) reported some knowledge that decks A and B were "bad" in the long run and decks C and D were "good."

When we scored the behavioral data (card selections) and anticipatory SCR data according to the four knowledge periods, a number of intriguing results emerged (figure 73.5). During the pre-hunch period, there was a significant increase in the magnitude of anticipatory SCRs in the normal subjects; i.e., they began to develop anticipatory SCRs *before* they had any clue as to what was happening in the game, and before their behavior changed clearly in favor of the good decks. During the hunch and conceptual periods, the controls exhibited sustained anticipatory SCR activity to the bad decks, but it began to wane for the good decks. The ventromedial prefrontal subjects failed to show the development of anticipatory SCRs; moreover, they continued to choose more frequently from the bad than the good desks throughout

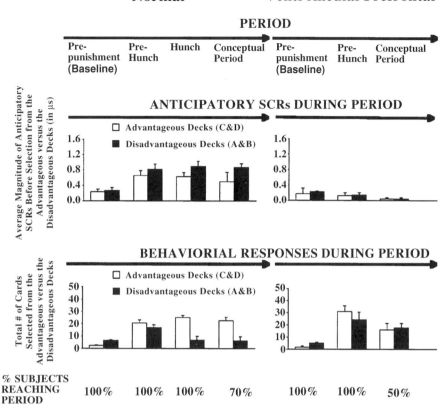

FIGURE 73.5 Psychophysiological (anticipatory SCRs) and behavioral (card selection) data for control subjects ($n = 10$) and ventromedial prefrontal subjects ($n = 6$), as a function of four knowledge periods. Even before they knew anything consciously about how the game worked (pre-hunch period), control subjects began to generate anticipatory SCRs and to shift their selections away from the bad decks. In the controls, anticipatory SCRs, especially to the bad decks, became more pronounced as the game progressed, and the subjects shifted almost exclusively to the good decks. The ventromedial prefrontal subjects never produced anticipatory SCRs, and they also continued to opt more frequently for the bad decks. This pattern occurred even in ventromedial subjects ($n = 3$) who knew how the game worked at conscious level (conceptual period), and were aware some decks were good and some were bad.

the task. Two additional findings were of particular importance (see figure 73.6): (1) The three controls who failed to reach the conceptual period continued to avoid the bad decks, and they generated anticipatory SCRs whenever they did opt for a bad deck. (2) Three of the six ventromedial prefrontal subjects actually reached the conceptual period; i.e., they produced accurate testimony about knowing the advantageous strategy for the game. Nonetheless, they continued to choose disadvantageously, and failed to generate anticipatory SCRs.

These results suggest that the sensory representation of a situation that requires a decision leads to two nonexclusive, interacting chains of events. (1) The sensory representation of a situation, and/or the facts evoked by it, activate neural systems holding nondeclarative dispositional knowledge related to one's previous emotional experience of similar situations. We believe the ventromedial prefrontal cortices are an important part of the structures holding such dispositional knowledge. Their activation produces consequent activation of autonomic and neurotransmitter nuclei (and of other regions). The ensuing signals, which remain nonconscious, act as covert biases on circuits that support processes of cognitive evaluation and reasoning. (2) The representation of a situation generates (a) overt recall of pertinent facts (e.g., potential response options and probable future outcomes) and (b) application of conscious reasoning strategies to facts and options. The results from our study suggest that in normal individuals, nonconscious biases guide reasoning and decision-making behavior before conscious knowledge does, and without the help of such biases, overt knowledge may be insufficient to ensure advantageous behavior. It is worth noting that studies in social psychology have led to a similar notion–specifically, that individuals can learn and make decisions with information that is not available to conscious awareness (e.g., Lewicki, Hill, and Czyzewska, 1992). We believe that the autonomic responses detected in our experiment (especially those

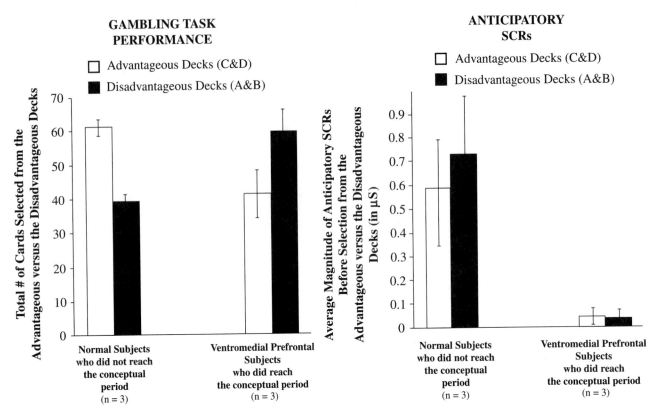

GAMBLING TASK PERFORMANCE

Advantageous Decks (C&D)
Disadvantageous Decks (A&B)

Normal Subjects who did not reach the conceptual period (n = 3)

Ventromedial Prefrontal Subjects who did reach the conceptual period (n = 3)

ANTICIPATORY SCRs

Advantageous Decks (C&D)
Disadvantageous Decks (A&B)

Normal Subjects who did not reach the conceptual period (n = 3)

Ventromedial Prefrontal Subjects who did reach the conceptual period (n = 3)

FIGURE 73.6 Gambling Task performance and anticipatory SCRs in 3 normal control subjects who *did not* reach the conceptual period (i.e., never developed an explicit notion of how the game worked) versus 3 ventromedial prefrontal subjects who *did* reach the period (i.e., who knew, and could articulate, the correct strategy for playing the game). Despite their lack of conceptual knowledge, the controls played the game correctly (i.e., they chose more from the advantageous decks) and continued to generate anticipatory SCRs, especially to the disadvantageous decks. Conversely, conceptual knowledge notwithstanding, the ventromedial prefrontal subjects still played the game incorrectly, and failed to produce anticipatory SCRs.

evident in the pre-hunch period) are evidence for a non-conscious signaling process, which reflects in turn access of records of previous experience shaped by reward, punishment, and apposed emotional states.

FURTHER CHARACTERIZATION OF DECISION-MAKING IMPAIRMENTS IN SUBJECTS WITH VENTROMEDIAL PREFRONTAL DAMAGE

The decision-making impairment is not attributable to working-memory deficits. Our investigations with the Gambling Task raise the question of the extent to which impairments on the task might be attributable to working-memory deficits, rather than to defective decision making per se–this, in spite of the fact that the majority of ventromedial prefrontal subjects are robustly normal in conventional neuropsychological working memory tasks such as digit span backward and trail-making. To test the question further, we designed an experiment in which working-memory tasks adapted from the nonhuman primate literature (the classic paradigms of delayed response and delayed nonmatching to sample, adapted to use with humans) were used to assess working memory, while the Gambling Task was used to assess decision making (Bechara et al., 1998a).

The working-memory and decision-making tasks were administered to 9 subjects with bilateral ventromedial prefrontal lesions. We also studied 10 subjects with dorsolateral prefrontal lesions (4 right, 6 left), and 21 normal controls. We found a split result in the ventromedial group: 4 subjects were impaired on the decision-making task, but not on the working-memory tasks, while 5 were impaired on both tasks. Detailed lesion analysis indicated that in the first 4 subjects, lesions were situated more anteriorly in the ventromedial region; in the 5 other subjects, lesions extended more posteriorly, probably into the basal forebrain region. The subjects with right-sided dorsolateral prefrontal lesions performed defectively on the working-memory tasks, but not on the decision-making tasks (the left dorsolateral subjects were normal on all tasks).

A double dissociation, cognitively and anatomically, is supported by the results from the anterior ventromedial subjects and the right dorsolateral subjects. This outcome indicates that decision-making impairments produced by ventromedial prefrontal damage are not directly or solely the result of a working-memory impairment. Not surprisingly, however, it probably is true that severely impaired working memory compromises the efficiency of decision making to some extent (the right dorsolateral subjects had relatively lower scores on the Gambling Task, albeit in the normal range). The findings also indicate that the most likely scenario for an isolated impairment in decision making is one involving an anteriorly situated ventromedial prefrontal lesion. With lesions that encompass the posterior sector, which often involve the basal forebrain, the decision-making defect is more likely to be accompanied, and perhaps exacerbated, by working-memory impairments.

Subjects with ventromedial prefrontal lesions are insensitive to future consequences. We have demonstrated that subjects with ventromedial prefrontal lesions utilize a risky strategy when executing the Gambling Task, selecting responses that yield higher short-term rewards but higher long-term punishment. We have interpreted this phenomenon as an indication that such subjects are insensitive to the future consequences of their behavior. But another interpretation is also plausible–that the subjects are simply insensitive to punishment, especially immediate punishment. To test this idea, we designed a variant on the Gambling Task, in which higher magnitudes of immediate punishment were connected to long-term reward, and lower magnitudes of immediate punishment were connected to long-term punishment (Anderson et al., 1996). Specifically, using the basic format of the Gambling Task, we rigged two decks (the good decks) so they would yield higher immediate punishment (monetary losses), but offer occasional large-magnitude rewards (monetary gains); these rewards would more than offset the immediate losses to yield long-term gain. The other two, bad, decks were rigged to yield lower immediate punishment, but also lower rewards; so the long-term outcome was, on balance, negative. We studied 9 ventromedial prefrontal subjects and 10 normal controls. The control subjects learned to select from the good decks as the task progressed; i.e., they opted for higher immediate punishment but higher long-term reward. Most of the ventromedial prefrontal subjects (6 of 9) played the opposite way; i.e., they opted for lower immediate punishment and hence higher long-term loss. All subjects, including controls and ventromedial prefrontals, generated normal SCRs to reward and punishment experiences.

The findings that the ventromedial prefrontal subjects avoided responses associated with lower immediate punishment, and that they generated normal SCRs to punishment experiences, are inconsistent with the interpretation that the subjects are simply insensitive to punishment. The experiment also showed that the subjects were not lured by occasional large-magnitude rewards (in decks with larger-magnitude immediate punishment), and that they had normal SCRs to reward experiences, suggesting that the subjects are not hypersensitive to reward. Together with findings from the original version of the Gambling Task, this experiment strongly implicates the explanation that the defective strategy of the ventromedial prefrontal subjects is attributable to an overall insensitivity to future consequences, whatever those consequences might be.

THE ROLE OF OTHER NEURAL STRUCTURES IN DECISION MAKING

The amygdala As suggested earlier, the somatic marker hypothesis proposes that the amygdala is another important structure comprising the neural network for somatic markers, although its specific functions may very well differ from those of the ventromedial prefrontal region. There is no question that the amygdala plays an important role in emotion, particularly negative emotion (e.g., fear, anger), as demonstrated repeatedly in recent lesion and functional imaging studies in humans (Adolphs et al., 1994, 1995; Adolphs, Tranel, and Damasio, 1998; Breiter et al., 1996; Broks et al., 1998; Calder et al., 1996; Morris et al., 1996, 1998; Scott et al., 1997; Whalen et al., 1998. See also *Science*, 1998, Vol. 280, pp. 1005–1008). Following the logic of the somatic marker hypothesis, then, we might also expect the amygdala to play a role in decision making. We tested this idea in the following experiment (Bechara et al., 1996a).

We administered our Gambling Task to 5 subjects with bilateral amygdala damage and to subjects with unilateral left ($n = 3$) or unilateral right ($n = 4$) amygdala damage. [*Note:* Here, and in the remainder of this chapter, we are referring to the standard version of the task–the one using immediate reward and delayed punishment.] We recorded electrodermal activity (SCRs) throughout the task, using the same procedures described earlier (see Bechara et al., 1996b).

All 5 subjects with bilateral amygdala lesions were impaired in the Gambling Task; i.e., they failed to learn to avoid the bad decks as the game progressed, and played by a strategy that yielded a net long-term loss (figure 73.7). Like the ventromedial prefrontal subjects, the bilateral amygdala subjects failed to generate anticipatory SCRs (despite having normal or near-normal SCRs to basic physical stimuli). Finally, the bilateral amygdala

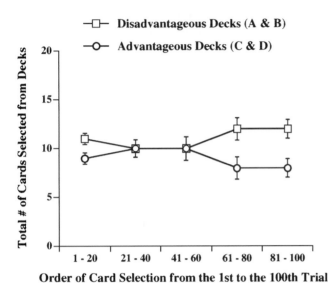

Bilateral Amygdala Subjects (N=5)

□ **Disadvantageous Decks (A & B)**
○ **Advantageous Decks (C & D)**

(y-axis) Total # of Cards Selected from Decks

(x-axis) Order of Card Selection from the 1st to the 100th Trial

FIGURE 73.7 Gambling Task performance in 5 subjects with bilateral amygdala damage, as a function of deck type and trial block. The subjects never evidenced the normal shift away from the disadvantageous decks and toward the advantageous decks, and in fact, on the last two trial blocks (trials 61–100), demonstrated a small but reliable preference for the bad decks.

subjects also failed to produce SCRs to punishment and reward. The latter finding differs from that obtained in ventromedial prefrontal subjects, who were capable of generating punishment and reward SCRs. We also found that none of the subjects with unilateral amygdala damage was impaired on the task, either in behavioral strategy or in anticipatory and response SCRs. The outcome in bilateral amygdala subjects was replicated and extended in another study (Bechara et al., 1997b).

These findings support the notion that the amygdala is also an important component of the neural network subserving somatic marker activation, albeit in a manner that differs somewhat from that of the ventromedial prefrontal cortices. We have interpreted these results as indicating that the decision-making impairment associated with bilateral amygdala damage is a consequence of a more basic defect in first-order conditioning, i.e., coupling a stimulus configuration (or its concept) with a somatic state triggered by primary reward or punishment (see Damasio, 1995a). Our interpretation derives from a variety of conditioning studies, which have shown that the amygdala is necessary for associating basic perceptual stimuli (e.g., a color or tone) with a somatic state induced by a primary unconditioned stimulus (e.g., an aversive sound, food, electric shock) (Bechara et al., 1995; Davis, 1992; Gaffan, 1992; Kim, Rison, and Fanselow, 1993; LaBar et al., 1995; LeDoux, 1996). As it

pertains to the Gambling Task, this explanation would work as follows. Throughout development, we learn to associate the concepts of "winning" and "losing" money with states of primary reward or punishment (e.g., food, sex, pain), and eventually, those concepts become associated in a more fundamental or primary way with somatic states of their own. When the amygdala is damaged, the concepts of winning and losing can no longer trigger appropriate somatic states. Accordingly, in the Gambling Task, subjects with bilateral amygdala lesions fail to generate SCRs when they win or lose money (i.e., they fail to generate reward and punishment SCRs); also, the subjects fail to activate somatic states when making complex decisions.

On the other hand, we believe the decision-making impairment associated with ventromedial prefrontal damage is a manifestation of a defect in higher-order conditioning, i.e., coupling a strategy or plan of action with a somatic state elicited by the concept of how that course of action may eventually turn out. Conditioning experiments have shown that the ventromedial prefrontal cortices are not required for the acquisition of fear conditioning in nonhuman animals (Morgan and LeDoux, 1995). Similarly, we have shown that in humans, the ventromedial prefrontal cortices (particularly the anterior sector) are not required for conditioning involving a basic perceptual stimulus, say a color or tone, associated with a primary unconditioned stimulus, such as an aversive loud sound (Tranel et al., 1996). This indicates that the ventromedial prefrontal region is not necessary for first-order conditioning, and its damage should not preclude the ability of a primary, basic-level concept to trigger an appropriate somatic state. Accordingly, ventromedial prefrontal subjects are capable of generating SCRs in response to winning or losing money in the Gambling Task. After experiencing punishment in connection with certain response selections, though, the ventromedial prefrontal subjects fail to link this experience with the disadvantageous response strategy; consequently, they fail to generate anticipatory SCRs when pondering their card selections.

Thus, while both the ventromedial prefrontal cortices and the amygdala are important components of the neural network for decision making, their roles are somewhat different. Both structures couple exteroceptive sensory information with interoceptive information concerning somatic states, but these coupling mechanisms involve different types of information. Specifically, the amygdala is necessary for first-order conditioning, whereas the ventromedial prefrontal region is necessary for higher-order conditioning. This interpretation is consistent with the claim that the human prefrontal cortex, particularly its anterior-most aspect, is the most advanced on the evolu-

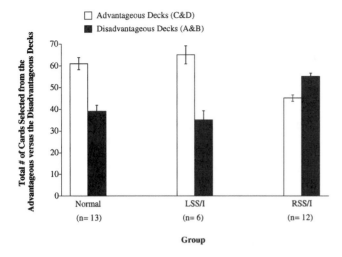

GAMBLING TASK PERFORMANCE

☐ Advantageous Decks (C&D)
■ Disadvantageous Decks (A&B)

FIGURE 73.8 Gambling Task performance in 13 normal control subjects, 6 subjects with left somatosensory/insular cortex lesions (LSS/I), and 12 subjects with right somatosensory/insular cortex lesions (RSS/I). The RSS/I subjects performed defectively, opting for the disadvantageous decks (A and B) more frequently than the advantageous decks (C and D). The LSS/I subjects, however, were normal.

tionary scale. In fact, first-order conditioning is more readily accomplished in "lower" animals, mediated by structures such as the amygdala. At the same time, higher-order conditioning is much more difficult to achieve in laboratory animals, and even when produced, is never as powerful as that accomplished in humans. Assuming the prefrontal cortices are important for higher-order conditioning, this helps account for the unique ability of humans to utilize concepts far removed from primary emotions (e.g., social feedback, praise, embarrassment) to guide decision making in everyday life (see Damasio, 1995a).

The right somatosensory/insular cortices Using the Gambling Task paradigm, we studied decision making in 12 subjects with right somatosensory/insular cortex (RSS/I) lesions, 6 subjects with left somatosensory/insular cortex (LSS/I) lesions, and 13 age- and education-matched normal controls (Bechara et al., 1997b). Eight of the RSS/I subjects were severely impaired on the task, and 4 were borderline (figure 73.8). By contrast, none of the LSS/I subjects was impaired; they played the game exactly the way the normal controls did, choosing more often from the advantageous decks. The results support the idea that the *right* somatosensory/insular region (but not the left) is another important component of the neural network subserving somatic marker activation and decision making.

The peripheral nervous system As outlined in the previous section, the somatic marker hypothesis proposes that body-related information, whether obtained directly from the body proper (the body loop) or indirectly from CNS-somatic–representing structures (the as-if-body loop), is critical for mechanisms of decision making. To investigate the part of the hypothesis related to the body-loop mode of operation, we tested the prediction that significant impairments of nervous system signaling, as seen in certain peripheral neuropathies, should be associated with impairments on the Gambling Task (Bechara et al., 1998b). The target subjects were 12 patients with peripheral neuropathy, mainly of the sensory type. They were compared with 7 demographically matched normal controls. We found that subjects with peripheral neuropathy performed defectively on the Gambling Task relative to controls, opting for the risky decks more frequently, especially as the task progressed. These results support the notion that on-line signaling concerning the body state is relevant for decision-making processes leveraged by reward and punishment.

Concluding comment

The somatic marker hypothesis provides a systems-level neuroanatomical and cognitive framework for reasoning, decision making, and emotional processing. A program of research aimed at testing various predictions from the hypothesis has yielded important new insights into the neural basis of decision making, some of the nonconscious and conscious operations that influence decision making, and some of the ways in which bioregulatory signals, including those that constitute emotion, play a role in decision making. The results thus far have been promising, and have supported several of the basic principles of the somatic marker hypothesis, including our emphasis on the role of neuroanatomical structures such as the ventromedial prefrontal cortex, the amygdala, and the right somatosensory/insular cortices in decision making and emotional processing.

ACKNOWLEDGMENTS Supported by Program Project Grant NINDS NS19632 and the Mathers Foundation. We thank Hanna Damasio and Ralph Adolphs for their collaboration in several of the studies reported here. We also thank Joseph Newman, University of Wisconsin, for a helpful approach to analyzing data from the Gambling Task.

NOTES

1. The discussion of connectional neuroanatomy here is based primarily on work in nonhuman primates, although we have every reason to believe that most of the key findings from this work would generalize accurately to humans.

2. This outcome may appear at odds with the finding reported earlier that the ventromedial prefrontal subjects failed to generate SCRs to emotionally charged pictures. We do not believe the outcomes are incompatible, though, because of the many differences in the nature of the stimuli and experimental paradigm, and the fact that the Gambling Task provides explicit feedback (reinforcement) to the subjects, whereas the previous paradigm did not.

REFERENCES

ADOLPHS, R., D. TRANEL, and A. R. DAMASIO, 1998. The human amygdala in social judgment. *Nature* 393:470–474.

ADOLPHS, R., D. TRANEL, H. DAMASIO, and A. R. DAMASIO, 1994. Impaired recognition of emotion in facial expressions following bilateral damage to the human amygdala. *Nature* 372:669–672.

ADOLPHS, R., D. TRANEL, H. DAMASIO, and A. R. DAMASIO, 1995. Fear and the human amygdala. *J. Neurosci.* 15:5879–5891.

AMARAL, D. G., and J. L. PRICE, 1984. Amygdalo-cortical projections in the monkey (*Macaca fascicularis*). *J. Comp. Neurol.* 230:465–496.

AMERICAN PSYCHIATRIC ASSOCIATION, 1994. *Diagnostic and Statistical Manual of Mental Disorders* (4th Ed.). Washington, D.C.: American Psychiatric Association.

ANDERSON, S. W., A. BECHARA, D. TRANEL, H. DAMASIO, and A. R. DAMASIO, 1996. Characterization of the decision-making defect of subjects with ventromedial frontal lobe damage. *Soc. Neurosci.* 22:1108.

BECHARA, A., A. R. DAMASIO, H. DAMASIO, and S. W. ANDERSON, 1994. Insensitivity to future consequences following damage to human prefrontal cortex. *Cognition* 50:7–15.

BECHARA, A., H. DAMASIO, D. TRANEL, and S. W. ANDERSON, 1998a. Dissociation of working memory from decision making within the human prefrontal cortex. *J. Neurosci.* 18:428–437.

BECHARA, A., H. DAMASIO, D. TRANEL, and A. R. DAMASIO, 1997a. Deciding advantageously before knowing the advantageous strategy. *Science* 275:1293–1295.

BECHARA, A., G. P. LEE, R. ADOLPHS, D. TRANEL, and A. R. DAMASIO, 1996a. Insensitivity to future consequences following bilateral damage to the human amygdala: Contrasts with ventromedial frontal lobe lesions. *Soc. Neurosci.* 22:1109.

BECHARA, A., D. TRANEL, H. DAMASIO, R. ADOLPHS, C. ROCKLAND, and A. R. DAMASIO, 1995. Double dissociation of conditioning and declarative knowledge relative to the amygdala and hippocampus in humans. *Science* 269:1115–1118.

BECHARA, A., D. TRANEL, H. DAMASIO, and A. R. DAMASIO, 1996b. Failure to respond autonomically to anticipated future outcomes following damage to prefrontal cortex. *Cereb. Cortex* 6:215–225.

BECHARA, A., D. TRANEL, H. DAMASIO, and A. R. DAMASIO, 1997b. An anatomical system subserving decision-making. *Soc. Neurosci.* 23:495.

BECHARA, A., D. TRANEL, J. WILSON, A. HEBERLEIN, M. ROSS, and A. R. DAMASIO, 1998b. Impaired decision making in peripheral neuropathy. *Soc. Neurosci.* 24:1176.

BENTON, A., 1991. The prefrontal region: Its early history. In *Frontal Lobe Function and Dysfunction*, H. S. Levin, H. M.

Eisenberg, and A. L. Benton, eds. New York: Oxford University Press, pp. 3–32.

BREITER, H. C., N. L. ETCOFF, P. J. WHALEN, W. A. KENNEDY, S. L. RAUCH, R. L. BUCKNER, M. M. STRAUSS, S. E. HYMAN, and B. R. ROSEN, 1996. Response and habituation of the human amygdala during visual processing of facial expression. *Neuron* 17:875–887.

BROKS, P., A. W. YOUNG, E. J. MARATOS, P. J. COFFEY, A. J. CALDER, C. ISAAC, A. R. MAYES, J. R. HODGES, D. MONTALDI, E. CEZAYIRLI, N. ROBERTS, and D. HADLEY, 1998. Face processing impairments after encephalitis: Amygdala damage and recognition of fear. *Neuropsychologia* 36:59–70.

CALDER, A. J., A. W. YOUNG, D. ROWLAND, D. I. PERRETT, J. R. HODGES, and N. L. ETCOFF, 1996. Facial emotion recognition after bilateral amygdala damage: Differentially severe impairment of fear. *Cogn. Neuropsychol.* 13:699–745.

CHAVIS, D. A., and D. N. PANDYA, 1976. Further observations on corticofrontal connections in the rhesus monkey. *Brain Res.* 117:369–386.

DAMASIO, A. R., 1979. The frontal lobes. In *Clinical Neuropsychology*, K. M. Heilman and E. Valenstein, eds. New York: Oxford University Press, pp. 360–412.

DAMASIO, A. R., 1989a. Time-locked multiregional retroactivation: A systems-level proposal for the neural substrates of recall and recognition. *Cognition* 33:25–62.

DAMASIO, A. R., 1989b. The brain binds entities and events by multiregional activation from convergence zones. *Neural Computation* 1:123–132.

DAMASIO, A. R., 1994. *Descartes' Error: Emotion, Reason and the Human Brain*. New York: Grosset/Putnam.

DAMASIO, A. R., 1995a. Toward a neurobiology of emotion and feeling: Operational concepts and hypotheses. *Neuroscientist* 1:19–25.

DAMASIO, A. R., 1995b. On some functions of the human prefrontal cortex. In *Structure and Functions of the Human Prefrontal Cortex*, J. Grafman, K. Holyoak, and F. Boller, eds. New York: New York Academy of Sciences, pp. 241–251.

DAMASIO, A. R., 1996. The somatic marker hypothesis and the possible functions of the prefrontal cortex. *Phil. Trans. R. Soc. Lond. B* 351:1413–1420.

DAMASIO, A. R., and S. W. ANDERSON, 1993. The frontal lobes. In *Clinical Neuropsychology* (3d Ed.), K. Heilman and E. Valenstein, eds. New York: Oxford University Press, pp. 409–460.

DAMASIO, A. R., D. TRANEL, and H. DAMASIO, 1990. Individuals with sociopathic behavior caused by frontal damage fail to respond autonomically to social stimuli. *Behav. Brain Res.* 41:81–94.

DAMASIO, A. R., D. TRANEL, and H. DAMASIO, 1991. Somatic markers and the guidance of behavior: Theory and preliminary testing. In *Frontal Lobe Function and Dysfunction*, H. S. Levin, H. M. Eisenberg, and A. L. Benton, eds. New York: Oxford University Press, pp. 217–229.

DAMASIO, H., T. GRABOWSKI, R. FRANK, A. M. GALABURDA, and A. R. DAMASIO, 1994. The return of Phineas Gage: Clues about the brain from the skull of a famous patient. *Science* 264:1102–1105.

DAVIS, M., 1992. The role of the amygdala in conditioned fear. In *The Amygdala: Neurobiological Aspects of Emotion, Memory, and Mental Dysfunction*, J. P. Aggleton, ed. New York: Wiley–Liss, pp. 255–305.

Eslinger, P. J., and A. R. Damasio, 1985. Severe disturbance of higher cognition after bilateral frontal lobe ablation: Patient EVR. *Neurology* 35:1731–1741.

Gaffan, D., 1992. Amygdala and the memory of reward. In *The Amygdala: Neurobiological Aspects of Emotion, Memory, and Mental Dysfunction*, J. P. Aggleton, ed. New York: Wiley–Liss, pp. 471–483.

Goldman-Rakic, P. S., L. D. Selemon, and M. L. Schwartz, 1984. Dual pathways connecting the dorsolateral prefrontal cortex with the hippocampal formation and parahippocampal cortex in the rhesus monkey. *Neuroscience* 12:719–743.

Hall, R. E., R. B. Livingston, and C. M. Bloor, 1977. Orbital cortical influences on cardiovascular dynamics and myocardial structure in conscious monkeys. *J. Neurosurg.* 46:638–647.

Jones, E. G., and T. P. S. Powell, 1970. An anatomical study of converging sensory pathways within the cerebral cortex of the monkey. *Brain* 93:793–820.

Kim, J. J., R. A. Rison, and M. S. Fanselow, 1993. Effects of amygdala, hippocampus, and periaqueductal gray lesions on short- and long-term contextual fear. *Behav. Neurosci.* 107:1093–1098.

LaBar, K. S., J. E. LeDoux, D. D. Spencer, and E. A. Phelps, 1995. Impaired fear conditioning following unilateral temporal lobectomy in humans. *J. Neurosci.* 15:6846–6855.

LeDoux, J. E., 1996. *The Emotional Brain*. New York: Simon and Schuster.

Lewicki, P., T. Hill, and M. Czyzewska, 1992. Nonconscious acquisition of information. *Amer. Psychologist* 47:796–801.

Morgan, M. A., and J. E. LeDoux, 1995. Differential contribution of dorsal and ventral medial prefrontal cortex to the acquisition and extinction of conditioned fear in rats. *Behav. Neurosci.* 109:681–688.

Morris, J. S., C. D. Frith, D. I. Perrett, D. Rowland, A. W. Young, A. J. Calder, and R. J. Dolan, 1996. A differential neural response in the human amygdala to fearful and happy facial expressions. *Nature* 383:812–815.

Morris, J. S., A. Ohman, and R. J. Dolan, 1998. Conscious and unconscious emotional learning in the human amygdala. *Nature* 393:467–470.

Nauta, W. J. H., 1971. The problem of the frontal lobe: A reinterpretation. *J. Psychiat. Res.* 8:167–187.

Pandya, D. N., and H. G. J. M. Kuypers, 1969. Cortico-cortical connections in the rhesus monkey. *Brain Res.* 13:13–36.

Porrino, L. J., A. M. Crane, and P. S. Goldman-Rakic, 1981. Direct and indirect pathways from the amygdala to the frontal lobe in rhesus monkeys. *J. Comp. Neurol.* 198:121–136.

Potter, H., and W. J. H. Nauta, 1979. A note on the problem of olfactory associations of the orbitofrontal cortex in the monkey. *Neuroscience* 4:316–367.

Scott, S. K., A. W. Young, A. J. Calder, D. J. Hellawell, J. P. Aggleton, and M. Johnson, 1997. Impaired auditory recognition of fear and anger following bilateral amygdala lesions. *Nature* 385:254–257.

Stuss, D. T., and D. F. Benson, 1986. *The Frontal Lobes*. New York: Raven Press.

Tranel, D., 1994. "Acquired sociopathy": The development of sociopathic behavior following focal brain damage. In *Progress in Experimental Personality and Psychopathology Research*, Vol. 17, D. C. Fowles, P. Sutker, and S. H. Goodman, eds. New York: Springer, pp. 285–311.

Tranel, D., in press. Nonconscious brain processes indexed by psychophysiological measures. In *The Biological Basis for Mind Body Interactions*, E. A. Mayer and C. Saper, eds. Amsterdam: Elsevier.

Tranel, D., S. W. Anderson, and A. L. Benton, 1994. Development of the concept of "executive function" and its relationship to the frontal lobes. In *Handbook of Neuropsychology*, Vol. 9, F. Boller and J. Grafman, eds. Amsterdam: Elsevier, pp. 125–148.

Tranel, D., A. Bechara, H. Damasio, and A. R. Damasio, 1996. Fear conditioning after ventromedial frontal lobe damage in humans. *Soc. Neurosci.* 22:1108.

Tranel, D., and H. Damasio, 1989. Intact electrodermal skin conductance responses after bilateral amygdala damage. *Neuropsychologia* 27:381–390.

Tranel, D., and H. Damasio, 1994. Neuroanatomical correlates of electrodermal skin conductance responses. *Psychophysiology* 31:427–438.

Van Hoesen, G. W., D. N. Pandya, and N. Butters, 1972. Cortical afferents to the entorhinal cortex of the rhesus monkey. *Science* 175:1471–1473.

Van Hoesen, G. W., D. N. Pandya, and N. Butters, 1975. Some connections of the entorhinal (area 28) and perirhinal (area 35) cortices of the rhesus monkey: II. Frontal lobe afferents. *Brain Res.* 95:25–38.

Whalen, P. J., S. L. Rauch, N. L. Etcoff, S. C. McInerney, M. B. Lee, and M. A. Jenike, 1998. Masked presentations of emotional facial expressions modulate amygdala activity without explicit knowledge. *J. Neurosci.* 18:411–418.

IX EMOTION

Introduction

JOSEPH E. LeDOUX

The study of emotion was neglected by brain and cognitive scientists for decades, but it is now one of the major growth areas in neuroscience research. Studies in experimental animals are mapping pathways in great detail, and human research, spurred on by new developments in functional imaging, is confirming that the animal work applies to the human brain and is extending the findings in new directions. These are exciting times for emotion research.

In the introduction to the Emotion section in the first edition of this book, I said that there was not really a coherent group of neuroscientists who identified themselves as primarily emotion researchers. This situation has changed. It was fairly easy to assemble the cast for the first edition, but pretty difficult for this second edition, because of the large increase in the number of researchers working in the area, the greater range of topics being worked on, and the rapid expansion of human research on brain and emotion.

The chapters included in the present volume, I believe, give a flavor for the range of work being today. Armony and LeDoux examine interactions between fear mechanisms and cognitive systems using neurobiological studies of rats and parallel connectionist modeling studies. McGaugh, Roozendaal, and Cahill examine the way emotionally arousing stimuli modulate declarative memory in rats and humans. Ono and Nishijo use single-unit recordings in primates to explore the neural systems involved in processing aversive and appetitive stimuli. Dolan focuses on the representation of fear in the brains of normal humans, using functional magnetic resonance imaging (fMRI) to map circuits. Pitman, Shalev, and Orr study abnormal fear, as in patients with post-trauamatic stress disorder, using functional imaging and other approaches. Finally, Davidson uses both functional imaging and electrophysiological recordings to study affective style in normal subjects and psychiatric patients.

Perhaps the overriding theme across all the chapters is the importance of the amygdala in emotional processes. This brain region is a central focus in each of the chapters, reflecting a remarkable degree of convergence of research findings about the neural basis of emotional processes across species and paradigms.

In hailing the progress that has been made though, it is important not to lose sight of several humbling facts. The first is that there is little agreement about what emotions are. Our crude conceptions have allowed us to move forward in identifying brain mechanisms, but surely we would be better off if we had a better understanding of what we are looking for.

Second, much of what we know about the detailed circuitry of emotion has come from studies of fear conditioning in rats. This has been a great way to jump-start the field, since subsequent research on humans, using fear conditioning and other fear-related tasks (for example, processing angry or threatening faces) has suggested that the animal findings are indeed relevant to the human brain. But much needs to be done in the study of fear. For example, the automatic fear reactions elicited by conditioned fear stimuli and threatening faces are just the beginning of an emotional episode. Once these responses have been elicited, typically without conscious participation, decision processes, and ultimately conscious experiences, come into play. Little is known about how these cognitive factors interact with more primitive emotion networks. And, in contrast to fear, work on even the basic mechanisms in other emotions has really just begun.

Third, it is conceptually appealing that the amygdala has been implicated in fear and some other emotions across paradigms and species, but we need to be cautious in interpreting these data. We have pretty much gotten rid of the limbic system theory of emotions and its overambitious explanation of all emotions as functions of one big system, and we should not replace it too quickly with the amygdala theory of emotion. We should not, in other words, generalize from the research on fear to other emotions and assume that the amygdala is involved. The amygdala could be involved in several emotions because it plays the same role in each or because it plays different roles. There are about 13 different nuclei of the amygdala, and each has several subnuclei with unique connections. For fear conditioning in rats, the anatomical resolution at this point is approaching the subnuclei. Until the circuitry underlying the amygdala's contribution in different emotions is known in similar detail, we have to be very careful about what we conclude.

Finally, it is important to realize that the neural mechanisms underlying the expression of emotional responses, like the defense responses associated with the fear system, are not necessarily the mechanisms that give rise to the subjective feelings, like the feeling of being afraid, that occur when these systems are active in the human brain. We know little at this point about the brain mechanisms of subjective emotional experience. It is possible that the topic of emotional experience is really more about the nature of consciousness than the nature of emotion (for more about this topic, see Armony and LeDoux, chapter 74).

Emotion research is likely to continue at a rapid pace. It is important for researchers in this area to keep asking themselves what it is they are studying and to be especially cognizant of the limitations of data they collect. By the time the next edition of this book is published, one may hope that some of the conceptual problems will have been solved and that a large body of research findings will have begun to give us a coherent picture of how our brains make emotions.

74 How Danger Is Encoded: Toward a Systems, Cellular, and Computational Understanding of Cognitive-Emotional Interactions in Fear

JORGE L. ARMONY AND JOSEPH E. LEDOUX

ABSTRACT   The neurobiology of cognitive-emotional interactions can be better understood by studying the neural mechanisms of well-defined and experimentally tractable aspects of particular emotions and by exploring their relationship with specific cognitive processes. In this chapter we focus on fear, because the neural bases of this emotion have been worked out better than any other. Specifically, we describe recent findings on behavioral and physiological aspects of fear conditioning. This issue is approached from both a systems and a cellular point of view, combining empirical studies with computational modeling. The interactions of the fear network with some of the neural systems associated with perception, attention, declarative memory, and consciousness are discussed.

Introduction

The relationship between cognition and emotion has been a central issue in the study of the mind throughout history. Nevertheless, the nature of this relation, especially at the neural level, is still poorly understood. Part of the problem, it would seem, is that the broad concepts of "cognition" and "emotion" refer to collections of disparate brain processes, rather than to real functions performed by the brain. For example, within the domain of "cognition," the terms *perception, memory, attention,* and *action* more closely characterize processes mediated by the brain. But each of these, in turn, is also a shorthand description of more fundamental processes that better approximate the neural functions in question—vision versus touch, implicit versus explicit memory, attention versus preattentive processes, and so on. And even these can be further broken down into more fundamental processes; visual perception, for instance, consists of distinc-

tive functional components, such as form, color, motion processing, and so on. Similarly, emotions are made up of component functions (subjective experience, stimulus evaluation, physiological responses, feedback, elicited behaviors, voluntary behavior, etc.). Though substantial progress has been made over the past several decades in understanding cognitive processes by studying the fundamental components as brain functions (as illustrated in the present volume), emotion has not been studied extensively in this way. There are historical and conceptual reasons why emotion was not included within cognitive science (see LeDoux, 1996) and, accordingly, was not a major research focus within cognitive neuroscience either. Nevertheless, there is no reason why emotions cannot also be explored as specific information-processing functions of the brain. In fact, segregating both "emotion" and "cognition" into elementary processes, grounded in neural systems, is likely to be a far more powerful approach to understanding how the processes in question work than one that ignores these considerations.

In this chapter, we will outline an approach to understanding cognitive-emotional interactions in the brain, examining the problem through explorations of one specific emotion—fear. We lay out what the neural components of the fear system are, as well as the processes subserved by these, and then ask how the processes in that neural system relate to components of systems that mediate various cognitive processes. We examine the problem from behavioral, neural-systems, and cellular points of view. By drawing upon different levels of analysis and ensuring that theories proposed at one level correspond with theories of other levels (see Churchland and Sejnowski, 1992), we hope to gain a better understanding of the neurobiological bases of cognitive-emotional interactions. Furthermore, although much of

JORGE L. ARMONY   Institute of Cognitive Neuroscience, University College, London, U.K.
JOSEPH E. LEDOUX   Center for Neural Science, New York University, New York, N.Y.

the work that rationalizes this approach is based on empirical findings, we have also recently explored some of the issues through computational modeling, and will draw on both kinds of studies here.

WHY FEAR?   Fear is an emotion that is particularly important to human and animal existence. It is a normal reaction to danger and occurs often in daily life. A number of psychiatric conditions that afflict humans (including panic attacks, phobias, generalized anxiety, and posttraumatic stress syndrome) are likely to represent disorders of the fear system (Charney et al., 1995; LeDoux, 1996; Öhman, Flykt, and Lundqvist, in press). Also, fear is particularly amenable to laboratory experimentation: It can be readily elicited, and a number of quantitative measures of fear can be used. Even if through studies of fear we were to learn only about fear-related processes, rather than about "emotion" in general, these findings would still be an important achievement.

FEAR CONDITIONING AS A MODEL APPROACH TO FEAR   There are a number of experimental tools for studying fear and anxiety in animals and humans. One of the simplest and most commonly used is classical aversive conditioning, or fear conditioning. With this procedure, meaningless stimuli acquire affective properties when they occur in conjunction with a biologically significant event. When a conditioned stimulus (CS), often a tone, is repeatedly presented to a rat in association with an aversive unconditioned stimulus (US), such as a mild electric shock to the feet, the rat will, when presented with the CS in the absence of the US, exhibit a complex set of fear responses. These responses include increases in heart rate and blood pressure, "freezing" (absence of all movements but those associated with breathing), and hormone release, among others. The responses are not themselves learned, but they are hardwired (genetically specified) reactions to naturally occurring threats. Through fear conditioning, novel environmental stimuli can gain access to neural circuits that control hardwired, evolutionarily acquired, defense responses. Fear conditioning is a very efficient form of learning. It can be acquired very quickly (in as little as a single trial) and is very difficult to extinguish. It occurs throughout the phyla, and within vertebrates, including humans, it appears to involve very similar neural mechanisms across species. Much of the background information about fear conditioning is summarized in LeDoux (1996).

NEURAL CIRCUITRY OF FEAR CONDITIONING   A large number of studies, using different experimental paradigms and measures of conditioned fear responses, have consistently supported the notion that the amygdala is the key structure in the neural system involved in learning about stimuli that signal threat (e.g., Davis, 1992; Fanselow, 1994; Kapp et al., 1992; LeDoux, 1996). The amygdala receives and integrates information about the CS, as well as information about context and internal states, and controls the various conditioned response networks in the brain stem. In this section, we summarize findings about the pathways involved in fear conditioning to auditory stimuli, since these are the best understood (more detailed descriptions can be found in Armony and LeDoux, 1997a; LeDoux, 1995, 1996).

An acoustic CS is transmitted through the auditory system to the auditory thalamus–the medial geniculate body (MGB). From there, information is conveyed to the amygdala by way of two parallel pathways. A direct projection originates primarily in the medial division of the MGB (MGm) and the associated posterior intralaminar nucleus (PIN). A second, indirect, pathway conveys information from all areas of the MGB to auditory cortex, from where, via several corticocortical links, it is transmitted to the amygdala. The direct thalamic pathway is believed to provide rapid but imprecise information, whereas the auditory cortex provides slower but more detailed representation to the amygdala (e.g., LeDoux, 1996). Lesion studies have demonstrated that either pathway is sufficient for conditioning to a simple stimulus, such as a pure tone (Romanski and LeDoux, 1992). Although auditory cortex appears not to be necessary for simple frequency discrimination (discussed later; Armony et al., 1997b), it may become crucial for higher levels of processing involving complex sounds (e.g., Whitfield, 1980).

Anatomical and physiological studies suggest that the lateral nucleus of the amygdala (LA) is a major site of termination of both thalamic and cortical auditory inputs (Amaral et al., 1992; Bordi and LeDoux, 1992; LeDoux et al., 1990; Romanski et al., 1993). In fact, single cells in LA receive convergent inputs from the auditory thalamus and cortex (Li, Stutzmann, and LeDoux, 1996). Information flows from LA to the central nucleus (CE) over well-defined intra-amygdala circuits (for a review, see Pitkänen, Savander, and LeDoux, 1997). The central nucleus appears to be the interface with the motor systems that are involved in controlling conditioned responses (Davis, 1992; Kapp et al., 1992). Thus, whereas lesions of CE interfere with the expression of fear responses of all types, lesions of areas to which CE projects interfere with select responses. For example, lesions of the lateral hypothalamus interfere with sympathetic-nervous-system-mediated responses (such as changes in blood pressure) whereas lesions of the central gray interfere with behaviorally conditioned re-

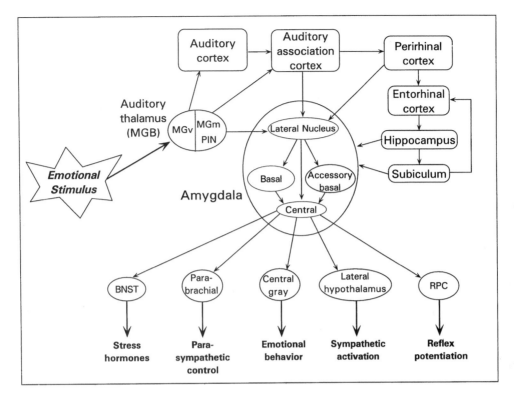

FIGURE 74.1 Schematic of the circuit underlying auditory fear conditioning. The lateral nucleus of the amygdala receives a hierarchical cascade of information from sensory areas in the thalamus and neocortex, as well as inputs from higher-order association neocortical regions and hippocampal formation. Through intra-amygdala processing, information reaches the central nucleus, which controls the expression of different emotional responses. BNST, bed nucleus of the stria terminalis; RPC, nucleus reticularis pontis caudalis. (Modified from Armony and LeDoux, 1997a.)

sponses (e.g., freezing). A schematic of the neural circuit underlying auditory fear conditioning is depicted in figure 74.1.

Although most of the findings about the neural basis of fear conditioning have been obtained from studies of animals, particularly rats, recent studies suggest that analogous brain regions and mechanisms are involved in human fear conditioning. For example, patients with temporal lobe lesions that include the amygdala (LaBar et al., 1995) or are restricted mainly to it (Bechara et al., 1995) have shown deficits in fear conditioning and in the perception of fear in facial expressions (Adolphs et al., 1994) and voices (Scott et al., 1997). In addition, functional imaging studies have now shown activation of the amygdala during fear conditioning (Büchel et al., 1998; LaBar et al., 1998) and while processing faces and other emotional stimuli (Whalen et al., 1998).

Simulating circuits: A computational model of the fear conditioning network

In our attempt to understand the neural mechanisms of fear processing, we have constructed a computational model of the fear conditioning system based on the em-

pirical findings described in the preceding section. The model has captured some functional aspects of the circuitry and underlying processes surprisingly well, and it has made some novel predictions that have been borne out by subsequent empirical studies.

THE MODEL   A diagram of the basic architecture of the network used in the simulations described here is shown in figure 74.2. The essential elements of the model are the following (more details can be found in Armony et al., 1995, 1997a, 1997b):

• Processing units: Simple, nonlinear summing units are used as a first approximation of the behavior of a single neuron (or a neuronal assembly that redundantly codes for the same piece of information). The response of a unit to a given input pattern is thought to represent the time-averaged neuronal firing rate.

• Architecture: Information is coded and processed in two parallel systems; one that involves more elaborate representations but less direct connections with response systems (the indirect, or "cortical," pathway) and another that involves cruder representations but more direct connections with the response systems (the direct, or "subcortical," pathway). These two systems

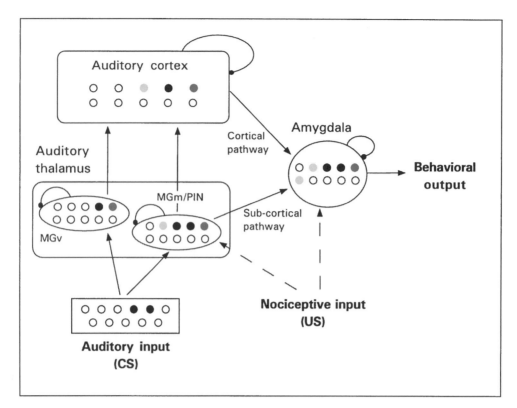

FIGURE 74.2 Architecture of the network used in the simulations of fear conditioning. Modules of nonlinear, mutually inhibitory units represent the main structures of the fear circuit. A typical pattern of activity is schematized by representing unit activation with gray shadings (solid circles, maximum activation; open circles, zero activation). Connections between modules are feedforward and excitatory, and are modified through an extended Hebbian learning rule (see text for details). Dashed arrows indicate positive, nonmodifiable connections. MGv, ventral division of the medial geniculate body (MGB); MGm, medial division of the MGB; PIN, posterior intralaminar nucleus; CS, conditioned stimulus; US, unconditioned stimulus. (Adapted from Armony et al., 1997b.)

converge on the amygdala–the effector system for fear responses. Units within a module are mutually inhibitory. The strength of this lateral inhibition is used to capture the differences in the response properties (broad versus narrow receptive fields) of the extralemniscal MGB (MGm/PIN) and amygdala on the one hand, and lemniscal MGB (MGv) and auditory cortex on the other hand.

• *Sensory input:* Auditory input is simulated by a set of overlapping patterns of activity, representing pure tones of contiguous frequencies (arranged along an arbitrary scale). During the conditioning phase, one of the stimuli serves as a CS. The US is a positive quantity directly added to the input term of all units in the MGm/PIN and amygdala modules during conditioning.

• *Learning:* We relied on a simple modification of the Hebbian learning rule, in which connection strengths are increased between correlated units and decreased for uncorrelated units. This, together with the lateral inhibitory connections, represents a variant of standard competitive learning rules (Rumelhart and Zipser, 1986).

EXPERIMENTS WITH THE MODEL
Conditioning-induced plasticity: From units to behavior Single-unit recording studies have shown that individual cells in the auditory thalamus, auditory cortex, and lateral amygdala have characteristic frequency receptive field profiles, and that these are altered through fear conditioning. We examined whether this pattern might also occur in the model. Prior to conditioning, and as a result of the presentation of simulated acoustic tones, units developed frequency receptive fields (RFs); that is, each unit responded only to a subset of contiguous inputs, centered on a best frequency (BF). Subsequent conditioning (CS-US pairing) resulted in some units showing frequency-specific retuning of their RFs, such that there was a shift of the BF toward the CS. An example of an amygdala RF shift is shown in figure 74.3A. In the model, as in real brains, the shifts occurred in the MGm, auditory cortex, and amygdala, but not in the MGv. The unit receptive-field changes in the model thus closely mirrored the changes observed in the exact same areas in animal experiments (Bordi and LeDoux, 1993; Weinberger, 1995). It should be noted that the model

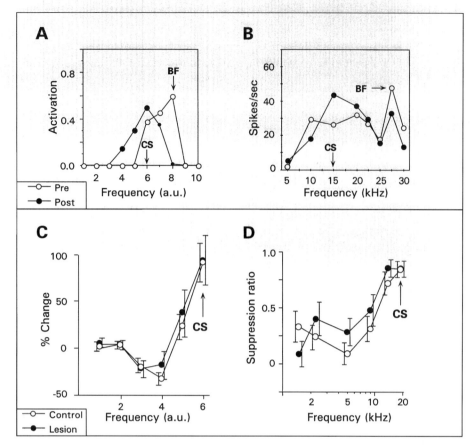

FIGURE 74.3 Examples of conditioning-induced plasticity in receptive fields (RFs) of amygdala units in the computational model (A), and of amygdala neurons in rats (B), before (Pre, open symbols) and after (Post, filled symbols) conditioning. In both cases, fear conditioning resulted in a shift of RFs, such that the conditioned stimulus (CS) became the new best frequency (BF). This stimulus re-representation, in turn, resulted in increases of fear responses to the CS and adjacent frequen- cies in the model (C; open symbols) and in rats (D; open sym- bols), in the form of a stimulus generalization gradient (SGG). Cortical lesions prior to conditioning did not have an effect on the width of the SGG in either case (C, D; filled symbols). a.u., arbitrary units. (A, adapted from Armony et al., 1995; B, based on data from Bordi and LeDoux, 1993; C and D, modified from Armony et al., 1997b.)

was in no way programmed to exhibit these changes. The changes instead occurred because of the network architecture: The areas that changed were areas that re- ceive inputs from the CS and US.

The re-representation of the input patterns at the sin- gle-unit level, based on their learned aversive value, is reflected in the behavioral output of the network as an increase in the response to the CS and adjacent frequen- cies in the form of a stimulus generalization gradient (SGG), shown in figure 74.3C (open symbols). Similar gradients are observed in animal experiments (figure 74.3D; see Armony et al., 1997b).

Auditory cortex lesions and stimulus generalization Once we found that the basic physiological and behavioral ob- servations were quantitatively reproduced by the model, it became possible to use the model to formulate new predictions. We were particularly interested in investi- gating the relative contributions of the thalamic and cor-

tical inputs to the amygdala in fear conditioning. Because the cells of origin in the direct thalamic path- way have broader receptive fields, we hypothesized that removal of the cortical input to the amygdala would cause fear responses to generalize more broadly to stim- uli other than the CS. However, the simulations showed that lesion of the corticoamygdala pathway in the model did not affect the stimulus generalization gradient (figure 74.3C). Further analysis indicated why this result oc- curred. Although individual thalamic units in the MGm/ PIN, which provide the direct projection to the amygdala, may not be capable of discriminating similar stimuli (because of their broad RF), the structure as a whole is a much better stimulus discriminator, because it relies on population coding. Interestingly, subsequent studies in rats confirmed the predictions of the model; that is, removal of auditory cortex did not have a signifi- cant effect on the conditioned SGG, as shown in figure 74.3D. This finding shows that, contrary to what was previously thought (see Jarrell et al., 1987; LeDoux, 1995), the direct thalamoamygdala pathway is capable of supporting some aspects of stimulus discrimination. Further studies are needed to realize the full capacity, and limitations, of the thalamic inputs to the amygdala. The key point though is that the modeling study gave an unexpected result that led us to perform studies in animals. The latter study showed that the modeling result, though unexpected, was correct.

Cellular mechanisms

With key aspects of the circuitry now understood in some detail, investigators have turned to an analysis of cellular mechanisms underlying conditioning. It is generally accepted that classical conditioning involves the neural intersection of pathways transmitting information about the CS and US. The US somehow changes the strength of the synaptic connections in the CS processing pathway, allowing the CS to have an amplified effect. The lateral amygdala (LA), the sensory interface of the amygdala, is a site of CS-US convergence. Thus it is important to understand how sensory information is represented in LA neurons—and how this representation is altered through fear conditioning.

STIMULUS PROCESSING IN THE LATERAL AMYGDALA Most studies of sensory processing by amygdala cells have involved auditory stimuli in rats (e.g., Bordi and LeDoux, 1992, 1993; Quirk, Repa, and LeDoux, 1995; Romanski et al., 1993) and visual stimuli in primates (reviewed in Rolls, 1992). In rats, LA cells have short latency responses to simple auditory stimuli. These latencies must correspond to direct transmission from the thalamus, since they are similar to the earliest latencies in areas in auditory cortex that project to the amygdala. Some cells habituate quickly to repeated unreinforced presentations of the same stimulus, but they respond strongly if the stimulus is changed or if it is paired with a US. That is, these cells act as novelty detectors: they learn to ignore stimuli that produce no consequences, and hence have no emotional meaning. Some cells in LA seem to respond preferentially to species-specific stimuli with intrinsic affective value. For example, in rats, LA cells with auditory responses have relatively high thresholds (about 30–50 dB above the primary auditory system) and tend to prefer high-frequency stimulation (16–30 kHz tones). This frequency range is similar to that of the warning calls that rats emit when threatened (Blanchard et al., 1991). In primates, face identity and expression play an important role in social behavior. A group of cells in the monkey amygdala responds primarily to faces (see Rolls, 1992),

and recent imaging studies in humans, mentioned earlier, show that emotional faces activate the amygdala. Finally, again in rats, most cells that respond to auditory stimuli also respond to somatosensory stimulation (Romanski et al., 1993) and, therefore, are potential sites of CS-US integration during auditory fear conditioning.

CONDITIONING-INDUCED NEURAL PLASTICITY IN LA Neurons in several components of the fear circuit exhibit changes in their response to the CS after conditioning. Specifically, cells in the MGm, auditory cortex, and amygdala develop conditioning-induced plasticity (Quirk, Armony, and LeDoux, 1997; Quirk, Repa, and LeDoux, 1995; Weinberger, 1995). In LA some cells develop short-latency increases to a tone CS after it has been paired with a foot-shock US. The earliest latency of this plasticity falls within 10–20 ms after tone onset (Quirk, Repa, and LeDoux, 1995). These changes cannot be accounted for by corticoamygdala projections, since the earliest plasticity observed in auditory association cortex does not occur until 20–40 ms after tone onset (Quirk, Armony, and LeDoux, 1997). Moreover, it is unlikely that plasticity in LA merely reflects active plasticity transmitted from the auditory thalamus either, as thalamic conditioning-induced plasticity appears to take longer (for a discussion, see Quirk et al., 1996). Neural plasticity in LA also develops in fewer trials (1–3 CS-US pairings) than auditory cortex (6–9 pairings) (Quirk, Armony, and LeDoux, 1997). Interestingly, amygdala lesions do not have an effect on onset plasticity in auditory cortex (Armony, Quirk, and LeDoux, 1998). These findings suggest that onset plasticity in both LA and auditory cortex develop independently, and that both are driven by direct inputs from the thalamus. Conditioning-induced plasticity is also observed in other amygdala subnuclei, such as the basal and central nuclei (Muramoto et al., 1993; Pascoe and Kapp, 1985). Plasticity in these areas, however, occurs at later times than in LA (e.g., 30–50 ms after CS onset in the central nucleus; Pascoe and Kapp, 1985). These latency differences between the input and output nuclei suggest that significant processing occurs within amygdala circuits.

Plasticity of synaptic transmission in LA has also been studied using long-term potentiation (LTP) in the thalamoamygdala pathway (Clugnet and LeDoux, 1990; Rogan and LeDoux, 1995); LTP induction results in an enhanced processing of auditory stimuli through this pathway (Rogan and LeDoux, 1995), indicating that natural stimuli can make use of artificially induced plasticity. Most important, though, natural learning (fear conditioning) also enhances the processing of auditory stimuli in the same way (Rogan, Stäubli, and LeDoux, 1997). Thus fear conditioning induces an LTP-like neural change in LA. Together with the unit-recording studies

FIGURE 74.4 (A) Schematic of the biophysical model of an amygdala neuron. The neuron receives excitatory inputs acting upon AMPA and NMDA receptors, and feedforward inhibition via GABA$_A$ and GABA$_B$ receptors. (B) Effects of AMPA and NMDA blockade on the model neuron's response to thalamic and cortical stimulations. Removal of AMPA currents blocks action potential generation in both cases, but blocking of NMDA receptors only has an effect on the thalamic pathway, consistent with experimental findings (see text for details). (C) Joint stimulation of the thalamic and cortical pathways (with a short delay, meant to represent the different latencies in normal auditory transmission) elicits suprathreshold response (action potential) in the model neuron, even when stimulation of each pathway individually only results in subthreshold responses.

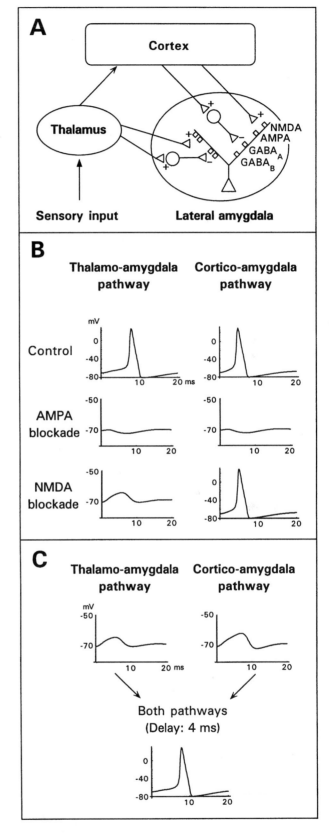

described previously, these findings point toward synaptic changes in the input pathways to the amygdala as being important in the learning experience.

BIOPHYSICAL MODELING OF AMYGDALA NEURONS With more information becoming available about cellular mechanisms within the amygdala, it is becoming possible to explore this region using neuronal models. In this spirit, we have recently begun to expand our network model to incorporate biophysical data. As a first step, we have explored interactions between thalamic and cortical auditory inputs to single LA cells.

We developed a simplified biophysical model of an amygdala neuron receiving convergent inputs from the thalamic and cortical pathways (Armony and LeDoux, 1997b; Li, Armony, and LeDoux, 1996) to explore how information arriving from both pathways is integrated within individual amygdala cells. The model neuron (see figure 74.4A), represented as a single compartment, has six ion-channel types: two of them, sodium and potassium, are voltage-gated and modeled using the standard Hodgkin-Huxley formalism; the other four are ligand-gated. They represent the excitatory and inhibitory synaptic currents activated by the glutamate receptors (AMPA and NMDA) and GABA receptors (GABA$_A$ and GABA$_B$), respectively. These channels are represented by a two-state model, proposed by Destexhe, Mainen, and Sejnowski (1994). The parameters for the AMPA and NMDA currents were derived from patch-clamp data from amygdala neurons (Weisskopf and LeDoux, 1997), whereas those for GABA currents were obtained from previously published hippocampus data (Otis and Mody, 1992), since no amygdala data were available. This simple model captured a number of physiological observations that have been previously reported:

1. Both thalamic and cortical pathways depend on AMPA receptors for synaptic transmission. The thala-

moamygdala pathway also requires NMDA activation for normal transmission (figure 74.4B; see Li, Phillips, and LeDoux, 1995; Li, Stutzmann, and LeDoux, 1996).

2. Blockade of GABA_A receptors results in an increase of evoked action potentials elicited by thalamic or cortical stimulation (cf. Li, Armony, and LeDoux, 1996).

3. The differential contributions of GABA_A and GABA_B to short- and long-delay inhibition, respectively, can be accounted for by a simple feedforward inhibitory circuit (see Li, Armony, and LeDoux, 1996).

4. Combined inputs from thalamic and cortical projections (with a short delay between them) can elicit suprathreshold responses in amygdala cells, when each input individually only evokes subthreshold responses (figure 74.4C; see Li, Woodson, and LeDoux, 1997).

As with the connectionist model described in previous sections, once the validity of the model is established by its capacity to account for several of the key phenomena observed in in-vivo and slice intracellular experiments, we can use the model to make new predictions that will guide future physiological studies. Moreover, we can use these simplified biophysical models of individual neurons as computational units in the systems model of the fear network described earlier, to further explore the relations between neural and behavioral processes. This approach is possible given the modular nature of the network model. In other words, the amygdala module can be replaced with a biophysically based module, leaving the connections from the other modules intact and allowing the biophysical properties in the amygdala to operate within a larger, realistic network. This model might prove useful as a means of testing hypotheses about the synaptic and cellular basis of fear learning.

Cognitive-emotional interactions in fear

Identification of the neural system involved in fear processing paves the way for considering how key elements of that system interact with brain systems involved in certain aspects of cognitive processing. In this section, therefore, we will examine how the amygdala interacts with brain systems involved in aspects of perception, attention, memory, and consciousness.

PERCEPTION AND FEAR   The amygdala receives inputs from cortical sensory processing regions of each sensory modality (Amaral et al., 1992; Turner, Mishkin, and Knapp, 1980) and can, as in the case of fear conditioning, determine whether stimuli processed through those channels are sources of potential danger. However, the amygdala also projects back to cortical sensory processing areas (Amaral et al., 1992). This anatomical arrangement suggests that in addition to

processing the emotional significance of external stimuli transmitted to the amygdala from cortical areas, the amygdala might also influence the processing that occurs in these areas. In contrast, while the amygdala also receives and processes the significance of sensory stimuli directly from sensory areas in the thalamus, it does not project back to these areas (see LeDoux, Ruggiero, and Reis, 1985).

The amygdala only receives inputs from the late stages of cortical sensory processing, but it projects back to the earliest stages (Amaral et al., 1992). As a result, once the amygdala is activated by a sensory event from the thalamus or cortex, it can begin to regulate the cortical areas that project to it, controlling the kinds of inputs it receives. The amygdala also influences the cortical sensory process indirectly, by way of projections to various "arousal" networks, including the basal forebrain cholinergic system, the brainstem cholinergic system, and the locus coeruleus noradrenergic system, each of which innervates widespread areas of the cortex. Thus, once the amygdala detects danger, it can activate these arousal systems, which could then influence sensory processing (e.g., Aston-Jones et al., 1996; Gallagher and Holland, 1994; Kapp et al., 1992; Weinberger, 1995).

FEAR AND SELECTIVE ATTENTION   Selective attention is believed to occur in cortical areas and to result from the allocation of processing resources so that task-relevant (i.e., attended) stimuli are focused on at the expense of competing (unattended) ones (Duncan, Humphreys, and Ward, 1997). However, if this mechanism operated unconditionally, deleterious consequences could occur in some situations. For example, if a predator appeared somewhere outside of the focus of attention, it would be ignored until it was too late, because of the reduced cortical representation given to it by attentional filtering processes. However, we are generally able to respond to threats arising outside our focus of attention (Öhman, Flykt, and Lundqvist, in press). The direct thalamo-amygdala pathway may hold the key.

Using a computational model, we tested the hypothesis that the thalamoamygdala pathway might constitute an attention-independent channel that provides the amygdala with information about threat signals that occur outside (or inside) the focus of attention. The model was based on the fear conditioning network described earlier, integrated with a model of selective attention proposed by Cohen, Dunbar, and McClelland (1990). The architecture of the network is shown in figure 74.5. Two parallel processing streams, representing different aspects of the environment (such as right and left auditory hemifields) or task demands (such as color naming

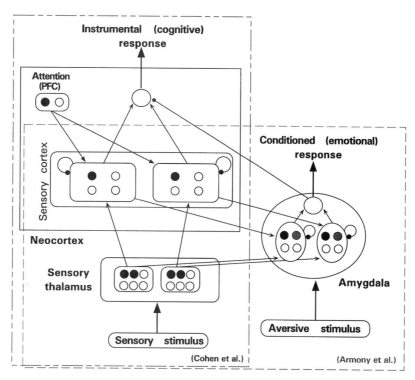

FIGURE 74.5 Architecture of the integrated network used in the simulations of attention-emotion interactions. The network combines the original fear network described in Armony et al. (1995, 1997b; see figure 74.2), and the model of selective attention of Cohen, Dunbar, and McClelland (1990). Sensory information flows along two parallel processing streams, representing different dimensions of the stimulus space. The two streams compete for cortical resources, which are allocated by externally set attentional inputs. Emotional (fear) responses have the capacity to inhibit instrumental responses. Connections with filled arrowheads correspond to nonmodifiable excitatory weights, open arrowheads represent modifiable excitatory connections, and circular arrowheads represent inhibitory connections. PFC, prefrontal cortex.

versus word reading in the Stroop task), compete for the limited pool of processing resources to determine behavioral responses. Selective attention units were externally set to bias one representation over the other, depending on where attention was allocated (Duncan, Humphreys, and Ward, 1997). The direct thalamo-amygdala pathway was not subject to attentional bias. The overall behavioral output of the network resulted from competition between instrumental (cognitive) responses, determined by output of the cortical module, and fear-related responses, elicited by amygdala activation. This response competition was implemented in an asymmetrical fashion, so that the fear response had the capacity to inhibit instrumental responses. This design was meant to represent, in a simplified manner, empirical observations that fear reactions can interrupt ongoing behavior in favor of danger-elicited survival responses (Bouton and Bolles, 1980). The results of the simulations predict that lesions of the direct thalamic projections to the amygdala will interfere with fear responses to an unattended CS. The model also suggests that significant interference in stimulus processing in cognitive-attentional tasks, such as the Stroop word-

color interference task, can occur when some of the stimuli have acquired strong negative affective value through fear conditioning (Armony et al., 1996). Thus the model shows how emotional processing can operate independently of, and modulate the focus of, attentional mechanisms.

Electrophysiological experiments support the view that the amygdala regulates cortical attentional/perceptual processing. Stimulation of the amygdala results in a desynchronization of cortical EEG, which typically occurs when attention is directed to some stimulus (Kapp, Supple, and Whalen, 1994). This effect is mediated by cholinergic projections from the basal forebrain. Furthermore, during fear conditioning some cells in the auditory cortex exhibit an increase in neural activity during the CS just before the occurrence of the US (figure 74.6; Quirk, Armony, and LeDoux, 1997). These cells may be involved in the direction of attention to the spatiotemporal aspects of the US. Damage to the amygdala prevents the emergence of this conditioned neural response (Armony, Quirk, and LeDoux, 1998). This fact does not imply that the amygdala is involved in all aspects of cortical attention, but rather that it may

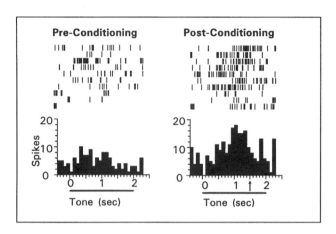

FIGURE 74.6   Example of an auditory cortex neuron showing long-latency conditioned tone responses. Before conditioning, the cell did not respond to the tone. Following CS-US pairings, however, the neuron developed a late significant tone response, starting at about 500 ms after tone onset, and reaching its peak at 1500 ms, which was the onset of the US during conditioning (indicated by the arrow). Bin size is 100 ms. (Adapted from Armony, Quirk, and LeDoux, 1998.)

be involved in the direction and focusing of attention toward dangerous stimuli or stimuli that predict danger. As we pointed out, amygdala regulation of the cortex could involve the facilitation of processing of stimuli that signal danger even if such stimuli occur outside of the attentional field (Armony et al., 1996, 1997a).

DECLARATIVE MEMORY AND FEAR   It is now widely recognized that there are a variety of memory systems in the brain, some of which work in parallel (see Cohen and Eichenbaum, 1993; Gaffan, 1994; Squire and Zola, 1996). For example, information about stimuli associated with painful or otherwise unpleasant experiences is stored in the amygdala and related brain regions. This system mediates the emotional reactions that are elicited when these stimuli are reencountered. It can operate at an implicit or unconscious level (LeDoux, 1996; Öhman, Flykt, and Lundqvist, in press). However, we usually have explicit or conscious memories about emotional situations as well. These, like other explicit memories, are mediated by the medial temporal lobe memory system involving the hippocampus, rhinal cortex, and related cortical areas (Gaffan, 1994). The implicit memories of emotional events have been called *emotional memories*, and the explicit memories have been termed *memories about emotions* (LeDoux, 1996). Implicit emotional memories are automatically elicited in the presence of trigger stimuli and do not require conscious retrieval or recall, whereas explicit memories of emotion are retrieved consciously. In humans, damage to the amygdala interferes with implicit emotional memories but not explicit memories about emotions, whereas damage to the medial temporal lobe memory system interferes with explicit memories about emotions but not with implicit emotional memories (Bechara et al., 1995; LaBar et al., 1995). For example, patients with amygdala lesions do not exhibit conditioned fear responses to the CS but remember that the CS was related to the US, while patients with hippocampal damage exhibit conditioned responses but have no memory of the CS-US pairing experience.

As described earlier, in a set of physiology studies of fear conditioning in rats, we determined that short-latency plasticity develops independently in neocortex and amygdala (see figure 74.7). These findings provide further support, at a cellular level, for the notion that the declarative and emotional memory systems may, to some extent, operate in parallel.

While explicit memories with and without emotional content are mediated by the medial temporal lobe system, those with emotional content differ from those without such content. The former tend to be longer lasting and more vivid (see Christianson, 1992). Studies by McGaugh and colleagues (McGaugh, Cahill, and Roozendal, 1996) have shown that stories with emotional content are remembered better than similar stories lacking emotional implications. Lesions of the amygdala or systemic administration of a beta-adrenergic antagonist prevent this effect (see McGaugh, Cahill, and Roozendal, 1996). In animal studies, lesions of the amygdala significantly accelerate the extinction rate of plasticity in auditory cortex neurons (Armony, Quirk, and LeDoux, 1998), as shown in figure 74.7. Thus both behavioral and physiological findings suggest a role for the amygdala in the enhancement and/or consolidation of declarative memories with affective content.

FEAR AND CONSCIOUSNESS   We have described findings about how the brain process emotions, particularly fear, without mentioning conscious feelings (i.e., the experience of being afraid). Nevertheless, consciousness is an important part of the study of emotion and other mental processes. Our hypothesis is that the mechanism of consciousness is the same for emotional and nonemotional subjective states and that what distinguishes these states is the brain system that consciousness is aware of at the time.

We are far from solving what consciousness is, but a number of theorists have proposed that it may be related to working memory, a serially organized mental workspace where things can be compared and contrasted and mentally manipulated (Baddeley, 1992). A variety of studies of humans and nonhuman primates point to the

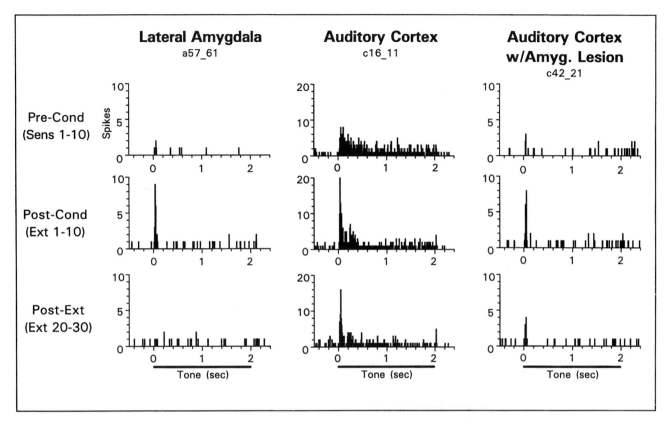

FIGURE 74.7 Poststimulus time histograms showing the effects of acquisition and extinction of onset tone responses in lateral amygdala, auditory cortex, and auditory cortex in animals with amygdala ablation. The auditory cortex cell from an intact rat developed onset-conditioned increases after conditioning (Post-Cond; extinction trials 1–10) that lasted through the entire extinction phase (Post-Ext; extinction trials 20–30).

In contrast, the amygdala cell and the auditory cortex cell of a lesioned animal developed short-latency conditioned increases that returned to preconditioning levels (Pre-Cond; sensitization trials 1–10) at the end of the extinction phase. Bin size 10 ms. (Adapted from Armony, Quirk, and LeDoux, 1998, and Quirk, Armony, and LeDoux, 1997.)

prefrontal cortex—especially the dorsolateral prefrontal areas, as well as the anterior cingulate and orbital cortical regions—as being involved in working memory (Goldman-Rakic, 1992). Immediately present stimuli and stored representations are integrated in working memory by way of interactions between prefrontal areas, sensory processing systems (which serve as short-term memory buffers, as well as perceptual processors), and the long-term explicit (declarative) memory system involving the hippocampus and related areas of the temporal lobe. In the case of an affectively charged stimulus, such as a trigger of fear, the same sorts of processes will be called upon as for stimuli without emotional implications, but in addition, working memory will become aware of the fact that the fear system of the brain has been activated. This additional information, when added to perceptual and mnemonic information about the object or event, could be the condition for the subjective experience of an emotional state of fear.

But what is the additional information that is added to working memory when the fear system is activated?

The amygdala projects to many cortical areas, even some that it does not receive inputs from (Amaral et al., 1992). It can thus influence the operation of perceptual and short-term memory processes, as well as processes in higher order areas. Although the amygdala does not have extensive connections with the dorsolateral prefrontal cortex, it does communicate with the anterior cingulate and orbital cortex, two other components of the working-memory network. But in addition, the amygdala projects to nonspecific systems involved in the regulation of cortical arousal. And the amygdala controls bodily responses (behavioral, autonomic, endocrine), which then provide feedback that can influence cortical processing indirectly. Thus working memory receives a greater number of inputs and receives inputs of a greater variety in the presence of an emotional stimulus than in the presence of other stimuli. These extra inputs may just be what is required to add affective charge to working-memory representations, and thus to turn subjective experiences into emotional experiences.

ACKNOWLEDGMENTS   This work was supported by U.S. Public Health Service grants MH38774, MH46516, and MH00956 awarded to Joseph E. LeDoux and by a grant from the Keck Foundation to New York University.

REFERENCES

ADOLPHS, R., D. TRANEL, H. DAMASIO, and A. R. DAMASIO, 1994. Impaired recognition of emotion in facial expressions following bilateral damage to the human amygdala. *Nature* 372:669-672.

AMARAL, D. G., J. L. PRICE, A. PITKÄNEN, and S. T. CARMICHAEL, 1992. Anatomical organization of the primate amygdaloid complex. In *The Amygdala: Neurobiological Aspects of Emotion, Memory, and Mental Dysfunction,* J. P. Aggleton, ed. New York: Wiley, pp. 1-66.

ARMONY, J. L., and J. E. LEDOUX, 1997a. How the brain processes emotional information. *Ann. N.Y. Acad. Sci.* 821:259-270.

ARMONY, J. L., and J. E. LEDOUX, 1997b. A simplified biophysical model of amygdala neurons. *Soc. Neurosci. Abstr.* 23:785.

ARMONY, J. L., G. J. QUIRK, and J. E. LEDOUX, 1998. Differential effects of amygdala lesions on early and late plastic components of auditory cortex spike trains during fear conditioning. *J. Neurosci.* 18:2592-2601.

ARMONY, J. L., D. SERVAN-SCHREIBER, J. D. COHEN, and J. E. LEDOUX, 1995. An anatomically constrained neural network model of fear conditioning. *Behav. Neurosci.* 109:246-257.

ARMONY, J. L., D. SERVAN-SCHREIBER, J. D. COHEN, and J. E. LEDOUX, 1996. Emotion and cognition interactions in the thalamo-cortico-amygdala network: Theory and model. *Cognit. Neurosci. Soc. Abstr.* 3:76.

ARMONY, J. L., D. SERVAN-SCHREIBER, J. D. COHEN, and J. E. LEDOUX, 1997a. Computational modeling of emotion: Explorations through the anatomy and physiology of fear conditioning. *Trends Cognit. Sci.* 1:28-34.

ARMONY, J. L., D. SERVAN-SCHREIBER, L. M. ROMANSKI, J. D. COHEN, and J. E. LEDOUX, 1997b. Stimulus generalization of fear responses: Effects of auditory cortex lesions in a computational model and in rats. *Cereb. Cortex* 7:157-165.

ASTON-JONES, G., J. RAJKOWSKI, P. KUBIAK, R. J. VALENTINO, and M. T. SHIPLEY, 1996. Role of the locus coeruleus in emotional activation. *Prog. Brain Res.* 107:379-402.

BADDELEY, A., 1992. Working memory. *Science* 255:556-559.

BECHARA, A., D. TRANEL, H. DAMASIO, R. ADOLPHS, C. ROCKLAND, and A. R. DAMASIO, 1995. Double dissociation of conditioning and declarative knowledge relative to the amygdala and hippocampus in humans. *Science* 269:1115-1118.

BLANCHARD, R. J., D. C. BLANCHARD, R. AGULLANA, and S. M. WEISS, 1991. Twenty-two kHz alarm cries to presentation of a predator, by laboratory rats living in visible burrow systems. *Physiol. Behav.* 50:967-972.

BORDI, F., and J. E. LEDOUX, 1992. Sensory tuning beyond the sensory system: An initial analysis of auditory properties of neurons in the lateral amygdaloid nucleus and overlying areas of the striatum. *J. Neurosci.* 12:2493-2503.

BORDI, F., and J. E. LEDOUX, 1993. Sensory-specific conditioned plasticity in lateral amygdala neurons. *Soc. Neurosci. Abstr.* 19:1227.

BOUTON, M. E., and R. C. BOLLES, 1980. Conditioned fear assessed by freezing and by the suppression of three different baselines. *Animal Learn. Behav.* 8:429-434.

BÜCHEL, C., J. MORRIS, R. J. DOLAN, and K. J. FRISTON, 1998. Brain systems mediating aversive conditioning: An event-related fMRI study. *Neuron* 20:947-957.

CHARNEY, D. S., A. Y. DEUTCH, S. M. SOUTHWICK, and J. H. KRYSTAL, 1995. Neural circuits and mechanisms of post-traumatic stress disorder. In *Neurobiological and Clinical Consequences of Stress: From Normal Adaptation to PTSD,* M. J. Friedman, D. S. Charney, and A. Y. Deutch, eds. Philadelphia: Lippincott-Raven, pp. 271-287.

CHRISTIANSON, S.-A., ed., 1992. *Handbook of Emotion and Memory: Research and Theory.* Hillsdale, N.J.: Erlbaum.

CHURCHLAND, P. S., and T. J. SEJNOWSKI, 1992. *The Computational Brain.* Cambridge, Mass.: MIT Press.

CLUGNET, M. C., and J. E. LEDOUX, 1990. Synaptic plasticity in fear conditioning circuits: Induction of LTP in the lateral nucleus of the amygdala by stimulation of the medial geniculate body. *J. Neurosci.* 10:2818-2824.

COHEN, J. D., K. DUNBAR, and J. L. MCCLELLAND, 1990. On the control of automatic processes: A parallel distributed processing account of the Stroop effect. *Psychol. Rev.* 97:332-361.

COHEN, N. J., and H. EICHENBAUM, 1993. *Memory, Amnesia, and the Hippocampal System.* Cambridge, Mass.: MIT Press.

DAVIS, M., 1992. The role of the amygdala in conditioned fear. In *The Amygdala: Neurobiological Aspects of Emotion, Memory, and Mental Dysfunction.* J. P. Aggleton, ed. New York: Wiley, pp. 255-306.

DESTEXHE, A., Z. F. MAINEN, and T. J. SEJNOWSKI, 1994. Synthesis of models for excitable membranes, synaptic transmission and neuromodulation using a common kinetic formalism. *J. Comput. Neurosci.* 1:195-231.

DUNCAN, J., G. HUMPHREYS, and R. WARD, 1997. Competitive brain activity in visual attention. *Curr. Opin. Neurobiol.* 7:255-261.

FANSELOW, M. S., 1994. Neural organization of the defensive behavior system responsible for fear. *Psychonom. Bull. Rev.* 1:429-438.

GAFFAN, D., 1994. Dissociated effects of perirhinal cortex ablation, fornix transection and amygdalectomy: Evidence for multiple memory systems in the primate temporal lobe. *Exp. Brain Res.* 99:411-422.

GALLAGHER, M., and P. H. HOLLAND, 1994. The amygdala complex: Multiple roles in associative learning and attention. *Proc. Natl. Acad. Sci. U.S.A.* 91:11771-11776.

GOLDMAN-RAKIC, P. S., 1992. Working memory and the mind. *Sci. Am.* 267:110-117.

JARRELL, T. W., C. G. GENTILE, L. M. ROMANSKI, P. M. MCCABE, and N. SCHNEIDERMAN, 1987. Involvement of cortical and thalamic auditory regions in retention of differential bradycardia conditioning to acoustic conditioned stimuli in rabbits. *Brain Res.* 412:285-294.

KAPP, B. S., W. F. SUPPLE, and P. J. WHALEN, 1994. Effects of electrical stimulation of the amygdaloid central nucleus on neocortical arousal in the rabbit. *Behav. Neurosci.* 108:81-93.

KAPP, B. S., P. J. WHALEN, W. F. SUPPLE, and J. P. PASCOE, 1992. Amygdaloid contributions to conditioned arousal and sensory information processing. In *The Amygdala: Neurobiological Aspects of Emotion, Memory, and Mental Dysfunction,* J. P. Aggleton, ed. New York: Wiley, pp. 229-254.

LABAR, K. S., J. C. GATENBY, J. C. GORE, J. E. LEDOUX, and E. A. PHELPS, 1998. Human amygdala activation during conditioned fear acquisition and extinction: A mixed-trial fMRI study. *Neuron* 20:937-945.

LABAR, K. S., J. E. LEDOUX, D. D. SPENCER, and E. A. PHELPS, 1995. Impaired fear conditioning following unilateral temporal lobectomy in humans. *J. Neurosci.* 15:6846–6855.

LEDOUX, J. E., 1995. Emotion: Clues from the brain. *Annu. Rev. Psychol.* 46:209–235.

LEDOUX, J., 1996. *The Emotional Brain.* New York: Simon & Schuster.

LEDOUX, J. E., P. CICCHETTI, A. XAGORARIS, and L. M. ROMANSKI, 1990. The lateral amygdaloid nucleus: Sensory interface of the amygdala in fear conditioning. *J. Neurosci.* 10: 1043–1054.

LEDOUX, J. E., D. A. RUGGIERO, and D. J. REIS, 1985. Projections to the subcortical forebrain from anatomically defined regions of the medial geniculate body in the rat. *J. Comp. Neurol.* 242:182–213.

LI, X. F., J. L. ARMONY, and J. E. LEDOUX, 1996. GABA$_A$ and GABA$_B$ receptors differentially regulate synaptic transmission in the auditory thalamo-amygdala pathway: An *in vivo* microiontophoretic study and a model. *Synapse* 24:115–124.

LI, X., R. G. PHILLIPS, and J. E. LEDOUX, 1995. NMDA and non-NMDA receptors contribute to synaptic transmission between the medial geniculate body and the lateral nucleus of the amygdala. *Exp. Brain Res.* 105:87–100.

LI, X. F., G. E. STUTZMANN, and J. E. LEDOUX, 1996. Convergent but temporally separated inputs to lateral amygdala neurons from the auditory thalamus and auditory cortex use different postsynaptic receptors: *In vivo* intracellular and extracellular recordings in fear conditioning pathways. *Learn. Mem.* 3:229–242.

LI, X. F., W. WOODSON, and J. E. LEDOUX, 1997. Physiologically and morphologically identified lateral amygdala neurons *in vivo*: Relationship to parvalbumin-containing interneurons. *Soc. Neurosci. Abstr.* 23:786.

MCGAUGH, J. L., L. CAHILL, and B. ROOZENDAL, 1996. Involvement of the amygdala in memory storage: Interaction with other brain systems. *Proc. Natl. Acad. Sci. U.S.A.* 93: 13508–13514.

MURAMOTO, K., T. ONO, H. NISHIJO, and M. FUKUDA, 1993. Rat amygdaloid neuron responses during auditory discrimination. *Neuroscience* 52:621–636.

ÖHMAN, A., A. FLYKT, and D. LUNDQVIST, in press. Unconscious emotion: Evolutionary perspectives, psychophysical data, and neuropsychological mechanisms. In *The Interface between Emotion and Cognitive Neuroscience*, R. D. Lane and L. Nadel, eds. New York: Oxford University Press.

OTIS, T. S., and I. MODY, 1992. Modulation of decay kinetics and frequency of GABA$_A$ receptor-mediated spontaneous inhibitory postsynaptic currents in hippocampal neurons. *Neuroscience* 49:13–32.

PASCOE, J. P., and B. S. KAPP, 1985. Electrophysiological characteristics of amygdaloid central nucleus neurons during Pavlovian fear conditioning in the rabbit. *Behav. Brain Res.* 16:117–133.

PITKÄNEN, A., V. SAVANDER, and J. L. LEDOUX, 1997. Organization of intra-amygdaloid circuitries: An emerging framework for understanding functions of the amygdala. *Trends Neurosci.* 20:517–523.

QUIRK, G. J., J. L. ARMONY, and J. E. LEDOUX, 1997. Fear conditioning enhances different temporal components of tone-evoked spike trains in auditory cortex and lateral amygdala. *Neuron* 19:613–624.

QUIRK, G. J., J. L. ARMONY, J. C. REPA, X. F. LI, and J. E. LEDOUX, 1996. Emotional memory: A search for sites of plasticity. *Cold Spring Harb. Symp. Quant. Biol.* 61:247–257.

QUIRK, G. J., J. C. REPA, and J. E. LEDOUX, 1995. Fear conditioning enhances short-latency auditory responses of lateral amygdala neurons: Parallel recordings in the freely behaving rat. *Neuron* 15:1029–1039.

ROGAN, M. T., and J. E. LEDOUX, 1995. LTP is accompanied by commensurate enhancement of auditory-evoked responses in a fear conditioning circuit. *Neuron* 15:127–136.

ROGAN, M. T., U. V. STÄUBLI, and J. E. LEDOUX, 1997. Fear conditioning induces associative long-term potentiation in the amygdala. *Nature* 390:604–607.

ROLLS, E. T., 1992. Neurophysiology and functions of the primate amygdala. In *The Amygdala: Neurobiological Aspects of Emotion, Memory, and Mental Dysfunction*, J. P. Aggleton, ed. New York: Wiley, pp. 143–165.

ROMANSKI, L. M., and J. E. LEDOUX, 1992. Equipotentiality of thalamo-amygdala and thalamo-cortico-amygdala projections as auditory conditioned stimulus pathways. *J. Neurosci.* 12:4501–4509.

ROMANSKI, L. M., J. E. LEDOUX, M. C. CLUGNET, and F. BORDI, 1993. Somatosensory and auditory convergence in the lateral nucleus of the amygdala. *Behav. Neurosci.* 107:444–450.

RUMELHART, D. E., and D. ZIPSER, 1986. Feature discovery by competitive learning. In *Parallel Distributed Processing: Explorations in the Microstructure of Cognition*, D. E. Rumelhart and J. L. McClelland, eds. Cambridge, Mass.: MIT Press, pp. 147–193.

SCOTT, S. K., A. W. YOUNG, A. J. CALDER, D. J. HELLAWELL, J. P. AGGLETON, and M. JOHNSON, 1997. Impaired auditory recognition of fear and anger following bilateral amygdala lesions. *Nature* 385:254–257.

SQUIRE, L. R., and S. M. ZOLA, 1996. Structure and function of declarative and nondeclarative memory systems. *Proc. Natl. Acad. Sci. U.S.A.* 93:13515–13522.

TURNER, B. H., M. MISHKIN, and M. KNAPP, 1980. Organization of the amygdalopetal projections from modality-specific cortical association areas in the monkey. *J. Comp. Neurol.* 191:515–543.

WEINBERGER, N. M., 1995. Retuning the brain by fear conditioning. In *The Cognitive Neurosciences*, 1st ed., M. S. Gazzaniga, ed. Cambridge, Mass.: MIT Press, pp. 1071–1089.

WEISSKOPF, M. G., and J. E. LEDOUX, 1997. *In-vitro* analysis of synaptic input to the dorsal subdivision of the lateral amygdala. *Soc. Neurosci. Abstr.* 23:786.

WHALEN, P. J., S. L. RAUCH, N. L. ETCOFF, S. C. MCINERNEY, M. B. LEE, and M. A. JENIKE, 1998. Masked presentations of emotional facial expressions modulate amygdala activity without explicit knowledge. *J. Neurosci.* 18:411–418.

WHITFIELD, I. C., 1980. Auditory cortex and the pitch of complex tones. *J. Acoust. Soc. Am.* 67:644–647.

75 Modulation of Memory Storage by Stress Hormones and the Amygdaloid Complex

JAMES L. McGAUGH, BENNO ROOZENDAAL, AND LARRY CAHILL

ABSTRACT It is well established that emotional arousal influences long-term explicit/declarative memory formation. The hypothesis guiding the research reviewed in this chapter is that this influence is mediated by activation of the amygdala by adrenergic and glucocorticoid stress hormones and that amygdala activation regulates memory consolidation occurring in other brain regions. This hypothesis is strongly supported by evidence that lesions of the amygdala block adrenal hormone influences on memory storage as well as evidence that drugs affecting adrenergic and glucocorticoid receptors modulate memory storage when infused directly into the amygdala after training. The memory-modulatory influences involve β-adrenergic activation in the basolateral nucleus of the amygdala. Other findings indicate that an intact amygdala is not required for expression of retention of memory influenced by amygdala activation. Findings of studies with human subjects confirm those of animal studies. Beta-adrenoceptor antagonists and lesions of the amygdala block the enhancing effects of emotional arousal on memory. Furthermore, long-term retention of emotional material is highly correlated with PET activation of the amygdala during learning. Such findings provide strong support for the hypothesis that the basolateral amygdala is part of a system that regulates the strength of explicit/declarative memories in relation to their emotional significance.

We remember most of the events in our lives rather poorly, and many of our experiences may be completely forgotten. However, memories for many experiences endure vividly. It has long been noted that emotionally arousing experiences are often the ones that are better remembered (James, 1890). Findings of studies in humans and animals provide compelling evidence that emotional experiences tend to be well remembered (Christianson, 1992). Significant personal experiences such as birthdays, weddings, special achievements, and awards tend to leave lasting memories. Studies investigating this issue report that people tend to remember rather well where they were and what they were doing when they experienced an earthquake (Neisser et al., 1996), witnessed an accident (Stratton, 1919; Bohannon, 1988), or learned surprising and important information

JAMES L. McGAUGH, BENNO ROOZENDAAL, and LARRY CAHILL Center for the Neurobiology of Learning and Memory and Department of Neurobiology and Behavior, University of California, Irvine, Calif.

(Conway et al., 1994). Rats remember where they were in an apparatus when they received a foot shock (Vazdarjanova and McGaugh, 1998). Unpleasant and shocking experiences are not the only ones that are well remembered. Winners of Nobel Prizes, Academy Awards, and lotteries no doubt remember when and where they learned of the award. Such observational, experimental, and anecdotal evidence strongly suggests that emotional responses elicited by arousing experiences influence the storage of long-term memory of the events. That is, emotional arousal appears to play a central role in enabling the significance of events to influence the strength of the memories of events (McGaugh, 1992). Through this selective and highly adaptive influence, memories of exciting experiences generally endure while those of little significance are generally weakly retained unless, of course, they are strengthened by repetition (Ebbinghaus, 1885).

This chapter reviews research investigating the neurobiological systems mediating the influence of emotional arousal on long-term memory for events. That is, our focus is primarily on emotionally influenced storage of lasting explicit (episodic/declarative) memory. Emotional experiences also create learned emotional responses (Schlosberg, 1934; Mowrer, 1947; Davis, 1992; LeDoux, 1995). The findings of our experiments emphasize the importance of distinguishing between these two mnemonic consequences of emotional arousal.

In an early effort to offer a neurobiological account of the influence of emotional arousal on memory, Livingston (1967) suggested that stimulation of the limbic system and brainstem reticular formation might promote the storage of recently activated brain events by initiating a "neurohormonal influence [favoring] future repetitions of the same neural activities" (p. 576). Kety (1972) subsequently offered the more specific suggestion that adrenergic catecholamines released in emotional states may serve "to reinforce and consolidate new and significant sensory patterns in the neocortex" (p. 73).

Although the specific details of our findings and theoretical interpretations differ in many ways from those early views offered by Livingston and Kety, they are consistent with their general hypotheses. Our findings indicate that stress-induced release of hormones from the adrenal medulla (epinephrine) and adrenal cortex (corticosterone in the rat) influence memory by activating noradrenergic systems projecting to the amygdala. The basic hypothesis that is suggested by these findings and that guides our current research is that emotionally arousing stimulation activates the amygdala, and that amygdala activity regulates the consolidation of long-term explicit memory of events by modulating neuroplasticity in other brain regions (McGaugh, Cahill, and Roozendaal, 1996; Cahill and McGaugh, 1998). That is, the amygdala is part of a system that serves to regulate the strength of memories in relation to their emotional significance. Furthermore, according to this view, the amygdala is not critically involved in the retrieval or behavioral expression of emotionally influenced explicit memory. This hypothesis is based on evidence from our studies examining the involvement of the amygdala in mediating stress hormone and drug influences on memory as well as studies of the effects of lesions and temporary inactivation of the amygdala. Although the conclusions are based primarily on findings of studies using rats, the conclusions are also supported by recent findings from studies using human subjects (Cahill, 1996).

Modulation of memory storage

Memory is, of course, inferred from changes in behavior; it is not directly observed. Experiments investigating the neural bases of learning and memory use many kinds of treatments, including lesions and drugs, that can and do directly affect behavior that is observed and used to make inferences about memory. Thus it is of critical importance to be able to distinguish the effects of the treatments on the inferred process of memory from the effects of the treatments on attentional, motivational, and motoric processes affecting the behavior used to assess memory.

The use of posttraining treatments to alter the brain functions shortly after training has provided an effective technique for dealing with this issue (McGaugh, 1966, 1989a; McGaugh and Herz, 1972). With the use of this paradigm brain functioning is experimentally altered only after learning has occurred, and with most treatments used the acute effects of the treatments are short-lasting and do not directly affect brain functioning when retention is tested a day or longer after the learning. This approach is based on the "consolidation hypothesis" originally proposed by Mueller and Pilzecker a century ago (1900) suggesting that memory traces are initially fragile and become consolidated over time. The consoli-

dation hypothesis has been strongly supported by extensive evidence from experimental as well as clinical findings (McGaugh and Herz, 1972; Weingartner and Parker, 1984). More importantly for the issues addressed in this chapter were the early findings that posttraining injections of stimulant drugs enhance memory when administered shortly after training (Breen and McGaugh, 1961; McGaugh, 1966, 1968, 1973) and are generally ineffective when administered several hours after learning (McGaugh and Herz, 1972). Such findings indicate that the drugs affect memory by modulating the consolidation of recently acquired information.

Hormonal modulation of memory storage

The susceptibility of memory storage processes to modulating influences induced after learning provides the opportunity for emotional activation to regulate the strength of memory traces representing important experiences (Gold and McGaugh, 1975; McGaugh, 1983a,b; McGaugh and Gold, 1989). It is well established that, in rats and mice, hormones of the adrenal medulla and adrenal cortex are released during and immediately after stressful stimulation of the kinds used in aversively motivated learning tasks (McCarty and Gold, 1981; McGaugh and Gold, 1989). Removal of adrenal hormones by adrenalectomy generally results in memory impairment (Borrell et al., 1983; Borrell, de Kloet, and Bohus, 1984; Oitzl and de Kloet, 1992; Roozendaal, Portillo-Marquez, and McGaugh, 1996).

EPINEPHRINE   Gold and van Buskirk (1975) were the first to report that, in adrenally intact rats, systemic posttraining injections of the adrenomedullary hormone epinephrine enhances long-term retention of inhibitory avoidance. As with stimulant drugs, the epinephrine effects were dose dependent and time dependent: Memory enhancement was greatest when the injections were administered shortly after training. Highly comparable effects have been obtained in experiments using many different types of training tasks, including inhibitory avoidance, active avoidance, discrimination learning, and appetitively motivated tasks (Introini-Collison and McGaugh, 1986; Izquierdo and Diaz, 1985; Liang, Juler, and McGaugh, 1986; Sternberg et al., 1985). Thus the epinephrine effects on memory do not depend upon any specific task or motivational requirements. The evidence strongly supports the view that epinephrine enhances consolidation of the memory of the training experience.

GLUCOCORTICOIDS   There is also extensive evidence that adrenocortical hormones are involved in modulating memory storage (for reviews see Bohus, 1994; de Kloet, 1991; Lupien and McEwen, 1997; McEwen and Sapolsky, 1995). As with epinephrine, single injections of moderate doses of glucocorticoids can enhance memory storage (Cottrell and Nakajima, 1977; Roozendaal and McGaugh, 1996a; Sandi and Rose, 1994). Because glucocorticoids are highly lipophilic, they readily enter the brain and bind directly to mineralocorticoid receptors (type I) and glucocorticoid receptors (type II) (McEwen, Weiss, and Schwartz, 1966; de Kloet, 1991). These two receptor types differ in their affinity for corticosterone and synthetic ligands. Mineralocorticoid receptors have a high affinity for the natural steroids corticosterone and aldosterone, whereas glucocorticoid receptors have a high affinity for synthetic ligands such as dexamethasone and RU 28362 (Reul and de Kloet, 1985; Reul et al., 1990; Sutanto and de Kloet, 1987). As a consequence, mineralocorticoid receptors are almost saturated during basal levels of corticosterone, whereas glucocorticoid receptors become occupied only during stress and at the circadian peak. Several findings suggest that the memory-modulating effects of glucocorticoids selectively involve activation of glucocorticoid receptors (Lupien and McEwen, 1997; Oitzl and de Kloet, 1992; Roozendaal, Portillo-Marquez, and McGaugh, 1996). Blockade of glucocorticoid receptors, but not mineralocorticoid receptors, shortly before or immediately after training impairs memory. Such findings strongly implicate the involvement of glucocorticoid receptors in memory storage and support the hypothesis that endogenously released glucocorticoids enhance memory storage.

ADRENERGIC-GLUCOCORTICOID INTERACTION   Other findings indicate that catecholamines and glucocorticoids interact in influencing memory storage. Borrell and colleagues reported that glucocorticoids alter the sensitivity of epinephrine in influencing memory storage in adrenalectomized rats (Borrell et al., 1983; Borrell, de Kloet, and Bohus, 1984). We examined glucocorticoid-adrenergic interactions on memory storage in adrenally intact rats injected with metyrapone, a drug that reduces the elevation of circulating corticosterone induced by aversive stimulation (Roozendaal, Carmi, and McGaugh, 1996). Rats received systemic injections of metyrapone or a control solution 90 minutes before training in an inhibitory avoidance task and posttraining injections of epinephrine, amphetamine, or 4-OH amphetamine (a peripherally acting derivative of amphetamine). Both amphetamine drugs are known to stimulate the release of epinephrine from the adrenal medulla (Weiner, 1985). As shown in figure 75.1, all three adrenergic drugs enhanced retention. Metyrapone

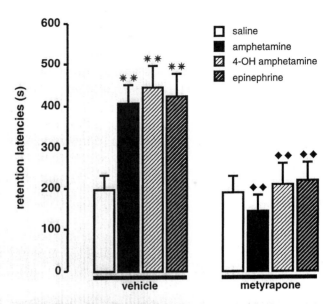

FIGURE 75.1   Step-through latencies (mean ± SEM) for a 48-hour inhibitory avoidance test. Effects of corticosteroid synthesis blockade with metyrapone (50 mg/kg) on the enhancement of memory produced by posttraining injections of amphetamine (1.0 mg/kg), 4-OH amphetamine (2.0 mg/kg), or epinephrine (0.1 mg/kg). **$p < .01$ as compared with the corresponding saline group; ◆◆ $p < .01$ as compared with the corresponding vehicle pretreatment group. (From Roozendaal, Carmi, and McGaugh, 1996.)

administration alone did not affect memory but completely blocked the memory-enhancing effects of the other three drugs. These findings indicate that stress-induced increases in plasma corticosterone and consequent activation of central glucocorticoid receptors are essential for enabling the memory-enhancing effects of epinephrine and amphetamine.

Amygdala involvement in neuromodulatory influences on memory consolidation

Extensive evidence indicates that epinephrine and glucocorticoid effects on memory are mediated by influences involving the amygdala. As epinephrine does not readily cross the blood-brain barrier, if at all, its influence on the amygdala *must* be mediated indirectly (Weil-Malherbe, Axelrod, and Tomchick, 1959). In contrast, it is well established that glucocorticoids readily enter the brain and bind directly to adrenal steroid receptors. Although these hormones differ in the way in which they influence the amygdala, they have remarkably similar effects on processes regulating memory consolidation. As will be discussed subsequently, activation of norepinephrine (NE) release in the amygdala appears to be an essential step in mediating the effects of peripheral catecholamines as well as those of glucocorticoids on memory storage.

ADRENERGIC INFLUENCES Our interest in the amygdala as a brain site mediating epinephrine effects on memory was guided by evidence that, in rats given inhibitory or active avoidance training, memory storage is modulated by electrical stimulation of the amygdala (McGaugh and Gold, 1976). Furthermore, adrenal demedullation and injections of epinephrine alter the memory-modulating effects of electrical stimulation of the amygdala (Liang, Bennett, and McGaugh, 1985). Additionally, lesions of either the amygdala or the stria terminalis, a major amygdala pathway, block epinephrine effects on memory storage (Cahill and McGaugh, 1991; Liang and McGaugh, 1983). Stria terminalis lesions alone do not block inhibitory avoidance performance, and amygdala lesions impair but do not block the learning (Liang and McGaugh, 1983; Cahill and McGaugh, 1990).

Posttraining intra-amygdala infusions of the β-adrenoceptor antagonist propranolol also block epinephrine effects on memory storage (Liang, Juler, and McGaugh, 1986). Such findings suggest that NE release in the amygdala is involved in mediating epinephrine effects on memory. In support of this implication, we and others have found that posttraining infusions of NE or the β-adrenoceptor agonist clenbuterol into the amygdala produce dose-dependent enhancement of memory storage (Introini-Collison, Miyazaki, and McGaugh, 1991; Introini-Collison, Dalmaz, and McGaugh, 1996; Liang, Juler, and McGaugh, 1986; Liang, McGaugh, and Yao, 1990; Liang, Chen, and Huang, 1995). Furthermore, posttraining intra-amygdala infusions of β-adrenoceptor antagonists impair retention and block the memory-enhancing effects of NE (Liang, Juler, and McGaugh, 1986; Liang, Chen, and Huang, 1995; Salinas et al., 1997).

Epinephrine effects on memory are also blocked by peripherally administered propranolol (Introini-Collison et al., 1992), a drug that readily enters the brain, as well as by sotalol, a β-adrenoceptor antagonist that does not readily enter the brain. The memory-modulating effects of other β-adrenoceptor agonists that enter the brain, including dipivefrin (DPE) and clenbuterol, are blocked by propranolol but not by sotalol (Introini-Collison et al., 1992). These findings, considered together with other evidence, suggest that epinephrine effects on memory storage are initiated by activation of peripheral β-adrenoceptor receptors located on vagal afferents (Schreurs, Seelig, and Schulman, 1986) that project to the nucleus of the solitary tract and that projections from the nucleus of the solitary tract release NE within the amygdala (Ricardo and Koh, 1978). Consistent with this hypothesis, inactivation of the nucleus of the solitary tract with lidocaine blocks epinephrine effects on memory (Will-

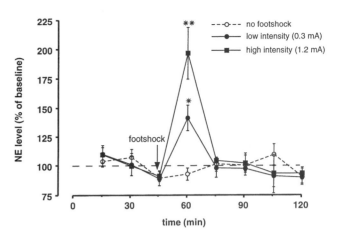

FIGURE 75.2 Effects of low- and high-intensity foot shock on norepinephrine (NE) release in the amygdala assessed by in vivo microdialysis and HPLC. NE levels are represented as mean (± SEM) of basal levels prior to foot shock. * $p < .05$; **$p < .01$ as compared with the no-foot-shock group. (From Quirarte et al., 1998.)

iams and McGaugh, 1993). Additionally, other investigators have found that memory is enhanced in an "inverted-U" manner by posttraining electrical stimulation of vagal afferents (Clark et al., 1995). These findings thus provide strong support for the hypothesis that epinephrine effects on memory storage are mediated by the amygdala and that the effects involve activation of the release of NE within the amygdala.

A major implication of this hypothesis is that stimulation comparable to that used in inhibitory avoidance training should induce the release of NE in the amygdala. In experiments using in vivo microdialysis and high-performance liquid chromatography (HPLC), we found that foot-shock stimulation of the kind typically used in inhibitory avoidance training induced NE release within the amygdala (Galvez, Mesches, and McGaugh, 1996). As is shown in figure 75.2, NE release in the amygdala following foot-shock stimulation varied with the intensity of stimulation: Low-intensity foot-shock stimulation (0.30 mA for 3 seconds) induced a 41% increase in NE release, whereas a high-intensity foot shock (1.20 mA for 3 seconds) induced a 96% increase (Quirarte et al., 1998). NE release returned to baseline levels 30 minutes after foot shock. Furthermore, NE release in the amygdala is influenced by hormones known to modulate memory storage. Peripheral injections of epinephrine (Williams et al., 1998) or the opiate antagonist naloxone potentiate NE release induced by foot shock (Quirarte et al., 1998). This latter finding is consistent with evidence that intra-amygdala infusions of β-adrenergic antagonists block naloxone effects on memory storage (Introini-Collison, Nagahara, and McGaugh, 1989; McGaugh, Introini-Collison, and Nagahara, 1988) as well as evidence that opiate agonists inhibit the release of NE in the brain (Arbilla and Langer, 1978).

GLUCOCORTICOID INFLUENCES Extensive evidence indicates that activation of adrenal steroid receptors in the hippocampus plays an important role in mediating the effects of glucocorticoids on memory (Bohus, 1994; McEwen and Sapolsky, 1995). Recent findings from our laboratory indicate that glucocorticoids also affect memory storage through influences involving the amygdala. The findings of our studies of the effects of glucocorticoids on memory for inhibitory avoidance training are similar to those of our studies of the effects of epinephrine. Lesions of the stria terminalis or amygdala block the memory-enhancing effects of post-training systemic injections of the synthetic glucocorticoid dexamethasone (Roozendaal and McGaugh, 1996a, 1996b). Furthermore, as will be discussed more extensively later, memory is modulated by intra-amygdala infusions of glucocorticoids (Roozendaal and McGaugh, 1997a), and these effects of glucocorticoids depend on noradrenergic activation in the amygdala.

INTERACTION OF NEUROMODULATORY SYSTEMS WITHIN THE AMYGDALA Activation of the noradrenergic system in the amygdala is also involved in mediating other neuromodulatory influences on memory, including those of opioid peptidergic and GABAergic systems. Posttraining systemic injections of opioid peptides and opiates generally impair memory, and as noted earlier, opiate antagonists enhance memory (Izquierdo and Diaz, 1983; McGaugh, 1989b; McGaugh, Introini-Collison, and Castellano, 1993). GABAergic antagonists and agonists enhance and impair retention, respectively (Brioni and McGaugh, 1988; Brioni, Nagahara, and McGaugh, 1989). Lesions of the amygdala or stria terminalis block opioid peptidergic and GABAergic influences on memory storage (Mc-Gaugh et al., 1986; Ammassari-Teule et al., 1991). Intra-amygdala infusions of propranolol block opiate and GABAergic influences on memory (McGaugh, Introini-Collison, and Nagahara, 1988; Introini-Collison, Naga-hara, and McGaugh, 1989). In experiments using both inhibitory avoidance and water-maze spatial tasks, intra-amygdala infusions of the β-adrenoceptor agonist clenbuterol blocked the memory-impairing effects of β-endorphin administered concurrently. Moreover, low and otherwise ineffective doses of β-endorphin and propranolol-impaired memory when infused concurrently into the amygdala (Introini-Collison, Ford, and McGaugh, 1995).

Most of our experiments have used inhibitory avoidance training. But, as noted earlier, comparable effects have been obtained in experiments using other training tasks. A series of experiments examined the involvement of the amygdala in memory for a change in reward magnitude (CRM). In these experiments rats were first trained for several days to run in a straight alley for a large reward (10 pellets of food). The reward was then reduced to 1 pellet, and changes in running speeds (i.e., slower running) assessed the next day indicated memory of the decrease in reward (CRM). Posttraining systemic administration of 4-OH amphetamine enhanced memory for CRM (Salinas, Williams, and McGaugh, 1996), and posttraining administration of the GABAergic agonist muscimol impaired memory for CRM (Salinas and McGaugh, 1995). Other findings indicate that, as with memory for other types of training, memory for CRM involves the amygdala. Posttraining intra-amygdala infusions of muscimol, lidocaine, or propranolol impaired memory for CRM (Salinas and McGaugh, 1995; Salinas, Packard, and McGaugh, 1993; Salinas et al., 1997). Additionally, posttraining intra-amygdala infusions of the GABAergic and agonist bicuculline enhanced memory for an *increase* in reward magnitude (Salinas and McGaugh, 1996). These latter findings, together with the findings that amygdala treatments affect spatial learning (e.g., Introini-Collison, Ford, and McGaugh, 1995), provide additional evidence strongly indicating that amygdala influences on memory storage are not restricted to the learning of aversive information. The neuromodulatory interactions found in our experiments are summarized schematically in figure 75.3. Additional glucocorticoid findings included in the figure are discussed in the next section.

Selective involvement of the basolateral nucleus of the amygdala

In the studies reviewed in the preceding section, the experiments involved lesions of the entire amygdaloid complex or intra-amygdala infusion volumes (0.5 or 1.0 μl) that spread throughout the amygdala. Many experiments have suggested that two of the amygdala nuclei, the basolateral (BLA) and central (CEA), are involved in aversively based learning (Davis, 1992; LeDoux, 1995). However, the findings of a series of experiments (see table 75.1) indicate that the BLA is selectively involved in mediating neuromodulatory influences on memory storage. Our initial findings of the selective involvement of the BLA came from studies investigating the effects of benzodiazepines (BZDs) on memory. It is well established that BZDs impair memory when

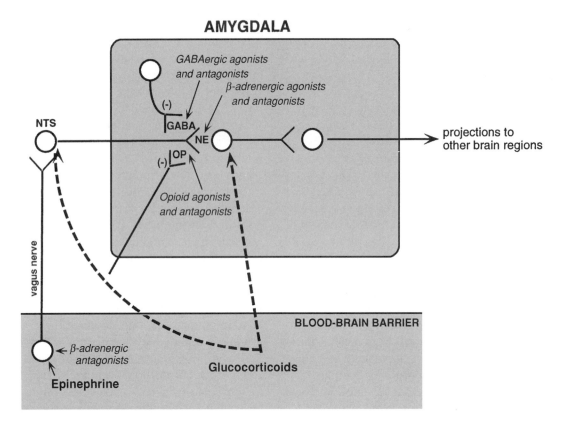

FIGURE 75.3   Schematic summarizing the interactions of neu-romodulatory influences on memory storage as suggested by the findings of our experiments.

TABLE 75.1
Basolateral amygdala is critical to memory modulation

Reference	Procedure	Basolateral Nucleus	Central Nucleus
Parent and McGaugh, 1994	Lidocaine infusion postlearning	Modulates memory	No effect
Roozendaal and McGaugh, 1997b	Infusions of glucocorticoid agonist or antagonist into AC nuclei	Modulates memory	No effect
Roozendaal and McGaugh, 1996a	Lesions of AC nuclei; systemic dexamethasone	Blocks modulation	No effect
Roozendaal, Portillo-Marquez, and McGaugh, 1996	Lesions of AC nuclei; adrenalectomy	Blocks modulation	No effect
Roozendaal and McGaugh, 1997b	Lesions of AC nuclei; infusion of glucocorticoid agonist or antagonist into hippocampus	Blocks modulation	No effect
Tomaz, Dickinson-Anson, and McGaugh, 1992	Lesions of AC nuclei; systemic diazepam	Blocks modulation	No effect
Quirarte, Roozendaal, and McGaugh, 1997a	Infusion of β-blocker into AC nuclei; systemic dexamethasone	Blocks modulation	No effect
Hatfield and McGaugh, 1999, and unpublished data	Infusion of norepinephrine into AC nuclei	Modulates memory	No effect
Da Cunha et al., 1999	Infusion of benzodiazepine antagonist into AC nuclei	Modulates memory	No effect

*All lesions excitotoxic

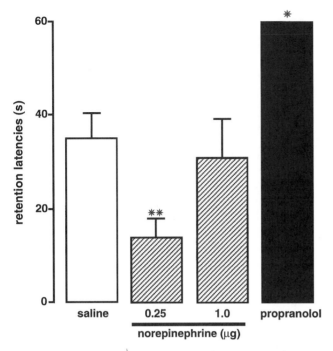

FIGURE 75.4   Retention swim latency (mean ± SEM) for 24 hours after training in a water-maze spatial task. Effects of immediate posttraining infusions of norepinephrine (NE) or the β-adrenoceptor antagonist propranolol (0.3 μg) into the basolateral amygdala. * $p < .05$; ** $p < .01$ as compared with the corresponding saline group. (From Hatfield and McGaugh, 1999.)

administered before learning (Lister, 1985) and that BZDs affect memory for inhibitory avoidance through influences on GABAergic mechanisms in the amygdala (Izquierdo, Da Cunha, and Medina, 1990; Izquierdo et al., 1990). The BLA appears to be the critical amygdala nucleus mediating the memory impairment. We found that lesions restricted to the BLA blocked BZD effects on memory for inhibitory avoidance training, whereas lesions of the CEA were ineffective. In contrast, CEA lesions alone impaired retention, whereas BLA lesions did not (Tomaz, Dickinson-Anson, and McGaugh, 1992). Additionally, when BZDs were infused selectively into the BLA or CEA, only BLA infusions impaired memory (de Souza-Silva and Tomaz, 1995). Furthermore, posttraining intra-amygdala infusions of the BZD antagonist flumazenil enhanced memory when administered into the BLA, whereas infusions into the CEA were ineffective (Da Cunha et al., in press).

Experiments examining the effects of inactivation of amygdala nuclei with posttraining infusions of lidocaine provide additional evidence that the BLA is selectively involved in modulating memory storage. Infusions of lidocaine selectively infused into the BLA

immediately after inhibitory avoidance training impaired inhibitory avoidance retention, whereas infusions administered into the CEA were ineffective (Parent and McGaugh, 1994). Thus, although, as we have just noted (Tomaz, Dickinson-Anson, and McGaugh, 1992), an intact BLA is not essential for inhibitory avoidance acquisition and retention, disruption of the functioning of the BLA shortly after learning impairs memory. Noradrenergic influences on memory storage also selectively involve the BLA. As is shown in figure 75.4, the BLA is involved in modulating memory for spatial training in a water maze (Hatfield and McGaugh, 1999). Posttraining infusions of NE into the BLA enhanced spatial memory, whereas infusions of propranolol into the BLA impaired spatial memory.

The findings of several recent experiments indicate that glucocorticoid influences on memory storage also selectively involve the BLA and that the effects require noradrenergic activation within the BLA. As is shown in figure 75.5A, lesions of the amygdala restricted selectively to the BLA block the memory-enhancing effects of posttraining systemic injections of dexamethasone (Roozendaal and McGaugh, 1996a). Furthermore, as is shown in figure 75.5B, posttraining infusions of a specific glucocorticoid receptor agonist (RU 28362) selectively enhance retention when administered into the BLA (Roozendaal and McGaugh, 1997a). In addition to disrupting the memory-modulatory effects of a glucocorticoid in an inhibitory avoidance task, lesions of the BLA also block glucocorticoid effects on memory for water-maze spatial learning (Roozendaal, Portillo-Marquez, and McGaugh, 1996). Adrenalectomy 4–5 days prior to training impaired memory in this task, and immediate posttraining dexamethasone attenuated the adrenalectomy-induced memory impairment. Additionally, BLA lesions block the effect of adrenalectomy and glucocorticoids on retention. In contrast, lesions of the CEA impaired acquisition and retention performance but did not block the glucocorticoid-induced modulation of memory storage. These findings indicate that the effects of glucocorticoids on memory storage are mediated, at least in part, by binding directly to adrenal steroid receptors in the BLA. Furthermore, as we will discuss, the BLA appears to modulate the effects, on memory storage, of activation of adrenal steroid receptors in the hippocampus (Roozendaal and McGaugh, 1997b).

Other findings from our laboratory indicate that glucocorticoid influences on memory storage depend critically on β-adrenoceptor activation within the BLA. As is shown in figure 75.6, microinfusions of β-adrenoceptor antagonists administered into the BLA blocked

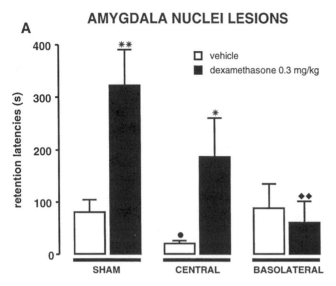

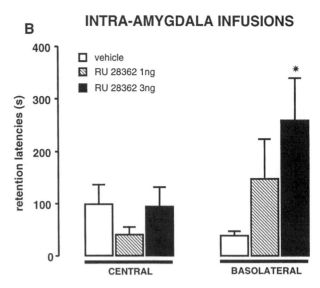

FIGURE 75.5   Step-through latencies (mean ± SEM) on a 48-hour inhibitory avoidance test. (A) Rats with sham lesions or lesions of either the central or basolateral nucleus of the amygdala had been treated with dexamethasone (0.3 mg/kg) or vehicle immediately after training. (B) Rats received post-training microinfusions of the glucocorticoid receptor agonist RU 28362 (1.0 or 3.0 ng in 0.2 µl) into the central or basolateral nucleus. * $p < .05$; ** $p < .01$ as compared with the corresponding vehicle group; • $p < .05$ as compared with the corresponding sham-lesion-vehicle group; ◆◆ $p < .01$ as compared with the corresponding sham-lesion-dexamethasone group. (From Roozendaal and McGaugh, 1996a, 1997a.)

the enhancing effects of posttraining systemic dexamethasone on inhibitory avoidance retention (Quirarte, Roozendaal, and McGaugh, 1997a). In contrast, β-adrenoceptor antagonist infusions administered into the CEA did not block dexamethasone effects on memory. Some of the effects can likely be explained by activation of glucocorticoid receptors in the ascending noradrenergic cell groups in the brain stem that are known to have high densities of glucocorticoid receptors (Harfstrand et al., 1986). As discussed earlier, noradrenergic projections from the nucleus of the solitary tract as well as the locus coeruleus activate the amygdala. In a recent study (Roozendaal, Williams, and McGaugh, 1999) we found that posttraining administration of the glucocorticoid receptor agonist RU 28362 into the nucleus of the solitary tract enhanced memory for inhibitory avoidance training. Moreover, this effect was blocked in animals given the β-adrenoceptor antagonist atenolol in the BLA. Other studies from our laboratory indicate that glucocorticoids may also interact with the noradrenergic system in the BLA in other ways. Recent findings suggest that the BLA is a locus of interaction between glucocorticoids and the noradrenergic system. As is shown in figure 75.7, blockade of glucocorticoid receptor in the BLA with the specific antagonist attenuated the dose-response memory-enhancing effect of the β-adrenoceptor agonist clenbuterol infused into the BLA posttraining (Quirarte, Roozendaal, and McGaugh, 1997b). Thus it appears that glucocorticoid receptor activation in the

BLA influences the effectiveness of β-adrenergic stimulation in modulating memory storage. Such a permissive role of glucocorticoids on the action of the noradrenergic system is consistent with findings of biochemical studies examining such interactions in hippocampal and cortical tissue (McEwen, 1987).

Amygdala interactions with other brain systems in modulating memory storage

The findings summarized in the previous section indicate that the amygdala is a site for integrating the interactions of neuromodulatory systems influencing memory storage and that the BLA is of critical importance. However, the findings do not reveal the brain sites at which amygdala activity modulates memory storage. Evidence from several kinds of studies has suggested that neural changes mediating fear conditioning may be located within the amygdala (Davis, 1992; LeDoux, 1995). Additionally, several studies have reported that long-term potentiation can be induced in the amygdala (Chapman et al., 1990; Clugnet and LeDoux, 1990; Maren and Fanselow, 1995; McKernan and Shinnick-Gallagher, 1997; Rogan, Stäubli, and LeDoux, 1997), and others have reported that drugs that block long-term potentiation also attenuate fear-based learning (Campeau, Miserendino, and Davis, 1992; Fanselow and Kim, 1994; Gewirtz and Davis, 1997; Kim and McGaugh, 1992). As yet, however, it cannot be concluded that long-term potentiation in the amygdala serves as a

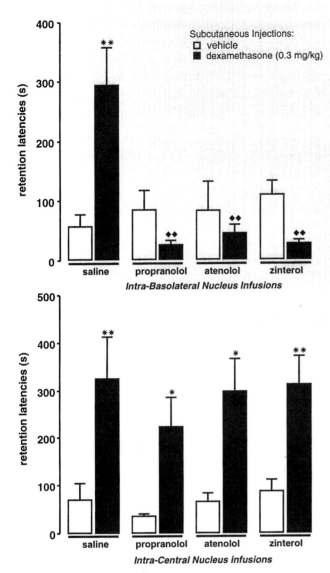

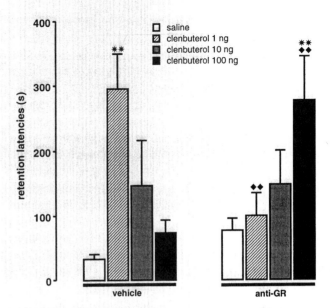

FIGURE 75.7 Step-through latencies (mean ± SEM) for a 48-hour inhibitory avoidance test. Effects of pretraining infusions of the specific glucocorticoid receptor antagonist RU 38486 (1.0 ng in 0.2 µl) into the basolateral amygdala and immediate posttraining infusions of the β-adrenoceptor agonist clenbuterol (1, 10, or 100 ng in 0.2 µl) into the BLA. ** $p < .01$ as compared with the corresponding saline group; ◆◆ $p < .01$ as compared with the corresponding vehicle-clenbuterol group. (From Quirarte, Roozendaal, and McGaugh, 1997b.)

FIGURE 75.6 Step-through latencies (mean ± SEM) for a 48-hour inhibitory avoidance test. Effects of pretraining infusions of either the nonspecific β-adrenoceptor antagonist propranolol (0.5 µg in 0.2 µl), the β_1-adrenoceptor antagonist atenolol (0.5 µg in 0.2 µl), or the β_2-adrenoceptor antagonist zinterol (0.5 µg in 0.2 µl) into the basolateral or central amygdala and immediate posttraining subcutaneous injections of dexamethasone (0.3 mg/kg). * $p < .05$; ** $p < .01$ as compared with the corresponding vehicle group; ◆◆ $p < .01$ as compared with the corresponding saline-dexamethasone group. (From Quirarte, Roozendaal, and McGaugh, 1997a.)

basis for fear-based memory (Stevens, 1998). Further, it is clear that amygdala involvement in memory is not restricted to effects involving fear conditioning. The amygdala is involved in mediating appetitive as well as aversive learning (Burns, Everitt, and Robbins, 1994). Additionally, as we have emphasized, there is extensive evidence that alteration of amygdala functioning influences memory for training involving different motivation as well as different kinds of learned information

(Burns, Everitt, and Robbins, 1994; Hatfield and Gallagher, 1995; Hatfield and McGaugh, 1999; Killcross, Robbins, and Everitt, 1997; McGaugh, Introini-Collison, and Nagahara, 1988; Salinas and McGaugh, 1996).

Other evidence strongly suggests that the amygdala is not a site of memory storage for the information acquired in the tasks typically used in our experiments, including inhibitory avoidance and water-maze spatial tasks. Lesions of the amygdala (Parent, Tomaz, and McGaugh, 1992; Parent, West, and McGaugh, 1994) or BLA (Parent and McGaugh, 1994; Parent, Avila, and McGaugh, 1995) induced one week or even one month after aversive training do not block inhibitory avoidance retention performance. Additionally, large lesions of the amygdaloid complex induced before training typically attenuate but do not block inhibitory avoidance retention performance (Cahill and McGaugh, 1990). Further, although amygdala lesions typically impair the expression of conditioned fear as assessed by fear-potentiated startle (Davis, 1992) or "freezing" behavior (LeDoux, 1995), overtraining of fear conditioning attenuates the freezing deficit (Maren, 1998) and enables reacquisition of fear-potentiated startle (Kim and Davis, 1993). Such findings clearly demonstrate that an intact amygdaloid complex is not essential for the acquisition and expression of fear conditioning.

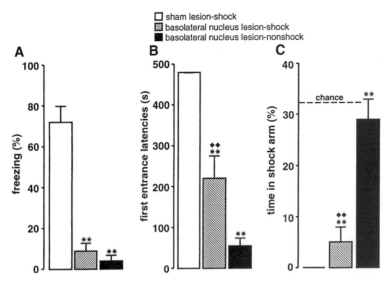

FIGURE 75.8 Effects of basolateral amygdala lesions on several measures of retention 24 hours after context foot-shock pairing in a three-arm maze. (A) Percent total time (mean ± SEM) rats spent in freezing behavior. (B) First entrance latency (mean ± SEM) to enter the former shock arm. (C) Percent total time (mean ± SEM) rats spent in the former shock arm. The dotted line depicts the level of chance. ** $p < .01$ as compared with the sham-lesion-shock group; ♦♦ $p < .01$ as compared between the basolateral nucleus lesion-nonshock and basolateral nucleus lesion-shock groups. (From Vazdarjanova and McGaugh, 1998.)

In such experiments it is, of course, essential to distinguish the effects of the lesions on performance of the response used as an index of fear from effects on learning of the significance of the cues inducing the fear. This issue can be addressed by using different behavioral measures to make inferences about learned fear. In a recent experiment in our laboratory (Vazdarjanova and McGaugh, 1998), BLA-lesioned and sham-lesioned control rats were given a series of foot shocks in one alley of a Y-maze. Other animals did not receive foot shocks. For retention testing 24 hours later the rats were placed in one of the other alleys, and several measures of behavior were recorded for 8 minutes (see figure 75.8). In comparison with the sham-lesioned controls, the lesioned rats displayed less "freezing" and entered the "shock" alley more quickly (i.e., were impaired in inhibitory avoidance). Additionally, and most importantly, in comparison with animals not given foot shock, the lesioned rats given foot shock, like the sham-lesioned controls, spent significantly less time in the alley where they had previously received foot shocks. Thus measures based on locomotor activity suggested that the behavior used to assess memory of the foot-shock training was blocked (freezing) or impaired (inhibitory avoidance) in the BLA-lesioned rats. However, it was clear that rats with BLA lesions, like nonlesioned controls, remembered the place in the maze where they had received the foot-shock stimulation. These findings indicate that an intact BLA is not required for expressing explicit/declarative memory of learned fear. Additionally, the findings emphasize the importance of using a variety of behavioral observations that enable assessment of memory for aversive stimulation.

Studies measuring conditioned neuroendocrine responses provide additional evidence that the amygdala is not a long-term site of memory for fear conditioning (Roozendaal, Koolhaas, and Bohus, 1992). In agreement with findings of others, lesions of the amygdala induced one day after training blocked rats' freezing behavior. However, conditioned neuroendocrine responses remained intact. Moreover, studies using strains of rats that differ in their tendencies to freeze in response to fearful stimulation indicated that, in both strains, posttraining intra-amygdala infusions of NE enhanced memory of an aversive event (mild shock delivered through a probe inserted into the cage). However, the expression of the enhanced memory depended on the rats' ability to freeze. In the strain of rats that normally displayed freezing, the posttraining NE enhanced freezing. In the other strain the posttraining NE did not enhance freezing but, instead, enhanced another natural defensive response (i.e., burying and biting of the probe) typically displayed by rats of this strain. Such findings indicate that amygdala NE has a comparable role in regulating memory storage for fear conditioning and inhibitory avoidance learning (Roozendaal, Koolhaas, and Bohus, 1993).

Findings of other recent experiments provide additional evidence suggesting that the lateral/basolateral nuclei have time-limited roles in modulating memory storage. Hess and colleagues (1997) examined c-fos expression induced by olfactory discrimination training and retention testing and found that c-fos in the BLA was selectively activated by the training. Quirk, Armony, and LeDoux (1997) recorded unit activity in the lateral amygdala and auditory cortex of rats given fear conditioning and extinction and reported that conditioned changes in cell firing in the auditory cortex generally occurred after changes in the amygdala. Furthermore, amygdala units extinguished relatively rapidly, whereas the cortical units persisted in responding during the extinction. A recent study (LaBar et al., 1998), using fMRI brain imaging to study changes induced by classical fear conditioning in human subjects, reported findings indicating a time-limited role for the amygdala for such learning. These findings suggested, "The amygdala, therefore, may preferentially signal the detection of affective signals when they are novel, or in the initial stages of learning when their emotional meaning is actively encoded" (LaBar et al., 1998, p. 940). Another study using fMRI to study brain changes induced by classical fear conditioning in humans (Buchel et al., 1998) reported finding habituation in the lateral amygdala nucleus during continued activation of cortical areas and concluded that "these observations suggest that with time, mnemonic representations of behaviorally salient contexts are expressed in *cortical* regions other than medial temporal lobe structures" (p. 954). Collectively, these findings provide additional support for our view that the amygdala has a temporally limited role in modulating memory storage occurring elsewhere in the brain (Cahill and McGaugh, 1998; McGaugh et al., 1984; McGaugh, 1989c; McGaugh, Cahill, and Roozendaal, 1996; Packard et al., 1995).

The findings of several experiments provide additional evidence that the amygdala is involved in regulating memory consolidation occurring in other brain regions. The amygdala sends efferent projections to many brain regions including direct projections to the striatum via the stria terminalis. Additionally, the finding that N-methyl-D-aspartate infused into the amygdala induces the expression of the proto-oncogene c-fos in the dentate gyrus of the dorsal hippocampus and the caudate nucleus indicates that the amygdala is functionally connected with both of these brain structures (Packard et al., 1995).

There is considerable evidence based on "double-dissociation" studies indicating that the caudate nucleus and hippocampus are involved in mediating different forms of memory (Packard and McGaugh, 1992, 1996). Hippocampal lesions selectively impair water-maze spatial learning (swimming to a submerged platform) (Morris et al., 1982; Moser, Moser, and Anderson, 1993; Olton,

Becker, and Handelman, 1979), whereas caudate lesions selectively impair water-maze visually cued learning (swimming to a visible platform) (Packard and McGaugh, 1992). The findings of several recent experiments indicate that the amygdala modulates memory storage for both hippocampal-dependent and caudate nucleus–dependent learning tasks (Packard, Cahill, and McGaugh, 1994; Packard and Teather, 1998). As is shown in table 75.2, unilateral posttraining infusions of amphetamine administered into the dorsal hippocampus immediately after a single training session enhanced memory storage for the spatial version of the water maze but not for the cued version, whereas amphetamine infused into the caudate nucleus after training enhanced memory for the cued but not the spatial task. However, amphetamine injected into the amygdala posttraining enhanced memory storage for both the spatial and the cued versions of the task. These findings clearly indicate that activation of the amygdala modulates memory storage processes for both hippocampal-dependent and caudate nucleus-dependent tasks. Additionally, inactivation of the amygdala prior to the retention tests did not block the enhanced retention induced by the posttraining intra-amygdala infusions of amphetamine (Packard, Cahill, and McGaugh, 1994). In other experiments examining the memory-enhancing effects of posttraining intra-amygdala infusions of amphetamine (Packard and Teather, 1998), infusions of lidocaine into the hippocampus prior to retention testing selectively blocked the memory enhancement obtained in the spatial task, whereas infusions of lidocaine into the caudate selectively blocked the enhanced memory for cued training. And, as was found in the earlier experiment (Packard, Cahill, and McGaugh, 1994), lidocaine infused into the amygdala prior to the retention test did not block amphetamine-induced memory enhancement in either task. The finding that an intact amygdala is not required for the expression of retention of either the spatial or the cued learning provides further evidence that the learning is not mediated by lasting neural changes located within the amygdala.

Other recent findings indicate that inputs from the BLA play a role in enabling the processing of hippocampally dependent memory (Roozendaal, Sapolsky, and McGaugh, 1998). Posttraining intrahippocampal administration of a glucocorticoid receptor agonist enhanced retention of inhibitory avoidance training. However, the memory enhancement was completely blocked in animals with BLA lesions. Lesions of the CEA were ineffective (Roozendaal and McGaugh, 1997b). Consistent with other studies indicating the importance of the BLA noradrenergic system in memory storage modulation, antagonism of β-adrenoceptors in the BLA with atenolol also blocked the memory-enhancing effects of glucocorticoid administration into the hippocampus. (Roozendaal et al., 1998).

These findings are of interest in relation to evidence indicating that selective lesions of the BLA, but not the CEA, attenuate the induction of long-term potentiation in the dentate gyrus in vivo (Ikegaya, Saito, and Abe, 1994, 1995a). A β-adrenoceptor antagonist infused into the BLA also blocked dentate-gyrus long-term potentiation (Ikegaya et al., 1997). Moreover, high-frequency stimulation of the BLA facilitates the induction of long-term potentiation in the dentate gyrus (Ikegaya, Saito, and Abe, 1995b). Thus these physiological findings are consistent with findings of behavioral studies indicating that modulation of memory storage involves noradrenergic influences in the BLA and that the BLA influences memory by modulating memory storage in other brain structures. Another important feature of a recent study (Roozendaal et al., 1998) and those by Ikegaya and colleagues is that the effects of the glucocorticoid receptor agonist on memory as well as electrical stimulation of the hippocampus on long-term potentiation were blocked only by manipulation of the ipsilateral BLA. Lesions or pharmacological inhibition of the contralateral BLA were not effective in altering the hippocampal effects. Although at present it is not known precisely how the BLA affects hippocampal function, some evidence indicates an involvement of the BLA–nucleus accumbens pathway. The nucleus accumbens receives projections from both the BLA and hippocampus (O'Donnell and Grace, 1995). As discussed previously, lesions of the stria terminalis, which carries the projections from the BLA to the nucleus accumbens, exert effects highly comparable to those induced by amygdala or selective BLA lesions. Moreover, excitotoxic lesions of the nucleus accumbens also block the memory-modulating effects of posttraining systemic injections of dexamethasone (Setlow, Roozendaal, and McGaugh, 1999).

Emotionally influenced memory storage in human subjects

Several recent studies of memory in human subjects provide additional evidence that drugs affecting adrenergic systems modulate memory storage and that the effects are mediated through influences involving the amygdala. As noted earlier, there is extensive evidence from animal experiments that posttraining systemic (or intra-amygdala) administration of amphetamine enhances memory storage. Consistent with those findings, Soetens and colleagues (Soetens, D'Hooge, and Hueting, 1993; Soetens et al., 1995) reported that administration of amphetamine to human subjects before or immediately after learning of word lists enhanced long-term retention of the words.

Other recent experiments examined the effects of β-adrenoceptor antagonists on memory in human subjects. One experiment (Cahill et al., 1994) examined in healthy volunteers the effect of the β-adrenoceptor antagonist propranolol or a placebo on long-term (i.e., 1-

TABLE 75.2

Amygdala modulation of hippocampal-dependent and caudate nucleus–dependent memory processes

	Spatial Task Retention	Cued Task Retention
Posttraining Infusions		
d-amphetamine, hippocampus[1]	Enhanced	No effect
d-amphetamine, caudate nucleus[1]	No effect	Enhanced
d-amphetamine, amygdala[1]	Enhanced	Enhanced
d-amphetamine, amygdala Lidocaine, hippocampus[2]	Enhancement blocked	Enhanced
d-amphetamine, amygdala Lidocaine, caudate nucleus[2]	Enhanced	Enhancement blocked
Posttraining and Pretesting Infusions		
Post: d-amphetamine, hippocampus Pre: lidocaine, hippocampus[2]	Enhancement blocked	(Not tested)
Post: d-amphetamine, caudate nucleus Pre: lidocaine, caudate nucleus[2]	(Not tested)	Enhancement blocked
Post: d-amphetamine, amygdala Pre: lidocaine, amygdala[1]	Enhanced	Enhanced

[1] Packard, Cahill, and McGaugh (1994); Packard and Teather (1998)
[2] Packard and Teather (1998)

week) memory for either an emotionally neutral story or a closely matched but more emotionally arousing story. Propranolol selectively impaired memory for the emotionally arousing story. The memory impairment could not be attributed to effects on attention, sedation, or emotional reactions of the subjects during story viewing. Another recent study confirmed the impairing effect of propranolol on memory for the emotional story and found that nadolol (a β-adrenoceptor antagonist that does not easily cross the blood-brain barrier) did not affect memory for either the emotionally arousing or neutral story (van Stegeren et al., 1998). The lack of effect of nadolol on memory suggests that the impairing effect of propranolol in this situation likely results from central, rather than peripheral, actions of the drug. Last, Nielson and Jensen (1994) examined the effect of β-adrenoceptor antagonists on enhanced memory induced by physical arousal (i.e., increased muscle tension). The arousal did not enhance retention in elderly subjects who were taking beta-blockers as medication. These experiments are consistent with extensive findings of animal studies indicating that modulation of explicit or declarative memory storage by emotional arousal involves activation of β-adrenoceptors.

In addition to β-adrenoceptor activation, amygdala function is now implicated in enhanced memory for emotional material in humans. Experiments using the same general procedures used in the experiment by Cahill and colleagues (1994) indicate that emotional arousal does not enhance long-term declarative memory in humans with selective, bilateral amygdala lesions (Cahill et al., 1995; Adolphs et al., 1997). Interestingly, the reactions of amygdala-damaged subjects to the emotional material in these studies appeared normal, suggesting therefore that the amygdala in humans may not be as critical for the production of an emotional reaction per se as for processes translating an emotional reaction into enhanced long-term memory. It is of interest that, in contrast to findings seen in subjects with damaged amygdalae, amnesic subjects with intact amygdalae demonstrate normal enhancement of memory for emotional material (Hamann, Cahill, and Squire, 1997; Hamann et al., 1997).

The results of a recent PET scan study of memory in human subjects provide further evidence that the amygdala is involved in emotionally influenced memory (Cahill et al., 1996). Subjects viewed a series of brief, emotionally arousing videos and, in a second session, a series of relatively emotionally neutral videos. Three weeks later memory of the videos was assessed with a surprise free-recall test. As is shown in figure 75.9, glucose metabolic rate of the right amygdala induced by viewing the emotional film clips correlated highly (+0.93) with the number of films recalled. Amygdala activity did

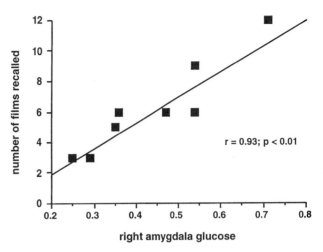

FIGURE 75.9 Amygdala activity in humans correlated with the formation of memory for emotionally arousing information. Graph shows correlation between glucose utilization in the right amygdala of 8 healthy subjects while viewing a series of relatively emotionally arousing (negative) films and long-term (3-week) recall of those films. (From Cahill et al., 1996.)

not correlate significantly with subjects' self-assessed emotional reactions to viewing the films. Consistent with the findings from patients with amygdala damage, these PET findings suggest greater involvement of the human amygdala in the formation of long-term memory for emotionally arousing events than in the production of emotion per se.

Conclusions

Collectively, these studies of emotionally influenced memory in human subjects are clearly consistent with findings of animal experiments indicating that β-adrenoceptor receptor activation and the amygdala participate in the formation of long-term, explicit/declarative memory for emotional events. Our findings based on studies of memory in animal and human subjects are consistent with those from other laboratories indicating that adrenal stress hormones and the amygdala, especially the BLA, are involved in regulating the consolidation of emotionally influenced explicit/declarative memory. Noradrenergic activation within that nucleus appears to be critical. Our findings also indicate that an intact amygdala is not required for the expression of emotionally influenced explicit/declarative memory and suggest that the amygdala regulates memory consolidation processes by modulating neural plasticity in other brain regions. The findings provide strong support for the hypothesis that the BLA is part of a neuromodulatory system that regulates the strength of explicit/declarative memories in relation to their emotional significance.

ACKNOWLEDGMENTS This research was supported by US-PHS Grant MH12526 from NIMH (JLM), an R.W. and Leona Gerard Family Trust (BR and LC) and USPHS MH57508 (LC).

REFERENCES

ADOLPHS, R., L. CAHILL, R. SCHUL, and R. BABINSKY, 1997. Impaired declarative memory for emotional stimuli following bilateral amygdala damage in humans. *Learn. Mem.* 4:291–300.

AMMASSARI-TEULE, M., F. PAVONE, C. CASTELLANO, and J. L. MCGAUGH, 1991. Amygdala and dorsal hippocampus lesions block the effects of GABAergic drugs on memory storage. *Brain Res.* 551:104–109.

ARBILLA, S., and S. Z. LANGER, 1978. Morphine and beta-endorphin inhibit release of noradrenaline from cerebral cortex but not of dopamine from rat striatum. *Nature* 271:559–561.

BOHANNON, J. N., 1988. Flashbulb memories of the space shuttle disaster: A tale of two theories. *Cognition* 29:179–196.

BOHUS B., 1994. Humoral modulation of learning and memory processes: Physiological significance of brain and peripheral mechanisms. In J. Delacour, *The Memory System of the Brain.* Advanced Series of Neuroscience, vol. 4. Singapore: World Scientific, pp. 337–364.

BORRELL, J., E. R. DE KLOET, and B. BOHUS, 1984. Corticosterone decreases the efficacy of adrenaline to affect passive avoidance retention of adrenalectomized rats. *Life Sci.* 34:99–105.

BORRELL, J., E. R. DE KLOET, D. H. G. VERSTEEG, and B. BOHUS, 1983. Inhibitory avoidance deficit following short-term adrenalectomy in the rat: The role of adrenal catecholamines. *Behav. Neural Biol.* 39:241–258.

BREEN, R. A., and J. L. MCGAUGH, 1961. Facilitation of maze learning with posttrial injections of picrotoxin. *J. Comp. Physiol. Psych.* 54:498–501.

BRIONI, J. D., and J. L. MCGAUGH, 1988. Posttraining administration of GABAergic antagonists enhance retention of aversively motivated tasks. *Psychopharmacology* 96:505–510.

BRIONI, J. D., A. H. NAGAHARA, and J. L. MCGAUGH, 1989. Involvement of the amygdala GABAergic system in the modulation of memory storage. *Brain Res.* 487:105–112.

BUCHEL, C., J. MORRIS, R. J. DOLAN, and K. J. FRISTON, 1998. Brain systems mediating aversive conditioning: An event-related fMRI study. *Neuron* 20:947–957.

BURNS, L. H., B. J. EVERITT, and T. W. ROBBINS, 1994. Intra-amygdala infusion of the *N*-methyl-D-aspartate receptor antigonist AP5 impairs acquisition but not performance of discriminated approach to an appetitive CS. *Behav. Neural Biol.* 61:242–250.

CAHILL, L., 1996. The neurobiology of memory for emotional events: Converging evidence from infra-human and human studies. In *Function and Dysfunction in the Nervous System, Symposium 61.* Cold Spring Harbor, N.Y.: Cold Spring Harbor Press, pp. 259–264.

CAHILL, L., R. BABINSKY, H. MARKOWITSCH, and J. L. MCGAUGH, 1995. The amygdala and emotional memory. *Nature* 377:295–296.

CAHILL, L., R. HAIER, J. FALLON, M. ALKIRE, C. TANG, D. KEATOR, J. WU, and J. L. MCGAUGH, 1996. Amygdala activity at encoding correlated with long-term, free recall of emotional information. *Proc. Natl. Acad. Sci. U.S.A.* 93:8016–8021.

CAHILL, L., and J. L. MCGAUGH, 1990. Amygdaloid complex lesions differentially affect retention of tasks using appetitive and aversive reinforcement. *Behav. Neurosci.* 104:532–543.

CAHILL, L., and J. L. MCGAUGH, 1991. NMDA-induced lesions of the amygdaloid complex block the retention enhancing effect of posttraining epinephrine. *Psychobiology* 19:206–210.

CAHILL, L., and J. L. MCGAUGH, 1998. Mechanisms of emotional arousal and lasting declarative memory. *Trends Neurosci.* 21:294–299.

CAHILL, L., B. PRINS, M. WEBER, and J. L. MCGAUGH, 1994. Beta-adrenergic activation and memory for emotional events. *Nature* 371:702–704.

CAMPEAU, S., M. J. D. MISERENDINO, and M. DAVIS, 1992. Intra-amygdala infusion of the n-methyl-d-aspartate receptor antignonist AP5 blocks acquisition but not expression of fear-potentiated startle to an auditory conditioned stimulus. *Behav. Neurosci.* 106:569–574.

CHAPMAN, P. F., E. W. KAIRISS, C. L. KEENAN, and T. H. BROWN, 1990. Long-term synaptic potentiation in the amygdala. *Synapse* 6:271–278.

CHRISTIANSON, S. A., ed., 1992. *The Handbook of Emotion and Memory: Research and Theory.* Hillsdale, N.J.: Lawrence Erlbaum.

CLARK, K. B., S. E. KRAHL, D. C. SMITH, and R. A. JENSEN, 1995. Post-training unilateral vagal stimulation enhances retention performance in the rat. *Neurobiol. Learn. Mem.* 63:213–216.

CLUGNET, M. C., and J. E. LEDOUX, 1990. Synaptic plasticity in fear conditioning circuits: Induction of LTP in the lateral nucleus of the amygdala by stimulation of the medial geniculate body. *Neuroscience* 10:2818–2824.

CONWAY, M. A., S. J. ANDERSON, S. F. LARSEN, C. M. DONNELLY, M. A. MCDANIEL, A. G. R. MCCLELLAND, R. E. RAWLES, and R. H. LOGIE, 1994. The formation of flashbulb memories. *Mem. Cogn.* 22:326–343.

COTTRELL, G. A., and S. NAKAJIMA, 1977. Effects of corticosteroids in the hippocampus on passive avoidance behavior in the rat. *Pharmacol. Biochem. Behav.* 7:277–280.

DA CUNHA, C., B. ROOZENDAAL, A. VAZDARJANOVA, and J. L. MCGAUGH, in press. Microinfusions of flumazenil into the basolateral but not central nucleus of the amygdala enhance memory consolidation in rats. *Neurobiol. Learn. Mem.*

DAVIS, M., 1992. The role of the amygdala in conditioned fear. In J. Aggleton, *The Amygdala.* New York: Wiley-Liss, pp. 255–306.

DE KLOET, E. R., 1991. Brain corticosteroid receptor balance and homeostatic control. *Front. Neuroendocrinol.* 12:95–164.

DE SOUZA-SILVA, M. A., and C. TOMAZ, 1995. Amnesia after diazepam infusion into basolateral but not central amygdala of *Rattus norvegicus. Neuropsychobiology* 32:31–36.

EBBINGHAUS, H., 1885. *Uber das Gedachtnis.* Leipzig: Duncker and Humbolt.

FANSELOW, M. S., and J. J. KIM, 1994. Acquisition of contextual Pavlovian fear conditioning is blocked by application of an NMDA receptor antagonist D,L-2-amino-5-phosphonovaleric acid to the basolateral amygdala. *Behav. Neuorsci.* 108:210–212.

GALVEZ, R., M. MESCHES, and J. L. MCGAUGH, 1996. Norepinephrine release in the amygdala in response to footshock stimulation. *Neurobiol. Learn. Mem.* 66:253–257.

GEWIRTZ, J. C., and M. DAVIS, 1997. Second-order fear conditioning prevented by blocking NMDA receptors in amygdala. *Nature* 388:471–474.

GOLD, P. E., and J. L. MCGAUGH, 1975. A single-trace, two process view of memory storage processes. In: D. Deutsch and J. A. Deutsch, *Short-Term Memory*. New York: Academic Press, pp. 355–378.

GOLD, P. E., and R. VAN BUSKIRK, 1975. Facilitation of time-dependent memory processes with posttrial epinephrine injections. *Behav. Biol.* 13:145–153.

HAMANN, S. B., L. CAHILL, J. L. MCGAUGH, and L. R. SQUIRE, 1997. Intact enhancement of declarative memory for emotional material in amnesia. *Learn. Mem.* 4:301–309.

HAMMAN, S. B., L. CAHILL, and L. R. SQUIRE, 1997. Emotional perception and memory in amnesia. *Neuropsychology* 11:1–10.

HARFSTRAND, A., K. FUXE, A. CINTRA, L. AGNATI, L. MZINI, A. C. WIKSTROM, S. OKRET, Z. Y. YU, M. GOLDSTEIN, H. STEINBUSCH, A. VERHOFSTAD, and J.-A. GUSTAFSSON, 1986. Glucocorticoid receptor immunoreactivity in monoaminergic neurons of rat brain. *Proc. Natl. Acad. Sci. U.S.A.* 83:9779–9783.

HATFIELD, T., and M. GALLAGHER, 1995. Taste-potentiated odor conditioning: Impairment produced by an infusion of an *N*-methyl-D-aspartate antagonist into the basolateral amygdala. *Behav. Neurosci.* 109:663–668.

HATFIELD, T., and J. L. MCGAUGH, 1999. Norepinephrine infused into the basolateral amygdala posttraining enhances retention in a spatial water maze task. *Neurobiol. Learn. Mem.* 91:232–239.

HESS, U. S., C. M. GALL, R. GRANGER, and G. LYNCH, 1997. Differential patterns of c-fos mRNA expression in amygdala during successive stages of odor discrimination learning. *Learn. Mem.* 4:262–283.

IKEGAYA, Y., H. SAITO, and K. ABE, 1994. Attenuated hippocampal long-term potentiation in basolateral amygdala-lesioned rats. *Brain Res.* 656:157–164.

IKEGAYA, Y., H. SAITO, and K. ABE, 1995a. Requirement of basolateral amygdala neuron activity for the induction of long-term potentiation in the dentate gyrus in vivo. *Brain Res.* 671:351–354.

IKEGAYA, Y., H. SAITO, and K. ABE, 1995b. High-frequency stimulation of the basolateral amygdala facilitates the induction of long-term potentiation in the dentate gyrus in vivo. *Neurosci. Res.* 22:203–207.

IKEGAYA, Y., H. SAITO, K. ABE, and K. NAKANISHI, 1997. Amygdala β-noradrenergic influence on hippocampal long-term potentiation in vivo. *NeuroReport* 8:3143–3146.

INTROINI-COLLISON, I., C. DALMAZ, and J. L. MCGAUGH, 1996. Amygdala β-noradrenergic influences on memory storage involve cholinergic activation. *Neurobiol. Learn. Mem.* 65:57–64.

INTROINI-COLLISON, I., L. FORD, and J. L. MCGAUGH, 1995. Memory impairment induced by intra-amygdala β-endorphin is mediated by noradrenergic influences. *Neurobiol. Learn. Mem.* 63:200–205.

INTROINI-COLLISON, I. B., and J. L. MCGAUGH, 1986. Interaction of adrenergic, cholinergic and opioid systems in modulation of memory storage. *Soc. Neurosci. Abstr.* 12:710.

INTROINI-COLLISON, I. B., and J. L. MCGAUGH, 1987. Naloxone and beta-endorphin alter the effects of posttraining epinephrine on retention of an inhibitory avoidance response. *Psychopharmacology* 92:229–235.

INTROINI-COLLISON, I., B. MIYAZAKI, and J. L. MCGAUGH, 1991. Involvement of the amygdala in the memory-enhancing effects of clenbuterol. *Psychopharmacology* 104:541–544.

INTROINI-COLLISON, I. B., A. H. NAGAHARA, and J. L. MCGAUGH, 1989. Memory-enhancement with intra-amygdala posttraining naloxone is blocked by concurrent administration of propranolol. *Brain Res.* 476:94–101.

INTROINI-COLLISON, I., D. SAGHAFT, G. NOVACK, and J. L. MCGAUGH, 1992. Memory-enhancing effects of posttraining dipivefrin and epinephrine: Involvement of peripheral and central adrenergic receptors. *Brain Res.* 572:81–86.

IZQUIERDO, I., C. DA CUNHA, C. H. HUANG, R. WALZ, C. WOLFMAN, and J. H. MEDINA, 1990. Posttraining down-regulation of memory consolidation by a GAMA-A mechanism in the amygdala modulated by endogenous benzodiazepines. *Behav. Neural Biol.* 54:105–109.

IZQUIERDO, I., C. DA CUNHA, and J. MEDINA, 1990. Endogenous benzodiazepine modulation of memory processes. *Neurosci. Biobehav. Rev.* 14:419–424.

IZQUIERDO, I., and R. D. DIAZ, 1983. Effect of ACTH, epinephrine, β-endorphin, naloxone, and of the combination of naloxone or β-endorphin with ACTH or epinephrine on memory consolidation. *Psychoneuroendocrinology* 8:81–87.

IZQUIERDO, I., and R. D. DIAZ, 1985. Influence on memory of posttraining or pre-test injections of ACTH, vasopressin, epinephrine or β-endorphin and their interaction with naloxone. *Psychoneuroendocrinology* 10:165–172.

JAMES, W., 1890. *The Principles of Psychology.* New York: Henry Holt.

KETY, S., 1972. Brain catecholamines, affective states and memory. In J. L. McGaugh, ed. *The Chemistry of Mood, Motivation and Memory.* New York: Plenum Press, pp. 65–80.

KILLCROSS, S., T. W. ROBBINS, and B. J. EVERITT, 1997. Different types of fear-conditioned behaviour mediated by separate nuclei within amygdala. *Nature* 388:377–380.

KIM, M., and M. DAVIS, 1993. Electrolytic lesions of the amygdala block acquisition and expression of fear-potentiated startle even with extensive training but do not prevent reacquisition. *Behav. Neurosci.* 7:580–595.

KIM, M., and J. L. MCGAUGH, 1992. Effects of intra-amygdala injections of NMDA receptor antagonists on acquisition and retention of inhibitory avoidance. *Brain Res.* 585:35–48.

LABAR, K. S., J. C. GATENBY, J. C. GORE, J. E. LEDOUX, and E. A. PHELPS, 1998. Human amygdala activation during conditioned fear acquisition and extinction: A mixed trial fMRI study. *Neuron* 20:937–945.

LEDOUX, J. E., 1995. Emotion: Clues from the brain. *Annu. Rev. Psychol.* 46:209–235.

LIANG, K. C., C. BENNETT, and J. L. MCGAUGH, 1985. Peripheral epinephrine modulates the effects of posttraining amygdala stimulation on memory. *Behav. Brain Res.* 15:93–100.

LIANG, K., L. CHEN, and T.-E. HUANG, 1995. The role of amygdala norepinephrine in memory formation: Involvement in the memory enhancing effect of peripheral epinephrine. *Chin. J. Physiol.* 38:81–91.

LIANG, K. C., R. JULER, and J. L. MCGAUGH, 1986. Modulating effects of posttraining epinephrine on memory: Involvement of the amygdala noradrenergic system. *Brain Res.* 368:125–133.

LIANG, K. C., and J. L. MCGAUGH, 1983. Lesions of the stria terminalis attenuate the enhancing effect of posttraining epinephrine on retention of an inhibitory avoidance response. *Behav. Brain Res.* 9:49–58.

LIANG, K. C., J. L. MCGAUGH, and H. YAO, 1990. Involvement of amygdala pathways in the influence of posttraining amygdala norepinephrine and peripheral epinephrine on memory storage. *Brain Res.* 508:225–233.

LISTER, R., 1985. The amnesic action of benzodiazepines in man. *Biobehav. Rev.* 9:87–94.

LIVINGSTON, R. B., 1967. Reinforcement: A study program. In G. C. Quarton, T. Melnechuk, and F. O. Schmitt, eds., *The Neurosciences.* New York: Rockefeller University Press, pp. 568–576.

LUPIEN, S. J., and B. S. MCEWEN, 1997. The acute effects of corticosteroids on cognition: Integration of animal and human model studies. *Brain Res. Rev.* 24:1–27.

MAREN, S., 1998. Overtraining does not mitigate contextual fear conditioning deficits produced by neurotoxic lesions of the basolateral amygdala. *J. Neurosci.* 18:3088–3097.

MAREN, S., and M. FANSELOW, 1995. Synaptic plasticity in the basolateral amygdala induced by hippocampal formation stimulation in vivo. *J. Neurosci.* 15:7548–7564.

MCCARTY, R., and P. E. GOLD, 1981. Plasma catecholamines: Effects of footshock level and hormonal modulators of memory storage. *Horm. Behav.* 15:168–182.

MCEWEN, B. S., 1987. Glucocorticoid-biogenic amine interactions in relation to mood and behavior. *Biochem. Pharmacol.* 36:1755–1763.

MCEWEN, B. S., and R. M. SAPOLSKY, 1995. Stress and cognitive function. *Curr. Opin. Neurobiol.* 5:205–216.

MCEWEN, B. S., J. M. WEISS, and L. S. SCHWARTZ, 1966. Selective retention of corticosterone by limbic structors in the rat brain. *Nature* 220:911–912.

MCGAUGH, J. L., 1966. Time-dependent processes in memory storage. *Science* 153:1351–1358.

MCGAUGH, J. L., 1968. Drug facilitation of memory and learning. In *Psychopharmacology: A Review of Progress.* PHS Publication 1836. Washington, DC: U.S. Government Printing Office, pp. 891–904.

MCGAUGH, J. L., 1973. Drug facilitation of learning and memory. *Annu. Rev. Pharmacol.* 13:229–241.

MCGAUGH, J. L., 1983a. Hormonal influences on memory. *Annu. Rev. Psychol.* 34:297–323.

MCGAUGH, J. L., 1983b. Preserving the presence of the past: Hormonal influences on memory storage. *Am. Psychol.* 38: 161–174.

MCGAUGH, J. L., 1989a. Dissociating learning and performance: Drug and hormone enhancement of memory storage. *Brain Res. Bull.* 23:339–345.

MCGAUGH, J. L., 1989b. Involvement of hormonal and neuromodulatory systems in the regulation of memory storage. *Annu. Rev. Neurosci.* 12:255–287.

MCGAUGH, J. L., 1989c. Modulation of memory storage processes. In P. R. Solomon, G. R. Goethels, C. M. Kelly, and B. R. Stevens, eds. *Memory: Interdisciplinary Approaches.* New York: Springer Verlag, pp. 33–64.

MCGAUGH, J. L., 1992. Affect, neuromodulatory systems and memory storage. In S. A. Christianson, ed. *Handbook of Emotion and Memory: Current Research and Theory.* Hillsdale, N.J.: Erlbaum, pp. 245–268.

MCGAUGH, J. L., L. CAHILL, and B. ROOZENDAAL, 1996. Involvement of the amygdala in memory storage: Interaction with other brain systems. *Proc. Natl. Acad. Sci. U.S.A.* 93: 13508–13514.

MCGAUGH, J. L., and P. E. GOLD, 1976. Modulation of memory by electrical stimulation of the brain. In M. R. Rosenzweig and E. L. Bennett, eds. *Neural Mechanisms of Learning and Memory.* Cambridge, Mass.: MIT Press, pp. 549–560.

MCGAUGH, J. L., and P. E. GOLD, 1989. Hormonal modulation of memory. In R. B. Brush and S. Levine, eds. *Psychoendocrinology.* New York: Academic Press, pp. 305–339.

MCGAUGH, J. L., and M. J. HERZ, 1972. *Memory Consolidation.* San Francisco: Albion.

MCGAUGH, J. L., I. INTROINI-COLLISON, and C. CASTELLANO, 1993. Involvement of opioid peptides in learning and memory. In A. Herz, H. Akil, and E. J. Simon, eds. *Handbook of Experimental Pharmacology, Opioids,* parts 1 and 2. Heidelberg, Germany: Springer-Verlag, pp. 419–477.

MCGAUGH, J. L., I. B. INTROINI-COLLISON, R. G. JULER, and I. IZQUIERDO, 1986. Stria terminalis lesions attenuate the effects of posttraining naloxone and β-endorphin on retention. *Behav. Neurosci.* 100:839–844.

MCGAUGH, J. L., I. B. INTROINI-COLLISON, and A. H. NAGAHARA, 1988. Memory-enhancing effects of posttraining naloxone: Involvement of β-noradrenergic influences in the amygdaloid complex. *Brain Res.* 446:37–49.

MCGAUGH, J. L., K. C. LIANG, C. BENNETT, and D. B. STERNBERG, 1984. Adrenergic influences on memory storage: Interaction of peripheral and central systems. In G. Lynch, J. L. McGaugh, and N. M. Weinberger, eds. *Neurobiology of Learning and Memory.* New York: Guilford Press, pp. 313–333.

MCKERNAN, M. G., and P. SHINNICK-GALLAGHER, 1997. Fear conditioning induces a lasting potentiation of synaptic currents in vitro. *Nature* 390:607–611.

MORRIS, R. G. M., P. GARRUD, J. N. P. RAWLINS, and J. O'KEEFE, 1982. Place navigation impaired in rats with hippocampal lesions. *Nature* 297:681–683.

MOSER, E., M.-B. MOSER, and P. ANDERSEN, 1993. Spatial learning impairment parallels the magnitude of dorsal hippocampal lesions, but is hardly present following ventral lesions. *J. Neurosci.* 13:3916–3925.

MOWRER, O. H., 1947. On the dual nature of learning—A reinterpretation of "conditioning" and "problem-solving." *Harv. Educ. Rev.* 17:102–148.

MUELLER, G. E., and A. PILZECKER, 1900. Experimentelle Beitrage zur Lehre vom Gedächtnis. *Z. Psychol.* 1:1–288.

NEISSER, U., E. WINOGRAD, E. BERGMAN, A. SCHREIBER, S. PALMER, and M. S. WELSOM, 1996. Remembering the earthquake: Direct experience versus hearing the news. *Memory* 4:337–357.

NIELSON, K., and R. JENSEN, 1994. Beta-adrenergic receptor antagonist antihypertensive medications impair arousal-induced modulation of working memory in elderly humans. *Behav. Neural Biol.* 62:190–200.

O'DONNELL, P., and A. A. GRACE, 1995. Synaptic interactions among excitatory afferents to nucleus accumbens neurons: Hippocampal gating of prefrontal cortical input. *J. Neurosci.* 15:3622–3639.

OITZL, M. S., and E. R. DE KLOET, 1992. Selective corticosteroid antagonists modulate specific aspects of spacial orientation learning. *Behav. Neurosci.* 106:62–71.

OLTON, D. S., J. T. BECKER, and G. E. HANDELMAN, 1979. Hippocampus, space, and memory. *Behav. Brain Sci.* 2:313–365.

PACKARD, M. G., L. CAHILL, and J. L. MCGAUGH, 1994. Amygdala modulation of hippocampal-dependent and caudate nucleus-dependent memory processes. *Proc. Natl. Acad. Sci. U.S.A.* 91:8477–8481.

PACKARD, M. G., and J. L. MCGAUGH, 1992. Double dissociation of fornix and caudate nucleus lesions on acquisition of two water maze tasks: Further evidence for multiple memory systems. *Behav. Neurosci.* 106:439–446.

PACKARD, M. G., and J. L. MCGAUGH, 1996. Inactivation of hippocampus or caudate nucleus with lidocaines differentially affects expression of place and response learning. *Neurobiol. Learn. Mem.* 65:65–72.

PACKARD, M. G., and L. TEATHER, 1998. Amygdala modulation of multiple memory systems: Hippocampus and caudate-putamen. *Neurobiol. Learn. Mem.* 69:163–203.

PACKARD, M. G., C. WILLIAMS, L. CAHILL, and J. L. MCGAUGH, 1995. The anatomy of a memory modulatory system: From periphery to brain. In N. Spear, L. Spear, and M. Woodruff, eds., *Neurobehavioral Plasticity: Learning, Development and Response to Brain Insults.* Hillsdale, N.J.: Lawrence Erlbaum, pp. 149–184.

PARENT, M., E. AVILA, and J. L. MCGAUGH, 1995. Footshock facilitates the expression of aversively motivated memory in rats given post-training amygdala basolateral complex lesions. *Brain Res.* 676:235–244.

PARENT, M., and J. L. MCGAUGH, 1994. Posttraining infusion of lidocaine into the amygdala basolateral complex impairs retention of inhibitory avoidance training. *Brain Res.* 661:97–103.

PARENT, M., C. TOMAZ, and J. L. MCGAUGH, 1992. Increased training in an aversively motivated task attenuates the memory impairing effects of posttraining N-methyl-D-aspartic acid–induced amygdala lesions. *Behav. Neurosci.* 106:791–799.

PARENT, M., M. WEST, and J. L. MCGAUGH, 1994. Memory of rats with amygdala lesions induced 30 days after footshock-motivated escape training reflects degree of original training. *Behav. Neurosci.* 6:1080–1087.

QUIRARTE, G. L., R. GALVEZ, B. ROOZENDAAL, and J. L. MCGAUGH, 1998. Norepinephrine release in the amygdala in response to footshock and opioid peptidergic drugs. *Brain Res.* 808:134–140.

QUIRARTE, G. L., B. ROOZENDAAL, and J. L. MCGAUGH, 1997a. Glucocorticoid enhancement of memory storage involves noradrenergic activation in the basolateral amygdala. *Proc. Natl. Acad. Sci. U.S.A.* 94:14048–14053.

QUIRARTE, G. L., B. ROOZENDAAL, and J. L. MCGAUGH, 1997b. Glucocorticoid receptor antagonist infused into the basolateral amygdala inhibits the memory enhancing effects of the noradrenergic agonist infused clenbuterol. *Soc. Neurosci. Abstr.* 23:1314.

QUIRK, G. J., J. L. ARMONY, and J. E. LEDOUX, 1997. Fear conditioning enhances different temporal components of tone-evoked spike trains in auditory cortex and lateral amygdala. *Neuron* 19:613–624.

REUL, J. M. H. M., and E. R. DE KLOET, 1985. Two receptors system for corticosterone in rat brain: Microdistribution and differential occupation. *Endocrinology* 117:2505–2512.

REUL, J. M. H. M., E. R. DE KLOET, F. J. VAN SLUYS, A. RIJNBERK, and J. ROTHUIZEN, 1990. Binding characteristics of mineralocorticoid and glucocorticoid receptors in dog brain and pituitary. *Endocrinology* 127:907–915.

RICARDO, J., and E. KOH, 1978. Anatomical evidence of direct projections from the nucleus of the solitary tract to the hypothalamus, amygdala, and other forebrain structures in the rat. *Brain Res.* 153:1–26.

ROGAN, M. T., U. V. STÄUBLI, and J. E. LEDOUX, 1997. Fear conditioning induces associative long-term potentiation in the amygdala. *Nature* 390:604–607.

ROOZENDAAL, B., O. CARMI, and J. L. MCGAUGH, 1996. Adrenocortical suppression blocks the memory-enhancing effects of amphetamine and epinephrine. *Proc. Natl. Acad. Sci. U.S.A.* 93:1429–1433.

ROOZENDAAL, B., J. M. KOOLHAAS, and B. BOHUS, 1992. Central amygdaloid involvement in neuroendocrine correlates of conditioned stress response. *J. Neuroendocrinol.* 4:483–489.

ROOZENDAAL, B., J. M. KOOLHAAS, and B. BOHUS, 1993. Posttraining norepinephrine infusion into the central amygdala differentially enhances later retention in roman high-avoidance and low-avoidance rats. *Behav. Neurosci.* 7:575–579.

ROOZENDAAL, B., and J. L. MCGAUGH, 1996a. Amygdaloid nuclei lesions differentially affect glucocorticoid-induced memory enhancement in an inhibitory avoidance task. *Neurobiol. Learn. Mem.* 65:1–8.

ROOZENDAAL, B., and J. L. MCGAUGH, 1996b. The memory-modulatory effects of glucocorticoids depend on an intact stria terminalis. *Brain Res.* 709:243–350.

ROOZENDAAL, B., and J. L. MCGAUGH, 1997a. Glucocorticoid receptor agonist and antagonist administration into the basolateral but not central amygdala modulates memory storage. *Neurobiol. Learn. Mem.* 67:176–179.

ROOZENDAAL, B., and J. L. MCGAUGH, 1997b. Basolateral amygdala lesions block the memory-enhancing effect of glucocorticoid administration in the dorsal hippocampus of rats. *Euro. J. Neurosci.* 9:76–83.

ROOZENDAAL, B., B. T. NGUYEN, A. E. POWER, and J. L. MCGAUGH, 1998. Basolateral amygdala noradrenergic influence on the memory-enhancing effect of glucocorticoid infusions into the hippocampus. *Soc. Neurosci Abstr.* 24:1901.

ROOZENDAAL, B., G. PORTILLO-MARQUEZ, and J. L. MCGAUGH, 1996. Basolateral amygdala lesions block glucocorticoid-induced modulation of memory for spatial learning. *Behav. Neurosci.* 110:1074–1083.

ROOZENDAAL, B., R. SAPOLSKY, and J. L. MCGAUGH, 1998. Basolateral amygdala lesions block the disruptive effects of long-term adrenalectomy on spatial memory. *Neuroscience* 84:453–465.

ROOZENDAAL, B., C. L. WILLIAMS, and J. L. MCGAUGH, in press. Glucocorticoid receptor activation of noradrenergic neurons within the rat nucleus of the solitary tract facilitates memory consolidation: Involvement of the basolateral amygdala. *Euro. J. Neurosci.*

SALINAS, J., I. B. INTROINI-COLLISON, C. DALMAZ, and J. L. MCGAUGH, 1997. Posttraining intra-amygdala infusion of oxotremorine and propranolol modulate storage of memory for reduction in reward magnitude. *Neurobiol. Learn. Mem.* 68:51–59.

SALINAS, J., and J. L. MCGAUGH, 1995. Muscimol induces retrograde amnesia for changes in reward magnitude. *Neurobiol. Learn. Mem.* 63:277–285.

SALINAS, J., and J. L. MCGAUGH, 1996. The amygdala modulates memory for changes in reward magnitude: Involvement of the amygdaloid gabaergic system. *Behav. Brain Res.* 80:87–98.

SALINAS, J., M. G. PACKARD, and J. L. MCGAUGH, 1993. Amygdala modulates memory for changes in reward magnitude: Reversible post-training inactivation with lidocaine attenuates the response to a reduction reward. *Behav. Brain Res.* 59:153–159.

SALINAS, J., C. L. WILLIAMS, and J. L. MCGAUGH, 1996. Peripheral posttraining administration of 4-OH amphetamine enhances retention of a reduction in reward magnitude. *Neurobiol. Learn. Mem.* 65:192–195.

SANDI, C., and S. P. R. ROSE, 1994. Corticosterone enhances long-term potentiation in one-day-old chicks trained in a weak passive avoidance learning paradigm. *Brain Res.* 647:106–112.

SCHREURS, J., T. SEELIG, and H. SCHULMAN, 1986. β_2-adrenergic receptors on peripheral nerves. *J. Neurochem.* 46:294–296.

SCHLOSBERG, H., 1934. Conditioned responses in the white rat. *J. Gen. Psychol.* 45:303–335.

SETLOW, B., B. ROOZENDAAL, and J. L. MCGAUGH, 1999. Involvement of a basolateral amygdala nucleus accumbens pathway in induced modulation of memory storage. Submitted.

SOETENS, E., R. D'HOOGE, and J. E. HUETING, 1993. Amphetamine enhances human-memory consolidation. *Neurosci. Lett.* 161:9–12.

SOETENS, E., S. CASAER, R. D'HOOGE, and J. E. HUETING, 1995. Effect of amphetamine on long-term retention of verbal material. *Psychopharmacology* 119:155–162.

STERNBERG, D. B., K. ISAACS, P. E. GOLD, and J. L. MCGAUGH, 1985. Epinephrine facilitation of appetitive learning: Attenuation with adrenergic receptor antagonists. *Behav. Neural Biol.* 44:447–453.

STEVENS, C. F., 1998. A million dollar question: Does LTP = memory? *Neuron* 20:1–2.

STRATTON, G., 1919. Retroactive hyperamnesia and other emotional effects on memory. *Psychol. Rev.* 26:474–486.

SUTANTO, W., and E. R. DE KLOET, 1987. Species-specificity of corticosteroid receptors in hamster and rat brains. *Endocrinology* 121:1405-1411.

TOMAZ, C., H. DICKINSON-ANSON, and J. L. MCGAUGH, 1992. Basolateral amygdala lesions block diazepam-induced anterograde amnesia in an inhibitory avoidance task. *Proc. Natl. Acad. Sci. U.S.A.* 89:3615–3619.

VAN STEGEREN, A. H., W. EVERAERD, L. CAHILL, J. L. MCGAUGH, and L. J. G. GOOREN, 1998. Memory for emotional events: Differential effects of centrally versus peripherally acting beta-blocking agents. *Psychopharmacology* 138:305–310.

VAZDARJANOVA, A., and J. L. MCGAUGH, 1998. Basolateral amygdala is not a critical locus for memory of contextual fear conditioning. *Proc. Natl. Acad. Sci. U.S.A.*, 95:15003–15007.

WEIL-MALHERBE, H., J. AXELROD, and R. TOMCHICK, 1959. Blood-brain barrier for adrenaline. *Science* 129:1226–1228.

WEINER, N., 1985. Norepinephrine, epinephrine, and the sympathomimetic amines. In A. G. Gilman, L. S. Goodman, T. W. Rall, and F. Murad, eds., *The Pharmacological Basis of Therapeutics.* New York: Macmillan, pp. 145–180.

WEINGARTNER, H., and E. S. PARKER, 1984. *Memory Consolidation.* Hillsdale, N.J.: Erlbaum.

WILLIAMS, C. L., and J. L. MCGAUGH, 1993. Reversible lesions of the nucleus of the solitary tract attenuate the memory-modulating effects of posttraining epinephrine. *Behav. Neurosci.* 107:1–8.

WILLIAMS, C. L., D. MEN, E. C. CLAYTON, and P. E. GOLD, 1998. Norepinephrine release in the amygdala following systemic injection of epinephrine or escapable foot shock: Contribution of the nucleus of the solitary tract. *Behav. Neurosci.* 112:1414–1422.

76 Neurophysiological Basis of Emotion in Primates: Neuronal Responses in the Monkey Amygdala and Anterior Cingulate Cortex

TAKETOSHI ONO AND HISAO NISHIJO

ABSTRACT Both the amygdala and anterior cingulate cortex, which are main components of the rhinencephalon, have been implicated in emotion. Neuronal responses in the amygdala and anterior cingulate cortex of the monkey to stimuli that were considered to be biologically significant were studied in behavioral tasks that involved the discrimination of different rewarding and aversive stimuli. Neurons in the amygdala displayed modulation of responses to objects in various situations including satiation and reversal, and in a specific context in which food delivery was expected. This finding suggests that the amygdala is involved in ongoing evaluation of sensory stimuli in a context-relevant manner. However, our results suggest that the anterior cingulate cortex integrates inputs from other emotion-related regions and from the frontal cortex, and sends the information to motor executive centers to behave appropriately in a variety of specific motivational or emotional behavioral contexts. The present results could provide neuronal bases for the involvement of these emotion-related areas in human emotional and motivated behaviors.

It has been reported that emotional responses are highly dependent on cognitive factors (Hebb, 1972). Extensive studies using Pavlovian conditioning indicate that animals such as rodents can well localize a relevant simple stimulus in the environment and display emotional responses to such a stimulus (i.e., conditioned emotional response). In higher mammals such as monkeys, a wider variety of complex stimuli can be recognized by the sophisticated cortical sensory systems. In turn, this ability enables higher mammals to display emotional responses to a wider variety of complex stimuli such as "death masks" to which rodents do not respond (Hebb, 1972). The amygdala (AM) and the anterior cingulate cortex (AC) as well as cortical sensory systems have been implicated in a variety of cognitive and emotional pro-

TAKETOSHI ONO and HISAO NISHIJO   Department of Physiology, Faculty of Medicine, Toyama Medical and Pharmaceutical University, Toyama, Japan

cesses, and their evolution and differentiation in mammals are parallel to the evolution of complex emotional and social behaviors (MacLean, 1986; Stephan, Frahm, and Baron, 1987). It has been suggested that sequential processing of sensory information occurs in the neocortex (Turner, Mishkin, and Knapp, 1980; Pons et al., 1987). The AM receives highly integrated sensory information from all modalities in a late stage of this sequential processing (Gloor, 1960; Aggleton, Burton, and Passingham, 1980; Turner, Mishkin, and Knapp, 1980; Amaral et al., 1992), and emotional and cognitive functions of the AM depend on such connections (Turner, Mishkin, and Knapp, 1980). The anterior part of area 24 (AC) receives inputs from the prefrontal cortex and the emotion-related areas including the AM as well as other association cortices (Vogt and Pandya, 1987).

Bilateral lesion of the temporal cortex including the AM produces Klüver-Bucy syndrome (Klüver and Bucy, 1939; Weiskrantz, 1956; Gloor, 1960). This syndrome consists of a complex set of several affective disorders: tameness; approach to normally fear-inducing stimuli such as humans, gloves, and bear models (loss of fear); increased and inappropriate sexual behavior (hypersexuality); and tendency to investigate orally and put inedible objects into mouth (oral tendency). Approach to aversive stimuli and deficits in discriminating food from nonfood are known as *psychic blindness*, which is an inability to identify the biological significance of stimuli. The AM is suggested to be a focal point of causes contributing to Klüver-Bucy syndrome (Gloor, 1960; Goddard, 1964). Electrical stimulation and unit recording as well as selective lesion studies also manifest the crucial role of the AM in emotional behavior (Kaada, 1972; Sanghera, Rolls, and Roper-Hall, 1979; Ono et al., 1980; LeDoux, 1987; Davis, 1992). However, animals with AM lesions had neither sensory deficits (Aggleton, 1992) nor deficits in executing motivated and emotional behaviors in response to unconditioned stimuli (i.e., primary reinforcement) (Gallagher, Graham, and Holland, 1990; Everitt, Cador, and Robbins, 1989; Everitt et al., 1991).

This evidence supports the idea that the AM is related to ongoing evaluation of the affective significance of learned conditioned sensory stimuli and of the learning processes that associate sensory stimuli with affective significance (stimulus-affect association) (Weiskrantz, 1956; Geschwind, 1965; Jones and Mishkin, 1972; Mishkin and Aggleton, 1981; Gaffan and Harrison, 1987; Nishijo, Ono, and Nishino, 1988a, 1988b; Cador, Robbins, and Everitt, 1989; Everitt, Cador, and Robbins, 1989; Everitt et al., 1991).

This conclusion leads to two important ways in which the AM is functionally significant. First, the amygdalectomized animals cannot appreciate the emotional significance of a stimulus, resulting in deficits in emotional expression due to inability to activate the executing systems for behavioral and autonomic responses. This function may depend on the sequential sensory pathway from sensory association cortices to the brainstem executive system including the hypothalamus for emotional expression through the AM. Second, the AM might contribute to plasticity of cortical neurons during learning through two pathways directed to the neocortex. One consists of the widespread direct cortical projections from the AM (Amaral and Price, 1984; Amaral et al., 1992), and the other, cholinergic projections to the neocortex by way of the substantia innominata, to which the AM projects (Russchen, Amaral, and Price, 1985). It has been reported that receptive fields of auditory-responsive neurons in the neocortex could be changed plastically by conditioned associative learning (Weinberger et al., 1990). Computational study suggested that this plasticity of receptive fields in the neocortex was attributed to neocortical inputs from a value-dependent learning system consisting of the AM and substantia innominata (Friston et al., 1994).

However, most works on the functional significance of the AC have been concerned with their role in "emotional activity" or responses to noxious stimuli (Papez, 1937; Vogt, David, and Olson, 1992). Papez (1937) viewed the cingulate cortex as the cortical receptive region for the experiencing of emotion and argued, "The cingulate cortex is the seat of dynamic vigilance by which environmental experiences are endowed with an emotional consciousness." Tumors of the cingulate cortex are known to produce apathy, drowsiness, memory defects, and stupor (Vogt, David, and Olson, 1992). Recent PET studies suggested that the obsessive-compulsive disorder of humans could be ascribed to hyperactivity of the AC (Sawle et al., 1991). Patients with

affective illness such as schizophrenics had abnormal $GABA_A$ receptor binding in the AC (Benes et al., 1992). Activity and volume of the AC of depressive patients was decreased (Drevets et al., 1997). All of these relations suggest AC involvement in emotion and complex behavioral control.

In this chapter, we first characterize the responses of AM and AC neurons to affective sensory stimuli that are related to ongoing evaluation of the affective significance of the stimuli. Amygdala and AC neuronal responses to stimuli that were considered to be biologically significant (Weiskrantz, 1956; Horel, Keating, and Misantone, 1975; Perrett, Rolls, and Caan, 1982) were studied in various behavioral tasks that involved the discrimination of different rewarding and aversive stimuli (Ono et al., 1980; Fukuda, Ono, and Nakamura, 1987; Nishijo et al., 1986, 1997; Nishijo, Ono, and Nishino, 1988a, 1988b). Comparison of AM and AC neuronal responsiveness to affective sensory stimuli may elucidate differences in the functions of these two structures. To characterize AM neuronal responsiveness indicating AM involvement in stimulus-affect association, some AM neurons were further tested by changing the affective significance of the stimuli presented. Second, since both disconnection of sensory inputs to the AM and disconnection of outputs from the AM to the hypothalamus resulted in Klüver-Bucy syndrome (Downer, 1961; Hilton and Zbrozyna, 1963; Horel, Keating, and Misantone, 1975; Gaffan, Gaffan, and Harrison, 1988), effects of disconnection of AM inputs and outputs were investigated (Fukuda, Ono, and Nakamura, 1987). Functional connections between the association cortex and the AM, which may underlie AM responsiveness to complex sensory stimuli, were investigated by analyzing neuronal response changes during reversible disconnection of the inferotemporal cortex (ITCx) from the AM. Disconnection of the AM from the hypothalamus, which receives AM outputs, was also tested by cooling the AM during recording of lateral hypothalamic (LHA) neurons.

Amygdalar neuronal responses during visual discrimination

TASK PARADIGMS *Macaca fuscata* monkeys were restrained painlessly in a stereotaxic apparatus by a previously prepared, surgically fixed head holder designed in our laboratory (Ono et al., 1980; Ono, Nishino, et al., 1981). They sat in a chair facing a panel that had two shutters (one opaque and one transparent) and a bar for operant responding. Liquid was accessible to the monkey through a small spout controlled by an electromagnetic valve [figure 76.1A,a] (Nishijo,

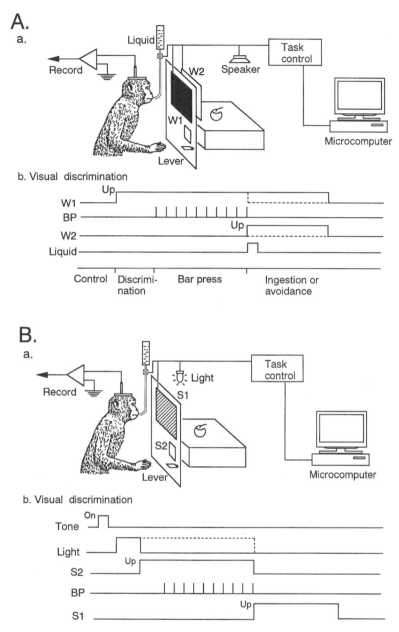

FIGURE 76.1 Schema of experimental setups and task paradigms of original (A) and modified (B) versions. (A) Original version. (a) A monkey sat in a chair facing a panel with a bar, and a window covered by two shutters (W1, an opaque shutter; W2, a transparent shutter in front of a stage). Liquid was delivered from a spout near the monkey's mouth. (b) Time sequence of visual discrimination tasks that involved presentation of food or nonfood objects (solid line), white and red cylinders associated with liquid (dashed line), and brown cylinder associated with avoidance (dashed line). Shutters opened at Up. BP: indications of individual bar presses and time during which they occurred. Liquid dispensed from spout after last bar press if a particular object was presented. (B) Modified version. (a) Schema of an ex-

perimental setup. The monkey could see an object on a stage through a one-way mirror (S1) in front of the stage when a light was turned on. However, another shutter (S2) prevented access to the bar. (b) Time sequence of visual discrimination task of the modified version. A trial was initiated by a warning tone (Tone). After a delay of at least 2 seconds, S2 was opened automatically. The S1 shutter was opened by the last bar press. The monkey's behavior and the neuronal responses were essentially the same in this and the previously described situation. The monkey can take a drop of juice dispensed from spout after the last bar press, or a cookie or raisin from the stage, which is made available by the opening of S1 after the last bar press; it can also avoid shock by bar pressing.

Ono, and Nishino, 1988a, 1988b). Aversive stimulation was administered as a weak electric shock applied between the earlobes. In the visual discrimination task an opaque shutter (W1) was opened at random intervals.

The monkey could see an object through a transparent shutter (W2) in front of the stage. The animal could then obtain the object if it wanted to, by pressing the bar a predetermined number of times (fixed ratio, FR

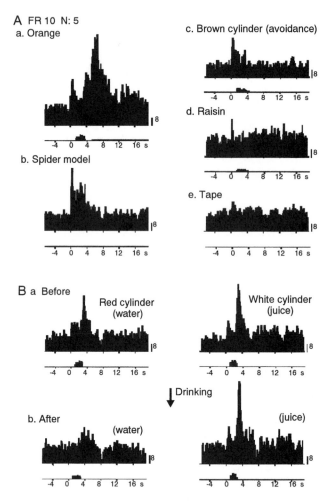

FIGURE 76.2 Modulation of responses of an evaluation-related neuron by satiation in the amygdala. (A) Activity increased in response to preferred food (a), aversion-related objects (c), and new object (b), but not in response to familiar less preferred food (d) or neutral nonfood (e). (B) Modulation of neuronal responses during discrimination and ingestion phases by satiety to water. Responses to sight of water-associated red cylinder and water ingestion decreased after drinking water (80 ml), but responses to sight of juice-associated white cylinder and juice ingestion did not change. Bar presses: histogram on time scale. Abscissas: time, seconds; zero, W1 open; each histogram bin, 200 ms. Ordinates: summed responses for N trials as indicated. FR: fixation ratio. Histogram pairs upper and lower show firing rates and bar presses totalled for N trials, respectively.

10-30). The last bar-press opened W2 and the animal could then take the object and ingest it if it was desirable food (figure 76.1A,b, solid line). Similarly, when the FR criterion was met in the drinking portion of the task, W1 was automatically closed and a drop of potable liquid (juice or water) portended by some symbolic object (white or red cylinder, cube, etc.) could be licked from a small spout (figure 76.1A,b, dashed line). A white or red cylinder was usually associated, respectively, with juice or water, for example. In the avoidance situation of the task, a brown cylinder, for example, was associated with a weak electric shock. If the animal saw the brown cylinder and heard the 1200-Hz tone, it had to complete an FR schedule within 4–6 seconds to avoid electric shock. The last bar press closed W1 (figure 76.1A,b, dashed line).

RESPONSE CHARACTERISTICS OF THE AM NEURONS
More than 1500 AM neurons were tested by recording activity changes in response to various objects or to stimulation of various sensory modalities that did or did not have affective significance. Since detailed sensory responsiveness of the AM neurons was reported previously (Nishijo et al., 1986; Nishijo, Ono, and Nishino, 1988a, 1988b), here we present the data showing that AM neurons are involved in ongoing evaluation of sensory stimuli.

About one-fourth of the AM neurons differentially responded to various objects with biological significance during visual stimulation (differential vision-responsive neurons). These AM neurons responded strongly to the sight of unfamiliar objects regardless of whether they were food or nonfood. Among these differential vision-responsive neurons, more than half responded consis-

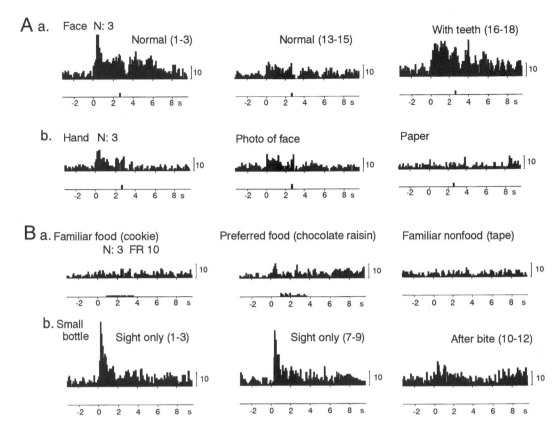

FIGURE 76.3 Responses of specific neurons displaying modulation of responses. (A) A specific neuron responded to certain objects including real human faces. (a) Neuronal responses to a real normal human face (Normal) gradually decreased in repeated trials. However, the activity of the neuron increased when a face with open mouth (With teeth) was presented. (b) The neuron responded to a real human hand and a photo of face, but not to a piece of paper. In a and b, the stimulus was presented by a shutter with an aperture of 15 cm. (B) Responses of a specific neuron that showed response habituation.

(a) The neuron did not respond to familiar regular food (cookie), familiar preferred food (chocolate raisin), or familiar nonfood (tape). (b) The neuron responded to a small bottle from the 1st to the 9th trials. Note that the neuron did not respond to it after the monkey took and bit it in the 10th to 12th trials. Numbers in parentheses indicate order of trials in sequential presentation. Abscissas: time, seconds; zero, shutter opening; each histogram bin, 100 ms. Histogram on time scale in A indicates accumulated trigger signals indicating shutter closing. Other descriptions as for figure 76.2.

tently to rewarding objects such as familiar food and the red or white cylinders associated with water or juice, as well as to aversive nonfood objects such as the brown cylinder that was associated with electric shock, a syringe, a glove, and so on, but not to neutral nonfood objects (tape) (evaluation-related neurons). The remaining differential vision-responsive neurons responded to not all but some of visual stimuli with biological significance (specific neurons).

The response magnitude of evaluation-related neurons was significantly different in response to different objects in that the neuron responded more strongly to more preferred food than to less preferred food. Another characteristic of these neurons was that response magnitudes of the neurons were modulated by satiation. A typical response of one neuron of this type, located in the corticomedial group of the AM, is shown in figure 76.2. This neuron responded strongly to preferred food (figure 76.2A,a, orange) and weakly to regular food (figure 76.2

A,d, raisin) and less to neutral nonfood (figure 76.2A,e, tape) although all of these were familiar to the animal. It also responded to a punishment-associated object (figure 76.2A,c, brown cylinder) and to an unfamiliar but potentially aversive object (figure 76.2A,b, spider model). Then, this neuron was tested with satiation. Before satiation, the neuron responded to sight of both red and white cylinders, and to ingestion of both water and juice (figure 76.2B,a). After the drinking of 80 ml of water, responses to the water-associated red cylinder and to water ingestion decreased, but responses to the juice-associated white cylinder did not change (figure 76.2B,b).

Most AM neurons including both evaluation-related and specific neurons display habituation of neuronal responses to the stimuli in repeated trials. Results suggest that response habituation to a given object is attributed to changes in biological significance of the object during the trials, rather than to simple sensory habituation. Figure 76.3A shows an example of such an AM

A. Evaluation-related

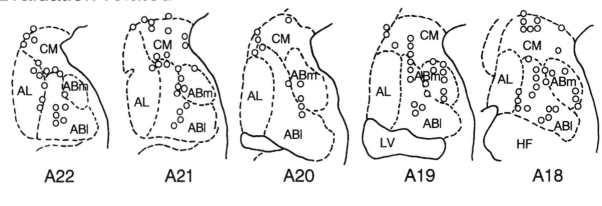

A22   A21   A20   A19   A18

B. Specific

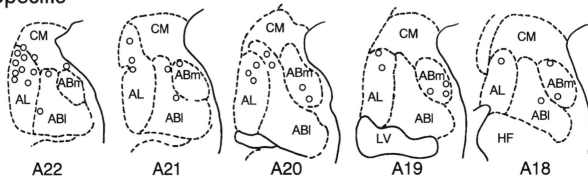

A22   A21   A20   A19   A18

FIGURE 76.4 Recording sites of the evaluation-related (A) and specific neurons (B) in the amygdala. Numbers below each section indicate distance (mm) anterior from interaural line.

CM, corticomedial group of the amygdala; AL, lateral nucleus; ABl, basolateral nucleus; ABm, basomedial nucleus; LV, lateral ventricle; HF, hippocampal formation.

neuron that responded to specific stimuli such as human faces. Although the neuron did not respond to familiar foods and nonfoods (data not shown), it responded strongly to a real human face with a closed mouth (figure 76.3A,a). It also responded to a human hand and a photo of a human face, but not to a plain piece of paper (figure 76.3A,b). When the neuron was tested repeatedly with the same human face, responses to the face gradually decreased from 1st to 15th trials. However, neuronal responses to the face increased again when the human face with open mouth was presented to the monkey (figure 76.3A,a). Figure 76.3B illustrates another example of a specific AM neuron that showed response habituation in repeated trials. The neuron responded specifically to a small bottle (figure 76.3B,b). The neuron continued to respond to the small bottle from the 1st to 9th trials (figure 76.3B,b). However, the responses to the small bottle suddenly decreased after the monkey took and bit it. These results suggest that a decrease in neuronal responses reflected a decrease in the biological significance of objects. This habituation of neuronal responses to objects including faces is consistent with a recent PET study in which an

increase in cerebral blood flow in the AM in response to fearful and happy faces rapidly habituated in repeated trials (Breiter et al., 1996). The recording sites of evaluation-related and specific neurons are depicted in figure 76.4. Although both types of AM neurons were located in the lateral, basolateral, basomedial, and corticomedial group of the AM, specific neurons were located mainly in the basal nuclei (i.e., lateral, basolateral, and basomedial nuclei of the AM).

Some AM neurons were further tested with either complex objects such as a walking human or specific situations (or contexts) in which food delivery was expected. Figure 76.5 illustrates an example of an evaluation-related neuron that was tested with human movements. The neuron was initially tested with several foods and nonfoods. The neuron responded to the sight of familiar food such as a cookie (figure 76.5A,a) and a piece of raisin (not shown). When the neuron was tested with a piece of raisin that was slightly salted on its hidden side, the monkey ate it in 3 successive trials. The neuron responded strongly to the sight and ingestion of the salted raisin during these trials (figure 76.5A,b). However, the neuronal responses to the

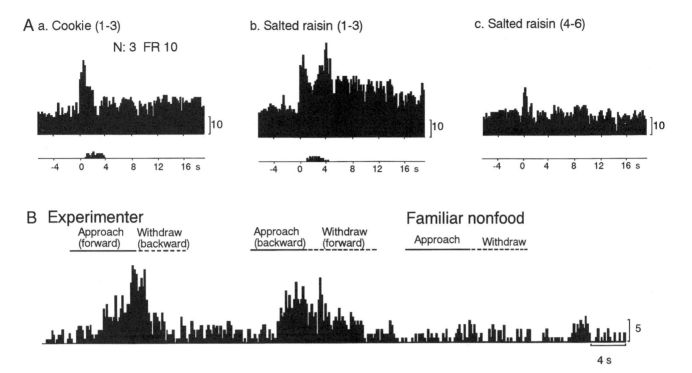

A
a. Cookie (1-3)
N: 3 FR 10

b. Salted raisin (1-3)

c. Salted raisin (4-6)

B Experimenter

Approach (forward) Withdraw (backward)

Approach (backward) Withdraw (forward)

Familiar nonfood

Approach Withdraw

FIGURE 76.5 Responses of an evaluation-related neuron that responded to various objects and human movements. (A) The neuron responded not only to familiar regular food (a, cookie), but also to sight and ingestion of a salted raisin (b). After the monkey ate it, responses to the sight of a salted raisin decreased (c). (B) Activity of the neuron increased in response to human movements. The activity of the neuron gradually increased when the experimenter approached by walking forward, toward the monkey, and decreased when the experimenter with-drew from the monkey by walking backward. When the experimenter approached by walking backward and withdrew by walking forward (i.e., walking toward and away from the monkey with the back toward the monkey), the activity of the neuron similarly changed. However, the activity of the neuron did not change when the familiar nonfood (tape) was moved toward and away from the monkey. Solid line, approaching; dashed line, withdrawing. Each histogram bin, 200 ms.

salted raisin suddenly decreased in the subsequent three trials, and the monkey did not eat it (figure 76.5A,c). Since the neuron also responded strongly to the sight and ingestion of familiar preferred foods such as a piece of orange (data not shown), these results suggest that the neuronal responses were related to evaluation of biological significance of the objects. The neuron was then tested with human movements (figure 76.5B). When the experimenter approached, by walking forward, toward the monkey, the activity of the neuron gradually increased. When the experimenter withdrew from the monkey by walking backward, the activity gradually decreased. Furthermore, when the experimenter approached by walking backward and withdrew by walking forward (i.e., walking toward and away from the monkey with the back toward the monkey), the activity of the neuron similarly changed. However, the activity of the neuron did not change when the familiar nonfood item (tape) was moved toward and away from the monkey. All of these data were consistent with the idea that this neuron was related to evaluation of biological significance of the stimuli in a context-dependent manner.

Figure 76.6 shows an example of a specific neuron displaying activity changes in relation to reward expectancy. The neuron responded to familiar food (A,a, cookie), but less to familiar nonfood (A,b, tape). Furthermore, the neuron responded to hand extension toward the stage behind the shutter by the experimenter (A,c, hand extension). Usually, food and nonfood trials followed hand extension. However, the responses to hand extension gradually decreased if the experimenter extended his hand repeatedly without food trials (data not shown). Figure 76.6B shows raw records of the same neuron during the trials. The activity of the neuron increased in response to the sight of food (cookie) after W1 and W2 opening (open triangles and last filled triangles, respectively, in B,a–c). When fixation ratio (FR) was suddenly increased to 20 in Bb, the activity increased not only after W1 and W2 opening, but also at the moment corresponding to W2 opening in the regular trials with FR 10 schedule in Ba. However, the activity did not increase at the same moment of the third trial with FR 20 schedule in Bc. These results suggest involvement of the AM neurons in evaluation of biological significance of objects in specific contexts.

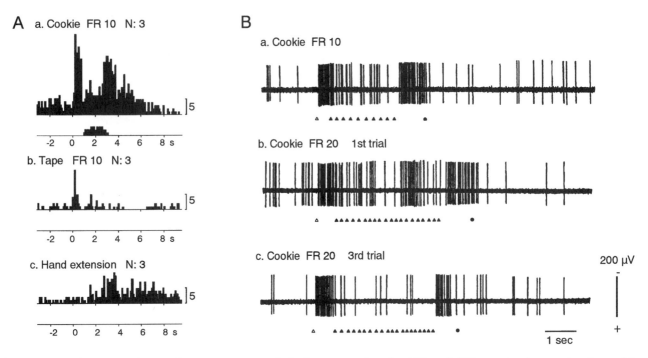

FIGURE 76.6 Responses of a specific neuron, activity of which increased in a specific context. (A) The neuron responded to a familiar regular food (a), but not to a tape (b). Activity of the neuron increased in response to hand extension by an experimenter (c). Each histogram bin, 100 ms. Other descriptions as for figure 76.2. (B) Responses of the neuron in food trials shown as raw records. Activity increased in response to sight of a cookie after W1 and W2 opening (open triangles and last filled triangles) in the trials with FR 10 and 20 schedules (a–c). Note that, in the 1st trial with FR 20 (b), the activity also increased during bar pressing at the moment corresponding to W2 opening in the regular trials with FR 10 schedule. Open triangles, times W1 opened; filled triangles, bar presses; filled circle, food put into mouth.

EFFECTS OF REVERSAL ON AM NEURONAL ACTIVITY
Some AM neurons were tested with alteration of affective significance of the food objects by salting foods. Not only visual but also ingestion responses of the neurons were attenuated by salting. Figure 76.7 shows such modulation of responses of the neuron that responded to both sight and ingestion of some foods. The neuron may have responded slightly in the late ingestion phase to a white cylinder associated with juice and to a cookie in trials 1 and 2. In the visual and ingestion phases, this neuron responded to apple, potato, raisin, and orange in trials 3–5, 9, and 13–15. The response differences to the various food stimuli showed no correlation with mouth movement and neuronal activity. In addition, in our feeding paradigm, mouth movement was slight or absent during the discrimination and bar-press phases. This fact suggests that the neuronal responses preceding ingestion were not preparatory to mouth movement. Similarly, bar-pressing behavior did not correlate with neural activity in trials 6, 13, and 14, but visual presentation of a normally ingested food did elicit activity in trials 9 and 15. The neuron represented in figure 76.7 did not respond to any known aversive or neutral objects such as the brown cylinder that was associated with electric shock, a syringe, tape, or salted orange (trials 6–8,

12, and others, not shown). Trials 9–15 show the effects of salting food. The attenuation was apparent during both the visual inspection and ingestion phases of the task. In the first salted food trial (trial 10), the response disappeared immediately after the animal put salted orange into its mouth. Salting of food was always done in such a way that the salt could not be seen, so it was first detected by the animal upon ingestion. The response to the sight of orange diminished in subsequent salted food trials (trials 11 and 12), as well as in the first two unsalted food trials that followed (trials 13 and 14). After the experimenter gave a piece of unsalted orange to the animal by hand, bar pressing to obtain orange began again in trials 13 to 15, and neuronal responses to the sight and ingestion of orange quickly recovered.

It should be noted that neuronal responses were first suppressed during the initial ingestion of salted food; suppression of visual responses then followed although the visual appearance of the food was the same. In preliminary experiments, we also observed suppression of gustatory responses by quinine that was similar to the suppression by salt that is reported here. The gustation phase of ingestion is an important factor in the evaluation of food palatability (Bartoshuk, 1989). All this evidence suggests that the suppression of neuronal activity

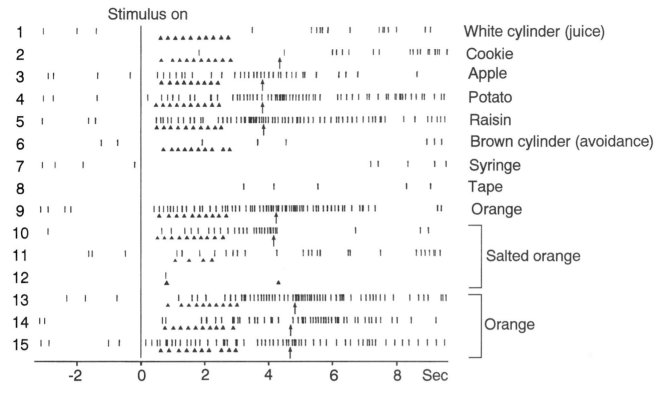

FIGURE 76.7 Modulation of responses of a specific neuron by reversal tests. Neuronal responses are shown by raster display. The neuron responded slightly to the ingestion of juice and cookie in trials 1 and 2. Activity increased primarily in and immediately preceding ingestion phase in trials 3–5. Note no neural response in bar press phase in avoidance trial (trial 6). Trials 9–15 show reversal associated with salted food. Note that neural response disappeared at the moment when the animal put salted orange into its mouth (arrow in trial 10). Abscissas: time, seconds; W1 opened at time 0. Each filled triangle below a raster display indicates one bar press.

discussed here is related to aversion to salted food. This speculation is reasonable, since behavioral responses were also suppressed after the first of a series of salted food trials. Thus the conclusion based on ingestion that salted food was aversive led to a judgment that visual appearance of the same food was aversive (suppression of visually dependent neural responses). This dependence of visual responses on ingestion sensation suggests that these neurons were involved in stimulus (visual stimulus)–affect (ingestion sensation, possibly gustatory) association (i.e., visual-oral sensory association) (Geschwind, 1965; Nishijo, Ono, and Nishino, 1988a,b).

RELATIONS TO BAR-PRESS BEHAVIORS The analysis of the relation between neuronal and behavioral responses indicates one important characteristic of AM neurons. There was not always a direct correlation between rate or amount of bar pressing and neuronal activity, and no direct correlation between individual bar presses and neuronal activity in the AM (direct, one-to-one motor-coupled response) was ever observed. Although spontaneous bar pressing during intertrial intervals was rare, when such spontaneous pressing did

occur, no concomitant neuronal activity change was ever observed. In high-FR(FR 20) trials the responses of the AM neurons returned to the control level during bar pressing and then reappeared when the shutter was opened after the last bar press (figure 76.6B,c, third trial). Even when there was no bar pressing, AM neurons would respond to the sight of biologically significant objects. In the bar-press phase, the animal usually looked at the window, and AM neuron responses in that phase depended on the affective nature of the objects. During the bar-press phase, responses of some neurons to the most preferred food were significantly stronger than responses of the same neurons to less preferred food. Nevertheless, differences in the duration of the bar-press phase, which was inversely related to the rapidity of bar pressing, were not statistically significant, except in reversal tests when some confusion might be expected. However, there was some apparent tendency toward indirect relations between neuronal and behavioral responses. For instance, stronger neuronal responses accompanied normal bar pressing, but the same neurons responded less vigorously when bar pressing was delayed or absent (figure 76.7)

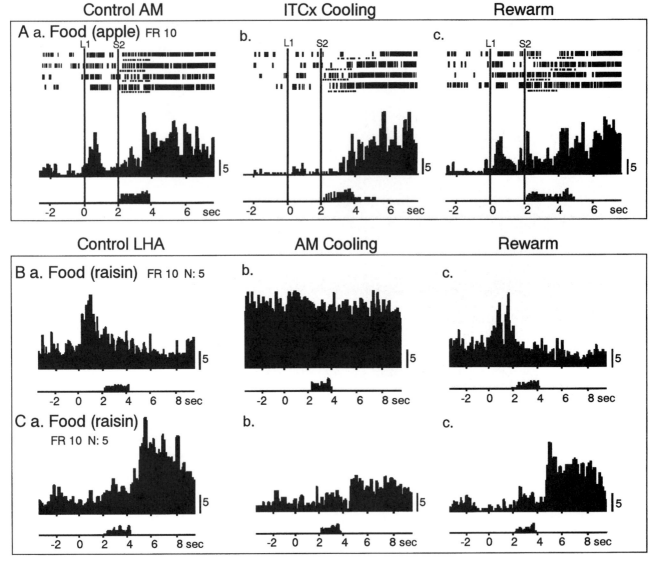

| Control AM | ITCx Cooling | Rewarm |

A a. Food (apple) FR 10
b.
c.

| Control LHA | AM Cooling | Rewarm |

B a. Food (raisin) FR 10 N: 5
b.
c.

C a. Food (raisin) FR 10 N: 5
b.
c.

FIGURE 76.8 Effects of cooling of the inferotemporal cortex (ITCx) and amygdala (AM) during a visual discrimination task. (A) Effects of ITCx cooling on AM food-predominant neurons. Raster displays and histograms (80-ms bins, 10.24 s) show neuronal responses to the sight of food (apple) before ITCx cooling (a), during cooling (b), and after rewarming (c), and bar presses (lower histogram of each set) for 4 trials. Time L1 (0), light on; S2, shutter in front of bar opened. Note no visual responses to the sight of food during ITCx cooling (b). (B) Effects of AM cooling on LHA food-predominant neurons. Histo-grams (100-ms bins, 12.8 s) represent responses for 5 trials during control (a), AM cooled (b), and rewarmed (c) states. No significant visual responses to sight of food during AM cooling, although spontaneous firing rate increased remarkably (b). (C) Effects of AM cooling on responses of ingestion-related LHA neurons. Neuron responded substantially before (a) and after (c), but less during AM cooling (b). Histograms: accumulated in 5 trials (100-ms bins, 12.8 s). Other descriptions as in figure 76.8A.

as in reversal trials. Our present results imply that neuronal activity in the AM is not directly related to sensory inputs nor to overt acts of the animals. Neuronal activity may, however, reflect evaluation of the biological significance of an object. Consequently, it may reflect motivational aspects of an animal's behavioral responses and an animal's attention to a biologically significant object among various exteroceptive stimuli.

Disconnection experiment by reversible cooling of ITCx or AM

To test disconnection of visual inputs to the AM, cooling probes were chronically implanted bilaterally over the dura of the anterior inferotemporal cortex (ITCx) in one monkey; and to disconnect between the AM and the hypothalamus, cooling probes were chronically implanted in the bilateral AM in two monkeys. In this experiment, the modified version of the task was used (figure 76.1B). The monkey could see an object on a stage through a one-way mirror (S1) in front of the stage when a light was turned on. However, another shutter (S2) prevented access to the bar. After a delay of at least 2 seconds, S2 was opened automatically. The S1 shutter was opened by the last bar press. The monkey's behavior and the neuronal responses were essentially the same in this and the previously described situation.

The ITCx cooling suppressed discriminative responses of some AM neurons to various objects. Figure 76.8A shows one example of such modulation by ITCx cooling. Before cooling, the neuron activity increased at the sight of food and during ingestion in all trials (A,a). About 3 minutes after the start of ITCx cooling, the visual responses to the sight of food disappeared in each of the four trials (A,b). Inferotemporal cortex cooling did not change responses of this particular neuron during ingestion (A,b). Thus the main AM responses to ITCx deficits were depression of vision-related neuronal responses and spontaneous firing rates. Previous recording studies indicated that some ITCx neurons responded to only one pattern regardless of size or color (Gross, Bender, and Rocha-Miranda, 1969; Sato, Kawamura, and Iwai, 1980; Desimone et al., 1984) or to specific colors (Fuster and Jervey, 1982; Desimone et al., 1984). The results reported here along with the previous studies strongly suggest that the ITCx is in one of the paths of object-related information passing from the visual cortex to the AM.

Effects of AM cooling on the LHA neuron responses are shown in figure 76.8B,C. The LHA neuron responded preferentially to the sight of food (B,a). During AM cooling, no excitatory visual response was significantly greater than the background activity, since the spontaneous firing rate was greatly increased by bilateral AM cooling (B,b). In contrast to the effects of ITCx cooling on AM responses in the ingestion phase, AM cooling depressed the responses of LHA neurons that responded in the ingestion phase (figure 76.8C). In summary, AM cooling mainly depressed excitatory or inhibitory LHA responses related to visual and ingestion signals, and decreased or increased the spontaneous firing rates of LHA neurons. This finding is consistent with our previous studies in which the effects of AM stimulation on LHA neurons were generally caused by either inhibition or disinhibition (Oomura, Ono, and Ooyama, 1970; Ono, Oomura, et al., 1981; Oomura and Ono, 1982). Taken together, our analysis of neural relations between the ITCx, AM, and LHA in the monkey indicates that the AM mediates integration and links between the ITCx and LHA. Rolls (1981) suggested a similar notion, since latency to visual stimuli increased from the ITCx to the LHA.

Neuronal responses of monkey anterior cingulate neurons to biologically significant objects

In this experiment, a modified version of the task was used (figure 76.1B) (Nishijo et al., 1997). Anterior cingulate neurons also responded to biologically significant objects. Figure 76.9A shows an example of an AC neuron that responded to certain foods. This neuron responded to rewarding objects, cookie (a) and apple (b), but not to the brown cylinder associated with avoidance (aversive electric shock) (c) or a yellow cylinder that had no association (d). Responses of this vision-related differentiating neuron to various food and nonfood objects are compared in figure 76.9B. Each histogram shows the mean firing rate for 2 seconds in 4 trials after the light was turned on minus spontaneous firing rate. This neuron responded to rewarding objects, such as familiar food (apple, raisin, cookie, and white cylinder associated with juice), but did not respond to familiar aversive objects (syringe, frog model, and brown cylinder associated with aversive electric shock), a neutral yellow cylinder, or an unfamiliar object (blue tape). In the reversal tests in which the meanings of objects were changed, responses of these neurons to rewarding or aversive objects were readily suppressed. Another type of AC neurons responded to both familiar rewarding objects, such as apple, raisin, cookie, and white cylinder associated with juice, and familiar aversive nonfood objects, such as syringe and familiar cylinder associated with electric shock, but not to a neutral object. These neurons also responded strongly to unfamiliar objects. The response magnitudes of these neurons to rewarding objects were correlated to the animal's preference (not shown). These results indicate AC neurons could encode emotional or motivational information. Suppression of neuronal responses in the reversal tests strongly suggests that the responses were related to the rewarding or aversive nature of a stimulus. Neurophysiological results in the former section as well as those in the previous lesion studies (Jones and Mishkin, 1972) suggest that the AM is involved in evaluation of biological significance of a stimulus, which is important in discrimination of food (rewarding) from nonfood (nonrewarding). Anatomical study indicates that the AC receives strong projections from the AM (Vogt and Pandya, 1987). Our present study suggests that responsiveness of a class of the AC neurons is very similar to that of AM neurons and that the AC is also involved in evaluation of the biological significance of a stimulus.

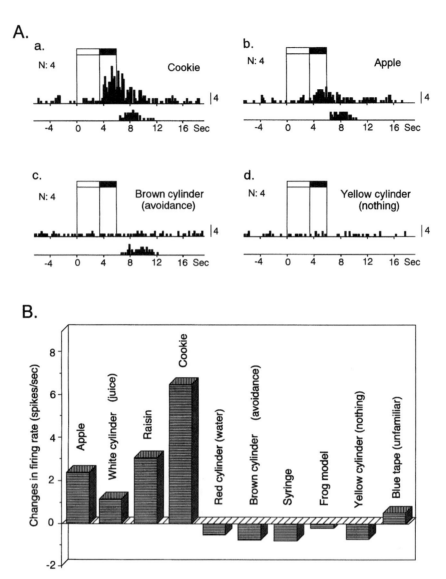

FIGURE 76.9   Responses of a differential vision-related neuron in the anterior cingulate cortex. (A) Responses to various objects with and without biological significance. The neuron responded to rewarding objects: cookie (a) and apple (b), but not to a brown cylinder associated with electric shock (c) or a yellow cylinder with no association (d) during visual discrimination phase. Upper histogram (200-ms bin), summed neuronal responses of 4 trials with the object indicated; lower histogram, bar presses. Zero on time scale, onset of start tone. Open strip, delay phase between the start tone and visual stimulation; black strip, visual discrimination phase. Calibration at right of each histogram: number of spikes per bin. (B) Summary of responses of the neuron shown in figure 76.9A to various food and nonfood objects. Each column shows response magnitude after the indicated object was presented, measured as mean discharge rate (spikes/second) for four 2-second intervals minus spontaneous rate.

However, there were substantial differences between the AM and AC. It should be emphasized that some AC neurons responded mainly in the bar-press phase (bar-press-related neurons). Such neurons were not observed in the AM. Figure 76.10 illustrates an example of a typical bar-press-related neuron. This neuron responded during bar pressing to obtain food (A, cookie; B, juice), but not during bar pressing to avoid shock (C) (differential bar-press-related neurons). These responses of the differential bar-press-related neurons cannot be attributed to simple motor response. However, neuronal responses of these neurons were correlated to the bar-press phase when delays were imposed before or after the bar-press phase (not shown). The results indicated that these neuronal responses were related to both bar presses and affective significance of the objects. This finding suggests that these neurons were related to positive or negative motivation for motor performance. Another type of bar-press-related neurons responded not only during bar pressing to obtain food, but also during bar pressing to avoid shock (nondifferential bar-press-related neurons). Shima and colleagues (1991) observed

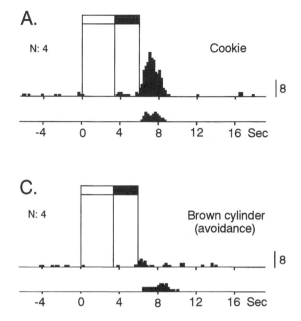

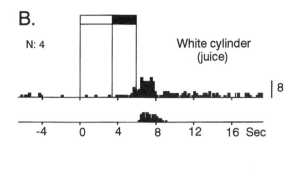

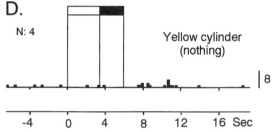

FIGURE 76.10 Responses of a differential bar-press-related neuron in the anterior cingulate cortex. The neuron responded mainly during the bar-press phase only for cookie (A) and juice (B), but not for avoidance (C) or a neutral object (D). Other descriptions as for figure 76.9.

two foci of movement-related neurons in the posterior part of the AC, with the anterior part being more significant in the self-paced than in the sensorily triggered movements. The loci of nondifferential bar-press-related neurons in the present study were comparable to the anterior sites of the movement-related neurons described by Shima and colleagues (1991). Anatomical studies suggest that these movement-related areas of the AC project to motor and premotor cortices and basal ganglia (Royce, 1982; Yeterian and Van Hoesen, 1978). The results in the present study, together with anatomical results, suggest that the cingulate cortex is important in motivation for motor performance.

Various types of AC neurons were located topographically. Differential vision-related neurons were located more anteriorly than bar-press-related neurons. Differential and nondifferential bar-press-related neurons were located in the mid and posterior portions of the AC, respectively. The anterior part of area 24 receives inputs from the prefrontal cortex and other emotion-related areas such as the AM (Vogt and Pandya, 1987), and projects to its posterior part, which in turn projects to motor and premotor cortices and basal ganglia (Royce, 1982; Yeterian and Van Hoesen, 1978). This anatomical and neurophysiological evidence suggests that sensory information is processed and transformed to motor command from the anterior to the posterior portions of the AC. Results of lesion and stimulation studies were consistent with this idea. Lesion of the AC results in deficits in the control of complex motor behavior such as emotional and active avoidance behaviors (Gabriel, 1990; Gabriel et al., 1991; Vogt, David, and Olson, 1992). Electrical stimulation of the AC in man elicits various types of highly integrated motor behavior (Thalairach et al., 1973). Our results suggest that the AC integrates inputs from other emotion-related areas and frontal cortex, and sends the information to motor executive centers to behave appropriately in a variety of specific motivational or emotional contexts.

Functional consideration of the amygdala and anterior cingulate cortex in humans

The present results strongly suggest that the AM is involved in evaluation of the biological significance of incoming sensory information. This conclusion is consistent with recent neuropsychological studies in humans. The patient with AM bilateral damage could evaluate neither facial expressions (Adolphs et al., 1994, 1995) nor emotional intonation of speech (Scott et al., 1997). Recent PET and fMRI studies have demonstrated that cerebral blood flow in the AM of normal humans increased when subjects looked at photos of faces with emotional expressions (Morris et al., 1996; Breiter et al., 1996), unpleasant pictures (Irwin et al., 1996), and human movements (Bonda et al., 1996). These results along with our neurophysiological results suggest that the AM is one of the receptive areas of emotion in the brain, although Papez supposed that the cingulate gyrus had such functions (Papez, 1937).

However, cerebral blood flow consistently increased not only in the AM but also in the AC of normal subjects who voluntarily recalled emotional events (George et al., 1995). Similarly, cerebral blood flow in those areas increased in normal subjects who experienced hallucination by intravenous injection of procaine (Ketter et al., 1996) and in normal subjects who dreamed during REM sleep (Maquet et al., 1996; Braun et al., 1998). These results suggest that activation of the AC might evoke emotional experience without external sensory inputs. Furthermore, cerebral blood flow in the AC as well as the AM increased in patients with emotional disturbances such as posttraumatic stress disorder, simple phobia, and obsessive-compulsive disorder who could not control their emotionally negative thinking (Rauch et al., 1994, 1995, 1996). This finding suggests that abnormally elevated activity of the AC might result in excessive thinking of negative ideas in these patients.

Taken together, all this evidence suggests some functional differences between the AM and AC; the AM is primarily involved in evaluation of incoming external sensory inputs, while the AC might be involved in internal or voluntary generation of emotion without external sensory inputs. We reported the existence of differential bar-press-related AC neurons involved in positive and negative motivation. These AC neurons might be involved in internal or voluntary generation of emotion. In the preceding section we suggested that inputs from the other emotion-related areas and the prefrontal cortex are transformed to motor behaviors in the AC by sending its outputs to motor executive centers. Similarly, the AC might integrate that information to generate appropriate emotion by sending its outputs to the AM. Taken together, the AM and AC are crucial in emotional and motivated behaviors of primates including humans. Understanding the functions of these areas will contribute to elucidation of various human emotional disorders associated with inappropriate behaviors.

ACKNOWLEDGMENTS We thank Dr. Patrick D. Martin, Toyama Medical and Pharmaceutical University, for advice and help with the manuscript. This work was supported partly by the Japanese Ministry of Education, Science and Culture Grants-in-Aid for Scientific Research (08279105, 11308033, 10680762, and 11145217), and by Funds for Comprehensive Research on Aging and Health.

REFERENCES

ADOLPHS, R., D. TRANEL, H. DAMASIO, and A. R. DAMASIO, 1994. Impaired recognition of emotion in facial expressions following bilateral damage to the human amygdala. *Nature* 372:669–672.

ADOLPHS, R., D. TRANEL, H. DAMASIO, and A. R. DAMASIO, 1995. Fear and the human amygdala. *J. Neurosci.* 15:5879–5891.

AGGLETON, J. P., 1992. The functional effects of amygdala lesions in humans: A comparison with findings from monkeys. In *The Amygdala: Neurobiological Aspects of Emotion, Memory, and Mental Dysfunction,* J. P. Aggleton, ed. New York: Wiley, pp. 485–503.

AGGLETON, J. P., M. J. BURTON, and R. E. PASSINGHAM, 1980. Cortical and subcortical afferents to the amygdala of the rhesus monkey (*Macaca mulatta*). *Brain Res.* 190:347–368.

AMARAL, D. G., and J. L. PRICE, 1984. Amygdalo-cortical projections in the monkey (*Macaca fascicularis*). *J. Comp. Neurol.* 230:465–496.

AMARAL, D. G., J. L. PRICE, A. PITKANEN, and S. T. CARMICHAEL, 1992. Anatomical organization of the primate amygdaloid complex. In *The Amygdala: Neurobiological Aspects of Emotion, Memory, and Mental Dysfunction,* J. P. Aggleton, ed. New York: Wiley, pp. 1–66.

BARTOSHUK, L. M., 1989. The functions of taste and olfaction. *Ann. N.Y. Acad. Sci.* 575:353–362.

BENES, F. M., S. L. VINCENT, G. ALSTERBERG, E. D. BIRD, and J. P. SANGIOVANNI, 1992. Increased GABA$_A$ receptor binding in superficial layers of cingulate cortex in schizophrenics. *J. Neurosci.* 12:924–929.

BONDA, E., M. PETRIDES, D. OSTRY, and A. EVANS, 1996. Specific involvement of human parietal systems and the amygdala in the perception of biological motion. *J. Neurosci.* 16:3737–3744.

BRAUN, A. R., T. J. BALKIN, N. J. WESENSTEN, F. GWADRY, R. E. CARSON, M. VARGA, P. BALDWIN, G. BELENKY, and P. HERSCOVITCH, 1998. Dissociated pattern of activity in visual cortices and their projections during human rapid eye movement sleep. *Science* 279:91–95.

BREITER, H. C., N. L. ETCOFF, P. J. WHALEN, W. A. KENNEDY, S. L. RAUCH, R. L. BUCKNER, M. M. STRAUSS, S. E. HYMAN, and B. R. ROSEN, 1996. Response and habituation of the human amygdala during visual processing of facial expression. *Neuron* 17:875–887.

CADOR, M., T. W. ROBBINS, and B. J. EVERITT, 1989. Involvement of the amygdala in stimulus-reward associations: Interaction with the ventral striatum. *Neuroscience* 30: 77–86.

DAVIS, M., 1992. The role of the amygdala in conditioned fear. In *The Amygdala: Neurobiological Aspects of Emotion, Memory, and Mental Dysfunction,* J. P. Aggleton, ed. New York: Wiley, pp. 255–305.

DESIMONE, R., T. D. ALBRIGHT, C. G. GROSS, and C. BRUCE, 1984. Stimulus-selective properties of inferior temporal neurons in the macaque. *J. Neurosci.* 4:2051–2062.

DOWNER, J. DE C., 1961. Changes in visual gnostic functions and emotional behavior following unilateral temporal lobe damage in 'split-brain' monkey. *Nature* 191:50–51.

DREVETS, W. C., J. L. PRICE, J. R. SIMPSON, JR., R. D. TODD, T. REICH, M. VANNIER, and M. E. RAICHLE, 1997. Subgenual prefrontal cortex abnormalities in mood disorders. *Nature* 386:824–827.

EVERITT, B. J., M. CADOR, and T. W. ROBBINS, 1989. Interactions between the amygdala and ventral striatum in stimulus-reward associations: Studies using second-order schedule of sexual reinforcement. *Neuroscience* 30:63–75.

EVERITT, B. J., K. A. MORRIS, A. O'BRIEN, and T. W. ROBBINS, 1991. The basolateral amygdala-ventral striatal system and conditioned place preference: Further evidence of limbic-striatal interactions underlying reward-related processes. *Neuroscience* 42: 1–18.

FRISTON, K. J., G. TONONI, G. N. REEKE, JR., O. SPORNS, and G. M. EDELMAN, 1994. Value-dependent selection in the brain: Simulation in a synthetic neural model. *Neuroscience* 59:229–243.

FUKUDA, M., T. ONO, and K. NAKAMURA, 1987. Functional relations among inferotemporal cortex, amygdala, and lateral hypothalamus in monkey operant feeding behavior. *J. Neurophysiol.* 57:1060–1077.

FUSTER, J. M., and J. P. JERVEY, 1982. Neuronal firing in the inferotemporal cortex of the monkey in a visual memory task. *J. Neurosci.* 2:361–375.

GABRIEL, M., 1990. Functions of anterior and posterior cingulate cortex during avoidance learning in rabbits. *Prog. Brain Res.* 85:467–483.

GABRIEL, M., Y. KUBOTA, S. SPARENBORG, K. STRAUBE, and B. A. VOGT, 1991. Effects of cingulate cortical lesions on avoidance learning and training-induced unit activity in rabbits. *Exp. Brain Res.* 86: 585–600.

GAFFAN, E. A., D. GAFFAN, and S. HARRISON, 1988. Disconnection of the amygdala from visual association cortex impairs visual reward association learning in monkeys. *J. Neurosci.* 8:3144–3150.

GAFFAN, D., and S. HARRISON, 1987. Amygdalectomy and disconnection in visual learning for auditory secondary reinforcement by monkeys. *J. Neurosci.* 7:2285–2292.

GALLAGHER, M., P. W. GRAHAM, and P. C. HOLLAND, 1990. The amygdala central nucleus and appetitive Pavlovian conditioning: Lesions impair one class of conditioned behavior. *J. Neurosci.* 10:1906–1911.

GEORGE, M. S., T. A. KETTER, P. I. PAREKH, B. HORWITZ, P. HERSCOVITCH, and R. M. POST, 1995. Brain activity during transient sadness and happiness in healthy women. *Am. J. Psychiatry* 152:341–351.

GESCHWIND, N. 1965. Disconnexion syndromes in animals and man. *Brain* 88:237–294.

GLOOR, P. 1960. Amygdala. In *Handbook of Physiology, Neurophysiology*, vol. 2, J. Field, ed. Washington, D.C.: American Physiological Society, pp. 1395–1420.

GODDARD, G. V., 1964. Functions of the amygdala. *Psychol. Bull.* 62:89–109.

GROSS, C. G., D. B. BENDER, and C. F. ROCHA-MIRANDA, 1969. Visual receptive fields of neurons in inferotemporal cortex of the monkey. *Science* 116:1303–1306.

HEBB, D. O., 1972. *A Textbook of Psychology*, 3rd ed. Philadelphia: Saunders.

HILTON, S. M., and A. W. ZBROZYNA, 1963. Amygdaloid region for defense reactions and its afferent pathways to the brain stem. *J. Physiol. (Lond.)* 165:160–173.

HOREL, J. A., E. G. KEATING, and L. J. MISANTONE, 1975. Partial Klüver-Bucy syndrome produced by destroying temporal neocortex or amygdala. *Brain Res.* 94: 347–359.

IRWIN, W., R. J. DAVIDSON, M. J. LOWE, B. J. MOCK, J. A. SORENSON, and P. A. TURSKI, 1996. Human amygdala activation detected with echo-planar functional magnetic resonance imaging. *Neuroreport* 7:1765–1769.

JONES, B., and M. MISHKIN, 1972. Limbic lesions and the problem of stimulus-reinforcement associations. *Exp. Neurol.* 36: 362–377.

KAADA, B. R., 1972. Stimulation and regional ablation of the amygdaloid complex with reference to functional represen-

tations. In *The Neurobiology of the Amygdala*, B .E. Eleftheriou, ed. New York: Plenum, pp. 205–281.

KETTER, T. A., P. J. ANDREASON, M. S. GEORGE, C. LEE, D. S. GILL, P. I. PAREKH, M. W. WILLIS, P. HERSCOVITCH, and R. M. POST, 1996. Anterior paralimbic mediation of procaine-induced emotional and psychosensory experiences. *Arch. Gen. Psychiatry* 53:59–69.

KLÜVER, H., and P. C. BUCY, 1939. Preliminary analysis of functions of the temporal lobes in monkeys. *Arch. Neurol. Psychiatry* 42:979–1000.

LEDOUX, J. E., 1987. Emotion. In *Handbook of Physiology. 1: The Nervous System*, vol. 5, V. B. Mountcastle, ed. Bethesda, Md.: American Physiological Society, pp. 419–459.

MACLEAN, P. D., 1986. Culminating developments in the evolution of the limbic system: The thalamocingulate division. In *The Limbic System: Functional Organization and Clinical Disorders*, B. K. Doane and K. E. Livingston, eds. New York: Raven Press, pp. 1–28.

MAQUET, P., J.-M. PETERS, J. AERTS, G. DELFIORE, C. DEGUELDRE, A. LUXEN, and G. FRANCK, 1996. Functional neuroanatomy of human rapid-eye-movement sleep and dreaming. *Nature* 383:163–166.

MISHKIN, M., and J. AGGLETON, 1981. Multiple functional contributions of the amygdala in the monkey. In *The Amygdaloid Complex*, Y. Ben-Ari, ed. Amsterdam: Elsevier/North-Holland Biomedical Press, pp. 409–420.

MORRIS, J. S., C. D. FRITH, D. I. PERRETT, D. ROWLAND, A. W. YOUNG, A. J. CALDER, and R. J. DOLAN, 1996. A differential neural response in the human amygdala to fearful and happy facial expressions. *Nature* 383: 812–815.

NISHIJO, H., T. ONO, K. NAKAMURA, M. KAWABATA, and K. YAMATANI, 1986. Neuron activity in and adjacent to the dorsal amygdala of monkey during operant feeding behavior. *Brain Res. Bull.* 17:847–854.

NISHIJO, H., T. ONO, and H. NISHINO, 1988a. Single neuron responses in amygdala of alert monkey during complex sensory stimulation with affective significance. *J. Neurosci.* 8: 3570–3583.

NISHIJO, H., T. ONO, and H. NISHINO, 1988b. Topographic distribution of modality-specific amygdalar neurons in alert monkey. *J. Neurosci.* 8:3556–3569.

NISHIJO, H., Y. YAMAMOTO, T. ONO, T. UWANO, J. YAMASHITA, and T. YAMASHIMA, 1997. Single neuron responses in the monkey anterior cingulate cortex during visual discrimination. *Neurosci. Lett.* 227:79–82.

ONO, T., H. NISHINO, K. SASAKI, M. FUKUDA, and K. MURAMOTO, 1980. Role of the lateral hypothalamus and the amygdala in feeding behavior. *Brain Res. Bull.* (Suppl. 4) 5:143–149.

ONO, T., H. NISHINO, K. SASAKI, M. FUKUDA, and K. MURAMOTO, 1981. Monkey lateral hypothalamic neuron response to sight of food, and during bar press and ingestion. *Neurosci. Lett.* 21:99–104.

ONO, T., Y. OOMURA, H. NISHINO, K. SASAKI, M. FUKUDA, and K. MURAMOTO, 1981. Neural mechanisms of feeding behavior. In *Brain Mechanisms of Sensation*, Y. Katsuki, R. Norgren, and M. Sato, eds. New York: Wiley, pp. 271–286.

OOMURA, Y., and T. ONO, 1982. Mechanism of inhibition by the amygdala in the lateral hypothalamic area of rats. *Brain Res. Bull.* 8:653–666.

OOMURA, Y., T. ONO, and H. OOYAMA, 1970. Inhibitory action of the amygdala on the lateral hypothalamic area in rats. *Nature* 228:1108–1110.

PAPEZ, J. W., 1937. A proposed mechanism of emotion. *Arch. Neurol. Psychiatry* 38:725–744.

PERRETT, D. I., E. T. ROLLS, and W. CAAN, 1982. Visual neurons responsive to faces in the monkey temporal cortex. *Exp. Brain Res.* 47:329–342.

PONS, T. P., P. E GARRAGHTY, D. P. FRIEDMAN, and M. MISHKIN, 1987. Physiological evidence for serial processing in somatosensory cortex. *Science* 237:417–420.

RAUCH, S. L., M. A. JENIKE, N. M. ALPERT, L. BAER, H. C. BREITER, C. R. SAVAGE, and A. J. FISCHMAN, 1994. Regional cerebral blood flow measured during symptom provocation in obsessive-compulsive disorder using oxygen 15–labeled carbon dioxide and position emission tomography. *Arch. Gen. Psychiatr.* 51:62–70.

RAUCH, S. L., C. R. SAVAGE, N. M. ALPERT, E. C. MIGUEL, L. BARE, H. C. BREITER, A. J. FISCHMAN, P. A. MANZO, C. MORETTI, and M. A. JENIKE, 1995. A positron emission tomographic study of simple phobic symptom provocation. *Arch. Gen. Psychiatr.* 52:20–28.

RAUCH, S. L., B. A. VAN DER KOLK, R. E. FISLER, N. M. ALPERT, S. P. ORR, C. R. SAVAGE, A. J. FISCHMAN, M. A. JENIKE, and R. K. PITMAN, 1996. A symptom provocation study of posttraumatic stress disorder using positron emission tomography and script-driven imagery. *Arch. Gen. Psychiatr.* 53:380–387.

ROLLS, E. T., 1981. Processing beyond the inferior temporal visual cortex related to feeding, memory, and striatal function. In *Brain Mechanisms of Sensation*, Y. Katsuki, R. Norgren, and M. Sato, eds. New York: Wiley, pp. 241–269.

ROYCE, G. J., 1982. Laminar origin of cortical neurons which project upon the caudate nucleus: A horseradish peroxidase investigation in the cat. *J. Comp. Neurol.* 205: 8–29.

RUSSCHEN, F. T., D. G. AMARAL, and J. L. PRICE, 1985. The afferent connections of the substantia innominata in the monkey, *Macaca fascicularis. J. Comp. Neurol.* 242:1–27.

SANGHERA, M. K., E. T. ROLLS, and A. ROPER-HALL, 1979. Visual responses of neurons in the dorsolateral amygdala of the alert monkey. *Exp. Neurol.* 63:610–626.

SATO, T., T. KAWAMURA, and E. IWAI, 1980. Responsiveness of inferotemporal single units to visual pattern stimuli in monkeys performing discrimination. *Exp. Brain Res.* 38:313–319.

SAWLE, G. V., N. F. HYMAS, A. J. LEES, and R. S. J. FRACKOWIAK, 1991. Obsessional slowness. Functional studies with positron emission tomography. *Brain* 114:2191–2202.

SCOTT, S. K., A. W. YOUNG, A. J. CALDER, D. J. HELLAWELL, J. P. AGGLETON, and M. JOHNSON, 1997. Impaired auditory recognition of fear and anger following bilateral amygdala lesions. *Nature* 385:254–257.

SHIMA, K., K. AYA, H. MUSHIAKE, M. INASE, H. AIZAWA, and J. TANJI, 1991. Two movement-related foci in the primate cingulate cortex observed in signal-triggered and self-paced forelimb movements. *J. Neurophysiol.* 65:188–202.

STEPHAN, H., H. D. FRAHM, and G. BARON, 1987. Comparison of brain structure volumes in insectivora and primates. 7. Amygdaloid components. *J. Hirnforsch.* 28:571–584.

THALAIRACH, J., J. BANCAUD, S. GEIGER, M. BORDAS-FERRER, A. BONIS, G. SZIKLA, and M. RUSU, 1973. The cingulate gyrus and human behavior. *Electroencephalogr. Clin. Neurophysiol.* 34:45–52.

TURNER, B. H., M. MISHKIN, and M. KNAPP, 1980. Organization of the amygdalopetal projections from modality-specific cortical association areas in the monkey. *J. Comp. Neurol.* 191:515–543.

VOGT, B. A., M. F. DAVID, and C. R. OLSON, 1992. Functional heterogeneity in cingulate cortex: The anterior executive and posterior evaluative regions. *Cereb. Cortex* 2:435–443.

VOGT, B. A., and D. N. PANDYA, 1987. Cingulate cortex of the rhesus monkey. 2. cortical afferents. *J. Comp. Neurol.* 262: 271–289.

WEINBERGER, N. M., J. H. ASHE, R. METHERATE, T. M. MCKENNA, D. M. DIAMOND, J. S. BAKIN, R. C. LENNARTZ, and J. M. CASSADY, 1990. Neural adaptive information processing: A preliminary model of receptive-field plasticity in auditory cortex during Pavlovian conditioning. In *Learning and Computational Neuroscience: Foundations of Adaptive Networks*, M. Gabriel and J. Moore, eds. Cambridge, Mass.: MIT Press, pp. 91–138.

WEISKRANTZ, L., 1956. Behavioral changes associated with ablation of the amygdaloid complex in monkeys. *J. Comp. Physiol. Psychol.* 49:381–391.

YETERIAN, E. H., and G. W. VAN HOESEN, 1978. Cortico-striate projections in the rhesus monkey: The organization of certain cortico-caudate connections. *Brain Res.* 139:43–63.

77 Emotional Processing in the Human Brain Revealed through Functional Neuroimaging

RAYMOND J. DOLAN

ABSTRACT The mechanisms by which sensory events that represent fear are processed in the human brain provides a general model for understanding emotional function. This chapter presents functional neuroimaging data from studies of fear processing and relates these to a neurobiological model of emotional processing. A critical role for the amygdala in processing sensory stimuli that signal fear is highlighted. The time course of an amygdala response to behaviorally relevant sensory inputs shows rapid habituation. When a previously neutral stimulus acquires an ability to elicit fear, this acquisition is expressed in plasticity changes in related sensory processing regions. This adaptive learning also involves context-specific changes in connectivity between sensory processing regions and regions such as the amygdala that mediate value. Using masking procedures, which disrupt conscious awareness of a target stimulus occurrence, privileged access to the amygdala for sensory stimuli that signal fear can be demonstrated.

This chapter provides a neurobiological perspective on emotional processing in the human brain informed principally by functional neuroimaging. The focus is on an exemplar emotion, fear. I begin with a psychological analysis of fear and its relation to other so-called basic emotions. I then present a neurobiological model of emotional processing, framed in terms of value-dependent learning. This model is subsequently used to formulate questions and interpret findings from empirical neuroimaging experiments. The type of questions addressed include the following: How does the brain process behaviorally relevant sensory stimuli? To what degree is processing of fear-inducing stimuli dependent on conscious awareness? What dynamic neural events ensue when a salient sensory stimulus activates a fear-processing system? What neural mechanisms enable a neutral sensory stimulus to acquire behavioral significance? What is the time course of activation in critical brain regions that process fear-inducing stimuli?

RAYMOND J. DOLAN Wellcome Department of Cognitive Neurology, Institute of Neurology, London, United Kingdom

Concepts and frameworks

Fear is a psychological trait that represents an adaptation to danger. More broadly, it is an evolved pancultural trait homologous to that seen in a wide range of species. Restricting a discussion of human emotion to a single instance, fear, might be considered limiting. However, this approach benefits from the fact that knowledge of fear processing in other species provides constraints for interpretation of human neurobiological data. The more ambitious program of elaborating a general neurobiological account of emotion is conceptually problematic. It is generally accepted that the concept of emotion subsumes a wide range of distinct linguistic categories largely derived from everyday discourse. There are no a priori grounds for assuming that these vernacular concepts necessarily reflect the operation of neurobiological systems. Conceptual imprecision, arising from overreliance on vernacular concepts of emotion, has recently resulted in trenchant calls for abandonment or radical reformulation of the entire emotion concept (Brothers, 1997; Griffiths, 1997).

The perspective adopted in this chapter is influenced by a psychoevolutionary approach that reflects a rediscovery of Darwin's views on emotion (Darwin, 1965; Griffiths, 1997). Crucial in this regard is the affect programs concept (Ekman, 1971, 1982; Ekman and Friesen, 1971). This proposes several distinct emotions, termed primary emotions, that include fear, anger, happiness, sadness, disgust, and surprise. These emotions, reflex like in their operation, are expressed in multicomponent behavior patterns including facial, motor, vocal, endocrine, and autonomic responses. It is beyond the present brief to review the relevant supportive evidence. However, critical observations include the recognition of distinct patterns of facial emotional expression, corresponding to primary emotion category labels, across cultures (Izard, 1998; Ekman and Friesen, 1971). The affect program concept does not exhaust the vernacular concept of emotion. Emotions such as envy, shame, and guilt, among others, do not readily fall within a primary emotion category. One proposal is that they represent a separate category of higher cognitive or secondary emotions (Griffiths, 1997; Damasio, 1995). Distinguishing features of this category are a greater involvement of higher cognition and the fact that they arise almost exclusively within the context of interpersonal relationships.

A model of emotional processing

A simplified model of emotional processing proposes input and output components. An emotional input refers to a sensory stimulus that elicits an emotional state. The high degree of variance in stimuli that elicit primary emotions indicates that most are learned. There is, nevertheless, substantial evidence for innate bias in emotional learning mechanisms. For example, there is facilitation of learning in relation to certain salient stimuli, such as conditioning to angry faces, a form of response preparedness (Öhman, Fredrikson, and Hugdahl, 1976; Seligman, 1971). This learning bias suggests the presence of systems with innate response dispositions to particular sensory inputs. By contrast, an emotional output is the behavioral sequel to engagement of an emotional processing system. Primary emotions, including fear, are relatively invariant in their expression, indicating encapsulation of the associated output systems. Whether interactions with other aspects of cognition, such as attention and memory, occur at input or output stages of processing is an unanswered question.

Many neurobiological models of emotion and emotional learning have been articulated based on animal data (LeDoux, 1996). The model that we apply is based upon that of value-dependent learning (Friston et al., 1994) outlined schematically in figure 77.1. The model assumes the existence of epigenetically specified neural systems that respond to signals that have innate adaptive value. Examples of innate value are responses to hunger and sex but might also include prepotent stimuli such as fearful faces. Although not explicitly specified, candidate components of value systems could include the amygdala and basal forebrain regions. Outputs from value systems are proposed to reflect responses to innately salient stimuli but also provide constraints, through selective consolidation of synaptic change, for acquisition of novel adaptive behaviors. Thus a key proposal of the model is

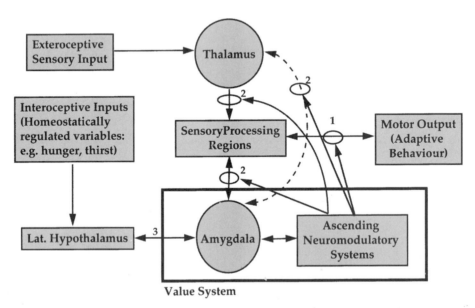

FIGURE 77.1 A schematic model of value-dependent neural selection adapted from Friston and colleagues (1994). The value system, outlined in the large rectangle, represents a mechanism that signals the consequence of behaviors vital for homeostasis. The value system can be engaged by feedback from interoceptive inputs or via sensory inputs to structures such as the amygdala. Activation of the value system sends neuromodulatory signals, which consolidate synaptic changes, to sensory and motor regions, as indicated by arrows and red circles. As a consequence, neural activity (and related behaviors) coincident with events possessing innate value elicit responses in the value system that mediate emotional or value-dependent learning. The mechanistic basis of this learning has three components designated 1, 2, and 3 in the figure. These correspond to (1) consolidation of adaptive responses (i.e., sensorimotor integration) that mediate procedural learning; (2) mediation of acquired value (i.e., salient cues become reinforcers by virtue of gaining access to the amygdala or value system); and (3) mediation of innate value (i.e., connections to the amygdala specified epigenetically and determined by evolution as opposed to experience-dependent mechanisms).

that stimuli acquire value or behavioral relevance through selective consolidation of afferents to value systems from sensory processing systems. This consolidation itself occurs under the influence of outputs from value systems. Emotional learning is therefore considered a "bootstrap" procedure where autodidactic acquisition of adaptive responses, to stimuli with acquired value, can be traced back to reinforcers with innate value selected on an evolutionary time scale. For example, in a classical conditioning experiment, an aversive noise (US) represents a stimulus with innate value. A conditioned stimulus (CS+) acquires value through consolidation of afferents, from sensory processing regions, to value systems through modulatory effects mediated by outputs from innately specified value systems.

How the brain processes fear-related visual stimuli

Innate salience or value refers to the ability of a stimulus to elicit emotional or adaptive responses in the absence of learning. Certain sensory stimuli, such as facial expressions that reflect basic emotions, are conjectured to possess innate salience or value determined by evolutionary selection (Darwin, 1965). Neuropsychological observations indicate a dissociation in processing facial identity involving extrastriate regions from regions involved in processing facial emotion (Young et al., 1993; Etcoff, 1984). Animal data suggest a role for the amygdala (and related subcortical structures) in emotional processing of faces (Rolls, 1995; LeDoux et al., 1990; LeDoux, 1993). Furthermore, human amygdala lesions lead to selective deficits in the recognition of fearful facial expressions (Adolphs et al., 1994; Calder et al., 1996) and impaired fear conditioning (Bechara et al., 1995; LaBar et al., 1995).

MEASURING NEURAL RESPONSES TO FEARFUL FACES What brain systems process fear in facial expressions? To address this question we carried out an experiment, using functional neuroimaging, that compared neural responses of subjects as they viewed exemplars of either happy or fearful facial expressions. As well as representing distinct categories of expression we also introduced a parametric variation into the degree of emotion expressed in the stimuli by a computer graphical manipulation of the faces (Perrett, May, and Yoshikawa, 1994) (see figure 77.2A). The task requirement was for subjects to make a sex classification without any explicit instruction to attend to the facial expressions per se. Comparing the neural response associated with processing fearful and happy expressions revealed activation of left amygdala and left periamygdaloid cortex specific to the fear condition (see figure 77.2B) (Morris et al., 1996). Us-

ing similar stimuli, but without an intensity variation or a specific task instruction, these findings have now been replicated by others (Breiter et al., 1996). However, the introduction of an intensity variation allowed us to extend our analysis to describe brain regions conjointly responsive to emotion category (fearful versus happy) and expression intensity (low versus high). The data indicated that neural responses in the left amygdala increased monotonically with increasing intensity of expressed fear, as illustrated in figure 77.2C (Morris et al., 1996).

In terms of our model, processing innately fearful stimuli involves obligatory access to value- or fear-processing mechanisms. Because faces were classified by sex, and not by expression, we can infer that amygdala activation does not depend upon explicit hedonic processing of a target stimulus. The unilateral response, though surprising, parallels findings during procaine-induced fear (Ketter et al., 1996) and in patients with unilateral amygdala damage who show lower emotional intensity ratings for facial expressions in association with left- compared to right-sided amygdala lesions (Adolphs et al., 1995).

The neuromodulatory role of the amygdala in visual processing

Connections of the amygdala to sensory, motor, and autonomic output systems provide an anatomical basis for adaptive responses to stimuli that signal fear (Amaral and Price, 1984; Jones and Burton, 1976; LeDoux et al., 1988). This conjecture is reinforced by specific projections from amygdala to emotional processing regions such as orbitofrontal cortex, anterior cingulate cortex, ventral striatum, nucleus basalis, and brainstem nuclei (Jones and Powell, 1970; Amaral et al., 1992; Mesulam et al., 1983; Russchen, Amaral, and Price, 1985). The survival value conferred by adaptive responses to danger should provide mechanisms that enhance processing of salient, for example fear-provoking, stimuli (Friston et al., 1994; LeDoux, 1996). Our model of value-dependent learning proposes that engagement of value systems results in neuromodulatory effects that reinforce processing of salient cues. An important source of afferent inputs to primate amygdala is from temporal and early visual association cortices that represent distinct features of environment (Aggleton, Burton, and Passingham, 1980; Iwai and Yukie, 1987). However, it is the more extensive amygdala efferents to early stages of visual processing that may, in part, mediate value-dependent neuromodulatory effects (Amaral and Price, 1984; Amaral et al., 1992; Iwai and Yukie, 1987).

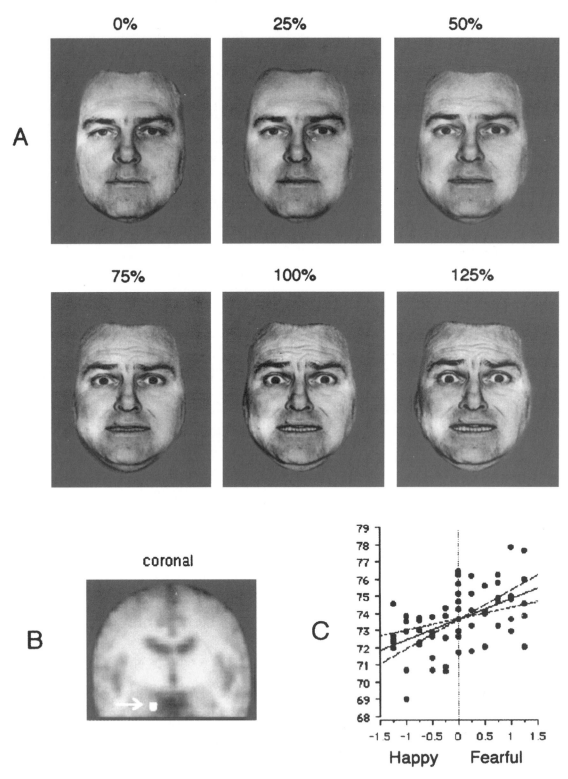

FIGURE 77.2 Fearful faces and the amygdala. (A) Different intensities of fearful expression produced by computer morphing. The 0% and 100% faces are prototypical neutral and fearful expressions, respectively. Faces 25%–75% are interpolations between these prototypes. The 125% face was created by shifting the shape of the fear prototype 25% further beyond 100% fearful. (B) The figure shows the left amygdala in which a significant area of activation is displayed on a coronal slice of a mean MRI image produced from all the subjects. (C) The graph plots the regional cerebral blood flow (rCBF) values in milliliters per deciliter per minute for all conditions and all subjects at the pixel of maximal activation in the left amygdala. The x-axis represents the proportion of the prototypical expression in the face stimuli, with fearful being positive (i.e., 100% = 1) and happy negative (i.e., 100% = −1). A regression line has been fitted to the data, with broken lines representing the 95% confidence interval for the gradient of the slope.

CONTEXT-DEPENDENT NEURAL RESPONSES TO EMOTIONAL FACES   To test a hypothesis that the amygdala selectively influences visual processing of salient stimuli, we examined its contribution to extrastriate activity under distinct psychological contexts (fear versus happy and vice versa). This approach is predicated on a concept of functional integration that emphasizes interactions between brain regions. The analysis involved measuring amygdala responses, under fearful and happy conditions, that are then regressed on activity in all other brain regions and directly contrasted using statistical parametric mapping (SPM) (Friston et al., 1997). What this type of analysis demonstrates is an aspect of effective connectivity between amygdala and other brain regions, where effective connectivity reflects "the influence one neural system exerts over another" (Friston, Frith, and Frackowiak, 1993). Strikingly, our analysis indicated an enhanced influence of the amygdala on extrastriate activity including bilateral inferior occipital gyri, right fusiform gyrus, and left lingual gyrus as well as the pulvinar, that was expressed solely during presentation of fearful stimuli (Morris, Friston, et al., 1998). Interestingly, the extrastriate regions with the strongest functional interactions with the amygdala subsume regions involved in face processing per se (Sergent et al., 1994; Dolan et al., 1997; Kanwisher, McDermott, and Chun, 1997). These context-dependent effects are illustrated in figure 77.3.

Processing salient visual stimuli

The behavioral values of sensory stimuli are not fixed but vary during the lifetime of an individual. Classical conditioning provides a simple model for this type of value-dependent learning. In essence, classical conditioning is a form of associative learning in which a neutral stimulus acquires value through close temporal pairing with an innately salient unconditioned stimulus. The amygdala is strongly implicated in this process with numerous studies highlighting dynamic changes in the interaction between auditory thalamus and amygdala during aversive noise conditioning (LeDoux, 1989, 1996). Neurobiological models have also proposed that the pulvinar may be crucial in early selective processing of salient sensory information (Olshausen, Anderson, and Van Essen, 1993), a proposal supported by electrophysiological recordings in monkeys (Robinson and Petersen, 1992).

CHANGES IN NEURAL RESPONSE TO FACES FOLLOWING CONDITIONING   We used aversive classical conditioning to manipulate the behavioral significance of human facial expressions (happy, fearful, and neutral) while subjects underwent functional neuroimaging (PET). An initial question was which brain regions alter their responses

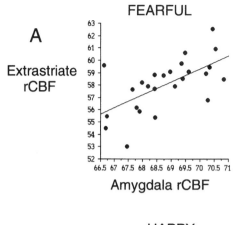

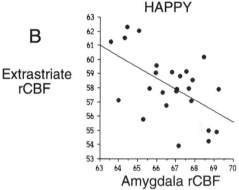

FIGURE 77.3   The context-specific nature of the connectivity between the amygdala and a region of the extrastriate cortex is illustrated graphically. It can be clearly seen that the regression of amygdala responses on extrastriate cortex has a positive slope in the fearful condition (A) and a negative slope in the happy condition (B). This type of influence can be formulated in terms of a condition-specific change in the effective connectivity between brain regions.

when the behavioral relevance, but not other aspects, of a stimulus alters through learning. In the experiment subjects viewed a sequence of gray-scale images of faces consisting of two different faces, each repeated 8 times, presented in a pseudorandom order. Within a sequence the faces had either happy, fearful, or neutral expressions. Subjects responded "yes" if there was a consecutive repeat of a face and "no" if not. One face (the CS+) was always followed by a noise stimulus; the other face (the CS–) was always followed by silence. Scanning coincided with the end of the conditioning sequence and involved repeated presentations of one of the preceding faces in the absence of noise. In half the scans this face was a CS+, while in the other half the face was a CS–.

Contrasting all paired (CS+) with all unpaired (CS–) conditions highlighted right hemisphere activations in the pulvinar, orbitofrontal cortex, and superior frontal gyrus (Morris, Friston, and Dolan, 1997). The interaction between emotional expression and conditioning, which tested for expression-specific activations, revealed augmented activation in the right pulvinar for happy expressions (see figure 77.4A). Activation of the right amygdala was also seen in the contrast of CS+ with CS– faces but at a lower significance than for the preceding activations. However, since this was the main predicted activation, the finding is nevertheless significant (see figure 77.4B). The overall findings accord with models that propose thalamic involvement in processing saliency within selected thalamocortical and corticothalamic circuits (Posner and Petersen, 1990; Petersen, Robinson, and Keys, 1985; Petersen, Robinson, and Morris, 1987; Robinson and Petersen, 1992; Rafal and Posner, 1989). The altered thalamic response reflects a form of stimulus-specific neural plasticity, where plasticity refers to experience-dependent changes in the physiological (hemodynamic) response to stimuli. Differential responses, elicited by the faces, were experience-dependent in the sense that they could only be explained by associative learning (prior to scanning). Recall that the only difference between the CS+ and CS– conditions was an experimental manipulation of salience. One question that arises concerns the mechanism of these experience-dependent changes in pulvinar response.

CHARACTERIZING FUNCTIONAL INTERACTIONS DURING CONDITIONING   Our model of value-dependent learning predicts that connections to regions such as the amygdala from sensory processing systems are selectively strengthened when sensory stimuli acquire value (Friston et al., 1994). In the context of the outlined conditioning experiment, activity in the amygdala, and other "value systems," should covary with thalamic activity during conditioning. The data accord with the prediction in that pulvinar activity, for all conditions expressed over the course of the entire experiment, showed significant covariation with activity in the right amygdala and basal forebrain regions (see figure 77.4C) (Morris, Friston, and Dolan, 1997). In this regard these functional neuroimaging findings complement animal data that stress the importance of thalamoamygdala interactions in emotional learning (LeDoux et al., 1990; LeDoux, 1995; Campeau and Davis, 1995; LeDoux et al., 1988; LaBar and LeDoux, 1996). However, it is important to emphasize that the analysis of covariation in our functional neuroimaging data does not speak to the directionality of influence between these regions.

Plasticity in sensory systems associated with emotional learning

Emotional learning has been extensively investigated in animal models using electrophysiological methods. For

FIGURE 77.4   Aversive conditioning of faces. (A) Selective activation of the right pulvinar together with a graphical representation of the rCBF values. The SPM is the result of two orthogonal contrasts, the first selecting regions with a greater response to CS+ than CS– faces, and the second selecting voxels that responded more to happy expressions than fearful. The activation is displayed on a coronal slice of a canonical MRI image. The associated graph displays the adjusted mean activity (with bars showing 2 standard errors) for the right pulvinar. (B) Responses in the right amygdala, indexed by mean adjusted rCBF values for the CS+ and CS– conditions. (C) The regions that covary in response with activity in the pulvinar are shown superimposed on a structural MRI image. A, bilateral fusiform; B, hippocampus; C, right amygdala; D, medial forebrain; E, orbitofrontal cortex.

example, there is modulation of tonotopic auditory cortical responses when an animal learns, through conditioning, that an auditory stimulus predicts a future aversive event (Ashe, McKenna, and Weinberger, 1989; Edeline and Weinberger, 1991; Metherate and Ashe, 1991). This learning-related plasticity is dependent upon afferent inputs from medial geniculate nucleus (MGN) of thalamus, amygdala, and basal nucleus of Meynert (Weinberger, 1995). Little is known concerning the neural changes that ensue in the human brain consequent upon this type of emotional learning. It can be conjectured that the underlying mechanisms may be important in relation to psychopathological states such as phobias and posttraumatic stress disorder (PTSD).

THE PRIMARY AUDITORY CORTEX IN DISCRIMINATORY CONDITIONING   To determine sensory changes associated with emotional learning, we used a discriminatory learning paradigm involving presentation of high-frequency (8000-Hz) and low-frequency (200-Hz) pure auditory tones. Three types of sequence were employed: *nonconditioning*, during which only pure tones were played; *unpaired* in which four 100-dB white-noise bursts (one second duration) were played midway between tones (equal frequency between low-high, high-low, high, and low consecutive tone pairs to ensure no differential conditioning to one frequency); and *conditioning*, in which four 100-dB white-noise bursts were played immediately after the offset of tones of one frequency to produce discriminatory classical conditioning to either high or low tones in a 4:10 partial reinforcement schedule. The tone frequency paired with noise represented the CS+; the tone frequency unpaired with noise was the CS–. An illustration of the experimental design is provided in figure 77.5.

Regions were first identified with tonotopic responses to the two distinct tone frequencies (200 Hz and 8000 Hz) independent of conditioning using nonconditioning sequence scans. Within these regions frequency-specific

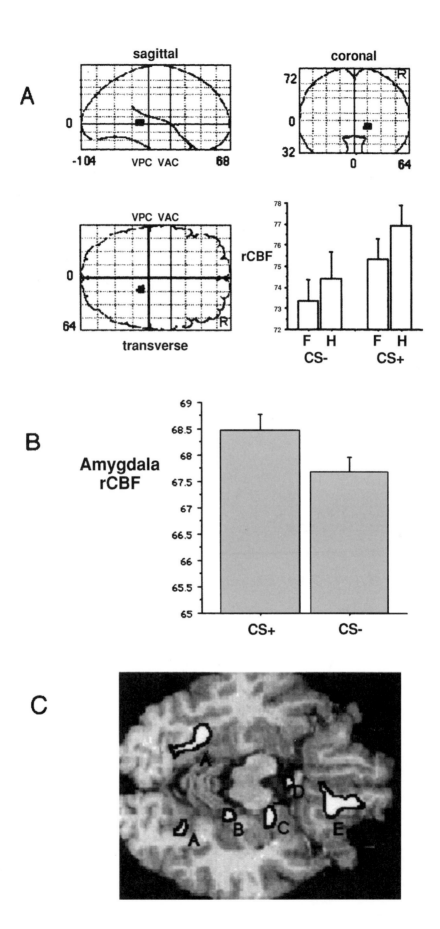

modulation of neural responses occurred with discriminatory conditioning (see figure 77.6A). Surprisingly, these modulations all involved decreases in neural response to conditioned tone (CS+). In other words, there was an apparent attenuation of neural response of low-frequency-selective auditory cortex regions by association of low tones with an aversive noise. Responses to high tones were unaffected in this region. Modulations identical to those seen for low tones occurred in high-frequency-selective regions.

Reversals of frequency selectivity in auditory cortex parallel the experience-dependent receptive-field plasticity demonstrated in a range of animal species (Scheich et al., 1993; Recanzone, Schreiner, and Merzenich, 1993; Edeline and Weinberger, 1992; Weinberger and Diamond, 1987). In these experiments there is a small and narrowly tuned increase in response of auditory cortex for the CS+ frequency with decreased responses to surrounding frequencies (Edeline and Weinberger, 1992). The surprising frequency-specific attenuation of neural responses to CS+ tones may reflect these intrinsic lateral inhibition effects. Frequency-specific augmented responses are spatially restricted and likely to be masked by a greater surround inhibition. Within the spatial resolution of PET, this surround inhibition would result in an overall net decrease in activity. An alternative explanation is that a learned expectancy of noise, in relation to the CS+ tone, results in a generalized attentional inhibition of responses to the CS+ tone. A final possibility is that the block design, involving repeated nonpaired presentation of the CS+ within a scanning window, results in auditory response profiles that reflect extinction. Consistent with this explanation are studies of auditory conditioning that report decreases in auditory cortex activity during extinction (Molchan et al., 1994; Schreurs et al., 1997).

MGB AND PRIMARY CORTEX CONNECTIVITY DURING DISCRIMINATORY LEARNING   In our model of value-dependent learning, stimuli that acquire salience are characterized by an ability to elicit responses in value systems. This effect occurs through a strengthening of connections between sensory systems and value systems. In auditory conditioning a crucial sensory processing region, in addition to primary auditory cortex, is the medial geniculate nucleus (MGN). When conditioning scans (CS+ and CS–) are contrasted with nonconditioning scans, increased activity is evident in a region of left inferoposterior thalamus that includes MGN and pulvinar. We reasoned that if conditioning-related modulation of auditory cortex responses was dependent on dynamic changes in the strength of inputs from MGN, then MGN activity should predict auditory cortex activ-

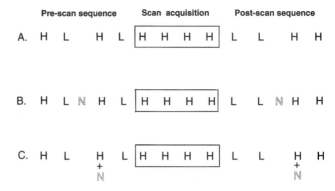

FIGURE 77.5 Diagrammatic representation of stimulus sequences in an auditory conditioning experiment. (A) A nonconditioning sequence during which no noises are played. (B) An unpaired sequence, identical to A, except that noise bursts are played midway between tones. (C) A conditioning sequence, identical to A and B, except that the noise bursts occur immediately following high-frequency tones. Note that noises never occur in any of the scanning windows (indicated by boxes). H, high-frequency tones; L, low-frequency tones: ℕ, noise-burst.

ity under the context of conditioning (compared to nonconditioning). As illustrated in figure 77.6B, the MGN contribution to activity in auditory cortex is significantly greater for the conditioning than nonconditioning sequences. This finding indicates that context-dependent alterations in the effective connectivity between MGN and auditory cortex accompany processing of stimuli with adaptive value (Friston et al., 1997). The similarity between conditioning-related dynamic interactions between MGN and auditory cortex in animals and humans is striking (McIntosh and Gonzalez-Lima, 1995).

Studying emotional learning with fMRI: An event-related approach

Studies using PET and fMRI have been limited by a necessity to use blocked designs in which target stimuli are repeatedly presented. In a typical experiment subjects are conditioned during one block by presenting a CS with a US and neural responses assessed in a second block when the CS is presented alone (Morris, Friston, and Dolan, 1997). However, this procedure is confounded by the fact that the second block, when a CS is presented alone, must reflect extinction as much as emotional learning. This distinction is critical given evidence that the neural systems implicated in learning acquisition and extinction differ (Rolls et al., 1994).

The optimal conditions to study emotional learning are met by event-related fMRI (Buckner et al., 1996; Dale and Buckner, 1997; Josephs, Turner, and Friston, 1997). This technique is similar to event-related potential

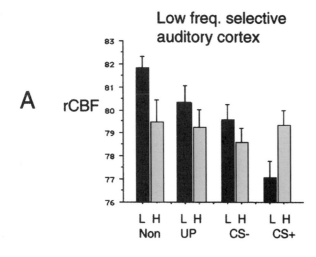

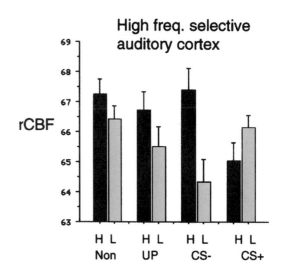

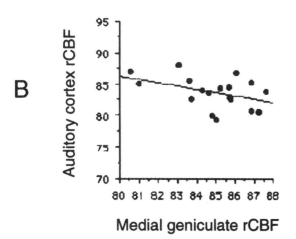

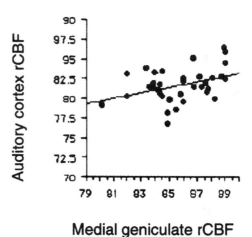

FIGURE 77.6 Learning-related modulation of auditory cortex. (A) Graphical displays of mean rCBF values for voxels in left auditory cortex with a selectivity for low-frequency and high-frequency tones. L, low-frequency tones; H, high-frequency tones; Non, nonconditioned scans; UP, scans in which both tone frequencies were unpaired with noise; CS+, scans in which the tone frequency associated with noise was presented; CS−, scans in which the tone frequency explicitly not associated with noise was presented. (B) Bivariate regression plots of rCBF values (in ml/dl/min) in auditory cortex ($x = -50$, $y = -12$, $z = -4$) and medial geniculate nucleus ($x = -12$, $y = -26$, $z = -2$) for conditioning and nonconditioning scans. Note the context-specific positive slope for conditioning and negative slope for nonconditioning sequences.

recordings in electrophysiology where responses to different stimuli are individually sampled and subsequently averaged. Recent technical advances have enabled a study of evoked hemodynamic responses for the whole brain, to conditioned and neutral reference stimuli, in a manner applicable to mixed-trial classical conditioning paradigms (Josephs, Turner, and Friston, 1997). In contrast to evoked responses in electrophysiology, the sampling rate (i.e., TR) in event-related fMRI is restricted. Consequently, to characterize hemodynamic responses to a target stimulus, it is necessary to sample data points after the onset of many stimuli at different peristimulus time points. This purpose can be achieved by the intro-

duction of a fixed or random jitter between the interstimulus interval (ISI) and TR.

MEASURING SINGLE NEURONAL RESPONSES DURING EMOTIONAL LEARNING   To assess neural responses to single events we chose four neutral faces, two male and two female from the Ekman series, as target stimuli (Ekman, 1982). Subjects were scanned during two distinct phases. During conditioning two of the four faces (one male, one female) were paired with an unpleasant tone, lasting 500 ms and adjusted to 10% above each subject's pain threshold, to become CS+. To assess evoked hemodynamic response to the CS+ in the absence of the

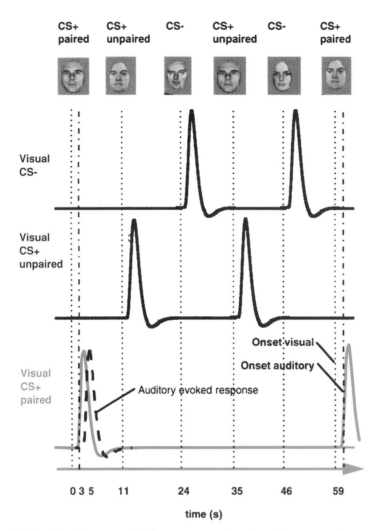

CS+ **CS+** **CS-** **CS+** **CS-** **CS+**
paired **unpaired** **unpaired** **paired**

Visual
CS-

Visual
CS+
unpaired

Visual
CS+
paired

Onset visual

Onset auditory

Auditory evoked response

0 3 5   11   24   35   46   59

time (s)

FIGURE 77.7   Single-event fMRI and conditioning. The figure describes the experimental design in which four images of faces were presented to subjects. Two faces were conditioned with an aversive tone using a 50% partial reinforcement schedule (i.e., half the presentations were followed by an aversive tone). Vertical dotted and dashed lines indicate the onset of the visual and auditory stimulus, respectively. The time course plots show the corresponding modeled hemodynamic responses time-locked to the onset of the face stimuli (CS−, unpaired CS+, and paired CS+). The time scale indicates that the ISI was randomized to introduce a phase shift between sampling and stimuli onset.

US (i.e., tone) a 50% partial reinforcement strategy was employed. In effect only half the presentations of the two CSs were paired with the tone. In total, 104 stimuli were presented over a period of approximately 20 minutes. Of these, 52 were neutral stimuli, 26 were CS paired with noise, and 26 were CS not paired with noise. Figure 77.7 provides an illustration of the experimental design.

Four event types were defined, three of which were time-locked to the onset of the presentation of the face and the fourth to the onset of the tone (Buechel et al., 1998). The three visual events were subdivided into (1) CS−, (2) CS+ unpaired, and (3) CS+ paired face stimuli (first three rows in figure 77.7). The comparisons of interest were between conditioning-evoked neural re-

sponses to the unpaired CS+ (i.e., no noise presentations) and the CS−. Differential activation of anterior cingulate gyrus and bilateral anterior insular cortex were seen for the CS+ conditions (figure 77.8; see color plate 47). Other differential responses, of lesser significance, were detected in motor output regions including the supplementary motor area (SMA), the left premotor cortex, and both red nuclei. Overall, these data implicate an extended neural system that includes insula as well as motor output regions, such as SMA, cingulate, and red nuclei in emotional learning.

The most robust activations were located in bilateral cingulate and insular cortices. The cingulate is a functionally heterogeneous region with known roles in regulating context-dependent behavior (Devinsky and

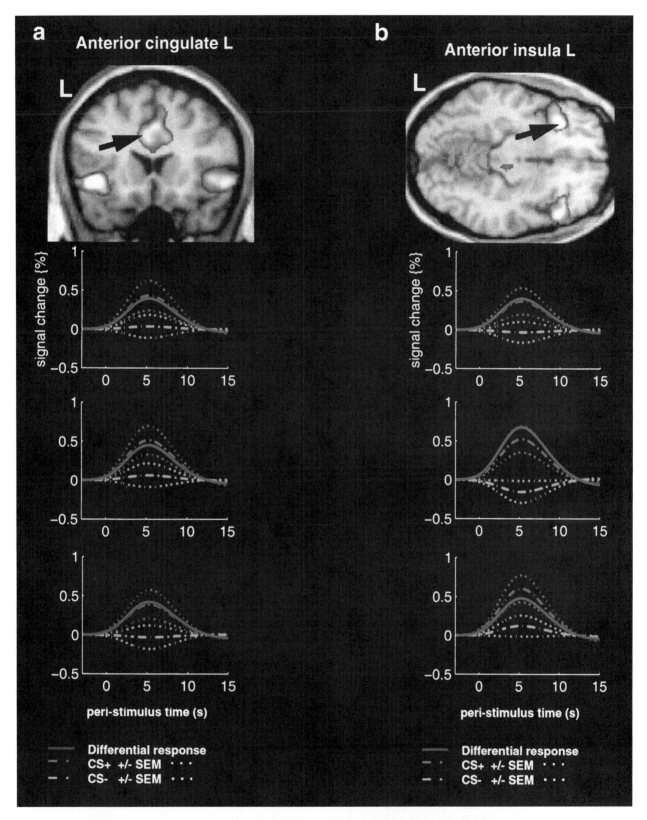

FIGURE 77.8 Averaged single event responses during acquisition. The top of the figure shows the focus of significant differential activations (CS+ > CS−) in anterior cingulate (circled) and bilateral anterior insula superimposed on a structural MRI scan. At the bottom the peristimulus time plots for all 6 subjects are displayed with reference to differential cingulate responses. The plots show the fitted response +/− the standard error of the mean (SEM) for CS− (blue) and unpaired CS+ (red) events. Dashed lines correspond to mean responses, and dotted lines are SEM. Statistical inference is based on the difference between the two responses, which is shown in green.

Luciano, 1993). Activation in a similar region has been reported in association with processing the affective component of painful stimuli (Rainville et al., 1997). Its activation with presentation of CS+ may reflect a predictive function with respect to the probability of occurrence of a future aversive event. Alternatively, its engagement may reflect adaptive sensorimotor responses to salient stimuli with activation of brainstem nuclei (red nuclei) reflecting a more downstream component. This latter region is also implicated in animal and human eye-blink conditioning paradigms (Logan and Grafton, 1995; Clark and Lavond, 1993; Desmond and Moore, 1991). The other highlighted region was the anterior insula. This is an area with projections to anterior cingulate, perirhinal, entorhinal, and peri-amygdaloid cortex and various amygdaloid nuclei that has led to its conceptualization as an area functionally associated with emotional processing (Augustine, 1996). Its strong connections to sensory regions may mean that its activation reflects changes in the bodily state that anticipate adversity, in this case an unpleasant noise (Mesulam and Mufson, 1982). In terms of our model the insula may mediate interoceptive inputs to value systems that reflect anticipatory homeostatic changes. Several functional neuroimaging studies suggest a role for the anterior insula in processing emotional contexts, for example pain (Casey et al., 1994) or the recollection of affect-laden autobiographical information (Fink et al., 1996). The mnemonic component of our study is that the CS+ is predictive of a future unpleasant sensory event (US).

Surprisingly, amygdala responses were not found in a categorical comparison of neural responses to a CS+ versus a CS−. One possible explanation is that amygdala response shows rapid habituation during emotional learning as indicated in animal experiments (Breiter et al., 1996). Temporal effects, where the magnitude of response changes over time, would not be revealed in a simple categorical analysis and need to be explicitly tested for using time-by-event-type interactions. In effect these test for areas in which neural responses to a CS+ decrease over time, and at the same time this pattern is significantly different for responses evoked by the CS−. In this analysis there were significant differential adaptations evident for the CS+ relative to the CS−, indicating rapid habituation of amygdalae responses for the CS+ that were significant for bilateral amygdalae (see figure 77.9). These data are remarkably similar to those seen in animal classical conditioning (Bordi et al., 1993; Quirk, Armony, and LeDoux, 1997) and neuroimaging experiments from other groups (LaBar et al., 1998). The transient response profile of the amygdala suggests a role in early phases of emotional learning. A similar early versus late dissociation during learning suggested for the hippocampus may also apply to the amygdala.

Conscious awareness and processing of learned fear

Ekman, in proposing the concept of affect programs, had little to say concerning their neurophysiological implementation. However, he was explicit in proposing that some elicitors "will activate the facial affect program with little or no prior cognitive processing" (Ekman, 1971). Important empirical research, consistent with this conjecture, includes evidence of discriminatory skin conductance responses (SCRs) to aversively conditioned stimuli that have been backwardly masked to prevent conscious awareness of their occurrence (Esteves, Dimberg, and Öhman, 1994; Öhman and Soares, 1994; Parra et al., 1997). An intriguing neurobiological question is how, in the absence of conscious awareness, the brain discriminates between physically equivalent stimuli when one of the stimuli has acquired salience through prior learning. A related question is whether level of awareness of an emotionally salient stimulus modulates the associated neural processing.

The ability of the brain to discriminate between salient stimuli without conscious awareness provides evidence that, in certain contexts, processing of inputs to value systems may be obligatory. It has been proposed that an integrated response to threat or danger, without higher level processing, can be mediated via the amygdala (Kling and Brothers, 1992) or thalamic-amygdala circuitry (LeDoux, 1996). In terms of emotional learning, patients with amygdala damage fail to acquire conditioned SCRs to stimuli paired with an aversive unconditioned stimulus (US) despite intact declarative knowledge concerning stimulus associations (Bechara et al., 1995; LaBar et al., 1995). Conversely, patients with intact amygdalae and damaged hippocampi acquire reliable discriminatory SCRs but cannot report which stimuli have been paired with the UCS (Bechara et al., 1995). The role of the amygdala is also highlighted by functional neuroimaging data (fMRI) where discriminatory responses to masked fearful and happy faces have been demonstrated in the absence of explicit awareness of their occurrence (Whalen et al., 1998).

CONSCIOUS AND UNCONSCIOUS PROCESSING OF FEARFUL FACES   To determine how the brain discriminates between salient stimuli in the absence of conscious awareness, we used a backward masking procedure involving presenting targets on a screen for 30 milliseconds immediately followed by a masking stimulus for 45 milliseconds (Morris, Öhman, and Dolan, 1998). This

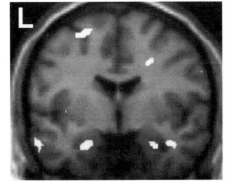

a

L

y = -3 mm

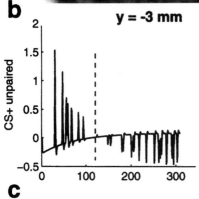

b

CS+ unpaired

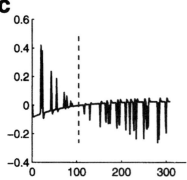

c

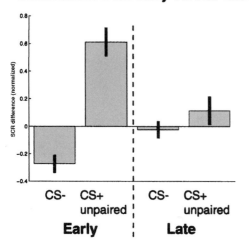

d Interaction: SCR early versus late

SCR difference (normalized)

CS- | CS+ unpaired | CS- | CS+ unpaired
Early | **Late**

FIGURE 77.9 (a) Bilateral activation of amygdalae for an analysis based on a time-by-condition (CS+ versus CS−) interaction. (b and c) Fitted responses for CS+ in the left amygdala from two individual subjects. It can be seen that responses are initially positive and then attenuate to become relative deactivations (relative to baseline). (d) Differences in SCRs for CS+ and CS− for first 8 minutes and last 12 minutes of conditioning corresponding to scanning data. This interaction between early and late phases is significant and mirrors that seen for the amygdala response in terms of early and late components.

procedure effectively prevents reportable awareness of the target stimulus (see figure 77.10A). Faces were again used and consisted of two angry and two neutral expressions. In a conditioning study phase, one of the angry faces (the CS+) was paired with a 1-second 100-dB white-noise burst. None of the neutral faces was ever paired with noise. During scanning, faces consisting of a target and mask were repeatedly shown at 5-second intervals for each experimental condition. In effect, for half the experimental conditions, subjects' awareness of the target angry faces, conditioned and unconditioned, was prevented by masking with neutral faces (see figure 77.10B). The subject's task was to report, by pressing a button, the occurrence of an angry face. The factorial design of the experiment is outlined in figure 77.10C.

Behaviorally, none of the angry faces were reported in the masked condition, whereas the detection rate of unmasked angry faces was 100%. Mean SCRs were significantly greater for CS+ than CS− faces, both for masked and unmasked presentations. Contrasting all CS+ (masked and unmasked) with all CS− scans (masked and unmasked) revealed bilateral amygdala responses. When neural responses to unmasked CS+ and CS− faces were contrasted, a significant response was evident in the region of the left amygdala (see figure 77.10D). To determine whether this amygdala response also occurred when subjects were not aware of the conditioned faces, we contrasted masked CS+ and CS− scans. This comparison revealed a highly significant effect in the right amygdala (see figure 77.10E). The interaction between conditioning and masking indicated that the right amygdala response to CS+ faces is significantly enhanced by masking while the left amygdala response is enhanced by unmasking. Note again that the only difference between the CS+ and CS− conditions was subjects' prior experience of the temporal association between CS+ faces and an aversive noise.

Two general conclusions can be drawn from these data. First, they indicate that the amygdala discriminates between perceptually similar stimuli solely on the basis of their prior history. This discrimination (at least for the right amygdala) occurs without conscious awareness of a

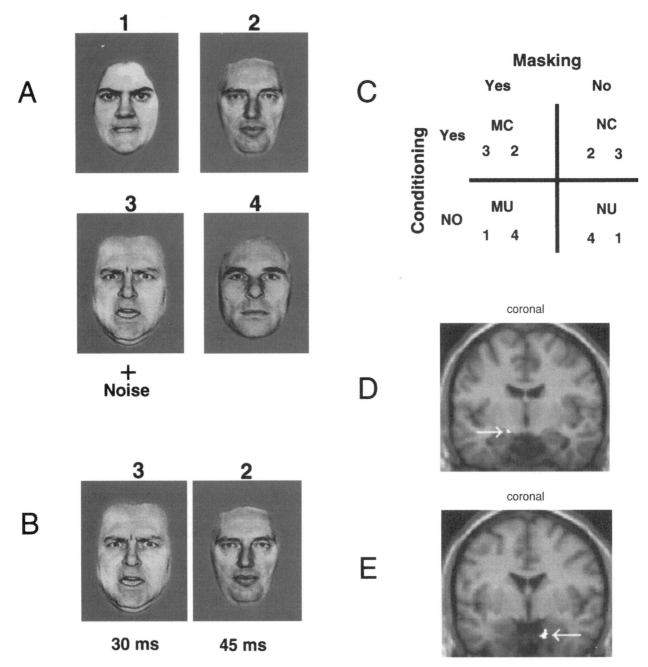

FIGURE 77.10 Masking of aversively conditioned faces. (A) In a prescanning conditioning sequence, 2 angry faces (1 and 3) and 2 neutral faces were shown sequentially for 75 ms at 15–25-s intervals. One of the angry faces (3) was always followed by a 100-dB white-noise burst. (B) During scanning, 2 faces were shown in rapid succession to produce backward masking of the first face by the second. In all conditions, the target face was displayed for 30-ms and immediately followed by a 45-ms mask. (C) There were 4 separate conditions, determined by whether the angry face was masked or conditioned. MC, masked conditioned; NC, nonmasked conditioned; MU, masked unconditioned; NU, nonmasked unconditioned. (D) The figure shows activation of left amygdala in the contrast of unmasked CS+ and CS– angry faces displayed on a coronal slice of a group averaged MRI image. (E) Activation of right amygdala in the contrast of masked CS+ and CS– angry faces.

target stimulus. These data also extend functional neuroimaging findings that the amygdala can discriminate between salient, but categorically distinct, facial emotions (Whalen et al., 1998). The data also provide a

mechanistic account of behavioral observations that indicate unconscious processing of previously learned aversive stimuli (Esteves, Dimberg, and Öhman, 1994; Öhman and Soares, 1994; Parra et al., 1997). Second, the pattern of lateralization is modulated by reportable awareness of the target stimulus. This finding suggests that factors related to conscious awareness, for example automatic engagement of language systems, influence processing of salience. "Split-brain" patients can verbally report stimuli shown to the isolated left hemisphere but deny awareness of the same stimuli presented to the right hemisphere (Gazzaniga, 1989). Conversely, the isolated right hemisphere shows superior performance in tasks involving facial and emotional processing (Gazzaniga, 1989; DeKosky et al., 1980). The lateralized amygdala responses indicate that the same segregation of reportable and unreportable processing observed in split-brain subjects is also manifest in the intact brain.

Conclusions

The account of emotional processing outlined has focused on a primary emotion, fear. A critical role for the amygdala is highlighted in discriminating between stimuli that represent danger and during emotional learning. Discriminatory emotional learning is associated with neural plasticity in primary sensory regions and changes in afferent connection strengths to these regions. The response profile of the amygdala, during emotional learning, is complex and is best characterized in terms of time-dependent changes involving early activation and late deactivations. The amygdala's role in processing behaviorally relevant stimuli would seem to be automatic and obligatory in that its response can discriminate between the behaviorally relevant sensory inputs independent of conscious awareness.

REFERENCES

ADOLPHS, R., D. TRANEL, H. DAMASIO, and A. DAMASIO, 1994. Impaired recognition of emotion in facial expressions following bilateral damage to the human amygdala. *Nature* 372:669–672.

ADOLPHS, R., D. TRANEL, H. DAMASIO, and A. R. DAMASIO, 1995. Fear and the human amygdala. *J. Neurosci.* 15:5879–5891.

AGGLETON, J. P., M. J. BURTON, and R. E. PASSINGAHAM, 1980. Cortical and subcortical afferents to the amygdala in the rhesus monkey (*Macaca mulatta*). *Brain Res.* 190:347–368.

AMARAL, D. G., and J. L. PRICE, 1984. Amygdalo-cortical projections in the monkey (*Macaca fascicularis*). *J. Comp. Neurol.* 230:465–496.

AMARAL, D., J. L. PRICE, A. PITKANEN, and S. T. CARMICHAEL, 1992. Anatomical organization of the primate amygdaloid complex. In *The Amygdala: Neurobiological Aspects of Emotion, Memory and Mental Dysfunction*, J. P. Aggleton, ed. New York: Wiley-Liss, pp. 1–66.

ASHE, J. H., T. M. MCKENNA, and N. M. WEINBERGER, 1989. Cholinergic modulation of frequency receptive fields in auditory cortex: Frequency-specific effects of anticholinesterases provide evidence for a modulatory action of endogenous ACH. *Synapse* 4:44–54.

AUGUSTINE, A. R., 1996. Circuitry and functional aspects of the insular lobe in primates including humans. *Brain Res. Rev.* 22:229–244.

BECHARA, A., D. TRANEL, H. DAMASIO, R. ADOLPHS, C. ROCKLAND, and A. R. DAMASIO, 1995. Double dissociation of conditioning and declarative knowledge relative to the amygdala and hippocampus in humans. *Science* 269:115–118.

BORDI, F., J. E. LEDOUX, M. C. CLUGNET, and C. PAVLIDES, 1993. Single-unit activity in the lateral nucleus of the amygdala and overlying areas of striatum in freely behaving rats: Rates, discharge patterns, and responses to acoustic stimuli. *Behav. Neurosci.* 107:757–769.

BREITER, H. C., N. L. ECTOFF, P. J. WHALEN, D. N. KENNEDY, S. L. RAUCH, R. L. BUCKNER, M. M. STRAUSS, S. E. HYMAN, and B. R. ROSEN, 1996. Response and habituation of the human amygdala during visual processing of facial expression. *Neuron* 2:875–887.

BROTHERS, L., 1997. *Friday's Footprint.* New York: Oxford University Press.

BUCKNER, R. L., P. A. BANDETTINI, K. M. OCRAVEN, R. L. SAVOY, S. E. PETERSEN, M. E. RAICHLE, and B. R. ROSEN, 1996. Detection of cortical activation during averaged single trials of a cognitive task using functional magnetic-resonance-imaging. *Proc. Natl. Acad. Sci. U.S.A.* 93:14878–14883.

BUECHEL, C., J. MORRIS, R. J. DOLAN, and K. J. FRISTON, 1998. Brain systems mediating aversive conditioning: An event related fMRI study. *Neuron* 20:947–957.

CALDER, A. J., A. W. YOUNG, D. ROWLAND, D. I. PERRETT, J. R. HODGES, and N. L. ETCOFF, 1996. Facial emotion recognition after bilateral amygdala damage: Differentially severe impairment of fear. *Cognit. Neuropsychol.* 13:699–745.

CAMPEAU, S., and M. DAVIS, 1995. Involvement of subcortical and cortical afferents to the lateral nucleus of the amygdala in fear conditioning measured with fear potentiated startle in rats trained concurrently with auditory and visual conditioned stimuli. *J. Neurosci.* 15:2301–2311.

CASEY, K. L., S. MINOSHIMA, K. L. BERGER, R. A. KOEPPE, T. J. MORROW, and K. A. FREY, 1994. Positron emission tomographic analysis of cerebral structures activated specifically by repetitive noxious heat stimuli. *J. Neurophysiol.* 71:802–807.

CLARK, R. E., and D. G. LAVOND, 1993. Reversible lesions of the red nucleus during acquisition and retention of a classically-conditioned behavior in rabbits. *Behav. Neurosci.* 107:264–270.

DALE, A. M., and R. L. BUCKNER, 1997. Selective averaging of rapidly presented individual trials using fMRI. *Hum. Brain Mapp.* 5:329–340.

DAMASIO, A. R., 1995. *Descartes Error.* London: Picador.

DARWIN, C., 1965. *The Expression of the Emotions in Man and Animals.* Chicago: University of Chicago Press.

DEKOSKY, S. T., K. M. HEILMAN, D. BOWERS, and E. VALENSTEIN, 1980. Recognition and discrimination of emotional faces and pictures. *Brain Lang.* 9:206–214.

DESMOND, J. E., and J. W. MOORE, 1991. Single-unit activity in red nucleus during the classically-conditioned rabbit nictitating-membrane response. *Neurosci. Res.* 10:260–279.

DEVINSKY, O., and D. LUCIANO, 1993. The contributions of the cingulate cortex to human behavior. In *Neurobiology of the*

Cingulate Cortex and Limbic Thalamus. B. A. Vogt and M. Gabriel, eds. Boston: Birkhauser, pp. 527–556.

DOLAN, R. J., G. R. FINK, E. ROLLS, M. BOOTH, A. HOLMES, R. S. J. FRACKOWIAK, and K. J. FRISTON, 1997. How the brain learns to see objects and faces in an impoverished context. *Nature* 389:596–599.

EDELINE, J.-M., and N. M. WEINBERGER, 1991. Thalamic short term plasticity in the auditory system: Associative retuning of receptive fields in the ventral medial geniculate body. *Behav. Neurosci.* 105:618–639.

EDELINE, J.-M., and N. M. WEINBERGER, 1992. Associative retuning in the thalamic source of input to the amygdala and auditory cortex: Receptive field plasticity in the medial division of the medial geniculate body. *Behav. Neurosci.* 106:81–105.

EKMAN, P., 1971. Universals and cultural differences in facial expressions of emotion. In *Nebraska Symposium on Motivation*, J. K. Cole, ed. Lincoln: University of Nebraska Press, pp. 207–284.

EKMAN, P., 1982. *Emotion in the Human Face.* Cambridge, England: Cambridge University Press.

EKMAN, P., and W. V. FRIESEN, 1971. Constants across cultures in the face and emotion. *J. Pers. Soc. Psychol.* 17:124–129.

ESTEVES, F., U. DIMBERG, and A. ÖHMAN, 1994. Automatically elicited fear: Conditioned skin conductance responses to masked facial expressions. *Cognit. Emotion* 9:99–108.

ETCOFF, N. L., 1984. Selective attention to facial identity and facial emotion. *Neuropsychologia* 22:281–295.

FINK, G. R., H. J. MARKOWITSCH, M. REINKEMEIER, T. BRUCKBAUER, J. KESSLER, and W.-D. HEISS, 1996. Cerebral representation of one's own past: Neural networks involved in autobiographical memory. *J. Neurosci.* 16:4275–4282.

FRIED, I., K. A. MACDONALD, and C. L. WILSON, 1997. Single neuron activity in hippocampus and amygdala during recognition of faces and objects. *Neuron* 18:875–887.

FRISTON, K. J., C. BUECHAL, G. FINK, J. S. MORRIS, E. T. ROLLS, and R. J. DOLAN, 1997. Psychophysiological and modulatory interactions in neuroimaging. *Neuroimage* 6:218–219.

FRISTON, K. J., C. D. FRITH, and R. S. J. FRACKOWIAK, 1993. Time-dependent changes in effective connectivity measured with PET. *Hum. Brain Mapp.* 1:69–79.

FRISTON, K. J., G. TONONI, G. N. REEKE, O. SPORNS, and G. M. EDELMAN, 1994. Value-dependent selection in the brain: Simulation in a synthetic neural model. *Neuroscience* 30:77–86.

GAZZANIGA, M. S., 1989. Organization of the Human Brain. *Science* 245:947–951.

GRIFFITHS, P. E., 1997. *What Emotions Really Are.* Chicago: University of Chicago Press.

IWAI, E., and M. YUKIE, 1987. Amygdalofugal and amygdalopetal connections with modality-specific visual cortical areas in macaques (*Macaca fuscata, M. mulatta, M. fascicularis*). *J. Comp. Neurol.* 261:362–387.

IZARD, C. E., 1998. *The Face of Emotion.* New York: Appleton-Century-Crofts.

JONES, E. G., and H. BURTON, 1976. A projection from the medial pulvinar to the amygdala in primates. *Brain Res.* 104:142–147.

JONES, E. G., and T. P. S. POWELL, 1970. An anatomical study of converging sensory pathways within the cerebral cortex of the monkey. *Brain* 93:793–820.

JOSEPHS, O., R. TURNER, and K. FRISTON, 1997. Event-related fMRI. *Hum. Brain Mapp.* 5:243–248.

KANWISHER, N., J. MCDERMOTT, and M. M. CHUN, 1997. The fusiform face area: A module in human extrastriate cortex specialized for face perception. *J. Neurosci.* 17:4302–4311.

KETTER, T. A., P. J. ANDREASON, M. S. GEORGE, C. LEE, D. S. GILL, P. I. PAREKH, M. W. WILLIS, P. HERSCOVITCH, and R. M. POST, 1996. Anterior paralimbic mediation of procaine-induced emotional and psychosensory experience. *Arch. Gen. Psychiatry* 53:59–69.

KLING, A. S., and L. A. BROTHERS, 1992. The amygdala and social behavior. In *The Amygdala: Neurobiological Aspects of Emotion, Memory and Mental Dysfunction.* J. P. Aggleton, ed. New York: Wiley-Liss.

LABAR, K. S., J. C. GATENBY, J. C. GORE, J. E. LEDOUX, and E. A. PHELPS, 1998. Human amygdala activation during conditioned fear acquisition and extinction: A mixed-trial fMRI study. *Neuron* 20:937–945.

LABAR, K. S., and J. E. LEDOUX, 1996. Partial disruption of fear conditioning in rat with unilateral amygdala damage–correspondence with unilateral temporal lobe damage in humans. *Behav. Neurosci.* 110:991–997.

LABAR, K. S., J. E. LEDOUX, D. D. SPENCER, and E. A. PHELPS, 1995. Impaired fear conditioning following unilateral temporal lobectomy. *J. Neurosci.* 15:6846–6855.

LEDOUX, J. E., 1989. Cognitive-emotional interactions in the brain. *Cognit. Emotion* 3:267–289.

LEDOUX, J. E., 1993. Emotional memory systems in the brain. *Behav. Brain Res.* 58:69–79.

LEDOUX, J. E., 1995. In search of an emotional system in the brain: Leaping from fear to emotion and consciousness. In *The Cognitive Neurosciences*, M. Gazzaniga, ed. Cambridge, Mass.: MIT Press, pp. 1049–1061.

LEDOUX, J., 1996. *The Emotional Brain.* New York: Simon and Schuster.

LEDOUX, J. E., P. CICCHETTI, A. XAGORARIS, and L. M. ROMANSKI, 1990. The lateral amygdaloid nucleus: Sensory interface of the amygdala in fear conditioning. *J. Neurosci.* 10:1062–1069.

LEDOUX, J. E., J. IWATA, P. CICCHETTI, and D. REIS, 1988. Differential projections of the central amygdaloid nucleus mediate autonomic and behavioral correlates of conditioned fear. *J. Neurosci.* 8:2517–2529.

LOGAN, C. G., and S. T. GRAFTON, 1995. Functional-anatomy of human eyeblink conditioning determined with regional cerebral glucose-metabolism and positron emission tomography. *Proc. Natl. Acad. Sci. U.S.A.* 92:7500–7504.

MCINTOSH, A. R., and F. GONZALEZ-LIMA, 1995. Functional network interactions between parallel auditory pathways during Pavlovian conditioned inhibition. *Brain Res.* 693:228–241.

MESULAM, M.-M., and E. J. MUFSON, 1982. Insula of the old world monkey. 3. Efferent cortical output and comments on its function. *J. Comp. Neurol.* 242:38–52.

MESULAM, M.-M., E. J. MUFSON, A. I. LEVEY, and B. H. WAINER, 1983. Cholinergic innervation of cortex by basal forebrain: Cytochemistry and cortical connections of the septal area, diagonal band nuclei, nucleus basalis (substantia innominata) and hypothalamus in the rhesus monkey. *J. Comp. Neurol.* 214:170–197.

METHERATE, R., and J. H. ASHE, 1991. Basal forebrain stimulation modifies auditory cortex responsiveness by an action at muscarinic receptors. *Brain Res.* 559:163–167.

MOLCHAN, S. E., T. SUNDERLAND, A. R. McINTOSH, O. HER-SCOVITCH, and B. G. SCHREURS, 1994. A functional anatomical study of associative learning in humans. *Proc. Natl. Acad. Sci. U.S.A.* 91:8122–8126.

MORRIS, J. S., K. J. FRISTON, C. BUECHEL, C. D. FRITH, A. W. YOUNG, A. J. CALDER, and R. J. DOLAN, 1998. A neuromodulatory role for the human amygdala in processing emotional facial expressions. *Brain* 121:47–55.

MORRIS, J., K. J. FRISTON, and R. J. DOLAN, 1997. Neural responses to salient visual stimuli. *Proc. R. Soc. Lond. B* 264: 769–775.

MORRIS, J., C. D. FRITH, D. PERRETT, D. ROWLAND, A. W. YOUNG, A. J. CALDER, and R. J. DOLAN, 1996. A differential neural response in the human amygdala to fearful and happy facial expressions. *Nature* 383:812–815.

MORRIS, J. S., A. ÖHMAN, and R. J. DOLAN, 1998. Conscious and unconscious emotional learning in the human amygdala. *Nature* 393:467–470.

ÖHMAN, A., M. FREDRIKSON, and K. HUGDAHL, 1976. Premise of equipotentiality in human classical conditioning. *J. Exp. Psychol.* 105:313–337.

ÖHMAN, A., and J. F. SOARES, 1994. "Unconscious anxiety": Phobic responses to masked stimuli. *J. Abnorm. Psychol.* 103: 231–240.

OLSHAUSEN, B. A., C. H. ANDERSON, and D. C. VAN ESSEN, 1993. A neurobiological model of visual attention and invariant pattern recognition based on dynamic routing of information. *J. Neurosci.* 13:4700–4719.

PARRA, C., F. ESTEVES, A. FLYKT, and A. ÖHMAN, 1997. Pavlovian conditioning to social stimuli: Backward masking and dissociation of implicit and explicit cognitive processes. *Eur. Psychol.* 2:106–117.

PERRETT, D., K. A. MAY, and S. YOSHIKAWA, 1994. Female shape and judgements of female attractiveness. *Nature* 368:239–242.

PETERSEN, S. E., D. L. ROBINSON, and W. KEYS, 1985. Pulvinar nuclei of the behaving rhesus monkey: Visual responses and their modulation. *J. Neurophysiol.* 54:867–886.

PETERSEN, S. E, D. L. ROBINSON, and J. D. MORRIS, 1987. Contributions of the pulvinar to visual spatial attention. *Neuropsychologia* 25:97–105.

POSNER, M. I., and S. E. PETERSEN, 1990. The attention system of the human brain. *Annu. Rev. Neurosci.* 13:25–42.

QUIRK, G. J., J. L. ARMONY, and J. E. LEDOUX, 1997. Fear conditioning enhances different temporal components of tone-evoked spike trains in auditory cortex and lateral amygdala. *Neuron* 19:613–624.

RAFAL, R. D., and M. I. POSNER, 1989. Deficits in human visual spatial attention following thalamic lesions. *Neuropsychologia* 27:1031–1041.

RAINVILLE, P., G. H. DUNCAN, D. D. PRICE, B. CARRIER, and M. C. BUSHNELL, 1997. Pain affect encoded in human anterior cingulate but not somatosensory cortex. *Science* 277: 968–971.

RECANZONE, G. H., C. E. SCHREINER, and M. M. MERZENICH, 1993. Plasticity in the frequency representation of primary auditory cortex following discrimination training in adult owl monkeys. *J. Neurosci.* 13:87–103.

ROBINSON, D. L., and S. E. PETERSEN, 1992. The pulvinar and visual salience. *Trends Neurosci.* 1:127–132.

ROLLS, E. T., 1995. A theory of emotion and consciousness, and its application to understanding the neural basis of emotion. In *The Cognitive Neurosciences*, M. S. Gazzaniga, ed. Cambridge, Mass.: MIT Press, pp. 1091–1106.

ROLLS, E. T., J. HORNAK, D. WADE, and J. McGRATH, 1994. Emotion-related learning in patients with social and emotional changes associated with frontal lobe damage. *J. Neurol. Neurosurg. Psychiatry* 57:1518–1524.

RUSSCHEN, F. T., D. G. AMARAL, and J. L. PRICE, 1985. The afferent connections of the substantia innominata in the monkey, *Macaca fascicularis. J. Comp. Neurol.* 242:1–27.

SCHEICH, H., C. SIMONIS, F. OHL, J. TILLEIN, and H. THOMAS, 1993. Functional organization and learning-related plasticity in auditory cortex of the Mongolian gerbil. *Prog. Brain Res.* 97:135–143.

SCHREURS, B. G., A. R. McINTOSH, M. BAHRO, P. HERSCOVITCH, T. SUNDERLAND, and S. E. MOLCHAN, 1997. Lateralisation and behavioral correlation of changes in regional cerebral blood flow with classical conditioning of the human eyeblink response. *J. Neurophysiol.* 77:2153–2163.

SELIGMAN, M. E. P., 1971. Phobias and preparedness. *Behav. Ther.* 2:307–320.

SERGENT, J., S. OHTA, B. MacDONALD, and E. ZUCK, 1994. Segregated processing of facial identity and emotion in the human brain: A PET study. *Vis. Cogn.* 1:349–369.

WEINBERGER, N. M., 1995. Retuning the brain by fear conditioning. In *The Cognitive Neurosciences*, M. Gazzaniga, ed. Cambridge, Mass.: MIT Press, pp. 1071–1090.

WEINBERGER, N. M., and D. M. DIAMOND, 1987. Physiological plasticity of single neurons in auditory cortex: Rapid induction by learning. *Prog. Neurobiol.* 29:1–55.

WHALEN, P. J., and B. S. KAPP, 1991. Contributions of the amygdaloid central nucleus to the modulation of the nictitating membrane reflex in the rabbit. *Behav. Neurosci.* 104:141–153.

WHALEN, P. J., S. L. RAUSCH, N. L. ETCOFF, S. C. McINERNEY, M. B. LEE, and M. A. JENIKE, 1998. Masked presentations of emotional facial expression modulate amygdala activity without explicit knowledge. *J. Neurosci.* 18:411–418.

YOUNG, A. W., F. NEWCOMBE, E. H. F. DE HAAN, M. SMALL, and D. C. HAY, 1993. Face perception after brain injury: Selective impairments affecting identity and expression. *Brain* 116:941–959.

78 Posttraumatic Stress Disorder: Emotion, Conditioning, and Memory

ROGER K. PITMAN, ARIEH Y. SHALEV, AND SCOTT P. ORR

ABSTRACT Posttraumatic stress disorder (PTSD) provides illustrations of human mechanisms of emotion, conditioning, and memory that can inform cognitive neuroscience. Because the etiologic event can be clearly identified, the role of Pavlovian conditioning is clearer in PTSD than in other mental disorders. Laboratory studies have confirmed the presence of peripheral physiologic reactivity upon exposure to internal or external cues that symbolize or resemble an aspect of the traumatic event in PTSD. Functional neuroimaging studies implicate the anterior paralimbic system, including the amygdala, as a key brain area in the formation and elaboration of posttraumatic conditioned fear responses. In contrast, structural neuroimaging and functional memory studies suggest posterior paralimbic (i.e., hippocampal) impairment in PTSD. Persons with PTSD appear to be more conditionable on a constitutional or acquired basis. They are also more reactive to nonconditioned, especially startling, stimuli. Facilitation of emotional memory by stress hormones (especially epinephrine) released at the time of the traumatic event is theoretically involved in the pathogenesis of PTSD.

Because psychopathologic phenomena often represent extreme forms of ordinarily adaptive human behavior, evolutionary neurobiologic mechanisms may be cast in higher relief in the mentally disordered. Darwin (1872) noted that the behavior of insane patients reveals the "brute nature" within human beings. Behavior associated with mental disorders constitutes potentially useful data that are often overlooked by basic scientists.

The recently rediscovered mental disorder known as posttraumatic stress disorder (PTSD) provides illustrations of human mechanisms of emotion, conditioning, and memory that can inform cognitive neuroscience. This chapter will examine some examples. Comprehensive reviews of the neurobiology of PTSD have appeared elsewhere (Friedman, Charney, and Deutch, 1995; Yehuda and McFarlane, 1997).

ROGER K. PITMAN and SCOTT P. ORR Veterans Affairs Research Service, Manchester, N.H.; Massachusetts General Hospital, Boston, Mass.; Department of Psychiatry, Harvard Medical School, Boston, Mass.

ARIEH Y. SHALEV Department of Psychiatry, Hadassah University Hospital; Hebrew University Medical School, Jerusalem, Israel

PTSD and conditioned fear

The current clinical definition of PTSD according to the *Diagnostic and Statistical Manual of Mental Disorders*, 4th ed. (DSM-IV; American Psychiatric Association, 1994) appears in abbreviated form in table 78.1. Readers of this chapter will readily recognize the basic elements of classical (or Pavlovian) conditioning that it incorporates. After a traumatic event (unconditioned stimulus, or UCS) has induced an intense emotional response of fear, helplessness, or horror (unconditioned response, or UCR), external and internal cues that were present at the time of the traumatic event (conditioned stimuli, or CSs) acquire the capacity through their association with the traumatic experience to evoke intense emotional responses (conditioned responses, or CRs) on subsequent occasions. Avoidance of emotionally distressing and arousing trauma-related cues reflects secondary operant conditioning.

In addition to the specific symptoms of PTSD (B.1–5, C.1–3 in table 78.1) that are related to conditioning and uniquely define this disorder, there are several general psychiatric symptoms (C.4–7, D.1–4) that PTSD shares with other anxiety and/or depressive disorders.

PERIPHERAL PHYSIOLOGIC RESPONSES TO TRAUMA-RELATED CUES DSM-IV PTSD criterion B.5, "physiological reactivity upon exposure to internal or external cues that symbolize or resemble an aspect of the traumatic event," has been amply supported in the laboratory. Several studies have shown that audiovisual cues of battle situations (e.g., pictures of ground troops unloading from helicopters, sounds of machine gun fire) produce larger increases in heart rate (HR) and blood pressure (BP) in veterans with PTSD (reviews in Blanchard, 1990; Orr, 1994; Shalev and Rogel-Fuchs, 1993). McNally and colleagues (1987) reported larger skin conductance (SC) responses to combat-related words in Vietnam veterans with PTSD.

When individuals with PTSD have recalled past traumatic events via internal, script-driven imagery, they have produced larger HR, SC, and facial electromyogram

1133

TABLE 78.1

Abridged DSM-IV diagnostic criteria for PTSD (American Psychiatric Association, 1994)

A. Traumatic event/response
   1. An event that threatens or inflicts serious injury to self or others
   2. A response of intense fear, helplessness, or horror

B. Reexperiencing criteria (one required)
   1. Recurrent, intrusive, distressing recollections of the traumatic event
   2. Recurrent, distressing dreams of the traumatic event
   3. Flashbacks to the traumatic event
   4/5. Intense psychological distress/physiological reactivity on exposure to traumatic event–related cues

C. Avoidance/numbing criteria (three required)
   1. Of thoughts and feelings associated with the trauma
   2. Of activities, places, or people associated with the trauma
   3. Inability to recall an important aspect of the trauma
   4. Markedly diminished interest in significant activities
   5. Feelings of detachment or estrangement from others
   6. Restricted range of affect (numbing)
   7. Sense of a foreshortened future

D. Arousal criteria (two required)
   1. Insomnia
   2. Irritability or outbursts of anger
   3. Difficulty concentrating
   4. Hypervigilance
   5. Exaggerated startle response

E. Duration at least one month

F. Distress/impairment, e.g., social, occupational

(EMG) responses than individuals who experienced similarly stressful events but did not develop the disorder (review in Orr, 1994). This finding has held for various types of traumatic events including combat in Vietnam (Pitman et al., 1987), Korea, and World War II (Orr et al., 1993); terrorist attacks and other traumatic events (Shalev, Orr, and Pitman, 1993); and childhood sexual abuse (Orr, Lasko, et al., 1998), all of which were studied under similar laboratory conditions using the same script-driven imagery technique (figure 78.1). The finding has also been replicated for PTSD resulting from motor vehicle accidents (Blanchard et al., 1996). Results of a large multisite study of 1328 Vietnam veterans that combined audiovisual cues and script-driven imagery (Keane et al., 1998) found heightened physiologic reactivity to trauma-related cues in the veterans with PTSD.

If classical conditioning is the mechanism by which emotional responses to trauma-related cues are acquired, then reactivity should be specific to trauma-related stimuli. Such specificity is supported by findings of comparable autonomic reactivity between PTSD and non-PTSD subjects to imagery of stressful life events unrelated to the event that caused the PTSD (Orr et al., 1993; Pitman et al., 1987; Shalev, Orr, and Pitman, 1993) and to mental arithmetic and other generic stressors (Blanchard et al., 1986; Orr, Meyerhoff, et al., 1998).

STRESS-INDUCED ANALGESIA Exposure to previously conditioned fear stimuli has been shown to produce analgesia in animals (Fanselow, 1986). In many instances, this effect is reversed or blocked by the opiate antagonists naloxone and naltrexone. If the emotional responses generated by trauma-related cues in PTSD veterans represent conditioned fear, then combat-related stimuli might be expected to produce an analgesic response in the laboratory. This expectation was tested in a study of eight Vietnam veterans with PTSD and eight non-PTSD veterans that measured pain responses to standardized heat stimuli after exposure to a videotape of dramatized combat in Vietnam. Subjects previously received either naloxone or placebo in a randomized, double-blind, crossover design (Pitman, van der Kolk, et al., 1990). Consistent with the hypothesis, PTSD subjects after viewing the combat videotape showed a 30% decrease in pain intensity ratings after receiving placebo but no decrease after naloxone. The non-PTSD subjects showed no decrease in pain ratings in either condition. Interestingly, degree of control over the stressful event has been found to mediate both stress-induced analgesia (Maier, 1986) and PTSD (Kushner et al., 1993).

TRAUMA-RELATED PET ACTIVATION STUDIES Recent studies of PTSD using positron emission tomography (PET) have more directly examined changes in brain

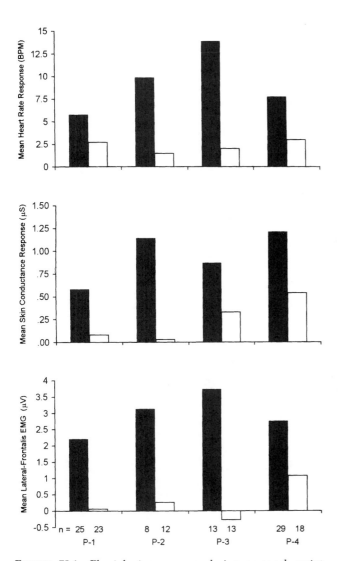

FIGURE 78.1 Physiologic responses during personal, script-driven, traumatic imagery of subjects with (black bars) and without (white bars) posttraumatic stress disorder recruited from various trauma-exposed populations. P = 1, male Vietnam combat veterans (Pitman et al., 1987; Pitman, Orr, et. al, 1990); P = 2, male World War II and Korean combat veterans (Orr et al., 1993); P = 3, male and female Israeli civilian trauma victims (Shalev, Orr, and Pitman, 1993); P = 4, female victims of childhood sexual abuse (Orr, Lasko, et al., 1998). BPM, beats per minute; μS, microsiemens; μV, microvolts; EMG, electromyogram.

activity that presumably underlie emotional reexperiencing in PTSD. Rauch and colleagues (1996) employed personal script-driven imagery to study eight individuals with PTSD (six women and two men) stemming from a variety of traumatic events. During traumatic imagery compared to neutral imagery, there were significant increases in regional cerebral blood flow (rCBF) in anterior paralimbic structures, including posterior medial orbitofrontal, insular, anterior temporal, medial temporal, and anterior cingulate cortex, as well as amygdala (figure 78.2; see color plate 48). An rCBF decrease was found in

Broca's area. However, because this study included neither non-trauma-related scripts nor a non-PTSD comparison group, it was not possible to determine the specificity of the findings to trauma-related stimuli or PTSD.

Shin, Kosslyn, and colleagues (1997) examined rCBF during PET in seven PTSD and seven non-PTSD Vietnam combat veterans during exposure to combat pictures and during imaginary recall of the same pictures. Increased rCBF was found in anterior cingulate cortex and amygdala in PTSD subjects, but not in non-PTSD subjects, during imagery of the combat pictures. Interestingly, imagery was more effective than direct perception in activating anterior paralimbic areas.

Recently, Shin, McNally, and colleagues (1999) examined rCBF during script-driven imagery in 16 women with histories of childhood sexual abuse, eight with PTSD, and eight without PTSD. Subjects with PTSD showed significantly greater activation than non-PTSD subjects during personal sexual abuse imagery compared to neutral imagery in orbitofrontal cortex and anterior temporal pole. Anterior cingulate cortex, however, was differentially activated in the non-PTSD group. The PTSD group showed a significantly greater deactivation of Broca's area. With the exception of anterior cingulate cortex, these results are consistent with the aforementioned studies regarding the role of anterior paralimbic regions in the mediation of emotional responses during imagery of traumatic events in PTSD. There were no significant activation peaks localizable to amygdala within either group.

In summary, PET activation studies converge to show increased activation of orbitofrontal cortex and anterior temporal pole, and decreased activation of Broca's area, during exposure to trauma-related cues in individuals with PTSD. Absence of amygdala activation in some studies could reflect technical difficulties in capturing rCBF changes in this small structure. Alternately, it might be that the amygdala is more critical in the acquisition of conditioned fear responses than in their later evocation. Findings from studies of normal humans have been inconsistent on this question (Hugdahl, 1998; Morris, Öhman, and Dolan, 1998).

BASIC CONDITIONING RESEARCH RELEVANT TO PTSD
In animal work, LeDoux (1996) has shown that connections from the thalamus to the amygdala constitute a "quick and dirty" pathway for the mediation of conditioned fear. The thalamocorticoamygdala pathway is a parallel system that allows more precise but slower elaboration and discrimination of sensory input. LeDoux has found that lesions of the thalamoamygdala connection prevent the acquisition of conditioned fear

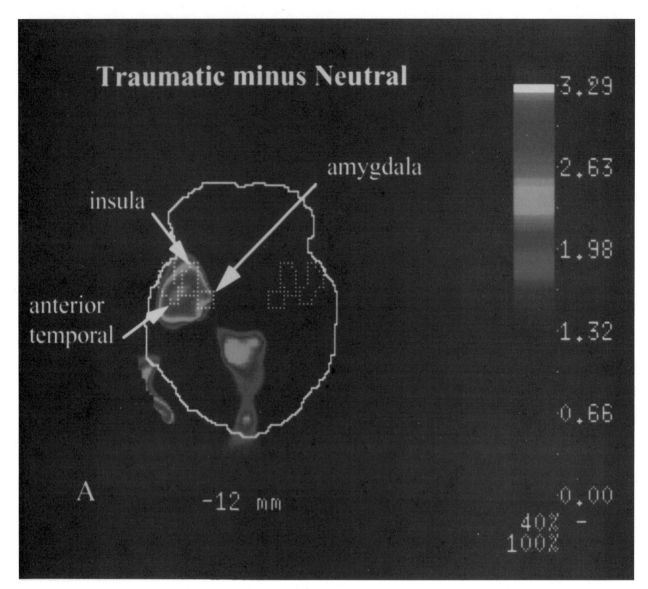

FIGURE 78.2 Positron-emission-tomography statistical parametric map of regional cerebral blood flow during traumatic minus neutral personal imagery in eight subjects with posttraumatic stress disorder, displayed with a Sokoloff color scale in units of *z* score. White dashed outlines reflecting the boundaries of specified brain regions, as defined via a digitized version of the Talairach atlas, are superimposed for anatomical reference. Whole-brain slice outlines are demarcated with solid lines. The tranverse section shown is parallel and 12 mm inferior to the intercommissural plane. Top, anterior; bottom, posterior; right, left; left, right. (Rauch et al., 1996; reprinted with permission from *Archives of General Psychiatry*, vol. 53, no. 5, May 1996, p. 385; Copyright © American Medical Association.)

responses. In contrast, certain lesions of medial prefrontal cortex in rats (roughly corresponding to anterior cingulate cortex in humans) enhance the acquisition and/ or retard the extinction of such responses (Morgan and LeDoux, 1995), implying that intact cortex inhibits acquisition and facilitates extinction. This pattern of findings suggests that extinction of conditioned emotional responses does not involve their undoing, but rather the superimposition of cortical inhibition on their behavioral expression. When this inhibition fails, the conditioned responses are there waiting to emerge. In humans, medial temporal lesions (LaBar et al., 1995), amygdala lesions in particular (Bechara et al., 1995), are associated with deficits in aversive electrodermal conditioning.

This research has led to the conclusion that once formed, "emotional memory may be forever" (LeDoux, 1990, p. 41). Posttraumatic stress disorder may represent an unhappy clinical manifestation of this proposition. The concept of indelible subcortical conditioned emotional responses, held in check with varying degrees of success by the cortex, can account for several clinical observations in PTSD. For example, delayed-onset PTSD, recognized in the DSM-IV, may represent the activated expression of latent conditioned fear responses upon the failure, for whatever reason, of cortical inhibitory control. Also, PTSD patients in clinical remission are vulnerable to the effect of further stress and may relapse upon exposure to it (Solomon et al., 1987). The prediction of a higher occurrence of PTSD in Vietnam veterans at times when their psychological defenses are compromised (Horowitz and Solomon, 1975) is in line with this viewpoint, as is the reemergence of traumatic memories in elderly holocaust survivors and veterans faced with fatal disease or senility (e.g., Holloway and Ursano, 1984).

CONDITIONABILITY   Conditioning theory provides an explanation as to how trauma-related cues might acquire the capacity to generate heightened physiologic responses in individuals with PTSD, but it does not explain why, upon exposure to comparably stressful events (i.e., comparable UCSs), some individuals develop PTSD whereas others do not. It may be that individuals who are prone to develop PTSD acquire CRs more readily or extinguish them more slowly, that is, are more "conditionable."

In a clinical sample of patients with generalized anxiety disorder, Pitman and Orr (1986) previously observed slower extinction of a conditioned SC response to angry facial expression CSs. Recently, Orr et al. (1999) examined conditionability in 33 trauma-exposed individuals, 15 with and 18 without PTSD. They employed a Pavlovian differential paradigm that used simple CSs (colored circles) that bore no conceivable relationship to any trauma-related stimuli, in order to test for de novo conditioning, as opposed to previously acquired conditioned responding. The UCS was a "highly annoying" electric pulse (shock) to the fingers. Results indicated that the PTSD subjects acquired the conditioned SC response more strongly and extinguished it less readily. The pattern of SC responses shown by the PTSD group during acquisition—namely, SC responses that became increasingly larger across CS+ acquisition trials—was strikingly different from that of the non-PTSD group. This finding is consistent with the proposition that fearfulness increased for the PTSD group as the CS+ acquired signal value for predicting the UCS, whereas for individuals without PTSD, fearfulness decreased as the UCS became more predictable. The PTSD group also showed elevated resting HR and SC levels, larger SC responses during the preconditioning habituation phase, a larger unconditioned HR response, and larger HR and corrugator EMG responses during the acquisition phase. These latter findings are consistent with greater anterior paralimbic and limbic (i.e., amygdala) activation during the conditionability experiment.

An important moderator of conditionability appears to be "emotionality," which has been variously conceptualized in terms of anxiety, neuroticism, electrodermal lability, and slower habituation. Individuals identified as more emotional typically have been found to condition more strongly, as indicated by more rapid acquisition and/or greater resistance to extinction of a CR (Boucsein, 1992; Eysenck, 1980; Öhman and Bohlin, 1973; Pitman and Orr, 1986). Eysenck's conditioning model of neurosis highlights the importance of neuroticism and extraversion. An individual who scores high on neuroticism and low on extraversion "is predisposed to neurosis because he reacts strongly to emotionally arousing stimuli and strongly conditions these stimuli" (Eysenck, 1980, p. 163). Neuroticism has been found to predict the development of PTSD following traumatic events (Breslau and Davis, 1992; McFarlane, 1988). Gray (1972) has suggested that the neurologic basis of extraversion-introversion includes the orbitofrontal cortex. As noted previously, PET studies of trauma-related imagery have found increased orbitofrontal (i.e., anterior paralimbic) activation in individuals with PTSD.

Pretrauma individual differences in conditionability could have either a genetic or an acquired basis. Brush (1985) noted that different genetic strains of rats show marked variations in their "emotionality," and that animals identified as having higher emotionality acquired a conditioned response more readily, that is, at lower UCS intensities (see also Owen et al., 1997). A meta-analysis of human twin studies conducted between 1967 and 1985 noted that both emotionality and anxiety have strong genetic influence (McCartney, Harris, and Bernieri, 1990). Results of a twin study of Vietnam veterans showed that PTSD symptoms have a substantial genetic component (True et al., 1993).

Early developmental experiences are also likely to influence emotionality. Research using animals has shown that maternal deprivation can produce adverse consequences in stress-related endocrinologic systems that persist into later life (Rasmusson and Charney, 1997). Increased responsivity to the α-2-adrenergic antagonist yohimbine has been reported for young adult monkeys exposed to early stress associated with variable foraging requirements on their mothers (Rosenblum et al., 1994). Exposure to earlier stressful life events has also been found to increase vulnerability to PTSD (Breslau and Davis, 1992). Finally, it is possible that increased conditionability could result from, and not precede, the stressful event that caused the PTSD.

Sensitization

Classical conditioning provides a powerful explanatory model for several specific features of PTSD. Yet some symptoms associated with PTSD seem to reflect response dispositions that are not a consequence of the immediate presence of any particular CS. For example, PTSD is characterized by self-reported hypervigilance, irritability, and exaggerated startle (table 78.1). Such symptoms could represent manifestations of heightened sensitivity to aversive UCSs, especially in threatening contexts. The amygdala could play a central role in the mediation of individual differences in either pretrauma sensitivity or posttrauma sensitization. Projections from the amygdala influence sympathetic nervous system activity, neuroendocrine responses, startle potentiation, defensive responses, and increased vigilance during fear (Davis, 1997). Each of these has been implicated in one way or another in PTSD.

The diagnostic criteria of DSM-IV for PTSD require that symptoms indicative of hyperarousal not have been present prior to the trauma. However, to the best of our knowledge, no explicit testing has ever been done in this area. Instead, the pretrauma presence of such symptoms could represent dispositions reflecting a heightened sensitivity to noxious stimuli and threatening situations. Individuals with such preexisting dispositions might be more vulnerable to developing PTSD after stressful events. Alternatively, such increased sensitization might result from exposure to the traumatic event. There is ample evidence from the animal literature demonstrating that exposure to a single, severe stressor can cause a range of structural and neurochemical changes consistent with sensitization (Yehuda and Antelman, 1993).

INCREASED SENSITIVITY TO THREAT   Individuals with PTSD appear to be more sensitive to threatening stimuli and contexts. Orr, Meyerhoff, et al. (1998) found no differences between PTSD and non-PTSD veterans' resting HR levels or responses to orthostatic, mental arithmetic, or cold pressor challenges, when these were assessed in the veterans' homes. In contrast, higher resting HR, SC, and BP levels frequently have been observed in contexts where PTSD subjects were anticipating exposure to trauma-related cues (reviews in Keane et al., 1998; Orr, 1994). Higher HR and BP levels also have been found in PTSD veterans seeking psychiatric help in a hospital emergency room (ER; Gerardi et al., 1994).

In the conditionability study described earlier (Orr et al., 1999), PTSD subjects showed higher resting SC and HR levels, indicative of heightened sympathetic arousal, before any UCSs were presented. This higher arousal

may have resulted from the PTSD group's greater sensitivity to a context made threatening by anticipation of the electric shock. In turn, this heightened arousal may have played a role in the PTSD subjects' greater conditionability. In fact, higher resting SC levels were found to be correlated with larger differential SC responses to CS+ versus CS− trials during acquisition across subjects. In a study of potentiated startle, Morgan and colleagues (1995) attributed larger fear-potentiated eye-blink startle responses observed in veterans with combat-related PTSD to heightened emotional arousal caused by the threat of shock. Research using animals has shown that amygdala kindling serves to increase fear-potentiated but not baseline startle (Rosen et al., 1996).

DEFENSIVE AUTONOMIC RESPONDING   When individuals with PTSD are exposed to sudden, intense acoustic stimuli, they produce larger HR responses. This finding has held in Israeli civilian trauma victims (Shalev et al., 1992), Vietnam veterans (Orr et al., 1995; Paige et al., 1990), Israeli war veterans (Orr, Solomon, et al., 1997), and childhood sexual abuse victims (Metzger et al., 1999), all studied under similar laboratory conditions with the same loud-tone technique (figure 78.3). Even tones of moderate intensity and slower rise time have been found to produce larger HR responses in PTSD subjects (Orr, Lasko, et al., 1997). Increased eye-blink EMG and SC responses, and a slower rate of decline of the latter have also been observed in persons with PTSD (review in Metzger et al., 1999).

An interpretation of increased autonomic responses to tones is that they represent defensive responses that

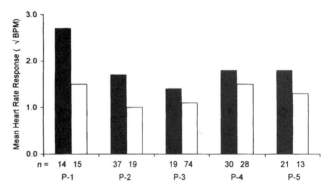

FIGURE 78.3   Heart rate responses (in square root beats per minute) to sudden 95-dB tones of subjects with (black bars) and without (white bars) posttraumatic stress disorder recruited from various trauma-exposed populations. P = 1, male and female Israeli civilian trauma victims (Shalev et al., 1992); P = 2, male Vietnam combat veterans (Orr et al., 1995); P = 3, male Israeli combat veterans (Orr, Solomon, et al., 1997); P = 4, male and female Israeli civilian trauma victims (Shalev et al., 1997); P = 5, female victims of childhood sexual abuse. (Metzger et al., 1999.)

serve to increase the organism's preparation for motor activity (Graham, 1979), as opposed to orienting responses, which are manifest in HR slowing. Hypervigilance, DSM-IV PTSD symptom D.4, reflects a defensive readiness to respond to threatening stimuli or situations. Observations in animals indicate that amygdala neurons are preferentially activated by high-intensity acoustic stimuli (Bordi and LeDoux, 1992).

Shalev and colleagues (1999) studied patients who presented to an ER following an acute psychologically stressful event. Those who went on to develop chronic PTSD did not show elevated HR responses to sudden, loud tones one week posttrauma, but they did one and four months posttrauma. This finding supports the proposition that defensive responding in PTSD is a consequence of the traumatic event, and that it requires some time to develop (or incubate) after the event's occurrence. In other words, the finding supports the evolution of posttrauma sensitization, as opposed to preexisting sensitivity in PTSD, at least with regard to HR responses to loud tones. Elevated HR responses to loud tones did not arise in patients who developed depression without PTSD, supporting the specificity of this laboratory sign for PTSD.

Paige and colleagues (1990) have provided data supporting defensive cortical responses in PTSD. When exposed to tones of increasing intensity, the P200 event-related potentials (ERPs) of individuals with PTSD showed a decrease in amplitude (i.e., reduction) at higher intensity levels, whereas non-PTSD veterans showed an opposite pattern (i.e., augmentation). Paige and colleagues suggested that the decreased P200 response at higher stimulus intensities resulted from greater nervous system sensitivity with a compensatory cortical reduction of stimulation. The finding has been replicated and extended by Lewine and colleagues (1997) using magnetoencephalography. This technique identified the source of the P200 reduction as reduced activation of the auditory association cortex in PTSD subjects. A normally augmenting N100 response in the PTSD group, found by both Lewine and colleagues and Paige and colleagues, indicated that primary auditory cortex was increasingly activated as stimulus intensity increased. This suggests that some type of sensory gating prevented information associated with high stimulus intensities from reaching association cortex in PTSD subjects.

RESPONSE TO YOHIMBINE CHALLENGE Individuals with PTSD have been found to show greater anxiety, panic attacks, and startle following infusion of yohimbine (which serves to stimulate noradrenaline activity). In response to yohimbine challenge, PTSD patients with panic attacks showed greater increases in HR, systolic BP, and the plasma noradrenergic metabolite 3-methoxy-4-hydroxy-phenylglycol (MHPG) (Southwick et al., 1993). Bremner, Innis, and colleagues (1997) used [^{18}F]fluorodeoxyglucose to measure brain metabolism following yohimbine administration in 10 PTSD Vietnam combat veterans and 10 healthy noncombat control subjects. Compared to controls, PTSD patients showed decreased metabolism in prefrontal, temporal, parietal, and orbitofrontal cortical areas. These findings support the proposition that the central noradrenergic system is more sensitive in individuals with PTSD.

HYPOTHALAMIC-PITUITARY-ADRENAL (HPA) SENSITIZATION Selye's general adaptation syndrome model predicts that cortisol should be elevated in human stress disorders, but the evidence in PTSD has generally suggested the opposite (Yehuda, Giller, et al., 1991). In contrast, lymphocyte glucocorticoid receptors (GRs) have been found to be increased in number and sensitivity in PTSD subjects (Yehuda, Lowy, et al., 1991). The finding of a larger number of GRs is consistent with observations of low cortisol in PTSD, in that low circulating levels of a hormone or neurotransmitter are typically associated with compensatory receptor up-regulation. Alternatively, GRs may exert a primary influence on cortisol level by mediating the strength of negative feedback (Yehuda, Boisoneau, et al., 1995). This is supported by the observation that cortisol following a low dose of dexamethasone is suppressed to a greater extent in patients with PTSD (Yehuda et al., 1993), the opposite of the classic nonsuppression of cortisol found in major depression. Nonsuppression of cortisol results from reduced negative feedback inhibition of dexamethasone on the release of CRH and ACTH. Stronger cortisol suppression suggests more effective negative feedback inhibition, also referred to as a sensitized HPA axis (Yehuda, 1997). Resnick and colleagues (1995) found that women who had experienced prior sexual victimization showed smaller cortisol responses to a subsequent rape incident, suggesting that previous trauma may have sensitized their HPA axes. Under certain conditions, experimental stress may induce a sensitized HPA axis in rats (Liberzon, Krstov, and Young, 1997).

PTSD, hormones, and memory

A substantial body of animal research has demonstrated that stress hormones, especially epinephrine but also glucocorticoids, ACTH, vasopressin, and CRH, can strengthen emotional memory or conditioned responses (De Wied, 1969; Gold and Van Buskirk, 1975; Roozendaal

TABLE 78.2
Probability of PTSD as a function of heart rate immediately after an acute traumatic event
(Shalev, Sahar, et al., 1998)

Heart Rate	PTSD Patients	non-PTSD Patients	Total	PTSD Percent
All	20	67	87	23
>70	20	63	83	24
>80	19	47	66	29
>90	15	16	31	48
>100	7	9	16	44
>110	5	1	6	83

and McGaugh, 1996). This effect has been found to require an intact amygdala in both animals and humans and is eliminated by β-adrenergic blockade with propranolol, given either systemically or injected into the amygdala (review in Cahill and McGaugh, 1998). Corticosteroids potentiate conditioned fear (Corodimas et al., 1994). Propranolol antagonizes the enhanced conditioned fear produced by CRH (Cole and Koob, 1988).

Based upon the above animal research, Pitman (1989) theorized that stress hormones and neuromodulators released in response to a traumatic event may overconsolidate memories of the event. These memories subsequently may manifest themselves as intrusive recollections and reexperiencing symptoms. Recalling the event may release additional stress hormones that further enhance the strength of the traumatic memory, creating a positive feedback loop that may eventuate in PTSD. An implication of this theory is that pharmacologic intervention—for example, administration of a β-blocker such as propranolol—soon after a traumatic event might block this cycle of events and prevent the development of PTSD.

NEUROPEPTIDE INFLUENCES ON TRAUMATIC MEMORY RETRIEVAL   Once PTSD has developed, it is too late to study traumatic memory consolidation. However, animal research has shown that hormonal effects on memory are biphasic, that is, exerted at the time of consolidation and again at the time of retrieval. Memory consolidation and retrieval are influenced by various hormonal interventions in parallel ways (Kovacs and Telegdy, 1982). In animals, the posterior pituitary neuropeptide vasopressin has been found to facilitate the acquisition and resistance to extinction of conditioned avoidance responses, whereas oxytocin (which exerts effects opposite to vasopressin) suppresses acquisition and enhances extinction (van Wimersma Greidanus, Jolles, and De Wied, 1985). The effects of vasopressin and oxytocin on physiologic responses during personal combat imagery were examined in 43 Vietnam veterans with PTSD (Pitman, Orr, and Lasko, 1993). Veterans were

randomly assigned to receive either double-blind, intranasal vasopressin, placebo, or oxytocin prior to the experiment. Mean physiologic responses during personal combat imagery were in the predicted direction, namely, vasopressin > placebo > oxytocin (figure 78.4). These results are consistent with enhancing and inhibiting effects exerted by vasopressin and oxytocin (respectively) on memory retrieval, and they support a role for hormonal modulation of memory in PTSD.

POSTTRAUMA HYPERADRENERGIC STATE   In patients presenting to a hospital ER following a psychologically stressful event, Shalev, Sahar, and colleagues (1998) found higher initial HRs in those who went on to develop PTSD but not depression without PTSD (Shalev, Freedman, et al., 1998) four months later. The PTSD effect persisted even when ER HRs were adjusted for differences in the severity of the psychological trauma

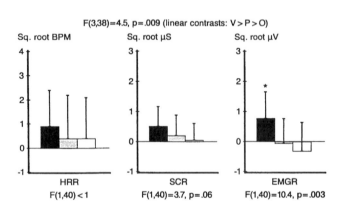

FIGURE 78.4   Mean physiologic responses of 43 Vietnam combat veterans with posttraumatic stress disorder during personal combat imagery one hour following intranasal study medication: V, vasopressin (black bars, $n = 13$); P = placebo (gray bars, $n = 15$); O, oxytocin (white bars, $n = 15$); HRR, heart rate response; SCR, skin conductance response; EMGR, left lateral frontalis electromyogram response; BPM, beats per minute; μS, microsiemens; μV, microvolts. Lines above bars indicate standard deviations. Star indicates response significantly different from placebo at $p = .02$. (Pitman, Orr, and Lasko, 1993; reprinted from *Psychiatry Research*, vol. 48, no. 2, August 1993, p. 113; in the public domain.)

or the subjective response. Table 78.2 presents the probability of PTSD, which rose rapidly as a function of ER HR. Not shown in this table is that 13 (72%) of the 18 patients with ER HRs ≤90 beats per minute (BPM) who had PTSD at one month remitted over the next three months. In sharp contrast, none (0%) of the 15 patients with ER HRs >90 BPM who had PTSD at one month showed remission at four months. A plausible explanation for this finding is that the patients who had higher HRs in the ER had released more circulating epinephrine in response to the traumatic event, and that this served to overconsolidate memories of it, leading to PTSD.

Memory and hippocampal structure in PTSD

The overly strong conditioned responses found in PTSD might be regarded as one form of so-called implicit memory, in that they do not necessarily require conscious recollection for their expression. In contrast to the overly strong emotional memories for traumatic events found in this disorder is a relative weakness of memory for nonemotional information. A number of studies have reported deficits in declarative memory for material unrelated to PTSD subjects' traumatic events (Bremner et al., 1995b; Bremner et al., 1993; Jenkins et al., 1998; Yehuda, Keefe, et al., 1995).

REDUCED HIPPOCAMPAL VOLUME Declarative, or explicit, memory is widely accepted to be mediated by the medial temporal lobe, especially the hippocampus. Animal research has indicated that this brain structure may be damaged by stress (Uno et al., 1989), an effect attributed to cortisol (Sapolsky et al., 1990). These findings motivated four recent studies of hippocampal volume, two in Vietnam combat veterans (Bremner et al., 1995a; Gurvits et al., 1996) and two in childhood physical and sexual abuse subjects (Bremner, Randall, et al., 1997; Stein et al., 1997). Each of these studies found significantly smaller hippocampal volumes in PTSD subjects than in non-PTSD subjects (examples in figure 78.5). A fifth study (Schuff et al., 1997), which combined MRI and magnetic resonance spectroscopy, noted 6% smaller right hippocampal volumes in veterans with combat-related PTSD. Although the group difference was not significant in the small sample sizes studied, the effect size was substantial (.71). Moreover, results of the spectroscopic imaging revealed less of the amino acid N-acetyl aspartate (NAA) in the PTSD group's right hippocampus, suggesting lower neuronal density in this structure.

The preceding findings raise the possibility that traumatic stress damages the human hippocampus (Sapolsky, 1996). In support, Gurvits and colleagues (1996)

found a strong negative correlation between severity of past combat exposure in Vietnam and hippocampal volume (figure 78.6). However, the absence of hypercortisolism in PTSD described earlier creates a formidable problem for this interpretation. Alternative explanations include the possibility that diminished hippocampal volume represents a risk factor for exposure to stressful events and/or a vulnerability factor for the development of PTSD upon such exposure. It is also possible that alcohol or other substance abuse associated with PTSD exerts a toxic effect, although most studies have attempted to control for this factor.

FUNCTIONAL NEUROIMAGING OF HIPPOCAMPUS Functional neuroimaging studies of the hippocampus in PTSD have lagged far behind structural studies and represent a needed area of investigation. Semple and colleagues (1993) measured rCBF in six PTSD combat veterans with recent substance abuse or dependence and seven normal (noncombat) controls at rest and during auditory continuous performance and word-generation tasks. PTSD subjects showed trends for increased rCBF in orbitofrontal cortex and decreased left/right hippocampal ratios across conditions. However, confounding of PTSD diagnosis with recent substance use, together with the absence of a trauma-exposed control group, cause the results of this study to be of uncertain significance. In their [18F]fluorodeoxyglucose PET study described previously, Bremner, Innis, and colleagues (1997) found that yohimbine challenge, which activates noradrenergic activity in the locus coeruleus, produced a significant reduction in rCBF in the hippocampus in Vietnam combat veterans with PTSD.

NON-MEMORY FUNCTIONS OF HIPPOCAMPUS In addition to its well-recognized role in the formation of declarative memory, the hippocampus plays a role in regulating behavior. Douglas (1972) described the hippocampus as "the organ of expression of internal inhibition," citing deficiencies of hippocampectomized animals in habituation, extinction, reversal learning, and other behaviors in which Pavlovian internal inhibition plays a prominent role (see also Kimble, 1968). In contrast, Douglas attributed Pavlovian excitation to the amygdala. In a similar vein, Devenport, Devenport, and Holloway (1981) found that the hippocampus functions to increase the animal's behavioral variability and resistance to stereotypy, noting that counterproductive habits are not readily discarded by hippocampal-lesioned rats. As noted in the psychophysiologic studies described earlier, PTSD subjects suffer from impaired habituation and extinction on either a preexisting or

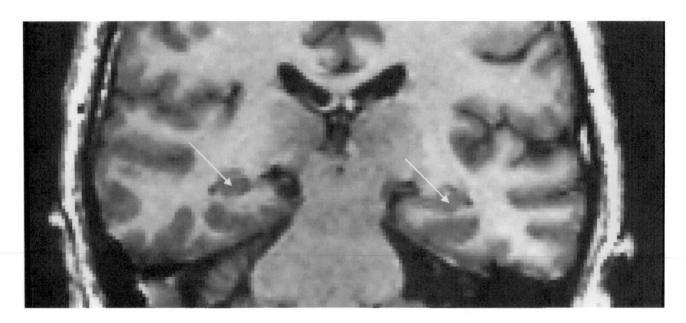

MR Image From Non-PTSD Veteran

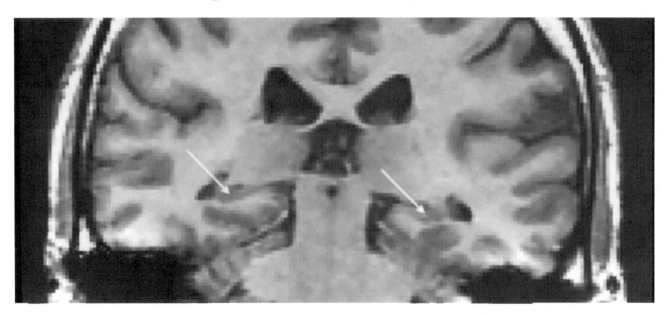

MR Image From PTSD Veteran

FIGURE 78.5 Magnetic resonance images illustrating smaller left and right hippocampi in a Vietnam combat veteran with PTSD (bottom) than in one without PTSD (top). (Gurvits et al., 1996; reprinted from *Biological Psychiatry,* vol. 40, no. 11, December 1, 1996, p. 1096; in the public domain.)

acquired basis. Reduced hippocampal function could offer an anatomic explanation for these phenomena in PTSD patients. As discussed previously, another candidate brain area for internal inhibition is anterior cingulate cortex.

Conclusions

"HOT" AND "COOL" MEMORY SYSTEMS IN PTSD In an overview of more than a decade of research by various authors, Metcalfe and Jacobs (1996) have dis-

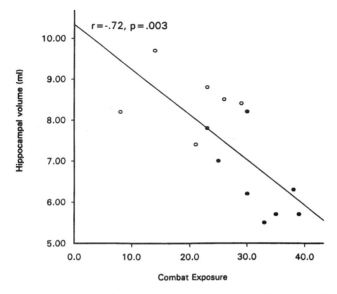

FIGURE 78.6 Total hippocampal volume as a function of Combat Exposure Scale score. Closed circles, PTSD subjects; open circles, non-PTSD subjects. (Gurvits et al., 1996; reprinted from *Biological Psychiatry*, vol. 40 no. 11, December 1, 1996, p. 1096; in the public domain.)

tinguished between an amygdala-centered (anterior paralimbic) emotional, "hot," memory system, and a hippocampus-centered (posterior paralimbic) cognitive, "cool" memory system. This distinction has received support from case studies of humans with selective amygdala and/or hippocampal damage (Bechara et al., 1995). Metcalfe and Jacobs theorized that the "hot" amygdala system is critically involved in traumatic memory formation and the pathogenesis of PTSD. The "cool" hippocampal system either is not active in traumatic memory formation, or it may even be deactivated under stress. As we have noted, the specific symptoms of PTSD may be fruitfully conceptualized as the products of fear conditioning. The critical role of the amygdala in this process has been amply demonstrated in preclinical research. Results of PTSD neuroimaging studies point to anterior paralimbic activation during traumatic reexperiencing. Indirect evidence suggests that hormonal potentiation of memory consolidation in the amygdala is involved in the pathogenesis of PTSD. Not all psychobiologic aspects of PTSD, however, can be subsumed under a conditioning model. Sensitization appears to represent a necessary additional dimension.

Findings of impaired declarative memory and diminished hippocampal volume in PTSD subjects lend support to the other half of Metcalfe and Jacobs' theory. A deficit in inhibitory functions due to functional posterior paralimbic (i.e., hippocampal) impairment, either on a preexisting or acquired basis, could have a permissive influence on the overdevelopment of anterior paralimbic excitation in the pathogenesis of PTSD.

GAPS AND CONTRADICTIONS Some patients with PTSD have detailed recollections that suggest enhanced, rather than impaired, declarative memory at the time of the traumatic event, which would imply heightened acute hippocampal function. Cahill and McGaugh (1998) have argued that the amygdala serves to activate various cortical brain areas, including the hippocampus. The implication is that the amygdala and the hippocampus may work in concert in the pathogenesis of PTSD.

The paradoxical finding of lower cortisol levels in PTSD is difficult to reconcile with the proposition that diminished hippocampal volume in this disorder represents a stress- or cortisol-induced phenomenon. It is tempting to speculate that cortisol levels immediately following the traumatic event are initially high in PTSD and then become lower in some compensatory manner. This result would be consistent with results from animal research indicating that corticosteroids potentiate conditioned fear and memory consolidation. However, the empirical PTSD data do not seem to be consistent with this proposition; if anything, immediate posttrauma cortisol levels appear to be lower in persons who go on to develop PTSD (McFarlane, Atchison, and Yehuda, 1997). A potential explanation of this contradiction is that increased GR sensitivity represents a pretrauma vulnerability factor for PTSD, either constitutional or acquired from prior stressful experience (Yehuda, 1997). According to this theory, cortisol stimulated at the time of the traumatic event would exert a greater initial physiologic impact at more sensitive brain GR sites before it was turned off by a supersensitive HPA negative feedback axis. Although tempting, this explanation is speculative and in need of supporting data.

Ultimately, the resolution of these and other questions will require prospective investigations, in which subjects are studied before and after the occurrence of a psychologically stressful event. Such studies will no doubt be difficult and expensive but have become essential to the advancement of the field.

Whatever data future research may yield, it is clear that the interchange between basic cognitive neuroscience and clinical investigation of PTSD will continue to yield exciting insights for both fields.

ACKNOWLEDGMENTS Work presented in this chapter was supported by Merit Review grants from the Veterans Affairs Medical Research Service and NIMH Grants R01MH48559, R01MH50379, and R01MH54636. We thank our collaborators cited in the references.

REFERENCES

AMERICAN PSYCHIATRIC ASSOCIATION, 1994. *Diagnostic and Statistical Manual of Mental Disorders*, 4th ed. Washington, DC: American Psychiatric Association.

BECHARA, A., D. TRANEL, H. DAMASIO, R. ADOLPHS, C. ROCKLAND, and A. R. DAMASIO, 1995. Double dissociation of conditioning and declarative knowledge relative to the amygdala and hippocampus in humans. *Science* 269:1115–1118.

BLANCHARD, E. B., 1990. Elevated basal levels of cardiovascular response in Vietnam veterans with PTSD: A health problem in the making? *J. Anxiety Disord.* 4:233–237.

BLANCHARD, E. B., E. J. HICKLING, T. C. BUCKLEY, A. E. TAYLOR, A. VOLLMER, and W. R. LOOS, 1996. The psychophysiology of motor vehicle accident related posttraumatic stress disorder: Replication and extension. *J. Consult. Clin. Psychol.* 64:742–751.

BLANCHARD, E. B., L. C. KOLB, R. J. GERARDI, P. RYAN, and T. P. PALLMEYER, 1986. Cardiac response to relevant stimuli as an adjunctive tool for diagnosing posttraumatic stress disorder in Vietnam veterans. *Behav. Ther.* 17:592–606.

BORDI, F., and J. LEDOUX, 1992. Sensory tuning beyond the sensory system: An initial analysis of auditory response properties of neurons in the lateral amygdaloid nucleus and overlying areas of the striatum. *J. Neurosci.* 12:2493–2503.

BOUCSEIN, W., 1992. *Electrodermal Activity.* New York: Plenum.

BREMNER, J. D., R. B. INNIS, C. K. NG, L. H. STAIB, R. M. SALOMON, R. A. BRONEN, J. DUNCAN, S. M. SOUTHWICK, J. H. KRYSTAL, D. RICH, G. ZUBAL, H. DEY, R. SOUFER, and D. S. CHARNEY, 1997. Positron emission tomography measurement of central metabolic correlates of yohimbine administration in combat-related posttraumatic stress disorder. *Arch. Gen. Psychiatry* 54:246–254.

BREMNER, J. D., P. RANDALL, T. N. SCOTT, R. A. BRONEN, J. P. SEIBYL, S. M. SOUTHWICK, R. C. DELANEY, G. MCCARTHY, D. S. CHARNEY, and R. B. INNIS, 1995a. MRI-based measurements of hippocampal volume in combat-related posttraumatic stress disorder. *Am. J. Psychiatry* 152:973–981.

BREMNER, J. D., P. RANDALL, T. M. SCOTT, S. CAPELLI, R. DELANEY, G. MCCARTHY, and D. S. CHARNEY, 1995b. Deficits in short-term memory in adult survivors of childhood abuse. *Psychiatry Res.* 59:97–107.

BREMNER, J. D., P. RANDALL, E. VERMETTEN, L. STAIB, R. A. BRONEN, C. MAZURE, S. CAPELLI, G. MCCARTHY, R. B. INNIS, and D. S. CHARNEY, 1997. Magnetic resonance imaging-based measurement of hippocampal volume in posttraumatic stress disorder related to childhood physical and sexual abuse–A preliminary report. *Biol. Psychiatry* 41:23–32.

BREMNER, J. D., T. M. SCOTT, R. C. DELANEY, S. M. SOUTHWICK, J. W. MASON, D. R. JOHNSON, R. B. INNIS, G. MCCARTHY, and D. S. CHARNEY, 1993. Deficits in short-term memory in posttraumatic stress disorder. *Am. J. Psychiatry* 150:1015–1019.

BRESLAU, N., and G. C. DAVIS, 1992. Posttraumatic stress disorder in an urban population of young adults: Risk factors for chronicity. *Am. J. Psychiatry* 149:671–675.

BRUSH, R. F., 1985. Genetic determinations of avoidance learning: mediation by emotionality. In *Affect, Conditioning, and Cognition: Essays on the Determinants of Behavior*, R. F. Brush, and J. B. Overmier, eds. Hillsdale, N.J.: Erlbaum, pp. 27–42.

CAHILL, L., and J. L. MCGAUGH, 1998. Mechanisms of emotional arousal and lasting declarative memory. *Trends Neurosci.* 21:294–299.

COLE, B. J., and G. F. KOOB, 1988. Propranolol antagonizes the enhanced conditioned fear produced by corticotropin releasing factor. *J. Pharmacol. Exp. Ther.* 247:902–910.

CORODIMAS, K. P., J. E. LEDOUX, P. W. GOLD, and J. SCHULKIN, 1994. Corticosterone potentiation of conditioned fear in rats. *Ann. N.Y. Acad. Sci.* 746:392–393.

DARWIN, C., 1872. *The Expression of the Emotions in Man and Animals.* London: John Murray.

DAVIS, M., 1997. The neurobiology of fear responses: The role of the amygdala. *J. Neuropsychiatry Clin. Neurosci.* 9:382–402.

DEVENPORT, L. D., J. A. DEVENPORT, and F. A. HOLLOWAY, 1981. Reward-induced stereotypy: Modulation by the hippocampus. *Science* 212:1288–1289.

DE WIED, D., 1969. Effects of peptide hormones on behavior. In *Frontiers in Neuroendocrinology*, W. S. Ganong and L. Martini, eds. London: Oxford University Press, pp. 97–140.

DOUGLAS, R. J., 1972. Pavlovian conditioning and the brain. In *Inhibition and Learning*, R. A. Boakes and M. S. Halliday, eds. London: Academic Press, pp. 529–553.

EYSENCK, H. J., 1980. The conditioning model of neurosis. *Behav. Brain Sci.* 2:155–199.

FANSELOW, M. S., 1986. Conditioned fear-induced opiate analgesia: A competing motivational state theory of stress analgesia. *Ann. N.Y. Acad. Sci.* 467:40–54.

FRIEDMAN, M. J., D. S. CHARNEY, and A. Y. DEUTCH, eds., 1995. *Neurobiological and Clinical Consequences of Stress: From Normal Adaptation to Post-Traumatic Stress Disorder.* Philadelphia: Lippincott-Raven.

GERARDI, R. J., T. M. KEANE, B. J. CAHOON, and G. W. KLAUMINIZER, 1994. An in vivo assessment of physiological arousal in posttraumatic stress disorder. *J. Abnorm. Psychol.* 103:825–827.

GOLD, P. E., and R. VAN BUSKIRK, 1975. Facilitation of time-dependent memory processes with posttrial epinephrine injections. *Behav. Biol.* 13:145–153.

GRAHAM, F. K., 1979. Distinguishing among orienting, defense, and startle reflexes. In *The Orienting Reflex in Humans*, H. D. Kimmel, E. H. Van Olst, and J. F. Orlebeke, eds. An International Conference Sponsored by the Scientific Affairs Division of the North Atlantic Treaty Organization. Hillsdale, N.J.: Erlbaum.

GRAY, J. A., 1972. The psychophysiological nature of introversion-extraversion: A modification of Eysenck's theory. In *Biological Basis of Individual Behavior*, V. D. Nebylitsyn and J. A. Gray, eds. New York: Academic Press, pp. 182–205.

GURVITS, T. V., M. E. SHENTON, H. HOKAMA, H. OHTA, N. B. LASKO, M. W. GILBERTSON, S. P. ORR, K. KIKINIS, F. A. JOLESZ, R. W. MCCARLEY, and R. K. PITMAN, 1996. Magnetic resonance imaging study of hippocampal volume in chronic, combat-related post-traumatic stress disorder. *Biol. Psychiatry* 40:1091–1099.

HOLLOWAY, H. C., and R. J. URSANO, 1984. The Vietnam veteran: Memory, social context, and metaphor. *Psychiatry* 47:103–108.

HOROWITZ, M. J., and G. F. SOLOMON, 1975. A prediction of stress response syndromes in Vietnam veterans: Observations and suggestions for treatment. *J. Soc. Issues* 31:67–80.

HUGDAHL, K., 1998. Cortical control of human classical conditioning: Autonomic and positron emission tomography data. *Psychophysiology* 35:170–178.

JENKINS, M. A., P. J. LANGLAIS, D. DELIS, and R. COHEN, 1998. Learning and memory in rape victims with posttraumatic stress disorder. *Am. J. Psychiatry* 155:278–279.

KEANE, T. M., L. C. KOLB, D. G. KALOUPEK, S. P. ORR, R. G. THOMAS, F. HSIEH, and P. LAVORI, 1998. Results of a multisite clinical trial on the psychophysiological assessment of posttraumatic stress disorder. *J. Consult. Clin. Psychol.* 66:914–923.

KIMBLE, D. P., 1968. Hippocampus and internal inhibition. *Psychol. Bull.* 70:285–295.

KOVACS, G. L., and G. TELEGDY, 1982. Role of oxytocin in memory and amnesia. *Pharmacol. Ther.* 18:375–395.

KUSHNER, M.G., D. S. RIGGS, E. B. FOA, and S. M. MILLER, 1993. Perceived controllability and the development of posttraumatic stress disorder in crime victims. *Behav. Res. Ther.* 31:105–110.

LABAR, K. S., J. E. LEDOUX, D. D. SPENCER, and E. A. PHELPS, 1995. Impaired fear conditioning following unilateral temporal lobectomy in humans. *J. Neurosci.* 15:6846–6855.

LEDOUX, J. E., 1990. Information flow from sensation to emotion: Plasticity in the neural computation of stimulus value. In *Learning Computational Neuroscience: Foundations of Adaptive Networks*, M. Gabriel and J. Moore, eds. Cambridge, Mass.: MIT Press, pp. 3–51.

LEDOUX, J. E., 1996. *The Emotional Brain.* New York: Simon and Schuster.

LEWINE, J. D., J. M. CANIVE, W. W. ORRISON, C. J. EDGAR, S. L. PROVENCAL, J. T. DAVIS, K. PAULSON, D. GRAEBER, B. ROBERTS, P. R. ESCALONA, and L. CALAIS, 1997. Electrophysiological abnormalities in PTSD. *Ann. N.Y. Acad. Sci.* 821:508–511.

LIBERZON, I., M. KRSTOV, and E. A. YOUNG, 1997. Stress-restress: Effects on ACTH and fast feedback. *Psychoneuroendocrinology* 22:443–453.

MAIER, S. F., 1986. Stressor controllability and stress-induced analgesia. *Ann. N.Y. Acad. Sci.* 467:55–72.

MCCARTNEY, K., M. J. HARRIS, and F. BERNIERI, 1990. Growing up and growing apart: A developmental meta-analysis of twin studies. *Psychol. Bull.* 107:226–237.

MCFARLANE, A. C., 1988. The aetiology of post-traumatic stress disorder following a natural disaster. *Br. J. Psychiatry* 152:116–121.

MCFARLANE, A. C., M. ATCHISON, and R. YEHUDA, 1997. The acute stress response following motor vehicle accidents and its relation to PTSD. *Ann. N.Y. Acad. Sci.* 821:437–441.

MCNALLY, R. J., D. L. LUEDKE, J. K. BESYNER, R. A. PETERSON, K. BOHM, and O. J. LIPS, 1987. Sensitivity to stress-relevant stimuli in posttraumatic stress disorder. *J. Anxiety Disord.* 1:105–116.

METCALFE, J., and W. J. JACOBS, 1996. A "hot-system/cool-system" view of memory under stress. *PTSD Res. Q.* 7(2):1–3.

METZGER, L. J., S. P. ORR, N. J. BERRY, C. E. AHERN, N. B. LASKO, and R. K. PITMAN, 1999. Physiologic reactivity to startling tones in women with PTSD. *J. Abnorm. Psychol.* 108:347–352.

MORGAN, C. A., C. GRILLON, S. M. SOUTHWICK, M. DAVIS, and D. S. CHARNEY, 1995. Fear-potentiated startle in posttraumatic stress disorder. *Biol. Psychiatry* 38:378–385.

MORGAN, M. A., and J. E. LEDOUX, 1995. Differential contribution of dorsal and ventral medial prefrontal cortex to the acquisition and extinction of conditioned fear in rats. *Behav. Neurosci.* 109:681–688.

MORRIS, J. S., A. ÖHMAN, and R. J. DOLAN, 1998. Conscious and unconscious emotional learning in the human amygdala. *Nature* 393:467–470.

ÖHMAN, A., and G. BOHLIN, 1973. The relationship between spontaneous and stimulus-correlated electrodermal responses in simple and discriminative conditioning paradigms. *Psychophysiology* 6:580–600.

ORR, S. P., 1994. An overview of psychophysiological studies of PTSD. *PTSD Res. Q.* 5(1):1–7.

ORR, S. P., N. B. LASKO, L. J. METZGER, N. J. BERRY, C. E. AHERN, and R. K. PITMAN, 1998. Psychophysiologic assessment of women with PTSD resulting from childhood sexual abuse. *J. Consult. Clin. Psychol.* 66:906–913.

ORR, S. P., N. B. LASKO, L. J. METZGER, and R. K. PITMAN, 1997. Physiologic responses to nonstartling tones in Vietnam veterans with post-traumatic stress disorder. *Psychiatry Res.* 73:103–107.

ORR, S. P., N. B. LASKO, A. SHALEV, and R. K. PITMAN, 1995. Physiologic responses to loud tones in Vietnam veterans with PTSD. *J. Abnorm. Psychol.* 104:75–82.

ORR, S. P., L. J. METZGER, N. B. LASKO, M. L. MACKLIN, T. PERI, and R. K. PITMAN, 1999. Conditionability in trauma-exposed individuals with and without post-traumatic stress disorder. Submitted.

ORR, S. P., J. L. MEYERHOFF, J. W. EDWARDS, and R. K. PITMAN, 1998. Heart rate and blood pressure resting levels and responses to generic stressors in Vietnam veterans with posttraumatic stress disorder. *J. Trauma. Stress* 11:155–164.

ORR, S. P., R. K. PITMAN, N. B. LASKO, and L. R. HERZ, 1993. Psychophysiologic assessment of posttraumatic stress disorder imagery in World War II and Korean combat veterans. *J. Abnorm. Psychol.* 102:152–159.

ORR, S. P., Z. SOLOMON, T. PERI, R. K. PITMAN, and A. Y. SHALEV, 1997. Physiologic responses to loud tones in Israeli veterans of the 1973 Yom Kippur war. *Biol. Psychiatry* 41:319–326.

OWEN, E. H., S. C. CHRISTENSEN, R. PAYLOR, and J. M. WEHNER, 1997. Identification of quantitative trait loci involved in contextual and auditory-cued fear conditioning in BXD recombinant inbred strains. *Behav. Neurosci.* 111:292–300.

PAIGE, S. R., G. M. REID, M. G. ALLEN, and J. E. O. NEWTON, 1990. Psychophysiological correlates of posttraumatic stress disorder in Vietnam veterans. *Biol. Psychiatry* 27:419-430.

PITMAN, R. K., 1989. Post-traumatic stress disorder, hormones, and memory. *Biol. Psychiatry* 26:221–223.

PITMAN, R. K., and S. P. ORR, 1986. Test of the conditioning model of neurosis: Differential aversive conditioning of angry and neutral facial expressions in anxiety disorder patients. *J. Abnorm. Psychol.* 95:208–213.

PITMAN, R. K., S. P. ORR, D. F. FORGUE, B. ALTMAN, J. B. DE JONG, and L. R. HERZ, 1990. Psychophysiologic responses to combat imagery of Vietnam veterans with post-traumatic stress disorder versus other anxiety disorders. *J. Abnorm. Psychol.* 99:49–54.

PITMAN, R. K., S. P. ORR, D. F. FORGUE, J. B. DE JONG, and J. M. CLAIBORN, 1987. Psychophysiologic assessment of posttraumatic stress disorder imagery in Vietnam combat veterans. *Arch. Gen. Psychiatry* 44:970–975.

PITMAN, R. K., S. P. ORR, and N. B. LASKO, 1993. Effects of intranasal vasopressin and oxytocin on physiologic responding during personal combat imagery in Vietnam veterans with post-traumatic stress disorder. *Psychiatry Res.* 48:107–117.

PITMAN, R. K., B. A. VAN DER KOLK, S. P. ORR, and M. S. GREENBERG, 1990. Naloxone-reversible analgesic response to combat-related stimuli in post-traumatic stress disorder: A pilot study. *Arch. Gen. Psychiatry* 47:541–544.

RASMUSSON, A. M., and D. CHARNEY, 1997. Animal models of relevance to PTSD. *Ann. N.Y. Acad. Sci.* 821:332–351.

RAUCH, S. L., B. A. VAN DER KOLK, R. E. FISLER, N. M. ALPERT, S. P. ORR, C. R. SAVAGE, A. J. FISCHMAN, M. A. JENIKE, and R. K. PITMAN, 1996. A symptom provocation study of posttraumatic stress disorder using positron emission tomography and script-driven imagery. *Arch. Gen. Psychiatry* 53:380–387.

RESNICK, H. S., R. YEHUDA, R. K. PITMAN, and D. W. FOY, 1995. Effect of previous trauma on acute plasma cortisol level following rape. *Am. J. Psychiatry* 152:1675–1677.

ROOZENDAAL, B., and J. L. MCGAUGH, 1996. Amygdaloid nuclei lesions differentially affect glucocorticoid-induced memory enhancement in an inhibitory avoidance task. *Neurobiol. Learn. Mem.* 65:1–8.

ROSEN, J. B., E. HAMERMAN, J. R. GLOWA, M. SITCOSKE, and J. SCHULKIN, 1996. Hyperexcitability: Exaggerated fear-potentiated startle produced by partial amygdala kindling. *Behav. Neurosci.* 110:43–50.

ROSENBLUM, L. A., J. D. COPLAN, S. FRIEDMAN, T. BASSOFF, J. M. GORMAN, and M. W. ANDREWS, 1994. Adverse early experiences affect noradrenergic and serotonergic functioning in adult primates. *Biol. Psychiatry* 35:221–227.

SAPOLSKY, R. M., 1996. Why stress is bad for your brain. *Science* 273:749–750.

SAPOLSKY, R. M., H. UNO, C. S. REBERT, and C. E. FINCH, 1990. Hippocampal damage associated with prolonged glucocorticoid exposure in primates. *J. Neurosci.* 10:2897–2902.

SCHUFF, N., C. R. MARMAR, D. S. WEISS, T. C. NEYLAN, F. SCHOENFELD, G. FEIN, and M. W. WEINER, 1997. Reduced hippocampal volume and *n*-acetyl aspartate in posttraumatic stress disorder. *Ann. N.Y. Acad. Sci.* 821:516–520.

SEMPLE, W. E., P. GOYER, R. MCCORMICK, E. MORRIS, B. COMPTON, G. MUSWICK, D. NELSON, B. DONOVAN, G. LEISURE, M. BERRIDGE, F. MIRALDI, and S. C. SCHULZ, 1993. Brain blood flow using PET in patients with posttraumatic stress disorder and substance-abuse histories. *Biol. Psychiatry* 34:115–118.

SHALEV, A. Y., S. FREEDMAN, T. PERI, D. BRANDES, T. SAHAR, S. P. ORR, and R. K. PITMAN, 1998. Prospective study of posttraumatic stress disorder and depression following trauma. *Am. J. Psychiatry* 155:630–637.

SHALEV, A. Y., S. P. ORR, P. PERI, S. SCHREIBER, and R. K. PITMAN, 1992. Physiologic responses to loud tones in Israeli post-traumatic stress disorder patients. *Arch. Gen. Psychiatry* 49:870–975.

SHALEV, A. Y., S. P. ORR, and R. K. PITMAN, 1993. Psychophysiologic assessment of traumatic imagery in Israeli civilian post-traumatic stress disorder patients. *Am. J. Psychiatry* 150:620–624.

SHALEV, A. Y., T. PERI, D. BRANDES, S. FREEDMAN, S. P. ORR, and R. K. PITMAN, 1999. Auditory startle responses in trauma survivors with PTSD: A prospective study. Submitted.

SHALEV, A. Y., T. PERI, E. GELPIN, S. P. ORR, and R. K. PITMAN, 1997. Psychophysiologic assessment of mental imagery of stressful events in Israeli civilian posttraumatic stress disorder patients. *Compr. Psychiatry* 38:269–273.

SHALEV, A. Y., and Y. ROGEL-FUCHS, 1993. Psychophysiology of the posttraumatic stress disorder: From sulfur fumes to behavioral genetics. *Psychosom. Med.* 55:413–423.

SHALEV, A. Y., T. SAHAR, S. FREEDMAN, T. PERI, N. GLICK, D. BRANDES, S. P. ORR, and R. K. PITMAN, 1998. A prospective study of heart rate response following trauma and the subsequent development of PTSD. *Arch. Gen. Psychiatry* 55:553–559.

SHIN, L. M., S. M. KOSSLYN, R. J. MCNALLY, N. M. ALPERT, W. L. THOMPSON, S. L. RAUCH, M. A. MACKLIN, and R. K. PITMAN, 1997. Visual imagery and perception in posttraumatic stress disorder: A positron emission tomographic investigation. *Arch. Gen. Psychiatry* 54:233–241.

SHIN, L. M., R. J. MCNALLY, S. M. KOSSLYN, W. L. THOMPSON, S. L. RAUCH, N. M. ALPERT, L. J. METZGER, N. B. LASKO, S. P. ORR, and R. K. PITMAN, 1999. Regional cerebral blood flow during script-driven imagery in childhood sexual abuse–related posttraumatic stress disorder: A positron emission tomographic investigation. *Am. J. Psychiatry* 156:575–584.

SOLOMON, Z., R. GARB, A. BLEICH, and D. GRUPPER, 1987. Reactivation of combat related posttraumatic stress disorder. *Am. J. Psychiatry* 144:51–55.

SOUTHWICK, S. M., J. H. KRYSTAL, C. A. MORGAN III, D. JOHNSON, L. M. NAGY, A. NICOLAOU, G. R. HENINGER, and D. S. CHARNEY, 1993. Abnormal noradrenergic function in posttraumatic stress disorder. *Arch. Gen. Psychiatry* 50:266–274.

STEIN, M. B., C. KOVEROLA, C. HANNA, M. G. TORCHIA, and B. MCCLARTY, 1997. Hippocampal volume in women victimized by childhood sexual abuse. *Psychol. Med.* 27:951–959.

TRUE, W. R., J. RICE, S. A. EISEN, A. C. HEATH, J. GOLDBERG, M. J. LYONS, and J. NOWAK, 1993. A twin study of genetic and environmental contributions to liability for posttraumatic stress symptoms. *Arch. Gen. Psychiatry* 50:257–264.

UNO, H., R. TARARA, J. ELSE, M. SULEMAN, and R. M. SAPOLSKY, 1989. Hippocampal damage associated with prolonged and fatal stress in primates. *J. Neurosci.* 9:1705–1711.

VAN WIMERSMA GREIDANUS, T. B., J. JOLLES, and D. DE WIED, 1985. Hypothalamic neuropeptides and memory. *Acta Neurochir. (Wien)* 75:99–105.

YEHUDA, R., 1997. Sensitization of the hypothalamic-pituitary-adrenal axis in posttraumatic stress disorder. *Ann. N.Y. Acad. Sci.* 821:57–75.

YEHUDA, R., and S. M. ANTELMAN, 1993. Criteria for rationally evaluating animal models of posttraumatic stress disorder. *Biol. Psychiatry* 33:479–486.

YEHUDA, R., D. BOISONEAU, M. T. LOWY, and E. L. GILLER, 1995. Dose-response changes in plasma cortisol and lymphocyte glucocorticoid receptors following dexamethasone administration in combat veterans with and without posttraumatic stress disorder. *Arch. Gen. Psychiatry* 52:583–593.

YEHUDA, R., E. L. GILLER, S. M. SOUTHWICK, M. T. LOWY, and J. W. MASON, 1991. Hypothalamic-pituitary-adrenal dysfunction in posttraumatic stress disorder. *Biol. Psychiatry* 30:1031–1048.

YEHUDA, R., S. E. KEEFE, P. D. HARVEY, R. A. LEVENGOOD, D. K. GERBER, J. GENI, and L. J. SIEVER, 1995. Learning and memory in combat veterans with posttraumatic stress disorder. *Am. J. Psychiatry* 152:137–139.

YEHUDA, R., M. T. LOWY, S. M. SOUTHWICK, S. SHAFFER, and E. L. GILLER, 1991. Increased lymphocyte glucocorticoid receptor number in posttraumatic stress disorder. *Am. J. Psychiatry* 149:499–504.

YEHUDA, R., and A. C. MCFARLANE, 1997. Psychobiology of Post-traumatic Stress Disorder. *Ann. N.Y. Acad. Sci.* 821.

YEHUDA, R., S. M. SOUTHWICK, J. H. KRYSTAL, D. BREMNER, D. S. CHARNEY, and J. W. MASON, 1993. Enhanced suppression of cortisol following dexamethasone administration in posttraumatic stress disorder. *Am. J. Psychiatry* 150:83–86.

79 The Neuroscience of Affective Style

RICHARD J. DAVIDSON

ABSTRACT Among the most striking features of human emotion is the pronounced variability across individuals in the quality and intensity of emotional reactions to the same elicitor. This chapter introduces a framework for the objective neuroscientific study of such individual differences in affective style. The constituents of affective style are first reviewed and methods for their objective study described. The circuitry underlying two major forms of emotion and motivation is then presented. The foundations of this analysis are derived from the animal literature, and such observations are complemented by recent human neuroimaging studies. Emphasis is placed on the prefrontal cortex, the amygdala, and the ventral striatum in the generation of certain forms of positive and negative affect. Next, individual differences in aspects of this circuitry are considered. Here the emphasis is on individual differences in activation asymmetry in regions of the prefrontal cortex that appear to play a fundamental role in approach and withdrawal motivational disposition. Data are reviewed that indicate that individual differences in baseline measures of prefrontal activation are stable over time and predict both psychological and biological measures that have been linked to affective style. Finally, the implications of these data for conceptualizing the affective dysfunction in certain forms of psychopathology are considered.

Among the most striking features of human emotion is the variability that is apparent across individuals in the quality and intensity of emotional reactions to similar incentives and challenges and in the intensity and valence of dispositional mood. The broad range of differences in these varied affective phenomena has been referred to as *affective style* (Davidson, 1992). Differences among people in affective style appear to be associated with temperament (Kagan, Reznick, and Snidman, 1988), personality (Gross, Sutton, and Ketelaar, 1998), health (Ryff and Singer, 1998), and vulnerability to psychopathology (Meehl, 1975). Moreover, such differences are not a unique human attribute but appear to be present in a number of different species (e.g., Davidson, Kalin, and Shelton, 1993; Kalin, 1993).

In the next section of this chapter, conceptual distinctions among the various components of affective style will be introduced and methodological challenges to their study will be highlighted. The third section will present a brief overview of the anatomy of two basic motivational/emotional systems—the approach and

RICHARD J. DAVIDSON Department of Psychology, University of Wisconsin, Madison, Wis.

withdrawal systems—and will review research using neuroimaging methods to make inferences about the circuitry associated with these affective dispositions. The fourth section will consider individual differences in these basic systems and indicate how such differences might be studied. The final section will consider some of the implications of the research on affective style for conceptualizing the dysfunctions in emotion regulation in psychopathology, particularly mood and anxiety disorders.

The constituents of affective style

Many phenomena are subsumed under the rubric of affective style. A concept featured in many discussions of affective development, affective disorders, and personality is *emotion regulation* (Thompson, 1994). Emotion regulation refers to a broad constellation of processes that serve to either amplify, attenuate, or maintain the strength of emotional reactions. Included among these processes are certain features of attention that regulate the extent to which an organism can be distracted from a potentially aversive stimulus (Derryberry and Reed, 1996) and the capacity for self-generated imagery to replace emotions that are unwanted with more desirable imagery scripts. Emotion regulation can be both automatic and controlled. Automatic emotion regulation may result from the progressive automization of processes that initially were voluntary and controlled and have evolved to become more automatic with practice. We hold the view that regulatory processes are an intrinsic part of emotional behavior, and rarely does an emotion get generated in the absence of recruiting associated regulatory processes. For this reason, it is often conceptually difficult to distinguish sharply between where an emotion ends and where regulation begins. Even more problematic is the methodological challenge of operationalizing these different components in the stream of affective behavior.

When considering the question of individual differences in affective behavior, one must specify the particular response systems in which the individual differences are being explored. It is not necessarily the case that the same pattern of individual differences would be found across response systems. Thus, for example, an individual may have a low threshold for the elicitation of the subjective experience (as reflected in self-reports) of a particular emotion but a relatively high threshold for the elicitation of a particular physiological change. It is important not to assume that individual differences in any parameter of affective responding will necessarily generalize across response systems, within the same emotion. Equally important is the question of whether individual differences associated with the generation of a particular specific emotion will necessarily generalize to other emotions. For example, are those individuals who are behaviorally expressive in response to a fear challenge also likely to show comparably high levels of expressivity in response to positive incentives? While systematic research on this question is still required, initial evidence suggests that at least certain aspects of affective style may be emotion specific, or at least valence specific (e.g., Wheeler, Davidson, and Tomarken, 1993).

In addition to emotion regulation, there are also likely to be intrinsic differences in certain components of emotional responding. There are likely to be individual differences in the *threshold* for eliciting components of an emotion, given a stimulus of a particular intensity. Thus some individuals are likely to produce facial signs of disgust upon presentation of a particular intensity of noxious stimulus, whereas other individuals may require a more intense stimulus for the elicitation of the same response at a comparable intensity. This suggestion implies that dose-response functions may reliably differ across individuals. Unfortunately, systematic studies of this kind have not been performed, in part because of the difficulty of creating stimuli that are graded in intensity and designed to elicit the same emotion. In the olfactory and gustatory modalities, there are possibilities of creating stimuli that differ systematically in the concentration of a disgust-producing component and then obtaining psychophysical threshold functions that would reveal such individual differences. However, the production of such intensity-graded stimuli in other modalities will likely be more complicated, though with the development of large, normatively rated complex stimulus sets, this may be possible. An example is the *International Affective Picture System* (Lang, Bradley, and Cuthbert, 1995) developed by Peter Lang and his colleagues. This set includes a large number of visual stimuli that have been rated on valence and arousal dimensions and that comprise locations throughout this two-dimensional space. The density of stimulus exemplars at all levels within this space allows for the possibility of selecting stimuli that are graded in intensity for dose-response studies of the sort described.

There are also likely to be individual differences in the *peak* or *amplitude* of the response. Upon presentation of a series of graded stimuli that differ in intensity, the maximum amplitude in a certain system (e.g., intensity of a facial contraction, change in heart rate, etc.) is likely to differ systematically across subjects. Some individuals will respond with a larger amplitude peak than will others. Again, such individual differences may well be quite specific to particular systems and will not necessarily generalize across systems, even within the same emotion. Thus the individual who is in the tail of the distribution in her heart-rate response to a fearful stimulus will not necessarily be in the tail of the distribution in her facial response.

Another parameter that is likely to differ systematically across individuals is the *rise time to peak*. Some individuals will rise quickly in a certain response system, whereas others will rise more slowly. There may be an association between the peak of the response and the rise time to the peak within certain systems for particular emotions. Thus it may be the case that for anger-related emotion, those individuals with higher peak vocal responses also show a faster rise time, but to the best of my knowledge, there are no systematic data related to such differences.

Finally, another component of intrinsic differences across individuals is the *recovery time*. Following perturbation in a particular system, some individuals recover quickly, and others recover slowly. For example, following a fear-provoking encounter, some individuals show a persisting heart-rate elevation that might last for minutes, whereas other individuals show a comparable peak and rise time but recover much more quickly. Of course, as with other parameters, there are likely to be differences in recovery time across different response systems. Some individuals may recover rapidly in their expressive behavior, while recovering slowly in certain autonomic channels. The potential significance of such dissociations has not been systematically examined.

The specific parameters of individual differences that are delineated in the preceding paragraphs describe *affective chronometry*–the temporal dynamics of affective responding. Very little is known about the factors that govern these individual differences and the extent to which such differences are specific to particular emotion response systems or generalize across emotions. (For example, is the heart-rate recovery following fear similar to that following disgust?) Moreover, the general issue of the extent to which these different parameters that have been identified are orthogonal or correlated features of emotional responding is an empirical question that has yet to be answered. For reasons that I hope to make clear, affective chronometry is a particularly important feature of affective style and is likely to play a key role in determining vulnerability to psychopathology. It is also a feature of affective style that is methodologically tractable and can yield to experimental study of its neural substrates.

We also hold that affective style is critical in understanding the continuity between normal and abnormal functioning and in the prediction of psychopathology and the delineation of vulnerability. On the opposite side of the spectrum, such individual differences in affective style will also feature centrally in any comprehensive theory of resilience. The fact that some individuals reside "off the diagonal" and appear to maintain very high levels of psychological well-being despite their exposure to objective life adversity is likely related to their affective style (Ryff and Singer, 1998). Some of these implications will be discussed at the end of this chapter.

We first consider some of the neural substrates of two fundamental emotion systems. This discussion provides the foundation for a consideration of individual differences in these systems and the neural circuitry responsible for such differences.

The anatomy of approach and withdrawal

Although the focus of my empirical research has been on measures of prefrontal brain activity, it must be emphasized at the outset that the circuit instantiating emotion in the human brain is complex and involves a number of interrelated structures. Precious few empirical studies using modern neuroimaging procedures that afford a high degree of spatial resolution have yet been performed (see George et al., 1995; Paradiso et al., 1997, for examples). Therefore, hypotheses about the set of structures that participate in the production of emotion must necessarily be speculative and based to a large extent on the information available from the animal literature (e.g., LeDoux, 1987, 1996) and from theoretical accounts of the processes involved in human emotion.

Based upon the available strands of theory and evidence, numerous scientists have proposed two basic circuits each mediating different forms of motivation and emotion (see, e.g., Gray, 1994; Lang, Bradley, and Cuthbert, 1990; Davidson, 1995). The approach system facilitates appetitive behavior and generates certain types of positive affect that are approach related—for example, enthusiasm, pride, and so on (see Depue and Collins, in press, for review). This form of positive affect is usually generated in the context of moving toward a desired goal (see Lazarus, 1991; Stein and Trabasso, 1992, for theoretical accounts of emotion that place a premium on goal states). The representation of a goal state in working memory is hypothesized to be implemented in dorsolateral prefrontal cortex. The medial prefrontal cortex

seems to play an important role in maintaining representations of behavioral-reinforcement contingencies in working memory (Thorpe, Rolls, and Maddison, 1983). In addition, output from the medial prefrontal cortex to nucleus accumbens (NA) neurons modulates the transfer of motivationally relevant information through the NA (Kalivas, Churchill, and Klitenick, 1993). The basal ganglia are hypothesized to be involved in the expression of the abstract goal in action plans and in the anticipation of reward (Schultz, Apicella, et al., 1995; Schultz, Romo, et al., 1995). The NA, particularly the caudomedial shell region of the NA, is a major convergence zone for motivationally relevant information from a myriad of limbic structures. Cells in this region of the NA increase their firing rate during reward expectation (see Schultz, Apicella, et al., 1995). There are likely other structures involved in this circuit that depend on a number of factors including the nature of the stimuli signaling appetitive information, the extent to which the behavioral-reinforcement contingency is novel or overlearned, and the nature of the anticipated behavioral response.

It should be noted that the activation of this approach system is hypothesized to be associated with one particular form of positive affect and not all forms of such emotion. It is specifically predicted to be associated with *pre-goal-attainment positive affect*, the form of positive affect that is elicited as an organism moves closer to an appetitive goal. *Post-goal-attainment positive affect* represents another form of positive emotion that is not expected to be associated with activation of this circuit (see Davidson, 1994, for a more extended discussion of this distinction). This latter type of positive affect may be phenomenologically experienced as contentment and is expected to occur when the prefrontal cortex goes offline after a desired goal has been achieved. Cells in the NA have also been shown to decrease their firing rate during post-goal-consummatory behavior (e.g., Henriksen and Giacchino, 1993).

Lawful individual differences can enter into many different stages of the approach system. Such individual differences will be considered in detail later. For the moment, it is important to underscore two issues. One is that there are individual differences in the tonic level of activation of the approach system that alters an individual's propensity to experience approach-related positive affect. Second, there are likely to be individual differences in the capacity to shift between pre- and post-goal attainment positive affect and in the ratio between these two forms of positive affect. Upon reaching a desired goal, some individuals will immediately replace the just-achieved goal with a new desired goal, and so will have little opportunity to experience post-goal-attainment positive affect, or contentment. There may be an optimal balance between these two forms of positive affect, though this issue has never been studied.

There appears to be a second system concerned with the neural implementation of withdrawal. This system facilitates the withdrawal of an individual from sources of aversive stimulation and generates certain forms of negative affect that are withdrawal related. Both fear and disgust are associated with increasing the distance between the organism and a source of aversive stimulation. From invasive animal studies and human neuroimaging studies, it appears that the amygdala is critically involved in this system (e.g., LeDoux, 1987, 1996). Using functional magnetic resonance imaging (fMRI) we have recently demonstrated for the first time activation in the human amygdala in response to aversive pictures compared with neutral control pictures (Irwin et al., 1996). Several experiments using both fMRI and the lesion method have further supported the idea that the amygdala is a key structure in the perception of facial expressions of fear (e.g., Adolphs et al., 1995; Breiter et al., 1996; Morris et al., 1996). Interestingly, recent evidence indicates that the perception of facial signs of disgust is associated with activation of the anterior insular cortex but not the amygdala (e.g., Phillips et al., 1997). These data imply that certain components of the circuit underlying the withdrawal emotions of fear and disgust may be the same, but other components appear to differ. The pronounced vagal response often associated with disgust may in part be responsible for the insular activation (see Cacioppo et al., 1993), though this conjecture has never been formally tested. The temporal polar region also appears to be activated during withdrawal-related emotion (e.g., Reiman et al., 1989; but see Drevets et al., 1992). Some evidence suggests that at least in humans, these effects appear to be more pronounced on the right side of the brain (see Davidson, 1992, 1993, for reviews). In the human electrophysiological studies, the right frontal region is also activated during withdrawal-related negative affective states including both fear and disgust (e.g., Davidson, Ekman, et al., 1990). At present it is not entirely clear whether this EEG change reflects activation at a frontal site or whether the activity recorded from the frontal scalp region is volume-conducted from other cortical loci. The resolution of this uncertainty must await additional studies using positron emission tomography (PET) or fMRI, which have sufficient spatial resolution to differentiate among different anterior cortical regions. In addition to the temporal polar region, the amygdala, and possibly the prefrontal cortex, it is also likely that the basal ganglia and hypothalamus are involved in the motor and autonomic components, respectively, of withdrawal-related negative affect (see Smith, DeVita, and Astley, 1990). In summary, from the evidence currently available, the right-sided anterior cortical activation appears to be common to both fear and disgust; activation of the amygdala appears to be more specific to fear; and activation of the insular cortex appears to be more specific to disgust. These findings are thus consistent with both discrete and dimensional views of emotion, suggesting that some circuitry may be unique to specific discrete emotions and other circuitry may code for broader dimensional characteristics.

The nature of the relation between these two hypothesized affect systems also remains to be delineated. The emotion literature is replete with different proposals regarding the interrelations among different forms of positive and negative affect. Some theorists have proposed a single bivalent dimension that ranges from unpleasant to pleasant affect, with a second dimension that reflects arousal (e.g., Russell, 1980). Other theorists have suggested that affect space is best described by two orthogonal positive and negative dimensions (e.g., Watson and Tellegen, 1985). Still other workers have suggested that the degree of orthogonality between positive and negative affect depends upon the temporal frame of analysis (Diener and Emmons, 1984). This formulation holds that when assessed in the moment, positive and negative affect are reciprocally related, but when examined over a longer time frame (e.g., dispositional affect), they are orthogonal. It must be emphasized that these analyses of the relation between positive and negative affect are all based exclusively on measures of self-report, and therefore the generalizability to other measures of affect is uncertain. However, based upon new data that will be described later, we believe that a growing corpus of data does indeed indicate that one function of positive affect is to inhibit concurrent negative affect.

What do individual differences in asymmetric prefrontal activation reflect?

This section will present a brief overview of recent work from my laboratory that was designed to examine individual differences in measures of prefrontal activation and their relation to different aspects of emotion, affective style, and related biological constructs. These findings will be used to address the question of what underlying constituents of affective style such individual differences in prefrontal activation actually reflect.

In both infants (Davidson and Fox, 1989) and adults (Davidson and Tomarken, 1989) there are large individual differences in baseline electrophysiological measures of prefrontal activation, and such individual variation is associated with differences in aspects of affective reactivity. In infants, Davidson and Fox (1989) reported that

10-month-old babies who cried in response to maternal separation were more likely to have less left- and greater right-sided prefrontal activation during a preceding resting baseline compared with those infants who did not cry in response to this challenge. In adults, we first noted that the phasic influence of positive and negative emotion elicitors (e.g., film clips) on measures of prefrontal activation asymmetry appeared to be superimposed on more tonic individual differences in the direction and absolute magnitude of asymmetry (Davidson and Tomarken, 1989).

During our initial explorations of this phenomenon, we needed to determine if baseline electrophysiological measures of prefrontal asymmetry were reliable and stable over time and thus could be used as a traitlike measure. Tomarken and colleagues (1992) recorded baseline brain electrical activity from 90 normal subjects on two occasions separately by approximately three weeks. At each testing session, brain activity was recorded during 8 one-minute trials, four with eyes open and four with eyes closed, presented in counterbalanced order. The data were visually scored to remove artifact and then Fourier-transformed. Our focus was on power in the alpha band (8–13 Hz), though we extracted power in all frequency bands. (See Davidson, Chapman, et al., 1990, for a discussion of power in different frequency bands and their relation to activation.) We computed coefficient alpha as a measure of internal consistency reliability from the data for each session. The coefficient alphas were quite high, with all values exceeding .85, indicating that the electrophysiological measures of asymmetric activation indeed showed excellent internal consistency reliability. The test-retest reliability was adequate with intraclass correlations ranging from .65 to .75 depending on the specific sites and methods of analysis. The major conclusion from this study was the demonstration that measures of activation asymmetry based on power in the alpha band from prefrontal scalp electrodes showed both high internal-consistency reliability and acceptable test-retest reliability to be considered a traitlike index.

On the basis of our prior data and theory, we reasoned that extreme left and extreme right frontally activated subjects would show systematic differences in dispositional positive and negative affect. We administered the trait version of the Positive and Negative Affect Scales (PANAS; Watson, Clark, and Tellegen, 1988) to examine this question and found that the left-frontally activated subjects reported more positive and less negative affect than their right-frontally activated counterparts (Tomarken et al., 1992; see figure 79.1). More recently with Sutton (Sutton and Davidson, 1997) we showed that scores on a self-report measure designed to operationalize Gray's concepts of Behavioral Inhibition

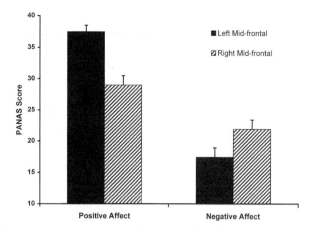

FIGURE 79.1 Dispositional positive affect (from scores on the PANAS–General Positive Affect Scale) in subjects who were classified as extreme and stable left-frontally active ($N = 14$) and extreme and stable right-frontally active ($N = 13$) on the basis of electrophysiological measures of baseline activation asymmetries on two occasions separated by three weeks. (From Tomarken et al., 1992.)

and Behavioral Activation (the BIS/BAS scales; Carver and White, 1994) were even more strongly predicted by electrophysiological measures of prefrontal asymmetry than were scores on the PANAS scales (see figure 79.2). Subjects with greater left-sided prefrontal activation reported more relative BAS to BIS activity than did subjects exhibiting more right-sided prefrontal activation.

We also hypothesized that our measures of prefrontal asymmetry would predict reactivity to experimental elicitors of emotion. The model that we have developed over the past several years (see Davidson, 1992, 1994, 1995, for background) features individual differences in prefrontal activation asymmetry as a reflection of a diathesis which modulates reactivity to emotionally significant events. According to this model, individuals who differ in prefrontal asymmetry should respond differently to an elicitor of positive or negative emotion, even when baseline mood is partialed out. We performed an experiment to examine this question (Wheeler, Davidson, and Tomarken, 1993; see also Tomarken, Davidson, and Henriques, 1990). We presented short film clips designed to elicit positive or negative emotion. Brain electrical activity was recorded prior to the presentation of the film clips. Just after the clips were presented, subjects were asked to rate their emotional experience during the preceding film clip. In addition, subjects completed scales that were designed to reflect their mood at baseline. We found that individual differences in prefrontal asymmetry predicted the emotional response to the films even after measures of baseline mood were statistically removed. Those individuals with more left-sided prefrontal activation at baseline reported more positive affect to the positive film clips, and those with more

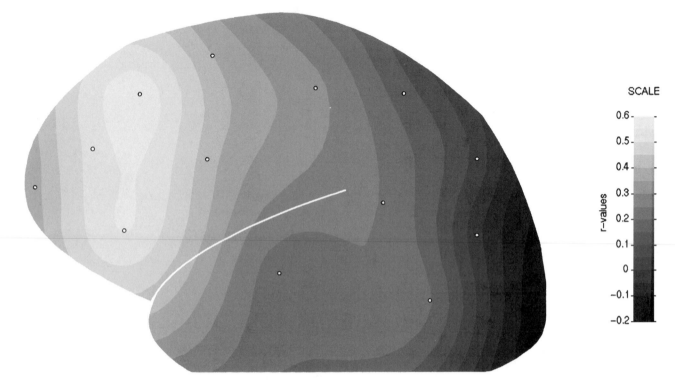

SCALE

0.6
0.5
0.4
0.3
0.2
0.1
0
-0.1
-0.2

r-values

FIGURE 79.2 Relations between electrophysiological measures of asymmetry and the difference between the standardized score on the Behavioral Activation and Behavioral Inhibition Scales (BIS/BAS scales; Carver and White, 1994), $N = 46$. Electrophysiological data were recorded from each subject on two separate occasions separated by 6 weeks. The BIS/BAS scales were also administered on these two occasions. Data were averaged across the two time periods prior to performing correlations. The topographic map displays the correlations between alpha power asymmetry (log right minus log left alpha power; higher values denote greater relative left-sided activation) and the difference score between the standardized BAS minus BIS scales. After correlations were per-

formed for each homologous region, a spline-interpolated map was created. The lighter values of the scale denote positive correlations. The figure indicates that the correlation between the BAS-BIS difference score and the electrophysiology asymmetry score is highly positive in prefrontal scalp regions, denoting that subjects with greater relative left-sided activation report more relative Behavioral Activation than Behavioral Inhibition tendencies. The relation between asymmetric activation and the BAS-BIS difference is highly specific to the anterior scalp regions, as the correlation drops off rapidly more posteriorly. The correlation in the prefrontal region is significantly larger than the correlation in the parieto-occipital region. (From Sutton and Davidson, 1997.)

right-sided prefrontal activation reported more negative affect to the negative film clips. These findings support the idea that individual differences in electrophysiological measures of prefrontal activation asymmetry mark some aspect of vulnerability to positive and negative emotion elicitors. The fact that such relations were obtained following the statistical removal of baseline mood indicates that any difference between left and right frontally activated subjects in baseline mood cannot account for the prediction of film-elicited emotion effects that were observed.

In a very recent study, we examined relations between individual differences in prefrontal activation asymmetry and the emotion-modulated startle (Davidson et al., in preparation). In this study, we presented pictures from the *International Affective Picture System* (Lang, Bradley, and Cuthbert, 1995) while acoustic startle probes were presented and the EMG-measured blink

response from the orbicularis oculi muscle region was recorded (see Sutton et al., 1997, for basic methods). Startle probes were presented both during the 6-second slide exposure and 500 ms following the offset of the pictures, on separate trials.[1] We interpreted startle magnitude during picture exposure as providing an index related to the peak of emotional response, while startle magnitude following the *offset* of the pictures was taken to reflect the recovery from emotional challenge. Used in this way, startle probe methods can potentially provide new information on the time course of emotional responding. We expected that individual differences during actual picture presentation would be less pronounced than individual differences following picture presentation, since an acute emotional stimulus is likely to pull for a normative response across subjects, yet individuals are likely to differ dramatically in the time to recover. Similarly, we predicted that individual differences in prefrontal asymmetry would account for more variance in predicting magnitude of recovery (i.e., startle magnitude poststimulus) than in predicting startle magnitude during the stimulus. Our findings were consistent with our predictions and indicated that subjects with greater right-sided prefrontal activation show a larger blink magnitude following the offset of the negative stimuli, after the variance in blink magnitude *during* the negative stimulus was partialed out. Measures of prefrontal asymmetry did not reliably predict startle magnitude during picture presentation. The findings from this study are consistent with our hypothesis and indicate that individual differences in prefrontal asymmetry are associated with the time course of affective responding, particularly the recovery following emotional challenge.

In addition to the studies using self-report and psychophysiological measures of emotion that have been described, we have also examined relations between individual differences in electrophysiological measures of prefrontal asymmetry and other biological indices that in turn have been related to differential reactivity to stressful events. Two recent examples from our laboratory include measures of immune function and cortisol. In the case of the former, we examined differences between left and right prefrontally activated subjects in natural killer cell activity, since declines in NK activity have been reported in response to stressful, negative events (Kiecolt-Glaser and Glaser, 1991). We predicted that subjects with right prefrontal activation would exhibit lower NK activity compared with their left-activated counterparts because the former type of subject has been found to report more dispositional negative affect, to show higher relative BIS activity, and to respond more intensely to negative emotional stimuli. We found that right-frontally activated subjects indeed had lower levels of NK activity compared with their left frontally activated counterparts (Kang et al., 1991).

In collaboration with Kalin, our laboratory has been studying similar individual differences in scalp-recorded measures of prefrontal activation asymmetry in rhesus monkeys (Davidson, Kalin, and Shelton, 1992, 1993). Recently we acquired measures of brain electrical activity from a large sample of rhesus monkeys ($N= 50$) (Kalin et al., 1998). EEG measures were obtained during periods of manual restraint. A subsample of 15 of these monkeys were tested on two occasions four months apart. We found that the test-retest correlation for measures of prefrontal asymmetry was .62, suggesting similar stability of this metric in monkey and man. In the group of 50 animals, we also obtained measures of plasma cortisol during the early morning. We hypothesized that if individual differences in prefrontal asymmetry were associated with dispositional affective

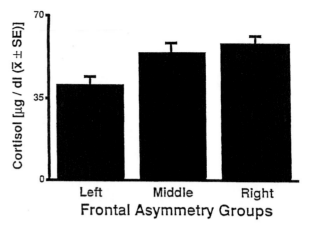

FIGURE 79.3 Basal morning plasma cortisol from one-year-old rhesus monkeys classified as left ($N= 12$), middle ($N= 16$), or right ($N= 11$) frontally activated based upon electrophysiological measurements. (From Kalin et al., 1998.)

style, such differences should be correlated with cortisol, since individual differences in baseline cortisol have been related to various aspects of trait-related stressful behavior and psychopathology (see, e.g., Gold, Goodwin, and Chrousos, 1988). We found that animals with right-sided prefrontal activation had higher levels of baseline cortisol than their left-frontally activated counterparts (see figure 79.3). Moreover, when blood samples were collected two years after our initial testing, animals classified as showing extreme right-sided prefrontal activation at age one year had significantly higher baseline cortisol levels when they were three years of age than animals who were classified at age one year as displaying extreme left-sided prefrontal activation. These findings indicate that individual differences in prefrontal asymmetry are present in nonhuman primates and that such differences predict biological measures that are related to affective style.

With the advent of neuroimaging, it has become possible to investigate the relation between individual differences in aspects of amygdala function and measures of affective style. We have used PET with fluorodeoxyglucose (FDG) as a tracer to investigate relations between individual differences in glucose metabolism in the amygdala and dispositional negative affect. Because the period of active uptake of tracer in the brain is approximately 30 minutes, FDG-PET is well suited to capture traitlike effects. Thus it is inherently more reliable than O15 blood-flow measures, since the FDG data reflect activity aggregated over a 30-minute period. We have used resting FDG-PET to examine individual differences in glucose metabolic rate in the amygdala and its relation to dispositional negative affect in depressed subjects (Abercrombie et al., 1998). We acquired a resting FDG-PET scan as well as a structural MR scan for

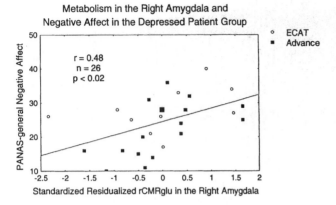

FIGURE 79.4 Scatter plot of the relation between metabolic rate in the right amygdala and dispositional negative affect. Metabolic rate in the amygdala was obtained by coregistering MRI and PET images and then drawing regions of interest (ROIs) on the MRIs around the amygdala. These ROIs were then automatically transferred to the PET images, and glucose metabolic rate for these regions was determined. ECAT and Advance refer to two different PET scanners that were used to collect the data. (From Abercrombie et al., 1998.)

each subject. The structural MR scans are used for anatomical localization by coregistering the two image sets. Thus, for each subject, we used an automated algorithm to fit the MR scan to the PET image. Regions of interest (ROIs) were then drawn on each subject's MR scan to outline the amygdala in each hemisphere. These ROIs were drawn on coronal sections of subjects' MR images, and the ROIs were then automatically transferred to the coregistered PET images. Glucose metabolism in the left and right amygdala ROIs were then extracted. The inter-rater reliability for the extracted glucose metabolic rate is highly significant with intraclass correlations between two independent raters $\geq .97$. We found that subjects with greater glucose metabolism in the right amygdala report greater dispositional negative affect on the PANAS scale (see figure 79.4). These findings indicate that individual differences in resting glucose metabolism in the amygdala are present and that they predict dispositional negative affect among depressed subjects.

In a small sample of 9 normal subjects, we have been able to examine the relation between the magnitude of MR signal change in the amygdala in response to aversive compared with neutral pictures and dispositional negative affect on the PANAS scale (Irwin et al., 1998). We correlated the average value of the pixels with the maximum Student's t from the left and right amygdala with dispositional negative affect. The correlation was $r = .75$. A pixel in the fusiform gyrus that revealed robust activation by the aversive pictures was selected as a control region. We correlated the magnitude of activation in the pixel showing the maximal response in this region to the aversive pictures with dispositional nega-

tive affect and found no relation $(p > .5)$. Moreover, the correlations in the amygdala and fusiform gyrus were found to be significantly different. The findings from the fMRI and PET studies of amygdala function indicate that individual differences in both tonic activation and phasic activation in response to aversive stimuli predict the intensity of dispositional negative affect.

Implications and conclusions

Earlier in this chapter, the constituents of affective style were described. We considered individual differences in threshold, peak amplitude, rise time to peak, and recovery time. Together these constitute parameters of affective chronometry and dictate important features of the time course of affective responding. Following a description of the functional neuroanatomy of the approach and withdrawal systems, individual differences in prefrontal activation asymmetry and amygdala function were discussed and their relation to affective style described. In light of this information, we now return to the question posed in the section titled "What do individual differences in asymmetric prefrontal activation reflect?"

On the basis of findings from several new studies in my laboratory, I suggest that at least one important component of what prefrontal cortex "does" in affective responding is to modulate the time course of emotional responding, particularly recovery time. There are several facts critical to making this claim. First, there are extensive reciprocal connections between amygdala and PFC, particularly the medial and orbital zones of prefrontal cortex (Amaral et al., 1992). The glutamatergic efferents from PFC likely synapse on GABA neurons (Amaral et al., 1992) and thus provide an important inhibitory input to the amygdala. Second, LeDoux and his colleagues (Morgan, Romanski, and LeDoux, 1993; but see Gewirtz, Falls, and Davis, 1997) demonstrated in rats that lesions of medial prefrontal cortex dramatically prolong the maintenance of a conditioned aversive response. In other words, animals with medial prefrontal lesions retain aversive associations for a much longer duration of time than normal animals. These findings imply that the medial PFC normally inhibits the amygdala as an active component of extinction. In the absence of this normal inhibitory input, the amygdala remains unchecked and continues to maintain the learned aversive response. Third, the data from my laboratory cited in the section that asks, "What do individual differences . . . reflect?," indicate that individual differences in prefrontal activation asymmetry significantly predict the magnitude of the poststimulus startle following removal of the variance attributable to startle magnitude during the presentation of the emotional picture. In particular, left prefrontal activation appears to facilitate two processes simultaneously: (1) It maintains representations of behavioral-reinforcement contingencies in working memory (Thorpe et al., 1983); and (2) It inhibits the amygdala. In this way, the time course of negative affect is shortened while the time course of positive affect is accentuated. And finally, new findings using PET from my laboratory indicate that in normal subjects, glucose metabolism in left medial and lateral prefrontal cortex is strongly reciprocally associated with glucose metabolic rate in the amygdala (Abercrombie et al., 1996). Thus subjects with greater left-sided prefrontal metabolism have lower metabolic activity in their amygdala. These findings are consistent with the lesion study of LeDoux and colleagues and imply that prefrontal cortex plays an important role in modulating activity in the amygdala. At the same time, left prefrontal cortex is also likely to play a role in the maintenance of reinforcement-related behavioral approach. Perhaps the damping of negative affect and shortening of its time course facilitate the maintenance of approach-related positive affect.

Data were also presented that indicate individual differences in both tonic glucose metabolism and phasic activation in response to aversive stimuli in the amygdala. These individual differences predict dispositional negative affect. Whatever modulatory influence the prefrontal cortex might have over the amygdala, it appears that the magnitude of phasic activation of the amygdala by aversive stimuli accounts for a substantial portion of variance in self-reported dispositional negative affect, considerably more than any of our measures of prefrontal function. Thus the proximal control of dispositional negative affect is likely to be more closely associated with amygdala function than with prefrontal function.

The questions that are featured in this chapter are more tractable now than ever before. With the advent of echoplanar methods for rapid functional MR imaging, sufficient data can be collected within individuals to examine functional connections among regions hypothesized to constitute important elements of the approach and withdrawal circuits discussed earlier. Individual differences in different aspects of these systems can then be studied with greater precision. In addition, fMRI methods lend themselves to address questions related to affective chronometry. In particular, we can calculate the slope of declines in MR signal intensity following the offset of an aversive stimulus to provide an index of the rapidity of recovery from activation in select brain regions. Also, PET methods using new radioligands that permit quantification of receptor density for specific neurotrans-

mitters in different brain regions are yielding new insights directly relevant to questions about affective style (see, e.g., Farde, Gustavsson, and Jönsson, 1997). Trait-like differences in affective style are likely reflected in relatively stable differences in characteristics of the underlying neurochemical systems. Using PET to examine such individual differences promises to provide important syntheses between neurochemical and neuroanatomical approaches to understanding the biological bases of affective style.

Affective neuroscience seeks to understand the underlying proximal neural substrates of elementary constituents of emotional processing. In this chapter, I have provided a model of the functional neuroanatomy of approach and withdrawal motivational/emotional systems and illustrated the many varieties of individual differences that might occur in these systems. Research on prefrontal asymmetries associated with affective style was used to illustrate the potential promise of some initial approaches to the study of these questions. Modern neuroimaging methods used in conjunction with theoretically sophisticated models of emotion and psychopathology offer great promise in advancing our understanding of the basic mechanisms that give rise to affective style and to affective and anxiety disorders.

NOTE

1. In this initial study on the recovery function assessed with startle probe measures, we had only a single poststimulus probe at 500 ms following the offset of the picture. Readers may be surprised that the interval between the offset of the picture and the presentation of the probe was so short. However, it should be noted that these emotional pictures are not particularly intense, and so the lingering effect of emotion following the presentation of such pictures is likely not to last very long in most individuals. Future studies will probe further out following the offset of the picture. Since at most only a single probe can be presented for each picture so that habituation effects are minimized, each new probe position requires a substantial increase in the overall number of pictures presented. There is a finite limit to the number of pictures contained in the IAPS. Even more importantly, we have found that it is critical to keep the picture viewing period to well under one hour to minimize fatigue and boredom.

REFERENCES

ABERCROMBIE, H. C., S. M. SCHAEFER, C. L. LARSON, T. R. OAKES, K. A. LINDGREN, J. E. HOLDEN, S. B. PERLMAN, P. A. TURSKI, D. D. KRAHN, R. M. BENCA, and R. J. DAVIDSON, 1998. Metabolic rate in the amygdala predicts negative affect in depressed patients. *NeuroReport* 9:3301–2207.
ABERCROMBIE, H. C., S. M. SCHAEFER, C. L. LARSON, R. T. WARD, J. F. HOLDEN, P. A. TURSKI, S. B. PERLMAN, R. J. DAVIDSON, 1996. Medial prefrontal and amygdalar glucose

metabolism in depressed and control subjects: An FDG-PET study. *Psychophysiology* 33:S17.

ADOLPHS, R., et al., 1995. Fear and the human amygdala. *J. Neurosci.* 16:7678–7687.

AMARAL, D. G., J. L. PRICE, A. PITKANEN, and S. T. CARMICHAEL, 1992. Anatomical organization of the primate amygdaloid complex. In J. P. Aggleton, ed., *The Amygdala: Neurobiological Aspects of Emotion, Memory and Mental Dysfunction.* New York: Wiley-Liss, pp. 1–66.

BREITER, H. C., N. L. ETCOFF, P. J. WHALEN, W. A. KENNEDY, S. L. RAUCH, R. L. BUCKNER, M. M. STRAUSS, S. E. HYMAN, and B. R. ROSEN, 1996. Response and habituation of the human amygdala during visual processing of facial expression. *Neuron* 17:875–887.

CACIOPPO, J. T., D. J. KLEIN, G. G. BERNTSON, and E. HATFIELD, 1993. The psychophysiology of emotion. In *Handbook of Emotion*, M. Lewis and J. Haviland, eds. New York: Guilford Press, pp. 119–142.

CARVER, C. S., and T. L. WHITE, 1994. Behavioral inhibition, behavioral activation and affective responses to impending reward and punishment: The BIS/BAS scales. *J. Pers. Soc. Psychol.* 67:319–333.

DAVIDSON, R. J., 1992. Emotion and affective style: Hemispheric substrates. *Psychol. Sci.* 3:39–43.

DAVIDSON, R. J., 1993. Cerebral asymmetry and emotion: Conceptual and methodological conundrums. *Cogn. Emotion* 7:115–138.

DAVIDSON, R. J., 1994. Asymmetric brain function, affective style and psychopathology: The role of early experience and plasticity. *Dev. Psychopathol.* 6:741–758.

DAVIDSON, R. J., 1995. Cerebral asymmetry, emotion and affective style. In R. J. Davidson and K. Hugdahl, eds., *Brain Asymmetry.* Cambridge, Mass.: MIT Press, pp. 361–387.

DAVIDSON, R. J., J. P. CHAPMAN, L. P. CHAPMAN, and J. B. HENRIQUES, 1990. Asymmetrical brain electrical activity discriminates between psychometrically-matched verbal and spatial cognitive tasks. *Psychophysiol.* 27:528–543.

DAVIDSON, R. J., I. DOLSKI, C. LARSON, and S. K. SUTTON, in preparation. Electrophysiological measures of prefrontal asymmetry predict recovery of emotion-modulated startle.

DAVIDSON, R. J., P. EKMAN, C. SARON, J. SENULIS, and W. V. FRIESEN, 1990. Approach/withdrawal and cerebral asymmetry: Emotional expression and brain physiology, I. *J. Pers. Soc. Psychol.* 58:330–341.

DAVIDSON, R. J., and N. A. FOX, 1989. Frontal brain asymmetry predicts infants' response to maternal separation. *J. Abnorm. Psychol.* 98:127–131.

DAVIDSON, R. J., N. H. KALIN, and S. E. SHELTON, 1992. Lateralized effects of diazepam on frontal brain electrical asymmetries in rhesus monkeys. *Biol. Psychiatry* 32:438–451.

DAVIDSON, R. J., N. H. KALIN, and S. E. SHELTON, 1993. Lateralized response to diazepam predicts temperamental style in rhesus monkeys. *Behav. Neurosci.* 107:1106–1110.

DAVIDSON, R. J., and A. J. TOMARKEN, 1989. Laterality and emotion: An electrophysiological approach. In F. Boller and J. Grafman, eds., *Handbook of Neuropsychology.* Amsterdam: Elsevier.

DEPUE, R. A., and P. F. COLLINS, in press. Neurobiology of the structure of personality: Dopamine, incentive motivation and extroversion. *Behav. Brain Sci.*

DERRYBERRY, D., and M. A. REED, 1996. Regulatory processes and the development of cognitive representations. *Dev. Psychopathol.* 8:215–234.

DIENER, V. E., and R. A. EMMONS, 1984. The independence of positive and negative affect. *J. Pers. Soc. Psychol.* 47:1105–1117.

DREVETS, W. C., T. O. VIDEEN, A. K. MACLEOD, J. W. HALLER, and M. E. RAICHLE, 1992. PET images of blood changes during anxiety: Correction. *Science* 256:1696.

FARDE, L., J. P. GUSTAVSSON, and E. JÖNSSON, 1997. D2 dopamine receptors and personality. *Nature* 385:590.

GEORGE, M. S., T. A. KETTER, P. I. PAREKH, B. HORWITZ, P. HERSCOVITCH, and R. M. POST, 1995. Brain activity during transient sadness and happiness in healthy women. *Am. J. Psychiatry* 152:341–351.

GEWIRTZ, J. C., W. A. FALLS, and M. DAVIS, 1997. Normal conditioned inhibition and extinction of freezing and fear-potentiated startle following electrolytic lesions of medical prefrontal cortex in rats. *Behav. Neurosci.* 111:712–726.

GOLD, P. W., F. K. GOODWIN, and G. P. CHROUSOS, 1988. Clinical and biochemical manifestations of depression: Relation to the neurobiology of stress. *N. Engl. J. Med.* 314:348–353.

GRAY, J. A., 1994. Three fundamental emotion systems. In P. Ekman and R. J. Davidson, eds., *The Nature of Emotion: Fundamental Questions.* New York: Oxford University Press, pp. 243–247.

GROSS, J. J., S. K. SUTTON, and T. V. KETELAAR, 1998. Relations between affect and personality: Support for the affect-level and affective-reactivity views. *Pers. Soc. Psychol. Bull.* 24:279–288.

HENRIKSEN, S. J., and J. GIACCHINO, 1993. Functional characteristics of nucleus accumbens neurons: Evidence obtained from *in vivo* electrophysiological recordings. In P. W. Kalivas and C. D. Barnes, eds. *Limbic Motor Circuits and Neuropsychiatry.* Boca Raton, Fl.: CRC Press, pp. 101–124.

IRWIN, W., R. J. DAVIDSON, M. J. LOWE, B. J. MOCK, J. A. SORENSON, and P. A. TURSKI, 1996. Human amygdala activation detected with echo-planar functional magnetic resonance imaging. *NeuroReport* 7:1765–1769.

IRWIN, W., B. J. MOCK, S. K. SUTTON, M. J. ANDERLE, N. H. KALIN, J. A. SORENSON, P. A. TURSKI, and R. J. DAVIDSON, 1998. Ratings of affective stimulus characteristics and measures of affective reactivity predict MR signal change in the human amygdala. *NeuroImage* 7:S908.

KAGAN, J., J. S. REZNICK, and N. SNIDMAN, 1988. Biological bases of childhood shyness. *Science* 240:167–171.

KALIN, N. H., 1993. The neurobiology of fear. *Sci. Am.* 268:94–107.

KALIN, N. H., C. LARSON, S. E. SHELTON, and R. J. DAVIDSON, 1998. Asymmetric frontal brain activity, cortisol, and behavior associated with fearful temperament in rhesus monkeys. *Behav. Neurosci.* 112:286–292.

KALIVAS, P. W., L. CHURCHILL, and M. A. KLITENICK, 1993. The circuitry mediating the translation of motivational stimuli into adaptive motor responses. In P. W. Kalivas and C. D. Barnes, eds., *Limbic Motor Circuits and Neuropsychiatry.* Boca Raton, Fl.: CRC Press, pp. 237–287.

KANG, D. H., R. J. DAVIDSON, C. L. COE, R. W. WHEELER, A. J. TOMARKEN, and W. B. ERSHLER, 1991. Frontal brain asymmetry and immune function. *Behav. Neurosci.* 105:860–869.

KIECOLT-GLASER, J. K., and R. GLASER, 1991. Stress and immune function in humans. In R. Ader, D. L. Felten, and N. Cohen, eds., *Psychoneuroimmunology*, 2nd ed. San Diego, Calif.: Academic Press, pp. 849–867.

LANG, P. J., M. M. BRADLEY, and B. N. CUTHBERT, 1990. Emotion, attention and the startle reflex. *Psychol. Rev.* 97: 377–398.

LANG, P. J., M. M. BRADLEY, and B. N. CUTHBERT, 1995. *International Affective Picture System (IAPS): Technical Manual and Affective Ratings*. Gainesville, Fl.: Center for Research in Psychophysiology, University of Florida.

LAZARUS, R. S., 1991. *Emotion and Adaptation*. Oxford: Oxford University Press.

LEDOUX, J. E., 1987. Emotion. In V. B. Mountcastle, ed., *Handbook of Physiology*, Section 1: *The Nervous System*, Vol. 5: *Higher Functions of the Brain*. Bethesda, Md.: American Physiological Society, pp. 419–460.

LEDOUX, J. E., 1996. *The Emotional Brain*. New York: Simon & Schuster.

MEEHL, P. E., 1975. Hedonic capacity: Some conjectures. *Bull. Menninger Clin.* 39:295–307.

MORGAN, M. A., L. ROMANSKI, and J. E. LEDOUX, 1993. Extinction of emotional learning: Contribution of medial prefrontal cortex. *Neurosci. Lett.* 163:109–113.

MORRIS, J., et al., 1996. A differential neural response in the human amygdala to fearful and happy facial expressions. *Nature* 383:812–815.

PARADISO, S., R. G. ROBINSON, N. C. ANDREASEN, J. E. DOWNHILL, R. J. DAVIDSON, P. T. KIRCHNER, G. L. WATKINS, L. L. BOLES, and R. D. HICHWA, 1997. Emotional activation of limbic circuitry in elderly and normal subjects in a PET study. *Am. J. Psychiatry* 154:382–389.

PHILLIPS, M. L., A. W. YOUNG, C. SENIOR, M. BRAMMER, C. ANDREWS, A. J. CALDER, E. T. BULLMORE, D. I. PERRETT, D. ROWLAND, S. C. R. WILLIAMS, J. A. GRAY, and A. S. DAVID, 1997. A specific neural substrate for perceiving facial expressions of disgust. *Nature* 389:495–498.

REIMAN, E. M., M. J. L. FUSSELMAN, B. J. FOX, and M. E. RAICHLE, 1989. Neuroanatomical correlates of anticipatory anxiety. *Science* 243:1071–1074.

RUSSELL, J. A., 1980. A circumplex model of emotion. *J. Pers. Soc. Psychol.* 39:1161–1178.

RYFF, C. D., and B. SINGER, 1998. The contours of positive human health. *Psychological Inquiry* 9:1–28.

SCHULTZ, W., P. APICELLA, R. ROMO, and E. SCARNATI, 1995. Context-dependent activity in primate striatum reflecting past and future behavioral events. In J. C. Houk, J. L. Davis, and D. G. Beiser, eds., *Models of Information Processing in the Basal Ganglia*. Cambridge, Mass.: MIT Press, pp. 11–28.

SCHULTZ, W., R. ROMO, T. LJUNGBERG, J. MIRENOWICZ, J. R. HOLLERMAN, and A. DICKINSON, 1995. Reward-related signals carried by dopamine neurons. In J. C. Houk, J. L. Davis, and D. G. Beiser, eds., *Models of Information Processing in the Basal Ganglia*. Cambridge, Mass.: MIT Press, pp. 233–248.

SMITH, O. A., J. L. DEVITA, and C. A. ASTLEY, 1990. Neurons controlling cardiovascular responses to emotion are located in lateral hypothalamus-perifornical region. *Am. J. Physiol.* 259:R943–R954.

STEIN, N. L., and T. TRABASSO, 1992. The organization of emotional experience: Creating links among emotion, thinking, language and intentional action. *Cogn. Emotion* 6:225–244.

SUTTON, S. K., and R. J. DAVIDSON, 1997. Prefrontal brain asymmetry: A biological substrate of the behavioral approach and inhibition systems. *Psychol. Sci.* 8:204–210.

SUTTON, S. K., R. J. DAVIDSON, B. DONZELLA, W. IRWIN, and D. A. DOTTL, 1997. Manipulating affective state using extended picture presentation. *Psychophysiology* 34:217–226.

THOMPSON, R. A., 1994. Emotion regulation: A theme in search of definition. In N. A. Fox, ed., *The Development of Emotion Regulation: Biological and Behavioral Aspects. Monographs of the Society for Research in Child Development*, 59 (Serial No. 240), pp. 25–52.

THORPE, S., E. ROLLS, and S. MADDISON, 1983. The orbitofrontal cortex: Neuronal activity in the behaving monkey. *Exp. Brain Res.* 49:93–113.

TOMARKEN, A. J., R. J. DAVIDSON, and J. B. HENRIQUES, 1990. Resting frontal brain asymmetry predicts affective responses to films. *J. Pers. Soc. Psychol.* 59:791–801.

TOMARKEN, A. J., R. J. DAVIDSON, R. E. WHEELER, and R. C. DOSS, 1992. Individual differences in anterior brain asymmetry and fundamental dimensions of emotion. *J. Pers. Soc. Psychol.* 62:676–687.

WATSON, D., L. A. CLARK, and A. TELLEGEN, 1988. Developmental and validation of brief measures of positive and negative affect: The PANAS scales. *J. Pers. Soc. Psychol.* 54:1063–1070.

WATSON, D., and A. TELLEGEN, 1985. Toward a consensual structure of mood. *Psychol. Bull.* 98:219–235.

WHEELER, R. E., R. J. DAVIDSON, and A. J. TOMARKEN, 1993. Frontal brain asymmetry and emotional reactivity: A biological substrate of affective style. *Psychophysiology* 30:82–89.

X EVOLUTION

Introduction

LEDA COSMIDES AND JOHN TOOBY

Most cognitive neuroscientists recognize the need for reliable sources of theoretical guidance. Many have taken a bottom-up approach, turning to cellular and molecular neurobiology. But there also is a top-down approach, which can be equally or more informative. Knowledge of evolved function can be used to identify functional units within the brain and mind and to guide investigation into their designs. Despite their sustained record of success in other areas of biology, evolutionary methods are only beginning to be understood or applied in the cognitive neurosciences. This section outlines this approach and illustrates its use.

Dissection implies function

When anatomists dissect an organism, they do not cut it randomly. Dissection–whether done by a real scalpel or a conceptual one–implies the search for functional units. Because the brain's function is to process information, correctly dissecting its neural architecture into functional units depends on correctly dissecting its cognitive architecture into corresponding, functionally meaningful computational units. Because human and nonhuman brains were constructed by the evolutionary process, these units were organized according to an underlying evolutionary logic–a logic that must be grasped if this process of dissection is to be successful. Because knowledge of adaptive problems and models of evolved functions provides the functional engineering specifications to which human and nonhuman brains were built to conform, evolutionary biology and psychology can help researchers to isolate, identify, activate, and map the important, functional design features of the cognitive architecture that otherwise would be lost among the maze of functionally irrelevant physical concomitants in which they are embedded (see chapter 80 for an overview of issues).

The cross-species diversity of brain architectures

Advocates of the bottom-up approach argue that the findings of neuroscience will place strong constraints on theory formation at the cognitive level. Such knowledge is very valuable, and it undoubtedly will contribute a great deal to theory formation in the long run. But one reason why many neglect the analysis of evolved function is because they believe that neural constraints will be sufficient for developing cognitive theories. This cannot be true.

Consider the fact that there are bird species that navigate by the stars or by the Earth's magnetic field, bats that echolocate and engage in reciprocal blood sharing, bees that compute the variance of flower patches and discriminate classes of kin, spiders that spin webs and extract social information from web movement, ant species that farm or defend host trees or dead reckon, elephant seals that forage hundreds of feet underwater, monogamous gibbons, polygynous gorillas, polyandrous seahorses, sex-changing coral reef fish, mole rats that form social-insect-like colonies, and so on. There are millions of animal species on earth, each with a different set of cognitive programs—programs that often are radically different from each other, even in closely related species. The same basic neural tissue embodies all of these programs, and it could support innumerable others as well. Facts about the properties of neurons, neurotransmitters, and cellular development cannot tell you which of these billions of programs will develop reliably in the human (or, e.g., the rhesus) mind.

Even if all neural computation turned out to be the expression of universally shared processes at the cellular level, it is the higher-order arrangement of neurons—into birdsong templates or web-spinning programs or facial emotion display programs—that matters computationally. The idea that low-level neuroscience unassisted can produce models of cognitive mechanisms is a physicalist expression of the ethologically naïve associationist doctrine that all animal brains are essentially the same (see chapter 81 [associationism] and chapter 84 and Preuss, 1995 [comparative neuroanatomy]). A related assumption—that a few computational principles underlie most

mechanisms in the brains of animal species—organizes the thinking of neoassociationists and connectionists (e.g., Quartz and Sejnowski, 1997). If this were true, then the adaptive problems encountered by species ancestrally would indeed be irrelevant: The neoassociationist assumption is that evolution selected for general-purpose brains that solved most or all problems using methods applicable to the broadest and most general class of problems. In this view, brains lack specializations reflecting the specific demands of a species' particular way of life. A logical corollary of this view is that all information necessary to solve problems must be acquirable ontogenetically, through the senses, because it is not being supplied phylogenetically, in the form of evolutionarily organized specializations.

The challenge from evolutionary biology

It is difficult to reconcile this view with the mass of data accumulated by behavioral ecologists and evolutionarily oriented psychologists about behavioral diversity and the array of problems that organisms are known to solve. By using theories of adaptive function to guide their investigations, behavioral ecologists have been able to document a range of animal behavior that is breathtaking in its adaptive problem-solving sophistication and whose generation often requires information that could not be supplied ontogenetically or perceptually. There is, for example, no perceptual data in the ontogenetic environment that specifies that a male langur monkey who has taken over a troop should kill all the infants born within the following several months whereas a titi monkey should not; or that a female ground squirrel should give more alarm calls when the neighboring ground squirrels are her sisters than when they are not, and so on. These rules must be in the adaptations, because they are not in stimuli.

Equally important, specialization of circuitry often greatly increases computational efficiency, and endows architectures with the capacity to solve problems that could not be solved at all by general-purpose methods, making architectures that operate primarily through general-purpose methods uncompetitive and unlikely to evolve. These and many other converging lines of evidence and argument collectively contradict the view that a few general-purpose computational principles could explain known behavioral phenomena or be capable of solving many of the adaptive problems that humans and other species faced during their evolutionary histories (Tooby and Cosmides, 1992). As Gallistel shows (chapter 81), even in the case of animal learning—the set of phenomena that associationism was explicitly developed to handle—associationistic theories are theoretical and empirical failures, incapable of being made consistent with the data, much less of accounting for it.

To free theorizing in cognitive neuroscience from the Procrustean bed of a one-solution-fits-all-problems approach, and to clear the ground for a new generation of theories of heterogeneous functional specializations, it would be helpful if cognitive neuroscientists became aware of the truly diverse nature of adaptive problems organisms solve. Toward this end, this section includes several chapters about nonhumans to give a textured feel for the kinds of adaptive tasks that other animals' minds are able to solve quickly and efficiently. These include the chapters by Fernald and White (chapter 82) on the social behavior of territorial fish, by Sherry (chapter 83) on the spatial cognition of parasitic cowbirds, polygynous meadow voles and monogamous pine voles, and by Gallistel (chapter 81) on dead-reckoning in ants, computation of the solar ephemeris by bees, and classical conditioning in pigeons and rats (see also Gaulin, 1995; Daly and Wilson, 1995). In every case in which the computational processes are known in any detail, they have turned out to be narrowly tailored to the demands of solving specific adaptive problems.

Constraints on hypotheses

Because efficient computational designs will almost always be specialized to fit the particular nature of the problems they solve, an investigation into the nature of adaptive problems is a very productive research strategy. For any given adaptive problem, only a highly restricted class of candidate program designs has the properties required to solve it. Thus, knowledge of the structure of the adaptive problem informs the researcher about large numbers of probable design features, greatly facilitating the construction of experiments that can probe for their presence.

For this reason, cognitive neuroscientists stand to profit greatly from formally describing the problems that the human cognitive architecture evolved to solve. The intuitive conceptions of function that are widely used instead–such as "learning" and "memory"–are simply too broad to be useful. As Gallistel (chapter 81) points out:

It is odd but true that most past and contemporary theorizing about learning does not assume that learning mechanisms are adaptively specialized for the solution of particular kinds of problems. Most theorizing assumes that there is a general purpose learning process in the brain, a process adapted only to solving the problem of learning. There is no attempt to formalize what the problem of learning is and thereby determine whether it can in fact be conceived of as a single or uniform problem. From a biological perspective, this assumption is equivalent to assuming that there is a general purpose sensory organ, which solves the problem of sensing.

In his chapter, Gallistel analyzes various learning problems solved by desert ants, bees, pigeons, and other animals, showing that (1) they are incommensurate; (2) each is solved by a different computational machine that is specialized for that task; and (3) associative theories of learning are incapable of explaining the animal learning data. According to Gallistel, there is no evidence in any species supporting the existence of the associative bond. If he is correct, then neuroscientists who hope to unlock the secrets of learning and memory by looking for the neural basis of the associative bond have had their time wasted by evolutionarily uninformed models of natural computational systems. This underlines how good research at the neural level depends on having a correct characterization of the computational level, which in turn depends on understanding the evolutionary principles responsible for organic design.

Humans also evolved

The chapters dealing with humans (chapters 83 and 85–87) also take a top-down approach. Although the hypothesis that there might be cognitive specializations for navigating the social world was once considered intuitively implausible by many, the adaptive problems posed by social life are both complex and have enormous fitness consequences. This led evolutionarily informed researchers to research the hypothesis that human brains–like those of other animals–contain a number of cognitive adaptations for understanding and negotiating social life. Following this logic, Baron-Cohen, Cosmides and Tooby, and Leslie have been finding evidence for domain-specific mechanisms specialized for reasoning about the contents of other minds and about cooperation. This research not only illuminates the computational structure of social cognitive adaptations, but it also illuminates the nature of neurological disorders, such as autism, which appear to involve selective deficits in particular computational subcomponents of social adaptations.

ACKNOWLEDGMENTS

The authors gratefully acknowledge the financial support of the James S. McDonnell Foundation, the National Science Foundation (NSF grant BNS9157-449 to John Tooby), and a Research Across Disciplines grant (Evolution and the Social Mind) from the UCSB Office of Research.

REFERENCES

DALY, M., and M. WILSON, 1995. Discriminative parental solicitude and the relevance of evolutionary models to the analysis of motivational systems. In *The Cognitive Neurosciences*, M. S. Gazzaniga, ed. Cambridge, Mass.: MIT Press, pp. 1269–1286.

GAULIN, S., 1995. Does evolutionary theory predict sex differences in the brain? In *The Cognitive Neurosciences*, M. S. Gazzaniga, ed. Cambridge, Mass.: MIT Press, pp. 1211–1225.

PREUSS, T., 1995. The argument from animals to humans in cognitive neuroscience. In *The Cognitive Neurosciences*, M. S. Gazzaniga, ed. Cambridge, Mass.: MIT Press, pp. 1227–1241.

QUARTZ, S. and T. SEJNOWSKI, 1997. The neural basis of cognitive development. *Behav. Brain Sci.* 20:537–555.

TOOBY, J., and L. COSMIDES, 1992. The psychological foundations of culture. In *The Adapted Mind: Evolutionary Psychology and the Generation of Culture*, J. Barkow, L. Cosmides, and J. Tooby, eds. New York: Oxford University Press.

80 Toward Mapping the Evolved Functional Organization of Mind and Brain

JOHN TOOBY AND LEDA COSMIDES

ABSTRACT   The human brain is a biological system produced by the evolutionary process, and thus, cognitive neuroscience is itself a branch of evolutionary biology. Accordingly, cognitive neuroscientists can benefit by learning about and applying the technical advances made in modern evolutionary biology. Among other things, evolutionary biology can supply researchers with (1) the biologically rigorous concept of function appropriate to neural and cognitive systems, (2) a growing list of the specialized functions the human brain evolved to perform, and (3) the ability to distinguish the narrowly functional aspects of the neural and cognitive architecture that are responsible for its organization from the much larger set of properties that are by-products or noise. With these and other tools, researchers can construct experimental stimuli and tasks that activate and are meaningful to functionally dedicated subunits of the brain. The brain is comprised of many such subunits: evolutionarily meaningful stimuli and tasks are far more likely than arbitrary ones to elicit responses that can illuminate their complex functional organization.

Nothing in biology makes sense except in the light of evolution.
– T. Dobzhansky

It is the theory which decides what we can observe.
– A. Einstein

Seeing with new eyes: Toward an evolutionarily informed cognitive neuroscience

The task of cognitive neuroscience is to map the information-processing structure of the human mind and to discover how this computational organization is implemented in the physical organization of the brain. The central impediment to progress is obvious: The human brain is, by many orders of magnitude, the most complex system that humans have yet investigated. Purely as a physical system, the vast intricacy of chemical and electrical interactions among hundreds of billions of neurons and glial cells defeats any straightforward attempt to build a comprehensive model, as one might at-

JOHN TOOBY   Center for Evolutionary Psychology and Department of Anthropology, University of California, Santa Barbara, Calif.
LEDA COSMIDES   Center for Evolutionary Psychology and Department of Psychology, University of California, Santa Barbara, Calif.

tempt to do with particle collisions, geological processes, protein folding, or host-parasite interactions. Combinatorial explosion makes the task of elucidating the brain's computational structure even more overwhelming: There is an indefinitely large number of specifiable inputs, measurable outputs, and possible relationships between them. Even worse, no one yet knows with certainty how computations are physically realized. They depend on individuated events within the detailed structure of neural microcircuitry largely beyond the capacity of current technologies to observe or resolve. Finally, the underlying logic of the system has been obscured by the torrent of recently generated data.

Historically, however, well-established theories from one discipline have functioned as organs of perception for others (e.g., statistical mechanics for thermodynamics). They allow new relationships to be observed and make visible elegant systems of organization that had previously eluded detection. It seems worth exploring whether evolutionary biology could provide a rigorous metatheoretical framework for the brain sciences, as they have recently begun to do for psychology (Shepard, 1984, 1987a, 1987b; Gallistel, 1990; Cosmides and Tooby, 1987; Pinker, 1994, 1997; Marr 1982; Tooby and Cosmides, 1992).

Cognitive neuroscience began with the recognition that the brain is an organ designed to process information and that studying it as such would offer important new insights. Cognitive neuroscientists also recognize that the brain is an evolved system, but few realize that anything follows from this second fact. Yet these two views of the brain are intimately related and, when considered jointly, can be very illuminating.

Why brains exist

The brain is an organ of computation that was built by the evolutionary process. To say that the brain is an organ of computation means that (1) its physical structure embodies a set of programs that process information, and (2) that physical structure is there *because* it embodies these programs. To say that the brain was built

1167

by the evolutionary process means that its functional components–its programs–are there *because* they solved a particular problem-type in the past. In systems designed by natural selection, function determines structure.

Among living things, there are whole kingdoms filled with organisms that lack brains (plants, Monera, fungi). The sole reason that evolution introduced brains into the designs of some organisms–the reason brains exist at all–is because brains performed computations that regulated these organisms' internal processes and external activities in ways that promoted their fitness. For a randomly generated modification in design to be selected–that is, for a mutation to be incorporated by means of a nonrandom process into a species-typical brain design–it had to improve the ability of organisms to solve adaptive problems. That is, the modification had to have a certain kind of effect: It had to improve the organisms' performance of some activity that systematically enhanced the propagation of that modification, summed across the species' range and across many generations. This means that the design of the circuits, components, systems, or modules that make up our neural architecture must reflect, to an unknown but high degree, (1) the computational task demands inherent in the performance of those ancestral activities and (2) the evolutionarily long-enduring structure of those task environments (Marr, 1982; Shepard, 1987a; Tooby and Cosmides, 1992).

Activities that promoted fitness in hominid ancestral environments differ in many ways from activities that capture our attention in the modern world, and they were certainly performed under radically different circumstances. (Consider: hunting *vs*. grocery shopping; walking everywhere *vs*. driving and flying; cooperating within a social world of ~200 relatives and friends *vs*. 50,000 strangers in a medium-sized city). The design features of the brain were built to specifications inherent in ancestral adaptive problems and selection pressures, often resulting in talents or deficits that seem out of place or irrational in our world. A baby cries–alerting her parents–when she is left to sleep alone in the dark, not because hyenas roam her suburban household, but because her brain is designed to keep her from being eaten under the circumstances in which our species evolved.

There is no single algorithm or computational procedure that can solve every adaptive problem (Cosmides and Tooby, 1987; Tooby and Cosmides, 1990a, 1992). The human mind (it will turn out) is composed of many different programs for the same reason that a carpenter's toolbox contains many different tools: Different problems require different solutions. To reverse-engineer the brain, one needs to discover functional units that are native to its organization. To do this, it is useful to know, as specifically as possible, what the brain is for–which specific families of computations it was built to accomplish and what counted as a biologically successful outcome for each problem-type. The answers to this question must be phrased in computational terms because that is the only language that can capture or express the functions that neural properties were naturally selected to embody. They must also refer to the ancestral activities, problems, selection pressures, and environments of the species in question because jointly these define the computational problems each component was configured to solve (Cosmides and Tooby 1987; Tooby and Cosmides, 1990a, 1992).

For these reasons, evolutionary biology, biological anthropology, and cognitive psychology (when integrated, called *evolutionary psychology*) have the potential to supply to cognitive neuroscientists what might prove to be a key missing element in their research program: a partial list of the native information-processing functions that the human brain was built to execute, as well as clues and principles about how to discover or evaluate adaptive problems that might be proposed in the future.

Just as the fields of electrical and mechanical engineering summarize our knowledge of principles that govern the design of human-built machines, the field of evolutionary biology summarizes our knowledge of the engineering principles that govern the design of organisms, which can be thought of as machines built by the evolutionary process (for overviews, see Daly and Wilson, 1984; Dawkins, 1976, 1982, 1986; Krebs and Davies, 1997). Modern evolutionary biology constitutes, in effect, a foundational "organism design theory" whose principles can be used to fit together research findings into coherent models of specific cognitive and neural mechanisms (Tooby and Cosmides, 1992). To apply these theories to a particular species, one integrates analyses of selection pressures with models of the natural history and ancestral environments of the species. For humans, the latter are provided by hunter–gatherer studies, biological anthropology, paleoanthropology, and primatology (Lee and DeVore, 1968).

First principles: Reproduction, feedback, and the antientropic construction of organic design

Within an evolutionary framework, an organism can be described as a self-reproducing machine. From this perspective, the defining property of life is the presence in a system of "devices" (organized components) that cause the system to construct new and similarly reproducing systems. From this defining property–self-reproduction–the entire deductive structure of modern Darwinism logically follows (Dawkins, 1976; Williams, 1985; Tooby and Cosmides, 1990a). Because the replication of the design of the parental machine is not always error free, randomly modified designs (i.e., mutants) are introduced into populations of reproducers. Because such machines are highly organized so that they cause the otherwise improbable outcome of constructing offspring machines, most random modifications interfere with the complex sequence of actions necessary for self-reproduction. Consequently, such modified designs will tend to remove themselves from the population–a case of negative feedback.

However, a small residual subset of design modifications will, by chance, happen to constitute improvements in the design's machinery for causing its own reproduction. Such improved designs (by definition) cause their own increasing frequency in the population–a case of positive feedback. This increase continues until (usually) such modified designs outreproduce and thereby replace all alternative designs in the population, leading to a new species-standard design. After such an event, the population of reproducing machines is different from the ancestral population: The population- or species-standard design has taken a step "uphill" toward a greater degree of functional organization for reproduction than it had previously. This spontaneous feedback process–natural selection–causes functional organization to emerge *naturally*, that is, without the intervention of an intelligent "designer" or supernatural forces.

Over the long run, down chains of descent, this feedback cycle pushes designs through state-space toward increasingly well-organized–and otherwise improbable–functional arrangements (Dawkins 1986; Williams, 1966, 1985). These arrangements are functional in a specific sense: the elements are improbably well organized to cause their own reproduction in the environment in which the species evolved. Because the reproductive fates of the inherited traits that coexist in the same organism are linked together, traits will be selected to enhance each other's functionality (however, see Cosmides and Tooby, 1981, and Tooby and Cosmides, 1990a, for the relevant genetic analysis and qualifications). As design features accumulate, they will tend to sequentially fit themselves together into increasingly functionally elaborated machines for reproduction, composed of constituent mechanisms–called *adaptations*–that solve problems that either are necessary for reproduction or increase its likelihood (Darwin, 1859; Dawkins, 1986; Thornhill, 1991; Tooby and Cosmides, 1990a; Williams, 1966, 1985). Significantly, in species like humans, genetic processes ensure that complex adaptations virtu-

ally always are species-typical (unlike nonfunctional aspects of the system). This means that *functional* aspects of the architecture will tend to be universal at the genetic level, even though their expression may often be sex or age limited, or environmentally contingent (Tooby and Cosmides, 1990b).[1]

Because design features are embodied in individual organisms, they can, generally speaking, propagate themselves in only two ways: by solving problems that increase the probability that offspring will be produced either by the organism they are situated in or by that organism's kin (Hamilton, 1964; Williams and Williams, 1957; however, see Cosmides and Tooby, 1981, and Haig, 1993, for intragenomic methods). An individual's relatives, by virtue of having descended from a recent common ancestor, have an increased likelihood of having the same design feature as compared to other conspecifics. This means that a design modification in an individual that causes an increase in the reproductive rate of that individual's kin will, by so doing, tend to increase its own frequency in the population. Accordingly, design features that promote both direct reproduction and kin reproduction, and that make efficient trade-offs between the two, will replace those that do not. To put this in standard biological terminology, design features are selected to the extent that they promote their inclusive fitness (Hamilton, 1964).

In addition to selection, mutations can become incorporated into species-typical designs by means of chance processes. For example, the sheer impact of many random accidents may cumulatively propel a useless mutation upward in frequency until it crowds out all alternative design features from the population. Clearly, the presence of such a trait in the architecture is not explained by the (nonexistent) functional consequences that it had over many generations on the design's reproduction; as a result, chance-injected traits will not tend to be coordinated with the rest of the organism's architecture in a functional way.

Although such chance events play a restricted role in evolution and explain the existence and distribution of many simple and trivial properties, organisms are not primarily chance agglomerations of stray properties. Reproduction is a highly improbable outcome in the absence of functional machinery designed to bring it about, and only designs that retain all the necessary machinery avoid being selected out. To be invisible to selection and, therefore, not organized by it a modification must be so minor that its effects on reproduction are negligible. As a result, chance properties do indeed drift through the standard designs of species in a random way, but they are unable to account for the complex organized design in organisms and are, correspondingly, usually peripheralized into those aspects that do not make a significant impact on the functional operation of the system (Tooby and Cosmides, 1990a, 1990b, 1992). Random walks do not systematically build intricate and improbably functional arrangements such as the visual system, the language faculty, face recognition programs, emotion recognition modules, food aversion circuits, cheater detection devices, or motor control systems, for the same reason that wind in a junkyard does not assemble airplanes and radar.

Brains are composed primarily of adaptive problem-solving devices

In fact, natural selection is the only known cause of and explanation for complex functional design in organic systems. Hence, all naturally occurring functional organization in organisms should be ascribed to its operation, and hypotheses about function are likely to be correct only if they are the kinds of functionality that natural selection produces.

This leads to the most important point for cognitive neuroscientists to abstract from modern evolutionary biology: Although not everything in the designs of organisms is the product of selection, all complex functional organization is. Indeed, selection can only account for functionality of a very narrow kind: approximately, design features organized to promote the reproduction of an individual and his or her relatives in ancestral environments (Williams, 1966; Dawkins, 1986). Fortunately for the modern theory of evolution, the only naturally occurring complex functionality that ever has been documented in undomesticated plants, animals, or other organisms is functionality of just this kind, along with its derivatives and by-products.

This has several important implications for cognitive neuroscientists:

1. *Technical definition of function.* In explaining or exploring the reliably developing organization of a cognitive device, the *function* of a design refers solely to how it systematically caused its own propagation in ancestral environments. It does not validly refer to any intuitive or folk definitions of function such as "contributing to personal goals," "contributing to one's well-being," or "contributing to society." These other kinds of usefulness may or may not exist as side effects of a given evolved design, but they can play no role in explaining how such designs came into existence or why they have the organization that they do.

It is important to bear in mind that the evolutionary standard of functionality is entirely independent of any ordinary human standard of desirability, social value, morality, or health (Cosmides and Tooby, in press).

2. *Adapted to the past.* The human brain, to the extent that it is organized to do anything functional at all, is organized to construct information, make decisions, and generate behavior that would have tended to promote inclusive fitness in the ancestral environments and behavioral contexts of Pleistocene hunter-gatherers and before. (The preagricultural world of hunter-gatherers is the appropriate ancestral context because natural selection operates far too slowly to have built complex information-processing adaptations to the post-hunter-gatherer world of the last few thousand years.)

3. *No evolved "reading modules."* The problems that our cognitive devices are designed to solve do not reflect the problems that our modern life experiences lead us to see as normal, such as reading, driving cars, working for large organizations, reading insurance forms, learning the oboe, or playing Go. Instead, they are the odd and seemingly esoteric problems that our hunter-gatherer ancestors encountered generation after generation over hominid evolution. These include such problems as foraging, kin recognition, "mind reading" (i.e., inferring beliefs, desires, and intentions from behavior), engaging in social exchange, avoiding incest, choosing mates, interpreting threats, recognizing emotions, caring for children, regulating immune function, and so on, as well as the already well-known problems involved in perception, language acquisition, and motor control.

4. *Side effects are personally important but scientifically misleading.* Although our architectures may be capable of performing tasks that are "functional" in the (nonbiological) sense that we may value them (e.g., weaving, playing piano), these are incidental side effects of selection for our Pleistocene competencies—just as a machine built to be a hair-dryer can, incidentally, dehydrate fruit or electrocute. But it will be difficult to make sense of our cognitive mechanisms if one attempts to interpret them as devices designed to perform functions that were not selectively important for our hunter-gatherer ancestors, or if one fails to consider the adaptive functions these abilities are side effects of.

5. *Adaptationism provides new techniques and principles.* Whenever one finds better-than-chance functional organization built into our cognitive or neural architecture, one is looking at adaptations—devices that acquired their distinctive organization from natural selection acting on our hunter-gatherer or more distant primate ancestors. Reciprocally, when one is searching for intelligible functional organization underlying a set of cognitive or neural phenomena, one is far more likely to discover it by using an adaptationist framework for organizing observations because adaptive organization is the only kind of functional organization that is there to be found.

Because the reliably developing mechanisms (i.e., circuits, modules, functionally isolable units, mental organs, or computational devices) that cognitive neuroscientists study are evolved adaptations, all the biological principles that apply to adaptations apply to cognitive devices. This connects cognitive neuroscience and evolutionary biology in the most direct possible way. This conclusion should be a welcome one because it is the logical doorway through which a very extensive body of new expertise and principles can be made to apply to cognitive neuroscience, stringently constraining the range of valid hypotheses about the functions and structures of cognitive mechanisms. Because cognitive neuroscientists are usually studying adaptations and their effects, they can supplement their present research methods with carefully derived adaptationist analytic tools.

6. *Ruling out and ruling in.* Evolutionary biology gives specific and rigorous content to the concept of function, imposing strict rules on its use (Williams, 1966; Dawkins, 1982, 1986). This allows one to rule out certain hypotheses about the proposed function of a given cognitive mechanism. But the problem is not just that cognitive neuroscientists sometimes impute functions that they ought not to. An even larger problem is that many fail to impute functions that they ought to. For example, an otherwise excellent recent talk by a prominent cognitive neuroscientist began with the claim that one would not expect jealousy to be a "primary" emotion–that is, a universal, reliably developing part of the human neural architecture (in contrast to others, such as disgust or fear). Yet there is a large body of theory in evolutionary biology–sexual selection theory–that predicts that sexual jealousy will be widespread in species with substantial parental investment in offspring (particularly in males); behavioral ecologists have documented mate-guarding behavior (behavior designed to keep sexual competitors away from one's mate) in a wide variety of species, including various birds, fish, insects, and mammals (Krebs and Davies, 1997; Wilson and Daly, 1992); male sexual jealousy exists in every documented human culture (Daly et al., 1982; Wilson and Daly, 1992); it is the major cause of spousal homicides (Daly and Wilson, 1988), and in experimental settings, the design features of sexual jealousy have been shown to differ between the sexes in ways that reflect the different adaptive problems faced by ancestral men and women (Buss, 1994). From the standpoint of evolutionary biology and behavioral ecology, the hypothesis that sexual jealousy is a primary emotion–more specifically, the hypothesis that the human brain includes neurocognitive mechanisms whose function is to regulate the conditions under which sexual jealousy is expressed and what its cognitive and behav-

ioral manifestations will be like–is virtually inescapable (for an evolutionary/cognitive approach to emotions, see Tooby and Cosmides, 1990a, 1990b). But if cognitive neuroscientists are not aware of this body of theory and evidence, they will not design experiments capable of revealing such mechanisms.

7. *Biological parsimony, not physics parsimony.* The standard of parsimony imported from physics, the traditional philosophy of science, or from habits of economical programming is inappropriate and misleading in biology, and hence, in neuroscience and cognitive science, which study biological systems. The evolutionary process never starts with a clean work board, has no foresight, and incorporates new features solely on the basis of whether they lead to systematically enhanced propagation. Indeed, when one examines the brain, one sees an amazingly heterogeneous physical structure. A correct theory of evolved cognitive functions should be no less complex and heterogeneous than the evolved physical structure itself and should map on to the heterogeneous set of recurring adaptive tasks faced by hominid foragers over evolutionary time. Theories of engineered machinery involve theories of the subcomponents. One would not expect that a general, unified theory of robot or automotive mechanism could be accurate.

8. *Many cognitive adaptations.* Indeed, analyses of the adaptive problems humans and other animals must have regularly solved over evolutionary time suggest that the mind contains a far greater number of functional specializations than is traditionally supposed, even by cognitive scientists sympathetic to "modular" approaches. From an evolutionary perspective, the human cognitive architecture is far more likely to resemble a confederation of hundreds or thousands of functionally dedicated computers, designed to solve problems endemic to the Pleistocene, than it is to resemble a single general purpose computer equipped with a small number of domain-general procedures, such as association formation, categorization, or production rule formation (for discussion, see Cosmides and Tooby, 1987, 1994; Gallistel, 1990; Pinker, 1997; Sperber, 1994; Symons, 1987; Tooby and Cosmides, 1992; see also chapter 81 of this volume).

9. *Cognitive descriptions are necessary.* Understanding the neural organization of the brain depends on understanding the functional organization of its computational relationships or cognitive devices. The brain originally came into existence and accumulated its particular set of design features only because these features functionally contributed to the organism's propagation. This contribution–that is, the evolutionary function of the brain–is obviously the adaptive regulation of behavior and physiology *on the basis of information* derived

from the body and from the environment. The brain performs no significant mechanical, metabolic, or chemical service for the organism–its function is purely informational, computational, and regulatory in nature. Because the function of the brain is informational in nature, its precise functional organization can only be accurately described in a language that is capable of expressing its informational functions–that is, in cognitive terms, rather than in cellular, anatomical, or chemical terms. Cognitive investigations are not some soft, optional activity that goes on only until the "real" neural analysis can be performed. Instead, the mapping of the computational adaptations of the brain is an unavoidable and indispensable step in the neuroscience research enterprise. It must proceed in tandem with neural investigations and provides one of the primary frameworks necessary for organizing the body of neuroscience results.

The reason is straightforward. Natural selection retained neural structures on the basis of their ability to create adaptively organized relationships between information and behavior (e.g., the sight of a predator activates inference procedures that cause the organism to hide or flee) or between information and physiology (e.g., the sight of a predator increases the organism's heart rate, in preparation for flight). Thus, it is the information-processing structure of the human psychological architecture that has been functionally organized by natural selection, and the neural structures and processes have been organized insofar as they physically realize this cognitive organization. Brains exist and have the structure that they do because of the computational requirements imposed by selection on our ancestors. The adaptive structure of our computational devices provides a skeleton around which a modern understanding of our neural architecture should be constructed.

Brain architectures consist of adaptations, by-products, and random effects

To understand the human (or any living species') computational or neural architecture is a problem in reverse engineering: We have working exemplars of the design in front of us, but we need to organize our observations of these exemplars into a systematic functional and causal description of the design. One can describe and decompose brains into properties according to any of an infinite set of alternative systems, and hence there are an indefinitely large number of cognitive and neural phenomena that could be defined and measured. However, describing and investigating the architecture in terms of its adaptations is a useful place

to begin, because (1) the adaptations are the cause of the system's organization (the reason for the system's existence), (2) organisms, properly described, consist largely of collections of adaptations (evolved problem-solvers), (3) an adaptationist frame of reference allows cognitive neuroscientists to apply to their research problems the formidable array of knowledge that evolutionary biologists have accumulated about adaptations, (4) all of the complex functionally organized subsystems in the architecture are adaptations, and (5) such a frame of reference permits the construction of economical and principled models of the important features of the system, in which the wealth of varied phenomena fall into intelligible, functional, and predictable patterns. As Ernst Mayr put it, summarizing the historical record, "the adaptationist question, 'What is the function of a given structure or organ?' has been for centuries the basis for every advance in physiology" (Mayr, 1983, p. 32). It should prove no less productive for cognitive neuroscientists. Indeed, all of the inherited design features of organisms can be partitioned into three categories: (1) adaptations (often, although not always, complex); (2) the by products or concomitants of adaptations; and (3) random effects. Chance and selection, the two components of the evolutionary process, explain different types of design properties in organisms, and all aspects of design must be attributed to one of these two forces. The conspicuously distinctive cumulative impacts of chance and selection allow the development of rigorous standards of evidence for recognizing and establishing the existence of adaptations and distinguishing them from the nonadaptive aspects of organisms caused by the nonselectionist mechanisms of evolutionary change (Williams, 1966, 1985; Pinker and Bloom, 1992; Symons, 1992; Thornhill, 1991; Tooby and Cosmides, 1990a, 1990b, 1992; Dawkins, 1986).

DESIGN EVIDENCE Adaptations are systems of properties ("mechanisms") crafted by natural selection to solve the specific problems posed by the regularities of the physical, chemical, developmental, ecological, demographic, social, and informational environments encountered by ancestral populations during the course of a species' or population's evolution (table 80.1). Adaptations are recognizable by "evidence of special design" (Williams, 1966)–that is, by recognizing certain features of the evolved species-typical design of an organism "as components of some special problem-solving machinery" (Williams, 1985, p. 1). Moreover, they are so well organized and such good engineering solutions to adaptive problems that a chance coordination between problem and solution is effectively ruled out

TABLE 80.1
The formal properties of an adaptation

An adaptation is:

1. A cross-generationally recurring set of characteristics of the phenotype

2. that is reliably manufactured over the developmental life history of the organism,

3. according to instructions contained in its genetic specification,

4. in interaction with stable and recurring features of the environment (i.e., it reliably develops normally when exposed to normal ontogenetic environments),

5. whose genetic basis became established and organized in the species (or population) over evolutionary time, because

6. the set of characteristics systematically interacted with stable and recurring features of the ancestral environment (the "adaptive problem"),

7. in a way that systematically promoted the propagation of the genetic basis of the set of characteristics better than the alternative designs existing in the population during the period of selection. This promotion virtually always takes place through enhancing the reproduction of the individual bearing the set of characteristics, or the reproduction of the relatives of that individual.

Adaptations. The most fundamental analytic tool for organizing observations about a species' functional architecture is the definition of an adaptation. To function, adaptations must evolve such that their causal properties rely on and exploit these stable and enduring statistical structural regularities in the world, and in other parts of the organism. Things worth noticing include the fact that an adaptation (such as teeth or breasts) can develop at any time during the life cycle, and need not be present at birth; an adaptation can express itself differently in different environments (e.g., speaks English, speaks Tagalog); an adaptation is not just any individually beneficial trait, but one built over evolutionary time and expressed in many individuals; an adaptation may not be producing functional outcomes currently (e.g., agoraphobia), but only needed to function well in ancestral environments; finally, an adaptation (like every other aspect of the phenotype) is the product of gene–environment interaction. Unlike many other phenotypic properties, however, it is the result of the interaction of the species-standard set of genes with those aspects of the environment that were present and relevant during the species' evolution. For a more extensive definition of the concept of adaptation, see Tooby and Cosmides, 1990b, 1992.

as a counter-hypothesis. Standards for recognizing special design include whether the problem solved by the structure is an evolutionarily long-standing adaptive problem, and such factors as economy, efficiency, complexity, precision, specialization, and reliability, which, like a key fitting a lock, render the design too good a solution to a defined adaptive problem to be coinci-

dence (Williams, 1966). Like most other methods of empirical hypothesis testing, the demonstration that something is an adaptation is always, at core, a probability assessment concerning how likely a set of events is to have arisen by chance alone. Such assessments are made by investigating whether there is a highly nonrandom coordination between the recurring properties of the phenotype and the structured properties of the adaptive problem, in a way that meshed to promote fitness (genetic propagation) in ancestral environments (Tooby and Cosmides, 1990b, 1992). For example, the lens, pupil, iris, retina, visual cortex, and other parts of the eye are too well coordinated, both with each other and with features of the world, such as the properties of light, optics, geometry, and the reflectant properties of surfaces, to have co-occurred by chance. In short, like the functional aspects of any other engineered system, they are recognizable as adaptations for analyzing scenes from reflected light by their organized and functional relationships to the rest of the design and to the structure of the world.

In contrast, concomitants or by products of adaptations are those properties of the phenotype that do not contribute to functional design per se, but that happen to be coupled to properties that are. Consequently, they were dragged along into the species-typical architecture because of selection for the functional design features to which they are linked. For example, bones are adaptations, but the fact that they are white is an incidental by-product. Bones were selected to include calcium because it conferred hardness and rigidity to the structure (and was dietarily available), and it simply happens that alkaline earth metals appear white in many compounds, including the insoluble calcium salts that are a constituent of bone. From the point of view of functional design, by-products are the result of "chance," in the sense that the process that led to their incorporation into the design was blind to their consequences (assuming that they were not negative). Accordingly, such by-products are distinguishable from adaptations by the fact that they are not complexly arranged to have improbably functional consequences (e.g., the whiteness of bone does nothing for the vertebrae).

In general, by-products will be far less informative as a focus of study than adaptations because they are consequences and not causes of the organization of the system (and hence are functionally arbitrary, unregulated, and may, for example, vary capriciously between individuals). Unfortunately, unless researchers actively seek to study organisms in terms of their adaptations, they usually end up measuring and investigating arbitrary and random admixtures of functional and functionless aspects of organisms, a situation that hampers the discovery of the underlying organization of the biological system. We do not yet, for example, even know which exact aspects of the neuron are relevant to its function and which are by-products, so many computational neuroscientists may be using a model of the neuron that is wildly inaccurate.

Finally, entropic effects of many types are always acting to introduce disorder into the design of organisms. Traits introduced by accident or by evolutionary random walks are recognizable by the lack of coordination that they produce within the architecture or between the architecture and the environment, as well as by the fact that they frequently cause uncalibrated variation between individuals. Examples of such entropic processes include genetic mutation, recent change in ancestrally stable environmental features, and developmentally anomalous circumstances.

How well-engineered are adaptations?

The design of our cognitive and neural mechanisms should only reflect the structure of the adaptive problems that our ancestors faced to the extent that natural selection is an effective process. Is it one? How well or poorly engineered are adaptations? Some researchers have argued that evolution primarily produces inept designs, because selection does not produce perfect optimality (Gould and Lewontin, 1979). In fact, evolutionary biologists since Darwin have been well aware that selection does not produce perfect designs (Darwin, 1859; Williams, 1966; Dawkins, 1976, 1982, 1986; for a recent convert from the position that organisms are optimally designed to the more traditional adaptationist position, see Lewontin, 1967, 1979; see Dawkins, 1982, for an extensive discussion of the many processes that prevent selection from reaching perfect optimality). Still, because natural selection is a hill-climbing process that tends to choose the best of the variant designs that actually appear, and because of the immense numbers of alternatives that appear over the vast expanse of evolutionary time, natural selection tends to cause the accumulation of very well-engineered functional designs.

Empirical confirmation can be gained by comparing how well evolved devices and human engineered devices perform on evolutionarily recurrent adaptive problems (as opposed to arbitrary, artificial modern tasks, such as chess). For example, the claim that language competence is a simple and poorly engineered adaptation cannot be taken seriously, given the total amount of time, engineering, and genius that has gone into the still unsuccessful effort to produce artificial systems that can remotely approach—let alone equal—human speech per-

ception, comprehension, acquisition, and production (Pinker and Bloom, 1992).

Even more strikingly, the visual system is composed of collections of cognitive adaptations that are well-engineered products of the evolutionary process, and although they may not be "perfect" or "optimal"—however these somewhat vague concepts may be interpreted—they are far better at vision than any human-engineered system yet developed.

Wherever the standard of biological functionality can be clearly defined—semantic induction, object recognition, color constancy, echolocation, relevant problem-solving generalization, chemical recognition (olfaction), mimicry, scene analysis, chemical synthesis—evolved adaptations are at least as good as and usually strikingly better than human engineered systems, in those rare situations in which humans can build systems that can accomplish them at all. It seems reasonable to insist that before a system is criticized as being poorly designed, the critic ought to be able to construct a better alternative—a requirement, it need hardly be pointed out, that has never been met by anyone who has argued that adaptations are poorly designed. Thus, although adaptations are certainly suboptimal in some ultimate sense, it is an empirically demonstrable fact that the short-run constraints on selective optimization do not prevent the emergence of superlatively organized computational adaptations in brains. Indeed, aside from the exotic nature of the problems that the brain was designed to solve, it is exactly this sheer functional intricacy that makes our architecture so difficult to reverse-engineer and to understand.

Cognitive adaptations reflect the structure of the adaptive problem and the ancestral world

Four lessons emerge from the study of natural competences, such as vision and language: (1) most adaptive information-processing problems are complex; (2) the evolved solution to these problems is usually machinery that is well engineered for the task; (3) this machinery is usually specialized to fit the particular nature of the problem; and (4) its evolved design often embodies substantial and contentful "innate knowledge" about problem-relevant aspects of the world.

Well-studied adaptations overwhelmingly achieve their functional outcomes because they display an intricately engineered coordination between their specialized design features and the detailed structure of the task and task environment. Like a code that has been torn in two and given to separate couriers, the two halves (the structure of the mechanism and the structure of the task) must be put together to be understood. To function, adaptations evolve such that their causal properties rely on and exploit these stable and enduring statistical and structural regularities in the world. Thus, to map the structures of our cognitive devices, we need to understand the structures of the problems that they solve and the problem-relevant parts of the hunter-gatherer world. If studying face recognition mechanisms, one must study the recurrent structure of faces. If studying social cognition, one must study the recurrent structure of hunter-gatherer social life. For vision, the problems are not so very different for a modern scientist and a Pleistocene hunter-gatherer, so the folk notions of function that perception researchers use are not a problem. But the more one strays from low-level perception, the more one needs to know about human behavioral ecology and the structure of the ancestral world.

Experimenting with ancestrally valid tasks and stimuli

Although bringing cognitive neuroscience current with modern evolutionary biology offers many new research tools (Preuss, 1995; see also chapter 84), we have out of necessity limited discussion to only one: an evolutionary functionalist research strategy (see chapter 87 and Tooby and Cosmides, 1992, for a description; for examples, see chapters in Barkow et al., 1992; Daly and Wilson, 1995; Gaulin, 1995; and chapter 81). The adoption of such an approach will modify research practice in many ways. Perhaps most significantly, researchers will no longer have to operate purely by intuition or guesswork to know which kinds of tasks and stimuli to expose subjects to. Using knowledge from evolutionary biology, behavioral ecology, animal behavior, and hunter–gatherer studies, they can construct ancestrally or adaptively valid stimuli and tasks. These are stimuli that would have had adaptive significance in ancestral environments, and tasks that resemble (at least in some ways) the adaptive problems that our ancestors would have been selected to be able to solve.

The present widespread practice of using arbitrary stimuli of no adaptive significance (e.g., lists of random words, colored geometric shapes) or abstract experimental tasks of unknown relevance to Pleistocene life has sharply limited what researchers have observed and can observe about our evolved computational devices. This is because the adaptive specializations that are expected to constitute the majority of our neural architecture are designed to remain dormant until triggered by cues of the adaptively significant situations that they were designed to handle. The Wundtian and British Empiricist methodological assumption that complex stimuli, behaviors, representations, and compe-

tences are compounded out of simple ones has been empirically falsified in scores of cases (see, e.g., Gallistel, 1990), and so, restricting experimentation to such stimuli and tasks simply restricts what researchers can find to a highly impoverished and unrepresentative set of phenomena. In contrast, experimenters who use more biologically meaningful stimuli have had far better luck, as the collapse of behaviorism and its replacement by modern behavioral ecology have shown in the study of animal behavior. To take one example of its applicability to humans, effective mechanisms for Bayesian inference–undetected by 20 years of previous research using "modern" tasks and data formats–were activated by exposing subjects to information formatted in a way that hunter–gatherers would have encountered it (Brase et al., 1998; Cosmides and Tooby, 1996; Gigerenzer and Hoffrage, 1995). Equally, when subjects were given ancestrally valid social inference tasks (cheater detection, threat interpretation), previously unobserved adaptive reasoning specializations were activated, guiding subjects to act in accordance with evolutionarily predicted but otherwise odd patterns (Cosmides, 1989; Cosmides and Tooby, 1992; see also chapter 87).

Everyone accepts that one cannot study human language specializations by exposing subjects to meaningless sounds: the acoustic stimuli must contain the subtle, precise, high level relationships that make sound language. Similarly, to move on to the study of other complex cognitive devices, subjects should be exposed to stimuli that contain the subtle, ancestrally valid relationships relevant to the diverse functions of these devices. In such an expanded research program, experimental stimuli and tasks would involve constituents such as faces, smiles, disgust expressions, foods, the depiction of socially significant situations, sexual attractiveness, habitat quality cues, animals, navigational problems, cues of kinship, rage displays, cues of contagion, motivational cues, distressed children, species-typical "body language," rigid object mechanics, plants, predators, and other functional elements that would have been part of ancestral hunter-gatherer life. Investigations would look for functional subsystems that not only deal with such low-level and broadly functional competences as perception, attention, memory, and motor control, but also with higher-level ancestrally valid competences as well—mechanisms such as eye direction detectors (Baron-Cohen, 1994), face recognizers (e.g. Johnson and Morton, 1991), food memory subsystems (e.g., Hart et al., 1985; Caramazza and Shelton, 1998), person-specific memory, child care motivators (Daly and Wilson, 1995), and sexual jealousy modules.

Although these proposals to look for scores of content-sensitive circuits and domain-specific specializations will strike many as bizarre and even preposterous, they are well grounded in modern biology. We believe that in a decade or so they will look tame. If cognitive neuroscience is anything like investigations in domain-specific cognitive psychology (Hirschfeld and Gelman, 1994) and in modern animal behavior, researchers will be rewarded with the materialization of a rich array of functionally patterned phenomena that have not been observed so far because the mechanisms were never activated in the laboratory by exposure to ecologically appropriate stimuli. Although presently, the functions of most brain structures are largely unknown, pursuing such research directions may begin to populate the empty regions of our maps of the brain with circuit diagrams of discrete, functionally intelligible computational devices.

In short, because theories and principled systems of knowledge can function as organs of perception, the incorporation of a modern evolutionary framework into cognitive neuroscience may allow the community to detect ordered relationships in phenomena that otherwise seem too complex to be understood.

Conclusion

The aforementioned points indicate why cognitive neuroscience is pivotal to the progress of the brain sciences. There are an astronomical number of physical interactions and relationships in the brain, and blind empiricism rapidly drowns itself among the deluge of manic and enigmatic measurements. Through blind empiricism, one can equally drown at the cognitive level in a sea of irrelevant things that our computational devices can generate, from writing theology or dancing the mazurka to calling for the restoration of the Plantagenets to the throne of France. However, evolutionary biology, behavioral ecology, and hunter-gatherer studies can be used to identify and supply descriptions of the recurrent adaptive problems humans faced during their evolution. Supplemented with this knowledge, cognitive research techniques can abstract out of the welter of human cognitive performance a series of maps of the functional information-processing relationships that constitute our computational devices and that evolved to solve this particular set of problems: our cognitive architecture. These computational maps can then help us abstract out of the ocean of physical relationships in the brain that exact and minute subset that implements those information-processing relationships because it is only these relationships that explain the existence and functional organization of the system. The immense number of other physical relationships in the brain are incidental by-products of those narrow aspects that implement the functional computational architecture. Consequently, an adaptationist inventory and functional mapping of our cognitive devices can provide the essential theoretical guidance for neuroscientists that will allow them to home in on these narrow but meaningful aspects of neural organization and to distinguish them from the sea of irrelevant neural phenomena.

ACKNOWLEDGMENTS The authors gratefully acknowledge the financial support of the James S. McDonnell Foundation, the National Science Foundation (NSF grant BNS9157-449 to John Tooby), and a Research Across Disciplines grant (Evolution and the Social Mind) from the UCSB Office of Research.

NOTE

1. The genes underlying complex adaptations cannot vary substantially between individuals because if they did, the obligatory genetic shuffling that takes place during sexual reproduction would break apart the complex adaptations that had existed in the parents when these are recombined in the offspring generation. All the genetic subcomponents necessary to build the complex adaptation rarely would reappear together in the same individual if they were not being supplied reliably by both parents in all matings (for a discussion of the genetics of sexual recombination, species-typical adaptive design, and individual differences, see Tooby, 1982; Tooby and Cosmides, 1990b).

REFERENCES

BARKOW, J., L. COSMIDES, and J. TOOBY, eds., 1992. *The Adapted Mind: Evolutionary Psychology and the Generation of Culture.* New York: Oxford University Press.

BARON-COHEN, S., 1994. The eye-direction detector: A case for evolutionary psychology. In *Joint-Attention: Its Origins and Role in Development,* C. Moore and P. Dunham, eds. Hillsdale, N.J.: Erlbaum.

BRASE, G., L. COSMIDES, and J. TOOBY, 1998. Individuation, counting, and statistical inference: The role of frequency and whole-object representations in judgment under uncertainty. *J. Exp. Psychol. Gen.* 127:3–21.

BUSS, D., 1994. *The Evolution of Desire.* New York: Basic Books.

CARAMAZZA, A., and J. SHELTON, 1998. Domain-specific knowledge systems in the brain: The animate-inanimate distinction. *J. Cogn. Neurosci.* 10:1–34.

COSMIDES, L., 1989. The logic of social exchange: Has natural selection shaped how humans reason? Studies with the Wason selection task. *Cognition* 31:187–276.

COSMIDES, L., and J. TOOBY, 1981. Cytoplasmic inheritance and intragenomic conflict. *J. Theor. Biol.* 89:83–129.

COSMIDES, L., and J. TOOBY, 1987. From evolution to behavior: Evolutionary psychology as the missing link. In *The Latest on the Best: Essays on Evolution and Optimality,* J. Dupre, ed. Cambridge: Mass.: MIT Press, pp. 277–306.

COSMIDES, L., and J. TOOBY, 1992. Cognitive adaptations for social exchange. In *The Adapted Mind: Evolutionary Psychology and the Generation of Culture,* J. Barkow, L. Cosmides, and J. Tooby, eds. New York: Oxford University Press, pp. 163–228.

COSMIDES, L., and J. TOOBY, 1994. Beyond intuition and instinct blindness: The case for an evolutionarily rigorous cognitive science. *Cognition* 50:41–77.

COSMIDES, L., and J. TOOBY, 1996. Are humans good intuitive statisticians after all? Rethinking some conclusions from the literature on judgment under uncertainty. *Cognition* 58: 1–73.

COSMIDES, L., and J. TOOBY, in press. Toward an evolutionary taxonomy of treatable conditions. *J. Abnorm. Psychol.*

DALY, M., and M. WILSON, 1984. *Sex, Evolution and Behavior*, Second Edition. Boston: Willard Grant.

DALY, M., and M. WILSON, 1988. *Homicide*. New York: Aldine.

DALY, M., and M. WILSON, 1995. Discriminative parental solicitude and the relevance of evolutionary models to the analysis of motivational systems. In *The Cognitive Neurosciences*, M. S. Gazzaniga, ed. Cambridge, Mass.: MIT Press, pp. 1269–1286.

DALY, M., M. WILSON, and S. J. WEGHORST, 1982. Male sexual jealousy. *Ethol. Sociobiol.* 3:11–27.

DARWIN, C., 1859. *On the Origin of Species*. London, Murray. New edition: Cambridge, Mass.: Harvard University Press.

DAWKINS, R., 1976. *The Selfish Gene*. New York: Oxford University Press.

DAWKINS, R., 1982. *The Extended Phenotype*. San Francisco: W. H. Freeman.

DAWKINS, R., 1986. *The Blind Watchmaker*. New York: Norton.

GALLISTEL, C. R., 1990. *The Organization of Learning*. Cambridge, Mass.: MIT Press.

GAULIN, S., 1995. Does evolutionary theory predict sex differences in the brain? In *The Cognitive Neurosciences*, M. S. Gazzaniga, ed. Cambridge, Mass.: MIT Press, pp. 1211–1225.

GIGERENZER, G., and U. HOFFRAGE, 1995. How to improve Bayesian reasoning without instruction: Frequency formats. *Psychol. Rev.* 102:684–704.

GOULD, S. J., and R. C. LEWONTIN, 1979. The spandrels of San Marco and the Panglossian program: A critique of the adaptationist programme. *Proc. R. Soc. Lond.* 205:281–288.

HAIG, D., 1993. Genetic conflicts in human pregnancy. *Q. Rev. Biol.* 68:495–532.

HAMILTON, W. D., 1964. The genetical evolution of social behavior. *J. Theor. Biol.* 7:1–52.

HART, J. JR., R. S. BERNDT, and A. CARAMAZZA, 1985. Category-specific naming deficit following cerebral infarction. *Nature* 316:439–440.

HIRSCHFELD, L., and S. GELMAN, eds. 1994. *Mapping the Mind: Domain Specificity in Cognition and Culture*. New York Cambridge University Press.

JOHNSON, M., and J. MORTON, 1991. *Biology and Cognitive Development: The Case of Face Recognition*. Oxford: Blackwell.

KREBS, J. R., and N. B. DAVIES, 1997. *Behavioural Ecology: An Evolutionary Approach*, 4th edition. London: Blackwell Science.

LEE, R. B., and I. DEVORE, 1968. *Man the Hunter*. Chicago: Aldine.

LEWONTIN, R., 1967. Spoken remark in *Mathematical Challenges to the Neo-Darwinian Interpretation of Evolution*, P. Moorhead and M. Kaplan, eds. *Wistar Institute Symposium Monograph* 5: 79.

LEWONTIN, R., 1979. Sociobiology as an adaptationist program. *Behav. Sci.* 24:5–14.

MARR, D., 1982. *Vision: A Computational Investigation into the Human Representation and Processing of Visual Information*. San Francisco: Freeman.

MAYR, E., 1983. How to carry out the adaptationist program. *Am. Naturalist* 121:324–334.

PINKER, S., 1994. T*he Language Instinct*. New York: Morrow.

PINKER, S., 1997. *How the Mind Works*. New York: Norton.

PINKER, S., and P. BLOOM, 1992. Natural language and natural selection. Reprinted in *The Adapted Mind: Evolutionary Psychology and the Generation of Culture*, J. Barkow, L. Cosmides, and J. Tooby, eds. New York Oxford University Press, pp. 451–493.

PREUSS, T., 1995. The argument from animals to humans in cognitive neuroscience. In *The Cognitive Neurosciences*, M. S. Gazzaniga, ed. Cambridge, Mass.: MIT Press, pp. 1227–1241.

SHEPARD, R. N., 1984. Ecological constraints on internal representation: Resonant kinematics of perceiving, imagining, thinking, and dreaming. *Psychol. Rev.* 91:417–447.

SHEPARD, R. N., 1987a. Evolution of a mesh between principles of the mind and regularities of the world. In *The Latest on the Best: Essays on Evolution and Optimality*, J. Dupre, ed. Cambridge, Mass.: MIT Press, pp. 251–275.

SHEPARD, R. N., 1987b. Towards a universal law of generalization for psychological science. *Science* 237:1317–1323.

SPERBER, D., 1994. The modularity of thought and the epidemiology of representations. In *Mapping the Mind: Domain Specificity in Cognition and Culture*, L. Hirschfeld and S. Gelman, eds. New York: Cambridge University Press, pp. 39–67.

SYMONS, D., 1987. If we're all Darwinians, what's the fuss about? In *Sociobiology and Psychology*, C. B. Crawford, M. F. Smith, and D. L. Krebs, eds. Hillsdale, N.J.: Erlbaum, pp. 121–146.

SYMONS, D., 1992. On the use and misuse of Darwinism in the study of human behavior. In *The Adapted Mind: Evolutionary Psychology and the Generation of Culture*, J. Barkow, L. Cosmides, and J. Tooby, eds. New York: Oxford University Press, pp. 137–159.

THORNHILL, R., 1991. The study of adaptation. In *Interpretation and Explanation in the Study of Behavior,* M. Bekoff and D. Jamieson, eds. Boulder, Colo.: Westview Press.

TOOBY J., 1982. Pathogens, polymorphism, and the evolution of sex. *J. Theor. Biol.* 97:557–576.

TOOBY, J., and L. COSMIDES, 1990a. The past explains the present: Emotional adaptations and the structure of ancestral environments. *Ethol. Sociobiol.* 11:375–424.

TOOBY, J., and L. COSMIDES, 1990b. On the universality of human nature and the uniqueness of the individual: The role of genetics and adaptation. *J. Pers.* 58:17–67.

TOOBY, J., and L. COSMIDES, 1992. The psychological foundations of culture. In *The Adapted Mind: Evolutionary Psychology and the Generation of Culture*, J. Barkow, L. Cosmides, and J. Tooby, eds. New York Oxford University Press, pp. 19–136.

WILLIAMS, G. C., 1966. *Adaptation and Natural Selection: A Critique of Some Current Evolutionary Thought*. Princeton, N.J.: Princeton University Press.

WILLIAMS, G. C., 1985. A defense of reductionism in evolutionary biology. *Oxford Surv. Biol.* 2:1–27.

WILLIAMS, G. C., and D. C. WILLIAMS, 1957. Natural selection of individually harmful social adaptations among sibs with special reference to social insects. *Evolution* 17:249–253.

WILSON, M., and M. DALY, 1992. The man who mistook his wife for a chattel. In *The Adapted Mind: Evolutionary Psychology and the Generation of Culture*, J. Barkow, L. Cosmides, and J. Tooby, eds. New York: Oxford University Press, pp. 289–322.

81 The Replacement of General-Purpose Learning Models with Adaptively Specialized Learning Modules

C. R. GALLISTEL

ABSTRACT Associative theories of learning assume a general-purpose learning process whose structure does not reflect the demands of a particular learning problem. By contrast, implicit in the studies of learning conducted by zoologists and, recently, by some experimental psychologists, is the assumption that learning mechanisms are specialized computationally for solving particular kinds of problems. Models of the latter kind have begun to be applied even to the results from experiments on classical and instrumental conditioning. These models imply that to understand learning neurobiologically, we must discover the cellular mechanisms by which the nervous system stores and retrieves the values of variables and carries out the elementary computational operations (the elementary operations of arithmetic and logic). At the systems level, we must discover the circuits that implement special-purpose computations using these universal elements of computation.

Theories of learning are and always have been predominantly associative theories. However, in the study of animal learning, where these theories historically have been most dominant, a different conception is gaining ground. Whereas associative theories have their historical roots in the empiricist philosophy of mind, the alternative conception has its roots in evolutionary biology, more particularly in zoology, that is, in the study of the natural history of animal behavior and of the mechanisms that enable animals to cope with the challenges posed by their habits of life.

Associative theories of learning assume a basic learning mechanism, or, in any event, a modest number of learning mechanisms. These mechanisms are distinguished by their properties–for example, whether they depend on temporal pairing–not by the particular kind of problem that their special structure enables them to solve. Indeed, people doing neural net modeling, which currently is the most widespread form of associative theorizing, often are at pains to point out that the network has solved a problem in the absence of an initial struc-

ture tailored to the solution of that problem (Becker and Hinton, 1992).

The alternative conceptualization, by contrast, takes for granted that biological mechanisms are hierarchically nested adaptive specializations, each mechanism constituting a particular solution to a particular problem. The foliated structure of the lung reflects its role as the organ of gas exchange, as does the specialized structure of the tissue that lines it. The structure of the hemoglobin molecule reflects its function as an oxygen carrier. The structure of the rhodopsin molecule reflects its function as a photon-activated enzyme. One cannot use a hemoglobin molecule as the first stage in light transduction and one cannot use a rhodopsin molecule as an oxygen carrier, any more than one can see with an ear or hear with an eye. Adaptive specialization of mechanism is so ubiquitous and so obvious in biology, at every level of analysis, and for every kind of function, that no one thinks it necessary to call attention to it as a general principle about biological mechanisms.

In this light, it is odd but true that most past and contemporary theorizing about learning does not assume that learning mechanisms are adaptively specialized for the solution of particular kinds of problems. Most theorizing assumes that there is a general-purpose learning process in the brain, a process adapted only to solving the problem of learning. There is no attempt to formalize what the problem of learning is and thereby determine whether it can in fact be conceived of as a single or uniform problem. From a biological perspective, this assumption is equivalent to assuming that there is a general-purpose sensory organ that solves the problem of sensing.

In this chapter, I review some of the evidence that whenever learning occurs, it is made possible by an adaptively specialized learning mechanism–a learning module–whose structure is as specific to a particular learning problem as the structure of a sensory organ like the eye or the ear is specific to a particular stimulus

C. R. GALLISTEL Department of Psychology, University of California, Los Angeles, Calif.

modality. Gould and Marler (1987) call these modules "learning instincts," emphasizing that they have the same problem-specific structure that we see in instinctive behaviors. The review focuses on the differences in computational structure between several distinct learning mechanisms that are important to an animal's ability to find its way about and a different set of mechanisms that enable it to learn and exploit the temporal structure of its experience. I finish with some observations on the implications of this view for research on the neural mechanisms of learning and memory.

Rozin and Kalat (1971) were among the first to argue for adaptive specializations of learning from a biological natural-history perspective, and Chomsky (1975) was among the first to argue for it on computational grounds. Early work focusing on the role of adaptive specialization in learning tended to formulate the problem in terms of the constraints (Hinde and Hinde, 1973) or boundaries (Seligman and Hager, 1972) that biological considerations placed on *the* learning process. By contrast, the argument advanced by Chomsky (1975), Gould and Marler (1987), Gelman and Williams (1998), and Gallistel (1990) is that there is no such thing as *the* learning process; rather, there are many different learning processes. While it is true that the structure of these processes constrain the outcome of learning in interesting ways, the more important point is that it is the problem-specific structure of these processes that makes learning possible.

Spatial learning mechanisms

LEARNING BY PATH INTEGRATION Our first example of a learning module is so far removed from what commonly is regarded as a learning mechanism that before I discuss it, I usually get people to agree that the pretheoretic definition of a learning mechanism is a mechanism by which we acquire knowledge of the world and our place in it. Then, I show them figure 81.1, which is the track of a long-legged fast-moving desert ant, *Cataglyphis bicolor*, foraging for and finding a morsel of food on the hot plain of the Tunisian desert. On the outward leg of its journey (solid tracing), the ant twists and turns this way and that searching for the carcass of an insect that has succumbed to the heat. When it finally finds one, it bites off a chunk, turns, and runs more or less straight toward its nest, a hole 1 mm in diameter, which may be as far as 50 m away. Its ability to orient homeward demonstrably depends on information it acquires during the outward journey. If the ant is deprived of this information by being picked up as it emerges from the nest and transported to an arbitrary point in the vicinity of its nest, it wanders in circles and

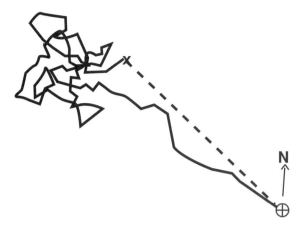

FIGURE 81.1 Track of a foraging ant. The outward (searching) journey is the solid line. It found food at X. Its homeward run is the broken line. (Redrawn from Harkness and Maroudas, 1985. Used with permission of the author and publisher.)

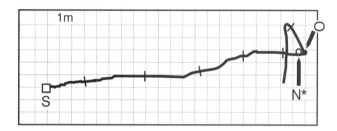

FIGURE 81.2 The homeward run of an ant displaced into unfamiliar territory on which the experimenters had previously marked off a 1-m gridwork. *S* indicates the point of release. *N** indicates the location of the fictive nest (where the ant's nest would have been had the ant not been displaced). *O* indicates the point at which the ant terminated its nestward run and entered a search pattern. (Redrawn from Wehner and Srinivasan, 1981. Used with permission of the author and publisher.)

makes it back to the nest only after a long time, if at all (Wehner and Flatt, 1972). A simple experiment by Wehner and Srinivasan (1981) reveals the nature of the learning mechanism that acquires the requisite position information. When the ant turns from a food source back toward its nest, it is picked up and transported more than half a kilometer across the desert; here it is released to run across a large grid the experimenter has marked in advance on the desert floor. The grid on the desert enables the experimenter to trace the ant's course on a graph-paper grid at a reduction of 100:1 (figure 81.2). Although the ant is now in territory it has never seen, it runs in a direction that lies within a degree or two of the compass direction of its nest from the site where it was picked up, the direction in which it would have run had it not been displaced. It runs in a straight line for a distance slightly longer than the distance of its nest from the point where it was picked up, then stops abruptly its straight run to begin a systematic search for the nonexistent nest.

The ant's ability to run over unfamiliar terrain a course whose direction and distance equal the direction and distance of its nest from the point of its capture implies that its navigation is based on some form of path integration or dead reckoning. Path integration is the integration of the velocity vector with respect to time to obtain the position vector, or a discrete approximation to this computation. The discrete approximation in traditional marine navigation is to record the direction and speed of travel (the velocity) at intervals, multiply each recorded velocity by the interval since the previous recording to get interval-by-interval displacements (e.g., making 5 knots on a northeast course for half an hour puts the ship 2.5 nautical miles northeast of where it was), and sum the successive displacements (changes in position) to get the net change in position. These running sums of the longitudinal and latitudinal displacements are the deduced reckoning of the ship's location (abbreviated "ded. reckoning," thus, "dead reckoning").

For this computation to be possible, the ant's nervous system must have elements capable of preserving the value of a variable over time. The essence of the ongoing summation that underlies path integration is the adding of values that specify the most recent displacement to the values that specify the cumulative prior displacement. To do this, one must be able to hold in memory the value of the sum, and add to that value.

Path integration is a process that computes and stores values that specify a quantifiable objective fact about the world—the ant's direction and distance from its nest. The use made of the values, if any, is determined by the decision process-controlling behavior at the moment. The integration of velocity to obtain position goes on throughout the ant's journey, but only when the decision to turn for home is made do the position coordinates stored in the dead-reckoning integrator lead to the well-oriented straight runs for a predetermined distance shown in figures 81.1 and 81.2. The position-specifying values (coordinates) in the nervous system are in no sense associative bonds: they were not created by temporal pairing and they do not function as conducting links in the circuitry that links sensory input to behavioral output, nor in circuitry that links the memory of one sensory input to the memory of a different sensory input. Rather, these coordinates are symbols. Their values (magnitudes) specify a fact about the world, which different decision processes may use in different ways. They are no more conducting links than are memory locations in a computer or genes on a chromosome. Like these two examples, they are repositories of information.

The values accumulated in the integrator at important points in the forager's journey may also be stored for later use– either in the direction of overt behavior or in computations that lead to the storing of other facts about the world. For example, the ant stores the coordinates of the location at which it finds the carcass, so that it can return directly there on its next foraging trip. We infer this because when we set up a food source in a fixed location, the ants soon come directly to it from their nest (Wehner and Srinivasan, 1981). These fast-moving ants do not lay an odor trail, so their ability to set a course directly for the food source from the nest implies that they have recorded its position relative to the nest.

The foraging bee gives direct evidence that it has stored the coordinates of a food source for later use. When it returns to its hive, it performs a symbolic dance. It runs in a figure-eight path, waggling when it runs the central segment where the two loops join. Other foragers follow behind the dancing bee to learn the location of the food source. The direction of the waggling part of the run relative to the gravitational vertical specifies the direction of the food source relative to the sun (the solar bearing of the source), whereas the number of waggles specifies the approximate distance of the source from the hive (Frisch, 1967). In this way, the bee communicates to others the position-specifying values computed and saved by its path-integrating mechanism. This is but one of several possible illustrations of the diverse uses to which values stored in memory may be put by different behavioral read-out systems.

If the adaptive specialization of the complex computations that mediate information acquisition is taken for granted, the only plausible elementary mechanisms that might be common to learning mechanisms in general are a mechanism for storing and retrieving the computed values of variables and the mechanisms that carry out the primitive elements of all computation (adding, subtracting, multiplying, dividing, ordination, conditional testing, and so on). Path integration is a notably simple and widespread neural computation that makes straightforward use of these elementary computational operations. It should, therefore, be of central interest to the large community of scientists who seek to discover the cellular-level mechanisms that make learning and higher cognitive function possible. In other words, it should be regarded as a paradigmatic learning process worthy of intensive study at the neurobiological level.

Why then do many people find the idea of path integration as a paradigmatic and notably simple instance of learning perverse? The reasons offered are revelatory. First, it is argued that it is a special-purpose innate mechanism designed to do this and only this. In short, it is an adaptive specialization. This is equivalent to arguing that the eye is not a representative example of a sensory organ because it is designed specifically for vision. The argument presupposes that there is such a thing as a general-purpose learning mechanism, which is the presupposition that the zoological approach to learning calls into question.

Another reason offered for regarding path integration as unusual is that the ant does not have to experience its outward journey repeatedly before it knows the way. A variant of this argument is that the ant does not get better at running home with repeated practice. These objections reify the basic assumption of associative theory, which is that learning involves the gradual strengthening of something. To be sure, the conditioned response in classical conditioning usually does not appear until there have been several co-occurrences of the conditioned and unconditioned stimuli, but the only apparent justification for making strengthening through repetition part of the definition of learning is the conviction that there is a general purpose learning mechanism and that the classical conditioning paradigm captures its essence. If we think that path integration captures the only essence of learning that is there to be captured, then we are not going to make strengthening by repetition part of the definition of learning. Moreover, as will be shown later in the chapter, the domain-specific approach to learning mechanisms offers an interpretation of classical conditioning in which the notion of strengthening a conductive connection through repeated pairing of stimuli plays no role.

LEARNING THE SOLAR EPHEMERIS Dead reckoning requires a fixed directional reference; the animal must know which way is north at all times. A wide variety of animals, including the ant, derive this information from the sun's azimuth, the point on the horizon above which the sun is positioned at a given moment. This is remarkable because to use the sun for directional reference, the animal must know the solar ephemeris, the sun's position as a function of the time of the year and the day. Because the sun's azimuth at a given time of day depends strongly on the animal's latitude and the time of year, the solar ephemeris must be learned. A recent experiment by Dyer and Dickinson (1994) sheds new light on the mechanism that is specialized to learn this.

It has long been known that one of the characteristics of the mechanism that learns the solar ephemeris is that it enables animals to judge the position of the sun at times of day when they have never seen–and will never see–the sun. Honeybees at mid-northern latitudes, for example, treat a sun substitute presented at midnight on their internal clock as if it were due north (Lindauer, 1957). Bees that have only experienced the sun in the af-

ternoon, when it is in the west, assume that it is nonetheless in the east in the morning (Lindauer, 1959). The most common explanation of this has been that bees learn the average angular velocity of the sun's azimuth (the number of degrees it moves along the horizon per hour) and extrapolate its position by multiplying its average velocity by the time elapsed since they last saw it. This explanation always has been somewhat problematic because at tropical latitudes, the sun's angular velocity is negligible throughout the late afternoon, and bees evolved in the tropics.

In any event, the Dyer and Dickinson experiments show that it is not extrapolation but rather curve fitting that enables the bees to know the sun's direction at times of day when they have never observed it. Dyer and Dickinson restricted the foraging experience of incubator-raised bees to the last 4 hours of daylight, during which the sun always was more or less in the west, with its azimuth moving through less than 20% of the angle it covers between dawn and dusk. The bees foraged from a single source due south of the hive. As already noted, the dance that the bees execute when they return to the hive indicates the solar bearing of the source. When the source is due south of the hive (compass bearing 180°) and the sun due west (compass bearing 270°), then the dance is at an angle of 180°–270° = –90°, or 90° to the left of vertical, the number of degrees that the source is counterclockwise from the current position of the sun. When the compass bearing of the source is fixed, the angle of the dance is the bee's estimate of the sun's azimuth.

On heavily overcast days, when bees cannot see the direction of the sun (Brines and Gould, 1982), returning foragers dance nonetheless. They can do so because they have learned the solar ephemeris. They know where the sun is when they cannot see it. In the early morning of such a day, Dyer and Dickinson released the bees that had seen the sun only in the afternoon. The released bees foraged from the fixed source throughout the day, and the changing angle of their dance indicated their changing estimate of where the sun was–the solar ephemeris that they had derived from their limited experience of the sun's movement. The results are in figure 81.3.

As in Lindauer's classic experiments, bees that had never experienced the sun except in the afternoon, when it is in the west, nonetheless believed it to be (or acted as though it were) in the east in the morning. But, as the morning wore on, they did not think that it moved steadily into the south, as they would if they extrapolated the previously observed motion of the sun in any of the ways that have been proposed previously (dashed lines in figure 81.3). In the solar ephemeris that these bees had derived from their limited experience, the sun stayed in the east until about noon, when it moved abruptly into the west, changing its azimuth by 180° in a very short time. In short, the mechanism for learning the solar ephemeris has built into it what is universally true about the sun, no matter where one is on the earth: it is somewhere in the east in the morning and somewhere in the west in the afternoon. Learning the solar ephemeris simply is a matter of adjusting the parameters of this universal ephemeris function to make it fit the locally observed motion of the sun.

This learning mechanism is reminiscent of the mechanism by which birds learn to sing a song appropriate to their species and region (Marler, 1991), despite the fact that they hear songs from many other species, some closely related, during the period when they are learning their own song. Built into the song-learning mechanism is a template or selective filter, which enables the birds to recognize the kind of song that they should be learning, the features that are universal in the song of that species. The ephemeris-learning mechanism also is reminiscent of contemporary theories of language learning, which assume that the learning of a human language is a matter of establishing through observation the parameter values that enable a universal grammar to generate the language spoken locally (Chomsky, 1981; Roeper and Williams, 1987). The universal grammar has built

into it what is universally true about human languages just as the solar ephemeris mechanism has built into it what is universally true about the sun's motion.

If problem-specific learning mechanisms are required to explain everything from the learning of the solar ephemeris in bees to song learning in birds and language learning in humans, should we nonetheless continue to imagine that there exists a general-purpose learning mechanism in addition to all these problem-specific learning mechanisms? What structure could it have? It is like trying to imagine the structure of a general-purpose organ, the organ that takes care of the problems not taken care of by adaptively specialized organs like the liver, the kidney, the heart, and the lungs.

Temporal learning mechanisms

Although there are no current proposals for a general-purpose organ, there is a centuries-old and still very popular proposal for a general-purpose learning mechanism—the mechanism of association formation. An association is a connection between two units of mental or neural activity (two ideas, two neurons, two nodes in a neural net, etc.). The associative connection arises either because the two units often have been active at nearly the same time (the temporal pairing of activation) or through the repeated operation of a feedback mechanism that is activated by errors in the output and adjusts associative strengths to reduce the error. In traditional animal learning theory, the process that forms associations by the first mechanism (temporal pairing of activation) is called the classical or Pavlovian conditioning process, whereas the process that forms associations through the agency of error-correcting feedback is called the instrumental or operant conditioning process. In neural net modeling, the first process is called an unsupervised learning mechanism (Becker and Hinton, 1992) in contrast to the more common second mechanism, which requires a supervisor or teacher who knows the correct output. The correct output is required for the error-actuated back-propagation algorithm, which selectively strengthens connections that lead to correct outputs and weakens those that do not. In theories of instrumental learning (Hull, 1943), the error-correcting feedback comes from the rewards and punishments generated by effective acts.

The Pavlovian and instrumental or operant experimental paradigms were created to study the principles of association formation. The creators shared with contemporary connectionist modelers the assumption that the general nature of learning already was known; it was associative. The problem was to determine the details of the associative process and how it explained whatever it

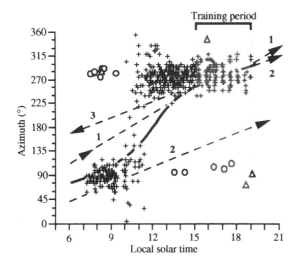

FIGURE 81.3 The solar azimuth indicated by the dances of returning foragers (+) as a function of the time of day. The bees could not see the sun. The foraging site was due south of the hive. The gray zone indicates the period during which the bees had been allowed to forage with a view of the sun on previous days. The solid curve is the actual solar azimuth. The numbered dashed lines indicate the sun's azimuth as extrapolated in various imaginable ways from the motion observed during the gray period. (Reproduced from Dyer and Dickinson, 1994, by permission of authors and publisher.)

was that subjects were observed to learn. Conditioning paradigms were not intended to be laboratory analogs of particular learning problems that animals had been observed to solve in the field. This does not mean, of course, that the paradigms do not in fact represent problems of a particular kind. In fact they do. From a mathematical perspective, they are examples of problems in *multivariate, nonstationary time-series* analysis.

They are *time-series* problems because what the animals are learning is the temporal dependence of one event on another, that is, temporal *contingency*. One of the most important discoveries to emerge from the modern study of conditioning is that temporal pairing is neither necessary nor sufficient for conditioning because it is contingency, not temporal pairing, that drives conditioning.

Contingency cannot be reduced to temporal pairing. Imagine, for example, an experimental protocol in which the opening of the grain hopper (the US) occurs only when a key on the wall of a pigeon's cage (the CS) is illuminated. (This is the standard classical conditioning protocol.) The opening of the hopper is contingent on the illumination of the key. The contingency is just as great if the hopper only opens when the key is not illuminated, never when it is illuminated. (This is called the explicitly unpaired protocol.) Both contingencies are learned equally readily (Colwill, 1991; Kaplan, 1984; LoLordo and Fairless, 1985; Rescorla, 1969), yet in the second, the CS and US are never paired (the hopper opens only when the key is not illuminated), whereas in the first, they always are paired (the hopper opens only when the key is illuminated). The fact that animals learn negative contingencies as readily as positive contingencies establishes that temporal pairing is not necessary for conditioning.

Conditioning protocols are *multivariate* time-series problems because there are many different events or time-varying conditions that may or may not predict the time or rate of US occurrence. An important challenge that the animal faces is figuring out what predicts what. This is the multivariate problem. The modern era in the study of conditioning began with the almost simultaneous discovery by three different laboratories of the fact that the learning mechanism operating during conditioning experiments solves the multivariate problem in ingenious and sophisticated ways (Kamin, 1969; Rescorla, 1968; Wagner et al., 1968). For example, imagine a rat that already has learned that the onset of noise predicts shock. If we give trials in which noise and light come on together, followed by shock, the rat does not learn that the onset of the light predicts shock–no matter how often the light and the shock are paired. This is called blocking. Intuitively, the light does not predict

anything new, anything that is not predicted already by the noise. The discovery of blocking and closely related phenomena (overshadowing, the effects of background conditioning, and the effects of the relative validity of the CSs) showed that temporal pairing is not sufficient for conditioning. Thus, conditioning by negative contingency and blocking between them establish the fundamental point that conditioning is not mediated by temporal pairing.

Conditioning protocols require solutions to the problem of *nonstationarity*, because the contingencies between CSs and USs commonly change from one phase of the experiment to another. In extinction experiments, for example, the rate of reinforcement (US delivery) is higher when the CS is present, but only during the training phase of the experiment. During a subsequent extinction phase, the rate of reinforcement is zero when the CS is present. This is an example of a nonstationary temporal dependency, a contingency that itself changes over time. It has been known since the early days of the study of both classical and operant conditioning that subjects detect these changes in contingency and alter their behavior appropriately. They cease responding to the CS during the extinction phase and resume responding to it if the extinction phase is followed by a reacquisition phase. The possibility that the contingency itself may change over time requires a particularly sophisticated kind of time-series analysis, one that detects and takes into account nonstationarity.

The fact that conditioning protocols present problems in multivariate, nonstationary time-series analysis is irrelevant from the perspective of associative models of the conditioning process because the associative process is not assumed to be specialized for this or any other particular sort of problem. For that very reason, it has proved difficult to elaborate a real-time[1] associative model of the conditioning process capable of explaining in an internally consistent, mathematically simple, and economical way the results from conditioning experiments (Gallistel and Gibbon, in press). In recent years, models that take as their point of departure the assumption that the results are generated by a learning mechanism specifically tailored to solve this kind of problem have been more successful (Gallistel and Gibbon, in press). They naturally explain fundamental features of the conditioning data that have challenged associative models for decades.

The problems that associative models confront in attempting to explain the results of classical and operant conditioning experiments are numerous (Gallistel and Gibbon, in press), but many of them stem from the *timescale invariance* of the conditioning process. This means that when one conducts the same experiment at differ-

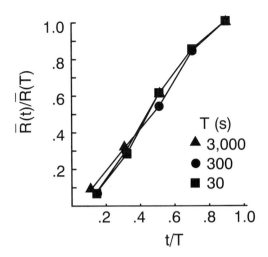

FIGURE 81.4 Dew's (1970) data on the normalized rate of responding during the inter-reward interval on fixed interval schedules ranging from 30 s to 3,000 s, as a function of the normalized time in the interval. The normalized rate is the average rate at elapsed time, t, since the most recent reward divided by the average rate at latency, T, just before the next reward. The normalized time is t/T. The responding in any one inter-reward interval is discontinuous. The seemingly smooth acceleration of responding seen here is an averaging artifact. These data show that the distribution of response onsets is time-scale invariant because the normalized distributions superimpose. (Reproduced with minor modifications from Gibbon, 1977, and used by permission of the author and publisher.)

ent scales—multiplying or dividing all the time intervals in the protocol by a common factor—one gets the same results. The results do not vary when the time scale of the experiment is varied by as much as one or even two orders of magnitude.

The simplest example of the time-scale invariance of conditioned behavior—and the first to be noted (Dews, 1970; Gibbon, 1972; Gibbon, 1977)—is in the timing of the operant (instrumental) response. If, as is commonly the case, the animal's response can elicit a reinforcement only after a fixed interval has elapsed since the onset of a conditioned stimulus or since the last reinforcement (e.g., on a fixed interval [FI] schedule), then the conditioned response (key pecking or lever pressing) begins on average at some fixed proportion of the reinforcement latency (the interval that must elapse before reinforcement can be obtained). Because the ratio between the reinforcement latency and the onset of responding is constant, the time scale for the experimental protocol does not matter. The moment at which responding begins varies substantially from one inter-reinforcement interval to the next (or from one CS presentation to the next), but this variability also is proportional to reinforcement latency. Thus, when the distributions of response onsets (and offsets) are normal-

ized, that is, when the time scale is taken out, they are superimposable (figure 81.4). Thus, the noise or variability in the timing of the conditioned response is time-scale invariant (Gibbon, 1977; Gibbon, Church, and Meck, 1984).

Explaining the fact that the timing of the onsets and offsets of conditioned responding is proportional to reinforcement latency is one of the challenges that associative models of the conditioning process have not confronted. It implies that the subjects remember the reinforcement latency and base their behavior on a comparison between this remembered interval and a currently elapsing interval. Because associative bonds are assumed to be conducting links whose current strengths depend on many different aspects of the subject's conditioning experience, they cannot readily be made to specify (code for) reinforcement latency. Reinforcement latency (the delay of reinforcement) usually is assumed to be one of several variables that *determine* increments in associative strength, rather than a variable whose value is *encoded by* associative strength.[2]

The acquisition process in conditioning also is time-scale invariant. This means that changing the duration of the intervals in a conditioning protocol (e.g., the delay of reinforcement) has no effect on the rate of conditioning (the inverse of reinforcements to acquisition) provided one does not change the temporal proportions—how much of one kind of interval there is relative to each other kind. It is these proportions that determine the rate of conditioning, not the intervals themselves.

It is commonly but erroneously taken for granted that delaying reinforcement retards or prevents the acquisition of conditioned responding (Usherwood, 1993, p. 427). Experiments that seemed to show this (Coleman and Gormezano, 1971; Schneiderman and Gormezano, 1964) did not change the intertrial interval (the interval between CS–US pairings) in proportion to the changes in the delay between CS onset and the US (the delay or reinforcement). When the intertrial interval is increased in proportion to the increase in the delay of reinforcement, delay of reinforcement has no effect on the rate of acquisition (figure 81.5).

The time-scale invariance of the acquisition process also is manifest in the surprising fact that partial reinforcement does not affect either the rate of acquisition or the rate of extinction. During training, the number of reinforcements required for acquisition (hence, the rate of acquisition) is not affected by mixing in as many as nine unreinforced trials for every one reinforced trial (see the more or less flat dashed lines in figure 81.6B). When the subjects then are shifted to extinction (no reinforcements at all), the proportion of reinforced trials

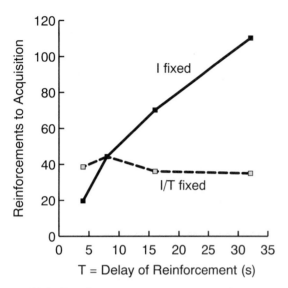

FIGURE 81.5 Reinforcements to acquisition in the pigeon autoshaping paradigm as a function of delay of reinforcement, with intertrial interval (I) fixed and with intertrial interval varying in proportion to the delay (I/T fixed). Note that delay of reinforcement (T) appears to have a strong affect on reinforcements to acquisition (hence, on the rate of conditioning) if the intertrial interval is not varied. But when the intertrial interval, I, is varied in proportion to the variations in the delay of reinforcement, delay of reinforcement is seen to have no effect. (From Gallistel and Gibbon, in press.)

during training has no effect on how many reinforcements must be omitted to induce the subject to stop responding (see the more or less flat dashed lines in figure 81.6C). (The rate of extinction is the inverse of this number, the number of reinforcements that must be omitted to extinguish the conditioned response to the CS.)

The failure of partial reinforcement to affect the rates of acquisition and extinction is profoundly puzzling from an associative perspective. Because the effects of unreinforced trials are assumed to antagonize the effects of reinforced trials (to weaken net excitatory strength), intermingling unreinforced trials with the reinforced trials during acquisition should augment the number of reinforced trials required for acquisition. It also should make the net excitatory strength of the associative bonds after any given number of reinforced trials weaker, so that it takes fewer unreinforced trials to produce extinction. Neither result is in fact seen. This directly challenges the fundamental idea that reinforcement and nonreinforcement have opposing effects on the strengths of associative connections.

The lack of an effect of partial reinforcement is an example of time-scale invariance because partial reinforcement does not change the relative amounts of exposure to the CS and to the background per reinforcement, and it is these proportions that determine the rate of acquisi-

tion. Consider, for example, the 1:1 schedule of reinforcement (one reinforcement at the termination of each illumination of the key) with the key illuminations (the "trials") each lasting T seconds. After the reinforcement (the opportunity to eat from the food hopper), there is a period of I seconds during which the background alone (the experimental chamber) is present. At the end of this intertrial interval, the cycle repeats itself–key illumination for T seconds, reinforcement, intertrial interval for I seconds. Thus, in each cycle, the subject gets T seconds of exposure to the CS and I seconds of exposure to the background alone. Now consider the case when there is a 2:1 schedule of reinforcement (the food hopper opens at the termination of, on average, every second illumination of the key). Now the subject sees the CS on average twice before the hopper opens, for an average of $2T$ seconds of CS exposure per CS reinforcement. But it also experiences the background alone for, on average, $2I$ seconds between each reinforcement of the CS. Thus, the relative amounts of exposure to the CS and to the background alone are not affected by the reinforcement schedule. Because conditioning depends only on these unaltered temporal proportions (the principle of time-scale invariance), partial reinforcement affects neither the rate of acquisition nor the rate of subsequent extinction.

Explaining the time-scale invariance of conditioning is difficult for associative models for three interrelated reasons: (1) they usually assume that temporal pairing is important; (2) they invariably assume that it is differences in probability of reinforcement that are important; and (3) they commonly divide continuous time into discrete trials. Each of these assumptions would appear to make time-scale invariance impossible. The notion of temporal pairing assumes that there is some time window within which the CS and the US both must occur if they are to be regarded as temporally paired. The width of this window imposes a time scale on the process. Increasing the delay of reinforcement to the point at which the CS and the US are separated by more than the window of associability alters the outcome of the experiment (a violation of time-scale invariance). Probabilities of reinforcement and differences in probabilities of reinforcement cannot be defined except by assuming some discrete finite interval of time within which the probability is measured. That is, they cannot be defined without assuming that continuous time is divided into discrete trials, because the probability of any event goes to zero as the intervals within which probabilities are measured become arbitrarily small (and so do differences in probability). The values of all probabilities entering into an associative analysis depend on the assumed duration of the trials. Thus, the assumed trial duration imposes a time scale. The predictions of an as-

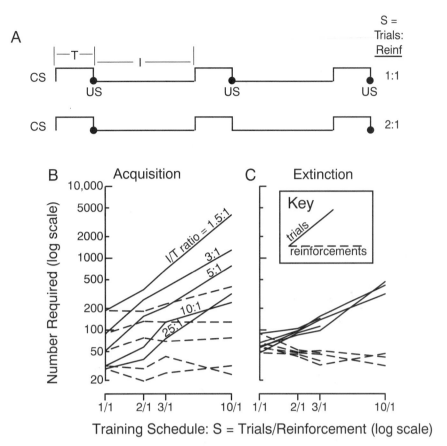

FIGURE 81.6 (A) The parameters of a simple conditioning protocol are *T* (the duration of a CS presentation, usually called a "trial"), *I* (the average interval between presentations, called the intertrial interval), and *S*, the reinforcement schedule (the ratio of trials to reinforcements). Dots indicate reinforcements, which are delivered at CS termination (on reinforced trials). Thus, *T*, the duration of each CS presentation also is the delay of reinforcement. (B) The effect of the partial reinforcement schedule (*x* axis) and the *I/T* ratio (between curves) on trials to acquisition (solid lines) and on reinforcements to acquisition (dashed lines). Note that partial reinforcement has no effect on reinforcements to acquisition (dashed lines), but the *I/T* ratio has a dramatic effect: the greater the *I/T* ratio, the fewer reinforcements are required for acquisition. (C) The effect of the partial reinforcement schedule in force during training on unreinforced trials to extinction (solid lines) and on the number of omitted reinforcements to extinction (dashed lines). An omitted reinforcement is a reinforcement that would have been delivered by the training schedule, but was not. The rate of extinction is the reciprocal of the number of reinforcements that must be omitted to produce extinction; the higher this number, the slower the rate of extinction. (Reproduced from Gallistel and Gibbon, in press, by permission of author and publisher.)

sociative model (for fixed values of its parameters) change as the time scale of the experiment changes because events that fall within a single trial at one time scale fall in different trials on a different time scale.

Suppose, however, that we assume the following: (1) The mechanism that underlies conditioning is specialized to compute the effects of various stimulus conditions on the relative *rates* (N.B. not probabilities) of reinforcement. (2) It also is sensitive to the limits on the certainty with which these effects can be known given a limited amount of experience. That is, it is sensitive to the statistical uncertainties inherent in limited observations. These are the distinctive features of the problem that confronts animals in conditioning experiments. These also are the features of the problem that confronts

a foraging animal in the wild. If it is to forage efficiently, it must be sensitive to the differences in rates of reward at different sites and under different foraging conditions. It must detect changes in these rates, and it must be sensitive to the statistical uncertainties inherent in a limited number of observations. If it relies too much on the evidence from too small a sample, it constantly will be misled by chance fluctuations. If, to avoid being misled, it relies on the average from a large sample, it will be slow to adjust to genuine changes.

These considerations suggest that the operation of any mechanism well tuned to a problem with the structure of conditioning problems should be time-scale invariant because time series analysis itself is time-scale invariant. Changing time scales affects neither the relative rates of reward, the limits on the certainty with which they can be known after a given number of reinforcements have been delivered, nor the number of interevent intervals that must be observed to detect a change in the rate of reinforcement. The simplest way to see that this must be so is to ask whether the units attached to the numbers going into a statistical analysis affect the outcome of that analysis.[3] Of course they do not, because it is the proportions among the numbers (quantities) that determine the outcome of the analysis, not the units attached to them. Changing the units attached to the numbers (e.g., from seconds to days) is the same as changing the time scale of the experiment. Thus, a time-series analysis and any process that mimics such an analysis must be time-scale invariant.

In short, two assumptions that arise naturally in a perspective that takes for granted the functional specialization of learning mechanisms predict the time-scale invariance seen in the results from conditioning experiments. The first is that conditioning experiments test properties of the learning mechanism that enables animals to forage efficiently from a variety of sources with varying rates of reward. This is an assumption about the natural context for the behavior whose mechanism is examined in the laboratory. The second assumption is that the learning mechanism is specialized to deal with the computational challenges inherent in this kind of problem.

The aforementioned assumptions predict time-scale invariance in the sense of "lead one to expect." It remains to elaborate a proposal for the computational structure of this learning mechanism that predicts in the sense of "generates," which is what rate estimation theory does (Gallistel, 1990). In this model, the acquisition of conditioned responding in simple conditioning is based on the ratio between the subject's estimate of the rate of reinforcement when the CS is present $(\hat{\lambda}_{cs})$ and its estimate of the rate of reinforcement when the background alone is present $(\hat{\lambda}_b)$.

In a simple or basic conditioning protocol, there are no background reinforcements, that is, no reinforcements during the intertrial intervals. Because there are nST seconds of exposure to the CS per n reinforcements, the subject's estimate of the rate of CS reinforcement, $(\hat{\lambda}_{cs})$ is $n/nST = 1/ST$ reinforcements per second, and this estimate does not change as n increases (i.e., as training goes on). But what about $\hat{\lambda}_b$, the subject's estimate of the background rate of reinforcement? Because there are no reinforcements in the intertrial intervals, $\hat{\lambda}_b$ is assumed to be the reciprocal of the subject's cumulative exposure to the background since the beginning of conditioning. For example, if the subject has experienced 1,000 seconds of unreinforced exposure to the chamber alone, then its estimate of the possible rate of background reinforcement is 1/1,000. In making this estimate, which is the upper limit on what the rate of background reinforcement might be, given the animal's experience so far, the learning module shows its sensitivity to the (objectively) important principle that "absence of evidence is not evidence of absence." One thousand seconds of exposure to the chamber with no opening of the hopper except when the key was illuminated does not justify the conclusion that the hopper never opens when the key light is not on. It only justifies the conclusion that such events happen no more often than once in 1,000 seconds.

The estimate of the rate of CS reinforcement $(\hat{\lambda}_{cs})$ remains constant as conditioning goes on, but the longer that conditioning continues without background reinforcements, the smaller the $\hat{\lambda}_b$ becomes. Thus, the ratio $\hat{\lambda}_{cs}/\hat{\lambda}_b$ grows as conditioning continues. In rate estimation theory, this ratio, which is called the decision variable, grows in proportion to the number of reinforced trials. When it exceeds a threshold (the decision threshold), the animal begins to respond to the CS. Acquisition in this model is time-scale invariant because the decision variable, $\hat{\lambda}_{cs}/\hat{\lambda}_b$, is the ratio of two rates. This ratio is a dimensionless quantity.

Rate estimation theory explains acquisition without positing anything that is strengthened by reinforcement. It takes several co-occurrences of the CS and the US in simple conditioning before a conditioned response is seen because the conditioned response is a consequence of a decision process that is sensitive to the ambiguity inherent in a limited number of observations. Put another way, the process that leads to conditioned responding is designed to detect contingency, and contingency cannot be recognized unambiguously in the absence of several occurrences of the events in question. (If you happened to be brushing your teeth when the earthquake struck, your sense of civic responsibility should not lead you to give up dental hygiene.)

Rate estimation theory also predicts one of the best-established quantitative facts about the acquisition process (at least in pigeon autoshaping, which is the most widely used appetitive Pavlovian paradigm), namely that the rate of acquisition is directly proportional to the I/T ratio (figures 81.6 and 81.7). The I/T ratio is the amount of exposure to the background alone relative to the amount of exposure to the CS. The greater this ratio, the more uncommon it is for the CS to be present. Thus, what figure 81.7 shows is that when the CS is only rarely present, reinforcing it from time to time leads rapidly to conditioned behavior, whereas when the CS is present a large percentage of the time, reinforcing it leads only slowly to acquisition. Intuitively, the higher I/T ratio, the

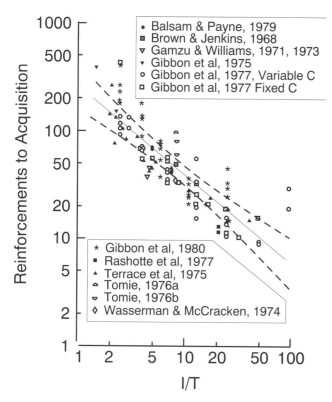

FIGURE 81.7 Reinforcements to acquisition as a function of the *I/T* ratio (double logarithmic coordinates). The data are from the 12 experiments listed in the key. (Reproduced from figure 2 in Gibbon and Balsam, 1981, which see for citations listed in the key.)

more rapidly it becomes evident that the rate of background reinforcement must be significantly less than the rate of CS reinforcement. In the Gallistel and Gibbon model (in press), the *I/T* ratio is the constant of proportionality relating the number of reinforcements to the decision variable, $\hat{\lambda}_{cs}/\hat{\lambda}_b$. The higher this constant of proportionality, the sooner the decision variable reaches the decision threshold.

The rate estimates in rate estimation theory are generated by a mechanism that solves simple systems of linear equations by the usual process of matrix inversion. The functional structure of this module is determined entirely by (is a mathematical consequence of) two simple principles: (1) rate additivity: the estimated rates of reinforcement for each CS must sum to the rates observed when various combinations of CSs are present, and (2) predictor minimization (Occam's razor): when there is more than one additive solution, the solution that minimizes the sum of the absolute values of the predicted rates, and hence the number of predictor variables, is the preferred solution. This rate-estimating structure, whose problem-specific nature is obvious, predicts well-known effects of background conditioning, blocking, overshadowing, and relative va-

lidity (Gallistel, 1990). Unlike the predictions of associative models (Rescorla and Wagner, 1972), its predictions do not depend on parametric assumptions. They follow directly from the basic ideas in the model. The operation of the rate-estimating mechanism is time-scale invariant because the coefficients of the matrices that are inverted to obtain the rate estimates are ratios of temporal intervals in the protocol. Thus, they, too, are dimensionless quantities.

In Gallistel and Gibbon's (in press) model of the mechanism that mediates extinction, the decision variable is the ratio of the cumulative amount of exposure to the CS since the last reinforcement of the CS and the expected amount of CS exposure per CS reinforcement. This ratio gets greater in proportion to the number of unreinforced presentations of the CS because each such presentation augments the cumulative unreinforced exposure to the CS. When this ratio reaches a critical value–the decision threshold in extinction–the animal stops responding to the CS. This decision mechanism also is time-scale invariant because the decision variable is the ratio of two time intervals. The thinner the reinforcement schedule during training, the longer the expected amount of CS exposure per reinforcement, which is the denominator of the decision ratio. Hence, the amount of exposure to the CS during extinction–the numerator of the decision ratio–must be proportionately greater before the decision criterion is reached. This explains why the number of trials to extinction increases in proportion to the degree of partial reinforcement during training–the partial reinforcement extinction effect. The result is that the number of reinforcements that must be omitted to produce extinction–hence, the rate of extinction–is unaffected by partial reinforcement during training.

In this model of extinction, nothing gets weaker as extinction progresses. On the contrary, the decision variable grows as extinction progresses. It takes many unreinforced trials to produce extinction because changes in contingency, like contingency itself, cannot be recognized without extended experience. Before it can be concluded reliably that the contingency between the CS and the US has changed, the interval without a reinforcement must get much longer than the training experience has led the subject to expect. Note that once again, the mechanism that mediates this aspect of conditioning is tuned to the inherent structure of the problem to be solved.

In short, models that assume adaptively specialized rather than general-purpose learning mechanisms provide a systematic alternative to the general-purpose associative framework within which the results from Pavlovian and instrumental conditioning experiments traditionally have been understood. These models explain in fundamentally different ways the basic phenomena of conditioning (e.g., the acquisition and extinction of the conditioned response). There is no notion of strengthening through repetition in these models. The associative bond is replaced by the concept of a decision variable whose magnitude depends on the ratio of two rate estimates.

Rate estimates are like the position coordinates generated by the dead-reckoning mechanism; they are symbolic quantities in the head, repositories of remembered information, not conducting links. They are computed from experience by a problem-specific learning module, a module adapted to the solution of multivariate, nonstationary time-series problems. The operation of this module is time-scale invariant because the problem that it solves is time-scale invariant.

The success of domain-specific modeling in the homeland of associative modeling suggests that learning mechanisms, like other biological mechanisms, invariably will exhibit adaptive specialization. We should no more expect to find a general-purpose learning mechanism than we should expect to find a general-purpose sensory organ.

The conclusion that learning is mediated by several different problem-specific modules, which compute symbolic representations of objectively specifiable properties of the animal's experience, has potentially profound consequences for neuroscience research. Temporal pairing does not appear to be relevant to the operation of any of these modules, including the modules that produce conditioned responses in Pavlovian and instrumental learning paradigms. Thus, efforts to find the cellular mechanism of learning based on the assumption that learning depends on temporal pairing may be searching for something that does not exist. For example, most of the interest in the cellular phenomena of long-term potentiation (LTP) and long-term depression (LTD) rests on the assumption that these mechanisms are the physical realization of changes in associative strength. If there is no such thing as an associative bond, then the significance of these cellular phenomena for neuroscience as a whole becomes problematic.

Despite long-standing and deeply entrenched views to the contrary, the brain no longer can be viewed as an amorphous plastic tissue that acquires its distinctive competencies from the environment acting on general purpose cellular-level learning mechanisms. Cognitive neuroscientists, as they trace out the functional circuitry of the brain, should be prepared to identify adaptive specializations as the most likely functional units they will find. At the circuit level, special-purpose circuitry is to be expected everywhere in the brain, just as it currently is expected routinely in the analysis of sensory and motor function. At the cellular level, the only processes likely to be universal are the elementary computational processes for manipulating neural signals in accord with the laws of arithmetic and logic and for storing and retrieving the values of variables. Thus, an important question for neurobiology is how nervous tissue stores and retrieves the values of variables.

NOTES

1. That is, a model that does not require that experience be imagined to occur in discrete "trials." The trial assumption is ubiquitous in associative modeling. It makes most associative models unsuitable as models of possible cellular mechanisms of learning, because it has so far proved impossible to operationalize the notion of a trial, that is, to specify a priori (in the absence of a particular experimental protocol) what constitutes a learning trial. Thus, the division of the animal's experience into trials in associative modeling is ad hoc (not governed by explicit, generally applicable principles).

2. The size of an increment in associative strength is a function of more than one aspect of the events on a given trial. In most models, the increment in associative strength is, for example, a function of (at least) the intensity or magnitude of the unconditioned stimulus and the duration of the interval between the onset of the conditioned stimulus (CS) and the delivery of the US. It also is a function of the internal state of the animal–the pretrial strength of the association, and the pretrial strengths of other associations to the same US. In many models, it also is a function of the extent to which the animal is attending to the CS and/or the US. Therefore, the resulting strength of an associative connection confounds several properties of the animal's past experience–among them, the intensity of the USs, the duration of the CS–US interval, and the number and kind of trials the animal has experienced. Because of this confounding, none of these properties is recoverable from the current strength of the connections forged by the animal's cumulative conditioning experience. Put more formally, the strength of an associative connection is a many-one function of different properties of the conditioning protocol. Many-one functions are not invertible; you cannot get from the one back to the many. That is why the connection weights in a neural net generally do not specify specific facts about the system's experience, they merely cause the system to respond more adaptively to subsequent inputs. These altered connection weights cause the system to behave "as if" it knew something when in fact it does not, which is why these nets are called subsymbolic. The net does not know anything because it is impossible to recover from the weights of its connections any objective property of the inputs that the net has been given. Thus, there is no symbolic knowledge. Facts about the world are not represented therein.

3. Assuming, of course, that the units are used consistently, that is, that milliseconds (msec) are not used for some intervals and seconds (s) for others.

REFERENCES

BECKER, S., and G. E. HINTON, 1992. Self-organizing neural network that discovers surfaces in random-dot stereograms. *Nature* 355:161–163.

BRINES, M. L., and J. L. GOULD, 1982. Skylight polarization patterns and animal orientation. *J. Exp. Biol.* 96:69–91.

CHOMSKY, N., 1975. *Reflections on language*. New York: Pantheon.

CHOMSKY, N., 1981. *Lectures on Government and Binding*. Dordrecht: Foris.

COLEMAN, S. R., and I. GORMEZANO, 1971. Classical conditioning of the rabbit's (*Oryctolagus cuniculus*) nictitating membrane response under symmetrical CS-US interval shifts. *J. Comp. Physiol. Psychol.* 77:447–455.

COLWILL, R. M., 1991. Negative discriminative stimuli provide information about the identity of omitted response-contingent outcomes. *Anim. Learn. Behav.* 19:326–336.

DEWS, P. B., 1970. The theory of fixed-interval responding. In *The Theory of Reinforcement Schedules*, W. N. Schoenfeld, ed. New York: Appleton-Century-Crofts.

DYER, F. C., and J. A. DICKINSON, 1994. Development of sun compensation by honeybees: How partially experienced bees estimate the sun's course. *Proc. Natl. Acad. Sci. U.S.A.* 91:4471–4474.

FRISCH, K. V., 1967. *The Dance-Language and Orientation of Bees*. Cambridge, Mass.: Harvard University Press.

GALLISTEL, C. R., 1990. *The Organization of Learning*. Cambridge, Mass.: Bradford Books/MIT Press.

GALLISTEL, C. R., and J. GIBBON, in press. Time, rate and conditioning. *Psychological Review*.

GELMAN, R., and E. WILLIAMS, 1998. Enabling constraints on cognitive development. In *Cognition, Perception, and Language. Vol. 2. Handbook of Child Psychology*, 5th ed., D. Kuhn and R. Siegler, eds. New York: Wiley, pp. 575–630.

GIBBON, J., 1972. Timing and discrimination of shock density in avoidance. *Psychol. Rev.* 79:68–92.

GIBBON, J., 1977. Scalar expectancy theory and Weber's law in animal timing. *Psychol. Rev.* 84:279–335.

GIBBON, J., R. M. CHURCH, and W. H. MECK, 1984. Scalar timing in memory. In *Timing and Time Perception*, J. Gibbon and L. Allan, eds. Vol. 423. New York: New York Academy of Sciences, pp. 52–77.

GIBBON, J., and P. BALSAM, 1981. Spreading associations in time. In *Autoshaping and Conditioning Theory*, C. M. Locurto, H. S. Terrace, and J. Gibbon, eds. New York: Academic Press, pp. 219–253.

GOULD, J. L., and P. MARLER, 1987. Learning by instinct. *Sci. Am.* 256:74–85.

HARKNESS, R. D., and N. G. MAROUDAS, 1985. Central place foraging by an ant (Cataglyphis bicolor Fab.): A model of searching. *Anim. Behav.* 33:916–928.

HINDE, R. A., and J. S. HINDE, eds., 1973. *Constraints on Learning*. New York: Academic Press.

HULL, C. L., 1943. *Principles of Behavior*. New York: Appleton-Century-Crofts.

KAMIN, L. J., 1969. Selective association and conditioning. In *Fundamental Issues in Associative Learning*, N. J. Mackintosh and W. K. Honig, eds. Halifax: Dalhousie University Press, pp. 42–64.

LINDAUER, M., 1957. Sonnenorientierung der Bienen unter der Aequatorsonne und zur Nachtzeit. *Naturwissenschaften* 44:1–6.

LINDAUER, M., 1959. Angeborene und erlernte Komponenten in der Sonnenorientierung der Bienen. *Zeitschrift für vergleichende Physiologie* 42:43–62.

LOLORDO, V. M., and J. L. FAIRLESS, 1985. Pavlovian conditioned inhibition: The literature since 1969. In *Information Processing in Animals*, R. R. Miller and N. E. Spear, eds. Hillsdale, N.J.: Lawrence Erlbaum Associates.

MARLER, P., 1991. The instinct to learn. In *The Epigenesis of Mind*, S. Carey and R. Gelman, eds. Hillsdale, N.J.: Lawrence Erlbaum Associates, pp. 37–66.

RESCORLA, R. A., 1968. Probability of shock in the presence and absence of CS in fear conditioning. *J. Comp. Physiol. Psychol.* 66:1–5.

RESCORLA, R. A., 1969. Pavlovian conditioned inhibition. *Psychol. Bull.* 72:77–94.

RESCORLA, R. A., and A. R. WAGNER, 1972. A theory of Pavlovian conditioning: Variations in the effectiveness of reinforcement and nonreinforcement. In *Classical conditioning II*, A. H. Black and W. F. Prokasy, eds. New York: Appleton-Century-Crofts, pp. 64–99.

ROEPER, T., and E. WILLIAMS, eds., 1987. *Parameter Setting*. Boston: Reidel.

ROZIN, P., and J. W. KALAT, 1971. Specific hungers and poison avoidance as adaptive specializations of learning. *Psychol. Rev.* 78:459–486.

SCHNEIDERMAN, N., and I. GORMEZANO, 1964. Conditioning of the nictitating membrane of the rabbit as a function of CS-US interval. *J. Comp. Physiol. Psychol.* 57:188–195.

SELIGMAN, M. E. P., and J. L HAGER, eds., 1972. *Biological Boundaries of Learning*. New York: Appleton-Century-Crofts.

USHERWOOD, P. N. R., 1993. Memories are made of this. *Trends Neurosci.* 16:427–429.

WAGNER, A. R., F. A. LOGAN, K. HABERLANDT, and T. PRICE, 1968. Stimulus selection in animal discrimination learning. *J. Exp. Psychol.* 76:171–180.

WEHNER, R., and I. FLATT, 1972. The visual orientation of desert ants, *Cataglyphis bicolor*, by means of territorial cues. In *Information Processing in the Visual System of Arthropods*, R. Wehner, ed. New York: Springer, pp. 295–302.

WEHNER, R., and M. V. SRINIVASAN, 1981. Searching behavior of desert ants, genus *Cataglyphis* (*Formicidae*, Hymenoptera). *J. Comp. Physiol.* 142:315–338.

82 Social Control of Brains: From Behavior to Genes

RUSSELL D. FERNALD AND STEPHANIE A. WHITE

ABSTRACT It seems self-evident that the brain controls behavior, but can behavior also "control" the brain? Behavior can and does influence specific aspects of brain structure and function over three different time frames. A causal link is easy to establish on an evolutionary time scale because the selective forces of the ecological niche of the animal typically are reflected in body shape, sensory and motor systems, and behavior. Similarly, on a developmental time scale, behavior acts in concert with the environment to establish structural changes in the brain that influence an organism throughout its lifetime. Surprisingly, there currently is evidence that in real time, social behavior also causes changes in the brain in adult animals. These alterations, caused by behavioral interactions, often are related to reproductive behavior and can be dramatic and reversible. Understanding the mechanisms responsible for such dynamic changes in the nervous systems of adult animals is a major challenge. How does behavior sculpt the brain, and how are these changes controlled? In this chapter, the authors review some key examples of the kinds of changes caused over evolutionary and developmental time scales and describe more specifically how behavior influences cellular and molecular processes in the brain. Their studies link molecular events with organism behavior by using a model system in which social behaviors regulate reproduction. Understanding the mechanisms through which social encounters cause changes in the brain of organisms is a significant challenge that is likely to yield important insights about how the reality of one's social world changes one's physiology.

Among social animals, the behavior of one individual or group of individuals influences the behavior of others (Lorenz, 1935). The nature of this influence depends on the species, the situation, and the specific interaction. However, the most reliable predictor of the behavior and outcome of such encounters is the social status of the individuals involved. A dominant animal threatened by a nondominant animal behaves differently than does a dominant animal threatened by another dominant individual. Correspondingly, behavioral actions by a female produce very different reactions in males depending on their social status. Indeed, in every social system that has been observed, the behavior of individuals depends in part on their social status and in part on their environment. For students of animal behavior, the fact that animals behave in a manner appropriate to their particular status provides an essential scientific framework for interpreting social behavior. But how does an animal recognize its status and then behave appropriately? How does it understand an opportunity to change its status upward or respond to an imposed change in status downward? Clearly, physiological and ultimately molecular processes must be matched with the external social status to allow the animal to act. Some of these physiological and molecular changes must precede behavioral change, but others are a consequence of that change. How are these controlled?

Von Uexküll (1909) first realized that every animal species experiences life differently, living in its own "Umwelt," or unique perceptual world. A bat using sonic echoes to understand the world in darkness surely perceives its surroundings differently than does a giraffe that relies on its eyes, looking down on the scene from above, or a fish depending entirely on weak electrical signals for information. Each animal species has different sensory capabilities that, in turn, restrict the stimuli it can sense. This restriction on the perceived world necessarily constrains the possible behavioral responses of any animal. Writing at the turn of the century, von Uexküll could not possibly have anticipated the discovery of magnetic, electric, or pressure senses, nor could he have imagined vision that extends into the infrared and ultraviolet, or even that light detection exists at some remarkable places other than the eye (Arikawa, Suyama, and Fujii, 1996). These discoveries make his writing all the more prescient, and the many interesting, unusual "umwelts" discovered to date reveal the many ways that natural selection has shaped animal perceptions. These are matched by the variation in animal forms and functions, which also illustrate adaptations to the environment. Together, physiological and behavioral adaptations are quite spectacular, and with every discovery comes renewed surprise.

In thinking about evolutionary change, it is clear that the ultimate arbiter of successful adaptations is behavior.

RUSSELL D. FERNALD Neuroscience Program and Department of Psychology, Stanford University, Stanford, Calif.
STEPHANIE A. WHITE Neurosciences Program, Duke University, Durham, N.C.

An animal that survives does so because it behaves successfully during a multitude of interactions with other animals in its environment. However, behavior, in turn, depends on intricate physiological, cellular, and ultimately molecular adaptations. Thus, one major challenge in biology is to understand the linkage across these levels as an animal interacts with its world. How is behavior controlled by means of physiological processes, and, correspondingly, how does behavior influence physiological, cellular, or molecular events? In this review, we discuss examples of such synergistic interactions between behavior and physiology that occur at different biological time scales: evolutionary time, developmental time, and real time.

Natural selection for shape

An animal's habitat is the major selective force shaping resident animal's form and function. Some adaptations are so striking that one can guess where the animal lives simply by observing its appearance. A wonderful example is the star-nosed mole *Condylura cristat*. Moles have adapted to their subterranean, nocturnal existence by developing a specialized sensory organ on their snouts, known as Eimer's organ, which provides tactile information. The star-nosed mole, however, has the premier of snouts: A paired set of 11 fleshy appendages is assembled in a starfish-like array around its nostrils. The entire structure contains some 30,000 Eimer's organs. This packing density makes the star-nosed mole's snout arguably one of the most sensitive detection devices for tactile cues. What accounts for this flamboyance compared with the humble snout of the common eastern mole? The differences very likely reflect the different habitats each species lives in (Catania and Kass, 1995). The eastern mole negotiates a substratum of dry soil and rocks, whereas the star-nosed mole lives amidst muddier terrain. The softer soil of the star-nosed mole's underground "umwelt" was selected for its more delicate and elaborate sensory structure.

The brain of the star-nosed mole reflects its extreme sensory bias because the area devoted to vision is comparatively small compared with the area devoted to somatosensory perception. Electrical recordings from the somatosensory cortex reveal a large and precise topographic representation of the snout (Catania et al., 1993; Catania and Kaas, 1995). Cytochrome oxidase staining of the sensory area in each hemisphere produces 11 dark stripes of dense tissue separated by narrow regions of lesser staining, suggesting that each stripe conforms to one of the fleshy rays on the snout. These orderly maps of the mole's tactile world are thought to develop in a manner similar to the way that topographic maps form in other sensory systems, namely through segregation of inputs that have temporally correlated activity. As the animal feels its way through its burrows, its vigorous behavior results in coactivation of neighboring regions on a single ray. This coactivation presumably leads to refinement of the map as correlated inputs are stabilized at the expense of discorrelated ones. Although such patterning occurs before birth, as best illustrated in the visual system (Meister et al., 1991), initial patterns still are malleable postnatally and behavior can influence that refinement (e.g., Nudo et al., 1996). Such a mechanism is a primary example of how behavior, resulting in sensory stimulation, can shape brain structure.

The star-nosed mole exemplifies the intricate relationship among sensory capacity, biological structure, and behavior as molded by natural selection. The fleshy fingers on the snout advertise how habitat, in this case, a muddy substratum, molds biological form and function during evolution. As a result of its sensory adaptation, the animal has a specialized capacity to "feel" its environment. The most important feature of the "Umwelt" for this animal is clearly in the tactile domain requiring tactile-oriented behavior which, in turn, influences the synaptic connections in the somatosensory cortex of the mole's brain.

Natural selection in development

Adaptation on an evolutionary time-scale occurs over the course of generations. The first and most important requirement for this is reproduction. Successful reproduction requires exquisitely timed developmental and physiological changes coupled with relatively precise social interactions. Maturational adaptations are triggered by hormones, which are powerful molecules that sculpt physiological and morphological change to enable reproduction. Surviving to puberty, attracting mates, conceiving, bearing, and parenting progeny all depend on these changes. In most vertebrates, the earliest actions of hormones, known as organizational effects, occur close to birth, when our complement of sex chromosomes or some environmental cue such as temperature dictates which molecules shape our anatomy and physiology.

SEXUAL DIMORPHISM When Phoenix and colleagues (1959) first framed the organizational hypothesis of hormonal effects, their terminology was meant to convey the fact that the very circuitry of the nervous system was being shaped by the action of these molecules. The contrasting term "activational" hormonal effects referred to the waxing or waning of hormonal flow in response to proximate stimuli within a fully formed structure. Although this dichotomous categorization has proven to be a useful heuristic, accumulating evidence revealed that hormones produce observable changes in neuronal structure both during development and in response to proximate stimuli.

A classic example of the extent to which hormones shape neural structure was the finding of Arnold, Nottebohm, and Pfaff (1976) that the size of key nuclei within the song circuit of songbirds was three to six times larger in males than in females. These size differences, visible in histological sections with the naked eye, are related to sex and seasonal differences in song behavior (but see also Brenowitz, Lent, and Kroodsma, 1995). To date, the list of sexual dimorphisms produced by hormonal effects is as diverse as our degree of knowledge about their significance. For example, in humans, there is a distinct difference in the shape of the splenium of the corpus callosum between men and women, although it is not known whether that morphological difference reflects a functional difference (deLacoste-Utamsing and Holloway, 1982; Holloway and deLacoste, 1986). In contrast, when differences in behaviors that are critical for the survival of the organism direct the research focus, it is easier to understand the relevance of the dimorphism.

This approach has been especially fruitful in studies on the electric fish, *Sternopygus* (reviewed in Zakon, 1996). In these visionless fish, electrical communication is used to detect and recognize conspecifics. Weak electric organ discharges (EODs) produced are sexually dimorphic such that adult females emit shorter duration pulses at higher frequencies than mature males. Androgen treatment lowers EOD frequency and duration, whereas estradiol 17β and human chorionic gonadotropin raise it. The mechanism that underlies this dimorphic behavior has been identified at the molecular level. Within the electric organ, the presence of dihydrotestosterone slows the inactivation kinetics of the electrocyte sodium channel, and this is correlated with longer duration action potentials and lower frequency discharge (Ferrari, McAnelly, and Zakon, 1995). This hormonal modulation of channel kinetics is a novel finding that ultimately explains how a sexually dimorphic behavior is produced that allows these fish to recognize one another's gender.

NEURONAL PLASTICITY UNDERLYING MOTHER–INFANT INTERACTIONS During development, hormonal secretions sculpt differences not only between the sexes but also within each gender. Pervasive examples may be found during the formation of a social bond between parent and offspring in early life. Here, changes in the molecular and cellular properties of discrete neuronal populations reflect an interaction among diverse factors, including sensory stimulation, endocrine priming, neuronal plasticity, and behavior during development. Consider the brief period when a young bird may have to learn what species it is and even the characteristics of a species-appropriate mate (Lorenz, 1935). Imprinting is the name given to the specialized, typically irreversible learning that occurs in early life resulting in a bond between mother and offspring or in mate choice often first observed years later. Stimuli appearing during a critical window of development acquire a potent valence for their influence on behavior. The surmise is that the sensitivity of the nervous system somehow is different during this critical period, heightening the impact of specific sensory cues on the cellular and molecular processes that underlie memory. The search for the biological basis for this brief learning process has produced a few candidates, but by and large, only the phenomenological features of these processes are well known (Lorenz, 1935).

Sensory systems play powerful roles in triggering hormonal flow and changes in adult stages of maturation as well. In pregnant sheep, the passage of the fetus through the birth canal provides cervicovaginal stimulation, triggering the release of oxytocin, a potent peptide for maternal behavior. For this to occur, the mother must be primed by the high levels of estrogen that are present during pregnancy. Simultaneously, the birthing sensation also changes the way that the mother perceives her lamb. Before birth, ewes are repelled by the odor of amniotic fluid and reject approaching lambs. Incredibly, after parturition, they find this same aroma attractive (Poindron, Levy, and Krehbiel, 1988) and lick and sniff the newborn, culminating in the formation of an enduring and highly selective bond between mother and lamb. The mechanistic basis for this phenomenon involves a change in the electrical activity of neurons in the olfactory bulb, where there are receptors for oxytocin. After birth, the number of mitral cells that respond to lamb odors increases (Kendrick, Levy, and Keverne, 1992), and recognition of her own lamb is accompanied by increased activity within a subset of these cells in the mother's olfactory bulb. It is not known just how oxytocin might influence the electrical properties of the mitral cells or how this might produce the bond that forms between mother and offspring (DaCosta et al., 1996). Interestingly, a similar perceptual shift to a pheromonal cue may be at work in humans where it has been reported that one chemical, andosterone, is found attractive or repellent by women depending on their reproductive state.

Oxytocin plays another major role during reproduction, namely to trigger lactation in mammals. Here the causal chain of events between an organism's behavior on another's physiology is understood somewhat better. Oxytocin is released by magnocellular neurons in the hypothalmoneurohypophysial system (HNS). This system undergoes dramatic structural alterations in response to gonadal steroids (reviewed in Hatton, 1995), including withdrawal of glia, synaptogenesis, and formation of dendrodendritic gap junctions. Significantly, all these changes occur during nursing of rat pups, and they reverse on weaning. The suckling of pups is a critical sensory input that initiates a neuroendocrine reflex arc. During suckling, short and intermittent high-frequency bursts of action potentials occur in oxytocinergic neurons in the mother's HNS. When these bursts become synchronized, a bolus of oxytocin is delivered to the mother's bloodstream where, on reaching the mammary glands, it promotes milk ejection.

Another dramatic plasticity produced by the suckling sensation occurs in the primary somatosensory cortex of the mother. Although there is no known link to hormonal circulation, the area devoted to the nursing mother's ventrum actually increases in representation by nearly twofold over that in nonlactating control and virgin animals. This cortical magnification is transient, reverting to its prior size after weaning (Xerri, Stern, and Merzenich, 1994). Thus, in both the triggering of a simple reflex arc as well as the more complex rewiring of regions of the cortex, the pups' behavior causes profound structural changes in the mother's brain.

Neuronal plasticity in real time

The aforementioned processes of parturition and lactation exemplify the complementary interaction between sensory stimuli, hormonal response, and behavior that unfold during development to ensure the survival of the newborn. Many examples of structural plasticity have been found beyond ontogeny, and our ability to recognize these events has benefited from their clear parallels with developmental processes. The mechanisms responsible for continued plasticity might be shared with normal development.

HORMONAL INFLUENCES ON SOCIAL DOMINANCE AND SEASONAL CHANGES   It is not surprising that hormones, the key regulators of developmental plasticity, also are essential for many types of plasticity in real time. In these instances, the endocrine system, acting as an integrative force, serves to match an organism's internal state to its specific situation. The context for this action depends on its physical and social environment. Hormonal mechanisms allow adaptive responses to social factors in their physical context. The following examples are meant to illustrate how hormonal mechanisms allow adaptive responses to social factors, circumstances that require flexibility not achievable with fixed neural wiring.

In many social systems, it has been tempting to think that steroid molecules completely predestine the behav-

ioral role of the animal, particularly where social dominance is concerned. One popular notion is that higher levels of testosterone lead to dominance through increased aggressive behavior. It is not so simple. For example, in some systems, it is the social environment, composed of behavioral interactions between individuals, that provides the cues from which an individual recognizes its chance for elevated social status. Work by Cardwell and Liley (1991) in the stoplight parrotfish and our own teleost model system demonstrate that increased androgen levels actually follow, rather than precede, the assumption of dominance. These examples suggest that the fish's brain initially integrates sensory cues from its social interactions to delimit an endogenous social set point and this, in turn, instructs the control of hormones.

In some systems, increases in androgen both precede and follow social interactions. Work by Wingfield in Gambel's sparrows (reviewed in Wingfield et al., 1990) shows that the seasonal increase in day length stimulates testosterone production. Indeed, testis weight increases up to 600-fold, priming the animal for its upcoming reproductive tasks. However, later in the season, when testosterone has declined, contact with an unfamiliar, intruding male can immediately re-elevate those levels. That the hormone itself is not required for aggressive behavior has been demonstrated in castrated birds that also exhibit territorial behavior. Once again, it is clear that behavior, either of an individual or its conspecific, can initiate changes in the endocrine state.

Another example of plasticity is the seasonal change in the morphology of telencephalic nuclei that control song behavior, which has been reported for diverse species of songbirds. For all cases studied to date (cf. Brenowitz et al., 1998), testis size and circulating testosterone concentrations were greater in spring versus fall birds. The absolute volumes of three song nuclei in the brain (HVc, RA, and Area X), and their volumes relative to those of either the total telencephalon or three thalamic nonsong nuclei, typically are significantly greater in the spring than in the fall. Typically, song behavior also changes seasonally, and seasonal plasticity can be regarded as a common feature of the seasonally breeding songbirds studied.

SOCIAL ENVIRONMENT SHAPES
NEURONAL STRUCTURE

Natural behavior of Haplochromis burtoni   To address the central question of how behavior influences the brain, our laboratory studies a cichlid fish, *Haplochromis burtoni* native to Lake Tanganyika in Africa. In their natural habitat, there are two kinds of males: those with

GnRH neuronal soma and gonad size

Large   Small

Source of cues

Social

Endogenous

FIGURE 82.1   Social and reproductive states in *H. burtoni.* Male and female *H. burtoni* each are shown in two distinct reproductive states. Nonterritorial males and brooding females each possess small preoptic gonadotropin-releasing hormone (GnRH)-containing neurons. Territorial males and spawning females have larger GnRH neurons. GnRH neurons in females change size according to their reproductive cycle when they shrink significantly in size during the 2-week period between spawning and brooding of fry. In contrast, neurons change size according to social signals in males. It takes more than 3 weeks for neurons to shrink in males undergoing a descent in social status but only 1 week to grow during social ascent.

territories and those without (Fernald and Hirata, 1977a, b). Territorial males, which make up only 10% of the males, are brightly colored, having a blue or yellow body color, dramatic black stripe through the eye, vertical black bars on the body, a black spot on the tip of the gill cover, and a large red patch just behind it. In contrast, nonterritorial males are cryptically colored, making them difficult to distinguish from the background and from females that are similarly camouflaged so that they appear nearly identical to females (figure 82.1). The animals live in a lek-like social system in which the brightly colored territorial males vigorously defend contiguous territories arrayed over a food supply (Fernald, 1977).

Social communication among these fish depends primarily on visual signals (Fernald, 1984). Territorial males are very active, performing at least 19 distinct behavioral acts during fast-paced social encounters (Fernald,

1977). They spend time digging a pit in the center of their territory, fighting with neighbors at their common territorial boundaries, chasing nonterritorial animals away, and soliciting and courting females. Solicitation and courtship behaviors are identified easily because the males display bright coloration patterns toward the courted female. Courtship includes "leading" the female toward the territory, and during "courting," the male quivers his spread, brightly colored anal fin in front of the female. Females led into the territory feed by nipping at and sifting through the bottom cover.

Interestingly, nonterritorial males mimic this female behavior accurately enough so that the territorial males allow them to eat in the territory. Soon enough, the deception is discovered, and the female impersonator is chased off. If a genetic female responds to the entreaties of a male, he leads her into his pit and continues the elaborate courtship movements, swimming to the front of the female and rapidly quivering his entire body with his anal fin spread in her view. As the pair disappears into the spawning pit out of direct view of the territory, other animals exploit this opportunity to feed energetically. The spawning male repeatedly interrupts his courtship behavior to chase intruders off his limited food supply. If physiologically ready and adequately stimulated, the female lays her eggs at the bottom of the pit, collecting them in her mouth almost immediately. After she lays several eggs, the male swims in front of her, again displaying the anal fins spots, his body quivering. The female then nips at the male's anal fin as though she mistakes his spots for uncollected ova. Thus, while attempting to "collect" the spots, the female ingests the milt ejected near them by the male and ensures fertilization. After several bouts of this alternating behavior, the female may go to the territory of another male to lay more eggs or depart from the territorial arena with the fertilized eggs to brood them (Fernald, 1984).

This brief description of the natural behavior of *H. burtoni* reveals the extensive role of visual signals in social interactions and how much the social scene governs the behavior of individual animals. Each behavioral act influences the next, both in the observed individual and in the animals involved in the interaction. During the behavior, a great deal of information is exchanged between individuals. What does the animal attend to and what are the consequences of that observation? Our studies have shown (Muske and Fernald, 1987) that the territorial males differ not only in their social displays, but also in the prominence of those signals to other viewers. Becoming and remaining socially dominant produces long-term physiological changes. Given the importance of the correct production and recognition of social signals, there must be mechanisms responsible for their development.

Developmental strategies in H. burtoni As young fish grow, social behavior of conspecifics regulates their growth (Fraley and Fernald, 1982). For the first 7 to 8 weeks of life, living in a group facilitates growth of males as compared with broodmates reared in total isolation. After this time, group-reared males that do not acquire and defend territories grow more slowly than those with territories do. Males that form territories develop their color patterns faster, weigh more, and have larger and more highly developed gonads than do animals reared under any other conditions. The growth of the animals under optimal conditions is dramatic and has resulted in novel developmental solutions over evolutionary time. This includes the addition of new cells to the lens and retina (Fernald and Wright, 1983; Fernald, 1993, 1989; Johns and Fernald, 1981). Such social control of matura-

tion and growth is widespread among animals and takes a variety of forms in different species. In *H. burtoni*, however, there are some unique effects of this social regulation of growth.

Males reared with adults show delayed maturation relative to those reared without adults, and moreover, these animals have smaller gonadotropin-releasing hormone (GnRH)-containing neurons in the preoptic area (POA) of the ventral hypothalamus (Davis and Fernald, 1990; figure 82.2). This finding suggests that the social control of maturation is reflected in changes in structures in the brain.

What are the salient sensory cues that a juvenile male fish perceives that influence its initial social state? In the laboratory, if juvenile males are reared alone, they develop into territorial males with all of the defining characteristics from large gonads to prominent lachrymal stripes. This shows that every male has the potential for social dominance, that this is the default developmental pathway, and that any genetic influence on dominance is negligible in comparison to social cues.

We have begun to dissect these social cues by sensory modality to determine the ones responsible for suppressing nonterritorial males and have discovered that, in addition to visual cues, tactile stimuli play a part (Davis and Fernald, unpublished observations, 1989). Thus, if a cohort of young fish is raised in the same aquarium as an older established community, the young males remain nonterritorial, as stated previously. If, however, the two groups are separated by a fine mesh net, one that allows visual and chemical contact and even permits threat displays across the barrier, they quickly learn that the would-be bullies on the other side of the tank are unable to chase and bite them. Freed from the threat of aggression by the big territorial males, the younger fish form their own communities where again, some 10% of the males escape maturational suppression and become territorial. In turn, these suppress the maturation of the remaining 90% of the males on their side of the net. Because both the older and younger communities have visual and chemical access to each other, these findings indicate that biting and nipping behaviors form some part of the suppressive signal imparted to nonterritorial fish.

Neuronal plasticity in adulthood In their natural environment, there are costs and benefits associated with territoriality. The benefits are that territorial males have a reliable food supply and through this, they are the only males that spawn. On the down side, the bright flashy colors and active behaviors of dominant males make them conspicuous to birds of prey. Predation of dominant males occurs at a significantly higher rate than does that of females and nonterritorial males (Fernald and

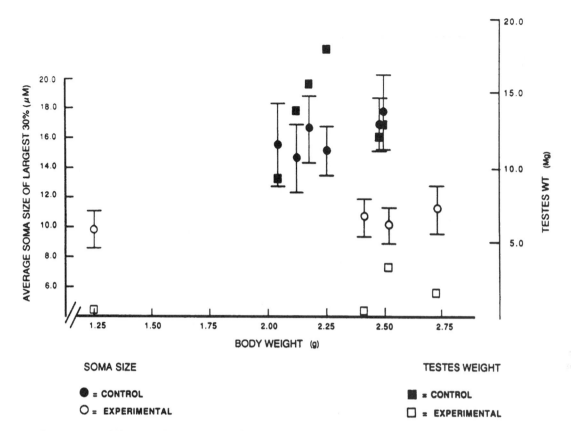

SOMA SIZE

● = CONTROL

○ = EXPERIMENTAL

TESTES WEIGHT

■ = CONTROL

□ = EXPERIMENTAL

FIGURE 82.2   Comparison of the size of preoptic area GnRH-containing cells between dominant and nondominant males. Preoptic irGnRH cell soma sizes are compared between control (early maturing) males and experimental (maturation-suppressed) males, illustrating that in control animals, the cells are approximately 50% larger. Average soma diameters for the largest 30% of preoptic irGnRH cells for the six controls and four experimental males are presented as a function of body weight. Bars indicate standard deviation. Testes weights are plotted on the same graph. The contrast in testes weights between the two groups is even more striking, with the low values for experimental males reflecting extreme hypogonadism. (Adapted from Davis and Fernald, 1990.)

Hirata, 1977b). When it occurs, the vacated territory is an open opportunity for a formerly suppressed nonterritorial male to make a dramatic switch in social state. Within seconds, the previously nonterritorial animal produces an eyebar and exhibits aggressive behavior. What endogenous changes accompany this outward transformation?

To understand the role of social status in determining reproductive state in older animals, adult males were changed from territorial (T) to nonterritorial (NT), or vice versa. To do this, T males were moved into communities with larger T males, as a result of which they became NT (T≡NT). Correspondingly, NT males were moved to new communities consisting of females and smaller males, which they could dominate, as a result of which they became T (NT≡T). In each case, the subjects remained in the altered social setting for 4 weeks, after which the size of GnRH-containing cells was measured (Francis, Soma, and Fernald, 1993).

Mean soma size of both the POA immunoreactive gonadotropin-releasing hormone (irGnRH)-containing neurons (figure 82.3) and gonadosomatic index (GSI) (figure 82.4) were significantly larger in the control T males than in the control NT males. In another irGnRH cell group located in the terminal nerve in the telencephalon, there was no difference in mean soma sizes between T and NT males, indicating that the status-linked variation in soma size is not a general property of GnRH-containing neurons but instead is confined to the POA population.

In fish subjected to social transitions, experimentally induced T males (NT≡T) showed GnRH neuronal soma sizes and GSIs similar to control territorial males. This indicates that within 1 month, endogenous changes occur that equip the newly dominant male with the physiological capacity appropriate to his new social state. Conversely, in animals undergoing a downgrade in social status (T≡NT), GnRH neurons shrank to sizes that were insignificantly different from control nonterritorial males, and so did their gonads. Thus, social status determines both soma size of POA irGnRH neurons and GSI, and these effects are reversible. The relatively

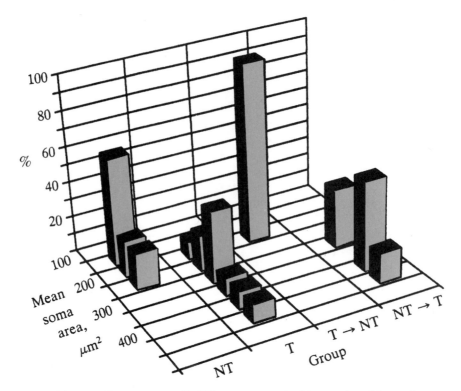

FIGURE 82.3 Comparison of the size of preoptic area GnRH-containing cells between males following a transition between different social states. Three-dimensional plot of mean soma sizes of preoptic area (POA) irGnRH neurons, showing significant differences between T and T≡NT males and between NT≡T males. Percentage of individuals with mean soma size in a given size bin are plotted for each treatment condition. There are no significant differences between T males and their experimental counterparts (NT≡T) or between NT males and their experimental counterparts (T≡NT). (Adapted from Francis, Soma, and Fernald, 1993.)

larger testes and irGnRH neurons characteristic of T males is a consequence of their social dominance, and when this dominance advantage is lost, both neurons and testes shrink.

Because the precipitating event in these studies was the experimentally manipulated change in social status, it is clear that in these teleosts, social state can initiate changes in endocrine state. However, such changes in social and endocrine systems interleave so fluently that they suggest a complex nexus of interactions rather than a linear chain of control. Thus, GnRH-containing neurons in the hypothalamus of adult territorial males both influence and are influenced by circulating gonadal hormones. We know this because castration of territorial males caused GnRH neurons to increase in size (Soma et al., 1996). This neuronal hypertrophy in castrated animals was prevented either by testosterone (T) or by 11-ketotestosterone (KT) treatment. Estradiol (E2) treatment did not reduce GnRH cell size in castrated animals. These results (figure 82.5) indicate that androgens reduce the size of GnRH cells through negative feedback. Because E2 had no effect, androgen influence on GnRH cell size appears to be independent of aromatization.

These data are consistent with the hypothesis that the set point for hypothalamic GnRH cell size is determined by social cues and that this set point is maintained by means of negative feedback by gonadal androgens. Territorial males have large GnRH-containing neurons *despite* high circulating androgens, not because of them (figure 82.6).

The aforementioned castration experiment was performed on territorial males. Enlarged GnRH neurons resulted, and although the mean soma sizes were even slightly bigger than those in control territorial males, their large size is in concert with the social dominance of the animal. To test whether GnRH neuronal cell size and social state can be dissociated, the castration experiment was replicated, this time using nonterritorial animals. After surgery to remove gonadal tissue, the fish were returned to the social settings from whence they came, ensuring that they remained nonterritorial. Behavioral observations confirmed that these animals indeed were submissive. Two weeks later, the fish were killed and the brains were examined for the sizes of the GnRH neurons in the POA. The number of animals that survived the surgical intervention followed by restoration to the community tank was small, and thus, the

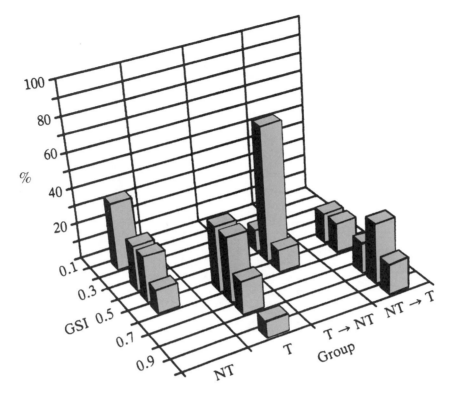

FIGURE 82.4 Comparison of the gonad size between males after a transition between different social states. Three-dimensional representation of gonadosomatic index (GSI) data showing significant differences between T and T≡NT males and between NT and NT≡T males. Percentage of animals within a given 0.2 magnitude range are plotted for each treatment condition. There are no significant differences between T males and their experimental counterparts (NT≡T) or between NT males and their experimental counterparts (T≡NT). (Adapted from Francis, Soma, and Fernald, 1993.)

results are preliminary. They suggest, however, that the GnRH neurons grew to be insignificantly different from those seen in territorial males (Yu and Fernald, unpublished observations, 1998). Thus, through experimental manipulation, it appears that GnRH neuronal soma size and social behavior can be uncoupled.

In *H. burtoni*, the regulation of growth and development may be adaptive in their habitat, where territorial space is limited. In the shore pools where these animals live, only a fraction of the males can breed at any time. As aforementioned, these breeding males appear to be particularly vulnerable to avian predators (Fernald and Hirata, 1977b), and hence territorial ownership may be relatively brief. Thus, there may be a selective advantage for males to have a retarded growth rate until they have an opportunity to become territorial, whereupon they grow rapidly.

Interestingly, after our original observation, we analyzed in more detail the rate at which social interactions influence the GnRH cell size. We recently have shown that the rate of cell size change is a function of the direction of the social transition (Nguyen et al., unpublished observations, 1996). Animals moving from nonterritorial to territorial status achieve the changes in GnRH-containing cell size (cf. figure 82.3) in just 7 days, whereas those animals moving from territorial to nonterritorial may require 4 weeks until completion. This result is intuitively satisfying because there is such a distinct selective advantage to being a territorial male. Preliminary analysis of the behavior of animals that are moving in either direction is quite instructive. Many territorial males that have lost status continue to act territorial, even if only in concealed locations and at times when they are not being scrutinized by the new dominant male.

In sum, these data suggest that external social signals are transduced into at least two different pathways in *H. burtoni* males—one hormonal, determining the reproductive state of the animal, and the other behavioral. While in intact animals, the two pathways are correlated and the hormonal one serves to maintain the relevant physiology that goes along with social state, it is possible to dissociate the circuitry by experimental intervention, for example, castration of nonterritorial males. Further support that the two systems can be dissociated comes from work in *H. burtoni* females in which the social circuit appears to be muted or missing while the endocrine circuitry shows parallel plasticity to that seen in males.

In contrast to males, female *H. burtoni* do not appear to have differences in social status. They spend most of their time at the fringes of the dominant male's territory

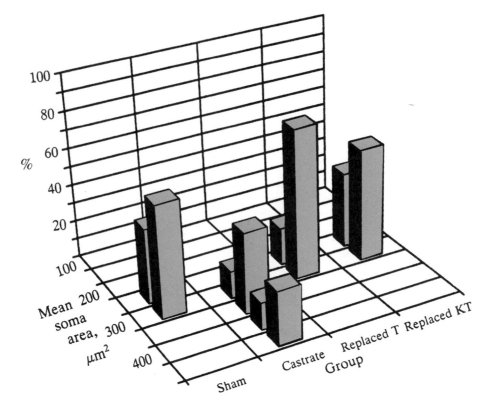

FIGURE 82.5 Relationship of hormonal and social treatments as seen in GnRH-containing cell sizes. Soma area of POA ir-GnRH neurons plotted as a function of experimental treatment. Values shown are mean ± SE. Castrated animals (Castrate, $n = 4$) had significantly larger mean soma areas than intact sham-operated controls (Sham, $n = 5$), and hormonal treatments in castrates had differential effects on POA irGnRH cell size. In castrates treated with testosterone (Castrate + T, $n = 4$) or 11-ketotestosterone (Castrate + KT, $n = 4$), androgen replacement significantly reduced neuronal hypertrophy. In contrast, castrates treated with estradiol (Castrate + E2, $n = 4$) had significantly larger mean somas than the sham group. For each subject, approximately 100 POA irGnRH cells were measured (see Soma et al., 1996, for methods). Groups that are significantly different from the sham group are indicated with an asterisk (*). (Mann-Whitney U test, $p < .05$). (Adapted from Soma et al., 1996.)

FIGURE 82.6 Integration of social and hormonal cues in regulating GnRH-containing cell sizes. Proposed model of GnRH regulation in male *H. burtoni*. Neurons in the hypothalamic preoptic area integrate both social and hormonal signals to regulate GnRH release. In this model, the set point for the GnRH level is determined by social signals, and the maintenance of the GnRH level at this setpoint is achieved by negative feedback from gonadal androgens. (Adapted from Soma et al., 1996.)

where they school with nonterritorial males. As described previously, they move into territorial waters territories only to feed or spawn. This absence of social difference among females prompted the question: Are GnRH neurons in female *H. burtoni* similarly plastic to males and, if so, what regulates changes in cell size? As aforementioned, a ripe female lays her eggs and then takes them into her mouth for fertilization and brooding. The brood is carried for approximately 2 weeks before being released. Changes in female appearance that accompany these reproductive states are due to physiological rather than social events. Thus, differences in body color, which in males reflects reproductive status, do not occur in females. Instead, a female that is ready to spawn has an enlarged abdomen, caused by the presence of ripe eggs. Later, after spawning, females with distinctively large mouth cavities filled with fry are not ready to spawn and avoid males.

Because females do not engage in the aggressive social interactions that drive male GnRH cell size, it is possible that they might not show the same plastic changes. GnRH cell size then would be sexually dimorphic, increasing in females simply as a function of development and becoming stable at maturity. This would contrast with the lifelong potential for plasticity seen in males.

Alternatively, because GnRH cell size in males is correlated with both social and reproductive status, cell size in females might fluctuate according to the female reproductive cycle.

To study possible changes in cell size in female *H. burtoni*, we analyzed cell size as a function of reproductive state in females (White and Fernald, 1993). Although there is some contribution of body size to the cell size changes, body size differences do not account for all the observed changes. Soma sizes in spawning females typically are twice as large as those in females carrying broods (figure 82.7), whereas postreproductive fish have the largest neuronal soma sizes. These changes occur within the 2 weeks it takes to brood a clutch, and the differences in GnRH neuronal soma size are comparable to those seen between dominant and subordinate males.

TRANSDUCTION OF SOCIAL SIGNALS INTO CELLULAR ACTION   It seems clear that social encounters in particular social contexts have a profound effect on the behavior, reproductive potential, and brain structures in *H. burtoni*. How are these behavioral acts transduced into the proper cellular and molecular signals? For social behavior to have consequences in the brain and reproductive system requires an endogenous mediator that fluidly tracks social events and produces a signal, that, when integrated over time, sculpts changes in gene expression. Several lines of evidence suggest that the glucocorticoid stress hormone cortisol might serve this function. First, increased secretion of cortisol is a primary indicator of stress in teleost fish (reviewed in Wendelaar Bonga, Balm, and Lamers, 1995). Changing social settings can produce changes in cortisol levels in mammals (Alberts, Altmann, and Sapolsky, 1992; Gust et al., 1993; Johnson et al., 1996; Manogue, Candland, and Leshner, 1975; Sapolsky, 1986, 1993), birds (Schwabl et al., 1988), and fish (Pottinger, 1992, and reviewed in Billiard, Bry, and Gillet, 1981; Schreck, 1981). Stress suppresses the reproductive axis (reviewed for mammals, Rivier and Rivest, 1991; Sapolsky, 1993; for newts, Moore and Miller, 1984; for fish, Leitz, 1987; Pickering et al., 1987). Finally, stress steroids can alter gene expression by binding to intracellular glucocorticoid receptors, leading to dimerization, nuclear entry, and transcriptional activation or repression of genes bearing consensus elements in their upstream promoter regions (Meisfeld et al., 1986). To understand how social opportunity translates into physiological change in male *H. burtoni*, we manipulated the social setting and measured stress response with cortisol production and reproductive potential with the production of GnRH and gonad size (Fox et al., 1997). Our results show that cortisol levels depend on both individual dominance and reproductive status and social stability,

and that the reproductive opportunity of any individual hinges on temporal features of the social situation.

Support for the hypothesis that cortisol may be a key intermediate factor responsible for converting social interactions into a physiological change is that territorial males have low basal levels of cortisol whereas nonterritorial individuals have more varied and generally higher levels (Fox et al., 1997). Although dominant animals must continuously defend their territories through aggressive interactions with their territorial neighbors, it appears that the ritualized nature of these displays spares them from stress relative to their harassed and nonreproducing counterparts.

To understand the interaction of social behavior and reproductive physiology and brain structure, we compared animals in a variety of social settings over time (Fox et al., 1997). Our results show that in *H. burtoni*, stress depends not only on the social state of the individual, but also on the stability of the social community in which the animal lives. In addition, our data extend previous reports on the relationship between social and reproductive states in male *H. burtoni* into more complex social arenas because in all social settings, Ts had larger irGnRH-containing neurons and GSIs than NTs. Taken together, these results suggest that cortisol may serve as an endogenous signal relating the social environment to an animal's social status or internal reproductive state.

The distinct stress profiles of male fish in different social contexts indicate that cortisol levels responded to social dynamics. In all stable settings, Ts had lower serum cortisol than NTs (figure 82.8), but the emergence of this difference varied depending on the experimental group and the degree of social stability. Among social pairs, the cortisol difference was significant only during the second week of pairing among older fish, suggesting that stress levels decreased in Ts and increased in NTs as social relationships became established. This idea is borne out in community settings, where the development of social stability was explicitly examined. In high-density tanks, fish acclimated for 2 months before the start of the experiment. As a result, societies already were stable when initial observations were made, as seen in the high stability index (1.54; figure 82.8). In these tanks, Ts and NTs had significantly different levels of cortisol overall. In contrast, observations of the low-density tank began early enough to document the establishment of the social hierarchy. Switches in social state initially were frequent as males struggled for dominance. When emergent Ts succeeded in maintaining their territories over several weeks, the stability index increased from below 0.5 to 1.33, close to the stabilized, high-density tanks. At the same time, significant differences between T and NT cortisol levels became apparent. Thus,

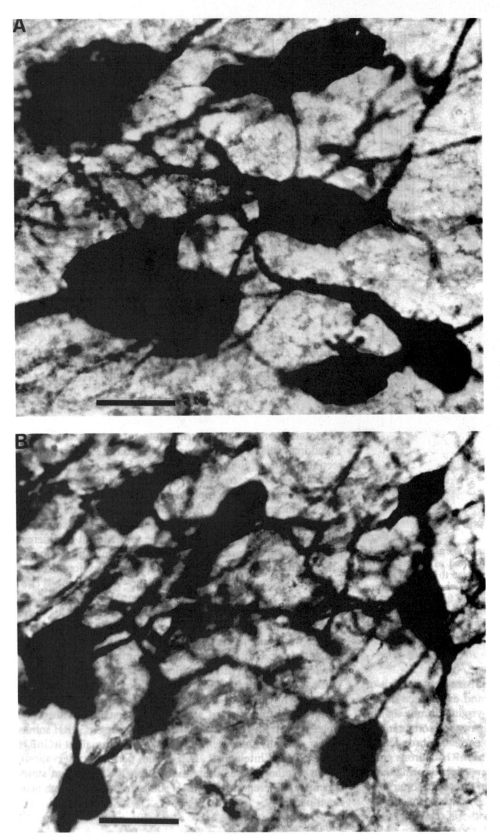

FIGURE 82.7 Comparison of GnRH-containing neurons between spawning and brooding females. Photomicrograph
showing irGnRH cells in a spawning (A) and a brooding (B)
fish. Immunoreactive GnRH cells were labeled with a primary
antibody to GnRH and visualized via a 3,3″-diaminobenzidine
reaction. Scale bars, 20 μm. (Adapted from White and Fernald,
1993).

early in the process of establishing a social hierarchy, both social relationships and rank-related stress levels stabilized.

In addition to corresponding to the social stability of a community, cortisol levels also reflected the social state of individual fish. This is highlighted in the 22 cases in which blood samples were taken before and after each spontaneous switch in social status (figure 82.9). In general, cortisol concentration is a noisy variable, varying widely *between* fish, so it is instructive to compare levels associated with the T and NT state in *the same* individual as it undergoes a social transition. In 18 of these cases, cortisol levels were lower within a male when he was T than when he was NT.

Because cortisol levels both track the dynamics of the overall social scene and correlate with individual social status, it is possible that integration of the cortisol signal could serve as an endogenous determinant of behavioral or reproductive state. If stress physiology predicts social status (Johnson et al., 1996), individuals with lowered cortisol responses should preferentially become dominant. Alternatively, if stress levels *result* from social status, once *any* individual becomes T, he may lead a less stressful life.

The size of GnRH-containing neurons in the POA of male *H. burtoni* also reflects social experience: Ts have significantly larger average neurons than NTs in each of the experimental set-ups tested (Fox et al., 1997). As with cortisol levels, the difference in GnRH neuronal magnitude appears to correspond both to individual social state and to overall social environment. Differences were most extreme when animals were maintained in pairs, followed by fish kept in high-density tanks with stable social structure. Maintenance of fish in a low-density tank showed the smallest, although still significant, difference. Interestingly, soma sizes for both Ts and NTs in community tanks tended to be larger than in the social pairs, raising the possibility that GnRH production scales with social setting. Because cortisol and GnRH cell size each reflect individual and overall social states, it is tempting to speculate that integration of the cortisol signal could lead to changes in GnRH neuronal size. In the hypothalamus, cortisol might produce effects on GnRH neurons directly (Ahima and Harlan, 1992; Chandran et al., 1994); alternatively, the hypothalamic stress factor corticotropin-releasing hormone could influence GnRH cell size (MacLusky, Naftolin, Leranth, 1988; Rivier and Vale, 1984). It should be noted that in birds (Hahn et al., 1995) and reptiles (Denardo and Licht, 1993), it has been proposed that glucocorticosteroids can influence reproductive behavior without inhibiting reproductive hormones. In *H. burtoni*, however, the soma size and behavior are both different between Ts and NTs, which is not consistent with independent action of cortisol directly on behavior.

Future studies using implants either to block or augment cortisol levels should resolve whether and how cortisol might play a role in relating behavioral change to brain change. Further, examining cortisol levels in females who exhibit reproductively regulated cyclical changes in GnRH neuronal soma size but do not exhibit

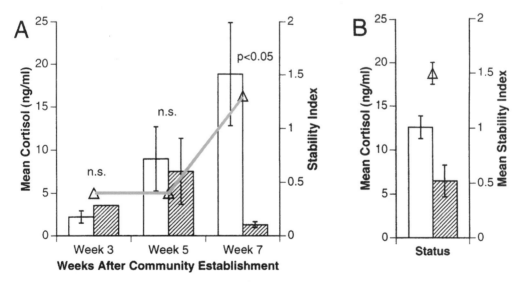

FIGURE 82.8 Stress levels in animals under different social conditions. Cortisol levels of NTs (open bars) and Ts (hatched bars) shown for (A) low-density communities and (B) high-density communities (averaged). In both cases, the stability index (see Materials and Methods) is superimposed on cortisol level data. In the low-density setting, differences in cortisol levels are plotted over the course of 7 weeks. High-density communities had been established for 2 months prior to blood sampling and are fully stabilized. (Redrawn from Fox et al., 1997.)

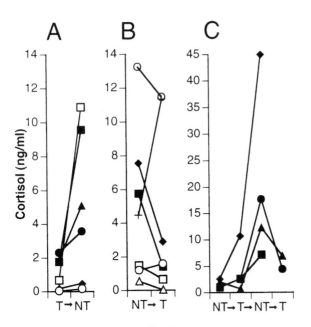

Switches in Status

FIGURE 82.9 Cortisol levels in individual fish that switched social status. (A) Single switches from T to NT. (B) Single switches from NT to T and (C) multiple switches (note different ordinate scale in [C]). Fish had significantly higher cortisol levels as NT than as T ($p < .05$, Wilcoxon signed rank, using last switch if multiple switches per fish). (Redrawn from Fox et al., 1997.)

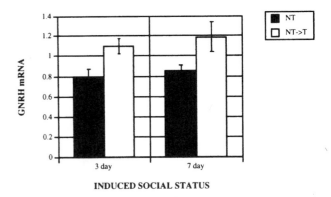

FIGURE 82.10 Levels of GnRH gene expression in males after experimentally induced switches in social state. The mean values of mRNA levels for GnRH-I for males switched from NT≡T status. At both 3 and 7 days after switching, NT≡T males have higher preoptic GnRH mRNA levels than their control NT counterparts.

differences in social rank (White and Fernald, 1993) also could distinguish effects restricted to reproductive, rather than social, states.

MOLECULAR CONSEQUENCES OF SOCIAL CHANGE
One necessary outcome of changes in social status is the regulation of GnRH gene expression. To test the hypothesis that social interactions ultimately regulate reproductive capacity through control of GnRH gene expression requires that social manipulations be combined with molecular measurements. We previously have shown that this fish has three distinct cDNAs that code for GnRH forms, each localized to a separate neuronal population (White et al., 1994, 1995). One of these three genes is expressed in the hypothalamic neurons that change size (GnRH-I), a second in the midbrain (GnRH-II), and a third in the forebrain (GnRH-III). Of these, only the function of GnRH-I, namely controlling reproduction, is known. With these genetic probes, we combined behavioral manipulations with measurement of gene expression to discover whether animals forced to change fate responded with changes in gene expression. In "undisturbed" colonies, T males have higher levels of GnRH-I mRNA than do NT males (White and Fernald, unpublished). Using a paradigm termed "certain fate," we examined the time course of any changes

in gene expression accompanying social change by switching the social states of males and then measuring changes in gene expression in individual animals using RNAse protection assays. Seven days after being moved into a social setting, animals that went from NT≡T had elevated levels of GnRH-I mRNA relative to their NT controls ($p < 0.002$, Mann-Whitney U test, one-tailed; figure 82.10). In contrast, there was no significant difference in expression levels of the other two GnRH forms (White and Fernald, unpublished). These preliminary data show that changing social status causes a change in gene expression that can be measured in individuals. This suggests that we may contemplate connecting behavior to molecular biology in a meaningful way.

This model system has revealed how changes in social state translate into changes at the cellular and molecular levels. However, we still do not know how many signals link the animal's perception of its social status to specific behavioral and endocrine changes.

Neuronal plasticity in the service of behavior

Understanding how behavior influences the brain requires analysis at three important time scales: evolutionary time, developmental time, and real time. The adaptive function of particular behavioral acts shaped over evolutionary and developmental time can suggest where to look for neuronal plasticity in real time, especially in brain regions controlling essential acts such as reproduction. We can expect social specializations in brains of all kinds of organisms. There are likely parts of all vertebrate brains that process social information so that unraveling the pathways that lead from social exchange to structural change within the brain should continue to yield surprising insights about how the environment sculpts behavioral, cellular, and, ultimately, molecular changes in the nervous system.

ACKNOWLEDGMENTS The authors thank their colleagues, Mark Davis, Helen Fox, Mimi Kao, Monica Peterson, Tuan Nguyen, Kenneth Yu, and Irene Yun, for their contributions. This work was supported by NIH NS 34950 to RDF.

REFERENCES

AHIMA, R. S., and R. E. HARLAN, 1992. Glucocorticoid receptors in LHRH neurons. *Neuroendocrinology* 56:845–850.

ALBERTS, S. C., J. ALTMANN, and R. M. SAPOLSKY, 1992. Behavioral, endocrine, and immunological correlates of immigration by an aggressive male into a natural primate group. *Horm. Behav.* 26:163–173.

ARIKAWA, K., D. SUYAMA, and D. FUJII, 1996. Light on butterfly mating. *Nature* 382:119.

ARNOLD, A.P., F. NOTTEBOHM, and D. W. PFAFF, 1976. Hormone concentrating cells in vocal control and other areas of the brain of the zebra finch *Poephila guttata. J. Comp. Neurol.* 165:487–512.

BILLIARD, R., C. BRY, and T. GILLET, 1981. Stress, environment, and reproduction in teleost fish. In *Stress and Fish*, A. D. Pickering, ed. London: Academic Press, pp. 185–208.

BRENOWITZ, E. A., K. LENT, and D. E. KROODSMA, 1995. Brain space for learned song in birds develops independently of song learning. *J. Neurosci.* 15:6281–6286.

BRENOWITZ, E. A., L. F. BAPTISTA, K. LENT, and J. C. WINGFIELD, 1998. Seasonal plasticity of the song control system in wild Nuttall's white-crowned sparrows. *J. Neurobiol.* 341:69–82.

CARDWELL, J. R., and N. R. LILEY, 1991. Androgen control of social status in males of a wild population of stoplight parrotfish, *Sparisome viride Scaridae. Horm. Behav.* 25:1–18.

CATANIA, K. C., and J. H. KAAS, 1995. Organization of the somatosensory cortex of the star-nosed mole. *J. Comp. Neurol.* 351:549–567.

CATANIA, K. C., R. G. NORTHCUTT, J. H. KAAS, and P. D. BECK, 1993. Nose stars and brain stripes. *Nature* 364:493.

CHANDRAN, U., B. ATTARDI, R. FRIEDMAN, K. W. DONG, J. L. ROBERTS, and D. B. DEFRANCO, 1994. Glucocorticoid receptor-mediated repression of gonadotropin-releasing hormone promoter activity in GT1 hypothalamic cell lines. *Endocrinology* 134:1467–1474.

DACOSTA, A. P. C., R. G. GUEVARA-GUZMAN, S. OHKURA, J. A. GOODE, and K. M. KENDRICK, 1996. The role of oxytocin release in the paraventricular nucleus in the control of maternal behaviour in the sheep. *J. Neuroendocrinol.* 8:163–177.

DAVIS, M. R., and R. D. FERNALD, 1990. Social control of neuronal soma size. *J Neurobiol.* 21:1180–1188.

DELACOSTE-UTAMSING, C., and R. L. HOLLOWAY, 1982. Sexual dimorphism in the human corpus callosum. *Science* 216:1431–1432.

DENARDO, D. F, and P. LICHT, 1993. Effects of corticosterone on social behavior of male lizards. *Horm. Behav.* 27:184–199.

FERNALD, R. D., 1977. Quantitative behavioural observations of *Haplochromis burtoni* under semi-natural conditions. *Anim. Behav.* 25:643–653.

FERNALD, R. D., 1984. Vision and behavior in an African cichlid fish. *Am. Sci.* 72:58–65.

FERNALD, R. D., 1989. Seeing through a growing eye. In *Perspectives in Neural Systems and Behavior*, T. J. Carew and D. B. Kelley, eds. New York: Liss, pp. 151–174.

FERNALD, R. D., 1993. Vision. In *The Physiology of Fishes*, D. H. Evans, ed. Boca Raton: CRC Press, pp. 161–189.

FERNALD, R. D, and S. E. WRIGHT, 1985. Growth of the visual system in the African cichlid fish, *Haplochromis burtoni. Vision Rese.* 25:163–170.

FERNALD, R. D., and N. HIRATA, 1977a. Field study of *Haplochromis burtoni*: Habitat and co-habitants. *Environ. Biol. F.* 2:299–308.

FERNALD, R. D., and N. HIRATA, 1977b. Field study of *Haplochromis burtoni*: Quantitative behavioral observations. *Anim. Behav.* 25:964–975.

FERRARI, M. B., M. L. MCANELLY, and H. H. ZAKON, 1995. Individual variation in and androgen-modulation of the sodium current in electric organ. *J. Neurosci.* 15:4023–4032.

FOX, H. E., S. A. WHITE, M. H. F. KAO, and R. D. FERNALD, 1997. Stress and dominance in a social fish. *J. Neurosci.* 17:6463–6469.

FRALEY, N. B., and R. D. FERNALD, 1982. Social control of developmental rate in the African cichlid, *Haplochromis burtoni. Z. Tierpsychol.* 60:66–82.

FRANCIS, R. C., K. K. SOMA, and R. D. FERNALD, 1993. Social regulation of the brain-pituitary-gonadal axis. *Proc. Natl. Acad. Sci. U.S.A.* 90:7794–7798.

GUST, D. A., T. P. GORDON, M. K. HAMBRIGHT, and M. E. WILSON, 1993. Relationship between social factors and pituitary-adrenocortical activity in female rhesus monkeys *Macaca mulatta. Horm. Behav.* 27:318–331.

HAHN, T. P., J. C. WINGFIELD, R. MULLEN, and P. J. DEVICHE, 1995. Endocrine bases of spatial and temporal opportunism in Arctic-breeding birds. *Am. Zool.* 35:259–273.

HATTON, G. I., 1995. Gonadal steroid influences on cell-cell interactions in the magnocellular hypothalamo-neurohypophysial system. In *Neurobiological Effects of Sex Steroid Hormones*, P. E. Micevych and R. P. Hammer, Jr., eds. New York: Cambridge University Press, pp. 412–431.

HOLLOWAY, R. L., and M. C. DELACOSTE, 1986. Sexual dimorphism in the human corpus callosum: An extension and replication study. *Hum. Neurobiol.* 5:87–91.

JOHNS, P. R., and R. D. FERNALD, 1981. Genesis of rods in teleost fish retina. *Nature* 293:141–142.

JOHNSON, E. O., T. C. KAMILARIS, C. S. CARTER, A. E. CALOGERO, P. W. GOLD, and G. P. CHROUSOS, 1996. The behavioral consequences of psychogenic stress in a small, social primate *Callithrix jacchus jaccus. Biol. Psychol.* 40:317–337.

KENDRICK, K.M., F. LEVY, and E. B. KEVERNE, 1992. Changes in the sensory processing of olfactory signals induced by birth in sleep. *Science* 256:833–836.

LEITZ, T. 1987. Social control of testicular steroidogenic capacities in the Siamese fighting fish *Betta splendens* Regan. *J. Exp. Zool.* 244:473–478.

LORENZ, K, 1935. Der Kumpan in der Umwelt des Vogels. *J. f. Ornithologie* 80, Heft 2.

MACLUSKY, N. J., F. NAFTOLIN, and C. LERANTH, 1988. Immunocytochemical evidence for direct synaptic connections between corticotropin-releasing factor CRF and gonadotropin-releasing hormone GnRH-containing neurons in the preoptic area of the rat. *Brain Res.* 439:391–395.

MANOGUE, K., D. CANDLAND, and A. LESHNER, 1975. Dominance status and adrenocortical reactivity to stress in squirrel monkeys *Saimiri scuireus. Primates* 16:457–463.

MEISFELD, R., S. RUSCONI, P. J. GODOWSKI, B. A. MALER, S. OKRET, A. C. WIKSTROM, J.-A. FUSTAFSSON, and K. R. YAMOMOTO, 1986. Genetic complementation of a glucocorticoid receptor deficiency by expression of cloned receptor cDNA. *Cell* 46:369–399.

MEISTER, R., R. O. L. WONG, D. A. BAYLOR, and C. J. SHATZ, 1991. Synchronous bursts of action potentials in ganglion cells of the developing mammalian retina. *Science* 252:939–943.

MOORE, F. L., and L. J. MILLER, 1984. Stress-induced inhibition of sexual behavior: corticosterone inhibits courtship behaviors of a male amphibian *Taricha graulosa. Horm. Behav.* 18:400–410.

MUSKE, L., and R. D. FERNALD, 1987. Control of a teleost social signal: II. Anatomical and physiological specializations of chromatophores. *J. Comp. Physiol. A* 160:99–107.

NUDO, R. J., G. W. MILLIKEN, W. M. JENKINS, and M. M. MERZENICH, 1996. Use-dependent alterations of movement representations in primary motor cortex of adult squirrel monkeys. *J. Neurosci.* 16:785–807.

PHOENIX, C. H., R. W. GOY, A. A. GERALL, and W. C. YOUNG, 1959. Organizing action of prenatally administered testosterone propionate on the tissues mediating mating behavior in the female guinea pig. *Endocrinology* 65:369–382.

PICKERING, A. D., T. G. POTTINGER, J. CARRAGHER, and J. P. SUMPTER, 1987. The effects of acute and chronic stress on the levels of reproductive hormones in the plasma of mature male brown trout. *Gen. Comp. Endocrinol.* 68:249–259.

POINDRON, P., F. LEVY, and D. KREHBIEL, 1988. Genital, olfactory, and endocrine interactions in the development of maternal-behavior in the parturient ewe. *Psychoneuroendocrinology* 13:99–125.

POTTINGER, T. G. 1992. The influence of social interaction on the acclimation of rainbow trout, *Oncorhynchus mykiss* Walbaum to chronic stress. *J. Fish Biol.* 41:435–447.

RIVIER, C., and S. RIVEST, 1991. Effect of stress on the activity of the hypothalamic-pituitary-gonadal axis: peripheral and central mechanisms. *Biol. Reprod.* 45:523–532.

RIVIER, C., and W. VALE, 1984. Influence of corticotropin-releasing factor on reproductive functions in the rat. *Endocrinology* 114:914–921.

SAPOLSKY, R. M., 1986. Endocrine and behavioral correlates of drought in wild olive baboons *Papio anubis. Am. J. Primatol.* 11:217–227.

SAPOLSKY, R. M., 1993. Endocrinology alfresco: Psychoendocrine studies of wild baboons. In *Recent Progress in Hormone Research*, Vol. 48, Laurentian Hormone Conference, C. W. Bardin, ed. San Diego, Calif.: Academic Press, pp. 437–468.

SCHRECK, C., 1981. Stress and compensation in teleostan fishes: Responses to social and physical factors. In *Stress and Fish*, A. D. Pickering, ed. London: Academic Press, pp. 295–321.

SCHWABL, H., M. RAMENOFSKY, I. SCHWABL-BENZINGER, D. S. FARNER, and J. C. WINGFIELD, 1988. Social status, circulating levels of hormones, and competition for food in winter flocks of the white-throated sparrow. *Behavior* 107:107–121.

SOMA, K. K., R. C. FRANCIS, J. C. WINGFIELD, and R. D. FERNALD, 1996. Androgen regulation of hypothalamic neurons containing gonadotropin-releasing hormone in a cichlid fish: Integration with social cues. *Horm. Behav.* 30:216–226.

VON UEXKÜLL, J., 1909. *Umwelt und Innenleben der Tiere.* Berlin: Springer-Verlag.

WENDELAAR-BONGA, S. E., P. H. M. BALM, and A. E. LAMERS, 1995. The involvement of ACTH and MSH in the stress response in teleost fish. *Neth. J. Zool.* 45:103–106.

WHITE, S. A., C. T. BOND, R. C. FRANCIS, T. L. KASTEN, R. D. FERNALD, and J. P. ADELMAN, 1994. A second gene for GnRH: cDNA and pattern of expression. *Proc. Natl. Acad. Sci. U.S.A.* 91:1423–1427.

WHITE, S. A., and R. D. FERNALD, 1993. Gonadotropin-releasing hormone-containing neurons change size with reproductive state in female *Haplochromis burtoni. J. Neurosci.* 13:434–441.

WHITE, S. A., T. L. KASTEN, C. T. BOND, J. P. ADELMAN, and R. D. FERNALD, 1995. Three gonadotropin-releasing hormone genes in one organism suggest novel roles for an ancient peptide. *Proc. Natl. Acad. Sci. U.S.A.* 92:8363–8367.

WINGFIELD, J. C., R. E. HEGNER, A. M. DUFTY, JR., and G. F. BALL, 1990. The "challenge hypothesis": Theoretical implications for patterns of testosterone secretion, mating systems, and breeding strategies. *Am. Naturalist* 136:829–847.

XERRI, C., J. M. STERN, and M. M. MERZENICH, 1994. Alterations of the cortical representation of the rat ventrum induced by nursing behavior. *J. Neurosci.* 14:1710–1721.

ZAKON, H. H. 1996. Hormonal modulation of communication signals in electric fish. *Devel. Neurosci.* 18:115–123.

83 What Sex Differences in Spatial Ability Tell Us about the Evolution of Cognition

DAVID F. SHERRY

ABSTRACT   Human cognition is a collection of adaptations shaped by the selective pressures to which we have been exposed during our evolutionary history. Identifying these selective pressures, however, and determining the selective advantages conferred by the properties of human cognition is not easy. Sex differences in human spatial ability provide an opportunity to test evolutionary hypotheses about the evolution of human cognition. Men tend to perform better than women do on some tests of spatial ability, and sex differences in spatial ability occur in a variety of nonhuman animals. Males tend to perform better than females on tests of spatial ability in species of mammals in which males possess larger home ranges than females during the breeding season. These sex differences in spatial behavior and cognition are accompanied by a sex difference, in favor of males, in the relative size of the hippocampus. In species in which females are more active in spatial search than males, females possess a larger hippocampus than males. These results suggest that spatial ability and relative size of the hippocampus are evolutionary adaptations associated with spatial behavior and orientation. Findings with animals raise the question of whether sex differences in humans also may be adaptations to sex differences in spatial behavior. Men have larger home ranges than women do, and spatial ability in humans is sensitive to the effects of both testosterone and estrogen. These results suggest that sex differences in human spatial ability are the product of both natural selection and sexual selection and provide some insight into the evolutionary pressures that influenced the evolution of human cognition.

Sex differences in human reproductive behavior and physiology are not particularly controversial. Their existence, at any rate, is not a matter of dispute. Sex differences in cognition are a different matter and are debated hotly (Caplan, MacPherson, and Tobin, 1985). In the area of spatial ability, however, the existence of a consistent sex difference in performance is well established (Voyer, Voyer, and Bryden, 1995). On some tests of spatial ability, such as the Vandenberg version of the Shepard-Metzler Mental Rotations Test (Vandenberg, 1971), the mean performance of men can be as much as one standard deviation greater than the mean performance of women.

DAVID F. SHERRY   Department of Psychology, University of Western Ontario, London, Ontario, Canada

Alleged sex differences in human behavior and cognition sometimes are solely in the eye of the beholder and reflect nothing more than societal expectations and biases. Sex differences with a firm empirical foundation, in contrast, invite a search for their origin. In this chapter, I introduce evolutionary arguments that sex differences in human spatial ability, like sex differences in spatial ability in other animals, are a consequence of evolved differences in the reproductive roles of the two sexes. Sex differences in spatial ability are one among many legacies of our evolutionary origin and can help us understand why our cognitive apparatus takes the form it does. Human cognition in all its complexity is an adaptation, or more accurately, a host of adaptations, shaped by natural selection to deal with specific problems in our environment of evolutionary adaptedness ([EEA]; Tooby and De Vore, 1987). Sex differences may be a window through which we can glimpse our long-vanished EEA. Sex differences in human spatial ability are consistent with some, but not all, conjectures about human origins and may in this way provide insights about the evolution of human cognition.

The chapter begins with a discussion of spatial orientation in animals that illustrates the relation between reproductive behavior, home range, and spatial ability. This example, taken from the work of Gaulin and colleagues on *Microtus* voles, also introduces the topic of sexual selection and sexual selection for spatial abilities. In some voles, as in humans, males perform better than females on laboratory tests of spatial ability. A correlated sex difference is found in voles in the size of the hippocampus, a structure involved in a variety of cognitive functions, including spatial orientation. Superior performance by males on spatial tests is by no means universal, however, as shown by the second example. In brood parasitic cowbirds, females search for host nests and experience greater demands on spatial ability than males. The consequences of this sex difference in behavior are reflected in a sex difference in the size of the hippocampus that is the reverse of that found in voles: Female cowbirds have a larger hippocampus than males. In the final part of the chapter, I return to human sex differences, present the evolutionary hypotheses that have been proposed for their origin, and describe how recent research on hormonal influences on human spatial abilities can be used to test these hypotheses.

Mating system, spatial ability, and the hippocampus

HOME RANGE SIZE AND SPATIAL ABILITY IN VOLES Most voles in the genus *Microtus* are polygynous. The meadow vole (*M. pennsylvanicus*) is typical. During the breeding season, males expand their home ranges to encompass the home ranges of a number of females. Males compete with each other for mating opportunities by ranging widely and thereby encountering greater numbers of females. Female meadow voles gain no reproductive advantage by increasing the number of their mates–additional matings do not produce additional offspring–and their home ranges are considerably smaller than those of breeding males, approximately 200 m^2 compared with male home ranges of 600 m^2 or more (Gaulin and FitzGerald, 1986). Outside the breeding season, male meadow vole home ranges are the same size as those of females.

A few species of *Microtus* voles, however, like the pine vole (*M. pinetorum*) and the prairie vole (*M. ochrogaster*), are monogamous. Male and female pine vole home ranges are the same size, approximately 40 m^2, and mated pairs remain together on a territory they share with juveniles and subadults (FitzGerald and Madison, 1983). Male and female prairie vole home ranges are likewise the same size, approximately 200 m^2, and are shared by a male and female, both of whom provide parental care and exclude other adult prairie voles from the territory (Gaulin and FitzGerald, 1989). In a monogamous mating system, males gain no reproductive advantage from having a larger home range than females. Females that they encounter likely are mated already, and male reproductive success in a monogamous mating system is influenced more by the quality of parental care provided to the young than by the number of mating opportunities.

These differences in breeding system led Steven Gaulin and his colleagues to make a number of predictions about the evolution of spatial ability in voles; voles were selected as study organisms because evolutionary thinking indicated that they might be a particularly informative group of animals to examine. It may be that sex differences in spatial ability are an intrinsic part of male and female development, a consequence of how male and female brains develop. Alternatively, and this was Gaulin's line of reasoning, sex differences in spatial ability might occur only when there is selection for spatial ability that is specific to one sex only. Only under

these conditions would superior spatial ability in one sex be expected. In the absence of sex-specific selection, there should be no sex difference in spatial ability. Thus, the predictions were that male meadow voles should have better spatial ability than females because of selection to navigate successfully their large home ranges, whereas in the monogamous species there should be no sex difference in spatial ability.

A series of studies showed that male meadow voles perform better than females on a variety of laboratory maze tasks, although there is no sex difference in maze performance in either pine voles or prairie voles (Gaulin and FitzGerald, 1986; Gaulin and FitzGerald, 1989; Gaulin, FitzGerald, and Wartell, 1990). Superior spatial performance by males is a typical mammalian pattern. What is particularly striking is that in a monogamous breeding system, in which there is no selection for greater home range size in males, there is no difference in spatial ability. Sex-specific selection for range size in the polygynous breeding system of meadow voles is likely to be the origin of the sex difference in spatial ability observed in this species. Further experiments have shown that sex and species differences in the level of activity in the mazes cannot account for the occurrence of a sex difference in the polygynous species and its absence in the monogamous species (Gaulin, FitzGerald, and Wartell, 1990). Experiments also showed that vastly different amounts of spatial experience in laboratory-reared and wild caught prairie voles did not affect their maze performance (Gaulin and Wartell, 1990). The performance of males and females (which does not differ in this monogamous species) was not affected by experience with different-sized home ranges.

The difference in spatial ability between male and female meadow voles has evolved by sexual selection. Sexual selection, according to Darwin, accounts for the evolution of traits that contribute little to survival or longevity but instead provide an advantage solely in competition for mates. Sexual selection can be of two forms–traits that provide an advantage in contests with members of the same sex for access to mates and traits that increase reproductive success because individuals with the trait are preferred as mates by members of the opposite sex. The antlers of deer may have evolved because they provide males with an advantage in direct competition with other males, a process called intrasexual selection. The elaborate displays of birds of paradise may have evolved because males performing these displays are preferred as mates by females, a process called intersexual or epigamic selection (Andersson, 1994). The spatial abilities of male meadow voles thus are likely to have evolved under the influence of intrasexual selection because males compete for mates in the polygynous meadow vole breeding system by traversing large home ranges in search of females.

Darwin proposed that if a trait had evolved by sexual selection, it would be expected to have some further properties. It obviously should develop to a greater degree in one sex than the other, it might be expected to appear at sexual maturity *not* before, its occurrence may be restricted to the breeding season, and it should be displayed to rivals or mates. These properties do not apply to all sexually selected traits. Sexually selected dimorphism in body size, for example, does not disappear outside the breeding season. The last property, concerning display, does not apply particularly well to male meadow voles' territories because the competition that male meadow voles engage in by having large home ranges is somewhat indirect. Indeed, competing males may never encounter each other. The first three properties expected under sexual selection, however, have been examined in some detail in voles. Territory size and spatial ability, as we have seen, are greater in male meadow voles than in females. Nonreproductive male meadow voles, as determined by examination of the testes, and males observed outside the breeding season, have territories approximately the same size as those of females (Gaulin and FitzGerald, 1988; Gaulin and FitzGerald, 1989).

In another polygynous breeding rodent, the deer mouse (*Peromyscus maniculatus*), males also have larger home ranges than females during the breeding season. Males in breeding condition acquire the Morris water maze task more quickly than females do, although outside the breeding season the sexes do not differ in their performance on the water maze (Galea et al., 1994; Galea, Kavaliers, and Ossenkopp, 1996). Galea and colleagues found, however, that the sex difference during breeding is due only in part to an improvement in male performance; part of the effect is due to a decline in performance by breeding females. The latter outcome is not predicted by sexual selection for spatial ability in males, although as we shall see later, it resembles one of the most interesting results in recent research on sex differences in human spatial ability.

SEX DIFFERENCES IN THE HIPPOCAMPUS Male meadow voles not only have larger home ranges and better spatial ability than females, they also have a different brain. In particular, they have a larger hippocampus than females, a sex difference that does not occur in the monogamous pine vole (Jacobs et al., 1990). This sex difference in hippocampal size, which is greater than expected on the basis of sex differences in brain size and body size, suggests that sexual selection on males in the polygynous meadow vole breeding system has had a se-

ries of propagating effects. Selection for increased home range size in males, spatial ability adequate to navigate this home range, and a hippocampus modified to cope with the navigational problems of a larger home range has produced a suite of interacting behavioral, cognitive, and neural traits. Merriam's and bannertail kangaroo rats (*Dipodomys merriami* and *D. spectabilis*) also breed polygynously and exhibit a sex difference in home range size, the home ranges of males being larger than those of females. As with meadow voles, males have a larger hippocampus than females in both species of kangaroo rat (Jacobs and Spencer, 1994). Male mongolian gerbils (*Meriones unguiculatus*) have a larger home range than females in the wild (Ågren, Zhou, and Zhong, 1989) and a larger hippocampus (Sherry, Galef, and Clark, 1996).

Brood parasitism and the hippocampus of cowbirds

The female brown-headed cowbird (*Molothrus ater*) is a very drab-looking bird, even by blackbird standards: grey-brown above with a hint of streaking on the breast and a throat slightly paler than the rest. The eponymous male is a striking iridescent black with a chocolate-brown head. The common names of birds typically show such male sex bias. But the brain and behavior of cowbirds exhibit a sex difference that not only runs counter to appearances, but also illustrates a general point about sex differences in spatial cognition.

Brown-headed cowbirds are brood parasites. Females lay approximately 40 eggs a year in the nests of other species (Scott and Ankney, 1980; Scott and Ankney, 1983) that then are hatched and raised by the host, usually at a cost to the host in the number of its own young that it can rear. Brown-headed cowbirds exploit more than 200 host species, capitalizing on the failure of the adoptive parents to discriminate a cowbird egg or nestling from their own. Female cowbirds search for potential host nests unassisted by males. Females have been observed sitting silently in the forest canopy watching nest building by potential hosts, walking on the forest floor scanning the canopy, and flying noisily into understorey shrubs, presumably to flush incubating birds from their nests (Norman and Robertson, 1975). Synchronizing laying with the stage of progress of the host nest is important for cowbirds. Placing an egg in a nest under construction can cause the host to simply cover it over with nest material, or desert the semicompleted nest and start another. Laying too late in the host's nesting cycle can result in the cowbird egg being abandoned when the host's young hatch and fledge. Female cowbirds evidently prefer a nest containing at least one but not more than two host eggs (King, 1979), although they are prolific layers and often place eggs in less than ideal sites.

Females lay at or before dawn, then spend the rest of the morning searching for host nests before leaving the forest and edge habitats, where most host nests are found, to feed with males in grain fields and livestock yards often far from areas with potential host nests. Females probably travel at dawn to a nest or nests that they have located on a previous day and lay an egg quickly during the incubating parent's absence. There is little time in the early light of day to search for a suitable host nest, and females likely lay in nests that they have located previously.

All this leads to the conclusion that female cowbirds probably remember for at least 1 day, and possibly many days, the spatial locations of some number of suitable host nests. Males do not participate in the search for host nests, but instead follow females in their daily routine. We hypothesized that natural selection for the ability to locate and remember the locations of potential host nests may have affected spatial ability and the brain of female cowbirds in a way that has not occurred in males (Sherry et al., 1993). Specifically, we proposed that the hippocampus of female cowbirds would be larger than that of males, after allowing for any sex difference in overall brain or body size.

To determine whether any sex difference in hippocampal size that might be found in cowbirds is related to search for host nests by females requires some further information. Perhaps the hippocampus is larger in females in all blackbirds, or in all birds for that matter. As with the effects of breeding system on spatial ability in voles, the appropriate way to answer this question is comparatively. We compared the hippocampi of males and females in two species of blackbirds that are not brood parasites, red-winged blackbirds (*Agelaius phoeniceus*) and common grackles (*Quiscalus quiscula*). Red-winged blackbirds, grackles, and cowbirds are all members of the same tribe, Agelaiini, within the same blackbird subfamily, the Icterinae. The logic of this comparative analysis is that with a shared phylogenetic history, differences between species can be attributed more readily to current ecological or behavioral differences between the species, in this case brood parasitism (Harvey and Krebs, 1990).

The results showed that the hippocampus of female brown-headed cowbirds was, in fact, significantly larger than that of males and that this difference was greater than could be attributed to sex differences in brain size or body size. Neither red-winged blackbirds nor common grackles showed any indication of a sex difference in hippocampal size (Sherry et al., 1993).

What is striking about this result is that the direction of the sex difference runs counter to all previously reported sex differences in hippocampal size. In meadow voles, deer mice, kangaroo rats, gerbils, and other mammals the sex differences that occur in hippocampal size favor males. As we saw earlier, this sex difference probably is a consequence of selection on males for large home ranges and matching spatial ability. The occurrence of greater hippocampal size in female cowbirds shows that it is not sex per se that determines hippocampal size, but an evolutionary history of differential use of space by the two sexes. When females are the sex with greater demands on spatial ability, as in cowbirds, they are the sex found with a relatively larger hippocampus.

Altogether, six species of cowbird are found in the New World. The shiny cowbird (*Molothrus bonariensis*) is a generalist parasite, like the brown-headed cowbird. Shiny cowbirds parasitize more than 150 different species of host, and females search for potential host nests without male assistance (Mason, 1987). The screaming cowbird (*M. rufoaxillaris*), in contrast, is a specialist. It parasitizes only one species, and this species is itself a cowbird, the bay-winged cowbird (*M. badius*). Male and female screaming cowbirds search together for bay-winged cowbird nests (Mason, 1987), and this cooperative search behavior, in contrast to search by females only in brown-headed and shiny cowbirds, reasonably might be expected to eliminate any sex difference in the hippocampus due to sex-specific spatial behavior. Bay-winged cowbirds, the sole host of screaming cowbirds, are not nest parasites but incubate their own eggs and raise their own young (Fraga, 1991). Bay-winged cowbirds nest colonially, however, and sometimes usurp the nests of other colony members. Two remaining species, the bronzed cowbird (*M. aeneus*) and the giant cowbird (*Scaphidura oryzivora*) parasitize intermediate numbers of hosts, approximately 40 to 50, but they play no further part in this story.

Shiny, screaming, and bay-winged cowbirds are all found in Argentina and were collected in the field during the breeding season by Reboreda and colleagues (1996). They determined the size of the hippocampus in males and females of all three species and found that, overall, the hippocampus was larger relative to the size of the forebrain in the two brood parasites than in the nonparasitic bay-winged cowbird. As predicted, females had a larger hippocampus than males only in the shiny cowbird, the generalist parasite in which females search alone for host nests. No sex difference in relative hippocampal size occurred in screaming cowbirds, the specialist brood parasite in which both sexes search for host nests, or in the nonparasitic bay-winged cowbird. Similarly, in other passerines birds in which there are no ecological or evolutionary reasons to expect a sex difference in spatial behavior, like the black-capped chickadee

THE TYPICAL SEX DIFFERENCE ON THE MENTAL ROTATION TEST

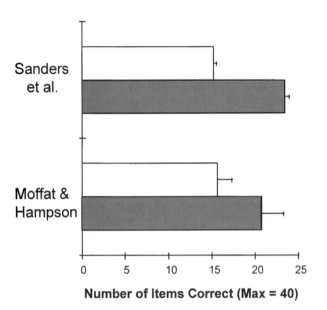

Number of Items Correct (Max = 40)

THE SEX DIFFERENCE IN HEIGHT OF ADULT MEN AND WOMEN

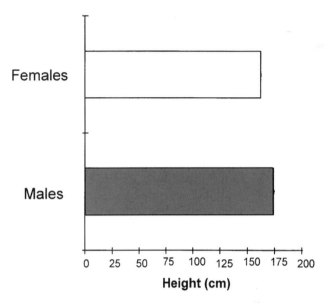

Height (cm)

FIGURE 83.1   The sex difference in human spatial ability can be large on some tests, even compared with morphological sex differences such as height. Performance of adult men and women on the Vandenberg version of the Shepard-Metzler mental rotation test is shown for two representative studies (left). The mean score for women ($N = 672$) was 65% of that for men ($N = 359$) in the study by Sanders and associates (1982).

The mean score for women ($N = 19$) was 75% of that for men ($N = 19$) in the study by Moffat and Hampson (1996). The mean height (right) of women is 93% that of men (Tanner, 1990). Error bars equal 1 standard error of the mean and are too small to appear in the height data. (Reprinted from Sherry and Hampson, 1997.)

(*Parus atricapillus*), no sex difference occurs in the size of the hippocampus (Petersen and Sherry, 1996).

Sex differences in human spatial ability

In humans, men and boys generally perform better on standardized tests of spatial ability than women and girls do. Although there is debate about the origin and correct interpretation of this difference, a meta-analysis by Voyer and associates (1995) shows that it is reported consistently in experimental work. Males typically perform better than females on tests such as the Shepard-Metzler task, which requires subjects to view a drawing of a three-dimensional object and then indicate in multiple-choice fashion which of several drawings portray possible rotations of the original object. Sex differences on tasks such as this are reliable and have remarkably large effect sizes (figure 83.1).

It probably is no coincidence that men and boys have greater home ranges than women and girls do (Gaulin and Hoffman, 1987). Fossil evidence of the modification of human limb bones by the loads due to locomotion and similar modification in the bones of contemporary humans, indicate greater ranges in males than in females from the middle Paleolithic to the present (Ruff, 1987).

In both contemporary urban societies and in developing countries, men have larger home ranges than women (Munroe and Munroe, 1971; Dab and Robert, 1997).

The relations among performance on standardized tests of spatial ability, range size, and navigation in humans is not entirely clear. Males could show better performance on standardized tasks because they have larger ranges and more real-world spatial experience, or males could have larger ranges and more spatial experience because they are better at the kind of problems measured in standard tests. It also should be emphasized that paper-and-pencil tests of spatial ability are not necessarily measures of the capacity for real-world orientation and navigation. They may measure spatial abilities that are quite independent of the cognitive capacities required for orientation and navigation within a home range. The picture is not entirely discouraging, however. Performance on standardized mental rotation tasks is correlated with performance on slightly more realistic navigation problems, such as navigation through a virtual environment presented on a computer screen (Moffat, Hampson, and Hatzpantelis, 1998), and range size is correlated, at least in males, with performance on standardized tests (Dab and Robert, 1997). Nevertheless, further research on the relation between paper-and-pencil tests of spatial ability and navigation and orientation by humans clearly is required.

With these provisos in mind, it nonetheless is notable that observations on sex differences in spatial ability and home range size in polygynous mammals raise the possibility that there may be an evolutionary explanation for sex differences in human spatial ability. It is possible that in the environment of evolutionary adaptedness, human males and females were exposed with some consistency to differential selection for spatial ability and that one effect of such selection is a sex difference among contemporary humans in performance on spatial tasks in the laboratory. Elizabeth Hampson and I recently assembled seven evolutionary hypotheses that have been advanced to account for sex differences in human spatial abilities (Sherry and Hampson, 1997). Three of these hypotheses propose that the sex difference is a consequence of sexual selection for increased range size in males. Two propose that the sex difference is the outcome of a division of labor between the sexes in foraging. Two further hypotheses propose that life history differences between the sexes, specifically dispersal and reproductive roles, have selected for a sex difference in spatial ability.

SEXUAL SELECTION Gaulin has extended ideas derived from work on rodent breeding systems to humans by noting that humans are polygynous to some degree, that increased mating opportunities may be available to human males by increasing their range size, and that males do indeed have larger home ranges than females (Gaulin, 1992). Competition among males for mates thus may have resulted in sexual selection for spatial ability in human males, an effect that has not occurred in human females. Females, unlike males, do not obtain an increase in the number of their offspring from an increase in the number of mates and so are less exposed to the effects of intrasexual competition for mates.

Another sexual selection hypothesis suggests that human males benefited evolutionarily from increased range size, but in this case, the function of increased range size was to attack other groups to decrease local competition for resources or to obtain mates (Alexander, 1979). Thus male warfare also might impose selection restricted to males on spatial ability and cognition.

Finally, epigamic sexual selection, based on female choice for mates, may have selected for male spatial ability. The anthropologist Kirsten Hawkes has made the interesting observation that in some societies, the benefit of male hunting success is not provision of meat to the hunter and his immediate family but instead an increase in status for the hunter, obtained by distributing meat to other members of the group (Hawkes, 1990; Hawkes, 1991). The nutritional benefits to the hunter and his family may be insignificant. What is significant is that successful male hunters enjoy high status and are sought after as mates. In this scenario, sexual selection acts through female choice. Hunting, with its associated ranging ability and spatial skills, becomes a sexually selected display, more akin to the display of male birds of paradise than to the competitive ranging behavior of male meadow voles.

FORAGING A division of labor between the sexes in foraging occurs in hunter–gather societies: males usually, but not always, range more widely to capture game whereas females search for nonmobile foods. Superior male spatial ability in this hypothesis is attributed to sex-specific selection on males for long-range navigation and possibly throwing skills (Lovejoy, 1981; Jardine and Martin, 1983).

An interesting variation on the foraging hypothesis proposes that females should show superiority on spatial tasks that correspond more closely to foraging tasks performed by females than do the usual tests of spatial ability (Silverman and Eals, 1992; Eals and Silverman, 1994). Silverman and colleagues have shown that women perform better than men on tests that require remembering the location of objects in a spatial array and detecting when the location of these objects has been changed. Tasks of this kind have not been widely used to examine sex differences in spatial ability but clearly suggest that spatial ability and sex differences in spatial ability may not be all of a kind.

LIFE HISTORY Dispersal from the place of birth to the eventual site of adult residence is sex biased in many birds and mammals (Greenwood, 1980). In mating systems in which defense of a resource, such as a territory, is essential for mating, females tend to disperse during the late juvenile or early adult period whereas males remain in the natal area. In mating systems that depend on the physical defence of mates rather than resources, males tend to disperse and females remain in the natal area. It thus has been suggested that sex-biased dispersal, and the demands it makes on orientation, may be responsible for sex differences in spatial ability. This hypothesis is difficult to sustain for humans because although it clearly supposes selection for superior spatial ability in the sex that disperses, in humans it is females that disperse farther than males between birth and adult mating and child-rearing (Koenig, 1989; Clarke and Low, 1992). This effect can be observed in a variety of cultures and is apparent even in contemporary North America. It is also probably an oversimplification to suppose that animal dispersal, in which late juvenile and early adult animals leave the natal area in search of suitable habitat elsewhere, is an appropriate model for human dispersal. In humans, dispersal by females is likely to always have occurred along established routes of contact between groups, probably under the control of male kin, and not by a process of cross-country orienteering.

Pregnancy, lactation, and parental care are life history traits that differ between the sexes in humans and may have had important effects on human spatial ability. Under this hypothesis, a large home range was selected against in women because a large home range and a high degree of mobility may impose energetic costs that reduce fertility, interfere with cyclicity, and compromise pregnancy and parental care (Sherry and Hampson, 1997). A reduction in mobility at critical times during the reproductive life of women might provide benefits in terms of reduced risk of predation, accident, encounter with males of other groups, and other possible hazards. This hypothesis thus supposes that spatial ability is not so much enhanced in males as reduced in females because of the sex-specific advantage to females of reduced range size.

TESTING THE HYPOTHESES   Although the evolutionary origins of sex-specific human spatial abilities are remote and seemingly inaccessible, recent research on development and hormonal influences on human spatial abilities provide data that can be used to test some of these ideas about the evolutionary origin of sex differences in human spatial ability.

As mentioned earlier, Darwin believed that traits that have evolved by sexual selection should tend to appear at sexual maturity, not before. Therefore, the sexual selection hypotheses all predict that the advantage in male spatial ability should emerge at sexual maturity and perhaps exhibit some effect of testosterone in males.

In their meta-analysis, Voyer and associates (1995) grouped subjects by age in three categories: under 13 years of age, 13 to 18 years, and older than 18 years of age. For mental rotation tasks, the sex difference is significant in all three age groups, but the effect size increases with age. For tests of spatial perception, the effect size also increases across the three groups. The sex difference is significant at 13 to 18 years, and older than 18 years, but not under 13 years. For spatial visualization, the effect size likewise increases across age groups, but the sex difference is only significant for the older than 18 years group. There thus appears to be some indication that the sexes diverge in spatial ability around the age of puberty, as predicted by the sexual selection hypotheses, although the data do not permit a positive identification of its onset with the timing of puberty in

males. If anything, the age of onset in early, rather than late, adolescence may correspond more closely to puberty in girls than in boys.

Hormonal data show that testosterone can have an enhancing effect on human spatial ability. Some of these androgenic effects are revealed by the effects on spatial ability in girls of high androgen levels experienced in utero. Androgen levels at the high end of the normal range of variation during pregnancy (Grimshaw, Sitarenios, and Finegan, 1995) and androgens produced by a male twin (Cole-Harding, Morstad, and Wilson, 1988) both lead to greater spatial abilities in girls. Abnormally high androgen levels produced by congenital adrenal hyperplasia (CAH) produce enhanced spatial abilities in girls (Hampson, Rovet, and Altmann, 1998) and adolescent women (Resnick et al., 1986). In adults, exogenous testosterone also can produce improved spatial abilities. Therapeutic administration of testosterone to adult transsexuals (Van Goozen et al., 1995) and to men aged 60 to 75 years (Janowsky, Oviatt, and Orwoll, 1994) both produced improved spatial abilities. All these data sources clearly indicate an effect of male hormones, as predicted by the sexual selection hypotheses.

The foraging hypotheses make no predictions about the pattern spatial abilities should show across the life span or how hormonal variation might influence the occurrence of a sex difference in human spatial abilities. Without additional assumptions about age-related changes in the division of labor for foraging or endocrine effects on foraging, the absence of any specific predictions for the foraging hypotheses means that they are unable to account for existing data on hormonal effects on the sex difference in human spatial abilities.

The dispersal hypothesis, as noted previously, predicts greater spatial ability in women than in men. It predicts that this female superiority should emerge in the late juvenile or early adult period, and if followed strictly, predicts that there may be little sex difference in human spatial ability after the dispersal phase. This hypothesis clearly is contradicted by the nature of the sex difference in human spatial ability and by data on hormonal effects on spatial ability.

The fertility and reproduction hypothesis holds that the sex difference in human spatial ability is due in part to selection against a large home range in women during the reproductive years. Its predictions are that emergence of the sex difference should coincide with puberty in girls and that pregnancy should have an inhibitory effect on spatial ability. There is some indication that range size is reduced in women during pregnancy (English and Hitchcock, 1968). In addition, spatial ability has been reported to decrease in women during pregnancy, when estrogen levels are high, then return to normal after delivery (Woodfield, 1984). Estrogen levels also fluctuate during the menstrual cycle, and a number of studies have shown that spatial ability in women is reduced during the high estrogen phase of the menstrual cycle (Komnenich et al., 1978; Hampson and Kimura, 1988; Hampson, 1990; Silverman and Phillips, 1993), although not all studies show this effect (Gordon and Lee, 1993). The interpretation of these results is not that variation in spatial ability across the menstrual cycle is necessarily adaptive, but rather that the effects of estrogen, which are adaptive during pregnancy, depress spatial ability during the menstrual cycle, too. These results, along with the indication of early pubertal onset of sex differences in spatial ability, are as predicted by the fertility and parental care hypothesis.

Hormonal effects on human spatial ability thus show an enhancing effect of testosterone on male spatial ability, as expected if sexual selection on males contributed to the evolution of a sex difference in human spatial ability, and also an inhibitory effect of estrogen on female spatial ability, as expected if natural selection for fertility and reproduction contributed to the evolution of this sex difference. As noted earlier, increased spatial ability in males and decreased spatial ability in females both are found during breeding in other mammals.

That the contemporary functioning of our cognitive apparatus bears the traces of our evolutionary past should not be surprising. On an evolutionary time scale, we have only very recently left our environment of evolutionary adaptedness. Lingering sex differences in spatial ability are a consequence of adaptation to this environment and the ecological problems it presented. Their existence encourages us to ask evolutionary questions about other aspects of cognitive organization and perhaps begin to understand more generally the adaptations that are human cognition.

ACKNOWLEDGMENTS   The author thanks Amy Gordon, Elizabeth Hampson, John Tooby, and Leda Cosmides for their many helpful comments on the manuscript. Preparation of this chapter and the author's research are supported by grants from the Natural Sciences and Engineering Research Council of Canada.

REFERENCES

ÅGREN, G., Q. ZHOU, and W. ZHONG, 1989. Ecology and social behaviour of Mongolian gerbils, *Meriones unguiculatus*, at Xilinhot, Inner Mongolia, China. *Anim. Behav.* 37:11–27.

ALEXANDER, R. D., 1979. *Darwinism and Human Affairs*. London: Pitman.

ANDERSSON, M., 1994. *Sexual Selection*. Princeton, N.J.: Princeton University Press.

CAPLAN, P. J., G. M. MACPHERSON, and P. TOBIN, 1985. Do sex-related differences in spatial abilities exist? A multilevel critique with new data. *Am. Psychol.* 40:786–799.

CLARKE, A. L., and B. S. LOW, 1992. Ecological correlates of human dispersal in 19th century Sweden. *Anim. Behav.* 44:677–693.

COLE-HARDING, S., A. L. MORSTAD, and J. R. WILSON, 1988. Spatial ability in members of opposite-sex twin pairs. *Behav. Genet.* 18:710.

DAB, I., and M. ROBERT, 1997. Home range and navigational skills: Stronger correlation in men than in women? Paper presented at the 9th annual convention of the American Psychological Society, Washington, D.C.

EALS, M., and I. SILVERMAN, 1994. The hunter-gatherer theory of spatial sex differences: Proximate factors mediating the female advantage in recall of object arrays. *Ethol. Sociobiol.* 15:95–105.

ENGLISH, R. M., and N. E. HITCHCOCK, 1968. Nutrient intakes during pregnancy, lactation and after the cessation of lactation in a group of Australian women. *Br. J. Nutr.* 22:615–624.

FITZGERALD, R. W., and D. M. MADISON, 1983. Social organization of a free-ranging population of pine voles, *Microtus pinetorum*. *Behav. Ecol. Sociobiol.* 13:183–187.

FRAGA, R. M., 1991. The social system of a communal breeder, the bay-winged cowbird, *Molothrus badius*. *Ethology* 89:195–210.

GALEA, L. A. M., M. KAVALIERS, and K.-P. OSSENKOPP, 1996. Sexually dimorphic spatial learning in meadow voles *Microtus pennsylvanicus* and deer mice *Peromyscus maniculatus*. *J. Exp. Biol.* 199:195–200.

GALEA, L. A. M., M. KAVALIERS, K.-P. OSSENKOPP, D. INNES, and E. L. HARGREAVES, 1994. Sexually dimorphic spatial learning varies seasonally in two populations of deer mice. *Brain Res.* 635:18–26.

GAULIN, S. J. C., 1992. Evolution of sex differences in spatial ability. *Yearbook Phys. Anthropol.* 35:125–151.

GAULIN, S. J. C., and R. W. FITZGERALD, 1986. Sex differences in spatial ability: An evolutionary hypothesis and test. *Am. Naturalist* 127:74–88.

GAULIN, S. J. C., and R. W. FITZGERALD, 1988. Home-range size as a predictor of mating systems in *Microtus*. *J. Mammalogy* 69:311–319.

GAULIN, S. J. C., and R. W. FITZGERALD, 1989. Sexual selection for spatial-learning ability. *Anim. Behav.* 37:322–331.

GAULIN, S. J. C., R. W. FITZGERALD, and M. S. WARTELL, 1990. Sex differences in spatial ability and activity in two vole species (*Microtus ochrogaster* and *M. pennsylvanicus*). *J. Comp. Psychol.* 104:88–93.

GAULIN, S. J. C., and H. A. HOFFMAN, 1987. Evolution and development of sex differences in spatial ability. In *Human Reproductive Behaviour: A Darwinian Perspective*, L. L. Betzig, M. Borgerhoff Mulder, and P. W. Turke, eds. Cambridge, U.K.: Cambridge University Press, pp. 129–151.

GAULIN, S. J. C., and M. S. WARTELL, 1990. Effects of experience and motivation on symmetrical-maze performance in the prairie vole (*Microtus ochrogaster*). *J. Comp. Psychol.* 104:183–189.

GORDON, H. W., and P. A. LEE, 1993. No difference in cognitive performance between phases of the menstrual cycle. *Psychoneuronendocrinology* 18:521–531.

GREENWOOD, P. J., 1980. Mating systems, philopatry and dispersal in birds and mammals. *Anim. Behav.* 28:1140–1162.

GRIMSHAW, G. M., G. SITARENIOS, and J. K. FINEGAN, 1995. Mental rotation at 7 years: Relations with prenatal testosterone levels and spatial play experiences. *Brain Cogn.* 29:85–100.

HAMPSON, E., 1990. Estrogen-related variations in human spatial and articulatory-motor skills. *Psychoneuroendocrinology* 15:97–111.

HAMPSON, E., and D. KIMURA, 1988. Reciprocal effects of hormonal fluctuations on human motor and perceptual-spatial skills. *Behav. Neurosci.* 102:456–459.

HAMPSON, E., J. F. ROVET, and D. ALTMANN, 1998. Spatial reasoning in children with congenital adrenal hyperplasia due to 21-hydroxylase deficiency. *Dev. Neuropsychol.* 14:299–320.

HARVEY, P. H., and J. R. KREBS, 1990. Comparing brains. *Science* 249:140–146.

HAWKES, K., 1990. Why do men hunt? Benefits for risky choices. In *Risk and Uncertainty in Tribal and Peasant Economies*, E. Cashdan, ed. Boulder, Co.: Westview Press, pp. 145–166.

HAWKES, K., 1991. Showing off: Tests of an hypothesis about men's foraging goals. *Ethol. Sociobiol.* 12:29–54.

JACOBS, L. F., S. J. C. GAULIN, D. F. SHERRY, and G. E. HOFFMAN, 1990. Evolution of spatial cognition: Sex-specific patterns of spatial behavior predict hippocampal size. *Proc. Natl. Acad. Sci. U.S.A.* 87:6349–6352.

JACOBS, L. F., and W. D. SPENCER, 1994. Natural space-use patterns and hippocampal size in kangaroo rats. *Brain Behav. Evol.* 44:125–132.

JANOWSKY, J. S., S. K. OVIATT, and E. S. ORWOLL, 1994. Testosterone influences spatial cognition in older men. *Behav. Neurosci.* 108:325–332.

JARDINE, R., and N. G. MARTIN, 1983. Spatial ability and throwing accuracy. *Behav. Genet.* 13:331–340.

KING, A. P., 1979. *Variables Affecting Parasitism in the North American Cowbird* (Molothrus ater). Ithaca, N.Y.: Cornell University. PhD Thesis.

KOENIG, W. D., 1989. Sex-biased dispersal in the contemporary United States. *Ethol. Sociobiol.* 10:263–278.

KOMNENICH, P., D. M. LANE, R. P. DICKEY, and S. C. STONE, 1978. Gonadal hormones and cognitive performance. *Physiol. Psychol.* 6:115–120.

LOVEJOY, C. O., 1981. The origin of man. *Science* 211:341–350.

MASON, P., 1987. Pair formation in cowbirds: Evidence found for screaming but not shiny cowbirds. *Condor* 89:349–356.

MOFFAT, S. D., and E. HAMPSON, 1996. A curvilinear relationship between testosterone and spatial cognition in humans: Possible influence of hand preference. *Psychoneuroendocrinology* 21:323–337.

MOFFAT, S. D., E. HAMPSON, and M. HATZIPANTELIS, 1998. Navigation in a "virtual" maze: Sex differences and correlation with psychometric measures of spatial ability in humans. *Evolution Hum. Behav.* 19:73–87.

MUNROE, R. L., and R. H. MUNROE, 1971. Effect of environmental experience on spatial ability in an East African society. *J. Soc. Psychol.* 83:15–22.

NORMAN, R. F., and R. J. ROBERTSON, 1975. Nest-searching behavior in the Brown-headed cowbird. *Auk* 92:610–611.

PETERSEN, K., and D. F. SHERRY, 1996. No sex difference occurs in hippocampus, food-storing, or memory for food caches in black-capped chickadees. *Behav. Brain Res.* 79:15–22.

REBOREDA, J. C., N. S. CLAYTON, and A. KACELNIK, 1996. Species and sex differences in hippocampus size in parasitic and non-parasitic cowbirds. *Neuroreport* 7:505–508.

RESNICK, S. M., S. A. BERENBAUM, I. GOTTESMAN, and T. J. BOUCHARD, 1986. Early hormonal influences on cognitive functioning in congenital adrenal hyperplasia. *Dev. Psychol.* 22:191–198.

RUFF, C., 1987. Sexual dimorphism in human lower limb bone structure: Relationship to subsistence strategy and sexual division of labour. *J. Hum. Evolution* 16:391–416.

SANDERS, B., M. P. SOARES, and J. M. D'AQUILA, 1982. The sex difference on one test of spatial visualization: A nontrivial difference. *Child Dev.* 53:1106–1110.

SCOTT, D. M., and C. D. ANKNEY, 1980. Fecundity of the brown-headed cowbird in southern Ontario. *Auk* 97:677–683.

SCOTT, D. M., and C. D. ANKNEY, 1983. The laying cycle of brown-headed cowbirds: Passerine chickens? *Auk* 100:583–592.

SHERRY, D. F., M. R. L. FORBES, M. KHURGEL, and G. O. IVY, 1993. Females have a larger hippocampus than males in the brood-parasitic brown-headed cowbird. *Proc. Natl. Acad. Sci. U.S.A.* 90:7839–7843.

SHERRY, D. F., B. G. G. GALEF, JR., and M. M. CLARK, 1996. Sex and intrauterine position influence the size of the gerbil hippocampus. *Physiol. Behav.* 60:1491–1494.

SHERRY, D. F., and E. HAMPSON, 1997. Evolution and the hormonal control of sexually-dimorphic spatial abilities in humans. *Trends Cogn. Sci.* 1:50–56.

SILVERMAN, I., and M. EALS, 1992. Sex differences in spatial abilities: Evolutionary theory and data. In *The Adapted Mind: Evolutionary Psychology and the Generation of Culture*, J. H. Barkow, L. Cosmides, and J. Tooby, eds. Oxford: Oxford University Press, pp. 533–549.

SILVERMAN, I., and K. PHILLIPS, 1993. Effects of estrogen changes during the menstrual cycle on spatial performance. *Ethol. Sociobiol.* 14:257–270.

TANNER, J. M., 1990. *Foetus into Man*. Cambridge, Mass.: Harvard University Press.

TOOBY, J., and I. DE VORE, 1987. The reconstruction of hominid behavioral evolution through strategic modeling. In *The Evolution of Human Behaviour: Primate Models*, W. G. Kinzey, ed. Albany, N.Y.: SUNY Press, pp. 183–237.

VANDENBERG, S. G., 1971. *Mental Rotations Test*. Department of Psychology, University of Colorado, Boulder.

VAN GOOZEN, S. H. M., P. T. COHEN-KETTENIS, L. J. G. GOOREN, N. H. FRIJDA, and N. E. VAN DE POLL, 1995. Gender differences in behavior: Activating effects of cross-sex hormones. *Psychoneuroendocrinology* 20:343–363.

VOYER, D., S. VOYER, and M. P. BRYDEN, 1995. Magnitude of sex differences in spatial abilities: A meta-analysis and consideration of critical variables. *Psychol. Bull.* 117:250–270.

WOODFIELD, R. L., 1984. Embedded Figures test performance before and after childbirth. *Br. J. Psychol.* 75:81–88.

84 What's Human about the Human Brain?

TODD M. PREUSS

ABSTRACT Understanding how human brain organization differs from that of other species is essential for understanding the neural bases of human cognitive and behavioral specializations. Nevertheless, neuroscientists have largely ignored this subject. A review of the small body of available evidence indicates that the human brain became enormously enlarged following the divergence of humans from African apes, with association cortex expanding disproportionately. There is, however, no evidence that humans evolved new cortical areas; indeed, a reasonable case can be made that classical language areas have homologs in nonhuman primates. Humans possess morphological characteristics (sylvian-fissure asymmetries) and features of cortical histology that monkeys lack, although apes are more similar to humans in these respects. We can improve our understanding of human brain specializations by directly comparing humans, apes, and other nonhuman primates using the wide array of available morphological and histological techniques that do not require invasive or terminal procedures.

Homo sapiens: The undiscovered primate

Given what we know about the human brain, two facts stand out as astonishing: (1) We know very little about what distinguishes the human brain from that of other species; and (2) apparently, few neuroscientists regard fact 1 as much of a problem. To be sure, we know a great deal about mammalian and primate brains generally; we also know quite a bit about the localization of function in the human brain, thanks to recent developments in imaging technology. Nonetheless, neuroscientists have devoted little effort to identifying the distinctively human features of the human brain. As a result, no well-developed theory of human mind–brain organization exists—not one that takes the distinctive characteristics of the human brain into account and explains how and why human cognition is different from that of, say, rhesus monkeys. To put the matter bluntly, cognitive neuroscience has very little to say about the specifically human aspects of human nature.

Why are we so ignorant about something so fundamental? This chapter considers the practical and theoretical difficulties posed by the study of human brain specializations, surveys the evidence regarding some

TODD M. PREUSS   Institute of Cognitive Science, University of Southwestern Louisiana–New Iberia Research Center, New Iberia, La.

proposed human brain specializations, and discusses some prospects for future discovery. One of the principal lessons of this review is that our ignorance of human brain specializations has more to do with prevailing (and erroneous) ideas about the nature of brain evolution than with the inherent difficulty of studying it.

Identifying human brain specializations

Is it even possible to study human brain specializations? At first glance, the task appears to entail insuperable difficulties. For one thing, there is relatively little we can learn about brain evolution from the study of fossils. Although fossils provide evidence about evolutionary changes in brain size and external morphology, fossils do not preserve information about the histology or internal organization of the brain. But the lack of fossils does not preclude an evolutionary analysis of internal brain structure. Molecular biologists are able, through comparative studies of living species, to reconstruct the evolutionary history of genomes in remarkable detail. To do so, they employ the standard "cladistic" techniques of modern evolutionary biology (Harvey and Pagel, 1991), an approach that can be applied to brain evolution as well (Nishikawa, 1997; Preuss, 1993; Preuss and Kaas, 1996).

It is difficult to overstate the importance of comparative studies—patently, one cannot understand human brain specializations simply by studying humans. Humans share many features of brain organization with other primate and mammalian species by virtue of common ancestry; but while these shared features are, without doubt, important in the functional economy of the human brain, they are not *distinctively* human. Our knowledge of the human brain may advance significantly as the result of, say, advances in imaging technology; however, we cannot enhance our knowledge of what is distinctively human about the human brain unless we can specify what it is humans possess that other species lack, and what other species possess that humans lack (Preuss, 1995a). Thus, from the perspective of cognitive neuroscience, understanding what it is to be human requires comparing human brains to those of other species.

Scientists seeking to undertake these comparisons encounter some genuine technical hurdles, however. As

Crick and Jones (1993) note, studies of human beings face technical limitations not encountered in studies of laboratory animal species. The most informative techniques available for tracing neural connections and studying neuronal activity require invasive and terminal experimental procedures. These techniques are, of course, unsuitable for use in humans. On the other hand, most modern human studies employ noninvasive imaging technologies. These provide much information about the localization of function in the brain and about cerebral morphology (the sizes of brain structures, patterns of cortical folding, etc.), but they tell us little about the connections or intrinsic organization of brain structures. Furthermore, scanning technologies are difficult to adapt for use with nonhuman species, especially in paradigms that involve behaving subjects. Thus, for the present at least, the noninvasive methods used to study humans and the invasive methods used to study laboratory animals provide us with different kinds of information.

Although this methodological gap is real, its magnitude should not be overstated. One can certainly use a variety of techniques to compare the cerebral morphology of humans and nonhuman species (Semendeferi et al., 1998; Zilles et al., 1996). Finer levels of organization can be investigated as well. The past two decades have seen the development of new histological techniques, including immunocytochemical, autoradiographic, and related procedures; and a fantastic array of antibodies and other ligands is now available for probing nervous system organization. With these tools, one can localize neurotransmitters and receptors, structural molecules (e.g., neurofilaments and microtubules), extracellular matrix components, calcium-binding proteins (e.g., calbindin and parvalbumin), and enzymes (e.g., acetylcholinesterase and cytochrome oxidase). One signal virtue of these techniques is that they can be used effectively with autopsied brain tissue from humans as well as from nonhuman species; they are therefore well suited for comprehensive comparative studies involving humans. Although current post-mortem histological techniques do not allow one to study long connections within the brain, they do make it possible to study aspects of laminar, modular, and cellular organization of the cortex in great detail. Also, because cortical areas differ in the density and laminar distribution of particular molecules, histochemical techniques can be used to map the location and extent of cortical areas, supplementing the classical cyto- and myeloarchitectonic techniques. Increasingly, these techniques are being applied to the study of the human brain, as well as to those of nonhuman species. Thus, even as we look forward to improvements in technique that will make it possible to do comparative, in

vivo studies of connectivity (Paus et al., 1997) and functional localization (Takechi et al., 1997), we already possess the means to carry out highly informative comparisons of human and nonhuman brains.

Continuity versus diversity in cerebral evolution

If we do not lack the means to study human brain specializations, why do we know so little about them? The answer, I believe, lies in the continuing influence of outdated ideas about brain evolution. Neuroscientists, as a group, hold firmly to the view that mammalian species differ little in internal brain organization, the main differences being matters of size. If one accepts this premise, the only specialization of the human brain worth considering is its peculiar size–human brains average about three times the volume of chimpanzee brains (Stephan, Baron, and Frahm, 1988), chimpanzees being our closest relatives and also quite similar to us in body size.

This emphasis on the *continuity* of brain organization across mammals has an impeccable lineage, deriving as it does from Charles Darwin. Darwin claimed that "the difference in mind between man and the higher animals, great as it is, is certainly one of degree and not of kind" (Darwin, 1871, p. 105). For Darwin, humans were essentially big-brained apes, greatly improved in intelligence and morals, perhaps, but not different in fundamental ways. T. H. Huxley, who was Darwin's ally and a neuroanatomical authority, specifically denied that humans possess features of brain organization that other primates lack (Huxley, 1863). Indeed, early Darwinians and anti-Darwinians both believed the theory of evolution by natural selection would be disproved if humans could be shown to possess unique features of brain organization (Preuss, 1993; Richards, 1987).

In keeping with Darwin's views, subsequent generations of psychologists and neuroscientists have typically emphasized the similarities between animal species and downplayed the differences (for historical reviews, see Povinelli, 1993; Preuss, 1993, 1995a; Preuss and Kaas, 1998). In psychology, for example, the doctrine of behaviorism held that vertebrate behavior was to be explained by reference to a small set of learning processes common to all species (Boakes, 1984). At the same time, neuroscientists such as the influential Karl Lashley (Lashley, 1949) were championing the view that the only important brain difference between species was size. Similarly, among modern neuroscientists it has been claimed that there is a "basic uniformity" of cortical organization among mammals, as Rockel, Hiorns, and Powell (1980) put it, a claim that has found much favor (e.g., Creutzfeldt, 1977; Eccles, 1984; Mountcastle,

1978; Phillips, Zeki, and Barlow, 1983; Szentágothai, 1975). The core idea is that the cortex is a collection of narrow, vertical cell columns, consisting of a specific complement of pyramidal cells and interneurons that span the six layers of cortex, these columns being interconnected in stereotyped ways. Columns are considered to be a fundamental information-processing unit of cortex and, given their supposedly stereotyped organization, perform the same transformation on incoming information, no matter what their location in the cortex. According to this view, evolution modifies brain structure mainly by adding new columns, while conserving column structure.

For neuroscientists, there are good reasons to hope that the doctrine of continuity is true. With its Darwinian imprimatur, it would seem to be on sound evolutionary footing. Moreover, it is compatible with the popular idea that living forms can be arranged along a phylogenetic scale, with us, the big-brained humans, at the top, the crowning achievement of evolution. At the same time, the doctrine of continuity affirms the qualitative similarity of animals. Thus we can regard rats and rhesus monkeys as simplified models of human beings, without having to worry about whether humans have evolved brain specializations those animals lack or, worse, whether rats and rhesus monkeys have specializations that humans lack.

The appeal of continuity notwithstanding, it is important to recognize that modern evolutionary biology has abandoned this part of Darwin's doctrine. Evolutionists are no longer troubled by the idea that a given species may possess structures that its close relatives lack; it is acknowledged, for example, that humans possess structures of the hands and feet that apes lack (Aiello and Dean, 1990). Furthermore, evolutionists today regard phylogeny as primarily a matter of diversification rather than ascent or progress (see especially Bowler, 1996, and Richards, 1987, 1992, for historical reviews). As a consequence, they have adopted the branching tree as the appropriate metaphor for evolution and have dispensed with the phylogenetic scale. These changes of perspective have profoundly affected the evolutionary view of humanity's place in nature: Whereas evolutionists once regarded humans as the near-inevitable product of a general evolutionary progression from the simplest to increasingly complex forms, today they regard the human species not as the apogee of evolution, but rather as one remarkable evolutionary outcome among many (figure 84.1).

Taking the modern view of evolution seriously, we should expect that mammals exhibit diverse psychological organizations. Under behaviorism, with its emphasis on just one or two basic learning processes, it is difficult to imagine how animals could evolve different psychologies. By contrast, modern cognitive science conceives the mind as a collection of specialized component processes; under this view, one can envision a diversity of minds, with species varying both in the cognitive processes they possess and in the interactions among those processes. Psychologists are now exploring how species differ in cognitive organization, and have begun to characterize the distinctive features of human cognition and behavior. Proposed human specializations include language (Tomasello and Call, 1997; Wallman, 1992), a strong population bias for left-hemisphere dominance for upper-limb control (i.e., right-handedness; McGrew and Marchant, 1997), and "theory of mind"–the propensity to interpret behavior by making inferences about mental states, rather than merely in terms of behavioral tendencies (Cheney and Seyfarth, 1990; Povinelli and Eddy, 1996; Povinelli and Preuss, 1995; Tomasello and Call, 1997). There are likely to be many additional human-specific cognitive characteristics.

If psychological organization varies across species, we should not be surprised to discover that brain organization varies as well. Indeed, there are now so many well-documented examples of nontrivial variations in mammalian brain structure–and especially in cortical organization–that the concept of "basic uniformity" has become untenable (Preuss, 1993, 1995a,b; Preuss and Kaas, 1998). Diversity is exhibited in many dimensions of cortical organization. The cell biology of the cortex is variable, with species exhibiting distinctive differences in the morphologies and biochemical phenotypes of pyramidal cells and interneurons (Brückner et al., 1994; Garey, Winkelmann, and Brauer, 1985; Glezer et al., 1993). Individual areas, such as the primary visual area (V1), exhibit species variations in the laminar distribution of thalamic afferents and in the connections between layers (reviewed by Casagrande and Kaas, 1994; Kaas and Preuss, 1993). There are also marked differences between mammalian groups in the laminar distribution of neurotransmitters and receptors within homologous areas (Berger and Gaspar, 1995; Gebhard et al., 1995). The manner in which areas are parceled into subdivisions can also vary dramatically. For instance, area V1 of primates is characterized by the presence of small, repeating territories of high metabolic activity in the upper layers of cortex. These are known as "blobs" (Horton and Hubel, 1981). Although blobs are also present in carnivores, they are absent in animals thought to be closely related to primates (tree shrews and bats) and many other mammals as well, suggesting that blobs evolved independently in primates and carnivores (Preuss and Kaas, 1996). Finally, the number of major structural subdivisions (areas) of the cortex differs

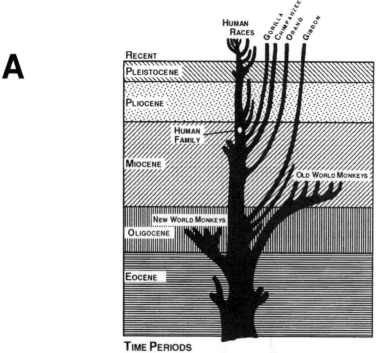

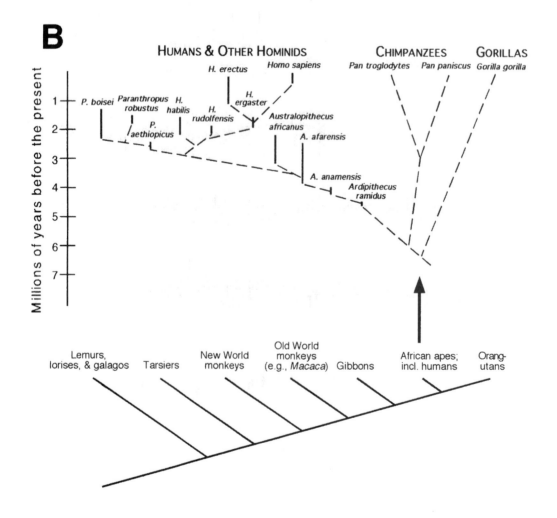

FIGURE 84.1 (A) Early views of human evolution, such as those of G. Elliot Smith (1924), a pioneering neuroanatomist and primatologist, depicted humans as the centerpiece of evolution. The path to humans is straight upward, while other species are set off on side branches. The Old World and New World monkeys are drawn as though they stopped evolving millions of years ago! (B) Modern views of human evolution depict humans as one of many diverse outcomes of primate evolution. The lower part of B shows the evolutionary relationships among living primate groups, as currently understood; the upper part expands the portion of the primate tree that contains the African ape group (gorillas, chimpanzees, and humans). The rich fossil record of human evolution indicates that modern humans are the survivors of what was once a remarkable radiation of human-like (hominid) primates. Comparative molecular and anatomical evidence indicates that humans are very closely related to the living African apes, the chimpanzees and gorilla, and chimpanzees are probably the closest relatives of humans. Humans are more distantly related to orangutans and gibbons, the other members of the ape-human superfamily (Hominoidea). Humans are even more distantly related to Old World monkeys, which include the familiar macaque monkeys (genus *Macaca*). As this diagram suggests, the fossil record of African ape evolution is extremely poor compared to the wealth of the hominid record. (Principal sources: Strait, Grine, and Moniz, 1997; Wood, 1996.)

---

among mammals. There appears to be a small set of areas (perhaps 20 or so) that are widely shared among extant mammals–and probably among ancestral mammals–but some mammalian groups have many more areas than others (Allman, 1990; Northcutt and Kaas, 1995). Primates and carnivores, for instance, have independently evolved many higher-order visual areas (Kaas and Krubitzer, 1991), and anthropoid primates possess dorsolateral prefrontal areas (and related connectional systems) that are not found in other mammals (Preuss, 1995b; Preuss and Goldman-Rakic, 1991a,b).

It is clear that evolution of mammalian brains was marked not only by changes in size, but by diversification of structure as well. It thus makes sense for neuroscientists to seek to identify the constellation of brain characteristics that are distinctive of particular mammalian lineages, including the human lineage. But, as the following section makes clear, much work remains to be done before we will have a detailed account of distinctively human brain systems.

Possible human brain specializations

In this section we consider current evidence pertaining to the ways human brain organization differs from that of other primates, particularly apes, our closest relatives, and Old World monkeys, the animals most closely related to the ape-human (hominoid) group (figure 84.1). In addition to the unusually great size of the human

brain, candidate human specializations include the differential enlargement of specific brain regions (namely the frontal lobe, association cortex, and portions of the cerebellum), the addition of new cortical areas, a unique pattern of cerebral asymmetries, and modifications of the cellular and connectional organization of the cortex.

ENLARGED ASSOCIATION CORTEX   Enlargement of the cerebral cortex accounts for most of the difference in brain volume between humans and other primates (Stephan, Frahm, and Baron, 1981). But was the evolutionary enlargement of human cerebral cortex a general enlargement, or did it entail the differential expansion of specific regions? Many have concluded that there was an expansion of specific cortical regions, notably the classical "association" regions of the parietal, temporal, and frontal lobes (e.g., Blinkov and Glezer, 1968; Brodmann, 1909, 1912; Elliot Smith, 1924; Le Gros Clark, 1959).

Frontal cortex has been singled out for special attention (for reviews, see Falk, 1992; Semendeferi et al., 1997). There are sound reasons for thinking that the frontal cortex was extensively modified during human evolution, given its role in language and evidence of its involvement in theory of mind (e.g., Fletcher et al., 1995). Based on his quantitative, comparative studies of the cortical mantle in primates, Brodmann (1912) maintained that one segment of the frontal cortex in particular, the prefrontal cortex ("Regio frontalis," in his terminology), underwent progressive evolution, being larger in apes than in monkeys, and larger in humans than in apes (figure 84.2). Blinkov and Glezer (1968) provided evidence that both the prefrontal cortex and the frontal cortex as a whole were enlarged in human evolution relative to posterior cortex.

Enlargement of frontal or prefrontal cortex in human evolution has not been universally accepted, however (see the review of Semendeferi et al., 1997). Semendeferi and colleagues, for instance, re-examined the issue, using structural MRI to compare frontal and nonfrontal cortical volumes and surface areas in humans, apes, and monkeys. They concluded that frontal cortex was *not* enlarged in recent human evolution, humans having about the same relative amount of frontal cortex as apes, about 31–37% of total hemispheric volume, although humans might still have more frontal cortex than monkeys (figure 84.2).

Why are there such pronounced discrepancies in published studies of frontal lobe size? Sampling error may contribute to the differences, as all the existing data sets are extremely small, particularly with regard to the number of ape individuals included. Also, different morphometric approaches have been used. Finally,

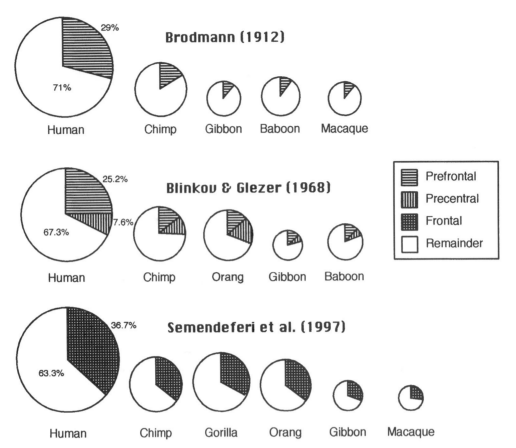

FIGURE 84.2 The fraction of the cerebral cortex occupied by the prefrontal, frontal, and nonfrontal cortex in humans, apes (chimpanzees, gorillas, orangutans, and gibbons), and Old World monkeys (macaques and baboons), as indicated by the studies of Brodmann (1912), Blinkov and Glezer (1968), and Semendeferi et al. (1997).

different structures were compared in these studies: Semendeferi and colleagues compared the entire frontal cortex (including prefrontal, precentral, and anterior cingulate cortex) to nonfrontal cortex; Brodmann compared prefrontal cortex (excluding the precentral and anterior cingulate regions) to non-prefrontal cortex; and Blinkov and Glezer considered prefrontal, premotor, and primary motor cortex surface areas as percentages of total cortical surface area.

The distinction between *frontal* cortex and *prefrontal* cortex may be critical in this regard. Even if we accept that the frontal lobes did not expand out of proportion to the rest of the cortex in human evolution, as Semendeferi and associates argue, it does not follow that the percentage of prefrontal cortex remained unchanged. There is, in fact, reason to think that humans possess a relatively large amount of higher-order frontal and posterior association cortex. In addition to the direct morphometric evidence for association cortex enlargement offered by Brodmann (1912) and Blinkov and Glezer (1968), there is substantial indirect evidence as well. Although human brains are about three times the volume

of great ape brains, the absolute amounts of cortex devoted to the primary visual area (Blinkov and Glezer, 1968; Frahm, Stephan, and Baron, 1984) and the primary motor area (Blinkov and Glezer, 1968) are similar in humans and apes. Consistent with this, we recently found that humans and chimpanzees differ in the location of primary motor cortex (area 4) with respect to cortical sulci: In humans, area 4 is largely confined to the anterior bank of the central sulcus; but in chimpanzees, area 4 occupies the anterior bank of the central sulcus, the precentral gyrus, and most of the precentral sulcus as well (Preuss et al., 1997a). Therefore, motor cortex probably occupies a smaller fraction of frontal cortex in humans than in chimpanzees, implying an expansion of premotor and/or prefrontal cortex in human evolution. Likewise, the primary visual area and other lower-order visual areas appear to have been displaced posteriorly in humans compared to other primates (Tootell et al., 1996; Ungerleider and Haxby, 1994), suggesting an expansion of posterior association cortex. Armstrong's comparative studies of thalamic nuclei (summarized in Armstrong, 1982) also provide evidence of the differential enlargement of human association cortex. Armstrong found that the thalamic nuclei that project to primary visual and auditory cortex (i.e., the lateral and medial geniculate nuclei) contain similar numbers of neurons in great apes and humans, whereas nuclei that project to the prefrontal, parietal, and temporal association cortex (including the mediodorsal nucleus and the pulvinar) contain approximately 2–3 times as many cells in humans as in great apes. In sum, the existing data clearly support the view that prefrontal cortex, and posterior association cortex as well, expanded differentially during human evolution.

ENLARGED CEREBELLUM There is no reason to expect that evolutionary changes have been restricted to the forebrain; indeed, there is evidence suggesting that the cerebellum was modified in ape and human evolution. Specifically, ape cerebella are relatively large for primates of their body size, and the human cerebellum is larger still (Passingham, 1975; Stephan, Baron, and Frahm, 1988). There is also evidence that one division of the deep cerebellar nuclei in particular, the dentate nucleus, is larger relative to body weight and hindbrain volume in humans than in apes (Matano and Hirasaki, 1997). The dentate receives projections from the lateral cerebellar cortex, and projects in turn to the cerebral cortex via the thalamus. Leiner, Leiner, and Dow (1986) argue that apes and humans possess a unique subdivision of the dentate that sends outputs to the prefrontal cortex (via the thalamus). These considerations are particularly interesting in view of the accumulating evidence that the cerebellum contributes to cognitive as well as motor functions (Ivry and Baldo, 1992; Leiner, Leiner, and Dow, 1986; Middleton and Strick, 1994; Schmahmann, 1991). Leiner and colleagues (1986), for example, argue that the cerebellum contributes to the routinization of complex cognitive procedures and hence to mental agility. If the emergence of higher-order representations depends on the routinization and consolidation of lower-order schemas, as posited by Karmiloff-Smith (1992), interactions between the cerebellum and cerebral cortex could play an important role in the development of higher-order cognitive representations.

NEW CORTICAL AREAS How has the organization of human cerebral cortex been modified during its evolutionary expansion? One very appealing possibility is that new areal subdivisions evolved. In mammals, there appears to be a relationship between brain size and number of cortical areas, such that larger-brained taxa tend to have more areas than smaller-brained forms (Allman, 1990; Brodmann, 1909; Kaas, 1987; Preuss and

Kaas, 1998). The expectation that humans possess new cortical areas becomes even stronger if one believes that the existence of human-specific psychological capacities, such as language or theory of mind, implies the existence of human-specific processing "modules," because we can readily cast cortical areas in the role of psychological modules. In this vein, it has been suggested that Broca's area and other language-related cortical regions are probably unique to humans (e.g., Brodmann, 1909; Crick and Jones, 1993; Killackey, 1995).

However appealing this picture, there is at present no good evidence that humans possess cortical areas in addition to those found in other primates (figure 84.3). Several recent frontal-lobe studies bear on this point. Petrides and Pandya (1994) concluded there is essentially a one-to-one match between the cytoarchitectonic areas of macaque frontal cortex and that of humans. Similarly, recent architectonic studies of human dorsolateral prefrontal cortex (Rajkowska and Goldman-Rakic, 1995) and dorsomedial premotor cortex (Baleydier, Achache, and Froment, 1997; Zilles et al., 1995) have identified areas known to be present in macaques, but not additional, human-specific areas.

It would be premature, nonetheless, to conclude that humans have exactly the same complement of frontal areas that macaques and other nonhuman primates have. Our understanding of cortical areal organization is far from complete, even in macaques, the primates about which we know most. The widely used architectonic maps of Brodmann (1909) and Walker (1940) certainly understate the number of frontal lobe areas in Old World monkeys: Areas unrecognized by these authors have recently been described in the dorsolateral, orbital, and medial prefrontal cortex of macaques (Carmichael and Price, 1994; Petrides and Pandya, 1994; Preuss and Goldman-Rakic, 1989, 1991a,b). Even the primary motor "area" can be subdivided in macaques based on variations in the distribution of neurofilaments (Preuss et al., 1997b). Nor is frontal cortex exceptional: The parcellation of the much-studied visual cortex in Old World and New World monkeys is still not fully settled (Kaas, 1993). Moreover, studies of *human* cortical parcellation are just beginning. Until we have relatively complete and accurate parcellations of the cortex of humans and other primate species, we will not be able to confidently conclude whether humans do or do not possess human-specific cortical areas.

ARE THERE NONHUMAN HOMOLOGS OF HUMAN LANGUAGE AREAS? If we cannot resolve the general question of at least whether humans possess new cortical areas at present, we can at least address the more limited question of whether the language areas are unique to

Brodmann (1909)

Petrides and Pandya (1994)

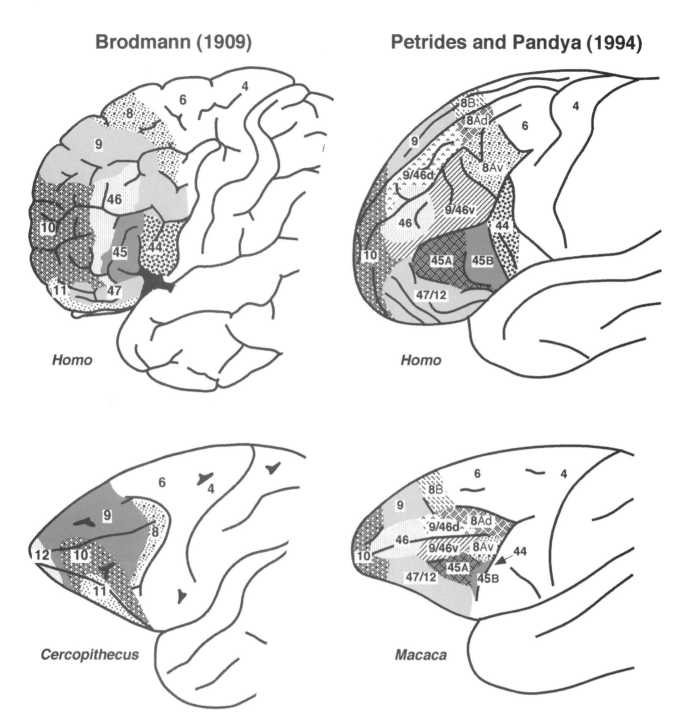

FIGURE 84.3 The frontal lobe areas of humans (*Homo*) and Old World monkeys (*Cercopithecus* and *Macaca*) according to the cytoarchitectonic studies of Brodmann (1909) and Petrides and Pandya (1994). Brodmann concluded that the number of areas in the cerebral cortex increased during human evolution, whereas Petrides and Pandya depict humans and macaques as having the same complement of frontal-lobe areas.

humans. If new functions require new cortical areas, and if language is a uniquely human function, then cortical areas specialized for language processing should indeed be found only in humans. Nonetheless, there are long-standing claims that homologs of both Broca's area and Wernicke's area are present in macaques and other non-human primates (figure 84.4).

Most interest has focused on Broca's area, which is usually identified with architectonic areas 44 and 45 of Brodmann (1909). While Brodmann indicated that these areas are unique to humans, others have identified architectonically similar areas in the ventral premotor region of nonhuman primates (see especially Bonin, 1944, and Bucy, 1944). Furthermore, electrical stimulation of the

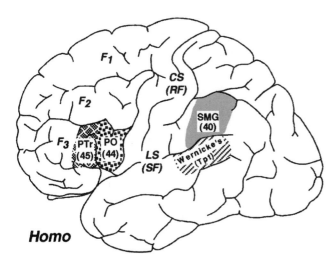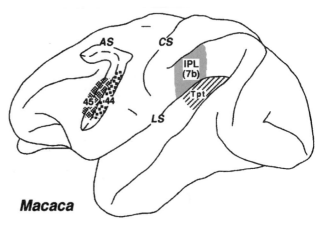

Homo **Macaca**

FIGURE 84.4   Human language areas and their suggested homologs in macaques, based on architectonic and functional similarities. Broca's area in humans is located in the posterior part of the third frontal gyrus (F3), and includes two smaller gyri, pars opercularis (PO) and pars triangularis (PTr). These small gyri are occupied by areas 44 and 45 of Brodmann, respectively. In macaques, the ventral limb of the arcuate sulcus (AS) contains cortex that resembles human areas 44 and 45 architectonically. Wernicke's area has been identified with architectonic area Tpt in humans, and there is a similar area in macaques. The cortex of the human supramarginal gyrus (SMG; Brodmann's area 40), which may be involved in language processing, resembles area 7b of macaques. Additional abbreviations: CS, central sulcus; LS, lateral sulcus; SF, sylvian fissure; RF, Rolandic fissure.

ventral premotor region in nonhuman primates produces oral and laryngeal movements (for review, see Stepniewska, Preuss, and Kaas, 1993). Many workers have therefore concluded that a portion of the ventral premotor region of nonhuman primates contains cortex homologous to Broca's area (e.g., Abbs, 1986; Bonin, 1944; Bucy, 1944; Deacon, 1992; Galaburda and Pandya, 1982; Jürgens, 1979; Lieberman, 1985).

Recent studies of ventral premotor cortex in nonhuman primates and Broca's area in humans provide additional evidence of homology (for discussion, see Preuss, 1995a; Preuss, Stepniewska, and Kaas, 1996; Stepniewska, Preuss, and Kaas, 1993). In nonhuman primates, it has been found that ventral premotor cortex represents hand movements as well as orofacial movements. In humans, likewise, the cortex of Broca's area is activated by simple movements of the hands and mouth, as well as during language tasks (Colebatch et al., 1991; Petersen et al., 1988). Rizzolatti, Gallese, and colleagues also suggest that neurons in the anterior ventral premotor cortex of macaques have properties suited for the analysis of orofacial and manual gesture, and propose that this area is preadapted for a role in language (Gallese et al., 1996; Rizzolatti et al., 1996).

Homologs of posterior language cortex—specifically Wernicke's area and the inferior parietal cortex (supramarginal and angular gyri)—may also exist in nonhuman primates (see figure 84.4). For example, Galaburda and Pandya (1982) have argued that macaques possess a cytoarchitectonic zone, area Tpt in the temporal cortex of the posterior sylvian fissure that resembles Wernicke's area in architecture and location. Eidelberg and Galaburda (1984) also note the architectonic similarity of the inferior parietal cortex of humans and nonhuman primates (area PG; angular gyrus). Functional imaging studies provide additional evidence for homology between the supramarginal gyrus of humans (Brodmann's area 40) and the anterior inferior parietal lobule (anterior area 7) of nonhuman primates. In nonhuman primates, anterior area 7 is known to represent the face and forelimb (Leinonen et al., 1979). In humans, the supramarginal gyrus is activated during linguistic tasks (Paulescu, Frith, and Frackowiak, 1993), but also during nonlinguistic forelimb movements (Colebatch et al., 1991). It is noteworthy that in macaques, the anterior parietal cortex, ventral premotor cortex, several somatic areas in the operculum and insula, and at least two ventral prefrontal areas are all interconnected (Preuss and Goldman-Rakic, 1989). Preuss and Goldman-Rakic (1989) proposed that these areas constitute a network of perisylvian somatic areas, representing preferentially the face and forelimb.

If nonhuman primates possess homologs of at least some of the major language-related cortical areas of humans, then we must consider the possibility that human-specific language functions evolved, not by the addition of new cortical areas, but by the modification of pre-existing structures and systems, as Bonin (1944) suggested long ago. Under this view, nonhuman primates possess areas and connectional systems that are preadapted for

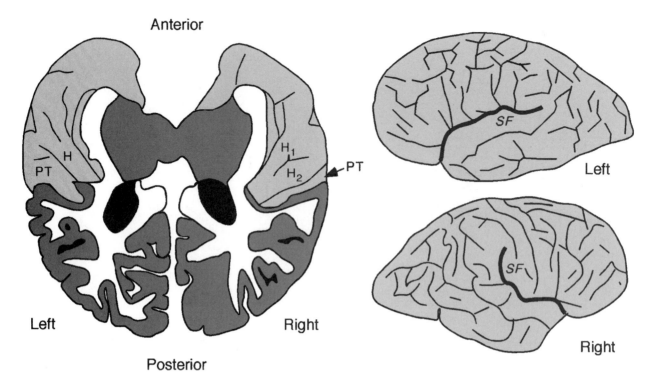

FIGURE 84.5   The left and right temporal lobes of humans are remarkably asymmetrical. The figure on the left shows a brain sectioned in the horizontal plane to reveal the superior aspect of the temporal lobes; anterior is to the top. (The cut surface of the cortex is represented by the dark gray fill.) The planum temporale (PT) is larger in the left hemisphere than the right in most people; in this individual, the right PT is scarcely evident. H_1 and H_2 are components of Heschl's gyrus, which corresponds to the primary auditory area. The figures on the right illustrate the asymmetry in the course of the sylvian fissure. In most individuals, the sylvian fissure is longer and flatter in the left hemisphere than in the right. (Figures are based on photographs in Galaburda, 1984.)

language, with functions that make them suitable for "recruitment," as Bonin put it, by language (see also Gallese et al., 1996; Kimura, 1976, 1993; Lieberman, 1985; Rizzolatti et al., 1996). It is intriguing that the perisylvian areas represent forelimb as well as orofacial function, for this may explain why humans can so readily acquire a manual sign language when deafness renders the auditory-verbal channel unavailable (Preuss, 1995a). It may also be germane to the many evolutionary scenarios of language origins that hold that humans passed through an evolutionary stage in which manual gesture was a far more important component of communication than it is in modern humans (Hewes, 1976).

Although one can make a reasonable case that homologs of human language areas exist in nonhuman primates, we probably should not regard the matter as settled. Until we have accurate charts of cortical areas in humans and other primates, and a very detailed mapping of the distribution of linguistic and nonlinguistic functions in the human perisylvian cortex, we cannot rule out the possibility that language is represented in areas adjacent to, but distinct from, the areas representing nonlinguistic functions. Nevertheless, it must be empha-

sized that there is currently no strong evidence that the classical language areas are unique to humans.

UNIQUE CEREBRAL ASYMMETRIES   The fact that the human left hemisphere is dominant for language and upper-limb control in most individuals suggests that the hemispheres should be structurally asymmetrical, and indeed they are. The region of temporal cortex usually identified with Wernicke's area—the so-called planum temporale, the posterior part of the temporal lobe buried within the sylvian fissure—is highly asymmetrical (figure 84.5). Geschwind and Levitsky (1968) reported that the left planum temporale was larger than the right in 65% of human brains examined, the remainder being about equal or larger on the right. Furthermore, the external appearance of the sylvian fissure shows marked asymmetry in a majority of individuals, the right sulcus being shorter than the left and showing a distinct upward bend at its posterior end (Foundas, Leonard, and Heilman, 1995; LeMay and Culebras, 1972) (figure 84.5). Broca's area, which corresponds to the posterior part of the third frontal convolution and includes gyri known as pars triangularis and pars opercularis, is also asymmetrical. Specifically, the sulci within Broca's region are deeper and longer on the left than on the right (Albanese et al., 1989; Falzi, Perrone, and Vignolo, 1982; Foundas et al., 1996; Foundas, Leonard, and Heilman, 1995), suggesting that the amount of cortex is greater on the left than the right. Consistent with this is a report that cytoarchitectonic area 44, which occupies pars triangularis, is larger on the left than the right (Galaburda, 1980). Cortical area Tpt within Wernicke's region is also reported to be larger on the left (Galaburda and Sanides, 1980). Finally, there are reports of left–right asymmetries of pyramidal cell size and dendritic morphology in the classical language regions (Hayes and Lewis, 1995; Hutsler and Gazzaniga, 1996; Scheibel et al., 1985).

Given that humans are distinctive among primates in their possession of language (which is localized mainly in the left hemisphere in most individuals) and in their preference for the right hand (control of which is localized in the left hemisphere in most persons), it is reasonable to suppose that the constellation of left–right perisylvian asymmetries is unique to humans. It is reported, however, that nonhuman primates possess at least some of the asymmetries found in humans. Asymmetries of sylvian fissure length (with the left longer than the right) are present in Old World monkeys and apes as well as in humans (see the review of Bradshaw and Rogers, 1993). Furthermore, in apes, but not monkeys, the tip of the sylvian fissure is usually higher on the right than on the left, as is the case in humans (LeMay and Geschwind, 1975; Yeni-Komshian and Benson, 1976). Finally, there are reports that chimpanzees possess planum temporale asymmetries similar to those of humans (Gannon et al., 1998; Hopkins et al., 1998). Thus, on current evidence, the pattern of asymmetries of the posterior sylvian fissure appears to be qualitatively similar in apes and humans. It remains possible that there are differences between apes and humans in the degree of fissural asymmetry (Yeni-Komshian and Benson, 1976) or differences in the cellular organization of language-related regions; these possibilities have not yet been adequately addressed empirically. The presence of human-like asymmetries in the posterior sylvian fissure of apes, which lack language and handedness, implies that there is no simple relationship between cerebral asymmetries and cognitive and hemispheric dominance for language and upper-limb control in humans (Gannon et al., 1998).

CHANGES AT FINER LEVELS OF ORGANIZATION To date, relatively little attention has been paid to the possibility that humans differ from other primates in the cellular and laminar organization of the cortex. Given the lack of evidence for human-specific cortical areas,

and the rapidly accumulating evidence of phyletic diversity in cortical histology, the search for human specializations at finer levels of cortical organization assumes new importance. As already noted, the development of modern histological techniques, especially immunocytochemistry, makes it possible to compare the cortical organization of humans and other species in considerable detail.

One well-documented difference in the cortical histology of macaques and humans concerns the primary visual area, V1 (figure 84.6). In primates, portions of layer IV stain densely for the metabolic enzyme cytochrome oxidase (CO). In macaques and many other Old and New World monkeys, CO staining occurs in two bands, a thick lower band, corresponding to layer IVC, and a thin upper band, corresponding to layer IVA (Horton, 1984). The dense CO staining in these bands presumably reflects the high level of metabolic activity of the terminals of thalamic afferent fibers, which are extremely numerous in layers IVC and IVA. Humans are different. Although they possess a layer IVA, as judged from cytoarchitecture, layer IVA does not stain densely for CO; humans have only a single CO-dense band, corresponding to layer IVC (Horton and Hedley-Whyte, 1984; Wong-Riley et al., 1993). This suggests that there may be fewer thalamic afferents in IVA of humans than in macaques, or that these afferents have lower firing rates (Wong-Riley et al., 1993). Macaques and humans also differ in the distribution of neurons containing the calcium-binding protein, calbindin: Layer IVA has very few calbindin-immunoreactive cells in macaques, but it has a dense population of these cells in humans (Hendry and Carder, 1993). These findings suggest that the pathway from the parvocellular (P) layers of the LGN, which terminates (in part) in layer IVA of primary visual cortex, was modified at some point in human evolution (Preuss, Qi, and Kaas, 1998).

Humans and macaques also differ in the biology of pyramidal cells. Campbell and Morrison (1989) reported that humans possess more pyramidal cells in the superficial cortical layers that express nonphosphorylated neurofilament protein (recognized by the SMI-32 antibody) than do macaques, this difference being evident across a number of cortical areas. It is not known why some pyramidal cells express the nonphosphorylated neurofilament epitope recognized by SMI-32 while others do not. However, these results suggest that the organization of the upper cortical layers of humans may differ in important ways from macaques. One possibility is that humans possess classes of pyramidal cells that are absent in macaques (Campbell and Morrison, 1989). Alternatively, the connectional organization of the superficial layers may be different in humans and

Macaca

Homo

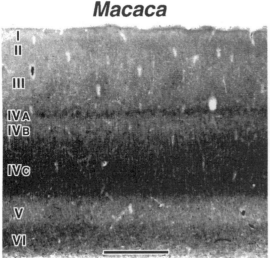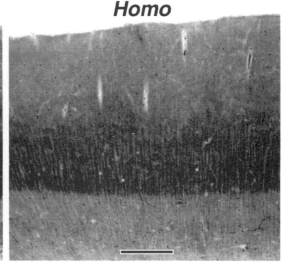

FIGURE 84.6   The laminar organization of the primary visual cortex (area V1 or 17) revealed by staining for cytochrome oxidase (CO). In macaques and other Old World and New World monkeys, there is a distinctive, narrow band of dense CO staining, corresponding to layer IVA, located above the main band of dense staining in layer IVC. In humans, layer IVA does not stain strongly for CO. Scale bars are 500 µm.

macaques. The latter suggestion follows from experimental studies in macaques indicating that pyramidal cells that stain for SMI-32 and those that do not project preferentially to different targets (Hof et al., 1996). The higher percentage of SMI-32 immunoreactive cells in humans as compared to macaques suggests that certain classes of corticocortical projections may be stronger in humans than in macaques. In addition to this difference in pyramidal cells, macaques and humans reportedly differ in the biochemistry of their chandelier cells, a class of cortical interneuron (del Río and DeFelipe, 1997).

The aforementioned studies provide evidence of differences in the cellular and laminar organization of macaque and human cortex. These results do not, however, allow us to determine whether the differences represent *human* specializations in the strict sense, or *hominoid* specializations—i.e., derived features that humans share with apes. To address this issue, my collaborators and I have begun a series of studies comparing the cortical histology of humans, chimpanzees (the animals most closely related to humans), and Old World and New World monkeys. Our initial results indicate that the primary visual cortex of chimpanzees resembles that of humans, and differs from those of macaques and other Old World and New World monkeys, in having a layer IVA that stains weakly for CO and contains a dense band of calbindin-immunoreactive cells (Preuss, Qi, and Kaas, 1998). In addition, we have examined the distribution of neurons expressing nonphosphorylated neurofilament in precentral motor cortex, using SMI-32 (Preuss et al., 1997a). Consistent with Campbell and

Morrison (1989), we found that humans have more SMI-32 immunoreactive pyramidal cells in the outer cortical layers than do macaques. Once again, however, we found that chimpanzees are more like humans than like macaques. Thus, in the aspects of cortical histology we have examined so far, the characteristics that distinguish humans from macaques appear to be hominoid specializations rather than true human specializations.

Conclusions

In order to build theory of human brain systems that can account for distinctively human behavioral and cognitive capacities, we need to understand how the human brain differs from that of other species. As the current survey makes clear, we do not yet have a deep understanding of human brain specializations, although we are in a position to draw certain significant conclusions. Humans have disproportionately enlarged association cortex compared to apes and monkeys; it remains an open question whether humans possess more cortical areas than other primates. Human brains are not merely bigger, better monkey brains, however; they display cerebral asymmetries and features of cortical histology that monkeys lack. Apes, which are more closely related to humans than are monkeys, share with humans a number of brain characteristics not present in monkeys. There is, however, no strong evidence that humans possess more cortical areas than other primates, although the evidence against new human areas remains less than compelling.

This review offers lessons for future research. First, identifying human brain specializations requires comparative studies that include apes, and especially chimpanzees, in addition to monkeys. Studies that compare monkeys and humans, but do not include apes, cannot in principle distinguish hominoid (ape-human) specializations from true human specializations. Second, we need much better maps of cortical areal organization both for humans and other primates if we want to determine definitively whether the evolutionary enlargement of human cortex was accompanied by the addition of new areas, by the enlargement of pre-existing areas (and if so, which areas), or by some combination of both. Third, it is evident that neuroscientists have focused too narrowly on the addition of cortical areas as *the* mode of evolutionary change, neglecting possible changes at finer levels of cortical organization.

Perhaps the most important lesson, however, is that it is possible to pursue the study of human brain specializations very profitably with currently available neuroscientific technologies. While the lack of adequate noninvasive techniques for studying connectivity poses a limitation on our understanding of human specializations, there is every reason to go forward with the techniques currently available for studying cerebral morphology and histology.

The main obstacle to understanding what is human about the human brain is not so much technological as ideological. The special appeal of cognitive neuroscience as a scientific enterprise derives from the widely held belief that there is something unusual about the human brain and cognition. Despite this, adherence to the doctrine of continuity and belief in the basic uniformity of cortical organization have led neuroscientists generally to stress the importance of features of brain organization that are shared widely among species, and to downplay the importance of species differences and the kind of research that is necessary to identify them. But what is distinctively human about the human brain is, after all, a species difference. Unless our profession makes a commitment to comparative studies, and most especially to comparative studies of humans and apes, our knowledge of the human brain will be limited to the ways in which humans resemble monkeys and rats. That would be an important contribution, to be sure, but it would leave cognitive neuroscience without much to say about the very subject that makes the enterprise so appealing in the first place.

ACKNOWLEDGMENTS   The author would like to thank the section editors, John Tooby and Leda Cosmides, and also Mary Anne Case, Emmanuel Gilessen, Jon Kaas, David Kornack, Daniel Povinelli, and Katerina Semendeferi, for providing critical comments on early drafts of this manuscript. The author's research is supported by the USL-New Iberia Research Center and by the McDonnell-Pew Program in Cognitive Neuroscience.

REFERENCES

ABBS, J. H., 1986. Invariance and variability in speech production: A distinction between linguistic intent and its neuromotor implementation. In *Invariance and Variability in Speech Process*, J. S. Perkell and D. S. Klatt, eds. Hillsdale, N.J.: Lawrence Erlbaum, pp. 202–219.

AIELLO, L., and C. DEAN, 1990. *Human Evolutionary Anatomy*. London: Academic Press.

ALBANESE, E., A. MERLO, A. ALBANESE, and E. GOMEZ, 1989. Anterior speech region: Asymmetry and weight–surface correlation. *Arch. Neurol.* 46:307–310.

ALLMAN, J., 1990. Evolution of neocortex. In *Cerebral Cortex. Vol. B: Comparative Structure and Evolution of Cerebral Cortex, Part II*, E. G. Jones and A. Peters, eds. New York: Plenum Press, pp. 269–283.

ARMSTRONG, E., 1982. Mosaic evolution in the primate brain: Differences and similarities in the hominoid thalamus. In *Primate Brain Evolution*, E. Armstrong and D. Falk, eds. New York: Plenum Press, pp. 131–161.

BALEYDIER, C., P. ACHACHE, and J. C. FROMENT, 1997. Neurofilament architecture of superior and mesial premotor cortex in the human brain. *Neuroreport* 8:1691–1696.

BERGER, B., and P. GASPAR, 1995. Comparative anatomy of the catecholaminergic innervation of rat and primate prefrontal cortex. In *Phylogeny and Ontogeny of Catecholamine Systems in the CNS of Vertebrates*, W. J. A. J. Smeets and A. Reiner, eds. Cambridge, Mass.: Cambridge University Press, pp. 293–324.

BLINKOV, S., and I. GLEZER, 1968. *The Human Brain in Figures and Tables*. New York: Basic Books.

BOAKES, R., 1984. *From Darwin to Behaviourism*. Cambridge: Cambridge University Press.

BONIN, G. V., 1944. The architecture. In *The Precentral Motor Cortex*, P. C. Bucy, ed. Urbana, Ill.: University of Illinois Press, pp. 7–82.

BOWLER, P. J., 1996. *Life's Splendid Drama*. Chicago: University of Chicago Press.

BRADSHAW, J. L., and L. J. ROGERS, 1993. *The Evolution of Lateral Asymmetries, Language, Tool Use, and Intellect*. San Diego: Academic Press.

BRODMANN, K., 1909. *Vergleichende Lokalisationslehre der Grosshirnrinde*. Leipzig: Barth (reprinted as Brodmann's *Localisation in the Cerebral Cortex*, translated and edited by L. J. Garey, London: Smith-Gordon, 1994).

BRODMANN, K., 1912. Neue Ergibnisse uber die vergleichende histologische Lokalisation der Grosshirnrinde mit besonderer Berucksichtigung des Stirnhirns. *Anat. Anzeiger (Suppl.)* 41:157–216.

BRÜCKNER, G., G. SEEGER, K. BRAUER, W. HÄRTIG, J. KACZA, and V. BIGL, 1994. Cortical areas are revealed by distribution patterns of proteoglycan components and parvalbumin in the Mongolian gerbil and rat. *Brain Res.* 658:67–86.

BUCY, P. C., 1944. Introduction. In *The Precentral Motor Cortex*, P. C. Bucy, ed. Urbana, Ill.: University of Illinois Press, pp. 1–6.

CAMPBELL, M. J., and J. H. MORRISON, 1989. Monoclonal antibody to neurofilament protein (SMI-32) labels a subpopulation of pyramidal neurons in the human and monkey neocortex. *J. Comp. Neurol.* 282:191–205.

CARMICHAEL, S. T., and J. L. PRICE, 1994. Architectonic subdivision of the orbital and medial prefrontal cortex in the macaque monkey. *J. Comp. Neurol.* 346:366–402.

CASAGRANDE, V. A., and J. H. KAAS, 1994. The afferent, intrinsic, and efferent connections of primary visual cortex in primates. In *Cerebral Cortex, Vol. 10, Primary Visual Cortex in Primates*, A. Peters and K. Rockland, eds. New York: Plenum Press, pp. 201–259.

CHENEY, D. L., and R. M. SEYFARTH, 1990. *How Monkeys See the World*. Chicago: University of Chicago Press.

COLEBATCH, J. G., M.-P. DEIBER, R. E. PASSINGHAM, K. J. FRISTON, and R. S. J. FRACKOWIAK, 1991. Regional cerebral blood flow during voluntary arm and hand movements in human subjects. *J. Neurophysiol.* 65:1392–1401.

CREUTZFELDT, O. D., 1977. Generality of functional structure of the neocortex. *Naturwiss.* 64:507–517.

CRICK, F., and E. G. JONES, 1993. Backwardness of human neuroanatomy. *Nature* 361:109–110.

DARWIN, C., 1871. *The Descent of Man, and Selection in Relation to Sex*. London: John Murray [Facsimile edition: Princeton, N.J.: Princeton University Press, 1981].

DEACON, T. W., 1992. Cortical connections of the inferior arcuate sulcus cortex in the macaque brain. *Brain Res.* 573:8–26.

DEL RÍO, M. R., and J. DEFELIPE, 1997. Colocalization of parvalbumin and calbindin D-28k in neurons including chandelier cells of the human temporal neocortex. *J. Chem. Neuroanat.* 12:165–173.

ECCLES, J. C., 1984. The cerebral neocortex: A theory of its operation. In *Cerebral Cortex. Vol. 2: Functional Properties of Cortical Cells*, E. G. Jones and A. Peters, eds. New York: Plenum Press, pp. 1–36.

EIDELBERG, D., and A. M. GALABURDA, 1984. Inferior parietal lobule: Divergent architectonic asymmetries in the human brain. *Arch. Neurol.* 41:843–852.

ELLIOT SMITH, G., 1924. *The Evolution of Man. Essays*. London: Oxford University Press.

FALK, D., 1992. *Evolution of the Brain and Cognition in Hominids. Sixty-Second James Arthur Lecture on the Evolution of the Human Brain*. New York: American Museum of Natural History.

FALZI, G., P. PERRONE, and L. A. VIGNOLO, 1982. Right-left asymmetry in the anterior speech region. *Arch. Neurol.* 39:239–240.

FLETCHER, P. C., F. HAPPÉ, U. FRITH, S. C. BAKER, R. J. DOLAN, R. S. J. FRACKOWIAK, and C. D. FRITH, 1995. Other minds in the brain: A functional imaging study of "theory of mind" in story comprehension. *Cognition* 57:109–128.

FOUNDAS, A. L., C. M. LEONARD, R. GILMORE, E. FENNELL, and K. M. HEILMAN, 1996. The pars triangularis and speech and language lateralization. *Proc. Natl. Acad. Sci. U.S.A.* 93:719–722.

FOUNDAS, A. L., C. M. LEONARD, and K. M. HEILMAN, 1995. Morphologic cerebral asymmetries and handedness: The pars triangularis and planum temporale. *Arch. Neurol.* 52:501–508.

FRAHM, H. D., H. STEPHAN, and G. BARON, 1984. Comparison of brain structure volumes in insectivora and primates. V. Area striata (AS). *J. Hirnforsch.* 25:537–557.

GALABURDA, A. M., 1980. La région de Broca: Observations anatomiques faites un siècle après la mort de son découvreur. *Rev. Neurol. (Paris)* 136:609–616.

GALABURDA, A. M., 1984. Anatomical asymmetries. In *Cerebral Dominance*, N. Geschwind and A. M. Galaburda, eds. Cambridge, Mass.: Harvard University Press, pp. 11–25.

GALABURDA, A. M., and D. N. PANDYA, 1982. Role of architectonics and connections in the study of brain evolution. In *Primate Brain Evolution*, E. Armstrong and D. Falk, eds. New York: Plenum Press, pp. 203–216.

GALABURDA, A. M., and F. SANIDES, 1980. Cytoarchitectonic organization of the human auditory cortex. *J. Comp. Neurol.* 190:597–610.

GALLESE, V., L. FADIGA, L. FOGASSI, and G. RIZZOLATTI, 1996. Action recognition in the premotor cortex. *Brain* 119:593–609.

GANNON, P. J., R. L. HOLLOWAY, D. C. BROADFIELD, and A. R. BRAIN, 1998. Asymmetry of chimpanzee planum temporale: Humanlike pattern of Wernicke's brain language area homolog. *Science* 279:220–222.

GAREY, L. J., E. WINKELMANN, and K. BRAUER, 1985. Golgi and Nissl studies of the visual cortex of the bottlenose dolphin. *J. Comp. Neurol.* 240:305–321.

GEBHARD, R., K. ZILLES, A. SCHLEICHER, B. J. EVERITT, T. W. ROBBINS, and I. DIVAC, 1995. Parcellation of the frontal cortex of the New World monkey *Callithrix jacchus* by eight neurotransmitter-binding sites. *Anat. Embryol.* 191:509–517.

GESCHWIND, N., and W. LEVITSKY, 1968. Left-right asymmetry in temporal speech region. *Science* 161:186–187.

GLEZER, I. I., P. R. HOF, C. LERANTH, and P. J. MORGANE, 1993. Calcium-binding protein-containing neuronal populations in mammalian visual cortex: A comparative study in whales, insectivores, bats, rodents, and primates. *Cereb. Cortex* 3:249–272.

HARVEY, P. H., and M. D. PAGEL, 1991. *The Comparative Method in Evolutionary Biology*. Oxford: Oxford University Press.

HAYES, T. L., and D. A. LEWIS, 1995. Anatomical specialization of the anterior motor speech area: Hemispheric differences in magnopyramidal neurons. *Brain Lang.* 49:289–308.

HENDRY, S. H., and R. K. CARDER, 1993. Neurochemical compartmentation of monkey and human visual cortex: Similarities and variations in calbindin immunoreactivity across species. *Vis. Neurosci.* 10:1109–1120.

HEWES, G., 1976. The current status of the gestural theory of language origin. *Ann. N.Y. Acad. Sci.* 280:482–504.

HOF, P. R., L. G. UNGERLEIDER, M. J. WEBSTER, R. GATTASS, M. M. ADAMS, C. A. SAILSTAD, and J. H. MORRISON, 1996. Neurofilament protein is differentially distributed in subpopulations of corticocortical projection neurons in the macaque monkey visual pathways. *J. Comp. Neurol.* 376:112–127.

HOPKINS, W. D., L. MARINO, J. K. RILLING, and L. A. MACGREGOR, 1998. Planum temporale asymmetries in great apes as revealed by magnetic resonance imaging (MRI). *Neuroreport* 9:2913–2918.

HORTON, J. C., 1984. Cytochrome oxidase patches: A new cytoarchitectonic feature of monkey visual cortex. *Phil. Trans. R. Soc. Lond.* B 304:199–253.

HORTON, J. C., and E. T. HEDLEY-WHYTE, 1984. Mapping of cytochrome oxidase patches and ocular dominance columns in human visual cortex. *Phil. Trans. R. Soc. Lond.* B 304:255–272.

HORTON, J. C., and D. H. HUBEL, 1981. Regular patchy distribution of cytochrome oxidase staining in primary visual cortex of macaque monkey. *Nature* 292:762–764.

HUTSLER, J. J., and M. S. GAZZANIGA, 1996. Acetylcholinesterase staining in human auditory and language cortices: Regional variation of structural features. *Cereb. Cortex* 6:260–270.

HUXLEY, T. H., 1863. *Evidence as to Man's Place in Nature.* London: Williams and Norgate [Re-issued 1959, Ann Arbor: University of Michigan Press].

IVRY, R. B., and J. V. BALDO, 1992. Is the cerebellum involved in learning and cognition? *Curr. Opin. Neurobiol.* 2:212–216.

JÜRGENS, U., 1979. Neural control of vocalization in nonhuman primates. In *Neurobiology of Social Communication in Primates*, H. D. Steklis and M. J. Raleigh, eds. New York: Academic Press, pp. 11–44.

KAAS, J. H., 1987. The organization and evolution of neocortex. In *Higher Brain Function: Recent Explorations of the Brain's Emergent Properties*, S. P. Wise, ed. New York: John Wiley, pp. 347–378.

KAAS, J. H., 1993. The organization of visual cortex in primates: Problems, conclusions, and the use of comparative studies in understanding the human brain. In *Functional Organization of the Human Visual System*, B. Gulyas, D. Ottoson, and P. E. Roland, eds. Oxford: Pergamon, pp. 1–11.

KAAS, J. H., and L. A. KRUBITZER, 1991. The organization of extrastriate cortex. In *Neuroanatomy of the Visual Pathways and Their Development*, B. Dreher and S. R. Robinson, eds. London: Macmillan, pp. 302–323.

KAAS, J. H., and T. M. PREUSS, 1993. Archontan affinities as reflected in the visual system. In *Mammal Phylogeny: Placentals*, F. S. Szalay, M. J. Novacek, and M. C. McKenna, eds. New York: Springer Verlag, pp. 115–128.

KARMILOFF-SMITH, A., 1992. *Beyond Modularity.* Cambridge, Mass.: MIT Press.

KILLACKEY, H. P., 1995. Evolution of the human brain: A neuroanatomical perspective. In *The Cognitive Neurosciences*, M. S. Gazzaniga, ed. Cambridge, Mass.: MIT Press, pp. 1243–1253.

KIMURA, D., 1976. The neural basis of language qua gesture. In *Studies in Neurolinguistics*, H. Whitaker and H. A. Whitaker, eds. New York: Academic Press, pp. 145–156.

KIMURA, D., 1993. *Neuromotor Mechanisms in Human Communications.* Oxford: Oxford University Press.

LASHLEY, K. S., 1949. Persistent problems in the evolution of mind. *Quart. Rev. Biol.* 24:28–42.

LE GROS CLARK, W. E., 1959. *The Antecedents of Man.* Edinburgh: Edinburgh University Press.

LEINER, H. C., A. L. LEINER, and R. S. DOW, 1986. Does the cerebellum contribute to mental skills? *Behav. Neurosci.* 100:443–454.

LEINONEN, L., J. HYVÄRINEN, G. NYMAN, and I. LINNANKOSKI, 1979. I. Functional properties of neurons in lateral part of associative area 7 in awake monkeys. *Exp. Brain Res.* 34:299–320.

LEMAY, M., and A. CULEBRAS, 1972. Human brain: Morphologic differences in the hemispheres demonstrable by carotid arteriography. *New Eng. J. Med.* 287:168–179.

LEMAY, M., and N. GESCHWIND, 1975. Hemispheric difference in the brains of great apes. *Brain Behav. Evol.* 11:48–52.

LIEBERMAN, P., 1985. On the evolution of human syntactic ability. Its pre-adaptive bases—Motor control and speech. *J. Hum. Evol.* 14:657–668.

MATANO, S., and E. HIRASAKI, 1997. Volumetric comparisons in the cerebellar complex of anthropoids, with special reference to locomotor types. *Amer. J. Physiol. Anthropol.* 103:173–183.

MCGREW, W. C., and L. F. MARCHANT, 1997. On the other hand: Current issues in and meta-analysis of the behavioral laterality of hand function in nonhuman primates. *Yrbk. Phys. Anthropol.* 40:201–232.

MIDDLETON, F. A., and P. L. STRICK, 1994. Anatomical evidence for cerebellar and basal ganglia involvement in higher cognitive function. *Science* 266:458–461.

MOUNTCASTLE, V. B., 1978. An organizing principle for cerebral function: The unit module and the distributed system. In *The Mindful Brain*, G. M. Edelman, ed. Cambridge, Mass.: MIT Press, pp. 7–50.

NISHIKAWA, K. C., 1997. Emergence of novel functions during brain evolution. *BioScience* 47:341–354.

NORTHCUTT, R. G., and J. H. KAAS, 1995. The emergence and evolution of mammalian neocortex. *Trends Neurosci.* 18:373–379.

PASSINGHAM, R. E., 1975. Changes in the size and organization of the brain in man and his ancestors. *Brain Behav. Evol.* 11:73–90.

PAULESCU, E., C. D. FRITH, and R. S. J. FRACKOWIAK, 1993. The neural correlates of the verbal component of working memory. *Nature* 362:342–344.

PAUS, T., R. JECH, C. J. THOMPSON, R. COMEAU, T. PETERS, and A. C. EVANS, 1997. Transcranial magnetic stimulation during positron emission tomography: A new method for studying connectivity of the human cerebral cortex. *J. Neurosci.* 17:3178–3184.

PETERSEN, S. E., P. T. FOX, M. I. POSNER, M. MINTUN, and M. E. RAICHLE, 1988. Positron emission tomographic studies of the cortical anatomy of single-word processing. *Nature* 331:585–589.

PETRIDES, M., and D. N. PANDYA, 1994. Comparative architectonic analysis of the human and the macaque frontal cortex. In *Handbook of Neuropsychology*, F. Booler and J. Grafman, eds. Amsterdam: Elsevier, pp. 17–58.

PHILLIPS, C. G., S. ZEKI, and H. B. BARLOW, 1983. Localization of function in the cerebral cortex: Past, present and future. *Brain* 107:328–361.

POVINELLI, D. J., 1993. Reconstructing the evolution of the mind. *Amer. Psychol.* 48:493–509.

POVINELLI, D. J., and T. J. EDDY, 1996. What young chimpanzees know about seeing. *Monogr. Soc. Res. Child Dev.* 61:i–vi, 1–152; discussion 153–191.

POVINELLI, D. J., and T. M. PREUSS, 1995. Theory of mind: Evolutionary history of a cognitive specialization. *Trends Neurosci.* 18:418–424.

PREUSS, T. M., 1993. The role of the neurosciences in primate evolutionary biology: Historical commentary and prospectus. In *Primates and Their Relatives in Phylogenetic Perspective*, R. D. E. MacPhee, ed. New York: Plenum Press, pp. 333–362.

PREUSS, T. M., 1995a. The argument from animals to humans in cognitive neuroscience. In *The Cognitive Neurosciences*, M. S. Gazzaniga, ed. Cambridge, Mass.: MIT Press, pp. 1227–1241.

PREUSS, T. M., 1995b. Do rats have prefrontal cortex? The Rose–Woolsey–Akert program reconsidered. *J. Cogn. Neurosci.* 7:1–24.

PREUSS, T. M., and P. S. GOLDMAN-RAKIC, 1989. Connections of the ventral granular frontal cortex of macaques with perisylvian premotor and somatosensory areas: Anatomical evidence for somatic representation in primate frontal association cortex. *J. Comp. Neurol.* 282:293–316.

PREUSS, T. M., and P. S. GOLDMAN-RAKIC, 1991a. Myelo- and cytoarchitecture of the granular frontal cortex and surrounding regions in the strepsirhine primate *Galago* and the anthropoid primate *Macaca. J. Comp. Neurol.* 310:429–474.

PREUSS, T. M., and P. S. GOLDMAN-RAKIC, 1991b. Ipsilateral cortical connections of granular frontal cortex in the strepsirhine primate *Galago*, with comparative comments on anthropoid primates. *J. Comp. Neurol.* 310:507–549.

PREUSS, T. M., and J. H. KAAS, 1996. Cytochrome oxidase "blobs" and other characteristics of primary visual cortex in a lemuroid primate, *Cheirogaleus medius. Brain Behav. Evol.* 47:103–112.

PREUSS, T. M., and J. H. KAAS, 1999. Human brain evolution. In *Fundamental Neuroscience*, F. E. Bloom, S. C. Landis, J. L. Robert, L. R. Squire, and M. J. Zigmond, eds. San Diego: Academic Press, pp. 1283–1311.

PREUSS, T. M., H.-X. QI, P. GASPAR, and J. H. KAAS, 1997a. Histochemical evidence for multiple subdivisions of primary motor cortex in chimpanzees. *Soc. Neurosci. Abstr.* 23:1273.

PREUSS, T. M., H.-X. QI, and J. H. KAAS, 1998. Chimpanzees and humans share specializations of primary visual cortex. *Soc. Neurosci. Abstr.* 24:1273.

PREUSS, T. M., I. STEPNIEWSKA, N. JAIN, and J. H. KAAS, 1997b. Multiple divisions of macaque precentral motor cortex identified with neurofilament antibody SMI-32. *Brain Res.* 767:148–153.

PREUSS, T. M., I. STEPNIEWSKA, and J. H. KAAS, 1996. Movement representation in the dorsal and ventral premotor areas of owl monkeys: A microstimulation study. *J. Comp. Neurol.* 371:649–676.

RAJKOWSKA, G., and P. S. GOLDMAN-RAKIC, 1995. Cytoarchitectonic definition of prefrontal areas in the normal human cortex: I. Remapping of areas 9 and 46 using quantitative criteria. *Cereb. Cortex* 5:307–322.

RICHARDS, R. J., 1987. *Darwin and the Emergence of Evolutionary Theories of Mind and Behavior.* Chicago: University of Chicago Press.

RICHARDS, R. J., 1992. *The Meaning of Evolution.* Chicago: University of Chicago Press.

RIZZOLATTI, G., L. FADIGA, V. GALLESE, and L. FOGASSI, 1996. Premotor cortex and the recognition of motor actions. *Cognit. Brain Res.* 3:131–141.

ROCKEL, A. J., R. W. HIORNS, and T. P. S. POWELL, 1980. The basic uniformity of structure of the neocortex. *Brain* 103:221–224.

SCHEIBEL, A. B., L. A. PAUL, I. FRIED, A. B. FORSYTHE, U. TOMIYASU, A. WECHSLER, A. KAO, and J. SLOTNICK, 1985. Dendritic organization of the anterior speech area. *Exp. Neurol.* 87:109–117.

SCHMAHMANN, J. D., 1991. An emerging concept. The cerebellar contribution to higher function. *Arch. Neurol.* 48:1178–1187.

SEMENDEFERI, K., E. ARMSTRONG, A. SCHLEICHER, K. ZILLES, and G. W. VAN HOESEN, 1998. Limbic frontal cor-

tex in hominoids: A comparative study of area 13. *Amer. J. Phys. Anthropol.* 106:129–155.

SEMENDEFERI, K., H. DAMASIO, R. FRANK, and G. W. VAN HOESEN, 1997. The evolution of the frontal lobes: A volumetric analysis based on three-dimensional reconstructions of magnetic resonance image scans of human and ape brains. *J. Human Evol.* 32:375–388.

STEPHAN, H., G. BARON, and H. D. FRAHM, 1988. Comparative size of brains and brain components. In *Comparative Primate Biology, Vol. 4: Neurosciences*, H. D. Steklis and J. Erwin, eds. New York: Liss, pp. 1–38.

STEPHAN, H., J. FRAHM, and G. BARON, 1981. New and revised data on volumes of brain structures in insectivores and primates. *Folia Primatol.* 35:1–29.

STEPNIEWSKA, I., T. M. PREUSS, and J. H. KAAS, 1993. Architectonics, somatotopic organization, and ipsilateral cortical connections of the primary motor area (M1) of owl monkeys. *J. Comp. Neurol.* 330:238–271.

STRAIT, D. S., F. E. GRINE, and M. A. MONIZ, 1997. A reappraisal of early hominid phylogeny. *J. Human Evol.* 32:17–82.

SZENTÁGOTHAI, J., 1975. The 'module-concept' in cerebral cortex architecture. *Brain Res.* 95:475–496.

TAKECHI, H., H. ONOE, H. SHIZUNO, E. YOSHIKAWA, N. SADATO, H. TSUKADA, and Y. WATANABE, 1997. Mapping of cortical areas involved in color vision in non-human primates. *Neurosci Lett.* 230:17–20.

TOMASELLO, M., and J. CALL, 1997. *Primate Cognition.* New York: Oxford University Press.

TOOTELL, R. B., A. M. DALE, M. I. SERENO, and R. MALACH, 1996. New images from human visual cortex. *Trends Neurosci.* 19:481–489.

UNGERLEIDER, L. G., and J. V. HAXBY, 1994. 'What' and 'where' in the human brain. *Curr. Opin. Neurobiol.* 4:157–165.

WALKER, A. E., 1940. A cytoarchitectural study of the prefrontal area of the macaque monkey. *J. Comp. Neurol.* 73:59–86.

WALLMAN, J., 1992. *Aping Language.* Cambridge, Mass.: Cambridge University Press.

WONG-RILEY, M. T. T., R. F. HEVNER, R. CUTLAN, M. EARNEST, R. EGAN, J. FROST, and T. NGUYEN, 1993. Cytochrome oxidase in the human visual cortex: Distribution in the developing and the adult brain. *Vis. Neurosci.* 10:41–58.

WOOD, B., 1996. Human evolution. *BioEssays* 18:945–954.

YENI-KOMSHIAN, G. H., and D. A. BENSON, 1976. Anatomical study of cerebral symmetry in the temporal lobe of humans, chimpanzees and rhesus monkeys. *Science* 192:387–389.

ZILLES, K., A. DABRINGHAUS, S. GEYER, K. AMUNTS, M. QÜ, A. SCHLEICHER, E. GILISSEN, G. SCHLAUG, and H. STEINMETZ, 1996. Structural asymmetries in the human forebrain and the forebrain of non-human primates and rats. *Neurosci. Biobehav. Res.* 20:593–605.

ZILLES, K., G. SCHLAUG, M. MATELLI, G. LUPPINO, A. SCHLEICHER, M. QÜ, A. DABRINGHAUS, R. SEITZ, and P. ROLAND, 1995. Mapping of human and macaque sensorimotor areas by integrating architectonic, transmitter receptor, MRI and PET data. *J. Anat.* 187:515–537.

85

"Theory of Mind" as a Mechanism of Selective Attention

ALAN M. LESLIE

ABSTRACT A key component of human intelligence is our ability to think about each other's mental states. This ability provides an interesting challenge for cognitive neuroscience attempts to understand the nature of abstract concepts and how the brain acquires them. Research over the past 15 years has shown that very young children and children of extremely limited intellectual ability can acquire mental state concepts with ease. Children with Kanner's syndrome have severe difficulty using these concepts, despite relatively great experience and ability. These discoveries have led to the development of the first information processing models of belief-desire reasoning.

The term "theory of mind" was coined by David Premack (Premack and Woodruff, 1978) to refer to our ability to explain, predict, and interpret behavior in terms of mental states, like *wanting, believing,* and *pretending.* Because the behavior of complex organisms is a result of their cognitive properties–their perceptions, goals, internal information structures, and so on–it may have been adaptive for our species to develop some sensitivity to these properties. The capacity to attend to mental state properties is probably based on a specialized representational system and is evident even in young children.

The term "theory of mind" is potentially misleading. It might suggest that the child really has a *theory* or that the child has a theory of *mind* as such. Although there are some writers who hold such views (Perner, 1991; Gopnik and Meltzoff, 1997; Gopnik and Wellman, 1995), I assume simply that the child is endowed with a representational system that captures cognitive properties underlying behavior. To better see what is meant by "theory of mind" ability, consider the following scenario (figure 85.1). Sally has a marble that she places in a basket and covers, and then departs. While she is gone, Ann removes the marble from the basket and places it in the box. A child to whom this scenario is presented then is asked to predict where Sally will look for her marble when she returns. To correctly predict Sally's behavior, it is necessary to take into account both Sally's desire for the marble and Sally's belief concerning the location of the marble. In this scenario, Sally's belief is

ALAN M. LESLIE Department of Psychology and Center for Cognitive Science, Rutgers University, Piscataway, N.J.

rendered false by Ann's tampering. Therefore, to succeed on this task, the child must attribute to Sally a belief that, from the attributer's point of view, is false.

There have been two major discoveries concerning the false-belief problem in figure 85.1. First, Wimmer and Perner (1983), using a somewhat more complex version of the task, found that the majority of 6-year-olds already could pass it, whereas Baron-Cohen and associates (1985), using the version depicted, found that the majority of 4-year-olds could succeed. Subsequently, a large number of studies have confirmed this finding: Whether predicting behavior or reporting where Sally thinks the object is, normally developing children typically solve the problem shortly after the fourth birthday. The second major finding is that autistic children typically fail to solve this task despite mental ages (MAs) well in excess of 4 years, whereas other disabled children–for example, those with Down syndrome–can succeed (Baron-Cohen, Leslie, and Frith, 1985). These two findings raise the following deeply challenging problem for the theorist of cognitive development. How is the young brain able to attend to mental states when mental states cannot be

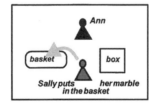

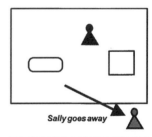

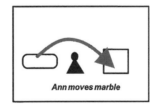

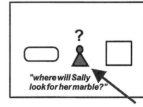

FIGURE 85.1 Illustration of the standard "Sally and Ann" false-belief task given to children to test their ability to attribute beliefs to other people and to calculate the contents of those beliefs correctly. (After Baron-Cohen, Leslie, and Frith, 1985.)

Mother's behavior:

talking to a banana...

Infer mental state:

**mother PRETENDS
(of) the banana (that)
"it is a telephone"**

FIGURE 85.2   The 2-year-old brain can attend to behavior and infer the mental state from which the behavior issues. To do this requires the development of the "M-representation." See this page for further explanation. (After Leslie, 1994.)

seen, heard, or felt? I call this the *fundamental* problem of "theory of mind" because if the child cannot attend to mental states, then how can he or she learn about them?

Previously (Leslie, 1987), I proposed a general answer to the fundamental question of how the young brain can attend to mental states: Attend to behavior and infer the mental state from which the behavior arises. For example, the 2-year-old child watches as mother talks to a banana. If the child were limited to representing simply the mother's behavior then he or she would be unable to recover the significance of the mother's behavior. This he or she can do only by inferring that the mother is pretending that the banana is a telephone (figure 85.2). In fact, 2-year-olds are quite capable of this feat (Harris and Kavanaugh, 1993; Leslie, 1987, 1994).

For the young brain to move attention from behavior to the mental state from which the behavior issues, appropriate processing mechanisms must deploy a system of representation capable of representing mental states. I call this system of representation the *M-representation*, and the associated processing mechanisms the *theory of mind mechanism* (ToMM).

The M-representation provides agent-centered descriptions of behavior using three-place relations that make explicit four kinds of information. The first piece of information specifies the agent involved. The second piece of information identifies an "informational relation" or attitude that the agent holds. The third piece of information identifies an aspect of the world that anchors

the agent's attitude, and the final piece of information identifies the content of the agent's attitude. For example, in the agent-centered description of the mother's behavior shown in figure 85.2, the M-representation shows the agent, **mother**, holding the attitude, **pretends-true**, toward the content, "**it is a telephone**," with regard to the **banana**. The M-representation system is highly flexible. The present example can be extended easily to cover: own pretend play, by having the child process an M-representation which identifies the agent as self (I **pretend-true** of **the banana** "it is a telephone"); different mental states, including false beliefs (**mother believes-true of the banana "it is a telephone"**); different anchors; and different contents. Forming and processing an M-representation requires the brain to integrate information from a number of very different sources.

These ideas led my colleagues and me to develop a neuropsychological perspective on autism, a perspective that also has helped us to understand the normal development of social intelligence (Baron-Cohen, 1995; Frith, Morton, and Leslie, 1991; Happé, 1995; Leslie, 1987, 1991, 1992, 1994; Leslie and German, 1995; Leslie and Roth, 1993; Leslie and Thaiss, 1992; Roth and Leslie, 1998; see also chapter 87). According to the model, the M-representation is deployed by a dedicated processor, ToMM. The ToMM is a specialized component of social intelligence providing the time-pressured, on-line intentional interpretations of behavior that are necessary for an agent to take part effectively in conversations and other real-time social interactions. The ToMM is a mechanism of selective attention, it operates postperceptually, it operates spontaneously whenever an agent's behavior is attended, it is domain specific, and it is subject to dissociable damage. In the limit, the ToMM may be modular. The ToMM employs a proprietary representational system, namely the M-representation. The ToMM is hypothesized to form the specific basis of our capacity to acquire "theory of mind." Finally, the ToMM is damaged in autism (Kanner's syndrome), resulting in the core signs of that neurodevelopmental disorder.

Background assumptions about autism

Autism is a disorder affecting at least 4 or 5 in 10,000 births; approximately 75% of those affected are mentally retarded. The evidence is overwhelming that the disorder has a biological etiology (Gillberg and Coleman, 1992) and is most likely genetic in origin (see chapter 87; also see Bailey et al., 1995).

At present, autism is diagnosed on behavioral grounds, including impaired social skills, language delay, lack of pretend play, and stereotypes, with onset before

36 months of age (American Psychiatric Association, 1994). Large-scale epidemiological studies by Wing and Gould (1979) showed that autistic children suffer a "triad of impairments" relative to nonautistic mentally retarded children matched on mental age. The triad of impairments includes social incompetence, poor verbal and nonverbal communicative skills, and a lack of pretend play. Although approximately 25% of children with autism are not mentally retarded, they still show the "triad of impairments" compared with their peers. This suggests that the triad, although central to the syndrome of autism, is not the result of general mental retardation but reflects a more specific impairment at the cognitive level (Leslie, 1987). Because "theory of mind" abilities underlie human social competence, communication, and pretending, the autistic triad might be the result of an impaired ToMM. These speculations led to the prediction that autistic children would be specifically impaired in their understanding of beliefs in other people.

Investigating the theory of mind mechanism hypothesis: Initial phase

To test the predicted impairment in belief understanding, Baron-Cohen, Leslie, and Frith (1985) studied three groups of children: normally developing 4-year-olds, children with autism, and children with Down syndrome. Subjects were tested on the Sally and Ann false-belief task (figure 85.1). To allow a conservative test of the hypothesis, the autistic children were older (12 years) and thus more experienced than the other two groups (10 years and 4 years) and had a higher mean IQ (82) than the children with Down syndrome (64). After an experimenter explained the scenario with the aid of props, subjects were asked three questions: a Memory question, "In the beginning, where did Sally put her marble?"; a Reality question, "Where is the marble now?"; and a Prediction test question, "Where will Sally look for her marble?"

The results were striking. Eighty-five percent of the normally developing children and 86% of the children with Down syndrome attributed Sally a false belief and predicted that she would look in the basket. Only 20% of the autistic children predicted Sally's behavior in this way, failing as a group to show their advantage in age, experience, and ability.

Leslie and Frith (1988) replicated these findings with a group of autistic children with mean verbal MAs of 7 years, 2 months, comparing them to MA-matched specific language impaired (SLI) children. All the SLI children passed the task; by contrast, only 28% of the autistic children passed. Leslie and Frith also showed that although autistic children were perfect in a "line of

sight" task, they performed poorly in a test of "seeing leads to knowing." Perner and associates (1989) investigated a second false-belief task with autistic children. In this task, the child is shown a container for a well-known candy and asked, "What's in here?" After the child names the candy, the container is opened and the child is shown that it contains only a pencil. The pencil then is replaced and the container again closed. The child is told that when his or her friend comes in, the friend too will be shown the container and asked what is inside. The child then is asked what the friend will say. The results on this task for normally developing children closely follow those obtained from the Sally and Ann task: typically, 3-year-olds fail to predict behavior by attributing a false belief, whereas 4-year-olds typically succeed. Perner and colleagues (1989) found that almost 100% of MA-matched SLI children passed the candies task, whereas 83% of their able autistic group failed.

These initial findings have been replicated and extended by different laboratories around the world (Baron-Cohen, 1995; Mitchell, Saltmarsh, and Russell, 1997; Naito, Komatsu, and Fuke, 1994; Ozonoff, Pennington, and Rogers, 1991; Prior, Dahlstrom, and Squires, 1990; Reed, 1994; Sodian and Frith, 1992; Tager-Flusberg, 1992). Autistic children are impaired in their understanding of beliefs relative to normal developmental milestones, relative to their own level of general intellectual functioning, and relative to other syndromes of mental retardation and language impairment. This pattern is consistent with impairment to their ToMM.

A key question and a key finding

How do we know that the failure of autistic children on false-belief tasks is not due to an impairment in general processing or general reasoning? It is easy to think of nonspecific impairments that would impact on these tasks, for example, impaired working memory, poor executive function, limited abstract reasoning, difficulties with counterfactual reasoning, or other nameless processing factors impaired in critical combinations.

To answer this question, a task that closely parallels the general problem-solving structure of false-belief tasks, but without engaging mental state concepts, would be useful. Zaitchik (1990) devised just such a task, the so-called "photographs" task, in which Sally is downsized, replaced by "hi-tech," namely a Polaroid camera. Sally's belief is replaced by a photograph: a mental representation is replaced by a public representation.

Because photographs and other pictures are easily attended to, can be picked up, pointed to, discussed with mother, and almost always are out of date, they should have a marked advantage in the development of the child over invisible, intangible, immaterial beliefs.

The task begins by ensuring that preschoolers understand the basics of the operation of the camera. After training, the children are asked to take a photograph of a toy cat sitting on a chair (figure 85.3). When the photograph emerges from the camera, the experimenter places it face down on a table. The child does not get to see the photograph; after all, the child did not get to see Sally's belief! The cat then is moved from the chair and placed on the bed. The child is asked the usual control questions, "When you took the photograph, where was the cat? Where is the cat now?" Finally, the child is asked the crucial test question, "In the photograph, where is the cat?"

When Zaitchik gave this task to preschoolers, the results resembled those obtained from the false-belief task: 3-year-olds typically failed, answering the test question with the current location of the cat, whereas 4-year-olds typically passed.

Leslie and Thaiss (1992) adapted this task for use with autistic children and compared their performance with that of normally developing 4-year-olds. Two standard false-belief tasks, the Sally and Ann and candies tasks, were given, along with two photographs tasks—the aforementioned task and a second task in which the photographed object subsequently is replaced with a different object. In this latter task, the test question is, "In the photograph, what is on the chair?" This asks for the identity of an object, as does the test question in the candies task.

The results showed that most of the normally developing 4-year-olds passed both the out-of-date belief tasks and their equivalent out-of-date photograph tasks. Although their performance on the belief and photograph tasks did not differ significantly, for children who passed only one of the tasks, there was a tendency to pass false belief. This tendency also was found by Zaitchik (1990) in her three experiments that allowed the comparison. Together with the pair of tasks from Leslie and Thaiss (1992), these five studies show the same small advantage for out-of-date beliefs over photographs, *using closely parallel task structures*. Experiment-wise, the effect is reliable ($p = .032$), with normally developing children finding false beliefs slightly easier than out-of-date photographs.[1]

If only general learning mechanisms are involved, it is surprising that photographs and other pictures are not easier to learn about than beliefs. Moreover, despite attempts to put a brave face on it (Perner, 1995; Leekam and Perner, 1991), these findings are a particular embarrassment for accounts in which the child comes to understand belief by discovering a "theory" about mental states, namely, the theory that *"mental states are represen-*

tations" (Perner, 1991). The failure to find a large advantage for pictures over beliefs supports the idea that something in the young brain compensates for the invisibility of belief. Apparently, if anything, beliefs are easier, not harder, to learn about. This highlights the proposed role of the ToMM as a mechanism that directs attention to otherwise unattendable mental states and thus promotes learning.

The results from the autistic subjects in the study by Leslie and Thaiss (1992) were strikingly different. Autistic children showed their characteristic poor performance on both false-belief tasks coupled with near perfect performance on the equivalent photographs tasks, reversing the pattern found in normally developing children.

Leslie and Thaiss ran a further study in which the camera and photograph were replaced by a "map." Subjects were familiarized with a simple diagrammatic map of a doll's house and were trained in how a puppet, placed on a piece of furniture, could have its position marked on the map with a colored sticker. During testing, the experimenter placed a puppet on the bed and placed a sticker on the map to show where the dog was. Again, the child did not get to see the marked map. The doll then was moved from the bed onto the toy box. After the usual control questions, the child was asked "In the map, where is the doll?" Again, the autistic children fared better on the public representation task than on false belief, whereas the normally developing children showed the opposite pattern.

Figure 85.4 puts these results together. It shows how the autistic children performed with the normal profile on public representation tasks, only with greater success— *as they should*, given their age and ability advantage over the other group. When a belief task enters the comparison, a crossover emerges.

These results help rule out a whole class of explanation for the poor performance of autistic children on false-belief tasks. For example, if autistic children perform poorly on false-belief tasks because of limited working memory, because of poor executive function, or because of impaired counterfactual reasoning, then why did the photographs/maps tasks not also demand these things? Similarly, for impaired event memory, for poor attention shifting, for poor mental imagery, and for other "general" impairments, it is hard to see why false-belief problems require the favored resource while other representation tasks do not. These findings challenge accounts that rely on an impairment in a general capacity.

The double dissociations in figure 85.4 suggest that although autistic children possess the general problem-solving resources required by the false-belief task, they are impaired in a specific representational competence,

FIGURE 85.3   The out-of-date photograph task. (Reproduced from Happé, 1995, by permission of the artist, Axel Scheffler.)

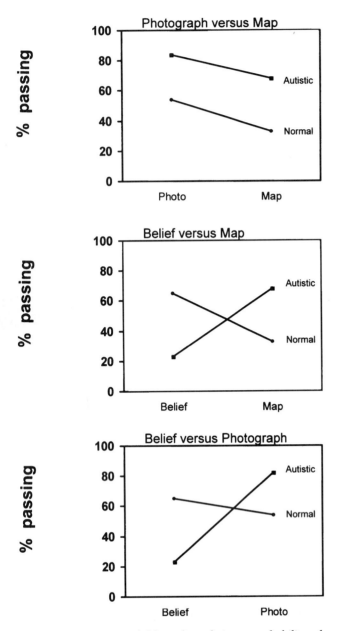

FIGURE 85.4 Autistic children show their age and ability advantage over normally developing 4-year-old children on tasks testing understanding of out-of-date public representations (top panel). When tasks with the same general structure but testing understanding of the mental state *belief* are introduced, autistic performance collapses, revealing a double dissociation between understanding public and mental representations (bottom two panels). (Data from Leslie and Thaiss, 1992.)

for example, the ToMM. The picture for normally developing children is crucially different and consistent with the idea that those who fail false-belief tasks do so because of limitations in general resources. Leslie and Thaiss proposed that the ToMM alone is not sufficient for the standard false-belief task, which requires a further mechanism. They called this extra mechanism selection processing (SP). They argued that the ToMM by

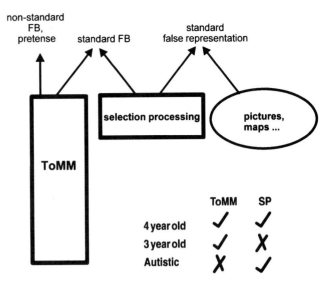

FIGURE 85.5 The theory of mind mechanism–selection processing (ToMM–SP) model of "theory of mind" development. Some problems require only the ToMM, for example, recognizing pretense and "modified" nonstandard false-belief tasks that typically are passed by normally developing 3-year-old children but are hard for autistic children. Standard false-belief tasks require the cooperation of SP with the ToMM, typically are failed by 3-year-olds and by autistic children, but typically are passed by 4-year-olds. Public representation tasks with the same task structure as standard false-belief tasks also require SP but do not involve the ToMM; these tasks are passed by normally developing 4-year-olds and autistic children. Normally developing children have an intact ToMM, but younger children have only weak SP. Autistic children are a mirror image of 3-year-olds with adequate SP but an impaired ToMM. (After Leslie and Thaiss, 1992.)

default attributes a belief with a content that reflects current reality. To succeed in a false-belief task, this default attribution must be *inhibited* and an alternative nonfactual content for the belief selected instead. Standard photograph tasks also demand SP. The normal 3-year-old fails both kinds of task because he or she has only weak SP. The successful 4-year-old has both an intact ToMM and sufficiently strong SP to pass standard tasks. The autistic child is a mirror image of the 3-year-old in so far as he or she has sufficiently strong SP (to pass photographs and maps) but an impaired ToMM. Figure 85.5 summarizes the ToMM-SP model of "theory of mind" development.

Examining failure on false belief: A second phase of research

Thus far, autistic children have been compared with normally developing 4-year-olds and nonautistic mentally retarded children who *pass* standard false-belief tasks. This work has established a specific impairment in "theory of mind" abilities in autistic children. More recently, we have been studying the reason for autistic failure by comparing autistic children with normally developing 3-year-olds who also *fail* standard false-belief tasks. Do these two groups fail for the same reasons?

A number of studies are showing that these groups fail for different reasons. In the first such study, Roth and Leslie (1991) modified a false-belief task so that it became easier for 3-year-olds. Although most of the 3-year-olds in this task successfully attributed a false belief, most of the older autistic subjects did not. Roth and Leslie (1998) found differences between normally developing 3-year-olds and older autistic subjects on a "seeing leads to knowing" task. In a further experiment, Roth and Leslie (1998) showed that a modified false-belief task was easier than a standard false-belief task for 3-year-olds but not for autistic subjects, and that selection processing demands were a limiting factor on 3-year-old performance but not on autistic performance.

A number of modifications to the standard false-belief task are known to help 3-year-olds achieve better performance. The most minimal modification to the standard false-belief task that helps 3-year-olds is to ask, "Where will Sally look *first* for her marble?" Siegal and Beattie (1991) found that the addition of the single word "first" dramatically improved performance in a task in which children are told explicitly what Sally thinks. Surian and Leslie (1999) applied this minimal modification to a standard Sally and Ann task. One potential problem with asking where Sally will look first is that children simply might respond with where the object had been placed *first.* They then would appear to pass the task without ever considering Sally's belief. Or children might assume, on being asked about a first look, that there will be a series of looks culminating in success and that the first look will therefore be a *failing* look. Again, responding with a failing look, children will appear to pass the task without ever considering Sally's belief. To control for these possibilities, Surian and Leslie tested children on a control task in which Sally does not go away but instead watches while Ann moves the marble from the basket to the box. In this case, Sally knows where the marble is. If children in this condition follow either of the placed-first or failing-look strategies, they again will indicate the empty location; however, in the true-belief condition, such a response is wrong.

Normally developing children approximately 3 years and 9 months of age were tested in one of four conditions: a standard false-belief condition; an equivalent "standard" true-belief condition in which Sally stays and watches; a "look first" false-belief condition; and an equivalent "look first" true-belief condition. Only 30% of children in the standard false-belief condition passed,

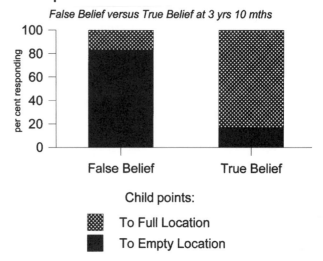

Responses to "Look first" Question

False Belief versus True Belief at 3 yrs 10 mths

Child points:
- To Full Location
- To Empty Location

FIGURE 85.6   Three-year-old children respond correctly to a "look first" prediction question in both false-belief and true-belief tasks, although correct responses are opposite in the two tasks. The "look first" modification therefore helps 3-year-old children to calculate belief. (After Surian and Leslie, 1999.)

a typical result, whereas all the children passed the corresponding true-belief version. In the "look first" conditions, 83% of the children passed false belief, whereas the same proportion passed the true-belief equivalent. The children in the latter two groups produced opposite responses when asked "Where will Sally look first for her marble?" depending on the belief status of Sally (figure 85.6).

The "look first" question helps younger children calculate a false belief. How does it do this? One possibility suggested by Siegal and Beattie (1991) is that it helps younger children recognize the questioner's intention to ask about a belief rather than about reality. This may well be correct, but it does not indicate how it helps younger children do this, nor does it indicate why slightly older children do not need such help. Surian and Leslie (1999) suggest that by directing children's attention to the first location of the object or to the possibility of failing looks, the question increases the salience of the first location *as the possible content* of Sally's belief. This increased salience of the nonfactual content relative to the default reduces the need for inhibition, and thus, the task places less load on SP.

Surian and Leslie (1999) carried out a second experiment to determine whether the "look first" question also would help autistic children with false belief. In this study, a "think" question was asked before the usual control questions. After the control questions, the children were asked the "look first" version of the "prediction" question. With this design, the same child can be

Think versus Look First Questions
Normally developing 3yr. 5m. old and Autistic children

FIGURE 85.7 The "look first" question improves younger 3-year-old performance over a standard "think" false-belief question. No such improvement is seen in older autistic children. (After Surian and Leslie, 1999).

asked a standard task "think" question followed by a nonstandard "look first" question. A comparison group of normally developing children of approximately 3 years and 5 months of age also was tested in this way. The normally developing children again were helped by the "look first" question, although not as much as before, presumably because they were younger. The children with autism, by contrast, were not helped at all (figure 85.7).

In summary, normally developing 3-year-olds and older autistic children fail false-belief tasks for different reasons. There is growing evidence that normally developing children's performance on false-belief problems is limited by processing resources rather than by an inability to represent belief states in others. These processing resources increase gradually over the preschool period and by the time the child is a little older than 4 years of age usually are sufficient to allow success on standard tasks. Older children with autism fail false-belief tasks for different reasons, apparently reflecting an impaired capacity to acquire normal "theory of mind" knowledge and skills. The emerging pattern supports the ToMM-SP model.

Inhibition in belief-desire reasoning

So far we have been considering why children fail false-belief tasks. It is equally important to develop models of how children pass these tasks. One requirement is the ability to represent the right kinds of information: information about agents, attitudes, anchors, and contents tied together in the relational structure modeled by the M-representation. But simply being able to deploy concepts, like *pretend, desire,* and *believe,* does not guarantee that the child is able to solve particular "theory of mind" problems or already knows particular "theory of mind" facts.

We saw earlier that default belief attributions need to be inhibited to solve a false-belief problem and suggested that producing and controlling this inhibition may be a problem for young children. Performance changes due to the maturation of prefrontal cortex may be ubiquitous in development (Diamond, 1988; Goldman-Rakic, 1987), and Carlson and associates (1998) provide independent evidence of inhibitory involvement in the development of "theory of mind" skills.

It is useful to understand why belief attribution has a default bias. If *desires* set an agent's goals, *beliefs* inform the agent about the state of the world. A belief that misinforms an agent is a useless, even dangerous, thing: beliefs *ought* to be true. Therefore, the best guess strategy for the naive belief attributer is to assume that an agent's beliefs *are* true. Apparently, this is the strategy followed by the 3-year-old. However, false-belief tasks require that the default strategy be over-ridden. According to the ToMM–SP model, to do so requires inhibition of the prepotent attribution. The older child's success shows that he manages this inhibition.

In a standard false-belief task, there are essentially two possible locations, the basket and the box, to which Sally's belief about the marble might refer or which might be targets of Sally's desire. The default belief attribution draws attention to one of these locations, namely, the current location of the object. To successfully solve the false-belief problem, the brain must disengage attention from this target and shift to the false-belief target. Inhibitory brain processes appear to be involved in other kinds of attention shifting, for example, in shifting covert visual attention (Posner and Presti, 1987; Rafal and Henik, 1994). According to the ToMM–SP model, belief-task target shifting also requires inhibitions.

Leslie and Polizzi (1998) tested the belief inhibition hypothesis by following up a finding of Cassidy (1995). Cassidy found that when the desire in a standard false-belief task is negative rather than positive, then 4-year-old children perform poorly. Typically, in false-belief task scenarios, Sally wants the target object; but in Cassidy's task, Sally did *not* want to find the target. Leslie and Polizzi argued that the critical feature was not negation as such but whether the negation produced target shifting. Suppose a protagonist has a desire for whichever location does not have property X, and the only way to identify the NOT(X) location is to first identify the X location, and then choose the other one, that is, NOT(X). Identifying the protagonist's desire target this way involves the brain in target shifting. For example, Sally has a box and a basket that both contain some wool. She does not want to put a fish in the basket because there is a sick kitten nestling in the wool there (the kitten might get worse if it eats the fish). To identify where Sally wants to put the fish, one first identifies which location has the kitten, then, because this is *not* what Sally wants, one shifts from this location to the alternative. This creates a target-shifting desire.

Leslie and Polizzi (1998) pointed out an interesting feature of inhibition models of belief-desire reasoning. With true belief and positive desire, there is no target shifting. A false belief (with positive desire) involves a single target-shifting inhibition; so does a target-shifting desire (with true belief). However, when a false belief is combined with a target-shifting desire to produce a double inhibition task, the two inhibitions cannot simply sum their inhibitions because this will produce the wrong answer. Working through figure 85.8 will clarify this last point.

The four panels in figure 85.8 correspond to four kinds of behavior prediction task. The first is the simple true-belief plus positive-desire task: Sally wants the object and knows where it is. The pointing hand represents a mental index that the brain uses to indicate the target of Sally's belief and desire, and therefore the answer to the prediction task. In this model, belief and desire targets are identified in parallel. The next panel is the standard false-belief task. Here the first belief-desire index again indicates the location that contains the object because the initial belief attribution always is the default true belief, that is, where someone *should* think the object is. But in this task, the protagonist's belief is false and so, to succeed, the subject must inhibit this index. In the second panel, the inhibition is visualized by the "inhibition arm" reaching in to weaken the index. Because the initial target is inhibited, the index moves across to the alternate location, yielding the correct prediction that the protagonist will look in the empty location.

The third panel in figure 85.8 shows a true-belief with target-shifting desire. Again, the initial belief index shows the default true-belief location. The initial desire index shows the same target because the protagonist desires the NOT(X) location and the only way to identify that is to first identify the X location, then cancel it in favor of NOT(X). So in this panel, the inhibition arm inhibits the desire target and again the index moves to the empty location, generating the correct prediction.

The final panel shows how to predict behavior when the protagonist's belief is false and desire "negative." Once again, the belief-desire index initially is placed against the full location. But now two inhibitions must

Inhibitory processing in belief tasks

Inhibition of inhibition

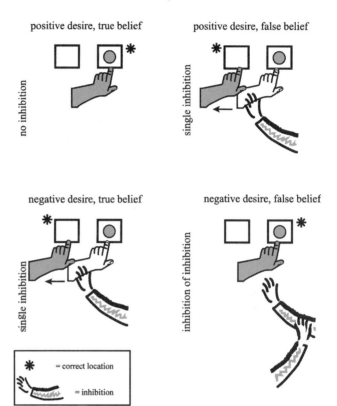

FIGURE 85.8   A model of selection processing in belief-desire reasoning. The panels are arranged to illustrate a 2×2 factorial design with rows ± desire and columns ± belief. The pointing hand represents a mental index indicating the target of belief desire and thus, the answer to a "prediction of behavior" question. The grabbing arm represents an inhibitory brain process that weakens an index to which it is applied (reduced shading). Indexes are set initially for true belief and positive desire but subsequently inhibited if the belief is false (second panel) or the desire "negative" (third panel). Weakening of an index causes the index to move to the alternate location. The final panel shows double inhibitions canceling out, rather than summing. This gives the correct answer to false-belief with "negative-desire" problems. (After Leslie and Polizzi, 1998.)

be mobilized, one for the belief because it is false and one for the desire because it is a desire for NOT(X). If both these inhibitions are applied, as before, to the initial target, then it will be inhibited doubly and the index again will move to the empty location. But this time, predicting the empty location is wrong. If Sally wrongly believes the sick kitten to be in the left-hand location and does not want to put the fish in with the kitten, then Sally will try to put the fish in the right-hand location, where the kitten is. To get the correct answer, the two inhibitions cannot be applied in the usual way. Instead, one inhibition must inhibit the other so that no inhibition reaches the initial target. The index then does not move, and Sally's behavior is predicted correctly. Even though logically, double inhibition problems have the same answer as simple true-belief + positive-desire tasks, the model predicts difficulty from marshaling an inhibition of inhibition.

Leslie and Polizzi (1998) tested the aforementioned prediction on a group of 4-year-olds who passed a standard false-belief task. One half of the children were given a true-belief with target-shifting desire task to measure how difficult it was for them to shift targets from a desire. Only a single child out of 16 tested failed the true-belief task, presumably because shifting from desire targets is easy for 4-year-olds who can target shift in a standard false-belief task. The other half of the subjects were tested with a false belief coupled with target-shifting desire. Here the results were dramatically different. Only 38% of this group correctly predicted which box Sally would approach with the fish.

To answer "think" questions requires calculating belief only; prediction of behavior requires taking into account both belief and desire. Despite this, children's success on "think" and "prediction" in standard tasks is tightly linked. So it is particularly interesting that all of the aforementioned children who failed "prediction" had, immediately before this, passed a "think" question.

The same pattern was found in a second experiment in which Leslie and Polizzi examined whether the aforementioned effects are caused by the linguistic demands of the negation used in stating the desire. Children were introduced to the "Mixed-up Man," a character who always does the opposite of what he wants: if he wants to pat a dog, he pats a cat; if he wants to eat ice cream, he eats a carrot. A scenario was constructed similar to the Sally-with-fish-and-kitten story but with the Mixed-up Man looking for a Mexican jumping bean which, unbeknownst to him, jumps from one box to the other. The key point is that the Mixed-up Man's desire was entirely positive but his behavior was opposite, so that negation did not appear in the protocol. Nevertheless, to predict his behavior, one first had to identify the target of a normal man's action, then shift to the alternate. From the point of view of selection-inhibition theory, what is critical is not negation but whether tasks are processed such that target shifting occurs. Indeed, the false beliefs in standard tasks always are positive but, according to the SP hypothesis, involve target shifting.

The novel Mixed-up Man introduced general difficulty because a substantial number of children failed the true-belief version of the task. Despite being far from ceiling on behavioral target shifting, significantly more

Prediction of behavior in belief tasks

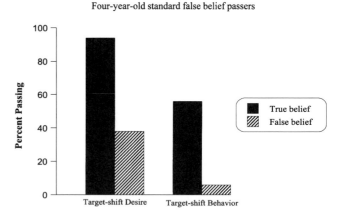

FIGURE 85.9 Four-year-old children who have passed a standard false-belief task can easily combine a "negative" (target-shift) desire with a true belief, but combination with a false belief is very hard. A "target-shift behavior" task was fairly difficult for these children, even with true belief but overwhelmingly difficult when combined with false belief. In both cases, false-belief calculations were difficult even though the false belief was available in memory as shown by ceiling performance on a "think" question. (After Leslie and Polizzi, 1998.)

children failed the double inhibition version. Results from both experiments are shown in figure 85.9.

One interpretation of these results is simply that 4-year-olds are so close to using up all their resources in solving a false-belief task that the addition of *any* further complexity pushes them below threshold. Even the tiny demand from desire-target shifting is sufficient to produce a catastrophic effect. However, this seems unlikely in view of the robustness of 4-year-old performance on a wide variety of standard false-belief tasks (Gopnik 1993), and the lack of reports of other minor modifications that seriously disrupt their performance. However, what is especially intriguing about our findings with double inhibition is that the false-belief calculation should contribute *any* difficulty at all to prediction. Recall that the child solved the false-belief problem to answer the "think" question. All the child has to do then is *remember the answer* for 3 seconds and combine it with *desire* to predict behavior. It is deeply puzzling on a resource model why this task should be any harder than the easy true-belief version: there too, the child simply has to remember the true belief attributed seconds earlier and combine it with desire to predict behavior. It is as if a child is asked to calculate 2 + 2 (hard), manages to get the right answer, then is asked to add 1 to that, and, in response, proceeds to calculate, not 4 +1 (easy), but 2 + 2 + 1 (extremely hard).

The inhibition of inhibition model explains the aforementioned effect only on the assumption that prediction mandates recalculation of belief despite the answer's availability in memory. Such rigid behavior might reflect the modular character of the ToMM. However, Leslie and Polizzi (1998) proposed a second inhibition model that accounts for these findings without assuming mandatory recalculation. The alternative model is based on the idea of *inhibition of return*. Inhibition of return is an effect familiar from studies of visual attention. It is harder to return attention to a visual target that has been previously attended then disengaged from than it is to attend to the target for the first time (Rafal and Henik, 1994). The model in figure 85.10 assumes that belief (and therefore the belief target) is calculated first and desire targets identified relative to belief. In the critical doubled case, the true-belief target is inhibited first, causing the index to shift to the other location. The desire target is set initially to this second location but, because the desire is "negative," this too must be inhibited, forcing return to the initial location. But the initial location still is inhibited, making return to it difficult. Now, because the first target was inhibited in the process of answering the "think" question correctly, even if the answer is remembered simply for a few seconds, the double inhibition prediction requires return to that still inhibited target. Even without mandatory recalculation, this will be difficult.

One recent study may indicate that recalculation is mandatory. Polizzi and Leslie (1999) tested a group of 4-year-old standard false-belief passers on the "double inhibition" task, outlined previously, but this time instead of asking where Sally would go with the fish, they asked where Sally would go *first*. Recall that asking a "look first" question helps 3-year-old children pass an otherwise standard false-belief task. Surian and Leslie (1999) hypothesized that this was because the word "first" made the nonfactual content more salient, reducing the need for inhibition of the default content. If "look first" works that way for 3-year-olds, might it also help 4-year-olds on double inhibition tasks? Polizzi and Leslie (1999) found that indeed it does: 81% of a group of 4-year-olds succeeded on the double inhibition task when asked the "look first" question. For 4-year-olds to be helped in this way, prediction must force recalculation of belief.

Summary

Rather than assume that because mental state concepts are abstract they can only be acquired by the child constructing a theory, I analyze "theory of mind" as a mechanism of selective attention. Mental state concepts

Inhibitory processing in belief tasks:
return to inhibited target

FIGURE 85.10 An alternative model of inhibitory processing in belief-desire reasoning. Instead of identifying the target of belief and desire in parallel, in this model belief targets are identified first and desire targets second. Desire targets are identified in relation to belief targets. Again, indexes are set initially for true belief and positive desire but, subsequently, the belief target is inhibited if the belief is false (second panel) and the desire target inhibited if the desire is "negative" (third panel). The final panel shows the resulting sequence in the double inhibition task. First, the target of true belief is identified and inhibited, causing the belief target to move to the alternative. The target of positive desire then is identified in relation to the new false belief target. Finally, the positive-desire target is inhibited, forcing return to the still inhibited true-belief target. (After Leslie and Polizzi, 1998).

simply allow the brain to attend selectively to corresponding mental state properties of agents and thus permit learning about those properties. Autistic children are impaired specifically in this attentional mechanism and find it hard to learn about the mental life of agents. Normally developing preschoolers acquire greater flexibility in attending to the contents of mental states, in particular, to the contents of beliefs that are false. The first information processing models of belief-desire reasoning were outlined.

NOTE

1. Leekam and Perner (1991) found exactly equal numbers of passers and failers, whereas Slaughter (1998) and Perner and associates (in press) used nonparallel task structures, voiding the comparison.

REFERENCES

AMERICAN PSYCHIATRIC ASSOCIATION, 1994. *Diagnostic and Statistical Manual of Mental Disorders*, 4th edition. Washington, D.C.: APA.

BAILEY, A., A. LeCOUTEUR, I. GOTTESMAN, P. BOLTON, E. SIMONOFF, E. YUZDA, and M. RUTTER, 1995. Autism as strongly genetic disorder: Evidence from a British twin study. *Psychol. Med.* 25:63–77.

BARON-COHEN, S., 1995. *Mindblindness: An essay on autism and theory of mind.* Cambridge, Mass.: MIT Press.

BARON-COHEN, S., A. M. LESLIE, and U. FRITH, 1985. Does the autistic child have a "theory of mind"? *Cognition* 21:37–46.

CARLSON, S. M., L. J. MOSES, and H. R. HIX, 1998. The role of inhibitory processes in young children's difficulties with deception and false belief. *Child Dev.* 69:672–691.

CASSIDY, K. W., 1995. Use of a desire heuristic in a theory of mind task. Paper presented to the *Biennial Meeting of the Society for Research in Child Development*, April 1995, Indianapolis, Ind.

DIAMOND, A., 1988. Differences between adult and infant cognition: Is the crucial variable presence or absence of language? In *Thought Without Language*, L. Weiskrantz, ed. Oxford: Oxford Science Publications, pp. 335–370.

FRITH, U., J. MORTON, and A. M. LESLIE, 1991. The cognitive basis of a biological disorder: Autism. *Trends Neurosci.* 14: 433–438.

GILLBERG, C., and M. COLEMAN, 1992. *The Biology of the Autistic Syndromes–2nd Edition. Clinics in Developmental Medicine No. 126.* New York: Cambridge University Press (Mac Keith Press).

GOLDMAN-RAKIC, P. S., 1987. Development of cortical circuitry and cognitive function. *Child Dev.* 58:601–622.

GOPNIK, A., 1993. How we know our minds: The illusion of first-person knowledge of intentionality. *Behav. Brain Sci.* 16: 1–14.

GOPNIK, A., and A. N. MELTZOFF, 1997. *Words, Thoughts, and Theories.* Cambridge, Mass.: MIT Press.

GOPNIK, A., and H. M. WELLMAN, 1995. Why the child's theory of mind really *is* a theory. In *Folk Psychology: The Theory of Mind Debate.* M. Davies and T. Stone, eds. Oxford: Blackwell, pp. 232–258.

HAPPÉ, F. G., 1995. *Autism: An Introduction to Psychological Theory.* Cambridge, Mass.: Harvard University Press.

HARRIS, P. L., and R. KAVANAUGH, 1993. The comprehension of pretense by young children. *Soc. Res. Child Dev. Monogr.* 231.

LEEKAM, S., and J. PERNER, 1991. Does the autistic child have a "metarepresentational" deficit? *Cognition* 40:203–218.

LESLIE, A.M., 1987. Pretense and representation: The origins of "theory of mind." *Psychol. Rev.* 94:412–426.

LESLIE, A. M., 1991. The theory of mind impairment in autism: Evidence for a modular mechanism of development? In *Natural Theories of Mind: Evolution, Development and Simulation of Everyday Mindreading*, A. Whiten, ed. Oxford: Blackwell, pp. 63–78.

LESLIE, A. M., 1992. Autism and the "Theory of Mind" module. *Curr. Dir. Psychol. Sci.* 1:18–21.

LESLIE, A. M., 1994. *Pretending* and *believing*: Issues in the theory of ToMM. *Cognition* 50:211–238.

LESLIE, A. M., and U. FRITH, 1988. Autistic children's understanding of seeing, knowing and believing. *Br. J. Dev. Psychol.* 6:315–324.

LESLIE, A. M., and T. P. GERMAN, 1995. Knowledge and ability in "theory of mind": One-eyed overview of a debate. In *Mental Simulation: Philosophical and Psychological Essays*, M. Davies and T. Stone, eds. Oxford: Blackwell, pp. 123–150.

LESLIE, A. M., and P., POLIZZI, 1998. Inhibitory processing in the false belief task: Two conjectures. *Dev. Sci.* 1:247–258.

LESLIE, A. M., and D. ROTH, 1993. What autism teaches us about metarepresentation. In *Understanding Other Minds: Perspectives from Autism*, S. Baron-Cohen, H. Tager-Flusberg, and D. Cohen, eds. Oxford: Oxford University Press, pp. 83–111.

LESLIE, A. M., and L. THAISS, 1992. Domain specificity in conceptual development: Neuropsychological evidence from autism. *Cognition* 43:225–251.

MITCHELL, P., R. SALTMARSH, and H. RUSSELL, 1997. Overly literal interpretations of speech in autism: Understanding that messages arise from minds. *J. Child Psychol. Psychiatry* 38:685–691.

NAITO, M., S. KOMATSU, and T. FUKE, 1994. Normal and autistic children's understanding of their own and others' false belief: A study from Japan. *Br. J. Dev. Psychol.* 12:403–416.

OZONOFF, S., B. F. PENNINGTON, and S. J. ROGERS, 1991. Executive function deficits in high-functioning autistic individuals: Relationship to theory of mind. *J. Child Psychol. Psychiatry* 32:1081–1105.

PERNER, J., 1991. *Understanding the Representational Mind.* Cambridge, Mass.: MIT Press.

PERNER, J., U. FRITH, A. M. LESLIE, and S. R. LEEKAM, 1989. Exploration of the autistic child's theory of mind: Knowledge, belief and communication. *Child Dev.* 60:689–700.

PERNER, J., S. LEEKAM, D. MYERS, S. DAVIS, and N. ODGERS, in press. Misrepresentation and referential confusion: Children's difficulty with false beliefs and outdated photographs. *Br. J. Dev. Psychol.*

POLIZZI, P. A., and A. M. LESLIE, 1999. "Look first" eases inhibitory demands in the false belief task. Paper presented to the Biennial Meeting of the Society for Research in Child Development, April, Albuquerque, N. Mex.

POSNER, M. I., and D. E. PRESTI, 1987. Selective attention and cognitive control. *Trends Neurosci.* 10:13–17.

PREMACK, D., and G. WOODRUFF, 1978. Does the chimpanzee have a theory of mind? *Behav. Brain Sci.* 4:515–526.

PRIOR, M., B. DAHLSTROM, and T. SQUIRES, 1990. Autistic children's knowledge of thinking and feeling states in other people. *J. Child Psychol. Psychiatry* 31:587–601.

RAFAL, R., and A. HENIK, 1994. The neurology of inhibition: Integrating controlled and automatic processes. In *Inhibitory Processes in Attention, Memory and Language.* D. Dagenbach and T. H. Carr, eds. New York: Academic Press, pp. 1–51.

REED, T., 1994. Performance of autistic and control subjects on three cognitive perspective-taking tasks. *J. Autism Dev. Disord.* 24:53–66.

ROTH, D., and A. M. LESLIE, 1991. The recognition of attitude conveyed by utterance: A study of preschool and autistic children. *Br. J. Dev. Psychol.* 9:315–330.

ROTH, D., and A. M. LESLIE, 1998. Solving belief problems: Toward a task analysis. *Cognition* 66:1–31.

SIEGAL, M., and K. BEATTIE, 1991. Where to look first for children's knowledge of false beliefs. *Cognition* 38:1–12.

SLAUGHTER, V., 1998. Children's understanding of pictorial and mental representations. *Child Dev.* 69:321–332.

SODIAN, B., and U. FRITH, 1992. Deception and sabotage in autistic, retarded and normal children. *J. Child Psychol. Psychiatry* 33:591–605.

SURIAN, L., and A. M. LESLIE, 1999. Competence and performance in false belief understanding: A comparison of autistic and three-year-old children. *Br. J. Dev. Psychol.* 17:141–155.

TAGER-FLUSBERG, H., 1992. Autistic children's talk about psychological states: Deficits in the early acquisition of a theory of mind. *Child Dev.* 63:161–172.

WIMMER, H., and J. PERNER, 1983. Beliefs about beliefs: Representation and constraining function of wrong beliefs in young children's understanding of deception. *Cognition* 13:103–128.

WING, L., and J. GOULD, 1979. Severe impairments of social interaction and associated abnormalities in children: Epidemiology and classification. *J. Autism Dev. Disord.* 9:11–29.

ZAITCHIK, D., 1990. When representations conflict with reality: The preschooler's problem with false beliefs and "false" photographs. *Cognition* 35:41–68.

86 The Cognitive Neuroscience of Autism: Evolutionary Approaches

SIMON BARON-COHEN

ABSTRACT   An evolutionary approach to the cognitive neuroscience of autism generated the "theory of mind" (ToM) hypothesis. Most of its predictions of selective deficits in this domain have been confirmed. Currently attempts are being made to isolate the brain basis of the ToM deficits in autism. The ToM hypothesis has considerable explanatory power in relation to the "triad symptoms" of autism (social, communication, and imagination abnormalities) but has little relevance to the nontriad symptoms (attention to detail, islets of ability, and obsessions). An evolutionary hypothesis to account for these in terms of superior folk physics is discussed.

This chapter illustrates how an evolutionary approach has generated a key hypothesis in the cognitive neuroscience of autism. It then reintroduces the evolutionary approach to generate a new hypothesis for those features that are not yet well understood. But first, what is autism?

Autism is considered to be the most severe of the childhood neuropsychiatric conditions. It is diagnosed on the basis of abnormal development of social behavior, communication, and imagination, often in the presence of marked obsessional, repetitive, or ritualistic behavior (APA, 1994). In an attempt to understand the so-called "triad" impairments in autism (social, communication, and imagination abnormalities), my colleagues and I adopted an evolutionary framework. We asked the following questions: (1) Might mechanisms for understanding and interacting with the social world be specialized adaptations, universal both to current hominids and ancestrally? (2) If so, what might such ancient cognitive mechanisms be? (3) Could such mechanisms become selectively impaired as a result of a genetic factor? (4) Might autism be such a case of genetic caused impairment to specialized social-cognitive mechanisms?

To answer these questions we turned to the philosophical, primatological, and human developmental literatures as pointers to the prerequisites for hominid social interaction. Three key texts led to the same clear conclusions: Human social life is characterized by the neces-

SIMON BARON-COHEN   Departments of Experimental Psychology and Psychiatry, University of Cambridge, Cambridge, U.K.

sary adoption of the "intentional stance" (Dennett, 1987), that is, understanding action by ascribing mental states (beliefs, desires, intentions, etc.) to agents; humans appear to do this universally, whilst chimpanzees (or other nonhuman primates) only do this in a very limited way, if at all (Premack and Woodruff, 1978); and in the normal case even a 4-year-old child can pass a shockingly complex test of social intelligence or mental state ascription, namely, a test of understanding *false beliefs* (Wimmer and Perner, 1983). This fundamental and apparently uniquely human ability has been called a *theory of mind* (ToM). My colleagues and I therefore set out to test the ToM hypothesis of autism–that such children might for genetic reasons have a selective deficit in this most essential of neurocognitive mechanisms (Baron-Cohen, Leslie, and Frith, 1985). The relevant evidence is summarized next.

The theory of mind hypothesis: Experimental evidence

FIRST-ORDER THEORY OF MIND TESTS   *First-order* tests involve inferring what one person thinks, knows, intends, or desires. There is a good deal of experimental evidence to review, so this section is necessarily concise. For clarity, different cognitive tests used are in italics.

Most children with autism are at chance on tests of the *mental-physical distinction* (Baron-Cohen, 1989a). They also have been shown to have an appropriate understanding of the functions of the brain but have a poor understanding of the *functions of the mind* (Baron-Cohen, 1989a). That is, they do not spontaneously mention the mind's mental function (in thinking, dreaming, wishing, deceiving, etc.). They also fail to make the *appearance-reality distinction* (Baron-Cohen, 1989a). They fail a range of *first-order false belief* tasks, that is, they fail to distinguish between their own current belief and that of someone else (Baron-Cohen, Leslie, and Frith, 1985; Baron-Cohen, Leslie, and Frith, 1986; Leekam and Perner, 1991; Perner et al., 1989; Reed and Peterson, 1990; Swettenham et al., 1996) They also fail tests assessing whether they understand the principle that "*seeing leads*

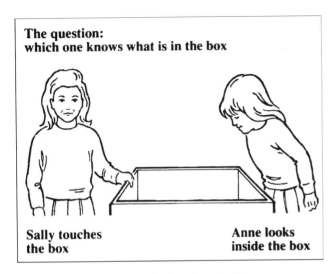

The question:
which one knows what is in the box

Sally touches
the box

Anne looks
inside the box

FIGURE 86.1   The "seeing leads to knowing" test.

to knowing" (Baron-Cohen and Goodhart, 1994; Leslie and Frith, 1988). For example, when presented with two dolls, one of which touches a box and the other of which *looks inside* the box, then asked "Which one *knows* what's inside the box?" they are at chance in their response (figure 86.1). In contrast, normal children of 3 to 4 years of age correctly judge that it is the one who looked who knows what's in the box.

Children with autism are at chance on a test of *recognizing mental state words* (like "think," "know," and "imagine") in a wordlist (Baron-Cohen et al., 1994). They also do not produce the same range of mental state words in their spontaneous speech (Baron-Cohen, Leslie, and Frith, 1986; Tager-Flusberg, 1992). They also are impaired in the production of spontaneous *pretend play* (Baron-Cohen, 1987; Lewis and Boucher, 1988; Wing and Gould, 1979; Ungerer et al., 1981). Pretend play is relevant here because it is thought to involve understanding the mental state of pretending. Although they can understand simple causes of emotion (such as situations and desires), most children with autism have difficulty on tests of understanding more *complex causes of emotion* (such as beliefs) (Baron-Cohen, 1991a; Baron-Cohen, Spitz, and Cross, 1993).

They also fail tests of recognizing *the eye-region of the face* as indicating when a person is thinking and what a person might want (Baron-Cohen et al., 1995; Baron-Cohen and Cross, 1992). Children and adults without autism use gaze to infer both of these mental states. They fail a test of being able to *monitor their own intentions* (Phillips, Baron-Cohen, and Rutter, 1998). That is, they are poor at distinguishing whether they "meant" to do something or whether they did something accidentally.

They also have problems on tests of *deception* (Baron-Cohen, 1992; Sodian and Frith, 1992; Yirmiya,

Solomonica-Levi, and Shulman, 1996), a result that would be expected if one was unaware that people's beliefs can differ and therefore can be manipulated. They also fail tests of *understanding metaphor, sarcasm, and irony*–these all being intentionally nonliteral statements (Happe, 1993). Indeed, they fail to produce most aspects of *pragmatics* in their speech (Baron-Cohen, 1988; Tager-Flusberg, 1993) and fail to recognize violations of pragmatic rules, such as the Gricean Maxims of conversational cooperation (Surian, Baron-Cohen, and Van der Lely, 1996). Because many pragmatic rules involve tailoring one's speech to what the listener needs to know, or might be interested in, this can be seen as intrinsically linked to a theory of mind. Most children with autism also have difficulties in tests of *imagination* (Scott and Baron-Cohen, 1996), for example, producing drawings of impossible or totally fictional entities such as two-headed men. This could reflect a difficulty in thinking about their own mental state of imagination or reflect difficulties in flexible behavior (Leevers and Harris, 1998). Supporting an imagination deficit, they also do not show the normal facilitation effect of imagination on logical reasoning (Scott, Baron-Cohen, and Leslie, in press), unlike normally developing children. Performance on ToM tasks by children with autism has been found to correlate with real-life social skills, as measured by a modified version of the Vineland Adaptive Behaviour Scale (Frith, Happ, and Siddons, 1994).

SECOND-ORDER, ADOLESCENT, AND ADULT THEORY OF MIND TESTS   A small minority of children or adults with autism pass first-order false belief tests. However, these individuals often fail *second-order false belief tests* (Baron-Cohen, 1989b), that is, tests of understanding what one character believes another character thinks. Such second-order reasoning usually is understood by normal children of 5 to 6 years of age (Sullivan, Zaitchik, and Tager-Flusberg, 1994), and yet individuals with autism with a mental age above this level may fail these tests. This suggests that there can be a *specific developmental delay* in theory of mind at a number of different points. Some individuals with autism who are very high functioning (in terms of intelligence quotient [IQ] and language level), and who are old enough, may pass even second-order tests (Bowler, 1992; Happe, 1993; Ozonoff, Pennington, and Rogers, 1991). Those who can pass second-order tests, however, may have difficulties in *understanding stories* in which characters are motivated by complex mental states such as bluff and double bluff (Happe, 1994). Equally, such able subjects have difficulties in decoding complex mental states from the expression in the eye-region of the face (Baron-Cohen, Jolliffe,

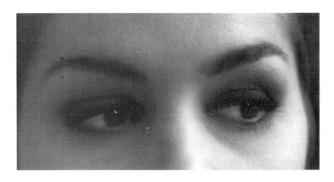

FIGURE 86.2   An item from the "reading the mind in the eyes" test. Is this face concerned or unconcerned?

Mortimore, and Robertson, 1997; Baron-Cohen, Wheelwright, and Jolliffe, 1997). Examples of the *Eyes Test* are shown in figure 86.2. Again, this suggests that the mind-reading deficit may only be detectable in such high-level, older subjects using sensitive, age-appropriate tests.

Similarly, children with Asperger's syndrome (AS) may pass first- and second-order ToM tests but fail to detect *faux pas* in speech (Baron-Cohen et al., in press). Detecting faux pas, of course, is all about detecting who said the "wrong" thing—that is, detecting who said something that the listener should not *know* about. Finally, parents of children with AS, at least one of whom presumably carries the genes for AS, also show difficulties in attributing mental states when just the eye-region of the face is available (Baron-Cohen and Hammer, 1997).

For this reason, autism has been conceptualized as involving "mindblindness" *to varying degrees* (Baron-Cohen, 1990, 1995).

UNIVERSALITY   To test whether the ToM deficit is universal in autism, more complex, subtle, or age-appropriate ToM tests may have to be used. When these have been used, ToM deficits do appear to be universal in autism and AS (Baron-Cohen, Joliffe, et al., 1997). A different approach to addressing the universality question is to adopt Uta Frith's suggestion (Frith, 1989) that there should be no cases of someone with an autism spectrum condition who passes a ToM test at the right chronological or mental age. (Thus, even a child with AS, if tested at 4 years old, should fail a false-belief test, even if he or she can pass it when retested at 6 years, for example. Such a pattern would fit the specific developmental delay hypothesis [Baron-Cohen, 1989b].)

VALIDITY   Some authors (Waterhouse, Fein, and Modahl, 1996) have claimed that no correlation between ToM deficits and social skills is found. In fact, when the *relevant* social skills are assessed (namely, social skills in-

volving mentalizing) strong correlations are found (Frith, Happe, and Siddons, 1994). A further point surrounding validity is that because ToM skills only appear in the preschool years, and yet autism develops by the end of the first year of life, this may mean that ToM deficits cannot be a core of the condition (Rutter and Bailey, 1993). This argument is wrong simply because it ignores the work on infancy precursors to ToM, which is reviewed next.

INFANCY PRECURSORS TO THEORY OF MIND   Leslie (1987) proposed that normally, a theory of mind already is evident in the capacity for pretense, and in children with autism, an early manifestation of the ToM deficit lies in their inability to pretend. Why? In his view, to understand that someone else might *pretend* that "this banana is real," the child (according to Leslie) would need to be able to represent the agent's *mental attitude* toward the proposition. One idea, then, is that ToM is first evident from approximately 18 to 24 months of age in the normal toddler's emerging pretend play.

However, there is some evidence that ToM might have *even earlier* developmental origins. There are severe deficits in *joint attention* skills in children with autism (Sigman et al., 1986). Joint attention skills are those behaviors produced by the child that involve monitoring or directing the target of attention of another person, so as to coordinate the child's own attention with that of somebody else (Bruner, 1983). Such behaviors include the pointing gesture, gaze-monitoring, and showing gestures, most of which are absent in most children with autism. Joint attention behaviors normally are fully developed by about 14 months of age (Butterworth, 1991; Scaife and Bruner, 1975), so their absence in autism signifies a very early-occurring deficit.

What is the evidence for lack of joint attention in autism? One study (Baron-Cohen, 1989d) found that young children (younger than 5 years old) with autism produced one form of the pointing gesture (imperative pointing, or pointing to request) while failing to produce another form of pointing (declarative pointing, or pointing to share interest). This dissociation was interpreted in terms of the declarative form of pointing alone being an indicator of the child monitoring another person's mental state—in this case, the mental state of "interest," or "attention." More recent laboratory studies have confirmed the lack of spontaneous gaze-monitoring (Charman et al., 1997; Leekam et al., 1997; Phillips, Baron-Cohen, and Rutter, 1992; Phillips et al., 1996). Absence of joint attention at 18 months of age, in combination with an absence of pretend play, is a very strong predictor of autism, both in a high-risk study of siblings who are undiagnosed (Baron-Cohen, Allen, and Gillberg, 1992) and in a random population study (Baron-Cohen et al., 1996). In the latter study, 16,000 children at 18 months of age were screened by their health visitors for these behaviors using the Checklist for Autism in Toddlers (CHAT). Just 12 children of the total population lacked joint attention and pretend play, 11 of whom were discovered to have an autism spectrum disorder.[1] The joint attention deficit in autism has received a great deal of research attention and currently is one of the best validated cognitive deficits in the condition (Mundy, 1995; Mundy and Crowson, 1997; Mundy, Sigman, and Kasari, 1990, 1994).

The finding of both joint attention and ToM deficits in autism may not be a coincidence if joint attention is a *precursor* to the development of a ToM. This is plausible because joint attention involves attending to another person's mental state of attention (Baron-Cohen, 1989c, 1989d, 1991b).

DOES THE THEORY OF MIND DEFICIT IMPLY MODULARITY?   One possibility is that there may be a particular part of the brain that normally is responsible for understanding mental states that is specifically impaired in autism. This may be modular, as in Leslie's proposal of an innate theory of mind mechanism (Leslie, 1987, 1991; Leslie and Roth, 1993). Leslie (see also chapter 85) suggests that the function of such a mechanism is to represent information in a data-structure of the following form: [Agent-Attitude-"Proposition"]–for example: [Fred-thinks-"the safe is behind the Picasso"]. Such a proposal is sufficient to allow representation of the full range of mental states, in the attitude slot. Leslie's computational analysis has been widely accepted, although the innate modularity claim is more controversial (Carruthers, 1996; Russell, 1997b). Future work needs to focus on testing this claim against alternatives. For example, lower level social-perception mechanisms (an Eye-Direction Detector [EDD], an Intentionality Detector [ID], and a Shared Attention Mechanism [SAM]) may provide input to ToM, so that what is innate may be an attentional bias to relevant social information (faces, actions, eyes) (Baron-Cohen, 1994). Russell (1997a) argues that the ToM deficit can be produced by nonmodular, executive dysfunction.

Note that the modularity thesis of ToM has been tested in a series of single cases of neurological patients: (1) A patient with severe specific language impairment (SLI) but with intact ToM demonstrates the potential independence of language and ToM (Van der Lely, 1997). (2) A patient with impaired executive function (EF) but intact ToM demonstrates the potential independence of

EF and ToM. Some patients with Tourette's syndrome meet these criteria (Baron-Cohen, Robertson, and Moriarty, 1994). (3) A patient with intact EF but impaired ToM also suggests the independence of these two cognitive domains (Baron-Cohen, et al., in press). (4) A person with a very high IQ but ToM impairments demonstrates the existence of pure deficits in social intelligence, independent of general intelligence (Baron-Cohen et al., in press). (5) Patients with low IQs but intact ToM prove the same point. Patients with Williams syndrome fulfill this criterion (Tager-Flusberg, Boshart, and Baron-Cohen, 1998).[2]

It is entirely possible that the ToM deficit in autism occurs for genetic reasons because autism appears to be strongly heritable (Bailey et al., 1995; Bolton and Rutter, 1990; Le Couteur et al., 1996). The idea that the development of ToM normally is under genetic/biological control is consistent with evidence from cross-cultural studies. Normally developing children from markedly different cultures seem to pass tests of theory of mind at roughly the same ages (Avis and Harris, 1991). Which brain areas might be involved in ToM?

THE NEURAL BASIS OF THEORY OF MIND   Exactly which part of the brain might subserve ToM is not yet clear, although candidate regions include the following: the right *orbitofrontal cortex*, which is active when subjects are thinking about mental state terms during functional imaging using single photon emission computed tomography (SPECT) (Baron-Cohen et al., 1994); and the *left medial frontal cortex*, which is active when subjects are drawing inferences about thoughts while undergoing positron-emission tomography (PET) scan (Fletcher et al., 1995; Goel et al., 1995). The first PET study to look at adults with autism/AS during a ToM task shows that such patients do not show the same patterns of neural activation when thinking about other minds (Happe et al., 1996); other candidate regions include the *amygdala* (Baron-Cohen and Ring, 1994). Ongoing studies suggest that adult patients with acquired amygdala lesions have difficulties with advanced (or adult-level) ToM tasks (Andy Young, personal communication, 1999), and a recent functional magnetic resonance imaging (fMRI) study of ToM using the Eyes Task (described earlier) found that although normal controls used areas of the frontotemporal cortex and the amygdala, high-functioning adults with autism or AS did not activate the amygdala during this task (Baron-Cohen et al., 1999). Finally, the demonstration of a joint attention deficit in autism and the role that the *superior temporal sulcus* in the monkey brain plays in the monitoring of gaze-direction (Perrett et al., 1985) has led to the idea that the superior temporal sulcus may be involved in the development of a ToM (Baron-Cohen and Ring, 1994).

SUMMARY The ToM deficit in autism is present to varying degrees in individuals of different ages with autism or AS. It can be seen at least as early as 18 months of age, in the form of an absence of joint attention and pretend play; and this is not only of interest to basic science but is of clinical significance in improving early diagnosis. Future research needs to explore the first year of life, using prospective studies of high-risk populations, to better understand the ontogenesis of both ToM and autism. The ToM hypothesis is successful in explaining the "triad" symptoms of autism (social, communication, and imagination deficits) but has almost no relevance to the "nontriad" symptoms (attention to detail, strong obsessions, islets of ability). What might explain these?

Reintroducing the evolutionary framework to explain the nontriad symptoms of autism

Existing attempts to account for the nontriad symptoms of autism essentially paint these symptoms in terms of deficits (central coherence is said to be "weak" [Frith, 1989], or executive control is said to be "dysfunctional" [Russell, 1997a]). In this section, I rethink the nontriad features to keep evolutionary considerations central and to emphasize these features as reflecting superior abilities, not deficits.

The evolutionary view of cognition is in terms of domain specificity. A number of theorists have suggested that rather than adopting the traditional ways of carving-up of cognition, one should instead study cognitive development in terms of a small set of "core domains of cognition," motivated by an evolutionary framework (Carey, 1985; Gelman and Hirschfield, 1994; Pinker, 1997; Sperber et al., 1995; Wellman and Gelman, 1998). This refers to domains of knowledge that develop very early in human infancy, with a universal pattern of ontogenesis, and an initial state that is likely to be in part innate. The universalist approach here immediately underlines that these aspects of cognition may be fundamental and result from evolutionary selection pressures at least as old as early hominids, if not older.

A consensus among these researchers is that two such core domains of cognition are *folk psychology* and *folk physics*. The term "folk" is intended to emphasize that this knowledge develops without any formal teaching. Some authors also use the terms "intuitive psychology" and "intuitive physics." Folk psychology is our everyday ability to understand and predict an agent's behavior in

terms of intentional states such as goals, beliefs, and desires. It is what we considered earlier, under the heading of theory of mind. Folk physics is our everyday ability to understand and predict the behavior of inanimate objects in terms of principles relating to physical causality.

As indicated in the section on the experimental evidence of the ToM hypothesis, an impaired folk psychology characterizing autism seems beyond any doubt. But it is plausible that there might also be an intact or even *superior* folk physics in autism. In the following discussion of this, we include the following within folk physics: understanding of objects, machines, physical-causality, and physical systems. How well are predictions from this view of autism confirmed?

There is a range of relevant evidence to consider. First, children with autism certainly understand physical causality (Baron-Cohen et al., 1986). They also seem to understand machines such as cameras (Leekam and Perner, 1991; Leslie and Thaiss, 1992), possibly better than mental age-matched controls. In addition, many of their obsessional interests center on machines and physical systems (Baron-Cohen, 1997; Baron-Cohen and Wheelwright, in press).

If *impaired folk psychology together with superior folk physics* were a good characterization of the cognitive phenotype of autism, then this also might constitute the "broader phenotype" of those first-degree relatives of children with autism who carry the relevant genes but express them to a lesser degree. Recent studies bear this out. First, parents of children with AS show impairments on an adult test of folk psychology (the Reading the Mind in the Eyes Test), together with a superiority on the Embedded Figures Test (Baron-Cohen and Hammer, 1997a). Exactly what the Embedded Figures Test is a test of is unclear, although at one level it measures how one analyzes wholes into their parts, and this may be a prerequisite of folk physics. Second, fathers of children with autism, as well as grandfathers, are over-represented in occupations such as engineering relative to occupations such as social work (Baron-Cohen, Wheelwright, et al., 1997). Engineering is a clear example of an occupation that requires good folk physics, whereas social work is a clear example of an occupation that requires good folk psychology. Similarly, students in the fields of math/physics/engineering are more likely to have a relative with autism than are students in the humanities (Baron-Cohen et al., 1998). These family studies all are consistent with the idea that the autistic spectrum phenotype at the cognitive level involves this *combination* of superior folk physics with impaired folk psychology. This is summarized in the model in figure 86.3 relating cognition to symptoms.

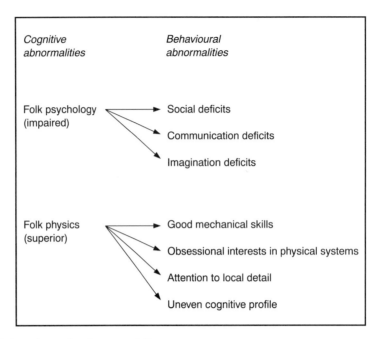

FIGURE 86.3 A model of the relationship between folk psychology and folk physics.

The extreme male brain theory of autism: A third evolutionary hypothesis

There is one more interesting evolutionary hypothesis to consider, and this picks up an old but undeveloped idea from Asperger (1944), who wrote "The autistic personality is an extreme variant of male intelligence. . . . In the autistic individual the male pattern is exaggerated to the extreme" (Frith, 1991). The extreme male brain (EMB) theory is explored in detail elsewhere (Baron-Cohen and Hammer, 1997b). One clue to the EMB theory is that in autism, the sex ratio is 4 males to 1 female (Rutter, 1978). The 4:1 sex ratio is true of autism when one includes individuals with this condition at all points on the IQ scale. If one restricts it to individuals with autism with an IQ in the normal range (referred to as either "high-functioning autism" or AS[3]), the sex ratio is even more dramatically biased against males: Wing (1988) estimates it as 9:1 (male:female), and Ehlers and associates (1997) recently documented a ratio of 40:0 (m:f). Because high-functioning autism or AS may be considered to be "pure autism" (i.e., not confounded by the effects of mental retardation; Frith, 1989), it may be that these sex ratios are more accurate estimates of how the sexes are affected differentially by this condition.

A second clue to the EMB theory is that superior folk physics skills (seen in autism and AS) also generally are associated with being male: the sex ratio in fields like engineering, math, and physics remains heavily biased toward males. Whether this reflects biological or social factors has not been established. A third clue is that three recent studies have found sex differences in the rate of development of folk psychology/ToM skills (Baron-Cohen, Joliffe, et al., 1997; Baron-Cohen et al., in press; Happe, 1995) in all cases showing a female superiority. The implication is that if the male brain[4] involves this combination of impaired folk psychology and superior folk physics to a mild degree, in autism spectrum disorders this combination occurs to a more marked extent.

Conclusions

The evolutionary framework used might help explain why a condition like autism persists in the gene pool: The very same genes that lead an individual to have a child with autism can lead to superior functioning in the domain of folk physics. Pinker (1997) argues that the evolution of the human mind should be considered in terms of its evolved adaptedness to the environment. In his view, the brain needed to be able to maximize the survival of its host body in response to at least two broad challenges: the physical environment and the social environment. The specialized cognitive domains of folk physics and folk psychology can be seen as adaptations to each of these. One possibility is that a cognitive profile of superior folk physics along with impaired folk psychology could arise for genetic reasons because some brains are better adapted to understanding the social environment whereas other brains are better adapted to understanding the physical environment. Exactly why this relationship should occur between these two domains is not clear: Is this neural compensation by one domain over another? Are these two independent domains that can dissociate from one another to a greater or lesser extent? How are such domains constructed in the first place? These are questions for the future.

ACKNOWLEDGMENTS   The author was supported by the Medical Research Council, the Wellcome Trust, and the Gatsby Foundation during the period of this work.

NOTES

1. In the paper reporting this result, the rate was 10 of 12 affected children. Subsequent follow-up of these cases reveals the rate is now 11 of 12.
2. Caution is needed to distinguish the innate modularity thesis of ToM from an acquired modularity thesis of ToM.
3. High-functioning autism is the term used when an individual of normal IQ meets criteria for autism, including a delay in the onset of speech; Asperger syndrome (AS) is the term used when an individual of normal IQ meets criteria for autism, but with no delay in the onset of speech (ICD-10, 1994).
4. Note that the theory therefore defines what constitutes the male brain. This cognitive profile does not have to be true of every biological male, of course. There are many individuals who are biologically male who do not have the male brain, as so defined. Equally, there are some individuals who are biologically female who have the male brain, so defined.

REFERENCES

APA, 1994. DSM-IV *Diagnostic and Statistical Manual of Mental Disorders*, 4th edition. Washington, D.C.: American Psychiatric Association.

ASPERGER, H., 1944. Die "Autistischen Psychopathen" im Kindesalter. *Archiv Psychiatrie Nervenkrankheiten* 117:76–136.

AVIS, J., and P. HARRIS, 1991. Belief-desire reasoning among Baka children: Evidence for a universal conception of mind. *Child Dev.* 62:460–467.

BAILEY, T., A. LE COUTEUR, I. GOTTESMAN, P. BOLTON, E. SIMONOFF, E. YUZDA, and M. RUTTER, 1995. Autism as a strongly genetic disorder: Evidence from a British twin study. *Psychol. Med.* 25:63–77.

BARON-COHEN, S., 1987. Autism and symbolic play. *Br. J. Dev. Psychol.* 5:139–148.

BARON-COHEN, S., 1988. Social and pragmatic deficits in autism: Cognitive or affective? *J. Autism Dev. Disord.* 18:379–402.

BARON-COHEN, S., 1989a. Are autistic children behaviourists? An examination of their mental-physical and appearance-reality distinctions. *J. Autism Dev. Disord.* 19:579–600.

BARON-COHEN, S., 1989b. The autistic child's theory of mind: A case of specific developmental delay. *J. Child Psychol. Psychiatry* 30:285–298.

BARON-COHEN, S., 1989c. Joint attention deficits in autism: Towards a cognitive analysis. *Dev. Psychopathol.* 1:185–189.

BARON-COHEN, S., 1989d. Perceptual role-taking and proto-declarative pointing in autism. *Br. J. Dev. Psychol.* 7:113–127.

BARON-COHEN, S., 1990. Autism: A specific cognitive disorder of "mindblindness." *Int. Rev. Psychiatry* 2:79–88.

BARON-COHEN, S., 1991a. Do people with autism understand what causes emotion? *Child Dev.* 62:385–395.

BARON-COHEN, S., 1991b. Precursors to a theory of mind: Understanding attention in others. In *Natural Theories of Mind*, A. Whiten, ed. Oxford: Basil Blackwell.

BARON-COHEN, S., 1992. Out of sight or out of mind: Another look at deception in autism. *J. Child Psychol. Psychiatry* 33:1141–1155.

BARON-COHEN, S., 1994. How to build a baby that can read minds: Cognitive mechanisms in mindreading. *Cahiers de Psychologie Cognitive/Current Psychology of Cognition* 13:513–552.

BARON-COHEN, S., 1995. *Mindblindness: An Essay on Autism and Theory of Mind*. Cambridge, Mass.: Bradford Books, MIT Press.

BARON-COHEN, S., 1997. Are children with autism superior at folk physics? In *Children's Theories. New Direction for Child Development Series*, H. Wellman and K. Inagaki, eds. San Francisco: Jossey-Bass, Inc.

BARON-COHEN, S., J. ALLEN, and C. GILLBERG, 1992. Can autism be detected at 18 months? The needle, the haystack, and the CHAT. *Br. J. Psychiatry* 161:839–843.

BARON-COHEN, S., P. BOLTON, S. WHEELWRIGHT, L. SHORT, G. MEAD, A. SMITH, and V. SCHILL, 1998. Autism occurs more often in families of physicists, engineers, and mathematicians. *Autism* 2:296–301.

BARON-COHEN, S., R. CAMPBELL, A. KARMILOFF-SMITH, J. GRANT, and J. WALKER, 1995. Are children with autism blind to the mentalistic significance of the eyes? *Br. J. Dev. Psychol.* 13:379–398.

BARON-COHEN, S., A. COX, G. BAIRD, J. SWETTENHAM, A. DREW, N. NIGHTINGALE, K. MORGAN, and T. CHARMAN, 1996. Psychological markers of autism at 18 months of age in a large population. *Br. J. Psychiatry* 168:158–163.

BARON-COHEN, S., and CROSS, P., 1992. Reading the eyes: Evidence for the role of perception in the development of a theory of mind. *Mind Lang.* 6:173–186.

BARON-COHEN, S., and F. GOODHART, 1994. The "seeing leads to knowing" deficit in autism: The Pratt and Bryant probe. *Br. J. Dev. Psychol.* 12:397–402.

BARON-COHEN, S., and J. HAMMER, 1997a. Parents of children with Asperger syndrome: What is the cognitive phenotype? *J. Cogn. Neurosci.* 9:548–554.

BARON-COHEN, S., and J. HAMMER, 1997b. Is autism an extreme form of the male brain? *Autism Res.* 11:193–207.

BARON-COHEN, S., T. JOLLIFFE, C. MORTIMORE, and M. ROBERTSON, 1997. Another advanced test of theory of mind: Evidence from very high functioning adults with autism or Asperger syndrome. *J. Child Psychol. Psychiatry* 38:813–822.

BARON-COHEN, S., A. M. LESLIE, and U. FRITH, 1985. Does the autistic child have a "theory of mind"? *Cognition* 21:37–46.

BARON-COHEN, S., A. M. LESLIE, and U. FRITH, 1986. Mechanical, behavioural and intentional understanding of picture stories in autistic children. *Br. J. Dev. Psychol.* 4:113–125.

BARON-COHEN, S., M. O'RIORDAN, R. JONES, V. STONE, and K. PLAISTEAD, in press. Can children with Asperger syndrome detect faux pas? *J. Autism Dev. Disord.*

BARON-COHEN, S., and H. RING, 1994. A model of the mind-reading system: Neuropsychological and neurobiological perspectives. In *Origins of an Understanding of Mind*, P. Mitchell and C. Lewis, eds. Hillsdale, N.J.: Erlbaum.

BARON-COHEN, S., H. RING, J. MORIARTY, P. SHMITZ, D. COSTA, and P. ELL, 1994. Recognition of mental state terms: A clinical study of autism, and a functional neuroimaging study of normal adults. *Br. J. Psychiatry* 165:640–649.

BARON-COHEN, S., H. RING, S. WILLIAMS, S. WHEELWRIGHT, E. BULLAMORE, M. BRAMMER, and C. ANDREW, 1999. Social intelligence in the normal and autistic brain: An fMRI study. *Euro. J. Neurosci.* 11:1891–1898.

BARON-COHEN, S., M. ROBERTSON, and J. MORIARTY, 1994. The development of the will: A neuropsychological analysis of Gilles de la Tourette's syndrome. In *The Self and Its Dysfunction: Proceedings of the Fourth Rochester Symposium*, D. Cicchetti and S. Toth, eds. Rochester: University of Rochester Press.

BARON-COHEN, S., A. SPITZ, and P. CROSS, 1993. Can children with autism recognize surprise? *Cognition Emotion* 7:507–516.

BARON-COHEN, S. S., and S. WHEELWRIGHT. in press. Obsessions in children with autism or Asperger syndrome: A context analysis in terms of core domains. *Br. J. Psychiatry.*

BARON-COHEN, S., S. WHEELWRIGHT, and T. JOLLIFFE, 1997. Is there a "language of the eyes"? Evidence from normal adults and adults with autism or Asperger syndrome. *Vis. Cogn.* 4:311–331.

BARON-COHEN, S., S. WHEELWRIGHT, V. STONE, and M. RUTHERFORD, in press. A mathematician, a physicist, and a computer scientist with Asperger syndrome. *Neurocase.*

BARON-COHEN, S., S. WHEELWRIGHT, C. STOTT, P. BOLTON, and I. GOODYER, 1997. Is there a link between engineering and autism? *Autism Int. J. Res. Pract.* 1:153–163.

BOLTON, P., and M. RUTTER, 1990. Genetic influences in autism. *Int. Rev. Psychiatry* 2:67–80.

BOWLER, D. M., 1992. Theory of mind in Asperger syndrome. *J. Child Psychol. Psychiatry.* 33:877–895.

BRUNER, J., 1983. *Child's Talk: Learning to Use Language*. Oxford: Oxford University Press.

BUTTERWORTH, G., 1991. The ontogeny and phylogeny of joint visual attention. In *Natural Theories of Mind*, A. Whiten, ed. Oxford: Oxford University Press.

CAREY, S., 1985. *Conceptual Change in Childhood*. Cambridge, Mass.: Bradford Books, MIT Press.

CARRUTHERS, P., 1996. Autism as mindblindness: An elaboration and partial defense. In *Theories of Theories of Mind*, P. Carruthers, ed. Cambridge: Cambridge University Press.

CHARMAN, T., J. SWETTENHAM, S. BARON-COHEN, A. COX, and G. BAIRD, 1997. Infants with autism: An investigation of empathy, joint attention, pretend play, and imitation. *Dev. Psychol.* 33:781–789.

DENNETT, D., 1987. *The Intentional Stance*. Cambridge, Mass.: Bradford Books, MIT Press.

EHLERS, S., A. NYDEN, C. GILLBERG, A. SANDBERG, S. DALGREN, E. HJELMQUIST, and A. ODEN, 1997. Asperger syndrome, autism, and attention disorders: A comparative study of the cognitive profiles of 120 children. *J. Child Psychol. Psychiatry* 38:207–218.

FLETCHER, P. C., F. HAPPE, U. FRITH, S. C. BAKER, R. J. DOLAN, R. S. J. FRACKOWIAK, and C. D. FRITH, 1995. Other minds in the brain: A functional imaging study of "theory of mind" in story comprehension. *Cognition* 57:109–128.

FRITH, U., 1989. *Autism: Explaining the Enigma*. Oxford: Basil Blackwell.

FRITH, U., 1991. *Autism and Asperger's Syndrome*. Cambridge: Cambridge University Press.

FRITH, U., F. HAPPE, and F. SIDDONS, 1994. Autism and theory of mind in everyday life. *Soc. Dev.* 3:108–124.

GELMAN, S., and L. HIRSCHFIELD, 1994. *Mapping the Mind*. Cambridge: Press Syndicate, University of Cambridge.

GOEL, V., J. GRAFMAN, N. SADATO, and M. HALLETT, 1995. Modeling other minds. *Neuroreport* 6:1741–1746.

HAPPE, F., 1993. Communicative competence and theory of mind in autism: A Test of Relevance Theory. *Cognition* 48:101–119.

HAPPE, F., 1994. An advanced test of theory of mind: Understanding of story characters' thoughts and feelings by able autistic, mentally handicapped, and normal children and adults. *J. Autism Dev. Disord.* 24:129–154.

HAPPE, F., 1995. The role of age and verbal ability in the theory of mind task performance of subjects with autism. *Child Dev.* 66:843–855.

HAPPE, F., S. EHLERS, P. FLETCHER, U. FRITH, M. JOHANSSON, C. GILLBERG, R. DOLAN, R. FRANCKOWIAK, and C. FRITH, 1996. "Theory of mind" in the brain: Evidence from a PET scan study of Asperger syndrome. *Neuroreport* 8:197–201.

LE COUTEUR, A., A. BAILEY, S. GOODE, A. PICKLES, S. ROBERTSON, I. GOTTESMAN, and M. RUTTER, 1996. A broader phenotype of autism: the clinical spectrum in twins. *J. Child Psychol. Psychiatry* 37:785–801.

LEEKAM, S., S. BARON-COHEN, S. BROWN, D. PERRETT, and M. MILDERS, 1997. Eye-Direction Detection: a dissociation between geometric and joint-attention skills in autism. *Br. J. Dev. Psychol.* 15:77–95.

LEEKAM, S., and J. PERNER, 1991. Does the autistic child have a metarepresentational deficit? *Cognition* 40:203–218.

LEEVERS, H., and P. HARRIS, 1998. Drawing impossible entities: A measure of the imagination in children with autism, children with learning disabilities, and normal 4-year-olds. *J. Child Psychol. Psychiatry* 39:399–410.

LESLIE, A., 1991. The theory of mind impairment in autism: Evidence for a modular mechanism of development? In *Natural Theories of Mind*, A. Whiten, ed. Oxford: Basil Blackwell, pp. 63–78.

LESLIE, A., and D. ROTH, 1993. What can autism teach us about metarepresentation? In *Understanding Other Minds: Perspectives from Autism*, S. Baron-Cohen, H. Tager-Flusberg, and D. Cohen, eds. Oxford: Oxford Medical Publications.

LESLIE, A. M., 1987. Pretence and representation: the origins of "theory of mind." *Psychol. Rev.* 94:412–426.

LESLIE, A. M., and U. FRITH, 1988. Autistic children's understanding of seeing, knowing, and believing. *Br. J. Dev. Psychol.* 6:315–324.

LESLIE, A. M., and L. THAISS, 1992. Domain specificity in conceptual development: Evidence from autism. *Cognition* 43:225–251.

LEWIS, V., and J. BOUCHER, 1988. Spontaneous, instructed and elicited play in relatively able autistic children. *Br. J. Dev. Psychol.* 6:325–339.

MUNDY, P., 1995. Joint attention, social emotional approach in children with autism. *Dev. Psychopathol.* 7:63–82.

MUNDY, P., and M. CROWSON, 1997. Joint attention and early social communication. *J. Autism Dev. Disord.* 27:653–676.

MUNDY, P., M. SIGMAN, and C. KASARI, 1990. A longitudinal study of joint attention and language development in autistic children. *J. Autism Dev. Disord.* 20:115–128.

MUNDY, P., M. SIGMAN, and C. KASARI, 1994. Joint attention, developmental level, and symptom presentation in young children with autism. *Dev. Psychopathol.* 6:389–401.

OZONOFF, S., B. PENNINGTON, and S. ROGERS, 1991. Executive function deficits in high-functioning autistic children: Relationship to theory of mind. *J. Child Psychol. Psychiatry* 32:1081–1106.

PERNER, J., U. FRITH, A. M. LESLIE, and S. LEEKAM, 1989. Exploration of the autistic child's theory of mind: knowledge, belief, and communication. *Child Dev.* 60:689–700.

PERRETT, D., P. SMITH, D. POTTER, A. MISTLIN, A. HEAD, A. MILNER, and M. JEEVES, 1985. Visual cells in the temporal cortex sensitive to face view and gaze direction. *Proc. R. Soc. Lond. B* 223:293–317.

PHILLIPS, W., S. BARON-COHEN, and M. RUTTER, 1992. The role of eye-contact in the detection of goals: Evidence from normal toddlers, and children with autism or mental handicap. *Dev. Psychopathol.* 4:375–383.

PHILLIPS, W., S. BARON-COHEN, and M. RUTTER, 1998. Can children with autism understand intentions? *Br. J. Dev. Psychol.* 16:337–348.

PHILLIPS, W., J.-C. GOMEZ, S. BARON-COHEN, A. RIVIERE, and V. LAA, 1996. Treating people as objects, agents, or subjects: How young children with and without autism make requests. *J. Child Psychol. Psychiatry* 36:1383–1398.

PINKER, S., 1997. *How the Mind Works.* New York: Penguin Books.

PREMACK, D., and G. WOODRUFF, 1978. Does the chimpanzee have a "theory of mind"? *Behav. Brain Sci.* 4:515–526.

REED, T., and C. PETERSON, 1990. A comparative study of autistic subjects' performance at two levels of visual and cognitive perspective taking. *J. Autism Dev. Disord.* 20:555–568.

RUSSELL, J., ed., 1997a. *Autism as an Executive Disorder.* Oxford: Oxford University Press.

RUSSELL, J., 1997b. Introduction. In *Autism as an Executive Disorder,* J. Russell, ed. Oxford: Oxford University Press.

RUTTER, M., 1978. Diagnosis and definition. In *Autism: A Reappraisal of Concepts and Treatment,* M. Rutter and E. Schopler, eds. New York: Plenum Press, pp. 1–26.

RUTTER, M., and A. BAILEY, 1993. Thinking and relationships: Mind and Brain. In *Understanding Other Minds: Perspectives from Autism,* S. Baron Cohen and H. Tager-Flusberg, eds. Oxford: Oxford University Press.

SCAIFE, M., and J. BRUNER, 1975. The capacity for joint visual attention in the infant. *Nature* 253:265–266.

SCOTT, F., and S. BARON-COHEN, 1996. Imagining real and unreal objects: An investigation of imagination in autism. *J. Cogn. Neurosci.* 8:400–411.

SCOTT, F., BARON-COHEN, S., and LESLIE, A., in press. "If pigs could fly": An examination of imagination and counterfactual reasoning in autism. *Br. J. Dev. Psychol.*

SIGMAN, M., P. MUNDY, J. UNGERER, and T. SHERMAN, 1986. Social interactions of autistic, mentally retarded, and normal children and their caregivers. *J. Child Psychol. Psychiatry* 27:647–656.

SODIAN, B., and U. FRITH, 1992. Deception and sabotage in autistic, retarded, and normal children. *J. Child Psychol. Psychiatry* 33:591–606.

SPERBER, D., D. PREMACK, and A. PREMACK, eds., 1995. *Causal Cognition: A Multidisciplinary Debate.* Oxford: Oxford University Press.

SULLIVAN, K., D. ZAITCHIK, and H. TAGER-FLUSBERG, 1994. Preschoolers can attribute second-order beliefs. *Dev. Psychol.* 30:395–402.

SURIAN, L., S. BARON-COHEN, and H. VAN DER LELY, 1996. Are children with autism deaf to Gricean Maxims? *Cognitive Neuropsychiatry,* 1:55–72.

SWETTENHAM, J., S. BARON-COHEN, J.-C. GOMEZ, and S. WALSH, 1996. What's inside a person's head? Conceiving of the mind as a camera helps children with autism develop an alternative theory of mind. *Cogn. Neuropsychiatry* 1:73–88.

TAGER-FLUSBERG, H., 1992. Autistic children's talk about psychological states: Deficits in the early acquisition of a theory of mind. *Child Dev.* 63:161–172.

TAGER-FLUSBERG, H., 1993. What language reveals about the understanding of minds in children with autism. In *Understanding Other Minds: Perspectives from Autism,* S. Baron-Cohen, H. Tager-Flusberg, and D. J. Cohen, eds. Oxford: Oxford University Press.

TAGER-FLUSBERG, H., J. BOSHART, and S. BARON-COHEN, 1998. Reading the windows of the soul: Evidence of domain specificity sparing in Williams syndrome. *J. Cogn. Neurosci.* 10:631–639.

VAN DER LELY, H., 1997. Language and cognitve development in a grammatical SLI boy: Modularity and innateness. *J. Neurolinguistics* 10:75–107.

WATERHOUSE, L., D. FEIN, and C. MOHAHL, 1996. Neurofunctional mechanisms in autism. *Psychol. Rev.* 103:457–489.

WELLMAN, H., and S. GELMAN, 1998. Knowledge acquisition in foundational domains. In *Cognition, Perception and Language:* Volume 2 of *The Handbook of Child Psychology,* 5th ed., D. Kuhn and R. Siegler, eds. New York: Wiley.

WIMMER, H., and J. PERNER, 1983. Beliefs about beliefs: Representation and constraining function of wrong beliefs in young children's understanding of deception. *Cognition* 13:103–28.

WING, L., 1988. The autistic continuum. In *Aspects of Autism: Biological Research,* L. Wing, ed. London: Gaskell/Royal College of Psychiatrists.

WING, L., and J. GOULD, 1979. Severe impairments of social interaction and associated abnormalities in children: Epidemiology and classification. *J. Autism Dev. Disord.* 9:11–29.

YIRMIYA, N., D. SOLOMONICA-LEVI, and C. SHULMAN, 1996. The ability to manipulate behaviour and to understand manipulation of beliefs: A comparison of individuals with autism, mental retardation, and normal development. *Dev. Psychol.* 32:62–69.

87 The Cognitive Neuroscience of Social Reasoning

LEDA COSMIDES AND JOHN TOOBY

ABSTRACT Cognitive scientists need theoretical guidance that is grounded in something beyond intuition. They need evolutionary biology's "adaptationist program": a research strategy in which theories of adaptive function are key inferential tools, used to identify and investigate the design of evolved systems. Using research on how humans reason about social exchange, the authors will (1) illustrate how theories of adaptive function can generate detailed and highly testable hypotheses about the design of computational machines in the human mind and (2) review research that tests for the presence of these machines. This research suggests that the human computational architecture contains an expert system designed for reasoning about cooperation for mutual benefit, with a subroutine specialized for cheater detection.

Natural competences

Scientists have been dissecting the neural architecture of the human mind for several centuries. Dissecting its computational architecture has proven more difficult, however. Our natural competences—our abilities to see, to speak, to find someone beautiful, to reciprocate a favor, to fear disease, to fall in love, to initiate an attack, to experience moral outrage, to navigate a landscape, and myriad others—are possible only because there is a vast and heterogeneous array of complex computational machinery supporting and regulating these activities. But this machinery works so well that we do not even realize that it exists. Our intuitions blur our scientific vision. As a result, we have neglected to study some of the most interesting machinery in the human mind.

Theories of adaptive function are powerful lenses that allow one to see beyond one's intuitions. Aside from those properties acquired by chance or imposed by engineering constraint, the mind consists of a set of information-processing circuits that were designed by natural selection to solve adaptive problems that our ancestors faced, generation after generation. If we

LEDA COSMIDES   Center for Evolutionary Psychology and Department of Psychology, University of California, Santa Barbara, Calif.
JOHN TOOBY Center for Evolutionary Psychology and Department of Anthropology, University of California, Santa Barbara, Calif.

know what these problems were, we can seek mechanisms that are well engineered for solving them.

The exploration and definition of adaptive problems is a major activity in evolutionary biology. By combining results derived from mathematical modeling, comparative studies, behavioral ecology, paleoanthropology, and other fields, evolutionary biologists try to identify (1) what problems the mind was designed to solve, (2) why it was designed to solve *those* problems rather than other ones, and (3) what information was available in ancestral environments that a problem-solving mechanism could have used. These are the components of what Marr (1982) called a "computational theory" of an information-processing problem: a task analysis defining what a computational device does and why it does it.

Because there are multiple ways of achieving any solution, experiments are always needed to determine which algorithms and representations actually evolved to solve a particular problem. But the more precisely you can define the goal of processing—the more tightly you can constrain what would count as a solution—the more clearly you can see what a program capable of producing that solution would have to look like. The more constraints you can discover, the more the field of possible solutions is narrowed, and the more you can concentrate your experimental efforts on discriminating between viable hypotheses.

In this way, theories of adaptive problems can guide the search for the cognitive programs that solve them. Knowing what cognitive programs exist can, in turn, guide the search for their neural basis. To illustrate this approach, we will show how it guided a research program of our own on how people reason about social interactions.

Some of the most important adaptive problems our ancestors had to solve involved navigating the social world, and some of the best work in evolutionary biology is devoted to analyzing constraints on the evolution of mechanisms that solve these problems. Constructing computational theories from these constraints led us to suspect that the human cognitive architecture contains expert systems specialized for reasoning about the social

1259

world. If these exist, then their inference procedures, representational primitives, and default assumptions should reflect the structure of adaptive problems that arose when our hominid ancestors interacted with one another. Our first task analysis was of the adaptive information-processing problems entailed by the human ability to engage in social exchange.

Social exchange and conditional reasoning

In categorizing social interactions, there are two basic consequences that humans can have on each other: helping or hurting, bestowing benefits or inflicting costs. Some social behavior is unconditional: One nurses an infant without asking it for a favor in return, for example. But most social acts are delivered conditionally. This creates a selection pressure for cognitive designs that can detect and understand social conditionals reliably, precisely, and economically (Cosmides, 1985, 1989; Cosmides and Tooby, 1989, 1992). Two major categories of social conditionals are social exchange and threat—conditional helping and conditional hurting—carried out by individuals or groups on individuals or groups. We initially focused on social exchange (for review, see Cosmides and Tooby, 1992). A social exchange involves a conditional of the approximate form: *If person A provides the requested benefit to or meets the requirement of person or group B, then B will provide the rationed benefit to A.* (Herein, a rule expressing this kind of agreement to cooperate will be referred to as a *social contract.*)

We elected to study reasoning about social exchange for several reasons:

1. Many aspects of the evolutionary theory of social exchange (sometimes called *cooperation, reciprocal altruism,* or *reciprocation*) are relatively well developed and unambiguous. Consequently, certain features of the functional logic of social exchange could be confidently relied on in constructing *a priori* hypotheses about the structure of the information-processing procedures that this activity requires.

2. Complex adaptations are constructed in response to evolutionarily long-enduring problems. Situations involving social exchange have constituted a long-enduring selection pressure on the hominid line: Evidence from primatology and paleoanthropology suggests that our ancestors have engaged in social exchange for at least several million years.

3. Social exchange appears to be an ancient, pervasive, and central part of human social life. The universality of a behavioral phenotype is not a *sufficient* condition for claiming that it was produced by a cognitive adaptation, but it is suggestive. As a behavioral phenotype, so-

cial exchange is as ubiquitous as the human heartbeat. The heartbeat is universal because the organ that generates it is everywhere the same. This is a parsimonious explanation for the universality of social exchange as well: the cognitive phenotype of the organ that generates it is everywhere the same. Like the heart, its development does not seem to require environmental conditions (social or otherwise) that are idiosyncratic or culturally contingent.

4. Social exchange is relatively rare across species, however. Many species have the ability to recognize patterns (as connectionist systems do) or change their behavior in response to rewards and punishments (see chapter 81 of this volume). Yet these abilities alone are insufficient for social exchange to emerge, despite the rewards it can produce. This suggests that social exchange behavior is generated by cognitive machinery specialized for that task.[1]

5. Finding procedures specialized for reasoning about social exchange would challenge a central assumption of the behavioral sciences: that the evolved architecture of the mind consists solely or predominantly of a small number of content-free, general-purpose mechanisms (Tooby and Cosmides, 1992).

Reasoning is among the most poorly understood areas in the cognitive sciences. Its study has been dominated by a pre-Darwinian view, championed by the British Empiricists and imported into the modern behavioral sciences in the form of the Standard Social Science Model (SSSM). According to this view, reasoning is accomplished by circuits designed to operate uniformly over every class of content (see chapter 81), and the mind has no content that was not derived from the perceptual data these circuits take as input. These circuits were thought to be few in number, content free, and general purpose, part of a hypothetical faculty that generates solutions to all problems: "general intelligence." Experiments were designed to reveal what computational procedures these circuits embodied; prime candidates were all-purpose heuristics and "rational" algorithms—ones that implement formal methods for inductive and deductive reasoning, such as Bayes's rule or the propositional calculus. These algorithms are jacks of all trades: Because they are content free, they can operate on information from any domain (their strength). They are also masters of none: To be content independent means that they lack any domain-specialized information that would lead to correct inferences in one domain but would not apply to others (their weakness).

This view of reasoning as a unitary faculty composed of content-free procedures is intuitively compelling to many people. But the discipline of asking what adaptive information-processing problems our minds evolved to solve changes one's scientific intuitions/sensibilities. One begins to appreciate (1) the complexity of most adaptive information-processing problems; (2) that the evolved solution to these problems is usually machinery that is well engineered for the task; (3) that this machinery is usually specialized to fit the particular nature of the problem; and (4) that its evolved design must embody "knowledge" about problem-relevant aspects of the world.

The human computational architecture can be thought of as a collection of evolved problem-solvers. Some of these may indeed embody content-free formalisms from mathematics or logic, which can act on any domain and acquire all their specific content from perceptual data alone (Gigerenzer, 1991; Brase, Cosmides, and Tooby, 1998). But many evolved problem-solvers are expert systems, equipped with "crib sheets": inference procedures and assumptions that embody knowledge specific to a given problem domain. These generate correct (or, at least, adaptive) inferences that would not be warranted on the basis of perceptual data alone. For example, there currently is at least some evidence for the existence of inference systems that are specialized for reasoning about objects (Baillergeon, 1986; Spelke, 1990), physical causality (Brown, 1990; Leslie, 1994), number (Gallistel and Gelman, 1992; Wynn, 1992, 1995), the biological world (Atran, 1990; Hatano and Inagaki, 1994; Keil, 1994; Springer, 1992), the beliefs and motivations of other individuals (Baron-Cohen, 1995; Leslie, 1987; see also chapters 85 and 86), and social interactions (Cosmides and Tooby, 1992; Fiske, 1991). These domain-specific inference systems have a distinct advantage over domain-independent ones, akin to the difference between experts and novices: Experts can solve problems faster and more efficiently than novices because they already know a lot about the problem domain.

So what design features might one expect an expert system that is well engineered for reasoning about social exchange to have?

Design features predicted by the computational theory

The evolutionary analysis of social exchange parallels the economist's concept of trade. Sometimes known as "reciprocal altruism," social exchange is an "I'll scratch your back if you scratch mine" principle. Economists and evolutionary biologists had already explored constraints on the emergence or evolution of social exchange using game theory, modeling it as a repeated Prisoners' Dilemma. Based on these analyses, and on data from paleoanthropology and primatology, we developed a computational theory (*sensu* Marr, 1982) specifying design features that algorithms capable of satisfying these constraints would have to have. For example:

1. To discriminate social contracts from threats and other kinds of conditionals, the algorithms involved would have to be sensitive to the presence of benefits and costs and be able to recognize a well-formed social contract (for a grammar of social exchange, see Cosmides and Tooby, 1989). Social exchange is cooperation for *mutual benefit*. The presence of a benefit is crucial for a situation to be recognized as involving social exchange. The presence of a cost is not a necessary condition: providing a benefit may cause one to incur a cost, but it need not. There must, however, be algorithms that can assess relative benefits and costs, to provide input to decision rules that cause one to accept a social contract only when the benefits outweigh the costs.

2. The game theoretic analyses indicated that social exchange cannot evolve in a species or be sustained stably in a social group unless the cognitive machinery of the participants allows a potential cooperator to detect individuals who cheat, so that they can be excluded from future interactions in which they would exploit cooperators (Axelrod, 1984; Axelrod and Hamilton, 1981; Boyd, 1988; Trivers, 1971; Williams, 1966). In this context, a *cheater* is an individual who accepts a benefit without satisfying the requirements that provision of that benefit was made contingent upon. This definition does not map onto content-free definitions of violation found in the propositional calculus and in most other reasoning theories (e.g., Rips, 1994; Johnson-Laird and Byrne, 1991). A system capable of detecting cheaters would need to define the concept using contentful representational primitives, referring to illicitly taken *benefits*. The definition also is perspective dependent because the item or action that one party views as a benefit, the other views as a requirement. Given "If you give me your watch, I'll give you $10," you would have cheated me if you took my $10 but did not give me your watch; I would have cheated you if I had taken your watch without giving you the $10. This means that the system needs to be able to compute a cost-benefit representation from the perspective of each participant, and define cheating with respect to that perspective-relative representation.

In short, what counts as cheating is so content dependent that a detection mechanism equipped with a domain-general definition of violation would not be able to solve the problem of cheater detection. Hence, an expert system designed for conditional reasoning about social exchange should have a subroutine *specialized* for detecting cheaters.

TABLE 87.1
Computational machinery that governs reasoning about social contracts

Design features predicted (and established)

1. It includes inference procedures specialized for detecting cheaters.
2. The cheater detection procedures cannot detect violations that do not correspond to cheating (e.g., mistakes when no one profits from the violation).
3. The machinery operates even in situations that are unfamiliar and culturally alien.
4. The definition of cheating varies lawfully as a function of one's perspective.
5. The machinery is just as good at computing the cost-benefit representation of a social contract from the perspective of one party as from the perspective of another.
6. It cannot detect cheaters unless the rule has been assigned the cost-benefit representation of a social contract.
7. It translates the surface content of situations involving the contingent provision of benefits into representational primitives, such as "benefit," "cost," "obligation," "entitlement," "intentional," and "agent."
8. It imports these conceptual primitives, even when they are absent from the surface content.
9. It derives the implications specified by the computational theory, even when these are not valid inferences of the propositional calculus (e.g., "If you take the benefit, then you are obligated to pay the cost" implies "If you paid the cost, then you are entitled to take the benefit").
10. It does not include procedures specialized for detecting altruists (individuals who have paid costs but refused to accept the benefits to which they are therefore entitled).
11. It cannot solve problems drawn from other domains (e.g., it will not allow one to detect bluffs and double-crosses in situations of threat).
12. It appears to be neurologically isolable from more general reasoning abilities (e.g., it is unimpaired in schizophrenic patients who show other reasoning deficits; Maljkovic, 1987).
13. It appears to operate across a wide variety of cultures (including an indigenous population of hunter-horticulturists in the Ecuadorian Amazon; Sugiyama, Tooby, and Cosmides, 1995).

Alternative (by-product) hypotheses eliminated

1. That familiarity can explain the social contract effect.
2. That social contract content merely activates the rules of inference of the propositional calculus.
3. That social contract content merely promotes (for whatever reason) "clear thinking."
4. That permission schema theory can explain the social contract effect.
5. That any problem involving payoffs will elicit the detection of violations.
6. That a content-independent deontic logic can explain the effect.

Based on evidence reviewed in Cosmides and Tooby, 1992.

3. Algorithms regulating social exchange should be able to operate even over unfamiliar contents and situations. Unlike other primates, who exchange only a limited array of favors (e.g., grooming, food, protection), humans trade an almost unlimited variety of goods and services. Moreover, one needs to be able to interpret each new situation that arises–not merely ones that have occurred in the past. Thus, the algorithms should be able to operate properly even in unfamiliar situations, as long as they can be interpreted as involving the conditional provision of benefits. This means the representational format of the algorithms cannot be tied to specific items with a fixed exchange rate (e.g., one could imagine the reciprocation algorithms of vampire bats, who share regurgitated blood, to specify an exchange rate in blood volume). From the surface content of a situation, the algorithms should compute an abstract level of representation, with representational primitives such as $benefit_{agent\ 1}$, $requirement_{agent\ 1}$, $agent\ 1$, $agent\ 2$, $cost_{agent\ 2}$, and so forth.

4. In the context of social exchange, modals such as "must" and "may" should be interpreted deontically, as referring to obligation and entitlement (rather than to necessity and possibility). As a result, cheating is taking a benefit one is not entitled to. It does not matter where terms such as "benefit taken" or "requirement not met" fall in the logical structure of a rule. In addition, there are constraints on when one should punish cheating, and by how much (Cosmides, 1985; Cosmides and Tooby, 1989).

Such analyses provided a principled basis for generating detailed hypotheses about reasoning procedures that, because of their domain-specialized structure, would be well designed for detecting social conditionals involving exchange, interpreting their meaning, and successfully solving the inference problems they pose (table 87.1). These hypotheses were tested using standard methods from cognitive psychology, as described below.

Part of your new job for the City of Cambridge is to study the demographics of transportation. You read a previously done report on the habits of Cambridge residents that says: **"If a person goes into Boston, then that person takes the subway."**

The cards below have information about four Cambridge residents. Each card represents one person. One side of a card tells where a person went, and the other side of the card tells how that person got there. Indicate only those card(s) you definitely need to turn over **to see if any of these people violate this rule.**

| Boston | Arlington | subway | cab |

FIGURE 87.1 The Wason selection task (descriptive rule, familiar content). In a Wason selection task, there is always a rule of the form *If P then Q*, and four cards showing the values *P*, *not-P*, *Q*, and *not-Q* (respectively) on the side that the subject can see. From a logical point of view, only the combination of *P* and *not-Q* can violate this rule, so the correct answer is to check the *P* card (to see whether it has a *not-Q* on the back), the *not-Q* card (to see whether it has a *P* on the back), and no others. Few subjects answer correctly, however, when given problems with descriptive rules, such as the problem in figure 87.1.

Computational theories (or task analyses) are important because they specify a mechanism's adaptive function: the problem it was designed by natural selection to solve. They are central to any evolutionary investigation of the mind, for a simple reason. To show that an aspect of the phenotype is an adaptation, one needs to demonstrate a fit between form and function: One needs *design evidence*. There are now a number of experiments on human reasoning comparing performance on tasks in which a conditional rule either did or did not express a social contract. These experiments—some of which are described below—have provided evidence for a series of domain-specific effects predicted by our analysis of the adaptive problems that arise in social exchange. Social contracts activate content-*dependent* rules of inference that appear to be complexly specialized for processing information about this domain. These rules include subroutines that are specialized for solving a particular problem within that domain: cheater detection. The programs involved do not operate so as to detect potential altruists (individuals who pay costs but do not take benefits), nor are they activated in social contract situations in which errors would correspond to innocent mistakes rather than intentional cheating. Nor are they designed to solve problems drawn from domains other than social exchange; for example, they do not allow one to detect bluffs and double-crosses in situations of threat, nor do they allow one to detect when a safety rule has been violated. The pattern of results elicited by social exchange content is so distinctive that we believe reasoning in this domain is governed by computational units that are domain specific and functionally distinct: what we have called *social contract algorithms* (Cosmides, 1985, 1989; Cosmides and Tooby, 1992).

To help readers track which hypotheses are tested by each experiment, we will refer to the list in table 87.1. For example, D1 = design feature #1 (inference procedures specialized for detecting cheaters); B1 = byproduct hypothesis #1 (that familiarity can explain the social contract effect).

Tests with the Wason selection task

To test for the presence of the design features predicted, we used an experimental paradigm called the Wason selection task (Wason, 1966; Wason and Johnson-Laird, 1972). For more than 30 years, psychologists have been using this paradigm (which was orginally developed as a test of logical reasoning) to probe the structure of human reasoning mechanisms. In this task, the subject is asked to look for violations of a conditional rule of the form *If P then Q*. Consider the Wason selection task presented in figure 87.1.

From a logical point of view, the rule has been violated whenever someone goes to Boston without taking the subway. Hence, the logically correct answer is to turn over the *Boston* card (to see if this person took the subway) and the *cab* card (to see if the person taking the cab went to Boston). More generally, for a rule of the form *If P then Q*, one should turn over the cards that represent the values *P* (a true antecedent) and *not-Q* (a false consequent).

If the human mind develops reasoning procedures specialized for detecting logical violations of conditional rules, this would be intuitively obvious. But it is not. In general, fewer than 25% of subjects spontaneously make this response. Moreover, even formal training in logical reasoning does little to boost performance on descriptive rules of this kind (Cheng et al., 1986; Wason and Johnson-Laird, 1972). Indeed, a large literature exists that shows that people are not very good at detecting logical violations of if-then rules in Wason selection tasks, *even when these rules deal with familiar content drawn from everyday life* (Manktelow and Evans, 1979; Wason, 1983).

The Wason selection task provided an ideal tool for testing hypotheses about reasoning specializations designed to operate on social conditionals, such as social exchanges, threats, permissions, obligations, and so on, because (1) it tests reasoning about conditional rules, (2) the task structure remains constant while the content of the rule is changed, (3) content effects are easily elicited, and (4) there was already a body of existing experimental results against which performance on new content domains could be compared.

For example, to show that people who ordinarily cannot detect violations of conditional rules can do so when that violation represents cheating on a social contract would constitute initial support for the view that people have cognitive adaptations specialized for detecting cheaters in situations of social exchange. To find that violations of conditional rules are spontaneously detected when they represent bluffing on a threat would, for similar reasons, support the view that people have reasoning procedures specialized for analyzing threats. Our general research plan has been to use subjects' inability to spontaneously detect violations of conditionals expressing a wide variety of contents as a comparative baseline against which to detect the presence of performance-boosting reasoning specializations. By seeing which content-manipulations switch on or off high performance, the boundaries of the domains within which reasoning specializations successfully operate can be mapped.

The results of these investigations were striking. People who ordinarily cannot detect violations of if-then rules can do so easily and accurately when that violation represents cheating in a situation of social exchange (Cosmides, 1985, 1989; Cosmides and Tooby, 1989, 1992). Given a rule of the general form, "If you take benefit B, then you must satisfy requirement R," subjects choose the *benefit accepted* card and the *requirement not met* card—the cards that represent potential cheaters. The adaptively correct answer is immediately obvious to almost all subjects, who commonly experience a "pop out" effect. No formal training is needed. Whenever the content of a problem asks one to look for cheaters in a social exchange, subjects experience the problem as simple to solve, and their performance jumps dramatically. In general, 65% to 80% of subjects get it right, the highest performance found for a task of this kind (supports D1).

This is true for familiar social contracts, such as, "If a person drinks beer, then that person must be over 19

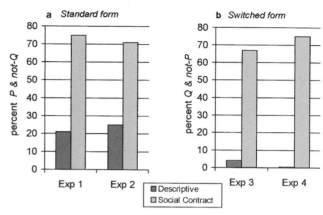

FIGURE 87.2 Detecting violations of unfamiliar conditional rules: social contracts versus descriptive rules. In these experiments, the same, unfamiliar rule was embedded either in a story that caused it to be interpreted as a social contract or in a story that caused it to be interpreted as a rule describing some state of the world. For social contracts, the correct answer is always to pick the *benefit accepted* card and the *requirement not met* card. (A) For standard social contracts, these correspond to the logical categories *P* and *not-Q. P and not-Q* also happens to be the logically correct answer. More than 70% of subjects chose these cards for the social contracts, but fewer than 25% chose them for the matching descriptive rules. (B) For switched social contracts, the *benefit accepted* and *requirement not met* cards correspond to the logical categories *Q* and *not-P*. This is not a logically correct response. Nevertheless, approximately 70% of subjects chose it for the social contracts; virtually no one chose it for the matching descriptive rule.

years old" (Griggs and Cox, 1982; Cosmides, 1985). According to our computational theory, however, performance also should be high for unfamiliar ones—such as, "If a man eats cassava root, then he must have a tattoo on his face," where cassava root is portrayed as a highly desirable aphrodisiac and having a facial tattoo is a sign of being married. As figure 87.2A shows, this is true. Subjects choose the *benefit accepted* card (e.g., "ate cassava root") and the *requirement not met* card (e.g., "no tattoo") for any social conditional that can be interpreted as a social contract and in which looking for violations can be interpreted as looking for cheaters (supports D1, D3, D7, D8; disconfirms B1; Cosmides, 1985, 1989; Gigerenzer and Hug, 1992; Platt and Griggs, 1993). Indeed, familiarity did not help at all. Cosmides (1985) found that performance was just as high on unfamiliar as on familiar social contracts—an uncomfortable result for any explanation that invokes domain-general learning, which depends on familiarity and repetition.

From a domain-general, formal view, investigating men eating cassava root and men without tattoos is logically equivalent to investigating people going to Boston and people taking cabs. But everywhere it has been tested (adults in the United States, United Kingdom, Germany, Italy, France, Hong-Kong, Japan; schoolchildren in Ecuador; Shiwiar hunter-horticulturists in the the Ecuadorian Amazon (Sugiyama, Tooby, and Cosmides, 1995), people do not treat social exchange problems as equivalent to other kinds of reasoning problems. Their minds distinguish social exchange contents and reason as if they were translating these situations into representational primitives such as "benefit," "cost," "obligation," "entitlement," "intentional," and "agent" (Cheng and Holyoak, 1985; Cosmides, 1989; Platt and Griggs, 1993; supports D13). Indeed, the relevant inference procedures are not activated unless the subject has represented the situation as one in which one is entitled to a benefit only if one has satisfied a requirement.

Do social contracts simply activate content-free logical rules?

The procedures activated by social contract rules do not behave as if they were designed to detect *logical* violations per se; instead, they prompt choices that track what would be useful for detecting cheaters, regardless of whether this happens to correspond to the logically correct selections. For example, by switching the order of requirement and benefit within the if-then structure of the rule (figure 87.3), one can elicit responses that are functionally correct from the point of view of cheater detection, but logically incorrect. Subjects choose the *benefit accepted* card and the *requirement not met* card–the adaptively correct response if one is looking for cheaters–*no matter what logical category these cards fall into* (figure 87.2B; supports D9, D8; disconfirms B2, B3, B1) This means that cheater detection is not accomplished by procedures embodying the content-free rules of logical inference. If it were, then subjects would choose the logically correct response–*P and not-Q*–even on switched rules, where these represent the *requirement met* card (P) and the *benefit not accepted* card (*not-Q*). Yet these represent people who cannot possibly have cheated. A person who has met a requirement without accepting the benefit this entitles one to is either an altruist or a fool, but not a cheater.

That content-free rules of logic are not responsible for cheater detection was demonstrated in a different way by Gigerenzer and Hug (1992) in experiments designed to test the prediction that what counts as cheating should depend on one's perspective (D4, D5, B2, B4). Subjects were asked to look for violations of rules such as, "If a previous employee gets a pension from a firm, then that person must have worked for the firm

for at least 10 years." For half of them, the surrounding story cued the subjects into the role of the employer, whereas for the other half, it cued them into the role of an employee.

If social contracts activate rules for detecting logical violations, then this manipulation should make no difference. Perspectives, such as that of employer versus employee, play no role in formal logic: To detect a logical violation, the P card ("employee got the pension") and the *not-Q* card ("employee worked for less than 10 years") should be chosen, no matter whose perspective you have taken. But in social contract theory, perspective matters. Because these two cards represent instances in which the employer may have been cheated, a cheater detection subroutine should choose them in the employer condition. But in the employee condition, the same cheater detection procedures ought to draw attention to situations in which an *employee* might have been cheated, that is, the "employee worked for more than 10 years" card (Q) and "employee got no pension" card (*not-P*). In the employee condition, Q *and not-P* is logically incorrect, but adaptively correct.

The results confirmed the social contract prediction. In the employer condition, 73% of subjects chose *P and not-Q* (which is both logically and adaptively correct), and less than 1% chose *Q and not-P* (which is both logically and adaptively incorrect). But in the employee condition, 66% chose *Q and not-P*–which is logically incorrect but adaptively correct–and only 8% chose *P and not-Q*–which is logically correct, but adaptively incorrect (supports D4, D7, D9; disconfirms B2, B4). Furthermore, the percent of subjects choosing the correct cheater detection response did not differ significantly in these two conditions (73% vs. 66%), indicating that it was just as easy for subjects to compute a cost-benefit representation from the perspective of the employer as from that of the employee (supports D5).

Are cheater detection procedures part of "general intelligence"?

Data from Maljkovic (1987) show that the ability to detect cheaters can remain intact even in individuals suffering large impairments in their more general intellectual functioning. Maljkovic tested the reasoning of patients suffering from positive symptoms of schizophrenia, comparing their performance to that of hospitalized controls. The schizophrenic patients were indeed impaired on more general tests of logical reasoning, in a way typical of individuals with frontal lobe dysfunction. But their ability to detect cheaters on Wason selection tasks was unimpaired (supports D1, D12; disconfirms

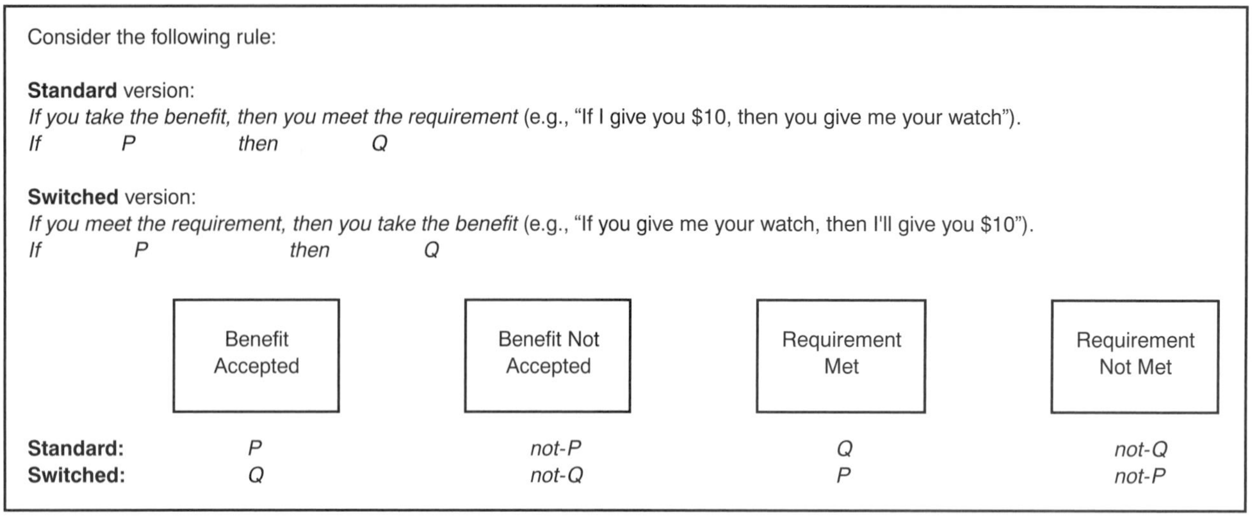

Consider the following rule:

Standard version:
If you take the benefit, then you meet the requirement (e.g., "If I give you $10, then you give me your watch").
If   P   then   Q

Switched version:
If you meet the requirement, then you take the benefit (e.g., "If you give me your watch, then I'll give you $10").
If   P   then   Q

Benefit Accepted	Benefit Not Accepted	Requirement Met	Requirement Not Met

	Benefit Accepted	Benefit Not Accepted	Requirement Met	Requirement Not Met
Standard:	P	not-P	Q	not-Q
Switched:	Q	not-Q	P	not-P

FIGURE 87.3   Generic structure of a social contract. A cheater detection subroutine always would cause one to look at instances in which the potential violator has taken the benefit and not met the requirement. But whether this corresponds to the logically correct answer (*P and not-Q*) depends on exactly how the exchange was expressed. The same social contract has been offered to you, whether the offerer says, "If I give you $10, then you give me your watch" (standard) or "If you give me your watch, I'll give you $10" (switched). But the benefit to you (getting the $10) is in the *P* clause in the standard version and in the

Q clause in the switched version. Likewise, your not meeting the requirement (not giving me the watch) would correspond to the logical category *not-Q* in the standard version and *not-P* in the switched version. By always choosing the *benefit accepted* and *requirement not met* cards, a cheater detection procedure would cause one to choose *P and not-Q* in the standard version—a logically correct response—and *Q and not-P* in the switched version—a logically incorrect response. By testing switched social contracts, one can see that the reasoning procedures activated cause one to detect cheaters, not logical violations.

B1, B3). This is all the more remarkable given that schizophrenics usually show impairments on virtually any test of intellectual functioning that they are given (McKenna, Clare, and Baddeley, 1995). Maljkovic argues that a dissociation of this kind is what one would expect if social exchange, which is a long-enduring adaptive problem, is generated by mechanisms in more evolutionarily ancient parts of the brain than the frontal lobes. Whether this conjecture is true or not, her results indicate that the algorithms responsible for cheater detection are different from those responsible for performance on the more general logical reasoning tasks these patients were given.

Are these effects produced by permission schemas?

The human cognitive phenotype has many features that appear to be complexly specialized for solving the adaptive problems that arise in social exchange. But demonstrating this is not sufficient for claiming that these features are cognitive adaptations *for* social exchange. One also needs to show that these features are not more parsimoniously explained as the by-product of mechanisms designed to solve some other adaptive problem or class of problems.

TABLE 87.2
The permission schema is composed of four production rules

1. Rule 1: If the action is to be taken, then the precondition must be satisfied.
2. Rule 2: If the action is not to be taken, then the precondition need not be satisfied.
3. Rule 3: If the precondition is satisfied, then the action may be taken.
4. Rule 4: If the precondition is not satisfied, then the action must not be taken.

From Cheng and Holyoak, 1985.

For example, Cheng and Holyoak (1985, 1989) also invoke content-dependent computational mechanisms to explain reasoning performance that varies across domains. But they attribute performance on social contract rules to the operation of a permission schema (and/or an obligation schema; these do not lead to different predictions on the kinds of rules usually tested; see Cosmides, 1989), which operates over a larger class of problems. They propose that this schema consists of four production rules (table 87.2) and that their scope is any permission rule, that is, any conditional rule to which the subject assigns the following abstract representation: "If action A is to be taken, then precondition P must be satisfied." All social contracts are permission rules, but not all permission rules are social contracts. The conceptual

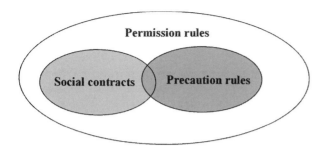

FIGURE 87.4 All social contracts are permission rules; all precaution rules are permission rules; but not all permission rules are social contracts or precautions. Many permission rules that have been tested fall into the white area (neither social contracts nor precautions): these do not elicit the high levels of performance that social contracts and precaution rules do. This argues against permission schema theory. By testing patients with focal brain damage and through priming studies, one can see whether reasoning about social contracts and precautions can be dissociated. These methods allow one to determine whether reasoning about social contracts and precaution rules is generated by one permission schema, or by two separate domain-specific mechanisms.

primitives of a permission schema have a larger scope than those of social contract algorithms. For example, a "benefit taken" is a kind of "action taken," and a "cost paid" (i.e., a benefit offered in exchange) is a kind of "precondition satisfied." They take evidence that people are good at detecting violations of precaution rules—rules of the form, "If hazardous action H is taken, then precaution P must be met"—as evidence for their hypothesis (on precautions, see Manktelow and Over, 1988, 1990). After all, a precaution rule is a kind of permission rule, but it is not a kind of social contract. We, however, have hypothesized that reasoning about precaution rules is governed by a functionally specialized inference system that differs from social contract algorithms and operates independently of them (Cosmides and Tooby, 1992, 1997; Fiddick, 1998; Fiddick, Cosmides, and Tooby, 1995; figure 87.4).

In other words, there are two competing proposals for how the computational architecture that causes reasoning in these domains should be dissected. Several lines of evidence speak to these competing claims.

ARE BENEFITS NECESSARY? According to the grammar of social exchange, a rule is not a social contract unless it contains a *benefit to be taken*. Transformations of input should not matter, as long as the subject continues to represent an action or state of affairs as beneficial to the potential violator and the violator as illicitly obtaining this benefit. The corresponding argument of the permission schema—an *action to be taken*—has a larger scope: Not

all "actions taken" are "benefits taken." If this construal of the rule's representational structure is correct, then the behavior of the reasoning system should be invariant over transformations of input that preserve it. But it is not. For example, consider two rules: (1) "If one goes out at night, then one must tie a small piece of red volcanic rock around one's ankle" and (2) "If one takes out the garbage at night, then one must tie a small piece of red volcanic rock around one's ankle." Most undergraduate subjects perceive the action to be taken in (1)—going out at night—as a benefit, and 80% of them answered correctly. But when one substitutes a different action—taking out the garbage—into the same place in the argument structure, then performance drops to 44% (supports D6, D7; disconfirms B4, B6; Cosmides and Tooby, 1992). This transformation of input preserves the *action to be taken* representational structure, but it does not preserve the *benefit to be taken* representational structure—most people think of taking out the garbage as a chore, not a benefit. If the syntax of the permission schema were correct, then performance should be invariant over this transformation. But a drop in performance is expected if the syntax of the social contract algorithms is correct.

We have been doing similar experiments with precaution rules (e.g., "If you make poison darts, then you must wear rubber gloves."). All precaution rules are permission rules (but not all permission rules are precaution rules). We have been finding that the degree of hazard does not affect performance, but the nature of the precaution does—even though all the *precautions taken* are instances of *preconditions satisfied*. Performance drops when the precaution is not perceived as a good safeguard given the hazard specified (Rutherford, Tooby, and Cosmides, 1996). This is what one would expect if the syntax of the rules governing reasoning in this domain take representations such as *facing a hazard* and *precaution taken*; it is not what one would expect if the representations were *action taken* and *precondition satisfied*.

DOES THE VIOLATION HAVE TO BE CHEATING? By hypothesis, social contract algorithms contain certain conceptual primitives that the permission schema lacks. For example, *cheating* is taking a benefit that one is not entitled to; we have proposed that social contract algorithms have procedures that are specialized for detecting *cheaters*. This conceptual primitive plays no role in the operation of the permission schema. For this schema, whenever the action has been taken but the precondition has not been satisfied, a *violation* has occurred. People should be good at detecting violations, whether that violation counts as cheating (the benefit has been illicitly taken by the violator) or a mistake (the violator does not get the benefit stipulated in the rule).

Given the same social contract rule, one can manipulate contextual factors to change the nature of the violation from cheating to a mistake. When we did this, performance changed radically, from 68% correct in the cheating condition to 27% correct in the mistake condition (supports D2; disconfirms B1-B6). Gigerenzer and Hug (1992) found the same drop in response to a similar context manipulation.

In bargaining games, experimental economists have found that subjects are twice as likely to punish defections when it is clear that the defector intended to cheat as when the defector is a novice who might have simply made a mistake (Hoffman, McCabe, and Smith, 1997). This provides interesting convergent evidence, using entirely different methods, for a conceptual distinction between mistakes and cheating, where intentionality also plays a role.

IS REASONING ABOUT SOCIAL CONTRACTS AND PRECAUTIONS GENERATED BY ONE MECHANISM OR TWO?

If reasoning about social contracts and precautions is caused by one and the same mechanism—a permission schema—then neurological damage to this schema should lower performance on both rules equally. But if reasoning about these two domains is caused by two, functionally distinct mechanisms, then one could imagine neurological damage to the social contract algorithms that leaves the precaution mechanisms unimpaired, and vice versa. Stone and colleagues (Stone, Cosmides, and Tooby, 1996; Stone, Cosmides, and Tooby, forthcoming; Stone et al., 1997) tested R. M., a patient with bilateral damage to his orbitofrontal and anterior temporal cortex, as well as to the left amygdala, on social contract and precaution problems that had been matched for difficulty on normal controls (who got 71% and 73% correct, respectively). R. M.'s performance on the precaution problems was 70% correct: equivalent to that of the normal controls. In contrast, his performance on the social contract problems was only 39% correct. This is a marked impairment, whether compared to the normal controls or to his own performance on the precaution problems (figure 87.5). R. M.'s difference score—his percent correct for precautions minus his percent correct for social contracts—was 31 percentage points. In contrast, the difference scores for individual normal subjects were all close to zero (mean = 0.14 percentage points). If reasoning on both social contracts and precautions were caused by a single mechanism—whether a permission schema or anything else—then one would not be able to find individuals who perform well on one class of content but not on the other. This pattern of results is best explained by the hypothesis that reasoning about these

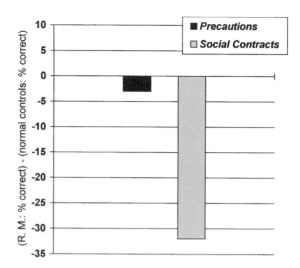

FIGURE 87.5 Performance of R.M. versus normal controls: precautions versus social contracts. Selective impairment of social contract reasoning in R. M., a patient with bilateral damage to the orbitofrontal and anterior temporal lobes and damage to the left amygdala. R. M. reasons normally when asked to look for violations of precaution rules but has difficulty when asked to look for (logically isomorphic) violations of social contracts (i.e., detecting cheaters). The *y*-axis plots the difference between R. M.'s percent correct and the mean performance of 37 normal controls. (Data from Stone, Cosmides, and Tooby, 1996.)

two types of content is governed by two separate mechanisms.

Although tests of this kind cannot conclusively establish the anatomical location of a mechanism, tests with other patients suggest that amygdalar damage was important in creating this selective deficit. Stone and associates tested two other patients who had no damage to the amygdala. One had bilateral orbitofrontal and anterior temporal damage; the other had bilateral anterior temporal damage, but no orbitofrontal damage. Neither patient exhibited a selective deficit; indeed, both scored extremely high on both classes of problems.

Convergent evidence for the single dissociation found by Stone and colleagues comes from a study by Fiddick and associates (Fiddick, Cosmides, and Tooby, 1995; Fiddick, 1998). Using a priming paradigm, they produced a functional dissociation in reasoning in normal, brain-intact subjects. Indeed, they were able to produce a *double* dissociation between social contract and precaution reasoning. More specifically, they found that: (1) when the problem used as a prime involved a clear social contract rule, performance on the target problem—an ambiguous social contract—increased. Moreover, this was due to the activation of social contract categories, not logical ones: when the prime was a switched social contract, in which the correct cheater detection answer is *not* the logically correct answer (see figure 87.3), subjects matched their answers on the target to the prime's benefit/requirement categories, not its logical categories. (2) When the prime was a clear precaution rule, performance on an ambiguous precaution target increased. Most importantly, (3) these effects were caused by the operation of two mechanisms, rather than one: the precaution prime produced little or no increase in performance on an ambiguous social contract target; similarly, the social contract prime produced little or no increase in performance on an ambiguous precaution target.

This should not happen if permission schema theory were correct. In that view, it should not matter which rule is used as a prime because the only way in which social contracts and precautions can affect the interpretation of ambiguous rules is through activating the more general permission schema. Because both types of rules strongly activate this schema, an ambiguous target should be primed equally by either one.

Conclusion

Many cognitive scientists believe that theories of adaptive function are an explanatory luxury–fanciful, unfalsifiable post-hoc speculations that one indulges in at the end of a project, after the hard work of experimentation has been done. Nothing could be farther from the truth. By using a computational theory specifying the adaptive problems entailed by social exchange, we and our colleagues were able to predict, in advance, that certain very subtle changes in content and context would produce dramatic differences in how people reason. Without this theory, it is unlikely that this very precise series of effects would have been found. Even if someone stumbled upon a few of them, it is unlikely that their significance would have been recognized. Indeed, the situation would be similar to that in 1982, when we started this work: cognitive scientists could not understand why some familiar content–such as the drinking-age problem–produced "logical" reasoning whereas other familiar content–such as the transportation problem–did not (Griggs and Cox, 1982). By applying the adaptationist program, we were able to explain what was already known and to discover design features that no one had thought to test for before.

To isolate a functionally organized mechanism within a complex system, one needs a theory of what function that mechanism was designed to perform. The goal of cognitive neuroscience is to dissect the computational architecture of the human mind into functional units. The adaptationist program is cognitive neuroscience's best hope for achieving this goal.

ACKNOWLEDGMENTS The authors gratefully acknowledge the financial support of the James S. McDonnell Foundation, the National Science Foundation (NSF Grant BNS9157-449 to John Tooby), and a Research Across Disciplines grant (Evolution and the Social Mind) from the UCSB office of Research.

NOTE

1. Its relative rarity also suggests that this machinery is unlikely to evolve unless certain other cognitive capacities–components of a theory of mind, perhaps–are already in place.

REFERENCES

ATRAN, S., 1990. *The Cognitive Foundations of Natural History.* New York: Cambridge University Press.

AXELROD, R., 1984. *The Evolution of Cooperation.* New York: Basic Books.

AXELROD, R., and W. D. HAMILTON, 1981. The evolution of cooperation. *Science* 221:1390–1396.

BAILLARGEON, R., 1986. Representing the existence and the location of hidden objects: Object permanence in 6- and 8-month old infants. *Cognition* 23:21–41.

BARON-COHEN, S., 1995. *Mindblindness: An Essay on Autism and Theory of Mind.* Cambridge, Mass.: MIT Press.

BOYD, R., 1988. Is the repeated prisoner's dilemma a good model of reciprocal altruism? *Ethol. Sociobiol.* 9:211–222.

BRASE, G., L. COSMIDES, and J. TOOBY, 1998. Individuation, counting, and statistical inference: The role of frequency and whole object representations in judgment under uncertainty. *J. Psychol. Gen.* 127:1–19.

BROWN, A., 1990. Domain-specific principles affect learning and transfer in children. *Cogn. Sci.* 14:107–133.

CHENG, P., and K. HOLYOAK, 1985. Pragmatic reasoning schemas. *Cogn. Psychol.* 17:391–416.

CHENG, P., and K. HOLYOAK, 1989. On the natural selection of reasoning theories. *Cognition* 33:285–313.

CHENG, P., K. HOLYOAK, R. NISBETT, and L. OLIVER, 1986. Pragmatic versus syntactic approaches to training deductive reasoning. *Cogn. Psychol.* 18:293–328.

COSMIDES, L., 1985. *Deduction or Darwinian algorithms? An Explanation of the "Elusive" Content Effect on the Wason Selection Task.* Doctoral dissertation, Department of Psychology, Harvard University, Cambridge, Mass., University Microfilms, #86 02206.

COSMIDES, L., 1989. The logic of social exchange: Has natural selection shaped how humans reason? Studies with the Wason selection task. *Cognition* 31:187–276.

COSMIDES, L., and J. TOOBY, 1989. Evolutionary psychology and the generation of culture, part II. Case study: A computational theory of social exchange. *Ethol. Sociobiol.* 10:51–97.

COSMIDES, L., and J. TOOBY, 1992. Cognitive adaptations for social exchange. In *The Adapted Mind*, J. Barkow, L. Cosmides, and J. Tooby, eds. New York: Oxford University Press, pp. 163–228.

COSMIDES, L., and J. TOOBY, 1997. Dissecting the computational architecture of social inference mechanisms. In *Characterizing Human Psychological Adaptations* (Ciba Foundation Symposium #208). Chichester: Wiley, pp. 132–156.

FIDDICK, L., 1988. *The Deal and the Danger: An Evolutionary Analysis of Deonitic Reasoning.* Doctoral dissertation, University of California, Santa Barbara, Calif.

FIDDICK, L., L. COSMIDES, and J. TOOBY, 1995. *Priming Darwinian Algorithms: Converging Lines of Evidence for Domain-Specific Inference Modules.* Presented at the Seventh Annual meeting of the Human Behavior and Evolution Society, Santa Barbara, Calif., June 28–July 2, 1995.

FISKE, A., 1991. *Structures of Social Life: The Four Elementary Forms of Human Relations.* New York: Free Press.

GALLISTEL, C., and R. GELMAN, 1992. Preverbal and verbal counting and computation. *Cognition* 44:43–74.

GIGERENZER, G., 1991. How to make cognitive illusions disappear: Beyond heuristics and biases. *Eur. Rev. Soc. Psychol.* 2:83–115.

GIGERENZER, G., and K. HUG, 1992. Domain-specific reasoning: Social contracts, cheating and perspective change. *Cognition* 43:127–171.

GRIGGS, R., and J. COX, 1982. The elusive thematic-materials effect in Wason's selection task. *Br. J. Psychol.* 73:407–420.

HATANO, G., and K. INAGAKI, 1994. Young children's naive theory of biology. *Cognition* 50:171–188.

HOFFMAN, E., MCCABE, K., and SMITH, V., 1997. Behavioral foundations of reciprocity: Experimental economics and evolutionary psychology. Economic Science Laboratory, University of Arizona. To appear in *Economic Inquiry.*

JOHNSON-LAIRD, P., and R. BYRNE, 1991. *Deduction.* Hillsdale, N.J.: Erlbaum.

KEIL, F., 1994. The birth and nurturance of concepts by domain: The origins of concepts of living things. In *Mapping the Mind: Domain Specificity and Culture,* L. Hirschfeld and S. Gelman, eds. New York: Cambridge University Press, pp. 234–254.

LESLIE, A., 1987. Pretense and representation: The origins of "theory of mind." *Psychol. Rev.* 94:412–426.

LESLIE, A., 1994. ToMM, ToBY, and agency: Core architecture and domain specificity. In *Mapping the Mind: Domain Specificity in Cognition and Culture,* L. Hirschfeld and S. Gelman, eds. New York: Cambridge University Press, pp. 119–148.

MALJKOVIC, V., 1987. *Reasoning in Evolutionarily Important Domains and Schizophrenia: Dissociation Between Content-Dependent and Content Independent Reasoning.* Unpublished undergraduate honors thesis, Department of Psychology, Harvard University, Cambridge, Mass.

MANKTELOW, K., and D. OVER, 1988. *Sentences, Stories, Scenarios, and the Selection Task.* Presented at the First International Conference on Thinking. Plymouth, U.K. July 1988.

MANKTELOW, K., and D. OVER, 1990. Deontic thought and the selection task. In *Lines of Thinking,* Vol. 1, K. J. Gilhooly, M. T. G. Keane, R. H. Logie, and G. Erdos, eds. London: Wiley.

MANKTELOW, K. I., and J. ST. B. T. EVANS, 1979. Facilitation of reasoning by realism: Effect or non-effect? *Br. J. Psychol.* 70:477–488.

MARR, D., 1982. *Vision: A Computational Investigation into the Human Representation and Processing of Visual Information.* San Francisco: Freeman.

MCKENNA, P., L. CLARE, and A. BADDELEY, 1995. Schizophrenia. In *Handbook of Memory Disorders,* A. D. Baddeley, B. A. Wilson, and F. N. Watts, eds. New York: Wiley.

PLATT, R., and R. GRIGGS, 1993. Darwinian algorithms and the Wason selection task: A factorial analysis of social contract selection task problems. *Cognition* 48:163–192.

RIPS, L., 1994. *The Psychology of Proof.* Cambridge, Mass.: MIT Press.

RUTHERFORD, M., J. TOOBY, and L. COSMIDES, 1996. *Adaptive Sex Differences in Reasoning About Self-Defense.* Presented at the Eighth Annual Meeting of the Human Behavior and Evolution Society, Northwestern University, Ill., June 26–30, 1996.

SPELKE, E., 1990. Principles of object perception. *Cogn. Sci.* 14:29–56.

SPRINGER, K., 1992. Children's awareness of the implications of biological kinship. *Child Dev.* 63:950–959.

STONE, V. E., S. BARON-COHEN, L. COSMIDES, J. TOOBY, and R. T. KNIGHT, 1997. Selective impairment of social inference abilities following orbitofrontal cortex damage. In *Proceedings of the Nineteenth Annual Conference of the Cognitive Science Society,* M. G. Shafto and P. Langley, eds. London: Lawrence Erlbaum, p. 1062.

STONE, V., L. COSMIDES, and J. TOOBY, 1996. *Selective Impairment of Cheater Detection: Neurological Evidence for Adaptive Specialization.* Presented at the Eighth Annual Meeting of the Human Behavior and Evolution Society, Northwestern University, Ill., June 26–30, 1996.

STONE, V., L. COSMIDES, and J. TOOBY, forthcoming. Selective impairment of social reasoning in an orbitofrontal and anterior temporal patient.

SUGIYAMA, L., J. TOOBY, and L. COSMIDES, 1995. *Cross-Cultural Evidence of Cognitive Adaptations for Social Exchange among the Shiwiar of Ecuadorian Amazonia.* Presented at the Seventh Annual Meetings of the Human Behavior and Evolution Society, University of California, Santa Barbara. Calif., June 28–July 2, 1995.

TOOBY, J., and L. COSMIDES, 1992. The psychological foundations of culture. In *The Adapted Mind,* J. Barkow, L. Cosmides, and J. Tooby, eds. New York: Oxford University Press, pp. 19–36.

TRIVERS, R., 1971. The evolution of reciprocal altruism. *Q. Rev. Biol.* 46 33–57.

WASON, P., 1983. Realism and rationality in the selection task. In *Thinking and Reasoning: Psychological Approaches,* J. St. B. T. Evans, ed. London: Routledge, pp. 44–75.

WASON, P., 1966. Reasoning. In *New Horizons in Psychology,* B. M. Foss, ed. Harmondsworth: Penguin.

WASON, P., and P. JOHNSON-LAIRD, 1972. *The Psychology of Reasoning: Structure and content.* Cambridge, Mass.: Harvard University Press.

WILLIAMS, G., 1966. *Adaptation and Natural Selection.* Princeton: Princeton University Press.

WYNN, K., 1992. Addition and subtraction by human infants. *Nature* 358:749–750.

WYNN, K., 1995. Origins of numerical knowledge. *Math. Cogn.* 1:35–60.

XI

CONSCIOUSNESS

Introduction

DANIEL L. SCHACTER

Human consciousness is just about the last surviving mystery.
—*Daniel C. Dennett (1991)*

Every period in the relatively brief history of neuroscience has considered that it had a special, sometimes even ultimate, insight into the neural mechanisms of conscious awareness. . . .
—*Lawrence Weiskrantz (1991)*

Mention the term "consciousness" to a cognitive neuroscientist, and you will probably elicit one of two very different reactions. Some will likely shrug or groan, mumbling uncomfortably that consciousness is a construct that we do not yet know how to approach sensibly or to investigate productively. Dennett (1991, p. 21) acknowledged the vexing "mystery" of consciousness: "A mystery is a phenomenon that people don't know how to think about—yet." Others, however, will probably respond with enthusiasm, even excitement, citing the latest experimental dissociations between conscious and unconscious processes in neuropsychology or electrophysiology as evidence that cognitive neuroscience is on the verge of finally "cracking" the riddle of consciousness. Weiskrantz (1991, p. 1) has noted that this enthusiasm is not without historical precedent.

Consciousness is a particularly challenging topic for cognitive neuroscience. The challenge begins with the fact that most investigators have a difficult time agreeing on an adequate definition of the term (e.g., Wilkes, 1988). Contemporary treatments of consciousness often begin with an acknowledgment that although we all have a subjective sense of what we mean when we use the expression, satisfactory formal definitions are difficult to come by. Indeed, a number of writers have argued that the term "consciousness" is simply too coarse to be useful theoretically. Block (1995), for instance, distinguished between "phenomenal consciousness" (the raw "feel" of experience) and "access consciousness" (the accessibility of experience to verbal report and use in intentional control), claiming that various analyses of consciousness run into difficulty because they fail to make such a distinction. Tulving (1985) had previously distinguished among three types of consciousness: anoetic (nonknowing), which entails simple awareness of external stimuli; noetic (knowing), which involves awareness of symbolic representations of the world; and autonoetic (self-knowing) consciousness, which involves awareness of self and personal experience extended in time. Farthing (1992) offered a distinction between primary consciousness–simple perceptual awareness of external and internal stimuli–and reflective consciousness–"thoughts about one's own conscious experiences per se" (1992, p. 13). Natsoulas (1978) distinguished among seven different ways in which the term "consciousness" has been used, and numerous other distinctions among forms or types of consciousness could be cited (cf. Chalmers, 1996; Marcel and Bisiach, 1988; Milner and Rugg, 1991; Weiskrantz, 1997).

Definitional problems notwithstanding, cognitive neuroscientists have approached phenomena of consciousness from a variety of perspectives. During the 1950s and 1960s there was great excitement about possibilities for understanding the neurophysiological basis of "states" of consciousness, spurred on by the groundbreaking discoveries by Moruzzi and Magoun (1949) concerning the reticular activating system and conscious awareness, and stimulated by the discovery of rapid eye movement sleep (Aserinsky and Kleitman, 1953). A new and startling perspective on consciousness was provided by observations of commissurotomy, or split-brain, patients that began to appear in the 1960s and 1970s. Led by such investigators as Sperry (1966), Bogen (1969), and Gazzaniga (1970), studies of split-brain patients produced striking observations that suggested the possible existence of independent systems of consciousness in each hemisphere. These observations provided fertile ground for theorizing about consciousness–much of it rather speculative–in neuroscience, psychology, and philosophy (cf. Popper and Eccles, 1977; Puccetti, 1981; Springer and Deutsch, 1985).

While much of the initial excitement surrounding split-brain studies developed during the 1960s and early 1970s, a different sort of phenomenon began to capture the attention of cognitive neuroscientists during the late 1970s and 1980s: Demonstrations that various kinds of brain-damaged patients exhibit preserved access to nonconscious or implicit knowledge despite a profound impairment of conscious or explicit knowledge. Perhaps the best known and most arresting example is that of blindsight, where patients with lesions to striate cortex who deny conscious perception of visual stimuli nonetheless can "guess" their location and other attributes (e.g., Weiskrantz, 1986, 1997). Similarly, amnesic patients who lack explicit or conscious memory for their recent experiences can exhibit nonconscious or implicit memory for aspects of those experiences, as exemplified by such phenomena as priming and skill learning (Schacter, 1987). Similar kinds of dissociations have been observed in patients with aphasia, alexia, and unilateral neglect, among others (Schacter, McAndrews, and Moscovitch, 1988), and have led to the discovery of analogous phenomena in normal subjects (for recent reviews, see Schacter and Buckner, 1998; Stadler and Frensch, 1997). These dissociations have led to a variety of proposals concerning the nature, function, and neural basis of consciousness (see Milner and Rugg, 1991).

The 1980s also witnessed renewed attention to another neuropsychological phenomenon with important implications for thinking about consciousness: unawareness of deficit, or anosognosia. The observation that some brain-damaged patients claim to be entirely unaware of the existence of deficits that are all too obvious to others was first reported in the late nineteenth and early twentieth centuries. Unfortunately, implications of the phenomenon for understanding the nature of conscious experience were not pursued systematically, perhaps because of the prevalence of psychodynamic approaches to the issue (for historical review, see McGlynn and Schacter, 1989). However, stimulated largely by the pioneering research of Bisiach and his colleagues concerning anosognosia in neglect patients (Bisiach and Geminiani, 1991), the central importance of anosognosia and related phenomena for theories of consciousness has come to be more widely appreciated (see Prigatano and Schacter, 1991, and more recent work by Ramachandran, 1995, 1998, for an overview of contemporary approaches).

With the rapid development of functional neuroimaging during the 1990s, we are beginning to witness the first applications of imaging technologies to consciousness-related issues, ranging from nonconscious aspects of perception (Sahraie et al., 1997; Whalen et al., 1998) to the development of automatic habits (Raichle et al., 1994) and distinctions among conscious and nonconscious forms of memory (Schacter et al., 1996; Squire et al., 1992). Although the use of neuroimaging to understand problems related to consciousness is just beginning, we can expect many more such studies in the future.

The chapters in this section provide a broad overview of approaches to consciousness in contemporary cognitive neuroscience that summarize in some depth the foregoing areas of investigation, and point the way to future research. The first two chapters focus on general conceptual and methodological issues. Güzeldere, Flanagan, and Hardcastle provide a philosophical treatment of various constructs that are central to discussions of consciousness, using the compelling phenomenon of blindsight as a "test case" to develop and explore their views concerning alternative philosophical approaches to consciousness. Koch and Crick consider fundamental aspects of visual consciousness and describe the logic of an approach that postulates the existence of a specific consciousness system. Merikle and Daneman focus on the ways in which consciousness and awareness have been defined and operationalized in studies of conscious vs. nonconscious perceptual functions. They examine a general distinction between "subjective" and "objective" criteria for distinguishing conscious from unconscious perception, and argue for the usefulness of focusing on qualitative differences between conscious and unconscious processes. These points have important implications for consciousness studies in general—implications that extend beyond the domain of perceptual functions treated in their chapter.

The subsequent chapters also address general conceptual and methodological issues in the context of more focused discussions of specific phenomena that are critical to the analysis of consciousness. Raichle outlines a research strategy in which functional neuroimaging is used to understand the nature of brain activity as people become increasingly practiced at carrying out various kinds of cognitive and motor tasks. Because these increasingly automatic functions make correspondingly fewer demands on conscious processes, studying them with functional neuroimaging can provide a potentially important window on particular aspects of consciousness. Knight and Grabowecky focus on the role of frontal regions in conscious experience, using both neuropsychological and electrophysiological observations to formulate a general perspective on the issue. They emphasize the crucial importance of various frontal regions for aspects of consciousness that are related to time—planning into the future and remembering back to the past. Baynes and Gazzaniga summarize and integrate numerous observations concerning consciousness and the cerebral hemispheres, including some striking new phenomena observed in split-brain patients that raise intriguing questions concerning the nature of consciousness in the cerebral hemispheres. They discuss these phenomena with respect to the notion of a left-hemisphere "interpreter" that plays a key role in generating aspects of conscious experience.

Hobson, Pace-Schott, and Stickgold consider problems of consciousness with respect to sleep and alterations in arousal. They approach issues of sleep and consciousness from the perspective of contemporary cognitive neuroscience, suggesting explicit linkages between underlying neurophysiology and conscious experience during sleep. Hobson and colleagues summarize a new wave of recent studies that have used functional neuroimaging techniques to explore brain involved with aspects of conscious experience during sleep and dreaming.

As we enter the twenty-first century, are scientists any closer to understanding consciousness than those of the preceding century? Only time will tell, but the ferment of activity surrounding the topic can at least assure us that the age-old enigma of consciousness will continue to occupy cognitive neuroscientists well into the new millennium.

REFERENCES

ASERINSKY, E., and N. KLEITMAN, 1953. Regularly occurring periods of ocular motility and concomitant phenomena during sleep. *Science* 118:361–375.

BISIACH, E., and G. GEMINIANI, 1991. Anosognosia related to hemiplegia and hemianopia. In *Awareness of Deficit after Brain Injury*, G. P. Prigatano and D. L. Schacter, eds. New York: Oxford University Press.

BLOCK, N., 1995. On a confusion about a function of consciousness. *Behav. Brain Sci.* 18:227–247.

BOGEN, J. E., 1969. The other side of the brain: An appositional mind. *Bull. Los Angeles Neurol. Soc.* 34:135–162.

CHALMERS, D., 1996. *The Conscious Mind.* New York: Oxford University Press.

DENNETT, D. C., 1991. *Consciousness Explained.* Boston: Little, Brown.

FARTHING, G. W., 1992. *The Psychology of Consciousness.* Englewood Cliffs, N.J.: Prentice Hall.

GAZZANIGA, M. S., 1970. *The Bisected Brain.* New York: Appleton-Century-Crofts.

MARCEL, A. J., and E. BISIACH (eds.), 1988. *Consciousness in Contemporary Science.* New York: Oxford University Press.

MCGLYNN, S. M., and D. L. SCHACTER, 1989. Unawareness of deficits in neuropsychological syndromes. *J. Clin. Exp. Neuropsychol.* 11:143–205.

MILNER, A. D., and M. D. RUGG (eds.), 1991. *The Neuropsychology of Consciousness.* San Diego: Academic Press.

MORUZZI, G., and H. W. MAGOUN, 1949. Brain stem reticular formation and activation of the EEG. *Electroencephalogr. Clin. Neurophysiol.* 1:455–478.

NATSOULAS, T., 1978. Consciousness. *Am. Psychol.* 33:906–914.

POPPER, K. R., and J. C. ECCLES, 1977. *The Self and Its Brain: An Argument for Interactionism.* Berlin: Springer.

PRIGATANO, G. P., and D. L. SCHACTER (eds.), 1991. *Awareness of Deficit after Brain Injury.* New York: Oxford University Press.

PUCCETTI, R., 1981. The case for mental duality: Evidence from split brain data and other considerations. *Behav. Brain Sci.* 4:93–123.

RAICHLE, M. E., J. A. FIEZ, T. O. VIDEEN, A. M. MACLEOD, J. V. PARDO, P. T. FOX, and S. E. PETERSEN, 1994. Practice-related changes in human brain functional anatomy during nonmotor learning. *Cereb. Cortex* 4:8–26.

RAMACHANDRAN, V. S., 1995. Anosognosia in parietal lobe syndrome. *Conscious. Cognit.* 4:22–51.

RAMACHANDRAN, V. S., 1998. Memory and the brain: New lessons from old syndromes. In *Memory, Brain, and Belief,* D. L. Schacter and E. Scarry, eds. Cambridge, Mass.: Harvard University Press.

SAHRAIE, A., L. WEISKRANTZ, J. L. BARBUR, A. SIMMONS, and S. C. R. WILLIAMS, 1997. Pattern of neuronal activity associated with conscious and unconscious processing of visual signals. *Proc. Natl. Acad. Sci. U.S.A.* 94:9406–9411.

SCHACTER, D. L., 1987. Implicit memory: History and current status. *J. Exp. Psychol.: Learn. Mem. Cogn.* 13:501–518.

SCHACTER, D. L., N. M. ALPERT, C. R. SAVAGE, S. L. RAUCH, and M. S. ALBERT, 1996. Conscious recollection and the human hippocampal formation: Evidence from positron emission tomography. *Proc. Natl. Acad. Sci. U.S.A.* 93:321–325.

SCHACTER, D. L., and R. L. BUCKNER, 1998. Priming and the brain. *Neuron* 20:185–195.

SCHACTER, D. L., M. P. MCANDREWS, and M. MOSCOVITCH, 1988. Access to consciousness: Dissociations between implicit and explicit knowledge. In *Thought without Language,* L. Weiskrantz, ed. New York: Oxford University Press, pp. 242–278.

SPERRY, R. W., 1966. Brain bisection and mechanisms of consciousness. In *Brain and Conscious Experience,* J. C. Eccles, ed. New York: Springer-Verlag, pp. 298–313.

SPRINGER, S. P., and G. DEUTSCH, 1985. *Left Brain, Right Brain.* New York: Freeman.

SQUIRE, L. R., J. G. OJEMANN, F. M. MIEZIN, S. E. PETERSEN, T. O. VIDEEN, and M. E. RAICHLE, 1992. Activation of the hippocampus in normal humans: A functional anatomical study of memory. *Proc. Natl. Acad. Sci. U.S.A.* 89:1837–1841.

STADLER, M. A., and P. A. FRENSCH (eds.), 1997. *Handbook of Implicit Learning.* Thousand Oaks, Calif.: Sage Publications.

TULVING, E., 1985. How many memory systems are there? *Am. Psychol.* 40:385–398.

WEISKRANTZ, L., 1986. *Blindsight: A Case Study and Implications.* Oxford: Clarendon Press.

WEISKRANTZ, L., 1991. Introduction: Dissociated issues. In *The Neuropsychology of Consciousness,* A. D. Milner and M. D. Rugg, eds. San Diego: Academic Press.

WEISKRANTZ, L., 1997. *Consciousness Lost and Found.* New York: Oxford University Press.

WHALEN P. J., S. L. RAUCH, N. L. ETCOFF, S. C. MCINERNEY, M. B. LEE, and M. A. JENIKE, 1998. Masked presentations of emotional facial expressions modulate amygdala activity without explicit knowledge. *J. Neurosci.* 18:411–418.

WILKES, K. V., 1988. ------, yìshì, duh, um, and consciousness. In *Consciousness in Contemporary Science,* A. J. Marcel and E. Bisiach, eds. New York: Oxford University Press.

88 The Nature and Function of Consciousness: Lessons from Blindsight

GÜVEN GÜZELDERE, OWEN FLANAGAN, AND VALERIE GRAY HARDCASTLE

ABSTRACT It is not easy to explain why consciousness exists or should exist. What does consciousness add to an intelligent system that high-performance information processing, storage, and retrieval capabilities don't? Blindsight, which is interesting both biologically and philosophically, is a phenomenon that brings to the fore questions about the role consciousness plays in our general cognitive economy. In this chapter, we discuss the much-debated topic of the function of consciousness in the light of blindsight, pointing out some of its implications for thinking about the nature of consciousness.

In 1866, the English biologist T. H. Huxley remarked, "What consciousness is, we know not; and how it is that anything so remarkable as a state of consciousness comes about as the result of irritating nervous tissue, is just as unaccountable as the appearance of the Djin when Aladdin rubbed his lamp in the story" (Huxley, 1866, p. 193). In 1999, many in the natural sciences and philosophy would scarcely disagree with Huxley, even though the geography of the dialectical space is more complicated today. Following a brief overview of some major philosophical positions on consciousness, this chapter focuses on a particular phenomenon–blindsight–to demonstrate how philosophical, psychological, and neuroscientific debates on the nature and function of consciousness can find a common platform for a fruitful exchange. (For a detailed "field guide" to the consciousness literature, see Güzeldere, 1997.)

Francis Crick and Cristof Koch (1990) called consciousness "the most mysterious aspect of the mind–body problem." What is the nature of this mystery? For some, consciousness is mysterious because it seems to have no place for the realm of physical magnitudes (Nagel, 1974, 1986). For others, consciousness is a natural phenomenon realized in biological systems, just as other biological and psychological phenomena are, but the nature of the relation between consciousness and its bodily underpinnings is bound to elude us forever. This is so because we human beings do not have the requisite cognitive capacities for reaching a full understanding of the mind–body problem epitomized by the problem of consciousness (McGinn, 1991).

These are related, but different positions. In the first line of reasoning, there is something inherently unique about the nature of consciousness that makes it different from all other kinds of physical, biological, or psychological phenomena. Thus, even an advanced science of the mind may never be able to explain consciousness in the same way chemistry explained the atomic structure of matter or biology explained the genetic structure of life. In the second line of reasoning, on the other hand, consciousness does not differ *in kind* from other biological and psychological phenomena. However, a scientific account of consciousness may be much more complicated than anything science has tackled thus far–so complicated, in fact, that the human mind will never be able to conquer it, even as cognitive reach of nonhuman animals will never stretch to an explanatory account of the motions of heavenly bodies.

Consciousness skeptics occupy yet a third position, suggesting that the term *consciousness* may be no more than a "dummy-term like 'thing' with no specific content" (Wilkes, 1984), in which case it should be discarded from the scientific and philosophical vocabulary. Or consciousness may be no more real than a scientifically defunct ghostly entity, in which case one would have good reasons for "doubting that oneself is conscious . . . and [thus] thinking that nothing is conscious" (Rey, 1988).

Many others, abjuring skepticism and mystery alike, have labored to develop various constructive explanatory accounts of consciousness. This group can be characterized by a common ontological denominator, say, a commitment to a materialist/naturalist framework; but here, too, we find differences of opinion. Consciousness is explained in terms of causal/functional roles (Lewis, 1966; Lycan, 1987), representational properties (Dretske, 1995; Tye, 1995), emergent biological properties

GÜVEN GÜZELDERE Department of Philosophy and Center for Cognitive Neuroscience, Duke University, Durham, N.C.
OWEN FLANAGAN Departments of Philosophy, Psychology (Experimental), and Neurobiology, Duke University, Durham, N.C.
VALERIE GRAY HARDCASTLE Department of Philosophy, Virginia Tech, Blacksburg, Va.

1277

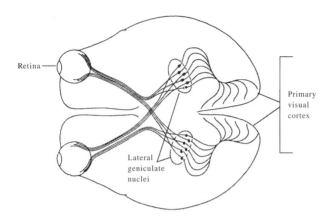

FIGURE 88.1   The primary visual pathway. This schematic illustrates the major projections from the retina, as viewed from the underside of the brain. The optic nerve connects retinal cells to the optic tract. The optic tract projects onto the lateral geniculate nuclei. Optic radiations from the lateral geniculate nucleus terminate in primary visual cortex, also known as area V1 or the striate cortex. Lesions in V1 result in the phenomenon of blindsight.

(Flanagan, 1992; Searle, 1992), higher-order mental states (Armstrong, 1980; Rosenthal, 1997), or computer-related metaphors (Dennett, 1991), or a combination of these.

Within this latter group, we find a certain group of philosophers characterized by an emerging commitment to a particular methodological strategy, a commitment shared by some psychologists and neuroscientists interested in explaining the nature and function of our subjective experiences. Research into the nature and function of consciousness has made some recent advances, especially in the field of cognitive neuroscience, on the basis of a triangulation of data coming from the phenomenological reports of patients, psychological testing at the cognitive/behavioral level, and neurophysiological and neuroanatomical findings. Churchland (1986) calls this strategy for studying the mind the "co-evolutionary strategy"; and Shallice (1988), Dennett (1978, 1991), and Flanagan (1985, 1991, 1992) each promote co-evolutionary methodologies that attempt to bring into equilibrium the phenomenological, the psychological, and the neurobiological in understanding the mind.

Here, using blindsight as an example, we present one way in which this methodology can be used to further our understanding of consciousness. Blindsight is one of the more curious deficits studied in cognitive neuroscience. Lesions in the primary visual cortex (V1) were thought to result in complete blindness. This was reasonable, as V1 was considered to be the terminal information processing station along the primary visual pathway that solely subserved vision (see figure 88.1). However, Weiskrantz and Cowey (1967) pointed out that monkeys whose striate cortex had been removed acted in some

ways as if they could see. These monkeys interacted with their environment in a fluid manner unexpected of completely blind animals. Similar effects are observed in humans, with an interesting twist. Patients with primary visual cortex damage complain that they are blind–that they lack visual experiences–in the field corresponding to the lesioned area. However, upon closer examination, it appears that they can make certain visual discriminations, despite protests that they can see nothing in their blindfield.

Since the publication of Pöppel, Held, and Frost's initial findings on residual visual function in four war veterans with cortical damage (1973), neuroscientists have been documenting the degree to which blind people can react to visual stimuli and trying to explain how they do so. Weiskrantz and colleagues (1974) coined the term "blindsight" for the phenomenon. And since then, its study (and related sensory deficits dubbed, similarly oxymoronically, "numb-sense" and "deaf-hearing") has been a thriving industry in neuroscience (cf. Weiskrantz, 1986, 1997).

Philosophers picked up on blindsight relatively soon after its discovery–though blindsight-type thought experiments had already anticipated the phenomenon (cf. Perkins, 1971). Mellor (1977) introduced blindsight into the literature when he noted, correctly, that blindsight represents an actual case in which function and experience come apart to some degree. Thus, he raised prospects for neuroscientific and philosophical cooperation on questions about the accuracy of first-person psychological reports, about the possibility–indeed the actuality–of nonconscious information–bearing states, and about the function of consciousness. Following Searle (1979) and Churchland (1980), the practice of using blindsight as a case study in discussions of consciousness, perception, and intentionality has become a lively pocket of philosophical literature as well (Güzeldere, 1998).

Blindsight is interesting, first and foremost, because it shows how visual function and visual experience can diverge, at least to some extent, in defiance of ordinary experience. It is a matter of common faith in cognitive neuroscience that not all cognitive processing is conscious. But it is no easy task to separate how unconscious and conscious processing systems divide mental labor. Investigating blindsight gives us one way of investigating the particular causal mechanisms that underlie conscious visual processing. More specifically, understanding blindsight is key to understanding alternative notions of visual capacities: Whether visual capacities are subserved solely by the primary visual pathway in which the primary visual cortex plays an indispensable role, so that all visual discriminations are made consciously; or whether certain visual functions are subserved by multiple pathways radiating toward various other cortical and subcortical areas in addition to V1 via different routes, so that some visual discriminations may be made unconsciously.

In this context, blindsight offers an actual example of what the dissociation of function and experience can be like—a thought experiment "made flesh." As such, blindsight promises new progress on questions of perennial concern to philosophers, psychologists, and neuroscientists. To what extent are we aware of the information received which affects performance? To what extent is performance consciously controlled? Is consciousness a particular component in the system of mental life, or is it a more general feature of the workings of the system? Does consciousness *necessarily* play a role in mental life, or could we do just as well without it?

Blindsight research

Continuing research for the past 25 years has considerably expanded our understanding of the scope of the residual functions present in cortically damaged blindsight patients, from spatial localization of visual targets in the field defect to spectral discrimination, to discrimination of form and movement. In addition, blindsight effects are also measured indirectly: The indirect tasks make use of the fact that visual stimuli falling in the field defect, while not noticeable or reportable by the subject, affect the subject's response to subsequent stimuli presented in the normal visual field. For example, light flashed in the blindfield speeds the reaction time to visual stimuli presented in the normal field (Marzi et al., 1986); words presented in the blindfield semantically prime word pairs in the normal visual field (Marcel, 1983); and figure-halves presented in the blindfield complete other figure-halves presented in the normal visual field (Marcel, as reported in Weiskrantz, 1990).

It is important to emphasize that blindsight patients in these studies do not perform as well as normal subjects on visual tasks. In all of these tasks, the patients are presented with a small set of relatively simple stimuli. They fail to discriminate more complex or subtle phenomena in any fashion. Furthermore, patients never initiate localization- or discrimination-related behavior themselves in the complete absence of consciousness of visual stimuli in their blindfield. Nevertheless, the residual visual capacities that remain comprise an impressive array of capacities exhibited by patients who paradoxically insist that they cannot see.

The first question to address is whether these capacities are residual of a damaged but nonetheless partially functioning primary visual pathway, or whether they

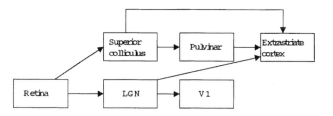

FIGURE 88.2 Alternate visual pathways. Evidence suggests that retinal information not only travels to V1 via the lateral geniculate nuclei (LGN), but also goes to extrastriate cortex via the superior colliculus and the pulvinar, or perhaps via the superior colliculus alone. It is also possible that there are some connections from LGN directly to extrastriate cortex, skipping V1 entirely.

provide evidence for alternative pathways for the visual system. Discovering the answer to this question would tell us something about the nature of visual consciousness vis-a-vis visual function. If losing part of our primary visual pathway means that we lose consciousness, then consciousness is likely to be a threshold effect. Without enough activation, we are not conscious of whatever information is being processed. If our primary visual pathway is completely disrupted and visual processing continues only subcortically, then consciousness might be area-specific. In particular, this would show that we need V1 to be conscious—other visual areas won't suffice. These two possibilities are not mutually exclusive, but knowing the details of the physiology underlying blindsight will give us clues about where to expend our research energy.

Whether the primary visual pathway is necessary for vision, and whether blindsight is a counterexample to this hypothesis, has been a puzzle for neuroscience. And the answer is not uncontroversial. Some have argued that residual functions in blindsight may all be attributable to methodological artifacts, such as the scattering of light onto the intact parts of the retina during the visual presentations (Campion, Lotto, and Smith, 1983). Another hypothesis is that thus far unnoticed islands of spared cortical tissue are responsible for the blindsight patients' discriminatory abilities (Fendrich et al., 1992; Gazzaniga, Fendrich, and Wessinger, 1994; cf. Barinaga, 1992). On the other hand, there are a number of radiations from the retina that extend to regions other than the striate cortex (see figure 88.2). For example, there are thalamic routes to the extrastriate cortex, via the superior colliculus and the pulvinar, as well as routes to subcortical areas (in monkeys) via the collicular route plus the accessory optic tract (Hernandez-Gonzalez and Reinoso-Suarez, 1994; Webster et al., 1993). These different pathways could subserve the residual capacities exemplified in blindsight as the absence of a properly functioning primary visual pathway "presses them into action" (Weiskrantz, 1997).

Final resolution of the debates in the neurophysiology of blindsight will require more data and further studies. At present, the competing hypotheses regarding alternative pathways that mediate the residual visual functions in blindsight patients are under investigation, and the jury is still out on the definitive verdict on the neurological mechanism of blindsight.

Implications for consciousness studies

Philosophers and scientists have approached blindsight primarily as an actual example of a mental phenomenon where functional aspects come apart from experiential aspects. This issue has a significant place in philosophy of mind and cognitive science owing to deep-rooted debates about the function of consciousness and the possibility of *epiphenomenalism*–the view that consciousness is just a causally inert by-product, much like, in T. H. Huxley's words, the steam of a steam engine with respect to the workings of the locomotive. There have also been some skeptical voices among philosophers who claimed that blindsight data should count for little in the debates concerning the nature and function of qualitative experience. To these issues we now turn.

THE FUNCTION OF CONSCIOUSNESS How is blindsight used in support of various theories of consciousness? Mainly, to support two claims: Consciousness facilitates our interpretation and comprehension of the world around us; and consciousness makes behavior more adaptive.

Blindsight patients claim to have no information about the goings-on in their blindfield. They are wrong in this, but we have to press them to get them to show what information they actually have. The case is altogether different with normal persons, and Flanagan (1992) argues that this difference is crucial from a functional point of view. Conscious awareness of a word that favors a particular interpretation, e.g., *river* bank over money *bank*, leads to better performance on disambiguation tasks than does the cruder sensitivity to the helpful clue in blindsight (see also Hardcastle, 1995; Vaina, 1995). The suggested conclusion here is that being conscious helps us process semantic information.

In addition, conscious awareness of objects in our environment contributes to voluntary action. The blindsighted person will make no move toward objects in his or her blindfield. Nonetheless, under forced-choice conditions, the blindsighted exhibit intriguing behavior. As Marcel reports, "Cortically blind patients who have no phenomenal experience of an object in the blindfield will nonetheless preadjust their hands appropriately to size, shape, orientation and 3-D location of that object in the blindfield when forced to attempt to grasp it. Yet such patients will make no spontaneous attempt to grasp a glass of water in their blind field even when thirsty. Voluntary actions often depend upon conscious perception" (Marcel, 1986, p. 41). This sort of evidence implies that conscious awareness of the environment also facilitates adaptive motor actions in creatures like us: "Information needs to be presented to us phenomenally for it to play a role in the choice, initiation, or direction of the intentional action" (Van Gulick, 1994, p. 33).

Van Gulick (1994) notes that this conclusion makes most sense if we assume that consciousness is a form of self-awareness in that we are consciously aware of objects only in relation to ourselves (see also Searle, 1983). My experience of my computer is as *my* computer in front of *me* which *I* am currently using in *my* world. Representing information in terms of how it affords us opportunities to move about or interact in our world makes it easily available to guide our actions in pursuit of our goals.

While this kind of reasoning about the function of consciousness seems too obvious to belabor, the issue vis-à-vis blindsight is not as clear as it might appear at first blush. Some philosophers suggest that since blindsight patients demonstrate both implicit semantic priming and pattern completion in a blindfield, the exact contribution of consciousness to the comprehension of word meaning, object recognition, and the initiation of action remains unclear. If blindsight patients can be trained to learn to act on the visual cues in their blindfield on their own, as Block (1995) suggests, they can become living examples of agents whose visual capacities remain entirely instantiated independently of their consciousness. This would show that visual consciousness is not necessary in the instantiation of visual function.

Note, however, that the performance of blindsight patients is always very limited, confined to simple tasks under forced-choice laboratory conditions. Thus, blindsight patients remain essentially impaired in their abilities to do in their blindfield what normally sighted patients can do. The fact that repeated exposures to the same visual stimuli has produced no blindsight patient who could act voluntarily on an unrestricted set of visual cues in the blindfield provides some evidence that visual consciousness is tied to visual function.

There is another possibility to consider. The egg may stick to the pan for want of heated butter, but butter isn't a necessary condition for nonstuck eggs. A Teflon pan will do. Might this be the case with consciousness? Blindsight patients are unaware of what is in their blindfield. It may be that imperfect performance is due to lack of awareness; but it may also be that whatever knocks out awareness also degrades performance, not that awareness is necessary for optimal performance. That is, awareness of visual stimuli may be related to behavioral performance toward those stimuli not directly, but only by means of a common cause.

These sorts of worries should not be trivialized, and we have to wait for further empirical evidence for definitive answers. Nevertheless, inference to best explanation from the data in hand suggests that consciousness has a crucial role in the initiation of voluntary actions and plasticity of behavioral performance. Whatever else consciousness may be discovered to add to our cognitive economy, the incoming evidence from blindsight continues to give us a valuable, albeit small, piece of that puzzle.

EPIPHENOMENALISM AND ZOMBIES Some philosophers take the residual capacities of blindsight patients very seriously, claiming that blindsight can potentially show that consciousness plays no role in cognition. We could be exactly the same as we are now, only lacking in conscious experience. The theoretical possibility of beings who are like humans in every behavioral and functional aspect except for the fact that they lack experience (dubbed "zombies") occupies a substantial space in contemporary philosophical literature. If this possibility is genuine, then consciousness is not necessary for intelligent life, hence one route to epiphenomenalism. And what can better show that such a possibility is indeed genuine than an actual case discovered by neuroscientists?

Some theoreticians have made claims along these lines, citing works on blindsight in support of the idea of epiphenomenalism. The earlier accounts suggest that because blindsight patients can show appropriate behaviors toward stimuli in their blindfields, we may conclude that consciousness plays no interesting causal role in our psychological life (Carruthers, 1989; see also Siewert, 1993). Later accounts, recognizing that blindsight patients are not as competent as normals in their behavior toward stimuli, maintain that the disability is not due to a lack of phenomenal consciousness, but to some other processing failure instead (Velmans, 1991).

Van Gulick (1994) remarks that epiphenomenalism is an implausible and unduly pessimistic position. We agree. The fact that conscious experience is regularly connected with certain abilities that blindsight patients lack is a fact that needs to be explained. There are numerous cases of neuropsychological deficits linked with deficits in consciousness, and in many of these cases the incapacitation of subjective awareness stands out as an explanatory factor. The simplest and most straightforward explanation of why blindsight patients cannot perform certain tasks is that they are not visually conscious of all the things that normally sighted people are. While epiphenomenalism might be a logical possibility, it has no empirical plausibility in explaining blindsight in the face of what we learn from cognitive neuroscience (Flanagan, 1992; Hardcastle, 1995; Tye 1993, 1995).

Part of the appeal of epiphenomenalism lies in how one ranks different types of evidence. We support a method of seeking reflective equilibrium among all relevant data—no datum, phenomenological, psychological, or neuroscientific, automatically trumps the rest. This method has not always been employed in the history of the science of the mind, nor is it always used today. At the turn of the century, when introspectionism reigned in psychology, first-person phenomenology was privileged. Later, with behaviorism, behavioral evidence ruled, and phenomenology was considered something of an embarrassment. Later still (in the late 1970s and early 1980s), brain circuits and brain chemistry trumped when eliminative materialism had its fifteen minutes of fame. But dismissing first-person reports of subjective experience and discounting performance data from psychology could lead one to the mistake of looking exclusively for alternative nonconscious processing routes. Instead, consciousness should be taken seriously as an important phenomenon to be explained in its own right, a phenomenon that plays an important explanatory role in our cognitive economy.

SKEPTICAL REACTIONS Several philosophers have discussed the possibility that patients with blindsight might be conscious of information arriving through the scotoma, despite their inability to report what the data are (Block, 1995; Chalmers, 1996; McGinn, 1991; Mellor, 1977; Wider, 1993). Ned Block's skeptical discussion advancing the possibility that blindsight patients may be, contrary to popular opinion, conscious of what is in their blindfield while lacking access to it for action or reportability is the most developed. Block bases his argument on the observation that the concept of consciousness is a mongrel and that not everyone means the same thing by the term. In particular, he distinguishes between "phenomenal" (P) consciousness and "access" (A) consciousness. P-consciousness refers to "the way it feels to have experiences, the qualitative character of experience." A-consciousness, in contrast, refers to mental states that can be used as a premise in reasoning or the rational control of action, including verbal reports.

Block (1995) charges those who use blindsight as evidence that consciousness has a performance-enhancing function (e.g., Farah, 1994; Flanagan, 1992; Marcel, 1986; Schacter, 1989; Schacter, McAndrews, and

Moscovitch, 1988; Van Gulick, 1994) of reasoning in the following way:

1. In blindsight patients, consciousness of the stimuli in the blindfield is missing.

2. As a result, blindsight patients fail to engage in some expected behavior.

3. Therefore, consciousness has the function of (or plays a causal role in) bringing about that behavior.

This inference (dubbed "target reasoning") is fallacious, Block claims, because it misses the distinction between the phenomenal and the access aspects of consciousness. Indeed, he claims that consciousness is used in one sense in the first premise and in the other sense in the conclusion. Examined more carefully the argument would look like this:

1. In blindsight patients, A-consciousness of the stimuli in the blindfield is missing.

2. As a result, blindsight patients fail to engage in some expected behavior.

3. Therefore, P-consciousness has the function of (or plays a causal role in) bringing about that behavior.

Put this way the argument is clearly invalid. According to Block it is A-consciousness that is missing in the blindsight patients, whereas the conclusion is drawn with regard to P-consciousness. Block claims that there is good evidence that A-consciousness plays a role in guiding voluntary action, whereas the (causal) status of P-consciousness remains entirely unclear. Any conclusion regarding P-consciousness based on this reasoning will be fallacious.

The validity of Block's fallacy charge, and other arguments like it, depends on, among other things, whether he is entitled to divide the concept of consciousness into his two types: A-consciousness and P-consciousness. One can agree that the concept of consciousness is not a perfectly well-defined term while denying that there is any notion of consciousness that does not involve P-consciousness. To put it another way, whatever we mean by consciousness, we mean a state that has phenomenal feel. This renders Block's A-consciousness, which isolated from any phenomenological feel, suspect as a concept of consciousness.

Ordinary usage supports this response to Block, as does common usage among those working on problems of consciousness. This includes those whom Block accuses of the fallacious "target reasoning," who deny that there is any useful independent concept of A-consciousness (Flanagan, 1992; Graham, 1995). In a telling remark, Block acknowledges that A-consciousness without P-consciousness is "conceptually possible" but "perhaps not actual." The concept of consciousness, no matter

how loosely defined, is used to name a familiar phenomenon, not a mere conceptual possibility. Again, the idea that there exists in the minds of those working in consciousness studies a concept of consciousness that is merely conceivable, and equally applicable to zombies, is worthy of suspicion.

Another problem with the A-consciousness/P-consciousness distinction presents itself in the reverse direction, in the implicit assumption that Block's P-consciousness (by itself) captures the notion of phenomenal consciousness commonly used by Block's target authors. But this assumption is false. The notion that phenomenal consciousness employed in target reasoning is typically laden with properties that belong to Block's A-consciousness; and this, too, makes the A-consciousness/P-consciousness distinction unacceptable from the beginning (cf. Güzeldere and Aydede, 1997; Harman, 1995; Kobes, 1995; Mangan, 1997).

Consider, for example, Marcel, whose "phenomenal consciousness" includes "more than qualia"; it is what "we refer to as known directly or non-inferentially when we report our states" (Marcel, 1988). Thus, for Marcel, it seems that a P-conscious state must involve elements of A-consciousness in Block's sense, e.g., availability to the subject for action. Similarly, Schacter uses the term "phenomenal consciousness" to mean "an ongoing awareness of specific mental activity . . . expressed knowledge that subjects are phenomenally aware that they possess" (Schacter, 1989, p. 356). Again, in Schacter's terms, phenomenal consciousness involves the sort of cognitive elements that belong to Block's A-consciousness, most notably verbal expressibility. In short, decoupling P-consciousness from A-consciousness in the way Block does goes against the intuitions that underlie the ordinary understanding of consciousness, and makes his two-type theory of consciousness stray from the one with which the target reasoning is operating.

Both the skeptics and the champions of the target reasoning think that blindsight patients possess some sort of information that drives their behavior in a certain way—making correct guesses in forced-choice situations, for example—even though they are not aware of possessing this information. According to Block, the patient's awareness of (the possession of) such information, or its lack thereof, is a matter of A-consciousness, not P-consciousness.

In contrast, according to us, and to others who maintain that blindsight is useful for understanding consciousness, the patient's (lack of) awareness of the information about the properties of the visual stimuli in her blindfield is a matter of P-consciousness. The problem is that what is being referred to as "P-consciousness" in arguments connecting blindsight to consciousness essentially involves some sort of "ongoing access" to the phenomenal properties of the state one is in–an "immediately present availability." In the case of humans, this becomes co-extensive with reportability under normal circumstances (but see Cam, 1985; Nelkin, 1993, 1995; Stoerig, 1997). To put the matter in another way, from our perspective, it is never the case that one is simultaneously P-conscious of certain qualities, while not "accessing" them–e.g., knowing about or being able to report their presence. In sum, when it comes to consciousness, *esse* has to be, if not *percipi*, then at least "access-related."

This is not the case for the skeptics like Block. For that reason, however, they cannot claim, as they want to do, to subscribe to an uncontroversial, common-sense conception of consciousness, and at the same time maintain that a person can have phenomenal consciousness while resolutely denying that she is having any sense experience. The notion of qualitative character is supposed to capture the ways things seem to us–not necessarily the way things actually are, but their "seemings." The skeptics' insistence that one can have seemings without anything seeming (or, seeming to seem, if you like) a certain way goes against the grain of subjective experience.

The information the blindsight patient is sensitive to may be degraded because only tiny islands of processing remain in V1. This may be part of the reason the blindsight patient lacks phenomenal awareness. Or it may be that the information is not degraded but is simply untransmissable to a consciousness-related "module" due to visual information traveling only subcortically. This may be the reason why the blindsight patient has no consciousness of this information. Regardless of whether consciousness is location-dependent or dependent upon the degree of activity, the inference to the best explanation is that if the information were to become conscious, performance would improve. By what we know from the knowledge-without-awareness literature and about what the blindsight patient has access to, we should infer that the lack of conscious awareness of the blindfield partly explains the inability to bring the knowledge the system possesses into normal, high-quality play in inference, reporting, and action.

REFERENCES

ARMSTRONG, D., 1980. What is consciousness? In *The Nature of Mind and Other Essays*. Ithaca: Cornell University Press, pp. 55–67.

BARINAGA, M., 1992. Unraveling the dark paradox of "blindsight." *Science* 258:1438–1439.

BLOCK, N., 1995. On a confusion about a function of consciousness. *Behav. Brain Sci.* 18:227–247.

CAM, P., 1985. Phenomenology and speech dispositions. *Phil. Studies*. 47:357–368.

CAMPION, J., R. LOTTO, and Y. M. SMITH, 1983. Is blindsight an effect of scattered light, spared cortex, and near-threshold vision? *Behav. Brain Sci.* 63:423–486.

CARRUTHERS, P., 1989. Brute experience. *J. Phil.* 86:258–269.

CHALMERS, D., 1996. *The Conscious Mind: In Search of a Fundamental Theory*. New York: Oxford University Press.

CHURCHLAND, P. S., 1980. A perspective on mind–brain research. *J. Phil.* 77:185–207.

CHURCHLAND, P. S., 1986. *Neurophilosophy: Toward a Unified Science of the Mind/Brain*. Cambridge, Mass.: MIT Press.

CRICK, F., and C. KOCH, 1990. Towards a neurobiological theory of consciousness. *Seminars in the Neurosciences* 2:263–275.

DENNETT, D. C., 1978. *Brainstorms*. Cambridge, Mass.: MIT Press.

DENNETT, D. C., 1991. *Consciousness Explained*. Boston, Mass.: Little, Brown.

DRETSKE, F., 1995. *Naturalizing the Mind*. Cambridge, Mass.: MIT Press.

FARAH, M., 1994. Visual perception and visual awareness after brain damage: A tutorial overview. In *Attention and Performance*, XV, C. Umilta and M. Moscovitch, eds. Cambridge, Mass.: MIT Press, pp. 37–75.

FENDRICH, R. F., C. M. Messinger, and M. Gazzaniga, 1992. Residual vision in a scotoma: Implications for blindsight. *Science* 258:1489–1491.

FLANAGAN, O., 1985. Consciousness, naturalism, and Nagel. *J. Mind Behav.* 6:373–390.

FLANAGAN, O., 1991. *The Science of the Mind* (2d Ed.). Cambridge, Mass.: MIT Press.

FLANAGAN, O., 1992. *Consciousness Reconsidered*. Cambridge, Mass.: MIT Press.

GAZZANIGA, M., R. F. FENDRICH, and C. M. WESSINGER, 1994. Blindsight reconsidered. *Curr. Direct. Psychol. Sci.* 3:93–96.

GRAHAM, G., 1995. Guilty consciousness. *Behav. Brain Sci.* 18:2.

GÜZELDERE, G. 1997. The many faces of consciousness: A field guide. In *The Nature of Consciousness*, N. Block, O. Flanagan, and G. Güzeldere, eds. Cambridge, Mass.: MIT Press, pp. 1–67.

GÜZELDERE, G., 1998. Blindsight and the function of consciousness. Presented at *Toward a Science of Consciousness III*, Tucson, Ariz.

GÜZELDERE, G., and M. AYDEDE, 1997. On the relation between phenomenal and representational properties. *Behav. Brain Sci.* 20:1.

HARDCASTLE, V. G., 1995. *Locating Consciousness*. Amsterdam: John Benjamins Press.

HARMAN, G., 1995. Phenomenal fallacies and conflations. *Behav. Brain Sci.* 18:2.

HUXLEY, T. H., 1866. *Lessons in Elementary Physiology*. London: Macmillan.

HERNANDEZ-GONZALEZ, C. C., and F. REINOSO-SUAREZ, 1994. The lateral geniculate nucleus projects to the inferior temporal cortex in the macaque monkey. *Neurology Rep.* 5:2692–2696.

KOBES, B., 1995. Access and what it is like. *Behav. Brain Sci.* 18:2.

LEWIS, D., 1966. An argument for the identity thesis. *J. Phil.* 63:17–25.

LYCAN, W., 1987. *Consciousness*. Cambridge, Mass.: MIT Press.

MANGAN, B., 1997. Empirical status of Block's phenomenal/access distinction. *Behav. Brain Sci.* 20:1.

MARCEL, A. J., 1983. Conscious and unconscious perception: An approach to the relations between phenomenal experience and perceptual processes. *Cogn. Psychol.* 15:197–237.

MARCEL, A. J., 1986. Consciousness and processing: Choosing and testing a null hypothesis. *Behav. Brain Sci.* 9:40–41.

MARCEL, A. J., 1988. Phenomenal experience and functionalism. In *Consciousness in Contemporary Science*, A. J. Marcel and E. Bisiach, eds. Oxford: Clarendon Press.

MARZI, C. A., G. TASSINARI, S. AGLIOT, and L. LUTZENBERGER, 1986. Spatial summation across the vertical meridian in hemianopics: A test of blindsight. *Neuropsychologia* 24:749–758.

McGINN, C., 1991. *The Problem of Consciousness*. Oxford: Blackwell Publishers.

MELLOR, D. H., 1977. Conscious belief. *Proc. Aristotelian Soc.* 78:87–101.

MILNER, A. D., and M. A. GOODALE, 1995. *The Visual Brain in Action*. Oxford: Oxford University Press.

NAGEL, T., 1974. What is it like to be a bat? Reprinted in *Mortal Questions*, Cambridge: Cambridge University Press, pp. 165–180.

NAGEL, T., 1986. *The View from Nowhere*. Oxford: Oxford University Press.

NELKIN, N., 1993. What is consciousness? *Phil. Sci.* 60:419–434.

NELKIN, N., 1995. The dissociation of phenomenal states from apperception. In *Conscious Experience*, T. Metzinger, ed. Patterborn: Ferdinand Schoningh, pp. 373–383.

PERKINS, M., 1971. Sentience. *J. Phil.* 68:329–337.

PÖPPEL, E., R. HELD, and D. FROST, 1973. Residual visual function after brain wounds involving the central visual pathways in man. *Nature* 243:295–296.

REY, G., 1988. A question about consciousness. In *Perspectives on Mind*, H. Otto and J. Tuedio, eds. Dordrecht: D. Reidel, pp. 5–24.

ROSENTHAL, D., 1997. A theory of consciousness. In *The Nature of Consciousness*, N. Block, O. Flanagan, and G. Güzeldere (eds.), Cambridge, Mass.: MIT Press.

SCHACTER, D., 1989. On the relation between memory and consciousness: Dissociable interactions and conscious experience. In *Varieties of Memory and Consciousness: Essays in Honour of Endel Tulving*, H. Roediger 3d and F. Craik, eds. Hillsdale, N.J.: Lawrence Erlbaum.

SCHACTER, D., M. McANDREWS, and M. MOSCOVITCH, 1988. Access to consciousness: Dissociable interactions and conscious experience. In *Thought without Language*, L. Weiskrantz, ed. Oxford: Oxford University Press.

SEARLE, J., 1979. *Expression and Meaning*. Cambridge: Cambridge University Press.

SEARLE, J., 1983. *Intentionality*. Cambridge: Cambridge University Press.

SEARLE, J., 1992. *The Rediscovery of the Mind*. Cambridge, Mass.: MIT Press.

SHALLICE, T., 1988. *From Neuropsychology to Mental Structure*. Cambridge: Cambridge University Press.

SIEWERT, C., 1993. What Dennett can't imagine and why. *Inquiry* 36:93–112.

STOERIG, P., 1997. Phenomenal vision and apperception: Evidence from blindsight. *Mind Lang.* 2:224–237.

TYE, M., 1993. Blindsight, the absent qualia hypothesis, and the mystery of consciousness. In *Philosophy and Cognitive Science*, C. Hookway and D. Peterson, eds. Royal Institute of Philosophy Supplement, Vol. 34, pp. 19–40.

TYE, M., 1995. *Ten Problems of Consciousness*. Cambridge, Mass.: MIT Press.

VAINA, L. M., 1995. Akinetopsia, achromatopsia and blindsight: Recent studies on perception without awareness. *Synthese* 105:253–271.

VAN GULICK, R., 1994. Deficit studies and the function of phenomenal consciousness. In *Philosophical Psychology*, G. Graham and L. Stephens, eds. Cambridge, Mass.: MIT Press, pp. 25–50.

VELMANS, M., 1991. Is human information processing conscious? *Behav. Brain Sci.* 14:651–669.

WEBSTER, M. J., J. BACHEVALIER, and L. G. UNGERLEIDER, 1993. Subcortical connections of inferior temporal areas TE and TEO in macaque monkeys. *J. Comp. Neurol.* 33:73–91.

WEISKRANTZ, L., 1986. *Blindsight: A Case Study and Implications*. Oxford: Oxford University Press.

WEISKRANTZ, L., 1990. Outlooks for blindsight: Explicit methodologies for implicit processes. *Proc. R. Soc. Lond. B.* 239:247–278.

WEISKRANTZ, L., 1997. *Consciousness Lost and Found: A Neuropsychological Exploration*. New York: Oxford University Press.

WEISKRANTZ, L., E. K. WARRINGTON, M. D. SANDERS, and J. MARSHALL, 1974. Visual capacity in the hemianotopic field following a restricted occipital ablation. *Brain* 97:709–728.

WEISKRANTZ, L., and A. COWEY, 1967. A comparison of the effects of striate cortex and retinal lesions on visual acuity in the monkey. *Science* 155:104–106.

WIDER, K., 1993. Sartre and the long distance truck driver: The reflexivity of consciousness. *J. Brit. Social Phenomenol.* 24:232–239.

WILKES, K. 1984. Is consciousness important? *Brit. J. Phil. Sci.* 35:223–243.

89 Some Thoughts on Consciousness and Neuroscience

CHRISTOF KOCH AND FRANCIS CRICK

ABSTRACT   We outline our approach to the problem of consciousness by focusing on the neuronal correlate of visual awareness in the primate brain. We seek to understand its function and the specific neuronal structures necessary to explain the phenomenology of conscious vision. We describe the relevant ongoing experimental work, focusing in particular on electrophysiological data in the awake macaque monkey. We argue that, at the moment, the most promising empirical approach is to discover the neuronal correlate of consciousness (NCC).

The aim of this chapter is to outline an experimental program for the elucidation of the neuronal basis of consciousness (much of this material is taken from Crick and Koch, 1998). We assume that when people talk about "consciousness," there is something to be explained. After all, one indubitable fact about the world is that, under certain circumstances, I can "see" or "smell" things, I can remember a friend's face, and I can imagine a future encounter with her. We assume that the reader has similar experiences, else there would be nothing to explain. We seek to understand the neuronal correlates of this brute fact. We can state bluntly the major question that neuroscience must ultimately answer: It is probable that, at any moment, some active neuronal processes in our heads correlate with consciousness while others do not. What, then, is the difference between them? We refer to the neuronal correlate of consciousness as the NCC. We believe that, at this time, it is empirically most profitable to seek to identify the NCC.

In approaching the problem, we made the tentative assumption (Crick and Koch, 1990) that all the different aspects of consciousness (pain, visual awareness, self-consciousness, and so forth) employ a basic common mechanism, or perhaps a few such mechanisms. We also think precise definitions of consciousness are premature but that any such definition is likely to include attention and some form of short-term memory. We assume that some species of animals—in particular the higher mammals—possess some of the essential features of consciousness, but not necessarily all. It follows that a language system is not essential for consciousness. This is not to say, however, that language does not enrich consciousness considerably.

How can one approach consciousness in a scientific manner? Consciousness takes many forms, but for an initial scientific attack it usually pays to concentrate on the form that appears easiest to study. We chose visual consciousness rather than other forms of consciousness, largely because our visual percepts are especially vivid and rich in information. Furthermore, the visual system of primates appears fairly similar to our own (Tootell et al., 1996), and many experiments on the visual systems have already been done on animals such as the macaque monkey.

Why are we conscious?

We have suggested (Crick and Koch, 1995) that the biological usefulness of visual consciousness in humans is to produce the best current interpretation of the visual scene in the light of past experience, either of ourselves or of our ancestors (embodied in our genes), and to make this interpretation directly available, for a sufficient time, to the parts of the brain that contemplate and plan voluntary motor output, of one sort or another, including speech.

Philosophers have invented a creature called a "zombie," which is supposed to act just as normal people do but to be completely unconscious (Chalmers, 1995). This seems to us to be an untenable scientific idea, but there is now suggestive evidence that part of the brain does behave like a zombie. That is, in some cases, a person uses the current visual input to produce a relevant motor output, without being able to say what was seen. Milner and Goodale (1995) point out that a frog has at least two independent systems for action. These may well be unconscious. One is used by the frog to snap at small, prey-like objects, and the other for jumping away from large, looming ones. Why does our brain not consist simply of a series of such specialized zombie systems

CHRISTOF KOCH   Computation and Neural Systems Program, California Institute of Technology, Pasadena, Calif.
FRANCIS CRICK   The Salk Institute, La Jolla, Calif.

1285

without any consciousness? Why do we have any conscious mental life at all?

We suggest that such an arrangement is inefficient when very many such systems are required. Better to produce a single but complex representation and make it available for a sufficient time to the parts of the brain that make a choice among many different but possible plans for action. This, in our view, is what "seeing" is about.

Milner and Goodale (1995) suggest that in primates there are two systems, which we have called the on-line and the seeing systems. The latter is conscious, while the former, acting more rapidly, is not. There is anecdotal evidence from sports. It is often stated, for example, that a trained tennis player reacting to a fast serve has no time to see the ball; the seeing comes afterwards. Similarly, a sprinter is believed to start to run before he or she consciously hears the starting pistol.

The nature of the visual representation

We have argued elsewhere (Crick and Koch, 1995) that to be aware of an object or event, the brain has to construct a multilevel, explicit, symbolic interpretation of part of the visual scene. By *multilevel*, we mean, in psychological terms, different levels such as those that correspond, for example, to lines or eyes or faces. In neurological terms, we mean, loosely, the different levels in the visual hierarchy (Felleman and Van Essen, 1991).

The important idea is that the representation should be explicit. We have had some difficulty getting this idea across. By an explicit representation, we mean a smallish group of neurons that employ coarse coding (Ballard, Hinton, and Sejnowski, 1983) to represent some aspect of the visual scene. In the case of a particular face, all of these neurons can fire to somewhat face-like objects (Young and Yamane, 1992). We postulate that one set of such neurons will be all of one type, will probably be fairly close together, and will all project to roughly the same place. If all such groups of neurons (there may be several of them, stacked one above the other) were destroyed, then the person would not see a face, though he or she might be able to see the parts of a face—the eyes, the nose, the mouth, etc. There are other places in the brain that explicitly represent other aspects of a face, such as the emotion the face is expressing or its angle of gaze.

Notice that while the information needed to represent a face is contained in the firing of the ganglion cells in the retina, it lacks an explicit representation for faces.

How many neurons are there likely to be in such a group? This is not yet known, but we would guess that the number to represent one aspect is likely to be closer to 10^2–10^3 than to 10^4–10^6.

A representation of an object or an event will usually consist of representations of many of the relevant aspects of it, and these are likely to be distributed, to some degree, over different parts of the visual system. The question of how these are bound together is known as the binding problem (von der Malsburg, 1995).

A great deal of neural activity, most of which is probably unconscious, is usually needed for the brain to construct a representation. It may prove useful to consider this unconscious activity as the computations needed to find the best interpretation, while the interpretation itself may be considered to be the results of the computations, only some of which we are then aware. To judge from our perception, the results probably have something of a winner-take-all character.

As a working hypothesis, we have assumed that only some types of specific neurons will express the NCC. It is already known (see the discussion under "Bistable Percepts") that the firing of many cortical cells does not correspond to what the animal is currently seeing. An alternative possibility is that the NCC is necessarily global, usually identified with some emergent property of very large and diffuse assemblies of neurons (e.g., Libet, 1993; Popper and Eccles, 1981; Sperry, 1969). In one extreme form this would mean that, at one time or another, any neuron in cortex and associated structures could express the NCC, and it would be foolish to locate consciousness at the level of single neurons. At this point, we feel it more fruitful to explore the simpler hypothesis—that only particular types of neurons express the NCC—before pursuing the more global hypothesis. Such "local" theories of consciousness, which emphasize specific neuronal or cognitive subsystems responsible for the genesis of consciousness, have been less popular (for an earlier perspective broadly compatible with ours, see Schacter, 1989). Note that such locality does not preclude global effects (think of the genes in the nucleus that control properties throughout the cell).

The conscious visual representation is likely to be distributed over more than one area of the cerebral cortex and possibly over certain subcortical structures as well. We have argued (Crick and Koch, 1995) that in primates, contrary to most received opinion, it is not located in primary visual cortex (V1). This is not to say that what goes on in V1 is not important; indeed, it may be crucial for most forms of vivid visual awareness. But we do suggest that the neural activity there is not directly correlated with what is seen.

What is essential for visual consciousness?

The term "visual consciousness" almost certainly covers a variety of processes. When one is actually looking at a visual scene, the experience is very vivid. In contrast, the visual images produced by trying to remember the same scene are much less vivid and detailed (a vivid recollection is usually called a hallucination). We are concerned here mainly with normal vivid experiences. (It is possible that our visual recollections are dimmer mainly because the back-pathways in the visual hierarchy act on the random activity in the earlier stages of the system.)

Some form of very short-term memory seems almost essential for consciousness, but this memory may be very transient, lasting only a fraction of a second. The existence of iconic memory, as it is called, is well established experimentally (Coltheart, 1983; Gegenfurtner and Sperling, 1993).

Psychophysical evidence for short-term memory (Potter, 1976) suggests that if we do not pay attention to some part or aspect of the visual scene, our memory of it is very transient and can be overwritten (masked) by the following visual stimulus. This probably explains many of our fleeting memories when we drive a car over a familiar route. If we do pay attention (noticing, for example, a child crossing the road), our recollection of this can be longer-lasting.

Our impression that at any moment we see all of a visual scene very clearly and in great detail is illusory. This is due in part to ever-present eye movements and in part to our ability to use the scene itself as a readily available form of memory, since in most circumstances the scene changes rather little over a short span of time (O'Regan, 1992).

Although working memory (Baddeley, 1992) expands the time frame of consciousness, it is not obvious that it is essential for consciousness. It seems to us that working memory is a mechanism for bringing an item, or a small sequence of items, into consciousness. In a similar way, the episodic memory enabled by the hippocampal system (Zola-Morgan and Squire, 1993) is not essential for consciousness, though a person without it is severely handicapped.

Consciousness, then, is enriched by visual attention, though attention may not be essential for visual consciousness to occur (Braun and Julesz, 1998; Rock et al., 1992). Attention is broadly of two types: bottom-up, which is saliency-driven and task-independent; and top-down, which is produced by the planning parts of the brain. Visual attention can be directed either to a location in the visual field or to one or more (moving) objects. The exact neural mechanisms that achieve this are still being debated. Attention is a complicated subject, and we cannot summarize here all the relevant work.

To interpret the visual input, the brain must arrive at a coalition of neurons whose firing represents the best interpretation of the visual scene, often in competition with other possible but less likely interpretations; and there is evidence that attentional mechanisms bias this competition (Luck et al., 1997).

Recent experimental results

We shall not attempt to describe all the various experimental results of direct relevance to the search for the neuronal correlates of visual consciousness in detail. Rather, we outline a few of them.

ACTION WITHOUT SEEING: CLASSICAL BLINDSIGHT Blindsight occurs in humans when there is extensive damage to cortical area V1 (Weiskrantz, 1997). It has been reproduced in monkeys by complete lesioning of primary visual cortex (Cowey and Stoerig, 1995). In a typical case, the patient can indicate, well above chance level, the direction of movement of a spot of light over a certain range of speed, while denying that he sees anything at all. If the movement is less salient, his performance falls to chance; if more salient (that is, brighter or faster), he may report that he had some ill-defined conscious percept ("waving your hand in front of your eyes when they are closed," Weiskrantz, 1997, p. 144), considerably different from the normal one. Other patients can respond to large, simple shapes or colors. While the existence of true blindsight (i.e., the possession of certain residual visual abilities in the absence of any acknowledged awareness) is no longer controversial, its neuronal substrate is (Kentridge, Heywood, and Weiskrantz, 1997; Wessinger, Fendrich, and Gazzaniga, 1997).

The pathways involved have not yet been established. A possible one goes from the superior colliculus to the pulvinar and from there to parts of visual cortex; several other known weak anatomical pathways from the retina and bypassing V1 are also possible. Recent functional magnetic resonance imaging (fMRI) of one blindsight patient, G.Y., directly implicates the superior colliculus as being active–specifically, when G.Y. correctly discriminates the direction of motion of some stimulus without being aware of it at all (Sahraie et al., 1997).

ACTION WITHOUT SEEING: THE ON-LINE SYSTEM The broad properties of the two hypothetical systems– the on-line system and the seeing system–are shown in table 89.1 (following Milner and Goodale, 1995; for a recent review, see Boussaoud, di Pellegrino, and Wise, 1996). The on-line system may have multiple subsystems (for eye movements, for arm movements, for body posture adjustment, and so on). Normally, the two systems work in parallel; indeed, there is evidence that,

TABLE 89.1
Comparison of the hypothetical on-line system and the seeing system*

	On-Line System	Seeing System
Visual inputs handled	Must be simple	Can be complex
Motor outputs produced	Stereotyped responses	Many possible responses
Minimum time needed for response	Short	Longer
Effect of a few seconds' delay	May not work	Can still work
Coordinates used	Egocentric	Object-centered
Certain perceptual illusions	Not effective	Seen
Conscious	No	Yes

*Based on Milner and Goodale, 1995.

in some circumstances, the seeing system can interfere with the on-line system (Rossetti, 1998).

One striking piece of evidence for an on-line system comes from studies on patient D.F. (Milner et al., 1991). Her brain has diffuse damage produced by carbon monoxide poisoning. She is able to see color and texture very well but is very deficient in seeing orientation and form. In spite of this, she is very good at catching a ball. She can "post" her hand or a card into an elongated slot without difficulty, though she is unable to report the slot's orientation.

It is obviously important to discover the difference between the on-line system, which is unconscious, and the seeing system, which is conscious. Milner and Goodale (1995) suggest that the on-line system mainly uses the dorsal visual stream. They propose that rather than being the "where" stream, as suggested by Ungerleider and Mishkin (1982), it is really the "how" stream. This might imply that all activity in the dorsal stream is unconscious. They consider the ventral stream, on the other hand, to be largely conscious. An alternative suggestion (Steven Wise, personal communication; and Boussaoud, di Pellegrino, and Wise, 1996) is that direct projections from parietal cortex into premotor areas are unconscious, whereas projections to them via prefrontal cortex are related to consciousness.

We suspect that, while these suggestions about two systems are on the right lines, they are probably oversimplified. The little that is known of the neuroanatomy hints of multiple cortical streams, with numerous anatomical connections between them (Distler et al., 1993). In short, the neuroanatomy does not suggest that the sole pathway goes up to the highest levels of the visual system, and from there to the highest levels of the prefrontal system and then down to the motor output. Rather, there are numerous pathways from intermediate levels of the visual system to intermediate frontal regions (see figure 89.1).

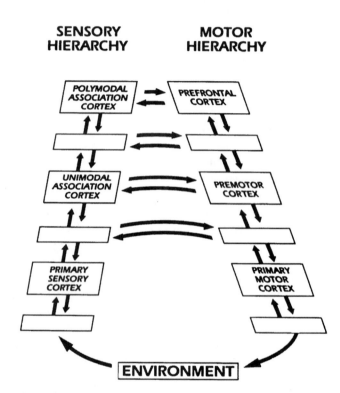

FIGURE 89.1 The fiber connections between cortical regions participating in the perception–action cycle. Empty rectangles stand for intermediate areas or subareas of the labeled regions. Notice that there are connections between the two hierarchies at several levels of the sensory and motor hierarchies, not just at the top level. (From Fuster, 1997; with permission by Lippincott-Raven Publishers.)

We therefore suggest the hypothesis that the brain always tries to use the quickest appropriate pathway for the situation at hand. Exactly how this idea works out in detail remains to be discovered. Perhaps there is competition, and the fastest stream wins. The postulated on-line system would be the quickest of these hypothetical cortical streams. This would be the zombie part of you.

BISTABLE PERCEPTS Perhaps the most important current experimental approach to finding the NCC is the study of the behavior of single neurons–specifically, single neurons in the monkey's brain when it is looking at something that produces a bistable percept. The visual input, apart from minor eye movements, is constant; but the subject's percept can take one of two alternative forms. This happens, for example, when one looks at a drawing of the well-known Necker cube.

A more practical alternative is to study binocular rivalry (Myerson, Miezin, and Allman, 1981). If the visual input into each eye is different, but perceptually overlapping, one usually sees the visual input as received by one eye alone, then by the other one, then by the first one, and so on. The input is constant, but the percept changes. Which neurons in the brain mainly follow the input, and which the percept?

This approach has been explored by Logothetis and his colleagues working on the macaque visual system. They trained the monkey to report which of two rivalrous inputs it saw. The fairly similar distribution of switching times strongly suggests that monkeys and humans perceive these bistable visual inputs in the same way. The first set of experiments (Logothetis and Schall, 1989) studied neurons in area MT. The stimuli were vertically drifting horizontal gratings. Of the relevant neurons, only about 35% were somewhat modulated according to the monkey's reported percept. Surprisingly, half of these responded in the opposite direction to the one expected.

The second set of experiments (Leopold and Logothetis, 1996) used stationary gratings. The orientation was chosen in each case to be optimal for the neuron studied, and orthogonal to it in the other eye. They recorded how the neuron fired during several alterations of the reported percept. While only a small fraction of foveal V1/V2 neurons followed the percept, about 40% of neurons in V4 did. Interestingly, about half of V4 cells were anticorrelated with the stimulus.

The results of the most recent set of experiments (Sheinberg and Logothetis, 1997) are striking (figure 89.2). In this case, the visual inputs include images of humans, monkeys, butterflies, reptiles, and various manmade objects. If a new image is flashed into one eye while the second eye was fixating another pattern, the new stimulus is the one that is always perceived ("flash suppression"). Recordings were made in the upper and lower banks of the superior temporal sulcus (STS) and inferior temporal cortex (IT). Overall, approximately 90% of the recorded neurons in STS and IT reliably predict the perceptual state of the animal. Moreover, many of these neurons respond in a near all-or-nothing fashion, firing strongly for one percept, yet only at noise level for the alternative one.

Bradley, Chang, and Andersen (1998) have studied a different bistable percept in macaque MT using a structure-from-motion paradigm. It is produced by showing the monkey on a TV screen the two-dimensional projection of a transparent, rotating cylinder with random dots "painted" on it, without providing any stereoscopic disparity information. Human subjects exploit structure-from-motion, seeing a three-dimensional cylinder rotating around its axis. But, without further clues, the direction of rotation is ambiguous; observers first report rotation in one direction, then, a few seconds later, rotation in the other direction, and so on. The trained monkey responds as if it saw the same alternation. In their studies on the monkey, about half the relevant MT neurons Bradley and colleagues recorded from followed the percept rather than the "constant" retinal stimulus.

These are all exciting experiments, but they are still in the early stages. Just because a particular neuron follows the percept, it does not automatically imply that its firing is part of the NCC. It is obviously important to discover, for each cortical area, which neurons are following the percept and, most important of all, where they project to. It is, at the moment, technically difficult to do this, but it is essential to have this knowledge, or it will be almost impossible to understand the neural nature of consciousness.

Evicting the NCC from V1

We have argued (Crick and Koch, 1995) that one is not directly conscious of the features represented by the neural activity in primary visual cortex. Activity in V1 may be necessary for vivid and veridical visual consciousness (as is activity in the retina), but we suggest that the firing of none of the neurons in V1 correlates directly with what we consciously see.

Our reasons are that at each stage in the visual hierarchy the explicit aspects of the representation we have postulated is always re-coded. We also assumed that any neurons expressing an aspect of the NCC must project directly, without re-coding, to at least some of the parts of the brain that plan voluntary action–that is what we have argued seeing is for. We think that these plans are made in some parts of frontal cortex.

The neuroanatomy of the macaque monkey shows that V1 cells do not project directly to any part of frontal cortex (Crick and Koch, 1995).

The strategy to verify or falsify this and similar hypotheses is to relate the receptive field properties of individual neurons in V1 or elsewhere to perception in a quantitative manner. Ultimately, this correlation has to be made on an individual trial-to-trial basis. If the structure of perception does not map to the receptive field

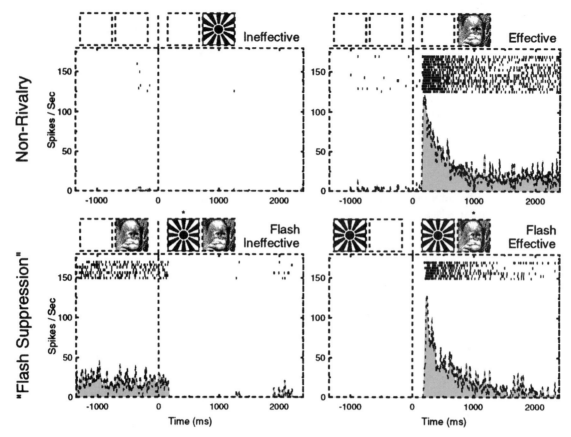

FIGURE 89.2 The activity of a single neuron in the STS of a macaque monkey in response to different stimuli presented to the two eyes. In the upper left panel a sunburst pattern is presented to the right eye without evoking any firing response (ineffective stimulus). The same cell will fire vigorously in response to its effective stimulus–here, the image of an ape's face (upper right panel). When the monkey is shown the face in one eye for awhile, and the sunburst pattern is flashed onto the monitor for the other eye, the monkey signals that it is "seeing" this new pattern and that the stimulus associated with the rivalrous eye is perceptually suppressed (flash suppression; lower left panel). At the neuronal level, the cell rapidly shuts down in response to the ineffective yet perceptually dominant stimulus following stimulus onset (at the dotted line) although the cell's preferred stimulus is still present on the retina. Conversely, if the monkey fixates on the sunburst pattern for a while, and the image of the face is flashed on, it reports perceiving the face, and the cell will now fire strongly (lower right panel). Neurons in V4 are largely unaffected by perceptual changes during flash suppression. (From Sheinberg and Logothetis, 1997.)

properties of V1 cells, it is unlikely that these neurons directly give rise to consciousness. In the presence of a correlation between perceptual experience and the receptive field properties of V1 cells, it is unclear whether these cells just correlate with consciousness or directly give rise to it. In that case, further experiments need to be carried out to untangle the exact relationship between neurons and perception.

An example may make this clearer. It is well known that the color we perceive at one particular visual location is influenced by the wavelengths of the light entering the eye from surrounding regions in the visual field (Land and McCann, 1971). It has been shown in the anesthetized monkey (Schein and Desimone, 1990; Zeki, 1983) that neurons in V4, but not in V1, exhibit this form of partial color constancy, also known as the Land effect. If the same results could be obtained in a behaving monkey, it would follow that it would not be directly aware of the "color" neurons in V1.

In the last several years, a number of psychophysical, physiological, and imaging studies have provided support for our V1 hypothesis, although this evidence falls short of proving it (Cumming and Parker, 1997; He, Smallman, and MacLeod, 1995; Kolb and Braun, 1995; but see Morgan, Mason, and Solomon, 1997). Let us briefly discuss two cases.

When two isoluminant colors are alternated at frequencies beyond 10 Hz, humans perceive only a single fused color with a minimal sensation of brightness flicker. In spite of the perception of color fusion, color opponent cells in primary visual cortex of two alert macaque monkeys follow high-frequency flicker well above heterochromatic fusion frequencies (Gur and Snodderly, 1997). In other words, neuronal activity in V1 can clearly represent certain retinal stimulation that is not perceived. This is supported by recent fMRI studies on human color perception by Engel, Zhang, and Wandell (1997).

The study by He, Cavanagh, and Intriligator (1996) exploits a common visual aftereffect. If a subject stares for a fraction of a minute at a horizontal grating, and is then tested with a faint grating at the same location to decide whether it is oriented vertically or horizontally, the subject's sensitivity for detecting a horizontal grating will be reduced. This adaptation is orientation-specific–the sensitivity for vertical gratings is almost unchanged–and disappears quickly. He and his colleagues projected a single patch of grating onto a computer screen some 25 degrees from the fixation point. It was clearly visible and their subjects showed the predictable orientation-selective adaptation effect. Adding one or more similar patches of gratings to either side of the original grating removes the lines of the grating from visibility; it is "masked." Subjectively, one still sees "something" at the location of the original grating, but one is unable to make out its orientation, even when given unlimited viewing time. Yet despite this inability to "see" the adapting stimulus, the aftereffect was as strong and as specific to the orientation of the "invisible" grating as when the grating was visible. What this shows is that visual awareness must occur at a higher stage in the visual hierarchy than orientation-specific adaptation. This aftereffect is thought to be mediated by oriented neurons in V1 and beyond, implying that the NCC must be located past this stage.

Our hypothesis is not disproved by PET experiments showing that V1 can be activated during visual imagery (Kosslyn et al., 1995), though severe damage to V1 is compatible with visual imagery in patients (Goldenberg, Müllbacker, and Nowak, 1995). There is no obvious reason why such top-down effects should not reach V1. This activity would not, by itself, prove that we are directly aware of it, any more than the V1 activity produced there when our eyes are open proves this. We hope that further neuroanatomical work will make our hypothesis plausible for humans. If correct, it would narrow the search to areas of the brain farther removed from the sensory periphery.

The frontal lobe hypothesis

As mentioned several times, we hypothesize that the NCC must have access to explicitly encoded visual information and directly project into the planning stages of the brain, associated with the frontal lobes in general and with prefrontal cortex in particular (Fuster, 1997). We would therefore predict that patients unfortunate enough to have lost their entire prefrontal cortex on both sides (including Broca's area) would not be visually conscious, although they might still have well-preserved, but unconscious, visual-motor abilities. No such patient is known to us (not even Brickner's famous patient; for an extensive discussion, see Damasio and Anderson, 1993). The visual abilities of any "frontal lobe" patient need to be carefully evaluated using a battery of appropriate psychophysical tests.

The fMRI study of the blindsight patient G.Y. (Sahraie et al., 1997) provides direct evidence for our view by revealing that prefrontal areas 46 and 47 are active when G.Y. is aware of a moving stimulus.

The recent findings of neurons in the inferior prefrontal cortex (IPC) of the macaque that respond selectively to faces–and that receive direct input from regions around STS and the inferior temporal gyrus that are well known to contain face-selective neurons–is very encouraging (Scalaidhe, Wilson, and Goldman-Rakic, 1997; figure 89.3). This raises the question of why face cells would be represented in both IT and IPC. It is unlikely that the same information is represented at two different locations, so it will be important to find out in what way they differ.

Large-scale lesion experiments carried out in the monkey suggest that the absence of frontal lobes leads to complete blindness (Nakamura and Mishkin, 1986; see also Gazzaniga, 1966). One would hope that future monkey experiments reversibly (by cooling and/or injection of GABA agonists) inactivate specific prefrontal areas and demonstrate the specific loss of abilities linked to visual perception while visual-motor behaviors–mediated by the on-line system–remain intact.

It will be important to study the pattern of connections between the highest levels of the visual hierarchy–such as inferotemporal cortex–and premotor and prefrontal cortex. In particular, does the anatomy reveal any feedback loops that might sustain activity between IT and prefrontal neurons? There is suggestive evidence (Webster, Bachevalier, and Ungerleider, 1994) that projections from prefrontal cortex back into IT might terminate in layer 4, but these need to be studied directly.

Some cognitive scientists (in particular Jackendoff, 1987) have argued for an "intermediate-level" theory of consciousness in which neither early sensory processing (the "outer world") nor high-level three-dimensional information or thoughts (the "inner world") are directly accessible to consciousness. The intermediate-level hypothesis raises the intriguing possibility that although much of the frontal lobes might be necessary

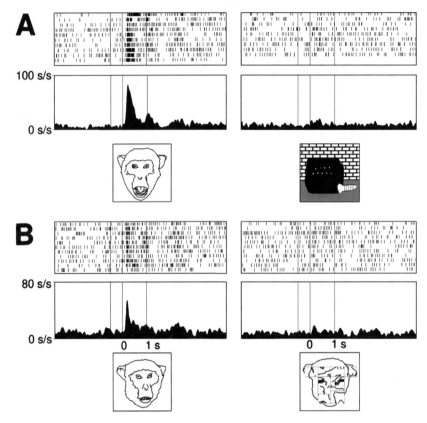

FIGURE 89.3   Face-specific neurons in the inferior prefrontal cortex of the macaque. (A) Firing response of one neuron to its most effective face and nonface stimulus, illustrated by trial rasters and the average spike density function. (B) Response of the same cell to a different face and a scrambled version of this face. The first vertical line denotes foveal fixation, the second line represents stimulus onset, and the third stimulus offset. Total stimulus duration is 1 s. (From Scalaidhe, Wilson, and Goldman-Rakic, 1997.)

for consciousness, the NCC might be preferentially located in more intermediate levels of cortex, such as the inferior temporal lobes (for a more detailed discussion of this and some experimental ramifications, see Crick and Koch, in press).

Future experiments

At the moment the most promising experiments are those on bistable percepts; these need to be expanded to include other brain areas (in particular prefrontal cortex) in both the monkey and in humans (Lumer, Friston, and Rees, 1998) as well as other percepts. It is important to discover which neurons express the NCC in each case (which neuronal subtype, in what layer, and so on), how they fire (do they fire in bursts), and, especially, to where they project. To assist this, more detailed neuroanatomy of the connectivity will be needed. This is relatively easy to do in the macaque, but difficult in humans (Crick and Jones, 1993). It is also important to discover how the various on-line systems work, so that one can contrast their (unconscious) neuronal activity with the NCC.

It will not be enough to show that certain neurons embody the NCC in certain–limited–visual situations. Rather, we need to locate the NCC for all types of visual inputs, or at least for a sufficiently large and representative sample of them. For example, when one blinks, the eyelids briefly (30–50 ms) cover the eyes, yet the visual percept is scarcely interrupted (blink suppression; Volkmann, Riggs, and Moore, 1980). We would therefore expect the NCC to be insensitive to eye-blinks (e.g., the firing activity should not drop noticeably during the blink) but not to blanking out of the visual scene for a similar duration due to artificial means. Another example is the large number of visual illusions. For instance, humans clearly perceive, under appropriate circumstances, a transient motion aftereffect. On the basis of fMRI, it has been found that the human equivalent of cortical area MT is activated by the motion aftereffect (in the absence of any moving stimuli; Tootell et al., 1995). The time course of this illusion parallels the time course of activity as assayed using fMRI. In order to pinpoint the NCC, one would need to identify individual cells expressing this, and similar, visual aftereffects.

In the long run, finding the NCC will not be enough. A complete theory of consciousness is required, including its functional role. With luck, this might illuminate the hard problem of qualia. It is likely that scientists will then stop using the term "consciousness," except in a very loose way. After all, biologists no longer worry whether a seed or a virus is "alive." They just want to know how it evolved, how it develops, and what it can do.

The explanation of consciousness is one of the major unsolved problems of modern science. After several thousand years of speculation, it would be very gratifying to find an answer to it.

ACKNOWLEDGMENTS   We thank the J.W. Kieckhefer Foundation, NIMH, ONR, and NSF for support. We thank David Chalmers and Larry Weiskrantz for helpful comments.

REFERENCES

BADDELEY, A., 1992. Working memory. *Science* 255:556–559.

BALLARD, D. H., G. E. HINTON, and T. J. SEJNOWSKI, 1983. Parallel visual computation. *Nature* 306:21–26.

BOUSSAOUD, D., G. DI PELLEGRINO, and S. P. WISE, 1996. Frontal lobe mechanisms subserving vision-for-action versus vision-for-perception. *Behav. Brain Res.* 72:1–15.

BRADLEY, D. C., G. C. CHANG, and R. A. ANDERSEN, 1998. Activities of motion-sensitive neurons in primate visual area MT reflect the perception of depth. *Nature* 392:714–717.

BRAUN, J., and B. JULESZ, 1998. Withdrawing attention at little cost: Detection and discrimination tasks. *Percept. Psychophys.* 60:1–23.

CHALMERS, D., 1995. *The Conscious Mind: In Search of a Fundamental Theory.* Oxford: Oxford University Press.

COLTHEART, M., 1983. Iconic memory. *Phil. Trans. R. Soc. Lond. B* 302:283–294.

COWEY, A., and P. STOERIG, 1995. Blindsight in monkeys. *Nature* 373:247–249.

CRICK, F., and E. JONES, 1993. Backwardness of human neuroanatomy. *Nature* 361:109–110.

CRICK, F., and C. KOCH, 1990. Towards a neurobiological theory of consciousness. *Sem. Neurosci.* 2:263–275.

CRICK, F., and C. KOCH, 1995. Are we aware of neural activity in primary visual cortex? *Nature* 375:121–123.

CRICK, F., and C. KOCH, 1998. Consciousness and neuroscience. *Cereb. Cortex* 8:97–107.

CRICK, F., and C. KOCH, in press. The unconscious homunculus. In *The Neuronal Correlates of Consciousness*, T. Metzinger, ed. Cambridge, Mass.: MIT Press.

CUMMING, B. G., and A. J. PARKER, 1997. Responses of primary visual cortical neurons to binocular disparity without depth perception. *Nature* 389:280–283.

DAMASIO, A. R., and S. W. ANDERSON, 1993. The frontal lobes. In *Clinical Neuropsychology* (3d Ed.), K. M. Heilman and E. Valenstein, eds. Oxford: Oxford University Press, pp. 409–460.

DISTLER, C., D. BOUSSAOUD, R. DESIMONE, and L. G. UNGERLEIDER, 1993. Cortical connections of inferior temporal area TEO in macaque monkeys. *J. Comp. Neurol.* 334:125–150.

ENGEL, S., X. ZHANG, and B. WANDELL, 1997. Colour tuning in human visual cortex measured with functional magnetic resonance imaging. *Nature* 388:68–71.

FELLEMAN, D. J., and D. VAN ESSEN, 1991. Distributed hierarchical processing in the primate cerebral cortex. *Cereb. Cortex* 1:1–47.

FUSTER, J. M., 1997. *The Prefrontal Cortex: Anatomy, Physiology, and Neuropsychology of the Frontal Lobe* (3d Ed.), Philadelphia: Lippincott-Raven.

GAZZANIGA, M. S., 1966. Visuomotor integration in split-brain monkeys with other cerebral lesions. *Exp. Neurol.* 16:289–298.

GEGENFURTNER, K. R., and G. SPERLING, 1993. Information transfer in iconic memory experiments. *J. Exp. Psychol.: Human Percept. Perform.* 19:845–866.

GOLDENBERG, G., W. MÜLLBACKER, and A. NOWAK, 1995. Imagery without perception–A case study of anosognosia for cortical blindsight. *Neuropsychologia* 33:1373–1382.

GUR, M., and D. M. SNODDERLY, 1997. A dissociation between brain activity and perception: Chromatically opponent cortical neurons signal chromatic flicker that is not perceived. *Vis. Res.* 37:377–382.

HE, S., P. CAVANAGH, and J. INTRILIGATOR, 1996. Attentional resolution and the locus of visual awareness. *Nature* 383:334–337.

HE, S., H. SMALLMAN, and D. MACLEOD, 1995. Neural and cortical limits on visual resolution. *Invest. Ophthalmol. Vis. Sci.* 36:2010.

JACKENDOFF, R., 1987. *Consciousness and the Computational Mind.* Cambridge, Mass.: MIT Press.

KENTRIDGE, R.W., C. A. HEYWOOD, and L. WEISKRANTZ, 1997. Residual vision in multiple retinal locations within a scotoma: Implications for blindsight. *J. Cogn. Neurosci.* 9:191–202.

KOLB, F. C., and J. BRAUN, 1995. Blindsight in normal observers. *Nature* 377:336–339.

KOSSLYN, S. M., W. L. THOMPSON, I. J. KIM, and N. M. ALPERT, 1995. Topographical representations of mental images in primary visual cortex. *Nature* 378:496–498.

LAND, E. H., and J. J. MCCANN, 1971. Lightness and retinex theory. *J. Opt. Soc. Am.* 61:1–11.

LEOPOLD, D. A., and N. K. LOGOTHETIS, 1996. Activity changes in early visual cortex reflect monkeys' percepts during binocular rivalry. *Nature* 379:549–553.

LIBET, B., 1993. *Neurophysiology and Consciousness: Selected Papers and New Essays.* Boston: Birkhauser.

LOGOTHETIS, N., and J. SCHALL, 1989. Neuronal correlates of subjective visual perception. *Science* 245:761–763.

LUCK, S. J., L. CHELAZZI, S. A. HILLYARD, and R. DESIMONE, 1997. Neural mechanisms of spatial selective attention in areas V1, V2, and V4 of macaque visual cortex. *J. Neurophysiol.* 77:24–42.

LUMER, E. D., K. J. FRISTON, and G. REES, 1998. Neural correlates of perceptual rivalry in the human brain. *Science* 280:1930–1934.

MILNER, D., and M. GOODALE, 1995. *The Visual Brain in Action.* Oxford: Oxford University Press.

MILNER, A. D., D. I. PERRETT, R. S. JOHNSTON, P. J. BENSON, T. R. JORDAN, and D. W. HEELEY, 1991. Perception and action in "visual form agnosia." *Brain* 114:405–428.

MORGAN, M. J., A. J. S. MASON, and J. A. SOLOMON, 1997. Blindsight in normal subjects? *Nature* 385:401–402.

MYERSON, J., F. MIEZIN, and J. ALLMAN, 1981. Binocular rivalry in macaque monkeys and humans: A comparative study in perception. *Behav. Anal. Lett.* 1:149–156.

NAKAMURA, R. K., and M. MISHKIN, 1986. Chronic blindness following lesions of nonvisual cortex in the monkey. *Exp. Brain Res.* 62:173–184.

O'REGAN, J. K., 1992. Solving the "real" mysteries of visual perception: The world as an outside memory. *Can. J. Psychol.* 46:461–488.

POPPER, K. R., and J. C. ECCLES, 1981. *The Self and the Brain.* Berlin: Springer Verlag.

POTTER, M. C., 1976. Short-term conceptual memory for pictures. *Exp. Psychol.: Hum. Learn. Mem.* 2:509–522.

ROCK, I., C. M. LINNETT, P. GRANT, and A. MACK, 1992. Perception without attention: Results of a new method. *Cogn. Psychol.* 24:502–534.

ROSSETTI, Y., 1998. Implicit perception in action: Short-lived motor representations of space evidenced by brain-damaged and healthy subjects. In *Finding Consciousness in the Brain*, P. G. Grossenbacher, ed. Philadelphia: J. Benjamins, in press.

SAHRAIE, A., L. WEISKRANTZ, J. L. BARBUR, A. SIMMONS, S. C. R. WILLIAMS, and M. J. BRAMMER, 1997. Pattern of neuronal activity associated with conscious and unconscious processing of visual signals. *Proc. Natl. Acad. Sci. U.S.A.* 94:9406–9411.

SCALAIDHE, S. P. O., F. A. W. WILSON, and P. S. GOLDMAN-RAKIC, 1997. Areal segregation of face-processing neurons in prefrontal cortex. *Science* 278:1135–1138.

SCHACTER, D. L., 1989. On the relation between memory and consciousness: Dissociable interactions and conscious experience. In *Varieties of Memory and Consciousness: Essays in Honor of Endel Tulving*, H. L. Roediger and F. I. M. Craik, eds. Hillsdale, N.J.: Lawrence Erlbaum Associates, pp. 355–389.

SCHEIN, S. J., and R. DESIMONE, 1990. Spectral properties of V4 neurons in the macaque. *J. Neurosci.* 10:3369–3389.

SHEINBERG, D. L., and N. K. LOGOTHETIS, 1997. The role of temporal cortical areas in perceptual organization. *Proc. Natl. Acad. Sci. U.S.A.* 94:3408–3413.

SPERRY, R.W., 1969. A modified concept of consciousness. *Psychol. Rev.* 76:532–536.

TOOTELL, R. B. H., A. M. DALE, M. I. SERENO, and R. MALACH, 1996. New images from human visual cortex. *Trends Neurosci.* 19:481–489.

TOOTELL, R. B. H., J. B. REPPAS, A. M. DALE, R. B. LOOK, M. I. SERENO, R. MALACH, T. J. BRADY, and B. R. ROSEN, 1995. Visual motion aftereffect in human cortical area MT revealed by functional magnetic resonance imaging. *Nature* 375:139–141.

UNGERLEIDER, L. G., and M. MISHKIN, 1982. Two cortical visual systems. In *Analysis of Visual Behavior*, D. J. Ingle, M. A. Goodale, and R. J. W. Mansfield, eds. Cambridge, Mass.: MIT Press, pp. 549–586.

VOLKMANN, F. C., L. A. RIGGS, and R. K. MOORE, 1980. Eyeblinks and visual suppression. *Science* 207:900–902.

VON DER MALSBURG, C., 1995. Binding in models of perception and brain function. *Curr. Opin. Neurobiol.* 5:520–526.

WEBSTER, M. J., J. BACHEVALIER, and L. G. UNGERLEIDER, 1994. Connections of inferotemporal areas TEO and TE with parietal and frontal cortex in macaque monkeys. *Cereb. Cortex* 5:470–483.

WEISKRANTZ, L., 1997. *Consciousness Lost and Found.* Oxford: Oxford University Press.

WESSINGER, C. M., R. FENDRICH, and M. S. GAZZANIGA, 1997. Islands of residual vision in hemianopic patients. *J. Cogn. Neurosci.* 9:203–221.

YOUNG, M. P., and S. YAMANE, 1992. Sparse population coding of faces in the inferotemporal cortex. *Science* 256:1327–1331.

ZEKI, S., 1983. Colour coding in the cerebral cortex: The reaction of cells in monkey visual cortex to wavelengths and colours. *Neuroscience* 9:741–765.

ZOLA-MORGAN, S., and L. R. SQUIRE, 1993. Neuroanatomy of memory. *Ann. Rev. Neurosci.* 16:547–563.

90 Conscious vs. Unconscious Perception

PHILIP M. MERIKLE AND MEREDYTH DANEMAN

ABSTRACT   In this chapter, we discuss three approaches for distinguishing conscious from unconscious perception. The oldest approach uses subjective measures based on people's self-reports regarding whether they are aware of perceiving. A more recent approach uses objective measures based on people's abilities to discriminate between stimulus states such as the presence or absence of a stimulus. Both of these approaches have been used to establish the existence of unconscious perception. With the third approach, the existence of unconscious perception is assumed and the goal is to show that conscious and unconscious perception of the same stimulus information can lead to qualitatively different consequences. The importance of qualitative differences is that they show that unconscious perception is not simply a weak form of conscious perception. We describe how these approaches have been used with neurologically intact individuals and neurological patients to demonstrate unconscious perception and to establish how unconscious perception differs from conscious perception.

Imagine that you are in a lecture hall and the lecturer holds up a series of white flash cards. All you see on each card is a dim, blurred spot, or nothing at all. However, the lecturer tells you that each card contains a single character—either a letter from the set B, Z, K, U, and H or a digit from the set 2, 4, 5, 7, and 9—and she asks you to report the character that you "see" on each card. You comply with her request, even though it feels as if you are guessing. Later, you are surprised to learn that your "guesses" were considerably more accurate than the chance level of performance. This classroom demonstration illustrates one of the earliest approaches to the study of unconscious perception. In fact, Sidis reported a number of similar experiments in 1898. The participants in his experiments also "complained that they could not see anything at all; that even the black, blurred, dim spot often disappeared from their field of vision" and "that they might as well shut their eyes and guess" (Sidis, 1898, p. 171). Despite these complaints, Sidis found that the participants in his studies performed consistently above chance. And on the basis of these findings, he concluded that his experiments indicated "the presence within us of a secondary subwaking self

that perceives things which the primary waking self is unable to get at" (p. 171).

The studies conducted by Sidis illustrate one approach for demonstrating unconscious perception. This approach, which relies on observers' self-reports regarding awareness, is still widely used today, and is one of the two major approaches for demonstrating unconscious perception discussed in this chapter. The other approach for demonstrating unconscious perception discussed in the chapter is an approach that relies on more objective measures of awareness. This alternative approach was developed because some investigators (e.g., Eriksen, 1960) have been reluctant to measure awareness solely on the basis of self-reports, given that so many factors other than awareness can influence self-reports of perceptual experiences. With this second approach, awareness is assessed on the basis of perceptual discriminations, and an inability to discriminate is assumed to indicate an absence of awareness. Although there has been considerable debate regarding the relative merits of subjective measures of awareness based on self-reports and objective measures of awareness based on perceptual discriminations (e.g., Holender, 1986), both approaches have been used successfully to demonstrate unconscious perception. In this chapter, we suggest that both approaches may assess the same underlying subjective awareness of perceiving.

By and large, the goal of the vast majority of studies based on subjective and objective measures of awareness has been simply to demonstrate unconscious perception. A more recent research strategy has been to ask how conscious and unconscious perceptual processes differ in their influence on thoughts, actions, and feelings. This alternative strategy has led to a third approach to the study of unconscious perception—one that emphasizes how unconscious and conscious perception can at times have different consequences. We describe examples of studies in which qualitative differences have been established, and we suggest that studies of qualitative differences provide stronger evidence both for unconscious perception per se and for the importance of the distinction between conscious and unconscious perception than is provided by any approach that simply attempts to demonstrate unconscious perception.

PHILIP M. MERIKLE   Department of Psychology, University of Waterloo, Waterloo, Ontario, Canada
MEREDYTH DANEMAN   Department of Psychology, University of Toronto, Mississauga, Ontario, Canada

Demonstrations of unconscious perception

SUBJECTIVE MEASURES OF AWARENESS One of the most reliable ways to demonstrate perception without awareness is simply to ask people whether or not they are aware of perceiving. If awareness is reported, conscious perception is assumed, whereas if no awareness is reported and perception can be demonstrated, unconscious perception is assumed. In the following sections, we review how self-reports have been used successfully to demonstrate perception in the absence of an awareness of perceiving. We first consider studies in which stimuli have been presented below a subjective threshold for awareness to neurologically intact individuals, then we consider studies in which stimuli have been presented to neurological patients who have no awareness of perceiving.

Subjective thresholds In studies based on subjective thresholds, the basic strategy is to systematically degrade the stimulus conditions until the quality of the stimulus information is so poor that observers claim not to be able to perceive the stimuli. The subjective threshold for awareness is defined in terms of the minimal stimulus conditions necessary for someone to experience the awareness of perceiving (cf. Cheesman and Merikle, 1986), and the primary question addressed by these studies is whether stimuli presented below the subjective threshold are nevertheless perceived.

Some of the best examples of studies based on subjective thresholds come from the earliest studies of unconscious perception. The studies conducted by Sidis (1898) are good examples of this general approach. Another example is a study conducted by Dunlap (1900) showing that the Müller-Lyer illusion can be induced by "stimulation of such low intensity as to be imperceptible" (p. 435). Examples of the stimuli used by Dunlap are shown in figure 90.1. The task for the participants was simply to indicate which line segment appeared to be longer. For line A, both the left and right segments are equal in length; and, not surprisingly, the participants showed no bias in judging either the left or right segment as being longer. However, when Dunlap added the faint angular lines shown in

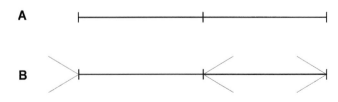

FIGURE 90.1   Examples of the stimuli used by Dunlap (1900).

line B, the participants were more likely to indicate that the left segment was longer than the right segment. Given that the angular lines were presented at an intensity below the level of conscious perception, Dunlap concluded that "we have evidence for the belief that under certain conditions things of which we are not . . . conscious have their immediate effects on consciousness" (p. 436).

Over the years, there have been countless studies demonstrating perception of information presented below a subjective threshold for awareness. Many of these studies were conducted during the late 1800s and early 1900s when consciousness was a central topic in psychology. These studies showed that the following types of information can be perceived without awareness: (1) visual characters such as letters or digits (e.g., Sidis, 1898); (2) names of letters whispered so faintly that "no sound whatever could be heard" (e.g., Stroh, Shaw, and Washburn, 1908); (3) small differences in the weight of two objects (e.g., Peirce and Jastrow, 1884); (4) geometric figures such as circles, triangles, and squares (e.g., Williams, 1938); and (5) orientations of lines as vertical, horizontal, or diagonal (e.g., Baker, 1937). In more recent studies, it has been shown that the meaning of words can be perceived under conditions that do not lead to the subjective experience of perceiving (e.g., Cheesman and Merikle, 1986; Debner and Jacoby, 1994; Merikle, Joordens, and Stolz, 1995) and that attention can be directed to locations in the visual field by visual cues presented below the subjective threshold for awareness (McCormick, 1997). In addition, in a recent study of the perception of the emotions expressed in pictures of human faces, fMRI has revealed that fearful and happy faces lead to differential activation in the amygdala even when the pictures are presented under conditions that make it impossible for participants to explicitly identify the emotion expressed in the faces (Whalen et al., 1998). Taken together, the results of both the older studies and the more recent studies show that a considerable amount of information is perceived even when observers do not report any awareness of perceiving.

Neurological patients A striking characteristic of a number of neurological syndromes is that even though patients may claim that they do not see particular stimuli, they can nevertheless respond on the basis of information conveyed by the very same stimuli that they claim not to see (cf. Schacter, McAndrews, and Moscovitch, 1988). Such dissociations between patients' self-reports and their performance define a number of neurological syndromes. Perhaps the best known example is the blindsight demonstrated when patients with damage to the primary visual cortex report no awareness of objects but correctly guess the size, shape, or orientation of objects presented within the "blind" area of the visual field (e.g., Weiskrantz, 1986). Other examples of perception in the absence of the subjective experience of perceiving are found in studies of prosopagnosia or face agnosia (cf. Young, 1994). Although prosopagnosics may consciously experience looking at a person's face in the sense that they report "I see a face," they are unable to identify the person even though the person may be well known to them. Thus, based on their self-reports, prosopagnosics have no awareness of perceiving any information regarding whose face they may be viewing. However, despite this inability to consciously identify faces, some prosopagnosics are able to choose which of two names goes with the face that they claim not to be able to identify (e.g., De Haan, Young, and Newcombe, 1991; Sergent and Poncet, 1990). Thus, despite their claims to the contrary, prosopagnosics are able to perceive faces, albeit unconsciously.

Visual neglect is another syndrome that provides evidence regarding the types of information that may be perceived despite patients' claims to the contrary. Patients with visual neglect claim not to see stimuli presented to the side of a visual display that is contralateral to their lesion. One way in which this deficit manifests itself is in situations in which stimuli are presented simultaneously to the left and right visual fields. For example, if patients with lesions in the parietal lobe of the right hemisphere are shown a picture of an apple to the left of fixation and a picture of a comb to the right of fixation, most patients will be able to name the comb, but few if any patients will be able to name the apple. But despite this absence of awareness of stimuli presented to the neglected visual field, patients with visual neglect perceive sufficient information to make accurate judgments regarding whether a word or picture presented to the neglected visual field is the same as or different from the consciously perceived word or picture presented to the normal visual field (Volpe, LeDoux, and Gazzaniga, 1979).

Stimuli presented to the neglected visual field can also influence a patient's reactions to the consciously perceived stimuli presented to the normal visual field. For example, Berti and Rizzolatti (1992) presented a picture of an animal (e.g., bird, rat) or a fruit (e.g., apple, pear) to the normal visual field, and the patients' task was to categorize each target picture as being either an animal or a fruit. Each target picture was preceded by one of three types of pictures presented to the neglected visual field. In the highly congruent condition, the picture presented to the neglected field (e.g., a duck) was identical to the target picture. In the congruent condi-

tion, the picture presented to the neglected field (e.g., a rat) was a different example from the same category as the target picture (e.g., a duck). In the noncongruent condition, the picture presented to the neglected field (e.g., a duck) was a picture from the other category (e.g., grapes). Berti and Rizzolatti found that the time taken to categorize a target was faster in both the highly congruent and congruent conditions relative to the noncongruent condition. These findings demonstrate that the neglect patients perceived the meaning of the pictures presented to the neglected visual field despite their inability to name the pictures.

These dissociations between the ability of patients to explicitly identify or name stimuli and their performance on tasks such as same/different judgments or semantic categorization are similar to the dissociations found when information is presented below the subjective threshold for awareness to neurologically intact individuals. Thus, the results from studies with neurological patients lead to a similar conclusion: Considerable information is perceived even when self-reports indicate an absence of an awareness of perceiving.

OBJECTIVE MEASURES OF AWARENESS In 1960, Eriksen suggested that the ability of observers to discriminate between alternative stimulus states is a better measure to distinguish conscious from unconscious perception than are observers' self-reports of awareness. This suggestion followed from Eriksen's concern that self-reports can be influenced by many factors other than a person's subjective awareness. It is always possible that statements indicating an absence of an awareness of perceiving simply reflect a person's preconceived ideas concerning the value of particular types of perceptual experiences for making decisions rather than a true absence of conscious perception (cf. Merikle, 1984). For this reason, Eriksen suggested that the distinction between conscious and unconscious perception is best defined in terms of an observer's ability to discriminate between alternative stimulus states. Thus, an inability to discriminate between two stimulus states, such as the presence or absence of a stimulus, indicates a complete absence of awareness of the perceptual characteristic(s) that distinguish one stimulus state from the other. Conversely, if it is possible to discriminate one stimulus state from another, then this indicates that the stimuli are consciously perceived. Eriksen's suggestion led to the idea that awareness should be defined objectively in terms of discriminative responding rather than subjectively in terms of self-reports of awareness.

Objective thresholds Perception below an objective threshold for awareness was first demonstrated by

Marcel (1974/1983). In a series of studies, he showed that semantic priming was produced by words presented under such poor stimulus conditions that observers could not tell when a word was present or absent. Marcel based his experiments on the well known finding that the time to respond to a target word is facilitated (i.e., primed) when it is preceded by a semantically related word (e.g., Meyer and Schvaneveldt, 1976). For example, the letter string *doctor* can be classified as a word faster when it follows the word *nurse* than when it follows the word *bread*. Marcel's important new variation was that he presented the words that served as primes under two different conditions. In one condition, the primes were clearly visible; in the other, the primes were so degraded by a visual mask that observers could not detect whether or not a prime had been presented. Marcel found that the magnitude of semantic priming was similar in the two conditions. In other words, the undetectable primes were as effective as the clearly visible primes. On the basis of these findings, Marcel concluded that the meaning of words can be perceived even under conditions in which there is no awareness of perceiving the words.

Marcel's basic methodology for demonstrating semantic priming without awareness has now been repeated in many different experiments. Many studies have demonstrated that unconsciously perceived words can prime decisions regarding consciously perceived words (e.g., Balota, 1983; Dagenbach, Carr, and Wihelmsen, 1989; Fowler et al., 1981; Groeger, 1984). Moreover, other studies have demonstrated that unconsciously perceived pictures (e.g., McCauley et al., 1980) and unconsciously perceived auditory stimuli (Groeger, 1988) can prime decisions regarding subsequently presented target words. In addition, there is evidence that the affective valence of unconsciously perceived words (e.g., love, grief) can prime evaluative decisions (i.e., good vs. bad) of target words (Greenwald, Klinger, and Liu, 1989), and that the emotion expressed in unconsciously perceived faces (e.g., happiness vs. anger) can influence subsequent evaluative judgments of unfamiliar Chinese ideographs (Murphy and Zajonc, 1993). Assuming that objective thresholds for awareness were successfully established in these studies, the combined results provide compelling evidence that stimuli are perceived even when it is not possible to discriminate between alternative stimulus states.

Neurological patients Given the success of experiments with neurologically intact individuals in demonstrating perception in the absence of discrimination, similar experiments have been conducted with prosopagnosics and patients with visual neglect. In general, the results of these studies with neurological patients lead to the same conclusion as the studies with neurologically intact individuals. They show that stimulus information is perceived even when the patients are unable to make overt discriminations between alternative stimulus states.

Bauer (1984) reported one of the first studies in which awareness was assessed by an objective measure of a patient's ability to discriminate between alternative stimulus states. In his study, a patient with prosopagnosia was shown two sets of photographs of faces. One set consisted of ten well-known people (e.g., actors, athletes) and the other set consisted of eight family members. While viewing each face in each set, the patient heard five spoken names, one of which corresponded to the face. The patient was asked to select the name that went with each face. Not surprisingly, the number of correct responses did not differ from chance, indicating that the patient was unaware of whose face he was viewing. But though the patient was unable to overtly recognize the correct names, his galvanic skin response (GSR) indicated that he was able to unconsciously recognize the names that corresponded with the faces. Bauer measured the patient's GSR to each of the names presented with each face, and found that the correct names elicited the largest change in GSR more often than would be expected on the basis of chance. The fact that the correct names elicited large GSRs even though the patient could not select the correct names provides strong evidence that faces can be unconsciously perceived by prosopagnosics (see also Tranel and Damasio, 1988).

Objective measures of discriminative responding have also been used with both prosopagnosic patients and patients with visual neglect to demonstrate that stimuli that cannot be discriminated can nevertheless prime decisions regarding targets. For example, Young and De Haan (1988) have found that a prosopagnosic patient, PH, is not able to discriminate familiar from unfamiliar faces. Nevertheless, PH can classify a printed name (e.g., *Prince Charles*) as being familiar more quickly when it follows the face of a related person (e.g., Princess Diana) than when it follows the face of an unrelated person (e.g., Nancy Reagan) (Young, Hellawell, and De Haan, 1988). Primes that cannot be discriminated have also been shown to facilitate neglect patients' subsequent decisions regarding targets (e.g., Ladavas, Paladini, and Cubelli, 1993; McGlinchey-Berroth et al., 1993; 1996). Consider, for example, the study reported by McGlinchey-Berroth and colleagues (1993). They compared the magnitude of priming produced by pictures presented to the neglected field or the normal field, measuring the speed with which patients were able to decide whether a centrally presented letter string was a word or nonword. They presented a picture (e.g., cup, hat) to one visual field immediately before a target word (e.g., *saucer*) or nonword (e.g., *spiger*) was presented. On some trials, the prime and target were semantically related (e.g., a picture of a cup followed by the word *saucer*), whereas on other trials the prime and target were unrelated (e.g., a picture of a pig followed by the word *saucer*). They found equivalent priming for pictures presented to either visual field, even though, as established in a separate experiment, the neglect patients could not make correct forced-choice decisions regarding the pictures presented to the neglected field. Similar results have been found when the primes are words rather than pictures (McGlinchey-Berroth et al., 1996). Taken together, the results of the studies with the prosopagnosic patient PH and the studies with neglect patients show that these patients perceive the meaning of stimuli even when they are unable to make correct forced-choice discriminations between the alternative stimuli.

SUBJECTIVE VS. OBJECTIVE MEASURES OF AWARENESS Studies based on subjective and objective measures assess awareness in very different ways. But despite these methodological differences, the results of studies based on both types of measures lead to similar conclusions. How can such apparently different measures of awareness lead to such similar conclusions? There are two possible answers to this question.

One answer is that objective measures of awareness are often influenced by subjective factors, such as a person's beliefs regarding the quality of the perceived information. For example, if someone is asked to discriminate between two stimulus states, such as the presence or absence of a stimulus, and there is no subjective awareness of perceiving, there is often a bias to say "absent" or "no stimulus" each time a decision is requested (cf. Merikle, 1982). More generally, when someone is asked to discriminate between alternative stimulus states and there is no subjective awareness of perceiving, there may be no motivation to perform the task. An unmotivated observer may show a bias to choose one of the response alternatives or a bias to choose a response alternative in an unsystematic manner each time a response is requested. In either case, the observed performance will simply reflect the observer's belief that no useful information was perceived; hence an objective measure of awareness will reveal nothing more than that which could be assessed by self-reports of awareness.

A second answer to the question is that objective measures of awareness are often based on so few trials that relatively high levels of discriminative responding do not differ statistically from the chance level of performance (cf. Macmillan, 1986; Merikle, 1982). Suppose, for example, an objective measure is based on a presence vs. absence discrimination and there is a total of 50 trials (25 present trials and 25 absent trials). Then the confidence interval ($p < .05$) around the chance level of performance (50% correct) ranges from 38% to 62% correct. With such a large confidence interval, one may conclude, incorrectly, that discriminative responding does not differ from chance. But if discriminative responding is actually above chance, the results may simply show that information is perceived under conditions in which perception is not accompanied by the subjective awareness of perceiving.

Despite the obvious methodological differences that distinguish objective and subjective measures, it is now clear that in many contexts objective and subjective measures assess the same underlying subjective awareness of perceiving. Furthermore, objective measures often do not provide any information that cannot be gained from the more straightforward approach of simply asking observers to report the presence or absence of awareness. In reaction to this state of affairs, some investigators have tried to find better objective measures that can then be used to show that perception does in fact occur below an objective threshold for awareness (e.g., Draine and Greenwald, 1998; Greenwald, Draine, and Abrams, 1996; Snodgrass, Shevrin, and Kopka, 1993). This approach can be successful for demonstrating unconscious perception; but unless it is possible to find objective measures that assess conscious perception *exclusively,* such an approach will inevitably underestimate the influence of unconsciously perceived information on thoughts and actions (cf. Merikle and Reingold, 1998). All measures of perception can, in principle, be influenced by both consciously and unconsciously perceived information. Hence any set of experimental conditions that leads to lower performance on an objective measure of perception will reduce not only the influence of consciously perceived information but the influence of unconsciously perceived information as well. The only alternative to finding better objective measures of awareness is to develop better ways to use self-reports of awareness. Notwithstanding a justified uneasiness about using self-reports as the sole basis for distinguishing conscious from unconscious perception, all things considered, self-reports of awareness offer both a direct and accurate indication of the presence or absence of the subjective awareness of perceiving in many contexts (cf. Chalmers, 1996; Merikle, 1992).

Qualitative differences between conscious and unconscious perception

The importance of the distinction between conscious and unconscious perception is sometimes overlooked. Surely, the distinction is much more significant and interesting if the consequences of conscious and unconscious perception are qualitatively different, so that unconscious perception is not simply a weak form of conscious perception (cf. Dixon, 1971; Merikle, 1992; Shevrin and Dickman, 1980). It has even been suggested that the distinction between conscious and unconscious perception would be of limited value if conscious and unconscious perception did *not* lead to different consequences (e.g., Reingold and Merikle, 1990). For this reason, it is important to assess the ways in which conscious perception differs from unconscious perception.

In the following sections we describe studies that show a qualitative difference in the influence of consciously and unconsciously perceived stimuli. These studies were based on subjective measures of awareness. The general research strategy in these studies was to use self-reports to establish the conditions under which perception is either accompanied or unaccompanied by the subjective awareness of perceiving, and then to show that information perceived under these two conditions leads to qualitatively different consequences. Although this research strategy has most often been used in studies with neurologically intact individuals, it has also been used in studies with neurological patients.

NEUROLOGICALLY INTACT INDIVIDUALS It is often assumed that conscious perception enables one to use perceived information to act on the world and to produce effects on the world (cf. Chalmers, 1996; Searle, 1992), whereas unconsciously perceived information leads to more automatic reactions that cannot be controlled by the perceiver. This distinction between the controlled use of consciously perceived information and the more automatic influences of unconsciously perceived information has been captured in a number of studies.

One example of this type of experiment is a study reported by Debner and Jacoby (1994). In their study, a single word was presented and masked on each trial. The interval between the onset of the word and the onset of the mask was either relatively short (e.g., 50 ms), so that most of the words were unconsciously perceived, or somewhat longer (e.g., 150 ms), so that most of the words were consciously perceived. Immediately following the mask, the first three letters of the word were presented once again. At this point, the participants were told to complete the word stem with any word that came to mind except the word that had just been presented. Thus, if the word presented on a trial was *dough*, the letter-stem *dou* was presented immediately thereafter, and the participants were instructed to use any word except *dough* to complete the word stem. For example, the participants could complete the word stem with *doubt* or *double* but not *dough*. Debner and Jacoby (1994) found that the par-

ticipants had difficulty following the instructions when the words that preceded the word stems were unconsciously perceived because of the short (50-ms) duration. Despite explicit instructions to the contrary, the participants used these words to complete the word stems. This failure to exclude unconsciously perceived words was not due to some perverse desire on the part of the participants not to cooperate: When the words were presented for the slightly longer duration (150 ms), the participants successfully excluded the words that were presented immediately before the word stems. These results are completely consistent with the idea that unconsciously perceived information leads to automatic reactions that cannot be controlled by a perceiver. In contrast, consciously perceived information allows individuals to use this information to guide their actions so that they are able to follow the instructions.

Another example of how unconscious perception leads to automatic reactions and conscious perception allows individuals to modify their reactions comes from a series of experiments showing that prediction based on stimulus redundancy occurs only when the predictive stimuli are consciously perceived (e.g., Merikle and Joordens, 1997). These experiments were based on a two-color variant of the Stroop (1935) color-word interference task. On each experimental trial, either the word *RED* or the word *GREEN* was presented so that it was either consciously or unconsciously perceived. A patch of color that was also either red or green was then shown. The task for the participants was simply to name the color of each color patch as fast as possible. The standard result found with this task is that it takes more time to name a color patch (e.g., green) when it follows an incongruent color word (e.g., *RED*) than when it follows a congruent color word (e.g., *GREEN*). Presumably, this occurs because participants are unable to avoid reading the word even though they are not required to read it, and reading a color word that represents a conflicting color concept (e.g., *RED*) interferes with naming the color patch (e.g., green). In the Merikle and Joordens experiments, this standard interference effect in color naming was found independent of whether the preceding words were consciously or unconsciously perceived. However, when the experimental conditions were changed so that 75% of the word/color-patch pairings were incongruent (i.e., *GREEN*/red or *RED*/green) and the remaining 25% of the word/color-patch pairings were congruent (i.e., *GREEN*/green or *RED*/red), the results depended on whether the words were consciously or unconsciously perceived. When the words were consciously perceived, it actually took LESS time to name a color patch when it followed an incongruent color word (e.g., *GREEN*/red) than when it followed a congruent color word (e.g., *GREEN*/green). What seems to have happened is that the participants capitalized on the predictive information provided by the words; they learned to expect that the color patch on each trial would be the color NOT named by the preceding word. This predictive strategy facilitated performance on the incongruent trials and slowed performance on the congruent trials, leading to a reversal of the standard result. In contrast, when the words were unconsciously perceived, the standard Stroop interference effect was found independent of the predictive relation between the words and color patches. In other words, the participants did not make use of the predictive information provided by the words to change their expectations. These results provide another demonstration of how unconscious perception leads to automatic reactions, whereas conscious perception allows individuals to use the perceived information to guide their actions so that they can react to stimuli in a more flexible manner.

NEUROLOGICAL PATIENTS   In general, there has been little emphasis on showing qualitative differences in the consequences of information perceived with and without awareness in neurological patients. However, there is at least one interesting example of the success of this approach in studies of one patient with visual form agnosia (Milner and Goodale, 1995). The patient, DF, has bilateral damage to the lateral occipital cortex and is not able to give an accurate report of the location of objects in space; nor is she able to describe other characteristics of objects such as their shape, size, or orientation. In fact, based on both her self-reports and her inability to discriminate between different objects, DF does not appear to have any awareness of perceiving objects in space. But despite what is clearly an absence of relevant conscious perceptual experiences, DF is able to reach successfully and pick up objects. In addition, when DF reaches for objects, she shapes her hand so that her grip is adjusted to accommodate different-sized objects even though her self-reports indicate that she has no awareness of how the objects may differ in size. These dissociations between DF's conscious perceptual experiences and her skilled actions directed toward objects have led Milner and Goodale to suggest that there are two quite separate visual pathways: the ventral stream which mediates conscious perception of objects, and the dorsal stream which mediates the guidance of skilled actions directed toward objects independent of whether or not the objects are consciously perceived.

The idea that the conscious perception of objects and the visuomotor control of reaching for objects are mediated by separate visual pathways gains strong support from studies of qualitative differences in reaching between DF and neurologically intact individuals. Goodale, Jakobson, and Keillor (1994) conducted a series of studies in which neurologically intact individuals and DF were either required to reach for a target object while the object was in view or to pantomime reaching for the object two seconds after viewing it. Not surprisingly, introducing a delay between viewing the object and reaching for it led to a number of differences in the reaching movements of both the neurologically intact individuals and DF. However, there was an important difference in the way normal individuals and DF scaled their grips to accommodate different-sized objects when there was a delay between viewing an object and reaching for it. For neurologically intact individuals, increases in object width led to corresponding increases in the maximum grip aperture exhibited when they mimed reaching for the objects. In contrast, when DF mimed reaching for different-sized objects following a delay, she did not scale her grip. Rather, her maximum grip aperture was basically the same irrespective of the actual size of the object.

These findings demonstrate a rather dramatic difference between the consequences of conscious and unconscious perception. When objects are in view and reaching is immediate, both DF and neurologically intact individuals can direct actions toward the objects on the basis of the unconsciously perceived information provided by the dorsal visual pathway which mediates the visuomotor control of reaching when objects are in view. However, the visuomotor systems operate in real time using current visual information. Thus, in order to mediate a temporal interval between viewing an object and reaching for the object, it is necessary to form a representation of the object based on different information than is provided by the dorsal pathway. Milner and Goodale (1995) suggest that the ventral pathway provides the information that allows neurologically intact individuals to form conscious perceptual representations of objects. These conscious representations can then be used to guide visuomotor actions, such as scaling grip size to object size, following a temporal delay between viewing and reaching. In contrast, DF is unable to form conscious representations of objects that provide sufficient information to guide her visuomotor actions. As a consequence, when she reaches for an object following a delay, she does not scale her grip to the size of the object.

Concluding comments

The question of whether unconscious perceptual processes play an important role in determining conscious experiences, feelings, thoughts, and actions has dominated much of the research on consciousness during the past 100 years. One reason for the fixation on this particular question is our intellectual heritage. Descartes' famous dictum "I think therefore I am" led to the belief that consciousness and mind are one and the same (cf. Rorty, 1979). Given this belief, any evidence for unconscious perception attracts attention because it challenges the conventional view of mind. Another reason that so much effort has been directed toward demonstrating the existence of unconscious mental processes is that our conscious experiences give us the illusion that all important mental processes are conscious. Our feelings, thoughts, and actions almost always occur in temporal contiguity with ongoing conscious experiences. This leads us to attribute our feelings, thoughts, and actions to these ongoing conscious experiences. Taken together, both our intellectual heritage suggesting that mind and consciousness are synonymous and our delusion that conscious mental processes are the only important mental processes probably account for the continual interest in and fascination with demonstrations of unconscious perception in both neurologically intact individuals and neurological patients. It also probably accounts for why so much effort has been devoted to demonstrating the existence of unconscious processes.

Given the evidence that has been amassed during the past 100 years, there is now little doubt that unconscious processes play an important role in determining feelings, thoughts, and actions. For this reason, research regarding conscious and unconscious perception is now beginning to focus on the differences that distinguish conscious from unconscious perception. Not only do the qualitative differences that have been established show how conscious and unconscious perception differ, but they also provide further confirmation of the importance of distinguishing between conscious and unconscious perceptual processes. Qualitative differences show that unconscious perception is not simply a weak form of conscious perception and that conscious perception and unconscious perception of the same stimuli can at times lead to qualitatively different consequences.

Now that the distinction between conscious and unconscious perception has been shown to have a firm empirical basis, future experimental studies can continue to explore the characteristics that distinguish conscious from unconscious perception. It will be important to determine exactly what types of information can and cannot be perceived unconsciously, what types of information may be more readily perceived unconsciously than consciously, what the duration of the impact of unconsciously perceived information may be, and whether some individuals are particularly sensitive to unconscious influences and conversely whether some individuals are particularly insensitive to unconscious influences. With the available tools, it should be possible to begin to tease apart the factors determining how different individuals and different contexts lead to different reactions to both consciously and unconsciously perceived information.

ACKNOWLEDGMENTS Preparation of this chapter was facilitated by grants from the Natural Sciences and Engineering Research Council of Canada.

REFERENCES

BAKER, L. E., 1937. The influence of subliminal stimuli on verbal behavior. *J. Exp. Psychol.* 20:84–100.

BALOTA, D. A., 1983. Automatic semantic activation and episodic memory. *J. Verb. Learn. Verb. Behav.* 22:88–104.

BAUER, R. M., 1984. Autonomic recognition of names and faces in prosopagnosia: A neuropsychological application of the guilty knowledge test. *Neuropsychologia* 22:457–469.

BERTI, A. and G. RIZZOLATTI, 1992. Visual processing without awareness: Evidence from unilateral neglect. *J. Cogn. Neurosci.* 4:345–351.

CHALMERS, D. J., 1996. *The Conscious Mind.* New York: Oxford University Press.

CHEESMAN, J., and P. M. MERIKLE, 1986. Distinguishing conscious from unconscious perceptual processes. *Canad. J. Psychol.* 40:343–367.

DAGENBACH, D., T. H. CARR, and A. WIHELMSEN, 1989. Task-induced strategies and near-threshold priming: Conscious influences on unconscious perception. *J. Mem. Lang.* 28:412–443.

DEBNER, J. A., and L. L. JACOBY, 1994. Unconscious perception: Attention, awareness, and control. *J. Exp. Psychol.: Learn. Mem. Cognit.* 20:304–317.

DE HAAN, E. H. F., A. W. YOUNG, and F. NEWCOMBE, 1991. Covert and overt recognition in prosopagnosia. *Brain* 114:2575–2591.

DIXON, N. F., 1971. *Subliminal Perception: The Nature of a Controversy.* New York: McGraw-Hill.

DRAINE, S. C., and A. G. GREENWALD, 1998. Replicable unconscious semantic priming. *J. Exp. Psychol.: Gen.*

DUNLAP, K., 1900. The effect of imperceptible shadows on the judgment of distance. *Psychol. Rev.* 7:435–453.

ERIKSEN, C. W., 1960. Discrimination and learning without awareness: A methodological survey and evaluation. *Psychol. Rev.* 67:279–300.

FOWLER, C. A., G. WOLFORD, R. SLADE, and L. TASSINARY, 1981. Lexical access with and without awareness. *J. Exp. Psychol.: Gen.* 110:341–362.

GOODALE, M. A., L. S. JAKOBSON, and J. KEILLOR, 1994. Differences in the visual control of pantomimed and natural grasping movements. *Neuropsychologia* 32:1159–1178.

GREENWALD, A. G., S. C. DRAINE, and R. L. ABRAMS, 1996. Three cognitive markers of unconscious semantic activation. *Science* 273:1699–1702.

GREENWALD, A. G., M. R. KLINGER, and T. J. LIU, 1989. Unconscious processing of dichoptically masked words. *Mem. Cognit.* 17:35–47.

GROEGER, J. A., 1984. Evidence of unconscious semantic processing from a forced-error situation. *Brit. J. Psychol.* 75:305–314.

GROEGER, J. A., 1988. Qualitatively different effects of undetected and unidentified auditory primes. *Quart. J. Exp. Psychol.* 40A:323–339.

HOLENDER, D., 1986. Semantic activation without conscious identification in dichotic listening, parafoveal vision, and visual masking: A survey and appraisal. *Behav. Brain Sci.* 9:1–23.

LADAVAS, E., R. PALADINI, and R. CUBELLI, 1993. Implicit associative priming in a patient with left visual neglect. *Neuropsychologia* 31:1307–1320.

MACMILLAN, N. A., 1986. The psychophysics of subliminal perception. *Behav. Brain Sci.* 9:38–39.

MARCEL, A. J., 1974. Perception with and without awareness. Paper presented at the meeting of the Experimental Psychology Society, Stirling, Scotland, July.

MARCEL, A. J., 1983. Conscious and unconscious perception: Experiments on visual masking and word recognition. *Cogn. Psychol.* 15:197–237.

MCCAULEY, C., C. M. PARMELEE, C. D. SPERBER, and T. H. CARR, 1980. Early extraction of meaning from pictures and its relation to conscious identification. *J. Exp. Psychol.: Hum. Percept. Perform.* 6:265–276.

MCCORMICK, P. A., 1997. Orienting attention without awareness. *J. Exp. Psychol.: Hum. Percept. Perform.* 23:168–180.

MCGLINCHEY-BERROTH, R., W. P. MILBERG, M. VERFAELLIE, M. ALEXANDER, and P. T. KILDUFF, 1993. Semantic processing in the neglected visual field: Evidence from a lexical decision task. *Cogn. Neuropsychol.* 10:79–108.

MCGLINCHEY-BERROTH, R., W. P. MILBERG, M. VERFAELLIE, L. GRANDE, M. D'ESPOSITO, and M. ALEXANDER, 1996. Semantic processing and orthographic specificity in hemispatial neglect. *J. Cogn. Neurosci.* 8:291–304.

MERIKLE, P. M., 1982. Unconscious perception revisited. *Percept. Psychophys.* 31:298–301.

MERIKLE, P. M., 1984. Toward a definition of awareness. *Bull. Psychon. Soc.* 22:449–450.

MERIKLE, P. M., 1992. Perception without awareness: Critical issues. *Am. Psychol.* 47:792–795.

MERIKLE, P. M., and S. JOORDENS, 1997. Parallels between perception without attention and perception without awareness. *Conscious. Cognit.* 6:219–236.

MERIKLE, P. M., S. JOORDENS, and J. A. STOLZ, 1995. Measuring the relative magnitude of unconscious influences. *Conscious. Cognit.* 4:422–439.

MERIKLE, P. M., and E. M. REINGOLD, 1998. On demonstrating unconscious perception. *J. Exp. Psychol.: Gen.*

MEYER, D. E., and R. W. SCHVANEVELDT, 1976. Meaning, memory structure, and mental processes. *Science* 192:27–33.

MILNER, A. D., and M. A. GOODALE, 1995. *The Visual Brain in Action.* New York: Oxford University Press.

MURPHY, S. T., and R. B. ZAJONC, 1993. Affect, cognition, and awareness: Affective priming with optimal and sub-

optimal stimulus exposures. *J. Pers. Soc. Psychol.* 64:723–739.

PEIRCE, C. S., and J. JASTROW, 1884. On small differences in sensation. *Memoirs Natl. Acad. Sci.* 3:73–83.

REINGOLD, E. M., and P. M. MERIKLE, 1990. On the interrelatedness of theory and measurement in the study of unconscious processes. *Mind Lang.* 5:9–28.

RORTY, R., 1979. *Philosophy and the Mirror of Nature.* Princeton: Princeton University Press.

SCHACTER, D. L., M. P. MCANDREWS, and M. MOSCOVITCH, 1988. Access to consciousness: Dissociations between implicit and explicit knowledge in neurological syndromes. In *Thought without Language,* L. Weiskrantz, ed. New York: Oxford University Press, pp. 242–278.

SEARLE, J. R., 1992. *The Rediscovery of the Mind.* Cambridge, Mass.: MIT Press.

SERGENT, J., and M. PONCET, 1990. From covert to overt recognition of faces in a prosopagnosic patient. *Brain* 113:989–1004.

SHEVRIN, H., and S. DICKMAN, 1980. The psychological unconscious: A necessary assumption for all psychological theory? *Amer. Psychol.* 35:421–434.

SIDIS, B., 1898. *The Psychology of Suggestion.* New York: D. Appleton and Company.

SNODGRASS, M., H. SHEVRIN, and M. KOPKA, 1993. The mediation of intentional judgments by unconscious perceptions: The influence of task strategy, task preference, word meaning, and motivation. *Conscious. Cognit.* 2:169–193.

STROH, M. A., M. SHAW, and M. F. WASHBURN, 1908. A study of guessing. *Amer. J. Psychol.* 19:243–245.

STROOP, J. R., 1935. Studies of interference in serial verbal reactions. *J. Exp. Psychol.* 18:643–662.

TRANEL, D., and A. R. DAMASIO, 1988. Non–conscious face recognition in patients with face agnosia. *Behav. Brain Res.* 30:235–249.

VOLPE, B. T., J. E. LEDOUX, and M. S. GAZZANIGA, 1979. Information processing in the "extinguished" visual field. *Nature* 282:722–724.

WHALEN, P. J., S. L. RAUCH, N. L. ETCOFF, S. C. MCINERNEY, M. B. LEE, and M. A. JENIKE, 1998. Masked presentations of emotional facial expressions modulate amygdala activity without explicit knowledge. *J. Neurosci.* 18:411–418.

WEISKRANTZ, L., 1986. *Blindsight: A Case Study and Implications.* New York: Oxford University Press.

WILLIAMS, A. C., JR., 1938. Perception of subliminal visual stimuli. *J. Psychol.* 6:187–199.

YOUNG, A. W., 1994. Covert recognition. In *The Neuropsychology of High-Level Vision,* M. J. Farah and G. Ratcliff, eds. Hillsdale, N.J.: Erlbaum, pp. 331–358.

YOUNG, A. W., and E. H. F. DE HAAN, 1988. Boundaries of covert recognition. *Cogn. Neuropsychol.* 5:317–336.

YOUNG, A. W., D. HELLAWELL, and E. H. F. DE HAAN, 1988. Cross-domain semantic priming in normal subjects and a prosopagnosic patient. *Quart. J. Exp. Psychol.* 40A:561–580.

91 The Neural Correlates of Consciousness: An Analysis of Cognitive Skill Learning

MARCUS E. RAICHLE

ABSTRACT This chapter presents a functional brain imaging strategy using positron emission tomography (PET) and functional magnetic resonance imaging (fMRI) to isolate neural correlates of consciousness in humans. This strategy is based on skill learning. In the example presented (rapidly generating verbs for visually presented nouns), a cognitive skill is examined before and after practice. As shown, there are marked qualitative differences in the neural circuitry supporting performance of this task before and after practice. These include both increases and decreases from a baseline level of activity in the brain. An important concept considered in this chapter is that of a baseline level of brain activity in conscious humans.

Two components of our conscious behavior are *content* and *arousal* (Plum and Posner, 1980). One of the great challenges of modern neurobiology is to identify the brain systems responsible for these components. As Damasio (1995) has stated, "[K]nowing *how* [the brain engenders consciousness], to a considerable extent, requires that we first know *where.*"

Much work points to systems ascending from the reticular core of the brainstem via the thalamus to the cortex as responsible for arousal or alert wakefulness (Steriade, 1996a,b). We are much less certain, once alert wakefulness has been achieved, which cortical systems are responsible for the content of our consciousness. One of the difficulties in identifying these cortical systems is distinguishing them from those concerned with the many nonconscious cognitive, attentional, and emotional processes that occur in support of our conscious experiences. Several approaches have been used.

One approach is to examine patients with lesions that deprive them of some aspect of their normal conscious experience. Typical of such an approach is the study of patients with blindsight (Weiskrantz, 1986, 1997). Such patients, fully awake and otherwise alert, have lost the conscious perception of visual information presented to their blind hemifield. However, information entering the blind hemifield still influences behavior. The inference to be drawn is that the area of the brain damaged by the lesion contributes to the content of conscious experience.

A second approach is to examine normal activities in which consciousness is transiently suspended. Francis Crick and Christof Koch (1998) have provided a recent review of this approach. A typical experiment might involve an analysis of the suppression of conscious visual experience during eye movements, or so-called saccadic suppression (Bridgeman, Hijiden, and Velichovsky, 1994). During saccadic suppression, visual perception is suspended, yet information presented during this period of time influences behavior. By identifying changes in the neural circuitry that occur when a conscious visual perception is momentarily suspended one would hope to identify regions that contribute to conscious experience. Functional brain imaging with positron emission tomography (PET) has been used to identify changes during saccadic suppression in humans (Paus et al., 1995).

According to William James, "Habit diminishes the conscious attention with which our acts are performed" (James, 1890). This comment captures the essence of a third approach. In some ways analogous to the second, this approach involves identifying the brain systems supporting a task when it is novel and effortful then comparing these systems to those engaged when the task is routine and reflexive. The performance demands of such a task must necessarily be sufficient to require conscious attention (or "willed action"; see Frith et al., 1991) for its initial performance. The brain systems unique to the novel state, if identified by comparison with the practiced state, then become candidate systems necessary for conscious experience.

Because tasks involving motor as well as cognitive skills can be transformed from reflective, effortful tasks to reflexive, seemingly effortless tasks within a short period of time (Petersen et al., 1998), it is feasible to employ this third approach with modern functional imaging techniques. We already know from such functional imaging studies in normal humans that this transformation is accompanied by dramatic changes in the underlying brain circuitry concerned with the task (Raichle et al., 1994a). These transformations provide important insights into

MARCUS E. RAICHLE Departments of Radiology and Neurology, Washington University School of Medicine, St. Louis, Mo.

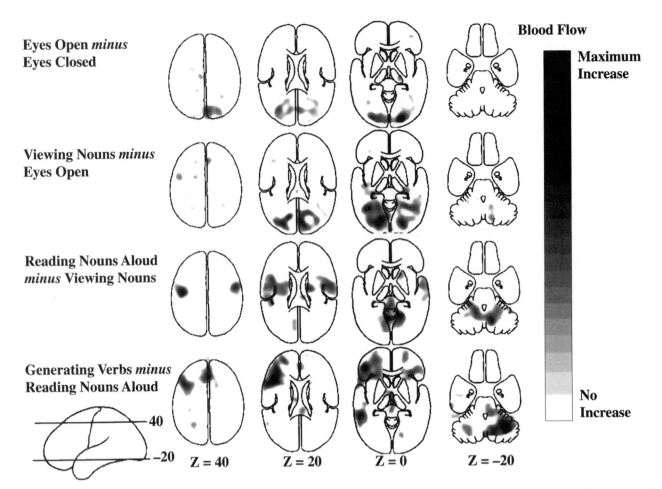

Eyes Open *minus* **Eyes Closed**

Viewing Nouns *minus* **Eyes Open**

Reading Nouns Aloud *minus* **Viewing Nouns**

Generating Verbs *minus* **Reading Nouns Aloud**

Z = 40   Z = 20   Z = 0   Z = –20

Blood Flow

Maximum Increase

No Increase

FIGURE 91.1 Four different hierarchically organized conditions are represented in these mean blood flow difference images obtained with PET. All of the changes shown in these images represent *increases* over the control state for each task. A group of normal subjects performed these tasks involving common English nouns (Petersen et al., 1988, 1989; Raichle et al., 1994b). These horizontal images are oriented with the front of the brain on top and the left side to the reader's left. Z = 40 indicates millimeters above and below a horizontal plane (Z = 0) through the brain (Fox, Perlmutter, and Raichle, 1985).

those brain systems concerned with conscious elements of naïve task performance.

It is the purpose of this chapter to explore the use of this approach in the context of a simple word reading paradigm involving cognitive skill learning in normal human subjects. As will become apparent, the results present a complex picture of widely distributed change (both increases and decreases) in the activity of brain systems uniquely associated with naïve task performance. The richness of the information provided should stimulate, as well as constrain, theories about brain systems serving consciousness.

The paradigm

Studies of word reading have played a central role in functional brain imaging studies of language over the past decade (for recent reviews see Fiez and Petersen, 1998; Posner and Pavese, 1998). This work has benefited from the large amount of information already known about this skill (for review see Rayner and Pollatsek, 1989). These extant behavioral data on word reading have provided the basis for the design of many imaging experiments with both positron emission tomography (PET) and functional magnetic resonance imaging (fMRI).

Beginning in the 1980s, the author and his colleagues Steven E. Petersen, Michael I. Posner, Peter T. Fox, Julie Fiez, and Mark Mintun began their own imaging and behavioral experiments of word reading (Petersen et al., 1988, 1989, 1990; Raichle et al., 1994a; Shulman et al., 1997b). It is from these published experiments that the data presented here have in part been culled.

A key feature of the experiments is their hierarchical design. In concert with most other functional imaging studies, the strategy here compares images of blood flow obtained with PET in a control state to those obtained when the brain is engaged in a task of interest (for a more detailed review of the strategy and its physiological basis

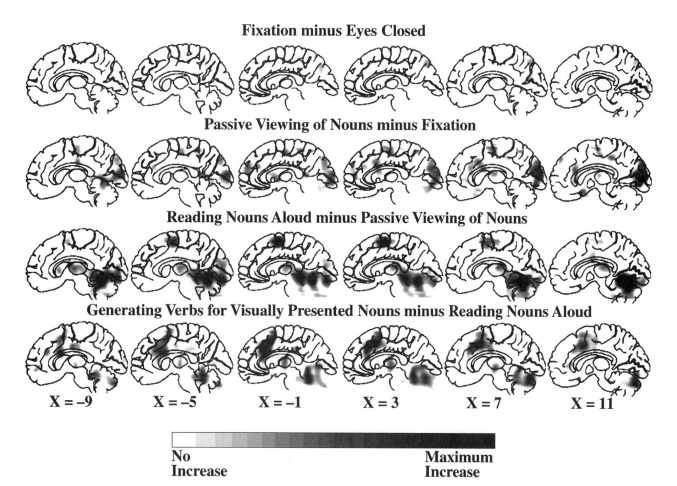

Fixation minus Eyes Closed

Passive Viewing of Nouns minus Fixation

Reading Nouns Aloud minus Passive Viewing of Nouns

Generating Verbs for Visually Presented Nouns minus Reading Nouns Aloud

X = –9   X = –5   X = –1   X = 3   X = 7   X = 11

**No
Increase**   **Maximum
Increase**

FIGURE 91.2   Data identical to that shown in figure 91.1 except that it is presented in the saggital plane. These images be-

gin 9 millimeters to the left of the midline $(X = -9)$ and end 11 millimeters to the right of the midline $(X = 11)$.

see Raichle, 1998). The five behavioral states include: (1) awake, alert, with eyes closed, performing no task; (2) maintaining visual fixation on a television monitor containing only a fixation point; (3) maintaining visual fixation on a television monitor while common English nouns are presented just below the point of fixation; (4) reading aloud the nouns as they are presented; and (5) speaking aloud an appropriate use or verb for each noun as it is presented. In the initial experiments (Petersen et al., 1988, 1989) the words were presented 60 times per minute and were on the monitor for 500 ms. In the later experiments (Raichle et al., 1994b) the words were presented 40 times per minute, again for 500 ms each. English was the native language of the subjects and they were all skilled readers. The behavioral state comparisons to be discussed in this chapter include 2 versus 1, 3 versus 2, 4 versus 3, 5 versus 4, and $5_{practiced}$ versus 5_{naive}.

Observations

Figure 91.1 illustrates, in horizontal sections, the areas of the brain that *increase* their activity (i.e., blood flow) in

association with incremental increases in the complexity of a simple word reading task. Figure 91.2 is a saggital representation of the information in figure 91.1 and more clearly depicts the changes occurring along the midline in parietal and frontal cortices.

As shown in the first row of figure 91.1, opening the eyes and maintaining fixation on a small crosshair on an otherwise blank television monitor results in activation of visual cortex as compared to resting quietly with eyes closed. The images in the second row of figures 91.1 and 91.2 represent those additional areas of the brain that become active when common English nouns appear on the screen. The subjects' instruction was simply to maintain fixation. Multiple areas within visual cortices become active when words are presented even though no specific processing of these words has been requested. Much effort has been devoted to an analysis of changes such as these (Fiez and Petersen, 1998; Howard et al., 1992; Petersen et al., 1990; Price, Wise, and Frackowiak, 1996; Price et al., 1994), but the results have so far been inconclusive.

The images in the third row of figures 91.1 and 91.2 reflect those areas of the brain associated with the motor

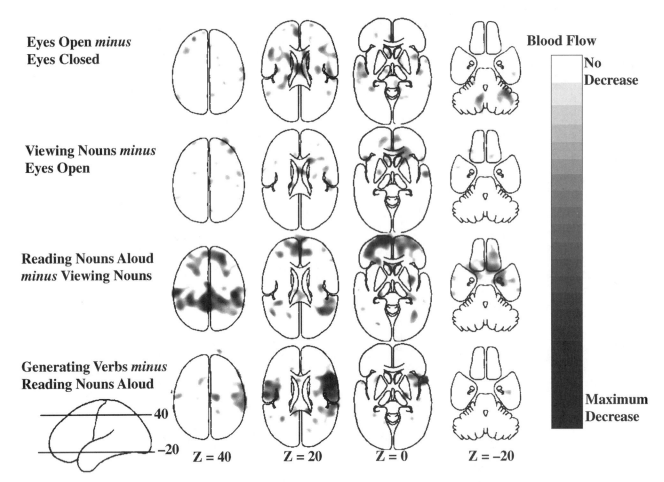

Eyes Open *minus* **Eyes Closed**

Viewing Nouns *minus* **Eyes Open**

Reading Nouns Aloud *minus* **Viewing Nouns**

Generating Verbs *minus* **Reading Nouns Aloud**

40

−20

Z = 40   Z = 20   Z = 0   Z = −20

Blood Flow

No Decrease

Maximum Decrease

FIGURE 91.3 Hierarchically organized subtractions involving the same task conditions as shown in figure 91.1, with the difference that these images represent areas of *decreased* activity in the task condition as compared with the control condition.

aspects of reading words aloud. Not surprisingly, these include the primary motor cortices bilaterally, the supplementary motor cortex (best seen along and anterior midline in figure 91.2) and the paramedian cerebellum. There was also prominent activity over sylvian-insular cortices bilaterally (figure 91.1, row 3, Z = 20).

Finally, the images in the fourth row of figures 91.1 and 91.2 reflect those additional areas of the brain active during verb generation. These include the anterior cingulate cortex (best seen in figure 91.2), the left prefrontal cortex, the left temporal cortex, and the right hemisphere of the cerebellum. The latter finding was a particular surprise because the subtraction producing this image had eliminated all of the motor aspects of speech production.

Reviewing all of the changes in figures 91.1 and 91.2, it is possible to appreciate those associated with the perfected skill of word reading (i.e., the first three rows) and those changes associated with the much more difficult and novel task of verb generation. It should be noted that all subjects performing verb generation initially found it difficult. This was reflected in a much slower voice onset

latency and a failure to supply verbs for all nouns in order to keep pace with the task (Raichle et al., 1994a).

The data presented in figures 91.1 and 91.2 illustrate nicely a hierarchical dissection of word reading in terms of the way regions of the brain increase their activity in support of the component processes involved. In keeping with the thesis of this chapter, it is tempting to assume that areas of the brain added in support of the verb generation task (i.e., row four, figures 91.1 and 91.2) become candidates for those concerned with task-associated consciousness. But before making such an assumption, it is important to appreciate a bit more fully additional changes taking place in brain organization–changes that are not revealed in these two figures. To set the stage for a presentation of these changes, we first examine one of the major criticisms of the subtractive logic leading to the images in figures 91.1 and 91.2.

The strategy employed in the experiments depicted in figures 91.1 and 91.2 was introduced in 1868 by the Dutch physiologist Franciscus C. Donders (cf. Donders, 1969). Donders proposed a general method to measure thought processes based on a simple logic. He

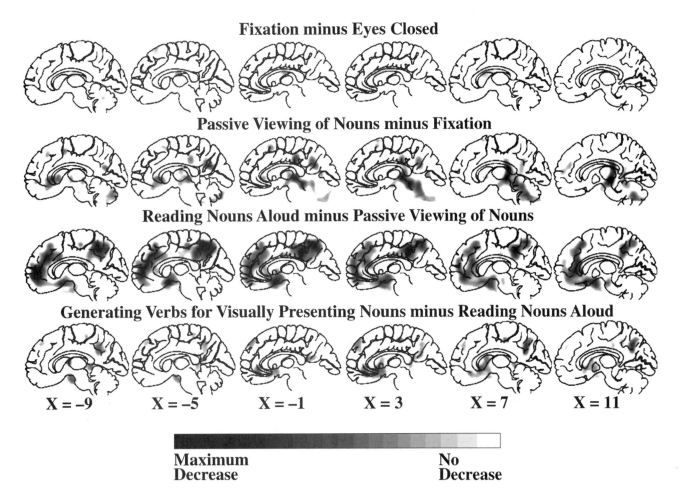

Fixation minus Eyes Closed

Passive Viewing of Nouns minus Fixation

Reading Nouns Aloud minus Passive Viewing of Nouns

Generating Verbs for Visually Presenting Nouns minus Reading Nouns Aloud

X = –9   X = –5   X = –1   X = 3   X = 7   X = 11

Maximum
Decrease

No
Decrease

FIGURE 91.4   Data identical to that shown in figure 91.3 except that it is presented in the saggital plane. The slices are positioned as noted in figure 91.2.

subtracted the time needed to respond to a light (say, by pressing a key) from the time needed to respond to a particular color of light. He found that identifying the color of the light required about 50 ms. In this way, Donders isolated and measured a mental process for the first time by subtracting a control state (i.e., responding to a light regardless of its color) from a task state (i.e., discriminating the color of the light). It is the same logic that is now applied in the experiments presented in figures 91.1 and 91.2.

One criticism of this approach has been that the time necessary to press a key after a decision to do so has been made is affected by the nature of the decision process itself. By implication, the nature of the processes underlying key press, in this example, may have been altered. Although this issue (known in cognitive science jargon as the *assumption of pure insertion*) has been the subject of continuing discussion in cognitive science, it finds a resolution in functional brain imaging, where changes in any process are directly signaled by changes in observable brain states.

Careful analysis of the changes in the functional images reveals whether processes (e.g., specific cognitive operations) can be added or removed without affecting ongoing processes (e.g., motor processes). This is accomplished by examining the data not only for areas activated during the course of a particular cognitive paradigm but also those that become deactivated. An analysis of regional deactivations is presented in figures 91.3 and 91.4. Figure 91.4 is a saggital representation of the information in figure 91.3 and more clearly presents changes occurring along the midline of the brain in parietal and orbital frontal cortices. By examining the images in figures 91.1–91.4 *together*, we gain a much more complete picture of the dramatic changes taking place in the word reading paradigm under analysis here.

Finally, in order to exploit fully the paradigm depicted in figures 91.1–91.4 for the purpose of identifying candidate regions of the brain concerned with task-related consciousness, it is important to assess the effect of practice on the regions uniquely recruited in the verb generation task (row 4, figure 91.1). As we have previously

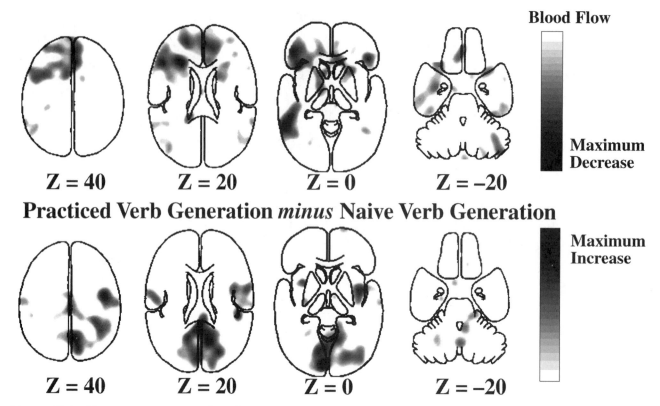

FIGURE 91.5 Changes in activity resulting from practice on the verb generation task include decreases (top row) and increases (bottom row) in brain activity.

demonstrated (Raichle et al., 1994a), a brief period of practice on the verb generation task results in a significant reduction in voice onset latency (i.e., subjects are simply able to respond more quickly when seeing the same noun on multiple occasions). In addition, responses become stereotyped, with the same verb being chosen each time a particular noun is presented. These changes in performance are associated with dramatic changes in the brain regions supporting task performance. The brain changes associated with practice are illustrated in figures 91.5 and 91.6. In these two figures it can be seen that anterior cingulate cortex (and associated dorsal medial frontal cortices), left prefrontal cortex (including the left and right frontal operculum), left temporal cortex, and right cerebellum (not as well shown; see Raichle et al., 1994a, for more details)—all active during naïve verb generation—return to baseline.

Activity in the ventral medial frontal cortex, reduced in the naïve condition (see figure 91.3, rows 3 and 4), is actually reduced even further after practice. Regional activity within sylvian-insular cortices, active during word reading (figure 91.1, row 3, $Z = 20$) yet inactivated during naïve verb generation (figure 91.3, row 4, $Z = 20$), are now reactivated, especially on the right side. Finally, midline activity within the region of the precuneus

and posterior cingulate cortex, while reduced from baseline during naïve word reading and verb generation (figure 91.4), increases in association with increased activity in visual cortices as the result of practice on the verb generation task (figure 91.6, row 2).

Discussion

The purpose of this exercise was to identify brain activity changes associated with task-related conscious behavior. The strategy involved comparing PET images of blood flow change obtained in a novel reading task (i.e., verb generation) with those obtained during a well-practiced task with identical perceptual and motor requirements (i.e., word reading). Additionally, comparisons were made between the naïve and practiced performance of the verb generation task itself. On these comparisons, it was hypothesized that regions of the brain concerned with conscious task performance could be isolated and identified. Consistent with this hypothesis, regional changes in brain activity associated with conscious, effortful performance of the verb generation task were identified. These included widely distributed regions of both increases and decreases in brain activity.

Practiced Verb Generation minus Naive Verb Generation

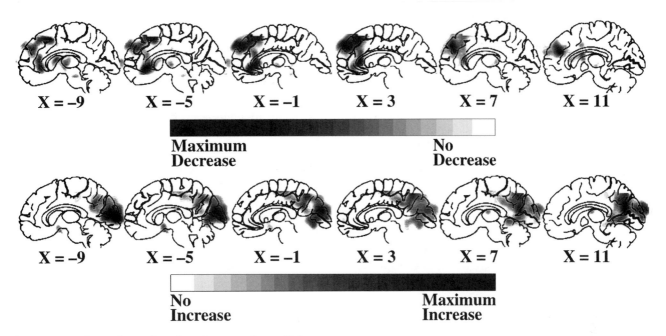

FIGURE 91.6   Data identical to that shown in figure 91.5 except that it is presented in the saggital plane. The slices are position as noted in figure 91.2.

REGIONS OF INCREASED ACTIVITY   When naïve performance of the verb generation task was compared to word reading, regions in anterior cingulate cortex, left prefrontal cortex, left temporal cortex, and the right cerebellar hemisphere were found to exhibit increased activity. Consistent with our hypothesis that these regions are uniquely associated with the conscious performance of this task, their activity ceased with practice, which both produced significant improvement in performance and elicited stereotyped responses (Raichle et al., 1994a). Changes in the opposite direction in sylvian-insular cortices bilaterally offered further support for the unique role of these regions in conscious task performance (Raichle et al., 1994a). Thus, regions active during naïve task performance disappeared with practice whereas regions within sylvian-insular cortices bilaterally, inactive during naïve task performance, become active with practice. The reciprocal nature of these changes makes it unlikely that practice simply results in a more efficient use of regions always devoted to task performance.

Thus, reading aloud familiar words utilizes a pathway from word perception regions to speech production regions via regions in sylvian-insular cortices bilaterally. Prior to practice, a completely different pathway connects word perception regions to speech production regions. How are we to think about these two pathways and the circumstances under which they are utilized? What is their relationship, if any, to the several instantia-

tions of dual route ideas in speech production? What, if anything, does this have to say about conscious versus nonconscious behaviors?

To begin, the two routes revealed by our studies of the verb generation task (Petersen et al., 1988, 1989; Raichle et al., 1994a) would qualify for the two routes envisioned in Lichtheim's original theoretical formulation (Lichtheim, 1885; McCarthy and Warrington, 1984). Although probably first suggested by John Hughlings Jackson (Jackson, 1874), the idea of two pathways was advanced most clearly by Lichtheim, a Swiss neurologist. In an attempt to provide a conceptual framework for the various forms of aphasia reported by Broca, Wernicke, and others, he devised a scheme centered around three brain systems: an auditory word-form area concerned with the perceptual aspects of language; a center for the motor representations of words, or a motor center of speech; and a very distributed system "for the elaboration of concepts." As he envisioned it, information coming from the auditory word-form system could advance to the motor center for speech either directly or via the concept system. The latter route via the concept system he characterized as more "conscious" and less fluent than the former (see Lichtheim, 1885, p. 474). One pathway utilized a direct route from perception to production whereas the other utilized a more indirect route involving a distributed system of widely separated areas of the cerebral cortex.

In a very telling discussion Lichtheim said:

[I]t would appear as if, in naming objects, the auditory representations once found had to react in consciousness. This variety of language is a much more "conscious" one than fluent speaking, in which *we are aware of the sense of what we are saying, rather than of every word we say* [italics added]. Under certain circumstances conversational language is carried on in a similar way to naming, as, for instance, when we use an idiom not quite familiar to us. Here we must seek the words by the complicated process just mentioned; the direct communication between concept and motor center without cooperation of sound-representation does not exist; the subconscious act of speaking is not yet possible. A greater psychical exertion is obviously required, and consequently more fatigue is entailed. (Lichtheim, 1885, p. 474.)

Lichtheim also envisioned, presciently, that acquisition of language occurred by imitation, "as observed in the child, and upon the reflex arc which this process presupposes." And he went on to say, "When intelligence of the imitated sounds is superimposed, a connection is established between the auditory center (for word-representations) and the part (of the brain) where concepts are elaborated."

Shallice and Norman formulate such issues more generally in terms of what they call "contention scheduling" and a "supervisory attention system" (Shallice, 1988). *Contention scheduling* is the process by which selection is made of routine actions or thought processes. It is considered to be a decentralized process involving a very large but finite set of discrete programs, hierarchically organized. Routine activities of our daily lives, such as driving a car back and forth to work, are managed in a nonconscious manner through contention scheduling (Lichtheim, I am sure, would have used spontaneous speech as an example). A particular set of programs or schema has a level of activation dependent upon the triggering inputs it receives. While summarized nicely in Norman and Shallice's model, this general idea has much support in the psychological literature (see the summary discussion, p. 333, in Shallice, 1988). We would suggest that, in the case of the verb generation paradigm (Raichle et al., 1994a), regions within sylvian-insular cortices represent some of the regions involved in the process of contention scheduling as formulated by Norman and Shallice.

This formulation of the functional organization of our mental lives is obviously incomplete. A moment's reflection suggests that, useful as they may be under most circumstances, routine actions and thought processes are sometimes inappropriate, occasionally embarrassing, and potentially dangerous (Reason and Mycielska, 1982). Therefore, there has to be a means by which routine, reflexive behaviors and thoughts can be inhibited

and replaced, either transiently or permanently, by more appropriate behaviors and thoughts (Reason and Mycielska, 1982). Norman and Shallice (Shallice, 1988) postulate the existence of a second system—the supervisory attention system—to accomplish this.

The *supervisory attention system* provides a mechanism whereby elements or schema within the lower-level contention scheduling system for routine, reflexive behaviors and thoughts can be temporarily modified by activating or inhibiting particular elements within it. This facilitates coping with novel situations in which the routine selections are unsatisfactory. As Shallice states, "The primary function of the Supervisory System is that of producing a response to novelty that is planned rather than one that is routine or impulsive" (Shallice, 1988, p. 345). In a general sense, this fits nicely with Lichtheim's concept of a center for the elaboration of concepts.

While both Lichtheim and Norman and Shallice envisioned a *superimposition* of higher centers for the conscious guidance of behavior over more routine, reflexive responses, our data would suggest a *substitution* of regions. In our example, regions guiding nonautomatic or conscious speech acts are preferentially selected, by a process yet to be defined, over those areas concerned with automatic or nonconscious speech acts when a well-learned, reflexive response like word reading is not appropriate. As a corollary, one must also envision circumstances in which the reverse is true: Automatic responses are preferred and, hence, selected. As Sutherland has pointed out, "[W]hen confronted by a predator, it is surely better to climb a non-optimal tree than to be eaten while weighing the respective merits of different trees" (Sutherland, 1996). The manner in which the brain is biased *either* way (i.e., toward or away from automatic behaviors) remains a most important and challenging question.

Lichtheim did not specify the neural correlates of his higher centers, but he was quite clear that he did not believe them to be housed in a single area. "Though in the diagram point B [see diagram 1, p. 436, in Lichtheim (1885)] is represented as a sort of center for the elaboration of concepts, this has been done for simplicities [sic] sake; with most writers, I do not consider the function to be localized in one spot of the brain, but rather to result from the combined action of the whole sensorial sphere. Hence, the point B should be distributed over many spots" (Lichtheim, 1885, p. 477).

Shallice and Norman were much more specific in drawing attention to the role of the frontal lobe in their supervisory attention system (Shallice, 1988). They review extensive evidence, primarily from neuropsychology, showing that patients with frontal lobe injury often act in an impulsive and reflexive manner as if they lacked a supervisory attention system.

Reviewing the evidence that has now been gained from functional imaging studies in normal subjects, one would have to conclude that both Lichtheim and Norman and Shallice were correct in anticipating brain regions uniquely involved in conscious, reflective behavior as distinct from regions concerned with reflexive, habitual performance. It is clear from the data presented in this chapter that multiple, widely distributed areas of the normal human brain—including the cerebellum—are involved in the performance of a novel speech production act, just as Lichtheim (1885) would have predicted. Likewise, it is also clear that the frontal lobe plays a role, although not an exclusive one, as Norman and Shallice implied.

The experiments used for illustrative purposes in this chapter and the work of Lichtheim (1885) focus specifically on language. The work of Norman and Shallice (Shallice, 1988) and of others (e.g., Passingham, 1993; Shiffrin and Schneider, 1977) suggests that the issues involved transcend any single domain of human performance.

Many analyses might conclude at this point with comments about the potential role of brain regions that *increase* their activity during reflective or novel task performance. However, our data suggest there is more to the story. To wit: While some regions of the brain increase their activity during novel task performance, others, just as dramatically, *decrease* their activity.

REGIONS OF DECREASED ACTIVITY   When subjects become actively involved in word reading, whether reading aloud or generating verbs, multiple regions across both cerebral hemispheres show a significant decrease in activity (figures 91.3–91.6). These include regions along the midline in orbitofrontal cortex, posterior cingulate cortex, and precuneus, which have been noted to decrease in a wide variety of tasks (for details of a large meta-analysis of such changes, see Shulman et al., 1997b). Characteristic of the experiments in which these particular decreases are regularly seen are ones in which subjects must actively process a visual stimulus. The control state is one in which the same stimulus is passively viewed. Additionally, decreases should also be noted in sylvian-insular cortices bilaterally. These appear only in naïve verb generation and not in word reading, where increases are actually observed (figure 91.1, row 3, $Z = 20$).

What are we to make of these reductions? Physiologists have long recognized that individual neurons in the cerebral cortex can both increase or decrease their activities from a resting, baseline firing pattern depending on task conditions. Decreases, however, seem to have received somewhat less attention. Nevertheless, examples

of decreases abound in the neurophysiological literature (e.g., Georgopoulos et al., 1982). A parsimonious view of these decreases in neuronal activity is that they reflect the activity of inhibitory interneurons acting within local neuronal circuits of the cerebral cortex. Because inhibition is energy-requiring (Ackerman et al., 1984; Batini et al., 1984; Biral et al., 1984), it should be impossible to distinguish inhibitory from excitatory cellular activity on the basis of changes in either blood flow or metabolism. Thus, on this view, a local increase in inhibitory activity is just as likely to increase blood flow and the fMRI BOLD signal as a local increase in excitatory activity. How, then, might decreases in blood flow as seen with PET (figures 91.3–91.6) or the fMRI BOLD signal arise?

To understand the significance of the decreases in blood flow in a functional imaging experiment, it is important to distinguish two separate conditions in which they might arise. The usual circumstance accounting for reductions in activity arises when two images are compared, one containing a regional increase in blood flow caused by some type of task-induced activity while the other does not.

Let us consider, for example, the increase in activity over the sylvian-insular cortices that occurs when individuals read a word aloud as compared to viewing the same word passively. This is seen bilaterally in figure 91.1, row 3, at $Z = 20$. Turning to figure 91.2, row 4, note that we now observe a reduction in activity in almost the same region as subjects perform, naïvely, verb generation as compared to reading aloud. What has occurred is that images in which the region is activated (i.e., word reading) are subtracted from images in which the region is not activated (i.e., verb generation). These results suggest that this region is used in automatic speech production such as word reading, not for a novel reading task like verb. However, as verb generation becomes more automatic, this region is reactivated (figure 91.4, row 2, $Z = 20$ and $Z = 0$).

The second circumstance in which decreases in blood flow and the fMRI BOLD signal are observed is not due to data manipulations of the type just described. Rather, blood flow and the fMRI BOLD signal actually decrease regionally from a *baseline state* for that region. The immediate question that arises is, how is such a baseline state defined. How, for instance, is it to be distinguished from just another activation state? The definition arises from a consideration of the metabolic and circulatory events surrounding the activation of a typical cortical region (for a recent review see Raichle, 1998) and how these differ from the metabolism and circulation of the baseline state of the awake human brain.

Measurements in the normal, adult, awake human reveal a brain that consumes approximately 0.27

micromoles of glucose and 1.54 micromoles of oxygen per gram of tissue per minute (Siesjo, 1978). This is supplied by a blood flow of approximately 0.55 milliliters of blood per gram of tissue per minute (Siesjo, 1978). While these values vary from one region of the brain to another (e.g., the average values in white matter are typically one-fourth that of gray matter), the *relationship* among them remains remarkably constant. As a consequence, the fraction of available oxygen removed by the cerebral cortex of the resting brain from circulating blood (i.e., the oxygen extraction fraction or OEF) is quite uniform.

What, then is so distinctive about areas of increased activity? The answer lies in the deviations from these baseline relationships. One might assume that an increase in local cellular activity in the cerebral cortex would be accompanied by a proportionate increase in blood flow and oxygen consumption. This would be reflected in an unchanged OEF. However, this is not observed (Fox and Raichle, 1986; Fox et al., 1988). Blood flow actually increases substantially in excess of any increase in oxygen consumption, leading to a significant decrease in the OEF. The direct correlate of this is a local increase in the ratio of oxyhemoglobin to deoxyhemoglobin as oxygen supply exceeds demand. It is the local increase in the oxyhemoglobin:deoxyhemoglobin ratio that forms the basis for the fMRI signal. This fMRI signal usually is referred to as the BOLD (blood oxygen level dependent contrast) (Ogawa et al., 1990; Ogawa et al., 1992; Kwong et al., 1992).

Positive BOLD contrast is now routinely seen by investigators worldwide doing functional brain imaging studies with fMRI. There is a remarkable correspondence between the location of BOLD contrast and changes in blood flow measured with PET when the same tasks are studied (for a recent review see Raichle, 1998). This correspondence has become routine confirmation of the fact that blood flow changes in excess of any change in oxygen consumption during changes in the functional activity of the cerebral cortex.

We are now in a position to ask a rather obvious question. What is the baseline-state metabolic and circulatory status of brain regions that exhibit a reduction in blood flow and a negative BOLD contrast when subjects actively engage in task performance? The regions of particular interest are those seen along the midline in figures 91.3–91.6 and previously noted to behave similarly across a wide variety of visual attention tasks (Shulman et al., 1997b). For these medial regions of orbital frontal and posterior cingulate/parietal cortex, the OEF does not differ significantly from the overall brain average in the baseline state (data from 20 normal adult controls; unpublished observations of M. E. Raichle, A.-M. Mac-

Leod, W. Drevets, and W. J. Powers) whereas the blood flow, oxygen consumption, and glucose utilization significantly exceed the brain average. Remarkably, the region of the posterior cingulate and adjacent precuneus is actually the metabolically most active region of the cerebral cortex in the resting brain (data from 20 normal adult controls; unpublished observations of M. E. Raichle, A.-M. MacLeod, W. Drevets, and W. J. Powers).

The above analysis leads to the inescapable conclusion that anterior as well as posterior regions of the cerebral hemispheres, particularly prominent but not exclusively along the midline, are intensely active during the baseline state of the awake brain (e.g., eyes closed or passive viewing of a television monitor and its contents). With focused attention on a variety of tasks (e.g., see Shulman et al., 1997b, and figures 91.3–91.6) these regions exhibit a conspicuous reduction in activity. What makes the active state of these regions so distinctive is that it is characterized by metabolic and circulatory relationships that typify baseline, not functionally activated cerebral cortex. It is as if these areas of the brain are uniquely active as a *default baseline state of the conscious resting brain*.

Several additional general comments about these decreases from a baseline state should be made. First, they are not, as some have informally suggested, merely the hemodynamic consequence of increases elsewhere (i.e., an intracerebral "steal" phenomenon). Such a hypothesis is very unlikely to be correct because of the tremendous hemodynamic reserve of the brain (Heistad and Kontos, 1983) and also because there is no one-to-one spatial or temporal correlation between increases and decreases (see figures 91.1–91.6).

Second, they are not confined to regions of the brain whose baseline activity significantly exceeds that of the overall brain average. For example, it has been shown that, in anticipation of stimulation, areas of somatosensory cortex outside the representation of the skin area that is the target of the expected stimulation exhibit marked reductions in activity as measured with PET (Drevets et al., 1995). These observations are thought to reflect a model of spatial attention in which potential signal enhancement relies on a generalized suppression or filtering of background activity (Whang, Burton, and Shulman, 1991).

Third, the relatively large spatial extent of these regional decreases suggests the inactivation of specific systems within the cerebral cortex. The mechanism(s) by which this is achieved remains to be determined. What is most important for our present purpose is identifying the functions with which these regions are associated. Whatever the functions, it seems reasonable to suggest that they must be suspended for proper task execution.

With regard to the posterior cingulate and adjacent precuneus, animal studies suggest that it is involved in orientation within and interpretation of the environment (for a review see Vogt, Finch, and Olson, 1992). The response of posterior cingulate neurons to visual stimuli, for example, is crucially dependent upon the physical characteristics of the stimulus. Small spots of light to which a monkey may be attending and responding do not elicit neuronal responses in this area. In contrast, large, brightly textured stimuli elicit responses even if they are totally irrelevant to tasks the animal is performing. Lesions of the posterior cingulate also disrupt spatial working memory. From the studies reviewed by Vogt and his colleagues (1992), it is not possible to separate, cleanly, spatial working memory functions from functions concerned with evaluation and interpretation of the environment.

Additional light is shed on the function of the posterior cingulate cortex and adjacent precuneus by the work of Carol Colby (Colby et al., 1988) and John Allman (Baker et al., 1981). Both of these studies call attention to the fact that elements of the dorsal stream of extrastriate visual cortex (area M in the owl monkey and area PO in the macaque) are part of a network of areas concerned with the representation of the visual periphery. These areas are primarily located along the dorsal midline and can be distinguished in various ways, experimentally, from those areas of the visual system of the monkey that represent the fovea (i.e., the central 10 degrees of the visual field). From these data and those reviewed by Vogt and colleagues (1992) emerges a specific hypothesis: Activity within the posterior cingulate cortex and adjacent precuneus in the baseline state in humans is associated with the representation (monitoring) of the world around us (i.e., our environment or our visual periphery). The hypothesis further predicts that efficient processing of items in the center of our visual field requires generalized suppression or filtering of this background activity (Whang et al., 1991). This is operationally achieved by reducing activity of the posterior cingulate and precuneus. As has been shown by Shulman and colleagues (1997a), attention to centrally presented stimuli is accompanied by enhanced responses in areas of the visual system concerned with their processing at the same time that posterior cingulate and precuneus are shut down (Shulman et al., 1997b).

Behavioral evidence in humans provides additional support for the above hypothesis. Mackworth (1965) has shown that increased foveal load leads to decreased extrafoveal information acquisition. He termed this phenomenon "tunnel vision." This work has been confirmed and extended by a number of workers (e.g., see Henderson and Ferreira, 1990). Older adults are actually more affected by foveal load than younger adults (Owsley, Ball, and Keeton, 1995). While no studies have been done to relate this decrement in performance with normal aging to reductions in the activity of the posterior cingulate and adjacent precuneus, recent studies in patients with Alzheimer's disease provide an intriguing perspective.

As reported recently by Kuhl and his associates (Minoshima, Foster, and Kuhl, 1994; Minoshima et al., 1997) reduction in the activity of the posterior cingulate gyrus is the earliest metabolic abnormality detected by PET in patients with Alzheimer's disease. Abnormalities in the processing of extrafoveal information have been noted in patients with dementia of the Alzheimer's type (Benson, Davis, and Snyder, 1988), but no systematic study has been performed on this group of patients in light of the recent findings of Kuhl and his associates (Minoshima et al., 1994, 1997).

Finally, severe damage to parietal cortex when it extends medially to include precuneus and the posterior cingulate produces a condition known as Balint's syndrome (Hecaen and Ajuriaguerra, 1954) whose cardinal feature is the inability to perceive the visual field as a whole (i.e., severe tunnel vision). This is known as simultanagnosia (Rizzo and Robin, 1990). It is of interest that simultanagnosia has been reported in patients with dementia of the Alzheimer's type (Benson et al., 1988). Of interest would be a study of the relationship between decrements in baseline metabolic activity in this region in patients with Alzheimer's disease and the development of simultanagnosia.

Thus, posterior cingulate and adjacent precuneus cortex can be hypothesized as a region of the brain associated with the continuous gathering of information about the world around us. It would appear to be a default condition of the brain with rather obvious evolutionary significance. Successful performance on tasks requiring focused attention demands that such broad information gathering be curtailed. We see this reflected in marked decreases in this region during focused attention. As a task becomes easier and requires less focused attention, activity in this area predictably resumes (figure 91.6, row 1).

The other midline region of the cortex exhibiting prominent decreases in activity during focused attention is orbitofrontal cortex. As with the posterior cingulate and adjacent precuneus, these changes have been observed not only in the tasks discussed in this chapter but also in a wide variety of other tasks requiring focused attention (Shulman et al., 1997b). In contrast to the behavior of the posterior cingulate and adjacent precuneus, the decreases we observe in orbitofrontal cortex not only decrease initially when reading tasks are novel and require focused attention, but actually decrease even further with practice (figure 91.6, row 2). Further analysis of these changes (Simpson et al., 1997) reveals a number of important features. First, the reductions observed in this region, as they increase with practice, are significantly correlated with improved performance as measured by improved reaction times on the verb generation task. Second, these changes represent correlated responses within a group of areas in orbital and medial inferior prefrontal cortex and the hypothalamus. This is consistent with the connectional anatomy of this region known from nonhuman primates (Carmichael and Price, 1994, 1995, 1996). Third, the likelihood that these changes are related to the emotional aspects of novel task performance is supported by a parallel study of anticipatory anxiety in normal subjects (Simpson et al., 1997). Reductions similar to those seen in the verb generation task were correlated with the degree of anxiety reported by the subjects. Less anxious subjects showed greater reductions in activity.

These observations occur against a background of considerable clinical and experimental data suggesting that orbital and medial prefrontal cortex plays an important role in emotional behavior (Drevets et al., 1997), especially fear (for a review see LeDoux, 1996) and decision making (Bechara et al., 1997; Damasio et al., 1994). These activities are based on converging information from multiple sensory modalities (Rolls and Baylis, 1994) and connections to amygdala, hypothalamus, brainstem, and basal ganglia (Carmichael and Price, 1996). Puzzling, of course, is the fact that the changes we observe are seen as reductions and, as discussed in detail earlier, they begin from a baseline level of activity which is significantly above the brain mean.

A broad view of the function of the prefrontal cortex suggests that it is active when new rules need to be learned and older ones rejected (Dias, Robbins, and Roberts, 1997; Wise, Murray, and Gerfen, 1996). The activation of regions within prefrontal cortex during the naïve performance of the verb generation task (figure 91.1, row 4) would certainly be consistent with that view. When this same reasoning is applied to orbital and medial prefrontal cortex, one must confront the fact that activity in this region may be greatest in the baseline state. Thus, as we come to associate general monitoring of incoming sensory information with the posterior cingulate and adjacent precuneus, we may also come to associate an evaluation of this information with the medial and orbital frontal cortices.

Conclusions

The main purpose of this chapter was to present a functional brain imaging strategy that isolates potential neural correlates of consciousness in humans. This strategy is based on skill learning. In the example presented (rapidly generating verbs for visually presented nouns), a cognitive skill is examined before and after practice. As shown, there are marked qualitative differences in the neural circuitry supporting performance of this task in the naïve and practiced state. As pointed out, William James succinctly captured the interpretation we wish to place on this transformation in performance and neural circuitry: "Habit diminishes the conscious attention with which our acts are performed" (James, 1890). Areas active during naïve performance become candidate neural correlates of consciousness.

The neural correlates of consciousness for one task may not correspond, region for region, to those for another task. This is most directly demonstrated in our own data when comparisons are made between verb generation and maze tracing (Petersen et al., 1998). Thus, while a common theme emerges from the work reviewed here in terms of principles governing the neural instantiation of conscious and nonconscious behavior of the same task, differences do exist among tasks in terms of the specific brain regions involved. Put another way, no single, unique architecture emerges as a unifying feature of conscious, reflective performance (see also Shulman et al., 1997b).

The cerebral cortex appears like the sections of a symphony orchestra. No one section or individual is at all times necessary for the production of the music. Likewise in the brain, no one region (system) necessarily specifies the content of consciousness under all circumstances. Rather, it is a distributed process with changing participants allocated by need. Some of those participants are identified through the strategy described. Relationships determine performance and performance can be infinitely variable.

The continuity of consciousness awareness must also be kept in mind in pursuing the type of analysis presented in this chapter. Consciousness is not terminated when naïve task performance ceases. In this regard, it is important to consider the role of brain regions whose activity ceases during naïve task performance only to resume under baseline conditions or practiced task performance. These task-induced deactivations from a baseline state provide equally important clues about the neural correlates of the content of consciousness. The recognition of these decreases and, as a consequence, a better understanding the baseline state, probably represent a unique contribution of functional brain imaging to our understanding of human cortical physiology. These findings should stimulate increased interest in the manner in which brain resources are allocated.

ACKNOWLEDGMENTS The material in this chapter was presented, in part, as the 1997 Thomas William Salmon Lecture of the New York Academy of Medicine. I thank my many colleagues whose published data I have reviewed in this chapter. I also thank the National Institutes of Health, The McDonnell Center for Studies of Higher Brain Function of Washington University, The John T. and Katherine T. MacArthur Foundation, and the Charles A. Dana Foundation for generous support over many years.

REFERENCES

ACKERMAN, R. F., D. M. FINCH, T. L. BABB, and J. ENGEL, JR., 1984. Increased glucose metabolism during long-duration recurrent inhibition of hippocampal cells. *J. Neurosci.* 4:251–264.

BAKER, J. F., S. E. PETERSEN, W. T. NEWSOME, and J. M. ALLMAN, 1981. Visual response properties of neurons in four extrastriate visual areas of the owl monkey (Aotus trivirgatus): A quantitative comparison of medial, dorsomedial, dorsolateral, and middle temporal areas. *J. Neurophysiol.* 45:397–416.

BATINI, C., F. BENEDETTI, C. BUISSERET-DELMAS, P. G. MONTAROLO, and P. STRATA, 1984. Metabolic activity of intracerebellar nuclei in the rat: Effects of inferior olive inactivation. *Exp. Brain Res.* 54:259–265.

BECHARA, A., H. DAMASIO, D. TRANEL, and A. R. DAMASIO, 1997. Deciding advantageously before knowing the advantageous strategy. *Science* 275:1293–1295.

BENSON, D. F., J. DAVIS, and B. D. SNYDER, 1988. Posterior cortical atrophy. *Arch. Neurol.* 45:789–793.

BIRAL, G., M. CAVAZZUTI, C. PORRO, R. FERRARI, and R. CORAZZA, 1984. [^{14}C]Deoxyglucose uptake of the rat visual centres under monocular optokinetic stimulation. *Behav. Brain Res.* 11:271–275.

BRIDGEMAN, B., A. H. C. VAN DER HIJIDEN, and B. M. VELICHOVSKY, 1994. A theory of visual stability across saccadic eye movements. *Behav. Brain Sci.* 17:247–292.

CARMICHAEL, S. T., and J. L. PRICE, 1994. Architectonic subdivision of the orbital and medial prefrontal cortex in the macaque monkey. *J. Comp. Neurol.* 346:366–402.

CARMICHAEL, S. T., and J. L. PRICE, 1995. Limbic connections of the orbital and medial prefrontal cortex of macaque monkeys. *J. Comp. Neurol.* 368:615–641.

CARMICHAEL, S. T., and J. L. PRICE, 1996. Connectional networks within the orbital and medial prefrontal cortex of macaque monkeys. *J. Comp. Neurol.* 371:179–207.

COLBY, C. L., R. GATTASS, C. R. OLSON, and C. G. GROSS, 1988. Topographic organization of cortical afferents to extrastriate visual area PO in the macaque: a dual tracer study. *J. Comp. Neurol.* 238:1257–1299.

CRICK, F., and C. KOCH, 1998. Consciousness and neuroscience. *Cereb. Cortex* 8:97–107.

DAMASIO, A. R., 1995. Knowing how, knowing where. *Nature* 375:106–107.

DAMASIO, H., T. GRABOWSKI, R. FRANK, A. M. GALABURDA, and A. R. DAMASIO, 1994. The return of Phineas Gage: Clues about the brain from the skull of a famous patient. *Science* 264:1102–1105.

DIAS, R., T. W. ROBBINS, and A. C. ROBERTS, 1997. Dissociable forms of inhibitory control within prefrontal cortex with an analog of the Wisconsin Card Sort Test: Restriction to novel situations and independence from "on-line" processing. *J. Neurosci.* 17:9285–9297.

DONDERS, F. C., 1969. On the speed of mental processes. *Acta Psychologia* 30:412–431.

DREVETS, W. C., H. BURTON, T. O. VIDEEN, A. Z. SNYDER, J. R. SIMPSON, JR., and M. E. RAICHLE, 1995. Blood flow changes in human somatosensory cortex during anticipated stimulation. *Nature* 373:249–252.

DREVETS, W. C., J. L. PRICE, J. R. SIMPSON, JR., R. D. TODD, T. REICH, V. VANNIER, and M. E. RAICHLE, 1997. Subgenual prefrontal cortex abnormalities in mood disorders. *Nature* 386:824–827.

FIEZ, J. A., and S. E. PETERSEN, 1998. Neuroimaging studies of word reading. *Proc. Natl. Acad. Sci. U.S.A.* 95:914–921.

FOX, P. T., J. S. PERLMUTTER, and M. E. RAICHLE, 1985. A stereotactic method of anatomical localization for positron emission tomography. *J. Computer Assisted Tomogr.* 9:141–153.

FOX, P. T., and M. E. RAICHLE, 1986. Focal physiological uncoupling of cerebral blood flow and oxidative metabolism during somatosensory stimulation in human subjects. *Proc. Natl. Acad. Sci. U.S.A.* 83:1140–1144.

FOX, P. T., M. E. RAICHLE, M. A. MINTUN, and C. DENCE, 1988. Nonoxidative glucose consumption during focal physiologic neural activity. *Science* 241:462–464.

FRITH, C. D., K. FRISTON, P. F. LIDDLE, and R. S. J. FRACKOWIAK, 1991. Willed action and the prefrontal cortex in man: a study with PET. *Proc. R. Soc. Lond. B* 244:241–246.

GEORGOPOULOS, A. P., J. F. KALASKA, R. CAMINITI, and J. T. MASSEY, 1982. On the relations between the direction of two-dimensional arm movements and cell discharge in primate motor cortex. *J. Neurosci.* 2:1527–1537.

HECAEN, H., and J. AJURIAGUERRA, 1954. Balint's syndrome (psychic paralysis of gaze) and its minor forms. *Brain* 77:373–400.

HEISTAD, D. D., and H. A. KONTOS, 1983. Cerebral circulation. In *Handbook of Physiology: The Cardiovascular System*, Vol. 3, J. T. Sheppard and F. M. Abboud, eds. Bethesda, Md.: American Physiological Society, pp. 137–182.

HENDERSON, J. M., and F. FERREIRA, 1990. Effects of foveal processing difficulty on the perceptual span in reading: Implications for attention and eye movement control. *J. Exp. Psychol.: Learn. Mem. Cognit.* 16:417–429.

HOWARD, D., K. PATTERSON, R. WISE, D. BROWN, K. FRISTON, C. WEILLER, and R. FRACKOWIAK, 1992. The cortical localizations of the lexicons: Positron emission tomography evidence. *Brain* 115:1769–1782.

JACKSON, J. H., 1874. On the nature of the duality of the brain. *Medical Press and Circular* 1:19, 41, 63.

JAMES, W., 1890. *Principles of Psychology*. New York: Henry Holt, pp. 97–99.

KWONG, K. K., J. W. BELLIVEAU, D. A. CHESLER, I. E. GOLDBERG, R. M. WEISKOFF, B. P. PONCELET, D. N. KENNEDY, B. E. HOPPEL, M. S. COHEN, R. TURNER, H. M. CHENG, T. J. BRADY, and B. R. ROSEN, 1992. Dynamic magnetic resonance imaging of human brain activity during primary sensory stimulation. *Proc. Natl. Acad. Sci. U.S.A.* 89:5675–5679.

LEDOUX, J., 1996. *The Emotional Brain*. New York: Simon and Schuster.

LICHTHEIM, L., 1885. On aphasia. *Brain* 7:433–484.

MACKWORTH, N. H., 1965. Visual noise causes tunnel vision. *Psychonom. Sci.* 3:67–70.

MCCARTHY, R., and E. K. WARRINGTON, 1984. A two-route model of speech production: Evidence from aphasia. *Brain* 107:463–485.

MINOSHIMA, S., N. L. FOSTER, and D. E. KUHL, 1994. Posterior cingulate cortex in Alzheimer's disease. *Lancet* 344:895.

MINOSHIMA, S., B. GIORDANI, S. BERENT, K. A. FREY, N. L. FOSTER, and D. E. KUHL, 1997. Metabolic reduction in the posterior cingulate cortex in very early Alzheimer's disease. *Ann. Neurol.* 42:85–94.

NORMAN, D. A., and T. SHALLICE, 1985. Attention to action: Willed and automatic control of behavior. In *Consciousness and Self-Regulation.* New York: Plenum Press, pp. 1–18.

OGAWA, S., T. M. LEE, A. R. KAY, and D. W. TANK, 1990. Brain magnetic resonance imaging with contrast dependent on blood oxygenation. *Proc. Natl. Acad. Sci. U.S.A.* 87:9868–9872.

OGAWA, S., D. W. TANK, R. MENON, J. M. ELLERMANN, S.-G. KIM, H. MERKLE, and K. UGURBIL, 1992. Intrinsic signal changes accompanying sensory stimulation: Functional brain mapping with magnetic resonance imaging. *Proc. Natl. Acad. Sci. U.S.A.* 89:5951–5955.

OWSLEY, C., K. BALL, and D. M. KEETON, 1995. Relationship between visual sensitivity and target localization in older adults. *Vis. Res.* 35:579–587.

PASSINGHAM, R. E., 1993. *The Frontal Lobes and Voluntary Action.* Oxford: Oxford University Press.

PAUS, T., S. MARRETT, K. J. WORSLEY, and A. C. EVANS, 1995. Extraretinal modulation of cerebral blood flow in the human visual cortex: Implications for saccadic suppression. *J. Neurophysiol.* 74:2179–2183.

PETERSEN, S. E., P. T. FOX, M. I. POSNER, M. MINTUN, and M. E. RAICHLE, 1988. Positron emission tomographic studies of the cortical anatomy of single-word processing. *Nature* 331:585–589.

PETERSEN, S. E., P. T. FOX, M. I. POSNER, M. A. MINTUN, and M. E. RAICHLE, 1989. Positron emission tomographic studies of the processing of single words. *J. Cogn. Neurosci.* 1:153–170.

PETERSEN, S. E., P. T. FOX, A. Z. SNYDER, and M. E. RAICHLE, 1990. Activation of extrastriate and frontal cortical areas by visual words and word-like stimuli. *Science* 249:1041–1044.

PETERSEN, S. E., H. VAN MIER, J. A. FIEZ, and M. E. RAICHLE, 1998. The effects of practice on the functional anatomy of task performance. *Proc. Natl. Acad. Sci. U.S.A.* 95:853–860.

PLUM, F., and J. B. POSNER, 1980. *The Diagnosis of Stupor and Coma* (3d Ed.). Philadelphia: F. A. Davis Company.

POSNER, M. I., and A. PAVESE, 1998. Anatomy of word and sentence meaning. *Proc. Natl. Acad. Sci. U.S.A.* 95:899–905.

PRICE, C. J., R. J. S. WISE, and R. S. J. FRACKOWIAK, 1996. Demonstrating the implicit processing of visually presented words and pseudowords. *Cereb. Cortex* 6:62–70.

PRICE, C. J., R. J. S. WISE, J. D. G. WATSON, K. PETTERSON, D. HOWARD, and R. S. J. FRACKOWIAK, 1994. Brain activity during reading: The effects of exposure duration and task. *Brain* 117:1255–1269.

RAICHLE, M. E., 1998. Behind the scenes of function brain imaging: A historical and physiological perspective. *Proc. Natl. Acad. Sci. U.S.A.* 95:765–772.

RAICHLE, M. E., J. A. FIEZ, T. O. VIDEEN, A. K. MACLEOD, J. V. PARDO, P. T. FOX, and S. E. PETERSEN, 1994a. Prac-tice-related changes in human brain functional anatomy during nonmotor learning. *Cereb. Cortex* 4:8–26.

RAICHLE, M. E., J. A. FIEZ, T. O. VIDEEN, A. M. MACLEOD, J. V. PARDO, P. T. FOX, and S. E. PETERSEN, 1994b. Practice-related changes in human brain functional anatomy during nonmotor learning. *Cereb. Cortex* 4:8–26.

RAYNER, K., and A. POLLATSEK, 1989. *The Psychology of Reading*, Englewood Cliffs, N.J.: Prentice Hall.

REASON, J., and K. MYCIELSKA, 1982. Absent-Minded? *The Psychology of Mental Lapses and Everyday Errors.* Englewood Cliffs, N.J.: Prentice Hall.

RIZZO, M., and D. A. ROBIN, 1990. Simultanagnosia: A defect of sustained attention yields insights on visual information processing. *Neurology* 40:447–455.

ROLLS, E. T., and L. L. BAYLIS, 1994. Gustatory, olfactory, and visual convergence within the primate orbitofrontal cortex. *J. Neurosci.* 14:5437–5452.

SHALLICE, T., 1988. *From Neuropsychology to Mental Structure.* Cambridge: Cambridge University Press.

SHIFFRIN, R., and W. SCHNEIDER, 1977. Controlled and automatic human information processing: II. Perceptual learning, automatic attending and a general theory. *Psychol. Rev.* 84:127–190.

SHULMAN, G. L., M. CORBETTA, R. L. BUCKNER, M. E. RAICHLE, J. A. FIEZ, F. M. MIEZIN, and S. E. PETERSEN, 1997a. Top-down modulation of early sensory cortex. *Cereb. Cortex* 7:193–206.

SHULMAN, G. L., J. A. FIEZ, M. CORBETTA, R. L. BUCKNER, F. M. MIEZIN, M. E. RAICHLE, and S. E. PETERSEN, 1997b. Common blood flow changes across visual tasks: II. Decreases in cerebral cortex. *J. Cogn. Neurosci.* 9:648–663.

SIESJO, B. K., 1978. *Brain Energy Metabolism.* New York: John Wiley and Sons.

SIMPSON, J. R. J., A. K. MACLEOD, J. A. FIEZ, W. C. DREVETS, and M. E. RAICHLE, 1997. Blood flow decreases in human medial inferior prefrontal cortex and hypothalamus correlate with anxiety self-rating and with practice-related changes on a cognitive task. *Soc. Neurosci. Abstr.* 23:1317.

STERIADE, M., 1996a. Arousal: Revisiting the reticular activating system. *Science* 272:225–226.

STERIADE, M., 1996b. Awakening the brain. *Nature* 383:24–25.

SUTHERLAND, N. S., 1996. The biological causes of irrationality. In *Research and Perspectives in Neurosciences*, Y. Christen, ed. Berlin: Springer, pp. 145–156.

VOGT, B. A., D. M. FINCH, and C. R. OLSON, 1992. Functional heterogeneity in cingulate cortex: The anterior executive and posterior evaluative regions. *Cereb. Cortex* 2:435–443.

WEISKRANTZ, L., 1986. *Blindsight: A Case Study and Implications.* Oxford: Oxford University Press.

WEISKRANTZ, L., 1997. *Consciousness Lost and Found: A Neuropsychological Exploration.* Oxford: Oxford University Press.

WHANG, K. C., H. BURTON, and G. L. SHULMAN, 1991. Selective attention in vibrotactile tasks: Detecting the presence and absence of amplitude change. *Percept. Psychophys.* 50:157–165.

WISE, S. P., E. A. MURRAY, and C. R. GERFEN, 1996. The frontal cortex–basal ganglia system in primates. *Crit. Rev. Neurobiol.* 10:317–356.

92 Prefrontal Cortex, Time, and Consciousness

ROBERT T. KNIGHT AND MARCIA GRABOWECKY

ABSTRACT   A central feature of consciousness is the ability to control the fourth dimension, time. Humans can effortlessly move their internal mental set from the present moment to a past remembrance and just as easily project themselves into a future event. It is proposed that this capacity to extract oneself from the present and fluidly move forward or backward in time is dependent on the evolution of the human prefrontal cortex. Prefrontal cortex modulates activity in multi-modal association and limbic cortices through widely distributed inhibitory and excitatory pathways. Prefrontal cortex also has a selective bias to novelty, crucial for detecting change and hence for the correct temporal coding of events. These extensive modulatory pathways coupled with an intrinsic link to temporal coding provide a mechanism for rapid engagement of distributed neural networks critical for seamless transitions through the time continuum. Support for this hypothesis is found in the fact that prefrontal damage results in a failure in the ability to extract oneself from the present. Indeed, the hallmark of the severe prefrontal syndrome is perseveratory and stimulus-bound behavior—a classic example of a failure in temporal control.

The massive evolution of the prefrontal cortex parallels the development of many distinctively human behaviors. One central feature of human cognition is the ability to go "off-line" to self-consciously monitor one's own behavior. Effective self-monitoring requires rapid comparison of behaviors and outcomes from one's past in order to make predictions about present and future situations. Through its extensive reciprocal connections, the human prefrontal cortex is uniquely suited to control self-monitoring processes. The prefrontal cortex has been shown to be involved in inhibitory and excitatory control of large-scale neural systems, and it exhibits a response bias toward novelty. Predictably, prefrontal damage results in deficits in both inhibitory gating and excitatory modulation together with failures in the detection and production of novelty. Thus, the prefrontal patient functions in a noisy internal milieu and is lacking in appropriate clues to new versus old information.

ROBERT T. KNIGHT   Department of Psychology, University of California, Berkeley; Veterans Medical Center, Martinez, Calif.

MARCIA GRABOWECKY   Department of Psychology, Northwestern University, Evanston, Ill.

In addition, the prefrontal patient's difficulties with excitatory modulation of connected brain regions lead to a breakdown in working-memory abilities (Baddeley, 1992a,b).

These physiological problems manifest behaviorally as reduced decision confidence, failure in sustaining neural activity over delays, and deficits in the proper ordering of past, present, and future events. Lack of executive control of internal and external events results in a variety of deficits in planning and memory organization. Perhaps as important a problem is the failure to effectively recruit large-scale neural ensembles for self-monitoring and self-direction across the time domain. It is proposed that consciousness is dependent on the ability to rapidly switch between an internal and external milieu—an ability that permits one to remove from the present and construct and compare alternative interpretations of past, present, and future events. This off-line ability to consciously evaluate and adjust behavior along the time continuum is crucially dependent on lateral prefrontal cortex.

Jacobsen's (1935) seminal report of delayed-response deficits in sulcus principalis–lesioned monkeys provided a landmark observation for insight into the role of prefrontal cortex in integrative behavior. The delayed-response deficit was initially thought to reflect a simple memory problem. Subsequent research in the 1940s revealed that a problem with the inhibition of extraneous inputs was a major contributor to the delayed-response deficit, leading to the formulation of the distractibility hypothesis of prefrontal function (Malmo, 1942; Bartus and Levere, 1977). This theory postulates that prefrontal patients are unable to suppress response to irrelevant stimuli during both sensory and cognitive processing. Inhibitory deficits are found in neurological patients with dorsolateral prefrontal damage and in schizophrenic patients with prefrontal hypometabolism, providing support for the prefrontal-distractibility hypothesis. In addition to inhibition of task-irrelevant distractors, successful delay performance requires selective excitatory engagement and integration of activity in diverse brain regions dependent on task-specific parameters. Single-unit data in monkeys, electrophysiological data in normal controls and prefrontal-lesioned patients, and cerebral blood flow data from normals have all shown that combined prefrontal-posterior association cortex activation is required to perform difficult tasks that entail bridging a delay.

Damage to dorsolateral prefrontal cortex (Rajkowska and Goldman-Rakic, 1995a,b) results in a distinct set of cognitive disturbances (Damasio, 1985; Knight, 1991). In early disease from tumors or degenerative disorders or in cases of unilateral structural damage from stroke or tumor, subtle deficits in creativity and mental flexibility can be observed. When unilateral disease progresses or becomes bilateral, pronounced behavioral deterioration emerges. Well characterized problems with attention, planning, temporal coding, metamemory, judgment, and insight predominate. In advanced bilateral dorsolateral prefrontal damage, perseveration (manifesting as being "stuck" in the present) and primitive reflexes (including snout, grasp, and palmomental reflexes) emerge.

An invariable consequence of prefrontal damage is a decreased confidence about many aspects of behavior. Prefrontal patients are often uncertain about their performance despite objective evidence to the contrary. The prefrontal patient's inability to selectively inhibit unwanted input results in a noisy internal milieu; and this, coupled with an inability to detect deviance, hampers the ability to properly code spatiotemporal information. Lacking the ability to maintain a temporal stream and reach decisions with appropriate levels of confidence, the prefrontal patient has no coherent past or future; he or she is locked in an uncertain present characterized by perseveration and stimulus-bound behavior. The neurophysiological and neuropsychological evidence supporting these conclusions will be reviewed in turn.

Neurophysiological studies

INHIBITORY CONTROL

Inhibition in animals Prefrontal inhibitory control of neural activity in multiple brain regions has been reported in a variety of mammalian preparations. Net inhibitory control to both subcortical (Edinger, Siegel, and Troiano, 1975) and cortical regions has been documented (Alexander, Norman, and Symmes, 1976; Skinner and Yingling, 1977). Sensory transmission is under constant modulation. Galambos (1956) provided the first physiological evidence of an inhibitory pathway in mammals with the description of the brainstem auditory olivo-cochlear bundle. The olivo-cochlear bundle projects from the olivary nucleus to the cochleus in the

inner ear. Stimulation of the bundle results in inhibition of transmission from the peripheral cochlea to the brainstem cochlear nucleus, as measured by reductions in evoked responses in the auditory nerve. This research revealed that mammalian nervous systems employ inhibitory connections to regulate sensory flow in small-scale systems. Subsequent studies reported evidence of inhibition in larger neuronal networks. Motor control studies revealed that movement induces sensory gating from the spinal cord to the primary cortical receptive zone (MacKay and Crammond, 1989). In an elegant series of experiments, Skinner and Yingling reported evidence of a multi-modal prefrontal-thalamic sensory gating system in cats. Cryogenic blockade of this prefrontal-thalamic gating system resulted in enhancement of amplitudes of evoked responses in primary sensory cortices (Skinner and Yingling, 1977; Yingling and Skinner, 1977).

This prefrontal-thalamic inhibitory system provides a mechanism for intermodality suppression of irrelevant inputs at an early stage of sensory processing. The system is modulated by an excitatory prefrontal projection to the nucleus reticularis thalami. This nucleus reticularis thalami in turn sends inhibitory GABA-ergic projections to all sensory relay nuclei, providing a potential neural substrate for selective sensory filtering (Guillery, Feig, and Lozsadi, 1998). This system provides a powerful neural substrate for early suppression of extraneous inputs, permitting more effective focusing of attention. In addition to obvious behavioral relevance, this gating system conserves energy expenditure since irrelevant inputs are blocked at an early level of processing.

Inhibition in prefrontal patients The attention deficits observed in prefrontal patients have been linked to problems with inhibitory control of posterior sensory and perceptual mechanisms (Lhermitte, 1986; Lhermitte, Pillon, and Serdaru, 1986). Event-related potential (ERP) studies document inhibitory failure in prefrontal lesioned patients. Recordings of ERPs to irrelevant auditory and somatosensory stimuli (monaural clicks or brief electric shocks to the median nerve) in patients with dorsolateral prefrontal damage provide physiological evidence of a deficit in inhibitory control. Evoked responses from primary auditory (Kraus, Ozdamar, and Stein, 1982) and somatosensory (Sutherling et al., 1988) cortices were recorded from these patients and age-matched and non–prefrontal-damaged controls (figure 92.1). Stimuli consisted of either monaural clicks or brief electric shocks to the median nerve eliciting a small opponens pollicis twitch. Prefrontal damage produced disinhibition of both the primary auditory and somato-

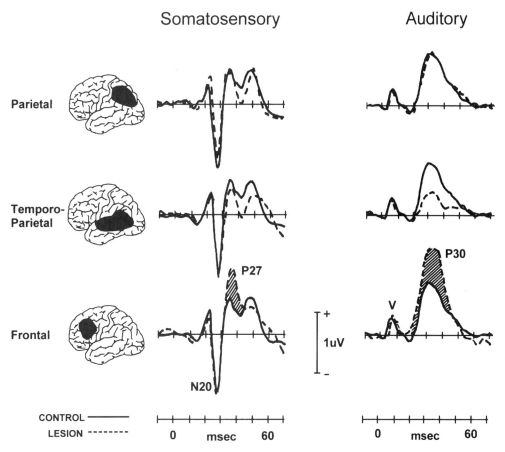

Somatosensory   Auditory

Parietal

Temporo-
Parietal

Frontal

P27

N20

P30

V

+

1uV

−

CONTROL ———
LESION --------

0   msec   60   0   msec   60

FIGURE 92.1 Primary cortical auditory and somatosensory evoked potentials are shown for controls (solid line) and patients (dashed line) with focal damage in the lateral parietal cortex (top, $n = 8$), temporal-parietal junction (middle, $n = 13$) or dorsolateral prefrontal cortex (bottom, $n = 13$). Reconstructions of the center of damage in each patient group are shown on the left. Somatosensory evoked responses were recorded from area 3b (N20) and areas 1 and 2 on the crown of the postcentral gyrus (P26). Stimuli were squarewave pulses of 0.15 ms duration delivered to the median nerve at the wrist. Stimulus intensity was set at 10% above opponens twitch threshold and stimuli were delivered at a rate of 3/s. Damage in posterior cortical regions sparing primary somatosensory cortex had no effect on the N20 or earlier spinal cord potentials. Prefrontal damage resulted in a selective increase in the amplitude of the P26 response (hatched area). Auditory stimuli were clicks delivered at a rate of 13/s at intensity levels of 50 dB HL. Unilateral damage in the temporal-parietal junction extending into primary auditory cortex reduces P30 responses. Lateral parietal damage sparing primary auditory has no effect on P30 responses. Dorsolateral prefrontal damage results in normal inferior collicular potentials (wave V) but an enhanced P30 primary cortical response (hatched area). The shaded area in each modality indicates the area of evoked potential amplitude enhancement. (Adapted from Knight, 1994.)

sensory evoked responses (Knight, Scabini, and Woods, 1989; Yamaguchi and Knight, 1990). Spinal cord and brainstem potentials were not affected by prefrontal damage, suggesting that the amplitude enhancement was due to abnormalities in either a prefrontal-thalamic or a prefrontal-sensory cortex mechanism. Damage to primary auditory or somatosensory cortex reduced the early latency (20–40 ms) evoked responses generated in these regions. Posterior association cortex lesions that spared the primary sensory regions had no effect on early sensory potentials and served as a brain-lesioned control group (see figure 92.1).

Chronic sensory disinhibition contributes to the behavioral sequelae noted after prefrontal damage. For in-

stance, decision confidence, a hallmark of prefrontal disease, is decremented by a noisy internal milieu. Distractibility has been proposed to be a major component of the delayed-response deficit in animals with prefrontal lesions (Bartus and Levere, 1977; Brutkowski, 1965; Malmo, 1942). Inability to suppress irrelevant information is associated with difficulties in target detection and match-to-sample paradigms in prefrontal patients. For example, patients with frontal resections are impaired at detecting multiple visual targets embedded among distractors (Richer et al., 1993) and in suppressing information in memory and Stroop tasks (Shimamura et al., 1995; Vendell et al., 1995). Likewise, patients with lesions confined to dorsolateral prefrontal cortex are

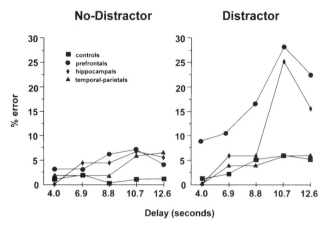

No-Distractor   **Distractor**

- controls
- prefrontals
- hippocampals
- temporal-parietals

% error

Delay (seconds)

FIGURE 92.2   Mean percentage error for the three patient groups and age-matched controls in the no-distractor and distractor conditions (from Chao and Knight, 1995). Note the marked decrement in performance of the prefrontal patients in the presence of distractors. Similar to monkeys, hippocampal region–damaged patients are affected by distractors only at longer ISIs.

impaired in simple delay tasks requiring matching of two environmental sounds only when distractors intervene between cue and target.

Prefrontal lesioned patients were tested on an auditory delayed match-to-sample task. Subjects reported whether a cue (S1) and a subsequent target sound (S2) were identical. On some trials, S1 and S2 were separated by a silent period. On other trials, the delay between S1 and S2 was filled with irrelevant tone pips. As noted above, prefrontal patients were impaired behaviorally by distractors and generated enhanced primary auditory cortex–evoked responses to these irrelevant tones (Chao and Knight, 1995, 1998; see figure 92.2).

Inhibition in psychiatric patients   There is extensive literature supporting prefrontal dysfunction in schizophrenics. Findings suggestive of altered dorsolateral prefrontal function include evidence from both cerebral blood flow (Weinberger, Berman, and Zec, 1986; Weinberger et al., 1992) and post-mortem studies (Akbarian et al., 1995, 1996). Schizophrenics are also reported to have a physiological deficit in inhibitory control. Freedman and colleagues developed the P50 auditory gating paradigm to study inhibitory control in schizophrenics. In normals, presentation of a pair of clicks at a short interstimulus interval decreases the amplitude of the evoked response to the second stimulus. Freedman reported that the second stimulus in a pair of auditory pulses did not habituate in schizophrenics (Freedman et al., 1983). This electrophysiological finding supported the long-standing proposal that schizophrenics fail to properly

filter extraneous inputs (McGhie and Chapman, 1961; Venables, 1964). The P50 gating deficit is reliably seen in a significant percentage of nonpsychotic relatives of schizophrenics and has been proposed to be a neurophysiological trait for schizophrenia. Phenotypic segregation of schizophrenics and first-order relatives using the P50 gating paradigm has been employed in recent genetic studies. This research has isolated a putative schizophrenia gene localized to chromosome 15q13-14 which controls alpha 7 nicotinic receptor expression (Freedman et al., 1997).

The neural network controlling P50 gating is of both theoretical and clinical relevance. We examined the P50 gating deficit in patients with dorsolateral prefrontal damage and in age-matched controls (see figure 92.3). An initial study has shown that elderly control subjects ($n = 9$) have normal suppression of the second stimulus in an auditory pulse pair. Prefrontal patients ($n = 8$) failed to suppress the amplitude of the second stimulus in the ear contralateral to prefrontal damage (Knight et al., 1998). This suggests that prefrontal cortex dysfunction may underlie or contribute to the P50 schizophrenic gating deficit.

EXCITATORY CONTROL

Excitation in prefrontal patients   In addition to suppressing response to irrelevant stimuli, subjects must sustain neural activity in distributed brain regions in order to attend to and correctly perform delay and working-memory tasks. Neural modeling employing prefrontal excitatory modulation of distributed brain regions has successfully modeled several prefrontally mediated behaviors and prefrontal dysfunction in schizophrenia (Cohen, Braver, and O'Reilly, 1996). Neurological patients with focal prefrontal damage provide further physiological evidence of failure in excitatory control of

FIGURE 92.3   (a) Topographic maps display the scalp voltage distribution of the N170 generated to targets in a visual detection task for controls and prefrontal patients. The extrastriate focus of the N170 is reduced ipsilateral to prefrontal damage. The shaded area on the brain shows the area of lesion overlap, while the star indicates a putative generator location of the N170 in extrastriate cortex. (b) Group-averaged ERPs for target stimuli in controls and prefrontal patients ($n = 11$); waveforms are from posterior temporal electrodes (T5/T6 in controls), and ipsilateral (ipsi) or contralateral (contra) to lesion. (c) Topographic maps and (d) waveforms from an auditory delayed match to sample paradigm in controls and frontals ($n = 10$). There is a prominent intrahemispheric decrease in the auditory N100 generated to the S1 and S2 stimuli in the matching paradigm. (Adapted from Swick and Knight, 1998.)

EXCITATORY MODULATION

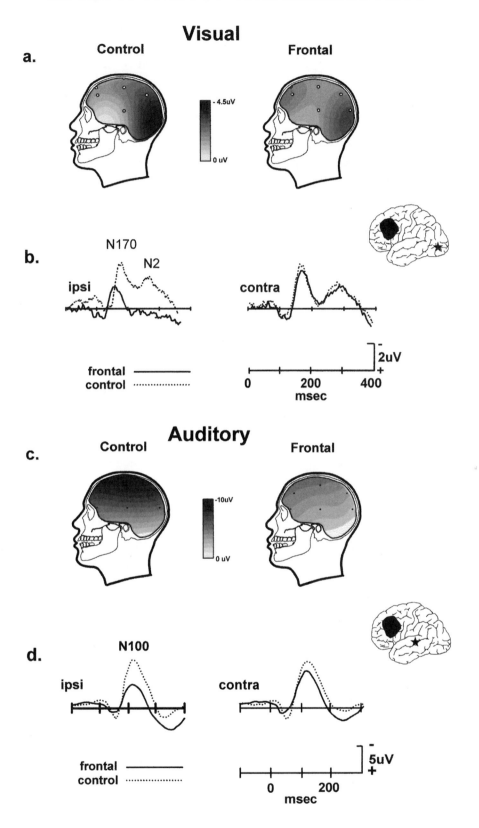

Visual

a.   Control   Frontal

- 4.5uV

0 uV

b.

N170

N2

ipsi   contra

frontal ——
control ⋯⋯⋯

-
2uV
+

0   200   400
msec

Auditory

c.   Control   Frontal

-10uV

0 uV

d.

N100

ipsi   contra

frontal ——
control ⋯⋯⋯

-
5uV
+

0   200
msec

posterior association cortex in patients with prefrontal damage.

Reduced neural activity in extrastriate visual association cortex is also observed after prefrontal damage (Knight, 1997a; Swick and Knight, 1998). Visual stimuli elicit a prominent, attention-sensitive N170 (N1) scalp potential maximal in amplitude over temporal-occipital sites (Mangun and Hillyard, 1988; Mangun, 1995). Topographic and dipole modeling studies indicate an N170 source in extrastriate cortex (Gomez-Gonzalez et al., 1994). The influence of prefrontal cortex on the visual N170 has been examined in both linguistic and nonlinguistic tasks. In one experiment, controls and frontal patients performed a visual detection task requiring detection of an infrequent target embedded in a series of irrelevant background and novel stimuli (Knight, 1997a). Dorsolateral prefrontal damage decreased visual N170 amplitude for all stimuli in the lesioned hemisphere. N170 was normal in the nonlesioned hemisphere. Maximal reductions were seen at posterior temporal sites over extrastriate cortex (figure 92.2b). N170 reductions in frontal patients are also observed for verbal stimuli (Swick and Knight, 1998). Subjects read words and pronounceable nonwords and performed either lexical decision or recognition memory tasks. As in the detection experiment, N170 amplitude was reduced over extrastriate recording sites ipsilateral to prefrontal damage.

The visual experiments indicate that dorsolateral prefrontal cortex provides an ipsilateral facilitory input to neural processing in extrastriate cortex which enhances neural activity within 120 ms post-stimulus. Further support for prefrontal modulation of visual processing in extrastriate areas during sustained attention and spatial memory performance comes from blood flow data in humans (Roland, 1982), network analyses of PET results (McIntosh et al., 1994), and single-unit and lesion data in monkeys (Fuster, 1985; Funahashi, Bruce, and Goldman-Rakic, 1993). Projections from prefrontal areas 45 and 8 to inferior temporal (IT) areas TE and TEO have been demonstrated in monkeys (Webster, Bachevalier, and Ungerleider, 1994). This provides a putative pathway by which prefrontal cortex could exert facilitory influence on activity in posterior visual association cortex. A similar failure of prefrontal excitatory modulation is observed in the auditory modality. In the delayed match-to-sample task discussed above, both the S1 and S2 stimuli generated a prominent N100 ERP response, which reflects neural activity in auditory association cortex (Woods, 1990). Prefrontal lesions markedly reduced the N100 component throughout the hemisphere ipsilateral to damage (figure 92.3c,d). There are well described prefrontal projections to the superior temporal plane

which may subserve this excitatory input (Alexander, Newman, and Symmes, 1976).

The auditory and visual data provide clear evidence that dorsolateral prefrontal cortex is crucial for maintaining distributed intrahemispheric neural activity during auditory and visual attention–dependent tasks. These results are also in accord with findings that patients with prefrontal lesions are impaired in their ability to focus attention on task-relevant stimuli (Fuster, 1989; Knight et al., 1981; Damasio, 1985; Woods and Knight, 1986).

Sustained attention in normals Hillyard and colleagues (1973; Hillyard and Picton, 1987) reported that focused attention to tones in one ear resulted in an enhancement of evoked potentials to all stimuli in that ear. This enhancement onset occurred at about 50 ms post-stimulation and was sustained for at least 200 to 500 ms. These electrophysiological results provided critical information to attention theorists. First, stimulus discriminability was shown to be dependent on the degree of attention-related evoked potential enhancements, providing a link between physiology and attention in humans. Second, the early onset of the attention modulation provided clear evidence of an early sensory filtering mechanism in humans, addressing the long-standing early vs. late selection controversy (Broadbent, 1958; Kahneman and Treisman, 1984; Treisman, 1960). Subsequent work has shown that the effects of attention can onset as early as 25 ms after stimulation, indicating that humans are able to exert attention effects on inputs to the primary auditory cortex (McCallum et al., 1983; Woldorff and Hillyard, 1991). Early onset selective attention effects have also been reported in the visual and somatosensory modalities (Desmedt, Hut, and Bourguet, 1983; Woods, 1990). In the visual modality attention may not modulate primary sensory activity in calcarine cortex, but instead acts on subsequent stages of processing in visual association cortices (Gomez-Gonzalez et al., 1994; Mangun, 1995).

Sustained attention in prefrontal patients Normal subjects generate robust attention effects for left- or right-ear stimulation. Left prefrontal patients have slightly reduced attention effects in both ears. A different pattern is observed after right prefrontal damage. Right prefrontal patients show electrophysiological and behavioral evidence of a dense hemi-inattention to left-ear stimuli (Knight et al., 1981). These data are in accord with the human hemi-neglect syndrome, which is more common after right prefrontal or temporal-parietal lesions (Kertesz and Dobrolowski, 1981; Mesulam, 1981). One theory states that the contralateral neglect observed after temporal-parietal or prefrontal right hemisphere lesions is due to innate hemispheric attention asymmetries. The left frontal lobe is proposed to be capable of allocating attention only to the contralateral right hemispace, whereas the right frontal lobe can allocate attention to both the contralateral and ipsilateral hemispace. Thus, neglect is mild or not apparent after left-hemisphere lesions, since the intact right hemisphere is capable of allocating attention to both hemi-spaces. Dense contralateral neglect is seen after right hemisphere damage since the left hemisphere is incapable of allocating attention to the left hemispace (Mesulam, 1981).

Increased size of the right frontal lobe in humans may provide the anatomical substrate for the hemi-inattention syndrome in humans (Wada, Clarke, and Hamm, 1975; Weinberger et al., 1982). Posterior association cortex lesions in the temporal-parietal junction have comparable attention deficits for left- and right-sided lesions, indicating that these areas are not asymmetrically organized for auditory selective attention (Woods, Knight, and Scabini, 1993). This suggests that the left hemineglect syndrome subsequent to right temporal-parietal damage may be due to remote effects of disconnection from asymmetrically organized prefrontal regions.

Attention capacity is enhanced at short versus long interstimulus intervals in prefrontal lesioned patients. This could be due either to a problem with temporal bridging or to a distractibility deficit. Prefrontal cortex is necessary for bridging temporal discontinuities (Fuster, 1989). Thus, attention deficits at longer interstimulus intervals might be due to temporal bridging problems. However, at longer interstimulus intervals prefrontal subjects are also more likely to encounter intervening irrelevant stimuli. ERP-behavioral experiments provide evidence supporting the distractibility hypothesis. In normal subjects, delivery of an irrelevant stimulus in a nonattended ear during a dichotic listening experiment has no effect on attention effects to a subsequent stimulus in the attended ear. However, presentation of an irrelevant stimulus in the nonattended ear impairs detection of a subsequent stimulus in the attended ear in prefrontal patients. This effect is particularly pronounced in the ear contralateral to a prefrontal lesion at long interstimulus intervals. Since attention performance at long interstimulus intervals improves in the absence of distracting irrelevant stimuli, the results favor distractibility as the major contributor to prefrontal attention deficits (Woods and Knight, 1986).

NOVELTY

Overview   The ability to detect and respond to new information is highly evolved in humans. In lower mammalian species, detection of and response to deviant environmental events are critical for survival (Sokolov,

1963). In humans, novelty detection remains crucial for the orienting response. However, the ability to process novelty has evolved into a central parameter for many other cognitive processes, such as memory and creativity. In the 1930s, Von Restorff reported that discrete novel stimuli are remembered better (Von Restorff, 1933). Subsequent behavioral-electrophysiological experiments confirmed that stimulus distinctiveness enhances recall (Karis, Fabiani, and Donchin, 1984).

Novelty has a powerful effect on memory for everyday events outside of the laboratory setting. Infrequent personal events—say, the birth of a child or a death—are deeply encoded. Similarly, rare but engaging external events, such as assassinations, are also better remembered. Several factors influence this effect. For instance, repetition of the news of Kennedy's assassination drives deep encoding. However, many individuals distinctly remember the first moments in which they were informed about Kennedy's death, often recalling exact details of what they were doing when they heard the news. Novelty influences other human behaviors, as well. Creative behavior is commonly defined in direct relation to the degree of novelty. The relationship between novelty and creativity extends to many endeavors, including art and science.

The neural mechanisms both of novelty detection and the generation of novel behaviors have stimulated increased interest in recent years. Multiple experimental approaches have focused on the biological mechanisms of novelty processing. Genetic studies of novelty-seeking behavior in humans have provided a link to the short arm of chromosome 11 and the dopamine D4 receptor gene (Benjamin et al., 1996; Ebstein et al., 1996). Neuropsychological, electrophysiological, and cerebral blood flow techniques (Knight and Scabini, 1998) have revealed that a distributed neural network including dorsolateral prefrontal cortex, temporal-parietal junction, hippocampus, and cingulate cortex is engaged both by novelty detection and during the production of novel behaviors. The data supporting these contentions will be reviewed.

ERPs, fMRI, and voluntary attention   In everyday life, humans continually detect and respond to discrete environmental events. Subjects may allocate attention to a discrete event either voluntarily or automatically. Examples of voluntary attention might include simple tasks, such as looking for a pencil on your desk, or more complicated tasks, such as finding one key reference in a large pile of papers. Both tasks involve the ability to maintain a template of what you are looking for and to mount an appropriate behavioral response when that template is matched. During voluntary attentive search, distinct scalp recorded ERPs are generated to a correctly detected stimulus. In the 1960s, researchers began to employ scalp-recorded event-related potentials (ERPs) to study a wide range of sensory and cognitive processes, including attention, motor performance, memory, and language. In 1965 two separate laboratories described the generation of a large positive parietal maximal scalp potential (P300), peaking in amplitude 300–500 ms after stimulus delivery, when a subject voluntarily detected a task-relevant event (Desmedt, Debecker, and Manil, 1965; Sutton et al., 1965). This ERP is referred to as a P3b response to distinguish it from scalp positive potentials (P3a) generated by novel stimuli. P300 responses to task-relevant targets (P3b) and task-irrelevant novel stimuli (P3a) are generated in all sensory modalities. P3b responses can even be recorded to the detection of a missing stimulus in a train of irrelevant stimuli.

Researchers studying voluntary attention have operationalized detection behavior to the "oddball task." In the oddball task a subject is asked to detect an infrequent and low-probability event. The detected or target stimulus is referred as the "oddball" stimulus in a series of background stimuli. Detection of the oddball generates a prominent parietal maximal P3b. Theories focused on attention and memory have been proposed to account for the cognitive basis of the P3b, although no clear consensus has emerged (Donchin and Coles, 1988; Verleger, 1988). The most widely held view is that the P3b indexes updating of activity in corticolimbic circuits during voluntary attention and working memory (Ruchkin et al., 1992). Other proposals such as those linking P3b and template matching may also be subsumed under the concept of context updating in working memory (Chao, Nielsen-Bohlman, and Knight, 1995). There is an extensive literature on the P3b, including electroencephalographic and magnetoencephalographic work in normals, intracranial ERP data from epileptic patients, and lesion and neuropharmacological studies in humans and animal models. These will not be reviewed in detail since several extensive reviews are available (Picton, 1995; Swick, Kutas, and Neville, 1994). The basic conclusion is that a distributed circuit including multi-modal posterior association cortex, hippocampus, cingulate cortex, and prefrontal cortex is engaged during voluntary detection tasks. The degree of prefrontal activation as measured by ERPs (Swick, 1998; Swick and Knight, 1999) or blood flow techniques (D'Esposito et al., 1994; Owen, Evans, and Petrides, 1996; Petrides et al., 1993a,b) increases with task difficulty and may be minimal when employing easy detection tasks.

Recent event-related fMRI studies have provided converging evidence on P3b sources. Visual or auditory studies have reported differing combinations of inferior parietal, superior temporal plane, thalamic, and cingulate activations to correctly detected oddballs. Inferior parietal activation was reported by all groups. The degree of prefrontal activation has varied between different laboratories independently of the size of the magnet (Kirino et al., 1997; McCarthy et al., 1997; Menon et al., 1997). Although intracranial recording has provided clear evidence of generation of large hippocampal electrical fields to voluntarily detected stimuli (Smith et al., 1990; McCarthy et al., 1989), this activation is not readily apparent with fMRI. One possibility may relate to magnetic susceptibility effects. The authors of one report suggested that differences in sensitivity between ERP and fMRI techniques or differential degrees of sustained versus phasic activation in cortical versus hippocampal regions might also contribute to lack of significant activation of the hippocampus (McCarthy et al., 1997).

ERPs and novelty For several decades after Von Restorff's seminal contribution on the relationship of novelty and memory performance, relatively little attention was directed to the underlying neural basis of this powerful effect. This changed in the mid-1970s with the publication of two papers reporting generation of scalp potentials to novel or deviant stimuli (Courchesne, Hillyard, and Galambos, 1975; Squires, Squires, and Hillyard, 1975). Involuntary orientation to an unexpected and novel stimulus generates a P300 response similar in some respects to that generated by a voluntarily detected stimulus. However, the novel response differs in three important aspects from the voluntary attention–related P3b. The novelty P300, referred to as a P3a, has a more frontocentral scalp distribution than the P3b, peaks 60–80 ms earlier in all sensory modalities, and undergoes rapid habituation over the first 5–10 stimulus presentations (Knight, 1984; Knight et al., 1989; Knight, 1997a; Yamaguchi and Knight, 1991a). Intracranial recordings of ERPs in the visual, auditory, and somatosensory modalities have documented that multiple neocortical and limbic regions are activated during tasks that generate scalp-recorded novelty-dependent P3a potentials (Bau-dena et al., 1995; Halgren et al., 1980, 1995a,b; Heit, Smith, and Halgren, 1990). Single-unit recording in humans has also reported novelty-related activity in the hippocampus (Fried, MacDonald, and Wilson, 1997).

Intracranial areas with novelty-related activity include frontal and posterior association cortex in addition to cingulate and mesial temporal regions. Scalp and intracranial novelty-related ERPs have been proposed to index neural activity in a distributed multi-modal corticolimbic orienting system that processes novel events (Courchesne, Hillyard, and Galambos, 1975; Knight, 1984; Squires, Squires, and Hillyard, 1975). Intracranial recordings in humans have revealed that limbic-recorded voluntary attention and novelty ERPs have differential habituation properties (Knight and Scabini, 1998; Scabini and McCarthy, 1993). The hippocampal-recorded target ERP, like the scalp target P3b response, does not habituate over repeated detection of the attended stimulus (Knight and Scabini, 1998). Conversely, the hippocampal novelty ERP response, similar to its scalp electrophysiological P3a counterpart, undergoes rapid amplitude reduction over repeated trials (Knight, 1984; Yamaguchi and Knight, 1991a). These data support the claim that the novelty P3a is a central nervous system marker of the orienting response.

P300 potentials to both voluntarily detected stimuli and to unexpected task-irrelevant novel stimuli are recorded in multiple mammalian species including rats (Ehlers, Wall, and Chapin, 1991; Yamaguchi, Globus, and Knight, 1993), cats (O'Connor and Starr; 1985; Wilder, Farley, and Starr, 1981), dolphins (Woods et al., 1986), and monkeys (Arthur and Starr, 1994; Neville and Foote, 1984; Paller et al., 1988, 1992), supporting a broad ethological significance. The animal and human ERP work employing single-unit, field potential, lesion modeling, and neuropharmacological approaches has the power to delineate both the neural network and neural activity underlying novelty detection (Acquas, Wilso, and Fibiger, 1996; Burns et al., 1996; Feenstra, Botterblom, and Van Uum, 1995; Kitchigina et al., 1997; Metcalfe, 1993; Pineda, Foote, and Neville, 1989; Thinus-Blanc et al., 1996; Treves and Rolls, 1994).

Novelty and prefrontal patients Prefrontal cortex patients show impairments in both sustained and phasic attention (Knight, 1994). Neuropsychological testing has documented additional problems with the solving of novel problems (Godfrey and Rousseaux, 1997; Goldberg, Podell, and Lovell, 1994). Simple attention tasks are typically performed normally, but in advanced disease classic problems including indifference, loss of creativity, and deficits in orienting to novel stimuli and events emerge. In accord with these clinical observations, prefrontal damage results in differential effects on scalp P3a and P3b responses. The parietal P3b and concomitant behavioral performance in simple sensory discrimination tasks are unaffected by prefrontal damage. However, P3b reductions after prefrontal damage are observed in more complex tasks (Swick, 1998; Swick and Knight, 1999), supporting the notion of increasing prefrontal involvement with difficult tasks. Conversely, P3a responses to unexpected novel stimuli are markedly reduced by prefrontal lesions in the auditory (Knight, 1984; Knight and Scabini, 1998), visual (Knight, 1997a), and somatosensory modalities (Yamaguchi and Knight, 1991b, 1992), support-

ing a central role of prefrontal cortex in the processing of novelty (Godfrey and Rousseaux, 1997; Kimble, Bagshaw, and Pribram, 1965).

Novelty and mesial temporal-prefrontal dysfunction The hippocampal region is well known to be involved in memory encoding. The observation that stimulus novelty enhances memory encoding suggests that the hippocampus is likely involved in novelty processing. There is a long animal research literature linking the hippocampus with novelty or mismatch detection (Honey, Watt, and Good, 1998; Sokolov, 1963; Vinogradova, 1975). To address the question of the relationship of novelty and the hippocampus, we examined novelty detection capacity in patients with focal damage in the hippocampal region. The artery of Uchimura is a branch of the posterior cerebral artery that perfuses the hippocampal region (Uchimura, 1928). Damage from artery of Uchimura occlusion centers in the posterior hippocampal region, including hippocampus proper, dentate gyrus, subiculum, parahippocampal gyri, entorhinal cortex, and fornix (Eichenbaum, Otto, and Cohen, 1994). The fornix infarction results in macroscopic post-mortem atrophy of the mammillary body unilateral to fornix damage (Efanov, Knight, and Amaral, 1997). Mesial temporal infarction results in verbal and spatial memory deficits after left mesial temporal infarction and predominantly spatial nonverbal deficits after right-sided infarction (De Renzi, Zambolin, and Crisi, 1987; von Cramon, Hebel, and Schuri, 1988). Other deficits include problems with recognition and familiarity memory (Yonelinas et al., 1998) and failures in the binding of memory elements resulting in illusory memory conjunctions (Kroll et al., 1996).

Patients with posterior hippocampal region damage have normal parietal P3b activity and intact behavioral indices of detection ability. Conversely, frontocentral P300 activity to both target and novel stimuli is markedly reduced by hippocampal damage in all sensory modalities (Knight, 1996; see figures 92.4 and 92.5). These reductions are comparable to, and in some instances greater in amplitude than, those observed after focal frontal damage. The findings in the neurological patients support involvement of a prefrontal-hippocampal network in the detection of novelty in the ongoing sensory stream and suggest that the hippocampal formation has facilitory input into prefrontal cortex. Resting-state PET scans have documented frontal hypometabolism in patients with medial temporal amnesia (Perani et al., 1993), although no data are available for memory-related activation studies. Reciprocal intra- and interhemispheric pathways (Amaral, Inausti, and Cowan, 1993; Goldman-Rakic, Selemon, and Schwartz, 1984; Suzuki and Amaral, 1994) coursing through retrospenial cortex or the cingulate (Shallice et

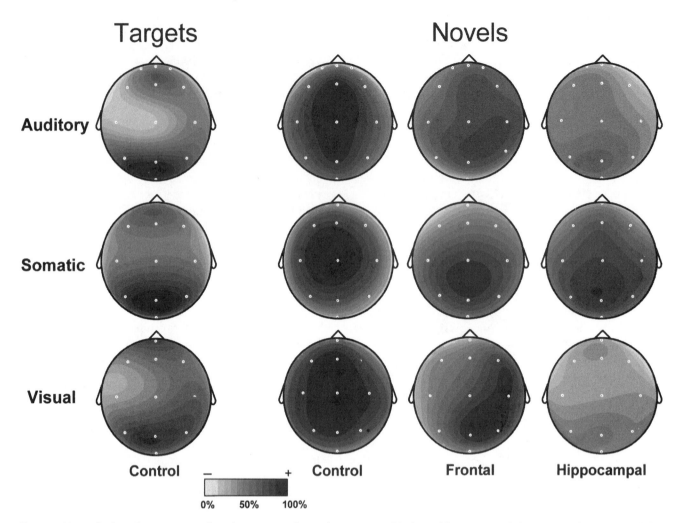

Targets

Auditory

Somatic

Visual

Control

Novels

Control   Frontal   Hippocampal

−   +

0%   50%   100%

FIGURE 92.4   Scalp voltage topographies for target and novel stimuli in controls on the left. Note the marked increase in prefrontal activity to the novel stimuli in all sensory modalities. The effects of prefrontal or hippocampal lesions on the brain novelty response are shown on the right. Unilateral prefrontal damage results in multi-modal decrease in the novelty re-

sponse. Unilateral hippocampal damage results in severe bilateral reductions in the novelty response maximal at prefrontal sites. These findings implicate a prefrontal-hippocampal network in the detection of perturbations in the environment. (Adapted from Knight, 1997b.)

al., 1994) may provide the critical anatomical substrates for prefrontal-hippocampal interactions during novelty detection and memory processing. However, contributions from corticolimbic connections through entorhinal cortex or fornix-mammilothalamic-cortical pathways cannot be eliminated. Single-unit data in monkeys reveals that novelty-related cells in inferior temporal cortex fire within 100 ms (Miller, Li, and Desimone, 1991), suggesting that stimulus processing antecedent to P3a generation may contribute to novelty-related activation in humans.

PET and fMRI studies of novelty   PET studies have shown that stimulus novelty activates distributed brain regions known to be engaged during memory storage (Tulving et al., 1996). Recently, fMRI has also been employed to study novelty. Generation of novel words activated the posterior hippocampus in the same area lesioned in the

hippocampal stroke patients with novelty ERP and SSR reductions (Stern et al., 1996). A study employing event-related fMRI techniques with a 1.5 T magnet failed to find significant visual novelty-related activation in either prefrontal or hippocampal regions, but did report posterior cortical activation (Kirino et al., 1997). Event-related fMRI research with a 4 T magnet has reported prefrontal and temporal activation to auditory novels (Turetsky, Alsop, and Gur, 1997), and a study on a 3 T magnet also found novelty-related prefrontal and posterior cortical activation (Knight and Nakada, 1998).

Neuropsychological studies

Clinical neuropsychological tests fail to capture the behavioral changes associated with prefrontal damage. For instance, patients with large prefrontal lesions often

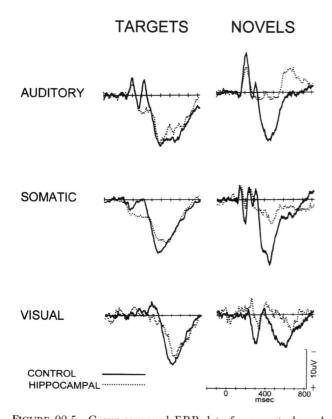

TARGETS   NOVELS

AUDITORY

SOMATIC

VISUAL

CONTROL ———
HIPPOCAMPAL ·············

10uV

0   400   800
msec

FIGURE 92.5 Group-averaged ERP data from controls and hippocampal-lesioned patients ($n = 7$) for auditory, visual, and somatosensory target and novel stimuli. Subjects were seated in a sound-attenuated booth and instructed to press a button upon detection of a designated target stimulus during each experiment. Auditory stimuli consisted of blocks of repetitive standard 1000-Hz monaural tone bursts (60 dB HL, 50 ms duration, 1 s ISI). Tone bursts of 1500 Hz occurred randomly on 10% of the trials and served as targets. Unexpected novel tones consisting of complex computer generated sounds and environmental noises such as bells or barks were randomly delivered on 10% of the trials. A similar paradigm was employed in the visual modality. Visual stimuli consisted of repetitive presentation of triangles. On 10% of the trials, inverted triangles served as target stimuli. On an additional 10% of trials, random line drawings or pictures of irrelevant stimuli served as novel events. Somatosensory stimuli consisted of repetitive taps to the index finger with targets being random taps to the ring finger that occurred on 10% of the trials. Novel stimuli consisted of brief random shocks to the median nerve on 6% of the trials. ERPs are shown from the electrode where maximal response were recorded (Pz for targets; Fz for novels). The novelty P3a is markedly reduced at prefrontal sites in all three modalities and the target P3b is spared. (From Knight, 1996.)

perform normally on standardized tests of memory and intelligence. Even the Wisconsin Card Sorting Test (WCST) commonly associated with frontal damage fails to effectively discriminate patients with frontal lesions from normals or those with lesions in other regions (Eslinger and Damasio, 1985; Grafman, Jonas, and Salazar, 1990). However, patients with prefrontal cortex damage are impaired in the conduct of their daily lives. How can this paradox of good performance on standardized tests be reconciled with impaired functioning in daily life? Developments in the field of cognitive neuropsychology are beginning to provide important insights into the "prefrontal syndrome."

THEORETICAL FRAMEWORK It is proposed that two classes of cognitive operations–simulation and reality checking–are disproportionately impaired after lateral prefrontal damage. *Simulation* refers to the process of generating internal models of external reality. These internal models may represent an accurate past or an alternative past, present, or future reality and can include models of the environment, of other people, and of the self. *Reality checking* refers to processes that monitor sources of information to develop accurate models of the form and context of internally and externally generated information. These monitoring processes are critical for discriminating between simulations of alternative possibilities and veridical models of the world. Simulation and reality checking can be considered "supervisory" (Shallice, 1988), "executive" (Baddeley and Wilson, 1988; Milner, 1982; Milner and Petrides, 1984; Stuss and Benson, 1986), or "organizational" functions (Duncan, 1986). Simulation and reality checking are essential for behavior to be integrated, coherent, and contextually appropriate–features that may be necessary for processing to become conscious (Allport, 1988). Both functions, acting in concert with other evaluative functions mediated by ventromedial and limbic structures, are required for behavior to be disengaged from current environmental constraints while simultaneously maintaining a representation of these constraints.

A patient lacking the ability to simulate alternatives to a situation is incapable of responding flexibly and becomes "stimulus-bound" (Luria, 1966; Luria and Homskaya, 1970). Without reality checking, a patient is incapable of discriminating between internally generated possible realities and the model of the external world as it currently exists. Simulation and reality checking work in concert, allowing humans to internally simulate manipulations of the external environment, evaluate the consequences of those manipulations, and act on the results of those simulations with a richer knowledge of potential outcomes. Rapid engagement of large-scale neural ensembles is required to achieve these goals. As previously posited, the prefrontal cortex is uniquely suited to perform this task.

It has been proposed that the frontal lobes are involved in decision making, goal-directed behavior, planning, and self-monitoring (Stuss and Benson, 1984, 1986; Stuss, 1991). Stuss and colleagues suggest that behavior is controlled by a hierarchical process with three levels of activity. The first includes sensory-perceptual mechanisms that are located in posterior regions of the brain and tend to be modality-specific. Routinized operations are the rule in guiding sensory-perceptual behavior and the course of action is based on the demands of stimuli immediately present in the environment. An example is Shallice's proposal of a "contention scheduling" mechanism to associate overlearned inputs with routine actions (Shallice, 1988). The second level is that of executive functions. This level receives input from the sensory-perceptual level and is responsible for the direction of lower-level subsystems toward achievement of a goal. Control by the executive level is effortful in novel situations but, given sufficient practice, executive functions may become automatized. Simulation processes lie in the domain of executive functions. The highest level in this framework is that of consciousness and self-awareness. At this level a person maintains a self-image, with information about self-generated behavior integrated both over time and with the environment. Inputs to the level of self-awareness may include representations of the options generated by simulation processes operating at the executive level. Reality-monitoring activities are important at this level to allow an integrated model of the self to be maintained. In the following sections, evidence related to simulation and reality monitoring from normals and patients with frontal lobe impairments will be reviewed.

SIMULATION AND COUNTERFACTUALS

Overview Simulation processes have been extensively studied in normal populations (Kahneman and Miller, 1986; Kahneman and Tversky, 1972, 1982; Kahneman and Varey, 1990; Tversky and Kahneman, 1973, 1983). Judgments, including assessments of degree of satisfaction with an outcome and decisions about appropriate future actions, are made based on an evaluation of a set of internally generated alternatives. These are called counterfactual scenarios because they are alternative realities to the one objectively experienced. Counterfactual alternatives are omnipresent in normal human cognition and form a large and important part of our conscious awareness. Counterfactual expressions occur often in everyday life, especially in situations involving regret or grief. For example, a distraught parent may say, "If only I hadn't given my son the keys to the car! Then the accident wouldn't have happened." Such expressions reflect internally generated alternatives that seem very real to the person generating them. Of course, counterfactual alternatives occur in more mundane and less emotionally weighted situations as well. When, for instance, I say to myself, "If I'd ordered marinara instead of white sauce, this stain on my tie would be even worse," I am generating a counterfactual scenario. Counterfactual alternatives play an important role in life satisfaction, with the most salient counterfactuals either increasing or decreasing satisfaction. For example, bronze medalists in Olympic competition tend to be happier than silver medalists, even though, objectively, the silver medalists have performed better (Medvec, Madey, and Gilovich, 1995). Presumably, this occurs because the most available counterfactual alternative for the bronze medalist is a worse outcome, finishing out of the medals, while the most available counterfactual outcome for the silver medalist is a better outcome, winning the gold.

According to Kahneman and Miller (1986), all events are compared to counterfactual alternatives. Events that recruit few alternatives, perhaps because they match the norm of similar events, are judged to have been predictable and unavoidable. Thus, even unanticipated events are seen as normal if they do not cause the generation of many counterfactual alternatives. It is proposed that patients with prefrontal damage are impaired in their ability to generate and evaluate counterfactuals, and that this problem may stem in part from a dysfunction in the automatic detection and generation of novelty. Because prefrontal patients do not respond appropriately to novel events, they may fail to process them appropriately. If the changes introduced by a new event are missed, the current situation will not be appropriately updated, and consequently, fewer counterfactual alternatives will be generated. Counterfactuals are constructed to compare what happened with what could have happened. Without such simulations, it is difficult to avoid making the same mistakes over and over again.

Stimulus-bound behavior Stimulus-bound behavior in patients with dorsolateral prefrontal lesions (Luria, 1966; Lhermitte, 1986) may be interpreted as a consequence of an inability to internally simulate situations differing from those specified by the current stimulus. For example, when objects are placed in front of a prefrontal patient, they are picked up and used without the patient's being asked to do so (termed "utilization behavior" by Lhermitte et al., 1986). In addition, the behavior of the experimenter may be imitated, even when this behavior is bizarre and socially inappropriate (Lhermitte, Pillon, and Serdaru, 1986). The visual grasp reflex may also reflect the stimulus-bound behavior of patients with frontal lesions. Guitton, Buchtel, and Douglas (1985) found that lesions anywhere in the frontal cortex caused difficulty in making a directed saccade in the direction away from a visual cue (an anti-saccade), due to both a difficulty in suppressing a reflexive saccade to the cue and to slowed initiation of a volitional saccade to the target. In short, patients with frontal lesions appeared excessively constrained by environmental cues.

Impairments in planning Patients with prefrontal cortex lesions have also been described as having little concern for either the past or for the future, lacking insight and foresight, as incapable of planning for the near or distant future, and as deficient in creativity (Ackerly and Benton, 1948; Eslinger and Damasio, 1985; Goldstein, 1944; Hebb and Penfield, 1940; Damasio, 1985). This set of abnormal behaviors may be a consequence of a deficit in the ability to simulate alternatives. In particular, patients with damage to the ventromedial portion of the prefrontal cortex appear to be insensitive to the future consequences of their actions and are excessively influenced by immediate reward (Bechara et al., 1994). Such deficits may occur because these patients have a diminished ability to simulate a future reality, including the consequences of a continued course of action; alternatively, they may simulate the outcome but be unable to attach an appropriate affective valence to it.

Deficits in estimation and frequency judgments Patients with frontal lesions are impaired at estimation. Smith and Milner (1984) showed that patients with focal frontal lesions performed poorly at a task involving estimating the price of common objects, with patients with right frontal lesions producing the greatest number of extreme errors. Shallice and Evans (1978) had frontal patients estimate the size of well known objects for which no ready size information was available, e.g., the length of the average man's spine. Frontal patients were seriously impaired at this task, at times giving wildly inaccurate and even impossible answers. To perform estimation tasks, subjects must recruit appropriate exemplars, construct category norms, and then select an appropriate size or price judgment. These processes all involve off-line simulation processes.

Temporal coding abnormalities Many empirical studies support specific impairments in the temporal coding of information, consistent with expectations from the animal literature. Patients with frontal lobe lesions are impaired in tasks involving temporal ordering, such as the sequencing of recent or remote events (McAndrews and Milner, 1991; Milner, Petrides, and Smith, 1985; Moscovich, 1989; Shimamura, Janowsky, and Squire, 1990), and temporal perception (Harrington, Halland, and Knight, 1998). In addition, these patients are impaired in making recency judgments (Janowsky, Shimamura, and Squire, 1989a,b; Milner, 1971; Milner, Petrides, and Smith, 1985; Janowsky et al., 1989), a process that prob-

ably relies on the correct temporal coding of events. Self-ordered pointing, a task in which the patient must remember the order in which objects have been indicated, is also impaired in patients with frontal lesions (Petrides and Milner, 1982). Temporal coding deficits are also influential in errors in planning and perhaps in extracting rules and developing heuristics to guide behavior. Planning may be defective in part because components of a plan are incorrectly ordered in time, and plans may terminate before end goals are reached (Sirigu et al., 1995). In a task involving the extraction of implicit rules, patients with lesions to the prefrontal cortex were impaired relative to controls with posterior lesions (Burgess and Shallice, 1996). Performance in this task is likely to be influenced by temporal coding errors. If a patient cannot confidently order both consequences and antecedents in time, forming an accurate representation of the reward and punishment structure of a task will be difficult, and this failure may lead to seemingly random and bizarre responses.

REALITY CHECKING

Overview The term "reality checking" refers to those aspects of monitoring the external world that have been called "reality *testing*" when they concern the present, and "reality *monitoring*" when they concern the past. Reality checking entails maintaining an awareness of the difference between an internally generated alternative reality and a current objective reality. This includes creating a representation of the context and modality of encoded information, termed source monitoring, and is consequently important for the construction of a detailed representation of an experience. Reality checking is essential for simulation processes to be carried out without compromising the ability to respond to the objective environment. Simulation processes generate an alternative reality that must be evaluated in relation to its divergence from the current reality. Depending on the affective valence of the counterfactual alternative, a plan may be created to change the current reality either toward or away from that alternative. Without the ability to maintain an up-to-date model of external reality, this process will fail. Likewise, if the internally generated reality is confused with the internal representation of the external reality, the process will also fail.

Reality monitoring Memories are created for events experienced in the world and for events experienced through internally constructed simulations. Given that both internal and external events create memory representations, what cues differentiate our internal models of reality from our internal simulations of reality? Johnson and Raye (1981) studied subjects' abilities to discriminate between memories of external events and of internal events. Rich memory traces with many sensory features were ascribed to external experience. Memories of external events tend to be more detailed and have more spatial and temporal contextual information. Internally generated memories tend to be abstract and schematic, lacking in detail, but may include richer information about the cognitive operations involved in their construction. The two types of memory representations form overlapping populations, such that internal and external events may become confused. Reality checking involves a continual assessment of the relationship between behavior and the environment. The detection of novelty is essential to this process in order to incorporate changes in the environment into a representation of the external world. As an individual acts on the environment, the consequences of the action must be incorporated into existing plans.

Frontal lobe impairments and reality monitoring in schizophrenia   Schizophrenic patients performed similarly to frontal lobe patients on a visuospatial working memory task and on planning in the Tower of London task, and performed worse on a measure of visuospatial memory span. Patients were also similar to controls with Parkinson's disease in terms of slower execution time subsequent to initiating the task, suggesting that both showed evidence of the cognitive slowing characteristic of basal ganglia disorders (Pantelis et al., 1997). These memory deficits suggest that schizophrenic patients, like patients with frontal lobe damage, may have difficulty in appropriately tagging events in time, and in protecting the ensuing representations from interference. Consequences of this failure may include both planning deficits and failures in reality monitoring. In fact, in a source memory task, both hallucinating and nonhallucinating psychiatric patients showed increased source attribution errors relative to controls after a delay of one week (Bentall, Baker, and Havers, 1991). Source attribution errors increased more for responses that were strongly associated with a cue than for those that were weakly associated. In addition, hallucinating psychotic patients were more likely to incorrectly attribute self-generated, low-probability (i.e., cognitively demanding) responses to the experimenter than were either nonhallucinating patients or normal controls, even though the hallucinating patients made an equivalent number of source attribution errors to the nonhallucinating patient controls. In another experiment, schizophrenic patients showed an increase in false alarms to new items relative to controls, misattributing them as having previously occurred when

they had not. In addition, they were also less accurate at making self-generated vs. other-generated decisions, with a bias toward attributing prior occurrences to an external source (Brebion et al., 1997). Thus, schizophrenic patients show clear evidence of impaired reality monitoring, which may be a consequence of frontal lobe dysfunction in their disease.

Source memory and confabulation   Patients with damage to prefrontal cortex show a disproportionate impairment in memory for the source of information (Janowsky, Shimamura, and Squire, 1989b; Schacter, Harbluk, and McLachlan, 1984; Shimamura and Squire, 1987; Shimamura, 1995) and a higher false recognition rate (Schacter et al., 1996). Factual information may be correctly recalled but the spatiotemporal context in which the information was acquired is forgotten. These patients also have a diminished ability to make metamemory judgments (Janowsky, Shimamura, and Squire, 1989b). Metamemory includes an ability to judge whether or not the answer to a factual question has been or will be correctly retrieved. Patients with frontal lesions were impaired at making these judgments even though their memory for the facts was intact.

An interesting subgroup of amnesics are those who confabulate. Not all amnesics confabulate, but those who do are likely to have damage to the prefrontal cortex (Mayes, 1988; Moscovich, 1989). For patients who confabulate, plausible memories are not discriminated from implausible ones. This may reflect a reality monitoring deficit. In combination with a deficit in the temporal coding of events, these impaired processes lead to the selection of an alternative from among many others retrieved in a memory search, but this choice is made with little confidence and consequently many errors. Confabulation does not correlate with degree of memory impairment, but is correlated with the ability to self-correct (Stuss and Benson, 1986).

Reality monitoring and development of the frontal lobe   Tertiary association areas including the prefrontal cortex are the last regions of cortex to complete development, with morphological development complete by adolescence (Orzhekhovskaya, 1981). Electrophysiological maturity of the brain starts in posterior regions and continues in a posterior-anterior direction (Hudspeth, 1985), with an increase in EEG coherence between frontal and posterior regions occurring during the period between 4 and 9 years of age (Thatcher, 1992). The prefrontal cortex is among the last regions to myelinize (Yakolev, 1962). Even within prefrontal cortex, developments occur at differing rates, with orbitofrontal cortex developing prior to the dorsolateral cortex. Full development of all aspects of the frontal cortex probably takes until about age 16, and changes continue well into adulthood, possibly allowing new cognitive skills to be continually added. In addition to the development of the frontal cortex, connectivity and interactions among the tertiary association areas may be essential for the development of higher cognitive operations such as simulation and reality checking.

There is evidence that children younger than 6 may perform like frontal patients on tests sensitive to frontal damage (Chelune and Baer, 1986; Schacter, Kagan, and Leichtman, 1995). Six-, seven-, and eight-year olds differed from adults in the number of categories achieved, the number of perseverative errors, and failures to maintain set. However, by age 9 children achieved adult levels in the number of categories achieved, and by age 10 children performed within the normal adult range on all measures. Further, children's test performance covaried with measures of their intellectual achievement. Of all the groups of children, the performance of 6-year olds was most similar to that of adults with focal frontal lesions. Children younger than 5 are also poor, relative to the performance of older children, at spatial memory span tasks, visual working memory tasks, and planning tasks (Luciana and Nelson, 1998).

The simulation and reality checking processes we have discussed are also fairly late to develop in children. Young children are poor at simulating another individual's point of view, including understanding that another person may hold a false belief. The ability to represent another person's belief correlates with performance on a working-memory task in children (Gordon and Olson, 1998) and with performance on a test of creativity (in 3- to 4-year olds; Suddendorf and Fletcher-Flinn, 1997). In another study, young children had difficulty with both a false belief task and with a task involving generating counterfactuals based on a change in some state of the world. This suggests the possibility that both tasks may depend on an ability to generate counterfactual alternatives (Riggs et al., 1998). Children aged 6 and younger also have difficulties with reality monitoring tasks. A group of 6-year olds performed poorly relative to 9- and 12-year olds in discriminating performed events from events that were watched or imagined (Markham, 1991). In a different task, 4-year olds who created a collage with an adult incorrectly remembered who placed which pieces, and misattributed the adult's actions as their own (Foley, Ratner, and Passalacqua, 1993).

It is tempting to speculate that the development of these processes may follow the time course of matura-tion of the prefrontal cortex. Of course, we cannot assume that similarity in the behavior of young children and of patients with focal frontal lesions arises from the same source; however, evidence that the behavior of humans with immature frontal lobes is similar to that of patients with frontal lesions provides converging evidence on the role of the frontal lobes in guiding complex behavior.

Conclusions

The extensive anatomical connections of prefrontal cortex led Nauta to propose that this region was involved in generating and evaluating internal models of action (Nauta, 1971). We propose that prefrontal cortex is crucial for detecting changes in both the internal and external environment and for discriminating internally and externally derived models of the world (Knight and Grabowecky, 1995). Extensive behavioral and physiological data have confirmed that prefrontal contributions are necessary for controlling neural activity in distributed neural networks. This flexibility of processing enables rapid and fluid mental movement through time as one's representation of the world is continually updated. Effortless movement through time occupies a major portion of conscious awareness and is linked to the massive evolution of human prefrontal cortex.

Many aspects of conscious awareness are altered in patients with prefrontal damage. Awareness of flow and change in the stream of internal and external events is impaired by deficits in novelty detection. Failures in inhibitory and excitatory regulation of neural networks critical for working memory contribute to impaired reality monitoring and impaired decision confidence. Inability to bridge temporal gaps and temporally sequence internal events alters coherent representations of counterfactual realities. Prefrontal damage does not eliminate the experience of consciousness, but it can ensnare the patient in a noisy and constrained present. Prefrontal patients suffer deficits in an ability that is a quintessential part of human experience—one we rarely appreciate since it is so effortless—the ability to escape from linear time.

ACKNOWLEDGMENTS Special thanks to Clay C. Clayworth for technical assistance in all phases of the work. Supported by NINDS grant NS21135 and PO17778 to RTK and the Veterans Administration Medical Research Service.

REFERENCES

ACKERLY, S. S., and A. L. BENTON, 1947. Report of a case of bilateral frontal lobe defect. *Res. Publ.: Assoc. Res. Nervous Mental Disease* 27:479–504.

ACQUAS, E., C. WILSO, and H. C. FIBIGER, 1996. Conditioned and unconditioned stimuli increase frontal cortical and hippocampal acetylcholine release: Effects of novelty, habituation, and fear. *J. Neurosci.* 16(9):3089–3096.

AKBARIAN, S., M. M. HUNTSMAN, J. J. KIM, A. TAFAZOLLI, S. G. POTKIN, W. E. BUNNEY, and E. G. JONES, 1995. GABAa receptor subunit gene expression in human prefrontal cortex: comparison of controls and schizophrenics. *Cereb. Cortex* 5:550–560.

AKBARIAN, S., J. J. KIM, S. G. POTKIN, W. P. HETRICK, W. E. BUNNEY, and E. G. JONES, 1996. Maldistribution of interstitial neurons in prefrontal white matter of the brains of schizophrenic patients. *Arch. Gen. Psychiat.* 53:425–436.

ALEXANDER, G. E., J. D. NEWMAN, and D. SYMMES, 1976. Convergence of prefrontal and acoustic inputs upon neurons in the superior temporal gyrus of the awake squirrel monkey. *Brain Res.* 116:334–338.

ALLPORT, A., 1988. What concept of consciousness? In *Consciousness in Contemporary Science*, A. J. Marcel and E. Bisiach, eds. Oxford: Clarendon Press, pp. 159–182.

AMARAL, D. G., R. INAUSTI, and W. M. COWAN, 1983. Evidence for a direct projection from the superior temporal gyrus to the entorhinal cortex in the monkey. *Brain Res.* 275:263–277.

ARTHUR, D. L., and A. STARR, 1994. Task-relevant late positive component of the auditory event-related potential in monkeys resembles P300 in humans. *Science* 223:186–188.

BADDELEY, A., 1992a. Working memory. *Science* 255:556–560.

BADDELEY, A., 1992b. Working memory: The interface between memory and cognition. *J. Cogn. Neurosci.* 4:281–288.

BADDELEY, A., and B. WILSON, 1988. Frontal amnesia and the dysexecutive syndrome. *Brain Cognit.* 7:212–230.

BARTUS, R. T., and T. E. LEVERE, 1977. Frontal decortication in Rhesus monkeys: A test of the interference hypothesis. *Brain Res.* 119:233–248.

BAUDENA, P., E. HALGREN, G. HEIT, and J. M. CLARKE, 1995. Intracerebral potentials to rare target and distractor auditory and visual stimuli: 3. Frontal cortex. *Electroencephalogr. Clin. Neurophysiol.* 94:251–264.

BECHARA, A., A. R. DAMASIO, H. DAMASIO, and S. W. ANDERSON, 1994. Insensitivity to future consequences following damage to human prefrontal cortex. *Cognition* 50:7–15.

BENJAMIN, J., L. LI, C. PATTERSON, B. D. GREENBERG, D. L. MURPHY, and D. H. HAMER, 1996. Population and familial association between the D4 dopamine receptor gene and measures of novelty seeking. *Nature Genet.* 12:81–84.

BENTALL, R. P., G. A. BAKER, and S. HAVERS, 1991. Reality monitoring and psychotic hallucinations. *Brit. J. Clin. Psychol.* 30:213–222.

BREBION, G., M. J. SMITH, J. M. GORMAN, and X. AMADOR, 1997. Discrimination accuracy and decision biases in different types of reality monitoring in schizophrenia. *J. Nervous Mental Disease* 185(4):247–253.

BROADBENT, D. E., 1958. *Perception and Communication.* London: Pergamon Press.

BRUTKOWSKI, S., 1965. Functions of prefrontal cortex in animals. *Physiol. Rev.* 45:721–746.

BURGESS, P. W., and T. SHALLICE, 1996. Bizarre responses, rule detection and frontal lobe lesions. *Cortex* 32:241–259.

BURNS, L. H., L. ANNETT, A. E. KELLEY, B. J. EVERITT, and T. W. ROBBINS, 1996. Effects of lesions to amygdala, ventral subiculum, medial prefrontal cortex, and nucleus accumbens on the reaction to novelty: Implication for limbic-striatal interactions. *Behav. Neurosci.* 110(1):60–73.

CHAO, L. L., and R. T. KNIGHT, 1995. Human prefrontal lesions increase distractibility to irrelevant sensory inputs. *Neuroreport* 6:1605–1610.

CHAO, L. L., and R. T. KNIGHT, 1998. Contribution of human prefrontal cortex to delay performance. *J. Cogn. Neurosci.* 10(2):167–177.

CHAO, L. L., L. NIELSEN-BOHLMAN, and R. T. KNIGHT, 1995. Auditory event-related potentials dissociate early and late memory processes. *Electroencephalogr. Clin. Neurophysiol.* 96:157–168.

CHELUNE, G. J., and R. A. BAER, 1986. Developmental norms for the Wisconsin Card Sorting Test. *J. Clin. Exp. Neuropsychol.* 8(3):219–228.

COHEN, J. D., S. B. BRAVER, and R. C. O'REILLY, 1996. A computational approach to prefrontal cortex, cognitive control and schizophrenia: Recent developments and current challenges. *Phil. Trans. R. Soc. Lond.* 351: 1515–1527.

COURCHESNE, E., S. A. HILLYARD, and R. GALAMBOS, 1975. Stimulus novelty, task relevance, and the visual evoked potential in man. *Electroencephalogr. Clin. Neurophysiol.* 39:131–143.

DAMASIO, A. S., 1985. The frontal lobes. In *Clinical Neuropsychology* (2d Ed.), K. M. Heilman and E. Valenstein, eds. New York: Oxford University Press, pp. 339–374.

DE RENZI, E., A. ZAMBOLIN, and G. CRISI, 1987. The pattern of neuropsychological impairment associated with left posterior cerebral artery infarcts. *Brain* 110:1099–1116.

DESMEDT, J. E., J. DEBECKER, and J. MANIL, 1965. Mise en evidence d'un signe electrique cerebral associe a la detection par le sujet d'un stimulus sensoriel tactile. *Bull. Acad. R. Med. Belg.* 5:887–936.

DESMEDT, J. E., N. T. HUT, and M. BOURGUET, 1983. The cognitive P40, N60 and P100 components of somatosensory evoked potentials and the earliest signs of sensory processing in man. *Electroencephalogr. Clin. Neurophysiol.* 56: 272–282.

D'ESPOSITO, M., J. DETRE, D. ALSOP, R. SHIN, S. ATLAS, and M. GROSSMAN, 1995. The neural basis of the central executive system of working memory. *Nature* 378:279–281.

DONCHIN, E., and M. G. H. COLES, 1988. Is the P300 component a manifestation of context updating? *Behav. Brain Sci.* 11:357–427.

DUNCAN, J., 1986. Disorganization of behavior after frontal lobe damage. *Cogn. Neuropsychol.* 3(3):271–290.

EBSTEIN, R. P., O. NOVIC, R. UMANSKY, B. PRIE, V. OSHER, D. BLAINE, E. R. BENNETT, L. NEMANOV, M. KATZ, and R. H. BELMAKER, 1996. Dopamine D4 receptor (D4DR) exon III polymorphism associated with the human personality trait of novelty seeking. *Nature Genet.* 12:78–80.

EDINGER, H. M., A. SIEGEL, and R. TROIANO, 1975. Effect of stimulation of prefrontal cortex and amygdala on diencephalic neurons. *Brain Res.* 97:17–31.

EFANOV, M., R. T. KNIGHT, and D. AMARAL, 1997. Effects of hippocampal lesions on the medial mammillary nucleus in humans and non-human primates. *Soc. Neurosci. (Abstr.)* 23: 774.

EHLERS, C. L., T. L. WALL, and R. I. CHAPIN, 1991. Long latency event-related potentials in rats: Effects of dopaminergic and serotonergic depletions. *Pharm. Biochem. Behav.* 38: 789–793.

EICHENBAUM, H., T. OTTO, and N. COHEN, 1994. Two functional components of the hippocampal memory system. *Behav. Brain Sci.* 17(3):449–518.

ESLINGER, P. J., and A. R. DAMASIO, 1985. Severe disturbance of higher cognition after bilateral frontal lobe ablation: Patient EVR. *Neurology* 35:1731–1741.

FEENSTRA, M. G. P., M. H. A. BOTTERBLOM, and J. F. M. VAN UUM, 1995. Novelty-induced increase in dopamine release in the rat prefrontal cortex in vivo: Inhibition by diazepam. *Neurosci. Lett.* 189:81–84.

FOLEY, M. A., H. H. RATNER, and C. PASSALACQUA, 1993. Appropriating the actions of another: Implications for children's memory and learning. *Cogn. Dev.* 8(4):373–401.

FREEDMAN, R., L. E. ADLER, M. C. WALDO, E. PACHTMAN, and R. D. FRANKS, 1983. Neurophysiological evidence for a defect in inhibitory pathways in schizophrenia: Comparison of medicated and drug-free patients. *Biol. Psych.* 18:537–551.

FREEDMAN, R., H. COON, M. MYLES-WORSLEY, A. ORR-URTREGER, A. OLINCY, A. DAVIS, M. POLYMEROPOULOS, J. HOLIK, J. HOPKINS, J. ROSENTHAL, M. C. WALDO, F. REIMHERR, P. WENDER, J. YAW, D. A. YOUNG, C. R. BREESE, C. ADAMS, D. PARRERSON, L. E. ADLER, L. KRUGLYAK, S. LEONARD, and W. BYERLY, 1997. Linkage of a neurophysiological deficit in schizophrenia to a chromosome 15 locus. *Proc. Natl. Acad. Sci.* 94:587–592.

FRIED, I., K. A. MACDONALD, and C. L. WILSON, 1997. Single neuron activity in human hippocampus and amygdala during recognition of faces and objects. *Neuron* 18(5):753–765.

FUNAHASHI, S., C. J. BRUCE, and P. S. GOLDMAN-RAKIC, 1993. Dorsolateral prefrontal lesions and oculomotor delayed-response performance: Evidence for mnemonic "scotomas." *J. Neurosci.* 13:1479–1497.

FUSTER, J. M., 1985. The prefrontal cortex, mediator of cross-temporal contingencies. *Human Neurobiol.* 4:169–179.

FUSTER, J. M., 1989. *The Prefrontal Cortex: Anatomy, Physiology, and Neuropsychology of the Frontal Lobe* (2d Ed.). New York: Raven Press.

GALAMBOS, R., 1956. Suppression of auditory nerve activity by stimulation of efferent fibers to the cochlea. *J. Neurophysiol.* 19:424–437.

GODFREY, O., and M. ROUSSEAUX, 1997. Novel decision making in patients with prefrontal or posterior brain damage. *Neurology* 49:695–701.

GOLDBERG, E., K. PODELL, and M. LOVELL, 1994. Lateralization of frontal lobe functions and cognitive novelty. *J. Neuropsychiat. Clin. Neurosci.* 6:371–378.

GOLDMAN-RAKIC, P. S., L. D. SELEMON, and M. L. SCHWARTZ, 1984. Dual pathways connecting the dorsolateral prefrontal cortex with the hippocampal formation and parahippocampal cortex in the Rhesus monkey. *Neuroscience* 12:719–743.

GOLDSTEIN, K., 1944. Mental changes due to frontal lobe damage. *J. Psychol.* 17:187–208.

GOMEZ-GONZALEZ, C. M. G., V. P. CLARK, S. FAN, S. J. LUCK, and S. A. HILLYARD, 1994. Sources of attention-sensitive visual event-related potentials. *Brain Topography* 7:41–51.

GORDON, A. C. L., and D. R. OLSON, 1998. The relation between acquisition of a theory of mind and the capacity to hold in mind. *J. Exp. Child Dev.* 68(1):70–83.

GRAFMAN, J., B. JONAS, and A. SALAZAR, 1990. Wisconsin Card Sorting Test performance based on location and size of neuroanatomical lesion in Vietnam veterans with penetrating head injury. *Percept. Motor Skills* 71:1120–1122.

GUILLERY, R. W., S. L. FEIG, and D. A. LOZSADI, 1998. Paying attention to the thalamic reticular nucleus. *Trends Neurosci.* 21:28–32.

GUITTON, D., H. A. BUCHTEL, and R. M. DOUGLAS, 1985. Frontal lobe lesions in man cause difficulties in suppressing reflexive glances and in generating goal-directed saccades. *Exp. Brain Res.* 58:455–472.

HALGREN, E., P. BAUDENA, J. M. CLARKE, G. HEIT, C. LIEGEOIS, P. CHAUVEL, and A. MUSOLINO, 1995a. Intracerebral potentials to rare target and distractor auditory and visual stimuli: 1. Superior temporal plane and parietal lobe. *Electroencephalogr. Clin. Neurophysiol.* 94:191–220.

HALGREN, E., P. BAUDENA, J. M. CLARKE, G. HEIT, K. MARINKOVIC, B. DEVAUX, J. VIGNAL, and A. BIRABIN, 1995b. Intracerebral potentials to rare target and distractor stimuli: 2. Medial, lateral and posterior temporal lobe. *Electroencephalogr. Clin. Neurophysiol.* 94:229–250.

HALGREN, E., N. K. SQUIRE, C. L. WILSON, J. W. ROHRBAUGH, T. L. BABB, and P. H. CRANDALL, 1980. Endogenous potentials generated in the human hippocampal formation and amygdala by infrequent events. *Science* 210:803–805.

HARRINGTON, D. L., K. Y. HALLAND, and R. T. KNIGHT, 1998. Cortical networks underlying mechanisms of time perception. *J. Neurosci.* 18(3):1085–1095.

HEBB, D. O., and W. PENFIELD, 1940. Human behavior after extensive bilateral removals from the frontal lobes. *Arch. Neurol. Psych.* 4:421–438.

HEIT, G., M. E. SMITH, and E. HALGREN, 1990. Neuronal activity in the human medial temporal lobe during recognition memory. *Brain* 113:1093–1112.

HILLYARD, S. A., R. F. HINK, U. L. SCHWENT, and T. W. PICTON, 1973. Electrical signs of selective attention in the human brain. *Science* 182:177–180.

HILLYARD, S. A., and T. W. PICTON, 1987. Electrophysiology of cognition. In *Handbook of Physiology: The Nervous System*, F. Plum, ed. Baltimore: American Physiol. Society, pp. 519–584.

HONEY, R. C., A. WATT, and M. GOOD, 1998. Hippocampal lesions disrupt an associative mismatch process. *J. Neurosci.* 18(6):2226–2230.

HUDSPETH, J. W., 1985. Developmental neuropsychology: Functional implications of quantitative EEG maturation. *J. Clin. Exp. Neuropsychol.* 7:606.

JACOBSEN, C. F., 1935. Functions of frontal association areas in primates. *Arch. Neurol. Psychiat.* 33:558–569.

JANOWSKY, J. S., A. P. SHIMAMURA, M. KRITCHEVSKY, and L. R. SQUIRE, 1989. Cognitive impairment following frontal lobe damage and its relevance to human amnesia. *Behav. Neurosci.* 103:548–560.

JANOWSKY, J. S., A. P. SHIMAMURA, and L. R. SQUIRE, 1989a. Memory and metamemory: Comparisons between patients with frontal lobe lesions and amnesic patients. *Psychobiology* 17:3–11.

JANOWSKY, J. S., A. P. SHIMAMURA, and L. R. SQUIRE, 1989b. Source memory impairment in patients with frontal lobe lesions. *Neuropsychologia* 27:1043–1056.

JOHNSON, M. K., and C. L. RAYE, 1981. Reality monitoring. *Psychol. Rev.* 88(1):67–85.

KAHNEMAN, D., and D. T. MILLER, 1986. Norm theory: Comparing reality to its alternatives. *Psychol. Rev.* 93(2):136–153.

KAHNEMAN, D., and A. TREISMAN, 1984. Changing views of attention and automaticity. In *Varieties of Attention*, R.

Parasuraman and R. Davies, eds. San Diego: Academic Press, pp. 29–61.

KAHNEMAN, D., and A. TVERSKY, 1972. Subjective probability: A judgement of representativeness. *Cogn. Psychol.* 3:430–454.

KAHNEMAN, D., and A. TVERSKY, 1982. The simulation heuristic. In *Judgement under Uncertainty: Heuristics and Biases*, D. Kahneman, P. Slovic, and A. Tversky, eds. New York: Cambridge University Press, pp. 201–208.

KAHNEMAN, D., and C. A. VAREY, 1990. Propensities and counterfactuals: The loser that almost won. *J. Personality Soc. Psychol.* 59(6):1101–1110.

KARIS, D., M. FABIANI, and E. DONCHIN, 1984. "P300" and memory: Individual differences in the Von Restorff effect. *Cogn. Psychol.* 16:177–216.

KERTESZ, A., and S. DOBROLOWSKI, 1981. Right-hemisphere deficits, lesion size and location. *J. Clin. Neurophysiol.* 3:283–299.

KIMBLE, D. P., M. H. BAGSHAW, and K. H. PRIBRAM, 1965. The GSR of monkeys during orienting and habituation after selective partial ablations of the cingulate and frontal cortex. *Neuropsychology* 3:121–128.

KIRINO, E., A. BELGER, J. C. GORE, P. S. GOLDMAN-RAKIC, and G. MCCARTHY, 1997. A comparison of prefrontal activation to infrequent visual targets and non-target novel stimuli: A functional MRI study. *Soc. Neurosci.* 23:493.

KITCHIGINA, V., A. VANKOV, C. HARLEY, and S. J. SARA, 1997. Novelty-elicited noradrenaline-dependent enhancement of excitability in the dentate gyrus. *Eur. J. Neurosci.* 9(1):41–47.

KNIGHT, R. T., 1984. Decreased response to novel stimuli after prefrontal lesions in man. *Electroencephalogr. Clin. Neurophysiol.* 59:9–20.

KNIGHT, R. T., 1991. Evoked potential studies of attention capacity in human frontal lobe lesions. In *Frontal Lobe Function and Dysfunction*, H. Levin, H. Eisenberg, and F. Benton, eds. London: Oxford University Press, pp. 139–153.

KNIGHT, R. T., 1994. Attention regulation and human prefrontal cortex. In *Motor and Cognitive Functions of the Prefrontal Cortex: Research and Perspectives in Neurosciences*, A. M. Thierry, J. Glowinski, P. Goldman-Rakic, and Y. Christen, eds. Paris: Springer-Verlag, pp. 160–173.

KNIGHT, R. T., 1996. Contribution of human hippocampal region to novelty detection. *Nature* 383:256–259.

KNIGHT, R. T., 1997a. Distributed cortical network for visual stimulus detection. *J. Cogn. Neurosci.* 9:75–91.

KNIGHT, R. T., 1997b. Electrophysiological methods in behavioral neurology and neuropsychology. In *Behavioral Neurology and Neuropsychology*, T. E. Feinberg and M. J. Farah, eds. New York: McGraw-Hill, pp. 101–119.

KNIGHT, R. T., and M. GRABOWECKY, 1995. Escape from linear time: Prefrontal cortex and conscious experience. In *The Cognitive Neurosciences*, M. Gazzaniga, ed. MIT Press, pp. 1357–1371.

KNIGHT, R. T., S. A. HILLYARD, D. L. WOODS, and H. J. NEVILLE, 1981. The effects of frontal cortex lesions on event-related potentials during auditory selective attention. *Electroencephalogr. Clin. Neurophysiol.* 52:571–582.

KNIGHT, R. T., and T. NAKADA, 1998. Cortico-limbic circuits and novelty: A review of the EEG and blood flow data. *Rev. Neurosci.* 9(1):57–70.

KNIGHT, R. T., and D. SCABINI, 1998. Anatomic bases of event-related potentials and their relationship to novelty detection in humans. *J. Clin. Neurophysiol.* 15(1):3–13.

KNIGHT, R. T., D. SCABINI, and D. L. WOODS, 1989a. Prefrontal cortex gating of auditory transmission in humans. *Brain Res.* 504:338–342.

KNIGHT, R. T., D. SCABINI, D. L. WOODS, and C. C. CLAYWORTH, 1989. Contribution of the temporal-parietal junction to the auditory P3. *Brain Res.* 502:109–116.

KNIGHT, R. T., W. R. STAINES, D. SWICK, and L. L. CHAO, 1998. Prefrontal cortex regulates inhibition and excitation in distributed neural networks. *Acta Psychologia* 101:159–178.

KRAUS, N., O. OZDAMAR, and L. STEIN, 1982. Auditory middle latency responses (MLRs) in patients with cortical lesions. *Electroencephalogr. Clin. Neurophysiol.* 54:275–287.

KROLL, N. E. A., R. T. KNIGHT, J. METCALFE, E. S. WOLF, and E. TULVING, 1996. Consolidation failure as a source of memory illusions. *J. Mem. Lang.* 35:176–196.

LHERMITTE, F., 1986. Human autonomy and the frontal lobes. Part II: Patient behavior in complex and social situations: The "environmental dependency syndrome." *Ann. Neurol.* 19:335–343.

LHERMITTE, F., B. PILLON, and M. SERDARU, 1986. Human anatomy and the frontal lobes. Part I: Imitation and utilization behavior: A neuropsychological study of 75 patients. *Ann. Neurol.* 19:326–334.

LUCIANA, M., and C. A. NELSON, 1998. The functional emergence of prefrontally-guided working memory systems in four- to eight-year-old children. *Neuropsychologia* 36(3):273–293.

LURIA, A. R., 1966/1980. *Higher Cortical Functions in Man*. New York: Basic Books.

LURIA, A. R., and E. D. HOMSKAYA, 1970. Frontal lobes and the regulation of arousal process. In *Attention: Contemporary Theory and Analysis*, D. I. Mostofsky, ed. New York: Appleton-Century-Crofts, pp. 303–330.

MACKAY, W. A., and D. J. CRAMMOND, 1989. Cortical modification of sensorimotor linkages in relation to intended action. In *Volitional Action*, W. A. Hershberger, ed. New York: Elsevier, pp. 169–193.

MALMO, R. R., 1942. Interference factors in delayed response in monkeys after removal of frontal lobes. *J. Neurophysiol.* 5:295–308.

MANGUN, G. R., 1995. Neural mechanisms of visual selective attention. *Psychophysiology* 32:4–18.

MANGUN, G. R., and S. A. HILLYARD, 1988. Spatial gradients of visual attention: Behavioral and electrophysiological evidence. *Electroencephalogr. Clin. Neurophysiol.* 70:417–428.

MARKHAM, R., 1991. Development of reality monitoring for performed and imagined actions. *Percept. Motor Skills* 72(3):1347–1354.

MAYES, A. R., 1988. *Human Organic Memory Disorders*. New York: Cambridge University Press.

MCANDREWS, M. P., and B. MILNER, 1991. The frontal cortex and memory for temporal order. *Neuropsychologia* 29(9):849–859.

MCCALLUM, W. C., S. H. CURRY, R. COOPER, P. V. POCOCK, and D. PAPAKOSTOPOULOS, 1983. Brain event-related potentials as indicators of early selective processes in auditory target localization. *Psychophysiology* 20:1–17.

MCCARTHY, G., M. LUBY, J. GORE, and P. S. GOLDMAN-RAKIC, 1997. Infrequent events transiently activate human prefrontal and parietal cortex as measured by functional MRI. *J. Neurophysiol.* 77:1630–1634.

MCCARTHY, G., C. C. WOOD, P. D. WILLIAMSON, and D. D. SPENCER, 1989. Task-dependent field potentials in human hippocampal formation. *J. Neurosci.* 9:4253–4260.

MCGHIE, A., and J. CHAPMAN, 1961. Disorders of attention and perception in early schizophrenia. *Brit. J. Med. Psychol.* 34:103–116.

MCINTOSH, A. R., C. L. GRADY, L. G. UNGERLEIDER, J. W. HAXBY, S. I. RAPOPORT, and B. HORWITZ, 1994. Network analysis of cortical visual pathways mapped with PET. *J. Neurosci.* 14:655–666.

MEDVEC, V. H., S. F. MADEY, and T. GILOVICH, 1995. When less is more: Counterfactual thinking and satisfaction among Olympic medalists. *J. Personality Soc. Psychol.* 69(4):603–610.

MENON, K., J. M. FORD, K. O. LIM, G. H. GLOVER, and A. PFEFFERBAUM, 1997. A combined event-related fMRI and EEG evidence for temporal-parietal activation during target detection. *Neuroreport* 8:3029–3037.

MESULAM, M. M., 1981. A cortical network for directed attention and unilateral neglect. *Ann. Neurol.* 10:309–325.

METCALFE, J., 1993. Novelty monitoring, metacognition, and control in a composite holographic associative recall model: implications for Korsakoff amnesia. *Psychol. Rev.* 100:3–22.

MILLER, E. K., L. LI, and R. DESIMONE, 1991. A neural mechanism for working and recognition memory in inferior temporal cortex. *Science* 254:1377–1379.

MILNER, B., 1971. Interhemispheric differences in the localization of psychological processes in man. *Brit. Med. Bull.* 27:272–277.

MILNER, B., 1982. Some cognitive effects of frontal lesions in man. *Phil. Trans. R. Soc. Lond.* 298:211–226.

MILNER, B., and M. PETRIDES, 1984. Behavioural effects of frontal-lobe lesions in man. *Trends Neurosci.* 7:403–407.

MILNER, B., M. PETRIDES, and M. L. SMITH, 1985. Frontal lobes and the temporal organization of memory. *Hum. Neurobiol.* 4:137–142.

MOSCOVICH, M., 1989. Confabulation and the frontal systems: Strategic versus associative retrieval in neuropsychological theories of memory. In *Varieties of Memory and Consciousness: Essays in Honour of Endel Tulving*, H. L. Roediger III and F. I. M. Craik, eds. Hillsdale, N.J.: Lawrence Erlbaum, pp. 133–160.

NAUTA, W. J. H., 1971. The problem of the frontal lobe: A reinterpretation. *J. Psychiatry Res.* 8:167–187.

NEVILLE, H. J., and S. L. FOOTE, 1984. Auditory event-related potentials in the squirrel monkey: Parallels to human late wave responses. *Brain Res.* 298:107–116.

O'CONNOR, T., and A. STARR, 1985. Intracranial potentials correlated with an event-related potential, P300, in the cat. *Science* 339:27–28.

ORZHEKHOVSKAYA, N. S., 1981. Fronto-striatal relationships in primate ontogeny. *Neurosci. Behav. Physiol.* 11:379–385.

OWEN, A. M., A. C. EVANS, and M. PETRIDES, 1996. Evidence for a two-staged model of spatial working memory processing within the lateral frontal cortex. *Cereb. Cortex* 6:31–38.

PALLER, K. A., G. MCCARTHY, E. ROESSLER, T. ALLISON, and C. C. WOOD, 1992. Potentials evoked in human and monkey medial temporal lobe during auditory and visual oddball paradigms. *Electroencephalogr. Clin. Neurophysiol.* 84:269–279.

PALLER, K. A., S. ZOLA-MORGAN, L. R. SQUIRE, and S. A. HILLYARD, 1988. P3-like brain wave in normal monkeys and in monkeys with medial temporal lesions. *Behav. Neurosci.* 102:714–725.

PANTELIS, C., T. R. E. BARNES, H. E. NELSON, S. TANNER, A. M. WEATHERLEY, A. M. OWEN, and T. W. ROBBINS, 1997. Frontal-striatal cognitive deficits in patients with chronic schizophrenia. *Brain* 120:1823–1843.

PERANI, D., S. BRESSI, S. F. CAPPA, G. VALLAR, M. ALBERONI, F. GRASSI, C. CALTAGIRONE, L. CIPOLOTTI, M. FRANCESCHI, G. L. LENZI, and F. FAZIO, 1993. Evidence of multiple memory systems in the human brain: A ^{18}F FDG PET metabolic study. *Brain* 116:903–919.

PETRIDES, M., B. ALIVASATOS, E. MEYER, and A. C. EVANS, 1993a. Dissociation of human mid-dorsolateral from posterior dorsolateral frontal cortex in memory processing. *Proc. Natl. Acad. Sci. U.S.A.* 90:873–877.

PETRIDES, M., B. ALIVISATOS, E. MEYER, and A. C. EVANS, 1993b. Functional activation of the human prefrontal cortex during the performance of verbal working memory tasks. *Proc. Natl. Acad. Sci. U.S.A.* 90:878–882.

PETRIDES, M., and B. MILNER, 1982. Deficits on subject-ordered tasks after frontal- and temporal-lobe lesions in man. *Neuropsychologia* 20:249–262.

PICTON, T. W., 1995. The P300 wave of the human event-related potential. *J. Clin. Neurophysiol.* 9(4):456–479.

PINEDA, J. A., S. L. FOOTE, and H. J. NEVILLE, 1989. Effects of locus coeruleus lesions on auditory, long-latency, event-related potentials in monkeys. *J. Neurosci.* 9:81–93.

RAJKOWSKA, G., and P. S. GOLDMAN-RAKIC, 1995a. Cytoarchitechtonic definition of prefrontal areas in the normal human cortex: I. Remapping of areas 9 and 46 using quantitative criteria. *Cereb. Cortex* 5:307–322.

RAJKOWSKA, G., and P. S. GOLDMAN-RAKIC, 1995b. Cytoarchitechtonic definition of prefrontal areas in the normal human cortex: II. Variability in locations of areas 9 and 46 and relationship to the Talairach coordinate system. *Cereb. Cortex* 5:323–337.

RICHER, F., A. DECARY, M. F. LAPIERRE, I. ROULEAU, G. BOUVIER, and J. M. SAINT-HILAIRE, 1993. Target detection deficits in frontal lobectomy. *Brain Cognit.* 21:203–211.

RIGGS, K. J., D. M. PETERSON, E. J. ROBINSON, and P. MITCHELL, 1998. Are errors in false belief tasks symptomatic of a broader difficulty with counterfactuality? *Cogn. Dev.* 13(1): 73–90.

ROLAND, P. E., 1982. Cortical regulation of selective attention in man. A regional cerebral blood flow study. *J. Neurophysiol.* 48:1059–1078.

RUCHKIN, D. S., R. JOHNSON, JR., J. GRAFMAN, H. CANOUNE, and W. RITTER, 1992. Distinctions and similarities among working memory processes: An event-related potential study. *Cogn. Brain Res.* 1:53–66.

SCABINI, D., and G. MCCARTHY, 1993. Hippocampal responses to novel somatosensory stimuli. *Soc. Neurosci. [Abstr.]* 19:564.

SCHACTER, D. L., T. CURRAN, L. GALLUCCIO, W. P. MILBERG, and J. F. BATES, 1996. False recognition and the right frontal lobe: A case study. *Neuropsychologia* 34(8):793–808.

SCHACTER, D. L., J. L. HARBLUK, and D. R. MCLACHLAN, 1984. Retrieval without recollection: An experimental analysis of source amnesia. *J. Verbal Learn. Verbal Behav.* 23:593–611.

SCHACTER, D. L., J. KAGAN, and M. D. LEICHTMAN, 1995. True and false memories in children and adults: A cognitive neuroscience approach. *Psychol. Public Policy Law.* 1(2):411–428.

SHALLICE, T., 1988. *From Neuropsychology to Mental Structure.* Cambridge: Cambridge University Press.

SHALLICE, T., and M. E. EVANS, 1978. The involvement of the frontal lobes in cognitive estimation. *Cortex* 14:294–303.

SHALLICE, T., P. FLETCHER, C. D. FRITH, P. GRASBY, R. S. FRACKOWIAK, and R. J. DOLAN, 1994. Brain regions associated with acquisition and retrieval of verbal episodic memory. *Nature* 368:633–635.

SHIMAMURA, A. P., 1995. Memory and the frontal lobe. In *The Cognitive Neurosciences*, M. Gazzaniga, ed. Cambridge, Mass.: MIT Press, pp. 803–813.

SHIMAMURA, A. P., F. B. GERSHBERG, P. J. JURICA, J. A. MANGELS, and R. T. KNIGHT, 1992. Intact implicit memory in patients with focal frontal lobe lesions. *Neuropsychol.* 30(10): 931–937.

SHIMAMURA, A. P., J. S. JANOWSKY, and L. R. SQUIRE, 1990. Memory for the temporal order of events in patients with frontal lobe lesions and amnesic patients. *Neuropsychologia* 28:803–813.

SHIMAMURA, A. P., P. J. JURICA, J. A. MANGELS, F. B. GERSHBERG, and R. T. KNIGHT, 1995. Susceptibility to memory interference effects following frontal lobe damage: Findings from tests of paired-associate learning. *J. Cogn. Neurosci.* 7:144–152.

SHIMAMURA, A. P., and L. R. SQUIRE, 1987. A neuropsychological study of fact memory and source amnesia. *J. Exp. Psychol.: Learn. Mem. Cognit.* 13:464–473.

SIRIGU, A., T. ZALLA, B. PILLON, J. GRAFMAN, Y. AGID, and B. DUBOIS, 1995. Selective impairments in managerial knowledge following pre-frontal cortex damage. *Cortex* 31:301–316.

SKINNER, J. E., and C. D. YINGLING, 1977. Central gating mechanisms that regulate event-related potentials and behavior. In *Progress in Clinical Neurophysiology*, Vol. 1, J. E. Desmedt, ed. Basel: S. Karger, pp. 30–69.

SMITH, M. E., E. HALGREN, M. E. SOKOLIK, P. BAUDENA, C. LIEGEOIS-CHAUVEL, A. MUSOLINO, and P. CHAUVEL, 1990. The intra-cranial topography of the P3 event-related potential elicited during auditory oddball. *Electroencephalogr. Clin. Neurophysiol.* 76:235–248.

SMITH, M. L., and B. MILNER, 1984. Differential effects of frontal lobe lesions on cognitive estimation and spatial memory. *Neuropsychologia* 22:697–705.

SOKOLOV, E. N., 1963. Higher nervous functions: The orienting reflex. *Ann. Rev. Physiol.* 25:545–580.

SQUIRES, N., K. SQUIRES, and S. A. HILLYARD, 1975. Two varieties of long-latency positive waves evoked by unpredictable auditory stimuli in man. *Electroencephalogr. Clin. Neurophysiol.* 38:387–401.

STERN, C. E., S. CORKIN, R. G. GONZALEZ, A. R. GUIMARES, J. R. BAKER, P. J. JENNINGS, C. A. CARR, R. M. SUGIURA, V. VEDANTHAM, and B. R. ROSENE, 1996. The hippocampal formation participates in novel picture encoding: Evidence from functional magnetic resonance imaging. *Proc. Natl. Acad. Sci. U.S.A.* 93:8660–8665.

STUSS, D. T., 1991. Self, awareness, and the frontal lobes: A neuropsychological perspective. In *The Self: Interdisciplinary Approaches*, J. Strauss and G. R. Goethals, eds. New York: Springer-Verlag, pp. 255–278.

STUSS, D. T., 1992. Biological and psychological development of executive functions. *Brain Cognit.* 20:8–23.

STUSS, D. T., and F. BENSON, 1984. Neuropsychological studies of the frontal lobes. *Psychol. Bull.* 95:3–28.

STUSS, D. T., and D. F. BENSON, 1986. *The Frontal Lobes.* New York: Raven Press.

SUDDENDORF, T., and C. M. FLETCHER-FLINN, 1997. Theory of mind and the origin of divergent thinking. *J. Creative Behav.* 31(3):169–179.

SUTHERLING, W. W., P. H. CRANDALL, T. M. DARCEY, D. P. BECKER, M. F. LEVESQUE, and D. S. BARTH, 1988. The magnetic and electric fields agree with intracranial localizations of somatosensory cortex. *Neurol.* 38:1705–1714.

SUTTON, S., M. BAREN, J. ZUBIN, and E. R. JOHN, 1965. Evoked potentials correlates of stimulus uncertainty. *Science* 150:1187–1188.

SUZUKI, W., and D. AMARAL, 1994. Perirhinal and parahippocampal cortices of the macaque monkey: Cortical afferents. *J. Comp. Neurol.* 350:497–533.

SWICK, D., 1998. Effects of prefrontal lesions on lexical processing and repetition priming: An ERP study. *Cogn. Brain Res.* 7(2):143–157.

SWICK, D., and R. T. KNIGHT, 1998. Lesion studies of prefrontal cortex and attention. In *The Attentive Brain*, R. Parasuraman, ed. Cambridge, Mass.: Bradford Books, MIT Press, pp. 143–162.

SWICK, D., and R. T. KNIGHT, 1999. Contributions of prefrontal cortex to recognition memory: Electrophysiological and behavioral evidence. *Neuropsychology* 13(2):155–170.

SWICK, D., M. KUTAS, and H. J. NEVILLE, 1994. Localizing the neural generators of event-related brain potentials. In *Localization in Neuroimaging in Neuropsychology*, A. Kertesz, ed. New York: Academic Press, pp. 73–121.

THATCHER, R.W., 1992. Cyclic cortical reorganization during early childhood. *Brain Cognit.* 20:24–50.

THINUS-BLANC, C., E. SAVE, C. ROSSI-ARNAUD, A. TOZZI, and M. AMMASSARI-TEULE, 1996. The differences shown by C57BL/6 and DBA/2 inbred mice in detecting spatial novelty are subserved by a different hippocampal and parietal cortex interplay. *Behav. Brain Res.* 80(1–2):33–40.

TREISMAN, A. M., 1960. Contextual cues in selective listening. *Quart. J. Exp. Psychol.* 12:242–248.

TREVES, A., and E. T. ROLLS, 1994. Computational analysis of the role of the hippocampus in memory. *Hippocampus* 4(3):374–391.

TULVING, E., H. J. MARKOWITSCH, F. E. CRAIK, R. HABIB, and S. HOULE, 1996. Novelty and familiarity activations in PET studies of memory encoding and retrieval. *Cereb. Cortex* 6(1):71–79.

TULVING, E., and D. L. SCHACTER, 1990. Priming and human memory systems. *Science* 247:301–306.

TURETSKY, B. L., D. ALSOP, and R. E. GUR, 1997. Functional magnetic imaging of the sources of the auditory P300. American College of Neuropsychopharmacology.

TVERSKY, A., and D. KAHNEMAN, 1973. Availability: A heuristic for judging frequency and probability. *Cogn. Psychol.* 5:207–232.

TVERSKY, A., and D. KAHNEMAN, 1983. Extensional versus intuitive reasoning: The conjunction fallacy in probability judgement. *Psychol. Rev.* 90(4):293–315.

UCHIMURA, J., 1928. Uber die gefassversorgung des Ammonshornes. *Z. Gesamte Neurol. Psychiatr.* 112:1–19.

VENABLES, P., 1964. Input dysfunction in schizophrenia. In *Progress in Experimental Personality Research*, B. A. Maher, ed. New York: Academic Press, pp. 1–47.

VENDRELL, P., C. JUNQUE, J. PUJOL, M. A. JURADO, J. MOLET, and J. GRAFMAN, 1995. The role of prefrontal regions in the Stroop task. *Neuropsychologia* 33:341–352.

VERLEGER, R., 1988. Event-related potentials and cognition: A critique of the context updating hypothesis and an alternative interpretation of P3. *Behav. Brain Sci.* 11:343–356.

VINOGRADOVA, O. S., 1975. Registration of information and the limbic system. In *Short-Term Changes in Neural Activity and Behavior*, G. Horn and R. A. Hinde, eds. Cambridge: Cambridge University Press, pp. 95–148.

VON CRAMON, D. Y., N. HEBEL, and U. SCHURI, 1988. Verbal memory and learning in unilateral posterior cerebral infarction: A report on 30 cases. *Brain* 111:1061–1077.

VON RESTORFF, H., 1933. Uber die Wirkung von Bereischsbildungen im spurenfeld. *Psychol. Forschung* 18:299–342.

WADA, J. A., R. CLARKE, and A. HAMM, 1975. Cerebral hemispheric asymmetry in humans. *Arch. Neurol.* 32:239–246.

WEBSTER, M. J., J. BACHEVALIER, and L. G. UNGERLEIDER, 1994. Connections of inferior temporal areas TEO and TE with parietal and frontal cortex in macaque monkeys. *Cereb. Cortex* 5:470–483.

WEINBERGER, D. R., K. F. BERMAN, and R. F. ZEC, 1986. Physiological dysfunction of dorsolateral prefrontal cortex in schizophrenia, I: Regional cerebral blood flow evidence. *Arch. Gen. Psychiatry* 43:114–124.

WEINBERGER, D. R., K. F. BERMAN, R. SUDDATH, and E. F. TORREY, 1992. Evidence of dysfunction of a prefrontal-limbic network in schizophrenia: A magnetic resonance imaging and regional blood flow study of discordant monozygotic twins. *Amer. J. Psychiatry* 149:890–897.

WEINBERGER, D. R., D. J. LUCHINS, J. MORISHA, and R. J. WYATT, 1982. Asymmetric volumes of the right and the left frontal and occipital regions of the human brain. *Ann. Neurol.* 11:97–100.

WILDER, M. B., G. R. FARLEY, and A. STARR, 1981. Endogenous late positive component of the evoked potential in cats corresponding to P300 in humans. *Science* 211:605–607.

WOLDORFF, M. G., and S. A. HILLYARD, 1991. Modulation of early auditory processing during selective listening to rapidly presented tones. *Electroencephalogr. Clin. Neurophysiol.* 79:170–191.

WOODS, D. L., 1990. The physiological basis of selective attention: Implications of event-related potential studies. In *Event-Related Brain Potentials*, J. Rohrbaugh, Jr., R. Johnson, and R. Parasurman, eds. New York: Oxford University Press, pp. 178–210.

WOODS, D. L., and R. T. KNIGHT, 1986. Electrophysiological evidence of increased distractibility after dorsolateral prefrontal lesions. *Neurol.* 36:212–216.

WOODS, D. L., R. T. KNIGHT, and D. SCABINI, 1993. Anatomical substrates of auditory selective attention: Behavioral and electrophysiological effects of temporal and parietal lesions. *Cogn. Brain Res.* 1:227–240.

WOODS, D. L., S. H. RIDGWAY, D. G. CARDER, and T. H. BULLOCK, 1986. Middle and long-latency auditory event-related potentials in the dolphin. In *Dolphin Cognition and Behavior: A Comparative Perspective*, R. Buhr, R. Schusterman, J. Thomas, and F. Wood, eds. New York: Lawrence Erlbaum Associates, pp. 61–78.

YAKOLEV, P. I., 1962. Morphological criteria of growth and maturation of the nervous system in man. *Res. Publ.: Res. Nervous Mental Disease* 39:3–46.

YAMAGUCHI, S., H. GLOBUS, and R. T. KNIGHT, 1993. P3-like potentials in rats. *Electroencephalogr. Clin. Neurophysiol.* 88:151–154.

YAMAGUCHI, S., and R. T. KNIGHT, 1990. Gating of somatosensory inputs by human prefrontal cortex. *Brain Res.* 521:281–288.

YAMAGUCHI, S., and R. T. KNIGHT, 1991a. P300 generation by novel somatosensory stimuli. *Electroencephalogr. Clin. Neurophysiol.* 78:50–55.

YAMAGUCHI, S., and R. T. KNIGHT, 1991b. Anterior and posterior association cortex contributions to the somatosensory P300. *J. Neurosci.* 11(7):2039–2054.

YAMAGUCHI, S., and R. T. KNIGHT, 1992. Effects of temporal-parietal lesions on the somatosensory P3 to lower limb stimulation. *Electroencephalogr. Clin. Neurophysiol.* 84:139–148.

YINGLING, C. D., and J. E. SKINNER, 1977. Gating of thalamic input to cerebral cortex by nucleus reticularis thalami. In *Progress in Clinical Neurophysiology*, Vol. I, J. E. Desmedt, ed. Basel: S. Karger, pp. 70–96.

YONELINAS, A. P., N. E. A. KROLL, I. G. DOBBINS, M. LAZZARA, and R. T. KNIGHT, 1998. Recollection and familiarity deficits in amnesia: Convergence of remember/know, process dissociation and ROC data. *Neuropsychology* 12(3):323–339.

93 Consciousness: Its Vicissitudes in Waking and Sleep

J. ALLAN HOBSON, EDWARD F. PACE-SCHOTT, AND ROBERT STICKGOLD

ABSTRACT Phenomenological, electrophysiological, and neuroimaging data show isomorphic differences between waking, non-REM (NREM), and REM consciousness states. Phenomenological data suggest that NREM sleep mentation is characterized by quantitative paucity and qualitative impoverishment in comparison to waking and REM sleep mentation. In comparison to waking mentation, REM sleep dreaming is characterized by motor and affective enhancement together with prominent executive deficits such as disorientation and amnesia. Electrophysiological data suggest that deepening NREM is characterized by the release of intrinsic thalamocortical rhythms such as spindle and delta waves as well as the onset of slower ($<$1 Hz) rhythms. By contrast, gamma-frequency (30–70 Hz) oscillations are ubiquitous in waking and REM sleep. Neuroimaging data indicate widespread deactivation of ascending arousal systems, subcortex, and cortex, with the transition from waking to NREM followed by preferential reactivation, in REM sleep, of the brainstem, diencephalic structures, striatum, limbic and paralimbic structures, and specific areas of association cortex but continuing deactivation of executive prefrontal structures and striate cortex. Dream changes in brain lesion patients largely complement neuroimaging findings, allowing construction of a preliminary integrated neuroanatomical model of brain regions involved in dreaming.

Few doubt that consciousness is a brain function. And there is now a great resurgence of interest in exactly how that function can be explained in terms of specific brain mechanisms. In this chapter, we review recent data on sleep and dreaming and attempt to integrate them with our previously published conceptualizations of the state-dependent aspects of consciousness. We begin with a brief review of recent findings on the phenomenology, electrophysiology, and neuroimaging of non-REM (NREM) sleep, but devote the bulk of our discussion to recent electrophysiological and neuroimaging studies of REM sleep and their integration with dream phenomenology and recent findings in dream neuropsychology. We conclude with an integrative model of the neuronal bases of REM sleep dreaming and a discussion of the biological bases for the cognitive differentiation between waking, NREM sleep, and REM sleep.

J. ALLAN HOBSON, EDWARD F. PACE-SCHOTT, and ROBERT STICKGOLD Laboratory of Neurophysiology, Department of Psychiatry, Harvard Medical School, Boston, Mass.

NREM sleep and the decline in level of consciousness

Neuroimaging (table 93.1) and electrophysiological studies strongly support a distinction between REM and NREM sleep as states whose differing activation patterns predict their observed psychological differences. The emerging picture is one of widespread cerebral deactivation during NREM, as compared to both waking and REM. Figure 93.1 illustrates this cycle of activation and deactivation in terms of its well-known behavioral and polysomnographic signs.

PHENOMENOLOGY OF NREM SLEEP MENTATION Substantial recall of mentation from NREM sleep negates an exclusive association of sleep mentation with REM (e.g., Cavallero et al., 1992; Foulkes, 1967; Herman, Ellman, and Roffwarg, 1978). Nevertheless, early dream studies found that REM reports were more frequent (e.g., Goodenough et al., 1965), longer (e.g., Antrobus, 1983), more bizarre (e.g., Ogilvie et al., 1982), more visual (e.g., Goodenough et al., 1965), more often containing movement (e.g., Foulkes, 1962), and more emotional (e.g., Rechtschaffen, Verdone, and Wheaton, 1963) than NREM reports. New findings confirm a quantitative and qualitative distinction between REM and NREM sleep mentation even when reports are normalized for length (Casagrande et al., 1996; Waterman Elton, and Kenemans, 1993).

PET IMAGING STUDIES OF NREM SLEEP (SEE TABLE 93.1) Relative to waking and REM, positron emission tomography (PET) studies of NREM sleep show a decrease in global cerebral energy metabolism (e.g., Maquet et al., 1997), global cerebral blood flow (e.g., Braun et al., 1997), and blood flow velocity (e.g., Kuboyama et al., 1997) of which at least energy metabolism decreases progressively with greater depth of NREM sleep (Maquet, 1995). In contrast, global cerebral energy metabolism in REM tends to be equal to (e.g., Braun et al., 1997) or greater than (e.g., Buchsbaum et al., 1989) that of waking. Regional declines in thalamic glucose or oxygen utilization relative to waking occur in NREM (Buchsbaum et al.,

TABLE 93.1

Subcortical and cortical regional brain activation and deactivation revealed by recent PET studies comparing REM sleep with waking and with NREM sleep and NREM sleep with waking

Sleep Stage	REM	REM	REM	REM	NREM (3 & 4)	NREM (delta)	NREM (3 & 4)
Study	Maquet et al., 1996	Nofzinger et al., 1996	Braun et al., 1997	Braun et al., 1997	Maquet et al., 1997	Hofle et al., 1997	Braun et al., 1997
Technique	$H_2{}^{15}O$	^{18}FDG	$H_2{}^{15}O$	$H_2{}^{15}O$	$H_2{}^{15}O$	$H_2{}^{15}O$	$H_2{}^{15}O$
Relative to	all other stages	waking	pre- (& post*)-sleep waking	NREM 3 & 4	all other stages	change with increase in delta	pre- or post-sleep waking
Subcortical Areas							
Brainstem							
Pontine tegmentum	increase		increase: (R*)	increase	decrease	decrease: R	decrease
Midbrain			increase*	increase			decrease
Dorsal mesencephalon	increase				decrease		
Diencephalon							
Thalamus	increase: L			increase	decrease	decrease: M	decrease
Hypothalamus		increase: R Lat.	increase: A-POA	increase: A-POA	decrease		decrease: A-POA
Basal forebrain					decrease		
Limbic system							
Left amygdala	increase	increase					
Right amygdala	increase						
Septal nuclei		increase					
Hippocampus			increase*	increase			
Basal ganglia/ striatum							
Caudate		increase: A, I, L	increase*	increase	decrease		decrease
Putamen				increase			decrease: P
Ventral striatum (n. accumbens, sub. innominata)		increase		increase			decrease
Lenticular nuclei					decrease		
Cerebellum			increase (vermis)*	increase (vermis)		decrease	decrease: I
Cortical Areas							
Frontal		decrease: L sm. areas increase: R					
Dorsolateral prefrontal	decrease: L: 10, 11, 46, 47 R: 8, 9, 10, 11, 46	increase	decrease: 46*				decrease: 46
Opercular			decrease: 45*				decrease: 45
Paraolfactory		increase					
Lateral orbital		increase: 11, 12	decrease: 11*		decrease: 11, 25	decrease: R 11	decrease: 11

TABLE 93.1 *Continued*

Sleep Stage	REM	REM	REM	REM	NREM (3 & 4)	NREM (delta)	NREM (3 & 4)
Study	Maquet et al., 1996	Nofzinger et al., 1996	Braun et al., 1997	Braun et al., 1997	Maquet et al., 1997	Hofle et al., 1997	Braun et al., 1997
Medial orbital							decrease: R
Caudal orbital			increase	increase			decrease
Gyrus rectus		increase					
Parietal							
Brodmann's area 40 (supramarginal gyrus)	increase: R A 40 decrease: L 40		decrease: 40*			increase: L 40	decrease: 40
Angular gyrus			decrease: 39*				decrease: 39
Precuneus	decrease				decrease: 7		
Cuneus					decrease: 19		
Pericentral						increase: L 3/4	
Temporal							
Mesiotemporal					decrease: R 28		
Middle		increase R				increase: A R & L 21	
Posterior superior					increase: 22	increase: L 22	
Inferior/fusiform			increase: 37, 19 (post-sleep only)	increase: 37, 19			
Occipital		decrease: sm. areas					
Medial						increase: R 17/18 increase: L 17	
Post-rolandic sensory			increase				
Limbic associated							
Medial (prelimbic) prefrontal		increase: R 32	increase: 10	increase: 10			decrease: 10
Anterior cingulate	increase: 24	increase: 24	increase: 32*	increase: 32	decrease: 24, 32	decrease: 24/32	decrease: 32
Posterior cingulate	decrease: 31	decrease: R sm. areas	decrease*				
Infralimbic		increase: 25					
Insula		increase: L	decrease: P	increase: A/I			decrease: A
Parahippocampal		increase	increase: 37*	increase: 37			
Entorhinal	increase	increase (in fusiform)					
Temporal pole				increase: 38			decrease: 38

*Change reported in post- as well as pre-sleep waking.

Abbreviations: PET, positron emission tomography; ^{18}FDG, ^{18}F-fluorodeoxyglucose; L, left hemisphere; R, right hemisphere; A, anterior; P, posterior; C, caudal; M, medial; Lat., lateral; I, inferior; S, superior; A/I, anteroinferior; A-POA, anterior preoptic area; sm., small; all numerals = Brodmann's area

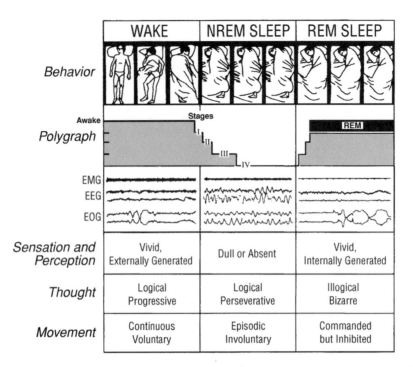

	WAKE	NREM SLEEP	REM SLEEP
Behavior			
Polygraph			
EMG			
EEG			
EOG			
Sensation and Perception	Vivid, Externally Generated	Dull or Absent	Vivid, Internally Generated
Thought	Logical Progressive	Logical Perseverative	Illogical Bizarre
Movement	Continuous Voluntary	Episodic Involuntary	Commanded but Inhibited

FIGURE 93.1   Behavioral states in humans. States of waking, NREM sleep, and REM sleep have behavioral, polygraphic, and psychological manifestations. In the behavior channel, posture shifts (detectable by time-lapse photography or video) can occur during waking and in concert with phase changes of the sleep cycle. Two different mechanisms account for sleep immobility: disfacilitation (during stages I–IV of NREM sleep) and inhibition (during REM sleep). In dreams, we imagine that we move but we do not. The sequence of these stages is represented in the polygraph channel. Sample tracings of three variables used to distinguish state are also shown: Electromyelogram (EMG), which is highest in waking, intermediate in NREM sleep, and lowest in REM sleep; and electroencephalogram (EEG) and electrooculogram (EOG), which are both activated in waking and REM sleep and inactivated in NREM sleep. Each sample record is 20 s. Three lower channels describe other subjective and objective state variables. (From Hobson and Steriade, 1986.)

1989; Maquet et al., 1990, 1992, 1997; Braun et al., 1997; Hofle et al., 1997), and this decline is correlated with increased delta EEG activity (Hofle et al., 1997). Regional deactivation during NREM is also seen in the pontine brain stem, orbitofrontal cortex, and anterior cingulate cortex (Braun et al., 1997; Hofle et al., 1997; Maquet et al., 1997).

NREM SLEEP AND SLOW EEG OSCILLATIONS   The decline in cerebral activation during NREM sleep probably reflects the progressive deactivation of the reticular activating system (RAS) which accompanies deepening NREM sleep and results in disfacilitation of thalamocortical relay neurons (Hofle et al., 1997; Maquet et al., 1997). This disfacilitation, in turn, allows the emergence of underlying thalamocortical oscillatory rhythms (Steriade, Contreras, and Amzica, 1994; Steriade, McCormick, and Sejnowski, 1993) such as spindle (12–14 Hz) and delta (1–4 Hz) frequency oscillations (Steriade et al., 1993; Steriade, Nunez, and Amzica, 1993a,b). The cortex may further entrain the spindle and delta-wave–generating thalamocortical bursts, as well as the K-complex, within a newly described slow (<1 Hz) oscillation seen in the cat

(Amzica and Steriade, 1998; Steriade, Nunez, and Amzica, 1993b; Contreras and Steriade, 1997; Marino, Martinez, and Canedo, 1996; Steriade, 1997). In humans, such slow oscillations include a novel 0.7 to 0.8 Hz rhythm as well as a periodicity in the grouping of spindle and delta-wave activity (Achermann and Borbely, 1997). In this deactivated state, intrinsic thalamocortical slow oscillations may be incompatible with the integrative demands of conscious experience that appear to be dependent upon much higher frequency synchronizing processes.

REM sleep and dreaming

If the cerebral machinery supporting consciousness is turned down in NREM sleep, how is it turned back up again in REM sleep so that dreaming is enhanced? And in what way does the REM sleep activation process differ from that of waking so as to account for heightened vividness and emotion and for the impaired critical thinking and memory of dreaming?

PHENOMENOLOGY OF REM SLEEP DREAMING   REM sleep dreams have several distinctive formal features

TABLE 93.2

The formal features of REM sleep dreaming *

Hallucinations: Especially visual and motoric hallucinations, but occasionally in any and all sensory modalities

Bizarreness: Incongruity (imagery is strange, unusual or impossible); discontinuity (imagery and plot can change, appear or disappear rapidly); uncertainty (persons, places, and events often bizarrely uncertain by waking standards)

Delusion: We are consistently duped into believing that we are awake (unless we cultivate lucidity)

Self-reflection: Absent or greatly reduced relative to waking

Lack of orientational stability: Persons, times, and places are fused, plastic, incongruous, and discontinuous

Narrative: Story lines explain and integrate all the dream elements in a confabulatory manner

Emotions: Increased, intensified, and dominated by fear/anxiety

Instinctual programs: Often incorporated–especially fight-or-flight

Volition: Volitional control greatly attenuated

Memory: Memory deficits across dream-wake, wake-dream, and dream-dream transitions

*Extensive references documenting each of the above features can be found in Hobson, Stickgold, and Pace-Schott (1998).

that the underlying brain state must somehow determine. These include sensorimotor hallucinations, bizarre imagery and events, the delusional belief that one is awake, diminished self-reflective awareness, orientational instability, narrative structure, intensification of emotion, instinctual behaviors, attenuated volition, and very poor memory. Table 93.2 summarizes these features (see Hobson, Pace-Schott, and Stickgold, 1998). Our discussion is based upon our psychophysiological theory of brain–mind isomorphism, as first specified in the activation-synthesis hypothesis of dreaming (Hobson and McCarley, 1977) and more recently elaborated in the AIM model of conscious state determination (Hobson 1997a; Hobson and Stickgold, 1995; Kahn, Pace-Schott, and Hobson, 1997).

We assume that any enhancement (or impairment) of any psychological function (e.g., dreaming) will be mirrored by enhancement (or impairment) of its physiological substrate's function (e.g., REM sleep). We have emphasized these formal aspects of dreaming because they are noted in all REM sleep dreams regardless of their specific narrative content. We expect that REM sleep neurobiology will be able to explain more about such generic formal features than it now can about specific dream content.

GAMMA-FREQUENCY (30–70 HZ) OSCILLATIONS IN WAKING AND REM   Studies on gamma-frequency oscillations reinforce the distinction between REM and NREM as well as the similarities between REM and waking that have been described in neurophysiological models of sleep-cycle control such as the reciprocal interaction hypothesis (figure 93.2). Such gamma-range oscillations have been widely interpreted to reflect cognitive processing both while awake or in REM during dreaming (Hari and Salmelin, 1997; Kahn, Pace-Schott,

and Hobson, 1997; Llinas and Ribary, 1993; Llinas et al., 1994; Steriade, 1996). Although gamma-frequency oscillations have recently been reported during slow-wave sleep in cats, these oscillations are strongly suppressed during the hyperpolarization phase of each slow wave (Steriade and Amzica, 1996; Steriade, Amzica, and Contreras, 1996).

In animal models, gamma-frequency oscillations become strongly synchronized following arousal, focused attention, or a salient external or internal stimulus (Amzica and Steriade, 1996; Gray and McCormick, 1996; Kreiter and Singer, 1996; Munk et al., 1996; Steriade and Amzica, 1996; Steriade et al., 1996). In extracellular recordings in the cat, PGO waves appear synchronously at multiple cortical sites and become increasingly synchronized over the course of a REM period (Amzica and Steriade, 1996). This finding highlights the important fact that endogenous, REM-related stimuli are effective in evoking the same synchronization of gamma oscillation as exogenous sensory stimuli (Amzica and Steriade, 1996).

In humans, EEG studies have shown gamma-frequency oscillations to be associated with visual stimuli (Lutzenberger et al., 1995; Muller et al., 1996; Tallon-Baudry et al., 1996) as well as with specific functions of working memory (Tallon-Baudry et al., 1997, 1998). Moreover, gamma-frequency oscillations have been observed to bear distinct relationships with hippocampal theta rhythms, suggesting an important role in learning and memory phenomena (Chrobak and Buzsaki, 1998).

With respect to the question of how the brain is reactivated in REM so that the off-line consciousness of dreaming is possible, the answer appears to be that the reticular neurons of the pontine tegmentum are activated, presumably via the same aminergic disinhibition found in cats. The pons activates the midbrain and, in turn, the

A. Structural Model

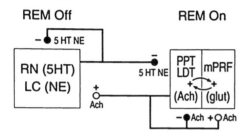

B. Dynamic Model

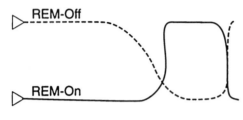

C. Activation Level

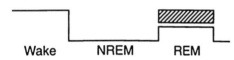

FIGURE 93.2 The reciprocal interaction model of physiological mechanisms determining alterations in activation level. (A) Structural model of reciprocal interaction with synaptic modifications of the original model (McCarley and Hobson, 1975) based upon recent findings of self-inhibitory cholinergic autoreceptors in mesopontine cholinergic nuclei and excitatory interactions between mesopontine cholinergic and noncholinergic neurons. In the original model, REM-on cells of the pontine reticular formation are cholinoceptively excited and/or cholinergically excitatory (ACH+) at their synaptic endings (open circles) while pontine REM-off cells are noradrenergically (NE) or serotonergically (5HT) inhibitory (–) at their synapses (filled circles). Note that the exponential magnification of cholinergic output predicted by the original model can also occur in this model, with mutually excitatory cholinergic–noncholinergic interactions taking the place of the previously postulated, mutually excitatory cholinergic–cholinergic interactions. In the revised model, inhibitory cholinergic autoreceptors would contribute to the inhibition of LDT and PPT cholinergic neurons, which is also caused by noradrenergic and serotonergic inputs to these nuclei. Therefore, the originally proposed shape of reciprocal interaction's dynamic model and its resultant alternation of behavioral state also result from this revised model. (See Hobson, Pace-Schott, and Stickgold, 1998, for more details and references.) (B) Dynamic model. During waking, the pontine aminergic (dashed line) system is tonically activated and inhibits the pontine cholinergic (solid line) system. During NREM sleep, aminergic inhibition gradually wanes and cholinergic excitation reciprocally waxes. At REM sleep onset, aminergic inhibition is shut off and cholinergic excitation reaches its high point. (C) Activation level. As a consequence of the interplay of the neuronal systems shown in A and B, the net activation level of the brain is at equally high levels in waking and REM sleep and at about half this peak level in NREM sleep. Symbols and abbreviations: Open circles, excitatory postsynaptic potentials; closed circles, inhibitory postsynaptic potentials; RN, dorsal raphe nucleus; LC, locus coeruleus; mPRF, medial pontine reticular formation; PPT, pedunculopontine tegmental nucleus; LDT, laterodorsal tegmental nucleus; 5HT, serotonin; NE, norepinephrine; Ach, acetylcholine; glut, glutamate.

thalamocortical system, such that its spontaneous slow oscillations are arrested and consciousness is reinstated. The cortical desynchronization seen in the surface EEG reflects this central core activation as does the high-frequency (30–70 Hz) gamma activity which, unlike slow oscillations, tends toward stimulus-evoked synchronization with greater activation (Munk et al., 1996; Steriade, 1996; Steriade and Amzica, 1996; Steriade, Amzica, and Contreras, 1996; Steriade et al., 1996). It is in these ways that the thalamocortical brain is similar in waking and REM sleep. Now, what about the differences?

PET IMAGING STUDIES OF REM SLEEP Recent PET imaging studies of REM sleep reveal many of the physiological differences underlying phenomenological differences between REM sleep dreaming and NREM and waking mentation. These findings, which are summarized in table 93.1, provide important new data for our understanding of dream synthesis by the forebrain, as summarized at the end of this section and in figure 93.4.

Compared to waking, the new imaging studies indicate a preferential activation of limbic and paralimbic regions of the forebrain in REM sleep (Braun et al., 1997; Maquet et al., 1996; Nofzinger et al., 1997) and, simultaneously, significant deactivation of the dorsolateral prefrontal cortex (Braun et al., 1997; Maquet et al., 1996). Two of these studies validate experimental animal data on the critical and specific role of the pontine brain stem

in REM sleep generation (Braun et al., 1997; Maquet et al., 1996). Moreover, instead of the global, regionally nonspecific picture of forebrain activation that had been suggested by older EEG studies, all of these new imaging studies indicate a preferential activation of limbic and paralimbic regions of the forebrain in REM sleep compared to waking or to NREM sleep (Braun et al., 1997; Maquet et al., 1996; Nofzinger et al., 1997).

Maquet and colleagues (1996) used an $H_2^{15}O$ positron source to compare REM sleep activation to other behavioral states in subjects who were subsequently awakened for the solicitation of dream reports. In addition to the pontine tegmentum, significant activation was seen in both amygdalae and in the anterior cingulate cortex (table 93.1). These authors also noted REM-associated deactivation of a vast area of the dorsolateral prefrontal cortex (table 93.1).

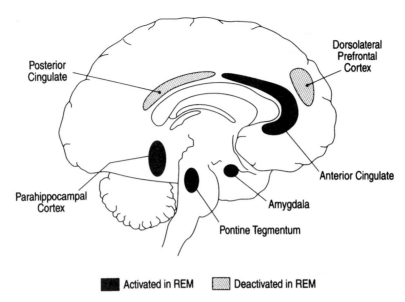

FIGURE 93.3   Convergent findings on relative regional brain activation and deactivation in REM compared to waking. A schematic sagittal view of the human brain shows those areas of relative activation and deactivation in REM sleep compared to waking and/or NREM sleep which were reported in two or more of three recent PET studies (Braun et al., 1997; Maquet et al., 1996; Nofzinger et al., 1997). Only those areas that could be easily matched between two or more studies are illustrated here and no realistic morphology of the depicted areas is implied. Note that considerably more extensive areas of activation and deactivation are reported in the individual studies; these more detailed findings are given in table 94.1. The areas depicted in this figure are thus most realistically viewed as representative portions of larger CNS areas subserving similar functions (e.g., limbic-related cortex, ascending activation pathways, and multimodal association cortex).

In another $H_2^{15}O$ PET study, Braun and colleagues (1997) replicated the Maquet group's findings of a consistent REM-related brainstem, limbic, and paralimbic activation. When REM sleep brain activity was compared to brain activity in delta NREM, pre-sleep waking, and post-sleep waking, the Braun group showed relative activation of the pons, the midbrain, the anterior hypothalamus, the hippocampus, the caudate, and the medial prefrontal, caudal orbital, anterior cingulate, parahippocampal, and inferior temporal cortices in REM sleep as compared to each of the above three conditions (table 93.1). These authors also noted a REM-associated decreased activation in dorsolateral prefrontal and parietal heteromodal association cortices (table 93.1). Braun and colleagues (1998) have recently expanded their findings to describe a unique pattern of striate cortex deactivation and extrastriate activation in REM sleep compared to waking as well as to NREM.

Using an ^{18}F-fluorodeoxyglucose (FDG) PET technique to compare REM sleep and waking, Nofzinger and colleagues (1997) confirmed the widespread limbic activation of the human brain in REM, showing increased glucose utilization in the lateral hypothalamic area, the amygdaloid complex, and a large "bilateral confluent paramedian zone which extends from the septal area into ventral striatum, infralimbic, prelimbic, orbitofrontal and anterior cingulate cortex" (p. 192). These authors, how-ever, did not observe the REM-associated decrease in dorsolateral prefrontal activation, a discrepancy possibly due to the poorer temporal resolution of ^{18}FDG compared to $H_2^{15}O$ techniques (Bootzin et al., 1998).

Figure 93.3 illustrates regions relatively activated and deactivated in two or more of these three recent PET studies (Braun et al., 1997; Maquet et al., 1996; Nofzinger et al., 1997).

Additional neuroimaging studies support the findings of the Braun, Maquet, and Nofzinger groups. For example, the anterior cingulate cortex has consistently shown increased activation in REM in other PET studies (Hong et al., 1995; Bootzin et al., 1998). In addition, FDG PET activation of anterior medial structures, including the anterior cingulate and medial frontal cortex, was found to correlate with REM density in the REM period during which FDG uptake occurred (Hong et al., 1995). Finally, REM-associated decreases in cerebral blood flow to frontal areas during REM have also been noted using single photon emission computed tomography (SPECT) (Madsen et al., 1991).

Lesion studies and the neuropsychology of dreaming

An important complement to recent neuroimaging findings is provided by the clinical neuropsychology of changes in the subjective experience of dreaming–and especially its formal properties—that are caused by localized brain lesions. Previous results of investigations using this method have provided tantalizing hypotheses of a critical disconnection in the left parieto-occipital region as the basis of cessation of dreaming following strokes (Doricchi and Violani, 1992; Greenberg and Farah, 1986), but these studies were limited by the small number of cases studied (e.g., Greenberg and Farah, 1986) or by the retrospective secondary nature of larger clinical series (Doricchi and Violani, 1992).

In a new study, Solms (1997) administered a 13-question dream interview to all patients referred to him over a four-year period to assess possible cerebral injury. Patients retrospectively compared pre- and post-illness dream features such as dream frequency, complexity, emotional valence, and visual imagery. Standard CT and MRI were used to localize lesions. Solms then statistically compared inventory responses with lesion locale. Based upon his findings and a review of 73 extant publications on the dreaming-related sequelae of cerebral injury, Solms proposes a new nosology for cerebral injury–related disorders of dreaming as well as a comprehensive model of the contributions and interactions of different brain regions in normal dreaming.

Solms has shown that two distinct syndromes comprise the classical Charcot-Wilbrand syndrome, which was previously defined as the cessation of dreaming, the inability to produce mental imagery in waking (visual irreminiscence), prosopagnosia, and topographical agnosia or amnesia. In one syndrome, "global anoneria," a global cessation of dreaming results from either posterior cortical or deep bilateral frontal lesions. In a second syndrome, "visual anoneria," bilateral medial occipitotemporal lesions produce full or partial loss of dream visual imagery. Among his own patients (which, importantly, included 29 controls found to lack any cerebral illness), Solms reports a strikingly different incidence of the two proposed symptom complexes, with only two patients (1.1%) showing attenuated visual dream imagery while 34.9% showed a global cessation of dreaming.

Solms's patients confirmed that either posterior cortical or deep medial frontal lesions produced global anoneria. The posterior global anoneria syndrome resulted from lesions of the inferior parietal lobes in either hemisphere, with lesions to Brodmann's areas 39 and 40 being the most restricted damage sufficient to produce the syndrome. For the anterior variant of global anoneria resulting from deep medial frontal damage, bilateral damage to white matter in the vicinity of the frontal horns of the lateral ventricles was the most restricted site causing the syndrome.

Solms's patients also supported the theory that bilateral medial occipitotemporal lesions produced visual anoneria in which dreaming continued to occur but in the absence of visual imagery. Notably, the cardinal waking correlate of visual anoneria was the classical Charcot-Wilbrand symptom of visual irreminiscence. Solms also identified further variants of partial visual anoneria by the particular visual element affected (e.g., "kinematic anoneria" or "facial anoneria").

In addition to disorders of attenuated dreaming, Solms reported another interrelated pair of symptom complexes that combined *increased* frequency and intensity of dreaming. He suggests that increased vivacity and frequency of dreaming is associated with anterior limbic lesions while recurring nightmares are associated with temporal seizures.

On the basis of these findings, Solms builds the following neuropsychological model of normal dreaming: Frontal dopaminergic mesolimbic reward circuits produce an instigating impetus for dreaming when activated by arousing stimuli (e.g., ascending brainstem arousal in REM). The passage of this subcortical stimulus to posterior heteromodal association areas in the inferior parietal lobe is gated by a reality-monitoring process in anterior limbic areas. These areas also interrupt voluntary motor signals and facilitate back projection processes. Back projection then continues from the inferior parietal lobe (which contributes the capacity for spatial cognition) to visual association areas in medial occipitotemporal cortex (which contribute visual imagery), but not as far back as primary visual cortex.

INTEGRATION OF IMAGING AND LESION FINDINGS   The recent PET findings are important in several ways. First, they bring the neurobiology of human REM sleep into alignment with animal studies (via the brainstem activation). Second, they help to explain such positive cognitive dream features as the emotional intensification (via activation of subcortical and cortical limbic structures), the visuospatial vividness (via parietal operculum and unimodal visual association cortex activation), and fictive movement (via activation of basal ganglia, cerebellar vermis, and anterior cingulate). Third, they help to explain such negative cognitive dream features as the orientational instability, loss of self-reflective awareness, lack of directed thought, and amnesia (via the dorsolateral prefrontal deactivation). Each region showing REM-associated activation by neuroimaging has a counterpart effect in Solms's lesion study of dreaming (table 93.3).

In most cases, lesions of areas activated in REM produce a global or partial deficit in dream experience. Particularly striking is the similarity between Solms's findings that visual anoneria is caused by damage to vi-

TABLE 93.3

Imaging of brain activation in REM and the effects of brain lesions on dreaming

Region	PET Studies of Activation in REM	Lesions Studies of Effects on Dreaming
Pontine tegmentum	↑	—
Limbic structures	↑	↑
Striate cortex	↓	—
Extrastriate cortex	↑	↓
Parietal operculum	↑(right)	↓
Dorsolateral prefrontal cortex	↓	—
Mediobasal frontal cortex	—	↓

Key: ↑ increase; ↓ decrease; — no change.

sual association but not primary visual cortex and PET findings by Braun and colleagues (1998) who found extrastriate activation but striate deactivation in the occipital lobes during REM sleep compared to waking.

Two exceptions to this general correspondence involve lesions of the brainstem (for which Solms reports no attenuation of dreaming) and lesions of the rostral limbic system (for which Solms reports an accentuation of dreaming). In the case of pontine lesions, based upon the difficulty of suppressing REM by experimental lesions of the pons in animals, we suggest that any lesion capable of destroying the pontine REM sleep generator mechanism would have to be so extensive as to eliminate consciousness altogether. In the case of the rostral limbic system, we speculate that there either could be irritative versus destructive lesions or that lesions in different areas of this functionally highly heterogeneous region (Devinsky, Morrell, and Vogt, 1995) could produce dramatically different effects.

An integrated model of REM sleep dreaming

Figure 93.4 presents a hypothetical model of normal dreaming that integrates findings from neuroimaging, neurophysiological, and lesion studies. In this model, dreaming consciousness results from processes of arousal impinging upon selectively facilitated, disfacilitated, or input/output-blockaded forebrain structures. The various elements of normal dreams are contributed by brain networks, which include structures known to contribute to analogous processes in waking–although, as the model suggests, dreaming is characterized by a deletion of certain circuits active in waking and, perhaps, the accentuation of others.

ASCENDING AROUSAL SYSTEMS (AREAS 1 AND 2 IN FIGURE 93.4) As in waking, activation of the forebrain occurs through ascending arousal systems located in the brainstem reticular activating system (Steriade, 1996), the basal forebrain (Szyusiak, 1995), and possibly the hypothalamus (Saper, Sherin, and Elmquist, 1997), which together may form an integrated ascending midline network (Woolf, 1996). Forebrain stimulation by such arousal systems probably allows "consciousness" (as opposed to unconsciousness) to exist in dreaming and such consciousness may be detected by the desynchronization of the traditionally measured cortical EEG frequencies (Hobson, 1988) as well as by the appearance and synchronization of gamma-frequency oscillatory rhythms (Hobson et al., 1998; Kahn, Pace-Schott, and Hobson, 1997; Llinas and Ribary, 1993; Steriade, 1997).

THALAMOCORTICAL RELAY CENTERS AND THALAMIC SUBCORTICAL CIRCUITRY (AREA 6 IN FIGURE 93.4) During REM sleep, activated thalamic nuclei, which occupy key sites in relay and other brain circuits, probably contribute to most of the psychological modalities and phenomena of dreaming, while the release in the thalamus of intrinsic oscillatory corticothalamic circuits may suppress the experience of perception and mentation during NREM sleep (see above). Diverse roles of different thalamic nuclei may include transmission to the cortex of PGO-associated signals containing corollary discharge information on gaze shifts or activated motor patterns (Hobson and McCarley, 1977), modulation of the sleep cycle (Mancia and Marini, 1997), or participation in subcortical circuitry of motor pathways (Braun et al., 1997).

SUBCORTICAL AND CORTICAL LIMBIC AND PARALIMBIC STRUCTURES (AREA 3 IN FIGURE 93.4) Medial forebrain structures, especially limbic and paralimbic areas of the cortex and subcortex, appear to be selectively activated during REM sleep dreaming (Braun et al., 1997, 1998;

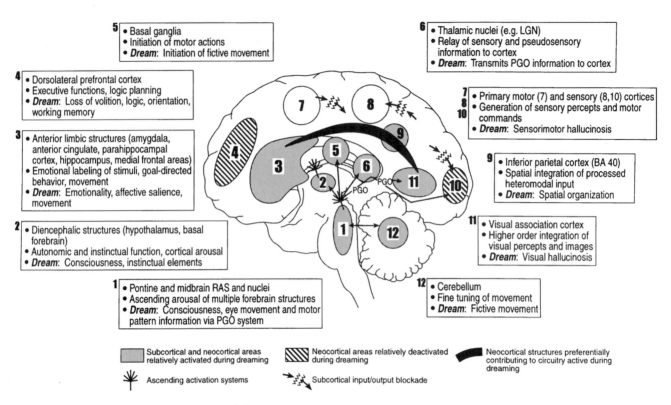

5
- Basal ganglia
- Initiation of motor actions
- *Dream*: Initiation of fictive movement

6
- Thalamic nuclei (e.g. LGN)
- Relay of sensory and pseudosensory information to cortex
- *Dream*: Transmits PGO information to cortex

4
- Dorsolateral prefrontal cortex
- Executive functions, logic planning
- *Dream*: Loss of volition, logic, orientation, working memory

7 8 10
- Primary motor (7) and sensory (8,10) cortices
- Generation of sensory percepts and motor commands
- *Dream*: Sensorimotor hallucinosis

3
- Anterior limbic structures (amygdala, anterior cingulate, parahippocampal cortex, hippocampus, medial frontal areas)
- Emotional labeling of stimuli, goal-directed behavior, movement
- *Dream*: Emotionality, affective salience, movement

9
- Inferior parietal cortex (BA 40)
- Spatial integration of processed heteromodal input
- *Dream*: Spatial organization

2
- Diencephalic structures (hypothalamus, basal forebrain)
- Autonomic and instinctual function, cortical arousal
- *Dream*: Consciousness, instinctual elements

11
- Visual association cortex
- Higher order integration of visual percepts and images
- *Dream*: Visual hallucinosis

1
- Pontine and midbrain RAS and nuclei
- Ascending arousal of multiple forebrain structures
- *Dream*: Consciousness, eye movement and motor pattern information via PGO system

12
- Cerebellum
- Fine tuning of movement
- *Dream*: Fictive movement

Subcortical and neocortical areas relatively activated during dreaming

Neocortical areas relatively deactivated during dreaming

Neocortical structures preferentially contributing to circuitry active during dreaming

Ascending activation systems

Subcortical input/output blockade

FIGURE 93.4   Forebrain processes in normal dreaming—an integration of neurophysiological, neuropsychological, and neuroimaging data.

Maquet et al., 1996; Nofzinger et al., 1997) and this activation may underlie dream emotionality (Braun et al., 1997; Hobson, Pace-Schott, and Stickgold, 1998; Maquet and Franck, 1997). Such activated limbic structures include the amygdala, which mediates anxiety (LeDoux, 1995), the most prevalent dream emotion (Domhoff, 1996; Merritt et al., 1994; Nielsen et al., 1991); the anterior cingulate, which mediates emotional valence biases, salience assessment, and integration with motor actions (Devinsky, Morrell, and Vogt, 1995); orbitofrontal, insular, and medial prefrontal cortices with abundant limbic connections (Braun et al., 1997), whose disruption may cause dream-like confabulatory syndromes (Braun et al., 1997; Solms, 1997); and the hippocampus, in which the amygdala may mediate storage of emotional memories (Cahill and McGaugh, 1998)—interactions which may underlie the oft-hypothesized role of REM and dreaming in processing emotional memories (Braun et al., 1997; Cartwright, 1990; Hobson, Pace-Schott, and Stickgold, 1998; Kramer, 1993; Maquet et al., 1996; Maquet and Franck, 1997; Nofzinger et al., 1997; Perlis and Nielsen, 1993).

MOTOR INITIATION AND CONTROL CENTERS (AREA 5 IN FIGURE 93.4)   Strong activation of the basal ganglia (Braun et al., 1997) may initiate the ubiquitous fictive

motion of dreams (Hobson, 1988; Porte and Hobson, 1996), and the striatum is extensively connected to the pedunculopontine area (Inglis and Winn, 1995; Rye, 1997), which also regulates REM phenomena (Hobson, Pace-Schott, and Stickgold, 1998). As in waking, other areas may modulate motion. For example: Vestibular dream sensations (Hobson et al., 1997; Leslie and Ogilvie, 1997) may arise via cerebellar connectivity with brainstem vestibular nuclei; motor cortices (area 7 in figure 93.4) participate in dream movement, as evidenced by the expression of dreamed action in REM sleep behavior disorder (Schenck, Hurwitz, and Mahowald, 1993); and premotor areas of the anterior cingulate cortex (Devinsky, Morrell, and Vogt, 1995) may integrate dream movement and emotion.

VISUAL ASSOCIATION CORTEX (AREA 11 IN FIGURE 93.4)   Areas of the medial occipital and temporal cortices involved in higher-order visual processing, as opposed to primary visual cortex (area 10 in figure 93.4), may generate the visual imagery of dreams (Braun et al., 1998; Solms, 1997). As in waking, specific areas of the visual association cortex may process specific visual features of dreaming. For example, the fusiform gyrus both mediates waking face recognition (Kanwisher, McDermott, and Chun, 1997; McCarthy et al., 1997) and is selectively activated in REM (Braun et al., 1997, 1998; Nofzinger et al., 1997). *Activation* of visual association (e.g., Brodmann areas 37 and 19) and paralimbic cortices with the *deactivation* of primary visual and dorsolateral prefrontal cortices has led Braun and colleagues (1997, 1998) to suggest that REM constitutes a unique cortical condition of internal information processing (between extrastriate and limbic cortices) functionally isolated from input (via striate cortex) or output (via frontal cortex) to the external world.

INFERIOR PARIETAL LOBE (AREA 9 IN FIGURE 93.4) The inferior parietal lobe, especially Brodmann's area 40, may generate the perception of a fictive dream space necessary for the global experience of dreaming (Solms, 1997; see also Doricchi and Violani, 1992) while PET scans show its activation despite widespread parietal deactivation (Maquet et al., 1996). Moreover, both lesion and PET studies suggest a greater importance of the right versus the left inferior parietal lobe (Maquet et al., 1996; Solms, 1997).

DORSOLATERAL PREFRONTAL EXECUTIVE ASSOCIATION CORTEX (AREA 4 IN FIGURE 93.4) Deactivation of frontal executive areas such as the dorsolateral prefrontal cortex during NREM (Braun et al., 1997, 1998; Hofle et al., 1997; Maquet et al., 1997) followed by their failure to reactivate along with medial paralimbic areas in REM (Braun et al., 1997, 1998; Maquet et al., 1996) may underlie the prominent executive deficiencies of dream mentation (Hobson, Pace-Schott, and Stickgold, 1998; Kahn, Pace-Schott, and Hobson, 1997). For example, in waking, prefrontal cortical areas are selectively activated during reasoning (Goel et al., 1998), episodic memory (Fletcher, Frith and Rugg, 1997), and working memory (Goldman-Rakic, 1996). Prefrontal deactivation in dreaming may, therefore, lead to illogical reasoning such as ad hoc explanations (Williams et al., 1992), prominent mnemonic deficits (Pace-Schott, Stickgold, and Hobson, 1997), and bizarre uncertainties (Hobson et al., 1987). Interestingly, hypoperfusion of the frontal cortex has been associated with pathological temporal limbic activation in epilepsy (Rabinowicz et al., 1997) and reciprocal inhibition between frontal and limbic areas has been hypothesized in theories on the etiology of schizophrenia (Weinberger, 1995). Possibly REM sleep dreaming involves a normal physiological state of the brain analogous to psychopathological conditions (Hobson, 1994, 1997b) in which limbic hyperactivation is combined with frontal hypoactivation.

DYNAMIC INTERACTIONS OF BRAIN REGIONS DURING NORMAL DREAMING–HYPOTHESES Component subsystems of global states of consciousness (like memory or visual processing) are physically instantiated in networks, each consisting of several to many discrete brain regions (e.g., see Cummings, 1993; Kolb and Whishaw, 1996; Nadel, 1994). At this early stage in dream neuropsychology research, a few generalizations are beginning to emerge. First, ascending arousal systems activate the many forebrain regions involved in dream construction but do so in a manner chemically and perhaps anatomically different from waking arousal processes. Second, cortical circuits activated in dreaming favor more medial circuits linking posterior association and paralimbic areas (represented by central crescent in figure 93.4) versus circuits including the primary sensory cortex and/or frontal executive regions (see Braun et al., 1998). Third, subcortical circuits involving the limbic structures, basal ganglia, diencephalon, and the brainstem contribute strongly to regional brain activation in REM and probably therefore also to the physiological substrate of dreaming.

Implications for changes in consciousness with changing behavioral state

DIFFERENCES BETWEEN NREM MENTATION AND WAKING Compared to waking, the deactivation of ascending arousal systems in the pons, midbrain, and diencephalon with the onset and progression of NREM sleep is likely to translate into a lower level of global forebrain activation (Braun et al., 1997; Hofle et al., 1997; Maquet et al., 1997) with a concomitant decrease in cognitive output from the cerebral cortex. In addition, the regional deactivation in NREM of multimodal association cortices in prefrontal and parietal areas compared to waking (Braun et al., 1997, 1998) might selectively constrain higher-level cognitive activity in NREM. As noted, gamma-frequency oscillations are continuous during REM and waking but, in NREM, are intermittent, being suppressed during the prolonged portions of slow waves corresponding to hyperpolarization (Steriade, 1997). Such periodic interference with those cortical rhythms associated with conscious processes may represent one example of a physiological isomorphism with the phenomenological observation that NREM mentation is more sporadic and limited than either REM or waking mentation.

DIFFERENCES BETWEEN REM AND NREM SLEEP MENTATION Previous publications have linked phenomenological differences between REM and NREM mentation in terms of neuromodulatory changes (e.g., Hobson, 1988, 1994, 1997a) as well as to patterns of neuronal oscillation (e.g., Kahn, Pace-Schott, and Hobson, 1997; Hobson et al., 1998). The current chapter adds striking neuroimaging findings to these other measures on the physiological substrate of psychological differences between mentation in these two states. In summary, the regional pattern of deactivation in NREM sharply contrasts with the regional *activation* of these same regions (i.e., thalamus, pontine brainstem, anterior cingulate cortex) in REM (table 93.1). The level of consciousness falls in parallel with brain deactivation in NREM sleep, and we hypothesize that it is the thalamocortical deactivation allowing emergence of intrinsic slow thalamocortical rhythms that may cause the depression of conscious experience in NREM sleep. Moreover, compared to REM sleep, the decreased activation of limbic-related cortical structures such as the anterior cingulate in NREM (Braun et al., 1997; Hofle et al., 1997; Maquet et al., 1997) may limit the affectively biased thought characteristic of REM-sleep dreaming.

DIFFERENCES BETWEEN REM AND WAKING MENTATION Taken together, the imaging, brain lesion, and electrophysiological results strongly suggest that the forebrain activation and synthesis processes underlying dreaming are very different from those of waking. Not only is REM sleep chemically biased but the preferential cholinergic neuromodulation is associated with selective activation of the subcortical and cortical limbic structures (which mediate emotion) while the aminergic demodulation is associated with relative inactivation of the frontal cortex (which mediates directed thought). This wake-to-REM sleep shift from the top to the bottom and from the front to the back of the brain may correspond, in a crude but compelling way, to the shift from the deliberate, environmentally integrated character of waking consciousness to the automatic, internally directed character of dream consciousness.

ACKNOWLEDGMENTS This project was funded by the MacArthur Foundation Mind Body Network and NIH MH-48,832, MH13923 and MH01287. The authors wish to thank Dr. Eric A. Nofzinger, Dr. Allen R. Braun, Dr. David Kahn, Dr. James Quattrochi, Dr. Rosalia Silvestri, Jill Gustafson, Dorothea Abbott, and April Malia for their collaboration.

REFERENCES

ACHERMANN, P., and A. A. BORBELY, 1997. Low Frequency (<1 Hz) oscillations in the human sleep electroencephalogram. *Neuroscience* 81:213–222.

AMZICA, F., and M. STERIADE, 1996. Progressive cortical synchronization of ponto-geniculo-occipital potentials during rapid eye movement in sleep. *Neuroscience* 72:309–314.

AMZICA, F., and M. STERIADE, 1998. Cellular substrates and laminar profile of sleep K-complex. *Neuroscience* 82:671–686.

ANTROBUS, J. S., 1983. REM and NREM sleep reports: Comparison of word frequencies by cognitive classes. *Psychophysiology* 20:562–568.

BOOTZIN, R. R., T. L. HUBBARD, E. M. REIMAN, D. BANDY, L. S. YUN, and T. MUNZLINGER, 1998. Brain regions preferentially affected during different stages of sleep and wakefulness: A PET study. *Sleep* 21(suppl.):272.

BRAUN, A. R., T. J. BALKIN, N. J. WESENSTEN, R. E. CARSON, M. VARGA, P. BALDWIN, S. SELBIE, G. BELENKY, and P. HERSCOVITCH, 1997. Regional cerebral blood flow throughout the sleep–wake cycle. *Brain* 120:1173–1197.

BRAUN, A. R., T. J. BALKIN, N. J. WESENSTEN, F. GWADRY, R. E. CARSON, M. VARGA, P. BALDWIN, G. BELENKY, and P. HERSCOVITCH, 1998. Dissociated pattern of activity in visual cortices and their projections during human rapid-eye-movement sleep. *Science* 279:91–95.

BUCHSBAUM, M. S., J. C. GILLIN, J. WU, E. HAZLETT, N. SICOTTE, R. M. DUPONT, and W. E. BUNNEY, 1989. Regional cerebral glucose metabolic rate in human sleep assessed by positron emission tomography. *Life Sci.* 45:1349–1356.

CAHILL, L., and J. L. MCGAUGH, 1998. Mechanisms of emotional arousal and lasting declarative memory. *Trends Neurosci.* 21:294–299.

CARTWRIGHT, R., 1990. A network model of dreams. In *Sleep and Cognition*, R. Bootzin, J. Kihlstrom, and D. Schacter, eds. Washington, D.C.: American Psychological Association.

CASAGRANDE, M., C. VIOLANI, F. LUCIDI, E. BUTTINELLI, and M. BERTINI, 1996. Variations in sleep mentation as a function of time of night. *Int. J. Neurosci.* 85:19–30.

CAVALLERO, C., P. CICOGNA, V. NATALE, M. OCCHIONERO, and A. ZITO, 1992. Slow wave sleep dreaming. *Sleep* 15:562–566.

CHROBAK, J. J., and G. BUZSAKI, 1998. Gamma oscillations in the entorhinal cortex of the freely behaving rat. *J. Neurosci.* 18:388–398.

CONTRERAS, D., and M. STERIADE, 1997. Synchronization of low-frequency rhythms in corticothalamic networks. *Neuroscience* 76:11–24.

CUMMINGS, J. L., 1993. Frontal-subcortical circuits and human behavior. *Arch. Neurol.* 50:873–880.

DEVINSKY, O., M. J. MORRELL, and B. A. VOGT, 1995. Contributions of anterior cingulate cortex to behavior. *Brain* 118:279–306.

DOMHOFF, G. W., 1996. *Finding Meaning in Dreams: A Quantitative Approach.* New York: Plenum.

DORICCHI, F., and C. VIOLANI, 1992. Dream recall in brain-damaged patients: A contribution to the neuropsychology of dreaming through a review of the literature. In *The Neuropsychology of Sleep and Dreaming*, J. S. Antrobus and M. Bertini, eds. Mahwah, N.J.: Lawrence Erlbaum Associates, pp. 99–129.

FLETCHER, P. C., C. D. FRITH, and M. D. RUGG, 1997. The functional neuroanatomy of episodic memory. *Trends Neurosci.* 20:213–218.

FOULKES, D., 1962. Dream reports from different stages of sleep. *J. Abn. Soc. Psychol.* 65:14–25.

FOULKES, D., 1967. Nonrapid eye movement mentation. *Exp. Neurol.* 19:28–38.

GOEL, V., B. GOLD, S. KAPUR, and S. HOULE, 1998. Neuroanatomical correlates of human reasoning. *J. Cogn. Neurosci.* 10:293–302.

GOLDMAN-RAKIC, P. S., 1996. The prefrontal landscape: Implications of functional architecture for understanding human mentation and the central executive. *Phil. Trans. R. Soc. Lond. B* 351:1445–1453.

GOODENOUGH, D. R., H. B. LEWIS, A. SHAPIRO, L. JARET, and I. SLESER, 1965. Dream reporting following abrupt and gradual awakenings from different types of sleep. *J. Pers. Soc. Psychol.* 2:170–179.

GRAY, C. M., and D. A. MCCORMICK, 1996. Chattering cells: Superficial pyramidal neurons contributing to the generation of synchronous oscillations in the visual system. *Science* 274:109–113.

GREENBERG, M. S., and M. J. FARAH, 1986. The laterality of dreaming. *Brain Cognit.* 5:307–321.

HARI R., and R. SALMELIN, 1997. Human cortical oscillations: A neuromagnetic view through the skull. *Trends Neurosci.* 20:44–49.

HERMAN, J. H., S. J. ELLMAN, and H. P. ROFFWARG, 1978. The problem of NREM recall re-examined. In *The Mind in Sleep*, A. M. Arkin, J. S. Antrobus, and S. J. Ellman, eds. Mahwah, N.J.: Lawrence Erlbaum Associates, pp. 59–92.

HOBSON, J. A., 1988. *The Dreaming Brain*. New York: Basic Books.

HOBSON, J. A., 1994. *The Chemistry of Conscious States*. Boston: Little, Brown.

HOBSON, J. A., 1997a. Consciousness as a state-dependent phenomenon. In *Scientific Approaches to the Question of Consciousness*, J. Cohen and J. Schooler, eds. Mahwah, N.J.: Lawrence Erlbaum Associates, pp. 379–396.

HOBSON, J. A., 1997b. Dreaming as delirium: A mental status exam of our nightly madness. *Sem. Neurol.* 17:121–128.

HOBSON, J. A., E. HOFFMAN, R. HELFAND, and D. KOSTNER, 1987. Dream bizarreness and the activation-synthesis hypothesis. *Hum. Neurobiol.* 6:157–164.

HOBSON, J. A., and R. W. MCCARLEY, 1977. The brain as a dream-state generator: An activation-synthesis hypothesis of the dream process. *Am. J. Psychiat.* 134:1335–1348.

HOBSON, J. A., E. F. PACE-SCHOTT, and R. STICKGOLD, 1998. The neuropsychology of REM sleep dreaming. *NeuroReport* 9:R1–R14.

HOBSON, J. A., E. F. PACE-SCHOTT, R. STICKGOLD, and D. KAHN, 1998. To dream or not to dream? Relevant data from new neuroimaging and electrophysiological studies. *Curr. Opin. Neurobiol.* 8:239–244.

HOBSON, J. A., and M. STERIADE, 1986. Neuronal basis of behavioral state control. In *Handbook of Physiology: The Nervous System*, Vol. 4, V. Mountcastle and F. E. Bloom, eds. Washington: American Physiological Society, pp. 701–823.

HOBSON, J. A., and R. STICKGOLD, 1995. The conscious state paradigm: A neurocognitive approach to waking, sleeping and dreaming. In *The Cognitive Neurosciences*, M. Gazzaniga, ed. Cambridge, Mass.: MIT Press, pp. 1373–1389.

HOBSON, J. A., R. STICKGOLD, E. F. PACE-SCHOTT, and K. R. LESLIE, 1997. Sleep and vestibular adaptation: Implications for function in microgravity. *J. Vestib. Res.* 8:1–13.

HOFLE, N., T. PAUS, D. REUTENS, P. FISET, J. GOTMAN, A. C. EVANS, and B. E. JONES, 1997. Regional cerebral blood flow changes as a function of delta and spindle activity during slow wave sleep in humans. *J. Neurosci.* 17:4800–4808.

HONG, C. C. H., J. C. GILLIN, B. M. DOW, J. WU, and M. S. BUCHSBAUM, 1995. Localized and lateralized cerebral glucose metabolism associated with eye movements during REM sleep and wakefulness: A positron emission tomography (PET) study. *Sleep* 18:570–580.

INGLIS, W. L., and P. WINN, 1995. The pedunculopontine tegmental nucleus: Where the striatum meets the reticular formation. *Prog. Neurobiol.* 47:1–29.

KAHN, D., E. F. PACE-SCHOTT, and J. A. HOBSON, 1997. Consciousness in waking and dreaming: The roles of neuronal oscillation and neuromodulation in determining similarities and differences. *Neuroscience* 78:13–38.

KANWISHER, N., J. MCDERMOTT, and M. M. CHUN, 1997. The fusiform face area: A module in human extrastriate cortex specialized for face perception. *J. Neurosci.* 17:4302–4311.

KOLB, B., and I. Q. WHISHAW, 1996. *Fundamentals of Human Neuropsychology*, 4th Ed. New York: W.H. Freeman.

KRAMER, M., 1993. The selective mood regulatory function of dreaming: An update and revision. In *The Functions of Dreaming*, A. Moffitt, M. Kramer, and R. Hoffman, eds. Albany: State University of New York Press, pp. 139–195.

KREITER, A. K., and W. SINGER, 1996. Stimulus-dependent synchronization of neuronal responses in the visual cortex of the awake macaque monkey. *J. Neurosci.* 16:2381–2396.

KUBOYAMA, T., A. HORI, T. SATO, T. NIKAMI, T. YAMAKI, and S. VEDA, 1997. Changes in cerebral blood flow velocity in healthy young men during overnight sleep and while awake. *Electroencephalogr. Clin. Neurophysiol.* 102:125–131.

LEDOUX, J. E., 1995. In search of an emotional system in the brain: Leaping from fear to emotion and consciousness. In *The Cognitive Neurosciences*, M. Gazzaniga, ed. Cambridge, Mass.: MIT Press, pp. 1049–1061.

LESLIE, K., and R. OGILVIE, 1996. Vestibular dreams: The effect of rocking on dream mentation. *Dreaming* 6:1–16.

LLINAS, R., and U. RIBARY, 1993. Coherent 40-Hz oscillation characterizes dream state in humans. *Proc. Natl. Acad. Sci. U.S.A.* 90:2078–2081.

LLINAS, R., U. RIBARY, M. JOLIOT, and X. J. WANG, 1994. Content and context in temporal thalamocortical binding. *Temporal Coding in the Brain*, G. Buzsaki, ed. Berlin: Springer-Verlag, pp. 251–272.

LUTZENBERGER, W., F. PULVERMULLER, T. EBERT, and N. BIRNBAUMER, 1995. Visual stimulation alters local 40 Hz responses in humans: an EEG study. *Neurosci. Lett.* 183:39–42.

MADSEN, P. C., S. HOLM, S. VORSTUP, L. FRIBERG, N. A. LASSEN, and L. F. WILDSCHIODTZ, 1991. Human regional cerebral blood flow during rapid eye movement sleep. *J. Cereb. Blood Flow Met.* 11:502–507.

MANCIA, M., and G. MARINI, 1997. Thalamic mechanisms in sleep control. In *Sleep and Sleep Disorders: From Molecule to Behavior*, O. Hayaishi and S. Inoue, eds. Tokyo: Academic Press, pp. 377–393.

MAQUET, P., 1995. Sleep function(s) and cerebral metabolism. *Behav. Brain Res.* 69:75–83.

MAQUET, P., D. DEGUELDRE, G. DELFIORE, J. AERTS, J. M. PETERS, A. LUXEN, and G. FRANCK, 1997. Functional neuroanatomy of human slow wave sleep. *J. Neurosci.* 17:2807–2812.

MAQUET, P., D. DIVE, E. SALMON, B. SADZOT, G. FRANCO, R. POIRRIER, and G. FRANCK, 1990. Cerebral glucose utilization during sleep-wake cycle in man determined by positron emission tomography and [18F]-2-fluoro-2 deoxy-d-glucose method. *Brain Res.* 513:136–143.

MAQUET, P., D. DIVE, E. SALMON, B. SADZOT, G. FRANCO, R. POIRRIER, and G. FRANCK, 1992. Cerebral glucose utilization during stage 2 sleep in man. *Brain Res.* 571:149–153.

MAQUET P., and G. FRANCK, 1997. REM sleep and the amygdala. *Molec. Psychiat.* 2:195–196.

MAQUET, P., J. M. PETERS, J. AERTS, G. DELFIORE, C. DEGUELDRE, A. LUXEN, and G. FRANCK, 1996. Functional neuroanatomy of human rapid-eye-movement sleep and dreaming. *Nature* 383:163–166.

MARINO, J., L. MARTINEZ, and A. CANEDO, 1996. Coupled slow and delta oscillations between cuneothalamic and thalamocortical neurons in the chloralose anaesthetized cat. *Neurosci. Lett.* 219:107–110.

McCARTHY, G., A. PUCE, J. C. GORE, and A. TRUETT, 1997. Face specific processing in the human fusiform gyrus. *J. Cogn. Neurosci.* 9:605–610.

MERRITT, J. M., R. STICKGOLD, E. F. PACE-SCHOTT, J. WILLIAMS, and J. A. HOBSON, 1994. Emotion profiles in the dreams of men and women. *Cons. Cognit.* 3:46–60.

MULLER, M. M., J. BOSCH, T. ELBERT, A. K. KRIETER, M. V. SOSA, P. V. SOSA, and B. ROCKSTROH, 1996. Visually induced gamma-based responses in human electroencephalographic activity: A link to animal studies. *Exp. Brain Res.* 112:96–102.

MUNK, M. H. J., P. R. ROELFSEMA, P. KONIG, A. K. ENGEL, and W. SINGER, 1996. Role of reticular activation in the modulation of intracortical synchronization. *Science* 272:271–274.

NADEL, L., 1994. Multiple memory systems: What and why, an update. In *Memory Systems 1994*, D. L. Schacter and E. Tulving, eds. Cambridge, Mass.: MIT Press, pp. 39–63.

NIELSEN, T. A., D. DESLAURIERS, and G. W. BAYLOR, 1991. Emotions in dream and waking event reports. *Dreaming* 1:287–300.

NOFZINGER, E. A., M. A. MINTUN, M. B. WISEMAN, D. J. KUPFER, and R. Y. MOORE, 1997. Forebrain activation in REM sleep: An FDG PET study. *Brain Res.* 770:192–201.

OGILVIE, R., H. HUNT, C. SAWICKI, and J. SAMAHALSKI, 1982. Psychological correlates of spontaneous MEMA during sleep. *Sleep* 11:11–27.

PACE-SCHOTT, E. F., R. STICKGOLD, and J. A. HOBSON, 1997. Memory processes within dreaming: Methodological issues. *Sleep Res.* 26:277.

PERLIS, L., and T. A. NIELSEN, 1993. Mood regulation, dreaming and nightmares: Evaluation of a desensitization function. *Dreaming* 3:243–257.

PORTE, H., and J. A. HOBSON, 1996. Physical motion in dreams: One measure of three theories. *J. Abn. Psychol.* 105:329–335.

RABINOWICZ, A. L., E. SALAS, F. BESERRA, R. C. LEIGUARDA, and S. E. VAZQUEZ, 1997. Changes in regional cerebral blood flow beyond the temporal lobe in unilateral temporal lobe epilepsy. *Epilepsia* 38:1011–1014.

RECHTSCHAFFEN, A., P. VERDONE, and J. WHEATON, 1963. Reports of mental activity during sleep. *Can. Psychiat.* 8:409–414.

RYE, D. B., 1997. Contributions of the pedunculopontine region to normal and altered REM sleep. *Sleep* 20:757–788.

SAPER, C. B., J. E. SHERIN, and J. K. ELMQUIST, 1997. Role of the ventrolateral preoptic area in sleep induction. In *Sleep and Sleep Disorders: From Molecule to Behavior*, O. Hayaishi and S. Inoue, eds. Tokyo: Academic Press, pp. 281–295.

SCHENCK, C. H., T. D. HURWITZ, and M. W. MAHOWALD, 1993. REM sleep behavior disorder: An update on a series of 96 patients and a review of the world literature. *J. Sleep Res.* 2:224–231.

SOLMS, M., 1997. *The Neuropsychology of Dreams: A Clinico-Anatomical Study.* Mahwah, N.J.: Lawrence Erlbaum Associates.

STERIADE, M., 1996. Arousal: Revisiting the reticular activating system. *Science* 272:225–226.

STERIADE, M., 1997. Synchronized activities of coupled oscillators in the cerebral cortex and thalamus at different levels of vigilance. *Cereb. Cortex* 7:583–604.

STERIADE, M., and F. AMZICA, 1996. Intracortical and corticothalamic coherency of fast spontaneous oscillations. *Proc. Natl. Acad. Sci. U.S.A.* 93:2533–2538.

STERIADE, M., F. AMZICA, and D. CONTRERAS, 1996. Synchronization of fast (30–40 Hz) spontaneous cortical rhythms during brain activation. *J. Neurosci.* 16:392–417.

STERIADE, M., D. CONTRERAS, and F. AMZICA, 1994. Synchronized sleep oscillations and their paroxysmal developments. *Trends Neurosci.* 17:199–208.

STERIADE, M., D. CONTRERAS, F. AMZICA, and I. TIMOFEEV, 1996. Synchronization of fast (30–40 Hz) spontaneous oscillations in intrathalamic and thalamocortical networks. *J. Neurosci.* 16:2788–2808.

STERIADE, M., D. CONTRERAS, C. DOSSI, and A. NUNEZ, 1993. The slow (<1 Hz) oscillation in reticular thalamic and thalamocortical neurons: Scenario of sleep rhythm generation in interacting thalamic and neocortical networks. *J. Neurosci.* 13:3284–3299.

STERIADE, M., D. A. McCORMICK, and T. SEJNOWSKI, 1993. Thalamocortical oscillations in the sleeping and aroused brain. *Science* 262:679–684.

STERIADE, M., A. NUNEZ, and F. AMZICA, 1993a. A novel slow (<1 Hz) oscillation of neocortical neurons in vivo: Depolarizing and hyperpolarizing components. *J. Neurosci.* 13:3252–3265.

STERIADE, M., A. NUNEZ, and F. AMZICA, 1993b. Intracellular analysis of relations between the slow (<1 Hz) neocortical oscillation and other sleep rhythms of the electroencephalogram. *J. Neurosci.* 13:3266–3283.

SZYMUSIAK, R., 1995. Magnocellular nuclei of the basal forebrain: Substrates of sleep and arousal regulation. *Sleep* 18:478–500.

TALLON-BAUDRY, C., O. BERTRAND, C. DELPUECH, and J. PERNIER, 1996. Stimulus specificity of phase-locked and non–phase locked 40 Hz visual responses in humans. *J. Neurosci.* 16:4240–4249.

TALLON-BAUDRY, C., O. BERTRAND, C. DELPUECH, and J. PERNIER, 1997. Oscillatory gamma-band (30–70 Hz) activity induced by a visual search task in humans. *J. Neurosci.* 17:722–734.

TALLON-BAUDRY, C., O. BERTRAND, F. PERONNET, and J. PERNIER, 1998. Induced gamma-band activity during the delay of a visual short-term memory task in humans. *J. Neurosci.* 18:4244–4254.

WATERMAN, D., M. ELTON, and J. L. KENEMANS, 1993. Methodological issues affecting the collection of dreams. *J. Sleep Res.* 2:8–12.

WEINBERGER, D. R., 1995. Neurodevelopmental perspectives on schizophrenia. In *Psychopharmacology: The Fourth Generation of Progress*, F. E. Bloom, ed. New York: Raven Press, pp. 1171–1183.

WILLIAMS, J., J. MERRITT, C. RITTENHOUSE, and J. A. HOBSON, 1992. Bizarreness in dreams and fantasies: Implications for the activation-synthesis hypothesis. *Cons. Cognit.* 1:172–185.

WOOLF, N. J., 1996. Global and serial neurons form a hierarchically arranged interface proposed to underlie memory and cognition. *Neuroscience* 74:625–651.

94 Consciousness, Introspection, and the Split-Brain: The Two Minds/One Body Problem

KATHLEEN BAYNES AND MICHAEL S. GAZZANIGA

ABSTRACT The history of split-brain research and its relation to our understanding of consciousness and modularity is reviewed briefly. Owing to the limited control of expressive language by the right hemisphere (RH), the problem of the level of consciousness in the RH is presented as approachable only through observation of behavioral changes that demonstrate its contribution to consciousness. The role of memory, emotion, and language in our understanding of conscious behavior in the RH is reviewed. Insight gained from data obtained from a new patient with anomalous language representation is presented. An evolutionary perspective is considered.

There are two mysteries regarding the sectioning of the corpus callosum. One emerges when the researcher observes the activity of two separate cognitive systems in one person, each acting out of the consciousness of the other. And the second emerges when the researcher observes the placid acceptance of this state by the split-brain patients themselves. Patients respond to requests for introspection with a curious lack of insight or interest. Don't we all believe that we would be dismayed by an apparent "other" inhabiting our brains? But perhaps not, depending upon how we understand the effect that sectioning of the corpus callosum has on the structure of our conscious selves.

The mystery of the status of consciousness in the split-brain may not be easily answered, as answering the question of the consciousness of the nondominant hemisphere is equivalent to defining consciousness itself. Neuroscience has made inroads into the concept of consciousness, reducing some of its aspects to empirically approachable chunks. What these chunks are depends in part on the perspective of the writer. Definitions of consciousness differ from the matter-of-fact assessment of the neurologist, eliciting an ability to respond and withdraw from pain, to the exquisite awareness of ourselves and our place in the world that troubles the

KATHLEEN BAYNES   Center for Neuroscience, University of California at Davis, Davis, Calif.
MICHAEL S. GAZZANIGA   Director, Program in Cognitive Neuroscience, Dartmouth College, Hanover, N.H.

philosopher. Contemporary theories of consciousness frequently recognize two, or perhaps three, kinds of consciousness (Tulving, 1985; Pinker, 1997). And many question whether the most interesting aspects of consciousness are tractable problems at all (Dennett, 1991). Whatever the ultimate solution to the problem of consciousness, it seems likely that it will be multifaceted, perhaps breaking apart in ways we have not yet begun to think about.

We want to use the idea that our skulls may house very different states of consciousness under different circumstances to examine the possible states of consciousness in the right and left hemispheres. It was our subjective notion of a unity of consciousness that made the first observations of split-brain behavior so astounding. There is clearly a separation of cognitive function after section of the callosum. But some have argued that the impression of two consciousnesses is illusory (Eccles, 1965). Dennett (1991), for example, has suggested that the right hemisphere (RH) has, at best, a "rudimentary self." We, too, believe that the RH has more limited cognitive abilities than the left; but we feel it is crucial to accurately assess the upper extent of its cognitive function.

Here, we review the progress made in the study of dual consciousness in the split-brain subject with an emphasis on the relation to language processing. Consciousness is not likely to be an all-or-nothing concept. Consciousness has multiple facets, and we may see some of them displayed more clearly in the split-brain and other neurological populations. But they are ultimately combined to form the totality of our conscious experience. Language is one of these aspects—an aspect that has been important to the study of the split-brain patient. But we wish to maintain that it is not sufficient of itself.

The early years

The ground-breaking observation in the 1960s that section of the corpus callosum in humans yielded a being in whom some forms of information could be isolated to

1355

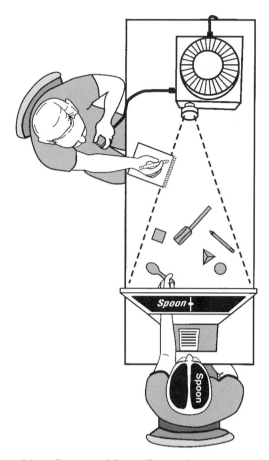

FIGURE 94.1 Cartoon of data collection from early split-brain studies. Words presented to the LVF/right hemisphere allowed the left hand to select the correct object by touch. (From Gazzaniga, 1983.)

one hemisphere and responded to only by that hemisphere was a remarkable one. In 1962 the surgical team led by Bogen and Vogel sectioned the callosum of a patient who, prior to surgery, could name stimuli presented in either visual field or placed in either hand (Gazzaniga, Bogen, and Sperry, 1962). After the surgery, he could not name items displayed in his left visual field or presented to his left hand (figure 94.1). However, when given a nonverbal method of response, the RH was indeed able to demonstrate knowledge to which the left hemisphere (LH) was not privy (Gazzaniga, Bogen, and Sperry, 1962, 1965).

These experiments and those that followed demonstrated that each hemisphere could have knowledge of things the other did not and could respond on the basis of this independent experience. Of the first six patients operated on, two patients, L.B. and N.G., showed language competence in their RHs (Gazzaniga and Sperry, 1967). Although the RH appeared helpless when spoken responses were required, allowing tactile or pointing responses permitted the RH to show it had a written and

auditory vocabulary with some level of "abstraction, generalization, and mental association" (ibid, p. 137). Further, this work confirmed that the LH in isolation could continue to carry out basic language functions, speaking, reading, and writing normally. The RH, too, appeared to be carrying out basic functions. Patients did not exhibit neglect of intrapersonal or extrapersonal space; they did not bump into objects in the left hemispace or fail to orient or attend to visual or auditory information in the normal situation. So, despite the dramatic differences that could be seen in special experimental situations, these people appeared to be going about their normal daily lives without disruption and did not report changes in their conscious perception of the world.

Recent research

In the years that followed, researchers in the Gazzaniga laboratory have tried to characterize the nature of conscious mechanisms in these patients. Gazzaniga (1995) tracked the major findings in split-brain research as they relate to the larger questions of how our brains enable everyday reality, how we incorporate experience into that reality, and the role and nature of the self within that context. Insights into emotion, memory, and the role of the left hemisphere in interpreting our actions will be reviewed here briefly before focusing on the relation between linguistic skill and conscious experience in the right hemisphere.

EMOTIONAL INTELLIGENCE Our short list of some of the components of a conscious life suggests that emotional valence is one of them. The RH does not have easy access to verbalization, but can it experience emotions? Early work with patient P.S. indicated that his RH had some emotional reactions to stimuli and was able to maintain some goals and opinions that differed between his hemispheres (LeDoux, Wilson, and Gazzaniga, 1977a; Gazzaniga, LeDoux, and Wilson, 1977).

There also appears to be some specificity to the emotion that the RH can experience. In an experiment done with patient V.P. (see table 94.1), there appears to be sufficient specificity in the emotional arousal of the RH that the LH is able to correctly discern the emotion experienced although uninformed as to the real cause. In one instance a frightening scene of a fire was shown to V.P.'s RH. After viewing this scene, she said, "I don't really know what I saw; I think just a white flash. Maybe some trees, red trees like in the fall. I don't know why, but I feel kind of scared. I feel jumpy. I don't like this room, or maybe it's you guys getting me nervous" (Gazzaniga and LeDoux, 1987). In this case, the response to the

TABLE 94.1
Ages of onset, time of surgery, and callosal damage of patients discussed here

ID	Sex	Handedness	Age at Onset (Years)	Age at Surgery (Years)	Callosal Damage	Post-Event IQ
P.S.	Male	Right	2	15	Callostomy: 2 stage, anterior first	89 (WAIS)
J.W.	Male	Right	19	25	Callostomy: 2 stage, posterior first	95 (WAIS-R)
V.P.	Female	Right	6	27	Callostomy: 2 stage, anterior first	91 (WAIS-R)
D.R.	Female	Right	17	38	Callostomy: Single stage	89 (WAIS-R)
V.J.	Female	Left	16	42	Callostomy: 2 stage, anterior first	88 (WAIS-R)
A.W.*	Female	Right	50	—	Vascular disease: Thinning of body of callosum	93 (WAIS-R)

*A.W. suffered anarchic or alien hand symptoms following a vascular lesion. There was no surgical intervention.

scene appears to have been physiological and specific enough that the LH identified it correctly. The cause was not known, so the immediate surroundings were seen as suddenly scary. In the context of this discussion, the point is that the RH saw a frightening scene and interpreted it correctly and specifically.

From another point of view, this experimental evidence illustrates an extreme case of a phenomenon that commonly occurs to all of us. A change in mood alters the physiological state of the brain. In response, the verbal system notes the mood and attributes cause to the feeling based on available evidence. Cognitive interpretations of physiological changes in normal subjects have been reported in experiments performed by social psychologists (i.e., Dutton and Aron, 1974). Those experiments were seen as evidence that all physiological responses are similar and that it is the cognitive interpretation that labels them as specific emotions. In the instance above, however, it appears the RH is capable of a specific emotional response to a simulated situation. The abstract visual presentation has a physiological result that the LH can recognize as fear. It may be that the LH interpreter is easily "tricked" by clever psychologists into re-interpreting a physiological response to fit the circumstances with which it is confronted; but in the case of V.P., the physiological response seems sufficiently specific to indicate that the RH was experiencing the emotion expected under the circumstances.

In the examples reviewed here, it appears that the RH not only makes an interpretive contribution to the world about which the LH speaks, but has a specific set of emotional reactions as well. One prediction from these results is that the isolated LH might be more easily "misled" about the emotional valence of a physiological response. For present purposes, however, it is the accurate emotional valence of the RH in response to a simulation that is relevant to evaluating its level of conscious behavior.

CALLOSOTOMY AND MEMORY It remains difficult to quantify the costs to cognitive ability incurred by callosal section. Early studies showed no change in reaction time for simple discriminations (Gazzaniga and Sperry, 1966), in the ability to form hypotheses (LeDoux, Wilson, and Gazzaniga, 1977b), or in verbal IQ (Campbell, Bogen, and Smith, 1981), suggesting no substantial contribution to psychometric intelligence from the RH. However, there are numerous reports that negative effects can be registered on memory function (Zaidel and Sperry, 1974; Phelps, Hirst, and Gazzaniga, 1991; Jha et al., 1997). There may be changes in cognitive functions that are not easily captured by standard psychometric means. One of these functions is memory.

There have been subjective reports from family members that patients may suffer some memory failures post-callosotomy (Gazzaniga and Sperry, 1967). Although psychometric results sometimes suggested a decline in memory function, it was unclear why this would occur. Phelps and Gazzaniga (1992) examined the role that the LH interpreter might play in memory. They showed two patients, V.P. and J.W., a sequence of pictures that made up vignettes of familiar activities when viewed in order. Later, the pictures were interspersed with distractors that were either consistent or inconsistent with the vignette. (If, for example, the vignette were about a man getting ready for work, a picture of him pouring coffee would be consistent, but a picture of him pouring lemonade would not.) The patients were then asked to accept pictures they had seen before and reject those they had not seen. Both the right and left hemispheres could accurately accept the pictures they had seen before; and both could reject, as things they had not seen, pictures that were inconsistent with the vignette. The hemispheric difference was seen in the pictures that were consistent with the vignette. The RH was able to reject such pictures more accurately than the LH. Rather than enhance memory, the

LH interpretive activity interfered with accurate recognition. The RH was better able to reflect accurately what it had seen before.

There is also reason to believe that encoding of simpler material may be less effective after callosotomy. Jha and colleagues (1997) compared J.W., V.P., and D.R. (table 94.1) with patients with hippocampal damage on a series of verbal and visual memory tasks (Kroll et al., 1996). The split-brain patients made a large number of false-positive responses to lures made of combinations of previously viewed features, suggesting a binding problem similar to that seen in patients with right hippocampal lesions. This result suggests that the RH is contributing to the normal encoding process via callosal fibers and that, when divided, the hemispheres cannot carry out this binding process at normal levels of accuracy.

These experiments suggest that memory performance may decline after callosotomy not because of a change in memory processes per se but because the right and left hemispheres may make unique contributions to a fully elaborated memory trace. Split patients can learn new material, but may not encode it as fully and hence may not have as many retrieval cues at their disposal as they did prior to surgery.

CEREBRAL DOMINANCE AND THE INTERPRETER   The demonstration of hemispheric specialization was perhaps less surprising than the persistence of the LH in explaining actions that it did not generate. Even in the early patients, the tendency of the LH to speak up in situations in which it was not informed was observed (Gazzaniga and Hillyard, 1971; Gazzaniga, LeDoux and Wilson, 1977). In a now-classic demonstration, P.S. (table 94.1)–one of the subjects with very well developed RH language–was being tested with bilaterally presented pictures (figure 94.2). After watching his right and left hands make disparate choices from an array of pictures, without batting an eyelash, his LH accounted verbally for the behavior it witnessed by combining that observation with the knowledge of the only display it had seen. No "Why did I do that?" but instead an automatic assumption of responsibility for the complete action it had just observed. This propensity of the LH to provide a rationale for disparate behaviors has led Gazzaniga to dub it the Interpreter (Gazzaniga, 1985).

This behavior in split-brain patients contrasts with that observed in alien (anarchic) hand patients with partial callosal lesions. These patients are mystified and distressed by the unintended actions of their nondominant (and sometimes dominant) hands. One patient, A.W., with a lesion of the central portion of the corpus callosum had no significant paralysis or sensory loss, but was unable to drive her car because her right hand grabbed

FIGURE 94.2   Patient P.S. confabulates about his left hand's choices when presented with bilateral picture displays. The right hand selects a rooster to match the claw seen by the left hemisphere, but P.S. states that the shovel selected by the left hand was needed to clean out the chicken house. The left hemisphere Interpreter had no knowledge of the snow scene seen by the right hemisphere. (From Gazzaniga and LeDoux, 1978.)

the wheel away from her left (Baynes et al., 1997). She complained that at the supermarket, her left hand has snatched back money she had just paid to the cashier with her right hand. This patient is aware of and distressed by her independently functioning left hand. What makes the difference between these two types of responses to left-hand actions outside the control of the LH? Why does A.W. not simply confabulate that she thought she had given the cashier the wrong amount of money or changed her mind about the purchase? In her case, the Interpreter sees the actions of that hand as strange and separate from itself. Hence, instead of trying to explain and incorporate the behavior, it rejects the actions and the limb itself.

Why doesn't A.W. confabulate about her behavior? Perhaps A.W.'s less precise callosal lesion interferes with the neural coding of the motor commands in a way that makes them impenetrable to the LH. In contrast, P.S.'s LH may receive appropriate feedback via ipsilateral fibers regarding the execution of the motor action to assume it has generated them. Bisiach, Luzzatti, and Perani (1979) in explaining neglect and denial have suggested that not only is function lost, but also *expectations* about function. A.W. may still have unfulfilled expectations about the behavior of her left hand that P.S. lacks.

It would appear that the LH confabulates only under specific conditions which may require failing to receive constraining information from the RH. If this is the case, it would provide support for the belief that the RH is not only conscious in the sense of aware but is capable of formulating some basic hypotheses regarding the relation of its actions to the world. It may be in some sense fact-checking for the LH (Gazzaniga, 1998).

The modular organization of the human brain is well-accepted. The functioning modules do have some kind of physical instantiation, but the precise nature of the neural networks that carry out those functions has not been specified. What is clear is that they operate largely outside the realm of awareness, and that they announce their computational products to various executive systems that result in behavior or cognitive states. It may be the level at which this processing breaks down in the examples above that determines whether the Interpreter is conscious that the behavior originates outside of its control or simply observes and incorporates it in its world view. We want to emphasize our belief that there are multiple executive systems that may have varying degrees of influence over behavior depending upon the situation. Managing and interpreting all of this constant and parallel activity is the role of the LH's interpreter module, but under normal conditions it is informed and constrained by the RH (Gazzaniga, 1998).

The language connection

Although we recognize that the acute awareness of our activities—our experience of the struggle to convey a complicated idea or the taste of cold water when we are thirsty—is an essential part of our humanity, we also recognize the problem of solipsism. How do we know that these experiences are shared with anyone else? Is your blue, my blue? Your tiramisu, my tiramisu? We can only be reassured by our observations of others. When you speak of blue, you point to the same color patch I do, with great reliability. In fact, even if you don't have a word for blue, you reliably demonstrate you can see it (Berlin and Kay, 1969; Heider, 1972). So when we think about whether or not the separated right and left hemisphere apprehends the world in a manner similar to the connected brain, we have the same lack of absolute assurance. Throughout the development of split-brain research, this problem is exacerbated by the silence of the

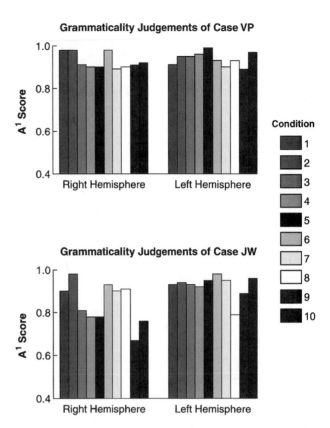

FIGURE 94.3   Percent correct on judgments of grammaticality in the right and left hemispheres of patients V.P. and J.W. Both subjects do well identifying grammatical sentences, but cannot use this information to guide sentence comprehension. (From Baynes and Gazzaniga, 1988.)

RH. It can seldom assure us that it thinks or feels without the language apparatus of the LH.

Moreover, there are marked differences among those RHs that possess some language (Baynes, 1990). P.S., one of the early patients in the Dartmouth series, displayed a sophisticated language system, with knowledge of subtle differences in meaning as well as an appreciation of some grammatical differences (Gazzaniga and LeDoux, 1978). P.S. was also one of the patients who proved to be able to generate speech from his RH. A similar profile was seen in V.P., who also demonstrated a good lexicon, some ability to identify aurally presented grammatical sentences but limited ability to use grammatical information to aid her sentence comprehension (figure 94.3), and early development of speech in her RH (Gazzaniga et al., 1984; Baynes and Gazzaniga, 1988). These are also the patients in whom some RH emotional valence has been documented. It remains unclear if the more well-developed language system contributes to the actual generation of the emotional valence or if it only makes it easier to observe.

In contrast, patient J.W. was for many years the prototype of the mute RH. Despite not producing spoken speech, J.W. displayed an excellent aural and visual vocabulary and could do a variety of semantic and grammatical tasks (figure 94.3), although generally not as accurately as V.P., despite psychometrically higher intelligence (Gazzaniga et al., 1984; Baynes and Gazzaniga, 1988; Baynes and Eliassen, 1998). He is skilled in drawing and even with his nondominant hand was often able to demonstrate recognition of stimuli displayed to his RH with his drawings. J.W.'s RH is skilled at a variety of nonlanguage tasks and has demonstrated relatively good attention and memory as well. These characteristics have been present since J.W.'s surgery, but more recently he has developed the ability to generate spoken responses to stimuli presented in his LVF (Baynes et al., 1995; Gazzaniga et al., 1996). This skill developed at a time well beyond the period associated with recovery of function after a neurological insult. How this apparent functional recovery occurred remains unknown. It is possible that the good auditory lexicon possessed by J.W.'s RH was sufficient for this process to occur, whereas other splits with language skills below a certain threshold are unable to develop in this way. However, a change of this nature implies a RH that is an active participant in the world, not a mere automaton.

Another problem in evaluating the status of language in the RH is the speed required to read tachistoscopic materials. Visual words are available for, at most, 150 milliseconds. Even the most verbally talented patients were slower to respond to words displayed to the RH, so perhaps some of our apparently nonverbal RH's could read, but not at tachistoscopic speeds. This was the case with D.R. (Baynes, Tramo, and Gazzaniga, 1992). D.R. was one of the brightest patients to undergo this surgery. She had a BA in accounting and had worked and traveled extensively. She enjoyed reading for pleasure. It seemed likely that, post-surgery, she would have a literate RH. However, after her surgery she was unable to respond accurately to many verbal experiments. It became apparent that if pictures were lateralized and D.R. was given the opportunity to read free-field, she could pick out the word that matched the picture she had seen. Since only her RH had seen the picture, this indicated that her RH could read when given sufficient time. Nonetheless, although D.R. can read free-field well enough to perform adequately on standardized tests, she no longer reads for pleasure, suggesting some change in language function following callosotomy.

A striking example of a loss of specific function due to section of callosal fibers occurred in patient V.J. Prior to surgery, V.J. was an avid reader who enjoyed corresponding with the members of her far-flung family. Post-surgery, V.J. became agraphic; i.e., she was unable to write at will or to take dictation with either hand. Although she has, over time, regained the ability to write

her signature, she remains unable to write despite extensive therapy. Unlike D.R., V.J. remains an avid reader; but now, almost three years post-surgery, she cannot write notes or lists or write words to dictation or the names of palpated objects. However, when words were lateralized tachistoscopically and her hands placed out of view, she was able to read out loud words displayed to her LH although she remained unable to write them (figure 94.4). More remarkably, when words were displayed to her RH, she was able to write them although she could not report them out loud (Baynes et al., 1998). In this patient, the motor commands for written language were isolated in her RH and could not be called into play by her dominant LH. Moreover, when asked to write the name of a picture or an object she had palpated, V.J. proved unable to do so. This ability to write words displayed to the LVF with the left hand, but to fail to write the names of pictures displayed to the LVF, suggested a slavish RH copying system that did not understand written language. But when asked to indicate whether words and pictures matched, V.J. proved very adept. Moreover, she also showed semantic priming in a lexical decision task in her RH, a task usually interpreted to indicate the presence of an intact semantic network. Her good, even excellent, performance on tasks that implied the presence of semantic knowledge was at odds with her apparent inability to write the name of a lateralized picture. She remained unable to write names, even when the pictures were displayed free field and she had as much time to respond as she needed.

The surprising lack of communication and integration in this system suggested that the language representation in V.J.'s right hemisphere might be a set of independent modules that lacked any productive capacity without the guidance of her dominant left hemisphere. Could we be observing a collection of modular components without any sense of self or conscious experience of its capacities? To answer this question, a series of paired questions, one correctly answered positively and one negatively, were posed to each hemisphere in writing. Answers were lateralized and presented randomly to each hemisphere so V.J. never knew which hemisphere would have to answer the questions. She demonstrated accurate knowledge about herself and her family in both hemispheres. So, although the loss of communication between her hemispheres has handicapped her RH, it may maintain an independent sense of self. However, even though the motor programs for writing are in her RH, it has not been able to use them to express independent thoughts and desires to date. It would be easy to conclude that the RH of this patient only supported preconscious modules that participated in reading and writing only at the behest of the dominant LH prior to surgery. These preliminary re-

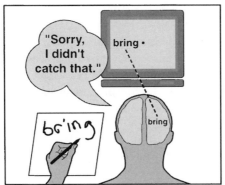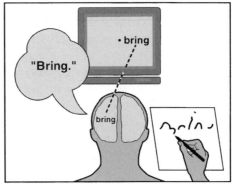

FIGURE 94.4   Examples of writing with the right and left hand of words lateralized to the ipsilateral visual field of patient V.J.

sults suggest this is a false picture of the isolated RH of V.J.; however, further studies are in progress to be certain whether this view can be correctly rejected.

Such behaviors indicate that RHs with varying language representation can exhibit goal-directed behavior and display the desire to cooperate with the experimenter to carry out experimental tasks. They demonstrate a variety of complex cognitive abilities that suggest the isolated RH is more than an automaton. Although these results have been obtained from some subjects with minimal RH language, RHs without language remain mysterious. Without a code for communication, we remain unable to engage those RHs so that we can be certain we are observing their optimum responses.

Consciousness and the cognitive basis of reality

Study of split-brain patients over the past forty years has helped change our understanding of the nature of consciousness. The left-brain Interpreter seems to be the executive, coordinating entity that enables all of the parts of a normal brain to interact with the environment in an integrated manner. But the status of the right brain continues to be a mystery. We can see some specialized capacities, hints of will and independence, but remain unable to positively characterize the RH or enlighten ourselves as to the experience of the world from the perspective of the RH. As we near the end of the Decade of the Brain, it appears George Bush may have been ahead of his time. It may be in the first decades of the 21st century that we see progress on the complex questions of human consciousness, will, and emotion built on the foundation of the more complete neurophysiological and neuropsychological understanding of brain function gained in this decade and on insights from the past.

In 1976, Rozin coined the term "cognitive unconscious" to describe the activity of the systems we have called "preconscious." Taking an evolutionary perspective, he suggested humans have evolved from creatures whose behavior was determined by modular systems with little integration. As these systems evolved and became more complex, consciousness emerged as a way of exerting executive control over diverse functions. One way of viewing the RH is as a less evolved entity with poor communication between modules, less sophisticated language, and debatable consciousness. Gazzaniga's (1983) view that a RH without language has cognitive skills that compare unfavorably with a chimpanzee may be consistent with such a view.

Perhaps we can re-invest the RH with some respectability by considering the evolutionary view of the implicit/explicit distinction proposed by Reber (1992). Reber does not find the arguments for modularity compelling, but he is sympathetic to the universality of the implicit/explicit distinction and suggests that implicit knowledge processes and explicit knowledge processes display similar phylogenic and ontogenic development. Further, he suggests that implicit knowledge may provide a basis for the kind of "intelligent" behavior that IQ tests fail to measure. As with most cognitive dichotomies, this one probably does not lateralize clearly into the hemispheres. But it may characterize one of the relevant differences between them. The LH may play a greater role in the expression of explicit knowledge and the right may be more adept at shaping behavior based on implicit knowledge—hence the lack of effect of callosotomy on psychometric intelligence, anecdotal changes in postoperative initiative and behavior notwithstanding.

Finally, the best examples of behavior that appear to represent consciousness in the RH come from those split-brain patients with at least some language capacity. Our newest patient, V.J., is anomalous in that she controls written and spoken output with different hemispheres. She is also unique in another way. She is the first split in my experience who is frequently dismayed by the independent performance of her right and left hands. She is discomfited by the fluent writing of her left hand to unseen stimuli and distressed by the inability of her right hand to write out words she can read out loud and spell. In the myriad articles discussing duality of consciousness, consciousness is sometimes considered as arising from the need for a single serial channel for motor output (Bradshaw, 1981; Güzeldere, Flanagan, and Hardcastle, this volume). In normally lateralized persons, the LH maintains control of output of both speech and writing. In V.J., we have two centers of control of the motor output of language, one partially disabled but still functional. One problem for this point of view is that some split-brain patients, notably J.W. and V.P., do have some control of motor speech from either hemisphere. However, in both of these cases, the control of spoken language developed after the surgical intervention, and this sequence of events may have different consequences for the conscious experience of it. If serial control of output is an important determinant of what we perceive as consciousness, and if the fluent shifting of control of output from one system to another is a part of that function, we may still have a good deal to learn from the split-brain model.

ACKNOWLEDGMENTS We gratefully acknowledge the support of NINDS P01 NS 17778 and the John S. McDonnell Foundation.

REFERENCES

BAYNES, K., 1990. Right hemisphere language and reading: Highways or byways of the brain? *J. Cogn. Neurosci.* 2:159–179.

BAYNES, K., and J. C. ELIASSEN, 1998. The visual word form: Its access and organization in commissurotomy patients. In *Right Hemisphere Language Comprehension: Perspectives from Cognitive Neuroscience*, C. Chiarello and M. Beeman, eds. Hillsdale, N.J.: Lawrence Erlbaum, pp. 79–104.

BAYNES, K., J. C. ELIASSEN, H. L. LUTSEP, and M. S. GAZZANIGA, 1998. Modular organization of cognitive systems masked by interhemispheric integration. *Science* 280:902–905.

BAYNES, K., and M. S. GAZZANIGA, 1988. Right hemisphere language: Insights into normal language mechanisms. In *Language, Communication and the Brain*, F. Plum, ed. New York: Raven Press.

BAYNES, K., M. J. TRAMO, and M. S. GAZZANIGA, 1992. Reading in the right hemisphere of a callosotomy patient. *Neuropsychologia* 30:187–200.

BAYNES, K., M. J. TRAMO, A. G. REEVES, and M. S. GAZZANIGA, 1997. Isolation of a right hemisphere cognitive system in a patient with anarchic (alien) hand sign. *Neuropsychologia* 35:1159–1173.

BAYNES, K., C. M. WESSINGER, R. FENDRICH, and M. S. GAZZANIGA, 1995. The emergence of the capacity of a disconnected right hemisphere to name LVF stimuli: Implications for functional plasticity. *Neuropsychologia* 31:1225–1242.

BERLIN, B., and P. KAY, 1969. *Basic Color Terms: Their Universality and Evolution.* Berkeley: University of California Press.

BISIACH, E., C. LUZZATTI, and D. PERANI, 1979. Unilateral neglect of representational schema and consciousness. *Brain* 102:609–618.

BRADSHAW, J., 1981. In two minds. *Behav. Brain Sci.* 4:101–102.

CAMPBELL, A. L., J. E. BOGEN, and A. SMITH, 1981. Disorganization and reorganization of cognitive and sensorimotor functions in cerebral commissurotomy: Compensatory roles of the forebrain commissures and cerebral hemispheres in man. *Brain* 104:493–511.

DENNETT, D., 1991. *Consciousness Explained.* Boston: Little, Brown.

DUTTON, D. G., and A. P. ARON, 1974. Some evidence for heightened sexual attraction under conditions of high anxiety. *J. Personality Soc. Psychol.* 30:510–517.

ECCLES, J., 1965. The brain and unity of conscious experience. *The 19th Arthur Stanley Eddington Memorial Lecture.* Cambridge: Cambridge University Press.

GAZZANIGA, M. S., 1983. Right hemisphere language following brain bisection: A 20-year perspective. *Am. Psychologist* 38:525–537.

GAZZANIGA, M. S., 1985. *The Social Brain.* New York: Basic Books.

GAZZANIGA, M. S., 1995. Consciousness and the cerebral hemispheres. In *The Cognitive Neurosciences,* M. S. Gazzaniga, ed. Cambridge, Mass.: MIT Press, pp. 1391–1400.

GAZZANIGA, M. S., 1998. *The Mind's Past.* Berkeley: University of California Press.

GAZZANIGA, M. S., J. E. BOGEN, and R. W. SPERRY, 1962. Some functional effects of sectioning the cerebral commissures in man. *Proc. Natl. Acad. Sci. U.S.A.* 48:1765–1769.

GAZZANIGA, M. S., J. E. BOGEN, and R. W. SPERRY, 1965. Observations on visual perception after disconnection of the cerebral commissures in man. *Brain* 88:221–236.

GAZZANIGA, M. S., J. C. ELIASSEN, L. NISENSON, R. FENDRICH, and K. BAYNES, 1996. Collaboration between the hemispheres of a callosotomy patient: Emerging right hemisphere speech and the left hemisphere interpreter. *Brain* 119:1255–1262.

GAZZANIGA, M. S., and S. A. HILLYARD, 1971. Language and speech capacity of the right hemisphere. *Neuropsychologia* 9:273–280.

GAZZANIGA, M. S., and J. E. LEDOUX, 1978. *The Integrated Mind.* New York: Plenum Press.

GAZZANIGA, M. S., J. E. LEDOUX, and D. H. WILSON, 1977. Language praxis and the right hemisphere: Clues to some mechanisms of consciousness. *Neurology* 27:1144–1147.

GAZZANIGA, M. S., C. SMYLIE, K. BAYNES, W. HIRST, and C. MCCLEARY, 1984. Profiles of right hemisphere language and speech following brain bisection. *Brain Lang.* 22:206–220.

GAZZANIGA, M. S., and R. W. SPERRY, 1966. Simultaneous double discrimination response following brain bisection. *Psychonomic Sci.* 4:261–262.

GAZZANIGA, M. S., and R. W. SPERRY, 1967. Language after section of the cerebral commissures. *Brain* 90:131–138.

HEIDER, E. R., 1972. Universals in color naming and memory. *J. Exp. Psychol.* 93:10–20.

JHA, A. P., N. KROLL, K. BAYNES, and M. S. GAZZANIGA, 1997. Memory encoding following complete commissurotomy. *J. Cogn. Neurosci.* 9:143–159.

KROLL, N. E. A., R. T. KNIGHT, J. METCALFE, E. S. WOLF, and E. TULVING, 1996. Cohesion failure as a source of memory illusions. *Mem. Lang.* 35:176–196.

LEDOUX, J. E., D. H. WILSON, and M. S. GAZZANIGA, 1977a. A divided mind: Observations on the conscious properties of the separated hemispheres. *Ann. Neurol.* 2:417–421.

LEDOUX, J. E., D. H. WILSON, and M. S. GAZZANIGA, 1977b. Manipulo-spatial aspects of cerebral lateralization: Clues to the origin of lateralization. *Neuropsychologia* 15:743–750.

PHELPS, E. A., and M. S. GAZZANIGA, 1992. Hemispheric differences in mnemonic processing: The effects of left hemisphere interpretation. *Neuropsychologia* 30:293–297.

PHELPS, E. A., W. HIRST, and M. S. GAZZANIGA, 1991. Deficits in recall following partial and complete commissurotomy. *Cereb. Cortex* 1(6):492–498.

PINKER, S., 1997. *How the Mind Works.* New York: Norton.

REBER, A. S., 1992. The cognitive unconscious: An evolutionary perspective. *Consciousness Cognit.* 1:93–133.

ROZIN, P., 1976. The evolution of intelligence and access to the cognitive unconscious. *Prog. Psychobiol. Physiol. Psychol.* 6:245–280.

TULVING, E., 1985. Memory and consciousness. *Canad. Psychol.* 25:1–12.

ZAIDEL, D., and R. W. SPERRY, 1974. Memory impairment after commissurotomy in man. *Brain* 97:263–272.

CONTRIBUTORS

ADELSON, EDWARD H.   Department of Brain and Cognitive Sciences, Massachusetts Institute of Technology, Cambridge, Massachusetts

ALLAN, KEVIN   Institute of Cognitive Neuroscience, University College London, London, England

ANDERSEN, R. A.   Division of Biology, California Institute of Technology, Pasadena, California

ARMONY, JORGE L.   Institute of Cognitive Neuroscience, University College, London, England

BAILEY, CRAIG H.   Center for Neurobiology and Behavior, College of Physicians and Surgeons of Columbia University, New York, New York

BARON-COHEN, SIMON   Departments of Experimental Psychology and Psychiatry, University of Cambridge, Cambridge, England

BARTSCH, DUSAN   Center for Neurobiology and Behavior, College of Physicians and Surgeons of Columbia University, New York, New York

BASSO, MICHELE A.   Laboratory of Sensorimotor Research, National Eye Institute, National Institutes of Health, Bethesda, Maryland

BATISTA, A. P.   Division of Biology, California Institute of Technology, Pasadena, California

BAVELIER, DAPHNE   University of Rochester, Rochester, New York

BAYNES, KATHLEEN   Center for Neuroscience, University of California at Davis, Davis, California

BECHARA, ANTOINE   Department of Neurology, Division of Behavioral Neurology and Cognitive Neuroscience, University of Iowa College of Medicine, Iowa City, Iowa

BEHRMANN, MARLENE   Department of Psychology, Carnegie Mellon University, Pittsburgh, Pennsylvania

BIZZI, EMILIO   Department of Brain and Cognitive Sciences, Massachusetts Institute of Technology, Cambridge, Massachusetts

BLACK, IRA B.   Department of Neuroscience and Cell Biology, Robert Wood Johnson Medical School, University of Medicine and Dentistry of New Jersey, Piscataway, New Jersey

BLAKEMORE, COLIN   University Laboratory of Physiology, Oxford University, Oxford, England

BOURGEOIS, JEAN-PIERRE   Laboratoire de Neurobiologie Moleculaire, Departement des Biotechnologies, Institut Pasteur, Paris, France

BRAINARD, MICHAEL S.   Departments of Physiology and Psychiatry and Keck Center for Integrative Neuroscience, University of California, San Francisco, California

BROWN, COLIN M.   Neurocognition of Language Processing Research Group, Max Planck Institute for Psycholinguistics, Nijmegen, The Netherlands

BUCKNER, RANDY L.   Departments of Psychology, Anatomy and Neurobiology, and Radiology, Washington University, St. Louis, Missouri

BUNEO, C. A.   Division of Biology, California Institute of Technology, Pasadena, California

CAHILL, LARRY   Center for the Neurobiology of Learning and Memory and Department of Neurobiology and Behavior, University of California, Irvine, California

CARAMAZZA, ALFONSO   Department of Psychology, Harvard University, Cambridge, Massachusetts

CHAFEE, MATTHEW V.   Brain Science Center, VA Medical Center, Minneapolis, Minnesota

CHALUPA, LEO M.   Section of Neurobiology, Physiology, and Behavior, University of California, Davis, California

CHELAZZI, LEONARDO   Dipartimento di Scienze Neurologiche e della Visione, University of Verona, Verona, Italy

CHRISTOPHE, ANNE   Laboratoire de Sciences Cognitives et Psycholinguistique, Ecole des Hautes Etudes en Sciences Sociales, CNRS, UMR 8554, Paris, France

COHEN, Y. E.   Division of Biology, California Institute of Technology, Pasadena, California

CORBETTA, MAURIZIO   Department of Neurology, Radiology, Anatomy and Neurobiology, and the McDonnell Center for Studies of Higher Brain Functions, Washington University, St. Louis, Missouri

COSMIDES, LEDA   Center for Evolutionary Psychology and Department of Psychology, University of California, Santa Barbara, California

CRICK, FRANCIS   The Salk Institute, La Jolla, California

CROWLEY, JUSTIN C.   Howard Hughes Medical Institute and Department of Neurobiology, Duke University Medical Center, Durham, North Carolina

CUMMING, BRUCE G.   University Laboratory of Physiology, Oxford University, Oxford, England

CURRAN, H. VALERIE   Clinical Health Psychology, University College London, London, England

CURRAN, TIM   Department of Psychology, Case Western Reserve University, Cleveland, Ohio

DAMASIO, ANTONIO R.   Department of Neurology, Division of Behavioral Neurology and Cognitive Neuroscience, University of Iowa College of Medicine, Iowa City, Iowa

DANEMAN, MEREDYTH   Department of Psychology, University of Toronto, Mississauga, Ontario, Canada

DAVIDSON, RICHARD J.   Department of Psychology, University of Wisconsin, Madison, Wisconsin

DEANGELIS, GREGORY C.   Howard Hughes Medical Institute and Department of Neurobiology, Stanford University School of Medicine, Stanford, California

DELL, GARY S.   Beckman Institute, University of Illinois at Urbana-Champaign, Urbana, Illinois

DEHAENE, STANISLAS   INSERM U. 334, Service Hospitalier Frédéric Joliot, CEA/DRM/DSV, Orsay, France

DESIMONE, ROBERT   Laboratory of Neuropsychology, National Institute of Mental Health, National Institutes of Health, Bethesda, Maryland

DIGIROLAMO, GREGORY J.   Beckman Institute, University of Illinois, Urbana, Illinois

DODD, JON V.   University Laboratory of Physiology, Oxford University, Oxford, England

DOLAN, RAYMOND J.   Wellcome Department of Cognitive Neurology, Institute of Neurology, London, England

DOUPE, ALLISON J.   Departments of Physiology and Psychiatry and Keck Center for Integrative Neuroscience, University of California, San Francisco, California

DOYA, KENJI   Kawato Dynamic Brain Project, ERATO, Japan Science and Technology Corporation, Kyoto, Japan, and Howard Hughes Medical Institute, Salk Institute for Biological Studies, La Jolla, California

DRONKERS, NINA F.   VA Northern California Health Care System and University of California, Davis, California

ERICKSON, CYNTHIA A.   Laboratory of Neuropsychology, National Institute of Mental Health, National Institutes of Health, Bethesda, Maryland

FARAH, MARTHA J.   Department of Psychology, University of Pennsylvania, Philadelphia, Pennsylvania

FERNALD, RUSSELL D.   Neuroscience Program and Department of Psychology, Stanford University, Stanford, California

FIEZ, JULIE A.   Department of Psychology, University of Pittsburgh, Pittsburgh, Pennsylvania

FLANAGAN, OWEN   Departments of Philosophy, Psychology (Experimental), and Neurobiology, Duke University, Durham, North Carolina

FOGASSI, LEONARDO   Istituto di Fisiologia Umana, Università di Parma, Parma, Italy

GALLESE, VITTORIO   Istituto di Fisiologia Umana, Università di Parma, Parma, Italy

GALLISTEL, C. R.   Department of Psychology, University of California, Los Angeles, California

GAZZANIGA, MICHAEL S.   Director, Program in Cognitive Neuroscience, Dartmouth College, Hanover, New Hampshire

GEORGOPOULOS, APOSTOLOS P.   Brain Sciences Center, Veterans Affairs Medical Center and Cognitive Sciences Center, Departments of Neuroscience, Physiology, Neurology, and Psychiatry, University of Minnesota, Minneapolis, Minnesota

GHEZ, CLAUDE   Center for Neurobiology and Behavior, N.Y.S. Psychiatric Institute, Columbia University, College of Physicians and Surgeons, New York, New York

GHILARDI, MARIA-FELICE   Center for Neurobiology and Behavior, Columbia University, New York, New York, and INB-CNR, Milan, Italy

GOLDMAN-RAKIC, PATRICIA S.   Section of Neurobiology, Yale University School of Medicine, New Haven, Connecticut

GOODALE, MELVYN A.   Department of Psychology and Graduate Program in Neuroscience, University of Western Ontario, London, Ontario, Canada

GRABOWECKY, MARCIA   Department of Psychology, Northwestern University, Evanston, Illinois

GÜZELDERE, GÜVEN   Department of Philosophy and Center for Cognitive Neuroscience, Duke University, Durham, North Carolina

HAGOORT, PETER   Neurocognition of Language Processing Research Group, Max Planck Institute for Psycholinguistics, Nijmegen, The Netherlands

HANDY, TODD C.   Department of Psychology and Center for Neuroscience, University of California, Davis, California

HARDCASTLE, VALERIE GRAY   Department of Philosophy, Virginia Tech, Blacksburg, Virginia

HAXBY, JAMES V.   National Institute of Mental Health, Laboratory of Brain and Cognition, Bethesda, Maryland

HESSLER, NEAL A.   Departments of Physiology and Psychiatry and Keck Center for Integrative Neuroscience, University of California, San Francisco, California

HIKOSAKA, O.   Department of Physiology, Juntendo University, School of Medicine, Tokyo, Japan

HILLYARD, STEVEN A.   Department of Neurosciences, University of California, San Diego, La Jolla, California

HOBSON, J. ALLAN   Laboratory of Neurophysiology, Department of Psychiatry, Harvard Medical School, Boston, Massachusetts

HOPFINGER, JOSEPH B.   Department of Psychology and Center for Neuroscience, University of California, Davis, California

INDEFREY, PETER   Max Planck Institute for Psycholinguistics, Nijmegen, The Netherlands

IVRY, RICHARD B.   Department of Psychology, University of California, Berkeley, California

JAGADEESH, BHARATHI   Laboratory of Neuropsychology, National Institute of Mental Health, National Institutes of Health, Bethesda, Maryland

JHA, AMISHI P.   Brain Imaging and Analysis Center, Duke University, Durham, North Carolina

JONIDES, JOHN   Department of Psychology, University of Michigan, Ann Arbor, Michigan

JORDAN, MICHAEL I.   Division of Computer Science and Department of Statistics, University of California, Berkeley, California

KAAS, JON H.   Department of Psychology, Vanderbilt University, Nashville, Tennessee

KANDEL, ERIC R.   Howard Hughes Medical Institute and Center for Neurobiology and Behavior, College of Physicians and Surgeons of Columbia University, New York, New York

KATZ, LAWRENCE C.   Howard Hughes Medical Institute and Department of Neurobiology, Duke University Medical Center, Durham, North Carolina

KERSTEN, DANIEL   Department of Psychology, University of Minnesota, Minneapolis, Minnesota

KING, ANDREW J.   University Laboratory of Physiology, Oxford University, Oxford, England

KNIGHT, ROBERT T.   Department of Psychology, University of California, Berkeley; Veterans Medical Center, Martinez, California

KNOWLTON, BARBARA J.   Department of Psychology, University of California, Los Angeles, California

KOCH, CHRISTOF   Computation and Neural Systems Program, California Institute of Technology, Pasadena, California

KOSSLYN, STEPHEN M.   Department of Psychology, Harvard University, Cambridge, Massachusetts

KRAKAUER, JOHN W.   Department of Neurology, Columbia University, College of Physicians and Surgeons, New York, New York

KUHL, PATRICIA K.   Department of Speech and Hearing Sciences, University of Washington, Seattle, Washington

KUTAS, MARTA   Department of Cognitive Science, University of California, San Diego, California

LABERGE, DAVID   Department of Cognitive Sciences, University of California, Irvine, California

LAMME, VICTOR A. F.   The Netherlands Ophthalmic Research Institute, Amsterdam, The Netherlands

LEDOUX, JOSEPH E.   Center for Neural Science, New York University, New York, New York

LESLIE, ALAN M.   Department of Psychology and Center for Cognitive Science, Rutgers University, Piscataway, New Jersey

LEVELT, WILLEM J. M.   Max Planck Institute for Psycholinguistics, Nijmegen, The Netherlands

LEVINE, ERIC S.   Department of Pharmacology, University of Connecticut Health Center, Farmington, Connecticut

LEVITT, PAT   Department of Neurobiology, University of Pittsburgh School of Medicine, Pittsburgh, Pennsylvania

LU, X.   Department of Physiology, Juntendo University, School of Medicine, Tokyo, Japan

LUCK, STEVEN J.   Department of Psychology, University of Iowa, Iowa City, Iowa

LYNCH, GARY   Department of Psychiatry and Human Behavior, University of California, Irvine, California

MANGUN, GEORGE R.   Center for Cognitive Neuroscience, Duke University, Durham, North Carolina

MARKOWITSCH, HANS J.   Physiological Psychology, University of Bielefeld, Bielefeld, Germany

MARTIN, ALEX   National Institute of Mental Health, Laboratory of Brain and Cognition, Bethesda, Maryland

MARTIN, KELSEY C.   Center for Neurobiology and Behavior, College of Physicians and Surgeons of Columbia University, New York, New York

MAUNSELL, JOHN H. R.   Howard Hughes Medical Institute and Division of Neuroscience, Baylor College of Medicine, Houston, Texas

MCADAMS, CARRIE J.   Division of Neuroscience, Baylor College of Medicine, Houston, Texas

MCCARTHY, GREGORY   Brain Imaging and Analysis Center, Duke University Medical Center, and Veterans Affairs Medical Center, Durham, North Carolina

MCEWEN, BRUCE S.   Harold and Margaret Milliken Hatch Laboratory of Neuroendocrinology, Rockefeller University, New York, New York

MCGAUGH, JAMES L.   Center for the Neurobiology of Learning and Memory and Department of Neurobiology and Behavior, University of California, Irvine, California

MEHLER, JACQUES   Laboratoire de Sciences Cognitives et Psycholinguistique, Ecole des Hautes Etudes en Sciences Sociales, CNRS, UMR 8554, Paris, France

MERIKLE, PHILIP M.   Department of Psychology, University of Waterloo, Waterloo, Ontario, Canada

MIDDLEBROOKS, JOHN C.   Kresge Hearing Research Institute, University of Michigan, Ann Arbor, Michigan

MIYACHI, S.   Department of Physiology, Juntendo University, School of Medicine, Tokyo, Japan

MIYASHITA, YASUSHI   Department of Physiology, The University of Tokyo School of Medicine, Hongo, Tokyo; Laboratory of Cognitive Neuroscience, National Institute for Physiological Sciences, Okazaki; Mind Articulation Project, ICORP, Japan Science and Technology Corporation, Yushima, Tokyo, Japan

MOVSHON, J. ANTHONY   Center for Neural Science, New York University, New York, New York

MURRAY, ELISABETH A.   Laboratory of Neuropsychology, National Institute of Mental Health, National Institutes of Health, Bethesda, Maryland

MUSSA-IVALDI, FERDINANDO A.   Department of Physiology, Northwestern University, Chicago, Illinois

NAKAHARA, H.   Department of Physiology, Juntendo University, School of Medicine, Tokyo, Japan

NAKAMURA, K.   Department of Physiology, Juntendo University, School of Medicine, Tokyo, Japan

NEVILLE, HELEN J.   University of Oregon, Eugene, Oregon

NEWSOME, WILLIAM T.   Howard Hughes Medical Institute and Department of Neurobiology, Stanford University School of Medicine, Stanford, California

NISHIJO, HISAO   Department of Physiology, Faculty of Medicine, Toyama Medical and Pharmaceutical University, Toyama, Japan

NORRIS, DENNIS   Medical Research Council Cognition and Brain Sciences Unit, Cambridge, England

ONO, TAKETOSHI   Department of Physiology, Faculty of Medicine, Toyama Medical and Pharmaceutical University, Toyama, Japan

ORR, SCOTT P.   Veterans Affairs Research Service, Manchester, New Hampshire; Massachusetts General Hospital, Boston, Massachusetts; Department of Psychiatry, Harvard Medical School, Boston, Massachusetts

Ó SCALAIDHE, SÉAMAS P.   Section of Neurobiology, Yale University School of Medicine, New Haven, Connecticut

PACE-SCHOTT, EDWARD F.   Laboratory of Neurophysiology, Department of Psychiatry, Harvard Medical School, Boston, Massachusetts

PARÉ, MARTIN   Laboratory of Sensorimotor Research, National Eye Institute, National Institutes of Health, Bethesda, Maryland

PARKER, ANDREW J.   University Laboratory of Physiology, Oxford University, Oxford, England

PITMAN, ROGER K.   Veterans Affairs Research Service, Manchester, New Hampshire; Massachusetts General Hospital, Boston, Massachusetts; Department of Psychiatry, Harvard Medical School, Boston, Massachusetts

POSNER, MICHAEL I.   Sackler Institute, Weill Medical College of Cornell University, Ithaca, New York

PREUSS, TODD M.   Institute of Cognitive Science, University of Southwestern Louisiana–New Iberia Research Center, New Iberia, Louisiana

RAFAL, ROBERT   University of Wales, Bangor, Wales

RAICHLE, MARCUS E.   Departments of Radiology and Neurology, Washington University School of Medicine, St. Louis, Missouri

RAKIC, PASKO   Section of Neurobiology, Yale University School of Medicine, New Haven, Connecticut

RAND, M. K.   Department of Physiology, Juntendo University, School of Medicine, Tokyo, Japan

RECANZONE, GREGG H.   Center for Neuroscience and Section of Neurobiology, Physiology, and Behavior, University of California, Davis, California

REDFERN, BRENDA B.   VA Northern California Health Care System and University of California, Davis, California

RINGACH, DARIO   Center for Neural Science, New York University, New York, New York

RIZZOLATTI, GIACOMO   Istituto di Fisiologia Umana, Universitá di Parma, Parma, Italy

ROBERTSON, LYNN C.   Veterans Affairs Neurology Research and Department of Psychology, University of California, Berkeley, California

ROOZENDAAL, BENNO   Center for the Neurobiology of Learning and Memory and Department of Neurobiology and Behavior, University of California, Irvine, California

RUGG, MICHAEL D.   Institute of Cognitive Neuroscience, University College London, London, England

SAFFRAN, ELEANOR M.   Center for Cognitive Neuroscience, Temple University School of Medicine, Philadelphia, Pennsylvania

SAINBURG, ROBERT L.   School of Health Related Professions, State University of New York at Buffalo, Buffalo, New York

SAKAI, K.   Department of Physiology, Juntendo University, School of Medicine, Tokyo, Japan

SCHACTER, DANIEL L.   Department of Psychology, Harvard University, Cambridge, Massachusetts

SCHNUPP, JAN W. H.   University Laboratory of Physiology, Oxford University, Oxford, England

SCHWARTZ, MYRNA F.   Moss Rehabilitation Research Institute, Philadelphia, Pennsylvania

SEJNOWSKI, TERRENCE J.   Department of Biology, University of California, San Diego, and Howard Hughes Medical Institute, Salk Institute for Biological Studies, La Jolla, California

SHALEV, ARIEH Y.   Department of Psychiatry, Hadassah University Hospital; Hebrew University Medical School, Jerusalem, Israel

SHAMMA, SHIHAB A.   Center for Auditory and Acoustic Research, Institute for Systems Research, Department of Electrical Engineering, University of Maryland, College Park, Maryland

SHAPLEY, ROBERT   Center for Neural Science, New York University, New York, New York

SHERRY, DAVID F.   Department of Psychology, University of Western Ontario, London, Ontario, Canada

SINGER, WOLF   Department of Neurophysiology, Max Planck Institute for Brain Research, Frankfurt, Germany

SMITH, EDWARD E.   Department of Psychology, University of Michigan, Ann Arbor, Michigan

SNYDER, L. H.   Division of Biology, California Institute of Technology, Pasadena, California

SOMMER, MARC A.   Laboratory of Sensorimotor Research, National Eye Institute, National Institutes of Health, Bethesda, Maryland

SPEKREIJSE, HENK   Graduate School of Neurosciences, AMC, University of Amsterdam, Amsterdam, The Netherlands

SQUIRE, LARRY R.   Department of Psychiatry and Neurosciences, University of California at San Diego, and Department of Veterans Affairs, San Diego, California

STANFORD, TERRENCE R.   Department of Neurobiology and Anatomy, Wake Forest University School of Medicine, Winston-Salem, North Carolina

STEIN, BARRY E.   Department of Neurobiology and Anatomy, Wake Forest University School of Medicine, Winston-Salem, North Carolina

STICKGOLD, ROBERT   Laboratory of Neurophysiology, Department of Psychiatry, Harvard Medical School, Boston, Massachusetts

STROMSWOLD, KARIN   Department of Psychology and Center for Cognitive Science, Rutgers University, New Brunswick, New Jersey

TELLER, DAVIDA Y.   Departments of Psychology and Physiology/Biophysics, University of Washington, Seattle, Washington

THOMPSON, WILLIAM L.   Department of Psychology, Harvard University, Cambridge, Massachusetts

TOOBY, JOHN   Center for Evolutionary Psychology and Department of Anthropology, University of California, Santa Barbara, California

TRANEL, DANIEL   Department of Neurology, Division of Behavioral Neurology and Cognitive Neuroscience, University of Iowa College of Medicine, Iowa City, Iowa

TULVING, ENDEL   Rotman Research Institute, Baycrest Centre for Geriatric Care, North York, Ontario, Canada

UNGERLEIDER, LESLIE G.   National Institute of Mental Health, Laboratory of Brain and Cognition, Bethesda, Maryland

WALLACE, MARK T.   Department of Neurobiology and Anatomy, Wake Forest University School of Medicine, Winston-Salem, North Carolina

WANDELL, BRIAN A.   Neuroscience Program and Department of Psychology, Stanford University, Stanford, California

WEFERS, CARA J.   Section of Neurobiology, Physiology, and Behavior, University of California, Davis, California

WELIKY, MICHAEL   Center for Visual Science, University of Rochester, Rochester, New York

WHITE, STEPHANIE A.   Neurosciences Program, Duke University, Durham, North Carolina

WILSON, M. A.   Departments of Brain and Cognitive Sciences and Biology, Center for Learning and Memory, Massachusetts Institute of Technology, Cambridge, Massachusetts

WISE, RICHARD   Medical Research Council Cyclotron Unit and Imperial College School of Medicine, Hammersmith Hospital, London, England

WOLPERT, DANIEL M.   Sobell Department of Neurophysiology, Institute of Neurology, University College, London, England

WURTZ, ROBERT H.   Laboratory of Sensorimotor Research, National Eye Institute, National Institutes of Health, Bethesda, Maryland

ZHOU, RENPING   Department of Chemical Biology, College of Pharmacy, Rutgers University, and Department of Neuroscience and Cell Biology, Robert Wood Johnson Medical School, Piscataway, New Jersey

INDEX

Brain Electrical Source Analysis (BESA) algorithm, 628, 702
Brain-mind isomorphism, during REM sleep, 1345
Brainstem, 1048
    activation/deactivation, during NREM/REM sleep, 1342, 1352
    attention mechanisms, 712
    and auditory localization, 425, 435
    axons in, origin of, 9
    in dreaming, 1349, 1351
    GABAergic neurons, 442–443
    lesions, and dreaming, 1349
    and neural correlates of consciousness, 1316
    neuromodulatory centers, and neuronal activity, 225
    nuclei, 1048
    olivo-cochlear bundle, inhibitory control, 1320
    prefrontal damage and, 1321
    REM sleep and, 1346, 1349–1350
    saccades, 486
    song-learning motor pathways in, 453, 471
Brightness, defined, 342
Brightness illusions, 343
Broca's aphasia, 951–952, 955–956
Broca's area, 859, 862, 890–892, 915, 949, 952, 1008, 1025
    activity, 1028
    asymmetry of, 1228–1229
    injuries to, 956
    involvement, 955
    nonhuman homologs to, 1225–1227
Brodmann numbers, 1019
Brodmann's area, 817, 824–825, 874, 991, 1019, 1023
    activation/deactivation, during NREM/REM sleep, 1343
Brood parasitism, 1211–1212
Buildup neurons, 486–487

C

Cadherin gene family, as guidance molecules in regionalization of cerebral cortex, 28
Cadherins, in long-term potentiation, 146
Calbindin, 1229–1230
Calcarine cortex. See Prefrontal cortex
Calcium
    fluctuations, in migrating neurons, 11
    and synaptic growth and stabilization, 466
Calcium channels
    in hippocampus, 187
    nerve growth factor and, 163, 165
Calculus of variations, 603
Callosotomy, split-brain research and, 1357–1358, 1362
Canonical babbling, in speech development, 102
Capacity reduction effect, 937
CAPS/CC READER, 934
Carnivores, retinocollicular pathway in, topographic organization of, 33, 42
Cartesian framework, kinematic cost models, 603–604
Caspases, in programmed cell death, 10
Castration, and hippocampus, 175
Cat(s)
    gamma-frequency oscillations in, 1345
    multisensory integration in, 59, 68
    neural response in, synchronization of, 333
    NREM sleep in, EEG oscillation during, 1344
    prefrontal-thalamic sensory system of, 1320
    retinocollicular pathway in, topographic organization of, 33, 42
    strabismic amblyopia in, 333
    superior colliculus of, postnatal development of, 62–63

Categories. See also Categorization; Semantic category-specific deficits
    functional, 913
    lexical, 913
    linguistic, 913
    mental representations of, 1013
    syntactic, acquisition of, 910–911
Categorization
    cognitive neuroscience of, 1013, 1019–1021
    dot-pattern, 1015–1016, 1021
    exemplar-based, 1014
    and explicit memory, 1016
    mechanisms of, 1013, 1020
    memory-based, 1018
    rule-based, 1018
Categorization tasks, 832
    performance of
        by amnesic patients, 1015–1016
        by neurological patients, 1017–1018
        by normal subjects, 1017–1019
    probabilistic, 1016
Category learning, 830, 832
    memory and, 773–775
Category numbers, 1028
Category prototypes, 102–103
Category-specific cerebral circuit, 996
Category-specific deficits, 1027, 1030, 1039, 1043–1044. See also Semantic category-specific deficits
Category-specific effects
    functional magnetic resonance imaging of, 1023
    positron emission tomography of, 1023
Category-specific knowledge disorders, 1029
Category-specific naming, 1029
Category-specific regions, 859
Category-specific semantic representation, 987, 1039
Caudal orbital activation/deactivation, during waking/NREM/REM sleep, 1347
Caudate activation/deactivation, during waking/NREM/REM sleep, 1347
Caudate nucleus
    left, 854
    right, 854
Causative constructions, 910
CCAAT enhancer-binding protein (C/EBP), 126, 128
Cell adhesion molecules (CAMs)
    down-regulation of, by serotonin, 129–131
    in long-term potentiation, 145–146
Cell-cell recognition, in neuronal migration, 11
Cell cycle, duration of, and cortical size, 9, 13
Cell death
    histogenetic, 10
    programmed. See Programmed cell death
Cell dispersion, and cortical specification, 27, 29
Cell fate
    alteration by transplantion of progenitor cells, 25–26
    in cortex, molecular determinants of, 25
    and cortical regionalization, 27, 29
    of mitotically active and postmitotic cells, 27
    of ventricular zone cells, 15
Cell nucleus, translocation during neuronal migration, 11
Cell perikarya, 11
Cell soma
    in formation of bilaminate cortical plate, 16
    synaptic localization on, 45, 51
    translocation during neuronal migration, 11

Cell transplants
    of cortical progenitor cells, 25–26
    of mitotically active cells, phenotypic fate of, 27
    to test differentiative potential of cortical material, 25–26
Cellular context and cellular differentiation, 24
Center of mass calculations, object-based neglect and, 660
Center-surround processing, 339–340
Central auditory system. *See* Auditory cortex
Central executive system. *See* Executive control
Central nervous system
    and computational motor control, 601
    cortical anomalies and, 29–30
    embryonic development of, 23, 30
    and motor skill restoration, 498
    parcellation of domains in, 23
    regionalization of, 23, 30
    representation of movement in, 489
Central nucleus, 1068
    of inferior colliculus, 446
Central pattern generators, 469
Cerebellar cortex, 1006, 1023
Cerebellar hemispheres, 1000
Cerebellar timing system, 1006
Cerebello-prefrontal pathways, 1000
Cerebellum, 848
    activation, 851, 860, 1002, 1004, 1007–1008
    activation/deactivation, during NREM/REM sleep, 1342
    blood flow difference images of, word reading studies and, 1310
    classicial conditioning and, 776
    cognitive functions of, 1225
        evidence for, 999–1002
    error signal, 1005
    evolutionary changes in, 1225
    function, 999, 1007
    left/medial, 860
    lesions of, 1003–1004
    medial lateral, 854
    midline, 859
    neurogenesis in, 9
    neurotrophins in, 162–164
    pathology of, 1000–1001. *See also* Neuropsychological tests
    right lateral, 854
    right medial, 854
    saccades, 486
    task domain, 1006
    working memory activation in, 402
Cerebral convolutions
    formation of, in mouse embryos, 10
    relationship to subplate zone, 9
Cerebral cortex. *See also entries under* Cortical
    asymmetries in, 1228–1229
    cellular constituents of
        early divergence of, 9
        formation of, 7, 18
    coding in. *See* Coding
    developmental anomalies of, consequences of, 29–30
    form information processing in, 85–86
    lesions, and auditory localization, 425
    and Lichtheim's brain formulation, 1311
    and memory storage, 789–790
    and neurocognitive development, 83, 96
    organization of, 253
    parcellation of, 1225
        cellular organization and, 45
    regionalization, molecular determinants of, 25, 30
    size of, 9, 13

synaptogenesis in, 45, 51
    vision projection systems in, 367–368
    and visuospatial attention, 667–682
Cerebral infarction, 954
Cerebral substrates, 992
Cerebrum
    germinal matrix of, neurogenesis in, 9
    structures of, 860
Change in reward magnitude, 1085
Charcot-Wilbrand syndrome, 1348
Chemical stimulation, of lumbar spinal cord, 493–494, 496
Chemoaffinity hypothesis, 214
Chemoarchitecture, of primate neocortex, 45
Chemotactic attractants, 15
Children
    abandoned, linguistic development of, 102
    behavior of
        reality checking and, 1333
        simulation and, 1333
    cerebral organization in, primary language acquisition and, 93, 96
    language-impaired, 919
    and prefrontal patients, similarities between, 1333
    specific language impairment in, 917, 923
    wild, 914
        linguistic development of, 102
Chimeric mice, 14, 27
Chloramphenicol acetyl-transferase (CAT) gene, 123–124
Cholinergic system
    agonists, and memory enhancement, 802–803
    autoreceptors, REM sleep and, 1346
    memory function and, 798–800
Chomsky, Noam, 99, 101
Chromaticity, infant sensitivity to, 77, 79
Chronometric studies, 988
Chunking, artificial grammar learning and, 771–772
Cingulate cortex. *See also* Anterior cingulate cortex; Posterior cingulate cortex
    activation of, 851
    and attention control, 627–628, 668–669
    blood flow difference images of, 1310, 1313
    novelty and, 1325–1326
    in spatially selective attention, 668–669
Cingulate gyrus, and emotion-specific facial expression, 404
Classical conditioning, 1016
    Aplysia studies of, 131–132
    aversive, emotional learning and, 1119–1120, 1124, 1128
    memory function and, 775–776
    neuronal effects of, 238–239
Classification tasks, 832
Clausal boundaries, 911
Clean-up units, 943–944
Clones, neuronal, 11, 13, 15
Cochlea, 414, 439, 471
    hair cells in, 412
    multiscale analysis, 417
    olivo-cochlear bundle and, 1320
Cochlear nucleus/nuclei, 412–414, 417, 425, 440–441
    lateral inhibition in, 413
    ventral, 440
Coding. *See also* Population coding
    discharge rates, 327
    face, 401, 406
    object-centered, 368
    odors, 335
    place, 437

Markers, molecular
  and differentiation of cortical tissue, 26
  and retinal decussation, 36, 38
Matching task. *See* Word-to-definition matching task
Maternal language, 902
Mathematical models
  exemplar-based, 1013
  prototype-based, 1013
Max-1 genes, in regionalization of forebrain, 24
Meaning-based deep encoding task, 819
Meaning-based task, 819
Meaningfulness, 853
Mean length of utterance, 924
Medial diencephalic amnesia, 783
Medial diencephalon, memory transfer and,
    788–789
Medial geniculate body, 413, 1068–1069
  medial division, 1068, 1070–1071
  ventral division, 1070
Medial geniculate nucleus, during value-dependent learning,
    1122
Medial occipital activations, 854
Medial temporal diencephalic system, 1016
Medial temporal lobe amnesia, 783
Medial temporal region, 834
Mediodorsal nucleus, and attention mechanisms, 714
Mediolateral segments, 851
Melody recognition, 420
Memories about emotions, 1076
Memorization, 820. *See also* Word(s)
Memory. *See also* Facilitation, synaptic; Implicit memory;
      Learning; Working memory
  acquisition of, 786–787
  affect and, 784–786
  anatomical bases of, 781–793
  areal specificity and, 737–738
  arousal and, 800–801
  and artificial grammar learning, 771–773
  associative, 379–391, 977
    object recognition and, 755–758
    pair-association tasks, 380–381
  associative networks, 470
  attention and, 801–802
  brain damage and, 783–784
  brain systems and, 733–740, 765–776
  category learning and, 773–775
  classical conditioning and, 775–776
  cognitive. *See* Cognitive memory
  cognitive neuroscience analyses of, 817, 819
  components
    conceptually driven, 806
    data-driven, 806
  conjunction errors, 834
  conscious awareness and, 729, 1287
  consolidation, 139–154, 509–512
    amygdala in, 1083–1085
    medial temporal lobe in, 390
    neuromodulatory influences on, 1083–1085
  declarative, 830, 1076. *See also* Fear
    definition of, 728
    medial temporal lobe components for,
      767–768
    versus nondeclarative, 729–730, 765
    remembering versus knowing and, 769
  disorders of. *See* Amnesia
  drug specificity and, 800

  emotional
    arousal and, 1081
      posttraumatic stress disorder and, 1136–1137
      stress hormones and, 1139–1140
    encoding, 820–821
    episodic. *See* Episodic memory(ies)
    event-related potentials in, 805–806
    explicit, 806, 832, 1076, 1274
      contamination of, 807
      definition of, 728
      versus implicit, 729–730, 765, 1016
      incidental, 806
      involuntary, 806, 831
      retrieval of, 824–825
      voluntary, 831
    faces and, 400–402
    false, 829, 833–836
    formation of, 820
      backward signal role in, 386, 390
    gene expression in, 122–128
    habits and, 771
    high vocal center (HVc), 471–472
    iconic, 1287
    illusory, 833
    long-term, 379–391, 509–510, 824, 850, 889, 1014, 1081, 1093
      acquisition processes for, 786–787
      anatomical bases of, 782
      encoding, 385, 819, 821
      Kornhuber's memory processing scheme for, 784, 785
      psychopharmacology and, 799–800
      retrograde amnesia and, 766
      transfer to, 787–789
    medial prefrontal cortex in, 1151
    medial temporal lobe function and
      neural network homogeneity and, 758–759
      retrograde amnesia and, 765–767
      specialization, 759–761
      system components, 767–768
    modification of synaptic connections and, 49
    modulatory influences and, 1081
    neuroimaging and, 817–818, 835–836
    neuropsychology of, 730–731
    NMDA receptors and, 803
    nondeclarative, 830
      and artificial grammar learning, 771–773
      and category learning, 773–775
      classical conditioning as, 775–776
      versus declarative memory, 729–730, 765
      and priming, 769–771
      and skills and habits, 771
    object, nonhuman primate studies of, 753–761
    olfactory recognition, studies of, 758–759
    PET scan study of, 1093
    pharmacological specificity and, 802–803
    in posttraumatic stress disorder
      and hippocampal structure, 1141–1142
      and systems of cool and hot, 1142–1143
    procedural, 728
    psychopharmacological approaches to, 797–802
    recall, 381
    recollection, 809
    remembering versus knowing and, 730, 768–769
    research, 829
    retrieval, 805, 812
      processes, 790–791
      theoretical background, 806

Memory (*continued*)
  sentential information, 937
  sex differences in, 172–173, 188
  short-term. *See* Short-term memory
  skills learning and, 771
  source, 769, 810
    in prefrontal patients, 1332
    remembering versus knowing and, 769
  stress and, 185–189, 731–732, 1139–1140
  studies of, 727–728
    in nonhuman primates, 731, 743–761, 822
  systems, 728, 1076
  tasks and processes, 728–729
  transfer of, 787–789
  traumatic, retrieval of, 1140
  visual, 977
    long-term, 380–381
  without remembering, 829–830
Memory abilities
  of children, 1333
  during dreaming, 1350–1351
  episodic/working, and dreaming, 1351
  hippocampus and, 1327–1328, 1345
  novelty detection and, 1325
  prefrontal syndrome and, 1319
  reality monitoring and, 1331–1332
  during REM sleep, 1345
  split-brain research and, 1357–1358
  voluntary attention and, 1326
Memory-based categorization, 1018
Memory fields, cellular specificity in, 733–736
Memory storage
  cerebral cortex and, 789–790
  emotionally influenced, in humans,
    1092–1093
  enhancement of, 1084
  mechanisms of, 789–791
  modulation, 1081–1082, 1088–1092
    hormonal, 1081–1083
Memory strategies, facilitated by ampakines, 153
Memory tasks, 818. *See also* Working memory
Mental imagery. *See also* Imagery
  debate about, 965–966, 970–971
  neural bases of, 965
  perception and, 968
Mental images
  brain bases for, 966–972
  contralesional sides and, 966
  format, 966–972
  generation, 972
  modality specificity of, 966–972
  transformations, 967
Mental retardation, 916
Mental rotation, 967
  and object-based neglect, 660–661
Mental rotation tasks, 997, 1213, 1215
Mental states, attending to, 1235–1236, 1250–1251
Mesencephalon, activation/deactivation, during NREM/REM
    sleep, 1342
Mesendodermal cells, as source of sonic hedgehog, 23–24
Mesiotemporal cortex, activation/deactivation, during NREM/
    REM sleep, 1343
Message-level representation, 886, 889
Messenger RNA
  in long-term memory, 123, 125, 134
  and synaptic integrins, 144–145

Metacontrast masking, 283
Metacontrast stimulus, 283
Metalinguistic skills, 918
Metalinguistic tasks, 869, 871–872
Metamemory, prefrontal cortex damage and, 1320, 1332
Metamer, 293
N-Methyl-D-aspartate
  activation, 1073
  and adrenal steroids, 178
  and androgens, 175
  and estrogen, 174
  in hippocampus, 172, 186
  iontophoresis, 493–494
  and neurotrophins, 161, 165–167
  and serotonin, 182
  synapses and, 466
N-Methyl-D-aspartate receptors, 438, 466, 472, 479, 1073
  antagonists, 445
  in calcium fluxes, 208
  memory function and, 803
  and sensorimotor learning, 473
  simulation, 474–475
Metyrapone, 1083
Microstimulation
  in area MT, 309–312
  spinal cord, 491–496
Midbrain
  activation/deactivation
    during NREM/REM sleep, 1342
    during waking/NREM/REM sleep, 1347
  caudal structures, 843, 848
  neuronal maps, 425
  REM sleep and, 1345–1346
  retinorecipient structure in, ocular connections to, 33
  song learning motor pathways, 453
  stimulus coding, 440–441
Midbrain nucleus AVT, 473
Middle ear, 412
Middle temporal activation, 1025
Middle temporal visual area. *See* Area V5 (MT)
Mid-level vision. *See* Vision
Migration, neuronal
  cellular dispersion and cortical specification in, 27
  during corticogenesis, 8, 11, 16, 18
  and synaptogenesis, relationship of, 46
Mineralocorticoid receptor (Type I) effects, 176–178,
    184–185
Minimum jerk model, 603–605, 616
Minimum variance theory, 605–606
Mismatched negativity, 111–112
Mis-selections, 940
Mitotic index, in region subjacent to visual cortex, 15
Mnemonic information, 1077
Mnestic block syndrome, 785–786, 790–791
Modal auxillaries, 912
Modality-specific subsystems, 1037–1040
Modular dissociations, 990–991
Modularity, and computational motor control, 614–616
Mole, star-nosed, 1194
Molecular basis of cortical regionalization, 23, 27,
    29–30
Molecular markers
  of differentiation of cortical tissue, 26
  and retinal decussation, 36, 38
Mondrians, 341
Monitoring tasks, 1002

Neuron(s) (*continued*)
  orientation tuning, 316–320
  pair-coding, object association memory and, 756–758
  perirhinal, 386
    and associative learning, 750–752
    and learning and memory, 743–744
    in object memory studies, 754–755
  in perirhinal cortex, 386
  plasticity, 159–168, 1195–1196, 1198–1207
  postmitotic
    fate of, 15–16
    migration of, 11, 14
  projection, in cortical regionalization, 25
  single
    neurophysiological response in, 274
    orientation preference of, 260
    in perception and behavior, 263, 270
    response of, 253, 268
    response properties of, 238–239
  smart, 328
  spatial order of, 213
  spatial selectivity, 440
  spiking simulations, 331
  subplate, 9
  temporal lobe, and face responses, 402
Neuronal correlate of consciousness, 1285–1293
Neuronal events, 818
Neuronal fate
  in cortex, molecular determinants of, 25
  of ventricular zone cells, 15
Neuronal migration
  cell-cell recognition in, 11
  cellular dispersion and cortical specification, 27
  during corticogenesis, 8, 11, 16, 18
  differential adhesion in, 11
  relationship to synaptogenesis, 46
  transmembrane signaling in, 11
Neuronal network(s)
  encoding rates, 325–327
  self-organization of assemblies in, 329
Neuronal perikarya, 11
Neuronal precursors, 16, 18
Neuronal response(s). *See also* Synchronization of neural responses
  attention effects
    stimulus sensitive, 316
    strength of, 315
Neuronal signals
  associative learning and, 748–752
  spatially selective attention and, 671–678
    ventral visual systems in, 679–681
  working memory and network specificity in, 736–737
Neuronal source-localization, 883
Neuronal synchronization. *See* Synchronization of neural responses
Neurophilic cell migration, 11
Neurophysiology
  of attention, 288
  of lexical access, 845
  of location-based attention, 673–678
  of postlexical processing, 844
Neuropil, density of synapses per unit volume of, 45–46
Neuropsychiatric disorders, and defects in cortical development, 29
Neuropsychological assessment, 1005
Neuropsychological data, 905
Neuropsychological deficits, 942

Neuropsychological studies, 988, 1004
Neuropsychological tests, 1048
  performance on, 1001
    cerebellar patients', 1001
Neuropsychological working memory, 1056
Neuropsychology, 942, 995, 1014
  of amnesia, 829
  of dreaming, 1347–1348
  of memory, 730–731
  of retrieval, 731
  teachings, 903
Neuroticism, and posttraumatic stress disorder, 1137
Neurotransmitters
  cellular specificity and memory function, 736
  modifications in, 232
  premotor nucleus (RA) simulation, 474–475
  regulation of, 223, 225
  species variation, 1221
  and trophic stimulation, 162–165
Neurotrophins, 159–168
  associated with learning, 167
  in cerebellum, 162–164
  in hippocampus, 159–162, 165–167
Newborn infants, multisensory integration in, 59, 65
Next-state equation, 609–610
Nicotine, and memory enhancement, 802
Nightmare(s), recurring, seizures and, 1348
Nkx2.1 genes, in regionalization of forebrain, 24–25
NMDA. *See* N-Methyl-D-aspartate
Noise, 420–421, 881
  bursts, 869
  increase, 933
  internal effects of, and selective attention, 694–695
  signal-correlated, 869
  signal-dependent, minimum variance theory, 605–606
Noncategorical patterns, processing, 832
Noncerebellar structures, 1004
Nonconscious biasing
  signal, 1048
  step, 1054
Nonconvexity problem, 610–611
Nonhuman primate studies
  of cellular specificity and memory function, 733–736
  of hemispatial neglect, 661–662
  of object memory, 753–761
Noninvasive imaging, 817, 883
Nonlinear summing units, 1069
Nonlinear systems, direct inverse modeling, 610–611
Nonlinguistic abilities, 910
Nonlinguistic defects, 917
Nonlinguistic domains, 909, 916
Nonlinguistic species, 872
Nonlinguistic variables, 890
Nonlinguistic visual features processing. *See* Word-like stimuli
Nonpreferred syntactic analysis, 888
Nonpresented semantic associate, 836
Non-REM sleep. *See* NREM sleep
Nonreversible sentences, 934
Nonsemantic direct naming route, 995
Nonsense syllables, 834, 902
Nonsilent word generation tasks, 848
Nonspeech, 869
Nonsyntactic information, 882
Nontarget object, 823
Nonverbal imagination, 860
Nonverbal materials, 820

Programmed cell death
  and cortical size, 9–10, 13
  elimination of inappropriate retinal projections, 13
Progressive participles, 912
Progressive supranuclear palsy, visual attention disorders and, 634–635
Proliferative zone
  cell death in, 9–10
  cortical plate development in, 11, 15–16
Propositional format, 846
Propositional memory, definition of, 728
Proprioception, 487, 511–512
  hand position, 503–506
  limb dynamics, 502
  motor planning, 501
  visual field rotation and, 508
Prosodic boundary information, 901
Prosodic correlates, 900
Prosodic edges, 902
Prosodic information, 898, 900
Prosodic patterns, in speech production, 102
Prosodic properties, 898
Prosody, 901
Prosopagnosia, 393–395, 400, 402–403, 1348
  and achromatopsia, 396
  objective awareness and, 1298–1299
  subjective awareness and, 1297–1299
Protein kinase A (PKA), in synaptic transmission, 122, 124, 126, 129
Protein synthesis, in long-term facilitation, 128–131
Protomap hypothesis, of cytoarchitectonic diversity, 15–16, 27
Prototype recognition procedure, 834
Prototypes, 1016
  phonetic, 102–103, 111
  retrieval, 1014
  similarity, 1013, 1020
Proximal development theory, 101
Pseudowords, 891–892, 900
  implicit processing, 859
  reading, 850, 854, 859
Pseudoword sentence repetition task, 862
Psychiatric disorders
  attention mechanisms and, 628
  prefrontal damage in, and inhibitory control, 1322
Psychoacoustics, 411
Psychoactive drugs, memory function and, 797–802
Psycholinguistics, 867, 871
Psychological refractory period paradigm, 697–698
Psychological variables, 869
Psychology, 950
  behaviorism doctrine, 1220–1221
  folk, 1253–1255
  and species variation in cognitive organization, 1221
Psychopathic personality profile, 1047
Psychopathology, and defects in cortical development, 29–30
Psychopharmacology, memory function and, 797–802
Psychophysiological data, 1055
Psychophysiological dependent variable, 1052
Psychophysiological responses, anticipatory, 1052–1054
PTSD. *See* Posttraumatic stress disorder
Puberty, synaptic loss during, 47
Pulvinar nucleus, 372
  attention mechanisms, 713–717
  and triangular-circuit theory of attention, 720
  and visual pathways, 1279
Punishment, 1052–1053

Pure alexia, 876
Purkinje cells, plasticity of, 162–164
Pursuit tracking, and posterior parietal cortex cells, 373
Putamen, activation/deactivation, during NREM/REM sleep, 1342
P3 wave, 697–698
Pyramidal cells
  asymmetries, left/right hemisphere, 1229
  species variation in, 1229

Q

Quantity representation
  notation-independent analogical, 988
  selective impairments in, 991–992
Question-sentence, 884

R

Rabbits, adult, stability of synapses in, 49
Radial glial cells, neuronal migration along, 11
Radial region of cortex
  development of, 7
  radial unit increase in mouse embryos, 10
Radial unit hypothesis of cortical development, 11, 15
Radiolabeled isotopes, 817
Rapid serial visual presentation, 935, 937
Rate coding, 437
  versus temporal coding, 326–328
Rate estimation theory, 1188–1189
Rats
  adult, synaptogenesis in, effect of experience on, 48–49
  retinocollicular pathway in, topographic organization of, 33, 42
Reaching dynamics, 507–508
Reaching movement(s)
  and optic ataxia, 368
  posterior parietal cortex cells and, 373
  visuospatial attention and, 678
Reaction speed, intersensory interactions and, 55, 68
Reaction times, 824
Reading model, 942
Reading span task, 934
Reality checking
  behavior of children and, 1333
  cognitive basis of, 1361–1362
  monitoring, 1331–1332
  prefrontal damage and, 1329, 1331–1333
  testing, 1331
Reasoning, social. *See* Social reasoning
Recall
  associative, 380–381
  direct memory tests and, 806
  stimulus conditions and, 1325
Recency judgment deficits, in prefrontal patients, 1331
Receptive field(s), 257, 279, 294–295, 297, 1070–1071
  alignment in superior colliculus
    of adult animals, 56, 58
    cross-modality, maturation of, 65, 68
  analysis, 279
  contextual modulation and, 287
  distributions in, 259
  generation of, 229
  geniculocortical afferents and, 204–207
  information encoding in, 280
  modular processing and, 280–281
  positions of, 282
  properties, 279, 283
    changes in, 225

Receptive field(s) (*continued*)
 stimulus, 693–694
  sensory response modulations, 671–673
  and spatial attention in ventral visual system, 678–681
 surround effects in, 285
 surround of, 257
 validity of, 259
 visual area function and, 279–280
Receptors, species variation, 1221
Reciprocal interaction model, NREM/REM sleep, 1346
Recoding, cognitive memory and, 729
Recognition. *See also* Face recognition; False recognition;
  Object(s), recognition of; Tools
 in animals, 1028–1029
 auditory, 845
  high vocal center (HVc), 471
  spatial encoding, 485
 cell-cell, in neuronal migration, 11
 color, Stroop effect and, 627
 direct memory tests, 806
 of fear, 404–405
 melody, 420
 misses, 808
 of negative emotions, 404
 old/new, 812
 olfactory, 759
 testing, 835
 true, 835
Recognition memory, 809, 1016
 familiarity-support, 809
 long-term, 1015
Recognition-memory task, 1016
Recognition molecules, 11
Recognition processes
 category learning and, 775
 hippocampal function and, 768
 object memory studies, 753–754
 priming and, 770–771
 rembering vs. knowing and, 768–769
Recollection
 event-related potentials in, 811–814
 familiarity comparison, 809–811
 operational definitions, 809
 true, 812
Recollective experience, 811, 833
Recording epoch, 813
Recurring utterances, 956
Red-green chromatic stimuli, infant sensitivity to, 77
Redundancy, of connections between auditory and visual cortex, 89
Reference task, 818
Reflectance, 291
 changes, 340
 definition of, 341
 in luminance formula, 342
Reflexive-antecedent gender agreement, 887
Reflexive orienting, spatial attention and, 705–707
Regional cerebral blood flow, 867
Regional cerebral metabolic changes, measurement, 850–851
Region-specific attractants, in cytoarchitectonic diversity, 15
Region-specific molecules, in formation of axonal pathways, 15
Reinforcement, 1185–1186, 1188–1189
Reinforcement learning, 470, 472–474
 motor learning systems, 613
 simulation, 477–480
 songbirds, 469–480
Relational processing, combinatorial problems in, 328

Relative clauses constructions, 910
Remembered responses, 812
Remembering
 events, 830
 versus knowing, 730, 768–769, 799–800
 without memory, 829
Remember/Know procedure/task, 811–812
Remote cortex, 876
REM sleep
 activation levels
  alterations of, 1346
  psychological aspects, 1351–1352
 behavioral state, electromyelogram and, 1344
 dreaming in
  integrated model of, 1349–1351
  phenomenology, 1344–1345
 formal dream features in, 1345
 gamma-frequency oscillations in, 1345–1346
 imaging techniques for, 1341
 and NREM sleep mentation, 1351–1352
 phenomenology, 1341
 positron emission tomography in, 1346–1347
  lesions and, 1348–1349
Repeating tasks, 874
Representational networks, 882
Representations, modality-specific, 977
Representative utterances, 910
Rescaling, 511–512
Residual vision, visual grasp reflex and, 635
Respiration, 453
Response-based sequences, 833
Response fields, 414–417
Response processing, selection during, 697–698
Responsibility predictor, multiple paired forward-inverse model, 616
Responsibility signals, multiple paired forward-inverse model, 616
Restricted word order, 910
Retention testing, 1091
Retina
 activity, patterns of, 200
 decussation patterns, 36–37
 development of, 33, 42
 ectopic cells in, 34
 nasal and temporal hemi-retinas in monkeys, 34–35
 signal transduction in, 325
 widespread retinocollicular projection, 34
Retinal ganglion cells, 33–34, 297–298
 activity of, 200
 axonal behavior and, 214, 217–219
 cortical neuron convergence of, 328
 innervation of target structures, 33–34
 molecular marking of, 37–38
 ON/OFF, 36, 201–202, 253
 in retinal response, 326
Retinal image, wavelength composition of, 291
Retinal positional markers, 36–37
Retinal projections
 binocular overlap of, 41
 binocular segregation of, 39, 41
 eye-specific, in primates, 34, 36, 39, 42
 fetal, 11, 33, 42
 formation of, 33, 42
 inappropriate, elimination in cell death, 13
 laminar-specific, in primates, 35, 37
 nasaltemporal, in primates, 34, 37
 in primates, 34, 37

Selective attention (*continued*)
  and fear, 1074–1076
  gain control mechanism in, 695
  gating mechanisms in, 623
  historical perspective on, 623
  internal noise effects and, 694–695
  locus-of-selection theory and, 687, 689–690
  multiple stages of, 688–689
  neural sites for, 690–691
  perceptual levels and, 689–691
  processing stages of, 687–699
  properties of, 711–712
  response processing in, 697–698
  working memory and, 695–697
Selective deficits, 1041
Selective impairments. *See* Quantity representation
Selectivity
  attention and, 623–624
  electrophysiology of, 687
Self-monitoring, 848, 862–863
  internal, 863
  post-articulatory, 874
  prefrontal cortex and, 1319–1320
  and time, 1319–1320
Self perception, 848
Self-report measures, 1054
Semantic arguments, 847
Semantic associates, 836
  nonpresented, 836
Semantic bootstrapping, 911
Semantic category-specific deficits, 1038–1042
  categories, 1040
  damaged semantic information subtype, 1040–1041
Semantic decision task, 822
Semantic errors, 941, 945
Semantic incongruities, 938
Semantic information
  network, 956
  sources, 938
Semantic integration processes, 882–883
Semantic knowledge, 889
  associative recall of, 380
  sensory/motor model, 1023, 1025–1030
Semantic layer, 942
Semantic memory
  definition of, 728
  psychopharmacology of, 800
Semantic nodes, 941
Semantic object representations, automatic activation, 1027–1028
Semantic priming, 1297–1299
  and awareness, objective measures, 1298–1299
Semantic primitives, 1032–1033
Semantic processes/processing, 882–884
  developmental specificity in, 91, 96
  development of, in deaf adults, 91, 93
  higher-order, 892
  second language acquisition and, 91
Semantic relations, 881
Semantic representations, 882
Semantic reversibility, 934
Semantics
  analysis, 1001
  modality-specific, 1037–1042
Semantic sensitivity, 885
Semantic space, 944
Semantic subsystems, modality-specific, 1039–1040

Semantic-syntactic properties, of words, 938
Semantic systems, 846
Semantic variables, 892
Semaphorin family, in regionalization of cerebral cortex, 28
Senescence, synaptic decline in, 47
Sensation, electrophysiology of, in waking/NREM/REM sleep, 1344
Senses, and subjective awareness, 1296
Sensitive period(s)
  for experience-dependent modifications to cortical organization, 83, 85, 89, 92
  hypothesis for, 914
  for learning, 107–108
Sensitization, 121–122, 129. *See also* Posttraumatic stress disorder
  defensive autonomic responding and, 1138–1139
  hypothalamic-pituitary-adrenal, 1139
  increased sensitivity to threat and, 1138
  response to yohimbine challenge and, 1139
Sensorimotor activations, 860
Sensorimotor integration model, 607–608
Sensorimotor learning, in songbirds, 451–466, 469, 473
Sensorimotor transformations, 601, 606–607
Sensory encoding, 252, 469
  and acoustic information, 412
Sensory epithelium, 425
Sensory error, 608
Sensory/functional theory, 1038–1042
Sensory information, sequential processing of, in neocortex, 1099
Sensory input, 1070
Sensory integration. *See* Multisensory convergence; Multisensory integration
Sensory maps
  auditory, 437
  dynamics of, 224–225
  neuronal circuitry in, 224–225
  plasticity of, 223
  reorganization of. *See* Sensory reorganization
  synaptic strength and, 225, 232
Sensory mechanisms, 251
Sensory modalities, 810
  cross-modality synthesis, 55, 68
  use of, early modality-specific experiences and, 62
Sensory/motor model, of semantic knowledge, 1023, 1025–1030
Sensory networks
  convergence of, 437–448
  spatiotemporal relationships, 437–448
Sensory processing, 437
  analysis of, 252
  binding functions in, 327
  computation and, 251
  deductions contributing to, 251
  speed, 326
  stimulus locking versus internal patterning in, 330
  temporal constraints, 325–326
Sensory reorganization, 223, 225–226, 228, 230, 233
  after deafferentations, 223
  of anterior parietal center, 228
  of auditory cortex, 229
  evidence for, 229
  of MT area, 228–229
  neuronal growth and, 224
  perception and, 230–233
  of primary motor cortex, 229
  types of, 233
  of visual cortex, 228
Sensory representations, motor function and, 252

Sleep. *See also* NREM sleep; REM sleep
   consciousness and, 1275
Slice intracellular experiments, 1074
Slow shifts, 889–890
Small clause constructions, 910
Smart errors, 940
Smoothness parameter, and kinematic cost models, 604
Snake illusion, 349
Social bonding, 843
Social contract, 1260–1269
   algorithms, 1263
   permission rules, 1266–1267
Social exchange, conditional reasoning and, 1260–1269
Social factors
   anterior forebrain and, 463–465
   and singing in birds, 451, 466
Social reasoning, 1259–1269
   adaptive function of, 1259–1269
   benefits, necessity of, 1267
   cheater detection, 1261, 1263–1268
   computational theory, 1259–1269
   design features predicted by, 1261–1263
   expert systems, 1259–1260
   permission rules, 1266–1267
   and schizophrenia, 1265–1266
   and social exchange, 1260–1269
   Standard Social Science Model, 1260
   Wason selection task, 1263–1265
Social status
   and behavior, 1193, 1196
   and gene expression, 1206
   and preoptic area neuron size, 1198–1205
   and reproductive state, 1199
Sociopathic personality profile, 1047
Sodium channels, nerve growth factor and, 163, 165
Solar ephemeris learning, 1182–1183
Solipsism, 1359
Soma, cell
   in formation of bilaminate cortical plate, 16
   synaptic localization on, 45, 51
   translocation during neuronal migration, 11
Somatic marker activation, 1058
Somatic marker hypothesis, 1047–1059
Somatic markers
   covert, 1054–1056
   neural network, 1048–1049
Somatic responses. *See* Emotionally charged stimuli
Somatosensory cortex, 848
   localization, 425, 428
   nursing and, 1196
   right, 1047
   in star-nosed mole, 1194
   synaptic density in, 47
Somatosensory maps, 240
Somatosensory pattern image, 1048
Somatosensory reorganization, 224–225, 231–232. *See also*
      Sensory reorganization
   after dorsal column lesions, 232
   after retinal lesions, 232
   and axonal collateral growth, 231
   compensation in, 244
   of hand representation, 225–227, 231–232
Somatosensory responses
   event-related potentials in, in prefrontal patients, 1320–1321
   filtering mechanisms and, 1324
Somatosensory stimuli, convergence, 437

Somatosensory system, 1004
Song behavior in birds, 1195. *See also* Song learning in birds
Songbirds
   auditory feedback in, 453–455
   brain lesions in, 453
   central pattern generators in, 451
   neural structures in, 452–453, 470–471
   social factors and, 463–465
   song learning in, 452, 465–466, 469–480
   song systems of, 451
   vocal behavior of, 451–466
   vocal learning in, 108
Song learning in birds, 452, 465–466, 469–480
   anterior forebrain and, 465–466
   area X and, 458–563
   lateral magnocellular nucleus of anterior neostriatum in, 453, 465–466
   simulation, 477–480
Song motor control nucleus. *See* High vocal center
Sonic hedgehog, in regionalization of central nervous system, 23, 25
Sonic hedgehog receptor, 24
Sound
   analysis of, 420–422
   features of, 411
   neural representations of, 411
Sound localization, 411, 425–448
   by barn owls, 107
   development of, 443–446
   lesions and, 425
   merged with visual localization, 437–448
   monaural spectral cues, 442–443
   specialized areas, 426
   visual cues and, 443–445
Source discrimination, 810, 812
Source memory, 769, 810
   in prefrontal patients, 1332
   remembering versus knowing and, 769
Source procedure, 813
Spatial ability
   home range size and, 1210–1214
   mental rotation tasks, 1213, 1215
   sex differences in, 1209–1216
      in cowbirds, 1211–1213
      home range and, 1210–1211, 1213–1214
      hormones and, 1215–1216
      in humans, 1213–1216
      in voles, 1210–1211
Spatial attention
   neuronal signals and, 671–678
   paradigms, 667–668
   reflexive orienting and, 705–707
   selective processing onset in, 689–690
   sensory response modulations and, 671–673
   ventral visual system and, 678–681
   working memory and, 707–709
Spatial contrast sensitivity function, 76, 79
Spatial encoding, 485
Spatial frequency hypothesis, and visual attention disorders, 643
Spatial imagery tasks, 966
Spatial indexing, in bottom-up attention control, 717–718
Spatial layout problems, 356
Spatial learning mechanism(s)
   in foraging ants/bees, 1180–1182
   for learning solar ephemeris, 1182–1183

Stimulus onset asynchrony, and working memory and spatial attention, 707–709
Stimulus/stimuli
    attention performance and, 1325
    auditory responses and, 1356
    cognitive simulation, prefrontal damage, 1329–1331
    conscious versus unconscious perception of, 1300, 1302
    discriminator, 1071
    and event-related potentials, in prefrontal patients, 1320
    generalization, 1071–1072
    language connection and, 1359–1361
    memory, prefrontal cortex and, 1319
    modality, 833
    novelty, 823–824
    objective awareness, discrimination ability and, 1297–1299
    perception determination and, minimal thresholds and, 1296–1297
    scalp potentials and, 1326
    sensory
        intensity of, effect on multisensory interaction, 58–59
        and postnatal cortical organization, 83, 85
        response enhancement or response depression to, 57, 59
        spatial relationship between, 57, 59
        timing of, effect on multisensory interaction, 58–59
    surround, 280
    temporal variables of, 326
    visual responses and, 1356
Strabismic rearing, 199
Strabismus, 333–334
Stress
    and adrenal steroids, 177–178, 180–183, 185–189
    and affect, 785–786
    and mossy fiber reorganization, 183–184
    and neurogenesis, 180–181
    and neuronal atrophy, 181–183, 185–189
Stress hormone(s)
    and emotional memory, 1139–1140
    and memory storage, 1081
Stress-induced analgesia, 1134. See also Posttraumatic stress disorder
Striate cortex
    left, 877
    lesions, and blindsight, 1274, 1278
    posterior, 876
Striate visual cortex. See Area V1
Striatum
    activation, REM sleep integrated model and, 1350
    activation/deactivation, during waking/NREM/REM sleep, 1347
    dysfunction of, 832
    lesions, and dreaming, 1348–1349
    neuropathology of, 832
    ventral, activation/deactivation, during NREM/REM sleep, 1342
Stroke
    and novelty response, 1328
    and visual attention disorders, 633–647
Stroop color-word interference task, conscious versus unconscious perception and, 1300–1301
Stroop effect
    attentional conflict and, 627–629
    Balint's syndrome and, 646–647
Structure-building operations, 892
Subcortical areas
    activation, REM sleep integrated model and, 1349–1350
    activation/deactivation, during NREM/REM sleep, 1341–1342
    in dreaming, 1351

Subcortical map recovery, 233
Subcortical plasticity, 226–227, 232
    feedback connections and, 227
Subcortical subsystems, 876
Subdural electrode grids, 850
    implanted, 850
Subject-initiated strategies, 819, 825
Subjective perception. See Unconscious perception
Subject-relative sentences, 889–890
Subject-verb number agreement, 887
Sublexical processing, 868
Sublexical representations, 900, 904
Subplate zone, 9, 15–16, 18
    synaptogenesis in, 46
Subtraction analysis, 876
Subtractive method. See Language
Subventricular zone, transient, 9, 16
Superior colliculus, 367, 372, 977
    and auditory localization, 425–426, 443–446
    auditory map in
        early visual-auditory experience and, 65
        visual map as template for, 65–66
    bimodal cells, 448
    innervation of, 440
    map alignment in, 56, 58, 67
    mapping templates in, 65, 67
    motor aspects of, maturation of, 63, 65
    motor map in, 56, 58, 65, 67
    and multisensory convergence, 55, 68, 437–439
    posterior parietal cortex and, 373
    postnatal development of, in cats, 62–63
    receptive field alignment in
        in adult animals, 56, 58
        cross-modality, maturation of, 65, 68
    saccades, 486–487
    sensorimotor aspects of, maturation of, 63, 65
    sensory map in, 56, 58, 65, 67, 439–443
    sensory networks, 437–448
    topography of, 56, 58
    visual map in, as template for auditory map, 65–66
    visual pathways, 1279, 1287
Superior medial cortex, 1008
Superior olivary complex, 413
    localization, auditory, 425
Superior olive
    lateral, 440
    medial, 440
Superior temporal sulcus (STS), 372, 1032
    and consciousness, 1289, 1291
    and gaze direction, 402
    object activation in, 395
Superposition principle, 420
Supervised learning systems, 609–614
Supervisory attention system, and contention scheduling, 1312
Supplementary motor area, 487, 1008
    activation, 860, 862
Supramarginal gyrus, 892
    activation/deactivation, during NREM/REM sleep, 1343
Surface judgment, 819
Surface structures, 845, 847
Surround region, 271
Surround stimuli, 280
Sustained field, 873
Syllabification, 847–850
Sylvian cortices, blood flow difference images of, 1313